Classics

of

Moral and
Political Theory

Classics

OF

Moral and Political Theory

Edited by
MICHAEL L. MORGAN

HACKETT PUBLISHING COMPANY

INDIANAPOLIS/CAMBRIDGE

Copyright © 1992 by Hackett Publishing Company, Inc.
All rights reserved
Printed in the United States of America

99 98 97 96 95 94 93 92   1 2 3 4 5 6 7 8

Cover art:
Cover design by Listenberger Design Associates
Interior design by James N. Rogers

For further information, please address

Hackett Publishing Company, Inc.
P.O. Box 44937
Indianapolis, Indiana 46244-0937

Library of Congress Cataloging-in-Publication Data

Classics of moral and political theory/edited by Michael Morgan.
   p.   cm.
  Includes bibliographical references.
  ISBN 0-87220-127-9 (cloth): ISBN 0-87220-126-0 (pbk.)
  1. Political ethics. 2. Political science. I. Morgan, Michael
L., 1944–
JA79.C59 1992
172—dc20
                                  91-38760
                                    CIP

Contents

Introduction   vii
Acknowledgments   ix

PLATO   1
  Apology   6
  Crito   22
  Republic   31

ARISTOTLE   232
  Nicomachean Ethics   235
  Politics (Bk I, 1–9; Bk II, 1–5, 9; Bk III, 1–2, 4–5; Bk VII, 1–3, 13–15)   382

EPICURUS   415
  Letter to Menoeceus   417
  Principal Doctrines   420

EPICTETUS   424
  The Handbook (Encheiridion)   426

AUGUSTINE   442
  City of God (Bk XIX, 1, 4–8, 14, 17, 19, 27)   444

AQUINAS   460
  On Kingship (I, 1)   463
  Summa Theologica (I–II, Q.90. 1–4, Q.91. 1–4, Q.94. 1–6; II-II, Q.40.1, Q42.2, Q.66. 1–2)   466

MACHIAVELLI   490
  The Prince   493
  Discourses (Bk I, 1–2; Bk II, 1–2, 20, 29; Bk III, 1, 9)   542
  Letter to Vettori   565

HOBBES   568
  Leviathan (Introduction, Parts I–II, Conclusion)   571

LOCKE   733
    Second Treatise of Government   736

HUME   818
    Treatise of Human Nature (Bk III, Pt I, i–ii; Pt II, i–ii)   820

ROUSSEAU   846
    Discourse on the Origin of Inequality   848
    On The Social Contract   913

KANT   988
    Grounding for the Metaphysics of Morals   991

MILL   1042
    On Liberty   1044
    Utilitarianism   1116

MARX   1157
    Estranged Labor   1159
    On the Jewish Question   1168
    Communist Manifesto   1190
    Critique of the Gotha Program   1216

NIETZSCHE   1230
    On the Genealogy of Morals (Preface, First and Second Essays)   1233

Each one of these classic texts, moreover, means and has meant many things. Each work meant something, surely many things, when it was written and published and initially read. Each came to mean much else as it was reread, cited, recalled, and reinterpreted in the years and decades thereafter. And each text now means many things to its many current readers, us among them, as it is read again and interpreted in the context of today's debates, issues, and events. Different readers will approach these works for different reasons and with different interests and presuppositions. In a way, then, each of these texts is not one text but many, a vast plurality.

These issues have guided the construction of this anthology. From a much larger list of classic texts of moral and political thought we carved the current table of contents, trying insofar as it was possible to include many of the most influential and significant classics that are currently taught and studied. Moreover, where we could, we chose to include entire works or at least very sizeable chunks. The more we excerpt, the more we limit the reader's perspective and options and hence the more we coopt the reader's role as interpreter and critic. We did not want to do that either to you, the teacher, or to you, the student. Finally, the introductions to each author are not intended as full-scale interpretations of the works; rather they aim to help the student by situating the author and the work historically and by saying some general things about the author's work and thought. In the end, these strategies all serve a single goal: to provide a useful and convenient resource for the critical study of moral and political thinking in the Western historical traditions.

In many ways this work is an empirical enterprise. It does not hope to shape a tradition so much as to respond to and express features of several. For this reason, as years go by and as interests change, it may be advisable, if not necessary, to alter its contents—to add, delete, and replace these classics with others. Your guidance in this process will be invaluable, and we invite it. In such a way, this anthology, which has thus far been a cooperative enterprise, will continue to be one, in a continually useful and significant way.

Introduction

We have called this anthology *Classics of Moral and Political Theory* in order to suggest by its title some of the volume's important features. First, it contains writings with a certain content. Some of the texts are about moral or ethical theory in the broad sense that includes reflection on the nature of morality and discussion of the content of the moral life, its principles and ideals, its characteristic virtues and vices. Other works deal with political matters, also in a broad way, often treating the relationships among political, legal, religious, philosophical, moral, and psychological issues, discussing the nature of political institutions, political practice, and much else. Some of these works, then, are classic moral texts; some are classic political texts; some are both. All, however, and this is my second point, are classics.

What is a classic? Surely there is no short and simple answer to this question. But perhaps this much will do: A classic text is one that reverberates within one or more traditions. It is a text that articulates powerfully influential views, positions, or conceptions; that exhibits in a paradigmatic way models, motifs, or arguments; and that is recalled, cited, and exhibited in subsequent discussion, inquiry, and debate. A classic, in short, is a work that makes an important difference or at least, from a particular vantage point, is thought to have made and to continue to make such a difference.

Not all texts of course are classics. But while others may be interesting or valuable or helpful, only classic texts are somehow necessary, both for understanding a tradition and for participating in one as well as for calling a tradition into question and seeking to deconstruct or subvert it. To say something significant and important within or against a tradition of discourse, one must, to some degree or other, call upon the resources that constitute that tradition, and classic texts are the chief written repositories of these resources—of the tradition's terms, its alternative views, its examples, formulations, arguments, and indeed all that make up its tools for discussion and debate. In this sense, the writings collected in this anthology are classics, not *the* classics, to be sure—for there are many others, and the very status of being a classic changes in the course of history—but *some of the classics* of the several traditions of reflection about moral and political matters in the West, from Greek antiquity to the late nineteenth century.

These classics, moreover, are of a limited kind. They are all works written by men, largely for men; their conceptions of human nature, the good life, political virtues, and so on exhibit a gender bias. Furthermore, they are Western, European classics that are featured in certain traditions of discussion and debate but should be compared and contrasted with other types—non-Western classics, classics by nonwhites, by women, by Native Americans, by non-Christian authors, and more. For many reasons, excluding such alternative classics is unfortunate, but it has been unavoidable and purposeful. What this volume contains is not a sample of everything; it is, rather, a selection that can serve as a common resource both for those who seek to understand and continue the Western traditions of debate and for those who seek to examine these traditions critically and, in the end, to oppose them.

Acknowledgments

In the fall of 1990 Jay Hullett approached me with a proposal for a major anthology of classic texts in the Western traditions of moral and political theory. At every stage, this has been a collegial and cooperative effort. Jay has supervised our work with sensitivity and wisdom; Brian Rak has been a thoughtful and meticulous editor. Dan Kirklin has guided the production process with tremendous attention to detail, constant encouragement, and a great understanding of our goals.

In making my editorial selections I was aided by a number of friends and colleagues—Jeff Isaac, Paul Eisenberg, Milton Fisk—but especially by Brian Rak, with his keen sense for what is used and what is useful in the teaching of ethics and political theory. In preparing the introductions I benefited from a vast amount of biographical, historical, and philosophical work. Jim Tully read all the introductions and made copious recommendations, virtually all of which I accepted and which directed me to avoid infelicities and inaccuracies. Gillian Parker read text and proofs as we tried to make the result as accurate as possible, and Mark Rooks of InteLex provided many texts on disk and scanned others, in order to facilitate the publication process. Audrey, Debbie, Sara, and our two cats, Blaze and Amanda, endured a good deal less attention than they deserved, sympathizing as I worried about deadlines and providing encouragement and distraction as needed.

PLATO

In 399 B.C.E., five years after the conclusion of the Peloponnesian War (431–404 B.C.E.), Socrates (469–399) was charged with impiety, tried by the Athenian court, and executed. To this day scholars debate the character and significance of this event. What were the real issues that led to Socrates' trial and execution? What was Athens like in 399, and why were the majority of dicasts (jurors) convinced of Socrates' guilt? Indeed, of what was Socrates really guilty? What kind of life did he live? How did he defend himself? Does the event teach us anything in general about the role of philosophy in society and the relation between philosophy and morality or philosophy and politics?

By the time this trial took place, Socrates was an old man of seventy. He had been born in Athens and left it only two, perhaps three times, for military service. We know very little of his life. He was a citizen of modest means, who had a deep commitment to Athens, who was married with young children at the time of the trial, and who had been associated, in the popular mind, with the Sophists, those itinerant educators of fifth-century Greece, teachers of language, rhetoric, oratory, argument, and political skills. There is reason to think that early in his life, when Athens flourished under Pericles and was the hub of Greek intellectual activity, Socrates had been interested in the investigations of nature of people like Democritus and Anaxagoras. At some point, however, probably prior to the outbreak of the Peloponnesian War in 431, he turned to other matters, to the examination of beliefs about ethical notions. He came to hold the primacy of the soul and its well-being and became committed to seeking knowledge of the good and the truth about the best human life. His fellow Athenians found him difficult, annoying, an enigma, and perhaps even a threat. Many of his associates and students, e.g., Alcibiades and Critias, were pro-Spartan, aristocratic, and antidemocratic, and it is possible that his characteristic conduct, the *elenchos* or critical interrogation, led many to think that he too opposed the democracy. At the very least, some took him to be a threat to Athenian values or disdainful of them. If Plato's *Apology* is an accurate portrayal of his defense, he was not able—or perhaps did not even try—to persuade them otherwise.

Modern students of Greek philosophy and culture have found Socrates to be a richly rewarding subject. He wrote nothing, but many of Plato's dialogues are taken to reflect with some fidelity his method of philosophical interrogation, his moral and religious views, and his political thought. But the picture we get from Plato, especially when it is supplemented from other ancient sources, e.g., Xenophon, Aristophanes, and Aristotle, is unclear and hard to fill in consistently. Socrates was committed to

1

the primacy of soul or character in living the best human life. Knowledge was central to that commitment, and hence philosophy, as the quest for moral knowledge, was also fundamental. Moreover, Socrates was convinced that the best character and knowledge were closely tied to right conduct, and that harmful or unjust action was self-destructive. But the intricacies of these and other of his views are complex and have led to much debate, as has the nature of Socrates' political thought and his primary political allegiance. One wonders how perspicuous was the average Athenian's understanding of this man.

While many Athenians may have been satisfied, if not pleased, with the verdict against Socrates and his execution, some clearly were not. Among this group of Socrates' friends, associates, and disciples was a young Athenian aristocrat who labored for a lifetime under the shadow of these events. Later in life he reports the disturbing effects that these events had on him and his thinking:

> When I was a young man I had the same ambitions as many others: I thought of entering public life as soon as I came of age. And certain happenings in public affairs favored me. . . . a new government was set up [the Thirty Tyrants]. Some of these men happened to be relatives and acquaintances of mine, and they invited me to join them. . . . I thought that they were going to lead the city out of the unjust life she had been living and establish her in the path of justice.

But this young aristocrat realized he was wrong when this government acted corruptly, on one occasion commanding "Socrates, an older friend of mine whom I should not hesitate to call the wisest and justest man of that time," to participate in the assassination of Leon of Salamis, "planning thereby to make Socrates willy-nilly a party to their actions." He refused, to his credit, but later, after the democracy had been reinstated in 403,

> certain powerful persons brought into court this same friend Socrates, . . . charged him with impiety, and the jury condemned and put to death the very man who, at the time when his accusers were themselves in misfortune and exile, had refused to have a part in the unjust arrest of one of their friends.

Here Plato (427–347), in his famous Seventh Letter, reflects on the pivotal role that Socrates' trial had had on his life and on his thinking about justice, human nature, and the state.

Plato was born in 427, probably in Athens. Both his father Ariston and his mother Perictione were of distinguished lineage; indeed, Perictione traced her descent from the great lawgiver Solon. Critias, Perictione's cousin, was one of the most violent and most hated of the Thirty Tyrants of 404, the oligarchic government which Sparta enforced at the conclusion of the war, while Charmides, her brother, was also a member of the Thirty and one of the overseers of the Piraeus, the Athenian port. Plato had two brothers, Glaucon and Adiemantus, who appear as major players in the *Republic*, and one sister, Potone, whose son Speusippus was appointed head of the Academy (see below) upon Plato's death.

We know nothing in detail of Plato's youth. Doubtless he would have had the normal Athenian education in culture and gymnastics that he describes in the *Republic*. Clearly he developed a high degree of literary skill and studied the various subjects taught by the Sophists and natural investigators. He became acquainted with Socrates no later than when he was twenty and, given his status, certainly had military service, probably in the cavalry.

After Socrates' death, Plato and some other disciples left Athens to join Euclides, a close associate of Socrates, in Megara, where he remained until 395 or so, when he would have been called to serve in the Corinthian War. During the next several years, we may surmise, Plato wrote many of the early, short dialogues in which Socrates is the chief character and which aim to clarify and portray the Socratic life. These dialogues include the *Apology*, *Crito*, *Laches*, *Lysis*, *Charmides*, *Euthyphro*, *Ion*, *Hippias Major*, and *Hippias Minor*.

When he was forty, in 387, Plato made the first of three visits to Italy and Sicily. Later sources claim that his trip was motivated by his desire to meet the Pythagorean philosophers and religious thinkers there, especially the important mathematician, Archytas of Tarentum, who became a lifelong friend and may have influenced Plato's belief in the immortality of the soul and the importance of mathematics to philosophy. While in Sicily, moreover, Plato met Dion, then twenty, the brother-in-law of the powerful tyrant of Syracuse, Dionysus I. With Dion Plato developed a close, indeed intimate relationship. Dion was a brilliant and receptive student who quickly became Plato's disciple and a convinced Socratic, committed to the life of virtue and goodness and opposed to the hedonistic, luxurious style of Italian and Sicilian life.

Once back in Athens, in 387, Plato purchased some buildings and a grove of trees nearly a mile outside the walls of Athens. There he founded a society or religious fellowship (*thiasos*), on the model of an Orphic-Pythagorean religious association, which he called the Academy, after the hero Hecademus, to whom the spot was sacred. Until his death he was its director, organizing and coordinating its activities, from meals held according to fairly strict rules, to lectures, discussions, guided research, and visits by foreign scholars. Among the many subjects studied and examined in the Academy, philosophical inquiry, mathematics, and moral-political thought were probably preeminent. During the 380s, moreover, Plato wrote further dialogues, but these dialogues develop his own thinking, on Socratic foundations, on matters such as moral character, virtue (*arete*), inquiry, knowledge, metaphysics, and more. These writings include the *Protagoras*, *Gorgias*, and *Meno*, followed by the middle dialogues, in which his own thinking emerges in full form, the *Phaedo*, *Symposium*, *Republic*, *Phaedrus*, and *Cratylus*. In these dialogues, he first displays his famous theory of Forms or Ideas, develops his understanding of philosophical inquiry, its stages and ultimate goal, sketches an account of philosophical education and moral development, identifies various capacities and states of the soul in an increasingly subtle psychology, and works out the features of his moral view and its political implications.

In 368 Dionysus I of Syracuse died and was replaced immediately by his inexperienced and insecure son Dionysus II. To Dion, who was dazzled by the possibilities of Plato's moral and political thinking and all too unrealistic in his expectations, the situation seemed propitious. He persuaded the young ruler to invite Plato to Syracuse, and he himself wrote to Plato suggesting that the young Dionysus might be an ideal subject for Plato's proposals about philosophy and political rule as expressed in the *Republic*. Whatever Plato's hopes or misgivings, he accepted the invitation but, upon arriving in Syracuse, found a situation of jealousy, conflict, and intrigue. Eventually, Dion was expelled from Sicily, and, when war broke out with

Carthage, Plato was sent home. By 365 Dion had joined Plato in Athens, where for four years Plato directed research, taught, and wrote, all the while keeping abreast of affairs in Sicily. By this time too Plato's disenchantment with politics had grown deeper; it was directed not only at Dionysus and Sicily but also at Athens and the city's misguided efforts to regain her power, her empire, and her prestige.

By 362 a new invitation had arrived from Dionysus II, who showed signs of the commitment to philosophy that Plato had long sought. Full of doubts, Plato once again sailed to Sicily, and once again his plans came to naught. The young Dionysus refused Plato's directions for philosophical education, began to sell off Dion's property while he was still a virtual exile, and in the end held Plato under house arrest. Only the intervention of Plato's old friend Archytas enabled him to escape and return to Athens.

Amid all this turmoil, Plato had begun a serious deepening of his own thinking about knowledge, inquiry, reality, politics, morality, and law. He wrote or at least began an extraordinarily rich set of dialogues, the *Parmenides*, *Theaetetus*, *Politicus*, and *Sophist*. In the remaining thirteen years of his life, he completed these works, began several new ones, and continued to direct the affairs of the Academy. He died in 347, leaving unfinished his last great work, the *Laws*. In it Plato's sense of political realism emerges in full force. He attempts to set out in detail the structure, goals, and character of a *polis* that is both ideal and realistic, a *polis* in which expert rulers play their roles alongside an elaborate legal order that coordinates philosophy, political life, religion, and ethics.

Since the 360s Plato had appreciated the demands on the worldly career of philosophy; already in the *Republic* he had tried to reconcile the philosopher's religious goals, his aspiration to transcendence, with his political responsibilities and the complex psychology of the embodied soul. By the time he begins the *Laws*, Plato is fully aware of the limitations on human hopes and possibilities. The prominence of law and all its accoutrements in his last work expresses that awareness and all that comes with it, the sober recognition that human life is a fragile but difficult blending of this world and beyond and that any genuine understanding of philosophy and the moral-political life must appreciate that blending to the fullest.

Recommended readings

Allen, R. E. *Socrates and Legal Obligation*. Minneapolis: University of Minnesota Press, 1980.

Annas, Julia. *An Introduction to Plato's Republic*. Oxford: Oxford University Press, 1981.

Brickhouse, Tom, and Nicholas Smith. *Socrates on Trial*. Princeton: Princeton University Press, 1989.

Cross, R. C., and A. D. Woozley. *Plato's Republic: A Philosophical Commentary*. London: Macmillan, 1964.

Dover, K. J. *Greek Popular Morality in the Time of Plato and Aristotle*. Oxford: Blackwell's, 1974.

Gulley, Norman. *The Philosophy of Socrates*. London: Macmillan, 1968.

Guthrie, W. K. C. *A History of Greek Philosophy*. Vols. III-IV. Cambridge: Cambridge University Press, 1969, 1975, 1978.

Irwin, T. H. *Classical Thought*. Oxford: Oxford University Press, 1989.

Irwin, T. H. *Plato's Moral Theory*. Oxford: Oxford University Press, 1977.

Kraut, Richard. *Socrates and the State*. Princeton: Princeton University Press, 1984.

Morgan, Michael L. *Platonic Piety: Philosophy and Ritual in Fourth Century Athens*. New Haven: Yale University Press, 1990.

Murphy, N. R. *The Interpretation of Plato's Republic*. Oxford: Oxford University Press, 1951.

Okin, Susan Moller. *Women in Western Political Thought*. Princeton: Princeton University Press, 1979.

Reeve, C.D.C. *Philosopher-Kings*. Princeton: Princeton University Press, 1988.

Reeve, C.D.C. *Socrates in the Apology*. Indianapolis: Hackett, 1989.

Santas, Gerismos. *Socrates*. London: Routledge, 1979.

Vlastos, Gregory (ed.). *The Philosophy of Socrates*. Garden City: Doubleday, 1971.

Vlastos, Gregory (ed.). *Plato*. Vol.II. Garden City: Doubleday, 1970.

Vlastos, Gregory. *Socrates, Ironist and Moral Philosopher*. Ithaca: Cornell, 1991.

White, N. P. *A Companion to Plato's Republic*. Indianapolis: Hackett, 1979.

Woozley, A. D. *Law and Obedience: The Arguments of Plato's Crito*. London: Duckworth, 1970.

APOLOGY[1]

17 I do not know, men of Athens, how my accusers affected you; as for me, I was almost carried away in spite of myself, so persuasively did they speak. And yet, hardly anything of what they said is true. Of the many lies they told, one in particular surprised me, namely that you should be careful not to be deceived by an accomplished speaker like me. That they are not ashamed to be immediately proved

b wrong by the facts, when I show myself not to be an accomplished speaker at all, that I think is most shameless on their part—unless indeed they call an accomplished speaker the man who speaks the truth. If they mean that, I would agree that I am an orator, but not after their manner, for indeed, as I say, practically nothing they said was true. From me you will hear the whole truth, though not, by Zeus,

c gentlemen, expressed in embroidered and stylized phrases like theirs, but things spoken at random and expressed in the first words that come to mind, for I put my trust in the justice of what I say, and let none of you expect anything else. It would not be fitting at my age, as it might be for a young man, to toy with words when I appear before you.

One thing I do ask and beg of you, gentlemen: if you hear me making my defence in the same kind of language as I am accustomed to use in the market place by the bankers' tables,[2] where many of you have heard me, and elsewhere, do not be surprised or create a disturbance on that account. The position is this: this is my

d first appearance in a lawcourt, at the age of seventy; I am therefore simply a stranger to the manner of speaking here. Just as if I were really a stranger, you would certainly excuse me if I spoke in that dialect and manner in which I had been

18 brought up, so too my present request seems a just one, for you to pay no attention to my manner of speech—be it better or worse—but to concentrate your attention on whether what I say is just or not, for the excellence of a judge lies in this, as that of a speaker lies in telling the truth.

It is right for me, gentlemen, to defend myself first against the first lying accusations made against me and my first accusers, and then against the later accusations and the later accusers. There have been many who have accused me to you for many

b years now, and none of their accusations are true. These I fear much more than I fear Anytus and his friends, though they too are formidable. These earlier ones, however, are more so, gentlemen; they got hold of most of you from childhood, persuaded you and accused me quite falsely, saying that there is a man called Socrates, a wise man, a student of all things in the sky and below the earth, who makes the

c worse argument the stronger. Those who spread that rumour, gentlemen, are my dangerous accusers, for their hearers believe that those who study these things do

---

Reprinted from *The Trial & Death of Socrates*, translated by G.M.A. Grube (Indianapolis: Hackett Publishing Company, 1975), by permission of the publisher.

1. [The word *apology* is a transliteration, not a translation, of the Greek *apologia* which means defence. There is certainly nothing apologetic about the speech.—G.M.A.G.]

2. [The bankers or money-changers had their counters in the market place. It seems that this was a favourite place for gossip.]

not even believe in the gods. Moreover, these accusers are numerous and have been at it a long time; also, they spoke to you at an age when you would most readily believe them, some of you being children and adolescents, and they won their case by default, as there was no defence.

What is most absurd in all this is that one cannot even know or mention their names unless one of them is a writer of comedies.[3] Those who maliciously and slanderously persuaded you, who, also, when persuaded themselves then persuaded others, all those are most difficult to deal with: one cannot bring one of them into court or refute him; one must simply fight with shadows as it were in making one's defence, and cross-examine when no one answers. I want you to realize too that my accusers are of two kinds: those who have accused me recently, and the old ones I mention; and to think that I must first defend myself against the latter, for you have also heard their accusations first, and to a much greater extent than the more recent.

Very well then. I must surely defend myself and attempt to uproot from your minds in so short a time the slander that has resided there so long. I wish this may happen, if it is in any way better for you and me, and that my defence may be successful, but I think this is very difficult and I am fully aware of how difficult it is. Even so, let the matter proceed as the god may wish, but I must obey the law and make my defence.

Let us then take up the case from its beginning. What is the accusation from which arose the slander in which Meletus trusted when he wrote out the charge against me? What did they say when they slandered me? I must, as if they were my actual prosecutors, read the affidavit they would have sworn. It goes something like this: Socrates is guilty of wrongdoing in that he busies himself studying things in the sky and below the earth; he makes the worse into the stronger argument, and he teaches these same things to others. You have seen this yourselves in the comedy of Aristophanes, a Socrates swinging about there, saying he was walking on air and talking a lot of other nonsense about things of which I know nothing at all. I do not speak in contempt of such knowledge, if someone is wise in these things—lest Meletus bring more cases against me—but, gentlemen, I have no part in it, and on this point I call upon the majority of you as witnesses. I think it right that all those of you who have heard me conversing, and many of you have, should tell each other if anyone of you has ever heard me discussing such subjects to any extent at all. From this you will learn that the other things said about me by the majority are of the same kind.

Not one of them is true. And if you have heard from anyone that I undertake to teach people and charge a fee for it, that is not true either. Yet I think it a fine thing to be able to teach people as Gorgias of Leontini does, and Prodicus of Ceos, and Hippias of Elis.[4] Each of these men can go to any city and persuade the young, who can keep company with anyone of their own fellow-citizens they want without pay-

---

3. [This refers in particular to Aristophanes, whose comedy, *The Clouds*, produced in 423 B.C., ridiculed the (imaginary) school of Socrates.]

4. [These were all well-known Sophists. Gorgias, after whom Plato named one of his dialogues, was a celebrated rhetorician and teacher of rhetoric. He came to Athens in 427 B.C., and his rhetorical tricks took the city by storm. Two dialogues, the authenticity of which has been doubted, are named after Hippias, whose knowledge was encyclopedic. Prodicus was known for his insistence on the precise meaning of words. Both he and Hippias are characters in the *Protagoras* (named after another famous Sophist).]

20 ing, to leave the company of these, to join with themselves, pay them a fee, and be grateful to them besides. Indeed, I learned that there is another wise man from Paros who is visiting us, for I met a man who has spent more money on Sophists than everybody else, Callias, the son of Hipponicus. So I asked him—he has two sons—"Callias," I said, "if your sons were colts or calves, we could find and engage

b a supervisor for them who would make them excel in their proper qualities, some horse breeder or farmer. Now since they are men, whom do you have in mind to supervise them? Who is an expert in this kind of excellence, the human and social kind? I think you must have given thought to this for your sons. Is there such a person," I asked, "or is there not?" "Certainly there is," he said. "Who is he?" I asked, "What is his name, where is he from? and what is his fee?" "His name, Socrates, is Evenus, he comes from Paros, and his fee is five minas." I thought Evenus a happy

c man, if he really possesses this art, and teaches for so moderate a fee. Certainly I would pride and preen myself if I had this knowledge, but I do not have it, gentlemen.

One of you might perhaps interrupt me and say: "But Socrates, what is your occupation? From where have these slanders come? For surely if you did not busy yourself with something out of the common, all these rumours and talk would not have arisen unless you did something other than most people. Tell us what it is, that

d we may not speak inadvisedly about you." Anyone who says that seems to be right, and I will try to show you what has caused this reputation and slander. Listen then. Perhaps some of you will think I am jesting, but be sure that all that I shall say is true. What has caused my reputation is none other than a certain kind of wisdom. What kind of wisdom? Human wisdom, perhaps. It may be that I really possess this, while those whom I mentioned just now are wise with a wisdom more than human;

e else I cannot explain it, for I certainly do not possess it, and whoever says I do is lying and speaks to slander me. Do not create a disturbance, gentlemen, even if you think I am boasting, for the story I shall tell does not originate with me, but I will refer you to a trustworthy source. I shall call upon the god at Delphi as witness to the existence and nature of my wisdom, if it be such. You know Chairephon. He

21 was my friend from youth, and the friend of most of you, as he shared your exile and your return. You surely know the kind of man he was, how impulsive in any course of action. He went to Delphi at one time and ventured to ask the oracle—as I say, gentlemen, do not create a disturbance—he asked if any man was wiser than I, and the Pythian replied that no one was wiser. Chairephon is dead, but his brother will testify to you about this.

b Consider that I tell you this because I would inform you about the origin of the slander. When I heard of this reply I asked myself: "Whatever does the god mean? What is his riddle? I am very conscious that I am not wise at all; what then does he mean by saying that I am the wisest? For surely he does not lie; it is not legitimate for him to do so." For a long time I was at a loss; then I very reluctantly turned to some such investigation as this: I went to one of those reputed wise, thinking that

c there, if anywhere, I could refute the oracle and say to it: "This man is wiser than I, but you said I was." Then, when I examined this man—there is no need for me to tell you his name, he was one of our public men—my experience was something like this: I thought that he appeared wise to many people and especially to himself, but he was not. I then tried to show him that he thought himself wise, but that he was

d not. As a result he came to dislike me, and so did many of the bystanders. So I withdrew and thought to myself: "I am wiser than this man; it is likely that neither of us knows anything worthwhile, but he thinks he knows something when he does not, whereas when I do not know, neither do I think I know; so I am likely to be wiser to this small extent, that I do not think I know what I do not know." After this I approached another man, one of those thought to be wiser than he, and I thought the same thing, and so I came to be disliked both by him and by many others.

After that I proceeded systematically. I realized, to my sorrow and alarm, that I was getting unpopular, but I thought that I must attach the greatest importance to the god's oracle, so I must go to all those who had any reputation for knowledge to examine its meaning. And by the dog,[5] gentlemen of the jury—for I must tell you the truth—I experienced something like this: in my investigation in the service of the god I found that those who had the highest reputation were nearly the most deficient, while those who were thought to be inferior were more knowledgeable. I must give you an account of my journeyings as if they were labours I had undertaken to prove the oracle irrefutable. After the politicians, I went to the poets, the writers of tragedies and dithyrambs and the others, intending in their case to catch myself being more ignorant than they. So I took up those poems with which they seemed to have taken most trouble and asked them what they meant, in order that I might at the same time learn something from them. I am ashamed to tell you the truth, gentlemen, but I must. Almost all the bystanders explained the poems better than their authors could. I soon realized that poets do not compose their poems with knowledge, but by some inborn talent and by inspiration, like seers and prophets who also say many fine things without any understanding of what they say. The poets seemed to me to have had a similar experience. At the same time I saw that, because of their poetry, they thought themselves very wise men in other respects, which they were not. So there again I withdrew, thinking that I had the same advantage over them as I had over the politicians.

Finally I went to the craftsmen, for I was conscious of knowing practically nothing, and I knew that I would find that they had knowledge of many fine things. In this I was not mistaken; they knew things I did not know, and to that extent they were wiser than I. But, gentlemen of the jury, the good craftsmen seemed to me to have the same fault as the poets: each of them, because of success at his craft, thought himself very wise in other most important pursuits, and this error of theirs overshadowed the wisdom they had, so that I asked myself, on behalf of the oracle, whether I should prefer to be as I am, with neither their wisdom nor their ignorance, or to have both. The answer I gave myself and the oracle was that it was to my advantage to be as I am.

As a result of this investigation, gentlemen of the jury, I acquired much unpopularity, of a kind that is hard to deal with and is a heavy burden; many slanders came from these people and a reputation for wisdom, for in each case the bystanders thought that I myself possessed the wisdom that I proved that my interlocutor did not have. What is probable, gentlemen, is that in fact that god is wise and that his oracular response meant that human wisdom is worth little or nothing, and that when he says this man, Socrates, he is using my name as an example, as if he said: "This man among you, mortals, is wisest who, like Socrates, understands that

e

22

b

c

d

e

23

b

---

5. [A curious oath, occasionally used by Socrates, it appears in a longer form in the *Gorgias* (482b) as "by the dog, the god of the Egyptians."]

his wisdom is worthless." So even now I continue this investigation as the gods bade me—and I go around seeking out anyone, citizen or stranger, whom I think wise. Then if I do not think he is, I come to the assistance of the god and show him that he is not wise. Because of this occupation, I do not have the leisure to engage in public affairs to any extent, nor indeed to look after my own, but I live in great poverty because of my service to the god.

c   Furthermore, the young men who follow me around of their own free will, those who have most leisure, the sons of the very rich, take pleasure in hearing people questioned; they themselves often imitate me and try to question others. I think they find an abundance of men who believe they have some knowledge but know little or nothing. The result is that those whom they question are angry, not with

d themselves but with me. They say: "That man Socrates is a pestilential fellow who corrupts the young." If one asks them what he does and what he teaches to corrupt them, they are silent, as they do not know, but, so as not to appear at a loss, they mention those accusations that are available against all philosophers, about "things in the sky and things below the earth," about "not believing in the gods" and "making the worse the stronger argument;" they would not want to tell the truth, that they have been proved to lay claim to knowledge when they know nothing. These

e people are ambitious, violent and numerous; they are continually and convincingly talking about me; they have been filling your ears for a long time with vehement slanders against me. From them Meletus attacked me, and Anytus and Lycon, Meletus being vexed on behalf of the poets, Anytus on behalf of the craftsmen and the politicians, Lycon on behalf of the orators, so that, as I started out by saying, I

24 should be surprised if I could rid you of so much slander in so short a time. That, gentlemen of the jury, is the truth for you. I have hidden or omitted nothing. I know well enough that this very conduct makes me unpopular, and this is proof that what

b I say is true, that such is the slander against me, and that such are its causes. If you look into this either now or later, this is what you will find.

    Let this suffice as a defence against the charges of my earlier accusers. After this I shall try to defend myself against Meletus, that good and patriotic man, as he says he is, and my later accusers. As these are a different lot of accusers, let us again take up their sworn deposition. It goes something like this: Socrates is guilty of corrupting the young and of not believing in the gods in whom the city believes, but in

c other new divinities. Such is their charge. Let us examine it point by point.

    He says that I am guilty of corrupting the young, but I say that Meletus is guilty of dealing frivolously with serious matters, of irresponsibly bringing people into court, and of professing to be seriously concerned with things about none of which he has ever cared, and I shall try to prove that this is so. Come here and tell me,

d Meletus. Surely you consider it of the greatest importance that our young men be as good as possible?[6] — Indeed I do.

    Come then, tell the jury who improves them. You obviously know, in view of your concern. You say you have discovered the one who corrupts them, namely me, and you bring me here and accuse me to the jury. Come, inform the jury and tell them who it is. You see, Meletus, that you are silent and know not what to say. Does this not seem shameful to you and a sufficient proof of what I say, that you have not

    6. [Socrates here drops into his usual method of discussion by question and answer. This, no doubt, is what Plato had in mind, at least in part, when he made him ask the indulgence of the jury if he spoke "in his usual manner."]

been concerned with any of this? Tell me, my good sir, who improves our young
men? — The laws. e

That is not what I am asking, but what person, who has knowledge of the laws to
begin with? — These jurymen, Socrates.

How do you mean, Meletus? Are these able to educate the young and improve
them? — Certainly.

All of them, or some but not others? — All of them.

Very good, by Hera. You mention a great abundance of benefactors. But what
about the audience? Do they improve the young or not? — They do, too. 25

What about the members of Council? — The Councillors, also.

But, Meletus, what about the assembly? Do members of the assembly corrupt the
young, or do they all improve them? —They improve them.

All the Athenians, it seems, make the young into fine good men, except me, and I
alone corrupt them. Is that what you mean? — That is most definitely what I mean.

You condemn me to a great misfortune. Tell me: does this also apply to horses do b
you think? That all men improve them and one individual corrupts them? Or is
quite the contrary true, one individual is able to improve them, or very few, namely
the horse breeders, whereas the majority, if they have horses and use them, corrupt
them? Is that not the case, Meletus, both with horses and all other animals? Of
course it is, whether you and Anytus say so or not. It would be a very happy state of
affairs if only one person corrupted our youth, while the others improved them.

You have made it sufficiently obvious, Meletus, that you have never had any con- c
cern for our youth; you show your indifference clearly; that you have given no
thought to the subjects about which you bring me to trial.

And by Zeus, Meletus, tell us also whether it is better for a man to live among
good or wicked fellow-citizens. Answer, my good man, for I am not asking a difficult question. Do not the wicked do some harm to those who are ever closest to
them, whereas good people benefit them? — Certainly.

And does the man exist who would rather be harmed than benefited by his associ- d
ates? Answer, my good sir, for the law orders you to answer. Is there any man who
wants to be harmed? — Of course not.

Come now, do you accuse me here of corrupting the young and making them
worse deliberately or unwillingly? — Deliberately.

What follows, Meletus? Are you so much wiser at your age than I am at mine that
you understand that wicked people always do some harm to their closest
neighbours while good people do them good, but I have reached such a pitch of ig- e
norance that I do not realize this, namely that if I make one of my associates wicked
I run the risk of being harmed by him so that I do such a great evil deliberately, as
you say? I do not believe you, Meletus, and I do not think anyone else will. Either I
do not corrupt the young or, if I do, it is unwillingly, and you are lying in either 26
case. Now if I corrupt them unwillingly, the law does not require you to bring people to court for such unwilling wrongdoings, but to get hold of them privately, to
instruct them and exhort them; for clearly, if I learn better, I shall cease to do what
I am doing unwillingly. You, however, have avoided my company and were unwilling to instruct me, but you bring me here, where the law requires one to bring those
who are in need of punishment, not of instruction.

And so, gentlemen of the jury, what I said is clearly true: Meletus has never been at all concerned with these matters. Nonetheless tell us, Meletus, how you say that I corrupt the young; or is it obvious from your deposition that it is by teaching them not to believe in the gods in whom the city believes but in other new divinities? Is this not what you say I teach and so corrupt them? — That is most certainly what I do say.

Then by those very gods about whom we are talking, Meletus, make this clearer to me and to the jury: I cannot be sure whether you mean that I teach the belief that there are some gods—and therefore I myself believe that there are gods and am not altogether an atheist, nor am I guilty of that—not, however, the gods in whom the city believes, but others, and that this is the charge against me, that there are others. Or whether you mean that I do not believe in gods at all, and that this is what I teach to others.

— This is what I mean, that you do not believe in gods at all.

You are a strange fellow, Meletus. Why do you say this? Do I not believe, as other men do, that the sun and the moon are gods?

— No by Zeus, jurymen, for he says that the sun is stone, and the moon earth.

My dear Meletus, do you think you are prosecuting Anaxagoras? Are you so contemptuous of the jury and think them so ignorant of letters as not to know that the books of Anaxagoras[7] of Clazomenae are full of those theories, and further, that the young men learn from me what they can buy from time to time for a drachma, at most, in the bookshops, and ridicule Socrates if he pretends that these theories are his own, especially as they are so absurd? Is that, by Zeus, what you think of me, Meletus, that I do not believe that there are any gods?

— That is what I say, that you do not believe in the gods at all.

You cannot be believed, Meletus, even, I think, by yourself. The man appears to me, gentlemen of the jury, highly insolent and uncontrolled. He has made an insolent, violent and unrestrained deposition. He is like one who composed a riddle and is trying it out: "Will the wise Socrates realize that I am jesting and contradicting myself, or shall I deceive him and others?" I think he contradicts himself in the affidavit, as if he said: "Socrates is guilty of not believing in the gods but believing in the gods," and surely that is the part of a jester!

Examine with me how he appears to contradict himself, and you, Meletus, answer us. Remember, gentlemen, what I asked you when I began, not to create a disturbance if I proceed in my usual manner.

Does any man, Meletus, believe in human affairs who does not believe in human beings? Make him answer, and not again and again create a disturbance. Does any man who does not believe in horses believe in equine affairs? Or in flute music but not flute-players? No, my good sir, no man could. If you are not willing to answer, I will tell you and the jury. Answer the next question, however. Does any man believe in divine activities who does not believe in divinities? — No one.

Thank you for answering, if reluctantly, when the jury made you. Now you say that I believe in divine activities and teach about them, whether new or old, but at

7. [Anaxagoras of Clazomenae, born about the beginning of the fifth century, came to Athens as a young man and spent time in the pursuit of natural philosophy. He claimed that the universe was directed by Nous (Mind), and that matter was indestructible but always combining in various ways. He left Athens after being prosecuted for impiety.]

any rate divine activities according to what you say, and to this you have sworn in your deposition. But if I believe in divine activities I must quite inevitably believe in divine beings. Is that not so? It is indeed. I shall assume that you agree, as you do not answer. Do we not believe divine beings to be either gods or the children of gods? — Of course.

Then since I do believe in divine beings, as you admit, if divine beings are gods, this is what I mean when I say you speak in riddles and in jest, as you state that I do not believe in gods and then again that I do, since I believe in divine beings. If on the other hand the divine beings are children of the gods, bastard children of the gods by nymphs or some other mothers, as they are said to be, what man would believe children of the gods to exist, but not gods? That would be just as absurd as to believe the young of horses and asses, namely mules, to exist, but not to believe in the existence of horses and asses. You must have made this deposition, Meletus, either to test us or because you were at a loss to find any true wrongdoing of which to accuse me. There is no way in which you could persuade anyone of even small intelligence that it is not the part of one and the same man to believe in the activities of divine beings and gods, and then again the part of one and the same man not to believe in the existence of divinities and gods and heroes.

I do not think, gentlemen of the jury, that it requires a prolonged defence to prove that I am not guilty of the charges in Meletus' deposition, but this is sufficient. On the other hand, you know that what I said earlier is true, that I am very unpopular with many people. This will be my undoing, if I am undone, not Meletus or Anytus but the slanders and envy of many people. This has destroyed many and will, I think, continue to do so. There is no danger that it will stop at me.

Someone might say: "Are you not ashamed, Socrates, to have followed the kind of occupation that has led to your being now in danger of death?" However, I should be right to reply to him: "You are wrong, sir, if you think that a man who is any good at all should take into account the risk of life or death; he should look to this only in his actions, whether what he does is right or wrong, whether he is acting like a good or a bad man." According to your view, all the heroes who died at Troy were inferior people, especially the son of Thetis who was so contemptuous of danger compared with disgrace.[8] When he was eager to kill Hector, his goddess mother warned him, as I believe, in some such words as these: "My child, if you avenge the death of your comrade, Patroclus, and you kill Hector, you will die yourself, for your death is to follow immediately after Hector's." Hearing this, he despised death and danger and was much more afraid to live a coward who did not avenge his friends. "Let me die at once," he said, "when once I have given the wrongdoer his deserts, rather than remain here, a laughingstock by the curved ships, a burden upon the earth." Do you think he gave thought to death and danger?

This is the truth of the matter, gentlemen of the jury: wherever a man has taken a position that he believes to be best, or has been placed by his commander, there he must I think remain and face danger, without a thought for death or anything else, rather than disgrace. It would have been a dreadful way to behave, gentlemen of the jury, if, at Potidaea, Amphipolis and Delium, I had, at the risk of death, like anyone else, remained at my post where those you had elected to command had ordered me, and then, when the god ordered me, as I thought and believed, to live the life of a philosopher, to examine myself and others, I had abandoned my post for fear of

8. [The scene between Thetis and Achilles is from the *Iliad* (18, 94ff.).]

29   death or anything else. That would have been a dreadful thing, and then I might truly have justly been brought here for not believing in the gods, disobeying the oracle, fearing death, and thinking I was wise when I was not. To fear death, gentlemen, is no other than to think oneself wise when one is not, to think one knows what one does not know. No one knows whether death may not be the greatest of all blessings for a man, yet men fear it as if they knew that it is the greatest of evils. And

b   surely it is the most blameworthy ignorance to believe that one knows what one does not know. It is perhaps on this point and in this respect, gentlemen, that I differ from the majority of men, and if I were to claim that I am wiser than anyone in anything, it would be in this, that, as I have no adequate knowledge of things in the underworld, so I do not think I have. I do know, however, that it is wicked and shameful to do wrong, to disobey one's superior, be he god or man. I shall never fear or avoid things of which I do not know, whether they may not be good rather than things that I know to be bad. Even if you acquitted me now and did not believe

c   Anytus, who said to you that either I should not have been brought here in the first place, or that now I am here, you cannot avoid executing me, for if I should be acquitted, your sons would practise the teachings of Socrates and all be thoroughly corrupted. If you said to me in this regard: "Socrates, we do not believe Anytus now; we acquit you, but only on condition that you spend no more time on this investigation and do not practise philosophy, and if you are caught doing so you will

d   die;" if, as I say, you were to acquit me on those terms, I would say to you: "Gentlemen of the jury, I am grateful and I am your friend, but I will obey the god rather than you, and as long as I draw breath and am able, I shall not cease to practise philosophy, to exhort you and to point out to anyone of you whom I happen to meet: Good Sir, you are an Athenian, a citizen of the greatest city with the greatest reputation for both wisdom and power; are you not ashamed of your eagerness to possess

e   as much wealth, reputation and honours as possible, while you do not care for nor give thought to wisdom or truth, or the best possible state of your soul?" Then, if one of you disputes this and says he does care, I shall not let him go at once or leave him, but I shall question him, examine him and test him, and if I do not think he has attained the goodness that he says he has, I shall reproach him because he at-

30   taches little importance to the most important things and greater importance to inferior things, I shall treat in this way anyone I happen to meet, young and old, citizen and stranger, and more so the citizens because you are more kindred to me. Be sure that this is what the god orders me to do, and I think there is no greater blessing for the city than my service to the god. For I go around doing nothing but per-

b   suading both young and old among you not to care for your body or your wealth in preference to or as strongly as for the best possible state of your soul, as I say to you: "Wealth does not bring about excellence, but excellence brings about wealth and all other public and private blessings for men."

Now if by saying this I corrupt the young, this advice must be harmful, but if anyone says that I give different advice, he is talking nonsense. On this point I would say to you, gentlemen of the jury: "Whether you believe Anytus or not, whether you acquit me or not, do so on the understanding that this is my course of

c   action, even if I am to face death many times." Do not create a disturbance, gentlemen, but abide by my request not to cry out at what I say but to listen, for I think it will be to your advantage to listen, and I am about to say other things at which you will perhaps cry out. By no means do this. Be sure that if you kill the sort of man I say I am, you will not harm me more than yourselves. Neither Meletus nor Anytus

can harm me in any way; he could not harm me, for I do not think it is permitted
that a better man be harmed by a worse; certainly he might kill me, or perhaps   d
banish or disfranchise me, which he and maybe others think to be great harm, but I
do not think so. I think he is doing himself much greater harm doing what he is
doing now, attempting to have a man executed unjustly. Indeed, gentlemen of the
jury, I am far from making a defence now on my own behalf, as might be thought,
but on yours, to prevent you from wrongdoing by mistreating the god's gift to you
by condemning me; for if you kill me you will not easily find another like me. I was   e
attached to this city by the god—though it seems a ridiculous thing to say—as upon
a great and noble horse which was somewhat sluggish because of its size and needed
to be stirred up by a kind of gadfly. It is to fulfill some such function that the god
has placed me in the city. I never cease to rouse everyone of you, to persuade and re-   31
proach you all day long and everywhere I find myself in your company.

   Another such man will not easily come to be among you, gentlemen, and if you
believe me you will spare me. You might easily strike out at me as people do when
they are aroused from a doze; if convinced by Anytus you could easily kill me, and
then you could sleep on for the rest of your days, unless the god, in his care for you,
sent you someone else. That I am the kind of person to be a gift of the god to the city   b
you might realize from the fact that it does not seem like human nature for me to
have neglected all my own affairs and to have tolerated this neglect now for so many
years while I was always concerned with you, approaching each one of you like a
father or an elder brother to persuade you to care for virtue. Now if I profited from
this by charging a fee for my advice, there would be some sense to it, but you can
see for yourselves that, for all their shameless accusations, my accusers have not
been able in their impudence to bring forward a witness to say that I have ever   c
received a fee or ever asked for one. I, on the other hand, have a convincing witness
that I speak the truth, my poverty.

   It may seem strange that while I go around and give this advice privately and
interfere in private affairs, I do not venture to go to the assembly and there advise
the city. You have heard me give the reason for this in many places. I have a divine
sign from the god which Meletus has ridiculed in his deposition. This began when I   d
was a child. It is a voice, and whenever it speaks it turns me away from something I
am about to do, but it never encourages me to do anything. This is what has prevented me from taking part in public affairs, and I think it was quite right to prevent me. Be sure, gentlemen of the jury, that if I had long ago attempted to take
part in politics, I should have died long ago, and benefited neither you nor myself.
Do not be angry with me for speaking the truth; no man will survive who genuinely   e
opposes you or any other crowd and prevents the occurrence of many unjust and
illegal happenings in the city. A man who really fights for justice must lead a pri-   32
vate, not a public, life if he is to survive for even a short time.

   I shall give you great proofs of this, not words but what you esteem, deeds. Listen
to what happened to me, that you may know that I will not yield to any man contrary to what is right, for fear of death, even if I should die at once for not yielding.
The things I shall tell you are commonplace and smack of the lawcourts, but they
are true. I have never held any other office in the city, but I served as a member of   b
the Council, and our tribe was presiding at the time when you wanted to try as a
body the ten generals who had failed to pick up the survivors of the naval battle.[9]

9. [This was the battle of Arginusae (south of Lesbos) in 406 B.C., the last Athenian victory of the war.

This was illegal, as you all recognized later. I was the only member of the presiding committee to oppose your doing something contrary to the laws, and I voted against it. The orators were ready to prosecute me and take me away, and your shouts were egging them on, but I thought I should run any risk on the side of law and justice rather than join you, for fear of prison or death, when you were engaged in an unjust course.

This happened when the city was still a democracy. When the oligarchy was established, the Thirty[10] summoned me to the Hall, along with four others, and ordered us to bring Leon from Salamis, that he might be executed. They gave many such orders to many people, in order to implicate as many as possible in their guilt. Then I showed again, not in words but in action, that, if it were not rather vulgar to say so, death is something I couldn't care less about, but that my whole concern is not to do anything unjust or impious. That government, powerful as it was, did not frighten me into any wrongdoing. When we left the Hall, the other four went to Salamis and brought in Leon, but I went home. I might have been put to death for this, had not the government fallen shortly afterwards. There are many who will witness to these events.

Do you think I would have survived all these years if I were engaged in public affairs and, acting as a good man must, came to the help of justice and considered this the most important thing? Far from it, gentlemen of the jury, nor would any other man. Throughout my life, in any public activity I may have engaged in, I am the same man as I am in private life. I have never come to an agreement with anyone to act unjustly, neither with anyone else nor with any one of those who they slanderously say are my pupils. I have never been anyone's teacher. If anyone, young or old, desires to listen to me when I am talking and dealing with my own concerns, I have never begrudged this to anyone, but I do not converse when I receive a fee and not when I do not. I am equally ready to question the rich and the poor if anyone is willing to answer my questions and listen to what I say. And I cannot justly be held responsible for the good or bad conduct of these people, as I never promised to teach them anything and have not done so. If anyone says that he has learned anything from me, or that he heard anything privately that the others did not hear, be assured that he is not telling the truth.

Why then do some people enjoy spending considerable time in my company? You have heard why, gentlemen of the jury, I have told you the whole truth. They enjoy hearing those being questioned who think they are wise, but are not. And this is not unpleasant. To do this has, as I say, been enjoined upon me by the god, by means of oracles and dreams, and in every other way that a divine manifestation has ever ordered a man to do anything. This is true, gentlemen, and can easily be established.

If I corrupt some young men and have corrupted others, then surely some of them who have grown older and realized that I gave them bad advice when they were

---

A violent storm prevented the Athenian generals from rescuing their survivors. For this they were tried in Athens and sentenced to death by the assembly. They were tried in a body, and it is this to which Socrates objected in the Council's presiding committee which prepared the business of the assembly. He obstinately persisted in his opposition, in which he stood alone, and was overruled by the majority. Six generals who were in Athens were executed.]

10. [This was the harsh oligarchy that was set up after the final defeat of Athens in 404 B.C. and that ruled Athens for some nine months in 404-3 before the democracy was restored.]

young should now themselves come up here to accuse me and avenge themselves. If they were unwilling to do so themselves, then some of their kindred, their fathers or brothers or other relations should recall it now if their family had been harmed by me. I see many of these present here, first Crito, my contemporary and fellow demesman, the father of Critoboulos here; next Lysanias of Sphettus, the father of Aeschines here; also Antiphon the Cephisian, the father of Epigenes; and others whose brothers spent their time in this way, Nicostratus, the son of Theozotides, brother of Theodotus, and Theodotus has died so he could not influence him; Paralios here, son of Demodocus, whose brother was Theages; there is Adeimantus, son of Ariston, brother of Plato here; Acantidorus, brother of Apollodorus here.

I could mention many others, some one of whom surely Meletus should have brought in as witness in his own speech. If he forgot to do so, then let him do it now; I will yield time if he has anything of the kind to say. You will find quite the contrary, gentlemen. These men are all ready to come to the help of the corruptor, the man who has harmed their kindred, as Meletus and Anytus say. Now those who were corrupted might well have reason to help me, but the uncorrupted, their kindred who are older men, have no reason to help me except the right and proper one, that they know that Meletus is lying and that I am telling the truth.

Very well, gentlemen of the jury. This, and maybe other similar things, is what I have to say in my defence. Perhaps one of you might be angry as he recalls that when he himself stood trial on a less dangerous charge, he begged and implored the jury with many tears, that he brought his children and many of his friends and family into court to arouse as much pity as he could, but that I do none of these things, even though I may seem to be running the ultimate risk. Thinking of this, he might feel resentful and angry and cast his vote in anger. If there is such a one among you—I do not deem there is, but if there is—I think it would be right to say in reply: "My good sir, I too have a household and, in Homer's phrase, I am not born from 'oak or rock' but from men, so that I have a family, indeed three sons, gentlemen of the jury, of whom one is an adolescent while two are children. Nevertheless, I will not beg you to acquit me by bringing them here. Why do I do none of these things? Not through arrogance, gentlemen, nor through lack of respect for you. Whether I am brave in the face of death is another matter, but with regard to my reputation and yours and that of the whole city, it does not seem right to me to do these things, especially at my age and with my reputation. For it is generally believed, whether it be true or false, that in certain respects Socrates is superior to the majority of men. Now if those of you who are considered superior, be it in wisdom or courage or whatever other virtue makes them so, are seen behaving like that, it would be a disgrace. Yet I have often seen them do this sort of thing when standing trial, men who are thought to be somebody, doing amazing things as if they thought it a terrible thing to die, and as if they were to be immortal if you did not execute them. I think these men bring shame upon the city so that a stranger, too, would assume that those who are outstanding in virtue among the Athenians, whom they themselves select from themselves to fill offices of state and receive other honours, are in no way better than women. You should not act like that, gentlemen of the jury, those of you who have any reputation at all, and if we do, you should not allow it. You should make it very clear that you will more readily convict a man who performs these pitiful dramatics in court and so makes the city a laughingstock, than a man who keeps quiet.

Quite apart from the question of reputation, gentlemen, I do not think it right to
c   supplicate the jury and to be acquitted because of this, but to teach and persuade
them. It is not the purpose of a juryman's office to give justice as a favour to
whomever seems good to him, but to judge according to law, and this he has sworn
to do. We should not accustom you to perjure yourselves, nor should you make a
habit of it. This is irreverent conduct for either of us.

Do not deem it right for me, gentlemen of the jury, that I should act towards you
d   in a way that I do not consider to be good or just or pious, especially, by Zeus, as I
am being prosecuted by Meletus here for impiety; clearly, if I convinced you by my
supplication to do violence to your oath of office, I would be teaching you not to believe in the gods, and my defence would convict me of not believing in them. This is
far from being the case, gentlemen, for I do believe in them as none of my accusers
do. I leave it to you and the god to judge me in the way that will be best for me and
for you.

[The jury now gives its verdict of guilty, and Meletus asks for the penalty of death.]

e   There are many other reasons for my not being angry with you for convicting me,
gentlemen of the jury, and what happened was not unexpected. I am much more
36   surprised at the number of votes cast on each side, for I did not think the decision
would be by so few votes but by a great many. As it is, a switch of only thirty votes
would have acquitted me. I think myself that I have been cleared on Meletus'
charges, and it is clear to all that, if Anytus and Lycon had not joined him in accus-
b   ing me, he would have been fined a thousand drachmas for not receiving a fifth of
the votes.

He assesses the penalty at death. What counter-assessment should I propose to you,
gentlemen of the jury? Clearly it should be a penalty I deserve, and what do I deserve
to suffer or to pay because I have deliberately not led a quiet life but have neglected
what occupies most people: wealth, household affairs, the position of general or public
orator or the other offices, the political clubs and factions that exist in the city? I
thought myself too honest to survive if I occupied myself with those things. I did not
c   follow that path that would have made me of no use either to you or to myself, but I
went to each of you privately and conferred upon him what I say is the greatest
benefit, by persuading him not to care for any of his belongings before caring that he
himself should be as good and as wise as possible, not to care for the city's possessions
d   more than for the city itself, and to care for other things in the same way. What do I
deserve for being such a man? Some good, gentlemen of the jury, if I must truly make
an assessment according to my deserts, and something suitable. What is suitable for a
poor benefactor who needs leisure to exhort you? Nothing is more suitable, gentlemen, than for such a man to be fed in the Prytaneum,[11] much more suitable for him
than for anyone of you who has won a victory at Olympia with a pair or a team of
e   horses. The Olympian victor makes you think yourself happy, I make you be happy.
Besides, he does not need food, but I do. So if I must make a just assessment of what I
37   deserve, I assess it at this: free meals in the Prytaneum.

When I say this you may think, as when I spoke of appeals to pity and entreaties,
that I speak arrogantly, but that is not the case, gentlemen of the jury, rather it is

---

11. [The Prytaneum was the magistrates' hall or town hall of Athens in which public entertainments
were given, particularly to Olympian victors on their return home.]

like this: I am convinced that I never willingly wrong anyone, but I am not convincing you of this, for we have talked together but a short time. If it were the law with us, as it is elsewhere, that a trial for life should not last one but many days, you would be convinced, but now it is not easy to dispel great slanders in a short time. Since I am convinced that I wrong no one, I am not likely to wrong myself, to say that I deserve some evil and to make some such assessment against myself. What should I fear? That I should suffer the penalty Meletus has assessed against me, of which I say I do not know whether it is good or bad? Am I then to choose in preference to this something that I know very well to be an evil and assess the penalty at that? Imprisonment? Why should I live in prison, always subjected to the ruling magistrates? A fine, and imprisonment until I pay it? That would be the same thing for me, as I have no money. Exile? For perhaps you might accept that assessment.

I should have to be inordinately fond of life, gentlemen of the jury, to be so unreasonable as to suppose that other men will easily tolerate my company and conversation when you, my fellow citizens, have been unable to endure them, but found them a burden and resented them so that you are now seeking to get rid of them. Far from it, gentlemen. It would be a fine life at my age to be driven out of one city after another, for I know very well that wherever I go the young men will listen to my talk as they do here. If I drive them away, they will themselves persuade their elders to drive me out; if I do not drive them away, their fathers and relations will drive me out on their behalf.

Perhaps someone might say: But Socrates, if you leave us will you not be able to live quietly, without talking? Now this is the most difficult point on which to convince some of you. If I say that it is impossible for me to keep quiet because that means disobeying the god, you will not believe me and will think I am being ironical. On the other hand, if I say that it is the greatest good for a man to discuss virtue every day and those other things about which you hear me conversing and testing myself and others, for the unexamined life is not worth living for man, you will believe me even less.

What I say is true, gentlemen, but it is not easy to convince you. At the same time, I am not accustomed to think that I deserve any penalty. If I had money, I would assess the penalty at the amount I could pay, for that would not hurt me, but I have none, unless you are willing to set the penalty at the amount I can pay, and perhaps I could pay you one mina of silver.[12] So that is my assessment.

Plato here, gentlemen of the jury, and Crito and Critoboulus and Apollodorus bid me put the penalty at thirty minae, and they will stand surety for the money. Well then, that is my assessment, and they will be sufficient guarantee of payment.

[The jury now votes again and sentences Socrates to death.]

It is for the sake of a short time, gentlemen of the jury, that you will acquire the reputation and the guilt, in the eyes of those who want to denigrate the city, of having killed Socrates, a wise man, for they will say that I am wise even if I am not. If you had waited but a little while, this would have happened of its own accord. You see my age, that I am already advanced in years and close to death. I am saying this

---

12. [One mina was 100 drachmas, equivalent to, say, twenty-five dollars, though in purchasing power probably five times greater. In any case, a ridiculously small sum under the circumstances.]

d   not to all of you but to those who condemned me to death, and to these same jurors I
       say: Perhaps you think that I was convicted for lack of such words as might have
       convinced you, if I thought I should say or do all I could to avoid my sentence. Far
       from it. I was convicted because I lacked not words but boldness and shamelessness
       and the willingness to say to you what you would most gladly have heard from me,
e   lamentations and tears and my saying and doing many things that I say are unwor-
       thy of me but that you are accustomed to hear from others. I did not think then that
       the danger I ran should make me do anything mean, nor do I now regret the nature
       of my defence. I would much rather die after this kind of defence than live after
       making the other kind. Neither I nor any other man should, on trial or in war, con-
39   trive to avoid death at any cost. Indeed it is often obvious in battle that one could
       escape death by throwing away one's weapons and by turning to supplicate one's
       pursuers, and there are many ways to avoid death in every kind of danger if one will
       venture to do or say anything to avoid it. It is not difficult to avoid death, gentlemen
       of the jury, it is much more difficult to avoid wickedness, for it runs faster than
b   death. Slow and elderly as I am, I have been caught by the slower pursuer, whereas
       my accusers, being clever and sharp, have been caught by the quicker, wickedness.
       I leave you now, condemned to death by you, but they are condemned by truth to
       wickedness and injustice. So I maintain my assessment, and they maintain theirs.
       This perhaps had to happen, and I think it is as it should be.

c   Now I want to prophesy to those who convicted me, for I am at the point when
       men prophesy most, when they are about to die. I say gentlemen, to those who
       voted to kill me, that vengeance will come upon you immediately after my death, a
       vengeance much harder to bear than that which you took in killing me. You did this
       in the belief that you would avoid giving an account of your life, but I maintain that
       quite the opposite will happen to you. There will be more people to test you, whom
d   I now held back, but you did not notice it. They will be more difficult to deal with as
       they will be younger and you will resent them more. You are wrong if you believe
       that by killing people you will prevent anyone from reproaching you for not living
       in the right way. To escape such tests is neither possible nor good, but it is best and
       easiest not to discredit others but to prepare oneself to be as good as possible. With
       this prophecy to you who convicted me, I part from you.

e   I should be glad to discuss what has happened with those who voted for my
       acquittal during the time that the officers of the court are busy and I do not yet have
       to depart to my death. So, gentlemen, stay with me awhile, for nothing prevents us
       from talking to each other while it is allowed. To you, as being my friends, I want to
40   show the meaning of what has occurred. A surprising thing has happened to me,
       judges — you I would rightly call judges. At all previous times my usual mantic sign
       frequently opposed me, even in small matters, when I was about to do something
       wrong, but now that, as you can see for yourselves, I was faced with what one might
       think and what is generally thought to be, the worst of evils, my divine sign has not
b   opposed me, either when I left home at dawn, or when I came into court, or at any
       time that I was about to say something during my speech. Yet in other talks it often
       held me back in the middle of my speaking, but now it has opposed no word or deed
       of mine. What do I think is the reason for this? I will tell you. What has happened to
       me may well be a good thing, and those of us who believe death to be an evil are cer-
       tainly mistaken. I have convincing proof of this, for it is impossible that my custom-
c   ary sign did not oppose me if I was not about to do what was right.

Let us reflect that there is good hope that death is a blessing, for it is one of two things: either the dead are nothing and have no perception of anything, or it is, as we are told, a change for the soul from here to another place. If it is complete lack of perception, like a dreamless sleep, then death would be a great advantage. For I think that if one had to pick out that night during which a man slept soundly and did not dream, put beside it the other nights and days of his life, and then see how many days and nights had been better and more pleasant than that night, not only a private person but the great king would find them easy to count compared with the other days and nights. If death is like this I say it is an advantage, for all eternity would then seem to be no more than a single night. If, on the other hand, death is a change from here to another place, and what we are told is true and all who have died are there, what greater blessing could there be, gentlemen of the jury? If anyone arriving in Hades will have escaped from those who call themselves judges here, and will find those true judges who are said to sit in judgment there, Minos and Radamanthus and Aeacus and Triptolemus and the other demi-gods who have been upright in their own life, would that be a poor kind of change? Again, what would one of you give to keep company with Orpheus and Musaeus, Hesiod and Homer? I am willing to die many times if that is true. It would be a wonderful way for me to spend my time whenever I met Palamedes and Ajax, the son of Telamon, and any other of the men of old who died through an unjust conviction, to compare my experience with theirs. I think it would be pleasant. Most important, I could spend my time testing and examining people there, as I do here, as to who among them is wise, and who thinks he is, but is not.

What would one not give, gentlemen of the jury, for the opportunity to examine the man who led the great expedition against Troy, or Odysseus, or Sisyphus, and innumerable other men and women one could mention. It would be an extraordinary happiness to talk with them, to keep company with them and examine them. In any case, they would certainly not put one to death for doing so. They are happier there than we are here in other respects, and for the rest of time they are deathless, if indeed what we are told is true.

You too must be of good hope as regards death, gentlemen of the jury, and keep this one truth in mind, that a good man cannot be harmed either in life or in death, and that his affairs are not neglected by the gods. What has happened to me now has not happened of itself, but it is clear to me that it was better for me to die now and to escape from trouble. That is why my divine sign did not oppose me at any point. So I am certainly not angry with those who convicted me, or with my accusers. Of course that was not their purpose when they accused and convicted me, but they thought they were hurting me, and for this they deserve blame. This much I ask from them: when my sons grow up, avenge yourselves by causing them the same kind of grief that I caused you, if you think they care for money or anything else more than they care for virtue, or if they think they are somebody when they are nobody. Reproach them as I reproach you, that they do not care for the right things and think they are worthy when they are not worthy of anything. If you do this, I shall have been justly treated by you, and my sons also.

Now the hour to part has come. I go to die, you go to live. Which of us goes to the better lot is known to no one, except the god.

CRITO

43   SOCRATES: Why have you come so early, Crito? Or is it not still early?

CRITO: It certainly is.

S: How early?

C: Early dawn.

S: I am surprised that the warder was willing to listen to you.

C: He is quite friendly to me by now, Socrates. I have been here often and I have given him something.

S: Have you just come, or have you been here for some time?

C: A fair time.

b   S: Then why did you not wake me right away but sit there in silence?

C: By Zeus no, Socrates. I would not myself want to be in distress and awake so long. I have been surprised to see you so peacefully asleep. It was on purpose that I did not wake you, so that you should spend your time most agreeably. Often in the past throughout my life, I have considered the way you live happy, and especially so now that you bear your present misfortune so easily and lightly.

S: It would not be fitting at my age to resent the fact that I must die now.

c   C: Other men of your age are caught in such misfortunes, but their age does not prevent them resenting their fate.

S: That is so. Why have you come so early?

C: I bring bad news, Socrates, not for you, apparently, but for me and all your friends the news is bad and hard to bear. Indeed, I would count it among the hardest.

d   S: What is it? Or has the ship arrived from Delos, at the arrival of which I must die?

C: It has not arrived yet, but it will, I believe, arrive today, according to a message brought by some men from Sunium, where they left it. This makes it obvious that it will come today, and that your life must end tomorrow.

S: May it be for the best. If it so please the gods, so be it. However, I do not think it will arrive today.

44   C: What indication have you of this?

S: I will tell you. I must die the day after the ship arrives.

C: That is what those in authority say.

S: Then I do not think it will arrive on this coming day, but on the next. I take to witness of this a dream I had a little earlier during this night. It looks as if it was the right time for you not to wake me.

C: What was your dream?

S: I thought that a beautiful and comely woman dressed in white approached

Reprinted from *The Trial & Death of Socrates*, translated by G.M.A. Grube (Indianapolis: Hackett Publishing Company, 1975), by permission of the publisher.

me. She called me and said: "Socrates, may you arrive at fertile Phthia[1] on the third   b
day."

C: A strange dream, Socrates.

S: But it seems clear enough to me, Crito

C: Too clear it seems, my dear Socrates, but listen to me even now and be
saved. If you die, it will not be a single misfortune only for me. Not only will I be
deprived of a friend, the like of whom I shall never find again, but many people who
do not know you or me very well will think that I could have saved you if I were   c
willing to spend money, but that I did not care to do so. Surely there can be no
worse reputation than to be thought to value money more highly than one's friends,
for the majority will not believe that you yourself were not willing to leave prison
while we were eager for you to do so.

S: My good Crito, why should we care so much for what the majority think?
The most reasonable people, to whom one should pay more attention, will believe
that things were done as they were done.

C: You see, Socrates, that one must also pay attention to the opinion of the ma-   d
jority. Your present situation makes clear that the majority can inflict not the least
but pretty well the greatest evils if one is slandered among them.

S: Would that the majority could inflict the greatest evils, for they would then
be capable of the greatest good, and that would be fine, but now they cannot do
either. They cannot make a man either wise or foolish, but they inflict things
haphazardly.

C: That may be so. But tell me this, Socrates, are you anticipating that I and   e
your other friends would have trouble with the informers if you escape from here, as
having stolen you away, and that we should be compelled to lose all our property or
pay heavy fines and suffer other punishment besides? If you have any such fear,   45
forget it. We would be justified in running this risk to save you, and worse, if necessary. Do follow my advice, and do not act differently.

S: I do have these things in mind, Crito, and also many others.

C: Have no such fear. It is not much money that some people require to save you
and get you out of here. Further, do you not see that those informers are cheap, and
that not much money would be needed to deal with them? My money is available and
is, I think, sufficient. If, because of your affection for me, you feel you should not spend   b
any of mine, there are those strangers here ready to spend money. One of them, Sim-
mias the Theban, has brought enough for this very purpose. Cebes, too, and a good
many others. So, as I say, do not let this fear make you hesitate to save yourself, nor let
what you said in court trouble you, that you would not know what to do with yourself
if you left Athens, for you would be welcomed in many places to which you might go.
If you want to go to Thessaly, I have friends there who will greatly appreciate you and   c
keep you safe, so that no one in Thessaly will harm you.

Besides, Socrates, I do not think that what you are doing is right, to give up your
life when you can save it, and to hasten your fate as your enemies would hasten it,

1. [A quotation from the ninth book of the *Iliad* (363). Achilles has rejected all the presents of
Agamemnon for him to return to the battle, and threatens to go home. He says his ships will sail in the
morning, and with good weather he might arrive on the third day "in fertile Phthia" (which is his
home). The dream means, obviously, that on the third day Socrates' soul, after death, will find its home.
As always, counting the first member of a series, the third day is the day after tomorrow. — G.M.A.G.]

d and indeed have hastened it in their wish to destroy you. Moreover, I think you are betraying your sons by going away and leaving them, when you could bring them up and educate them. You thus show no concern for what their fate may be. They will probably have the usual fate of orphans. Either one should not have children, or one should share with them to the end the toil of upbringing and education. You seem to me to choose the easiest path, whereas one should choose the path a good and courageous man would choose, particularly when one claims throughout one's life to care for virtue.

e I feel ashamed on your behalf and on behalf of us, your friends, lest all that has happened to you be thought due to cowardice on our part: the fact that your trial came to court when it need not have done so, the handling of the trial itself, and now this absurd ending which will be thought to have got beyond our control through some
46 cowardice and unmanliness on our part, since we did not save you, or you save yourself, when it was possible and could be done if we had been of the slightest use. Consider, Socrates, whether this is not only evil, but shameful, both for you and for us. Take counsel with yourself, or rather the time for counsel is past and the decision should have been taken, and there is no further opportunity, for this whole business must be ended tonight. If we delay now, then it will no longer be possible, it will be too late. Let me persuade you on every count, Socrates, and do not act otherwise.

S: My dear Crito, your eagerness is worth much if it should have some right aim;
b if not, then the greater your keenness the more difficult it is to deal with. We must therefore examine whether we should act in this way or not, as not only now but at all times I am the kind of man who listens only to the argument that on reflection seems best to me. I cannot, now that this fate has come upon me, discard the arguments I used; they seem to me much the same. I value and respect the same principles as
c before, and if we have no better arguments to bring up at this moment, be sure that I shall not agree with you, not even if the power of the majority were to frighten us with more bogeys, as if we were children, with threats of incarcerations and executions and confiscation of property. How should we examine this matter most reasonably? Would it be by taking up first your argument about the opinions of men, whether it is sound in every case that one should pay attention to some opinions, but not to others? Or was
d that well-spoken before the necessity to die came upon me, but now it is clear that this was said in vain for the sake of argument, that it was in truth play and nonsense? I am eager to examine together with you, Crito, whether this argument will appear in any way different to me in my present circumstances, or whether it remains the same, whether we are to abandon it or believe it. It was said on every occasion by those who thought they were speaking sensibly, as I have just now been speaking, that one
e should greatly value some people's opinions, but not others. Does that seem to you a sound statement?

You, as far as a human being can tell, are exempt from the likelihood of dying
47 tomorrow, so the present misfortune is not likely to lead you astray. Consider then, do you not think it a sound statement that one must not value all the opinions of men, but some and no others, nor the opinions of all men, but those of some and not of others? What do you say? Is this not well said?

C: It is.

S: One should value the good opinions, and not the bad ones?

C: Yes.

S: The good opinions are those of wise men, the bad ones those of foolish men?

C: Of course.

S: Come then, what of statements such as this: Should a man professionally
engaged in physical training pay attention to the praise and blame and opinion of   b
any man, or to those of one man only, namely a doctor or trainer?

C: To those of one only.

S: He should therefore fear the blame and welcome the praise of that one man,
and not those of the many?

C: Obviously.

S: He must then act and exercise, eat and drink in the way the one, the trainer
and the one who knows, thinks right, not all the others?

C: That is so.

S: Very well. And if he disobeys the one, disregards his opinion and his praises   c
while valuing those of the many who have no knowledge, will he not suffer harm?

C: Of course.

S: What is that harm, where does it tend, and what part of the man who disobeys does it affect?

C: Obviously the harm is to his body, which it ruins.

S: Well said. So with other matters, not to enumerate them all, and certainly
with actions just and unjust, shameful and beautiful, good and bad, about which we
are now deliberating, should we follow the opinion of the many and fear it, or that of
the one, if there is one who has knowledge of these things and before whom we feel   d
fear and shame more than before all the others. If we do not follow his directions, we
shall harm and corrupt that part of ourselves that is improved by just actions and
destroyed by unjust actions. Or is there nothing in this?

C: I think there certainly is, Socrates.

S: Come now, if we ruin that which is improved by health and corrupted by
disease by not following the opinions of those who know, is life worth living for us
when that is ruined? And that is the body, is it not?   e

C: Yes.

S: And is life worth living with a body that is corrupted and in bad condition?

C: In no way.

S: And is life worth living for us with that part of us corrupted that unjust
action harms and just action benefits? Or do we think that part of us, whatever it is,
that is concerned with justice and injustice, is inferior to the body?   48

C: Not at all.

S: It is more valuable?

C: Much more.

S: We should not then think so much of what the majority will say about us,
but what he will say who understands justice and injustice, the one, that is, and the
truth itself. So that, in the first place, you were wrong to believe that we should care
for the opinion of the many about what is just, beautiful, good, and their opposites.
"But," someone might say, "the many are able to put us to death."

C: That too is obvious, Socrates, and someone might well say so.   b

S: And, my admirable friend, that argument that we have gone through remains, I think, as before. Examine the following statement in turn as to whether it

stays the same or not, that the most important thing is not life, but the good life.

C: It stays the same.

S: And that the good life, the beautiful life, and the just life are the same; does that still hold, or not?

C: It does hold.

S: As we have agreed so far, we must examine next whether it is right for me to try to get out of here when the Athenians have not acquitted me. If it is seen to be right, we will try to do so; if it is not, we will abandon the idea. As for those questions you raise about money, reputation, the upbringing of children, Crito, those considerations in truth belong to those people who easily put men to death and would bring them to life again if they could, without thinking; I mean the majority of men. For us, however, since our argument leads to this, the only valid consideration, as we were saying just now, is whether we should be acting rightly in giving money and gratitude to those who will lead me out of here, and ourselves helping with the escape, or whether in truth we shall do wrong in doing all this. If it appears that we shall be acting unjustly, then we have no need at all to take into account whether we shall have to die if we stay here and keep quiet, or suffer in another way, rather than do wrong.

C: I think you put that beautifully, Socrates, but see what we should do.

S: Let us examine the question together, my dear friend, and if you can make any objection while I am speaking, make it and I will listen to you, but if you have no objection to make, my dear Crito, then stop now from saying the same thing so often, that I must leave here against the will of the Athenians. I think it important to persuade you before I act, and not to act against your wishes. See whether the start of our enquiry is adequately stated, and try to answer what I ask you in the way you think best.

C: I shall try.

S: Do we say that one must never in any way do wrong willingly, or must one do wrong in one way and not in another? Is to do wrong never good or admirable, as we have agreed in the past, or have all these former agreements been washed out during the last few days? Have we at our age failed to notice for some time that in our serious discussions we were no different from children? Above all, is the truth such as we used to say it was, whether the majority agree or not, and whether we must still suffer worse things than we do now, or will be treated more gently, that nonetheless, wrongdoing is in every way harmful and shameful to the wrongdoer? Do we say so or not?

C: We do.

S: So one must never do wrong.

C: Certainly not.

S: Nor must one, when wronged, inflict wrong in return, as the majority believe, since one must never do wrong.

C: That seems to be the case.

S: Come now, should one injure anyone or not, Crito?

C: One must never do so.

S: Well then, if one is oneself injured, is it right, as the majority say, to inflict an injury in return, or is it not?

C: It is never right.

S: Injuring people is no different from wrongdoing.

C: That is true.

S: One should never do wrong in return, nor injure any man, whatever injury one has suffered at his hands. And Crito, see that you do not agree to this, contrary to your belief. For I know that only a few people hold this view or will hold it, and there is no common ground between those who hold this view and those who do not, but they inevitably despise each other's views. So then consider very carefully whether we have this view in common, and whether you agree, and let this be the basis of our deliberation, that neither to do wrong or to return a wrong is ever right, not even to injure in return for an injury received. Or do you disagree and do not share this view as a basis for discussion? I have held it for a long time and still hold it now, but if you think otherwise, tell me now. If, however, you stick to our former opinion, then listen to the next point.

C: I stick to it and agree with you. So say on.

S: Then I state the next point, or rather I ask you: when one has come to an agreement that is just with someone, should one fulfill it or cheat on it?

C: One should fulfill it.

S: See what follows from this: if we leave here without the city's permission, are we injuring people whom we should least injure? And are we sticking to a just agreement, or not?

C: I cannot answer your question, Socrates. I do not know.

S: Look at it this way. If, as we were planning to run away from here, or whatever one should call it, the laws and the state came and confronted us and asked: "Tell me, Socrates, what are you intending to do? Do you not by this action you are attempting intend to destroy us, the laws, and indeed the whole city, as far as you are concerned? Or do you think it possible for a city not to be destroyed if the verdicts of its courts have no force but are nullified and set at naught by private individuals?" What shall we answer to this and other such arguments? For many things could be said, especially by an orator on behalf of this law we are destroying, which orders that the judgments of the courts shall be carried out. Shall we say in answer, "The city wronged me, and its decision was not right." Shall we say that, or what?

C: Yes, by Zeus, Socrates, that is our answer.

S: Then what if the laws said: "Was that the agreement between us, Socrates, or was it to respect the judgments that the city came to?" And if we wondered at their words, they would perhaps add: "Socrates, do not wonder at what we say but answer, since you are accustomed to proceed by question and answer. Come now, what accusation do you bring against us and the city, that you should try to destroy us? Did we not, first, bring you to birth, and was it not through us that your father married your mother and begat you? Tell us, do you find anything to criticize in those of us who are concerned with marriage?" And I would say that I do not criticize them. "Or in those of us concerned with the nurture of babies and the education that you too received? Were those assigned to that subject not right to instruct your father to educate you in the arts and in physical culture?" And I would say that they were right. "Very well," they would continue, "and after you were born and nurtured and educated, could you, in the first place, deny that you are our

offspring and servant, both you and your forefathers? If that is so, do you think that
we are on an equal footing as regards the right, and that whatever we do to you it is
right for you to do to us? You were not on an equal footing with your father as regards the right, nor with your master if you had one, so as to retaliate for anything
51   they did to you, to revile them if they reviled you, to beat them if they beat you, and
so with many other things. Do you think you have this right to retaliation against
your country and its laws? That if we undertake to destroy you and think it right to
do so, you can undertake to destroy us, as far as you can, in return? And will you say
that you are right to do so, you who truly care for virtue? Is your wisdom such as
not to realize that your country is to be honoured more than your mother, your
father and all your ancestors, that it is more to be revered and more sacred, and that
b   it counts for more among the gods and sensible men, that you must worship it, yield
to it and placate its anger more than your father's? You must either persuade it or
obey its orders, and endure in silence whatever it instructs you to endure, whether
blows or bonds, and if it leads you into war to be wounded or killed, you must obey.
To do so is right, and one must not give way or retreat or leave one's post, but both
c   in war and in courts and everywhere else, one must obey the commands of one's city
and country, or persuade it as to the nature of justice. It is impious to bring violence
to bear against your mother or father, it is much more so to use it against your country." What shall we say in reply, Crito, that the laws speak the truth, or not?

C: I think they do.

S: "Reflect now, Socrates," the laws might say, "that if what we say is true, you
are not treating us rightly by planning to do what you are planning. We have given
d   you birth, nurtured you, educated you, we have given you and all other citizens a
share of all the good things we could. Even so, by giving every Athenian the opportunity, after he has reached manhood and observed the affairs of the city and us the
laws, we proclaim that if we do not please him, he can take his possessions and go
wherever he pleases. Not one of our laws raises any obstacle or forbids him, if he is not
satisfied with us or the city, if one of you wants to go and live in a colony or wants to go
anywhere else, and keep his property. We say, however, that whoever of you remains,
when he sees how we conduct our trials and manage the city in other ways, has in fact
e   come to an agreement with us to obey our instructions. We say that the one who disobeys does wrong in three ways, first because in us he disobeys his parents, also those
who brought him up, and because, in spite of his agreement, he neither obeys us nor, if
we do something wrong, does he try to persuade us to do better. Yet we only propose
52   things, we do not issue savage commands to do whatever we order; we give two alternatives, either to persuade us or to do what we say. He does neither. We do say that
you too, Socrates, are open to those charges if you do what you have in mind; you
would be among not the least but the most guilty of the Athenians." And if I should
say "Why so?" they might well be right to upbraid me and say that I am among the
Athenians who most definitely came to that agreement with them. They might well
b   say: "Socrates, we have convincing proofs that we and the city were congenial to you.
You would not have dwelt here most consistently of all the Athenians if the city had
not been exceedingly pleasing to you. You have never left the city, even to see a
festival, nor for any other reason except military service; you have never gone to stay
in any other city, as people do; you have had no desire to know another city or other
c   laws; we and our city satisfied you.

"So decisively did you choose us and agree to be a citizen under us. Also, you
have had children in this city, thus showing that it was congenial to you. Then at

your trial you could have assessed your penalty at exile if you wished, and you are now attempting to do against the city's wishes what you could then have done with her consent. Then you prided yourself that you did not resent death, but you chose, as you said, death in preference to exile. Now, however, those words do not make you ashamed, and you pay no heed to us, the laws, as you plan to destroy us, and you act like the meanest type of slave by trying to run away, contrary to your undertakings and your agreement to live as a citizen under us. First then, answer us on this very point, whether we speak the truth when we say that you agreed, not only in words but by your deeds, to live in accordance with us." What are we to say to that, Crito? Must we not agree?

C: We must, Socrates.

S: "Surely," they might say, "you are breaking the undertakings and agreements that you made with us without compulsion or deceit, and under no pressure of time for deliberation. You have had seventy years during which you could have gone away if you did not like us, and if you thought our agreements unjust. You did not choose to go to Sparta or to Crete, which you are always saying are well governed, nor to any other city, Greek or foreign. You have been away from Athens less than the lame or the blind or other handicapped people. It is clear that the city has been outstandingly more congenial to you than to other Athenians, and so have we, the laws, for what city can please without laws? Will you then not now stick to our agreements? You will, Socrates, if we can persuade you, and not make yourself a laughingstock by leaving the city.

"For consider what good you will do yourself or your friends by breaking our agreements and committing such a wrong. It is pretty obvious that your friends will themselves be in danger of exile, disfranchisement and loss of property. As for yourself, if you go to one of the nearby cities—Thebes or Megara, both are well governed—you will arrive as an enemy to their government; all who care for their city will look on you with suspicion, as a destroyer of the laws. You will also strengthen the conviction of the jury that they passed the right sentence on you, for anyone who destroys the laws could easily be thought to corrupt the young and the ignorant. Or will you avoid cities that are well governed and men who are civilized? If you do this, will your life be worth living? Will you have social intercourse with them and not be ashamed to talk to them? And what will you say? The same as you did here, that virtue and justice are man's most precious possession, along with lawful behaviour and the laws? Do you not think that Socrates would appear to be an unseemly kind of person? One must think so. Or will you leave those places and go to Crito's friends in Thessaly? There you will find the greatest license and disorder, and they may enjoy hearing from you how absurdly you escaped from prison in some disguise, in a leather jerkin or some other things in which escapees wrap themselves, thus altering your appearance. Will there be no one to say that you, likely to live but a short time more, were so greedy for life that you transgressed the most important laws? Possibly, Socrates, if you do not annoy anyone, but if you do, many disgraceful things will be said about you.

"You will spend your time ingratiating yourself with all men, and be at their beck and call. What will you do in Thessaly but feast, as if you had gone to a banquet in Thessaly? As for those conversations of yours about justice and the rest of virtue, where will they be? You say you want to live for the sake of your children, that you may bring them up and educate them. How so? Will you bring them up and educate them by taking them to Thessaly and making strangers of them, that they may enjoy that too? Or not so, but they will be better brought up and educated here, while you are alive, though absent? Yes, your friends will look after them. Will they look after them if you go and live in Thessaly, but not if you go away to the underworld? If those who profess themselves your friends are any good at all, one must assume that they will.

"Be persuaded by us who have brought you up, Socrates. Do not value either your children or your life or anything else more than goodness, in order that when you arrive in Hades you may have all this as your defence before the rulers there. If you do this deed, you will not think it better or more just or more pious here, nor will any one of your friends, nor will it be better for you when you arrive yonder. As it is, you depart, if you depart, after being wronged not by us, the laws, but by men; but if you depart after shamefully returning wrong for wrong and injury for injury, after breaking your agreement and contract with us, after injuring those you should injure least—yourself, your friends, your country and us—we shall be angry with you while you are still alive, and our brothers, the laws of the underworld, will not receive you kindly, knowing that you tried to destroy us as far as you could. Do not let Crito persuade you, rather than us, to do what he says."

Crito, my dear friend, be assured that these are the words I seem to hear, as the Corybants hear the music of their flutes, and the echo of these words resounds in me, and makes it impossible for me to hear anything else. As far as my present beliefs go, if you speak in opposition to them, you will speak in vain. However, if you think you can accomplish anything, speak.

C: I have nothing to say, Socrates.

S: Let it be then, Crito, and let us act in this way, since this is the way the god is leading us.

REPUBLIC

BOOK I

I went down to the Piraeus yesterday with Glaucon, the son of Ariston. I intended   327
to say a prayer to the goddess,[1] and I also wanted to see how they would manage
the festival, since this was its first celebration. I thought our own procession was a
fine one and that which the Thracians had sent was no less outstanding. After we   b
had said our prayer and witnessed the procession we started back toward the city.
Polemarchus saw us from a distance as we were setting off for home and he told his
slave to run and bid us wait for him. So the slave caught hold of my cloak from
behind: Polemarchus, he said, bids you wait for him. I turned around and asked
where Polemarchus was. There he is, coming up behind you, he said, please wait
for him. And Glaucon said: All right, we'll wait.

Just then Polemarchus caught up with us. Adeimantus, the brother of Glaucon,[2]   c
was with him, and so were Niceratus, the son of Nicias, and some others, presumably
on their way from the procession.

Then Polemarchus said: Socrates, it looks to me as if you had started on your way
back to the city.

Quite right, said I.

Do you see how many we are? he said.

Of course I do.

Well, he said, you must either be stronger than we are, or you must stay here.

Is there not another alternative, said I, namely that we may persuade you to let
us go?

Could you, said he, persuade men who do not listen?

Not possibly, said Glaucon.

Well, you can take it that we are certainly not going to listen.

Adeimantus intervened: Do you really not know that there is to be a torch race   328
on horseback this evening in honour of the goddess?

Reprinted from *Plato's Republic*, translated by G. M. A. Grube (Indianapolis: Hackett Publishing Company,
1974), by permission of the publisher.

1. ["The goddess" in an Athenian writer, especially when the scene is laid in Athens, usually means Athena,
and it may do so here. However, we know from 354a, and the mention of the Thracians here, that the festival
was that of Bendis, a Thracian goddess whose worship had recently been introduced in the Piraeus, and the
reference may be to her.—G.M.A.G.]

2. [Glaucon and Adeimantus are the brothers of Plato, who is not present. They carry the main burden of
the conversation with Socrates from the beginning of the second book to the end of the work. The scene is the
house of old Cephalus, father of Polemarchus, Lysias, and Euthydemus. Lysias is a well-known writer of
speeches of the late fifth century, and a number of them are extant. He later became the model of the simple
style. He takes no part. We have a dialogue named after Euthydemus. Thrasymachus was a Sophist of the
younger generation, known for his powerful emotional appeals. He is the main objector in the first book, but
after that says very little. The whole discussion is probably supposed to have taken place about 411 B.C.]

On horseback? said I, that is a novelty. Are they going to race on horseback and hand the torches on in relays, or how do you mean?

That's it, said Polemarchus, and there will be an all night festival besides, which will be worth seeing, and which we intend to watch after dinner. We shall be joined

b by many of our young men here and talk with them. So please do stay.

And Glaucon said: It seems that we'll have to stay.

If you think so, said I, then we must.

So we went to the home of Polemarchus, and there we found Lysias and Euthydemus, the brothers of Polemarchus, also Thrasymachus of Chalcedon, Charmantides of Paiania, and Cleitophon the son of Aristonymus. Polemarchus' father Cephalus

c was also in the house. I thought he looked quite old, as I had not seen him for some time. He was sitting on a seat with a cushion, a wreath on his head, for he had been offering a sacrifice in the courtyard. There was a circle of seats there, and we sat down by him.

As soon as he saw me Cephalus welcomed me and said: Socrates, you don't often come down to the Piraeus to see us. You should. If it were still easy for me to walk

d to the city you would not need to come here, we would come to you, but now you should come more often. You should realize that, to the extent that my physical pleasures get feebler, my desire for conversation, and the pleasure I take in it, increase. So be sure to come more often and talk to these youngsters, as you would to good friends and relations.

I replied: Indeed, Cephalus, I do enjoy conversing with men of advanced years.

e As from those who have travelled along a road which we too will probably have to follow, we should enquire from them what kind of a road it is, whether rough and difficult or smooth and easy, and I should gladly learn from you what you think about this, as you have reached the point in life which the poets call "the threshold of old age,"[3] whether it is a difficult part of life, or how your experience would describe it to us.

329 Yes by Zeus, Socrates, he said, I will tell you what I think of old age. A number of us who are more or less the same age often get together in accordance with the old adage.[4] When we meet, the majority of us bemoan their age: they miss the pleasures which were theirs in youth; they recall the pleasures of sex, drink, and feasts, and some other things that go with them, and they are angry as if they were deprived of important things, as if they then lived the good life and now were not

b living at all. Some others deplore the humiliations which old age suffers in the household, and because of this they repeat again and again that old age is the cause of many evils. However, Socrates, I do not think that they blame the real cause. For if old age were the cause, then I should have suffered in the same way, and so would all others who have reached my age. As it is, I have met other old men who do not feel like that, and indeed I was present at one time when someone asked the poet

c Sophocles: "How are you in regard to sex, Sophocles? Can you still make love to a woman?" "Hush man, the poet replied, I am very glad to have escaped from this, like a slave who has escaped from a mad and cruel master." I thought then that he was right, and I still think so, for a great peace and freedom from these things come

---

3. [The phrase occurs several times in Homer (e.g. *Iliad* 22, 60).]

4. [The old saying that like consorts with like.]

with old age: after the tension of one's desires relaxes and ceases, then Sophocles' d
words certainly apply, it is an escape from many mad masters. As regards both sex
and relations in the household there is one cause, Socrates, not old age but the
manner of one's life: if it is moderate and contented, then old age too is but
moderately burdensome; if it is not, then both old age and youth are hard to bear.

I wondered at his saying this and I wanted him to say more, so I urged him on by
saying: Cephalus, when you say this, I don't think most people would agree with e
you; they think you endure old age easily not because of your manner of life but
because you are wealthy, for the wealthy, they say, have many things to encourage
them.

What you say is true, he said. They would not agree. And there is something in
what they say, but not as much as they think. What Themistocles said is quite right:
when a man from Seriphus[5] was insulting him by saying that his high reputation 330
was due to his city and not to himself, he replied that, had he been a Seriphian, he
would not be famous, but neither would the other had he been an Athenian. The
same can be applied to those who are not rich and find old age hard to bear—namely
that a good man would not very easily bear old age in poverty, nor would a bad man,
even if wealthy, be at peace with himself.

Did you inherit most of your wealth, Cephalus, I asked, or did you acquire it?

How much did I acquire, Socrates? As a moneymaker I stand between my grand- b
father and my father. My grandfather and namesake inherited about the same
amount of wealth which I possess but multiplied it many times. My father, Lysanias,
however, diminished that amount to even less than I have now. As for me, I am
satisfied to leave to my sons here no less but a little more than I inherited.

The reason I asked, said I, is that you did not seem to me to be overfond of money,
and this is generally the case with those who have not made it themselves. Those c
who have acquired it by their own efforts are twice as fond of it as other men. Just
as poets love their own poems and fathers love their children, so those who have
made their money are attached to it as something they have made themselves, besides
using it as other men do. This makes them poor company, for they are unwilling to
give their approval to anything but money.

What you say is true, he said.

It surely is, said I. Now tell me this much more: What is the greatest benefit you d
have received from the enjoyment of wealth?

I would probably not convince many people in saying this, Socrates, he said, but
you must realize that when a man approaches the time when he thinks he will die,
he becomes fearful and concerned about things which he did not fear before. It is
then that the stories we are told about the underworld, which he ridiculed before— e
that the man who has sinned here will pay the penalty there—torture his mind lest
they be true. Whether because of the weakness of old age, or because he is now
closer to what happens there and has a clearer view, the man himself is filled with
suspicion and fear, and he now takes account and examines whether he has wronged
anyone. If he finds many sins in his own life, he awakes from sleep in terror, as
children do, and he lives with the expectation of evil. However, the man who knows 331
he has not sinned has a sweet and good hope as his constant companion, a nurse to

---

5. [Seriphus was a small island of little importance.]

his old age, as Pindar too puts it. The poet has expressed this charmingly, Socrates, that whoever lives a just and pious life

> Sweet is the hope that nurtures his heart,
> companion and nurse to his old age,
> a hope which governs the rapidly changing thoughts of mortals.

b This is wonderfully well said. It is in this connection that I would say that wealth has its greatest value, not for everyone but for a good and well-balanced man. Not to have lied to or deceived anyone even unwillingly, not to depart yonder in fear, owing either sacrifices to a god or money to a man: to this wealth makes a great contribution. It has many other uses, but benefit for benefit I would say that its greatest usefulness lies in this for an intelligent man, Socrates.

c Beautifully spoken, Cephalus, said I, but are we to say that justice or right[6] is simply to speak the truth and to pay back any debt one may have contracted? Or are these same actions sometimes right and sometimes wrong? I mean this sort of thing, for example: everyone would surely agree that if a friend has deposited weapons with you when he was sane, and he asks for them when he is out of his mind, you should not return them. The man who returns them is not doing right, nor is one who is willing to tell the whole truth to a man in such a state.

d What you say is correct, he answered.

This then is not a definition of right or justice, namely to tell the truth and pay one's debts.

It certainly is, said Polemarchus interrupting, if we are to put any trust in Simonides.[7]

And now, said Cephalus, I leave the argument to you, for I must go back and look after the sacrifice.

Do I then inherit your role? asked Polemarchus.

You certainly do, said Cephalus laughing, and as he said it he went off to sacrifice.

e Then do tell us, Polemarchus, said I, as the heir to the argument, what it is that Simonides stated about justice which you consider to be correct.

He stated, said he, that it is just to give to each what is owed to him, and I think he was right to say so.

Well now, I said, it is hard not to believe Simonides, for he is a wise and inspired man, but what does he mean? Perhaps you understand him, but I do not. Clearly he does not mean what we were saying just now, that anything he has deposited must be returned to a man who is not in his right mind; yet anything he has deposited 332 is owing to him. Is that not so?—Yes.

---

6. [It should be kept in mind throughout the *Republic* that the Greek word *dikaios* and the noun *dikaiosyne* are often used, as here, in a much wider sense than our word "just" and "justice" by which we must usually translate them. They then mean "right" or "righteous," i.e. good conduct in relation to others, and the opposite *adikia* then has the general sense of wrongdoing.]

7. [Simonides was a well-known lyric and elegiac poet, and author of many epigrams. He died about 468 B.C., around the time of Socrates' birth.]

But it is not to be returned to him at all if he is out of his mind when he asks for it?—That's true.

Certainly Simonides meant something different from this when he says that to return what is owed is just.

He did indeed mean something different by Zeus, said he. He believes that one owes it to one's friends to do good to them, and not harm.

I understand, said I, that one does not give what is owed or due if one gives back gold to a depositor, when giving back and receiving are harmful, and the two are   b
friends. Is that not what you say Simonides meant?—Quite.

Well then, should one give what is due to one's enemies?

By all means, said he, what is in fact due to them, and I believe that is what is properly due from an enemy to an enemy, namely something harmful.

It seems, I said, that Simonides was suggesting the nature of the just poetically and in riddles. For he thought this to be just, to give to each man what is proper to   c
him, and he called this what is due.—Surely.

Then by Zeus, I said, if someone asked him: "Simonides, what does the craft[8] which we call medicine give that is due, and to whom?" What do you think his answer would be?

Clearly, it is the craft which prescribes medicines and food and drink for our bodies.

And what does the craft which we call cooking give that is due and fitting, and to whom?—It adds flavor to food.   d

Very well. What, and to whom, does that craft give which we would call justice?

It must follow from what was said before, Socrates, that it is that which benefits one's friends and harms one's enemies.

He means then that to benefit one's friends and harm one's enemies is justice?— I think so.

And who is most capable of benefiting his friends and harming his enemies in matters of health and disease?—A physician.

And who can do so best when they are sailing and heading into a storm?—A pilot.   e

What about the just man? In what activity and what task is he most able to benefit his friends and harm his enemies?—In waging war and in alliances, I think.

Very well. Now when people are not ill, my dear Polemarchus, the physician is no use to them?—True.

Nor is the pilot when they are not sailing?—That is so.

So to people who are not fighting a war the just man is useless?—I do not think so at all.

Justice then is useful also in peace time?—It is.   333

And so is farming, is it not?—Yes.

For the producing of a harvest?—Yes.

And the cobbler's craft too?—Yes.

I think you would say for getting shoes?—Certainly.

---

8. [By *technē*, here translated "craft," Socrates refers to any art or craft which requires special knowledge.]

Well then, what is it which justice helps one to use or acquire in peace time?—Contracts, Socrates.

By contracts you mean dealings between people, or something else?—That is what I mean.

b   Is the just man a good and useful associate in a game of checkers, or is the checkers player?—The checkers player.

And for putting together bricks and stones, is the just man a better and more useful associate than the builder?—Not at all.

In what kind of dealings then is the just man a better associate than the builder or the musician, as the musician is better than the just man in matters of music?—In money matters, I think.

Except perhaps, Polemarchus, when money is to be used, for whenever one needs to buy or sell a horse together, I think the horse breeder is a more useful associate.
c   Is that not so?—Apparently.

And when one needs to buy a boat, the shipbuilder or the captain of a ship?—So it seems.

In what joint use of silver and gold is the just man a more useful associate than the others?—Whenever one needs to deposit it and keep it safe.

You mean whenever there is no need to use it, but to keep it?—Quite so.

d   So it is whenever money is not being used that justice is useful?—I'm afraid so.

And whenever one needs to keep a pruning knife safe, but not to use it, justice is useful both in associations and in private. When you need to use it, however, it is the craft of vine dressing that is useful.—So it seems.

You will agree then that when one needs to keep a shield or a lyre safe and not use them, justice is a useful thing, but when you need to use them, it is the hoplite's or the musician's craft which is useful.—That necessarily follows.

So with all other things, justice is useless in their use, but useful when they are not in use.—I fear so.

e   In that case, my friend, justice is not a very important thing if it is only useful for things not in use. Let us, however, investigate the following point: is not the man most capable of landing a blow in a fight, be it boxing or any other kind, also the most capable of guarding against blows?—Certainly.

And the man most able to guard against disease is also the man most able to inflict it unnoticed?—So it seems.

334   Further, the same man is a good guardian of a camp who is also able to steal the plans of the enemy and be aware of their actions?—Quite so.

Whenever a man is a good guardian of anything, he is also a good thief of it.—Apparently.

If then the just man is good at guarding money, he is also good at stealing it.—So our argument shows.

The just man then has turned out to be a kind of thief. You may well have learned
b   this from Homer, for he likes Odysseus' maternal grandfather Autolycus, and at the same time he says that he excelled all men in thieving and perjury. It follows that justice, according to you and Homer and Simonides, appears to be a craft of

thieving, of course to the advantage of one's friends and to the harm of one's enemies. Is this not what you meant?

No, by Zeus, he said, I don't any longer know what I meant, but this I still believe to be true, that justice is to benefit one's friends and harm one's enemies.

When you say friends, do you mean those whom a man believes to be helpful to   c
him, or those who are helpful even if they do not appear to be so, and so with enemies?

Probably, he said, one is fond of those whom one thinks to be good and helpful to one, and one hates those whom one considers bad and harmful.

Surely people make mistakes about this, and consider many to be helpful when they are not, and often make the opposite mistake about enemies?—They do.

Then good men are their enemies, and bad people their friends?—Quite so.

And so it is just and right for these mistaken people to benefit the bad and harm   d
the good?—It seems so.

But the good are just and able to do no wrong?—True.

But according to your argument it is just to harm those who do no wrong.

Never, Socrates, he said. It is the argument that is wrong.

It is just to harm the wrongdoers and to benefit the just?

That statement, Socrates, seems much more attractive than the other.

Then, Polemarchus, for many who are mistaken in their judgment it follows that it is just to harm their friends, for these are bad, and to benefit their enemies, who   e
are good, and so we come to a conclusion which is the opposite of what we said was the meaning of Simonides.

That certainly follows, he said, but let us change our assumption; we have probably not defined the friend and the enemy correctly.

Where were we mistaken, Polemarchus?

—When we said that a friend was one who was thought to be helpful.

How shall we change this now? I asked.

Let us state, he said, that a friend is one who is both thought to be helpful and also is; one who is thought to be, but is not, helpful is thought to be a friend but is   335
not. And so also with the enemy.

According to this argument then, the good man will be a friend, and the bad man an enemy.—Yes.

You want us to add to what we said before about the just, namely that it is just to benefit one's friend and harm one's enemy; to this you want us to make an addition and say that it is just to benefit the friend who is good and to harm the enemy who is bad?

Quite so, he said. This seems to me to be well said.   b

But, I said, is it the part of the just man to harm anyone at all?

Why certainly, he said, those who are bad and one's enemies.

Do horses become better or worse when they are harmed?—Worse.

Do they deteriorate in their excellence as dogs or as horses?—As horses.

And when dogs are harmed, they deteriorate in their excellence as dogs, not in that of horses?—Necessarily.

c Shall we not say so about men too, that when they are harmed they deteriorate in their human excellence?—Quite so.

And is not justice a human excellence?—Of course.

Then men who are harmed, my friend, necessarily become more unjust.—So it appears.

Can musicians, by practising music, make men unmusical?—Not possibly.

Or can teachers of horsemanship, by the practice of their craft, make them into non-horsemen?—Impossible.

Well then, can the just, by the practice of justice, make men unjust? Or, in a word, d can good men, by the practice of their virtue, make men bad?—They cannot.

It is not the function of heat to cool things, but the opposite?—Yes.

Nor of dryness to make things wet but the opposite?—Quite so.

And it is not the function of the good to harm people, but the opposite?—It seems so.

And the just man is good?—Certainly.

It is not then the function of the just man, Polemarchus, to do harm to a friend or anyone else, but it is that of his opposite, the unjust man?—I think that you are entirely right, Socrates.

e If, then, anyone tells us that it is just to give everyone his due, and he means by this that from the just man harm is due to his enemies and benefit due to his friends—the man who says that is not wise, for it is not true. We have shown that it is never just to harm anyone.—I agree.

You and I, I said, will therefore together fight anyone who tells us that Simonides said this, or Bias or Pittacus or any other of our wise and blessed men.—Yes, and I am quite willing to join that fight.

336 Do you know, I said, to whom I think this saying belongs, that it is just to benefit one's friends and harm one's enemies?—To whom?

I think Periander said that, or Perdiccas, or Xerxes, or Ismenias of Corinth, or some other wealthy man who believed himself to have great power.[9]—What you say is very true.

Very well, said I. Since neither justice nor the just appears to be that either, what else might one say it is?

b While we were speaking Thrasymachus often started to interrupt, but he was restrained by those who were sitting by him, for they wanted to hear the argument to the end. But when we paused after these last words of mine he could no longer keep quiet. He gathered himself together like a wild beast about to spring, and he came at us as if to tear us to pieces.

Polemarchus and I were afraid and flustered as he roared into the middle of our company: What nonsense have you two been talking, Socrates? Why do you play the c fool in thus giving way to each other? If you really want to know what justice is, don't only ask questions and then score off anyone who answers, and refute him.

---

9. [Bias of Priene in Ionia and Pittacus of Mytilene (both early sixth century) were counted among the seven wise men of Greece. Periander (650–570) was tyrant of Corinth. Perdiccas probably refers to the first king of Macedonia (eighth century) and Xerxes was the king of Persia who invaded Greece in the second Persian war.]

You know very well that it is much easier to ask questions than to answer them. Give an answer yourself and tell us what you say justice is. And don't tell me that it is the needful, or the advantageous, or the beneficial, or the gainful, or the useful, but tell me clearly and precisely what you mean, for I will not accept it if you utter such rubbish.

His words startled me, and glancing at him I was afraid. I think if I had not looked at him before he looked at me, I should have been speechless. As it was I had glanced at him first when our discussion began to exasperate him, so I was able to answer him and I said, trembling: do not be hard on us, Thrasymachus, if we have erred in our investigation, he and I; be sure that we err unwillingly. You surely do not believe that if we were searching for gold we would be unwilling to give way to each other and thus destroy our chance of finding it, but that when searching for justice, a thing more precious than much gold, we mindlessly give way to one another, and that we are not thoroughly in earnest about finding it. You must believe that, my friend, for I think we could not do it. So it is much more seemly that you clever people should pity us than that you should be angry with us.

When he heard that he gave a loud and bitter laugh and said: By Heracles, that is just Socrates' usual irony. I knew this, and I warned these men here before that you would not be willing to answer any questions but would pretend ignorance, and that you would do anything rather than give an answer, if anyone questioned you.

You are clever, Thrasymachus, I said, for you knew very well that if you asked anyone how much is twelve, and as you asked him you warned him: "Do not, my man, say that twelve is twice six, or three times four, or six times two, or four times three, for I will not accept such nonsense," it would be quite clear to you that no one can answer a question asked in those terms. And if he said to you: "What do you mean, Thrasymachus? Am I not to give any of the answers you mention, not even, you strange man, if it happens to be one of those things, but am I to say something which is not the truth, or what do you mean?" What answer would you give him?

Well, he said, do you maintain that the two cases are alike?

They may well be, said I. Even if they are not, but the person you ask thinks they are, do you think him less likely to answer what he believes to be true, whether we forbid him or not?

And you will surely do the same, he said. Will you give one of the forbidden answers?

I shouldn't wonder, said I, if after investigation that was my opinion.

What, he said, if I show you a different answer about justice from all these and a better one? What penalty do you think you should pay then?

What else, said I, but what is proper for an ignorant man to pay? It is fitting for him to learn from one who knows. And that is what I believe I would deserve.

You amuse me, he said. You must not only learn but pay the fee.

Yes, when I have the money, I said.

We have the money, said Glaucon. If it is a matter of money, speak, Thrasymachus, for we shall all contribute for Socrates.

Quite so, said he, so that Socrates can carry on as usual: he gives no answer himself, and then, when someone else does give one, he takes up the argument and refutes it.

My dear man, I said, how could one answer, when in the first place he does not know and does not profess to know, and then, if he has an opinion, an eminent man forbids him to say what he believes? It is much more seemly for you to answer, since 338 you say you know and have something to say. Please do so. Do me that favour, and do not begrudge your teaching to Glaucon and the others.

While I was saying this, Glaucon and the others begged him to speak. It was obvious that Thrasymachus was eager to do so and earn their admiration, and that he thought he had a beautiful answer, but he pretended that he wanted to win his b   point that I should be the one to answer. However, he agreed in the end, and then said: "There you have Socrates' wisdom; he himself is not willing to teach but he goes around learning from others, and then he is not even grateful."

When you say that I learn from others you are right, Thrasymachus, said I, but when you say that I am not grateful, that is not true. I show what gratitude I can, but I can only give praise. I have no money, but how enthusiastically I praise when someone seems to me to speak well is something you will realize quite soon after you have given your answer, for I think you will speak well.

c   Listen then, said he. I say that the just is nothing else than the advantage of the stronger. Well, why don't you praise me? But you will not want to.

I must first understand your meaning, said I, for I do not know it yet. You say that the advantage of the stronger is just. What do you mean, Thrasymachus? Surely you do not mean such a thing as this: Poulydamas, the pancratist athlete, is stronger than we are; it is to his advantage to eat beef to build up his physical strength. Do you mean that this food is also advantageous and just for us who are weaker than d   he is?

You disgust me, Socrates, he said. Your trick is always to take up the argument at the point where you can damage it most.

Not at all, my dear sir, I said, but tell us more clearly what you mean.

Do you not know, he said, that some cities are ruled by a despot, others by the people, and others again by the aristocracy?—Of course.

And this element has the power and rules in every city?—Certainly.

e   Yes, and each government makes laws to its own advantage: democracy makes democratic laws, a despotism makes despotic laws, and so with the others, and when they have made these laws they declare this to be just for their subjects, that is, their own advantage, and they punish him who transgresses the laws as lawless and unjust. 339 This then, my good man, is what I say justice is, the same in all cities, the advantage of the established government, and correct reasoning will conclude that the just is the same everywhere, the advantage of the stronger.

Now I see what you mean, I said. Whether it is true or not I will try to find out. But you too, Thrasymachus, have given as an answer that the just is the advantageous whereas you forbade that answer to me. True, you have added the words "of the stronger."

b   Perhaps, he said, you consider that an insignificant addition!

It is not clear yet whether or not it is significant. Obviously, we must investigate whether what you say is true. I agree that the just is some kind of advantage, but you add that it is the advantage of the stronger. I do not know. We must look into this.—Go on looking, he said.

We will do so, said I. Tell me, do you also say that obedience to the rulers is just?—I do.

And are the rulers in all cities infallible, or are they liable to error?—No doubt they are liable to error.   c

When they undertake to make laws, therefore, they make some correctly and make others incorrectly?—I think so.

"Correctly" means that they make laws to their own advantage, and "incorrectly" not to their own advantage. Or how would you put it?—As you do.

And whatever laws they make must be obeyed by their subjects, and this is just?—Of course.

Then, according to your argument, it is just to do not only what is to the advantage of the stronger, but also the opposite, what is not to their advantage.   d

What is that you are saying? he asked.

The same as you, I think, but let us examine it more fully. Have we not agreed that, in giving orders to their subjects, the rulers are sometimes in error as to what is best for themselves, yet it is just for their subjects to do whatever their rulers order. Is that much agreed?—I think so.

Think then also, said I, that you have agreed that it is just to do what is to the disadvantage of the rulers and the stronger whenever they unintentionally give orders which are bad for themselves, and you say it is just for the others to obey their given orders. Does it not of necessity follow, my wise Thrasymachus, that it is just to do the opposite of what you said? The weaker are then ordered to do what is to the disadvantage of the stronger.   e

Yes by Zeus, Socrates, said Polemarchus, that is quite clear.   340

Yes, if you bear witness for him, interrupted Cleitophon.

What need of a witness? said Polemarchus. Thrasymachus himself agrees that the rulers sometimes give orders that are bad for themselves, and that it is just to obey them.

Thrasymachus maintained that it is just to obey the orders of the rulers, Polemarchus.

He also said that the just was the advantage of the stronger, Cleitophon. Having established those two points he went on to agree that the stronger sometimes ordered the weaker, their subjects, to do what was disadvantageous to themselves. From these agreed premises it follows that what is of advantage to the stronger is no more just than what is not.   b

But, Cleitophon replied, he said that the advantage of the stronger is what the stronger believes to be of advantage to him. This the weaker must do, and that is what he defined the just to be.

That is not how he stated it, said Polemarchus.

It makes no difference, Polemarchus, I said. If Thrasymachus now wants to put it that way, let us accept it. Tell me, Thrasymachus, was this what you intended to say justice is, namely that which appears to the stronger to be to his advantage, whether it is so or not? Shall we say that this is what you mean?   c

Not in the least, said he. Do you think that I would call stronger a man who is in error at the time he errs?

I did think you meant that, said I, when you said that the rulers were not infallible but were liable to error.

d   You are being captious, Socrates, he said. Do you call a man a physician when he is in error in the treatment of patients, at the moment of, and in regard to this very error? Or would you call a man an accountant when he makes a miscalculation at the moment of, and with regard to this miscalculation? I think that we express ourselves in words which, taken literally, do say that the physician is in error, or the accountant, or the grammarian. But each of these, in so far as he is what we call

e   him, never errs, so that, if you use language with precision—and you want to be precise—no practitioner of a craft ever errs. It is when the knowledge of his craft leaves him that he errs, and at that time he is not a practitioner of it. No craftsman,

341   wise man, or ruler is in error at the time that he is a ruler in the precise sense. However, everyone will say that the physician or the ruler is in error. Take it then that this is now my answer to you. To speak with precision, the ruler, in so far as he is a ruler, unerringly decrees what is best for himself and this the subject must do. The just then is, as I said from the first, to do what is advantageous to the stronger.

Very well, Thrasymachus, said I. You think I am captious?

You certainly are, he said.

And you think that it was deliberate trickery on my part to ask you the questions I did ask?

I know it very well, he said, but it will not do you any good, for I would be well

b   aware of your trickery; nor would you have the ability to force my agreement in open debate.

I would not even try, my good sir, I said, but in order to avoid a repetition of this, do define clearly whether it is the ruler in the ordinary or the precise sense whose advantage is to be pursued as that of the stronger.

I mean, he said, the ruler in the most exact sense. Now practise your trickery and your captiousness on this if you can, for I will not let any statement of yours pass, and you certainly won't be able to.

c   Do you think, I said, that I am crazy enough to try to shave a lion or trick Thrasymachus?

You certainly tried just now, he said, though you are no good at it.

Enough of this sort of thing, I said. But tell me: is the physician in the strict sense, whom you mentioned just now, a moneymaker or one who treats the sick? Tell me about the real physician.—He is one who treats the sick, said he.

What about the ship's captain? Is he, to speak correctly, a ruler of sailors or a sailor?—A ruler of sailors.

d   We should not, I think, take into account the fact that he sails in a ship, and we should not call him a sailor, for it is not on account of his sailing that he is called a ship's captain, but because of his craft and his authority over sailors.—True.

And there is something which is advantageous to each of these, that is: patients and sailors?—Certainly.

And is not the purpose of a craft's existence to seek and secure the advantageous in each case?—That's right.

Now is there any other advantage to each craft, except that it be as perfect as

e   possible?—What is the meaning of that question?

It is this, said I. If you asked me whether our body is sufficient unto itself, or has a further need I should answer: "It certainly has needs, and for this purpose the craft of medicine exists and has now been discovered, because the body is defective, not self-sufficient. So to provide it with things advantageous to it the craft of medicine has been developed." Do you think I am correct in saying this or not?—Correct.

Well then, is the craft of medicine itself defective, or is there any other craft which needs some further excellence—as the eyes are in need of sight, the ears of hearing, and, because of this need, they require some other craft to investigate and provide for this?—is there in the craft itself some defect, so that each craft requires another craft which will investigate what is beneficial to it, and then the investigating craft needs another such still, and so ad infinitum? Or does a craft investigate what is beneficial to it, or does it need neither itself nor any other to investigate what is required because of imperfections? There is in fact no defect or error of any kind in any craft, nor is it proper to any craft to seek what is to the advantage of anything but the object of its concern; it is itself pure and without fault, being itself correct, as long as it is wholly itself in the precise sense. Consider this with that preciseness of language which you mentioned. Is it so or otherwise?—It appears to be so.

The craft of medicine, I said, does not seek its own advantage but that of the body.—Yes.

Nor does horse-breeding seek its own advantage but that of horses. Nor does any other craft seek its own advantage—it has no further need—but that of its object.— That seems to be the case.

And surely, Thrasymachus, the crafts govern and have power over their object.

He agreed, but with great reluctance at this point.

No science of any kind seeks or orders its own advantage, but that of the weaker which is subject to it and governed by it.

He tried to fight this conclusion, but he agreed to this too in the end. And after he had, I said: Surely no physician either, in so far as he is a physician, seeks or orders what is advantageous to himself, but to his patient? For we agreed that the physician in the strict sense of the word is a ruler over bodies and not a moneymaker. Was this not agreed?

He said yes.

So the ship's captain in the strict sense is a ruler over sailors, and not a sailor?— That has been agreed.

Does it not follow that the ship's captain and ruler will not seek and order what is advantageous to himself, but to the sailor, his subject.

He agreed, but barely.

So then, Thrasymachus, I said, no other ruler in any kind of government, in so far as he is a ruler, seeks what is to his own advantage or orders it, but that which is to the advantage of his subject who is the concern of his craft; it is this he keeps in view; all his words and actions are directed to this end.

When we reached this point in our argument and it was clear to all that the definition of justice had turned into its opposite, Thrasymachus, instead of answering, said: Tell me, Socrates, do you have a nanny?

What's this? said I. Had you not better answer than ask such questions?

Because, he said, she is letting you go around with a snotty nose and does not wipe it when she needs to, if she leaves you without any knowledge of sheep or shepherds.

What is the particular point of that remark? I asked.

b   You think, he said, that shepherds and cowherds seek the good of their sheep or cattle, whereas their sole purpose in fattening them and looking after them is their own good and that of their master. Moreover, you believe that rulers in the cities, true rulers that is, have a different attitude towards their subjects than one has

c   towards sheep, and that they think of anything else, night and day, than their own advantage. You are so far from understanding the nature of justice and the just, of injustice and the unjust, that you do not realize that the just is really another's good, the advantage of the stronger and the ruler, but for the inferior who obeys it is a personal injury. Injustice on the other hand exercises its power over those who are truly naive and just, and those over whom it rules do what is of advantage to the

d   other, the stronger, and, by obeying him, they make him happy, but themselves not in the least.

You must look at it in this way, my naive Socrates: the just is everywhere at a disadvantage compared with the unjust. First, in their contracts with one another: wherever two such men are associated you will never find, when the partnership ends, the just man to have more than the unjust, but less. Then, in their relation to the city: when taxes are to be paid, from the same income the just man pays more,

e   the other less; but, when benefits are to be received, the one gets nothing while the other profits much; whenever each of them holds a public office, the just man, even if he is not penalized in other ways, finds that his private affairs deteriorate through neglect while he gets nothing from the public purse because he is just; moreover, he is disliked by his household and his acquaintances whenever he refuses them an

344   unjust favour. The opposite is true of the unjust man in every respect. I repeat what I said before: the man of great power gets the better deal. Consider him if you want to decide how much more it benefits him privately to be unjust rather than just. You will see this most easily if you turn your thoughts to the most complete form of injustice which brings the greatest happiness to the wrongdoer, while it makes those whom he wronged, and who are not willing to do wrong, most wretched. This most complete form is despotism; it does not appropriate other people's property little by little, whether secretly or by force, whether public or private, whether sacred

b   objects or temple property, but appropriates it all at once.

When a wrongdoer is discovered in petty cases, he is punished and faces great opprobrium, for the perpetrators of these petty crimes are called temple robbers, kidnappers, housebreakers, robbers, and thieves, but when a man, besides appropri-

c   ating the possessions of the citizens, manages to enslave the owners as well, then, instead of those ugly names he is called happy and blessed, not only by his fellow-citizens but by all others who learn that he has run through the whole gamut of injustice. Those who give injustice a bad name do so because they are afraid, not of practising but of suffering injustice.

And so, Socrates, injustice, if it is on a large enough scale, is a stronger, freer, and more powerful thing than justice and, as I said from the first, the just is what is advantageous to the stronger, while the unjust is to one's own advantage and benefit.

d   Having said this and poured this mass of close-packed words into our ears as a bathman might a flood of water, Thrasymachus intended to leave, but those present did not let him, and made him stay for a discussion of his views. I too begged him to stay and I said: My dear Thrasymachus, after throwing such a speech at us, you want to leave before adequately instructing us or finding out whether you are right or not? Or do you think it a small thing to decide on a whole way of living, which, if each of us adopted it, would make him live the most profitable life? e

Do I think differently? said Thrasymachus.

You seem to, said I, or else you care nothing for us nor worry whether we'll live better or worse, in ignorance of what you say you know. Do, my good sir, show some 345 keenness to teach us. It will not be without value to you to be the benefactor of so many of us. For my own part, I tell you that I do not believe that injustice is more profitable than justice, not even if one gives it full scope and does not put obstacles in its way. No, my friend. Let us assume the existence of an unjust man with every opportunity to do wrong, either because his misdeeds remain secret or because he has the power to battle things through; nevertheless he does not persuade me that injustice is more profitable than justice. Perhaps some other of us feels the same, b and not only I. Come now, my good sir, really persuade us that we are wrong to esteem justice more highly than injustice in planning our life.

And how, said he, shall I persuade you, if you are not convinced by what I said just now? What more can I do? Am I to take my argument and pour it into your mind?

Zeus forbid! Don't you do that, but first stick to what you have said and, if you change your position, do so openly and do not deceive us. You see now, Thrasyma- c chus—let us examine again what went before—that, while you first defined the true physician, you did not think it necessary later to observe the precise definition of the true shepherd, but you think that he fattens sheep, in so far as he is a shepherd, not with what is best for the sheep in mind, but like a guest about to be entertained at a feast, with a banquet in view, or again a sale, like a moneymaker, not a shepherd. The shepherd's craft is concerned only to provide what is best for the object of its d care; as for the craft itself, it is sufficiently provided with all it needs to be at its best, as long as it does not fall short of being the craft of the shepherd. That is why I thought it necessary for us to agree just now that every kind of rule, as far as it truly rules, does not seek what is best for anything else than the subject of its rule and care, and this is true both of public and private kinds of rule. Do you think that e those who rule over cities, the true rulers, rule willingly?—I don't think it, by Zeus, I know it, he said.

Well but, Thrasymachus, said I, do you not realize that in other kinds of rule no one is willing to rule, but they ask for pay, thinking that their rule will benefit not themselves but their subjects. Tell me, does not every craft differ from every other in that it has a different function? Please do not give an answer contrary to what 346 you believe, so that we can come to some conclusion.

Yes, that is what makes it different, he said.

And each craft benefits us in its own particular way, different from the others. For example, medicine gives us health, navigation safety while sailing, and so with the others.—Quite so.

And the craft of earning pay gives us wages, for that is its function. Or would you b call medicine the same craft as navigation? Or, if you wish to define with precision as you proposed, if the ship's captain becomes healthy because sailing benefits his health, would you for that reason call his craft medicine?—Not at all, he said.

Nor would you call wage-earning medicine if someone is healthy while earning wages?—Certainly not.

Nor would you call medicine wage-earning if someone earns pay while healing?—
c   No.

So we agree that each craft brings its own benefit?—Be it so.

Whatever benefit all craftsmen receive in common must then result clearly from some craft which they pursue in common, and so are benefited by it.—It seems so.

We say then that if the practitioners of these crafts are benefited by earning a wage, this results from their practising the wage earning craft.

He reluctantly agreed.

d   So this benefit to each, the receiving of pay, does not result from the practice of their own craft, but if we are to examine this precisely, medicine provides health while the craft of earning provides pay; house building provides a house, and the craft of earning which accompanies it provides a wage, and so with the other crafts; each fulfills its own function and benefits that with which it is concerned. If pay is not added, is there any benefit which the practitioner gets from his craft?—Apparently not.

e   Does he even provide a benefit when he works for nothing?—Yes, I think he does.

Is this not clear now, Thrasymachus, that no craft or rule provides its own advantage, but, as we have been saying for some time, it procures and orders what is of advantage to its subject; it aims at his advantage, that of the weaker, not of the stronger. That is why, my dear Thrasymachus, I said just now that no one willingly
347   wants to rule, to handle and straighten out the affairs of others. They ask for pay because the man who intends to practise his craft well never does what is best for himself, nor, when he gives such orders, does he give them in accordance with his craft, but he pursues the advantage of his subject. For that reason, then, it seems one must provide remuneration if they are to be willing to rule, whether money or honour, or a penalty if he does not rule.

What do you mean, Socrates? said Glaucon. I understand the two kinds of remuneration, but I do not understand what kind of penalty you mean, which you mention under the heading of remuneration.

Then you do not understand the remuneration of the best men, I said, which
b   makes them willing to rule. Do you not know that the love of honour and money are made a reproach, and rightly so?—I know that.

Therefore good men will not be willing to rule for the sake of either money or honour. They do not want to be called hirelings if they openly receive payment for ruling, nor, if they provide themselves with it secretly, to be called thieves. Nor will
c   they do it for honour's sake, for they have no love for it. So, if they are to be willing to rule, some compulsion or punishment must be brought to bear on them. That is perhaps why to seek office willingly, before one must, is thought shameful. Now the greatest punishment is to be ruled by a worse man than oneself if one is not willing to rule. I think it is the fear of this which makes men of good character rule whenever
d   they do. They approach office not as something good or something to be enjoyed, but as something necessary because they cannot entrust it to men better than, or even equal to, themselves. In a city of good men, if there were such, they would probably vie with each other in order not to rule, not, as now, in order to be rulers. There it would be quite clear that the nature of the true ruler is not to seek his own

advantage but that of his subjects, and everyone, knowing this, would prefer to receive benefits rather than take the trouble to benefit others. In this matter I do not at all agree with Thrasymachus that the just is the advantage of the stronger, but we will look into this matter another time. What seems to me of greater importance is what Thrasymachus is saying now, namely that the life of the unjust man is to be preferred to that of the just. Which will you choose, Glaucon, and which of our views do you consider the more truly spoken? e

I certainly think that the life of the just is more profitable.

You have heard, said I, all the blessings of the unjust life which Thrasymachus enumerated just now? 348

I heard, said he, but I am not convinced.

Do you want us to persuade him, if we could find the means to do so, that what he says is not true?

Of course I want it, he said.

If we were to oppose him, I said, with a parallel set speech on the blessings of the just life, then another speech from him in turn, then another from us, we should have to count and measure the blessings mentioned on each side, and we should need some judges to decide the case. If, on the other hand, we investigate the question, as we were doing, by seeking agreement with each other, then we can ourselves be both the judges and the advocates.—Quite so. b

Which method do you prefer? I asked.—The second.

Come then, Thrasymachus, I said, answer us from the beginning. You say that complete injustice is more profitable than complete justice?

I certainly do say that, he said, and I have told you why. c

Well then, what about this: you call one of the two a virtue and the other a vice?—Of course.

That is, you call justice a virtue, and injustice a vice?

Is that likely, my good man, said he, since I say that injustice is profitable, and justice is not?

What then?—The opposite.

Do you call being just a vice?—No, but certainly high-minded foolishness.

And you call being unjust low-minded?—No, I call it good judgment. d

You consider the unjust then, Thrasymachus, to be good and knowledgeable?

Yes, he said, those who are able to carry injustice through to the end, who can bring cities and communities of men under their power. Perhaps you think I mean purse-snatchers? Not that those actions too are not profitable, if they are not found out, but they are not worth mentioning in comparison with what I am talking about.

I am not unaware of what you mean, I said, but this point astonishes me: do you include injustice under virtue and wisdom, and justice among their opposites?—I certainly do. e

That makes it harder, my friend, and it is not easy now to know what to say. If you had declared that injustice was more profitable, but agreed that it was a vice or shameful as some others do, we could have discussed it along the lines of general opinion. Now, obviously, you will say that it is fine and strong, and apply to it all the

349   attributes which we used to apply to justice, since you have been so bold as to include it under virtue and wisdom.—Your guess, he said, is quite right.

We must not, however, shrink from pursuing our argument and looking into this, so long as I am sure that you mean what you say. For I do not think you are joking now, Thrasymachus, but are saying what you believe to be true.

What difference, said he, does it make to you whether I believe it or not? Is it not my argument you are refuting?

No difference, said I, but try to answer this further question: do you think that b   the just man wants to get the better of the just?

Never, said he, for he would not then be well mannered and simple, as he is now.

Does he want to overreach a just action?[10]

Not a just action either, he said.

Would he want to get the better of an unjust man, and would he deem that just or not?

He would want to, he said, and he would deem it right, but he would not be able to.

That was not my question, said I, but whether the just man wants and deems it c   right to outdo not a just man, but an unjust one?—That is so.

What about the unjust man? Would he deem it right to outdo the just man and the just action?

Of course he does, he said, since he deems it right to get the better of everybody.

So the unjust man will get the better of another unjust man or an unjust action and he will strive to get all he can from everyone?—That is so.

Let us put it this way, I said. The just man does not try to get the better of one d   like him but of one unlike him, whereas the unjust man overreaches the like and the unlike?—Very well put.

The unjust man, I said, is knowledgeable and good, and the just man is neither?— That is well said too.

It follows, I said, that the unjust man is like the knowledgeable and the good, while the just man is unlike them?

Of course that will be so, he said, being such a man he will be like such men, while the other is not like them.

Good. Each of them has the qualities of those he is like?—Why not?

Very well, Thrasymachus. Now you speak of one man as musical, of another as e   unmusical?—I do indeed.

Which is knowledgeable and which is not?

Of course the musical man is knowledgeable, the unmusical is not.

What he has knowledge of he is good at, and he who has no knowledge is bad?— Yes.

Is not the same true of the physician?—The same.

Do you think, my dear sir, that any musician, when tuning his lyre, desires, in the

10. [*pleon echein* or *pleonexia*, literally to have more, comes to mean "to outdo, to overreach, to do better than."]

tightening and relaxing of the strings, to do better than another musician or deems it right to get the better of him?—I don't think so.

But he wants to do better than a non-musician?—Necessarily.

What of a physician? When prescribing food or drink, does he want to do better   350 than another medical man or action?—Certainly not.

But better than the non-medical?—Yes.

In matters involving any kind of knowledge or ignorance, do you think that any expert would wish to achieve more than any other expert would do or say, rather than, in respect to the same action, achieve the same as anyone like himself?—Well perhaps, it must be as you say.

What about the non-expert? Does he not want to outdo the expert and the non-   b expert equally?—Perhaps.

The man with knowledge is wise?—I agree.

And the wise is good?—I agree.

So the good and wise does not wish to get the better of one like himself, but of the unlike and opposite?—Apparently.

But the bad and ignorant would want to get the better of his like and his opposite?—So it appears.

Now Thrasymachus, I said, we found that the unjust man tries to get the better of both those like and those unlike him. Did you not say so?—I did.

Yes, and the just man will not get the better of his like, but of one unlike him?—   c Yes.

The just man then, I said, resembles the wise and good, while the unjust resembles the bad and ignorant?—It may be so.

Further, we agreed that each will be such as the man he resembles?—We did so agree.

So we find that the just man has turned out to be good and wise, and the unjust man ignorant and bad.

Thrasymachus agreed to all this, not easily as I am telling it, but reluctantly and after being pushed. It was summer and he was perspiring profusely. And then I saw   d something I had never seen before: Thrasymachus blushing. After we had agreed that justice was virtue and wisdom, and injustice vice and ignorance, I said: Very well, let us consider this as established, but we also said that injustice was powerful, or don't you remember, Thrasymachus?

I remember, he said, but then I am not satisfied with what you are now saying. I could make a speech about it, but if I should speak I know that you would say I am delivering a public oration. So either allow me to speak or, if you want to ask   e questions, ask them, and I will say "very well," and nod yes and no, as one does to old wives' tales.

Don't ever do that, I said, against your own opinion.

Just to please you, he said, since you won't let me speak. What else do you want?

Nothing at all, said I. If you will do this, do it. I will ask my questions.—Ask them then.

I am asking what I asked before, so that we may proceed with our argument about the relation of justice and injustice in an orderly way. It was said that injustice is   351 more powerful and stronger than justice. But now, I said, since justice is wisdom and virtue, it will easily be shown to be also stronger than injustice which is ignorance; nobody could still not know that. However, I do not want to state this thus simply, Thrasymachus, but to look into it in some such way as this: would you say that it is unjust for a city to undertake to enslave other cities unjustly and hold them in subjection, having enslaved many cities to its power?

Of course, he said, this is what the best city will do, the most completely unjust.

I understand that this was your argument, I said, but let me examine this point: will the city which has become stronger than another achieve this power without justice, or must it do so with the help of justice?

If what you said just now stands—that justice is wisdom—with the help of justice, but if things are as I stated them, with injustice.

I am delighted, Thrasymachus, that you do not merely nod yes or no, but that you answer in a very fine manner.

I am doing it to please you, he said.

You are doing well. Now please me also by answering this question: do you think that a city, an army, a band of robbers or thieves, or any other body of men which engages unjustly upon a common course, could achieve anything if they wrong one another?—No indeed.

What if they do not wrong one another? Would they not achieve more?—Certainly.

Yes, for injustice, Thrasymachus, causes factions and hatreds and fights with one another, while justice brings a sense of common purpose and friendship. Is that not so?—Be it so, to agree with you.

You are doing well my good friend. Tell me this: if it is the result of injustice to bring hatred wherever it occurs, then its presence, whether among free men or slaves, will make them hate each other and quarrel, and be unable to achieve any common purpose?—Quite so.

What if it occurs between two men? Will they not be at odds, hate each other, and be hostile to each other as well as to the just?—They will be.

Does injustice, my good sir, lose this capacity for dissension when it occurs within one individual, or will it preserve it intact?

Let it be preserved intact, he said.

It seems to follow that injustice, wherever it occurs, be it in a city, a family, an army, or anything else results in making it incapable of achieving anything as a unit because of the dissensions and differences it creates, and, further, it makes that unit hostile to itself, to its every enemy, and to the just. Is that not so?—Quite.

Even in one individual it has the same effect, which follows from its nature. First, it makes that individual incapable of achievement because he is at odds with himself and not of one mind. It makes him his own enemy, as well as the enemy of the just, does it not?—It does.

The gods too, my friend, are just.—Be it so.

So the unjust man is also an enemy of the gods, while the just man is their friend.

Bravely enjoy your feast of words, he said. I will not oppose you, to avoid unpopularity in this company.

Come then, said I, complete the feast for me by answering as you are now doing.

The just are shown to be wiser and more able in action, while the unjust are not even able to act together, for surely, when we speak of a powerful achievement by unjust men acting in common, we are altogether far from the truth. They could not have kept their hands off each other if they had been completely bad, but clearly they had some justice which forbade them to wrong each other and their enemies at the same time. It was this which enabled them to do what they did. They started on their unjust course being half evil with injustice, for those who are completely evil and completely unjust are also completely incapable of achievement. I can see that this is so, and not as you at first assumed.

We must now examine whether the just also live a better life than the unjust and are happier, a point which we deferred for later investigation.[11] I think it is clear even now that they are, yet we must look into this further, for the argument concerns no casual topic, but one's whole manner of living.—Look into it, then.

I am looking, said I. Do you think there is such a thing as the function of a horse?— I do.

And would you define the function of a horse, or of anything else, as to do that which can be done only, or be done best, by means of it?

I do not understand your question, he said.

Put it like this: is it possible to see by any other means than the eyes?—Certainly not.

Further, could you hear by any other means than the ears?—Not possibly.

Then we are right to say that these are the functions of eyes and ears?—Quite so.

Further, would you use a dagger or a carving knife to trim the branches of a vine, or many other instruments?—Of course.

But you would not do it as well with any other instrument as with a pruning knife which was made for the purpose?—That is true.

Then shall we put it that this is the function of a pruning knife?—We shall.

Now I think you will understand my recent question better, when I inquired whether the function of each thing is to do that which it alone can perform, or perform better than anything else could.—I understand, he said, and I think that is the function of each.

Very well, said I. Does each thing to which a particular task is assigned also have its excellence? Let us go over the same ground again. We say that the eyes have a particular task?—Yes.

They also have their own excellence?—They have.

The ears too have a function?—Yes.

So they have their excellence?—That too.

Is that not the case with all other things?—It is.

Moreover, could the eyes perform their function well if they did not possess their own excellence or virtue, but their own vice instead?

How could they? he said. You mean blindness instead of sight?

Whatever their virtue is, for I am not now asking that, but whether any agent

---

11. [See 347e.]

performs its function well by means of its own excellence or virtue, or badly through its own badness or vice.—What you say is true.

So the ears, too, deprived of their own virtue, would perform their function badly.—Quite so.

d   And we could say the same about all other things?—I think so.

Come now, consider this point next: There is a function of the soul which you could not fulfill by means of any other thing, as for example: to take care of things, to rule, to deliberate, and other things of the kind; could we entrust these things to any other agent than the soul and say that they belong to it?—To no other.

What of living? Is that not a function of the soul?—It most certainly is.

So there is also an excellence of the soul?—We say so.

e   And, Thrasymachus, will the soul ever fulfill its function well if it is deprived of its own particular excellence, or is this impossible?—Impossible.

It is therefore inevitable that the bad soul rules and looks after things badly and that the good soul does all these things well.—Inevitable.

Now we have agreed that justice is excellence of the soul, and that injustice is vice of soul?—We have so agreed.

The just soul and the just man, then, will live well, and the unjust man will live badly.—So it seems, according to your argument.

354   Surely the one who lives well is blessed and happy, and the one who does not is the opposite.—Of course.

So the just man is happy, and the unjust one is wretched.—So be it.

It profits no one to be wretched, but to be happy.—Of course.

And so, my good Thrasymachus, injustice is never more profitable than justice.

Let that be your banquet of words, he said, at the feast of Bendis, Socrates.

Given by you, Thrasymachus, I said, after you became gentle and ceased to be
b   angry with me. Yet I have not had a good banquet, but that was my fault, not yours. I seem to have behaved as gluttons do, snatching at every dish that passes them and tasting it before they have reasonably enjoyed the one before. So I, before finding the answer to our first enquiry into the nature of justice, let that go and turned to investigate whether it was vice and ignorance or wisdom and virtue. Another argument came up after, that injustice was more profitable than justice, and I could not refrain from following this up and abandoning the previous one so that the result of our discussion for me is that I know nothing; for, when I do not know what justice
c   is, I shall hardly know whether it is a kind of virtue or not, or whether the just man is unhappy or happy.

BOOK II

357   When I had said this I thought I had done with the discussion, but evidently this was only a prelude. Glaucon on this occasion too showed that boldness which is characteristic of him, and refused to accept Thrasymachus' abandoning the argu-

ment. He said: Do you, Socrates, want to appear to have persuaded us, or do you   b
want truly to convince us that it is better in every way to be just than unjust?

I would certainly wish to convince you truly, I said, if I could.

Well, he said, you are certainly not attaining your wish. Tell me, do you think
there is a kind of good which we welcome not because we desire its consequences
but for its own sake: joy, for example, and all the harmless pleasures which have no
further consequences beyond the joy which one finds in them?

Certainly, said I, I think there is such a good.

Further, there is the good which we welcome for its own sake and also for its   c
consequences, knowledge for example and sight and health. Such things we somehow welcome on both counts.

Yes, said I.

Are you also aware of a third kind, he asked, such as physical training, being
treated when ill, the practice of medicine, and other ways of making money? We
should say that these are wearisome but beneficial to us; we should not want them
for their own sake, but because of the rewards and other benefits which result from   d
them.

There is certainly such a third kind, I said, but why do you ask?

Under which of these headings do you put justice? he asked.

I would myself put it in the finest class, I said, that which is to be welcomed both   358
for itself and for its consequences by any man who is to be blessed with happiness.

That is not the opinion of the many, he said; they would put it in the wearisome
class, to be pursued for the rewards and popularity which come from a good reputation, but to be avoided in itself as being difficult.

I know that is the general opinion, I said. Justice has now for some time been
objected to by Thrasymachus on this score while injustice was extolled, but it seems
I am a slow learner.

Come then, he said, listen to me also to see whether you are still of the same   b
opinion, for I think that Thrasymachus gave up before he had to, charmed by you
as by a snake charmer. I am not yet satisfied by the demonstration on either side. I
am eager to hear the nature of each, of justice and injustice, and what effect its
presence has upon the soul. I want to leave out of account the rewards and consequences of each. So, if you agree, I will do the following: I will renew the argument   c
of Thrasymachus; I will first state what people consider the nature and origin of
justice; secondly, that all who practise it do so unwillingly as being something necessary but not good; thirdly, that they have good reason to do so, for, according to
what people say, the life of the unjust man is much better than that of the just.

It is not that I think so, Socrates, but I am perplexed and my ears are deafened
listening to Thrasymachus and innumerable other speakers; I have never heard   d
from anyone the sort of defence of justice that I want to hear, proving that it is
better than injustice. I want to hear it praised for itself, and I think I am most likely
to hear this from you. Therefore I am going to speak at length in praise of the
unjust life and in doing so I will show you the way I want to hear you denouncing
injustice and praising justice. See whether you want to hear what I suggest.

I want it more than anything else, I said. Indeed, what subject would a man of
sense talk and hear about more often with enjoyment?

e   Splendid, he said, then listen while I deal with the first subject I mentioned: the
nature and origin of justice.

They say that to do wrong is naturally good, to be wronged is bad, but the suffering
of injury so far exceeds in badness the good of inflicting it that when men have done
wrong to each other and suffered it, and have had a taste of both, those who are
359   unable to avoid the latter and practise the former decide that it is profitable to come
to an agreement with each other neither to inflict injury nor to suffer it. As a result
they begin to make laws and covenants, and the law's command they call lawful and
just. This, they say, is the origin and essence of justice; it stands between the best
and the worst, the best being to do wrong without paying the penalty and the worst
to be wronged without the power of revenge. The just then is a mean between two
b   extremes; it is welcomed and honoured because of men's lack of the power to do
wrong. The man who has that power, the real man, would not make a compact with
anyone not to inflict injury or suffer it. For him that would be madness. This then,
Socrates, is, according to their argument, the nature and origin of justice.

Even those who practise justice do so against their will because they lack the power
to do wrong. This we could realize very clearly if we imagined ourselves granting to
c   both the just and the unjust the freedom to do whatever they liked. We could then
follow both of them and observe where their desires led them, and we would catch
the just man redhanded travelling the same road as the unjust. The reason is the
desire for undue gain which every organism by nature pursues as a good, but the
law forcibly sidetracks him to honour equality. The freedom I just mentioned would
most easily occur if these men had the power which they say the ancestor of the
d   Lydian Gyges possessed. The story is that he was a shepherd in the service of the
ruler of Lydia. There was a violent rainstorm and an earthquake which broke open
the ground and created a chasm at the place where he was tending sheep. Seeing
this and marvelling, he went down into it. He saw, besides many other wonders of
which we are told, a hollow bronze horse. There were window-like openings in it;
he climbed through them and caught sight of a corpse which seemed of more than
e   human stature, wearing nothing but a ring of gold on its finger. This ring the
shepherd put on and came out. He arrived at the usual monthly meeting which
reported to the king on the state of the flocks, wearing the ring. As he was sitting
among the others he happened to twist the hoop of the ring towards himself, to the
360   inside of his hand, and as he did this he became invisible to those sitting near him
and they went on talking as if he had gone. He marvelled at this and, fingering the
ring, he turned the hoop outward again and became visible. Perceiving this he tested
whether the ring had this power and so it happened: if he turned the hoop inwards
he became invisible, but was visible when he turned it outwards. When he realized
this, he at once arranged to become one of the messengers to the king. He went,
committed adultery with the king's wife, attacked the king with her help, killed him,
b   and took over the kingdom.

Now if there were two such rings, one worn by the just man, the other by the
unjust, no one, as these people think, would be so incorruptible that he would stay
on the path of justice or bring himself to keep away from other people's property
and not touch it, when he could with impunity take whatever he wanted from the
c   market, go into houses and have sexual relations with anyone he wanted, kill anyone,
free all those he wished from prison, and do the other things which would make
him like a god among men. His actions would be in no way different from those of

the other and they would both follow the same path. This, some would say, is a great proof that no one is just willingly but under compulsion, so that justice is not one's private good, since wherever either thought he could do wrong with impunity he would do so. Every man believes that injustice is much more profitable to himself   d than justice, and any exponent of this argument will say that he is right. The man who did not wish to do wrong with that opportunity, and did not touch other people's property, would be thought by those who knew it to be very foolish and miserable. They would praise him in public, thus deceiving one another, for fear of being wronged. So much for my second topic.

As for the choice between the lives we are discussing, we shall be able to make a   e correct judgment about it only if we put the most just man and the most unjust man face to face; otherwise we cannot do so. By face to face I mean this: let us grant to the unjust the fullest degree of injustice and to the just the fullest justice, each being perfect in his own pursuit. First, the unjust man will act as clever craftsmen do—a top navigator for example or physician distinguishes what his craft can do and what it cannot; the former he will undertake, the latter he will pass by, and when he slips   361 he can put things right. So the unjust man's correct attempts at wrongdoing must remain secret; the one who is caught must be considered a poor performer, for the extreme of injustice is to have a reputation for justice, and our perfectly unjust man   b must be granted perfection in injustice. We must not take this from him, but we must allow that, while committing the greatest crimes, he has provided himself with the greatest reputation for justice; if he makes a slip he must be able to put it right; he must be a sufficiently persuasive speaker if some wrongdoing of his is made public; he must be able to use force, where force is needed, with the help of his courage, his strength, and the friends and wealth with which he has provided himself.

Having described such a man, let us now in our argument put beside him the just man, simple as he is and noble, who, as Aeschylus put it,[12] does not wish to appear just but to be so. We must take away his reputation, for a reputation for justice   c would bring him honour and rewards, and it would then not be clear whether he is what he is for justice's sake or for the sake of rewards and honour. We must strip him of everything except justice and make him the complete opposite of the other. Though he does no wrong, he must have the greatest reputation for wrongdoing so that he may be tested for justice by not weakening under ill repute and its conse- quences. Let him go his incorruptible way until death with a reputation for injustice   d throughout his life, just though he is, so that our two men may reach the extremes, one of justice, the other of injustice, and let them be judged as to which of the two is the happier.

Whew! My dear Glaucon, I said, what a mighty scouring you have given those two characters, as if they were statues in a competition.

I do the best I can, he replied. The two being such as I have described, there should be no difficulty in following the argument through as to what kind of life awaits each of them, but it must be said. And if what I say sounds rather boorish,   e Socrates, realize that it is not I who speak, but those who praise injustice as preferable

---

12. [In *Seven Against Thebes*, 592–4, it is said of Amphiaraus that "he did not wish to appear but to be the best," and it continues with the words quoted below: "He harbours in his heart a deep furrow, from which good counsels grow."]

362 to justice. They will say that the just man in these circumstances will be whipped, stretched on the rack, imprisoned, have his eyes burnt out, and, after suffering every kind of evil, he will be impaled and realize that one should not want to be just but to appear so. Indeed, Aeschylus' words are far more correctly applied to the unjust than to the just, for we shall be told that the unjust man pursues a course which is based on truth and not on appearances; he does not want to appear but to be unjust:

b
> He harvests in his heart a deep furrow
> from which good counsels grow.

He rules his city because of his reputation for justice, he marries into any family he wants to, he gives his children in marriage to anyone he wishes, he has contractual and other associations with anyone he may desire, and, beside all these advantages, he benefits in the pursuit of gain because he does not scruple to practise injustice.

c In any contest, public or private, he is the winner, getting the better of his enemies and accumulating wealth; he benefits his friends and does harm to his enemies. To the gods he offers grand sacrifices and gifts which will satisfy them, he can serve the gods much better than the just man, and also such men as he wants to, with the result that he is likely to be dearer to the gods. This is what they say, Socrates, that both from gods and men the unjust man secures a better life than the just.

d After Glaucon has thus spoken I again had it in mind to say something in reply, but his brother Adeimantus intervened: You surely do not think that enough has been said from this point of view, Socrates?

Why not? said I.

The most important thing, that should have been said, has not been said, he replied.

Well then, I said, let brother stand by brother. If Glaucon has omitted something, you come to his help. Yet what he has said is sufficient to throw me and to make me incapable of coming to the help of justice.

e Nonsense, he said. Hear what more I have to say, for we should also go fully into the arguments opposite to those he mentioned, those which praise justice and censure injustice, so that what I take to be Glaucon's intention may be clearer. When fathers speak to their sons, they say one must be just—and so do all who care for

363 them, but they do not praise justice itself, only the high reputations it leads to, in order that the son, thought to be just, shall enjoy those public offices, marriages, and the rest which Glaucon mentioned, as they belong to the just man because of his high repute; they lay even greater emphasis on the results of reputation. They add popularity granted by the gods, and mention abundant blessings which, they say, the gods grant to the pious. So too the noble Hesiod and Homer declare,[13] the

b one that for the just the gods make "the oak trees bear acorns at the top and bees in the middle and their fleecy sheep are heavy with their burden of wool" and many other blessings of like nature. The other says similar things:

---

13. [The two quotations which immediately follow are from Hesiod's *Works and Days,* 232–3, and Homer, *Odyssey,* 19, 109.]

<blockquote>
(like the fame) of a goodly king who, in his piety,
upholds justice; for him the black earth bears wheat
and barley and the trees are heavy with fruit; his
sheep bear lambs continually and the sea provides its
fish.
</blockquote>

c

Musaeus[14] and his son grant from the gods more robust pleasures to the just. Their words lead the just to the underworld, and, seating them at table, provide them with a banquet of the saints, crown them with wreaths, and make them spend all their time drinking, as if they thought that the finest reward of virtue was perpetual drunkenness. Others stretch the rewards of virtue from the gods even further, for they say that the children and the children's children and the posterity of the pious man who keeps his oaths will survive into the future. Thus, and in other such ways, do they praise justice. The impious and unjust they bury in mud in the underworld, they force them to carry water in a sieve, they bring them into disrepute while still living, and they attribute to them all the punishments which Glaucon enumerated in the case of the just with a reputation for injustice, but they have nothing else to say. This then is the way people praise and blame justice and injustice.

d

e

Besides this, Socrates, look at another kind of argument which is spoken in private, and also by the poets, concerning justice and injustice. All go on repeating with one voice that justice and moderation are beautiful, but certainly difficult and burdensome, while incontinence and injustice are sweet and easy, and shameful only by repute and by law. They add that unjust deeds are for the most part more profitable than just ones. They freely declare, both in private and in public, that the wicked who have wealth and other forms of power are happy. They honour them but pay neither honour nor attention to the weak and the poor, though they agree that these are better men than the others.

364

b

What men say about the gods and virtue is the most amazing of all, namely that the gods too inflict misfortunes and a miserable life upon many good men, and the opposite fate upon their opposites. Begging priests and prophets frequent the doors of the rich and persuade them that they possess a god-given power to remedy by sacrifices and incantations at pleasant festivals any crime that the rich man or one of his ancestors may have committed. Moreover, if one wishes to harass some enemy, then at little expense he will be able to harm the just and the unjust alike, for by means of spells and enchantments they can persuade the gods to serve them. They bring the poets as witnesses to all this, some harping on the easiness of vice, that

c

<blockquote>
Vice is easy to choose in abundance, the path is
smooth and it dwells very near, but sweat is placed by
the gods on the way to virtue,
</blockquote>

d

and a path which is long, rough, and steep;[15] others quote Homer as a witness that the gods can be influenced by men, for he too said:[16]

---

14. [Musaeus was a legendary poet closely connected with the mystery religion of Orphism.]

15. [Hesiod, *Work and Days*, 287–89.]

16. [Homer, *Iliad*, 9, 497–501.]

the gods themselves can be swayed by prayer, for
suppliant men can turn them from their purpose by
sacrifices and gentle prayers, by libations and burnt offerings
e   whenever anyone has transgressed and sinned.

They offer in proof a mass of writings by Musaeus and Orpheus, offspring, as they
say, of Selene and the Muses. In accordance with these they perform their ritual
365   and persuade not only individuals but whole cities that, both for the living and for
the dead, there are absolutions and purifications for sin by means of sacrifices and
pleasurable, playful rituals. These they call initiations which free from punishment
yonder, where a dreadful fate awaits the uninitiated.

When all such sayings about the attitudes of men and gods toward virtue and vice
are so often repeated, what effect, my dear Socrates, do we think they have upon
the minds of our youth? One who is naturally talented and able, like a bee flitting
from flower to flower gathering honey, to flit over these sayings and to gather from
them an impression of what kind of man he should be and of how best to travel
b   along the road of life, would surely repeat to himself the saying of Pindar: should
I by justice or by crooked deceit scale this high wall and thus live my life fenced off
from other men? The advantages said to be mine if I am just are of no use, I am
told, unless I also appear so; while the troubles and penalties are obvious. The unjust
man, on the other hand, who has secured for himself a reputation for justice, lives,
c   they tell me, the life of a god. Therefore, since appearance, as the wise men tell me,
forcibly overwhelms truth and controls happiness, this is altogether the way I should
live. I should build around me a facade that gives the illusion of justice to those
who approach me and keep behind this the greedy and crafty fox of the wise
Archilochus.[17]

"But surely" someone objects, "it is not easy for vice to remain hidden always."
We shall reply that nothing is easy which is of great import. Nevertheless, this is the
d   way we must go if we are to be happy, and follow along the lines of all we have been
told. To protect our secret we shall form sworn conspiratorial societies and political
clubs. Besides, there are teachers of persuasion who make one clever in dealing with
assemblies and with the courts. This will enable us to use persuasion here and force
there, so that we can secure our own advantage without penalty.

"But one cannot force the gods nor have secrets from them." Well, if either they
do not exist or do not concern themselves with human affairs, why should we worry
e   about secrecy? If they do exist and do concern themselves, we have heard about
them and know them from no other source than our laws and our genealogising
poets, and these are the very men who tell us that the gods can be persuaded and
influenced by gentle prayers and by offerings. We should believe both or neither.
If we believe them, we should do wrong and then offer sacrifices from the proceeds.
366   If we are just, we shall not be punished by the gods but we shall lose the profits of
injustice. If we are unjust we shall get the benefit of sins and transgressions, and
afterwards persuade the gods by prayer and escape without punishment. "But in
Hades we will pay the penalty for the crimes committed here, either ourselves or
our children's children." "My friend," the young man will reply as he does his

---

17. [I.e. the fox mentioned by Archilochus. The fable in question is not extant.]

reckoning, "mystery rites have great potency, and so have the gods of absolution, as the greatest cities tell us, and the children of the gods who have become poets and prophets tell us that this is so."

b

For what reason then should we still choose justice rather than the greatest injustice? If we practise the latter with specious decorum we shall do well at the hands of gods and of men; we shall live and die as we intend, for so both the many and the eminent tell us. From all that has been said, Socrates, what possibility is there that any man of power, be it the power of mind or of wealth, of body or of birth, will be willing to honour justice and not laugh aloud when he hears it praised? And surely any man who can show that what we have said is untrue and has full knowledge that justice is best, will be full of forgiveness, and not of anger, for the unjust. He knows that only a man of godlike character whom injustice disgusts, or one who has superior knowledge, avoids injustice, and that no other man is willingly just, but through cowardice or old age or some other weakness objects to injustice, because he cannot practise it. That this is so is obvious, for the first of these men to acquire power is the first to do wrong as much as he is able.

c

d

The only reason for all this talk, Socrates, which led to Glaucon's speech and mine, is to say to you: Socrates, you strange man, not one of all of you who profess to praise justice, beginning with the heroes of old, whose words are left to us, to the present day—not one has ever blamed injustice or praised justice in any other way than by mentioning the reputations, honours, and rewards which follow justice. No one has ever adequately described, either in poetry or in private conversation, what the very presence of justice or injustice in his soul does to a man even if it remains hidden from gods and men; one is the greatest evil the soul can contain, while the other, justice, is the greatest good. If you had treated the subject in this way and had persuaded us from youth, we should then not be watching one another to see we do no wrong, but every man would be his own best guardian and he would be afraid lest, by doing wrong, he live with the greatest evil.

e

367

Thrasymachus or anyone else might say what we have said, and perhaps more in discussing justice and injustice. I believe they would be vulgarly distorting the effect of each. To be quite frank with you, it is because I am eager to hear the opposite from you that I speak with all the emphasis I can muster. So do not merely give us a theoretical proof that justice is better than injustice, but tell us how each, in and by itself, affects a man, the one for good, the other for evil. Follow Glaucon's advice and do not take reputations into account, for if you do not deprive them of true reputation and attach false reputations to them, we shall say that you are not praising justice but the reputation for it, or blaming injustice but the appearance of it, that you are encouraging one to be unjust in secret, and that you agree with Thrasymachus that the just is another's good, the advantage of the stronger, while the unjust is one's own advantage and profit, though not the advantage of the weaker.

b

c

Since you have agreed that justice is one of the greatest goods, those which are worthy of attainment for their consequences, but much more for their own sake—sight, hearing, knowledge, health, and all other goods which are creative by what they are and not by what they seem—do praise justice in this regard: in what way does its very possession benefit a man and injustice harm him? Leave rewards and reputations for others to praise.

d

For others would satisfy me if they praised justice and blamed injustice in this way, extolling the rewards of the one and denigrating those of the other, but from

you, unless you tell me to, I will not accept it, because you have spent your whole
e   life investigating this and nothing else. Do not, therefore, give us a merely theoretical
proof that justice is better than injustice, but tell us what effect each has in and by
itself, the one for good, the other for evil, whether or not it be hidden from gods
and men.

I had always admired the character of Glaucon and Adeimantus, and on this
368   occasion I was quite delighted with them as I listened and I said: You are the sons
of a great man, and Glaucon's lover began his elegy well when he wrote, celebrating
the repute you gained at the battle of Megara:

Sons of Ariston, godlike offspring of a famous man.

That seems well deserved, my friends; you must be divinely inspired if you are not
convinced that injustice is better than justice, and yet can speak on its behalf as you
b   have done. And I do believe that you are really unconvinced by your own words. I
base this belief on my knowledge of the way you live, for, if I had only your words
to go by, I would not trust you. The more I trust you, however, the more I am at a
loss what to do. I do not see how I can be of help; I feel myself incapable. I see a
proof of this in the fact that I thought what I said to Thrasymachus showed that
justice is better than injustice, but you refuse to accept this as adequate. On the other
hand I do not see how I can refuse my help, for I fear it is even impious to be present
c   when justice is being charged and to fail to come to her help as long as there is
breath in one's body and one is still able to speak. So the best course is to give her
any assistance I can.

Glaucon and the others begged me to give any help I could, not to abandon the
argument but to track down the nature of justice and injustice, and where the truth
lay as regards the benefits of both. So I said what I had in mind: This investigation
d   we are undertaking is not easy, I think, but requires keen eyesight. As we are not
very clever, I said, I think we should adopt a method like this: if men who did not
have keen eyesight were told to read small letters from a distance, and then someone
noticed that these same letters were to be found somewhere else on a larger scale
and on a larger object, it would, I think, be considered a piece of luck that they
could read these first and then examine the smaller letters to see if they were the
same.

That is certainly true, said Adeimantus, but what relevance do you see in it to our
e   present search for justice?

I will tell you, I said. There is, we say, the justice of one man, and also the justice
of a whole city?—Certainly.

And a city is larger than one man?—It is.

Perhaps there is more justice in the larger unit, and it may be easier to grasp. So,
369   if you are willing, let us first investigate what justice is in the cities, and afterwards
let us look for it in the individual, observing the similarities to the larger in the
smaller.—Your proposal seems sound.

Well then, I said, if we observed the birth of a city in theory, we would also see its
justice and injustice beginning to exist.—Probably.

And as the process went on, we may hope that the object of our search would be
b   easier to discover.—Much easier.

Do you think we should attempt to carry this through? It is no small task, I think. Think it over.

We have, said Adeimantus. Carry on.

I think a city comes to be, I said, because not one of us is self-sufficient, but needs many things. Do you think a city is founded on any other principle?—On no other.

As they need many things, people make use of one another for various purposes. c They gather many associates and helpers to live in one place, and to this settlement we give the name of city. Is that not so?—It is.

And they share with one another, both giving and taking, in so far as they do, because they think this better for themselves?—Quite so.

Come then, I said, let us create a city from the beginning in our discussion. And it is our needs, it seems, that will create it.—Of course.

Surely our first and greatest need is to provide food to sustain life.—It certainly d is.

Our second need is for shelter, our third for clothes and such things.— Quite so.

Consider then, said I, how the city will adequately provide for all this. One man obviously must be a farmer, another a builder, and another a weaver. Or should we add a cobbler and some other craftsman to look after our physical needs?—All right.

So the essential minimum for the city is four or five men.—Apparently.

A further point: must each of them perform his own work as common for them e all, for example the one farmer provide food for them all, and spend four times as much time and labour to provide food which is shared by the others, or will he not 370 care for this but provide for himself a quarter of such food in a quarter of the time and spend the other three quarters, one in building a house, one in the production of clothes, and one to make shoes, and not trouble to associate with the others but for and by himself mind his own business?

Perhaps, Socrates, Adeimantus replied, the way you suggested first would be easier than the other.

By Zeus, said I, there is nothing surprising in this, for even as you were speaking I was thinking that, in the first place, each one of us is born somewhat different from the others, one more apt for one task, one for another. Don't you think so?— b I do.

Further, does a man do better if he practises many crafts, or if, being one man, he restricts himself to one craft.—When he restricts himself to one.

This at any rate is clear, I think, that if one misses the proper time to do something, the opportunity to do it has gone.—Clear enough.

For I do not think that the thing to be done awaits the leisure of the doer, but the doer must of necessity adjust himself to the requirements of his task, and not consider this of secondary importance.—He must. c

Both production and quality are improved in each case, and easier, if each man does one thing which is congenial to him, does it at the right time, and is free of other pursuits.—Most certainly.

We shall then need more than four citizens, Adeimantus, to provide the things we have mentioned. It is likely that the farmer will not make his own plough if it is to be a good one, nor his mattock, nor other agricultural implements. Neither will d   the builder, for he too needs many things; and the same is true of the weaver and the cobbler, is it not?—True.

Carpenters, metal workers, and many such craftsmen will share our little city and make it bigger.—Quite so.

Yet it will not be a very big settlement if we add cowherds, shepherds, and other
e   herdsmen in order that our farmers have oxen to do their ploughing, and the builders will join the farmers in the use of them as beasts of burden to transport their materials, while the weavers and cobblers will use their wool and hides.

Neither will it be a small city, said he, if it has to hold all these things.

And further, it is almost impossible to establish the city in the kind of place that will need no imports.—Impossible.

So we shall still need other people to bring what is needed from other cities.—We shall.

371   Now if one who serves in this way goes to the other city without a cargo of the things needed by those from whom he is to bring what his own people need, he will come away empty-handed, will he not?—I think so.

Therefore our citizens must not only produce enough for themselves at home, but also the things these others require, of the right quality and in the right quantity.—They must.

So we need more farmers and other craftsmen in our city.—We do.

Then again we need more people to service imports and exports. These are merchants, are they not?—Yes.

So we shall need merchants too.—Quite so.

And if the trade is by sea, we shall need a number of others who know how to sail
b   the seas.—A good many, certainly.

A further point: how are they going to share the things that each group produces within the city itself? This association with each other was the very purpose for which we established the city.

Clearly, he said, they must do this by buying and selling.

It follows that we must have a market place and a currency for this exchange.—Certainly.

c   If the farmer brings some of his produce to market, or any other craftsman, and he does not arrive at the same time as those who want to exchange things with him, will he be sitting idly in the market place, away from his own work?

Not at all, he said. There will be people who realize this and engage in this service. In well-organized cities this will be pretty well those of feeble physique who are not
d   fit for other work. They must stay around the market, buying for money from those who have something to sell, and then again selling at a price to those who want to buy.

To fill this need there will be retailers in our city. Do we not call retailers those who establish themselves in the market place for this service of buying and selling, while those who travel between cities are called merchants? Quite so.

e   There are some others to serve, as I think, who are not worth admitting into our society for their intelligence, but they have sufficient physical strength for heavy labour. These sell the use of their strength; their reward for this is a wage and they are, I think, called wage-earners. Is that not so?—Certainly.

So the wage-earners complete our city.—I think so.

Well, Adeimantus, has our city now grown to its full size?—Perhaps.

Where then would justice and injustice be in it? With which of the parts we have examined have they come to be?

I do not notice them, Socrates, he said, unless it is in the relations of these very people to one another.   372

You may be right, I said, but we must look into it and not grow weary. First then let us see what kind of life our citizens will lead when they have thus been provided for. Obviously they will produce grain and wine and clothes and shoes. They will build their houses. In the summer they will strip for their work and go without shoes, though they will be adequately clothed and shod in the winter. For food they   b will make flour from wheat and meal from barley; they will bake the former and knead the latter; they will put their excellent cakes and loaves upon reeds or clean leaves; then, reclining upon a bed of strewn bryony and myrtle leaves, they will feast together with their children, drinking of their wine. Crowned with wreaths they will hymn the gods and enjoy each other, bearing no more children than their means allow, cautious to avoid poverty and war.

Glaucon interrupted and said: You make your people feast, it seems, without   c cooked dishes or seasoning.

True enough, I said, I was forgetting that they will need these, salt obviously and olives and cheese; they will boil roots and vegetables such as are found in the fields. We shall put sweetmeats before them consisting of figs and chickpeas and beans, and they will bake myrtles and acorns before the fire, drinking moderately. So they   d will live at peace and in good health, and when they die at a ripe age they will bequeath a similar life to their offspring.

And he said: If you were founding a city of pigs, Socrates, what else would you fatten them on?

And how should I feed them, Glaucon? said I.

In the conventional way, he said. If they are not to be miserable they should recline on proper couches and dine at a table, with the cooked foods and delicacies which people have nowadays.   e

Very well, I said, I understand. We should examine not only the birth of a city, but of a luxurious city. This may not be a bad idea, for in examining such a one we might very well see how justice and injustice grow in the cities. Yet to me the true city is that which we described, like a healthy individual. However, if you wish, let us also observe the feverish city. There is nothing to prevent us. The things I   373 mentioned would not, it seems, satisfy some people, nor would that kind of life. There will be couches, then, and tables and the other kinds of furniture. They must have cooked dishes and unguents and perfumes, and courtesans and pastries—various kinds of all these. We must no longer provide them only with the necessities we mentioned at first, houses and clothes and shoes, but we must call in painting and embroidery; we must acquire gold and ivory and all such things. Is that not so?—Yes.   b

We must then again enlarge our city. That healthy community is no longer adequate, but it must be swollen in bulk and filled with a multitude of things which are no longer necessities, as, for example, all kinds of hunters and artists,[18] many of them concerned with shapes and colours, many with music; poets and their auxiliaries, actors, choral dancers, and contractors; and makers of all kinds of instruments, including those needed for the beautification of women. And further we shall require more services in the city, or do you not think we shall need tutors, wet nurses, dry nurses, beauty parlours, barbers, and again chefs and cooks, also swineherds? These were not needed in our earlier city, but in this one there is need of them, as there will be for many other fatted beasts, once one eats them. Is that not so?—Of course.

And if we live like this we shall have far greater need of physicians than before.—Much greater.

The land which was adequate to feed the earlier population will become small and inadequate instead, shall we say?—That is so.

We must therefore annex a portion of our neighbours' land if we are to have sufficient pasture and ploughland, and they will want to annex part of ours if they too have surrendered themselves to the limitless acquisition of wealth and overstepped the boundaries of the necessary.—Inevitably, Socrates.

So our next step is war, Glaucon, or what will be the situation?—As you describe it.

Let us say nothing as yet whether the effects of war are good or evil, I said, but only this, that we have now found the origin of war. It originates from the same source from which many evils both public and private come in their own time upon the state.—Quite so.

Again, my friend, we shall need a city larger by not a little, in fact larger by a whole army, which will go out and fight on behalf of all this property and of the people we have mentioned, against the invaders.

Why? he said, are the citizens themselves not able to do so?[19]

Not, I said, if you and all of us were right to agree when we fashioned our city: we agreed, if you remember, that it was impossible for one man to practise many crafts successfully.—That is true.

Well then, I said, do you not think that the contest of war is a craft?—Definitely.

And does the cobbler's craft require more care than that of the soldier?—Not at all.

We prevented the cobbler trying to be at the same time a farmer or a weaver or a builder, and we said that he must remain a cobbler so that the product of his craft be good; so with the others, each was to have one trade for which he had a natural aptitude, stick to it for life, and keep away from other crafts so as not to miss the opportunities to practise his own craft well. Is it not of the greatest importance that matters of war be well performed? Or is fighting a war so easy that a farmer can at the same time be a soldier and so with the cobbler and any other craftsman? Yet no

18. [Hunters are needed because the people are no longer vegetarians. The Greek word translated artists is *mimētai*, literally "imitators."]

19. [Citizen armies were the rule in earlier Greek history, but professional and mercenary armies came into their own in the fourth century.]

one can become an adequate draughts or dice player if he does not practise at it
from childhood and only considers it a sideline. Can a man then pick up a shield or   d
any other arm or instrument of war and on the same day be an adequate performer
in a hoplite battle or any other kind? No other instrument makes any man a craftsman or champion by just being picked up, nor will it be of any use except to one
who has acquired the necessary knowledge and had sufficient practice.

If instruments could do this, they would be valuable indeed, he said.

Therefore, I said, as the task of the guardian is most important, so he should have
the most freedom from all other pursuits, for he requires technical knowledge and   e
the greatest diligence.—I think so.

He also needs a nature which is suited to his pursuit, does he not?—Of course.

It is then our task to select, if we can, the man whose nature is most suited to
guard the city.—So it is.

By Zeus, I said, this is no small matter we have raised. However, we must not
weaken, so far as our ability permits.—We must not.   375

Do you think, said I, that the nature of a pedigree puppy[20] differs from that of a
well-born youth as regards his capacity to guard things?—What do you mean?

In so far as each of them must be quick to see things and swift in the pursuit of
what he has seen and also strong if it is necessary to catch up with the enemy and
fight to the end.—They need all these qualities.

And he must be brave, if he is to fight well.—Of course.

And will a horse, a dog, or any other animal be brave, if he is not high-spirited?
Or have you noticed that a high spirit is invincible and unbeatable? Its presence
makes the whole soul fearless and unconquerable.—I have noticed it.   b

The physical qualities of the guardian are clear.—Yes.

And as far as the soul is concerned, he must be high-spirited.—That too.

How then, Glaucon, said I, being of such a nature, will they not be savage in their
behavior to each other and to the rest of the citizens?

That, by Zeus, will not be easy, he said.

Yet certainly they must be gentle to their own people, but hard for the enemy to   c
deal with. Else they will not wait for others to destroy the city but destroy it themselves
first.—True.

What shall we do then? said I. Where shall we find a character which is both gentle
and high-spirited at the same time? For a gentle nature is the opposite of a spirited
one.—So it seems.

And surely if either of these qualities is missing, he cannot be a good guardian.
The combination seems impossible, so it follows that a good guardian cannot exist.—   d
I am afraid so.

So I was at a loss, but on reexamining what we had said: My friend, I said, we
deserve to be in difficulties, for we have neglected the image we put forward.—How
do you mean?

---

20. [The humour of the comparison is enhanced in the Greek by the play on the words *skylax* (puppy) and
phylax (guardian) which is of course untranslatable.]

We have failed to notice that there exists such natures as we thought did not exist, combining these opposite qualities.—Where?

e One might see this in other animals too, but not least in the one we compared to the guardian. You know that this type of character exists by nature in the pedigree dog. He is as gentle as one can be to those he is used to and knows, but the opposite to those he does not know.—Yes, I know that.

So the thing is possible, and our search for the good guardian is not against nature.—Apparently not.

376 Do you think that our future guardian, besides being high-spirited, must also naturally love wisdom?—How so? I do not understand.

You will see this also in dogs, which makes one marvel at the animal.—See what?

That whenever he sees a stranger he is angry, even though no harm has been done to him, but whomsoever he knows he welcomes even if he has never received anything good from him. Have you not wondered at this?

I have never, he said, paid any attention to the matter, but obviously this is how a dog behaves.

b This is a smart way for a dog to behave, and his nature seems truly wisdom-loving.[21]—In what way?

In that he judges anything he sees as being friendly or hostile by no other criterion than that he knows the former and does not know the latter. Surely anyone who distinguishes what he feels to be akin to him and its opposite by this criterion of knowledge and ignorance must be a lover of knowledge?—That must follow.

Surely loving knowledge and loving wisdom are the same thing? I said.—They are the same.

c We are therefore encouraged to assume in the case of a man also, that if he is to be gentle toward his familiars and his acquaintances, he must be a lover of wisdom and a lover of knowledge.—Let us assume it.

So he who is to be a fine and good guardian of our city must be a lover of wisdom, high-spirited, swift and strong by nature.—That is altogether so.

d This type of man would be available, as we saw, but how is he to be brought up and educated? The question is highly relevant to our investigation, since our primary purpose is to see how justice and injustice come to be in our city. We do not want to omit a necessary argument, nor speak at too great length.

At this point Glaucon's brother said: Certainly I expect that this inquiry will be very relevant to our purpose.

Then, by Zeus, Adeimantus, I said, we must not leave it out, even if its discussion may be somewhat long.—No indeed.

21. [The Greek word is *philosophos*. Both it and the corresponding verb occur but rarely in our texts before Plato; their meaning is quite general: intellectual curiosity, wanting to know things, without ulterior motive. The two best-known earlier examples occur in Herodotus (1, 30) where we are told that Solon did a lot of travelling "wanting to know things," and also Pericles' famous phrase in the funeral speech (Thucydides 2, 40), "we love beauty without extravagance and we love knowledge without being soft." The word is here introduced in its general sense, and the jest is less startling in Greek than in English. As the discussion proceeds the meaning deepens, and Plato uses the word in the central books of his philosopher who is there fully described. Then "philosopher" is the only possible translation, but even so a Greek reader would, I think, have remained conscious of the etymological meaning, and it will help us to remember it.]

Come then, let us in theory educate our guardians as if we were telling a story and had the leisure to do so.—We must.   e

What will this education be? Or is it hard to find a better one than that which has been developed over a long period of time? It is in part physical training for the body and training in the arts[22] for the soul.—That is so.

Do we not start education in the arts before physical training?—Of course.

Under the arts you include literature, or not?—I do.

There are two kinds of discourse, the true and the untrue—Yes.

They must be educated in both, but first in the untrue?—I do not understand   377
your meaning, he said.

Do you not understand, I said, that we first tell stories to children. These are, in general, untrue, though there is some truth in them. And we tell stories to small children before we give them physical training.—That is so.

That is what I meant, that we must deal with the arts before physical training.—Correct.

You know that the beginning of any process is most important, especially for anything young and tender. For it is at that time that it takes shape, and any mould   b
one may want can be impressed upon it.—Very true.

Shall we then carelessly allow the children to hear any kind of stories composed by anybody, and to take into their souls beliefs which are for the most part contrary to those we think they should hold in maturity?—We shall certainly not allow that.

Then we must first of all, it seems, control the story tellers. Whatever noble story they compose we shall select, but a bad one we must reject. Then we shall persuade   c
nurses and mothers to tell their children those we have selected and by those stories to fashion their minds far more than they can shape their bodies by handling them. The majority of the stories they now tell must be thrown out.—Which do you mean?

We shall be able to examine the lesser by observing the larger. For they must all have much the same mould and the same effect, whether they be large or small. Do   d
you not think so?

I do, he said, but I do not know which you call large.

Those told, I said, by Hesiod and Homer and the other poets, for they put together fictitious stories and told them to men, and still do.

Which stories do you mean? said he, and why do you object to them?

Because of what one should object to first and most, especially if the fictitious is not well told.—As for instance?

Whenever any story gives a bad image of the nature of gods[23] and heroes, like a   e
painter drawing a bad picture, unlike the model he is wanting to portray.

---

22. [The reference is to the conventional Greek education in *gymnastikē* and *mousikē*. The meaning of the first, physical training, is quite clear; *mousikē* is more difficult: sometimes the fine arts seem to be included, but the word refers mostly to both poetry and music. Moreover, music, in Plato's time, was only beginning to be thought of as a separate art, and it was the combination of music and poetry which made up the song and was inspired by the Muses. "Music" is therefore a misleading translation, and I have chosen the more general "education in the arts" which includes all literature and, in Plato, even the "reasoned speech" of philosophy.]

23. [It should be noted that throughout the *Republic*, as indeed elsewhere, Plato uses the singular *theos* and the plural *theoi* quite indifferently, a god, gods, or the gods. He even uses the singular with the article, the god. This, however, is the generic use of the article and does not refer to any particular god unless the context makes

You are right to object to that, he said, but how shall we proceed and what shall we say?

First, I said, the greatest lie[24] about the most important matters was that of the man who told bad fiction when he said that Ouranos did what Hesiod tells us he did, and how Cronos punished him for it.[25] Then again, even if the deeds of Cronos and what he suffered from his son were true,[26] I do not think this should be told to foolish and young people; it should be passed over in silence. If there were some necessity to tell it, only a very few people should hear it, and in secret, after sacrificing not a pig but some great and scarce victim, so that as few people as possible should hear it.—Yes, he said, these stories are hard to deal with.

And they should not be told, Adeimantus, I said, in our city. Nor should a young man hear it said that in committing the worst crimes he is not doing anything out of the way, or that, if he inflicts every kind of punishment upon an erring father, he is only doing the same as the first and greatest of the gods.—No by Zeus, he said, I myself do not think these things are fit to be told.

Nor indeed, said I, any tales of gods warring and plotting and fighting against each other—these things are not true—if those who are to guard our city are to think it shameful to be easily driven to hate each other. Certainly stories of battles of giants must not be told nor embroidered, nor all the various stories of gods hating their kindred or friends. If we are to persuade our people that no citizen has ever hated another and that this is impious, then that is the kind of tale we should tell right away to small children, and to old men and women also, and to the middle-aged, and we must compel our poets to follow those guidelines. We shall not admit into our city stories about Hera being chained by her son, or of Hephaestus being hurled from heaven by his father when he intended to help his mother who was being beaten,[27] nor the battle of the gods in Homer, whether these stories are told allegorically or without allegory. The young cannot distinguish what is allegorical from what is not, and the beliefs they acquire at that age are hard to expunge and usually remain unchanged. That may be the reason why it is most important that the first stories they hear should be well told and dispose them to virtue.

That is reasonable, he said, but if someone were to ask us what these stories are, what should we say?

I answered: You and I, Adeimantus, are not poets now, but we are founding a city, and it is proper that founders should know the general lines which the poets must follow in telling their stories. These lines they will not be allowed to cross. We are not to compose their poems for them.

Correct, he said, but on this very point, what would be the general lines about the gods?

378

b

c

d

e

379

---

this obvious. It certainly does not imply any kind of monotheism, as a modern reader might think. All these expressions are equivalent, and refer to the gods or the divine nature generally.]

24. [The Greek word *pseudos* means untruth, and need not imply a deliberate lie, though it frequently does.]

25. [The story of Ouranos and his castration by his son Cronos is told by Hesiod in *Theogony*, 154–210.]

26. [For the birth of Zeus and his revenge on his father Cronos see *Theogony*, 453–506.]

27. [There is a reference to this myth in *Iliad* I, 590–4. The battle of the gods is in *Iliad* 20 and 21.]

Something like this, I said: the god must always be represented as he is, whether in epic, lyric, or tragedy.—That must be.

Now the god is good in truth and must be so presented.—What then?   b

Surely nothing good is harmful, or is it?—I don't think so.

And what is not harmful does no harm?—Not ever.

Does what does no harm work any evil?—No.

And what works no evil could not be the cause of evil.—How could it?

Further, the good is beneficial.—Yes.

It is the cause of well-being.—Yes.

The good then is not the cause of all things, but of good only; it is guiltless of evils.—I agree entirely.   c

Neither is the god, since he is good, the cause of all things, as the many say, but of only a few things for men, of many he is guiltless. For good things are fewer than bad things in our life. For the good things no one else is responsible, but for evil things we must find some other cause, not the god.—I think what you say is very true.

Therefore we shall not accept from Homer or any other this foolish mistake about the gods when he says: d

> There are two urns by the threshold of Zeus
> one filled with good, the other with evil fates ....

and the man to whom Zeus grants a mixture of these two

at one time meets with evil, at another with good

but the one who is given purely from the second urn,

evil famine drives him over the goodly earth,[28]

nor shall we grant that Zeus is for us   e

of evil and good the distributor.

And if anyone tells us that the breaking of oaths and truce as Pandarus broke them, was brought about by Athena and Zeus we shall not approve, nor that the quarrel and judgment came about through Themis and Zeus. Again, we must not allow our youth to hear the words of Aeschylus: 380

---

28. [All three quotations are from *Iliad* 24, 527–32, but for the following the reference is unknown, as it is for the quotation from Aeschylus. The story of Athena urging Pandarus to break the truce is told in *Iliad* 4, 73–126.]

> a god makes mortals guilty
> when he wants utterly to destroy a house.

And if anyone composes a poem in which these lines occur, or the sufferings of Niobe, or the fate of the house of Pelops, or the Trojan tale, or anything else of that kind, we must allow him to say either that these are not the work of a god or, if they are, then the poets must find the kind of explanation we are seeking, and say that the actions of the god are good and just, and that those who receive punishment are benefited thereby. We shall not allow the poet to say that those who pay the penalty are wretched and that it was a god who did this. If, on the other hand, they say that the wicked are wretched because they stand in need of punishment, and that in paying the penalty they are benefited by the gods, that we must allow. But to say that the god, himself good, is the cause of evil for anyone, that we shall fight in every way, and we shall not allow anyone to say it in his own city, if it is to be well governed, nor must anyone hear it said, neither young nor old, neither in verse or prose. It is impious to say these things; they do us no good, and they are inconsistent with themselves.—I like your law, he said, and I will vote for it.

This then is one of the rules and guidelines about the gods within which speakers must speak and poets compose, that the god is not the cause of all things but only of the good.—That is very satisfactory.

What about this second rule? Do you think that the god is a sorcerer, able to appear in different forms at different times, at times as himself yet changing his appearance into different shapes, sometimes deceiving us and making us think him different, or that he has one single form and is least likely to step out of it?—I cannot say offhand, he said.

What about this? Must he not, if he step out of his own form, be changed either of his own volition, or by another's?—Necessarily.

Now the best things are least liable to change or alteration. For example, the body by food or drink or labour, or any plant by sunshine and wind and the like; does not the healthiest and strongest change least?—Of course.

The strongest and most knowledgeable soul would be least disturbed and changed by any outside experience.—Yes.

So with all artifacts, furniture, and houses and clothes, those which are well made and good are least changed by time or anything else that happens to them.—That is so.

Anything then which is in good condition, either by nature or as the product of a craft, or both, is least changed by anything else.—That is likely.

Surely the god, and all that is his, are in every way best?—Of course.

Then the god would be the least likely to have many shapes.—Least of all.

Would he change and alter himself?—Clearly he does, if he changes at all.

Would he change himself into something better and more beautiful, or into something worse and uglier than himself?

The change must be for the worse, he said, if there is change, for we shall not say that the god is deficient in beauty or virtue.

Quite correct, I said, and do you think, Adeimantus, that anyone who was in such a perfect state, be he man or god, would deliberately make himself in any way worse?—Impossible.

It is then impossible, said I, for a god to want to change himself, but being, as is fitting, each of them as far as is possible best and most beautiful, he remains always simply in his own form.—That seems to me quite inevitable.

Then, my dear sir, I said, let no poet tell us that   d

> like unto strangers from every land
> the gods in various shapes frequent our towns[29]

nor tell us lies about Proteus and Thetis; neither in their tragedies nor other poems bring on Hera in altered form, as a priestess begging for

> the life-giving sons of the river, Argive Inachus,[30]

and many other such lies they must not tell. Nor must our mothers, believing them,   e
terrify their children by telling bad stories, saying that some gods wander at night in the shape of strangers from many lands.

These stories slander the gods, and at the same time make children more cowardly.—They must not be told.

Or do the gods themselves, though unable to change, make us believe that they appear in many forms, thus deceiving and beguiling us?—Perhaps.

How so? said I. Would a god be willing to lie, either in word or deed, by projecting   382
a false appearance?—I do not know.

Do you not know, I said, that the true lie, if one may call it so, is hated by all gods and men?—What do you mean?

I mean this, I said: no one is willing to speak untruth with the most important part of himself about the most important subjects, but of all things he is most afraid to have untruth in that part.

I still do not understand, he said.

You think, I said, that I am saying something mysterious. I mean to lie and to be   b
in a state of untruth about reality in one's soul, to be ignorant, and there to have and to hold untruth. This is what men most want to avoid, and they hate this state of soul most.—Quite so.

Surely, as I said just now, this would most correctly be called the true lie, the ignorance in the soul of the man who has been deceived. The verbal lie is a mere reflection of that which exists in the soul, a reflection of it which comes later, and is not completely untrue. Is that not so?—Certainly.   c

And the real lie is hated not only by the gods, but also by men.—I think so.

What about the verbal lie? When and to whom is it useful and not deserving hatred? Is it not useful against one's enemies and those of one's so-called friends

29. [*Odyssey* 17, 485–6.]

30. [Inachus was the father of Io who was persecuted by Hera, but the part of the story here referred to is unknown.]

d who, through madness or ignorance, are attempting to do some wrong, in order to turn them away from it? The lie then becomes useful, like a drug. It is also useful in the case of those stories we mentioned just now, because of our ignorance of what truly happened of old. We then make the fiction as like the truth as we can, and so make the lie or untruth useful.—That certainly is the case.

In which of these ways can the lie be useful to the god? Is it because of his ignorance of the past, making fiction as like truth as possible?—That would be ridiculous.

There is nothing of the fictional poet in the god?—I do not think so.

e Would he lie for fear of his enemies?—Far from it.

Because of the ignorance or madness of his kindred?

None of the foolish or mad are friends of the gods, he said.

There is then no reason for the god to lie.—None.

Therefore the divine and the godlike do not lie at all.—Not at all.

The god then is simple and true in word and deed; he does not change himself nor deceive others, either by images or by words or by sending signs, either in visions

383 or in dreams.

That is what I thought, he said, even as you spoke.

You agree then that this is our second rule according to which one should speak or compose poetry about the gods, that neither are they sorcerers who change, nor do they mislead us by lies in word or deed?—I agree.

We praise many things in Homer, but we will not approve of the dream which
b Zeus sent to Agamemnon,[31] nor of Aeschylus when he makes Thetis say that Apollo prophesied in song at her wedding the good fortune of her offspring:

> their long lives of disease quite free,
> and my good fortunes pleasing to the gods,
> he sang a paean and encouraged me.
> I hoped the lips of Phoebus would be truthful
> those divine lips, with prophecy endowed.
> Himself he sang, was present at the feast,
> himself he said this, yet himself it is,
> this same god, who killed my child.[32]

c Whenever anyone says such things about a god, we shall be angry and refuse him a chorus, nor allow his poetry to be used in the education of the young, if our guardians are to be god-fearing and godlike, as far as man can be.

I altogether agree with these rules, he said, and I would make them into laws.

31. [In the second book of the *Iliad* Zeus sends a dream to Agamemnon to promise his success if he attacks Troy now. The promise is a lie.]

32. [From an unknown play of Aeschylus. The point of the quotation is that Achilles, the son of Thetis, died very young, and Apollo's promise was false.]

BOOK III

Such then are the kinds of stories which should be heard about the gods, and the   386
kinds that should not be heard from childhood on, by those who are to honour both
their gods and their parents, and who will attach no little importance to friendship
with one another.—I certainly think our view is correct.

What if they are to be brave? Should one not tell them things that will make them
least afraid of death? Or do you think anyone ever becomes brave if this fear
possesses him?—No, by Zeus, I do not.   b

Further, can he be without fear of death, and prefer it to defeat in battle and to
slavery, if he believes in an underworld full of terrors?—In no way.

We must then, it seems, supervise such tales and those who undertake to tell them,
and beg them not to rail at things in the underworld in the unrestrained manner
they do, but rather to praise them, as their stories are neither true nor beneficial to   c
future warriors.—We must.

We shall expunge all that sort of thing, I said, beginning with these lines:[33]

> I would rather labour on earth in service to another,
> to a man who is landless, with little to live on,
> than be king over all the dead.

and also:

> lest his home should appear to gods and men
> fearful, dank, hated even by gods.   d

and:

> Alas, there survives in the halls of Hades
> a soul, a mere wraith, with no mind at all.

and:

> and he alone could think, the shades rushing around him.

and:

33. [The seven quotations which follow are all from Homer: (1) Odysseus addressing the ghost of Achilles
when the latter visits the underworld, in *Odyssey* 11, 489–91; (2) the gods take up battle positions as Zeus
thunders and Poseidon shakes the earth, and Hades is afraid that the earth might split open and expose the
underworld, in *Iliad* 20, 64–5; (3) words of Achilles as the ghost of Patroclus leaves him, in *Iliad* 23, 103–4; (4)
Circe speaking to Odysseus, referring to the prophet Teiresias in the underworld, in *Odyssey* 10, 493–5; (5)
words of Patroclus whom Hector has just mortally wounded, in *Iliad* 16, 856–7; (6) words of the ghost of
Patroclus as he leaves Achilles, in *Iliad* 23, 100; (7) description of the souls of the suitors killed by Odysseus, as
they follow Hermes to Hades, in *Odyssey* 24, 6–9.]

> the soul, leaving his limbs, made its way to Hades,
> lamenting its fate, leaving manhood and youth.

and again:

387

> his soul went below the earth like smoke,
> screeching as it went . . .

and:

> as when bats in the corner of a goodly cave
> fly about screeching if one of them falls
> from the mass at the roof, all holding together,
> so their souls went screeching . . . .

b   We shall ask Homer and the other poets not to be angry if we delete these and all similar passages. They are poetic and pleasing to the majority of hearers, but the more poetic they are the less they should be heard by children and by men who must be free and fear slavery more than death.—Most certainly.

So too all those fearful and dreadful names about the underworld must be struck out: the Cokytuses (rivers of mourning), and the Styxes (hateful rivers), and names
c   of the dead such as "those underground," and "the sapless ones," and all those names of things in the underworld which make every hearer shudder. And perhaps it is right to delete them for another reason: we are fearful on behalf of our guardians, lest such shudders make them more malleable and soft than they should be.

That fear is justified, he said.

Such passages are to be struck out?—Yes.

Poets must follow the opposite pattern in speaking and composing.—Clearly so.

d   We shall also delete lamentations and pitiful speeches on the part of famous men?—This necessarily follows.

Look then, I said, whether we are right to take out the following. We surely assert that the good man does not think death to be a dreadful thing for another good man, his friend.—We do.

And he will not mourn for him as for one who has suffered a terrible thing.—Certainly not.

We also assert that such a man is most self-sufficient in living the good life and,
e   above all others, has least need of another person.—True.

Then it is less dreadful for him than for another to be deprived of a son or a brother, of possessions and any other such things.—Certainly less.

He will therefore give least way to lamentations, and bear it most quietly when such a misfortune hits him.—Certainly.

We would be right then to delete the lamentations of famous men, to leave them to women, and not even to good women, and to cowardly men, so that those whom

we say we are training to guard our city will disdain to act in a similar manner.—   388
Right.

   Again we shall beg Homer and the other poets not to represent Achilles, the son
of a goddess[34]

> lying now on his side, now on his back, and then
> again face down . . .

and then, having got up,

> wandering this way and that on the shore of the
> harvestless sea . . .   b

nor make him pick up ashes in both hands and pour them over his head, weeping
and lamenting in the ways he does in Homer; nor to make Priam, a near descendent
of the gods, pray rolling in dung and calling upon each man by name. Even more
earnestly shall we beg them not to represent the gods lamenting, and saying:

> Alas, unfortunate that I am, the wretched mother of a great son[35]   c

and if they must so represent the gods, at least not to venture to represent the
greatest of the gods so unlike his true nature as to say:[36]

> Alas, with my own eyes I see a man to me most dear
> chased round the city, and my heart laments

and also:[37]

> Ah me! that it be the fate of Sarpedon, to me most dear,
> to be killed by Patroclus, the son of Menoetius . . .   d

For if, my dear Adeimantus, our young men should hear such things in all earnest
and not ridicule them as unworthily spoken, not one of them could easily consider
himself, a mere man, to be above such behaviour, and rebuke himself for saying or
doing this when misfortune comes upon him; rather he would not be ashamed to
lose his self-control and utter many groans and laments for small misfortunes.—   e
What you say is very true.

---

   34. [Both the quotations are taken from the scene where Achilles is mourning for Patroclus in *Iliad* 24, 3–
12. The pouring of ashes occurs when he first gets the news of Patroclus' death at 18, 23–4. Priam's lamentation
at the death of Hector is at 22, 414–5.]

   35. [Thetis among the Nereids at *Iliad* 18, 54.]

   36. [Zeus, as he watches Hector pursued by Achilles in *Iliad* 22, 168–9.]

   37. [Zeus mourns the fate of Sarpedon at *Iliad* 16, 433–4.]

Our discussion has just shown that this must not happen, and we must believe it until someone persuades us with a better argument.—No, it must not happen.

Further, they must not be overfond of laughter either, for whenever anyone indulges in violent laughter, a violent change of mood is likely to follow.—I think so.

389   So we shall not approve if someone represents worthy men overcome by laughter, and much less the gods.—Much less, he said.

Therefore we shall not approve of Homer saying such things about the gods as:

> And unquenchable laughter arose among the blessed gods
> as they saw Hephaestus limping through the hall.[38]

Such things must be rejected, according to your argument.—If you want to, call it mine, he said, but in any case they must be rejected.

b   Moreover, truth must also be highly esteemed. If what we said just now is correct and untruth is of no use to the gods, though useful to men as a kind of medicine, clearly we must allow physicians to use it, but not private citizens.—Obviously.

So it is fitting for the rulers, if for anyone, to use lies for the good of the city because of certain actions of the enemy or of citizens, but everyone else must keep
c   away from them. For a private citizen to lie to such rulers is as wrong or worse than for a sick man to lie to his physician or an athlete to his trainer about his physical condition, or for a sailor not to tell the navigator the truth about the condition of the ship or how he himself or a fellow sailor is behaving.—Very true.

d   And if the ruler catches anyone else lying in the city

> of those who are public workers
> be it a prophet, a healer of evils, or a maker of spears[39]

he will punish him as one who is introducing into the city as subversive and destructive an element as it would be in a ship.—Yes, he said, if his actions follow his words.

Then again, our young men will need moderation.—Of course.

And are not these the most important aspects of moderation for the majority: to be obedient to the rulers, and oneself to rule over the pleasures of drink, sex, and
e   food?—I think so.

And we shall say, I think, that the words of Diomede in Homer are well spoken:

> Sit down in silence my friend, be persuaded by me.[40]

---

38. [*Iliad*, 1, 599–600.]

39. [*Odyssey* 17, 384.]

40. [At *Iliad* 4, 412, Agamemnon has quite undeservedly rebuked Diomede for cowardice. Diomede's squire protests but Diomede quiets him with these words. This is therefore an example of self-control and respect for the commander-in-chief. The lines which Plato quotes as following this do not in fact follow in our text; one is found at 3, 8, while the other occurs at 4, 443, which of course is shortly after the incident quoted.]

and what follows:

> The Achaeans, breathing power,
> marched silently, fearing their commanders,

and all the other things of that kind.—Fine.

But what of this kind of thing?

> Wine-bibber, with the eyes of a dog and the heart of a deer.[41]

And what follows, is this well spoken? or whatever other headstrong words are   390
spoken by private citizens against their rulers, whether in prose or verse?—They
are bad.

I do not think they are suitable for our youth to hear with a view to moderation,
though it is not surprising that they are pleasing enough in other ways. How does
this strike you?—Just as you say.

What about making the cleverest of men say that he thinks the finest spectacle of
all is when

> the tables are well laden   b
> with cereals and meat, and the winebearer
> draws wine from the mixing bowl and pours it in the cups.[42]

Do you think such things make for self-control in our young men? or

> Death by starvation is the most pitiful fate.[43]

Or to have Zeus, when all other gods and men are asleep and he alone is awake,
easily forget all his plans through sexual desire, and so struck by the sight of Hera   c
that he is not even willing to go inside but wants to possess her there on the ground,
saying that the urgency of his desire is greater than even when they first came
together without their dear parents' knowledge;[44] or the chaining of Ares and
Aphrodite together for similar reasons.[45]—No, by Zeus, that does not seem suitable
to me.

On the other hand if there are examples of self-control in all things, in word or   d

41. [These insulting words are spoken by Achilles to Agamemnon at *Iliad* 1, 225, during their famous
quarrel.]

42. [Odysseus to Alcinous while entertained in Phaeacia, *Odyssey* 9, 8-10.]

43. [At *Odyssey* 12, 342, Eurylochus urges the men to slay the cattle of the Sun in Odysseus' absence.]

44. [The temptation of Zeus by Hera to divert his attention from the battlefield in the fourteenth book of
Iliad.]

45. [The story of Ares and Aphrodite caught in adultery by Hephaestus and chained to the bed for all the
gods to see is told in the eighth book of the *Odyssey.*]

deed, on the part of famous men, these must be seen and heard, as for example Odysseus

> struck his chest and spoke unto his heart:
> "Endure, my heart, you have suffered more shameful things
> than this."[46]

—Most certainly this should be heard.

But we must not allow men to be depicted as open to bribery or as money lovers.—Certainly not.

e   Nor must the poets sing to our youth that:

> Gifts persuade the gods, and gifts the revered kings.[47]

Nor must Phoenix, the tutor of Achilles, be praised as speaking with moderation when he advises him to take the gifts and defend the Achaeans but not to cease from anger without gifts.[48] And we shall not deem it worthy of Achilles himself, or think

391 him so fond of possessions that he accepts the gifts of Agamemnon, or that he will release the corpse of Hector for ransom, but not otherwise.—It is not right to praise such things.

Indeed I hesitate, said I, out of respect for Homer, to say that it is impious to accuse Achilles of such things, or to believe others who say them, and again to make him address Apollo in these words:

> You have injured me, Farshooter, most deadly of the gods;
> and I would punish you, had I the power[49]

b   and also that he disobeyed the river, a god, and was ready to fight him, or again that he consecrated to the dead Patroclus the hair that was consecrated to that other river, Spercheios; that he did this is not to be believed; then again the dragging of the dead Hector round the tomb of Patroclus, or the massacre of the captives on the

c   pyre; we shall deny the truth of these things. We shall not allow our people to believe that Achilles, the son of a goddess and of that most moderate man Peleus, the grandson of Zeus, brought up as he was by the very wise Cheiron, was so full of inner tumult as to have two contrary diseases in his soul, meanness and the love of money on the one hand, and arrogance toward gods and men on the other.—You are quite right.

d   We will certainly not believe these things, nor allow it to be said that Theseus, the

---

46. [*Odyssey* 20, 17–18.]

47. [These exact words are not found in our texts, but the sentiment is common. See 346b.]

48. [The advice of Phoenix is in the ninth book of the *Iliad*. See especially 602–3. The release of Hector's body is the main episode of book 24.]

49. [*Iliad* 22, 15 and 20. For Achilles and the river see *Iliad* 21, 232ff.; the dedication of Achilles' hair at 23, 141–52; the dragging of Hector's body at 24, 14–8; and the sacrifice on Patroclus' pyre at 23, 175.]

son of Poseidon, and Peirithous, the son of Zeus, engaged in dreadful kidnappings,[50] or that any other hero, son of a god, ventured upon dreadful and impious deeds as they now untruthfully tell against them. We shall compel the poets to deny that these deeds were theirs or to deny that they were children of the gods; they must not say both or attempt to persuade our young men that the gods beget evil and that heroes are not better than ordinary men. As we said earlier, these things are both impious and untrue, for we have shown that evils cannot originate with the gods.—Of course.   e

And indeed these tales are harmful to those who hear them, for every man will be ready to excuse his own evil conduct if he believes these things are done, and have been done in the past, by

> close descendants of the gods,
> those near to Zeus, to whom belongs
> the ancestral altar high up on Mount Ida,
> with divine blood unweakened in their veins.[51]

These are the reasons why we must stop such tales, lest they produce in our youth   392
a considerable tolerance of evil.—Quite so, he said.

Now then, I said, there is still a class of tales about which we are to determine which are to be told and which are not. The manner in which gods are to be treated has been dealt with, and also spirits and heroes and things in the underworld.—It has indeed.

What is left is how to deal with tales about men.—Obviously.

But my friend, we cannot settle this at present.—Why not?

Because I think that we shall say that both poets and prose-writers tell bad tales about men in most important matters; they say that many unjust men are happy   b
and many just men wretched, that injustice is profitable if it escapes notice, that justice is another's good and one's own punishment. I think we will forbid these tales and order them to compose the opposite kind of poetry and tell the opposite kind of tales. Don't you think so?—I know we shall. *authoritarian censorship*

Then if you agree that I am right in this, I shall say that you have agreed to the conclusion of what we have been seeking for some time.—Your assumption is correct.

Therefore we shall agree what tales must be told about men when we have discov-   c
ered the nature of justice, that it is by nature beneficial to its possessor, whether he is reputed to be just or not.—Very true.

Let our discussion of content end here, and we should now, I think, investigate the diction, then we shall have examined fully both what should be said and the manner of saying it.

Adeimantus said: I do not understand what you mean.

Surely you must, I said, but perhaps you will understand it better if I put it this   d

---

50. [According to certain legends, Theseus and Peirithous together abducted Helen and tried to abduct Persephone from the underworld.]

51. [Apparently a quotation from the *Niobe*, a lost play of Aeschylus.]

way: is not everything said by poets and story-tellers narrative about past, present or future events.—What else?

And do they not proceed by simple narration, or narrative through imitation[52] or both.—This too I want to understand more clearly.

And I said: As a teacher I seem to be ridiculous and obscure. Like those who cannot make a speech, I will not deal with the matter as a whole but I will take up a part separately, and by means of this show you what I want. Tell me. You know the beginning of the *Iliad*, the passage where the poet tells us that Chryses begs Agamemnon to release his daughter. One of them gets angry and the other, having failed in his object, prays to the god against the Achaeans?—I do.

You know then that up to the lines:

> and he begged all the Achaeans,
> But especially the two sons of Atreus, commanders of the host,

the poet himself is speaking and does not attempt to turn our attention elsewhere as if the speaker were someone other than himself. After this, however, he speaks as if he were Chryses and tries as far as possible to make us think that the speaker is not Homer but the priest, an old man. And he composes pretty well the whole of the rest of his narrative in this way about the events in Troy or in Ithaca and throughout the *Odyssey*.—Quite so.

Now it is narrative[53] both when he makes speeches and also the parts between the speeches?—Of course.

But when he makes a speech as if he were someone else, shall we not say that he makes his language as like as possible to that of whatever person he has told us is about to speak?—We shall say that.

Now to make oneself like somebody else in voice or form is to imitate or impersonate the person one makes oneself resemble?—Certainly.

In these passages, it seems, he and the other poets tell their narrative through impersonation.—Quite so.

If the poet nowhere hid himself, the whole of his poem would be narration without impersonation. In order that you should not say again that you do not understand, I will show you how this would be. When Homer had said that Chryses came, bearing a ransom for his daughter, as a suppliant to the Achaens and especially to the kings, if after this he did not speak as if he had become Chryses but as being Homer still, there would be no impersonation but simple narration. It would have gone something like this—I will speak without the metre, for I am no poet: And the priest came and prayed that the gods grant them to capture Troy and safety thereafter, and that they might accept the ransom and free his daughter and thus show

52. [The Greek word for imitation is *mimēsis*. We have already seen (373b) that, in the general sense of imitation, all art is *mimēsis*. In this book, however, the word is used in the more restricted sense of impersonation, and will often be so translated. This takes place wherever direct speech is used, as Plato explains. We know from the *Ion* that rhapsodes acted the speeches when reciting the epic.]

53. [A certain confusion arises because Plato uses the word *diēgēsis* both for narrative in general, as here, including both direct and indirect speech, and also for narrative without direct speech. Perhaps we may avoid it by using narrative for the general meaning, and narration where there is no direct speech at all.]

respect for the god. When he had spoken the others showed their respect for the priest and approved of this, but Agamemnon was angry and ordered him to leave forthwith and never to return lest his priestly wand and the wreaths of the god be insufficient protection. He said that before freeing the daughter he would grow old in Argos by her side, told him to go and not make him angry if he wanted to get home safely. When the old man heard this he was afraid and went away in silence. On leaving the camp he prayed at length to Apollo, calling upon him by his various titles, reminding him of his services, and asking him that, if ever he had given the god a pleasing gift either in a temple building or at a sacrifice, as a return for this, the arrows of the god make the Achaeans pay for his tears. In this way, my friend, I said, it becomes simple narration without impersonation.—I understand, he said.

 Understand also, I said, that the opposite occurs when one leaves out the words between the speeches and leaves the dialogue.

 I understand, too, he said, that tragedy is like that.

 You are quite correct, I said, in that assumption, and I think that I have made clear to you what I could not make clear before, namely that one kind of poetry and story-telling is wholly through impersonation—tragedy and comedy, as you say; another kind is through narration by the poet himself—you would find this mostly in dithyrambs; and a third kind uses both, as in epic poetry and frequently elsewhere, if you follow me.—I do understand what you meant to say.

 Remember also what we said before, that we had dealt with content, but that the manner in which it was presented was still to be investigated.—I remember.

 This is the very thing I meant, that we need to agree whether we will allow imitative poets to narrate things to us, or are they to imitate some things and not others, and what kind of things in each case, or whether they are not to use impersonation at all.

 I presume, he said, that you are examining whether we shall accept tragedy or comedy into our city, or whether we shall not.

 Perhaps so, I said, or perhaps even more than that, but we must follow the argument wherever, like a wind, it may lead us.—Right.

 Consider this point, Adeimantus, whether our guardians should be imitative or not. Or does this too follow from our earlier statement that every individual should follow one occupation well, not many, for if he tries to do that, he will touch upon many pursuits and fail in them all, at least to the extent of attaining repute in any.— He will indeed.

 Does then the same argument hold for imitation, that the same man cannot imitate many things as well as he could imitate one?—He cannot.

 He will then hardly be able to pursue one worthwhile occupation and at the same time imitate many things and be imitative, since the same people are not able at the same time to engage in two kinds of imitation which are thought to be closely akin, such as comedy and tragedy. Did you not just now call these two forms of imitation.— I did, and, you are quite right, the same people cannot do both.

 Nor can they be both rhapsodes and actors.—True.

 Not even the same actors are used for comedy and tragedy, yet all these are imitations, are they not?—They are.

 Moreover, Adeimantus, human nature seems to be fragmented by even smaller differences, so that it is incapable of giving a successful imitation of many things, or to perform those very actions of which their imitations are likenesses.—Very true, he said.

If then we are to preserve our first principle, that our guardians must be kept

c   away from all other kinds of work, but work strictly for the freedom of our city, and do no other work which does not contribute to this, they must neither do nor imitate anything else. If they do or imitate anything else it must be, from childhood on, what is suitable to them, namely brave, self-controlled, pious, and free men and all their actions. They must not be clever at doing or imitating mean actions or anything shameful, lest from enjoying the imitation they come to enjoy the reality. Have you

d   not noticed that imitations, if they last from youth for some time, become part of one's nature and settle into habits of gesture, voice, and thought?—Yes indeed.

We shall then not allow those for whom we profess to care and who must grow up into good men to imitate, being men, a young or older woman who is railing at a

e   man, or quarreling with the gods, or bragging while thinking herself happy, or one in misfortune and sorrows and lamentations, even less one in illness or in love or in labour.—Absolutely.

Nor must they imitate slaves, female or male, performing slavish tasks.—Not that either.

Nor evil men, it seems, cowards, or people doing the opposite of those we mentioned just now, libelling and ridiculing each other, using bad language whether

396   drunk or sober, or erring in any other way that such men do in word or deed, towards themselves or towards others. They must not become accustomed to making themselves like madmen in word or deed. They must have knowledge of men and women who are mad and evil, but none of their actions should be performed or imitated.—Very true.

Should they imitate metal workers or other craftsmen, or those who row in tri-

b   remes, or their time-keepers, or anything else connected with ships?—How could they? he said, since they are not to concern themselves with any of those occupations.

Will they imitate neighing horses or bellowing bulls, roaring rivers or the clashing sea and all such things?—They are forbidden to be mad or to imitate mad people, he said.

Then, I said, if I understand what you say, there is one kind of style of narration

c   which the true gentleman would use to express himself and another different style which his opposite by nature and education would favour, and in which he would narrate.—What are they?

Well, I said, I think that when a moderate man in his narrative comes upon the words or actions of a good man he will be willing to expound it in character and not

d   be ashamed of that kind of imitation; he will impersonate this good man acting in a faultless and intelligent manner, but he will do so much less when the good man is overcome by disease or sexual passion, or by drunkenness or some other misfortune. When he comes upon a character unworthy of himself, he will be unwilling to make himself seriously like that worse character, except perhaps briefly when he is doing a good deed. He will be ashamed to do so, and also he is unpractised in the imitation of these types; he will resent shaping and moulding himself after

e   those worse than himself, since he despises them in his mind, except perhaps for the sake of play.—That seems likely.

He will therefore use the kind of narrative which we described when we were dealing with the Homeric epic a short time ago. His style will use both impersonation and the other kind of narrative, though impersonation will be but a small part of a long tale, or am I wrong?—That will inevitably be the style of such a speaker, he said.

A different speaker, however, in so far as he is an inferior person, will tell everything and think nothing unworthy of himself. As a result he will attempt to imitate everything in earnest and before a large audience, including the things we mentioned just now, thunder and the noise of wind and of hail, of axles and of wheels, of trumpets and flutes and pipes, even the cries of dogs and sheep and birds. That man's style will consist entirely of imitation in voice and gesture, or at least have very little straight narration.—That too is inevitable.

These then, I said, are the two kinds of style I spoke of.—And they certainly exist.

The first of these two has few variations, and if someone gives a musical mode and a rhythm suited to it, the correct speaker will remain pretty well within that mode throughout—the changes are few—and also he will stay with a similar rhythm.—That is surely so.

What about the other kind? Does it not require the opposite, namely all kinds of musical modes, all kinds of rhythms, if it is to be spoken in a suitable manner, because it contains every form of variation?—That certainly is so.

All poets and speakers make use of one or the other kind of style, or of a mixture of both.—Necessarily, he said.

What then shall we do? said I, shall we admit all these into our city, or only one of the pure kinds, or the mixed one?

If my opinion is to prevail, he said, we will accept only the pure style which imitates the good man only.

And yet, Adeimantus, the mixed style, the opposite to the one you have chosen, is pleasant, and gives most pleasure to children and their slave-tutors, and to the mob.—Most pleasant to them.

But perhaps, I said, you do not think that it fits into our community because with us a man is not two or more persons at once, but each one has but one occupation.— It is not suitable.

And for this reason it is only in our city that we shall find a cobbler who is a cobbler and not a pilot besides, and a farmer who is a farmer and not a juryman as well, and a warrior who is a warrior and not a moneymaker in addition, and so with them all?—True.

It seems then that if a man who in his cleverness can become many persons and imitate all things should arrive in our city and want to give a performance of his poems, we should bow down before him as being holy, wondrous, and sweet, but we should tell him that there is no such man in our city and that it is not lawful that there should be. We would pour myrrh on his head and crown him with wreaths, and send him away to another city. We ourselves would employ a more austere and less pleasure-giving poet and story-teller for our own good, one who would imitate the speech of a good man and would express himself in accordance with the patterns we laid down when we first undertook the education of our soldiers.—That, he said, is certainly what we would do if it were within our power.

Now, I said, we have probably completed, my friend, our discussion of that part of the literary art which concerns discourse and stories, for we have spoken both of content and of the manner of expressing it.—I think so myself.

c   What is left after this is the manner of expressing lyric odes and songs?—Clearly.

Could not anyone discover what we should say it ought to be if we are to remain in tune with our previous statements?

Glaucon laughed and said: I'm afraid, Socrates, that I am not included under "anyone." I have at the moment no adequate idea of the kind of thing we are to say. True, I have my suspicions.

d   Surely, I said, you can state this first point, that a song consists of three elements: words, musical mode, and rhythm.—Yes, he said, I can state that.

As far as words go, there is no difference with speech which is not set to music; it must conform to the patterns which we enunciated just now and in the same way.—True, he said.

Further, the mode and the rhythm must fit the words.—Of course.

And we certainly said that we needed no dirges and lamentations in our discourses.—No indeed.

e   What are the lamenting modes, then? You tell me, for you are musical.

The mixo-Lydian, the syntono-Lydian, and some others of that kind, he said.

Shall we then ban those? They are useless even for women who are to be good, let alone men.—Certainly.

Drunkenness is most improper for our guardians, and softness and idleness as well.—Of course.

Which are the soft and drinking modes?

The Ionian, he said, and some Lydian are called relaxed.

399   Could you ever make use of these for warriors?

Never, he said, and I fear that the only modes left are the Dorian and the Phyrgian.

I do not know the musical modes, I said, but leave me that mode which would suitably imitate the tone and voice changes of a brave man in battle action or any
b   violent deed, also when he is failing and on his way to wounds or death, or falling into some other misfortune, and is, in all these circumstances, fighting off his fate steadily and with self-control. Leave me also another mode, that of a man engaged in peaceful, nonviolent, and willing action, either persuading someone and asking a favour, either from a god in prayer or from a mortal by teaching and exhortation; or again, on the contrary, submitting himself to the supplications of another who is teaching him or wanting him to change his mind, and in all these circumstances
c   acting as he thinks he should, without arrogance but reasonably and moderately, and being content with the consequences. Leave me those two modes, the violent and the willing, which will best imitate the accents of brave and moderate men both in misfortune and prosperity.

The modes you ask for, he said, are the very ones I was mentioning.

We will then, I said, have no need for many-stringed instruments or varied modes in our odes and songs.—I don't think so.

We shall therefore not provide for makers of triangular lyres or Lydian pipes or
d   any many-stringed instruments of many varied modes.—It seems not.

Further, will you admit flute makers and flute players into the city? Does the flute not sound like the instrument with the most strings and are not many changes of mode an imitation of the flute?—Clearly.

The lyre and the cithara then are left to you as useful in the city, I said, and the pipes for herdsmen in the country.—As our argument shows.

We are certainly not doing anything new, my friend, said I, in preferring Apollo and his instruments to Marsyas and his.[54]—By Zeus, said he, I don't think we are.   e

And by the dog[55] I said, we have, without noticing it, purified again the city which we recently declared to be luxurious.—A reasonable thing for us to do.

Come then, I said, let us continue the purification. The next topic after musical modes should be meters. We should not seek all kinds of feet and variations but ascertain what are the rhythms of an ordered and brave life and then adapt the metrical feet and the tune to the words of that kind of person, not adapt his words   400
to the foot and the tune. What these rhythms are it is for you to say, as in the case of the modes.

No, by Zeus, he said, I don't know what to say. I do know from observation that there are three basic kinds on which the feet are built, just as there are four bases of modes, but I cannot say which kind imitates which kind of life.[56]

We will, I said, consult Damon[57] as to which metrical feet are suited to meanness   b
and insolence or madness and other wickedness, and which are suited to the opposite. I think I have heard him name one kind of composite metrical phrase an enoplion, and speak of dactylic and heroic meters, but I am not clear about this. I do not know how he arranged them but he made the arsis and the thesis equal, ending with a short and long syllable, and, I think, he named one the iambus, while   c
another foot he called the trochee, and fitted in the long and short syllables. Then I believe he approved or disapproved of the tempo of a foot as much as of the rhythms themselves, or something which was both, for I do not know. But, as I said, we will leave this to Damon, for to define these things would require a long discussion, or do you think we should do it?—No, by Zeus, not I.

But this is a distinction you can make, that gracefulness or the reverse follow upon a good or bad rhythm.—Of course.

Now a good rhythm follows beautiful language and is similar to it, while a bad   d
rhythm follows the opposite, and so with musical harmony or discord, if, as we said

---

54. [When Athena had invented the flute, she discarded it because it distorted her features when she played it. It was picked up by a satyr Marsyas who learned to play it and was foolish enough to challenge Apollo to a musical contest. He was defeated, and Apollo flayed him alive.]

55. [A curious oath sometimes affected by Socrates. In the *Gorgias* (482b) it occurs in the form: "by the dog, the god of the Egyptians." It is thought to be a euphemism to avoid the name of a god, but Socrates does not hesitate to swear by Zeus. It seems to be used in moments of ironic emphasis.]

56. [The three kinds of feet are probably: (1) those in which one part of the foot is to the other in the ratio of 2/2 such as the dactyl or the spondee —˘˘ and——; (2) in the ratio of 3/2, such as the paeon, ˘˘˘—; and (3) in a ratio of 2/1 such as the iambus ˘— or the trochee—˘. The enoplion is a metrical phrase, namely ˘—˘˘—˘˘—.]

57. [Damon was a fifth-century writer on music and meter. The views expressed here may owe a good deal to him.]

just now, the rhythm and the tune must conform to the words, and not vice versa.—Certainly, these things must conform to the words.

What of the manner of expression and the content? Do these not adapt to the character of the speaker's soul?—Of course.

And the rest conform to the words?—Yes.

So fine speech, fine music, gracefulness, and fine rhythm are all adapted to a simplicity of character, and I do not mean simplicity in the sense we use it as a euphemism for foolishness, but where the mind has established a truly good and fine character.—Most certainly.

And should our young men not aim at this everywhere, if they are to fulfill the task that is theirs?—They must indeed.

Painting is full of these qualities, and all such artistic works; so is weaving and embroidery and architecture and the making of furniture; so is our bodily nature and that of other growing things; in all these there is seemliness and unseemliness. Unseemliness, poor rhythm, and discord are closely akin to poor language and poor character, while their opposites are closely akin to, and imitations of, the opposite, a good and moderate character.—This is altogether true.

Is it then the poets only whom we shall command and compel to represent the image of good character in their poems or else not practise among us, or are we to give orders also to other craftsmen, and forbid them to represent, whether in pictures or in buildings or in any other works, character that is vicious, mean, unrestrained, or graceless? We must not allow one who cannot do this to work among us, that our guardians may not, bred among images of evil as in an evil meadow, culling and grazing much every day from many sources, little by little collect all unawares a great evil in their own soul. We must seek out such artists as have the talent to pursue the beautiful and the graceful in their work, in order that our young men shall be benefited from all sides like those who live in a healthy place, whence something from these beautiful works will strike their eyes and ears like a breeze that brings health from salubrious places, and lead them unawares from childhood to love of, resemblance to, and harmony with, the beauty of reason.—This, he said, would be by far the best nurture for them.

Are these not the reasons, Glaucon, I said, why nurture in the arts is most important, because their rhythm and harmony permeate the inner part of the soul, bring graciousness to it, and make the strongest impression, making a man gracious if he has the right kind of upbringing; if he has not, the opposite is true. The man who has been properly nurtured in this area will be keenly aware of things which are neglected, things not beautifully made by art or nature. He will rightly resent them, he will praise beautiful things, rejoice in them, receive them into his soul, be nurtured by them and become both good and beautiful in character. He will rightly object to what is ugly and hate it while still young before he can grasp the reason, and when reason comes he who has been reared thus will welcome it and easily recognize it because of its kinship with himself.—Yes, he said, I agree those are the reasons for education in the arts.

Just as earlier in the case of letters of the alphabet, I said, we only had an adequate grasp of them when we paid attention to them, that there were but few in whatever combinations they occurred, and we did not neglect them either in small things or in great, or think they need not be noticed, but were keen to distinguish them everywhere, knowing that we would not be competent readers until we could do so.—True.

And we shall not recognize the images of letters which may appear in water or mirrors before we know the letters themselves, this being part of the same craft and practice.—Most certainly.

What I mean, by the gods, is that we shall not be educated in the arts, neither ourselves nor those whom we say we must educate to be our guardians, before   c we recognize the different forms[58] of moderation and courage, of generosity and munificence, their kindred qualities and their opposites too, as they occur every-where, and perceive wherein they occur, both themselves and their images, and do not despise them in small things or in great, but realize that this is part of the same craft and training.—That is very necessary.

When a man's soul has a beautiful character, and his body matches it in beauty   d and is thus in harmony with it, that harmonizing combination, sharing the same mould, is the most beautiful spectacle for anyone who has eyes to see.—It certainly is.

And that which is most beautiful is most lovable.—Of course.

A cultured man would love such people, but would not love one lacking in such harmony.

Not, he said, if he had some defect in the soul, yet a physical defect he might   e overlook and be fond of him.

I understand, said I, that you have, or have had, such a beloved, and I agree with you. Tell me this, however, is excessive pleasure compatible with moderation?—How can it be, since it drives one to frenzy?

Or with the other virtues?—In no way.   403

Well then, is it compatible with violence and lack of restraint?—Very much so.

Can you think of a greater and sharper pleasure than the sexual?—No, nor a madder one.

But the right kind of love is to love a well-behaved and beautiful person with moderation and restraint?—Certainly, he said.

The right kind of love has nothing frenzied or licentious about it?—Nothing.

That sexual pleasure we mentioned must therefore not be brought into it, and   b the right lovers and beloved must have no share of it.—No, by Zeus, Socrates, that pleasure must not be brought into it.

You will therefore lay it down in our city which is being established that the lover, if he can persuade him, can kiss his beloved, keep company with him, and touch him as a father would his son for the sake of good conduct and associate with one of whom he is genuinely fond in such a manner that their relationship will never   c appear to go beyond this; otherwise he will incur the reproach of vulgarity and lack of taste.—That is so.

Do you agree that we have now completed our discussion of education in the arts,

---

58. [The word for forms here is *eidos* which will be used later in the *Republic* as the technical name of the Platonic Form or Idea, but it is here used in its common, nontechnical meaning of "forms" or "kinds" of moderation, courage etc.]

I said, and that it has ended as it should? For a discussion of the arts must end in the love of the beautiful.—I agree.

After education in the arts, our young men must have physical training.—Quite so.

d In this too they must have careful training from childhood throughout life. The matter stands, it seems to me, something like this. You too consider the point. It seems to me that a fit body does not by its own excellence ensure a good soul, but on the contrary it is a good soul which by its own excellence ensures that the body shall be as fit as possible. What do you think?—I think as you do.

e Therefore, if we have devoted sufficient care to the mind, we would be right to entrust to it the detailed supervision of physical matters, and here only lay down the general lines, to avoid talking at excessive length.—Certainly.

Drunkenness we said that our youths must avoid. It is less proper for a guardian than for anybody else to be drunk and not to know where on earth he is.—It would be absurd, he said, for the guardian to need a guardian.

What about food? These men are athletes in the greatest contest, are they not?—Yes.

404 Would the present regimen of athletes in training suit them?—Perhaps.

It seems, I said, somewhat soporific, and of doubtful value to health. Do you not see that these trainees sleep their life away, and if they move a small step away from their prescribed regimen, they are seriously and violently ill.—I do see that.

b Our warrior-athletes need a more sophisticated kind of training. They must, like dogs, be quick to wake and have very good eyesight and hearing; on campaigns they have to endure frequent changes of drinking water and food, of summer and winter weather. They cannot afford to be easily tripped up in matters of health.—I think the same.

Is not the best physical training closely akin to that simplicity in the arts which we discussed previously?—How do you mean?

That simple physical training is also good training, especially in training for war.—How so?

c One might learn this from Homer, I said. You know that on the campaign he does not feast his heroes on fish at their banquets, in spite of the fact that they are by the sea on the Hellespont, nor on boiled meat but only on roasted, which is most easily available to soldiers, for everywhere, one might say, it is easier to use fire than to carry vessels along.—Yes indeed.

Nor does Homer anywhere mention seasonings. Or do other trainees too know that if the body is to be sound one should keep away from all such things?—They are right to know it and to keep away from them.

d Then you do not approve, my friend, of a Syracusan cuisine, nor of Sicilian variety of dishes, it seems, if you think this right.—I do not.

You object then also to having a Corinthian girl friend for men who are to be in good physical shape.—Most certainly I do.

And also to those Attic pastries which are thought to be such a delight?—It follows of necessity.

I believe we would be right to compare this whole kind of diet and way of living

to the kind of lyric odes and songs which are composed in all sorts of modes and   e
rhythms.—Of course.

Just as these variations produced licentiousness there, so here they bring disease.
Simplicity in poetry and music makes for moderation in the soul, so in physical
culture it makes for health.—Very true.

And as licentiousness and diseases propagate in the city, many lawcourts and   405
hospitals are opened. Skill in pleading and medicine give themselves solemn airs
when even many free men pursue them eagerly.—What is to prevent it?

Yet could you find a better proof of bad and shameful education in a city than
that the need for highly skilled physicians and jurists is felt not only by inferior men
and artisans, but even by those who profess to have received a liberal education? Do   b
you not think it shameful and a great sign of vulgarity to be forced to make use of
a justice imposed upon one by others, as by masters and judges, because of one's
lack of inner resources?—I think it of all things the most shameful.

But is it not even more shameful not only to spend a good part of one's life in
lawcourts as defendant or plaintiff but to believe one should preen oneself on this,
that one is clever at wrongdoing, that one is skilled in taking advantage of all
the twists and turns and of every trick to escape conviction, and that in the most   c
unimportant and worthless cases—in ignorance that it is much better and finer to
arrange one's own life so that one never stands in need of a sleepy judge?—That is
even more shameful than the other.

And to need medical help, except for wounds and an attack of seasonable diseases,
because we live in idleness and in the manner we have described, like stagnant pools   d
full of winds and currents, thereby forcing sophisticated physicians to use the words
"blasts" and "torrents" as names for diseases, does not that seem shameful to you?—
It certainly does, he said, and these are indeed novel and strange names for diseases.

And I said: They did not, I think, exist in the time of Asclepius. I take it as a proof
of this that his sons at Troy did not reproach the woman who gave to the wounded   e
Eurypylus Pramnian wine to drink with much barley meal and cheese grated on top   406
of it, though this is thought to be feverous, nor did they make an objection to
Patroclus who was treating him.[59]—Yet it is a strange drink to give a man in that
condition.

Not so if you realize, I replied, that the kind of modern medicine which cossets
the disease was not used by the Asclepiads, they say, before Herodicus. He was a
gymnastic trainer who became ill and mixed physical culture with medicine and   b
wore out first himself and then many others.—How? he said.

By making his dying a lengthy process, he followed the course of his deadly
disease; he was not, I believe, able to cure himself, and so he lived out his life under
medical treatment, doing nothing else whatever; he was quite worn out if he took
the slightest step away from his customary regimen. So his skill allowed him to reach
old age, dying a hard death the while.—A fine prize for his skill!

One which is likely, said I, for a man who did not understand that it was not   c
through ignorance or inexperience of this type of medicine that Asclepius did not

---

59. [Plato seems to have two Homeric passages in mind, one from *Iliad* 4, 210 ff., where Machaon treats the
wounded Menelaus, and the other at 11, 580 ff. where Eurypylus is wounded and cared for, but in neither case
are the circumstances as here described. However, the passages generally support his main point.]

teach it to his sons, but because he knew that every man in a well-governed community has his own prescribed task to fulfill, and that no one has the leisure to be ill and under treatment all his life. We see such a life to be ridiculous for the workers, but we do not realize that it is equally ridiculous for those who are reputed to be rich and prosperous.—How?

d When a carpenter is ill, I said, he expects to receive from his physician an emetic or a purge or to get rid of his disease by cautery or surgery. If anyone should prescribe a long regimen to him, that he should rest with his head on pillows and all that goes with this, he would soon say that he has no leisure to be ill and that life is no use to him if he must always be concerned with his illness and neglect the task
e before him. After that he would bid his physician good-bye, resume his usual manner of life, and recover his health. If his body could not tolerate the illness, he would die and escape from his troubles.—For such a man to use medicine in this way is thought fitting.

407 Is that because if he does not perform the task which is his, life is of no benefit to him?—Obviously.

But the rich man, we say, has no such set task, the non-performance of which makes life not worth living.—People say he has not.

Have you not heard the saying of Phocylides that after a man makes his living, he ought to practice virtue?—Before too, I should think.

We will not quarrel with him about this, but let us teach ourselves whether the
b rich man must practise this, and whether his life is not worth living if he does not. Or is cosseting an illness an obstacle to applying oneself to carpentry and the other crafts, but something which does not interfere in any way with the advice of Phocylides?

By Zeus it does, he said. Excessive concern for the body beyond physical training is pretty well the greatest obstacle of all; it puts difficulties in the way of managing a household, of military service, or of holding a sedentary public office.

The worst of it is that it makes difficulties with regard to learning of any kind, or
c thought, or self-training, always suspecting some headache or dizziness and accusing the love of wisdom of causing it. The result is that in whatever way this love leads to the practice or testing of virtue, this excessive care for the body stands in the way; it always makes a man think he is ill and gives him no respite from bodily pain.— This is likely to happen.

We shall say that Asclepius understood this. He taught medicine for those who were healthy in their nature and their habits but were suffering from a specific
d disease; he rid them of it by drugs or surgery and then ordered them to live as usual in order not to upset the social system. For those, however, whose bodies were always in a state of inner sickness he did not attempt to prescribe a regimen, or, drawing off a little here and pouring in a little there, to make their life a prolonged misery and let them produce offspring like themselves as they were likely to do. He did not
e think he should treat those who could not live the regular course of life, as they were useless to themselves and to the community.—Your Asclepius was quite a sociologist!

Clearly, said I, and because he was such a man, do you not see how his sons at
408 Troy proved themselves to be good warriors and to practise medicine as I say they did? Do you not remember that from the wound which Pandarus inflicted on

Menelaus "they sucked out the blood and applied gentle potions to it,"[60] but after
that they did not prescribe what he should eat or drink any more than they did for
Eurypylus. They considered their remedies sufficient to cure men who, before being
wounded, were healthy and lived an orderly life, even if they drank a posset at that   b
moment. They did not consider the life of those who were inherently sick and
unrestrained to be beneficial either to themselves or to anyone else; medicine was
not intended for them and they should not be treated, even if they were richer than
Midas.

The sons of Asclepius, according to you, he said, were certainly sophisticated!

That is fitting, I said, but the tragedians and Pindar do not believe us. They say
that Asclepius was the son of Apollo and that he was bribed with gold to heal a rich
man who was already dying, for which he was killed by lightning. Now in accordance   c
with what we said before we shall not believe both their statements; if he was the
son of a god he was not, we shall say, a money-grubber or, if he was that, he was not
the son of a god.

That is quite correct, he said, but, Socrates, what do you say about the following?
Do we not need to have good physicians in the city? These would surely be the men
who have visited the greatest number of healthy and the greatest number of sick   d
people. In the same way the best judges would be those who have associated with all
kinds of human nature.

I quite agree, I said, that they must be good, but do you know whom I consider
as such?—If you tell me.

I will try, I said, but you include different things in the same question.—How so?

The cleverest physicians, I said, would be those who from childhood on have been
in contact with the greatest number of very sick bodies, have themselves experienced
every illness, and are not very healthy by nature. They do not, I think, treat bodies   e
with their body—for in that case their body should not be or become bad—but with
their mind, which could not give good care to anything if it were itself bad or became
so.—Correct.

As for the judge,[61] my friend, it is with his soul that he rules another soul, and it   409
is not possible for a soul to be nurtured among evil souls, associate with them,
indulge itself in all kinds of wrongdoing, and come through in the end so as to be
able to judge other people's crimes from its own experience as it can with physical
diseases. It must itself remain pure and without experience of vice when it is young,
if it is to be beautiful and good itself and have a healthy judgment of just actions.
That is why good people, when young, appear simple-minded and easily deceived,   b
because they do not have within themselves any model of evil feelings.—They
certainly have that experience.

Therefore, I said, a good judge must not be a young but an old man, who has
learned late the nature of injustice. He cannot recognize it as anything of his own,
he must have studied it as something alien, present in other people. It is only after

60. [From *Iliad* 4, except that in our text Machaon is acting alone.]

61. [The Greek word is *dikastēs*, a member of a jury panel. These were very large (500 in Socrates' trial) and
they combined the duties of jury and judge, as they decided both the question of guilt and the penalty. Here
Plato is obviously thinking of the act of judging, and the translation "judge" is unavoidable.]

c   a long time that he fully recognizes its nature, intellectually, and not from his own experience.

Such a judge, he said, is likely to be a very noble character.

And good too, which was what you asked, for he who has a good soul is good. That other character, the clever and suspicious one who has committed many wrongs himself, the rascal who thinks himself wise, appears clever in the company of his like because of his caution and because he refers things to a model within himself, but when he meets with good, older people, he is seen to be foolish, distrustful at

d   the wrong time, and ignorant of moral health, as he has no model of this within himself. Too often, however, whether the people he meets are good or bad, he is thought to be wise rather than ignorant by others as well as by himself.—That is altogether true.

It is not such a man that we must seek to be a good and wise judge, but the former type. Wickedness could never know either itself or virtue, whereas virtue, as one's

e   nature is being educated, will at the same time acquire the knowledge of itself and of wickedness. It is that man who becomes wise, as I believe, not the bad man.—I agree with you.

Therefore you will legislate in our city for the kind of medicine we have mentioned and for this kind of judicial system. Together they will look after the well endowed

410   in body and soul. Those not so endowed physically will be allowed to die, and those who are incurably evil in their soul will be executed.

That seems to be best, he said, both for the victims and for the city.

The young, I said, will obviously be wary of coming into court because theirs is that simple culture in the arts which we said engenders modesty.—Quite so.

b   And will not the cultured man if he is willing to pursue physical culture in the same way, choose to have no need of medicine except when unavoidable?—I think so.

He will labour at physical exercises in order to arouse the spirited part of his nature rather than to acquire that physical strength for the sake of which the other athletes diet and exercise.—Quite right.

And I said: Those, Glaucon, who establish education in the arts and physical

c   training do not do so with the aim that people attribute to them, namely to take care of the body by means of the one, and of the soul by means of the other.—What then?

They may well, I said, establish both in large part to look after the soul.—How so?

Do you not realize, I said, the state of mind of those who practise physical culture throughout their life but do not touch the arts, and of those in the opposite case?—What are you talking about?

d   I am talking of harshness and rigidity, I said, and also of softness and gentleness.

I get the point, he said. You mean that those who devote themselves exclusively to physical culture turn out to be harsher than they should be, while those who devote themselves to the arts become softer than is good for them.

And further, said I, it is the spirited part of one's nature which provides the harshness; rightly nurtured it becomes courageous, but if strained too far it would be likely to become rigid and harsh to deal with.—I think so.

And is it not the wisdom-loving nature which provides the gentleness, and, if e
relaxed too far, becomes softer than it should, though if properly nurtured it is
gentle and orderly?—That is so.

We said that our guardians must have both these natures.—They must.

These must then be harmonized with each other?—Of course.

If this harmony is achieved the soul is both moderate and brave?—Certainly. 411

If not, it becomes cowardly and boorish?—Yes indeed.

Therefore, when a man gives music an opportunity to charm his soul with the
flute, and to pour through his ears as through a funnel those sweet, soft, and
plaintive tunes we have mentioned, when he spends his whole life humming them
and delighting in them, then at first, if he has any spirit, it is softened as iron is b
tempered and, from being hard and useless, is made useful. But if he keeps on, does
not desist, but is beguiled by this music, after a time his spirit is melted and dissolved
until it vanishes, cut out of his soul like a tendon, and he becomes "a feeble warrior."[62]—Quite so.

And if, I said, he had a spiritless nature from the first, this process is soon
accomplished. If he had a spirited nature, this spirit becomes weak and unstable,
flaring up for trifles and as quickly quenched. So men become quick-tempered and c
prone to anger instead of spirited, and they are full of peevishness.—That is certainly
true.

What if a man labours much at physical exercises and lives well but is quite out of
touch with the arts and philosophy? Is he not in good physical condition at first, full
of resolution and spirit, and becomes braver than he was before? Certainly.

But if he does nothing else and never associates with the Muse? He never has a
taste of any learning or any investigation; he has no share in any reasoned discussion d
or any other form of culture; even if he had some love of learning in his soul it soon
becomes enfeebled, deaf, and blind as it is not aroused or nurtured; and even his
senses are not sharpened.—That is so, he said.

I believe that such a man comes to hate reasoned discussion and the arts; he makes
no further use of persuasion but bulls his way through every situation by force and
fierceness like a wild beast; he lives in ignorance and ineptitude with a total lack of e
harmony and grace.—That is most certainly the case.

It seems then that a god has given men these two means, artistic and physical
education, to deal with these two parts of themselves, not the body and the soul
except incidentally but the spirited and the wisdom-loving parts, in order that these 412
be in harmony with each other, each being stretched and relaxed to the proper
point.—It seems so.

We should then quite correctly call the man who achieves the most beautiful blend
of physical and artistic culture, and in due measure impresses this upon his soul,
the completely Muse-inspired and harmonious man, far more so than the musician
who harmonizes the strings of his instrument.—That is very likely, Socrates.

Therefore in our city too, Glaucon, we shall always need this kind of man as an
overseer, if our community is to be preserved?—We shall certainly have the greatest b
need of him.

---

62. [The phrase is used of Menelaus by Apollo who is encouraging Hector to fight him, in *Iliad* 17, 588.]

These then are the outlines of our education and upbringing, but why should one enumerate the dances of our youth, their hunts and chases with hounds, their gymnastic and horse-riding contests? These must pretty clearly follow our outlines and are no longer hard to discover.—Perhaps not.

Very well, I said. Shall we choose as our next topic of discussion which of these
c   same men shall rule, and which be ruled?—Why not?

Now it is obvious that the rulers must be older men and that the younger must be ruled.—Obviously.

And that the rulers must be the best of them?—That too.

The best farmers are those who have to the highest degree the qualities required for farming?—Yes.

Now as the rulers must be the best among the guardians, they must have to the highest degree the qualities required to guard the city—Yes.

d   And for this they must be intelligent, able, and also care for the city?—That is so.

Now one cares most for that which one loves.—Necessarily.

And one loves something most when one believes that what is good for it is good for oneself, and that when it is doing well the same is true of oneself, and so with the opposite.—Quite so, he said.

We must therefore select from among our guardians those who, as we test them, hold throughout their lives to the belief that it is right to pursue eagerly what they
e   believe to be to the advantage of the city, and who are in no way willing to do what is not.—Yes, for they are good men.

I think we must observe them at all ages to see whether they are guardians of this principle, and make sure that they cannot be tempted or forced to discard or forget the belief that they must do what is best for the city.—What, he said, do you mean by discarding?

I will tell you, I said. I think the discarding of a belief is either voluntary or involuntary; voluntary when the belief is false, and as a result of learning one
413 changes one's mind, involuntary when the belief is true.—I understand the voluntary discarding, but not the involuntary.

Really? Do you not think that men are unwilling to be deprived of good things, but willingly deprived of bad things? Is not untruth and missing the truth a bad thing, while to be truthful is good? And is not to have a true opinion to be truthful?— You are right, he said, and people are unwilling to be deprived of a true opinion.

b   But they can be so deprived by theft, or compulsion, or under a spell?—I do not understand even now.

I fear I must be talking like a tragic poet! I apply the word "theft" to those who change their mind or those who forget, not realizing that time or argument has robbed them of their belief. Do you understand now?—Yes.

By compulsion I mean those whom pain or suffering causes to change their mind.—That too I understand and you are right.

c   Those under a spell I think you would agree are those who change their mind because they are bewitched by pleasure or fear.—It seems to me, he said, that anything which deceives bewitches.

As I said just now, we must find out who are the best guardians of their belief that they must always do whatever they think to be in the best interest of the city. We must keep them under observation from childhood and set them tasks which would most easily lead one to forget this belief, or to be deceived. We must select the one who keeps on remembering and is not easily deceived, the other we will reject. Do you agree?—Yes.

We must also subject them to labours, sufferings, and contests in which to observe this.—Right.

Then, I said, for the third kind we must observe how they face bewitchment. Like those who lead colts into noise and tumult to see if they are fearful, so we must expose our young to fears and pleasures to test them, much more thoroughly than one tests gold in fire, and see whether a guardian is hard to bewitch and behaves well in all circumstances as a good guardian of himself and of the cultural education he has received, always showing himself a gracious and harmonious personality, the best man for himself and for the city. The one who is thus tested as a child, as a youth, and as an adult, and comes out of it untainted, is to be made a ruler as well as a guardian. He is to be honoured both in life and after death and receive the most esteemed rewards in the form of tombs and memorials. The one who does not prove himself in this way is to be rejected. It seems to me, Glaucon, I said, that rulers and guardians must be selected and established in some such way as this, to speak in a general way and not in exact detail.—I also think it must be done in some such way.

These are the men whom it is most correct to call proper guardians, so that the enemies without shall not have the power, and their friends within shall not have the desire, to harm the city. Those young men whom we have called guardians hitherto we shall call auxiliaries to help the rulers in their decisions.—I agree.

What device could we find to make our rulers, or at any rate the rest of the city, believe us if we told them a noble fiction, one of those necessary untruths of which we have spoken?—What kind of fiction?

Nothing new, I said, but a Phoenician story which the poets say has happened in many places and made people believe them; it has not happened among us, though it might, and it will take a great deal of persuasion to have it believed.

You seem hesitant to tell your story, he said.

When you hear it you will realize that I have every reason to hesitate.

Speak without fear.

This is the story—yet I don't know that I am bold enough to tell it or what words I shall use. I shall first try to persuade the rulers and the soldiers, and then the rest of the city, that the upbringing and the education we gave them, and the experience that went with them, were a dream as it were, that in fact they were then being fashioned and nurtured inside the earth, themselves and their weapons and their apparel. Then, when they were quite finished, the earth, being their mother, brought them out into the world. So even now they must take counsel for, and defend, the land in which they live as their mother and nurse, if someone attacks it, and they must think of their fellow-citizens as their earth-born brothers.

It is not for nothing that you were shy, he said, of telling your story.

Yes, I said, I had very good reason. Nevertheless, hear the rest of the tale. "All of you in the city are brothers" we shall tell them as we tell our story, "but the god who fashioned you mixed some gold in the nature of those capable of ruling because they are to be honoured most. In those who are auxiliaries he has put silver, and iron and bronze in those who are farmers and other workers. You will for the most b   part produce children like yourself, but, as you are all related, a silver child will occasionally be born from a golden parent, and vice versa, and all the others from each other. So the first and most important command of the god to the rulers is that there is nothing they must guard better or watch more carefully than the mixture in the souls of the next generation. If their own offspring should be found to have

c   iron or bronze in his nature, they must not pity him in any way, but give him the esteem appropriate to his nature; they must drive him out to join the workers and farmers. Then again, if an offspring of these is found to have gold or silver in his nature they will honour him and bring him up to join the rulers or guardians, for there is an oracle that the city will be ruined if ever it has an iron or bronze guardian. Can you suggest any device which will make our citizens believe this story?

d   I cannot see any way, he said, to make them believe it themselves, but the sons and later generations might, both theirs and those of other men.

Even that, I said, would help to make them care more for their city and each other, for I do understand what you mean. But let us leave this matter to later tradition. Let us now arm our earthborn and lead them forth with their rulers in charge. And as they march let them look for the best place in the city to have their

e   camp, a site from which they could most easily control those within, if anyone is unwilling to obey the laws, and ward off any outside enemy who came like a wolf upon the flock. When they had established their camp and made the right sacrifices, let them see to their sleeping quarters, or what do you suggest?—I agree.

These must protect them adequately both in winter and summer.

Of course, he said, you mean their dwellings.

Yes, I said, dwellings for soldiers, not for money-makers.

416   What would you say is the difference? he asked.

I will try to tell you, I said. The most terrible and shameful thing for a shepherd is to train his dogs, who should help the flocks, in such a way that, through lack of discipline or hunger or bad habit, those very dogs maltreat the animals and behave like wolves rather than dogs.—Quite true.

b   We must therefore take every precaution to see that our auxiliaries, since they are the stronger, do not behave like that toward the citizens, and become cruel masters instead of kindly allies.—We must watch this.

And a really good education would endow them with the greatest caution in this regard?—But surely they have had that.

And I said: Perhaps we should not assert this dogmatically, my dear Glaucon. What we can assert is what we were saying just now, that they must have the correct

c   education, whatever that is, in order to attain the greatest degree of gentleness toward each other and toward those whom they are protecting.—Right.

Besides this education, an intelligent man might say that they must have the amount of housing and of other property which would not prevent them from being

d   the best guardians and would not encourage them to maltreat the other citizens.— That would be true.

Consider then, said I, whether they should live in some such way as this if they are to be the kind of men we described: First, not one of them must possess any private property beyond what is essential. Further, none of them should have a house or a storeroom which anyone who wishes is not permitted to enter. Whatever

moderate and courageous warrior-athletes require will be provided by taxation   e
upon the other citizens as a salary for their guardianship, no more and no less than
they need over the year. They will have common messes and live together as soldiers
in a camp. We shall tell them that the gold and silver they always have in their nature
as a gift from the gods makes the possession of human gold unnecessary, indeed
that it is impious for them to defile this divine possession by any admixture of the
human kind of gold, because many an impious deed is committed in connection   417
with the currency of the majority, and their own must remain pure. For them alone
among the city's population it is unlawful to touch or handle gold or silver; they
must not be under the same roof with it, or wear any, or drink from gold or silver
goblets; in this way they may preserve themselves and the city. If they themselves
acquire private land and houses and currency, they will be household managers and
farmers instead of guardians, hostile masters of the other citizens instead of their   b
allies; they will spend their whole life hating and being hated, plotting and being
plotted against; they will be much more afraid of internal than of external enemies,
and they will rush themselves and their city very close to ruin. For all these reasons,
I said, let us say that the guardians must be provided with housing and other matters
in this way, and these are the laws we shall establish.

Certainly, said Glaucon.

BOOK IV

Adeimantus took up the argument and said: What defense, Socrates, would you   419
offer against the charge that you are not making your guardians very happy, and
that through their own fault? The city is really in their power, yet they derive
no good from this. Others own land, build grand and beautiful houses, acquire
furnishings appropriate to them, make their own private sacrifices to the gods,
entertain, also, as you mentioned just now, have gold and silver and all the possessions which are thought to belong to people who will be happy. One might well say
that your guardians are simply settled in the city like paid mercenaries, with nothing
to do but to watch over it.   420

Yes, said I. Moreover, they work for their keep and get no extra wages as the
others do, so that if they want to leave the city privately they cannot do so; they have
nothing to give their mistresses, nothing to spend in whatever other way they wish,
as men do who are considered happy. You have omitted these and other such things
from the charge.—Let these accusations be added, he said.

Now you ask what defence we shall offer?—Yes.   b

I think we shall discover what to say if we follow the same path as before, I said.
We shall say that it would not be at all surprising if these men too were very happy.
In any case, in establishing our city, we are not aiming to make any one group
outstandingly happy, but to make the whole city so, as far as possible. We thought
that in such a city we would most easily find justice, find injustice in a badly governed
one, and then decide what we have been looking for all the time. Now we think we   c
are fashioning the happy city not by separating a few people in it and making them

happy, but by making the whole city so. We shall look at the opposite kind of city presently. If someone came to us while we were painting a statue[63] and objected because we did not apply the finest colours to the finest parts of the body, for the eyes are the most beautiful part, and they are not made purple but black, we should appear to offer a reasonable defence if we said: "My good sir, do not think that we must make the eyes so beautiful that they no longer appear to be eyes at all, and so with the other parts, but look to see whether by dealing with each part appropriately we are making the whole statue beautiful." And so now, do not force us to give our guardians the kind of happiness which would make them anything but guardians.

d

We know how to clothe our farmers too in purple robes, surround them with gold and tell them to work the land at their pleasure, and how to settle our potters on couches by the fire, feasting and passing the wine, put their wheel by them and tell them to make pots as much as they want; we know how to make all the others also happy in the same way, so that the whole city is happy. Do not exhort us to do this, however. If we do, the farmer will not be a farmer, nor the potter a potter; nor would anyone else fulfill any of the functions which make up the state. For the others this is less important: if shoemakers become inferior and corrupt, and claim to be what they are not, the state is not in peril, but, if the guardians of our laws and city only appear to be guardians and are not, you surely see that they destroy the city utterly, as they alone have the opportunity to govern it well and to make it happy.

e

421

If then we are making true guardians who are least likely to work wickedness upon the city, whereas our accuser makes some farmers into banqueters, happy as at some festival but not in a city, he would be talking about something else than a city. We should examine then, with this in mind, whether our aim in establishing our guardians should be to give them the greatest happiness, or whether we should in this matter look to the whole city and see how its greatest happiness can be secured. We must compel and persuade the auxiliaries and the guardians to be excellent performers of their own task, and so with all the others. As the whole city grows and is well governed, we must leave it to nature to provide each group with its share of happiness.

b

c

I think, he said, that you put that very well.

Will you also, said I, think that I speak reasonably when I make the next point which is closely akin to this?—What is that?

d

Consider whether these factors corrupt the other workers also, so that they become bad at their job?—What factors?

Wealth, I said, and poverty.—How do you mean?

Like this. Do you think that a potter who has become wealthy will still be willing to pay attention to his craft?—Not in any way.

He will become more idle and careless than he was?—Much.

And therefore become a worse potter?—Far worse.

And surely if poverty prevents him having the tools or anything else his craft needs, he will produce poorer work, and his sons or any others he may teach will not be as good workers.—Of course.

e

---

63. [There is no doubt that the Greeks painted their statues, at times only certain parts of them.]

So both poverty and wealth make the products of the crafts worse, and the craftsmen too.—Apparently.

We have, it seems, found other dangers against which our guardians must guard most carefully, lest these should penetrate the city unnoticed.—What are these?

Both wealth and poverty, I said. The former makes for luxury, idleness, and political change, the latter for meanness, bad work, and change as well. 422

That is certainly true, he said, but please consider this point, Socrates: how will our city be able to fight a war, since it has not acquired wealth, especially if it has to fight against a mighty and wealthy opponent?

Obviously, I said, it will be harder to fight one such city than two,—How do you mean? said he. b

First of all, said I, if they must fight, will they not be fighting as warrior-athletes against rich men?—As far as that goes, yes.

Well then, Adeimantus, I said, do you not think that one boxer who has had the best possible training could easily fight two rich and fat non-boxers?—Perhaps not at the same time.

Not even, said I, if he could run off and then turn round and hit the one close to him, and did this again and again in the stifling heat of the sun? Would he not be c able, in his condition, to tackle even more than two?—That would certainly not be surprising.

And do you not think that the rich have more knowledge and experience of boxing than of fighting in war?—I do.

Our athletes would then most likely be able to fight with ease twice or three times their own numbers.—I will agree with you, for I think you are talking sense.

What if they sent envoys to the other city and said, which is the truth: "We have d no use for gold or silver and it is not lawful for us to possess them, but you can. So join us in this war and make the other side's possessions your own." Do you think that any people on hearing this would choose to fight against hardened and spare dogs rather than, with the dogs on their side, fight against sleek and soft sheep?

No, I do not think so, he said, but if the wealth of the others came to be gathered together in one city, take care that this does not imperil your non-wealthy city. e

You are fortunate, I said, if you think that any other city than the kind we are founding deserves the name.—What do you mean?

We must find a grander name for the others, as each of them is a cluster of cities, not one city, as they say in the game.[64] Each of them, in any case, consists of two hostile cities, that of the poor and that of the rich, and each of these contains many. 423 It would be a grave mistake to approach them as one, but if you approach them as many and give the possessions of one to the other, their wealth, their power, and even their persons, you will always have many allies and few enemies. As long as your city is governed with moderation as we have just established it, it will itself have greatness. I do not mean great repute but true greatness, even if it have only one thousand men to fight for it. You will not easily find one great city in this sense either among Greeks or barbarians, though you will find a very large number that b are thought to be great. Do you think differently?—By Zeus no.

---

64. [The reference is obscure; it may be to an unknown saying or proverb, or to a game.]

This then would be the best limitation which our guardians should put upon the size of the city; they should then mark off the amount of land required for its size, and let the rest go.—What is this limitation?

c I think, I said, that it is this: to let the city grow as long as it is willing to retain its unity, but not beyond that point.—Quite right.

This then is another order we shall give our guardians: to watch most carefully that the city should not appear either small or big, but sufficient, and remain one.— This, he said, is indeed an easy order we shall give them!

d Even easier than that, I said, is the one we mentioned before when we said that, if an offspring of the guardian is inferior, he must be sent off to join the other citizens, and if the others have an able offspring, he must be taken into the guardian group. This was meant to make clear that the other citizens must each be directed to the one task for which each is naturally fitted, so that he should pursue that one task which is his own and be himself one person and not many, and the city itself be a unity and not a plurality.—That is an even easier order than the other!

These orders we give them, my good Adeimantus, I said, are not, as one might think, either numerous or important; they are all secondary, provided that they guard the one great thing, as people say, though rather than great I would call it sufficient.—What is that?

Their education and their upbringing, I said. If they become cultured, moderate men, they will easily see these things for themselves, and other things too which we are now omitting, the acquiring of wives and children which must all accord with

424 the old proverb, that the possessions of friends must be held in common.—That would be the best way.

Surely, I said, once our city gets a good start, it would go on growing in a circle. Good education and upbringing, if preserved, will lead to men of a better nature, and these in turn, if they cling to their education, will improve with each generation

b both in other respects and also in their children, just like other animals.—Quite likely.

To put it briefly, those in charge of our city must cling to this and see that education is not corrupted without their noticing it, guard above all else that there should be no innovations in physical and artistic education as established, and be as careful as they can. They should be fearful when they hear anyone say:

> Men care most for the song,
> which is newest to the singer,[65]

c lest anyone should praise this, thinking that the poet meant not new songs but new ways of singing. One should not praise such a thing nor take it up; one should be cautious in adopting a new kind of poetry and music, for this endangers the whole system. The ways of poetry and music are not changed anywhere without change in the most important laws of a city, as Damon affirms and I believe.—You can count me too among the believers.

---

65. [From *Odyssey* 1, 351–2, but our texts read: "men always praise that song most which is new to those who hear it." Plato is probably quoting from memory, or he may have had a different text.]

It is here, said I, in music and the arts,, that our guardians must build their   d
bulwark against change.

Yes, he said, for lawlessness easily creeps in there unawares.

Yes, said I, as if it was just play and did no harm at all.

Nor does it, he said, except that, after establishing itself there, lawlessness quietly
flows over into the character and pursuits of men. Then, greatly increased, it steps
out into private contracts, and from private contracts it makes its way insolently into   e
the laws and the government, until in the end it upsets everything public and private.

Very well, I said, is that how it works?—I think so.

Then, as we said at the beginning, our children's games must be more law-abiding,
for if their games become lawless and the children follow suit, it is impossible for
them to grow up into good and law-abiding men.—How could they?   425

When children play the right games from the first, they absorb obedience to the
law through their training in the arts, quite the opposite of what happens to those
who play lawless games. This lawfulness follows them in everything, fosters their
growth, and can correct anything that has gone wrong before in the city.—This is
indeed true.

They then discover those conventions which seem unimportant, all of which those
who came before them have destroyed.—What conventions?

Things like this: when it is proper for the young to be silent in the company of   b
their elders, how they should sit at table, when to give up their seat, care for their
parents, hair styles, what clothes and shoes to wear, deportment, and the other
things of that kind. Do you not think so?—I do.

I think it is foolish to legislate about such things. Verbal or written decrees will
never make them come about or last.—How could they?

They are likely to follow as necessary consequences from the direction one's   c
education takes. Does not like always call to like?—Quite so.

And we might say that it ends in one complete and vigorous product which is itself
either good or the opposite.—Quite so.

For these reasons, I said, I would not go on to attempt legislation about such
things.—That seems right.

Then by the gods what about market business, the private contracts which they   d
make with one another in the market place; add, if you wish, cases of insulting
behavior, ill treatment, the bringing of lawsuits, the establishment of juries, the
payment and assessment of dues that may be necessary in markets or harbours, and
all the regulations in the market, the city, or the harbour, and all other such—shall
we venture to legislate for any of these?

It is not worthwhile, he said, to make orders about these for good men and true;
they will easily discover most of those which need legislation.   e

Yes, my friend, I said, if a god grant the preservation of the laws which we have
already described.

And if not, he said, they will spend their lives enacting many laws and amending
them, believing that they are thus attaining what is best.

You mean, I said, that they will live the same sort of life as those sick people who,
through lack of self-control, cannot give up their bad diet?—Quite so.

426   They too live a pleasant life! Their treatment achieves nothing, except that their complaints become worse and more varied; they are always hoping, when someone advises a new medicine, that this will cure them.—That is certainly the experience of that kind of sick people, he said.

Further, I said, is this not charming of them, that they consider as their worst enemy the man who tells them the truth, namely that until they give up drunkenness,
b   overeating, lechery, and idleness, no medicine, cautery, or surgery, no charms or amulets or anything of the kind will do them any good.

Not charming at all, for to quarrel with one who is saying the right thing has no charm.

You do not approve, it seems, of such men, I said.—By Zeus, I certainly do not.

Nor will you approve if, as we said, a whole city behaves in this way. Don't you think that those which are badly governed behave like this when they warn their
c   citizens not to disturb the whole political establishment on pain of death? Thus governed, people will consider as good and wise in important matters, and greatly honour, the man who serves them most pleasantly, who indulges them, flatters them, anticipates their wishes, and is clever at fulfilling them.

Certainly they seem to behave in the same way, he said, and I do not approve at all.

d   What about those who are willing and eager to serve such cities? Do you not admire their courage and complaisance?

I do, he said, except for those who are deceived by the approval of the majority into believing that they are true statesmen.

How do you mean, I asked, do you not forgive them? or do you think it possible for a man ignorant of measurement not to believe it himself when many other
e   ignorant people tell him that he is six feet tall?—No, I do not think that either.

Do not be hard on them; they are of all men the most engaging. They pass laws on those subjects which we were just enumerating, and amend them, and they always think they will find a way to put a stop to cheating on contracts and the other things
427   I was mentioning. They do not realize that this is, in fact, like cutting off a hydra's head.[66]—That is surely what they are doing.

I should have thought, said I, that the true lawgiver must not bother with that kind of law and administration either in a well governed or in a badly governed city—in the latter, because it is useless and accomplishes nothing, in the former, because anyone at all could discover some of these laws for himself, while other laws follow automatically from the pursuits we laid down earlier.

b   What, he asked, is now left for us to deal with under the heading of legislation?

I answered: For us nothing, but for the Delphic Apollo the greatest, the finest, and the first enactments.—What are these?

The establishing of temples, sacrifices, and other forms of service to the gods, spirits, and heroes; then again the burials of the dead and the services which ensure their favour. We have no knowledge of these things and in establishing our city we
c   shall not, if we are wise, accept any other advice or use any other than our ancestral

---

66. [The Hydra was a primeval monster with many heads. As soon as one head was cut off, two or three new heads grew in its place. The slaying of the Hydra was one of the labours of Heracles.]

guide. This god is the ancestral interpreter of these things for all men as he sits upon the rock which is the center of the earth.[67]—You are quite right, he said, and we must do so.

Well, son of Ariston, I said, your city might now be said to be established. The next step is for you to look inside it with what light you can procure, to call upon your brother and Polemarchus and the others, if we can somehow see where justice resides in it, and where injustice, what the difference is between them, and which of the two the man who intends to be happy should possess, whether gods and men recognize it or not.

Nonsense, said Glaucon. You promised to look for them yourself because you said it was impious for you not to come to the rescue of justice in every way you could.

True, I said, as you remind me; I must do so, but you must help.—We will, he said.

I hope to find it, I said, in this way. I think our city, if it is rightly founded, is completely good.—Necessarily so, he said.

Clearly then it is wise, brave, moderate, and just.—Clearly.

Therefore whichever of these we find in the city, the rest will be what we have not found?—You mean?

As with any four things, if we were looking for any one of them in anything, if we first recognize it, that would be enough, but if we recognize the other three first, then by that very fact we recognize what we are looking for. For clearly it can be no other than what is left.—Correct, he said.

So with these, since there are four, we must look for them in the same way.—Obviously.

Now the first of them which I believe to be clear is wisdom; and there seems to be something strange about it.—What is that? he said.

I think that the city which we have described is wise in fact because it has sound judgment, is it not so?—Yes.

Now this very thing, sound judgment, is clearly some kind of knowledge, for it is through knowledge, not ignorance, that people judge soundly.—Clearly.

There are many kinds of knowledge in the city.—Of course.

Would we call the city wise and sound in judgment because of the knowledge of its carpenters?—Never through that, he said; we would then call it sound in carpentry.

Nor through the knowledge by which it judges which wooden furniture is best would we call the city wise.—No indeed.

Nor because of its knowledge of brazen things or of any similar things.—Nor through any of them.

Nor through the knowledge of how to raise a harvest from the earth, but then we should call it agricultural.—I think so.

Well then, I said, is there some knowledge in the city we have just founded and among some of the citizens, which does not deliberate about any particular matter

d

e

428

b

c

d

---

67. [I.e. Apollo at Delphi: a rock in the sanctuary was said to be the navel of the earth.]

but about the city as a whole, how best to maintain good relations both internally and with other cities?—There is.

What is this knowledge, I asked, and in whom does it reside?

It is the knowledge of guardianship, he said, and it resides in those rulers whom just now we named the complete guardians.

Then what does this knowledge entitle us to call the city?

Really wise, he said, and of good judgment.

e   Do you think, I asked, that the metal-workers or these true guardians are the more numerous in our city?—The metal-workers, he said, by far.

Of all those who are called by a certain name because they have some knowledge, the guardians would be the least numerous?—They are by far the fewest.

Then a whole city which is established according to nature would be wise because of the smallest group or part of itself, the commanding or ruling group. This group seems to be the smallest by nature and to it belongs a share in that knowledge which, alone of them all, must be called wisdom.—What you say is very true, he said.

We have now found, I don't know how, this to be itself one of the four, and also where in the city it resides.—Our way of finding it, he said, seems good enough to me.

It is surely not very difficult to see courage itself, through which the city is to be called brave, and where in the city it is to be found.—How?

b   Who, I said, when calling the city cowardly or brave, would look anywhere else but to that part of it which makes war and campaigns on its behalf?—No one, he said, would look anywhere else.

I do not think, I said, that whether the other citizens were cowardly or brave would cause the city to be called one or the other.—It would not.

The city then is brave because of a part of itself which has the capacity always to preserve its belief about things to be feared, that they are those things and those kinds
c   of things which the lawgiver declared to be such in the course of their education. Or don't you call that courage?—I do not, he said, quite understand what you mean. Please repeat it.

I mean, said I, that courage is a kind of preservation.—What kind?

The preservation of the belief which has been inculcated by the law through one's education as to what things and what kinds of things are to be feared, and by always
d   I meant to preserve this belief and not to lose it when one is in pain, beset by pleasures and desires, and by fears. I will, if you like, make clear what I think this resembles by a simile.—I should like you to do so.

You know, I said, that dyers who want to dye wool purple, first of all pick out from many colours the natural white, and then prepare this in a number of ways so
e   that it will absorb the colour as well as possible, and only then dye it. In what is dyed in this way the colour is fast; no washing with or without soap can take it away. You also know what becomes of material which has not been dyed in this way, whether someone dyes it other colours or does not prepare the wool beforehand.—I know, he said, that it looks washed out and ridiculous.

Understand then, I said, that, as far as we could, we were doing something similar
430   when we were selecting our soldiers and were educating them in the arts and physical culture. What we were in fact contriving was that, in obeying us, they should absorb

Courage found in city's soldiers

the laws most beautifully like a dye, so that, as they had the right nature and the proper education, their belief as to what they should fear and so on should become fast and that the detergents which are extremely effective should not wash it out: pleasure, which is much more potent than any powder or soda or soap, and pain, and fear and appetite. Now this capacity to preserve through everything the right and lawful belief as to what is to be feared and what is not, this is what I call and define as courage, unless you say otherwise.

b

I have, he said, nothing to say, for I assume that the right opinion about these same things which is not the result of education, such as you find in animals and slaves, you do not consider to be inculcated by law, and you do not call it courage but something else.

Very true, I said.—Then I accept your description of courage.

c

Accept also, I said, that it is civic courage, and your acceptance will be sound. We shall discuss this subject more fully some other time, if you want to, but it is not the object of our investigation; justice is, and for that purpose I think this is sufficient.—You are quite right, he said.

There are now two qualities left for us to find in the city: moderation and that at which our whole investigation is aimed, justice.—Quite so.

d

How could we find justice, so that we need not bother with moderation[68] any further?

I do not know, he said, and I should not want it to appear first, if that means that we do not investigate moderation. If you want to please me, look for moderation before the other.

e

I am certainly willing, I said; it would be wrong not to be.—Look then.

We must do so, I said. Looked at from here, it is more like a consonance or harmony than the others we have considered hitherto.—How?

Moderation is a certain orderliness, I said, and mastery over certain pleasures and appetites, as people somehow indicate by using the phrase self-control and other expressions which give a clue to its nature. Is that not so?—Most certainly.

Yet the expression self-control is laughable, for the controller of self and the self that is weaker and controlled is the same person, and so with all those expressions. It is the same person that is referred to.—Of course.

431

But, I said, the expression seems to want to indicate that in the soul of the man himself there is a better and a worse part; whenever what is by nature the better part is in control of the worse, this is expressed by saying that the man is self-controlled or master of himself, and this is a term of praise. When, on the other hand, the smaller and better part, because of poor upbringing or bad company, is overpowered by the larger and worse, this is made a reproach and called being defeated by oneself, and a man in that situation is called uncontrolled.—Properly so.

b

Look now, I said, at our new city and you will find one of those alternatives in it. You will say that it is rightly called self-controlled, since that in which the better

68. [The Greek word translated moderation is *sōphrosunē*. It has a very wide meaning: self-control, temperance, reasonableness, in some contexts chastity. Etymologically it seems to mean a man who remains equable under strain or, to use a slang expression, one who "keeps his cool."]

rules the worse should be called moderate and self-controlled.—I am looking at it, and what you say is true.

c   Further, one would mostly find many and various appetites and pleasures of all kinds as well as pains in children and women and household slaves, and in the many and the inferior among those called free men.—Quite so.

But those that are simple and measured and directed by reasoning with intelligence and right belief you will meet with in but few people who are the best by nature and the best educated.—True.

You will see this also in your city; there the desires of the inferior many are
d   controlled by the desires and the knowledge of the fewer and better?—I do indeed.

If any city is to be called in control of its pleasures and desires and of itself, this city is.—Most certainly.

And will it not be called moderate in all these respects?—Definitely.

Further, if the same opinion exists in any city among the rulers and also the ruled
e   as to who should rule, it will be found in this city, do you not think?—Definitely.

And when that is the case, in which of the two kinds of citizens will you say that moderation exists, among the rulers or the ruled?—Among both, I suppose.

You see now how right we were to foresee that moderation resembles a kind of harmony?—How so?

Because, unlike courage and wisdom, each of which resided in one part of the city
432   and made it, the one brave, the other wise, moderation spreads throughout the whole, among the weakest and the strongest and those who are in between, be it in regard to knowledge or, if you wish, in physical strength or in numbers or in wealth or in anything else, and it makes them all sing the same tune. This unanimity would rightly be called moderation, agreement, that is, between the naturally worse and the naturally better as to which of the two must rule, both in the city and in each
b   individual.—I quite agree.

Very well, I said. We have now found three of the four in the city, as far as our present discussion takes us. What would the remaining kind be which still makes the city share in virtue? Or is it clear that this is justice?—Quite clear.

So now we must concentrate our attention like hunters surrounding a coppice, lest justice escape us and vanish without our seeing it, for obviously it is somewhere
c   around here. Look eagerly, now, in case you see it before I do, and tell me.

I wish I could, he said, but you will make a more sensible use of me if you take me to be a follower who can see things when you point them out.

Follow then, I said, and join me in a prayer.—I will do that, but you lead.

Indeed, I said, the place seems impenetrable and full of shadows; it is certainly dark and hard to hunt in. However, go on we must.—We must indeed.

d   As I looked I exclaimed: Aha! Glaucon, it looks as if there was a track, and I don't think our prey will altogether escape us.—Good news.

Surely, I said, we are being stupid.—In what way?

My good friend, it seems to have been rolling about right in front of our feet for some time, in fact from the beginning, and we did not see it. This was quite ridiculous of us. As people sometimes look for the very thing they are holding in their hands,
e   so we paid no attention to it, but were looking away in the distance, which accounts for our not seeing it.—What do you mean?

I mean, I said, that we have been mentioning it, and hearing it mentioned, for a long time without understanding ourselves that we were, in a way, speaking of it.—This is a long prelude for someone who is impatient to hear.

Well, I said, listen whether I am talking sense. I think that justice is the very thing,   433
or some form of the thing which, when we were beginning to found our city, we said had to be established throughout. We stated, and often repeated, if you remember, that everyone must pursue one occupation of those in the city, that for which his nature best fitted him.—Yes, we kept saying that.

Further, we have heard many people say, and have often said ourselves, that justice is to perform one's own task and not to meddle with that of others.—We have   b
said that.

This then, my friend, I said, when it happens, is in some way justice, to do one's own job. And do you know what I take to be a proof of this?—No, tell me.

I think what is left over of those things we have been investigating, after moderation and courage and wisdom have been found, was that which made it possible for those three qualities to appear in the city and to continue as long as it is present. We   c
also said that what remained after we found the other three was justice.—It had to be.

And surely, I said, if we had to decide which of the four will make the city good by its presence, it would be hard to judge whether it is a common belief among the rulers and the ruled, or the preservation among the soldiers of a law-inspired belief as to the nature of what is, and what is not, to be feared, or the knowledge and   d
guardianship of the rulers, or whether it is, above all, the presence of this fourth in child and woman, slave and free, artisan, ruler and subject, namely that each man, a unity in himself, performed his own task and was not meddling with that of others.—How could this not be hard to judge?

It seems then that the capacity for each of the city to perform his own task rivals   e
wisdom, moderation, and courage as a source of excellence for the city.—It certainly does.

You would then describe justice as a rival to them for excellence in the city?—Most certainly.

Look at it this way and see whether you agree: you will order your rulers to act as judges in the courts of the city?—Surely.

And will their exclusive aim in delivering judgment not be that no citizen should have what belongs to another or be deprived of what is his own?—That would be their aim.

That being just?—Yes.

In some way then possession of one's own and the performance of one's own task could be agreed to be justice.—That is so.   434

Consider then whether you agree with me in this: if a carpenter attempts to do the work of a cobbler, or a cobbler that of a carpenter, and they exchange their tools and the esteem that goes with the job, or the same man tries to do both, and all the other exchanges are made, do you think that this does any great harm to the city?—No.

But I think that when one who is by nature a worker or some other kind of moneymaker is puffed up by wealth, or by the mob, or by his own strength, or some   b other such thing, and attempts to enter the warrior class, or one of the soldiers tries to enter the group of counsellors and guardians, though he is unworthy of it, and these exchange their tools and the public esteem, or when the same man tries to perform all these jobs together, then I think you will agree that these exchanges and this meddling bring the city to ruin.—They certainly do.

c   The meddling and exchange between the three established orders does very great harm to the city and would most correctly be called wickedness.—Very definitely.

And you would call the greatest wickedness worked against one's own city injustice?—Of course.

That then is injustice. And let us repeat that the doing of one's own job by the moneymaking, auxiliary, and guardian groups, when each group is performing its own task in the city, is the opposite, it is justice and makes the city just.—I agree d   with you that this is so.

Do not let us, I said, take this as quite final yet. If we find that this quality, when existing in each individual man, is agreed there too to be justice, then we can assent to this—for what can we say?—but if not, we must look for something else. For the present, let us complete that examination which we thought we should make, that if we tried to observe justice in something larger which contains it, this would make e   it easier to observe it in the individual. We thought that this larger thing was a city, and so we established the best city we could, knowing well that justice would be present in the good city. It has now appeared to us there, so let us now transfer it to the individual and, if it corresponds, all will be well. But if it is seen to be something different in the individual, then we must go back to the city and examine this new 435   notion of justice. By thus comparing and testing the two, we might make justice light up like fire from the rubbing of firesticks, and when it has become clear, we shall fix it firmly in our own minds.—You are following the path we set, and we must do so.

Well now, when you apply the same name to a thing whether it is big or small, are these two instances of it like or unlike with regard to that to which the same name applies?—They are alike in that, he said.

b   So the just man and the just city will be no different but alike as regards the very form of justice.—Yes, they will be.

Now the city was thought to be just when the three kinds of men within it each performed their own task, and it was moderate and brave and wise because of some other qualities and attitudes of the same groups.—True.

And we shall therefore deem it right, my friend, that the individual have the same c   parts in his own soul, and through the same qualities in those parts will correctly be given the same names.—That must be so.

Once again, my good man, I said, we have come upon an easy inquiry whether the soul has these three parts or not!

It does not look easy to me, he said. Perhaps the old saying is true, that all fine things are difficult.

So it seems, said I. I want you to know, Glaucon, that in my opinion we shall d   certainly not attain any precise answer by following our present methods. There is another longer and fuller way which leads to such an answer. However, this way is perhaps good enough to accord with our previous statements and inquiries.

Is it not satisfactory? he asked. It is enough for me at the present time.

And indeed, I said, it will quite satisfy me.—Do not weary, he said, but continue.

Well then, I said, we are surely compelled to agree that each of us has within   e
himself the same parts and characteristics as the city? Where else would they come
from? It would be ridiculous for anyone to think that spiritedness has not come to
be in the city from individuals who are held to possess it, like the inhabitants of
Thrace and Scythia and others who live in the north of us, or that the same is not
true of the love of learning which one would attribute most to our part of the   436
world, or the love of money which one might say is conspicuously displayed by the
Phoenicians and the Egyptians.—Certainly, he said.

This then is the case, I said, and it is not hard to understand.—No indeed.

But this is: whether we do everything with the same part of our soul, or one thing
with one of the three parts, and another with another. Do we learn with one part of
ourselves, get angry with another, and with some third part desire the pleasures of
food and procreation and other things closely akin to them, or, when we set out   b
after something, do we act with the whole of our soul in each case? This will be hard
to determine satisfactorily.—I think so too.

Let us try to determine in this way whether these parts are the same or different.—
How?

It is clear that one thing cannot act in opposite ways or be in opposite states at the
same time and in the same part of itself in relation to the same other thing; so if we
find this happening we shall know that we are not dealing with one thing but with
several.—Be it so.   c

Examine then what I am about to say.—Say on.

Is it possible for the same thing to stand still and to move at the same time in the
same part of itself?—In no way.

Let us go into this more precisely to avoid disagreements later on. If someone
were to say that a man is standing still but moving his hands and his head, and that
therefore he is moving and standing still at the same time, I think we would not
deem that the proper way to put it, but that one part of him is standing still and   d
another part is moving. Is not that the way to express it?—It is.

Then if our interlocutor carried the objection further, and was smart enough to say
that whole spinning tops stand still and move at the same time for, while remaining in
the same spot, they turn round their axis, and so with anything else moving in a
circular motion while staying in the same place, we would not agree because the
parts of them in respect to which they stand still and move are not the same. We   e
should say that these objects have an axis and a circumference; in their axis they
stand still, for they do not wobble in any way, and their circumference moves in a
circle; then, when the axis inclines left or right, frontward or backward, while the
top goes round, it is not still at all.—And we would be right.

No such statements shall disturb us or make us believe that anything, while
remaining itself, can ever be affected, or be, or act, in opposite ways at the same
time, in the same part of itself in relation to the same other object.—They will not   437
make me believe it at any rate.

Nevertheless, I said, in order to avoid having to go through all these objections
one by one and taking a long time proving them untrue, let us assume that it is so

and carry on. We agree that if the matter should ever be shown to be otherwise, all the consequences we have drawn from it will also be invalidated.—We must do so.

b   Would you not, I said, consider all the following as pairs of opposites: assent and dissent, to want to have something and to deny oneself, to take something to oneself and to cast it off? Whether they are actions or passive states makes no difference in this respect.—They are opposites.

Further, I said, thirst and hunger and the appetites as a whole, then again inclination and willingness, would you not include all these among the class of things we c   were mentioning? Would you not say that the soul of one who desires something longs for the object of his desire, or wants to take to itself what he wants to have, or again, in so far as he wants to be provided with something, the soul nods assent to itself as if someone were questioning it, because it yearns for it to be?—Yes.

Then we would include among what is altogether the opposite of these: being unwilling, lacking desire, since these lead to driving away or casting off from the d   soul.—Of course.

That being so, we will say that there is a class of things named appetites and that the most obvious of these are hunger and thirst?—We agree.

One of these is for drink, the other for food?—Yes.

Now in so far as it is mere thirst, is it a desire in the soul for something more than what we mentioned? For example, is thirst a thirst for a hot drink or a cold drink, a long or a short one, or, in a word, is it for a drink of a certain kind? Or is it that e   if you feel hot as well as thirsty, this adds a desire for cold or, if you feel cold, for hot. If the desire is great because of the presence of quantity it will make it a desire for much, and if it is little, for a little one, but thirst itself is never for anything different from its natural object, drink unqualified, and so too with hunger, for food.

That's it, he said, each desire itself is only for its natural object in each case, and additional circumstances add the qualifications, that is, for such and such an object.

438   Do not let us be disturbed, I said, because we are unprepared for it, by someone saying that no one just wants a drink but a good drink, or any food but good food. All men want good things. So that if thirst is a desire, it will be a desire for good, be it a drink or anything else for which it is a desire, and so with the other desires.— Perhaps the man who says this has a point, he said.

But surely, I said, in the case of all things that are related to another, when the b   first is qualified by a predicate, the second is too, but each in itself is unqualified and directed to an unqualified object.—I do not understand.

You do not understand that the greater is such as to be greater than something?— Quite so.

It is greater than the smaller?—Yes.

And that which is much greater is related to something much smaller?—Yes.

c   And that which is sometimes greater is related to that which is sometimes smaller.—Certainly.

So is the more numerous to the less numerous, the double to the half, and so with all things of the kind, the heavier to the lighter, the swifter to the slower, also the hot to the cold, and all similar things. Is that not so?—Quite.

Then what about knowledge? Does the same apply? Knowledge itself is directed to the thing itself which is learned, or whatever one should say that knowledge is related to, and, when knowledge is qualified, it is of a qualified object. I mean this: d when knowledge is of building a house it is called building-knowledge?—Yes indeed.

And is this not qualified as no other knowledge is?—Yes.

So when it becomes knowledge of a certain object, it becomes a certain kind of knowledge, and this is true of all crafts and sciences?—That is so.

This is what I was wanting to say, I said, if you understand now. In a relation between two things, when the first is unqualified by a predicate, so is the second, and when the first is qualified by a predicate, the second is too. I do not mean that   e the predicate need be the same for them both—for example, knowledge of health or disease is not healthy or diseased, or the knowledge of good and evil does not itself become good or evil—but that when knowledge is no longer of its simple object but a qualification is added to the object, it follows that the knowledge itself is qualified. It is then no longer simply called knowledge but is qualified, as in this case it becomes medical knowledge.—I understand and I think that it is so.

As for thirst, I said, would you not include it as something which in itself is related   439 to something else? Thirst is related to . . .—I know, to drink.

Therefore when a predicate is added to the drink, one is also added to the thirst, but in itself thirst is not for a long drink or a short one, a good drink or a bad one, in a word not for a qualified drink, but thirst in itself is by nature for a drink without any qualification.—Quite true.

The soul of the thirsty, in so far as he is thirsty, does not want anything else, only to drink; this is what it longs for and sets out to get.—Obviously.   b

Therefore if anything pulls it back when it is thirsty, there must be a different part in the soul from the part that is thirsty and, like an animal, leads him to drink: for we say that the same thing cannot act in contrary ways with the same part of itself toward the same object at the same time.—It cannot.

Just as I think it wrong to say that a man's hands at the same time push the bow away and draw it toward him. One ought to say that one hand pushes it away and the other draws it toward him.—Most certainly one should.   c

Shall we say that there are times when thirsty people are not willing to drink?—Certainly it happens often and to many people.

What then, I said, should one say about this? Is there not in their soul that which bids them drink, and also that which prevents them, that the latter is different and overrules the other part?—I think so, he said.

And the preventing part comes into play as a result of reasoning, whereas the impulses that lead and drag him are due to emotive states and diseases?—Apparently.   d

It is therefore not unreasonable for us to say that these are two distinct parts, to call that with which it reasons the rational part of the soul, and that with which it lusts and feels hungry and thirsty and gets excited with other desires the irrational and appetitive part, the companion of repletions and pleasures.—That is a natural way for us to think.   e

Let these two then be described as two parts existing in the soul. Now is the spirited part by which we get angry a third part, or is it of the same nature as either of the other two?—Perhaps it is like the appetitive part.

I have, I said, heard a story which I believe, that Leontius, the son of Aglaion, as he came up from the Piraeus on the outside of the northern wall, saw the executioner with some corpses lying near him. Leontius felt a strong desire to look at them, but at the same time he was disgusted and turned away. For a time he struggled with himself and covered his face, but then, overcome by his desire, pushing his eyes wide open and rushing toward the corpses: "Look for yourselves," he said, "you evil things, get your fill of the beautiful sight!"—I've heard that story myself.

It certainly proves, I said, that anger sometimes wars against the appetites as one thing against another.—It does.

Besides, I said, we often see this elsewhere, when his appetites are forcing a man to act contrary to reason, and he rails at himself and is angry with that within himself which is compelling him to do so; of the two civic factions at odds, as it were, the spirited part becomes the ally of reason. I do not think that you can say that when reason has decided that it must not be opposed, you have ever perceived the spirited part associating itself with the appetites, either in yourself or in anyone else.—No by Zeus I have not.

What happens, I said, when anyone thinks he is doing wrong? Is it not true that the nobler a man is, the less he can resent it if he suffers hunger or cold or anything of that kind at the hands of one whom he believes to be inflicting this on him justly, and as I say, does not his spirited part refuse to be aroused?—True.

What if a man believes himself wronged? I asked. Is the spirit within him not boiling and angry, fighting for what he believes to be just? Will he not endure hunger and cold and such things and carry on till he wins out? and not cease from noble actions until he either wins out or dies, or, like a dog by his shepherd, is called to heel by the reason within himself and quieted down?

The spirit certainly behaves as you say, he said. Moreover, in our city we made the auxiliaries, like dogs, obey the rulers, the shepherds of the city.

You understand very well, I said, what I want to convey. In addition, reflect on this further point.—What point?

The position of the spirited part seems the opposite of what we thought a short time ago. Then we thought of it as something appetitive, but now we say it is far from being that; in the civil war of the soul it aligns itself far more with the reasonable part.—Very much so.

Is it different from that also, or is it some part of reason, so that there are two parts of the soul instead of three, the reasonable and the appetitive? Or, as we had three separate parts holding our city together, the money-making, the auxiliary and the deliberative, so in the soul the spirited is a third part, by nature the helper of reason, if it has not been corrupted by a bad upbringing?—It must be a third part.

Yes, I said, if it now appears to be different from the reasonable part, as earlier from the appetitive part.

It is not difficult, he said, to show that it is different. One can see this in children; they are full of spirit from birth, whereas a few of them seem to me never to acquire a share of reason, while the majority do not do so until late.

By Zeus, I said, that is very well put. One can see this also in animals. Besides, our earlier quotation from Homer bears witness to it, where he says:

Striking his chest, he addressed his heart,[69]

69. [*Odyssey* 20, 17, already quoted more fully above at III, 390d.]

for clearly Homer represents the part which reasons about the better and the worse   c
course, and which strikes his chest, as different from that which is angry without
reasoning.—You are definitely right.

We have now made our difficult way through a sea of argument to reach this
point, and we have fairly agreed that the same kinds of parts, and the same number
of parts, exist in the soul of each individual as in our city.—That is so.

It necessarily follows that the individual is wise in the same way, and in the same
part of himself, as the city.—Quite so.

And the part which makes the individual brave is the same as that which makes   d
the city brave, and in the same manner, and everything which makes for virtue[70] is
the same in both?—That necessarily follows.

Moreover, Glaucon, I think we shall say that a man is just in the same way as the
city is just.—That too is inevitable.

We have surely not forgotten that the city was just because each of the three classes
in it was fulfilling its own task.—I do not think, he said, that we have forgotten that.

We must remember then that each one of us within whom each part is fulfilling
its own task will himself be just and do his own work.—We must certainly remember   e
this.

Therefore it is fitting that the reasonable part should rule, it being wise and
exercising foresight on behalf of the whole soul, and for the spirited part to obey it
and be its ally.—Quite so.

Is it not then, as we were saying,[71] a mixture of artistic and physical culture which
makes the two parts harmonious, stretching and nurturing the reasonable part with
fine speech and learning, relaxing and soothing the spirited part, and making it   442
gentle by means of harmony and rhythm.—Very definitely, he said.

These two parts, then, thus nurtured and having truly learned their own role and
being educated in it, will exercise authority over the appetitive part which is the
largest part in any man's soul and is insatiable for possessions. They will watch it to
see that it is not filled with the so-called pleasures of the body, and by becoming   b
enlarged and strong thereby no longer does its own job but attempts to enslave and
to rule over those over whom it is not fitted to rule, and so upsets everybody's whole
life.—Quite so, he said.

These two parts will also most effectively stand on guard on behalf of the whole
soul and the body, the one by planning, the other by fighting, following its leader,
and by its courage fulfilling his decisions.—That is so.

It is this part which causes us to call an individual brave, when his spirit preserves
in the midst of pain and pleasure his belief in the declarations of reason as to what   c
he should fear and what he should not.—Right.

70. [Plato uses the word *aretē* in two somewhat different senses. It can refer to the quality, or combination of
qualities, which makes a person, an animal, or even an object good at doing something which nothing else can do,
or at least do as well (above 1, 353b ff., cp.335b–c), and it is then best translated by excellence (cp. below 444a). Each
of the virtues, however, is also an *aretē*, and it is then best translated "virtue." Of course, the two senses merge at
times; we may note, however, that in this discussion Plato does not use the term to describe the individual virtues.]

71. [The reference is to the discussion of the effects of education in the arts and physical culture above at
410–11. There both are said to have a good effect, but here Plato refers only to the effect of the arts upon both
reason and spirit.]

And we shall call him wise because of that small part of himself which ruled in him and made those declarations, which possesses the knowledge of what is beneficial to each part, and of what is to the common advantage of all three.—Quite so.

Further, shall we not call him moderate because of the friendly and harmonious relations between these same parts, when the rulers and the ruled hold a common belief that reason should rule, and they do not rebel against it?—Moderation, he said, is surely just that, both in the individual and the city.

And he will be just in the way we have often described.—Necessarily.

Now, I said, has our notion of justice become at all indistinct? Does it appear to be something different from what it was seen to be in the city?—I do not think so.

If any part of our soul still disputes this, we could altogether confirm it by bringing up common arguments.—What are they?

For example, concerning the city and the man similar to it by nature and training, if we had to come to an agreement whether we think that this man has embezzled a deposit of gold and silver, who, do you think, would consider him to have done this rather than men of a different type?—No one would.

And he would have nothing to do with temple robberies, thefts, or betrayals, either of friends in his private life, or, in public life, of cities?—Nothing.

Further, he would be in no way untrustworthy in keeping an oath or any other agreement.—How could he be?

Adultery too, disrespect for parents, neglect of the gods would suit his character less than any other man's.—Much less.

And the reason for all this is that every part within him fulfills its own function, be that ruling or being ruled?—Certainly that, and nothing else.

Are you still looking for justice to be anything else than this power which produces such men and such cities as we have described?—By Zeus, he said, not I.

We have then completely realized the dream we had when we suspected[72] that, by the grace of god, we came upon a principle and mould of justice right at the beginning of the founding of our city.—Very definitely.

Indeed, Glaucon—and this is why it is useful—it was a sort of image of justice, namely that it was right for one who is by nature a cobbler to cobble and to do nothing else, and for the carpenter to carpenter, and so with the others.—Apparently.

And justice was in truth, it appears, something like this. It does not lie in a man's external actions, but in the way he acts within himself, really concerned with himself and his inner parts. He does not allow each part of himself to perform the work of another, or the sections of his soul to meddle with one another. He orders what are in the true sense of the word his own affairs well; he is master of himself, puts things in order, is his own friend, harmonizes the three parts like the limiting notes of a musical scale, the high, the low, and the middle, and any others there may be between. He binds them all together, and himself from a plurality becomes a unity. Being thus moderate and harmonious, he now performs any action, be it about the acquisition of wealth, the care of his body, some public actions, or private contract. In all these fields he thinks the just and beautiful action, which he names as such, to be that which preserves this inner harmony and indeed helps to achieve it, wisdom

---

72. [The reference seems to be to 432d–433a.]

to be the knowledge which oversees this action, an unjust action to be that which   444
always destroys it, and ignorance the belief which oversees that.—Socrates you are
altogether right.

Very well, I said, we would then not be thought to be lying if we claim that we
have found the just man, the just city, and the justice that is in them.—No by Zeus,
we would not.

Shall we say so then?—Yes, let us.

Let that stand then, I said. After this we must, I think, look for injustice.—
Obviously.

Surely it must be a kind of civil war between the three parts, a meddling and a   b
doing of other people's task, a rebellion of one part against the whole soul in order
to rule it, though this is not fitting, as the rebelling part is by nature fitted to serve,
while the other part is by nature not fit to serve, for it is of the ruling kind. We shall
say, I think, that such things, the turmoil and the straying, are injustice and license
and cowardice and ignorance and, in a word, every kind of wickedness.—That is
what they are.

If justice and injustice are now sufficiently clear to us, then so are unjust actions   c
and wrongdoing on the one hand, just actions on the other, and all such things.—
How so?

Because they are no different from healthy and diseased actions; what those are
in the body, these are in the soul.—In what way?

Healthy actions produce health, diseased ones, disease.—Yes.

Therefore just actions produce justice in a man, and unjust actions, injustice?—
Inevitably.   d

To produce health in the body is to establish the parts of the body as ruler and
ruled according to nature, while disease is that they rule and are ruled contrary to
nature.—That is so. health → body

Therefore to produce justice is to establish the parts of the soul as ruler and ruled
according to nature, while injustice means they rule and are ruled contrary to
nature.—Most certainly. justice → soul

Excellence then seems to be a kind of health and beauty and well-being of the
soul, while vice is disease and ugliness and weakness.—That is so.   e

Then do not fine pursuits lead one to acquire virtue, ugly ones to acquire vice?—
Of necessity.

It is left for us to enquire, it seems, if it is more profitable to act justly, to engage
in fine pursuits and be just, whether one is known to be so or not, or to do wrong   445
and be unjust, provided one does not pay the penalty and is not improved by
punishment.

But Socrates, he said, this enquiry strikes me as becoming ridiculous now that
justice and injustice have been shown to be such as we described. It is generally
thought that life is not worth living when the body's nature is ruined, even if every
kind of food and drink, every kind of wealth and power are available; yet we are to
enquire whether life will be worth living when our soul, the very thing by which we
live, is confused and ruined, if only one can do whatever one wishes, except that   b
one cannot do what will free one from vice and injustice and make one acquire
justice and virtue.

Ridiculous indeed, I said, but as we have reached the point from which we can see the state of these things most clearly, we must not give up.

No by Zeus, he said, least of all must we give up.

c   Join me at this point, I said, that you may see how many forms of vice there are, as I think, that are worth looking at.—I follow you, only proceed.

Well now, I said, as it appears to me from this vantage point which we have reached in our discussion, there is one form of excellence and infinite number of forms of vice, four of them worth calling to mind.—How do you mean?

It is likely, I said, that there are as many types of soul as there are specific forms of government.—How many then?

d   Five forms of government, I said, and five of soul.—Tell us which they are.

I mean, I said, that one is the form of government we have been describing; and it could have two names: if there is one outstanding among the rulers it is called kingship; if there are more, aristocracy.[73]—True.

That then, I said I call one form; whether the rulers be one or more they would not disturb the worthwhile laws of the city, and to ensure this they would make use of the upbringing and education we have described.—It is not likely that they would change them, he said.

BOOK V

449   This then is the kind of city and government which I call good and right, and so too this kind of man. And if this is the right kind, then the others are bad and wrong, both in the management of the cities and the manner of life of the individual soul. Their badness is of four kinds.—What are these?

I was going to enumerate them and say how I thought they developed out of one b   another, but Polemarchus—he was sitting a little further away than Adeimantus— extended his hand and took hold of the other's cloak from above at the shoulder, drew him toward himself while he leaned forward and said something to him of which I only heard the words "Shall we let it pass, or what shall we do?"

Certainly not, said Adeimantus, now speaking aloud.

And I asked: What is it which you won't let pass?—You, he said.

c   Why in particular? I asked.

We think that you are getting slack, he said, and that you have filched away a whole section of the argument and one of some importance, in order to avoid dealing with it. You thought we would not notice when you said casually that as regards wives and children anyone could see that the possessions of friends should be held in common.[74]—Was that not right Adeimantus? said I.

___

73. [I.e. aristocracy in the original Greek sense of the rule of the best.]

74. [The enumeration and description of the bad forms of governments and individual characters is not taken up again until the eighth book.]

Yes, he said, but that "right," like the other things, requires explanation as to the manner of this holding in common, for there could be many ways; so do not fail to tell us which you mean. We have been waiting for some time for you to mention how they will beget children and bring them up, and this whole subject of the holding in common of wives and children. We believe that the right or the wrong way of it makes a considerable difference, indeed all the difference, to the government of your city. At this point, since you are going on to deal with another kind of government before you have adequately dealt with these matters, we thought, as you heard, that we would not let you off until you deal fully with all this as you have with the other matters.

And Glaucon said: Count me as associating myself with this proposal.

In fact, added Thrasymachus, consider this, Socrates, as the vote of us all.

What a thing you have done, I said, in stopping me! What an argument you have started up again as if from the beginning about the administration of our city! I joyfully thought I had completed this, and I was quite glad that anyone would accept what was then said on the subject and let me go on. You do not realize what a swarm of arguments you have stirred up by now calling me to account. I was aware of this when I passed it by, for fear it might give us much trouble.

Come now, said Thrasymachus, do you think these men have come here to smelt ore for gold[75] and not to hear a discussion?

They have come for discussion, I said, but discussion within reason.

It is within reason, Socrates, said Glaucon, for intelligent men to listen to a discussion of this kind their whole life long. So never mind about us, but do not weary of telling us at length what your thoughts are on the subject about which we enquired, namely what this common ownership of wives and children will be for the guardians, and how the children will be brought up while they are small, from the time of their birth until they begin their education, which seems the most difficult period. Try to tell us what the manner of this upbringing must be.

It is not, my dear friend, said I, an easy subject to explain for it raises even more doubts than the subjects we have expounded before. People may not believe that what we say is possible or that, if it should come to pass, it would be for the best. Hence my hesitation in broaching the subject, lest our discussion should seem to be mere wishful thinking.

Do not hesitate, he said, for your audience is neither inconsiderate, nor incredulous, nor ill-disposed.

And I said: Do you wish to encourage me by saying this?—I do.

Well, I said, you are doing the opposite. Your encouragement would be fine if I trusted myself to speak with knowledge, for one can feel both safe and bold if one speaks among intelligent friends about the most important and cherished subjects with knowledge of the truth, but to speak at a time when one is still in doubt and searching, which is what I am doing, is both frightening and unsafe. I am not afraid of being laughed at—that indeed would be childish—but I fear that I may not only miss my footing in my search for the truth, but also drag down my friends in my

75. [A proverbial expression applied to those who neglect their proper tasks to follow some fascinating but vain hope of immediate gain. It also reminds one of I, 336e.]

fall where a false step should least occur. So I bow to Adrasteia[76] for what I am going to say, as I expect it is a lesser crime to kill someone involuntarily than to deceive people about beautiful, good, and just institutions. It is better then to run that risk

b   among enemies than among friends, so you do indeed encourage me!

Glaucon laughed and said: Well, Socrates, if we suffer anything untoward as a result of this conversation, then, as if it were murder, we free you of any guilt; we declare you pure and no deceiver. So speak boldly.

Surely, I said, as the law declares a man to be pure who is freed from guilt in the case of homicide, this is likely to apply here also.—As far as that goes speak then, he said.

We must now, said I, go back to what should have been said earlier in sequence.

c   However, this may well be the right way: after we have completed the parts that men must play, we turn to those of women, especially as you call on me to do so.

For men of such a nature and education as we have described there is, in my opinion, no other right way to deal with wives and children than following the road upon which we started them. We attempted, in our argument, to establish the men as guardians of the flock.—Yes.

d   Let us then give them for the birth and upbringing of children a system appropriate to that function and see whether it suits us or not.—How?

Like this: do we think that the wives of our guardian watchdogs should join in whatever guardian duties the men fulfill, join them in the hunt, and do everything else in common, or should we keep the women at home as unable to do so because they must bear and rear their young, and leave to the men the labour and the whole care of the flock?

e   All things, he said, should be done in common, except that the women are physically weaker and the men stronger.

And is it possible, I asked, to make use of living creatures for the same purposes unless you give them the same upbringing and education?—It is not possible.

So if we use the women for the same tasks as the men, they must be taught the

452   same things.—Yes.

Now we gave the men artistic and physical culture.—Yes.

So we must give both also to the women, as well as training in war, and use them for the same tasks.—That seems to follow from what you say.

Perhaps, I said, many of the things we are saying, being contrary to custom, would stir up ridicule, if carried out in practice in the way we are telling them.—They certainly would, he said.

What, I asked, is the most ridiculous feature you see in this? Or is it obviously that women should exercise naked in the palaestra along with the men, not only the

b   young women but the older women too, as the old men do in the gymnasia when their bodies are wrinkled and not pleasant to look at and yet they are fond of physical exercise?—Yes, by Zeus, he said, it would appear ridiculous as things stand now.

Surely, I said, now that we have started on this argument, we must not be afraid of all the jokes of the kind that the wits will make about such a change in physical

---

76. [Adrasteia was a kind of Nemesis, a punisher of pride and proud words. The "bow to Adrasteia" is therefore a kind of apology for a bold statement to follow.]

and artistic culture, and not least about the women carrying arms and riding   c
horses.—You are right, he said.

As we have begun this discussion we must go on to the tougher part of the law
and beg these people not to practice their own trade of comedy at our expense but
to be serious and to remember that it is not very long since the Greeks thought it
ugly and ridiculous, as the majority of barbarians still do, for men to be seen naked.
When first the Cretans and then the Lacedaemonians started their physical training,   d
the wits of those days could have ridiculed it all, or do you not think so?—I do.

But I think that after it was found in practice to be better to strip than to cover
up all those parts, then the spectacle ceased to be looked on as ridiculous because
reasonable argument had shown that it was best. This showed that it is foolish to
think anything ridiculous except what is bad, or to try to raise a laugh at any other
spectacle than that of ignorance and evil as being ridiculous, as it is foolish to be in   e
earnest about any other standard of beauty than that of the good.—Most certainly.

Must we not first agree whether our proposals are possible or not? And we must
grant an opportunity for discussion to anyone who, in jest or seriously, wishes to
argue the point whether female human nature can share all the tasks of the male   453
sex, or none at all, or some but not others, and to which of the two waging war
belongs. Would this not be the best beginning and likely to lead to the best conclusion?—Certainly.

Do you then want us to dispute among ourselves on behalf of those others, lest
the other side of the argument fall by default?—There is nothing to stop us.   b

Let us then speak on their behalf: "Socrates and Glaucon, there is no need for
others to argue with you. You yourselves, when you began to found your city, agreed
that each person must pursue the one task for which he is fitted by nature." I think
we did agree to this, of course.—"Can you deny that a woman is by nature very
different from a man?—Of course not. "And is it not proper to assign a different
task to each according to their nature?"—Certainly. "How then are you not wrong   c
and contradicting yourselves when you say that men and women must do the same
things, when they have quite separate natures?" Do you have any defence against
that argument, my good friend?

That is not very easy offhand, he said, but I ask and beg you to explain the
argument on our side, whatever it is.

It is these and many other difficulties that I foresaw, Glaucon, I said, when I was
afraid and hesitated to tackle the law concerning the acquiring of wives and the   d
upbringing of children.—By Zeus, he said, it does not seem at all easy.

It is not, said I, but the fact is that whether a man falls into a small swimming pool
or in the middle of the ocean, he must swim all the same.—Certainly.

So then we must swim too and try to save ourselves from the sea of our argument,
hoping that a dolphin will pick us up or we may find some other miraculous deliverance.—It seems so.   e

Come now, said I, let us see if we can find a way out. We have agreed that a
different nature must follow a different occupation and that the nature of man and
woman is different, and we now say that different natures must follow the same
pursuits. This is the accusation brought against us.—Surely.

How grand is the power of disputation, Glaucon.—Why?   454

Because, I said, many people fall into it unwittingly and think they are not disputing but conversing because they cannot analyze their subject into its parts, but they pursue mere verbal contradictions of what has been said, thus engaging in a dispute rather than in a conversation.

Many people, he said, have that experience, but does this also apply to us at the present moment?

b   It most certainly does, I said. I am afraid we have indeed unwittingly fallen into disputation.—How?

We are bravely, but in a disputatious and verbal fashion, pursuing the principle that a nature which is not the same must not engage in the same pursuits, but when we assigned different tasks to a different nature and the same to the same nature, we did not examine at all what kind of difference and sameness of nature we had in mind and in what regard we were distinguishing them.—No, we did not look into that.

c   We might therefore just as well, it seems, ask ourselves whether the nature of bald men and long-haired men is the same and not opposite, and then, agreeing that they are opposite, if we allow bald men to be cobblers, not allow long-haired men to be, or again if long-haired men are cobblers, not allow the others to be.—That would indeed be ridiculous.

Is it ridiculous for any other reason than because we did not fully consider their same or different natures in every respect but we were only watching the kind of
d   difference and sameness which applied to those particular pursuits? For example, a male and a female physician, we said, have the same nature of soul, or do you not think so?—I do.

But a physician and a carpenter have a different nature?—Surely.

Therefore, I said, if the male and the female are seen to be different as regards a particular craft or other pursuit we shall say this must be assigned to one or the other. But if they seem to differ in this particular only, that the female bears children while the male begets them, we shall say that there has been no kind of proof that
e   a woman is different from a man as regards the duties we are talking about, and we shall still believe that our guardians and their wives should follow the same pursuits.—And rightly so.

Next we shall bid anyone who holds the contrary view to instruct us in this: with
455   regard to what craft or pursuit concerned with the establishment of the city is the nature of man and woman not the same but different?—That is right.

Someone else might very well say what you said a short time ago, that it is not easy to give an immediate reply, but that it would not be at all difficult after considering the question.—He might say that.

Do you then want us to beg the one who raises these objections to follow us to see
b   whether we can show him that no pursuit connected with the management of the city belongs in particular to a woman?—Certainly.

Come now, we shall say to him, give us an answer: did you mean that one person had a natural ability for a certain pursuit, while another had not, when the first learned it easily, the latter with difficulty? The one, after a brief period of instruction, was able to find things out for himself from what he had learned, while the other, after much instruction, could not even remember what he had learned; the former's
c   body adequately served his mind, while the other's physical reactions opposed his.

Are there any other ways in which you distinguished the naturally gifted in each case from those who were not?—No one will say anything else.

Do you know of any occupation practised by mankind in which the male sex is not superior to the female in all these respects? Or shall we pursue the argument at length by mentioning weaving, baking cakes, cooking vegetables, tasks in which the female sex certainly seems to distinguish itself, and in which it is most laughable of all for women to be inferior to men?   d

What you say is true, he said, namely that one sex is much superior to the other in almost everything, yet many women are better than many men in many things, but on the whole it is as you say.

There is therefore no pursuit connected with city management which belongs to woman because she is a woman, or to a man because he is a man, but various natures are scattered in the same way among both kinds of persons. Woman by nature shares all pursuits, and so does man, but in all of them woman is a physically weaker   e
creature than man.—Certainly.

Shall we then assign them all to men, and none to a woman?—How can we?

One woman, we shall say, is a physician, another is not, one is by nature artistic, another is not.—Quite so.

One may be athletic or warlike, while another is not warlike and has no love of   456
athletics.—I think so.

Further, may not one woman love wisdom, another hate it, or one may be high-spirited, another be without spirit?—That too.

So one woman may have a guardian nature, the other not. Was it not a nature with these qualities which we selected among men for our male guardians too?—We did.

Therefore the nature of man and woman is the same as regards guarding the city, except in so far as she is physically weaker, and the man's nature stronger.—So it seems.

Such women must then be chosen along with such men to live with them and share   b
their guardianship, since they are qualified and akin to them by nature.—Certainly.

Must we not assign the same pursuits to the same natures?—The same.

We have come round then to what we said before, and we agree that it is not against nature to give to the wives of the guardians an education in the arts and physical culture.—Definitely not.

We are not legislating against nature or indulging in mere wishful thinking since the law we established is in accord with nature. It is rather the contrary present   c
practice which is against nature as it seems.—It appears so.

Now we were to examine whether our proposals were possible and the best.—We were.

That they are possible is now agreed?—Yes.

After this we must seek agreement whether they are the best.—Clearly.

With a view to having women guardians, we should not have one kind of education to fashion the men, and another for the women, especially as they have the same   d
nature to begin with.—No, not another.

What is your opinion of this kind of thing?—Of what?

About thinking to yourself that one man is better and another worse, or do you think that they are all alike?—Certainly not.

In the city we were establishing, do you think the guardians are made better men by the education they have received, or the cobblers who were educated for their craft?—Your question is ridiculous.

e   I know, said I. Well, are these guardians not the best of all the citizens?—By far.

Will then these women guardians not be the best of women?—That too by far.

Is there anything better for a city than to have the best possible men and women?—Nothing.

457   And it is the arts and physical culture, as we have described them, which will achieve this?—Of course.

So the institution we have established is not only possible but also the best.—That is so.

The women then must strip for their physical training, since they will be clothed in excellence. They must share in war and the other duties of the guardians about the city, and have no other occupation; the lighter duties will be assigned to them because of the weakness of their sex. The man who laughs at the sight of naked women exercising for the best of reasons is "plucking the unripe fruit of laughter",[77] he understands nothing of what he is laughing at, it seems, nor what he is doing. For it is and always will be a fine saying that what is beneficial is beautiful, what is harmful is ugly.—Very definitely.

Let us say then that we have escaped from one wave of criticism in our discussion of the law about women, and we have not been altogether swamped when we laid it down that male and female guardians must share all their duties in common, and our argument is consistent when it states that this is both possible and beneficial.—It is, he said, certainly no small wave from which you are escaping.

You will not say this was a big one when you see the one that follows, I said.—Speak up, then, he said, and let me see it.

I think, I said, that the law follows from the last and those that have gone before.—What law?

d   All these women shall be wives in common to all the men, and not one of them shall live privately with any man; the children too should be held in common so that no parent shall know which is his own offspring, and no child shall know his parent.

This proposal raises far more doubts than the last, both as to its possibility and its usefulness, he said.

I do not think its usefulness will be disputed, I said, namely that it is not a great blessing to hold wives in common, and children too, provided it is possible. I think that most controversy will arise on the question of its possibility.—Both points, he said, will certainly be disputed.

e   You mean that I will have to fight a combination of arguments. I thought I could

77. [Plato is here adapting a phrase of Pindar, to us a fragment. The text is uncertain. As it stands in the text it means "They pluck from wisdom the unripe fruit of laughter," which does not seem to make much sense. The Pindaric phrase was "they pluck the unripe fruit of wisdom," i.e., their wisdom is not wisdom; it seems likely that Plato simply replaced *sophias* (of wisdom) by *geloiou* "they pluck the unripe fruit of laughter." As the original meant that their wisdom was no wisdom, the adaptation then means that their laughter is no true laughter, because what they laugh at is not laughable.]

escape by running away from one of them, if you thought the proposal beneficial, and that it would only remain for me to argue its possibility.—I saw you running away, he said, but you must explain both.

Well, I said, I must take my punishment. Allow me, however, to indulge myself   458
as if on holiday, as lazy-minded people feast on their own thoughts whenever they take a walk alone. Instead of finding out how something they desire may become a reality, such people pass over that question to avoid wearying themselves by deliberating on what is possible and what is not; they assume that what they desire is available; they arrange the details and enjoy themselves thinking about all they will do when it has come to pass, thus making a lazy mind even lazier. I am myself at   b
this moment getting soft, and I want to delay consideration of the feasibility of our proposal until later. I will assume that it is feasible and examine, if you will allow me, how the rulers will arrange these things when they happen and I will argue that this will be most beneficial to the city and to the guardians. This I will try to examine along with you, and deal with the other question later, if you permit.—I permit it, he said, carry on with your examination.

I think that surely our rulers, if indeed they are worthy of the name, and their auxiliaries as well, will be willing, the latter to do what they are told, the former to   c
give the orders, in part by obeying the laws themselves, and in part, in such matters as we have entrusted to them, by imitating these laws.—That is likely.

You then, as their lawgiver, just as you chose the men, will in the same manner choose the women and provide as far as possible those of the same nature. Since they have their dwellings and meals together and none of them possess anything of the kind as private property, they will be together and mix together both in the   d
gymnasia and in the rest of their education and they will, I think, be driven by inborn necessity to have intercourse with one another. Or do you not think that what I say will of necessity happen?

The necessity is not of a mathematical but of an erotic kind, he said, and this is probably stronger in persuading and compelling the mass of the people.

Yes indeed, I said. The next point is, Glaucon, that promiscuity is impious in a city of fortunate people, nor will the rulers allow it.—It is not right.   e

After this we must obviously make marriage as sacred as possible, and sacred marriages will be those which are the most beneficial.—Most certainly.

How then will they be most beneficial? Tell me, Glaucon: I see that at home you   459
have hunting dogs and quite a number of pedigree birds. Did you then, by Zeus, pay any attention to their unions and breeding?—In what way? he asked.

In the first place, though they are all of good stock, are there not some who are and prove themselves to be best?—There are.

Do you breed equally from them all, or are you anxious to breed most from the best?—From the best.

Further, do you breed from the youngest, or from the oldest, or from those in   b
their prime?—From those in their prime.

And do you think that if they were not bred in this way, your stock of birds and dogs would deteriorate considerably?—I do.

Do you think things are any different in the case of horses and the other animals?—That would indeed be absurd.

Good gracious, my friend, I said, how great is our need for extremely able rulers
c   if the same is true for the human race.—It is, but what about it?

Because they will need to use a good many drugs. For people who do not need
drugs but are willing to follow a diet even an inferior physician will be sufficient,
but when drugs are needed, we know that a bolder physician is required.—True,
but what do you have in mind?

This, I said: our rulers will probably have to make considerable use of lies and
d   deceit for the good of their subjects. We said that all such things are useful as a kind
of drug.—And rightly so.

This "rightly" will occur frequently in matters of marriage and the bearing of
children.—How so?

It follows from our previous agreement that the best men must have intercourse
with the best women as frequently as possible, and the opposite is true of the very
e   inferior men and women; the offspring of the former must be reared, but not the
offspring of the latter, if our herd is to be of the highest possible quality. Only the
rulers should know of these arrangements, if our herd of guardians is to avoid all
dissension as far as possible.—Quite right.

Therefore certain festivals will be established by law at which we shall bring the
460 brides and grooms together; there will also be sacrifices, and our poets must compose
hymns to celebrate the marriages. The number of marriages we shall leave to the
rulers to decide, in such a way as to keep the number of males as stable as possible,
taking into account war, disease, and similar factors so that our city shall, as far as
possible, become neither too big nor too small.—Right.

There will have to be some clever lots introduced, so that at each marriage celebration the inferior man we mentioned will blame chance but not the rulers.—Quite
so.

b   The young men who have distinguished themselves in war or in other ways must
be given awards consisting of other prizes and also more abundant permission to
sleep with women, so that we may have a good excuse to have as many children as
possible begotten by them.—Right.

As the children are born, officials appointed for the purpose—be they men or
women or both, since our offices are open to both women and men—will take
them.—Yes.

c   The children of good parents they will take to a rearing pen in the care of nurses
living apart in a certain section of the city; the children of inferior parents, or any
child of the others born defective, they will hide, as is fitting, in a secret and unknown
place.[78]—Yes, he said, if the breed of the guardians is to remain pure.

The nurses will also see to it that the mothers are brought to the rearing pen when
d   their breasts have milk, but take every precaution that no mother shall know her
own child; they will provide wet nurses if the number of mothers is insufficient;
they will take care that the mothers suckle the children for only a reasonable time;

78. [There can be no doubt that Plato is here recommending infanticide by exposure for these babies, a
practice which was quite common even in classical times (cp. 459d–e and 461b–c). Presumably the point of
exposure rather than direct infanticide was that the responsibility was felt to be thrown upon the gods, for the
child might be saved, as Oedipus was.]

the care of sleepless children and all other troublesome duties will belong to the wet nurses and other attendants.

You are making it very easy, he said, for the wives of the guardians to have children.

And that is fitting, I said. Let us take up the next point of our proposal: We said that the children's parents should be in their prime.—True.

Do you agree that a reasonable interpretation of this is twenty years for a woman and thirty years for a man?—Which years?   e

A woman, I said, is to bear children for the state from the age of twenty to the age of forty, a man after he has passed "his peak as a racer" begets children for the state till he reaches fifty.—This, he said, is the physical and mental peak for both.   461

If a man either younger or older than this meddles with procreation for the state, we shall declare his offence to be neither pious nor right as he begets for the city a child which, if it remains secret, will be born without benefit of the sacrifices and prayers which priests and priestesses and the whole city utter at every marriage festival, that the children of good and useful parents may always prove themselves better and more useful; but this child is born in darkness, the result of dangerous incontinence.—Right.   b

The same law will apply, I said, if a man still of begetting years unites with a woman of child-bearing age without the sanction of the rulers; we shall say that he brings to the city an unauthorized and unhallowed bastard.—Quite right.

However, I think that when women and men have passed the age of having children, we shall leave them free to have intercourse with anyone they wish, with   c
these exceptions: for a man, his daughter or mother, or the daughter's daughters, or his mother's female progenitors; for a woman, a son or father, their male issue or progenitors. Having received these instructions they should be very careful not to bring a single child into the light, but if one should be conceived, and forces its way to the light, they must deal with it knowing that no nurture is available for it.

This too, he said, is sensibly spoken, but how shall they know their fathers and daughters and those other relationships you mentioned?   d

They have no means of knowing, I said, but all the children who are born in the tenth and seventh month after a man became a bridegroom he will call sons if they are male, daughters if they are female, and they will call him father, and so too he will call their offspring his grandchildren who in turn will call the first group their grandfathers and grandmothers. Those born during the time when their fathers and mothers were having children they will call their brothers and sisters, so that, as I said, these groups will have no sexual relations with each other. But the law will   e
allow brothers and sisters to live together if the lot so falls and the Pythian approves.—Quite right.

This then is the holding in common of wives and children for the guardians of your city. We must now confirm in our argument that it conforms with the rest of our constitution and is by far the best. Or how are we to proceed?—In that way, by Zeus.   462

Is not the first step towards agreement to ask ourselves what we say is the greatest good in the management of the city? At this the lawgiver must aim in making his laws. Also what is the greatest evil. Then we should examine whether the system we have just described follows the tracks of the good and not those of evil.—By all means.

Is there any greater evil we can mention for a city than whatever tears it apart
b   into many communities instead of one?—There is not.

Do not common feelings of pleasure and pain bind the city together, when as nearly as possible all the citizens equally rejoice or feel pain at the same successes and failures?—Most certainly.

For such feelings to be isolated and private dissolves the city's unity, when some
c   suffer greatly while others greatly rejoice at the same public or private events.—Of course.

And that sort of thing happens whenever such words as "mine" and "not mine"—and so with "another's"—are not used in unison.—Most certainly.

And the city which most closely resembles the individual? When one of us hurts his finger, the whole organism which binds body and soul together into the unitary system managed by the ruling part of it shares the pain at once throughout when
d   one part suffers. This is why we say that the man has a pain in his finger, and the same can be said of any part of the man, both about the pain which any part suffers, and its pleasure when it finds relief.

Certainly, he said. As for your question, the best managed city certainly closely resembles such an organism.

And whenever anything good or bad happens to a single one of its citizens, such
e   a city will certainly say that this citizen is a part of itself, and the whole city will rejoice or suffer with him.—That must be so, if it has good laws.

It is time now, I said, for us to return to our own city and to look there for the features we have agreed on, whether it, or any other city, possesses them to the greatest degree.—We must do so.

463   Well then. There are rulers and people in the other cities as well as in this one?—There are.

And they all call each other fellow-citizens.—Of course.

Besides the word fellow-citizens, what do the people call the rulers in the other cities?

In many they call them masters, but in democracies they call them by this very name, rulers.[79]

What do the people call them in our city? Besides fellow citizens, what do they call
b   the rulers?—Saviours and helpers.

And what do the rulers call the people?—Providers of food and wages.

What do the rulers call the people in the other cities?—Slaves.

And what do the rulers call each other?—Fellow rulers.

And ours?—Fellow guardians.

Can you tell me whether a ruler in the other cities might address one of his fellow rulers as his kinsman and another as an outsider?—Certainly, many could.

_____

79. [The Greek word is archōn, a general term for ruler, but also in Athens the board of archons were the chief magistrates.]

He then considers his kinsman, and addresses him, as his own, but not the outsider?—That is so.   c

What about your guardians? Can any of them consider any other of his fellow guardians an outsider and address him as such?

Not in any way, he said, for when he meets any one of them he will think he is meeting a brother or a sister, a father or a mother, a son or a daughter, their offspring or progenitors.

You put that very well, I said, but, further, tell me this: will you legislate these family relationships as names only, or must they act accordingly in all they do? Must   d
a man show to his fathers the respect, solicitude, and obedience to parents required by law? Otherwise, if he acts differently, he will fare worse at the hands of gods and men as one whose actions are neither pious nor just. Will these be the sayings that ring in his ears on the part of all citizens from childhood both about their fathers, those pointed out to them as such, and about their other kindred—or will there be other voices?

It will be those, he said; it would be absurd if their lips spoke these names of   e
kindred without appropriate action following.

So in our city more than any other, when any individual fares well or badly, they would all speak in unison the words we mentioned just now, namely that "mine" is doing well, or "mine" is doing badly.—That also is very true.

And we said that such a belief and its expression are followed by common feelings   464
of pleasure and pain.—And we were right.

So our citizens will to the greatest extent share the same thing which they call "mine," with the result that they in the highest degree share common feelings of pleasure and pain.—Surely.

And besides other arrangements, the reason for this is the holding of wives and children in common among the guardians.—More than anything else.

This we agreed was the greatest blessing for a city, and we compared a well run   b
city to the body's reactions to pain or pleasure in any part of it.—And we were right to agree on that.

So then the cause of the greatest good for our city has been shown to be the common ownership of wives and children among the auxiliaries.—Certainly.

And in this we are consistent with what went before, for we said somewhere that they must have no private houses or land or any private possessions, that they receive their upkeep from the other citizens as a wage for their guardianship, and that they must all spend it in common, if they are to be real guardians.—Right.   c

Does not what we said before and what we are saying now make them even more real guardians, and prevent them from tearing the city apart by not calling the same thing "mine," one man applying the word to one thing and another to another? One man would then drag into his own house whatever he could get hold of away from   d
the others; another drag things into his different house to another wife and other children. This would make for private pleasures and pains at private events. Our people, on the other hand, will think of the same thing as their own, aim at the same goal, and, as far as possible, feel pleasure and pain in unison.—Most certainly.

What follows? Will not lawsuits and mutual accusations disappear from among them, one might say, since they own nothing but their body, everything else being e   held in common? Hence they will be spared all the dissension which is due to the possession of wealth, children, and families?—They will inevitably be spared them.

Nor could cases of violence or assault rightly occur among them, for we shall declare that it is a fine and just thing to defend oneself against those of the same age, thus compelling them to keep in good physical condition.—Right.

465   The law is right in this also, that if an angry man satisfied his anger in a personal encounter of this kind, he is less likely to turn to more important quarrels.—Certainly.

An older man will have authority over all the young, and be allowed to chastise them.—Obviously.

It is surely also obvious that a younger man, except by order of the rulers, shall not apply violence of any kind to, nor strike, an older man, nor fail to respect him in other ways. There are two adequate guardians to prevent this, namely shame and

b   fear; shame will prevent him laying hands on his parents, fear because the others will come to the rescue of the victim, some as his sons, some as his brothers, and some as his fathers.—That follows, he said.

So the laws will induce people to live at peace with each other.—Very much so.

And if there is no discord among the guardians there is no danger that the rest of the city will start factions against them or among themselves.—No danger.

c   I hesitate to mention the petty evils they will escape: the poor man's flattery of the rich, the perplexities and sufferings involved in bringing up children and in making the necessary money to feed the household, sometimes borrowing, sometimes denying the debt, in one way or another providing enough money to hand over to their wives and household slaves to dispense; all the various troubles which men endure in these matters are quite obvious and sordid and not worth discussing.—They are

d   clear even to the blind.

They will be free of all these, and they will live a life more blessed than that of Olympian victors.—How?

Olympian victors are considered happy on account of only a small part of the blessings available to our guardians, whose victory is even finer and their upkeep from public funds more complete. The victory they gain is the safety of the whole city and the victor's crown they and their children receive is their nurture and all the necessities of life; they receive rewards from their own city while they live, and

e   at their death they are given a worthy funeral.—Certainly fine rewards.

Remember, said I, that earlier in our discussion someone—I forget who[80]—shocked us by saying that we did not make our guardians happy, that while it was

466   in their power to own all the possessions of our citizens, yet they possessed nothing. We said at the time that we would investigate later whether this would happen, but that our concern at the time was to make our guardians true guardians and the city as happy as we could, and that we would not concentrate our attention upon one group and make them happy in our city.—I remember.

Well now, if the life of the auxiliaries is indeed much finer and better than that of Olympian victors, it is not to be compared to that of the cobblers or other

b   craftsmen, or with that of the farmers?—I do not think so.

---

80. [The objection was actually made by Adeimantus at the beginning of the fourth book (419a).]

It is surely right to repeat here what I said then, that, if a guardian seeks happiness in such a way as not even to be a guardian nor to be satisfied with a life so stable and moderate and, as we maintain, so much the best; if a silly and youthful idea of happiness should come into his mind and set him off to use his power to appropriate everything in the city as his own, he will realize the true wisdom of Hesiod's saying   c that somehow "the half is more than the whole."[81]

If he takes my advice, he said, he will stay with this kind of life.

You agree then, I said, that the women should be associated with the men in the way we have described in matters of education and child bearing, and in the guarding of the other citizens. Both when they remain in the city and when they go to war they must share the guardians' duties, hunt with them like hounds, share as far as   d possible in everything in every way. In doing so they will be acting for the best, and in no way contrary to woman's nature as compared with man's, as they were born to associate with one another.—I agree.

It now remains, I said, for us to determine whether this association can be brought about among human beings as it can among animals, and how it can be brought about.—You took the words out of my mouth.

As far as war is concerned, I said, the way they will wage it is clear, I think.—How   e so?

Men and women will campaign together; moreover they will take the sturdy among their children with them, in order that, like the children of other craftsmen, they may observe the actions which they will perform when they grow up. Moreover,   467 in addition to observing these, they can assist and help in all the duties of war and attend upon their fathers and mothers. Have you not noticed in the other crafts how the children of potters for example assist and observe for a long time before they engage in making pots?—Yes indeed.

Should those craftsmen take more care than the guardians in training their children by suitable experience and observation?—That would be quite ridiculous.

Besides, every living creature will fight better in the presence of its young.—That   b is true, but, Socrates, there is a considerable danger that, if they are defeated, as happens frequently in war, they will lose their children's lives as well as their own, thus making it impossible for the rest of the city to recover.

What you say is true, I said, but do you think that the first thing we should aim at is to take measures to avoid danger?—Certainly not.

Well then, if risks must be run, should one not run them where success will improve people?—Obviously.

And do you think that it makes little difference, and is not worth the risk, that the   c children, who are the future warriors, should observe matters of war?—No. It does make a difference with regard to what you are mentioning.

We must then make opportunities for the children to observe war while contriving to keep them safe, and all will be well, will it not?—Yes.

Well, said I, in the first place their fathers will know, as far as men can, which expeditions are dangerous and which are not.—That is likely.   d

---

81. [Hesiod, *Works and Days* 40.]

So they will take them on some expeditions, but be cautious about others.—Rightly.

And they will put in charge of them officers whose age and experience qualifies them to be leaders and tutors.—That is fitting.

However, many things have happened unexpectedly to many people.—Yes indeed.

With this in view, my friend, we must provide the children with wings while they are small, so that they can fly away and escape.—How do you mean?

e   They must as early as possible be mounted on horses and learn to ride before they are taken to observe warfare on horseback. Their horses should not be high-spirited or fond of fighting, but very swift and easy to manage. In this way they will observe their own future task best as well as most safely and, if the need arises, they will find safety in following their older commanders.—I think what you say is right.

468   What about the waging of war? What should be the attitude of the soldiers to each other and to the enemy? Are my ideas right or not?—What ideas?

Should not any soldier who, through cowardice, deserts his post, throws away his arms, or behaves in any such manner be reduced to be a craftsman or a farmer?—Quite so.

b   And should not one who is captured alive be left to his captors as a gift to do with as they please?—Most certainly.

Do you not think that one who has distinguished himself and earned high esteem should first of all, while still on the campaign, be crowned with wreaths in turn by every youth and child who accompany the expedition?—I do.

Further, shaken by the hand?—That too.

But this, said I, I think you will no longer agree to?—What?

That he should kiss and be kissed by each of them.

That most of all, he said, and I would add this to the law: that as long as the c   campaign lasts, no one whom he wants to kiss shall be allowed to refuse, the purpose being that if any one should be in love with another, whether male or female, he would be all the keener to carry off the prize for valour.

Excellent, I said, and we have already stated that, as a good man, more marriages will be available to him and that such men will be chosen as bridegrooms more often than the others, in order that a man of that kind may beget as many children as possible.—We have said so.

Indeed, according to Homer too it is right to honour by such means the brave d   among the young. He said that Ajax, who was distinguished in war, "was rewarded with the long cut of the chine." This is a proper way to honour a young and brave man as, beside the honour, it will also increase his strength.—Quite right.

Let us then, I said, follow Homer in these matters. We too shall, at our sacrifices and on all such occasions, honour good men according to their bravery, with hymns and in the other ways we were just mentioning, also with "seats of honour, meats e   and well-filled wine cups," so that along with the honour we may continue to train our good men and women.—What you say is excellent.

As for those who died on the campaign, first we shall declare anyone who distinguished himself to belong to the golden race, shall we not?—That above all.

And shall we not believe Hesiod, whenever any of the golden race die, that they are

> Sacred spirits living upon the earth   469
> Noble, warding off evil, guardians of mortal men.[82]

—We shall believe him.

We shall therefore enquire from the god what kind of distinguished burial we should give to those inspired and godlike men, and we shall follow his instructions.—Of course we shall.

Then, for the rest of time, we shall care for, and worship at, their graves as at   b
those of divine spirits. We shall follow the same rites for anyone of those who have been judged to have lived an outstandingly good life, whether they die of old age or in any other way.—That is right.

Again, how will our soldiers act towards the enemy?—What do you have in mind?

First about enslavement. Do you think it right for Greeks to enslave Greek cities, or should they, as far as they can, not even allow any other city to do so, and make a habit of sparing the Greek race as a precaution against being enslaved by the   c
barbarians?—It is altogether and in every way best, he said, to spare one another.

And they should not themselves acquire a Greek as a slave, and advise the other Greeks not to do so?—Definitely, he said, for in this way they would be better able to turn against the barbarian and keep from fighting each other.

Further, I said, should they despoil the dead of anything but their armour after a victory, or is stripping the dead a good thing? Do not cowards make this an excuse   d
for not facing the enemy as if they were doing something essential when they keep skulking about a corpse, and has not many an army been lost through such greed?—Yes indeed.

Do you not think it mean and greedy to strip a corpse? Is it not womanish and small-minded to regard the body as your enemy, when the enemy himself has flitted away and left behind only the instruments with which he fought? Do you think such   e
behavior any different from that of dogs who are angry with the stone that hits them and leave the thrower alone?—Not different at all.

They must therefore not strip corpses, nor refuse the enemy permission to pick up their dead.—By Zeus, he said, they certainly must not.

Nor shall we take the arms of the enemy to the temples to dedicate them, especially not the arms of other Greeks, if we care at all for goodwill among the Greeks. We should rather be afraid of polluting the temples if we bring them such things from   470
our own people, unless the god tells us to do so.—Quite right.

What about ravaging Greek land and burning the houses? How are your soldiers to behave to the enemy?—I would be glad to hear your opinion on this subject, he said.

I think they should do neither of those things, but destroy the year's harvest only. Do you want me to tell you why?—Surely I do.   b

---

82. [*Works and Days* 122. The above reference to Ajax is in *Iliad* 7, 321.]

It seems to me that as we have two terms, war and civil strife, so there are two things, and the terms apply to differences in two fields, one of one's own kindred, the other of outside strangers. Enmity with one's own is called civil strife, whereas enmity to strangers is called war.—What you say is to the point.

c   See then whether this too is to the point: I say that the Greek race is related and akin, while the barbarians are outsiders and strangers.—You are right.

We shall say then that Greeks fighting barbarians or barbarians fighting Greeks are at war, that they are natural enemies, and this enmity is to be called war; but when Greeks fight Greeks, they are by nature friends, and in those circumstances

d   Greece is sick and in a state of civil strife, and this enmity is to be called civil strife.— Yes, I agree to think of it that way.

Note that in civil strife, as the term is generally used, wherever something of the kind occurs, and a city is divided against itself, if either party ravages the land of the others and burns their houses, this is considered an outrage and both parties unpatriotic, for if they loved their land they would never ravage it, their nurse and mother, though it is considered reasonable for the victors to carry off the harvest

e   of the defeated. They should, however, keep in mind that they will not always be at war, and that peace will return.—This attitude is much more civilized than the other, he said.

Now, I said, the city you are founding is Greek, is it not?—It must be.

So your citizens will be good and civilized?—Yes indeed.

And will they not love Greece? Will they not consider Greece to be their own? Will they not share the religion of the other Greeks?—Very much so.

471   They will therefore consider their differences with Greeks, their kindred, as civil strife and will not call it war?—They will not.

They will then quarrel as people who one day will be reconciled?—Certainly.

They will therefore chasten their foes in a friendly spirit; they will not punish them with enslavement and destruction. They are chastisers, not enemies at war.— Quite so.

Being Greeks, they will not ravage Greece, they will not burn the houses, nor will they maintain that all the inhabitants of each city are their foes, men, women and

b   children, but only a few, those who caused the quarrel. For all these reasons, as the majority are their friends, they will not ravage the country or destroy the houses. They will carry their quarrel to the point of compelling those who caused it to be punished by those who were guiltless and the victims of it.

I agree, he said, that this is how our citizens must behave toward their enemies, and toward barbarians they must behave as the Greeks now do toward each other.

c   Let us then make this a law for our guardians, neither to ravage the country nor to burn the houses.

Let us, he said, and let us also say that these things are well, as is what went before. But I think, Socrates, that if one lets you talk on these subjects, you will never remember the subject you postponed before you said all this, namely, that it is possible for this city to exist and how it can be brought about. I agree that, if it existed, all the things we have mentioned would be good for the city in which they

d   occurred, including things you are leaving out: they would be excellent fighters against an enemy because they would be least likely to desert each other, since they know each other as, and call each other by the name of, brothers, fathers, sons. Moreover, if their women joined their campaigns, whether in the same ranks or drawn up behind as reserves, either to frighten the enemy or as reinforcements, should they ever be needed, I know that this would make them quite unbeatable. I also see that a number of good things would ensue for them at home which have not been mentioned. Take it that I agree that all these things would happen as well as innumerable others, if this kind of government were to exist. Say no more on this subject but let us now try to convince ourselves of this, namely that it is possible and how it is possible. Let the rest go.

This is a sudden attack you have made upon my argument, I said, and you show no leniency towards my loitering. You may not realize that I have barely escaped from the first two waves of objections as you bring the third upon me, the biggest and most difficult to deal with. When you hear and see it you will surely be more lenient towards my natural hesitation and my fear to state, and attempt thoroughly to examine, such a paradox.

The more you speak like this, he said, the less we shall let you off from telling us how this city is possible. So speak and do not waste time.

Well then, I said, we must first remember that we have come to this point while we were searching for the natures of justice and injustice.—We must, but what of it?

Nothing, but if we find out what justice is, shall we require that the just man be in no way different from that justice itself, and be like justice in every respect, or shall we be satisfied if he comes as close to it as possible, and share in it far more than others?—That will satisfy us.

It was then to have a model, I said, that we were seeking the nature of justice itself, and of the completely just man, if he should exist, and what kind of man he would be if he did, and so with injustice and the most unjust man. Our purpose was, with these models before us, to see how they turned out as regards happiness and its opposite. Thus we would be forced to come to an agreement about ourselves, that he who was as like them as possible would also have a life most like theirs. It was not our purpose to prove that these could exist.—What you say is true.

Do you think a man is any less a good painter if, having painted a model of what the most beautiful man would be, and having rendered all the details satisfactorily in his picture, he could not prove that such a man can come into being?—By Zeus, I do not.

Well then, do we not also say that we were making a model of a good city in our argument?—Certainly.

Do you think our discussion less worthwhile if we cannot prove that it is possible to found a city such as we described?—Not at all.

And indeed, I said, that is the truth. But if we must, to please you, exert ourselves to pursue this topic, namely to show how and in what respect this might best be possible, then you in turn should agree that the same thing applies to this demonstration.—What thing?

Is it possible to realize anything in practice as it can be formulated in words or is it natural for practice to have a lesser grip on truth than theory, even if some people do not think so? Will you first agree to this or not?—I agree.

Then do not compel me to show that the things we have described in theory can

exist precisely in practice. If we are able to discover how the administration of a city can come closest to our theories, shall we say that we have found that those things
b are possible which you told us to prove so? Or will you not be satisfied with that measure of success? For I would be satisfied.—So would I.

Next, it seems, we should try to find out and to show what is now badly done in the cities which prevents them from being governed in this way, and what is the smallest change which would enable a city to reach our type of government—one change if possible, or, if not one, then two, or at any rate as few changes and as
c insignificant in their effects as possible.—By all means.

There is one change to which I think we could point which would accomplish this. It is certainly neither small nor easy, but it is possible.—What is it?

I have now come, I said, to what we likened to the greatest wave. However, it shall be said even if, like a wave of laughter, it will simply drown me in ridicule and contempt.—Say on.

And I said: Cities will have no respite from evil, my dear Glaucon, nor will the
d human race, I think, unless philosophers[83] rule as kings in the cities, or those whom we now call kings and rulers genuinely and adequately study philosophy, until, that is, political power and philosophy coalesce, and the various natures of those who now pursue the one to the exclusion of the other are forcibly debarred from doing so. Otherwise the city we have been describing will never grow into a possibility or
e see the light of day. It is because I saw how very paradoxical this statement would be that I have for some time hesitated to make it. It is hard to realize that there can be no happiness, public or private, in any other city.

Socrates, he said, you have uttered such a speech and statement that after speaking it you must expect a great many not undistinguished people to cast off their cloak
474 at once and, thus stripped for action, to snatch any available weapon, make a determined rush at you and do astonishing things to you. Unless you can hold them off by argument and escape, you will really pay the penalty of general derision.

Well, I said, it is you who brought this on me.

And I was quite right, he said. However, I will not betray you but defend you by any means I can, by good will, by urging you on, and perhaps I could give you more appropriate answers than another. Try, with this assistance, to show the unbelievers
b that things are as you state them.

I must try, I said, with the considerable support that you offer. If we are to escape from the people you mention, I think we need to define for them whom we mean by philosophers when we venture to say that they must rule. Once this is clear, one
c should be able to defend oneself by showing that some people have a natural aptitude for philosophy and for leading the state, while others have not that aptitude and must follow the leader.—This would be the time for that definition.

Come then, follow me in this, if we can somehow explain it.—Lead on.

Will it be necessary to remind you, or do you remember, that when we say that a man loves something, it must be shown, if the word is properly applied to him, that

83. [It is important to remember in this context that the word *philosophos*, which was not in common use before this time, retained its etymological meaning as a lover of truth and wisdom rather than a philosopher in our more restricted sense. The rest of this book and the next two are largely devoted to explaining the character and necessary training of the Platonic *philosophos*, and this includes practical experience.]

he loves not one part of it and the other not, but that he is fond of all of it?—It
seems, he said, that I need to be reminded, for I do not remember very well.   d

Your reply suited another man rather than you. An amorous man should not
forget that all those in the bloom of youth stir and excite a boy lover and amorous
man in some way, as all of them appear to deserve his care and attentions. Is that
not how you people behave to beautiful youths? You will praise the snub-nosed
as being charming, the hook-nosed you say is regal, the one in between is well   e
proportioned, dark ones are manly in appearance, and the pale are children of the
gods. As for the "honey-hued," do you think this very term is anything but the
euphemistic invention of a lover who found it easy to tolerate sallowness as long as
the boy was young? In a word, you will find all kinds of terms and excuses not to   475
reject anyone in the flower of his youth.

If, he said, you must take me as your example of how lovers behave, I will agree
for the sake of the argument.

Further, I said, do you not see wine-lovers behave in the same way? They love
every kind of wine and find every excuse to welcome it.—Certainly.

And I think you see lovers of honour, if they cannot be generals, be captains; if
they cannot be honoured by men of importance and dignity, they are content to be   b
honoured by insignificant and inferior men, for they have a passion for honour at
any price.—Definitely so.

Do you agree, or not, that when we say that a man has a passion for something,
we shall say that he desires that whole kind of thing, not just one part of it and not
the other?—Yes, the whole of it.

The lover of wisdom, we shall say, has a passion for wisdom, not for this kind of
wisdom and not that, but for every kind of wisdom?—True.

As for one who is choosy about what he learns, especially if he is young and cannot
yet give a reasoned account of what is useful and what is not, we shall not call him   c
a lover of learning or a philosopher, just as we shall not say that a man who is difficult
about his food is hungry or has an appetite for food. We shall not call him a lover
of food but a bad feeder.—And we should be right.

But we shall rightly call a philosopher the man who is easily willing to learn every
kind of knowledge, gladly turns to learning things, and is insatiable in this respect.
Is that not so?

And Glaucon said: That will include many strange people: the lovers of spectacles   d
seem to be included because of the pleasure they take in learning things, and the
lovers of sounds seem to be the strangest folk to include among philosophers; they
would never willingly attend a serious discussion or spend their time that way, but
they run around to all the Dionysiac festivals omitting none, either in the city or the
villages, as if their ears were under contract to listen to every chorus. Are we to say
that all these people, and those who learn similar things, and those who learn petty
crafts, are philosophers?   e

No, I said, but they do resemble philosophers.

Whom then, he asked, do you call the true philosophers?

Those who love the spectacle of truth, I said.

That is correct, he said, but what do you mean by it?

It would not be easy to explain to anyone else, but I think you will agree to this.—
What?

476   Since the beautiful is the opposite of the ugly, they are two things.—Of course.

And since they are two, each is one?—I grant that too.

The same is true of the just and the unjust, the good and the bad, and all the Forms[84] each is itself one, but because they appear everywhere in association with actions, and bodies, and each other, each appear to be many.—You are right.

So, I said, I make this distinction: on one side are those whom you just now called lovers of spectacles and lovers of crafts and practical men, on the other side are those whom we are discussing, and whom alone one would call philosophers.—How
b   do you mean?

The lovers of sights and sounds, I said, like beautiful sounds and colours and shapes, and all the objects fashioned from them, but their thought is unable to see and welcome the nature of Beauty itself.—That is surely the case, he said.

Those who can reach Beauty itself and see it in itself would be only a few, would
c   they not?—Certainly.

As for the man who believes in beautiful things but not in the existence of Beauty itself, nor is able to follow one who leads him to the knowledge of it, do you not think that his life is a dream rather than a reality? Consider: is this not dreaming, namely, whether asleep or awake, to think that a likeness is not a likeness but the reality which it resembles?—I certainly think that the man who does this is dreaming.

The man who, on the contrary, believes that there is such a thing as Beauty itself,
d   who can see both it and the things which share in it, and does not confuse the two, does he seem to you to live in a dream or in reality?—In reality certainly, he said.

His thought, since he knows, we could correctly call knowledge; that of the other we would call opinion, since he merely opines.—Quite so.

What if the man who has opinion but not knowledge is angry with us and disputes the truth of what we are saying? Shall we have some way to appease him and gently persuade him, while hiding from him that he is not in his right mind?—We must
e   have.

Come now, consider what we shall say to him. Or do you want us to enquire from him as follows—first telling him that nobody would grudge him any knowledge he may have, but that we should be glad to see that he knows something—"Tell us this: does the man who has knowledge know something or nothing?" You answer for him.—I will answer, he said, that he knows something.

Something that is, or is not?—Something that is, for how could that which is not
477   be known?

In however many ways we examine the question, we can hold this to be certain: what fully is, is fully knowable, and what in no way is, is altogether unknowable.— That is quite certain.

Very well, now if anything is in such a state as to be and also not to be, will it not be intermediate between that which purely is and that which in no way is?—Yes, it will be between them.

Then, as knowledge is directed to what is, while ignorance is of necessity directed

84. [It seems clear that the theory of Forms is here introduced as familiar to Glaucon. I shall, in the translation, capitalize words like Beauty, the Good and the like when, and only when, they refer specifically to a Platonic Form.]

to what is not, we must find something intermediate between ignorance and knowledge for that which lies between them, if there is such a thing.—Certainly.   b

Do we say that opinion is something?—Of course.

Is it a different capacity from knowledge or the same?—A different one.

Opinion then is directed to one object, and knowledge to another, according to the capacity of each?—That is so.

Knowledge then is by its nature directed to what is, to know it as it is—but I think it necessary first to make this distinction.—What distinction?

We shall say that capacities are a certain class of realities which enable us to do   c
what we are capable of doing, and so with anything else which is capable of doing anything. I mean sight for example, or hearing, are among the capacities, if you understand the class of things to which I want to refer.—I understand.

Listen to what I think about them. I cannot see any colour or shape of a capacity, or any such attribute as I see in many other things, looking to a few of which I distinguish some things from others for myself. In the case of a capacity I can look only to this: to what it is directed and what it achieves, and in this way I called it a   d
capacity; if it is related to the same object and achieves the same result I call it the same, while that which is related to a different object and achieves a different result I call a different capacity. How do you proceed?—In the same way.

Let us now go back, my good friend, I said. Would you say that knowledge is a capacity, or how do you classify it?—Among the capacities, he said, and the most powerful of all.

Further, do you count opinion as a capacity, or in what class do you put it?   e

In no other class, he said, for opinion is that by which we opine.

A short time ago you agreed that knowledge and opinion are not the same.

How, he answered, can any intelligent man say that a fallible thing is the same as an infallible one?

Right, said I. We clearly agree that opinion is different from knowledge.—It is   478
different.

Each of these two is by its nature directed to a different object and achieves a different result.—Necessarily so.

Knowledge is directed to what is, to know it as it is.—Yes.

And we say that opinion opines?—Yes.

Does it opine on the same subject which knowledge knows; are the knowable and the opinable the same, or is this impossible?

It is impossible, he said, following from our agreement. If a different capacity is directed to a different object, and opinion and knowledge are capacities, but different, it follows that the knowable and the opinable cannot be the same.   b

Then if what is, is knowable, the opinable must be something other than what is?—Clearly, it is different.

Does one then opine what is not? Or is it impossible to opine what is not? Think about this. Does not the man who opines direct his opinion to something? Or is it possible to opine, yet to opine nothing?—Impossible.

But the man who opines, opines some one thing?—Yes.

Surely that which is not, is not correctly called one, but nothing?—Quite so.   c

But we had to assign ignorance to what is not, and knowledge to what is?—Correct, he said.

So a man opines neither what is nor what is not?—Quite so.

Yet opinion is neither ignorance nor knowledge?—It does not appear so.

Is it outside these, exceeding either knowledge in clarity or ignorance in obscurity?—Neither.

Does opinion appear to you, I asked, to be more shadowy than knowledge but clearer than ignorance?—Very much so, he said.

d   Then it lies between the two?—Yes.

Opinion then is intermediate between those two?—Most certainly.

Now we said before that if something was shown to be and not to be at the same time, this would lie between what purely is and what completely is not, and that neither knowledge nor ignorance was directed to it, but that which appeared to be between ignorance and knowledge.—Correct.

And now what we call opinion has appeared between those two.—So it has.

e   It is now left for us, it seems, to find that which partakes of both being and nonbeing, and correctly cannot be called one or the other absolutely, in order that, if it appears, we can rightly call it the opinable, thus applying the extreme terms to the extremes, and the intermediate to the intermediate. Is that not so?—It is.

479   These things being established, I shall say, I want a word with, and an answer from, the good fellow who does not believe that there is a Beautiful itself or any Form of Beauty itself, which remains externally the same in all respects, but who believes that many beautiful things exists, that lover of spectacles who would not allow anyone to say that the Beautiful is one, and so with the Just and the rest. We shall say to him: "My dear sir, of all those many beautiful things, is there one which will not also appear ugly? And is there one of those just actions which will not also appear unjust? and of pious actions, one that will not appear impious?"

b   Not one, he said, for inevitably those beautiful things will appear ugly under certain circumstances, and so with the other things included in your question.

What about the many things that are double? Are they any less half than double?—Not one of them.

So with things big and small, light and heavy, does any predicate we apply to them apply to them any more than its opposite?—No, he said, each of these things partakes of both opposites.

Is then each of the many things, more than it is not, that which anyone might call it?

c   This, he said, is like those double meanings one is entertained with at banquets, and the children's riddle about the eunuch and his throw at the bat; they riddle about what he hit it with and what it was settled on.[85] Those things too are ambiguous and one cannot know for certain either that they are or that they are not, or that they are both or neither.

Well, I said, have you any better way of dealing with them? Can you put them in

---

85. [The riddle seems to have been: a man who is not a man saw and did not see a bird which was not a bird sitting on a bough that was not a bough; he pelted and did not pelt it with a stone which was not a stone. The answer is: a eunuch with imperfect eyesight saw a bat sitting on a reed, threw a pumice stone at it, and missed.]

a better place than between being and nonbeing? They will not appear more obscure
or less real than what is not, nor are they clearer and more real than what is.—Very
true, he said.   d

We have now discovered, it seems, that the many conventional opinions of the
majority about Beauty and the other things are rolling around between nonbeing
and pure being.—We have.

And we agreed previously that if anything of the kind appeared it would have to
be spoken of as the opinable but not knowable, the wandering intermediate grasped
by the intermediate capacity.—We did.

As for those who contemplate many beautiful things but do not see Beauty itself   e
and are incapable of following another who leads them to it, who see many just
actions but not Justice itself, and so with everything—these people, we shall say,
opine everything but have no knowledge of anything they opine.—Of necessity.

What about those who in each case contemplate the things themselves which are
always in every way the same? Do these have knowledge, not opinion?—That too
necessarily follows.

Shall we then say that these love and welcome the objects of knowledge, as the   480
others do the objects of opinion? Do we not remember that we said that these latter
loved and contemplated beautiful sounds and colours and such things, but they
would not allow that Beauty itself was an existent?—We remember.

We shall then not be out of line if we call them lovers of opinion rather than lovers
of wisdom. Will they be very angry with us for calling them that?—Not if they take
my advice, he said, for it is not lawful to be angry with those who speak the truth.

And those who welcome that itself which truly is in each case we must call philosophers or lovers of knowledge, and not lovers of opinion?—Most definitely.

BOOK VI

And so, I said, Glaucon, after a somewhat lengthy discussion, the philosophers,   484
and those who are not, have each of them with some difficulty revealed who they
are.

Perhaps, he said, it was not easy to do this briefly.

It seems not, said I, but I certainly still think that they would have been seen more
clearly if we had only this subject to discuss, and not the many other topics which
are necessary if one is to realize the difference between the just and the unjust life.   b

What is now our next topic of discussion? he asked.

What else, said I, but that which follows? Since those who can apprehend that
which remains in all respects ever the same are philosophers, while those who cannot
do this are not philosophers but wander among the many phenomena which exist
in multifarious ways, which of the two must we establish as rulers of our city?

How shall we proceed, he asked, to deal with this question at a suitable length?

We should establish as guardians, I said, those who appear competent to guard   c
the laws and ways of cities.—Correct.

This much is clear, I said, whether a blind man or one with keen eyesight should be a guardian to watch over anything.—Of course that is clear.

Do you think that there is any difference between the blind and those who are really deprived of the knowledge of every reality, who have no clear model of it in their soul and cannot, as painters can, look to that which is most true, always refer

d   to it, contemplate it as exactly as possible, and so establish here on earth lawful notions about things beautiful, just, and good where they need establishing, or guard and preserve them once established?—No, by Zeus, these are not very different from the blind.

Should we then make these people our guardians rather than those who have knowledge of every reality and are not inferior to the others in experience, or indeed in any other aspect of excellence?

It would be absurd, he said, to choose others if these are not inferior in other respects, for in this respect they are superior in what is probably the most important matter.

485   Let us then discuss how men can be qualified in both knowledge and experience.—By all means.

As we said at the beginning of this discussion,[86] it is first necessary to understand their nature. I think that, if we can reach adequate agreement on their nature, we shall also agree that the same men can possess both qualifications, and that none but they must be leaders in cities.—How so?

b   Let us agree on this aspect of the philosophic nature, that it is always in love with any knowledge which makes clear to them that everlasting reality which does not wander to and fro through generation and decay.—Let that be agreed.

Further, I said, that their passion is for the whole of that reality, and that they will not willingly give up any part of it, small or large, whether more or less honoured, just as we stated before[87] in the case of ambitious and erotic men.—What you say is correct.

Consider next whether those who are to be such as we described must in addition

c   also have this in their nature . . .—What?

Truthfulness, and never willingly to tolerate untruth but to hate it, and to love the truth.—That is likely.

It is not only likely, my friend, but it is quite unavoidable that one who naturally has a passion for something should love everything which is akin to, or belongs to, the object of his love.—Correct.

Could you find anything closer to wisdom than truth?—How could one?

Is it then possible for the same nature to love wisdom and to love untruth?—Not

d   possible at all.

The man who loves learning must therefore, from childhood on, long for every kind of truth.—That is altogether so.

When a man's passions are strongly directed to one object, we know that they are

86. [With this discussion of the philosophic nature compare V, 474d–476d.]

87. [The reference is to V, 474c–475c.]

thereby weakened in other directions, like a stream which has been canalized.—
Surely.

In one whose passions flow toward knowledge and all that kind of thing, they would concentrate, I think, upon the pleasures of the mind alone and by itself, and he would give up the pleasures of the body, if he is a true philosopher and does not merely pretend to be one.—Inevitably so.

Surely such a man is moderate and not at all a lover of money, for the objects requiring lavish expenditures for which the money is sought are suited to be taken seriously by others, but not by him.—That is so.

You must also look to the following when you are about to decide which is a philosophic nature and which is not.—To what?

You must notice whether it has any share of meanness, for pettiness is altogether incompatible with a soul that will long to grasp the divine and the human as a whole and in its totality.—Very true.

Do you think that a mind which is lofty enough to contemplate all time and all existence will consider life to be of great importance?—Not possibly.

Neither will such a man consider death a terrible thing?—Least of all.

Then a cowardly and mean nature will have no share, it seems, in true philosophy.—I do not think so.

Further, can a well-balanced man, neither money-loving nor mean, neither a boaster nor a coward, possibly become unreliable or unjust?—Not possibly.

And when you are examining a philosophic or unphilosophic soul, you will note at once in a young subject whether his soul is just and gentle, or wild and hard to deal with.—Quite so.

And you will surely not omit this quality, I think.—What quality?

Whether he is quick or slow to learn. Or do you ever expect anyone to be keen on something of which the practice is painful to him, and in which he with great difficulty achieves very little?—He could not be.

What if he could retain nothing of what he learned, being full of forgetfulness? Could he avoid being without knowledge?—How could he?

Thus labouring in vain, do you not think that in the end he would inevitably come to hate himself and the practice of that subject?—Of course he would.

Let us then never include a forgetful soul among the philosophers, but let us look for one that must have a good memory.—By all means.

Certainly, we would say that an uncouth and ungracious soul only drags one into excesses.—Quite so.

Do you think that truthfulness is akin to excesses or to proper measure?—To the latter.

Let us then look for a mind which, besides its other qualities, is by nature measured and gracious, and which will easily be led to a perception of the Form of each reality.—Of course.

Well, do you think that we have enumerated all the necessary and compatible qualities for a soul which will have an adequate and complete grasp of reality?—They are certainly most necessary.

And can you in any way object to a pursuit which no one is able to follow adequately unless he by nature has a good memory, is a quick learner, is generous, gracious, and friend of and akin to truth, justice, courage, and moderation?—Not even Momus,[88] he said, could object to such a pursuit.

And when such men have reached maturity in age and education, would you not entrust the city to them and to them alone?

b   Adeimantus said: No one, Socrates, could contradict the things you say, but on each occasion that you say them your hearers are affected in some such way as this: they think that because of their inexperience in asking and answering questions they are led astray by the argument, a little at each of your questions and when all their small concessions are added together at the end of the discussion, a great fallacy appears which contradicts what they said at first. Just as inexperienced checkers
c   players are in the end trapped by the experts and cannot make a move, so they too are trapped in the end and have nothing they can say in this different kind of checkers which is played not with counters but with words; yet they do not believe the conclusion to be in any way more true for that. I say this with reference to our present position. Someone might well say now that he cannot, as each question is asked, oppose you in argument, yet he sees that in fact, of those who turn to
d   philosophy, not taking up the subject as young people for the sake of education and then giving it up, but who continue to spend a great deal of time on it, of these the greatest number become quite queer, not to say altogether vicious, while those who seem the best of them suffer from this pursuit which you praise to the extent of becoming quite useless to the state.

When I had heard him out I said: Do you think that what these people say is untrue?

I do not know, he said, and I should like to hear what you think.

You would hear that to me they seem to speak the truth.

e   How then, he said, can it be right to say that there will be no end to evils in our cities before the philosophers rule in them, men who, we agree, are useless?

The question you ask needs to be answered through a parable.

And you, I suppose, are not accustomed to speak in parables!

Very well, I said, you are making fun of me after involving me in an argument
488   that is very hard to prove. Listen then to my parable, that you may better understand how niggardly I am in their use. What the best among men experience in relation to their city is so difficult that there is no single other experience like it, and one must gather together features from many quarters for comparison, and make a defence on their behalf as painters make pictures of goat-stags and other such mixtures.

Imagine something like this happening on board one or many ships: the owner
b   surpasses all on board in size and strength, but he is hard of hearing, somewhat short-sighted and his knowledge of seafaring is of the same quality. The sailors are quarreling about the steering, each of them thinking that he should be the pilot, though he has never learned the art of navigation; he cannot point to anyone who taught him or to a time when he learned it; moreover, they maintain that navigation cannot be taught and are ready to cut to pieces anyone who says it can. They are

88. [Momus is a personification of blame or censure. In Hesiod (*Theogony* 214) he is a child of Night.]

always crowding round the owner begging him and doing everything they can to   c
get him to entrust the rudder to them. Sometimes, if they do not succeed while
others do, they execute these others or throw them overboard, and they overpower
their noble owner with drugs, or wine, or in some other way. Then they rule over
the ship and enjoy its stores; drinking and feasting they sail as such men are likely
to do. Further, the man who is clever at devising how they may rule by persuading   d
or forcing the owner they call a navigator and a pilot who knows ships; anyone else
they blame as useless. They do not even understand that a true navigator must pay
attention to the seasons of the year, the sky, the stars, the winds, and all that pertains
to his craft if he really is to be the master of a ship. Nor do they think it possible to   e
acquire the art and practice of navigation whether people want one to steer or not
and therewith the art of navigation. When this happens on ships, do you not think
that the true pilot will be called a stargazer, a prattler, a good-for-nothing by those
who sail on ships managed in that way?—I certainly do, said Adeimantus.   489

I do not think you require us to examine this parable in detail to see that it
resembles the attitude of cities towards the true philosophers, but you understand
my meaning.—I certainly do.

Then to begin with, teach this parable to the man who wondered that philosophers
are not esteemed in the cities, and try to persuade him that it would be much more
surprising if they were.—I will teach him.   b

Then say to him: "What you say is true, that the best among the philosophers are
useless to the majority," and bid him blame for this uselessness not these good men
but those who do not make use of them. It is not the natural thing for the navigator
to beg the sailors to be ruled by him, nor for the wise to knock at the doors of the
rich, but the man who originated that smart saying was not telling the truth.[89] The
natural thing is for a sick man, be he rich or poor, to knock at the physician's door,   c
and for anyone who needs to be governed to knock at that of the man who can
govern him. It is not for the ruler, if he is in truth any good, to beg the others to
accept his rule. As for our present rulers in the cities, you would not be wrong to
compare them to the sailors we mentioned just now, or to compare those whom they
declare to be useless stargazers to the true navigators.—Quite right.

As a result, it is not easy for the best of pursuits to be highly esteemed in these
circumstances by those who follow the opposite course. But by far the greatest and   d
most serious libel on philosophy comes from those who profess to practice it, those
of whom the accuser of philosophy declared that the greatest number of its followers
are thoroughly wicked. He also said that the best of them were useless, and I agreed
that he was right. Is that not so?—Yes.

Then we discussed the reason for the uselessness of the good philosophers?—
Quite so.

Do you want us to discuss next why the greater number are inevitably wicked, and
shall we try to show, if we can, that philosophy is not responsible for this either?—
By all means.   e

Shall we then remind ourselves, as we speak and listen in turn, of the point at
which we started to discuss what nature one who is to become a good and noble man

89. [Aristotle (*Rhetoric* 2, 1391a) says it was the poet Simonides who, when asked whether it was better to be
rich or wise, replied: "Rich, because the wise spend their time at the doors of the rich."]

490   must have? First of all, he was to be guided by the truth; this he was always and in every way to pursue; else he would be an imposter and have no share at all in true philosophy.—That is what was said.

Now this one point is certainly quite contrary to the general opinion about him?—It certainly is.

Will it not be reasonable for us to plead in his defence that the true lover of learning has the inborn capacity to consort with reality, and not to remain living

b   among the multiplicity of particular things which are the objects of opinion? As he goes his way, his passion will not be blunted nor will he cease from it before he grasps the nature of the true reality in each case with that part of his soul which is fitted to grasp it because of its kinship with it; approaching it with this and mixing with true reality, he begets intelligence and truth. He would then, but not before, have knowledge, truly live, be nourished, and cease from travail.—This is the most reasonable defence possible.

Will it be the part of that man to love untruth, or quite the contrary, to hate it?—

c   To hate it.

When truth is one's guide we deny, I think, that any company of evils ever follows?—How could it?

The character is healthy and just, and moderation follows.—Correct.

What need is there to marshal again in their inevitable array from the beginning the company of other qualities which belong to the philosophic nature? Remember that courage belongs to it, as well as generosity, ease in learning, and a good memory.

d   You then interposed that everyone would be compelled to agree with what we said, but if he abandoned the argument and looked at the actual facts which the argument was about, he would say that some philosophers were useless while the majority had every kind of vice. So we examined the reason for this slander and have now arrived at the point of enquiring why the majority of them are vicious. For this reason we have again taken up, and necessarily defined, the inborn characteristics of the true

e   philosophers.—That is so.

We must now observe the ways in which this nature is corrupted, how it is destroyed in many while a small number escape, those whom they do not call bad but useless.

491   After this we must observe the type of natures which imitate the philosophic, establish themselves in the pursuit of philosophy and thus engage in a pursuit too high and too great for them; they are again and again out of tune with it, and bring upon philosophy everywhere and among all men the reputation you mention.—In what ways are they corrupted?

I will try to enumerate them for you if I can, I said. This much surely everyone will agree to, that such a nature, with all the qualities which we have attributed to it if it is to be completely philosophic, is rare among men and occurs but rarely.

b   Don't you think so?—I surely do.

Consider then the many important ways in which these few can be corrupted.—What are they?

What will surprise you most, when you hear it, is that every one of the qualities we have praised in this nature tends to destroy the soul which possesses it and drags it away from philosophy. I mean courage, moderation, and all the others we have mentioned.—That does sound strange.

c   Besides, I said, all those things which are said to be blessings corrupt it and drag

it away: beauty, health, physical strength, noble birth in the city, and all that goes
with these. That tells you the kind of things I mean.

It does, he said, and I would be glad to hear more precisely what you mean.

If you understand my notion correctly as a general principle, I said, it will be clear
to you, and what I have said on the subject will not seem strange.—What, he said,
do you want me to do?

We know that every seed, I said, every growing thing, whether plant or animal,   d
must receive the nurture proper to it, its proper soil and season, and that the more
powerful it is the more it requires a suitable environment, for the bad is more
contrary to the good than to the merely not good.—Of course.

It is then reasonable to say that the best nature fares worse, when unsuitably
nurtured, than the inferior.—It is.

Therefore, Adeimantus, I said, may we say that the same is true of the most gifted   e
souls: when they receive a bad upbringing they become outstandingly bad? Or do
you think that great crimes and unalloyed wickedness originate in an inferior and
not in a vigorous nature corrupted by its upbringing, and that a weak nature is ever
the cause of either great good or great evil?—No, you are right.

Now I think that the philosophic nature as we defined it, provided it receive its   492
proper instruction, will inevitably grow to reach every excellence, but if it is sown
and grows in an unsuitable environment, it will develop in quite the opposite way
unless some god come to its rescue. Or do you agree with the general opinion that
certain young men are corrupted by sophists, that private sophists corrupt them to
any extent worth mentioning? Are the people who say this not themselves the
greatest sophists, who educate most effectively and make young and old, men and   b
women, into the kind of people they want them to be?—When do they do this?

Whenever, I said, many of them are sitting together in assemblies, in courts, in
camps, or in some other public gathering of the crowd, they object very noisily to
some of the things that are said or done, and approve others, in both cases to excess,
by shouting and clapping. Moreover, the rocks and the place of meeting re-echos   c
and doubles the din of their blame or praise. During such a scene, what is the effect
on the young man's psyche,[90] as they say? What private training can hold out against
this and not be drowned by that kind of censure or approval, not be swept along by
the current whithersoever it may carry it, and not declare the same things to be
beautiful or ugly as the crowd does. Our young man will then follow the same
pursuits as the crowd, and be the same kind of man?—Quite inevitably, Socrates.   d

And yet, I said, we have not mentioned the strongest compulsion.—What is that?

It is that which these educators and sophists add by their actions if their words
fail to persuade. Or do you not know that they punish the recalcitrant with disfranchisement and fines and death?—They most certainly do.

What other sophist, do you think, or what private exhortations which tend in the
opposite direction can prevail?—None, I think.   e

No indeed, I said, and it would be great folly to try. There is not now, has not
been in the past, nor ever will be in the future, a man of a character so unusual that
he has been educated to virtue in spite of the education he received from the mob,

90. [Literally: "What heart will the young man have, as the saying goes."]

a human character that is, for the divine, as the proverb goes, we exclude from our argument, my friend. We must realize that if any character is saved and becomes

493 what it should, in the present state of our societies, you would not be wrong to say that it has been saved by a god's intervention.—I agree with you.

Then, I said, you should also think this.—What?

Not one of those private paid teachers, whom the people call sophists and consider to be their rivals, teaches anything different from the beliefs which the many express whenever they are gathered together, and this he calls wisdom. It is as if its keeper

b studied the moods and desires of a mighty and powerful beast, how to approach it, how to handle it, how it becomes most difficult and most gentle and what makes it so, what sounds it utters on each occasion, and what sounds addressed to it soothe or anger it. Having learned all this by tending the brute over a period of time he calls this wisdom, gathers his information together as if it were an art, and starts to teach it. The truth is that he knows nothing about these beliefs and desires, as to

c which of them is beautiful or ugly, good or bad, just or unjust, but he gives them these names in accordance with the brute's reactions: what it enjoys he calls good, what angers it he calls bad, and he can give no other account of them. What he must do, he calls just and beautiful, but he has never observed, nor can he show to another, the nature of the necessary or the beautiful or the difference between them. Do you not think, by Zeus, that such a man is a weird kind of educator?—I do indeed.

Is there then any difference between him and the man who believes that it is

d wisdom to understand the temper and pleasures of a crowd gathered from all quarters, be it about painting, music and poetry, or indeed about politics. If anyone approaches the crowd to exhibit his poetry, or some other work of his, or his service to the city, and gives the many mastery over himself beyond the degree that is unavoidable, he will be under the Diomedean necessity,[91] as it is called, to compose the sort of thing of which the crowd approves. But have you ever heard any one of them present an argument which was not utterly ridiculous to the effect that such things are truly good and beautiful?—Nor do I expect ever to hear such an ar-

e gument.

Keeping all this in mind, recall this question also: can the crowd in any way tolerate, or believe in, the existence of Beauty itself, and not only of the many beautiful things, or of what truly is in each case and not only of many particular

494 things?—No way at all.

The crowd then can never be philosophers?—It cannot.

And it inevitably disapproves of those who practise philosophy?—Inevitably.

So do all those private citizens who associate with the mob and are eager to please it.—Clearly.

As a result of this, do you see any salvation for one who is by nature a philosopher so that he can stay with his pursuit to the end? Reflect on what we said before. It is

b agreed that ease in learning, a good memory, courage, and loftiness are his inborn characteristics.—Yes.

It follows that such a boy will straightaway be leader among the children in all things, especially if his physique matches his soul?—How could he not be?

---

91. [The origin of the phrase is doubtful, but it refers to an inescapable compulsion.]

Then, as he gets older, his kindred and his fellow citizens will, I think, want to use him for their own purposes.—Of course they will.

They will be at him with their requests and honours, trying by flattery to secure   c
beforehand for themselves the power that will be his.—This does usually happen.

What do you think, I said, that such a youth will do under these circumstances, especially if he happens to live in a mighty city, is rich, of noble birth, tall, and beautiful? Will he not be filled with an impossible expectation that he will be capable of settling the affairs of both the Greeks and the barbarians? Will he not exalt himself to great heights, be full of self-importance and foolish pride?—He certainly will.   d

If someone then comes to a man in that condition and gently tells him the truth, that there is no sense in him and that he stands in need of it, but that it cannot be acquired unless one works like a slave to attain it, do you think it will be easy for him to listen in the midst of so many evils?—Far from it.

If then, I said, because of his noble nature and its kinship with reasonable discourse he should somehow see the point and be influenced and led to philosophy, what do   e
we think those people will do who believe they are losing the use of him as well as his comradeship? Will they not take any action and say anything, both to him to prevent his being persuaded, and against his persuader, privately plotting against him and publicly bringing him to court to prevent him from persuading the youth?—
They must certainly do so.   495

Is there any chance for such a man to practise philosophy?—Indeed no.

You see then, I said, that we were right to say that the characteristics of the philosophic nature were, if the upbringing was bad, themselves somehow the cause of his falling away, as well as the so-called goods: wealth and all those other advantages.—That was quite correct.

We say then that these are the many ways in which the best nature, rare enough in any case as we pointed out, is destroyed and corrupted with regard to the best of   b
pursuits. It is among these men that we shall find those who bring the greatest evils upon cities and individuals, and also the greatest good, if the current takes them that way. A petty nature will never do anything great either to an individual or a city.—Very true.

When these men, to whom it properly belongs, fall away from philosophy, they leave her desolate and unwed, and their own life becomes unsuited and untrue to   c
them. As for philosophy, other men unworthy of her come upon her as upon an orphan deprived of the protection of kinsmen, bring shame upon her, and also those reproaches which you say are cast upon her by those who revile her, namely that some of those who consort with her are useless, but the greater number deserve many evils.—Certainly these things are said.

And, I said, it is natural that they should be said. For other little men, seeing the home of philosophy empty, full as it is of fine names and ornaments, leap gladly   d
from their little trades to philosophy, like prisoners escaping from jail and taking refuge in the temples. These are the cleverest at their own little trade, for, compared with other crafts, philosophy, in spite of its present poor state, still has a more grandiose reputation. This, in spite of their imperfect nature, many desire to possess, though their bodies are debased by their crafts and services, and similarly their souls are crushed and fragmented by the sordidness of their work. Is that not inevitable?—   e
It certainly is.

Do you think these people look any different from a small and bald tinker who has come into money and, just released from jail, has taken a bath, put on a new cloak, and is got up like a bridegroom to marry the boss's daughter because of her poverty and loneliness?—No different.

496

What kind of children will that marriage produce? Will they not be base-born and of inferior nature?—Quite unavoidably.

So when those unfit for education approach philosophy and consort with her, what kind of thoughts and opinions are we to say they will produce? Will they not be such as to deserve to truly be called sophistry, that is, nothing genuine or partaking of wisdom.—This is altogether certain.

There remains but a very small group of those who deservedly consort with philosophy: a noble and well brought up character, caught up in exile, who remains with philosophy according to his nature because the corrupting influences are absent; a great soul living in a small city, who disdains its public affairs; a small number naturally talented come from other trades which they rightly do not honour; there also might be the bridle which holds back our friend Theages, for he is in every way qualified to be tempted away from philosophy but his physical illness keeps him out of politics; my own case is not worth mentioning, my divine sign, for this has hardly happened to anyone before. Of this small group, those who have become philosophers and have tasted how sweet and blessed a possession philosophy is, when they have fully realized also the madness of the majority, that practically never does anyone act sanely in public affairs, that there is no ally with whom one might go to the help of justice and live— then, like a man who has fallen among wild beasts, being unwilling to join in wrongdoing and not being strong enough to oppose the general savagery alone, for he would perish, useless both to himself and to others, before he could benefit either his country or his friends, of no use to himself or anyone else; taking all this into account he keeps quiet and minds his own business. Like a man who takes refuge under a small wall from a storm of dust or hail driven by the wind, and seeing other men filled with lawlessness, the philosopher is satisfied if he can somehow live his present life free from injustice and impious deeds, and depart from it with a beautiful hope, blameless and content.—Indeed, he said, that would be no small achievement before departure.

497

Nor is it the greatest, I said, as he does not live under a constitution that suits him. Under a suitable one, his own growth will be fuller, and he will save the community as well as himself. It seems to me that we have now discussed at reasonable length why philosophy is slandered and that the slander is unjust, unless you have something to add.

Nothing on this subject, he said, but which of our present constitutions do you say is congenial to philosophy?

b

None at all, I said, and this is what I complain of, that not one of our present constitutions is worthy of the philosophic nature, and that in consequence this nature is twisted and altered, like a foreign seed which is sown in alien ground is usually overcome and fades away in the native flora. Similarly, the philosophic nature fails to develop its full power, but is altered into a different character. If it were to find the best constitution, as it is itself the best, it would be clearly seen to be truly divine while other natures and pursuits are but human. Obviously you are going to ask next which constitution that is.

You are wrong there, he said. I was not going to ask that, but whether it was the constitution we described when we were founding our city, or another.

In other respects it is that one, I said, but we said even then that there must always be some people in the city who understand the rational principle on which the constitution is based, the same which guided you, the lawgiver, when you made the laws.—We did say that.   d

Yes, I said, but we did not emphasize it sufficiently, for fear that the proof of it would be long and difficult, as your interventions showed it to be. Indeed, what remains is not the easiest thing to discuss.—What is that?

How a city can engage in philosophy without being destroyed? All great things are risky and, as the saying goes, what is beautiful is difficult.

Nevertheless, he said, our exposition must continue to the end, and this must be made clear.   e

It is not unwillingness, I said, but lack of ability which will prevent us, if we fail. You will yourself witness my eagerness. Look how eager I am to speak, in spite of the risk, that the city must deal with the pursuit of philosophy in a manner contrary to what it does at present.—How?

Now, I said, those who study it do so as young men who have just left childhood behind, before they engage in housekeeping and money making and, just as they approach its most difficult part, they give it up, and they are regarded as fully trained in philosophy. By the most difficult part I mean the study of rational discourse. In later life they think it much if they are willing to listen by invitation to a lecture on philosophy by others who practise it, but they think one should study it as a sideline. When they reach old age, with a few exceptions, their eagerness is quenched more thoroughly than the sun of Heraclitus,[92] for it is never rekindled.—   b
What should be done?   498

Quite the opposite. As youths and children their education and philosophy should be suited to their age; they should concentrate their care upon their bodies which are growing into manhood at this time, while acquiring the habit to serve philosophy. As they grow older and their soul begins to reach maturity, they should extend their philosophical exercises; then, when their physical powers are failing, and they have retired from public life and military service, they should graze freely in the pastures   c
of philosophy and have no other occupation except as a sideline—those, that is, who are to live happily, and in death add a fitting destiny yonder to the life they have lived.

You seem to speak with true enthusiasm, Socrates, he said, but I am sure that most of your hearers will oppose you with even greater enthusiasm, and not be in any way convinced, beginning with Thrasymachus.

Don't slander me and Thrasymachus just as we have become friends, not that we were enemies before. We will not relax our efforts until we either convince him and   d
others, or at any rate do something which may benefit them in a later incarnation when, born again, they happen on a similar discussion.

You are taking a short view, aren't you?

92. [According to Heraclitus the sun burned out in the West every evening and a new sun was kindled in the East every morning.]

Not such a long one either, compared with the whole of time. But it is no wonder that our words do not convince the majority, for they have never yet seen that upon which we are now insisting[93] as existing (much more often have they heard such word-chimes deliberately planned and not occurring by chance as is the case here). They have never yet seen a man chiming with, and completely assimilated to, virtue, as far as is humanly possible, both in words and deeds, reigning in a city of the same kind, neither one nor more. Or do you think they have?—No, never.

Nor have they sufficiently listened, my good friend, to fine and free discussions which eagerly seek in every way to find the truth for the sake of knowledge, and which keep away from clever debating points that only aim at opinion and disputation, both in the courts and in private discussions.—They have not.

It is for this reason, I said, that, foreseeing these difficulties and full of apprehension, we were nevertheless compelled by truth to say then that no perfect city or constitution, and equally no perfect individual, would ever come to be until these philosophers, the few who are not wicked but are now said to be useless, are compelled by chance, whether they wish it or not, to take charge of a city and that city is compelled to obey them, or unless by divine inspiration a genuine passion for true philosophy come upon the sons of the present rulers or kings, or upon those rulers themselves. That either or both of these things is impossible cannot, I say, be reasonably maintained. If it were, we would rightly be ridiculed for indulging in wishful thinking. Is that not so?—It is.

Whether men most gifted for philosophy have ever been forced to take charge of a city in the infinity of past time, or whether it is happening now in some foreign place far beyond our ken, or will happen in the future, let us be ready to struggle to maintain in argument that the city we described has existed, exists now, and will exist whenever the Muse of philosophy controls a city. It is not impossible, and our talk is not of impossible things. That it is difficult we ourselves agree.—I think so too.

But, I said, you will say that the majority do not?—Perhaps.

My dear friends, I said, do not make these wholesale charges against the many. They will change their opinion if you show them, not contentiously but encouragingly, whom you mean by philosophers and thus remove their slanderous prejudice against the love of learning, if you define the philosophic nature and its vocation as you did just now, so that they realize that you do not mean the same people as they do. If they once see it your way, you will say that they hold a different opinion and will give different answers. Do you think that anyone who is gentle and without malice is irritated with one who shows no irritation, or malicious to one who has no malice? I anticipate your answer and say that such a difficult nature is, I believe, found in a few people, but not in the majority.—Yes, I certainly think so too.

Think this also then, namely that the intolerance of the many towards philosophy is caused by those outsiders who come to philosophy, where they do not belong, like

---

93. [Plato is here ridiculing the rhetoricians who were overfond of word jingles, similarities of sound at the beginning and end of clauses etc. Hence the Greek word jingle in the text, namely *genomenon to nun legomenon* which he claims is purely accidental, not sought as the rhetoricians seek it. The translation in*sisting* as e*xisting* is an attempt to imitate the effect, as well as an approximation to the meaning. Then Plato goes on using rhetorical terms throughout the paragraph.]

a band of revellers. They are continually abusing each other and being quarrelsome; they always talk in personalities, which is quite unsuited to philosophy.—Yes indeed.

The man whose thoughts are truly directed to real existences, Adeimantus, does not have the time to look down upon the affairs of men, and by contending with them to be filled with malice and ill-will. As he looks upon and contemplates things that are ordered and ever the same, that do no wrong to, and are not wronged by, each other, being all in a rational order, he imitates them and tries to become as like them as he can. Or do you think one can consort with things one admires without imitating them in one's own person?—Not possibly.

c

So the philosopher, who consorts with what is divine and ordered, himself becomes godlike and ordered as far as a man can, but there is much slander everywhere.— That is certainly true.

d

And if it becomes necessary for him to put into practice the things he sees yonder by applying them to the characters of men both in private and in public life instead of only moulding his own, do you think he will be a poor craftsman of moderation and justice, and of popular virtue generally?—Least of all men.

Further, when the many realize that we speak the truth about him, will they be irritated with the philosophers and will they distrust us when we say that the city will never find happiness unless the painters who use the divine model sketch its outline?

e

They will not be angry, he said, if they realize this. But what manner of outline?

501

They would take the city and men's characters as a draughting board, and first of all they would clean it, which is not at all easy. Know then that the immediate difference between them and others is that they would refuse to touch a city or an individual, or to write laws, unless they either take over a clean board or clean it themselves.—Quite right.

After that, do you think, they would sketch out the shape of the constitution?— Quite.

Then I think that, as they work, they would keep looking back and forth, to Justice, Beauty, Moderation, and all such things as by nature exist, and they would compose human life with reference to these, mixing and mingling the human like-ness from various pursuits, basing their judgment on what Homer too called the divine and godlike existing in man.[94]—Rightly.

b

They would erase one thing and draw in another, I think, until they had made human characters as dear to the gods as possible.—That would indeed be a most beautiful picture.

c

Are we, said I, in any way persuading those people who, you said, were straining to attack us, that the man whom we were praising to them and to whom they resented our entrusting our cities is that kind of draughtsman of constitutions? Are they at all appeased when they hear what we are now saying?—Considerably, if they are in their right mind.

What grounds will they find for dispute? Will they say that philosophers are not lovers of reality and truth?—That would be quite absurd.

d

---

94. [Homer uses the adjective *theoeikelos* (godlike) which Plato uses here in *Iliad* 1, 131 (of Achilles) and elsewhere.]

Or that their nature as we have described it is not close to the best?—Not that either.

What then? That such a nature, if it follows its own pursuits, is not completely good and loves wisdom if any nature does? Or will they say that those people whom we have excluded do so more?—Certainly not.

Will they then still be angry when we say that until the philosophers attain power in a city there will be no respite from evil for either city or citizens, nor will the constitution which we have imagined in our argument ever be realized in fact.—Perhaps they will be less angry.

Are you willing for us not to say "less so," but that they have become altogether gentle and are convinced, if only for shame of disagreeing?—Certainly.

Let us assume that they are convinced on this point; but will anyone dispute that the sons of kings and dynasts could be born with a philosophic nature?—No one could.

And could anyone maintain that, once born, they must quite inevitably be corrupted? We would ourselves agree that it is hard for them to be saved from corruption, but could anyone maintain that, in the fullness of time, not one of them could ever be saved?—How could one?

And surely one such individual, if his city obeyed him, would be sufficient to bring about all the measures which now seem incredible?—He would be sufficient.

If he was in power, I said, and established those laws and institutions which we have described, it is not impossible that the citizens would be willing to act accordingly.—Not at all impossible.

Would it be astonishing and impossible that others should think as we do?—I do not think so.

And we have given sufficient proof earlier in our discussion that, if these things are possible, they are for the best.—Quite so.

So we may now properly conclude that the laws we suggest are the best, if they are possible, and we agree that it is hard to realize them, but not that they are impossible.—We may so conclude.

Since we have with some difficulty concluded that argument, we must now deal with what remains, namely how the saviours of our constitution will develop, what studies and pursuits they must follow, and at what age they must severally take up each of these.—We must do so.

It was not clever of me in our previous discussion to omit the difficult subjects of acquiring wives and begetting children and the appointment of rulers, because I knew that the method which was completely in accordance with the truth would cause difficulties and resentment, for now I have to deal with it just the same. The subject of women and children has been fully dealt with, but that of the rulers must be taken up again from the beginning. We said, if you remember, that they must be seen to love their city, that they must be tested by pleasure and pain, and that neither in toil nor fear, nor in any change of circumstances must they lose that love. The one who was incapable of this was to be rejected, while the one who came through unaltered, like gold tested in fire, was to be established as ruler and receive prizes both while he lived and after death. We said something like this, but our argument

veiled its face and passed along, for fear of stirring up the question which is facing   b
us now.—Very true, I remember it.

We hesitated, my friend, I said, to say the things which have now been boldly
stated. So let us now boldly say that those who are our guardians in the most precise
sense must be philosophers.—Let us say this.

Consider then that these are likely to be very few, for they must have the nature
we have described and its qualities rarely occur in the same person; for the most
part they are scattered.—What do you mean?   c

You know that men who learn easily, have a good memory, are quick-witted and
sharp, and have the other qualities which go with these, are not usually able to be
at the same time both vigorous and liberal-minded, and also able to live quietly in
an orderly and stable manner; their sharpness carries them hither and thither and
all stability escapes them.—That is true.

On the other hand the stable characters who do not change easily, whom one
would consider more trustworthy, and who are not easily moved to fear in battle,   d
have the same attitude to learning: they are hard to move, they learn with difficulty
as if benumbed, they are full of sleep and yawns whenever any intellectual work is
required.—That is so.

Yet we say that a man must have a fair and goodly share of both temperaments
if he is to receive the most exact education as well as honour and power.—We are
right.

And you think this mixture is rare?—Of course.

We must test this nature in those toils, fears, and pleasures we mentioned before   e
and also—this we omitted before but are adding now—it must be exercised in many
kinds of studies to see whether it can tolerate the greatest studies, or whether it will
shrink from them, like those who fail in other tests.   504

It is proper, he said, to examine them like this, but what do you mean by the most
important studies?

You remember, I said, that when we had distinguished three parts of the soul, we
discussed with reference to these parts the nature of each of justice, moderation,
courage and wisdom.

If I did not remember that, he said, I should not deserve to hear the rest.

And also what we said before that?—What was that?

We spoke as best we could at the time, and we said that to see these things most   b
clearly there was a longer way round which would make them plain to anyone who
travelled it, but that it was possible to deal with them on a level of proof compatible
with what had been said up to then. You said that this was satisfactory; however, I
thought that what was said then in that way was lacking in precision, but you might
tell me if it satisfied you.[95]—I thought you gave us good measure, he said, and so,
apparently, did the others.

Any measure, my friend, I said, which, in these matters, falls short of reality to   c
any degree, is not good measure. Nothing which is incomplete is a measure of

---

95. [The reference is to IV, 435d. The longer way requires the education of the philosopher which Plato is
about to describe.]

anything, though sometimes people think it is already enough and that there is no need to search further.—They do this because they are lazy.

Laziness, however, is a quality that the guardian of a city and of laws can do without.—Very likely.

d   That sort of man should go round the longer way, my friend, I said, and put as much effort into his studies as into physical training; otherwise he will never reach the end of the most important and most appropriate study.

Are these virtues then, he said, not the most important subject of study? Is there anything still more important than justice and the things we discussed?

There is, I said. Also, we should not observe a mere outline of these things themselves, as we are doing now, and neglect the most finished picture. Is it not ridiculous to strain every nerve to have a most exact and pure picture of other things

e   of little value, and not to require the greatest accuracy for the greatest subjects?

It certainly is, he said, but do you think that anyone is going to let you off without asking you what this greatest study is, and what you say it is about?

No indeed, I said, you too can ask me. You have certainly heard it often enough, but now either you are not thinking, or you again intend to make trouble for me by

505 your intervention. I rather think that the latter is the case, for you have often heard it said that the Form of the Good is the greatest object of study, and that it is by their relation to it that just actions and the other things become useful and beneficial. You probably knew that I was about to say this and, besides, that our knowledge of it is inadequate. If we do not know it, even the fullest possible knowledge of other things

b   is no help to us, any more than if we acquire any possession without the good. Do you think there is any advantage to have acquired every kind of possession, if it is not good, or to have every kind of knowledge without that of the Good, thus knowing nothing beautiful or good?—No, by Zeus, I do not.

Furthermore, you certainly know that the many believe that pleasure is the Good, while the more sophisticated believe it is knowledge.—Of course.

And, my friend, that those who believe this cannot tell us what knowledge, but in the end they are compelled to say that it is the knowledge of the Good.—And very ridiculous that is.

c   Of course it is, I said. They blame us for not knowing the Good and then again they talk to us as if we did know the Good. For they say that it is knowledge of the Good, as if we knew what they mean once they have uttered the word good.—Very true.

What about those who define the Good as pleasure? Are they less confused in mind than the others? Are not even they compelled to admit that there are bad pleasures?—Definitely.

So, I think, they have to conclude that the same things are good and bad. Is that
d   not so?—Of course.

So then this is a subject of great and frequent controversies?—It certainly is.

Further, is it not clear that in the case of just and beautiful things, many are content with what seems so, even if it is not, yet they act, acquire, and think on that basis; but when it comes to good things nobody is satisfied to acquire what seems to be so, but they seek the things that really are good, and everybody in this case disdains appearances.—Quite so.

This every soul pursues, and all its actions are done for its sake. It divines that it is something but is perplexed and cannot adequately grasp what it is, nor does it have about this the firm opinion which it has about other things, and because of this it misses the benefit, if any, even of those other things. Should we say that even the best men in the city to whom we entrust everything must remain in such darkness about so great and so important a subject?—Least of all.

When it is not known how just and beautiful things come to be good, these things will not find it much use to secure a guardian over themselves who does not have this knowledge. And I surmise that no one will understand those just and beautiful things adequately before he knows this.—A fine surmise.

Our constitution then will be perfectly ordered when such a man looks after it— that is, a man who has this knowledge.

Necessarily, he said, but you also, Socrates, must tell us whether you consider the good to be knowledge, or pleasure, or something else.

What a man! I said. It has been clear for some time that the opinion of others on this subject would not satisfy you.

Well, Socrates, he said, it does not seem right to me to be able to tell the opinions of others and not one's own, especially for a man who has spent so much time as you have occupying himself with this subject.

Why? said I. Do you think it right to talk about things one does not know as if one knew them?

Not as if one knew them, he said, but for a man who has an opinion to say what that opinion is.

And have you not noticed that opinions not based on knowledge are ugly things? The best of them are blind; or do you think that those who express a true opinion without knowledge are any different from blind people who yet follow the right road?—They are no different.

Do you want to contemplate ugly, blind, and crooked things when you can hear bright and beautiful things from others?

By Zeus, Socrates, said Glaucon, do not stand off as if you had come to the end. We shall be satisfied if you discuss the Good in the same fashion as you did justice, moderation, and the other things.

That, my friend, I said, would also quite satisfy me, but I fear I shall not be able to do so, and that in my eagerness I shall disgrace myself and make myself ridiculous. But, my excellent friends, let us for the moment abandon the quest for the nature of the Good itself, for that I think is a larger question than what we started on, which was to ascertain my present opinion about it. I am willing to tell you what appears to be the offspring of the Good and most like it, if that is agreeable to you. If not, we must let the question drop.

Well, he said, tell us. The story of the parent remains a debt which you will pay us some other time.

I wish, I said, that I could pay it in full now, and you could exact it in full and not, as now, only receive the interest.[96] However, accept then this offspring and child of

---

96. [Plato is punning on the Greek word *tokos* which means a child, and in the plural was used also of the interest on capital, a pleasant and common metaphor.]

the Good. Only be careful that I do not somehow deceive you unwillingly by giving a counterfeit account of this offspring.—We shall be as careful as we can. Only tell us.

b I will, I said, after coming to an agreement with you and reminding you of the things we said before, and also many times elsewhere.—What are these things?

We speak of many beautiful things and many good things, and we say that they are so and so define them in speech.—We do.

And Beauty itself and Goodness itself, and so with all the things which we then classed as many; we now class them again according to one Form of each, which is one and which we in each case call that which is.—That is so.

And we say that the many things are the objects of sight but not of thought, while the Forms are the objects of thought but not of sight.—Altogether true.

c With what part of ourselves do we see the objects that are seen?—With our sight.

And so things heard are heard by our hearing, and all that is perceived is perceived by our other senses?—Quite so.

Have you considered how very lavishly the maker of our senses made the faculty of seeing and being seen?—I cannot say I have.

Look at it this way: do hearing and sound need another kind of thing for the former to hear and the latter to be heard, and in the absence of this third element
d the one will not hear and the other not be heard.—No, they need nothing else.

Neither do many other senses, if indeed any, need any such other thing, or can you mention one?—Not I.

But do you not realize that the sense of sight and that which is seen do have such a need?—How so?

Sight may be in the eyes, and the man who has it may try to use it, and colours may be present in the objects, but unless a third kind of thing is present, which is
e by nature designed for this very purpose, you know that sight will see nothing and the colours remain unseen.—What is this third kind of thing?

What you call light, I said.—Right.

So to no small extent the sense of sight and the power of being seen are yoked
508 together by a more honourable yoke than other things which are yoked together, unless light is held in no honour.—That is far from being the case.

Which of the gods in the heavens can you hold responsible for this, whose light causes our sight to see as beautifully as possible, and the objects of sight to be seen?— The same as you would, he said, and as others would; obviously the answer to your question is the sun.

And is not sight naturally related to the sun in this way?—Which way?

b Sight is not the sun, neither itself nor that in which it occurs which we call the eye.—No indeed.

But I think it is the most sunlike of the organs of sense.—Very much so.

And it receives from the sun the capacity to see as a kind of outflow.—Quite so.

The sun is not sight, but is it not the cause of it, and is also seen by it?—Yes.

Say then, I said, that it is the sun which I called the offspring of the Good, which the Good begot as analogous to itself. What the Good itself is in the world of thought

in relation to the intelligence and things known, the sun is in the visible world, in   c
relation to sight and things seen.—How? Explain further.

You know, I said, that when one turns one's eyes to those objects of which the
colours are no longer in the light of day but in the dimness of the night, the eyes
are dimmed and seem nearly blind, as if clear vision was no longer in them.—Quite
so.

Yet whenever one's eyes are turned upon objects brightened by sunshine, they   d
see clearly, and clear vision appears in those very same eyes?—Yes indeed.

So too understand the eye of the soul: whenever it is fixed upon that upon which
truth and reality shine, it understands and knows and seems to have intelligence,
but whenever it is fixed upon what is mixed with darkness—that which is subject to
birth and destruction—it opines and is dimmed, changes its opinions this way and
that, and seems to have no intelligence.—That is so.

Say that what gives truth to the objects of knowledge, and to the knowing mind   e
the power to know, is the Form of Good. As it is the cause of knowledge and truth,
think of it also as being the object of knowledge. Both knowledge and truth are
beautiful, but you will be right to think of the Good as other and more beautiful
than they. As in the visible world light and sight are rightly considered sun-like, but   509
it is wrong to think of them as the sun, so here it is right to think of knowledge and
truth as Good-like, but wrong to think of either as the Good, for the Good must be
honoured even more than they.

This is an extraordinary beauty you mention, he said, if it provides knowledge
and truth and is itself superior to them in beauty. You surely do not mean this to
be pleasure!

Hush! said I, rather examine the image of it in this way.—How?   b

You will say, I think, that the sun not only gives to the objects of sight the capacity
to be seen, but also that it provides for their generation, increase, and nurture,
though it is not itself the process of generation.—How could it be?

And say that as for the objects of knowledge, not only is their being known due
to the Good, but also their reality being, though the Good is not being but superior
to and beyond being in dignity and power.

Glaucon was quite amused and said: By Apollo, a miraculous superiority!   c

It is your own fault, I said, you forced me to say what I thought about it.

Don't you stop, he said, except for a moment, but continue to explain the similarity
to the sun in case you are leaving something out.

I am certainly leaving out a good deal, I said.—Don't omit the smallest point.

Much is omitted, I said. However, as far as the explanation can go at present, I
will not omit anything.—Don't you!

Understand then, I said, that, as we say, there are those two, one reigning over   d
the intelligible kind and realm, the other over the visible (not to say heaven, that I
may not appear to play the sophist about the name).[97] So you have two kinds, the
visible and the intelligible.—Right.

---

97. [He means play on the similarity of sound between *ouranos*, the sky, and *horaton*, visible.]

It is like a line divided[98] into two unequal parts, and then divide each section in the same ratio, that is, the section of the visible and that of the intelligible. You will then have sections related to each other in proportion to their clarity and obscurity.

e

510

The first section of the visible consists of images—and by images I mean shadows in the first instance, then the reflections in water and all those on close-packed, smooth, and bright materials, and all that sort of thing, if you understand me.—I understand.

In the other section of the visible, place the models of the images, the living creatures around us, all plants, and the whole class of manufactured things.—I so place them.

Would you be willing to say that, as regards truth and untruth, the division is made in this proportion: as the opinable is to the knowable so the image is to the model it is made like?—Certainly.

b

Consider now how the section of the intelligible is to be divided.—How?

In such a way that in one section the soul, using as images what before were models, is compelled to investigate from hypotheses, proceeding from these not to a first principle but to a conclusion. In the second section which leads to a first principle that is not hypothetical, the soul proceeds from a hypothesis without using the images of the first section, by means of the Forms themselves and proceeding through these.—I do not, he said, quite understand what you mean.

c

Let us try again, I said, for you will understand more easily because of what has been said. I think you know that students of geometry, calculation, and the like assume the existence of the odd and the even, of figures, of three kinds of angles, and of kindred things in each of their studies, as if they were known to them. These they make their hypotheses and do not deem it necessary to give any account of them either to themselves or to others as if they were clear to all; these are their

d

starting points, and going through the remaining steps they reach an agreed conclusion on what they started out to investigate.—Quite so, I understand that.

98. [It is clear that Plato visualizes a vertical line (511d and throughout) with B as the highest point and A as the lowest. The main division is at C. AC is the visible, CB being the intelligible world.

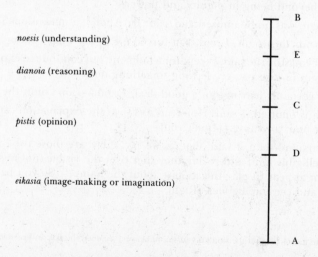

noesis (understanding)

dianoia (reasoning)

pistis (opinion)

eikasia (image-making or imagination)

You know also that they use visible figures and talk about them, but they are not thinking about them but about the models of which these are likenesses; they are making their points about the square itself, the diameter itself, not about the diame-   e
ter which they draw, and similarly with the others. These figures which they fashion and draw, of which shadows and reflections in the water are images, they now in turn use as images, in seeking to understand those others in themselves, which one cannot see except in thought.—That is true.   511

This is what I called the intelligible class, and said that the soul is forced to use hypotheses in its search for it, not travelling up to a first principle, since it cannot reach beyond its hypotheses, but it uses as images those very things which at a lower level were models and which, in comparison with their images, were thought to be clear and honoured as such.—I understand, he said, that you mean what happens   b
in geometry and kindred sciences.

Understand also that by the other section of the intelligible I mean that which reason itself grasps by the power of dialectic. It does not consider its hypotheses as first principles, but as hypotheses in the true sense of stepping stones and starting points, in order to reach that which is beyond hypothesis, the first principle of all that exists. Having reached this and keeping hold of what follows from it, it does   c
come down to a conclusion without making use of anything visible at all, but proceeding by means of Forms and through Forms to its conclusions which are Forms.

I understand, he said, but not completely, for you seem to be speaking of a mighty task—that you wish to distinguish the intelligible reality contemplated by the science of dialectic as clearer than that viewed by the so-called sciences, for which their hypotheses are first principles. The students of these so-called sciences are, it is true, compelled to study them by thought and not by sense perception, yet because they   d
do not go back to a first principle but proceed from hypotheses, you do not think that they have any clear understanding of their subjects, although these can be so understood if approached from a first principle. You seem to me to call the attitude of mind of geometers and such reasoning but not understanding, reasoning being midway between opinion and understanding.

You have grasped this very satisfactorily, I said. There are four such processes in the soul, corresponding to the four sections of our line: understanding for the highest, reasoning for the second; give the name of opinion to the third, and   e
imagination to the last. Place these in the due terms of a proportion and consider that each has as much clarity as the content of its particular section shares in truth.—
I understand, and I agree and arrange them as you say.

BOOK VII

Next, I said, compare the effect of education and the lack of it upon our human   514
nature to a situation like this: imagine men to be living in an underground cave-like dwelling place, which has a way up to the light along its whole width, but the entrance is a long way up. The men have been there from childhood, with their neck and legs in fetters, so that they remain in the same place and can only see ahead of them, as   b

their bonds prevent them turning their heads. Light is provided by a fire burning some way behind and above them. Between the fire and the prisoners, some way behind them and on a higher ground, there is a path across the cave and along this a low wall has been built, like the screen at a puppet show in front of the performers who show their puppets above it.—I see it.

c
515

See then also men carrying along that wall, so that they overtop it, all kinds of artifacts, statues of men, reproductions of other animals in stone or wood fashioned in all sorts of ways, and, as is likely, some of the carriers are talking while others are silent.—This is a strange picture, and strange prisoners.

b

They are like us, I said. Do you think, in the first place, that such men could see anything of themselves and each other except the shadows which the fire casts upon the wall of the cave in front of them?—How could they, if they have to keep their heads still throughout life?

And is not the same true of the objects carried along the wall?—Quite.

If they could converse with one another, do you not think that they would consider these shadows to be the real things?—Necessarily.

What if their prison had an echo which reached them from in front of them? Whenever one of the carriers passing behind the wall spoke, would they not think that it was the shadow passing in front of them which was talking? Do you agree?—By Zeus I do.

c

Altogether then, I said, such men would believe the truth to be nothing else than the shadows of the artifacts?—They must believe that.

Consider then what deliverance from their bonds and the curing of their ignorance would be if something like this naturally happened to them. Whenever one of them was freed, had to stand up suddenly, turn his head, walk, and look up toward the light, doing all that would give him pain, the flash of the fire would make it impossible for him to see the objects of which he had earlier seen the shadows.

d

What do you think he would say if he was told that what he saw then was foolishness, that he was now somewhat closer to reality and turned to things that existed more fully, that he saw more correctly? If one then pointed to each of the objects passing by, asked him what each was, and forced him to answer, do you not think he would be at a loss and believe that the things which he saw earlier were truer than the things now pointed out to him?—Much truer.

e

If one then compelled him to look at the fire itself, his eyes would hurt, he would turn round and flee toward those things which he could see, and think that they were in fact clearer than those now shown to him.—Quite so.

And if one were to drag him thence by force up the rough and steep path, and did not let him go before he was dragged into the sunlight, would he not be in

516

physical pain and angry as he was dragged along? When he came into the light, with the sunlight filling his eyes, he would not be able to see a single one of the things which are now said to be true.—Not at once, certainly.

I think he would need time to get adjusted before he could see things in the world above; at first he would see shadows more easily, then reflections of men and other things in water, then the things themselves. After this he would see objects in the

b

sky and the sky itself more easily at night, the light of the stars and the moon more easily than the sun and the light of the sun during the day.—Of course.

Then, at last, he would be able to see the sun, not images of it in water or in some alien place, but the sun itself in its own place, and be able to contemplate it.—That must be so.

After this he would reflect that it is the sun which provides the seasons and the years, which governs everything in the visible world, and is also in some way the cause of those other things which he used to see.—Clearly that would be the next stage.

What then? As he reminds himself of his first dwelling place, of the wisdom there and of his fellow prisoners, would he not reckon himself happy for the change, and pity them?—Surely.

And if the men below had praise and honours from each other, and prizes for the man who saw most clearly the shadows that passed before them, and who could best remember which usually came earlier and which later, and which came together and thus could most ably prophesy the future, do you think our man would desire those rewards and envy those who were honoured and held power among the prisoners, or would he feel, as Homer put it, that he certainly wished to be "serf to another man without possessions upon the earth"[99] and go through any suffering, rather than share their opinions and live as they do?—Quite so, he said, I think he would rather suffer anything.

Reflect on this too, I said. If this man went down into the cave again and sat down in the same seat, would his eyes not be filled with darkness, coming suddenly out of the sunlight?—They certainly would.

And if he had to contend again with those who had remained prisoners in recognizing those shadows while his sight was affected and his eyes had not settled down— and the time for this adjustment would not be short—would he not be ridiculed? Would it not be said that he had returned from his upward journey with his eyesight spoiled, and that it was not worthwhile even to attempt to travel upward? As for the man who tried to free them and lead them upward, if they could somehow lay their hands on him and kill him, they would do so.—They certainly would.

This whole image, my dear Glaucon, I said, must be related to what we said before. The realm of the visible should be compared to the prison dwelling, and the fire inside it to the power of the sun. If you interpret the upward journey and the contemplation of things above as the upward journey of the soul to the intelligible realm, you will grasp what I surmise since you were keen to hear it. Whether it is true or not only the god knows, but this is how I see it, namely that in the intelligible world the Form of the Good is the last to be seen, and with difficulty; when seen it must be reckoned to be for all the cause of all that is right and beautiful, to have produced in the visible world both light and the fount of light, while in the intelligible world it is itself that which produces and controls truth and intelligence, and he who is to act intelligently in public or in private must see it.—I share your thought as far as I am able.

Come then, share with me this thought also: do not be surprised that those who have reached this point are unwilling to occupy themselves with human affairs, and that their souls are always pressing upward to spend their time there, for this is natural if things are as our parable indicates.—That is very likely.

---

99. [*Odyssey* 11, 489–90, where Archilles says to Odysseus, on the latter's visit to the underworld, that he would rather be a servant to a poor man on earth than king among the dead.]

Further, I said, do you think it at all surprising that anyone coming to the evils of human life from the contemplation of the divine behaves awkwardly and appears very ridiculous while his eyes are still dazzled and before he is sufficiently adjusted to the darkness around him, if he is compelled to contend in court or some other place about the shadows of justice or the objects of which they are shadows, and to

e   carry through the contest about these in the way these things are understood by those who have never seen Justice itself?—That is not surprising at all.

518   Anyone with intelligence, I said, would remember that the eyes may be confused in two ways and from two causes, coming from light into darkness as well as from darkness into light. Realizing that the same applies to the soul, whenever he sees a soul disturbed and unable to see something, he will not laugh mindlessly but will consider whether it has come from a brighter life and is dimmed because unadjusted, or has come from greater ignorance into greater light and is filled with a brighter

b   dazzlement. The former he would declare happy in its life and experience, the latter he would pity, and if he should wish to laugh at it, his laughter would be less ridiculous than if he laughed at a soul that has come from the light above.—What you say is very reasonable.

We must then, I said, if these things are true, think something like this about them, namely that education is not what some declare it to be; they say that knowledge is not present in the soul and that they put it in, like putting sight into blind eyes.—

c   They surely say that.

Our present argument shows, I said, that the capacity to learn and the organ with which to do so are present in every person's soul. It is as if it were not possible to turn the eye from darkness to light without turning the whole body; so one must turn one's whole soul from the world of becoming until it can endure to contemplate

d   reality, and the brightest of realities, which we say is the Good.—Yes.

Education then is the art of doing this very thing, this turning around, the knowledge of how the soul can most easily and most effectively be turned around; it is not the art of putting the capacity of sight into the soul; the soul possesses that already but it is not turned the right way or looking where it should. This is what education has to deal with.—That seems likely.

Now the other so-called virtues of the soul seem to be very close to those of the

e   body—they really do not exist before and are added later by habit and practice— but the virtue of intelligence belongs above all to something more divine, it seems, which never loses its capacity but, according to which way it is turned, becomes

519   useful and beneficial or useless and harmful. Have you never noticed in men who are said to be wicked but clever, how sharply their little soul looks into things to which it turns its attention? Its capacity for sight is not inferior, but it is compelled to serve evil ends, so that the more sharply it looks the more evils it works.—Quite so.

Yet if a soul of this kind has been hammered at from childhood and those excrescences had been knocked off it which belong to the world of becoming and have

b   been fastened upon it by feasting, gluttony, and similar pleasures, and which like leaden weights draw the soul to look downward—if, being rid of these, it turned to look at things that are true, then the same soul of the same man would see these just as sharply as it now sees the things towards which it is directed.—That seems likely.

Further, is it not likely, I said, indeed it follows inevitably from what was said before, that the uneducated who have no experience of truth would never govern a city satisfactorily, nor would those who are allowed to spend their whole life in the process of educating themselves; the former would fail because they do not have a single goal at which all their actions, public and private, must aim; the latter because they would refuse to act, thinking that they have settled, while still alive, in the faraway islands of the blessed.—True.

It is then our task as founders, I said, to compel the best natures to reach the study which we have previously said to be the most important, to see the Good and to follow that upward journey. When they have accomplished their journey and seen it sufficiently, we must not allow them to do what they are allowed to do today.— What is that?

To stay there, I said, and to refuse to go down again to the prisoners in the cave, there to share both their labours and their honours, whether these be of little or of greater worth.

Are we then, he said, to do them an injustice by making them live a worse life when they could live a better one?

You are again forgetting, my friend, I said, that it is not the law's concern to make some one group in the city outstandingly happy but to contrive to spread happiness throughout the city, by bringing the citizens into harmony with each other by persuasion or compulsion, and to make them share with each other the benefits which each group can confer upon the community. The law has not made men of this kind in the city in order to allow each to turn in any direction they wish but to make use of them to bind the city together.—You are right, I had forgotten.

Consider then, Glaucon, I said, that we shall not be doing an injustice to those who have become philosophers in our city, and that what we shall say to them, when we compel them to care for and to guard the others, is just. For we shall say: "Those who become philosophers in other cities are justified in not sharing the city's labours, for they have grown into philosophy of their own accord, against the will of the government in each of those cities, and it is right that what grows of its own accord, as it owes no debt to anyone for its upbringing, should not be keen to pay it to anyone. But we have made you in our city kings and leaders of the swarm, as it were, both to your own advantage and to that of the rest of the city; you are better and more completely educated than those others, and you are better able to share in both kinds of life. Therefore you must each in turn go down to live with other men and grow accustomed to seeing in the dark. When you are used to it you will see infinitely better than the dwellers below; you will know what each image is and of what it is an image, because you have seen the truth of things beautiful and just and good, and so, for you as for us, the city will be governed as a waking reality and not as in a dream, as the majority of cities are now governed by men who are fighting shadows and striving against each other in order to rule as if this were a great good." For this is the truth: a city in which the prospective rulers are least keen to rule must of necessity be governed best and be most free from civil strife, whereas a city with the opposite kind of rulers is governed in the opposite way.—Quite so.

Do you think that those we have nurtured will disobey us and refuse to share the labours of the city, each group in turn, though they may spend the greater part of their time dwelling with each other in a pure atmosphere?

They cannot, he said, for we shall be giving just orders to just men, but each of them will certainly go to rule as to something that must be done, the opposite attitude from that of the present rulers in every city.

That is how it is, my friend, I said. If you can find a way of life which is better than governing for the prospective governors, then a well-governed city can exist for you. Only in that city will the truly rich rule, not rich in gold but in the wealth which the happy man must have, a life with goodness and intelligence. If beggars hungry for private goods go into public life, thinking that they must snatch their good from it, the well-governed city cannot exist, for then office is fought for, and such a war at home inside the city destroys them and the city as well.—Very true.

Can you name, I said, any other life than that of true philosophy which disdains political office?—No, by Zeus.

And surely it is those who are no lovers of governing who must govern. Otherwise, rival lovers of it will fight them.—Of course.

What other men will you compel to become guardians of the city rather than those who have the best knowledge of the principles that make for the best government of a city and who also know honours of a different kind, and a better life than the political?—No one else.

Do you want us to examine how such men will come to be in our city, and how one will lead them to the light, as some are said to have gone up from the underworld to join the gods?—Of course I want it.

This is not a matter of spinning a coin[100] but of turning a soul from a kind of day that is night to the true day, being the upward way to reality which we say is true philosophy.—Quite so.

We must therefore examine what study has the power to do so.—Of course.

What study would it be, Glaucon, which draws the soul from the world of that which becomes to the world of that which is? This occurs to me as I am speaking; did we not say that these men, in youth, must be athletes in war?—We did say that.

The study we seek must therefore also have this characteristic, besides the other.— Which characteristic?

It must not be useless to men at war.—That must be so, if possible.

We educated them before this in the arts and physical culture.—We did.

Now physical culture is concerned with what comes to be and dies, since it oversees the growth and decay of the body.—So it seems.

It could not therefore be the study we seek.—No.

Is it then that education in the arts which we described?

But that, he said, was the counterpart of physical training. It educated the guardians through habits; its melodies gave them a certain inner harmony, not knowledge, and its rhythms gave them a certain grace; moreover its stories, whether fictional or nearer the truth, cultivated certain habits akin to those, but there was no knowledge in it which would lead to what you are looking for now.

---

100. [A proverbial saying, referring to a children's game in which the players were divided into two groups. A shell or potsherd, white on one side and black on the other, was then thrown in the space between them to the cry of "night or day" (note the reference to night and day which immediately follows) and, according as the white or black fell uppermost, one group ran away pursued by the other.]

You remind me most precisely, I said. In fact it has nothing of the sort. But, my **b** good Glaucon, what would such a study be? For all the crafts seemed to be too base.

Of course. Yet what study is there left, apart from the arts and physical training and the crafts?

Come, I said, if we can find nothing outside these, let us take something which bears upon them all.—What kind of thing?

For example, the common thing which is used by all crafts, all modes of thought, **c** and all sciences, and which everybody of necessity must learn to begin with.—What is it?

That trifling thing, said I, namely to distinguish one and two and three, or, to give it one name, I call it number and calculation. Is it not true that every craft and science must have a share in this?—Certainly.

War then also shares in it?—It cannot avoid it.

Palamedes[101] in the tragedies shows up Agamemnon every time as a quite ridicu- **d** lous general, or have you not noticed that he says he invented numbers which men did not know before, then arrayed the companies in the camp in Ilium and counted the ships and everything else. Agamemnon apparently did not even know how many feet he had, since he did not know how to count. What sort of a general do you think that made him?

A very strange one, he said, in my opinion, if that was true.

Shall we say then, I said, that this study is very necessary for a warrior, that is, to **e** be able to count and calculate?

More necessary than anything else, he said, if he is to understand anything about marshalling troops, indeed if he is to be a man at all.

Do you think the same as I do about this study?—What?

It is likely to be one of those we are seeking, which leads to intelligent thought, **523** but no one uses it correctly, though in every way it draws one to reality.—How do you mean?

I will try, I said, to make clear what I think. As I distinguish for myself the studies which lead in the direction we mentioned and those that do not, you must observe them along with me and agree or disagree, so that we may know more clearly whether it is as I surmise.—Show me.

Among our sense impressions there are some that do not call upon the intelligence to examine them because the decision of our perception is sufficient, while others **b** certainly summon the help of intelligence to examine them because the sensation does not achieve a sensible result.

You are, he said, obviously referring to things appearing in the distance and to shadow-painting.

You are not quite getting my meaning, I said.—What is it then?

They do not call for help, I said, if they do not at the same time give a contrary **c** impression; I describe those that do as calling for help whenever the sense perception does not point to one thing rather than its opposite, whether its object be far or

---

101. [In legend a clever Greek hero of the Trojan war. The invention of the alphabet and of arithmetic was credited to him. When Odysseus feigned madness to avoid going to Troy, Palamedes exposed him. In revenge Odysseus faked evidence of treason against him and he was put to death.]

near. You will understand my meaning better if I put it this way: here, we say, are three fingers, the smallest, the second, and the middle finger.—Quite so.

Assume that I am talking about them as being seen quite close. Now examine this about them.—What?

d   Each of them equally appears to be a finger, and in this respect it makes no difference whether it is seen to be at the end or in the middle, whether it is white or black, thick or thin, and all that sort of thing. In all this the soul of the many is not compelled to ask the intelligence what a finger is, for the sense of sight does not indicate to it that the finger is the opposite of a finger.—Certainly not.

e   Therefore this sense perception would not be likely to call on the intelligence or arouse it.—Not likely.

What about their bigness or smallness? Does the sense of sight have a sufficient perception of them, and does it make no difference to it whether the finger is in the middle or at one end? or their thickness and thinness, their hardness or softness in the case of the sense of touch? And do our other senses not lack clearness in their perception of these qualities? Does not each sense behave in the following way: in 524   the first place the sense concerned with the hard is of necessity also concerned with the soft and it declares to the soul that it perceives the same object to be both hard and soft.—That is so.

Then in those cases the soul in turn is puzzled as to what this perception means by hard, if it says that the same thing is also soft; and so with the perception of the light and the heavy, the soul is puzzled as to what is the meaning of the light and the heavy, if sense perception indicates that what is light is also heavy, and what is heavy, light.

b   Yes, he said, these indications are strange to the soul, and need investigation.

It is likely then, I said, that in these cases the soul will attempt, by calling upon calculation and intelligence, to examine whether each of the things announced to it is one or two.—Of course.

Then if they appear to be two, each appears as different and one.—Yes.

If each is one while both are two, it will think of the two as separate, for if they c   were not separate, it would not be thinking of them as two, but as one.—Correct.

But we say that the sense of sight saw big and small not as separate but as commingled. Is that not so?—Yes.

So in order to clarify this, intelligence is compelled to see big and small not as commingled but as separate, the opposite way from sight.—True.

And it is from some such circumstances that it first occurs to us to ask: "What is the nature of bigness, and again of smallness?"—That is surely true.

d   And so we called the one intelligible and the other visible.—Quite correct.

This is what I was trying to express before when I said that some things call upon thought, and others do not. Those which affect the senses in contrary ways at the same time I defined as calling on thought, while those which do not I described as not rousing the intelligence.—I understand now and I think that is right.

Well then, to which of these two classes do number and the unit seem to belong?—I do not know.

Reason it out from what was said before. If the unit, in and by itself, is adequately seen or perceived by any other sense, then, as we were saying in the case of the

fingers, it would not draw one toward reality. If, however, something contrary to it
is always seen at the same time so that it does not appear to be one more than the
opposite, it would stand in need of a judge. The soul would then be at a loss, search
for an answer, stir up intelligence within itself, and ask what is the nature of the
unit in itself, and so the study of the unit would be one of those which leads the soul 525
and turns it toward the contemplation of reality.

Certainly, he said, the sight of the unit possesses this characteristic to a remarkable
degree, for we see the same object to be both one and an infinite number.

Then if the one has this quality, every number has it too.—Of course.

Now calculation and arithmetic are wholly concerned with number.—Definitely.

Then indeed they appear to lead one to the truth.—Remarkably so.   b

They would then belong, it seems, to the studies we seek. The warrior must learn
them to marshal his troops, and also the philosopher because he must emerge from
the world of becoming and grasp reality, or never be a rational thinker.—That is
so.

And our guardian must be both a warrior and a philosopher.—Definitely.

This study would then be a suitable one, Glaucon. We should legislate and persuade those who will share the highest offices in our city to turn to arithmetic
and to pursue it in no amateur spirit, but until they reach by pure thought the   c
contemplation of the nature of numbers. They do not pursue this study for the sake
of buying and selling like merchants and retailers, but both for the sake of war and
to attain ease in turning the soul itself from the world of becoming to truth and
reality.—A fine statement.

Moreover it occurs to me, since the study of calculation has been mentioned, what   d
a subtle study it is and in how many ways it is useful to our purpose, if one studies
it for the sake of knowledge and not to buy and sell.—In what way?

In the way we were mentioning. It forcibly leads the soul upward and compels it
to discuss the numbers themselves. Nor does the soul allow one to discuss them by
presenting numbers with visible and touchable bodies. You know how experts in
these matters, if someone tries to divide the unit in argument, laugh at him and do   e
not allow it; if you divide it, they multiply, taking care that the unit should never
appear to be many parts and not to be one.—Very true indeed.

Then what do you think they would answer if one asked them: "You strange   526
people, what kind of numbers are you talking about, in which the one is as you
postulate it, each unit equal to every other without the smallest difference, and
containing no parts?"

I think they would answer that they are talking about things which can only be
grasped by thought and which cannot be dealt with in any other way.

You see, my friend, I said, that the study is likely to be really essential for us since
it appears to compel the soul to use intelligence alone to discover truth itself.—   b
Indeed, he said, it certainly does this.

Further, have you yet noticed that those who are by nature good at calculation[102]
are, as one might say, naturally sharp in every other study, and that those who are

---

102. [The Greek word which means calculation also means reasoning, so that the man who is good at
calculation (*logistikos*) is also good at reasoning.]

slow at it, if they are educated and exercised in this study, nevertheless improve and become sharper than they were?—That is so.

c   Moreover, I do not think that you will easily find studies which give more trouble to the practising pupil, or not many of them.—No indeed.

For all these reasons, this study is not to be neglected, and the best natures must be educated in it.—I agree.

Let that then, I said, be one of our studies. In the second place let us look at that which is next to it.

What study is that, he said, or are you thinking of geometry?—The very one.

d   In so far as it pertains to war, he said, it is obviously suitable. As regards encampments, occupation of positions, concentration and deployment of troops, and all the other formations employed both in the battles themselves and on the march, being a geometer or not makes all the difference to a man.

Yes, I said, but for those purposes even a small amount of geometry and calculation would suffice. We must examine whether the greater portion of it which is more e   advanced tends to make it easier to see the Form of the Good. All things tend in that direction which compel the soul to turn itself toward the place in which the most blessed part of reality exists, which the soul must see at any cost.—You are right.

Therefore if it compels the soul to contemplate reality it is suitable, if to see only what comes to be, it is not.—So we have said.

527   No one who has even a little experience of geometry will dispute that the science itself contradicts the expressions used by those who practise it.—How do you mean?

They use ridiculous terms, and indeed must do so. They speak like men of action and all their words point to actions. They talk of "squaring" and "applying" and "adding" and do so throughout, whereas the whole study is pursued for the sake of b   knowledge.—By all means.

This then must be agreed on.—What?

That it is pursued for the knowledge of that which exists forever, not of that which at some time comes to birth and is destroyed.—That is easily agreed, for geometry is knowledge of that which exists forever.

It would then, my noble friend, draw the soul toward truth and produce philosophic thought, and make us direct upward those parts of ourselves which we now direct downward when we should not.—It does this as much as is possible.

c   So we must, I said, prescribe as much as possible that the inhabitants of your beautiful city should in no way neglect geometry. And its side benefits are also considerable.—What are they?

Those which you mentioned, I said, as concerned with war, and also, with regard to all other studies and greater success in them, we know that there is a world of difference between the man who has studied geometry and the man who has not.— A world of difference indeed.

Shall we then put this down as a second study for our youth?—Let us.

d   Well then, shall we make astronomy the third, or don't you think so?

That suits me, he said. A better perception of the seasons and the months and the years concerns not only the farmer and the navigator, but no less the general.

You amuse me, I said, you are so like a man who is afraid of appearing to the many to prescribe useless studies. The other reason for this study is not unimportant though hard to credit, that by pursuing it a certain organ in every student's soul is cleansed and rekindled, which has been blinded and destroyed by his other pursuits, yet it is more worth saving than a thousand eyes, for by this organ alone is the truth perceived. Those who agree with you will think that you are speaking incredibly well, but those who have never been aware of this fact are likely to think that you are talking nonsense, for they see no other benefit in those studies worth mentioning. Consider then right now which group you are addressing. Or are you addressing neither, but discussing mostly for your own sake, though you will not begrudge anyone else whatever benefit he may gain from your words.

I prefer that, he said, to speak, question, and answer mostly for my own sake.

Fall back then, I said, to our previous position, for we were wrong just now about the study which comes after geometry.—How so?

In taking up, I said, solid bodies in motion before taking the solid by itself. It is correct to take the third dimension after the second, that is the dimension of cubes and that which shares in depth.

You are right, Socrates, he said, but those studies have not been discovered yet.

There are two reasons for this, I said. No city honours these studies, they are difficult and weakly researched and the researchers need a leader, without whom they would not make discoveries. Now it is difficult for such a man to be found, and then, even if he were, the people who occupy themselves with this research are proud and would not follow him. However, if the whole city helped him to supervise this study and held it in honour, he would be followed and, if the subject was consistently and vigorously pursued, its problems would soon become clear. Even now, when it is without honour, discredited by the many, and pursued by investigators who can give no account of its usefulness, nevertheless, in spite of all these handicaps, the charm of this study compels its development, and it is no wonder that its problems are being solved.

The study, he said, has unusual charm, but explain more clearly what you were saying just now. You have put down the study of plane surfaces as geometry.—Yes.

Then at first, he said, you put astronomy after it, but later you went back on that.

In my haste to enumerate them all, I said, I have progressed the more slowly. The study of the dimension of depth was next, but because the investigation of it is in a ridiculous state, I passed it by and spoke of astronomy after geometry, that is, the motion of things which have depth.—Correct.

Let us then, I said, put astronomy as the fourth study, since that which we now omit is available, if the city should take it up.

That seems reasonable, he said. You reproached me just now for praising astronomy in a vulgar manner, so now I praise it in the way you approach it, for I think it is obvious to anyone that it compels the soul to look upward and leads it from things here to things yonder.

Perhaps, I said, that is obvious to anyone but me, for I do not think so.—How so?

As those who lead us to philosophy practise it today, it certainly makes one look downward.—How do you mean?

You seem to have no mean idea of the study of things above. If someone were b contemplating ornaments on a ceiling and learned something with his head bent back, you would probably say that he is looking not with his eyes but with his intelligence. Perhaps you are right and I am foolish, for I cannot conceive of any study making the soul look upward except that which concerns itself with reality and the invisible. If anyone tries to acquire knowledge about any object of sense, whether he is gaping upward with his mouth open or looking down with his mouth

c shut, I say he cannot learn anything, for there is no knowledge of such things, and his soul is not looking upward but downward, even if he is lying on his back on land or in the sea.

Your rebuke is deserved, he said, and I take my punishment, but what did you mean when you said that astronomy must be studied in a different way, if the study is to be useful for our purpose?

It is like this, I said: these ornaments which brighten the sky, since they are
d embroidered in the visible world, we should consider as the most beautiful and the most exact of visible things, but they fall far short of true existences, of the motions by which true speed and true slowness are carried along in true number and true shapes, both in relation to each other and carrying along what these true shapes contain. These things can be perceived by reason and thought, but not by sight, or do you think they can?—In no way.

Therefore, I said one should use the embroidery of the sky as models in the study of those other things. Just as if one came upon plans most carefully drawn and
e excellently worked out by Daedalus, or some other craftsman or artist. A man versed in geometry, on seeing these, would think them beautifully worked out, but that it was absurd to examine them with any serious hope of finding the truth there about
530 the equal, or the double, or any other ratio.—It surely would be absurd.

Do you not think that a real astronomer will feel the same when he looks upon the movements of the stars? He will think them of the most beautiful workmanship, that the maker of the sky and all that it contains has put it together in the most beautiful manner possible for such things, but, as for the relation of night to day, of these to month, and month to year, and of the other stars to these and to each
b other, will he not, do you think, consider it strange to believe that they are ever the same and do not deviate at all anywhere, since they are material and visible, and he will undertake, in every way he can, to understand the real truth of these things?— It does indeed seem so to me, as I listen to you now.

Let us then study astronomy by means of problems as we do geometry and let the things in the sky go, if the study of astronomy is to make the naturally intelligent
c part of the soul useful instead of useless.

You are prescribing, he said, a task many times harder than the present practice of astronomy.

I think, I said, that our other prescriptions will be of the same kind if we are to be of any benefit as lawgivers. But have you any other suitable study to suggest?— Not offhand.

Well, motion is not of one but of several kinds. Perhaps a wise man could tell them
d all; however, two kinds are clear to us.—What are they?

Beside the one we have discussed, we have its counterpart.—What is that?

It is likely that, as the eyes are fixed upon astronomy, so the ears are fixed upon the movements of harmony, and that these sciences are closely akin, as the Pythagoreans say and we agree with them, Glaucon, or do we?—We do.[103]

Then, since this is a considerable task, let us enquire from them what they have   e
to say about this, and whether there is anything to add. And all along we shall keep our aim in view.—And what is that?

That they should not make those whom we are nurturing learn something which leads nowhere and which does not reach the end which everything should reach, as we saw just now in the case of astronomy. Do you not realize that they do something   531
similar with harmony? The consonances and sounds which they hear they measure against each other and so labour in vain, as do the astronomers.

Yes by the gods, he said, and they do so to a ridiculous degree. They talk of something they call a quarter-tone and lay their ears to their instruments like someone trying to hear what the neighbours are saying; then some say they hear a sound in between and that this is the shortest interval by which they must measure, while others argue that the sounds are the same. Both place the ear before the mind.   b

You are talking, I said, about those good people who give trouble to their strings, torturing them and stretching them on the pegs; but, lest our image become tedious by speaking of blows delivered by the plectrum, accusations, and denials and boastings of strings, I am cutting it short, and I say that those are not the people I refer to, but those whom we said just now that we would question about harmony, for they seek for numbers in the consonances they hear but do not make their way up   c
to problems to examine which numbers are consonant and which are not, and what is the reason in each case.

This you mention is a superhuman task, he said.

But a useful one, I said, in respect to the search for the Beautiful and the Good, while pursued in a different way the study is useless.—Quite likely.

I certainly think, I said, that if the practice of all the pursuits we have mentioned   d
reaches the study of their association and kinship with one another, and they are studied together to show how closely related they are, then the investigation of them does make some contribution to what we want, and the labour is not in vain, but otherwise it is vain.

I too, he said, predict this to be true, but it is a mighty labour you speak of, Socrates.

You mean that of the prelude, or what? Do we not know that all these studies are but preludes to the song[104] that must be learned? For surely you do not think that those who are clever at these studies are dialecticians?[105]—No, by Zeus, he said,   e
except a few of those I have met.

---

103. [Pythagoras had discovered that musical consonances could be expressed by mathematical ratios. He did this by varying the length of the string on a one-string instrument.]

104. [In this and the next paragraph, Plato is playing on the double meaning of the Greek word *nomos* which means both a song and law.]

105. [The word *dialegesthai* simply means to converse. It was applied to the Socratic method of question and answer, that is, of proceeding step by step, each step being based on mutual agreement, as seen in the first book (e.g. 348 a–b). Plato derives the word dialectic from this, and he continues to use the vocabulary of Socratic conversation, even when the word dialectic has acquired for him a much deeper significance.]

Further, I said, do those who cannot give and exact a reasoned account of what is said know anything at all of the things we say they must know?—No again.

532　　This now, Glaucon, I said, is the law which dialectic fulfills. The law is intelligible, and the power of sight would be imitating it when we described it as attempting to look at actual living creatures, then at the actual stars, and finally at the actual sun. So whenever one tries through dialectic, and without any help from the senses but by means of reason, to set out to find each true reality and does not give up before

b　　apprehending the Good itself with reason alone, one reaches the final goal of the intelligible as the prisoner escaping from the cave reached the final goal of the visible.—That is altogether so.

Well then, do you not call this journey dialectic?—I do.

The deliverance from bonds and the turning around from the shadows to the images and the firelight, and then the way up out of the cave to the sunlight, and there the continuing inability to look at living creatures and plants and the light of

c　　the sun but only at divine images of them in water and shadows of actual things—no longer at shadows of images thrown by another source of light which is itself an image as compared to the sun—the practice of every study we have described has this power to rouse the best part of the soul and lead it upward to the contemplation of that which is the best among the existents, just as then the clearest sense in the body was driven to the contemplation of the brightest thing in the physical and

d　　visible world.

I accept that it is so, he said, and yet these things seem hard to accept, but then in another way they are hard to reject. Nevertheless—for we must hear this not only at the present moment but must return often to the subject again—assuming them to be as you now say, let us turn to the law itself and discuss it in the same way as we did the prelude. Tell us the way in which the power of dialectic works, what its

e　　parts are, and what paths it follows. For these, it would seem, lead to the very place arriving where a man may find rest from travelling and the end and purpose of his journey.

533　　Not yet, my dear Glaucon, I said, will you be able to follow—it is not that keenness is lacking on my part—for you would no longer be seeing an image of what we are discussing but the truth itself, or so it seems to me. It is not worthwhile insisting that it is so in fact, but we must maintain that one would see something of this kind. Is that not so?—It surely is.

And that the power of dialectic will only appear to one who is experienced in the studies we have described, and cannot ever appear otherwise.—That too is worth insisting on.

b　　No one will dispute with us when we say that dialectic is a different study which attempts to apprehend methodically, with regard to each thing, what each really is. All the other crafts are concerned with the opinions of men and their passions, or with the process of generation and composition, or the care of plants and composite things. The remainder which we said grasp at reality to some extent, namely geome-

c　　try and those which follow it, we see as dreaming about reality, unable to have a waking view of it so long as they make use of hypotheses and leave them undisturbed and cannot give a reasoned account of them. What begins with an unknown has its conclusion and the steps in between put together from the unknown, so how could any agreed conclusion it comes to ever become knowledge?—It cannot.

Now dialectic is the only subject which travels this road, doing away with hypotheses and proceeding to the first principle where it will find certainty. It gently draws the eye of the soul, which is really buried in a kind of barbaric mire, and leads it   d upwards, using the sciences we have described as assistants and helpers in the process of turning the soul around. We have often called these by the name of science through force of habit, but they need another name, clearer than opinion and more obscure than science—we described it as reasoning somewhere before—but it seems to me that people who have as many things to investigate as we have do not dispute   e about a name.—Certainly not.

It will therefore be enough, I said, as before, to call the first section knowledge, the second reasoning, the third belief, and the fourth imagination. The last two   534 together we call opinion, the other two intelligence.[106] Opinion is concerned with the process of generation while intelligence is concerned with being. As being is to generation, so intelligence is to opinion, and as intelligence is to opinion, so knowledge is to belief and reasoning to imagination. We pass over the proportions between the objects to which they apply, and the division of either section, the opinable and the knowable, into two, Glaucon, lest it involve us in a great many more arguments than those which went before.—I agree, he said, with the rest, in so far as I am able   b to follow.

And you also call a dialectician the man who can give a reasoned account of the reality of each thing? To the man who can give no such account, either to himself or another, you will to that extent deny knowledge of his subject?—How could I say he had it?

And the same applies to the Good. The man who cannot by reason distinguish the Form of the Good from all others, who does not, as in a battle, survive all refutations, eager to argue according to reality and not according to opinion, and who does not come through all the tests without faltering in reasoned discourse—   c such a man you will say does not know the Good itself, nor any kind of good. If he gets hold of some image of it, it is by opinion, not knowledge; he is dreaming and asleep throughout his present life, and, before he wakes up here, he will arrive in Hades and go to sleep forever.—Yes, by Zeus, I will declare all this to be true.   d

As for those boys of yours whom you are nurturing and educating in theory, if you ever were doing this in fact, I do not think you would allow them, while they are as irrational as irrational quantities, to rule in your city and be responsible for the most important matters.—Certainly not.

You will then legislate for them to follow this study which will enable them to ask and answer questions with the greatest of knowledge?—I will do so, with your help.   e

Is dialectic, then, do you think, I said, placed at the top of your studies like a coping stone, and no other study can rightly be placed above it, but our account of   535 studies has now come to an end?—I think so.

There now remains, I said, for you to deal with the question of their distribution, namely to whom we shall assign these studies and in what manner.—Clearly.

---

106. [Before (i.e. at the end of Book Six, 511d–3) Plato called the highest mental process *noēsis*, which we translated as "understanding." Now he calls it *epistēmē* (knowledge), and he applies the term *noēsis* to both the higher sections, that is, to the whole intelligible world, which we here translate as "intelligence."]

Do you remember what kind of men we chose in our earlier selection of rulers?—Of course I remember.

b   In other respects, I said, the same natures have to be chosen, for we have to select the most stable and the most brave, and as far as possible the most beautiful. Beside these qualities we must seek not only men of noble and tough moral character, but they must also have the natural characteristics conducive to this education of ours.—What characteristics precisely?

They must be quick to learn and learn without difficulty, for people's souls give up much more easily in hard study than in physical exercises, because the labour of learning belongs more closely to the soul: it is private to it and not shared with the body.—True.

c   We must also look for a man with a good memory, who is persistent and loves hard work in every way, for how else do you think he will be willing to carry out certain physical tasks and also complete so much study and practice.—No one would, except someone with great natural talent.

The present mistaken view of philosophy, and the lack of esteem for it are due, as we said before, to the fact that people pursue it unworthily. No pretenders but only genuine students should take it up.—How so?

d   In the first place no student should limp in his approach, half of him keen, the other half work-shy. This happens when a man loves physical exercise and the hunt, is very keen on all physical effort but not on learning, listening, or research; in all those exercises he hates effort. However, the opposite half-heartedness is also a kind of limping lameness.—What you say is very true.

So in its attitude to truth, I said, we shall similarly declare to be maimed a soul
e   which hates the willing lie, finds it hard to bear in itself, and is overly angry when others tell lies, but it quite easily accepts the unwilling lie, nor is it angry when it is caught in ignorance; it bears that easily, wallowing in its ignorance like a pig.—Yes indeed.

536   With regard to moderation too, I said, to courage, liberality, and all the parts of excellence, it is very necessary to distinguish the genuine from the pretender. Whenever one does not know how to do this, whether as a city or an individual, people unwittingly make use of lame pretenders as friends or rulers for whatever service they want.—That is certainly the case.

So we must be careful, I said, in all these matters as, if we bring men sound of
b   limb and mind to so much learning and so much training and thus educate them, even Justice herself will not blame us and we shall preserve the city and the constitution, but if we bring to them a different kind of man we shall do the opposite and set loose an even greater flood of ridicule upon philosophy.—That would be a shame indeed.

It certainly would be, I said, and I seem likely to be ridiculous right now.—In what way?

c   I forgot, I said, that we were merely diverting ourselves, and I spoke too emotionally. For I looked upon philosophy as I spoke, and seeing her undeservedly besmirched, I seem to have lost my temper and, like one angry with those who are the cause of it, I spoke too intensely.

No by Zeus, he said, that was not my impression when I heard you.

But it was mine, I said, as the speaker. Let us not forget that in our earlier selection we chose older men, but this is not possible this time, for we shall not believe Solon   d
that as a man grows old he can learn many things. He can do that even less than he can run, and all great and numerous labours belong to the young.—Necessarily.

Calculation and geometry and the whole of the preliminary studies which must precede dialectic must be offered to them in boyhood, but our method of teaching must not be by compulsion.—How so?

Because, I said, no free man must learn anything under compulsion like a slave.   e
Physical labour performed under duress does no harm to the body, but nothing learned under compulsion stays in the mind.—True.

Do not, therefore, my excellent friend, I said, instruct the boys in these studies by force, but in play, so that you will also see better what each of them is by nature   537
fitted for.—That seems reasonable.

You remember, I said, that we stated the boys were to be led even into war, as observers on horseback and, wherever it is safe to do so, they should be brought close and taste blood, like puppies.—I remember.

In all these things, I said, in physical labours, in studies, in circumstances provoking fear, whoever is seen to be always very skillful is to be inscribed on a list.—
At what age?   b

When they give up compulsory physical training, I said. For during that period whether it be two or three years, youth is unable to do anything else. Physical labour and sleep are the enemies of study. At the same time this physical training is itself one of the tests, and not the least important, as to how each of them performs in physical exercises.—Of course.

After that time, that is, from the age of twenty, those who are chosen will also receive more honours than the others. The studies which have been indiscriminately taught in the education of the boys must now be brought together for them in order   c
to give them a synoptic view of their kinship with each other and with the nature of reality.—Indeed, only the kind of instruction in which this takes place will remain with them. It is also, I said, the best test of the dialectical nature, for the man who sees things as a whole is a dialectician; the man who does not, is not.—I think so too.

You will have to oversee these things to discover those among them who show   d
these qualities and who remain steadfast in their studies, steadfast in war and other lawful activities. These, after they complete their thirtieth year, you will in turn choose from among the chosen group and award them greater honours and then find out, testing them by the power of dialectic, who can relinquish the eyes and the other senses and take the way of truth to reality itself, a task which requires great care, my friend.—Why mostly?

Do you not realize, I said, the great evil which has now come upon dialectic?—   e
What is that?

Those who practise it are filled with lawlessness, I said.—They surely are.

Do you think that what is happening to them is surprising, and do you not forgive them?—In what way particularly?

It is, I said, as if some child were brought up among great wealth, in a numerous and great family with many flatterers, and when he had grown to manhood he   538
discovered that he was not the child of his professed parents, but he did not find

out who his real parents were. Do you think you can foretell his attitude toward the flatterers and his supposed parents both at the time he did not know about his parentage, and again at the time when he did know, or do you want to hear what I surmise?—I do indeed.

b   I expect that, during the time when he did not know the truth, he would honour his father and mother and his other supposed relations more than the flatterers, that he would pay greater attention to their needs, that he would be less likely to treat them lawlessly in word or deed, more likely to be persuaded by them than by the flatterers in any matters of importance.—That is likely.

When he learned the truth, however, he would honour and care for them less, while his relations with the flatterers would become more intense, he would be c   persuaded by them far more than before, he would now live in the way they did and keep company with them openly, and, unless he had a very fine nature indeed, he would not care at all for that father of his and his other supposed relatives.

All this, he said, might well happen as you say, but what relevance has this image to those who concern themselves with reasoned discourse?

The following: we hold from childhood certain beliefs about just and beautiful things; we are brought up in these beliefs as by parents, we obey and honour them.—That is so.

d   However, there are other pursuits contrary to these which give pleasure, flatter our soul, and attract it toward themselves, but they do not persuade those who are at all moderate. These honour the principles of their fathers which we mentioned and obey them.—That is so.

And then, I said, a questioner comes along and asks a man in those circumstances what is the beautiful, and, when he answers what he has heard from the lawgiver, the argument refutes him, and does this often and in many places. This reduces e   him to the belief that this thing is no more beautiful than it is ugly, and the same with what is just and good and the things he honoured most. What do you think his attitude would be about honouring and obeying his early beliefs?—Of necessity, he said, he will not honour and obey them as much.

Then, I said, when he no longer believes these principles to be his own nor to be obeyed, as he did before, and he does not discover true ones, is he likely to adopt 539   any other kind of life than the flattering kind?—Not likely.

And so from law abiding he becomes lawless.—Inevitably.

That is why the experience of those who come to reasoned discourse in this way is, as I said just now, both probable and deserving much forgiveness.—And pity too.

It is also why, in order not to feel pity for your thirty-year-olds, you must be extremely careful how you introduce them to dialectic.—Yes indeed.

b   Is not one lasting precaution not to let them have a taste of it while young? I do not think it has escaped your notice that when youths get their first taste of reasoned discourse they take it as a game and always use it to contradict. They imitate those who cross-examined them and themselves cross-examine others, rejoicing like puppies to drag along and tear to bits in argument whoever is near them.—Yes, to excess.

And when they have themselves cross-examined many people and been cross-c   examined by many, they fall vehemently and quickly into disbelieving what they believed before. As a result, they themselves and the whole of philosophy are discredited in the eyes of other men.—Very true.

An older man, I said, would not want to take part in such folly; he will imitate one who is willing to converse in order to discover the truth rather than one who is merely playing and contradicting for play; he will himself be more measured and will bring honour rather than discredit to the pursuit of philosophy.—Quite right.   d

Indeed, all that we said before this was said for the sake of caution, that those whom one allows to partake in reasoned discourse should by nature be orderly and steady, not as now when anyone engages in it, even if he is quite unfit.—Quite so.

It will be enough to stay with the study of dialectic continuously and intensely, doing nothing else, in a similar way to the time spent in physical training, but for twice the number of years.—Do you mean four or six?   e

No matter, I said, make it five, for after that they must go down into that cave for you, and they must be compelled to rule on matters of war and the government of youth, so that they shall not be inferior to others in experience. And even in those years they must be tested as to whether they will remain steadfast as they are pulled this way and that, or whether they will change anything.—And how long do you fix   540 that period? he asked.

Fifteen years, I said. Then, at the age of fifty, those who have survived the tests and have been successful both in action and in the scientific studies must be led to the goal and must be compelled to lift up the eyes of their soul to what itself provides light to all and, as they look upon the Good itself and taking it as their model, they must put in order the city and its citizens as well as themselves for the remainder of   b their life, each in turn. They will spend much of their time with philosophy, but, when their turn comes, they must each labour and rule in public affairs, and they will do this not as something splendid but as a duty. Thus, having educated others to be men of their kind, and leaving other guardians to take their place, they will depart to the islands of the blessed and dwell there. The city will publicly establish memorials and sacrifices for them as for divine spirits, if the Pythian agrees, or if   c not, then for happy and divinely inspired men.

Like a sculptor, Socrates, he said, you fashioned these rulers as magnificent statues of men.

And of women too, Glaucon, I said, for you must not think that what I have said applies to men any more than it applies to women, those that may be born sufficiently able by nature.

You are right, he said, if they share equally, as we said they should, all the activities of men.

You agree then that what we have said about the city and its constitution is not   d altogether wishful thinking, that these things are difficult, but somehow possible, though only in the way we indicated, whenever true philosophers, be it one or more, become rulers in a city. They will despise the present honours as mean and worthless; they will attach the greatest importance to doing what is right and to the honours   e deriving from that; they will regard justice as the greatest and most essential thing; they will serve it and increase it as they set their city in order.—How will they do that?

All in the city, I said, over ten years of age they will send into the country. Then   541 they will take the children in hand, away from their parents' way of life, and bring them up in their own ways and by their own laws which will be such as we have described. This is the quickest and the easiest way to establish the city and constitution we have discussed, for it to be happy and to confer the greatest benefits upon the people among whom it may be established.

b Much the easiest way, he said, and you seem to me, Socrates, to have described very well how it should arise, if it ever does.

Have we now said enough about the city and about the man who resembles it? It is surely clear what kind of man we shall declare he must be.

Quite clear, he said. As for your question, I think we have come to the end of this topic.

BOOK VIII

543 Very well. These things then, Glaucon, are agreed. If a city is to be well governed, wives, children, and all education must be in common, and so too their occupations in peace and war must be common to both sexes; their kings must be those who are best in the practice of philosophy and the waging of war.—That is agreed.

b We have further agreed that as soon as the rulers are established they will lead the soldiers and settle them in such dwellings as we have mentioned, in which there is no private property but which are common to all. Besides the houses, we have also agreed, if you remember, what kind of possessions they will have.

I remember, he said, that we thought that no one should acquire any of the things c that other people now do, but that, as athletes of war and guardians, they should receive their yearly keep from the other citizens as wages of their guardianship, their duty being to look after themselves and the rest of the city.

That is correct, I said. But come, since we have completed this discussion, let us recall the point at which we digressed to reach our present position, so that we may continue along the same path.

That offers no difficulty, he said, for then, much the same as now, you were talking as if you had completed the discussion of the city; you said that you would class as good the city which you had described, and that the good man was he who d resembled it, although it seems that you still had a finer city and man about which 544 to tell us. You then mentioned the other cities which were of the wrong kind, if this one was right. You said, as I remember, that there were four kinds of other cities which would be worth discussing, observing their errors, as well as the men corresponding to them. Our aim was to observe them all, to agree which was the best man and which the worst, and then to examine whether the best man was the happiest and the worst most wretched, or whether matters stood otherwise. I was asking you b to say which were these four kinds of cities when Polemarchus and Adeimantus interrupted,[107] and so you took up the argument again and have now arrived at this point.—Your recollection, I said, is quite correct.

---

107. [At the beginning of the fifth book.]

Well then, like a wrestler, give me the same hold again and, as I ask the same question, do you try to give the answer which you were about to give then.—If indeed I can, said I.

Indeed, he said, I am myself eager to hear what four cities you meant.

You will hear these without difficulty, for they are those which have names. There   c
is that which is praised by most people, the Cretan or Laconian. The second kind, which is also second in the praise it receives, is called oligarchy and it is full of many evils. Then there is a different one which comes into existence next, namely democracy. Then the noble dictatorship[108] which stands out from all these is the fourth and last diseased city. Or can you name another kind which is in a clearly different class? For hereditary dynasties and bought kingships and some such other   d
forms of rule are somewhere between these named kinds and one can find as many of them among the barbarians as among the Greeks.—One hears of many strange kinds, he said.

You realize, I said, that there are of necessity as many ways of life for men as there are types of cities? Or do you think that governments are born "from oak or rock"[109]   e
and not from the characters of the men who live in the cities, which characters tip the scales and drag other things after them?

I do not believe, he said, that they have any other origin.

Then if the cities are of five kinds, the dispositions of the individuals' souls must be five also.—Quite so.

We have already described the man who is like aristocracy, whom we correctly state to be the good and just man.—We have.   545

After this we must describe the worse types: the lover of victory and honour who corresponds to the Laconian city, then the oligarchic man, the democratic, and the dictatorial, in order to observe the most unjust man and contrast him with the most just. Thus we will complete our investigation of the relation between pure justice and pure injustice with regard to the happiness and wretchedness of the men who possess these qualities. We shall then be persuaded either by Thrasymachus to practise injustice, or, in the light of our present argument, to pursue justice.—This   b
we must certainly do.

Shall we then, just as we began by seeking moral qualities in the cities, as being clearer, before we did so in individuals, also now examine the city which loves honour—I have no other name for it, or should we call it a timocracy or timarchy— and then examine that kind of individual, then oligarchy and the oligarchic man, then again after examining democracy we shall observe the democratic man; then   c

108. [The Greek words *tyrannis* and *tyrannos* do not mean tyranny or tyrant in our sense, though they are usually so translated through this book and the next. The *tyrannos* is one who seizes power for himself without legal justification, by some sort of coup, and the most exact modern equivalent seems to be dictator, and I have so translated it. Actually, a Greek *tyrannos* was sometimes a very good ruler. Plato is of course well aware that the "tyrannies" often preceded full democracy in Greek history. He is using a time sequence to illustrate what is really a psychological analysis of different kinds of states and different types of characters corresponding to them.]

109. [A Homeric expression as for example *Odyssey* 19, 163, where Penelope asks the supposed stranger (who is Odysseus) who he is and his ancestry "for you were not born from an oak or a rock."]

fourthly we shall come to the city under a dictator and observe it, and then look into the dictatorial soul? Thus we shall try to become well-qualified judges of the problem which we set ourselves.—It would be reasonable for our investigation and decision to proceed in this way, he said.

d
Come now, I said, let us try to explain how timocracy emerges from aristocracy. Or is it a simple principle that the cause of change in any government is to be found in the ruling group itself, whenever discord breaks out in this very group. While it remains of one mind, even if it be quite small, it cannot be removed.—That is so.

e
How then, Glaucon, I asked, will our city be changed? How will discord arise among the auxiliaries and the guardians, both between the two and among them-selves? Do you want us to do like Homer and to pray to the Muses that they may tell us "how discord first broke out,"[110] and shall we say that they express themselves to us, as to children, in tragic language, playfully and in banter, though their language is lofty, as if in earnest.—How so?

546
In some such way as this: "It is hard for a city composed in this way to change. But everything that is born must perish. Not even a constitution such as this will last forever but it must face dissolution, and its dissolution will be as follows. Not only all plants which grow in the earth but all animals which grow upon it have periods of birth and barrenness of both soul and body whenever the cycles of their existence complete the circumference of their circles. These are short for the short-lived, and the opposite for their opposites. Those whom you have educated to be leaders in

b
your city, though they are wise, still will not, as their reasoning is involved with sense perception, achieve the right production and nonproduction of your race. This will escape them, and they will at some time bring children to birth when they should not.

"For a divine creature which is born there is a cycle contained in a perfect number; for man it is the first number in which are found root and square increases, taking three dimensions and four limits, of the numbers that make things like and unlike, cause them to increase and decrease and which make all things correspond and

c
rational in relation to one another. Of these the lowest numbers in the ratio of four to three, married to five, give two harmonies when multiplied three times, the one a square, so many times a hundred, the other of equal length one way, but oblong, the one side a hundred numbers obtained from the rational diameters of five, each reduced by one, or from the irrational diameters reduced by two, the other side being a hundred cubes of three.[111]

110. [This is not a Homeric quotation but an imitation of his epic style. Compare his invocation of the Muses at *Iliad* 16, 112.]

111. [The mock heroic invocation to the Muses and their talking in tragic language should warn us not to take the mathematical myth which follows too seriously or too literally. It is perhaps the most obscure and controversial passage in the whole of Plato's works. Scholars are not even agreed as to whether there is one Platonic number or two. The latter seems to be the case since he speaks of a number for the "divinely created thing" (which it is admitted must be the universe) and one for the human creature. The actual world-number is again pretty well agreed on. It is three multiplied by four multiplied by five (i.e. 60), multiplied three times by itself, which is 12,960,000. This represented geometrically can be thought of as a square of which the side is 3600, or as a rectangle of which the longer side is 4800 and the shorter 2700. That much is clear. The human number seems to be the addition of the cubes of 3, 4, and 5, which is 216 (which Adam points out is the shortest period of human gestation in days, seven months each reckoned as 30 days, plus the Pythagorean marriage number 6).

The numbers 3, 4, and 5 were the sides of the first right angled triangle of which the sides are whole numbers.

"This whole geometric number controls this kind of thing, namely better and   d
worse births. Whenever your rulers, in ignorance of this, join brides and grooms at
the wrong time, the children will be neither talented nor fortunate. The older
generation will make the best of these rulers, they are nevertheless unworthy, and
when they acquire their fathers' powers they will as guardians neglect us, the Muses,
first of all, thinking the arts less important then they ought. Then, in the second
place, they will neglect physical training, and so your young people will become less
cultured. As a result you will have rulers who do not have the proper guardians'
character to test the races of Hesiod[112] and your own—the golden, silver, copper,   e
and iron races. Iron will then be mixed with silver and copper with gold, and a lack   547
of homogeneity will arise in the city, and discordant differences, and whenever
these things happen they breed war and hostility. From such parentage,[113] we must
declare, civil discord is born wherever it occurs."

We shall, he said, declare the Muses' answer to be correct.

And so it must be, said I, since they are Muses.

And what, he asked, do the Muses go on to say?   b

As civil discord arises, I said, two kinds, the copper and the bronze, draw men
along to money-making and the acquisition of land, a house, gold, and silver, while
the other two kinds, the gold and the silver, not being poor but rich by nature, draw
men's souls to virtue and the old order. Violently opposed to each other, they agree
to a compromise: they distribute the land and houses as private property, and those   c
whom they previously guarded and considered as free men, friends, and providers,
they now enslave and hold as serfs and servants, while they themselves still take care
of their protection and defense in war.

I think, he said, that this is how the change started.

This government then, I said, stands between aristocracy and oligarchy?—Certainly.

This is how it will change. And, having changed, how will it be managed? Clearly,
it will be like the earlier government in some respects, and like oligarchy in others,   d
being between the two, and it will also have some features of its own.—That is so.

It will honour the rulers; the fighting section of the state will take no part in
agriculture, manual labour, or other ways of making money; it will eat communally
and devote itself to physical exercise and training for war; in all these ways it will be
like the earlier city?—Yes.

This is the triangle of which the Pythagoreans made much mystical use. They are obviously basic to both the
Platonic numbers and are here the numbers which make things "like and unlike." The sides of the rectangle
are 2700 and 4800, the latter being "obtained from" the diameter of 5, i.e. the diameter of a square whose side
is 5, which is the root of 50, which is irrational, and the nearest rational number is 7 and the number "obtained
from" this is 49, from which we are told to subtract 1 (i.e. 48) while the number obtained from the irrational
diameter is of course fifty, and from this we are told to subtract 2 (i.e. 48) and a hundred times this is 4800.
Plato is obviously playing with numbers and the details are probably not of great importance.

Behind it all, however, is the serious conviction that the laws of the universe can be expressed mathematically;
the totality of those laws, had we sufficient knowledge, would be the mathematical aspect of the supreme reality,
one aspect of the Form of Good. Those who want to pursue the "harmonies" that can be extracted from these
numbers should consult Adam's notes and Appendix 1 to Book VIII.]

112. [The reference is to Hesiod's myth of the five races of men which succeed each other at *Works and Days*
109–202.]

113. [A Homeric expression. (*Iliad* 6, 211.)]

e   On the other hand it will be afraid to appoint wise men to office, because such
         men are no longer simple and earnest, but of mixed nature; it then turns to spirited
548   and simpler-minded men who are born for war rather than for peace; the tricks and
         devices of war are now held in high esteem, and the city spends all its time in making
         war. Most of these features will be all its own.—Yes.

         Such men, I said, will be greedy for money, as men are in oligarchies; they will
         prize gold and silver without restraint but in secret; they will have private treasuries
         and storing places where they can keep it hidden; their houses will enclose them,
b   like private nests where they can spend a great deal of money on women and anyone
         else they may wish.—Very true.

         They will also be mean with money, since they prize it and do not acquire it openly,
         but they will be ready to spend other people's money because of their passion for it.
         They will enjoy their pleasures in secret, escaping from the law as sons from their
         father. They have not been educated by persuasion but by force, because they have
c   neglected the true Muse, that of discussion and philosophy, and have honoured
         physical training more highly than the arts.

         The city you mention, he said, is altogether a mixture of good and bad.

         Yes, I said, it is indeed a mixture. There is only one thing which appears in it
         most clearly under the rule of the spirited part, namely the love of victory and of
         honours.—Very definitely.

         This then, I said, is the kind of government it would be and how it would arise,
d   to sketch the shape of it without working it out in detail, for even from a sketch we
         shall discern the most just and the most unjust man, and it would be an intolerably
         long task to describe every kind of city and every kind of character without omitting
         any detail.—Correct.

         Who is now the man who corresponds to this city? How does he come to be and
         what kind of a man is he?

         I think, said Adeimantus, that he would be very like Glaucon here as far as the
         love of victory goes.

e   Perhaps in that respect, I said, but in the following respects he would be very
         different.—In what respects? he said.

         He must be rather obstinate and somewhat uncultured, though he likes the arts;
         he must like to hear things, but is in no way a speaker; he would be harsh to his
549   slaves, but not because he looks down on them as a man of good education does;
         toward free men, however, he would be gentle and quite obedient to those in power,
         being himself a lover of power and honours. He does not believe that the capacity
         to express oneself, or anything of that kind, should lead to power, but rather deeds
         in war and concerning war, as he is a lover of physical training and the hunt.—Yes,
         he said, that is the character of that city.

         Such a man, I said, would despise money while young, but welcome it more and
b   more as he grows older, for he has his share of the money-loving nature. He is not
         pure in his attitude to virtue because he lacks the best of guardians.—What is that?

         Reasonable discourse, I said, with an admixture of the arts, for this dwells in a
         man as the sole preserver of his virtue throughout his life.—Well said.

c   This then is the timocratic youth, and he resembles this kind of city.—Quite so.

         And he comes to be, I said, in some such manner as this. He is the son of a good father who lives in a city which is not well governed. The father avoids honours and office and lawsuits and all that kind of business; he is even willing to be put at a disadvantage in order to avoid trouble.

How, he said, does the timocrat come to be?

He becomes such in the first instance, I said, when he hears his mother being angry because her husband is not one of the rulers and she is less esteemed among other women on that account. Then she sees that he is not very concerned about money, that he does not fight back when he is insulted in private or in the courts or in public, and that he bears all this with indifference. She also sees him always concentrating his mind upon his own thoughts, neither greatly honouring nor slighting her. Angered by all this, she tells her son that his father is unmanly and too easygoing, and all the things which women repeat over and over again about such men.—Yes, said Adeimantus, they do say many things which are characteristic of them.

You know too, I said, that these men's servants sometimes say similar things to the sons covertly, those servants who are thought to be well disposed. When they see the father failing to prosecute someone who owes him money or wrongs him in some other way, they advise the son that when he grows up he must take vengeance on all those people and be more of a man than his father. The boy hears and sees the same kind of thing when he goes out, that those who restrict themselves to their own affairs are called foolish in the city and held in low esteem, while those who meddle with the affairs of others are honoured and praised. The young man hears and sees all this, but on the other hand he also listens to what his father says, observes what he does from close at hand, and compares his actions with those of the others. So he is pulled both ways; his father nourishes the reasonable part of his soul and makes it grow, the others foster the spirited and the appetitive parts. As he is not a bad man by nature but keeps bad company, pulled both ways he has settled in the middle and has surrendered the rule over himself to the middle part, the victory-loving and spirited part, and becomes a proud and ambitious man.

I certainly think, he said, that you have given a full account of the birth of this type.

We have then, I said, the second type of city and the second type of man.—We have.

After this then, to quote Aeschylus, let us talk of "another man placed over against another city,"[114] or rather, according to our plan, talk of the city first.—Quite so.

The one to come after this city is, as I think, oligarchy.

And what kind of constitution would you call oligarchy? he asked.

The constitution based on income, I said, in which the rich rule, while the poor have no share of power.—I understand.

So now we must first tell how the timarchy changes into an oligarchy?—Yes.

Surely, I said, the manner of this change is clear even to the blind.—How?

That private treasury, I said, which each man has, becomes filled with gold and destroys the constitution. First they find ways of spending it on themselves, they

d

e

550

b

c

d

---

114. [The line does not occur in the extant plays, but it may be an adaptation of *Seven Against Thebes* 451, where Eteocles is assigning a defender to each gate.]

twist the laws for this purpose, and they themselves disobey it along with their wives.—Likely enough.

e   Then as one man sees another doing this and envies him, they make the masses like themselves in this.—That is probable.

Then as they proceed further into money-making, the more they honour this the less they honour virtue. Or does not virtue stand in such opposition to wealth that if each were in the scale of a balance, they would ever incline in opposite directions?—Certainly.

551   When wealth and the wealthy are honoured in a city, virtue and the virtuous are prized less.—Clearly.

What is honoured is always practised, and what is slighted is neglected.—That is so.

In the end the lovers of victory and honours become money-lovers and money-makers; they praise and admire the wealthy man and appoint him to office while they disregard the poor man.—Quite so.

b   Then they pass a law which is the characteristic of oligarchy by establishing a wealth qualification, higher where the government is more oligarchic, of a lesser amount where it is less so, having previously declared that those whose possessions do not reach the stated amount are not qualified for office. They either enforce this by force of arms, or else they have terrorized people before they established this kind of government. Is that not so?—It is.

This, in general terms, is how this kind of government is established.

c   Yes, he said, but how does it work? And what are the flaws which we said it had?

First of all, I said, is the very nature of the characteristic we mentioned. For look, would anyone appoint the pilots of a ship this way, by their wealth, and not entrust the ship to a poor man even if he was a better pilot?

People who did that, he said, would make a poor voyage.

Is that not also true of the rule of anything else?—I think so.

Except a city? I said, or does it also apply to a city?

More than to anything else, he said, in so far as this is the most difficult and the most important kind of rule.

d   This then is one considerable flaw of oligarchy?—So it appears.

Further, is the following flaw less than this?—What?

The fact that it is of necessity not one city but two, one of the poor and the other of the rich, living in the same place and always plotting against each other.—This, by Zeus, is just as big a flaw.

And this is not a fine feature either, that they are probably unable to fight a war,
e   because they would be compelled either to arm the people and use them, and be more afraid of them than of the enemy, or, if they did not do so, they would indeed be oligarchs, being so few, in the actual fighting. At the same time they would be unwilling to pay taxes, being lovers of money.—Not a fine feature.

Moreover, there is also what we strongly disapproved of before, that the same men in such a state would fulfill many functions, being farmers and money-makers
552   and warriors all at the same time. Or do you think this right?—Not right at all.

But look whether of all the evils this is not the greatest, which is first found in this city.—What evil?

That a man may sell all his possessions and another may buy them, and, having sold them, he lives in the city without being any part of the community, neither a money-maker nor a craftsman, neither cavalry man nor hoplite, but one they call a pauper without means.—Yes, and this is the first city to allow this.

Yet this is not forbidden in an oligarchy. If it were, some would not be excessively rich and others utter paupers.—Correct.

However, consider this: when this man was rich and spending his money, was he of any greater use to the city in the ways we have just mentioned? He appeared to be one of the rulers, but in fact was neither ruler nor subject in the city, but merely someone who was spending money that was ready to hand.—That is so, he said. He appeared to be part of the community, but he was nothing but a spender.

Should we say then, I said, that, as a drone exists in a cell and is an affliction to the hive, so this man is a drone in the house and an affliction to the city?—Quite so, Socrates.

The god, Adeimantus, has fashioned all the winged drones without stings, but of these two-footed drones some are stingless, while others have dangerous stings. The stingless ones continue as beggars into old age, but it is from among those endowed with stings that all those we call criminals come.—Very true.

Clearly then, in any city where you see beggars there are thieves hidden in the place, and footpads and temple robbers, and the doers of all such evil deeds.—Clearly.

And do you not notice the presence of beggars in oligarchies?—Almost everyone, he said, except the rulers.

Shall we not believe then that there are many criminals with stings in these cities, whom those in office deliberately keep in check by force?—We think so.

And shall we not say that it is the lack of education and a poor upbringing, as well as the condition of the city, that are the cause of the drones' presence?—We shall.

This then, or something like this, is the oligarchic city; it contains these many evils, and perhaps even more.—I think so.

That completes our picture of this city which they call oligarchy, where the rulers are chosen for their wealth. Let us now examine the man who is like it, how he comes to be and the sort of man he is.—By all means.

Does he change from the timocrat we described to an oligarchic man mostly in this way?—Which way?

The timocrat's son at first emulates his father and follows in his footsteps; then he suddenly sees him crashing against the city like a ship against a reef and spilling all his possessions and even his life. He had been a general or held some other high office, then he is brought to court by informers and put to death or exiled or disfranchised and loses all his property.—That is likely to happen.

The son sees all this, suffers from it, and loses all his property. Then, fearing for his life, right away he drives from the throne in his own soul the love of honours and the spirited part which ruled there. Humbled by poverty he turns greedily to making money; little by little he saves, works, and gathers property. Do you not think that this man would establish his appetitive and money-making part on that inner throne and make this a great king within himself, adorning him with golden tiaras and collars and girding him with Persian swords?—I do think so.

d   The reasonable and spirited parts he makes sit upon the ground beneath the king, one on either side, reducing them to slaves, the first he will not allow to reason about or examine anything else than how little money can be made into much; while he does not allow the other part to honour or admire anything but wealth and wealthy men, or to have any other ambition than the acquisition of wealth or of anything which may contribute to this.

No other change, he said, will as quickly or as certainly turn a young lover of honours into a lover of money.

e   And he then, I said, is the oligarchic man?

The change in the man is surely the same as that which made for an oligarchy in the city.

554   Let us look then whether he is similar to the city.—Let us.

He is like the city in the first place in that he attaches the greatest importance to money.—Of course.

Further, in that he is thrifty and a worker, satisfying only his necessary appetites, and makes no other expenditures, but he enslaves his other desires as vain.—Quite so.

He is somewhat squalid, I said, making a profit from everything; the sort of man
b   the crowd approves of. Is this not the man who resembles such a city?

I certainly think so, he said. Possessions are certainly held in honour by both the city and the man.

I do not think, I said, that such a man pays any attention to education.

I think not, he said. If he did he would not have chosen a blind leader of his dance and honoured him most.[115]

Good, said I, but consider this: shall we not say that dronish appetites exist in him
c   because of his lack of education: some are beggarly, others are evil, but they are forcibly held in check by his other preoccupation?—Definitely.

Do you know where you should look to see their malpractices?—Where?

If he happens to be the guardian of orphans, or something of the kind, where he would have great opportunities to do wrong.—True.

Does this not make it clear that in his other associations where he has a good reputation and is thought to be just, he forcibly holds his other evil appetites in
d   check by means of some good part of himself? He does not persuade himself that it is better not to indulge them, nor does he tame them by reasoning, but he acts under the compulsion of fear, trembling for his other possessions.—Quite so.

And by Zeus, my friend, I said, you will find that when other people's money has to be spent, they have appetites which are akin to those of the drone.—That is most certainly true.

Such a man would not, then, be without discord within himself, he is not one man

115. [The blind leader is Plutus, the god of wealth, who is represented as blind, e.g. in the *Plutus* of Aristophanes.]

but two, though generally his better appetites are in control of his worse.—That is   e
so.

For this reason the man would be more respectable than many, but the true
excellence of a harmonious soul, of one mind within itself, escapes him by far.—I
think so.

Further, this thrifty man is a poor antagonist in any private contest for victory or   555
some other fine rivalry, as he is not willing to spend money for the sake of renown
or for any contest of that kind. He is afraid to arouse his spending appetites or to
call on them as allies to obtain victory, so he fights with only a small part of himself
in the oligarchic manner, and so he is mostly defeated—and remains rich.—Quite
so.

Have we any further doubt that the thrifty money-maker corresponds to the
oligarchic city and is like it?—No doubt at all.   b

After this we must consider democracy, how it originated and how it functions
once it has come into existence, in order that we should know the manner of life of
the democratic man and put him beside the city for judgment.—We would be
proceeding consistently in doing so.

Well, I said, the city changes from an oligarchy to a democracy in some such way
as this, because of its insatiable desire to attain what it has set before itself as the
good, namely the need to become as rich as possible.—How so?

I think that, in as much as those who rule in the city do so because they have   c
accumulated great possessions, they are not willing to prevent by law the intemperate
among the young from spending and wasting their substance. Their intention is to
buy them up and lend them money so that they themselves will become even richer
and more honoured.

Now this is quite clear: it is impossible to honour wealth in a city and at the same
time for the citizens to acquire sufficient moderation; one or the other is inevitably
neglected.—Quite clear.

Because of this neglect, and because they do not restrain the intemperate, men of   d
good birth are often reduced to poverty in oligarchies.—Quite so.

So there they are in the city, with their stings and their weapons; some of them
are in debt; some are disfranchised, some are both; they hate those who have
acquired their property and plot against them as well as against others, and they
long for revolution.—That is so.   e

The money-makers on the other hand keep their eyes on the ground and do not
appear to see them, but they injure anyone of the others who yields to them by
providing him with money and exacting as interest many times the principal sum,   556
and so they create a considerable number of drones and beggars in the city.—
Certainly a good many.

And as this evil flares up in the city they do not wish to quench it either in the way
we mentioned, by preventing people doing whatever they please with their own, or
by another law which might solve the problem.—What law?

One which is a second best but which compels people to pay attention to virtue,
if it prescribes that the majority of private contracts be entered into at one's own   b
risk; they would then be less shameless in their pursuit of money in the city and
fewer of those evils we were mentioning just now would develop.—Far fewer.

But as it is now, I said, for all these reasons this is the condition to which the rulers reduce their subjects in the city. As for themselves and their children, do they not
c   make the young fond of luxury, incapable of effort either physical or mental, soft in the face of pleasure and pain, and lazy besides?—Surely.

They neglect everything except making money, and care no more for virtue than the poor do.—Indeed they do not.

When rulers and subjects in this condition meet each other on a journey or on some other common pursuit, at festivals or on an embassy or on a campaign, on
d   shipboard or in the army, and observe each other facing danger, on those occasions the poor are not despised by the rich. Often a poor man, spare and suntanned, stands in battle next to a rich man who is pale for lack of sun with much superfluous flesh, and sees him panting and at a loss. Do you not think that he would consider that it is through the cowardice of the poor that people like that are rich, and one
e   poor man would say to the other as they met privately: "These men are at our mercy; they are no good."—I know very well that they do this.

Then, as a sick body needs only a slight shock from outside to fall into illness and sometimes even without this it is in a state of civil strife, so a city which is in the same plight needs but a small excuse and, as one side brings in allies from an oligarchic city or the other from a democracy, the city is ill and fights itself, and sometimes a
557   revolution occurs even without outside help.—Most certainly.

I think democracy comes when the poor are victorious, kill some of the other side, expel others, and to the rest they give an equal share of political power and offices, and generally the offices are filled by lot in this city.

Yes, he said, that is how democracy is established, be it by force of arms or because those on the other side are frightened into exile.

b   How do they live then? I asked. Of what kind is this city? For clearly a man of this kind will turn out to be a democratic man.—Clearly.

First of all they are free, and the city becomes full of liberty and freedom of speech, and in it one can do anything one pleases.—So they say.

Where this opportunity exists, everyone will arrange his own life in any manner that pleases him.—Obviously.

c   And in this city above all others there would, I think, be all sorts of people.—Of course.

This is probably the most beautiful of all constitutions. Like a cloak embroidered with every kind of ornament, so this city, embroidered with every kind of character, would seem the most beautiful, and perhaps many would judge it to be so, like children and women gazing at embroideries of many colours.—They certainly would.

d   It is also, my good friend, I said, a convenient place to look for a constitution.— How do you mean?

It contains all kinds of constitutions because of its permissiveness, and the man who wants to establish a city, as we were doing, should probably go to a democracy as if it were an emporium of constitutions, pick out whatever type pleases him and
e   establish that.—Perhaps he would not be at a loss for models.

In this city, I said, there is no compulsion to rule, even if you are capable of it, or again to be ruled if you do not want to be, or to be at war when the others are, or at peace unless you desire peace. If some law forbids you to hold office or to go to law, you nevertheless do both if it occurs to you to do so. Is that not a divine and pleasant life for the time being?—Perhaps, he said, for the time being.

And is the placidity of some of their condemned criminals not civilized? Or have you not seen in this city men who have been condemned to death or exile stay in the city in spite of this? The criminal strolls around like a hero's ghost, without anyone seeing him or giving him a thought.—Yes, I have seen many such.

The tolerance in such a city! It certainly does not show any petty concern for b trifles. Indeed it despises those things we solemnly spoke of when we were founding our city, as that, unless a man had an exceedingly fine nature, he would never become a good man unless from early childhood he played fine games and followed fine pursuits. How magnificently this city tramples all this underfoot and does not give a thought to what a man was doing before he enters public life. It honours him if only he says that he wishes the crowd well.—An altogether noble city! c

These are the qualities of democracy, and others like these, and it would seem to be a pleasant constitution without any rulers and with much variety, distributing a kind of equality to the equal and the unequal alike.—We certainly know what you mean.

Look now, I said, what is a man like that in his private life? Or should we first enquire, as we did with the city, how he comes to be?—Yes.

Well, does it not happen like this? The son of that thrifty oligarch would be brought up by his father in his way of life.—Of course. d

So he too controls his pleasures by force, repressing the spendthrift ones that do not make money. These he calls unnecessary.—Clearly.

Should we first define the necessary and the unnecessary desires to avoid discussing in the dark?—We should.

Those we are unable to deny we would be right to call necessary or those of which the satisfaction benefits us, for we are by nature compelled to satisfy them. Is that e not so?—Certainly.

So we would be right to apply the term necessary to them.—Yes.

As for those which one could avoid if one trained oneself to avoid them from youth, which lead to no good or indeed to the opposite, would we not rightly call these unnecessary?—We certainly would.

Let us pick an example of each, so that we may grasp them as a type.—We must do so.

Is not the desire to eat to the point of health and well-being, the desire for bread and cooked food, necessary?—I think so. b

The desire for bread is necessary on both counts; it is useful and it keeps one alive.—Yes.

That for cooked food is necessary too, if it contributes in any way to well-being.— Certainly.

What of the desire which goes beyond this, for strange foods and the like. This can be restrained from youth, and schooled to leave most people; it is harmful to the body, and to the soul also as regards thought and moderation. Would it not be correct to call this unnecessary?—Very correct. c

Shall we say that these are also the spendthrift pleasures, while the others are profitable because they are good for doing work?—Surely.

And so with the pleasures of sex and the others.—Quite so.

d   When we called a man a drone, we meant one who is full of such pleasures and desires and ruled by those which are unnecessary, while we called one who is ruled by necessary desires thrifty and oligarchic.—Quite so.

Let us then repeat that the democratic man evolves from the oligarchic, and it seems to happen for the most part as follows.—How?

e   Whenever a youth who was brought up in the miserly manner we described, and without real education, has a taste of the honey of the drones and frequents wild and dangerous creatures who can provide all kinds of varied pleasures from all sources, think that there is the beginning of the change of the oligarchy within him to democracy.—Quite inevitably.

Just as the city changed when one faction received help from like-minded people outside, so the young man changes when help comes from the same type of desires outside to one of the factions within himself.—Definitely.

560   And, I think, if any contrary help comes to the oligarchic faction in him, either from his father or the rest of the household who exhort and reproach him, then there is faction and counterfaction within him and he battles against himself.—Quite so.

Sometimes the democratic element yields to the oligarchic, and some of his appetites are overcome, some are expelled, a kind of shame arises in the young man's soul, and order is restored.—That does sometimes happen.

b   But then again as desires are cast out, other desires akin to them are nurtured unawares, and because of the father's ignorance of proper upbringing, they grow numerous and strong.—Yes, that often happens.

They draw him into the same bad company, and while they are with him they breed another crowd of desires unnoticed.—Surely.

c   In the end they occupy the citadel of the young man's soul, as they see it empty of knowledge, fine pursuits, and true reasoning, which are the best guards and guardians in the minds of men whom the gods love.—Very much so.

Instead of these, false and boastful reasonings and beliefs rush up and occupy this same part of such a youth.—Definitely.

d   Will he then not return to these lotus-eaters and live with them openly? And if some help comes from his household for the thrifty part of his soul, these boastful discourses close the gates of the royal wall within him and will not allow those allies to enter, nor will they admit as envoys the wiser discourses which are emissaries of older persons, while they themselves fight and conquer; reverence they call foolishness, and cast it out beyond the frontiers as a disfranchised exile; moderation they call cowardice; they abuse it and throw it out; they persuade him that measured and orderly expenditure is boorish and mean; and with the help of many useless desires they expel it over the border.—They do indeed.

e   Having thus emptied and cleansed the soul of their victim, which is being initiated with splendid rites, they now introduce into it insolence and anarchy and extravagance and shamelessness wreathed and radiant among many followers, eulogizing them and calling them by fair names; insolence they call good breeding, anarchy

freedom, extravagance munificence, shamelessness courage. Is it not in some such   561
way, I said, that, being young, he changes from one brought up among necessary
desires to one who lets loose and indulges in unnecessary and useless pleasures.—
Yes indeed, that is clearly the case.

After this, I think, such a man spends his money, effort, and time no less upon
unnecessary than upon necessary pleasures. If he is lucky and does not overstep the
boundary of frenzy, then, as he grows older and the great tumult has spent itself,   b
he welcomes back some of the exiles and does not surrender himself completely to
the newcomers, he puts pleasures on an equal footing and so spends his life, always
surrendering the government of himself to one, as if chosen by lot, until he is
satisfied and then to another, not disdaining any but fulfilling them all equally.—
Quite so.

He does not welcome true reasoning or allow it into the guardhouse; if someone
tells him that some pleasures belong to good and beautiful desires, but others belong   c
to evil ones, that one should prize and pursue the former while the latter must be
restrained and mastered, he denies all this and declares that all pleasures are equal
and must be equally prized.—A man in that condition would certainly do so.

And he lives on, yielding day by day to the desire at hand. At one time he drinks
heavily to the accompaniment of the flute, at another he drinks only water and is
wasting away; at one time he goes in for physical exercise, then again he does nothing   d
and cares for nothing; at times he pretends to spend his time on philosophy; often
he takes part in public affairs; he then leaps up from his seat and says and does
whatever comes into his mind; if he happens to admire military men, he is carried
in that direction, if moneyed men, he turns to making money; there is no plan or
discipline in his life but he calls it pleasant, free, and blessed, and he follows it
throughout his time.—You have certainly described the life of a man who believes
in legal equality.   e

I also think, I said, that he is a fine man of great variety full of all sorts of
characters, just like that city. Many men and many women might envy his life, for
it contains the greatest number of governments and ways of living. Shall we then   562
place this man beside democracy as being correctly called the democratic man?—
Let him so be placed.

The finest government and the finest kind of man remain for us to discuss,
dictatorship and the dictatorial man.—They certainly do remain.

Come, my dear friend, what is dictatorship like? That it evolves from democracy
is pretty clear.—Obviously.

Does it not evolve from democracy in much the same way as democracy does from   b
oligarchy?—How?

What they put before them as the good, which was the basis of oligarchy, was
wealth, was it not?—Yes.

Then their insatiable desire for wealth, and their neglect of other things for
money-making was what destroyed it, was it not?—True.

Now insatiability for what democracy defines as the good also destroys it.—And
what do you say it defines as such?

Liberty, I said. This is what you would hear in a democracy is its finest possession
and that this is the reason why it is the only city worth living in for a man who is by   c
nature free.—That too is very often said.

Well, this is just what I was going to say, that insatiability regarding this, and neglect of other things because of it, is the thing which changes this government too, and puts it in a condition in which it needs dictatorship.—How so?

d   I think that whenever a democracy athirst for liberty has bad cup-bearers to preside over it and drinks too deeply of the pure wine of liberty, then the rulers, unless they are very accommodating and give plenty of liberty, are punished by the city and accused of being foul oligarchs.—Yes, that is so.

It abuses those who obey the rulers as willing slaves and of no account, but it praises and honours, both in public and in private, rulers who behave like subjects and subjects who behave like rulers. Must not such a city reach the extreme of

e   liberty?—Of course.

Liberty makes its way into private households and in the end it breeds anarchy even among the animals.—What do you mean?

I mean, for example, that a father will accustom himself to behave like a child and to fear his sons, while the son behaves like a father, and feels neither shame nor fear before his parents, in order to be free. A resident alien is the equal of a citizen and a citizen the equal of a resident alien, and so too a foreign visitor.—That is what

563   happens.

Yes it does, I said, and so do other such small matters. A teacher in such a community is afraid of his pupils and flatters them, while the pupils think little of their teachers or their tutors. Altogether the young are thought to be the equals of the old and compete with them in word and deed, while the old accommodate

b   themselves to the young, and are full of playfulness and pleasantries, thus aping the young for fear of appearing disagreeable and authoritarian.

The uttermost liberty for the crowd is reached, my friend, I said, in such a city when bought slaves, both male and female, are no less free than those who bought them. And I almost forgot to mention what great equality exists between women and men.—Well then, to quote Aeschylus, shall we speak what now comes to our

c   lips?

Certainly, I said, and I put it this way: No one who has not experienced it would believe how much freer the animals who serve man are here than anywhere else. As the proverb says, dogs are literally the equals of their mistresses, and indeed so are horses and donkeys, accustomed as they are to making their way freely and proudly along the streets, bumping into anyone they meet if he does not get out of their way,

d   and everything else too is full of liberty.

You are telling me what I know, he said, for I often experience this when I walk in the country.

To sum up, I said. All these things together, you notice, make the soul of the citizens so sensitive that if anyone brings up a word about slavery, they become angry and cannot endure it. And you know that in the end they take no notice of the laws, written or unwritten, in order that there should in no sense be a master

e   over them.—Quite so.

That then, my friend, I said, is that so fine and vigorous government from which dictatorship seems to me to evolve.—Vigorous certainly, he said, but what follows?

The same disease, I said, which developed in oligarchy develops here also, more widespread and virulent because of the permissiveness, and it enslaves democracy. In fact, excessive action in one direction usually sets up a reaction in the opposite

direction. This happens in weather, in plants, in bodies, and not least in politics. So   564
excessive liberty, whether in the individual or the state, is likely to change to excessive
servitude and nothing else.—Likely enough.

So, I said, dictatorship is likely to evolve from democracy, the most severe and
cruel servitude from pure liberty.—That is reasonable.

I do not think that was your question, however, but you asked what was the disease   b
which developed in oligarchy and also in democracy and enslaved it.—That is true.

I mentioned that class of idle and extravagant men, some of whom were very brave
leaders while others were their more cowardly followers. This class we compared to
drones, the former endowed with stings, the latter stingless.—Quite correct.

Now these two groups cause disturbances in any city they inhabit, as phlegm and
bile do in the body. The good physician therefore, and the lawgiver of a city, must,   c
no less than the good beekeeper, take precautions ahead of time, in the first instance
to prevent their presence, and if they should be present, to cut them out of the hive
as quickly as possible, cells and all.—Yes, by Zeus, he must certainly do that.

Shall we take up the question in this way, so that we may see our way more clearly
to decide what we want?—Which way?

Let us divide a democracy into three parts in our argument as it is in reality. One
part is this class of idlers, and it grows here no less than in oligarchy because of the   d
permissiveness.—That is so.

And it is much more bitter here than there.—How so?

There it is bitter because it is disdained but, as it is kept out of office, it is lacking
in experience and does not become strong. In a democracy, however, this class is
the presiding element, with few exceptions. The most bitter speak and act, while the
rest of them settle, buzzing around the speakers' platform, and will not tolerate the
opposition of another speaker so that everything is managed by them in this city,   e
with a few exceptions.—That is certainly so.

Then there is also the following group which can be distinguished in the crowd.—
Which is that?

When everybody is trying to make money, those who are the most steady by nature
generally become the wealthiest.—Probably so.

They would provide the most and the most easily available honey for the drones.—
Yes, for how can one take honey from those who have very little?

So I think that these rich are called the drones' pasture.—Pretty well.

The people would be a third part, those who work with their own hands. They   565
take no part in politics and have but few possessions. This is the most numerous and
the most powerful element in a democracy whenever they are assembled.

It is, he said, but they are not willing to gather often, unless they get a share of
the honey.

They always do take a share, I said, as much as their leaders can give them as they
take it from the prosperous and distribute it to the people, though they keep the
greater share of it to themselves.—Yes, he said, that is how the people get their
share.   b

And those from whom it is taken are compelled to defend themselves by speaking
and acting before the people in so far as they can.—Of course.

They are accused by the other side of plotting against the people and of being oligarchs, even when they have no desire for revolution.—Quite so.

So in the end, when they see the people trying to harm them, not of its own free will but through ignorance and being deceived by their accusers, then indeed they truly do become oligarchs, not willingly but that drone stings them with this evil too.—Definitely.

Then there are impeachments and judgments and trials on both sides.—Quite.

Now the people are always in the habit of elevating one man as their champion above all others, and they nurture him and make him great.—That is the custom.

It is clear that this championship of the people is the one and only root from which dictatorship and the dictator can grow.—Quite clear.

What is the beginning of the change from people's champion to dictator? Or does it clearly come when the champion begins to behave like the man in the story which is told about the temple of Lycaean Zeus in Arcadia?—What story?

That the man who has tasted human flesh, a single piece of it cut up among the pieces from other sacrificial victims, must inevitably become a wolf. Have you not heard that story?—I have heard it.

So too the man who has become the people's champion and dominates the mob that obeys him, does not abstain from spilling kindred blood. He brings his enemy to trial on false charges, as they often do, and blots out a human life. His impious tongue and lips taste the murder of kindred. He drives his enemy into exile, kills him, while he throws out hints to the people of the cancellation of debts and the redistribution of land. Is not such a man inevitably fated either to be killed by his enemies or to become a dictator and from being a man become a wolf?—Quite inevitably.

He is the one who stirs up factions against the owners of property.—He is.

If he is exiled and returns despite his enemies, he comes back as a full-fledged dictator.—Obviously.

If they are unable to expel him or to kill him by denouncing him to the city, then they plot secretly to kill him.—Yes, that usually happens.

All who have reached this point on the road to dictatorship discover the often quoted request of the dictator, namely to ask the people for a bodyguard, so that the safety of their helper may be assured.—Quite so.

They give it to him because, I believe, they are afraid for his safety but quite confident about themselves.—Yes indeed.

Then, when a man of property sees this and, with his property, is accused of being an enemy of the people, he, as the oracle to Croesus put it, "flees to the banks of the many-pebbled Hermus; he does not stay, and is not ashamed of being a coward."[116]

He would not, he said, have another chance of being ashamed.

True, I said, for if he was caught he would be executed.—He most certainly would.

---

116. [The story of Croesus' oracle is found in Herodotus 1, 55.]

As for the champion, mighty he is but he does not mightily lie in the dust:[117] having brought down many others, he takes his stand as driver on the chariot of state, having now become from a champion a complete dictator.—What is to stop him?

Shall we now, I said, describe the happiness of the man, and of the city in which such a mortal arises?—Certainly, let us describe it.

Will he not, during the first days, and indeed for some time, smile in welcome at anyone he meets. He says he is no dictator and makes many promises both in private and in public. He has freed people from debt and redistributed the land to the people and to his own entourage, and he pretends to be gracious and gentle to all.—He must do that.

But I think that when he has dealt with his outside enemies by making peace with some and destroying others, and all is quiet on the external fronts, the first thing he always does is to stir up a war, so that the people shall feel the need of a leader.—That is likely.

Also in order that by paying war taxes they become poor and are compelled to concern themselves with their daily needs and thus are less likely to plot against him.—Obviously.

Besides, if he suspects some of having thoughts of freedom and of not favouring his rule, he would have an excuse to destroy them by giving them up to the enemy. For all these reasons a dictator must always stir up war.—He must.

And because he does this, he is the more readily hated by the citizens?—Of course.

Then some of those who have helped to establish the dictatorship and hold positions of power speak freely to him and to each other; that is, the bravest of them reproach him for what is happening.—That is likely. The dictator must eliminate them all if he is intending to rule, until he leaves no one who is of any account among his friends or his enemies.—Clearly.

He must therefore keep a sharp lookout for anyone who is brave, proud, wise, or rich; so happy is he that he must be the enemy of them all, whether he wants to be or not, and plot against them until he has purged the city.—A fine purge!

Yes, I said, the opposite of that which the physicians apply to the body. They eliminate the worst and leave the best, he does the opposite.—He is compelled to do this, it seems, if he is to rule.

A happy kind of necessity! said I, which binds him and orders him to live with a crowd of inferior people and to be hated by them, or not live at all.—That is how he must live.

And the more his actions make the citizens hate him, the more numerous and loyal a bodyguard he needs.—Of course.

Who will these loyal people be, and where will he get them from?

They will come flocking of their own accord, he said, if he pays them.

Drones by the dog! I think you mean foreign drones, I said, from all kinds of places.—You are right.

But whom will he get from the city? For he would not want to . . .—Do what?

---

117. [See Homer, *Iliad* 16, 776, the fight around the body of Cebriones who "in his might mightily lay in the whirling dust, his horsemanship forgotten."]

Deprive citizens of their slaves by freeing them and enlisting them in his body-guard.

He certainly will, he said, since they will also be the most loyal to him.

568   What a blessed sort of person you make the dictator out to be, I said, if those are the kind of friends and loyal followers he has, after doing away with his earlier ones.—Anyway, that is the kind he has.

These friends admire him, I said, and the new citizens associate with him while the good citizens hate him and avoid him.—How could they not do so?

It is not for nothing that tragedy as a whole is thought to be wise, and Euripides is outstanding in it.—How so?

b   Because he said, and this shows a subtle mind, that "dictators are wise who keep company with the wise"; and he clearly meant that the wise are the company they keep.[118] Also, he said, he eulogizes dictatorship as something godlike, and both he and the other poets say many things like that.

Surely, I said, being wise, the tragic poets will forgive us and those whose government is close to ours, if we do not admit them into our city because they praise dictatorship.

c   I think, he said, that the more subtle among them will.

I believe, I said, that they go round the other cities, collect crowds, hire men with beautiful, resounding, and persuasive voices, and draw the cities to dictatorship and democracy.—They do indeed.

Besides this they receive pay and honours, especially from the dictators, as is natural, then from the democracies, but the higher they go on the ascending scale

d   of governments, the more their honours fail, as if unable to keep up with them for lack of breath.—That is certainly true.

But, I said, we have digressed here. Let us say again from what source the dictator's army, that beautiful, numerous, and varied body which never remains the same, draws its sustenance.

Clearly, he said, if there are sacred treasures in the city, he will spend them, as well as the property of his victims, for as long as these last, thus necessitating smaller taxes from the people.

e   What when these give out?

Obviously, he said, he and his fellow revellers and companions and mistresses will have to be fed from his father's estate.

I understand, I said. You mean that the people, who fathered the dictatorship, will have to feed him and his companions.—They will certainly be compelled to do so.

How do you mean? said I. If the people get angry and say that it is not right for a young son to be kept by his father, but on the contrary for the father to be kept

569   by the son, and that they did not father the dictatorship and put him in power, in order that, when he had grown great, they should be enslaved to their own slaves and feed him and his slaves and the other rabble; but they hoped that his champion-

---

118. [An otherwise unknown fragment, but Euripides obviously meant that it is wise for dictators to keep company with the wise—and he probably meant rulers in general, for the word *tyrannos* is often used in tragedy in this more general sense.]

ship would free them from the rich, the so-called best people in the city. They now order him and his companions to leave the city, like a father driving a son with his mob of fellow revellers from the house.

Then by Zeus, he said, the people will learn what kind of creature they fathered, welcomed, and caused to grow, and that they are the weaker trying to drive out the   b stronger.

How do you mean? I said. Will he dare to use violence against his father, and to strike him if he does not obey?

Yes, he said, after he has taken away his arms.

You are saying that the dictator is a parricide, I said, and a cruel nurse to old age. This is now an acknowledged tyranny and, as the saying goes, the people, in trying   c to avoid the smoke of servitude to free men, have fallen into the fire of having slaves as their masters, and, in the place of that vast and pure liberty, they have put upon themselves the harshest and most bitter slavery to slaves.—That indeed is what happened.

Well then, I said, shall we not be justified in saying that we have adequately described how dictatorship evolves from democracy, and what its nature is when it has so evolved?—Quite adequately.

BOOK IX

The dictatorial man himself is left to be considered, how the change from the   571 democratic man takes place, then what kind of a man he is, the manner of his life, and whether he is miserable or happy.—Yes, we still have to consider him.

Do you know what I still feel is lacking?—What?

I do not think we have dealt adequately with the question of our appetites, their number and qualities, and if that subject is not adequately dealt with, our whole   b investigation will be obscured.

Well, he said, we are still in good time to do so.

Certainly. Consider what I want to know about them. It is this: some of our unnecessary pleasures and desires seem to me lawless; they are probably present in everyone, but they are held in check by the laws and by the better desires with the help of reason. In a few men they have been eliminated or a small number are left in a weakened state, while in others they are stronger and more numerous.—What   c desires do you mean?

Those that are aroused during sleep, I said, whenever the rest of the soul, the reasonable, gentle, and ruling part, is slumbering; whereas the wild and animal part, full of food and drink, skips about, casts off sleep, and seeks to find a way to its gratification. You know that there is nothing it will not dare to do at that time, free of any control by shame or prudence. It does not hesitate, as it thinks, to attempt   d sexual intercourse with a mother or anyone else—man, god, or beast; it will commit any foul murder and does not refrain from any kind of food. In a word, it will not fall short of any folly or shameless deed.—What you say is true.

On the other hand, when a healthy and moderate man who has come to understand himself goes to sleep after rousing his reasonable part and feasting it on fine discussions and speculations but neither starving nor surfeiting his appetites, these appetites will slumber, and neither their pleasure nor their pain will disturb his best part, but they will allow it, pure and by itself, to look for and reach toward the perception of what he does not know, be it past, present, or future; if he has further, in the same manner, soothed his spirited part and has not gone to sleep with ruffled feelings after an outburst of anger, then, having quieted both spirit and appetites, he arouses his third part in which intelligence resides and thus takes his rest; you know that it is then that he best grasps reality, and the visions which appear in his dreams are the least lawless.—I agree with you entirely.

We have been led to speak at some length on this subject, but what we want to establish is this: that there is a dangerous, wild, and lawless kind of desire in everyone, even the few of us who appear moderate. This becomes obvious in our sleep. See whether you think I am talking sense and whether you agree with me.—I do.

Recall then what kind of person we declared the democratic man to be. He grew up from a young man brought up by a thrifty father who respected only those desires which made money but despised the unnecessary desires which aimed at play and beautification. Is that not so?—Yes.

As he kept company with more sophisticated men who were full of the desires we have described, his hatred of his father's stinginess impelled him toward every kind of excess and their way of life. However, he had a better nature than his corrupters; he was pulled both ways and settled down in the middle between the two ways of life, moderately, as he thought, enjoying both. So he led a life which was neither mean nor lawless, and from an oligarchic became a democratic man.—He did, and that was our opinion of the man.

Suppose now that he too has become older, and that he has a son who was brought up in his way of life.—I am supposing it.

Suppose further that the same things which happened to the boy's father now happen to him. He is led to every kind of lawlessness which those who influence him call liberty in every case. His father and the rest of the household come to the rescue of the middle desires, the others to the help of the other side. When those dangerous wizards and dictator-makers have no hope of mastering the young man in any other way, they contrive to implant in his soul as champion of those idle desires which spend whatever is at hand, a great Lust, for what else do you think Love is in such men?—Nothing else but that.

His other desires buzz around him, full of incense and myrrh and wreaths and wine and the loose pleasures found in such company. In the end they develop and nurture in the drone the sting of longing. Then, with madness as his bodyguard, this champion of the soul becomes frenzied; if he finds in the man some beliefs or desires which are thought to be good and still have some feeling of shame, he destroys them and throws them out, until he has cleansed him of moderation and filled him with imported madness.—You have accounted perfectly for the origin of the dictatorial man.

Is this not the reason why Love has of old been said to be a tyrant?—Probably.

And so, my friend, I said, a drunken man has something of a dictatorial or tyrannical mind.—He has.

Moreover, a man who is mad expects to be able to rule not only over men but over the gods, and attempts to do so.—He certainly does.

This, my dear friend, I said, is precisely how a man becomes dictatorial, when his nature or his pursuits or both make him intoxicated, lustful, and mad.—That is altogether so.

In this manner the dictatorial man originates. Now how does he live?—You tell me, as people say playfully.   d

I am telling you, I said. I think the next stage is that those in whose soul dwells the tyrant Lust who directs everything, go in for feasts, revelries, banquets, mistresses, and all that sort of thing.—They must.

And do not many dire new desires shoot up every day and every night beside the old ones?—Many indeed.

Any income such men have is soon spent.—Of course.

Borrowing follows, and encroachment on capital.—What else?   e

And when everything has gone, must not the violent crowd of appetites which has nested within shout in protest, and the men, driven by the stings of the other desires, and especially by Lust itself who leads all the others as his bodyguard, become frenzied, and look to see who possesses anything that can be taken from him by   574
force or guile.—Very much so.

They must either acquire property from somewhere or live in great pain and suffering.—Inevitably.

And just as the pleasures that are latecomers have the advantage over the older and steal away their satisfactions, so the man himself, though he is younger, deems it right to have more than his father and mother and, when he has spent his own, deprives them of their property by spending from his father's estate.—Of course.

If they do not allow it, will he not at first try to steal it and deceive his parents?—   b
Surely.

And whenever he could not do so, would he not snatch it by force?—I think so.

If the old man and the old woman put up a fight, would he be cautious and refrain from violence?—I am not very sanguine about the fate of those parents.

But by Zeus, Adeimantus, do you think he would sacrifice his long beloved and irreplaceable mother for a recently acquired mistress whom he can do without, or, for the sake of a young boy recently become dear to him, sacrifice his aged and   c
irreplaceable father, his oldest friend, beat him, and make his parents slaves of those others if he brought them under the same roof?—Yes, by Zeus, he would.

It seems a great blessing to produce a dictatorial son!—It certainly does!

Further, when the possessions of his father and mother fail him, with that great   d
swarm of pleasures within him, will he not first try to lay hands on property in a private house or snatch someone's coat late at night, and after that rob a temple?[119]
In all this the old traditional beliefs which he has held from childhood as to what is fine and what is shameful are overcome by new beliefs which have recently been freed from servitude, are now Lust's bodyguard, and share his power. They used to be freed in dreams when he himself was subject to the laws and to his father and   e

---

119. [The temples acted as public treasuries, so that a temple robber is almost equivalent to a bank robber.]

575 was a democratic man. Now, however, under the tyranny of Lust, he has permanently become in fact what he occasionally became in a dream. He will not refrain from any terrible murder, from any kind of food or deed. Lust lives like a dictator within him in complete anarchy and lawlessness as the sole ruler, and drives his victim as he does a city to dare anything which will provide sustenance for himself and the unruly crowd around him, a part of which has come from outside through bad company while a part has come from within, liberated and let loose by the same bad habits of the man himself. Is this not the kind of life such a man leads?—It is indeed.

b Now if there are only a few such men in a city and the rest of the people are moderate, these men will leave the city to act as bodyguard to some other dictator or to serve as mercenaries in a war somewhere, but if they live in a quiet time of peace they will commit many petty crimes there in the city.—What crimes do you mean?

They are thieves, burglars, purse snatchers. footpads, temple robbers, slave traders; sometimes, if they are sufficiently good speakers they are informers; they bear false witness and accept bribes.[120]

c These evils may be small, he said, if there are only a few such men.

Small things are small in comparison with big things, I said. All these crimes do not come within a mile, as the saying goes, of the rule of a dictator in wickedness and misery for a city. For when this type of men and their followers become numerous and conscious of their numbers, it is they who create the dictator we spoke of, helped by the people's folly, and the dictator more than any of them has within d himself the greatest and strongest dictator.—Naturally, he said, for he would be the most dictatorial man.

They may yield to him willingly, but if the city does not support him, then just as he once chastised his mother and father, so now he will, if he can, castigate his country by bringing in new friends and make his fatherland (or motherland, as the e Cretans say) subject to them and keep it so. That is the ultimate aim of such a man's desire.—It most certainly is.

Now in private life, before they attain power, their character is like this: all those with whom they keep company either flatter them and are ready to obey them in everything, or, if they are themselves in need of something, they cringe and readily adopt any form of supplication as friends, but once they have obtained what they 576 wanted they are strangers again.—They certainly do that.

So they live their whole life without being friends with anyone; their relations with other men are either those of a master or a slave, and the dictatorial nature never has a taste of freedom and true friendship.—Quite so.

Would we be right to call these men untrustworthy?—Of course.

And as unjust as man can be, if we were right when we agreed on the nature of b justice.—We certainly were right.

Let us then sum up the worst type of man, I said. He is in reality such as we said a man was in his dreams.—Quite so.

---

120. [As there were no public prosecutors in Athens, trials had to be initiated by the ordinary citizens. A number of people almost made a profession of this, for profit. They were the "*sycophants*," a word the origin of which is obscure.]

That is what the man becomes who is most dictatorial by nature and who is sole ruler, and the longer he rules the more like this he becomes.

Inevitably, said Glaucon, taking over the argument.

Well then, I said, is the man who is seen to be the most wicked also the most miserable? And the man who rules longest as a dictator and is the most tyrannical becomes in truth the most miserable, and for the longest time? The majority, however, have many opinions about this.—That indeed is certainly true.   c

Surely, I said, the despotic man is like the dictator-ruled city, as the democratic man is like the democratic city, and so with the others?—Of course.

And the relation between the cities in respect of excellence and happiness is the same as that between the individuals?—Definitely.   d

How then does the city ruled by a dictator compare with the city ruled by kings which we described first?

They are direct opposites, he said, one is the best, the other the worst.

I will not ask you which you mean, for it is obvious, I said, but do you give the same decision as regards happiness and misery? Do not let us be dazzled by looking only at the dictator, for he is only one man, or the few who surround him, but let us, as we must, go into the city and observe the whole of it. Let us take the plunge, look at all of it, and then voice a clear opinion.   e

You are right to call on us, he said; it is obvious to anyone that there is no more miserable city than a dictatorship and no happier one than that ruled by kings.

Would I be right then to make the same challenge about the individuals, assuming that the man who judges should be one who can in thought enter the character of a man and look thoroughly, not like a child looking from the outside. He must not be dazzled by the image of themselves which dictators adopt for the outside world but see right through it.   577

Would I not be right to think we should all listen to the man who can give a proper judgment because he has lived in the same house with a dictator and has witnessed his behaviour at home and his relations to the whole of his household where he is stripped of his theatrical paraphernalia, and again has observed how he behaves when in danger from the people: could we not bid this man, who has seen all that, to declare to us how the dictator compares with other men in happiness and misery?[121]—You would be quite right to call on him, he said.   b

Do you then, I said, want us to profess that we are among those who can give such a judgement and that we have met people so qualified in order that we may have someone to answer our questions?—I do indeed.

Come now, I said, look at it in this way: remembering how city and individual resemble each other, look at each in turn and tell us what happens to each.—What kinds of things?   c

First, I said, speaking of the city, would you say that a city under a dictator is free or enslaved?—As enslaved as it is possible to be.

Yet you see in it men who are masters and free.

---

121. [Plato's first visit to Syracuse had already taken place, and he had had every opportunity to observe the "tyrant" Dionysius I in action. He is here in fact claiming to speak with full knowledge. (His second visit to Syracuse, to Dionysius II, did not take place until much later.)]

I do, he said, but they are very few; one might say that the city as a whole and the best elements in it are wretched slaves without civic rights.

d   If then, I said, the individual is like the city, the same structure must prevail in him, and his soul must be full of servitude and lack freedom, and it is the best parts of it which are enslaved, and a small part, the most wicked and mad, which is master.—That follows of necessity.

And will you say that such a soul is free or slave?—Certainly slave.

So the enslaved and dictator-ruled city is least likely to do what it wants?—Quite so.

e   And the dictator-ruled soul will also be the least likely to do what it may want—that is, the soul as a whole; it will always be driven by violent frenzy and is full of disorder and remorse.—Of course.

Must a city under dictatorship be rich or poor?—Poor.

578   So then the despotically ruled soul must always be poor and unsatisfied.—That is so.

Further, must not such a city and such an individual be full of fear?—Quite inevitably.

Is there, do you think, more lamenting, complaining, and grieving to be found in any other city?—Definitely not.

And are such things more common in any other individual than the dictatorial man maddened by desires and lusts?—How could they be?

b   It is in view of all this, I think, and other things of the kind, that you judged this to be the most miserable of all cities.—And was I not right?

Certainly, I said, and what, looking at all this, do you say about the dictatorial individual?—He is by far the most miserable of men.

There, I said, you are no longer right.—How do you mean?

I do not think, I said, that this man has yet reached the extreme of misery.—Who has then?

Well the following may perhaps seem to you even more miserable.—Who?

c   The man of a dictatorial nature who does not live out his life in private, but some misfortune compels him to become a dictator.

I judge from what was said before that what you say is true, he said.

Yes, I said, but in matters of this kind we should not assume things; we greatly need to examine them by an argument such as ours, for we are investigating something of supreme importance, namely the good and the bad life.—Quite right.

See whether I am talking sense, for I think our investigation will be helped by the
d   following considerations.—What are they?

We should look at all the wealthy private citizens in our cities who have many slaves. They have this in common with the dictator, that they rule over many, and the difference lies in the number of the dictator's subjects.—That is so.

You know that these rich people live without fear and that they are not afraid of their household slaves.—What should they fear?

Nothing, I said, but do you realize the reason?—Yes, it is because the whole city will come to the help of every private citizen.

You are right, I said, but then if this one man with his fifty or more slaves were   e
lifted out of the city by some god, together with his wife and children, and deposited
with his slaves and other property in a deserted place where no free man could come
to his assistance, how frightened would he be on his own behalf and that of his wife
and children, lest they be killed by the slaves?—Very frightened indeed.

Would he not be compelled to flatter some of his own slaves, to promise them   579
many things, to free some of them though he did not want to do so, and to turn out
to be the flatterer of servants?—He would have to be, or else perish.

What then if the god settled many neighbours around him who would not tolerate
anyone to claim mastery over anyone else, and who would inflict the worst punishments upon anyone they caught doing this?—He would have even more troubles of   b
every kind, being ringed round by watching enemies.

Is this not the kind of prison in which the dictator is held? His nature is such as
we have described it, full of many fears and lusts of all kinds; greedy as his soul is,
he alone of the whole city cannot go abroad anywhere or see the sights which all
free men are eager to see; he takes refuge in his house and lives there for the
most part like a woman, envying any citizen who goes abroad and sees something   c
worthwhile.—That is certainly the case.

By such evils then does the man who is badly governed within himself, whom you
just now judged to be the most miserable, reap an even greater harvest of ills if he
does not live as a private citizen but is compelled by some chance to be a dictator
and, while not master of himself, to attempt to rule over others. He is like a man
with a sick and uncontrolled body who, instead of living a private life is compelled
to contend with others in physical contests and battles all his life.—They are very   d
alike, Socrates, and what you say is very true.

And so, my dear Glaucon, the life of the reigning dictator is altogether wretched,
and he is more miserable than the one you judged to be most miserable.—Quite.

In truth, even if people do not think so, the actual dictator is in reality enslaved
in the worst kind of slavery and in the greatest need to flatter, a flatterer of the most
wicked men. He cannot in any way satisfy his appetites; he is in the greatest need,   e
and is truly poor if one knows how to observe his soul as a whole; he is full of fear,
convulsions, and pain throughout his life, if indeed his condition is similar to that
of the city over which he rules. And it is, is it not?—It certainly is.

Besides all this, we shall assign to him the qualities we mentioned before; he   580
inevitably is, and his rule makes him even more so, envious, untrustworthy, unjust,
friendless, impious, and host and nurse to every kind of vice; all these qualities make
him extremely miserable, and he goes on to make those near him like himself.—No
man in his senses will contradict you.

Come then, I said, like a final judge declaring,[122] declare to me who of our five
men, the kingly, the timocrat, the oligarch, the democrat and the dictator is first in   b
the matter of happiness, who comes second, and so on in order.

---

122. [This probably refers to the judging of plays at festivals. From a list of chosen persons for each tribe
one was drawn by lot. These were the ten judges. Of these ten votes five were again drawn by lot, and it was
this last judgment which was announced by a herald. The singular "final judge," however, is obscure in meaning
and reference.]

That judgment is easy to make, he said; I judge them regarding virtue and vice, happiness and the opposite, as I might judge choruses in the order of their appearance.

Shall we then hire a herald, or shall I myself announce that the son of Ariston has given as his verdict that the best, most happy, and most just is the most kingly who rules like a king over himself, that the worst, most unjust, and most miserable, is the most dictatorial who tyrannizes most over himself and over his city.—Be it so announced.

And, I said, shall I add to the announcement that this is so whether their character is known or not known to all men and gods?—Yes, make that addition.

Very well, I said. This would be one of our proofs. The second one is this, if you think there is anything in it.—What is that?

Since, like the city, the soul of each individual is divided into three parts, this admits of another proof.—What is it?

This: As there are three parts, there are also, it seems to me, three kinds of pleasure, one peculiar to each part, and so with desires and kinds of rule.—How do you mean?

One part, we say, is that by which a man learns; the second is that with which he gets angry; as for the third part, because of its manifold aspects we had no one special name to give it, but we have named it after the biggest and strongest thing in it and have called it the appetitive part because of the violence of the appetites for food, drink, sex, and other things which follow from these. We have also called it the money-loving part because such appetites are most easily satisfied by means of money.—And that is right.

If we said that its pleasure and love are concentrated on profit we would be mostly relying on one chief feature to clarify our meaning whenever we mentioned this part. So we would be right to call it money-loving and profit-loving.—I think so at any rate.

Further, do we not say that the spirited part is wholly dedicated to the pursuit of power, victory, and high repute?—Certainly.

It would be appropriate then for us to call it victory-loving and honour-loving?—Most appropriate.

It is obvious to anyone that the part with which we learn is always wholly straining to know where the truth lies, and that of the three it cares least for money and reputation.—Quite so.

So to call it a lover of learning and philosophic would be in tune with its ways.—Of course.

Of these three, one rules in the soul of one man, I said, another in another's, whichever it happens to be.—That is so.

That is why we say that there are three primary kinds of men, the philosophic, the lover of victory, and the lover of profit.—There certainly are.

And there are three kinds of pleasures, one for each of these?—Definitely.

Do you realize, I said, that if you wanted to ask these three kinds of men in turn which of these three kinds of lives is the most pleasant, each would give the highest praise to his own? The money-maker would say that compared with making a profit the pleasure of being honoured or of learning is valueless, unless it contains something that makes money.—True.

What about the lover of honour, I asked. Does he not think the pleasure of making money to be vulgar, and the pleasure of learning to be smoke and nonsense, in so far as learning brings no honour?—That is so.

And, I said, what are we to think the philosopher considers the other pleasures are worth compared with that of knowing where the truth lies and of always learning in this field? Are they not far behind? In fact he calls these pleasures necessary because he would feel no need of them if they were not necessary to live.

This question requires clear knowledge, he said.

When the pleasures of each kind, and the very way of life is in dispute, not as to which is the more beautiful or ugly, or the better or the worse, but which is actually the more pleasant and less painful, how can we know which man is speaking most truly?—I have no answer to give to that.

Look at it this way: what enables us to give a good answer? Is it not experience, knowledge, and discussion? Or could anyone give a better criterion than these?—How could one?

Consider then which of the three men has most experience of the pleasures we mentioned. Does the profit-lover have more experience of the pleasure to be derived from learning the nature of truth itself than the philosopher has of the pleasure to be derived from making a profit?

There is a considerable difference, he said. The philosopher has of necessity tasted the other pleasures, beginning in childhood, but the profit-lover did not necessarily taste the sweet pleasure of learning the nature of things or become experienced in this. Rather, even if he was eager, it would be hard for him to do so.

Then the philosopher, I said, is superior to the profit-lover in his experience of both their pleasures.—He surely is.

How does he relate to the lover of honour? Has he less experience of the pleasures to be got from being honoured than the other has of the pleasure derived from knowledge?

Honour, he said, comes to them all, provided they reach the goal for which they set out. The rich man is honoured by many, so is the brave man and also the wise, so that they are all aware of the pleasure of being honoured, but the pleasure to be gained from the contemplation of reality cannot be tasted by anyone except the philosopher.

So then, as far as experience goes, he makes the best judgment of the three.—Very much so.

And he alone has experience of intelligence.—Of course.

Moreover, the instrument through which one must judge is not one which belongs to the profit-lover or the lover of honour, but to the philosopher.—What is that?

We said one must make a judgment through discussion, and discussion is very much the philosopher's tool.—Of course.

Now if wealth and profit were the means of making a judgment, what the profit-lover said in praise or blame would necessarily be very true.—Quite so.

If honour, victory, and bravery were the means of judging, would it not be what the lover of honour and victory said?—Obviously.

But since the means are experience, intelligence, and discussion—?—Necessarily it is the praise of the philosopher, the lover of discussion, which is most true.

583   Then of the three kinds of pleasure it is the pleasure of that part of the soul by means of which we learn which is the sweetest, and so is the life of the man in whom this part rules.—It surely will be, since he is the best judge, and he praises his own life.

To what life and what pleasure, I asked, does the judge give second place?

Clearly, he said, to that of the warrior and the lover of honours, for it is closer to the first than that of the money-maker.

Then that of the profit-lover comes last, as it seems.—Of course.

b   These then are two proofs in a row, and twice the just man has defeated the unjust. The third, as at Olympia, is dedicated to Olympian Zeus the Saviour.[123] Observe that the pleasure of the others, apart from that of the man of intellect, is not entirely true or pure, but illusory like a shadow image, as I think I have heard one of our wise men say. Now this will be the main and decisive bout.—Certainly, but what is your meaning?

c   I shall discover it like this, by searching for it with you as you answer my questions.—Ask your questions then.

Tell me, I said, do we not say that pain is the opposite of pleasure?—Certainly.

Is there such a thing as feeling neither pleasure nor pain?—There is.

Being a mean between those two, it is a kind of calm of the soul in this regard. Do you not call it that?—I do.

Do you recall what sick people say when they are ill?—What?

d   That nothing gives more pleasure than health, but that they had not realized this before they were ill.—I recall it.

And you hear those who are in great pain say that nothing is as pleasureable as cessation from pain.—I do.

And there are many other circumstances in which you find men, whenever they are in pain, praise relief and freedom from pain, not the feeling of pleasure, to be the most pleasant.—Perhaps at that time a state of calm becomes most sweet and desirable to them.

e   And whenever anyone ceases to feel pleasure, this calm will be painful to him.— Perhaps.

So what we said stands between the two, this calm, will at times be both pain and pleasure.—So it seems.

Now is it possible for that which is neither to be both?—I do not think so.

Surely the feeling of pleasure in the soul and the feeling of pain are both some kind of movement, are they not?—Yes.

584   And did not what is neither painful nor pleasant appear to be a calm in between the two?—It did.

---

123. [The third toast at a banquet was to Zeus the Saviour, and the phrase "the third to Zeus the Saviour" became proverbial. The addition "Olympian" is not so clear, as it was the first libation which was addressed to him.]

How then can it be right to think that the absence of pain is pleasure and the absence of pleasure is pain?—It cannot be at all right.

Then this cannot be so, I said, but at such times the calm, when side by side with pain, seems to be pleasant, while beside pleasure it seems to be pain, but there is nothing sound about these appearances as regards the truth; they are a kind of illusion.—So the argument shows.

Look at the pleasures which are not preceded by pain that you may not, in the present case, be repeatedly led to believe that the nature of pleasure is absence from pain, and the nature of pain is absence of pleasure.—Look where? Which pleasures?   b

There are many others, I said, but you will realize this best if you are willing to take note of the pleasures of smell. They are not preceded by pain but they suddenly become extraordinarily intense, and when they cease they leave no pain behind.— Very true.

Then let no one persuade us that pure pleasure is the absence of pain, or pure pain the absence of pleasure.—They will not.   c

Yet most of the so-called pleasures which reach the soul through the body, and the most intense, are of this kind, some kind of escape from pain.—Yes, they are.

So too with the pleasures and pains of anticipation which arises from the expectation of pleasure and pain to be; they are of the same kind.—They are.

Do you know the nature of them and what they resemble most?—What?   d

You believe, I said that there is in nature an above, a below, and a middle?—I do.

Do you not think that a man who was carried from below to the middle would believe that he was carried to the above. And if he stood in the middle and saw whence he had come could he think anything else but that he was in the above, not having seen the true above?—By Zeus, I do not see how he could think anything else.

Then again, if he was carried back, he would think he was being carried below, and he would be right.—Of course.   e

All this would happen to him because he has no experience of what is truly above, in the middle and below?—Obviously.

Can you wonder then if those who have no experience of truth have many unsound opinions about many other things as well as about pleasure and pain and what is between them? When they descend to pain they believe what is true, namely that   585
they are in pain, but when, after pain, they ascend to the middle they firmly believe that they have reached fulfillment and pleasure; it's just as if, not having any experience of white, they were comparing grey with black—so, not having any experience of pleasure, they compare pain with the absence of pain and are misled.—
By Zeus, I would wonder much more if it were not so.   b

Think of it this way, I said: are not hunger and thirst and the like a sort of emptiness in the body?—Quite so.

And ignorance and lack of sense are an emptiness in the soul.—Of course.

So the man who takes his share of food and the man who acquires wisdom would be filled?—Very much so.

Which kinds of filling do you think have a greater share of reality, those which fill with bread, drink, meat, and every other kind of food, or the kind which fills   c
with true opinion and knowledge and intelligence and, in a word, with every kind

of virtue. Judge it this way: do you think that what is concerned with the unchanging and immortal and with truth, being itself of the same kind and existing in a receptacle of the same nature, is more real than what is concerned with the mortal and ever changing, being itself of that kind and existing in a receptacle of the same nature?—That which is concerned with the unchanging is by far the more real.

And does the reality of the unchanging partake to any greater extent of reality than of knowledge?—Not at all.

Or partake more of truth?—Not that either.

d   If it partook less of truth, it would partake less of reality?—Necessarily.

Therefore the kinds of filling concerned with the care of the body have less share in truth and reality than those concerned with the care of the soul?—Much less.

Do you not think that the same difference applies to the body itself and the soul?—Certainly.

It follows that what is filled with things more real, and is itself more real, is more truly filled than that which is filled with things less real and is itself less real?—Of course.

If to be filled with things appropriate to our nature is pleasureable, that which is in fact more filled with real things will make one rejoice more really and more truly
e   in true pleasure, while that which partakes of things less real will be less truly and lastingly filled and partake of a less reliable and less true pleasure.—Quite inevitable.

586   Now those who have no experience of wisdom and virtue but are always occupied with feasts and the like are carried down and then back up to the middle, and so they wander throughout their life but they never reach beyond to what is the true above. They never look up to it nor are carried thither; they have never been truly filled with what truly exists, nor tasted any stable and pure pleasure. They look down always with their heads bent to the ground like cattle; at the banquet tables
b   they feed, fatten, and fornicate. To get their fill of such things they kick and butt each other with iron horns and hoofs and kill each other. They are insatiable as they do not fill the real and continent part of themselves with true realities.

Socrates, said Glaucon, you describe the life of the majority like an oracle.

Must they not live with pleasures that are mixed with pain, illusory images of true
c   pleasures, which take their colour from the juxtaposition, so that both appear intense? They implant in the foolish mad passions for themselves and they are fought for as Stesichorus tells us that the wraith of Helen was fought for at Troy by men who did not know the truth.[124]—It must certainly be something like that.

Must not similar things happen to the man who satisfies his spirited part at all cost? His love of honours makes him envious, his love of victory makes him violent,
d   his irritability makes him angry, and he pursues the satisfaction of honours, victory, and anger without reasoning or intelligence.—Such things must happen to him also.

But then, I said, let us confidently assert that those desires of even the profit-loving and honour-loving parts, which follow knowledge and reason and pursue with their help those pleasures which intelligence prescribes, will attain the truest

124. [The story, referred to by Plato in the *Phaedrus* (243a), was that Stesichorus had written a poem defaming Helen and was struck with blindness. He then wrote a palinode and recovered his sight. The palinode was that Helen herself was never at Troy, but only a wraith or shadow of her. The *Helen* of Euripides is based on this story.]

pleasures possible for them, since they are following the truth. These pleasures are their own, if that which is best for each thing may be said to be fully its own.—Indeed it is.

If the whole soul follows the wisdom-loving part and there is no internal dissension, then each part will be able to fulfill its own task and be just in other respects, and also each will reap its own pleasures, the best and the truest as far as possible.—Very definitely.

But when one of the other parts rules in the soul to any extent, it cannot find its own pleasure and it compels the other parts to pursue a pleasure that is alien to them and false.—That is so.

And those parts which are most remote from philosophy and reason are most likely to do this sort of thing.—Very much so.

Is not that which is most remote from reason also remote from law and order?—Clearly.

The most remote have been shown to be the lustful and dictatorial appetites.—By far.

The least remote are the kingly and well ordered?—Yes.

So I think the dictator will be furthest away from enjoying true pleasure, and his own, while the king will be nearest to this.—It must be so.

So the dictator will lead the least pleasant life, and the king the most pleasant.—Definitely.

Do you know, I said, by how much the dictator's life is less pleasant than the king's?—If you tell me.

There are, it seems, one genuine and two bastard pleasures, and the dictator is at the extreme end of the latter. He avoids both law and reason, and lives with certain slave pleasures as his bodyguard. It is not easy to say by how much he is inferior except perhaps in the following manner.—How?

The dictator was third distant from the oligarch, for the democratic man was between them.—Yes.

So he lives with an image of pleasure which is thrice[125] removed from the oligarch as to its truth, if what we said before is true?—Quite so.

Now the oligarch in turn was third from the king, if we identify the king and aristocrat.—Third he is.

So the dictator is three times three times removed from true pleasure.—So it appears.

The image of dictatorial pleasure, according to the number of its dimensions, is a plane.[126] By squaring and cubing this number it will become clear how large is the distance between the dictator and the king.—Clear at any rate to a mathematician.

Turning this around, if one wants to know how far the king is superior to the dictator in the truth of his pleasure, he will find, if he completes his multiplication,

e

587

b

c

d

e

---

125. [Three times because the Greeks always counted the first as well as the last number of a series, e.g. the day after tomorrow was the third day.]

126. [9 can be said to be a plane because it is the square of 3, but Plato does not say why he then cubes 9. In any case he wants the dictator to be as far removed from the king as possible.]

that the king lives seven hundred and twenty-nine times more pleasantly than the dictator, and that the dictator is the same number of times more miserable.[127]

588   You have brought up an extraordinary calculation, he said, of the difference between the two men, the just and the unjust, as regards pleasure and pain.

Yet it is a true one, I said, and a number appropriate to human life, if days and nights and months and years are appropriate to them.—They surely are.

Then if the good and just man wins out over the bad and unjust to such an extent in pleasure, by how much more will he surpass him in the graciousness of his life, its beauty and excellence.—By Zeus yes, he certainly will.

b   Very well, I said. As we have come to this point in our discussion, let us take up again what was said at first, which has led us to this. It was said at some point that injustice was to the benefit of the completely unjust man who had a reputation for justice, was it not?[128]—It certainly was.

Since we have fully agreed, I said, upon the effect of each, that is, of just and unjust behaviour, let us now talk to the man who maintains this point of view.— How?

Let us in our argument fashion an image of the soul, so that he may understand
c   the kind of thing he was saying.—What kind of image?

One of the kind that are told in ancient legends about creatures like the Chimera, Scylla, Cerberus, and many others in whose natures many different kinds had grown into one.—We are told of such creatures.

Fashion me then one kind of multiform beast with many heads, a ring of heads of both tame and wild animals, who is able to change these and grow them all out of himself.

d   A work for a clever modeller, he said. However, as words are more malleable than wax and such things, take it as fashioned.

Then one other form, that of a lion, and another of a man, but the first form of all is much the largest, and the second second.—That is easy and it is done.

Gather the three into one, so that they somehow grow together.—All right.

Model around them on the outside the appearance of being one, a man, so that anyone who cannot see what is inside but only the outside cover will think it is one
e   creature, a man.—Done.

Let us now tell the one who maintains that injustice benefits this man, and that justice brings him no advantage, that his words simply mean that it benefits the man
589   to feed the multiform beast well and make it strong, as well as the lion and all that pertains to him, but to starve and weaken the man within so that he is dragged along whithersoever one of the other two leads. He does not accustom one part to the other or make them friendly, but he leaves them alone to bite and fight and kill each other.—This is most certainly what one who praises injustice means.

On the other hand, one who maintains that justice is to our advantage would say that all our words and deeds would tend to make the man within the man the

---

127. [If Plato is following Philolaus who counted 364½ days in the year, there are 729 days *and* nights in the year, and the dictator is more miserable every day and every night. Plato may mean no more than that, though it seems that Philolaus also had a great year of 729 months.]

128. [The point was made at some length by Glaucon in Book Two, 361a ff.]

strongest. He would look after the many-headed beast as a farmer looks after his   b
animals, fostering and domesticating the gentle heads and preventing the wild ones
from growing. With the lion's nature as his ally, he will care for all of them and rear
them by making them all friendly with each other and with himself.—This is most
definitely the meaning of him who praises justice.

What is said of justice is true in every way, and what is said on the other side is
false, whether one examines it from the point of view of pleasure, of good repute,   c
or of advantage; whereas he who condemns justice has nothing sound to say, and
he does not know what he is condemning.—I don't think he does at all.

Let us then gently persuade him—he is not willingly wrong—by asking him: "My
good sir, should we not say that beautiful and ugly traditions have originated as
follows: the beautiful are those which subordinate the beastlike parts of our nature   d
to the human, or perhaps we should say to the divine, while the ugly enslave the
gentler side to the wilder?" Will he agree or what?—He will agree if, he takes my
advice.

Can it benefit anyone, I said, to acquire gold unjustly if when he takes the gold
he enslaves the best part of himself to the most vicious part? Or, if by taking the
gold he should make a slave of his son or daughter in the house of wild and evil   e
men, it would certainly not benefit him to acquire even a great deal of gold on those
terms.

If then he enslaves the most divine part of himself to the most ungodly and
disgusting part and feels no pity for it, is he not wretched and is he not accepting
a bribe of gold for a more terrible death than Eriphyle when she accepted the   590
necklace for her husband's life?—Much more, said Glaucon. I will answer for him.

Then do you think that licentiousness has long been condemned because in a
licentious man that terrible, that big, that multiform beast is let loose more than it
should be?—Clearly.

Obstinacy and irritability are condemned whenever the lion and snakelike part is
increased and stretched disproportionately?—Surely.   b

Are luxury and softness condemned because the slackening and looseness of this
same part produce cowardice?—Of course.

And do not flattery and meanness come when this same spirited part is subordinated to the turbulent beast which accustoms it from youth to being abused for the
sake of money and the beast's insatiability, and to become an ape instead of a lion?—   c
Certainly.

Why do you think the mechanical work of one's own hands is subject to reproach?
Shall we say that it is so only when the best part of one's soul is naturally weak and
cannot rule the animals within but pampers them and can learn nothing except ways
to flatter them.—That is likely.

Therefore, in order that such a man be ruled by a principle similar to that which
rules the best man, we say he must be enslaved to the best man, who has a divine
ruler within himself. It is not to harm the slave that we believe he must be ruled, as   d
Thrasymachus thought subjects should be, but because it is better for everyone to
be ruled by divine intelligence. It is best that he should have this within himself, but
if he has not, then it must be imposed from outside, so that, as far as possible, we
should all be alike and friendly and governed by the same principle.—Quite right.

This, I said, is clearly the aim of the law which is the ally of everyone in the city,   e

and of our rule over children. We should not allow them to be free until we establish a government within them, as we did in the city, fostering the best in them with what
591 is best in ourselves and securing within the child a similar guardian and ruler, and then let him go free.—The law does make that clear.

How then and by what argument can we maintain, Glaucon, that injustice, licentiousness, and shameful actions are profitable, since they make a man more wicked, though he may acquire more riches or some other form of power?—We cannot.

Or that to do wrong without being discovered and not to pay the penalty is
b profitable? Does not one who remains undiscovered become even more vicious, whereas within the man who is discovered and punished the beast is calmed down and tamed; his whole soul, settling into its best nature, as it acquires moderation and justice together with wisdom, attains a more honoured condition than a strong, beautiful, and healthy body, in so far as the soul is to be honoured more than the body.—Most certainly.

c The man of sense then will direct all his efforts to this end; firstly, he will prize such studies as make his soul like this, and he will disregard the others.—Obviously.

Then, I said, he will see to his bodily condition and nurture it in such a way that he does not entrust it to the irrational pleasure of the beast, turn himself that way, and live on that level. It is not even health he aims at, nor does he consider it
d most important that he should be strong, healthy, or beautiful, unless he acquires moderation as a result, but he will cultivate harmony in his body for the sake of consonance in his soul.—That is altogether true, if he is truly to be a cultured man.

To the same end, there will be order and measure in his acquisition of wealth. He will not be panicked by the numbers of the crowd into accepting their idea of blessedness and increase his wealth without limit, and so have unlimited ills.—I do not think he will do so.

e Looking to the government within, I said, he will guard against disturbances being caused there by too much wealth or too little, and he will direct, as far as he can, both the acquiring and spending of his possessions.—Very definitely.

592 He will have the same end in view as regards honours. He will share in, and willingly taste, those which he believes will make him a better man, but he will avoid both public and private honours which he believes will destroy the existing condition of his soul.

He will not then, he said, if that is his concern, be willing to go into politics.

Yes, by the dog, he will, I said, at least in his own kind of city, but not in his fatherland perhaps, unless divine good luck should be his.

I understand, he said, you mean in the city which we were founding and described,
b our city of words, for I do not believe it exists anywhere on earth.

Perhaps, I said, it is a model laid up in heaven, for him who wishes to look upon, and as he looks, set up the government of his soul. It makes no difference whether it exists anywhere or will exist. He would take part in the public affairs of that city only, not of any other.—That is probable, he said.

BOOK X

I am sure, I said, that when we founded the city we were entirely right about many   595
of its features, and when I say this I am especially thinking of poetry.—How so?

The fact that we did not admit such poetry as is imitative.[129] Now that the parts
of the soul have each been separately described, it is even clearer, I think, that such   b
poetry should most certainly be excluded.—What do you mean?

To speak between ourselves—for you will not denounce me to the tragic and all
the other imitative poets—all such poetry is likely to damage the minds of the
audience unless these have knowledge of its nature, as an antidote.—What do you
have in mind when you say this?

Speak I must, I said, even though the love and respect which I have had since
childhood for Homer prevents me from talking about him. He seems to be the first,
the teacher and leader of all those fine tragedians, but no man must be honoured   c
more than the truth and so, as I say, I must speak out.—Quite so.

Listen then, or rather answer.—Ask your questions.

Could you tell me what is the general nature of imitation, for I do not myself quite
understand what meaning that word is trying to express.—Am I then likely to
understand it?

There would be nothing strange about that, I said, for people with poor eyesight
have often seen things before those with keener eyesight.   596

That is so, he said, but I would not be eager to speak in your presence even if
something occurred to me. You look yourself.

Do you want us to start looking in our usual way? We are accustomed to assuming
one Form in each case for the many particulars to which we give the same name. Or
do you not understand?—Yes, I do.

Let us then take any set of particulars you like. For example, there are many beds
and tables.—Of course.   b

But there are only two Forms for these two articles, one of the bed and one of the
table.—Yes.

We also usually say that the makers of these articles look to the Form when they
make, one the beds, the other the tables, which we use. And so with other things.
The Form itself is not the work of any craftsman, for how could it be?—It could
not.

Now consider what you call this kind of maker.—What kind?   c

The one who makes all the things which any and every artisan makes.—You are
talking of a clever and wonderful man!

Not yet, but you will soon have more reason to say so, for this same artisan is able
to make not only all kinds of furniture but also all plants that grow from the earth,
all animals including himself and, besides, the earth and the heavens and the gods,

---

129. [The reference is of course to the discussion of poetry in the third book, and in particular to 396b to
398b.]

d   all things in heaven and all things in Hades below the earth.—A marvelously clever man.

You don't believe me? I said. Tell me, do you think such a craftsman does not exist at all, or that in one way there is a maker of all these things, and in another way there is not. Do you not see that in one way you could make all these things yourself?—And what way is that?

Not a difficult one. You could do it quickly and in many places. The quickest way
e   is to carry a mirror with you everywhere; you will then quickly make the sun and things in the heavens, the earth as quickly, yourself and the other living creatures, manufactured articles, plants, and all that was mentioned just now.

Yes, he said, I could make them appear, but I could not make them as they truly are.

True, I said, and you have come to the necessary point in the argument, for I think that the painter too belongs to this class of makers,[130] does he not?—Of course.

You will say that he does not make true things; yet in a way the painter too makes a bed, does he not?—Yes, he does, but only the appearance of a bed.

597   What about the carpenter? Did you not say just now that he does not make the Form, what we call the truly existent bed, but he makes a bed?—I did say that.

Now if he does not make that which is, he would not be making what is, but something which is like what is, but is not that. If one said that the work of the carpenter or that of any other craftsman is completely real, one would risk saying what is not true.

That, he said, would be the opinion of those who busy themselves with this kind of discussion.

Let us not be surprised then if his bed too is somewhat obscure in comparison
b   with the truth.—We should not be.

Do you want us to seek the nature of the imitator in these same examples?—If you wish.

There are then three beds of a kind; one which exists in nature, which we would say, as I think, is the work of a god, or is it that of someone else?—Of no one else, I think.

One which is the work of a carpenter.—Yes.

And one which the painter makes, does he not?—Be it so.

Painter, carpenter, god; these three, corresponding to three kinds of bed.—Yes, three.

The god, either because he did not wish to make more than one bed in nature, or
c   because he was compelled not to do so, thus made only that one bed which is the real bed. Neither two nor more of these have been created by the god or ever will be.—How so?

Because, I said, if he were to make only two, there would again appear one of

---

130. [Throughout the following passage Plato takes advantage of the fact that the Greek word *poiein* means both "to make" generally and also "to compose poetry." Indeed the word *poiētēs* means both poet and maker, so that to class the poet (and the painter) as "makers" is much more natural in Greek.]

which the two would have the Form, and this would be the truly real bed, not the two.—Correct.

The god knew this, I think, and wishing to be the real creator of the truly real bed, not a particular maker of a particular bed, created this as the one bed in nature.—That seems likely.   d

Shall we then call him the natural maker of this, or some such name?—That would be right, since he made the true nature of this and everything else.

What about the carpenter? Is he not the maker of a bed?—Yes.

Can we also call the painter a craftsman and maker of such a thing?—Not at all.

Then what will you say he is in relation to the bed?

This, he said, seems to me the most reasonable name to give him, namely he is an imitator of that which the others made.   e

Very well, I said, you call an imitator one whose product is at three removes from nature.—Quite so.

This will be true also of the tragedian, as he is an imitator; he is naturally third from the king and the truth, and so are all other imitators.—Probably so.

We are agreed on the imitator. But tell me this about the painter. Do you think he tries to imitate what is real, in nature in each case, or the works of the craftsmen?—   598
The works of the craftsmen.

Such as they are or such as they appear? Define this too.—How do you mean?

Like this: is a bed any different if you look at it from the side or from the front or from any other point? Or is it not different but appears different, and so with other things?—That is how it is; it appears different, but it is not.

On this very point: what does the picture relate to? Does it imitate the reality of   b
the model as it is, or its appearance as it appears? Is it an imitation of the truth or of an image?—Of an image.

Imitative art, then, is far removed from the truth, and that is why, it seems, it can make everything, because it touches only a small part of each thing, and that an image. The painter, we say, will make a picture of a cobbler, of a carpenter, of other   c
craftsmen, though he knows nothing of these crafts. Nevertheless, if he should be a good painter and display his picture of a carpenter at a distance, he could deceive children and foolish men into believing that it is really a carpenter.—Why not?

I think, my friend, that we should have this in mind about all such things: if someone declares to us in connection with anybody that he has met a man who knows all the crafts and everything else that anybody knows, and that there is nothing which he does not know better than anyone, we must assume that the   d
speaker is a simple-minded individual, that he apparently met some magician and imitator and was deceived into believing him all-wise because he himself could not distinguish between knowledge, ignorance, and imitation.—Very true.

We should therefore examine tragedy next, and Homer its leader, since we hear some people say that those poets know all the crafts, all human affairs concerned with virtue and vice, and all about the gods as well. For these people say that if the   e
good poet is to compose fine poetry, he must have knowledge of his subject; else he cannot compose at all. We must therefore investigate whether they have been deceived on meeting these imitators, and when they see their works they do not realize that these are at a third remove from reality and are easy to compose without   599

knowledge of the truth; they are but images, not reality, or whether there is something in what these people say, and the good poets really do have knowledge of the subjects about which the majority thinks they speak so well.—We must certainly examine this question.

Do you think that a man who could make both the model and the image would allow himself to be in earnest about the making of images and put this in the
b   forefront of his life as the best talent he had?—I do not.

I think that, if he truly had knowledge of the things he imitates, he would much rather devote himself to actions than to the imitation of them, and that he would try to leave behind many fine actions as memorials of himself and be eager to be the subject of a eulogy rather than the author of it.—I think so, for they are not equal either in honour or in usefulness.

We shall not require from Homer or any other poet an account of other things,
c   such as whether any one of them has medical knowledge and is not merely an imitator of medical language, or whom any poet of the old or the new school has made healthy as Asclepius did, or what disciples of his medical craft he has left behind as Asclepius did his sons, nor shall we question them about other crafts. All that we will pass over. About the most important and most beautiful subjects of which Homer undertakes to speak—wars, generalship, the government of cities,
d   men's education—about these we are right to question him and to inquire: Dear Homer, if you are not third from the truth as regards virtue, a maker of images whom we have described as an imitator, but are even second and capable of knowing what pursuits make men better in private and in public life, then tell us to the betterment of what city's government you have contributed, as Lycurgus did to that
e   of Sparta, and many other men have done in many cities large and small. What city gives you credit for being a good lawgiver and having benefited them, as Italy and Sicily give credit to Charondas,[131] and we do to Solon? Who gives credit to you?" Will he be able to name one?—I do not think so, said Glaucon. Even the Homeridae[132] do not claim this for him.

600   Well then, is any war in his time remembered which was won by his generalship or advice?—None.

Or such contributions as a practically wise man makes, skillful inventions in crafts or other practices, as we are told Thales of Miletus and Anacharsis the Scythian did?[133]—There is nothing of that kind at all.

Then if there is nothing of a public nature, is Homer himself, while alive, said to have been, in his private life, a leader in the education of some people who loved
b   him for his company and left to posterity a Homeric manner of life? Pythagoras was

---

131. [Charondas probably lived in the sixth century B.C., and gave laws to Catane and other cities in Italy.]

132. [The name Homeridae may at first have been restricted to the descendants of Homer, but it came to be applied more generally to the rhapsodes who recited and expounded Homer throughout the Greek world.]

133. [Thales was the oldest philosopher of the Milesian school who were the originators of physical science. He predicted the solar eclipse of 585 B.C. He regarded water as the basic material of all things. Ancharsis lived around 600 B.C., was well travelled in the Greek world, and was often regarded as one of the seven sages. He is also credited with the beginnings of Greek geometry and is said to have been able to calculate the distance of ships at sea.]

himself particularly loved for this, and even today his followers are conspicuous for what they call the Pythagorean way of life.

Again, he said, we are told nothing of the kind about Homer. Creophylus,[134] his companion, Socrates, would appear to have been even more ridiculous than his name in matters of education, if what is said about Homer is true, namely that he was very much neglected in his day, while he was alive.

c

So we are told, I said, but, Glaucon, do you think that, if Homer had really been able to educate men and make them better, if he could have had knowledge about such things and not merely imitated them, he would not have had many companions and been honoured and loved by them? Protagoras of Abdera, Prodicus of Ceos, and a great many others are able to convince those around them in private that they would not be able to manage their household or their city unless these sophists were put in charge of their education; they are so beloved because of this wisdom of theirs that their disciples all but carry them around on their shoulders. Surely, if Homer had been able to benefit men and make them more virtuous, his contemporaries would not have allowed him, or Hesiod either, to wander around as rhapsodes. Would they not have clung to them closer than to gold and compelled them to stay at home with them; or, if they failed to persuade them to do so, would they not have followed them wherever they went until they had sufficiently partaken of that education?—I think, Socrates, that what you say is absolutely true.

d

e

Shall we then assume that all poetic imitators, beginning with Homer, imitate images of virtue and of everything else they write about and have no contact with the truth? We said just now that the painter, though he knows nothing about leatherwork, makes a picture which appears to be a cobbler to those who have no knowledge either and judge by colour and shape.—Quite so.

601

In the same way, I think that the poetic imitator though he knows nothing except how to imitate, gives colour to certain crafts with words and phrases so that others without knowledge, who judge by the words, believe that anything said with meter, rhythm, and tune, be it on cobbling or generalship or anything else whatever, is right—so great is the natural charm of poetry, for if you strip the works of the poets of their artistic colouring, you know what they are like without these ornaments. Indeed you have seen this.—I have.

b

They are like the faces of those who were young but not beautiful after the bloom of youth has left them.—Definitely.

Come now, consider this: the maker of the image, we say, knows nothing of the reality; he only knows the appearance. Is that not so?—Yes.

c

Let us not leave the discussion of this point halfway, but examine it fully.—Say on.

A painter, we say, will make a picture of reins and bridle?—Yes.

A cobbler and a metal-worker will make them?—Certainly.

Now does the painter know what kind of reins and bridle they must be? Or do even the metal-worker and the cobbler, who make them, not know this, but only the man who knows how to use them, that is the horseman, and he alone?—Very true.

---

134. [Creophilus was sometimes said to have been an epic poet as well as the friend of Homer. His name means "of the meat tribe." Nothing is really known about him.]

Shall we then not say that this is the case with everything?—How so?

d   In each case there are these three crafts; one will use the article, one will make it, and one will imitate it.—Yes.

Then the excellence, beauty, and rightness of each article, living creature, or action aim at nothing else than its use, and it is with this in view that each thing is manufactured or adapted by nature?—That is so.

It is quite inevitable that the user of each article has most experience of it; it is he who tells the maker which of his products performs well or badly in the use he makes e   of it. The flute-player, for example, tells the flute-maker about the flutes which respond well in the playing, and he prescribes what kind of flutes the other should make, while the other will follow instructions.—Of course.

The man who knows gives instructions about good and bad flutes; the other will rely on him in making them.—Yes.

So with regard to the same article the maker will have right opinion about its beauty and quality; he consorts with the one who knows and has to listen to him, 602 but the user has knowledge.—Quite so.

Does the imitator have either the knowledge derived from the use of the things he depicts as to whether they are beautiful or right, or has he the right opinion because he must consort with the one who knows and be told what to depict?— Neither.

So the imitator will have neither knowledge nor right opinion about the beauty or quality of the things he imitates?—He does not appear to have.

Then the poetic imitator would be a smart fellow as regards his knowledge of the subjects of his poetry!—Not so very smart.

b   Nevertheless he will make his imitations, though he does not know whether a particular subject is good or bad, and he seems likely to imitate what appears beautiful to the ignorant majority.—What else?

So we are fairly well agreed on this, namely that the imitator has no worthwhile knowledge of his subject, that imitation is a kind of game and not to be taken seriously, that the tragic poets, whether they write in iambics or in hexameters, are imitators to the greatest possible extent.—Quite so.

c   By Zeus, I said, this imitating is concerned with something at a third remove from the truth is it not?—Yes.

And upon what in a man does it have the effect it has?—What kind of thing are you talking about?

This kind of thing: the same magnitude does not appear to our sight to be of the same size when we look at it from nearby or from a distance.—It does not.

And the same things seem crooked when we see them in water and straight when we see them out of it; the same things appear concave or convex because our eyes are confused by colours, and every confusion of this kind clearly exists in our soul. d   Scene painting relies upon this weakness in our nature and is nothing short of magic; so does conjuring and other such trickery.—True.

However, do not measuring, counting, and weighing give us most welcome assistance in preventing illusions about greater or lesser size, number, or weight from ruling in our soul, and insuring that part of us will rule which has calculated, measured, and weighed?—Of course.

And that would be the function of the reasoning part in the soul.—It is indeed.   e

When this part has measured and indicated that some objects are larger and some smaller than others, or that they are equal, the opposite impression also appears at the same time about the same objects.—Yes.

We have said that it is impossible for the same thing to have contrary opinions about the same thing at the same time.—And we were right.

That part of the soul which gives an opinion contrary to the measurements could   603
not be the same as the part of which the opinion is in accordance with them.—It could not.

Now the part which relies on measurement and calculation would be the best part of the soul.—Of course.

And that which opposes it would be among the inferior parts within us.—It must be.

As I wished to reach agreement on this, I said that painting, and imitation generally, produces a work that is far from the truth; it consorts with a part of ourselves which is far from intelligence and is its companion and friend for no healthy or true   b
purpose.—That is quite definitely so.

Imitation, then, being an inferior thing and consorting with an inferior part, produces inferior offspring.—That is likely.

Does this apply only to imitations we see, or also to those we hear, which we call poetry?—It is likely to apply to them also.

Let us not, I said, rely on a likely analogy from painting but let us tackle directly   c
that part of our minds with which the imitation of poetry consorts, and let us see whether it is good or inferior.—We must do so.

Let us face the question this way. We say that imitative poetry imitates men acting voluntarily or under compulsion, and believing that as a result of these actions they have fared well or ill, also suffering or rejoicing in all this. Does it imitate anything else apart from this?—Nothing.

Now is a man under all these circumstances of one mind? Or, just as he was at odds with himself in matters of sight and held contrary opinions at the same time   d
about the same objects, so also in his actions he is at odds with himself and fights himself. But I remember that we need not seek agreement on this point now, for we have already agreed on all this in our previous discussion,[135] namely that our soul is full of innumerable such contradictions at the same time.—Right.

Right indeed, I said, but I think that we must now discuss what we omitted then.—
What was that?   e

We said then somewhere,[136] I said, that if a good man with a soul of the same quality lost a son or some other most prized possession, he would bear this far more easily than others.—Quite so.

Let us now enquire whether he would not grieve at all, or whether, this being impossible, he would somehow be measured in his sorrow.—The latter is nearer the truth.

135. [The reference is to IV, 439b ff.]

136. [At III, 387e.]

604   Now tell me this about him: would he fight his pain and resist it more when his equals can see him, or when he is alone and by himself, in solitude?—When he is seen, and the difference will be considerable.

He will venture to say many things when alone which he would be ashamed to be heard saying, and also do many things which he would not like to be seen doing.—That is so.

b   That which bids him resist pain is reason, also the law, whereas it is the suffering itself which draws him to give way to grief.—True.

As he is pulled in opposite directions at the same time in relation to the same thing, we say that these impulses within the man must be two.—Of course.

One part of him is ready to obey the law wherever it leads him.—How so?

The law says that the best thing is to remain as quiet as possible in misfortune and not to resent it because it is not clear whether such events are good or bad, also
c   because to take it hard makes the future no better, because no human experience is worth taking very seriously, and because grieving is an obstacle to attaining as soon as possible that which we must attain in the circumstances.—What do you refer to?

One should think over what has happened and, as with a fall of dice, arrange one's affairs in whatever way reason chooses as the best, and not, as children do when they trip, hug the stricken part and spend one's time crying. One should
d   always accustom one's soul to turn as quickly as possible to healing the stricken or sick part and replace lamentation by therapy.—One would be quite right to face misfortune that way.

We say then that it is the best part of us which is willing to follow this reasoning.—Obviously.

And shall we not say that the part which leads one to dwell on one's misfortune, to lamentations—and of these it never has its fill—is unreasonable, idle and friendly to cowardice?—We shall say that.

e   Now this peevish part gives many opportunities for all sorts of imitations, while the wise and quiet character which always remains pretty well the same is neither easy to imitate nor easy to understand when imitated, especially for a festival crowd, people of all sorts gathered in the theatres. For them the imitation is one of suffering
605   alien to them.—That is definitely true.

Clearly, the imitative poet does not relate naturally to this part of the soul, nor is his cleverness directed to please it if he is to attain high repute among the many, but he relates to the excitable and varied character because it is easy to imitate.—Obviously.

Therefore we would be right to take him and put him beside the painter. Like him, he produces work inferior as regards truth, and he appeals to a part of the
b   soul of a similar nature and not to the best, and in this too they are alike. So we are right not to admit him into a city which is to be well governed because he arouses this part of the soul and strengthens it, and by so doing he destroys the reasonable part, just as when one makes the vicious strong in the city and surrenders it to them, one destroys the better sort of citizens. We shall say that the imitative poet does the same; he sets up a bad government in the soul of every private individual by
c   gratifying the mindless part which cannot distinguish the small from the large but

thinks that the same things are at one time small, at another large. He is a maker of images which are very far removed from the truth.—Quite so.

We have not yet, however, brought the most serious charge against imitation, namely that it is able to corrupt even good men, with very few exceptions, and that is a terribly dangerous thing.—Terrible indeed, if it does that.

Listen and reflect: when even the best of us hear Homer or some other tragedian imitating one of the heroes sorrowing and stretching out a long speech of lamentation or a chorus beating their breasts you know that we enjoy it, surrender ourselves, share their feelings, and earnestly praise as a good poet the one who affects us most in this way.—I know; of course we do.   d

But when one of us suffers a private loss, then, as you know, we pride ourselves on the opposite behaviour, if we can keep quiet and master our grief; this we think to be the part of a man, and the other behaviour, which we then praised, to be womanish.—I realize it.   e

Can that praise in the theatre be right? To see a man behaving as one would not deem it right to behave oneself, indeed as one would be ashamed to behave, to enjoy and praise the spectacle and not be disgusted by it?—No by Zeus, it does not seem sensible.

It does though, I said, if you look at it in this way.—How?   606

If you reflect that the part which is forcibly controlled in our private misfortunes and has been pining to weep and adequately lament, as it is by nature desirous of this, is the very part which receives satisfaction from the poets in the theatre and enjoys it. That part of ourselves which is the best by nature has not been sufficiently educated either by reason or habit, and it relaxes its watch over the lachrymose part because it is watching another's suffering and there is no shame involved for itself   b
in praising and pitying another man who, in spite of his claim to goodness, grieves excessively. Moreover, there is, he thinks, a definite gain, namely pleasure, and he would not welcome being deprived of it by despising the whole drama. Only a few will reflect that the enjoyment will be transferred from the spectacle of another's sufferings to one's own, and that one who has nurtured and strengthened the part of him that feels pity at those spectacles will not find it easy to hold it in check at the time of his own misfortunes.—Very true.   c

Does not the same argument hold about ridicule? You greatly enjoy on the comic stage, or even in private conversation, things at which you would be ashamed to provoke laughter yourself, and there you do not hate them as wicked. Indeed you do the same as in the case of the pitiful, for that part of you which wants to provoke laughter was held back by your reason, for fear of being thought a buffoon, but you let it loose in the theatre, not realizing that, by making that part strong there, you will be led to being a comedian in your own life.—Yes indeed.

So too with sex, anger, and all the desires, pleasures, and pains which we say   d
follow us in every activity. Poetic imitation fosters these in us. It nurtures and waters them when they ought to wither; it places them in command in our soul when they ought to obey in order that we might become better and happier men instead of worse and more miserable.—I cannot disagree.

And so, Glaucon, I said, when you meet those who praise Homer and say that the   e
poet educated Greece, that he deserves that one should take up his works, learn from them the management of human affairs and of education, and arrange one's

life in accordance with his teaching, you must welcome these people and treat them
607   as friends, for they are as good as they are capable of being. You can agree that
Homer is most poetic and that he stands first among the tragedians, but you must
know for sure that hymns to the gods and eulogies of good men are the only poetry
which we can admit into our city. If you admit the Muse of sweet pleasure, whether
in lyrics or epic, pleasure and pain will rule as monarchs in your city, instead of the
law and that rational principle which is always and by all thought to be the best.—
Very true.

b   Let this be our defence as we have returned to the subject of poetry, that it was
reasonable for us to banish poetry from the city earlier, considering its nature, for
the argument compelled us to do so. However, lest we be charged with a certain
harshness and boorishness, let us tell poetry that there is an ancient quarrel between
it and philosophy, as is proved by phrases like "the dog yelping at its master" or
c   "baying" and "great in the empty talk of fools" and "the crowd of over-wise heads"
or "subtle thinkers" and that they are "beggars" and innumerable other signs of the
old opposition between them.[137] Nevertheless it should be said that we at least, if
poetry that aims at pleasure and imitation has any argument to bring forward to
prove that it must have a place in a well-governed city, should be glad to welcome
it, for we are aware of the charm it exercises, but it is impious to betray what one
d   believes to be the truth. Are you not yourself, my friend, charmed by poetry,
especially when you see it through Homer?—Very much so.

Therefore it is right that it should come back from exile after making its defence
in lyric or any other meter.—Certainly.

We should also give its champions who are not poets the opportunity to speak on
its behalf in prose to the effect that it not only gives pleasure but is useful to cities
and to human life. We shall listen to them in a friendly spirit, for we shall certainly
e   benefit if poetry is shown to be not only pleasant but useful.—How could we not
benefit?

However, as long as such a defence is not made, my dear friend, we shall behave
like people who have fallen in love but realize that their passion is not beneficial.
They force themselves to stay away from their loved one; so, because of the love of
such poetry which has been implanted in us by the upbringing we received from
608   our beautiful governments, we shall be well disposed to any proof that poetry is an
excellent and very true thing. But as long as it is not able to put up such a defence,
we shall listen to it but repeat to ourselves like an incantation the argument we now
put forward and be careful not to fall again into that childish and popular love. We
b   shall go on repeating that such poetry must not be taken seriously as if it had any
contact with truth and were an earnest matter, but that the man who is anxious
about the government of his soul must be careful when he hears it, and that what
we have said about poetry must be believed.—I entirely agree with you.

The struggle to be good or bad is important, my dear Glaucon, I said, much more
important than people think, so that it is not worth being led on by honours, wealth,
or any office, nor indeed by poetry, to neglect justice and the other virtues.—After
what we have said I agree with you, and I think so would anyone else.

---

137. [The philosophers, long before Plato, had attacked Homer for his immoral tales about the gods. The
phrases here quoted are presumably from poetry, but their sources are unknown.]

And yet, I said, we have not described the greatest prizes at hand and available to virtue.—Their greatness must be tremendous, he said, if there are other prizes greater than those already mentioned.

What, I said, could become great in quite a short time? For what is the whole time from childhood to old age compared with eternity?—Nothing at all.

Well, I said, do you think that what is immortal should seriously be concerned with that short time, and not with eternity?—I agree with you, but why do you say this?

Have you not realized, I said, that our soul is immortal and is never destroyed?[138]

He looked at me in wonder and said: No by Zeus I have not. Can you assert that?

I should be wrong to deny it, I said, and you can assert it too, for it is in no way difficult.—I should be glad to hear you on this "in no way difficult" subject.

You could hear it, I said.—Speak then.

There is something you call good and something you call bad?—There is.

And do you think about them as I do?—What?

That which destroys and corrupts is the bad, that which preserves and benefits is the good?—I agree.

Further, do you say that there is an evil and a good for everything? For example, ophthalmia for the eyes, sickness for the whole body, mildew for grain, rot for wood, rust for iron or bronze, and we may say that all things have each their natural evil and sickness.—I do say so.

So that whenever one of these evils attaches itself to something, it makes it defective and finally disintegrates and destroys it wholly.—Of course.

The natural evil and defect of each thing destroy each thing, but if they do not destroy it, no other thing will do so, for its good will never destroy it, nor again will anything which is neither good nor bad.—How could it?

If then we should discover something which has its peculiar evil, and this makes it bad but cannot disintegrate or destroy it, shall we not know that a thing of such a nature cannot be destroyed?—That is likely.

Well now, I said, is there not an evil of the soul which makes it bad?

Certainly, he said, the things we were mentioning: injustice, license, cowardice, and ignorance.

Does any one of these disintegrate and destroy the soul? And reflect lest we be deceived into thinking that when the unjust and foolish man is caught in wrongdoing, his soul, which is bad, is destroyed by its injustice. Think of it this way: just as disease which is the evil of the body wears it out, destroys it, and drives it to being a body no longer, so all the things we mentioned just now cease to exist through their own peculiar evil which attaches itself to them, is present in them, and destroys them until they cease to exist—is that not so?—Yes.

Come now, look at the soul in the same way: does injustice which exists in it, and

---

138. [All living creatures have a *psyche*, which we must translate by soul, but, as this passage makes clear, it is not necessarily thought of as immortal. While the argument here professes to prove the soul immortal, Plato does not tackle the question of which part of the soul is immortal, though he more than hints that it is not immortal in all its parts (611b–612a), but only in its pure state, and that seems to refer to its reasoning part only.]

the other vices, by their presence and by attaching themselves to it, corrupt and make it waste away until they cause its death and separate it from the body?—Not at all.

And surely it is unreasonable to suppose that the evil of another thing destroys that which its own evil does not destroy?—It is unreasonable.

e   For reflect, Glaucon, I said, that we do not think that the body must be destroyed even by the badness of foods, whatever it be—staleness or rottenness or whatever else—but if the badness of the food implants in the body its own evil, we shall say

610 that the body was destroyed by its own evil, namely disease caused by the food. We shall never deem that the body died of the badness of the food, which is a different thing from the body, and thus by an alien badness, unless it implants in the body its own natural and peculiar evil.—This is again quite correct.

By the same argument, I said, unless the evil of the body cause the soul's own evil in the soul, we shall never believe that the soul is destroyed by an alien evil without the presence of its own peculiar evil.—That too is reasonable.

So either we must refute our argument and show that we are wrong, or, as long

b   as it remains unrefuted, we must never say that the soul is destroyed by a fever or any other disease, nor even by murder, not even if the body were cut up into tiny pieces. We must not say that the soul is destroyed through these things until some-body shows us that these sufferings of the body have made the soul more unjust and more impious. When the evil of one thing is present in another, but its own peculiar

c   evil is absent, we shall not allow it to be said that anything is destroyed, be it the soul or anything else.

To be sure, he said, no one will ever prove that the souls of the dying become more unjust because of death.

But if anyone, I said, should venture to come to grips with our argument in order to avoid agreeing that our souls are immortal, and says that a dying man becomes more vicious and unjust, we shall reply that, if what he says is true, then injustice

d   must be deadly to the unjust like a disease, and that those who catch it die of it because of its own deadly nature; those who get it worst die more quickly and those who have it less die more slowly, but the unjust would not die then as they do now because others inflict a penalty upon them.

By Zeus, he said, injustice will not then seem to be a very terrible thing if it brings death to the unjust—for that would be an escape from their troubles—but I think

e   it will be seen to be quite the opposite; it brings death to other people if it can, but it makes the unjust very lively, and besides being lively they are very much awake. Thus it is very far from being deadly.

You are right, I said, for when its own evil and its own badness is insufficient to kill the soul and destroy it, then an evil which is directed to the destruction of something else will hardly kill the soul, or indeed anything else except the thing which it is ordained to destroy.—"Hardly" is right, it seems.

611 Now if it is not destroyed by any one evil, either its own or another's, clearly it must always exist, and, if it always exists, it is immortal.—Inevitably.

So be it, I said. And if it is so, you realize that the souls would always be the same, for they could not be made less by the death of one soul, nor become more numerous, for if anything immortal is increased, the increase must come from what is mortal, and everything would be immortal in the end.—That is true.

We must not think that, for the argument does not allow it, nor that in its truest nature the soul is in itself full of great variety and unlikeness and difference.—How do you mean?   b

It is not easy for anything composed of many parts to be everlasting if it is not put together in the fairest manner, yet that is how the soul now appeared to us.—It is certainly unlikely to be.

That the soul is immortal both our recent argument and others would compel us to believe, but to see it in its true nature one should not observe it as we do now, maimed by its association with the body and other evils, but in its pure state, and as c such it must be contemplated by reason which will find it far more beautiful and will also see more clearly justices and injustices and all that we have now discussed. What we have said about it is true, as it appears at present. We have observed it in this state like those who saw the sea-god Glaucus and would no longer easily see his d original nature because some of the old parts of his body had been broken off, others had been crushed, and his whole body marred by the waves, while other accretions—shells and seaweeds, and stones—had grown upon him so that he was more like a wild animal than he was like himself. This is how we observe the soul beset by countless evils. This is where we must look, Glaucon.—Where?

To the soul's love of wisdom, and realize what things it apprehends, what company e it longs for as it is akin to the divine, the immortal, and the ever existing, what it would become if it followed this with the whole of its being and if that impulse lifted it out of the sea in which it now dwells, if the many stones and shells, the many stony 612 and wild things which have been encrusted all over it by those so-called happy feasts as it feeds on earth, were scraped off. Then one would see its true nature, whether it is multiform or simple, the way and manner of its being. However, we have now rightly described its experiences and its parts, I think, as it exists in human life.— We certainly have.

Well, I said, our argument has dealt with the other objections, and we have not invoked the rewards and the reputation of justice, as you said Homer and Hesiod b did,[139] but we have found that justice in itself is best for the soul itself, and that it must do what is right, whether it has the ring of Gyges or not, and besides that ring the cap of Hades as well.[140]

What you say is quite true.

Then, Glaucon, I said, it cannot now be resented if in addition we now return to justice and the rest of virtue the many kinds of rewards which they provide to the c soul from both gods and men, while a man is still alive and after his death.—It certainly cannot be resented.

Will you then return to me what you borrowed in the course of the argument?— What in particular?

I granted your request that the just man should be reputed unjust, and the unjust man just, even though it would be impossible that the falseness of their reputations should escape both gods and men. I yielded in this for the sake of the argument, so

139. [This passage refers back to the speeches of Glaucon and Adeimantus at the beginning of the second book, specifically to 358d and 367b–e.]

140. [For the ring of Gyges see Book Two, 359d–360a. The cap of Hades also made its wearer invisible.]

d   that justice and injustice could be judged in themselves, or do you not remember?—It would be very wrong of me not to remember.

Since that judgment has now been made, I ask on behalf of justice the return of the reputation it has in fact among gods and men, and that we agree it has this reputation, in order that it may carry off the prizes which follow from it and give them to the just, since we have now seen it give the blessings which follow from its

e   very presence and that it does not deceive those who possess it.—Your request is just.

Then grant me this first, that the nature of each of the two men does not escape the gods.—We will grant that.

Then if neither of them escapes the notice of the gods, one would be loved by the gods and the other hated by them, as we agreed at the beginning.—That is so.

And shall we not agree that, as far as gifts from the gods are concerned, all will

613   happen as well as possible for the friend of the gods, unless some necessary evil was due to him owing to some previous wrongdoing?—Certainly.

We must suppose this about the just man who falls into poverty or disease or some other apparent evil, that this will end well for him either during his lifetime or afterwards, for the gods never neglect a man who is eagerly wanting to be just and to become as like a god as it is possible for a man to be by practising virtue.—It is

b   likely, he said, that such a man would not be neglected by one like himself.

And we must think the opposite about the unjust man?—Definitely.

So the prizes the just man gets from the gods are something like that.—Certainly, in my opinion.

What about rewards from men? Is this not in fact the case? Do not clever but unjust men act like runners who run well for the first part of the course, but not for the second part? At first they leap away sharply, but they become ridiculous by the

c   end with their ears sunk into their shoulders and they leave the track without being crowned, whereas true runners get to the end, take the prizes, and are crowned. Does not the same generally happen to just men? By the end of each action or association, and by the end of their life, they enjoy a high reputation and carry off the human prizes.—Surely.

Will you then allow me to say about them what you yourself said about the unjust?

d   I shall say that, when they get older, just men fill the public offices of their own city if they wish, marry into any family they want to, give their children in marriage to anyone they wish, and all you said about the unjust I now say about the just. As for the unjust, the majority of them, even if they escape detection when young, by the end of the race are caught and are covered with ridicule, and as they get old they become miserable, they are insulted by both strangers and citizens, are beaten with

e   the lash, and suffer those punishments which you rightly called cruel—the rack and the burning. Imagine that I have said they suffer them all; see whether you will allow what I say.—Certainly, for what you say is just.

So these are, I said, the prizes and rewards and gifts which gods and men give to

614   the just man while he lives, in addition to those which justice itself provides for him.—They are fine and lasting awards.

They are as nothing in number and magnitude compared with those that await each of the two after death. These should be heard, in order that both should receive

in full what the argument owes them.—Tell us, he said, for there are few things I   b
would more gladly hear.

It is not a tale of Alcinous I shall tell you, but that of a brave man, Er the son of
Armenias, a Pamphylian by race who once died in war. When the dead were picked
up ten days later, putrefaction had already set in but his corpse was quite fresh. He
was picked up and taken home and preparations were made for his funeral. On the
twelfth day, as he was already laid out on the funeral pyre, he revived. When he had
revived he told what he had seen yonder. He said that after his soul had left him it
travelled with many others until they came to a marvellous place, where there were   c
two openings side by side into the earth, and opposite them two others upward
into heaven, and between them sat judges. These, when they had given judgment,
ordered the just to go upward through the heavens by the opening on the right,
and they attached signs of the judgment on them in front. The unjust they ordered
to travel downward by the opening on the left with signs of all their deeds on their
back. When Er himself came forward they told him that he was to be a messenger   d
to mankind of what happened there, and that he was to listen and to observe
everything in the place. He said he saw souls leaving by either opening into the
heavens and into the earth after their judgment. As for the other two openings,
from one souls emerged from the earth covered with dust and dirt, by the other
souls came down from heaven clean. And all the time those who arrived appeared   e
to have been on a long journey; they gladly went and camped in the meadow, like
a festival crowd. Those who knew each other exchanged greetings and enquiries. If
they had come up from the earth they asked what happened in the other place, and
if they came from heaven what had happened to the others. They recounted it to   615
each other, those from the earth wailing and weeping as they recalled all they had
suffered and seen on their journey below the earth—it lasted a thousand years—
while those who came down from heaven told how well they had fared and the
incredibly beautiful sights they had seen. There was much to tell, Glaucon, and it
took a long time, but the main point was this: for all the wrongs they had done to
any person they paid a tenfold penalty one after the other, that is, once in every
century of their journey, as human life is reckoned of that length, so that they should   b
pay a tenfold price for every injustice. If, for example, some of them had caused
many deaths by betraying a city or an army and had thrown many people into
slavery, or had been accomplices in other misdeeds, they had to suffer ten times the
pain they had caused to each individual. Then again, if they had done good deeds
and had become just and pious, they would receive a reward on the same scale. He
said some other things about the stillborn and those who had lived but a short time,   c
but these are not worth mentioning. He also spoke of even greater penalties or
rewards for piety and impiety toward the gods and parents, and for the murder of
kindred.

For he said he was present when a man was asked where the great Ardiaius was.
This Ardiaius was said to have been dictator in a city of Pamphylia a thousand years
before, had killed his father and his elder brother, and committed many other   d
impious deeds. Er said he heard the answer: "He has not come, and never will, for
this was one of the dreadful sights we saw: when we came near the opening on our
way out after all our sufferings, we suddenly saw him and others, most of them were
dictators but there were some private people who had been great sinners. They
thought they were now going to get out but the opening did not admit them; it   e
roared whenever one of those incurably wicked men, or someone who had not paid

a sufficient penalty, tried to come out, and then, he said, some savage men, all fiery
to look at, who were standing by and recognised the roar, took hold of them and
616   led them away. They bound the feet, hands, and head of Adriaius and others, threw
them down and beat them, took them out of our path and by the side of the road,
tortured them on thorny bushes, and indicated to those who were continually passing
by why this was done, and that they would be led away and dropped into Tartarus."
Of their many fears, he said that this was the greatest, lest the roar should be heard
as each of them came up, and each was immensely relieved if silence greeted him.
b   Such were the penalties and retributions and the rewards corresponding to them.

When those in the meadow had each been there seven days, on the eighth they
had to get up and go on a journey, and on the fourth day of that journey they came
to a place where they could look down from above upon a light stretching straight
through the whole of heaven and earth like a column,[141] very like a rainbow but
c   brighter and more pure. They went on and arrived there after another day and
from there in the middle of the light they saw the extremities of the bonds stretched
from heaven, for the light holds together its whole revolution in the same way
as the cables underpinning a trireme. From the extremities hangs the spindle of
Necessity, by means of which all the orbits revolve; its staff and hook are made of
adamant, whereas in the whorl adamant is mixed with other materials. The nature
d   of the whorl was as follows:[142]

Its shape was like that of an ordinary whorl, but we must understand Er's account
of the parts which composed it. It was as if in one big whorl which had been
thoroughly scooped out, another smaller one had been closely fitted like boxes fitting
into one another, so there was a third and a fourth and four more, eight whorls
e   altogether inside one another, their rims showing in a circle and a continuous surface
of one whorl round the shaft which was driven right through the middle of the
eighth circle.

The first and outside whorl had the widest circular rim, that of the sixth was
second in width, the fourth was third, the eighth was fourth, the seventh was fifth,
the fifth was sixth, the third was seventh, and the second was eighth. The circle of
the largest was spangled; the circle of the seventh was the brightest; that of the
617   eighth took its colour from the brightest; the seventh, the second, and the fifth were
about equal in brightness, more yellow than the others; the third was the whitest in
colour; the fourth was rather red; and the sixth was second in whiteness. The whole

141. [The first stop of the souls seems to be at the top of the universe, conceived of as a sphere, and the light
here is spoken of as a shaft going from top to bottom through the center, and they look at it from above. A day
later they seem to arrive at the center. Some think that the light also goes around the sphere, and the mention
of the underpinning cables of a trireme seems to favour this view.]

142. [Where the spindle of Necessity hangs from is not at all clear. The whorl consists of concentric half
spheres which fit into one another; their lips or rims fit together on one plane. As the whorl obviously is meant
to represent the dome of heaven, with the fixed stars in the outside one, and the eight spheres contain the other
heavenly bodies, these half spheres clearly are not material, for wherever the observing souls are placed they
are meant to see the heavenly bodies in their orbits, that is in their half spheres, and the various speeds are
meant to represent the movements of the sun, moon, and planets. The width of the half spheres represents the
distance of these from one another. Proceeding inward from the first and outside half sphere, the second, with
the narrowest rim, is the orbit of Saturn, the third that of Jupiter, the fourth of Mars, the fifth of Mercury, the
sixth of Venus, the seventh of the sun, the eighth of the moon. The earth, of course, is in the middle. Further
details and conjectures will be found in Adam's notes and Appendix 6 to Book X.]

spindle turned at the same speed, but as the whole turned the inner circles were carried round at a slower pace in a motion contrary to that of the whole. Of these the eighth was the swiftest; then second were seventh, sixth, and fifth at an equal pace; third in speed as it appeared to them as it turned was the fourth; fourth was the third; and the second was fifth. The spindle turned on the knees of Necessity. On each of the circles stood a Siren who was carried along with it and uttered one note, and the eight notes made up a concordance. Three others were sitting around at equal distances: the daughters of Necessity, the Fates, dressed in white with garlands on their heads; Lachesis and Clotho and Atropos; and they sang to the music of the Sirens—Lachesis sang of the past, Clotho of the present, and Atropos of the future. Clotho with her right hand touched the outer part of the spindle and helped it turn, and then left off for a time; Atropos did the same to the inner circles with her left hand; Lachesis would help both motions in turn, one with one hand and one with the other.

When the souls arrived, they had to go to Lachesis right away, and an interpreter of the divine first arranged them in order, then took from Lachesis a number of lots and samples of lives, ascended a high platform and spoke: "This is the message of Lachesis, the maiden daughter of Necessity. Souls of a day, this is the beginning of another mortal round which will bring death. Your guardian spirit will not be assigned to you, you will choose him. Let him who has the first lot be the first to choose a life which will of necessity be his. Virtue knows no master, each will possess it in greater or lesser degree according as he honours or disdains it. The responsibility is his who makes the choice, the god has none."

When he had said this he threw the lots to them all and each one picked up that which fell at his feet, except Er who was not allowed to do so. As each man picked it up his place in the order of choice was made clear to him. Next after this the samples of lives were placed on the ground before them, far more numerous than the souls present. They were of all kinds, for the lives of animals were there as well as all kinds of human lives. There were dictatorships, some that lasted throughout life, others that lasted half way through and ended in poverty, exile, and beggary. There were lives of men famous for their physical powers, for beauty and strength and athletic success, others famed for high birth and the virtues of ancestors, also the lives of men of no fame at all for these things, and the same with lives of women. The state of the soul was not included, for this unavoidably depended upon the kind of life one chose. The other qualities were mixed with wealth and poverty, with health and disease, and some too were moderate in these respects.

It is here, my dear Glaucon, that man faces every danger, and because of this we should be most concerned that each of us neglect other studies in order to seek for and learn the knowledge which will enable him to discover who will enable him to distinguish the good life from the bad, and always to make the best possible choice everywhere. He should think over all that has now been said about the nature of the virtuous life, separately and together, and know what good or evil physical beauty can accomplish mixed with wealth and poverty and with what state of the soul.

He should know the effects of high or low birth, of private life and public office, of physical strength or weakness, of ease and difficulty in learning, of all such things as affect the soul by nature or as acquired characteristics, and what they achieve when mixed with one another, so that with all this in mind he should be able to make a thoughtful choice, while considering the nature of the soul, between the better

e   life and the worse. He will call the worse that which leads the soul to being more
        unjust, the better that which leads it to being more just; for we have seen that this
        is the best choice for a man, both in life and after. Everything else he will ignore.
619   One should hold on to this belief with adamantine determination as one goes down
        to the underworld, so that there too one should not be dazzled by wealth and similar
        evils and should not stumble into a dictator's life and actions of that kind, and
        perform many incurable evils and suffer even worse oneself, but know how always
        to choose the mean in such lives, avoid excesses both ways, and live as far as possible
b   such a life forever. That is where a man will find the greatest happiness.

            Then our messenger from the other world reported that the interpreter spoke as
        follows: "Even for the one who comes last a life which is not bad but satisfactory is
        available if he chooses intelligently and lives consistently. Let not the first be careless
        in his choice nor the last be discouraged." When the interpreter had thus spoken,
        Er said, the one who came up first chose the mightiest dictatorship. In his folly and
        greed he chose without a careful look and did not notice that he was fated to devour
c   his own children and other evils, but when he examined his chosen life at leisure,
        he beat his breast and bemoaned his choice, nor did he abide by the warning of the
        interpreter for he did not blame himself for these evils, but fortune and the gods,
        and everyone but himself. He was one of those who had come down from heaven;
        he had lived his previous life in a well-ordered city, and had been virtuous by habit
        without philosophy. One might say that among those who were caught that way the
d   souls who had come down from heaven were not in a minority because they had no
        experience of evil. The majority of those who had come up from the earth, having
        suffered themselves and seen others suffer, were in no rush to make their choice.
        There was thus an interchange of evils and blessings for the majority of souls, and
        also because of the chance of the lot.

            Therefore if someone, whenever he comes to live here on earth, pursues philoso-
e   phy soundly, and the lot of the choice does not place him among the last, he is likely
        to be happy here, according to the message received from the other world, and his
        journey from here to there and back again will not be along the rough path below
        the earth, but along the smooth and heavenly.

620   Er said that It was a spectacle worth seeing how the souls each chose their lives.
        It was pitiful, ridiculous, and surprising. For the most part their choice depended
        upon the character of their previous life. He said that he saw the soul which had
        once been that of Orpheus choosing the life of a swan in his hatred of women;
        because of his death at their hands he did not want to be born of a woman. He saw
        the soul of Thamyris[143] choosing the life of a nightingale, and on the other hand a
        swan changing to choose the life of a man, and so with other musical birds. The
b   twentieth soul chose the life of a lion. This was the soul of Ajax, son of Telamon,[144]
        avoiding human life because he remembered the judgment about the armour. The
        soul which came after him was that of Agamemnon. His sufferings too made him
        hate the human race and he changed to the life of an eagle. The lot had assigned

---

143. [Thamyris was a legendary poet and singer who boasted that he could defeat the Muses in a contest of
song. For this they blinded him and took away his voice. He is mentioned in *Iliad* 2, 596–600.]

144. [Ajax was the great Homeric hero, always the last to retreat on the Greek side. After the death of
Achilles his armour was allotted to Odysseus and the disappointed Ajax went mad and finally killed himself.
See the *Ajax* of Sophocles.]

a place about the middle to the soul of Atalanta;[145] as she saw great honours being paid to an athlete she could not pass it by and chose it. After her he saw the soul of Epeius the son of Panopeus[146] entering the life of a craftswoman. Far on among the last the soul of the ridiculous Thersites[147] entered the life of a monkey. By chance the soul of Odysseus had been allotted the very last place to make its choice. Remembering its former ills and taking a rest from ambition it went around for a long time looking for the quiet life of a private individual and had difficulty finding it as it lay neglected by everybody. He gladly chose it and said he would have made the same choice if he had been first. As for the others, animals chose men's lives and each other's, the unjust ones choosing the life of wild beasts, the just ones choosing the tame lives, and all sorts of mixtures occurred.

After all the souls had chosen their lives, they went forward to Lachesis in the same order in which they had chosen, and she sent with each the genius he had chosen as guardian of his life and to fulfill his choice. This genius first led the soul to Clotho, under her hand, and the rotation of the spindle confirming the fate which the lot and his choice had given him. After contacting her he led the soul to the spinning of Atropos, making what had been spun irreversible. Thence they went under the throne of Necessity without turning round and after passing through there, when all had gone through, they all went to the plain of forgetfulness in burning, choking, terrible heat, for it was empty of trees and of the plants that grow from the earth. There they camped, as it was now evening, by the stream of Oblivion whose water no vessel can hold.

All had to drink a measure of this water, but those who were not preserved by wisdom drank more, and as each drank they forgot everything. After they had slept and it was the middle of the night, there was a clap of thunder and an earthquake, and suddenly they were carried upward to birth in different directions, rushing like stars. Er himself was forbidden to drink of the water. He did not know how and in what way he arrived back in his body, but looking up suddenly he saw himself lying on the pyre at dawn.

And so, Glaucon, the story was preserved and not lost. It could save us if we believe it, and we shall safely cross the stream of Forgetfulness and not be defiled in our soul. If we are persuaded by me to believe that the soul is immortal and that it can endure all evils and all blessings, we shall always hold on to the upward journey and we shall in every way practise justice with wisdom, in order that we may be at peace with ourselves and with the gods while we remain here on earth, and in order that afterwards we may receive the rewards of justice like the victors at the games who collect their pay, and may fare well both here and on the thousand-year journey we have described.

---

145. [Atalanta was a legendary huntress who would marry only a man who could beat her in the footrace, and in most versions the loser was killed. Melanion received three golden apples from Aphrodite which he dropped in the race and Atalanta stopped to pick them up, thus losing the race to him.]

146. [Epeius is mentioned by Homer (*Odyssey* 8, 493) as the man who, with the help of Athena, made the Wooden Horse.]

147. [Thersites is the rank and filer who abuses Agamemnon in the second book of the *Iliad* (211–277) and is silenced by Odysseus. What he says is true enough, but his companions laugh at him and Odysseus beats him up.]

ARISTOTLE

Augustine tells us that, in reading Cicero's dialogue *Hortensius*, he was led to turn to a life of philosophy and ultimately to faith and a sense of utter dependence upon divine grace. For Augustine, then, philosophy was the vehicle to a recognition of human finitude and the unrestricted character of God's power. But the *Hortensius* was itself inspired by Cicero's reading of Aristotle's dialogue, the *Protrepticus or Exhortation to Philosophy*. In this work, of which only fragments remain, the young Aristotle (384–322 B.C.E.) calls the reader to a life of searching for knowledge, a life of inquiry, research, and the investigation of all things.

Aristotle himself lived such a life, as one commentator puts it, "driven throughout his life by a single overmastering desire—the desire for knowledge." Later, in the famous first sentence of his *Metaphysics*, Aristotle would acknowledge that he shared this desire with all people: "all men by nature desire to know." Ultimately, it is a desire that would result in Aristotle's remarkable achievements in the study of biology, psychology, logic, physics, ethics, politics, and much else. It would also find its place at the core of his ethics and politics. The relation between virtuous conduct and intellectual activity is a controversial feature of Aristotle's moral thinking, but one interpretation is that he conceived of the good life, which we all desire above all else, as a self-sufficient life devoted to inquiry and contemplation. For Aristotle, then, philosophy or the search for knowledge and understanding will enable man to become as divine as he can ever be; it involves the human recognition of all that human beings can attain and of the way in which divinity is within human grasp. Ironically, the roots of Augustine's life of grace and dependence upon God lie in Aristotle's humanistic and naturalistic conception of the self-sufficient philosophical quest for divine knowledge and thereby for the good life.

Aristotle was born in 384 B.C.E., in Stagira, a small town in Chalcidice in northern Greece. His father, Nicomachus, was a physician in the court of Amyntas, king of Macedon, and a member of a guild devoted to Asclepius, the god of medicine. Although Nicomachus died when Aristotle was still very young, he had probably begun to teach his son something of Greek medicine and biology. These interests had a long-lasting impact on Aristotle.

In 367, at the age of seventeen, Aristotle made the most important move of his life. He left Stagira for Athens, where he became a member of Plato's intellectual and religious fellowship, the Academy. Plato was probably the most dominant intellectual influence on Aristotle throughout his life. He remained in the Academy—studying, teaching, lecturing, and writing—for twenty years, until Plato's death. It was during these years that Aristotle wrote a number of literary dialogues, in the Platonic style, among them the *Protrepticus* and the *Eudemus or On the Soul*, which deals with the separate existence and immortality of the soul. Only fragments of some of these dialogues exist today. It was in this period too that Aristotle tried out radically anti-Platonic views and strategies in works such as the *Categories*.

In 347 Aristotle left the Academy and Athens. Plato had died; his nephew Speusippus had been appointed to replace him, perhaps to keep the property in the family or perhaps for ideological reasons; and in 348 Philip of Macedon sacked the town of Olynthus, provoking a wave of anti-Macedonian feeling, spurred on by the oratory of Demosthenes and his supporters. Aristotle, with a few fellow philosophers, fled Athens, sailing east to the coast of Asia Minor and arriving at Atarneus, at the invitation of its ruler, Hermeias, who settled them in the town of Assos. After two or three years, Aristotle moved to Mytilene, near Lesbos, where he met Theophrastus, who was to become his most important companion and pupil. Aristotle also married Hermeias' niece, Pythias, who bore him two children, a daughter, Pythia, and a son, Nicomachus, after whom the *Nicomachean Ethics* is named.

Two years later, in 342, Aristotle accepted Philip's invitation to settle in Pella, capital of Macedonia, and later in the royal castle at Mieza, to tutor the king's thirteen-year-old son, Alexander. We know little concerning their relationship or about the content of Alexander's education. Subsequent events make it hard to believe that Aristotle taught Alexander anything about ethics or politics. Alexander was strongly committed to a blending of Greek and foreign cultures and conceived of a vast, disparate empire without the centrality of the *polis* (city-state); Aristotle would have differed on both matters. Aristotle is thought to have composed for Alexander a work on monarchy and one on colonies, but we know nothing of their content or influence on Alexander.

In 340 Alexander was made regent, and Aristotle probably settled in Stagira until Philip's death, in 335, when he returned to Athens. The next dozen years were the richest and most productive of Aristotle's life. First, he sought to establish his own school or fellowship (*thiasos*), the Lyceum, renting some buildings in a grove northeast of the city, a site sacred to Apollo Lyceius and, as tradition has it, a favorite spot of Socrates. Second, Aristotle engaged in a vast array of investigations. These were based on prior and ongoing research and the collection of data, views, and positions, conducted by himself and his associates. He lectured, taught, and cultivated an environment of study that yielded writings on biology, logic, rhetoric, physics, metaphysics, ethics, politics, the arts, and more. Only twenty per cent of this output remains, but it is sufficient to establish Aristotle as a giant of Western intellectual culture.

In 323 Alexander died. Once again anti-Macedonian feeling erupted in Athens, and Aristotle saw charges of impiety fabricated against him. He fled to Chalcis, in Euboea, "to save the Athenians," as he put it, "from sinning twice against philosophy." There he died a year later, at the age of sixty-two. Diogenes Laertius, the third-century doxographer, preserves his will, in which he arranges his affairs and those of his family with sensitivity, kindness, and generosity. It is a rare opportunity to glimpse the humanity that existed so delicately alongside an incomparable, unrelenting intellect and an all-consuming desire for knowledge.

It is hard to understand with any depth the concrete person whose life spanned these turbulent years. This much, however, is clear, that Aristotle's life and his thinking were joined in an attempt to live the best life possible for a human being.

This is the life that he examines, defends, and endorses in his great ethical and political works, especially the *Nicomachean Ethics* and the *Politics*. There he locates the core of human life in the enrichment of our character; there he associates this goal of *eudaimonia* (human flourishing or well-being) with the functioning of soul at its highest level, the level of reason; and there he explores how reason functions, together with desire, pleasure, deliberation, and decision, in everyday life and in the life of inquiry and contemplation. Moreover, the good life is the object of our most important and strongest desire, and the political is the context of associations and structures best suited to enable its achievement.

Aristotle's account rises out of a tradition of natural philosophy in the fifth and fourth centuries; it attempts to unite religious, scientific, and moral aspiration in such a way that human life in fourth-century Greece is seen to take on meaning and purpose. Later, in the Middle Ages and in the modern world, Aristotle's theory loosed itself from the ancient *polis* and found new adherents who agreed with Aristotle that moral character is a complex interplay of rational judgement, deliberation, desire, decision, community, law, and much else. Whether this conception of moral character and the good life could be freed from Aristotelian science and its teleological order was and is a difficult question. But it does nothing to discredit Aristotle's own attempt to practice philosophy and thereby to articulate and to live the best life possible for human beings.

Recommended readings

Barker, Ernest. *The Politics of Aristotle*. Oxford: Oxford University Press, 1946.

Barnes, J., M. Schofield, and R. Sorabji (eds.). *Articles on Aristotle*. Vol. 2. *Ethics and Politics*. London: Duckworth, 1977.

Broadie, Sarah. *Ethics with Aristotle*. Oxford: Oxford University Press, 1991.

Cooper, John. *Reason and Human Good in Aristotle*. Cambridge: Harvard University Press, 1975; Hackett, 1986.

Hardie, W.F.R. *Aristotle's Ethical Theory*. 2nd ed. Oxford: Oxford University Press, 1980.

Irwin, T. H. *Aristotle's First Principles*. Oxford: Oxford University Press, 1988.

Keyt, David, and Fred Miller (eds.). *Essays on Aristotle's Politics*. Oxford: Blackwell's, 1991.

Kraut, Richard. *Aristotle on the Human Good*. Princeton: Princeton University Press, 1989.

Moravcsik, J. (ed.). *Aristotle*. Garden City: Doubleday, 1967.

Mulgan, R. G. *Aristotle's Political Theory*. Oxford: Oxford University Press, 1977.

Nussbaum, Martha C. *The Fragility of Goodness*. Cambridge: Cambridge University Press, 1986.

Okin, Susan Moller. *Women in Western Political Thought*. Princeton: Princeton University Press, 1979.

Reeve, C.D.C. *Aristotle's Ethics*. Oxford: Oxford University Press, (forthcoming).

Rorty, A. O. (ed.). *Essays on Aristotle's Ethics*. Berkeley: University of California Press, 1980.

Sherman, N. *The Fabric of Character*. Oxford: Oxford University Press, 1988.

NICOMACHEAN ETHICS

BOOK ONE

1

Every craft and every investigation, and likewise every action and decision, seems   1094a
to aim at some good; hence the good has been well described as that at which
everything aims.

However, there is an apparent difference among the ends aimed at. For the end
is sometimes an activity, sometimes a product beyond the activity; and when there   5
is an end beyond the action, the product is by nature better than the activity.

Since there are many actions, crafts and sciences, the ends turn out to be many as
well; for health is the end of medicine, a boat of boatbuilding, victory of generalship,
and wealth of household management.   10

But whenever any of these sciences are subordinate to some one capacity—as
e.g. bridlemaking and every other science producing equipment for horses are
subordinate to horsemanship, while this and every action in warfare are in turn
subordinate to generalship, and in the same way other sciences are subordinate to
further ones—in each of these the end of the ruling science is more choiceworthy   15
than all the ends subordinate to it, since it is the end for which those ends are also
pursued. And here it does not matter whether the ends of the actions are the
activities themselves, or some product beyond them, as in the sciences we have
mentioned.

2

Suppose, then, that (a) there is some end of the things we pursue in our actions
which we wish for because of itself, and because of which we wish for the other
things; and (b) we do not choose everything because of something else, since (c) if   20
we do, it will go on without limit, making desire empty and futile; then clearly (d)
this end will be the good, i.e. the best good.

Then surely knowledge of this good is also of great importance for the conduct
of our lives, and if, like archers, we have a target to aim at, we are more likely to hit
the right mark. If so, we should try to grasp, in outline at any rate, what the good   25
is, and which science or capacity is concerned with it.

It seems to concern the most controlling science, the one that, more than any
other, is the ruling science. And political science apparently has this character.

(1) For it is the one that prescribes which of the sciences ought to be studied in
cities, and which ones each class in the city should learn, and how far.   1094b

(2) Again, we see that even the most honoured capacities, e.g. generalship, household management and rhetoric, are subordinate to it.

Reprinted by permission of the translator, Terence Irwin, from Aristotle, *Nicomachean Ethics* (Indianapolis:
Hackett Publishing Company, 1985).

(3) Further, it uses the other sciences concerned with action, and moreover legislates what must be done and what avoided.

Hence its end will include the ends of the other sciences, and so will be the human
good.

[This is properly called political science;] for though admittedly the good is the
same for a city as for an individual, still the good of the city is apparently a greater
and more complete good to acquire and preserve. For while it is satisfactory to
acquire and preserve the good even for an individual, it is finer and more divine to
acquire and preserve it for a people and for cities. And so, since our investigation
aims at these [goods, for an individual and for a city], it is a sort of political science.

3

Our discussion will be adequate if its degree of clarity fits the subject-matter; for
we should not seek the same degree of exactness in all sorts of arguments alike, any
more than in the products of different crafts.

Moreover, what is fine and what is just, the topics of inquiry in political science,
differ and vary so much that they seem to rest on convention only, not on nature.
Goods, however, also vary in the same sort of way, since they cause harm to many
people; for it has happened that some people have been destroyed because of their
wealth, others because of their bravery.

Since these, then, are the sorts of things we argue from and about, it will be
satisfactory if we can indicate the truth roughly and in outline; since [that is to say]
we argue from and about what holds good usually [but not universally], it will be
satisfactory if we can draw conclusions of the same sort.

Each of our claims, then, ought to be accepted in the same way [as claiming to
hold good usually], since the educated person seeks exactness in each area to the
extent that the nature of the subject allows; for apparently it is just as mistaken
to demand demonstrations from a rhetorician as to accept [merely] persuasive
arguments from a mathematician.

Further, each person judges well what he knows, and is a good judge about that;
hence the good judge in a particular area is the person educated in that area, and
the unconditionally good judge is the person educated in every area.

This is why a youth is not a suitable student of political science; for he lacks
experience of the actions in life which political science argues from and about.

Moreover, since he tends to be guided by his feelings, his study will be futile and
useless; for its end is action, not knowledge. And here it does not matter whether
he is young in years or immature in character, since the deficiency does not depend
on age, but results from being guided in his life and in each of his pursuits by his
feelings; for an immature person, like an incontinent person, gets no benefit from
his knowledge.

If, however, we are guided by reason in forming our desires and in acting, then
this knowledge will be of great benefit.

These are the preliminary points about the student, about the way our claims are
to be accepted, and about what we intend to do.

4

Let us, then, begin again. Since every sort of knowledge and decision pursues some good, what is that good which we say is the aim of political science? What [in   15 other words] is the highest of all the goods pursued in action?

As far as its name goes, most people virtually agree [about what the good is], since both the many and the cultivated call it happiness, and suppose that living well and doing well are the same as being happy. But they disagree about what happiness is,   20 and the many do not give the same answer as the wise.

For the many think it is something obvious and evident, e.g. pleasure, wealth or honour, some thinking one thing, others another; and indeed the same person keeps changing his mind, since in sickness he thinks it is health, in poverty wealth. And when they are conscious of their own ignorance, they admire anyone who speaks of   25 something grand and beyond them.

[Among the wise,] however, some used to think that besides these many goods there is some other good that is something in itself, and also causes all these goods to be goods.

Presumably, then, it is rather futile to examine all these beliefs, and it is enough to examine those that are most current or seem to have some argument for them.   30

We must notice, however, the difference between arguments from origins and arguments towards origins. For indeed Plato was right to be puzzled about this, when he used to ask if [the argument] set out from the origins or led towards them— just as on a race course the path may go from the starting-line to the far end, or   1095b back again.

For while we should certainly begin from origins that are known, things are known in two ways; for some are known to us, some known unconditionally [but not necessarily known to us]. Presumably, then, the origin *we* should begin from is what is known to *us*.

This is why we need to have been brought up in fine habits if we are to be adequate   5 students of what is fine and just, and of political questions generally. For the origin we begin from is the belief that something is true, and if this is apparent enough to us, we will not, at this stage, need the reason why it is true in addition; and if we have this good upbringing, we have the origins to begin from, or can easily acquire them. Someone who neither has them nor can acquire them should listen to Hesiod:[1] 'He who understands everything himself is best of all; he is noble also who listens   10 to one who has spoken well; but he who neither understands it himself nor takes to heart what he hears from another is a useless man.'

5

But let us begin again from [the common beliefs] from which we digressed. For, it would seem, people quite reasonably reach their conception of the good, i.e. of   15

---

1. [Aristotle frequently quotes ancient sources, from Hesiod and Homer to Sophocles, Euripides, Epicharmus, and Simonides. For a comprehensive list of Aristotle's literary references see Terence Irwin, *Aristotle Nichomachean Ethics* (Hackett Publishing Company, 1985), 433–36.—M.L.M.]

17, 18   happiness, from the lives [they lead]; for there are roughly three most favoured
19, 16   lives—the lives of gratification, of political activity, and, third, of study.

17   The many, the most vulgar, would seem to conceive the good and happiness as
19   pleasure, and hence they also like the life of gratification. Here they appear com-
20   pletely slavish, since the life they decide on is a life for grazing animals; and yet they
       have some argument in their defence, since many in positions of power feel the
       same way as Sardanapallus[2] [and also choose this life].

           The cultivated people, those active [in politics], conceive the good as honour, since
       this is more or less the end [normally pursued] in the political life. This, however,
25   appears to be too superficial to be what we are seeking, since it seems to depend
       more on those who honour than on the one honoured, whereas we intuitively believe
       that the good is something of our own and hard to take from us.

           Further, it would seem, they pursue honour to convince themselves that they are
       good; at any rate, they seek to be honoured by intelligent people, among people
       who know them, and for virtue. It is clear, then, that in the view of active people at
30   least, virtue is superior [to honour].

           Perhaps, indeed, one might conceive virtue more than honour to be the end of
       the political life. However, this also is apparently too incomplete [to be the good].
       For, it seems, someone might possess virtue but be asleep or inactive throughout his
1096a life; or, further, he might suffer the worst evils and misfortunes; and if this is the
       sort of life he leads, no one would count him happy, except to defend a philosopher's
       paradox. Enough about this, since it has been adequately discussed in the popular
       works also.

5   The third life is the life of study, which we will examine in what follows.

           The money-maker's life is in a way forced on him [not chosen for itself]; and
       clearly wealth is not the good we are seeking, since it is [merely] useful, [choiceworthy
       only] for some other end. Hence one would be more inclined to suppose that [any
       of] the goods mentioned earlier is the end, since they are liked for themselves. But
10   apparently they are not [the end] either; and many arguments have been presented
       against them. Let us, then, dismiss them.

       6

           Presumably, though, we had better examine the universal good, and puzzle out
       what is meant in speaking of it. This sort of inquiry is, to be sure, unwelcome to us,
       when those who introduced the Forms were friends of ours; still, it presumably
15   seems better, indeed only right, to destroy even what is close to us if that is the way
       to preserve the truth. And we must especially do this when we are philosophers,
       [lovers of wisdom]; for though we love both the truth and our friends, piety requires
       us to honour the truth first.

           Those who introduced this view did not mean to produce an Idea for any [series]
       in which they spoke of prior and posterior [members]; that was why they did not
       mean to establish an Idea [of number] for [the series of] numbers. But the good is
20   spoken of both in the [category of] what-it-is [i.e. substance], and in [the categories

---

2. [An Assyrian king (669–626) who lived in legendary luxury.—T.I.]

of] quality and relative; and what is in itself, i.e. substance, is by nature prior to what is relative, since a relative would seem to be an appendage and coincident of being. And so there is no common Idea over these.

Further, good is spoken of in as many ways as being is spoken of. For it is spoken of in [the category of] what-it-is, as god and mind; in quality, as the virtues; in quantity, as the measured amount; in relative, as the useful; in time, as the opportune moment; in place, as the [right] situation; and so on. Hence it is clear that the good cannot be some common [nature of good things] that is universal and single; for if it were, it would be spoken of in only one of the categories, not in them all.   25

Further, if a number of things have a single Idea, there is also a single science of them; hence [if there were an Idea of Good] there would also be some single science of all goods. But in fact there are many sciences even of the goods under one category; for the science of the opportune moment, e.g. in war is generalship, in disease medicine. And similarly the science of the measured amount in food is medicine, in exertion gymnastics. [Hence there is no single science of the good, and so no Idea.]   30

One might be puzzled about what [the believers in Ideas] really mean in speaking of The So-and-So Itself, since Man Itself and man have one and the same account of man; for in so far as each is man, they will not differ at all. If that is so, then [Good Itself and good have the same account of good]; hence they also will not differ at all in so far as each is good, [hence there is no point in appealing to Good Itself].   35
            1096b

Moreover, Good Itself will be no more of a good by being eternal; for a white thing is no whiter if it lasts a long time than if it lasts a day.   5

The Pythagoreans seemingly have a more plausible view about the good, since they place the One in the column of goods. Indeed, Speusippus[3] seems to have followed them. But let us leave this for another discussion.

A dispute emerges about what we have said: 'The arguments [in favour of the Idea] are not concerned with every sort of good. Goods pursued and liked in themselves are spoken of as one species of goods, while those that in some way tend to produce or preserve these goods, or to prevent their contraries, are spoken of as goods because of these and in a different way; clearly, then, goods are spoken of in two ways, and some are goods in themselves, others goods because of these. [And it is claimed only that there is a single Form for all goods in themselves.]'   10

Let us, then, separate the goods in themselves from the [merely] useful goods, and consider whether goods in themselves are spoken of in correspondence to a single Idea.   15

Well, what sorts of goods may be regarded as goods in themselves? (a) Perhaps they are those that are pursued even on their own, e.g. intelligence, seeing, some types of pleasures, and honours; for even if we also pursue these because of something else, they may still be regarded as goods in themselves. (b) Or perhaps nothing except the Idea is good in itself.   20

[If (b) is true], then the Form will be futile, [since it will not explain the goodness of anything. But if (a) is true], then, since these other things are also goods in themselves, the same account of good will have to turn up in all of them, just as the

---

3. [Plato's nephew; succeeded Plato in 347 as head of the Academy.—M.L.M.]

same account of whiteness turns up in snow and in chalk. In fact, however, honour,
25   intelligence and pleasure have different and dissimilar accounts, precisely in so far
        as they are goods. Hence the good is not something common which corresponds to
        a single Idea.

But how after all, then, is good spoken of? For [these goods have different
accounts, i.e. are homonymous, and yet] are seemingly not homonymous by mere
chance. Perhaps they are homonymous by all being derived from a single source,
or by all referring to a single focus. Or perhaps instead they are homonymous by
analogy; for example, as sight is to body, so understanding is to soul, and so on for
other cases.

30   Presumably, though, we should leave these questions for now, since their exact
treatment is more appropriate for another [branch of] philosophy. And the same is
true about the Idea. For even if the good predicated in common is some single thing,
or something separated, itself in itself, clearly it is not the sort of good a human
35   being can pursue in action or possess; but that is just the sort we are looking for in
our present inquiry.

'But,' it might seem to some, 'it is better to get to know the Idea with a view to the
1097a   goods that we can possess and pursue in action; for if we have this as a sort of
pattern, we shall also know better about the goods that are goods for us, and if we
know about them, we shall hit on them.'

This argument does indeed have some plausibility, but it would seem to clash with
5   the sciences. For each of these, though it aims at some good and seeks to supply
what is lacking, proceeds without concern for knowledge of the Idea; and if the
Idea were such an important aid, surely it would not be reasonable for all craftsmen
to be ignorant and not even to look for it.

Moreover, it is a puzzle to know what the weaver or carpenter will gain for his
10   own craft from knowing this Good Itself, or how anyone will be better at medicine
or generalship from having gazed on the Idea Itself. For what the doctor appears
to consider is not even health [universally, let alone good universally], but human
beings' health, and even more than that, presumably, this human being's health,
since it is particular patients he treats.

So much, then, for these questions.

7

15   But let us return once again to the good we are looking for, and consider just
what it could be, since it is apparently one thing in one action or craft, and another
thing in another; for it is one thing in medicine, another in generalship, and so on
for the rest.

What, then, is the good in each of these cases? Surely it is that for the sake of
which the other things are done; and in medicine this is health, in generalship
20   victory, in housebuilding a house, in another case something else, but in every action
and decision it is the end, since it is for the sake of the end that everyone does the
other things.

And so, if there is some end of everything that is pursued in action, this will be
the good pursued in action; and if there are more ends than one, these will be the
goods pursued in action.

Our argument has progressed, then, to the same conclusion [as before, that the highest end is the good]; but we must try to clarify this still more.   25

Though apparently there are many ends, we choose some of them, e.g. wealth, flutes and, in general, instruments, because of something else; hence it is clear that not all ends are complete. But the best good is apparently something complete. Hence, if only one end is complete, this will be what we are looking for; and if more than one are complete, the most complete of these will be what we are looking for.   30

An end pursued in itself, we say, is more complete than an end pursued because of something else; and an end that is never choiceworthy because of something else is more complete than ends that are choiceworthy both in themselves and because of this end; and hence an end that is always [choiceworthy, and also] choiceworthy in itself, never because of something else, is unconditionally complete.

Now happiness more than anything else seems unconditionally complete, since we always [choose it, and also] choose it because of itself, never because of something   1097b
else.

Honour, pleasure, understanding and every virtue we certainly choose because of themselves, since we would choose each of them even if it had no further result, but we also choose them for the sake of happiness, supposing that through them we   5
shall be happy. Happiness, by contrast, no one ever chooses for their sake, or for the sake of anything else at all.

The same conclusion [that happiness is complete] also appears to follow from self-sufficiency, since the complete good seems to be self-sufficient.

Now what we count as self-sufficient is not what suffices for a solitary person by himself, living an isolated life, but what suffices also for parents, children, wife and   10
in general for friends and fellow-citizens, since a human being is a naturally political [animal]. Here, however, we must impose some limit; for if we extend the good to parents' parents and children's children and to friends of friends, we shall go on without limit; but we must examine this another time.

Anyhow, we regard something as self-sufficient when all by itself it makes a life choiceworthy and lacking nothing; and that is what we think happiness does.   15

Moreover, we think happiness is most choiceworthy of all goods, since it is not counted as one good among many. If it were counted as one among many, then, clearly, we think that the addition of the smallest of goods would make it more choiceworthy; for [the smallest good] that is added becomes an extra quantity of goods [so creating a good larger than the original good], and the larger of two goods is always more choiceworthy. [But we do not think any addition can make happiness more choiceworthy; hence it is most choiceworthy.]   20

Happiness, then, is apparently something complete and self-sufficient, since it is the end of the things pursued in action.

But presumably the remark that the best good is happiness is apparently something [generally] agreed, and what we miss is a clearer statement of what the best good is.

Well, perhaps we shall find the best good if we first find the function of a human being. For just as the good, i.e. [doing] well, for a flautist, a sculptor, and every   25
craftsman, and, in general, for whatever has a function and [characteristic] action, seems to depend on its function, the same seems to be true for a human being, if a human being has some function.

30 Then do the carpenter and the leatherworker have their functions and actions, while a human being has none, and is by nature idle, without any function? Or, just as eye, hand, foot and, in general, every [bodily] part apparently has its functions, may we likewise ascribe to a human being some function besides all of theirs?

1098a What, then, could this be? For living is apparently shared with plants, but what we are looking for is the special function of a human being; hence we should set aside the life of nutrition and growth. The life next in order is some sort of life of sense-perception; but this too is apparently shared, with horse, ox and every animal. The remaining possibility, then, is some sort of life of action of the [part of the soul] that has reason.

5 Now this [part has two parts, which have reason in different ways], one as obeying the reason [in the other part], the other as itself having reason and thinking. [We intend both.] Moreover, life is also spoken of in two ways [as capacity and as activity], and we must take [a human being's special function to be] life as activity, since this seems to be called life to a fuller extent.

(a) We have found, then, that the human function is the soul's activity that expresses reason [as itself having reason] or requires reason [as obeying reason]. (b) Now the function of F, e.g. of a harpist, is the same in kind, so we say, as the function
10 of an excellent F, e.g. an excellent harpist. (c) The same is true unconditionally in every case, when we add to the function the superior achievement that expresses the virtue; for a harpist's function, e.g. is to play the harp, and a good harpist's is to do it well. (d) Now we take the human function to be a certain kind of life, and take this life to be the soul's activity and actions that express reason. (e) [Hence by (c) and (d)] the excellent man's function is to do this finely and well. (f) Each function
15 is completed well when its completion expresses the proper virtue. (g) Therefore [by (d), (e) and (f)] the human good turns out to be the soul's activity that expresses virtue.

And if there are more virtues than one, the good will express the best and most complete virtue. Moreover, it will be in a complete life. For one swallow does not
20 make a spring, nor does one day; nor, similarly, does one day or a short time make us blessed and happy.

This, then, is a sketch of the good; for, presumably, the outline must come first, to be filled in later. If the sketch is good, then anyone, it seems, can advance and articulate it, and in such cases time is a good discoverer or [at least] a good co-
25 worker. That is also how the crafts have improved, since anyone can add what is lacking [in the outline].

However, we must also remember our previous remarks, so that we do not look for the same degree of exactness in all areas, but the degree that fits the subject-matter in each area and is proper to the investigation. For the carpenter's and the
30 geometer's inquiries about the right angle are different also; the carpenter's is confined to the right angle's usefulness for his work, whereas the geometer's concerns what, or what sort of thing, the right angle is, since he studies the truth. We must do the same, then, in other areas too, [seeking the proper degree of exactness], so that digressions do not overwhelm our main task.

1098b Nor should we make the same demand for an explanation in all cases. Rather, in some cases it is enough to prove that something is true without explaining why it is true. This is so, e.g. with origins, where the fact that something is true is the first principle, i.e. the origin.

Some origins are studied by means of induction, some by means of perception, some by means of some sort of habituation, and others by other means. In each case we should try to find them out by means suited to their nature, and work hard to define them well. For they have a great influence on what follows; for the origin seems to be more than half the whole, and makes evident the answer to many of our questions.

8

However, we should examine the origin not only from the conclusion and premises [of a deductive argument], but also from what is said about it; for all the facts harmonize with a true account, whereas the truth soon clashes with a false one.

Goods are divided, then, into three types, some called external, some goods of the soul, others goods of the body; and the goods of the soul are said to be goods to the fullest extent and most of all, and the soul's actions and activities are ascribed to the soul. Hence the account [of the good] is sound, to judge by this belief anyhow—and it is an ancient belief agreed on by philosophers.

Our account is also correct in saying that some sort of actions and activities are the end; for then the end turns out to be a good of the soul, not an external good.

The belief that the happy person lives well and does well in action also agrees with our account, since we have virtually said that the end is a sort of living well and doing well in action.

Further, all the features that people look for in happiness appear to be true of the end described in our account. For to some people it seems to be virtue; to others intelligence; to others some sort of wisdom; to others again it seems to be these, or one of these, involving pleasure or requiring its addition; and others add in external prosperity as well.

Some of these views are traditional, held by many, while others are held by a few reputable men; and it is reasonable for each group to be not entirely in error, but correct on one point at least, or even on most points.

First, our account agrees with those who say happiness is virtue [in general] or some [particular] virtue; for activity expressing virtue is proper to virtue. Presumably, though, it matters quite a bit whether we suppose that the best good consists in possessing or in using, i.e. in a state or in an activity [that actualizes the state]. For while someone may be in a state that achieves no good, if, e.g., he is asleep or inactive in some other way, this cannot be true of the activity; for it will necessarily do actions and do well in them. And just as Olympic prizes are not for the finest and strongest, but for contestants, since it is only these who win; so also in life [only] the fine and good people who act correctly win the prize.

Moreover, the life of these [active] people is also pleasant in itself. For being pleased is a condition of the soul, [hence included in the activity of the soul]. Further, each type of person finds pleasure in whatever he is called a lover of, so that a horse, e.g. pleases the horse-lover, a spectacle the lover of spectacles, and similarly what is just pleases the lover of justice, and in general what expresses virtue pleases the lover of virtue. Hence the things that please most people conflict, because they are not pleasant by nature, whereas the things that please lovers of what is fine are

things pleasant by nature; and actions expressing virtue are pleasant in this way;
15   and so they both please lovers of what is fine and are pleasant in themselves.

Hence their life does not need pleasure to be added [to virtuous activity] as some
sort of ornament; rather, it has its pleasure within itself. For besides the reasons
already given, someone who does not enjoy fine actions is not good; for no one
would call him just, e.g., if he did not enjoy doing just actions, or generous if he did
20   not enjoy generous actions, and similarly for the other virtues. If this is so, then
actions expressing the virtues are pleasant in themselves.

Moreover, these actions are good and fine as well as pleasant; indeed, they are
good, fine and pleasant more than anything else, since on this question the excellent
person has good judgment, and his judgment agrees with our conclusions.

Happiness, then, is best, finest and most pleasant, and these three features are
25   not distinguished in the way suggested by the Delian inscription: 'What is most just
is finest; being healthy is most beneficial; but it is most pleasant to win our heart's
desire.' For all three features are found in the best activities, and happiness we say
30   is these activities, or [rather] one of them, the best one.

Nonetheless, happiness evidently also needs external goods to be added [to the
activity], as we said, since we cannot, or cannot easily, do fine actions if we lack the
resources.

1099b   For, first of all, in many actions we use friends, wealth and political power just as
we use instruments. Further, deprivation of certain [externals]—e.g. good birth,
good children, beauty—mars our blessedness; for we do not altogether have the
character of happiness if we look utterly repulsive or are ill-born, solitary or childless,
5   and have it even less, presumably, if our children or friends are totally bad, or were
good but have died.

And so, as we have said, happiness would seem to need this sort of prosperity
added also; that is why some people identify happiness with good fortune, while
others [reacting from one extreme to the other] identify it with virtue.

9

This [question about the role of fortune] raises a puzzle: Is happiness acquired
10   by learning, or habituation, or by some other form of cultivation? Or is it the result
of some divine fate, or even of fortune?

First, then, if the gods give any gift at all to human beings, it is reasonable for
them to give happiness also; indeed, it is reasonable to give happiness more than
any other human [good], in so far as it is the best of human [goods]. Presumably,
however, this question is more suitable for a different inquiry.

15   But even if it is not sent by the gods, but instead results from virtue and some sort
of learning or cultivation, happiness appears to be one of the most divine things,
since the prize and goal of virtue appears to be the best good, something divine and
blessed.

Moreover [if happiness comes in this way] it will be widely shared; for anyone who
is not deformed [in his capacity] for virtue will be able to achieve happiness through
20   some sort of learning and attention.

And since it is better to be happy in this way than because of fortune, it is reasonable for this to be the way [we become] happy. For whatever is natural is naturally in the finest state possible, and so are the products of crafts and of every other cause, especially the best cause; and it would be seriously inappropriate to entrust what is greatest and finest to fortune.

The answer to our question is also evident from our account [of happiness]. For we have said it is a certain sort of activity of the soul expressing virtue, [and hence not a product of fortune]; and some of the other goods are necessary conditions [of happiness], others are naturally useful and cooperative as instruments [but are not parts of it].   25

Further, this conclusion agrees with our opening remarks. For we took the goal of political science to be the best good; and most of its attention is devoted to the character of the citizens, to make them good people who do fine actions, [which is reasonable if happiness depends on virtue, not on fortune].   30

It is not surprising, then, that we regard neither ox nor horse nor any other kind of animal as happy, since none of them can share in this sort of activity. And for the same reason a child is not happy either, since his age prevents him from doing these sorts of actions; and if he is called happy, he is being congratulated because of anticipated blessedness, since, as we have said, happiness requires both complete virtue and a complete life.   1100a

[Happiness needs a complete life.] For life includes many reversals of fortune, good and bad, and the most prosperous person may fall into a terrible disaster in old age, as the Trojan stories tell us about Priam; but if someone has suffered these sorts of misfortunes and comes to a miserable end, no one counts him happy.   5

10

Then should we count no human being happy during his lifetime, but follow Solon's[4] advice to wait to see the end? And if we should hold that, can he really be happy during the time after he has died? Surely that is completely absurd, especially when we say happiness is an activity.   10

We do not say, then, that someone is happy during the time he is dead, and Solon's point is not this [absurd one], but rather that when a human being has died, we can safely pronounce [that he was] blessed [before he died], on the assumption that he is now finally beyond evils and misfortunes.   15

Still, even this claim is disputable. For if a living person has good or evil of which he is not aware, then a dead person also, it seems, has good or evil when, e.g., he receives honours or dishonours, and his children, and descendants in general, do well or suffer misfortune. [Hence, apparently, what happens after his death can affect whether or not he was happy before his death.]   20

However, this view also raises a puzzle. For even if someone has lived in blessedness until old age, and has died appropriately, many fluctuations of his descendants' fortunes may still happen to him; for some may be good people and get the life they deserve, while the contrary may be true of others, and clearly they may be as distantly related to their ancestor as you please. Surely, then, it would be an absurd result if   25

4. [Important Athenian statesman and sage about 600; when he saw the vast wealth of Croesus, king of Lydia, Solon refused to call him the happiest man until he saw how his life ended.—M.L.M.]

the dead person's condition changed along with the fortunes of his descendants, so that at one time he became happy [in his lifetime] and at another time miserable.
30   But it would also be absurd if the condition of descendants did not affect their ancestors at all or for any length of time.

But we must return to the previous puzzle, since that will perhaps also show us the answer to our present question.

If, then, we must wait to see the end, and must then count someone blessed, not as being blessed [during the time he is dead] but because he previously was blessed,
35   surely it is absurd if at the time when he is happy we will not truly ascribe to him the happiness he has.

1100b [We hesitate] out of reluctance to call him happy during his lifetime, because of the variations, and because we suppose happiness is enduring and definitely not prone to fluctuate, whereas the same person's fortunes often turn to and fro. For
5   clearly, if we are guided by his fortunes, so that we often call him happy and then miserable again, we will be representing the happy person as a kind of chameleon, insecurely based.

But surely it is quite wrong to be guided by someone's fortunes. For his doing well or badly does not rest on them; though a human life, as we said, needs these added,
10   it is the activities expressing virtue that control happiness, and the contrary activities that control its contrary.

Indeed, the present puzzle is further evidence for our account [of happiness]. For no human achievement has the stability of activities that express virtue, since these seem to be more enduring even than our knowledge of the sciences; and the most
15   honourable of the virtues themselves are more enduring [than the others] because blessed people devote their lives to them more fully and more continually than to anything else—for this [continual activity] would seem to be the reason we do not forget them.

It follows, then, that the happy person has the [stability] we are looking for and keeps the character he has throughout his life. For always, or more than anything
20   else, he will do and study the actions expressing virtue, and will bear fortunes most finely, in every way and in all conditions appropriately, since he is truly 'good, foursquare and blameless'.

However, many events are matters of fortune, and some are smaller, some greater.
25   Hence, while small strokes of good or ill fortune clearly will not influence his life, many great strokes of good fortune will make it more blessed, since in themselves they naturally add adornment to it, and his use of them proves to be fine and excellent. Conversely, if they are great misfortunes, they oppress and spoil his
30   blessedness, since they involve pain and impede many activities.

And yet, even here what is fine shines through, whenever someone bears many severe misfortunes with good temper, not because he feels no distress, but because he is noble and magnanimous.

And since it is activities that control life, as we said, no blessed person could ever
35   become miserable, since he will never do hateful and base actions. For a truly good
1101a and intelligent person, we suppose, will bear strokes of fortune suitably, and from his resources at any time will do the finest actions, just as a good general will make
5   the best use of his forces in war, and a good shoemaker will produce the finest shoe from the hides given him, and similarly for all other craftsmen.

If this is so, then the happy person could never become miserable. Still, he will not be blessed either, if he falls into misfortunes as bad as Priam's. Nor, however, will he be inconstant and prone to fluctuate, since he will neither be easily shaken from his happiness nor shaken by just any misfortunes. He will be shaken from it, though, by many serious misfortunes, and from these a return to happiness will take no short time; at best, it will take a long and complete length of time that includes great and fine successes. 10

Then why not say that the happy person is the one who expresses complete virtue in his activities, with an adequate supply of external goods, not for just any time but for a complete life? Or should we add that he will also go on living this way and will come to an appropriate end? 15

The future is not apparent to us, and we take happiness to be the end, and altogether complete in every way; hence we will say that a living person who has, and will keep, the goods we mentioned is blessed, but blessed as a human being is. So much for a determination of this question. 20

11

Still, it is apparently rather unfriendly and contrary to the [common] beliefs to claim that the fortunes of our descendants and all our friends contribute nothing. But since they can find themselves in many and various circumstances, some of which affect us more, some less, it is apparently a long, indeed endless, task to differentiate all the particular cases, and perhaps a general outline will be enough of an answer. 25

Misfortunes, then, even to the person himself, differ, and some have a certain weight and influence on his life, while others would seem to be lighter. The same is true for the misfortunes of his friends; and it matters whether they happen to living or to dead people—much more than it matters whether lawless and terrible crimes are committed before a tragic drama begins or in the course of it. In our reasoning, then, we should also take account of this difference, and even more, presumably, of the puzzle about whether the dead share in any good or evil. 30

35
1101b

For if we consider this, anything good or evil penetrating to the dead would seem to be weak and unimportant, either unconditionally or for them; and even if it is not, still its size and character are not enough to make people happy who are not happy, or to take away the blessedness of those who are happy. And so, when friends do well, and likewise when they do badly, it appears to contribute something to the dead, but of a character and size that neither makes happy people not happy nor anything else of this sort. 5

12

Now that we have determined these points, let us consider whether happiness is something praiseworthy, or instead something honourable; for clearly it is not a capacity [which is neither praiseworthy nor honourable]. 10

Whatever is praiseworthy appears to be praised for its character and its state in relation to something. We praise, e.g., the just and the brave person, and in general the good person and virtue, for their actions and achievements; and we praise the 15 strong person, the good runner and each of the others because he naturally has a certain character and is in a certain state in relation to something good and excellent. This is clear also from praises of the gods; for these praises appear ridiculous because they are referred to us, but they are referred to us because, as we said, praise depends on such a reference.

If praise is for these sorts of things, then clearly for the best things there is no praise, but something greater and better. And indeed this is how it appears. For the gods and the most godlike of men are [not praised, but] congratulated for their blessedness and happiness. And the same is true of goods; for we never praise happiness, as we praise justice, but count it blessed, as something better and more godlike [than anything that is praised].

Indeed, Eudoxus[5] seems to have used the correct argument for the victory of pleasure. By not praising pleasure though it is a good, we indicate, so he thought, that it is superior to everything praiseworthy; and [only] the god and the good have this superiority since the other goods are [praised] by reference to them.

[Here he seems to have argued correctly.] For praise is given to virtue, since it makes us do fine actions; but celebrations are for [successful] achievements, either of body or of soul. But an exact treatment of this is presumably more proper for specialists in celebrations. For us, anyhow, it is clear from what has been said that happiness is something honourable and complete.

A further reason why this would seem to be correct is that happiness is an origin; for the origin is what we all aim at in all our other actions; and we take the origin and cause of goods to be something honourable and divine.

13

Since happiness is an activity of the soul expressing complete virtue, we must examine virtue; for that will perhaps also be a way to study happiness better.

Moreover, the true politician seems to have spent more effort on virtue than on anything else, since he wants to make the citizens good and law-abiding. We find an example of this in the Spartan and Cretan legislators and in any others with their concerns. Since, then, the examination of virtue is proper for political science, the inquiry clearly suits our original decision [to pursue political science].

It is clear that the virtue we must examine is human virtue, since we are also seeking the human good and human happiness. And by human virtue we mean virtue of the soul, not of the body, since we also say that happiness is an activity of the soul. If this is so, then it is clear that the politician must acquire some knowledge about the soul, just as someone setting out to heal the eyes must acquire knowledge about the whole body as well. This is all the more true to the extent that political science is better and more honourable than medicine—and even among doctors the cultivated ones devote a lot of effort to acquiring knowledge about the body. Hence the politician as well [as the student of nature] must study the soul.

But he must study it for the purpose [of inquiring into virtue], as far as suffices for what he seeks; for a more exact treatment would presumably take more effort

5. [Famous mathematician and member of Plato's academy.—M.L.M.]

than his purpose requires. [We] have discussed the soul sufficiently [for our purposes] in [our] popular works as well [as our less popular], and we should use this discussion.

We have said, e.g., that one [part] of the soul is nonrational, while one has reason. Are these distinguished as parts of a body and everything divisible into parts are? Or are they two only in account, and inseparable by nature, as the convex and the concave are in a surface? It does not matter for present purposes.

Consider the nonrational [part]. One [part] of it, i.e. the cause of nutrition and growth, is seemingly plant-like and shared [with other living things]: for we can ascribe this capacity of the soul to everything that is nourished, including embryos, and the same one to complete living things, since this is more reasonable than to ascribe another capacity to them.

Hence the virtue of this capacity is apparently shared, not [specifically] human. For this part and capacity more than others seem to be active in sleep, and here the good and the bad person are least distinct, which is why happy people are said to be no better off than miserable people for half their lives.

And this lack of distinction is not surprising, since sleep is inactivity of the soul in so far as it is called excellent or base, unless to some small extent some movements penetrate [to our awareness], and in this way the decent person comes to have better images [in dreams] than just any random person has. Enough about this, however, and let us leave aside the nutritive part, since by nature it has no share in human virtue.

Another nature in the soul would also seem to be nonrational, though in a way it shares in reason.

[Clearly it is nonrational.] For in the continent and the incontinent person we praise their reason, i.e. the [part] of the soul that has reason, because it exhorts them correctly and towards what is best; but they evidently also have in them some other [part] that is by nature something besides reason, conflicting and struggling with reason.

For just as paralysed parts of a body, when we decide to move them to the right, do the contrary and move off to the left, the same is true of the soul; for incontinent people have impulses in contrary directions. In bodies, admittedly, we see the part go astray, whereas we do not see it in the soul; nonetheless, presumably, we should suppose that the soul also has a [part] besides reason, contrary to and countering reason. The [precise] way it is different does not matter.

However, this [part] as well [as the rational part] appears, as we said, to share in reason. At any rate, in the continent person it obeys reason; and in the temperate and the brave person it presumably listens still better to reason, since there it agrees with reason in everything.

The nonrational [part], then, as well [as the whole soul] apparently has two parts. For while the plant-like [part] shares in reason not at all, the [part] with appetites and in general desires shares in reason in a way, in so far as it both listens to reason and obeys it.

It listens in the way in which we are said to 'listen to reason' from father or friends, not in the way in which we ['give the reason'] in mathematics.

The nonrational part also [obeys and] is persuaded in some way by reason, as is shown by chastening, and by every sort of reproof and exhortation.

30

1102b

5

10

15

20

25

30

1103a

If we ought to say, then, that this [part] also has reason, then the [part] that has reason, as well [as the nonrational part] will have two parts, one that has reason to the full extent by having it within itself, and another [that has it] by listening to reason as to a father.

The distinction between virtues also reflects this difference. For some virtues are called virtues of thought, other virtues of character; wisdom, comprehension and intelligence are called virtues of thought, generosity and temperance virtues of character.

For when we speak of someone's character we do not say that he is wise or has good comprehension, but that he is gentle or temperate. [Hence these are the virtues of character.] And yet, we also praise the wise person for his state, and the states that are praiseworthy are the ones we call virtues. [Hence wisdom is also a virtue.]

BOOK TWO

1

Virtue, then, is of two sorts, virtue of thought and virtue of character. Virtue of thought arises and grows mostly from teaching, and hence needs experience and time. Virtue of character [i.e. of *ēthos*] results from habit [*ethos*]; hence its name 'ethical', slightly varied from '*ethos*'.

Hence it is also clear that none of the virtues of character arises in us naturally.

For if something is by nature [in one condition], habituation cannot bring it into another condition. A stone, e.g., by nature moves downwards, and habituation could not make it move upwards, not even if you threw it up ten thousand times to habituate it; nor could habituation make fire move downwards, or bring anything that is by nature in one condition into another condition.

Thus the virtues arise in us neither by nature nor against nature. Rather, we are by nature able to acquire them, and reach our complete perfection through habit.

Further, if something arises in us by nature, we first have the capacity for it, and later display the activity. This is clear in the case of the senses; for we did not acquire them by frequent seeing or hearing, but already had them when we exercised them, and did not get them by exercising them.

Virtues, by contrast, we acquire, just as we acquire crafts, by having previously activated them. For we learn a craft by producing the same product that we must produce when we have learned it, becoming builders, e.g., by building and harpists by playing the harp; so also, then, we become just by doing just actions, temperate by doing temperate actions, brave by doing brave actions.

What goes on in cities is evidence for this also. For the legislator makes the citizens good by habituating them, and this is the wish of every legislator; if he fails to do it well he misses his goal. [The right] habituation is what makes the difference between a good political system and a bad one.

Further, just as in the case of a craft, the sources and means that develop each virtue also ruin it. For playing the harp makes both good and bad harpists, and it

is analogous in the case of builders and all the rest; for building well makes good   10
builders, building badly, bad ones. If it were not so, no teacher would be needed,
but everyone would be born a good or a bad craftsman.

It is the same, then, with the virtues. For actions in dealings with [other] human
beings make some people just, some unjust; actions in terrifying situations and the   15
acquired habit of fear or confidence make some brave and others cowardly. The
same is true of situations involving appetites and anger; for one or another sort
of conduct in these situations makes some people temperate and gentle, others   20
intemperate and irascible.

To sum up, then, in a single account: A state [of character] arises from [the
repetition of] similar activities. Hence we must display the right activities, since
differences in these imply corresponding differences in the states. It is not unimportant, then, to acquire one sort of habit or another, right from our youth; rather, it   25
is very important, indeed all-important.

2

Our present inquiry does not aim, as our others do, at study; for the purpose of
our examination is not to know what virtue is, but to become good, since otherwise
the inquiry would be of no benefit to us. Hence we must examine the right way to   30
act, since, as we have said, the actions also control the character of the states we
acquire.

First, then, actions should express correct reason. That is a common [belief], and
let us assume it; later we will say what correct reason is and how it is related to the
other virtues.

But let us take it as agreed in advance that every account of the actions we must   1104a
do has to be stated in outline, not exactly. As we also said at the start, the type of
accounts we demand should reflect the subject-matter; and questions about actions
and expediency, like questions about health, have no fixed [and invariable answers].

And when our general account is so inexact, the account of particular cases is all   5
the more inexact. For these fall under no craft or profession, and the agents themselves must consider in each case what the opportune action is, as doctors and
navigators do.

The account we offer, then, in our present inquiry is of this inexact sort; still, we   10
must try to offer help.

First, then, we should observe that these sorts of states naturally tend to be ruined
by excess and deficiency. We see this happen with strength and health, which we
mention because we must use what is evident as a witness to what is not. For both
excessive and deficient exercises ruin strength; and likewise, too much or too little   15
eating or drinking ruins health, while the proportionate amount produces, increases
and preserves it.

The same is true, then, of temperance, bravery and the other virtues. For if,
e.g., someone avoids and is afraid of everything, standing firm against nothing, he   20
becomes cowardly, but if he is afraid of nothing at all and goes to face everything,
he becomes rash. Similarly, if he gratifies himself with every pleasure and refrains
from none, he becomes intemperate, but if he avoids them all, as boors do, he

25   becomes some sort of insensible person. Temperance and bravery, then, are ruined by excess and deficiency but preserved by the mean.

The same actions, then, are the sources and causes both of the emergence and growth of virtues and of their ruin; but further, the activities of the virtues will be
30   found in these same actions. For this is also true of more evident cases, e.g. strength, which arises from eating a lot and from withstanding much hard labour, and it is the strong person who is most able to do these very things. It is the same with the virtues. Refraining from pleasures make us become temperate, and when we have
35   become temperate we are most able to refrain from pleasures. And it is similar with
1104b bravery; habituation in disdaining what is fearful and in standing firm against it makes us become brave, and when we have become brave we shall be most able to stand firm.

3

But [actions are not enough]; we must take as a sign of someone's state his pleasure
5   or pain in consequence of his action. For if someone who abstains from bodily pleasures enjoys the abstinence itself, then he is temperate, but if he is grieved by it, he is intemperate. Again, if he stands firm against terrifying situations and enjoys it, or at least does not find it painful, then he is brave, and if he finds it painful, he is cowardly.

[Pleasures and pains are appropriately taken as signs] because virtue of character is concerned with pleasures and pains.

10   (1) For it is pleasure that causes us to do base actions, and pain that causes us to abstain from fine ones. Hence we need to have had the appropriate upbringing— right from early youth, as Plato says—to make us find enjoyment or pain in the right things; for this is the correct education.

(2) Further, virtues are concerned with actions and feelings; but every feeling and
15   every action implies pleasure or pain; hence, for this reason too, virtue is concerned with pleasures and pains.

(3) Corrective treatment [for vicious actions] also indicates [the relevance of plea-sure and pain], since it uses pleasures and pains; it uses them because such correction is a form of medical treatment, and medical treatment naturally operates through contraries.

(4) Further, as we said earlier, every state of soul is naturally related to and
20   concerned with whatever naturally makes it better or worse; and pleasures and pains make people worse, from pursuing and avoiding the wrong ones, at the wrong time, in the wrong ways, or whatever other distinctions of that sort are needed in an account.

These [bad effects of pleasure and pain] are the reason why people actually define
25   the virtues as ways of being unaffected and undisturbed [by pleasures and pains]. They are wrong, however, because they speak [of being unaffected] unconditionally, not of being unaffected in the right or wrong way, at the right or wrong time, and the added specifications.

We assume, then, that virtue is the sort of state [with the appropriate specifications] that does the best actions concerned with pleasures and pains, and that vice is the

contrary. The following points will also make it evident that virtue and vice are
concerned with the same things.   30

(5) There are three objects of choice—fine, expedient and pleasant—and three
objects of avoidance—their contraries, shameful, harmful and painful. About all
these, then, the good person is correct and the bad person is in error, and especially   35
about pleasure. For pleasure is shared with animals, and implied by every object of   1105a
choice, since what is fine and what is expedient appear pleasant as well.

(6) Further, since pleasure grows up with all of us from infancy on, it is hard to
rub out this feeling that is dyed into our lives; and we estimate actions as well [as
feelings], some of us more, some less, by pleasure and pain. Hence, our whole   5
inquiry must be about these, since good or bad enjoyment or pain is very important
for our actions.

(7) Moreover, it is harder to fight pleasure than to fight emotion, [though that is
hard enough], as Heracleitus says. Now both craft and virtue are concerned in every
case with what is harder, since a good result is even better when it is harder. Hence,   10
for this reason also, the whole inquiry, for virtue and political science alike, must
consider pleasures and pains; for if we use these well, we shall be good, and if badly,
bad.

In short, virtue is concerned with pleasures and pains; the actions that are its
sources also increase it or, if they are done differently, ruin it; and its activity is   15
concerned with the same actions that are its sources.

4

However, someone might raise this puzzle: 'What do you mean by saying that to
become just we must first do just actions and to become temperate we must first do
temperate actions? For if we do what is grammatical or musical, we must already be
grammarians or musicians. In the same way, then, if we do what is just or temperate,   20
we must already be just or temperate.'

But surely this is not so even with the crafts, for it is possible to produce something
grammatical by chance or by following someone else's instructions. To be a grammarian, then, we must both produce something grammatical and produce it in the
way in which the grammarian produces it, i.e. expressing grammatical knowledge   25
that is in us.

Moreover, in any case what is true of crafts is not true of virtues. For the products
of a craft determine by their own character whether they have been produced well;
and so it suffices that they are in the right state when they have been produced. But
for actions expressing virtue to be done temperately or justly [and hence well] it
does not suffice that they are themselves in the right state. Rather, the agent must   30
also be in the right state when he does them. First, he must know [that he is
doing virtuous actions]; second, he must decide on them, and decide on them for
themselves; and, third, he must also do them from a firm and unchanging state.

As conditions for having a craft these three do not count, except for the knowing   1105b
itself. As a condition for having a virtue, however, the knowing counts for nothing,
or [rather] for only a little, whereas the other two conditions are very important,
indeed all-important. And these other two conditions are achieved by the frequent
doing of just and temperate actions.   5

Hence actions are called just or temperate when they are the sort that a just or temperate person would do. But the just and temperate person is not the one who [merely] does these actions, but the one who also does them in the way in which just or temperate people do them.

10   It is right, then, to say that a person comes to be just from doing just actions and temperate from doing temperate actions; for no one has even a prospect of becoming good from failing to do them.

The many, however, do not do these actions but take refuge in arguments, thinking that they are doing philosophy, and that this is the way to become excellent
15   people. In this they are like a sick person who listens attentively to the doctor, but acts on none of his instructions. Such a course of treatment will not improve the state of his body; any more than will the many's way of doing philosophy improve the state of their souls.

5

Next we must examine what virtue is. Since there are three conditions arising in
20   the soul—feelings, capacities and states—virtue must be one of these.

By feelings I mean appetite, anger, fear, confidence, envy, joy, love, hate, longing, jealousy, pity, in general whatever implies pleasure or pain.

By capacities I mean what we have when we are said to be capable of these
25   feelings—capable of, e.g., being angry or afraid or feeling pity.

By states I mean what we have when we are well or badly off in relation to feelings. If, e.g., our feeling is too intense or slack, we are badly off in relation to anger, but if it is intermediate, we are well off; and the same is true in the other cases.

30   First, then, neither virtues nor vices are feelings. (a) For we are called excellent or base in so far as we have virtues or vices, not in so far as we have feelings. (b) We are neither praised nor blamed in so far as we have feelings; for we do not praise the angry or the frightened person, and do not blame the person who is simply
1106a   angry, but only the person who is angry in a particular way. But we are praised or blamed in so far as we have virtues or vices. (c) We are angry and afraid without decision; but the virtues are decisions of some kind, or [rather] require decision. (d)
5   Besides, in so far as we have feelings, we are said to be moved; but in so far as we have virtues or vices, we are said to be in some condition rather than moved.

For these reasons the virtues are not capacities either; for we are neither called good nor called bad in so far as we are simply capable of feelings. Further, while we
10   have capacities by nature, we do not become good or bad by nature; we have discussed this before.

If, then, the virtues are neither feelings nor capacities, the remaining possibility is that they are states. And so we have said what the genus of virtue is.

6

But we must say not only, as we already have, that it is a state, but also what sort
15   of state it is.

It should be said, then, that every virtue causes its possessors to be in a good state and to perform their functions well; the virtue of eyes, e.g., makes the eyes and their functioning excellent, because it makes us see well; and similarly, the virtue of a horse makes the horse excellent, and thereby good at galloping, at carrying its rider   20 and at standing steady in the face of the enemy. If this is true in every case, then the virtue of a human being will likewise be the state that makes a human being good and makes him perform his function well.

We have already said how this will be true, and it will also be evident from our   25 next remarks, if we consider the sort of nature that virtue has.

In everything continuous and divisible we can take more, less and equal, and each of them either in the object itself or relative to us; and the equal is some intermediate between excess and deficiency.

By the intermediate in the object I mean what is equidistant from each extremity;   30 this is one and the same for everyone. But relative to us the intermediate is what is neither superfluous nor deficient; this is not one, and is not the same for everyone.

If, e.g., ten are many and two are few, we take six as intermediate in the object,   35 since it exceeds [two] and is exceeded [by ten] by an equal amount, [four]; this is what is intermediate by numerical proportion. But that is not how we must take the   1106b intermediate that is relative to us. For if, e.g., ten pounds [of food] are a lot for someone to eat, and two pounds a little, it does not follow that the trainer will prescribe six, since this might also be either a little or a lot for the person who is to take it—for Milo [the athlete] a little, but for the beginner in gymnastics a lot; and   5 the same is true for running and wrestling. In this way every scientific expert avoids excess and deficiency and seeks and chooses what is intermediate—but intermediate relative to us, not in the object.

This, then, is how each science produces its product well, by focusing on what is intermediate and making the product conform to that. This, indeed, is why people   10 regularly comment on well-made products that nothing could be added or sub- tracted, since they assume that excess or deficiency ruins a good [result] while the mean preserves it. Good craftsmen also, we say, focus on what is intermediate when they produce their product. And since virtue, like nature, is better and more exact   15 than any craft, it will also aim at what is intermediate.

By virtue I mean virtue of character; for this [pursues the mean because] it is concerned with feelings and actions, and these admit of excess, deficiency and an intermediate condition. We can be afraid, e.g., or be confident, or have appetites, or get angry, or feel pity, in general have pleasure or pain, both too much and too   20 little, and in both ways not well; but [having these feelings] at the right times, about the right things, towards the right people, for the right end, and in the right way, is the intermediate and best condition, and this is proper to virtue. Similarly, actions also admit of excess, deficiency and the intermediate condition.

Now virtue is concerned with feelings and actions, in which excess and deficiency   25 are in error and incur blame, while the intermediate condition is correct and wins praise, which are both proper features of virtue. Virtue, then, is a mean, in so far as it aims at what is intermediate.

Moreover, there are many ways to be in error, since badness is proper to what is unlimited, as the Pythagoreans pictured it, and good to what is limited; but there is   30 only one way to be correct. That is why error is easy and correctness hard, since it is easy to miss the target and hard to hit it. And so for this reason also excess and

35   deficiency are proper to vice, the mean to virtue; 'for we are noble in only one way, but bad in all sorts of ways.'

1107a   Virtue, then, is (a) a state that decides, (b) [consisting] in a mean, (c) the mean relative to us, (d) which is defined by reference to reason, (e) i.e., to the reason by reference to which the intelligent person would define it. It is a mean between two vices, one of excess and one of deficiency.

5   It is a mean for this reason also: Some vices miss what is right because they are deficient, others because they are excessive, in feelings or in actions, while virtue finds and chooses what is intermediate.

Hence, as far as its substance and the account stating its essence are concerned, virtue is a mean; but as far as the best [condition] and the good [result] are concerned, it is an extremity.

10   But not every action or feeling admits of the mean. For the names of some automatically include baseness, e.g. spite, shamelessness, envy [among feelings], and adultery, theft, murder, among actions. All of these and similar things are called by these names because they themselves, not their excesses or deficiencies, are base.

15   Hence in doing these things we can never be correct, but must invariably be in error. We cannot do them well or not well—e.g. by committing adultery with the right woman at the right time in the right way; on the contrary, it is true unconditionally that to do any of them is to be in error.

20   [To think these admit of a mean], therefore, is like thinking that unjust or cowardly or intemperate action also admits of a mean, an excess and a deficiency. For then there would be a mean of excess, a mean of deficiency, an excess of excess and a deficiency of deficiency.

Rather, just as there is no excess or deficiency of temperance or of bravery, since the intermediate is a sort of extreme [in achieving the good], so also there is no mean of these [vicious actions] either, but whatever way anyone does them, he is in

25   error. For in general there is no mean of excess or of deficiency, and no excess or deficiency of a mean.

7

30   However, we must not only state this general account but also apply it to the particular cases. For among accounts concerning actions, though the general ones are common to more cases, the specific ones are truer, since actions are about particular cases, and our account must accord with these. Let us, then, find these from the chart.

(1) First, in feelings of fear and confidence the mean is bravery. The excessively

1107b   fearless person is nameless (and in fact many cases are nameless), while the one who is excessively confident is rash; the one who is excessively afraid and deficient in confidence is cowardly.

5   (2) In pleasures and pains, though not in all types, and in pains less than in pleasures, the mean is temperance and the excess intemperance. People deficient in pleasure are not often found, which is why they also lack even a name; let us call them insensible.

(3) In giving and taking money the mean is generosity, the excess wastefulness

and the deficiency ungenerosity. Here the vicious people have contrary excesses and defects; for the wasteful person spends to excess and is deficient in taking, whereas the ungenerous person takes to excess and is deficient in spending. At the moment we are speaking in outline and summary, and that suffices; later we shall define these things more exactly.

(4) In questions of money there are also other conditions. Another mean is magnificence; for the magnificent person differs from the generous by being concerned with large matters, while the generous person is concerned with small. The excess is ostentation and vulgarity, and the deficiency niggardliness, and these differ from the vices related to generosity in ways we shall describe later.

(5) In honour and dishonour the mean is magnanimity, the excess something called a sort of vanity, and the deficiency pusillanimity.

(6) And just as we said that generosity differs from magnificence in its concern with small matters, similarly there is a virtue concerned with small honours, differing in the same way from magnanimity, which is concerned with great honours. For honour can be desired either in the right way or more or less than is right. If someone desires it to excess, he is called an honour-lover, and if his desire is deficient he is called indifferent to honour, but if he is intermediate he has no name. The corresponding conditions have no name either, except the condition of the honour-lover, which is called honour-loving.

This is why people at the extremes claim the intermediate area. Indeed, we also sometimes call the intermediate person an honour-lover, and sometimes call him indifferent to honour; and sometimes we praise the honour-lover, sometimes the person indifferent to honour. We will mention later the reason we do this; for the moment, let us speak of the other cases in the way we have laid down.

(7) Anger also admits of an excess, deficiency and mean. These are all practically nameless; but since we call the intermediate person mild, let us call the mean mildness. Among the extreme people let the excessive person be irascible, and the vice be irascibility, and let the deficient person be a sort of inirascible person, and the deficiency be inirascibility.

There are three other means, somewhat similar to one another, but different. For they are all concerned with association in conversations and actions, but differ in so far as one is concerned with truth-telling in these areas, the other two with sources of pleasure, some of which are found in amusement, and the others in daily life in general. Hence we should also discuss these states, so that we can better observe that in every case the mean is praiseworthy, while the extremes are neither praiseworthy nor correct, but blameworthy. Most of these cases are also nameless, and we must try, as in the other cases also, to make names ourselves, to make things clear and easy to follow.

(8) In truth-telling, then, let us call the intermediate person truthful, and the mean truthfulness; pretence that overstates will be boastfulness, and the person who has it boastful; pretence that understates will be self-deprecation, and the person who has it self-deprecating.

(9) In sources of pleasure in amusements let us call the intermediate person witty, and the condition wit; the excess buffoonery and the person who has it a buffoon; and the deficient person a sort of boor and the state boorishness.

(10) In the other sources of pleasure, those in daily life, let us call the person who

30 is pleasant in the right way friendly, and the mean state friendliness. If someone goes to excess with no [further] aim he will be ingratiating; if he does it for his own advantage, a flatterer. The deficient person, unpleasant in everything, will be a sort of quarrelsome and ill-tempered person.

(11) There are also means in feelings and concerned with feelings: shame, e.g., is not a virtue, but the person prone to shame as well as the virtuous person we have described receives praise. For here also one person is called intermediate, and another—the person excessively prone to shame, who is ashamed about every-

35 thing—is called excessive; the person who is deficient in shame or never feels shame at all is said to have no sense of disgrace; and the intermediate one is called prone

1108b to shame.

(12) Proper indignation is the mean between envy and spite; these conditions are concerned with pleasure and pain at what happens to our neighbours. For the properly indignant person feels pain when someone does well undeservedly; the

5 envious person exceeds him by feeling pain when anyone does well, while the spiteful person is so deficient in feeling pain that he actually enjoys [other people's misfortunes].

There will also be an opportunity elsewhere to speak of these [means that are not virtues].

We must consider justice after these other conditions, and, because it is not spoken of in one way only, we shall distinguish its two types and say how each of them is a mean.

10 Similarly, we must consider the virtues that belong to reason.

8

Among these three conditions, then, two are vices—one of excess, one of deficiency—and one—the mean—is virtue. In a way each of them is opposed to each of the others, since each extreme is contrary both to the intermediate condition and to the other extreme, while the intermediate is contrary to the extremes. For as the

15 equal is greater in comparison to the smaller, and smaller in comparison to the greater, so also the intermediate states are excessive in comparison to the deficiencies and deficient in comparison to the excesses—both in feelings and in actions.

20 For the brave person, e.g., appears rash in comparison to the coward, and cowardly in comparison to the rash person; similarly, the temperate person appears intemperate in comparison to the insensible person, and insensible in comparison with the intemperate person, and the generous person appears wasteful in comparison to the ungenerous, and ungenerous in comparison to the wasteful person. That is why each of the extreme people tries to push the intermediate person to the other

25 extreme, so that the coward, e.g., calls the brave person rash, and the rash person calls him a coward, and similarly in the other cases.

Because these conditions of soul are opposed to each other in these ways, the extremes are more contrary to each other than to the intermediate. For they are further from each other than from the intermediate, just as the large is further from

30 the small, and the small from the large, than either is from the equal.

Moreover, sometimes one extreme, e.g. rashness or wastefulness, appears somewhat like the intermediate state, e.g. bravery or generosity; but the extremes are

most unlike one another; and the things that are furthest apart from each other are
defined as contraries. Hence also the things that are further apart are more contrary.   35

In some cases the deficiency, in others the excess, is more opposed to the interme-   1109a
diate condition; e.g. it is cowardice, the deficiency, not rashness, the excess, that is
more opposed to bravery; on the other hand, it is intemperance, the excess, not
insensibility, the deficiency, that is more opposed to temperance. This happens for   5
two reasons.

One reason is derived from the object itself. Since sometimes one extreme is closer
and more similar to the intermediate condition, we oppose the contrary extreme,
more than this closer one, to the intermediate condition. Since rashness, e.g., seems
to be closer and more similar to bravery, and cowardice less similar, we oppose
cowardice more than rashness to bravery; for what is further from the intermediate   10
condition seems to be more contrary to it. This, then, is one reason, derived from
the object itself.

The other reason is derived from ourselves. For when we ourselves have some
natural tendency to one extreme more than the other, this extreme appears more
opposed to the intermediate condition; since, e.g., we have more of a natural tendency to pleasure, we drift more easily towards intemperance than towards orderli-   15
ness. Hence we say that an extreme is more contrary if we naturally develop more
in that direction; and this is why intemperance is more contrary to temperance,
since it is the excess.

9

We have said enough, then, to show that virtue of character is a mean and what   20
sort of mean it is; that it is a mean between two vices, one of excess and one of
deficiency; and that it is a mean because it aims at the intermediate condition in
feelings and actions.

Hence it is hard work to be excellent, since in each case it is hard work to find
what is intermediate; e.g. not everyone, but only one who knows, finds the midpoint   25
in a circle. So also getting angry, or giving and spending money, is easy and anyone
can do it; but doing it to the right person, in the right amount, at the right time, for
the right end, and in the right way is no longer easy, nor can everyone do it. Hence
[doing these things] well is rare, praiseworthy and fine.   30

Hence if we aim at the intermediate condition we must first of all steer clear of
the more contrary extreme, following the advice that Calypso also gives—'Hold the
ship outside the spray and surge.' For since one extreme is more in error, the other
less, and since it is hard to hit the intermediate extremely accurately, the second-
best tack, as they say, is to take the lesser of the evils. We shall succeed best in this   35
by the method we describe.   1109b

We must also examine what we ourselves drift into easily. For different people
have different natural tendencies towards different goals, and we shall come to
know our own tendencies from the pleasure or pain that arises in us. We must drag   5
ourselves off in the contrary direction; for if we pull far away from error, as they
do in straightening bent wood, we shall reach the intermediate condition.

And in everything we must beware above all of pleasure and its sources; for we
are already biased in its favour when we come to judge it. Hence we must react to

10   it as the elders reacted to Helen, and on each occasion repeat what they said; for if
we do this, and send it off, we shall be less in error.

In summary, then, if we do these things we shall best be able to reach the intermediate condition. But no doubt this is hard, especially in particular cases, since it is not
15   easy to define the way we should be angry, with whom, about what, for how long;
for sometimes, indeed, we ourselves praise deficient people and call them mild, and
sometimes praise quarrelsome people and call them manly. Still, we are not blamed
20   if we deviate a little in excess or deficiency from doing well, but only if we deviate
a long way, since then we are easily noticed.

But how far and how much we must deviate to be blamed is not easy to define in
an account; for nothing perceptible is easily defined, and [since] these [circumstances
of virtuous and vicious action] are particulars, the judgment about them depends
on perception.

All this makes it clear, then, that in every case the intermediate state is praised,
25   but we must sometimes incline towards the excess, sometimes towards the deficiency;
for that is the easiest way to succeed in hitting the intermediate condition and [doing]
well.

BOOK THREE

1

30   Virtue, then, is about feelings and actions. These receive praise or blame when
they are voluntary, but pardon, sometimes even pity, when they are involuntary.
Hence, presumably, in examining virtue we must define the voluntary and the
35   involuntary. This is also useful to legislators, both for honours and for corrective
treatments.

1110a   What comes about by force or because of ignorance seems to be involuntary. What
is forced has an external origin, the sort of origin in which the agent or victim
contributes nothing—if, e.g., a wind or human beings who control him were to carry
him off.

But now consider actions done because of fear of greater evils, or because of
5   something fine. Suppose, e.g., a tyrant tells you to do something shameful, when he
has control over your parents and children, and if you do it, they will live, but if
not, they will die. These cases raise dispute about whether they are voluntary or
involuntary.

However, the same sort of thing also happens with throwing cargo overboard in
10   storms; for no one willingly throws cargo overboard, unconditionally, but anyone
with any sense throws it overboard [under some conditions] to save himself and the
others.

These sorts of actions, then, are mixed. But they would seem to be more like
voluntary actions. For at the time they are done they are choiceworthy, and the goal
of an action reflects the occasion; hence also we should call the action voluntary or
involuntary with reference to the time when he does it. Now in fact he does it
15   willingly; for in these sorts of actions he has within him the origin of the movement

of the limbs that are the instruments [of the action], and when the origin of the actions is in him, it is also up to him to do them or not to do them. Hence actions of this sort are voluntary, though presumably the actions without [the appropriate] condition are involuntary, since no one would choose any action of this sort in itself.

For such [mixed] actions people are sometimes actually praised, whenever they   20
endure something shameful or painful as the price of great and fine results; and if they do the reverse, they are blamed, since it is a base person who endures what is most shameful for nothing fine or for only some moderately fine result.

In some cases there is no praise, but there is pardon, whenever someone does a wrong action because of conditions of a sort that overstrain human nature, and that   25
no one would endure. But presumably there are some things we cannot be compelled to do, and rather than do them we should suffer the most terrible consequences and accept death; for the things that [allegedly] compelled Euripides' Alcmaeon to kill his mother appear ridiculous.

It is sometimes hard, however, to judge what [goods] should be chosen at the price   30
of what [evils], and what [evils] should be endured as the price of what [goods]. And it is even harder to abide by our judgment, since the results we expect [when we endure] are usually painful, and the actions we are compelled [to endure, when we choose] are usually shameful. That is why those who have been compelled or not   1110b
compelled receive praise and blame.

What sorts of things, then, should we say are forced? Perhaps we should say that something is forced unconditionally whenever its cause is external and the agent contributes nothing. Other things are involuntary in themselves, but choiceworthy on this occasion and as the price of these [goods], and their origin is in the agent.   5
These are involuntary in themselves, but, on this occasion and as the price of these [goods], voluntary. Still, they would seem to be more like voluntary actions, since actions involve particular [conditions], and [in mixed actions] these [conditions] are voluntary. But what sort of thing should be chosen as the price of what [good] is not easy to answer, since there are many differences in particular [conditions].

But suppose someone says that pleasant things and fine things force us, since they   10
are outside us and compel us. It will follow that for him everything is forced, since everyone in every action aims at something fine or pleasant.

Moreover, if we are forced and unwilling to act, we find it painful; but if something pleasant or fine is its cause, we do it with pleasure.

It is ridiculous, then, for [our opponent] to ascribe responsibility to external [causes] and not to himself, when he is easily snared by such things; and ridiculous   15
to take responsibility for fine actions himself, but to hold pleasant things responsible for his shameful actions.

What is forced, then, would seem to be what has its origin outside the person forced, who contributes nothing.

Everything caused by ignorance is non-voluntary, but what is involuntary also   20
causes pain and regret. For if someone's action was caused by ignorance, but he now has no objection to the action, he has done it neither willingly, since he did not know what it was, nor unwillingly, since he now feels no pain. Hence, among those who act because of ignorance, the agent who now regrets his action seems to be unwilling, while the agent with no regrets may be called non-willing, since he is another case— for since he is different, it is better if he has his own special name.

25   Further, action caused by ignorance would seem to be different from action done in ignorance. For if the agent is drunk or angry, his action seems to be caused by drunkenness or anger, not by ignorance. though it is done in ignorance, not in knowledge.

[This ignorance does not make an action involuntary.] Certainly every vicious person is ignorant of the actions he must do or avoid, and this sort of error makes
30   people unjust, and in general bad. But talk of involuntary action is not meant to apply to [this] ignorance of what is beneficial.

For the cause of involuntary action is not [this] ignorance in the decision, which causes vice; it is not [in other words] ignorance of the universal, since that is a cause
1111a   for blame. Rather, the cause is ignorance of the particulars which the action consists in and is concerned with; for these allow both pity and pardon, since an agent acts involuntarily if he is ignorant of one of these particulars.

Presumably, then, it is not a bad idea to define these particulars, and say what they are, and how many. They are: (1) who is doing it; (2) what he is doing; (3) about
5   what or to what he is doing; (4) sometimes also what he is doing it with, e.g. the instrument; (5) for what result, e.g. safety; (6) in what way, e.g. gently or hard.

Now certainly someone could not be ignorant of *all* of these unless he were mad. Nor, clearly, (1) could he be ignorant of who is doing it, since he could hardly be ignorant of himself. But (2) he might be ignorant of what he is doing, as when someone says that [the secret] slipped out while he was speaking, or, as Aeschylus said about the mysteries, that he did not know it was forbidden to reveal it; or, like
10   the person with the catapult, that he let it go when he [only] wanted to demonstrate it. (3) Again, he might think that his son is an enemy, as Merope did; or (4) that the barbed spear has a button on it, or that the stone is pumice-stone. (5) By giving someone a drink to save his life we might kill him; (6) and wanting to touch someone,
15   as they do in sparring, we might wound him.

There is ignorance about all of these [particulars] that the action consists in. Hence someone who was ignorant of one of these seems to have done an action unwillingly, especially when he was ignorant of the most important of them; these seem to be (2) what he is doing, and (5) the result for which he does it.

20   Hence it is action called involuntary with reference to *this* sort of ignorance [that we meant when we said that] the agent must, in addition, feel pain and regret for his action.

Since, then, what is involuntary is what is forced or is caused by ignorance, what is voluntary seems to be what has its origin in the agent himself when he knows the particulars that the action consists in.

[Our definition is sound.] For, presumably, it is not correct to say that action
25   caused by emotion or appetite is involuntary.

For, first of all, on this view none of the other animals will ever act voluntarily; nor will children. [But clearly they do.]

Next, among all the actions caused by appetite or emotion do we do none of them voluntarily? Or do we do the fine actions voluntarily and the shameful involuntarily? Surely [the second answer] is ridiculous when one and the same thing [i.e. appetite
30   or emotion] causes [both fine and shameful actions]. And presumably it is also absurd to say [as the first answer implies] that things we ought to desire are involuntary;

and in fact we ought both to be angry at some things and to have an appetite for some things, e.g. for health and learning.

Again, what is involuntary seems to be painful, whereas what expresses our appetite seems to be pleasant.

Moreover, how are errors that express emotion any less voluntary than those that express rational calculation? For both sorts of errors are to be avoided; and since nonrational feelings seem to be no less human [than rational calculation], actions resulting from emotion or appetite are also proper to a human being; it is absurd, then, to regard them as involuntary.

1111b

2

Now that we have defined what is voluntary and what involuntary, the next task is to discuss decision; for decision seems to be most proper to virtue, and to distinguish characters from one another better than actions do.

5

Decision, then, is apparently voluntary, but not the same as what is voluntary, which extends more widely. For children and the other animals share in what is voluntary, but not in decision; and the actions we do on the spur of the moment are said to be voluntary, but not to express decision.

10

Those who say decision is appetite or emotion or wish or some sort of belief would seem to be wrong.

For decision is not shared with nonrational [animals], but appetite and emotion are shared with them.

Further, the incontinent person acts on appetite, not on decision, but the continent person does the reverse and acts on decision, not on appetite.

15

Again, appetite is contrary to decision, but not to appetite.

Further, appetite's concern is what is pleasant and what is painful, but neither of these is the concern of decision.

Still less is emotion decision; for actions caused by emotion seem least of all to express decision.

But further, it is not wish either, though it is apparently close to it.

20

For, first, we do not decide to do what is impossible, and anyone claiming to decide to do it would seem a fool; but we do wish for what is impossible, e.g. never to die, as well [as for what is possible].

Further, we wish [not only for results we can achieve], but also for results that are [possible, but] not achievable through our own agency, e.g. victory for some actor or athlete. But what we decide to do is never anything of that sort, but what we think would come about through our own agency.

25

Again, we wish for the end more [than for what promotes it], but we decide to do what promotes the end. We wish, e.g. to be healthy, but decide to do what will make us healthy; and we wish to be happy, and say so, but could not appropriately say we decide to be happy, since in general what we decide to do would seem to be what is up to us.

30

Nor is it belief.

For, first, belief seems to be about everything, no less about what is eternal and what is impossible [for us] than about what is up to us.

Moreover, beliefs are divided into true and false, not into good and bad, but decisions are divided into good and bad more than into true and false.

1112a   Now presumably no one even claims that decision is the same as belief in general. But it is not the same as any kind of belief either.

For it is our decisions to do what is good or bad, not our beliefs, that make the characters we have.

Again, we decide to take or avoid something good or bad. We believe what it is, whom it benefits or how; but we do not exactly believe to take or avoid.

5

Further, decision is praised more for deciding on what is right, whereas belief is praised for believing rightly.

Moreover, we decide on something [even] when we know most completely that it is good; but [what] we believe [is] what we do not quite know.

Again, those who make the best decisions do not seem to be the same as those with the best beliefs; on the contrary, some seem to have better beliefs, but to make the wrong decisions because of vice.

10

We can agree that decision follows or implies belief. But that is irrelevant, since it is not the question we are asking; our question is whether decision is the *same* as some sort of belief.

Then what, or what sort of thing, is decision, since it is none of the things mentioned? Well, apparently it is voluntary, but not everything voluntary is decided. Then perhaps what is decided is the result of prior deliberation. For decision involves reason and thought, and even the name itself would seem to indicate that [what is decided, *prohaireton*] is chosen [*haireton*] before [*pro*] other things.

15

3

But do we deliberate about everything, and is everything open to deliberation, or is there no deliberation about some things? By 'open to deliberation', presumably, we should mean what someone with some sense, not some fool or madman, might deliberate about.

20

Now no one deliberates about eternal things, e.g. about the universe, or about the incommensurability of the sides and the diagonal; nor about things that are in movement but always come about the same way, either from necessity or by nature or by some other cause, e.g. the solstices or the rising of the stars; nor about what happens different ways at different times, e.g. droughts and rains; nor about what results from fortune, e.g. the finding of a treasure. For none of these results could be achieved through our agency.

25

30

We deliberate about what is up to us, i.e. about the actions we can do; and this is what is left [besides the previous cases]. For causes seem to include nature, necessity and fortune, but besides them mind and everything [operating] through human agency.

33

28, 29   However, we do not deliberate about all human affairs; no Spartan, e.g., deliber-

ates about how the Scythians might have the best political system. Rather, each group   33
of human beings deliberates about the actions *they* can do.

Now there is no deliberation about the sciences that are exact and self-sufficient,   1112b
e.g. about letters, since we are in no doubt about how to write them [in spelling a
word]. Rather, we deliberate about what results through our agency, but in different
ways on different occasions, e.g. about questions of medicine and money-making;
more about navigation than about gymnastics, to the extent that it is less exactly   5
worked out, and similarly with other [crafts]; and more about beliefs than about
sciences, since we are more in doubt about them.

Deliberation concerns what is usually [one way rather than another], where the
outcome is unclear and the right way to act is undefined. And we enlist partners in   10
deliberation on large issues when we distrust our own ability to discern [the right
answer].

We deliberate not about ends, but about what promotes ends; a doctor, e.g., does
not deliberate about whether he will cure, or an orator about whether he will
persuade, or a politician about whether he will produce good order, or any other
[expert] about the end [that his science aims at].   15

Rather, we first lay down the end, and then examine the ways and means to achieve
it. If it appears that any of several [possible] means will reach it, we consider which
of them will reach it most easily and most finely; and if only one [possible] means
reaches it, we consider how that means will reach it, and how the means itself is
reached, until we come to the first cause, the last thing to be discovered.

For a deliberator would seem to inquire and analyse in the way described, as   20
though analysing a diagram. [The comparison is apt, since], apparently, all deliberation is inquiry, though not all inquiry, e.g. in mathematics, is deliberation. And the
last thing [found] in the analysis is the first that comes to be.

If we encounter an impossible step—e.g. we need money but cannot raise it—we   25
desist; but if the action appears possible, we undertake it. What is possible is what
we could achieve through our agency [including what our friends could achieve for
us]; for what our friends achieve is, in a way, achieved through our agency, since
the origin is in us. [In crafts] we sometimes look for instruments, sometimes [for the
way] to use them; so also in other cases we sometimes look for the means to the end,   30
sometimes for the proper use of the means or for the means to that proper use.

As we have said, then, a human being would seem to originate action; deliberation
is about the actions he can do; and actions are for the sake of other things; hence
we deliberate about what promotes an end, not about the end.

Nor do we deliberate about particulars, e.g. about whether this is a loaf or is   1113a
cooked the right amount; for these are questions for perception, and if we keep on
deliberating at each stage we shall go on without end.

What we deliberate about is the same as what we decide to do, except that by the
time we decide to do it, it is definite; for what we decide to do is what we have judged
[to be right] as a result of deliberation. For each of us stops inquiring how to act as   5
soon as he traces the origin to himself, and within himself to the dominant part; for
this is the part that decides. This is also clear from the ancient political systems
described by Homer; there the kings would first decide and then announce their
decision to the people.

10   We have found, then, that what we decide to do is whatever action among those up to us we deliberate about and desire to do. Hence also decision will be deliberative desire to do an action that is up to us; for when we have judged [that it is right] as a result of deliberation, our desire to do it expresses our wish.

So much, then, for an outline of the sort of thing decision is about; it is about what promotes the end.

4

15   Wish, we have said, is for the end. But to some it seems that wish is for the good, to others that it is for the apparent good.

For those who say the good is what is wished, it follows that what someone wishes if he chooses incorrectly is not wished at all. For if it is wished, then [on this view] it is good; but what he wishes is in fact bad, if it turns out that way. [Hence what he
20   wishes is not wished, which is self-contradictory.]

For those, on the other hand, who say the apparent good is wished, it follows that there is nothing wished by nature. To each person what is wished is what seems [good to him]; but different things, and indeed contrary things, if it turns out that way, appear good to different people. [Hence contrary things will be wished and nothing will be wished by nature.]

If, then, these views do not satisfy us, should we say that, unconditionally and in reality, what is wished is the good, but to each person what is wished is the apparent good?

25   To the excellent person, then, what is wished will be what is wished in reality, while to the base person what is wished is whatever it turns out to be [that appears good to him]. Similarly in the case of bodies, really healthy things are healthy to people in good condition, while other things are healthy to sickly people, and the same is true of what is bitter, sweet, hot, heavy and so on.

30   For the excellent person judges each sort of thing correctly, and in each case what is true appears to him. For each state [of character] has its own special [view of] what is fine and pleasant, and presumably the excellent person is far superior because he sees what is true in each case, being a sort of standard and measure of what is fine and pleasant.

In the many, however, pleasure would seem to cause deception, since it appears
1113b   good when it is not; at any rate, they choose what is pleasant because they assume it is good, and avoid pain because they assume it is evil.

5

We have found, then, that we wish for the end, and deliberate and decide about what promotes it; hence the actions concerned with what promotes the end will
5   express a decision and will be voluntary. Now the activities of the virtues are concerned with [what promotes the end]; hence virtue is also up to us, and so is vice.

For when acting is up to us, so is not acting, and when No is up to us, so is Yes. Hence if acting, when it is fine, is up to us, then not acting, when it is shameful, is
10   also up to us; and if not acting, when it is fine, is up to us, then acting, when it is

shameful, is also up to us. Hence if doing, and likewise not doing, fine or shameful actions is up to us; and if, as we saw, [doing or not doing them] is [what it is] to be a good or bad person; then it follows that being decent or base is up to us.

The claim that no one is willingly bad or unwillingly blessed would seem to be   15
partly true but partly false. For while certainly no one is unwillingly blessed, vice is voluntary. If it is not, we must dispute the conclusion just reached, that a human being originates and fathers his own actions as he fathers his children. But if our conclusion appears true, and we cannot refer [actions] back to other origins beyond   20
those in ourselves, then it follows that whatever has its origin in us is itself up to us and voluntary.

There would seem to be testimony in favour of our views not only in what each of us does as a private citizen, but also in what legislators themselves do. For they impose corrective treatments and penalties on anyone who does vicious actions, unless his action is forced or is caused by ignorance that he is not responsible for;   25
and they honour anyone who does fine actions; they assume that they will encourage the one and restrain the other. But no one encourages us to do anything that is not up to us and voluntary; people assume it is pointless to persuade us not to get hot or distressed or hungry or anything else of that sort, since persuasion will not stop it happening to us.

Indeed, legislators also impose corrective treatments for the ignorance itself, if   30
the person seems to be responsible for the ignorance. A drunk, e.g., pays a double penalty; for the origin is in him, since he controls whether he gets drunk, and his getting drunk is responsible for his ignorance.

They also impose corrective treatment on someone who [does a vicious action] in ignorance of some provision of law that he is required to know and that is not hard [to know]. And they impose it in other cases likewise for any other ignorance that   1114a
seems to be caused by the agent's inattention; they assume it is up to him not to be ignorant, since he controls whether he pays attention.

But presumably his character makes him inattentive. Still, he is himself responsible for having this character, by living carelessly, and similarly for being unjust by   5
cheating, or being intemperate by passing his time in drinking and the like; for each type of activity produces the corresponding character. This is clear from those who train for any contest or action, since they continually practise the appropriate activities. [Only] a totally insensible person would not know that each type of activity   10
is the source of the corresponding state; hence if someone does what he knows will   12
make him unjust, he is willingly unjust.   13

Moreover, it is unreasonable for someone doing injustice not to wish to be unjust,   11
or for someone doing intemperate action not to wish to be intemperate. This does   12
not mean, however, that if he is unjust and wishes to stop, he will stop and will be   13
just.

For neither does a sick person recover his health [simply by wishing]; nonetheless,   15
he is sick willingly, by living incontinently and disobeying the doctors, if that was how it happened. At that time, then, he was free not to be sick, though no longer free once he has let himself go, just as it was up to us to throw a stone, since the origin was in us, though we can no longer take it back once we have thrown it.

Similarly, then, the person who is [now] unjust or intemperate was originally free   20
not to acquire this character, so that he has it willingly, though once he has acquired the character, he is no longer free not to have it [now].

It is not only vices of the soul that are voluntary; vices of the body are also voluntary for some people, and we actually censure them. For we never censure someone if nature causes his ugliness; but if his lack of training or attention causes

25   it, we do censure him. The same is true for weakness or maiming; for everyone would pity, not reproach someone if he were blind by nature or because of a disease or a wound, but would censure him if his heavy drinking or some other form of intemperance made him blind.

Hence bodily vices that are up to us are censured, while those not up to us are not

30   censured. If so, then in the other cases also the vices that are censured will be up to us.

But someone may say, 'Everyone aims at the apparent good, and does not control

1114b how it appears; on the contrary, his character controls how the end appears to him.'

First, then, if each person is in some way responsible for his own state [of character], then he is also himself in some way responsible for how [the end] appears.

Suppose, on the other hand, that no one is responsible for acting badly, but one

5   does so because one is ignorant of the end, and thinks this is the way to gain what is best for oneself. One's aiming at the end will not be one's own choice, but one needs a sort of natural, inborn sense of sight, to judge finely and to choose what is really good. Whoever by nature has this sense in a fine condition has a good nature. For this sense is the greatest and finest thing, and one cannot acquire it or learn it

10   from another; rather, its natural character determines his later condition, and when it is naturally good and fine, that is true and complete good nature.

If all this is true, then, surely virtue will be no more voluntary than vice? For how

15   the end appears is laid down, by nature or in whatever way, for the good and the bad person alike, and they trace all the other things back to the end in doing whatever actions they do.

Suppose, then, that it is not nature that makes the end appear however it appears to each person, but something also depends on him; or, alternatively, suppose that [how] the end [appears] is natural, but virtue is voluntary because the virtuous

20   person does the other things voluntarily. In either case vice will be no less voluntary than virtue; for the bad person, no less than the good, is responsible for his own actions, even if not for [how] the end [appears].

Now the virtues, as we say, are voluntary, since in fact we are ourselves in a way jointly responsible for our states of character, and by having the sort of character

25   we have we lay down the sort of end we do. Hence the vices will also be voluntary, since the same is true of them.

We have now discussed the virtues in general. We have described their genus in outline; they are means, and they are states. Certain actions produce them, and they cause us to do these same actions, expressing the virtues themselves, in the way that correct reason prescribes. They are up to us and voluntary.

30   Actions and states, however, are not voluntary in the same way. For we are in control of actions from the origin to the end, when we know the particulars. With

1115a states, however, we are in control of the origin, but do not know, any more than with sicknesses, what the cumulative effect of particular actions will be; none the less, since it was up to us to exercise a capacity either this way or another way, states are voluntary.

Let us now take up the virtues again, and discuss each singly. Let us say what they 5
are, what sorts of thing they are concerned with, and how they are concerned with
them; it will also be clear at the same time how many virtues there are.

6

First let us discuss bravery. We have already made it apparent that there is a mean
about feelings of fear and confidence. What we fear, clearly, is what is frightening,
and such things are, speaking without qualification, bad things; hence people define
fear as expectation of something bad.

Now while we certainly fear all bad things, e.g. bad reputation, poverty, sickness, 10
friendlessness, death, they do not all seem to concern the brave person. For fear of
some bad things, e.g. bad reputation, is actually right and fine, and lack of fear is
disgraceful; for if someone fears bad reputation, he is decent and properly prone
to shame, and if he has no fear of it, he has no feeling of disgrace. Some, however,
call this fearless person brave, by a transference [of the name], since he has some 15
similarity to the brave person, in that the brave person is also a type of fearless
person.

Presumably, though, it is wrong to fear poverty or sickness or, in general, [bad
things] that are not the results of vice or caused by ourselves; still, someone who is
fearless about these is not thereby brave. He also is called brave by similarity, since
some people who are cowardly in the dangers of war are nonetheless generous, and 20
face with confidence the [danger of] losing money.

Again, if someone is afraid of committing wanton aggression on children or
women, or of being envious or anything of that sort, that does not make him
cowardly. Nor again, if someone is confident when he is going to be whipped [for
his crimes] does that make him brave.

Then what sorts of frightening conditions concern the brave person? Surely the 25
most frightening; for no one stands firmer against terrifying conditions. Now death
is most frightening of all, since it is a boundary, and when someone is dead nothing
beyond it seems either good or bad for him any more. Still, not even death in all
conditions, e.g. on the sea or in sickness, seems to be the brave person's concern.

In what conditions, then, is death his concern? Surely in the finest conditions. 30
Now such deaths are those in war, since they occur in the greatest and finest danger;
and this judgment is endorsed by the honours given in cities and by monarchs.
Hence someone is called brave to the fullest extent if he is intrepid in facing a fine
death and the immediate dangers that bring death—and this is above all true of the 35
dangers of war.

Certainly the brave person is also intrepid on the sea and in sicknesses, but not in 1115b
the same way as seafarers are. For he has given up hope of safety, and objects to
this sort of death [with nothing fine in it], but seafarers' experience makes them
hopeful. Moreover, we act like brave men on occasions when we can use our strength, 5
or when it is fine to be killed; and neither of these is true when we perish on the sea.

7

Now what is frightening is not the same for everyone. We do say, however,
that some things are too frightening for a human being to resist; these, then, are

10   frightening for everyone, at least for everyone with any sense. What is frightening, but not irresistible for a human being, varies in its seriousness and degree; and the same is true of what inspires confidence.

Now the brave person is unperturbed, as far as a human being can be. Hence, though he will fear even the sorts of things that are not irresistible, he will stand firm against them, in the right way, as prescribed by reason, for the sake of what is fine, since this is the end aimed at by virtue.

15   It is possible to be more or less afraid of these frightening things, and also possible to be afraid of what is not frightening as though it were frightening. The cause of error may be fear of the wrong thing, or in the wrong way, or at the wrong time, or something of that sort; and the same is true for things that inspire confidence.

Hence whoever stands firm against the right things and fears the right things, for the right end, in the right way, at the right time, and is correspondingly confident, is the brave person; for the brave person's actions and feelings reflect what something is worth and what reason [prescribes].

20   Every activity aims at actions expressing its state of character, and to the brave person bravery is fine; hence the end it aims at is also fine, since each thing is defined by its end. The brave person, then, aims at what is fine when he expresses bravery in his standing firm and acting.

Consider now those who go to excess.

25   The person who is excessively fearless has no name—we said earlier that many states have no names. He would be some sort of madman, or incapable of feeling distress, if he feared nothing, neither earthquake nor waves, as they say about the Celts.

The person who is excessively confident about frightening things is rash. The rash

30   person also seems to be a boaster, and a pretender to bravery. At any rate, the attitude to frightening things that the brave person really has is the attitude that the rash person wants to appear to have; hence he imitates the brave person where he can. That is why most of them are rash cowards; for rash though they are on

1116a7   these [occasions for imitation], they do not stand firm against anything frightening.

8   Moreover, rash people are impetuous, and wish for dangers before they arrive, but

9   shrink from them when they come; brave people, on the contrary, are eager when in action, but keep quiet until then.

1115b34   The person who is excessively afraid is the coward, since he fears the wrong things,

35   and in the wrong way, and so on. Though indeed he is also deficient in confidence,

1116a   it is more his excessive pain that clearly distinguishes him. Hence, since he is afraid of everything, he is a despairing sort. The brave person, on the contrary, is hopeful, since [he is confident and] confidence is proper to a hopeful person.

5   Hence the coward, the rash person and the brave person are all concerned with the same things, but have different states related to them; the others are excessive

7   or defective, but the brave person has the intermediate and right state.

10   As we have said, then, bravery is a mean about what inspires confidence and about what is frightening in the conditions we have described; it chooses and stands firm because that is fine or because anything else is shameful. Dying to avoid poverty or erotic passion or something painful is proper to a coward, not to a brave person;

15   for trying to avoid burdens is softness, and such a person stands firm [in the face of death] to avoid an evil, not because it is fine.

8

Bravery, then, is something of this sort. But other states, five of them, are also called bravery.

Citizens' bravery comes first, since it looks most like bravery. For citizens seem to stand firm against dangers with the aim of avoiding reproaches and legal penalties and of winning honours; that is why the bravest seem to be those who hold cowards   20
in dishonour and do honour to brave people. That is how Homer also describes them when he speaks of Diomede and Hector. [Hector says,] 'Polydamas will be the first to heap disgrace on me', and [Diomede says,] 'For sometime Hector speaking   25
among the Trojans will say "The son of Tydeus fled from me." '

This is most like the [genuine] bravery described above, since it is caused by a virtue; for its cause is shame and desire for something fine—for honour—and aversion from reproach, which is disgraceful.

In this class we might also place those compelled by their superiors. However,   30
they are worse to the extent that their behaviour is caused by fear, not by shame, by aversion from what is painful, not from what is disgraceful. For those who control them compel them, as Hector does; 'If I notice anyone shrinking back from the   35
battle, nothing will help him to escape the dogs.' Commanders who strike the troops if they give ground and those who post them in front of ditches and suchlike do the   1116b
same thing, since they all compel them. However, we must be brave because it is fine, not because we are compelled.

Experience about each situation also seems to be bravery; that is why Socrates actually thought that bravery is scientific knowledge. Different people in different   5
conditions have this sort [of apparent courage], and in the conditions of war the professional soldiers have it; for there seem to be many groundless alarms in war, and the professionals are the most familiar with these, and hence appear brave, since others do not know that the alarms are groundless.

Moreover, their experience makes them most capable in attack and defence, since   10
they are capable users of their weapons, and have the weapons that are best for attack and defence. The result is that in fighting non-professionals they are like armed troops fighting unarmed, or like trained athletes fighting ordinary people; for in these contests also the best fighters are the strongest and physically fittest, not the bravest.   15

However, professional soldiers turn out to be cowards when the danger overstrains them and they are inferior in numbers and equipment. For they are the first to run, whereas the citizen troops stand firm and get killed; this was what happened at the temple of Hermes.[6] For the citizens find it shameful to run, and find death more   20
choiceworthy than safety at this cost. But the professionals from the start were facing the danger on the assumption of their superiority, and once they learn their mistake, they run, since they are more afraid of being killed than of doing something shameful; and that is not the brave person's character.

Emotion is also counted as bravery; for those who act on emotion also seem to be brave—as beasts seem to be when they attack those who have wounded them—   25
because brave people are also full of emotion. For emotion is most eager to run and

---

6. [When, in 353, mercenary soldiers were engaged to help the citizens in Coronea, they ran away.—M.L.M.]

30 face dangers; hence Homer's words, 'put strength in his emotion', 'aroused strength and emotion', and 'his blood boiled'. All these would seem to signify the arousal and the impulse of emotion.

Now brave people act because of what is fine, and their emotion cooperates with them. But beasts act because of pain; for [they attack only] because they have been wounded or frightened, since they do not approach us in a forest. They are not brave, then, since distress and emotion drives them in an impulsive rush to meet 35 danger, foreseeing none of the terrifying prospects. For if they were brave, hungry 1117a asses would also be brave, since they stay feeding even if they are beaten; and adulterers also do many daring actions because of appetite.

5 Human beings as well [as beasts] find it painful to be angered, and pleasant to exact a penalty. But those who fight for these reasons are not brave, though they are good fighters; for they fight because of their feelings, not because of what is 4 fine or as reason [prescribes]. Still, they have something similar [to bravery]. The [bravery] caused by emotion would seem to be the most natural sort, and is [real] 5 bravery once decision and the goal have been added to it.

9 Hopeful people are not brave either, since it is their many victories over many 10 opponents that make them confident in dangers. They are somewhat similar to brave people, since both are confident; but while brave people are confident for the reason given earlier, the hopeful are confident because they think they are stronger 15 and nothing could happen to them—and drunks do the same sort of thing, since they become hopeful. And when things turn out differently for them, they run; but, as we saw, it is proper to the brave person to stand firm against what is and appears frightening to a human being, because it is fine to stand firm and shameful to fail.

Indeed, that is why someone who is unafraid and unperturbed in a sudden alarm seems braver than [someone who is unafraid only] in dangers that are obvious in 20 advance; for what he does is more the result of his state of character, since it is less the outcome of preparation. If an action is foreseen, we might decide to do it [not only because of our state of character, but] also by reason and rational calculation; but when we have no warning, [our decision to act] expresses our state of character.

Those who act in ignorance also appear brave, and indeed they are close to hopeful people, though inferior to them in so far as they lack hopeful people's self-esteem. 25 That is why the hopeful stand firm for some time, whereas if ignorant people have been deceived and then realize or suspect that things are different, they run—that was what happened to the Argives when they stumbled on the Spartans and took them for Sicyonians.[7]

We have described, then, the character of brave people and of the people who seem to be brave.

9

30 Bravery is about feelings of confidence and fear, not, however, about both in the same way, but more about frightening things; for someone is brave if he is undisturbed and in the right state about these, more than if he is in this state about things

---

7. [In 392, during battle in Corinth, Spartan cavalry took up Sicyonian shields and were confused for them.—M.L.M.]

inspiring confidence. As we said, then, standing firm against what is painful makes us call people brave; that is why bravery is both painful and justly praised, since it is harder to stand firm against something painful than to refrain from something pleasant.   35

None the less, the end that bravery aims at seems to be pleasant, though obscured   1117b
by its surroundings. This is what happens in athletic contests. For boxers find that the end they aim at, the crown and the honours, is pleasant, but, being made of flesh, they find it distressing and painful to take the punches and to bear all the hard   5
work; and because there are so many of these painful things, the end, being small, appears to have nothing pleasant in it. And so, if this is also true for bravery, the brave person will find death and wounds painful, and suffer them unwillingly, but he will stand firm against them because that is fine or because failure is shameful.

Indeed, the more he has every virtue and the happier he is, the more pain he will   10
feel at the prospect of death. For this sort of person, more than anyone, finds it worth while to be alive, and is knowingly deprived of the greatest goods, and this is painful. But he is no less brave for all that; presumably, indeed, he is all the braver, because he chooses what is fine in war at the cost of all these goods.   15

Hence it is not true that the active exercise of every virtue is pleasant; it is pleasant only in so far as we attain the end.

However, it is quite possible for brave people not to be the best soldiers. Perhaps the best will be those who are less brave, but possess no other good; for they are ready to face dangers, and they sell their lives for small gains.   20

So much for bravery. It is easy to grasp what it is, in outline at least, from what we have said.

10

Let us discuss temperance next, since bravery and temperance seem to be the virtues of the non-rational parts. Temperance, then, is a mean concerned with   25
pleasures, as we have already said; for it is concerned less, and in a different way, with pains. Intemperance appears in this same area too. Let us, then, now distinguish the specific pleasures that concern them.

First, let us distinguish pleasures of the soul from those of the body. Love of honour and of learning, e.g., are among the soul's pleasures; for though a lover of one of these enjoys it, only his thought, not his body, is at all affected. Those   30
concerned with such pleasures are called neither temperate nor intemperate. The same applies to those concerned with any of the other non-bodily pleasures; for lovers of tales, story-tellers, those who waste their days on trivialities, are called   35
babblers, but not intemperate. Nor do we call people intemperate if they feel pain   1118a
over money or friends.

Temperance, then, will be about bodily pleasures, but not even about all of these. For those who enjoy what they notice through sight, e.g. colours, shapes, a painting, are called neither temperate nor intemperate, even though it would also seem   5
possible to enjoy these both in the right way and excessively or deficiently. The same is true for hearing; no one is ever called intemperate for the excessive enjoyment of songs or play-acting, or temperate for the right enjoyment of them.

Nor is this said about someone enjoying smells, except coincidentally. For someone

10   is called intemperate not for enjoying the smell of apples or roses or incense, but
rather for enjoying the smell of perfumes or cooked delicacies. For these are the
smells an intemperate person enjoys because they remind him of the objects of his
15   appetite; and we can see that others also enjoy the smells of food if they are hungry.
It is the enjoyment of the things [that he is reminded of by these smells] that is
proper to an intemperate person, since these are the objects of his appetite.

Nor do other animals find pleasures from these senses, except coincidentally.
What a hound enjoys, e.g., is not the smell of a hare, but eating it; but the hare's
20   smell made the hound perceive it. And what a lion enjoys is not the sound of the
ox, but eating it; but since the ox's sound made the lion perceive that it was near,
the lion appears to enjoy the sound. Similarly, what pleases him is not the sight of
'a deer or a wild goat', but the prospect of food.

The pleasures that concern temperance and intemperance are those that are
25   shared with the other animals, and so appear slavish and bestial. These pleasures
are touch and taste. However, they seem to deal even with taste very little or not at
all. For taste discriminates flavours—the sort of thing that wine-tasters and cooks
30   savouring food do; but people, or intemperate people at any rate, do not much
enjoy this. Rather, they enjoy the gratification that comes entirely through touch,
in eating and drinking and in what are called the pleasures of sex. That is why a
glutton actually prayed for his throat to become longer than a crane's, showing that
1118b   he took pleasure in the touching.

And so the sense that concerns intemperance is the most widely shared, and seems
justifiably open to reproach, since we have it in so far as we are animals, not in so
far as we are human beings. To enjoy these things, then, and to like them most of
5   all is bestial. For indeed the most civilized of the pleasures coming through touch,
e.g. those produced by rubbing and warming in gymnasia, are excluded from intemperance, since the touching that is proper to the intemperate person concerns only
some parts of the body, not all of it.

11

Some appetites seem to be shared [by everyone], while others seem to be additions
10   that are special [to different people]. The appetite for nourishment, e.g., is natural,
since everyone who lacks nourishment, dry or liquid, has an appetite for it, sometimes for both; and, as Homer says, the young in their prime [all] have an appetite
for sex. On the other hand, not everyone has an appetite for a particular sort of
food or drink or sex, or for the same things; hence that sort of appetite seems to be
special to [each of] us. Still, this also includes a natural element, since different sorts
of people find different sorts of things pleasanter, and there are some things that
are pleasanter for everyone than things chosen at random would be.

15   In natural appetites few people are in error, and only in one direction, towards
excess. Eating indiscriminately or drinking until we are too full is exceeding the
quantity that suits nature, since [the object of] natural appetite is the filling of a lack.
20   Hence these people are called 'gluttons', showing that they glut their bellies past
what is right; that is how extra-slavish people turn out.

With the pleasures that are special to different people, many make errors and in
many ways; for people are called lovers of something if they enjoy the wrong things,

or if they enjoy something more than most people enjoy it, or if they enjoy something in the wrong way. And in all these ways intemperate people go to excess. For some of the things they enjoy are hateful, and hence the wrong things; and any special pleasures it is right to enjoy they enjoy more than is right, and more than most people enjoy them. 25

Clearly, then, with pleasures excess is intemperance, and is blameworthy. With pains, however, we are not called temperate, as we are called brave, for standing firm against them, or intemperate for not standing firm. Rather, someone is intemperate because he feels more pain than is right at failing to get pleasant things; and even this pain is produced by the pleasure [he takes in them]. And someone is temperate because he does not feel pain at the absence of what is pleasant, or at refraining from it. 30

The intemperate person, then, has an appetite for all pleasant things, or rather for the pleasantest of them, and his appetite leads him to choose these at the cost of everything else. Hence he also feels pain both when he fails to get something and when he has an appetite for it, since appetite is associated with pain; it would seem absurd, though, to suffer pain because of pleasure. 1119a 5

People who are deficient in pleasures and enjoy them less than is right are not found very much. For that sort of insensibility is not human; indeed, even the other animals discriminate among foods, enjoying some but not others; and if someone finds nothing pleasant, or preferable to anything else, he is far from being human. And the reason he has no name is that he is not found much. 10

The temperate person has an intermediate state in relation to these [bodily pleasures]. For he finds no pleasure in what most pleases the intemperate person, but finds it disagreeable; he finds no pleasure at all in the wrong things; and he finds no intense pleasure in any [bodily pleasures], suffers no pain at their absence, and has no appetite for them, or only a moderate appetite, not to the wrong degree or at the wrong time or anything else at all of that sort. 15

If something is pleasant and conducive to health or fitness, he will desire this moderately and in the right way; and he will desire in the same way anything else that is pleasant if it is no obstacle to health and fitness, does not deviate from what is fine, and does not exceed his means. For the [opposite] sort of person likes these pleasures more than they are worth, and that is not the temperate person's character; on the contrary, he likes them as correct reason [prescribes]. 20

12

Intemperance looks more like a voluntary condition than cowardice does, since it is caused by pleasure, which is choiceworthy, while cowardice is caused by pain, which is to be avoided. Moreover, pain disturbs and ruins the nature of the sufferer, while pleasure does nothing of the sort; intemperance, then, is more voluntary. 25

Hence it is also more open to reproach. For it is also easier to acquire the habit of facing pleasant things, since our life includes many of them and we can acquire the habit with no danger; but with frightening things the reverse is true.

However, cowardice seems to be more voluntary than particular cowardly actions. For cowardice itself involves no pain, but the particular actions disturb us because of the pain [that causes them], so that we actually throw away our weapons and do 30 all the other disgraceful actions; and hence these actions even seem to be forced [and hence involuntary].

For the intemperate person the reverse is true. The particular actions are the result of his appetite and desire, and so they are voluntary; but the whole condition is less voluntary [than the actions], since no one has an appetite to be intemperate.

1119b We also apply the name of intemperance to the errors of children, since they have some similarity. Which gets its name from which does not matter for present purposes, but clearly the posterior is called after the prior.

5 The name would seem to be quite appropriately transferred. For what needs to be tempered is what desires shameful things and tends to grow large; and this is the character of appetites and of children above all, since children also live by appetite, and the desire for what is pleasant is found more in them than in anyone else.

If, then, [the child or the appetitive part] is not obedient and subordinate to its rulers, it will go far astray. For when someone lacks understanding, his desire for what is pleasant is insatiable, and seeks its satisfaction from anywhere; the [repeated]
10 active exercise of appetite increases the appetite he already had from birth; and if the appetites are large and intense, they actually expel rational calculation.

This is why appetites must be moderate and few, and never contrary to reason; this is the condition we call obedient and temperate. And just as the child's life must
15 follow the instructions of his guide, so too the appetitive part must follow reason.

Hence the temperate person's appetitive part must agree with reason; for both [his appetitive part and his reason] aim at what is fine, and the temperate person's appetites are for the right things, in the right ways, at the right times, which is just what reason also prescribes.

So much, then, for temperance.

BOOK FOUR

1

Next let us discuss generosity. It seems, then, to be the mean about wealth; for the generous person is praised not in conditions of war, nor in the conditions in
25 which the temperate person is praised, nor in judicial verdicts, but in the giving and taking of wealth, and more especially in the giving. We call wealth anything whose worth is measured by money.

Each one of wastefulness and ungenerosity is both an excess and a deficiency about
30 wealth. Ungenerosity is always ascribed to those who take wealth more seriously than is right. But when wastefulness is attributed to someone, several vices are sometimes combined. For incontinent people and those who spend money on intemperance are called wasteful; and since these have many vices at the same time, they make wasteful people seem the basest.

In fact, however, these people are not properly called wasteful. For the wasteful
1120a person is meant to have the single vicious feature of ruining his property; for someone who causes his own destruction ['lays waste' to himself, and so] is wasteful,

and ruining one's own property seems to be a sort of self-destruction, on the assumption that our living depends on our property. This, then, is how we understand wastefulness.

Whatever has a use can be used either well or badly; riches are something useful; and the best user of something is the person who has the virtue concerned with it. Hence the best user of riches will be the person who has the virtue concerned with wealth; and this is the generous person.

Now using wealth seems to consist in spending and giving, while taking and keeping seem to be possessing rather than using. Hence it is more proper to the generous person to give to the right people than to take from the right sources and not from the wrong sources. For it is more proper to virtue to do good than to receive good, and more proper to do fine actions than not to do shameful ones; and clearly [the right sort of] giving implies doing good and doing fine actions, while [the right sort of] taking implies receiving well or not doing something shameful.

Moreover, thanks go to the one who gives, not to the one who fails to take, and praise goes more [to the giver].

Besides, not taking is easier than giving, since people part with what is their own less readily than they avoid taking what is another's.

Further, those who are called generous are those who give [rightly]. Those who avoid taking [wrongly] are not praised for generosity, though they are praised none the less for justice, while those who take [rightly] are not much praised at all.

Besides, generous people are loved more than practically any others who are loved because of their virtue; that is because they are beneficial; and they are beneficial in their giving.

Actions expressing virtue are fine, and aim at what is fine. Hence the generous person as well [as every other virtuous person] will aim at what is fine in his giving and will give correctly; for he will give to the right people, the right amounts, at the right time, and all the other things that are implied by correct giving.

He will do this, moreover, with pleasure or [at any rate] without pain; for action expressing virtue is pleasant or [at any rate] painless, and least of all is it painful. If someone gives to the wrong people, or does not aim at what is fine, but gives for some other reason, he will not be called generous, but some other sort of person. Nor will he be called generous if he finds it painful to give; for such a person would choose wealth over fine action, and that is not proper to the generous person.

Nor will he take wealth from the wrong sources; since he does not honour wealth, this way of taking it is not for him. Nor will he be ready to ask for favours; since he is the one who benefits others, receiving benefits readily is not for him.

He will, however, acquire wealth from the right sources, e.g. from his own possessions, regarding taking not as fine, but as necessary to provide something to give. Nor will he neglect his own possessions, since he wants to use them to assist people. And he will avoid giving to just anyone, so that he will have something to give to the right people, at the right time, and where it is fine.

It is also very definitely proper to the generous person to exceed so much in giving that he leaves less for himself, since it is proper to a generous person not to look out for himself.

However, [the reference to 'exceeding' must not mislead us. For] in speaking of generosity we refer to generosity that fits one's property. For what is generous does not depend on the quantity of what is given, but on the state of the giver, and that kind of giving fits one's property. Hence one who gives less [than another] may still be more generous, if he has less to give.

Those who have not acquired their property by their own efforts, but have inherited it, seem to be more generous; for they have had no experience of shortage, and, besides, everyone likes his own products more than [other people's], as parents and poets do.

It is not easy for a generous person to grow rich, since he is ready to spend, not to take or keep, and honours wealth for the sake of giving, not for itself. Indeed fortune is denounced for this reason, that those who most deserve to grow rich actually do so least. In fact, however, this is not an unreasonable result, since someone cannot possess wealth, any more than other things, if he pays no attention to possessing it.

Still, he does not give to the wrong people, at the wrong time and so on. For if he did, his actions would no longer express generosity, and if he spent his resources on the wrong sort of giving, he would have nothing left to spend for the right purposes. For, as we have said, the generous person is the one whose spending fits his means, and for the right purposes, while the one who spends to excess is wasteful. Hence tyrants are not called wasteful, since it seems they will have difficulty giving and spending in excess of their possessions.

Since generosity, then, is a mean concerned with the giving and the taking of wealth, the generous person will both give and spend the right amount for the right purposes, in small and large matters alike, and do this with pleasure. He will also take the right amounts from the right sources; for since the virtue is a mean about both giving and taking, he will do both in the right way. For decent giving implies decent taking, and the other sort of taking is contrary to the decent sort; hence the states implying each other are present at the same time in the same subject, while the contrary states clearly are not.

If the generous person does find that his spending deviates from what is fine and right, he will feel pain, but moderately and in the right way; for it is proper to virtue to feel both pleasure and pain in the right things and in the right way.

The generous person is also an easy partner to associate with in dealings that involve money; for he can easily be treated unjustly, since he does not honour money, and is more grieved if he has failed to spend what it was right to spend than if he has spent what it was wrong to spend—here he disagrees with Simonides.

The wasteful person is in error here too, since he feels neither pleasure nor pain at the right things or in the right way; this will be more evident as we go on.

We have said that wastefulness and ungenerosity are excesses and deficiencies in two things, in giving and taking—for we also count spending as giving. Now wastefulness is excessive in giving and not taking, but deficient in taking. Ungenerosity is deficient in giving and excessive in taking, but in small matters.

Now the features of wastefulness are not very often combined; for it is not easy to take from nowhere and give to everyone, since private citizens soon outrun their resources in giving, and private citizens are the ones who seem to be wasteful. However, such a person seems to be quite a lot better than the ungenerous person, since he is easily cured, both by growing older and by poverty, and is capable of

reaching the intermediate condition. For he has the features proper to the generous person, since he gives and does not take, though he does neither rightly or well. If, then, he is changed, by habituation or some other means, so that he does them rightly and well, he will be generous; for then he will give to the right people and will not take from the wrong sources. This is why the wasteful person seems not to   25
be base in his character; for excess in giving without taking is proper to a foolish person, not to a vicious or ignoble one.

Someone who is wasteful in this way, then, seems to be much better than the ungenerous person, both for the reasons we have given and because he benefits many, whereas the ungenerous person benefits no one, not even himself.

Most wasteful people, however, as we have said, [not only give wrongly, but] also   30
take from the wrong sources, and to this extent are ungenerous. They become acquisitive because they wish to spend, but cannot do this readily, since they soon exhaust all they have; hence they are compelled to provide from elsewhere. At the same time they care nothing for what is fine, and so take from any source without   1121b
scruple; for they have an appetite for giving, and the way or source does not matter to them.

This is why their ways of giving are not generous either, since they are not fine, do not aim at what is fine, and are not done in the right way. Rather, these people   5
sometimes enrich people who ought to be poor, and would give nothing to people with sound characters, but would give much to flatterers or to those providing some other pleasure.

Hence most of these people are also intemperate. For since they part with money lightly, they also spend it lavishly on intemperance; and because their lives do not   10
aim at what is fine, they decline towards pleasures.

If, then, the wasteful person has been left without a guide, he changes into this; but if he receives attention, he might reach the intermediate and the right state.

Ungenerosity, on the other hand, is incurable, since old age and every incapacity seem to make people ungenerous. And it comes more naturally to human beings than wastefulness; for the many are money-lovers rather than givers.   15

Moreover, it extends widely and has many species, since there seem to be many ways of being ungenerous. For it consists in two conditions, deficiency in giving and excess in taking; but it is not found as a whole in all cases. Sometimes the two conditions are separated, and some people go to excess in taking while others are   20
deficient in giving.

The people called misers, tight-fisted, skinflints and so on, are all deficient in giving, but they do not go after other people's goods and do not wish to take them.

With some people the reason for this is some sort of decency in them, and a concern to avoid what is shameful. For some people seem—at least, this is what they   25
say—to hold on to their money so that they will never be compelled to do anything shameful. These include the cheeseparer, and everyone like that; he is so called from his excessive refusal to give anything.

Others refrain from other people's property because they are afraid, supposing that it is not easy for them to take other people's property without other people   30
taking theirs too; hence, they say, they are content if they neither take from others nor give to them.

Other people, by contrast, go to excess in taking, by taking anything from any

source—those, e.g., who work at degrading occupations, pimps and all such people,
1122a   and usurers who lend small amounts at high interest; for all of these take the wrong
amounts from the wrong sources.

Shameful love of gain is apparently their common feature, since they all put up
with reproaches for some gain, indeed for a small gain. For those who take the
5   wrong things from the wrong sources on a large scale, e.g. tyrants who sack cities
and plunder temples, are called wicked, impious and unjust, but not ungenerous.

The ungenerous, however, include the gambler and the robber, since these are
shameful lovers of gain. For in pursuit of gain both go to great efforts and put up
10   with reproaches; the robber faces the greatest dangers to get his haul, while the
gambler takes his gains from his friends, when they are the ones he ought to be
giving to. Both of them, then, are shameful lovers of gain, because they wish to
acquire gains from the wrong sources; and all these methods of acquisition are
ungenerous.

It is plausibly said that ungenerosity is contrary to generosity. For it is a greater
15   evil than wastefulness; and error in this direction is more common than the error
of wastefulness, as we have described it.

So much, then, for generosity and the vices opposed to it.

2

Next, it seems appropriate to discuss magnificence also. For it seems to be, like
20   generosity, a virtue concerned with wealth, but it extends not, as generosity does,
to all the actions involving wealth, but only to those involving heavy expenses, and
in them it exceeds generosity in its large scale.

For just as the name [*megaloprepeia*] itself suggests, magnificence is expenditure
that is fitting [*prepousa*] in its large scale [*megethos*]. But large scale is large relative to
something; for the expenses of a warship-captain and of a leader of a delegation
25   are not the same. Hence what is fitting is also relative to oneself, the circumstances
and the purpose.

Someone is called magnificent only if he spends the worthy amount on a large
purpose, not on a trivial or an ordinary purpose like the one who 'gave to many a
wanderer'; for the magnificent person is generous, but generosity does not imply
magnificence.

30   The deficiency of this state is called niggardliness. The excess is called vulgarity,
poor taste and such things. These are excesses not because they spend an excessively
great amount on the right things, but because they show off in the wrong circumstances and in the wrong way. We shall discuss these vices later.

The magnificent person, in contrast to these, is like a scientific expert, since he is
35   able to observe what will be the fitting amount, and to spend large amounts in an
appropriate way.

1122b   For, as we said at the start, a state is defined by its activities and its objects; now
the magnificent person's expenditures are large and fitting; so also, then, must the
achievements be, since that is what makes the expense large and fitting to the
5   achievement. Hence the achievement must be worthy of the expense, and the expense worthy of, or even in excess of, the achievement.

In this sort of spending the magnificent person will aim at what is fine, since that is a common feature of the virtues. Moreover, he will spend gladly and readily, since it is niggardly to count every penny; and he will think more about the finest and most fitting way to spend than about the cost or about the cheapest way to do it. 10

Hence the magnificent person must also be generous; for the generous person too will spend what is right in the right way. But it is in this spending that the large scale of the magnificent person, his greatness, is found, since his magnificence is a sort of large scale of generosity in these things; and from an expense that is equal [to a non-magnificent person's] he will make the achievement more magnificent.

[The achievement may be more magnificent even if the expense is equal.] For a 15 possession and an achievement have different sorts of excellence; the most honoured [and hence most excellent] possession is the one worth most, for example gold, but the most honoured achievement is the one that is great and fine, since that is what is admirable to behold. Now what is magnificent is admirable, and the excellence of the achievement consists in its large scale.

This sort of excellence is found in the sorts of expenses called honourable, e.g. in expenses for the gods—dedications, temples, sacrifices and so on for everything 20 divine—and in expenses that provoke a good competition for honour, to the benefit of the community—if, e.g., some city thinks a splendid chorus or warship or a feast for the city must be provided.

But in all cases, as we have said, we fix the right amount by reference to the agent [as well as the task]—by who he is and what resources he has; for the amounts must 25 be worthy of these, fitting the producer as well as the product.

Hence a poor person could not be magnificent, since he lacks the means for large and fitting expenditures; and if he attempts it, he is foolish, since he spends more than what is worthy and right for him, when in fact it is correct spending that expresses virtue.

But large spending befits those who have the means, acquired through their own 30 efforts or their ancestors or connections, or are well-born or reputable, and so on; for each of these conditions includes greatness and reputation for worth.

This, then, above all is the character of the magnificent person, and magnificence is found in these sorts of expenses, as we have said, since these are the largest and 35 most honoured.

It is found also in those private expenses that arise only once, e.g. a wedding and the like, and in those that concern the whole city, or the people in it with a reputation 1123a for worth—the receiving of foreign guests and sending them off, gifts and exchanges of gifts; for the magnificent person spends money on the common good, not on 5 himself, and the gifts have some similarity to dedications.

It is also proper to the magnificent person to build a house befitting his riches, since this is also a suitable adornment; and to spend more readily on long-lasting achievements, since these are the finest, and in each case on what is fitting. For what suits gods does not suit human beings, and what suits a temple does not suit a tomb. 10

And since each great expense is great in relation to a particular kind of object, the most magnificent will be a great expense on a great object, and what is magnificent in a particular area will be what is great in relation to the particular kind of object. Moreover, greatness in the achievements is not the same as greatness in an expense, since the finest ball or oil-bottle has the magnificence proper to a gift for a child, 15 but its value is small and paltry. And so it is proper to the magnificent person, whatever kind of thing he produces, to produce it magnificently, since this is not easily exceeded, and to produce something worthy of the expense.

This, then, is what the magnificent person is like.

The vulgar person who exceeds [the mean] exceeds by spending more than is right, as has been said. For in small expenses he spends a lot, and puts on an inappropriate display. He gives his club a dinner party in the style of a wedding banquet, and when he supplies a chorus for a comedy, he brings them on stage dressed in purple, as they do at Megara. In all this he aims not at what is fine, but at the display of his wealth and at the admiration he thinks he wins in this way. And so where a large expense is right, he spends a little, and spends a lot where a small expense is right.

The niggardly person will be deficient in everything. After spending the largest amounts, he will refuse a small amount, and so destroy a fine result. Whatever he does, while he is doing it he will hesitate and consider how he can spend the smallest possible amount; he will even moan about spending this, and will always think he is doing something on a larger scale than is right.

These states, vulgarity and niggardliness, are vices. But they do not bring reproaches, since they do no harm to one's neighbours and are not too disgraceful.

3

Magnanimity seems, even going by the name alone, to be concerned with great things. Let us see first the sorts of things it is concerned with. It does not matter whether we consider the state itself or the person who expresses it.

The magnanimous person, then, seems to be the one who thinks himself worthy of great things and is really worthy of them. For if someone is not worthy of them but thinks he is, he is foolish, and no virtuous person is foolish or senseless; hence the magnanimous person is the one we have mentioned. Someone who is worthy of little and thinks so is temperate, but not magnanimous; for magnanimity is found in greatness, just as beauty is found in a large body, and small people can be attractive and well-proportioned, but not beautiful.

Someone who thinks he is worthy of great things when he is not is vain; but not everyone who thinks he is worthy of greater things than he is worthy of is vain.

Someone who thinks he is worthy of less than he is worthy of is pusillanimous, whether he is worthy of great or of moderate things; and even if he is worthy of little, he thinks he is worthy of still less than that. The one who seems most pusillanimous is the one who is worthy of great things; for consider how little he would think of himself if he were worthy of less.

The magnanimous person, then, is at the extreme in so far as he makes great claims. But in so far as he makes them rightly, he is intermediate; for what he thinks he is worthy of reflects his real worth, while the others are excessive or deficient. The pusillanimous person is deficient both in relation to himself [i.e. his worth] and in relation to the magnanimous person's estimate of his own worth, while the vain person makes claims that are excessive for himself, but not for the magnanimous person.

If, then, he thinks he is worthy of great things, and is worthy of them, especially 15
of the greatest things, he has one concern above all. Worth is said to [make one
worthy of] external goods; and we would suppose that the greatest of these is the
one we award to the gods, the one above all that is the aim of people with a reputation
for worth, the prize for the finest [achievements]. All this is true of honour, since it 20
is called the greatest of the external goods. Hence the magnanimous person has the
right concern with honours and dishonours.

And even without argument it appears that magnanimous people are concerned
with honour. For the great think themselves worthy of honour most of all, and
honour befits their worth. 25

Since the magnanimous person is worthy of the greatest things, he is the best
person. For in every case the better person is worthy of something greater, and the
best person is worthy of the greatest things; and hence the truly magnanimous
person must be good.

Greatness in each virtue also seems proper to the magnanimous person. And 30
surely it would not at all fit a magnanimous person to run away [from danger when
a coward would], swinging his arms [to get away faster], or to do injustice. For what
goal will make him do shameful actions, when none [of their goals] is great to
him? And examination of particular cases makes the magnanimous person appear
altogether ridiculous if he is not good.

Nor would he be worthy of honour if he were base. For honour is the prize of 35
virtue, and is awarded to good people.

Magnanimity, then, looks like a sort of adornment of the virtues; for it makes 1124a
them greater, and it does not arise without them. Hence it is hard to be truly
magnanimous, since it is not possible without being fine and good.

The magnanimous person, then, is concerned especially with honours and dishon- 5
ours. And when he receives great honours from excellent people, he will be moderately pleased, thinking he is getting what is proper to him, or even less. For there
can be no honour worthy of complete virtue; but still he will accept [excellent
people's] honours, since they have nothing greater to award him.

But if he is honoured by just anyone, or for something small, he will entirely 10
disdain it; for that is not what he is worthy of. And similarly he will disdain dishonour; for it will not be justly attached to him.

As we have said, then, the magnanimous person is concerned especially with
honours. Still, he will also have a moderate attitude to riches and power and every
sort of good and bad fortune, however it turns out. He will be neither excessively 15
pleased by good fortune nor excessively distressed by ill fortune, since he does not
even regard honour as the greatest good.

For positions of power and riches are choiceworthy for their honour; at any rate
their possessors wish to be honoured on account of them. Hence the magnanimous
person who counts honour for little will also count these other goods for little, which
is why he seems arrogant. 20

The results of good fortune, however, seem to contribute to magnanimity. For
the well-born and the powerful or rich are thought worthy of honour, since they
are in a superior position, and everything superior in some good is more honoured.
Hence these things also make people more magnanimous, since some people honour
their possessors for these goods.

25   In reality, however, it is only the good person who is honourable. Still, anyone who has both virtue and these goods is more readily thought worthy of honour.

Those who lack virtue but have these other goods are not justified in thinking themselves worthy of great things, and are not correctly called magnanimous; that is impossible without complete virtue. However, they become arrogant and wantonly
30   aggressive when they have these other goods. For without virtue it is hard to bear
1124b   the results of good fortune suitably, and when these people cannot do it, but suppose they are superior to other people, they despise everyone else, and do whatever they please.

They do this because they are imitating the magnanimous person though they are not really like him. They imitate him where they can; hence they do not do actions
5   expressing virtue, but they despise other people. For the magnanimous person is justified when he despises, since his beliefs are true; but the many despise with no good reason.

He does not face dangers in a small cause, and does not face them frequently, since he honours few things, and is no lover of danger. But he faces them in a great cause, and whenever he faces them he is unsparing of his life, since he does not think life at all costs is worthwhile.

10   He is the sort of person who does good but is ashamed when he receives it; for doing good is proper to the superior person, and receiving it to the inferior. He returns more good than he has received; for in this way the original giver will be repaid, and will also have incurred a new debt to him, and will be the beneficiary.

Magnanimous people seem to remember the good they do, but not what they receive, since the recipient is inferior to the giver, and the magnanimous person
15   wishes to be superior. And they seem to find pleasure in hearing of the good they do, and none in hearing what they receive—that also seems to be why Thetis[8] does not tell Zeus of the good she has done him, and the Spartans do not tell of the good they have done the Athenians, but only of the good received from them.

Again, it is proper to the magnanimous person to ask for nothing, or hardly anything, but to help eagerly.

When he meets people with good fortune or a reputation for worth, he displays
20   his greatness, since superiority over them is difficult and impressive, and there is nothing ignoble in trying to be impressive with them. But when he meets ordinary people he is moderate, since superiority over them is easy, and an attempt to be impressive among inferiors is as vulgar as a display of strength against the weak.

He stays away from what is commonly honoured, and from areas where others
25   lead; he is inactive and lethargic except for some great honour or achievement. Hence his actions are few, but great and renowned.

Moreover, he must be open in his hatreds and his friendships, since concealment is proper to a frightened person. He is concerned for the truth more than for people's opinion. He is open in his speech and actions, since his disdain makes him
30   speak freely. And he speaks the truth, except [when he speaks less than the truth] to the many, [because he is moderate,] not because he is self-deprecating.

---

8. [Thetis, Zeus' daughter, does not remind him that she intervened when the other gods wanted to put him in chains.—M.L.M.]

He cannot let anyone else, except a friend, determine his life. For that would be   1125a
slavish; and this is why all flatterers are servile and inferior people are flatterers.

He is not prone to marvel, since he finds nothing great; or to remember evils,
since it is not proper to a magnanimous person to nurse memories, especially not of
evils, but to overlook them.   5

He is no gossip. For he will not talk about himself or about another, since he is
not concerned to have himself praised or other people blamed. Nor is he given to
praising people. Hence he does not speak evil even of his enemies, except [when he
responds to their] wanton aggression.

He especially avoids laments or entreaties about necessities or small matters, since   10
these attitudes are proper to someone who takes these things seriously.

He is the sort of person whose possessions are fine and unproductive rather than
productive and advantageous, since that is more proper to a self-sufficient person.

The magnanimous person seems to have slow movements, a deep voice and calm
speech. For since he takes few things seriously, he is in no hurry, and since he counts
nothing great, he is not strident; and these [attitudes he avoids] are the causes of a   15
shrill voice and hasty movements.

This, then, is the character of the magnanimous person.

The deficient person is pusillanimous, and the person who goes to excess is vain.
[Like the vulgar and the niggardly person] these also seem not to be evil people,
since they are not evil-doers, but to be in error.

For the pusillanimous person is worthy of goods, but deprives himself of the goods   20
he is worthy of, and would seem to have something bad in him because he does not
think he is worthy of the goods. Indeed he would seem not to know himself; for if
he did, he would aim at the things he is worthy of, since they are goods. For all that,
such people seem hesitant rather than foolish.

But this belief of theirs actually seems to make them worse. For each sort of person
seeks what [he thinks] he is worth; and these people hold back from fine actions and   25
practices, and equally from external goods, because they think they are unworthy
of them.

Vain people, on the other hand, are foolish and do not know themselves; and they
make this obvious. For they undertake commonly honoured exploits, but are not
worthy of them, and then they are found out. They adorn themselves with clothes   30
and ostentatious style and that sort of thing; and since they both wish for good
fortune and wish it to be evident, they talk about it, thinking it will bring them
honour.

Pusillanimity is more opposed than vanity to magnanimity; for it arises more
often, and is worse.

Magnanimity, then, as has been said, is the virtue concerned with *great* honour.   35

4

But, as we said in the first discussion, [just as there is a virtue for small-scale   1125b
giving], there would also seem to be a virtue concerned with honour whose relation
to magnanimity seems similar to the relation of generosity to magnificence.

For it abstains, just as generosity does, from anything great, but forms the right

5   attitude in us on medium and small matters; and just as the taking and giving of money admits of a mean, an excess and a deficiency, so also we can desire honour more or less than is right, and we can desire it from the right sources and in the right way.

10   For we blame the honour-lover for aiming at honour more than is right, and from the wrong sources; and we blame someone indifferent to honour for deciding not to be honoured even for fine things. Sometimes, however, we praise the honour-lover for being manly and a lover of what is fine; and again we praise the indifferent person for being moderate and temperate, as we said in the first discussion.

Clearly, however, since we speak in several ways of loving something, what we
15   regard as love of honour is not the same attitude in every case. Rather, when we praise it, we regard it as loving honour more than the many do; and when we blame it, we regard it as loving honour more than is right.

But when the mean has no name, the extremes look like rivals for it, as though it were unclaimed.

Nonetheless, where there is excess and deficiency there is also an intermediate
20   condition; and since people desire honour both more and less than is right, it is also possible to desire it in the right way. This state, then, a nameless mean concerned with honour, is praised.

When compared with love of honour, it appears as indifference to honour; when compared with indifference, it appears as love of honour; and when compared with both, it appears in a way as both. This would seem to be true with the other virtues
25   too; but in this case the extreme people appear to be opposed [only to each other] because the intermediate person has no name.

5

Mildness is the mean concerned with anger. Since the mean is nameless, and the extremes are practically nameless too, we call the intermediate condition mildness, inclining towards the deficiency, which is also nameless. The excess might be called
30   a kind of irascibility; for the relevant feeling is anger, though its sources are many and varied.

The person who is angry at the right things and towards the right people, and also in the right way, at the right time and for the right length of time, is praised. This, then, will be the mild person, since it is his mildness that is praised; for being
35   a mild person means being undisturbed, not led by feeling, but irritated at whatever
1126a reason prescribes and for the length of time it prescribes. And he seems to err more in the direction of deficiency, since the mild person is ready to pardon, not eager to exact a penalty.

The deficiency—a sort of inirascibility or whatever it is—is blamed, since people
5   who are not angered by the right things, or in the right way, or at the right times, or towards the right people, all seem to be foolish. For such a person seems to be insensible and to feel no pain. Since he is not angered, he does not seem to be the sort to defend himself; and such willingness to accept insults to oneself and to overlook insults to one's family and friends is slavish.

10   The excess arises in all these ways—in anger towards the wrong people, at the wrong times, more than is right, more hastily than is right, and for a longer time.

However, they are not all found in the same person; for they could not all exist together, since evil destroys itself as well as other things, and if it is present as a whole it becomes unbearable.

Irascible people get angry quickly, towards the wrong people, at the wrong times and more than is right; but they stop soon, and this is their best feature. They do all this because they do not contain their anger, but their quick temper makes them pay back the offence without concealment, and then stop.   15

Choleric people are quick-tempered to extreme, and irascible about everything and at everything; that is how they get their name.

Bitter people, however, are hard to reconcile, and stay angry for a long time, since they contain their emotion. It stops, however, when they pay back the offence; for the exaction of the penalty produces pleasure in place of pain, and so puts a stop to the anger. But if this does not happen, they hold their grudge; for no one else persuades them out of it, since it is not obvious, and digesting anger in oneself takes time. This sort of person is most troublesome to himself and to his closest friends.   20

                                       25

The people we call irritable are those who are irritated by the wrong things, more severely and for longer than is right, and are not reconciled until [the offender has suffered] a penalty and corrective treatment.

We regard the excess as more opposed [than the deficiency] to mildness. For it is more widespread, since it comes more naturally to human beings to exact a penalty from the offender [than to overlook an offence]; and moreover irritable people are harder to live with.   30

These remarks also make clear a previous point of ours. For it is hard to define how, against whom, about what, and how long we should be angry, and up to what point someone is acting correctly or in error.

For someone who deviates a little towards either excess or deficiency is not blamed. For sometimes we praise deficient people and say they are mild; and sometimes we say that people who get irritated are manly because we think they are capable of ruling others.   35
                                       1126b

How far, then, and in what way must someone deviate to be open to blame? It is not easy to answer in a [general] account, since these are particular cases, and the judgment depends on perception.

However, this much at least is clear: the intermediate state is to be praised, and it is expressed in being angry towards the right people, about the right things, in the right way and so on. The excesses and deficiencies are to be blamed, lightly if they go a little way, more if they go further, and strongly if they go far. Clearly, then, we must keep to the intermediate state.   5

So much, then, for the states concerned with anger.   10

6

In meeting people, living together and associating in conversations and actions, some people seem to be ingratiating; these are the ones who praise everything to please us and never cross us, but think they must cause no pain to those they meet. In contrast to these, people who oppose us on every point and do not care in the least about causing pain are called cantankerous and quarrelsome.   15

Clearly, the states we have mentioned are blameworthy, and the state intermediate between them is praiseworthy; this state is expressed in accepting and objecting to things when it is right and in the right way.

20   This state has no name, but it would seem to be most like friendship; for the character of the person in the intermediate state is just what we mean in speaking of a decent friend, except that the friend is also fond of us. It differs from friendship in not requiring any special feeling or any fondness for the people we meet. For this person takes each thing in the right way because that is his character, not because he is a friend or an enemy.

25   For he will behave this way to new and old acquaintances, to familiar companions and strangers without distinction, except that he will also do what is suitable for each; for the proper ways to spare or to hurt the feelings of familiar companions are not the proper ways to treat strangers.

We have said, then, that in general he will treat people in the right way when he meets them. [More exactly], he will aim to avoid causing pain or to share pleasure, while always referring to what is fine and beneficial.

30   For he would seem to be concerned with the pleasures and pains that arise in meeting people; and if it is not fine, or it is harmful, for him to share one of these pleasures, he will object and will decide to cause pain instead. Further, if the other person will suffer no slight disgrace or harm from doing an action, and only slight pain if he is opposed, the virtuous person will object to the action and not accept it.

35
1127a   When he meets people with a reputation for worth his attitude will be different from his attitude to just anyone; he will take different attitudes to those he knows better and those he knows less well; and similarly with the other differences, according what is suitable to each sort of person.

What he will choose in itself [if he need not consider the consequences], is to share
5   pleasure and avoid causing pain. But he will be guided by consequences—i.e. by what is fine and what is expedient—if they are greater; and, moreover, to secure great pleasure in the future he will cause slight pain.

This, then, is the character of the intermediate person, though he has no name.

Among those who share pleasure the person who tries to be pleasant with no ulterior purpose is ingratiating, and the one who does it for some advantage in
10   money and what money can buy is the flatterer. The one who objects to everything is, as we have said, the cantankerous and quarrelsome person. However, the extremes appear to be opposite [only] to each other, because the intermediate condition has no name.

7

The mean belonging to boastfulness is also concerned with practically these same [conditions of social life]; and it too is nameless.

15   It is a good idea to examine the nameless virtues as well as the others. For if we discuss particular aspects of character one at a time, we will acquire a better knowledge of them; and if we survey the virtues and see that in each case the virtue is a mean, we will have more confidence in our belief that the virtues are means.

As concerns social life, then, having discussed those who aim at giving pleasure or pain when they meet people, let us now discuss those who are truthful and false, both in words and in actions, i.e. in their claims [about themselves]. 20

First, then, the boaster seems to claim qualities that win reputation, when he either lacks them altogether or has less than he claims. And the self-deprecator, by contrast, denies or belittles his actual qualities. The intermediate person, however, is straight-forward, truthful in what he says and does, since he acknowledges the qualities he 25 has without belittling or exaggerating.

Each of these things may be done with or without an ulterior purpose; and someone's character determines what he says and does and the way he lives, if he is not acting for an ulterior purpose. Now in itself [when no ulterior purpose is involved], falsehood is base and blameworthy, and truth is fine and praiseworthy; hence the truthful person, like other intermediate people, is praiseworthy, and both 30 the tellers of falsehoods are blameworthy, the boaster to a higher degree.

Before we discuss each type of blameworthy person let us discuss the truthful person. Here we do not mean someone who is truthful in agreements and in matters of justice and injustice, since these concern a different virtue, but someone who is 1127b truthful both in what he says and in how he lives, when nothing about justice is at stake, simply because that is his state of character.

Someone with this character seems to be a decent person. For a lover of the truth who is truthful even when nothing is at stake will be still keener to tell the truth when 5 something is at stake, since he will avoid falsehood as shameful [when something is at stake], having already avoided it in itself [when nothing was at stake]. And this sort of person is praiseworthy.

He inclines to tell less, rather than more, than the truth; for this appears more suitable, since excesses are oppressive.

If someone claims to have more than he has, with no ulterior purpose, he certainly 10 looks as though he is a base person, since otherwise he would not enjoy telling falsehoods; but apparently he is pointlessly foolish rather than bad.

Among those who do it with an ulterior purpose, the one who does it for reputation or honour is not to be blamed too much as a boaster. But the one who does it for money or for means to making money is more disgraceful.

It is not a person's capacity, but his decision, that makes him a boaster; for his 15 state of character makes a person a boaster, just as it makes a person a liar. And [boasters differ in their states of character]; one is a boaster because he enjoys telling falsehoods in itself, another because he pursues reputation or gain.

Boasters who aim at reputation, then, claim the qualities that win praise or win congratulation for happiness. Boasters who aim at profit claim the qualities that gratify other people and that allow someone to avoid detection when he claims to 20 be what he is not, e.g. a wise diviner or doctor. That is why most people claim these sorts of things and boast about them; for they have the features just mentioned.

Self-deprecators underestimate themselves in what they say, and so appear to have more cultivated characters. For they seem to be avoiding bombast, not looking for profit, in what they say; and the qualities that win reputation are the ones that 25 these people especially disavow, as Socrates also used to do.

On the other hand, those who disavow small and obvious qualities are called humbugs, and are more readily despised; sometimes, indeed, this even appears a

30 form of boastfulness, as the Spartans' [austere] dress does—for the extreme deficiency, as well as the excess, is boastful.

But those who are moderate in their self-deprecation and confine themselves to
qualities that are not too commonplace or obvious appear sophisticated.

It is the boaster [rather than the self-deprecator] who appears to be opposed to
the truthful person, since he is the worse [of the two extremes].

8

Since life also includes relaxation, and in this we pass our time with some form of
1128a amusement, here also it seems possible to behave appropriately in meeting people,
and to say and listen to the right things and in the right way. The company we are
in when we speak or listen also makes a difference. Clearly, then, it is possible here
also to exceed the intermediate condition or to be deficient.

5   Those who go to excess in raising laughs seem to be vulgar buffoons. They stop
at nothing to raise a laugh, and care more about that than about saying what is
seemly and avoiding pain to the victims of the joke.

10   Those who would never say anything themselves to raise a laugh, and even object
when other people do it, seem to be boorish and stiff.

Those who joke in appropriate ways are called witty, or, in other words, agile-
witted, since these sorts of jokes seem to be movements of someone's character, and
characters are judged, as bodies are, by their movements. Since there are always
opportunities at hand for raising a laugh, and most people enjoy amusements and
15   jokes more than they should, buffoons are also called witty because they are thought
cultivated; nonetheless, they differ, and differ considerably, from witty people, as
our account has made clear.

Dexterity is also proper to the intermediate state. It is proper to the dexterous
person to say and listen to what suits the decent and civilized person. For some
20   things are suitable for this sort of person to say and listen to by way of amusement;
and the civilized person's amusement differs from the slavish person's, and the
educated person's from the uneducated person's. This can also be seen from old
and new comedies; for what people used to find funny was shameful abuse, but what
25   they now find funny instead is innuendo, which is considerably more seemly.

Then should the person who jokes well be defined by his making remarks not
unsuitable for a civilized person, or by his avoiding pain and even giving pleasure
to the hearer? Perhaps, though, this [avoiding pain and giving pleasure] is indefinable, since different people find different things hateful or pleasant.

The remarks he is willing to hear made are of the same sort, since those he is
prepared to hear made seem to be those he is prepared to make himself.

Hence he will not be indiscriminate in his remarks. For since a joke is a type of
30   abuse, and legislators prohibit some types of abuse, they would presumably be right
to prohibit some types of joke too. Hence the cultivated and civilized person, as a
sort of law to himself, will take this [discriminating] attitude.

This, then, is the character of the intermediate person, whether he is called
dexterous or witty.

The buffoon cannot resist raising a laugh, and spares neither himself nor anyone

else if he can cause laughter, even by making remarks that the sophisticated person 35
would never make, and some that the sophisticated person would not even be willing 1128b
to hear made.

The boor is useless when he meets people in these circumstances. For he contributes nothing himself, and objects to everything, even though relaxation and amusement seem to be necessary in life.

We have spoken, then, of three means in life, all concerned with association in 5
certain conversations and actions. They differ in so far as one is concerned with
truth, the others with what is pleasant. One of those concerned with pleasure is
found in amusements, and the other in our behaviour in the other aspects of life
when we meet people.

9

Shame is not properly regarded as a virtue, since it would seem to be more like 10
a feeling than like a state [of character]. It is defined, at any rate, as a sort of fear
of disrepute, and its expression is similar to that of fear of something terrifying; for
a feeling of disgrace makes people blush, and fear of death makes them turn pale.
Hence both [types of fear] appear to be in some way bodily [reactions], which seem 15
to be more characteristic of feelings than of states.

Further, the feeling of shame is suitable for youth, not for every time of life. For
we think it right for young people to be prone to shame, since they live by their
feelings, and hence often go astray, but are restrained by shame; and hence we
praise young people who are prone to shame. No one, by contrast, would praise an 20
older person for readiness to feel disgrace, since we think it wrong for him to do
any action that causes a feeling of disgrace.

For a feeling of disgrace is not proper to the decent person either, if it is caused
by base actions; for these should not be done. And if some actions are really disgraceful and others are base [only] in [his] belief, that does not matter, since neither
should be done, and so he should not feel disgrace. It is proper to a base person to 25
have a character that makes him do disgraceful action.

Further, if someone is in a state that would make him feel disgrace if he were to
do a disgraceful action, and because of this thinks he is decent, that is absurd. For
shame is concerned with what is voluntary, and the decent person will never willingly
do base actions. Shame might, however, be decent on an assumption; for if [the
decent person] were to do [these disgraceful actions], he would feel disgrace; but 30
this does not apply to the virtues.

And if we grant that it is base to feel no disgrace or shame at disgraceful actions,
it still does not follow that to do such actions and then to feel disgrace at them is
decent.

Continence is not a virtue either. It is a sort of mixed state. We will explain about 35
it in what we say later. Now let us discuss justice.

BOOK FIVE

1

1129a   The questions we must examine about justice and injustice are these: What sorts
5   of actions are they concerned with? What sort of mean is justice? What are the
extremes between which justice is intermediate? Let us examine them by the same
type of investigation that we used in the topics discussed before.

We see that the state everyone means in speaking of justice is the state that makes
us doers of just actions, that makes us do justice and wish what is just. In the same
10   way they mean by injustice the state that makes us do injustice and wish what is
unjust. Let us also, then, [follow the common beliefs and] begin by assuming this in
outline.

For what is true of sciences and capacities is not true of states. For while one and
the same capacity or science seems to have contrary activities, a state that is a contrary
15   has no contrary activities. Health, e.g., only makes us do healthy actions, not their
contraries; for we say we are walking in a healthy way if [and only if] we are walking
in the way a healthy person would.

Often one of a pair of contrary states is recognized from the other contrary; and
often the states are recognized from their subjects. For if, e.g., the good state is
20   evident, the bad state becomes evident too; and moreover the good state becomes
evident from the things that have it, and the things from the state. For if, e.g., the
good state is thickness of flesh, then the bad state will necessarily be thinness of
flesh, and the thing that produces the good state will be what produces thickness of
flesh.

It follows, usually, that if one of a pair of contraries is spoken of in more ways
25   than one, so is the other; if, e.g., what is just is spoken of in more ways than one, so
is what is unjust.

Now it would seem that justice and injustice are both spoken of in more ways than
one, but since the different ways are closely related, their homonymy is unnoticed,
and is less clear than it is with distant homonyms where the distance in appearance
30   is wide (e.g., the bone below an animal's neck and what we lock doors with are called
keys homonymously).

Let us, then, find the number of ways an unjust person is spoken of. Both the
lawless person and the greedy and unfair person seem to be unjust; and so, clearly,
both the lawful and the fair person will be just. Hence what is just will be both what
1129b   is lawful and what is fair, and what is unjust will be both what is lawless and what is
unfair.

Since the unjust person is greedy, he will be concerned with goods—not with all
goods, but only with those involved in good and bad fortune, goods which are,
[considered] unconditionally, always good, but for this or that person not always
5   good. Though human beings pray for these and pursue them, they are wrong; the
right thing is to pray that what is good unconditionally will also be good for us, but
to choose [only] what is good for us.

Now the unjust person [who chooses these goods] does not choose more in every
case; in the case of what is bad unconditionally he actually chooses less. But since
10   what is less bad also seems to be good in a way, and greed aims at more of what is

good, he seems to be greedy. In fact he is unfair; for unfairness includes [all these actions], and is a common feature [of his choice of the greater good and of the lesser evil].

Since, as we saw, the lawless person is unjustified and the lawful person is just, it clearly follows that whatever is lawful is in some way just; for the provisions of legislative science are lawful, and we say that each of them is just. Now in every matter they deal with the laws aim either at the common benefit of all, or at the benefit of those in control, whose control rests on virtue or on some other such basis. And so in one way what we call just is whatever produces and maintains happiness and its parts for a political community.

15

Now the law instructs us to do the actions of a brave person—not to leave the battle-line, e.g., or to flee, or to throw away our weapons; of a temperate person—not to commit adultery or wanton aggression; of a mild person—not to strike or revile another; and similarly requires actions that express the other virtues, and prohibits those that express the vices. The correctly established law does this correctly, and the less carefully framed one does this worse.

20

25

This type of justice, then, is complete virtue, not complete virtue unconditionally, but complete virtue in relation to another. And this is why justice often seems to be supreme among the virtues, and 'neither the evening star nor the morning star is so marvellous', and the proverb says 'And in justice all virtue is summed up.'

30

Moreover, justice is complete virtue to the highest degree because it is the complete exercise of complete virtue. And it is the complete exercise because the person who has justice is able to exercise virtue in relation to another, not only in what concerns himself; for many are able to exercise virtue in their own concerns but unable in what relates to another.

And hence Bias seems to have been correct in saying that ruling will reveal the man, since a ruler is automatically related to another, and in a community. And for the same reason justice is the only virtue that seems to be another person's good, because it is related to another; for it does what benefits another, either the ruler or the fellow-member of the community.

1130a

5

The worst person, therefore, is the one who exercises his vice towards himself and his friends as well [as towards others]. And the best person is not the one who exercises virtue [only] towards himself, but the one who [also] exercises it in relation to another, since this is a difficult task.

This type of justice, then, is the whole, not a part, of virtue, and the injustice contrary to it is the whole, not a part, of vice.

10

At the same time our discussion makes clear the difference between virtue and this type of justice. For virtue is the same as justice, but what it is to be virtue is not the same as what it is to be justice. Rather, in so far as virtue is related to another, it is justice, and in so far as it is a certain sort of state unconditionally it is virtue.

2

But we are looking for the type of justice, since we say there is one, that consists in a part of virtue, and correspondingly for the type of injustice that is a part [of vice].

15

Here is evidence that there is this type of justice and injustice:

First, if someone's activities express the other vices—if, e.g., cowardice made him throw away his shield, or irritability made him revile someone, or ungenerosity made him fail to help someone with money—what he does is unjust, but not greedy. But when one acts from greed, in many cases his action expresses none of these vices—certainly not all of them; but it still expresses some type of wickedness, since we blame him, and [in particular] it expresses injustice. Hence there is another type of injustice that is a part of the whole, and a way for a thing to be unjust that is a part of the whole that is contrary to law.

Moreover, if A commits adultery for profit and makes a profit, while B commits adultery because of his appetite, and spends money on it to his own loss, B seems intemperate rather than greedy, while A seems unjust, not intemperate. Clearly, then, this is because A acts to make a profit.

Further, we can refer every other unjust action to some vice—to intemperance if he committed adultery, to cowardice if he deserted his comrade in the battle-line, to anger if he struck someone. But if he made an [unjust] profit, we can refer it to no other vice except injustice.

Hence evidently (a) there is another type of injustice, special injustice, besides the whole of injustice; and (b) it is synonymous with the whole, since the definition is in the same genus. For (b) both have their area of competence in relation to another. But (a) special injustice is concerned with honour or wealth or safety, or whatever single name will include all these, and aims at the pleasure that results from making a profit; but the concern of injustice as a whole is whatever concerns the excellent person.

Clearly, then, there is more than one type of justice, and there is another type besides [the type that is] the whole of virtue; but we must still grasp what it is, and what sort of thing it is.

What is unjust is divided into what is lawless and what is unfair, and what is just into what is lawful and what is fair. The [general] injustice previously described, then, is concerned with what is lawless. But what is unfair is not the same as what is lawless, but related to it as part to whole, since whatever is unfair is lawless, but not everything lawless is unfair. Hence also the type of injustice and the way for a thing to be unjust [that expresses unfairness] are not the same as the type [that expresses lawlessness], but differ as parts from wholes. For this injustice [as unfairness] is a part of the whole of injustice, and similarly justice [as fairness] is a part of the whole of justice.

Hence we must describe special [as well as general] justice and injustice, and equally this way for a thing to be just or unjust.

Let us, then, set to one side the type of justice and injustice that corresponds to the whole of virtue, justice being the exercise of the whole of virtue, and injustice of the whole of vice, in relation to another.

And it is evident how we must distinguish the way for a thing to be just or unjust that expresses this type of justice and injustice; for the majority of lawful actions, we might say, are the actions resulting from virtue as a whole. For the law instructs us to express each virtue, and forbids us to express each vice, in how we live. Moreover, the actions producing the whole of virtue are the lawful actions that the laws prescribe for education promoting the common good.

We must wait till later, however, to determine whether the education that makes an individual an unconditionally good man is a task for political science or for another science; for, presumably, being a good man is not the same as being every sort of good citizen.

Special justice, however, and the corresponding way for something to be just [must be divided].

One species is found in the distribution of honours or wealth or anything else that can be divided among members of a community who share in a political system; for here it is possible for one member to have a share equal or unequal to another's.

Another species concerns rectification in transactions. This species has two parts, since one sort of transaction is voluntary, and one involuntary. Voluntary transactions include selling, buying, lending, pledging, renting, depositing, hiring out— these are called voluntary because the origin of these transactions is voluntary. Some involuntary ones are secret, e.g. theft, adultery, poisoning, pimping, slave-deception, murder by treachery, false witness; others are forcible, e.g. assault, imprisonment, murder, plunder, mutilation, slander, insult.

3

Since the unjust person is unfair, and what is unjust is unfair, there is clearly an intermediate between the unfair [extremes], and this is what is fair; for in any action where too much and too little are possible, the fair [amount] is also possible. And so if what is unjust is unfair, what is just is fair (*ison*), as seems true to everyone even without argument.

And since what is equal (*ison*) [and fair] is intermediate, what is just is some sort of intermediate. And since what is equal involves at least two things [equal to each other], it follows that what is just must be intermediate and equal, and related to some people. In so far as it is intermediate, it must be between too much and too little; in so far as it is equal, it involves two things; and in so far as it is just, it is just for some people. Hence what is just requires four things at least; the people for whom it is just are two, and the [equal] things that are involved are two.

Equality for the people involved will be the same as for the things involved, since [in a just arrangement] the relation between the people will be the same as the relation between the things involved. For if the people involved are not equal, they will not [justly] receive equal shares; indeed, whenever equals receive unequal shares, or unequals equal shares, in a distribution, that is the source of quarrels and accusations.

This is also clear from considering what fits a person's worth. For everyone agrees that what is just in distributions must fit some sort of worth, but what they call worth is not the same; supporters of democracy say it is free citizenship, some supporters of oligarchy say it is wealth, others good birth, while supporters of aristocracy say it is virtue.

Hence what is just [since it requires equal shares for equal people] is in some way proportionate. For proportion is special to number as a whole, not only to numbers consisting of [abstract] units, since it is equality of ratios and requires at least four terms.

Now divided proportion clearly requires four terms. But so does continuous proportion, since here we use one term as two, and mention it twice. When, e.g.,

30

1131a

5

10

15

20

25

30

1131b

line A is to line B as B is to C, B is mentioned twice; and so if B is introduced twice, the terms in the proportion will be four.

5   What is just will also require at least four terms, with the same ratio [between the pairs], since the people [A and B] and the items [C and D] involved are divided in the same way. Term C, then, is to term D as A is to B, and, taking them alternately, B is to D as A is to C. Hence there will also be the same relation of whole [A and C] to whole [B and D]; this is the relation in which the distribution pairs them, and it pairs them justly if this is how they are combined.

Hence the combination of term A with C and of B with D is what is just in
10   distribution, and this way of being just is intermediate, while what is unjust is contrary to what is proportionate. For what is proportionate is intermediate, and what is just is proportionate.

This is the sort of proportion that mathematicians call geometrical, since in geometrical proportion the relation of whole to whole is the same as the relation of each
15   [part] to each [part]. But this proportion [involved in justice] is not continuous, since there is no single term for both the person and the item.

What is just, then, is what is proportionate, and what is unjust is what is counterproportionate. Hence [in an unjust action] one term becomes more and the other less; and this is indeed how it turns out in practice, since the one doing injustice has
20   more of the good, and the victim less. With an evil the ratio is reversed, since the lesser evil, compared to the greater, counts as a good; for the lesser evil is more choiceworthy than the greater, what is choiceworthy is good, and what is more choiceworthy is a greater good.

This, then, is the first species of what is just.

4

25   The other way of being just is the rectificatory, found in transactions both voluntary and involuntary; and this way of being just belongs to a different species from the first.

For what is just in distribution of common assets will always fit the proportion
30   mentioned above, since distribution from common funds will also fit the ratio to one another of different people's deposits. Similarly, the way of being unjust that is opposed to this way of being just is what is counter-proportionate. On the other
1132a   hand, what is just in transactions is certainly equal in a way, and what is unjust is unequal; but still it fits numerical proportion, not the [geometrical] proportion of the other species.

For here it does not matter if a decent person has taken from a base person, or a base person from a decent person, or if a decent or a base person has committed adultery. Rather, the law looks only at differences in the harm [inflicted], and treats
5   the people involved as equals, when one does injustice while the other suffers it, and one has done the harm while the other has suffered it. Hence the judge tries to restore this unjust situation to equality, since it is unequal.

For [not only both when one steals from another but also] and when one is wounded and the other wounds him, or one kills and the other is killed, the action and the suffering are unequally divided [with profit for the offender and loss for

the victim]; and the judge tries to restore the [profit and] loss to a position of equality, 10
by subtraction from [the offender's] profit. For in such cases, stating it without
qualification, we speak of profit for, e.g., the attacker who wounded his victim, even
if that is not the proper word for some cases, and of loss for the victim who suffers
the wound. At any rate, when what was suffered has been measured, one part is
called the [victim's] loss, and the other the [offender's] profit.

In fact, however, these names 'loss' and 'profit' are derived from voluntary ex- 1132b11
change. For having more than one's own share is called making a profit, and having
less than what one had at the beginning is called suffering a loss, e.g. in buying and 15
selling and in other transactions permitted by law. And when people get neither
more nor less, but precisely what belongs to them, they say they have their own
share, and make neither a loss nor a profit.

Hence what is equal is intermediate between more and less; profit and loss are 1132a14
more and less in contrary ways, since more good and less evil is profit, and the
contrary is loss; and the intermediate area between [profit and loss], we have found,
is what is equal, which we say is just. Hence what is just in rectification is what is
intermediate between loss and profit.

Hence parties to a dispute resort to a judge, and an appeal to a judge is an appeal 20
to what is just; for the judge is intended to be a sort of living embodiment of what
is just. Moreover, they seek the judge as an intermediary, and in some cities they
actually call judges mediators, assuming that if they are awarded an intermediate
amount, the award will be just. If, then, the judge is an intermediary, what is just is
in some way intermediate.

The judge restores equality, as though a line [AB] had been cut into unequal parts 25
[AC and CB], and he removed from the larger part [AC] the amount [DC] by which
it exceeds the half [AD] of the line [AB], and added this amount [DC] to the smaller
part [CB]. And when the whole [AB] has been halved [into AD and DB], then they
say that each person has what is properly his own, when he has got an equal share.
This is also why it is called just (*dikaion*), because it is a bisection (*dicha*), as though 31
we said bisected (*dichaion*), and the judge (*dikastes*) is a bisector (*dichastes*).

What is equal [in this case] is intermediate, by numerical proportion, between the 29
larger [AC] and the smaller line [CB]. For when [the same amount] is subtracted 30, 32
from one of two equal things and added to the other, then the one part exceeds the
other by the two parts; for if a part had been subtracted from the one, but not added
to the other, the larger part would have exceeded the smaller by just one part. Hence 1132b
the larger part exceeds the intermediate by one part, and the intermediate from
which [a part] was subtracted [exceeds the smaller] by one part.

In this way, then, we will recognize what we must subtract from the one who has
more and add to the one who has less [to restore equality]; for to the one who has
less we must add the amount by which the intermediate exceeds what he has, and
from the greatest amount [which the one who has more has] we must subtract the 5
amount by which it exceeds the intermediate. Let lines AA', BB' and CC' be equal;
let AE be subtracted from AA' and CD be added to CC', so that the whole line DCC'
will exceed the line EA' by the parts CD and CF [where CF equals AE]; it follows
that DCC' exceeds BB' by CD.

Hence what is just is intermediate between a certain kind of loss and gain, since 18
it is having the equal amount both before and after [the transaction.] 20

5

It seems to some people, however, that reciprocity is also unconditionally just. This was the Pythagoreans' view, since their definition stated unconditionally that what is just is reciprocity with another.

25 The truth is that reciprocity suits neither distributive nor rectificatory justice, though people take even Rhadamanthys' [primitive] conception of justice to describe rectificatory justice: 'If he suffered what he did, upright justice would be done.'[9]

For in many cases reciprocity conflicts [with rectificatory justice]. If, e.g., a ruling official [exercising his office] wounded someone else, he must not be wounded in 30 retaliation, but if someone wounded a ruling official, he must not only be wounded but also receive corrective treatment. Moreover, the voluntary or involuntary character of the action makes a great difference.

In associations for exchange, however, this way of being just, reciprocity that is proportionate rather than equal, holds people together; for a city is maintained by proportionate reciprocity. For people seek to return either evil for evil, since other- 1133a wise [their condition] seems to be slavery, or good for good, since otherwise there is no exchange; and they are maintained [in an association] by exchange.

Indeed, that is why they make a temple of the Graces prominent, so that there will be a return of benefits received. For this is what is special to grace; when someone has been gracious to us, we must do a service for him in return, and also ourselves 5 take the lead in being gracious again.

It is diagonal combination that produces proportionate exchange. Let A be a builder, B a shoemaker, C a house, D a shoe. The builder must receive the shoemak- 10 er's product from him, and give him the builder's own product in return. If, then, first of all, proportionate equality is found, and, next, reciprocity is also achieved, then the proportionate return will be reached. Otherwise it is not equal, and the exchange will not be maintained, since the product of one may well be superior to the product of the other. These products, then, must be equalized.

This is true of the other crafts also; for they would have been destroyed unless 15 the producer produced the same thing, of the same quantity and quality as the thing affected underwent.

For no association [for exchange] is formed from two doctors. It is formed from a doctor and a farmer, and, in general, from people who are different and unequal and who must be equalized.

This is why all items for exchange must be comparable in some way. Currency 20 came along to do exactly this, and in a way it becomes an intermediate, since it measures everything, and so measures excess and deficiency—how many shoes are equal to a house.

Hence, as builder is to shoemaker, so must the number of shoes be to a house; for 25 if this does not happen, there will be no exchange and no association, and the proportionate equality will not be reached unless they are equal in some way. Every- thing, then, must be measured by some one measure, as we said before.

In reality, this measure is need, which holds everything together; for if people

---

9. [In mythology a judge in the underworld.—T.I.]

required nothing, or needed things to different extents, there would be either no exchange or not the same exchange. And currency has become a sort of pledge of need, by convention; in fact it has its name (*nomisma*) because it is not by nature, but   30
by the current law (*nomos*), and it is within our power to alter it and to make it useless.

Reciprocity will be secured, then, when things are equalized, so that the shoemaker's product is to the farmer's as the farmer is to the shoemaker. However, they   1133b
must be introduced into the figure of proportion not when they have already exchanged and one extreme has both excesses, but when they still have their own; in that way they will be equals and associates, because this sort of equality can be found in them. Let A be a farmer, C food, B a shoemaker and D his product that has been   5
equalized; if this sort of reciprocity were not possible, there would be no association.

Now clearly need holds [an association] together as a single unit, since people with no need of each other, both of them or either one, do not exchange, as they exchange whenever another requires what one has oneself, e.g. wine, when they allow the export of corn. This, then, must be equalized.   10

If an item is not required at the moment, currency serves to guarantee us a future exchange, guaranteeing that the item will be there for us if we require it; for it must be there for us to take if we pay. Now the same thing happens to currency [as to other goods], and it does not always count for the same; still, it tends to be more stable. Hence everything must have a price; for in that way there will always be   15
exchange, and then there will be association.

Currency, then, by making things commensurate as a measure does, equalizes them; for there would be no association without exchange, no exchange without equality, no equality without commensurability. And so, though things so different cannot become commensurate in reality, they can become commensurate enough   20
in relation to our needs. Hence there must be some single unit fixed [as current] by a stipulation. This is why it is called currency; for this makes everything commensurate, since everything is measured by currency.

Let A, for instance, be a house, B ten minae, C a bed. A is half of B if a house is worth five minae or equal to them; and C, the bed, is a tenth of B. It is clear, then,   25
how many beds are equal to one house—five. This is clearly how exchange was before there was currency; for it does not matter whether a house is exchanged for five beds or for the currency for which five beds are exchanged.

6

We have previously described, then, the relation of reciprocity to what is just. We   1134a23
must now notice that we are looking not only for what is just unconditionally but   25
also for what is just in a political association. This is found among associates in a life aiming at self-sufficiency, who are free and either proportionately or numerically equal.

Hence those who lack these features have nothing politically just in their relations, though they have something just in so far as it is similar [to what is politically just].

For what is just is found among those who have law in their relations. Where there   30
is law, there is injustice, since the judicial process is judgment that distinguishes what is just from what is unjust. Where there is injustice there is also doing injustice, though where there is doing injustice there need not also be injustice. And doing

injustice is awarding to oneself too many of the things that, [considered] unconditionally, are good, and too few of the things that, [considered] unconditionally, are
bad.

35
1134b
This is why we allow only reason, not a human being, to be ruler; for a human
being awards himself too many goods and becomes a tyrant, but a ruler is a guardian
of what is just and hence of what is equal [and so must not award himself too many
goods].

If a ruler is just, he seems to profit nothing by it. For since he does not award
himself more of what, [considered] unconditionally, is good if it is not proportionate
5   to him, he seems to labour for another's benefit; that is why justice is said, as we also
remarked before, to be another person's good. Hence some payment [for ruling]
should be given; this is honour and privilege, and the people who are unsatisfied by
these are the ones who become tyrants.

What is just for a master and a father is similar to this, not the same. For there is
10 no unconditional injustice in relation to what is one's own; one's own possession, or
one's child until it is old enough and separated, is as though it were a part of oneself,
and no one decides to harm himself. Hence there is no injustice in relation to them,
and so nothing politically unjust or just either. For we found that what is politically
15 just must conform to law, and apply to those who are naturally suited for law,
hence to those who have equality in ruling and being ruled. [Approximation to this
equality] explains why relations with a wife more than with children or possessions
allow something to count as just—for that is what is just in households; still, this too
is different from what is politically just.

7

One part of what is politically just is natural, and the other part legal. What is
20 natural is what has the same validity everywhere alike, independent of its seeming
so or not. What is legal is what originally makes no difference [whether it is done]
one way or another, but makes a difference whenever people have laid down the
rule—e.g. that a mina is the price of a ransom, or that a goat rather than two sheep
should be sacrificed; and also laws passed for particular cases, e.g. that sacrifices
should be offered to Brasidas,[10] and enactments by decree.

Now it seems to some people that everything just is merely legal, since what is
25 natural is unchangeable and equally valid everywhere—fire, e.g, burns both here
and in Persia—while they see that what is just changes [from city to city].

This is not so, though in a way it is so. With us, though presumably not at all with
30 the gods, there is such a thing as what is natural, but still all is changeable; despite
the change there is such a thing as what is natural and what is not.

What sort of thing that [is changeable and hence] admits of being otherwise is
natural, and what sort is not natural, but legal and conventional, if both natural and
legal are changeable? It is clear in other cases also, and the same distinction [between
the natural and the unchangeable] will apply; for the right hand, e.g., is naturally
35 superior, even though it is possible for everyone to become ambidextrous.

---

10. [Brasidas was a Spartan general who after his death received sacrifices in Amphipolis as a liberator; his
cult is introduced as an example of a strictly local observance initiated by decree.—T.I.]

The sorts of things that are just by convention and expediency are like measures. 1135a
For measures for wine and for corn are not of equal size everywhere, but in wholesale
markets they are bigger, and in retail smaller. Similarly, the things that are just by
human [enactment] and not by nature differ from place to place, since political 5
systems also differ; still, only one system is by nature the best everywhere.

We have now said what it is that is unjust and just. And now that we have defined 1133b29
them, it is clear that doing justice is intermediate between doing injustice and
suffering injustice, since doing injustice is having too much and suffering injustice
is having too little.

Justice is a mean, not as the other virtues are, but because it concerns an intermediate condition, while injustice concerns the extremes. Justice is the virtue that the 1134a
just person is said to express in the just actions expressing his decision, distributing
good things and bad, both between himself and others and between others. He does
not award too much of what is choiceworthy to himself and too little to his neighbour 5
(and the reverse with what is harmful), but awards what is proportionately equal;
and he does the same in distributing between others.

Injustice, on the other hand, is related [in the same way] to what is unjust. What
is unjust is disproportionate excess and deficiency in what is beneficial or harmful;
hence injustice is excess and deficiency because it concerns excess and deficiency.
The unjust person awards himself an excess of what is beneficial, [considered] 10
unconditionally, and a deficiency of what is harmful, and speaking as a whole, he
acts similarly [in distributions between] others, but deviates from proportion in
either direction. In an unjust action getting too little good is suffering injustice, and
getting too much is doing injustice.

So much, then, for the nature of justice and the nature of injustice, and similarly 15
for what is just and unjust in general.

Since it is possible to do injustice without thereby being unjust, what sort of
injustice must someone do to be unjust by having one of the different types of
injustice, e.g. as a thief or adulterer or brigand?

But perhaps it is not the type of action that makes the difference [between merely
doing injustice and being unjust]. For someone might lie with a woman and know 20
who she is, but the origin might be feeling rather than decision; in that case he is
not unjust, though he does injustice—e.g. not a thief, though he stole, not an
adulterer though he committed adultery, and so on in the other cases.

Each [type of] just and lawful [action] is related as a universal to the particulars 1135a5
[that embody it]; for the [particular] actions that are done are many, but each [type]
is one, since it is universal.

An act of injustice is different from what is unjust, and an act of justice from what
is just. For what is unjust is unjust by nature or enactment; and when this has been 10
done, it is an act of injustice, but until then it is only unjust.

The same applies to an act of justice [in contrast to what is just]. Here, however,
the general [type of action contrary to an act of injustice] is more usually called a
just act, and what is called an act of justice is the [specific type of just act] that rectifies
an act of injustice.

Later we must examine each of these actions, to see what sorts of species, and how
many, they have, and what they are concerned with. 15

8

Given this account of just and unjust actions, someone does injustice or does justice whenever he does them willingly, and does neither justice nor injustice whenever he does them unwillingly, except coincidentally, since the actions he does are coincidentally just or unjust.

20 Further, an act of injustice and a just act are defined by what is voluntary and what is involuntary. For when the action is voluntary, the agent is blamed, and thereby also it is an act of injustice. Hence something will be injust without thereby being an act of injustice, if it is not also voluntary.

And as I said before, I say that an action is voluntary under these conditions:

(1) It is up to the agent.

25 (2) He does it in knowledge, and [hence] not in ignorance of the person, instrument and goal, e.g. whom he is striking, with what, and for what goal.

(3) He [does] each of these neither coincidentally nor by force; if, e.g., someone seized your hand and struck another [with it] you [would not have struck the other] willingly, since it was not up to you.

However [the question about knowledge is more complicated. For] it is possible that the victim is your father, and you know he is a human being or a bystander, but 30 do not know he is your father. The same distinction must be made for the goal and for the action as a whole.

Actions are involuntary, then, if they are done in ignorance; or not done in 1135b ignorance, but not up to the agent; or done by force. For we also do or undergo many of our natural [actions and processes], e.g. growing old and dying, in knowledge; but none of them is either voluntary or involuntary.

Both unjust and just actions may also be coincidental in the same way. For if 5 someone returned a deposit unwillingly and because of fear, we should say that he neither does anything just nor does justice, except coincidentally. And similarly if someone is under compulsion and unwilling when he fails to return the deposit, we should say that he coincidentally does injustice and does something unjust.

In some of our voluntary actions we act on a previous decision, and in some we 10 act without any; we act on a previous decision when we act on previous deliberation, and without any when we act without previous deliberation.

Among the three ways of inflicting harms in an association, actions done with ignorance are errors if someone does neither the action he supposed, nor to the person, nor with the instrument, nor for the result he supposed. For he thought, e.g., that he was not hitting, or not hitting this person, or not for this result; but 15 coincidentally the result that was achieved was not what he thought (e.g. [he hit him] to graze, not to wound), or the victim or the instrument was not the one he thought.

If the infliction of harm violates reasonable expectation, the action is a misfortune. If it does not violate reasonable expectation, but is done without vice, it is an error. For someone is in error if the origin of the cause is in him, and unfortunate when it is outside.

20 If he does it in knowledge, but without previous deliberation, it is an act of injustice—e.g. actions caused by emotion and other feelings that are natural or necessary for human beings. For when someone inflicts these harms and commits

these errors, he does injustice and these are acts of injustice; but he is not thereby unjust or wicked, since it is not vice that causes him to inflict the harm.

But when his decision is the cause, he is unjust and vicious. Hence it is a sound judgment that actions caused by emotion do not result from forethought [and hence do not result from decision], since the origin is not the agent who acted on the emotion, but the person who provoked him to anger.   25

Moreover [in these cases] the dispute is not about whether [the action caused by anger] happened or not, but about whether it was just, since anger is a response to apparent injustice.

For they do not dispute about whether it happened or not, as they do in commercial   30
transactions, where one party or the other must be vicious, unless forgetfulness is the cause of the dispute. Rather [in cases of anger] they agree about the fact and dispute about which action was just; but [in commercial transactions] the [cheater] who has plotted against his victim knows very well [that what he is doing is unjust]. Hence [in cases of anger the agent] thinks he is suffering injustice, while [in transac-   1136a
tions the cheater] does not think so.

And if [the cheater's] decision causes him to inflict the harm, he does injustice, and in doing *this* sort of act of injustice the agent is unjust, if it violates proportion or equality. In the same way, a person is just if his decision causes him to do justice; but he [merely] does justice if he merely does it voluntarily.

Some involuntary actions are to be pardoned, and some are not. For when some-   5
one's error is not only committed in ignorance, but also caused by ignorance, it is to be pardoned. But when it is committed in ignorance, but is caused by some feeling that is neither natural nor human, and not by ignorance, it is not to be pardoned.

9

If we have adequately defined suffering injustice and doing injustice, some puzzles   10
might be raised.

First of all, are those bizarre words of Euripides correct, where he writes, ' "I killed my mother—a short tale to tell." "Were both of you willing or both unwilling?" ' ? For   15
is it really possible to suffer injustice willingly, or is it always involuntary, as doing injustice is always voluntary? And is it always one way or the other, or is it sometimes voluntary and sometimes involuntary?

The same question arises about receiving justice. Since doing justice is always voluntary [as doing injustice is], it is reasonable for the same opposition to apply in   20
both cases, so that both receiving justice and suffering injustice will be either alike voluntary or alike involuntary. Now it seems absurd in the case of receiving justice as well [as in the case of suffering injustice] for it to be always voluntary, since some people receive justice, but not willingly.

We might also raise the following puzzle: Does everyone who has received some-thing unjust suffer injustice, or is it the same with receiving as it is with doing? For   25
certainly it is possible, in the case both of doing and of receiving, to have a share in just things coincidentally; and clearly the same is true of unjust things, since doing something unjust is not the same as doing injustice, and suffering something unjust is not the same as suffering injustice. The same is true of doing justice and receiving

30   it; for it is impossible to suffer injustice if no one does injustice and impossible to receive justice if no one does justice.

Now if doing injustice is simply harming someone willingly (and doing something willingly is doing it with knowledge of the victim, the instrument and the way) with no further conditions; and if the incontinent person harms himself willingly; then he suffers injustice willingly. Hence someone can do injustice to himself; and one

1136b   of our puzzles was just this, whether someone can do injustice to himself.

Moreover, someone's incontinence might cause him to be willingly harmed by another who is willing, so that it would be possible to suffer injustice willingly.

Perhaps, however, our definition [of doing injustice] was incorrect, and we should add to 'harming with knowledge of the victim, the instrument and the way', the

5   condition 'against the wish of the victim'. If so, then someone is harmed and suffers something unjust willingly, but no one suffers injustice willingly. For no one wishes it, not even the incontinent, but he acts against his wish; for no one wishes for what he does not think is excellent, and what the incontinent does is not what he thinks it is right [and hence excellent] to do.

10   And if someone gives away what is his own, as Homer says Glaucus gave to Diomede 'gold for bronze, a hundred cows' worth for nine cows' worth', he does not suffer injustice. For it is up to him to give them, whereas suffering injustice is not up to him, but requires someone to do him injustice.

Clearly, then, suffering injustice is not voluntary.

15   Two further questions that we decided to discuss still remain: If A distributes to B more than B deserves, is it A, the distributor, or B, who has more, who does injustice? And is it possible to do injustice to oneself?

For if the first alternative is possible, and A rather than B does injustice, then if

20   A knowingly and willingly distributes more to B than to himself, A does injustice to himself. And indeed this is what a moderate person seems to do; for the decent person tends to take less than his share.

Perhaps, however, it is not true without qualification that he takes less. For perhaps he is greedy for some other good, e.g. for reputation or for what is unconditionally fine.

Moreover, our definition of doing injustice allows us to solve the puzzle. For since he suffers nothing against his own wish, he does not suffer injustice, at least not

25   from his distribution, but, at most, is merely harmed.

But it is evidently the distributor who does injustice, and the one who has more does not always do it. For the one who receives an unjust share does not do injustice, but rather the one who willingly does what is unjust, i.e. the one who originates the

30   action; and he is the distributor, not the recipient. Besides, doing is spoken of in many ways, and there is a way in which soulless things, or hands, or servants at someone else's order, kill; the recipient, then, does not do injustice, but does something that is unjust.

Further, if the distributor judged in ignorance, he does not do injustice in violation of what is legally just, and his judgment is not unjust; in a way, though, it is unjust, since what is legally just is different from what is primarily just.

If, however, he judged unjustly, and did it knowingly, then he himself as well [as

1137a   the recipient] is greedy—to win gratitude or exact a penalty. So someone who had judged unjustly for these reasons has also got more, exactly as though he got a share of the [profits of] the act of injustice. For if he gave judgment about some land, e.g., on this condition [that he would share the profits], and what he got was not land, but money.

Since human beings think that doing injustice is up to them, they think that being just is also easy, when in fact it is not. For while lying with a neighbour's wife, wounding a neighbour, bribing, are all easy and up to us, being in a certain state when we do them is not easy, and not up to us.

Similarly, people think it takes no wisdom to know the things that are just and unjust, because it is not hard to comprehend what the laws speak of. But these are not the things that are just, except coincidentally. Knowing how actions must be done, and how distributions must be made, if they are to be just, takes more work than it takes to know about healthy things. And even in the case of healthy things, knowing about honey, wine, hellebore, burning and cutting is easy, but knowing how these must be distributed to produce health, and to whom and when, takes all the work that it takes to be a doctor.

For the same reason they think that doing injustice is no less proper to the just than to the unjust person, because the just person is no less, and even more, able to do each of the actions. For he is able to lie with a woman, and to wound someone; and the brave person, similarly, is able to throw away his shield, and to turn and run this way or that.

In fact, however, doing acts of cowardice or injustice is not doing these actions, except coincidentally; it is being in a certain state when we do them. Similarly, practising medicine or healing is not cutting or not cutting, giving drugs or not giving them, but doing all these things in a certain way.

What is just is found among those who have a share in things that [considered] unconditionally are good, who can have an excess or a deficiency of them. Some (as, presumably, the gods) can have no excess of them; others, the incurably evil, benefit from none of them, but are harmed by them all; others again benefit from these goods up to a point; and this is why what is just is something human.

10

The next task is to discuss how decency is related to justice and how what is decent is related to what is just.

For on examination they appear as neither unconditionally the same nor as states of different kinds. Sometimes we praise what is decent and the decent person, so that even when we praise someone for other things we transfer the term 'decent' and use it instead of 'good', making it clear that what is more decent is better.

And yet, sometimes, when we reason about the matter, it appears absurd for what is decent to be something beyond what is just, and still praiseworthy. For [apparently] either what is just is not excellent or what is decent is not excellent, if it is something other than what is just, or else, if they are both excellent, they are the same.

These, then, are roughly the claims that raise the puzzle about what is decent; but in fact they are all correct in a way, and none is contrary to any other. For what is decent is better than one way of being just, but it is still just, and not better than

10   what is just by being a different genus. Hence the same thing is just and decent, and
       while both are excellent, what is decent is superior.

       The puzzle arises because what is decent is just, but is not what is legally just, but
       a rectification of it. The reason is that all law is universal, but in some areas no
15   universal rule can be correct; and so where a universal rule has to be made, but
       cannot be correct, the law chooses the [universal rule] that is usually [correct], well
       aware of the error being made. And the law is no less correct on this account; for
       the source of the error is not the law or the legislator, but the nature of the object
       itself, since that is what the subject-matter of actions is bound to be like.

20   Hence whenever the law makes a universal rule, but in this particular case what
       happens violates the [intended scope of] the universal rule, here the legislator falls
       short, and has made an error by making an unconditional rule. Then it is correct to
       rectify the deficiency; this is what the legislator would have said himself if he had
       been present there, and what he would have prescribed, had he known, in his
       legislation.

       Hence what is decent is just, and better than a certain way of being just—not
25   better than what is unconditionally just, but better than the error resulting from the
       omission of any condition [in the rule]. And this is the nature of what is decent—
       rectification of law in so far as the universality of law makes it deficient.

       This is also the reason why not everything is guided by law. For on some matters
       legislation is impossible, and so a decree is needed. For the standard applied to what
30   is indefinite is itself indefinite, as the lead standard is in Lesbian building, where it
       is not fixed, but adapts itself to the shape of the stone; likewise, a decree is adapted
       to fit its objects.

       It is clear from this what is decent, and clear that it is just, and better than a certain
35   way of being just. It is also evident from this who the decent person is; for he is the
1138a one who decides for and does such actions, not an exact stickler for justice in the
       bad way, but taking less than he might even though he has the law on his side. This
       is the decent person, and his state is decency; it is a sort of justice, and not some
       state different from it.

11

       Is it possible to do injustice to oneself or not? The answer is evident from what
       has been said.

5   First of all, some just actions are the legal prescriptions expressing each virtue;
       e.g., we are legally forbidden to kill ourselves. Moreover, if someone illegally and
       willingly inflicts harm on another, not returning harm for harm, he does injustice
10   (a person acting willingly is one who knows the victim and the instrument). Now if
       someone murders himself because of anger, he does this willingly, in violation of
       correct reason, when the law forbids it; hence he does injustice. But injustice to
       whom? Surely to the city, not to himself, since he suffers it willingly, and no one
       willingly suffers injustice. That is why the city both penalizes him and inflicts further
       dishonour on him for destroying himself, on the assumption that he is doing injustice
       to the city.

       Now consider the type of injustice doing which makes the agent only unjust, not
15   base generally. Clearly this type of unjust action is different from the first type. For

one type of unjust person is wicked in the same [special] way as the coward is, not by having total wickedness; hence his acts of injustice do not express total wickedness either.

Here also one cannot do injustice to oneself. For if one could, the same person could lose and get the same thing at the same time. But this is impossible; on the   20
contrary, what is just or unjust must always involve more than one person.

Moreover, doing injustice is voluntary, and results from a decision, and strikes first, since a victim who retaliates does not seem to do injustice; but if someone does injustice to himself, he does and suffers the same thing at the same time.

Further, on this view, it would be possible to suffer injustice willingly.

Besides, no one does injustice without doing one of the particular acts of injustice.   25
But no one commits adultery with his own wife, or burgles his own house, or steals his own possessions.

And in general the puzzle about doing injustice to oneself is also solved by the distinction about voluntarily suffering injustice.

Besides, it is evident that both doing and suffering injustice are bad, since one is having more, one having less, than the intermediate amount, in the same way as   30
with what is healthy in medicine and what is fit in gymnastics [both more and less than the intermediate amount are bad]. But doing injustice is worse; for it is blameworthy, involving vice that is either complete and unconditional or close to it (since not all voluntary doing of injustice is combined with [the state of] injustice). Suffering injustice, however, involves no vice or injustice.   35

In itself, then, suffering injustice is less bad; and though it might still be coinciden-   1138b
tally a greater evil, that is no concern of a craft. Rather, the craft says that pleurisy is a worse illness than a stumble, even though a stumble might sometimes coincidentally turn out worse, e.g. if someone stumbled and by coincidence was captured by the   5
enemy or killed because he fell.

It is possible for there to be a justice, by similarity and transference, not of a person to himself, but of certain parts of a person—not every kind of justice, but the kind that belongs to masters or households. For in these discussions the part of the soul that has reason is distinguished from the non-rational part. People look at   10
these and it seems to them that there is injustice to oneself, because in these parts it is possible to suffer something against one's own desire. Hence it is possible for those parts to be just to each other, as it is for ruler and ruled.

So much, then, for our definitions of justice and the other virtues of character.

BOOK SIX

1

Since we have said previously that we must choose the intermediate condition, not the excess or the deficiency, and that the intermediate condition is as correct reason   20
says, let us now determine this, [i.e. what it says].

For in all the states of character we have mentioned, as well as in the others, there is a target which the person who has reason focuses on and so tightens or relaxes; and there is a definition of the means, which we say are between excess and deficiency because they express correct reason.

To say this is admittedly true, but it is not at all clear. For in other pursuits directed by a science it is equally true that we must labour and be idle neither too much nor too little, but the intermediate amount prescribed by correct reason. But knowing only this, we would be none the wiser, e.g. about the medicines to be applied to the body, if we were told we must apply the ones that medical science prescribes and in the way that the medical scientist applies them.

Similarly, then, our account of the states of the soul must not only be true up to this point; we must also determine what correct reason is, i.e. what its definition is.

After we divided the virtues of the soul we said that some are virtues of character and some of thought. And so, having finished our discussion of the virtues of character, let us now discuss the others as follows, after speaking first about the soul.

Previously, then, we said there are two parts of the soul, one that has reason, and one nonrational. Now we should divide in the same way the part that has reason.

Let us assume there are two parts that have reason; one with which we study beings whose origins do not admit of being otherwise than they are, and one with which we study beings whose origins admit of being otherwise. For when the beings are of different kinds, the parts of the soul naturally suited to each of them are also of different kinds, since the parts possess knowledge by being somehow similar and appropriate [to their objects].

Let us call one of these the scientific part, and the other the rationally calculating part, since deliberating is the same as rationally calculating, and no one deliberates about what cannot be otherwise. Hence the rationally calculating part is one part of the part of the soul that has reason.

Hence we should find the best state of the scientific and the best state of the rationally calculating part; for this state is the virtue of each of them. And since something's virtue is relative to its own proper function [we must consider the function of each part].

2

There are three [capacities] in the soul—perception, understanding, desire—that control action and truth. Of these three perception clearly originates no action, since beasts have perception, but no share in action.

As assertion and denial are to thought, so pursuit and avoidance are to desire. Now virtue of character is a state that decides; and decision is a deliberative desire. If, then, the decision is excellent, the reason must be true and the desire correct, so that what reason asserts is what desire pursues.

This, then, is thought and truth concerned with action. By contrast, when thought is concerned with study, not with action or production, its good or bad state consists [simply] in being true or false. For truth is the function of whatever thinks; but the function of what thinks about action is truth agreeing with correct desire.

Now the origin of an action—the source of the movement, not the action's goal—is decision, and the origin of decision is desire together with reason that aims at some goal. Hence decision requires understanding and thought, and also a state of character, since doing well or badly in action requires both thought and character. 35

Thought by itself, however, moves nothing; what moves us is thought aiming at some goal and concerned with action. For this is the sort of thought that also 1139b originates productive thinking; for every producer in his production aims at some [further] goal, and the unconditional goal is not the product, which is only the [conditional] goal of some [production], and aims at some [further] goal. [An unconditional goal is] what we achieve in *action*, since doing well in action is the goal.

Now desire is for the goal. Hence decision is either understanding combined with desire or desire combined with thought; and what originates movement in this way 5 is a human being.

We do not decide to do what is already past; no one decides, e.g., to have sacked Troy. For neither do we deliberate about what is past, but only about what will be and admits [of being or not being]; and what is past does not admit of not having happened. Hence Agathon[11] is correct to say 'Of this alone even a god is deprived— to make what is all done to have never happened.' 10

Hence the function of each of the understanding parts is truth; and so the virtue of each part will be the state that makes that part grasp the truth most of all.

3

Then let us begin over again, and discuss these states of the soul. Let us say, then, that there are five states in which the soul grasps the truth in its affirmations or 15 denials. These are craft, scientific knowledge, intelligence, wisdom and understanding; for belief and supposition admit of being false.

What science is is evident from the following, if we must speak exactly and not be guided by [mere] similarities.

For we all suppose that what we know scientifically does not even admit of being 20 otherwise; and whenever what admits of being otherwise escapes observation, we do not notice whether it is or is not, [and hence we do not know about it]. Hence what is known scientifically is by necessity. Hence it is eternal; for the things that are by unconditional necessity are all eternal, and eternal things are ingenerable and indestructible.

Further, every science seems to be teachable, and what is scientifically knowable 25 is learnable. But all teaching is from what is already known, as we also say in the *Analytics*; for some teaching is through induction, some by deductive inference, [which both require previous knowledge].

Induction [reaches] the origin, i.e. the universal, while deductive inference proceeds from the universals. Hence deductive inference has origins from which it 30 proceeds, but which are not themselves [reached] by deductive inference. Hence they are [reached] by induction.

Scientific knowledge, then, is a demonstrative state, and has all the other features that in the *Analytics* we add to the definition. For someone has scientific knowledge

11. [A fifth-century dramatist; his victory is being celebrated in Plato's *Symposium*.—M.L.M.]

when he has the appropriate sort of confidence, and the origins are known to him;
35   for if they are not better known to him than the conclusion, he will have scientific
knowledge only coincidentally.

So much for a definition of scientific knowledge.

4

1140a   What admits of being otherwise includes what is produced and what is done in
action. Production and action are different; about them we rely also on [our] popular
discussions. Hence the state involving reason and concerned with action is different
from the state involving reason and concerned with production. Nor is one included
5   in the other; for action is not production, and production is not action.

Now building, e.g., is a craft, and is essentially a certain state involving reason
concerned with production; there is no craft that is not a state involving reason
concerned with production, and no such state that is not a craft. Hence a craft is the
10   same as a state involving true reason concerned with production.

Every craft is concerned with coming to be; and the exercise of the craft is the
study of how something that admits of being and not being comes to be, something
whose origin is in the producer and not in the product. For a craft is not concerned
with things that are or come to be by necessity; or with things that are by nature,
15   since these have their origin in themselves.

And since production and action are different, craft must be concerned with
production, not with action.

In a way craft and fortune are concerned with the same things, as Agathon says:
20   'Craft was fond of fortune, and fortune of craft.'

A craft, then, as we have said, is a state involving true reason concerned with
production. Lack of craft is the contrary state involving false reason and concerned
with production. Both are concerned with what admits of being otherwise.

5

25   To grasp what intelligence is we should first study the sort of people we call
intelligent.

It seems proper, then, to an intelligent person to be able to deliberate finely about
what is good and beneficial for himself, not about some restricted area—e.g. about
what promotes health or strength—but about what promotes living well in general.

A sign of this is the fact that we call people intelligent about some [restricted area]
30   whenever they calculate well to promote some excellent end, in an area where there
is no craft. Hence where [living well] as a whole is concerned, the deliberative person
will also be intelligent.

Now no one deliberates about what cannot be otherwise or about what cannot be
achieved by his action. Hence, if science involves demonstration, but there is no
35   demonstration of anything whose origins admit of being otherwise, since every such
1140b   thing itself admits of being otherwise; and if we cannot deliberate about what is by
necessity; it follows that intelligence is not science nor yet craft-knowledge. It is not

science, because what is done in action admits of being otherwise; and it is not craft-knowledge, because action and production belong to different kinds.

The remaining possibility, then, is that intelligence is a state grasping the truth,   5
involving reason, concerned with action about what is good or bad for a human
being.

For production has its end beyond it; but action does not, since its end is doing
well itself, [and doing well is the concern of intelligence].

Hence Pericles and such people are the ones whom we regard as intelligent,
because they are able to study what is good for themselves and for human beings;   10
and we think that household managers and politicians are such people.

This is also how we come to give temperance (*sōphrosunē*) its name, because we
think that it preserves intelligence, (*sōzousan tēn phronēsin*). This is the sort of supposition that it preserves. For the sort of supposition that is corrupted and perverted by
what is pleasant or painful is not every sort—not, e.g., the supposition that the   15
triangle does or does not have two right angles—but suppositions about what is done
in action.

For the origin of what is done in action is the goal it aims at; and if pleasure or
pain has corrupted someone, it follows that the origin will not appear to him. Hence
it will not be apparent that this must be the goal and cause of all his choice and
action; for vice corrupts the origin.   20

Hence [since intelligence is what temperance preserves, and what temperance
preserves is a true supposition about action], intelligence must be a state grasping
the truth, involving reason, and concerned with action about human goods.

Moreover, there is virtue [or vice in the use] of craft, but not [in the use] of
intelligence. Further, in a craft, someone who makes errors voluntarily is more
choiceworthy; but with intelligence, as with the virtues, the reverse is true. Clearly,
then, intelligence is a virtue, not craft-knowledge.   25

There are two parts of the soul that have reason. Intelligence is a virtue of one of
them, of the part that has belief; for belief is concerned, as intelligence is, with what
admits of being otherwise.

Moreover, it is not only a state involving reason. A sign of this is the fact that such
a state can be forgotten, but intelligence cannot.

6

Scientific knowledge is supposition about universals, things that are by necessity.   30
Further, everything demonstrable and every science have origins, since scientific
knowledge involves reason.

Hence there can be neither scientific knowledge nor craft-knowledge nor intelligence about the origins of what is scientifically known. For what is scientifically   35
known is demonstrable, [but the origins are not]; and craft and intelligence are
about what admits of being otherwise. Nor is wisdom [exclusively] about origins; for   1141a
it is proper to the wise person to have a demonstration of some things.

[The states of the soul] by which we always grasp the truth and never make
mistakes, about what can or cannot be otherwise, are scientific knowledge, intelli-   5
gence, wisdom and understanding. But none of the first three—intelligence, scien-

tific knowledge, wisdom—is possible about origins. The remaining possibility, then, is that we have understanding about origins.

7

We ascribe wisdom in crafts to the people who have the most exact expertise in the crafts, e.g. we call Pheidias a wise stone-worker and Polycleitus a wise bronze-worker, signifying nothing else by wisdom than excellence in a craft. But we also think some people are wise in general, not wise in some [restricted] area, or in some other [specific] way, as Homer says in the *Margites:* 'The gods did not make him a digger or a ploughman or wise in anything else.' Clearly, then, wisdom is the most exact [form] of scientific knowledge.

Hence the wise person must not only know what is derived from the origins of a science, but also grasp the truth about the origins. Therefore wisdom is understanding plus scientific knowledge; it is scientific knowledge of the most honourable things that has received [understanding as] its copingstone.

For it would be absurd for someone to think that political science or intelligence is the most excellent science, when the best thing in the universe is not a human being [and the most excellent science must be of the best things].

Moreover, what is good and healthy for human beings and for fish is not the same, but what is white or straight is always the same. Hence everyone would also say that the content of wisdom is always the same, but the content of intelligence is not. For the agent they would call intelligent is the one who studies well each question about his own [good], and he is the one to whom they would entrust such questions. Hence intelligence is also ascribed to some of the beasts, the ones that are evidently capable of forethought about their own life.

It is also evident that wisdom is not the same as political science. For if people are to say that science about what is beneficial to themselves [as human beings] counts as wisdom, there will be many types of wisdom [corresponding to the different species of animals]. For if there is no one medical science about all beings, there is no one science about the good of all animals, but a different science about each specific good. [Hence there will be many types of wisdom, contrary to our assumption that it has always the same content].

And it does not matter if human beings are the best among the animals. For there are other beings of a far more divine nature than human beings; e.g., most evidently, the beings composing the universe.

What we have said makes it clear that wisdom is both scientific knowledge and understanding about what is by nature most honourable. That is why people say that Anaxagoras or Thales or that sort of person is wise, but not intelligent, when they see that he is ignorant of what benefits himself. And so they say that what he knows is extraordinary, amazing, difficult and divine, but useless, because it is not human goods that he looks for.

Intelligence, by contrast, is about human concerns, about what is open to deliberation. For we say that deliberating well is the function of the intelligent person more than anyone else; but no one deliberates about what cannot be otherwise, or about what lacks a goal that is a good achievable in action. The unconditionally good deliberator is the one whose aim expresses rational calculation in pursuit of the best good for a human being that is achievable in action.

Nor is intelligence about universals only. It must also come to know particulars,   15
since it is concerned with action and action is about particulars. Hence in other areas also some people who lack knowledge but have experience are better in action than others who have knowledge. For someone who knows that light meats are digestible and healthy, but not which sorts of meats are light, will not produce health; the one   20
who knows that bird meats are healthy will be better at producing health. And since intelligence is concerned with action, it must possess both [the universal and the particular knowledge] or the [particular] more [than the universal]. Here too, however, [as in medicine] there is a ruling [science].

8

Political science and intelligence are the same state, but their being is not the same.

One part of intelligence about the city is the ruling part; this is legislative science.   25

The part concerned with particulars [often] monopolizes the name 'political science' that [properly] applies to both parts in common. This part is concerned with action and deliberation, since [it is concerned with decrees and] the decree is to be acted on as the last thing [reached in deliberation]. Hence these people are the only ones who are said to be politically active; for these are the only ones who practise [politics] in the way that handcraftsmen practise [their craft].

Now likewise intelligence concerned with the individual himself seems most of all   30
to be counted as intelligence; and this [part of intelligence often] monopolizes the name 'intelligence' that [properly] applies [to all parts] in common. Of the other parts one is household science, another legislative, another political, one part of which is deliberative and another judicial.

In fact knowledge of what is [good] for oneself is one species [of intelligence]. But there is much difference [in opinions] about it.

Someone who knows about himself, and spends his time on his own concerns,   1142a
seems to be intelligent, while politicians seem to be too active. Hence Euripides says, 'Surely I cannot be intelligent, when I could have been inactive, numbered among all the many in the army, and have had an equal share. . . . For those who go too far   5
and are too active. . . .'

For people seek what is good for themselves, and suppose that this [inactivity] is the action required [to achieve their good]. Hence this belief has led to the view that these are the intelligent people.

Presumably, however, one's own welfare requires household management and a   10
political system.

Moreover, [another reason for the difference of opinion is this]: it is unclear, and should be examined, how one must manage one's own affairs.

A sign of what has been said [about the unclarity of what intelligence requires] is the fact that whereas young people become accomplished in geometry and mathematics, and wise within these limits, intelligent young people do not seem to be found. The reason is that intelligence is concerned with particulars as well as univer-

15   sals, and particulars become known from experience, but a young person lacks experience, since some length of time is needed to produce it.

Indeed [to understand the difficulty and importance of experience] we might consider why a boy can become accomplished in mathematics, but not in wisdom or natural science. Surely it is because mathematical objects are reached through abstraction, whereas the origins in these other cases are reached from experience.
20   Young people, then, [lacking experience], have no real conviction in these other sciences, but only say the words, whereas the nature of mathematical objects is clear to them.

Moreover [intelligence is difficult because it is deliberative and] deliberation may be in error about either the universal or the particular. For [we may wrongly suppose] either that all sorts of heavy water are bad or that this water is heavy.

Intelligence is evidently not scientific knowledge; for, as we said, it concerns the
25   last thing [i.e. the particular], since this is what is done in action. Hence it is opposed to understanding. For understanding is about the [first] terms, [those] that have no account of them; but intelligence is about the last thing, an object of perception, not of scientific knowledge.

This is not the perception of special objects, but the sort by which we perceive that the last among mathematical objects is a triangle; for it will stop here too. This is
30   another species [of perception than perception of special objects]; but it is still perception more than intelligence is.

9

Inquiry and deliberation are different, since deliberation is a type of inquiry. We must also grasp what good deliberation is, and see whether it is some sort of scientific knowledge, or belief, or good guessing, or some other kind of thing.

First of all, then, it is not scientific knowledge. For we do not inquire for what we
1142b already know; but good deliberation is a type of deliberation, and a deliberator inquires and rationally calculates.

Moreover, it is not good guessing either. For good guessing involves no reasoning, and is done quickly; but we deliberate a long time, and it is said that we must act
5   quickly on the result of our deliberation, but deliberate slowly. Moreover, quick thinking is different from good deliberation, and quick thinking is a kind of good guessing.

Nor is good deliberation any sort of belief. Rather, since the bad deliberator is in error, and the good deliberator deliberates correctly, good deliberation is clearly some sort of correctness.

But it is not correctness in scientific knowledge or in belief. For there is no
10   correctness in scientific knowledge, since there is no error in it either; and correctness in belief consists in truth, [but correctness in deliberation does not].

Further, everything about which one has belief is already determined, [but what is deliberated about is not yet determined].

However, good deliberation requires reason; hence the remaining possibility is that it belongs to thought. For thought is not yet assertion; [and this is why it is not belief]. For belief is not inquiry, but already an assertion; but in deliberating, either well or badly, we inquire for something and rationally calculate about it. 15

But since good deliberation is a certain sort of correctness in deliberation, we must inquire what [this correctness] is and what it is [correctness] about.

Now since correctness has several types, clearly good deliberation will not be every type. For the incontinent or base person will use rational calculation to reach what he proposes to see, and so will have deliberated correctly [if that is all it takes], but will have got himself a great evil. Having deliberated well seems, on the contrary, 20 to be some sort of good; for the sort of correctness in deliberation that makes it good deliberation is the sort that reaches a good.

However, we can reach a good by a false inference, as well [as by correct deliberation], so that we reach the right thing to do, but by the wrong steps, when the middle term is false. Hence this type of deliberation, leading us by the wrong steps to the 25 right thing to do, is not enough for good deliberation either.

Moreover, one person may deliberate a long time before reaching the right thing to do, while another reaches it quickly. Nor, then, is the first condition enough for good deliberation; good deliberation is correctness that reflects what is beneficial, about the right thing, in the right way and at the right time.

Further, our deliberation may be unconditionally good or good only to the extent that it promotes some [limited] end. Hence unconditionally good deliberation is the 30 sort that correctly promotes the unconditional end [i.e. the highest good], while the [limited] sort is the sort that correctly promotes some [limited] end.

Hence, if having deliberated well is proper to an intelligent person, good deliberation will be the type of correctness that expresses what is expedient for promoting the end about which intelligence is true supposition.

10

Comprehension, i.e. good comprehension, makes people, as we say, comprehend and comprehend well. It is not the same as scientific knowledge in general. Nor is 1143a it the same as belief, since, if it were, everyone would have comprehension. Nor is it any one of the specific sciences [with its own specific area], in the way that medicine is about what is healthy or geometry is about magnitudes.

For comprehension is neither about what always is and is unchanging nor about just anything that comes to be. It is about what we might be puzzled about and might 5 deliberate about. Hence it is about the same things as intelligence.

Still, comprehension is not the same as intelligence. For intelligence is prescriptive, since its end is what must be done or not done in action, whereas comprehension only judges. (For comprehension and good comprehension are the same; and so are 10 people with comprehension and with good comprehension.)

Comprehension is neither having intelligence nor acquiring it. Rather, it is similar to the way learning is called comprehending when someone applies scientific knowledge. In the same way comprehension consists in the application of belief to judge someone else's remarks on a question that concerns intelligence, and moreover it must judge them finely since judging well is the same as judging finely. And that is 15 how the name 'comprehension' was attached to the comprehension that makes people have good comprehension. It is derived from the comprehension found in learning; for we often call learning comprehending.

11

20   The [state] called consideration makes people, as we say, considerate and makes them have consideration; it is the correct judgment of the decent person. A sign of this is our saying that the decent person more than others is considerate, and that it is decent to be considerate about some things. Considerateness is the correct consideration that judges what is decent; and correct consideration judges what is true.

25   It is reasonable for all these states to tend to the same point. For we ascribe consideration, comprehension, intelligence and understanding to the same people, and say that these have consideration, and thereby understanding, and that they are intelligent and comprehending. For all these capacities are about the last things, i.e. particulars. Moreover, someone has comprehension and good consideration, or

30   has considerateness, in being able to judge about the matters that concern the intelligent person; for what is decent is the common concern of all good people in relations with other people.

        [These states are all concerned with particulars because] whatever is done in action is one of the particular and last things. For the intelligent person also must recognize [what is done in action], while comprehension and consideration are concerned with

35   what is done in action, and this is one of the last things.

        Understanding is also concerned with the last things, and in both directions. For there is understanding, not a rational account, about the first terms and the last.

1143b   In demonstrations understanding is about the unchanging terms that are first.

        In [premises] about what is done in action understanding is about the last term, the one that admits of being otherwise, and hence about the minor premise. For these last terms are the origins of the end to be aimed at, since universals are reached

5   from particulars. We must, then, have perception of these particulars, and this perception is understanding.

        Hence these states actually seem to grow naturally, so that while no one seems to have natural wisdom, people seem to have natural consideration, comprehension and judgment. A sign [of their apparent natural character] is our thinking that they also correspond to someone's age, and the fact that understanding and consideration

10   belong to a certain age, as though nature were the cause.

        We must attend, then, to the undemonstrated remarks and beliefs of experienced and older people or of intelligent people, no less than to demonstrations. For these people see correctly because experience has given them their eye.

15   We have said, then, what intelligence and wisdom are; what each is about; and that each is the virtue of a different part of the soul.

12

        Someone might, however, be puzzled about what use they are.

20   For wisdom is not concerned with any sort of coming into being, and hence will not study any source of human happiness.

Admittedly intelligence will study this; but what do we need it for?   25

For knowledge of what is healthy or fit—i.e. of what results from the state of   26
health, not of what produces it—makes us no readier to act appropriately if we are
already healthy; for having the science of medicine or gymnastics makes us no   27
readier to act appropriately. Similarly, intelligence is the science of what is just and 21
what is fine, and what is good for a human being; but this is how the good man
acts; and if we are already good, knowledge of them makes us no readier to act   25
appropriately, since virtues are states [activated in actions].

If we concede that intelligence is not useful for this, should we say it is useful for   28
becoming good? In that case it will be no use to those who are already excellent.   30
Nor, however, will it be any use to those who are not. For it will not matter to them
whether they have it themselves or take the advice of others who have it. The advice
of others will be quite adequate for us, just as it is with health: we wish to be healthy,
but still do not learn medical science.

Besides, it would seem absurd for intelligence, inferior as it is to wisdom, to control
it [as a superior. But this will be the result], since the science that produces also rules 35
and prescribes about its product.

We must discuss these questions; for so far we have only gone through the puzzles
about them.

First of all, let us state that both intelligence and wisdom must be choiceworthy in   1144a
themselves, even if neither produces anything at all; for each is the virtue of one of
the two [rational] parts [of the soul].

Second, they do produce something. Wisdom produces happiness, not in the way
that medical science produces health, but in the way that health produces [health].   5
For since wisdom is a part of virtue as a whole, it makes us happy because it is a state
that we possess and activate.

Further, we fulfil our function in so far as we have intelligence and virtue of
character; for virtue makes the goal correct, and intelligence makes what promotes
the goal [correct]. The fourth part of the soul, the nutritive part, has no such virtue   10
[related to our function], since no action is up to it to do or not to do.

To answer the claim that intelligence will make us no readier to do fine and just
actions, we must begin from a little further back [in our discussion].

Here is where we begin. We say that some people who do just actions are not yet
thereby just, if, e.g., they do the actions prescribed by the laws, either unwillingly   15
or because of ignorance or because of some other end, not because of the actions
themselves, even though they do the right actions, those that the excellent person
ought to do. Equally, however, it would seem to be possible for someone to do each
type of action in the state that makes him a good person, i.e. because of decision
and for the sake of the actions themselves.   20

Now virtue makes the decision correct; but the actions that are naturally to be
done to fulfil the decision are the concern not of virtue, but of another capacity. We
must get to know them more clearly before continuing our discussion.

There is a capacity, called cleverness, which is such as to be able to do the actions
that tend to promote whatever goal is assumed and to achieve it. If, then, the goal   25
is fine, cleverness is praiseworthy, and if the goal is base, cleverness is unscrupu-
lousness; hence both intelligent and unscrupulous people are called clever.

30   Intelligence is not the same as this capacity [of cleverness], though it requires it.
Intelligence, this eye of the soul, cannot reach its fully developed state without
virtue, as we have said and as is clear. For inferences about actions have an origin:
'Since the end and the best good is this sort of thing', whatever it actually is—let it
be any old thing for the sake of argument. And this [best good] is apparent only to
35   the good person; for vice perverts us and produces false views about the origins of
actions.

1144b   Evidently, then, we cannot be intelligent without being good.

13

We must, then, also examine virtue over again. For virtue is similar [in this way]
to intelligence; as intelligence is related to cleverness, not the same but similar, so
natural virtue is related to full virtue.

For each of us seems to possess his type of character to some extent by nature,
5   since we are just, brave, prone to temperance, or have another feature, immediately
from birth. However, we still search for some other condition as full goodness, and
expect to possess these features in another way.

For these natural states belong to children and to beasts as well [as to adults], but
10   without understanding they are evidently harmful. At any rate, this much would
seem to be clear: just as a heavy body moving around unable to see suffers a heavy
fall because it has no sight, so it is with virtue. [A naturally well-endowed person
without understanding will harm himself.] But if someone acquires understanding,
he improves in his actions; and the state he now has, though still similar [to the
natural one], will be virtue to the full extent.

And so, just as there are two sorts of conditions, cleverness and intelligence, in
15   the part of the soul that has belief, so also there are two in the part that has character,
natural virtue and full virtue. And of these full virtue cannot be acquired without
intelligence.

This is why some say that all the virtues are [instances of] intelligence, and why
Socrates' inquiries were in one way correct, and in another way in error. For in that
20   he thought all the virtues are [instances of] intelligence, he was in error; but in that
he thought they all require intelligence, he was right.

Here is a sign of this: Whenever people now define virtue, they all say what state
it is and what it is related to, and then add that it is the state that expresses correct
reason. Now correct reason is reason that expresses intelligence; it would seem,
25   then, that they all in a way intuitively believe that the state expressing intelligence
is virtue.

But we must make a slight change. For it is not merely the state expressing correct
reason, but the state involving correct reason, that is virtue. And it is intelligence
that is correct reason in this area. Socrates, then, thought that the virtues are
30   [instances of] reason because he thought they are all [instances of] knowledge,
whereas we think they involve reason.

What we have said, then, makes it clear that we cannot be fully good without
intelligence, or intelligent without virtue of character.

In this way we can also solve the dialectical argument that someone might use to

show that the virtues are separated from each other. For, [it is argued], since the same person is not naturally best suited for all the virtues, someone will already have   35
one virtue before he has got another.

This is indeed possible with the natural virtues. It is not possible, however, with the [full] virtues that someone must have to be called unconditionally good; for as   1145a
soon as he has intelligence, which is a single state, he has all the virtues as well.

And clearly, even if intelligence were useless in action, we would need it because it is the virtue of this part of the soul, and because the decision will not be correct without intelligence or without virtue. For virtue makes us reach the end in our   5
action, while intelligence makes us reach what promotes the end.

Moreover, intelligence does not control wisdom or the better part of the soul, just as medical science does not control health. For it does not use health, but only aims to bring health into being; hence it prescribes for the sake of health, but does not prescribe to health. Besides, [saying that intelligence controls wisdom] would be like   10
saying that political science rules the gods because it prescribes about everything in the city.

BOOK SEVEN

1

Next we should make a new beginning, and say that there are three conditions of   15
character to be avoided—vice, incontinence and bestiality. The contraries of two of these are clear; we call one virtue and the other continence.

The contrary to bestiality is most suitably called virtue superior to us, a heroic, indeed divine, sort of virtue. Thus Homer made Priam say that Hector was remark-   20
ably good; 'nor did he look as though he were the child of a mortal man, but of a god.' Moreover, so they say, human beings become gods because of exceedingly great virtue.

Clearly, then, this is the sort of state that would be opposite to the bestial state. For indeed, just as a beast has neither virtue nor vice, so neither does a god, but the   25
god's state is more honourable than virtue, and the beast's belongs to some kind different from vice.

Now it is rare that a divine man exists. (This is what the Spartans habitually call him; whenever they very much admire someone, they say he is a divine man.) Similarly, the bestial person is also rare among human beings. He is most often found   30
in foreigners; but some bestial features also result from diseases and deformities. We also use 'bestial' as a term of reproach for people whose vice exceeds the human level.

We must make some remarks about this condition later. We have discussed vice earlier. We must now discuss incontinence, softness and self-indulgence, and also   35
continence and resistance; for we must not suppose that continence and inconti-   1145b
nence are concerned with the same states as virtue and vice, or that they belong to a different kind.

As in the other cases we must set out the appearances, and first of all go through

5 the puzzles. In this way we must prove the common beliefs about these ways of being affected—ideally, all the common beliefs, but if not all, then most of them, and the most important. For if the objections are solved, and the common beliefs are left, it will be an adequate proof.

10 Continence and resistance seem to be good and praiseworthy conditions, while incontinence and softness seem to be base and blameworthy conditions.

The continent person seems to be the same as one who abides by his rational calculation; and the incontinent person seems to be the same as one who abandons it.

The incontinent person knows that his actions are base, but does them because of his feelings, while the continent person knows that his appetites are base, but because of reason does not follow them.

15 People think the temperate person is continent and resistant. Some think that every continent and resistant person is temperate, while others do not. Some people say the incontinent person is intemperate and the intemperate incontinent, with no distinction; others say they are different.

Sometimes it is said that an intelligent person cannot be incontinent; but sometimes it is said that some people are intelligent and clever, but still incontinent.

20 Further, people are called incontinent about emotion, honour and gain.

These, then, are the things that are said.

2

We might be puzzled about the sort of correct supposition someone has when he acts incontinently.

First of all, some say he cannot have knowledge [at the time he acts]. For it would be terrible, Socrates thought, for knowledge to be in someone, but mastered by
25 something else, and dragged around like a slave. For Socrates fought against the account [of incontinence] in general, in the belief that there is no incontinence; for no one, he thought, supposes while he acts that his action conflicts with what is best; our action conflicts with what is best only because we are ignorant [of the conflict].

This argument, then, contradicts things that appear manifestly. If ignorance causes the incontinent person to be affected as he is, then we must look for the type
30 of ignorance that it turns out to be; for it is evident, at any rate, that before he is affected the person who acts incontinently does not think [he should do the action he eventually does].

Some people concede some of [Socrates' points], but reject some of them. For they agree that nothing is superior to knowledge, but deny that no one's action conflicts with what has seemed better to him. Hence they say that when the incontinent
35 person is overcome by pleasure he has only belief, not knowledge.

In that case, however, if he has belief, not knowledge, and what resists is not a
1146a strong supposition, but only a mild one, such as people have when they are in doubt, we will pardon failure to abide by these beliefs against strong appetites. In fact, however, we do not pardon vice, or any other blameworthy condition [and incontinence is one of these].

5 Then is it intelligence that resists, since it is the strongest? This is absurd. For on

this view the same person will be both intelligent and incontinent; and no one would say that the intelligent person is the sort to do the worst actions willingly.

Besides, we have shown earlier that the intelligent person acts [on his knowledge], since he is concerned with the last things, [i.e. particulars], and that he has the other virtues.

Further, if the continent person must have strong and base appetites, the temper-   10
ate person will not be continent nor the continent person temperate. For the temperate person is not the sort to have either excessive or base appetites; but [the continent person] must have both.

For if his appetites are good, the state that prevents him from following them must be base, so that not all continence is excellent. If, on the other hand, the   15
appetites are weak and not base, continence is nothing impressive; and if they are base and weak, it is nothing great.

Besides, if continence makes someone prone to abide by every belief, it is bad, if, e.g., it makes him abide by a false as well [as a true] belief.

And if incontinence makes someone prone to abandon every belief, there will be an excellent type of incontinence. Neoptolemus, e.g., in Sophocles' *Philoctetes* is   20
praiseworthy when, after being persuaded by Odysseus, he does not abide by his resolve, because he feels pain at lying.

Besides, the sophistical argument is a puzzle. For [the sophists] wish to refute an [opponent, by showing] that his views have paradoxical results, so that they will be clever in encounters. Hence the inference that results is a puzzle; for thought is tied up, since it does not want to stand still because the conclusion is displeasing, but it   25
cannot advance because it cannot solve the argument.

A certain argument, then, concludes that foolishness combined with incontinence is virtue. For incontinence makes someone act contrary to what he supposes [is right]; but since he supposes that good things are bad and that it is wrong to do   30
them, he will do the good actions, not the bad.

Further, someone who acts to pursue what is pleasant because this is what he is persuaded and decides to do, seems to be better than someone who acts not because of rational calculation, but because of incontinence.

For the first person is the easier to cure, because he might be persuaded otherwise;   35
but the incontinent person illustrates the proverb 'If water chokes us, what must we   1146b
drink to wash it down?' For if he had been persuaded to do the action he does, he would have stopped when he was persuaded to act otherwise; but in fact, though already persuaded to act otherwise, he still acts [wrongly].

Further, is there incontinence and continence about everything? If so, who is the simply incontinent? For no one has all the types of incontinence, but we say that some people are simply incontinent.   5

These, then, are the sorts of puzzles that arise. We must undermine some of these claims, and leave others intact; for the solution of the puzzle is the discovery [of what we are seeking].

3

First, then, we must examine whether the incontinent has knowledge or not, and in what way he has it. Second, what should we take to be the incontinent and the   10 continent person's area of concern—every pleasure and pain, or some definite subclass? Are the continent and the resistant person the same or different? Similarly we must deal with the other questions that are relevant to this study.

15 We begin the examination with this question: Are the continent and the incontinent person distinguished [from others] (i) by their concerns, or (ii) by their attitudes to them? In other words, is the incontinent person incontinent (i) only by having these concerns, or instead (ii) by having this attitude; or instead (iii) by both?

[Surely (iii) is right.] For [(i) is insufficient] since the simple incontinent is not 20 concerned with everything, but with the same things as the intemperate person. Moreover, [(ii) is insufficient] since he is not incontinent simply by being inclined towards these things—that would make incontinence the same as intemperance. Rather [as (iii) implies], he is incontinent by being inclined towards them in this way. For the intemperate person acts on decision when he is led on, since he thinks it is right in every case to pursue the pleasant thing at hand; but the incontinent person thinks it is wrong to pursue it, yet still pursues it.

25 It is claimed that the incontinent person's action conflicts with true belief, not with knowledge. But whether it is knowledge or belief that he has does not matter for this argument. For some people with belief are in no doubt, but think they have exact knowledge.

If, then, it is the weakness of their conviction that makes people with belief, not people with knowledge, act in conflict with their supposition, it follows that knowledge will [for these purposes] be no different from belief; for, as Heracleitus 30 makes clear, some people's convictions about what they believe are no weaker than other people's convictions about what they know.

But we speak of knowing in two ways, and ascribe it both to someone who has it without using it and to someone who is using it. Hence it will matter whether someone has the knowledge that his action is wrong, without attending to his knowledge, or 35 both has and attends to it. For this second case seems extraordinary, but wrong action when he does not attend to his knowledge does not seem extraordinary.

1147a Besides, since there are two types of premises, someone's action may well conflict with his knowledge if he has both types of premises, but uses only the universal premise and not the particular premise. For [the particular premise states the particulars and] it is particular actions that are done.

Moreover, [in both types of premises] there are different types of universal, (a) 5 one type referring to the agent himself, and (b) the other referring to the object. Perhaps, e.g., someone knows that (a1) dry things benefit every human being, and that (a2) he himself is a human being, or that (b1) this sort of thing is dry; but he either does not have or does not activate the knowledge that (b2) this particular thing is of this sort.

Hence these ways [of knowing and not knowing] make such a remarkable difference that it seems quite intelligible [for someone acting against his knowledge] to have the one sort of knowledge [i.e. without (b2)], but astounding if he has the other sort [including (b2)].

10 Besides, human beings may have knowledge in a way different from those we have described. For we see that having without using includes different types of having; hence some people, e.g. those asleep or mad or drunk, both have knowledge in a way and do not have it.

Moreover, this is the condition of those affected by strong feelings. For emotions, sexual appetites and some conditions of this sort clearly [both disturb knowledge and] disturb the body as well, and even produce fits of madness in some people. 15

Clearly, then [since incontinents are also affected by strong feelings], we should say that they have knowledge in a way similar to these people.

Saying the words that come from knowledge is no sign [of fully having it]. For people affected in these ways even recite demonstrations and verses of Empedocles. 20 Further, those who have just learnt something do not yet know it, though they string the words together; for it must grow into them, and this needs time.

Hence we must suppose that incontinents say the words in the way that actors do.

Further, we may also look at the cause in the following way, referring to [human] nature. One belief (a) is universal; the other (b) is about particulars, and because 25 they are particulars perception controls them. And in the cases where these two beliefs result in (c) one belief, it is necessary in purely theoretical beliefs for the soul to affirm what has been concluded, and in beliefs about production (d) to act at once on what has been concluded.

If, e.g., (a) everything sweet must be tasted, and (b) this, some one particular thing, is sweet, it is necessary (d) for someone who is able and unhindered also to 30 act on this at the same time.

Suppose, then, that someone has (a) the universal belief, and it hinders him from tasting; he has (b) the second belief, that everything sweet is pleasant and this is sweet, and this belief (b) is active; and he also has appetite. Hence the belief (c) tells him to avoid this, but appetite leads him on, since it is capable of moving each of 35 the [bodily] parts.

The result, then, is that in a way reason and belief make him act incontinently. 1147b The belief (b) is contrary to correct reason (a), but only coincidentally, not in itself. For it is the appetite, not the belief, that is contrary [in itself to correct reason].

Hence beasts are not incontinent, because they have no universal supposition, but [only] appearance and memory of particulars. 5

How is the ignorance resolved, so that the incontinent person recovers his knowledge? The same account that applies to someone drunk or asleep applies here too, and is not special to this way of being affected. We must hear it from the natural scientists.

And since the last premise (b) is a belief about something perceptible, and controls action, this must be what the incontinent person does not have when he is being 10 affected. Or rather the way he has it is not knowledge of it, but, as we saw, [merely] saying the words, as the drunk says the words of Empedocles.

Further, since the last term does not seem to be universal, or expressive of knowledge in the same way as the universal term, even the result Socrates was looking for 15 would seem to come about. For the knowledge that is present when someone is affected by incontinence, and that is dragged about because he is affected, is not the sort that seems to be knowledge to the full extent [in (c)], but only perceptual knowledge [in (b)].

So much, then, for knowing and not knowing, and for how it is possible to know and still to act incontinently.

4

20   Next we must say whether anyone is simply incontinent, or all incontinents are incontinent in some particular way; and if someone is simply incontinent, we must say what sorts of things he is incontinent about.

First of all, both the continent and resistant person and the incontinent and soft person are evidently concerned with pleasures and pains.

Some sources of pleasure are necessary; others are choiceworthy in themselves,
25   but can be taken to excess. The necessary ones are the bodily conditions, i.e. those that concern food, sexual intercourse, and the sorts of bodily conditions that we took to concern temperance and intemperance. Other sources of pleasure are not
30   necessary, but are choiceworthy in themselves, e.g. victory, honour, wealth and similar good and pleasant things.

When people go to excess, in conflict with the correct reason in them, in the pursuit of these sources of pleasure, we do not call them simply incontinent, but add the condition that they are incontinent about wealth, gain, honour or emotion, and not simply incontinent. For we assume that they are different, and called
35   incontinent [only] because of a similarity, just as the Olympic victor named Human[12]
1148a was different, since for him the common account [of human being] was only a little different from his special one, but it was different none the less.

A sign in favour of what we say is the fact that incontinence is blamed not only as an error but as a vice, either unconditional or partial, while none of these conditions is blamed as a vice.

5   Now consider the people concerned with the bodily gratifications, those that we take to concern the temperate and the intemperate person. Some of these people go to excess in pursuing these pleasant things and avoiding painful things—hunger, thirst, heat, cold and all that concerns touch and taste—not, however, because they have decided on it, but in conflict with their decision and thought.

10   These are the people called simply incontinent, not with the added condition that they are incontinent about, e.g., anger.

A sign of this is the fact that people are also called soft about these [bodily] pleasures, but not about any of the nonnecessary ones.

This is also why we include the incontinent and the intemperate person, and the continent and the temperate person, in the same class, but do not include any of
15   those who are incontinent in some particular way. It is because the incontinent and the intemperate person are concerned in a way with the same pleasures and pains. In fact they are concerned with the same things, but not in the same way; the intemperate person decides on them, but the incontinent person does not.

Hence, if someone has no appetites, or slight ones, for excesses, but still pursues them and avoids moderate pains, we will take him to be more intemperate than the
20   person who does it because he has intense appetites. For think of the lengths he would go to if he also acquired vigorous appetites and felt severe pains at the lack of necessities.

Some pleasant things are naturally choiceworthy, some naturally the opposite,

12. [The winning boxer in the Olympics of 456 was called Anthropos.—T.I.]

some in between, as we divided them earlier. Hence some appetites and pleasures are for fine and excellent kinds of things, e.g. wealth, profit, victory and honour. About all these and about the things in between people are blamed not for feeling an appetite and love for them, but for doing so in a particular way, namely to excess. 25

Some people are overcome by, or pursue, some of these naturally fine and good things to an extent that conflicts with reason, e.g. they take honour or children or parents more seriously than is right. For though these are certainly good and people are praised for taking them seriously, still excess about them is also possible. It is excessive if someone fights, as Niobe[13] did [for her children], even with the gods, or regards his father as Satyrus,[14] nicknamed the Fatherlover, did—for he seemed to be excessively silly about it. 30 1148b

There is no vice here, for the reason we have given, since each of these things is naturally choiceworthy for itself, though excess about them is bad and to be avoided. Similarly, there is no incontinence here either, since incontinence is not merely to be avoided, but also blameworthy [and these conditions are not]. 5

But because it is a similar way of being affected, people call it incontinence, adding the condition that it is incontinence about this or that. Just so they call someone a bad doctor or a bad actor, though they would never call him simply bad, since each of these conditions is not vice, but only similar to it by analogy. 10

It is likewise clear that the only condition we should take to be continence or incontinence is the one concerned with what concerns temperance and intemperance. We speak of incontinence about emotion because of the similarity [to simple incontinence], and hence add the condition that someone is incontinent about emotion, as we do with honour or gain.

5

Some things are naturally pleasant, and some of these are unconditionally pleasant, while others correspond to differences between kinds of animals and of human beings. Other things are not naturally pleasant, but deformities or habits or degenerate natures make them pleasant; and we can see states concerned with each of these that are similar to [states concerned with naturally pleasant things]. 15

By bestial states I mean e.g. the female human being who is said to tear pregnant women apart and devour the children; or the pleasures of some of the savage people around the Black Sea who are reputed to enjoy raw meat and human flesh, while some trade their children to each other to feast on; or what is said about Phalaris. These states are bestial. 20

Other states are caused by attacks of disease, and in some cases by fits of madness—e.g. the person who sacrificed his mother and ate her, and the one who ate the liver of his fellow-slave. 25

Other states result from diseased conditions or from habit—e.g. plucking hairs, chewing nails, even coal and earth, and besides these sexual intercourse between

13. [Claimed that her children were more beautiful than those of Leto.—M.L.M.]

14. [Stories are told of Satyrus that he committed suicide in grief when his father died.—M.L.M.]

30   males. For in some people these result from [a diseased] nature, in others from habit, as, e.g., in those who have suffered wanton [sexual] assault since their childhood.

Whenever nature is the cause, no one would call these people incontinent, any more than women would be called incontinent for being mounted rather than mounting. The same applies to those who are in a diseased state because of habit.

1149a   Each of these states, then, is outside the limits of vice, just as bestiality is. If someone who has them overcomes them or is overcome by them, that is not simple [continence or] incontinence, but the type so called from similarity, just as someone who is overcome by emotion should be called incontinent in relation to his feelings, but not [simply] incontinent.

5   Among all the excesses of foolishness, cowardice, intemperance and irritability some are bestial, some diseased. If, e.g., someone's natural character makes him afraid of everything, even the noise of a mouse, he is a coward with a bestial sort of cowardice. Another person was afraid of a weasel because of an attack of disease.

Among foolish people also those who naturally lack reason and live only by
10   perception are bestial, as some races of distant foreigners do. Those who are foolish because of attacks of disease, e.g. epilepsy, or because of fits of madness, are diseased.

Sometimes it is possible to have some of these conditions without being overcome—
15   e.g. if Phalaris had an appetite to eat a child or for some bizarre sexual pleasure, but restrained it. It is also possible to be overcome by these conditions and not merely to have them.

One sort of vice is human, and this is called simple vice; another sort is called vice with an added condition, and is said to be bestial or diseased vice, but not simple vice. Similarly, then, it is also clear that one sort of incontinence is bestial, another
20   diseased, but only the incontinence corresponding to human intemperance is simple incontinence.

It is clear, then, that incontinence and continence apply only to the concerns of intemperance and temperance, and for other things there is another form of incontinence, so called by transference of the name, and not simply.

6

Moreover, let us observe, incontinence about emotion is less shameful than incon-
25   tinence about appetites.

For, first of all, emotion would seem to hear reason a bit, but to mishear it. It is like over-hasty servants who run out before they have heard all their instructions, and then carry them out wrongly, or dogs who bark at any noise at all, before
30   investigating to see if it is a friend. In the same way, since emotion is naturally hot and hasty, it hears, but does not hear the instruction, and rushes off to exact a penalty. For reason or appearance has shown that we are being slighted or wantonly insulted; and emotion, as though it had inferred that it is right to fight this sort of
35   thing, is irritated at once. Appetite, however, only needs reason or perception to say that this is pleasant, and it rushes off for gratification.

1149b   Hence emotion follows reason in a way, but appetite does not. Therefore [incontinence about appetite] is more shameful. For if someone is incontinent about emotion, he is overcome by reason in a way; but if he is incontinent about appetite, he is overcome by appetite, not by reason.

Besides, it is more pardonable to follow natural desires, since it is also more pardonable to follow those natural appetites that are shared by everyone and to the extent that they are shared. Now emotion and irritability are more natural than the excessive and unnecessary appetites. It is just as the son said in his defence for beating his father: 'Yes, and he beat his father, and his father beat *his* father before that'; and pointing to his young son, he said, 'And he will beat me when he becomes a man; it runs in our family.' Similarly, the father being dragged by his son kept urging him to stop at the front door, since that was as far as he had dragged his own father.

Moreover, those who plot more are more unjust. But the emotional person does not plot, and neither does emotion; it is open. Appetite, however, is like what they say about Aphrodite, 'trick-weaving Cypris', and what Homer says about her embroidered girdle: 'Blandishment, which steals the wits even of the very intelligent.'

If, then, incontinence about appetite is more unjust and more shameful than incontinence about emotion, it is simple incontinence, and vice in a way.

Further, no one feels pain when he commits wanton aggression; but whatever someone does from anger, he does feeling pain when he does it, whereas the wanton aggressor does what he does with pleasure. Now if whatever more justly provokes anger is more unjust, incontinence caused by appetite is more unjust, since emotion involves no wanton aggression.

It is clear, then, how incontinence about appetites is more shameful than incontinence about emotion, and that continence and incontinence are about bodily appetites and pleasures. Now we must grasp the varieties of these appetites and pleasures.

As we said at the beginning, some appetites are human and natural in kind and degree, some bestial, some caused by deformities and diseases. Temperance and intemperance are concerned only with the first of these.

This is also why we do not call beasts either temperate or intemperate, except by transference of the name, if one kind of animal exceeds another altogether in wanton aggression, destructiveness and ravenousness. For beasts have neither decision nor rational calculation, but are outside [rational] nature, as the madmen among human beings are.

Bestiality is less grave than vice, but more frightening; for the best part is not corrupted, as it is in a human being, but absent altogether. Hence a comparison between the two is like a comparison between an inanimate and an animate being to see which is worse. For in each case the badness of something that lacks an internal origin of its badness is less destructive than the badness of something that has such an internal origin; and understanding is such an internal origin. It is similar, then, to a comparison between the injustice [of a beast] and an unjust human being; for in a way each [of these] is worse, since a bad human being can do innumerably more bad things than a beast.

7

Now consider the pleasures and pains arising through touch and taste, and consider the appetites for these pleasures, and the aversions from these pains. Earlier we defined temperance and intemperance as concerned with these. It is possible for someone to be in the state where he is overcome, even by [pleasure and pains] which most people overcome, and possible to overcome even those that overcome most people. The person who is prone to be overcome by pleasures is incontinent; the one who overcomes is continent; the one overcome by pains is soft; and the one who overcomes them is resistant. The state of most people is in between, though indeed they may lean more towards the worse states.

Now some pleasures are necessary and some are not. [The necessary ones are necessary] to a certain extent, while their excesses and deficiencies are not. The same is true for appetites and pains.

One person pursues excesses of pleasant things because they are excesses and because he decides on it, for themselves and not for some further result. He is intemperate; for he is bound to have no regrets, and so is incurable, since someone without regrets is incurable.

The one who is deficient is his opposite, while the intermediate one is temperate. The same is true for the one who avoids bodily pains not because he is overcome; but because he decides on it.

One of those who do not [act on] decision is led on because of pleasure; the other is led on because he is avoiding the pain that comes from appetite; hence these two differ from each other.

Now it would seem to everyone that someone who does a shameful action from no appetite or a weak one is worse than if he does it from an intense appetite; and similarly if he strikes another not from anger, he is worse than if he strikes from anger. For [if he can do such evil when he is unaffected by feeling], what would he have done if he had been strongly affected? Hence the intemperate person is worse than the incontinent.

One of the states mentioned [being overcome by pain] is more a species of softness, while the other person is intemperate. The continent person is opposed to the incontinent, and the resistant to the soft. For resistance consists in holding out, and continence in overcoming, but holding out is different from overcoming, just as not being defeated differs from winning; hence continence is more choiceworthy than resistance.

1150b   Someone who is deficient in withstanding what most people withstand, and are capable of withstanding, is soft and self-indulgent; for self-indulgence is a kind of softness. This person trails his cloak to avoid the labour and pain of lifting it, and imitates an invalid, though he does not think he is miserable—he is [merely] similar to a miserable person.

It is similar with continence and incontinence also. For it is not surprising if someone is overcome by strong and excessive pleasures or pains; on the contrary, this is pardonable, provided he struggles against them—like Theodectes' Philoctetes bitten by the snake, or Carcinus' Cercyon in the *Alope,* and like those who are trying to restrain their laughter and burst out laughing all at once, as happened to Xenophantes. But it is surprising if someone is overcome by what most people can resist, and is incapable of withstanding it, not because of his hereditary nature or because of disease—as, e.g., the Scythian kings' softness is hereditary, and as the female is distinguished [by softness] from the male.

The lover of amusements also seems to be intemperate, but in fact he is soft. For amusement is a relaxation, since it is a release, and the lover of amusement is one of those who go to excess here.

One type of incontinence is impetuosity, while another is weakness. For the weak person deliberates, but then his feeling makes him abandon the result of his deliberation; but the impetuous person is led on by his feelings because he has not deliberated. For some people are like those who do not get tickled themselves if they tickle someone else first; if they see and notice something in advance, and rouse themselves and their rational calculation, they are not overcome by feelings, no matter whether something is pleasant or painful.

20

25

Quick-tempered and ardent people are most prone to be impetuous incontinents. For in quick-tempered people the appetite is so fast, and in ardent people so intense, that they do not wait for reason, because they tend to follow appearance.

8

The intemperate person, as we said, is not prone to regret, since he abides by his decision [when he acts]. But every incontinent is prone to regret. Hence the truth is not what we said in raising the puzzles, but in fact the intemperate person is incurable, and the incontinent curable.

30

For vice resembles diseases such as dropsy or consumption, while incontinence is more like epilepsy; vice is a continuous bad condition, while incontinence is not. For the incontinent is similar to those who get drunk quickly from a little wine, and from less than it takes for most people.

1151a3
4
5

And in general incontinence and vice are of different kinds, for the vicious person does not notice that he is vicious, while the incontinent person notices that he is incontinent.

1150b35

Among the incontinent people themselves those who abandon themselves [to desire, i.e. the impetuous] are better than those [i.e. the weak] who have reason but do not abide by it. For the second type are overcome by a less strong feeling, and do not act without having deliberated, as the first type do.

1151a

Evidently, then, incontinence is not a vice, though presumably it is one in a way. For incontinence conflicts with decision, while vice expresses decision. All the same, it is similar to vice in its actions. Thus Demodocus attacks the Milesians: 'The Milesians are not stupid, but they do what stupid people would do'; and in the same way incontinents are not unjust, but will do injustice.

5

10

Moreover, the incontinent person is the sort to pursue excessive bodily pleasures that conflict with correct reason, but not because he is persuaded [it is best]. The intemperate person, however, is persuaded, because he is the sort of person to pursue them. Hence the incontinent person is easily persuaded out of it, while the intemperate person is not.

For virtue preserves the origin, while vice corrupts it; and in action the end we act for is the origin, as the assumptions are the origins in mathematics. Reason does not teach the origins either in mathematics or in actions; [with actions] it is virtue, either natural or habituated, that teaches correct belief about the origin.

15

The sort of person [with this virtue] is temperate, and the contrary sort intemperate. But there is also someone who because of his feelings abandons himself contrary

20

to correct reason. They overcome him far enough so that his actions do not express correct reason, but not so far as to make him the sort of person to be persuaded that it is right to pursue such pleasures without restraint. This is the incontinent person.
25   He is better than the intemperate person, and is not unconditionally bad, since the best thing, the origin, is preserved in him.

Another sort of person is contrary to him. [This is the continent person] who abides [by reason] and does not abandon himself, not because of his feelings at least. It is evident from this that the continent person's state is excellent, and the incontinent person's state is base.

9

Now is someone continent if he abides by just any sort of reason and any sort of
30   decision, or must he abide by the correct decision? And is someone incontinent if he fails to abide by just any decision and any reason, or must it be reason that is not false, and the correct decision? This was the puzzle raised earlier.

Perhaps in fact the continent person abides, and the incontinent fails to abide, by just any decision coincidentally, but abides by the true reason and the correct
35   decision in itself. For if someone chooses or pursues one thing because of a second,
1151b   he pursues and chooses the second in itself and the first coincidentally. Now when we speak of something unconditionally, we speak of it in itself. Hence in one way [i.e. coincidentally] the continent person abides by just any opinion, and the incontinent abandons it; but unconditionally the continent person abides by the true opinion and the incontinent person abandons it.

5   Now there are some other people who tend to abide by their belief. These are the people called stubborn, who are hard to persuade into something and not easy to persuade out of it. These have some similarity to continent people, just as the wasteful person has to the generous, and the rash to the confident. But they are different on many points.

The continent person is not swayed because of feeling and appetite; [but he is
10   not inflexible about everything] since he will be easily persuaded whenever it is appropriate. But stubborn people are not swayed by reason; for they acquire appetites, and many of them are led on by pleasures.

The stubborn include the opinionated, the ignorant and the boorish. The opinionated are as they are because of pleasure and pain. For they find enjoyment in winning
15   [the argument] if they are not persuaded to change their views, and they feel pain if their opinions are voided, like decrees in the Assembly. Hence they are more like incontinent than like continent people.

There are also some people who do not abide by their resolutions, but not because they are incontinent—Neoptolemus, e.g., in Sophocles' *Philoctetes*. Though certainly it was pleasure that made him abandon his resolution, it was a fine pleasure, since
20   he found telling the truth pleasant, and Odysseus had persuaded him to lie. [He is not incontinent;] for not everyone who does something because of pleasure is either intemperate or base or incontinent, but only someone who does it because of a shameful pleasure.

Now there is also the sort of person who enjoys bodily things less than is right,
25   and does not abide by reason; hence the continent person is intermediate between

this person and the incontinent. For the incontinent fails to abide by reason because of too much [enjoyment]; and the other person fails because of too little; while the continent person abides and is not swayed because of too much or too little.

If continence is excellent, then both of these contrary states must be base, as indeed they appear. However, the other state is evident in only a few people on a   30
few occasions; and hence continence seems to be contrary only to incontinence, just as temperance seems to be contrary only to intemperance.

Now many things are called by some name because of similarity [to genuine cases]; this has happened also to the continence of the temperate person, because of similarity. For the continent and the temperate person are both the sort to do   35
nothing in conflict with reason because of bodily pleasures; but the continent person has base appetites, and the temperate person lacks them. The temperate person is   1152a
the sort to find nothing pleasant that conflicts with reason; the continent is the sort to find such things pleasant but not to be led by them.

The incontinent and the intemperate person are similar too; though they are different, they both pursue bodily sources of pleasure, but the intemperate person   5
[pursues them because he] also thinks it is right, while the incontinent person does not think so.

10

Nor can the same person be at once both intelligent and incontinent.

For we have shown that an intelligent person must also at the same time be   8
excellent in character, [and the incontinent person is not]. However, a clever person   10
may well be incontinent. Indeed, the reason people sometimes seem to be intelligent   11
but incontinent is that [really they are only clever and] cleverness differs from   12
intelligence in the way we described in our first discussion; though they are closely   13
related in definition, they differ in [so far as intelligence requires the right] decision.   14

Moreover, someone is not intelligent simply by knowing; he must also act on his   8
knowledge. But the incontinent person does not.   9

Further, the incontinent person is not in the condition of someone who knows   14
and is attending [to his knowledge, as he would have to be if he had intelligence],   15
but in the condition of one asleep or drunk.

He acts willingly; for in a way he acts in knowledge both of what he is doing and of the end he is doing it for. But he is not base, since his decision is decent; hence he is half base.

Nor is he unjust, since he is not a plotter. For one type of incontinent person [i.e. the weak] does not abide by the result of his deliberation, while the ardent [i.e. impetuous] person is not even prone to deliberate at all.

In fact the incontinent person is like a city that votes for all the right decrees and   20
has good laws, but does not apply them, as in Anaxandrides' taunt, 'The city willed it, that cares nothing for laws.' The base person, by contrast, is like a city that applies its laws, but applies bad ones.

Incontinence and continence are concerned with what exceeds the state of most   25
people; the continent person abides [by reason] more than most people are capable of doing, the incontinent person less.

The [impetuous] type of incontinence found in ardent people is more easily cured than the [weak] type of incontinence found in those who deliberate but do not abide by it.

30 Incontinents through habituation are more easily cured than the natural incontinents; for habit is easier than nature to change. Indeed the reason why habit is also difficult to change is that it is like nature, as Euenus says, 'Habit, I say, is longtime training, my friend, and in the end training is nature for human beings.'

35 We have said, then, what continence and incontinence, resistance and softness are, and how these states are related to each other.

11

1152b It is proper to the political philosopher to study pleasure and pain, since he is the ruling craftsman of the end which we refer to in calling something unconditionally bad or good.

5 Moreover, we must also examine them because we have laid it down that virtue and vice of character are concerned with pains and pleasures, and because most people think happiness involves pleasure; hence they call the blessed person by that name (*makarios*) from enjoyment (*chairein*).

(1) Now it seems to some people that no pleasure is a good, either in itself or coincidentally, on the ground that the good is not the same as pleasure.

10 (2) To others it seems that some pleasures are good, but most are bad.

(3) Further, the third view is that even if every pleasure is a good, the best good still cannot be pleasure.

(1) Their reasons for thinking it is not a good at all are these:

(a) Every pleasure is a perceived becoming towards [the fulfillment of something's] nature; but no becoming is of the same kind as its end, e.g. no [process of] building

15 is of the same kind as a house.

(b) Besides, the temperate person avoids pleasures.

(c) Besides, the intelligent person pursues what is painless, not what is pleasant.

(d) Besides, pleasures impede intelligent thinking, and impede it more the more we enjoy them; no one, e.g., while having sexual intercourse can think about anything.

(e) Besides, every good is the product of a craft, but there is no craft of pleasure.

20 (f) Besides, children and animals pursue pleasure.

(2) To show that not all pleasures are excellent things, people say (a) that some are shameful and reproached, and (b) that some are harmful, since some pleasant things cause disease.

(3) To show that the best good is not pleasure, people say that pleasure is not an end, but a becoming.

These, then, are roughly the things said about it.

12

25 These arguments, however, do not show that pleasure is not a good, or even that it is not the best good. This will be clear as follows.

First of all, since what is good may be good in either of two ways, as unconditionally good or as good for some particular thing or person, this will also be true for natures and states, and hence also for processes and becomings. And so among the [processes and becomings] that seem bad (i) some are bad unconditionally, but for some person not bad, and for this person actually choiceworthy. (ii) Some are not choiceworthy 30 for him either, except sometimes and for a short time, not on each occasion. (iii) Some are not even pleasures, but appear to be; these are the [processes], e.g. in sick people, that involve pain and are means to medical treatment.

Further, since one sort of good is an activity and another sort is a state, the processes that restore us to our natural state are pleasant coincidentally. Here the 35 activity in the appetites belongs to the rest of our state and nature [i.e. the part that is still undisturbed]. For there are also pleasures without pain and appetite, e.g. the 1153a pleasures of studying, those in which our nature lacks nothing.

A sign [that supports our distinction between pleasures] is the fact that we do not enjoy the same thing when our nature is being refilled that we enjoy when it is eventually fully restored. When it is fully restored, we enjoy things that are unconditionally pleasant; but when it is being refilled, we enjoy even the contrary things.

For we even enjoy sharp or bitter things, though none of these is pleasant by 5 nature or unconditionally pleasant. Hence [these pleasures] are not [unconditional] pleasures either; for as pleasant things differ from each other, so the pleasures arising from them differ too.

Further, it is not necessary for something else to be better than pleasure, as the end, some say, is better than the becoming. For pleasures are not becomings, nor do they all even involve a becoming. They are activities, and an end [in themselves], 10 and arise when we exercise [a capacity], not when we are coming to be [in some state]. And not all pleasures have something else as their end, but only those in people who are being led towards the completion of their nature.

Hence it is also a mistake to call pleasure a perceived becoming. It should instead be called an activity of the natural state, and should be called not perceived, but unimpeded. The reason it seems to some people to be a becoming is that it is a good to the full extent [and hence an activity]; for they think activities are becomings, 15 though in fact these are different things.

To say that pleasures are bad because some pleasant things cause disease is the same as saying that some healthy things are bad for money-making. To this extent both are bad; but that is not enough to make them bad, since even study is sometimes 20 harmful to health.

Neither intelligence nor any state is impeded by the pleasures arising from it, but only by alien pleasures. For the pleasures arising from study and learning will make us study and learn all the more.

The fact that pleasure is not the product of a craft is quite reasonable; for a craft does not belong to any other activity either, but to a capacity. And yet, the crafts of 25 perfumery and cooking do seem to be crafts of pleasure.

The claim that the temperate person avoids pleasure, that the intelligent person pursues the painless life, and that children and beasts pursue pleasure—all these are solved by the same reply. For we have explained in what ways pleasures are good, and in what ways not all are unconditionally good; and it is these pleasures 30 [that are not unconditionally good] that beasts and children pursue, while the intelligent person pursues painlessness in relation to these. These are the pleasures associated with appetite and pain and the bodily pleasures (since these are associated with appetite and pain) and their excesses, whose pursuit makes the intemperate person intemperate. Hence the temperate person avoids these pleasures [but not all pleasures], since there are pleasures of the temperate person too.

13

1153b   Moreover, it is also agreed that pain is an evil, and is to be avoided; for one kind of pain is unconditionally bad, and another is bad in a particular way, by impeding [activities]. But the contrary to what is to be avoided, in so far as it is bad and to be avoided, is a good; hence pleasure must be a good.

For Speusippus' solution—[that pleasure is contrary both to pain and to the good] as the greater is contrary both to the lesser and to the equal—does not succeed. For he would not say [as his solution requires] that pleasure is essentially an evil.

Besides, just as one science might well be the best good, even though some sciences are bad, some pleasure might well be the best good, even though most pleasures are bad.

Moreover, if each state has its unimpeded activities, and happiness is the activity, if the activity is unimpeded, of all states or of some one of them, then presumably it necessarily follows that some unimpeded activity is most choiceworthy. But pleasure is an unimpeded activity; hence some type of pleasure might be the best good even if most pleasures turn out to be unconditionally bad.

This is why all think the happy life is pleasant and weave pleasure into happiness, quite reasonably, since no activity is complete if it is impeded, and happiness is something complete.

Hence the happy person needs to have goods of the body and external goods added [to good activities], and needs fortune also, so that he will not be impeded in these ways. Some maintain, on the contrary, that we are happy when we are broken on the wheel, or fall into terrible misfortunes, provided that we are good. Willingly or unwillingly, these people are talking nonsense.

And because happiness needs fortune added, good fortune seems to some people to be the same as happiness. But it is not. For when it is excessive, it actually impedes happiness; and then, presumably, it is no longer rightly called *good* fortune, since the limit [up to which it is good] is defined in relation to happiness.

The fact that all, both beasts and human beings, pursue pleasure is some sign of its being in some way the best good: 'No rumour is altogether lost which many peoples [spread]. . . .' But since the best nature and state neither is nor seems to be the same for all, they also do not all pursue the same pleasure, though they all pursue pleasure. Presumably in fact they do pursue the same pleasure, and not the one they think or would say they pursue; for all things by nature have something divine [in them].

However, the bodily pleasures have taken over the name because people most often aim at them, and all share in them; and so, since these are the only pleasures they know, people suppose that they are the only pleasures.

Evidently, moreover, if pleasure is not a good and an activity, it will not be true that the happy person lives pleasantly. For what will he need pleasure for if it is not a good? Indeed, it will even be possible for him to live painfully; for pain is neither an evil nor a good if pleasure is not, and why then would he avoid it? So the life of the excellent person will not be pleasanter if his activities are not also pleasanter. 5

14

Those who maintain that some pleasures, e.g. the fine ones, are highly choiceworthy, but the bodily pleasures that concern the intemperate person are not, should examine bodily pleasures. If what they say is true, why are the pains contrary to these pleasures awful? For it is a good that is contrary to an evil. 10

Then are the necessary [bodily pleasures] good only in the way that what is not bad is good? Or are they good up to a point?

[In fact they are good up to a point.] For though some states and processes allow no excess of what is better, and hence no excess of the pleasure [in them] either, others do allow excess of what is better, and hence also allow excess of the pleasure in them too. Now the bodily goods allow excess. The base person is base because he pursues the excess, but not because he pursues the necessary pleasures; for all enjoy delicacies and wines and sexual relations in some way, though not all in the right way. 15

The contrary is true for pains. The base person avoids pain in general, not [only] an excess of it. For not [all] pain is contrary to excess [of pleasure], except to someone who pursues the excess [of pleasure]. 20

We must, however, not only state the true view, but also explain the false view, since an explanation of that promotes confidence. For when we have an apparently reasonable explanation of why a false view appears true, that makes us more confident of the true view. Hence we should say why bodily pleasures appear more choiceworthy. 25

First, then, it is because bodily pleasure pushes out pain. Excesses of pain make people seek a cure in the pursuit of excessive pleasure and of bodily pleasure in general. And these cures become intense—that is why they are pursued—because they appear next to their contraries. 30

Indeed these are the two reasons why pleasure seems to be no excellent thing, as we have said.

First, some pleasures are the actions of a base nature—either base from birth, as in a beast, or base because of habit, e.g. the actions of base human beings.

Second, others are cures of something deficient, and it is better to be in a good state than to be coming into it. In fact these pleasures coincide with our restoration to complete health, and so are excellent coincidentally. 1154b

Further, bodily pleasures are pursued because they are intense, by people who are incapable of enjoying other pleasures. At any rate, these people induce some kinds of thirst in themselves, which is blameless whenever the thirsts are harmless, but base whenever they are harmful. And they do this because they enjoy nothing else, and many people's nature makes the neutral condition painful to them. 5

For an animal is always suffering, as the natural scientists also testify, since they maintain that seeing and hearing are painful. However, we are used [to seeing and hearing] by now, so they say, [and so feel no intense pain]. Indeed, the [process of] growth makes young people's condition similar to an intoxicated person's and hence youth is pleasant.

Naturally ardent people, by contrast, are always requiring a cure, since their constitution causes their body continual turmoil, and they are always having intense desires. A pain is driven out by its contrary pleasure, indeed by any pleasure at all that is strong enough; and this is why such people become intemperate and base.

Pleasures without pains, however, have no excess. These are pleasant by nature and not coincidentally. By coincidentally pleasant things I mean pleasant things that are curative; for the [process of] being cured coincides with some action of the part of us that remains healthy, and hence undergoing a cure seems to be pleasant. Things are pleasant by nature, however, when they produce action of a healthy nature.

The reason why no one thing is always pleasant is that our nature is not simple, but has more than one constituent, in so far as we are perishable; hence the action of one part is contrary to nature for the other nature in us, and when they are equally balanced, the action seems neither pleasant nor painful. For if something has a simple nature the same action will always be pleasantest.

That is why the god always enjoys one simple pleasure [without change]. For activity belongs not only to change but also to unchangingness, and indeed there is pleasure in rest more than in change. 'Variation in everything is sweet', as the poet says, because of some inferiority; for just as it is the inferior human being who is prone to variation, so also the nature that needs variation is inferior, since it is not simple or decent.

So much, then, for continence and incontinence and for pleasure and pain, what each of them is, and in what ways some [aspects] of them are good and others bad. It remains for us to discuss friendship as well.

BOOK EIGHT

1

After that the next topic to discuss is friendship; for it is a virtue, or involves virtue, and besides is most necessary for our life.

For no one would choose to live without friends even if he had all the other goods. For in fact rich people and holders of powerful positions, even more than other people, seem to need friends. For how would one benefit from such prosperity if one had no opportunity for beneficence, which is most often displayed, and most highly praised, in relation to friends? And how would one guard and protect prosperity without friends, when it is all the more precarious the greater it is? In poverty also, and in the other misfortunes, people think friends are the only refuge.

Moreover, the young need it to keep them from error. The old need it to care for them and support the actions that fail because of weakness. And those in their prime

need it, to do fine actions; for 'when two go together . . .', they are more capable of 15
understanding and acting.

Further, a parent would seem to have a natural friendship for a child, and a child
for a parent, not only among human beings but also among birds and most kinds of
animals. Members of the same race, and human beings most of all, have a natural 20
friendship for each other; that is why we praise friends of humanity. And in our
travels we can see how every human being is akin and beloved to a human being.

Moreover, friendship would seem to hold cities together, and legislators would
seem to be more concerned about it than about justice. For concord would seem to 25
be similar to friendship and they aim at concord above all, while they try above all
to expel civil conflict, which is enmity.

Further, if people are friends, they have no need of justice, but if they are just
they need friendship in addition; and the justice that is most just seems to belong
to friendship.

However, friendship is not only necessary, but also fine. For we praise lovers of
friends, and having many friends seems to be a fine thing. Moreover, people think 30
that the same people are good and also friends.

Still, there are quite a few disputed points about friendship.

For some hold it is a sort of similarity and that similar people are friends. Hence
the saying 'Similar to similar', and 'Birds of a feather', and so on. On the other hand 35
it is said that similar people are all like the proverbial potters, quarrelling with each
other.

On these questions some people inquire at a higher level, more proper to natural 1155b
science. Euripides says that when earth gets dry it longs passionately for rain, and
the holy heaven when filled with rain longs passionately to fall into the earth; and
Heracleitus says that the opponent cooperates, the finest harmony arises from 5
discordant elements, and all things come to be in struggle. Others, e.g. Empedocles,
oppose this view, and say that similar aims for similar.

Let us, then, leave aside the puzzles proper to natural science, since they are not
proper to the present examination; and let us examine the puzzles that concern
human [nature], and bear on characters and feelings. 10

For instance, does friendship arise among all sorts of people, or can people not
be friends if they are vicious?

Is there one species of friendship, or are there more? Some people think there is
only one species because friendship allows more and less. But here their confidence
rests on an inadequate sign; for things of different species also allow more and less. 15

2

Perhaps these questions will become clear once we find out what it is that is lovable.
For, it seems, not everything is loved, but [only] what is lovable, and this is either
good or pleasant or useful. However, it seems that what is useful is the source of
some good or some pleasure; hence what is good and what is pleasant are lovable as 20
ends.

Do people love what is good, or what is good for them? For sometimes these
conflict; and the same is true of what is pleasant. Each one, it seems, loves what is

25 good for him; and while what is good is lovable unconditionally, what is lovable for each one is what is good for him. In fact each one loves not what *is* good for him, but what *appears* good for him; but this will not matter, since [what appears good for him] will be what appears lovable.

Hence there are these three causes of love.

Love for a soulless thing is not called friendship, since there is no mutual loving, and you do not wish good to it. For it would presumably be ridiculous to wish good

30 things to wine; the most you wish is its preservation so that you can have it. To a friend, however, it is said, you must wish goods for his own sake.

If you wish good things in this way, but the same wish is not returned by the other, you would be said to have [only] goodwill for the other. For friendship is said to be *reciprocated* goodwill.

But perhaps we should add that friends are aware of the reciprocated goodwill.

35 For many a one has goodwill to people whom he has not seen but supposes to be
1156a decent or useful, and one of these might have the same goodwill towards him. These people, then, apparently have goodwill to each other, but how could we call them friends when they are unaware of their attitude to each other?

5 Hence, [to be friends] they must have goodwill to each other, wish goods and be aware of it, from one of the causes mentioned above.

3

Now since these causes differ in species, so do the types of loving and types of friendship. Hence friendship has three species, corresponding to the three objects of love. For each object of love has a corresponding type of mutual loving, combined with awareness of it, and those who love each other wish goods to each other in so

10 far as they love each other.

Those who love each other for utility love the other not in himself, but in so far as they gain some good for themselves from him. The same is true of those who love for pleasure; for they like a witty person not because of his character, but because he is pleasant to themselves.

And so those who love for utility or pleasure are fond of a friend because of what

15 is good or pleasant for themselves, not in so far as the beloved is who he is, but in so far as he is useful or pleasant.

Hence these friendships as well [as the friends] are coincidental, since the beloved is loved not in so far as he is who he is, but in so far as he provides some good or pleasure.

And so these sorts of friendships are easily dissolved, when the friends do not

20 remain similar [to what they were]; for if someone is no longer pleasant or useful, the other stops loving him.

What is useful does not remain the same, but is different at different times. Hence, when the cause of their being friends is removed, the friendship is dissolved too, on the assumption that the friendship aims at these [useful results]. This sort of friend-

25 ship seems to arise especially among older people, since at that age they pursue what

is advantageous, not what is pleasant, and also among those in their prime or youth who pursue what is expedient.

Nor do such people live together very much. For sometimes they do not even find each other pleasant. Hence they have no further need to meet in this way if they are not advantageous [to each other]; for each finds the other pleasant [only] to the extent that he expects some good from him. The friendship of hosts and guests is   30
taken to be of this type too.

The cause of friendship between young people seems to be pleasure. For their lives are guided by their feelings, and they pursue above all what is pleasant for themselves and what is near at hand. But as they grow up [what they find] pleasant changes too. Hence they are quick to become friends, and quick to stop; for their   35
friendship shifts with [what they find] pleasant, and the change in such pleasure is   1156b
quick. Young people are prone to erotic passion, since this mostly follows feelings, and is caused by pleasure; that is why they love and quickly stop, often changing in a single day.

These people wish to spend their days together and to live together; for this is how they gain [the good things] corresponding to their friendship.   5

But complete friendship is the friendship of good people similar in virtue; for they wish goods in the same way to each other in so far as they are good, and they are good in themselves. [Hence they wish goods to each other for each other's own sake.] Now those who wish goods to their friend for the friend's own sake are   10
friends most of all; for they have this attitude because of the friend himself, not coincidentally. Hence these people's friendship lasts as long as they are good; and virtue is enduring.

Each of them is both good unconditionally and good for his friend, since good people are both unconditionally good and advantageous for each other. They are pleasant in the same ways too, since good people are pleasant both unconditionally   15
and for each other. [They are pleasant for each other] because each person finds his own actions and actions of that kind pleasant, and the actions of good people are the same or similar.

It is reasonable that this sort of friendship is enduring, since it embraces in itself all the features that friends must have. For the cause of every friendship is good or   20
pleasure, either unconditional or for the lover; and every friendship reflects some similarity. And all the features we have mentioned are found in this friendship because of [the nature of] the friends themselves. For they are similar in this way [i.e. in being good]. Moreover, their friendship also has the other things—what is unconditionally good and what is unconditionally pleasant; and these are lovable most of all. Hence loving and friendship are found most of all and at their best in these friends.

These kinds of friendships are likely to be rare, since such people are few. More-   25
over, they need time to grow accustomed to each other; for, as the proverb says, they cannot know each other before they have shared the traditional [peck of] salt, and they cannot accept each other or be friends until each appears lovable to the other and gains the other's confidence. Those who are quick to treat each other in   30
friendly ways wish to be friends, but are not friends, unless they are also lovable, and know this. For though the wish for friendship comes quickly, friendship does not.

4

This sort of friendship, then, is complete both in time and in the other ways. In every way each friend gets the same things and similar things from each, and this is what must be true of friends. Friendship for pleasure bears some resemblance to this complete sort, since good people are also pleasant to each other. And friendship for utility also resembles it, since good people are also useful to each other.

With these [incomplete friends] also, the friendships are most enduring when they get the same thing—e.g. pleasure—from each other, and, moreover, get it from the same source, as witty people do. They must not be like the erotic lover and the boy he loves. For these do not take pleasure in the same things; the lover takes pleasure in seeing his beloved, while the beloved takes pleasure in being courted by his lover. When the beloved's bloom is fading, sometimes the friendship fades too; for the lover no longer finds pleasure in seeing his beloved, while the beloved is no longer courted by the lover.

Many, however, remain friends if they have similar characters and come to be fond of each other's characters from being accustomed to them. Those who exchange utility rather than pleasure in their erotic relations are friends to a lesser extent and less enduring friends.

Those who are friends for utility dissolve the friendship as soon as the advantage is removed; for they were never friends of each other, but of what was expedient for them.

Now it is possible for bad people as well [as good] to be friends to each other for pleasure or utility, for decent people to be friends to base people, and for someone with neither character to be a friend to someone with any character. Clearly, however, only good people can be friends to each other because of the other person himself; for bad people find no enjoyment in one another if they get no benefit.

Moreover, it is only the friendship of good people that is immune to slander. For it is hard to trust anyone speaking against someone whom we ourselves have found reliable for a long time; and among good people there is trust, the belief that he would never do injustice [to a friend], and all the other things expected in a true friendship. But in the other types of friendship [distrust] may easily arise.

[These must be counted as types of friendship.] For people include among friends [not only the best type, but] also those who are friends for utility, as cities are—since alliances between cities seem to aim at expediency—and those who are fond of each other, as children are, for pleasure. Hence we must presumably also say that such people are friends, but say that there are more species of friendship than one.

On this view, the friendship of good people in so far as they are good is friendship in the primary way, and to the full extent; and the others are friendships by similarity. They are friends in so far as there is something good, and [hence] something similar to [what one finds in the best kind]; for what is pleasant is good to lovers of pleasure. But these [incomplete] types of friendship are not very regularly combined, and the same people do not become friends for both utility and pleasure. For things that [merely] coincide with each other are not very regularly combined.

Friendship has been assigned, then, to these species. Base people will be friends for pleasure or utility, since they are similar in that way. But good people will be friends because of themselves, since they are friends in so far as they are good.

These, then, are friends unconditionally; the others are friends coincidentally and
by being similar to these.   5

5

Just as with the virtues some people are called good in their state of character,
others good in their activity, the same is true of friendship. For some people find
enjoyment in each other by living together, and provide each other with good things.
Others, however, are asleep or separated by distance, and so are not active in these
ways, but are in the state that would result in the friendly activities; for distance   10
does not dissolve the friendship unconditionally, but only its activity. But if the
absence is long, it also seems to cause the friendship to be forgotten; hence the
saying, 'Lack of conversation has dissolved many a friendship'.

Older people and sour people do not appear to be prone to friendship. For there
is little pleasure to be found in them, and no one can spend his days with what is   15
painful or not pleasant, since nature appears to avoid above all what is painful and
to aim at what is pleasant.

Those who welcome each other but do not live together would seem to have
goodwill rather than friendship. For nothing is as proper to friends as living to-   20
gether; for while those who are in want desire benefit, blessedly happy people [who
want for nothing], no less than the others, desire to spend their days together, since
a solitary life fits them least of all. But people cannot spend their time with each
other if they are not pleasant and do not enjoy the same things, as they seem to in
the friendship of companions.

It is the friendship of good people that is friendship most of all, as we have often   25
said. For what is lovable and choiceworthy seems to be what is unconditionally good
or pleasant, and what is lovable and choiceworthy for each person seems to be what
is good or pleasant for him; and both of these make one good person lovable and
choiceworthy for another good person.

Loving would seem to be a feeling, but friendship a state. For loving occurs no
less towards soulless things, but reciprocal loving requires decision, and decision   30
comes from a state; and what makes [good people] wish good to the beloved for his
own sake is their state, not their feeling.

Moreover, in loving their friend they love what is good for themselves; for when
a good person becomes a friend he becomes a good for his friend. Each of them   35
loves what is good for himself, and repays in equal measure the wish and the
pleasantness of his friend; for friendship is said to be equality. And this is true above 1158a
all in the friendship of good people.

6

Among sour people and older people friendship is found less often, since they
are worse tempered and enjoy meeting people less, [and so lack] what seems to be
most typical and most productive of friendship. That is why young people become   5
friends quickly, but older people do not, since they do not become friends with

people in whom they find no enjoyment—nor do sour people. These people have goodwill to each other, since they wish goods and give help in time of need; but they scarcely count as friends, since they do not spend their days together or find

10   enjoyment in each other, and these things seem to be above all typical of friendship.

No one can have complete friendship for many people, just as no one can have an erotic passion for many at the same time; for [complete friendship, like erotic passion,] is like an excess, and an excess is naturally directed at a single individual. Moreover, just as it is hard for the same person to please many people intensely at the same time, it is also hard, presumably, to be good towards many people at the same time.

15   Besides, he must gain experience of the other too, and become accustomed to him, which is very difficult.

It is possible, however, to please many people when the friendship is for utility or pleasure, since many people can be pleased in these ways, and the services take little time.

Of these other two types of friendship the friendship for pleasure is more like [real] friendship; for they get the same thing from each other, and they find enjoy-

20   ment in each other or in the same things. This is what friendships are like among young people; for a generous [attitude] is found here more [than among older people], whereas it is mercenary people who form friendships for utility.

Moreover, blessedly happy people have no need of anything useful, but do need sources of pleasure. For they want to spend their lives with companions, and though

25   what is painful is borne for a short time, no one could continuously endure even The Good Itself if it were painful to him; hence they seek friends who are pleasant. But, presumably, they must also seek friends who are good as well [as pleasant], and good for them too; for then they will have everything that friends must have.

Someone in a position of power appears to have separate groups of friends; for

30   some are useful to him, others pleasant, but the same ones are not often both. For he does not seek friends who are both pleasant and virtuous, or useful for fine actions, but seeks one group to be witty, when he pursues pleasure, and the other group to be clever in carrying out instructions; and the same person rarely has both features.

Though admittedly, as we have said, an excellent person is both pleasant and useful, he does not become a friend to a superior [in power and position] unless the

35   superior is also superior in virtue; otherwise he does not reach [proportionate] equality by having a proportionate superior. And this superiority both in power and in virtue is not often found.

1158b   The friendships we have mentioned involve equality, since both friends get the same and wish the same to each other, or exchange one thing for another, e.g. pleasure for benefit. But, as we have said, they are friendships to a lesser extent,

5   and less enduring. Because they are both similar and dissimilar to the same thing they seem both to be and not to be friendships. For in so far as they are similar to the friendship of virtue, they appear to be friendships; for that type of friendship includes both utility and pleasure, and one of these types includes utility, the other pleasure. On the other hand, since the friendship of virtue is enduring and immune

10   to slander, while these change quickly and differ from it in many other ways as well, they do not appear to be friendships, in so far as they are dissimilar to that [best] type.

7

A different species of friendship is the one that corresponds to superiority, e.g. of a father towards his son, and in general of an older person towards a younger, of a man towards a woman, and of any sort of ruler towards the one he rules.

These friendships also differ from each other. For friendship of parents to children is not the same as that of rulers to ruled; nor is friendship of father to son the same as that of son to father, or of man to woman as that of woman to man. 15

For each of these friends has a different virtue and a different function, and there are different causes of love. Hence the ways of loving are different, and so are the friendships. Each does not get the same thing from the other, then, and must not seek it; but whenever children accord to their parents what they must accord to those who gave them birth, and parents accord what they must to their children, their friendship is enduring and decent. 20

In all the friendships corresponding to superiority, the loving must also be proportional, e.g. the better person, and the more beneficial, and each of the others likewise, must be loved more than he loves; for when the loving reflects the comparative worth of the friends, equality is achieved in a way, and this seems to be proper to friendship. 25

Equality, however, does not appear to be the same in friendship as in justice. For in justice equality is equality primarily in worth and secondarily in quantity; but in friendship it is equality primarily in quantity and secondarily in worth. 30

This is clear if friends come to be separated by some wide gap in virtue, vice, wealth, or something else; for then they are friends no more, and do not even expect to be. This is most evident with gods, since they have the greatest superiority in all goods. But it is also clear with kings, since far inferior people do not expect to be their friends; nor do worthless people expect to be friends to the best or wisest. 35 1159a

Now in these cases there is no exact definition of how long people are friends. For even if one of them loses a lot, the friendship still endures; but if one is widely separated [from the other], as a god is [from a human being], it no longer endures. 5

Hence there is this puzzle: do friends really wish their friend to have the greatest good, e.g. to be a god? For [if he becomes a god], *he* will no longer have friends, and hence no longer have goods, since friends are goods.

If, then, we have been right to say that one friend wishes good things to the other for the sake of the other *himself*, the other must remain whatever sort of being he is. Hence it is to the other as a human being that a friend will wish the greatest goods—though presumably not all of them, since each person wishes goods most of all to himself. 10

8

It is because they love honour that the many seem to prefer being loved to loving; that is why they love flatterers. For the flatterer is a friend in an inferior position, or [rather] pretends to be one, and pretends to love more than he is loved; and being loved seems close to being honoured, which the many do indeed pursue. 15

It would seem, however, that they choose honour coincidentally, not in itself. For

20   the many enjoy being honoured by powerful people because they expect to get
      whatever they need from them, and so enjoy the honour as a sign of this good
      treatment. Those who want honour from decent people with knowledge are seeking
      to confirm their own view of themselves, and so they are pleased because the judg-
      ment of those who say they are good makes them confident that they are good.

25   Being loved, on the contrary, they enjoy in itself. Hence it seems to be better than
      being honoured, and friendship seems choiceworthy in itself.

            But friendship seems to consist more in loving than in being loved. A sign of this
      is the enjoyment a mother finds in loving. For sometimes she gives her child away
30   to be brought up, and loves him as long as she knows about him; but she does not
      seek the child's love, if she cannot both [love and be loved]. She would seem to be
      satisfied if she sees the child doing well, and she loves the child even if ignorance
      prevents him from according to her what befits a mother.

            Friendship, then, consists more in loving; and people who love their friends are
35   praised; hence, it would seem, loving is the virtue of friends. And so friends whose
1159b love corresponds to their friends' worth are enduring friends and have an enduring
      friendship. This above all is the way for unequals as well as equals to be friends,
      since this is the way for them to be equalized.

            Equality and similarity, and above all the similarity of those who are similar
      in being virtuous, is friendship. For virtuous people are enduringly [virtuous] in
5   themselves, and enduring [friends] to each other. They neither request nor provide
      assistance that requires base actions, but, you might even say, prevent this. For it is
      proper to good people to avoid error themselves and not to permit it in their friends.

            Vicious people, by contrast, have no firmness, since they do not even remain
10   similar to what they were, but become friends for a short time, enjoying each other's
      vice.

            Useful or pleasant friends, however, last longer, for as long as they supply each
      other with pleasures or benefits.

            The friendship that seems to arise most from contraries is friendship for utility,
      e.g. of poor to rich or ignorant to knowledgeable; for we aim at whatever we find
15   we lack, and give something else in return.

            Here we might also include the erotic lover and his beloved, and the beautiful and
      the ugly. Hence an erotic lover also sometimes appears ridiculous, when he expects
      to be loved in the same way as he loves; that would presumably be a proper expecta-
      tion if he were lovable in the same way, but it is ridiculous when he is not.

20   Presumably, however, contrary seeks contrary coincidentally, not in itself, and
      desire is for the intermediate. For what is good, e.g., for the dry is to reach the
      intermediate, not to become wet, and the same is true for the hot and so on. Let us,
      then, dismiss these questions, since they are rather extraneous to our concern.

9

25   As we said at the beginning, friendship and justice would seem to have the same
      area of concern and to be found in the same people. For in every community there
      seems to be some sort of justice, and some type of friendship also. At any rate,
      fellow-voyagers and fellow-soldiers are called friends, and so are members of other

communities. And the extent of their community is the extent of their friendship, 30
since it is also the extent of the justice found there. The proverb 'What friends have
is common' is correct, since friendship involves community. But while brothers and
companions have everything in common, what people have in common in other
types of community is limited, more in some communities and less in others, since
some friendships are also closer than others, some less close. 35

What is just is also different, since it is not the same for parents towards children 1160a
as for one brother towards another, and not the same for companions as for fellow-
citizens, and similarly with the other types of friendship. Similarly, what is unjust
towards each of these is also different, and becomes more unjust as it is practised
on closer friends. It is more shocking, e.g., to rob a companion of money than to 5
rob a fellow-citizen, to fail to help a brother than a stranger, and to strike one's
father than anyone else. What is just also naturally increases with friendship, since
it involves the same people and extends over an equal area.

All communities would seem to be parts of the political community. For people 10
keep company for some advantage and to supply something contributing to their
life. Moreover, the political community seems both to have been originally formed
and to endure for advantage; for legislators also aim at advantage, and the common
advantage is said to be just.

The other types of community aim at partial advantage. Sea-travellers, e.g. seek
the advantage proper to a journey, in making money or something like that, while 15
fellow-soldiers seek the advantage proper to war, desiring either money or victory
or a city; and the same is true of fellow-tribesmen and fellow-demesmen. Some
communities—religious societies and dining clubs—seem to arise for pleasure, since 20
these are, respectively, for religious sacrifices and for companionship.

All these communities would seem to be subordinate to the political community,
since it aims not at some advantage close at hand, but at advantage for the whole of
life . . . [For] in performing sacrifices and arranging gatherings for these, people
both accord honours to the gods and provide themselves with pleasant relaxations. 25
For the long-established sacrifices and gatherings appear to take place after the
harvesting of the crops, as a sort of first-fruits, since this was the time when people
used to be most at leisure [and the time when relaxation would be most advantageous
for the whole of life].

All the types of community, then, appear to be parts of the political community,
and these sorts of communities imply the appropriate sorts of friendships. 30

10

There are three species of political system (*politeia*), and an equal number of
deviations, which are a sort of corruption of them. The first political system is
kingship; the second aristocracy; and since the third rests on property (*timēma*) it
appears proper to call it a timocratic system, though most people usually call it a 35
polity (*politeia*). The best of these is kingship and the worst timocracy.

The deviation from kingship is tyranny. For, though both are monarchies, they 1160b
show the widest difference, since the tyrant considers his own advantage, but the
king considers the advantage of his subjects. For someone is a king only if he is self-
sufficient and superior in all goods; and since such a person needs nothing more, 5

he will consider the subjects' benefit, not his own. For a king who is not like this would be only some sort of titular king. Tyranny is contrary to this; for the tyrant pursues his own good.

It is more evident that [tyranny] is the worst [deviation than that timocracy is the worst political system]; but the worst is contrary to the best; [hence kingship is the best].

10 The transition from kingship is to tyranny. For tyranny is the degenerate condition of monarchy, and the vicious king becomes a tyrant.

The transition from aristocracy [rule of the best people] is to oligarchy [rule of the few], resulting from the badness of the rulers. They distribute the city's goods in conflict with people's worth, so that they distribute all or most of the goods to

15 themselves, and always assign ruling offices to the same people, counting wealth for most. Hence the rulers are few, and they are vicious people instead of the most decent.

The transition from timocracy is to democracy [rule by the people], since these border on each other. For timocracy is also meant to be rule by the majority, and all those with the property-qualification are equal; [and majority-rule and equality are

20 the marks of democracy]. Democracy is the least vicious [of the deviations]; for it deviates only slightly from the form of a [genuine] political system.

These, then, are the most frequent transitions from one political system to another, since they are the smallest and easiest.

Resemblances to these—indeed, a sort of pattern of them—can also be found in

25 households. For the community of a father and his sons has the structure of kingship, since the father is concerned for his children. Indeed that is why Homer also calls Zeus father, since kingship is meant to be paternal rule.

Among the Persians, however, the father's rule is tyrannical, since he treats his

30 sons as slaves. The rule of a master over his slaves is also tyrannical, since it is the master's advantage that is achieved in it. This, then, appears a correct form of rule, whereas the Persian form appears erroneous, since the different types of rule suit different subjects.

The community of man and woman appears aristocratic. For the man's rule in the area where it is right corresponds to the worth [of each], and he commits to the

35 woman what is fitting for her. If, however, the man controls everything, he changes
1161a it into an oligarchy; for then his action conflicts with the worth [of each], and does not correspond to his superiority. Sometimes, indeed, women rule because they are heiresses; and these cases of rule do not reflect virtue, but result from wealth and power, as is true in oligarchies.

The community of brothers is like a timocratic [system], since they are equal

5 except in so far as they differ in age; and hence, if they differ very much in age, the friendship is no longer brotherly.

Democracy is found most of all in dwellings without a master, since everyone there is on equal terms; and also in those where the ruler is weak and everyone is free [to do what he likes].

11

10 Friendship appears in each of the political systems, to the extent that justice appears also. A king's friendship to his subjects involves superior beneficence. For

he benefits his subjects, since he is good and attends to them to ensure that they do well, as a shepherd attends to his sheep; hence Homer also called Agamemnon shepherd of the peoples.　　　　　　　　　15

Paternal friendship resembles this, but differs in conferring a greater benefit, since the father is the cause of his children's being, which seems to be the greatest benefit, and of their nurture and education. These benefits are also ascribed to ancestors; and by nature father is ruler over sons, ancestors over descendants, and king over subjects.

All these are friendships of superiority; that is why parents are also honoured. 20 And what is just in these friendships is not the same in each case, but corresponds to worth; for so does the friendship.

The friendship of man to woman is the same as in an aristocracy. For it reflects virtue, in assigning more good to the better, and assigning what is fitting to each. 25 The same is true for what is just here.

The friendship of brothers is similar to that of companions, since they are equal and of an age, and such people usually have the same feelings and characters. Friendship in a timocracy is similar to this. For there the citizens are meant to be equal and decent, and so rule in turn and on equal terms. The same is true, then, of their friendship.　　　　　　　　　30

In the deviations, however, justice is found only to a slight degree; and hence the same is true of friendship. There is least of it in the worst deviation; for in a tyranny there is little or no friendship.

For where ruler and ruled have nothing in common, they have no friendship, since they have no justice either. This is true for a craftsman in relation to his tool, 35 and for the soul in relation to the body. For in all these cases the user benefits what 1161b he uses, but there is neither friendship nor justice towards soulless things.

Nor is there any towards a horse or cow, or towards a slave, in so far as he is a slave. For master and slave have nothing in common, since a slave is a tool with a soul, while a tool is a slave without a soul. In so far as he is a slave, then, there is no 5 friendship with him.

But there is friendship with him in so far as he is a human being. For every human being seems to have some relations of justice with everyone who is capable of community in law and agreement. Hence there is also friendship, to the extent that a slave is a human being.

Hence there are friendships and justice to only a slight degree in tyrannies also, but to a much larger degree in democracies; for there people are equal, and so have 10 much in common.

12

As we have said, then, every friendship is found in a community. But we should set apart the friendship of families and that of companions. The friendship of citizens, tribesmen, voyagers and suchlike are more like friendships in a community, since they appear to reflect some sort of agreement; and among these we may include 15 the friendship of host and guest.

Friendship in families also seems to have many species, but they all seem to depend on paternal friendship. For a parent is fond of his children because he regards them as something of himself; and children are fond of a parent because they regard themselves as coming from him.

20   A parent knows better what has come from him than the children know that they are from the parent; and the parent regards his children as his own more than the product regards the maker as its own. For a person regards what comes from him as his own, as the owner regards his tooth or hair or anything; but what has come from him regards its owner as its own not at all, or to a lesser degree.

25   The length of time also matters. For a parent becomes fond of his children as soon as they are born, while children become fond of the parent when time has passed and they have acquired some comprehension or [at least] perception. And this also makes it clear why mothers love their children more [than fathers do].

    A parent loves his children as [he loves] himself. For what has come from him is a sort of other himself; [it is other because] it is separate. Children love a parent because they regard themselves as having come from him.

30   Brothers love each other because they have come from the same [parents]. For the same relation to the parents makes the same thing for both of them; hence we speak of the same blood, the same stock and so on. Hence they are the same thing in a way, in different [subjects]. Being brought up together and being of an age
35 contributes largely to friendship; for 'two of an age' [get on well], and those with the same character are companions. That is why the friendship of brothers and that
1162a of companions are similar.

    Cousins and other relatives are akin by being related to brothers, since that makes them descendants of the same parents [i.e. the parents of these brothers]. Some are more akin, others less, by the ancestor's being near to or far from them.

5   The friendship of children to a parent, like the friendship of human beings to a god, is friendship towards what is good and superior. For the parent conferred the greatest benefits, since he is the cause of their being and nurture and of their education once they have been born. This sort of friendship also includes pleasure and utility, more than the friendship of unrelated people does, to the extent that [parents and children] have more of a life in common.

10   Friendship between brothers has the features of friendship between companions, especially when [the companions] are decent, or in general similar. For brothers are that much more akin to each other [than ordinary companions], and are fond of each other from birth; they are that much more similar in character when they are from the same parents, nurtured together and educated similarly; and the proof of
15 their reliability over time is fullest and firmest.

    Among other relatives too the features of friendship are proportional [to the relation].

    The friendship of man and woman also seems to be natural. For human beings naturally tend to form couples more than to form cities, to the extent that the household is prior to the city, and more necessary, and child-bearing is shared more widely among the animals.

20   With the other animals this is the extent of the community. Human beings, however, share a household not only for child-bearing, but also for the benefits in their life. For from the start their functions are divided, with different ones for the man and the woman; hence each supplies the other's needs by contributing a special

function to the common good. Hence their friendship seems to include both utility and pleasure.

And it may also be friendship for virtue, if they are decent. For each has a proper virtue, and this will be a source of enjoyment for them. Children seem to be another bond, and that is why childless unions are more quickly dissolved; for children are a common good for both, and what is common holds them together.

How should a man conduct his life towards his wife, or, in general, toward a friend? That appears to be the same as asking what the just conduct of their lives is. For what is just is not the same for a friend towards a friend as towards a stranger, or the same towards a companion as towards a classmate.

13

There are three types of friendship, as we said at the beginning; and within each type some friendships rest on equality, while others correspond to superiority. For equally good people can be friends, but also a better and a worse person; and the same is true of friends for pleasure or utility, since they may be either equal or unequal in their benefits. Hence equals must equalize in loving and in the other things, because of their equality; and unequals must make the return that is proportionate to the types of superiority.

Accusations and reproaches arise only or most often in friendship for utility. And this is reasonable. For friends for virtue are eager to benefit each other, since this is proper to virtue and to friendship; and if this is the achievement they compete for, there are no accusations or fights. For no one objects if the other loves and benefits him; if he is gracious, he retaliates by benefiting the other. And if the superior gets what he aims at, he will not accuse his friend of anything, since each of them desires what is good.

Nor are there many accusations among friends for pleasure. For both of them get what they want at the same time if they enjoy spending their time together; and someone who accused his friend of not pleasing him would appear ridiculous, when he is free to spend his days without the friend's company.

Friendship for utility, however, is liable to accusations. For these friends deal with each other in the expectation of gaining benefits. Hence they always require more, thinking they have got less than is fitting; and they reproach the other because they get less than they require and deserve. And those who confer benefits cannot supply as much as the recipients require.

There are two ways of being just, one unwritten, and one governed by rules of law. And similarly one type of friendship of utility would seem to depend on character, and the other on rules. Accusations arise most readily if it is not the same sort of friendship when they dissolve it that it was when they formed it.

Friendship dependent on rules is the type that is on explicit conditions. One type of this is entirely mercenary and requires immediate payment. The other is more generous and postpones the time [of repayment], but conforms to an agreement [requiring] one thing in return for another. In this sort of friendship it is clear and unambiguous what is owed, but the postponement is a friendly aspect of it. That is why some cities do not allow legal actions in these cases, but think that people who have formed an arrangement on the basis of trust must put up with the outcome.

Friendship [for utility] that depends on character is not on explicit conditions. Someone makes a present or whatever it is, as to a friend, but expects to get back as much or more, since he assumes that it is not a free gift, but a loan. And if he does not dissolve the friendship on the terms on which he formed it, he will accuse the other.

35
1163a
This happens because all or most people wish for what is fine, but decide to do what is beneficial; and while it is fine to do someone a good turn without the aim of receiving one in return, it is beneficial to receive a good turn.

We should, if we can, make a return worthy of what we have received, [if the other has undertaken the friendship] willingly. For we should never make a friend of someone who is unwilling, but must suppose that we were in error at the beginning,

5
and received a benefit from the wrong person; for since it was not from a friend, and this was not why he was doing it, we must dissolve the arrangement as though we had received a good turn on explicit conditions. And we will agree to repay if we can. If we cannot repay, the giver would not even expect it. Hence we should repay if we can. We should consider at the beginning who is doing us a good turn, and on what conditions, so that we can put up with it on these conditions, or else decline it.

10
It is disputable whether we must measure [the return] by the benefit accruing to the recipient, and make the return proportional to that, or instead by the good turn done by the benefactor. For a recipient says that what he got was a small matter for the benefactor, and that he could have got it from someone else instead, and so he

15
belittles it. But the benefactor says it was the biggest thing he had, that it could not be got from anyone else, and that he gave it when he was in danger or similar need.

Since the friendship is for utility, surely the benefit to the recipient must be the measure [of the return]. For he was the one who required it, and the benefactor supplies him on the assumption that he will get an equal return. Hence the aid has

20
been as great as the benefit received, and the recipient should return as much as he gained, or still more, since that is finer.

But in friendships of virtue, there are no accusations. Rather, the decision of the benefactor would seem to be the measure, since the controlling element in virtue and character is found in decision.

14

25
There are also disputes in friendships that correspond to superiority, since each friend expects to have more than the other, but whenever this happens the friendship is dissolved.

For the better person thinks it is fitting for him to have more, on the ground that more is fittingly accorded to the good person. And the more beneficial person thinks the same. For it is wrong, people say, for someone to have an equal share when he

30
is useless; a public service, not a friendship, is the result if the benefits from the friendship do not correspond to the worth of the actions. [Each superior party says this] because he notices that in a financial association the larger contributors gain more, and he thinks the same thing is right in a friendship.

But the needy person, the inferior party in the friendship, takes the opposite view, saying it is proper to a virtuous friend to supply his needy [friends]. For what use

is it, as they say, to be an excellent or powerful person's friend if you are not going   35
to gain anything by it?

Well, each of them would seem to be correct in what he expects, and it is right for   1163b
each of them to get more from the friendship—but not more of the same thing.
Rather, the superior person should get more honour, and the needy person more
profit, since honour is the reward of virtue and beneficence, while profit is what
supplies need.

This also appears to be true in political systems. For someone who provides   5
nothing for the community receives no honour, since what is common is given to
someone who benefits the community, and honour is something common. For it is
impossible both to make money off the community and to receive honour from it at
the same time; for no one endures the smaller share of everything. Hence someone   10
who suffers a monetary loss [by holding office] receives honour in return, while
someone who accepts bribes [in office] receives money [but not honour]; for distribution that corresponds to worth equalizes and preserves the friendship, as we have
said.

This, then, is how we should treat unequals. If we are benefited in virtue or in
money, we should return honour, and thereby make what return we can. For   15
friendship seeks what is possible, not what corresponds to worth, since that is
impossible in some cases, e.g. with honour to gods and parents. For no one could
ever make a return corresponding to their worth, but someone who attends to them
as far as he is able seems to be a decent person.

That is why it seems that a son is not free to disavow his father, but a father is free
to disavow his son. For a debtor should return what he owes, and since no matter   20
what a son has done he has not made a worthy return for what his father has done
for him, he is always the debtor. But the creditor is free to remit the debt, and hence
the father is free to remit.

At the same time, however, it presumably seems that no one would ever withdraw
from a son who was not far gone in vice. For, quite apart from their natural
friendship, it is human not to repel aid. The son, however, if he is vicious, will want   25
to avoid helping his father, or will not be keen on it. For the many wish to receive
benefits, but they avoid doing them because they suppose it is unprofitable. So much,
then, for these things.

BOOK NINE

1

In all friendships of friends with dissimilar aims it is proportion that equalizes
and preserves the friendship, as we said; e.g. in political friendship the cobbler   35
receives a worthy exchange for his shoes, and so do the weaver and the others. Here
money is supplied as a common measure; everything is related to this and measured   1164a
by it.

In erotic friendships, however, sometimes the lover charges that he loves the
beloved deeply and is not loved in return; and in fact perhaps he has nothing lovable   5

in him. The beloved, however, often charges that previously the lover was promising him everything, and now fulfils none of his promises.

These sorts of charges arise whenever the lover loves his beloved for pleasure while the beloved loves his lover for utility, and they do not both provide these. For when the friendship has these causes, it is dissolved whenever they do not get what they were friends for; for each was not fond of the other himself, but only of what the other had, and since this was unstable, the friendships are unstable too.

Friendship of character, however, is friendship in itself, and endures, as we have said.

Friends quarrel when they get results different from those they want; for when someone does not get what he aims at, it is like getting nothing. It is like the person who promised the lyre player a reward, and a greater reward the better he played; in the morning, when the player asked him to deliver on his promise, the other said he had paid pleasure for pleasure. Now if this was what each of them had wished, it would be quite enough. But if one wished for delight and the other for profit, and one has got his delight and the other has not made his profit, the association is in no good state. For each person sets his mind on what he finds he requires, and this will be his aim when he gives what he gives.

Who should fix the worth [of a benefit], the giver or the receiver? The giver would seem to leave it to the receiver, as Protagoras is said to have done. For whenever he taught anything at all, he used to tell the pupil to estimate how much the knowledge was worth, and that amount would be his payment. In such cases, however, some prefer the rule 'A man should have his payment'.

But those who take the money first, and then do nothing that they said they would do, because their promises were excessive, are predictably accused, since they do not carry out what they agreed to. And presumably the sophists are compelled to make excessive promises. For no one would pay them money for the knowledge they really have; hence they take the payment, and then do not do what they were paid to do, and predictably are accused.

But where no agreement about services is made, friends who give services because of the friend himself are not open to accusation, as we have said, since this is the character of the friendship that reflects virtue. And the return should reflect the decision [of the original giver], since decision is proper to a friend and to virtue.

And it would seem that the same sort of return should also be made to those who have shared philosophy in common with us. For its worth is not measured by money, and no equivalent honour can be paid; but it is enough, presumably, to do what we can, as we do towards gods and parents.

If the giving is not of this sort, but on some specified condition, then presumably the repayment must be, ideally, what each of them thinks matches the worth of the gift. But if they do not agree on this, then it would seem not merely necessary, but also just, for the party who benefits first to fix the repayment. For if the other receives in return as much benefit as the first received, or as much as he would have paid for the pleasure, he will have got the worthy return from him.

Indeed this is also how it appears in buying and selling. For in some cities there are actually laws prohibiting legal actions in voluntary bargains, on the assumption that if we have trusted someone we must dissolve the association with him on the

same terms on which we formed it. The law does this because it supposes that it is   15
more just for the recipient to fix repayment than for the giver to fix it.

For usually those who have something and those who want it do not put the same
price on it, since what they own and what they are giving appears to givers to be
worth a lot. But nonetheless the return is made in the amount fixed by the initial
recipient. Presumably, however, the price must be not what it appears to be worth   20
when he has got it, but the price he put on it before he got it.

2

Here are some other questions that raise a puzzle. Must one accord [authority in]
everything to his father, and obey him in everything? Or must he trust the doctor
when he is sick, and should he vote for a military expert to be general? Similarly,
should someone serve his friend rather than an excellent person, and return a   25
favour to a benefactor rather than do a favour for a companion, if he cannot do
both?

Surely it is not easy to define all these matters exactly. For they include many
differences of all sorts—in importance and unimportance and in what is fine and
what is necessary. Clearly, however, not everything should be given to the same   30
person, and usually we should return favours rather than do favours for our companions, just as we should return a loan to a creditor rather than lend to a companion.

But presumably this is not always true. If, e.g., someone has rescued you from
pirates, should you ransom him in return, no matter who he is? Or if he does not   35
need to be ransomed, but asks for his money back, should you return it, or should   1165a
you ransom your father instead? Here it seems that you should ransom your father,
rather than even yourself.

As we have said, then, generally speaking we should return what we owe. But if
making a gift [to B] outweighs [returning the money to A] by being finer or more
necessary, we should incline to [making the gift to B] instead.

For sometimes even a return of a previous favour is not fair [but an excessive   5
demand], whenever [the original giver] knows he is benefiting an excellent person,
but [the recipient] would be returning the benefit to someone he thinks is vicious.

For sometimes you should not even lend in return to someone who has lent to
you. For he expected repayment when he lent to a decent person, whereas you have
no hope of it from a bad person. If that is really so, then, the demand [for reciprocity]   10
is not fair; and even if it is not so, but you think it is so, your refusal of the demand
seems not at all absurd.

As we have often said, then, arguments about acting and being affected are no
more definite than their subject matter.

Clearly, then, we should not give the same thing to everyone, and we should not
give our fathers everything, just as we should not make all our sacrifices to Zeus.   15
And since different things should be given to parents, brothers, companions and
benefactors, we should accord to each what is proper and suitable. This is what
actually appears to be done; e.g. kinsfolk are the people invited to a wedding, since
they share the same family, and hence share in actions that concern it; and for the   20
same reason it is thought that kinsfolk more than anyone must come to funerals.

It seems that we must supply means of support to parents more than anyone. For we suppose that we owe them this, and that it is finer to supply those who are the causes of our being than to supply ourselves in this way. And we should accord honour to our parents, just as we should to the gods, but not every sort of honour; for we should not accord the same honour to father and to mother, nor accord them the honour due a wise person or a general. We should accord a father's honour to a father, and likewise a mother's to a mother.

We should accord to every older person the honour befitting his age, by standing up, giving up seats and so on. With companions and brothers we should speak freely, and have everything in common. To kinsfolk, fellow-tribesmen, fellow-citizens and all the rest we should always try to accord what is proper, and should compare what belongs to each, as befits closeness of relation, virtue or usefulness. Comparison is easier with people of the same kind, and more difficult with people of different kinds, but the difficulty is no reason for giving up the comparison; rather, we should define as far as we can.

3

There is also a puzzle about dissolving or not dissolving friendships with friends who do not remain the same. With friends for utility or pleasure perhaps there is nothing absurd in dissolving the friendship whenever they are no longer pleasant or useful. For they were friends of pleasure or utility; and if these give out, it is reasonable not to love.

However, we might accuse a friend if he really liked us for utility or pleasure, and pretended to like us for our character. For, as we said at the beginning, friends are most at odds when they are not friends in the way they think they are. And so, if we mistakenly suppose we are loved for our character, when our friend is doing nothing to suggest this, we must hold ourselves responsible. But if we are deceived by his pretence, we are justified in accusing him—even more justified than in accusing debasers of the currency, to the extent that his evildoing debases something more precious.

But if we accept a friend as a good person, and then he becomes vicious, and seems so, should we still love him? Surely we cannot, if not everything, but only what is good, is lovable. What is bad is not lovable, and must not be loved; for we ought neither to love what is bad nor to become similar to a bad person, and we have said that similar is friend to similar.

Then should the friendship be dissolved at once [as soon as the friend becomes bad]? Surely not with everyone, but only with an incurably vicious person. If someone can be set right, we should try harder to rescue his character than his property, in so far as character is both better and more proper to friendship.

However, the friend who dissolves the friendship seems to be doing nothing absurd. For he was not the friend of a person of this sort; hence, if the friend has altered, and he cannot save him, he leaves him.

But if one friend stayed the same and the other became more decent and far excelled his friend in virtue, should the better person still treat the other as a friend? Surely he cannot. This becomes clear in a wide separation, such as we find in friendships beginning in childhood. For if one friend still thinks as a child, while the other becomes a most superior man, how could they still be friends, when they neither approve of the same things nor find the same things enjoyable or painful? For they do not even find it so in their life together and without that they cannot be   30 friends, since they cannot live together—we have discussed this.

Then should the better person regard the other as though he had never become his friend? Surely he must keep some memory of the familiarity they had; and just as we think we must do kindnesses for friends more than for strangers, so also we should accord something to past friends because of the former friendship, whenever   35 excessive vice does not cause the dissolution.

4

The defining features of friendship that are found in friendships to one's   1166a neighbours would seem to be derived from features of friendship towards oneself.

For a friend is taken to be (1) someone who wishes and does goods or apparent goods to his friend for the friend's own sake; or (2) one who wishes the friend to be and to live for the friend's own sake—this is how mothers feel towards their children,   5 and how friends who have been in conflict feel [towards each other]. (3) Others take a friend to be one who spends his time with his friend, and (4) makes the same choices; or (5) one who shares his friend's distress and enjoyment—and this also is true especially of mothers. And people define friendship by one of these features.

Each of these features is found in the decent person's relation to himself, and it   10 is found in other people in so far as they suppose they are decent. As we have said, virtue and the excellent person would seem to be the standard in each case.

(4) The excellent person is of one mind with himself, and desires the same things in his whole soul.

(1) Hence he wishes goods and apparent goods to himself, and does them in his   15 actions, since it is proper to the good person to achieve the good. He wishes and does them for his own sake, since he does them for the sake of his thinking part, and that is what each person seems to be.

(2) He wishes himself to live and to be preserved. And he wishes this for the part by which he has intelligence more than for any other part. For being is a good for the good person, and each person wishes for goods for himself. And no one chooses   20 to become another person even if that other will have every good when he has come into being; for, as it is, the god has the good [but no one chooses to be replaced by a god]. Rather [each of us chooses goods] on condition that he remains whatever he is; and each person would seem to be the understanding part, or that most of all. [Hence the good person wishes for goods for the understanding part.]

(3) Further, such a person finds it pleasant to spend time with himself, and so wishes to do it. For his memories of what he has done are agreeable, and his   25 expectations for the future are good, and hence both are pleasant. And besides, his thought is well supplied with topics for study.

(5) Moreover, he shares his own distresses and pleasures, more than other people share theirs. For it is always the same thing that is painful or pleasant, not different things at different times. This is because he practically never regrets [what he has done].

30   The decent person, then, has each of these features in relation to himself, and is related to his friend as he is to himself, since the friend is another himself. Hence friendship seems to be one of these features, and people with these features seem to be friends.

Is there friendship towards oneself, or is there not? Let us dismiss that question
35   for the present. However, there seems to be friendship in so far as someone is two or more parts. This seems to be true from what we have said, and because an extreme
1166b   degree of friendship resembles one's friendship to oneself.

The many, base though they are, also appear to have these features. But perhaps they share in them only in so far as they approve of themselves and suppose they
5   are decent. For no one who is utterly bad and unscrupulous either has these features or appears to have them.

Indeed, even base people hardly have them.

(4) For they are at odds with themselves, and, like incontinent people, have an appetite for one thing and a wish for another.

(1) For they do not choose things that seem to be good for them, but instead
10   choose pleasant things that are actually harmful. And cowardice or laziness causes others to shrink from doing what they think best for themselves.

(2) Those who have done many terrible actions hate and shun life because of their vice, and destroy themselves.

(3) Besides, vicious people seek others to pass their days with, and shun themselves.
15   For when they are by themselves they remember many disagreeable actions, and expect to do others in the future; but they manage to forget these in other people's company. These people have nothing lovable about them, and so have no friendly feelings for themselves.

(5) Hence such a person does not share his own enjoyments and distresses. For
20   his soul is in conflict, and because he is vicious one part is distressed at being restrained, and another is pleased [by the intended action]; and so each part pulls in a different direction, as though they were tearing him apart. Even if he cannot be distressed and pleased at the same time, still he is soon distressed because he was pleased, and wishes these things had not become pleasant to him; for base people
25   are full of regret.

Hence the base person appears not to have a friendly attitude even towards himself, because he has nothing lovable about him.

If this state is utterly miserable, everyone should earnestly shun vice and try to be decent; for that is how someone will have a friendly relation to himself and will become a friend to another.

5

30   Goodwill would seem to be a feature of friendship, but still it is not friendship. For it arises even towards people we do not know, and without their noticing it, whereas friendship does not. We have said this before also.

Nor is it loving, since it lacks intensity and desire, which are implied by loving.
35   Moreover, while loving requires familiarity, goodwill can also arise in a moment, as
1167a   it arises, e.g., [in a spectator] for contestants. For [the spectator] acquires goodwill

for them, and wants what they want, but would not cooperate with them in any action; for, as we said, his good will arises in a moment and his fondness is superficial.

In fact goodwill would seem to originate friendship in the way that pleasure coming through sight originates erotic passion. For no one has erotic passion for another without previous pleasure in his appearance. But still enjoyment of his appearance does not imply erotic passion for him; passion consists also in longing for him in his absence and an appetite for his presence. Similarly, though people cannot be friends without previous goodwill, goodwill does not imply friendship; for when they have goodwill people only wish goods to the other, and will not cooperate with him in any action, or go to any trouble for him.

Hence we might transfer [the name 'friendship'], and say that goodwill is inactive friendship, and that when it lasts some time and they grow accustomed to each other, it becomes friendship.

It does not, however, become friendship for utility or pleasure, since these aims do not produce goodwill either.

For a recipient of a benefit does what is just when he returns goodwill for what he has received. But those who wish for another's welfare because they hope to enrich themselves through him would seem to have goodwill to themselves, rather than to him. Likewise, they would seem to be friends to themselves rather than to him, if they attend to him because he is of some use to them.

But in general goodwill results from some sort of virtue and decency, whenever one person finds another to be apparently fine or brave or something similar. As we said, this also arises in the case of contestants.

6

Now concord also appears to be a feature of friendship. Hence it is not merely sharing a belief, since this might happen among people who do not know each other. Nor are people said to be in concord when they agree about just anything, e.g. on astronomical questions, since concord on these questions is not a feature of friendship. Rather, a city is said to be in concord when [its citizens] agree about what is advantageous, make the same decision, and act on their common resolution.

Hence concord concerns questions for action, and, more exactly, large questions where both or all can get what they want. A city, e.g., is in concord whenever all the citizens resolve to make offices elective, or to make an alliance with the Spartans, or to make Pittacus[15] ruler, when he is willing too.

Whenever each person wants the same thing all to himself, as the people in the *Phoenissae*[16] do, they are in conflict. For it is not concord when each merely has the same thing in mind, whatever it is, but each must also have the same thing in mind for the same person; this is true, e.g., whenever both the common people and the

---

15. [After serving as dictator of Mitylene for fourteen years in the early sixth century, he gave up his office, although the citizens unanimously wanted him to continue.—M.L.M.]

16. [Euripides' *Phoenissae* is about the bitter and unscrupulous struggle between Eteocles and Polyneices for absolute power in Thebes.—T.I.]

1167b   decent party want the best people to rule, since when that is so both sides get what
they seek.

Concord, then, is apparently political friendship, as indeed it is said to be; for it
is concerned with advantage and with what affects life [as a whole].

5   This sort of concord is found in decent people. For they are in concord with
themselves and with each other, since they are practically of the same mind; for
their wishes are stable, not flowing back and forth like a tidal strait. They wish for
what is just and advantageous, and also seek it in common.

10   Base people, however, cannot be in concord, except to a small extent, just as they
can be friends only to a small extent; for they are greedy for more benefits, and
shirk labours and public services. And since each wishes this for himself, he interro-
gates and obstructs his neighbour; for when people do not look out for the common
15   good, it is ruined. The result is that they are in conflict, trying to compel each other
to do what is just, but not wishing to do it themselves.

7

Now benefactors seem to love their beneficiaries more than the beneficiaries love
them [in return], and this is discussed as though it were an unreasonable thing to
happen.

20   Here is how it appears to most people. It is because the beneficiaries are debtors
and the benefactors creditors: the debtor in a loan wishes the creditor did not exist,
while the creditor even attends to the safety of the debtor. So also, then, a benefactor
25   wants the beneficiary to exist because he expects gratitude in return, while the
beneficiary is not attentive about making the return.

Now Epicharmus might say that most people say this because they 'take a bad
person's point of view'. Still, it would seem to be a human point of view, since the
many are indeed forgetful, and seek to receive benefits more than to give them.

However, it seems that the cause is more proper to [human] nature, and the case
30   of creditors is not even similar. For they do not love their debtors, but in wishing
for their safety simply seek repayment; whereas benefactors love and like their
beneficiaries even if they are of no present or future use to them.

35   The same is true with craftsmen; for each likes his own product more than it
would like him if it acquired a soul. Perhaps this is true of poets most of all, since
1168a they dearly like their own poems, and are fond of them as though they were
their children. This, then, is what the case of the benefactor resembles; here the
5   beneficiary is his product, and hence he likes him more than the product likes its
producer.

The cause of this is as follows:

1. Being is choiceworthy and lovable for all.

2. We are in so far as we are actualized, since we are in so far as we live and act.

3. The product is, in a way, the producer in his actualization.

4. Hence the producer is fond of the product, because he loves his own being.
And this is natural, since what he is potentially is what the product indicates in
actualization.

10   At the same time, the benefactor's action is fine for him, so that he finds enjoyment

in the person he acts on; but the person acted on finds nothing fine in the agent, but only, at most, some advantage, which is less pleasant and lovable.

What is pleasant is actualization in the present, expectation for the future, and memory of the past; but what is pleasantest is the [action we do] in so far as we are actualized, and this is also most lovable. For the benefactor, then, his product endures, since what is fine is long-lasting; but for the person acted on, what is useful passes away.

Besides, memory of something fine is pleasant, while memory of [receiving] something useful is not altogether pleasant, or is less pleasant—though the reverse would seem to be true for expectation.

Moreover, loving is like production, while being loved is like being acted on; and [the benefactor's] love and friendliness is the result of his greater activity.

Besides, everyone is fond of what has needed effort to produce it; e.g. people who have made money themselves are fonder of it than people who have inherited it. And while receiving a benefit seems to take no effort, giving one is hard work.

This is also why mothers love their children more [than fathers do], since giving birth is more effort for them, and they know better that the children are theirs. And this also would seem to be proper to benefactors.

8

There is also a puzzle about whether one ought to love oneself or someone else most of all; for those who like themselves most are criticized and denounced as self-lovers, as though this were something shameful.

Indeed, the base person does seem to go to every length for his own sake, and all the more the more vicious he is; hence he is accused, e.g., of doing nothing of his own accord. The decent person, on the contrary, acts for what is fine, all the more the better he is, and for his friend's sake, disregarding his own good.

The facts, however, conflict with these claims, and that is not unreasonable.

For it is said that we must love most the friend who is most a friend; and one person is most a friend to another if he wishes goods to the other for the other's sake, even if no one will know about it. But these are features most of all of one's relation to oneself; and so too are all the other defining features of a friend, since we have said that all the features of friendship extend from oneself to others.

All the proverbs agree with this too, e.g. speaking of 'one soul', 'what friends have is common', 'equality is friendship' and 'the knee is closer than the shin'. For all these are true most of all in someone's relations with himself, since one is a friend to himself most of all. Hence he should also love himself most of all.

It is not surprising that there is a puzzle about which view we ought to follow, since both inspire some confidence; hence we must presumably divide these sorts of arguments, and distinguish how far and in what ways those on each side are true.

Perhaps, then, it will become clear, if we grasp how those on each side understand self-love.

Those who make self-love a matter for reproach ascribe it to those who award the biggest share in money, honours and bodily pleasures to themselves. For these are the goods desired and eagerly pursued by the many on the assumption that they are best; and hence they are also contested.

Those who are greedy for these goods gratify their appetites and in general their feelings and the non-rational part of the soul; and since this is the character of the many, the application of the term ['self-love'] is derived from the most frequent [kind of self-love], which is base. This type of self-lover, then, is justifiably reproached.

And plainly it is the person who awards himself these goods whom the many habitually call a self-lover. For if someone is always eager to excel everyone in doing just or temperate actions or any others expressing the virtues, and in general always gains for himself what is fine, no one will call him a self-lover or blame him for it.

However, it is this more than the other sort of person who seems to be a self-lover. At any rate he awards himself what is finest and best of all, and gratifies the most controlling part of himself, obeying it in everything. And just as a city and every other composite system seems to be above all its most controlling part, the same is true of a human being; hence someone loves himself most if he likes and gratifies this part.

Similarly, someone is called continent or incontinent because his understanding is or is not the master, on the assumption that this is what each person is. Moreover, his own voluntary actions seem above all to be those involving reason. Clearly, then, this, or this above all, is what each person is, and the decent person likes this most of all.

Hence he most of all is a self-lover, but a different kind from the self-lover who is reproached, differing from him as much as the life guided by reason differs from the life guided by feelings, and as much as the desire for what is fine differs from the desire for what seems advantageous.

Those who are unusually eager to do fine actions are welcomed and praised by everyone. And when everyone competes to achieve what is fine and strains to do the finest actions, everything that is right will be done for the common good, and each person individually will receive the greatest of goods, since that is the character of virtue.

Hence the good person must be a self-lover, since he will both help himself and benefit others by doing fine actions. But the vicious person must not love himself, since he will harm both himself and his neighbours by following his base feelings.

For the vicious person, then, the right actions conflict with those he does. The decent person, however, does the right actions, since every understanding chooses what is best for itself and the decent person obeys his understanding.

Besides, it is true that, as they say, the excellent person labours for his friends and for his native country, and will die for them if he must; he will sacrifice money, honours and contested goods in general, in achieving what is fine for himself. For he will choose intense pleasure for a short time over mild pleasure for a long time; a year of living finely over many years of undistinguished life; and a single fine and great action over many small actions.

This is presumably true of one who dies for others; he does indeed choose something great and fine for himself. He is ready to sacrifice money as long as his friends profit; for the friends gain money, while he gains what is fine, and so he awards himself the greater good. He treats honours and offices the same way; for he will sacrifice them all for his friends, since this is fine and praiseworthy for him.

It is not surprising, then, that he seems to be excellent, when he chooses what is fine at the cost of everything. It is also possible, however, to sacrifice actions to his friend, since it may be finer to be responsible for his friend's doing the action than to do it himself. In everything praiseworthy, then, the excellent person awards himself what is fine.

In this way, then, we must be self-lovers, as we have said. But in the way the many are, we ought not to be.

9

There is also a dispute about whether the happy person will need friends or not.

For it is said that blessedly happy and self-sufficient people have no need of friends. For they already have [all] the goods, and hence, being self-sufficient, need nothing added. But your friend, since he is another yourself, supplies what your own efforts cannot supply. Hence it is said, 'When the god gives well, what need is there of friends?'

However, in awarding the happy person all the goods it would seem absurd not to give him friends; for having friends seems to be the greatest external good.

And it is more proper to a friend to confer benefits than to receive them, and proper to the good person and to virtue to do good; and it is finer to benefit friends than to benefit strangers. Hence the excellent person will need people for him to benefit. Indeed, that is why there is a question about whether friends are needed more in good fortune than in ill-fortune; for it is assumed that in ill-fortune we need people to benefit us, and in good fortune we need others for us to benefit.

Surely it is also absurd to make the blessed person solitary. For no one would choose to have all [other] goods and yet be alone, since a human being is political, tending by nature to live together with others. This will also be true, then, of the happy person; for he has the natural goods, and clearly it is better to spend his days with decent friends than with strangers of just any character. Hence the happy person will need friends.

Then what are the other side saying, and in what way is it true? Surely they say what they say because the many think that it is the useful people who are friends. Certainly the blessedly happy person will have no need of these, since he has [all] goods. Similarly, he will have no need, or very little, of friends for pleasure; for since his life is pleasant, it has no need of imported pleasures. Since he does not need these sorts of friends, he does not seem to need friends at all.

However, this conclusion is presumably not true:

(1) For we said at the beginning that happiness is a kind of activity; and clearly activity comes into being, and does not belong [to someone all the time], as a possession does. Being happy, then, is found in living and being active.

(2) The activity of the good person is excellent, and [hence] pleasant in itself, as we said at the beginning.

(3) Moreover, what is our own is pleasant.

(4) We are able to observe our neighbours more than ourselves, and to observe their actions more than our own.

(5) Hence a good person finds pleasure in the actions of excellent people who are

1170a his friends, since these actions have both the naturally pleasant [features, i.e. they are good, and they are his own].

(6) The blessed person decides to observe virtuous actions that are his own; and the actions of a virtuous friend are of this sort.

(7) Hence he will need virtuous friends.

Further, it is thought that the happy person must live pleasantly. But the solitary
5 person's life is hard, since it is not easy for him to be continuously active all by himself; but in relation to others and in their company it is easier, and hence his activity will be more continuous. It is also pleasant in itself; as it must be in the blessedly happy person's case. For the excellent person, in so far as he is excellent, enjoys actions expressing virtue, and objects to actions caused by vice, just as the
10 musician enjoys fine melodies and is pained by bad ones.

Further, good people's life together allows the cultivation of virtue, as Theognis says.

If we examine the question more from the point of view of [human] nature, an excellent friend would seem to be choiceworthy by nature for an excellent person.

15 (1) For, as we have said, what is good by nature is good and pleasant in itself for an excellent person.

(2) For animals life is defined by the capacity for perception; for human beings it is defined by the capacity for perception or understanding.

(3) Every capacity refers to an activity, and a thing is present to its full extent in its activity.

(4) Hence living to its full extent would seem to be perceiving or understanding.

20 (5) Life is good and pleasant in itself. For it has definite order, which is proper to the nature of what is good.

(6) What is good by nature is also good for the decent person. That is why life would seem to be pleasant for everyone. Here, however, we must not consider a life that is vicious and corrupted, or filled with pains; for such a life lacks definite order,
25 just as its proper features do. (The truth about pain will be more evident in what follows.)

(7) Life itself, then, is good and pleasant. So it looks, at any rate, from the fact that everyone desires it, and decent and blessed people desire it more than others do; for their life is most choiceworthy for them, and their living is most blessed.

(8) Now someone who sees perceives that he sees; one who hears perceives that
30 he hears; and one who walks perceives that he walks.

(9) Similarly in the other cases also there is some [element] that perceives that we are active.

(10) Hence, if we are perceiving, we perceive that we are perceiving; and if we are understanding, we perceive that we are understanding.

(11) Now perceiving that we are perceiving or understanding is the same as perceiving that we are, since we agreed [in (4)] that being is perceiving or understanding.

1170b (12) Perceiving that we are alive is pleasant in itself. For life is by nature a good [from (5)], and it is pleasant to perceive that something good is present in us.

(13) And living is choiceworthy, for a good person most of all, since being is good

and pleasant for him; for he is pleased to perceive something good in itself together   5
[with his own being].

(14) The excellent person is related to his friend in the same way as he is related
to himself, since a friend is another himself.

(15) Therefore, just as his own being is choiceworthy for him, his friend's being
is choiceworthy for him in the same or a similar way.

We agreed that someone's own being is choiceworthy because he perceives that
he is good, and this sort of perception is pleasant in itself. He must, then, perceive   10
his friend's being together [with his own], and he will do this when they live together
and share conversation and thought. For in the case of human beings what seems
to count as living together is this sharing of conversation and thought, not sharing
the same pasture, as in the case of grazing animals.

If, then, for the blessedly happy person, being is choiceworthy, since it is naturally   15
good and pleasant; and if the being of his friend is closely similar to his own; then
his friend will also be choiceworthy. Whatever is choiceworthy for him he must
possess, since otherwise he will to this extent lack something, [and hence will not be
self-sufficient]. Anyone who is to be happy, then, must have excellent friends.

10

Then should we have as many friends as possible? Or is it the same as with the   20
friendship of host and guest, where it seems to be good advice to 'have neither many
nor none'? Is this also good advice in friendship, to have neither no friends nor
many?

With friends for utility the advice seems very apt, since it is hard work to return   25
many people's services, and life is too short for it. Indeed, more [such] friends than
are adequate for one's own life are superfluous, and a hindrance to living finely;
hence we have no need of them. A few friends for pleasure are enough also, just as
a little seasoning on food is enough.

Of excellent people, however, should we have as many as possible as friends, or   30
is there some proper measure of their number, as of the number in a city? For a city
could not be formed from ten human beings, but it would be a city no longer if it
had ten myriads; presumably, though, the right quantity is not just one number, but
anything between certain defined limits. Hence there is also some limit defining the   1171a
number of friends.

Presumably, this is the largest number with whom you could live together, since
we found that living together seems to be most characteristic of friendship. And
clearly you cannot live with many people and distribute yourself among them.

Besides, these many people must also be friends to each other, if they are all to
spend their days together; and this is hard work for many people to manage. It also   5
becomes difficult for many to share each other's enjoyments and distresses as their
own, since you are quite likely to find yourself sharing one friend's pleasure and
another friend's grief at the same time.

Presumably, then, it is good not to seek as many friends as possible, and good to
have no more than enough for living together; indeed it even seems impossible to
be an extremely close friend to many people. For the same reason it also seems   10

impossible to be passionately in love with many people, since passionate erotic love tends to be an excess of friendship, and one has this for one person; hence also one has extremely close friendship for a few people.

15 This would seem to be borne out in what people actually do. For the friendship of companions is not found in groups of many people, and the friendships celebrated in song are always between two people. By contrast, those who have many friends and treat everyone as close to them seem to be friends to no one, except in a fellow-citizen's way. These people are regarded as ingratiating.

Certainly it is possible to be a friend of many in a fellow-citizen's way, and still to be a truly decent person, not ingratiating; but it is impossible to be many people's 20 friend for their virtue and for themselves. We have reason to be satisfied if we can find even a few such friends.

11

Have we more need of friends in good fortune or in ill fortune? For in fact we seek them in both, since in ill fortune we need assistance, while in good fortune we need friends to live with and to benefit, since then we wish to do good.

25 Certainly it is more necessary to have friends in ill fortune, and hence useful friends are needed here. But it is finer to have them in good fortune, and hence we also seek decent friends; for it is more choiceworthy to do good to them and spend our time with them.

The very presence of friends is also pleasant, in ill fortune as well as good fortune; 30 for we have our pain lightened when our friends share our distress. Hence indeed one might be puzzled about whether they take a part of it from us, as though helping us to lift a weight, or, alternatively, their presence is pleasant and our awareness that they share our distress makes the pain smaller. Well, we need not discuss whether it is this or something else that lightens our pain; at any rate, what we have mentioned does appear to occur.

35 However, the presence of friends would seem to be a mixture [of pleasure and 1171b pain]. For certainly the sight of our friends in itself is pleasant, especially when we are in ill fortune, and it gives us some assistance in removing our pain. For a friend consoles us by the sight of him and by conversation, if he is dexterous, since he knows our character and what gives us pleasure and pain. Nonetheless, awareness 5 of his pain at our ill fortune is painful to us, since everyone tries to avoid causing pain to his friends.

That is why someone with a manly nature tries to prevent his friend from sharing his pain. Unless he is unusually immune to pain, he cannot endure pain coming to his friends; and he does not allow others to share his mourning at all, since he is not 10 prone to mourn himself either. Females, however, and effeminate men enjoy having people to wail with them; they love them as friends who share their distress. But in everything we clearly must imitate the better person.

In good fortune, by contrast, the presence of friends makes it pleasant to pass our time and to notice that they take pleasure in our own goods.

15 Hence it seems that we must eagerly call our friends to share our good fortune, since it is fine to do good. But we must hesitate to call them to share our ill fortune, since we must share bad things with them as little as possible; hence the saying 'My

misfortune is enough'. We should invite them most of all whenever they will benefit   20
us greatly, with little trouble to themselves.

Conversely, it is presumably appropriate to go eagerly, without having to be called,
to friends in misfortune. For it is proper to a friend to benefit, especially to benefit
a friend in need who has not demanded it, since this is finer and pleasanter for both
friends. In good fortune he should come eagerly to help him, since friends are
needed for this also; but he should be slow to come to receive benefits, since eagerness
to be benefitted is not fine. Presumably, though, one should avoid getting a reputa-   25
tion for being a killjoy, as sometimes happens, by refusing benefits.

Hence the presence of friends is apparently choiceworthy in all conditions.

12

What the erotic lover likes most is the sight of his beloved, and this is the sort of
perception he chooses over the others, supposing that this above all is what makes   30
him fall in love and remain in love. In the same way, surely, what friends find most
choiceworthy is living together. For friendship is community, and we are related to
our friend as we are related to ourselves. Hence, since the perception of our own
being is choiceworthy, so is the perception of our friend's being. Perception is active   35
when we live with him; hence, not surprisingly, this is what we seek.   1172a

Whatever someone [regards as] his being, or the end for which he chooses to be
alive, that is the activity he wishes to pursue in his friend's company. Hence some
friends drink together, others play dice, while others do gymnastics and go hunting,
or do philosophy. They spend their days together on whichever pursuit in life they   5
like most; for since they want to live with their friends, they share the actions in
which they find their common life.

Hence the friendship of base people turns out to be vicious. For they are unstable,
and share base pursuits; and by becoming similar to each other, they grow vicious.   10
But the friendship of decent people is decent, and increases the more often they
meet. And they seem to become still better from their activities and their mutual
correction. For each moulds the other in what they approve of, so that '[you will
learn] what is noble from noble people'.

So much, then, for friendship. The next task will be to discuss pleasure.   15

BOOK TEN

1

The next task, presumably, is to discuss pleasure. For it seems to be especially   20
proper to our [animal] kind, and hence when we educate children we steer them by
pleasure and pain. Besides, enjoying and hating the right things seems to be most
important for virtue of character. For pleasure and pain extend through the whole
of our lives, and are of great importance for virtue and the happy life, since people   25

decide to do what is pleasant, and avoid what is painful. Least of all, then, it seems, should these topics be neglected.

This is especially true because they arouse much dispute. For some say pleasure is the good, while others, on the contrary, say it is altogether base.

Now presumably some who say it is base say so because they are persuaded that it is so. Others, however, say it because they think it is better for the conduct of our lives to present pleasure as base even if it is not. For, they say, since the many lean towards pleasure and are slaves to pleasures, we must lead them in the contrary direction, because that is the way to reach the intermediate condition.

Surely, however, this is wrong. For arguments about actions and feelings are less credible than the facts; hence any conflict between arguments and perceptible [facts] arouses contempt for the arguments, and moreover undermines the truth as well [as the arguments]. For if someone blames pleasure, but then has been seen to seek it on *some* occasions, the reason for his lapse seems to be that he approves of *every* type of pleasure; for the many are not the sort to make distinctions.

True arguments, then, would seem to be the most useful, not only for knowledge but also for the conduct of life. For since they harmonize with the facts, they are credible, and so encourage those who comprehend them to live by them.

Enough of this, then; let us now consider what has been said about pleasure.

2

Eudoxus thought that pleasure is the good.

(1) This was because (a) he saw that all [animals], both rational and non-rational, seek it. (b) In everything, he says, what is choiceworthy is decent, and what is most choiceworthy is supreme. (c) Each thing finds its own good, just as it finds its own nourishment. (d) Hence, when all are drawn to the same thing [i.e. pleasure], this indicates that it is best for all. (e) And what is good for all, what all aim at, is the good.

Eudoxus' arguments were found credible because of his virtuous character, rather than on their own [merits]. For since he seemed to be outstandingly temperate, he did not seem to be saying this because he was a friend of pleasure; rather, it seemed, what he said was how it really was.

(2) He thought it was no less evident from consideration of the contrary. (a) Pain in itself is to be avoided for all. (b) Similarly, then, its contrary is choiceworthy for all. (c) What is most choiceworthy is what we choose not because of, or for the sake of, anything else. (d) And it is agreed that this is the character of pleasure, since we never ask anyone what his end is in being pleased, on the assumption that pleasure is choiceworthy in itself.

(3) Moreover, [he argued], when pleasure is added to any other good, e.g. to just or temperate action, it makes that good more choiceworthy; and good is increased by the addition of itself.

This [third] argument, at least, would seem to present pleasure as one good among others, no more a good than any other. For the addition of *any* other good makes a good more choiceworthy than it is all by itself.

Indeed Plato uses this sort of argument when he undermines the claim of pleasure

to be the good. For, he argues, the pleasant life is more choiceworthy when combined   30
with intelligence than it is without it; and if the mixed [good] is better, pleasure is
not the good, since nothing can be added to the good to make it more choiceworthy.

Nor, clearly, could anything else be the good if it is made more choiceworthy by
the addition of anything that is good in itself. Then what is the good that meets this   35
condition, and that we share in also? That is what we are looking for.

When some object that what everything aims at is not good, surely there is nothing
in what they say. For if things seem [good] to all, we say they *are* [good]; and if   1173a
someone undermines confidence in these, what he says will hardly inspire more
confidence in other things. For if [only] beings without understanding desired these
things, there would be something in the objection; but if intelligent beings also
desire them, how can there be anything in it? And presumably even in inferior
[animals] there is something superior to themselves, that seeks their own proper   5
good.

The argument [offered against Eudoxus] about the contrary would also seem to
be incorrect. For they argue that if pain is an evil, it does not follow that pleasure
is a good, since evil is also opposed to evil, and both are opposed to the neutral
condition [without pleasure or pain].

The objectors' general point here is right, but what they say in the case mentioned
is false. For if both pleasure and pain were evils, we would also have to avoid both,   10
and if both were neutral, we would have to avoid neither, or else avoid both equally.
Evidently, however, we avoid pain as an evil and choose pleasure as a good; hence
this must also be the opposition between them.

3

Again, if [as the objectors argue] pleasure is not a quality, it does not follow [as
they suppose] that it is not a good. For neither are virtuous activities or happiness   15
qualities.

They say that the good is definite, whereas pleasure is indefinite because it admits
of more and less.

If their judgment rests on the actual condition of being pleased, it must also hold
for justice and the other virtues, where evidently we are said to have a certain
character more and less, and to express the virtues more and less in our actions. For   20
we may be more [and less] just or brave, and may do just or temperate actions more
and less.

If, on the other hand, their judgment rests on the [variety of] pleasures, then
surely they fail to state the reason [why pleasures admit of more and less], namely
that some are unmixed [with pain] and others are mixed.

Moreover, just as health admits of more and less, though it is definite, why should   25
pleasure not be the same? For not every [healthy person] has the same proportion
[of bodily elements], nor does the same person always have the same, but it may be
relaxed and still remain up to a certain limit, and may differ in more and less. The
same is quite possible, then, for pleasure also.

They hold that what is good is complete, whereas processes and becomings are

30   incomplete; and they try to show that pleasure is a process and a becoming. It would
       seem, however, that they are wrong, and pleasure is not even a process.

             For quickness or slowness seems to be proper to every process—if not in itself (as,
       e.g., with the universe), then in relation to something else. But neither of these is
       true of pleasure. For though certainly it is possible to become pleased quickly, as it
1173b is possible to become angry quickly, it is not possible to be pleased quickly, not even
       in relation to something else. But this is possible for walking and growing and all
       such things [i.e. for processes]. It is possible, then, to pass quickly or slowly into
       pleasure, but not possible to be [quickly or slowly] in the corresponding activity, i.e.
       to be pleased quickly [or slowly].

5   And how could pleasure be a becoming? For not just any random thing, it seems,
       comes to be from any other; but what something comes to be from is what it is
       dissolved into. Hence whatever pleasure is the becoming of, pain should be the
       perishing of it.

             They do indeed say that pain is the emptying of the natural [condition, and hence
       the perishing], and that pleasure is its refilling, [and hence the becoming]. Emptying
       and filling happen to the body; if, then, pleasure is the refilling of something natural,
10   what has the refilling will also have the pleasure. Hence it will be the body that has
       pleasure.

             This does not seem to be true, however. The refilling, then, is not pleasure, though
       someone might be pleased while a refilling is going on, and pained when he is
       becoming empty.

             This belief [that pleasure is refilling] seems to have arisen from pains and pleasures
15   in connection with food; for first we are empty and suffer pain, and then take
       pleasure in the refilling. However, the same is not true for all pleasures; for pleasures
       in mathematics, and among pleasures in perception those through the sense of
       smell, and many sounds, sights, memories and expectations as well, all arise without
       [previous] pain. If this is so, what will they be comings-to-be of? For since no
20   emptiness of anything has come to be, there is nothing whose refilling might come
       to be.

             Some people cite the disgraceful pleasures [to show that pleasure is not a good].

             (1) To them we might reply that these [sources of disgraceful pleasures] are not
       pleasant. If things are healthy or sweet or bitter to sick people, we should not suppose
       that they are also healthy, or sweet, or bitter, except to them; nor should we suppose
       that things appearing white to people with eye disease are white, except to them.
       Similarly, if things are pleasant to people in bad condition, we should not suppose
       that they are also pleasant, except to these people.

25   (2) Or we might say that the pleasures are choiceworthy, but not when they come
       from these sources, just as wealth is desirable, but not if you have to betray someone
       to get it, and health is desirable, but not if it requires you to eat anything and
       everything.

             (3) Or perhaps pleasures differ in species. For those from fine sources are different
30   from those from shameful sources; and we cannot have the just person's pleasure
       without being just, any more than we can have the musician's without being musi-
       cians, and similarly in the other cases.

             The difference between a friend and a flatterer seems to indicate that pleasure is
       not good, or else that pleasures differ in species. For in dealings with us the friend

seems to aim at what is good, but the flatterer at what is pleasant; and the flatterer is reproached, whereas the friend is praised, on the assumption that in their dealings they have different aims.   1174a

Besides, no one would choose to live with a child's [level of] thought for his whole life, taking as much pleasure as possible in what pleases children, or to enjoy himself while doing some utterly shameful action, even if he would never suffer pain for it.

Moreover, there are many things that we would be eager for even if they brought no pleasure, e.g. seeing, remembering, knowing, having the virtues. Even if pleasures necessarily follow on them, that does not matter, since we would choose them even if no pleasure resulted from them.   5

It would seem to be clear, then, that pleasure is not the good, that not every pleasure is choiceworthy, and that some are choiceworthy in themselves, differing in species or in their sources [from those that are not]. So much, then, for the things that are said about pleasure and pain.   10

4

What, then, or what kind of thing, is pleasure? This will become clearer if we take it up again from the beginning.

Seeing seems to be complete at any time, since it has no need for anything else to complete its form by coming to be at a later time. And pleasure is also like this, since it is some sort of whole, and no pleasure is to be found at any time that will have its form completed by coming to be for a longer time. Hence pleasure is not a process either.   15

For every process, e.g. constructing a building, takes time, and aims at some end, and is complete when it produces the product it seeks, or, [in other words, is complete] in the whole time [that it takes].   20

Moreover, each process is incomplete during the processes that are its parts, i.e. during the time it goes on; and it consists of processes that are different in form from the whole process and from each other.

For laying stones together and fluting a column are different processes; and both are different from the [whole] production of the temple. For the production of the temple is a complete production, since it needs nothing further [when it is finished] to achieve the proposed goal; but the production of the foundation or the triglyph is an incomplete production, since [when it is finished] it is [the production] of a part.   25

Hence [processes that are parts of larger processes] differ in form; and we cannot find a process complete in form at any time [while it is going on], but [only], if at all, in the whole time [that it takes].

The same is true of walking and the other [processes]. For if locomotion is a process from one place to another, it includes locomotions differing in form—flying, walking, jumping and so on. And besides these differences, there are differences in walking itself. For the place from which and the place to which are not the same in the whole racecourse as they are in a part of it, or the same in one part as in another; nor is traveling along one line the same as traveling along another, since what we   30

1174b cover is not just a line, but a line in a [particular] place, and this line and that line are in different places.

Now we have discussed process exactly elsewhere. But, at any rate, a process, it would seem, is not complete at every time; and the many [constituent] processes are

5   incomplete, and differ in form, since the place from which and the place to which make the form of a process [and different processes begin and end in different places].

The form of pleasure, by contrast, is complete at any time. Clearly, then, it is different from a process, and is something whole and complete. This also seems true because a process must take time, but being pleased need not; for what [takes no time and hence is present] in an instant is a whole.

10   This also makes it clear that it is wrong to say there is a process or a coming-to-be of pleasure. For this is not said of everything, but only of what is divisible and not a whole; for seeing, or a point, or a unit, has no coming to be, and none of these is either a process or a becoming. But pleasure is a whole; hence it too has no coming to be.

Every faculty of perception is active in relation to its perceptible object, and

15   completely active when it is in good condition in relation to the finest of its perceptible objects. For this above all seems to be the character of complete activity, whether it is ascribed to the faculty or to the subject that has it. Hence for each faculty the best activity is the activity of the subject in the best condition in relation to the best object of the faculty.

20   This activity will also be the most complete and the pleasantest. For every faculty of perception, and every sort of thought and study, has its pleasure; the pleasantest activity is the most complete; and the most complete is the activity of the subject in good condition in relation to the most excellent object of the faculty. Pleasure completes the activity.

But the way in which pleasure completes the activity is not the way in which the

25   perceptible object and the faculty of perception complete it when they are both excellent—just as health and the doctor are not the cause of being healthy in the same way. For clearly a pleasure arises that corresponds to each faculty of perception, since we say that sights and sounds are pleasant; and clearly it arises above all whenever the faculty of perception is best, and is active in relation to the best sort

30   of object. When this is the condition of the perceptible object and of the perceiving subject, there will always be pleasure, when the producer and the subject to be affected are both present.

Pleasure completes the activity—not, however, as the state does, by being present [in the activity], but as a sort of consequent end, like the bloom on youths.

Hence as long as the objects of understanding or perception and the subject that

1175a   judges or attends are in the right condition, there will be pleasure in the activity. For as long as the subject affected and the productive [cause] remain similar and in the same relation to each other, the same thing naturally arises.

Then how is it that no one is continuously pleased? Is it not because we get tired?

5   For nothing human is capable of continuous activity, and hence no continuous pleasure arises either, since pleasure is a consequence of the activity.

Again, some things delight us when they are new to us, but less later, for the same reason. For at first our thought is stimulated and intensely active towards them, as our sense of sight is when we look closely at something; but later the activity becomes lax and careless, so that the pleasure fades also.   10

We might think that everyone desires pleasure, since everyone aims at being alive. Living is a type of activity, and each of us is active towards the objects he likes most and in the ways he likes most. The musician, e.g., activates his hearing in hearing melodies; the lover of learning activates his thought in thinking about objects of study; and so on for each of the others. Pleasure completes their activities, and   15 hence completes life, which they desire. It is reasonable, then, that they also aim at pleasure, since it completes each person's life for him, and life is choiceworthy.

Do we choose life because of pleasure, or pleasure because of life? Let us set aside this question for now, since the two appear to be yoked together, and to allow no   20 separation; for pleasure never arises without activity, and, equally, it completes every activity.

5

Hence pleasures also seem to be of different species. For we suppose that things of different species are completed by different things. That is how it appears, both with natural things and with artifacts, e.g. with animals, trees, a painting, a statue, a house or an implement; and similarly, activities that differ in species are also   25 completed by things that differ in species. Activities of thought differ in species from activities of the faculties of perception, and so do these from each other; so also, then, do the pleasures that complete them.

This is also apparent from the way each pleasure is proper to the activity that it completes. For the proper pleasure increases the activity. For we judge each thing   30 better and more exactly when our activity is associated with pleasure. If, e.g., we enjoy doing geometry, we become better geometers, and understand each question better; and similarly lovers of music, building and so on improve at their proper   35 function when they enjoy it.

Each pleasure increases the activity; what increases it is proper to it; and since the activities are different in species, what is proper to them is also different in species.   1175b

This is even more apparent from the way some activities are impeded by pleasures from others. For lovers of flutes, e.g., cannot pay attention to a conversation if they catch the sound of someone playing the flute, because they enjoy flute-playing more than their present activity; and so the pleasure proper to flute-playing destroys the   5 activity of conversation.

The same is true in other cases also, whenever we are engaged in two activities at once. For the pleasanter activity pushes out the other one, all the more if it is much pleasanter, so that we no longer even engage in the other activity. Hence if we are   10 enjoying one thing intensely, we do not do another very much. It is when we are only mildly pleased that we do something else, e.g. people who eat nuts in theatres do this most when the actors are bad.

Since, then, the proper pleasure makes an activity more exact, longer and better,   15 while an alien pleasure damages it, clearly the two pleasures differ widely.

For an alien pleasure does virtually what a proper pain does. The proper pain destroys activity, so that if, e.g., writing or rational calculation has no pleasure and is in fact painful for us, we do not write or calculate, since the activity is painful.

20   Hence the proper pleasures and pains have contrary effects on an activity; and the proper ones are those that arise from the activity in itself. And as we have said, the effect of alien pleasures is similar to the effect of pain, since they ruin the activity, though not in the same way as pain.

25   Since activities differ in degrees of decency and badness, and some are choiceworthy, some to be avoided, some neither, the same is true of pleasures; for each activity has its own proper pleasure. Hence the pleasure proper to an excellent activity is decent, and the one proper to a base activity is vicious; for, similarly, appetites for fine things are praiseworthy, and appetites for shameful things are blameworthy.

30   And in fact the pleasure in an activity is more proper to it than the desire for it. For the desire is distinguished from it in time and in nature; but the pleasure is close to the activity, and so little distinguished from it that disputes arise about whether the activity is the same as the pleasure.

35   Still, pleasure is seemingly neither thought nor perception, since that would be absurd. Rather, it is because [pleasure and activity] are not separated that to some people they appear the same.

1176a   Hence, just as activities differ, so do the pleasures. Sight differs from touch in purity, as hearing and smell do from taste; hence the pleasures also differ in the same way. So also do the pleasures of thought differ from these [pleasures of sense]; and both sorts have different kinds within them.

Each kind of animal seems to have its own proper pleasure, just as it has its own proper function; for the proper pleasure will be the one that corresponds to its activity.

5   This is apparent if we also study each kind. For a horse, a dog and a human being have different pleasures; and, as Heracleitus says, an ass would choose chaff over gold, since asses find food pleasanter than gold. Hence animals that differ in species also have pleasures that differ in species; and it would be reasonable for animals of the same species to have the same pleasures also.

10   In fact, however, the pleasures differ quite a lot, in human beings at any rate. For the same things delight some people, and cause pain to others; and while some find them painful and hateful, others find them pleasant and lovable. The same is true of sweet things. For the same things do not seem sweet to a feverish and to a healthy person, or hot to an enfeebled and to a vigorous person; and the same is true of other things.

But in all such cases it seems that what is really so is what appears so to the excellent person. If this is correct, as it seems to be, and virtue, i.e. the good person in so far as he is good, is the measure of each thing, then what appear pleasures to him will also *be* pleasures, and what is pleasant will be what he enjoys.

20   And if what he finds objectionable appears pleasant to someone, that is nothing surprising, since human beings suffer many sorts of corruption and damage. It is not pleasant, however, except to these people in these conditions.

Clearly, then, we should say that the pleasures agreed to be shameful are not pleasures at all, except to corrupted people.

But what about those pleasures that seem to be decent? Of these, which kind, or

25   which particular pleasure, should we take to be the pleasure of a human being? Surely it will be clear from the activities, since the pleasures are consequences of these.

Hence the pleasures that complete the activities of the complete and blessedly happy man, whether he has one activity or more than one, will be called the human pleasures to the fullest extent. The other pleasures will be human in secondary and even more remote ways corresponding to the character of the activities.

6

We have now finished our discussion of the types of virtue; of friendship; and of   30
pleasure. It remains for us to discuss happiness in outline, since we take this to be the end of human [aims]. Our discussion will be shorter if we first take up again what we said before.

We said, then, that happiness is not a state. For if it were, someone might have it   35
and yet be asleep for his whole life, living the life of a plant, or suffer the greatest   1176b
misfortunes. If we do not approve of this, we count happiness as an activity rather than a state, as we said before.

Some activities are necessary, i.e. choiceworthy for some other end, while others are choiceworthy in themselves. Clearly, then, we should count happiness as one of those activities that are choiceworthy in themselves, not as one of those choiceworthy   5
for some other end. For happiness lacks nothing, but is self-sufficient; and an activity is choiceworthy in itself when nothing further beyond it is sought from it.

This seems to be the character of actions expressing virtue; for doing fine and excellent actions is choiceworthy for itself.

But pleasant amusements also [seem to be choiceworthy in themselves]. For they are not chosen for other ends, since they actually cause more harm than benefit, by   10
causing neglect of our bodies and possessions.

Moreover, most of those people congratulated for their happiness resort to these sorts of pastimes. Hence people who are witty participants in them have a good reputation with tyrants, since they offer themselves as pleasant [partners] in the   15
tyrant's aims, and these are the sort of people the tyrant requires. And so these amusements seem to have the character of happiness because people in supreme power spend their leisure in them.

However, these sorts of people are presumably no evidence. For virtue and understanding, the sources of excellent activities, do not depend on holding supreme power. Further, these powerful people have had no taste of pure and civilized   20
pleasure, and so they resort to bodily pleasures. But that is no reason to think these pleasures are most choiceworthy, since boys also think that what they honour is best. Hence, just as different things appear honourable to boys and to men, it is reasonable that in the same way different things appear honourable to base and to decent people.

As we have often said, then, what is honourable and pleasant is what is so to the   25
excellent person; and to each type of person the activity expressing his own proper state is most choiceworthy; hence the activity expressing virtue is most choiceworthy to the excellent person [and hence is most honourable and pleasant].

Happiness, then, is not found in amusement; for it would be absurd if the end were amusement, and our lifelong efforts and sufferings aimed at amusing ourselves. For   30
we choose practically everything for some other end—except for happiness, since it is [the] end; but serious work and toil aimed [only] at amusement appears stupid

and excessively childish. Rather, it seems correct to amuse ourselves so that we can do something serious, as Anacharsis says; for amusement would seem to be relaxation, and it is because we cannot toil continuously that we require relaxation. Relaxation, then, is not [the] end, since we pursue it [to prepare] for activity.

Further, the happy life seems to be a life expressing virtue, which is a life involving serious actions, and not consisting in amusement.

Besides, we say that things to be taken seriously are better than funny things that provide amusement, and that in each case the activity of the better part and the better person is more serious and excellent; and the activity of what is better is superior, and thereby has more the character of happiness.

Moreover, anyone at all, even a slave, no less than the best person, might enjoy bodily pleasures; but no one would allow that a slave shares in happiness, if one does not [also allow that the slave shares in the sort of] life [needed for happiness]. Happiness, then, is found not in these pastimes, but in the activities expressing virtue, as we also said previously.

7

If happiness, then, is activity expressing virtue, it is reasonable for it to express the supreme virtue, which will be the virtue of the best thing.

The best is understanding, or whatever else seems to be the natural ruler and leader, and to understand what is fine and divine, by being itself either divine or the most divine element in us.

Hence complete happiness will be its activity expressing its proper virtue; and we have said that this activity is the activity of study. This seems to agree with what has been said before, and also with the truth.

For this activity is supreme, since understanding is the supreme element in us, and the objects of understanding are the supreme objects of knowledge.

Besides, it is the most continuous activity, since we are more capable of continuous study than of any continuous action.

We think pleasure must be mixed into happiness; and it is agreed that the activity expressing wisdom is the pleasantest of the activities expressing virtue. At any rate, philosophy seems to have remarkably pure and firm pleasures; and it is reasonable for those who have knowledge to spend their lives more pleasantly than those who seek it.

Moreover, the self-sufficiency we spoke of will be found in study above all.

For admittedly the wise person, the just person and the other virtuous people all need the good things necessary for life. Still, when these are adequately supplied, the just person needs other people as partners and recipients of his just actions; and the same is true of the temperate person and the brave person and each of the others.

But the wise person is able, and more able the wiser he is, to study even by himself; and though he presumably does it better with colleagues, even so he is more self-sufficient than any other [virtuous person].

Besides, study seems to be liked because of itself alone, since it has no result beyond having studied. But from the virtues concerned with action we try to a greater or lesser extent to gain something beyond the action itself.

Happiness seems to be found in leisure, since we accept trouble so that we can be at leisure, and fight wars so that we can be at peace. Now the virtues concerned with action have their activities in politics or war, and actions here seem to require trouble. 5

This seems completely true for actions in war, since no one chooses to fight a war, and no one continues it, for the sake of fighting a war; for someone would have to be a complete murderer if he made his friends his enemies so that there could be battles and killings. 10

But the actions of the politician require trouble also. Beyond political activities themselves these actions seek positions of power and honours; or at least they seek happiness for the politician himself and for his fellow-citizens, which is something different from political science itself, and clearly is sought on the assumption that it is different. 15

Hence among actions expressing the virtues those in politics and war are preeminently fine and great; but they require trouble, aim at some [further] end, and are choiceworthy for something other than themselves.

But the activity of understanding, it seems, is superior in excellence because it is the activity of study, aims at no end beyond itself and has its own proper pleasure, which increases the activity. Further, self-sufficiency, leisure, unwearied activity (as far as is possible for a human being), and any other features ascribed to the blessed person, are evidently features of this activity. 20

Hence a human being's complete happiness will be this activity, if it receives a complete span of life, since nothing incomplete is proper to happiness. 25

Such a life would be superior to the human level. For someone will live it not in so far as he is a human being, but in so far as he has some divine element in him. And the activity of this divine element is as much superior to the activity expressing the rest of virtue as this element is superior to the compound. Hence if understanding is something divine in comparison with a human being, so also will the life that expresses understanding be divine in comparison with human life. 30

We ought not to follow the proverb-writers, and 'think human, since you are human', or 'think mortal, since you are mortal'. Rather, as far as we can, we ought to be pro-immortal, and go to all lengths to live a life that expresses our supreme element; for however much this element may lack in bulk, by much more it surpasses everything in power and value. 1178a

Moreover, each person seems to be his understanding, if he is his controlling and better element; it would be absurd, then, if he were to choose not his own life, but something else's.

And what we have said previously will also apply now. For what is proper to each thing's nature is supremely best and pleasantest for it; and hence for a human being the life expressing understanding will be supremely best and pleasantest, if understanding above all is the human being. This life, then, will also be happiest. 5

8

The life expressing the other kind of virtue [i.e. the kind concerned with action] is [happiest] in a secondary way because the activities expressing this virtue are human. 10

For we do just and brave actions, and the others expressing the virtues, in relation to other people, by abiding by what fits each person in contracts, services, all types of actions, and also in feelings; and all these appear to be human conditions.

15   Indeed, some feelings actually seem to arise from the body; and in many ways virtue of character seems to be proper to feelings.

Besides, intelligence is yoked together with virtue of character, and so is this virtue with intelligence. For the origins of intelligence express the virtues of character; and correctness in virtues of character expresses intelligence. And since these virtues 20   are also connected to feelings, they are concerned with the compound. Since the virtues of the compound are human virtues, the life and the happiness expressing these virtues is also human.

The virtue of understanding, however, is separated [from the compound]. Let us say no more about it, since an exact account would be too large a task for our present project.

Moreover, it seems to need external supplies very little, or [at any rate] less than 25   virtue of character needs them. For grant that they both need necessary goods, and to the same extent, since there will be only a very small difference even though the politician labours more about the body and suchlike. Still, there will be a large difference in [what is needed] for the [proper] activities [of each type of virtue].

For the generous person will need money for generous actions; and the just person 30   will need it for paying debts, since wishes are not clear, and people who are not just pretend to wish to do justice. Similarly, the brave person will need enough power, and the temperate person will need freedom [to do intemperate actions], if they are to achieve anything that the virtue requires. For how else will they, or any other virtuous people, make their virtue clear?

35   Moreover, it is disputed whether it is decision or actions that is more in control of virtue, on the assumption that virtue depends on both. Well, certainly it is clear that 1178b   what is complete depends on both; but for actions many external goods are needed, and the greater and finer the actions the more numerous are the external goods needed.

But someone who is studying needs none of these goods, for that activity at least; indeed, for study at least, we might say they are even hindrances.

5   In so far as he is a human being, however, and [hence] lives together with a number of other human beings, he chooses to do the actions expressing virtue. Hence he will need the sorts of external goods [that are needed for the virtues], for living a human life.

In another way also it appears that complete happiness is some activity of study. 10   For we traditionally suppose that the gods more than anyone are blessed and happy; but what sorts of actions ought we to ascribe to them? Just actions? Surely they will appear ridiculous making contracts, returning deposits and so on. Brave actions? Do they endure what [they find] frightening and endure dangers because it is fine? Generous actions? Whom will they give to? And surely it would be absurd for them 15   to have currency or anything like that. What would their temperate actions be? Surely it is vulgar praise to say that they do not have base appetites. When we go through them all, anything that concerns actions appears trivial and unworthy of the gods.

However, we all traditionally suppose that they are alive and active, since surely

they are not asleep like Endymion. Then if someone is alive, and action is excluded,   20
and production even more, what is left but study? Hence the gods' activity that is
superior in blessedness will be an activity of study. And so the human activity that
is most akin to the gods' will, more than any others, have the character of happiness.

A sign of this is the fact that other animals have no share in happiness, being
completely deprived of this activity of study. For the whole life of the gods is blessed,   25
and human life is blessed to the extent that it has something resembling this sort of
activity; but none of the other animals is happy, because none of them shares in
study at all. Hence happiness extends just as far as study extends, and the more
someone studies, the happier he is, not coincidentally but in so far as he studies,   30
since study is valuable in itself. And so [on this argument] happiness will be some
kind of study.

However, the happy person is a human being, and so will need external prosperity
also; for his nature is not self-sufficient for study, but he needs a healthy body, and   35
needs to have food and the other services provided.

Still, even though no one can be blessedly happy without external goods, we must   1179a
not think that to be happy we will need many large goods. For self-sufficiency and
action do not depend on excess, and we can do fine actions even if we do not rule
earth and sea; for even from moderate resources we can do the actions expressing
virtue. This is evident to see, since many private citizens seem to do decent actions   5
no less than people in power do—even more, in fact. It is enough if moderate
resources are provided; for the life of someone whose activity expresses virtue will
be happy.

Solon[17] surely described happy people well, when he said they had been moder-   10
ately supplied with external goods, had done what he regarded as the finest actions,
and had lived their lives temperately. For it is possible to have moderate possessions
and still to do the right actions.

And Anaxagoras would seem to have supposed that the happy person was neither
rich nor powerful, since he said he would not be surprised if the happy person   15
appeared an absurd sort of person to the many. For the many judge by externals,
since these are all they perceive.

Hence the beliefs of the wise would seem to accord with our arguments.

These considerations do indeed produce some confidence. The truth, however,
in questions about action is judged from what we do and how we live, since these   20
are what control [the answers to such questions]. Hence we ought to examine what
has been said by applying it to what we do and how we live; and if it harmonizes
with what we do, we should accept it, but if it conflicts we should count it [mere]
words.

The person whose activity expresses understanding and who takes care of understanding would seem to be in the best condition, and most loved by the gods. For if
the gods pay some attention to human beings, as they seem to, it would be reasonable   25
for them to take pleasure in what is best and most akin to them, namely understand-
ing; and reasonable for them to benefit in return those who most of all like and

---

17. [According to Solon, Tellus of Athens was the happiest man he knew; he was wealthy, lived to see his
grandchildren, and died honorably in battle.—M.L.M.]

honour understanding, on the assumption that these people attend to what is beloved by the gods, and act correctly and finely.

30   Clearly, all this is true of the wise person more than anyone else; hence he is most
loved by the gods. And it is likely that this same person will be happiest; hence the
wise person will be happier than anyone else on this argument too.

9

          We have now said enough in outlines about happiness and the virtues, and about
35   friendship and pleasure also. Should we then think that our decision [to study these]
1179b has achieved its end? On the contrary, the aim of studies about action, as we say, is
surely not to study and know about each thing, but rather to act on our knowledge.
Hence knowing about virtue is not enough, but we must also try to possess and
exercise virtue, or become good in any other way.

5   Now if arguments were sufficient by themselves to make people decent, the rewards they would command would justifiably have been many and large, as Theognis
says, and rightly bestowed. In fact, however, arguments seem to have enough influence to stimulate and encourage the civilized ones among the young people, and
perhaps to make virtue take possession of a well-born character that truly loves what
10   is fine; but they seem unable to stimulate the many towards being fine and good.

          For the many naturally obey fear, not shame; they avoid what is base because of
the penalties, not because it is disgraceful. For since they live by their feelings, they
pursue their proper pleasures and the sources of them, and avoid the opposed
15   pains, and have not even a notion of what is fine and [hence] truly pleasant, since
they have had no taste of it.

          What argument could reform people like these? For it is impossible, or not easy,
to alter by argument what has long been absorbed by habit; but, presumably, we
should be satisfied to achieve some share in virtue when we already have what we
seem to need to become decent.

20   Some think it is nature that makes people good; some think it is habit; some that
it is teaching.

          The [contribution] of nature clearly is not up to us, but results from some divine
cause in those who have it, who are the truly fortunate ones.

          Arguments and teaching surely do not influence everyone, but the soul of the
25   student needs to have been prepared by habits for enjoying and hating finely, like
ground that is to nourish seed. For someone whose life follows his feelings would
not even listen to an argument turning him away, or comprehend it [if he did listen];
and in that state how could he be persuaded to change? And in general feelings
seem to yield to force, not to argument.

30   Hence we must already in some way have a character suitable for virtue, fond of
what is fine and objecting to what is shameful.

          But it is hard for someone to be trained correctly for virtue from his youth if he
has not been brought up under correct laws, since the many, especially the young,
do not find it pleasant to live in a temperate and resistant way. Hence laws must
35   prescribe their upbringing and practices; for they will not find these things painful
when they get used to them.

Presumably, however, it is not enough to get the correct upbringing and attention   1180a
when they are young; rather, they must continue the same practices and be habituated to them when they become men. Hence we need laws concerned with these
things also, and in general with all of life. For the many yield to compulsion more   5
than to argument, and to sanctions more than to what is fine.

This, some think, is why legislators should urge people towards virtue and exhort
them to aim at what is fine, on the assumption that anyone whose good habits have
prepared him decently will listen to them, but should impose corrective treatments
and penalties on anyone who disobeys or lacks the right nature, and completely
expel an incurable. For the decent person, it is assumed, will attend to reason because   10
his life aims at what is fine, while the base person, since he desires pleasure, has to
receive corrective treatment by pain, like a beast of burden; that is why it is said that
the pains imposed must be those most contrary to the pleasures he likes.

As we have said, then, someone who is to be good must be finely brought up and   15
habituated, and then must live in decent practices, doing nothing base either willingly or unwillingly. And this will be true if his life follows some sort of understanding and correct order that has influence over him.

A father's instructions, however, lack this influence and compelling power; and
so in general do the instructions of an individual man, unless he is a king or someone   20
like that. Law, however, has the power that compels; and law is reason that proceeds
from a sort of intelligence and understanding. Besides, people become hostile to an
individual human being who opposes their impulses even if he is correct in opposing
them; whereas a law's prescription of what is decent is not burdensome.

And yet, only in Sparta, or in a few other cities as well, does the legislator seem   25
to have attended to upbringing and practices. In most other cities they are neglected,
and each individual citizen lives as he wishes, 'laying down the rules for his children
and wife', like a Cyclops.

It is best, then, if the community attends to upbringing, and attends correctly. If,   30
however, the community neglects it, it seems fitting for each individual to promote
the virtue of his children and his friends—to be able to do it, or at least to decide
to do it.

From what we have said, however, it seems he will be better able to do it if he
acquires legislative science. For, clearly, attention by the community works through   35
laws, and decent attention works through excellent laws; and whether the laws are   1180b
written or unwritten, for the education of one or of many, seems unimportant, as
it is in music, gymnastics and other practices. For just as in cities the provisions of
law and the [prevailing] types of character have influence, similarly a father's words
and habits have influence, and all the more because of kinship and because of the   5
benefits he does; for his children are already fond of him and naturally ready to
obey.

Moreover, education adapted to an individual is actually better than a common
education for everyone, just as individualized medical treatment is better. For
though generally a feverish patient benefits from rest and starvation, presumably
some patient does not; nor does the boxing instructor impose the same way of   10
fighting on everyone. Hence it seems that treatment in particular cases is more
exactly right when each person gets special attention, since he then more often gets
the suitable treatment.

Nonetheless a doctor, a gymnastics trainer and everyone else will give the best
individual attention if they also know universally what is good for all, or for these
sorts. For sciences are said to be, and are, of what is common [to many particular
cases].

Admittedly someone without scientific knowledge may well attend properly to a
single person, if his experience has allowed him to take exact note of what happens
in each case, just as some people seem to be their own best doctors, though unable
to help anyone else at all. None the less, presumably, it seems that someone who
wants to be an expert in a craft and a branch of study should progress to the
universal, and come to know that, as far as possible; for that, as we have said, is what
the sciences are about.

Then perhaps also someone who wishes to make people better by his attention,
many people or few, should try to acquire legislative science, if we will become good
through laws. For not just anyone can improve the condition of just anyone, or the
person presented to him; but if anyone can it is the person with knowledge, just as
in medical science and the others that require attention and intelligence.

Next, then, should we examine whence and how someone might acquire legislative
science? Just as in other cases [we go to the practitioner], should we go to the
politicians? For, as we saw, legislative science seems to be a part of political science.

But is the case of political science perhaps apparently different from the other
sciences and capacities? For evidently in others the same people, e.g. doctors or
painters, who transmit the capacity to others actively practise it themselves. By
contrast, it is the sophists who advertise that they teach politics but none of them
practises it. Instead, those who practise it are the political activists, and they seem
to act on some sort of capacity and experience rather than thought.

For evidently they neither write nor speak on such questions, though presumably
it would be finer to do this than to compose speeches for the law courts or the
Assembly; nor have they made politicians out of their own sons or any other friends
of theirs. And yet it would be reasonable for them to do this if they were able; for
there is nothing better than the political capacity that they could leave to their cities,
and nothing better that they could decide to produce in themselves, or, therefore,
in their closest friends.

Certainly experience would seem to contribute quite a lot; otherwise people would
not have become better politicians by familiarity with politics. Hence those who aim
to know about political science would seem to need experience as well.

By contrast, those of the sophists who advertise [that they teach political science]
appear to be a long way from teaching; for they are altogether ignorant about the
sort of thing political science is, and the sorts of things it is about. For if they had
known what it is, they would not have taken it to be the same as rhetoric, or something
inferior to it, or thought it an easy task to assemble the laws with good reputations
and then legislate. For they think they can select the best laws, as though the selection
itself did not require comprehension, and as though correct judgment were not the
most important thing, as it is in music.

It is those with experience in each area who judge the products correctly and who
comprehend the method or way of completing them, and what fits with what; for if
we lack experience, we must be satisfied with noticing that the product is well or
badly made, as with painting. Now laws would seem to be the products of political

science; how, then, could someone acquire legislative science, or judge which laws are best, from laws alone? For neither do we appear to become experts in medicine by reading textbooks.

And yet doctors not only try to describe the [recognized] treatments, but also distinguish different [physical] states, and try to say how each type of patient might be cured and must be treated. And what they say seems to be useful to the experi- 5 enced, though useless to the ignorant.

Similarly, then, collections of laws and political systems might also, presumably, be most useful if we are capable of studying them and of judging what is done finely or in the contrary way, and what sorts of [elements] fit with what. Those who lack the [proper] state [of experience] when they go through these collections will not 10 manage to judge finely, unless they can do it all by themselves [without training], though they might come to comprehend them better by going through them.

Since, then, our predecessors have left the area of legislation uncharted, it is presumably better to examine it ourselves instead, and indeed to examine political systems in general, and so to complete the philosophy of human affairs, as far as we 15 are able.

First, then, let us try to review any sound remarks our predecessors have made on particular topics. Then let us study the collected political systems, to see from them what sorts of things preserve and destroy cities, and political systems of differ- ent types; and what causes some cities to conduct politics well, and some badly. 20

For when we have studied these questions, we will perhaps grasp better what sort of political system is best; how each political system should be organized so as to be best; and what habits and laws it should follow.

Let us discuss this, then, starting from the beginning.

POLITICS

(Bk. I [1–9], II [1–5, 9], III [1–2, 4–5], VII [1–3, 13–15])

BOOK ONE

1

Every state is a community of some kind, and every community is established with a view to some good; for everyone always acts in order to obtain that which they think good. But, if all communities aim at some good, the state or political community, which is the highest of all, and which embraces all the rest, aims at good in a greater degree than any other, and at the highest good.

Some people think that the qualifications of a statesman, king, householder, and master are the same, and that they differ, not in kind, but only in the number of their subjects. For example, the ruler over a few is called a master; over more, the manager of a household; over a still larger number, a statesman or king, as if there were no difference between a great household and a small state. The distinction which is made between the king and the statesman is as follows: When the government is personal, the ruler is a king; when, according to the rules of the political science, the citizens rule and are ruled in turn, then he is called a statesman.

But all this is a mistake, as will be evident to any one who considers the matter according to the method which has hitherto guided us. As in other departments of science, so in politics, the compound should always be resolved into the simple elements or least parts of the whole. We must therefore look at the elements of which the state is composed, in order that we may see in what the different kinds of rule differ from one another, and whether any scientific result can be attained about each one of them.

2

He who thus considers things in their first growth and origin, whether a state or anything else, will obtain the clearest view of them. In the first place there must be a union of those who cannot exist without each other; namely, of male and female, that the race may continue (and this is a union which is formed, not of choice, but because, in common with other animals and with plants, mankind have a natural desire to leave behind them an image of themselves), and of natural ruler and subject, that both may be preserved. For that which can foresee by the exercise of mind is by nature lord and master, and that which can with its body give effect to such foresight is a subject, and by nature a slave; hence master and slave have the same interest. Now nature has distinguished between the female and the slave. For she is not niggardly, like the smith who fashions the Delphian knife for many uses; she makes each thing for a single use, and every instrument is best made when intended for one and not for many uses. But among barbarians no distinction is made between women and slaves, because there is no natural ruler among them: they are a community of slaves, male and female. That is why the poets say,—

> It is meet that Hellenes should rule over barbarians;

as if they thought that the barbarian and the slave were by nature one.

Out of these two relationships the first thing to arise is the family, and Hesiod is right when he says,—

> First house and wife and an ox for the plough,

for the ox is the poor man's slave. The family is the association established by nature for the supply of men's everyday wants, and the members of it are called by Charondas, 'companions of the cupboard', and by Epimenides the Cretan, 'companions of the manger'. But when several families are united, and the association aims at something more than the supply of daily needs, the first society to be formed is the village. And the most natural form of the village appears to be that of a colony from the family, composed of the children and grandchildren, who are said to be 'suckled with the same milk'. And this is the reason why Hellenic states were originally governed by kings; because the Hellenes were under royal rule before they came together, as the barbarians still are. Every family is ruled by the eldest, and therefore in the colonies of the family the kingly form of government prevailed because they were of the same blood. As Homer says:

> Each one gives law to his children and to his wives.

For they lived dispersedly, as was the manner in ancient times. That is why men say that the Gods have a king, because they themselves either are or were in ancient times under the rule of a king. For they imagine not only the forms of the Gods but their ways of life to be like their own.

When several villages are united in a single complete community, large enough to be nearly or quite self-sufficing, the state comes into existence, originating in the bare needs of life, and continuing in existence for the sake of a good life. And therefore, if the earlier forms of society are natural, so is the state, for it is the end of them, and the nature of a thing is its end. For what each thing is when fully developed, we call its nature, whether we are speaking of a man, a horse, or a family. Besides, the final cause and end of a thing is the best, and to be self-sufficing is the end and the best.

Hence it is evident that the state is a creation of nature, and that man is by nature a political animal. And he who by nature and not by mere accident is without a state, is either a bad man or above humanity; he is like the

> Tribeless, lawless, hearthless one,

whom Homer denounces—the natural outcast is forthwith a lover of war; he may be compared to an isolated piece at draughts.

Now, that man is more of a political animal than bees or any other gregarious animals is evident. Nature, as we often say, makes nothing in vain, and man is the only animal who has the gift of speech. And whereas mere voice is but an indication of pleasure or pain, and is therefore found in other animals (for their nature attains to the perception of pleasure and pain and the intimation of them to one another, and no further), the power of speech is intended to set forth the expedient and inexpedient, and therefore likewise the just and the unjust. And it is a characteristic of man that he alone has any sense of good and evil, of just and unjust, and the like, and the association of living beings who have this sense makes a family and a state.

Further, the state is by nature clearly prior to the family and to the individual, since the whole is of necessity prior to the part; for example, if the whole body be destroyed, there will be no foot or hand, except homonymously, as we might speak of a stone hand; for when destroyed the hand will be no better than that. But things are defined by their function and power; and we ought not to say that they are the same when they no longer have their proper quality, but only that they are homonymous. The proof that the state is a creation of nature and prior to the individual is that the individual, when isolated, is not self-sufficing; and therefore he is like a part in relation to the whole. But he who is unable to live in society, or who has no need because he is sufficient for himself, must be either a beast or a god: he is no part of a state. A social instinct is implanted in all men by nature, and yet he who first founded the state was the greatest of benefactors. For man, when perfected, is the best of animals, but, when separated from law and justice, he is the worst of all; since armed injustice is the more dangerous, and he is equipped at birth with arms, meant to be used by intelligence and excellence, which he may use for the worst ends. That is why, if he has not excellence, he is the most unholy and the most savage of animals, and the most full of lust and gluttony. But justice is the bond of men in states; for the administration of justice, which is the determination of what is just, is the principle of order in political society.

3

Seeing then that the state is made up of households, before speaking of the state we must speak of the management of the household. The parts of household management correspond to the persons who compose the household, and a complete household consists of slaves and freemen. Now we should begin by examining everything in its fewest possible elements; and the first and fewest possible parts of a family are master and slave, husband and wife, father and children. We have therefore to consider what each of these three relations is and ought to be:—I mean the relation of master and servant, the marriage relation (the conjunction of man and wife has no name of its own), and thirdly, the paternal relation (this also has no proper name). And there is another element of a household, the so-called art of getting wealth, which, according to some, is identical with household management, according to others, a principal part of it; the nature of this art will also have to be considered by us.

Let us first speak of master and slave, looking to the needs of practical life and also seeking to attain some better theory of their relation than exists at present. For some are of the opinion that the rule of a master is a science, and that the management of a household, and the mastership of slaves, and the political and royal rule, as I was saying at the outset, are all the same. Others affirm that the rule of a master over slaves is contrary to nature, and that the distinction between slave and freeman exists by convention only, and not by nature; and being an interference with nature is therefore unjust.

4

Property is a part of the household, and the art of acquiring property is a part of the art of managing the household; for no man can live well, or indeed live at all, unless he is provided with necessaries. And as in the arts which have a definite sphere the workers must have their own proper instruments for the accomplishment of their work, so it is in the management of a household. Now instruments are of various sorts; some are living, others lifeless; in the rudder, the pilot of a ship has a lifeless, in the look-out man, a living instrument; for in the arts the servant is a kind of instrument. Thus, too, a possession is an instrument for maintaining life. And so, in the arrangement of the family, a slave is a living possession, and property a number of such instruments; and the servant is himself an instrument for instruments. For if every instrument could accomplish its own work, obeying or anticipating the will of others, like the statues of Daedalus, or the tripods of Hephaestus, which, says the poet,

> of their own accord entered the assembly of the Gods;

if, in like manner, the shuttle would weave and the plectrum touch the lyre, chief workmen would not want servants, nor masters slaves. Now the instruments commonly so called are instruments of production, whilst a possession is an instrument of action. From a shuttle we get something else besides the use of it, whereas of a garment or of a bed there is only the use. Further, as production and action are different in kind, and both require instruments, the instruments which they employ must likewise differ in kind. But life is action and not production, and therefore the slave is the minister of action. Again, a possession is spoken of as a part is spoken of; for the part is not only a part of something else, but wholly belongs to it; and this is also true of a possession. The master is only the master of the slave; he does not belong to him, whereas the slave is not only the slave of his master, but wholly belongs to him. Hence we see what is the nature and office of a slave; he who is by nature not his own but another's man, is by nature a slave; and he may be said to be another's man who, being a slave, is also a possession. And a possession may be defined as an instrument of action, separable from the possessor.

5

But is there any one thus intended by nature to be a slave, and for whom such a condition is expedient and right, or rather is not all slavery a violation of nature?

There is no difficulty in answering this question, on grounds both of reason and of fact. For that some should rule and others be ruled is a thing not only necessary, but expedient; from the hour of their birth, some are marked out for subjection, others for rule. And there are many kinds both of rulers and subjects (and that rule is the better which is exercised over better subjects—for example, to rule over men is better than to rule over wild beasts; for the work is better which is executed by better workmen, and where one man rules and another is ruled, they may be said to have a work); for in all things which form a composite whole and which are made up of parts, whether continuous or discrete, a distinction between the ruling and the subject element comes to light. Such a duality exists in living creatures, originating from nature as a whole; even in things which have no life there is a ruling principle, as in a musical mode. But perhaps this is matter for a more popular investigation. A living creature consists in the first place of soul and body, and of these two, the one is by nature the ruler and the other the subject. But then we must look for the intentions of nature in things which retain their nature, and not in things which are corrupted. And therefore we must study the man who is in the most perfect state both of body and soul, for in him we shall see the true relation of the two; although in bad or corrupted natures the body will often appear to rule over the soul, because they are in an evil and unnatural condition. At all events we may firstly observe in living creatures both a despotical and a constitutional rule; for the soul rules the body with a despotical rule, whereas the intellect rules the appetites with a constitutional and royal rule. And it is clear that the rule of the soul over the body, and of the mind and the rational element over the passionate, is natural and expedient; whereas the equality of the two or the rule of the inferior is always hurtful. The same holds good of animals in relation to men; for tame animals have a better nature than wild and all tame animals are better off when they are ruled by man; for then they are preserved. Again, the male is by nature superior, and the female inferior; and the one rules, and the other is ruled; this principle, of necessity, extends to all mankind. Where then there is such a difference as that between soul and body, or between men and animals (as in the case of those whose business is to use their body, and who can do nothing better), the lower sort are by nature slaves, and it is better for them as for all inferiors that they should be under the rule of a master. For he who can be, and therefore is, another's, and he who participates in reason enough to apprehend, but not to have, is a slave by nature. Whereas the lower animals cannot even apprehend reason;[1] they obey their passions. And indeed the use made of slaves and of tame animals is not very different; for both with their bodies minister to the needs of life. Nature would like to distinguish between the bodies of freemen and slaves, making the one strong for servile labour, the other upright, and although useless for such services, useful for political life in the arts both of war and peace. But the opposite often happens—that some have the souls and others have the bodies of freemen. And doubtless if men differed from one another in the mere forms of their bodies as much as the statues of the Gods do from men, all would acknowledge that the inferior class should be slaves of the superior. And if this is true of the body, how much more just that a similar distinction should exist in the soul? But the beauty of the body is seen, whereas the beauty of the soul is not seen. It is clear, then, that some men are by nature free, and others slaves, and that for these latter slavery is both expedient and right.

---

1. [Reading *logou*.—J.B.]

6

But that those who take the opposite view have in a certain way right on their side, may be easily seen. For the words slavery and slave are used in two senses. There is a slave or slavery by convention as well as by nature. The convention is a sort of agreement—the convention by which whatever is taken in war is supposed to belong to the victors. But this right many jurists impeach, as they would an orator who brought forward an unconstitutional measure: they detest the notion that, because one man has the power of doing violence and is superior in brute strength, another shall be his slave and subject. Even among philosophers there is a difference of opinion. The origin of the dispute, and what makes the views invade each other's territory, is as follows: in some sense excellence, when furnished with means, has actually the greatest power of exercising force: and as superior power is only found where there is superior excellence of some kind, power seems to imply excellence, and the dispute to be simply one about justice (for it is due to one party identifying[2] justice with goodwill, while the other identifies it with the mere rule of the stronger). If these views are thus set out separately, the other views have no force or plausibility against the view that the superior in excellence ought to rule, or be master. Others, clinging, as they think, simply to a principle of justice (for convention is a sort of justice), assume that slavery in accordance with the custom of war is just, but at the same moment they deny this. For what if the cause of the war be unjust? And again, no one would ever say that he is a slave who is unworthy to be a slave. Were this the case, men of the highest rank would be slaves and the children of slaves if they or their parents chanced to have been taken captive and sold. That is why people do not like to call themselves slaves, but confine the term to foreigners. Yet, in using this language, they really mean the natural slave of whom we spoke at first; for it must be admitted that some are slaves everywhere, others nowhere. The same principle applies to nobility. People regard themselves as noble everywhere, and not only in their own country, but they deem foreigners noble only when at home, thereby implying that there are two sorts of nobility and freedom, the one absolute, the other relative. The Helen of Theodectes says:

> Who would presume to call me servant who am on both sides sprung
> from the stem of the Gods?

What does this mean but that they distinguish freedom and slavery, noble and humble birth, by the two principles of good and evil? They think that as men and animals beget men and animals, so from good men a good man springs. Nature intends to do this often but cannot.

We see then that there is some foundation for this difference of opinion, and that all are not either slaves by nature or freemen by nature, and also that there is in some cases a marked distinction between the two classes, rendering it expedient and right for the one to be slaves and the others to be masters: the one practising obedience, the others exercising the authority and lordship which nature intended them to have. The abuse of this authority is injurious to both; for the interests of

2. [Reading *to* . . . *eynoian dokein.*]

part and whole, of body and soul, are the same, and the slave is a part of the master, a living but separated part of his bodily frame. Hence, where the relation of master and slave between them is natural they are friends and have a common interest, but where it rests merely on convention and force the reverse is true.

7

The previous remarks are quite enough to show that the rule of a master is not a constitutional rule, and that all the different kinds of rule are not, as some affirm, the same as each other. For there is one rule exercised over subjects who are by nature free, another over subjects who are by nature slaves. The rule of a household is a monarchy, for every house is under one head: whereas constitutional rule is a government of freemen and equals. The master is not called a master because he has science, but because he is of a certain character, and the same remark applies to the slave and the freeman. Still there may be a science for the master and a science for the slave. The science of the slave would be such as the man of Syracuse taught, who made money by instructing slaves in their ordinary duties. And such a knowledge may be carried further, so as to include cookery and similar menial arts. For some duties are of the more necessary, others of the more honourable sort; as the proverb says, 'slave before slave, master before master'. But all such branches of knowledge are servile. There is likewise a science of the master, which teaches the use of slaves; for the master as such is concerned, not with the acquisition, but with the use of them. Yet this science is not anything great or wonderful; for the master need only know how to order that which the slave must know how to execute. Hence those who are in a position which places them above toil have stewards who attend to their households while they occupy themselves with philosophy or with politics. But the art of acquiring slaves, I mean of justly acquiring them, differs both from the art of the master and the art of slave, being a species of hunting or war. Enough of the distinction between master and slave.

8

Let us now inquire into property generally, and into the art of getting wealth, in accordance with our usual method, for a slave has been shown to be a part of property. The first question is whether the art of getting wealth is the same as the art of managing a household or a part of it, or instrumental to it; and if the last, whether in the way that the art of making shuttles is instrumental to the art of weaving, or in the way that the casting of bronze is instrumental to the art of the statuary, for they are not instrumental in the same way, but the one provides tools and the other material; and by material I mean the substratum out of which any work is made; thus wool is the material of the weaver, bronze of the statuary. Now it is easy to see that the art of household management is not identical with the art of getting wealth, for the one uses the material which the other provides. For the art which uses household stores can be no other than the art of household management. There is, however, a doubt whether the art of getting wealth is a part of household management or a distinct art. If the getter of wealth has to consider whence wealth and property can be procured, but there are many sorts of property and riches, then are husbandry, and the care and provision of food in general, parts of the art of household management or distinct arts? Again, there are many sorts of food, and therefore there are many kinds of lives both of animals and men; they must all have food, and the differences in their food have made differences in their ways of life. For of beasts, some are gregarious, others are solitary; they live in the way which is best adapted to sustain them, accordingly as they are carnivorous or herbivorous or omnivorous: and their habits are determined for them by nature with regard to their ease and choice of food. But the same things are not naturally pleasant to all of them; and therefore the lives of carnivorous or herbivorous animals further differ among themselves. In the lives of men too there is a great difference. The laziest are shepherds, who lead an idle life, and get their subsistence without trouble from tame animals; their flocks having to wander from place to place in search of pasture, they are compelled to follow them, cultivating a sort of living farm. Others support themselves by hunting, which is of different kinds. Some, for example, are brigands, others, who dwell near lakes or marshes or rivers or a sea in which there are fish, are fishermen, and others live by the pursuit of birds or wild beasts. The greater number obtain a living from the cultivated fruits of the soil. Such are the modes of subsistence which prevail among those whose industry springs up of itself, and whose food is not acquired by exchange and retail trade—there is the shepherd, the husbandman, the brigand, the fisherman, the hunter. Some gain a comfortable maintenance out of two employments, eking out the deficiencies of one of them by another: thus the life of a shepherd may be combined with that of a brigand, the life of a farmer with that of a hunter. Other modes of life are similarly combined in any way which the needs of men may require. Property, in the sense of a bare livelihood, seems to be given by nature herself to all, both when they are first born, and when they are grown up. For some animals bring forth, together with their offspring, so much food as will last until they are able to supply themselves; of this the vermiparous or oviparous animals are an instance; and the viviparous animals have up to a certain time a supply of food for their young in themselves, which is called milk. In like manner we may infer that, after the birth of animals, plants exist for their sake, and that the other animals exist for the sake of man,[3] the tame for use and food, the wild, if not all, at least the greater part of them, for food, and for the provision of clothing and various instruments. Now if nature makes nothing incomplete, and nothing in vain, the inference must be that she has made all animals for the sake of man. And so, from one point of view, the art of war is a natural art of acquisition, for the art of acquisition includes hunting, an art which we ought to practise against wild beasts, and against men who, though intended by nature to be governed, will not submit; for war of such a kind is naturally just.

Of the art of acquisition then there is one kind which by nature is a part of the management of a household, in so far as the art of household management must either find ready to hand, or itself provide, such things necessary to life, and useful for the community of the family or state, as can be stored. They are the elements of true riches; for the amount of property which is needed for a good life is not unlimited, although Solon in one of his poems says that

No bound to riches has been fixed for man.

---

3. [Retaining *zōa tōn anthrōpōn*.]

But there is a boundary fixed, just as there is in the other arts; for the instruments of any art are never unlimited, either in number or size, and riches may be defined as a number of instruments to be used in a household or in a state. And so we see that there is a natural art of acquisition which is practised by managers of households and by statesmen, and the reason for this.

9

There is another variety of the art of acquisition which is commonly and rightly called an art of wealth-getting, and has in fact suggested the notion that riches and property have no limit. Being nearly connected with the preceding, it is often identified with it. But though they are not very different, neither are they the same. The kind already described is given by nature, the other is gained by experience and art.

Let us begin our discussion of the question with the following considerations. Of everything which we possess there are two uses: both belong to the thing as such, but not in the same manner, for one is the proper, and the other the improper use of it. For example, a shoe is used for wear, and is used for exchange; both are uses of the shoe. He who gives a shoe in exchange for money or food to him who wants one, does indeed use the shoe as a shoe, but this is not its proper use, for a shoe is not made to be an object of barter. The same may be said of all possessions, for the art of exchange extends to all of them, and it arises at first from what is natural, from the circumstance that some have too little, others too much. Hence we may infer that retail trade is not a natural part of the art of getting wealth; had it been so, men would have ceased to exchange when they had enough. In the first community, indeed, which is the family, this art is obviously of no use, but it begins to be useful when the society increases. For the members of the family originally had all things in common; later, when the family divided into parts, the parts shared in many things, and different parts in different things, which they had to give in exchange for what they wanted, a kind of barter which is still practised among barbarous nations who exchange with one another the necessaries of life and nothing more; giving and receiving wine, for example, in exchange for corn, and the like. This sort of barter is not part of the wealth-getting art and is not contrary to nature, but is needed for the satisfaction of men's natural wants. The other form of exchange grew, as might have been inferred, out of this one. When the inhabitants of one country became more dependent on those of another, and they imported what they needed, and exported what they had too much of, money necessarily came into use. For the various necessaries of life are not easily carried about, and hence men agreed to employ in their dealings with each other something which was intrinsically useful and easily applicable to the purposes of life, for example, iron, silver, and the like. Of this the value was at first measured simply by size and weight, but in process of time they put a stamp upon it, to save the trouble of weighing and to mark the value.

When the use of coin had once been discovered, out of the barter of necessary articles arose the other art of wealth-getting, namely, retail trade; which was at first probably a simple matter, but became more complicated as soon as men learned by experience whence and by what exchanges the greatest profit might be made. Originating in the use of coin, the art of getting wealth is generally thought to be chiefly concerned with it, and to be the art which produces riches and wealth, having to consider how they may be accumulated. Indeed, riches is assumed by many to be only a quantity of coin, because the arts of getting wealth and retail trade are concerned with coin. Others maintain that coined money is a mere sham, a thing not natural, but conventional only, because, if the users substitute another commodity for it, it is worthless, and because it is not useful as a means to any of the necessities of life, and, indeed, he who is rich in coin may often be in want of necessary food. But how can that be wealth of which a man may have a great abundance and yet perish with hunger, like Midas in the fable, whose insatiable prayer turned everything that was set before him into gold?

Hence men seek after a better notion of riches and of the art of getting wealth, and they are right. For natural riches and the natural art of wealth-getting are a different thing; in their true form they are part of the management of a household; whereas retail trade is the art of producing wealth, not in every way, but by exchange. And it is thought to be concerned with coin; for coin is the unit of exchange and the limit of it. And there is no bound to the riches which spring from this art of wealth-getting. As in the art of medicine there is no limit to the pursuit of health; and as in the other arts there is no limit to the pursuit of their several ends, for they aim at accomplishing their ends to the uttermost (but of the means there is a limit, for the end is always the limit), so, too, in this art of wealth-getting there is no limit of the end, which is riches of the spurious kind, and the acquisition of wealth. But the art of wealth-getting which consists in household management, on the other hand, has a limit;[4] the unlimited acquisition of wealth is not its business. And, therefore, from one point of view, all riches must have a limit; nevertheless, as a matter of fact, we find the opposite to be the case; for all getters of wealth increase their hoard of coin without limit. The source of the confusion is the near connexion between the two kinds of wealth-getting; in both, the instrument is the same, although the use is different, and so they pass into one another; for each is a use of the same property, but with a difference: accumulation is the end in the one case, but there is a further end in the other. Hence some persons are led to believe that getting wealth is the object of household management, and the whole idea of their lives is that they ought either to increase their money without limit, or at any rate not to lose it. The origin of this disposition in men is that they are intent upon living only, and not upon living well; and, as their desires are unlimited, they also desire that the means of gratifying them should be without limit. Those who do aim at a good life seek the means of obtaining bodily pleasures; and, since the enjoyment of these appears to depend on property, they are absorbed in getting wealth: and so there arises the second species of wealth-getting. For, as their enjoyment is in excess, they seek an art which produces the excess of enjoyment; and, if they are not able to supply their pleasures by the art of getting wealth, they try other causes, using in turn every faculty in a manner contrary to nature. The quality of courage, for example, is not intended to make wealth, but to inspire confidence; neither is this the aim of the general's or of the physician's art; but the one aims at victory and the other at health. Nevertheless, some men turn every quality or art into a means of getting wealth; this they conceive to be the end, and to the promotion of the end they think all things must contribute.

Thus, then, we have considered the art of wealth-getting which is unnecessary,

4. [Reading *au* for *ou*.]

and why men want it; and also the necessary art of wealth-getting, which we have seen to be different from the other, and to be a natural part of the art of managing a household, concerned with the provision of food, not, however, like the former kind, unlimited, but having a limit.

BOOK TWO

1

Our purpose is to consider what form of political community is best of all for those who are most able to realize their ideal of life. We must therefore examine not only this but other constitutions, both such as actually exist in well-governed states, and any theoretical forms which are held in esteem, so that what is good and useful may be brought to light. And let no one suppose that in seeking for something beyond them we are anxious to make a sophistical display at any cost; we only undertake this inquiry because all the constitutions which now exist are faulty.

We will begin with the natural beginning of the subject. The members of a state must either have all things or nothing in common, or some things in common and some not. That they should have nothing in common is clearly impossible, for the constitution is a community, and must at any rate have a common place—one city will be in one place, and the citizens are those who share in that one city. But should a well-ordered state have all things, as far as may be, in common, or some only and not others? For the citizens might conceivably have wives and children and property in common, as Socrates proposes in the *Republic* of Plato. Which is better, our present condition, or one conforming to the law laid down in the *Republic*?

2

There are many difficulties in the community of women. And the principle on which Socrates rests the necessity of such an institution evidently is not established by his arguments. Further, as a means to the end which he ascribes to the state, the scheme, taken literally, is impracticable, and how we are to interpret it is nowhere precisely stated. I am speaking of the supposition from which the argument of Socrates proceeds, that it is best for the whole state to be as unified as possible. Is it not obvious that a state may at length attain such a degree of unity as to be no longer a state?—since the nature of a state is to be a plurality, and in tending to greater unity, from being a state, it becomes a family, and from being a family, an individual; for the family may be said to be more one than the state, and the individual than the family. So that we ought not to attain this greatest unity even if we could, for it would be the destruction of the state. Again, a state is not made up only of so many men, but of different kinds of men; for similars do not constitute a state. It is not like a military alliance. The usefulness of the latter depends upon its quantity even where there is no difference in quality (for mutual protection is the end aimed at), just as a greater weight depresses the scale more (in like manner, a state differs from a nation, when the nation has not its population organized in villages, but lives an Arcadian sort of life); but the elements out of which a unity is to be formed differ in kind. That is why the principle of reciprocity, as I have already remarked in the *Ethics,* is the salvation of states. Even among freemen and equals this is a principle which must be maintained, for they cannot all rule together, but must change at the end of a year or some other period of time or in some order of succession. The result is that upon this plan they all govern; just as if shoemakers and carpenters were to exchange their occupations, and the same persons did not always continue shoemakers and carpenters. And since it is better that this should be so in politics as well, it is clear that while there should be continuance of the same persons in power where this is possible, yet where this is not possible by reason of the natural equality of the citizens, and at the same time it is just that all should share in the government (whether to govern be a good thing or a bad),—in these cases this is imitated.[5] Thus the one party rules and the others are ruled in turn, as if they were no longer the same persons. In like manner when they hold office there is a variety in the offices held. Hence it is evident that a city is not by nature one in that sense which some persons affirm; and that what is said to be the greatest good of cities is in reality their destruction; but surely the good of things must be that which preserves them. Again, from another point of view, this extreme unification of the state is clearly not good; for a family is more self-sufficing than an individual, and a city than a family, and a city only comes into being when the community is large enough to be self-sufficing. If then self-sufficiency is to be desired, the lesser degree of unity is more desirable than the greater.

3

But, even supposing that it were best for the community to have the greatest degree of unity, this unity is by no means proved to follow from the fact of all men saying 'mine' and 'not mine' at the same instant of time, which, according to Socrates, is the sign of perfect unity in a state. For the word 'all' is ambiguous. If the meaning be that every individual says 'mine' and 'not mine' at the same time, then perhaps the result at which Socrates aims may be in some degree accomplished; each man will call the same person his own son and the same person his own wife, and so of his property and of all that falls to his lot. This, however, is not the way in which people would speak who had their wives and children in common; they would say 'all' but not 'each'. In like manner their property would be described as belonging to them, not severally but collectively. There is an obvious fallacy in the term 'all': like some other words, 'both', 'odd', 'even', it is ambiguous, and even in abstract argument becomes a source of logical puzzles. That all persons call the same thing mine in the sense in which each does so may be a fine thing, but it is impracticable; or if the words are taken in the other sense, such a unity in no way conduces to harmony. And there is another objection to the proposal. For that which is common to the greatest number has the least care bestowed upon it. Everyone thinks chiefly of his own, hardly at all of the common interest; and only when he is himself concerned as an individual. For besides other considerations, everybody is more inclined to neglect something which he expects another to fulfil; as in families many attendants are often less useful than a few. Each citizen will have a thousand sons

---

5. [The text is uncertain.]

who will not be his sons individually, but anybody will be equally the son of anybody, and will therefore be neglected by all alike. Further, upon this principle, every one will use the word 'mine' of one who is prospering or the reverse, however small a fraction he may himself be of the whole number; the same boy will be my son, so and so's son, the son of each of the thousand, or whatever be the number of the citizens; and even about this he will not be positive; for it is impossible to know who chanced to have a child, or whether, if one came into existence, it has survived. But which is better—for each to say 'mine' in this way, making a man the same relation to two thousand or ten thousand citizens, or to use the word 'mine' as it is now used in states? For usually the same person is called by one man his own son whom another calls his own brother or cousin or kinsman—blood relation or connexion by marriage—either of himself or of some relation of his, and yet another his clansman or tribesman; and how much better is it to be the real cousin of somebody than to be a son after Plato's fashion! Nor is there any way of preventing brothers and children and fathers and mothers from sometimes recognizing one another; for children are born like their parents, and they will necessarily be finding indications of their relationship to one another. Geographers declare such to be the fact; they say that in part of Upper Libya, where the women are common, nevertheless the children who are born are assigned to their respective fathers on the ground of their likeness. And some women, like the females of other animals—for example, mares and cows—have a strong tendency to produce offspring resembling their parents, as was the case with the Pharsalian mare called Honest Wife.

4

Other difficulties, against which it is not easy for the authors of such a community to guard, will be assaults and homicides, voluntary as well as involuntary, quarrels and slanders, all of which are most unholy acts when committed against fathers and mothers and near relations, but not equally unholy when there is no relationship. Moreover, they are much more likely to occur if the relationship is unknown than if it is known and, when they have occurred, the customary expiations of them can be made if the relationship is known, but not otherwise. Again, how strange it is that Socrates, after having made the children common, should hinder lovers from carnal intercourse only, but should permit love and familiarities between father and son or between brother and brother, than which nothing can be more unseemly, since even without them love of this sort is improper. How strange, too, to forbid intercourse for no other reason than the violence of the pleasure, as though the relationship of father and son or of brothers with one another made no difference.

This community of wives and children seems better suited to the husbandmen than to the guardians, for if they have wives and children in common, they will be bound to one another by weaker ties, as a subject class should be, and they will remain obedient and not rebel. In a word, the result of such a law would be just the opposite of that which good laws ought to have, and the intention of Socrates in making these regulations about women and children would defeat itself. For friendship we believe to be the greatest good of states and what best preserves them against revolutions; and Socrates particularly praises the unity of the state which seems and is said by him to be created by friendship. But the unity which he commends would be like that of the lovers in the *Symposium*, who, as Aristophanes says, desire to grow together in the excess of their affection, and from being two to become one, in which case one or both would certainly perish. Whereas in a state having women and children common, love will be diluted; and the father will certainly not say 'my son', or the son 'my father'. As a little sweet wine mingled with a great deal of water is imperceptible in the mixture, so, in this sort of community, the idea of relationship which is based upon these names will be lost; there is no reason why the so-called father should care about the son, or the son about the father, or brothers about one another. Of the two qualities which chiefly inspire regard and affection—that a thing is your own and that it is precious—neither can exist in such a state as this.

Again, the transfer of children as soon as they are born from the rank of husbandmen or of artisans to that of guardians, and from the rank of guardians into a lower rank, will be very difficult to arrange; the givers or transferrers cannot but know whom they are giving and transferring, and to whom. And the previously mentioned assaults, unlawful loves, homicides, will happen more often among them; for they will no longer call the members of the class they have left brothers, and children, and fathers, and mothers, and will not, therefore, be afraid of committing any crimes by reason of consanguinity. Touching the community of wives and children, let this be our conclusion.

5

Next let us consider what should be our arrangements about property: should the citizens of the perfect state have their possessions in common or not? This question may be discussed separately from the enactments about women and children. Even supposing that the women and children belong to individuals, according to the custom which is at present universal, may there not be an advantage in having and using possessions in common? E.g. (1) the soil may be appropriated, but the produce may be thrown for consumption into the common stock; and this is the practice of some nations. Or (2), the soil may be common, and may be cultivated in common, but the produce divided among individuals for their private use; this is a form of common property which is said to exist among certain foreigners. Or (3), the soil and the produce may be alike common.

When the husbandmen are not the owners, the case will be different and easier to deal with; but when they till the ground for themselves the question of ownership will give a world of trouble. If they do not share equally in enjoyments and toils, those who labour much and get little will necessarily complain of those who labour little and receive or consume much. But indeed there is always a difficulty in men living together and having all human relations in common, but especially in their having common property. The partnerships of fellow-travellers are an example to the point; for they generally fall out over everyday matters and quarrel about any trifle which turns up. So with servants: we are most liable to take offence at those with whom we most frequently come into contact in daily life.

These are only some of the disadvantages which attend the community of property; the present arrangement, if improved as it might be by good customs and laws, would be far better, and would have the advantages of both systems. Property should be in a certain sense common, but, as a general rule, private; for, when everyone has a distinct interest, men will not complain of one another, and they will make more progress, because everyone will be attending to his own business. And yet by reason of goodness, and in respect of use, 'Friends', as the proverb says, 'will have all things common'. Even now there are traces of such a principle, showing that it is not impracticable, but, in well-ordered states, exists already to a certain extent and may be carried further. For, although every man has his own property, some things he will place at the disposal of his friends, while of others he shares the use with them. The Lacedaemonians, for example, use one another's slaves, and horses, and dogs, as if they were their own; and when they lack provisions on a journey, they appropriate what they find in the fields throughout the country. It is clearly better that property should be private, but the use of it common; and the special business of the legislator is to create in men this benevolent disposition. Again, how immeasurably greater is the pleasure, when a man feels a thing to be his own; for surely the love of self is a feeling implanted by nature and not given in vain, although selfishness is rightly censured; this, however, is not the mere love of self, but the love of self in excess, like the miser's love of money; for all, or almost all, men love money and other such objects in a measure. And further, there is the greatest pleasure in doing a kindness or service to friends or guests or companions, which can only be rendered when a man has private property. These advantages are lost by excessive unification of the state. The exhibition of two excellences, besides, is visibly annihilated in such a state: first, temperance towards women (for it is an honourable action to abstain from another's wife for temperance sake); secondly, liberality in the matter of property. No one, when men have all things in common, will any longer set an example of liberality or do any liberal action; for liberality consists in the use which is made of property.

Such legislation may have a specious appearance of benevolence; men readily listen to it, and are easily induced to believe that in some wonderful manner everybody will become everybody's friend—especially when someone is heard denouncing the evils now existing in states, suits about contracts, convictions for perjury, flatteries of rich men and the like, which are said to arise out of the possession of private property. These evils, however, are due not to the absence of communism but to wickedness. Indeed, we see that there is much more quarrelling among those who have all things in common, though there are not many of them when compared with the vast numbers who have private property.

Again, we ought to reckon not only the evils from which the citizens will be saved, but also the advantages which they will lose. The life which they are to lead appears to be quite impracticable. The error of Socrates must be attributed to the false supposition from which he starts. Unity there should be, both of the family and of the state, but in some respects only. For there is a point at which a state may attain such a degree of unity as to be no longer a state, or at which, without actually ceasing to exist, it will become an inferior state, like harmony passing into unison, or rhythm which has been reduced to a single foot. The state, as I was saying, is a plurality, which should be united and made into a community by education; and it is strange that the author of a system of education which he thinks will make the state virtuous, should expect to improve his citizens by regulations of this sort, and not by philosophy or by customs and laws, like those which prevail at Sparta and Crete respecting common meals, whereby the legislator has made property common. Let us remember that we should not disregard the experience of ages; in the multitude of years these things, if they were good, would certainly not have been unknown; for almost everything has been found out, although sometimes they are not put together; in other cases men do not use the knowledge which they have. Great light would be thrown on this subject if we could see such a form of government in the actual process of construction; for the legislator could not form a state at all without distributing and dividing its constituents into associations for common meals, and into phratries and tribes. But all this legislation ends only in forbidding agriculture to the guardians, a prohibition which the Lacedaemonians try to enforce already.

But, indeed, Socrates has not said, nor is it easy to decide, what in such community will be the general form of the state. The citizens who are not guardians are the majority, and about them nothing has been determined: are the husband men, too, to have their property in common? Or is each individual to have his own? and are their wives and children to be individual or common? If, like the guardians, they are to have all things in common, in what do they differ from them, or what will they gain by submitting to their government? Or upon what principle would they submit, unless indeed the governing class adopt the ingenious policy of the Cretans, who give their slaves the same institutions as their own, but forbid them gymnastic exercises and the possession of arms. If, on the other hand, the inferior classes are to be like other cities in respect of marriage and property, what will be the form of the community? Must it not contain two states in one, each hostile to the other? He makes the guardians into a mere occupying garrison, while the husbandmen and artisans and the rest are real citizens. But if so the suits and quarrels, and all the evils which Socrates affirms to exist in other states, will exist equally among them. He says indeed that, having so good an education, the citizens will not need many laws, for example laws about the city or about the markets; but then he confines his education to the guardians. Again, he makes the husbandmen owners of the property upon condition of their paying a tribute. But in that case they are likely to be much more unmanageable and conceited than the Helots, or Penestae, or slaves in general. And whether community of wives and property be necessary for the lower equally with the higher class or not, and the questions akin to this, what will be the education, form of government, laws of the lower class, Socrates has nowhere determined: neither is it easy to discover this, nor is their character of small importance if the common life of the guardians is to be maintained.

Again, if Socrates makes the women common, and retains private property, the men will see to the fields, but who will see to the house? And who will do so if the agricultural class have both their property and their wives in common? Once more: it is absurd to argue, from the analogy of animals, that men and women should follow the same pursuits, for animals have not to manage a household. The government, too, as constituted by Socrates, contains elements of danger; for he makes the same persons always rule. And if this is often a cause of disturbance among the meaner sort, how much more among high-spirited warriors? But that the persons whom he makes rulers must be the same is evident; for the gold which the God mingles in the souls of men is not at one time given to one, at another time to another, but always to the same: as he says, God mingles gold in some, and silver in others, from their very birth; but brass and iron in those who are meant to be artisans and husbandmen. Again, he deprives the guardians even of happiness, and says that the legislator ought to make the whole state happy. But the whole cannot be happy unless most, or all, or some of its parts enjoy happiness. In this respect happiness is not like the even principle in numbers, which may exist only in the whole, but in neither of the parts; not so happiness. And if the guardians are not happy, who are? Surely not the artisans, or the common people. The Republic of which Socrates discourses has all these difficulties, and others quite as great.

9

In the governments of Lacedaemon and Crete, and indeed in all governments, two points have to be considered: first, whether any particular law is good or bad, when compared with the perfect state; secondly, whether it is or is not consistent with the idea and character which the lawgiver has set before his citizens. That in a well-ordered state the citizens should have leisure and not have to provide for their daily wants is generally acknowledged, but there is a difficulty in seeing how this leisure is to be attained. The Thessalian Penestae have often risen against their masters, and the Helots in like manner against the Lacedaemonians, for whose misfortunes they are always lying in wait. Nothing, however, of this kind has as yet happened to the Cretans; the reason probably is that the neighboring cities, even when at war with one another, never form an alliance with rebellious serfs, rebellions not being for their interest, since they themselves have a dependent population. Whereas all the neighbours of the Lacedaemonians, whether Argives, Messenians, or Arcadians, were their enemies. In Thessaly, again, the original revolt of the slaves occurred because the Thessalians were still at war with the neighbouring Achaeans, Perrhaebians and Magnesians. Besides, if there were no other difficulty, the treatment or management of slaves is a troublesome affair; for, if not kept in hand, they are insolent, and think that they are as good as their masters, and, if harshly treated, they hate and conspire against them. Now it is clear that when these are the results the citizens of a state have not found out the secret of managing their subject population.

Again, the license of the Lacedaemonian women defeats the intention of the Spartan constitution, and is adverse to the happiness of the state. For, a husband and a wife being each a part of every family, the state may be considered as about equally divided into men and women; and, therefore, in those states in which the condition of the women is bad, half the city may be regarded as having no laws. And this is what has actually happened at Sparta; the legislator wanted to make the whole state hardy, and he has carried out his intention in the case of the men, but he has neglected the women, who live in every sort of intemperance and luxury. The consequence is that in such a state wealth is too highly valued, especially if the citizens fall under the dominion of their wives, after the manner of most warlike races, except the Celts and a few others who openly approve of male homosexuality. The old mythologer would seem to have been right in uniting Ares and Aphrodite, for all warlike races are prone to the love either of men or of women. This was exemplified among the Spartans in the days of their greatness; many things were managed by their women. But what difference does it make whether women rule, or the rulers are ruled by women? The result is the same. Even in regard to boldness, which is of no use in daily life, and is needed only in war, the influence of the Lacedaemonian women has been most mischievous. The evil showed itself in the Theban invasion, when, unlike the women in other cities, they were utterly useless and caused more confusion than the enemy. This license of the Lacedaemonian women existed from the earliest times, and was only what might be expected. For, during the wars of the Lacedaemonians, first against the Argives, and afterwards against the Arcadians and Messenians, the men were long away from home, and, on the return of peace, they gave themselves into the legislator's hand, already prepared by the discipline of a soldier's life (in which there are many elements of excellence), to receive his enactments. But, when Lycurgus, as tradition says, wanted to bring the women under his laws, they resisted, and he gave up the attempt. These then are the causes of what then happened, and this defect in the constitution is clearly to be attributed to them. We are not, however, considering what is or is not to be excused, but what is right or wrong, and the disorder of the women, as I have already said, not only gives an air of indecorum to the constitution considered in itself, but tends in a measure to foster avarice.

The mention of avarice naturally suggests a criticism on the inequality of property. While some of the Spartan citizens have quite small properties, others have very large ones: hence the land has passed into the hands of a few. And this is due also to faulty laws; for, although the legislator rightly holds up to shame the sale or purchase of an inheritance, he allows anybody who likes to give or bequeath it. Yet both practices lead to the same result. And nearly two-fifths of the whole country are held by women; this is owing to the number of heiresses and to the large dowries which are customary. It would surely have been better to have given no dowries at all, or, if any, but small or moderate ones. As the law now stands, a man may bestow his heiress on any one whom he pleases, and, if he die intestate, the privilege of giving her away descends to his heir. Hence, although the country is able to maintain 1500 cavalry and 30,000 hoplites, the whole number of Spartan citizens fell below 1000. The result proves the faulty nature of their laws respecting property; for the city sank under a single defeat; the want of men was their ruin. There is a tradition that, in the days of their ancient kings, they were in the habit of giving the rights of citizenship to strangers, and therefore, in spite of their long wars, no lack of population was experienced by them; indeed, at one time Sparta is said to have numbered not less than 10,000 citizens. Whether this statement is true or not, it would certainly have been better to have maintained their numbers by the equalization of property. Again, the law which relates to the procreation of children is adverse to the correction of this inequality. For the legislator, wanting to have as many Spartans as he could, encouraged the citizens to have large families; and there is a law at Sparta that the father of three sons shall be exempt from military service, and he who has four from all the burdens of the state. Yet it is obvious that, if there were many children, the land being distributed as it is, many of them must necessarily fall into poverty.

The Lacedaemonian constitution is defective also in respect of the Ephorate. This magistracy has authority in the highest matters, but the Ephors are chosen from the whole people, and so the office is apt to fall into the hands of very poor men, who, being badly off, are open to bribes. There have been many examples at Sparta of this evil in former times; and quite recently, in the matter of the Andrians, certain of the Ephors who were bribed did their best to ruin the state. And so great and tyrannical is their power, that even the kings have been compelled to court them, so that, in this way as well, together with the royal office the whole constitution has deteriorated, and from being an aristocracy has turned into a democracy. The Ephorate certainly does keep the state together; for the people are contented when they have a share in the highest office, and the result, whether due to the legislator or to chance, has been advantageous. For if a constitution is to be permanent, all the parts of the state must wish that it should exist and these arrangements be maintained. This is the case at Sparta, where the kings desire its permanence because they have due honour in their own persons; the nobles because they are represented in the council of elders (for the office of elder is a reward of excellence); and the people, because all are eligible for the Ephorate. The election of Ephors out of the whole people is perfectly right, but ought not to be carried on in the present fashion, which is too childish. Again, they have the decision of great causes, although they are quite ordinary men, and therefore they should not determine them merely on their own judgement, but according to written rules, and to the laws. Their way of life, too, is not in accordance with the spirit of the constitution—they have a deal too much license; whereas, in the case of the other citizens, the excess of strictness is so intolerable that they run away from the law into the secret indulgence of sensual pleasures.

Again, the council of elders is not free from defects. It may be said that the elders are good men and well trained in manly virtue; and that, therefore, there is an advantage to the state in having them. But that judges of important causes should hold office for life is a disputable thing, for the mind grows old as well as the body. And when men have been educated in such a manner that even the legislator himself cannot trust them, there is real danger. Many of the elders are well known to have taken bribes and to have been guilty of partiality in public affairs. And therefore they ought not to be non-accountable; yet at Sparta they are so. All magistracies are accountable to the Ephors. But this prerogative is too great for them, and we maintain that the control should be exercised in some other manner. Further, the mode in which the Spartans elect their elders is childish; and it is improper that the person to be elected should canvass for the office; the worthiest should be appointed, whether he chooses or not. And here the legislator clearly indicates the same intention which appears in other parts of his constitution; he would have his citizens ambitious, and he has reckoned upon this quality in the election of the elders; for no one would ask to be elected if he were not. Yet ambition and avarice, almost more than any other passions, are the motives of voluntary injustices.

Whether kings are or are not an advantage to states, I will consider at another time; they should at any rate be chosen, not as they are now, but with regard to their personal life and conduct. The legislator himself obviously did not suppose that he could make them really good men; at least he shows a great distrust of their virtue. For this reason the Spartans used to join enemies with them in the same embassy, and the quarrels between the kings were held to preserve the state.

Neither did the first introducer of the common meals, called 'phiditia', regulate them well. The entertainment ought to have been provided at public cost, as in Crete; but among the Lacedaemonians everyone is expected to contribute, and some of them are too poor to afford the expense; thus the intention of the legislator is frustrated. The common meals were meant to be a democratic institution, but the existing manner of regulating them is the reverse of democratic. For the very poor can scarcely take part in them; and, according to ancient custom, those who cannot contribute are not allowed to retain their rights of citizenship.

The law about the Spartan admirals has often been censured, and with justice; it is a source of dissension, for the kings are perpetual generals, and this office of admiral is but the setting up of another king.

The charge which Plato brings, in the *Laws*, against the intention of the legislator, is likewise justified; the whole constitution has regard to one part of excellence only—the excellence of the soldier, which gives victory in war. So long as they were at war, therefore, their power was preserved, but when they had attained empire they fell, for of the arts of peace they knew nothing, and have never engaged in any employment higher than war. There is another error, equally great, into which they have fallen. Although they truly think that the goods for which men contend are to be acquired by excellence rather than by vice, they err in supposing that these goods are to be preferred to the excellence which gains them.

Again, the revenues of the state are ill-managed; there is no money in the treasury, although they are obliged to carry on great wars, and they are unwilling to pay taxes. The greater part of the land being in the hands of Spartans, they do not look closely into one another's contributions. The result which the legislator has produced is the reverse of beneficial; for he has made his city poor, and his citizens greedy.

Enough respecting the Spartan constitution, of which these are the principal defects.

BOOK THREE

1

He who would inquire into the essence and attributes of various kinds of government must first of all determine what a state is. At present this is a disputed question. Some say that the state has done a certain act; others, not the state, but the oligarchy or the tyrant. And the legislator or statesman is concerned entirely with the state, a government being an arrangement of the inhabitants of a state. But a state is composite, like any other whole made up of many parts—these are the citizens, who compose it. It is evident, therefore, that we must begin by asking, Who is the citizen, and what is the meaning of the term? For here again there may be a difference of opinion. He who is a citizen in a democracy will often not be a citizen in an oligarchy. Leaving out of consideration those who have been made citizens, or who have obtained the name of citizen in any other accidental manner, we may say, first, that a citizen is not a citizen because he lives in a certain place, for resident aliens and slaves share in the place; nor is he a citizen who has legal rights to the extent of suing and being sued; for this right may be enjoyed under the provisions of a treaty. Resident aliens in many places do not possess even such rights completely, for they are obliged to have a patron, so that they do but imperfectly participate in the community, and we call them citizens only in a qualified sense, as we might apply the term to children who are too young to be on the register, or to old men who have been relieved from state duties. Of these we do not say quite simply that they are citizens, but add in the one case that they are not of age, and in the other, that they are past the age, or something of that sort; the precise expression is immaterial, for our meaning is clear. Similar difficulties to those which I have mentioned may be raised and answered about disfranchised citizens and about exiles. But the citizen whom we are seeking to define is a citizen in the strictest sense, against whom no such exception can be taken, and his special characteristic is that he shares in the administration of justice, and in offices. Now of offices some are discontinuous, and the same persons are not allowed to hold them twice, or can only hold them after a fixed interval; others have no limit of time—for example, the office of juryman or member of the assembly. It may, indeed, be argued that these are not magistrates at all, and that their functions give them no share in the government. But surely it is ridiculous to say that those who have the supreme power do not govern. Let us not dwell further upon this, which is a purely verbal question; what we want is a common term including both juryman and member of the assembly. Let us, for the sake of distinction, call it 'indefinite office', and we will assume that those who share in such office are citizens. This is the most comprehensive definition of a citizen, and best suits all those who are generally so called.

But we must not forget that things of which the underlying principles differ in kind, one of them being first, another second, another third, have, when regarded in this relation, nothing, or hardly anything, worth mentioning in common. Now we see that governments differ in kind, and that some of them are prior and that others are posterior; those which are faulty or perverted are necessarily posterior to those which are perfect. (What we mean by perversion will be hereafter explained.) The citizen then of necessity differs under each form of government; and our definition is best adapted to the citizen of a democracy; but not necessarily to other states. For in some states the people are not acknowledged, nor have they any regular assembly, but only extraordinary ones; and law-suits are distributed by sections among the magistrates. At Lacedaemon, for instance, the Ephors determine suits about contracts, which they distribute among themselves, while the elders are judges of homicide, and other causes are decided by other magistrates. A similar principle prevails at Carthage; there certain magistrates decide all causes. We may, indeed, modify our definition of the citizen so as to include these states. In them it is the holder of a definite, not an indefinite office, who is juryman and member of the assembly, and to some or all such holders of definite offices is reserved the right of deliberating or judging about some things or about all things. The conception of the citizen now begins to clear up.

He who has the power to take part in the deliberative or judicial administration of any state is said by us to be a citizen of that state; and, speaking generally, a state is a body of citizens sufficing for the purposes of life.

2

But in practice a citizen is defined to be one of whom both the parents are citizens (and not just one, i.e. father or mother); others insist on going further back; say to two or three or more ancestors. This is a short and practical definition; but there are some who raise the further question of how this third or fourth ancestor came to be a citizen. Gorgias of Leontini, partly because he was in a difficulty, partly in irony, said that mortars are what is made by the mortar-makers, and the citizens of Larissa are those who are made by the magistrates; for it is their trade to 'make Larissaeans'. Yet the question is really simple, for, if according to the definition just given they shared in the government, they were citizens. This is a better definition than the other. For the words, 'born of a father or mother who is a citizen', cannot possibly apply to the first inhabitants or founders of a state.

There is a greater difficulty in the case of those who have been made citizens after a revolution, as by Cleisthenes at Athens after the expulsion of the tyrants, for he enrolled in tribes many metics, both strangers and slaves. The doubt in these cases is, not who is, but whether he who is ought to be a citizen; and there will still be a further doubt, whether he who ought not to be a citizen, is one in fact, for what ought not to be is what is false. Now, there are some who hold office, and yet ought not to hold office, whom we describe as ruling, but ruling unjustly. And the citizen was defined by the fact of his holding some kind of rule or office—he who holds a certain sort of office fulfils our definition of a citizen. It is evident, therefore, that the citizens about whom the doubt has arisen must be called citizens.

4

There is a point nearly allied to the preceding: Whether the excellence of a good man and a good citizen is the same or not. But before entering on this discussion, we must certainly first obtain some general notion of the excellence of the citizen. Like the sailor, the citizen is a member of a community. Now, sailors have different functions, for one of them is a rower, another a pilot, and a third a look-out man, a fourth is described by some similar term; and while the precise definition of each individual's excellence applies exclusively to him, there is, at the same time, a common definition applicable to them all. For they have all of them a common object, which is safety in navigation. Similarly, one citizen differs from another, but the salvation of the community is the common business of them all. This community is the constitution; the excellence of the citizen must therefore be relative to the constitution of which he is a member. If, then, there are many forms of government, it is evident that there is not one single excellence of the good citizen which is perfect excellence. But we say that the good man is he who has one single excellence which is perfect excellence. Hence it is evident that the good citizen need not of necessity possess the excellence which makes a good man.

The same question may also be approached by another road, from a consideration of the best constitution. If the state cannot be entirely composed of good men, and yet each citizen is expected to do his own business well, and must therefore have excellence, still, inasmuch as all the citizens cannot be alike, the excellence of the citizen and of the good man cannot coincide. All must have the excellence of the good citizen— thus, and thus only, can the state be perfect; but they will not have the excellence of a good man, unless we assume that in the good state all the citizens must be good.

Again, the state, as composed of unlikes, may be compared to the living being: as the first elements into which a living being is resolved are soul and body, as soul is made up of rational principle and appetite, the family of husband and wife, property of master and slave, so of all these, as well as other dissimilar elements, the state is composed; and therefore the excellence of all the citizens cannot possibly be the same, any more than the excellence of the leader of a chorus is the same as that of the performer who stands by his side. I have said enough to show why the two kinds of excellence cannot be absolutely the same.

But will there then be no case in which the excellence of the good citizen and the excellence of the good man coincide? To this we answer that the good ruler is a good and wise man, but the citizen need not be wise. And some persons say that even the education of the ruler should be of a special kind; for are not the children of kings instructed in riding and military exercises? As Euripides says:

No subtle arts for me, but what the state requires.

As though there were a special education needed for a ruler. If the excellence of a good ruler is the same as that of a good man, and we assume further that the subject is a citizen as well as the ruler, the excellence of the good citizen and the excellence of the good man cannot be absolutely the same, although in some cases they may; for the excellence of a ruler differs from that of a citizen. It was the sense of this difference which made Jason say that 'he felt hungry when he was not a tyrant', meaning that he could not endure to live in a private station. But, on the other hand, it may be argued that men are praised for knowing both how to rule and how to obey, and he is said to be a citizen of excellence who is able to do both well. Now if we suppose the excellence of a good man to be that which rules, and the excellence of the citizen to include ruling and obeying, it cannot be said that they are equally worthy of praise. Since, then, it is sometimes thought that the ruler and the ruled must learn different things and not the same, but that the citizen must know and share in them both, the inference is obvious. There is, indeed, the rule of a master, which is concerned with menial offices—the master need not know how to perform these, but may employ others in the execution of them: the other would be degrading; and by the other I mean the power actually to do menial duties, which vary much in character and are executed by various classes of slaves, such, for example, as handicraftsmen, who, as their name signifies, live by the labour of their hands—under these the mechanic is included. Hence in ancient times, and among some nations, the working classes had no share in the government—a privilege which they only acquired under extreme democracy. Certainly the good man and the statesman and the good citizen ought not to learn the crafts of inferiors except for their own occasional use; if they habitually practise them, there will cease to be a distinction between master and slave.

But there is a rule of another kind, which is exercised over freemen and equals by birth—a constitutional rule, which the ruler must learn by obeying, as he would learn the duties of a general of cavalry by being under the orders of a general of cavalry, or the duties of a general of infantry by being under the orders of a general of infantry, and by having had the command of a regiment and of a company. It has been well said that he who has never learned to obey cannot be a good commander. The excellence of the two is not the same, but the good citizen ought to be capable of both; he should know how to govern like a freeman, and how to obey like a freeman—these are the excellences of a citizen. And, although the temperance and justice of a ruler are distinct from those of a subject, the excellence of a good man will include both; for the excellence of the good man who is free and also a subject, e.g. his justice, will not be one but will comprise distinct kinds, the one qualifying him to rule, the other to obey, and differing as the temperance and courage of men and women differ. For a man would be thought a coward if he had no more courage than a courageous woman, and a woman would be thought loquacious if she imposed no more restraint on her conversation than the good man; and indeed their part in the management of the household is different, for the duty of the one is to acquire, and of the other to preserve. Practical wisdom is the only excellence peculiar to the ruler: it would seem that all other excellences must equally belong to ruler and subject. The excellence of the subject is certainly not wisdom, but only true opinion; he may be compared to the maker of the flute, while his master is like the flute-player or user of the flute.

From these considerations may be gathered the answer to the question, whether the excellence of the good man is the same as that of the good citizen, or different, and how far the same, and how far different.

5

There still remains one more question about the citizen: Is he only a true citizen who has a share of office, or is the mechanic to be included? If they who hold no office are to be deemed citizens, not every citizen can have this excellence: for this man is a citizen. And if none of the lower class are citizens, in which part of the state are they to be placed? For they are not resident aliens, and they are not foreigners. May we not reply, that as far as this objection goes there is no more absurdity in them than in excluding slaves and freedmen from any of the above-mentioned classes? It must be admitted that we cannot consider all those to be citizens who are necessary to the existence of the state; for example, children are not citizens equally with grown-up men, who are citizens absolutely, but children, not being grown up, are only citizens on a certain assumption. In ancient times, and among some nations, the artisan class were slaves or foreigners, and therefore the majority of them are so now. The best form of state will not admit them to citizenship; but if they are admitted, then our definition of the excellence of a citizen will not apply to every citizen, nor to every free man as such, but only to those who are freed from necessary services. The necessary people are either slaves who minister to the wants of individuals, or mechanics and labourers who are the servants of the community. These reflections carried a little further will explain their position; and indeed what has been said already is of itself, when understood, explanation enough.

Since there are many forms of government there must be many varieties of citizens, and especially of citizens who are subjects; so that under some governments the mechanic and the labourer will be citizens, but not in others, as, for example, in so-called aristocracies, if there are any, in which honours are given according to excellence and merit; for no man can practise excellence who is living the life of a mechanic or labourer. In oligarchies the qualification for office is high, and therefore no labourer can ever be a citizen; but a mechanic may, for an actual majority of them are rich. At Thebes there was a law that no man could hold office who had not retired from business for ten years. But in many states the law goes to the length of admitting aliens; for in some democracies a man is a citizen though his mother only be a citizen; and a similar principle is applied to illegitimate children among many. Nevertheless they make such people citizens because of the dearth of legitimate citizens (for they introduce this sort of legislation owing to lack of population); so when the number of citizens increases, first the children of a male or a female slave are excluded; then those whose mothers only are citizens; and at last the right of citizenship is confined to those whose fathers and mothers are both citizens.

Hence, as is evident, there are different kinds of citizens; and he is a citizen in the fullest sense who shares in the honours of the state. Compare Homer's words 'like some dishonoured stranger';[6] he who is excluded from the honours of the state is no better than an alien. But when this exclusion is concealed, then its object is to deceive their fellow inhabitants.

As to the question whether the excellence of the good man is the same as that of the good citizen, the considerations already adduced prove that in some states the

6. [*Iliad* IX 648.]

good man and the good citizen are the same, and in others different. When they are the same it is not every citizen who is a good man, but only the statesman and those who have or may have, alone or in conjunction with others, the conduct of public affairs.

BOOK SEVEN

1

He who would duly inquire about the best form of a state ought first to determine which is the most eligible life; while this remains uncertain the best form of the state must also be uncertain; for, in the natural order of things, those men may be expected to lead the best life who are governed in the best manner of which their circumstances admit. We ought therefore to ascertain, first of all, which is the most generally eligible life, and then whether the same life is or is not best for the state and for individuals. Assuming that enough has been already said in discussions outside the school concerning the best life, we will now only repeat what is contained in them. Certainly no one will dispute the propriety of that partition of goods which separates them into three classes, viz. external goods, goods of the body, and goods of the soul, or deny that the happy man must have all three. For no one would maintain that he is happy who has not in him a particle of courage or temperance or justice or practical wisdom, who is afraid of every insect which flutters past him, and will commit any crime, however great, in order to gratify his lust for meat or drink, who will sacrifice his dearest friend for the sake of half a farthing, and is as feeble and false in mind as a child or a madman. These propositions are almost universally acknowledged as soon as they are uttered, but men differ about the degree or relative superiority of this or that good. Some think that a very moderate amount of excellence is enough, but set no limit to their desires for wealth, property, power, reputation, and the like. To them we shall reply by an appeal to facts, which easily prove that mankind does not acquire or preserve the excellences by the help of external goods, but external goods by the help of the excellences, and that happiness, whether consisting in pleasure or excellence, or both, is more often found with those who are most highly cultivated in their mind and in their character, and have only a moderate share of external goods, than among those who possess external goods to a useless extent but are deficient in higher qualities; and this is not only a matter of experience, but, if reflected upon, will easily appear to be in accordance with reason. For, whereas external goods have a limit, like any other instrument, and all things useful are useful for a purpose, and where there is too much of them they must either do harm, or at any rate be of no use, to their possessors, every good of the soul, the greater it is, is also of greater use, if the epithet useful as well as noble is appropriate to such subjects. No proof is required to show that the best state of one thing in relation to another corresponds in degree of excellence to the interval between the natures of which we say that these very states are states: so that, if the soul is more noble than our possessions or our bodies, both absolutely and in relation to us, it must be admitted that the best state of either has a similar ratio to the other. Again, it is for the sake of the soul that goods external and goods of the body are desirable at all, and all wise men ought to choose them for the sake of the soul, and not the soul for the sake of them.

Let us acknowledge then that each one has just so much of happiness as he has of excellence and wisdom, and of excellent and wise action. The gods are a witness to us of this truth, for they are happy and blessed, not by reason of any external good, but in themselves and by reason of their own nature. And herein of necessity lies the difference between good fortune and happiness; for external goods come of themselves, and chance is the author of them, but no one is just or temperate by or through chance. In like manner, and by a similar train of argument, the happy state may be shown to be that which is best and which acts rightly; and it cannot act rightly without doing right actions, and neither individual nor state can do right actions without excellence and wisdom. Thus the courage, justice, and wisdom of a state have the same form and nature as the qualities which give the individual who possesses them the name of just, wise or temperate.

Thus much may suffice by way of preface: for I could not avoid touching upon these questions, neither could I go through all the arguments affecting them; these are the business of another science.

Let us assume then that the best life, both for individuals and states, is the life of excellence, when excellence has external goods enough for the performance of good actions. If there are any who dispute our assertion, we will in this treatise pass them over, and consider their objections hereafter.

2

There remains to be discussed the question, whether the happiness of the individual is the same as that of the state, or different. Here again there can be no doubt— no one denies that they are the same. For those who hold that the well-being of the individual consists in his wealth, also think that riches make the happiness of the whole state, and those who value most highly the life of a tyrant deem that city the happiest which rules over the greatest number; while they who approve an individual for his excellence say that the more excellent a city is, the happier it is. Two points here present themselves for consideration: first, which is the more desirable life, that of a citizen who is a member of a state, or that of an alien who has no political ties; and again, which is the best form of constitution or the best condition of a state, either on the supposition that political privileges are desirable for all, or for a majority only? Since the good of the state and not of the individual is the proper subject of political thought and speculation, and we are engaged in a political discussion, while the first of these two points has a secondary interest for us, the latter will be the main subject of our inquiry.

Now it is evident that that form of government is best in which every man, whoever he is, can act best and live happily. But even those who agree in thinking that the life of excellence is the most desirable raise a question, whether the life of business and politics is or is not more desirable than one which is wholly independent of external goods, I mean than a contemplative life, which by some is maintained to be the only one worthy of a philosopher. For these two lives—the life of the philosopher and the life of the statesman—appear to have been preferred by those who have been most keen in the pursuit of excellence, both in our own and in other ages.

Which is the better is a question of no small moment; for the wise man, like the wise state, will necessarily regulate his life according to the best end. There are some who think that while a despotic rule over others is the greatest injustice, to exercise a constitutional rule over them, even though not unjust, is a great impediment to a man's individual well-being. Others take an opposite view; they maintain that the true life of man is the practical and political, and that every excellence admits of being practised, quite as much by statesmen and rulers as by private individuals. Others, again, are of the opinion that arbitrary and tyrannical rule alone makes for happiness; indeed, in some states the entire aim both of the laws and of the constitution is to give men despotic power over their neighbours. And, therefore, although in most cities the laws may be said generally to be in a chaotic state, still, if they aim at anything, they aim at the maintenance of power: thus in Lacedaemon and Crete the system of education and the greater part of the laws are framed with a view to war. And in all nations which are able to gratify their ambition military power is held in esteem, for example among the Scythians and Persians and Thracians and Celts. In some nations there are even laws tending to stimulate the warlike virtues, as at Carthage, where we are told that men obtain the honour of wearing as many armlets as they have served campaigns. There was once a law in Macedonia that he who had not killed an enemy should wear a halter, and among the Scythians no one who had not slain his man was allowed to drink out of the cup which was handed round at a certain feast. Among the Iberians, a warlike nation, the number of enemies whom a man has slain is indicated by the number of obelisks which are fixed in the earth round his tomb; and there are numerous practices among other nations of a like kind, some of them established by law and others by custom. Yet to a reflecting mind it must appear very strange that the statesman should be always considering how he can dominate and tyrannize over others, whether they are willing or not. How can that which is not even lawful be the business of the statesman or the legislator? Unlawful it certainly is to rule without regard to justice, for there may be might where there is no right. The other arts and sciences offer no parallel; a physician is not expected to persuade or coerce his patients, nor a pilot the passengers in his ship. Yet most men appear to think that the art of despotic government is statesmanship, and what men affirm to be unjust and inexpedient in their own case they are not ashamed of practising towards others; they demand just rule for themselves, but where other men are concerned they care nothing about it. Such behaviour is irrational; unless the one party is, and the other is not, born to serve, in which case men have a right to command, not indeed all their fellows, but only those who are intended to be subjects; just as we ought not to hunt men, whether for food or sacrifice, but only those animals which may be hunted for food or sacrifice, that is to say, such wild animals as are eatable. And surely there may be a city happy in isolation, which we will assume to be well-governed (for it is quite possible that a city thus isolated might be well-administered and have good laws); but such a city would not be constituted with any view to war or the conquest of enemies—all that sort of thing must be excluded. Hence we see very plainly that warlike pursuits, although generally to be deemed honourable, are not the supreme end of all things, but only means. And the good lawgiver should inquire how states and races of men and communities may participate in a good life, and in the happiness which is attainable by them. His enactments will not be always the same; and where there are neighbours he will have to see what sort of studies should be practised in relation to their several characters, or how the measures appropriate in relation to each are to be adopted. The end at which the best form of government should aim may be properly made a matter of future consideration.

3

Let us now address those who, while they agree that the life of excellence is the most desirable, differ about the manner of practising it. For some renounce political power, and think that the life of the freeman is different from the life of the statesman and the best of all; but others think the life of the statesman best. The argument of the latter is that he who does nothing cannot do well, and that acting well is identical with happiness. To both we say: 'you are partly right and partly wrong.' The first class are right in affirming that the life of the freeman is better than the life of the despot; for there is nothing noble in having the use of a slave, in so far as he is a slave; or in issuing commands about necessary things. But it is an error to suppose that every sort of rule is despotic like that of a master over slaves, for there is as great a difference between rule over freemen and rule over slaves as there is between slavery by nature and freedom by nature, about which I have said enough at the commencement of this treatise. And it is equally a mistake to place inactivity above action, for happiness is activity, and the actions of the just and wise are the realization of much that is noble.

But perhaps someone, accepting these premises, may still maintain that supreme power is the best of all things, because the possessors of it are able to perform the greatest number of noble actions. If so, the man who is able to rule, instead of giving up anything to his neighbour, ought rather to take away his power; and the father should care nothing for his son, nor the son for his father, nor friend for friend; they should not bestow a thought on one another in comparison with this higher object, for the best is the most desirable and 'acting well' is the best. There might be some truth in such a view if we assume that robbers and plunderers attain the chief good. But this can never be; their hypothesis is false. For the actions of a ruler cannot really be honourable, unless he is as much superior to other men as a man is to a woman, or a father to his children, or a master to his slaves. And therefore he who violates the law can never recover by any success, however great, what he has already lost in departing from excellence. For equals the honourable and the just consist in sharing alike, as is just and equal. But that the unequal should be given to equals, and the unlike to those who are like, is contrary to nature, and nothing which is contrary to nature is good. If, therefore, there is anyone superior in excellence and in the power of performing the best actions, he is the man we ought to follow and obey, but he must have the capacity for action as well as excellence.

If we are right in our view, and happiness is assumed to be acting well, the active life will be the best, both for every city collectively, and for individuals. Not that a life of action must necessarily have relation to others, as some persons think, nor are those ideas only to be regarded as practical which are pursued for the sake of practical results, but much more the thoughts and contemplations which are independent and complete in themselves; since acting well, and therefore a certain kind of action, is an end, and even in the case of external actions the directing mind is most truly said to act. Neither, again, is it necessary that states which are cut off from others and choose to live alone should be inactive; for activity, as well as other things, may take place by sections; there are many ways in which the sections of a state act upon one another. The same thing is equally true of every individual. If this were otherwise, the gods and the universe, who have no external actions over and above their own energies, would be far enough from perfection. Hence it is evident that the same life is best for each individual, and for states and for mankind collectively.

13

Returning to the constitution itself, let us seek to determine out of what and what sort of elements the state which is to be happy and well-governed should be composed. There are two things in which all well-being consists: one of them is the choice of a right end and aim of action, and the other the discovery of the actions which contribute towards it; for the means and the end may agree or disagree. Sometimes the right end is set before men, but in practice they fail to attain it; in other cases they are successful in all the contributory factors, but they propose to themselves a bad end; and sometimes they fail in both. Take, for example, the art of medicine; physicians do not always understand the nature of health, and also the means which they use may not effect the desired end. In all arts and sciences both the end and the means should be equally within our control.

The happiness and well-being which all men manifestly desire, some have the power of attaining, but to others, from some accident or defect of nature, the attainment of them is not granted; for a good life requires a supply of external goods, in a less degree when men are in a good state, in a greater degree when they are in a lower state. Others again, who possess the conditions of happiness, go utterly wrong from the first in the pursuit of it. But since our object is to discover the best form of government, that, namely, under which a city will be best governed, and since the city is best governed which has the greatest opportunity of obtaining happiness, it is evident that we must clearly ascertain the nature of happiness.

We maintain, and have said in the *Ethics*, if the arguments there adduced are of any value, that happiness is the realization and perfect exercise of excellence, and this not conditional, but absolute. And I use the term 'conditional' to express that which is indispensable, and 'absolute' to express that which is good in itself. Take the case of just actions; just punishments and chastisements do indeed spring from a good principle, but they are good only because we cannot do without them—it would be better that neither individuals nor states should need anything of the sort—but actions which aim at honour and advantage are absolutely the best. The conditional action is only the choice of a lesser evil; whereas these are the foundation and creation of good. A good man may make the best even of poverty and disease, and the other ills of life; but he can only attain happiness under the opposite conditions (for this also has been determined in the *Ethics*, that the good man is he for whom, because he is excellent, the things that are absolutely good are good; it is also plain that his use of these goods must be excellent and in the absolute sense good). This makes men fancy that external goods are the cause of happiness, yet we might as well say that a brilliant performance on the lyre was to be attributed to the instrument and not to the skill of the performer.

It follows then from what has been said that some things the legislator must find ready to his hand in a state, others he must provide. And therefore we can only say:

may our state be constituted in such a manner as to be blessed with the goods of which fortune disposes (for we acknowledge her power): whereas excellence and goodness in the state are not a matter of chance but the result of knowledge and choice. A city can be excellent only when the citizens who have a share in the government are excellent, and in our state all the citizens share in the government; let us then inquire how a man becomes excellent. For even if we could suppose the citizen body to be excellent, without each of them being so, yet the latter would be better, for in the excellence of each the excellence of all is involved.

There are three things which make men good and excellent; these are nature, habit, reason. In the first place, every one must be born a man and not some other animal; so, too, he must have a certain character, both of body and soul. But some qualities there is no use in having at birth, for they are altered by habit, and there are some gifts which by nature are made to be turned by habit to good or bad. Animals lead for the most part a life of nature, although in lesser particulars some are influenced by habit as well. Man has reason, in addition, and man only. For this reason nature, habit, reason must be in harmony with one another; for they do not always agree; men do many things against habit and nature, if reason persuades them that they ought. We have already determined what natures are likely to be most easily moulded by the hands of the legislator. All else is the work of education; we learn some things by habit and some by instruction.

14

Since every political society is composed of rulers and subjects, let us consider whether the relations of one to the other should interchange or be permanent. For the education of the citizens will necessarily vary with the answer given to this question. Now, if some men excelled others in the same degree in which gods and heroes are supposed to excel mankind in general (having in the first place a great advantage even in their bodies, and secondly in their minds), so that the superiority of the governors was undisputed and patent to their subjects, it would clearly be better that once for all the one class should rule and the others serve. But since this is unattainable, and kings have no marked superiority over their subjects, such as Scylax affirms to be found among the Indians, it is obviously necessary on many grounds that all the citizens alike should take their turn of governing and being governed. Equality consists in the same treatment of similar persons, and no government can stand which is not founded upon justice. For if the government is unjust everyone in the country unites with the governed in the desire to have a revolution, and it is an impossibility that the members of the government can be so numerous as to be stronger than all their enemies put together. Yet that governors should be better than their subjects is undeniable. How all this is to be effected, and in what way they will respectively share in the government, the legislator has to consider. The subject has been already mentioned. Nature herself has provided the distinction when she made a difference between old and young within the same species, of whom she fitted the one to govern and the other to be governed. No one takes offence at being governed when he is young, nor does he think himself better than his governors, especially if he will enjoy the same privilege when he reaches the required age.

We conclude that from one point of view governors and governed are identical, and from another different. And therefore their education must be the same and also different. For he who would learn to command well must, as men say, first of all learn to obey. As I observed in the first part of this treatise, there is one rule which is for the sake of the rulers and another rule which is for the sake of the ruled; the former is a despotic, the latter a free government. Some commands differ not in the thing commanded, but in the intention with which they are imposed. That is why many apparently menial offices are an honour to the free youth by whom they are performed; for actions do not differ as honourable or dishonourable in themselves so much as in the end and intention of them. But since we say that the excellence of the citizen and ruler is the same as that of the good man, and that the same person must first be a subject and then a ruler, the legislator has to see that they become good men, and by what means this may be accomplished, and what is the end of the perfect life.

Now the soul of man is divided into two parts, one of which has a rational principle in itself, and the other, not having a rational principle in itself, is able to obey such a principle. And we call a man in any way good because he has the excellences of these two parts. In which of them the end is more likely to be found is no matter of doubt to those who adopt our division; for in the world both of nature and of art the inferior always exists for the sake of the superior, and the superior is that which has a rational principle. This principle, too, in our ordinary way of making the division, is divided into two kinds, for there is a practical and a speculative principle. This part, then, must evidently be similarly divided. And there must be a corresponding division of actions; the actions of the naturally better part are to be preferred by those who have it in their power to attain to two out of the three or to all, for that is always to everyone the most desirable which is the highest attainable by him. The whole of life is further divided into two parts, business and leisure, war and peace, and of actions some aim at what is necessary and useful, and some at what is honourable. And the preference given to one or the other class of actions must necessarily be like the preference given to one or other part of the soul and its actions over the other; there must be war for the sake of peace, business for the sake of leisure, things useful and necessary for the sake of things honourable. All these points the statesman should keep in view when he frames his laws; he should consider the parts of the soul and their functions, and above all the better and the end; he should also remember the diversities of human lives and actions. For men must be able to engage in business and go to war, but leisure and peace are better; they must do what is necessary and indeed what is useful, but what is honourable is better. On such principles children and persons of every age which requires education should be trained. Whereas even the Greeks of the present day who are reputed to be best governed, and the legislators who gave them their constitutions, do not appear to have framed their governments with a regard to the best end, or to have given them laws and education with a view to all the excellences, but in a vulgar spirit have fallen back on those which promised to be more useful and profitable. Many modern writers have taken a similar view: they commend the Lacedaemonian constitution, and praise the legislator for making conquest and war his sole aim, a doctrine which may be refuted by argument and has long ago been refuted by facts. For most men desire empire in the hope of accumulating the goods of fortune; and on this ground Thibron and all those who have written about the Lacedaemonian constitution have praised their legislator, because the Lacedaemonians, by being trained to meet dangers, gained great power. But surely they are not a happy people now that their empire has passed away, nor was their legislator right. How ridiculous is the result, if, while they are continuing in the observance of his laws and no one interferes with them, they have lost the better part of life! These writers further err about the sort of government which the legislator should approve, for the government of freemen is nobler and implies more excellence than despotic government. Neither is a city to be deemed happy or a legislator to be praised because he trains his citizens to conquer and obtain dominion over their neighbours, for there is great harm in this. On a similar principle any citizen who could, should obviously try to obtain the power in his own state—the crime which the Lacedaemonians accuse king Pausanias of attempting, although he had such great honour already. No such principle and no law having this object is either statesmanlike or useful or right. For the same things are best both for individuals and for states, and these are the things which the legislator ought to implant in the minds of his citizens. Neither should men study war with a view to the enslavement of those who do not deserve to be enslaved; but first of all they should provide against their own enslavement, and in the second place obtain empire for the good of the governed, and not for the sake of exercising a general despotism, and in the third place they should seek to be masters only over those who deserve to be slaves. Facts, as well as arguments, prove that the legislator should direct all his military and other measures to the provision of leisure and the establishment of peace. For most of these military states are safe only while they are at war, but fall when they have acquired their empire; like unused iron they lose their edge in time of peace. And for this the legislator is to blame, he never having taught them how to lead the life of peace.

15

Since the end of individuals and of states is the same, the end of the best man and of the best constitution must also be the same; it is therefore evident that there ought to exist in both of them the excellences of leisure; for peace, as has been often repeated, is the end of war, and leisure of toil. But leisure and cultivation may be promoted not only by those excellences which are practised in leisure, but also by some of those which are useful to business. For many necessaries of life have to be supplied before we can have leisure. Therefore a city must be temperate and brave, and able to endure: for truly, as the proverb says, 'There is no leisure for slaves,' and those who cannot face danger like men are the slaves of any invader. Courage and endurance are required for business and philosophy for leisure, temperance and justice for both, and more especially in times of peace and leisure, for war compels men to be just and temperate, whereas the enjoyment of good fortune and the leisure which comes with peace tend to make them insolent. Those then who seem to be the best-off and to be in the possession of every good, have special need of justice and temperance—for example, those (if such there be, as the poets say) who dwell in the Islands of the Blest; they above all will need philosophy and temperance and justice, and all the more the more leisure they have, living in the midst of abundance. There is no difficulty in seeing why the state that would be happy and good ought to have these excellences. If it is disgraceful in men not to be able to use the goods of life, it is peculiarly disgraceful not to be able to use them in time of leisure—to show excellent qualities in action and war, and when they have peace and leisure to be no better than slaves. That is why we should not practise excellence after the manner of the Lacedaemonians. For they, while agreeing with other men in their conception of the highest goods, differ from the rest of mankind in thinking that they are to be obtained by the practice of a single excellence. And since these goods and the enjoyment of them are greater than the enjoyment derived from the excellences . . . and that for its own sake, is evident from what has been said; we must now consider how and by what means it is to be attained.

We have already determined that nature and habit and reason are required, and, of these, the proper nature of the citizens has also been defined by us. But we have still to consider whether the training of early life is to be that of reason or habit, for these two must accord, and when in accord they will then form the best of harmonies. Reason may be mistaken and fail in attaining the highest ideal of life, and there may be a like influence of habit. Thus much is clear in the first place, that, as in all other things, birth implies an antecedent beginning, and that there are beginnings whose end is relative to a further end. Now, in men reason and mind are the end towards which nature strives, so that the birth and training in custom of the citizens ought to be ordered with a view to them. In the second place, as the soul and body are two, we see also that there are two parts of the soul, the rational and the irrational, and two corresponding states—reason and appetite. And as the body is prior in order of generation to the soul, so the irrational is prior to the rational. The proof is that anger and wishing and desire are implanted in children from their very birth, but reason and understanding are developed as they grow older. For this reason, the care of the body ought to precede that of the soul, and the training of the appetitive part should follow: none the less our care of it must be for the sake of the reason, and our care of the body for the sake of the soul.

EPICURUS

Often, in the course of Western culture, morality and politics overlap. In the thought of Epicurus (341–271 B.C.E.), they do not, and this fact alone makes him an especially interesting figure, for in the ancient Greek world ethics and the good life were generally conceived in political terms. Hence, it would be surprising if Epicurus' rejection of political involvement were not in part a reaction to the thought of Plato and Aristotle and a return, in a sense, to Socratic thinking and an intense type of psychological therapy. Moreover, it would also be surprising if Epicurus' denial of the political, the avoidance of turbulence and fear, and the striving for psychological equilibrium were not in part a reaction to the pressures of the times—the achievements of Alexander, his death, the fragmentation of the empire, the increased familiarity among diverse cultures, and political crisis.

Epicurus was born on the island of Samos, off the coast of Asia Minor. His father was an Athenian citizen, and Epicurus at eighteen travelled to Athens to perform his military service. At about that time Alexander died, Aristotle left Athens and died a year later, and the Lyceum, Aristotle's school, came under new leadership. Epicurus seems to have returned to live with his family in Colophon and then to have organized his own philosophical circle first in Lesbos and then in Lampsacus, before moving to Athens in 307/306 B.C.E. He remained in Athens until his death in 271.

Upon his return to Athens, Epicurus purchased a house outside the city gates and founded a school, the "Garden," a kind of religious fellowship or society of friends. Apparently Epicurus had followers throughout the Greek world, and he kept in touch with many of them by means of letters, of which some fragments have survived. Epicurus wrote a great deal; Diogenes Laertius, the third-century doxographer, records forty-one of Epicurus' 'best books' and notes that no previous writer had greater productivity. Of this massive corpus, however, only a small portion remains, principally three letters quoted by Diogenes (*To Herodotus*, *To Pythocles*, and *To Menoeceus*), a collection of forty maxims or "principal doctrines" also quoted in Diogenes, and the quantity of Epicurean teaching cited and employed in Lucretius' *De rerum natura* (*On the Nature of Things*).

As A. A. Long has put it, "Epicurus' philosophy is a strange mixture of hardheaded empiricism, speculative metaphysics, and rules for the attainment of a tranquil life." That is, he develops a theory of knowledge that is grounded in sensation and sensory evidence. On this basis, Epicurus accounts for concepts, statements, truth, and rules of logic. He then proceeds to draw on the pre-Socratic atomists, Leucippus and Democritus, to develop his own theory of atoms and the void. From this theory he gives an account of the gods, fate, free will, and such matters. Finally, Epicurus uses these accounts to show how one should live in order to reduce pain and anxiety and thereby to maximize psychic tranquility (*ataraxia*) and pleasure. For example, he argues, tranquility occurs when the knowledge of nature removes our fear of the gods and of death itself. Human beings, Epicurus claims, can dissolve illusion and prejudice and thereby achieve the freedom from pain and the peace of mind that characterize the best life. There is no voluptuary hedonism in this; Epicurus does not fit the later parody of his thought. Rather there is dignity, moderation, and detachment, born of strife and worry but seeking nobility in a world riddled with turbulence, conflict, and superstition.

Recommended readings

Gerson, L., and B. Inwood (trans.), *Hellenistic Philosophy*. Indianapolis: Hackett, 1988.

Irwin, T. H. *Classical Thought*. Oxford: Oxford University Press, 1989.

Long, A. A. *Hellenistic Philosophy*. London: Duckworth, 1974.

Long, A. A., and David Sedley (trans. and commentary). *The Hellenistic Philosophers*. Vols. I and II. Cambridge: Cambridge University Press, 1987.

Prior, William. *Virtue and Knowledge: An Introduction to Ancient Greek Ethics*. London: Routledge, 1991.

Rist, John. *Epicurus*. Cambridge: Cambridge University Press, 1972.

LETTER TO MENOECEUS:

Epicurus to Menoeceus, greetings:

Let no one delay the study of philosophy while young nor weary of it when old. For no one is either too young or too old for the health of the soul. He who says either that the time for philosophy has not yet come or that it has passed is like someone who says that the time for happiness has not yet come or that it has passed. Therefore, both young and old must philosophize, the latter so that although old he may stay young in good things owing to gratitude for what has occurred, the former so that although young he too may be like an old man owing to his lack of fear of what is to come. Therefore, one must practise the things which produce happiness, since if that is present we have everything and if it is absent we do everything in order to have it.

Do and practise what I constantly told you to do, believing these to be the elements of living well. First, believe that god is an indestructible and blessed animal, in accordance with the general conception of god commonly held, and do not ascribe to god anything foreign to his indestructibility or repugnant to his blessedness. Believe of him everything which is able to preserve his blessedness and indestructibility. For gods do exist, since we have clear knowledge of them. But they are not such as the many believe them to be. For they do not adhere to their own views about the gods. The man who denies the gods of the many is not impious, but rather he who ascribes to the gods the opinions of the many. For the pronouncements of the many about the gods are not basic grasps but false suppositions. Hence come the greatest harm from the gods to bad men and the greatest benefits [to the good]. For the gods always welcome men who are like themselves, being congenial to their own virtues and considering that whatever is not such is uncongenial.

Get used to believing that death is nothing to us. For all good and bad consists in sense-experience, and death is the privation of sense-experience. Hence, a correct knowledge of the fact that death is nothing to us makes the mortality of life a matter for contentment, not by adding a limitless time [to life] but by removing the longing for immortality. For there is nothing fearful in life for one who has grasped that there is nothing fearful in the absence of life. Thus, he is a fool who says that he fears death not because it will be painful when present but because it is painful when it is still to come. For that which while present causes no distress causes unnecessary pain when merely anticipated. So death, the most frightening of bad things, is nothing to us; since when we exist, death is not yet present, and when death is present, then we do not exist. Therefore, it is relevant neither to the living nor to the dead, since it does not affect the former, and the latter do not exist. But the many sometimes flee death as the greatest of bad things and sometimes choose it as a relief from the bad things of life. But the wise man neither rejects life nor fears death. For living does not offend him, nor does he believe not living to be something bad. And just as he does not unconditionally choose the largest amount of food but the most pleasant food, so he savours not the longest time but the most pleasant. He

Reprinted from *Hellenistic Philosophy*, translated and edited by Brad Inwood and L. P. Gerson (Indianapolis: Hackett Publishing Company, 1988).

who advises the young man to live well and the old man to die well is simple-minded, not just because of the pleasing aspects of life but because the same kind of practice produces a good life and a good death. Much worse is he who says that it is good not to be born, "but when born to pass through the gates of Hades as quickly as possible."[1] For if he really believes what he says, why doesn't he leave life? For it is easy for him to do, if he has firmly decided on it. But if he is joking, he is wasting his time among men who don't welcome it. We must remember that what will happen is neither unconditionally within our power nor unconditionally outside our power, so that we will not unconditionally expect that it will occur nor despair of it as unconditionally not going to occur.

One must reckon that of desires some are natural, some groundless; and of the natural desires some are necessary and some merely natural; and of the necessary, some are necessary for happiness and some for freeing the body from troubles and some for life itself. The unwavering contemplation of these enables one to refer every choice and avoidance to the health of the body and the freedom of the soul from disturbance, since this is the goal of a blessed life. For we do everything for the sake of being neither in pain nor in terror. As soon as we achieve this state every storm in the soul is dispelled, since the animal is not in a passion to go after some need nor to seek something else to complete the good of the body and the soul. For we are in need of pleasure only when we are in pain because of the absence of pleasure, and when we are not in pain, then we no longer need pleasure.

And this is why we say that pleasure is the starting-point and goal of living blessedly. For we recognized this as our first innate good, and this is our starting point for every choice and avoidance and we come to this by judging every good by the criterion of feeling. And it is just because this is the first innate good, that we do not choose every pleasure; but sometimes we pass up many pleasures when we get a larger amount of what is uncongenial from them. And we believe many pains to be better than pleasures when a greater pleasure follows for a long while if we endure the pains. So every pleasure is a good thing, since it has a nature congenial [to us], but not every one is to be chosen. Just as every pain too is a bad thing, but not every one is such as to be always avoided. It is, however, appropriate to make all these decisions by comparative measurement and an examination of the advantages and disadvantages. For at some times we treat the good things as bad and conversely, the bad things as good.

And we believe that self-sufficiency is a great good, not in order that we might make do with few things under all circumstances, but so that if we do not have a lot we can make do with few, being genuinely convinced that those who least need extravagance enjoy it most; and that everything natural is easy to obtain and whatever is groundless is hard to obtain; and that simple flavours provide a pleasure equal to that of an extravagant life-style when all pain from want is removed, and barley cakes and water provide the highest pleasure when someone in want takes them. Therefore, becoming accustomed to simple, not extravagant, ways of life makes one completely healthy, makes man unhesitant in the face of life's necessary duties, puts us in a better condition for the times of extravagance which occasionally come along, and makes us fearless in the face of chance. So when we say that pleasure is the goal we do not mean the pleasures of the profligate or the pleasures of

1. [Theognis 425, 427.—B.I. and L.P.G.]

consumption, as some believe, either from ignorance and disagreement or from deliberate misinterpretation, but rather the lack of pain in the body and disturbance in the soul. For it is not drinking bouts and continuous partying and enjoying boys and women, or consuming fish and the other dainties of an extravagant table, which produce the pleasant life, but sober calculation which searches out the reasons for every choice and avoidance and drives out the opinions which are the source of the greatest turmoil for men's souls.

Prudence is the principle of all these things and is the greatest good. That is why prudence is a more valuable thing than philosophy. For prudence is the source of all the other virtues, teaching that it is impossible to live pleasantly without living prudently, honourably, and justly, and impossible to live prudently, honourably, and justly without living pleasantly. For the virtues are natural adjuncts of the pleasant life and the pleasant life is inseparable from them.

For who do you believe is better than a man who has pious opinions about the gods, is always fearless about death, has reasoned out the natural goal of life and understands that the limit of good things is easy to achieve completely and easy to provide, and that the limit of bad things either has a short duration or causes little trouble?

As to [Fate], introduced by some as the mistress of all, ⟨he is scornful, saying rather that some things happen of necessity,⟩ others by chance and others by our own agency, and that he sees that necessity is not answerable [to anyone], that chance is unstable, while what occurs by our own agency is autonomous, and that it is to this that praise and blame are attached. For it would be better to follow the stories told about the gods than to be a slave to the fate of the natural philosophers. For the former suggests a hope of escaping bad things by honouring the gods, but the latter involves an inescapable and merciless necessity. And he [the wise man] believes that chance is not a god, as the many think, for nothing is done in a disorderly way by god; nor that it is an uncertain cause. For he does not think that anything good or bad with respect to living blessedly is given by chance to men, although it does provide the starting points of great good and bad things. And he thinks it better to be unlucky in a rational way than lucky in a senseless way; for it is better for a good decision not to turn out right in action than for a bad decision to turn out right because of chance.

Practise these and the related precepts day and night, by yourself and with a like-minded friend, and you will never be disturbed either when awake or in sleep, and you will live as a god among men. For a man who lives among immortal goods is in no respect like a mere mortal animal.

THE PRINCIPAL DOCTRINES

I. What is blessed and indestructible has no troubles itself, nor does it give trouble to anyone else, so that it is not affected by feelings of anger or gratitude. For all such things are a sign of weakness.[1]

II. Death is nothing to us. For what has been dissolved has no sense-experience, and what has no sense-experience is nothing to us.

III. The removal of all feeling of pain is the limit of the magnitude of pleasures. Wherever a pleasurable feeling is present, for as long as it is present, there is neither a feeling of pain nor a feeling of distress, nor both together.

IV. The feeling of pain does not linger continuously in the flesh; rather, the sharpest is present for the shortest time, while what merely exceeds the feeling of pleasure in the flesh lasts only a few days. And diseases which last a long time involve feelings of pleasure which exceed feelings of pain.

V. It is impossible to live pleasantly without living prudently, honourably, and justly and impossible to live prudently, honourably, and justly without living pleasantly. And whoever lacks this cannot live pleasantly.

VI. The natural good of public office and kingship is for the sake of getting confidence from [other] men, [at least] from those from whom one *is* able to provide this.

VII. Some men want to become famous and respected, believing that this is the way to acquire security against [other] men. Thus if the life of such men is secure, they acquire the natural good; but if it is not secure, they do not have that for the sake of which they strove from the beginning according to what is naturally congenial.

VIII. No pleasure is a bad thing in itself. But the things which produce certain pleasures bring troubles many times greater than the pleasures.

IX. If every pleasure were condensed and were present, both in time and in the whole compound [body and soul] or in the most important parts of our nature, then pleasures would never differ from one another.

X. If the things which produce the pleasures of profligate men dissolved the intellect's fears about the phenomena of the heavens and about death and pains and, moreover, if they taught us the limit of our desires, then we would not have reason to criticize them, since they would be filled with pleasures from every source and would contain no feeling of pain or distress from any source—and that is what is bad.

XI. If our suspicions about heavenly phenomena and about death did not trouble us at all and were never anything to us, and, moreover, if not knowing the limits of pains and desires did not trouble us, then we would have no need of natural science.

XII. It was impossible for someone ignorant about the nature of the universe but still suspicious about the subjects of the myths to dissolve his feelings of fear about

---

1. [Scholiast: "Elsewhere he says that the gods are contemplated by reason, and that some exist 'numerically' [i.e., are numerically distinct, each being unique in kind] while others are similar in form, because of a continuous flow of similar images to the same place; and that they are anthropomorphic."—B.I. and L.P.G.]

the most important matters. So it was impossible to receive unmixed pleasures without knowing natural science.

XIII. It was useless to obtain security from men while the things above and below the earth and, generally, the things in the unbounded remained as objects of suspicion.

XIV. The purest security is that which comes from a quiet life and withdrawal from the many, although a certain degree of security from other men does come by means of the power to repel [attacks] and by means of prosperity.

XV. Natural wealth is both limited and easy to acquire. But wealth [as defined by] groundless opinions extends without limit.

XVI. Chance has a small impact on the wise man, while reasoning has arranged for, is arranging for, and will arrange for the greatest and most important matters throughout the whole of his life.

XVII. The just life is most free from disturbance, but the unjust life is full of the greatest disturbance.

XVIII. As soon as the feeling of pain produced by want is removed, pleasure in the flesh will not increase but is only varied. But the limit of mental pleasures is produced by a reasoning out of these very pleasures [of the flesh] and of the things related to these, which used to cause the greatest fears in the intellect.

XIX. Unlimited time and limited time contain equal [amounts of] pleasure, if one measures its limits by reasoning.

XX. The flesh took the limits of pleasure to be unlimited, and [only] an unlimited time would have provided it. But the intellect, reasoning out the goal and limit of the flesh and dissolving the fears of eternity, provided us with the perfect way of life and had no further need of unlimited time. But it [the intellect] did not flee pleasure, and even when circumstances caused an exit from life it did not die as though it were lacking any aspect of the best life.

XXI. He who has learned the limits of life knows that it is easy to provide that which removes the feeling of pain owing to want and makes one's whole life perfect. So there is no need for things which involve struggle.

XXII. One must reason about the real goal and every clear fact, to which we refer mere opinions. If not, everything will be full of indecision and disturbance.

XXIII. If you quarrel with all your sense-perceptions you will have nothing to refer to in judging even those sense-perceptions which you claim are false.

XXIV. If you reject unqualifiedly any sense-perception and do not distinguish the opinion about what awaits confirmation, and what is already present in the sense-perception, and the feelings, and every application of the intellect to presentations, you will also disturb the rest of your sense-perceptions with your pointless opinions; as a result you will reject every criterion. If, on the other hand, in your conceptions formed by opinion, you affirm everything that awaits confirmation as well as what does not, you will not avoid falsehood, so that you will be in the position of maintaining every disputable point in every decision about what is and is not correct.

XXV. If you do not, on every occasion, refer each of your actions to the goal of nature, but instead turn prematurely to some other [criterion] in avoiding or pursuing [things], your actions will not be consistent with your reasoning.

XXVI. The desires which do not bring a feeling of pain when not fulfilled are not necessary, but the desire for them is easy to dispel when they seem to be hard to achieve or to produce harm.

XXVII. Of the things which wisdom provides for the blessedness of one's whole life, by far the greatest is the possession of friendship.

XXVIII. The same understanding produces confidence about there being nothing terrible which is eternal or [even] long-lasting and has also realized that security amid even these limited [bad things] is most easily achieved through friendship.

XXIX. Of desires, some are natural and necessary, some natural and not necessary, and some neither natural nor necessary but occurring as a result of a groundless opinion.[2]

XXX. Among natural desires, those which do not lead to a feeling of pain if not fulfilled and about which there is an intense effort, these are produced by an groundless opinion and they fail to be dissolved not because of their own nature but because of the groundless opinions of mankind.

XXXI. The justice of nature is a pledge of reciprocal usefulness, [i.e.,] neither to harm one another nor be harmed.

XXXII. There was no justice or injustice with respect to all those animals which were unable to make pacts about neither harming one another nor being harmed. Similarly, [there was no justice or injustice] for all those nations which were unable or unwilling to make pacts about neither harming one another nor being harmed.

XXXIII. Justice was not a thing in its own right, but [exists] in mutual dealings in whatever places there [is] a pact about neither harming one another nor being harmed.

XXXIV. Injustice is not a bad thing in its own right, but [only] because of the fear produced by the suspicion that one will not escape the notice of those assigned to punish such actions.

XXXV. It is impossible for someone who secretly does something which men agreed [not to do] in order to avoid harming one another or being harmed to be confident that he will escape detection, even if in current circumstances he escapes detection ten thousand times. For until his death it will be uncertain whether he will continue to escape detection.

XXXVI. In general outline justice is the same for everyone; for it was something useful in mutual associations. But with respect to the peculiarities of a region or of other [relevant] causes, it does not follow that the same thing is just for everyone.

XXXVII. Of actions believed to be just, that whose usefulness in circumstances of mutual associations is supported by the testimony [of experience] has the attribute of serving as just whether it is the same for everyone or not. And if someone passes a law and it does not turn out to be in accord with what is useful in mutual associations, this no longer possesses the nature of justice. And if what is useful in the sense of being just changes, but for a while fits our basic grasp [of justice],

2. [Scholiast: "Epicurus thinks that those which liberate us from pains are natural and necessary, for example drinking in the case of thirst; natural and not necessary are those which merely provide variations of pleasure but do not remove the feeling of pain, for example expensive foods; neither natural nor necessary are, for example, crowns and the erection of statues."]

nevertheless it was just for that length of time, [at least] for those who do not disturb themselves with empty words but simply look to the facts.

XXXVIII. If objective circumstances have not changed and things believed to be just have been shown in actual practice not to be in accord with our basic grasp [of justice], then those things were not just. And if objective circumstances do change and the same things which had been just turn out to be no longer useful, then those things were just as long as they were useful for the mutual associations of fellow citizens; but later, when they were not useful, they were no longer just.

XXXIX. The man who has made the best arrangements for confidence about external threats is he who has made the manageable things akin to himself, and has at least made the unmanageable things not alien to himself. But he avoided all contact with things for which not even this could be managed and he drove out of his life everything which it profited him to drive out.

XL. All those who had the power to acquire the greatest confidence from [the threats posed by] their neighbours also thereby lived together most pleasantly with the surest guarantee; and since they enjoyed the fullest sense of belonging they did not grieve the early death of the departed, as though it called for pity.

EPICTETUS

Around 300 B.C.E., two short decades after the death of Alexander the Great and the breakup of the vast Alexandrian empire, there emerged in Athens a philosophical school that became the most influential in the Graeco-Roman world. Stoicism, named after the "porch" or *Stoa poikile* on the Athenian acropolis, where its earliest members convened, was at once a system of logic, a theory of knowledge, a natural philosophy or physics, and an ethics. But most of all it was a way of life, an attempt to confront and deal with the turbulent times and the deep anxiety that arose with the demise of the *polis* as the fixed parameter of moral and political life, and with the limitless horizons of world-wide diversity, competing cultures, and forms of knowledge.

Moreover, Stoic philosophy and the Stoic way of life are not only ancient phenomena. Chiefly through the works of Cicero, Diogenes Laertius, Seneca, Epictetus, and Marcus Aurelius, Stoicism permeated the writings of the Church Fathers and the literature of the Middle Ages. It influenced as well Renaissance thought and modern thinkers as diverse as John Calvin, Richard Hooker, Michel de Montaigne, Descartes, Spinoza, and Kant. Often stoicism was revived in situations as riddled with strain and anxiety as those which first gave rise to it, such as the remarkable neo-stoicism initiated by Justus Lipsius at the end of the sixteenth century.

Epictetus (ca. 55–135 C.E.) is one of three moral philosophers who comprise the Stoic movement known as late or Roman Stoicism. The other two representatives of this movement are Lucius Annaeus Seneca, a wealthy Roman orator, statesman, and author of the first century, and Marcus Aurelius, Emperor of Rome from 161 to 180 C.E. Although the earlier stages of Stoicism—developed by its founder, Zeno of Citium, and the major figures, Chrysippus, Panaetius, and Posidonius—involved sophisticated thinking about language, concepts, reasoning, physics, and much else, Roman Stoicism is primarily a moral doctrine and even a set of moral directives. It clearly relies on the philosophical developments of the Stoic tradition, but it was not itself engaged in serious argumentation and critical analysis. As we indicated above, this moral attractiveness is not surprising. There are doubtless social and political reasons why, in periods of crisis, many turned to Stoicism for solace and guidance. In troubled times its eulogy to philosophical rationality and devotion to self-control provided compelling vehicles for personal tranquility and salvation.

It is not true, however, that Stoicism began as a philosophical inquiry into logic, science, and such things, only later to become a moral doctrine. Indeed, from the beginning, in the hands of Zeno and his disciples, the aim of Stoicism was to determine how best to live. All along, the Stoic interest in technical subjects like logic was propaedeutic to this moral goal. Its materialism, its empiricism, its understanding of nature and fate, all these were intended to lead the Stoic to principles about what human agents can and should do in order to control their lives, reduce anxiety, practice virtue, free themselves from passion, and ultimately gain peace for themselves. For the Stoic, natural philosophy is so coherent that it provides the foundation for a life of harmony with nature, which the Stoic conceived as divine. In this way, the Stoic ideal was a life lived in harmony with the divine. This was an old goal, newly interpreted. Seeking the same freedom from anxiety that Epicurus sought, the Stoics found it in virtue and political participation and ultimately in kinship with rather than in rejection of the divine.

Epictetus was a Phrygian slave from Asia Minor. His master, Epaphroditus, who was Nero's freedman, let Epictetus study with Musonius Rufus, an important Stoic teacher. In 92 the Emperor Domitian banished the philosophers from Rome, and Epictetus settled in Nicopolis, in northwestern Greece, where he taught until his death. He wrote nothing, but one of his students, the future historian Arrian, took notes on his lectures in 115 C.E. and later published them as eight volumes of *Discourses*. These *Discourses*, rhetorical and sermonic, give the best sense of Epictetus' style. Of them four are extant, together with the *Encheiridion* (the *Manual*), which includes 53 extracts, often modified, from the larger work. It is this manual that was so influential in the sixteenth and seventeenth centuries and which Frederick the Great, emperor of Prussia in the eighteenth century, carried wherever he went.

Recommended readings

Gerson, L., and B. Inwood (eds. & trans.). *Hellenistic Philosophy*. Indianapolis: Hackett, 1988.

Inwood, B. *Ethics and Human Action in Early Stoicism*. Oxford: Oxford University Press, 1985.

Long. A. A. *Hellenistic Philosophy*. London: Duckworth, 1974.

Long. A. A. (ed.). *Problems of Stoicism*. London: The Athlone Press, 1971.

Long, A. A., and David Sedley (eds. and commentary). *The Hellenistic Philosophers*. Vols. I and II. Cambridge: Cambridge University Press, 1987.

Rist, John. *Stoic Philosophy*. Cambridge: Cambridge University Press, 1969.

Rist, John (ed.). *The Stoics*. Berkeley: University of California Press, 1978.

Sandbach, F. H. *The Stoics*. London: Chetto and Windus, 1975.

White, N. (trans.). *The Handbook of Epictetus*. Indianapolis: Hackett, 1983.

ENCHEIRIDION

1

Some things are up to us and some are not up to us. Our opinions are up to us, and our impulses, desires, aversions—in short, whatever is our own doing. Our bodies are not up to us, nor are our possessions, our reputations, or our public offices, or, that is, whatever is not our own doing. The things that are up to us are by nature free, unhindered, and unimpeded; the things that are not up to us are weak, enslaved, hindered, not our own. So remember, if you think that things naturally enslaved are free or that things not your own are your own, you will be thwarted, miserable, and upset, and will blame both gods and men. But if you think that only what is yours is yours, and that what is not your own is, just as it is, not your own, then no one will ever coerce you, no one will hinder you, you will blame no one, you will not accuse anyone, you will not do a single thing unwillingly, you will have no enemies, and no one will harm you, because you will not be harmed at all.

As you aim for such great goals, remember that you must not undertake them by acting moderately,[1] but must let some things go completely and postpone others for the time being. But if you want both those great goals and also to hold public office and to be rich then you may perhaps not get even the latter just because you aim at the former too; and you certainly will fail to get the former, which are the only things that yield freedom and happiness.[2]

From the start, then, work on saying to each harsh appearance,[3] "You are an appearance, and not at all the thing that has the appearance." Then examine it and assess it by these yardsticks that you have, and first and foremost by whether it concerns the things that are up to us or the things that are not up to us. And if it is about one of the things that is not up to us, be ready to say, "You are nothing in relation to me."

2

Remember, what a desire proposes is that you gain what you desire, and what an aversion proposes is that you not fall into what you are averse to. Someone who fails to get what he desires is *un*fortunate, while someone who falls into what he is averse to has met *mis*fortune. So if you are averse only to what is against nature among the things that are up to you, then you will never fall into anything that you are averse

Reprinted from *The Handbook of Epictetus,* translated, with introduction and annotations, by Nicholas White (Indianapolis: Hackett Publishing Company, 1983).

1. [This may mean simply that the proposed undertaking is difficult. (Oldfather's translation suggests this), or it may mean (as I believe) that the aim cannot be achieved by the Aristotelian policy of pursuing a mean or middle course between extremes.—N.W.]

2. [Epictetus recommends aiming to have one's state of mind in accord with nature, in the sense explained in the previous paragraph and in c. 8. His point here is that if you aim for that and also simultaneously for certain "externals" like wealth, you will probably have neither and clearly will not have the former.]

3. [The word "appearance" translates *phantasia*, which some translators render by "impression" or "presentation". An appearance is roughly the immediate experience of sense or feeling, which may or may not represent an external state of affairs. (The Stoics held, against the Sceptics, that some appearances self-evidently do represent external states of affairs correctly.)]

to; but if you are averse to illness or death or poverty, you will meet misfortune. So detach your aversion from everything not up to us, and transfer it to what is against nature among the things that are up to us. And for the time being eliminate desire completely, since if you desire something that is not up to us, you are bound to be unfortunate, and at the same time none of the things that are up to us, which it would be good to desire, will be available to you. Make use only of impulse and its contrary, rejection,[4] though with reservation, lightly, and without straining.

3

In the case of everything attractive or useful or that you are fond of, remember to say just what sort of thing it is, beginning with the least little things. If you are fond of a jug, say "I am fond of a jug!" For then when it is broken you will not be upset. If you kiss your child or your wife, say that you are kissing a human being; for when it dies you will not be upset.

4

When you are about to undertake some action, remind yourself what sort of action it is. If you are going out for a bath, put before your mind what happens at baths— there are people who splash, people who jostle, people who are insulting, people who steal. And you will undertake the action more securely if from the start you say of it, "I want to take a bath and to keep my choices in accord with nature;" and likewise for each action. For that way if something happens to interfere with your bathing you will be ready to say, "Oh, well, I wanted not only this but also to keep my choices in accord with nature, and I cannot do that if I am annoyed with things that happen."

5

What upsets people is not things themselves but their judgments about the things. For example, death is nothing dreadful (or else it would have appeared dreadful to Socrates), but instead the judgment about death that it is dreadful—*that* is what is dreadful. So when we are thwarted or upset or distressed, let us never blame someone else but rather ourselves, that is, our own judgments. An uneducated person accuses others when he is doing badly; a partly educated person accuses himself, an educated person accuses neither someone else nor himself.

6

Do not be joyful about any superiority that is not your own. If the horse were to say joyfully, "I am beautiful," one could put up with it. But certainly you, when you say joyfully, "I have a beautiful horse," are joyful about the good of the horse. What, then, is your own? Your way of dealing with appearances. So whenever you are in accord with nature in your way of dealing with appearances, then be joyful, since then you are joyful about a good of your own.

---

4. [Impulse and rejection (*hormē* and *aphormē*) are, in Stoic terms, natural and non-rational psychological movements, so to speak, that are respectively toward or away from external objects.]

7

On a voyage when your boat has anchored, if you want to get fresh water you may pick up a small shellfish and a vegetable by the way, but you must keep your mind fixed on the boat and look around frequently in case the captain calls. If he calls you must let all those other things go so that you will not be tied up and thrown on the ship like livestock. That is how it is in life too: if you are given a wife and a child instead of a vegetable and a small shellfish, that will not hinder you; but if the captain calls, let all those things go and run to the boat without turning back; and if you are old, do not even go very far from the boat, so that when the call comes you are not left behind.

8

Do not seek to have events happen as you want them to, but instead want them to happen as they do happen, and your life will go well.

9

Illness interferes with the body, not with one's faculty of choice,[5] unless that faculty of choice wishes it to. Lameness interferes with the limb, not with one's faculty of choice. Say this at each thing that happens to you, since you will find that it interferes with something else, not with you.

10

At each thing that happens to you, remember to turn to yourself and ask what capacity you have for dealing with it. If you see a beautiful boy or woman, you will find the capacity of self-control for that. If hardship comes to you, you will find endurance. If it is abuse, you will find patience. And if you become used to this, you will not be carried away by appearances.

11

Never say about anything, "I have lost it," but instead, "I have given it back." Did your child die? It was given back. Did your wife die? She was given back. "My land was taken." So this too was given back. "But the person who took it was bad!" How does the way the giver[6] asked for it back concern you? As long as he gives it, take care of it as something that is not your own, just as travelers treat an inn.

12

If you want to make progress,[7] give up all considerations like these: "If I neglect my property I will have nothing to live on," "If I do not punish my slave boy he will

---

5. ["Faculty of choice" translates *"proairesis"*, which designates a rational faculty of the soul (cf. n. 4).]

6. [The "giver" can be taken to be nature, or the natural order of the cosmos, or god, which the Stoics identified with each other.]

7. ["Making progress" (*prokoptein*) is the Stoic expression for movement in the direction of the ideal condition for a human being, embodied by the Stoic "sage" (cf. c. 15, n.).]

be bad." It is better to die of hunger with distress and fear gone than to live upset in the midst of plenty. It is better for the slave boy to be bad than for you to be in a bad state. Begin therefore with little things. A little oil is spilled, a little wine is stolen: say, "This is the price of tranquillity; this is the price of not being upset." Nothing comes for free. When you call the slave boy, keep in mind that he is capable of not paying attention, and even if he does pay attention he is capable of not doing any of the things that you want him to. But he is not in such a good position that your being upset or not depends on him.

13

If you want to make progress, let people think you are a mindless fool about externals, and do not desire a reputation for knowing about them. If people think you amount to something, distrust yourself. Certainly it is not easy to be on guard both for one's choices to be in accord with nature and also for externals, and a person who concerns himself with the one will be bound to neglect the other.

14

You are foolish if you want your children and your wife and your friends to live forever, since you are wanting things to be up to you that are not up to you, and things to be yours that are not yours. You are stupid in the same way if you want your slave boy to be faultless, since you are wanting badness not to be badness but something else. But wanting not to fail to get what you desire—*this* you are capable of. A person's master is someone who has power over what he wants or does not want, either to obtain it or take it away. Whoever wants to be free, therefore, let him not want or avoid anything that is up to others. Otherwise he will necessarily be a slave.

15

Remember, you must behave as you do at a banquet. Something is passed around and comes to you: reach out your hand politely and take some. It goes by: do not hold it back. It has not arrived yet: do not stretch your desire out toward it, but wait until it comes to you. In the same way toward your children, in the same way toward your wife, in the same way toward public office, in the same way toward wealth, and you will be fit to share a banquet with the gods. But if when things are set in front of you, you do not take them but despise them, then you will not only share a banquet with the gods but also be a ruler along with them. For by acting in this way Diogenes and Heraclitus[8] and people like them were deservedly gods and were deservedly called gods.

8. [Diogenes the Cynic (the one who with his lantern looked for an honest man) and Heraclitus of Ephesus, the presocratic philosopher, were along with Socrates and Zeno people whom the Stoics said might possibly have reached the perfect condition of being sages, which the Stoics took to be conceptually no different from the perfect condition of a god.]

16

When you see someone weeping in grief at the departure of his child or the loss of his property, take care not to be carried away by the appearance that the externals he is involved in are bad, and be ready to say immediately, "What weighs down on this man is not what has happened (since it does not weigh down on someone else), but his judgment about it." Do not hesitate, however, to sympathise with him verbally, and even to moan with him if the occasion arises; but be careful not to moan inwardly.

17

Remember that you are an actor in a play, which is as the playwright wants it to be: short if he wants it short, long if he wants it long. If he wants you to play a beggar, play even this part skillfully, or a cripple, or a public official, or a private citizen. What is yours is to play the assigned part well. But to choose it belongs to someone else.

18

When a raven gives an unfavorable sign by croaking,[9] do not be carried away by the appearance, but immediately draw a distinction to yourself and say, "None of these signs is for me, but only for my petty body or my petty property or my petty judgments or children or wife. For all signs are favorable if I wish, since it is up to me to be benefited by whichever of them turns out correct.

19

You can be invincible if you do not enter any contest in which victory is not up to you. See that you are not carried away by the appearance, in thinking that someone is happy when you see him honored ahead of you or very powerful or otherwise having a good reputation. For if the really good things are up to us, neither envy nor jealousy has a place, and you yourself will want neither to be a general or a magistrate or a consul, but to be free. And there is one road to this: despising what is not up to us.

20

Remember that what is insulting is not the person who abuses you or hits you, but the judgment about them that they *are* insulting. So when someone irritates you be aware that what irritates you is your own belief. Most importantly, therefore, try not to be carried away by appearance, since if you once gain time and delay you will control yourself more easily.

9. [Most people in antiquity believed in fortune-telling of various kinds, involving bird-calls, the flight of birds, inspection of entrails, stars, and whatnot. Many Stoics, notably Chrysippus, believed in such things, not least because they saw in them manifestations of the order of the cosmos and the tight and intricate interconnections within it, and thus saw them as scientific rather than superstitious.]

21

Let death and exile and everything that is terrible appear before your eyes every day, especially death; and you will never have anything contemptible in your thoughts or crave anything excessively.

22

If you crave philosophy prepare yourself on the spot to be ridiculed, to be jeered at by many people who will say, "Here he is again, all of a sudden turned philosopher on us!" and "Where did he get that high brow?" But don't *you* put on a high brow, but hold fast to the things that appear best to you, as someone assigned by god to this place. And remember that if you hold to these views, those who previously ridiculed you will later be impressed with you, but if you are defeated by them you will be doubly ridiculed.

23

If it ever happens that you turn outward to want to please another person, certainly you have lost your plan of life. Be content therefore in everything to be a philosopher, and if you want to seem to be one, make yourself appear so to yourself, and you will be capable of it.

24

Do not be weighed down by the consideration, "I shall live without any honor, everywhere a nobody!" For if lack of honors is something bad, I cannot be in a bad state because of another person any more than I can be in a shameful one. It is not your task[10] to gain political office, or be invited to a banquet, is it? Not at all. How then is that a lack of honor? And how will you be a nobody everywhere, if you need to be a somebody only in things that are up to you—in which it is open to you to be of the greatest worth? "But your friends will be without help!" What do you mean, "without help?" Well, they will be without a little cash from you, and you will not make them Roman citizens. Who told you, then, that these things are up to you and not the business of someone else? Who can give to someone else what he does not have himself? "Get money," someone says, "so that we may have some." If I can get it while keeping self-respect and trustworthiness and high-mindedness, show me the way and I will get it. But if you demand that I lose the good things that are mine so that you may acquire things that are not good, see for yourselves how unfair and inconsiderate you are. Which do you want more, money or a self-respecting and trustworthy friend? Then help me more toward this, and do not expect me to do things that will make me lose these qualities. "But my country," he says, "will be without help, in so far as it depends on me!" Again, what sort of "help" is this? So it will not have porticos and baths by your efforts. What does that amount to? For it does not have shoes because of the blacksmith or weapons because of the cobbler, but it is enough if each person fulfills his own task. And if you furnished for it

10. [The word translated "task" here and below is *ergon*, which might also be translated by "function."]

another citizen who was trustworthy and self-respecting, would you in no way be helpful to it? "Yes, I would be." Then neither would you yourself be unhelpful to it. "Then what place," he says "will I have in the city?" The one you can have by preserving your trustworthiness and self-respect. And if while wanting to help it you throw away these things, what use will you be to it if you turn out shameless and untrustworthy?

25

Has someone been given greater honor than you at a banquet or in a greeting or by being brought in to give advice? If these things are good, you should be glad that he has got them. If they are bad, do not be angry that you did not get them. And remember, you cannot demand an equal share if you did not do the same things, with a view to getting things that are not up to us. For how can someone who does not hang around a person's door have an equal share with someone who does, or someone who does not escort him with someone who does, or someone who does not praise him with someone who does? You will be unjust and greedy, then, if you want to obtain these things for free when you have not paid the price for which they are bought. Well, what is the price of heads of lettuce? An obol, say. So if someone who has paid an obol takes the heads of lettuce, and you who do not pay do not take them, do not think that you are worse off than the one who did. For just as he has the lettuce, you have the obol that you did not pay. It is the same way in this case. You were not invited to someone's banquet? You did not give the host the price of the meal. He sells it for praise; he sells it for attention. Then give him the balance for which it is sold, if that is to your advantage. But you are greedy and stupid if you want both not to pay and also to take. Have you got nothing, then, in place of the meal? Indeed you do have something; you did not praise someone you did not wish to praise, and you did not have to put up with the people around his door.

26

It is possible to learn the will of nature from the things in which we do not differ from each other. For example, when someone else's little slave boy breaks his cup we are ready to say, "It's one of those things that just happen." Certainly, then, when your own cup is broken you should be just the way you were when the other person's was broken. Transfer the same idea to larger matters. Someone else's child is dead, or his wife. There is no one would not say, "It's the lot of a human being." But when one's own dies, immediately it is, "Alas! Poor me!" But we should have remembered how we feel when we hear of the same thing about others.

27

Just as a target is not set up to be missed, in the same way nothing bad by nature happens in the world.[11]

---

11. [According to the Stoic view, the universe as a whole is perfect and everything in it has a place in its overall design, so that nothing can exist or occur that is bad in its relation to that overall design.]

28

If someone turned your body over to just any person who happened to meet you, you would be angry. But are you not ashamed that you turn over your own faculty of judgment to whoever happens along, so that if he abuses you it is upset and confused?

29

For each action, consider what leads up to it and what follows it, and approach it in the light of that. Otherwise you will come to it enthusiastically at first, since you have not borne in mind any of what will happen next, but later when difficulties turn up you will give up disgracefully. You want to win an Olympic victory? I do too, by the gods, since that is a fine thing. But consider what leads up to it and what follows it, and undertake the action in the light of that. You must be disciplined, keep a strict diet, stay away from cakes, train according to strict routine at a fixed time in heat and in cold, not drink cold water, not drink wine when you feel like it, and in general you must have turned yourself over to your trainer as to a doctor, and then in the contest "dig in,"[12] sometimes dislocate your hand, twist your ankle, swallow a lot of sand, sometimes be whipped, and, after all that, lose. Think about that and then undertake training, if you want to. Otherwise you will be behaving the way children do, who play wrestlers one time, gladiators another time, blow trumpets another time, then act a play. In this way you too are now an athlete, now a gladiator, then an orator, then a philosopher, yet you are nothing wholeheartedly, but like a monkey you mimic each sight that you see, and one thing after another is to your taste, since you do not undertake a thing after considering it from every side, but only randomly and half-heartedly.

In the same way when some people watch a philosopher and hear one speaking like Euphrates[13] (though after all who can speak like him?), they want to be philosophers themselves. Just you consider, as a human being, what sort of thing it is; then inspect your own nature and whether you can bear it. You want to do the pentathlon, or to wrestle? Look at your arms, your thighs, inspect your loins. Different people are naturally suited for different things. Do you think that if you do those things you can eat as you now do, drink as you now do, have the same likes and dislikes? You must go without sleep, put up with hardship, be away from your own people, be looked down on by a little slave boy, be laughed at by people who meet you, get the worse of it in everything, honor, public office, law course, every little thing. Think about whether you want to exchange these things for tranquillity, freedom, calm. If not, do not embrace philosophy, and do not like children be a philosopher at one time, later a tax-collector, than an orator, then a procurator of the emperor. These things do not go together. You must be one person, either good or bad. You must either work on your ruling principle,[14] or work on externals, practise the art either

---

12. [Nobody knows just what this expression means in this context.]

13. [Euphrates was a Stoic lecturer noted for his eloquence.]

14. [The "ruling principle" (or "governing principle"), the *hēgemonikon*, in the rather complicated psychological theory adopted by the Stoics, is that central part of the soul that can understand what is good and decide to act on that understanding. Cf. c. 38, n.]

of what is inside or of what is outside, that is, play the role either of a philosopher or of a non-philosopher.

30

Appropriate actions[15] are in general measured by relationships. He is a father: that entails taking care of him, yielding to him in everything, putting up with him when he abuses you or strikes you. "But he is a bad father." Does nature then determine that you have a good father? No, only that you have a father.[16] My brother has done me wrong." Then keep your place in relation to him; do not consider his action, but instead consider what you can do to bring your own faculty of choice[17] into accord with nature. Another person will not do you harm unless you wish it; you will be harmed at just that time at which you take yourself to be harmed. In this way, then, you will discover the appropriate actions to expect from a neighbor, from a citizen, from a general, if you are in the habit of looking at relationships.

31

The most important aspect of piety toward the gods is certainly both to have correct beliefs about them, as beings that arrange the universe well and justly, and to set yourself to obey them and acquiesce in everything that happens and to follow it willingly, as something brought to completion by the best judgment. For in this way you will never blame the gods or accuse them of neglecting you. And this piety is impossible unless you detach the good and the bad from what is not up to us and attach it exclusively to what is up to us, because if you think that any of what is not up to us is good or bad, then when you fail to get what you want and fall into what you do not want, you will be bound to blame and hate those who cause this. For every animal by nature flees and turns away from things that are harmful and from what causes them, and pursues and admires things that are beneficial and what causes them. There is therefore no way for a person who thinks he is being harmed to enjoy what he thinks is harming him, just as it is impossible to enjoy the harm itself. Hence a son even abuses his father when the father does not give him a share of things that he thinks are good; and thinking that being a tyrant was a good thing is what made enemies of Polyneices and Eteocles.[18] This is why the farmer too abuses the gods, and the sailor, and the merchant, and those who have lost their wives and children. For wherever someone's advantage lies, there he also shows piety. So whoever takes care to have desires and aversions as one should also in the same instance takes care about being pious. And it is always appropriate to make libations and sacrifices and give firstfruits according to the custom of one's forefathers, in a

---

15. ["Appropriate actions" are *kathēkonta*, which Cicero called *officia*, and are in English translations often called "duties," though the notion is actually somewhat different from that of duty. They are the actions that are of a type generally in accord with nature, or with a particular sort of person's place in it.]

16. [The idea here is, roughly, that there are certain relationships of affinity established by the natural order, and that having a father represents one of them, but that having a good father is not entailed by it.]

17. [Cf. c. 9, n., and c. 29, n.]

18. [The story of the conflict between the brothers Polyneices and Eteocles is best known to modern readers from Sophocles' tragedy, *Antigone*.]

manner that is pure and neither slovenly nor careless, nor indeed cheaply nor beyond one's means.

32

When you make use of fortune-telling, remember that you do not know what will turn out and have gone to the fortune-teller to find out, but that if you really are a philosopher you have gone already knowing what sort of thing it is. For if it is one of the things that is not up to us, it is bound to be neither good nor bad. Therefore do not bring desire or aversion to the fortune-teller and do not approach him trembling but instead realizing that everything that turns out is indifferent[19] and nothing in relation to you, and that whatever sort of thing it may be, you will be able to deal with it well and no one will hinder that. So go confidently to the gods as advisers, and thereafter when some particular advice has been given to you remember who your advisers are and whom you will be disregarding if you disobey. Approach fortune-telling as Socrates thought a person should, in cases where the whole consideration has reference to the outcome, and no resource is available from reason or any other technique to find out about the matter. So, when it is necessary to share a danger with a friend or with your country, do not use fortune-telling about whether you should share the danger. For if the fortune-teller says that the omens are unfavorable, clearly death is signified or the injury of a part of your body or exile. But reason chooses to stand by your friend and to share danger with your country even under these conditions. For this reason pay attention to the greater fortune-teller, Pythian Apollo, who threw out of the temple the man who did not help his brother when he was being murdered.[20]

33

Set up right now a certain character and pattern for yourself which you will preserve when you are by yourself and when you are with people. Be silent for the most part, or say what you have to in a few words. Speak rarely, when the occasion requires speaking, but not about just any topic that comes up, not about gladiators, horse-races, athletes, eating or drinking—the things that always come up; and especially if it is about people, talk without blaming or praising or comparing. Divert by your own talk, if you can, the talk of those with you to something appropriate. If you happen to be stranded among strangers, do not talk. Do not laugh a great deal or at a great many things or unrestrainedly. Refuse to swear oaths, altogether if possible, or otherwise as circumstances allow. Avoid banquets given by those outside philosophy. But if the appropriate occasion arises, take great care not to slide into their ways, since certainly if a person's companion is dirty the person who spends time with him, even if he happens to be clean, is bound to become dirty too. Take what has to do with the body to the point of bare need, such as food, drink, clothing, house, household slaves, and cut out everything that is for reputation or

19. [Things that are "indifferent" in the Stoic view are all things that are external and not up to oneself (cf. c. 1, e.g.).]

20. [The idea is that one does not need a fortune-teller to tell one whether one should defend one's country or one's friends, and that this fact was recognized by the oracle of Apollo at Delphi.]

luxury. As for sex stay pure as far as possible before marriage, and if you have it do only what is allowable. But do not be angry or censorious toward those who do engage in it, and do not always be making an exhibition of the fact that you do not.

If someone reports back to you that so-and-so is saying bad things about you, do not reply to them but answer, "Obviously he didn't know my other bad characteristics, since otherwise he wouldn't just have mentioned these."

For the most part there is no need to go to public shows, but if ever the right occasion comes do not show your concern to be for anything but yourself; that is to say, wish to have happen only what does happen, and for the person to win who actually does win, since that way you will not be thwarted. But refrain completely from shouting or laughing at anyone or being very much caught up in it. After you leave, do not talk very much about what has happened, except what contributes to your own improvement, since that would show that the spectacle had impressed you.

Do not go indiscriminately or readily to people's public lectures, but when you do be on guard to be dignified and steady and at the same time try not to be disagreeable.

When you are about to meet someone, especially someone who seems to be distinguished, put to yourself the question, "What would Socrates or Zeno have done in these circumstances?" and you will not be at a loss as to how to deal with the occasion. When you go to see someone who is important, put to yourself the thought that you will not find him at home, that you will be shut out, that the door will be slammed, that he will pay no attention to you. If it is appropriate to go even under these conditions, go and put up with what happens, and never say to yourself, "It wasn't worth all that!" For that is the way of a non-philosopher, someone who is misled by externals.

In your conversations stay away from making frequent and longwinded mention of what you have done and the dangers that you have been in, since it is not as pleasant for others to hear about what has happened to you as it is for you to remember your own dangers.

Stay away from raising a laugh, since this manner slips easily into vulgarity and at the same time is liable to lessen your neighbors' respect for you. It is also risky to fall into foul language. So when anything like that occurs, if a good opportunity arises, go so far as to criticize the person who has done it, and otherwise by staying silent and blushing and frowning you will show that you are displeased by what has been said.

34

Whenever you encounter some kind of apparent pleasure, be on guard, as in the case of other appearances, not to be carried away by it, but let the thing wait for you and allow yourself to delay. Then bring before your mind two times, both the time when you enjoy the pleasure and the time when after enjoying it you later regret it and berate yourself; and set against these the way you will be pleased and will praise yourself if you refrain from it. But if the right occasion appears for you to undertake the action, pay attention so that you will not be overcome by its attractiveness and pleasantness and seductiveness, and set against it how much better it is to be conscious of having won this victory against it.

35

When you do something that you determine is to be done, never try not to be seen doing it, even if most people are likely to think something bad about it. If you are not doing it rightly, avoid the act itself; if you are doing it rightly, why do you fear those who will criticize you wrongly?

36

Just as the propositions "It is day" and "It is night" have their full value when disjoined [*sc.,* in "It is day *or* it is night"] but have negative value when conjoined [*sc.,* in "It is day *and* it is night"], in the same way, granted that taking the larger portion has value for one's body, it has negative value for preserving the fellowship of a banquet in the way one should.[21] So when you eat with another, remember not merely to see the value for your body of what lies in front of you, but also to preserve your respect for your host.

37

If you undertake some role beyond your capacity, you both disgrace yourself by taking it and also thereby neglect the role that you were unable to take.

38

Just as in walking about you pay attention so as not to step on a nail or twist your foot, pay attention in the same way so as not to harm your ruling principle.[22] And if we are on guard about this in every action, we shall set about it more securely.

39

The measure of possessions for each person is the body, as the foot is of the shoe. So if you hold to this principle you will preserve the measure; but if you step beyond it, you will in the end be carried as if over a cliff; just as in the case of the shoe, if you go beyond the foot, you get a gilded shoe, and then a purple embroidered one. For there is no limit to a thing once it is beyond its measure.

40

Women are called ladies by men right after they are fourteen. And so when they see that they have nothing else except to go to bed with men, they begin to make themselves up and place all their hopes in that. It is therefore worthwhile to pay attention so that they are aware that they are honored for nothing other than appearing modest and self-respecting.

21. [Very roughly, the idea is that the value of an action has to be judged from all features of the context. The parallel is that allegedly the meaningfulness of a sentence depends in a way on its context.]

22. [Cf. c. 29, n. 14.]

41

It shows lack of natural talent to spend time on what concerns the body, as in exercising a great deal, eating a great deal, drinking a great deal, moving one's bowels or copulating a great deal. Instead you must do these things in passing, but turn your whole attention toward your faculty of judgment.[23]

42

When someone acts badly toward you or speaks badly of you, remember that he does or says it in the belief that it is appropriate for him to do so. Accordingly he cannot follow what appears to you but only what appears to him, so that if things appear badly to him, he is harmed in as much as he has been deceived. For if someone thinks that a true conjunctive proposition[24] is false, the conjunction is not harmed but rather the one who is deceived. Starting from these considerations you will be gentle with the person who abuses you. For you must say on each occasion, "That's how it seemed to him."

43

Everything has two handles, one by which it may be carried and the other not. If your brother acts unjustly toward you, do not take hold of it by this side, that he has acted unjustly (since this is the handle by which it may not be carried), but instead by this side, that he is your brother and was brought up with you, and you will be taking hold of it in the way that it can be carried.

44

These statements are not valid inferences: "I am richer than you; therefore I am superior to you", or "I am more eloquent than you; therefore I am superior to you." But rather these are valid: "I am richer than you; therefore my property is superior to yours", or "I am more eloquent than you; therefore my speaking is superior to yours." But you are identical neither with your property nor with your speaking.

45

Someone takes a bath quickly; do not say that he does it badly but that he does it quickly. Someone drinks a great deal of wine; do not say that he does it badly but that he does a great deal of it. For until you have discerned what his judgment was, how do you know whether he did it badly? In this way it will not turn out that you

23. [Cf. c. 29, n. 14. The claim is in effect that one should be concerned wholly with the state of the ruling part of one's soul, and not with external states of affairs or with those aspects of the soul, such as one's affective feelings or desires, that are directly dependent on external states of affairs. One can see here the Stoic view, which seems paradoxical to many, that one's feelings and non-rational desires are in a crucial sense external to one's true self (cf. c. 6 and Introd.).]

24. [Cf. c. 36. A proposition of this sort consists of two component propositions conjoined by "and".]

receive convincing appearances of some things but give assent to quite different ones.[25]

46

Never call yourself a philosopher and do not talk a great deal among non-philosophers about philosophical propositions, but do what follows from them. For example, at a banquet do not say how a person ought to eat, but eat as a person ought to. Remember that Socrates had so completely put aside ostentation that people actually went to him when they wanted to be introduced to philosophers, and he took them.[26] He was that tolerant of being overlooked. And if talk about philosophical propositions arises among non-philosophers, for the most part be silent, since there is a great danger of your spewing out what you have not digested. And when someone says to you that you know nothing and you are not hurt by it, then you know that you are making a start at your task. Sheep do not show how much they have eaten by bringing the feed to the shepherds, but they digest the food inside themselves, and outside themselves they bear wool and milk. So in your case likewise do not display propositions to non-philosophers but instead the actions that come from the propositions when they are digested.

47

When you have become adapted to living cheaply as far as your body is concerned, do not make a show of it, and if you drink water do not say at every opening that you drink water. If you wish to train yourself to hardship, do it for yourself and not for those outside. Do not throw your arms around statues.[27] Instead, when you are terribly thirsty, take cold water into your mouth, and spit it out, and do not tell anyone about it.

48

The position and character of a non-philosopher: he never looks for benefit or harm to come from himself but from things outside. The position and character of a philosopher: he looks for all benefit and harm to come from himself.

Signs of someone's making progress: he censures no one; he praises no one; he blames no one; he never talks about himself as a person who amounts to something or knows something. When he is thwarted or prevented in something, he accuses himself. And if someone praises him he laughs to himself at the person who has praised him; and if someone censures him he does not respond. He goes around like an invalid, careful not to move any of his parts that are healing before they have

---

25. [A "convincing appearance" is a *katalēptikē phantasia*, the sort of appearance that according to the Stoics is a self-evidently correct representation of the way things actually are (cf. n. 3). "Assent" is *synkatathesis*. Correct assent would of course be assent to self-evidently correct appearances. The line of thought here is, however, quite compressed, and the student will find it a difficult exercise to explain it.]

26. [The allusion is perhaps to the events in the early part of Plato's *Protagoras*.]

27. [According to a story in Diog. Laert. 6.23, Diogenes, the Cynic did this nude in cold weather, to toughen himself. But the statues were outdoors, and Diogenes was a bit of a show-off (but cf. n. 8!).]

become firm. He has kept off all desire from himself, and he has transferred all aversion onto what is against nature among the things that are up to us. His impulses toward everything are diminished. If he seems foolish or ignorant, he does not care. In a single phrase, he is on guard against himself as an enemy lying in wait.

49

When someone acts grand because he understands and can expound the works of Chrysippus,[28] say to yourself, "If Chrysippus had not written unclearly, this man would have nothing to be proud of."

But what do *I* want? To learn to understand nature and follow it. So I try to find out who explains it. And I hear that Chrysippus does, and I go to him. But I do not understand the things that he has written, so I try to find the person who explains them. Up to this point there is nothing grand. But when I do find someone who explains them, what remains is to carry out what has been conveyed to me. This alone is grand. But if I am impressed by the explaining itself, what have I done but ended up a grammarian instead of a philosopher—except that I am explaining Chrysippus instead of Homer. Instead, when someone says to me, "Read me some Chrysippus," I turn red when I cannot exhibit actions that are similar to his words and in harmony with them.

50

Abide by whatever task is set before you as if it were a law, and as if you would be committing sacrilege if you went against it. But pay no attention to whatever anyone says about you, since that falls outside what is yours.

51

How long do you put off thinking yourself worthy of the best things, and never going against the definitive capacity of reason?[29] You have received the philosophical propositions that you ought to agree to and you have agreed to them. Then what sort of teacher are you still waiting for, that you put off improving yourself until he comes? You are not a boy any more, but already a full-grown man. If you now neglect things and are lazy and are always making delay after delay and set one day after another as the day for paying attention to yourself, then without realizing it you will make no progress but will end up a non-philosopher all through life and death. So decide now that you are worthy of living as a full-grown man who is making progress, and make everything that seems best be a law that you cannot go against. And if you meet with any hardship or anything pleasant or reputable or disreputable, then remember that the contest is *now* and the Olympic games are *now* and you cannot put things off any more and that your progress is made or destroyed by a single day and a single action. Socrates became fully perfect in this way, by not

28. [On Chrysippus, see the Introduction.]

29. [In brief, the capacity of reason here is that of distinguishing different things from each other and defining them.]

paying attention to anything but his reason in everything that he met with. You, even if you are not yet Socrates, ought to live as someone wanting to be Socrates.

52

The first and most necessary aspect of philosophy is that of dealing with philosophical propositions, such as "not to hold to falsehood." The second is that of demonstrations, for example, "How come one must not hold to falsehood?" The third is that of the confirmation and articulation of these, for example. "How come this is a demonstration? What is demonstration? What is entailment? What is conflict? What is truth? What is falsity?" Therefore the third is necessary because of the second, and the second because of the first; but the most necessary, and the one where one must rest, is the first. We, however, do it backwards, since we spend time in the third and all of our effort goes into it, and we neglect the first completely. Therefore we hold to falsehood, but we are ready to explain how it is demonstrated that one must not hold to falsehood.

53

On every occasion you must have these thoughts ready:

> Lead me, Zeus, and you too, Destiny,
> Wherever I am assigned by you;
> I'll follow and not hesitate,
> But even if I do not wish to,
> Because I'm bad, I'll follow anyway.

> Whoever has complied well with necessity
> Is counted wise by us, and understands divine affairs.

> Well, Crito, if it is pleasing to the gods this way, then
>   let it happen this way.

> Anytus and Meletus can kill me, but they can't harm
>   me.[30]

30. [These four bits of poetry have the following origins. The first is by Cleanthes, who was head of the Stoic school at Athens between Zeno and Chrysippus. The second is a fragment of Euripides (fr. 965 Nauck). The third is Plato, *Crito* 43d, and the fourth is Plato, *Apology* 30c–d (slightly modified as compared with our manuscript texts), both purporting to be quotations from Socrates (cf. n. 8).]

AUGUSTINE

Like the Thirty Years' War (1618–1648) and the French Revolution (1789–1795), the sack of Rome by the Visigoths in 410 C.E. and the destruction of the Roman Empire was an event of momentous significance. At the time many Romans saw their world in ruins and sought to understand the event and to explain it, in part to assign blame and thereby to indict those responsible. Among these were pagan thinkers who ascribed Rome's downfall to Christianity. In 312 Rome had become Christian, under Constantine; the results, these pagans claimed, were the weakened loyalty of its citizens, an otherworldly abandonment of civic responsibility, and desertion of the gods of the city. All this led to Rome's weakness and her destruction and provided an historical refutation of the Church. By 413, Augustine (354–430), the Bishop of Hippo in North Africa, had written the first three books of his reply to these charges, his sweeping panorama of history and eschatology, of the goal of history and the role of the state in it, of the nature of society and the two cities—the City of God and the earthly city—that constitute it, and of the two types of love that ground these two cities. *De Civitate Dei* (*The City of God*), begun in 413 and completed in 426, speaks out of the dramatic encounter between Augustine and the critics of Christianity in the early fifth century, but it is a work that transcends this situation and addresses all subsequent attempts to understand the complex relations among politics, religion, history, and the moral ends of human life. In it, moreover, Augustine not only responds to the critics of Christianity; he also incorporates into his own conception of the "city of man" many central political values of his republican, stoic, and Roman law opponents, thereby providing a vehicle for transmitting these values to medieval Europe.

Augustine was born in 354 in Thagaste, in North Africa. His father was pagan, his mother, Monica, a Christian. As a youngster Augustine studied Latin and the Latin classics. By 370 he was in Carthage, mastering the works of classical rhetoric and becoming increasingly estranged from his mother's Christianity. In 374 he moved back to Thagaste to teach rhetoric, and then returned to Carthage, where he established a school of rhetoric.

During this period Augustine read Cicero's dialogue *Hortensius* (a work now lost) and was stimulated by it to pursue wisdom and truth through philosophy, in place of the irrational Christian doctrines he had rejected. He found an alternative in Manichaeism, a doctrine of two principles, the forces of light and darkness, of good and evil, that are eternally engaged in battle over the soul of each person and over the world itself. Augustine was especially drawn to this dualistic theory as a solution to the problem of the existence of evil, which the theory ascribed to the force of evil and not to God, and the problem of base human desires and passions.

In 383 Augustine moved to Rome, once again to teach rhetoric, and in 384 took the position of municipal professor of rhetoric in Milan. There Augustine was introduced to a neo-Platonic interpretation of Christianity in the sermons of Ambrose, the Bishop of Milan, and through acquaintance with other Christian intellectuals in Ambrose's circle. Here, finally, was the true philosophy which he had been seeking. By 386 Augustine was converted, and in 387 Ambrose baptized him into the Church.

Augustine returned to Thagaste in 388, where he established with friends a small monastic community. Within a few years and against his wishes, he was ordained a priest and called upon to aid the pastoral affairs of the aged Bishop of Hippo, a seaport town one hundred fifty miles west of Carthage. When the Bishop died in 396, Augustine replaced him, a position which he held until his death. During the years of his episcopacy, Augustine wrote extensively—Scriptural commentaries, theological treatises, letters, and much else. He engaged in polemics and controversies, with the Donatists and Pelagians, among others, delivered sermons, and conducted the affairs of his diocese. In 410 he completed his most important doctrinal work, *De Trinitate* (*On the Trinity*), and in 400 he published his greatest work, the *Confessions*, in which he recounts the spiritual journey of his first thirty-three years.

In 430, twenty years after the Visigoths had sacked Rome, the Vandals, under Genseric, flooded into Northern Africa from Spain and besieged Hippo. In the midst of the crisis, on August 28, 430, Augustine died, in time to avoid seeing the invaders burn his city.

Recommended readings

Brown, Peter. *Augustine of Hippo*. Berkeley: University of California Press, 1967.

Burns, James (ed.). *Cambridge History of Medieval Political Thought, 350–1450*. Cambridge: Cambridge University Press, 1989.

Gilson, Etienne. *The Christian Philosophy of St. Augustine*. New York: Random House, 1968.

Kirwan, Christopher. *Augustine*. London: Routledge, 1979.

Markus, R. A. (ed.). *Augustine*. Garden City: Doubleday, 1972.

CITY OF GOD

PART FIVE
THE ENDS OF THE TWO CITIES

BOOK XIX

Chapter 1

From this point on, I see that I must discuss the appointed ends of the two cities of earth and of heaven. But first I must set forth, within the limits which my work allows, the kind of philosophical efforts men have made in their search for happiness amid the sorrows of this mortal life. My purpose is, first, to point out the difference between their hollow aspirations and the holy assurances which God has given us; second, to make clear what is meant by the true beatitude which He will grant. For this latter purpose I shall appeal not only to divine Revelation but to such natural reasoning as will appeal to those who do not share our faith.

In regard to what is supremely good and supremely evil, philosophers have taken many different stands—all striving with the highest earnestness to determine what it is that makes men happy. By definition, our supreme end is that good which is sought for its own sake, and on account of which all other goods are sought. In the same way, the supreme evil is that on account of which other evils are avoided, whereas it is to be avoided on its own account. For the moment, we shall say that the ultimate good is not so much a good to end all goods as, rather, one by which goodness reaches its fullest consummation. In the same way, the ultimate evil is not one in which evil comes to an end, but the one in which evil reaches the very height of harm. It is in this sense that the greatest good and the worst evil are called ends or ultimates.

To determine what these ultimates are and then, in this life, to obtain the supreme good and avoid the supreme evil—such has been the aim and effort of all who have professed a zeal for wisdom in this world of shadows. Of course, for all their aberrations, the nature of man has set limits to men's deviations from the right track, seeing that the ultimate good and evil must be found either in the soul, or in the body, or in both. It was under these three general heads that Marcus Varro, in his work, *On Philosophy*, listed the immense variety of opinions which he examined with such careful and subtle scrutiny; he remarked that, by the application of various differentiating notes, he could easily reach no less than 288 possible species of opinions—not, of course, that there were that many schools in existence.

For the purpose of my exposition, I shall begin with an observation of Varro in the work just mentioned, namely, that there are four ends which men naturally pursue, irrespective of any teacher, formal education, or training in that purposeful art of living which we call virtue, and which is indubitably a matter of learning. These ends are: first, pleasure aroused by the pleasant stirring of our bodily senses;

second, calm, in the sense of the absence of all bodily vexation; third, that combination of pleasure and serenity which Epicurus called, in a single word, pleasure; fourth, the primary demands of nature which include, besides pleasure and calm, such needs of our body as wholeness, health, security, and such needs of our soul as man's innate spiritual powers, whether great or small. These four—pleasure, serenity, their combination, and the primary exigencies of nature—are so much a part of us that it is either on their account that we pursue the virtue which education brings us; or else they are sought on account of virtue; or else these four and virtue are sought, each on its own account. Hence, we get twelve schools of thought, since each of the four ends can be looked at in three ways. A single illustration will make this whole matter clear.

Take bodily pleasure. This can be either subordinated or preferred or merely joined to virtue in the soul. Hence, we get three different schools of thought. Pleasure is subordinate to virtue when it is a means to the practice of virtue. For example, it is a part of virtue to live in one's native land and to beget children for the sake of the fatherland—neither of which is possible without bodily pleasure, since we cannot eat to live without pleasure nor, without pleasure, take the means to propagate a family. On the other hand, when pleasure is preferred to virtue, it is sought for its own sake and virtue is pursued as a means for the sake of pleasure. This is to say that virtue makes no effort save to procure or to make secure some bodily pleasure. Strange life, indeed, where pleasure is the mistress and virtue is the handmaid! No such handmaid could, in fact, be called a virtue; yet this shameless and revolting theory has found philosophers to back and defend it.

Pleasure is combined with virtue when each is sought for itself and neither for the other. Thus, just as pleasure is subordinated to, or preferred to, or co-ordinated with, virtue—making three schools—so calm, a combination of pleasure and calm, and the primary needs of nature can each be taken as a criterion to produce three distinct schools. According to the variety of human opinions, these ends are sometimes subordinated to, sometimes preferred to, and sometimes made coordinate with, virtue; thus, the number of schools becomes twelve. But this number, in turn, is doubled the moment we introduce another distinction, that between individual and social life; for, anyone who follows one or other of the twelve schools mentioned above does so either for himself alone, or because of some neighbor for whom he ought to wish what he wishes for himself. Hence, there are twelve schools of those who hold that each of the opinions is to be held for purely personal reasons, and a second twelve made up of those who think they should philosophize in this way or that, not merely with a view to their own personal living, but because of others whose good they seek as they seek their own. And these twenty-four schools become twice as many, namely, forty-eight, by introducing a distinction from the philosophy of the New Academy;[1] for, each of the twenty-four opinions can be held and defended as certain (as the Stoics defended as certain their opinion that the good which makes a man happy is to be found solely in the virtue of the soul), or each of them can be held as being uncertain (much as the members of the New Academy defended their view merely as a probability). Thus, there are twenty-four schools of those who hold their views as certain because they are true, and another twenty-four made up of

1. [Or, as we would say today, Middle Academy.—Trans.]

those who think they should follow their views because they seem probable, although not certain.

Again, each of these forty-eight schools may be followed either after the manner of the Cynics, or after the manner of other philosophers; and by this distinction the forty-eight becomes ninety-six. Moreover, any of these opinions can be so followed and defended either with a view to the life of contemplative leisure (as in the case of those who would and could devote all their time to the study of the truth), or with a view to an active life (as in the case of those who, though philosophers, are actually engaged in the administration of State affairs or other human enterprises), or, finally with a view to a mixed life, both active and contemplative (as in the case of those who find time to alternate periods of scholarly leisure with periods of necessary business). By such differences the number of the schools can be tripled and brought up to 288.

All this is in Varro's book, but I have summarized what he says as clearly as I could in language of my own. Varro goes on to refute all the other views save the one he thinks to be the view of the Old Academy, as founded by Plato and adhered to up to the time of Polemon, the fourth leader of the school. It seemed to Varro that this school held their views as certain, and thus he distinguishes it from the New Academy (the kind of philosophy that began with Arcesilaus, the successor of Polemon, according to which everything is open to doubt). It seemed to Varro that the school of the Old Academy was free from all doubt and all error. Just how he reached these conclusions it would take me too long to show in detail. I cannot, however, forego all discussion of this matter.

What Varro first does is to remove all those distinguishing marks which merely multiply the number of schools but fail to include what is essential, namely, the supreme good. For, he thinks that no school of philosophy is worthy of the name unless it differs from others in what it regards as the ultimate good and the ultimate evil. The reason for this is that no one has any right to philosophize except with a view to happiness. Now, what makes a man happy is the supreme good. Hence, there is no reason for philosophizing apart from the supreme good. From this it follows that no school of philosophy is properly so called unless its search is for the supreme good.

Take the matter of social life. Is it to be entered upon by a philosopher as the supreme good by which he is both rendered happy and also seeks and procures his neighbor's good as he does his own, or should he cultivate it purely out of consideration for his own happiness? When we raise these questions we do not touch the matter of the supreme good itself, but merely ask whether or not our neighbor is to be reckoned as a sharer in this good on our account or on account of the neighbor himself, in the sense that we rejoice in his good as we do in our own.

So, too, with the question of the New Academy and its universal skepticism. When we ask whether all those matters which are the concern of philosophy are to be considered doubtful or whether we should consider them certain as other philosophers do, there is no question here as to what is to be sought as the supreme good, but merely whether or not we should have doubts as to the reality of the supreme good which we think should be pursued. In plain words, the question here is whether the person pursuing the supreme good should so pursue it as to call it a real good, or pursue it in such wise that he is willing to say that it is probably an objective good, although it may not be so—one and the same good, meanwhile, being pursued in both cases.

So, too, there is the distinction drawn from the dress and ways of the Cynics. Here the question raised is not the nature of the supreme good. The question is whether a person pursuing the supreme good—whatever he happens to think is the good that is both true and to be pursued—should pursue it in the dress and ways of the Cynics.

Finally, there have been philosophers who pursued quite different ends as being ultimates—some, virtue; others, pleasure—yet observed the idiosyncrasies of life that gave the Cynics their name. Hence, whatever it was that distinguished the Cynics from other philosophers, certainly it had nothing to do with choosing and holding to a good which might make them happy. For, if manners had anything to do with this matter, then similarity of manners would compel men to pursue the same end, and any variety would make this impossible.

Chapter 4

If I am asked what stand the City of God would take on the issues raised and, first, what this City thinks of the supreme good and ultimate evil, the answer would be: She holds that eternal life is the supreme good and eternal death the supreme evil, and that we should live rightly in order to obtain the one and avoid the other. Hence the Scriptural expression, 'the just man lives by faith'[2]—by faith, for the fact is that we do not now behold our good and, therefore, must seek it by faith; nor can we of ourselves even live rightly, unless He who gives us faith helps us to believe and pray, for it takes faith to believe that we need His help.

Those who think that the supreme good and evil are to be found in this life are mistaken. It makes no difference whether it is in the body or in the soul or in both—or, specifically, in pleasure or virtue or in both—that they seek the supreme good. They seek in vain whether they look to serenity, to virtue, or to both; whether to pleasure plus serenity, or to virtue, or to all three; or to the satisfaction of our innate exigencies, or to virtue, or to both. It is in vain that men look for beatitude on earth or in human nature. Divine Truth, as expressed in the Prophet's words, makes them look foolish: 'The Lord knows the thoughts of men'[3] or, as the text is quoted by St. Paul: 'The Lord knows the thoughts of the wise that they are vain.'[4]

For, what flow of eloquence is sufficient to set forth the miseries of human life? Cicero did the best he could in his *Consolatio de morte filiae*, but how little was his very best? As for the primary satisfactions of our nature, when or where or how can they be so securely possessed in this life that they are not subject to the ups and downs of fortune? There is no pain of body, driving out pleasure, that may not befall the wise man; no anxiety that may not banish calm. A man's physical integrity is ended by the amputation or crippling of any of his limbs; his beauty is spoiled by deformity, his health by sickness, his vigor by weariness, his agility by torpor and sluggishness.

2. [Gal. 3.11.]

3. [Ps. 93.11.]

4. [1 Cor. 3.20.]

There is not one of these that may not afflict the flesh even of a philosopher. Among our elementary requirements we reckon a graceful and becoming erectness and movement; but what happens to these as soon as some sickness brings on palsy or, still worse, a spinal deformity so severe that a man's hands touch the ground as though he were a four-footed beast? What is then left of any beauty or dignity in a man's posture or gait? Turn, now, to the primary endowments of the soul: senses to perceive and intelligence to understand the truth. How much sensation does a man have left if, for example, he goes deaf and blind? And where does the reason or intelligence go, into what strange sleep, when sickness unsettles the mind? We can hardly hold back our tears when mad men say or do extravagant things—things wholly unlike their customary behavior and normal goodness. To witness such things, even to recall them, makes a decent man weep. Still worse is the case of those possessed by demons. Their intelligence seems driven away, not to say destroyed, when an evil spirit according to its will makes use of their body and soul. And who can be sure that even a philosopher will not be such a victim at some time in his life?

Further, what is to be said of our perception of the truth, at the very best? What kind of truth and how much of it can we reach through our bodily senses? Do we not read in the truth-speaking Book of Wisdom: 'For the corruptible body is a load upon the soul, and the earthly habitation presseth down the mind that museth upon many things'?[5]

And what of the urge and appetite for action—*hormé*, as the Greeks call it—which is reckoned among the primary goods of our nature? Is not this the root, too, of those restless energies of the madmen who fill us with tears and fears when their senses deceive them and their reason refuses to function?

So much for the elementary endowments of nature. Look, now, at virtue herself, which comes later with education and claims for herself the topmost place among human goods. Yet, what is the life of virtue save one unending war with evil inclinations, and not with solicitations of other people alone, but with evil inclinations that arise within ourselves and are our very own.

I speak especially of temperance—*sōphrosynē*, as the Greeks call it—which must bridle our fleshly lusts if they are not to drag our will to consent to abominations of every sort. The mere fact that, as St. Paul says, 'the flesh is at war with the spirit,' is no small flaw in our nature; and virtue is at war with this evil inclination when, in the same Apostle's words, 'the spirit lusts against the flesh.' These are opposed to each other to such a degree that 'we do not the things that we would.'[6] And when we seek final rest in the supreme good, what do we seek save an end to this conflict between flesh and spirit, freedom from this propensity to evil against which the spirit is at war? Yet, will as we may, such liberty cannot be had in mortal life.

This much, however, we can do with the help of God—not yield by surrender of the spirit and be dragged into sin willingly. Meanwhile, we must not fondly imagine that, so long as we wage this inward war, we may achieve that longed-for beatitude which can be solely the prize of the victor. For there lives no man so perfected in wisdom as not to have some conflict with excessive desires.

Take, next, the virtue called prudence. Is not this virtue constantly on the lookout

5. [Wisd. 9.15.]

6. [Gal. 5.17.]

to distinguish what is good from what is evil, so that there may be no mistake made in seeking the one and avoiding the other? So it bears witness to the fact that we are surrounded by evil and have evil within us. This virtue teaches that it is evil to consent to desires leading to sin and good to resist them. And what prudence preaches temperance puts into practice. Yet, neither prudence nor temperance can rid this life of the evils that are their constant concern.

Finally, there is justice. Its task is to see that to each is given what belongs to each. And this holds for the right order within man himself, so that it is just for the soul to be subordinate to God, and the body to the soul, and thus for body and soul taken together to be subject to God. Is there not abundant evidence that this virtue is unremittingly struggling to effect this internal order—and is far from finished? For, the less a man has God in his thoughts, the less is his soul subject to God; the more the flesh lusts counter to the spirit, the less the flesh is subject to the soul. So long, then, as such weakness, such moral sickliness remains within us, how can we dare to say that we are out of danger; and, if not yet out of danger, how can we say that our happiness is complete?

Look, now, at the great virtue called fortitude. Is not its very function—to bear patiently with misfortune—overwhelming evidence that human life is beset with unhappiness, however wise a man may be? It is beyond my comprehension how the Stoics can boldly argue that such ills are not really ills, meanwhile allowing that, if a philosopher should be tried by them beyond his obligation or duty to bear, he may have no choice but to take the easy way out by committing suicide. So stultifying is Stoic pride that, all evidences to the contrary, these men still pretend to find the ultimate good in this life and to hold that they are themselves the source of their own happiness. Their kind of sage—an astonishingly silly sage, indeed—may go deaf, dumb and blind, may be crippled, wracked with pain, visited with every imaginable affliction, driven at last to take his own life, yet have the colossal impertinence to call such an existence the happy life! Happy life, indeed, which employs death's aid to end it! If such a life is happy, then I say, live it! Why pretend that evils are not evils, when they not only overcome the virtue of fortitude and force it to yield to evil, but make a man so irrational as to call one and the same life both happy and unlivable? How can anyone be so blind as not to see that if life is happy it should not be shunned? Yet, the moment sickness opens her mouth they say one must choose a way out. If so, why do they not bow their stiff necks and admit life's unhappiness? Now, let me ask: Was it courage or cowardice that made their hero Cato kill himself?[7] Certainly, he would not have done what he did had he not been too cowardly to endure the victory of Caesar. Where, then, was his fortitude? It was a fortitude that yielded, that surrendered, that was so beaten that Cato ran away, deserted, abandoned the happy life. Or, maybe it was no longer the happy life? In that case, it was unhappy. If so, how can anyone deny that the ills that made Cato's life unhappy and unlivable were real evils?

From this it follows that those who admit that such things are evils, so do the Aristotelians and those of the Old Academy whom Varro defends, are nearer the truth than the Stoics, even though Varro also makes the egregious mistake of maintaining that this life is still the happy life in spite of evils so grievous that, for one who suffers them, suicide becomes imperative. 'The pains and afflictions of the

---

7. [Cf. Plutarch, *Cato Minor*, 66–70.]

body,' Varro admits, 'are evils; and the worse the pains, the greater the evil. To escape them you should end your life.' I ask: Which life? He answers: 'This life which is made grievous by so many evils.' Life, then, is the happy life in the midst of evils which drive a man to escape from life? Is it, perhaps, the happy life precisely because you are allowed to escape its unhappiness by death? Suppose you should be bound by a divine law to remain in its evils and be permitted neither to die nor ever to be free from such misfortunes? Then, at least, you would have to say that such a life would be unhappy. And, surely, if you admit it would be unhappy if unending, you cannot say that it is not unhappy just because there is a quick way out. You cannot maintain that just because unhappiness is short-lived it is really not unhappiness at all; or, what is more preposterous, that because unhappiness is short-lived it deserves to be called happiness.

No, these ills of life must be very real indeed if they can drive even a sage of their type to take his life. For, these philosophers say—and rightly say—that the first and most fundamental command of nature is that a man should cherish his own human life and, by his very nature, shun death; that a man should be his own best friend, wanting and working with all his might and main to keep himself alive and to preserve the union of his body and soul. These ills must be very real indeed if they can subdue the very instinct of nature that struggles in every possible way to put death off; overwhelm it so utterly that death, once shunned, is now desired, sought, and, when all else fails, is self-inflicted. Yes, very real, when they can turn courage into a killer, if, indeed, there be any question of genuine courage, when this virtue, devised to support and steel a man, is so battered down by misfortune that—having failed to sustain him—it is driven, against its very function, to finish him off. It is true, of course, that a philosopher should face death as well as all other trials, with fortitude, but that means death coming upon him from without.

If then, as these philosophers held, even a wise man must yield to suicide, they ought logically to admit that there are evils—even insufferable evils—that account for this tragic compulsion; and that a life so burdensome, so exposed to fortune's ebb and flow, should not be called happy! Nor would those who talk of 'the happy life' ever have called life happy if they had yielded to the truth and the cogency of reason in their search for the happy life as readily as they yield to unhappiness and the weight of evils when they lose their life by suicide; and if, further, they had given up the idea that they could enjoy the supreme good in this mortal life. They would have realized that man's very virtues, his best and most useful possessions, are the most solid evidences of the miseries of life, precisely because their function is to stand by him in perils and problems and pains.

For, when virtues are genuine virtues—and that is possible only when men believe in God—they make no pretense of protecting their possessors from unhappiness, for that would be a false promise; but they do claim that human life, now compelled to feel the misery of so many grievous ills on earth, can, by the hope of heaven, be made both happy and secure. If we are asked how a life can be happy before we are saved, we have the answer of St. Paul: 'For in hope were we saved. But hope that is seen is not hope. For how can a man hope for what he sees? But if we hope for what we do not see, we wait for it with patience.'[8]

---

8. [Rom. 8.24, 25.]

Of course, the Apostle was not speaking of men lacking prudence, fortitude, temperance, and justice, but of men whose virtues were true virtues because the men were living by faith. Thus, as 'we are saved by hope,' so we are made happy by hope. Neither our salvation nor our beatitude is here present, but 'we wait for it' in the future, and we wait 'with patience,' precisely because we are surrounded by evils which patience must endure until we come to where all good things are sources of inexpressible happiness and where there will be no longer anything to endure. Such is to be our salvation in the hereafter, such our final blessedness. It is because the philosophers will not believe in this beatitude which they cannot see that they go on trying to fabricate here below an utterly fraudulent felicity built on virtue filled with pride and bound to fail them in the end.

Chapter 5

So much for the philosophers' 'happy life.' What we Christians like better is their teaching that the life of virtue should be a social life. For, if the life of the saints had not been social, how could the City of God (which we have been discussing in all these nineteen Books) have a beginning, make progress, and reach its appointed goal? Yet, social living, given the misery of our mortality, has enormous drawbacks— more than can be easily counted, or known for what they really are. Just recall the words of a character in one of the pagan comedies who is applauded for expressing everyone's feeling:

> A wife I wed. What a worry, the shrew!
> The babies were born, and the worries grew.[9]

And remember the troubles of lovers listed by the same Terence:

> Slights and fights and spirits vexed,
> War today and peace the next.[10]

All human relationships are fraught with such misunderstandings. Not even the pure-hearted affection of friends is free from them. All history is a tale of 'slights and fights and spirits vexed,' and we must expect such unpleasantness as an assured thing, whereas peace is a good unguaranteed—dependent upon the unknowable interior dispositions of our friends. Even if we could read their hearts today, anything might happen tomorrow. Take the members of a single family. Who are as fond of one another as, in general, they are or, at least, are expected to be? Yet, who can rely utterly even on family affection? How much unhappiness has sprung from the ambush of domestic disloyalties! And how galling the disillusionment after peace had been so sweet—or seemed to be, though in fact it was nothing but a clever counterfeit. That is why no one can read, without a sigh, those touching words of Cicero: 'No snares are ever so insidious as those lurking as dutiful devotion or labeled as family affection. You can easily escape from an open foe, but when hatred

9. [Terence, *Adelphi* 5.4.13, 14.]

10. [*Eunuchus* 1.1.14, 15.]

lurks in the bosom of a family it has taken a position and has pounced upon you before it can be spied out or recognized for what it is.'[11]

Even divine Revelation reminds us: 'And a man's enemies will be those of his own household.'[12] It breaks the heart of any good man to hear this, for, even if he be brave enough to bear, or vigilant enough to beware of, the ruses of faithless friends, he must suffer greatly just the same when he discovers how treacherous they are. And it makes no difference whether they were genuine friends who have turned traitors, or traitorous men who had been trading on pretended affection all along.

If, then, the home, every man's haven in the storms of life, affords no solid security, what shall one say of the civic community? The bigger a city is, the fuller it is of legal battles, civil and criminal, and the more frequent are wild and bloody seditions or civil wars. Even when the frays are over, there is never any freedom from fear.

Chapter 6

Even when a city is enjoying the profoundest peace, some men must be sitting in judgment on their fellow men. Even at their best, what misery and grief they cause! No human judge can read the conscience of the man before him. That is why so many innocent witnesses are tortured to find what truth there is in the alleged guilt of other men. It is even worse when the accused man himself is tortured to find out if he be guilty. Here a man still unconvicted must undergo certain suffering for an uncertain crime—not because his guilt is known, but because his innocence is unproved. Thus it often happens that the ignorance of the judge turns into tragedy for the innocent party. There is something still more insufferable—deplorable beyond all cleansing with our tears. Often enough, when a judge tries to avoid putting a man to death whose innocence is not manifest, he has him put to torture, and so it happens, because of woeful lack of evidence, that he both tortures and kills the blameless man whom he tortured lest he kill him without cause. And if, on Stoic principles, the innocent man chooses to escape from life rather than endure such torture any longer, he will confess to a crime he never committed. And when it is all over, the judge will still be in the dark whether the man he put to death was guilty or not guilty, even though he tortured him to save his innocent life, and then condemned him to death. Thus, to gather evidence, he tortures an innocent man and, lacking evidence, kills him.

Such being the effect of human ignorance even in judicial procedure, will any philosopher-judge dare to take his place on the bench? You may be sure, he will. He would think it very wrong indeed to withdraw from his bounden duty to society. But that innocent men should be tortured as witnesses in trials not their own; that accused men should be so overcome by pain as falsely to plead guilty and then die, as they were tortured, in innocence; that many men should die as a result of or during their torturings, prior to any verdict at all—in all this our philosopher-judge sees nothing wrong. So, too, a judge in his ignorance will condemn to death, as sometimes happens, men who had nothing but the good of society at heart. To prevent crimes from going unpunished, such men go to court; but the witnesses lie

11. [*In Verrem* 2.1.15.]

12. [Matt. 10.36.]

and the guilty party holds out inhumanly under the torture and makes no confession; the accusation, in spite of the facts, is not sustained and it is the accuser who is condemned. No, our philosopher-judge does not reckon such abuses as burdens on his conscience because he has no intention of doing harm. Often, he would say, he cannot get at the truth, yet the good of society demands that he hand down decisions. My only point is that, as a man, surely his cannot be the 'happy life' even though his philosophy may save him from a sense of wrongdoing. Granted that his ignorance and his office are to blame for the torture and death of innocent men, is it any consolation to feel free of responsibility unless he is also happy? Surely there is something finer and more humane in seeing and detesting his wretchedness in this necessity and, if he is a Christian, in crying out to God: 'Deliver me from my necessities.'[13]

Chapter 7

After the city comes the world community. This is the third stage in the hierarchy of human associations. First, we have the home; then the city; finally, the globe. And, of course, as with the perils of the ocean, the bigger the community, the fuller it is of misfortunes.

The first misfortune is the lack of communication resulting from language differences. Take two men who meet and find that some common need calls on them to remain together rather than to part company. Neither knows the language of the other. As far as intercommunication goes, these two, both men, are worse off than two dumb animals, even of different kinds. For all its identity in both, their human nature is of no social help, so long as the language barrier makes it impossible for them to tell each other what they are thinking about. That is why a man is more at home with his dog than with a foreigner.

It will be answered that the Roman Empire, in the interests of peaceful collaboration, imposes on nations it has conquered the yoke of both law and language, and thus has an adequate, or even an overflowing, abundance of interpreters. True enough. But at what cost! There is one war after another, havoc everywhere, tremendous slaughterings of men.

All this for peace. Yet, when the wars are waged, there are new calamities brewing. To begin with, there never has been, nor, is there today, any absence of hostile foreign powers to provoke war. What is worse, the very development of the empire accruing from their incorporation has begotten still worse wars within. I refer to the civil wars and social uprisings that involve even more wretched anxieties for human beings, either shaken by their actual impact, or living in fear of their renewal. Massacres, frequent and sweeping, hardships too dire to endure are but a part of the ravages of war. I am utterly unable to describe them as they are, and as they ought to be described; and even if I should try to begin, where could I end?

I know the objection that a good ruler will wage wars only if they are just. But, surely, if he will only remember that he is a man, he will begin by bewailing the necessity he is under of waging even just wars. A good man would be under compulsion to wage no wars at all, if there were not such things as just wars. A just war, moreover, is justified only by the injustice of an aggressor; and that injustice ought

13. [Ps. 24.17.]

to be a source of grief to any good man, because it is human injustice. It would be deplorable in itself, apart from being a source of conflict.

Any man who will consider sorrowfully evils so great, such horrors and such savagery, will admit his human misery. And if there is any man who can endure such calamities, or even contemplate them without feeling grief, his condition is all the more wretched for that. For it is only the loss of all humane feeling that could make him call such a life 'the happy life.'

Chapter 8

Another of the not uncommon miseries of our human life is to mistake, by a misunderstanding close to madness, enemies for friends and friends for enemies. This apart, even granted the ordinary miseries and mistakes, of which all human relationship is full, there is no greater consolation than the unfeigned loyalty and mutual love of good men who are true friends. Yet, the more friends we have, and the more scattered they are locally, the more widely stretched are our heartfelt fears, lest any of the mountainous miseries of life befall them. We become apprehensive not only about possible afflictions of famine, war, sickness, imprisonment, or such unimaginable sufferings as may be their lot in slavery. What is far harder to swallow is our fear that they may fail us in faithfulness, turn to hate us and work us harm. If and when our fear becomes a fact, and we find it out (and the more friends we have, the more sources of such heartbreak), the fire of pain is whipped to such a blazing in our heart as none can guess who has not felt the smart. Indeed, we would rather hear that our friends are dead.

Yet here is another source of sadness, for the death of those can never leave us free from grief whose friendship during life was a solace and delight. There are some who say men should not grieve. Then, let them try, if they can, to ban all loving interchange of thoughts, cut off and outlaw all friendly feelings, callously break the bonds of all human fellowship, or claim that such human relationships must be emptied of all tenderness. And if this is utterly impossible, it is no less impossible for us not to taste as bitter the death of those whose life for us was such a source of sweetness. It is, in fact, because such grief, in a broken heart, is like a wound or open sore that men feel it a duty to offer us the balm of their condolences. And if the heart is more easily and quickly healed the more virtuous a man is, that does not mean that there was no wound to heal.

There is no escape, then, from that misery of human life which is caused, in varying degrees, by the deaths of very close friends, especially if they have played some important role in public life. Yet it is easier to watch any of our loved ones die, in this sense, than to learn that they have lost their faith, or have fallen into grievous sin, and thus are spiritually dead. It is because of the immensity of this misery filling the earth that the Scripture asks: 'Is not the life of man upon earth a trial?'[14] No wonder the Lord said: 'Woe to the world because of scandals,'[15] and again: 'Because iniquity hath abounded, the charity of many shall grow cold.'[16]

14. [Job 7.1, reading *tentatio* in place of the Vulgate *militia*.]

15. [Matt. 18.7.]

16. [Matt. 24.12.]

That is why we Christians can feel a real joy when our friends die a holy death. Their death, of course, afflicts our heart, but faith gives us the surer consolation, that they are now freed from those evils of this present life which threaten the best of men with either failure or defilement—and sometimes with both.

Chapter 14

In the earthly city, then, temporal goods are to be used with a view to the enjoyment of earthly peace, whereas, in the heavenly City, they are used with a view to the enjoyment of eternal peace. Hence, if we were merely unthinking brutes, we would pursue nothing beyond the orderly interrelationship of our bodily part and the appeasing of our appetites, nothing, that is, beyond the comfort of the flesh and plenty of pleasures, so that the peace of body might contribute to peace of the soul. For, if order in the body be lacking, the peace of an irrational soul is checked, since it cannot attain the satisfaction of its appetites. Both of these forms of peace meanwhile subserve that other form of peace which the body and soul enjoy between them, the peace of life and health in good order.

For, just as brutes show that they love the peace or comfort of their bodies by shunning pain, and the peace of their souls by pursuing pleasure to satisfy their appetites, so, too, by running from death, they make clear enough how much they love the peace which keeps body and soul together.

Because, however, man has a rational soul, he makes everything he shares with brutes subserve the peace of his rational soul, so that he first measures things with his mind before he acts, in order to achieve that harmonious correspondence of conduct and conviction which I called the peace of the rational soul. His purpose in desiring not to be vexed with pain, nor disturbed with desire, nor disintegrated by death is that he may learn something profitable and so order his habits and way of life. However, if the infirmity of his human mind is not to bring him in his pursuit of knowledge to some deadly error, he needs divine authority to give secure guidance, and divine help so that he may be unhampered in following the guidance given.

And because, so long as man lives in his mortal body and is a pilgrim far from the Lord, he walks, not by vision, but by faith. Consequently, he refers all peace of body or soul, or their combination, to that higher peace which unites a mortal man with the immortal God and which I defined as 'ordered obedience guided by faith, under God's eternal law.'

Meanwhile, God teaches him two chief commandments, the love of God and the love of neighbor. In these precepts man finds three beings to love, namely, God, himself, and his fellow man, and knows that he is not wrong in loving himself so long as he loves God. As a result, he must help his neighbor (whom he is obliged to love as himself) to love God. Thus, he must help his wife, children, servants, and all others whom he can influence. He must wish, moreover, to be similarly helped by his fellow man, in case he himself needs such assistance. Out of all this love he will arrive at peace, as much as in him lies, with every man—at that human peace which is regulated fellowship. Right order here means, first, that he harm no one, and, second, that he help whomever he can. His fundamental duty is to look out for his own home, for both by natural and human law he has easier and readier access to their requirements.

St. Paul says: 'But if any does not take care of his own, and especially of his household, he has denied the faith and is worse than an unbeliever.'[17] From this care arises that peace of the home which lies in the harmonious interplay of authority and obedience among those who live there. For, those who have the care of the others give the orders—a man to his wife, parents to their children, masters to their servants. And those who are cared for must obey—wives their husbands, children their parents, servants their masters. In the home of a religious man, however, of a man living by faith and as yet a wayfarer from the heavenly City, those who command serve those whom they appear to rule—because, of course, they do not command out of lust to domineer, but out of a sense of duty—not out of pride like princes but out of solicitude like parents.

Chapter 17

While the homes of unbelieving men are intent upon acquiring temporal peace out of the possessions and comforts of this temporal life, the families which live according to faith look ahead to the good things of heaven promised as imperishable, and use material and temporal goods in the spirit of pilgrims, not as snares or obstructions to block their way to God, but simply as helps to ease and never to increase the burdens of this corruptible body which weighs down the soul. Both types of homes and their masters have this in common, that they must use things essential to this mortal life. But the respective purposes to which they put them are characteristic and very different.

So, too, the earthly city which does not live by faith seeks only an earthly peace, and limits the goal of its peace, of its harmony of authority and obedience among its citizens, to the voluntary and collective attainment of objectives necessary to mortal existence. The heavenly City, meanwhile—or, rather, that part that is on pilgrimage in mortal life and lives by faith—must use this earthly peace until such time as our mortality which needs such peace has passed away. As a consequence, so long as her life in the earthly city is that of a captive and an alien (although she has the promise of ultimate delivery and the gift of the Spirit as a pledge), she has no hesitation about keeping in step with the civil law which governs matters pertaining to our existence here below. For, as mortal life is the same for all, there ought to be common cause between the two cities in what concerns our purely human living.

Now comes the difficulty. The city of this world, to begin with, has had certain 'wise men' of its own mold, whom true religion must reject, because either out of their own daydreaming or out of demonic deception these wise men came to believe that a multiplicity of divinities was allied with human life, with different duties, in some strange arrangement, and different assignments: this one over the body, that one over the mind; in the body itself, one over the head, another over the neck, still others, one for each bodily part; in the mind, one over the intelligence, another over learning, another over temper, another over desire; in the realities, related to life, that lie about us, one over flocks and one over wheat, one over wine, one over oil, and another over forests, one over currency, another over navigation, and still another over warfare and victory, one over marriage, a different one over fecundity and childbirth, so on and so on.

17. [1 Tim. 5.8.]

The heavenly City, on the contrary, knows and, by religious faith, believes that it must adore one God alone and serve Him with that complete dedication which the Greeks call *latreía* and which belongs to Him alone. As a result, she has been unable to share with the earthly city a common religious legislation, and has had no choice but to dissent on this score and so to become a nuisance to those who think otherwise. Hence, she has had to feel the weight of their anger, hatred, and violence, save in those instances when, by sheer numbers and God's help, which never fails, she has been able to scare off her opponents.

So long, then, as the heavenly City is wayfaring on earth, she invites citizens from all nations and all tongues, and unites them into a single pilgrim band. She takes no issue with that diversity of customs, laws, and traditions whereby human peace is sought and maintained. Instead of nullifying or tearing down, she preserves and appropriates whatever in the diversities of divers races is aimed at one and the same objective of human peace, provided only that they do not stand in the way of the faith and worship of the one supreme and true God.

Thus, the heavenly City, so long as it is wayfaring on earth, not only makes use of earthly peace but fosters and actively pursues along with other human beings a common platform in regard to all that concerns our purely human life and does not interfere with faith and worship. Of course, though, the City of God subordinates this earthly peace to that of heaven. For this is not merely true peace, but, strictly speaking, for any rational creature, the only real peace, since it is, as I said, 'the perfectly ordered and harmonious communion of those who find their joy in God and in one another in God.'

When this peace is reached, man will be no longer haunted by death, but plainly and perpetually endowed with life, nor will his body, which now wastes away and weighs down the soul, be any longer animal, but spiritual, in need of nothing, and completely under the control of our will.

This peace the pilgrim City already possesses by faith and it lives holily and according to this faith so long as, to attain its heavenly completion, it refers every good act done for God or for his fellow man. I say 'fellow man' because, of course, any community life must emphasize social relationships.

Chapter 19

The City of God does not care in the least what kind of dress or social manners a man of faith affects, so long as these involve no offense against the divine law. For it is faith and not fashions that brings us to God. Hence, when philosophers become Christians, the Church does not force them to give up their distinctive attire or mode of life which are no obstacle to religion, but only their erroneous teachings. She is entirely indifferent to that special mark which, in Varro's reckoning, distinguishes the Cynics, so long as it connotes nothing shameful or unbalanced.

Or take the three modes of life: the contemplative, the active, the contemplative-active. A man can live the life of faith in any of these three and get to heaven. What is not indifferent is that he love truth and do what charity demands. No man must be so committed to contemplation as, in his contemplation, to give no thought to his neighbor's needs, nor so absorbed in action as to dispense with the contemplation of God.

The attraction of leisure ought not to be empty-headed inactivity, but in the quest or discovery of truth, both for his own progress and for the purpose of sharing ungrudgingly with others. Nor should the man of action love worldly position or power (for all is vanity under the sun), but only what can be properly and usefully accomplished by means of such position and power, in the sense which I have already explained[18] of contributing to the eternal salvation of those committed to one's care. Thus, as St. Paul wrote: 'If anyone is eager for the office of bishop, he desires a good work.'[19] He wanted to make clear that the office of bishop, *episcopatus,* implies work rather than dignity. The word is derived from *epískopos,* which is Greek for 'superintendent.' Thus, a bishop is supposed to superintend those over whom he is set in the sense that he is to 'oversee' or 'look out for' those under him. The word, *skopein,* like the Latin *intendere,* means to look; and so *episkopein,* like *superintendere,* means 'to oversee' or 'to look out for those who are under one.' Thus, no man can be a good bishop if he loves his title but not his task.

In the same way, no man is forbidden to pursue knowledge of the truth, for that is the purpose of legitimate leisure. But it is the ambition for the position of dignity which is necessary for government that is unbecoming, although, of course, the dignity itself and its use are not wrong in themselves. Thus, it is the love of study that seeks a holy leisure; and only the compulsion of charity that shoulders necessary activity. If no such burden is placed on one's shoulders, time should be passed in study and contemplation. But, once the burden is on the back, it should be carried, since charity so demands. Even so, however, no one should give up entirely his delight in learning, for the sweetness he once knew may be lost and the burden he bears overwhelm him.

Chapter 27

The City of God, however, has a peace of its own, namely, peace with God in this world by faith and in the world to come by vision. Still, any peace we have on earth, whether the peace we share with Babylon or our own peace through faith, is more like a solace for unhappiness than the joy of beatitude. Even our virtue in this life, genuine as it is because it is referred to the true goal of every good, lies more in the pardoning of sins than in any perfection of virtues. Witness the prayer of God's whole City, wandering on earth and calling out to Him through all her members: 'Forgive us our debts as we also forgive our debtors.'[20]

This prayer is effective, not on the lips of those whose faith without works is dead,[21] but only on the lips of men whose faith works through charity.[22] This prayer is necessary for the just because their reason, though submissive to God, has only imperfect mastery over their evil inclinations so long as they live in this world and in a corruptible body that 'is a load upon the soul.'[23] Reason may give commands, but can exercise no control without a struggle. And, in this time of weakness,

18. [Cf. above, 19.6.]

19. [1 Tim. 3.1.]

20. [Matt. 6.12.]

21. [Cf. James 2.17.]

22. [Cf. Gal. 5.6.]

23. [Wisd. 9.15.]

something will inevitably creep in to make the best of soldiers—whether in victory or still in battle with such foes—offend by some small slip of the tongue, some passing thought, if not by habitual actions. This explains why we can know no perfect peace so long as there are evil inclinations to master. Those which put up a fight are put down only in perilous conflict; those that are already overcome cannot be kept so if one relaxes, but only at the cost of vigilant control. These are the battles which Scripture sums up in the single phrase: 'The life of man upon earth is a warfare.'[24]

Who, then, save a proud man, will presume that he can live without needing to ask God: 'Forgive us our debts'? Not a great man, you may be sure, but one blown up with the wind of self-reliance—one whom God in His justice resists while He grants His grace to the humble. Hence, it is written: 'God resists the proud, but gives grace to the humble.'[25]

This, then, in this world, is the life of virtue. When God commands, man obeys; when the soul commands, the body obeys; when reason rules, our passions, even when they fight back, must be conquered or resisted; man must beg God's grace to win merit and the remission of his sins and must thank God for the blessings he receives.

But, in that final peace which is the end and purpose of all virtue here on earth, our nature, made whole by immortality and incorruption, will have no vices and experience no rebellion from within or without. There will be no need for reason to govern non-existent evil inclinations. God will hold sway over man, the soul over the body; and the happiness in eternal life and law will make obedience sweet and easy. And in each and all of us this condition will be everlasting, and we shall know it to be so. That is why the peace of such blessedness or the blessedness of such peace is to be our supreme good.

24. [Job 7.1.]

25. [James 4.6; 1 Peter 5.5.]

THOMAS AQUINAS

In 1277, three years after the death of Thomas Aquinas (1224–1274), Pope John XXI asked Stephen Tempier, the bishop of Paris, to investigate the dispute between philosophy and theology that had flourished during the thirteenth century, after the rediscovery of Aristotle's works. The result was a set of 219 propositions that were held by the philosophers and that opposed the Christian faith, including, for example, that the world is eternal and that there is no freedom of choice. On March 7, 1277, the bishop condemned these propositions, which included some of Aquinas's attempts to harmonize Aristotelianism and Christian faith. With this act of condemnation the great task of uniting faith and reason, theology and philosophy, reached a turning point. What Aquinas had tried to achieve, both philosophers and theologians began to reject in their different ways, and his grand synthesis, later to be canonized as official Catholic doctrine, came to generate diverse criticisms.

Aquinas was born at the castle of Roccasecca, near Naples, Italy, the youngest son of Landalfo, the count of Aquino. At the age of five, he began his education under the Benedictine monks at nearby Monte Cassino, where he remained until 1239. He then went to the University of Naples and soon became acquainted with a vigorous young group of Dominicans, students of philosophy and theology. By 1244 Aquinas had joined this local convent of Dominican friars, against his family's wishes. When the Dominicans arranged for him to accompany them on a trip to Cologne, with the plan to send him on to study for a Dominican novitiate at the University of Paris, Aquinas's brothers kidnapped him and held him prisoner at Aquino for a year.

In 1245 Aquinas escaped and made his way to Paris, where he remained until 1248. From 1248 to 1252 he was a member of a Dominican house of studies in Cologne and became the student of the famous German Dominican Aristotelian, Albert the Great. In 1252 Aquinas returned to Paris, where he taught until 1259. He then moved to Italy, where, until 1268, he taught in and around Rome. Once again, he returned to Paris and engaged in controversy with the Latin Averroists and followers of Siger of Brabant, who argued for a pure Aristotelianism, and, on the other side, with the followers of Saint Bonaventure, who sought to establish an ultra–Augustinian (or voluntaristic) Christianity and ban Aristotelianism altogether. In 1272 he was sent to Naples to establish a Dominican house of study. By this time, his health was not good; indeed, some conjecture that he had suffered a stroke. When he was called to Lyons by Pope Gregory X to participate in a council, he struck his head and died of complications on the way, on March 7, 1274, at a monastery between Naples and Rome.

Aquinas's life was intellectually rich, filled with study, teaching, and writing. He left an enormous corpus of work. While teaching in Paris from 1252 to 1259, he wrote his commentary on the *Sentences* of Peter Lombard and his treatises *On the Principles of Nature, On Being and Essence*, and *On Truth*. The *Summa Contra Gentiles*, a work intended to help Dominican missionaries in Spain and North Africa, was completed while he was in Italy between 1259 and 1268, and the great *Summa Theologica* was written between 1265 and 1273. During his relatively brief lifetime, he also published a variety of other treatises and commentaries on no less than twelve Aristotelian treatises.

Aquinas was both a theologian and a philosopher. As a theologian, he wrote about God and the world based on rational inquiry and the evidence of faith. As a philosopher, he was an Aristotelian who employed the data of the senses, examined and understood in the light of first principles. He sought to understand God in terms of an inquiry into nature and then to return to understand nature with new thoughts based on his grasp of the divine. The twofold character of his thought, moreover, influenced his ethics; in his understanding of man, the soul, human will, appetite, and moral purpose, he used the teleological notions of capacities, potentialities, and purposes. For Aquinas, man's ultimate goal is happiness, which he takes to be the joyful knowledge of God and a life which attempts to realize the nature which God has given to man. It is a goal that can be achieved in a variety of ways; his moral theory focuses on these ways. On the one hand, Aquinas is concerned with virtue and the cultivation of character, as these facilitate human happiness; on the other, he is concerned with law as it directs our conduct from the outside but toward the same goal.

In a way, this dichotomy between internal and external control is also reflected in Aquinas's political theory. His family had imperial connections in southern Italy, and hence he grew up with monarchist sensibilities. But he cast his lot with the democratic-style practices of the Dominican order. The result, in Aquinas's thought, is a commitment to a kind of mixed form of government, a constitutional monarchy. Such a society, he argued, is the most conducive to the best human life, and that means to the life of virtue. The best government is government by law for the common good, the community's well-being. It governs a society that best enables people to achieve happiness, which is a society both political in character and religious in purpose. Moreover, the mixed constitution does this through law, which helps people to prevent evil and to seek the good. For Aquinas, then, the state arises out of religious and moral purposes, and morality emerges from human nature and its tendencies, the object of God's beneficent purposes.

Aquinas's life coincides with a period when Christian faith and Aristotelian philosophy confronted each other and achieved as comfortable a synthesis as they would ever attain. His remarkable collection of works exemplifies that synthesis in a uniquely powerful way. Within two decades Aquinas crystallized the deep mood of an epoch, but his success was short-lived. By 1277, with the Condemnation of Paris, the unity was shattered and the main lines of response already plotted; the nominalist and conciliarist responses of Duns Scotus and William of Ockham were developed in the following generation in opposition to Aquinas's synthesis. Aquinas was, in short, a monumental figure, whose life, works, and intellect blend together as a decisive turning point in medieval thought.

Recommended readings

Burns, James (ed.). *Cambridge History of Medieval Political Thought, 350–1450*. Cambridge: Cambridge University Press, 1989.

Coppleston, Frederick. *Aquinas*. London: Penguin, 1955.

Finnis, John. *Natural Law and Natural Rights*. Oxford: Oxford University Press, 1982.

Gilson, Etienne. *The Christian Philosophy of St. Thomas Aquinas*. New York: Random House, 1956.

Kenny, Antony (ed.). *Aquinas*. Notre Dame: Notre Dame Press, 1976.

Maritain, J. *Man and the State*. Chicago: University of Chicago Press, 1951.

Sigmund, Paul (ed.). *St. Thomas Aquinas on Politics and Ethics*. New York: W. W. Norton, 1988.

STATESMANSHIP
ON KINGSHIP

TO THE KING OF CYPRUS

BOOK ONE

Chapter One

It is necessary for men living together to be ruled diligently by a king.

Our primary intention requires that we explain what is to be understood by the name "king." In all things, however, which are ordered to some goal, by which we can proceed in more than one way, there is a need for some directing principle, by which the task may be brought rightly to completion. For even a ship, randomly moved to and fro by different winds, will not reach her destined goal unless she is directed by the effort of the helmsman to her port. There is a certain goal for man toward which his whole life and deeds are ordered, since he acts by his intelligence, which is clearly to act with some goal in mind. It happens that people proceed towards their intended goal in different ways, which the very diversity of human endeavors and actions makes clear.

Therefore, man needs some directing principle to attain that goal. However, every man is endowed by nature with the light of reason, by which he may be directed in his actions to his goal. So, if it were fitting for man to live alone, as in the case of many animals, no other direction would be needed regarding that goal, but each would be a king unto himself under God, the highest king, inasmuch as in his actions he would direct himself by the light of reason divinely given to him.

Man is by nature, however, a social and political animal, living amid a multitude of his kind; more so, indeed, than is the case with all other animals, which natural necessity itself makes clear. For nature prepares for other animals their food, their covering of fur, their means of defense (such as teeth, horns, claws, or at least swiftness of flight). For man, however, none of these were provided by nature, but instead of all of these, reason was given to him, by which, through the labor of his hands, he would be able to fashion for himself all these things, but for the fashioning of all of which one man alone would not suffice. For one man alone, by his own devices, could not sufficiently make his way through life. It is, therefore, natural for man that he live in the companionship of many of his kind.

Moreover, instinct is given to other animals by which they discover all those things which are useful or dangerous, as the sheep instinctively recognizes the wolf as its enemy. Certain animals know instinctively that some herbs are medicinal and know instinctively other things necessary for their life. Man has a natural knowledge of those things which are necessary for survival, but only in a general way, insofar as, so to speak, being gifted by reason, he can pass from natural principles to the recognition of those particulars which are necessary for human life. It is not possible,

Reprinted from *On Law, Morality, and Politics*, edited by William P. Baumgarth and Richard J. Regan, s.j. (Indianapolis: Hackett Publishing Company, 1988, by permission of the publisher.)

though, that a single person could achieve all this knowledge by his own power of reason. It is, therefore, necessary for man to live in society with his fellows, so that one may be aided by another and that different persons may be engaged in making different discoveries through their respective powers of reason; one, for example, in medicine, another in this field, another in that. This point is made most clearly evident by this—that it is man's distinctive trait to speak, whereby one man can fully express his thought to others. Other animals can express to each other in a general way their feelings, as dogs express anger when they bark and other animals express their feelings in diverse ways. Man communicates with his fellows more than any other animal we see living in a group, such as cranes, ants, and bees. Reflecting upon this Solomon says, "It is better to be two than to be one. They have been enriched in one another's company." If it is natural that man live in society with his fellows, it is necessary that there be some power in men by which that group be ruled. If there be a group of people, with each one looking solely after his own interest, that group would break up into many parts unless, indeed, there were also someone taking care of those things pertaining to the good of the group, just as the body of a man or of any animal would fall apart unless there were some general ruling principle in the body which has as its interest the common good of all the members. Reflecting upon this Solomon says, "Where there is no governor, the people scatter." This happens reasonably enough. The particular and the common are not the same: the particular differentiates; the common unites. Different things, however, are the result of different causes. It is necessary, therefore, that, besides that which moves each towards his own private good, there be something else that moves towards the common good of the group. Therefore, in all things which are ordered to one goal, there is to be found some ruling principle. Thus, in the universe of bodies, divine Providence rules, by a certain order, other bodies by the first (that is, the heavenly) body and by that order all bodies are ruled by the rational creature. In every man, the soul rules the body, and, between the spirited and desiring parts of the soul, reason assigns an order. Again, among the members of the body, one is the chief, and it moves the others, whether it be the heart or the head. There has to be, therefore, some ruling principle in every group.

Even so, in those things which are directed to a goal, things can proceed rightly or not rightly. So, in ruling a group, it may be found that such is done rightly or not rightly. Each thing is directed rightly when it is brought to its fitting goal and not rightly when the goal is not fitting. The goal befitting a community of free men is different from that befitting a community of slaves. For the free man is the cause of his own actions; the slave, as such, belongs to another. If, therefore, a community of free men be ordered by a governor to the common good of that group, that will be a rule both right and just, as befits free men. If, in fact, his rule is directed, not to the common good of the group, but to the private advantage of the ruler, that will be a rule both unjust and perverse; wherefore the Lord warns such rulers through Ezechiel, saying, "Woe to the shepherds who feed themselves" (as if seeking their private advantage), "Should not the flocks be fed by the shepherds?" However, shepherds should seek the good of the flock, and, indeed, rulers the good of that group subject to them.

If, therefore, an unjust rule is exercised by one man alone, who seeks his own advantage from that rule, not the good of the group subject to him, such a ruler is called a tyrant, a name derived from strength, since, indeed, he oppresses by his power; he does not rule by justice. Therefore, among the ancients, powerful men were called tyrants. If, though, an unjust rule be exercised not by one alone but by several who are few, it is called oligarchy, that is, rule by the few, insofar as the few indeed oppress the common people for the sake of wealth, distinguishing themselves from the tyrant solely by being more than one. If wicked rule is exercised by many, it is termed democracy, that is, rule by the people, insofar as indeed the mass of common folk, by the force of numbers, oppresses the rich. Thus the whole of the people will be, as it were, one tyrant.

We must, in like manner, distinguish different just constitutions. If things are administered by some group, it is called by the common name "polity," as, for instance, when a group of soldiers rules a city or a province. If things are administered by few, this constitution is called aristocracy, that is, the best rule or rule by the best, who, therefore, are termed "the best men." If, indeed, a just constitution is exercised by one man alone, he is properly called king; therefore, the Lord through Ezechiel says, "My servant David will be a king over all, and he will be the one shepherd of all of them." Hence it is obvious that the very concept of a king entails that there be one who presides, and that he be the shepherd seeking the common good of the group and not his own advantage.

Since, then, it is necessary for man to live in society with his fellows, because by himself he could not secure those things necessary for life if he would remain in a solitary existence, it is a consequence that the companionship of many would be more complete to the extent that it will be more sufficient in itself for the necessities of life. There is, however, a certain sufficiency for life in the single family of one household (as much, that is, as suffices for the natural acts of nutrition and procreation and similar things); in one quarter of a city, there is as much sufficiency as is required for a single craft. In a city, however, (which is a complete community), there is as much as suffices for all the necessities of life, yet still much more in a province because of the need for defense and of the mutual aid of allies against the public enemy. Therefore, he who rules a complete community, that is, a city or a province, is justly termed king; he who rules a household is called father of the family, but not king.

A father has a certain likeness to a king, because of which kings are sometimes called the fathers of peoples.

It is clear from our discussion that a king is one who rules the multitude in a city or a province for the common good; therefore, Solomon says, "The king rules all lands which are subject to him."

SUMMA THEOLOGICA

LAW

ST I-II

QUESTION 90

OF THE ESSENCE OF LAW

[In Four Articles]

We have now to consider the extrinsic principles of acts. Now the extrinsic principle inclining to evil is the devil, of whose temptations we have spoken in the First Part. But the extrinsic principle moving to good is God, Who both instructs us by means of His law and assists us by His grace; wherefore, in the first place, we must speak of law; in the second place, of grace.

Concerning law, we must consider (1) law itself in general; (2) its parts. Concerning law in general, three points offer themselves for our consideration: (1) its essence; (2) the different kinds of law; (3) the effects of law.

Under the first head, there are four points of inquiry: (1) Whether law is something pertaining to reason? (2) concerning the end of law; (3) its cause; (4) the promulgation of law.

First Article

IS LAW SOMETHING PERTAINING TO REASON?

We proceed thus to the First Article:

Objection 1. It would seem that law is not something pertaining to reason. For the Apostle says: "I see another law in my members," etc. But nothing pertaining to reason is in the members, since the reason does not make use of a bodily organ. Therefore, law is not something pertaining to reason.

Obj. 2. Further, in the reason there is nothing else but power, habit, and act. But law is not the power itself of reason. In like manner, neither is it a habit of reason, because the habits of reason are the intellectual virtues of which we have spoken above. Nor, again, is it an act of reason because then law would cease when the act of reason ceases, for instance, while we are asleep. Therefore, law is nothing pertaining to reason.

Obj. 3. Further, the law moves those who are subject to it to act aright. But it belongs properly to the will to move to act, as is evident from what has been said

Reprinted from *On Law, Morality, and Politics,* edited by William P. Baumgarth and Richard J. Regan, s.j. (Indianapolis: Hackett Publishing Company, 1988, by permission of the publisher.

above. Therefore, law pertains not to the reason but to the will, according to the words of the Jurist: "Whatever pleases the ruler has the force of law."

On the contrary, It belongs to the law to command and to forbid. But it belongs to reason to command, as stated above. Therefore, law is something pertaining to reason.

I answer that Law is a certain rule and measure of acts whereby man is induced to act or is restrained from acting; for *lex* (law) is derived from *ligare* (to bind) because it binds one to act. Now the rule and measure of human acts is reason, which is the first principle of human acts, as is evident from what has been stated above, since it belongs to reason to direct to the end, which is the first principle in all matters of action, according to the Philosopher. Now, that which is the principle in any genus is the rule and measure of that genus, for instance, unity in the genus of numbers, and the first movement in the genus of movements. Consequently, it follows that law is something pertaining to reason.

Reply Obj. 1. Since law is a kind of rule and measure, it may be in something in two ways. First, as in that which measures and rules; and since this is proper to reason, it follows that, in this way, law is in reason alone. Second, as in that which is measured and ruled. In this way, law is in all those things that are inclined to something by reason of some law, so that any inclination arising from a law may be called a law, not essentially but by participation as it were. And thus the inclination of the members to concupiscence is called "the law of the members."

Reply Obj. 2. Just as, in external action, we may consider the work and the work done—for instance, the work of building and the house built, so in the acts of reason we may consider the act itself of reason, i.e., to understand and to reason, and something produced by this act. With regard to the speculative reason, this is first of all the definition; secondly, the proposition; thirdly, the syllogism or argument. And since also the practical reason makes use of a kind of syllogism in respect to the work to be done, as stated above and as the Philosopher teaches, hence we find in the practical reason something that holds the same position in regard to operations as, in the speculative intellect, the proposition holds in regard to conclusions. Such-like universal propositions of the practical intellect that are directed to actions have the nature of law. And these propositions are sometimes under our actual consideration, while sometimes they are retained in the reason by means of a habit.

Reply Obj. 3. Reason has its power of moving from the will, as stated above, for it is due to the fact that one wills the end that the reason issues its commands as regards things ordained to the end. But in order that the volition of what is commanded may have the nature of law, it needs to be in accord with some rule of reason. And in this sense is to be understood the saying that the will of the ruler has the force of law; otherwise, the ruler's will would savor of lawlessness rather than of law.

Second Article

Is the Law Always Directed to the Common Good?

We proceed thus to the Second Article:

Obj. 1. It would seem that the law is not always directed to the common good as to its end. For it belongs to law to command and to forbid. But commands are directed to certain individual goods. Therefore, the end of the law is not always the common good.

Obj. 2. Further, the law directs man in his actions. But human actions are concerned with particular matters. Therefore, the law is directed to some particular good.

Obj. 3. Further, Isidore says, "If the law is based on reason, whatever is based on reason will be a law." But reason is the foundation not only of what is ordained to the common good but also of that which is directed to private good. Therefore, the law is not only directed to the common good but also to the private good of an individual.

On the contrary, Isidore says that "Laws are enacted for no private profit but for the common benefit of the citizens."

I answer that, As stated above, the law belongs to that which is a principle of human acts because it is their rule and measure. Now, as reason is a principle of human acts, so in reason itself there is something which is the principle in respect of all the rest; wherefore to this principle chiefly and mainly law must needs be referred. Now the first principle in practical matters, which are the object of the practical reason, is the last end, and the last end of human life is bliss or happiness, as stated above. Consequently, the law must needs regard principally the relationship to happiness. Moreover, since every part is ordained to the whole as imperfect to perfect, and since a single man is a part of the perfect community, the law must needs regard properly the relationship to universal happiness. Wherefore the Philosopher, in the above definition of legal matters, mentions both happiness and the body politic, for he says that we call those legal matters just "which are adapted to produce and preserve happiness and its parts for the body politic" since the political community is a perfect community, as he says in Politics I, 1.

Now, in every genus, that which belongs to it most of all is the principle of the others, and the others belong to that genus in subordination to that thing; thus fire, which is chief among hot things, is the cause of heat in mixed bodies, and these are said to be hot insofar as they have a share of fire. Consequently, since the law is chiefly ordained to the common good, any other precept in regard to some individual work must needs be devoid of the nature of a law, save insofar as it is ordered to the common good. Therefore, every law is ordained to the common good.

Reply Obj. 1. A command denotes an application of a law to matters regulated by the law. Now the order to the common good, at which the law aims, is applicable to particular ends. And in this way, commands are given even concerning particular matters.

Reply Obj. 2. Actions are indeed concerned with particular matters, but those particular matters are referable to the common good, not as to a common genus or species, but as to a common final cause, according as the common good is said to be the common end.

Reply Obj. 3. Just as nothing stands firm with regard to the speculative reason except that which is traced back to the first indemonstrable principles, so nothing stands firm with regard to the practical reason unless it be directed to the last end which is the common good, and whatever stands to reason in this sense has the nature of a law.

Third Article

IS THE REASON OF ANY PERSON COMPETENT TO MAKE LAWS?

We proceed thus to the Third Article:

Obj. 1. It would seem that the reason of any person is competent to make laws. For the Apostle says that "when the Gentiles, who have not the law, do by nature those things that are of the law, . . . they are a law to themselves." Now he says this of all in general. Therefore, anyone can make a law for himself.

Obj. 2. Further, as the Philosopher says, "The intention of the lawgiver is to lead men to virtue." But every man can lead another to virtue. Therefore, the reason of any man is competent to make laws.

Obj. 3. Further, just as the ruler of a political community governs the political community, so every father of a family governs his household. But the ruler of a political community can make laws for the political community. Therefore, every father of a family can make laws for his household.

On the contrary, Isidore says, "A law is an ordinance of the people, whereby something is sanctioned by nobles together with commoners." Not everyone, therefore, is competent to make law.

I answer that Law, properly speaking, regards first and chiefly an ordering to the common good. Now to order anything to the common good belongs either to the whole people or to someone who is the vicegerent of the whole people. And, therefore, the making of law belongs either to the whole people or to a public personage who has care of the whole people, since, in all other matters, the directing of anything to the end concerns him to whom the end belongs.

Reply Obj. 1. As stated above, law is in a person not only as in one that rules but also by participation as in one that is ruled. In the latter way, each one is a law to himself, insofar as he shares the direction that he receives from one who rules him. Hence the same text goes on, "who show the work of the law written in their hearts."

Reply Obj. 2. A private person cannot lead another to virtue efficaciously, for he can only advise, and if his advice be not taken, it has no coercive power, such as the law should have in order to prove an efficacious inducement to virtue, as the Philosopher says. But this coercive power is vested in the whole people or in some public personage to whom it belongs to inflict penalties, as we shall state further on. Wherefore, the framing of laws belongs to him alone.

Reply Obj. 3. As one man is a part of the household, so a household is a part of the political community, and the political community is a perfect community, according to Politics I, 1. And, therefore, as the good of one man is not the last end but is ordained to the common good, so too the good of one household is ordained to the good of a single political community, which is a perfect community. Consequently, he that governs a family can indeed make certain commands or ordinances but not such as to have properly the nature of law.

Fourth Article

IS PROMULGATION ESSENTIAL TO A LAW?

We proceed thus to the Fourth Article:

Obj. 1. It would seem that promulgation is not essential to a law. For the natural law above all has the nature of law. But the natural law needs no promulgation. Therefore, it is not essential to a law that it be promulgated.

Obj. 2. Further, it belongs properly to a law to bind one to do or not to do something. But the obligation of fulfilling a law touches not only those in whose presence it is promulgated but also others. Therefore, promulgation is not essential to a law.

Obj. 3. Further, the obligation of a law extends even to the future since "laws are binding in matters of the future," as the jurists say. But promulgation is made to those who are present. Therefore, it is not essential to a law.

On the contrary, It is laid down in the *Decretum,* dist. 4, that "Laws are established when they are promulgated."

I answer that, As stated above, a law is imposed on others by way of a rule and measure. Now a rule or measure is imposed by being applied to those who are to be ruled and measured by it. Wherefore, in order that a law obtain the binding force which is proper to a law, it must needs be applied to the men who have to be ruled by it. Such application is made by its being notified to them by promulgation. Wherefore promulgation is necessary for the law to obtain its force.

Thus, from the four preceding articles, the definition of law may be gathered, and it is nothing else than a certain ordinance of reason for the common good, made by him who has care of the community, and promulgated.

Reply Obj. 1. The natural law is promulgated by the very fact that God instilled it into men's minds so as to be known by them naturally.

Reply Obj. 2. Those who are not present when a law is promulgated are bound to observe the law, insofar as it is notified or can be notified to them by others after it has been promulgated.

Reply Obj. 3. The promulgation that takes place now extends to future time by reason of the durability of written characters, by which means it is continually promulgated. Hence Isidore says that "*lex* (law) is derived from *legere* (to read) because it is written."

QUESTION 91

OF THE VARIOUS KINDS OF LAW

[In Six Articles]

We must now consider the various kinds of law, under which head there are six points of inquiry: (1) Whether there is an eternal law? (2) Whether there is a natural law? (3) Whether there is a human law? (4) Whether there is a divine law? (5) Whether there is one divine law or several? (6) Whether there is a law of sin?

First Article

Is There an Eternal Law?

We proceed thus to the First Article:

Obj. 1. It would seem that there is no eternal law because every law is imposed on someone. But there was not someone from eternity on whom a law could be imposed since God alone was from eternity. Therefore, no law is eternal.

Obj. 2. Further, promulgation is essential to law. But promulgation could not be from eternity because there was no one to whom it could be promulgated from eternity. Therefore, no law can be eternal.

Obj. 3. Further, a law implies order to an end. But nothing ordained to an end is eternal, for the last end alone is eternal. Therefore, no law is eternal.

On the contrary, Augustine says, "That law which is the supreme reason cannot be understood to be otherwise than unchangeable and eternal."

I answer that, As stated above, a law is nothing else but a dictate of practical reason in the ruler who governs a perfect community. Now it is evident, granted that the world is ruled by divine providence, as was stated in the First Part, that the whole community of the universe is governed by divine reason. Wherefore, the very idea of the government of things in God the Ruler of the universe has the nature of a law. And since the divine reason's conception of things is not subject to time but is eternal, according to Pr. 8:23, therefore it is that this kind of law must be called eternal.

Reply Obj. 1. Those things that are not in themselves exist with God inasmuch as they are foreknown and preordained by Him, according to Rom. 4:17, "Who calls those things that are not, as those that are." Accordingly, the eternal concept of the divine law bears the nature of an eternal law insofar as it is ordained by God to the government of things foreknown by Him.

Reply Obj. 2. Promulgation is made by word of mouth or in writing, and in both ways the eternal law is promulgated, because both the divine word and the writing of the Book of Life are eternal. But the promulgation cannot be from eternity on the part of the creature that hears or reads.

Reply Obj. 3. The law implies order to an end actively, insofar as it directs certain things to an end, but not passively—that is to say, the law itself is not ordained to an end—except accidentally, in a governor whose end is extrinsic to him, and to which end his law must needs be ordained. But the end of the divine government is God Himself, and His law is not distinct from Himself. Wherefore the eternal law is not ordained to another end.

Second Article

Is There a Natural Law in Us?

We proceed thus to the Second Article:

Obj. 1. It would seem that there is no natural law in us because man is governed sufficiently by the eternal law; for Augustine says that "the eternal law is that by which it is right that all things should be most orderly." But nature does not abound in superfluities, as neither does it fail in necessaries. Therefore, there is no natural law in man.

Obj. 2. Further, by the law man is directed in his acts to the end, as stated above. But the directing of human acts to their end is not by nature, as is the case in irrational creatures, which act for an end solely by their natural appetite, whereas man acts for an end by his reason and will. Therefore, there is no natural law for man.

Obj. 3. Further, the more a man is free, the less is he under the law. But man is freer than all other animals on account of his free will, with which he is endowed above all other animals. Since, therefore, other animals are not subject to a natural law, neither is man subject to a natural law.

On the contrary, A gloss on Rom. 2:14 ("When the Gentiles, who have not the law, do by nature those things that are of the law") comments as follows: "Although they have no written law, yet they have the natural law, whereby each one knows, and is conscious of, what is good and what is evil."

I answer that, As stated above, law, being a rule and measure, can be in a person in two ways: in one way, as in him that rules and measures; in another way, as in that which is ruled and measured, since a thing is ruled and measured insofar as it partakes of the rule or measure. Wherefore, since all things subject to divine providence are ruled and measured by the eternal law, as was stated above, it is evident that all things partake somewhat of the eternal law insofar as, namely, from its being imprinted on them, they derive their respective inclinations to their proper acts and ends. Now among all others, the rational creature is subject to divine providence in a more excellent way, insofar as it partakes of a share of providence, by being provident both for itself and for others. Wherefore it has a share of the eternal reason, whereby it has a natural inclination to its proper act and end, and this participation of the eternal law in the rational creature is called the natural law. Hence the Psalmist, after saying "offer up the sacrifice of justice," as though someone asked what the works of justice are, adds: "Many say, 'Who shows us good things?',", in answer to which question he says: "The light of Your countenance, O Lord, is signed upon us"; thus implying that the light of natural reason, whereby we discern what is good and what is evil, which pertains to the natural law, is nothing else than an imprint on us of the divine light. It is therefore evident that the natural law is nothing else than the rational creature's participation of the eternal law.

Reply Obj. 1. This argument would hold if the natural law were something different from the eternal law, whereas it is nothing but a participation thereof, as stated above.

Reply Obj. 2. Every act of reason and will in us is derived from that which is according to nature, as stated above; for every act of reasoning is based on principles that are known naturally, and every act of appetite in respect of the means is derived from the natural appetite in respect of the last end. Accordingly, the first direction of our acts to their end must needs be in virtue of the natural law.

Reply Obj. 3. Even irrational animals partake in their own way of the eternal reason, just as the rational creature does. But because the rational creature partakes thereof in an intellectual and rational manner, therefore the participation of the eternal law in the rational creature is properly called a law, since a law is something pertaining to reason, as stated above. Irrational creatures, however, do not partake thereof in a rational manner; wherefore, there is no participation of the eternal law in them, except by way of similitude.

Third Article

Is There a Human Law?

We proceed thus to the Third Article:

Obj. 1. It would seem that there is not a human law. For the natural law is a participation of the eternal law, as stated above. Now, through the eternal law, "all things are most orderly," as Augustine states. Therefore, the natural law suffices for the ordering of all human affairs. Consequently, there is no need for a human law.

Obj. 2. Further, a law has the nature of a measure, as stated above. But human reason is not a measure of things, but vice versa, as stated in *Metaphysics* IX, 1. Therefore, no law can emanate from human reason.

Obj. 3. Further, a measure should be most certain, as stated in *Metaphysics* 10. But the dictates of human reason in matters of conduct are uncertain, according to Wisdom 9:14: "The thoughts of mortal men are fearful, and our counsels uncertain." Therefore, no law can emanate from human reason.

On the contrary, Augustine distinguishes two kinds of law: the one eternal; the other temporal, which he calls human.

I answer that, As stated above, a law is a certain dictate of practical reason. Now it is to be observed that the same procedure takes place in the practical and in the speculative reason, for each proceeds from principles to conclusions, as stated above (ibid.). Accordingly, we conclude that just as, in the speculative reason, from naturally know indemonstrable principles we draw the conclusions of the various sciences, the knowledge of which is not imparted to us by nature but acquired by the efforts of reason, so too it is from the precepts of the natural law, as from general and indemonstrable principles, that the human reason needs to proceed to certain particular determinations of the laws. These particular determinations, devised by human reason, are called human laws, provided the other essential conditions of law be observed, as stated above. Wherefore, Tully says in his *Rhetoric* that "justice has its source in nature; thence certain things came into custom by reason of their utility; afterward these things which emanated from nature and were approved by custom were sanctioned by fear and reverence for the law."

Reply Obj. 1. The human reason cannot have a full participation of the dictate of the divine reason but according to its own mode and imperfectly. Consequently, as on the part of the speculative reason, by a natural participation of divine wisdom, there is in us the knowledge of certain general principles but not proper knowledge of each single truth, such as that contained in the divine wisdom, so too on the part of the practical reason, man has a natural participation of the eternal law according to certain general principles but not as regards the particular determinations of individual cases, which are, however, contained in the eternal law. Hence the need for human reason to proceed further to particular legal sanctions.

Reply Obj. 2. Human reason is not of itself the rule of things, but the principles impressed on it by nature are general rules and measures of all things relating to human conduct, whereof the natural reason is the rule and measure, although it is not the measure of things that are from nature.

Reply Obj. 3. The practical reason is concerned with practical matters, which are singular and contingent, but not with necessary things, with which the speculative reason is concerned. Wherefore human laws cannot have that inerrancy that belongs to the demonstrated conclusions of sciences. Nor is it necessary for every measure to be altogether unerring and certain but according as it is possible in its own particular genus.

Fourth Article

WAS THERE ANY NEED FOR A DIVINE LAW?

We proceed thus to the Fourth Article:

Obj. 1. It would seem that there was no need for a divine law because, as stated above, the natural law is a participation in us of the eternal law. But the eternal law is a divine law, as stated above. Therefore, there is no need for a divine law in addition to the natural law and human laws derived therefrom.

Obj. 2. Further, it is written that "God left man in the hand of his own counsel." Now counsel is an act of reason, as stated above. Therefore, man was left to the direction of his reason. But a dictate of human reason is a human law, as stated above. Therefore, there is no need for man to be governed also by a divine law.

Obj. 3. Further, human nature is more self-sufficing than irrational creatures. But irrational creatures have no divine law besides the natural inclination impressed on them. Much less, therefore, should the rational creature have a divine law in addition to the natural law.

On the contrary, David prayed God to set His law before him, saying: "Set before me for a law the way of Your justifications, O Lord."

I answer that, Besides the natural and the human law, it was necessary for the directing of human life to have a divine law. And this for four reasons. First, because it is by law that man is directed how to perform his proper acts in view of his last end. And, indeed, if man were ordained to no other end than that which is proportionate to his natural faculty, there would be no need for man to have any further direction on the part of his reason beyond the natural law and human law which is derived from it. But since man is ordained to an end of eternal happiness which is inproportionate to man's natural faculty, as stated above, therefore it was necessary that, besides the natural and the human law, man should be directed to his end by a law given by God.

Secondly, because, on account of the uncertainty of human judgment, especially on contingent and particular matters, different people form different judgments on human acts, whence also different and contrary laws result. In order, therefore, that man may know without any doubt what he ought to do and what he ought to avoid, it was necessary for man to be directed in his proper acts by a law given by God, for it is certain that such a law cannot err.

Thirdly, because man can make laws in those matters of which he is competent to judge. But man is not competent to judge of interior movements that are hidden but only of exterior acts which appear, and yet, for the perfection of virtue, it is necessary for man to conduct himself aright in both kinds of acts. Consequently, human law could not sufficiently curb and direct interior acts, and it was necessary for this purpose that a divine law should supervene.

Fourthly, because, as Augustine says, human law cannot punish or forbid all evil deeds, since, while aiming at doing away with all evils, it would do away with many good things and would hinder the advance of the common good, which is necessary for human intercourse. In order, therefore, that no evil might remain unforbidden and unpunished, it was necessary for the divine law to supervene, whereby all sins are forbidden.

And these four causes are touched upon in Ps. 118:8, where it is said: "The law of the Lord is unspotted," i.e., allowing no foulness of sin, "converting souls" because it directs not only exterior but also interior acts, "the testimony of the Lord is faithful" because of the certainty of what is true and right, "giving wisdom to little ones" by directing man to an end supernatural and divine.

Reply Obj. 1. By natural law, the eternal law is participated in in proportion to the capacity of human nature. But to his supernatural end, man needs to be directed in a yet higher way. Hence the additional law given by God whereby man shares more perfectly in the eternal law.

Reply Obj. 2. Counsel is a kind of inquiry; hence it must proceed from some principles. Nor is it enough for it to proceed from principles imparted by nature, which are the precepts of the natural law, for the reasons given above, but there is need for certain additional principles, namely, the precepts of the divine law.

Reply Obj. 3. Irrational creatures are not ordained to an end higher than that which is proportionate to their natural powers; consequently, the comparison fails.

QUESTION 94

OF THE NATURAL LAW

[In Six Articles]

We must now consider the natural law, concerning which there are six points of inquiry: (1) What is the natural law? (2) What are the precepts of the natural law? (3) Whether all acts of virtue are prescribed by the natural law? (4) Whether the natural law is the same in all? (5) Whether it is changeable? (6) Whether it can be abolished from the heart of man?

First Article

IS THE NATURAL LAW A HABIT?

We proceed thus to the First Article:

Obj. 1. It would seem that the natural law is a habit because, as the Philosopher says, "there are three things in the soul: power, habit, and passion." But the natural law is not one of the soul's powers, nor is it one of the passions, as we may see by going through them one by one. Therefore, the natural law is a habit.

Obj. 2. Further, Basil says that the conscience or "*synderesis* is the law of our mind," which can only apply to the natural law. But *synderesis* is a habit, as was shown in the First Part. Therefore, the natural law is a habit.

Obj. 3. Further, the natural law abides in man always, as will be shown further on. But man's reason, to which the law pertains, does not always think about the natural law. Therefore, the natural law is not an act but a habit.

On the contrary, Augustine says that "a habit is that whereby something is done when necessary." But such is not the natural law since it is in infants and in the damned who cannot act by it. Therefore, the natural law is not a habit.

I answer that A thing may be called a habit in two ways. First, properly and essentially, and thus the natural law is not a habit. For it has been stated above that the natural law is something appointed by reason, just as a proposition is a work of reason. Now, that which a man does is not the same as that whereby he does it, for he makes a becoming speech by the habit of grammar. Since, then, a habit is that by which we act, a law cannot be a habit properly and essentially.

Secondly, the term "habit" may be applied to that which we hold by a habit; thus faith may mean that which we hold by faith. And accordingly, since the precepts of the natural law are sometimes considered by reason actually, while sometimes they are in the reason only habitually, in this way the natural law may be called a habit. Thus, in speculative matters, the indemonstrable principles are not the habit itself whereby we hold those principles but are the principles the habit of which we possess.

Reply Obj. 1. The Philosopher proposes there to discover the genus of virtue, and since it is evident that virtue is a principle of action, he mentions only those things which are principles of human acts, viz., powers, habits, and passions. But there are other things in the soul besides these three: there are acts; thus to will is in the one that wills; again, things known are in the knower. Moreover, its own natural properties are in the soul, such as immortality and the like.

Reply Obj. 2. Synderesis is said to be the law of our mind because it is a habit containing the precepts of the natural law, which are the first principles of human actions.

Reply Obj. 3. This argument proves that the natural law is held habitually, and this is granted.

To the argument advanced in the contrary sense we reply that sometimes a man is unable to make use of that which is in him habitually on account of some impediment; thus, on account of sleep, a man is unable to use the habit of reasoning. In like manner, through the deficiency of his age, a child cannot use the habit of understanding principles, or the natural law, which is in him habitually.

Second Article

DOES THE NATURAL LAW CONTAIN SEVERAL PRECEPTS OR ONE ONLY?

We proceed thus to the Second Article:

Obj. 1. It would seem that the natural law contains, not several precepts, but one only. For law is a kind of precept, as stated above. If, therefore, there were many precepts of the natural law, it would follow that there are also many natural laws.

Obj. 2. Further, the natural law is consequent to human nature. But human nature as a whole is one, though, as to its parts, it is manifold. Therefore, either there is but one precept of the law of nature, on account of the unity of nature as a whole, or there are many by reason of the number of parts of human nature. The result would be that even things relating to the inclination of the concupiscible faculty belong to the natural law.

Obj. 3. Further, law is something pertaining to reason, as stated above. Now, reason is but one in man. Therefore, there is only one precept of the natural law.

On the contrary, The precepts of the natural law in man stand in relation to practical matters as the first principles to matters of demonstration. But there are several first indemonstrable principles. Therefore, there are also several precepts of the natural law.

I answer that, As stated above, the precepts of the natural law are to the practical reason what the first principles of demonstrations are to the speculative reason because both are self-evident principles. Now a thing is said to be self-evident in two ways: first, in itself; secondly, in relation to us. Any proposition is said to be self-evident in itself if its predicate is contained in the notion of the subject, although, to one who knows not the definition of the subject, it happens that such a proposition is not self-evident. For instance, this proposition, "Man is a rational being," is in its very nature self-evident, since who says "man" says "a rational being," and yet to one who knows not what a man is, this proposition is not self-evident. Hence it is that, as Boethius says, certain axioms or propositions are universally self-evident to all, and such are those propositions whose terms are known to all, as, "Every whole is greater than its part," and, "Things equal to one and the same are equal to one another." But some propositions are self-evident only to the wise who understand the meaning of the terms of such propositions; thus to one who understands that an angel is not a body, it is self-evident that an angel is not circumscriptively in a place, but this is not evident to the unlearned, for they cannot grasp it.

Now, a certain order is to be found in those things that are apprehended universally. For that which, before aught else, falls under apprehension, is "being," the notion of which is included in all things whatsoever a man apprehends. Wherefore the first indemonstrable principle is that the same thing cannot be affirmed and denied at the same time, which is based on the nature of "being" and "not-being," and on this principle all others are based, as it is stated in *Metaphysics* IV. Now, as "being" is the first thing that falls under the apprehension simply, so "good" is the first thing that falls under the apprehension of the practical reason, which is directed to action, since every agent acts for an end under the aspect of good. Consequently, the first principle in the practical reason is one founded on the notion of good, viz., that good is that which all things seek after. Hence this is the first precept of law, that good is to be done and pursued, and evil is to be avoided. All other precepts of the natural law are based upon this, so that whatever the practical reason naturally apprehends as man's good (or evil) belongs to the precepts of the natural law as something to be done or avoided.

Since, however, good has the nature of an end, and evil the nature of a contrary, hence it is that all those things to which man has a natural inclination are naturally apprehended by reason as being good and, consequently, as objects of pursuit, and their contraries as evil and objects of avoidance. Wherefore the order of the precepts of the natural law is according to the order of natural inclinations. Because in man there is first of all an inclination to good in accordance with the nature which he has in common with all substances, inasmuch as every substance seeks the preservation of its own being according to its nature, and by reason of this inclination, whatever is a means of preserving human life and of warding off its obstacles belongs to the natural law. Secondly, there is in man an inclination to things that pertain to him more specially according to that nature which he has in common with other animals, and in virtue of this inclination, those things are said to belong to the natural law "which nature has taught to all animals," such as sexual intercourse, education of offspring, and so forth. Thirdly, there is in man an inclination to good according to the nature of his reason, which nature is proper to him; thus man has a natural inclination to know the truth about God and to live in society, and in this respect, whatever pertains to this inclination belongs to the natural law, for instance, to shun ignorance, to avoid offending those among whom one has to live, and other such things regarding the above inclination.

Reply Obj. 1. All these precepts of the law of nature have the character of one natural law inasmuch as they flow from one first precept.

Reply Obj. 2. All the inclinations of any parts whatsoever of human nature, e.g., of the concupiscible and irascible parts, insofar as they are ruled by reason, belong to the natural law and are reduced to one first precept, as stated above, so that the precepts of the natural law are many in themselves but are based on one common foundation.

Reply Obj. 3. Although reason is one in itself, yet it directs all things regarding man, so that whatever can be ruled by reason is contained under the law of reason.

Third Article

Are All Acts of Virtue Prescribed by the Natural Law?

We proceed thus to the Third Article:

Obj. 1. It would seem that not all acts of virtue are prescribed by the natural law because, as stated above, it is essential to a law that it be ordained to the common good. But some acts of virtue are ordained to the private good of the individual, as is evident especially in regard to acts of temperance. Therefore, not all acts of virtue are the subject of natural law.

Obj. 2. Further, every sin is opposed to some virtuous act. If, therefore, all acts of virtue are prescribed by the natural law, it seems to follow that all sins are against nature, whereas this applies to certain special sins.

Obj. 3. Further, those things which are according to nature are common to all. But acts of virtue are not common to all, since a thing is virtuous in one and vicious in another. Therefore, not all acts of virtue are prescribed by the natural law.

On the contrary, Damascene says that "virtues are natural." Therefore, virtuous acts also are a subject of the natural law.

I answer that We may speak of virtuous acts in two ways: first, under the aspect of virtuous; secondly, as such and such acts considered in their proper species. If, then, we speak of acts of virtue considered as virtuous, thus all virtuous acts belong to the natural law. For it has been stated that to the natural law belongs everything to which a man is inclined according to his nature. Now each thing is inclined naturally to an operation that is suitable to it according to its form; thus fire is inclined to give heat. Wherefore, since the rational soul is the proper form of man, there is in every man a natural inclination to act according to reason, and this is to act according to virtue. Consequently, considered thus, all acts of virtue are prescribed by the natural law, since each one's reason naturally dictates to him to act virtuously. But if we speak of virtuous acts considered in themselves, i.e., in their proper species, thus not all virtuous acts are prescribed by the natural law; the many things are done virtuously to which nature does not incline at first, but which, through the inquiry of reason, have been found by men to be conducive to well-living.

Reply Obj. 1. Temperance is about the natural concupiscences of food, drink, and sexual matters, which are indeed ordained to the natural common good, just as other matters of law are ordained to the moral common good.

Reply Obj. 2. By human nature we may mean either that which is proper to man—and in this sense all sins, as being against reason, are also against nature, as Damascene states—or we may mean that nature which is common to man and other animals, and in this sense certain special sins are said to be against nature; thus, contrary to heterosexual intercourse, which is natural to all animals, is male homosexual union, which has received the special name of the unnatural vice.

Reply Obj. 3. This argument considers acts in themselves. For it is owing to the various conditions of men that certain acts are virtuous for some as being proportionate and becoming to them, while they are vicious for others as being out of proportion to them.

Fourth Article

Is the Natural Law the Same in All Men?

We proceed thus to the Fourth Article:

Obj. 1. It would seem that the natural law is not the same in all. For it is stated in the *Decretum* that "the natural law is that which is contained in the Law and the Gospel." But this is not common to all men because, as it is written, "all do not obey the gospel." Therefore, the natural law is not the same in all men.

Obj. 2. Further, "Things which are according to the law are said to be just," as stated in *Ethics* V. But it is stated in the same book that nothing is so universally just as not to be subject to change in regard to some men. Therefore, even the natural law is not the same in all men.

Obj. 3. Further, as stated above, to the natural law belongs everything to which a man is inclined according to his nature. Now, different men are naturally inclined to different things, some to the desire of pleasures, others to the desire of honors, and other men to other things. Therefore, there is not one natural law for all.

On the contrary, Isidore says, "The natural law is common to all nations."

I answer that, As stated above, to the natural law belong those things to which a man is inclined naturally, and among these, it is proper to man to be inclined to act according to reason. Now the process of reason is from the common to the proper, as stated in *Phys.* I. The speculative reason, however, is differently situated in this matter from the practical reason. For, since the speculative reason is concerned chiefly with necessary things, which cannot be otherwise than they are, its proper conclusions, like the universal principles, contain the truth without fail. The practical reason, on the other hand, is concerned with contingent matters, about which human actions are concerned, and consequently, although there is necessity in the general principles, the more we descend to matters of detail, the more frequently we encounter deviations. Accordingly, then, in speculative matters, truth is the same for all men both as to principles and as to conclusions, although the truth is not known to all as regards the conclusions but only as regards the principles which are called common notions. But in matters of action, truth or practical rectitude is not the same for all as to matters of detail but only as to the general principles, and where there is the same rectitude in matters of detail, it is not equally known to all.

It is, therefore, evident that, as regards the general principles, whether of speculative or practical reason, truth or rectitude is the same for all and is equally known by all. As to the proper conclusions of the speculative reason, the truth is the same for all but is not equally known to all; thus it is true for all that the three angles of a triangle are together equal to two right angles, although it is not known to all. But as to the proper conclusions of the practical reason, neither is the truth or rectitude the same for all, nor, where it is the same, is it equally known by all. Thus it is right and true for all to act according to reason, and from this principle, it follows as a proper conclusion that goods entrusted to another should be restored to their owner. Now this is true for the majority of cases, but it may happen in a particular case that it would be injurious, and therefore unreasonable, to restore goods held in trust, for instance, if they are claimed for the purpose of fighting against one's country. And this principle will be found to fail the more according as we descend further into detail, e.g., if one were to say that goods held in trust should be restored with such and such a guarantee or in such and such a way, because the greater the number of conditions added, the greater the number of ways in which the principle may fail, so that it be not right to restore or not to restore. Consequently, we must say that the natural law as to general principles is the same for all both as to rectitude and as to knowledge. But as to certain matters of detail, which are conclusions, as it were, of those general principles, it is the same for all in the majority of cases both as to rectitude and as to knowledge, and yet, in some few cases, it may fail both as to rectitude by reason of certain obstacles (just as natures subject to generation and corruption fail in some few cases on account of some obstacle) and as to knowledge, since, in some, the reason is perverted by passion or evil habit or an evil disposition of nature; thus, formerly, theft, although it is expressly contrary to the natural law, was not considered wrong among the Germans, as Julius Caesar relates.

Reply Obj. 1. The meaning of the sentence quoted is not that whatever is contained in the Law and the Gospel belongs to the natural law, since they contain many things that are above nature, but that whatever belongs to the natural law is fully contained in them. Wherefore Gratian, after saying that "the natural law is what is contained in the Law and the Gospel," adds at once, by way of example, "by which everyone is commanded to do to others as he would be done by."

Reply Obj. 2. The saying of the Philosopher is to be understood of things that are naturally just, not as general principles but as conclusions drawn from them, having rectitude in the majority of cases but failing in a few.

Reply Obj. 3. As, in man, reason rules and commands the other powers, so all the natural inclinations belonging to the other powers must needs be directed according to reason. Wherefore it is universally right for all men that all their inclinations should be directed according to reason.

Fifth Article

CAN THE NATURAL LAW BE CHANGED?

We proceed thus to the Fifth Article:

Obj. 1. It would seem that the natural law can be changed because, on Sir. 17:9, "He gave them instructions, and the law of life," a gloss says: "He wished the law of the letter to be written in order to correct the law of nature." But that which is corrected is changed. Therefore, the natural law can be changed.

Obj. 2. Further, the slaying of the innocent, adultery, and theft are against the natural law. But we find these things changed by God, as when God commanded Abraham to slay his innocent son, and when He ordered the Jews to borrow and purloin the vessels of the Egyptians, and when He commanded Hosea to take to himself "a wife of fornications." Therefore, the natural law can be changed.

Obj. 3. Further, Isidore says that "the possession of all things in common and universal freedom are matters of natural law." But these things are seen to be changed by human laws. Therefore, it seems that the natural law is subject to change.

On the contrary, It is said in the *Decretum*: "The natural law dates from the creation of the rational creature. It does not vary according to time but remains unchangeable."

I answer that A change in the natural law may be understood in two ways. First, by way of addition. In this sense, nothing hinders the natural law from being changed, since many things, for the benefit of human life, have been added over and above the natural law both by the divine law and by human laws.

Secondly, a change in the natural law may be understood by way of subtraction, so that what previously was according to the natural law ceases to be so. In this sense, the natural law is altogether unchangeable in its first principles, but in its secondary principles, which, as we have said, are like certain proper conclusions closely related to the first principles, the natural law is not changed so that what it prescribes be not right in most cases. But it may be changed in some particular cases of rare occurrence through some special causes hindering the observance of such precepts, as stated above.

Reply Obj. 1. The written law is said to be given for the correction of the natural law, either because it supplies what was wanting to the natural law or because the natural law was perverted in the hearts of some men as to certain matters, so that they esteemed those things good which are naturally evil, which perversion stood in need of correction.

Reply Obj. 2. All men alike, both guilty and innocent, die the death of nature, which death of nature is inflicted by the power of God on account of original sin, according to 1 Kings: "The Lord kills and makes alive." Consequently, by the command of God, death can be inflicted on any man, guilty or innocent, without any injustice whatever. In like manner, adultery is intercourse with another's wife, who is allotted to him by the law handed down by God. Consequently, intercourse with any woman, by the command of God, is neither adultery nor fornication. The same applies to theft, which is the taking of another's property. For whatever is taken by the command of God, to Whom all things belong, is not taken against the will of its owner, whereas it is in this that theft consists. Nor is it only in human things that whatever is commanded by God is right but also in natural things— whatever is done by God is, in some way, natural, as stated in the First Part.

Reply Obj. 3. A thing is said to belong to the natural law in two ways. First, because nature inclines thereto, e.g., that one should not do harm to another. Secondly, because nature did not bring in the contrary; thus we might say that for man to be naked is of the natural law because nature did not give him clothes, but art invented them. In this sense, "the possession of all things in common and universal freedom" are said to be of the natural law because, to wit, the distinction of possessions and slavery were not brought in by nature but devised by human reason for the benefit of human life. Accordingly, the law of nature was not changed in this respect except by addition.

Sixth Article

Can the Law of Nature Be Abolished from the Heart of Man?

We proceed thus to the Sixth Article:

Obj. 1. It would seem that the natural law can be abolished from the heart of man because, on Rom. 2:14, "When the Gentiles who have not the law," etc., a gloss says that "the law of righteousness, which sin had blotted out, is graven on the heart of man when he is restored by grace." But the law of righteousness is the law of nature. Therefore, the law of nature can be blotted out.

Obj. 2. Further, the law of grace is more efficacious than the law of nature. But the law of grace is blotted out by sin. Much more, therefore, can the law of nature be blotted out.

Obj. 3. Further, that which is established by law is made just. But many things are legally established which are contrary to the law of nature. Therefore, the law of nature can be abolished from the heart of man.

On the contrary, Augustine says, "Thy law is written in the hearts of men, which iniquity itself effaces not." But the law which is written in men's hearts is the natural law. Therefore, the natural law cannot be blotted out.

I answer that, As stated above, there belong to the natural law, first, certain most general precepts that are known to all; and secondly, certain secondary and more detailed precepts which are, as it were, conclusions following closely from first principles. As to those general principles, the natural law, in the abstract, can nowise be blotted out from men's hearts. But it is blotted out in the case of particular action insofar as reason is hindered from applying the general principles to a particular point of practice on account of concupiscence or some other passion, as stated above. But as to the other, i.e., the secondary precepts, the natural law can be blotted out from the human heart either by evil persuasions, just as in speculative matters errors occur in respect of necessary conclusions, or by vicious customs and corrupt habits, as among some men theft and even unnatural vices, as the Apostle states, were not esteemed sinful.

Reply Obj. 1. Sin blots out the law of nature in particular cases, not universally, except perchance in regard to the secondary precepts of the natural law, in the way stated above.

Reply Obj. 2. Although grace is more efficacious than nature, yet nature is more essential to man and therefore more enduring.

Reply Obj. 3. The argument is true of the secondary precepts of the natural law, against which some legislators have framed certain enactments which are unjust.

WAR AND KILLING

ST II-II

QUESTION 40

OF WAR

[In Four Articles, of Which Article One Is Included]

First Article

Is It Always Sinful to Wage War?

We proceed thus to the First Article:

Objection 1. It would seem that it is always sinful to wage war, because punishment is not inflicted except for sin. Now, those who wage war are threatened by Our Lord with punishment, according to Mt. 26:52: "All that take up the sword shall perish by the sword." Therefore, all wars are unlawful.

Obj. 2. Further, whatever is contrary to a divine precept is a sin. But war is contrary to a divine precept, for it is written: "But I say to you not to resist evil," and "Do not defend yourselves, my dearly beloved, but yield to [God's] wrath." Therefore, war is always sinful.

Obj. 3. Further, nothing except sin is contrary to an act of virtue. But war is contrary to peace. Therefore, war is always a sin.

Obj. 4. Further, the exercise of a lawful thing is itself lawful, as is evident in scientific exercises. But the warlike exercises which take place in tournaments are forbidden by the Church, since those who are slain in these trials are deprived of ecclesiastical burial. Therefore, it seems that war is a sin in itself.

On the contrary, Augustine says in a sermon on the servant of the centurion, "If Christian discipline forbad war altogether, those who sought salutary counsel in the Gospel would have been advised to cast aside their arms and to give up soldiering altogether. On the contrary, they were told: 'Do violence to no man, . . . and be content with your pay.' If He commanded them to be content with their pay, He did not forbid soldiering."

I answer that, In order for a war to be just, three things are necessary. First, the authority of the ruler, by whose command the war is to be waged; it is not the business of a private individual to declare war, because he can seek redress of his rights from the tribunal of his superior. Similarly, it is not the business of a private individual to summon together the people, something which has to be done in wars. But since the care of the common weal is committed to those who are in authority, it is their business to watch over the common weal of the city, kingdom, or province subject to them. And just as it is lawful for them to have recourse to the sword in defending that common weal against internal disturbances, when they punish evil-doers, according to the words of the Apostle: "He bears not the sword without cause, for he is God's minister, an avenger to execute wrath upon him that does evil," so too it is their business to have recourse to the sword of war in defending the common weal against external enemies. Hence it is said to those who are in authority: "Rescue the poor and deliver the needy out of the hand of the sinner," and for this reason Augustine says, "The natural order conducive to peace among mortals demands that the power to declare and counsel war should be in the hands of those who hold the supreme authority."

Secondly, a just cause is required, namely, that those who are attacked, should be attacked because they deserve it on account of some fault. Wherefore, Augustine says, "A just war is wont to be described as one that avenges wrongs, when a nation or state has to be punished for refusing to make amends for the wrongs inflicted by its subjects or to restore what it has seized unjustly."

Thirdly, it is necessary that the belligerents should have a rightful intention, so that they intend the advancement of good or the avoidance of evil. Hence Augustine says, "True religion looks upon as peaceful those wars that are waged not for motives of aggrandizement or cruelty but with the object of securing peace, of punishing evil-doers, and of uplifting the good." For it may happen that, even if war be declared by legitimate authority and for a just cause, it is nonetheless rendered unlawful through a wicked intention. Hence Augustine says, "The passion for inflicting harm, the cruel thirst to vengeance, an unpacific and relentless spirit, the fever of revolt, the lust of power, and such like things, all these are rightly condemned in war."

Reply Obj. 1. As Augustine says, "To take up the sword is to arm oneself in order to take the life of someone without the command or permission of superior or lawful authority." On the other hand, to have recourse to the sword (as a private person) by the authority of the ruler or judge or (as a public person) through zeal for justice and by the authority, so to speak, of God, is not to "take up the sword" but to use it as commissioned by another; wherefore it does not deserve punishment. And yet even those who make sinful use of the sword are not always slain by the sword, yet they always perish by their own sword, because, unless they repent, they are punished eternally for their sinful use of the sword.

Reply Obj. 2. Such like precepts, as Augustine observes, should always be borne in readiness of mind, so that we be ready to obey them and, if necessary, to refrain from resistance or self-defense. Nevertheless, it is necessary sometimes for a man to act otherwise for the common good or for the good of those with whom he is fighting. Hence Augustine says, "Those whom we have to punish with a kindly severity it is necessary to handle in many ways against their will. For when we are stripping a man of the lawlessness of sin, it is good for him to be vanquished, since nothing is more hopeless than the happiness of sinners, whence arises a guilty impunity and an evil will, like an internal enemy."

Reply Obj. 3. Those who wage war justly aim at peace, and so they are not opposed to peace, except to the evil peace which Our Lord "came not to send upon earth." Hence Augustine says, "We do not seek peace in order to be at war, but we go to war that we may have peace. Be peaceful, therefore, in warring, so that you may vanquish those whom you war against and bring them to the prosperity of peace."

Reply Obj. 4. Not all exercises by men in warlike feats of arms are forbidden but those which are inordinate and perilous and end in slaying or plundering. In older times, warlike exercises presented no such danger, and hence they were called "exercises of arms" or "bloodless wars," as Jerome states in an epistle.

SEDITION AND OBEDIENCE

ST II-II

QUESTION 42

OF SEDITION

[In Two Articles, of Which Article Two Is Included]

Second Article

IS SEDITION ALWAYS A MORTAL SIN?

We proceed thus to the Second Article:

Objection 1. It would seem that sedition is not always a mortal sin. For sedition denotes "a tumult leading to fighting," according to the gloss quoted above. But fighting is not always a mortal sin; indeed, it is sometimes just and lawful, as stated above. Much more, therefore, can sedition be without a mortal sin.

Obj. 2. Further, sedition is a kind of discord, as stated above. Now, discord can be without mortal sin and sometimes without any sin at all. Therefore, sedition can be also.

Obj. 3. Further, it is praiseworthy to deliver a community from tyrannical rule. Yet this cannot easily be done without some dissension in the community, if one part of the community seeks to retain the tyrant, while the rest strive to dethrone him. Therefore, there can be sedition without mortal sin.

On the contrary, The Apostle forbids seditions together with other things that are mortal sins. Therefore, sedition is a mortal sin.

I answer that, As stated above, sedition is contrary to the unity of the multitude, viz., the people of a political community or kingdom. Now, Augustine says that "wise men understand the word 'people' to designate, not any crowd of persons, but the assembly of those who are united together in fellowship recognized by law and for the common good." Wherefore it is evident that the unity to which sedition is opposed is the unity of law and the common good; whence it follows manifestly that sedition is opposed to justice and the common good. Therefore, by reason of its genus, it is a mortal sin, and its gravity will be all the greater as the common good which it assails surpasses the private good which is assailed by strife.

Accordingly, the sin of sedition is first and chiefly in its authors, who sin most grievously, and secondly, it is in those who are led by them to disturb the common good. Those, however, who defend the common good and withstand the seditious party are not themselves seditious, as neither is a man to be called quarrelsome because he defends himself, as stated above.

Reply Obj. 1. It is lawful to fight, provided it be for the common good, as stated above. But sedition runs counter to the common good of the multitude, so that it is always a mortal sin.

Reply Obj. 2. Discord from what is not manifestly good may be without sin, but discord from what is manifestly good cannot be without sin. And sedition is discord of this kind, for it is contrary to the unity of the multitude, which is manifestly good.

Reply Obj. 3. A tyrannical government is not just, because it is directed, not to the common good, but to the private good of the ruler, as the Philosopher states. Consequently, there is no sedition in disturbing a government of this kind, unless, indeed, the tyrant's rule be disturbed so inordinately that his subjects suffer greater harm from the consequent disturbance than from the tyrant's government. Indeed, it is the tyrant, rather, that is guilty of sedition, since he encourages discord and sedition among his subjects, that he may lord over them more securely; for this is tyranny, being conducive to the private good of the ruler and to the injury of the multitude.

PROPERTY

ST II-II

QUESTION 66

OF THEFT AND ROBBERY

[In Nine Articles]

We must now consider the sins opposed to justice whereby a man injures his neighbor in his belongings: namely theft and robbery.

Under this head there are nine points of inquiry: (1) Whether it is natural to man to possess external things? (2) Whether it is lawful for a man to possess something as his own? (3) Whether theft is the secret taking of another's property? (4) Whether robbery is a species of sin distinct from theft? (5) Whether every theft is a sin? (6) Whether theft is a mortal sin? (7) Whether it is lawful to thieve in a case of necessity? (8) Whether every robbery is a mortal sin? (9) Whether robbery is a more grievous sin than theft?

First Article

Is It Natural for Man to Possess External Things?

We proceed thus to the First Article:

Objection 1. It would seem that it is not natural for man to possess external things. For no man should ascribe to himself that which is God's. Now, the dominion over all creatures is proper to God, according to Ps. 23:1, "The earth is the Lord's," etc. Therefore, it is not natural for man to possess external things.

Obj. 2. Further, Basil, in expounding the words of the rich man, "I will gather together all my crops and my possessions," says, "Tell me: Which are yours? Where did you take them from and bring them into being?" Now, whatever man possesses naturally, he can fittingly call his own. Therefore, man does not naturally possess external things.

Obj. 3. Further, according to Ambrose, "dominion denotes power." But man has no power over external things, since he can work no change in their nature. Therefore, the possession of external things is not natural to man.

On the contrary, It is written: "You have subjected all things under his feet."

I answer that External things can be considered in two ways. First, as regards their nature, and this is not subject to the power of man but only to the power of God, Whose mere will all things obey. Secondly, as regards their use, and in this way man has a natural dominion over external things because, by his reason and will, he is able to use them for his own profit, as they were made on his account, for the imperfect is always for the sake of the perfect, as stated above. It is by this argument that the Philosopher proves that the possession of external things is natural to man. Moreover, this natural dominion of man over other creatures, which is competent to man in respect to his reason, wherein God's image resides, is shown forth in man's creation by the words: "Let us make man to Our image and likeness, and let him have dominion over the fishes of the sea," etc.

Reply Obj. 1. God has sovereign dominion over all things, and He, according to His providence, directed certain things to the sustenance of man's body. For this reason, man has a natural dominion over things as regards the power to make use of them.

Reply Obj. 2. The rich man is reproved for deeming external things to belong to him principally, as though he had not received them from another, namely, from God.

Reply Obj. 3. This argument considers the dominion over external things as regards their nature. Such a dominion belongs to God alone, as stated above.

Second Article

Is It Lawful for a Man to Possess a Thing as His Own?

We proceed thus to the Second Article:

Obj. 1. It would seem unlawful for a man to possess a thing as his own. For whatever is contrary to the natural law is unlawful. Now, according to the natural law, all things are common property, and the possession of property is contrary to this community of goods. Therefore, it is unlawful for any man to appropriate any external thing to himself.

Obj. 2. Further, Basil in expounding the words of the rich man quoted above, says, "The rich who deem as their own property the common goods they have seized upon are like to those who by going beforehand to the play prevent others from coming, and appropriate to themselves what is intended for common use." Now, it would be unlawful to prevent others from obtaining possession of common goods. Therefore, it is unlawful to appropriate to oneself what belongs to the community.

Obj. 3. Further, Ambrose says, and his words are quoted in the *Decretum*, "Let no man call his own that which is common property," and by common he means external things, as is clear from the context. Therefore, it seems unlawful for a man to appropriate an external thing to himself.

On the contrary, Augustine says, "The 'Apostolics' are those who with extreme arrogance have given themselves that name, because they admit into their communion only persons who are not married or possess nothing of their own, such as both the monks and clerics who in considerable number are to be found in the Catholic Church." Now, the reason these people are heretics is that, severing themselves from the Church, they think that those who enjoy the use of the above things, which they themselves lack, have no hope of salvation. Therefore, it is erroneous to maintain that it is unlawful for a man to possess property.

I answer that Two things are competent to man in respect of exterior things. One is the power to procure and dispense them, and in this regard it is lawful for man to possess property. Moreover, this is necessary to human life for three reasons. First, because every man is more careful to procure what is for himself alone than that which is common to many or to all, since each one would shirk the labor and leave to another that which concerns the community, as happens where there is a great number of servants. Secondly, because human affairs are conducted in more orderly fashion if each man is charged with taking care of some particular thing himself, whereas there would be confusion if everyone had to look after any one thing indeterminately. Thirdly, because a more peaceful state is ensured to man if each one is contented with his own. Hence it is to be observed that quarrels arise more frequently where there is no division of the things possessed.

The second thing that is competent to man with regard to external things is their use. In this respect man ought to possess external things, not as his own, but as common, so that, to wit, he is ready to communicate them to others in their need. Hence the Apostle says, "Charge the rich of this world . . . to give easily, to share," etc.

Reply Obj. 1. Community of goods is ascribed to the natural law, not because the natural law dictates that all things should be possessed in common, and that nothing should be possessed as one's own, but because there is division of possessions, not according to the natural law, but rather according to human agreement, which belongs to positive law, as stated above. Hence, the ownership of possessions is not contrary to the natural law but an addition thereto devised by human reason.

Reply Obj. 2. A man would not act unlawfully if by going beforehand to the play he prepared the way for others, but he acts unlawfully if by doing so he hinders others from going. In like manner, a rich man does not act unlawfully if he anticipates someone in taking possession of something which at first was common property and gives others a share, but he sins if he excludes others indiscriminately from using it. Hence Basil says, "Why are you rich while another is poor, unless it be that you may have the merit of a good stewardship, and he the reward of patience?"

Reply Obj. 3. When Ambrose says: "Let no man call his own that which is common," he is speaking of ownership as regards use; wherefore he adds: "He who spends too much is a robber."

NICCOLÒ MACHIAVELLI

Niccolò Machiavelli (1469–1527) was born, lived, and died in Renaissance Florence, but his thought was immersed in antiquity, in the Sparta of Lycurgus, the Athens of Solon and Pericles, and most of all in Republican Rome. And it is this immersion that establishes Machiavelli as the central political thinker in the tradition of Renaissance humanism. Its results are reflections about political ideals and political practice, about Fortune and *virtù* (ingenuity, skill, excellence), about honor, reputation, and power. But Machiavelli's thoughts are not mere fantasies; they are meant to be effective, to order political life, and to renew the past for the present. Writing to his friend Francesco Vettori in Rome, Machiavelli describes himself as a student of just this kind:

> When evening comes, I return to my home, and I go into my study; and on the threshold, I take off my everyday clothes, which are covered with mud and mire, and I put on regal and curial robes; and dressed in a more appropriate manner I enter into the ancient courts of ancient men and am welcomed by them kindly, and there I taste the food that alone is mine, and for which I was born. . . . I have noted down what I have learned from their conversation, and I composed a little work, *De principatibus* [*The Prince*]. . . .

Machiavelli was born on May 3, 1469, into a respectable middle-class family. His father had a deep commitment to the Latin classics, a devotion which he obviously conveyed to his son. In 1498, shortly after the execution of the Dominican prophetic prior Girolamo Savonarola, the unknown and inexperienced Machiavelli was installed as chancellor of the Second Chancery of the city, a position which he held for fourteen years. It was not a prestigious or powerful role but one that involved him with the nitty-gritty of domestic and especially foreign affairs. In the course of those years, he served as secretary to the board assigned to establish a citizens' militia, assisted Piero Soderini, his mentor and the city's chief executive after 1502, and participated in a number of foreign diplomatic missions. On many occasions, Machiavelli was able to observe major political figures, who subsequently in his writings became models for types of political conduct and leadership. These include Cesare Borgia, whom he observed three times between 1502 and 1503, Pope Julius II, and the Emperor Maximilian.

When Soderini was forced to leave Florence and the republic dissolved, Machiavelli was arrested, tortured, and exiled to his country estate. These political events, as one commentator puts it, were "a personal misfortune" but also a "catalyst for his political imagination." Forced into retirement, Machiavelli turned to study and writing. He joined a circle of Florentine intellectuals who met for conversation about literary and political matters at the Oricellari Gardens, owned by Cosimo Rucellai. It was here that he presented ideas that eventually became part of his extensive defense of republican liberty or self-government, the causes and nature of political corruption, the need for a civil religion, and the benefits of mixed constitution, the *Discourses on the First Ten Books of Titius Livius.*

The Prince, Machiavelli's most famous work, was written in this historical setting and for precise purposes. The son of Lorenzo de Medici had been elected Pope Leo X in 1513. With the republic under Soderini in ruins, the Medicis were destined to return to control Florence. The times were propitious for a union of Italian leadership under the Medicis, which would rule both Rome and Florence. In July to December of 1513, Machiavelli interrupted work on his commentary on Livy's *Histories* and set out in *The Prince* his conception of daring political rule, a form of leadership that would exploit the prince's skill (*virtù*) to take advantage of what Fortune provided in order to gain power, glory, and security. It was a conception of instrumental morality, ancient in design, that directly conflicted with Christian morality, but that at the same time was tailored to appeal to the Medicis' needs and aspirations. It was a conception of human excellence appreciating and coping with the changing contingencies of circumstance in such a way that the prince's ultimate goals could be achieved.

The Prince, then, was Machiavelli's handbook for the strategies required to capitalize on the rare opportunity the Medicis faced. It was also his way of showing fidelity to that goal and of advancing himself as a candidate for a political role in the Medician government. He hoped that his friend Vettori, the Florentine ambassador to Rome, would intercede with the Medicis on his behalf, and so he wrote to Vettori about his work. But Vettori never did so, and the plan to seek Medician patronage and political office failed.

For the remainder of his life, Machiavelli lived in exile and neglect. He wrote extensively on war, language, and history. But he was never invited to return to public life. In 1527 he died, living long enough to see the Medici driven out of Florence and the republic reestablished. Four years later, in 1531, the *Discourses* were published, and then in 1532 *The Prince*, the works on which his fame rests to this day. To some, *The Prince* is a work of realism and practical sensitivity; to many, a cynical, immoral treatise that borders on the diabolical; to others, however, *The Prince* exemplifies a return to an early ethic, a morality, born in antiquity, that acknowledges the changes of Fortune, the variety of abilities and skills required to cope with contingencies, and the role of power, boldness, and even violence in political life.

Recommended readings

Berlin, Isaiah. "The Originality of Machiavelli," in *Against the Current.* ed. H. Hardy. London, 1979, 25–79.

Bok, Sissela (ed.). *Machiavelli and Republicanism.* Cambridge: Cambridge University Press, 1990.

Burns, James (ed.) *Cambridge History of Political Thought, 1450–1700*. Cambridge: Cambridge University Press, 1991.

Gilbert, Felix. *Machiavelli and Guicciardini*. Princeton: Princeton University Press, 1965.

Pocock, J.G.A. *The Machiavellian Moment*. Princeton: Princeton University Press, 1975.

Skinner, Quentin. *The Foundations of Modern Political Thought*. Vol. II. Cambridge: Cambridge University Press, 1978.

Skinner, Quentin. *Machiavelli*. Oxford: Oxford University Press, 1981.

Wolin, Sheldon. *Politics and Vision*. New York: Little, Brown and Co., 1960.

THE PRINCE

Niccolò Machiavelli to
Lorenzo de' Medici, the Magnificent

In most instances, it is customary for those who desire to win the favor of a Prince to present themselves to him with those things they value most or which they feel will most please him; thus, we often see Princes given horses, arms, vestments of gold cloth, precious stones, and similar ornaments suited to their greatness. Wishing, therefore, to offer myself to Your Magnificence with some evidence of my devotion to you, I have not found among my belongings anything that I might value more or prize so much as the knowledge of the deeds of great men, which I learned from a long experience in modern affairs and a continuous study of antiquity; having with great care and for a long time thought about and examined these deeds, and now having set them down in a little book, I am sending them to Your Magnificence.

And although I consider this work unworthy of your station, I am sure, nevertheless, that your humanity will move you to accept it, for there could not be a greater gift from me than to give you the means to be able, in a very brief time, to understand all that I, in many years and with many hardships and dangers, came to understand and to appreciate. I have neither decorated nor filled this work with fancy sentences, with rich and magnificent words, or with any other form of rhetorical or unnecessary ornamentation which many writers normally use in describing and enriching their subject matter; for I wished that nothing should set my work apart or make it pleasing except the variety of its material and the seriousness of its contents. Neither do I wish that it be thought presumptuous if a man of low and inferior station dares to debate and to regulate the rule of princes; for, just as those who paint landscapes place themselves in a low position on the plain in order to consider the nature of the mountains and the high places and place themselves high atop mountains in order to study the plains, in like manner, to know well the nature of the people one must be a prince, and to know well the nature of princes one must be of the people.

Accept, therefore, Your Magnificence, this little gift in the spirit that I send it; if you read and consider it carefully, you will discover in it my most heartfelt desire that you may attain that greatness which Fortune and all your own capacities promise you. And if Your Magnificence will turn your eyes at some time from the summit of your high position toward these lowlands, you will realize to what degree I unjustly suffer a great and continuous malevolence of Fortune.

Chapter I

How Many Kinds of Principalities There Are and the Way They Are Acquired

All states and all dominions that have had and continue to have power over men were and still are either republics or principalities. And principalities are either hereditary, in which instance the family of the prince has ruled for generations, or they are new. And the new ones are either completely new, as was Milan for Francesco Sforza, or they are like members added to the hereditary state of the prince who acquires them, as is the Kingdom of Naples for the King of Spain. Dominions taken in this way are either used to living under a prince or are accustomed to being free; and they are gained either by the arms of others or by one's own, either through Fortune or through cleverness.

Chapter II
On Hereditary Principalities

I shall set aside any discussion of republics, because I treated them elsewhere at length. I shall consider solely the principality, developing as I go the topics mentioned above; and I shall discuss how these principalities can be governed and maintained.

I say, then, that in hereditary states accustomed to the rule of their prince's family there are far fewer difficulties in maintaining them than in new states; for it suffices simply not to break ancient customs, and then to suit one's actions to unexpected events; in this manner, if such a prince is of ordinary ability, he will always maintain his state, unless some extraordinary and inordinate force deprive him of it; and although it may be taken away from him, he will regain it with the slightest mistake of the usurper.

As an example, we have in Italy the Duke of Ferrara, who withstood the assaults of the Venetians in 1484 and those of Pope Julius in 1510 for no other reason than the tradition of his rule in that dominion. Because a prince by birth has fewer reasons and less need to offend his subjects, it is natural that he should be more loved; and if no unusual vices make him hated, it is reasonable that he be naturally well liked by them. And in the course and continuity of his rule, memories and the causes for innovations die out, because one change always leaves space for the construction of another.

Chapter III
On Mixed Principalities

But it is the new principality that causes difficulties. In the first place, if it is not completely new but is instead an acquisition (so that the two parts together may be called mixed), its difficulties derive from one natural problem inherent in all new principalities: men gladly change their masters, thinking to better themselves; and this belief causes them to take arms against their ruler; but they fool themselves in this, since with experience they see that things have become worse. This stems from another natural and ordinary necessity, which is that a new prince must always offend his new subjects with both his soldiers and other countless injuries that accompany his new conquest; thus, you have made enemies of all those you injured in occupying the principality and you are unable to maintain as friends those who helped you to rise to power, since you cannot satisfy them in the way that they had supposed, nor can you use strong measures against them, for you are in their debt; because, although one may have the most powerful of armies, he always needs the support of the inhabitants to seize a province. For these reasons, Louis XII, King of France, quickly occupied Milan and just as quickly lost it; and the first time, the troops of Ludovico alone were needed to retake it from him, because those citizens who had opened the gates of the city to the king, finding themselves deceived in their opinions and in that future improvement they had anticipated, could not support the offenses of the new prince.

It is indeed true that when lands which have rebelled once are taken a second time, it is more difficult to lose them; for the lord, taking advantage of the revolt, is less reticent about punishing offenders, ferreting out suspects, and shoring up weak positions. So that, if only a Duke Ludovico threatening the borders was sufficient for France to lose Milan the first time, the whole world had to oppose her and destroy her armies or chase them from Italy to cause her to lose it the second time; and this happened for the reasons mentioned above. Nevertheless, it was taken from her both the first and the second time.

The general explanations for the first loss have been discussed; now there remains to specify those for the second, and to see what remedies the King of France had, and those that one in the same situation might have, so that he might be able to maintain a stronger grip on his conquest than did France. Therefore, I say that those dominions which, upon being conquered, are added to the long-established state of him who acquires them are either of the same province and language or they are not. When they are, it is easier to hold them, especially when they are unaccustomed to freedom; and to possess them securely, it is only necessary to have extinguished the family line of the prince who ruled them, because insofar as other things are concerned, men live peacefully as long as their old way of life is maintained and there is no change in customs: thus, we have seen what happened in the case of Burgundy, Brittany, Gascony, and Normandy, which have been part of France for such a long time; and although there is a slight difference in the language, nevertheless the customs are similar and they have been able to get along together easily. And anyone who acquires these lands and wishes to maintain them must bear two things in mind: first, that the family line of the old prince must be extinguished; second, that neither their laws nor their taxes be altered; as a result they will become in a very brief time one body with the old principality.

But when dominions are acquired in a province that is not similar in language, customs, and laws, it is here that difficulties arise; and it is here that one needs much good fortune and much diligence to hold on to them. And one of the best and most efficacious remedies would be for the person who has taken possession of them to go and live there. This would make that possession more secure and durable, as the Turks did with Greece; for with all the other precautions they took to retain that dominion, if they had not gone there to live, it would have been impossible for them to hold on to it. Because, by being on the spot, one sees trouble at its birth and one can quickly remedy it; not being there, one hears about it after it has grown and there is no longer any remedy. Moreover, the province would not be plundered by one's own officers; the subjects would be pleased in having direct recourse to their prince; thus, wishing to be good subjects, they have more reason to love him and, wanting to be otherwise, more reason to fear him. Anyone who might wish to invade that dominion from abroad would be more hesitant; so that, living right there, the prince can only with the greatest of difficulties lose it.

The other and better solution is to send colonies into one or two places that will act as supports for your own state; for it is necessary that either the prince do this or maintain a large number of infantry and cavalry. Colonies do not cost much, and with little or no expense a prince can send and maintain them; and in so doing he offends only those whose fields and houses have been taken and given to the new inhabitants, who are only a small part of that state; and those that he offends, being dispersed and poor, cannot ever threaten him, and all the others remain on the one hand unharmed (and because of this, they should remain silent), and on the other afraid of making a mistake, for fear that what happened to those who were dispossessed might happen to them. I conclude that these colonies are not expensive, they are more faithful, and they create fewer difficulties; and those who are hurt cannot pose a threat, since they are poor and scattered, as I have already said. Concerning this, it should be noted that one must either pamper or do away with men, because they will avenge themselves for minor offenses while for more serious ones they cannot; so that any harm done to a man must be the kind that removes any fear of revenge. But by maintaining soldiers there instead of colonies, one spends much more, being obliged to consume all the revenues of the state in guarding its borders, so that the profit becomes a loss; and far greater offense is committed, since the entire state is harmed by the army changing quarters from one place to another; everybody resents this inconvenience, and everyone becomes an enemy; and these are enemies that can be harmful, since they remain, although conquered, in their own homes. And so, in every respect, this kind of defense is as useless as the other kind, colonization, is useful.

Moreover, anyone who is in a province that is unlike his own in the ways mentioned above should make himself the leader and defender of the less powerful neighbors and do all he can to weaken those who are more powerful, and he should be careful that, for whatever reason, no foreigner equal to himself in strength enter there. And it will always happen that the outsider will be brought in by those who are dissatisfied, either because of too much ambition or because of fear, as was once seen when the Aetolians brought the Romans into Greece; and in every other province that the Romans entered, they were brought in by the inhabitants. What occurs is that as soon as a powerful foreigner enters a province, all who are less powerful cling to him, moved by the envy they have for the one who has ruled over them; so that, concerning these weaker powers, he has no trouble whatsoever in winning them over, since all of them will immediately and willingly become part of the state that he has acquired. He has only to be on his guard that they do not seize too much power and authority; and he can, very easily, with his force and their support, put down those who are powerful in order to remain, in everything, arbiter of that province. And anyone who does not follow this procedure will quickly lose what he has taken, and while he holds it, he will find it full of infinite difficulties and worries.

In the provinces that they seized, the Romans observed these procedures very carefully; they sent colonies, kept the less powerful at bay without increasing their strength, put down the powerful, and did not allow powerful foreigners to gain prestige there. And I shall cite only the province of Greece as an example: the Romans kept the Achaeans and the Aetolians in check; the Macedonian kingdom was put down; Antiochus was driven out; nor were they ever persuaded by the merits of the Achaeans or the Aetolians to allow them any gain of territory; nor did the persuasion of Philip of Macedonia ever convince them to make him their friend without first humbling him; nor could the power of Antiochus force their consent to his having any authority whatsoever in that province. For the Romans did in these instances what all wise princes should do: these princes have not only to watch out for present problems but also for those in the future, and try diligently to avoid them; for once problems are recognized ahead of time, they can be easily cured; but if you wait for them to present themselves, the medicine will be too late, for the disease will have become incurable. And what physicians say about disease is applicable here: that at the beginning a disease is easy to cure but difficult to diagnose; but as time passes, not having been recognized or treated at the outset, it becomes easy to diagnose but difficult to cure. The same thing occurs in affairs of state; for by recognizing from afar the diseases that are spreading in the state (which is a gift given only to the prudent ruler), they can be cured quickly; but when, not having been recognized, they are left to grow to the extent that everyone recognizes them, there is no longer any cure.

Thus, seeing from afar any difficulties, the Romans always found a remedy; and they never let them develop in order to avoid a war, because they knew that war cannot be avoided but can only be put off to the advantage of others; therefore, they wanted to go to war with Philip and Antiochus in Greece in order not to have to combat them in Italy; and they could have, at the time, avoided the one and the other, but they did not want to. Nor did they ever like what is always on the tongues of our wise men today, to enjoy the benefits of time, but they enjoyed instead the benefits of their strength and prudence; for time brings with it all things, and it can bring with it the good as well as the bad and the bad as well as the good.

But let us return to France and determine if she did any of the things we have just mentioned; and I shall speak of Louis and not of Charles, and therefore about the one whose progress has been observed better because he held territory in Italy for a longer period; and you will see that he did the contrary of those things that must be done in order to hold one's rule in a foreign province.

King Louis was installed in Italy because of the ambition of the Venetians, who wanted by his coming to gain for themselves half of Lombardy. I will not criticize the enterprise the King undertook; for, wishing to establish a first foothold in Italy and not having any friends in this land and, furthermore, having all the gates closed to him because of the actions of King Charles, he was forced to strike up whatever friendships he could; and this worthy undertaking would have succeeded if he had not erred in his other moves. After having taken Lombardy, then, the King immediately regained the prestige that Charles had lost him: Genoa surrendered; the Florentines became his allies; the Marquis of Mantua, the Duke of Ferrara, the Bentivogli, the Countess of Forlì, the lords of Faenza, Pesaro, Rimini, Camerino, and Piombino, and the people of Lucca, Pisa, and Siena all rushed to gain his friendship. And at that point the Venetians could see the recklessness of the enterprise they had undertaken; in order to acquire a bit of Lombardy, they had made the King the master of a third of Italy.

Consider, now, with what little trouble the King might have maintained his reputation in Italy if he had followed the rules listed above and kept secure and defended all those friends of his who, there being a goodly number of them, both weak and fearful, some of the Church, others of the Venetians, were always forced to be his allies; and through them he could have easily secured himself against the remaining great powers. But no sooner was he in Milan than he did the contrary, giving assistance to Pope Alexander so that he could seize Romagna. Nor did he realize that with this decision he had made himself weaker, abandoning his allies and those who had thrown themselves into his lap, and made the Church stronger by adding to it so much temporal power in addition to the spiritual power from which it derives so much authority. And having made one first mistake, he was obliged to make others; so that in order to put an end to the ambition of Alexander and to keep him from becoming lord of Tuscany, he was forced to come to Italy. He was not satisfied to have made the Church powerful and to have lost his allies, for, coveting the Kingdom of Naples, he divided it with the King of Spain; and where he first had been the arbiter of Italy, he brought in a partner so that the ambitious and the malcontents of that province had someone else to turn to; and where he could have left a figurehead king to rule that kingdom, he replaced him, establishing one there who could, in turn, drive Louis out.

The desire to acquire is truly a very natural and normal thing; and when men who can do so, they will always be praised and not condemned; but when they cannot and wish to do so at any cost, herein lies the error and the blame. If France, therefore, could have assaulted Naples with her own troops, she should have done so; if she could not, she should not have shared it. And if the division of Lombardy with the Venetians deserves to be overlooked, since it allowed Louis to gain a foothold in Italy, the other division deserves to be criticized, since it cannot be excused by necessity.

Thus, Louis had made these five mistakes: he had destroyed the weaker powers; he increased the power of another force in Italy; he had brought into that province a powerful foreigner; he did not come there to live; and he did not send colonies there. In spite of this, these mistakes, had he lived, might not have damaged him if he had not made a sixth: that of reducing the Venetians' power; for if he had not made the Church stronger, nor brought Spain into Italy, it would have been most reasonable and necessary to put them down; but, having taken those first initiatives, he should never have agreed to their ruin; for as long as they were powerful they would have always kept the others from trying to seize Lombardy, partly because the Venetians would not have allowed this unless they themselves became the rulers of Lombardy, and partly because the others would not have wanted to take it away from France to give it to the Venetians; and they would not have had the nerve to provoke both of them. And if someone were to say: King Louis relinquished Romagna to Alexander and the Kingdom of Naples to Spain in order to avoid a war, I would reply with the arguments given above: that one should never allow chaos to develop in order to avoid going to war, because one does not avoid a war but instead puts it off to his disadvantage. And if some others were to note the promise that the King had made the Pope to undertake that enterprise in return for the annulment of his marriage and for the Cardinal's hat of Rouen, I should answer with what I shall say further on about the promises of princes and how they should be observed.

King Louis lost Lombardy, therefore, by not following any of the principles observed by others who had taken provinces and who wished to retain them. Nor is this in any sense a miracle, but very ordinary and reasonable. And I spoke about this at Nantes with the Cardinal of Rouen when Valentino (for this was what Cesare Borgia, son of Pope Alexander, was commonly called) occupied Romagna; for when the Cardinal of Rouen told me that Italians understood little about war, I replied to him that the French understood little about politics; for if they did understand, they would not permit the Church to gain so much power. And we have learned through experience that the power of the Church and of Spain in Italy has been caused by France, and that her downfall has been brought about by them. From this one can derive a general rule which rarely, if ever, fails: that anyone who is the cause of another's becoming powerful comes to ruin himself, because that power is the result either of diligence or of force, and both of these two qualities are suspect to the one who has become powerful.

Chapter IV

Why the Kingdom of Darius, Occupied by Alexander, Did Not Rebel Against His Successors After the Death of Alexander

Considering the difficulties one has in maintaining a newly acquired state, one might wonder how it happened that when Alexander the Great, having become lord of Asia in a few years and having hardly occupied it, died—wherefore it would have seemed reasonable for the whole state to revolt—Alexander's successors nevertheless managed to hold on to it; and they had, in keeping it, no other difficulty than that which was born among themselves from their own ambition. Let me reply that all principalities known to us are governed in one of two different ways: either by one prince with the others as his servants, who, as ministers, through his grace and permission, assist in governing that kingdom; or by a prince and barons who hold that position not because of any grace of their master but because of the nobility of their birth. Such barons as these have their own dominions and subjects who recognize them as masters and are naturally fond of them. Those dominions governed by a prince and his ministers hold their prince in greater authority, for in all his province there is no one that may be recognized as superior to him; and if they do obey any other, they do so as his minister and officer, and they do not harbor any special affection for him.

Examples of these two different kinds of governments in our own times are the Turkish Emperor and the King of France. The entire kingdom of the Turk is ruled by one master; the others are his servants; and dividing his kingdom into parts, he sends various administrators there, and he moves them and changes them as he pleases. But the King of France is placed among a group of established nobles who are recognized in that state by their subjects and who are loved by them; they have their hereditary rights; the King cannot remove them without danger to himself. Anyone, therefore, who considers these two states will find that the difficulty lies in taking possession of the Turkish state, but once it has been conquered, it is very simple to retain it. And therefore, on the contrary, you will find that in some ways it is easier to seize the French state, but it is extremely difficult to hold on to it.

The reasons for the difficulty in being able to occupy the Turkish kingdom are that it is not possible to be summoned there by the prince of that kingdom, nor to hope to make your enterprise easier with the rebellion of those the ruler has around him. This is because of the reasons mentioned above: since they are all slaves and dependent on the ruler, it is more difficult to corrupt them; and even if they were corrupted, you cannot hope that they will be very useful, not being able to attract followers for the reasons already discussed. Therefore, anyone who attacks the Turks must consider that he will find them completely united, and it is best that he rely more on his own strength than on their lack of unity. But once beaten and broken in battle so that they cannot regroup their troops, there is nothing else to be feared but the family of the prince; once it is extinguished, there remains no one else to be feared, for the others have no credit with the people; and just as the victor before the victory could not place hope in them, so he need not fear them afterward.

The opposite occurs in kingdoms governed like that of France, because you can enter them with ease once you have won to your side some baron of the kingdom; for you always find malcontents and those who desire changes; these people, for the reasons already given, can open the way to that state and facilitate your victory. Then, wishing to hold on to it is accompanied by endless problems, problems with those that have aided you and with those you have suppressed; nor does it suffice to do away with the family of the prince, because the lords who make themselves heads of new factions still remain; and you lose that state at the first occasion, for you are neither able to make them happy nor are you able to do away with them.

Now, if you will consider the type of government Darius established, you will find it similar to the kingdom of the Turks; and therefore Alexander first had to overwhelm it totally and defeat it in battle; after this victory, Darius being dead, that state remained securely in Alexander's hands for the reasons discussed above. And his successors would have enjoyed it without effort had they been united; for in that kingdom no disorders arose other than those they themselves had caused. But in states organized like that of France, it is impossible to hold them with such ease. Because of this, there arose the frequent revolts of Spain, France, and Greece against the Romans, all because of the numerous principalities that were in those states; as long as the memory of them lasted, the Romans were always unsure of their power; but once that memory had been extinguished, they became completely theirs. Afterward, when the Romans fought among themselves, each one was able to draw a following from those provinces, according to the authority he enjoyed there; and since the families of their former rulers had been extinguished, they recognized only the Romans. Taking all these things into account, therefore, no one at all should marvel at the ease with which Alexander retained the state of Asia, or at the problems that others suffered in preserving their acquisition, such as Pyrrhus and others. This is not caused by the greater or lesser skill of the victor but rather by the difference of the situations.

Chapter V
How Cities or Principalities Should Be Governed That Lived By Their Own Laws
Before They Were Occupied

As I have said, when those states that are acquired are used to living by their own laws and in freedom, there are three methods of holding on to them: the first is to destroy them; the second is to go there in person to live; the third is to allow them to live with their own laws, forcing them to pay a tribute and creating therein a government made up of a few people who will keep the state friendly toward you. For such a government, having been created by that prince, knows that it cannot last without his friendship and his power, and it must do everything possible to maintain them; and a city used to living in freedom is more easily maintained through the means of its own citizens than in any other way, if you decide to preserve it. As examples, there are the Spartans and the Romans. The Spartans held Athens and Thebes by building therein a government consisting of a few people; eventually they lost them both. The Romans, in order to hold Capua, Carthage, and Numantia, destroyed them and did not lose them; they wished to hold Greece by almost the same manner as the Spartans held it, making it free and leaving it under its own laws, and they did not succeed; thus, they were obliged to destroy many of the cities in that province in order to retain it. For, in truth, there is no secure means of holding on to them except by destroying them. And anyone who becomes lord of a city used to living in liberty and does not destroy it may expect to be destroyed by it; because such a city always has as a refuge, in any rebellion, the name of liberty and its ancient institutions, neither of which are ever forgotten either because of the passing of time or because of the bestowal of benefits. And it matters little what one does or foresees, since if one does not separate or scatter the inhabitants, they will not forget that name or those institutions; and immediately, in every case, they will return to them just as Pisa did after one hundred years of being held in servitude by the Florentines. But when cities or provinces are accustomed to living under a prince and the family of that prince has been extinguished, they, being on the one hand used to obedience and, on the other, not having their old prince and not being able to agree on choosing another from amongst themselves, yet not knowing how to live as free men, are as a result hesitant in taking up arms, and a prince can win them over and assure himself of their support with greater ease. But in republics there is greater vitality, greater hatred, greater desire for revenge; the memory of ancient liberty does not and cannot allow them to rest, so that the most secure way is either to destroy them or to go there to live.

Chapter VI
On New Principalities Acquired By One's Own Arms and By Skill

No one should marvel if, in speaking of principalities that are totally new as to their prince and organization, I use the most illustrious examples; since men almost always tread the paths made by others and proceed in their affairs by imitation, although they are not completely able to stay on the path of others nor reach the skill of those they imitate, a prudent man should always enter those paths taken by great men and imitate those who have been most excellent, so that if one's own skill does not match theirs, at least it will have the smell of it; and he should proceed like those prudent archers who, aware of the strength of their bow when the target they are aiming at seems too distant, set their sights, much higher than the designated target, not in order to reach to such a height with their arrow but rather to be able, with the aid of such a high aim, to strike their target.

I say, therefore, that in completely new principalities, where there is a new prince, one finds in maintaining them more or less difficulty according to the greater or lesser skill of the one who acquires them. And because this act of transition from private citizen to prince presupposes either ingenuity or Fortune, it appears that either the one or the other of these two things should, in part, mitigate many of the problems; nevertheless, he who has relied upon Fortune less has maintained his position best. Things are also facilitated when the prince, having no other dominions to govern, is constrained to come to live there in person. But to come to those who, by means of their own skill and not because of Fortune, have become princes, I say that the most admirable are Moses, Cyrus, Romulus, Theseus, and the like. And although we should not discuss Moses, since he was a mere executor of things ordered by God, nevertheless he must be admired, if for nothing but that grace which made him worthy of talking with God. But let us consider Cyrus and the others who have acquired or founded kingdoms; you will find them all admirable; and if their deeds and their particular institutions are considered, they will not appear different from those of Moses, who had so great a guide. And examining their deeds and their lives, one can see that they received nothing but the opportunity from Fortune, which then gave them the material they could mold into whatever form they desired; and without that opportunity the strength of their spirit would have been extinguished, and without that strength the opportunity would have come in vain.

It was therefore necessary for Moses to find the people of Israel slaves in Egypt and oppressed by the Egyptians in order that they might be disposed to follow him to escape this servitude. It was necessary for Romulus not to stay in Alba and to be exposed at birth so that he might become King of Rome and founder of that nation. It was necessary for Cyrus to find the Persians discontented with the empire of the Medes and the Medes soft and effeminate after a lengthy peace. Theseus could not have shown his skill if he had not found the Athenians scattered. These opportunities, therefore, made these men successful, and their outstanding ingenuity made that opportunity known to them, whereby their nations were ennobled and became prosperous.

Like these men, those who become princes through their skill acquire the principality with difficulty, but they hold on to it easily; and the difficulties they encounter in acquiring the principality grow, in part, out of the new institutions and methods they are obliged to introduce in order to found their state and their security. And one should bear in mind that there is nothing more difficult to execute, nor more dubious of success, nor more dangerous to administer than to introduce a new system of things: for he who introduces it has all those who profit from the old system as his enemies, and he has only lukewarm allies in all those who might profit from the new system. This lukewarmness partly stems from fear of their adversaries, who have the law on their side, and partly from the skepticism of men who do not truly believe in new things unless they have actually had personal experience of them. Therefore, it happens that whenever those who are enemies have the chance to attack, they do so in a partisan manner, and those others defend hesitantly, so that they, together with the prince, are in danger.

It is necessary, however, if we desire to examine this subject thoroughly, to note whether these innovators act on their own or are dependent on others: that is, if they are forced to beg or are able to use power in conducting their affairs. In the first case, they always end up badly and never accomplish anything; but when they lean on their own resources and can use power, then only seldom do they find themselves in peril. From this comes the fact that all armed prophets were victorious and the unarmed came to ruin. Besides what has been said, people are fickle by nature; and it is simple to convince them of something but difficult to hold them in that conviction; and, therefore, affairs should be managed in such a way that when they no longer believe, they can be made to believe by force. Moses, Cyrus, Theseus, and Romulus could not have made their institutions long respected if they had been unarmed; as in our times it befell Brother Girolamo Savonarola, who was ruined by his new institutions when the populace began no longer to believe in them; and he had no way of holding steady those who had believed nor of making the disbelievers believe. Therefore, such men have great problems in getting ahead, and they meet all their dangers as they proceed, and they must overcome them with their skill; but once they have overcome them and have begun to be respected, having removed those who were envious of their merits, they remain powerful, secure, honored, and happy.

To such noble examples I should like to add a minor one; but it will have some relation to the others, and I should like it to suffice for all similar cases: and this is Hiero of Syracuse. From a private citizen, this man became the prince of Syracuse; he did not receive anything from Fortune except the opportunity, for since the citizens of Syracuse were oppressed, they elected him as their leader; and from that he earned the right to be their prince. And he was so skillful that while still a private citizen someone who wrote about him said "that he lacked nothing save a kingdom to reign." He abolished the old militia and established a new one; he left behind old friendships and made new ones; and since he had allies and soldiers that depended on him, he was able to construct whatever building he wished on such a foundation; so that this required of him great effort to acquire but little to maintain.

Chapter VII
On New Principalities Acquired With the Arms and Fortunes of Others

Those private citizens who become princes through Fortune alone do so with little effort, but they maintain their position only with a great deal; they meet no obstacles along their way since they fly to success, but all their problems arise when they have arrived. And these are the men who are granted a state either because they have money or because they enjoy the favor of him who grants it: this occurred to many in Greece in the cities of Ionia and the Hellespont, where Darius created princes in order that he might hold these cities for his security and glory; in like manner were set up those emperors who from private citizens came to power by bribing the soldiers. Such men depend solely upon two very uncertain and unstable things: the will and the fortune of him who granted them the state; they do not know how and are not able to maintain their position. They do not know how, since if men are not of great intelligence and ingenuity, it is not reasonable that they know how to rule, having always lived as private citizens; they are not able to, since they do not have forces that are friendly and faithful. Besides, states that rise quickly, just as all the other things of nature that are born and grow rapidly, cannot have roots and ramifications; the first bad weather kills them, unless these men who have suddenly become princes, as I have noted, are of such ability that they know how to prepare themselves quickly and to preserve what Fortune has put in their laps, and to construct afterward those foundations that others have built before becoming princes.

Regarding the two methods just listed for becoming a prince, by skill or by Fortune, I should like to offer two examples from our own day: these are Francesco Sforza and Cesare Borgia. Francesco, through the required means and with a great deal of ingenuity, became Duke of Milan from his station as a private citizen, and that which he had acquired with a thousand efforts he maintained with little trouble. On the other hand, Cesare Borgia (commonly called Duke Valentino) acquired the state because of his father's fortune and lost it in the same manner, and this despite the fact that he did everything and used every means that a prudent and skillful man ought to use in order to root himself securely in those states that the arms and fortune of others had granted him. Because, as stated above, anyone who does not lay his foundations beforehand could do so later only with great skill, although this would be done with inconvenience to the architect and danger to the building. If, therefore, we consider all the steps taken by the Duke, we shall see that he laid sturdy foundations for his future power; and I do not judge it useless to discuss them, for I would not know of any better precepts to give to a new prince than the example of his deeds; and if he did not succeed in his plans, it was not his fault but was instead the result of an extraordinary and extreme instance of ill fortune.

Alexander VI, in his attempts to advance his son, the Duke, had many problems, both present and future. First, he saw no means of making him master of any state that did not already belong to the Church; and if he attempted to seize anything belonging to the Church, he knew that the Venetians and the Duke of Milan would not agree to it because Faenza and Rimini were already under the protection of the Venetians. Moreover, he saw that the troops of Italy, and especially those he would have to use, were in the hands of those who had reason to fear the Pope's power; and he could not count on them, since they were all Orsini, Colonnesi, and their allies. Therefore, he had to disturb the order of things and cause turmoil among these states in order securely to make himself master of a part of them. This was easy for him to do, for he found that the Venetians, moved by other motives, had decided to bring the French back into Italy; not only did he not oppose this, but he rendered it easier by annulling King Louis' first marriage. The King, therefore, entered Italy with the aid of the Venetians and the consent of Alexander; and no sooner was he in Milan than the Pope procured troops from him for the Romagna campaign; these were granted to him because of the reputation of the King.

Having seized, then, Romagna and having beaten the Colonna, the Duke, wishing to maintain his gain and to advance further, was held back by two things: first, his troops' lack of loyalty; second, the will of France; that is, the troops of the Orsini, which he had been using, might let him down and not only keep him from acquiring more territory but even take away what he had already conquered; and the King, as well, might do the same. He had one experience like this with the Orsini soldiers, when, after the seizure of Faenza, he attacked Bologna and saw them go reluctantly into battle; as for the King, he learned his purpose when he invaded Tuscany after the capture of the Duchy of Urbino; the King forced him to abandon that campaign. As a consequence, the Duke decided to depend no longer upon the arms and fortune of others. And his first step was to weaken the Orsini and Colonna factions in Rome; he won over all their followers who were noblemen, making them his own noblemen and giving them huge subsidies; and he honored them, according to their rank, with military commands and civil appointments; as a result, in a few months their affection for the factions died out in their hearts and all of it was turned toward the Duke. After this, he waited for the opportunity to do away with the Orsini leaders, having already scattered those of the Colonna family; and good opportunity arose and the use he put it to was even better; for when the Orsini later realized that the greatness of the Duke and of the Church meant their ruin, they called together a meeting at Magione, in Perugian territory. From this resulted the rebellion of Urbino and the uprisings in Romagna, and endless dangers for the Duke, all of which he overcame with the aid of the French. And when his reputation had been regained, placing no trust either in France or other outside forces, in order not to have to test them, he turned to deceptive methods. And he knew how to falsify his intentions so well that the Orsini themselves, through Lord Paulo, made peace with him; the Duke did not fail to use all kinds of gracious acts to reassure Paulo, giving him money, clothing, and horses, so that the stupidity of the Orsini brought them to Sinigaglia and into his hands. Having removed these leaders and having changed their allies into his friends, the Duke had laid very good foundations for his power, having all of Romagna along with the Duchy of Urbino, and, more important, it appeared that he had befriended Romagna and had won the support of all of its populace once the people began to taste the beneficial results of his rule.

And because this matter is notable and worthy of imitation by others, I shall not pass it over. After the Duke had taken Romagna and had found it governed by powerless lords who had been more anxious to plunder their subjects than to govern them and had given them reason for disunity rather than unity, so that the entire province was full of thefts, fights, and of every other kind of insolence, he decided that if he wanted to make it peaceful and obedient to the ruler's law it would be necessary to give it good government. Therefore, he put Messer Remirro de Orco, a cruel and able man, in command there and gave him complete authority. This man, in little time, made the province peaceful and united, and in doing this he made for himself a great reputation. Afterward, the Duke decided that such excessive authority was no longer required, for he was afraid that it might become despised; and he set up in the middle of the province a civil court with a very distinguished president, wherein each city had its own counselor. And because he realized that the rigorous measures of the past had generated a certain amount of hatred, he wanted to show, in order to purge men's minds and to win them to his side completely, that if any form of cruelty had arisen, it did not originate from him but from the harsh nature of his minister. And having come upon the opportunity to do this, one morning at Cesena he had Messer Remirro placed on the piazza in two pieces with a block of wood and a bloody sword beside him. The ferocity of such a spectacle left those people satisfied and amazed at the same time.

But let us return to where we digressed. I say that the Duke, finding himself very powerful and partially secured from present dangers, having armed himself the way he wanted to, and having in large measure destroyed those nearby forces that might have harmed him, still had to take into account the King of France if he wished to continue his conquests, for he realized that the King, who had become aware of his error too late, would not support further conquest. And because of this, he began to seek out new allies and to temporize with France during the campaign the French undertook in the Kingdom of Naples against the Spaniards who were besieging Gaeta. His intent was to make himself secure against them; and he would have quickly succeeded in this if Alexander had lived.

And these were his methods concerning present things. But as for future events, he had first to fear that a new successor in control of the Church might not be his friend and might try to take away from him what Alexander had given him. Against this possibility he thought to secure himself in four ways: first, by putting to death all the relatives of those lords that he had dispossessed in order to prevent the Pope from employing that opportunity; second, by gaining the friendship of all the noblemen of Rome, as already mentioned, in order to hold the Pope in check by means of them; third, by making the College of Cardinals as much his own as he could; fourth, by acquiring such a large territory before the Pope died that he would be able to resist an initial attack without need of allies. Of these four things, he had achieved three by the time of Alexander's death; the fourth he had almost achieved, for he killed as many of the dispossessed noblemen as he could seize, and very few saved themselves; and he had won over the Roman noblemen; and he had a great following in the College of Cardinals; and as for the acquisition of new territory, he had planned to become lord of Tuscany and was already in possession of Perugia and Piombino and had taken Pisa under his protection. And as soon as he no longer needed to respect the wishes of France (for he no longer had to, since the French had already been deprived of the kingdom by the Spaniards, so that it was necessary for both of them to purchase his friendship), he would attack Pisa. After this, Lucca and Siena would have immediately surrendered, partly to spite the Florentines and partly out of fear, and the Florentines would have had no means of preventing it. If he had carried out these designs (and he would have brought them to fruition during the same year that Alexander died), he would have gathered together so many forces and such a reputation that he would have been able to stand alone and would no longer have had to rely upon the fortune and forces of others, but rather on his own power and ingenuity. But Alexander died five years after he had drawn his sword. He left his son, gravely ill, with only the state of Romagna secured and with all the others up in the air, between two very powerful enemy armies. And there was in the Duke so much ferocity and so much ability, and so well did he understand how men can be won or lost, and so firm were the foundations that he had laid in such a short time, that if he had not had those armies upon him or if he had been healthy, he would have overcome every difficulty. And that his foundations were good is witnessed by the fact that Romagna waited more than a month for him; in Rome, still half alive, he was safe; and although the Baglioni, the Vitelli, and the Orsini came to Rome, they found none of their allies opposed to him; if he could not set up a Pope he wanted, at least could act to ensure that it would not be a man he did not want. But if he had been healthy at the time of Alexander's demise, everything would have been simple. And he himself said to me, on the day when Julius II was crowned Pope, that he had thought of what might happen on his father's death, and he had found a remedy for everything, except he never dreamed that at the time of his father's death he too would be at death's door.

   Now, having summarized all of the Duke's actions, I would not know how to censure him; on the contrary, I believe I am correct in proposing that he be imitated by all those who have risen to power through Fortune and with the arms of others. Because he, possessing great courage and noble intentions, could not have conducted himself in any other manner; and his plans were frustrated solely by the brevity of Alexander's life and by his own illness. Anyone, therefore, who determines it necessary in his newly acquired principality to protect himself from his enemies, to win friends, to conquer either by force or by fraud, to make himself loved and feared by the people, to be followed and respected by his soldiers, to put to death those who can or should do him harm, to replace ancient institutions with new ones, to be severe and gracious, magnanimous and generous, to do away with unfaithful soldiers and to select new ones, to maintain the friendship of kings and of princes in such a way that they must assist you gladly or offend you with caution—that person cannot find more recent examples than this man's deeds. One can only censure him for making Julius Pope; in this he made a bad choice, since, as I said before, not being able to elect a Pope of his own, he could have kept anyone he wished from the papacy; and he should have never agreed to raising to the papacy any cardinal he might have offended or who, upon becoming Pope, might have cause to fear him. For men do harm either out of fear or hatred. Those he had injured were, among others, San Pietro ad Vincula, Colonna, San Giorgio, Ascanio; any of the others, upon becoming Pope, would have to fear him, except for Rouen and the Spaniards: the latter because they were related to him and were in his debt, the former because of his power, since he was joined to the kingdom of France. Therefore, the Duke, above all else, should have made a Spaniard Pope; failing in that, he should have agreed to the election of Rouen and not to that of San Pietro ad Vincula. And anyone who believes that new benefits make men of high station forget old injuries is deceiving himself. The Duke, then, erred in this election, and it was the cause of his ultimate downfall.

Chapter VIII
On Those Who Have Become Princes Through Wickedness

But because there are yet two more ways one can from an ordinary citizen become prince, which cannot completely be attributed to either Fortune or skill, I believe they should not be left unmentioned, although one of them will be discussed at greater length in a treatise on republics. These two are: when one becomes prince through some wicked and nefarious means or when a private citizen becomes prince of his native city through the favor of his fellow citizens. And in discussing the first way, I shall cite two examples, one from classical times and the other from recent days, without otherwise entering into the merits of this method, since I consider them sufficient for anyone forced to imitate them.

Agathocles the Sicilian, not only from being an ordinary citizen but from being of low and abject status, became King of Syracuse. This man, a potter's son, lived a wicked life at every stage of his career; yet he joined to his wickedness such strength of mind and of body that, when he entered upon a military career, he rose through the ranks to become commander of Syracuse. Once placed in such a position, having considered becoming prince and holding with violence and without any obligations to others what had been granted to him by universal consent, and having made an agreement with Hamilcar the Carthaginian, who was waging war with his armies in Sicily, he called together one morning the people and the senate of Syracuse as if he were going to discuss things concerning the state; and with a prearranged signal, he had his troops kill all the senators and the richest members of the populace; and when they were dead, he seized and held the rule of the city without any opposition from the citizenry. And although he was twice defeated by the Carthaginians and eventually besieged, not only was he able to defend his city but, leaving part of his troops for the defense of the siege, with his other men he attacked Africa, and in a short time he freed Syracuse from the siege and forced the Carthaginians into dire straits: they were obliged to make peace with him and to be content with possession of Africa and to leave Sicily to Agathocles.

Anyone, therefore, who examines the deeds and the life of this man will observe nothing or very little that can be attributed to Fortune; since, as was said earlier, not with the aid of others but by rising through the ranks, which involved a thousand hardships and dangers, did he come to rule the principality which he then maintained by many brave and dangerous efforts. Still, it cannot be called skill to kill one's fellow citizens, to betray friends, to be without faith, without mercy, without religion; by these means one can acquire power but not glory. For if one were to consider Agathocles's ability in getting into and out of dangers, and his greatness of spirit in supporting and in overcoming adversities, one can see no reason why he should be judged inferior to any most excellent commander; nevertheless, his vicious cruelty and inhumanity, along with numerous wicked deeds, do not permit us to honor him among the most excellent of men. One cannot, therefore, attribute to either Fortune or skill what he accomplished without either the one or the other.

In our own days, during the reign of Alexander VI, Oliverotto of Fermo, who many years before had been left as a child without a father, was brought up by his maternal uncle, Giovanni Fogliani. In the early days of his youth he was sent to serve as a soldier under Paulo Vitelli so that, once he was versed in that skill, he might attain some outstanding military position. Then, after Paulo died, he served under his brother, Vitellozzo; and in a very brief time, because of his intelligence and his vigorous body and mind, he became the commander of his troops. But since he felt it was servile to work for others, he decided to seize Fermo with the aid of some citizens of Fermo who preferred servitude to the liberty of their native city, and with the assistance of the followers of Vitellozzo; and he wrote to Giovanni Fogliani about how, having been away many years from home, he wished to come to see him and his city and to inspect his inheritance; and since he had exerted himself for no other reason than to acquire glory, he wanted to arrive in honorable fashion, accompanied by an escort of a hundred horsemen from among his friends and servants so that his fellow citizens might see that he had not spent his time in vain; and he begged his uncle to arrange for an honorable reception from the people of Fermo, one which might bring honor not only to Giovanni but also to himself, being his pupil. Giovanni, therefore, in no way failed in his duty toward his nephew: he had him received in honorable fashion by the people of Fermo, and he gave him rooms in his own house. Oliverotto, after a few days had passed and he had secretly made the preparations necessary for his forthcoming wickedness, gave a magnificent banquet to which he invited Giovanni Fogliani and all of the first citizens of Fermo. And when the meal and all the other entertainment customary at such banquets were completed, Oliverotto, according to plan, began to discuss serious matters, speaking of the greatness of Pope Alexander and his son, Cesare, and of their undertakings. After Giovanni and the others had replied to his comments, he suddenly rose up, announcing that these were matters to be discussed in a more secluded place; and he retired into another room, followed by Giovanni and all the other citizens. No sooner were they seated than from secret places in the room out came soldiers who killed Giovanni and all the others. After this murder, Oliverotto mounted his horse, paraded through the town, and besieged the chief officials in the government palace; so that out of fear they were forced to obey him and to constitute a government of which he made himself prince. And when all those were killed who, if they had been discontent, might have threatened him, he strengthened himself by instituting new civil and military laws; so that, in the space of the year that he held the principality, not only was he secure in the city of Fermo, but he had become feared by all its neighbors. His expulsion would have been as difficult as that of Agathocles if he had not permitted himself to be tricked by Cesare Borgia, when at Sinigaglia, as was noted above, the Duke captured the Orsini and the Vitelli; there he, too, was captured, a year after he committed the parricide, and together with Vitellozzo, who had been his teacher in ingenuity and wickedness, he was strangled.

One might wonder how Agathocles and others like him, after so many betrayals and cruelties, could live for such a long time secure in their cities and defend themselves from outside enemies without being plotted against by their own citizens; many others, using cruel means, were unable even in peaceful times to hold on to their state, not to speak of the uncertain times of war. I believe that this depends on whether cruelty be well or badly used. Well used are those cruelties (if it is permitted to speak well of evil) that are carried out in a single stroke, done out of necessity to protect oneself, and are not continued but are instead converted into the greatest possible benefits for the subjects. Badly used are those cruelties which, although being few at the outset, grow with the passing of time instead of disappearing. Those who follow the first method can remedy their condition with God and with men as Agathocles did; the others cannot possibly survive.

Wherefore it is to be noted that in taking a state its conqueror should weigh all the harmful things he must do and do them all at once so as not to have to repeat them every day, and in not repeating them to be able to make men feel secure and to win them over with the benefits he bestows upon them. Anyone who does otherwise, either out of timidity or because of poor advice, is always obliged to keep his knife in his hand; nor can he ever count upon his subjects, who, because of their fresh and continual injuries, cannot feel secure with him. Injuries, therefore, should be inflicted all at the same time, for the less they are tasted, the less they offend; and benefits should be distributed a bit at a time in order that they may be savored fully. And a prince should, above all, live with his subjects in such a way that no unforeseen event, either good or bad, may make him alter his course; for when emergencies arise in adverse conditions, you are not in time to resort to cruelty, and that good you do will help you little, since it will be judged a forced measure and you will earn from it no thanks whatsoever.

Chapter IX
On the Civil Principality

But coming to the second instance, when a private citizen, not through wickedness or any other intolerable violence, but with the favor of his fellow citizens, becomes prince of his native city (this can be called a civil principality, the acquisition of which neither depends completely upon skill nor upon Fortune, but instead upon a mixture of shrewdness and luck), I maintain that one reaches this princedom either with the favor of the common people or with that of the nobility. For these two different humors are found in every body politic; and they arise from the fact that the people do not wish to be commanded or oppressed by the nobles, and the nobles desire to command and to oppress the people; and from these two opposed appetites there arises one of three effects: either a principality or liberty or anarchy.

A principality is brought about either by the common people or by the nobility, depending on which one of the two parties has the opportunity. For when the nobles see that they cannot resist the populace, they begin to support one among them and make him prince in order to be able, under his shadow, to satisfy their appetites. The common people as well, seeing that they cannot resist the nobility, give their support to one man and make him prince in order to have the protection of his authority. He who attains the principality with the aid of the nobility maintains it with more difficulty than he who becomes prince with the assistance of the common people, for he finds himself a prince amidst many who feel themselves to be his equals, and because of this he can neither govern nor manage them as he might wish. But he who attains the principality because of popular favor finds himself alone and has around him either no one or very few who are not ready to obey him. Moreover, one cannot honestly satisfy the nobles without harming others, but the common people can surely be satisfied: their desire is more honest than that of the nobles—the former wishing not to be oppressed and the latter wishing to oppress.

Moreover, a prince can never make himself secure when the people are his enemy because they are so many; he can make himself secure against the nobles because they are so few. The worst that a prince can expect from a hostile people is to be abandoned by them; but with a hostile nobility not only does he have to fear being abandoned but also that they will unite against him; for, being more perceptive and shrewder, they always have time to save themselves, to seek the favors of the side they believe will win. Furthermore, a prince must always live with the same common people; but he can easily do without the same nobles, having the power to create them and to destroy them from day to day and to take away and give back their reputation as he sees fit.

And in order to clarify this point better, I say that the nobles should be considered chiefly in two ways: either they govern themselves in such a way that they commit themselves completely to your fortunes or they do not. Those who commit themselves and are not greedy should be honored and loved; those who do not are to be examined in two ways. They act in this manner out of fear and a natural lack of courage, and then you make use of them, especially those who are wise advisers, since in prosperous times they will gain you honor and in adverse times you need not fear them. But when, deliberately and influenced by ambition, they refrain from committing themselves to you, this is a sign that they think more of themselves than of you; and the prince should be wary of such men and fear them as if they were open enemies, because they will always, in adverse times, help to ruin him.

However, one who becomes prince with the support of the common people must keep them as his friends; this is easy for him, since the only thing they ask of him is that they not be oppressed. But one who, against the will of the common people, becomes prince with the assistance of the nobility must, before all else, seek to win the people's support, which should be easy if he takes them under his protection. And because men, when they are well treated by those from whom they expected harm, are more obliged to their benefactor, the common people quickly become better disposed toward him than if he had become prince with their support. And a prince can gain their favor in various ways, but because they vary according to the situation no fixed rules can be given for them, and therefore I shall not talk about them. I shall conclude by saying only that a prince must have the friendship of the common people; otherwise he will have no support in times of adversity.

Nabis, prince of the Spartans, withstood the attacks of all of Greece and of one of Rome's most victorious armies, and he defended his city and his state against them; and when danger was near he needed only to protect himself from a few of his subjects; but if he had had the common people against him, this would not have been sufficient. And let no one dispute my opinion by citing that trite proverb: "He who builds upon the people builds upon the mud" because that is true when a private citizen lays his foundations and allows himself to believe that the common people will free him if he is oppressed by enemies or by the public officials (in this case a man might often find himself fooled, like the Gracchi of Rome or like Messer Giorgio Scali of Florence); but when the prince who builds his foundations on the people is one who is able to command and is a man of spirit, not confused by adversities, and does not lack other necessities, and through his courage and his institutions keeps up the spirits of the populace, he will never find himself deceived by the common people, and he will discover that he has laid sound foundations.

Principalities of this type usually are endangered when they are about to change from a republic to an absolute form of government. For these princes either rule by themselves or by means of public officials; in the latter case their position is weaker and more dangerous since they depend entirely upon the will of those citizens who are appointed to hold the offices; these men, especially in adverse times, can very easily seize the state either by open opposition or by disobedience. And in such times of danger the prince has no time for taking absolute control, for the citizens and subjects who are used to receiving their orders from public officials are, in these crises, not willing to obey his orders; and in doubtful times he will always find a scarcity of men he can trust. Such a prince cannot rely upon what he sees during periods of calm, when the citizens need his rule, because then everyone comes running, makes promises, and each one is willing to die for him—since death is unlikely; but in times of adversity, when the state needs its citizens, then few are to be found. And this experiment is so much the more dangerous in that it cannot be made but once. And, therefore, a wise prince should think of a method by which his citizens, at all times and in every circumstance, will need the assistance of the state and of himself and then they will always be loyal to him.

Chapter X
How the Strength of All Principalities Should Be Measured

In analyzing the qualities of these principalities, another consideration must be discussed; that is, whether the prince has so much power that he can, if necessary, stand on his own, or whether he always needs the protection of others. And in order to clarify this section, I say that I judge those princes self-sufficient who, either through abundance of troops or of money, are able to gather together a suitable army and fight a good battle against whoever should attack them; and I consider those who always need the protection of others to be those who cannot meet their enemy in the field, but must seek refuge behind their city walls and defend them. The first case has already been treated, and later on I shall say whatever else is necessary on the subject. Nothing more can be added to the second instance than to encourage such princes to fortify and provision their cities and not to concern themselves with the surrounding countryside. And anyone who has well fortified his city and has well managed his affairs with his subjects in the manner I detailed above (and discuss below) will be besieged only with great caution; for men are always enemies of undertakings that reveal their difficulties, and it cannot seem easy to attack someone whose city is well fortified and who is not despised by his people.

The cities of Germany are completely free, they have little surrounding territory, they obey the emperor when they wish, and they fear neither him nor any other nearby power, as they are fortified in such a manner that everyone thinks their capture would be a tedious and difficult affair. For they all have sufficient moats and walls; they have adequate artillery; they always store in their public warehouses enough to drink and to eat and to burn for a year; and besides all this, in order to be able to keep the lower classes fed without exhausting public funds, they always have in reserve a year's supply of raw materials sufficient to give these people work at those trades which are the nerves and the lifeblood of that city and of the industries from which the people earn their living. Moreover, they hold the military arts in high regard, and they have many regulations for maintaining them.

Therefore, a prince who has a strong city and who does not make himself hated cannot be attacked; and even if he were to be attacked, the enemy would have to depart in shame, for human affairs are so changeable that it is almost impossible that one maintain a siege for a year with his troops idle. And to anyone who might answer me: if the people have their possessions outside the city and see them destroyed, they will lose patience, and the long siege and self-interest will cause them to forget their prince, I reply that a powerful and spirited prince will always overcome all such difficulties, inspiring his subjects now with the hope that the evil will not last long, now with the fear of the enemy's cruelty, now by protecting himself with clever maneuvers against those who seem too outspoken. Besides this, the enemy will naturally burn and waste the surrounding country on arrival, just when the spirits of the defenders are still ardent and determined on the city's defense; and thus the prince needs to fear so much the less, because after a few days, when their spirits have cooled down a bit, the damage has already been inflicted and the evils suffered, and there is no means of correcting the matter; and now the people will rally around their prince even more, for it would appear that he is bound to them by obligations, since their homes were burned and their possessions wasted in his defense. And the nature of men is such that they find themselves obligated as much for the benefits they confer as for those they receive. Thus, if everything is taken into consideration, it will not be difficult for a prudent prince to keep high the spirits of his citizens from the beginning to the conclusion of the siege, so long as he does not lack enough food and the means for his defense.

Chapter XI
On Ecclesiastical Principalities

There remain now only the ecclesiastical principalities to be discussed: concerning these, all the problems occur before they are acquired; for they are acquired either through ability or through Fortune and are maintained without either; they are sustained by the ancient institutions of religion, which are so powerful and of such a kind that they keep their princes in power in whatever manner they act and live their lives. These princes alone have states and do not defend them, subjects and do not rule them; and the states, remaining undefended, are never taken away from them; and the subjects, being ungoverned, never sense any concern, and they do not think about, nor are they able to sever, their ties with them. These principalities, then, are the only secure and happy ones. But since they are protected by higher causes that the human mind is unable to reach, I shall not discuss them; for, being exalted and maintained by God, it would be the act of a presumptuous and foolhardy man to discuss them. Nevertheless, someone might ask me why it is that the Church, in temporal matters, has arrived at such power when, until the time of Alexander, the Italian powers—not just those who were the established rulers, but every baron and lord, no matter how weak considered her temporal power as insignificant, and now a King of France trembles before it and it has been able to throw him out of Italy and to ruin the Venetians; although this situation may already be known, it does not seem superfluous to me to recall it to memory in some detail.

Before Charles, King of France, came into Italy, this country was under the rule of the Pope, the Venetians, the King of Naples, the Duke of Milan, and the Florentines. These rulers had to keep two major problems in mind: first, that a foreigner could enter Italy with his armies; second, that no one of them increase his territory. Those whom they needed to watch most closely were the Pope and the Venetians. And to restrain the Venetians the alliance of all the rest was necessary, as was the case in the defense of Ferrara; and to keep the Pope in check they made use of the Roman barons, who, divided into two factions, the Orsini and the Colonna, always had a reason for squabbling amongst themselves; they kept the papacy weak and unstable, standing with their weapons in hand right under the Pope's eyes. And although from time to time there arose a courageous Pope like Pope Sixtus, neither Fortune nor wisdom could ever free him from these inconveniences. And the brevity of the reigns of the popes was the cause; for in ten years, the average life expectancy of a papacy, he might with difficulty put down one of the factions; and if, for example, one Pope had almost extinguished the Colonna, a new Pope who was the enemy of the Orsini would emerge, enabling the Colonna to grow powerful again, and yet he would not have time enough to destroy the Orsini.

As a consequence, the temporal powers of the Pope were little respected in Italy. Then Alexander VI came to power, and he, more than any of the popes who ever reigned, showed how well a Pope, with money and troops, could succeed; and he achieved, with Duke Valentino as his instrument and the French invasion as his opportunity, all those things that I discussed earlier in describing the actions of the Duke. And although his intention was not to make the Church great but rather the Duke, nevertheless what he did resulted in the increase of the power of the Church, which, after his death and once the Duke was destroyed, became the heir of his labors. Then came Pope Julius, and he found the Church strong, possessing all of Romagna, having destroyed the Roman barons, and, by Alexander's blows, having snuffed out their factions; and he also found the way open for the accumulation of wealth by a method never before used by Alexander or his predecessors. These practices Julius not only continued but intensified; and he was determined to take Bologna, to crush the Venetians, and to drive the French from Italy, and he succeeded in all these undertakings; and he is worthy of even more praise, since he did everything for the increased power of the Church and not for any special individual. He also managed to keep the Orsini and the Colonna factions in the same condition in which he found them; and although there were some leaders among them who wanted to make changes, there were two things which held them back: one, the power of the Church, which frightened them; and, two, not having any of their own family as cardinals, who were the source of the conflicts among them. For these factions will never be at peace as long as they have cardinals, since such men foster factions, both in Rome and outside it, and those barons are compelled to defend them; and thus, from the ambitions of the priests are born the discords and the tumults among the barons. Therefore, His Holiness Pope Leo has found the papacy very powerful indeed; and it is to be hoped that if his predecessors made it great by feats of arms, he, through his kindness and countless other virtues, will make it even greater and respected.

Chapter XII
On the Various Kinds of Troops and Mercenary Soldiers

Having treated in detail all the characteristics of those principalities which I proposed to discuss at the beginning, and having considered, to some extent, the reasons for their success or shortcomings, and having demonstrated the ways by which many have tried to acquire them and to maintain them, it remains for me now to speak in general terms of the kinds of offense and defense that can be adopted by each of the previously mentioned principalities. We have said above that a prince must have laid firm foundations; otherwise he will of necessity come to grief. And the principal foundations of all states, the new as well as the old or mixed, are good laws and good armies. And since there cannot exist good laws where there are no good armies, and where there are good armies there must be good laws, I shall leave aside the treatment of laws and discuss the armed forces.

Let me say, therefore, that the armies with which a prince defends his state are made up of either his own people or of mercenaries, either auxiliary or mixed troops. The mercenaries and the auxiliaries are useless and dangerous. And if a prince holds on to his state by means of mercenary armies, he will never be stable or secure; for they are disunited, ambitious, without discipline, disloyal; they are brave among friends; among enemies they are cowards; they have no fear of God and no faith in men; and your downfall is deferred only so long as the attack is deferred; and in peace you are plundered by them, in war by your enemies. The reason for this is that they have no other love nor other motive to keep them in the field than a meager wage, which is not enough to make them want to die for you. They love being your soldiers when you are not making war, but when war comes they either desert or depart. This would require little effort to demonstrate, since the present ruin of Italy is caused by nothing other than her dependence for a long period of time on mercenary forces. These forces did, at times, help some get ahead, and they appeared courageous in combat with other mercenaries; but when the invasion of the foreigner came they showed themselves for what they were; and thus, Charles, King of France, was permitted to take Italy with a piece of chalk.[1] And the man who said that our sins were the cause of this disaster spoke the truth; but they were not at all those that he thought, but rather these that I have described; and because they were the sins of princes, the princes in turn have suffered the penalty for them.

I wish to demonstrate more fully the sorry nature of such armies. Mercenary captains are either excellent soldiers or they are not; if they are, you cannot trust them, since they will always aspire to their own greatness either by oppressing you, who are their master, or by oppressing others against your intent; but if the captain is without skill, he usually ruins you. And if someone were to reply that anyone who bears arms will act in this manner, mercenary or not, I would answer that armies have to be commanded either by a prince or by a republic: the prince must go in person and perform the duties of a captain himself; the republic must send its own citizens; and when they send one who does not turn out to be an able man, they must replace him; and if he is capable, they ought to restrain him with laws so that he does not go beyond his authority. And we see from experience that only princes and armed republics make very great advances, and that mercenaries do nothing but harm; and a republic armed with its own citizens is less likely to come under the rule of one of its citizens than a city armed with foreign soldiers.

Rome and Sparta for many centuries stood armed and free. The Swiss are extremely well armed and are completely free. An example from antiquity of the use of mercenary troops is the Carthaginians; they were almost overcome by their own

---

1. [This expression refers to the practice Charles followed in marking the houses that were to be used to quarter his troops during the invasion of Italy in 1494–1495. Machiavelli implies by this that Italian resistance to Charles' invasion was nonexistent.]

mercenary soldiers after the first war with the Romans, even though the Carthaginians had their own citizens as officers. Philip of Macedonia was made captain of their army by the Thebans after the death of Epaminondas; and after the victory he took their liberty from them. The Milanese, after the death of Duke Philip, employed Francesco Sforza to war against the Venetians; having defeated the enemy at Caravaggio, he joined with them to oppress the Milanese, his employers. Sforza, his father, being in the employ of Queen Giovanna of Naples, all at once left her without defenses; hence, in order not to lose her kingdom, she was forced to throw herself into the lap of the King of Aragon. And if the Venetians and the Florentines have in the past increased their possessions with such soldiers, and their captains have not yet made themselves princes but have instead defended them, I answer that the Florentines have been favored in this matter by luck; for among their able captains whom they could have had reason to fear, some were defeated, others met with opposition, and others turned their ambition elsewhere. The one who did not win was John Hawkwood, whose loyalty, since he did not succeed, will never be known; but anyone will admit that had he succeeded, the Florentines would have been at his mercy. Sforza always had the Bracceschi as enemies so that each checked the other. Francesco turned his ambition to Lombardy; Braccio against the Church and the Kingdom of Naples.

But let us come to what has occurred just recently. The Florentines made Paulo Vitelli their captain, a very prudent man and one who rose from private life to achieve great fame. If this man had taken Pisa, no one would deny that the Florentines would have had to become his ally; for, if he had become employed by their enemies, they would have had no defense, and if they had kept him on, they would have been obliged to obey him. As for the Venetians, if we examine the course they followed, we see that they operated securely and gloriously as long as they fought with their own troops (this was before they started fighting on land); with their nobles and their common people armed, they fought courageously. But when they began to fight on land, they abandoned this successful strategy and followed the usual practices of waging war in Italy. As they first began to expand their territory on the mainland, since they did not have much territory there and enjoyed a high reputation, they had little to fear from their captains; but when these men grew in power, as they did under Carmagnola, the Venetians had a taste of this mistake; for, having found him very able, since under his command they had defeated the Duke of Milan, and knowing, on the other hand, that he had lost some of his fighting spirit, they judged that they could no longer conquer under him, for he had no wish to do so; yet they could not dismiss him for fear of losing what they had acquired; so in order to secure themselves against him, they were forced to execute him. Then they had as their captains Bartolomeo da Bergamo, Roberto da San Severino, the Count of Pitigliano, and the like; with such as these they had to fear their losses, not their acquisitions, as occurred later at Vailà, where, in a single day, they lost what had cost them eight hundred years of exhausting effort to acquire. From these soldiers, therefore, come only slow, tardy, and weak conquests and sudden and astonishing losses. And because with these examples I have begun to treat of Italy, which has for many years been ruled by mercenary soldiers, I should like to discuss the matter more thoroughly, in order that when their origins and developments are evident they can be more easily corrected.

You must, then, understand how in recent times, when the Empire began to be driven out of Italy and the Pope began to win more prestige in temporal affairs, Italy was divided into more states; for many of the large cities took up arms against their nobles, who, at first backed by the Emperor, had kept them under their control; and the Church supported these cities to increase its temporal power; in many other cities citizens became princes. Hence, Italy having come almost entirely into the hands of the Church and of several republics, those priests and those other citizens who were not accustomed to bearing arms began to hire foreigners. The first to give prestige to such troops was Alberigo of Conio, a Romagnol. From this man's school emerged, among others, Braccio and Sforza, who in their day were the arbiters of Italy. After them came all the others who, until the present day, have commanded these soldiers. And the result of their ability has been that Italy has been overrun by Charles, plundered by Louis, violated by Ferdinand, and insulted by the Swiss. Their method was first to increase the reputation of their own forces by taking away the prestige of the infantry. They did so because they were men without a state of their own who lived by their profession; a small number of foot soldiers could not give them prestige, and they could not afford to hire a large number of them; and so they relied completely upon cavalry, since for having only a reasonable number of horsemen they were provided for and honored. And they reduced things to such a state that in an army of twenty thousand troops, one could hardly find two thousand foot soldiers. Besides this, they had used every means to spare themselves and their soldiers hardship and fear, not killing each other in their battles but rather taking each other prisoner without demanding ransom; they would not attack cities at night; and those in the cities would not attack the tents of the besiegers; they built neither stockades nor trenches around their camps; they did not campaign in the winter. And all these things were permitted by their military institutions and gave them a means of escaping, as was stated, hardships and dangers: so that these condottieri have led Italy into slavery and humiliation.

Chapter XIII
On Auxiliary, Mixed, and Citizen Soldiers

Auxiliary troops, the other kind of worthless armies, are those that arrive when you call a powerful man to bring his forces to your aid and defense, as was done in recent days by Pope Julius, who, having witnessed in the campaign of Ferrara the sorry test of his mercenary soldiers, turned to auxiliary soldiers and made an agreement with Ferdinand, King of Spain, that he assist him with his troops and his armies. These soldiers can be useful and good in themselves, but for the man who summons them they are almost always harmful; for, if they lose you remain defeated; if they win you remain their prisoner. And although ancient histories are full of such instances, nevertheless I am unwilling to leave unexamined this recent example of Pope Julius II, whose policy could not have been more poorly considered, for, in wanting to take Ferrara, he threw himself completely into the hands of a foreigner. But his good fortune brought about a third development so that he did not gather the fruit of his poor decision: for after his auxiliaries were routed at Ravenna, the Swiss rose up and, to the consternation of Pope Julius as well as everyone else, chased out the victors. Thus, he was neither taken prisoner by his enemies, since they had fled, nor by his auxiliaries, since he triumphed with arms other than theirs. And the Florentines, completely unarmed, hired ten thousand French soldiers to take Pisa; such a plan endangered them more than any of their previous predicaments. The emperor of Constantinople, in order to oppose his neighbors, brought ten thousand Turkish troops into Greece, who, when the war was over, did not want to leave; this was the beginning of Greek servitude under the infidel.

Anyone, therefore, who does not wish to conquer should make use of these soldiers, for they are much more dangerous than mercenary troops. Because with them defeat is certain: they are completely united and all under the command of others; but the mercenaries need more time and a greater opportunity if they are to harm you after they have been victorious, for they are not a united body and are hired and salaried by you; a third party whom you may make their leader cannot immediately seize enough authority to harm you. And so, with mercenaries the greatest danger is their cowardice, with auxiliaries their courage.

A wise prince has always rejected these soldiers and has relied upon his own men; and he has chosen to lose with his own troops rather than to conquer with those of others, judging no true victory one gained by means of foreign armies. I shall never hesitate to cite Cesare Borgia and his deeds as an example. This duke entered Romagna with auxiliary forces, leading an army composed entirely of Frenchmen; and with them he captured Imola and Forlì. But not thinking such troops reliable, he turned to mercenary forces, judging them to be less dangerous, and he hired the Orsini and Vitelli. When he found out that they were doubtful, unfaithful, and treacherous, he destroyed them and turned to his own men. And it is easy to see the difference between these two sorts of troops if we examine the difference between the Duke's reputation when he had only French troops and when he had the Orsini and Vitelli, as opposed to when he was left with his own troops and himself to depend on: we find that his reputation always increased; never was he esteemed so highly than when everyone saw that he was complete master of his own army.

I did not wish to depart from citing recent Italian examples; yet I do not want to omit Hiero of Syracuse, one of those I mentioned above. This man, as I said previously, having been named by the Syracusans captain of their armies, immediately realized that mercenary forces were useless, composed, as they were, of men resembling our own Italian condottieri; and it seemed to him that he could neither keep them on nor dismiss them, so he had them all cut into little pieces: and afterward he made war with his own troops and not with those of foreigners. I would also like to recall to memory an example from the Old Testament that fits this argument. David offered himself to Saul to battle against Goliath, the Philistine challenger; Saul, in order to give him courage, armed him with his own armor, which David, when he had put it on, cast off, declaring that with it he could not test his true worth; he therefore wished to meet the enemy with his own sling and his own sword.

In short, the arms of another man either slide off your back, weigh you down, or tie you up. Charles VII, father of Louis XI, having freed France of the English by means of his good fortune and his ability, recognized the necessity of arming himself with his own men, and he set up in his kingdom an ordinance to procure cavalry and infantry. Later, his son, King Louis, abolished the ordinance of the infantry and began to hire Swiss troops; this mistake, followed by others as we can now witness, is the cause of the many threats to that kingdom. By giving prestige to the Swiss, he discredited his own troops; for he completely abolished his foot soldiers and obliged his cavalry to depend upon the soldiers of others; being accustomed to fighting with the Swiss, the French horsemen felt that they could not conquer without them. From this it came about that the French were not strong enough to match the Swiss, and without the Swiss they did not dare to meet others. The armies of France have, therefore, been mixed, partly mercenaries and partly citizen troops; armies combined together in such a fashion are much better than a purely auxiliary force or a purely mercenary army, and are greatly inferior to one's own troops. And the example just cited should suffice, for the kingdom of France would be invincible if Charles' policy had been developed or retained. But the shortsightedness in human nature will begin a policy that seems good at the outset but does not notice the poison that is underneath, as I said earlier in connection with consumptive fevers.

And thus anyone who does not diagnose the ills when they arise in a principality is not really wise; and this skill is given to few men. And if the primary cause of the downfall of the Roman Empire is examined, one will find it to be only when the Goths began to be hired as mercenaries; because from that beginning the strength of the Roman Empire began to be weakened, and all that strength was drained from it and was given to the Goths.

I conclude, therefore, that without having one's own soldiers, no principality is safe; on the contrary, it is completely subject to Fortune, not having the power and the loyalty to defend it in times of adversity. And it was always the opinion and belief of wise men that "nothing is so unhealthy or unstable as the reputation for power that is not based upon one's own power." And one's own troops are those which are composed either of subjects or of citizens or your own dependents; all others are either mercenaries or auxiliaries. And the means to organize a citizen army are easily discovered if the methods followed by those four men I have cited above are examined, and if one observes how Philip, father of Alexander the Great, and many republics and princes have armed and organized themselves: in such methods I have full confidence.

Chapter XIV
A Prince's Duty Concerning Military Matters

A prince, therefore, must not have any other object nor any other thought, nor must he take anything as his profession but war, its institutions, and its discipline; because that is the only profession which befits one who commands; and it is of such importance that not only does it maintain those who were born princes, but many times it enables men of private station to rise to that position; and, on the other hand, it is evident that when princes have given more thought to personal luxuries than to arms, they have lost their state. And the first way to lose it is to neglect this art; and the way to acquire it is to be well versed in this art.

Francesco Sforza became Duke of Milan from being a private citizen because he was armed; his sons, since they avoided the inconveniences of arms, became private citizens after having been dukes. For, among the other bad effects it causes, being disarmed makes you despised; this is one of those infamies a prince should guard himself against, as will be treated below: for between an armed and an unarmed man there is no comparison whatsoever, and it is not reasonable for an armed man to obey an unarmed man willingly, nor that an unarmed man should be safe among armed servants; since, when the former is suspicious and the latter are contemptuous, it is impossible for them to work well together. And therefore, a prince who does not understand military matters, besides the other misfortunes already noted, cannot be esteemed by his own soldiers, nor can he trust them.

He must, therefore, never raise his thought from this exercise of war, and in peacetime he must train himself more than in time of war; this can be done in two ways: one by action, the other by the mind. And as far as actions are concerned, besides keeping his soldiers well disciplined and trained, he must always be out hunting, and must accustom his body to hardships in this manner; and he must also learn the nature of the terrain, and know how mountains slope, how valleys open, how plains lie, and understand the nature of rivers and swamps; and he should devote much attention to such activities. Such knowledge is useful in two ways: first, one learns to know one's own country and can better understand how to defend it; second, with the knowledge and experience of the terrain, one can easily comprehend the characteristics of any other terrain that it is necessary to explore for the first time; for the hills, valleys, plains, rivers, and swamps of Tuscany, for instance, have certain similarities to those of other provinces; so that by knowing the lay of the land in one province one can easily understand it in others. And a prince who lacks this ability lacks the most important quality in a leader; because this skill teaches you to find the enemy, choose a campsite, lead troops, organize them for battle, and besiege towns to your own advantage.

Philopoemen, Prince of the Achaeans, among the other praises given to him by writers, is praised because in peacetime he thought of nothing except the means of waging war; and when he was out in the country with his friends, he often stopped and reasoned with them: "If the enemy were on that hilltop and we were here with our army, which of the two of us would have the advantage? How could we attack them without breaking formation? If we wanted to retreat, how could we do this? If they were to retreat, how could we pursue them?" And he proposed to them, as they rode along, all the contingencies that can occur in an army; he heard their opinions, expressed his own, and backed it up with arguments; so that, because of these continuous deliberations, when leading his troops no unforeseen incident could arise for which he did not have the remedy.

But as for the exercise of the mind, the prince must read histories and in them study the deeds of great men; he must see how they conducted themselves in wars; he must examine the reasons for their victories and for their defeats in order to avoid the latter and to imitate the former; and above all else he must do as some distinguished man before him has done, who elected to imitate someone who had been praised and honored before him, and always keep in mind his deeds and actions; just as it is reported that Alexander the Great imitated Achilles; Caesar, Alexander; Scipio, Cyrus. And anyone who reads the life of Cyrus written by Xenophon then realizes how important in the life of Scipio that imitation was to his glory and how much, in purity, goodness, humanity, and generosity, Scipio conformed to those characteristics of Cyrus that Xenophon had written about.

Such methods as these a wise prince must follow, and never in peaceful times must he be idle; but he must turn them diligently to his advantage in order to be able to profit from them in times of adversity, so that, when Fortune changes, she will find him prepared to withstand such times.

Chapter XV

On Those Things For Which Men, and Particularly Princes, Are Praised or Blamed

Now there remains to be examined what should be the methods and procedures of a prince in dealing with his subjects and friends. And because I know that many have written about this, I am afraid that by writing about it again I shall be thought of as presumptuous, since in discussing this material I depart radically from the procedures of others. But since my intention is to write something useful for anyone who understands it, it seemed more suitable to me to search after the effectual truth of the matter rather than its imagined one. And many writers have imagined for themselves republics and principalities that have never been seen nor known to exist in reality; for there is such a gap between how one lives and how one ought to live that anyone who abandons what is done for what ought to be done learns his ruin rather than his preservation: for a man who wishes to make a vocation of being good at all times will come to ruin among so many who are not good. Hence it is necessary for a prince who wishes to maintain his position to learn how not to be good, and to use this knowledge or not to use it according to necessity.

Leaving aside, therefore, the imagined things concerning a prince, and taking into account those that are true, I say that all men, when they are spoken of, and particularly princes, since they are placed on a higher level, are judged by some of these qualities which bring them either blame or praise. And this is why one is considered generous, another miserly (to use a Tuscan word, since "avaricious" in our language is still used to mean one who wishes to acquire by means of theft; we call "miserly" one who excessively avoids using what he has); one is considered a giver, the other rapacious; one cruel, another merciful; one treacherous, another faithful; one effeminate and cowardly, another bold and courageous; one humane, another haughty; one lascivious, another chaste; one trustworthy, another cunning; one harsh, another lenient; one serious, another frivolous; one religious, another unbelieving; and the like. And I know that everyone will admit that it would be a very praiseworthy thing to find in a prince, of the qualities mentioned above, those that are held to be good; but since it is neither possible to have them nor to observe them all completely, because human nature does not permit it, a prince must be prudent enough to know how to escape the bad reputation of those vices that would lose the state for him, and must protect himself from those that will not lose it for him, if this is possible; but if he cannot, he need not concern himself unduly if he ignores these less serious vices. And, moreover, he need not worry about incurring the bad reputation of those vices without which it would be difficult to hold his state; since, carefully taking everything into account, one will discover that something which appears to be a virtue, if pursued, will end in his destruction; while some other thing which seems to be a vice, if pursued, will result in his safety and his well-being.

Chapter XVI
On Generosity and Miserliness

Beginning, therefore, with the first of the above-mentioned qualities, I say that it would be good to be considered generous; nevertheless, generosity used in such a manner as to give you a reputation for it will harm you; because if it is employed virtuously and as one should employ it, it will not be recognized and you will not avoid the reproach of its opposite. And so, if a prince wants to maintain his reputation for generosity among men, it is necessary for him not to neglect any possible means of lavish display; in so doing such a prince will always use up all his resources and he will be obliged, eventually, if he wishes to maintain his reputation for generosity, to burden the people with excessive taxes and to do everything possible to raise funds. This will begin to make him hateful to his subjects, and, becoming impoverished, he will not be much esteemed by anyone; so that, as a consequence of his generosity, having offended many and rewarded few, he will feel the effects of any slight unrest and will be ruined at the first sign of danger; recognizing this and wishing to alter his policies, he immediately runs the risk of being reproached as a miser.

A prince, therefore, unable to use this virtue of generosity in a manner which will not harm himself if he is known for it, should, if he is wise, not worry about being called a miser; for with time he will come to be considered more generous once it is evident that, as a result of his parsimony, his income is sufficient, he can defend himself from anyone who makes war against him, and he can undertake enterprises without overburdening his people, so that he comes to be generous with all those from whom he takes nothing, who are countless, and miserly with all those to whom he gives nothing, who are few. In our times we have not seen great deeds accomplished except by those who were considered miserly; all others were done away with. Pope Julius II, although he made use of his reputation for generosity in order to gain the papacy, then decided not to maintain it in order to be able to wage war; the present King of France has waged many wars without imposing extra taxes on his subjects, only because his habitual parsimony has provided for the additional expenditures; the present King of Spain, if he had been considered generous, would not have engaged in nor won so many campaigns.

Therefore, in order not to have to rob his subjects, to be able to defend himself, not to become poor and contemptible, and not to be forced to become rapacious, a prince must consider it of little importance if he incurs the name of miser, for this is one of those vices that permits him to rule. And if someone were to say: Caesar with his generosity came to rule the empire, and many others, because they were generous and known to be so, achieved very high positions; I reply: you are either already a prince or you are on the way to becoming one; in the first instance such generosity is damaging; in the second it is very necessary to be thought generous. And Caesar was one of those who wanted to gain the principality of Rome; but if, after obtaining this, he had lived and had not moderated his expenditures, he would have destroyed that empire. And if someone were to reply: there have existed many princes who have accomplished great deeds with their armies who have been reputed to be generous; I answer you: a prince either spends his own money and that of his subjects or that of others; in the first case he must be economical; in the second he must not restrain any part of his generosity. And for that prince who goes out with his soldiers and lives by looting, sacking, and ransoms, who controls the property of others, such generosity is necessary; otherwise he would not be followed by his troops. And with what does not belong to you or to your subjects you can be a more liberal giver, as were Cyrus, Caesar, and Alexander; for spending the wealth of others does not lessen your reputation but adds to it; only the spending of your own is what harms you. And there is nothing that uses itself up faster than generosity, for as you employ it you lose the means of employing it, and you become either poor or despised or, in order to escape poverty, rapacious and hated. And above all other things a prince must guard himself against being despised and hated; and generosity leads you to both one and the other. So it is wiser to live with the reputation of a miser, which produces reproach without hatred, than to be forced to incur the reputation of rapacity, which produces reproach along with hatred, because you want to be considered as generous.

Chapter XVII
On Cruelty and Mercy and Whether It Is Better To Be Loved Than To Be Feared or the Contrary

Proceeding to the other qualities mentioned above, I say that every prince must desire to be considered merciful and not cruel; nevertheless, he must take care not to misuse this mercy. Cesare Borgia was considered cruel; nonetheless, his cruelty had brought order to Romagna, united it, restored it to peace and obedience. If we examine this carefully, we shall see that he was more merciful than the Florentine people, who, in order to avoid being considered cruel, allowed the destruction of Pistoia. Therefore, a prince must not worry about the reproach of cruelty when it is a matter of keeping his subjects united and loyal; for with a very few examples of cruelty he will be more compassionate than those who, out of excessive mercy, permit disorders to continue, from which arise murders and plundering; for these usually harm the community at large, while the executions that come from the prince harm one individual in particular. And the new prince, above all other princes, cannot escape the reputation of being called cruel, since new states are full of dangers. And Virgil, through Dido, states: "My difficult condition and the newness of my rule make me act in such a manner, and to set guards over my land on all sides."[2]

Nevertheless, a prince must be cautious in believing and in acting, nor should he be afraid of his own shadow; and he should proceed in such a manner, tempered by prudence and humanity, so that too much trust may not render him imprudent nor too much distrust render him intolerable.

From this arises an argument: whether it is better to be loved than to be feared, or the contrary. I reply that one should like to be both one and the other; but since it is difficult to join them together, it is much safer to be feared than to be loved when one of the two must be lacking. For one can generally say this about men: that they are ungrateful, fickle, simulators and deceivers, avoiders of danger, greedy for gain; and while you work for their good they are completely yours, offering you their blood, their property, their lives, and their sons, as I said earlier, when danger is far away; but when it comes nearer to you they turn away. And that prince who bases his power entirely on their words, finding himself stripped of other preparations, comes to ruin; for friendships that are acquired by a price and not by greatness and nobility of character are purchased but are not owned, and at the proper moment they cannot be spent. And men are less hesitant about harming someone who makes himself loved than one who makes himself feared because love is held together by a chain of obligation which, since men are a sorry lot, is broken on every occasion in which their own self-interest is concerned; but fear is held together by a dread of punishment which will never abandon you.

A prince must nevertheless make himself feared in such a manner that he will avoid hatred, even if he does not acquire love; since to be feared and not to be hated can very well be combined; and this will always be so when he keeps his hands off the property and the women of his citizens and his subjects. And if he must take someone's life, he should do so when there is proper justification and manifest cause; but, above all, he should avoid the property of others; for men forget more quickly the death of their father than the loss of their patrimony. Moreover, the reasons for seizing their property are never lacking; and he who begins to live by stealing always finds a reason for taking what belongs to others; on the contrary, reasons for taking a life are rarer and disappear sooner.

But when the prince is with his armies and has under his command a multitude of troops, then it is absolutely necessary that he not worry about being considered

2. [*Aeneid*, II, 563–564.]

cruel; for without that reputation he will never keep an army united or prepared for any combat. Among the praiseworthy deeds of Hannibal is counted this: that, having a very large army, made up of all kinds of men, which he commanded in foreign lands, there never arose the slightest dissention, neither among themselves nor against their prince, both during his good and his bad fortune. This could not have arisen from anything other than his inhuman cruelty, which, along with his many other abilities, made him always respected and terrifying in the eyes of his soldiers; and without that, to attain the same effect, his other abilities would not have sufficed. And the writers of history, having considered this matter very little, on the one hand admire these deeds of his and on the other condemn the main cause of them.

And that it be true that his other abilities would not have been sufficient can be seen from the example of Scipio, a most extraordinary man not only in his time but in all recorded history, whose armies in Spain rebelled against him; this came about from nothing other than his excessive compassion, which gave to his soldiers more liberty than military discipline allowed. For this he was censured in the senate by Fabius Maximus, who called him the corruptor of the Roman militia. The Locrians, having been ruined by one of Scipio's officers, were not avenged by him, nor was the arrogance of that officer corrected, all because of his tolerant nature; so that someone in the senate who tried to apologize for him said that there were many men who knew how not to err better than they knew how to correct errors. Such a nature would have, in time, damaged Scipio's fame and glory if he had maintained it during the empire; but, living under the control of the senate, this harmful characteristic of his not only concealed itself but brought him fame.

I conclude, therefore, returning to the problem of being feared and loved, that since men love at their own pleasure and fear at the pleasure of the prince, a wise prince should build his foundation upon that which belongs to him, not upon that which belongs to others: he must strive only to avoid hatred, as has been said.

Chapter XVIII
How A Prince Should Keep His Word

How praiseworthy it is for a prince to keep his word and to live by integrity and not by deceit everyone knows; nevertheless, one sees from the experience of our times that the princes who have accomplished great deeds are those who have cared little for keeping their promises and who have known how to manipulate the minds of men by shrewdness; and in the end they have surpassed those who laid their foundations upon honesty.

You must, therefore, know that there are two means of fighting: one according to the laws, the other with force; the first way is proper to man, the second to beasts; but because the first, in many cases, is not sufficient, it becomes necessary to have recourse to the second. Therefore, a prince must know how to use wisely the natures of the beast and the man. This policy was taught to princes allegorically by the ancient writers, who described how Achilles and many other ancient princes were given to Chiron the Centaur to be raised and taught under his discipline. This can only mean that, having a half-beast and half-man as a teacher, a prince must know how to employ the nature of the one and the other; and the one without the other cannot endure.

Since, then, a prince must know how to make good use of the nature of the beast, he should choose from among the beasts the fox and the lion; for the lion cannot defend itself from traps and the fox cannot protect itself from wolves. It is therefore necessary to be a fox in order to recognize the traps and a lion in order to frighten the wolves. Those who play only the part of the lion do not understand matters. A wise ruler, therefore, cannot and should not keep his word when such an observance of faith would be to his disadvantage and when the reasons which made him promise are removed. And if men were all good, this rule would not be good; but since men are a sorry lot and will not keep their promises to you, you likewise need not keep yours to them. A prince never lacks legitimate reasons to break his promises. Of this one could cite an endless number of modern examples to show how many pacts, how many promises have been made null and void because of the infidelity of princes; and he who has known best how to use the fox has come to a better end. But it is necessary to know how to disguise this nature well and to be a great hypocrite and a liar: and men are so simpleminded and so controlled by their present necessities that one who deceives will always find another who will allow himself to be deceived.

I do not wish to remain silent about one of these recent instances. Alexander VI did nothing else, he thought about nothing else, except to deceive men, and he always found the occasion to do this. And there never was a man who had more forcefulness in his oaths, who affirmed a thing with more promises, and who honored his word less; nevertheless, his tricks always succeeded perfectly since he was well acquainted with this aspect of the world.

Therefore, it is not necessary for a prince to have all of the above-mentioned qualities, but it is very necessary for him to appear to have them. Furthermore, I shall be so bold as to assert this: that having them and practicing them at all times is harmful; and appearing to have them is useful; for instance, to seem merciful, faithful, humane, forthright, religious, and to be so; but his mind should be disposed in such a way that should it become necessary not to be so, he will be able and know how to change to the contrary. And it is essential to understand this: that a prince, and especially a new prince, cannot observe all those things by which men are considered good, for in order to maintain the state he is often obliged to act against his promise, against charity, against humanity, and against religion. And therefore, it is necessary that he have a mind ready to turn itself according to the way the winds of Fortune and the changeability of affairs require him; and, as I said above, as long as it is possible, he should not stray from the good, but he should know how to enter into evil when necessity commands.

A prince, therefore, must be very careful never to let anything slip from his lips which is not full of the five qualities mentioned above: he should appear, upon seeing and hearing him, to be all mercy, all faithfulness, all integrity, all kindness, all religion. And there is nothing more necessary than to seem to possess this last quality. And men in general judge more by their eyes than their hands; for everyone can see but few can feel. Everyone sees what you seem to be, few perceive what you are, and those few do not dare to contradict the opinion of the many who have the majesty of the state to defend them; and in the actions of all men, and especially of princes, where there is no impartial arbiter, one must consider the final result.[3] Let

3. [The Italian original, *si guarda al fine,* has often been mistranslated as "the ends justify the means," something Machiavelli never wrote. For another important statement concerning ends and means, see Machiavelli's remarks about Romulus in *Discourses,* I, ix.]

a prince therefore act to seize and to maintain the state; his methods will always be judged honorable and will be praised by all; for ordinary people are always deceived by appearances and by the outcome of a thing; and in the world there is nothing but ordinary people; and there is no room for the few, while the many have a place to lean on. A certain prince of the present day, whom I shall refrain from naming, preaches nothing but peace and faith, and to both one and the other he is entirely opposed; and both, if he had put them into practice, would have cost him many times over either his reputation or his state.

Chapter XIX

On Avoiding Being Despised and Hated

But since, concerning the qualities mentioned above, I have spoken about the most important, I should like to discuss the others briefly in this general manner: that the prince, as was noted above, should think about avoiding those things which make him hated and despised; and when he has avoided this, he will have carried out his duties and will find no danger whatsoever in other vices. As I have said, what makes him hated above all else is being rapacious and a usurper of the property and the women of his subjects; he must refrain from this; and in most cases, so long as you do not deprive them of either their property or their honor, the majority of men live happily; and you have only to deal with the ambition of a few, who can be restrained without difficulty and by many means. What makes him despised is being considered changeable, frivolous, effeminate, cowardly, irresolute; from these qualities a prince must guard himself as if from a reef, and he must strive to make everyone recognize in his actions greatness, spirit, dignity, and strength; and concerning the private affairs of his subjects, he must insist that his decision be irrevocable; and he should maintain himself in such a way that no man could imagine that he can deceive or cheat him.

That prince who projects such an opinion of himself is greatly esteemed; and it is difficult to conspire against a man with such a reputation and difficult to attack him, provided that he is understood to be of great merit and revered by his subjects. For a prince must have two fears: one, internal, concerning his subjects; the other, external, concerning foreign powers. From the latter he can defend himself by his good troops and friends; and he will always have good friends if he has good troops; and internal affairs will always be stable when external affairs are stable, provided that they are not already disturbed by a conspiracy; and even if external conditions change, if he is properly organized and lives as I have said and does not lose control of himself, he will always be able to withstand every attack, just as I said that Nabis the Spartan did. But concerning his subjects, when external affairs do not change, he has to fear that they may conspire secretly: the prince secures himself from this by avoiding being hated or despised and by keeping the people satisfied with him; this is a necessary matter, as was treated above at length. And one of the most powerful remedies a prince has against conspiracies is not to be hated by the masses; for a man who plans a conspiracy always believes that he will satisfy the people by killing the prince; but when he thinks he might anger them, he cannot work up the courage to undertake such a deed; for the problems on the side of the conspirators are countless. And experience demonstrates that conspiracies have been many but few have been concluded successfully; for anyone who conspires cannot be alone, nor can he find companions except from amongst those whom he believes to be dissatisfied; and as soon as you have uncovered your intent to one dissatisfied man, you give him the means to make himself happy, since he can have everything he desires by uncovering the plot; so much is this so that, seeing a sure gain on the one hand and one doubtful and full of danger on the other, if he is to maintain faith with you he has to be either an unusually good friend or a completely determined enemy of the prince. And to treat the matter briefly, I say that on the part of the conspirator there is nothing but fear, jealousy, and the thought of punishment that terrifies him; but on the part of the prince there is the majesty of the principality, the laws, the defenses of friends and the state to protect him; so that, with the good will of the people added to all these things, it is impossible for anyone to be so rash as to plot against him. For, where usually a conspirator has to be afraid before he executes his evil deed, in this case he must be afraid, having the people as an enemy, even after the crime is performed, nor can he hope to find any refuge because of this.

One could cite countless examples on this subject; but I want to satisfy myself with only one which occurred during the time of our fathers. Messer Annibale Bentivogli, prince of Bologna and grandfather of the present Messer Annibale, was murdered by the Canneschi family, who conspired against him; he left behind no heir except Messer Giovanni, then only a baby. As soon as this murder occurred, the people rose up and killed all the Canneschi. This came about because of the good will that the house of the Bentivogli enjoyed in those days; this good will was so great that with Annibale dead, and there being no one of that family left in the city who could rule Bologna, the Bolognese people, having heard that in Florence there was one of the Bentivogli blood who was believed until that time to be the son of a blacksmith, went to Florence to find him, and they gave him the control of that city; it was ruled by him until Messer Giovanni became of age to rule.

I conclude, therefore, that a prince must be little concerned with conspiracies when the people are well disposed toward him; but when the populace is hostile and regards him with hatred, he must fear everything and everyone. And well-organized states and wise princes have, with great diligence, taken care not to anger the nobles and to satisfy the common people and keep them contented; for this is one of the most important concerns that a prince has.

Among the kingdoms in our times that are well organized and well governed is that of France: in it one finds countless good institutions upon which depend the liberty and the security of the king; of these the foremost is the parliament and its authority. For he who organized that kingdom, recognizing the ambition of the nobles and their insolence, and being aware of the necessity of keeping a bit in their mouths to hold them back, on the one hand, while, on the other, knowing the hatred, based upon fear, of the populace for the nobles, and wanting to reassure them, did not wish this to be the particular obligation of the king. In order to relieve himself of the burden he might incur from the nobles if he supported the common people, and from the common people if he supported the nobles, he established a third judicial body that might restrain the nobles and favor the masses without burdening the king. This institution could neither be better nor more prudent, nor could there be a better reason for the safety of the king and the kingdom. From this one can extract another notable observation: that princes must delegate distasteful tasks to others; pleasant ones they should keep for themselves. Again I conclude that a prince must respect the nobles but not make himself hated by the common people.

It could possibly seem to many who have studied the lives and deaths of some Roman emperors that they represent examples contrary to my point of view; for we shall find that some of them have always lived nobly and have demonstrated great strength of character yet have nevertheless lost their empire or have been killed by their own subjects who have plotted against them. Wishing, therefore, to reply to these objections, I shall discuss the traits of several emperors, showing the reasons for their ruin, which are not different from those which I myself have already deduced; and I shall bring forward for consideration those things which are worthy of note for anyone who reads about the history of those times. And I shall let it suffice to choose all those emperors who succeeded to the throne from Marcus the philosopher to Maximinus: these were Marcus, his son Commodus, Pertinax, Julian, Severus, Antoninus Caracalla his son, Macrinus, Heliogabalus, Alexander, and Maximinus. And it is first to be noted that where in other principalities one has only to contend with the ambition of the nobles and the arrogance of the people, the Roman emperors had a third problem: they had to endure the cruelty and the avarice of the soldiers. This was such a difficult thing that it was the cause of the downfall of many of them, since it was hard to satisfy both the soldiers and the populace; for the people loved peace and quiet and because of this loved modest princes, while the soldiers loved the prince who had a military character and who was arrogant, cruel, and rapacious; they wanted him to practice such qualities on the people so that they might double their salary and unleash their avarice and cruelty. As a result of this situation, those emperors always came to ruin who by nature or by guile did not have so great a reputation that they could keep both the people and the soldiers in check; and most of them, especially those who came to power as new princes, recognizing the difficulty resulting from these two opposing factions, turned to appeasing the soldiers, caring little about injuring the people. Such a decision was necessary; since princes cannot avoid being hated by somebody, they must first seek not to be hated by the bulk of the populace; and when they cannot achieve this, they must try with every effort to avoid the hatred of the most powerful group. And therefore, those emperors who had need of extraordinary support because of their newness in power allied themselves with the soldiers instead of the people; nevertheless, this proved to their advantage or not, according to whether the prince knew how to maintain his reputation with the soldiers.

For the reasons listed above, it came about that, of Marcus, Pertinax, and Alexander, all of whom lived modest lives, were lovers of justice, enemies of cruelty, humane, and kindly, all except Marcus came to an unhappy end. Marcus alone lived and died with the greatest of honor, for he succeeded to the empire by birthright, and he did not have to recognize any obligation for it either to the soldiers or to the people; then, being endowed with many characteristics which made him revered, he always held, while he was living, both the one party and the other within their limits, and he was never either hated or despised. But Pertinax was made emperor against the will of the soldiers, who, being used to living licentiously under Commodus, could not tolerate the righteous manner of life to which Pertinax wished to return them; whereupon, having made himself hated, and since to this hatred was added contempt for his old age, he came to ruin at the initial stage of his rule.

And here one must note that hatred is acquired just as much by means of good actions as by bad ones; and so, as I said above, if a prince wishes to maintain the state, he is often obliged not to be good; because whenever that group which you believe you need to support you is corrupted, whether it be the common people, the soldiers, or the nobles, it is to your advantage to follow their inclinations in order to satisfy them; and then good actions are your enemy. But let us come to Alexander.

He was of such goodness that among the other laudable deeds attributed to him is this: in the fourteen years that he ruled the empire he never put anyone to death without a trial; nevertheless, since he was considered effeminate and a man who let himself be ruled by his mother, because of this he was despised, and the army plotted against him and murdered him.

Considering now, in contrast, the characteristics of Commodus, Severus, Antoninus Caracalla, and Maximinus, you will find them extremely cruel and greedy; in order to satisfy their troops, they did not hesitate to inflict all kinds of injuries upon the people; and all except Severus came to a sorry end. For in Severus there was so much ability that, keeping the soldiers as his friends even though the people were oppressed by him, he was always able to rule happily; for those qualities of his made him so esteemed in the eyes of both the soldiers and the common people that the former were awestruck and stupefied and the latter were respectful and satisfied.

And since the actions of this man were great and noteworthy for a new prince, I wish to demonstrate briefly how well he knew how to use the masks of the fox and the lion, whose natures, as I say above, a prince must imitate. As soon as Severus learned of the indecisiveness of the emperor Julian, he convinced the army of which he was in command in Slavonia that it would be a good idea to march to Rome to avenge the death of Pertinax, who had been murdered by the Praetorian Guards. And under this pretext, without showing his desire to rule the empire, he moved his army to Rome, and he was in Italy before his departure was known. When he arrived in Rome, the senate, out of fear, elected him emperor, and Julian was killed. After this beginning, there remained two obstacles for Severus if he wanted to make himself master of the whole state: the first in Asia, where Pescennius Niger, commander of the Asiatic armies, had himself named emperor; and the other in the West, where Albinus was, who also aspired to the empire. And since he judged it dangerous to reveal himself as an enemy to both of them, he decided to attack Niger and to deceive Albinus. He wrote to the latter that, having been elected emperor by the senate, he wanted to share that honor with him; and he sent him the title of Caesar and, by decree of the senate, he made him his coequal: these things were accepted by Albinus as the truth. But after Severus had conquered and executed Niger and had pacified affairs in the East, upon returning to Rome, he complained to the senate that Albinus, ungrateful for the benefits received from him, had treacherously sought to kill him, and for this he was obliged to go and punish his ingratitude. Then he went to find him in France and took both his state and his life.

Anyone, therefore, who will carefully examine the actions of this man will find him a very ferocious lion and a very shrewd fox; and he will see him feared and respected by everyone and not hated by his armies; and one should not be amazed that he, a new man, was able to hold so great an empire; for his outstanding reputation always defended him from that hatred which the common people could have produced on account of his plundering. But Antoninus, his son, was also a man who had excellent abilities which made him greatly admired in the eyes of the people and pleasing to the soldiers, for he was a military man, most able to support any kind of hardship, a despiser of all delicate foods and soft living; this made him loved by all the armies; nevertheless, his ferocity and cruelty were so great and so unusual—since he had, after countless individual killings, put to death a large part of the populace of Rome and all that of Alexandria—that he became most despised all over the world. And he aroused the fears even of those whom he had around him; so that he was murdered by a centurion in the midst of his army. From this it is to be noted that such deaths as these, which result from the deliberation of a determined individual, are unavoidable for princes, since anyone who does not fear death can harm them; but the prince must not be too afraid of such men, for they are very rare. He must only guard against inflicting serious injury on anyone who serves him and anyone he has about him in the administration of the principality: Antoninus had done this, for he had shamefully put to death a brother of that centurion, and he threatened the man every day; yet he kept him as a bodyguard. This was a dangerous decision and one that would ruin him, just as it did.

But let us come to Commodus, who held the empire with great ease, having inherited it by birth, being the son of Marcus; and it would have been enough for him to follow in the footsteps of his father in order to satisfy the soldiers and the common people. But being a cruel and bestial person by nature, in order to practice his greed upon the common people, he turned to pleasing the armies and to making them undisciplined; on the other hand, by not maintaining his dignity, frequently descending into the arenas to fight with the gladiators and doing other degrading things unworthy of the imperial majesty, he became contemptible in the sight of the soldiers. And being hated, on the one hand, and despised, on the other, he was plotted against and murdered.

The qualities of Maximinus remain to be described. He was a very warlike man; and because the armies were angered by Alexander's softness, which I explained above, after Alexander's death they elected him to the empire. He did not retain it very long, for two things made him hated and despised: the first was his base origin, having herded sheep once in Thrace (this fact was well known everywhere and it caused him to lose considerable dignity in everyone's eyes); the second was that at the beginning of his reign he deferred going to Rome to take possession of the imperial throne, and he had given himself the reputation of being very cruel, having through his prefects, in Rome and in all other parts of the empire, committed many cruelties. As a result, the entire world was moved by disgust for his ignoble birth and by the hatred brought about by fear of his cruelty; first Africa revolted, then the senate with the entire populace of Rome, and finally all of Italy conspired against him. To this was added even his own army; for, while besieging Aquileia and finding the capture difficult, angered by his cruelty and fearing him less, seeing that he had many enemies, they murdered him.

I do not wish to discuss Heliogabalus or Macrinus or Julian, who, since they were universally despised, were immediately disposed of; but I shall come to the conclusion of this discourse. And I say that the princes of our times suffer less from this problem of satisfying their soldiers by extraordinary means in their affairs; for, although they have to observe some consideration toward them, yet they resolve the question quickly, for none of these princes has standing armies which have evolved along with the government and the administration of the provinces as did the armies of the Roman empire. And therefore, if it was then necessary to satisfy the soldiers more than the common people, it was because the soldiers could do more than the common people; now it is more necessary for all princes, except the Turk and the Sultan, to satisfy the common people more than the soldiers, since the people can do more than the soldiers. I make an exception of the Turk, for he always maintains near him twelve thousand infantrymen and fifteen thousand cavalrymen, upon whom depend the safety and the strength of his kingdom, and it is necessary that, setting aside all other concerns, that ruler maintain them as his friends. Likewise, the kingdom of the Sultan being entirely in the hands of the soldiers, it is fitting that he, too, should maintain them as his friends without respect to the people. And you must note that this state of the Sultan is unlike all the other principalities, since it is similar to a Christian pontificate, which cannot be called either a hereditary principality or a new principality; for it is not the sons of the old prince that are the heirs and that remain as lords, but instead the one who is elected to that rank by those who have the authority to do so. And because this system is an ancient one, it cannot be called a new principality, for in it are none of these difficulties that are to be found in new ones; since, although the prince is new, the institutions of that state are old and are organized to receive him as if he were their hereditary ruler.

But let us return to our subject. Let me say that anyone who will consider the discourse written above will see how either hatred or contempt has been the cause of the ruin of these previously mentioned emperors; and he will also recognize how it comes to pass that, although some acted in one way and others in a contrary manner, in each of these groups one man had a happy end and the others an unhappy one. Because for Pertinax and Alexander, being new princes, it was useless and damaging to wish to imitate Marcus, who was installed in the principality by hereditary right; and likewise for Caracalla, Commodus, and Maximinus, it was disastrous to imitate Severus, since they did not have enough ability to follow in his footsteps. Therefore, a new prince in a new principality cannot imitate the deeds of Marcus, nor yet does he need to follow those of Severus; instead, he should take from Severus those attributes which are necessary to found his state and from Marcus those which are suitable and glorious in order to conserve a state which is already established and stable.

Chapter XX
On Whether Fortresses and Many Things That Princes Employ Every Day Are Useful or Harmful

Some princes have disarmed their subjects in order to hold the state securely; others have kept their conquered lands divided; some have encouraged hostilities against themselves; others have turned to winning the support of those who were suspect at the beginning of their rule; some have built fortresses; others have torn them down and destroyed them. And although one cannot give a definite rule concerning these matters without knowing the particular details of those states wherein one had to take some similar decision, nevertheless I shall speak in as general a manner as the subject matter will allow.

There has never been, therefore, a time when a new prince disarmed his subjects; on the contrary, when he has found them unarmed he has always armed them, because when armed those arms become yours; those whom you suspect become faithful, and those who were faithful remain so, and they become your partisans rather than your subjects. And since all of your subjects cannot be armed, when those you arm are favored you can deal more securely with the others; and that distinction in treatment which they recognize toward themselves makes them obliged to you; the others excuse you, judging it necessary that those who are in more danger and who hold more re-sponsibility should have more reward. But when you disarm them you begin to offend them; you demonstrate that you have no trust in them, either out of cowardice or from little confidence in them; and the one and the other of these opinions breed hatred against you. And since you cannot be unarmed, you will have to turn to mercenary soldiers who have the characteristics explained above; and even if they were good, they could not be strong enough to defend you from powerful enemies and from unfaithful subjects. Therefore, as I have said, a new prince in a new principality has always instituted an army; and histories are full of such examples.

But when a prince acquires a new state that, like a member, is joined to his old one, then it is necessary to disarm that state, except for those who have been your partisans in its acquisition; and they as well, with time and the appropriate opportunity, must be rendered weak and effeminate; and things must be organized in such a fashion that the armed strength of your entire state will be concentrated in your own troops who live near to you in your older state.

Our ancestors, and those who were considered wise, used to say that it was necessary to hold Pistoia by factions and Pisa by fortresses; and because of this they would encourage factional strife in some of their subject towns in order to control them more easily. This advice, during those times when Italy had, to a certain extent, a balance of power, may have been a good policy; but I do not believe that today it can be given as a rule, since I do not think that factions ever did any good. On the contrary, when the enemy approaches, divided cities are, of necessity, always lost; for the weaker factions will always join the external forces and the others will not be able to resist.

The Venetians, moved by the reasons stated above, as I believe, encouraged the Guelf and Ghibelline factions in their subject cities; and although they never permitted matters to come to bloodshed, they still fostered these quarrels between them so that those citizens, busy with their own disputes, would not unite against them. This, as we have seen, did not result in their gain; for, having been defeated at Vailà, one faction of these cities immediately took courage and seized the entire territory from them. Methods such as these, however, imply weakness in a prince; for in a strong principality such divisions will never be allowed, since they are profitable only in peacetime, allowing the subjects to be more easily controlled by their means; but when war comes such a policy shows its defects.

Without a doubt, princes become great when they overcome difficulties and obstacles that are imposed on them; and therefore Fortune, especially when she wishes to increase the reputation of a new prince, who has a greater need to acquire prestige than a hereditary prince does, creates enemies for him and has them take action against him so that he will have the chance to overcome them and to climb higher up the ladder his enemies have brought him. Therefore many judge that a wise prince must, whenever he has the occasion, foster with cunning some hostility so that in stamping it out his greatness will increase as a result.

Princes, and especially those who are new, have discovered more loyalty and more utility in those men who, at the beginning of their rule, were considered suspect than in those who were at first trusted. Pandolfo Petrucci, prince of Siena, ruled his state more with the assistance of men who had been held in suspicion than by others. But on this issue one cannot speak in generalities, for it varies according to the case. I shall only say this: that the prince will always easily win the support of those men who had been enemies at the start of a principality, the kind who must have support in order to maintain themselves; and they are even more obliged to serve him faithfully inasmuch as they recognize the need, through their actions, to cancel the suspicious opinion that the prince had of them. And thus, the prince will always derive more profit from them than from those who, serving him with too much security, neglect his affairs.

And since the subject requires it, I do not wish to fail to remind princes who have conquered a state recently by means of assistance from its inhabitants to consider carefully what cause may have moved those who have helped him to do so; and if it is not natural affection for him, but simply because they were not happy with the preceding state, he will be able to keep them as his allies only with hard work and the greatest of difficulty, since it will be impossible for him to satisfy them. And considering carefully the reason for this, with the examples taken from antiquity and from modern times, he will see that he can more easily win friends for himself from among those men who were content with the preceding state, and therefore were his enemies, than from those who, since they were not satisfied with it, became his allies and helped him to occupy it.

In order to hold their states more securely, princes have been accustomed to build fortresses that may serve as the bridle and bit for those who might plot an attack against them, and to have a secure shelter from a sudden rebellion. I praise this method, since it was used in ancient times; nevertheless, Messer Niccolò Vitelli, in our own times, was seen to demolish two fortresses in Città di Castello in order to hold that state; Guido Ubaldo, Duke of Urbino, on returning to the rule from which Cesare Borgia had driven him, completely destroyed all the fortresses of that province, and he decided that without them it would be more difficult to recapture that state; the Bentivogli, having returned to power in Bologna, took similar measures. Fortresses, then, are either useful or not, according to the circumstances: if they benefit you in one way they injure you in another. This matter may be dealt with as follows: that prince who is more afraid of his own people than of foreigners should build fortresses; but one who is more afraid of foreigners than of his people should not consider constructing them. The castle of Milan, which Francesco Sforza built there, has caused and will cause more wars against the Sforza family than any other disorder in that state. However, the best fortress that exists is not to be hated by the people; because, although you may have fortresses, they will not save you if the people hate you; for once the people have taken up arms, they never lack for foreigners who will aid them. In our times we have not seen that they have benefited any prince except the Countess of Forlì after her husband, Count Girolamo, was killed; for because of her castle she was able to escape the popular uprising and to wait until help arrived from Milan in order to regain her state. And the times were such at that moment that no foreigner could give assistance to her people. But then fortresses were of little use to her when Cesare Borgia attacked her and when her hostile populace joined with the foreigner. Therefore, then and earlier, it would have been safer for her not to have been despised by her people than to have had the fortresses.

Considering all these matters, therefore, I shall praise both those princes who build fortresses and those who do not; and I shall criticize any prince who, trusting in fortresses, considers the hatred of the people to be of little importance.

Chapter XXI
How A Prince Should Act To Acquire Esteem

Nothing makes a prince more esteemed than great undertakings and examples of his unusual talents. In our own times we have Ferdinand of Aragon, the present

King of Spain. This man can be called almost a new prince, since from being a weak ruler he became, through fame and glory, the first king of Christendom; and if you will consider his accomplishments, you will find them all very grand and some even extraordinary. In the beginning of his reign he attacked Granada, and that enterprise was the basis of his state. First, he acted while things were peaceful and when he had no fear of opposition: he kept the minds of the barons of Castile busy with this, and they, concentrating on that war, did not consider reforms at home. And he acquired, through that means, reputation and power over them without their noticing it; he was able to maintain armies with money from the Church and the people, and with that long war he laid a basis for his own army, which has since brought him honor. Besides this, in order to be able to undertake greater enterprises, always using religion for his own purposes, he turned to a pious cruelty, hunting down and clearing out the Moors from his kingdom: no example could be more pathetic or more unusual than this. He attacked Africa, under the same cloak of religion; he undertook the invasion of Italy; he finally attacked France. And in such a manner, he has always done and planned great deeds which have always kept the minds of his subjects in suspense and amazed and occupied with their outcome. And these actions of his are born from each other in such a way that between one and another he would never give men enough time to be able to work calmly against him.

It also helps a prince a great deal to display rare examples of his skills in dealing with internal affairs, such as those which are reported about Messer Bernabò Visconti of Milan. When the occasion arises that a person in public life performs some extraordinary act, be it good or evil, he should find a way of rewarding or punishing him that will provoke a great deal of discussion. And above all, a prince should strive in all of his deeds to give the impression of a great man of superior intelligence.

A prince is also respected when he is a true friend and a true enemy; that is, when he declares himself on the side of one prince against another without any reservation. Such a policy will always be more useful than that of neutrality; for if two powerful neighbors of yours come to blows, they will be of the type that, when one has emerged victorious, you will either have cause to fear the victor or you will not have. In either of these two cases, it will always be more useful for you to declare yourself and to fight an open war; for, in the first case, if you do not declare your intentions, you will always be the prey of the victor to the delight and satisfaction of the vanquished, and you will have no reason why anyone would come to your assistance; because whoever wins does not want reluctant allies who would not assist him in times of adversity; and whoever loses will not give you refuge since you were unwilling to run the risk of coming to his aid.

Antiochus came into Greece, sent there by the Aetolians to drive out the Romans. Antiochus sent envoys to the Achaeans, who were friends of the Romans, to encourage them to adopt a neutral policy; and, on the other hand, the Romans were urging them to take up arms on their behalf. This matter came up for debate in the council of the Achaeans, where the legate of Antiochus persuaded them to remain neutral; to this the Roman legate replied: "The counsel these men give you about not entering the war is indeed contrary to your interests; without respect, without dignity, you will be the prey of the victors."

And it will always happen that he who is not your friend will request your neutrality and he who is your friend will ask you to declare yourself by taking up your arms. And irresolute princes, in order to avoid present dangers, follow the neutral road most of the time, and most of the time they are ruined. But when the prince declares himself vigorously in favor of one side, if the one with whom you have joined wins, although he may be powerful and you may be left to his discretion, he has an obligation to you and there does exist a bond of friendship; and men are never so dishonest that they will crush you with such a show of ingratitude; and then, victories are never so sure that the victor need be completely free of caution, especially when justice is concerned. But if the one with whom you join loses, you will be taken in by him; and while he is able, he will help you, and you will become the comrade of a fortune which can rise up again.

In the second case, when those who fight together are of such a kind that you need not fear the one who wins, it is even more prudent to join his side, since you go to the downfall of a prince with the aid of another prince who should have saved him if he had been wise; and in winning he is at your discretion, and it is impossible for him not to win with your aid.

And here it is to be noted that a prince should avoid ever joining forces with one more powerful than himself against others unless necessity compels it, as was said above; for you remain his prisoner if you win, and princes should avoid, as much as possible, being left at the mercy of others. The Venetians allied themselves with France against the Duke of Milan; and they could have avoided that alliance, which resulted in their ruin. But when such an alliance cannot be avoided (as happened to the Florentines when the Pope and Spain led their armies to attack Lombardy), then a prince should join in, for the reasons given above. Nor should any state ever believe that it can always choose safe courses of action; on the contrary, it should think that they will all be doubtful; for we find this to be in the order of things: that we never try to avoid one disadvantage without running into another; but prudence consists in knowing how to recognize the nature of disadvantages and how to choose the least bad as good.

A prince also should demonstrate that he is a lover of talent by giving recognition to men of ability and by honoring those who excel in a particular field. Furthermore, he should encourage his subjects to be free to pursue their trades in tranquillity, whether in commerce, agriculture, or in any other trade a man may have. And he should act in such a way that a man is not afraid to increase his goods for fear that they will be taken away from him, while another will not be afraid to engage in commerce for fear of taxes; instead, he must set up rewards for those who wish to do these things, and for anyone who seeks in any way to aggrandize his city or state. He should, besides this, at the appropriate times of the year, keep the populace occupied with festivals and spectacles. And because each city is divided into guilds or clans, he should take account of these groups, meet with them on occasion, offer himself as an example of humanity and munificence, always, nevertheless, maintaining firmly the dignity of his position, for this should never be lacking in any way.

Chapter XXII
On The Prince's Private Advisers

The choice of advisers is of no little import to a prince; and they may be good or not, according to the wisdom of the prince. The first thing one does to evaluate the wisdom of a ruler is to examine the men that he has around him; and when they are capable and faithful one can always consider him wise, for he has known how to recognize their ability and to keep them loyal; but when they are otherwise one can always form a low impression of him; for the first error he makes is made in this choice of advisers.

There was no one who knew Messer Antonio da Venafro, adviser of Pandolfo Petrucci, Prince of Siena, who did not judge Pandolfo to be a very worthy man for having him as his minister. For there are three types of intelligence: one understands on its own, the second discerns what others understand, the third neither understands by itself nor through the intelligence of others; that first kind is most excellent, the second excellent, the third useless; therefore, it was necessary that if Pandolfo's intelligence were not of the first sort it must have been of the second: for, whenever a man has the intelligence to recognize the good or the evil that a man does or says, although he may not have original ideas of his own, he recognizes the sorry deeds and the good ones of the adviser, and he is able to praise the latter and to correct the others; and the adviser cannot hope to deceive him and thus he maintains his good behavior.

But as to how a prince may know the adviser, there is this way which never fails. When you see that the adviser thinks more about himself than about you, and that in all his deeds he seeks his own self-interest, such a man as this will never be a good adviser and you will never be able to trust him; for a man who has the state of another in his hand must never think about himself but always about his prince, and he must never be concerned with anything that does not concern his prince. And on the other hand, the prince should think of the adviser in order to keep him good—honoring him, making him wealthy, putting him in his debt, giving him a share of the honors and the responsibilities—so that the adviser sees that he cannot exist without the prince and so his abundant wealth will not make him desire more riches, or his many duties make him fear innovations. When, therefore, advisers and princes are of such a nature in their dealings with each other, they can have faith in each other; and when they are otherwise, the outcome will always be harmful either to the one or to the other.

Chapter XXIII
On How To Avoid Flatterers

I do not wish to omit an important matter and an error from which princes protect themselves with difficulty if they are not very clever or if they do not have good judgment. And these are the flatterers which fill the courts; for men delight so much in their own concerns, deceiving themselves in this manner, that they protect themselves from this plague with difficulty; and wishing to defend oneself from them brings with it the danger of becoming despised. For there is no other way to guard yourself against flattery than by making men understand that telling you the truth will not offend you; but when each man is able to tell you the truth you lose their respect. Therefore, a wise prince should take a third course, choosing wise men for his state and giving only those free rein to speak the truth to him, and only on those matters as he inquires about and not on others. But he should ask them about everything and should hear their opinions, and afterward he should deliberate by himself in his own way; and with these counsels and with each of his advisers he should conduct himself in such a manner that all will realize that the more freely they speak the more they will be acceptable to him; besides these things, he should not want to hear any others, he should follow through on the policy decided upon, and he should be firm in his decisions. Anyone who does otherwise is either prey for flatterers or changes his mind often with the variance of opinions: because of this he is not respected.

I wish, in this regard, to cite a modern example. Father Luca, the representative of the present Emperor Maximilian, explained, speaking about His Majesty, how the emperor never sought advice from anyone, nor did he ever do anything in his own way; this came about because of the emperor's secretive nature, a policy contrary to the one discussed above. He communicates his plans to no one, he accepts no advice about them; but as they begin to be recognized and discovered as they are put into effect, they begin to be criticized by those around him; and he, being easily influenced, is drawn away from his plans. From this results the fact that those things he achieves in one day he destroys during the next, and no one ever understands what he wishes or plans to do, and one cannot rely upon his decisions.

A prince, therefore, should always seek counsel, but when he wishes and not when others wish it; on the contrary, he should discourage anyone from giving him counsel unless it is requested. But he should be a great inquisitor and then, concerning the matters inquired about, a patient listener to the truth; furthermore, if he learns that anyone, for any reason, does not tell him the truth, he should become angry. And although many feel that any prince who is considered clever is so reputed not because of his own character but because of the good advisers he has around him, without a doubt they are deceived. For this is a general rule which never fails: that a prince who is not wise in his own right cannot be well advised, unless by chance he has submitted himself to a single person who governed him in everything and who was a very prudent individual. In this case he could well receive good advice, but it would not last long because that adviser would in a brief time take the state away from him. But if he seeks advice from more than one, a prince who is not wise will never have consistent advice, nor will he know how to make it consistent on his own; each of his advisers will think about his own interests; he will not know either how to correct or to understand them. And one cannot find advisers who are otherwise, for men always turn out badly for you unless some necessity makes them good. Therefore, it is to be concluded that good advice, from whomever it may come, must arise from the prudence of the prince and not the prince's prudence from the good advice.

Chapter XXIV
Why Italian Princes Have Lost Their States

The things written above, if followed prudently, make a new prince seem well established and render him immediately safer and more established in his state than if he had been in it for some time. For a new prince is far more closely observed in his activities than is a hereditary prince; and when his deeds are recognized as skillful they attract men much more and bind them to him more strongly than does ancient blood. For men are much more taken by present concerns than by those of the past; and when they find the present good they enjoy it and seek nothing more; in fact, they will seize every measure to defend the new prince as long as he is not lacking in his other responsibilities. And thus he will have a double glory: that of having given birth to a new principality and of having decorated it and strengthened it with good laws, good arms, and good examples; as that one will have double shame who, having been born a prince, loses his principality on account of his lack of prudence.

And if one will consider those rulers in Italy that have lost their states in our times, such as the King of Naples, the Duke of Milan, and others, one will discover in them, first, a common defect insofar as arms are concerned, for the reasons that were discussed at length earlier; and then, one will see that some of them either will have had the people as their enemy or, if they have had the people as their friend, they will not have known how to secure themselves against the nobles; for without these defects states are not lost which have enough nerve to take an army into battle. Philip of Macedonia—not the father of Alexander but the one who was defeated by Titus Quintius—did not have much of a state compared to the greatness of the Romans and of Greece that attacked him; nonetheless, because he was a good soldier and knew how to hold the people and to secure himself from the nobility, he carried on war against them for many years; and if at the end he lost the control of several cities, he was nevertheless left with the kingdom.

Therefore, these princes of ours who have been in their principalities for many years, and who have then lost them, must not blame Fortune but instead their own idleness: for, never having thought in peaceful times that things might change (which is a common defect in men, not to consider in good weather the possibility of a tempest), when adverse times finally arrived they thought about running away and not about defending themselves; and they hoped that the people, after having been angered by the insolence of the victors, would recall them. This policy, when others are lacking, is good; but it is indeed bad to have disregarded all other solutions for this one; for you should never wish to fall, believing that you will find someone else to pick you up; because whether this occurs or not, it does not increase your security, that method being a cowardly defense and one not dependent upon your own resources. And only those defenses are good, certain, and lasting that depend on yourself and on your own ability.

Chapter XXV
On Fortune's Role In Human Affairs and How She Can Be Dealt With

It is not unknown to me that many have held, and still hold, the opinion that the things of this world are, in a manner, controlled by Fortune and by God, that men with their wisdom cannot control them, and, on the contrary, that men can have no remedy whatsoever for them; and for this reason they might judge that they need not sweat much over such matters but let them be governed by fate. This opinion has been more strongly held in our own times because of the great variation of affairs that has been observed and that is being observed every day which is beyond human conjecture. Sometimes, as I think about these things, I am inclined to their opinion to a certain extent. Nevertheless, in order that our free will not be extinguished, I judge it to be true that Fortune is the arbiter of one half of our actions, but that she still leaves the control of the other half, or almost that, to us. And I compare her to one of those ruinous rivers that, when they become enraged, flood the plains, tear down the trees and buildings, taking up earth from one spot and placing it upon another; everyone flees from them, everyone yields to their onslaught, unable to oppose them in any way. And although they are of such a nature, it does not follow that when the weather is calm we cannot take precautions with embankments and dikes, so that when they rise up again either the waters will be channeled off or their impetus will not be either so disastrous or so damaging. The same things happen where Fortune is concerned: she shows her force where there is no organized strength to resist her; and she directs her impact there where she knows that dikes and embankments are not constructed to hold her. And if you will consider Italy, the seat of these changes and the nation which has set them in motion, you will see a country without embankments and without a single bastion: for if she were defended by the necessary forces, like Germany, Spain, and France, either this flood would not have produced the great changes that it has or it would not have come upon us at all. And this I consider enough to say about Fortune in general terms.

But, limiting myself more to particulars, I say that one sees a prince prosper today and come to ruin tomorrow without having seen him change his character or any of his traits. I believe that this comes about, first, because of the reasons that have been discussed at length earlier; that is, that a prince who relies completely upon Fortune will come to ruin as soon as she changes; I also believe that the man who adapts his course of action to the nature of the times will succeed and, likewise, that the man who sets his course of action out of tune with the times will come to grief. For one can observe that men, in the affairs which lead them to the end that they seek—that is, glory and wealth—proceed there in different ways; one by caution, another with impetuousness; one through violence, another with guile; one with patience, another with its opposite; and each one by these various means can attain his goals. And we also see, in the case of two cautious men, that one reaches his goal while the other does not; and, likewise, two men equally succeed using two different means, one being cautious and the other impetuous: this arises from nothing else than the nature of the times that either suit or do not suit their course of action. From this results that which I have said, that two men, working in opposite ways, can produce the same outcome; and of two men working in the same fashion one achieves his goal and the other does not. On this also depends the variation of what is good; for, if a man governs himself with caution and patience, and the times and conditions are turning in such a way that his policy is a good one, he will prosper; but if the times and conditions change, he will be ruined because he does not change his method of procedure. Nor is there to be found a man so prudent that he knows how to adapt himself to this, both because he cannot deviate from that to which he is by nature inclined and also because he cannot be persuaded to depart from a path, having always prospered by following it. And therefore the cautious man, when it is time to act impetuously, does not know how to do so, and he is ruined; but if he had changed his conduct with the times, Fortune would not have changed.

Pope Julius II acted impetuously in all his affairs; and he found the times and conditions so apt to this course of action that he always achieved successful results. Consider the first campaign he waged against Bologna while Messer Giovanni Bentivogli was still alive. The Venetians were unhappy about it; so was the King of Spain; Julius still had negotiations going on about it with France; and nevertheless, he started personally on this expedition with his usual ferocity and lack of caution. Such a move kept Spain and the Venetians at bay, the latter out of fear and the former out of a desire to regain the entire Kingdom of Naples; and at the same time it drew the King of France into the affair, for when the king saw that the Pope had already made this move, he judged that he could not deny him the use of his troops without obviously harming him, since he wanted his friendship in order to defeat the Venetians. And therefore Julius achieved with his impetuous action what no other pontiff would ever have achieved with the greatest of human wisdom; for, if he had waited to leave Rome with agreements settled and things in order, as any other pontiff might have done, he would never have succeeded, because the King of France would have found a thousand excuses and the others would have aroused in him a thousand fears. I wish to leave unmentioned his other deeds, which were all similar and which were all successful. And the brevity of his life did not let him experience the opposite, since if times which necessitated caution had come his ruin would have followed from it: for never would he have deviated from those methods to which his nature inclined him.

I conclude, therefore, that since Fortune changes and men remain set in their ways, men will succeed when the two are in harmony and fail when they are not in accord. I am certainly convinced of this: that it is better to be impetuous than cautious, because Fortune is a woman, and it is necessary, in order to keep her down, to beat her and to struggle with her. And it is seen that she more often allows herself to be taken over by men who are impetuous than by those who make cold advances; and then, being a woman, she is always the friend of young men, for they are less cautious, more aggressive, and they command her with more audacity.

Chapter XXVI
An Exhortation To Liberate Italy From the Barbarians

Considering, therefore, all of the things mentioned above, and thinking to myself about whether the times are suitable, at present, to honor a new prince in Italy, and if there is the material that might give a skillful and prudent prince the opportunity to form his own creation that would bring him honor and good to the people of Italy, it seems to me that so many circumstances are favorable to such a new prince that I know of no other time more appropriate. And if, as I said, it was necessary that the people of Israel be slaves in Egypt in order to recognize Moses' ability, and it was necessary that the Persians be oppressed by the Medes to recognize the greatness of spirit in Cyrus, and it was necessary that the Athenians be dispersed to realize the excellence of Theseus, then, likewise, at the present time, in order to recognize the ability of an Italian spirit, it was necessary that Italy be reduced to her present condition and that she be more enslaved than the Hebrews, more servile than the Persians, more scattered than the Athenians; without a leader, without organization, beaten, despoiled, ripped apart, overrun, and prey to every sort of catastrophe.

And even though before now some glimmer of light may have shown itself in a single individual, so that it was possible to believe that God had ordained him for Italy's redemption, nevertheless it was witnessed afterward how at the height of his career he was rejected by Fortune. So now Italy remains without life and awaits the man who can heal her wounds and put an end to the plundering of Lombardy, the ransoms in the Kingdom of Naples and in Tuscany, and who can cure her of those sores which have been festering for so long. Look how she now prays to God to send someone to redeem her from these barbaric cruelties and insolence; see her still ready and willing to follow a banner, provided that there be someone to raise it up. Nor is there anyone in sight, at present, in whom she can have more hope than in your illustrious house, which, with its fortune and ability, favored by God and by the Church, of which it is now prince, could make itself the head of this redemption. This will not be very difficult if you keep before you the deeds and the lives of those named above. And although those men were out of the ordinary and marvelous, they were nevertheless men; and each of them had less opportunity than the present one; for their enterprises were no more just, nor easier, nor was God more a friend to them than to you. Here justice is great: "Only those wars that are necessary are just, and arms are sacred when there is no hope except through arms."[4] Here there is a great willingness; and where there is a great willingness there cannot be great difficulty, if only you will use the institutions of those men I have proposed as your target. Besides this, we now see extraordinary, unprecedented signs brought about by God: the sea has opened up; a cloud has shown you the path; the rock pours forth water; it has rained manna here; everything has converged for your greatness. The rest you must do yourself. God does not wish to do everything, in order not to take from us our free will and that part of the glory which is ours.

And it is no surprise if some of the Italians mentioned previously were not capable of doing what it is hoped may be done by your illustrious house, and if, during the many revolutions in Italy and the many campaigns of war, it always seems that her military ability is spent. This results from the fact that her ancient institutions were not good and that there was no one who knew how to discover new ones; and no other thing brings a new man on the rise such honor as the new laws and the new institutions discovered by him. These things, when they are well founded and have in themselves a certain greatness, make him revered and admirable. And in Italy there is no lack of material to be given a form: here there is great ability in her members, were it not for the lack of it in her leaders. Consider how in duels and skirmishes involving just a few men the Italians are superior in strength, dexterity, and cunning; but when it comes to armies they do not match others. And all this comes from the weakness of her leaders; for those who know are not followed; and with each one seeming to know, there has not been to the present day anyone who has known how to set himself above the others, either because of ingenuity or fortune, so that others might yield to him. As a consequence, during so much time and many wars fought over the past twenty years, whenever there has been an army made up completely of Italians it has always made a poor showing. As proof of this, there is first Taro, then Alexandria, Capua, Genoa, Vailà, Bologna, and Mestri.[5]

Therefore, if your illustrious house desires to follow these excellent men who redeemed their lands, it is necessary before all else, as a true basis for every undertaking, to provide yourself with your own native troops, for one cannot have either more faithful, more loyal, or better troops. And although each one separately may be brave, all of them united will become even braver when they find themselves commanded, honored, and well treated by their own prince. It is necessary, therefore, to prepare yourself with such troops as these, so that with Italian strength you will be able to defend yourself from foreigners. And although Swiss and Spanish infantry may be reputed terrifying, nevertheless both have defects, so that a third army could not only oppose them but be confident of defeating them. For the Spanish cannot withstand cavalry and the Swiss have a fear of foot soldiers they meet in combat who are as brave as they are. Therefore, it has been witnessed and experience will demonstrate that the Spanish cannot withstand French cavalry and

---

4. [Livy, IX, i.]

5. [Here Machiavelli refers to the battle of Fornovo (1495) and the taking of Alexandria (1499), Capua (1501), Genoa (1507), Vailà (1509), Bologna (1511), and Mestri (1513).]

the Swiss are ruined by Spanish infantrymen. And although this last point has not been completely confirmed by experience, there was nevertheless a hint of it at the battle of Ravenna,[6] when the Spanish infantry met the German battalions, who follow the same order as the Swiss; and the Spanish, with their agile bodies, aided by their spiked shields, entered between and underneath the Germans' long pikes and were safe, without the Germans having any recourse against them; and had it not been for the cavalry charge that broke them, the Spaniards would have slaughtered them all. Therefore, as the defects of both these kinds of troops are recognized, a new type can be instituted which can stand up to cavalry and will have no fear of foot soldiers: this will come about by creating new armies and changing battle formations. And these are among those matters that, when newly organized, give reputation and greatness to a new prince.

This opportunity, therefore, must not be permitted to pass by so that Italy, after so long a time, may behold its redeemer. Nor can I express with what love he will be received in all those provinces that have suffered through these foreign floods; with what thirst for revenge, with what obstinate loyalty, with what compassion, with what tears! What doors will be closed to him? Which people will deny him obedience? What jealousy could oppose him? What Italian would deny him homage? This barbarian dominion stinks to everyone! Therefore, may your illustrious house take up this mission with that spirit and with that hope in which just undertakings are begun; so that under your banner this country may be ennobled and, under your guidance, those words of Petrarch may come true:

> Discipline over rage
> Will take up arms; and the battle will be short.
> For ancient valor
> In Italian hearts is not yet dead.[7]

6. [On April 11, 1512, the French were victorious under the leadership of Gaston de Foix.]

7. [From Petrarch's famous *canzone*, "Italia mia" (ll. 93–96).]

DISCOURSES ON THE FIRST TEN BOOKS OF TITUS LIVIUS

Niccolò Machiavelli to
Zanobi Buondelmonti and Cosimo Rucellai,
Greetings

I am sending you a gift which, even though it may not match the obligations I have to you, is, without a doubt, the best that Niccolò Machiavelli can send to you; in it I have expressed all I know and all that I have learned from long experience and continuous study of worldly affairs. And since it is not possible for you or anyone else to ask more of me, you cannot complain if I have not given you more. You may very well complain about the poverty of my wit when my arguments are weak, and about the fallacious quality of my judgment if, in the course of my reasonings, I often manage to deceive myself. This being the case, I do not know which of us should be less obliged to the other: whether I should be so to you, who have encouraged me to write what I never would have written by myself, or you to me, since I may have written without satisfying you. Take this, then, as you would accept something from a friend: there one considers the intention of the sender more than the quality of the thing which is sent. And rest assured that in this venture I have one consolation, for I believe that although I may have deceived myself in many of its particulars, in one matter I know that I have not made an error; that is, to have chosen you above all others to whom I should dedicate these *Discourses* of mine, both because in so doing I believe that I have shown my gratitude for the benefits I have received and because I felt that I had departed from the common practice of those who write and always address their works to some prince and, blinded by ambition and by avarice, praise him for all his virtuous qualities when they ought to be blaming him for all his bad qualities. So, to avoid this mistake, I have chosen not those who are princes but those who, because of their numerous good qualities, deserve to be princes; not those who might shower me with offices, honors, and wealth, but those who, although unable, would like to do so. If men wish to judge correctly, they must esteem those who are generous, not those who are potentially generous; and, in like manner, they must esteem those who know how to rule a kingdom, not those who, without knowing how, have the power to do so. Thus, historians praise Hiero the Syracusan more when he was a private citizen than they do Perseus of Macedonia when he was king: for Hiero lacked nothing to be prince save a kingdom, while the other had no attribute of a king except his kingdom. Therefore, enjoy this good or bad work which you yourselves have requested; and if you persist in erroneously finding pleasure in my opinions, I shall not fail to follow this with the rest of the history, as I promised you in the beginning. Farewell.

BOOK I

INTRODUCTION

Because of the envious nature of men, it has always been no less dangerous to discover new methods and institutions than to explore unknown oceans and lands, since men are quicker to criticize than to praise the deeds of others. Nevertheless, driven by that natural desire I have always felt to work on whatever might prove beneficial to everyone, I have determined to enter a path which has not yet been taken by anyone; although it may bring me worry and difficulty, yet I may find my reward among those who study kindly the goal of these labors of mine. And if my feeble intelligence, my limited experience of current events, and my weak knowledge of ancient ones should make this attempt of mine defective and of little use, it may, at least, show the way to someone with more ability, more eloquence, and more judgment who will be able to fulfill my intention; so that if I do not earn praise, I should not receive blame.

When we consider, then, how much honor is attributed to antiquity, and how many times (leaving aside numerous other examples) a fragment of an ancient statue has been bought at a great price so that the buyer may have it near him to decorate his house or to have it imitated by those who take pleasure in that art; and when we see, on the other hand, the powerful examples which history shows us that have been accomplished by ancient kingdoms and republics, by kings, captains, citizens, and legislators who have exhausted themselves for their fatherland, examples that have been more often admired than imitated (or so much ignored that not the slightest trace of this ancient ability remains), I cannot but be at the same time both amazed and sorry. And I am even more amazed when I see that in civil disputes which arise among citizens, or in sicknesses that break out, men always have recourse to those judgments or remedies which were pronounced or prescribed by the ancients. For civil law is nothing other than the judgments given by ancient jurists which, organized into a system, instruct our jurists today. Nor is medicine anything other than the experiments carried out by ancient doctors on which the doctors of today base their diagnoses. Nevertheless, in instituting republics, maintaining states, governing kingdoms, organizing the army and administering a war, dispensing justice to subjects, and increasing an empire one cannot find a prince or a republic that has recourse to the examples of the ancients.

This, in my opinion, arises not so much from the weakness into which the present religion has brought the world or from the harm done to many Christian provinces and cities by an idle ambition as from not possessing a proper knowledge of histories, for in reading them we do not draw out of them that sense or taste that flavor which they have in themselves. Hence it happens that an infinite number of people read them and take pleasure in hearing about the variety of incidents which are contained in them without thinking to imitate them, for they consider imitation not only difficult but impossible; as if the heavens, the sun, the elements, and men had varied in their motion, their order, and their power from what they were in ancient times. Wishing, therefore, to free men of this erroneous way of thinking, I deemed it necessary to write about all those books by Livy which the malignity of time has not taken from us; I wish to write what I, according to my knowledge of ancient and modern affairs, judge necessary for a better understanding of them, so that those who read these statements of mine may more easily draw from them that practical knowledge one should seek from an acquaintance with history books. And although this undertaking is difficult, nevertheless, aided by those who have encouraged me to shoulder this burden, I believe I can carry it in such a manner that only a short distance will remain for another to bring it to the destined goal.

Chapter I

What the Beginnings of All Cities Have Been and What, In Particular, Was the Beginning of Rome

Those who read of the origin of the city of Rome, its lawgivers, and how it was organized will not be surprised that so much ability was preserved in that city for so many centuries, and that afterward there developed from it the empire which that republic achieved. And wishing first to discuss its origin, let me say that all cities are built either by men native to a region or by foreigners. The first situation occurs when inhabitants, dispersed in many small groups, feel they cannot live securely, since each single group, because of its location or its small number, cannot resist the assault of anyone who may attack it, and if the enemy arrives, they are not in time to unite for their defense; if there is time, they have to abandon many of their strong fortifications, and thus they remain at the mercy of their enemies. Hence, to escape these dangers, moved either by their own decision or by someone among them of greater authority, they join together to live as a group in a place chosen by them that is more convenient to live in and easier to defend.

This was what happened to Athens and Venice, among many others. The first of these cities, under the authority of Theseus, was built for such reasons by the inhabitants, who were a scattered people. As to the other city, many sought refuge on various small islands which were at the edge of the Adriatic Sea in order to escape the wars that arose each day as a result of the arrival of new barbarians after the decline of the Roman empire. The second city was built by its people without a particular prince to establish law and order, and they began on their own to live under those laws which appeared to them to be most suitable for their maintenance. This turned out well for them because of the lengthy peace which their location afforded them, for that sea had no harbor and the peoples who were molesting Italy had no ships with which to invade them; thus, this meager beginning was such that they were able to arrive at their present greatness.

The second instance occurs when a city is built by foreigners and originates either from free men or from those who depend on others, such as the colonies sent either by a republic or by a prince to relieve their lands of the inhabitants, or for the defense of a land which, newly acquired, they wish to maintain securely and without expenditure. The Roman people built many such cities throughout their empire. They may also be built by a prince, not in order to live there but rather for his own glorification, as was the case with the city of Alexandria for Alexander. And since these cities are not by origin free, it rarely happens that they make great progress and can be numbered among the chief capitals of kingdoms. The building of Florence was similar to that of such cities, for (either built by the soldiers of Sulla or perhaps by the inhabitants of the mountains of Fiesole, who came to live in the Arno plain because they had faith in the long peace that was born in the world under Octavian) she was built under the Roman empire, and she could not, in the beginning, experience any growth except that which the goodwill of her prince allowed her.

The builders of cities are free men when any people, either under the rule of a prince or on their own, are forced to abandon their native land and to find themselves a new home, either because of pestilence, famine, or war. Such men either inhabit the cities that they find in the lands which they conquer, as Moses did, or they build new ones, as Aeneas did. In this case we are able to see the ability of the builder in the fortune of what he builds, for the city is more or less remarkable according to whether he who has been its cause is more or less able. The ability of the man is recognized in two ways: the first is in his selection of a site, the second in the organization of the laws. And since men act either out of necessity or by choice, and since we know that there is more ability where free choice has less authority, it must be considered whether it might be best to select barren places for the building of cities so that men, forced to become industrious and less idle, will live more united, having less cause for discord because of the poverty of the site—as happened in Ragusa and in many other cities built in similar spots. Such a selection would, without a doubt, be most wise and useful if men were content to live on what they had and did not wish to try to govern others. Nevertheless, since men cannot make themselves secure without power, it is necessary for them to avoid the barren places in the country and to establish themselves in very fertile places where, the fruitfulness of the site permitting expansion of the city, men can both defend themselves from anyone who attacks them and overcome anyone who opposes their greatness. And as for that idleness which the site invites, one should organize the laws in such a way that they force upon the city those necessities which the location does not impose; and one should imitate the wise men who have lived in the most beautiful and fertile of lands, lands more apt to produce idle men unfit for any vigorous activity; in order to avoid the harm which the pleasant nature of the land might have caused because of idleness, they constrained their soldiers to undergo such training and exercise that better soldiers are produced there than in lands which are naturally harsh and barren. Among kingdoms like these was the kingdom of the Egyptians, where, notwithstanding the fact that the land was very pleasant, the necessity imposed by the laws was so powerful that it produced very excellent men; and if their names had not been destroyed by time, we would see that they merit more praise than Alexander the Great and many others still fresh in our memory. And if one considers the Kingdom of the Sultan, or the organization of the Mamelukes and that of their army before they were destroyed by Selim the Great Turk, one will see that there were many kinds of training exercises that the troops underwent, and one would also see how much they feared that idleness which the beneficence of the land might have brought upon them if they had not prevented it with the strictest of laws.

I say, therefore, that it is more prudent to select a fertile site when that fertility's influence is kept within certain bounds by the laws. When Alexander the Great wanted to construct a city to his glory, the architect Dinocrates came to him and showed him how he could build a city on top of Mount Athos, a place which, besides being strong, could be shaped in such a way that a human form would be given to that city, a most marvelous and rare thing and one worthy of his greatness. And when Alexander asked him how its inhabitants would live, he answered that he had not thought about that; at this Alexander laughed and put that mountain site aside and built Alexandria, where the inhabitants were happy to live because of the fertility of the land and the convenience of the sea and the Nile. Anyone who examines, then, the building of Rome, taking Aeneas as her first founder, will count her as one of those cities built by foreigners: if Romulus is taken as her first founder, he will consider her as one of those cities constructed by men native to the site; and in any case, he will see her as having had a free beginning, with no dependence upon anyone; and furthermore, he will see how many necessities were imposed upon her by the laws instituted by Romulus, Numa, and others so that the fertility of the location, the convenience of the sea, the frequent victories, and the grandeur of her empire were not able to corrupt her for many centuries; these laws kept her very rich in ability, richer than any other city or republic that was as well adorned.

And because the deeds she accomplished (of which Livy preserves the memory) were done either by public decree or private initiative, either inside or outside the city, I shall begin by discussing those internal affairs which happened as a result of public decree, which I judge to be most worthy of attention, adding to them everything that depended upon them; to these Discourses this first book, or rather this first part, will be limited.

Chapter II
Of How Many Kinds Of Republics There Are and Of What Kind the Roman Republic Was

I wish to put aside a discussion of those cities which, at their beginnings, were subject to others; and I shall speak about those which have had their beginnings far from any foreign servitude and have been governed from the beginning by their own judgment, either as republics or as principalities, and which have had different laws and institutions just as they have had different origins. Some of them, either at their start or after very little time, were given laws by a single man and at one time, as Lycurgus did with the Spartans; others acquired their laws by chance, at different times and according to circumstances, as occurred in Rome. A republic can, indeed, be called fortunate if it produces a man so prudent that he gives it laws organized in such a manner that it can live securely under them without needing to revise them. And it seems that Sparta observed its laws more than eight hundred years without corrupting them or without any dangerous upheaval. Unfortunate, on the contrary, is the city which is forced to reorganize itself, not having chanced to encounter a prudent organizer. And of these cities, the one which is the furthest from order is the most unfortunate; and that one is furthest from it which in its institutions is completely off the straight path which could lead it to its perfect and true goal, because for those who find themselves in this state it is almost impossible that by any happening they can be set on the right path again. Those other cities that have had a good beginning and are capable of becoming better, even if they have not had a perfect constitution, can, by means of an unexpected course of events, become perfect. But it is very true that institutions are never established without danger; for most men never agree to a new law that concerns a new order in the city unless a necessity demonstrates to them that it is required; and since this necessity cannot arise without danger, the republic may easily be destroyed before it is brought to a perfection of organization. The Republic of Florence testifies to this: reorganized after what occurred at Arezzo in 1502, it was disorganized by what occurred at Prato in 1512.[1]

Since I wish to discuss what the institutions of the city of Rome were and the circumstances which led to their perfection, let me say that those who have written about republics declare that there are in them three kinds of governments, which they call principality, aristocracy, and democracy; and that those who organize a city most often turn to one of these, depending upon whichever seems more appropriate to them. Others—and wiser men, according to the judgment of many—are of the opinion that there are six types of government: three of these are very bad; three others are good in themselves but are so easily corruptible that they, too, can become pernicious. Those which are good are the three mentioned above; those which are bad are three others which depend upon the first three, and each of them is, in a way, similar to its good counterpart, so that they easily jump from one form to another. For the principality easily becomes tyrannical; aristocrats can very easily produce an oligarchy; democracy is converted into anarchy with no difficulty. So that if a founder of a republic organizes one of these three governments in a city, he organizes it there for a brief period of time only, since no precaution can prevent it from slipping into its contrary on account of the similarity, in such a case, of the virtue and the vice.

These variations of government are born among men by chance: for in the beginning of the world, when its inhabitants were few, they lived at one time dispersed and like wild beasts; then, when their numbers multiplied, they gathered together and, in order to defend themselves better, they began to search among themselves for one who was stronger and braver, and they made him their leader and obeyed him. From this sprang the knowledge of what things are good and honorable, as distinct from the pernicious and the evil: for if someone were to harm his benefactor, this aroused hatred and compassion among men, since they cursed the ungrateful and honored those who showed gratitude; and thinking that the same injuries could also be committed against themselves, they made laws to avoid similar evils and instituted punishments for transgressors. Thus, the recognition of justice came about. The result was that, later on, when they had to elect a prince, they did not select the bravest man but rather the one who was most prudent and most just. But when they began to choose the prince by hereditary succession rather than by election, the heirs immediately began to degenerate from the level of their ancestors and, putting aside acts of valor, they thought that princes had nothing to do but to surpass other princes in luxury, lasciviousness, and in every other form of pleasure. So, as the prince came to be hated he became afraid of this hatred and quickly passed from fear to violent deeds, and the immediate result was tyranny.

From this there came next the destructions, the conspiracies, and the plots against princes, carried out not by those who were either timid or weak but by those who surpassed others in generosity, greatness of spirit, wealth, and nobility: these men could not stand the disreputable life of such a prince. The masses, therefore, following the authority of these powerful men, took up arms against the prince, and after

---

1. [Machiavelli here refers both to the constitutional changes in Florence after the suppression of a rebellion at Arezzo and to the return of the Medici and the fall of Soderini's republic after the sack of Prato.]

he had been eliminated they obeyed those men as their liberators. And since those men hated the very idea of a single ruler, they constituted for themselves a government, and in the beginning, since they remembered the past tyranny, they governed according to the laws instituted by themselves, subordinating their own interests to the common good, and they managed and maintained both their private and public affairs with the greatest of care. When this administration later passed to their sons, who did not understand the changeability of Fortune, had never experienced bad times, and could not be satisfied with equality among citizens, they turned to avarice, ambition, and the violation of other men's women, and they caused a government of the aristocrats to become a government of the few, with no regard to any civil rights; so that in a short time they experienced the same fate as the tyrant, for as the masses were sick of their rule, they assisted, in any way they could, anyone who might plan to attack these rulers, and thus there soon arose someone who, with the aid of the masses, destroyed them. And since the memory of the prince and of the injuries received from him was still fresh, they turned to a democratic form of government, having destroyed the government ruled by a few men and not wishing to return to that ruled by a prince; and they organized it in such a way that neither the few powerful men nor a prince might have any authority whatsoever in it. And because all governments are, at the outset, respected, this democratic government was maintained awhile, but not for a long time, particularly after the generation that organized it passed away; it immediately turned to anarchy, where neither the individual citizen nor the public official is feared; each individual lived according to his own wishes, so that every day a thousand wrongs were done; and so, constrained by necessity, either because of the suggestion of some good man or in order to flee such anarchy, it returned again to the principality; and from that, step by step, the government moved again in the direction of anarchy, in the manner and for the reasons just given.

And this is the cycle through which all states that have governed themselves or that now govern themselves pass; but rarely do they return to the same forms of government, for virtually no state can possess so much vitality that it can sustain so many changes and remain on its feet. But it may well happen that while a state lacking counsel and strength is in difficulty, it becomes subject to a neighboring state which is better organized; but if this were not the case, then a state might be liable to pass endlessly through the cycle of these governments.

Let me say, therefore, that all the forms of government listed are defective: the three good ones because of the brevity of their lives, the three bad ones because of their inherent harmfulness. Thus, those who were prudent in establishing laws recognized this fact and, avoiding each of these forms in themselves, chose one that combined them all, judging such a government to be steadier and more stable, for when there is in the same city-state a principality, an aristocracy, and a democracy, one form keeps watch over the other.

Among those who have deserved great praise for having established such constitutions is Lycurgus, who organized his laws in Sparta in such a manner that, assigning to the king, the aristocrats, and the people their respective roles, he created a state which lasted more than eight hundred years, to his everlasting credit, and resulted in the tranquillity of that city. The contrary happened to Solon, who organized the laws in Athens: for in organizing only a democratic state there he made it of such a brief existence that before he died he saw arise the tyranny of Pisistratus; and although forty years later the latter's heirs were driven away and Athens returned to its freedom, having reestablished the democratic state according to the institutions of Solon, it did not last more than a hundred years. In spite of the fact that many laws which were not foreseen by Solon were established in Athens in order to restrain the insolence of the upper class and the anarchy of the populace, nevertheless Athens lived a very brief time in comparison to Sparta because Solon did not mix democracy with the power of the principality and with that of the aristocrats.

But let us come to Rome. In spite of the fact that she never had a Lycurgus to organize her at the beginning so that she might exist free for a long time, nevertheless, because of the friction between the plebeians and the senate, so many circumstances attended her birth that chance brought about what a lawgiver had not accomplished. If Rome did not receive Fortune's first gift, she received the second: for her early institutions, although defective, nevertheless did not deviate from the right path that could lead them to perfection. Romulus and all the other kings passed many good laws in accordance with a free government; but since their goal was to found a kingdom and not a republic, when that city became free she lacked many institutions which were necessary to organize her under freedom, institutions which had not been set up by those kings. And when it happened that her kings lost their power for the reasons and in the ways described earlier, nonetheless those who drove them out, having immediately established two consuls in place of the king, drove out only the title of king and not royal power; so that, as there were in that republic the consuls and the senate, it came to be formed by only two of the three above-mentioned elements, that is, the principality and the aristocrats. There remained only to make a place for the democratic part of the government. When the Roman nobility became insolent, for the reasons that will be listed below, the people rose up against them; in order not to lose everything, the nobility was forced to concede to the people their own share; and on the other hand, the senate and the consuls retained enough authority so that they could maintain their rank in that republic. And thus there came about the creation of the tribunes of the plebeians, after which the government of the republic became more stable, since each of the three elements of government had its share. And Fortune was so favorable to Rome that even though she passed from a government by kings and aristocrats to one by the people, through those same steps and because of those same reasons which were discussed above, nevertheless the kingly authority was never entirely abolished to give authority to the aristocrats, nor was the authority of the aristocrats diminished completely to give it to the people; but since these elements remained mixed, Rome was a perfect state; and this perfection was produced through the friction between the plebeians and the senate, as the two following chapters will demonstrate at greater length.

BOOK II

INTRODUCTION

Men always praise ancient times and condemn the present, but not always with good reason; they are such advocates of the past that they celebrate not merely those ages which they know only through the memory of the historians but also those that they, now being old, remember having seen in their youth. And when this opinion of theirs is mistaken, as it is most of the time, I am persuaded that there are several reasons which lead them to make this mistake. First, I believe that we do not know the complete truth about antiquity; most often the facts that would discredit those times are hidden and other matters which bestow glory upon them are reported magnificently and most thoroughly. Most writers submit to the fortune of conquerors, and in order to render their victories glorious they not only exaggerate what they have ably achieved but also embellish the deeds of their enemies in such a way that anyone born afterward in either of the two lands—that of the victor or that of the vanquished—has reason to marvel at those men and those times and is forced to praise them and to love them to the greatest degree. Besides this, since men hate things either out of fear or envy, two very powerful reasons for hatred of things in the past are eliminated, for they cannot hurt you or give you cause for envy. But the contrary applies to those things you deal with and observe: they are known to you in every detail, you see in them what is good as well as the many things that displease you, and you are obliged to judge them most inferior to things of the past; while, in truth, those of the present may deserve even more glory and fame—I am not speaking of things pertaining to the arts here, for in themselves they possess so much brilliance that the times take away from them little and cannot bestow upon them much more glory than they intrinsically merit; I am speaking rather of those matters pertaining to the lives and customs of men, about which we do not witness such clear evidence.

I repeat, then, that this aforementioned custom of praising the old and condemning the new does exist, but it is not always wrong. Sometimes such a judgment has to be correct since human affairs are always in motion, either rising or declining. And so, one city or province can be seen to possess a government that was well organized by an excellent man; and for a time it may keep improving because of the ability of the founder. Anyone, then, who is born in such a state and praises ancient times more than modern times deceives himself, and his deception is caused by those things mentioned above. But those who are born afterward in that city or region, at the time of its decline, do not, then, deceive themselves. As I reflect on why these matters proceed as they do, I believe that the world has always been in the same state and that there has always been as much good as evil in it; but this evil and this good changes from country to country, as we can see from what we know of ancient kingdoms that were different from each other according to the differences in their customs, while the world remained the same as it always had been. There is only this difference: the world's talents first found a home in Assyria, then moved to Media, later to Persia, and, in time, came into Italy and Rome; and if, after the Roman empire, no succeeding empire has lasted, nor has there been one where the world has retained all its talents in one place, nevertheless we can still see them scattered among many nations where men live ably, as in the kingdom of the Franks, the Turks—that of the Sultan—and today among the peoples of Germany; earlier there was that Turkish group which achieved so many grand things and seized so much of the world once it had destroyed the Eastern Roman Empire. In all these lands, then, after the Romans came to ruin, and in all those groups of people, such talents existed and still exist in some of them where they are desired and truly praised. And anyone who is born there and praises past times more than present ones may be deceiving himself, but anyone who is born in Italy or Greece and has not become an Ultramontane in Italy or a Turk in Greece has reason to condemn his own times and to praise others, for in them there were many things that made them marvelous, but in the present ones there is nothing to be seen but utter misery, infamy, and vituperation. There is no observance of religion, laws, or military discipline; all is stained with every kind of filth. Furthermore, these vices are the more detestable as they are found among those who sit on tribunals, command others, and expect to be worshiped.

But, returning to our subject, let me say that if the judgment of men is unfair in deciding which is better—the present age or the past—the latter of which, because of its antiquity, men cannot have as perfect a knowledge of as they can of their own times, this should not corrupt the judgment of old men in assessing the time of their youth and their old age, since they have known and observed both one and the other equally well. This would be true if men were all of the same opinion and had the same desires in all phases of their lives; but since these desires change, and the times do not, things cannot appear to men to be the same, since they have other desires, other pleasures, and other concerns in their old age than they had in their youth. For as men grow older they lose in vigor and gain in judgment and prudence, and the things that seemed acceptable and good to them in their youth become, later on, as they grow older, intolerable and bad; and although they should place the blame for this on their own judgment, they blame the times instead. Besides this, human desires are insatiable, for we are endowed by Nature with the power and the wish to desire everything and by Fortune with the ability to obtain little of what we desire. The result is an unending discontent in the minds of men and a weariness with what they possess: this makes men curse the present, praise the past, and hope in the future, even though they do this with no reasonable motive. I do not know, therefore, if I deserve to be considered among those who deceive themselves if, in these discourses of mine, I am too lavish with my praise of ancient Roman times and condemn our own. And certainly, if the excellence that existed then and the vice that rules now were not clearer than the sun, I would speak more hesitantly for fear that I might fall into the same error of which I accuse others. But since the matter is clear enough for all to see, I shall boldly declare in plain terms what I understand of those ancient times and of our own times, so that the minds of young men who read these writings of mine may be able to reject the present and prepare themselves to imitate the past whenever Fortune provides them with an occasion. For it is your duty as a good man to teach others whatever good you yourself have not been able to do, either because of the malignity of the times or because of Fortune, in order that—since many will thus be made aware of it—someone more beloved by Heaven may be prepared to put your truth into action.

In the discourse of the preceding book I have discussed the decisions the Romans made in matters concerning their internal affairs; now, in this one, I shall discuss what it was that the Roman people did concerning the expansion of their empire.

Chapter I

Whether Ability Or Fortune Was the Main Reason the Romans Conquered Their Empire

Many have held the opinion—among them Plutarch, a most serious writer—that the Roman people, in acquiring their empire, were favored more by Fortune than by their own ability. And among the other reasons he brings forth, he says that the people, by their own admission, attributed all their victories to Fortune, since they built more temples to Fortune than to any other god. And it seems that Livy holds this opinion, for he seldom has any Roman deliver a speech in which he speaks of ability without mentioning Fortune. But I do not accept this argument in any way, nor do I believe that it can be supported, for if no republic produced such results as Rome did, it is obvious that there never has been a republic so organized that she could acquire as Rome did. For the ability of her armies caused her to acquire her empire, and the institution of her conduct and her individual way of living, which were discovered by her first lawgiver, allowed her to keep her conquests, as will be explained in more detail in successive chapters.

These same writers declare that it was a consequence of Fortune, and not because of the innate ability of the Roman people, that they never had to fight two great wars at the same time; that they never waged war on the Latins unless they had completely vanquished the Samnites and, in fact, were even waging war in their defense; they never fought with the Tuscans unless they had first subjugated the Latins and had almost exhausted the Samnites through frequent defeats. However, if two of these powers had united when they were fresh and at full strength, without a doubt one might say that the ruin of the Roman republic would have been inevitable. But no matter how things turned out, they never waged two important wars at the same time; on the contrary, the case was always such that either one came to an end at the beginning of another or the other was begun when one was finished. This is surely evident from the order in which their wars took place: putting aside those wars waged before Rome was sacked by the Gauls, it is clear that while they fought with the Aequi and the Volsci—and those peoples were powerful—other nations never rose up against them. When they were defeated, the war against the Samnites broke out, and although the Latin peoples revolted against the Romans before the war ended, nevertheless, when this rebellion occurred the Samnites were allied with Rome; their army helped them to tame the Latin insolence. When the Latins were defeated, the war with Samnium broke out again, and when the Samnite troops were broken by the many defeats they suffered, the war against the Tuscans began; when this was settled, the Samnites again rose up because of the crossing of Pyrrhus into Italy. When he was repulsed and driven back into Greece, they instigated the First Carthaginian War; no sooner was that war over than all the Gauls, from both sides of the Alps, joined together against the Romans until, between Popolonia and Pisa, where the tower of Saint Vincent stands today, they were destroyed in a great slaughter. When this war was over, the Romans waged wars of little consequence over a space of twenty years, for they fought with no one except the Ligurians and the remainder of the Gauls, who were in Lombardy. And they continued in this manner until the Second Carthaginian War broke out, which kept Italy occupied for sixteen years. This war having ended with the greatest glory for Rome, the Macedonian War broke out; and, after that was over, there followed the war against Antiochus and Asia. After that victory, there remained in all the world neither prince nor republic that could, either by itself or together with others, oppose the Roman forces.

But before this last victory, one who carefully examines the order of these wars and the way the Romans proceeded will see in them good fortune mixed with great ability and prudence. Thus, if one looks for the cause of such good fortune one will discover it easily, for it is certainly true that when a prince or a people attains such a reputation that every prince or people nearby is afraid to attack singly and is in a state of fear, it always happens that none will ever attack unless driven to it by necessity; as a result, that power will have, as it were, the choice of waging war upon whichever of its neighbors it chooses, while keeping the others at peace with its diplomatic skill. And they will easily be kept at peace, partly because of their respect for this power and partly because they are deceived by the means employed to lull them to sleep. Other powers, which are far away and have no dealings with them, consider the matter a remote one, of no concern to them; they remain in this error until the fire draws near, and when it does, they have no remedy to extinguish it except their own forces, which, by then, will not suffice, since the other forces have become so very powerful.

I shall not discuss how the Samnites watched while the Roman people conquered the Volsci and the Aequi, and in order not to be too wordy I shall mention only the Carthaginians, who were very powerful and enjoyed a great reputation while the Romans were fighting with the Samnites and the Tuscans, for they already held all of Africa, Sardinia, and Sicily, and had conquered part of Spain. Their power, plus the fact that they were situated far from the borders of the Roman people, never made them think of attacking Rome or of giving aid to the Samnites and the Tuscans; on the contrary, they acted as a prosperous person would act when all goes well, making treaties with the Romans and seeking their friendship. They never realized their error until the Romans, having now conquered all the peoples between themselves and the Carthaginians, began to fight with the latter over the rule of Sicily and Spain. The same thing happened to the Gauls that happened to the Carthaginians, as well as to Philip, King of the Macedonians, and to Antiochus: all of them believed that while the Roman people were occupied with another power, the other power would defeat Rome and they would have the time to defend themselves against the Romans in either peace or war. Therefore, I believe that the Fortune the Romans enjoyed in this regard would have been possible for those rulers who acted in the same way as the Romans and possessed the same ability.

In this regard, I would talk about the method used by the Roman people in entering the territories of others if it were not for the fact that in my treatise on principalities I spoke of this at some length; this question is discussed fully in that work. To be brief, I shall say only this: they always tried to have some friend in a new province who might serve as a ladder to climb up or a gate through which to enter or as a means to hold onto it, as is evident when they entered Samnium with the aid of the Capuans, Tuscany with the support of the Camertines, Sicily with the assistance of the Mamertines, Spain with the help of the Saguntians, Africa with the aid of Masinissa, Greece with the Aetolians, Asia with the support of Eumenes as well as other princes, and Gaul with the assistance of the Aedui. And so, they never lacked support to facilitate their undertakings in acquiring and maintaining such provinces. The peoples who observe this practice discover that they have less need of Fortune than those who do not observe it well, and in order that everyone may better understand how much more effective was their ability than their Fortune in acquiring their empire, we shall discuss in the following chapter the characteristics of the peoples with whom they had to fight and how stubborn they were in defending their liberty.

Chapter II

With What Kinds Of Peoples the Romans Had To Fight, and How Stubbornly Those People Defended Their Liberty

Nothing made it more difficult for the Romans to conquer the peoples around them and the provinces some distance from them than the love such peoples had in those times for liberty, which they defended so stubbornly that they would never have been defeated except for the extraordinary amount of strength employed against them; and in many instances we know in what dangers they placed themselves in order to maintain or regain that liberty, and what revenge they took against those who had deprived them of it. We also learn from reading their histories about the harm servitude caused these people and their cities. Whereas in our own times there is only one country that can be said to contain within it free cities,[2] in ancient times there were in all lands many peoples who lived completely free. It is clear that in the times of which we are now speaking, from the Apennines which divided Tuscany from Lombardy all the way to the tip of Italy, all the peoples were free, as were the Tuscans, the Romans, the Samnites, and many others who inhabited that section of Italy. Nor do we ever read that any kings existed there besides the ones that reigned in Rome and Porsenna, King of Tuscany, the extinction of whose lineage history does not explain. But it is most clear that in the time when the Romans went to besiege Veii, Tuscany was free, and it enjoyed its liberty so much and so hated the very name of prince that when the people of Veii created a king for their protection and asked the Tuscans to help them against the Romans, the Tuscans, after holding many meetings, decided not to aid the people of Veii so long as they lived under a king, believing that it was not a good idea to defend the native city of those who had already subjected it to someone else.

It is an easy matter to understand the origin of this love for free government among peoples, for experience shows that cities have never enlarged their dominion nor increased their wealth except while they have existed in freedom. It is truly a marvelous thing to consider to what greatness Athens arrived in the space of one hundred years after she freed herself from the tyranny of Pisistratus; but, above all, it is even more marvelous to consider the greatness Rome reached when she freed herself from her kings. The reason is easy to understand, for it is the common good and not private gain that makes cities great. Yet, without a doubt, this common good is observed only in republics, for in them everything that promotes it is practiced, and however much damage it does to this or that private individual, those who benefit from the said common good are so numerous that they are able to advance it in spite of the inclination of the few citizens who are oppressed by it.

The contrary happens when there is a prince; in general, what he does in his own interest harms the city and what he does for the city's benefit harms him. For this reason, when a tyranny replaces a free government the least amount of evil that results in cities so affected is that they no longer advance or increase in power and riches; but, in most cases—in truth, always—they decline. And if fate brings about the rise of an able tyrant who, through courage and force of arms, increases his dominion, the republic derives no benefit from this; it is he who benefits, for he cannot honor any of the brave and strong citizens whom he tyrannizes unless he is willing to fear them. Nor can he subjugate or make the cities he conquers tributaries to the city in which he is tyrant, for making the city powerful does not benefit him; but it is in his interest to keep the state disunited and to have each city and province acknowledge his personal rule. Thus, he alone profits from his conquests and not

---

2. [Here Machiavelli refers not to the republics of Italy, such as his native Florence, but to north European city-states in Germany and Switzerland.]

his native city. And anyone wishing to confirm this opinion with countless other arguments should read Xenophon's treatise entitled *On Tyranny*.[3]

It is no wonder, then, that ancient peoples prosecuted tyrants with so much hatred and loved free government, and that the very name of liberty was so revered by them. This was the case when Hieronymus, the grandson of Hiero of Syracuse, was murdered in Syracuse, for when the news of his death reached his army, which was far from the city, the soldiers first began to riot and to take up arms against his murderers; but when they heard that in Syracuse the word liberty was being shouted, they calmed down completely and, delighted by that word, put aside their anger against the tyrannicides and began thinking about how a free government might be organized in their city.

It is also no wonder that the people take extraordinary revenge on those who deprive them of their liberty. There are many cases of this, but I will refer to only one of them: it happened in Corcyra, a Greek city, during the Peloponnesian War. Greece was at that time divided into two factions, one of which followed the Athenians, the other the Spartans; thus, in many cities that were so divided one faction sought the friendship of Sparta and the other that of Athens. And when it happened that in Corcyra the nobles prevailed and deprived the people of liberty, the popular party regrouped its forces with Athenian assistance, seized the nobles, and shut them up in a prison capable of holding all of them; then they took them out eight or ten at a time, and under the pretence of sending them into exile in various places they had them tortured in memorable fashion and then killed. When those still inside the prison became aware of this, they decided to escape this ignominious death if at all possible: armed with whatever they could find, they defended the entrance of the prison, fighting off all those who tried to enter. As soon as the people heard the noise, they removed the upper part of the building and smothered the prisoners with the debris. Many other events took place in that country of a similarly horrible and noteworthy nature; thus, it is evidently true that liberty that has actually been taken from you is avenged with greater ferocity than is liberty that someone tries to take from you.

Considering, therefore, why it is that in ancient times the people were greater lovers of liberty than in our own times, I believe this arises from the same cause that makes men less strong today—and this, I believe, is due to the difference between our education and ancient education, based upon the difference between our religion and ancient religion. Since our religion has shown us the truth and the true path, it makes us value the honor of this world less; whereas the pagans,[4] who valued it very much and considered it the highest good, were more fierce in their actions. This can be seen in many of their institutions, beginning with the magnificence of their sacrifices as compared to the meagerness of our own. In our sacrifices there is some ceremony (more delicate than magnificent) but no act that is fierce or brave. Theirs lacked neither pomp nor ceremonial magnificence; in addition, there was the act of sacrifice, full of blood and ferocity, involving the killing of a multitude of animals—this spectacle was awesome, and it produced similarly awesome men.

3. [The *Hiero*, an imaginary Socratic dialogue on tyranny with Hiero of Syracuse, a figure frequently cited by Machiavelli, serving as one of the interlocutors.]

4. [Machiavelli actually uses the Italian word *gentile* to mean "pagan" here and elsewhere.]

Besides this, ancient religion glorified only men who were endowed with worldly glory, such as generals of armies and rulers of republics; our religion has glorified humble and contemplative men rather than active ones. Furthermore, it has established as the supreme good humility, abjection, and contempt for human affairs, while ancient religion defined it as grandeur of spirit, strength of body, and all the other things likely to make men most vigorous. If it is true that our religion also requires strength, it is the kind of strength that makes you willing to suffer rather than to undertake bold deeds.

So this way of living, then, seems to have rendered the world weak and handed it over as prey to wicked men, who can safely manage it when they see that most men think more of going to Heaven by enduring their injuries than by avenging them. If it would appear that the world has become effeminate and Heaven disarmed, this, without a doubt, is the result of the cowardice of men who have interpreted our religion according to sloth and not according to strength. For if they would consider that religion permits us to defend and better the fatherland, they would see that it intends us to love and honor it and to prepare ourselves to be the kind of men who can defend it.

Such education and such false interpretations as these, then, explain the fact that there are not as many republics today as there were in ancient times and, as a result, that people do not have as much love for liberty now as they did then; yet I believe that the cause of this was, rather, that the Roman empire, with its forces and its greatness, wiped out all the republics and all the self-governing states. And although this empire was later dissolved, the cities have not yet been able to unite or to reorganize themselves in a self-governing body except for very few places in the empire; however this may be, the Romans did encounter in the very remotest part of the globe a confederation of extremely well-armed republics that were most stubborn in the defense of their liberty. This demonstrates that the Roman people would never have been able to overcome such republics without rare and immense ability.

And as an illustration of a member of these confederations, the example of the Samnites should suffice: it seems a marvelous thing (and Livy admits it) that because they were so powerful and their armies so strong they were able to resist the Romans until the time of Papirius Cursor, consul and son of the first Papirius—a space of forty-six years—after the many defeats, ruins, and massacres they had suffered in their country; especially when one observes that a country where there were once so many cities and men is now almost uninhabited; at that time there was such order and force there that it would have been unconquerable if it had not been for the skill of the Romans. It is easy to see where that earlier order came from and how this present disorder arose: it all resulted from living in freedom then and living in servitude now. For, as I said above, all countries and provinces living in freedom make very great progress; for wherever there is a growing population marriages are freer and more desired by men, since every man willingly procreates the children he believes he can provide for without fear that this patrimony will be taken away; he is assured that they will be born free, not slaves, and that they may, through their own ability, become great men. Wealth derived from agriculture as well as from trade increases more rapidly in a free country, for all men gladly increase those things and seek to acquire those goods which they believe they can enjoy once they have acquired them. Thus, it comes about that men in competition with each other think about both private and public benefits, and both one and the other continue to grow miraculously.

The contrary of all these things occurs in countries that live in servitude: the further they move away from their accustomed good, the harsher is their servitude. And of all the harsh forms of slavery, the harshest is that which subjects you to a republic—first, because it is more lasting and there is less hope of escaping from it; second, because the goal of a republic is to enervate and weaken all other bodies in order to strengthen its own body. This is not done by a prince to whom you are subjugated unless the prince is some barbarian ruler or a destroyer of lands and a devastator of all human civilization, as are oriental rulers. But if he possesses humane and normal qualities, he is usually fond of all his subject cities and allows them all their industries and almost all their ancient institutions, so that if they cannot prosper like free men they will not come to ruin like slaves—and here I mean the kind of servitude which comes to cities subject to a foreigner, since I spoke earlier of those cities subject to one of their own citizens.

Anyone, then, who considers all that has been said will not wonder at the power of the Samnites when they were free and at their weakness when they later became slaves. Livy testifies to this fact in more than one passage, especially in his description of the war with Hannibal, where he shows that when the Samnites were oppressed by a legion of men stationed in Nola, they sent ambassadors to Hannibal begging him to come to their rescue. In their speech they said that they had fought with the Romans for a hundred years, using their own soldiers and their own generals; they had resisted two consular armies and two consuls on a number of occasions, and they had now come to such a shameful state that they could hardly defend themselves against one small Roman legion stationed in Nola.

Chapter XX
What Sort Of Danger a Prince or a Republic Employing Auxiliary or Mercenary Troops Incurs

If I had not discussed at length in another work of mine the question of how useless mercenary or auxiliary troops are and how useful are one's own soldiers, I would extend my discussion in this chapter further than I plan to do, but since I have spoken of the matter elsewhere at length I shall be brief here. Yet I do not think that it is a matter to pass over lightly, since I have found so much concerning auxiliary troops in Livy. Auxiliary soldiers are those that a prince or a republic sends to your aid at their own expense and command. Turning to Livy's text, let me say that the Romans defeated two of the Samnites' armies in two different places by using their own troops, which they sent to the aid of the Capuans, and thus liberated the Capuans from the war which the Samnites were waging against them; then, wishing to return to Rome, they left behind two legions in the city of Capua to defend them, so that the Capuans would not again be deprived of a garrison and again be the victims of the Samnites. Rotting in idleness, these legions began to enjoy this city, so much so that they forgot their fatherland and reverence for the senate and began thinking about taking up arms and making themselves the rulers of that land which they had defended with their strength, since they felt that the inhabitants were not worthy to own property they did not know how to defend. The Romans, who foresaw all this, took measures to crush and correct it, as will be discussed at length when I deal with conspiracies.

Let me say again that of all the many kinds of troops, auxiliaries are the most harmful: for the prince or republic that employs them has no authority over them whatsoever; only the one who sends them has authority over them, for auxiliaries are troops sent to your aid by a prince, as I have said, under his own generals, his own flags, and are paid by him—as was the army that the Romans sent to Capua. When they have conquered, such soldiers as these in most cases plunder the one who has hired them as well as the one against whom they are hired, and they do this either because of the wickedness of the prince who sends them or because of their own ambition. And while the intention of the Romans was not to break the treaty and the other agreements they had made with the Capuans, the conquest of the city nevertheless appeared so simple to these soldiers that they were persuaded to consider taking from the Capuans their land and their state. One could give many examples of this, but I wish this one to suffice: that of the people of Reggio, whose lives and city were taken by a legion that the Romans had sent there as a garrison. A prince (or a republic) should therefore adopt any policy except that of bringing auxiliaries into his state for his defense when he has to rely completely upon them; for any pact or agreement with the enemy, no matter how harsh, will be lighter on him when compared to the other means. And if past events are studied closely and present ones are reviewed, it will be discovered that for everyone who has succeeded in this, there are countless others who have been disappointed. And a prince or an ambitious republic cannot have a better opportunity to seize a city or a province than to be invited to send its own armies to the latter's defense. Therefore, anyone who is so ambitious that he calls in such assistance not only to defend himself but also to attack others seeks to acquire what he cannot hold and what can easily be taken from him by the very persons who acquire it for him. But the ambition of men is so great that in order to satisfy a desire of the moment they fail to consider the evil that may result from it in a brief period of time. Nor are they moved by ancient examples in this matter any more than in the others that have been discussed; for if they were moved by them they would see that the more generosity they show toward their neighbors and the less inclined they are to seize their territory, the more likely these neighbors are to throw themselves into their lap, as will be explained below by the example of the Capuans.

Chapter XXIX

Fortune Blinds Men's Minds When She Does Not Want Them To Oppose
Her Plans

If we consider carefully how human affairs proceed, we will see that many times things happen and incidents occur against which the heavens do not wish any provision to be made. And if what I am discussing happened in Rome, where there was so much ability, religion, and order, it is no wonder that it occurs much more frequently in a city or province that lacks these three above-mentioned qualities. Since this instance is very noteworthy in illustrating the power of Heaven over human affairs, Livy explains it at length and with the most effective language, saying that since Heaven, for some reason, wanted the Romans to recognize its power, it first caused those Fabii who went to the Gauls as envoys to make a mistake, and as a result of their action the Gauls were incited to wage war upon Rome; then it commanded that nothing worthy of the Roman people be done in Rome to stop that war; before this it had arranged for Camillus, perhaps the sole remedy for such a great evil, to be exiled to Ardea; then, when the Gauls came toward Rome, those who had created a dictator many times to deal with the attack of the Volscians and other nearby enemies of theirs failed to do so on this occasion. Also, in choosing their soldiers they did so in a feeble manner, without much care, and they were so slow in taking up arms that they barely managed to meet the Gauls on the river Allia, only ten miles away from Rome. There the tribunes set up their camp without any of their usual caution: without first inspecting the spot or surrounding it with a trench or stockade; not using any precautions, human or divine. And in drawing up the order of battle they allowed their ranks to be thin and weak so that neither the soldiers nor the generals accomplished anything worthy of Roman discipline. Then they fought without bloodshed, for they fled before they were attacked; the greater part of them went to Veii, while the rest retreated to Rome, where, without even going to their homes, they immediately entered the Capitol; the senate, not thinking of defending Rome, did not even close the city gates—not to mention anything else—and part of the people fled while others went with the soldiers to the Capitol. Yet, in defending the Capitol they used methods that were not disorderly, for they did not burden it with useless people; they stocked it with all the grain they could so that they might survive during a siege. As for the useless crowd of old people, women, and children, the greater number fled to surrounding cities and the rest remained inside Rome at the mercy of the Gauls. Thus, one who reads about the deeds accomplished by the Roman people so many years earlier and then reads about these later times would not, under any circumstance, believe that it was the same people. When Livy described all the aforementioned disorders, he concluded with these words: "Fortune blinds men's minds to such an extent when she does not wish them to oppose her gathering might."[5] This conclusion could not be more true; thus, men who normally live under great adversity, or with success, deserve less praise or blame, for in most cases it is evident that they have been driven to a grand or a disastrous action by a great opportunity that the heavens have granted them by giving or taking away from them the chance to act effectively.

Fortune certainly does this, for when she wishes to bring about great things she chooses a man of such spirit and ability that he recognizes the opportunities she offers him. In like manner, when she wishes to bring about great disasters, she puts men there who will contribute to that downfall. And should there be someone present who could oppose her, she either kills him or has him deprived of all means to achieve anything good.

We see from this passage that in order to make Rome greater and to lead her to the grandeur she attained, Fortune found it necessary to strike her down (as we shall discuss at length in the beginning of the following book) even though she did not wish to ruin her completely. Therefore, we see that she had Camillus exiled but not executed; she had Rome, but not the Capitol, taken; she commanded the Romans not to think of any good measure to protect Rome, but later not to overlook any good preparation in the defense of the Capitol. In order that Rome might be taken, she arranged for the majority of the soldiers who had been defeated at the river Allia to go to Veii, thus cutting off all avenues for the defense of the city of Rome. Yet in arranging this she prepared everything for Rome's recovery, having brought an entire Roman army to Veii and Camillus to Ardea in order to be able to achieve

5. [Livy, V, xxxvii (cited by Machiavelli in Latin).]

a great undertaking under a general untarnished by any disgrace of defeat and with a reputation intact for the recovery of his native city.

In confirmation of the things discussed, some modern examples might be cited, but we shall omit them, not judging them necessary, as this should be enough to satisfy anyone. Again, let me affirm as true, according to what is evident from all the histories, that men can assist Fortune but not oppose her; they can weave her schemes but they cannot break them. They should never give up, for not knowing her goals as she travels through crooked and unknown roads, men always have hope, and with hope they should never despair in whatever fortune and whatever difficulty they find themselves.

BOOK III

Chapter I
In Order For a Religious Group or a Republic To Exist For a Long Time, It Is Necessary Often To Bring It Back To Its Beginnings

It is a sure fact that all things of this world have a limit to their existence; but those which complete the entire life cycle ordained for them by Heaven are those which do not let their bodies fall into disorder but, rather, keep them in an orderly fashion so that no change occurs, or, if it does, it is a healthy change and not a damaging one. And since I am speaking of mixed bodies, such as republics and religious groups, let me say that those changes are healthy which bring such bodies back to their beginnings. It follows that among such states or groups, those having the best organization and longest life span are those that can often renew themselves through their own institutions or can arrive at such a renewal through some incident outside their own operation. And it is clearer than the light of the sun that without such renewals these bodies do not endure.

The means of renewing them is to bring them back to their beginnings, for all the origins of religious groups, republics, and kingdoms contain within themselves some goodness by means of which they have gained their initial reputation and their first growth. Since, in the course of time, this goodness becomes corrupted, if nothing intervenes that may bring it up to the proper mark, that body is, of necessity, killed by such corruption. And doctors of medicine say, when speaking of the body of man: "Every day it absorbs something that requires a remedy from time to time." This return to beginnings, in the case of republics, is accomplished either by an external event or as a result of internal foresight. As for the first method, it is evident that Rome had to be captured by the Gauls in order for her to be reborn; and in being reborn she had to take on new life and new strength and adopt once more the observance of religion and justice, both of which were becoming corrupt. This point is made very clear in Livy's history, where he demonstrates that in calling out their army against the Gauls, and in creating tribunes with consular authority, the Romans observed no religious ceremony. And, in the same way, they not only failed to punish the three Fabii, who had fought against the Franks "contrary to the law of nations," but they made them tribunes. And one may presume, too, that they were taking less account of the good laws instituted by Romulus and other prudent rulers than was reasonable and necessary for maintaining a free government. This external reversal occurred so that all the institutions of that city might be revived, as well as to show the people that it was not only necessary to maintain religion and justice but that they should also honor their good citizens and count their abilities for more than those conveniences which they felt were lacking on account of their actions. We see that this was precisely what occurred: for as soon as Rome was recaptured, the Romans renewed all the institutions of their ancient religion and punished the Fabii who had fought "contrary to the law of nations"; they then honored the ability and virtue of Camillus, so much so that the senate and the others put their envy aside and placed in his hands all the responsibility of the republic. It is necessary, therefore, as has been mentioned, that men living together under any kind of institution should often come to know themselves, either because of such external events or because of internal ones. As for the latter, they usually arise either from a law, which often obliges the men who reside in that body to examine their affairs, or, more often, by one good man born among them who, with his exemplary deeds and his able works, produces the same effect as does that law.

This benefit, then, arises in republics either through the ability of one man or through the strength of a law; as for the latter, the institutions that brought the Roman republic back toward its beginnings were the tribunes of the plebeians, the censors, and all the laws that checked the ambition and the insolence of the citizens. Such laws needed to be given life by the ability of one citizen who would courageously fight for their application against the power of those who might transgress against them. Concerning the application of such laws before the capture of Rome by the Gauls, the most notable examples were the death of the sons of Brutus, the death of the decemvirs,[6] and the death of Spurius Melius, the grain dealer. After the taking of Rome, we may cite the death of Manlius Capitolinus, the death of the son of Manlius Torquatus, the punishment by Papirius Cursor of Fabius, his master of cavalry, and the accusations brought against the Scipios. Because of their extraordinary and striking nature, the occurrence of each of these events made men return to their proper position; and as they became more rare, they gave men more time to become corrupted and to behave in a more dangerous and disorderly fashion. For this reason, not more than ten years should pass between one act of enforcement of the law and the next because after that amount of time has elapsed men begin to change their habits and to break the laws; and if nothing arises that recalls the penalty to their minds and renews the fear in their hearts, the delinquents will multiply in such a short time that they will not be punishable without danger. Those who governed the Florentine state from 1434 until 1494 used to say, in this regard, that it was necessary to reorganize the state every five years; otherwise it would be very difficult to maintain it; and by "reorganizing the state" they meant striking that same terror and fear into the hearts of men that they had instilled when they first constituted it, at which time they punished those men who, according to that old way of ruling, governed badly. When the memory of such punishment disappears, men grow bold and attempt to devise new plans to spread sedition; it is therefore necessary to make provision against this by bringing the state back toward its beginnings.

This return to origins in republics also arises from the simple ability of one man, without the necessity of any law moving people to action; his conduct will be of such

---

6. [The decemvirs were actually exiled, not put to death.]

renown and of such an exemplary character that good men will desire to imitate it and evil men will be ashamed to lead a life contrary to it. Those in Rome who provided particularly good examples were Horatius Cocles, Scaevola, Fabricius, the two Decii, Regulus Atilius, and several others; with their unusual and virtuous examples, these men created almost the same effect in Rome that its laws and institutions had created. And if the aforementioned punishments, together with these individual examples, had occurred at least every ten years in that city, it would have necessarily followed that the city would have never been corrupted; but since both of these occurred less frequently, the corrupting influences began to multiply, for after Marcus Regulus no similar example was witnessed in the city; and although there were the two Catos in Rome, there was such a space of time between Marcus Regulus and the two of them, and then between the two of them themselves, and they remained so isolated, that they could not achieve any good effect with their good examples—especially the last Cato, who, finding the better part of the city corrupted, could not, with his example, improve the citizens. And this should suffice as far as republics are concerned.

As for religious groups, these renewals are still seen to be necessary, as is evident from the example of our own religion, which would have been completely extinguished if it had not been brought back to its beginnings by Saint Francis and Saint Dominic: for with their poverty and the example of the life of Christ these two saints restored religion to the hearts of men whence it had vanished; and their new institutions were so powerful that they prevented the dishonesty of priests and the heads of the religion from ruining it. They continued to live in poverty and had such a reputation with the people in the confessional and in their preaching that they made them understand that it is evil to speak evil of what is evil and that it was good to live in obedience under the priests' control, and that the errors of priests should be left for God to punish: and thus, these church rulers do their worst, for they can have no fear of a punishment they do not see and in which they do not believe; therefore, this renewal has maintained, and still maintains, our religion.

Kingdoms also need to be renewed and to bring back their laws to their beginnings. What a good effect this achieves can be seen in the Kingdom of France, which lives under laws and regulations more than any other kingdom. The parliaments are the upholders of these laws and regulations, especially that of Paris, which is renewed every time it takes an action against a prince of that kingdom or goes against the king in its judgments. And it has maintained itself until now by being the obstinate opponent of the nobility of that kingdom; but should it, at any time, fail to punish the nobility and allow such offenses to increase, then the consequence will doubtless be that either these offenses will have to be corrected amidst great disorder or the kingdom will fall apart.

It may be concluded, then, that there is nothing more necessary in a political community, whether it be a religious group, a kingdom, or a republic, than to restore to it the reputation that it had at its beginnings and to strive to see that there are either good laws or good men to produce this effect without having to resort to external forces; although this may sometimes be the best remedy, as it was in Rome, it is such a dangerous one that there is no reason to desire it. In order to demonstrate to everyone to what extent the accomplishments of individual men made Rome great and brought about many good effects in that city, I shall now narrate and discuss these actions: this third book and last section of the commentary on these first ten books of Livy will conclude within the framework of this topic. Although the actions of kings were great and noteworthy, since history treats of them in great detail I shall nevertheless leave them aside, discussing them only when kings did something pertaining to their own personal interests; we shall begin, then, with Brutus, the father of Roman freedom.

Chapter IX

How It Is Necessary To Change With the Times In Order Always To Enjoy Good Fortune

I have often observed that the reason for the bad as well as good fortune of men is to be found in the way in which their way of working fits the times: for it is clear that in their actions some men proceed with impetuosity, others with care and caution. And since men go beyond the proper limits in both these methods, they make errors in both, not being able to follow the true path. But that man whose method of procedure, as I have said, fits the times makes fewer mistakes and enjoys a prosperous fortune, for you always act as Nature inclines you. Everyone knows how Fabius Maximus proceeded carefully and cautiously with his army, refraining from every act of impetuosity or Roman boldness, and good fortune caused this method of his to fit well with the times. At the time Hannibal came into Italy as a young man with fresh fortune, having already twice defeated the Roman people, and while that republic was almost totally deprived of her good soldiers and was terrified, no better fortune could arise for her than to have a general who, with his hesitation and caution, might delay the enemy. Nor could Fabius have found times more suitable to his methods, which caused him to become famous. And that Fabius did this naturally and not by choice is evident, for when Scipio wished to cross over into Africa with his armies to end the war, Fabius spoke out against it, as a man who was unable to give up his methods and his practices. In fact, if it had been left to him, Hannibal would still be in Italy, for Fabius was a man who did not understand that the times had changed and that it was also necessary to change the methods of warfare. And if Fabius had been king of Rome, he could have easily lost that war, for he would not have known how to change his ways to suit the times; however, since he was born in a republic where there were different citizens and different opinions, just as Rome once had Fabius as the best leader in times requiring that the war be drawn out, so later she had Scipio in times suitable for winning it.

Therefore, the truth is that a republic is of longer duration and has a much better fortune than a principality, for a republic, by virtue of its diverse citizenry, can better accommodate itself to the changeability of conditions than can a prince. For, as I have said, a man who is used to acting in one way never changes; he must come to ruin when the times, in changing, no longer are in harmony with his ways.

Piero Soderini, cited on other occasions, proceeded in all his affairs with humanity and patience. He and his native city prospered when the times were in harmony with his way of acting; but later, when the time came for him to put aside his patience and humility, he did not know how to do so, and the result was that, together with his native city, he came to ruin. Pope Julius II proceeded with impetuosity and haste throughout the entire span of his pontificate; and because the times went along with him every one of his undertakings succeeded. But if other times requiring different methods had come, he would have necessarily come to ruin, for he could not have changed either his method or his way of governing. And there are two reasons why we cannot change ourselves: first, because we cannot oppose the ways in which Nature inclines us; second, because once a man has truly prospered by means of one method of procedure it is impossible to convince him that he can benefit by acting otherwise. As a result, it happens that Fortune varies for a single man, for she changes the times while he does not change his ways. The downfall of cities also arises from this fact, for republics do not modify their methods with the times (as we have discussed above at length); rather, they are slow since it is more difficult for them to change. For change results from times in which the entire republic is shaken; and for this to occur, it is not sufficient for one man alone to modify his method of procedure.

And since we have mentioned Fabius Maximus, who kept Hannibal at bay, it seems appropriate for me to discuss, in the following chapter, whether a general eager to give battle to the enemy at any cost can be prevented from doing so by the enemy.

TO FRANCESCO VETTORI IN ROME

Magnificent Ambassador. Divine favors were never late.[1] I say this because it appears that I have not lost—but have rather misplaced your favor, since you have not written to me for quite a long time, and I was in doubt as to the cause. And I paid little attention to all the reasons that came to mind, except for one: I feared that you had stopped writing to me because you heard that I was not a good guardian for your letters; and I knew that outside of Filippo [Casavecchia] and Paolo [Vettori], no one else, as far as I know, has seen them. But now I have found your favor once again in your last letter of the twenty-third of the past month. I am very happy to see how regularly and calmly you carry on your public office, and urge you to continue in this way, since anyone who loses his own interests for those of others sacrifices his own and receives no thanks from the others. And since it is Fortune that does everything, it is she who wishes us to leave her alone, to be quiet and not to give her trouble, and to wait until she allows us to act again; then you will do well to strive harder, to observe things more closely, and it will be time for me to leave my country home and say: "Here I am!" In the meantime, I can only tell you in this letter of mine what my life is like, wishing to match favor with favor, and if you think you would like to exchange yours for mine, I would be very happy to do so.

I live in the country, and since my recent misadventures in Florence I have not spent, in total, twenty days there. Until recently, I have been snaring thrushes with my own hands. Rising before daybreak, I prepare the birdlime and go out with such a bundle of bird cages on my back that I look like Geta when he returned from port with the books of Amphitryon;[2] I usually catch at least two, at the most six thrushes. I spent all of September doing this. Then this pastime, vile and foreign to my nature as it is, came to an end, to my displeasure; let me tell you what my life is like now: I rise in the morning with the sun and go into a wood that I am having cut, where I remain two hours in order to check the work done the day before and to pass the time with the woodcutters, who always have some argument at hand among themselves or with their neighbors. And concerning this wood, I could tell you a thousand entertaining things that have happened to me in my affairs with Frosino da Panzano and with others who wanted part of it. And Frosino, especially—he sent for several cords of wood without even saying anything, and on payment he wanted to hold back ten lire which he says he should have had from me four years ago when he beat me at cards at Antonio Guicciardini's. I began to raise the devil and was going to accuse the carter who had come to steal the wood, but Giovanni Machiavelli entered the matter and made peace. Batista Guicciardini, Filippo Ginori, Tommaso del Bene, and some other citizens each bought a cord from me when that north

1. [A reference to Petrarch's *Triumphs* ("Triumph of Eternity," 1.13).—P. B. and M. M.]

2. [An allusion to a popular novella of the fifteenth century, *Geta and Birria*.]

wind was blowing.[3] I made promises to them all and sent one cord to Tommaso, which, by the time it reached Florence, turned out to be half a cord because he and his wife, his children, and the help piled it, so that it looked like Gabburra[4] and his boys butchering an ox on a Thursday. So, when I saw who was making a profit on this, I told the others that I had no more wood left, and they all made a big thing of it, especially Batista, who adds this to his other misfortunes of Prato.

Leaving the wood, I go to a spring, and from there to my bird-snare. I have a book with me, either Dante or Petrarca or one of the lesser poets like Tibullus, Ovid, and the like: I read about their amorous passions and about their loves, I remember my own, and I revel for a moment in this thought. I then move on up the road to the inn, I speak with those who pass, and I ask them for news of their area; I learn many things and note the different and diverse tastes and ways of thinking of men. Lunchtime comes, when my family and I eat that food which this poor farm and my meager patrimony permit. After eating, I return to the inn: there I usually find the innkeeper, a butcher, a miller, and two bakers. With these men I waste my time playing cards all day and from these games a thousand disagreements and countless offensive words arise, and most of the time our arguments are over a few cents; nevertheless, we can be heard yelling from San Casciano. Caught this way among these lice I wipe the mold from my brain and release my feeling of being ill-treated by Fate; I am happy to be driven along this road by her, as I wait to see if she will be ashamed of doing so.

When evening comes, I return to my home, and I go into my study; and on the threshold, I take off my everyday clothes, which are covered with mud and mire, and I put on regal and curial robes; and dressed in a more appropriate manner I enter into the ancient courts of ancient men and am welcomed by them kindly, and there I taste the food that alone is mine, and for which I was born; and there I am not ashamed to speak to them, to ask them the reasons for their actions; and they, in their humanity, answer me; and for four hours I feel no boredom, I dismiss every affliction, I no longer fear poverty nor do I tremble at the thought of death: I become completely part of them. And as Dante says that knowledge does not exist without the retention of it by memory,[5] I have noted down what I have learned from their conversation, and I composed a little work, *De principatibus*, where I delve as deeply as I can into thoughts on this subject, discussing what a principality is, what kinds there are, how they are acquired, how they are maintained, why they are lost. And if any of my fantasies has ever pleased you, this should not displease you; and to a prince, and especially to a new prince, it should be welcomed; therefore, I am dedicating it to his Magnificence, Giuliano.[6] Filippo Casavecchia has seen it; he can give you some idea both of the work itself and of the discussion we have had concerning it, although I am still enlarging it and polishing it up.

3. [An allusion either to Machiavelli's difficulties with the Medici after the collapse of the Florentine republic in 1512 or to the sack of Prato in 1512, which was administered at the time by Batista Guicciardini.]

4. [Gabburra was probably a well-known butcher.]

5. [*Paradiso*, V, 41–42.]

6. [Initially *The Prince* was dedicated to Giuliano de' Medici, but after his death in 1516 the work was addressed to his successor, Lorenzo de' Medici, Duke of Urbino.]

You would like me, Magnificent Ambassador, to leave this life here and to come to enjoy yours with you. I shall do it, come what may, but what keeps me back at present are certain affairs of mine which I shall settle within six weeks. What makes me hesitate is that the Soderini[7] are there, and I would be obliged, coming there, to visit them and speak to them. I would not be surprised if on my return I might have to stay at the Bargello prison rather than at home, since although this state has very strong foundations and great security, it is also new and, because of this, suspicious, and there are plenty of sly men who, to appear like Pagolo Bertini,[8] would put others in debt and leave the worries to me. I beg you to relieve me of this fear, and then, whatever happens, I shall come within the time established to find you.

I talked with Filippo about this little book of mine: whether or not I should present it to him [Giuliano], and whether, giving it to him, I should bring it myself or have it delivered to you. Giving it makes me afraid that Giuliano won't read it and that Ardinghelli[9] will take the credit for this, my latest labor. I am urged to give it by the necessity that drives me: I am wearing myself away, and I cannot remain in this state for long without being despised for my poverty, not to mention my desire that these Medici lords begin to make use of me, even if they start me off by rolling stones. If I could not win their favor with this work, then I should have myself to blame; and in this work, if it were read, they would see that I have been at the study of statecraft for fifteen years and have not slept nor played about; and each one of them should be happy to obtain the services of one who is full of experience at another man's expense. And they should not doubt my loyalty, for always having kept my word, I have not now learned to break it; and anyone who has been faithful and honest for forty-three years, as I have been, cannot change his character; and my poverty is witness to my honesty and goodness.

I should like you, therefore, to write me what you think about this matter, and I commend myself to you. *Sis felix*. December 10, 1513.

Niccolò Machiavelli in Florence

7. [Machiavelli here refers to his former superior, Piero Soderini, and his brother, Cardinal Francesco Soderini, both of whom had received permission from the Medici Pope, Leo X, to reside in Rome. Machiavelli's visit might have aroused Medici suspicion that he was in league with a Soderini-led republican plot.]

8. [One of the ardent Medici supporters and, therefore, a potential enemy of Machiavelli.]

9. [Pietro Ardinghelli, a papal secretary at Leo X's court.]

THOMAS HOBBES

Thomas Hobbes (1588–1679) was born in Malmesbury on April 5, 1588, the son of a poor minor clergyman who abandoned his family when Hobbes was sixteen. According to Hobbes, his mother went into labor when she heard that the Spanish Armada was approaching, so that, as he put it, "fear and I were born twins together." This familiar tale indicates how Hobbes himself appreciated the central conjunction of mortal fear and human nature in his own thinking and in his life as well.

After excelling in classical languages and poetry as a youngster and studying at Oxford, Hobbes took a position in the household of William Lord Cavendish, the Earl of Devonshire. There and in similar positions throughout his life he served as secretary, tutor, and advisor. This was a common vocation for intellectuals in seventeenth-century England; John Locke was to play a similar role later in the century. From 1610 to 1615, Hobbes accompanied the Lord's son on the Grand Tour of Europe; he returned to the Continent in 1634–36 with Cavendish's grandson. On the early tour, Hobbes visited Venice and became acquainted with the tradition of classical rhetoric; later he would draw on this background as he considered the role of rhetoric in political argument. On the latter tour, he met the leading philosophers of the day, from Galileo to Pierre Gassendi and Marin Mersenne, who put him in touch with René Descartes, then in the Netherlands. By then Hobbes had already been captivated by the rigor of geometry, to which he added a fascination with the new science. During this period, then, Hobbes's interests turned from classical literature to contemporary science and its applications, especially optics and ballistics. In 1629 he had produced his first publication, a translation of Thucydides, whom he revered for his sense of prudence and his sensitivity to the dangers of democracy. By the end of 1640 his scientific thinking had matured and joined with his political interests, resulting in a draft of a large, systematic work which he called the *Elements of Law, Natural and Political*. Among other things, the *Elements* is a work that grounded politics in a conception of natural law derived in part from the Dutch political theorist Hugo Grotius, whose great work *The Laws of War and Peace* had been published in 1625.

In 1640 Charles I was forced to call two Parliaments, and events occurred that eventually would lead to the English Civil War. Hobbes's associations were with the King and his ministers, and hence, as tensions escalated, he feared for his life. In November he fled to France and remained there until 1651–52. In 1642 Hobbes published in Latin a reworked version of the political section of the *Elements* under the title *De Cive* (*Of the Citizen*), a work that was issued in England in an unauthorized translation in 1651, at about the same time that his first English and most famous work, *Leviathan*, appeared. The earlier sections of the *Elements*, *De Corpore* (*Of Matter*) and *De Homine* (*Of Man*), were not published until 1655 and 1658, respectively.

Leviathan has been influential far beyond the historical context of its writing and publication. In its first two parts Hobbes sketches his physics and psychology, outlines his famous account of the state of nature and its laws, develops his version of the social contract, and argues for an undivided sovereignty with all its functions, agencies, and prerogatives. These parts constitute one of the founding texts of modern moral and political theory.

But *Leviathan* does not end here. In parts three and four, Hobbes turns to issues of immediate historical concern. He attacks Roman Catholicism, Aristotelianism in the universities and in general intellectual culture, and the Anglican Church, while defending Erastianism, the doctrine of the political control of religion, and religious Independency, the movement that advocated the independence and control of individual congregations against the claims of a strong, central episcopacy. At the same time, Hobbes's materialism, exhibited especially in part four, seemed to many to imply atheism. It is no wonder that, with the publication of *Leviathan*, Hobbes gained the reputation of a materialist and atheist and came to be known as the "beast of Malmesbury."

With *Leviathan*'s publication in 1651, Hobbes returned to England and once again to the service of the Earl of Devonshire. For the remainder of his long life he played the role of a prominent intellectual and controversialist. In the 1650s he confronted John Wallis, an important Presbyterian and mathematician, on a variety of religious and scientific matters, and in the 1660s he debated Robert Boyle on issues of physics and experimentation. During the Restoration, moreover, Hobbes was the subject of severe criticism for his defense of Independency and his abandonment of the Anglicanism renewed under Charles II. His final years, the decades of the 1660s and 1670s, were years of threat and fear, as his religious opponents massed against him. But before they could overtake him, illness did; Hobbes died on December 3, 1679, having found, as he said, a hole whereby to leave the world.

Recommended readings

Baumgold, Deborah. *Hobbes's Political Theory*. Cambridge: Cambridge University Press, 1988.

Brown, K. C. (ed.). *Hobbes Studies*. Oxford: Oxford University Press, 1965.

Burns, James (ed.). *Cambridge History of Political Thought, 1450–1700*. Cambridge: Cambridge University Press, 1991.

Cranston, M., and R. S. Peters (eds.). *Hobbes and Rousseau*. Garden City: Doubleday, 1972.

Dietz, Mary G. (ed.). *Thomas Hobbes and Political Theory*. Lawrence: University of Kansas Press, 1990.

Gauthier, David. *The Logic of Leviathan*. Oxford: Oxford University Press, 1969.

Goldsmith, M. M. *Hobbes's Science of Politics*. New York: Columbia University Press, 1966.

Hampton, Jean. *Hobbes and the Social Contract Tradition*. Cambridge: Cambridge University Press, 1986.

Hood, F. C. *The Divine Politics of Thomas Hobbes*. Oxford: Oxford University Press, 1964.

Johnston, David. *The Rhetoric of Leviathan*. Princeton: Princeton University Press, 1986.

Kavka, Gregory. *Hobbesian Moral and Political Theory*. Princeton: Princeton University Press, 1986.

McNeilly, F. S. *The Anatomy of Leviathan*. London: Macmillan, 1968.

Macpherson, C. B. *The Political Theory of Possessive Individualism*. Oxford: Oxford University Press, 1962.

Oakeshott, Michael. *Hobbes on Civil Association*. Oxford: Blackwell's, 1975.

Pocock, J. G. A. "Time, History, and Eschatology in the Thought of Thomas Hobbes," in *Politics, Language, and Time*. New York: Atheneum, 1973.

Rogers, G. A. J., and Alan Ryan (eds.). *Perspectives on Thomas Hobbes*. Oxford: Oxford University Press, 1988.

Skinner, Quentin. "Conquest and Consent: Thomas Hobbes and the Engagement Controversy," in *The Interregnum: the Quest for Settlement*. ed. G. E. Aylmer. London: Macmillan, 1974, 79–98.

Skinner, Quentin. "The Ideological Context of Hobbes's Political Thought," *Historical Journal* 9 (1966), 286–317.

Strauss, Leo. *Natural Right and History*. Chicago: University of Chicago Press, 1953.

Strauss, Leo. *The Political Philosophy of Hobbes*. Oxford: Oxford University Press, 1936.

Tuck, Richard. *Hobbes*. Oxford: Oxford University Press, 1989.

Warrender, Richard. *The Political Philosophy of Hobbes*. Oxford: Oxford University Press, 1957.

Wolin, Sheldon. *Politics and Vision*. New York: Little, Brown and Co., 1960.

LEVIATHAN

Dedicatory

Introduction

THE CONTENTS OF THE CHAPTERS.

THE FIRST PART.—OF MAN.
1. Of Sense.
2. Of Imagination.
3. Of the Consequence or Train of Imaginations.
4. Of Speech.
5. Of Reason and Science.
6. Of the Interior Beginnings of Voluntary Motions, commonly called the Passions; and the Speeches by which they are expressed.
7. Of the Ends or Resolutions of Discourse.
8. Of the Virtues, commonly called Intellectual; and their contrary Defects.
9. Of the Several Subjects of Knowledge.
10. Of Power, Worth, Dignity, Honour, and Worthiness.
11. Of the Difference of Manners.
12. Of Religion.
13. Of the Natural Condition of Mankind as concerning their Felicity and Misery.
14. Of the First and Second Natural Laws, and of Contract.
15. Of other Laws of Nature.
16. Of Persons, Authors, and Things Personated.

THE SECOND PART.—OF COMMONWEALTH.
17. Of the Causes, Generation, and Definition of a Commonwealth.
18. Of the Rights of Sovereigns by Institution.
19. Of several kinds of Commonwealth by Institution; and of Succession to the Sovereign Power.
20. Of Dominion Paternal, and Despotical.
21. Of the Liberty of Subjects.
22. Of Systems Subject, Political, and Private.
23. Of the Public Ministers of Sovereign Power.
24. Of the Nutrition, and Procreation of a Commonwealth.
25. Of Counsel.
26. Of Civil Law.
27. Of Crimes, Excuses, and Extenuations.
28. Of Punishments, and Rewards.
29. Of those things that weaken, or tend to the Dissolution of a Commonwealth.
30. Of the Office of the Sovereign Representative.
31. Of the Kingdom of God by Nature.
    A Review, and Conclusion

THE INTRODUCTION

Nature (the art whereby God hath made and governs the world) is by the *art* of man, as in many other things, so in this also imitated, that it can make an artificial animal. For seeing life is but a motion of limbs, the beginning whereof is in some principal part within; why may we not say, that all *automata* (engines that move themselves by springs and wheels as doth a watch) have an artificial life? For what is the *heart*, but a *spring;* and the *nerves*, but so many *strings;* and the *joints*, but so many *wheels*, giving motion to the whole body, such as was intended by the artificer? *Art* goes yet further, imitating that rational and most excellent work of nature, *man*. For by art is created that great LEVIATHAN called a COMMONWEALTH, or STATE, (in Latin CIVITAS) which is but an artificial man; though of greater stature and strength than the natural, for whose protection and defence it was intended; and in which, the *sovereignty* is an artificial *soul*, as giving life and motion to the whole body; the *magistrates*, and other *officers* of judicature and execution, artificial *joints;* *reward* and *punishment* (by which fastened to the seat of the sovereignty every joint and member is moved to perform his duty) are the *nerves*, that do the same in the body natural; the *wealth* and *riches* of all the particular members, are the *strength;* *salus populi* (the *people's safety*) its *business; counsellors*, by whom all things needful for it to know are suggested unto it, are the *memory; equity*, and *laws*, an artificial *reason* and *will; concord, health; sedition, sickness;* and *civil war, death*. Lastly, the *pacts* and *covenants*, by which the parts of this body politic were at first made, set together, and united, resemble that *fiat*, or the *let us make man*, pronounced by God in the creation.

To describe the nature of this artificial man, I will consider

First, the *matter* thereof, and the *artificer;* both which is *man*.

Secondly, *how*, and by what *covenants* it is made; what are the *rights* and just *power* or *authority* of a sovereign; and what it is that *preserveth* and *dissolveth* it.

Thirdly, what is a *Christian commonwealth*.

Lastly, what is the *kingdom of darkness*.

Concerning the first, there is a saying much usurped of late, that *wisdom* is acquired, not by reading of *books*, but of *men*. Consequently whereunto, those persons, that for the most part can give no other proof of being wise, take great delight to show what they think they have read in men, by uncharitable censures of one another behind their backs. But there is another saying not of late understood, by which they might learn truly to read one another, if they would take the pains; and that is, *nosce teipsum, read thyself:* which was not meant, as it is now used, to countenance, either the barbarous state of men in power, towards their inferiors; or to encourage men of low degree, to a saucy behaviour towards their betters; but to teach us, that for the similitude of the thoughts and passions of one man, to the thoughts and passions of another, whosoever looketh into himself, and considereth what he doth, when he does *think, opine, reason, hope, fear*, &c. and upon what grounds; he shall thereby read and know, what are the thoughts and passions of all other men upon the like occasions. I say the similitude of passions, which are the same in all men, *desire, fear, hope*, &c; not the similitude of the objects of the passions, which are the things *desired, feared, hoped*, &c: for these the constitution individual, and particular education, do so vary, and they are so easy to be kept from our knowledge, that the characters of man's heart, blotted and confounded as they are with dissembling, lying, counterfeiting, and erroneous doctrines, are legible only to him that searcheth hearts. And though by men's actions we do discover their design sometimes; yet to do it without comparing them with our own, and distinguishing all circumstances, by which the case may come to be altered, is to decypher without a key, and be for the most part deceived, by too much trust, or by too much diffidence; as he that reads, is himself a good or evil man.

But let one man read another by his actions never so perfectly, it serves him only with his acquaintance, which are but few. He that is to govern a whole nation, must read in himself, not this or that particular man; but mankind: which though it be hard to do, harder than to learn any language or science; yet when I shall have set down my own reading orderly, and perspicuously, the pains left another, will be only to consider, if he also find not the same in himself. For this kind of doctrine admitteth no other demonstration.

PART 1
OF MAN

CHAPTER 1
Of Sense

Concerning the thoughts of man, I will consider them first *singly,* and afterwards in *train*, or dependence upon one another. *Singly*, they are every one a *representation* or *appearance*, of some quality, or other accident of a body without us; which is commonly called an *object*. Which object worketh on the eyes, ears, and other parts of a man's body; and by diversity of working, produceth diversity of appearances.

The original of them all, is that which we call SENSE; (For there is no conception in a man's mind, which hath not at first, totally, or by parts, been begotten upon the organs of sense.) The rest are derived from that original.

To know the natural cause of sense, is not very necessary to the business now in hand; and I have elsewhere written of the same at large. Nevertheless, to fill each part of my present method, I will briefly deliver the same in this place.

The cause of sense, is the external body, or object, which presseth the organ proper to each sense, either immediately, as in the taste and touch; or mediately, as in seeing, hearing, and smelling: which pressure, by the mediation of nerves, and other strings and membranes of the body, continued inwards to the brain and heart, causeth there a resistance, or counter-pressure, or endeavour of the heart, to deliver it self: which endeavour, because *outward*, seemeth to be some matter without. And this *seeming*, or, *fancy*, is that which men call *sense;* and consisteth, as to the eye, in a *light*, or *colour figured;* to the ear, in a *sound;* to the nostril, in an *odour;* to the tongue and palate, in a *savour;* and to the rest of the body, in *heat, cold, hardness, softness*, and such other qualities as we discern by *feeling*. All which qualities called *sensible*, are in the object, that causeth them, but so many several motions of the matter, by which it presseth our organs diversely. Neither in us that are pressed, are they any thing else, but divers motions; (for motion produceth nothing but motion.) But their appearance to us is fancy, the same waking, that dreaming. And as pressing, rubbing, or striking the eye, makes us fancy a light; and pressing the ear, produceth a din; so do the bodies also we see, or hear, produce the same by their strong, though unobserved action. For if those colours and sounds were in the bodies, or objects that cause them, they could not be severed from them, as by glasses, and in echoes by reflection, we see they are; where we know the thing we see, is in one place; the appearance in another. And though at some certain distance, the real and very object seem invested with the fancy it begets in us; yet still the object is one thing, the image or fancy is another. So that sense in all cases, is nothing else but original fancy, caused (as I have said) by the pressure, that is, by the motion, of external things upon our eyes, ears, and other organs thereunto ordained.

But the philosophy-schools, through all the universities of Christendom, grounded upon certain texts of *Aristotle,* teach another doctrine; and say, for the cause of *vision,* that the thing seen, sendeth forth on every side a *visible species* (in English) a *visible show, apparition,* or *aspect,* or *a being seen;* the receiving whereof into the eye, is *seeing.* And for the cause of *hearing,* that the thing heard, sendeth forth an *audible species,* that is, an *audible aspect,* or *audible being seen;* which entering at the ear, maketh *hearing.* Nay for the cause of *understanding* also, they say the thing understood, sendeth forth *intelligible species,* that is, an *intelligible being seen;* which coming into the understanding, makes us understand. I say not this, as disapproving the use of universities: but because I am to speak hereafter of their office in a commonwealth, I must let you see on all occasions by the way, what things would be amended in them; amongst which the frequency of insignificant speech is one.

CHAPTER 2
Of Imagination

That when a thing lies still, unless somewhat else stir it, it will lie still for ever, is a truth that no man doubts of. But that when a thing is in motion, it will eternally be in motion, unless somewhat else stay it, though the reason be the same, (namely, that nothing can change it self,) is not so easily assented to. For men measure, not only other men, but all other things, by themselves: and because they find themselves subject after motion to pain, and lassitude, think every thing else grows weary of motion, and seeks repose of its own accord; little considering, whether it be not some other motion, wherein that desire of rest they find in themselves, consisteth. From hence it is, that the schools say, heavy bodies fall downwards, out of an appetite to rest, and to conserve their nature in that place which is most proper for them; ascribing appetite and knowledge of what is good for their conservation, (which is more than man has) to things inanimate, absurdly.

When a body is once in motion, it moveth (unless something else hinder it) eternally; and whatsoever hindreth it, cannot in an instant, but in time, and by degrees quite extinguish it: And as we see in the water, though the wind cease, the waves give not over rolling for a long time after; so also it happeneth in that motion, which is made in the internal parts of a man, then, when he sees, dreams, &c. For after the object is removed, or the eye shut, we still retain an image of the thing seen, though more obscure than when we see it. And this is it, the Latins call *imagination,* from the image made in seeing; and apply the same, though improperly, to all the other senses. But the Greeks call it *fancy;* which signifies *appearance,* and is as proper to one sense, as to another. IMAGINATION therefore is nothing but *decaying sense;* and is found in men, and many other living creatures, as well sleeping, as waking.

The decay of sense in men waking, is not the decay of the motion made in sense; but an obscuring of it, in such manner as the light of the sun obscureth the light of the stars; which stars do no less exercise their virtue, by which they are visible, in the day, than in the night. But because amongst many strokes, which our eyes, ears, and other organs receive from external bodies, the predominant only is sensible; therefore the light of the sun being predominant, we are not affected with the action of the stars. And any object being removed from our eyes, though the impression it made in us remain; yet other objects more present succeeding, and working on us, the imagination of the past is obscured, and made weak, as the voice of a man is in the noise of the day. From whence it followeth, that the longer the time is, after the sight or sense of any object, the weaker is the imagination. For the continual change of man's body destroys in time the parts which in sense were moved: so that distance of time, and of place, hath one and the same effect in us. For as at a great distance of place, that which we look at appears dim, and without distinction of the smaller parts; and as voices grow weak, and inarticulate: so also, after great distance of time, our imagination of the past is weak; and we lose (for example) of cities we have seen, many particular streets, and of actions, many particular circumstances. This *decaying sense*, when we would express the thing it self, (I mean *fancy* it self,) we call *imagination*, as I said before: but when we would express the *decay*, and signify that the sense is fading, old, and past, it is called *memory*. So that *imagination* and *memory* are but one thing, which for divers considerations hath divers names.

Much memory, or memory of many things, is called *experience*. Again, imagination being only of those things which have been formerly perceived by sense, either all at once, or by parts at several times; the former, (which is the imagining the whole object, as it was presented to the sense) is *simple imagination;* as when one imagineth a man, or horse, which he hath seen before. The other is *compounded*; as when from the sight of a man at one time, and of a horse at another, we conceive in our mind a Centaur. So when a man compoundeth the image of his own person, with the image of the actions of another man; as when a man imagines himself a *Hercules* or an *Alexander,* (which happeneth often to them that are much taken with reading of romances) it is a compound imagination, and properly but a fiction of the mind. There be also other imaginations that rise in men, (though waking) from the great impression made in sense: as from gazing upon the sun, the impression leaves an image of the sun before our eyes a long time after; and from being long and vehemently attent upon geometrical figures, a man shall in the dark, (though awake) have the images of lines and angles before his eyes: which kind of fancy hath no particular name; as being a thing that doth not commonly fall into men's discourse.

The imaginations of them that sleep are those we call *dreams*. And these also (as all other imaginations) have been before, either totally or by parcels in the sense. And because in sense, the brain and nerves, which are the necessary organs of sense, are so benumbed in sleep, as not easily to be moved by the action of external objects, there can happen in sleep no imagination; and therefore no dream, but what proceeds from the agitation of the inward parts of man's body; which inward parts, for the connexion they have with the brain, and other organs, when they be distempered, do keep the same in motion; whereby the imaginations there formerly made, appear as if a man were waking; saving that the organs of sense being now benumbed, so as there is no new object, which can master and obscure them with a more vigorous impression, a dream must needs be more clear, in this silence of sense, than are our waking thoughts. And hence it cometh to pass, that it is a hard matter, and by many thought impossible to distinguish exactly between sense and dreaming. For my part, when I consider that in dreams, I do not often, nor constantly think of the same persons, places, objects, and actions that I do waking; nor remember so long a train of coherent thoughts, dreaming, as at other times; and because waking I often observe the absurdity of dreams, but never dream of the absurdities of my waking thoughts; I am well satisfied, that being awake, I know I dream not; though when I dream I think myself awake.

And seeing dreams are caused by the distemper of some of the inward parts of the body; divers distempers must needs cause different dreams. And hence it is, that lying cold breedeth dreams of fear, and raiseth the thought and image of some fearful object (the motion from the brain to the inner parts, and from the inner parts to the brain being reciprocal;) and that as anger causeth heat in some parts of the body, when we are awake; so when we sleep the over heating of the same parts causeth anger, and raiseth up in the brain the imagination of an enemy. In the same manner, as natural kindness, when we are awake, causeth desire; and desire makes heat in certain other parts of the body; so also, too much heat in those parts, while we sleep, raiseth in the brain an imagination of some kindness shown. In sum, our dreams are the reverse of our waking imaginations; the motion when we are awake, beginning at one end; and when we dream, at another.

The most difficult discerning of a man's dream, from his waking thoughts, is then, when by some accident we observe not that we have slept: which is easy to happen to a man full of fearful thoughts; and whose conscience is much troubled; and that sleepeth, without the circumstances, of going to bed, or putting off his clothes, as one that noddeth in a chair. For he that taketh pains, and industriously lays himself to sleep, in case any uncouth and exorbitant fancy come unto him, cannot easily think it other than a dream. We read of *Marcus Brutus*, (one that had his life given him by *Julius Caesar,* and was also his favourite, and notwithstanding murdered him), how at *Philippi,* the night before he gave battle to *Augustus Caesar,* he saw a fearful apparition, which is commonly related by historians as a vision; but considering the circumstances, one may easily judge to have been but a short dream. For sitting in his tent, pensive and troubled with the horror of his rash act, it was not hard for him, slumbering in the cold, to dream of that which most affrighted him; which fear, as by degrees it made him wake; so also it must needs make the apparition by degrees to vanish; and having no assurance that he slept, he could have no cause to think it a dream, or any thing but a vision. And this is no very rare accident; for even they that be perfectly awake, if they be timorous, and superstitious, possessed with fearful tales, and alone in the dark, are subject to the like fancies; and believe they see spirits and dead men's ghosts walking in churchyards; whereas it is either their fancy only, or else the knavery of such persons, as make use of such superstitious fear, to pass disguised in the night, to places they would not be known to haunt.

From this ignorance of how to distinguish dreams, and other strong fancies, from vision and sense, did arise the greatest part of the religion of the Gentiles in time past, that worshipped satyrs, fawns, nymphs, and the like; and now-a-days the opinion that rude people have of fairies, ghosts, and goblins, and of the power of witches. For as for witches, I think not that their witchcraft is any real power; but yet that they are justly punished, for the false belief they have, that they can do such mischief, joined with their purpose to do it if they can: their trade being nearer to a new religion than to a craft or science. And for fairies, and walking ghosts, the opinion of them has I think been on purpose, either taught, or not confuted, to keep in credit the use of exorcism, of crosses, of holy water, and other such inventions of ghostly men. Nevertheless, there is no doubt, but God can make unnatural apparitions: But that he does it so often, as men need to fear such things, more than they fear the stay, or change, of the course of nature, which he also can stay, and change, is no point of Christian faith. But evil men under pretext that God can do any thing, are so bold as to say any thing when it serves their turn, though they think it untrue; it is the part of a wise man, to believe them no further, than right reason makes that which they say, appear credible. If this superstitious fear of spirits were taken away, and with it, prognostics from dreams, false prophecies, and many other things depending thereon, by which, crafty ambitious persons abuse the simple people, men would be much more fitted than they are for civil obedience.

And this ought to be the work of the schools: but they rather nourish such doctrine. For (not knowing what imagination, or the senses are), what they receive, they teach: some saying, that imaginations rise of themselves, and have no cause; others, that they rise most commonly from the will; and that good thoughts are blown (inspired) into a man by God, and evil thoughts by the Devil; or that good thoughts are poured (infused) into a man by God, and evil ones by the Devil. Some say the senses receive the species of things, and deliver them to the common sense; and the common sense delivers them over to the fancy, and the fancy to the memory, and the memory to the judgment, like handing of things from one to another, with many words making nothing understood.

The imagination that is raised in man (or any other creature indued with the faculty of imagining) by words, or other voluntary signs, is that we generally call *understanding*; and is common to man and beast. For a dog by custom will understand the call, or the rating of his master; and so will many other beasts. That understanding which is peculiar to man, is the understanding not only his will, but his conceptions and thoughts, by the sequel and contexture of the names of things into affirmations, negations, and other forms of speech; and of this kind of understanding I shall speak hereafter.

CHAPTER 3
Of the Consequence or Train of Imaginations

By *Consequence*, or TRAIN of thoughts, I understand that succession of one thought to another, which is called (to distinguish it from discourse in words) *mental discourse*.

When a man thinketh on any thing whatsoever, his next thought after, is not altogether so casual as it seems to be. Not every thought to every thought succeeds indifferently. But as we have no imagination, whereof we have not formerly had sense, in whole, or in parts; so we have no transition from one imagination to another, whereof we never had the like before in our senses. The reason whereof is this. All fancies are motions within us, relics of those made in the sense: and those motions that immediately succeeded one another in the sense, continue also together after sense: insomuch as the former coming again to take place, and be predominant, the latter followeth, by coherence of the matter moved, in such manner, as water upon a plain table is drawn which way any one part of it is guided by the finger. But because in sense, to one and the same thing perceived, sometimes one thing, sometimes another succeedeth, it comes to pass in time, that in the imagining of any thing, there is no certainty what we shall imagine next; only this is certain, it shall be something that succeeded the same before, at one time or another.

This train of thoughts, or mental discourse, is of two sorts. The first is *unguided, without design,* and inconstant; wherein there is no passionate thought, to govern and direct those that follow, to it self, as the end and scope of some desire, or other passion: in which case the thoughts are said to wander, and seem impertinent one to another, as in a dream. Such are commonly the thoughts of men, that are not only without company, but also without care of any thing; though even then their thoughts are as busy as at other times, but without harmony; as the sound which a lute out of tune would yield to any man; or in tune, to one that could not play. And yet in this wild ranging of the mind, a man may oft-times perceive the way of it, and the dependance of one thought upon another. For in a discourse of our present civil war, what could seem more impertinent, than to ask (as one did) what was the value of a Roman penny? Yet the coherence to me was manifest enough. For the thought of the war, introduced the thought of the delivering up the king to his enemies; the thought of that, brought in the thought of the delivering up of Christ; and that again the thought of the 30 pence, which was the price of that treason; and thence easily followed that malicious question, and all this in a moment of time; for thought is quick.

The second is more constant; as being *regulated* by some desire, and design. For the impression made by such things as we desire, or fear, is strong, and permanent, or, (if it cease for a time,) of quick return: so strong it is sometimes, as to hinder and break our sleep. From desire, ariseth the thought of some means we have seen produce the like of that which we aim at; and from the thought of that, the thought of means to that mean; and so continually, till we come to some beginning within our own power. And because the end, by the greatness of the impression, comes often to mind, in case our thoughts begin to wander, they are quickly again reduced into the way: which observed by one of the seven wise men, made him give men this precept, which is now worn out, *Respice finem*; that is to say, in all your actions, look often upon what you would have, as the thing that directs all your thoughts in the way to attain it.

The train of regulated thoughts is of two kinds; one, when of an effect imagined, we seek the causes, or means that produce it: and this is common to man and beast. The other is, when imagining any thing whatsoever, we seek all the possible effects, that can by it be produced; that is to say, we imagine what we can do with it, when we have it. Of which I have not at any time seen any sign, but in man only; for this is a curiosity hardly incident to the nature of any living creature that has no other passion but sensual, such as are hunger, thirst, lust, and anger. In sum, the discourse of the mind, when it is governed by design, is nothing but *seeking,* or the faculty of invention, which the Latins called *sagacitas,* and *solertia*; a hunting out of the causes, of some effect, present or past; or of the effects, of some present or past cause. Sometimes a man seeks what he hath lost; and from that place, and time, wherein he misses it, his mind runs back, from place to place, and time to time, to find where, and when he had it; that is to say, to find some certain, and limited time and place, in which to begin a method of seeking. Again, from thence, his thoughts run over the same places and times, to find what action, or other occasion might make him lose it. This we call *remembrance,* or calling to mind: the Latins call it *reminiscentia,* as it were a *re-conning* of our former actions.

Sometimes a man knows a place determinate, within the compass whereof he is to seek; and then his thoughts run over all the parts thereof, in the same manner as one would sweep a room, to find a jewel; or as a spaniel ranges the field, till he find a scent; or as a man should run over the alphabet, to start a rhyme.

Sometime a man desires to know the event of an action; and then he thinketh of some like action past, and the events thereof one after another; supposing like events will follow like actions. As he that foresees what will become of a criminal, recons what he has seen follow on the like crime before; having this order of thoughts, the crime, the officer, the prison, the judge, and the gallows. Which kind of thoughts, is called *foresight*, and *prudence*, or *providence*; and sometimes *wisdom*; though such conjecture, through the difficulty of observing all circumstances, be very fallacious. But this is certain; by how much one man has more experience of things past, than another; by so much also he is more prudent, and his expectations the seldomer fail him. The *present* only has a being in nature; things *past* have a being in the memory only, but things *to come* have no being at all; the *future* being but a fiction of the mind, applying the sequels of actions past, to the actions that are present; which with most certainty is done by him that has most experience; but not with certainty enough. And though it be called prudence, when the event answereth our expectation; yet in its own nature, it is but presumption. For the foresight of things to come, which is providence, belongs only to him by whose will they are to come. From him only, and supernaturally, proceeds prophecy. The best prophet naturally is the best guesser; and the best guesser, he that is most versed and studied in the matters he guesses at: for he hath most *signs* to guess by.

A *sign* is the event antecedent of the consequent; and contrarily, the consequent of the antecedent, when the like consequences have been observed, before: and the oftener they have been observed, the less uncertain is the sign. And therefore he that has most experience in any kind of business, has most signs, whereby to guess at the future time; and consequently is the most prudent: and so much more prudent than he that is new in that kind of business, as not to be equalled by any advantage of natural and extemporary wit: though perhaps many young men think the contrary.

Nevertheless it is not prudence that distinguisheth man from beast. There be beasts, that at a year old observe more, and pursue that which is for their good, more prudently, than a child can do at ten.

As prudence is a *presumption* of the *future*, contracted from the *experience* of time *past:* so there is a presumption of things past taken from other things (not future but) past also. For he that hath seen by what courses and degrees, a flourishing state hath first come into civil war, and then to ruin; upon the sight of the ruins of any other state, will guess, the like war, and the like courses have been there also. But this conjecture, has the same uncertainty almost with the conjecture of the future; both being grounded only upon experience.

There is no other act of man's mind, that I can remember, naturally planted in him, so as to need no other thing, to the exercise of it, but to be born a man, and live with the use of his five senses. Those other faculties, of which I shall speak by and by, and which seem proper to man only, are acquired, and increased by study and industry; and of most men learned by instruction, and discipline; and proceed all from the invention of words, and speech. For besides sense, and thoughts, and the train of thoughts, the mind of man has no other motion; though by the help of speech, and method, the same faculties may be improved to such a height, as to distinguish men from all other living creatures.

Whatsoever we imagine is *finite*. Therefore there is no idea, or conception of any thing we call *infinite*. No man can have in his mind an image of infinite magnitude; nor conceive infinite swiftness, infinite time, or infinite force, or infinite power. When we say any thing is infinite, we signify only, that we are not able to conceive the ends, and bounds of the things named; having no conception of the thing, but of our own inability. And therefore the name of God is used, not to make us conceive him; (for he is *incomprehensible;* and his greatness, and power are unconceivable;) but that we may honour him. Also because whatsoever (as I said before,) we conceive, has been perceived first by sense, either all at once, or by parts; a man can have no thought, representing any thing, not subject to sense. No man therefore can conceive any thing, but he must conceive it in some place; and indued with some determinate magnitude; and which may be divided into parts; nor that any thing is all in this place, and all in another place at the same time; nor that two, or more things can be in one, and the same place at once: for none of these things ever have, or can be incident to sense; but are absurd speeches, taken upon credit (without any significa-tion at all,) from deceived philosophers, and deceived, or deceiving schoolmen.

CHAPTER 4
Of Speech

The invention of *printing*, though ingenious, compared with the invention of *letters*, is no great matter. But who was the first that found the use of letters, is not known. He that first brought them into *Greece*, men say was *Cadmus*, the son of *Agenor*, king of Phoenicia. A profitable invention for continuing the memory of time past, and the conjunction of mankind, dispersed into so many, and distant regions of the earth; and withal difficult, as proceeding from a watchful observation of the divers motions of the tongue, palate, lips, and other organs of speech; whereby to make as many differences of characters, to remember them. But the most noble and profitable invention of all other, was that of SPEECH, consisting of *names* or *appellations*, and their connexion; whereby men register their thoughts; recall them when they are past; and also declare them one to another for mutual utility and conversation; without which, there had been amongst men, neither commonwealth, nor society, nor contract, nor peace, no more than amongst lions, bears, and wolves. The first author of speech was God himself, that instructed Adam how to name such creatures as he presented to his sight; for the Scripture goeth no further in this matter. But this was sufficient to direct him to add more names, as the experience and use of the creatures should give him occasion; and to join them in such manner by degrees, as to make himself understood; and so by succession of time, so much language might be gotten, as he had found use for; though not so copious, as an orator or philosopher has need of. For I do not find any thing in the Scripture, out of which, directly or by consequence can be gathered, that *Adam* was taught the names of all figures, numbers, measures, colours, sounds, fancies, relations; much less the names of words and speech, as *general, special, affirmative, negative, interroga-tive, optative, infinitive,* all which are useful; and least of all, of *entity, intentionality, quiddity,* and other insignificant words of the school.

But all this language gotten, and augmented by *Adam* and his posterity, was again lost at the tower of *Babel*, when, by the hand of God, every man was stricken, for his rebellion, with an oblivion of his former language. And being hereby forced to disperse themselves into several parts of the world, it must needs be, that the diversity of tongues that now is, proceeded by degrees from them, in such manner as need (the mother of all inventions) taught them; and in tract of time grew every where more copious.

The general use of speech, is to transfer our mental discourse, into verbal; or the train of our thoughts, into a train of words; and that for two commodities, whereof one is the registering of the consequences of our thoughts; which being apt to slip out of our memory, and put us to a new labour, may again be recalled, by such words as they were marked by. So that the first use of names is to serve for *marks*, or *notes* of remembrance. Another is, when many use the same words, to signify (by their connexion and order,) one to another, what they conceive, or think of each matter; and also what they desire, fear, or have any other passion for. And for this use they are called *signs*. Special uses of speech are these; first, to register, what by cogitation, we find to be the cause of any thing, present or past; and what we find things present or past may produce, or effect: which in sum, is acquiring of arts. Secondly, to show to others that knowledge which we have attained; which is, to counsel and teach one another. Thirdly, to make known to others our wills, and purposes, that we may have the mutual help of one another. Fourthly, to please and delight ourselves and others, by playing with our words, for pleasure or ornament, innocently.

To these uses, there are also four correspondent abuses. First, when men register their thoughts wrong, by the inconstancy of the signification of their words; by which they register for their conceptions, that which they never conceived, and so deceive themselves. Secondly, when they use words metaphorically; that is, in other sense than that they are ordained for; and thereby deceive others. Thirdly, when by words they declare that to be their will, which is not. Fourthly, when they use them to grieve one another: for seeing nature hath armed living creatures, some with teeth, some with horns, and some with hands, to grieve an enemy, it is but an abuse of speech, to grieve him with the tongue, unless it be one whom we are obliged to govern; and then it is not to grieve, but to correct and amend.

The manner how speech serveth to the remembrance of the consequence of causes and effects, consisteth in the imposing of *names*, and the *connexion* of them.

Of names, some are *proper*, and singular to one only thing, as *Peter, John, this man, this tree:* and some are *common* to many things, as *man, horse, tree*; every of which though but one name, is nevertheless the name of divers particular things; in respect of all which together, it is called an *universal*; there being nothing in the world universal but names; for the things named, are every one of them individual and singular.

One universal name is imposed on many things, for their similitude in some quality, or other accident; and whereas a proper name bringeth to mind one thing only, universals recall any one of those many.

And of names universal, some are of more, and some of less extent; the larger comprehending the less large: and some again of equal extent, comprehending each other reciprocally. As for example, the name *body* is of larger signification than the word *man*, and comprehendeth it; and the names *man* and *rational*, are of equal extent, comprehending mutually one another. But here we must take notice, that by a name is not always understood, as in grammar, one only word; but sometimes by circumlocution many words together. For all these words, *he that in his actions observeth the laws of his country*, make but one name, equivalent to this one word, *just*.

By this imposition of names, some of larger, some of stricter signification, we turn the reckoning of the consequences of things imagined in the mind, into a reckoning of the consequences of appellations. For example, a man that hath no use of speech at all, (such as is born and remains perfectly deaf and dumb,) if he set before his eyes a triangle, and by it two right angles, (such as are the corners of a square figure,) he may by meditation compare and find, that the three angles of that triangle, are equal to those two right angles that stand by it. But if another triangle be shown him, different in shape from the former, he cannot know without a new labour, whether the three angles of that also be equal to the same. But he that hath the use of words, when he observes, that such equality was consequent, not to the length of the sides, nor to any other particular thing in his triangle; but only to this, that the sides were straight, and the angles three; and that that was all, for which he named it a triangle; will boldly conclude universally, that such equality of angles is in all triangles whatsoever; and register his invention in these general terms, *every triangle hath its three angles equal to two right angles*. And thus the consequence found in one particular, comes to be registered and remembered, as an universal rule, and discharges our mental reckoning, of time and place, and delivers us from all labour of the mind, saving the first, and makes that which was found true *here*, and *now*, to be true in *all times* and *places*.

But the use of words in registering our thoughts is in nothing so evident as in numbering. A natural fool that could never learn by heart the order of numeral words, as *one, two*, and *three*, may observe every stroke of the clock, and nod to it, or say *one, one, one*, but can never know what hour it strikes. And it seems, there was a time when those names of number were not in use; and men were fain to apply their fingers of one or both hands, to those things they desired to keep account of; and that thence it proceeded, that now our numeral words are but ten, in any nation, and in some but five, and then they begin again. And he that can tell ten, if he recite them out of order, will lose himself, and not know when he has done. Much less will he be able to add, and subtract, and perform all other operations of arithmetic. So that without words there is no possibility of reckoning of numbers; much less of magnitudes, of swiftness, of force, and other things, the reckonings whereof are necessary to the being, or well-being of mankind.

When two names are joined together into a consequence, or affirmation, as thus, *a man is a living creature*; or thus, *if he be a man, he is a living creature*, if the latter name *living creature*, signify all that the former name *man* signifieth, then the affirmation, or consequence is *true*; otherwise *false*. For *true* and *false* are attributes of speech, not of things. And where speech is not, there is neither *truth* nor *falsehood*. *Error* there may be, as when we expect that which shall not be, or suspect what has not been: but in neither case can a man be charged with untruth.

Seeing then that *truth* consisteth in the right ordering of names in our affirmations, a man that seeketh precise *truth* had need to remember what every name he uses stands for, and to place it accordingly; or else he will find himself entangled in words, as a bird in lime twigs, the more he struggles the more belimed. And therefore in geometry, (which is the only science that it hath pleased God hitherto to bestow on mankind,) men begin at settling the significations of their words; which settling of significations they call *definitions*, and place them in the beginning of their reckoning.

By this it appears how necessary it is for any man that aspires to true knowledge, to examine the definitions of former authors; and either to correct them, where they are negligently set down, or to make them himself. For the errors of definitions multiply themselves according as the reckoning proceeds, and lead men into absurdities, which at last they see, but cannot avoid, without reckoning anew from the beginning, in which lies the foundation of their errors. From whence it happens, that they which trust to books do as they that cast up many little sums into a greater, without considering whether those little sums were rightly cast up or not; and at last finding the error visible, and not mistrusting their first grounds, know not which way to clear themselves, but spend time in fluttering over their books; as birds that entering by the chimney, and finding themselves enclosed in a chamber, flutter at the false light of a glass window, for want of wit to consider which way they came in. So that in the right definition of names lies the first use of speech; which is the acquisition of science: and in wrong, or no definitions, lies the first abuse; from which proceed all false and senseless tenets; which make those men that take their instruction from the authority of books, and not from their own meditation, to be as much below the condition of ignorant men, as men endued with true science are above it. For between true science and erroneous doctrines, ignorance is in the middle. Natural sense and imagination are not subject to absurdity. Nature itself cannot err; and as men abound in copiousness of language, so they become more wise, or more mad than ordinary. Nor is it possible without letters for any man to become either excellently wise, or (unless his memory be hurt by disease or ill constitution of organs) excellently foolish. For words are wise men's counters, they do but reckon by them; but they are the money of fools, that value them by the authority of an *Aristotle*, a *Cicero*, or a *Thomas*, or any other doctor whatsoever, if but a man.

Subject to names, is whatsoever can enter into or be considered in an account, and be added one to another to make a sum, or subtracted one from another and leave a remainder. The Latins called accounts of money *rationes*, and accounting *ratiocinatio*; and that which we in bills or books of account call *items*, they call *nomina*, that is *names*; and thence it seems to proceed, that they extended the word *ratio* to the faculty of reckoning in all other things. The Greeks have but one word, λόγος, for both *speech* and *reason*; not that they thought there was no speech without reason, but no reasoning without speech: and the act of reasoning they called *syllogism*, which signifieth summing up of the consequences of one saying to another. And because the same things may enter into account for divers accidents, their names are (to show that diversity) diversly wrested and diversified. This diversity of names may be reduced to four general heads.

First, a thing may enter into account for *matter* or *body*; as *living, sensible, rational, hot, cold, moved, quiet*; with all which names the word *matter*, or *body*, is understood; all such being names of matter.

Secondly, it may enter into account, or be considered, for some accident or quality, which we conceive to be in it; as for *being moved*, for *being so long*, for *being hot*, &c.; and then, of the name of the thing it self, by a little change or wresting, we make a name for that accident, which we consider; and for *living* put into the account *life*; for *moved, motion*; for *hot, heat*; for *long, length*, and the like: and all such names are the names of the accidents and properties by which one matter and body is distinguished from another. These are called *names abstract*, because severed (not from matter, but) from the account of matter.

Thirdly, we bring into account the properties of our own bodies, whereby we make such distinction; as when any thing is *seen* by us, we reckon not the thing it self, but the *sight*, the *colour*, the *idea* of it in the fancy: and when any thing is *heard*, we reckon it not, but the *hearing* or *sound* only, which is our fancy or conception of it by the ear; and such are names of fancies.

Fourthly, we bring into account, consider, and give names, to *names* themselves, and to *speeches:* For *general, universal, special, equivocal,* are names of names. And *affirmation, interrogation, commandment, narration, syllogism, sermon, oration,* and many other such, are names of speeches. And this is all the variety of names *positive;* which are put to mark somewhat which is in nature, or may be feigned by the mind of man, as bodies that are, or may be conceived to be; or of bodies, the properties that are, or may be feigned to be; or words and speech.

There be also other names, called *negative,* which are notes to signify that a word is not the name of the thing in question; as these words *nothing, no man, infinite, indocible, three want four,* and the like; which are nevertheless of use in reckoning, or in correcting of reckoning, and call to mind our past cogitations, though they be not names of any thing, because they make us refuse to admit of names not rightly used.

All other names are but insignificant sounds; and those of two sorts. One when they are new, and yet their meaning not explained by definition; whereof there have been abundance coined by schoolmen, and puzzled philosophers.

Another, when men make a name of two names, whose significations are contradictory and inconsistent; as this name, an *incorporeal body,* or (which is all one) an *incorporeal substance,* and a great number more. For whensoever any affirmation is false, the two names of which it is composed, put together and made one, signify nothing at all. For example, if it be a false affirmation to say *a quadrangle is round,* the word *round quadrangle* signifies nothing, but is a mere sound. So likewise, if it be false to say that virtue can be poured, or blown up and down, the words *in-poured virtue, in-blown virtue,* are as absurd and insignificant as a *round quadrangle.* And therefore you shall hardly meet with a senseless and insignificant word, that is not made up of some Latin or Greek names. A Frenchman seldom hears our Saviour called by the name of *parole,* but by the name of *verbe* often; yet *verbe* and *parole* differ no more, but that one is Latin, the other French.

When a man, upon the hearing of any speech, hath those thoughts which the words of that speech, and their connexion, were ordained and constituted to signify, then he is said to understand it; *understanding* being nothing else but conception caused by speech. And therefore if speech be peculiar to man (as for aught I know it is,) then is understanding peculiar to him also. And therefore of absurd and false affirmations, in case they be universal, there can be no understanding; though many think they understand then, when they do but repeat the words softly, or con them in their mind.

What kinds of speeches signify the appetites, aversions, and passions of man's mind; and of their use and abuse, I shall speak when I have spoken of the passions.

The names of such things as affect us, that is, which please and displease us, because all men be not alike affected with the same thing, nor the same man at all times, are in the common discourses of men of *inconstant* signification. For seeing all names are imposed to signify our conceptions, and all our affections are but conceptions, when we conceive the same things differently, we can hardly avoid different naming of them. For though the nature of that we conceive, be the same; yet the diversity of our reception of it, in respect of different constitutions of body, and prejudices of opinion, gives every thing a tincture of our different passions.

And therefore in reasoning a man must take heed of words; which besides the signification of what we imagine of their nature, have a signification also of the nature, disposition, and interest of the speaker; such as are the names of virtues and vices; for one man calleth *wisdom,* what another calleth *fear*; and one *cruelty,* what another *justice*; one *prodigality,* what another *magnanimity*; and one *gravity,* what another *stupidity,* &c. And therefore such names can never be true grounds of any ratiocination. No more can metaphors, and tropes of speech; but these are less dangerous, because they profess their inconstancy; which the other do not.

CHAPTER 5
Of Reason and Science

When a man *reasoneth,* he does nothing else but conceive a sum total, from *addition* of parcels; or conceive a remainder, from *subtraction* of one sum from another; which (if it be done by words,) is conceiving of the consequence of the names of all the parts, to the name of the whole; or from the names of the whole and one part, to the name of the other part. And though in some things, (as in numbers,) besides *adding* and *subtracting,* men name other operations, as *multiplying* and *dividing,* yet they are the same; for multiplication, is but adding together of things equal; and division, but subtracting of one thing, as often as we can. These operations are not incident to numbers only, but to all manner of things that can be added together, and taken one out of another. For as arithmeticians teach to add and subtract in *numbers*; so the geometricians teach the same in *lines, figures* (solid and superficial,) *angles, proportions, times, degrees of swiftness, force, power,* and the like; the logicians teach the same in *consequences of words*; adding together *two names* to make an *affirmation,* and *two affirmations* to make a *syllogism*; and *many syllogisms* to make a *demonstration*; and from the *sum,* or *conclusion* of a *syllogism,* they subtract one *proposition* to find the other. Writers of politics add together *pactions* to find men's *duties*; and lawyers, *laws* and *facts,* to find what is *right* and *wrong* in the actions of private men. In sum, in what matter soever there is place for *addition* and *subtraction,* there also is place for *reason*; and where these have no place, there *reason* has nothing at all to do.

Out of all which we may define, (that is to say determine,) what that is, which is meant by this word *reason,* when we reckon it amongst the faculties of the mind. For REASON, in this sense, is nothing but *reckoning* (that is, adding and subtracting) of the consequences of general names agreed upon for the *marking* and *signifying* of our thoughts; I say *marking* them when we reckon by ourselves, and *signifying,* when we demonstrate or approve our reckonings to other men.

And as in arithmetic, unpractised men must, and professors themselves may often err, and cast up false; so also in any other subject of reasoning, the ablest, most attentive, and most practised men may deceive themselves, and infer false conclusions; not but that reason itself is always right reason, as well as arithmetic is a certain and infallible art: but no one man's reason, nor the reason of any one number of men, makes the certainty; no more than an account is therefore well cast up, because a great many men have unanimously approved it. And therefore, as when there is a controversy in an account, the parties must by their own accord, set up for right reason, the reason of some arbitrator, or judge, to whose sentence they will both stand, or their controversy must either come to blows, or be undecided, for want of a right reason constituted by nature; so is it also in all debates of what kind soever.

And when men that think themselves wiser than all others, clamour and demand right reason for judge, yet seek no more, but that things should be determined, by no other men's reason but their own, it is as intolerable in the society of men, as it is in play after trump is turned, to use for trump on every occasion, that suite whereof they have most in their hand. For they do nothing else, that will have every of their passions, as it comes to bear sway in them, to be taken for right reason, and that in their own controversies: bewraying their want of right reason, by the claim they lay to it.

The use and end of reason, is not the finding of the sum and truth of one, or a few consequences, remote from the first definitions, and settled significations of names, but to begin at these, and proceed from one consequence to another. For there can be no certainty of the last conclusion, without a certainty of all those affirmations and negations, on which it was grounded and inferred. As when a master of a family, in taking an account, casteth up the sums of all the bills of expense into one sum, and not regarding how each bill is summed up, by those that give them in account; nor what it is he pays for; he advantages himself no more, than if he allowed the account in gross, trusting to every of the accountants' skill and honesty: so also in reasoning of all other things, he that takes up conclusions on the trust of authors, and doth not fetch them from the first items in every reckoning, (which are the significations of names settled by definitions,) loses his labour; and does not know any thing, but only believeth.

When a man reckons without the use of words, which may be done in particular things, (as when upon the sight of any one thing, we conjecture what was likely to have preceded, or is likely to follow upon it;) if that which he thought likely to follow, follows not, or that which he thought likely to have preceded it, hath not preceded it, this is called *error*; to which even the most prudent men are subject. But when we reason in words of general signification, and fall upon a general inference which is false, though it be commonly called error, it is indeed an *absurdity*, or senseless speech. For error is but a deception, in presuming that somewhat is past, or to come; of which, though it were not past, or not to come, yet there was no impossibility discoverable. But when we make a general assertion, unless it be a true one, the possibility of it is inconceivable. And words whereby we conceive nothing but the sound, are those we call *absurd, insignificant,* and *nonsense.* And therefore if a man should talk to me of a *round quadrangle*; or, *accidents of bread in cheese*; or *immaterial substances*; or of *a free subject; a free will*; or any *free*, but free from being hindered by opposition, I should not say he were in an error, but that his words were without meaning, that is to say, absurd.

I have said before, (in the second chapter,) that a man did excel all other animals in this faculty, that when he conceived any thing whatsoever, he was apt to inquire the consequences of it, and what effects he could do with it. And now I add this other degree of the same excellence, that he can by words reduce the consequences he finds to general rules, called *theorems,* or *aphorisms*; that is, he can reason, or reckon, not only in number, but in all other things, whereof one may be added unto, or subtracted from another.

But this privilege is allayed by another; and that is, by the privilege of absurdity; to which no living creature is subject, but man only. And of men, those are of all most subject to it, that profess philosophy. For it is most true that Cicero saith of them somewhere; that there can be nothing so absurd, but may be found in the books of philosophers. And the reason is manifest. For there is not one of them that begins his ratiocination from the definitions, or explications of the names they are to use; which is a method that hath been used only in geometry; whose conclusions have thereby been made indisputable.

I. The first cause of absurd conclusions I ascribe to the want of method; in that they begin not their ratiocination from definitions; that is, from settled significations of their words: as if they could cast account, without knowing the value of the numeral words, *one, two,* and *three.*

And whereas all bodies enter into account upon divers considerations, (which I have mentioned in the precedent chapter;) these considerations being diversely named, divers absurdities proceed from the confusion, and unfit connexion of their names into assertions. And therefore,

II. The second cause of absurd assertions, I ascribe to the giving of names of *bodies* to *accidents;* or of *accidents* to *bodies;* as they do, that say, *faith is infused,* or *inspired;* when nothing can be *poured,* or *breathed* into any thing, but body; and that, *extension* is *body;* that *phantasms* are *spirits,* &c.

III. The third I ascribe to the giving of the names of the *accidents* of *bodies without us,* to the *accidents* of our *own bodies;* as they do that say, the *colour is in the body; the sound is in the air,* &c.

IV. The fourth, to the giving of the names of *bodies* to *names,* or *speeches;* as they do that say, that *there be things universal;* that *a living creature is genus,* or *a general thing,* &c.

V. The fifth, to the giving of the names of *accidents* to *names* and *speeches;* as they do that say, *the nature of a thing is its definition; a man's command is his will;* and the like.

VI. The sixth, to the use of metaphors, tropes, and other rhetorical figures, instead of words proper. For though it be lawful to say, (for example) in common speech, *the way goeth, or leadeth hither, or thither; the proverb says this or that* (whereas ways cannot go, nor proverbs speak;) yet in reckoning, and seeking of truth, such speeches are not to be admitted.

VII. The seventh, to names that signify nothing; but are taken up, and learned by rote from the schools, as *hypostatical, transubstantiate, consubstantiate, eternal-now,* and the like canting of schoolmen.

To him that can avoid these things it is not easy to fall into any absurdity, unless it be by the length of an account; wherein he may perhaps forget what went before. For all men by nature reason alike, and well, when they have good principles. For who is so stupid, as both to mistake in geometry, and also to persist in it, when another detects his error to him?

By this it appears that reason is not, as sense and memory, born with us; nor gotten by experience only, as prudence is; but attained by industry; first in apt imposing of names; and secondly by getting a good and orderly method in proceeding from the elements, which are names, to assertions made by connexion of one of them to another; and so to syllogisms, which are the connexions of one assertion to another, till we come to a knowledge of all the consequences of names appertaining to the subject in hand; and that is it, men call SCIENCE. And whereas sense and memory are but knowledge of fact, which is a thing past, and irrevocable; *Science* is the knowledge of consequences, and dependance of one fact upon another: by which, out of that we can presently do, we know how to do something else when we will, or the like, another time; because when we see how any thing comes about, upon what causes, and by what manner; when the like causes come into our power, we see how to make it produce the like effects.

Children therefore are not endued with reason at all, till they have attained the use of speech; but are called reasonable creatures, for the possibility apparent of having the use of reason in time to come. And the most part of men, though they have the use of reasoning a little way, as in numbering to some degree; yet it serves them to little use in common life; in which they govern themselves, some better, some worse, according to their differences of experience, quickness of memory, and inclinations to several ends; but specially according to good or evil fortune, and the errors of one another. For as for *science,* or certain rules of their actions, they are so far from it, that they know not what it is. Geometry they have thought conjuring: but for other sciences, they who have not been taught the beginnings and some progress in them, that they may see how they be acquired and generated, are in this point like children, that having no thought of generation, are made believe by the women that their brothers and sisters are not born, but found in the garden.

But yet they that have no *science,* are in better, and nobler condition, with their natural prudence; than men, that by mis-reasoning, or by trusting them that reason wrong, fall upon false and absurd general rules. For ignorance of causes, and of rules, does not set men so far out of their way, as relying on false rules, and taking for causes of what they aspire to, those that are not so, but rather causes of the contrary.

To conclude, the light of human minds is perspicuous words, but by exact definitions first snuffed, and purged from ambiguity; *reason* is the *pace;* increase of *science,* the *way;* and the benefit of mankind, the *end.* And on the contrary, metaphors, and senseless and ambiguous words, are like *ignes fatui;* and reasoning upon them is wandering amongst innumerable absurdities; and their end, contention and sedition, or contempt.

As much experience, is *prudence;* so, is much science *sapience.* For though we usually have one name of wisdom for them both, yet the Latins did always distinguish between *prudentia* and *sapientia;* ascribing the former to experience, the latter to science. But to make their difference appear more clearly, let us suppose one man endued with an excellent natural use and dexterity in handling his arms; and another to have added to that dexterity, an acquired science, of where he can offend, or be offended by his adversary, in every possible posture or guard: the ability of the former, would be to the ability of the latter, as prudence to sapience; both useful; but the latter infallible. But they that trusting only to the authority of books, follow the blind blindly, are like him that, trusting to the false rules of a master of fence, ventures presumptuously upon an adversary, that either kills or disgraces him.

The signs of science are some, certain and infallible; some, uncertain. Certain, when he that pretendeth the science of any thing, can teach the same, that is to say, demonstrate the truth thereof perspicuously to another; uncertain, when only some particular events answer to his pretence, and upon many occasions prove so as he says they must. Signs of prudence are all uncertain; because to observe by experience, and remember all circumstances that may alter the success, is impossible. But in any business, whereof a man has not infallible science to proceed by; to forsake his own natural judgment, and be guided by general sentences read in authors, and subject to many exceptions, is a sign of folly, and generally scorned by the name of pedantry.

And even of those men themselves, that in councils of the commonwealth love to show their reading of politics and history, very few do it in their domestic affairs, where their particular interest is concerned; having prudence enough for their private affairs: but in public they study more the reputation of their own wit, than the success of another's business.

CHAPTER 6

Of the Interior Beginnings of Voluntary Motions; Commonly Called the Passions; and the Speeches by Which They Are Expressed

There be in animals, two sorts of *motions* peculiar to them: one called *vital*; begun in generation, and continued without interruption through their whole life; such as are the *course* of the *blood*, the *pulse*, the *breathing*, the *concoction, nutrition, excretion,* &c; to which motions there needs no help of imagination: the other is *animal motion,* otherwise called *voluntary motion*; as to *go*, to *speak*, to *move* any of our limbs, in such manner as is first fancied in our minds. That sense is motion in the organs and interior parts of man's body, caused by the action of the things we see, hear, &c.; and that fancy is but the relics of the same motion, remaining after sense, has been already said in the first and second chapters. And because *going, speaking,* and the like voluntary motions, depend always upon a precedent thought of *whither, which way,* and *what*; it is evident, that the imagination is the first internal beginning of all voluntary motion. And although unstudied men do not conceive any motion at all to be there, where the thing moved is invisible; or the space it is moved in, is (for the shortness of it) insensible; yet that doth not hinder, but that such motions are. For let a space be never so little, that which is moved over a greater space, whereof that little one is part, must first be moved over that. These small beginnings of motion, within the body of man, before they appear in walking, speaking, striking, and other visible actions, are commonly called ENDEAVOUR.

This endeavour, when it is toward something which causes it, is called APPETITE, or DESIRE; the latter, being the general name; and the other, oftentimes restrained to signify the desire of food, namely *hunger* and *thirst*. And when the endeavour is fromward something, it is generally called AVERSION. These words, *appetite* and *aversion,* we have from the *Latins;* and they both of them signify the motions, one of approaching, the other of retiring. So also do the Greek words for the same, which are ὁρμή and ἀφορμή. For nature itself does often press upon men those truths, which afterwards, when they look for somewhat beyond nature, they stumble at. For the Schools find in mere appetite to go, or move, no actual motion at all: but because some motion they must acknowledge, they call it metaphorical motion; which is but an absurd speech: for though words may be called metaphorical; bodies and motions cannot.

That which men desire, they are also said to LOVE: and to HATE those things for which they have aversion. So that desire and love are the same thing; save that by desire, we always signify the absence of the object; by love, most commonly the presence of the same. So also by aversion, we signify the absence; and by hate, the presence of the object.

Of appetites and aversions, some are born with men; as appetite of food, appetite of excretion, and exoneration, (which may also and more properly be called aversions, from somewhat they feel in their bodies;) and some other appetites, not many. The rest, which are appetites of particular things, proceed from experience, and trial of their effects upon themselves or other men. For of things we know not at all, or believe not to be, we can have no further desire, than to taste and try. But aversion we have for things, not only which we know have hurt us, but also that we do not know whether they will hurt us, or not.

Those things which we neither desire, nor hate, we are said to *contemn*; CONTEMPT being nothing else but an immobility, or contumacy of the heart, in resisting the action of certain things; and proceeding from that the heart is already moved otherwise, by other more potent objects; or from want of experience of them.

And because the constitution of a man's body is in continual mutation, it is impossible that all the same things should always cause in him the same appetites, and aversions: much less can all men consent, in the desire of almost any one and the same object.

But whatsoever is the object of any man's appetite or desire, that is it which he for his part calleth *good:* and the object of his hate and aversion, *evil*; and of his contempt, *vile* and *inconsiderable*. For these words of good, evil, and contemptible, are ever used with relation to the person that useth them: there being nothing simply and absolutely so; nor any common rule of good and evil, to be taken from the nature of the objects themselves; but from the person of the man (where there is no commonwealth;) or, (in a commonwealth,) from the person that representeth it; or from an arbitrator or judge, whom men disagreeing shall by consent set up, and make his sentence the rule thereof.

The Latin tongue has two words, whose significations approach to those of good and evil; but are not precisely the same; and those are *pulchrum* and *turpe*. Whereof the former signifies that, which by some apparent signs promiseth good; and the latter, that which promiseth evil. But in our tongue we have not so general names to express them by. But for *pulchrum* we say in some things, *fair*; in others, *beautiful*, or *handsome*, or *gallant*, or *honourable*, or *comely*, or *amiable*; and for *turpe, foul, deformed, ugly, base, nauseous,* and the like, as the subject shall require; all which words, in their proper places, signify nothing else but the *mine*, or countenance, that promiseth good and evil. So that of good there be three kinds; good in the promise, that is *pulchrum*; good in effect, as the end desired, which is called *jucundum, delightful*; and good as the means, which is called *utile, profitable*; and as many of evil: for *evil* in promise, is that they call *turpe*; evil in effect, and end, is *molestum, unpleasant, troublesome*; and evil in the means, *inutile, unprofitable, hurtful*.

As, in sense, that which is really within us, is, (as I have said before,) only motion, caused by the action of external objects, but in apparence; to the sight, light and colour; to the ear, sound; to the nostril, odour, &c.: so, when the action of the same object is continued from the eyes, ears, and other organs to the heart, the real effect there is nothing but motion, or endeavour; which consisteth in appetite, or aversion, to or from the object moving. But the apparence, or sense of that motion, is that we either call *delight*, or *trouble of mind*.

This motion, which is called appetite, and for the apparence of it *delight,* and *pleasure,* seemeth to be a corroboration of vital motion, and a help thereunto; and therefore such things as caused delight, were not improperly called *jucunda, (a juvando,)* from helping or fortifying; and the contrary, *molesta, offensive,* from hindering, and troubling the motion vital.

Pleasure therefore, (or *delight,*) is the apparence, or sense of good; and *molestation* or *displeasure,* the apparence, or sense of evil. And consequently all appetite, desire, and love, is accompanied with some delight more or less; and all hatred and aversion, with more or less displeasure and offence.

Of pleasures or delights, some arise from the sense of an object present; and those may be called *pleasures of sense,* (the word *sensual,* as it is used by those only that condemn them, having no place till there be laws.) Of this kind are all onerations and exonerations of the body; as also all that is pleasant, in the *sight, hearing, smell, taste, or touch.* Others arise from the expectation, that proceeds from foresight of the end, or consequence of things; whether those things in the sense please or displease. And these are *pleasures of the mind* of him that draweth those consequences, and are generally called JOY. In the like manner, displeasures are some in the sense, and called PAIN; others in the expectation of consequences, and are called GRIEF.

These simple passions called *appetite, desire, love, aversion, hate, joy,* and *grief,* have their names for divers considerations diversified. As first, when they one succeed another, they are diversely called from the opinion men have of the likelihood of attaining what they desire. Secondly, from the object loved or hated. Thirdly, from the consideration of many of them together. Fourthly, from the alteration or succession it self.

For *appetite,* with an opinion of attaining, is called HOPE.

The same, without such opinion, DESPAIR.

Aversion, with opinion of *hurt* from the object, FEAR.

The same, with hope of avoiding that hurt by resistance, COURAGE.

Sudden *courage,* ANGER.

Constant *hope,* CONFIDENCE of ourselves.

Constant *despair,* DIFFIDENCE of ourselves.

Anger for great hurt done to another, when we conceive the same to be done by injury, INDIGNATION.

Desire of good to another, BENEVOLENCE, GOOD WILL, CHARITY. If to man generally, GOOD NATURE.

Desire of riches, COVETOUSNESS: a name used always in signification of blame; because men contending for them, are displeased with one another's attaining them; though the desire in itself, be to be blamed, or allowed, according to the means by which those riches are sought.

Desire of office, or precedence, AMBITION: a name used also in the worse sense, for the reason before mentioned.

Desire of things that conduce but a little to our ends, and fear of things that are but of little hindrance, PUSILLANIMITY.

Contempt of little helps and hindrances, MAGNANIMITY.

Magnanimity, in danger of death or wounds, VALOUR, FORTITUDE.

Magnanimity, in the use of riches, LIBERALITY.

Pusillanimity, in the same, WRETCHEDNESS, MISERABLENESS, or PARSIMONY; as it is liked or disliked.

Love of persons for society, KINDNESS.

Love of persons for pleasing the sense only, NATURAL LUST.

Love of the same, acquired from rumination, that is, imagination of pleasure past, LUXURY.

Love of one singularly, with desire to be singularly beloved, THE PASSION OF LOVE. The same, with fear that the love is not mutual, JEALOUSY.

Desire, by doing hurt to another, to make him condemn some fact of his own, REVENGEFULNESS.

Desire to know why, and how, CURIOSITY; such as is in no living creature but *man:* so that man is distinguished, not only by his reason, but also by this singular passion from other *animals;* in whom the appetite of food, and other pleasures of sense, by predominance, take away the care of knowing causes; which is a lust of the mind, that by a perseverance of delight in the continual and indefatigable generation of knowledge, exceedeth the short vehemence of any carnal pleasure.

Fear of power invisible, feigned by the mind, or imagined from tales publicly allowed, RELIGION; not allowed, SUPERSTITION. And when the power imagined, is truly such as we imagine, TRUE RELIGION.

Fear, without the apprehension of why, or what, PANIC TERROR, called so from the fables, that make *Pan* the author of them; whereas in truth, there is always in him that so feareth, first, some apprehension of the cause, though the rest run away by example, every one supposing his fellow to know why. And therefore this passion happens to none but in a throng, or multitude of people.

Joy, from apprehension of novelty, ADMIRATION; proper to man, because it excites the appetite of knowing the cause.

Joy, arising from imagination of a man's own power and ability, is that exultation of the mind which is called GLORYING: which if grounded upon the experience of his own former actions, is the same with *confidence:* but if grounded on the flattery of others; or only supposed by himself, for delight in the consequences of it, is called VAINGLORY: which name is properly given; because a well grounded *confidence* begetteth attempt; whereas the supposing of power does not, and is therefore rightly called *vain.*

Grief, from opinion of want of power, is called DEJECTION of mind.

The *vain-glory* which consisteth in the feigning or supposing of abilities in ourselves, which we know are not, is most incident to young men, and nourished by the histories, or fictions of gallant persons; and is corrected oftentimes by age, and employment.

Sudden glory, is the passion which maketh those *grimaces* called LAUGHTER; and is caused either by some sudden act of their own, that pleaseth them; or by the apprehension of some deformed thing in another, by comparison whereof they suddenly applaud themselves. And it is incident most to them, that are conscious of the fewest abilities in themselves; who are forced to keep themselves in their own favour, by observing the imperfections of other men. And therefore much laughter at the defects of others, is a sign of pusillanimity. For of great minds, one of the proper works is, to help and free others from scorn; and compare themselves only with the most able.

On the contrary, *sudden dejection,* is the passion that causeth WEEPING; and is caused by such accidents, as suddenly take away some vehement hope, or some prop of their power: and they are most subject to it, that rely principally on helps external, such as are women, and children. Therefore some weep for the loss of friends; others for their unkindness; others for the sudden stop made to their thoughts of revenge, by reconciliation. But in all cases, both laughter, and weeping, are sudden motions; custom taking them both away. For no man laughs at old jests; or weeps for an old calamity.

Grief, for the discovery of some defect of ability, is SHAME, or the passion that discovereth itself in BLUSHING; and consisteth in the apprehension of some thing dishonourable; and in young men, is a sign of the love of good reputation, and commendable: in old men it is a sign of the same; but because it comes too late, not commendable.

The *contempt* of good reputation is called IMPUDENCE.

Grief, for the calamity of another, is PITY; and ariseth from the imagination that the like calamity may befall himself; and therefore is called also COMPASSION, and in the phrase of this present time a FELLOW-FEELING: and therefore for calamity arriving from great wickedness, the best men have the least pity; and for the same calamity, those have least pity, that think themselves least obnoxious to the same.

Contempt, or little sense of the calamity of others, is that which men call CRUELTY; proceeding from security of their own fortune. For, that any man should take pleasure in other men's great harms, without other end of his own, I do not conceive it possible.

Grief, for the success of a competitor in wealth, honour, or other good, if it be joined with endeavour to enforce our own abilities to equal or exceed him, is called EMULATION: but joined with endeavour to supplant, or hinder a competitor, ENVY.

When in the mind of man, appetites, and aversions, hopes, and fears, concerning one and the same thing, arise alternately; and divers good and evil consequences of the doing, or omitting the thing propounded, come successively into our thoughts; so that sometimes we have an appetite to it; sometimes an aversion from it; sometimes hope to be able to do it; sometimes despair, or fear to attempt it; the whole sum of desires, aversions, hopes and fears continued till the thing be either done, or thought impossible, is that we call DELIBERATION.

Therefore of things past, there is no *deliberation*; because manifestly impossible to be changed: nor of things known to be impossible, or thought so; because men know, or think such deliberation vain. But of things impossible, which we think possible, we may deliberate; not knowing it is in vain. And it is called *deliberation*; because it is a putting an end to the *liberty* we had of doing, or omitting, according to our own appetite, or aversion.

This alternate succession of appetites, aversions, hopes and fears, is no less in other living creatures than in man: and therefore beasts also deliberate.

Every *deliberation* is then said to *end,* when that whereof they deliberate, is either done, or thought impossible; because till then we retain the liberty of doing, or omitting, according to our appetite, or aversion.

In *deliberation,* the last appetite, or aversion, immediately adhering to the action, or to the omission thereof, is that we call the WILL; the act, (not the faculty,) of *willing.* And beasts that have *deliberation,* must necessarily also have *will.* The definition of the *will,* given commonly by the Schools, that it is a *rational appetite,* is not good. For if it were, then could there be no voluntary act against reason. For a *voluntary act* is that, which proceedeth from the *will,* and no other. But if instead of a rational appetite, we shall say an appetite resulting from a precedent deliberation, then the definition is the same that I have given here. *Will* therefore *is the last appetite in deliberating.* And though we say in common discourse, a man had a will once to do a thing, that nevertheless he forbore to do; yet that is properly but an inclination, which makes no action voluntary; because the action depends not of it, but of the last inclination, or appetite. For if the intervenient appetites, make any action voluntary; then by the same reason all intervenient aversions, should make the same action involuntary; and so one and the same action, should be both voluntary and involuntary.

By this it is manifest, that not only actions that have their beginning from covetousness, ambition, lust, or other appetites to the thing propounded; but also those that have their beginning from aversion, or fear of those consequences that follow the omission, are *voluntary actions*.

The forms of speech by which the passions are expressed, are partly the same, and partly different from those, by which we express our thoughts. And first, generally all passions may be expressed *indicatively*; as *I love, I fear, I joy, I deliberate, I will, I command:* but some of them have particular expressions by themselves, which nevertheless are not affirmations, unless it be when they serve to make other inferences, besides that of the passion they proceed from. Deliberation is expressed *subjunctively*; which is a speech proper to signify suppositions, with their consequences; as, *if this be done, then this will follow*; and differs not from the language of reasoning, save that reasoning is in general words; but deliberation for the most part is of particulars. The language of desire, and aversion, is *imperative*; as *do this, forbear that*; which when the party is obliged to do, or forbear, is *command;* otherwise *prayer*; or else *counsel.* The language of vain-glory, of indignation, pity and revengefulness, *optative:* but of the desire to know, there is a peculiar expression, called *interrogative*; as, *what is it, when shall it, how is it done*, and *why so?* other language of the passions I find none: for cursing, swearing, reviling, and the like, do not signify as speech; but as the actions of a tongue accustomed.

These forms of speech, I say, are expressions, or voluntary significations of our passions: but certain signs they be not; because they may be used arbitrarily, whether they that use them, have such passions or not. The best signs of passions present, are either in the countenance, motions of the body, actions, and ends, or aims, which we otherwise know the man to have.

And because in deliberation, the appetites, and aversions, are raised by foresight of the good and evil consequences, and sequels of the action whereof we deliberate; the good or evil effect thereof dependeth on the foresight of a long chain of consequences, of which very seldom any man is able to see to the end. But for so far as a man seeth, if the good in those consequences be greater than the evil, the whole chain is that which writers call *apparent*, or *seeming good*. And contrarily, when the evil exceedeth the good, the whole is *apparent*, or *seeming evil:* so that he who hath by experience, or reason, the greatest and surest prospect of consequences, deliberates best himself; and is able when he will, to give the best counsel unto others.

Continual success in obtaining those things which a man from time to time desireth, that is to say, continual prospering, is that men call FELICITY; I mean the felicity of this life. For there is no such thing as perpetual tranquillity of mind, while we live here; because life itself is but motion, and can never be without desire, nor without fear, no more than without sense. What kind of felicity God hath ordained to them that devoutly honour Him, a man shall no sooner know, than enjoy; being joys, that now are as incomprehensible, as the word of school-men *beatifical vision* is unintelligible.

The form of speech whereby men signify their opinion of the goodness of any thing, is PRAISE. That whereby they signify the power and greatness of any thing, is MAGNIFYING. And that whereby they signify the opinion they have of a man's felicity, is by the Greeks called μακαρισμός, for which we have no name in our tongue. And thus much is sufficient for the present purpose, to have been said of the PASSIONS.

CHAPTER 7
Of the Ends, or Resolutions of Discourse

Of all *discourse*, governed by desire of knowledge, there is at last an *end*, either by attaining, or by giving over. And in the chain of discourse, wheresoever it be interrupted, there is an end for that time.

If the discourse be merely mental, it consisteth of thoughts that the thing will be, and will not be, or that it has been, and has not been, alternately. So that wheresoever you break off the chain of a man's discourse, you leave him in a presumption of *it will be*, or, *it will not be*; or *it has been*, or, *has not been*. All which is *opinion*. And that which is alternate appetite, in deliberating concerning good and evil; the same is alternate opinion, in the enquiry of the truth of *past*, and *future*. And as the last appetite in deliberation, is called the *will*; so the last opinion in search of the truth of past, and future, is called the JUDGMENT, or *resolute* and *final sentence* of him that *discourseth*. And as the whole chain of appetites alternate, in the question of good, or bad, is called *deliberation*; so the whole chain of opinions alternate, in the question of true, or false, is called DOUBT.

No discourse whatsoever, can end in absolute knowledge of fact, past, or to come. For, as for the knowledge of fact, it is originally, sense; and ever after, memory. And for the knowledge of consequence, which I have said before is called science, it is not absolute, but conditional. No man can know by discourse, that this, or that, is, has been, or will be; which is to know absolutely: but only, that if this be, that is; if this has been, that has been; if this shall be, that shall be: which is to know conditionally; and that not the consequence of one thing to another; but of one name of a thing, to another name of the same thing.

And therefore, when the discourse is put into speech, and begins with the definitions of words, and proceeds by connexion of the same into general affirmations, and of these again into syllogisms; the end or last sum is called the conclusion; and the thought of the mind by it signified, is that conditional knowledge, or knowledge of the consequence of words, which is commonly called SCIENCE. But if the first ground of such discourse, be not definitions; or if the definitions be not rightly joined together into syllogisms, then the end or conclusion, is again OPINION, namely of the truth of somewhat said, though sometimes in absurd and senseless words, without possibility of being understood. When two, or more men, know of one and the same fact, they are said to be CONSCIOUS of it one to another; which is as much as to know it together. And because such are fittest witnesses of the facts of one another, or of a third; it was, and ever will be reputed a very evil act, for any man to speak against his *conscience:* or to corrupt or force another so to do: insomuch that the plea of conscience, has been always hearkened unto very diligently in all times. Afterwards, men made use of the same word metaphorically, for the knowledge of their own secret facts, and secret thoughts; and therefore it is rhetorically said, that the conscience is a thousand witnesses. And last of all, men, vehemently in love with their own new opinions, (though never so absurd,) and obstinately bent to maintain them, gave those their opinions also that reverenced name of conscience, as if they would have it seem unlawful, to change or speak against them; and so pretend to know they are true, when they know at most, but that they think so.

When a man's discourse beginneth not at definitions, it beginneth either at some other contemplation of his own, and then it is still called opinion; or it beginneth at some saying of another, of whose ability to know the truth, and of whose honesty in not deceiving, he doubteth not; and then the discourse is not so much concerning the thing, as the person; and the resolution is called BELIEF, and FAITH: *faith, in* the man; *belief,* both *of* the man, and *of* the truth of what he says. So that in belief are two opinions; one of the saying of the man; the other of his virtue. To *have faith in,* or *trust to,* or *believe a man,* signify the same thing; namely, an opinion of the veracity of the man: but to *believe what is said,* signifieth only an opinion of the truth of the saying. But we are to observe that this phrase, *I believe in*; as also the Latin, *credo in*; and the Greek, πιστένω ἔις, are never used but in the writings of divines. Instead of them, in other writings are put, *I believe him; I trust him; I have faith in him; I rely on him;* and in Latin, *credo illi: fido illi:* and in Greek, πιστένω αὐτῷ: and that this singularity of the ecclesiastic use of the word hath raised many disputes about the right object of the Christian faith.

But by *believing in,* as it is in the creed, is meant, not trust in the person; but confession and acknowledgment of the doctrine. For not only Christians, but all manner of men do so believe in God, as to hold all for truth they hear him say, whether they understand it, or not; which is all the faith and trust can possibly be had in any person whatsoever: but they do not all believe the doctrine of the creed.

From whence we may infer, that when we believe any saying whatsoever it be, to be true, from arguments taken, not from the thing it self, or from the principles of natural reason, but from the authority, and good opinion we have, of him that hath said it; then is the speaker, or person we believe in, or trust in, and whose word we take, the object of our faith; and the honour done in believing, is done to him only. And consequently, when we believe that the Scriptures are the word of God, having no immediate revelation from God himself, our belief, faith, and trust is in the church; whose word we take, and acquiesce therein. And they that believe that which a prophet relates unto them in the name of God, take the word of the prophet, do honour to him, and in him trust, and believe, touching the truth of what he relateth, whether he be a true, or a false prophet. And so it is also with all other history. For if I should not believe all that is written by historians, of the glorious acts of *Alexander,* or *Caesar*; I do not think the ghost of *Alexander,* or *Caesar,* had any just cause to be offended; or any body else, but the historian. If *Livy* say the Gods made once a cow speak, and we believe it not; we distrust not God therein, but *Livy.* So that it is evident, that whatsoever we believe, upon no other reason, than what is drawn from authority of men only, and their writings; whether they be sent from God or not, is faith in men only.

CHAPTER 8
Of the Virtues Commonly Called Intellectual; and Their Contrary Defects

Virtue generally, in all sorts of subjects, is somewhat that is valued for eminence; and consisteth in comparison. For if all things were equally in all men, nothing would be prized. And by *virtues* INTELLECTUAL, are always understood such abilities of the mind, as men praise, value, and desire should be in themselves; and go commonly under the name of a *good wit;* though the same word *wit,* be used also, to distinguish one certain ability from the rest.

These *virtues* are of two sorts; *natural,* and *acquired.* By natural, I mean not, that which a man hath from his birth: for that is nothing else but sense; wherein men differ so little one from another, and from brute beasts, as it is not to be reckoned amongst virtues. But I mean, that *wit,* which is gotten by use only, and experience; without method, culture, or instruction. This NATURAL WIT, consisteth principally in two things; *celerity of imagining,* (that is, swift succession of one thought to another;) and *steady direction* to some approved end. On the contrary a slow imagination, maketh that defect, or fault of the mind, which is commonly called DULLNESS, *stupidity,* and sometimes by other names that signify slowness of motion, or difficulty to be moved.

And this difference of quickness, is caused by the difference of men's passions; that love and dislike, some one thing, some another: and therefore some men's thoughts run one way, some another; and are held to, and observe differently the things that pass through their imagination. And whereas in this succession of men's thoughts, there is nothing to observe in the things they think on, but either in what they be *like one another,* or in what they be *unlike,* or *what they serve for,* or *how they serve to such a purpose*; those that observe their similitudes, in case they be such as are but rarely observed by others, are said to have a *good wit*; by which, in this occasion, is meant a *good fancy.* But they that observe their differences, and dissimilitudes; which is called *distinguishing,* and *discerning,* and *judging* between thing and thing; in case, such discerning be not easy, are said to have a *good judgment:* and particularly in matter of conversation and business; wherein, times, places, and persons are to be discerned, this virtue is called DISCRETION. The former, that is, fancy, without the help of judgment, is not commended as a virtue: but the latter which is judgment, and discretion, is commended for it self, without the help of fancy. Besides the discretion of times, places, and persons, necessary to a good fancy, there is required also an often application of his thoughts to their end; that is to say, to some use to be made of them. This done; he that hath this virtue, will be easily fitted with similitudes, that will please, not only by illustration of his discourse, and adorning it with new and apt metaphors; but also, by the rarity of their invention. But without steadiness, and direction to some end, a great fancy is one kind of madness; such as they have, that entering into any discourse, are snatched from their purpose, by every thing that comes in their thought, into so many, and so long digressions, and parentheses, that they utterly lose themselves: which kind of folly, I know no particular name for: but the cause of it is, sometimes want of experience; whereby that seemeth to a man new and rare, which doth not so to others: sometimes pusillanimity; by which that seems great to him, which other men think a trifle: and whatsoever is new, or great, and therefore thought fit to be told, withdraws a man by degrees from the intended way of his discourse.

In a good poem, whether it be *epic,* or *dramatic*; as also in *sonnets, epigrams,* and other pieces, both judgment and fancy are required: but the fancy must be more eminent; because they please for the extravagancy; but ought not to displease by indiscretion.

In a good history, the judgment must be eminent; because the goodness consisteth, in the method, in the truth, and in the choice of the actions that are most profitable to be known. Fancy has no place, but only in adorning the style.

In orations of praise, and in invectives, the fancy is predominant; because the design is not truth, but to honour or dishonour; which is done by noble, or by vile comparisons. The judgment does but suggest what circumstances make an action laudable, or culpable.

In hortatives, and pleadings, as truth, or disguise serveth best to the design in hand; so is the judgment, or the fancy most required.

In demonstration, in counsel, and all rigorous search of truth, judgment does all; except sometimes the understanding have need to be opened by some apt similitude; and then there is so much use of fancy. But for metaphors, they are in this case utterly excluded. For seeing they openly profess deceit; to admit them into counsel, or reasoning, were manifest folly.

And in any discourse whatsoever, if the defect of discretion be apparent, how extravagant soever the fancy be, the whole discourse will be taken for a sign of want of wit; and so will it never when the discretion is manifest, though the fancy be never so ordinary.

The secret thoughts of a man run over all things, holy, profane, clean, obscene, grave, and light, without shame, or blame; which verbal discourse cannot do, farther than the judgment shall approve of the time, place, and persons. An anatomist, or a physician may speak, or write his judgment of unclean things; because it is not to please, but profit: but for another man to write his extravagant, and pleasant fancies of the same, is as if a man, from being tumbled into the dirt, should come and present himself before good company. And it is the want of discretion that makes the difference. Again, in professed remissness of mind, and familiar company, a man may play with the sounds, and equivocal significations of words; and that many times with encounters of extraordinary fancy: but in a sermon, or in public, or before persons unknown, or whom we ought to reverence; there is no gingling of words that will not be accounted folly: and the difference is only in the want of discretion. So that where wit is wanting, it is not fancy that is wanting, but discretion. Judgment therefore without fancy is wit, but fancy without judgment, not.

When the thoughts of a man, that has a design in hand, running over a multitude of things, observes how they conduce to that design; or what design they may conduce unto; if his observations be such as are not easy, or usual, this wit of his is called PRUDENCE; and dependeth on much experience, and memory of the like things, and their consequences heretofore. In which there is not so much difference of men, as there is in their fancies and judgments; because the experience of men equal in age, is not much unequal, as to the quantity; but lies in different occasions; every one having his private designs. To govern well a family, and a kingdom, are not different degrees of prudence; but different sorts of business; no more than to draw a picture in little, or as great, or greater than the life, are different degrees of art. A plain husbandman is more prudent in affairs of his own house, than a privy councillor in the affairs of another man.

To prudence, if you add the use of unjust, or dishonest means, such as usually are prompted to men by fear, or want; you have that crooked wisdom, which is called CRAFT; which is a sign of pusillanimity. For magnanimity is contempt of unjust, or dishonest helps. And that which the Latins call *versutia*, (translated into English, *shifting*,) and is a putting off of a present danger or incommodity, by engaging into a greater, as when a man robs one to pay another, is but a shorter sighted craft, called *versutia*, from *versura*, which signifies taking money at usury for the present payment of interest.

As for *acquired wit*, (I mean acquired by method and instruction,) there is none but reason; which is grounded on the right use of speech, and produceth the sciences. But of reason and science, I have already spoken in the fifth and sixth chapters.

The causes of this difference of wits, are in the passions; and the difference of passions proceedeth, partly from the different constitution of the body, and partly from different education. For if the difference proceeded from the temper of the brain, and the organs of sense, either exterior or interior, there would be no less difference of men in their sight, hearing, or other senses, than in their fancies and discretions. It proceeds therefore from the passions; which are different, not only from the difference of mens' complexions; but also from their difference of customs, and education.

The passions that most of all cause the differences of wit, are principally, the more or less desire of power, of riches, of knowledge, and of honour. All which may be reduced to the first, that is, desire of power. For riches, knowledge, and honour are but several sorts of power.

And therefore, a man who has no great passion for any of these things; but is as men term it indifferent; though he may be so far a good man, as to be free from giving offence; yet he cannot possibly have either a great fancy, or much judgment. For the thoughts are to the desires, as scouts, and spies, to range abroad, and find the way to the things desired: all steadiness of the mind's motion and all quickness of the same, proceeding from thence: for as to have no desire, is to be dead: so to have weak passions, is dullness; and to have passions indifferently for every thing, GIDDINESS, and *distraction*; and to have stronger and more vehement passions for any thing, than is ordinarily seen in others, is that which men call MADNESS.

Whereof there be almost as many kinds, as of the passions themselves. Sometimes the extraordinary and extravagant passion, proceedeth from the evil constitution of the organs of the body, or harm done them; and sometimes the hurt, and indisposition of the organs, is caused by the vehemence, or long continuance of the passion. But in both cases the madness is of one and the same nature.

The passion, whose violence, or continuance, maketh madness, is either great *vain-glory*; which is commonly called *pride*, and *self-conceit*; or great *dejection* of mind.

Pride, subjecteth a man to anger, the excess whereof, is the madness called RAGE and FURY. And thus it comes to pass that excessive desire of revenge, when it becomes habitual, hurteth the organs, and becomes rage: that excessive love, with jealousy, becomes also rage: excessive opinion of a man's own self, for divine inspiration, for wisdom, learning, form and the like, becomes distraction and giddiness: the same, joined with envy, rage: vehement opinion of the truth of any thing, contradicted by others, rage.

Dejection subjects a man to causeless fears; which is a madness commonly called MELANCHOLY, apparent also in divers manners; as in haunting of solitudes and graves; in superstitious behaviour; and in fearing some one, some another particular thing. In sum, all passions that produce strange and unusual behaviour, are called by the general name of madness. But of the several kinds of madness, he that would take the pains, might enrol a legion. And if the excesses be madness, there is no doubt but the passions themselves, when they tend to evil, are degrees of the same.

(For example,) though the effect of folly, in them that are possessed of an opinion of being inspired, be not visible always in one man, by any very extravagant action, that proceedeth from such passion; yet when many of them conspire together, the rage of the whole multitude is visible enough. For what argument of madness can there be greater, than to clamour, strike, and throw stones at our best friends? Yet this is somewhat less than such a multitude will do. For they will clamour, fight against, and destroy those, by whom all their lifetime before, they have been protected, and secured from injury. And if this be madness in the multitude, it is the same in every particular man. For as in the midst of the sea, though a man perceive no sound of that part of the water next him; yet he is well assured, that part contributes as much to the roaring of the sea, as any other part of the same quantity; so also, though we perceive no great unquietness in one or two men, yet we may be well assured, that their singular passions, are parts of the seditious roaring of a troubled nation. And if there were nothing else that bewrayed their madness; yet that very arrogating such inspiration to themselves, is argument enough. If some man in Bedlam should entertain you with sober discourse; and you desire in taking leave, to know what he were, that you might another time requite his civility; and he should tell you, he were God the Father; I think you need expect no extravagant action for argument of his madness.

This opinion of inspiration, called commonly, private spirit, begins very often, from some lucky finding of an error generally held by others; and not knowing, or not remembering, by what conduct of reason, they came to so singular a truth, (as they think it, though it be many times an untruth they light on,) they presently admire themselves, as being in the special grace of God Almighty, who hath revealed the same to them supernaturally, by his Spirit.

Again, that madness is nothing else, but too much appearing passion, may be gathered out of the effects of wine, which are the same with those of the evil disposition of the organs. For the variety of behaviour in men that have drunk too much, is the same with that of madmen: some of them raging, others loving, others laughing, all extravagantly, but according to their several domineering passions: for the effect of the wine, does but remove dissimulation, and take from them the sight of the deformity of their passions. For, (I believe) the most sober men, when they walk alone without care and employment of the mind, would be unwilling the vanity and extravagance of their thoughts at that time should be publicly seen; which is a confession, that passions unguided, are for the most part mere madness.

The opinions of the world, both in ancient and later ages, concerning the cause of madness, have been two. Some deriving them from the passions; some, from demons, or spirits, either good or bad, which they thought might enter into a man, possess him, and move his organs in such strange and uncouth manner, as madmen use to do. The former sort therefore, called such men, madmen: but the latter, called them sometimes *demoniacs*, (that is, possessed with spirits;) sometimes *enurgumeni*, (that is, agitated or moved with spirits;) and now in *Italy* they are called not only *pazzi*, madmen; but also *spiritati*, men possessed.

There was once a great conflux of people in *Abdera*, a city of the Greeks, at the acting of the tragedy of *Andromeda*, upon an extreme hot day; whereupon, a great many of the spectators falling into fevers, had this accident from the heat, and from the tragedy together, that they did nothing but pronounce iambics, with the names of *Perseus* and *Andromeda;* which, together with the fever, was cured by the coming on of winter; and this madness was thought to proceed from the passion imprinted by the tragedy. Likewise there reigned a fit of madness in another Grecian city, which seized only the young maidens; and caused many of them to hang themselves. This was by most then thought an act of the Devil. But one that suspected, that contempt of life in them, might proceed from some passion of the mind, and supposing they did not contemn also their honour, gave counsel to the magistrates, to strip such as so hanged themselves, and let them hang out naked. This, the story says, cured that madness. But on the other side, the same Grecians, did often ascribe madness to the operation of the Eumenides, or Furies; and sometimes of *Ceres, Phoebus,* and other gods; so much did men attribute to phantasms, as to think them aereal living bodies; and generally to call them spirits. And as the Romans in this, held the same opinion with the Greeks, so also did the Jews; for they called madmen prophets, or (according as they thought the spirits good or bad) demoniacs; and some of them called both prophets and demoniacs, madmen; and some called the same man both demoniac, and madman. But for the Gentiles it is no wonder, because diseases and health, vices and virtues, and many natural accidents, were with them termed, and worshipped as demons. So that a man was to understand by demon, as well, (sometimes) an ague, as a devil. But for the Jews to have such opinion, is somewhat strange. For neither *Moses* nor *Abraham* pretended to prophecy by possession of a spirit; but from the voice of God; or by a vision or dream: nor is there any thing in his law, moral or ceremonial, by which they were taught, there was any such enthusiasm, or any possession. When God is said, *Numb.* 11. 25. to take from the spirit that was in *Moses,* and give to the 70 elders, the Spirit of God (taking it for the substance of God) is not divided. The Scriptures, by the Spirit of God in man, mean a man's spirit, inclined to godliness. And where it is said, *Exod.* 28. 3. *whom I have filled with the spirit of wisdom to make garments for Aaron,* is not meant a spirit put into them, that can make garments; but the wisdom of their own spirits in that kind of work. In the like sense, the spirit of man, when it produceth unclean actions, is ordinarily called an unclean spirit, and so other spirits, though not always, yet as often as the virtue or vice so styled, is extraordinary, and eminent. Neither did the other prophets of the old Testament pretend enthusiasm; or, that God spake in them; but to them, by voice, vision, or dream; and the *burthen of the Lord* was not possession, but command. How then could the Jews fall into this opinion of possession? I can imagine no reason, but that which is common to all men; namely, the want of curiosity to search natural causes; and their placing felicity in the acquisition of the gross pleasures of the senses, and the things that most immediately conduce thereto. For they that see any strange, and unusual ability, or defect in a man's mind; unless they see withal, from what cause it may probably proceed, can hardly think it natural; and if not natural, they must needs think it supernatural, and then what can it be, but that either God or the Devil is in him? And hence it came to pass, when our Saviour (*Mark* 3. 21.) was compassed about with the multitude, those of the house doubted he was mad, and went out to hold him: but the Scribes said he had *Beelzebub,* and that was it, by which he cast out devils; as if the greater madman had awed the lesser. And that (*John* 10. 20.) some said, *he hath a devil, and is mad;* whereas others holding him for a prophet, said, *these are not the words of one that hath a devil.* So in the old Testament he that came to anoint *Jehu,* 2 *Kings* 9. 11. was a prophet; but some of the company asked *Jehu, what came that madman for?* So that in sum, it is manifest, that whosoever behaved himself in extraordinary manner, was thought by the Jews to be possessed either with a good, or evil spirit; except by the Sadducees, who erred so far on the other hand, as not to believe there were at all any spirits, (which is very near to direct atheism;) and thereby perhaps the more provoked others, to term such men demoniacs, rather than madmen.

But why then does our Saviour proceed in the curing of them, as if they were possessed; and not as if they were mad? To which I can give no other kind of answer, but that which is given to those that urge the Scripture in like manner against the opinion of the motion of the earth. The Scripture was written to shew unto men the kingdom of God, and to prepare their minds to become his obedient subjects; leaving the world, and the philosophy thereof, to the disputation of men, for the exercising of their natural reason. Whether the earth's, or sun's motion make the day, and night; or whether the exorbitant actions of men, proceed from passion, or from the devil, (so we worship him not) it is all one, as to our obedience, and subjection to God Almighty; which is the thing for which the Scripture was written. As for that our Saviour speaketh to the disease, as to a person; it is the usual phrase of all that cure by words only, as Christ did, (and enchanters pretend to do, whether they speak to a devil or not.) For is not Christ also said (*Matt.* 8. 26.) to have rebuked the winds? Is not he said also (*Luke* 4. 39.) to rebuke a fever? Yet this does not argue that a fever is a devil. And whereas many of those devils are said to confess Christ; it is not necessary to interpret those places otherwise, than that those madmen confessed him. And whereas our Saviour (*Matt.* 12. 43.) speaketh of an unclean spirit, that having gone out of a man, wandereth through dry places, seeking rest, and finding none, and returning into the same man, with seven other spirits worse than himself; it is manifestly a parable, alluding to a man, that after a little endeavour to quit his lusts, is vanquished by the strength of them; and becomes seven times worse than he was. So that I see nothing at all in the Scripture, that requireth a belief, that demoniacs were any other thing but madmen.

There is yet another fault in the discourses of some men; which may also be numbered amongst the sorts of madness; namely, that abuse of words, whereof I have spoken before in the fifth chapter, by the name of absurdity. And that is, when men speak such words, as put together, have in them no signification at all; but are fallen upon by some, through misunderstanding of the words they have received, and repeat by rote; by others from intention to deceive by obscurity. And this is incident to none but those, that converse in questions of matters incomprehensible, as the School-men; or in questions of abstruse philosophy. The common sort of men seldom speak insignificantly, and are therefore, by those other egregious persons counted idiots. But to be assured their words are without any thing correspondent to them in the mind, there would need some examples; which if any man require, let him take a School-man into his hands and see if he can translate any one chapter concerning any difficult point, as the Trinity; the Deity; the nature of Christ; transubstantiation; free-will, &c. into any of the modern tongues, so as to make the same intelligible; or into any tolerable Latin, such as they were acquainted withal, that lived when the Latin tongue was vulgar. What is the meaning of these words. *The first cause does not necessarily inflow any thing into the second, by force of the essential subordination of the second causes, by which it may help it to work?* They are the translation of the title of the sixth chapter of *Suarez'* first book, *Of the Concourse, Motion, and Help of God.* When men write whole volumes of such stuff, are they not mad, or intend to make others so? And particularly, in the question of transubstantiation; where after certain words spoken, they that say, the white*ness*, round*ness*, magni*tude,* quali*ty*, corruptibili*ty*, all which are incorporeal, &c. go out of the wafer, into the body of our blessed Saviour, do they not make those *nesses, tudes,* and *ties,* to be so many spirits possessing his body? For by spirits, they mean always things, that being incorporeal, are nevertheless moveable from one place to another. So that this kind of absurdity, may rightly be numbered amongst the many sorts of madness; and all the time that guided by clear thoughts of their worldly lust, they forbear disputing, or writing thus, but lucid intervals. And thus much of the virtues and defects intellectual.

CHAPTER 9
Of the Several Subjects of Knowledge

There are of KNOWLEDGE two kinds; whereof one is *knowledge of fact:* the other *knowledge of the consequence of one affirmation to another.* The former is nothing else, but sense and memory, and is *absolute knowledge*; as when we see a fact doing, or remember it done: and this is the knowledge required in a witness. The latter is called *science;* and is *conditional;* as when we know, that, *if the figure shown be a circle, then any straight line through the center shall divide it into two equal parts.* And this is the knowledge required in a philosopher; that is to say, of him that pretends to reasoning.

The register of *knowledge of fact* is called *history.* Whereof there be two sorts: one called *natural history*; which is the history of such facts, or effects of nature, as have no dependence on man's *will;* such as are the histories of *metals, plants, animals, regions,* and the like. The other, is *civil history;* which is the history of the voluntary actions of men in commonwealths.

The registers of science, are such *books* as contain the *demonstrations* of consequences of one affirmation, to another; and are commonly called *books of philosophy;* whereof the sorts are many, according to the diversity of the matter; and may be divided in such manner as I have divided them in the following table.

CHAPTER 10
Of Power, Worth, Dignity, Honour, and Worthiness

The power *of a man,* (to take it universally,) is his present means, to obtain some future apparent good; and is either *original* or *instrumental.*

Natural power, is the eminence of the faculties of body, or mind: as extraordinary strength, form, prudence, arts, eloquence, liberality, nobility. *Instrumental* are those powers, which acquired by these, or by fortune, are means and instruments to acquire more: as riches, reputation, friends, and the secret working of God, which men call good luck. For the nature of power, is in this point, like to fame, increasing as it proceeds; or like the motion of heavy bodies, which the further they go, make still the more haste.

The greatest of human powers, is that which is compounded of the powers of most men, united by consent, in one person, natural, or civil, that has the use of all their powers depending on his will; such as is the power of a common-wealth: or depending on the wills of each particular; such as is the power of a faction or of divers factions leagued. Therefore to have servants, is power; to have friends, is power: for they are strengths united.

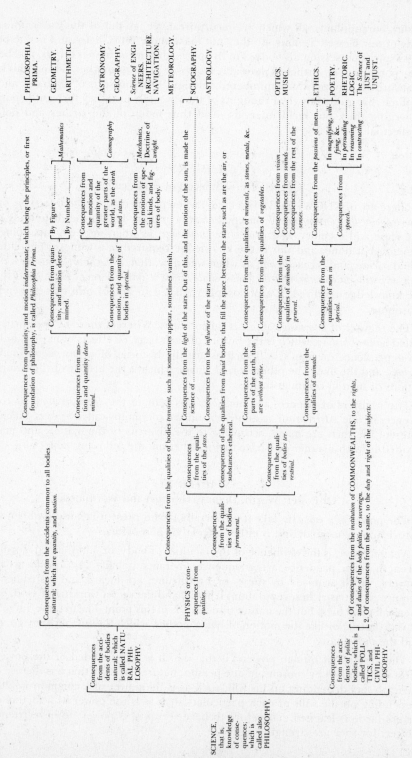

SCIENCE, that is, knowledge of consequences; which is called also PHILOSOPHY.

Consequences from the accidents of bodies natural; which is called NATURAL PHILOSOPHY.

Consequences from the accidents common to all bodies natural; which are *quantity,* and *motion.*

Consequences from quantity, and motion *indeterminate;* which being the principles, or first foundation of philosophy, is called *Philosophia Prima.* — PHILOSOPHIA PRIMA.

Consequences from motion and quantity *determined.*

Consequences from quantity, and motion determined. — *Mathematics*
- By Figure — GEOMETRY.
- By Number — ARITHMETIC.

Consequences from the motion, and quantity of bodies in *special.*

Consequences from the motion and quantity of the greater parts of the world, as the *earth* and *stars.* — *Cosmography*
- ASTRONOMY.
- GEOGRAPHY.

Consequences from the motions of special kinds, and figures of body. — *Mechanics,* Doctrine of *weight*
- *Science* of ENGINEERS.
- ARCHITECTURE.
- NAVIGATION.

PHYSICS or consequences from *qualities.*

Consequences from the qualities of bodies *transient,* such as sometimes appear, sometimes vanish. — METEOROLOGY.

Consequences from the qualities of bodies *permanent.*

Consequences from the qualities of the *stars.*
- Consequences from the *light* of the stars. Out of this, and the motion of the sun, is made the science of — SCIOGRAPHY.
- Consequences from the *influence* of the stars. — ASTROLOGY.

Consequences of the qualities from *liquid* bodies, that fill the space between the stars; such as are the *air,* or substances ethereal.

Consequences from the qualities of *bodies terrestrial.*

Consequences from the parts of the earth, that are *without sense.*
- Consequences from the qualities of *minerals,* as *stones, metals,* &c.
- Consequences from the qualities of *vegetables.*

Consequences from the qualities of *animals.*

Consequences from the qualities of *animals in general.*
- Consequences from *vision* — OPTICS.
- Consequences from *sounds* — MUSIC.
- Consequences from the rest of the senses.

Consequences from the qualities of *men in special.*
- Consequences from the *passions* of men. — ETHICS.
- Consequences from *speech.*
  - In *magnifying, vilifying,* &c. — POETRY.
  - In *persuading* — RHETORIC.
  - In *reasoning* — LOGIC.
  - In *contracting* — The *Science* of JUST and UNJUST.

Consequences from the accidents of *politic* bodies; which is called POLITICS, and CIVIL PHILOSOPHY.

1. Of consequences from the *institution* of COMMONWEALTHS, to the *rights,* and *duties* of the *body politic,* or *sovereign.*
2. Of consequences from the same, to the *duty* and *right* of the *subjects.*

Also riches joined with liberality, is power; because it procureth friends, and servants: without liberality, not so; because in this case they defend not; but expose men to envy, as a prey.

Reputation of power, is power; because it draweth with it the adherence of those that need protection.

So is reputation of love of a man's country, (called popularity,) for the same reason.

Also, what quality soever maketh a man beloved, or feared of many; or the reputation of such quality, is power; because it is a means to have the assistance, and service of many.

Good success is power; because it maketh reputation of wisdom, or good fortune; which makes men either fear him, or rely on him.

Affability of men already in power, is increase of power; because it gaineth love.

Reputation of prudence in the conduct of peace or war, is power; because to prudent men, we commit the government of ourselves, more willingly than to others.

Nobility is power, not in all places, but only in those commonwealths, where it has privileges: for in such privileges consisteth their power.

Eloquence is power, because it is seeming prudence.

Form is power; because being a promise of good, it recommendeth men to the favour of women and strangers.

The sciences, are small power; because not eminent; and therefore, not acknowledged in any man; nor are at all, but in a few, and in them, but of a few things. For science is of that nature, as none can understand it to be, but such as in a good measure have attained it.

Arts of public use, as fortification, making of engines, and other instruments of war; because they confer to defence, and victory, are power: and though the true mother of them, be science, namely the mathematics; yet, because they are brought into the light, by the hand of the artificer, they be esteemed (the midwife passing with the vulgar for the mother,) as his issue.

The *value*, or WORTH of a man, is as of all other things, his price; that is to say, so much as would be given for the use of his power: and therefore is not absolute; but a thing dependant on the need and judgment of another. An able conductor of soldiers, is of great price in time of war present, or imminent; but in peace not so. A learned and uncorrupt judge, is much worth in time of peace; but not so much in war. And as in other things, so in men, not the seller, but the buyer determines the price. For let a man (as most men do,) rate themselves at the highest value they can; yet their true value is no more than it is esteemed by others.

The manifestation of the value we set on one another, is that which is commonly called honouring, and dishonouring. To value a man at a high rate, is to *honour* him; at a low rate, is to *dishonour* him. But high, and low, in this case, is to be understood by comparison to the rate that each man setteth on himself.

The public worth of a man, which is the value set on him by the commonwealth, is that which men commonly call DIGNITY. And this value of him by the commonwealth, is understood, by offices of command, judicature, public employment; or by names and titles, introduced for distinction of such value.

To pray to another, for aid of any kind, is to HONOUR; because a sign we have an opinion he has power to help; and the more difficult the aid is, the more is the honour.

To obey, is to honour, because no man obeys them, whom they think have no power to help, or hurt them. And consequently to disobey, is to *dishonour*.

To give great gifts to a man, is to honour him; because it is buying of protection, and acknowledging of power. To give little gifts, is to dishonour; because it is but alms, and signifies an opinion of the need of small helps.

To be sedulous in promoting another's good; also to flatter, is to honour; as a sign we seek his protection or aid. To neglect, is to dishonour.

To give way, or place to another, in any commodity, is to honour; being a confession of greater power. To arrogate, is to dishonour.

To show any sign of love, or fear of another, is to honour; for both to love, and to fear, is to value. To contemn, or less to love or fear, than he expects, is to dishonour; for it is undervaluing.

To praise, magnify, or call happy, is to honour; because nothing but goodness, power, and felicity is valued. To revile, mock, or pity, is to dishonour.

To speak to another with consideration, to appear before him with decency, and humility, is to honour him; as signs of fear to offend. To speak to him rashly, to do any thing before him obscenely, slovenly, impudently, is to dishonour.

To believe, to trust, to rely on another, is to honour him; sign of opinion of his virtue and power. To distrust, or not believe, is to dishonour.

To hearken to a man's counsel, or discourse of what kind soever, is to honour; as a sign we think him wise, or eloquent, or witty. To sleep, or go forth, or talk the while, is to dishonour.

To do those things to another, which he takes for signs of honour, or which the law or custom makes so, is to honour; because in approving the honour done by others, he acknowledgeth the power which others acknowledge. To refuse to do them, is to dishonour.

To agree with in opinion, is to honour; as being a sign of approving his judgment, and wisdom. To dissent, is dishonour, and an upbraiding of error; and (if the dissent be in many things) of folly.

To imitate, is to honour; for it is vehemently to approve. To imitate one's enemy, is to dishonour.

To honour those another honours, is to honour him; as a sign of approbation of his judgment. To honour his enemies, is to dishonour him.

To employ in counsel, or in actions of difficulty, is to honour; as a sign of opinion of his wisdom, or other power. To deny employment in the same cases, to those that seek it, is to dishonour.

All these ways of honouring, are natural; and as well within, as without commonwealths. But in commonwealths, where he, or they that have the supreme authority, can make whatsoever they please, to stand for signs of honour, there be other honours.

A sovereign doth honour a subject, with whatsoever title, or office, or employment, or action, that he himself will have taken for a sign of his will to honour him.

The king of *Persia,* honoured *Mordecai,* when he appointed he should be conducted through the streets in the king's garment, upon one of the king's horses, with a crown on his head, and a prince before him, proclaiming, *thus shall it be done to him that the king will honour.* And yet another king of *Persia,* or the same another time, to one that demanded for some great service, to wear one of the king's robes, gave him leave so to do; but with this addition, that he should wear it as the king's fool; and then it was dishonour. So that of civil honour, the fountain is in the person of the commonwealth, and dependeth on the will of the sovereign; and is therefore temporary, and called *civil honour;* such as are magistracy, offices, titles; and in some places coats and scutcheons painted: and men honour such as have them, as having so many signs of favour in the commonwealth; which favour is power.

Honourable is whatsoever possession, action, or quality, is an argument and sign of power.

And therefore to be honoured, loved, or feared of many, is honourable; as arguments of power. To be honoured of few or none, *dishonourable.*

Dominion, and victory is honourable; because acquired by power; and servitude, for need, or fear, is dishonourable.

Good fortune (if lasting,) honourable, as a sign of the favour of God. Ill fortune, and losses, dishonourable. Riches, are honourable; for they are power. Poverty, dishonourable. Magnanimity, liberality, hope, courage, confidence, are honourable; for they proceed from the conscience of power. Pusillanimity, parsimony, fear, diffidence, are dishonourable.

Timely resolution, or determination of what a man is to do, is honourable; as being the contempt of small difficulties, and dangers. And irresolution, dishonourable; as a sign of too much valuing of little impediments, and little advantages: for when a man has weighed things as long as the time permits, and resolves not, the difference of weight is but little; and therefore if he resolve not, he overvalues little things, which is pusillanimity.

All actions, and speeches, that proceed, or seem to proceed from much experience, science, discretion, or wit, are honourable; for all these are powers. Actions, or words that proceed from error, ignorance, or folly, dishonourable.

Gravity, as far forth as it seems to proceed from a mind employed on something else, is honourable; because employment is a sign of power. But if it seem to proceed from a purpose to appear grave, it is dishonourable. For the gravity of the former, is like the steadiness of a ship laden with merchandise; but of the latter, like the steadiness of a ship ballasted with sand, and other trash.

To be conspicuous, that is to say, to be known, for wealth, office, great actions, or any eminent good, is honourable; as a sign of the power for which he is conspicuous. On the contrary, obscurity, is dishonourable.

To be descended from conspicuous parents, is honourable; because they the more easily attain the aids, and friends of their ancestors. On the contrary, to be descended from obscure parentage, is dishonourable.

Actions proceeding from equity, joined with loss, are honourable; as signs of magnanimity: for magnanimity is a sign of power. On the contrary, craft, shifting, neglect of equity, is dishonourable.

Covetousness of great riches, and ambition of great honours, are honourable; as signs of power to obtain them. Covetousness, and ambition, of little gains, or preferments, is dishonourable.

Nor does it alter the case of honour, whether an action (so it be great and difficult, and consequently a sign of much power,) be just or unjust: for honour consisteth only in the opinion of power. Therefore the ancient heathen did not think they dishonoured, but greatly honoured the Gods, when they introduced them in their poems, committing rapes, thefts, and other great, but unjust, or unclean acts: insomuch as nothing is so much celebrated in *Jupiter,* as his adulteries; nor in *Mercury,* as his frauds, and thefts: of whose praises, in a hymn of *Homer,* the greatest is this, that being born in the morning, he had invented music at noon, and before night, stolen away the cattle of *Apollo,* from his herdsmen.

Also amongst men, till there were constituted great commonwealths, it was thought no dishonour to be a pirate, or a highway thief; but rather a lawful trade, not only amongst the Greeks, but also amongst all other nations; as is manifest by the histories of ancient time. And at this day, in this part of the world, private duels are, and always will be honourable, though unlawful, till such time as there shall be honour ordained for them that refuse, and ignominy for them that make the challenge. For duels also are many times effects of courage; and the ground of courage is always strength or skill, which are power; though for the most part they be effects of rash speaking, and of the fear of dishonour, in one, or both the combatants; who engaged by rashness, are driven into the lists to avoid disgrace.

Scutcheons, and coats of arms hereditary, where they have any eminent privileges, are honourable; otherwise not: for their power consisteth either in such privileges, or in riches, or some such thing as is equally honoured in other men. This kind of honour, commonly called gentry, has been derived from the ancient Germans. For there never was any such thing known, where the German customs were unknown. Nor is it now any where in use where the Germans have not inhabited. The ancient Greek commanders, when they went to war, had their shields painted with such devices as they pleased; insomuch as an unpainted buckler was a sign of poverty, and of a common soldier; but they transmitted not the inheritance of them. The Romans transmitted the marks of their families: but they were the images, not the devices of their ancestors. Amongst the people of *Asia, Africa,* and *America,* there is not, nor was ever, any such thing. The Germans only had that custom; from whom it has been derived into *England, France, Spain,* and *Italy,* when in great numbers they either aided the Romans, or made their own conquests in these western parts of the world.

For *Germany,* being anciently, as all other countries, in their beginnings, divided amongst an infinite number of little lords, or masters of families, that continually had wars one with another; those masters, or lords, principally to the end they might, when they were covered with arms, be known by their followers; and partly for ornament, both painted their armour, or their scutcheon, or coat, with the picture of some beast, or other thing; and also put some eminent and visible mark upon the crest of their helmets. And this ornament both of the arms, and crest, descended by inheritance to their children; to the eldest pure, and to the rest with some note of diversity, such as the old master, that is to say in Dutch, the *Here-alt* thought fit. But when many such families, joined together, made a greater monarchy, this duty of the Hereailt, to distinguish scutcheons, was made a private office apart. And the issue of these lords, is the great and ancient gentry; which for the most part bear living creatures, noted for courage, and rapine; or castles, battlements, belts, weapons, bars, palisadoes, and other notes of war; nothing being then in honour, but virtue military. Afterwards, not only kings, but popular commonwealths, gave divers manners of scutcheons, to such as went forth to the war, or returned from it, for encouragement, or recompense to their service. All which, by an observing reader, may be found in such ancient histories, Greek and Latin, as make mention of the German nation and manners, in their times.

Titles of *honour*, such as are duke, count, marquis, and baron, are honourable; as signifying the value set upon them by the sovereign power of the commonwealth: which titles, were in old time titles of office, and command, derived some from the Romans, some from the Germans and French. Dukes, in Latin *duces,* being generals in war: counts, *comites,* such as bare the general company out of friendship, and were left to govern and defend places conquered, and pacified: marquises, *marchiones,* were counts that governed the marches, or bounds of the empire. Which titles of duke, count, and marquis, came into the empire, about the time of *Constantine* the Great, from the customs of the German *militia.* But baron, seems to have been a title of the Gauls, and signifies a great man; such as were the king's, or prince's men, whom they employed in war about their persons; and seems to be derived from *vir,* to *ber,* and *bar,* that signified the same in the language of the Gauls, that *vir* in Latin; and thence to *bero,* and *baro:* so that such men were called *berones,* and after barones; and (in Spanish) *varones.* But he that would know more particularly the original of titles of honour, may find it, as I have done this, in Mr. Selden's most excellent treatise of that subject. In process of time these offices of honour, by occasion of trouble, and for reasons of good and peaceable government, were turned into mere titles; serving for the most part, to distinguish the precedence, place, and order of subjects in the commonwealth: and men were made dukes, counts, marquises, and barons of places, wherein they had neither possession, nor command: and other titles also, were devised to the same end.

WORTHINESS, is a thing different from the worth, or value of a man; and also from his merit, or desert; and consisteth in a particular power, or ability for that, whereof he is said to be worthy: which particular ability, is usually named FITNESS, or *aptitude.*

For he is worthiest to be a commander, to be a judge, or to have any other charge, that is best fitted, with the qualities required to the well discharging of it; and worthiest of riches, that has the qualities most requisite for the well using of them: any of which qualities being absent, one may nevertheless be a worthy man, and valuable for something else. Again, a man may be worthy of riches, office, and employment, that nevertheless, can plead no right to have it before another; and therefore cannot be said to merit or deserve it. For merit presupposeth a right, and that the thing deserved is due by promise: of which I shall say more hereafter, when I shall speak of contracts.

Chapter 11
Of the Difference of Manners

By manners, I mean not here, decency of behaviour; as how one man should salute another, or how a man should wash his mouth, or pick his teeth before company, and such other points of the *small morals;* but those qualities of mankind, that concern their living together in peace, and unity. To which end we are to consider, that the felicity of this life, consisteth not in the repose of a mind satisfied. For there is no such *finis ultimus,* (utmost aim,) nor *summum bonum,* (greatest good,) as is spoken of in the books of the old moral philosophers. Nor can a man any more live, whose desires are at an end, than he, whose senses and imaginations are at a stand. Felicity is a continual progress of the desire, from one object to another; the attaining of the former, being still but the way to the latter. The cause whereof is, that the object of man's desire, is not to enjoy once only, and for one instant of time; but to assure for ever, the way of his future desire. And therefore the voluntary actions, and inclinations of all men, tend, not only to the procuring, but also to the assuring of a contented life; and differ only in the way: which ariseth partly from the diversity of passions, in divers men; and partly from the difference of the knowledge, or opinion each one has of the causes, which produce the effect desired.

So that in the first place, I put for a general inclination of all mankind, a perpetual and restless desire of power after power, that ceaseth only in death. And the cause of this, is not always that a man hopes for a more intensive delight, than he has already attained to; or that he cannot be content with a moderate power: but because he cannot assure the power and means to live well, which he hath present, without the acquisition of more. And from hence it is, that kings, whose power is greatest, turn their endeavours to the assuring it at home by laws, or abroad by wars: and when that is done, there succeedeth a new desire; in some, of fame from new conquest; in others, of ease and sensual pleasure; in others, of admiration, or being flattered for excellence in some art, or other ability of the mind.

Competition of riches, honour, command, or other power, inclineth to contention, enmity, and war: because the way of one competitor, to the attaining of his desire, is to kill, subdue, supplant, or repel the other. Particularly, competition of praise, inclineth to a reverence of antiquity. For men contend with the living, not with the dead; to these ascribing more than due, that they may obscure the glory of the other.

Desire of ease, and sensual delight, disposeth men to obey a common power: because by such desires, a man doth abandon the protection might be hoped for from his own industry, and labour. Fear of death, and wounds, disposeth to the same; and for the same reason. On the contrary, needy men, and hardy, not contented with their present condition; as also, all men that are ambitious of military command, are inclined to continue the causes of war; and to stir up trouble and sedition: for there is no honour military but by war; nor any such hope to mend an ill game, as by causing a new shuffle.

Desire of knowledge, and arts of peace, inclineth men to obey a common power: For such desire, containeth a desire of leisure; and consequently protection from some other power than their own.

Desire of praise, disposeth to laudable actions, such as please them whose judgment they value; for of those men whom we contemn, we contemn also the praises. Desire of fame after death does the same. And though after death, there be no sense of the praise given us on earth, as being joys, that are either swallowed up in the unspeakable joys of Heaven, or extinguished in the extreme torments of hell: yet is not such fame vain; because men have a present delight therein, from the foresight of it, and of the benefit that may redound thereby to their posterity: which though they now see not, yet they imagine; and any thing that is pleasure in the sense, the same also is pleasure in the imagination.

To have received from one, to whom we think ourselves equal, greater benefits than there is hope to requite, disposeth to counterfeit love; but really secret hatred; and puts a man into the estate of a desperate debtor, that in declining the sight of his creditor, tacitly wishes him there, where he might never see him more. For benefits oblige, and obligation is thraldom; and unrequitable obligation, perpetual thraldom; which is to one's equal, hateful. But to have received benefits from one, whom we acknowledge for superior, inclines to love; because the obligation is no new depression: and cheerful acceptation, (which men call *gratitude*,) is such an honour done to the obliger, as is taken generally for retribution. Also to receive benefits, though from an equal, or inferior, as long as there is hope of requital, disposeth to love: for in the intention of the receiver, the obligation is of aid, and service mutual; from whence proceedeth an emulation of who shall exceed in benefiting; the most noble and profitable contention possible; wherein the victor is pleased with his victory, and the other revenged by confessing it.

To have done more hurt to a man, than he can, or is willing to expiate, inclineth the doer to hate the sufferer. For he must expect revenge, or forgiveness; both which are hateful.

Fear of oppression, disposeth a man to anticipate, or to seek aid by society: for there is no other way by which a man can secure his life and liberty.

Men that distrust their own subtlety, are in tumult and sedition, better disposed for victory, than they that suppose themselves wise, or crafty. For these love to consult, the other (fearing to be circumvented,) to strike first. And in sedition, men being always in the precincts of battle, to hold together, and use all advantages of force, is a better stratagem, than any that can proceed from subtlety of wit.

Vain-glorious men, such as without being conscious to themselves of great sufficiency, delight in supposing themselves gallant men, are inclined only to ostentation; but not to attempt: because when danger or difficulty appears, they look for nothing but to have their insufficiency discovered.

Vain-glorious men, such as estimate their sufficiency by the flattery of other men, or the fortune of some precedent action, without assured ground of hope from the true knowledge of themselves, are inclined to rash engaging; and in the approach of danger, or difficulty, to retire if they can: because not seeing the way of safety, they will rather hazard their honour, which may be salved with an excuse; than their lives, for which no salve is sufficient.

Men that have a strong opinion of their own wisdom in matter of government, are disposed to ambition. Because without public employment in council or magistracy, the honour of their wisdom is lost. And therefore eloquent speakers are inclined to ambition; for eloquence seemeth wisdom, both to themselves and others.

Pusillanimity disposeth men to irresolution, and consequently to lose the occasions, and fittest opportunities of action. For after men have been in deliberation till the time of action approach, if it be not then manifest what is best to be done, it is a sign, the difference of motives, the one way and the other, are not great: therefore not to resolve then, is to lose the occasion by weighing of trifles; which is pusillanimity.

Frugality, (though in poor men a virtue,) maketh a man unapt to achieve such actions, as require the strength of many men at once: for it weakeneth their endeavour, which is to be nourished and kept in vigour by reward.

Eloquence, with flattery, disposeth men to confide in them that have it; because the former is seeming wisdom, the latter seeming kindness. Add to them military reputation, and it disposeth men to adhere, and subject themselves to those men that have them. The two former, having given them caution against danger from him; the latter gives them caution against danger from others.

Want of science, that is, ignorance of causes, disposeth, or rather constraineth a man to rely on the advice, and authority of others. For all men whom the truth concerns, if they rely not on their own, must rely on the opinion of some other, whom they think wiser than themselves, and see not why he should deceive them.

Ignorance of the signification of words, which is want of understanding, disposeth men to take on trust, not only the truth they know not; but also the errors; and which is more, the non-sense of them they trust: for neither error nor non-sense, can without a perfect understanding of words, be detected.

From the same it proceedeth, that men give different names, to one and the same thing, from the difference of their own passions: as they that approve a private opinion, call it opinion; but they that mislike it, heresy: and yet heresy signifies no more than private opinion; but has only a greater tincture of choler.

From the same also it proceedeth, that men cannot distinguish, without study and great understanding, between the one action of many men, and many actions of one multitude; as for example, between one action of all the senators of *Rome* in killing *Cataline*, and the many actions of a number of senators in killing *Caesar;* and therefore are disposed to take for the action of the people, that which is a multitude of actions done by a multitude of men, led perhaps by the persuasion of one.

Ignorance of the causes, and original constitution of right, equity, law, and justice, disposeth a man to make custom and example the rule of his actions; in such manner, as to think that unjust which it hath been the custom to punish; and that just, of the impunity and approbation whereof they can produce an example, or (as the lawyers which only use this false measure of justice barbarously call it) a precedent; like little children, that have no other rule of good and evil manners, but the correction they receive from their parents and masters; save that children are constant to their rule, whereas, men are not so; because grown strong, and stubborn, they appeal from custom to reason, and from reason to custom, as it serves their turn; receding from custom when their interest requires it, and setting themselves against reason, as oft as reason is against them: which is the cause, that the doctrine of right and wrong, is perpetually disputed, both by the pen and the sword: whereas the doctrine of lines, and figures, is not so; because men care not, in that subject, what be truth, as a thing that crosses no man's ambition, profit or lust. For I doubt not, but if it had been a thing contrary to any man's right of dominion, or to the interest of men that have dominion, *that the three angles of a triangle, should be equal to two angles of a square;* that doctrine should have been, if not disputed, yet by the burning of all books of geometry, suppressed, as far as he whom it concerned was able.

Ignorance of remote causes, disposeth men to attribute all events, to the causes immediate, and instrumental: for these are all the causes they perceive. And hence it comes to pass, that in all places, men that are grieved with payments to the public, discharge their anger upon the publicans, that is to say, farmers, collectors, and other officers of the public revenue; and adhere to such as find fault with the public government; and thereby, when they have engaged themselves beyond hope of justification, fall also upon the supreme authority, for fear of punishment, or shame of receiving pardon.

Ignorance of natural causes disposeth a man to credulity, so as to believe many times impossibilities: for such know nothing to the contrary, but that they may be

true; being unable to detect the impossibility. And credulity, because men love to be hearkened unto in company, disposeth them to lying: so that ignorance it self without malice, is able to make a man both to believe lies, and tell them; and sometimes also to invent them.

Anxiety for the future time, disposeth men to inquire into the causes of things: because the knowledge of them, maketh men the better able to order the present to their best advantage.

Curiosity, or love of the knowledge of causes, draws a man from consideration of the effect, to seek the cause; and again, the cause of that cause; till of necessity he must come to this thought at last, that there is some cause, whereof there is no former cause, but is eternal; which is it men call God. So that it is impossible to make any profound inquiry into natural causes, without being inclined thereby to believe there is one God eternal; though they cannot have any idea of him in their mind, answerable to his nature. For as a man that is born blind, hearing men talk of warming themselves by the fire, and being brought to warm himself by the same, may easily conceive, and assure himself, there is somewhat there, which men call *fire*, and is the cause of the heat he feels; but cannot imagine what it is like; nor have an idea of it in his mind, such as they have that see it: so also, by the visible things of this world, and their admirable order, a man may conceive there is a cause of them, which men call God; and yet not have an idea, or image of him in his mind.

And they that make little, or no inquiry into the natural causes of things, yet from the fear that proceeds from the ignorance it self, of what it is that hath the power to do them much good or harm, are inclined to suppose, and feign unto themselves, several kinds of powers invisible; and to stand in awe of their own imaginations; and in time of distress to invoke them; as also in the time of an expected good success, to give them thanks; making the creatures of their own fancy, their gods. By which means it hath come to pass, that from the innumerable variety of fancy, men have created in the world innumerable sorts of gods. And this fear of things invisible, is the natural seed of that, which every one in himself calleth religion; and in them that worship, or fear that power otherwise than they do, superstition.

And this seed of religion, having been observed by many; some of those that have observed it, have been inclined thereby to nourish, dress, and form it into laws; and to add to it of their own invention, any opinion of the causes of future events, by which they thought they should be best able to govern others, and make unto themselves the greatest use of their powers.

Chapter 12
Of Religion

Seeing there are no signs, nor fruit of *religion*, but in man only; there is no cause to doubt, but that the seed of *religion*, is also only in man; and consisteth in some peculiar quality, or at least in some eminent degree thereof, not to be found in other living creatures.

And first, it is peculiar to the nature of man, to be inquisitive into the causes of the events they see, some more, some less; but all men so much, as to be curious in the search of the causes of their own good and evil fortune.

Secondly, upon the sight of any thing that hath a beginning, to think also it had a cause, which determined the same to begin, then when it did, rather than sooner or later.

Thirdly, whereas there is no other felicity of beasts, but the enjoying of their quotidian food, ease, and lusts; as having little or no foresight of the time to come, for want of observation, and memory of the order, consequence, and dependence of the things they see; man observeth how one event hath been produced by another; and remembereth in them antecedence and consequence; and when he cannot assure himself of the true causes of things, (for the causes of good and evil fortune for the most part are invisible,) he supposes causes of them, either such as his own fancy suggesteth; or trusteth to the authority of other men, such as he thinks to be his friends, and wiser than himself.

The two first, make anxiety. For being assured that there be causes of all things that have arrived hitherto, or shall arrive hereafter; it is impossible for a man, who continually endeavoureth to secure himself against the evil he fears, and procure the good he desireth, not to be in a perpetual solicitude of the time to come; so that every man, especially those that are over provident, are in an estate like to that of *Prometheus*. For as *Prometheus*, (which interpreted, is, *the prudent man,)* was bound to the hill *Caucasus*, a place of large prospect, where, an eagle feeding on his liver, devoured in the day, as much as was repaired in the night: so that man, which looks too far before him, in the care of future time, hath his heart all the day long, gnawed on by fear of death, poverty, or other calamity; and has no repose, nor pause of his anxiety, but in sleep.

This perpetual fear, always accompanying mankind in the ignorance of causes, as it were in the dark, must needs have for object something. And therefore when there is nothing to be seen, there is nothing to accuse, either of their good, or evil fortune, but some *power,* or agent *invisible:* in which sense perhaps it was, that some of the old poets said, that the gods were at first created by human fear: which spoken of the gods, (that is to say, of the many gods of the Gentiles) is very true. But the acknowledging of one God, eternal, infinite, and omnipotent, may more easily be derived, from the desire men have to know the causes of natural bodies, and their several virtues, and operations; than from the fear of what was to befall them in time to come. For he that from any effect he seeth come to pass, should reason to the next and immediate cause thereof, and from thence to the cause of that cause, and plunge himself profoundly in the pursuit of causes; shall at last come to this, that there must be (as even the heathen philosophers confessed) one first mover; that is, a first, and an eternal cause of all things; which is that which men mean by the name of God: and all this without thought of their fortune; the solicitude whereof, both inclines to fear, and hinders them from the search of the causes of other things; and thereby gives occasion of feigning of as many gods, as there be men that feign them.

And for the matter, or substance of the invisible agents, so fancied; they could not by natural cogitation, fall upon any other conceit, but that it was the same with that of the soul of man; and that the soul of man, was of the same substance, with that which appeareth in a dream, to one that sleepeth; or in a looking-glass, to one that is awake; which, men not knowing that such apparitions are nothing else but creatures of the fancy, think to be real, and external substances; and therefore call them ghosts; as the Latins called them *imagines,* and *umbrae,* and thought them spirits, that is, thin aerial bodies; and those invisible agents, which they feared, to be like them; save that they appear, and vanish when they please. But the opinion that such spirits were incorporeal, or immaterial, could never enter into the mind

of any man by nature; because, though men may put together words of contradictory signification, as *spirit*, and *incorporeal;* yet they can never have the imagination of any thing answering to them: and therefore, men that by their own meditation, arrive to the acknowledgment of one infinite, omnipotent, and eternal God, choose rather to confess he is incomprehensible, and above their understanding, than to define his nature by *spirit incorporeal*, and then confess their definition to be unintelligible: or if they give him such a title, it is not *dogmatically*, with intention to make the divine nature understood; but *piously*, to honour him with attributes, of significations, as remote as they can from the grossness of bodies visible.

Then, for the way by which they think these invisible agents wrought their effects; that is to say, what immediate causes they used, in bringing things to pass, men that know not what it is that we call *causing*, (that is, almost all men) have no other rule to guess by, but by observing, and remembering what they have seen to precede the like effect at some other time, or times before, without seeing between the antecedent and subsequent event, any dependence or connexion at all: and therefore from the like things past, they expect the like things to come; and hope for good or evil luck, superstitiously, from things that have no part at all in the causing of it: as the Athenians did for their war at *Lepanto*, demand another *Phormio;* the Pompeian faction for their war in *Africa*, another *Scipio;* and others have done in divers other occasions since. In like manner they attribute their fortune to a stander by, to a lucky or unlucky place, to words spoken, especially if the name of God be amongst them; as charming and conjuring (the liturgy of witches;) insomuch as to believe, they have power to turn a stone into bread, bread into a man, or any thing into any thing.

Thirdly, for the worship which naturally men exhibit to powers invisible, it can be no other, but such expressions of their reverence, as they would use towards men; gifts, petitions, thanks, submission of body, considerate addresses, sober behaviour, premeditated words, swearing (that is, assuring one another of their promises,) by invoking them. Beyond that reason suggesteth nothing; but leaves them either to rest there; or for further ceremonies, to rely on those they believe to be wiser than themselves.

Lastly, concerning how these invisible powers declare to men the things which shall hereafter come to pass, especially concerning their good or evil fortune in general, or good or ill success in any particular undertaking, men are naturally at a stand; save that using to conjecture of the time to come, by the time past, they are very apt, not only to take casual things, after one or two encounters, for prognostics of the like encounter ever after, but also to believe the like prognostics from other men, of whom they have once conceived a good opinion.

And in these four things, opinion of ghosts, ignorance of second causes, devotion towards what men fear, and taking of things casual for prognostics, consisteth the natural seed of *religion;* which by reason of the different fancies, judgments, and passions of several men, hath grown up into ceremonies so different, that those which are used by one man, are for the most part ridiculous to another.

For these seeds have received culture from two sorts of men. One sort have been they, that have nourished, and ordered them, according to their own invention. The other have done it, by God's commandment, and direction: but both sorts have done it, with a purpose to make those men that relied on them, the more apt to obedience, laws, peace, charity, and civil society. So that the religion of the former sort, is a part of human politics; and teacheth part of the duty which earthly kings require of their subjects. And the religion of the latter sort is divine politics; and containeth precepts to those that have yielded themselves subjects in the kingdom of God. Of the former sort, were all the founders of commonwealths, and the lawgivers of the Gentiles: of the latter sort, were *Abraham, Moses,* and our *blessed Saviour;* by whom have been derived unto us the laws of the kingdom of God.

And for that part of religion, which consisteth in opinions concerning the nature of powers invisible, there is almost nothing that has a name, that has not been esteemed amongst the Gentiles, in one place or another, a god, or devil; or by their poets feigned to be inanimated, inhabited, or possessed by some spirit or other.

The unformed matter of the world, was a god, by the name of *Chaos.*

The heaven, the ocean, the planets, the fire, the earth, the winds, were so many gods.

Men, women, a bird, a crocodile, a calf, a dog, a snake, an onion, a leek, deified. Besides that, they filled almost all places, with spirits called *demons:* the plains, with *Pan,* and *Panises,* or Satyrs; the woods, with Fawns, and Nymphs; the sea, with Tritons, and other Nymphs; every river, and fountain, with a ghost of his name, and with Nymphs; every house with its *Lares,* or familiars; every man with his *Genius;* hell with ghosts, and spiritual officers, as *Charon, Cerberus,* and the *Furies;* and in the night time, all places with *larvae, lemures,* ghosts of men deceased, and a whole kingdom of fairies and bugbears. They have also ascribed divinity, and built temples to meer accidents, and qualities; such as are time, night, day, peace, concord, love, contention, virtue, honour, health, rust, fever, and the like; which when they prayed for, or against, they prayed to, as if there were ghosts of those names hanging over their heads, and letting fall, or withholding that good, or evil, for, or against which they prayed. They invoked also their own wit, by the name of *Muses;* their own ignorance, by the name of *Fortune;* their own lust, by the name of *Cupid;* their own rage, by the name *Furies;* their own privy members, by the name of *Priapus,* and attributed their pollutions, to *Incubi,* and *Succubae:* insomuch as there was nothing, which a poet could introduce as a person in his poem, which they did not make either a *god,* or a *devil.*

The same authors of the religion of the Gentiles, observing the second ground for religion, which is men's ignorance of causes; and thereby their aptness to attribute their fortune to causes, on which there was no dependence at all apparent, took occasion to obtrude on their ignorance, instead of second causes, a kind of second and ministerial gods; ascribing the cause of fecundity, to *Venus;* the cause of arts, to *Apollo;* of subtlety and craft, to *Mercury;* of tempests and storms, to *Aeolus;* and of other effects, to other gods; insomuch as there was amongst the heathen almost as great variety of gods, as of business.

And to the worship, which naturally men conceived fit to be used towards their gods, namely, oblations, prayers, thanks, and the rest formerly named; the same legislators of the Gentiles have added their images, both in picture, and sculpture; that the more ignorant sort (that is to say, the most part or generality of the people,) thinking the gods for whose representation they were made, were really included, and as it were housed within them, might so much the more stand in fear of them: and endowed them with lands, and houses, and officers, and revenues, set apart from all other human uses; that is, consecrated, and made holy to those their idols; as caverns, groves, woods, mountains, and whole islands; and have attributed to them, not only the shapes, some of men, some of beasts, some of monsters; but also the faculties, and passions of men and beasts; as sense, speech, sex, lust, generation, (and this not only by mixing one with another, to propagate the kind of gods; but also by mixing with men, and women, to beget mongrel gods, and but inmates of heaven, as *Bacchus, Hercules,* and others;) besides anger, revenge, and other passions of living creatures, and the actions proceeding from them, as fraud, theft, adultery, sodomy, and any vice that may be taken for an effect of power, or a cause of pleasure; and all such vices, as amongst men are taken to be against law, rather than against honour.

Lastly, to the prognostics of time to come; which are naturally, but conjectures upon the experience of time past; and supernaturally, divine revelation; the same authors of the religion of the Gentiles, partly upon pretended experience, partly upon pretended revelation, have added innumerable other superstitious ways of divination; and made men believe they should find their fortunes, sometimes in the ambiguous or senseless answers of the priests at *Delphi, Delos, Ammon,* and other famous oracles; which answers, were made ambiguous by design, to own the event both ways; or absurd, by the intoxicating vapour of the place, which is very frequent in sulphurous caverns: sometimes in the leaves of the Sybils; of whose prophecies (like those perhaps of *Nostradamus*; for the fragments now extant seem to be the invention of later times) there were some books in reputation in the time of the Roman republic: sometimes in the insignificant speeches of madmen, supposed to be possessed with a divine spirit, which possession they called enthusiasm; and these kinds of foretelling events, were accounted theomancy, or prophecy: sometimes in the aspect of the stars at their nativity; which was called horoscopy, and esteemed a part of judiciary astrology: sometimes in their own hopes and fears, called thumomancy, or presage: sometimes in the prediction of witches, that pretended conference with the dead; which is called necromancy, conjuring, and witchcraft; and is but juggling and confederate knavery: sometimes in the casual flight, or feeding of birds; called augury: sometimes in the entrails of a sacrificed beast; which was *aruspicina:* sometimes in dreams: sometimes in croaking of ravens, or chattering of birds: sometimes in the lineaments of the face; which was called metoposcopy; or by palmistry in the lines of the hand; in casual words, called *omina:* sometimes in monsters, or unusual accidents; as eclipses, comets, rare meteors, earthquakes, inundations, uncouth births, and the like, which they called *portenta,* and *ostenta,* because they thought them to portend, or foreshow some great calamity to come; sometimes, in mere lottery, as cross and pile; counting holes in a sieve; dipping of verses in *Homer,* and *Virgil;* and innumerable other such vain conceits. So easy are men to be drawn to believe any thing, from such men as have gotten credit with them; and can with gentleness, and dexterity, take hold of their fear, and ignorance.

And therefore the first founders, and legislators of commonwealths among the Gentiles, whose ends were only to keep the people in obedience, and peace, have in all places taken care; first, to imprint in their minds a belief, that those precepts which they gave concerning religion, might not be thought to proceed from their own device, but from the dictates of some god, or other spirit; or else that they themselves were of a higher nature than mere mortals, that their laws might the more easily be received: so *Numa Pompilius* pretended to receive the ceremonies he instituted amongst the Romans, from the nymph *Egeria:* and the first king and founder of the kingdom of *Peru,* pretended himself and his wife to be the children of the Sun: and *Mahomet,* to set up his new religion, pretended to have conferences with the Holy Ghost, in form of a dove. Secondly, they have had a care, to make it believed, that the same things were displeasing to the gods, which were forbidden by the laws. Thirdly, to prescribe ceremonies, supplications, sacrifices, and festivals, by which they were to believe, the anger of the gods might be appeased; and that ill success in war, great contagions of sickness, earthquakes, and each man's private misery, came from the anger of the gods, and their anger from the neglect of their worship, or the forgetting, or mistaking some point of the ceremonies required. And though amongst the ancient Romans, men were not forbidden to deny, that which in the poets is written of the pains, and pleasures after this life; which divers of great authority, and gravity in that state have in their *harangues* openly derided; yet that belief was always more cherished, than the contrary.

And by these, and such other institutions, they obtained in order to their end, (which was the peace of the commonwealth,) that the common people in their misfortunes, laying the fault on neglect, or error in their ceremonies, or on their own disobedience to the laws, were the less apt to mutiny against their governors. And being entertained with the pomp, and pastime of festivals, and public games, made in honour of the gods, needed nothing else but bread to keep them from discontent, murmuring, and commotion against the state. And therefore the Romans, that had conquered the greatest part of the then known world, made no scruple of tolerating any religion whatsoever in the city of *Rome* itself, unless it had something in it, that could not consist with their civil government; nor do we read, that any religion was there forbidden, but that of the Jews; who (being the peculiar kingdom of God) thought it unlawful to acknowledge subjection to any mortal king or state whatsoever. And thus you see how the religion of the Gentiles was a part of their policy.

But where God himself, by supernatural revelation, planted religion; there he also made to himself a peculiar kingdom; and gave laws, not only of behaviour towards himself, but also towards one another; and thereby in the kingdom of God, the policy, and laws civil, are a part of religion; and therefore the distinction of temporal, and spiritual domination, hath there no place. It is true, that God is king of all the earth: yet may he be king of a peculiar, and chosen nation. For there is no more incongruity therein, than that he that hath the general command of the whole army, should have withal a peculiar regiment, or company of his own. God is king of all the earth by his power: but of his chosen people, he is king by covenant. But to speak more largely of the kingdom of God, both by nature, and covenant, I have in the following discourse assigned another place.

From the propagation of religion, it is not hard to understand the causes of the resolution of the same into its first seeds, or principles; which are only an opinion of a deity, and powers invisible, and supernatural; that can never be so abolished out of human nature, but that new religions may again be made to spring out of them, by the culture of such men, as for such purpose are in reputation.

For seeing all formed religion, is founded at first, upon the faith which a multitude hath in some one person, whom they believe not only to be a wise man, and to labour to procure their happiness, but also to be a holy man, to whom God himself vouchsafeth to declare his will supernaturally; it followeth necessarily, when they that have the government of religion, shall come to have either the wisdom of those men, their sincerity, or their love suspected; or that they shall be unable to show any probable token of divine revelation; that the religion which they desire to uphold, must be suspected likewise; and (without the fear of the civil sword) contradicted and rejected.

That which taketh away the reputation of wisdom, in him that formeth a religion, or addeth to it when it is already formed, is the enjoining of a belief of contradictories: for both parts of a contradiction cannot possibly be true: and therefore to enjoin the belief of them, is an argument of ignorance; which detects the author in that; and discredits him in all things else he shall propound as from revelation supernatural: which revelation a man may indeed have of many things above, but of nothing against natural reason.

That which taketh away the reputation of sincerity, is the doing or saying of such things, as appear to be signs, that what they require other men to believe, is not believed by themselves; all which doings, or sayings are therefore called scandalous, because they be stumbling blocks, that make men to fall in the way of religion: as injustice, cruelty, profaneness, avarice, and luxury. For who can believe, that he that doth ordinarily such actions as proceed from any of these roots, believeth there is any such invisible power to be feared, as he affrighteth other men withal, for lesser faults?

That which taketh away the reputation of love, is the being detected of private ends: as when the belief they require of others, conduceth or seemeth to conduce to the acquiring of dominion, riches, dignity, or secure pleasure, to themselves only, or specially. For that which men reap benefit by to themselves, they are thought to do for their own sakes, and not for love of others.

Lastly, the testimony that men can render of divine calling, can be no other, than the operation of miracles; or true prophecy, (which also is a miracle;) or extraordinary felicity. And therefore, to those points of religion, which have been received from them that did such miracles; those that are added by such, as approve not their calling by some miracle, obtain no greater belief, than what the custom and laws of the places, in which they be educated, have wrought into them. For as in natural things, men of judgment require natural signs, and arguments; so in supernatural things, they require signs supernatural, (which are miracles,) before they consent inwardly, and from their hearts.

All which causes of the weakening of men's faith, do manifestly appear in the examples following. First, we have the example of the children of Israel; who when *Moses,* that had approved his calling to them by miracles, and by the happy conduct of them out of *Egypt,* was absent but 40 days, revolted from the worship of the true God, recommended to them by him; and setting up (*Exod.* 32. 1, 2.) a golden calf for their god, relapsed into the idolatry of the Egyptians; from whom they had been so lately delivered. And again, after *Moses, Aaron, Joshua,* and that generation which had seen the great works of God in Israel, (*Judges* 2. 11.) were dead; another generation arose, and served *Baal.* So that miracles failing, faith also failed.

Again, when the sons of *Samuel,* (1 *Sam.* 8. 3.) being constituted by their father judges in *Bersabee,* received bribes, and judged unjustly, the people of Israel refused any more to have God to be their king, in other manner than he was king of other people; and therefore cried out to Samuel, to choose them a king after the manner of the nations. So that justice failing, faith also failed: insomuch, as they deposed their God, from reigning over them.

And whereas in the planting of Christian religion, the oracles ceased in all parts of the Roman empire, and the number of Christians increased wonderfully every day, and in every place, by the preaching of the Apostles, and Evangelists; a great part of that success, may reasonably be attributed, to the contempt, into which the priests of the Gentiles of that time, had brought themselves, by their uncleanness, avarice, and juggling between princes. Also the religion of the church of *Rome,* was partly, for the same cause abolished in *England,* and many other parts of Christendom; insomuch, as the failing of virtue in the pastors, maketh faith fail in the people: and partly from bringing of the philosophy, and doctrine of *Aristotle* into religion, by the Schoolmen; from whence there arose so many contradictions, and absurdities, as brought the clergy into a reputation both of ignorance, and of fraudulent intention; and inclined people to revolt from them, either against the will of their own princes, as in *France* and *Holland;* or with their will, as in *England.*

Lastly, amongst the points by the church of *Rome* declared necessary for salvation, there be so many, manifestly to the advantage of the Pope, and of his spiritual subjects, residing in the territories of other Christian princes, that were it not for the mutual emulation of those princes, they might without war, or trouble, exclude all foreign authority, as easily as it has been excluded in *England.* For who is there that does not see, to whose benefit it conduceth, to have it believed, that a king hath not his authority from Christ, unless a bishop crown him? That a king, if he be a priest, cannot marry? That whether a prince be born in lawful marriage, or not, must be judged by authority from *Rome?* That subjects may be freed from their allegiance, if by the court of *Rome,* the king be judged an heretic? That a king (as *Chilperic* of *France*) may be deposed by a pope (as Pope *Zachary*) for no cause; and his kingdom given to one of his subjects? That the clergy and regulars, in what country soever, shall be exempt from the jurisdiction of their king, in cases criminal? Or who does not see, to whose profit redound the fees of private masses, and vales of purgatory; with other signs of private interest, enough to mortify the most lively faith, if (as I said) the civil magistrate, and custom did not more sustain it, than any opinion they have of the sanctity, wisdom, or probity of their teachers? So that I may attribute all the changes of religion in the world, to one and the same cause; and that is, unpleasing priests; and those not only amongst Catholics, but even in that church that hath presumed most of reformation.

CHAPTER 13
Of the Natural Condition of Mankind as Concerning Their Felicity, and Misery

Nature hath made men so equal, in the faculties of body, and mind; as that though there be found one man sometimes manifestly stronger in body, or of quicker mind than another; yet when all is reckoned together, the difference between man, and man, is not so considerable, as that one man can thereupon claim to himself any benefit, to which another may not pretend, as well as he. For as to the strength of body, the weakest has strength enough to kill the strongest, either by secret machination, or by confederacy with others, that are in the same danger with himself.

And as to the faculties of the mind, (setting aside the arts grounded upon words, and especially that skill of proceeding upon general, and infallible rules, called science; which very few have, and but in few things; as being not a native faculty, born with us; nor attained, (as prudence,) while we look after somewhat else,) I find yet a greater equality amongst men, than that of strength. For prudence, is but experience; which equal time, equally bestows on all men, in those things they equally apply themselves unto. That which may perhaps make such equality incredible, is but a vain conceit of one's own wisdom, which almost all men think they have in a greater degree, than the vulgar; that is, than all men but themselves, and a few others, whom by fame, or for concurring with themselves, they approve. For such is the nature of men, that howsoever they may acknowledge many others to be more witty, or more eloquent, or more learned; yet they will hardly believe there be many so wise as themselves: For they see their own wit at hand, and other men's at a distance. But this proveth rather that men are in that point equal, than unequal. For there is not ordinarily a greater sign of the equal distribution of any thing, than that every man is contented with his share.

From this equality of ability, ariseth equality of hope in the attaining of our ends. And therefore if any two men desire the same thing, which nevertheless they cannot both enjoy, they become enemies; and in the way to their end, (which is principally their own conservation, and sometimes their delectation only,) endeavour to destroy, or subdue one another. And from hence it comes to pass, that where an invader hath no more to fear, than another man's single power; if one plant, sow, build, or possess a convenient seat, others may probably be expected to come prepared with forces united, to dispossess, and deprive him, not only of the fruit of his labour, but also of his life, or liberty. And the invader again is in the like danger of another.

And from this diffidence of one another, there is no way for any man to secure himself, so reasonable, as anticipation; that is, by force, or wiles, to master the persons of all men he can, so long, till he see no other power great enough to endanger him: and this is no more than his own conservation requireth, and is generally allowed. Also because there be some, that taking pleasure in contemplating their own power in the acts of conquest, which they pursue farther than their security requires; if others, that otherwise would be glad to be at ease within modest bounds, should not by invasion increase their power, they would not be able, long time, by standing only on their defence, to subsist. And by consequence, such augmentation of dominion over men, being necessary to a man's conservation, it ought to be allowed him.

Again, men have no pleasure, (but on the contrary a great deal of grief) in keeping company, where there is no power able to over-awe them all. For every man looketh that his companion should value him, at the same rate he sets upon himself: and upon all signs of contempt, or undervaluing, naturally endeavours, as far as he dares (which amongst them that have no common power to keep them in quiet, is far enough to make them destroy each other), to extort a greater value from his contemners, by damage; and from others, by the example.

So that in the nature of man, we find three principal causes of quarrel. First, competition; secondly, diffidence; thirdly, glory.

The first, maketh men invade for gain; the second, for safety; and the third, for reputation. The first use violence, to make themselves masters of other men's persons, wives, children, and cattle; the second, to defend them; the third, for trifles, as a word, a smile, a different opinion, and any other sign of undervalue, either direct in their persons, or by reflection in their kindred, their friends, their nation, their profession, or their name.

Hereby it is manifest, that during the time men live without a common power to keep them all in awe, they are in that condition which is called war; and such a war, as is of every man, against every man. For WAR, consisteth not in battle only, or the act of fighting; but in a tract of time, wherein the will to contend by battle is sufficiently known: and therefore the notion of *time*, is to be considered in the nature of war; as it is in the nature of weather. For as the nature of foul weather, lieth not in a shower or two of rain; but in an inclination thereto of many days together: so the nature of war, consisteth not in actual fighting; but in the known disposition thereto, during all the time there is no assurance to the contrary. All other time is PEACE.

Whatsoever therefore is consequent to a time of war, where every man is enemy to every man; the same is consequent to the time, wherein men live without other security, than what their own strength, and their own invention shall furnish them withal. In such condition, there is no place for industry; because the fruit thereof is uncertain: and consequently no culture of the earth; no navigation, nor use of the commodities that may be imported by sea; no commodious building; no instruments of moving, and removing such things as require much force; no knowledge of the face of the earth; no account of time; no arts; no letters; no society; and which is worst of all, continual fear, and danger of violent death; and the life of man, solitary, poor, nasty, brutish, and short.

It may seem strange to some man, that has not well weighed these things; that nature should thus dissociate, and render men apt to invade, and destroy one another: and he may therefore, not trusting to this inference, made from the passions, desire perhaps to have the same confirmed by experience. Let him therefore consider with himself, when taking a journey, he arms himself, and seeks to go well accompanied; when going to sleep, he locks his doors; when even in his house he locks his chests; and this when he knows there be laws, and public officers, armed, to revenge all injuries shall be done him; what opinion he has of his fellow subjects, when he rides armed; of his fellow citizens, when he locks his doors; and of his children, and servants, when he locks his chests. Does he not there as much accuse mankind by his actions, as I do by my words? But neither of us accuse man's nature in it. The desires, and other passions of man, are in themselves no sin. No more are the actions, that proceed from those passions, till they know a law that forbids them: which till laws be made they cannot know: nor can any law be made, till they have agreed upon the person that shall make it.

It may peradventure be thought, there was never such a time, nor condition of war as this; and I believe it was never generally so, over all the world: but there are many places, where they live so now. For the savage people in many places of *America*, except the government of small families, the concord whereof dependeth on natural lust, have no government at all; and live at this day in that brutish manner, as I said before. Howsoever, it may be perceived what manner of life there would be, where there were no common power to fear; by the manner of life, which men that have formerly lived under a peacefull government, use to degenerate into, in a civil war.

But though there had never been any time, wherein particular men were in a condition of war one against another; yet in all times, kings, and persons of sovereign authority, because of their independency, are in continual jealousies, and in the state and posture of gladiators; having their weapons pointing, and their eyes fixed on one another; that is, their forts, garrisons, and guns upon the frontiers of their kingdoms; and continual spies upon their neighbours; which is a posture of war. But because they uphold thereby, the industry of their subjects; there does not follow from it, that misery, which accompanies the liberty of particular men.

To this war of every man against every man, this also is consequent; that nothing can be unjust. The notions of right and wrong, justice and injustice have there no place. Where there is no common power, there is no law: where no law, no injustice. Force, and fraud, are in war the two cardinal virtues. Justice, and injustice are none of the faculties neither of the body, nor mind. If they were, they might be in a man that were alone in the world, as well as his senses, and passions. They are qualities, that relate to men in society, not in solitude. It is consequent also to the same condition, that there be no propriety, no dominion, no *mine* and *thine* distinct; but only that to be every man's, that he can get; and for so long, as he can keep it. And thus much for the ill condition, which man by mere nature is actually placed in; though with a possibility to come out of it, consisting partly in the passions, partly in his reason.

The passions that incline men to peace, are fear of death; desire of such things as are necessary to commodious living; and a hope by their industry to obtain them. And reason suggesteth convenient articles of peace, upon which men may be drawn to agreement. These articles, are they, which otherwise are called the Laws of Nature: whereof I shall speak more particularly, in the two following chapters.

CHAPTER 14
Of the First and Second Natural Laws, and of Contracts

The RIGHT OF NATURE, which writers commonly call *jus naturale*, is the liberty each man hath, to use his own power, as he will himself, for the preservation of his own nature; that is to say, of his own life; and consequently, of doing any thing, which in his own judgment, and reason, he shall conceive to be the aptest means thereunto.

By LIBERTY, is understood, according to the proper signification of the word, the absence of external impediments: which impediments, may oft take away part of a man's power to do what he would; but cannot hinder him from using the power left him, according as his judgment, and reason shall dictate to him.

A LAW OF NATURE, (*lex naturalis,*) is a precept, or general rule, found out by reason, by which a man is forbidden to do that, which is destructive of his life, or taketh away the means of preserving the same; and to omit that, by which he thinketh it may be best preserved. For though they that speak of this subject, use to confound *jus*, and *lex, right* and *law;* yet they ought to be distinguished; because RIGHT, consisteth in liberty to do, or to forbear; whereas LAW, determineth, and bindeth to one of them: so that law, and right, differ as much, as obligation, and liberty; which in one and the same matter are inconsistent.

And because the condition of man, (as hath been declared in the precedent chapter) is a condition of war of every one against every one; in which case every one is governed by his own reason; and there is nothing he can make use of, that may not be a help unto him, in preserving his life against his enemies; it followeth, that in such a condition, every man has a right to every thing; even to one another's body. And therefore, as long as this natural right of every man to every thing endureth, there can be no security to any man, (how strong or wise soever he be,) of living out the time, which nature ordinarily alloweth men to live. And consequently it is a precept, or general rule of reason, *that every man, ought to endeavour peace, as far as he has hope of obtaining it; and when he cannot obtain it, that he may seek, and use, all helps, and advantages of war.* The first branch of which rule, containeth the first, and fundamental law of nature; which is, *to seek peace, and follow it.* The second, the sum of the right of nature; which is, *by all means we can, to defend ourselves.*

From this fundamental law of nature, by which men are commanded to endeavour peace, is derived this second law; *that a man be willing, when others are so too, as far-forth, as for peace, and defence of himself he shall think it necessary, to lay down this right to all things; and be contented with so much liberty against other men, as he would allow other men against himself.* For as long as every man holdeth this right, of doing any thing he liketh; so long are all men in the condition of war. But if other men will not lay down their right, as well as he; then there is no reason for any one, to divest himself of his: for that were to expose himself to prey, (which no man is bound to) rather than to dispose himself to peace. This is that law of the Gospel; *whatsoever you require that others should do to you, that do ye to them.* And that law of all men, *quod tibi fieri non vis, alteri ne feceris.*

To *lay down* a man's *right* to any thing, is to *divest* himself of the *liberty,* of hindering another of the benefit of his own right to the same. For he that renounceth, or passeth away his right, giveth not to any other man a right which he had not before; because there is nothing to which every man had not right by nature: but only standeth out of his way, that he may enjoy his own original right, without hindrance from him; not without hindrance from another. So that the effect which redoundeth to one man, by another man's defect of right, is but so much diminution of impediments to the use of his own right original.

Right is laid aside, either by simply renouncing it; or by transferring it to another. By *simply* RENOUNCING; when he cares not to whom the benefit thereof redoundeth. By TRANSFERRING; when he intendeth the benefit thereof to some certain person, or persons. And when a man hath in either manner abandoned, or granted away his right; then is he said to be OBLIGED, or BOUND, not to hinder those, to whom such right is granted, or abandoned, from the benefit of it: and that he *ought,* and it is his DUTY, not to make void that voluntary act of his own: and that such hindrance is INJUSTICE, and INJURY, as being *sine jure;* the right being before renounced, or transferred. So that *injury,* or *injustice,* in the controversies of the world, is somewhat like to that, which in the disputations of scholars is called *absurdity.* For as it is there called an absurdity, to contradict what one maintained in the beginning: so in the world, it is called injustice, and injury, voluntarily to undo that, which from the beginning he had voluntarily done. The way by which a man either simply renounceth, or transferreth his right, is a declaration, or signification, by some voluntary and sufficient sign, or signs, that he doth so renounce, or transfer; or hath so renounced, or transferred the same, to him that accepteth it. And these signs are either words only, or actions only; or (as it happeneth most often) both words, and actions. And the same are the BONDS, by which men are bound, and obliged: bonds, that have their strength, not from their own nature, (for nothing is more easily broken than a man's word,) but from fear of some evil consequence upon the rupture.

Whensoever a man transferreth his right, or renounceth it; it is either in consideration of some right reciprocally transferred to himself; or for some other good he hopeth for thereby. For it is a voluntary act: and of the voluntary acts of every man, the object is some *good to himself.* And therefore there be some rights, which no man can be understood by any words, or other signs, to have abandoned, or transferred. As first a man cannot lay down the right of resisting them, that assault him by force, to take away his life; because he cannot be understood to aim thereby, at any good to himself. The same may be said of wounds, and chains, and imprisonment; both because there is no benefit consequent to such patience; as there is to the patience of suffering another to be wounded, or imprisoned: as also because a man cannot tell, when he seeth men proceed against him by violence, whether they intend his death or not. And lastly the motive, and end for which this renouncing, and transferring of right is introduced, is nothing else but the security of a man's person, in his life, and in the means of so preserving life, as not to be weary of it. And therefore if a man by words, or other signs, seem to despoil himself of the end, for which those signs were intended; he is not to be understood as if he meant it, or that it was his will; but that he was ignorant of how such words and actions were to be interpreted.

The mutual transferring of right, is that which men call CONTRACT.

There is difference between transferring of right to the thing; and transferring, or tradition, that is, delivery of the thing it self. For the thing may be delivered together with the translation of the right; as in buying and selling with ready money; or exchange of goods, or lands: and it may be delivered some time after.

Again, one of the contractors, may deliver the thing contracted for on his part, and leave the other to perform his part at some determinate time after, and in the mean time be trusted; and then the contract on his part, is called PACT, or COVENANT: or both parts may contract now, to perform hereafter: in which cases, he that is to perform in time to come, being trusted, his performance is called *keeping of promise*, or faith; and the failing of performance (if it be voluntary) *violation of faith*.

When the transferring of right, is not mutual; but one of the parties transferreth, in hope to gain thereby friendship, or service from another, or from his friends; or in hope to gain the reputation of charity, or magnanimity; or to deliver his mind from the pain of compassion; or in hope of reward in heaven; this is not contract, but GIFT, FREE-GIFT, GRACE: which words signify one and the same thing.

Signs of contract, are either *express*, or *by inference*. Express, are words spoken with understanding of what they signify: and such words are either of the time *present*, or *past;* as, *I give, I grant, I have given, I have granted, I will that this be yours:* or of the future; as, *I will give, I will grant:* which words of the future are called PROMISE.

Signs by inference, are sometimes the consequence of words; sometimes the consequence of silence; sometimes the consequence of actions; sometimes the consequence of forbearing an action: and generally a sign by inference, of any contract, is whatsoever sufficiently argues the will of the contractor.

Words alone, if they be of the time to come, and contain a bare promise, are an insufficient sign of a free-gift and therefore not obligatory. For if they be of the time to come, as, *tomorrow I will give*, they are a sign I have not given yet, and consequently that my right is not transferred, but remaineth till I transfer it by some other act. But if the words be of the time present, or past, as, *I have given, or do give to be delivered tomorrow*, then is my tomorrow's right given away to day; and that by the virtue of the words, though there were no other argument of my will. And there is a great difference in the signification of these words, *volo hoc tuum esse cras,* and *cras dabo;* that is, between *I will that this be thine tomorrow,* and, *I will give it thee tomorrow:* for the word *I will,* in the former manner of speech, signifies an act of the will present; but in the latter, it signifies a promise of an act of the will to come: and therefore the former words, being of the present, transfer a future right; the latter, that be of the future, transfer nothing. But if there be other signs of the will to transfer a right, besides words; then, though the gift be free, yet may the right be understood to pass by words of the future: as if a man propound a prize to him that comes first to the end of a race, the gift is free; and though the words be of the future, yet the right passeth: for if he would not have his words so be understood, he should not have let them run.

In contracts, the right passeth, not only where the words are of the time present, or past, but also where they are of the future: because all contract is mutual translation, or change of right; and therefore he that promiseth only, because he hath already received the benefit for which he promiseth, is to be understood as if he intended the right should pass: for unless he had been content to have his words so understood, the other would not have performed his part first. And for that cause, in buying, and selling, and other acts of contract, a promise is equivalent to a covenant; and therefore obligatory.

He that performeth first in the case of a contract, is said to MERIT that which he is to receive by the performance of the other; and he hath it as *due.* Also when a prize is propounded to many, which is to be given to him only that winneth; or money is thrown amongst many, to be enjoyed by them that catch it; though this be a free gift; yet so to win, or so to catch, is to *merit,* and to have it as DUE. For the right is transferred in the propounding of the prize, and in throwing down the money; though it be not determined to whom, but by the event of the contention. But there is between these two sorts of merit, this difference, that in contract, I merit by virtue of my own power, and the contractor's need; but in this case of free gift, I am enabled to merit only by the benignity of the giver: in contract, I merit at the contractor's hand that he should depart with his right; in this case of gift, I merit not that the giver should part with his right; but that when he has parted with it, it should be mine, rather than another's. And this I think to be the meaning of that distinction of the Schools, between *meritum congrui,* and *meritum condigni.* For God Almighty, having promised Paradise to those men (hoodwinked with carnal desires,) that can walk through this world according to the precepts, and limits prescribed by him; they say, he that shall so walk, shall merit Paradise *ex congruo.* But because no man can demand a right to it, by his own righteousness, or any other power in himself, but by the free grace of God only; they say, no man can merit Paradise *ex condigno.* This I say, I think is the meaning of that distinction; but because disputers do not agree upon the signification of their own terms of art, longer than it serves their turn; I will not affirm any thing of their meaning: only this I say; when a gift is given indefinitely, as a prize to be contended for, he that winneth meriteth, and may claim the prize as due.

If a covenant be made, wherein neither of the parties perform presently, but trust one another; in the condition of mere nature, (which is a condition of war of every man against every man,) upon any reasonable suspicion, it is void: but if there be a common power set over them both, with right and force sufficient to compel performance, it is not void. For he that performeth first, has no assurance the other will perform after; because the bonds of words are too weak to bridle men's ambition, avarice, anger, and other passions, without the fear of some coercive power; which in the condition of mere nature, where all men are equal, and judges of the justness of their own fears, cannot possibly be supposed. And therefore he which performeth first, does but betray himself to his enemy; contrary to the right (he can never abandon) of defending his life, and means of living.

But in a civil estate, where there is a power set up to constrain those that would otherwise violate their faith, that fear is no more reasonable; and for that cause, he which by the covenant is to perform first, is obliged so to do.

The cause of fear, which maketh such a covenant invalid, must be always something arising after the covenant made; as some new fact, or other sign of the will not to perform: else it cannot make the covenant void. For that which could not hinder a man from promising, ought not to be admitted as a hindrance of performing.

He that transferreth any right, transferreth the means of enjoying it, as far as lieth in his power. As he that selleth land, is understood to transfer the herbage, and whatsoever grows upon it; nor can he that sells a mill turn away the stream that drives it. And they that give to a man the right of government in sovereignty, are understood to give him the right of levying money to maintain soldiers; and of appointing magistrates for the administration of justice.

To make covenants with brute beasts, is impossible; because not understanding our speech, they understand not, nor accept of any translation of right; nor can translate any right to another: and without mutual acceptation, there is no covenant.

To make covenant with God, is impossible, but by mediation of such as God speaketh to, either by revelation supernatural, or by his lieutenants that govern under him, and in his name: for otherwise we know not whether our covenants be accepted, or not. And therefore they that vow any thing contrary to any law of nature, vow in vain; as being a thing unjust to pay such vow. And if it be a thing commanded by the law of nature, it is not the vow, but the law that binds them.

The matter, or subject of a covenant, is always something that falleth under deliberation; (for to covenant, is an act of the will; that is to say an act, and the last act, of deliberation;) and is therefore always understood to be something to come; and which is judged possible for him that covenanteth, to perform.

And therefore, to promise that which is known to be impossible, is no covenant. But if that prove impossible afterwards, which before was thought possible, the covenant is valid, and bindeth, (though not to the thing it self,) yet to the value; or, if that also be impossible, to the unfeigned endeavour of performing as much as is possible: for to more no man can be obliged.

Men are freed of their covenants two ways; by performing; or by being forgiven. For performance, is the natural end of obligation; and forgiveness, the restitution of liberty; as being a retransferring of that right, in which the obligation consisted.

Covenants entered into by fear, in the condition of mere nature, are obligatory. For example, if I covenant to pay a ransom, or service for my life, to an enemy; I am bound by it. For it is a contract, wherein one receiveth the benefit of life; the other is to receive money, or service for it; and consequently, where no other law (as in the condition, of mere nature) forbiddeth the performance, the covenant is valid. Therefore prisoners of war, if trusted with the payment of their ransom, are obliged to pay it: and if a weaker prince, make a disadvantageous peace with a stronger, for fear; he is bound to keep it; unless (as hath been said before) there ariseth some new, and just cause of fear, to renew the war. And even in commonwealths, if I be forced to redeem myself from a thief by promising him money, I am bound to pay it, till the civil law discharge me. For whatsoever I may lawfully do without obligation, the same I may lawfully covenant to do through fear: and what I lawfully covenant, I cannot lawfully break.

A former covenant, makes void a later. For a man that hath passed away his right to one man today, hath it not to pass tomorrow to another: and therefore the later promise passeth no right, but is null.

A covenant not to defend myself from force, by force, is always void. For (as I have showed before) no man can transfer, or lay down his right to save himself from death, wounds, and imprisonment, (the avoiding whereof is the only end of laying down any right, and therefore the promise of not resisting force, in no covenant transferreth any right; nor is obliging. For though a man may covenant thus, *unless I do so, or so, kill me;* he cannot covenant thus, *unless I do so, or so, I will not resist you, when you come to kill me.* For man by nature chooseth the lesser evil, which is danger of death in resisting; rather than the greater, which is certain and present death in not resisting. And this is granted to be true by all men, in that they lead criminals to execution, and prison, with armed men, notwithstanding that such criminals have consented to the law, by which they are condemned.

A covenant to accuse one self, without assurance of pardon, is likewise invalid. For in the condition of nature, where every man is judge, there is no place for accusation: and in the civil state, the accusation is followed with punishment; which being force, a man is not obliged not to resist. The same is also true, of the accusation of those, by whose condemnation a man falls into misery; as of a father, wife, or benefactor. For the testimony of such an accuser, if it be not willingly given, is presumed to be corrupted by nature; and therefore not to be received: and where a man's testimony is not to be credited, he is not bound to give it. Also accusations upon torture, are not to be reputed as testimonies. For torture is to be used but as means of conjecture, and light, in the further examination, and search of truth: and what is in that case confessed, tendeth to the ease of him that is tortured, not to the informing of the torturers: and therefore ought not to have the credit of a sufficient testimony: for whether he deliver himself by true, or false accusation, he does it by the right of preserving his own life.

The force of words, being (as I have formerly noted) too weak to hold men to the performance of their covenants; there are in man's nature, but two imaginable helps to strengthen it. And those are either a fear of the consequence of breaking their word; or a glory, or pride in appearing not to need to break it. This latter is a generosity too rarely found to be presumed on, especially in the pursuers of wealth, command, or sensual pleasure; which are the greatest part of mankind. The passion to be reckoned upon, is fear; whereof there be two very general objects: one, the power of spirits invisible; the other, the power of those men they shall therein offend. Of these two, though the former be the greater power, yet the fear of the latter is commonly the greater fear. The fear of the former is in every man, his own religion: which hath place in the nature of man before civil society. The latter hath not so; at least not place enough, to keep men to their promises; because in the condition of mere nature, the inequality of power is not discerned, but by the event of battle. So that before the time of civil society, or in the interruption thereof by war, there is nothing can strengthen a covenant of peace agreed on, against the temptations of avarice, ambition, lust, or other strong desire, but the fear of that invisible power, which they every one worship as God; and fear as a revenger of their perfidy. All therefore that can be done between two men not subject to civil power, is to put one another to swear by the God he feareth: which *swearing*, or OATH, is a *form of speech, added to a promise; by which he that promiseth, signifieth, that unless he perform, he renounceth the mercy of his God, or calleth to him for vengeance on himself.* Such was the heathen form, *Let* Jupiter *kill me else, as I kill this beast.* So is our form, *I shall do thus, and thus, so help me God.* And this, with the rites and ceremonies, which every one useth in his own religion, that the fear of breaking faith might be the greater.

By this it appears, that an oath taken according to any other form, or rite, than his, that sweareth, is in vain; and no oath: and that there is no swearing by any thing which the swearer thinks not God. For though men have sometimes used to swear by their kings, for fear, or flattery; yet they would have it thereby understood, they attributed to them divine honour. And that swearing unnecessarily by God, is but prophaning of his name: and swearing by other things, as men do in common discourse, is not swearing, but an impious custom, gotten by too much vehemence of talking.

It appears also, that the oath adds nothing to the obligation. For a covenant, if lawful, binds in the sight of God, without the oath, as much as with it: if unlawful, bindeth not at all; though it be confirmed with an oath.

CHAPTER 15
Of Other Laws of Nature.

From that law of nature, by which we are obliged to transfer to another, such rights, as being retained, hinder the peace of mankind, there followeth a third; which is this, *that men perform their covenants made:* without which, covenants are in vain, and but empty words; and the right of all men to all things remaining, we are still in the condition of war.

And in this law of nature, consisteth the fountain and original of JUSTICE. For where no covenant hath preceded, there hath no right been transferred, and every man has right to every thing; and consequently, no action can be unjust. But when a covenant is made, then to break it is *unjust:* and the definition of INJUSTICE, is no other than *the not performance of covenant.* And whatsoever is not unjust, is *just.*

But because covenants of mutual trust, where there is a fear of not performance on either part, (as hath been said in the former chapter,) are invalid; though the original of justice be the making of covenants; yet injustice actually there can be none, till the cause of such fear be taken away; which while men are in the natural condition of war, cannot be done. Therefore before the names of just, and unjust can have place, there must be some coercive power, to compel men equally to the performance of their covenants, by the terror of some punishment, greater than the benefit they expect by the breach of their covenant; and to make good that propriety, which by mutual contract men acquire, in recompense of the universal right they abandon: and such power there is none before the erection of a common-wealth. And this is also to be gathered out of the ordinary definition of justice in the Schools: for they say, that *justice is the constant will of giving to every man his own.* And therefore where there is no *own,* that is, no propriety, there is no injustice; and where there is no coercive power erected, that is, where there is no commonwealth, there is no propriety; all men having right to all things: therefore where there is no commonwealth, there nothing is unjust. So that the nature of justice, consisteth in keeping of valid covenants: but the validity of covenants begins not but with the constitution of a civil power, sufficient to compel men to keep them: and then it is also that propriety begins.

The fool hath said in his heart, there is no such thing as justice; and sometimes also with his tongue; seriously alleging, that every man's conservation, and contentment, being committed to his own care, there could be no reason, why every man might not do what he thought conduced thereunto: and therefore also to make, or not make; keep, or not keep covenants, was not against reason, when it conduced to one's benefit. He does not therein deny, that there be covenants; and that they are sometimes broken, sometimes kept; and that such breach of them may be called injustice, and the observance of them justice: but he questioneth, whether injustice, taking away the fear of God, (for the same fool hath said in his heart there is no God,) may not sometimes stand with that reason, which dictateth to every man his own good; and particularly then, when it conduceth to such a benefit, as shall put a man in a condition, to neglect not only the dispraise, and revilings, but also the power of other men. The kingdom of God is gotten by violence: but what if it could be gotten by unjust violence? were it against reason so to get it, when it is impossible to receive hurt by it? and if it be not against reason, it is not against justice; or else justice is not to be approved for good. From such reasoning as this, successful wickedness hath obtained the name of virtue: and some that in all other things have disallowed the violation of faith; yet have allowed it, when it is for the getting of a kingdom. And the heathen that believed, that *Saturn* was deposed by his son *Jupiter,* believed nevertheless the same *Jupiter* to be the avenger of injustice: somewhat like to a piece of law in *Coke's Commentaries on Littleton;* where he says, if the right heir of the crown be attainted of treason; yet the crown shall descend to him, and *eo instante* the attainder be void: from which instances a man will be very prone to infer; that when the heir apparent of a kingdom, shall kill him that is in possession, though his father; you may call it injustice, or by what other name you will; yet it can never be against reason, seeing all the voluntary actions of men tend to the benefit of themselves; and those actions are most reasonable, that conduce most to their ends. This specious reasoning is nevertheless false.

For the question is not of promises mutual, where there is no security of performance on either side; as when there is no civil power erected over the parties promising; for such promises are no covenants: but either where one of the parties has performed already; or where there is a power to make him perform; there is the question whether it be against reason, that is, against the benefit of the other to perform, or not. And I say it is not against reason. For the manifestation whereof, we are to consider; first, that when a man doth a thing, which notwithstanding any thing can be foreseen, and reckoned on, tendeth to his own destruction, howsoever some accident which he could not expect, arriving may turn it to his benefit; yet such events do not make it reasonably or wisely done. Secondly, that in a condition of war, wherein every man to every man, for want of a common power to keep them all in awe, is an enemy, there is no man can hope by his own strength, or wit, to defend himself from destruction, without the help of confederates; where every one expects the same defence by the confederation, that any one else does: and therefore he which declares he thinks it reason to deceive those that help him, can in reason expect no other means of safety, than what can be had from his own single power. He therefore that breaketh his covenant, and consequently declareth that he thinks he may with reason do so, cannot be received into any society, that unite themselves for peace and defence, but by the error of them that receive him; nor when he is received, be retained in it, without seeing the danger of their error; which errors a man cannot reasonably reckon upon as the means of his security: and therefore if he be left, or cast out of society, he perisheth; and if he live in society, it is by the errors of other men, which he could not foresee, nor reckon upon; and consequently against the reason of his preservation; and so, as all men that contribute not to his destruction, forbear him only out of ignorance of what is good for themselves.

As for the instance of gaining the secure and perpetual felicity of heaven, by any way; it is frivolous: there being but one way imaginable; and that is not breaking, but keeping of covenant.

And for the other instance of attaining sovereignty by rebellion; it is manifest, that though the event follow, yet because it cannot reasonably be expected, but rather the contrary; and because by gaining it so, others are taught to gain the same in like manner, the attempt thereof is against reason. Justice therefore, that is to say, keeping of covenant, is a rule of reason, by which we are forbidden to do any thing destructive to our life; and consequently a law of nature.

There be some that proceed further; and will not have the law of nature, to be those rules which conduce to the preservation of man's life on earth; but to the attaining of an eternal felicity after death; to which they think the breach of covenant may conduce; and consequently be just and reasonable; (such are they that think it a work of merit to kill, or depose, or rebel against, the sovereign power constituted over them by their own consent.) But because there is no natural knowledge of man's estate after death; much less of the reward that is then to be given to breach of faith; but only a belief grounded upon other men's saying, that they know it supernaturally, or that they know those, that knew them, that knew others, that knew it supernaturally; breach of faith cannot be called a precept of reason, or nature.

Others, that allow for a law of nature, the keeping of faith, do nevertheless make exception of certain persons; as heretics, and such as use not to perform their covenant to others: and this also is against reason. For if any fault of a man, be sufficient to discharge our covenant made; the same ought in reason to have been sufficient to have hindered the making of it.

The names of just, and injust, when they are attributed to men, signify one thing; and when they are attributed to actions, another. When they are attributed to men, they signify conformity, or inconformity of manners, to reason. But when they are attributed to actions, they signify the conformity, or inconformity to reason, not of manners, or manner of life, but of particular actions. A just man therefore, is he that taketh all the care he can, that his actions may be all just: and an unjust man, is he that neglecteth it. And such men are more often in our language styled by the names of righteous, and unrighteous; than just, and unjust; though the meaning be the same. Therefore a righteous man, does not lose that title, by one, or a few unjust actions, that proceed from sudden passion, or mistake of things, or persons: nor does an unrighteous man, lose his character, for such actions, as he does, or forbears to do, for fear: because his will is not framed by the justice, but by the apparent benefit of what he is to do. That which gives to human actions the relish of justice, is a certain nobleness or gallantness of courage, (rarely found,) by which a man scorns to be beholding for the contentment of his life, to fraud, or breach of promise. This justice of the manners, is that which is meant, where justice is called a virtue; and injustice a vice.

But the justice of actions denominates men, not just, but *guiltless:* and the injustice of the same, (which is also called injury,) gives them but the name of *guilty.*

Again, the injustice of manners, is the disposition, or aptitude to do injury; and is injustice before it proceed to act; and without supposing any individual person injured. But the injustice of an action, (that is to say injury,) supposeth an individual person injured; namely him, to whom the covenant was made: and therefore many times the injury is received by one man, when the damage redoundeth to another. As when the master commandeth his servant to give money to a stranger; if it be not done, the injury is done to the master, whom he had before covenanted to obey; but the damage redoundeth to the stranger, to whom he had no obligation; and therefore could not injure him. And so also in commonwealths, private men may remit to one another their debts; but not robberies or other violences, whereby they are endamaged; because the detaining of debt, is an injury to themselves; but robbery and violence, are injuries to the person of the commonwealth.

Whatsoever is done to a man, conformable to his own will signified to the doer, is no injury to him. For if he that doeth it, hath not passed away his original right to do what he please, by some antecedent covenant, there is no breach of covenant; and therefore no injury done him. And if he have; then his will to have it done being signified, is a release of that covenant: and so again there is no injury done him.

Justice of actions, is by writers divided into *commutative,* and *distributive:* and the former they say consisteth in proportion arithmetical; the latter in proportion geometrical. Commutative therefore, they place in the equality of value of the things contracted for; and distributive, in the distribution of equal benefit, to men of equal merit. As if it were injustice to sell dearer than we buy; or to give more to a man than he merits. The value of all things contracted for, is measured by the appetite of the contractors: and therefore the just value, is that which they be contented to give. And merit, (besides that which is by covenant, where the performance on one part, meriteth the performance of the other part, and falls under justice commutative, not distributive,) is not due by justice; but is rewarded of grace only. And therefore this distinction, in the sense wherein it useth to be expounded, is not right. To speak properly, commutative justice, is the justice of a contractor; that is, a performance of covenant, in buying, and selling; hiring, and letting to hire; lending, and borrowing; exchanging, bartering, and other acts of contract.

And distributive justice, the justice of an arbitrator; that is to say, the act of defining what is just. Wherein, (being trusted by them that make him arbitrator,) if he perform his trust, he is said to distribute to every man his own: and this is indeed just distribution, and may be called, (though improperly,) distributive justice; but more properly equity; which also is a law of nature, as shall be shown in due place.

As justice dependeth on antecedent covenant; so does GRATITUDE depend on antecedent grace; that is to say, antecedent free-gift: and is the fourth law of nature; which may be conceived in this form, *that a man which receiveth benefit from another of mere grace, endeavour that he which giveth it, have no reasonable cause to repent him of his good will.* For no man giveth, but with intention of good to himself; because gift is voluntary; and of all voluntary acts, the object is to every man his own good; of which if men see they shall be frustrated, there will be no beginning of benevolence, or trust; nor consequently of mutual help; nor of reconciliation of one man to another; and therefore they are to remain still in the condition of *war;* which is contrary to the first and fundamental law of nature, which commandeth men to *seek peace.* The breach of this law, is called *ingratitude;* and hath the same relation to grace, that injustice hath to obligation by covenant.

A fifth law of nature, is COMPLAISANCE; that is to say, *that every man strive to accommodate himself to the rest.* For the understanding whereof, we may consider, that there is in men's aptness to society, a diversity of nature, rising from their diversity of affections; not unlike to that we see in stones brought together for building of an edifice. For as that stone which by the asperity, and irregularity of figure, takes more room from others, than itself fills; and for the hardness, cannot be easily made plain, and thereby hindereth the building, is by the builders cast away as unprofitable, and troublesome: so also, a man that by asperity of nature, will strive to retain those things which to himself are superfluous, and to others necessary; and for the stubbornness of his passions, cannot be corrected, is to be left, or cast out of society, as cumbersome thereunto. For seeing every man, not only by right, but also by necessity of nature, is supposed to endeavour all he can, to obtain that which is necessary for his conservation; he that shall oppose himself against it, for things superfluous, is guilty of the war that thereupon is to follow; and therefore doth that, which is contrary to the fundamental law of nature, which commandeth *to seek peace.* The observers of this law, may be called SOCIABLE, (the Latins call them *commodi;*) the contrary, *stubborn, insociable, froward, intractable.*

A sixth law of nature, is this, *that upon caution of the future time, a man ought to pardon the offences past of them that repenting, desire it.* For PARDON, is nothing but granting of peace; which though granted to them that persevere in their hostility, be not peace, but fear; yet not granted to them that give caution of the future time, is sign of an aversion to peace; and therefore contrary to the law of nature.

A seventh is, *that in revenges,* (that is, retribution of evil for evil,) *men look not at the greatness of the evil past, but the greatness of the good to follow.* Whereby we are forbidden to inflict punishment with any other design, than for correction of the offender, or direction of others. For this law is consequent to the next before it, that commandeth pardon, upon security of the future time. Besides, revenge without respect to the example, and profit to come, is a triumph, or glorying in the hurt of another, tending to no end; (for the end is always somewhat to come;) and glorying to no end, is vain-glory, and contrary to reason; and to hurt without reason, tendeth to the introduction of war; which is against the law of nature; and is commonly styled by the name of *cruelty.*

And because all signs of hatred, or contempt, provoke to fight; insomuch as most men choose rather to hazard their life, than not to be revenged; we may in the eighth place, for a law of nature, set down this precept, *that no man by deed, word, countenance, or gesture, declare hatred, or contempt of another.* The breach of which law, is commonly called *contumely.*

The question who is the better man, has no place in the condition of mere nature; where, (as has been shewn before,) all men are equal. The inequality that now is, has been introduced by the laws civil. I know that *Aristotle* in the first book of his

Politics, for a foundation of his doctrine, maketh men by nature, some more worthy to command, meaning the wiser sort, (such as he thought himself to be for his philosophy;) others to serve, (meaning those that had strong bodies, but were not philosophers as he;) as if master and servant were not introduced by consent of men, but by difference of wit: which is not only against reason; but also against experience. For there are very few so foolish, that had not rather govern themselves, than be governed by others: nor when the wise in their own conceit, contend by force, with them who distrust their own wisdom, do they always, or often, or almost at any time, get the victory. If nature therefore have made men equal, that equality is to be acknowledged: or if nature have made men unequal; yet because men that think themselves equal, will not enter into conditions of peace, but upon equal terms, such equality must be admitted. And therefore for the ninth law of nature, I put this, *that every man acknowledge other for his equal by nature.* The breach of this precept is *pride.*

On this law, dependeth another, *that at the entrance into conditions of peace, no man require to reserve to himself any right, which he is not content should be reserved to every one of the rest.* As it is necessary for all men that seek peace, to lay down certain rights of nature; that is to say, not to have liberty to do all they list: so is it necessary for man's life, to retain some; as right to govern their own bodies; enjoy air, water, motion, ways to go from place to place; and all things else without which a man cannot live, or not live well. If in this case, at the making of peace, men require for themselves, that which they would not have to be granted to others, they do contrary to the precedent law, that commandeth the acknowledgment of natural equality, and therefore also against the law of nature. The observers of this law, are those we call *modest,* and the breakers *arrogant* men. The Greeks call the violation of this law πλεονεξια; that is, a desire of more than their share.

Also if *a man be trusted to judge between man and man,* it is a precept of the law of nature, *that he deal equally between them.* For without that, the controversies of men cannot be determined but by war. He therefore that is partial in judgment, doth what in him lies, to deter men from the use of judges, and arbitrators; and consequently, (against the fundamental law of nature,) is the cause of war.

The observance of this law, from the equal distribution to each man, of that which in reason belongeth to him, is called EQUITY, and (as I have said before) distributive justice: the violation, *acception of persons,* προσωποληψία.

And from this followeth another law, *that such things as cannot be divided, be enjoyed in common, if it can be; and if the quantity of the thing permit, without stint; otherwise proportionably to the number of them that have right.* For otherwise the distribution is unequal, and contrary to equity.

But some things there be, that can neither be divided, nor enjoyed in common. Then, the law of nature, which prescribeth equity, requireth, *that the entire right; or else, (making the use alternate,) the first possession, be determined by lot.* For equal distribution, is of the law of nature; and other means of equal distribution cannot be imagined.

Of *lots* there be two sorts, *arbitrary,* and *natural.* Arbitrary, is that which is agreed on by the competitors: natural, is either *primogeniture,* (which the Greek calls κληρονομία, which signifies, *given by lot;*) or *first seizure.*

And therefore those things which cannot be enjoyed in common, nor divided, ought to be adjudged to the first possessor; and in some cases to the first-born, as acquired by lot.

It is also a law of nature, *that all men that mediate peace, be allowed safe conduct.* For the law that commandeth peace, as the *end,* commandeth intercession, as the *means;* and to intercession the means is safe conduct.

And because, though men be never so willing to observe these laws, there may nevertheless arise questions concerning a man's action; first, whether it were done, or not done; secondly, (if done,) whether against the law, or not against the law; the former whereof, is called a question *of fact;* the latter a question *of right;* therefore unless the parties to the question, covenant mutually to stand to the sentence of another, they are as far from peace as ever. This other, to whose sentence they submit, is called an ARBITRATOR. And therefore it is of the law of nature, *that they that are at controversy, submit their right to the judgment of an arbitrator.*

And seeing every man is presumed to do all things in order to his own benefit, no man is a fit arbitrator in his own cause: and if he were never so fit; yet equity allowing to each party equal benefit, if one be admitted to be judge, the other is to be admitted also; and so the controversy, that is, the cause of war, remains, against the law of nature.

For the same reason no man in any cause ought to be received for arbitrator, to whom greater profit, or honour, or pleasure apparently ariseth out of the victory of one party, than of the other: for he hath taken (though an unavoidable bribe, yet) a bribe; and no man can be obliged to trust him. And thus also the controversy, and the condition of war remaineth, contrary to the law of nature.

And in a controversy of *fact,* the judge being to give no more credit to one, than to the other, (if there be no other arguments,) must give credit to a third; or to a third and fourth; or more: for else the question is undecided, and left to force, contrary to the law of nature.

These are the laws of nature, dictating peace, for a means of the conservation of men in multitudes; and which only concern the doctrine of civil society. There be other things tending to the destruction of particular men; as drunkenness, and all other parts of intemperance; which may therefore also be reckoned amongst those things which the law of nature hath forbidden; but are not necessary to be mentioned, nor are pertinent enough to this place.

And though this may seem too subtle a deduction of the laws of nature, to be taken notice of by all men; whereof the most part are too busy in getting food, and the rest too negligent to understand; yet to leave all men inexcusable, they have been contracted into one easy sum, intelligible, even to the meanest capacity; and that is, *Do not that to another, which thou wouldest not have done to thyself;* which sheweth him, that he has no more to do in learning the laws of nature, but, when weighing the actions of other men with his own, they seem too heavy, to put them into the other part of the balance, and his own into their place, that his own passions, and self-love, may add nothing to the weight; and then there is none of these laws of nature that will not appear unto him very reasonable.

The laws of nature oblige *in foro interno;* that is to say, they bind to a desire they should take place: but *in foro externo;* that is, to the putting them in act, not always. For he that should be modest, and tractable, and perform all he promises, in such time, and place, where no man else should do so, should but make himself a prey to others, and procure his own certain ruin, contrary to the ground of all laws of nature, which tend to nature's preservation. And again, he that having sufficient security, that others shall observe the same laws towards him, observes them not himself, seeketh not peace, but war; and consequently the destruction of his nature by violence.

And whatsoever laws bind *in foro interno,* may be broken, not only by a fact contrary to the law, but also by a fact according to it, in case a man think it contrary. For though his action in this case, be according to the law; yet his purpose was against the law; which, where the obligation is *in foro interno,* is a breach.

The laws of nature are immutable and eternal; for injustice, ingratitude, arrogance, pride, iniquity, acception of persons, and the rest, can never be made lawful. For it can never be that war shall preserve life, and peace destroy it.

The same laws, because they oblige only to a desire, and endeavour, I mean an unfeigned and constant endeavour, are easy to be observed. For in that they require nothing but endeavour; he that endeavoureth their performance, fulfilleth them; and he that fulfilleth the law, is just.

And the science of them, is the true and only moral philosophy. For moral philosophy is nothing else but the science of what is *good,* and *evil,* in the conversation, and society of mankind. *Good,* and *evil,* are names that signify our appetites, and aversions; which in different tempers, customs, and doctrines of men, are different: and divers men, differ not only in their judgment, on the senses of what is pleasant, and unpleasant to the taste, smell, hearing, touch, and sight; but also of what is conformable, or disagreeable to reason, in the actions of common life. Nay, the same man, in divers times, differs from himself; and one time praiseth, that is, calleth good, what another time he dispraiseth, and calleth evil: from whence arise disputes, controversies, and at last war. And therefore so long a man is in the condition of mere nature, (which is a condition of war,) as private appetite is the measure of good, and evil: and consequently all men agree on this, that peace is good, and therefore also the way, or means of peace, which, (as I have shewed before) are *justice, gratitude, modesty, equity, mercy,* and the rest of the laws of nature, are good; that is to say, *moral virtues;* and their contrary *vices,* evil. Now the science of virtue and vice, is moral philosophy; and therefore the true doctrine of the laws of nature, is the true moral philosophy. But the writers of moral philosophy, though they acknowledge the same virtues and vices; yet not seeing wherein consisted their goodness; nor that they come to be praised, as the means of peaceable, sociable, and comfortable living; place them in a mediocrity of passions: as if not the cause, but the degree of daring, made fortitude; or not the cause, but the quantity of a gift, made liberality.

These dictates of reason, men use to call by the name of laws; but improperly: for they are but conclusions, or theorems concerning what conduceth to the conservation and defence of themselves; whereas law, properly, is the word of him, that by right hath command over others. But yet if we consider the same theorems, as delivered in the word of God, that by right commandeth all things; then are they properly called laws.

CHAPTER 16
Of Persons, Authors, and Things Personated

A person, is he, *whose words or actions are considered, either as his own, or as representing the words or actions of another man, or of any other thing to whom they are attributed, whether truly or by fiction.*

When they are considered as his own, then is he called a *natural person:* and when they are considered as representing the words and actions of another, then is he a *feigned* or *artificial person.*

The word person is Latin: instead whereof the Greeks have πρόσωπον, which signifies the *face,* as *persona* in Latin signifies the *disguise,* or *outward appearance* of a man, counterfeited on the stage; and sometimes more particularly that part of it, which disguiseth the face, as a mask or vizard: and from the stage, hath been translated to any representer of speech and action, as well in tribunals, as theatres. So that a *person,* is the same that an *actor* is, both on the stage and in common conversation; and to *personate,* is to *act,* or *represent* himself, or another; and he that acteth another, is said to bear his person, or act in his name; (in which sense Cicero useth it where he says, *Unus sustineo tres personas; mei, adversarii, et judicis,* I bear three persons; my own, my adversary's, and the judge's;) and is called in divers occasions, diversly; as a *representer,* or *representative,* a *lieutenant,* a *vicar,* an *attorney,* a *deputy,* a *procurator,* an *actor,* and the like.

Of persons artificial, some have their words and actions *owned* by those whom they represent. And then the person is the *actor;* and he that owneth his words and actions, is the AUTHOR: in which case the actor acteth by authority. For that which in speaking of goods and possessions, is called an *owner,* and in Latin *dominus,* in Greek κύριος; speaking of actions, is called author. And as the right of possession, is called dominion; so the right of doing any action, is called AUTHORITY. So that by authority, is always understood a right of doing any act: and *done by authority,* done by commission, or licence from him whose right it is.

From hence it followeth, that when the actor maketh a covenant by authority, he bindeth thereby the author, no less than if he had made it himself; and no less subjecteth him to all the consequences of the same. And therefore all that hath been said formerly, (*chap.* 14) of the nature of covenants between man and man in their natural capacity, is true also when they are made by their actors, representers, or procurators, that have authority from them, so far forth as is in their commission, but no farther.

And therefore he that maketh a covenant with the actor, or representer, not knowing the authority he hath, doth it at his own peril. For no man is obliged by a covenant, whereof he is not author; nor consequently by a covenant made against, or beside the authority he gave.

When the actor doth any thing against the law of nature by command of the author, if he be obliged by former covenant to obey him, not he, but the author breaketh the law of nature: for though the action be against the law of nature; yet it is not his: but contrarily, to refuse to do it, is against the law of nature, that forbiddeth breach of covenant.

And he that maketh a covenant with the author, by mediation of the actor, not knowing what authority he hath, but only takes his word; in case such authority be not made manifest unto him upon demand, is no longer obliged: for the covenant made with the author, is not valid, without his counter-assurance. But if he that so covenanteth, knew beforehand he was to expect no other assurance, than the actor's word; then is the covenant valid; because the actor in this case maketh himself the author. And therefore, as when the authority is evident, the covenant obligeth the author, not the actor; so when the authority is feigned, it obligeth the actor only; there being no author but himself.

There are few things, that are incapable of being represented by fiction. Inanimate things, as a church, an hospital, a bridge, may be personated by a rector, master, or overseer. But things inanimate, cannot be authors, nor therefore give authority to their actors: yet the actors may have authority to procure their maintenance, given them by those that are owners, or governors of those things. And therefore, such things cannot be personated, before there be some state of civil government.

Likewise children, fools, and madmen that have no use of reason, may be personated by guardians, or curators; but can be no authors, (during that time) of any action done by them, longer than (when they shall recover the use of reason) they shall judge the same reasonable. Yet during the folly, he that hath right of governing them, may give authority to the guardian. But this again has no place but in a state civil, because before such estate, there is no dominion of persons.

An idol, or mere figment of the brain, may be personated; as were the gods of the heathen; which by such officers as the state appointed, were personated, and held possessions, and other goods, and rights, which men from time to time dedicated, and consecrated unto them. But idols cannot be authors: for an idol is nothing. The authority proceeded from the state: and therefore before introduction of civil government, the gods of the heathen could not be personated.

The true God may be personated. As he was; first, by Moses; who governed the Israelites, (that were not his, but God's people,) not in his own name, with *hoc dicit Moses;* but in God's name, with *hoc dicit Dominus.* Secondly, by the Son of man, his own Son, our blessed Saviour Jesus Christ, that came to reduce the Jews, and induce all nations into the kingdom of his father; not as of himself, but as sent from his father. And thirdly, by the Holy Ghost, or Comforter, speaking, and working in the Apostles: which Holy Ghost, was a Comforter that came not of himself; but was sent, and proceeded from them both.

A multitude of men, are made *one* person, when they are by one man, or one person, represented; so that it be done with the consent of every one of that multitude in particular. For it is the *unity* of the representer, not the *unity* of the represented, that maketh the person *one.* And it is the representer that beareth the person, and but one person: and *unity,* cannot otherwise be understood in multitude.

And because the multitude naturally is not *one,* but *many;* they cannot be understood for one; but many authors, of every thing their representative saith, or doth in their name; every man giving their common representer, authority from himself in particular; and owning all the actions the representer doth, in case they give him authority without stint: otherwise, when they limit him in what, and how far he shall represent them, none of them owneth more, than they gave him commission to act.

And if the representative consist of many men, the voice of the greater number, must be considered as the voice of them all. For if the lesser number pronounce (for example) in the affirmative, and the greater in the negative, there will be negatives more than enough to destroy the affirmatives; and thereby the excess of negatives, standing uncontradicted, are the only voice the representative hath.

And a representative of even number, especially when the number is not great, whereby the contradictory voices are oftentimes equal, is therefore oftentimes mute, and incapable of action. Yet in some cases contradictory voices equal in number, may determine a question; as in condemning, or absolving, equality of votes, even in that they condemn not, do absolve; but not on the contrary condemn, in that they absolve not. For when a cause is heard; not to condemn, is to absolve: but on the contrary, to say that not absolving, is condemning, is not true. The like it is in a deliberation of executing presently, or deferring till another time: for when the voices are equal, the not decreeing execution, is a decree of dilation.

Or if the number be odd, as three, or more, (men, or assemblies;) whereof every one has by a negative voice, authority to take away the effect of all the affirmative voices of the rest, this number is no representative; because by the diversity of opinions, and interests of men, it becomes oftentimes, and in cases of the greatest consequence, a mute person, and unapt, as for many things else, so for the government of a multitude, especially in time of war.

Of authors there be two sorts. The first simply so called; which I have before defined to be him, that owneth the action of another simply. The second is he, that owneth an action, or covenant of another conditionally; that is to say, he undertaketh to do it, if the other doth it not, at, or before a certain time. And these authors conditional, are generally called SURETIES, in Latin *fidejussores*, and *sponsores;* and particularly for debt, *praedes;* and for appearance before a judge, or magistrate, *vades.*

PART 2
OF COMMONWEALTH

CHAPTER 17
Of the Causes, Generation, and Definition of a Commonwealth

The final cause, end, or design of men, (who naturally love liberty, and dominion over others,) in the introduction of that restraint upon themselves, (in which we see them live in commonwealths,) is the foresight of their own preservation, and of a more contented life thereby; that is to say, of getting themselves out from that miserable condition of war, which is necessarily consequent (as hath been shown), to, the natural passions of men, when there is no visible power to keep them in awe, and tie them by fear of punishment to the performance of their covenants, and observation of those laws of nature set down in the fourteenth and fifteenth chapters.

For the laws of nature (as *justice, equity, modesty, mercy,* and (in sum) *doing to others, as we would be done to,*) of themselves, without the terror of some power, to cause them to be observed, are contrary to our natural passions, that carry us to partiality, pride, revenge, and the like. And covenants, without the sword, are but words, and of no strength to secure a man at all. Therefore notwithstanding the laws of nature, (which every one hath then kept, when he has the will to keep them, when he can do it safely,) if there be no power erected, or not great enough for our security; every man will, and may lawfully rely on his own strength and art, for caution against all other men. And in all places, where men have lived by small families, to rob and spoil one another, has been a trade, and so far from being reputed against the law of nature, that the greater spoils they gained, the greater was their honour; and men observed no other laws therein, but the laws of honour; that is, to abstain from cruelty, leaving to men their lives, and instruments of husbandry. And as small families did then; so now do cities and kingdoms which are but greater families (for their own security) enlarge their dominions, upon all pretences of danger, and fear of invasion, or assistance that may be given to invaders, endeavour as much as they can, to subdue, or weaken their neighbours, by open force, and secret arts, for want of other caution, justly; and are remembered for it in after ages with honour.

Nor is it the joining together of a small number of men, that gives them this security; because in small numbers, small additions on the one side or the other, make the advantage of strength so great, as is sufficient to carry the victory; and therefore gives encouragement to an invasion. The multitude sufficient to confide in for our security, is not determined by any certain number, but by comparison with the enemy we fear; and is then sufficient, when the odds of the enemy is not of so visible and conspicuous moment, to determine the event of war, as to move him to attempt.

And be there never so great a multitude; yet if their actions be directed according to their particular judgments, and particular appetites, they can expect thereby no defence, nor protection, neither against a common enemy, nor against the injuries of one another. For being distracted in opinions concerning the best use and application of their strength, they do not help, but hinder one another; and reduce their strength by mutual opposition to nothing: whereby they are easily, not only subdued by a very few that agree together; but also when there is no common enemy, they make war upon each other, for their particular interests. For if we could suppose a great multitude of men to consent in the observation of justice, and other laws of nature, without a common power to keep them all in awe; we might as well suppose all mankind to do the same; and then there neither would be, nor need to be any civil government, or commonwealth at all; because there would be peace without subjection.

Nor is it enough for the security, which men desire should last all the time of their life, that they be governed, and directed by one judgment, for a limited time; as in one battle, or one war. For though they obtain a victory by their unanimous endeavour against a foreign enemy; yet afterwards, when either they have no common enemy, or he that by one part is held for an enemy, is by another part held for a friend, they must needs by the difference of their interests dissolve, and fall again into a war amongst themselves.

It is true, that certain living creatures, as bees, and ants, live sociably one with another, (which are therefore by *Aristotle* numbered amongst political creatures;) and yet have no other direction, than their particular judgments and appetites; nor speech, whereby one of them can signify to another, what he thinks expedient for the common benefit: and therefore some man may perhaps desire to know, why mankind cannot do the same. To which I answer,

First, that men are continually in competition for honour and dignity, which these creatures are not; and consequently amongst men there ariseth on that ground, envy and hatred, and finally war; but amongst these not so.

Secondly, that amongst these creatures, the common good differeth not from the private; and being by nature inclined to their private, they procure thereby the common benefit. But man, whose joy consisteth in comparing himself with other men, can relish nothing but what is eminent.

Thirdly, that these creatures, having not, (as man) the use of reason, do not see, nor think they see any fault, in the administration of their common business; whereas amongst men, there are very many, that think themselves wiser, and abler to govern the public, better than the rest; and these strive to reform and innovate, one this way, another that way; and thereby bring it into distraction and civil war.

Fourthly, that these creatures, though they have some use of voice, in making known to one another their desires, and other affections; yet they want that art of words, by which some men can represent to others, that which is good, in the likeness of evil; and evil, in the likeness of good; and augment, or diminish the apparent greatness of good and evil; discontenting men, and troubling their peace at their pleasure.

Fifthly, irrational creatures cannot distinguish between *injury*, and *damage;* and therefore as long as they be at ease, they are not offended with their fellows: whereas man is then most troublesome, when he is most at ease: for then it is that he loves to shew his wisdom, and control the actions of them that govern the commonwealth.

Lastly, the agreement of these creatures is natural; that of men, is by covenant only, which is artificial: and therefore it is no wonder if there be somewhat else required (besides covenant) to make their agreement constant and lasting; which is a common power, to keep them in awe, and to direct their actions to the common benefit.

The only way to erect such a common power, as may be able to defend them from the invasion of foreigners, and the injuries of one another, and thereby to secure them in such sort, as that by their own industry, and by the fruits of the earth, they may nourish themselves and live contentedly; is, to confer all their power and strength upon one man, or upon one assembly of men, that may reduce all their wills, by plurality of voices, unto one will: which is as much as to say, to appoint one man, or assembly of men, to bear their person; and every one to own, and acknowledge himself to be author of whatsoever he that so beareth their person, shall act, or cause to be acted, in those things which concern the common peace and safety; and therein to submit their wills, every one to his will, and their judgments, to his judgment. This is more than consent, or concord; it is a real unity of them all, in one and the same person, made by covenant of every man with every man, in such manner, as if every man should say to every man, *I authorise and give up my right of governing myself, to this man, or to this assembly of men, on this condition, that thou give up thy right to him, and authorize all his actions in like manner.* This done, the multitude so united in one person, is called a COMMONWEALTH, in Latin CIVITAS. This is the generation of that great LEVIATHAN, or rather (to speak more reverently) of that *mortal god,* to which we owe under the *immortal God,* our peace and defence. For by this authority, given him by every particular man in the commonwealth, he hath the use of so much power and strength conferred on him, that by terror thereof, he is enabled to form the wills of them all, to peace at home, and mutual aid against their enemies abroad. And in him consisteth the essence of the commonwealth; which (to define it,) is *one person, of whose acts a great multitude, by mutual covenants one with another, have made themselves every one the author, to the end he may use the strength and means of them all, as he shall think expedient, for their peace and common defence.*

And he that carrieth this person, is called SOVEREIGN, and said to have sovereign power; and every one besides, his SUBJECT.

The attaining to this sovereign power, is by two ways. One, by natural force; as when a man maketh his children, to submit themselves, and their children to his government, as being able to destroy them if they refuse; or by war subdueth his enemies to his will, giving them their lives on that condition. The other, is when men agree amongst themselves, to submit to some man, or assembly of men, voluntarily, on confidence to be protected by him against all others. This latter, may be called a political commonwealth, or commonwealth by *institution;* and the former, a commonwealth by *acquisition.* And first, I shall speak of a commonwealth by institution.

CHAPTER 18

Of the Rights of Sovereigns by Institution

A *commonwealth* is said to be *instituted,* when a *multitude* of men do agree, and *covenant, every one, with every one,* that to whatsoever *man,* or *assembly of men,* shall be given by the major part, the *right* to *present* the person of them all, (that is to say, to be their *representative;*) every one, as well he that *voted for it,* as he that *voted against it,* shall *authorize* all the actions and judgments, of that man, or assembly of men, in the same manner, as if they were his own, to the end, to live peaceably amongst themselves, and be protected against other men.

From this institution of a commonwealth are derived all the *rights,* and *faculties* of him, or them, on whom the sovereign power is conferred by the consent of the people assembled.

First, because they covenant, it is to be understood, they are not obliged by former covenant to any thing repugnant hereunto. And consequently they that have already instituted a commonwealth, being thereby bound by covenant, to own the actions, and judgments of one, cannot lawfully make a new covenant, amongst themselves, to be obedient to any other, in any thing whatsoever, without his permission. And therefore, they that are subjects to a monarch, cannot without his leave cast off monarchy, and return to the confusion of a disunited multitude; nor transfer their person from him that beareth it, to another man, or other assembly of men: for they are bound, every man to every man, to own, and be reputed author of all, that he that already is their sovereign, shall do, and judge fit to be done: so that any one man dissenting, all the rest should break their covenant made to that man, which is injustice: and they have also every man given the sovereignty to him that beareth their person; and therefore if they depose him, they take from him that which is his own, and so again it is injustice. Besides, if he that attempteth to depose his sovereign, be killed, or punished by him for such attempt, he is author of his own punishment, as being by the institution, author of all his sovereign shall do: and because it is injustice for a man to do any thing, for which he may be punished by his own authority, he is also upon that title, unjust. And whereas some men have pretended for their disobedience to their sovereign, a new covenant, made, not with men, but with God; this also is unjust: for there is no covenant with God, but by mediation of somebody that representeth God's person; which none doth but God's lieutenant, who hath the sovereignty under God. But this pretence of covenant with God, is so evident a lie, even in the pretenders' own consciences, that it is not only an act of an unjust, but also of a vile, and unmanly disposition.

Secondly, because the right of bearing the person of them all, is given to him they make sovereign, by covenant only of one to another, and not of him to any of them; there can happen no breach of covenant on the part of the sovereign; and consequently none of his subjects, by any pretence of forfeiture, can be freed from his subjection. That he which is made sovereign maketh no covenant with his subjects beforehand, is manifest; because either he must make it with the whole multitude, as one party to the covenant; or he must make a several covenant with every man. With the whole, as one party, it is impossible; because as yet they are not one person: and if he make so many several covenants as there be men, those covenants after he hath the sovereignty are void, because what act soever can be pretended by any one of them for breach thereof, is the act both of himself, and of all the rest, because done in the person, and by the right of every one of them in particular. Besides, if any one, or more of them, pretend a breach of the covenant made by the sovereign at his institution; and others, or one other of his subjects, or himself alone, pretend there was no such breach, there is in this case, no judge to decide the controversy; it returns therefore to the sword again; and every man recovereth the right of protecting himself by his own strength, contrary to the design they had in the institution. It is therefore in vain to grant sovereignty by way of precedent covenant. The opinion that any monarch receiveth his power by covenant, that is to say, on condition, proceedeth from want of understanding this easy truth, that covenants being but words and breath, have no force to oblige, contain, constrain, or protect any man, but what it has from the public sword; that is, from the untied hands of that man, or assembly of men that hath the sovereignty, and whose actions are avouched by them all, and performed by the strength of them all, in him united. But when an assembly of men is made sovereign; then no man imagineth any such covenant to have passed in the institution; for no man is so dull as to say, for example, the people of Rome made a covenant with the Romans, to hold the sovereignty on such or such conditions; which not performed, the Romans might lawfully depose the Roman people. That men see not the reason to be alike in a monarchy, and in a popular government, proceedeth from the ambition of some, that are kinder to the government of an assembly, whereof they may hope to participate, than of monarchy, which they despair to enjoy.

Thirdly, because the major part hath by consenting voices declared a sovereign; he that dissented must now consent with the rest; that is, be contented to avow all the actions he shall do, or else justly be destroyed by the rest. For if he voluntarily entered into the congregation of them that were assembled, he sufficiently declared thereby his will, (and therefore tacitly covenanted) to stand to what the major part should ordain: and therefore if he refuse to stand thereto, or make protestation against any of their decrees, he does contrary to his covenant, and therefore unjustly. And whether he be of the congregation, or not; and whether his consent be asked, or not, he must either submit to their decrees, or be left in the condition of war he was in before; wherein he might without injustice be destroyed by any man whatsoever.

Fourthly, because every subject is by this institution author of all the actions, and judgments of the sovereign instituted; it follows, that whatsoever he doth, it can be no injury to any of his subjects; nor ought he to be by any of them accused of injustice. For he that doth any thing by authority from another, doth therein no injury to him by whose authority he acteth: but by this institution of a commonwealth, every particular man is author of all the sovereign doth; and consequently he that complaineth of injury from his sovereign, complaineth of that whereof he himself is author; and therefore ought not to accuse any man but himself; no nor himself of injury; because to do injury to one's self, is impossible. It is true that they that have sovereign power, may commit iniquity; but not injustice, or injury in the proper signification.

Fifthly, and consequently to that which was said last, no man that hath sovereign power can justly be put to death, or otherwise in any manner by his subjects punished. For seeing every subject is author of the actions of his sovereign; he punisheth another, for the actions committed by himself.

And because the end of this institution, is the peace and defence of them all; and whosoever has right to the end, has right to the means; it belongeth of right, to whatsoever man, or assembly that hath the sovereignty, to be judge both of the means of peace and defence; and also of the hindrances, and disturbances of the same; and to do whatsoever he shall think necessary to be done, both beforehand, for the preserving of peace and security, by prevention of discord at home, and hostility from abroad; and, when peace and security are lost, for the recovery of the same. And therefore,

Sixthly, it is annexed to the sovereignty, to be judge of what opinions and doctrines are averse, and what conducing to peace; and consequently, on what occasions, how far, and what, men are to be trusted withal, in speaking to multitudes of people; and who shall examine the doctrines of all books before they be published. For the actions of men proceed from their opinions; and in the well-governing of opinions, consisteth the well-governing of men's actions, in order to their peace, and concord. And though in matter of doctrine, nothing ought to be regarded but the truth; yet this is not repugnant to regulating of the same by peace. For doctrine repugnant to peace, can no more be true, than peace and concord can be against the law of nature. It is true, that in a commonwealth, where by the negligence, or unskilfulness of governors, and teachers, false doctrines are by time generally received; the contrary truths may be generally offensive: Yet the most sudden, and rough busling in of a new truth, that can be, does never break the peace, but only sometimes awake the war. For those men that are so remissly governed, that they dare take up arms, to defend, or introduce an opinion, are still in war; and their condition not peace, but only a cessation of arms for fear of one another; and they live as it were, in the precincts of battle continually. It belongeth therefore to him that hath the sovereign power, to be judge, or constitute all judges of opinions and doctrines, as a thing necessary to peace; thereby to prevent discord and civil war.

Seventhly, is annexed to the sovereignty, the whole power of prescribing the rules, whereby every man may know, what goods he may enjoy, and what actions he may do, without being molested by any of his fellow-subjects; and this is it men call *propriety*. For before constitution of sovereign power (as hath already been shown) all men had right to all things; which necessarily causeth war: and therefore this propriety, being necessary to peace, and depending on sovereign power, is the act of that power, in order to the public peace. These rules of propriety (or *meum* and *tuum*) and of *good, evil, lawful,* and *unlawful* in the actions of subjects, are the civil laws; that is to say, the laws of each commonwealth in particular; though the name of civil law be now restrained to the ancient civil laws of the city of *Rome;* which being the head of a great part of the world, her laws at that time were in these parts the civil law.

Eighthly, is annexed to the sovereignty, the right of judicature; that is to say, of hearing and deciding all controversies, which may arise concerning law, either civil, or natural; or concerning fact. For without the decision of controversies, there is no protection of one subject, against the injuries of another; the laws concerning *meum* and *tuum* are in vain; and to every man remaineth, from the natural and necessary appetite of his own conservation, the right of protecting himself by his private strength, which is the condition of war; and contrary to the end for which every commonwealth is instituted.

Ninthly, is annexed to the sovereignty, the right of making war and peace with other nations, and commonwealths; that is to say, of judging when it is for the public good, and how great forces are to be assembled, armed, and paid for that end; and to levy money upon the subjects, to defray the expenses thereof. For the power by which the people are to be defended, consisteth in their armies; and the strength of an army, in the union of their strength under one command; which command the sovereign instituted, therefore hath; because the command of the *militia*, without other institution, maketh him that hath it sovereign. And therefore whosoever is made general of an army, he that hath the sovereign power is always generalissimo.

Tenthly, is annexed to the sovereignty, the choosing of all counsellors, ministers, magistrates, and officers, both in peace, and war. For seeing the sovereign is charged with the end, which is the common peace and defence, he is understood to have power to use such means, as he shall think most fit for his discharge.

Eleventhly, to the sovereign is committed the power of rewarding with riches, or honour; and of punishing with corporal, or pecuniary punishment, or with ignominy every subject according to the law he hath formerly made; or if there be no law made, according as he shall judge most to conduce to the encouraging of men to serve the commonwealth, or deterring of them from doing disservice to the same.

Lastly, considering what values men are naturally apt to set upon themselves; what respect they look for from others; and how little they value other men; from whence continually arise amongst them, emulation, quarrels, factions, and at last war, to the destroying of one another, and diminution of their strength against a common enemy; it is necessary that there be laws of honour, and a public rate of the worth of such men as have deserved, or are able to deserve well of the commonwealth; and that there be force in the hands of some or other, to put those laws in execution. But it hath already been shown, that not only the whole *militia*, or forces of the commonwealth; but also the judicature of all controversies, is annexed to the sovereignty. To the sovereign therefore it belongeth also to give titles of honour; and to appoint what order of place, and dignity, each man shall hold; and what signs of respect, in public or private meetings, they shall give to one another.

These are the rights, which make the essence of sovereignty; and which are the marks, whereby a man may discern in what man, or assembly of men, the sovereign power is placed, and resideth. For these are incommunicable, and inseparable. The power to coin money; to dispose of the estate and persons of infant heirs; to have praeemption in markets; and all other statute prerogatives, may be transferred by the sovereign; and yet the power to protect his subjects be retained. But if he transfer the *militia*, he retains the judicature in vain, for want of execution of the laws: or if he grant away the power of raising money; the *militia* is in vain: or if he give away the government of doctrines, men will be frighted into rebellion with the fear of spirits. And so if we consider any one of the said rights, we shall presently see, that the holding of all the rest will produce no effect, in the conservation of peace and justice, the end for which all commonwealths are instituted. And this division is it, whereof it is said, *a kingdom divided in itself cannot stand:* for unless this division precede, division into opposite armies can never happen. If there had not first been an opinion received of the greatest part of England, that these powers were divided between the King, and the Lords, and the House of Commons, the people had never been divided and fallen into this civil war; first between those that disagreed in politics; and after between the dissenters about the liberty of religion; which have so instructed men in this point of sovereign right, that there be few now (in *England,*) that do not see, that these rights are inseparable, and will be so generally acknowledged at the next return of peace; and so continue, till their miseries are forgotten; and no longer, except the vulgar be better taught than they have hitherto been.

And because they are essential and inseparable rights, it follows necessarily, that in whatsoever words any of them seem to be granted away, yet if the sovereign power itself be not in direct terms renounced, and the name of sovereign no more given by the grantees to him that grants them, the grant is void: for when he has granted all he can, if we grant back the sovereignty, all is restored, as inseparably annexed thereunto.

This great authority being indivisible, and inseparably annexed to the sovereignty, there is little ground for the opinion of them, that say of sovereign kings, though they be *singulis majores,* of greater power than every one of their subjects, yet they be *universis minores,* of less power than them all together. For if by *all together,* they mean not the collective body as one person, then *all together,* and *every one,* signify the same; and the speech is absurd. But if by *all together,* they understand them as one person, (which person the sovereign bears,) then the power of all together, is the same with the sovereign's power; and so again the speech is absurd: which absurdity they see well enough, when the sovereignty is in an assembly of the people; but in a monarch they see it not; and yet the power of sovereignty is the same in whomsoever it be placed.

And as the power, so also the honour of the sovereign, ought to be greater, than that of any, or all the subjects. For in the sovereignty is the fountain of honour. The dignities of lord, earl, duke, and prince are his creatures. As in the presence of the master, the servants are equal, and without any honour at all; so are the subjects, in the presence of the sovereign. And though they shine some more, some less, when they are out of his sight; yet in his presence, they shine no more than the stars in presence of the sun.

But a man may here object, that the condition of subjects is very miserable; as being obnoxious to the lusts, and other irregular passions of him, or them that have so unlimited a power in their hands. And commonly they that live under a monarch, think it the fault of monarchy; and they that live under the government of democracy, or other sovereign assembly, attribute all the inconvenience to that form of commonwealth; whereas the power in all forms, if they be perfect enough to protect them, is the same; not considering that the estate of man can never be without some incommodity or other; and that the greatest, that in any form of government can possibly happen to the people in general, is scarce sensible, in respect of the miseries, and horrible calamities, that accompany a civil war, or that dissolute condition of masterless men, without subjection to laws, and a coercive power to tie their hands from rapine and revenge: nor considering that the greatest pressure of sovereign governors, proceedeth not from any delight, or profit they can expect in the damage or weakening of their subjects, in whose vigour, consisteth their own strength and glory; but in the restiveness of themselves, that unwillingly contributing to their own defence, make it necessary for their governors to draw from them what they can in time of peace, that they may have means on any emergent occasion, or sudden need, to resist, or take advantage on their enemies. For all men are by nature provided of notable multiplying glasses, (that is their passions and self-love,) through which, every little payment appeareth a great grievance; but are destitute of those prospective glasses, (namely moral and civil science,) to see afar off the miseries that hang over them, and cannot without such payments be avoided.

CHAPTER 19

Of the Several Kinds of Commonwealth by Institution, and of Succession to the Sovereign Power

The difference of commonwealths, consisteth in the difference of the sovereign, or the person representative of all and every one of the multitude. And because the sovereignty is either in one man, or in an assembly of more than one; and into that assembly either every man hath right to enter, or not every one, but certain men distinguished from the rest; it is manifest, there can be but three kinds of commonwealth. For the representative must needs be one man, or more: and if more, then it is the assembly of all, or but of a part. When the representative is one man, then is the commonwealth a MONARCHY: when an assembly of all that will come together, then it is a DEMOCRACY, or popular commonwealth: when an assembly of a part only, then it is called an ARISTOCRACY. Other kind of commonwealth there can be none: for either one, or more, or all, must have the sovereign power (which I have shown to be indivisible) entire.

There be other names of government, in the histories, and books of policy; as *tyranny,* and *oligarchy:* But they are not the names of other forms of government, but of the same forms misliked. For they that are discontented under *monarchy,* call it *tyranny;* and they that are displeased with *aristocracy,* call it *oligarchy:* so also, they which find themselves grieved under a *democracy,* call it *anarchy,* (which signifies want of government;) and yet I think no man believes, that want of government, is any new kind of government: nor by the same reason ought they to believe, that the government is of one kind, when they like it, and another, when they mislike it, or are oppressed by the governors.

It is manifest, that men who are in absolute liberty, may, if they please, give authority to one man, to represent them every one; as well as give such authority to any assembly of men whatsoever; and consequently may subject themselves, if they think good, to a monarch, as absolutely, as to any other representative. Therefore, where there is already erected a sovereign power, there can be no other representative of the same people, but only to certain particular ends, by the sovereign limited. For that were to erect two sovereigns; and every man to have his person represented by two actors, that by opposing one another, must needs divide that power, which (if men will live in peace) is indivisible; and thereby reduce the multitude into the condition of war, contrary to the end for which all sovereignty is instituted. And therefore as it is absurd, to think that a sovereign assembly, inviting the people of their dominion, to send up their deputies, with power to make known their advice, or desires, should therefore hold such deputies, rather than themselves, for the absolute representative of the people: so it is absurd also, to think the same in a monarchy. And I know not how this so manifest a truth, should of late be so little observed; that in a monarchy, he that had the sovereignty from a descent of 600 years, was alone called sovereign, had the title of Majesty from every one of his subjects, and was unquestionably taken by them for their king, was notwithstanding never considered as their representative; that name without contradiction passing for the title of those men, which at his command were sent up by the people to carry their petitions, and give him (if he permitted it) their advice. Which may serve as an admonition, for those that are the true, and absolute representative of a people, to instruct men in the nature of that office, and to take heed how they admit of any other general representation upon any occasion whatsoever, if they mean to discharge the trust committed to them.

The difference between these three kinds of commonwealth, consisteth not in the difference of power; but in the difference of convenience, or aptitude to produce the peace, and security of the people; for which end they were instituted. And to compare monarchy with the other two, we may observe; first, that whosoever beareth the person of the people, or is one of that assembly that bears it, beareth also his own natural person. And though he be careful in his politic person to procure the common interest; yet he is more, or no less careful to procure the private good of himself, his family, kindred and friends; and for the most part, if the public interest chance to cross the private, he prefers the private: for the passions of men, are commonly more potent than their reason. From whence it follows, that where the public and private interest are most closely united, there is the public most advanced. Now in monarchy, the private interest is the same with the public. The riches, power, and honour of a monarch arise only from the riches, strength and reputation of his subjects. For no king can be rich, nor glorious, nor secure, whose subjects are either poor, or contemptible, or too weak through want, or dissention, to maintain a war against their enemies: whereas in a democracy, or aristocracy, the public prosperity confers not so much to the private fortune of one that is corrupt, or ambitious, as doth many times a perfidious advice, a treacherous action, or a civil war.

Secondly, that a monarch receiveth counsel of whom, when, and where he pleaseth; and consequently may hear the opinion of men versed in the matter about which he deliberates, of what rank or quality soever, and as long before the time of action, and with as much secrecy, as he will. But when a sovereign assembly has need of counsel, none are admitted but such as have a right thereto from the beginning; which for the most part are of those who have been versed more in the acquisition of wealth than of knowledge; and are to give their advice in long discourses, which may, and do commonly excite men to action, but not govern them in it. For the *understanding* is by the flame of the passions, never enlightened, but dazzled: Nor is there any place, or time, wherein an assembly can receive counsel with secrecy, because of their own multitude.

Thirdly, that the resolutions of a monarch, are subject to no other inconstancy, than that of human nature; but in assemblies, besides that of nature, there ariseth an inconstancy from the number. For the absence of a few, that would have the resolution once taken, continue firm, (which may happen by security, negligence, or private impediments,) or the diligent appearance of a few of the contrary opinion, undoes to day, all that was concluded yesterday.

Fourthly, that a monarch cannot disagree with himself, out of envy, or interest; but an assembly may; and that to such a height, as may produce a civil war.

Fifthly, that in monarchy there is this inconvenience; that any subject, by the power of one man, for the enriching of a favourite or flatterer, may be deprived of all he possesseth; which I confess is a great and inevitable inconvenience. But the same may as well happen, where the sovereign power is in an assembly: for their power is the same; and they are as subject to evil counsel, and to be seduced by orators, as a monarch by flatterers; and becoming one another's flatterers, serve one another's covetousness and ambition by turns. And whereas the favourites of monarchs, are few, and they have none else to advance but their own kindred; the favourites of an assembly, are many; and the kindred much more numerous, than of any monarch. Besides, there is no favourite of a monarch, which cannot as well succour his friends, as hurt his enemies: but orators, that is to say, favourites of sovereign assemblies, though they have great power to hurt, have little to save. For to accuse, requires less eloquence (such is man's nature) than to excuse; and condemnation, than absolution more resembles justice.

Sixthly, that it is an inconvenience in monarchy, that the sovereignty may descend upon an infant, or one that cannot discern between good and evil: and consisteth in this, that the use of his power, must be in the hand of another man, or of some assembly of men, which are to govern by his right, and in his name; as curators, and protectors of his person, and authority. But to say there is inconvenience, in putting the use of the sovereign power, into the hand of a man, or an assembly of men; is to say that all government is more inconvenient, than confusion, and civil war. And therefore all the danger that can be pretended, must arise from the contention of those, that for an office of so great honour, and profit, may become competitors. To make it appear, that this inconvenience, proceedeth not from that form of government we call monarchy, we are to consider, that the precedent monarch, hath appointed who shall have the tuition of his infant successor, either expressly by testament, or tacitly, by not controlling the custom in that case received: and then such inconvenience, (if it happen) is to be attributed, not to the monarchy, but to the ambition, and injustice of the subjects; which in all kinds of government, where the people are not well instructed in their duty, and the rights of sovereignty, is the same. Or else the precedent monarch hath not at all taken order for such tuition; and then the law of nature hath provided this sufficient rule, that the tuition shall be in him, that hath by nature most interest in the preservation of the authority of the infant, and to whom least benefit can accrue by his death, or diminution. For seeing every man by nature seeketh his own benefit, and promotion; to put an infant into the power of those, that can promote themselves by his destruction, or damage, is not tuition, but treachery. So that sufficient provision being taken, against all just quarrel, about the government under a child, if any contention arise to the disturbance of the public peace, it is not to be attributed to the form of monarchy, but to the ambition of subjects, and ignorance of their duty. On the other side, there is no great commonwealth, the sovereignty whereof is in a great assembly, which is not, as to consultations of peace, and war, and making of laws, in the same condition, as if the government were in a child. For as a child wants the judgment to dissent from counsel given him, and is thereby necessitated to take the advice of them, or him, to whom he is committed: so an assembly wanteth the liberty, to dissent from the counsel of the major part, be it good, or bad. And as a child has need of a tutor, or protector, to preserve his person and authority: so also (in great commonwealths,) the sovereign assembly, in all great dangers and troubles, have need of *custodes libertatis;* that is of dictators, or protectors of their authority; which are as much as temporary monarchs; to whom for a time, they may commit the entire exercise of their power; and have (at the end of that time) been oftener deprived thereof, than infant kings, by their protectors, regents, or any other tutors.

Though the kinds of sovereignty be, as I have now shown, but three; that is to say, monarchy, where one man has it; or democracy, where the general assembly of subjects hath it; or aristocracy, where it is in an assembly of certain persons nominated, or otherwise distinguished from the rest: yet he that shall consider the particular commonwealths that have been, and are in the world, will not perhaps easily reduce them to three, and may thereby be inclined to think there be other forms, arising from these mingled together. As for example, elective kingdoms; where kings have the sovereign power put into their hands for a time; or kingdoms, wherein the king hath a power limited: which governments, are nevertheless by most writers called monarchy. Likewise if a popular, or aristocratical commonwealth, subdue an enemy's country, and govern the same, by a president, procurator, or other magistrate; this may seem perhaps at first sight, to be a democratical, or aristocratical government. But it is not so. For elective kings, are not sovereigns, but ministers of the sovereign; nor limited kings sovereigns, but ministers of them that have the sovereign power: nor are those provinces which are in subjection to a democracy, or aristocracy of another commonwealth, democratically, or aristocratically governed, but monarchically.

And first, concerning an elective king, whose power is limited to his life, as it is in many places of Christendom at this day; or to certain years or months, as the dictator's power amongst the Romans; if he have right to appoint his successor, he is no more elective but hereditary. But if he have no power to elect his successor, then there is some other man, or assembly known, which after his decease may elect anew, or else the commonwealth dieth, and dissolveth with him, and returneth to the condition of war. If it be known who have the power to give the sovereignty after his death, it is known also that the sovereignty was in them before: for none have right to give that which they have not right to possess, and keep to themselves, if they think good. But if there be none that can give the sovereignty, after the decease of him that was first elected; then has he power, nay he is obliged by the law of nature, to provide, by establishing his successor, to keep those that had trusted him with the government, from relapsing into the miserable condition of civil war. And consequently he was, when elected, a sovereign absolute.

Secondly, that king whose power is limited, is not superior to him, or them that have the power to limit it; and he that is not superior, is not supreme; that is to say not sovereign. The sovereignty therefore was always in that assembly which had the right to limit him; and by consequence the government not monarchy, but either democracy, or aristocracy; as of old time in *Sparta;* where the kings had a privilege to lead their armies; but the sovereignty was in the *Ephori.*

Thirdly, whereas heretofore the Roman people governed the land of *Judea* (for example) by a president; yet was not *Judea* therefore a democracy; because they were not governed by any assembly, into the which, any of them, had right to enter; nor by an aristocracy; because they were not governed by any assembly, into which, any man could enter by their election: but they were governed by one person, which though as to the people of *Rome* was an assembly of the people, or democracy; yet as to people of *Judea,* which had no right at all of participating in the government, was a monarch. For though where the people are governed by an assembly, chosen by themselves out of their own number, the government is called a democracy, or aristocracy; yet when they are governed by an assembly, not of their own choosing, it is a monarchy; not of *one* man, over another man; but of one people, over another people.

Of all these forms of government, the matter being mortal, so that not only monarchs, but also whole assemblies die, it is necessary for the conservation of the peace of men, that as there was order taken for an artificial man, so there be order also taken, for an artificial eternity of life; without which, men that are governed by an assembly, should return into the condition of war in every age; and they that are governed by one man, as soon as their governor dieth. This artificial eternity, is that which men call the right of *succession*.

There is no perfect form of government, where the disposing of the succession is not in the present sovereign. For if it be in any other particular man, or private assembly, it is in a person subject, and may be assumed by the sovereign at his pleasure; and consequently the right is in himself. And if it be in no particular man, but left to a new choice; then is the commonwealth dissolved; and the right is in him that can get it; contrary to the intention of them that did institute the commonwealth, for their perpetual, and not temporary security.

In a democracy, the whole assembly cannot fail, unless the multitude that are to be governed fail. And therefore questions of the right of succession, have in that form of government no place at all.

In an aristocracy, when any of the assembly dieth, the election of another into his room belongeth to the assembly, as the sovereign, to whom belongeth the choosing of all counsellors and officers. For that which the representative doth, as actor, every one of the subjects doth, as author. And though the sovereign assembly may give power to others, to elect new men, for supply of their court; yet it is still by their authority, that the election is made; and by the same it may (when the public shall require it) be recalled.

The greatest difficulty about the right of succession, is in monarchy: and the difficulty ariseth from this, that at first sight, it is not manifest who is to appoint the successor; nor many times, who it is whom he hath appointed. For in both these cases, there is required a more exact ratiocination, than every man is accustomed to use. As to the question, who shall appoint the successor, of a monarch that hath the sovereign authority; that is to say, who shall determine of the right of inheritance, (for elective kings and princes have not the sovereign power in propriety, but in use only,) we are to consider, that either he that is in possession, has right to dispose of the succession, or else that right is again in the dissolved multitude. For the death of him that hath the sovereign power in propriety, leaves the multitude without any sovereign at all; that is, without any representative in whom they should be united, and be capable of doing any one action at all: and therefore they are incapable of election of any new monarch; every man having equal right to submit himself to such as he thinks best able to protect him; or if he can, protect himself by his own sword, which is a return to confusion, and to the condition of a war of every man against every man, contrary to the end for which monarchy had its first institution. Therefore it is manifest, that by the institution of monarchy, the disposing of the successor, is always left to the judgment and will of the present possessor.

And for the question (which may arise sometimes) who it is that the monarch in possession, hath designed to the succession and inheritance of his power; it is determined by his express words, and testament; or by other tacit signs sufficient.

By express words, or testament, when it is declared by him in his lifetime, *viva voce,* or by writing; as the first emperors of *Rome* declared who should be their heirs. For the word heir does not of itself imply the children, or nearest kindred of a man; but whomsoever a man shall any way declare, he would have to succeed him in his estate. If therefore a monarch declare expressly, that such a man shall be his heir, either by word or writing, then is that man immediately after the decease of his predecessor, invested in the right of being monarch.

But where testament, and express words are wanting, other natural signs of the will are to be followed: whereof the one is custom. And therefore where the custom is, that the next of kindred absolutely succeedeth, there also the next of kindred hath right to the succession; for that, if the will of him that was in possession had been otherwise, he might easily have declared the same in his life time. And likewise where the custom is, that the next of the male kindred succeedeth, there also the right of succession is in the next of the kindred male, for the same reason. And so it is if the custom were to advance the female. For whatsoever custom a man may by a word control, and does not, it is a natural sign he would have that custom stand.

But where neither custom, nor testament hath preceded, there it is to be understood, first, that a monarch's will is, that the government remain monarchical; because he hath approved that government in himself. Secondly, that a child of his own, male, or female, be preferred before any other; because men are presumed to be more inclined by nature, to advance their own children, than the children of other men; and of their own, rather a male than a female; because men, are naturally fitter than women, for actions of labour and danger. Thirdly, where his own issue faileth, rather a brother than a stranger; and so still the nearer in blood, rather than the more remote; because it is always presumed that the nearer of kin, is the nearer in affection; and it is evident that a man receives always, by reflection, the most honour from the greatness of his nearest kindred.

But if it be lawful for a monarch to dispose of the succession by words of contract, or testament, men may perhaps object a great inconvenience: for he may sell, or give his right of governing to a stranger; which, because strangers (that is, men not used to live under the same government, nor speaking the same language) do commonly undervalue one another, may turn to the oppression of his subjects; which is indeed a great inconvenience: but it proceedeth not necessarily from the subjection to a stranger's government, but from the unskilfulness of the governors, ignorant of the true rules of politics. And therefore the Romans when they had subdued many nations, to make their government digestible, were wont to take away that grievance, as much as they thought necessary, by giving sometimes to whole nations, and sometimes to principal men of every nation they conquered, not only the privileges, but also the name of Romans; and took many of them into the senate, and offices of charge, even in the Roman city. And this was it our most wise king, king *James,* aimed at, in endeavouring the union of his two realms of *England* and *Scotland.* Which if he could have obtained, had in all likelihood prevented the civil wars, which make both those kingdoms, at this present, miserable. It is not therefore any injury to the people, for a monarch to dispose of the succession by will; though by the fault of many princes, it hath been sometimes found inconvenient. Of the lawfulness of it, this also is an argument, that whatsoever inconvenience can arrive by giving a kingdom to a stranger, may arrive also by so marrying with strangers, as the right of succession may descend upon them: yet this by all men is accounted lawful.

CHAPTER 20
Of Dominion Paternal, and Despotical

A *commonwealth by acquisition*, is that, where the sovereign power is acquired by force; and it is acquired by force, when men singly, or many together by plurality of voices, for fear of death, or bonds, do authorize all the actions of that man, or assembly, that hath their lives and liberty in his power.

And this kind of dominion, or sovereignty, differeth from sovereignty by institution, only in this, that men who choose their sovereign, do it for fear of one another, and not of him whom they institute: but in this case, they subject themselves, to him they are afraid of. In both cases they do it for fear: which is to be noted by them, that hold all such covenants, as proceed from fear of death, or violence, void: which if it were true, no man, in any kind of commonwealth, could be obliged to obedience. It is true, that in a commonwealth once instituted, or acquired, promises proceeding from fear of death or violence, are no covenants, nor obliging, when the thing promised is contrary to the laws; but the reason is not, because it was made upon fear, but because he that promiseth, hath no right in the thing promised. Also, when he may lawfully perform, and doth not, it is not the invalidity of the covenant, that absolveth him, but the sentence of the sovereign. Otherwise, whensoever a man lawfully promiseth, he unlawfully breaketh: but when the sovereign, who is the actor, acquitteth him, then he is acquitted by him that extorted the promise, as by the author of such absolution.

But the rights, and consequences of sovereignty, are the same in both. His power cannot, without his consent, be transferred to another: he cannot forfeit it: he cannot be accused by any of his subjects, of injury: he cannot be punished by them: he is judge of what is necessary for peace; and judge of doctrines: he is sole legislator; and supreme judge of controversies; and of the times, and occasions of war, and peace: to him it belongeth to choose magistrates, counsellors, commanders, and all other officers, and ministers; and to determine of rewards, and punishments, honour, and order. The reasons whereof, are the same which are alleged in the precedent chapter, for the same rights, and consequences of sovereignty by institution.

Dominion is acquired two ways; by generation, and by conquest. The right of dominion by generation, is that, which the parent hath over his children; and is called PATERNAL. And is not so derived from the generation, as if therefore the parent had dominion over his child because he begat him; but from the child's consent, either express, or by other sufficient arguments declared. For as to the generation, God hath ordained to man a helper; and there be always two that are equally parents: the dominion therefore over the child, should belong equally to both; and he be equally subject to both, which is impossible; for no man can obey two masters. And whereas some have attributed the dominion to the man only, as being of the more excellent sex; they misreckon in it. For there is not always that difference of strength, or prudence between the man and the woman, as that the right can be determined without war. In commonwealths, this controversy is decided by the civil law: and for the most part, (but not always) the sentence is in favour of the father; because for the most part commonwealths have been erected by the fathers, not by the mothers of families. But the question lieth now in the state of mere nature; where there are supposed no laws of matrimony; no laws for the education of children; but the law of nature, and the natural inclination of the sexes, one to another, and to their children. In this condition of mere nature, either the parents between themselves dispose of the dominion over the child by contract; or do not dispose thereof at all. If they dispose thereof, the right passeth according to the contract. We find in history that the *Amazons* contracted with the men of the neighbouring countries, to whom they had recourse for issue, that the issue male should be sent back, but the female remain with themselves: so that the dominion of the females was in the mother.

If there be no contract, the dominion is in the mother. For in the condition of mere nature, where there are no matrimonial laws, it cannot be known who is the father, unless it be declared by the mother: and therefore the right of dominion over the child dependeth on her will, and is consequently hers. Again, seeing the infant is first in the power of the mother, so as she may either nourish, or expose it; if she nourish it, it oweth its life to the mother; and is therefore obliged to obey her, rather than any other; and by consequence the dominion over it is hers. But if she expose it, and another find and nourish it, the dominion is in him that nourisheth it. For it ought to obey him by whom it is preserved; because preservation of life being the end, for which one man becomes subject to another, every man is supposed to promise obedience, to him, in whose power it is to save, or destroy him.

If the mother be the father's subject, the child, is in the father's power: and if the father be the mother's subject, (as when a sovereign queen marrieth one of her subjects,) the child is subject to the mother; because the father also is her subject.

If a man and woman, monarchs of two several kingdoms, have a child, and contract concerning who shall have the dominion of him, the right of the dominion passeth by the contract. If they contract not, the dominion followeth the dominion of the place of his residence. For the sovereign of each country hath dominion over all that reside therein.

He that hath the dominion over the child, hath dominion also over the children of the child; and over their children's children. For he that hath dominion over the person of a man, hath dominion over all that is his; without which, dominion were but a title, without the effect.

The right of succession to paternal dominion, proceedeth in the same manner, as doth the right of succession to monarchy; of which I have already sufficiently spoken in the precedent chapter.

Dominion acquired by conquest, or victory in war, is that which some writers call DESPOTICAL, from Δεσπότης, which signifieth a *lord,* or *master;* and is the dominion of the master over his servant. And this dominion is then acquired to the victor, when the vanquished, to avoid the present stroke of death, covenanteth either in express words, or by other sufficient signs of the will, that so long as his life, and the liberty of his body is allowed him, the victor shall have the use thereof, at his pleasure. And after such covenant made, the vanquished is a SERVANT, and not before: for by the word *servant,* (whether it be derived from *servire,* to serve, or from *servare,* to save, which I leave to grammarians to dispute) is not meant a captive, which is kept in prison, or bonds, till the owner of him that took him, or bought him of one that did, shall consider what to do with him: (for such men, (commonly called slaves,) have no obligation at all; but may break their bonds, or the prison; and kill, or carry away captive their master, justly:) but one, that being taken, hath corporal liberty allowed him; and upon promise not to run away, nor to do violence to his master, is trusted by him.

It is not therefore the victory, that giveth the right of dominion over the vanquished, but his own covenant. Nor is he obliged because he is conquered; that is to say, beaten, and taken, or put to flight; but because he cometh in, and submitteth to the victor; nor is the victor obliged by an enemy's rendering himself, (without promise of life,) to spare him for this his yielding to discretion; which obliges not the victor longer, than in his own discretion he shall think fit.

And that which men do, when they demand (as it is now called) *quarter*, (which the Greeks called Ζωγρία, *taking alive*,) is to evade the present fury of the victor, by submission, and to compound for their life, with ransom, or service: and therefore he that hath quarter, hath not his life given, but deferred till farther deliberation; for it is not an yielding on condition of life, but to discretion. And then only is his life in security, and his service due, when the victor hath trusted him with his corporal liberty. For slaves that work in prisons, or fetters, do it not of duty, but to avoid the cruelty of their task-masters.

The master of the servant, is master also of all he hath; and may exact the use thereof; that is to say, of his goods, of his labour, of his servants, and of his children, as often as he shall think fit. For he holdeth his life of his master, by the covenant of obedience; that is, of owning, and authorizing whatsoever the master shall do. And in case the master, if he refuse, kill him, or cast him into bonds, or otherwise punish him for his disobedience, he is himself the author of the same; and cannot accuse him of injury.

In sum, the rights and consequences of both *paternal* and *despotical* dominion, are the very same with those of a sovereign by institution; and for the same reasons: which reasons are set down in the precedent chapter. So that for a man that is monarch of divers nations, whereof he hath, in one the sovereignty by institution of the people assembled, and in another by conquest, that is by the submission of each particular, to avoid death or bonds; to demand of one nation more than of the other, from the title of conquest, as being a conquered nation, is an act of ignorance of the rights of sovereignty. For the sovereign is absolute over both alike; or else there is no sovereignty at all; and so every man may lawfully protect himself, if he can, with his own sword, which is the condition of war.

By this it appears; that a great family if it be not part of some commonwealth, is of itself, as to the rights of sovereignty, a little monarchy; whether that family consist of a man and his children; or of a man and his servants; or of a man, and his children, and servants together: wherein the father or master is the sovereign. But yet a family is not properly a commonwealth; unless it be of that power by its own number, or by other opportunities, as not to be subdued without the hazard of war. For where a number of men are manifestly too weak to defend themselves united, every one may use his own reason in time of danger, to save his own life, either by flight, or by submission to the enemy, as he shall think best; in the same manner as a very small company of soldiers, surprised by an army, may cast down their arms, and demand quarter, or run away, rather than be put to the sword. And thus much shall suffice; concerning what I find by speculation, and deduction, of sovereign rights, from the nature, need, and designs of men, in erecting of commonwealths, and putting themselves under monarchs, or assemblies, entrusted with power enough for their protection.

Let us now consider what the Scripture teacheth in the same point. To Moses, the children of *Israel* say thus: *Speak thou to us, and we will hear thee; but let not God speak to us, lest we die.* (*Exod.* 20. 19.) This is absolute obedience to Moses. Concerning the right of kings, God himself by the mouth of Samuel, saith, (1 *Sam.* 8. 11, 12, &c.) *This shall be the right of the king you will have to reign over you. He shall take your sons, and set them to drive his chariots, and to be his horsemen, and to run before his chariots; and gather in his harvest; and to make his engines of war, and instruments of his chariots; and shall take your daughters to make perfumes, to be his cooks, and bakers. He shall take your fields, your vine-yards, and your olive-yards, and give them to his servants. He shall take the tithe of your corn and wine, and give it to the men of his chamber, and to his other servants. He shall take your man-servants, and your maid-servants, and the choice of your youth, and employ them in his business. He shall take the tithe of your flocks; and you shall be his servants.* This is absolute power, and summed up in the last words, *you shall be his servants*. Again, when the people heard what power their king was to have, yet they consented thereto, and say thus, (*verse* 19) *we will be as all other nations, and our king shall judge our causes, and go before us, to conduct our wars.* Here is confirmed the right that sovereigns have, both to the *militia,* and to all *judicature;* in which is contained as absolute power, as one man can possibly transfer to another. Again, the prayer of king Solomon to God, was this (1 *Kings,* 3. 9): *Give to thy servant understanding, to judge thy people, and to discern between good and evil.* It belongeth therefore to the sovereign to be judge, and to prescribe the rules of *discerning good* and *evil:* which rules are laws; and therefore in him is the legislative power. Saul sought the life of *David;* yet when it was in his power to slay *Saul,* and his servants would have done it, *David* forbad them, saying, (1 *Sam.* 24. 9) *God forbid I should do such an act against my Lord, the anointed of God.* For obedience of servants St. *Paul* saith; (*Col.* 3. 20) *Servants obey your masters in all things;* and, (*Verse* 22) *children obey your parents in all things.* There is simple obedience in those that are subject to paternal, or despotical dominion. Again, (*Matt.* 23. 2, 3) *The Scribes and Pharisees sit in Moses' chair, and therefore all that they shall bid you observe, that observe and do.* There again is simple obedience. And St. *Paul,* (*Titus* 3. 2) *Warn them that they subject themselves to princes, and to those that are in authority, and obey them.* This obedience is also simple. Lastly, our Saviour himself acknowledges, that men ought to pay such taxes as are by kings imposed, where he says, *Give to Caesar that which is Caesar's;* and paid such taxes himself. And that the king's word, is sufficient to take any thing from any subject, when there is need; and that the king is judge of that need: for he himself, as king of the Jews, commanded his disciples to take the ass, and ass's colt to carry him into Jerusalem, saying, (*Matth.* 21. 2, 3) *Go into the village over against you, and you shall find a she ass tied, and her colt with her, untie them, and bring them to me. And if any man ask you, what you mean by it, say the Lord hath need of them: and they will let them go.* They will not ask whether his necessity be a sufficient title; nor whether he be judge of that necessity; but acquiesce in the will of the Lord.

To these places may be added also that of *Genesis,* (*Genesis* 3. 5) *Ye shall be as gods, knowing good and evil.* And *verse* 11. *Who told thee that thou wast naked? hast thou eaten of the tree, of which I commanded thee thou shouldest not eat?* For the cognizance or judicature of good and evil, being forbidden by the name of the fruit of the tree of knowledge, as a trial of *Adam's* obedience; the devil to inflame the ambition of the woman, to whom that fruit already seemed beautiful, told her that by tasting it, they should be as gods, knowing *good* and *evil*. Whereupon having both eaten, they did indeed take upon them God's office, which is judicature of good and evil; but acquired no new ability to distinguish between them aright. And whereas it is said, that having eaten, they saw they were naked; no man hath so interpreted that place, as if they had been formerly blind, and saw not their own skins: the meaning is plain, that it was then they first judged their nakedness (wherein it was God's will to create them) to be uncomely; and by being ashamed, did tacitly censure God himself. And thereupon God saith, *Hast thou eaten, &c.* as if he should say, doest thou that owest me obedience, take upon thee to judge of my commandments? Whereby it is clearly, (though allegorically,) signified, that the commands of them that have the right to command, are not by their subjects to be censured, nor disputed.

So that it appeareth plainly, to my understanding, both from reason, and Scripture, that the sovereign power, whether placed in one man, as in monarchy, or in one assembly of men, as in popular, and aristocratical commonwealths, is as great, as possibly men can be imagined to make it. And though of so unlimited a power, men may fancy many evil consequences, yet the consequences of the want of it, which is perpetual war of every man against his neighbour, are much worse. The condition of man in this life shall never be without inconveniences; but there happeneth in no commonwealth any great inconvenience, but what proceeds from the subject's disobedience, and breach of those covenants, from which the commonwealth hath its being. And whosoever thinking sovereign power too great, will seek to make it less, must subject himself, to the power, that can limit it; that is to say, to a greater.

The greatest objection is, that of the practice; when men ask, where, and when, such power has by subjects been acknowledged. But one may ask them again, when, or where has there been a kingdom long free from sedition and civil war. In those nations, whose commonwealths have been long-lived, and not been destroyed but by foreign war, the subjects never did dispute of the sovereign power. But howsoever, an argument from the practice of men, that have not sifted to the bottom, and with exact reason weighed the causes, and nature of commonwealths, and suffer daily those miseries, that proceed from the ignorance thereof, is invalid. For though in all places of the world, men should lay the foundation of their houses on the sand, it could not thence be inferred, that so it ought to be. The skill of making, and maintaining commonwealths, consisteth in certain rules, as doth arithmetic and geometry; not (as tennis-play) on practice only: which rules, neither poor men have the leisure, nor men that have had the leisure, have hitherto had the curiosity, or the method to find out.

CHAPTER 21
Of the Liberty of Subjects

LIBERTY, or FREEDOM, signifieth (properly) the absence of opposition; (by opposition, I mean external impediments of motion;) and may be applied no less to irrational, and inanimate creatures, than to rational. For whatsoever is so tied, or environed, as it cannot move, but within a certain space, which space is determined by the opposition of some external body, we say it hath not liberty to go further. And so of all living creatures, whilst they are imprisoned, or restrained, with walls, or chains; and of the water whilst it is kept in by banks, or vessels, that otherwise would spread itself into a larger space, we use to say, they are not at liberty, to move in such manner, as without those external impediments they would. But when the impediment of motion, is in the constitution of the thing itself, we use not to say, it wants the liberty; but the power to move; as when a stone lieth still, or a man is fastened to his bed by sickness.

And according to this proper, and generally received meaning of the word, *a* FREEMAN, *is he, that in those things, which by his strength and wit he is able to do, is not hindered to do what he has a will to.* But when the words *free,* and *liberty,* are applied to any thing but *bodies,* they are abused; for that which is not subject to motion, is not subject to impediment: and therefore, when it is said (for example) the way is free, no liberty of the way is signified, but of those that walk in it without stop. And when we say a gift is free, there is not meant any liberty of the gift, but of the giver, that was not bound by any law, or covenant to give it. So when we *speak freely,* it is not the liberty of voice, or pronunciation, but of the man, whom no law hath obliged to speak otherwise than he did. Lastly, from the use of the word *free-will,* no liberty can be inferred of the will, desire, or inclination, but the liberty of the man; which consisteth in this, that he finds no stop, in doing what he has the will, desire, or inclination to do.

Fear, and liberty are consistent; as when a man throweth his goods into the sea for *fear* the ship should sink, he doth it nevertheless very willingly, and may refuse to do it if he will: it is therefore the action of one that was *free:* so a man sometimes pays his debt, only for *fear* of imprisonment, which because nobody hindered him from detaining, was the action of a man at *liberty.* And generally all actions which men do in commonwealths, for *fear* of the law, are actions, which the doers had *liberty* to omit.

Liberty, and *necessity* are consistent: as in the water, that hath not only *liberty,* but a *necessity* of descending by the channel; so likewise in the actions which men voluntarily do: which, because they proceed from their will, proceed from *liberty;* and yet, because every act of man's will, and every desire, and inclination proceedeth from some cause, and that from another cause, in a continual chain, (whose first link is in the hand of God the first of all causes,) they proceed from *necessity.* So that to him that could see the connexion of those causes, the *necessity* of all men's voluntary actions, would appear manifest. And therefore God, that seeth, and disposeth all things, seeth also that the *liberty* of man in doing what he will, is accompanied with the *necessity* of doing that which God will, and no more, nor less. For though men may do many things, which God does not command, nor is therefore author of them; yet they can have no passion, nor appetite to any thing, of which appetite God's will is not the cause. And did not his will assure the *necessity* of man's will, and consequently of all that on man's will dependeth, the *liberty* of men would be a contradiction, and impediment to the omnipotence and *liberty* of God. And this shall suffice, (as to the matter in hand) of that natural *liberty,* which only is properly called *liberty.*

But as men, for the attaining of peace, and conservation of themselves thereby, have made an artificial man, which we call a commonwealth; so also have they made artificial chains, called *civil laws,* which they themselves, by mutual covenants, have fastened at one end, to the lips of that man, or assembly, to whom they have given the sovereign power; and at the other end to their own ears. These bonds in their own nature but weak, may nevertheless be made to hold, by the danger, though not by the difficulty of breaking them.

In relation to these bonds only it is, that I am to speak now, of the *liberty* of *subjects*. For seeing there is no commonwealth in the world, wherein there be rules enough set down, for the regulating of all the actions, and words of men, (as being a thing impossible:) it followeth necessarily, that in all kinds of actions, by the laws praetermitted, men have the liberty, of doing what their own reasons shall suggest, for the most profitable to themselves. For if we take liberty in the proper sense, for corporal liberty; that is to say, freedom from chains, and prison, it were very absurd for men to clamour as they do, for the liberty they so manifestly enjoy. Again, if we take liberty, for an exemption from laws, it is no less absurd, for men to demand as they do, that liberty, by which all other men may be masters of their lives. And yet as absurd as it is, this is it they demand; not knowing that the laws are of no power to protect them, without a sword in the hands of a man, or men, to cause those laws to be put in execution. The liberty of a subject, lieth therefore only in those things, which in regulating their actions, the sovereign hath praetermitted: such as is the liberty to buy, and sell, and otherwise contract with one another; to choose their own abode, their own diet, their own trade of life, and institute their children as they themselves think fit; and the like.

Nevertheless we are not to understand, that by such liberty, the sovereign power of life and death, is either abolished, or limited. For it has been already shown, that nothing the sovereign representative can do to a subject, on what pretence soever, can properly be called injustice, or injury; because every subject is author of every act the sovereign doth; so that he never wanteth right to any thing, otherwise, than as he himself is the subject of God, and bound thereby to observe the laws of nature. And therefore it may, and doth often happen in commonwealths, that a subject may be put to death, by the command of the sovereign power; and yet neither do the other wrong: as when *Jephtha* caused his daughter to be sacrificed: in which, and the like cases, he that so dieth, had liberty to do the action, for which he is nevertheless, without injury put to death. And the same holdeth also in a sovereign prince, that putteth to death an innocent subject. For though the action be against the law of nature, as being contrary to equity, (as was the killing of *Uriah*, by *David;*) yet it was not an injury to *Uriah;* but to *God.* Not to *Uriah,* because the right to do what he pleased, was given him by *Uriah* himself: and yet to *God,* because *David* was *God's* subject; and prohibited all iniquity by the law of nature. Which distinction, *David* himself, when he repented the fact, evidently confirmed, saying, *To thee only have I sinned.* In the same manner, the people of *Athens,* when they banished the most potent of their commonwealth for ten years, thought they committed no injustice; and yet they never questioned what crime he had done; but what hurt he would do: nay they commanded the banishment of they knew not whom; and every citizen bringing his oystershell into the market place, written with the name of him he desired should be banished, without actual accusing him, sometimes banished an *Aristides,* for his reputation of justice; and sometimes a scurrilous jester, as *Hyperbolus,* to make a jest of it. And yet a man cannot say, the sovereign people of *Athens* wanted right to banish them; or an *Athenian* the liberty to jest, or to be just.

The liberty, whereof there is so frequent and honourable mention, in the histories, and philosophy of the ancient Greeks, and Romans, and in the writings, and discourse of those that from them have received all their learning in the politics, is not the liberty of particular men; but the liberty of the commonwealth: which is the same with that, which every man then should have, if there were no civil laws, nor commonwealth at all. And the effects of it also be the same. For as amongst masterless men, there is perpetual war, of every man against his neighbour; no inheritance, to transmit to the son, nor to expect from the father; no propriety of goods, or lands; no security; but a full and absolute liberty in every particular man: so in states, and commonwealths not dependent on one another, every commonwealth, (not every man) has an absolute liberty, to do what it shall judge (that is to say, what that man, or assembly that representeth it, shall judge) most conducing to their benefit. But withal, they live in the condition of a perpetual war, and upon the confines of battle, with their frontiers armed, and cannons planted against their neighbours round about. The *Athenians*, and *Romans* were free; that is, free commonwealths: not that any particular men had the liberty to resist their own representative; but that their representative had the liberty to resist, or invade other people. There is written on the turrets of the city of *Lucca* in great characters at this day, the word *LIBERTAS;* yet no man can thence infer, that a particular man has more liberty, or immunity from the service of the commonwealth there, than in *Constantinople*. Whether a commonwealth be monarchical, or popular, the freedom is still the same.

But it is an easy thing, for men to be deceived, by the specious name of *liberty*, and for want of judgment to distinguish, mistake that for their private inheritance, and birth right, which is the right of the public only. And when the same error is confirmed by the authority of men in reputation for their writings in this subject, it is no wonder if it produce sedition, and change of government. In these western parts of the world, we are made to receive our opinions concerning the institution, and rights of commonwealths, from *Aristotle, Cicero,* and other men, Greeks and Romans, that living under popular states, derived those rights, not from the principles of nature, but transcribed them into their books, out of the practice of their own commonwealths, which were popular; as the grammarians describe the rules of language, out of the practice of the time; or the rules of poetry, out of the poems of *Homer* and *Virgil*. And because the Athenians were taught, (to keep them from desire of changing their government,) that they were freemen, and all that lived under monarchy were slaves; therefore Aristotle puts it down in his *Politics, (lib.* 6. *cap.* 2.) *In democracy,* Liberty *is to be supposed: for it is commonly held, that no man is* Free *in any other government*. And as Aristotle; so Cicero, and other writers have grounded their civil doctrine, on the opinions of the Romans, who were taught to hate monarchy, at first, by them that having deposed their sovereign, shared amongst them the sovereignty of *Rome;* and afterwards by their successors. And by reading of these Greek, and Latin authors, men from their childhood have gotten a habit (under a false show of liberty,) of favouring tumults, and of licentious controlling the actions of their sovereigns; and again of controlling those controllers, with the effusion of so much blood; as I think I may truly say, there was never any thing so dearly bought, as these western parts have bought the learning of the Greek and Latin tongues.

To come now to the particulars of the true liberty of a subject; that is to say, what are the things, which though commanded by the sovereign, he may nevertheless, without injustice, refuse to do; we are to consider, what rights we pass away, when we make a commonwealth; or (which is all one,) what liberty we deny ourselves, by owning all the actions (without exception) of the man, or assembly we make our sovereign. For in the act of our *submission,* consisteth both our *obligation,* and our *liberty;* which must therefore be inferred by arguments taken from thence; there being no obligation on any man, which ariseth not from some act of his own; for all men equally, are by nature free. And because such arguments, must either be drawn from the express words, *I authorise all his actions,* or from the intention of him that submitteth himself to his power, (which intention is to be understood by the end for which he so submitteth;) the obligation, and liberty of the subject, is to be derived, either from those words, (or others equivalent;) or else from the end of the institution of sovereignty, namely, the peace of the subjects within themselves, and their defence against a common enemy.

First therefore, seeing sovereignty by institution, is by covenant of every one to every one; and sovereignty by acquisition, by covenants of the vanquished to the victor, or child to the parent; it is manifest, that every subject has liberty in all those things, the right whereof cannot by covenant be transferred. I have shewn before in the 14th chapter, that covenants, not to defend a man's own body, are void. Therefore,

If the sovereign command a man (though justly condemned,) to kill, wound, or maim himself; or not to resist those that assault him; or to abstain from the use of food, air, medicine, or any other thing, without which he cannot live; yet hath that man the liberty to disobey.

If a man be interrogated by the sovereign, or his authority, concerning a crime done by himself, he is not bound (without assurance of pardon) to confess it; because no man (as I have shown in the same chapter) can be obliged by covenant to accuse himself.

Again, the consent of a subject to sovereign power, is contained in these words, *I authorize, or take upon me, all his actions;* in which there is no restriction at all, of his own former natural liberty: for by allowing him to *kill me,* I am not bound to kill myself when he commands me. It is one thing to say, *kill me, or my fellow, if you please;* another thing to say, *I will kill myself, or my fellow.* It followeth therefore, that

No man is bound by the words themselves, either to kill himself, or any other man; and consequently, that the obligation a man may sometimes have, upon the command of the sovereign to execute any dangerous, or dishonourable office, dependeth not on the words of our submission; but on the intention, which is to be understood by the end thereof. When therefore our refusal to obey, frustrates the end for which the sovereignty was ordained; then there is no liberty to refuse: otherwise there is.

Upon this ground, a man that is commanded as a soldier to fight against the enemy, though his sovereign have right enough to punish his refusal with death, may nevertheless in many cases refuse, without injustice; as when he substituteth a sufficient soldier in his place: for in this case he deserteth not the service of the commonwealth. And there is allowance to be made for natural timorousness; not only to women, (of whom no such dangerous duty is expected,) but also to men of feminine courage. When armies fight, there is on one side, or both, a running away; yet when they do it not out of treachery, but fear, they are not esteemed to do it unjustly, but dishonourably. For the same reason, to avoid battle, is not injustice, but cowardice. But he that inrolleth himself a soldier, or taketh imprest money, taketh away the excuse of a timorous nature; and is obliged, not only to go to the battle, but also not to run from it, without his captain's leave. And when the defence of the commonwealth, requireth at once the help of all that are able to bear arms, every one is obliged; because otherwise the institution of the commonwealth, which they have not the purpose, or courage to preserve, was in vain.

To resist the sword of the commonwealth, in defence of another man, guilty, or innocent, no man hath liberty; because such liberty, takes away from the sovereign, the means of protecting us; and is therefore destructive of the very essence of government. But in case a great many men together, have already resisted the sovereign power unjustly, or committed some capital crime, for which every one of them expecteth death, whether have they not the liberty then to join together, and assist, and defend one another? Certainly they have: for they but defend their lives, which the guilty man may as well do, as the innocent. There was indeed injustice in the first breach of their duty; their bearing of arms subsequent to it, though it be to maintain what they have done, is no new unjust act. And if it be only to defend their persons, it is not unjust at all. But the offer of pardon taketh from them, to whom it is offered, the plea of self-defence, and maketh their perseverance in assisting, or defending the rest, unlawful.

As for other liberties, they depend on the silence of the law. In cases where the sovereign has prescribed no rule, there the subject hath the liberty to do, or forbear, according to his own discretion. And therefore such liberty is in some places more, and in some less; and in some times more, in other times less, according as they that have the sovereignty shall think most convenient. As for example, there was a time, when in *England* a man might enter into his own land, (and dispossess such as wrongfully possessed it,) by force. But in aftertimes, that liberty of forcible entry, was taken away by a statute made (by the king,) in parliament. And in some places of the world, men have the liberty of many wives: in other places, such liberty is not allowed.

If a subject have a controversy with his sovereign, of debt, or of right of possession of lands or goods, or concerning any service required at his hands, or concerning any penalty, corporal, or pecuniary, grounded on a precedent law; he hath the same liberty to sue for his right, as if it were against a subject; and before such judges, as are appointed by the sovereign. For seeing the sovereign demandeth by force of a former law, and not by virtue of his power; he declareth thereby, that he requireth no more, than shall appear to be due by that law. The suit therefore is not contrary to the will of the sovereign; and consequently the subject hath the liberty to demand the hearing of his cause; and sentence, according to that law. But if he demand, or take any thing by pretence of his power; there lieth, in that case, no action of law: for all that is done by him in virtue of his power, is done by the authority of every subject, and consequently, he that brings an action against the sovereign, brings it against himself.

If a monarch, or sovereign assembly, grant a liberty to all, or any of his subjects, which grant standing, he is disabled to provide for their safety, the grant is void; unless he directly renounce, or transfer the sovereignty to another. For in that he might openly, (if it had been his will,) and in plain terms, have renounced, or transferred it, and did not; it is to be understood it was not his will; but that the grant proceeded from ignorance of the repugnancy between such a liberty and the sovereign power: and therefore the sovereignty is still retained; and consequently all those powers, which are necessary to the exercising thereof; such as are the power of war, and peace, of judicature, of appointing officers, and councillors, of levying money, and the rest named in the 18th chapter.

The obligation of subjects to the sovereign, is understood to last as long, and no longer, than the power lasteth, by which he is able to protect them. For the right men have by nature to protect themselves, when none else can protect them, can by no covenant be relinquished. The sovereignty is the soul of the commonwealth; which once departed from the body, the members do no more receive their motion from it. The end of obedience is protection; which, wheresoever a man seeth it, either in his own, or in another's sword, nature applieth his obedience to it, and his endeavour to maintain it. And though sovereignty, in the intention of them that make it, be immortal; yet is it in its own nature, not only subject to violent death, by foreign war; but also through the ignorance, and passions of men, it hath in it, from the very institution, many seeds of a natural mortality, by intestine discord.

If a subject be taken prisoner in war; or his person, or his means of life be within the guards of the enemy, and hath his life and corporal liberty given him, on condition to be subject to the victor, he hath liberty to accept the condition; and having accepted it, is the subject of him that took him; because he had no other way to preserve himself. The case is the same, if he be detained on the same terms, in a foreign country. But if a man be held in prison, or bonds, or is not trusted with the liberty of his body; he cannot be understood to be bound by covenant to subjection; and therefore may, if he can, make his escape by any means whatsoever.

If a monarch shall relinquish the sovereignty, both for himself, and his heirs; his subjects return to the absolute liberty of nature; because, though nature may declare who are his sons, and who are the nearest of his kin; yet it dependeth on his own will, (as hath been said in the precedent chapter,) who shall be his heir. If therefore he will have no heir, there is no sovereignty, nor subjection. The case is the same, if he die without known kindred, and without declaration of his heir. For then there can no heir be known, and consequently no subjection be due.

If the sovereign banish his subject; during the banishment, he is not subject. But he that is sent on a message, or hath leave to travel, is still subject; but it is, by contract between sovereigns, not by virtue of the covenant of subjection. For whosoever entereth into another's dominion, is subject to all the laws thereof; unless he have a privilege by the amity of the sovereigns, or by special licence.

If a monarch subdued by war, render himself subject to the victor; his subjects are delivered from their former obligation, and become obliged to the victor. But if he be held prisoner, or have not the liberty of his own body; he is not understood to have given away the right of sovereignty; and therefore his subjects are obliged to yield obedience to the magistrates formerly placed, governing not in their own name, but in his. For, his right remaining, the question is only of the administration; that is to say, of the magistrates and officers; which, if he have not means to name, he is supposed to approve those, which he himself had formerly appointed.

CHAPTER 22
Of Systems Subject, Political, and Private

Having spoken of the generation, form, and power of a commonwealth, I am in order to speak next of the parts thereof. And first of systems, which resemble the similar parts, or muscles of a body natural. By SYSTEMS, I understand any numbers of men joined in one interest, or one business. Of which, some are *regular,* and some *irregular. Regular* are those, where one man, or assembly of men, is constituted representative of the whole number. All other are *irregular.*

Of regular, some are *absolute,* and *independent,* subject to none but their own representative: such are only commonwealths; of which I have spoken already in the 5 last precedent chapters. Others are dependent; that is to say, subordinate to some sovereign power, to which every one, as also their representative is *subject*.

Of systems subordinate, some are *political,* and some *private. Political,* (otherwise called *bodies politic,* and *persons in law,*) are those, which are made by authority from the sovereign power of the commonwealth. *Private,* are those, which are constituted by subjects amongst themselves, or by authority from a stranger. For no authority derived from foreign power, within the dominion of another, is public there, but private.

And of private systems, some are *lawful;* some *unlawful. Lawful,* are those which are allowed by the commonwealth: all other are *unlawful. Irregular* systems, are those which having no representative, consist only in concourse of people; which if not forbidden by the commonwealth, nor made on evil design, (such as are conflux of people to markets, or shows, or any other harmless end,) are lawful. But when the intention is evil, or (if the number be considerable), unknown, they are unlawful.

In bodies politic, the power of the representative is always limited: and that which prescribeth the limits thereof, is the power sovereign. For power unlimited, is absolute sovereignty. And the sovereign, in every commonwealth, is the absolute representative of all the subjects; and therefore no other, can be representative of any part of them, but so far forth, as he shall give leave. And to give leave to a body politic of subjects, to have an absolute representative to all intents and purposes, were to abandon the government of so much of the commonwealth, and to divide the dominion, contrary to their peace and defence, which the sovereign cannot be understood to do, by any grant, that does not plainly, and directly discharge them of their subjection. For consequences of words, are not the signs of his will, when other consequences are signs of the contrary; but rather signs of error, and misreckoning; to which all mankind is too prone.

The bounds of that power, which is given to the representative of a body politic, are to be taken notice of, from two things. One is their writ, or letters from the sovereign: the other is the law of the commonwealth.

For though in the institution or acquisition of a commonwealth, which is independent, there needs no writing, because the power of the representative has there no other bounds, but such as are set out by the unwritten law of nature; yet in subordinate bodies, there are such diversities of limitation necessary, concerning their businesses, times, and places, as can neither be remembered without letters, nor taken notice of, unless such letters be patent, that they may be read to them, and withal sealed, or testified, with the seals, or other permanent signs of the authority sovereign.

And because such limitation is not always easy, or perhaps possible to be described in writing; the ordinary laws, common to all subjects, must determine, what the representative may lawfully do, in all cases, where the letters themselves are silent. And therefore

In a body politic, if the representative be one man, whatsoever he does in the person of the body, which is not warranted in his letters, nor by the laws, is his own act, and not the act of the body, nor of any other member thereof besides himself: because further than his letters, or the laws limit, he representeth no man's person, but his own. But what he does according to these, is the act of every one: for of the act of the sovereign every one is author, because he is their representative unlimited;

and the act of him that recedes not from the letters of the sovereign, is the act of the sovereign, and therefore every member of the body is author of it.

But if the representative be an assembly; whatsoever that assembly shall decree, not warranted by their letters, or the laws, is the act of the assembly, or body politic, and the act of every one by whose vote the decree was made; but not the act of any man that being present voted to the contrary; nor of any man absent, unless he voted it by procuration. It is the act of the assembly, because voted by the major part; and if it be a crime, the assembly may be punished, as far forth as it is capable, as by dissolution, or forfeiture of their letters (which is to such artificial, and fictitious bodies, capital) or (if the assembly have a common stock, wherein none of the innocent members have propriety,) by pecuniary mulct. For from corporal penalties nature hath exempted all bodies politic. But they that gave not their vote, are therefore innocent, because the assembly cannot represent any man in things unwarranted by their letters, and consequently are not involved in their votes.

If the person of the body politic being in one man, borrow money of a stranger, that is, of one that is not of the same body, (for no letters need limit borrowing, seeing it is left to men's own inclinations to limit lending), the debt is the representative's. For if he should have authority from his letters, to make the members pay what he borroweth, he should have by consequence the sovereignty of them; and therefore the grant were either void, as proceeding from error, commonly incident to human nature, and an insufficient sign of the will of the granter; or if it be avowed by him, then is the representer sovereign, and falleth not under the present question, which is only of bodies subordinate. No member therefore is obliged to pay the debt so borrowed, but the representative himself: because he that lendeth it, being a stranger to the letters, and to the qualification of the body, understandeth those only for his debtors, that are engaged: and seeing the representer can engage himself, and none else, has him only for debtor; who must therefore pay him, out of the common stock (if there be any), or (if there be none) out of his own estate.

If he come into debt by contract, or mulct, the case is the same.

But when the representative is an assembly, and the debt to a stranger; all they, and only they are responsible for the debt, that gave their votes to the borrowing of it, or to the contract that made it due, or to the fact for which the mulct was imposed; because every one of those in voting did engage himself for the payment: for he that is author of the borrowing, is obliged to the payment, even of the whole debt, though when paid by any one, he be discharged.

But if the debt be to one of the assembly, the assembly only is obliged to the payment, out of their common stock (if they have any:) for having liberty of vote, if he vote the money, shall be borrowed, he votes it shall be paid; if he vote it shall not be borrowed, or be absent, yet because in lending, he voteth the borrowing, he contradicteth his former vote, and is obliged by the latter, and becomes both borrower and lender, and consequently cannot demand payment from any particular man, but from the common treasure only; which failing he hath no remedy, nor complaint, but against himself, that being privy to the acts of the assembly, and to their means to pay, and not being enforced, did nevertheless through his own folly lend his money.

It is manifest by this, that in bodies politic subordinate, and subject to a sovereign power, it is sometimes not only lawful, but expedient, for a particular man to make open protestation against the decrees of the representative assembly, and cause their dissent to be registered, or to take witness of it; because otherwise they may be obliged to pay debts contracted, and be responsible for crimes committed by other men. But in a sovereign assembly, that liberty is taken away, both because he that protesteth there, denies their sovereignty; and also because whatsoever is commanded by the sovereign power, is as to the subject (though not so always in the sight of God) justified by the command; for of such command every subject is the author.

The variety of bodies politic, is almost infinite: for they are not only distinguished by the several affairs, for which they are constituted, wherein there is an unspeakable diversity; but also by the times, places, and numbers, subject to many limitations. And as to their affairs, some are ordained for government; as first, the government of a province may be committed to an assembly of men, wherein all resolutions shall depend on the votes of the major part; and then this assembly is a body politic, and their power limited by commission. This word province signifies a charge, or care of business, which he whose business it is, committeth to another man, to be administered for, and under him; and therefore when in one commonwealth there be divers countries, that have their laws distinct one from another, or are far distant in place, the administration of the government being committed to divers persons, those countries where the sovereign is not resident, but governs by commission, are called provinces. But of the government of a province, by an assembly residing in the province itself, there be few examples. The Romans who had the sovereignty of many provinces; yet governed them always by presidents, and praetors; and not by assemblies, as they governed the city of *Rome,* and territories adjacent. In like manner, when there were colonies sent from *England,* to plant *Virginia,* and *Sommer-islands;* though the government of them here, were committed to assemblies in *London,* yet did those assemblies never commit the government under them to any assembly there; but did to each plantation send one governor. For though every man, where he can be present by nature, desires to participate of government; yet where they cannot be present, they are by nature also inclined, to commit the government of their common interest rather to a monarchical, than a popular form of government: which is also evident in those men that have great private estates; who when they are unwilling to take the pains of administering the business that belongs to them, choose rather to trust one servant, than an assembly either of their friends or servants. But howsoever it be in fact, yet we may suppose the government of a province, or colony committed to an assembly: and when it is, that which in this place I have to say, is this; that whatsoever debt is by that assembly contracted; or whatsoever unlawful act is decreed, is the act only of those that assented, and not of any that dissented, or were absent, for the reasons before alleged. Also that an assembly residing out of the bounds of that colony whereof they have the government, cannot execute any power over the persons, or goods of any of the colony, to seize on them for debt, or other duty, in any place without the colony itself, as having no jurisdiction, nor authority elsewhere, but are left to the remedy, which the law of the place alloweth them. And though the assembly have right, to impose a mulct upon any of their members, that shall break the laws they make; yet out of the colony itself, they have no right to execute the same. And that which is said here, of the rights of an assembly, for the government of a province, or a colony, is appliable also to an assembly for the government of a town, an university, or a college, or a church, or for any other government over the persons of men.

And generally, in all bodies politic, if any particular member conceive himself injured by the body itself, the cognizance of his cause belongeth to the sovereign, and those the sovereign hath ordained for judges in such causes, or shall ordain for that particular cause; and not to the body itself. For the whole body is in this case his fellow subject, which in a sovereign assembly, is otherwise: for there, if the sovereign be not judge, though in his own cause, there can be no judge at all.

In a body politic, for the well ordering of foreign traffic, the most commodious representative is an assembly of all the members; that is to say, such a one, as every one that adventureth his money, may be present at all the deliberations, and resolutions of the body, if they will themselves. For proof whereof, we are to consider the end, for which men that are merchants, and may buy and sell, export, and import their merchandise according to their own discretions, do nevertheless bind themselves up in one corporation. It is true, there be few merchants, that with the merchandise they buy at home, can freight a ship, to export it; or with that they buy abroad, to bring it home; and have therefore need to join together in one society; where every man may either participate of the gain, according to the proportion of his adventure; or take his own, and sell what he transports, or imports, at such prices as he thinks fit. But this is no body politic, there being no common representative to oblige them to any other law, than that which is common to all other subjects. The end of their incorporating, is to make their gain the greater; which is done two ways; by sole buying, and sole selling, both at home, and abroad. So that to grant to a company of merchants to be a corporation, or body politic, is to grant them a double monopoly, whereof one is to be sole buyers; another to be sole sellers. For when there is a company incorporate for any particular foreign country, they only export the commodities vendible in that country; which is sole buying at home, and sole selling abroad. For at home there is but one buyer, and abroad but one that selleth: both which is gainful to the merchant, because thereby they buy at home at lower, and sell abroad at higher rates: and abroad there is but one buyer of foreign merchandise, and but one that sells them at home; both which again are gainful to the adventurers.

Of this double monopoly one part is disadvantageous to the people at home, the other to foreigners. For at home by their sole exportation they set what price they please on the husbandry, and handy-works of the people; and by the sole importation, what price they please on all foreign commodities the people have need of; both which are ill for the people. On the contrary, by the sole selling of the native commodities abroad, and sole buying the foreign commodities upon the place, they raise the price of those, and abate the price of these, to the disadvantage of the foreigner: for where but one selleth, the merchandise is the dearer; and where but one buyeth the cheaper. Such corporations therefore are no other than monopolies; though they would be very profitable for a commonwealth, if being bound up into one body in foreign markets they were at liberty at home, every man to buy, and sell at what price he could.

The end then of these bodies of merchants, being not a common benefit to the whole body, (which have in this case no common stock, but what is deducted out of the particular adventures, for building, buying, victualling and manning of ships,) but the particular gain of every adventurer, it is reason that every one be acquainted with the employment of his own; that is, that every one be of the assembly, that shall have the power to order the same; and be acquainted with their accounts. And therefore the representative of such a body must be an assembly, where every member of the body may be present at the consultations, if he will.

If a body politic of merchants, contract a debt to a stranger by the act of their representative assembly, every member is liable by himself for the whole. For a stranger can take no notice of their private laws, but considereth them as so many particular men, obliged every one to the whole payment, till payment made by one dischargeth all the rest: but if the debt be to one of the company, the creditor is debtor for the whole to himself, and cannot therefore demand his debt, but only from the common stock, if there be any.

If the commonwealth impose a tax upon the body, it is understood to be laid upon every member proportionably to his particular adventure in the company. For there is in this case no other common stock, but what is made of their particular adventures.

If a mulct be laid upon the body for some unlawful act, they only are liable by whose votes the act was decreed, or by whose assistance it was executed; for in none of the rest is there any other crime but being of the body; which if a crime, (because the body was ordained by the authority of the commonwealth,) is not his.

If one of the members be indebted to the body, he may be sued by the body; but his goods cannot be taken, nor his person imprisoned by the authority of the body; but only by authority of the commonwealth: for if they can do it by their own authority, they can by their own authority give judgment that the debt is due; which is as much as to be judge in their own cause.

These bodies made for the government of men, or of traffic, be either perpetual, or for a time prescribed by writing. But there be bodies also whose times are limited, and that only by the nature of their business. For example, if a sovereign monarch, or a sovereign assembly, shall think fit to give command to the towns, and other several parts of their territory, to send to him their deputies, to inform him of the condition, and necessities of the subjects, or to advise with him for the making of good laws, or for any other cause, as with one person representing the whole country, such deputies, having a place and time of meeting assigned them, are there, and at that time, a body politic, representing every subject of that dominion; but it is only for such matters as shall be propounded unto them by that man, or assembly, that by the sovereign authority sent for them; and when it shall be declared that nothing more shall be propounded, nor debated by them, the body is dissolved. For if they were the absolute representative of the people, then were it the sovereign assembly; and so there would be two sovereign assemblies, or two sovereigns, over the same people; which cannot consist with their peace. And therefore where there is once a sovereignty, there can be no absolute representation of the people, but by it. And for the limits of how far such a body shall represent the whole people, they are set forth in the writing by which they were sent for. For the people cannot choose their deputies to other intent, than is in the writing directed to them from their sovereign expressed.

Private bodies regular, and lawful, are those that are constituted without letters, or other written authority, saving the laws common to all other subjects. And because they be united in one person representative, they are held for regular; such as are all families, in which the father, or master ordereth the whole family. For he obligeth his children, and servants, as far as the law permitteth, though not further, because none of them are bound to obedience in those actions, which the law hath forbidden to be done. In all other actions, during the time they are under domestic government, they are subject to their fathers, and masters, as to their immediate sovereigns. For the father, and master, being before the institution of commonwealth, absolute sovereigns in their own families, they lose afterward no more of their authority, than the law of the commonwealth taketh from them.

Private bodies regular, but unlawful, are those that unite themselves into one person representative, without any public authority at all; such as are the corporations of beggars, thieves and gipsies, the better to order their trade of begging, and stealing; and the corporations of men, that by authority from any foreign person, unite themselves in another's dominion, for the easier propagation of doctrines, and for making a party, against the power of the commonwealth.

Irregular systems, in their nature, but leagues, or sometimes mere concourse of people, without union to any particular design, not by obligation of one to another, but proceeding only from a similitude of wills and inclinations, become lawful, or unlawful, according to the lawfulness, or unlawfulness of every particular man's design therein: and his design is to be understood by the occasion.

The leagues of subjects, (because leagues are commonly made for mutual defence,) are in a commonwealth (which is no more than a league of all the subjects together) for the most part unnecessary, and savour of unlawful design; and are for that cause unlawful, and go commonly by the name of factions, or conspiracies. For a league being a connexion of men by covenants, if there be no power given to any one man, or assembly (as in the condition of mere nature) to compel them to performance, is so long only valid, as there ariseth no just cause of distrust: and therefore leagues between commonwealths, over whom there is no human power established, to keep them all in awe, are not only lawful, but also profitable for the time they last. But leagues of the subjects of one and the same commonwealth, where every one may obtain his right by means of the sovereign power, are unnecessary to the maintaining of peace and justice, and (in case the design of them be evil, or unknown to the commonwealth) unlawful. For all uniting of strength by private men, is, if for evil intent, unjust; if for intent unknown, dangerous to the public, and unjustly concealed.

If the sovereign power be in a great assembly, and a number of men, part of the assembly, without authority, consult apart, to contrive the guidance of the rest; this is a faction, or conspiracy unlawful, as being a fraudulent seducing of the assembly for their particular interest. But if he, whose private interest is to be debated and judged in the assembly, make as many friends as he can; in him it is no injustice; because in this case he is no part of the assembly. And though he hire such friends with money, (unless there be an express law against it,) yet it is not injustice. For sometimes, (as men's manners are,) justice cannot be had without money; and every man may think his own cause just, till it be heard, and judged.

In all commonwealths, if a private man entertain more servants, than the government of his estate, and lawful employment he has for them requires, it is faction, and unlawful. For having the protection of the commonwealth, he needeth not the defence of private force. And whereas in nations not thoroughly civilized, several numerous families have lived in continual hostility, and invaded one another with private force; yet it is evident enough, that they have done unjustly; or else that they had no commonwealth.

And as factions for kindred, so also factions for government of religion, as of Papists, Protestants, &c. or of state, as patricians, and plebeians of old time in *Rome*, and of aristocraticals and democraticals of old time in *Greece*, are unjust, as being contrary to the peace and safety of the people, and a taking of the sword out of the hand of the sovereign.

Concourse of people, is an irregular system, the lawfulness, or unlawfulness, whereof dependeth on the occasion, and on the number of them that are assembled. If the occasion be lawful, and manifest, the concourse is lawful; as the usual meeting of men at church, or at a public show, in usual numbers: for if the numbers be extraordinarily great, the occasion is not evident; and consequently he that cannot render a particular and good account of his being amongst them, is to be judged conscious of an unlawful, and tumultuous design. It may be lawful for a thousand men, to join in a petition to be delivered to a judge, or magistrate; yet if a thousand men come to present it, it is a tumultuous assembly; because there needs but one or two for that purpose. But in such cases as these, it is not a set number that makes the assembly unlawful, but such a number, as the present officers are not able to suppress, and bring to justice.

When an unusual number of men, assemble against a man whom they accuse; the assembly is an unlawful tumult; because they may deliver their accusation to the magistrate by a few, or by one man. Such was the case of St. *Paul* at *Ephesus;* where *Demetrius,* and a great number of other men, brought two of *Paul's* companions before the magistrate, saying with one voice, *Great is Diana of the Ephesians;* which was their way of demanding justice against them for teaching the people such doctrine, as was against their religion, and trade. The occasion here, considering the laws of that people, was just; yet was their assembly judged unlawful, and the magistrate reprehended them for it, in these words (*Acts* 19. 40.) *If Demetrius and the other workmen can accuse any man, of any thing, there be pleas, and deputies, let them accuse one another. And if you have any other thing to demand, your case may be judged in an assembly lawfully called. For we are in danger to be accused for this day's sedition; because, there is no cause by which any man can render any reason of this concourse of people.* Where he calleth an assembly, whereof men can give no just account, a sedition, and such as they could not answer for. And this is all I shall say concerning *systems,* and assemblies of people, which may be compared (as I said,) to the similar parts of man's body; such as be lawful, to the muscles; such as are unlawful, to wens, biles, and apostems, engendered by the unnatural conflux of evil humours.

CHAPTER 23
Of the Public Ministers of Sovereign Power

In the last chapter I have spoken of the similar parts of a commonwealth: in this I shall speak of the parts organical, which are public ministers.

A PUBLIC MINISTER, is he, that by the sovereign, (whether a monarch, or an assembly,) is employed in any affairs, with authority to represent in that employment, the person of the commonwealth. And whereas every man, or assembly that hath sovereignty, representeth two persons, or (as the more common phrase is) has two capacities, one natural, and another politic, (as a monarch, hath the person not only of the commonwealth, but also of a man; and a sovereign assembly hath the person not only of the commonwealth, but also of the assembly); they that be servants to them in their natural capacity, are not public ministers; but those only that serve them in the administration of the public business. And therefore neither ushers, nor sergeants, nor other officers that wait on the assembly, for no other purpose, but for the commodity of the men assembled, in an aristocracy, or democracy; nor stewards, chamberlains, cofferers, or any other officers of the household of a monarch, are public ministers in a monarchy.

Of public ministers, some have charge committed to them of a general administration, either of the whole dominion, or of a part thereof. Of the whole, as to a protector, or regent, may be committed by the predecessor of an infant king, during his minority, the whole administration of his kingdom. In which case, every subject is so far obliged to obedience, as the ordinances he shall make, and the commands he shall give be in the king's name, and not inconsistent with his sovereign power. Of a part, or province; as when either a monarch, or a sovereign assembly, shall give the general charge thereof to a governor, lieutenant, praefect or viceroy: and in this case also, every one of that province, is obliged to all he shall do in the name of the sovereign, and that not incompatible with the sovereign's right. For such protectors, viceroys, and governors, have no other right, but what depends on the sovereign's will; and no commission that can be given them, can be interpreted for a declaration of the will to transfer the sovereignty, without express and perspicuous words to that purpose. And this kind of public ministers resembleth the nerves, and tendons that move the several limbs of a body natural.

Others have special administration; that is to say, charges of some special business, either at home, or abroad: as at home; first, for the economy of a commonwealth, they that have authority concerning the *treasure*, as tributes, impositions, rents, fines, or whatsoever public revenue, to collect, receive, issue, or take the accounts thereof, are public ministers: ministers, because they serve the person representative, and can do nothing against his command, nor without his authority: public, because they serve him in his political capacity.

Secondly, they that have authority concerning the *militia;* to have the custody of arms, forts, ports; to levy, pay, or conduct soldiers; or to provide for any necessary thing for the use of war, either by land or sea, are public ministers. But a soldier without command, though he fight for the commonwealth, does not therefore represent the person of it; because there is none to represent it to. For every one that hath command, represents it to them only whom he commandeth.

They also that have authority to teach, or to enable others to teach the people their duty to the sovereign power, and instruct them in the knowledge of what is just, and unjust, thereby to render them more apt to live in godliness, and in peace amongst themselves, and resist the public enemy, are public ministers: ministers, in that they do it not by their own authority, but by another's; and public, because they do it (or should do it) by no authority, but that of the sovereign. The monarch, or the sovereign assembly only hath immediate authority from God, to teach and instruct the people; and no man but the sovereign, receiveth his power *Dei gratia* simply; that is to say, from the favour of none but God: all other, receive theirs from the favour and providence of God, and their sovereigns; as in a monarchy *Dei gratia et regis;* or *Dei providentia et voluntate regis.*

They also to whom jurisdiction is given, are public ministers. For in their seats of justice they represent the person of the sovereign; and their sentence, is his sentence; for, (as hath been before declared) all judicature is essentially annexed to the sovereignty; and therefore all other judges are but ministers of him, or them that have the sovereign power. And as controversies are of two sorts, namely of *fact* and of *law;* so are judgments, some of fact, some of law: and consequently in the same controversy, there may be two judges, one of fact, another of law.

And in both these controversies, there may arise a controversy between the party judged, and the judge; which because they be both subjects to the sovereign, ought in equity to be judged by men agreed on by consent of both; for no man can be judge in his own cause. But the sovereign is already agreed on for judge by them both, and is therefore either to hear the cause, and determine it himself, or appoint for judge such as they shall both agree on. And this agreement is then understood to be made between them divers ways; as first, if the defendant be allowed to except against such of his judges, whose interest maketh him suspect them, (for as to the complainant he hath already chosen his own judge), those which he excepteth not against, are judges he himself agrees on. Secondly, if he appeal to any other judge, he can appeal no further; for his appeal is his choice. Thirdly, if he appeal to the sovereign himself, and he by himself, or by delegates which the parties shall agree on, give sentence; that sentence is final: for the defendant is judged by his own judges, that is to say, by himself.

These properties of just and rational judicature considered, I cannot forbear to observe the excellent constitution of the courts of justice, established both for Common, and also for Public Pleas in England. By Common Pleas, I mean those, where both the complainant and defendant are subjects: and by public, (which are also called Pleas of the Crown) those, where the complainant is the sovereign. For whereas there were two orders of men, whereof one was Lords, the other Commons; the Lords had this privilege, to have for judges in all capital crimes, none but Lords; and of them, as many as would be present; which being ever acknowledged as a privilege of favour, their judges were none but such as they had themselves desired. And in all controversies, every subject (as also in civil controversies the Lords) had for judges, men of the country where the matter in controversy lay; against which he might make his exceptions, till at last twelve men without exception being agreed on, they were judged by those twelve. So that having his own judges, there could be nothing alleged by the party, why the sentence should not be final. These public persons, with authority from the sovereign power, either to instruct, or judge the people, are such members of the commonwealth, as may fitly be compared to the organs of voice in a body natural.

Public ministers are also all those, that have authority from the sovereign, to procure the execution of judgments given; to publish the sovereign's commands; to suppress tumults; to apprehend, and imprison malefactors; and other acts tending to the conservation of the peace. For every act they do by such authority, is the act of the commonwealth; and their service, answerable to that of the hands, in a body natural.

Public ministers abroad, are those that represent the person of their own sovereign, to foreign states. Such are ambassadors, messengers, agents, and heralds, sent by public authority, and on public business.

But such as are sent by authority only of some private party of a troubled state, though they be received, are neither public, nor private ministers of the commonwealth; because none of their actions have the commonwealth for author. Likewise, an ambassador sent from a prince, to congratulate, condole, or to assist at a solemnity, though the authority be public; yet because the business is private, and belonging to him in his natural capacity; is a private person. Also if a man be sent into another country, secretly to explore their counsels, and strength; though both the authority, and the business be public; yet because there is none to take notice of any person in him, but his own; he is but a private minister; but yet a minister of the commonwealth; and may be compared to an eye in the body natural. And those that are appointed to receive the petitions or other informations of the people, and are as it were the public ear, are public ministers, and represent their sovereign in that office.

Neither a councillor, nor a council of state, if we consider it with no authority of judicature or command, but only of giving advice to the sovereign when it is required, or of offering it when it is not required, is a public person. For the advice is addressed to the sovereign only, whose person cannot in his own presence, be represented to him, by another. But a body of councillors, are never without some other authority, either of judicature, or of immediate administration: as in a monarchy, they represent the monarch, in delivering his commands to the public ministers: in a democracy, the council, or senate propounds the result of their deliberations to the people, as a council; but when they appoint judges, or hear causes, or give audience to ambassadors, it is in the quality of a minister of the people: and in an aristocracy, the council of state is the sovereign assembly itself; and gives counsel to none but themselves.

CHAPTER 24
Of the Nutrition, and Procreation of a Commonwealth

The Nutrition of a commonwealth consisteth, in the *plenty,* and *distribution* of *materials* conducing to life: in *concoction,* or *preparation;* and, (when concocted) in the *conveyance* of it, by convenient conduits, to the public use.

As for the plenty of matter, it is a thing limited by nature, to those commodities, which from (the two breasts of our common mother) land, and sea, God usually either freely giveth, or for labour selleth to mankind.

For the matter of this nutriment, consisting in animals, vegetals, and minerals, God hath freely laid them before us, in or near to the face of the earth; so as there needeth no more but the labour, and industry of receiving them. Insomuch as plenty dependeth (next to God's favour) merely on the labour and industry of men.

This matter, commonly called commodities, is partly *native,* and partly *foreign: native,* that which is to be had within the territory of the commonwealth: *foreign,* that which is imported from without. And because there is no territory under the dominion of one commonwealth, (except it be of very vast extent,) that produceth all things needful for the maintenance, and motion of the whole body; and few that produce not something more than necessary; the superfluous commodities to be had within, become no more superfluous, but supply these wants at home, by importation of that which may be had abroad, either by exchange, or by just war, or by labour: for a man's labour also, is a commodity exchangeable for benefit, as well as any other thing: and there have been commonwealths that having no more territory, than hath served them for habitation, have nevertheless, not only maintained, but also encreased their power, partly by the labour of trading from one place to another, and partly by selling the manufactures, whereof the materials were brought in from other places.

The distribution of the materials of this nourishment, is the constitution of *mine,* and *thine,* and *his;* that is to say, in one word *propriety;* and belongeth in all kinds of commonwealth to the sovereign power. For where there is no commonwealth, there is (as hath been already shown) a perpetual war of every man against his neighbour; and therefore every thing is his that getteth it, and keepeth it by force; which is neither *propriety,* nor *community;* but *uncertainty.* Which is so evident, that even *Cicero,* (a passionate defender of liberty,) in a public pleading, attributeth all propriety to the law civil. *Let the civil law,* saith he, *be once abandoned, or but negligently guarded, (not to say oppressed,) and there is nothing, that any man can be sure to receive from his ancestor, or leave to his children.* And again; *Take away the civil law, and no man knows what is his own, and what another man's.* Seeing therefore the introduction of *propriety* is an effect of commonwealth; which can do nothing but by the person that represents it, it is the act only of the sovereign; and consisteth in the laws, which none can make that have not the sovereign power. And this they well knew of old, who called that Νόμος, (that is to say, *distribution,*) which we call law; and defined justice, by *distributing* to every man *his own.*

In this distribution, the first law, is for division of the land itself: wherein the sovereign assigneth to every man a portion, according as he, and not according as any subject, or any number of them, shall judge agreeable to equity, and the common good. The children of Israel, were a commonwealth in the wilderness; but wanted the commodities of the earth, till they were masters of the Land of Promise; which afterward was divided amongst them, not by their own discretion, but by the discretion of *Eleazar* the Priest, and *Joshua* their General, who, when there were twelve tribes, making them thirteen by subdivision of the tribe of *Joseph;* made nevertheless but twelve portions of the land; and ordained for the tribe of *Levi* no land; but assigned them the tenth part of the whole fruits; which division was therefore arbitrary. And though a people coming into possession of a land by war, do not always exterminate the ancient inhabitants, (as did the Jews,) but leave to many, or most, or all of them their estates; yet it is manifest they hold them afterwards, as of the victors' distribution; as the people of *England* held all theirs of *William* the *Conqueror.*

From whence we may collect, that the propriety which a subject hath in his lands, consisteth in a right to exclude all other subjects from the use of them; and not to exclude their sovereign, be it an assembly, or a monarch. For seeing the sovereign, that is to say, the commonwealth (whose person he representeth,) is understood to do nothing but in order to the common peace and security, this distribution of lands, is to be understood as done in order to the same: and consequently, whatsoever distribution he shall make in prejudice thereof, is contrary to the will of every subject, that committed his peace, and safety to his discretion, and conscience; and therefore by the will of every one of them, is to be reputed void. It is true, that a sovereign monarch, or the greater part of a sovereign assembly, may ordain the doing of many things in pursuit of their passions, contrary to their own consciences, which is a breach of trust, and of the law of nature; but this is not enough to authorize any subject, either to make war upon, or so much as to accuse of injustice, or any way to speak evil of their sovereign; because they have authorized all his actions, and in bestowing the sovereign power, made them their own. But in what cases the commands of sovereigns are contrary to equity, and the law of nature, is to be considered hereafter in another place.

In the distribution of land, the commonwealth itself, may be conceived to have a portion, and possess, and improve the same by their representative; and that such portion may be made sufficient, to sustain the whole expense to the common peace, and defence necessarily required: Which were very true, if there could be any representative conceived free from human passions, and infirmities. But the nature of men being as it is, the setting forth of public land, or of any certain revenue for the commonwealth, is in vain; and tendeth to the dissolution of government, and to the condition of mere nature, and war, as soon as ever the sovereign power falleth into the hands of a monarch, or of an assembly, that are either too negligent of money, or too hazardous in engaging the public stock, into a long or costly war. Commonwealths can endure no diet: for seeing their expense is not limited by their own appetite, but by external accidents, and the appetites of their neighbours, the public riches cannot be limited by other limits, than those which the emergent occasions shall require. And whereas in *England,* there were by the Conqueror, divers lands reserved to his own use, (besides forests, and chases, either for his recreation, or for preservation of woods,) and divers services reserved on the land he gave his subjects; yet it seems they were not reserved for his maintenance in his public, but in his natural capacity. For he, and his successors did for all that, lay arbitrary taxes on all subjects' land, when they judged it necessary. Or if those public lands, and services, were ordained as a sufficient maintenance of the commonwealth, it was contrary to the scope of the institution; being (as it appeared by those ensuing taxes) insufficient, and (as it appears by the late small revenue of the crown) subject to alienation and diminution. It is therefore in vain, to assign a portion to the commonwealth; which may sell, or give it away; and does sell and give it away when it is done by their representative.

As the distribution of lands at home; so also to assign in what places, and for what commodities, the subject shall traffic abroad, belongeth to the sovereign. For if it did belong to private persons to use their own discretion therein, some of them would be drawn for gain, both to furnish the enemy with means to hurt the common-wealth, and hurt it themselves, by importing such things, as pleasing men's appetites, be nevertheless noxious, or at least unprofitable to them. And therefore it belongeth to the commonwealth, (that is, to the sovereign only,) to approve, or disapprove both of the places, and matter of foreign traffic.

Further, seeing it is not enough to the sustentation of a commonwealth, that every man have a propriety in a portion of land, or in some few commodities, or a natural property in some useful art, and there is no art in the world, but is necessary either for the being, or well being almost of every particular man; it is necessary, that men distribute that which they can spare, and transfer their propriety therein, mutually one to another, by exchange, and mutual contract. And therefore it belongeth to the commonwealth, (that is to say, to the sovereign,) to appoint in what manner, all kinds of contract between subjects, (as buying, selling, exchanging, borrowing, lending, letting, and taking to hire,) are to be made; and by what words and signs they shall be understood for valid. And for the matter, and distribution of the nourishment, to the several members of the commonwealth, thus much (considering the model of the whole work) is sufficient.

By concoction, I understand the reducing of all commodities, which are not presently consumed, but reserved for nourishment in time to come, to some thing of equal value, and withal so portable, as not to hinder the motion of men from place to place; to the end a man may have in what place soever, such nourishment as the place affordeth. And this is nothing else but gold, and silver, and money. For gold and silver, being (as it happens) almost in all countries of the world highly valued, is a commodious measure of the value of all things else between nations; and money (of what matter soever coined by the sovereign of a commonwealth,) is a sufficient measure of the value of all things else, between the subjects of that commonwealth. By the means of which measures, all commodities, moveable, and immoveable, are made to accompany a man, to all places of his resort, within and without the place of his ordinary residence; and the same passeth from man to man, within the commonwealth; and goes round about, nourishing (as it passeth) every part thereof; in so much as this concoction, is as it were the sanguification of the commonwealth: for natural blood is in like manner made of the fruits of the earth; and circulating, nourisheth by the way, every member of the body of man.

And because silver and gold, have their value from the matter itself; they have first this privilege, that the value of them cannot be altered by the power of one, nor of a few commonwealths; as being a common measure of the commodities of all places. But base money, may easily be enhanced, or abased. Secondly, they have the privilege to make commonwealths move, and stretch out their arms, when need is, into foreign countries; and supply, not only private subjects that travel, but also whole armies with provision. But that coin, which is not considerable for the matter, but for the stamp of the place, being unable to endure change of air, hath its effect at home only; where also it is subject to the change of laws, and thereby to have the value diminished, to the prejudice many times of those that have it.

The conduits, and ways by which it is conveyed to the public use, are of two sorts; one, that conveyeth it to the public coffers; the other, that issueth the same out again for public payments. Of the first sort, are collectors, receivers, and treasurers; of the second are the treasurers again, and the officers appointed for payment of several public or private ministers. And in this also, the artificial man maintains his resemblance with the natural; whose veins receiving the blood from the several parts of the body, carry it to the heart; where being made vital, the heart by the arteries sends it out again, to enliven, and enable for motion all the members of the same.

The procreation, or children of a commonwealth, are those we call *plantations,* or *colonies;* which are numbers of men sent out from the commonwealth, under a conductor, or governor, to inhabit a foreign country, either formerly void of inhabitants, or made void then, by war. And when a colony is settled, they are either a commonwealth of themselves, discharged of their subjection to their sovereign that sent them, (as hath been done by many commonwealths of ancient time,) in which case the commonwealth from which they went, was called their metropolis, or mother, and requires no more of them, than fathers require of the children, whom they emancipate and make free from their domestic government, which is honour, and friendship; or else they remain united to their metropolis, as were the colonies of the people of *Rome;* and then they are no commonwealths themselves, but provinces, and parts of the commonwealth that sent them. So that the right of colonies (saving honour, and league with their metropolis,) dependeth wholly on their licence, or letters, by which their sovereign authorized them to plant.

CHAPTER 25
Of Counsel

How fallacious it is to judge of the nature of things, by the ordinary and inconstant use of words, appeareth in nothing more, than in the confusion of counsels, and commands, arising from the imperative manner of speaking in them both, and in many other occasions besides. For the words *do this,* are the words not only of him that commandeth; but also of him that giveth counsel; and of him that exhorteth; and yet there are but few, that see not, that these are very different things; or that cannot distinguish between them, when they perceive who it is that speaketh, and to whom the speech is directed, and upon what occasion. But finding those phrases in men's writings, and being not able, or not willing to enter into a consideration of the circumstances, they mistake sometimes the precepts of counsellors, for the precepts of them that command; and sometimes the contrary; according as it best agreeth with the conclusions they would infer, or the actions they approve. To avoid which mistakes, and render to those terms of commanding, counselling, and exhorting, their proper and distinct significations, I define them thus.

COMMAND is where a man saith, *do this*, or *do not this*, without expecting other reason than the will of him that says it. From this it followeth manifestly, that he that commandeth, pretendeth thereby his own benefit: for the reason of his command is his own will only, and the proper object of every man's will, is some good to himself.

COUNSEL, is where a man saith, *do*, or *do not this*, and deduceth his reasons from the benefit that arriveth by it to him to whom he saith it. And from this it is evident, that he that giveth counsel, pretendeth only (whatsoever he intendeth) the good of him, to whom he giveth it.

Therefore between counsel and command, one great difference is, that command is directed to a man's own benefit; and counsel to the benefit of another man. And from this ariseth another difference, that a man may be obliged to do what he is commanded; as when he hath covenanted to obey: but he cannot be obliged to do as he is counselled, because the hurt of not following it, is his own; or if he should covenant to follow it, then is the counsel turned into the nature of a command. A third difference between them is, that no man can pretend a right to be of another man's counsel; because he is not to pretend benefit by it to himself: but to demand right to counsel another, argues a will to know his designs, or to gain some other good to himself; which (as I said before) is of every man's will the proper object.

This also is incident to the nature of counsel; that whatsoever it be, he that asketh it, cannot in equity accuse, or punish it: for to ask counsel of another, is to permit him to give such counsel as he shall think best; and consequently, he that giveth counsel to his sovereign, (whether a monarch, or an assembly) when he asketh it, cannot in equity be punished for it, whether the same be conformable to the opinion of the most, or not, so it be to the proposition in debate. For if the sense of the assembly can be taken notice of, before the debate be ended, they should neither ask, nor take any further counsel; for the sense of the assembly, is the resolution of the debate, and end of all deliberation. And generally he that demandeth counsel, is author of it; and therefore cannot punish it; and what the sovereign cannot, no man else can. But if one subject giveth counsel to another, to do any thing contrary to the laws, whether that counsel proceed from evil intention, or from ignorance only, it is punishable by the commonwealth; because ignorance of the law, is no good excuse, where every man is bound to take notice of the laws to which he is subject.

EXHORTATION, and DEHORTATION, is counsel, accompanied with signs in him that giveth it, of vehement desire to have it followed; or to say it more briefly, *counsel vehemently pressed.* For he that exhorteth, doth not deduce the consequences of what he adviseth to be done, and tie himself therein to the rigour of true reasoning; but encourages him he counselleth, to action: as he that dehorteth, deterreth him from it. And therefore they have in their speeches, a regard to the common passions, and opinions of men, in deducing their reasons; and make use of similitudes, metaphors, examples, and other tools of oratory, to persuade their hearers of the utility, honour, or justice of following their advice.

From whence may be inferred, first, that exhortation and dehortation, is directed to the good of him that giveth the counsel, not of him that asketh it, which is contrary to the duty of a counsellor; who (by the definition of counsel) ought to regard, not his own benefit, but his whom he adviseth. And that he directeth his counsel to his own benefit, is manifest enough, by the long and vehement urging, or by the artificial giving thereof; which being not required of him, and consequently proceeding from his own occasions, is directed principally to his own benefit, and but accidentally to the good of him that is counselled, or not at all.

Secondly, that the use of exhortation and dehortation lieth only where a man is to speak to a multitude; because when the speech is addressed to one, he may interrupt him, and examine his reasons more rigorously, than can be done in a multitude; which are too many to enter into dispute, and dialogue with him that speaketh indifferently to them all at once.

Thirdly, that they that exhort and dehort, where they are required to give counsel, are corrupt counsellors, and as it were bribed by their own interest. For though the counsel they give be never so good; yet he that gives it, is no more a good counsellor, than he that giveth a just sentence for a reward, is a just judge. But where a man may lawfully command, as a father in his family, or a leader in an army, his exhortations and dehortations, are not only lawful, but also necessary, and laudable: But then they are no more counsels, but commands; which when they are for execution of sour labour; sometimes necessity, and always humanity requireth to be sweetened in the delivery, by encouragement, and in the tune and phrase of counsel, rather than in harsher language of command.

Examples of the difference between command and counsel, we may take from the forms of speech that express them in Holy Scripture. *Have no other Gods but me; make to thyself no graven image; take not God's name in vain; sanctify the sabbath; honour thy parents; kill not; steal not, &c.* are commands; because the reason for which we are to obey them, is drawn from the will of God our king, whom we are obliged to obey. But these words, *Sell all thou hast; give it to the poor; and follow me,* are counsel; because the reason for which we are to do so, is drawn from our own benefit; which is this, that we shall have *treasure in Heaven.* These words, *Go into the village over against you, and you shall find an ass tied, and her colt; loose her, and bring her to me,* are a command: for the reason of their fact is drawn from the will of their Master: but these words, *Repent and be baptized in the name of Jesus,* are counsel; because the reason why we should so do, tendeth not to any benefit of God Almighty, who shall still be king in what manner soever we rebel; but of ourselves, who have no other means of avoiding the punishment hanging over us for our sins.

As the difference of counsel from command, hath been now deduced from the nature of counsel, consisting in a deducing of the benefit, or hurt that may arise to him that is to be counselled, by the necessary or probable consequences of the action he propoundeth; so may also the differences between *apt,* and *inept* counsellors be derived from the same. For experience, being but memory of the consequences of like actions formerly observed, and counsel but the speech whereby that experience is made known to another; the virtues, and defects of counsel, are the same with the virtues, and defects intellectual: and to the person of a commonwealth, his counsellors serve him in the place of memory, and mental discourse. But with this resemblance of the commonwealth, to a natural man, there is one dissimilitude joined, of great importance; which is, that a natural man receiveth his experience, from the natural objects of sense, which work upon him without passion, or interest of their own; whereas they that give counsel to the representative person of a commonwealth, may have, and have often their particular ends, and passions, that render their counsels always suspected, and many times unfaithful. And therefore we may set down for the first condition of a good counsellor, *that his ends, and interest, be not inconsistent with the ends and interest of him he counselleth.*

Secondly, because the office of a counsellor, when an action comes into delibera- tion, is to make manifest the consequences of it, in such manner, as he that is counselled may be truly and evidently informed; he ought to propound his advice, in such form of speech, as may make the truth most evidently appear; that is to say, with as firm ratiocination, as significant and proper language, and as briefly, as the evidence will permit. And therefore *rash, and unevident inferences;* (such as are fetched only from examples, or authority of books, and are not arguments of what is good, or evil, but witnesses of fact, or of opinion,) *obscure, confused, and ambiguous expressions, also all metaphorical speeches, tending to the stirring up of passion,* (because such reasoning, and such expressions, are useful only to deceive, or to lead him we counsel towards other ends than his own) *are repugnant to the office of a counsellor.*

Thirdly, because the ability of counselling proceedeth from experience, and long study; and no man is presumed to have experience in all those things that to the administration of a great commonwealth are necessary to be known, *no man is presumed to be a good counsellor, but in such business, as he hath not only been much versed in, but hath also much meditated on, and considered.* For seeing the business of a commonwealth is this, to preserve the people in peace at home, and defend them against foreign invasion, we shall find, it requires great knowledge of the disposition of mankind, of the rights of government, and of the nature of equity, law, justice, and honour, not to be attained without study; and of the strength, commodities, places, both of their own country, and their neighbours; as also of the inclinations, and designs of all nations that may any way annoy them. And this is not attained to, without much experience. Of which things, not only the whole sum, but every one of the particulars requires the age, and observation of a man in years, and of more than ordinary study. The wit required for counsel, as I have said before (chap. 8.) is judgment. And the differences of men in that point come from different educa- tion, of some to one kind of study, or business, and of others to another. When for the doing of any thing, there be infallible rules, (as in engines and edifices, the rules of geometry,) all the experience of the world cannot equal his counsel, that has learnt, or found out the rule. And when there is no such rule, he that hath most experience in that particular kind of business, has therein the best judgment, and is the best counsellor.

Fourthly, to be able to give counsel to a commonwealth, in a business that hath reference to another commonwealth, *it is necessary to be acquainted with the intelligences, and letters* that come from thence, *and with all the records of treaties, and other transactions of state* between them; which none can do, but such as the representative shall think fit. By which we may see, that they who are not called to counsel, can have no good counsel in such cases to obtrude.

Fifthly, supposing the number of counsellors equal, a man is better counselled by hearing them apart, than in an assembly; and that for many causes. First, in hearing them apart, you have the advice of every man; but in an assembly many of them deliver their advice with *aye,* or *no,* or with their hands, or feet, not moved by their own sense, but by the eloquence of another, or for fear of displeasing some that have spoken, or the whole assembly, by contradiction; or for fear of appearing duller in apprehension, than those that have applauded the contrary opinion. Secondly, in an assembly of many, there cannot choose but be some whose interests are contrary to that of the public; and these their interests make passionate, and passion eloquent, and eloquence draws others into the same advice. For the passions of men, which asunder are moderate, as the heat of one brand; in assembly are like many brands, that inflame one another, (especially when they blow one another with orations) to the setting of the commonwealth on fire, under pretence of counselling it. Thirdly, in hearing every man apart, one may examine (when there is need) the truth, or probability of his reasons, and of the grounds of the advice he gives, by frequent interruptions, and objections; which cannot be done in an assembly, where (in every difficult question) a man is rather astonied, and dazzled with the variety of discourse upon it, than informed of the course he ought to take. Besides, there cannot be an assembly of many, called together for advice, wherein there be not some, that have the ambition to be thought eloquent, and also learned in the politics; and give not their advice with care of the business propounded, but of the applause of their motley orations, made of the divers coloured threds, or shreads of authors; which is an impertinence at least, that takes away the time of serious consultation, and in the secret way of counselling apart, is easily avoided. Fourthly, in deliberations that ought to be kept secret, (whereof there be many occasions in public business,) the counsels of many, and especially in assemblies, are dangerous; and therefore great assemblies are necessitated to commit such affairs to lesser numbers, and of such persons as are most versed, and in whose fidelity they have most confidence.

To conclude, who is there that so far approves the taking of counsel from a great assembly of counsellors, that wisheth for, or would accept of their pains, when there is a question of marrying his children, disposing of his lands, governing his household, or managing his private estate, especially if there be amongst them such as wish not his prosperity? A man that doth his business by the help of many and prudent counsellors, with every one consulting apart in his proper element, does it best, as he that useth able seconds at tennis play, placed in their proper stations. He does next best, that useth his own judgment only; as he that has no second at all. But he that is carried up and down to his business in a framed counsel, which cannot move but by the plurality of consenting opinions, the execution whereof is commonly (out of envy, or interest) retarded by the part dissenting, does it worst of all, and like one that is carried to the ball, though by good players, yet in a wheel-barrow, or other frame, heavy of itself, and retarded also by the inconcurrent judgments, and endeavours of them that drive it; and so much the more, as they be more that set their hands to it; and most of all, when there is one, or more amongst them, that desire to have him lose. And though it be true, that many eyes see more than one; yet it is not to be understood of many counsellors; but then only, when the final resolution is in one man. Otherwise, because many eyes see the same thing in divers lines, and are apt to look asquint towards their private benefit; they that desire not to miss their mark, though they look about with two eyes, yet they never aim but with one; and therefore no great popular commonwealth was ever kept up; but either by a foreign enemy that united them; or by the reputation of some one eminent man amongst them; or by the secret counsel of a few; or by the mutual fear of equal factions; and not by the open consultations of the assembly. And as for very little commonwealths, be they popular, or monarchical, there is no human wisdom can uphold them, longer than the jealousy lasteth of their potent neighbours.

CHAPTER 26
Of Civil Laws

By CIVIL LAWS, I understand the laws, that men are therefore bound to observe, because they are members, not of this, or that commonwealth in particular, but of a commonwealth. For the knowledge of particular laws belongeth to them, that profess the study of the laws of their several countries; but the knowledge of civil law in general, to any man. The ancient law of *Rome* was called their *civil law*, from the word *civitas*, which signifies a commonwealth: and those countries, which having been under the Roman empire, and governed by that law, retain still such part thereof as they think fit, call that part the civil law, to distinguish it from the rest of their own civil laws. But that is not it I intend to speak of here; my design being not to show what is law here, and there; but what is law; as *Plato, Aristotle, Cicero,* and divers others have done, without taking upon them the profession of the study of the law.

And first it is manifest, that law in general, is not counsel, but command; nor a command of any man to any man; but only of him, whose command is addressed to one formerly obliged to obey him. And as for civil law, it addeth only the name of the person commanding, which is *persona civitatis,* the person of the commonwealth.

Which considered, I define civil law in this manner. CIVIL LAW, *is to every subject, those rules, which the commonwealth hath commanded him, by word, writing, or other sufficient sign of the will, to make use of, for the distinction of right, and wrong; that is to say, of what is contrary, and what is not contrary to the rule.*

In which definition, there is nothing that is not at first sight evident. For every man seeth, that some laws are addressed to all the subjects in general; some to particular provinces; some to particular vocations; and some to particular men; and are therefore laws, to every of those to whom the command is directed; and to none else. As also, that laws are the rules of just, and unjust; nothing being reputed unjust, that is not contrary to some law. Likewise, that none can make laws but the commonwealth; because our subjection is to the commonwealth only: and that commands, are to be signified by sufficient signs; because a man knows not otherwise how to obey them. And therefore, whatsoever can from this definition by necessary consequence be deduced, ought to be acknowledged for truth. Now I deduce from it this that followeth.

1. The legislator in all commonwealths, is only the sovereign, be he one man, as in a monarchy, or one assembly of men, as in a democracy, or aristocracy. For the legislator is he that maketh the law. And the commonwealth only, prescribes, and commandeth the observation of those rules, which we call law: therefore the commonwealth is the legislator. But the commonwealth is no person, nor has capacity to do any thing, but by the representative, (that is, the sovereign;) and therefore the sovereign is the sole legislator. For the same reason, none can abrogate a law made, but the sovereign; because a law is not abrogated, but by another law, that forbiddeth it to be put in execution.

2. The sovereign of a commonwealth, be it an assembly, or one man, is not subject to the civil laws. For having power to make, and repeal laws, he may when he

pleaseth, free himself from that subjection, by repealing those laws that trouble him, and making of new; and consequently he was free before. For he is free, that can be free when he will: nor is it possible for any person to be bound to himself; because he that can bind, can release; and therefore he that is bound to himself only, is not bound.

3. When long use obtaineth the authority of a law, it is not the length of time that maketh the authority, but the will of the sovereign signified by his silence, (for silence is sometimes an argument of consent;) and it is no longer law, than the sovereign shall be silent therein. And therefore if the sovereign shall have a question of right grounded, not upon his present will, but upon the laws formerly made; the length of time shall bring no prejudice to his right; but the question shall be judged by equity. For many unjust actions, and unjust sentences, go uncontrolled a longer time, than any man can remember. And our lawyers account no customs law, but such as are reasonable, and that evil customs are to be abolished: But the judgment of what is reasonable, and of what is to be abolished, belongeth to him that maketh the law, which is the sovereign assembly, or monarch.

4. The law of nature, and the civil law, contain each other, and are of equal extent. For the laws of nature, which consist in equity, justice, gratitude, and other moral virtues on these depending, in the condition of mere nature (as I have said before in the end of the 15th chapter,) are not properly laws, but qualities that dispose men to peace and to obedience. When a commonwealth is once settled, then are they actually laws, and not before; as being then the commands of the commonwealth; and therefore also civil laws: for it is the sovereign power that obliges men to obey them. For in the differences of private men, to declare, what is equity, what is justice, and what is moral virtue, and to make them binding, there is need of the ordinances of sovereign power, and punishments to be ordained for such as shall break them; which ordinances are therefore part of the civil law. The law of nature therefore is a part of the civil law in all commonwealths of the world. Reciprocally also, the civil law is a part of the dictates of nature. For justice, that is to say, performance of covenant, and giving to every man his own, is a dictate of the law of nature. But every subject in a commonwealth, hath covenanted to obey the civil law, (either one with another, as when they assemble to make a common representative, or with the representative it self one by one, when subdued by the sword they promise obedience, that they may receive life;) and therefore obedience to the civil law is part also of the law of nature. Civil, and natural law are not different kinds, but different parts of law; whereof one part being written, is called civil, the other unwritten, natural. But the right of nature, that is, the natural liberty of man, may by the civil law be abridged, and restrained: nay, the end of making laws, is no other, but such restraint; without the which there cannot possibly be any peace. And law was brought into the world for nothing else, but to limit the natural liberty of particular men, in such manner, as they might not hurt, but assist one another, and join together against a common enemy.

5. If the sovereign of one commonwealth, subdue a people that have lived under other written laws, and afterwards govern them by the same laws, by which they were governed before; yet those laws are the civil laws of the victor, and not of the vanquished commonwealth. For the legislator is he, not by whose authority the laws were first made, but by whose authority they now continue to be laws. And therefore where there be divers provinces, within the dominion of a commonwealth, and in

those provinces diversity of laws, which commonly are called the customs of each several province, we are not to understand that such customs have their force, only from length of time; but that they were anciently laws written, or otherwise made known, for the constitutions, and statutes of their sovereigns; and are now laws, not by virtue of the prescription of time, but by the constitutions of their present sovereigns. But if an unwritten law, in all the provinces of a dominion, shall be generally observed, and no iniquity appear in the use thereof; that law can be no other but a law of nature, equally obliging all mankind.

6. Seeing then all laws, written and unwritten, have their authority, and force, from the will of the commonwealth; that is to say, from the will of the representative; which in a monarchy is the monarch, and in other commonwealths the sovereign assembly; a man may wonder from whence proceed such opinions, as are found in the books of lawyers of eminence in several commonwealths, directly, or by consequence making the legislative power depend on private men, or subordinate judges. As for example, *that the common law, hath no controller but the parliament;* which is true only where a parliament has the sovereign power, and cannot be assembled, nor dissolved, but by their own discretion. For if there be a right in any else to dissolve them, there is a right also to control them, and consequently to control their controllings. And if there be no such right, then the controller of laws is not *parliamentum,* but *rex in parliamento.* And where a parliament is sovereign, if it should assemble never so many, or so wise men, from the countries subject to them, for whatsoever cause; yet there is no man will believe, that such an assembly hath thereby acquired to themselves a legislative power. *Item,* that the two arms of a commonwealth, are *force, and justice; the first whereof is in the king; the other deposited in the hands of the parliament.* As if a commonwealth could consist, where the force were in any hand, which justice had not the authority to command and govern.

7. That law can never be against reason, our lawyers are agreed; and that not the letter, (that is, every construction of it,) but that which is according to the intention of the legislator, is the law. And it is true: but the doubt is of whose reason it is, that shall be received for law. It is not meant of any private reason; for then there would be as much contradiction in the laws, as there is in the Schools; nor yet, (as Sir *Edward Coke* makes it,) an *artificial perfection of reason, gotten by long study, observation, and experience,* (as his was.) For it is possible long study may increase, and confirm erroneous sentences: and where men build on false grounds, the more they build, the greater is the ruin: and of those that study, and observe with equal time, and diligence, the reasons and resolutions are, and must remain discordant: and therefore it is not that *juris prudentia,* or wisdom of subordinate judges; but the reason of this our artificial man the commonwealth, and his command, that maketh law: and the commonwealth being in their representative but one person, there cannot easily arise any contradiction in the laws; and when there doth, the same reason is able, by interpretation, or alteration, to take it away. In all courts of justice, the sovereign (which is the person of the commonwealth,) is he that judgeth: the subordinate judge, ought to have regard to the reason, which moved his sovereign to make such law, that his sentence may be according thereunto; which then is his sovereign's sentence; otherwise it is his own, and an unjust one.

8. From this, that the law is a command, and a command consisteth in declaration, or manifestation of the will of him that commandeth, by voice, writing, or some other sufficient argument of the same, we may understand, that the command of

the commonwealth is law only to those, that have means to take notice of it. Over natural fools, children, or madmen there is no law, no more than over brute beasts; nor are they capable of the title of just, or unjust; because they had never power to make any covenant, or to understand the consequences thereof; and consequently never took upon them to authorize the actions of any sovereign, as they must do that make to themselves a commonwealth. And as those from whom nature, or accident hath taken away the notice of all laws in general; so also every man, from whom any accident, not proceeding from his own default, hath taken away the means to take notice of any particular law, is excused, if he observe it not; and to speak properly, that law is no law to him. It is therefore necessary, to consider in this place, what arguments, and signs be sufficient for the knowledge of what is the law; that is to say, what is the will of the sovereign, as well in monarchies, as in other forms of government.

And first, if it be a law that obliges all the subjects without exception, and is not written, nor otherwise published in such places as they may take notice thereof, it is a law of nature. For whatsoever men are to take knowledge of for law, not upon other men's words, but every one from his own reason, must be such as is agreeable to the reason of all men; which no law can be, but the law of nature. The laws of nature therefore need not any publishing, nor proclamation; as being contained in this one sentence, approved by all the world, *Do not that to another, which thou thinkest unreasonable to be done by another to thyself.*

Secondly, if it be a law that obliges only some condition of men, or one particular man, and be not written, nor published by word, then also it is a law of nature; and known by the same arguments, and signs, that distinguish those in such a condition, from other subjects. For whatsoever law is not written, or some way published by him that makes it law, can be known no way, but by the reason of him that is to obey it; and is therefore also a law not only civil, but natural. For example, if the sovereign employ a public minister, without written instructions what to do; he is obliged to take for instructions the dictates of reason; as if he make a judge, the judge is to take notice, that his sentence ought to be according to the reason of his sovereign, which being always understood to be equity, he is bound to it by the law of nature: or if an ambassador, he is (in all things not contained in his written instructions) to take for instruction that which reason dictates to be most conducing to his sovereign's interest; and so of all other ministers of the sovereignty, public and private. All which instructions of natural reason may be comprehended under one name of *fidelity;* which is a branch of natural justice.

The law of nature excepted, it belongeth to the essence of all other laws, to be made known, to every man that shall be obliged to obey them, either by word, or writing, or some other act, known to proceed from the sovereign authority. For the will of another, cannot be understood, but by his own word, or act, or by conjecture taken from his scope and purpose; which in the person of the commonwealth, is to be supposed always consonant to equity and reason. And in ancient time, before letters were in common use, the laws were many times put into verse; that the rude people taking pleasure in singing, or reciting them, might the more easily retain them in memory. And for the same reason *Solomon* adviseth a man, to bind the ten commandments upon his ten fingers. And for the law which *Moses* gave to the people of Israel at the renewing of the covenant, he biddeth them to teach it their children, by discoursing of it both at home, and upon the way; at going to bed, and at rising

from bed; and to write it upon the posts, and doors of their houses; and (*Deut.* 31. 12) to assemble the people, man, woman, and child, to hear it read.

Nor is it enough the law be written, and published; but also that there be manifest signs, that it proceedeth from the will of the sovereign. For private men, when they have, or think they have force enough to secure their unjust designs, and convoy them safely to their ambitious ends, may publish for laws what they please, without, or against the legislative authority. There is therefore requisite, not only a declaration of the law, but also sufficient signs of the author, and authority. The author, or legislator is supposed in every commonwealth to be evident, because he is the sovereign, who having been constituted by the consent of every one, is supposed by every one to be sufficiently known. And though the ignorance, and security of men be such, for the most part, as that when the memory of the first constitution of their commonwealth is worn out, they do not consider, by whose power they use to be defended against their enemies, and to have their industry protected, and to be righted when injury is done them; yet because no man that considers, can make question of it, no excuse can be derived from the ignorance of where the sovereignty is placed. And it is a dictate of natural reason, and consequently an evident law of nature, that no man ought to weaken that power, the protection whereof he hath himself demanded, or wittingly received against others. Therefore of who is sovereign, no man, but by his own fault, (whatsoever evil men suggest,) can make any doubt. The difficulty consisteth in the evidence of the authority derived from him; the removing whereof, dependeth on the knowledge of the public registers, public counsels, public ministers, and public seals; by which all laws are sufficiently verified; verified, I say, not authorized: for the verification, is but the testimony and record; not the authority of the law; which consisteth in the command of the sovereign only.

If therefore a man have a question of injury, depending on the law of nature; that is to say, on common equity; the sentence of the judge, that by commission hath authority to take cognizance of such causes, is a sufficient verification of the law of nature in that individual case. For though the advice of one that professeth the study of the law, be useful for the avoiding of contention; yet it is but advice: it is the judge must tell men what is law, upon the hearing of the controversy.

But when the question is of injury, or crime, upon a written law; every man by recourse to the registers, by himself or others, may (if he will) be sufficiently informed, before he do such injury, or commit the crime, whether it be an injury, or not: nay he ought to do so: for when a man doubts whether the act he goeth about, be just, or unjust; and may inform himself, if he will; the doing is unlawful. In like manner, he that supposeth himself injured, in a case determined by the written law, which he may by himself, or others see and consider; if he complain before he consults with the law, he does unjustly, and bewrayeth a disposition rather to vex other men, than to demand his own right.

If the question be of obedience to a public officer; to have seen his commission, with the public seal, and heard it read; or to have had the means to be informed of it, if a man would, is a sufficient verification of his authority. For every man is obliged to do his best endeavour, to inform himself of all written laws, that may concern his own future actions.

The legislator known; and the laws, either by writing, or by the light of nature, sufficiently published; there wanteth yet another very material circumstance to make them obligatory. For it is not the letter, but the intendment, or meaning; that is to say, the authentic interpretation of the law (which is the sense of the legislator,) in which the nature of the law consisteth; and therefore the interpretation of all laws dependeth on the authority sovereign; and the interpreters can be none but those, which the sovereign, (to whom only the subject oweth obedience) shall appoint. For else, by the craft of an interpreter, the law may be made to bear a sense, contrary to that of the sovereign; by which means the interpreter becomes the legislator.

All laws, written, and unwritten, have need of interpretation. The unwritten law of nature, though it be easy to such, as without partiality, and passion, make use of their natural reason, and therefore leaves the violators thereof without excuse; yet considering there be very few, perhaps none, that in some cases are not blinded by self love, or some other passion; it is now become of all laws the most obscure; and has consequently the greatest need of able interpreters. The written laws, if they be short, are easily misinterpreted, from the divers significations of a word, or two: if long they be more obscure by the divers significations of many words: insomuch as no written law, delivered in few, or many words, can be well understood, without a perfect understanding of the final causes, for which the law was made; the knowledge of which final causes is in the legislator. To him therefore there cannot be any knot in the law, insoluble; either by finding out the ends, to undo it by; or else by making what ends he will, (as *Alexander* did with his sword in the Gordian knot,) by the legislative power; which no other interpreter can do.

The interpretation of the laws of nature, in a commonwealth, dependeth not on the books of moral philosophy. The authority of writers, without the authority of the commonwealth, maketh not their opinions law, be they never so true. That which I have written in this treatise, concerning the moral virtues, and of their necessity, for the procuring, and maintaining peace, though it be evident truth, is not therefore presently law; but because in all commonwealths in the world, it is part of the civil law: For though it be naturally reasonable; yet it is by the sovereign power that it is law: otherwise, it were a great error, to call the laws of nature unwritten law; whereof we see so many volumes published, and in them so many contradictions of one another, and of themselves.

The interpretation of the law of nature, is the sentence of the judge constituted by the sovereign authority, to hear and determine such controversies, as depend thereon; and consisteth in the application of the law to the present case. For in the act of judicature, the judge doth no more but consider, whether the demand of the party, be consonant to natural reason, and equity; and the sentence he giveth, is therefore the interpretation of the law of nature; which interpretation is authentic; not because it is his private sentence; but because he giveth it by authority of the sovereign, whereby it becomes the sovereign's sentence; which is law for that time, to the parties pleading.

But because there is no judge subordinate, nor sovereign, but may err in a judgment of equity; if afterward in another like case he find it more consonant to equity to give a contrary sentence, he is obliged to do it. No man's error becomes his own law; nor obliges him to persist in it. Neither (for the same reason) becomes it a law to other judges, though sworn to follow it. For though a wrong sentence given by authority of the sovereign, if he know and allow it, in such laws as are mutable, be a constitution of a new law, in cases, in which every little circumstance is the same; yet in laws immutable, such as are the laws of nature, they are no laws to the same, or other judges, in the like cases for ever after. Princes succeed one another; and one judge passeth, another cometh; nay, heaven and earth shall pass; but not one title of the law of nature shall pass; for it is the eternal law of God. Therefore all the sentences of precedent judges that have ever been, cannot all together make a law contrary to natural equity: nor any examples of former judges, can warrant an unreasonable sentence, or discharge the present judge of the trouble of studying what is equity (in the case he is to judge,) from the principles of his own natural reason. For example sake, it is against the law of nature, *to punish the innocent;* and innocent is he that acquitteth himself judicially, and is acknowledged for innocent by the judge. Put the case now, that a man is accused of a capital crime, and seeing the power and malice of some enemy, and the frequent corruption and partiality of judges, runneth away for fear of the event, and afterwards is taken, and brought to a legal trial, and maketh it sufficiently appear, he was not guilty of the crime, and being thereof acquitted, is nevertheless condemned to lose his goods; this is a manifest condemnation of the innocent. I say therefore, that there is no place in the world, where this can be an interpretation of a law of nature, or be made a law by the sentences of precedent judges, that had done the same. For he that judged it first, judged unjustly; and no injustice can be a pattern of judgment to succeeding judges. A written law may forbid innocent men to fly, and they may be punished for flying: but that flying for fear of injury, should be taken for presumption of guilt, after a man is already absolved of the crime judicially, is contrary to the nature of a presumption, which hath no place after judgment given. Yet this is set down by a great lawyer for the common law of *England. If a man,* (saith he) *that is innocent, be accused of felony, and for fear flyeth for the same; albeit he judicially acquitteth himself of the felony; yet if it be found that he fled for the felony; he shall notwithstanding his innocency, forfeit all his goods, chattels, debts, and duties. For as to the forfeiture of them, the law will admit no proof against the presumption in law, grounded upon his flight.* Here you see, *an innocent man judicially acquitted, notwithstanding his innocency,* (when no written law forbad him to fly) after his acquittal, *upon a presumption in law,* condemned to lose all the goods he hath. If the law ground upon his flight a presumption of the fact, (which was capital,) the sentence ought to have been capital: if the presumption were not of the fact, for what then ought he to lose his goods? This therefore is no law of *England;* nor is the condemnation grounded upon a presumption of law, but upon the presumption of the judges. It is also against law, to say that no proof shall be admitted against a presumption of law. For all judges, sovereign and subordinate, if they refuse to hear proof, refuse to do justice: for though the sentence be just, yet the judges that condemn without hearing the proofs offered, are unjust judges; and their presumption is but prejudice; which no man ought to bring with him to the seat of justice, whatsoever precedent judgments, or examples he shall pretend to follow. There be other things of this nature, wherein men's judgments have been perverted, by trusting to precedents: but this is enough to show, that though the sentence of the judge, be a law to the party pleading, yet it is no law to any judge, that shall succeed him in that office.

In like manner, when question is of the meaning of written laws, he is not the interpreter of them, that writeth a commentary upon them. For commentaries are commonly more subject to cavil, than the text; and therefore need other commentaries; and so there will be no end of such interpretation. And therefore unless there be an interpreter authorized by the sovereign, from which the subordinate judges are not to recede, the interpreter can be no other than the ordinary judges, in the same manner, as they are in cases of the unwritten law; and their sentences are to be taken by them that plead, for laws in that particular case; but not to bind other judges, in like cases to give like judgments. For a judge may err in the interpretation even of written laws; but no error of a subordinate judge, can change the law, which is the general sentence of the sovereign.

In written laws, men use to make a difference between the letter, and the sentence of the law: and when by the letter, is meant whatsoever can be gathered from the bare words, it is well distinguished. For the significations of almost all words, are either in themselves, or in the metaphorical use of them, ambiguous; and may be drawn in argument, to make many senses; but there is only one sense of the law. But if by the letter, be meant the literal sense, then the letter, and the sentence or intention of the law, is all one. For the literal sense is that, which the legislator intended, should by the letter of the law be signified. Now the intention of the legislator is always supposed to be equity: for it were a great contumely for a judge to think otherwise of the sovereign. He ought therefore, if the word of the law do not fully authorize a reasonable sentence, to supply it with the law of nature; or if the case be difficult, to respite judgment till he have received more ample authority. For example, a written law ordaineth, that he which is thrust out of his house by force, shall be restored by force: it happens that a man by negligence leaves his house empty, and returning is kept out by force, in which case there is no special law ordained. It is evident, that this case is contained in the same law: for else there is no remedy for him at all; which is to be supposed against the intention of the legislator. Again, the word of the law, commandeth to judge according to the evidence: a man is accused falsely of a fact, which the judge saw himself done by another; and not by him that is accused. In this case neither shall the letter of the law be followed to the condemnation of the innocent, nor shall the judge give sentence against the evidence of the witnesses; because the letter of the law is to the contrary: but procure of the sovereign that another be made judge, and himself witness. So that the incommodity that follows the bare words of a written law, may lead him to the intention of the law, whereby to interpret the same the better; though no incommodity can warrant a sentence against the law. For every judge of right, and wrong, is not judge of what is commodious, or incommodious to the commonwealth.

The abilities required in a good interpreter of the law, that is to say, in a good judge, are not the same with those of an advocate; namely the study of the laws. For a judge, as he ought to take notice of the fact, from none but the witnesses; so also he ought to take notice of the law, from nothing but the statutes, and constitutions of the sovereign, alleged in the pleading, or declared to him by some that have authority from the sovereign power to declare them; and need not take care beforehand, what he shall judge; for it shall be given him what he shall say concerning the fact, by witnesses; and what he shall say in point of law, from those that shall in their pleadings show it, and by authority interpret it upon the place. The Lords of parliament in *England* were judges, and most difficult causes have been heard and determined by them; yet few of them were much versed in the study of the laws, and fewer had made profession of them: and though they consulted with lawyers, that were appointed to be present there for that purpose; yet they alone had the authority of giving sentence. In like manner, in the ordinary trials of right, twelve men of the common people, are the judges, and give sentence, not only of the fact, but of the right; and pronounce simply for the complainant, or for the defendant; that is to say, are judges not only of the fact, but also of the right: and in a question of crime, not only determine whether done, or not done; but also whether it be *murder, homicide, felony, assault,* and the like, which are determinations of law: but because they are not supposed to know the law of themselves, there is one that hath authority to inform them of it, in the particular case they are to judge of. But yet if they judge not according to that he tells them, they are not subject thereby to any penalty; unless it be made appear, they did it against their consciences, or had been corrupted by reward.

The things that make a good judge, or good interpreter of the laws, are, first, *a right understanding* of that principal law of nature called *equity;* which depending not on the reading of other men's writings, but on the goodness of a man's own natural reason, and meditation, is presumed to be in those most, that have had most leisure, and had the most inclination to meditate thereon. Secondly, *contempt of unnecessary riches, and preferments.* Thirdly, *to be able in judgment to divest himself of all fear, anger, hatred, love, and compassion.* Fourthly, and lastly, *patience to hear; diligent attention in hearing; and memory to retain, digest and apply what he hath heard.*

The difference and division of the laws, has been made in divers manners, according to the different methods, of those men that have written of them. For it is a thing that dependeth not on nature, but on the scope of the writer; and is subservient to every man's proper method. In the Institutions of *Justinian,* we find seven sorts of civil laws.

1. The *edicts, constitutions,* and *epistles of the prince,* that is, of the emperor; because the whole power of the people was in him. Like these, are the proclamations of the kings of *England.*

2. *The decrees of the whole people of Rome,* (comprehending the senate,) when they were put to the question by the *senate.* These were laws, at first, by the virtue of the sovereign power residing in the people; and such of them as by the emperors were not abrogated, remained laws, by the authority imperial. For all laws that bind, are understood to be laws by his authority that has power to repeal them. Somewhat like to these laws, are the acts of parliament in England.

3. *The decrees of the common people,* (excluding the senate,) when they were put to the question by the *tribune* of the people. For such of them as were not abrogated by the emperors, remained laws by the authority imperial. Like to these, were the orders of the House of Commons in *England.*

4. *Senatus consulta,* the *orders of the senate;* because when the people of *Rome* grew so numerous, as it was inconvenient to assemble them; it was thought fit by the emperor, that men should consult the senate, instead of the people: and these have some resemblance with the acts of council.

5. *The edicts of praetors,* and (in some cases) of the *aediles:* such as are the chief justices in the courts of *England.*

6. *Responsa prudentum;* which were the sentences, and opinions of those lawyers, to whom the emperor gave authority to interpret the law, and to give answer to such as in matter of law demanded their advice; which answers, the judges in giving judgment were obliged by the constitutions of the emperor to observe: and should be like the reports of cases judged, if other judges be by the law of *England* bound to observe them. For the judges of the common law of *England,* are not properly judges, but *juris consulti;* of whom the judges, who are either the lords, or twelve men of the country, are in point of law to ask advice.

7. Also, *unwritten customs,* (which in their own nature are an imitation of law,) by the tacit consent of the emperor, in case they be not contrary to the law of nature, are very laws.

Another division of laws, is into *natural* and *positive. Natural* are those which have been laws from all eternity; and are called not only *natural,* but also *moral* laws; consisting in the moral virtues, as justice, equity, and all habits of the mind that conduce to peace, and charity; of which I have already spoken in the fourteenth and fifteenth chapters.

Positive, are those which have not been from eternity; but have been made laws by the will of those that have had the sovereign power over others; and are either written, or made known to men, by some other argument of the will of their legislator.

Again, of positive laws, some are *human,* some *divine;* and of human positive laws, some are *distributive,* some *penal. Distributive* are those that determine the rights of the subjects, declaring to every man what it is, by which he acquireth and holdeth a propriety in lands, or goods, and a right or liberty of action: and these speak to all the subjects. *Penal* are those, which declare, what penalty shall be inflicted on those that violate the law; and speak to the ministers and officers ordained for execution. For though every one ought to be informed of the punishments ordained beforehand for their transgression; nevertheless the command is not addressed to the delinquent, (who cannot be supposed will faithfully punish himself,) but to public ministers appointed to see the penalty executed. And these penal laws are for the most part written together with the laws distributive; and are sometimes called judgments. For all laws are general judgments, or sentences of the legislator; as also every particular judgment, is a law to him, whose case is judged.

Divine positive laws (for natural laws being eternal, and universal, are all divine,) are those, which being the commandments of God, (not from all eternity, nor universally addressed to all men, but only to a certain people, or to certain persons,) are declared for such, by those whom God hath authorized to declare them. But this authority of man to declare what be these positive laws of God, how can it be known? God may command a man by a supernatural way, to deliver laws to other men. But because it is of the essence of law, that he who is to be obliged, be assured of the authority of him that declareth it, which we cannot naturally take notice to be from God, *how can a man without supernatural revelation be assured of the revelation received by the declarer?* and *how can he be bound to obey them?* For the first question, how a man can be assured of the revelation of another, without a revelation particularly to himself, it is evidently impossible. For though a man may be induced to believe such revelation, from the miracles they see him do, or from seeing the extraordinary sanctity of his life, or from seeing the extraordinary wisdom, or extraordinary felicity of his actions, all which are marks of God's extraordinary favour; yet they are not assured evidences of special revelation. Miracles are marvellous works: but that which is marvellous to one, may not be so to another. Sanctity may be feigned; and the visible felicities of this world, are most often the work of God by natural, and ordinary causes. And therefore no man can infallibly know by natural reason, that another has had a supernatural revelation of God's will; but only a belief; every one (as the signs thereof shall appear greater, or lesser) a firmer, or a weaker belief.

But for the second, how he can be bound to obey them; it is not so hard. For if the law declared, be not against the law of nature (which is undoubtedly God's law) and he undertake to obey it, he is bound by his own act; bound I say to obey it, but not bound to believe it: for men's belief, and interior cogitations, are not subject to the commands, but only to the operation of God, ordinary, or extraordinary. Faith of supernatural law, is not a fulfilling, but only an assenting to the same; and not a duty that we exhibit to God, but a gift which God freely giveth to whom he pleaseth; as also unbelief is not a breach of any of his laws; but a rejection of them all, except the laws natural. But this that I say, will be made yet clearer, by the examples and testimonies concerning this point in holy Scripture. The covenant God made with *Abraham* (in a supernatural manner) was thus, (*Gen.* 17. 10) *This is the covenant which thou shalt observe between me and thee and thy seed after thee.* *Abraham's* seed had not this revelation, nor were yet in being; yet they are a party to the covenant, and bound to obey what *Abraham* should declare to them for God's law; which they could not be, but in virtue of the obedience they owed to their parents; who (if they be subject to no other earthly power, as here in the case of *Abraham*) have sovereign power over their children and servants. Again, where God saith to *Abraham, In thee shall all nations of the earth be blessed; for I know thou wilt command thy children, and thy house after thee to keep the way of the Lord, and to observe righteousness and judgment,* it is manifest, the obedience of his family, who had no revelation, depended on their former obligation to obey their sovereign. At Mount *Sinai Moses* only went up to God; the people were forbidden to approach on pain of death; yet were they bound to obey all that Moses declared to them for God's law. Upon what ground, but on this submission of their own, *Speak thou to us, and we will hear thee; but let not God speak to us, lest we die?* By which two places it sufficiently appeareth, that in a commonwealth, a subject that has no certain and assured revelation particularly to himself concerning the will of God, is to obey for such, the command of the commonwealth: for if men were at liberty, to take for God's commandments, their own dreams, and fancies, or the dreams and fancies of private men; scarce two men would agree upon what is God's commandment; and yet in respect of them, every man would despise the commandments of the commonwealth. I conclude therefore, that in all things not contrary to the moral law, (that is to say, to the law of nature,) all subjects are bound to obey that for divine law, which is declared to be so, by the laws of the commonwealth. Which also is evident to any man's reason; for whatsoever is not against the law of nature, may be made law in the name of them that have the sovereign power; and there is no reason men should be the less obliged by it, when it is propounded in the name of God. Besides, there is no place in the world where men are permitted to pretend other commandments of God, than are declared for such by the commonwealth. Christian states punish those that revolt from Christian religion, and all other states, those that set up any religion by them forbidden. For in whatsoever is not regulated by the commonwealth, it is equity, (which is the law of nature, and therefore an eternal law of God) that every man equally enjoy his liberty.

There is also another distinction of laws, into *fundamental* and *not fundamental*, but I could never see in any author, what a fundamental law signifieth. Nevertheless one may very reasonably distinguish laws in that manner.

For a fundamental law in every commonwealth is that, which being taken away, the commonwealth faileth, and is utterly dissolved; as a building whose foundation is destroyed. And therefore a fundamental law is that, by which subjects are bound to uphold whatsoever power is given to the sovereign, whether a monarch, or a sovereign assembly, without which the commonwealth cannot stand; such as is the power of war and peace, of judicature, of election of officers, and of doing whatsoever he shall think necessary for the public good. Not fundamental is that, the abrogating whereof, draweth not with it the dissolution of the commonwealth; such as are the laws concerning controversies between subject and subject. Thus much of the division of laws.

I find the words *lex civilis*, and *jus civile*, that is to say, *law* and *right civil*, promiscuously used for the same thing, even in the most learned authors; which nevertheless ought not to be so. For *right* is *liberty*, namely that liberty which the civil law leaves us: but *civil law* is an *obligation;* and takes from us the liberty which the law of nature gave us. Nature gave a right to every man to secure himself by his own strength, and to invade a suspected neighbour, by way of prevention: but the civil law takes away that liberty, in all cases where the protection of the law may be safely stayed for. Insomuch as *lex* and *jus*, are as different as *obligation* and *liberty*.

Likewise *laws* and *charters* are taken promiscuously for the same thing. Yet charters are donations of the sovereign; and not laws, but exemptions from law. The phrase of a law is, *jubeo, injungo, I command*, and *enjoin:* the phrase of a charter is, *dedi, concessi, I have given, I have granted:* but what is given or granted, to a man, is not forced upon him, by a law. A law may be made to bind all the subjects of a commonwealth: a liberty, or charter is only to one man, or some one part of the people. For to say all the people of a commonwealth, have liberty in any case whatsoever; is to say, that in such case, there hath been no law made; or else having been made, is now abrogated.

CHAPTER 27
Of Crimes, Excuses, and Extenuations

A *sin*, is not only a transgression of a law, but also any contempt of the legislator. For such contempt, is a breach of all his laws at once. And therefore may consist, not only in the *commission* of a fact, or in the speaking of words by the laws forbidden, or in the *omission* of what the law commandeth, but also in the *intention*, or purpose to transgress. For the purpose to break the law, is some degree of contempt of him, to whom it belongeth to see it executed. To be delighted in the imagination only, of being possessed of another man's goods, servants, or wife, without any intention to take them from him by force or fraud, is no breach of the law, that saith, *Thou shalt not covet:* nor is the pleasure a man may have in imagining, or dreaming of the death of him, from whose life he expecteth nothing but damage, and displeasure, a sin; but the resolving to put some act in execution, that tendeth thereto. For to be pleased in the fiction of that, which would please a man if it were real, is a passion so adherent to the nature both of man, and every other living creature, as to make it a sin, were to make sin of being a man. The consideration of this, has made me think them too severe, both to themselves, and others, that maintain, that the first motions of the mind, (though checked with the fear of God) be sins. But I confess it is safer to err on that hand, than on the other.

A CRIME, is a sin, consisting in the committing (by deed, or word) of that which the law forbiddeth, or the omission of what it hath commanded. So that every crime is a sin; but not every sin a crime. To intend to steal, or kill, is a sin, though it never appear in word, or fact: for God that seeth the thoughts of man, can lay it to his charge: but till it appear by something done, or said, by which the intention may be argued by a human judge, it hath not the name of crime: which distinction the Greeks observed, in the word ἁμάρτημα, and ἔγκλημα, or ἀιτία; whereof the former, (which is translated *sin*,) signifieth any swerving from the law whatsoever; but the two latter, (which are translated *crime*,) signify that sin only, whereof one man may accuse another. But of intentions, which never appear by any outward act, there is no place for human accusation. In like manner the Latins by *peccatum*, which is *sin*, signify all manner of deviation from the law; but by *crimen*, (which word they derive from *cerno*, which signifies to perceive,) they mean only such sins, as may be made appear before a judge; and therefore are not mere intentions.

From this relation of sin to the law, and of crime to the civil law, may be inferred, first, that where law ceaseth, sin ceaseth. But because the law of nature is eternal, violation of covenants, ingratitude, arrogance, and all facts contrary to any moral virtue, can never cease to be sin. Secondly, that the civil law ceasing, crimes cease: for there being no other law remaining, but that of nature, there is no place for accusation; every man being his own judge, and accused only by his own conscience, and cleared by the uprightness of his own intention. When therefore his intention is right, his fact is no sin: if otherwise, his fact is sin; but not crime. Thirdly, that when the sovereign power ceaseth, crime also ceaseth: for where there is no such power, there is no protection to be had from the law; and therefore every one may protect himself by his own power: for no man in the institution of sovereign power can be supposed to give away the right of preserving his own body; for the safety whereof all sovereignty was ordained. But this is to be understood only of those, that have not themselves contributed to the taking away of the power that protected them: for that was a crime from the beginning.

The source of every crime, is some defect of the understanding; or some error in reasoning; or some sudden force of the passions. Defect in the understanding, is *ignorance;* in reasoning, *erroneous opinion*. Again, ignorance is of three sorts; of the *law*, and of the *sovereign*, and of the *penalty*. Ignorance of the law of nature excuseth no man; because every man that hath attained to the use of reason, is supposed to know, he ought not to do to another, what he would not have done to himself. Therefore into what place soever a man shall come, if he do any thing contrary to that law, it is a crime. If a man come from the *Indies* hither, and persuade men here to receive a new religion, or teach them any thing that tendeth to disobedience of the laws of this country, though he be never so well persuaded of the truth of what he teacheth, he commits a crime, and may be justly punished for the same, not only because his doctrine is false, but also because he does that which he would not approve in another, namely, that coming from hence, he should endeavour to alter the religion there. But ignorance of the civil law, shall excuse a man in a strange country, till it be declared to him; because, till then no civil law is binding.

In the like manner, if the civil law of a man's own country, be not so sufficiently declared, as he may know it if he will; nor the action against the law of nature; the ignorance is a good excuse: in other cases ignorance of the civil law, excuseth not.

Ignorance of the sovereign power, in the place of a man's ordinary residence, excuseth him not; because he ought to take notice of the power, by which he hath been protected there.

Ignorance of the penalty, where the law is declared, excuseth no man: for in breaking the law, which without a fear of penalty to follow, were not a law, but vain words, he undergoeth the penalty, though he know not what it is; because, whosoever voluntarily doth any action, accepteth all the known consequences of it; but punishment is a known consequence of the violation of the laws, in every commonwealth; which punishment, if it be determined already by the law, he is subject to that; if not, then is he subject to arbitrary punishment. For it is reason, that he which does injury, without other limitation than that of his own will, should suffer punishment without other limitation, than that of his will whose law is thereby violated.

But when a penalty, is either annexed to the crime in the law itself, or hath been usually inflicted in the like cases; there the delinquent is excused from a greater penalty. For the punishment foreknown, if not great enough to deter men from the action, is an invitement to it: because when men compare the benefit of their injustice, with the harm of their punishment, by necessity of nature they choose that which appeareth best for themselves: and therefore when they are punished more than the law had formerly determined, or more than others were punished for the same crime; it is the law that tempted, and deceiveth them.

No law, made after a fact done, can make it a crime: because if the fact be against the law of nature, the law was before the fact; and a positive law cannot be taken notice of, before it be made; and therefore cannot be obligatory. But when the law that forbiddeth a fact, is made before the fact be done; yet he that doth the fact, is liable to the penalty ordained after, in case no lesser penalty were made known before, neither by writing, nor by example, for the reason immediately before alleged.

From defect in reasoning, (that is to say, from error,) men are prone to violate the laws, three ways. First, by presumption of false principles: as when men from having observed how in all places, and in all ages, unjust actions have been authorized by the force, and victories of those who have committed them; and that potent men, breaking through the cobweb laws of their country, the weaker sort, and those that have failed in their enterprises, have been esteemed the only criminals; have thereupon taken for principles, and grounds of their reasoning, *that justice is but a vain word: that whatsoever a man can get by his own industry, and hazard, is his own: that the practice of all nations cannot be unjust: that examples of former times are good arguments of doing the like again;* and many more of that kind: which being granted, no act in itself can be a crime, but must be made so (not by the law, but) by the success of them that commit it; and the same fact be virtuous, or vicious, as fortune pleaseth; so that what *Marius* makes a crime, *Sylla* shall make meritorious, and *Caesar,* (the same laws standing) turn again into a crime, to the perpetual disturbance of the peace of the commonwealth.

Secondly, by false teachers, that either misinterpret the law of nature, making it thereby repugnant to the law civil; or by teaching for laws, such doctrines of their own, or traditions of former times, as are inconsistent with the duty of a subject.

Thirdly, by erroneous inferences from true principles; which happens commonly to men that are hasty, and precipitate in concluding, and resolving what to do; such as are they, that have both a great opinion of their own understanding, and believe that things of this nature require not time and study, but only common experience, and a good natural wit; whereof no man thinks himself unprovided: whereas the knowledge, of right and wrong, which is no less difficult, there is no man will pretend to, without great and long study. And of those defects in reasoning, there is none that can excuse (though some of them may extenuate) a crime, in any man, that pretendeth to the administration of his own private business; much less in them that undertake a public charge; because they pretend to the reason, upon the want whereof they would ground their excuse.

Of the passions that most frequently are the causes of crime, one, is vain glory, or a foolish overrating of their own worth; as if difference of worth, were an effect of their wit, or riches, or blood, or some other natural quality, not depending on the will of those that have the sovereign authority. From whence proceedeth a presumption that the punishments ordained by the laws, and extended generally to all subjects, ought not to be inflicted on them, with the same rigour they are inflicted on poor, obscure, and simple men, comprehended under the name of the *vulgar*.

Therefore it happeneth commonly, that such as value themselves by the greatness of their wealth, adventure on crimes, upon hope of escaping punishment, by corrupting public justice, or obtaining pardon by money, or other rewards.

And that such as have multitude of potent kindred; and popular men, that have gained reputation amongst the multitude, take courage to violate the laws, from a hope of oppressing the power, to whom it belongeth to put them in execution.

And that such as have a great, and false opinion of their own wisdom, take upon them to reprehend the actions, and call in question the authority of them that govern, and so to unsettle the laws with their public discourse, as that nothing shall be a crime, but what their own designs require should be so. It happeneth also to the same men, to be prone to all such crimes, as consist in craft, and in deceiving of their neighbours; because they think their designs are too subtle to be perceived. These I say are effects of a false presumption of their own wisdom. For of them that are the first movers in the disturbance of commonwealth, (which can never happen without a civil war,) very few are left alive long enough, to see their new designs established: so that the benefit of their crimes, redoundeth to posterity, and such as would least have wished it: which argues they were not so wise, as they thought they were. And those that deceive upon hope of not being observed, do commonly deceive themselves, (the darkness in which they believe they lie hidden, being nothing else but their own blindness;) and are no wiser than children, that think all hid, by hiding their own eyes.

And generally all vain-glorious men, (unless they be withal timorous,) are subject to anger; as being more prone than others to interpret for contempt, the ordinary liberty of conversation: and there are few crimes that may not be produced by anger.

As for the passions, of hate, lust, ambition, and covetousness, what crimes they are apt to produce, is so obvious to every man's experience and understanding, as there needeth nothing to be said of them, saving that they are infirmities, so annexed to the nature, both of man, and all other living creatures, as that their effects cannot be hindered, but by extraordinary use of reason, or a constant severity in punishing them. For in those things men hate, they find a continual, and unavoidable molestation; whereby either a man's patience must be everlasting, or he must be eased by removing the power of that which molesteth him. The former is difficult; the latter is many times impossible, without some violation of the law. Ambition, and covetousness are passions also that are perpetually incumbent, and pressing; whereas reason is not perpetually present, to resist them: and therefore whensoever the hope of impunity appears, their effects proceed. And for lust, what it wants in the lasting, it hath in the vehemence, which sufficeth to weigh down the apprehension of all easy, or uncertain punishments.

Of all passions, that which inclineth men least to break the laws, is fear. Nay, (excepting some generous natures,) it is the only thing, (when there is apparence of profit or pleasure by breaking the laws,) that makes men keep them. And yet in many cases a crime may be committed through fear.

For not every fear justifies the action it produceth, but the fear only of corporeal hurt, which we call *bodily fear,* and from which a man cannot see how to be delivered, but by the action. A man is assaulted, fears present death, from which he sees not how to escape, but by wounding him that assaulteth him; if he wound him to death, this is no crime; because no man is supposed at the making of a commonwealth, to have abandoned the defence of his life, or limbs, where the law cannot arrive time enough to his assistance. But to kill a man, because from his actions, or his threatenings, I may argue he will kill me when he can, (seeing I have time, and means to demand protection, from the sovereign power,) is a crime. Again, a man receives words of disgrace, or some little injuries, (for which they that made the laws, had assigned no punishment, nor thought it worthy of a man that hath the use of reason, to take notice of,) and is afraid, unless he revenge it, he shall fall into contempt, and consequently be obnoxious to the like injuries from others; and to avoid this, breaks the law, and protects himself for the future, by the terror of his private revenge. This is a crime: for the hurt is not corporeal, but phantastical, and (though in this corner of the world, made sensible by a custom not many years since begun, amongst young and vain men,) so light, as a gallant man, and one that is assured of his own courage, cannot take notice of. Also a man may stand in fear of spirits, either through his own superstition, or through too much credit given to other men, that tell him of strange dreams and visions; and thereby be made believe they will hurt him, for doing, or omitting divers things, which nevertheless, to do, or omit, is contrary to the laws; and that which is so done, or omitted, is not to be excused by this fear; but is a crime. For (as I have shown before in the second chapter) dreams be naturally but the fancies remaining in sleep, after the impressions our senses had formerly received waking; and when men are by any accident unassured they have slept, seem to be real visions; and therefore he that presumes to break the law upon his own, or another's dream, or pretended vision, or upon other fancy of the power of invisible spirits, than is permitted by the commonwealth, leaveth the law of nature, which is a certain offence, and followeth the imagery of his own, or another private man's brain, which he can never know whether it signifieth any thing, or nothing, nor whether he that tells his dream, say true, or lie; which if every private man should have leave to do, (as they must by the law of nature, if any one have it) there could no law be made to hold, and so all commonwealth would be dissolved.

From these different sources of crimes, it appears already, that all crimes are not (as the Stoics of old time maintained) of the same allay. There is place, not only for EXCUSE, by which that which seemed a crime, is proved to be none at all; but also for EXTENUATION, by which the crime, that seemed great, is made less. For though all crimes do equally deserve the name of injustice, as all deviation from a straight line is equally crookedness, which the Stoics rightly observed; yet it does not follow that all crimes are equally unjust, no more than that all crooked lines are equally crooked; which the Stoics not observing, held it as great a crime, to kill a hen, against the law, as to kill one's father.

That which totally excuseth a fact, and takes away from it the nature of a crime, can be none but that, which at the same time, taketh away the obligation of the law.

For the fact committed once against the law, if he that committed it be obliged to the law, can be no other than a crime.

The want of means to know the law, totally excuseth: For the law whereof a man has no means to inform himself, is not obligatory. But the want of diligence to inquire, shall not be considered as a want of means; nor shall any man, that pretendeth to reason enough for the government of his own affairs, be supposed to want means to know the laws of nature; because they are known by the reason he pretends to: only children, and madmen are excused from offences against the law natural.

Where a man is captive, or in the power of the enemy (and he is then in the power of the enemy, when his person, or his means of living, is so,) if it be without his own fault, the obligation of the law ceaseth; because he must obey the enemy, or die; and consequently such obedience is no crime: for no man is obliged (when the protection of the law faileth,) not to protect himself, by the best means he can.

If a man, by the terror of present death, be compelled to do a fact against the law, he is totally excused; because no law can oblige a man to abandon his own preservation. And supposing such a law were obligatory; yet a man would reason thus, *If I do it not, I die presently; if I do it, I die afterwards; therefore by doing it, there is time of life gained;* nature therefore compels him to the fact.

When a man is destitute of food, or other thing necessary for his life, and cannot preserve himself any other way, but by some fact against the law; as if in a great famine he take the food by force, or stealth, which he cannot obtain for money, nor charity; or in defence of his life, snatch away another man's sword, he is totally excused, for the reason next before alleged.

Again, facts done against the law, by the authority of another, are by that authority excused against the author; because no man ought to accuse his own fact in another, that is but his instrument: but it is not excused against a third person thereby injured; because in the violation of the law, both the author and actor are criminals. From hence it followeth that when that man, or assembly, that hath the sovereign power, commandeth a man to do that which is contrary to a former law, the doing of it is totally excused: for he ought not to condemn it himself, because he is the author; and what cannot justly be condemned by the sovereign, cannot justly be punished by any other. Besides, when the sovereign commandeth any thing to be done against his own former law, the command, as to that particular fact, is an abrogation of the law.

If that man, or assembly, that hath the sovereign power, disclaim any right essential to the sovereignty, whereby there accrueth to the subject, any liberty inconsistent with the sovereign power, that is to say, with the very being of a commonwealth, if the subject shall refuse to obey the command in any thing, contrary to the liberty granted, this is nevertheless a sin, and contrary to the duty of the subject: for he ought to take notice of what is inconsistent with the sovereignty, because it was erected by his own consent, and for his own defence; and that such liberty as is inconsistent with it, was granted through ignorance of the evil consequence thereof. But if he not only disobey, but also resist a public minister in the execution of it, then it is a crime; because he might have been righted, (without any breach of the peace,) upon complaint.

The degrees of crime are taken on divers scales, and measured, first, by the malignity of the source, or cause: secondly, by the contagion of the example: thirdly, by the mischief of the effect: and fourthly, by the concurrence of times, places, and persons.

The same fact done against the law, if it proceed from presumption of strength, riches, or friends to resist those that are to execute the law, is a greater crime than if it proceed from hope of not being discovered, or of escape by flight: for presumption of impunity by force, is a root, from whence springeth, at all times, and upon all temptations, a contempt of all laws; whereas in the latter case, the apprehension of danger, that makes a man fly, renders him more obedient for the future. A crime which we know to be so, is greater than the same crime proceeding from a false persuasion that it is lawful: for he that committeth it against his own conscience, presumeth on his force, or other power, which encourages him to commit the same again: but he that doth it by error, after the error shewn him, is conformable to the law.

He, whose error proceeds from the authority of a teacher, or an interpreter of the law publicly authorized, is not so faulty, as he whose error proceedeth from a peremptory pursuit of his own principles, and reasoning: for what is taught by one that teacheth by public authority, the commonwealth teacheth, and hath a resemblance of law, till the same authority controlleth it; and in all crimes that contain not in them a denial of the sovereign power, nor are against an evident law, excuseth totally: whereas he that groundeth his actions on his private judgment, ought according to the rectitude, or error thereof, to stand, or fall.

The same fact, if it have been constantly punished in other men, is a greater crime, than if there have been many precedent examples of impunity. For those examples are so many hopes of impunity, given by the sovereign himself: and because he which furnishes a man with such a hope, and presumption of mercy, as encourageth him to offend, hath his part in the offence; he cannot reasonably charge the offender with the whole.

A crime arising from a sudden passion, is not so great, as when the same ariseth from long meditation: for in the former case there is a place for extenuation, in the common infirmity of human nature: but he that doth it with premeditation, has used circumspection, and cast his eye, on the law, on the punishment, and on the consequence thereof to human society; all which in committing the crime, he hath contemned, and postposed to his own appetite. But there is no suddenness of passion sufficient for a total excuse: for all the time between the first knowing of the law, and the commission of the fact, shall be taken for a time of deliberation; because he ought by meditation of the law, to rectify the irregularity of his passions.

Where the law is publicly, and with assiduity, before all the people read and interpreted; a fact done against it, is a greater crime, than where men are left without such instruction, to enquire of it with difficulty, uncertainty, and interruption of their callings, and be informed by private men: for in this case, part of the fault is discharged upon common infirmity; but in the former, there is apparent negligence, which is not without some contempt of the sovereign power.

Those facts which the law expressly condemneth, but the law-maker by other manifest signs of his will tacitly approveth, are less crimes, than the same facts, condemned both by the law and lawmaker. For seeing the will of the law-maker is a law, there appear in this case two contradictory laws; which would totally excuse, if men were bound to take notice of the sovereign's approbation, by other arguments, than are expressed by his command. But because there are punishments consequent, not only to the transgression of his law, but also to the observing of it, he is in part a cause of the transgression, and therefore cannot reasonably impute the whole crime to the delinquent. For example, the law condemneth duels; the punishment is made capital: on the contrary part, he that refuseth duel, is subject to contempt and scorn, without remedy; and sometimes by the sovereign himself thought unworthy to have any charge, or preferment in war. If thereupon he accept duel, considering all men lawfully endeavour to obtain the good opinion of them that have the sovereign power, he ought not in reason to be rigorously punished; seeing part of the fault may be discharged on the punisher: which I say, not as wishing liberty of private revenges, or any other kind of disobedience; but a care in governors, not to countenance any thing obliquely, which directly they forbid. The examples of princes, to those that see them, are, and ever have been, more potent to govern their actions, than the laws themselves. And though it be our duty to do, not what they do, but what they say; yet will that duty never be performed, till it please God to give men an extraordinary, and supernatural grace to follow that precept.

Again, if we compare crimes by the mischief of their effects, first, the same fact, when it redounds to the damage of many, is greater, than when it redounds to the hurt of few. And therefore, when a fact hurteth, not only in the present, but also, (by example) in the future, it is a greater crime, than if it hurt only in the present: for the former, is a fertile crime, and multiplies to the hurt of many; the latter is barren. To maintain doctrines contrary to the religion established in the commonwealth, is a greater fault, in an authorized preacher, than in a private person: so also is it, to live profanely, incontinently, or do any irreligious act whatsoever. Likewise in a professor of the law, to maintain any point, or do any act, that tendeth to the weakening of the sovereign power, is a greater crime, than in another man: also in a man that hath such reputation for wisdom, as that his counsels are followed, or his actions imitated by many, his fact against the law, is a greater crime, than the same fact in another: for such men not only commit crime, but teach it for law to all other men. And generally all crimes are the greater, by the scandal they give; that is to say, by becoming stumbling-blocks to the weak, that look not so much upon the way they go in, as upon the light that other men carry before them.

Also facts of hostility against the present state of the commonwealth, are greater crimes, than the same acts done to private men: for the damage extends itself to all: such are the betraying of the strengths, or revealing of the secrets of the commonwealth to an enemy; also all attempts upon the representative of the commonwealth, be it a monarch, or an assembly; and all endeavours by word, or deed to diminish the authority of the same, either in the present time, or in succession: which crimes the Latins understand by *crimina laesae majestatis,* and consist in design, or act, contrary to a fundamental law.

Likewise those crimes, which render judgments of no effect, are greater crimes, than injuries done to one, or a few persons; as to receive money to give false judgment, or testimony, is a greater crime, than otherwise to deceive a man of the like, or a greater sum; because not only he has wrong, that falls by such judgments; but all judgments are rendered useless, and occasion ministered to force, and private revenges.

Also robbery, and depeculation of the public treasure, or revenues, is a greater crime, than the robbing, or defrauding of a private man; because to rob the public, is to rob many at once.

Also the counterfeit usurpation of public ministry, the counterfeiting of public seals, or public coin, than counterfeiting of a private man's person, or his seal; because the fraud thereof, extendeth to the damage of many.

Of facts against the law, done to private men, the greater crime, is that, where the damage in the common opinion of men, is most sensible. And therefore

To kill against the law, is a greater crime, than any other injury, life preserved.

And to kill with torment, greater, than simply to kill.

And mutilation of a limb, greater, than the spoiling a man of his goods.

And the spoiling a man of his goods, by terror of death, or wounds, than by clandestine surreption.

And by clandestine surreption, than by consent fraudulently obtained.

And the violation of chastity by force, greater, than by flattery.

And of a woman married, than of a woman not married.

For all these things are commonly so valued; though some men are more, and some less sensible of the same offence. But the law regardeth not the particular, but the general inclination of mankind.

And therefore the offence men take, from contumely, in words, or gesture, when they produce no other harm, than the present grief of him that is reproached, hath been neglected in the laws of the Greeks, Romans, and other both ancient, and modern commonwealths; supposing the true cause of such grief to consist, not in the contumely, (which takes no hold upon men conscious of their own virtue,) but in the pusillanimity of him that is offended by it.

Also a crime against a private man, is much aggravated by the person, time, and place. For to kill one's parent, is a greater crime, than to kill another: for the parent ought to have the honour of a sovereign, (though he have surrendered his power to the civil law,) because he had it originally by nature. And to rob a poor man, is a greater crime, than to rob a rich man; because it is to the poor a more sensible damage.

And a crime committed in the time or place appointed for devotion, is greater, than if committed at another time or place: for it proceeds from a greater contempt of the law.

Many other cases of aggravation, and extenuation might be added: but by these I have set down, it is obvious to every man, to take the altitude of any other crime proposed.

Lastly, because in almost all crimes there is an injury done, not only to some private men, but also to the commonwealth; the same crime, when the accusation is in the name of the commonwealth, is called public crime: and when in the name of a private man, a private crime; and the pleas according thereunto called public, *judicia publica*, Pleas of the Crown; or Private Pleas. As in an accusation of murder, if the accuser be a private man, the plea is a Private Plea; if the accuser be the sovereign, the plea is a Public Plea.

CHAPTER 28

Of Punishments, and Rewards

A PUNISHMENT, *is an evil inflicted by public authority, on him that hath done, or omitted that which is judged by the same authority to be a transgression of the law; to the end that the will of men may thereby the better be disposed to obedience.*

Before I infer any thing from this definition, there is a question to be answered, of much importance; which is, by what door the right, or authority of punishing in any case, came in. For by that which has been said before, no man is supposed bound by covenant, not to resist violence; and consequently it cannot be intended, that he gave any right to another to lay violent hands upon his person. In the making of a commonwealth, every man giveth away the right of defending another; but not of defending himself. Also he obligeth himself, to assist him that hath the sovereignty, in the punishing of another; but of himself not. But to covenant to assist the sovereign, in doing hurt to another, unless he that so covenanteth have a right to do it himself, is not to give him a right to punish. It is manifest therefore that the right which the commonwealth (that is, he, or they that represent it) hath to punish, is not grounded on any concession, or gift of the subjects. But I have also showed formerly, that before the institution of commonwealth, every man had a right to every thing, and to do whatsoever he thought necessary to his own preservation; subduing, hurting, or killing any man in order thereunto. And this is the foundation of that right of punishing, which is exercised in every commonwealth. For the subjects did not give the sovereign that right; but only in laying down theirs, strengthened him to use his own, as he should think fit, for the preservation of them all: so that it was not given, but left to him, and to him only; and (excepting the limits set him by natural law) as entire, as in the condition of mere nature, and of war of every one against his neighbour.

From the definition of punishment, I infer, first, that neither private revenges, nor injuries of private men, can properly be styled punishment; because they proceed not from public authority.

Secondly, that to be neglected, and unpreferred by the public favour, is not a punishment; because no new evil is thereby on any man inflicted; he is only left in the estate he was in before.

Thirdly, that the evil inflicted by public authority, without precedent public condemnation, is not to be styled by the name of punishment; but of an hostile act; because the fact for which a man is punished, ought first to be judged by public authority, to be a transgression of the law.

Fourthly, that the evil inflicted by usurped power, and judges without authority from the sovereign, is not punishment; but an act of hostility; because the acts of power usurped, have not for author, the person condemned; and therefore are not acts of public authority.

Fifthly, that all evil which is inflicted without intention, or possibility of disposing the delinquent, or (by his example) other men, to obey the laws, is not punishment; but an act of hostility; because without such an end, no hurt done is contained under that name.

Sixthly, whereas to certain actions, there be annexed by nature, divers hurtful consequences; as when a man in assaulting another, is himself slain, or wounded; or when he falleth into sickness by the doing of some unlawful act; such hurt, though in respect of God, who is the author of nature, it may be said to be inflicted, and therefore a punishment divine; yet it is not contained in the name of punishment in respect of men, because it is not inflicted by the authority of man.

Seventhly, if the harm inflicted be less than the benefit, or contentment that naturally followeth the crime committed, that harm is not within the definition; and is rather the price, or redemption, than the punishment of a crime: because it is of the nature of punishment, to have for end, the disposing of men to obey the law; which end (if it be less than the benefit of the transgression) it attaineth not, but worketh a contrary effect.

Eighthly, if a punishment be determined and prescribed in the law itself, and after the crime committed, there be a greater punishment inflicted, the excess is not punishment, but an act of hostility. For seeing the aim of punishment is not a revenge, but terror; and the terror of a great punishment unknown, is taken away by the declaration of a less, the unexpected addition is no part of the punishment. But where there is no punishment at all determined by the law, there whatsoever is inflicted, hath the nature of punishment. For he that goes about the violation of a law, wherein no penalty is determined, expecteth an indeterminate, that is to say, an arbitrary punishment.

Ninthly, harm inflicted for a fact done before there was a law that forbade it, is not punishment, but an act of hostility: for before the law, there is no transgression of the law: but punishment supposeth a fact judged, to have been a transgression of the law; therefore harm inflicted before the law made, is not punishment, but an act of hostility.

Tenthly, hurt inflicted on the representative of the commonwealth, is not punishment, but an act of hostility: because it is of the nature of punishment, to be inflicted by public authority, which is the authority only of the representative itself.

Lastly, harm inflicted upon one that is a declared enemy, falls not under the name of punishment: because seeing they were either never subject to the law, and therefore cannot transgress it; or having been subject to it, and professing to be no longer so, by consequence deny they can transgress it, all the harms that can be done them, must be taken as acts of hostility. But in declared hostility, all infliction of evil is lawful. From whence it followeth, that if a subject shall by fact, or word, wittingly, and deliberately deny the authority of the representative of the commonwealth (whatsoever penalty hath been formerly ordained for treason,) he may lawfully be made to suffer whatsoever the representative will: For in denying subjection, he denies such punishment as by the law hath been ordained; and therefore suffers as an enemy of the commonwealth; that is, according to the will of the representative. For the punishments set down in the law, are to subjects, not to enemies; such as are they, that having been by their own act subjects, deliberately revolting, deny the sovereign power.

The first, and most general distribution of punishments, is into *divine,* and *human.* Of the former I shall have occasion to speak, in a more convenient place hereafter.

Human, are those punishments that be inflicted by the commandment of man; and are either *corporal,* or *pecuniary,* or *ignominy,* or *imprisonment,* or *exile,* or mixed of these.

Corporal punishment is that, which is inflicted on the body directly, and according to the intention of him that inflicteth it: such as are stripes, or wounds, or deprivation of such pleasures of the body, as were before lawfully enjoyed.

And of these, some be *capital,* some *less* than *capital.* Capital, is the infliction of death; and that either simply, or with torment. Less than capital, are stripes, wounds, chains, and any other corporal pain, not in its own nature mortal. For if upon the infliction of a punishment death follow not in the intention of the inflictor, the punishment is not to be esteemed capital, though the harm prove mortal by an accident not to be foreseen; in which case death is not inflicted, but hastened.

Pecuniary punishment, is that which consisteth not only in the deprivation of a sum of money, but also of lands, or any other goods which are usually bought and sold for money. And in case the law, that ordaineth such a punishment, be made with design to gather money, from such as shall transgress the same, it is not properly a punishment, but the price of privilege and exemption from the law, which doth not absolutely forbid the fact, but only to those that are not able to pay the money: except where the law is natural, or part of religion; for in that case it is not an exemption from the law, but a transgression of it. As where a law exacteth a pecuniary mulct, of them that take the name of God in vain, the payment of the mulct, is not the price of a dispensation to swear, but the punishment of the transgression of a law indispensable. In like manner if the law impose a sum of money to be paid, to him that has been injured; this is but a satisfaction for the hurt done him; and extinguisheth the accusation of the party injured, not the crime of the offender.

Ignominy, is the infliction of such evil, as is made dishonourable; or the deprivation of such good, as is made honourable by the commonwealth. For there be some things honourable by nature; as the effects of courage, magnanimity, strength, wisdom, and other abilities of body and mind: others made honourable by the commonwealth; as badges, titles, offices, or any other singular mark of the sovereign's favour. The former, (though they may fail by nature, or accident,) cannot be taken away by a law; and therefore the loss of them is not punishment. But the latter, may be taken away by the public authority that made them honourable, and are properly punishments: such are degrading men condemned, of their badges, titles, and offices; or declaring them incapable of the like in time to come.

Imprisonment, is when a man is by public authority deprived of liberty; and may happen from two divers ends; whereof one is the safe custody of a man accused; the other is the inflicting of pain on a man condemned. The former is not punishment; because no man is supposed to be punished, before he be judicially heard, and declared guilty. And therefore whatsoever hurt a man is made to suffer by bonds, or restraint, before his cause be heard, over and above that which is necessary to assure his custody, is against the law of nature. But the latter is punishment, because evil, and inflicted by public authority, for somewhat that has by the same authority been judged a transgression of the law. Under this word imprisonment, I comprehend all restraint of motion, caused by an external obstacle, be it a house, which is called by the general name of a prison; or an island, as when men are said to be confined to it; or a place where men are set to work, as in old time men have been condemned to quarries, and in these times to galleys; or be it a chain, or any other such impediment.

Exile (banishment) is when a man is for a crime, condemned to depart out of the dominion of the commonwealth, or out of a certain part thereof; and during a prefixed time, or for ever, not to return into it: and seemeth not in its own nature, without other circumstances, to be a punishment; but rather an escape, or a public commandment to avoid punishment by flight. And *Cicero* says, there was never any such punishment ordained in the city of *Rome;* but calls it a refuge of men in danger. For if a man banished, be nevertheless permitted to enjoy his goods, and the revenue of his lands, the mere change of air is no punishment; nor does it tend to that benefit of the commonwealth, for which all punishments are ordained, (that is to say, to the forming of men's wills to the observation of the law;) but many times to the damage of the commonwealth. For a banished man, is a lawful enemy of the commonwealth that banished him; as being no more a member of the same. But if he be withal deprived of his lands, or goods, then the punishment lieth not in the exile, but is to be reckoned amongst punishments pecuniary.

All punishments of innocent subjects, be they great or little, are against the law of nature: For punishment is only for transgression of the law, and therefore there can be no punishment of the innocent. It is therefore a violation, first, of that law of nature, which forbiddeth all men, in their revenges, to look at any thing but some future good: For there can arrive no good to the commonwealth, by punishing the innocent. Secondly, of that, which forbiddeth ingratitude: For seeing all sovereign power, is originally given by the consent of every one of the subjects, to the end they should as long as they are obedient, be protected thereby; the punishment of the innocent, is a rendering of evil for good. And thirdly, of the law that commandeth equity; that is to say, an equal distribution of justice; which in punishing the innocent is not observed.

But the infliction of what evil soever, on an innocent man, that is not a subject, if it be for the benefit of the commonwealth, and without violation of any former covenant, is no breach of the law of nature. For all men that are not subjects, are either enemies, or else they have ceased from being so by some precedent covenants. But against enemies, whom the commonwealth judgeth capable to do them hurt, it is lawful by the original right of nature to make war; wherein the sword judgeth not, nor doth the victor make distinction of nocent, and innocent, as to the time past; nor has other respect of mercy, than as it conduceth to the good of his own people. And upon this ground it is, that also in subjects, who deliberately deny the authority of the commonwealth established, the vengeance is lawfully extended, not only to the fathers, but also to the third and fourth generation not yet in being, and consequently innocent of the fact, for which they are afflicted: because the nature of this offence, consisteth in the renouncing of subjection; which is a relapse into the condition of war, commonly called rebellion; and they that so offend, suffer not as subjects, but as enemies. For *rebellion,* is but war renewed.

Reward, is either of *gift,* or by *contract.* When by contract, it is called *salary,* and *wages;* which is benefit due for service performed, or promised. When of gift, it is benefit proceeding from the *grace* of them that bestow it, to encourage, or enable men to do them service. And therefore when the sovereign of a commonwealth appointeth a salary to any public office, he that receiveth it, is bound in justice to perform his office; otherwise, he is bound only in honour, to acknowledgment, and an endeavour of requital. For though men have no lawful remedy, when they be commanded to quit their private business, to serve the public, without reward or salary; yet they are not bound thereto, by the law of nature, nor by the institution of the commonwealth, unless the service cannot otherwise be done; because it is supposed the sovereign may make use of all their means, insomuch as the most common soldier, may demand the wages of his warfare, as a debt.

The benefits which a sovereign bestoweth on a subject, for fear of some power, and ability he hath to do hurt to the commonwealth, are not properly rewards; for they are not salaries; because there is in this case no contract supposed, every man being obliged already not to do the commonwealth disservice: nor are they graces; because they be extorted by fear, which ought not to be incident to the sovereign power: but are rather sacrifices, which the sovereign (considered in his natural person, and not in the person of the commonwealth) makes, for the appeasing the discontent of him he thinks more potent than himself; and encourage not to obedience, but on the contrary, to the continuance, and increasing of further extortion.

And whereas some salaries are certain, and proceed from the public treasure; and others uncertain, and casual, proceeding from the execution of the office for which the salary is ordained; the latter is in some cases hurtful to the commonwealth; as in the case of judicature. For where the benefit of the judges, and ministers of a court of justice, ariseth for the multitude of causes that are brought to their cognizance, there must needs follow two inconveniences: one, is the nourishing of suits; for the more suits, the greater benefit: and another that depends on that, which is contention about jurisdiction; each court drawing to itself, as many causes as it can. But in offices of execution there are not those inconveniences; because their employment cannot be increased by any endeavour of their own. And thus much shall suffice for the nature of punishment and reward; which are, as it were, the nerves and tendons, that move the limbs and joints of a commonwealth.

Hitherto I have set forth the nature of man, (whose pride and other passions have compelled him to submit himself to government;) together with the great power of his governor, whom I compared to *Leviathan*, taking that comparison out of the two last verses of the one and fortieth of *Job;* where God having set forth the great power of *Leviathan,* calleth him king of the proud. *There is nothing,* saith he, *on earth, to be compared with him. He is made so as not to be afraid. He seeth every high thing below him; and is king of all the children of pride.* But because he is mortal, and subject to decay, as all other earthly creatures are; and because there is that in heaven, (though not on earth) that he should stand in fear of, and whose laws he ought to obey; I shall in the next following chapters speak of his diseases, and the causes of his mortality; and of what laws of nature he is bound to obey.

CHAPTER 29

Of Those Things That Weaken, or Tend to the Dissolution of a Commonwealth

Though nothing can be immortal, which mortals make; yet, if men had the use of reason they pretend to, their commonwealths might be secured, at least, from perishing by internal diseases. For by the nature of their institution, they are designed to live, as long as mankind, or as the laws of nature, or as justice itself, which gives them life. Therefore when they come to be dissolved, not by external violence, but intestine disorder, the fault is not in men, as they are the *matter;* but as they are the *makers,* and orderers of them. For men, as they become at last weary of irregular jostling, and hewing one another, and desire with all their hearts, to conform themselves into one firm and lasting edifice; so for want, both of the art of making fit laws, to square their actions by, and also of humility, and patience, to suffer the rude and cumbersome points of their present greatness to be taken off, they cannot without the help of a very able architect, be compiled, into any other than a crazy building, such as hardly lasting out their own time, must assuredly fall upon the heads of their posterity.

Amongst the *infirmities* therefore of a commonwealth, I will reckon in the first place, those that arise from an imperfect institution, and resemble the diseases of a natural body, which proceed from a defectuous procreation.

Of which, this is one, *that a man to obtain a kingdom, is sometimes content with less power, than to the peace, and defence of the commonwealth is necessarily required*. From whence it cometh to pass, that when the exercise of the power laid by, is for the public safety to be resumed, it hath the resemblance of an unjust act; which disposeth great numbers of men (when occasion is presented) to rebel; in the same manner as the bodies of children, gotten by diseased parents, are subject either to untimely death, or to purge the ill quality, derived from their vicious conception, by breaking out into biles and scabs. And when kings deny themselves some such necessary power, it is not always (though sometimes), out of ignorance of what is necessary to the office they undertake; but many times out of a hope to recover the same again at their pleasure: Wherein they reason not well; because such as will hold them to their promises, shall be maintained against them by foreign commonwealths; who in order to the good of their own subjects let slip few occasions to *weaken* the estate of their neighbours. So was *Thomas Becket,* archbishop of *Canterbury,* supported against *Henry* the Second, by the Pope; the subjection of ecclesiastics to the commonwealth, having been dispensed with by *William the Conqueror* at his reception, when he took an oath, not to infringe the liberty of the church. And so were the *barons,* whose power was by *William Rufus* (to have their help in transferring the succession from his elder brother, to himself,) increased to a degree, inconsistent with the sovereign power, maintained in their rebellion against *King John,* by the French.

Nor does this happen in monarchy only. For whereas the style of the ancient Roman commonwealth, was, *the senate, and people of Rome;* neither senate, nor people pretended to the whole power; which first caused the seditions, of *Tiberius Gracchus, Caius Gracchus, Lucius Saturninus,* and others; and afterwards the wars between the senate and the people, under *Marius* and *Sylla;* and again under *Pompey* and *Caesar,* to the extinction of their democracy, and the setting up of monarchy.

The people of *Athens* bound themselves but from one only action; which was, that no man on pain of death should propound the renewing of the war for the island of *Salamis;* and yet thereby, if *Solon* had not caused to be given out he was mad, and afterwards in gesture and habit of a madman, and in verse, propounded it to the people that flocked about him, they had had an enemy perpetually in readiness, even at the gates of their city; such damage, or shifts, are all commonwealths forced to, that have their power never so little limited.

In the second place, I observe the *diseases* of a commonwealth, that proceed from the poison of seditious doctrines, whereof one is, *That every private man is judge of good and evil actions.* This is true in the condition of mere nature, where there are no civil laws; and also under civil government, in such cases as are not determined by the law. But otherwise, it is manifest, that the measure of good and evil actions, is the civil law; and the judge the legislator, who is always representative of the commonwealth. From this false doctrine, men are disposed to debate with themselves, and dispute the commands of the commonwealth; and afterwards to obey, or disobey them, as in their private judgments they shall think fit. Whereby the commonwealth is distracted and *weakened.*

Another doctrine repugnant to civil society, is, that *whatsoever a man does against his conscience, is sin;* and it dependeth on the presumption of making himself judge of good and evil. For a man's conscience, and his judgment is the same thing; and as the judgment, so also the conscience may be erroneous. Therefore, though he that is subject to no civil law, sinneth in all he does against his conscience, because he has no other rule to follow but his own reason; yet it is not so with him that lives in a commonwealth; because the law is the public conscience, by which he hath already undertaken to be guided. Otherwise in such diversity, as there is of private consciences, which are but private opinions, the commonwealth must needs be distracted, and no man dare to obey the sovereign power, farther than it shall seem good in his own eyes.

It hath been also commonly taught, *that faith and sanctity, are not to be attained by study and reason, but by supernatural inspiration, or infusion,* which granted, I see not why any man should render a reason of his faith; or why every Christian should not be also a prophet; or why any man should take the law of his country, rather than his own inspiration, for the rule of his action. And thus we fall again into the fault of taking upon us to judge of good and evil; or to make judges of it, such private men as pretend to be supernaturally inspired, to the dissolution of all civil government. Faith comes by hearing, and hearing by those accidents, which guide us into the presence of them that speak to us; which accidents are all contrived by God Almighty; and yet are not supernatural, but only, for the great number of them that concur to every effect, unobservable. Faith and sanctity, are indeed not very frequent; but yet they are not miracles, but brought to pass by education, discipline, correction, and other natural ways, by which God worketh them in his elect, at such time as he thinketh fit. And these three opinions, pernicious to peace and government, have in this part of the world, proceeded chiefly from the tongues, and pens of unlearned divines; who joining the words of Holy Scripture together, otherwise than is agreeable to reason, do what they can, to make men think, that sanctity and natural reason, cannot stand together.

A fourth opinion, repugnant to the nature of a commonwealth, is this, *that he that hath the sovereign power, is subject to the civil laws.* It is true, that sovereigns are all subject to the laws of nature; because such laws be divine, and cannot by any man, or commonwealth be abrogated. But to those laws which the sovereign himself, that is, which the commonwealth maketh, he is not subject. For to be subject to laws, is to be subject to the commonwealth, that is to the sovereign representative, that is to himself; which is not subjection, but freedom from the laws. Which error, because it setteth the laws above the sovereign, setteth also a judge above him, and a power to punish him; which is to make a new sovereign; and again for the same reason a third, to punish the second; and so continually without end, to the confusion, and dissolution of the commonwealth.

A fifth doctrine, that tendeth to the dissolution of a commonwealth, is, *that every private man has an absolute propriety in his goods; such, as excludeth the right of the sovereign.* Every man has indeed a propriety that excludes the right of every other subject: and he has it only from the sovereign power; without the protection whereof, every other man should have equal right to the same. But if the right of the sovereign also be excluded, he cannot perform the office they have put him into; which is, to defend them both from foreign enemies, and from the injuries of one another; and consequently there is no longer a commonwealth.

And if the propriety of subjects, exclude not the right of the sovereign representative to their goods; much less to their offices of judicature, or execution, in which they represent the sovereign himself.

There is a sixth doctrine, plainly, and directly against the essence of a commonwealth; and it is this, *that the sovereign power may be divided.* For what is it to divide the power of a commonwealth, but to dissolve it; for powers divided mutually destroy each other. And for these doctrines, men are chiefly beholding to some of those, that making profession of the laws, endeavour to make them depend upon their own learning, and not upon the legislative power.

And as false doctrine, so also oftentimes the example of different government in a neighbouring nation, disposeth men to alteration of the form already settled. So the people of the Jews were stirred up to reject God, and to call upon the prophet *Samuel*, for a king after the manner of the nations: so also the lesser cities of *Greece*, were continually disturbed, with seditions of the aristocratical, and democratical factions; one part of almost every commonwealth, desiring to imitate the Lacede-monians; the other, the Athenians. And I doubt not, but many men, have been contented to see the late troubles in *England*, out of an imitation of the Low Coun-tries; supposing there needed no more to grow rich, than to change, as they had done, the form of their government. For the constitution of man's nature, is of itself subject to desire novelty: When therefore they are provoked to the same, by the neighbourhood also of those that have been enriched by it, it is almost impossible for them, not to be content with those that solicit them to change; and love the first beginnings, though they be grieved with the continuance of disorder; like hot bloods, that having gotten the itch, tear themselves with their own nails, till they can endure the smart no longer.

And as to rebellion in particular against monarchy; one of the most frequent causes of it, is the reading of the books of policy, and histories of the ancient Greeks, and Romans; from which, young men, and all others that are unprovided of the antidote of solid reason, receiving a strong, and delightful impression, of the great exploits of war, achieved by the conductors of their armies, receive withal a pleasing idea, of all they have done besides; and imagine their great prosperity, not to have proceeded from the emulation of particular men, but from the virtue of their popular form of government: not considering the frequent seditions, and civil wars, produced by the imperfection of their policy. From the reading, I say, of such books, men have undertaken to kill their kings, because the Greek and Latin writers, in their books and discourses of policy, make it lawful, and laudable, for any man so to do; provided, before he do it, he call him tyrant. For they say not *regicide*, that is, killing of a king, but *tyrannicide*, that is, killing of a tyrant is lawful. From the same books, they that live under a monarch conceive an opinion, that the subjects in a popular commonwealth enjoy liberty; but that in a monarchy they are all slaves. I say, they that live under a monarchy conceive such an opinion; not they that live under a popular government: for they find no such matter. In sum, I cannot imagine, how any thing can be more prejudicial to a monarchy, than the allowing of such books to be publicly read, without present applying such correctives of discreet masters, as are fit to take away their venom: which venom I will not doubt to compare to the biting of a mad dog, which is a disease the physicians call *hydrophobia*, or *fear of water*. For as he that is so bitten, has a continual torment of thirst, and yet abhorreth water; and is in such an estate, as if the poison endeavoured to convert him into a dog: so when a monarchy is once bitten to the quick, by those democratical writers, that continually snarl at that estate; it wanteth nothing more than a strong monarch, which nevertheless out of a certain *tyrannophobia*, or fear of being strongly governed, when they have him, they abhor.

As there have been doctors, that hold there be three souls in a man; so there be also that think there may be more souls, (that is, more sovereigns,) than one, in a commonwealth; and set up a *supremacy* against the *sovereignty; canons* against *laws;* and a *ghostly authority* against the *civil;* working on men's minds, with words and distinctions, that of themselves signify nothing, but bewray (by their obscurity) that there walketh (as some think invisibly) another kingdom, as it were a kingdom of fairies, in the dark. Now seeing it is manifest, that the civil power, and the power of the commonwealth is the same thing; and that supremacy, and the power of making canons, and granting faculties, implieth a commonwealth; it followeth, that where one is sovereign, another supreme; where one can make laws, and another make canons; there must needs be two commonwealths, of one and the same subjects; which is a kingdom divided in itself, and cannot stand. For notwithstanding the insignificant distinction of *temporal,* and *ghostly,* they are still two kingdoms, and every subject is subject to two masters. For seeing the *ghostly* power challengeth the right to declare what is sin it challengeth by consequence to declare what is law, (sin being nothing but the transgression of the law;) and again, the civil power challenging to declare what is law, every subject must obey two masters, who both will have their commands be observed as law; which is impossible. Or, if it be but one kingdom, either the *civil,* which is the power of the commonwealth, must be subordinate to the *ghostly,* and then there is no sovereignty but the *ghostly;* or the *ghostly* must be subordinate to the *temporal,* and then there is no *supremacy* but the *temporal.* When therefore these two powers oppose one another, the commonwealth cannot but be in great danger of civil war, and dissolution. For the *civil* authority being more visible, and standing in the clearer light of natural reason, cannot choose but draw to it in all times a very considerable part of the people: and the *spiritual,* though it stand in the darkness of School distinctions, and hard words; yet because the fear of darkness, and ghosts, is greater than other fears, cannot want a party sufficient to trouble, and sometimes to destroy a commonwealth, and this is a disease which not unfitly may be compared to the epilepsy, or falling sickness (which the Jews took to be one kind of possession by spirits) in the body natural. For as in this disease, there is an unnatural spirit, or wind in the head that obstructeth the roots of the nerves, and moving them violently, taketh away the motion which naturally they should have from the power of the soul in the brain, and thereby causeth violent, and irregular motions (which men call convulsions) in the parts; insomuch as he that is seized therewith, falleth down sometimes into the water, and sometimes into the fire, as a man deprived of his senses; so also in the body politic, when the spiritual power, moveth the members of a commonwealth, by the terror of punishments, and hope of rewards (which are the nerves of it,) otherwise than by the civil power (which is the soul of the commonwealth), they ought to be moved; and by strange, and hard words suffocates their understanding, it must needs thereby distract the people, and either overwhelm the commonwealth with oppression, or cast it into the fire of a civil war.

Sometimes also in the merely civil government, there be more than one soul: as when the power of levying money, (which is the nutritive faculty,) has depended on a general assembly; the power of conduct and command, (which is the motive faculty,) on one man; and the power of making laws, (which is the rational faculty,) on the accidental consent, not only of those two, but also of a third; this endangereth the commonwealth, sometimes for want of consent to good laws; but most often for want of such nourishment, as is necessary to life, and motion. For although few perceive, that such government, is not government, but division of the common-wealth into three factions, and call it mixed monarchy; yet the truth is, that it is not one independent commonwealth, but three independent factions; nor one representative person, but three. In the kingdom of God, there may be three persons independent, without breach of unity in God that reigneth; but where men reign, that be subject to diversity of opinions, it cannot be so. And therefore if the king bear the person of the people, and the general assembly bear also the person of the people, and another assembly bear the person of a part of the people, they are not one person, nor one sovereign, but three persons, and three sovereigns.

To what disease in the natural body of man I may exactly compare this irregularity of a commonwealth, I know not. But I have seen a man, that had another man growing out of his side, with an head, arms, breast, and stomach, of his own: if he had had another man growing out of his other side, the comparison might then have been exact.

Hitherto I have named such diseases of a commonwealth, as are of the greatest, and most present danger. There be other, not so great; which nevertheless are not unfit to be observed. As first, the difficulty of raising money, for the necessary uses of the commonwealth; especially in the approach of war. This difficulty ariseth from the opinion, that every subject hath of a propriety in his lands and goods, exclusive of the sovereign's right to the use of the same. From whence it cometh to pass, that the sovereign power, which foreseeth the necessities and dangers of the commonwealth, (finding the passage of money to the public treasure obstructed, by the tenacity of the people,) whereas it ought to extend itself, to encounter, and prevent such dangers in their beginnings, contracteth itself as long as it can, and when it cannot longer, struggles with the people by stratagems of law, to obtain little sums, which not sufficing, he is fain at last violently to open the way for present supply, or perish; and being put often to these extremities, at last reduceth the people to their due temper; or else the commonwealth must perish. Insomuch as we may compare this distemper very aptly to an ague; wherein, the fleshy parts being congealed, or by venomous matter obstructed; the veins which by their natural course empty themselves into the heart, are not (as they ought to be) supplied from the arteries, whereby there succeedeth at first a cold contraction, and trembling of the limbs; and afterwards a hot, and strong endeavour of the heart, to force a passage for the blood; and before it can do that, contenteth itself with the small refreshments of such things as cool for a time, till (if nature be strong enough), it break at last the contumacy of the parts obstructed, and dissipateth the venom into sweat; or (if nature be too weak) the patient dieth.

Again, there is sometimes in a commonwealth, a disease, which resembleth the pleurisy; and that is, when the treasure of the commonwealth, flowing out of its due course, is gathered together in too much abundance in one, or a few private men, by monopolies, or by farms of the public revenues; in the same manner as the blood in a pleurisy, getting into the membrane of the breast, breedeth there an inflammation, accompanied with a fever, and painful stitches.

Also the popularity of a potent subject, (unless the commonwealth have very good caution of his fidelity,) is a dangerous disease; because the people (which should receive their motion from the authority of the sovereign,) by the flattery, and by the reputation of an ambitious man, are drawn away from their obedience to the laws, to follow a man, of whose virtues, and designs they have no knowledge. And this is commonly of more danger in a popular government, than in a monarchy; because an army is of so great force, and multitude, as it may easily be made believe, they are the people. By this means it was, that *Julius Caesar,* who was set up by the people against the senate, having won to himself the affections of his army, made himself master, both of senate and people. And this proceeding of popular, and ambitious men, is plain rebellion; and may be resembled to the effects of witchcraft.

Another infirmity of a commonwealth, is the immoderate greatness of a town, when it is able to furnish out of its own circuit, the number, and expense of a great army: as also the great number of corporations; which are as it were many lesser commonwealths in the bowels of a greater, like worms in the entrails of a natural man. To which may be added, the liberty of disputing against absolute power, by pretenders to political prudence; which though bred for the most part in the lees of the people; yet animated by false doctrines, are perpetually meddling with the fundamental laws, to the molestation of the commonwealth; like the little worms, which physicians call *ascarides*.

We may further add, the insatiable appetite, or Bulimia, of enlarging dominion; with the incurable *wounds* thereby many times received from the enemy; and the *wens*, of ununited conquests, which are many times a burthen, and with less danger lost, than kept; as also the *lethargy* of ease, and *consumption* of riot and vain expense.

Lastly, when in a war (foreign or intestine,) the enemies get a final victory; so as (the forces of the commonwealth keeping the field no longer), there is no farther protection of subjects in their loyalty; then is the commonwealth DISSOLVED, and every man at liberty to protect himself by such courses as his own discretion shall suggest unto him. For the sovereign, is the public soul, giving life and motion to the commonwealth; which expiring, the members are governed by it no more, than the carcase of a man, by his departed (though immortal) soul. For though the right of a sovereign monarch cannot be extinguished by the act of another; yet the obligation of the members may. For he that wants protection, may seek it any where; and when he hath it, is obliged (without fraudulent pretence of having submitted himself out of fear,) to protect his protection as long as he is able. But when the power of an assembly is once suppressed, the right of the same perisheth utterly; because the assembly itself is extinct; and consequently, there is no possibility for the sovereignty to re-enter.

CHAPTER 30
Of the Office of the Sovereign Representative

The office of the sovereign, (be it a monarch, or an assembly,) consisteth in the end, for which he was trusted with the sovereign power, namely the procuration of *the safety of the people;* to which he is obliged by the law of nature, and to render an account thereof to God, the author of that law, and to none but him. But by safety here, is not meant a bare preservation, but also all other contentments of life, which every man by lawful industry, without danger, or hurt to the commonwealth, shall acquire to himself.

And this is intended should be done, not by care applied to individuals, further than their protection from injuries, when they shall complain; but by a general providence, contained in public instruction, both of doctrine, and example; and in the making, and executing of good laws, to which individual persons may apply their own cases.

And because, if the essential rights of sovereignty (specified before in the eighteenth chapter) be taken away, the commonwealth is thereby dissolved, and every man returneth into the condition, and calamity of a war with every other man, (which is the greatest evil that can happen in this life;) it is the office of the sovereign, to maintain those rights entire; and consequently against his duty, first, to transfer to another, or to lay from himself any of them. For he that deserteth the means, deserteth the ends; and he deserteth the means, that being the sovereign, acknowledgeth himself subject to the civil laws; and renounceth the power of supreme judicature; or of making war, or peace by his own authority; or of judging of the necessities of the commonwealth; or of levying money, and soldiers, when, and as much as in his own conscience he shall judge necessary; or of making officers, and ministers both of war and peace; or of appointing teachers, and examining what doctrines are conformable, or contrary to the defence, peace, and good of the people. Secondly, it is against his duty, to let the people be ignorant, or misinformed of the grounds, and reasons of those his essential rights; because thereby men are easy to be seduced, and drawn to resist him, when the commonwealth shall require their use and exercise.

And the grounds of these rights, have the rather need to be diligently, and truly taught; because they cannot be maintained by any civil law, or terror of legal punishment. For a civil law, that shall forbid rebellion (and such is all resistance to the essential rights of sovereignty), is not (as a civil law) any obligation, but by virtue only of the law of nature, that forbiddeth the violation of faith; which natural obligation if men know not, they cannot know the right of any law the sovereign maketh. And for the punishment, they take it but for an act of hostility; which when they think they have strength enough, they will endeavour by acts of hostility, to avoid.

As I have heard some say, that justice is but a word, without substance; and that whatsoever a man can by force, or art, acquire to himself (not only in the condition of war, but also in a commonwealth,) is his own, which I have already showed to be false: so there be also that maintain, that there are no grounds, nor principles of reason, to sustain those essential rights, which make sovereignty absolute. For if there were, they would have been found out in some place, or other; whereas we see, there has not hitherto been any commonwealth, where those rights have been acknowledged, or challenged. Wherein they argue as ill, as if the savage people of America, should deny there were any grounds, or principles of reason, so to build a house, as to last as long as the materials, because they never yet saw any so well built. Time, and industry, produce every day new knowledge. And as the art of well building, is derived from principles of reason, observed by industrious men, that had long studied the nature of materials, and the divers effects of figure, and proportion, long after mankind began (though poorly) to build: so, long time after men have begun to constitute commonwealths, imperfect, and apt to relapse into disorder, there may principles of reason be found out, by industrious meditation, to make their constitution (excepting by external violence) everlasting. And such are those which I have in this discourse set forth: which whether they come not into the sight of those that have power to make use of them, or be neglected by them, or not, concerneth my particular interest, at this day, very little. But supposing that these of mine are not such principles of reason; yet I am sure they are principles from authority of Scripture; as I shall make it appear, when I shall come to speak of the kingdom of God, (administered by *Moses*,) over the Jews, his peculiar people by covenant.

But they say again, that though the principles be right, yet common people are not of capacity enough to be made to understand them. I should be glad, that the rich, and potent subjects of a kingdom, or those that are accounted the most learned, were no less incapable than they. But all men know, that the obstructions to this kind of doctrine, proceed not so much from the difficulty of the matter, as from the interest of them that are to learn. Potent men, digest hardly any thing that setteth up a power to bridle their affections; and learned men, any thing that discovereth their errors, and thereby lesseneth their authority: whereas the common people's minds, unless they be tainted with dependance on the potent, or scribbled over with the opinions of their doctors, are like clean paper, fit to receive whatsoever by public authority shall be imprinted in them. Shall whole nations be brought to *acquiesce* in the great mysteries of Christian religion, which are above reason; and millions of men be made believe, that the same body may be in innumerable places, at one and the same time, which is against reason; and shall not men be able, by their teaching, and preaching, protected by the law, to make that received, which is so consonant to reason, that any unprejudicated man, needs no more to learn it, than to hear it? I conclude therefore, that in the instruction of the people in the essential rights (which are the natural, and fundamental laws) of sovereignty, there is no difficulty, (whilst a sovereign has his power entire,) but what proceeds from his own fault, or the fault of those whom he trusteth in the administration of the commonwealth; and consequently, it is his duty, to cause them so to be instructed; and not only his duty, but his benefit also, and security, against the danger that may arrive to himself in his natural person, from rebellion.

And (to descend to particulars) the people are to be taught, first, that they ought not to be in love with any form of government they see in their neighbour nations, more than with their own, nor, (whatsoever present prosperity they behold in nations that are otherwise governed than they,) to desire change. For the prosperity of a people ruled by an aristocratical, or democratical assembly, cometh not from aristocracy, nor from democracy, but from the obedience, and concord of the subjects: nor do the people flourish in a monarchy, because one man has the right to rule them, but because they obey him. Take away in any kind of state, the obedience, (and consequently the concord of the people,) and they shall not only not flourish, but in short time be dissolved. And they that go about by disobedience, to do no more than reform the commonwealth, shall find they do thereby destroy it; like the foolish daughters of *Peleus,* (in the fable;) which desiring to renew the youth of their decrepid father, did by the counsel of *Medea,* cut him in pieces, and boil him, together with strange herbs, but made not of him a new man. This desire of change, is like the breach of the first of God's commandments: for there God says, *Non habebis Deos alienos;* Thou shalt not have the Gods of other nations; and in another place concerning *kings,* that they are *Gods.*

Secondly, they are to be taught, that they ought not to be led with admiration of the virtue of any of their fellow subjects, how high soever he stand, nor how conspicuously soever he shine in the commonwealth; nor of any assembly, (except the sovereign assembly,) so as to defer to them any obedience, or honour, appropriate to the sovereign only, whom (in their particular stations) they represent; nor to receive any influence from them, but such as is conveyed by them from the sovereign authority. For that sovereign, cannot be imagined to love his people as he ought, that is not jealous of them, but suffers them by the flattery of popular men, to be seduced from their loyalty, as they have often been, not only secretly, but openly, so as to proclaim marriage with them *in facie ecclesiciae* by preachers; and by publishing the same in the open streets: which may fitly be compared to the violation of the second of the ten commandments.

Thirdly, in consequence to this, they ought to be informed, how great a fault it is, to speak evil of the sovereign representative, (whether one man, or an assembly of men;) or to argue and dispute his power; or any way to use his name irreverently, whereby he may be brought into contempt with his people, and their obedience (in which the safety of the commonwealth consisteth) slackened. Which doctrine the third commandment by resemblance pointeth to.

Fourthly, seeing people cannot be taught this, nor when it is taught, remember it, nor after one generation past, so much as know in whom the sovereign power is placed, without setting apart from their ordinary labour, some certain times, in which they may attend those that are appointed to instruct them; it is necessary that some such times be determined, wherein they may assemble together, and (after prayers and praises given to God, the sovereign of sovereigns) hear those their duties told them, and the positive laws, such as generally concern them all, read and expounded, and be put in mind of the authority that maketh them laws. To this end had the *Jews* every seventh day, a *sabbath*, in which the law was read and expounded; and in the solemnity whereof they were put in mind, that their king was God; that having created the world in six days, he rested the seventh day; and by their resting on it from their labour, that that God was their king, which redeemed them from their servile, and painful labour in *Egypt*, and gave them a time, after they had rejoiced in God, to take joy also in themselves, by lawful recreation. So that the first table of the commandments, is spent all in setting down the sum of God's absolute power; not only as God, but as king by pact, (in peculiar) of the Jews; and may therefore give light, to those that have sovereign power conferred on them by the consent of men, to see what doctrine they ought to teach their subjects.

And because the first instruction of children, dependeth on the care of their parents; it is necessary that they should be obedient to them, whilst they are under their tuition; and not only so, but that also afterwards (as gratitude requireth,) they acknowledge the benefit of their education, by external signs of honour. To which end they are to be taught, that originally the father of every man was also his sovereign lord, with power over him of life and death; and that the fathers of families, when by instituting a commonwealth, they resigned that absolute power, yet it was never intended, they should lose the honour due unto them for their education. For to relinquish such right, was not necessary to the institution of sovereign power; nor would there be any reason, why any man should desire to have children, or take the care to nourish, and instruct them, if they were afterwards to have no other benefit from them, than from other men. And this accordeth with the fifth commandment.

Again, every sovereign ought to cause justice to be taught, which (consisting in taking from no man what is his,) is as much as to say, to cause men to be taught not to deprive their neighbours, by violence, or fraud, of any thing which by the sovereign authority is theirs. Of things held in propriety, those that are dearest to a man are his own life, and limbs; and in the next degree (in most men,) those that concern conjugal affection; and after them riches and means of living. Therefore the people are to be taught, to abstain from violence to one another's person, by private revenges; from violation of conjugal honour; and from forcible rapine, and fraudulent surreption of one another's goods. For which purpose also it is necessary they be showed the evil consequences of false judgment, by corruption either of judges or witnesses, whereby the distinction of propriety is taken away, and justice becomes of no effect: all which things are intimated in the sixth, seventh, eighth, and ninth commandments.

Lastly, they are to be taught, that not only the unjust facts, but the designs and intentions to do them, (though by accident hindered,) are injustice; which consisteth in the pravity of the will, as well as in the irregularity of the act. And this is the intention of the tenth commandment, and the sum of the second table; which is reduced all to this one commandment of mutual charity, *thou shalt love thy neighbour as thyself:* as the sum of the first table is reduced to *the love of God;* whom they had then newly received as their king.

As for the means, and conduits, by which the people may receive this instruction, we are to search, by what means so many opinions, contrary to the peace of mankind, upon weak and false principles, have nevertheless been so deeply rooted in them. I mean those, which I have in the precedent chapter specified: as that men shall judge of what is lawful and unlawful, not by the law itself, but by their own consciences; that is to say, by their own private judgments: that subjects sin in obeying the commands of the commonwealth, unless they themselves have first judged them to be lawful: that their propriety in their riches is such, as to exclude the dominion, which the commonwealth hath over the same: that it is lawful for subjects to kill such, as they call tyrants: that the sovereign power may be divided, and the like; which come to be instilled into the people by this means. They whom necessity, or covetousness keepeth attent on their trades, and labour; and they, on the other side, whom superfluity, or sloth carrieth after their sensual pleasures, (which two sorts of men take up the greatest part of mankind,) being diverted from the deep meditation, which the learning of truth, not only in the matter of natural justice, but also of all other sciences necessarily requireth, receive the notions of their duty, chiefly from divines in the pulpit, and partly from such of their neighbours, or familiar acquaintance, as having the faculty of discoursing readily, and plausibly, seem wiser and better learned in cases of law, and conscience, than themselves. And the divines, and such others as make show of learning, derive their knowledge from the universities, and from the schools of law, or from the books, which by men eminent in those schools, and universities have been published. It is therefore manifest, that the instruction of the people, dependeth wholly, on the right teaching of youth in the universities. But are not (may some man say) the universities of *England* learned enough already to do that? or is it you will undertake to teach the universities? Hard questions. Yet to the first, I doubt not to answer; that till towards the latter end of *Henry the Eighth,* the power of the Pope, was always upheld against the power of the commonwealth, principally by the universities; and that the doctrines maintained by so many preachers, against the sovereign power of the king, and by so many lawyers, and others, that had their education there, is a sufficient argument, that though the universities were not authors of those false doctrines, yet they knew not how to plant the true. For in such a contradiction of opinions, it is most certain, that they have not been sufficiently instructed; and it is no wonder, if they yet retain a relish of that subtle liquor, wherewith they were first seasoned, against the civil authority. But to the latter question, it is not fit, nor needful for me to say either aye, or no: for any man that sees what I am doing, may easily perceive what I think.

The safety of the people, requireth further, from him, or them that have the sovereign power, that justice be equally administered to all degrees of people; that is, that as well the rich and mighty, as poor and obscure persons, may be righted of the injuries done them; so as the great, may have no greater hope of impunity, when they do violence, dishonour, or any injury to the meaner sort, than when one of these, does the like to one of them: For in this consisteth equity; to which, as being a precept of the law of nature, a sovereign is as much subject, as any of the meanest of his people. All breaches of the law, are offences against the commonwealth: but there be some, that are also against private persons. Those that concern the commonwealth only, may without breach of equity be pardoned; for every man may pardon what is done against himself, according to his own discretion. But an offence against a private man, cannot in equity be pardoned, without the consent of him that is injured; or reasonable satisfaction.

The inequality of subjects, proceedeth from the acts of sovereign power; and therefore has no more place in the presence of the sovereign; that is to say, in a court of justice, than the inequality between kings, and their subjects, in the presence of the King of kings. The honour of great persons, is to be valued for their beneficence and the aids they give to men of inferior rank, or not at all. And the violences, oppressions, and injuries they do, are not extenuated, but aggravated by the greatness of their persons; because they have least need to commit them. The consequences of this partiality towards the great, proceed in this manner. Impunity maketh insolence; insolence hatred; and hatred, an endeavour to pull down all oppressing and contumelious greatness, though with the ruin of the commonwealth.

To equal justice, appertaineth also the equal imposition of taxes; the equality whereof dependeth not on the equality of riches, but on the equality of the debt, that every man oweth to the commonwealth for his defence. It is not enough, for a man to labour for the maintenance of his life; but also to fight, (if need be,) for the securing of his labour. They must either do as the Jews did after their return from captivity, in re-edifying the temple, build with one hand, and hold the sword in the other; or else they must hire others to fight for them. For the impositions, that are laid on the people by the sovereign power, are nothing else but the wages, due to them that hold the public sword, to defend private men in the exercise of several trades, and callings. Seeing then the benefit that every one receiveth thereby, is the enjoyment of life, which is equally dear to poor and rich; the debt which a poor man oweth them that defend his life, is the same which a rich man oweth for the defence of his; saving that the rich, who have the service of the poor, may be debtors not only for their own persons, but for many more. Which considered, the equality of imposition, consisteth rather in the equality of that which is consumed, than of the riches of the persons that consume the same. For what reason is there, that he which laboureth much, and sparing the fruits of his labour, consumeth little, should be more charged, than he that living idly, getteth little, and spendeth all he gets; seeing the one hath no more protection from the commonwealth, than the other? But when the impositions, are laid upon those things which men consume, every man payeth equally for what he useth: nor is the commonwealth defrauded by the luxurious waste of private men.

And whereas many men, by accident inevitable, become unable to maintain themselves by their labour; they ought not to be left to the charity of private persons; but to be provided for, (as far-forth as the necessities of nature require,) by the laws of the commonwealth. For as it is uncharitableness in any man, to neglect the impotent; so it is in the sovereign of a commonwealth, to expose them to the hazard of such uncertain charity.

But for such as have strong bodies, the case is otherwise: they are to be forced to work; and to avoid the excuse of not finding employment, there ought to be such laws, as may encourage all manner of arts; as navigation, agriculture, fishing, and all manner of manufacture that requires labour. The multitude of poor, and yet strong people still increasing, they are to be transplanted into countries not sufficiently inhabited: where nevertheless, they are not to exterminate those they find there; but constrain them to inhabit closer together, and not range a great deal of ground, to snatch what they find; but to court each little plot with art and labour, to give them their sustenance in due season. And when all the world is overcharged with inhabitants, then the last remedy of all is war; which provideth for every man, by victory, or death.

To the care of the sovereign, belongeth the making of good laws. But what is a good law? By a good law, I mean not a just law: for no law can be unjust. The law is made by the sovereign power, and all that is done by such power, is warranted, and owned by every one of the people; and that which every man will have so, no man can say is unjust. It is in the laws of a commonwealth, as in the laws of gaming: whatsoever the gamesters all agree on, is injustice to none of them. A good law is that, which is *needful*, for the *good of the people*, and withal *perspicuous*.

For the use of laws, (which are but rules authorized) is not to bind the people from all voluntary actions; but to direct and keep them in such a motion, as not to hurt themselves by their own impetuous desires, rashness, or indiscretion; as hedges are set, not to stop travellers, but to keep them in the way. And therefore a law that is not needful, having not the true end of a law, is not good. A law may be conceived to be good, when it is for the benefit of the sovereign; though it be not necessary for the people; but it is not so. For the good of the sovereign and people, cannot be separated. It is a weak sovereign, that has weak subjects; and a weak people, whose sovereign wanteth power to rule them at his will. Unnecessary laws are not good laws; but traps for money: which where the right of sovereign power is acknowledged, are superfluous; and where it is not acknowledged, insufficient to defend the people.

The perspicuity, consisteth not so much in the words of the law itself, as in a declaration of the causes, and motives, for which it was made. That is it, that shows us the meaning of the legislator; and the meaning of the legislator known, the law is more easily understood by few, than many words. For all words, are subject to ambiguity; and therefore multiplication of words in the body of the law, is multiplication of ambiguity: besides it seems to imply, (by too much diligence,) that whosoever can evade the words, is without the compass of the law. And this is a cause of many unnecessary processes. For when I consider how short were the laws of ancient times; and how they grew by degrees still longer; methinks I see a contention between the penners, and pleaders of the law; the former seeking to circumscribe the latter; and the latter to evade their circumscriptions; and that the pleaders have got the victory. It belongeth therefore to the office of a legislator, (such as is in all commonwealths the supreme representative, be it one man, or an assembly,) to make the reason perspicuous, why the law was made; and the body of the law itself, as short, but in as proper, and significant terms, as may be.

It belongeth also to the office of the sovereign, to make a right application of punishments, and rewards. And seeing the end of punishing is not revenge, and discharge of choler; but correction, either of the offender, or of others by his example; the severest punishments are to be inflicted for those crimes, that are of most danger to the public; such as are those which proceed from malice to the government established; those that spring from contempt of justice; those that provoke indignation in the multitude; and those, which unpunished seem authorized, as when they are committed by sons, servants, or favourites of men in authority: For indignation carrieth men, not only against the actors, and authors of injustice; but against all power that is likely to protect them; as in the case of *Tarquin;* when for the insolent act of one of his sons, he was driven out of *Rome,* and the monarchy itself dissolved. But crimes of infirmity; such as are those which proceed from great provocation, from great fear, great need, or from ignorance whether the fact be a great crime, or not, there is place many times for lenity, without prejudice to the commonwealth; and lenity when there is such place for it, is required by the law of nature. The punishment of the leaders, and teachers in a commotion; not the poor seduced people, when they are punished, can profit the commonwealth by their example. To be severe to the people, is to punish that ignorance, which may in great part be imputed to the sovereign, whose fault it was, they were no better instructed.

In like manner it belongeth to the office, and duty of the sovereign, to apply his rewards always so, as there may arise from them benefit to the commonwealth: wherein consisteth their use, and end; and is then done, when they that have well served the commonwealth, are with as little expense of the common treasure, as is possible, so well recompensed, as others thereby may be encouraged, both to serve the same as faithfully as they can, and to study the arts by which they may be enabled to do it better. To buy with money, or preferment, from a popular ambitious subject, to be quiet, and desist from making ill impressions in the minds of the people, has nothing of the nature of reward; (which is ordained not for disservice, but for service past;) nor a sign of gratitude, but of fear: nor does it tend to the benefit, but to the damage of the public. It is a contention with ambition, like that of *Hercules* with the monster *Hydra,* which having many heads, for every one that was vanquished, there grew up three. For in like manner, when the stubbornness of one popular man, is overcome with reward, there arise many more (by the example) that do the same mischief, in hope of like benefit: and as all sorts of manufacture, so also malice encreaseth by being vendible. And though sometimes a civil war, may be deferred, by such ways as that, yet the danger grows still the greater, and the public ruin more assured. It is therefore against the duty of the sovereign, to whom the public safety is committed, to reward those that aspire to greatness by disturbing the peace of their country, and not rather to oppose the beginnings of such men, with a little danger, than after a longer time with greater.

Another business of the sovereign, is to choose good counsellors; I mean such, whose advice he is to take in the government of the commonwealth. For this word counsel, *consilium,* corrupted from *considium,* is of a large signification, and comprehendeth all assemblies of men that sit together, not only to deliberate what is to be done hereafter, but also to judge of facts past, and of law for the present. I take it here in the first sense only: and in this sense, there is no choice of counsel, neither in a democracy, nor aristocracy; because the persons counselling are members of the person counselled. The choice of counsellors therefore is proper to monarchy; in which, the sovereign that endeavoureth not to make choice of those, that in every kind are the most able, dischargeth not his office as he ought to do. The most able counsellors, are they that have least hope of benefit by giving evil counsel, and most knowledge of those things that conduce to the peace, and defence of the commonwealth. It is a hard matter to know who expecteth benefit from public troubles; but the signs that guide to a just suspicion, is the soothing of the people in their unreasonable, or irremediable grievances, by men whose estates are not sufficient to discharge their accustomed expenses and may easily be observed by any one whom it concerns to know it. But to know, who has most knowledge of the public affairs, is yet harder; and they that know them, need them a great deal the less. For to know, who knows the rules almost of any art, is a great degree of the knowledge of the same art; because no man can be assured of the truth of another's rules, but he that is first taught to understand them. But the best signs of knowledge of any art, are, much conversing in it, and constant good effects of it. Good counsel comes not by lot, nor by inheritance; and therefore there is no more reason to expect good advice from the rich, or noble, in matter of state, than in delineating the dimensions of a fortress; unless we shall think there needs no method in the study of the politics, (as there does in the study of geometry,) but only to be lookers on; which is not so. For the politics is the harder study of the two. Whereas in these parts of *Europe,* it hath been taken for a right of certain persons, to have place in the highest council of state by inheritance; it is derived from the conquests of the ancient Germans; wherein many absolute lords joining together to conquer other nations, would not enter into the confederacy, without such privileges, as might be marks of difference in time following, between their posterity, and the posterity of their subjects; which privileges being inconsistent with the sovereign power, by the favour of the sovereign, they may seem to keep; but contending for them as their right, they must needs by degrees let them go, and have at last no further honour, than adhereth naturally to their abilities.

And how able soever be the counsellors in any affair, the benefit of their counsel is greater, when they give every one his advice, and the reasons of it apart, than when they do it in an assembly, by way of orations; and when they have premeditated, than when they speak on the sudden; both because they have more time, to survey the consequences of action; and are less subject to be carried away to contradiction, through envy, emulation, or other passions arising from the difference of opinion.

The best counsel, in those things that concern not other nations, but only the ease, and benefit the subjects may enjoy, by laws that look only inward, is to be taken from the general informations, and complaints of the people of each province, who are best acquainted with their own wants, and ought therefore, when they demand nothing in derogation of the essential rights of sovereignty, to be diligently taken notice of. For without those essential rights, (as I have often before said,) the commonwealth cannot at all subsist.

A commander of an army in chief, if he be not popular, shall not be beloved, nor feared as he ought to be by his army; and consequently cannot perform that office with good success. He must therefore be industrious, valiant, affable, liberal and fortunate, that he may gain an opinion both of sufficiency, and of loving his soldiers. This is popularity, and breeds in the soldiers both desire, and courage, to recommend themselves to his favour; and protects the severity of the general, in punishing (when need is) the mutinous, or negligent soldiers. But this love of soldiers, (if caution be not given of the commander's fidelity,) is a dangerous thing to sovereign power; especially when it is in the hands of an assembly not popular. It belongeth therefore to the safety of the people, both that they be good conductors, and faithful subjects, to whom the sovereign commits his armies.

But when the sovereign himself is popular; that is, reverenced and beloved of his people, there is no danger at all from the popularity of a subject. For soldiers are never so generally unjust, as to side with their captain; though they love him, against their sovereign, when they love not only his person, but also his cause. And therefore those, who by violence have at any time suppressed the power of their lawful sovereign, before they could settle themselves in his place, have been always put to the trouble of contriving their titles, to save the people from the shame of receiving them. To have a known right to sovereign power, is so popular a quality, as he that has it needs no more, for his own part, to turn the hearts of his subjects to him, but that they see him able absolutely to govern his own family: nor, on the part of his enemies, but a disbanding of their armies. For the greatest and most active part of mankind, has never hitherto been well contented with the present.

Concerning the offices of one sovereign to another, which are comprehended in that law, which is commonly called the *law of nations,* I need not say any thing in this place; because the law of nations, and the law of nature, is the same thing. And every sovereign hath the same right, in procuring the safety of his people, that any particular man can have, in procuring the safety of his own body. And the same law, that dictateth to men that have no civil government, what they ought to do, and what to avoid in regard of one another, dictateth the same to commonwealths, that is, to the consciences of sovereign princes, and sovereign assemblies; there being no court of natural justice, but in the conscience only; where not man, but God reigneth; whose laws, (such of them as oblige all mankind,) in respect of God, as he is the author of nature, are *natural;* and in respect of the same God, as he is King of kings, are *laws.* But of the kingdom of God, as King of kings, and as King also of a peculiar people, I shall speak in the rest of this discourse.

CHAPTER 31

Of the Kingdom of God by Nature

That the condition of mere nature, that is to say, of absolute liberty, such as is theirs, that neither are sovereigns, nor subjects, is anarchy, and the condition of war: that the precepts, by which men are guided to avoid that condition, are the laws of nature: that a commonwealth, without sovereign power, is but a word, without substance, and cannot stand: that subjects owe to sovereigns, simple obedience, in all things, wherein their obedience is not repugnant to the laws of God, I have sufficiently proved, in that which I have already written. There wants only, for the entire knowledge of civil duty, to know what are those laws of God. For without that, a man knows not, when he is commanded any thing by the civil power, whether it be contrary to the law of God, or not: and so, either by too much civil obedience, offends the Divine Majesty, or through fear of offending God, transgresses the commandments of the commonwealth. To avoid both these rocks, it is necessary to know what are the laws divine. And seeing the knowledge of all law, dependeth on the knowledge of the sovereign power; I shall say something in that which followeth, of the KINGDOM OF GOD.

God is king, let the earth rejoice, saith the psalmist. (*Psalm* 96. 1). And again, (*Psalm* 98. 1) *God is king though the nations be angry; and he that sitteth on the cherubims, though the earth be moved.* Whether men will or not, they must be subject always to the divine power. By denying the existence, or providence of God, men may shake off their ease, but not their yoke. But to call this power of God, which extendeth itself not only to man, but also to beasts, and plants, and bodies inanimate, by the name of kingdom, is but a metaphorical use of the word. For he only is properly said to reign, that governs his subjects by his word, and by promise of rewards to those that obey it, and by threatening them with punishment that obey it not. Subjects therefore in the kingdom of God, are not bodies inanimate, nor creatures irrational; because they understand no precepts as his: nor atheists; nor they that believe not that God has any care of the actions of mankind; because they acknowledge no word for his, nor have hope of his rewards, or fear of his threatenings. They therefore that believe there is a God that governeth the world, and hath given precepts, and propounded rewards, and punishments to mankind, are God's subjects; all the rest, are to be understood as enemies.

To rule by words, requires that such words be manifestly made known; for else they are no laws: for to the nature of laws belongeth a sufficient, and clear promulgation, such as may take away the excuse of ignorance; which in the laws of men is but of one only kind, and that is, proclamation, or promulgation by the voice of man. But God declareth his laws three ways; by the dictates of *natural reason*, by *revelation*, and by the *voice* of some *man*, to whom by the operation of miracles, he procureth credit with the rest. From hence there ariseth a triple word of God, *rational, sensible*, and *prophetic*: to which correspondeth a triple hearing; *right reason, sense supernatural*, and *faith*. As for sense supernatural, which consisteth in revelation, or inspiration, there have not been any universal laws so given, because God speaketh not in that manner, but to particular persons, and to divers men divers things.

From the difference between the other two kinds of God's word, *rational*, and *prophetic*, there may be attributed to God, a twofold kingdom, *natural*, and *prophetic*: natural, wherein he governeth as many of mankind as acknowledge his providence, by the natural dictates of right reason; and prophetic, wherein having chosen out one peculiar nation (the Jews) for his subjects, he governed them, and none but them, not only by natural reason, but by positive laws, which he gave them by the mouths of his holy prophets. Of the natural kingdom of God I intend to speak in this chapter.

The right of nature, whereby God reigneth over men, and punisheth those that break his laws, is to be derived, not from his creating them, as if he required obedience, as of gratitude for his benefits; but from his *irresistible power*. I have formerly shown, how the sovereign right ariseth from pact: to show how the same right may arise from nature, requires no more, but to show in what case it is never taken away. Seeing all men by nature had right to all things, they had right every one to reign over all the rest. But because this right could not be obtained by force, it concerned the safety of every one, laying by that right, to set up men (with sovereign authority) by common consent, to rule and defend them: whereas if there had been any man of power irresistible; there had been no reason, why he should not by that power have ruled, and defended both himself, and them, according to his own discretion. To those therefore whose power is irresistible, the dominion of all men adhereth naturally by their excellence of power; and consequently it is from that power, that the kingdom over men, and the right of afflicting men at his pleasure, belongeth naturally to God Almighty; not as Creator, and gracious; but as omnipotent. And though punishment be due for sin only, because by that word is understood affliction for sin; yet the right of afflicting, is not always derived from men's sin, but from God's power.

This question, *why evil men often prosper, and good men suffer adversity*, has been much disputed by the ancient, and is the same with this of ours, *by what right God dispenseth the prosperities and adversities of this life;* and is of that difficulty, as it hath shaken the faith, not only of the vulgar, but of philosophers, and which is more, of the Saints, concerning the Divine Providence. *How good,* (saith *David*) (*Psalm* 72. 1, 2, 3) *is the God of Israel to those that are upright in heart; and yet my feet were almost gone, my treadings had well-nigh slipt; for I was grieved at the wicked, when I saw the ungodly in such prosperity.* And *Job,* how earnestly does he expostulate with God, for the many afflictions he suffered, notwithstanding his righteousness? This question in the case of *Job,* is decided by God himself, not by arguments derived from *Job's* sin, but his own power. For whereas the friends of *Job* drew their arguments from his affliction to his sin, and he defended himself by the conscience of his innocence, God himself taketh up the matter, and having justified the affliction by arguments drawn from his power, such as this, (*Job* 38. 4) *Where wast thou, when I laid the foundations of the earth,* and the like, both approved Job's innocence, and reproved the erroneous doctrine of his friends. Conformable to this doctrine is the sentence of our Saviour, concerning the man that was born blind, in these words, *Neither hath this man sinned, nor his fathers; but that the works of God might be made manifest in him.* And though it be said, *that death entered into the world by sin,* (by which is meant that if *Adam* had never sinned, he had never died, that is, never suffered any separation of his soul from his body,) it follows not thence, that God could not justly have afflicted him, though he had not sinned, as well as he afflicteth other living creatures, that cannot sin.

Having spoken of the right of God's sovereignty, as grounded only on nature; we are to consider next, what are the Divine laws, or dictates of natural reason; which laws concern either the natural duties of one man to another, or the honour naturally due to our Divine Sovereign. The first are the same laws of nature, of which I have spoken already in the 14th and 15th chapters of this treatise; namely, equity, justice, mercy, humility, and the rest of the moral virtues. It remaineth therefore that we consider, what precepts are dictated to men, by their natural reason only, without other word of God, touching the honour and worship of the Divine Majesty.

Honour consisteth in the inward thought, and opinion of the power, and goodness of another: and therefore to honour God, is to think as highly of his power and goodness, as is possible. And of that opinion, the external signs appearing in the words, and actions of men, are called *worship;* which is one part of that which the Latins understand by the word *cultus:* For *cultus* signifieth properly, and constantly, that labour which a man bestows on any thing, with a purpose to make benefit by it. Now those things whereof we make benefit, are either subject to us, and the profit they yield, followeth the labour we bestow upon them, as a natural effect; or they are not subject to us, but answer our labour, according to their own wills. In the first sense the labour bestowed on the earth, is called *culture;* and the education of children, a *culture* of their minds. In the second sense, where men's wills are to be wrought to our purpose, not by force, but by complaisance, it signifieth as much as courting, that is, a winning of favour by good offices; as by praises, by acknowledging their power, and by whatsoever is pleasing to them from whom we look for any benefit. And this is properly *worship:* in which sense *Publicola,* is understood for a worshipper of the people; and *cultus Dei,* for the worship of God.

From internal honour, consisting in the opinion of power and goodness, arise three passions; *love,* which hath reference to goodness; and *hope,* and *fear,* that relate to power: and three parts of external worship; *praise, magnifying,* and *blessing:* the subject of praise, being goodness; the subject of magnifying and blessing, being power, and the effect thereof felicity. Praise, and magnifying are signified both by words, and actions: by words, when we say a man is good, or great: by actions, when we thank him for his bounty, and obey his power. The opinion of the happiness of another, can only be expressed by words.

There be some signs of honour, (both in attributes and actions,) that be naturally so; as amongst attributes, *good, just, liberal,* and the like; and amongst actions, *prayers, thanks,* and *obedience.* Others are so by institution, or custom of men; and in some times and places are honourable; in others, dishonourable; in others indifferent: such as are the gestures in salutation, prayer, and thanksgiving, in different times and places, differently used. The former is *natural;* the latter *arbitrary* worship.

And of arbitrary worship, there be two differences: for sometimes it is a *commanded,* sometimes *voluntary* worship: commanded, when it is such as he requireth, who is worshipped: free, when it is such as the worshipper thinks fit. When it is commanded, not the words, or gesture, but the obedience is the worship. But when free, the worship consists in the opinion of the beholders: for if to them the words, or actions by which we intend honour, seem ridiculous, and tending to contumely; they are no worship; because no signs of honour; and no signs of honour; because a sign is not a sign to him that giveth it, but to him to whom it is made; that is, to the spectator.

Again, there is a *public,* and a *private* worship. Public, is the worship that a commonwealth performeth, as one person. Private, is that which a private person exhibiteth. Public, in respect of the whole commonwealth, is free; but in respect of particular men it is not so. Private, is in secret free; but in the sight of the multitude, it is never without some restraint, either from the laws, or from the opinion of men; which is contrary to the nature of liberty.

The end of worship amongst men, is power. For where a man seeth another worshipped, he supposeth him powerful, and is the readier to obey him; which makes his power greater. But God has no ends: the worship we do him, proceeds from our duty, and is directed according to our capacity, by those rules of honour, that reason dictateth to be done by the weak to the more potent men, in hope of benefit, for fear of damage, or in thankfulness for good already received from them.

That we may know what worship of God is taught us by the light of nature, I will begin with his attributes. Where, first, it is manifest, we ought to attribute to him *existence.* For no man can have the will to honour that, which he thinks not to have any being.

Secondly, that those philosophers, who said the world, or the soul of the world was God, spake unworthily of him; and denied his existence. For by God, is understood the cause of the world; and to say the world is God, is to say there is no cause of it, that is, no God.

Thirdly, to say the world was not created, but eternal, (seeing that which is eternal has no cause,) is to deny there is a God.

Fourthly, that they who attributing (as they think) ease to God, take from him the care of mankind; take from him his honour: for it takes away men's love, and fear of him; which is the root of honour.

Fifthly, in those things that signify greatness, and power; to say he is *finite,* is not to honour him: for it is not a sign of the will to honour God, to attribute to him less than we can; and finite, is less than we can; because to finite, it is easy to add more.

Therefore to attribute *figure* to him, is not honour; for all figure is finite:

Nor to say we conceive, and imagine, or have an *idea* of him, in our mind: for whatsoever we conceive is finite:

Nor to attribute to him *parts,* or *totality;* which are the attributes only of things finite:

Nor to say he is in this, or that *place:* for whatsoever is in place, is bounded, and finite:

Nor that he is *moved,* or *resteth:* for both these attributes ascribe to him place:

Nor that there be more Gods than one; because it implies them all finite: for there cannot be more than one infinite:

Nor to ascribe to him (unless metaphorically, meaning not the passion but the effect) passions that partake of grief; as *repentance, anger, mercy:* or of want; as *appetite, hope, desire;* or of any passive faculty: for passion, is power limited by somewhat else.

And therefore when we ascribe to God a *will,* it is not to be understood, as that of man, for a *rational appetite;* but as the power, by which he effecteth every thing.

Likewise when we attribute to him *sight,* and other acts of sense; as also *knowledge,* and *understanding;* which in us is nothing else, but a tumult of the mind, raised by external things that press the organical parts of man's body: for there is no such thing in God; and being things that depend on natural causes, cannot be attributed to him.

He that will attribute to God, nothing but what is warranted by natural reason, must either use such negative attributes, as *infinite, eternal, incomprehensible;* or superlatives, as *most high, most great,* and the like; or indefinite, as *good, just, holy, creator;* and in such sense, as if he meant not to declare what he is, (for that were to circumscribe him within the limits of our fancy,) but how much we admire him, and how ready we would be to obey him; which is a sign of humility, and of a will to honour him as much as we can: For there is but one name to signify our conception of his nature, and that is, I AM: and but one name of his relation to us, and that is *God;* in which is contained Father, King, and Lord.

Concerning the actions of divine worship, it is a most general precept of reason, that they be signs of the intention to honour God; such as are, first, *prayers:* For not the carvers, when they made images, were thought to make them gods; but the people that *prayed* to them.

Secondly, *thanksgiving;* which differeth from prayer in divine worship, no otherwise, than that prayers precede, and thanks succeed the benefit; the end both of the one, and the other, being to acknowledge God, for author of all benefits, as well past, as future.

Thirdly, *gifts;* that is to say, *sacrifices,* and *oblations,* (if they be of the best,) are signs of honour: for they are thanksgivings.

Fourthly, *not to swear by any but God,* is naturally a sign of honour: for it is a confession that God only knoweth the heart; and that no man's wit, or strength can protect a man against God's vengeance on the perjured.

Fifthly, it is a part of rational worship, to speak considerately of God; for it argues a fear of him, and fear, is a confession of his power. Hence followeth, that the name of God is not to be used rashly, and to no purpose; for that is as much, as in vain: and it is to no purpose unless it be by way of oath, and by order of the commonwealth, to make judgments certain; or between commonwealths, to avoid war. And that disputing of God's nature is contrary to his honour: for it is supposed, that in this natural kingdom of God, there is no other way to know any thing, but by natural reason; that is, from the principles of natural science; which are so far from teaching us any thing of God's nature, as they cannot teach us our own nature, nor the nature of the smallest creature living. And therefore, when men out of the principles of natural reason, dispute of the attributes of God, they but dishonour him: for in the attributes which we give to God, we are not to consider the signification of philosophical truth; but the signification of pious intention, to do him the greatest honour we are able. From the want of which consideration, have proceeded the volumes of disputation about the nature of God, that tend not to his honour, but to the honour of our own wits, and learning; and are nothing else but inconsiderate, and vain abuses of his sacred name.

Sixthly, in *prayers, thanksgivings, offerings* and *sacrifices,* it is a dictate of natural reason, that they be every one in his kind the best, and most significant of honour. As for example, that prayers and thanksgiving, be made in words and phrases, not sudden, nor light, nor plebeian; but beautiful, and well composed; For else we do not God as much honour as we can. And therefore the heathens did absurdly, to worship images for gods: but their doing it in verse, and with music, both of voice, and instruments, was reasonable. Also that the beasts they offered in sacrifice, and the gifts they offered, and their actions in worshipping, were full of submission, and commemorative of benefits received, was according to reason, as proceeding from an intention to honour him.

Seventhly, reason directeth not only to worship God in secret; but also, and especially, in public, and in the sight of men: For without that, (that which in honour is most acceptable) the procuring others to honour him, is lost.

Lastly, obedience to his laws (that is, in this case to the laws of nature,) is the greatest worship of all. For as obedience is more acceptable to God than sacrifice; so also to set light by his commandments, is the greatest of all contumelies. And these are the laws of that divine worship, which natural reason dictateth to private men.

But seeing a commonwealth is but one person, it ought also to exhibit to God but one worship; which then it doth, when it commandeth it to be exhibited by private men, publicly. And this is public worship; the property whereof, is to be *uniform:* for those actions that are done differently, by different men, cannot be said to be a public worship. And therefore, where many sorts of worship be allowed, proceeding from the different religions of private men, it cannot be said there is any public worship, nor that the commonwealth is of any religion at all.

And because words (and consequently the attributes of God) have their signification by agreement, and constitution of men; those attributes are to be held significative of honour, that men intend shall so be; and whatsoever may be done by the wills of particular men, where there is no law but reason, may be done by the will of the commonwealth, by laws civil. And because a commonwealth hath no will, nor makes no laws, but those that are made by the will of him, or them that have the sovereign power; it followeth, that those attributes which the sovereign ordaineth, in the worship of God, for signs of honour, ought to be taken and used for such, by private men in their public worship.

But because not all actions are signs by constitution, but some are naturally signs of honour, others of contumely, these latter (which are those that men are ashamed to do in the sight of them they reverence) cannot be made by human power a part of Divine worship; nor the former (such as are decent, modest, humble behaviour) ever be separated from it. But whereas there be an infinite number of actions, and gestures, of an indifferent nature; such of them as the commonwealth shall ordain to be publicly and universally in use, as signs of honour, and part of God's worship, are to be taken and used for such by the subjects. And that which is said in the Scripture, *It is better to obey God than men*, hath place in the kingdom of God by pact, and not by nature.

Having thus briefly spoken of the natural kingdom of God, and his natural laws, I will add only to this chapter a short declaration of his natural punishments. There is no action of man in this life, that is not the beginning of so long a chain of consequences, as no human providence, is high enough, to give a man a prospect to the end. And in this chain, there are linked together both pleasing and unpleasing events; in such manner, as he that will do any thing for his pleasure, must engage himself to suffer all the pains annexed to it; and these pains, are the natural punishments of those actions, which are the beginning of more harm than good. And hereby it comes to pass, that intemperance is naturally punished with diseases; rashness, with mischances; injustice, with the violence of enemies; pride, with ruin; cowardice, with oppression: negligent government of princes, with rebellion; and rebellion, with slaughter. For seeing punishments are consequent to the breach of laws; natural punishments must be naturally consequent to the breach of the laws of nature; and therefore follow them as their natural, not arbitrary effects.

And thus far concerning the constitution, nature, and right of sovereigns; and concerning the duty of subjects, derived from the principles of natural reason. And now, considering how different this doctrine is, from the practice of the greatest part of the world, especially of these western parts, that have received their moral learning from *Rome*, and *Athens;* and how much depth of moral philosophy is required, in them that have the administration of the sovereign power; I am at the point of believing this my labour, as useless, as the commonwealth of *Plato;* For he also is of opinion that it is impossible for the disorders of state, and change of governments by civil war, ever to be taken away, till sovereigns be philosophers. But when I consider again, that the science of natural justice, is the only science necessary for sovereigns, and their principal ministers; and that they need not be charged with the sciences mathematical, (as by *Plato* they are,) further, than by good laws to encourage men to the study of them; and that neither *Plato*, nor any other philosopher hitherto, hath put into order, and sufficiently or probably proved all the theorems of moral doctrine, that men may learn thereby, both how to govern, and how to obey; I recover some hope, that one time or other, this writing of mine, may fall into the hands of a sovereign, who will consider it himself, (for it is short, and I think clear,) without the help of any interested, or envious interpreter; and by the exercise of entire sovereignty, in protecting the public teaching of it, convert this truth of speculation, into the utility of practice.

A REVIEW, AND CONCLUSION

From the contrariety of some of the natural faculties of the mind, one to another, as also of one passion to another, and from their reference to conversation, there has been an argument taken, to infer an impossibility that any one man should be sufficiently disposed to all sorts of civil duty. The severity of judgment, they say, makes men censorious, and unapt to pardon the errors and infirmities of other men:

and on the other side, celerity of fancy, makes the thoughts less steady than is necessary, to discern exactly between right and wrong. Again, in all deliberations, and in all pleadings, the faculty of solid reasoning, is necessary: for without it, the resolutions of men are rash, and their sentences unjust: and yet if there be not powerful eloquence, which procureth attention and consent, the effect of reason will be little. But these are contrary faculties; the former being grounded upon principles of truth; the other upon opinions already received, true, or false; and upon the passions and interests of men, which are different, and mutable.

And amongst the passions, *courage,* (by which I mean the contempt of wounds, and violent death) inclineth men to private revenges, and sometimes to endeavour the unsettling of the public peace: and *timorousness,* many times disposeth to the desertion of the public defence. Both these they say cannot stand together in the same person.

And to consider the contrariety of men's opinions, and manners in general, it is, they say, impossible to entertain a constant civil amity with all those, with whom the business of the world constrains us to converse: which business, consisteth almost in nothing else but a perpetual contention for honour, riches, and authority.

To which I answer, that these are indeed great difficulties, but not impossibilities: for by education, and discipline, they may be, and are sometimes reconciled. Judgment and fancy may have place in the same man; but by turns; as the end which he aimeth at requireth. As the Israelites in Egypt, were sometimes fastened to their labour of making bricks, and other times were ranging abroad to gather straw: so also may the judgment sometimes be fixed upon one certain consideration, and the fancy at another time wandering about the world. So also reason, and eloquence, (though not perhaps in the natural sciences, yet in the moral) may stand very well together. For wheresoever there is place for adorning and preferring of error, there is much more place for adorning and preferring of truth, if they have it to adorn. Nor is there any repugnancy between fearing the laws, and not fearing a public enemy; nor between abstaining from injury, and pardoning it in others. There is therefore no such inconsistence of human nature, with civil duties, as some think. I have known clearness of judgment, and largeness of fancy; strength of reason, and graceful elocution; a courage for the war, and a fear for the laws, and all eminently in one man; and that was my most noble and honoured friend, Mr. Sidney Godolphin; who hating no man, nor hated of any, was unfortunately slain in the beginning of the late civil war, in the public quarrel, by an undiscerned, and an undiscerning hand.

To the Laws of Nature, declared in Chapter 15, I would have this added, *that every man is bound by nature, as much as in him lieth, to protect in war, the authority, by which he is himself protected in time of peace.* For he that pretendeth a right of nature to preserve his own body, cannot pretend a right of nature to destroy him, by whose strength he is preserved: it is a manifest contradiction of himself. And though this law may be drawn by consequence, from some of those that are there already mentioned; yet the times require to have it inculcated, and remembered.

And because I find by divers English books lately printed, that the civil wars have not yet sufficiently taught men in what point of time it is, that a subject becomes obliged to the conqueror; nor what is conquest; nor how it comes about, that it obliges men to obey his laws: therefore for further satisfaction of men therein, I say, the point of time, wherein a man becomes subject to a conqueror, is that point, wherein having liberty to submit to him, he consenteth, either by express words, or by other sufficient sign, to be his subject. When it is that a man hath the liberty to submit, I have showed before in the end of Chapter 21; namely, that for him that hath no obligation to his former sovereign but that of an ordinary subject, it is then, when the means of his life is within the guards and garrisons of the enemy; for it is then, that he hath no longer protection from him, but is protected by the adverse party for his contribution. Seeing therefore such contribution is every where, as a thing inevitable, (notwithstanding it be an assistance to the enemy,) esteemed lawful; a total submission, which is but an assistance to the enemy, cannot be esteemed unlawful. Besides, if a man consider that they who submit, assist the enemy but with part of their estates, whereas they that refuse, assist him with the whole, there is no reason to call their submission, or composition an assistance; but rather a detriment to the enemy. But if a man, besides the obligation of a subject, hath taken upon him a new obligation of a soldier, then he hath not the liberty to submit to a new power, as long as the old one keeps the field, and giveth him means of subsistence, either in his armies, or garrisons: for in this case, he cannot complain of want of protection, and means to live as a soldier. But when that also fails, a soldier also may seek his protection wheresoever he has most hope to have it; and may lawfully submit himself to his new master. And so much for the time when he may do it lawfully, if he will. If therefore he do it, he is undoubtedly bound to be a true subject: for a contract lawfully made, cannot lawfully be broken.

By this also a man may understand, when it is, that men may be said to be conquered; and in what the nature of conquest, and the right of a conqueror consisteth: for this submission is it implieth them all. Conquest, is not the victory itself; but the acquisition by victory, of a right, over the persons of men. He therefore that is slain, is overcome, but not conquered: he that is taken, and put into prison, or chains, is not conquered, though overcome; for he is still an enemy, and may save himself if he can: but he that upon promise of obedience, hath his life and liberty allowed him, is then conquered, and a subject; and not before. The Romans used to say, that their general had *pacified* such a *province,* that is to say, in English, *conquered* it; and that the country was *pacified* by victory, when the people of it had promised *imperata facere,* that is, *to do what the Roman people commanded them:* this was to be conquered. But this promise may be either express, or tacit: express, by promise: tacit, by other signs. As for example, a man that hath not been called to make such an express promise, (because he is one whose power perhaps is not considerable;) yet if he live under their protection openly, he is understood to submit himself to the government: but if he live there secretly, he is liable to any thing that may be done to a spy, and enemy of the state. I say not, he does any injustice, (for acts of open hostility bear not that name); but that he may be justly put to death. Likewise, if a man, when his country is conquered, be out of it, he is not conquered, nor subject: but if at his return, he submit to the government, he is bound to obey it. So that *conquest* (to define it) is the acquiring of the right of sovereignty by victory. Which right, is acquired, in the people's submission, by which they contract with the victor, promising obedience, for life and liberty.

In Chapter 29, I have set down for one of the causes of the dissolutions of commonwealths, their imperfect generation, consisting in the want of an absolute and arbitrary legislative power; for want whereof, the civil sovereign is fain to handle the sword of justice unconstantly, and as if it were too hot for him to hold. One reason whereof (which I have not there mentioned) is this, that they will all of them justify the war, by which their power was at first gotten, and whereon (as they think) their right dependeth, and not on the possession. As if, for example, the right of the kings of England did depend on the goodness of the cause of William the Conqueror, and upon their lineal, and directest descent from him; by which means, there would perhaps be no tie of the subjects' obedience to their sovereign at this day in all the world: wherein whilst they needlessly think to justify themselves, they justify all the successful rebellions that ambition shall at any time raise against them, and their successors. Therefore I put down for one of the most effectual seeds of the death of any state, that the conquerors require not only a submission of men's actions to them for the future, but also an approbation of all their actions past; when there is scarce a commonwealth in the world, whose beginnings can in conscience be justified.

And because the name of tyranny, signifieth nothing more, nor less, than the name of sovereignty, be it in one, or many men, saving that they that use the former word, are understood to be angry with them they call tyrants; I think the toleration of a professed hatred of tyranny, is a toleration of hatred to commonwealth in general, and another evil seed, not differing much from the former. For to the justification of the cause of a conqueror, the reproach of the cause of the conquered, is for the most part necessary: but neither of them necessary for the obligation of the conquered. And thus much I have thought fit to say upon the review of the first and second part of this discourse.

In Chapter 35, I have sufficiently declared out of the Scripture, that in the commonwealth of the Jews, God himself was made the sovereign, by pact with the people; who were therefore called his *peculiar people,* to distinguish them from the rest of the world, over whom God reigned not by their consent, but by his own power: and that in this kingdom Moses was God's lieutenant on earth; and that it was he that told them what laws God appointed them to be ruled by. But I have omitted to set down who were the officers appointed to do execution; especially in capital punishments; not then thinking it a matter of so necessary consideration, as I find it since. We know that generally in all commonwealths, the execution of corporal punishments, was either put upon the guards, or other soldiers of the sovereign power; or given to those, in whom want of means, contempt of honour, and hardness of heart, concurred, to make them sue for such an office. But amongst the Israelites it was a positive law of God their sovereign, that he that was convicted of a capital crime, should be stoned to death by the people; and that the witnesses should cast the first stone, and after the witnesses, then the rest of the people. This was a law that designed who were to be the executioners; but not that any one should throw a stone at him before conviction and sentence, where the congregation was judge. The witnesses were nevertheless to be heard before they proceeded to execution, unless the fact were committed in the presence of the congregation itself, or in sight of the lawful judges; for then there needed no other witnesses but the judges themselves. Nevertheless, this manner of proceeding being not thoroughly understood, hath given occasion to a dangerous opinion, that any man may kill another, in some cases, by a right of zeal; as if the executions done upon offenders in the kingdom of God in old time, proceeded not from the sovereign command, but from the authority of private zeal: which, if we consider the texts that seem to favour it, is quite contrary.

First, where the Levites fell upon the people, that had made and worshipped the Golden Calf, and slew three thousand of them; it was by the commandment of

Moses, from the mouth of God; as is manifest, *Exod.* 32. 27. And when the son of a woman of Israel had blasphemed God, they that heard it, did not kill him, but brought him before Moses, who put him under custody, till God should give sentence against him; as appears, *Levit.* 25. 11, 12. Again, (*Numb.* 25. 6, 7) when Phinehas killed Zimri and Cosbi, it was not by right of private zeal: their crime was committed in the sight of the assembly; there needed no witness; the law was known, and he the heir apparent to the sovereignty; and which is the principal point, the lawfulness of his act depended wholly upon a subsequent ratification by Moses, whereof he had no cause to doubt. And this presumption of a future ratification, is sometimes necessary to the safety [of] a commonwealth; as in a sudden rebellion, any man that can suppress it by his own power in the country where it begins, without express law or commission, may lawfully do it, and provide to have it ratified, or pardoned, whilst it is in doing, or after it is done. Also *Numb.* 35. 30, it is expressly said, *Whosoever shall kill the murderer, shall kill him upon the word of witnesses:* but witnesses suppose a formal judicature, and consequently condemn that pretence of *jus zelotarum.* The law of Moses concerning him that enticeth to idolatry, that is to say, in the kingdom of God to a renouncing of his allegiance, (*Deut.* 13. 8) forbids to conceal him, and commands the accuser to cause him to be put to death, and to cast the first stone at him; but not to kill him before he be condemned. And (*Deut.* 17. 4, 5, 6) the process against idolatry is exactly set down: for God there speaketh to the people, as judge, and commandeth them, when a man is accused of idolatry, to enquire diligently of the fact, and finding it true, then to stone him; but still the hand of the witness throweth the first stone. This is not private zeal, but public condemnation. In like manner when a father hath a rebellious son, the law is (*Deut.* 21. 18) that he shall bring him before the judges of the town, and all the people of the town shall stone him. Lastly, by pretence of these laws it was, that St. Stephen was stoned, and not by pretence of private zeal: for before he was carried away to execution, he had pleaded his cause before the high priest. There is nothing in all this, nor in any other part of the Bible, to countenance executions by private zeal; which being oftentimes but a conjunction of ignorance and passion, is against both the justice and peace of a commonwealth.

In chapter 36, I have said, that it is not declared in what manner God spake supernaturally to Moses: not that he spake not to him sometimes by dreams and visions, and by a supernatural voice, as to other prophets: for the manner how he spake unto him from the mercy-seat, is expressly set down *Numbers* 7. 89, in these words, *From that time forward, when Moses entered into the Tabernacle of the congregation to speak with God, he heard a voice which spake unto him from over the mercy-seat, which is over the Ark of the testimony, from between the cherubims he spake unto him.* But it is not declared in what consisted the preeminence of the manner of God's speaking to Moses, above that of his speaking to other prophets, as to Samuel, and to Abraham, to whom he also spake by a voice, (that is, by vision) unless the difference consist in the clearness of the vision. For *face to face,* and *mouth to mouth,* cannot be literally understood of the infiniteness, and incomprehensibility of the Divine nature.

And as to the whole doctrine, I see not yet, but the principles of it are true and proper; and the ratiocination solid. For I ground the civil right of sovereigns, and both the duty and liberty of subjects, upon the known natural inclinations of mankind, and upon the articles of the law of nature; of which no man, that pretends but reason enough to govern his private family, ought to be ignorant. And for the power ecclesiastical of the same sovereigns, I ground it on such texts, as are both evident in themselves, and consonant to the scope of the whole Scripture. And therefore am persuaded, that he that shall read it with a purpose only to be informed, shall be informed by it. But for those that by writing, or public discourse, or by their eminent actions, have already engaged themselves to the maintaining of contrary opinions, they will not be so easily satisfied. For in such cases, it is natural for men, at one and the same time, both to proceed in reading, and to lose their attention, in the search of objections to that they had read before: Of which in a time wherein the interests of men are changed (seeing much of that doctrine, which serveth to the establishing of a new government, must needs be contrary to that which conduced to the dissolution of the old,) there cannot choose but be very many.

In that part which treateth of a Christian commonwealth, there are some new doctrines, which, it may be, in a state where the contrary were already fully determined, were a fault for a subject without leave to divulge, as being an usurpation of the place of a teacher. But in this time, that men call not only for peace, but also for truth, to offer such doctrines as I think true, and that manifestly tend to peace and loyalty, to the consideration of those that are yet in deliberation, is no more, but to offer new wine, to be put into new cask, that both may be preserved together. And I suppose, that then, when novelty can breed no trouble, nor disorder in a state, men are not generally so much inclined to the reverence of antiquity, as to prefer ancient errors, before new and well proved truth.

There is nothing I distrust more than my elocution, which nevertheless I am confident (excepting the mischances of the press) is not obscure. That I have neglected the ornament of quoting ancient poets, orators, and philosophers, contrary to the custom of late time, (whether I have done well or ill in it,) proceedeth from my judgment, grounded on many reasons. For first, all truth of doctrine dependeth either upon *reason,* or upon *Scripture;* both which give credit to many, but never receive it from any writer. Secondly, the matters in question are not of *fact,* but of *right,* wherein there is no place for *witnesses.* There is scarce any of those old writers, that contradicteth not sometimes both himself and others; which makes their testimonies insufficient. Fourthly, such opinions as are taken only upon credit of antiquity, are not intrinsically the judgment of those that cite them, but words that pass (like gaping) from mouth to mouth. Fifthly, it is many times with a fraudulent design that men stick their corrupt doctrine with the cloves of other men's wit. Sixthly, I find not that the ancients they cite, took it for an ornament, to do the like with those that wrote before them. Seventhly, it is an argument of indigestion, when Greek and Latin sentences unchewed come up again, as they use to do, unchanged. Lastly, though I reverence those men of ancient time, that either have written truth perspicuously, or set us in a better way to find it out ourselves; yet to the antiquity itself I think nothing due: For if we will reverence the age, the present is the oldest. If the antiquity of the writer, I am not sure, that generally they to whom such honour is given, were more ancient when they wrote, than I am that am writing: But if it be well considered, the praise of ancient authors, proceeds not from the reverence of the dead, but from the competition, and mutual envy of the living.

To conclude, there is nothing in this whole discourse, nor in that I writ before of the same subject in Latin, as far as I can perceive, contrary either to the Word of God, or to good manners; or to the disturbance of the public tranquillity. Therefore I think it may be profitably printed, and more profitably taught in the Universities, in case they also think so, to whom the judgment of the same belongeth. For seeing the Universities are the fountains of civil, and moral doctrine, from whence the preachers, and the gentry, drawing such water as they find, use to sprinkle the same (both from the pulpit, and in their conversation) upon the people, there ought certainly to be great care taken, to have it pure, both from the venom of heathen politicians, and from the incantation of deceiving spirits. And by that means the most men, knowing their duties, will be the less subject to serve the ambition of a few discontented persons, in their purposes against the state; and be the less grieved with the contributions necessary for their peace, and defence; and the governors themselves have the less cause, to maintain at the common charge any greater army, than is necessary to make good the public liberty, against the invasions and encroachments of foreign enemies.

And thus I have brought to an end my Discourse of Civil and Ecclesiastical Government, occasioned by the disorders of the present time, without partiality, without application, and without other design, than to set before men's eyes the mutual relation between protection and obedience; of which the condition of human nature, and the laws divine, (both natural and positive) require an inviolable observation. And though in the revolution of states, there can be no very good constellation for truths of this nature to be born under, (as having an angry aspect from the dissolvers of an old government, and seeing but the backs of them that erect a new,) yet I cannot think it will be condemned at this time, either by the public judge of doctrine, or by any that desires the continuance of public peace. And in this hope I return to my interrupted speculation of bodies natural; wherein, (if God give me health to finish it,) I hope the novelty will as much please, as in the doctrine of this artificial body it useth to offend. For such truth, as opposeth no man's profit, nor pleasure, is to all men welcome.

JOHN LOCKE

A number of recent interpretations of the political writings of John Locke (1632–1704) situate them in the context of the Exclusion Controversy of 1679–1683 and the Glorious Revolution of 1688–1689. This portrait of Locke as a radical activist reminds us that his political and religious writings, like those of Hobbes before him, are intimately associated with the turbulent events of seventeenth-century England. His discussions of toleration, property, civil authority, rebellion, and much else are not detached reflections on perennial themes; rather, they are engaged contributions to real political debate and concrete events. Yet, while these events occasioned many arguments in the *Two Treatises*, it is equally true that Locke was dealing with problems of the origin, extent, and limits to government that were central to political thought in England and Europe since the 1620s and remain central today. Moreover, as with his predecessors, his thinking reverberated well beyond these boundaries, especially in the next century in America, where his account of property, his argument for political obligation, and his justification for the right of a people to rebel against an oppressive government were widely cited in the years preceding the American Revolution. Locke, then, was both a living and a posthumous revolutionary, a defender of liberal government in his own world and in years and places far from his own. There is nothing belated about Locke's importance to the tradition of Western political theory and philosophy.

Locke was born in Somerset in 1632, went to Westminster, an excellent school near London, and matriculated at Christ Church, Oxford, where, as Peter Laslett tells us, he was "urbane, idle, unhappy, and unremarkable." Locke took a medical degree, in order to avoid the clergy, and studied philosophy. His interest in the science of his day continued throughout his life; in 1668 he was elected to the Royal Society, and he was a friend of Robert Boyle, Isaac Newton, Thomas Sydenham, and other figures central to the development of the new science. Like Hobbes, shortly after his graduation Locke became associated with a wealthy, powerful patron. Anthony Ashley Cooper, the first Earl of Shaftesbury, played a major role in Restoration politics and religious life. He strongly advocated toleration, vigorously opposed the threat of Catholic influence in England, and was a leader in the movement to exclude Charles II's brother, James, a Catholic, from the line of succession to the throne. Locke became, first, Shaftesbury's physician, then his research associate, coauthor, and political advisor. In the years of the Exclusion Controversy, Locke was active in Shaftesbury's revolutionary group, and even during Shaftesbury's imprisonment in 1680 and after his death in 1683, Locke continued his participation in this radical political movement.

In 1683, after the failure of the famous Rye House Plot to assassinate Charles II, Locke fled to Holland. There he played an active role in the community of exiled revolutionaries, negotiating transfers of funds, writing, and working in behalf of the aborted attempt to place the Duke of Monmouth on the throne. Prior to his flight to the Continent, Locke deposited with his old friend James Tyrrell a manuscript on political matters. Most likely it was the first of the *Two Treatises*, a detailed critique of the patriarchalism and doctrine of the Adamite right of kings presented in the recently republished work of Robert Filmer. During these years of the Exclusion Controversy and the debate over the rights of government, Locke, like Algernon Sydney (regicide and author of *Discourses Concerning Government*), Tyrrell (author of *Patriarcha Non Monarcha*), and Shaftesbury himself, was absorbed with the notion of political power and the rights of the people. This fragment, the *First Treatise*, was the initial product of these early reflections. But it was not the last. In the 1680s Locke added to his earlier work and by the decade's end had completed a second treatise to accompany the first. In it he developed his famous account of the state of nature in terms of his conception of property and labor, his argument for the role and authority of government, and his defense of the right of resistance and the rights of the people against an oppressive government. The two treatises were published anonymously in 1689, one year after the installation of William and Mary and in the same year as Locke's *Letter on Toleration*.

After his return to England in 1689, Locke became a celebrity. By the end of the year appeared his most famous and influential work, the result of twenty years' labor and the foundation of his intellectual prominence, *An Essay Concerning Human Understanding*. Here Locke registers his important critique of Descartes's doctrine of innate ideas, argues for the empirical foundation of all of our concepts, beliefs, and judgements, and clarifies the nature and extent of our knowledge. Along the way, he discusses those ideas which ground the notion of natural law, which is so fundamental for his account of government in the second *Treatise*. For his remaining years, Locke was revered as the author of the *Essay*. He produced a stream of works, on education, money, religion, and much else, engaged in public controversies over his work, and served as a public official. In 1696 he became a member of the Board of Trade; later he was to arrange for his friend, Isaac Newton, to be appointed Warden of the Mint.

In 1702 Locke suffered an attack that left him largely deaf, and then, on October 29, 1704, in Essex, in the home of his closest friend, the wife of Francis Masham, Damaris Cudworth, who had cared for him during his final dozen years, he died quietly. Locke the radical had made peace with his notoriety. He had become an intellectual giant and a respected political participant in a world that knew only part of him. For virtually all of his life, it was unknown by most that the great philosopher was also the author of the *Two Treatises of Government*.

Recommended readings

Ashcraft, Richard. *Locke's Two Treatises of Government*. London: Unwin, 1987.

Ashcraft, Richard. *Revolutionary Politics and Locke's Two Treatises of Government*. Princeton: Princeton University Press, 1986.

Burns, James (ed.). *Cambridge History of Political Thought, 1450–1700*. Cambridge: Cambridge University Press, 1991.

Cranston, Maurice. *John Locke*. Oxford: Oxford University Press, 1957, 1985.

Dunn, John. *John Locke*. Oxford: Oxford University Press, 1983.

Dunn, John. *The Political Thought of John Locke*. Cambridge: Cambridge University Press, 1969.

Macpherson, C. B. *The Political Theory of Possessive Individualism*. Oxford: Oxford University Press, 1962.

Strauss, Leo. *Natural Right and History*. Chicago: University of Chicago Press, 1953.

Tuck, Richard. *Natural Rights Theories*. Cambridge: Cambridge University Press, 1979.

Tully, James. *A Defense of Property*. Cambridge: Cambridge University Press, 1980.

Tully, James (ed.). *John Locke, A Letter on Toleration*. Indianapolis: Hackett, 1983.

TWO TREATISES OF
CIVIL GOVERNMENT

PREFACE

READER,

Thou hast here the beginning and end of a discourse concerning government; what fate has otherwise disposed of the papers that should have filled up the middle, and were more than all the rest, it is not worth while to tell thee. These, which remain, I hope are sufficient to establish the throne of our great restorer, our present King William; to make good his title in the consent of the people; which being the only one of all lawful governments, he has more fully and clearly than any prince in Christendom; and to justify to the world the people of England, whose love of their just and natural rights, with their resolution to preserve them, saved the nation when it was on the very brink of slavery and ruin. If these papers have that evidence I flatter myself is to be found in them, there will be no great miss of those which are lost, and my reader may be satisfied without them. For I imagine, I shall have neither the time nor inclination to repeat my pains, and fill up the wanting part of my answer, by tracing Sir Robert again, through all the windings and obscurities which are to be met with in the several branches of his wonderful system. The king, and body of the nation, have since so thoroughly confuted his hypothesis, that I suppose no body hereafter will have either the confidence to appear against our common safety, and be again an advocate for slavery; or the weakness to be deceived with contradictions dressed up in a popular style, and well turned periods. For if any one will be at the pains himself, in those parts which are here untouched, to strip Sir Robert's discourses of the flourish of doubtful expressions, and endeavour to reduce his words to direct, positive, intelligible propositions, and then compare them one with another, he will quickly be satisfied there was never so much glib nonsense put together in well sounding English. If he think it not worth while to examine his works all through, let him make an experiment in that part where he treats of usurpation; and let him try whether he can, with all his skill, make Sir Robert intelligible, and consistent with himself, or common sense. I should not speak so plainly of a gentleman, long since past answering, had not the pulpit, of late years, publicly owned his doctrine, and made it the current divinity of the times. It is necessary those men, who, taking on them to be teachers, have so dangerously misled others, should be openly shewed of what authority this their patriarch is, whom they have so blindly followed; that so they may either retract what upon so ill grounds they have vented, and cannot be maintained; or else justify those principles which they preached up for gospel, though they had no better an author than an English courtier. For I should not have writ against Sir Robert, or taken the pains to shew his mistakes, inconsistencies, and want of (what he so much boasts of, and pretends wholly to build on) scripture-proofs, were there not men amongst us, who, by crying up his books, and espousing his doctrine, save me from the reproach of writing against a dead adversary. They have been so zealous in this point, that, if I have done him any wrong, I cannot hope they should spare me. I wish, where they have done the truth and the public wrong, they would be as ready to redress it, and allow its just weight to this reflection, viz. that there cannot be done a greater mischief to prince and people, than the propagating wrong notions concerning government; that so at last all times might not have reason to complain of the *drum ecclesiastic.* If any one, really concerned for truth, undertake the confutation of my hypothesis, I promise him either to recant my mistake, upon fair conviction; or to answer his difficulties. But he must remember two things,

First, That cavilling here and there, at some expression, or little incident of my discourse, is not an answer to my book.

Secondly, That I shall not take railing for arguments, nor think either of these worth my notice. Though I shall always look on myself as bound to give satisfaction to any one, who shall appear to be conscientiously scrupulous in the point, and shall shew any just grounds for his scruples.

I have nothing more, but to advertise the reader that A. stands for our author. O. for his Observations on Hobbes, Milton, &c. And that a bare quotation of pages always means pages of his *Patriarcha,* edit. 1680.

SECOND TREATISE OF GOVERNMENT

BOOK II

Chap.

1. The introduction
2. Of the state of nature
3. Of the state of war
4. Of slavery
5. Of property
6. Of paternal power
7. Of political or civil society
8. Of the beginning of political societies
9. Of the ends of political society and government
10. Of the forms of a commonwealth
11. Of the extent of the legislative power
12. Of the legislative, executive, and federative power of the commonwealth
13. Of the subordination of the powers of the commonwealth
14. Of prerogative
15. Of paternal, political and despotical power, considered together
16. Of conquest
17. Of usurpation
18. Of tyranny
19. Of the dissolution of government

OF CIVIL GOVERNMENT

BOOK II

CHAPTER I

1. It having been shewn in the foregoing discourse,

1. That Adam had not, either by natural right of fatherhood, or by positive donation from God, any such authority over his children, or dominion over the world, as is pretended:
2. That if he had, his heirs, yet, had no right to it:
3. That if his heirs had, there being no law of nature, nor positive law of God, that determines, which is the right heir in all cases that may arise, the right of succession, and consequently of bearing rule, could not have been certainly determined:
4. That if even that had been determined, yet the knowledge of which is the eldest line of Adam's posterity, being so long since utterly lost, that in the races of mankind and families of the world, there remains not to one above another the least pretence to be the eldest house, and to have the right of inheritance:

All these premises having, as I think, been clearly made out, it is impossible that the rulers now on earth, should make any benefit, or derive any the least shadow of authority from that, which is held to be the fountain of all power, *Adam's private dominion and paternal jurisdiction;* so that he that will not give just occasion to think that all government in the world is the product only of force and violence, and that men live together by no other rules but that of beasts, where the strongest carries it, and so lay a foundation for perpetual disorder and mischief, tumult, sedition, and rebellion (things that the followers of that hypothesis so loudly cry out against) must of necessity find out another rise of government, another original of political power, and another way of designing and knowing the persons that have it, than what Sir Robert Filmer hath taught us.

2. To this purpose, I think it may not be amiss, to set down what I take to be political power; that the power of a *magistrate* over a subject may be distinguished from that of a *father* over his children, a *master* over his servant, a *husband* over his *wife,* and a *lord* over his slave. All which distinct powers happening sometimes together in the same man, if he be considered under these different relations, it may help us to distinguish these powers one from another, and shew the difference betwixt a ruler of a commonwealth, a father of a family, and a captain of a galley.

3. *Political power,* then, I take to be a *right* of making laws and penalties of death, and consequently all less penalties for the regulating and preserving of property, and of employing the force of the community, in the execution of such laws, and in the defence of the commonwealth from foreign injury; and all this only for the public good.

CHAPTER II
Of the State of Nature

4. To understand political power, right, and derive it from its original, we must consider what state all men are naturally in, and that is, a *state of perfect freedom* to order their actions, and dispose of their possessions and persons, as they think fit,

within the bounds of the law of nature; without asking leave, or depending upon the will of any other man.

A *state* also of *equality*, wherein all the power and jurisdiction is reciprocal, no one having more than another; there being nothing more evident, than that creatures of the same species and rank, promiscuously born to all the same advantages of nature, and the use of the same faculties, should also be equal one amongst another without subordination or subjection; unless the lord and master of them all should, by any manifest declaration of his will, set one above another, and confer on him, by an evident and clear appointment, an undoubted right to dominion and sovereignty.

5. This *equality* of men by nature, the judicious Hooker looks upon as so evident in itself, and beyond all question, that he makes it the foundation of that obligation to mutual love amongst men, on which he builds the duties we owe one another, and from whence he derives the great maxims of *justice* and *charity*. His words are, "The like natural inducement hath brought men to know, that it is no less their duty to love others than themselves; for seeing those things which are equal, must needs all have one measure; if I cannot but wish to receive good, even as much at every man's hands, as any man can wish unto his own soul, how should I look to have any part of my desire herein satisfied, unless myself be careful to satisfy the like desire, which is undoubtedly in other men, being of one and the same nature? To have any thing offered them repugnant to this desire, must needs in all respects grieve them as much as me; so that if I do harm, I must look to suffer, there being no reason that others should shew greater measure of love to me, than they have by me shewed unto them: my desire therefore to be loved of my equals in nature, as much as possibly may be, imposeth upon me a natural duty of bearing to them-ward fully the like affection: From which relation of equality between ourselves and them that are as ourselves, what several rules and canons natural reason hath drawn, for direction of life, no man is ignorant." Eccl. Pol. L. I.

6. But though this be *a state of liberty,* yet *it is not a state of licence:* though man in that state have an uncontrolable liberty to dispose of his person or possessions, yet he has not liberty to destroy himself, or so much as any creature in his possession, but where some nobler use than its bare preservation calls for it. The *state of nature* has a law of nature to govern it, which obliges every one: And reason, which is that law, teaches all mankind, who will but consult it, that being all *equal and independent,* no one ought to harm another in his life, health, liberty, or possessions. For men being all the workmanship of one omnipotent and infinitely wise Maker; all the servants of one sovereign master, sent into the world by his order, and about his business; they are his property, whose workmanship they are, made to last during his, not another's pleasure. And being furnished with like faculties, sharing all in one community of nature, there cannot be supposed any such subordination among us, that may authorize us to destroy another, as if we were made for one another's uses, as the inferior ranks of creatures are for ours. Every one, as he is *bound to preserve himself,* and not to quit his station wilfully, so by the like reason, when his own preservation comes not in competition, ought he, as much as he can, *to preserve the rest of mankind,* and may not, unless it be to do justice to an offender, take away or impair the life, or what tends to the preservation of life, the liberty, health, limb, or goods of another.

7. And that all men may be restrained from invading others rights, and from doing hurt to one another, and the law of nature be observed, which willeth the

peace and *preservation of all mankind,* the *execution* of the law of nature is, in that state, put into every man's hands, whereby every one has a right to punish the transgressors of that law to such a degree as may hinder its violation. For the *law of nature* would, as all other laws that concern men in this world, be in vain, if there were no body that in the state of nature had a *power to execute* that law, and thereby preserve the innocent and restrain offenders. And if any one in the state of nature may punish another for any evil he has done, every one may do so. For in that *state of perfect equality,* where naturally there is no superiority or jurisdiction of one over another, what any may do in prosecution of that law, every one must needs have a right to do.

8. And thus, in the state of nature, *one man comes by a power over another;* but yet no absolute or arbitrary power, to use a criminal, when he has got him in his hands, according to the passionate heats, or boundless extravagancy of his own will; but only to retribute to him, so far as calm reason and conscience dictate, what is proportionate to his *transgression;* which is so much as may serve for *reparation* and *restraint.* For these two are the only reasons, why one man may lawfully do harm to another, which is that we call *punishment.* In transgressing the law of nature, the offender declares himself to live by another rule than that of reason and common equity, which is that measure God has set to the actions of men, for their mutual security; and so he becomes dangerous to mankind, the tye, which is to secure them from injury and violence, being slighted and broken by him. Which being a trespass against the whole species, and the peace and safety of it, provided for by the law of nature; every man upon this score, by the right he hath to preserve mankind in general, may restrain, or, where it is necessary, destroy things noxious to them, and so may bring such evil on any one, who hath transgressed that law, as may make him repent the doing of it, and thereby deter him, and by his example others, from doing the like mischief. And in this case, and upon this ground, *every man hath a right to punish the offender, and be executioner of the law of nature.*

9. I doubt not but this will seem a very strange doctrine to some men: but before they condemn it, I desire them to resolve me, by what right any prince or state can put to death, or *punish an alien,* for any crime he commits in their country. It is certain their laws, by virtue of any sanction they receive from the promulgated will of the legislative, reach not a stranger. They speak not to him, nor, if they did, is he bound to hearken to them. The legislative authority, by which they are in force over the subjects of that commonwealth, hath no power over him. Those who have the supreme power of making laws in England, France, or Holland, are to an Indian but like the rest of the world, men without authority: And therefore, if by the law of nature every man hath not a power to punish offences against it, as he soberly judges the case to require, I see not how the magistrates of any community can *punish an alien* of another country; since in reference to him, they can have no more power, than what every man naturally may have over another.

10. Besides the crime which consists in violating the law, and varying from the right rule of reason, whereby a man so far becomes degenerate, and declares himself to quit the principles of human nature, and to be a noxious creature, there is commonly injury done to some person or other, and some other man receives damage by his transgression, in which case he who hath received any damage, has besides the right of punishment common to him with other men, a particular right to seek *reparation* from him that has done it. And any other person who finds it just,

may also join with him that is injured, and assist him in recovering from the offender so much as may make satisfaction for the harm he has suffered.

11. From these *two distinct rights,* the one of *punishing* the *crime for restraint,* and preventing the like offence, which right of punishing is in every body; the other of taking reparation, which belongs only to the injured party; comes it to pass that the magistrate, who by being magistrate, hath the common right of punishing put into his hands, can often, where the public good demands not the execution of the law, *remit* the punishment of criminal offences by his own authority, but yet cannot *remit* the satisfaction due to any private man, for the damage he has received. That, he who has suffered the damage has a right to demand in his own name, and he alone can remit: The damnified person has this power of appropriating to himself the goods or service of the offender, *by right of self-preservation,* as every man has a power to punish the crime, to prevent its being committed again, *by the right he has of preserving all mankind;* and doing all reasonable things he can in order to that end: And thus it is, that every man, in the state of nature, has a power to kill a murderer, both to deter others from doing the like injury, which no reparation can compensate, by the example of the punishment that attends it from every body, and also *to secure* men from the attempts of a criminal, who having renounced reason, the common rule and measure, God hath given to mankind, hath by the unjust violence and slaughter he hath committed upon one, declared war against all mankind; and therefore may be destroyed as a *lion* or a *tiger,* one of those wild savage beasts, with whom men can have no society nor security: And upon this is grounded the great law of nature, "Whoso sheddeth mans blood, by man shall his blood be shed." And Cain was so fully convinced, that every one had a right to destroy such a criminal, that after the murder of his brother, he cries out, "Every one that findeth me, shall slay me;" so plain was it writ in the hearts of all mankind.

12. By the same reason may a man in the state of nature *punish the lesser breaches* of that law. It will perhaps be demanded, with death? I answer, each transgression may be *punished* to that *degree,* and with so much *severity,* as will suffice to make it an ill bargain to the offender, give him cause to repent, and terrify others from doing the like. Every offence that can be committed in the state of nature, may in the state of nature be also punished equally, and as far forth as it may, in a commonwealth: for though it would be besides my present purpose, to enter here into the particulars of the law of nature, or its *measures of punishment;* yet it is certain there is such a law, and that too, as intelligible and plain to a rational creature, and a studier of that law, as the positive laws of commonwealths, nay possibly plainer; as much as reason is easier to be understood, than the fancies and intricate contrivances of men, following contrary and hidden interests put into words; for so truly are a great part of the *municipal laws* of countries, which are only so far right, as they are founded on the law of nature, by which they are to be regulated and interpreted.

13. To this strange doctrine, viz. That *in the state of nature every one has the executive power* of the law of nature, I doubt not but it will be objected, that it is unreasonable for men to be judges in their own cases, that self-love will make men partial to themselves and their friends: And on the other side, that ill nature, passion and revenge will carry them too far in punishing others; and hence nothing but confusion and disorder will follow, and that therefore God hath certainly appointed government to restrain the partiality and violence of men. I easily grant, that civil government is the proper remedy for the inconveniencies of the state of nature, which

must certainly be great, where men may be judges in their own case, since it is easy to be imagined, that he who was so unjust as to do his brother an injury, will scarce be so just as to condemn himself for it: But I shall desire those who make this objection, to remember, that *absolute monarchs* are but men, and if government is to be the remedy of those evils, which necessarily follow from men's being judges in their own cases, and the state of nature is therefore not to be endured, I desire to know what kind of government that is, and how much better it is than the state of nature, where one man commanding a multitude, has the liberty to be judge in his own case, and may do to all his subjects whatever he pleases, without the least liberty to any one to question or control those who execute his pleasure? and in whatsoever he doth, whether led by reason, mistake or passion, must be submitted to? Much better it is in the state of nature, wherein men are not bound to submit to the unjust will of another: And if he that judges, judges amiss in his own, or any other case, he is answerable for it to the rest of mankind.

14. It is often asked as a mighty objection, *where are,* or ever were, there any *men in such a state of nature?* To which it may suffice as an answer at present: That since all princes and rulers of *independent* governments, all through the world, are in a state of nature, it is plain the world never was, nor ever will be, without numbers of men in that state. I have named all governors of *independent* communities, whether they are, or are not, in league with others. For it is not every compact that puts an end to the state of nature between men, but only this one of agreeing together mutually to enter into one community, and make one body politic; other promises and compacts men may make one with another, and yet still be in the state of nature. The promises and bargains for truck, &c. between the two men in the desert island, mentioned by Garcilasso de la Vega, in his history of Peru; or between a Swiss and an Indian, in the woods of America, are binding to them, though they are perfectly in a state of nature, in reference to one another. For truth and keeping of faith belongs to men as men, and not as members of society.

15. To those that say, there were never any men in the state of nature, I will not only oppose the authority of the judicious Hooker, *Eccl. Pol. lib. I. sect. 10,* where he says, "The laws which have been hitherto mentioned," i.e. the laws of nature, "do bind men absolutely, even as they are men, although they have never any settled fellowship, never any solemn agreement amongst themselves what to do or not to do, but for as much as we are not by our selves sufficient to furnish ourselves with competent store of things, needful for such a life, as our nature doth desire, a life fit for the dignity of man; therefore to supply those defects and imperfections which are in us, as living singly and solely by ourselves, we are naturally induced to seek communion and fellowship with others. This was the cause of men's uniting themselves at first in politic societies." But I moreover affirm, that all men are naturally in that state, and remain so, till by their own consents they make themselves members of some politic society; and I doubt not in the sequel of this discourse to make it very clear.

CHAPTER III
Of the State of War

16. The *state of war* is a state of *enmity* and *destruction:* And therefore declaring by word or action, not a passionate and hasty, but a sedate settled design upon another man's life, *puts him in a state of war* with him against whom he has declared such an

intention, and so has exposed his life to the other's power to be taken away by him, or any one that joins with him in his defence, and espouses his quarrel: it being reasonable and just I should have a right to destroy that which threatens me with destruction. For *by the fundamental law of nature, man being to be preserved* as much as possible, when all cannot be preserved, the safety of the innocent is to be preferred: And one may destroy a man who makes war upon him, or has discovered an enmity to his being, for the same reason that he may kill a *wolf* or a *lion;* because such men are not under the ties of the common law of reason, have no other rule, but that of force and violence, and so may be treated as beasts of prey, those dangerous and noxious creatures, that will be sure to destroy him whenever he falls into their power.

17. And hence it is, that he who attempts to get another man into his absolute power, does thereby *put himself into a state of war* with him; it being to be understood as a declaration of a design upon his life. For I have reason to conclude, that he who would get me into his power without my consent, would use me as he pleased when he got me there, and destroy me too when he had a fancy to it; for no body can desire to *have me in his absolute power* unless it be to compel me by force to that which is against the right of my freedom, i.e. make me a slave. To be free from such force is the only security of my preservation; and reason bids me look on him, as an enemy to my preservation, who would take away that freedom which is the fence to it; so that he who makes an *attempt to enslave* me, thereby puts himself into a state of war with me. He that, in the state of nature, *would take away the freedom* that belongs to any one in that state, must necessarily be supposed to have a design to take away every thing else, that *freedom* being the foundation of all the rest: As he that, in the state of society, would take away the freedom belonging to those of that society or commonwealth, must be supposed to design to take away from them every thing else, and so be looked on as *in a state of war.*

18. This makes it lawful for a man to *kill a thief,* who has not in the least hurt him, nor declared any design upon his life, any farther, than by the use of force, so to get him in his power, as to take away his money, or what he pleases, from him; because using force, where he has no right, to get me into his power, let his pretence be what it will, I have no reason to suppose, that he, who would *take away my liberty,* would not, when he had me in his power, take away every thing else. And therefore it is lawful for me to treat him as one who has put *himself into a state of war* with me, i.e. kill him if I can; for to that hazard does he justly expose himself, whoever introduces a state of war, and is aggressor in it.

19. And here we have the plain *difference between the state of nature and the state of war;* which however some men have confounded, are as far distant, as a state of peace, good will, mutual assistance and preservation, and a state of enmity, malice, violence and mutual destruction, are one from another. Men living together according to reason, without a common superior on earth, with authority to judge between them, is *properly the state of nature.* But force, or a declared design of force, upon the person of another, where there is no common superior on earth to appeal to for relief, *is the state of war:* And it is the want of such an appeal gives a man the right of war even against an aggressor, though he be in society and a fellow subject. Thus a *thief,* whom I cannot harm, but by appeal to the law, for having stolen all that I am worth, I may kill, when he sets on me to rob me but of my horse or coat; because the law, which was made for my preservation, where it cannot interpose to

secure my life from present force, which, if lost, is capable of no reparation, permits me my own defence, and the right of war, a liberty to kill the aggressor, because the aggressor allows not time to appeal to our common judge, nor the decision of the law, for remedy in a case where the mischief may be irreparable. *Want of a common judge with authority, puts all men in a state of nature: Force without right, upon a man's person, makes a state of war,* both where there is, and is not, a common judge.

20. But when the actual force is over, the *state of war ceases* between those that are in society, and are equally on both sides subjected to the fair determination of the law; because then there lies open the remedy of appeal for the past injury, and to prevent future harm: but where no such appeal is, as in the state of nature, for want of positive laws, and judges with authority to appeal to, *the state of war once begun, continues* with a right to the innocent party to destroy the other whenever he can, until the aggressor offers peace, and desires reconciliation on such terms as may repair any wrongs he has already done, and secure the innocent for the future: nay, where an appeal to the law, and constituted judges, lies open, but the remedy is denied by a manifest perverting of justice, and a barefaced wresting of the laws to protect or indemnify the violence or injuries of some men, or party of men, *there* it *is* hard to imagine any thing but *a state of war.* For wherever violence is used, and injury done, though by hands appointed to administer justice, it is still violence and injury, however coloured with the name, pretences, or forms of law, the end whereof being to protect and redress the innocent, by an unbiassed application of it, to all who are under it; wherever that is not *bona fide* done, *war is made* upon the sufferers, who having no appeal on earth to right them, they are left to the only remedy in such cases, an appeal to heaven.

21. To avoid this *state of war* (wherein there is no appeal but to heaven, and wherein every the least difference is apt to end, where there is no authority to decide between the contenders) is one great *reason of men's putting themselves into society,* and quitting the state of nature. For where there is an authority, a power on earth, from which relief can be had by *appeal,* there the continuance of the *state of war* is excluded, and the controversy is decided by that power. Had there been any such court, any superior jurisdiction on earth, to determine the right between Jephthah and the Ammonites, they had never come to a *state of war:* But we see he was forced to appeal to heaven. "The Lord the Judge," says he, "be judge this day, between the children of Israel and the children of Ammon," *Judg.* xi. 27, and then prosecuting, and relying on his appeal, he leads out his army to battle: and therefore in such controversies, where the question is put, *who shall be judge?* it cannot be meant, who shall decide the controversy; every one knows what Jephthah here tells us, that "the Lord the Judge" shall judge. Where there is no judge on earth, the appeal lies to God in heaven. That question then cannot mean, who shall judge? whether another hath put himself in a *state of war* with me, and whether I may, as Jephthah did, *appeal to heaven* in it? of that I myself can only be judge in my own conscience, as I will answer it, at the great day, to the supreme judge of all men.

CHAPTER IV
Of Slavery

22. The *natural liberty* of man is to be free from any superior power on earth, and not to be under the will or legislative authority of man, but to have only the law of nature for his rule. The *liberty of man,* in society, is to be under no other legislative

power, but that established, by consent, in the commonwealth; nor under the dominion of any will, or restraint of any law, but what that legislative shall enact, according to the trust put in it. Freedom then is not what Sir Robert Filmer tells us, O, A. 55. "a liberty for every one to do what he lists, to live as he pleases, and not to be tied by any laws:" But *freedom of men under government,* is, to have a standing rule to live by, common to every one of that society, and made by the legislative power erected in it; a liberty to follow my own will in all things, where the rule prescribes not; and not to be subject to the inconstant, uncertain, unknown, arbitrary will of another man: As *freedom of nature* is, to be under no other restraint but the law of nature.

23. This freedom from absolute, arbitrary power, is so necessary to, and closely joined with a man's preservation, that he cannot part with it, but by what forfeits his preservation and life together. For a man, not having the power of his own life, cannot, by compact, or his own consent, enslave himself to any one, nor put himself under the absolute, arbitrary power of another, to take away his life, when he pleases. No body can give more power than he has himself; and he that cannot take away his own life, cannot give another power over it. Indeed, having by his fault forfeited his own life, by some act that deserves death; he, to whom he has forfeited it, may (when he has him in his power) delay to take it, and make use of him to his own service, and he does him no injury by it. For, whenever he finds the hardship of his slavery outweigh the value of his life, it is in his power, by resisting the will of his master, to draw on himself the death he desires.

24. This is the perfect condition of *slavery,* which is nothing else, but *the state of war continued, between a lawful conqueror and a captive.* For, if once compact enter between them, and make an agreement for a limited power on the one side, and obedience on the other, the state of war and slavery ceases, as long as the compact endures. For, as has been said, no man can, by agreement, pass over to another that which he hath not in himself, a power over his own life.

I confess, we find among the Jews, as well as other nations, that men did sell themselves; but, it is plain, this was only to *drudgery, not to slavery.* For it is evident, the person sold was not under an absolute, arbitrary, despotical power. For the master could not have power to kill him, at any time, whom, at a certain time, he was obliged to let go free out of his service: and the master of such a servant was so far from having an arbitrary power over his life, that he could not, at pleasure, so much as maim him, but the loss of an eye, or tooth, set him free, *Exod.* xxi.

CHAPTER V
Of Property

25. Whether we consider natural *reason,* which tells us, that men, being once born, have a right to their preservation, and consequently to meat and drink, and such other things as nature affords for their subsistence: or *revelation,* which gives us an account of those grants God made of the world to Adam, and to Noah, and his sons, it is very clear, that God, as King David says, *Psal.* cxv. 16, "has given the earth to the children of men," given it to mankind in common. But this being supposed, it seems to some a very great difficulty how any one should ever come to have a *property* in any thing: I will not content myself to answer, that if it be difficult to make out *property,* upon a supposition, that God gave the world to Adam, and his posterity in common; it is impossible that any man, but one universal monarch, should have any property upon a supposition, that God gave the world to Adam, and his heirs in

succession, exclusive of all the rest of his posterity. But I shall endeavour to shew, how men might come to have a *property* in several parts of that which God gave to mankind in common, and that without any express compact of all the commoners.

26. God, who hath given the world to men in common, hath also given them reason to make use of it to the best advantage of life, and convenience. The earth, and all that is therein, is given to men for the support and comfort of their being. And though all the fruits it naturally produces, and beasts it feeds, belong to mankind in common, as they are produced by the spontaneous hand of nature; and no body has originally a private dominion, exclusive of the rest of mankind, in any of them, as they are thus in their natural state: yet being given for the use of men, there must of necessity be *a means to appropriate* them some way or other, before they can be of any use, or at all beneficial to any particular man. The fruit, or venison, which nourishes the wild Indian, who knows no enclosure, and is still a tenant in common, must be his, and so his, i.e. a part of him, that another can no longer have any right to it, before it can do him any good for the support of his life.

27. Though the earth, and all inferior creatures, be common to all men, yet every man has a property in his own person: this no body has any right to but himself. The labour of his body, and the work of his hands, we may say, are properly his. Whatsoever then he removes out of the state that nature hath provided, and left it in, he hath mixed his labour with, and joined to it something that is his own, and thereby makes it his property. It being by him removed from the common state nature hath placed it in, it hath by this labour something annexed to it, that excludes the common right of other men. For this labour being the unquestionable property of the labourer, no man but he can have a right to what that is once joined to, at least where there is enough, and as good, left in common for others.

28. He that is nourished by the acorns he picked up under an oak, or the apples he gathered from the trees in the wood, has certainly appropriated them to himself. No body can deny but the nourishment is his. I ask then, when did they begin to be his? When he digested? Or when he eat? Or when he boiled? Or when he brought them home? Or when he picked them up? And it is plain, if the first gathering made them not his, nothing else could. That *labour* put a distinction between them and common: that added something to them more than nature, the common mother of all, had done; and so they became his private right. And will any one say he had no right to those acorns or apples he thus appropriated, because he had not the consent of all mankind to make them his? Was it a robbery thus to assume to himself what belonged to all in common? If such a consent as that was necessary, man had starved, notwithstanding the plenty God had given him. We see in *commons,* which remain so by compact, that it is the taking any part of what is common, and removing it out of the state nature leaves it in, which *begins the property;* without which the common is of no use. And the taking of this or that part does not depend on the express consent of all the commoners. Thus the grass my horse has bit; the turfs my servant has cut; and the ore I have digged in any place, where I have a right to them in common with others, become my *property,* without the assignation or consent of any body. The *labour* that was mine, removing them out of that common state they were in, hath *fixed* my *property* in them.

29. By making an explicit consent of every commoner necessary to any one's appropriating to himself any part of what is given in common, children or servants could not cut the meat, which their father or master had provided for them in common, without assigning to every one his peculiar part. Though the water running

in the fountain be every one's, yet who can doubt, but that in the pitcher is his only who drew it out? His *labour* hath taken it out of the hands of nature, where it was common, and belonged equally to all her children, and *hath* thereby *appropriated* it to himself.

30. Thus this law of reason makes the deer that Indian's who hath killed it; it is allowed to be his goods, who hath bestowed his labour upon it, though before it was the common right of every one. And amongst those who are counted the civilized part of mankind, who have made and multiplied positive laws to determine *property,* this original law of nature, for the *beginning of property,* in what was before common, still takes place; and by virtue thereof, what fish any one catches in the ocean, that great and still remaining common of mankind; or what ambergreise any one takes up here, is *by* the *labour* that removes it out of that common state nature left it in, *made* his *property,* who takes that pains about it. And even amongst us, the hare that any one is hunting, is thought his who pursues her during the chase. For being a beast that is still looked upon as common, and no man's private possession; whoever has employed so much *labour* about any of that kind, as to find and pursue her, has thereby removed her from the state of nature, wherein she was common, and hath *begun a property.*

31. It will perhaps be objected to this, that *if gathering the acorns, or other fruits of the earth, &c.* makes a right to them, then any one may engross as much as he will." To which I answer, Not so. The same law of nature, that does by this means give us property, does also *bound* that *property* too. "God has given us all things richly," 1 *Tim;* vi. 17, is the voice of reason confirmed by inspiration. But how far has he given it us? *To enjoy.* As much as any one can make use of to any advantage of life before it spoils, so much he may by his labour fix a property in: whatever is beyond this, is more than his share, and belongs to others. Nothing was made by God for man to spoil or destroy. And thus, considering the plenty of natural provisions there was a long time in the world, and the few spenders; and to how small a part of that provision the industry of one man could extend itself, and engross it to the prejudice of others; especially keeping within the *bounds,* set by reason, *of* what might serve for his *use;* there could be then little room for quarrels or contentions about property so established.

32. But the *chief matter of property* being now not the fruits of the earth, and the beasts that subsist on it, but the *earth it self;* as that which takes in, and carries with it all the rest: I think it is plain, that *property* in that too is acquired as the former. *As much land* as a man tills, plants, improves, cultivates, and can use the product of, so much is his *property.* He by his labour does, as it were, enclose it from the common. Nor will it invalidate his right, to say every body else has an equal title to it; and therefore he cannot appropriate, he cannot enclose, without the consent of all his fellow commoners, all mankind. God, when he gave the world in common to all mankind, commanded man also to labour, and the penury of his condition required it of him. God and his reason commanded him to subdue the earth, i.e. improve it for the benefit of life, and therein lay out something upon it that was his own, his labour. He that, in obedience to this command of God, subdued, tilled, and sowed any part of it, thereby annexed to it something that was his *property,* which another had no title to, nor could without injury take from him.

33. Nor was this *appropriation* of any parcel of *land,* by improving it, any prejudice to any other man, since there was still enough, and as good left; and more than the yet unprovided could use. So that, in effect, there was never the less left for others

because of his enclosure for himself. For he that leaves as much as another can make use of, does as good as take nothing at all. No body could think himself injured by the drinking of another man, though he took a good draught, who had a whole river of the same water left him to quench his thirst: And the case of land and water, where there is enough of both, is perfectly the same.

34. God gave the world to men in common; but since he gave it them for their benefit, and the greatest conveniences of life they were capable to draw from it, it cannot be supposed he meant it should always remain common and uncultivated. He gave it to the use of the industrious and rational, (and *labour* was to be *his title* to it) not to the fancy or covetousness of the quarrel some and contentious. He that had as good left for his improvement, as was already taken up, needed not complain, ought not to meddle with what was already improved by another's labour: If he did, it is plain he desired the benefit of another's pains, which he had no right to, and not the ground which God had given him in common with others to labour on, and whereof there was as good left, as that already possessed, and more than he knew what to do with, or his industry could reach to.

35. It is true, in *land* that is *common* in England, or any other country, where there is plenty of people under government, who have money and commerce, no one can enclose or appropriate any part, without the consent of all his fellow-commoners: Because this is left common by compact, i.e. by the law of the land, which is not to be violated. And though it be common, in respect of some men, it is not so to all mankind, but is the joint property of this country, or this parish. Besides, the remainder, after such enclosure, would not be as good to the rest of the commoners, as the whole was when they could all make use of the whole: whereas in the beginning and first peopling of the great common of the world, it was quite otherwise. The law man was under, was rather for appropriating. God commanded, and his wants forced him to *labour*. That was his *property* which could not be taken from him wherever he had fixed it. And hence subduing or cultivating the earth, and having dominion, we see are joined together. The one gave title to the other. So that God, by commanding to subdue, gave authority so far to *appropriate:* And the condition of human life, which requires labour and materials to work on, necessarily introduces private possessions.

36. The *measure of property* nature has well set by the extent of men's *labour, and the conveniences of life:* No man's labour could subdue or appropriate all; nor could his enjoyment consume more than a small part; so that it was impossible for any man, this way, to intrench upon the right of another, or acquire to himself a property, to the prejudice of his neighbour, who would still have room for as good, and as large a possession (after the other had taken out his) as before it was appropriated. This *measure* did confine every man's *possession* to a very moderate proportion, and such as he might appropriate to himself, without injury to any body, in the first ages of the world, when men were more in danger to be lost, by wandering from their company, in the then vast wilderness of the earth, than to be straitened for want of room to plant in. And the same measure may be allowed still without prejudice to any body, as full as the world seems. For supposing a man, or family, in the state they were at first peopling of the world by the children of Adam, or Noah; let him plant in some inland, vacant places of America, we shall find that the *possessions* he could make himself, upon the *measures* we have given, would not be very large, nor, even to this day, prejudice the rest of mankind, or give them reason to complain, or

think themselves injured by this man's encroachment, though the race of men have now spread themselves to all the corners of the world, and do infinitely exceed the small number was at the beginning. Nay, the extent of *ground* is of so little value, *without labour*, that I have heard it affirmed, that in Spain itself a man may be permitted to plough, sow, and reap, without being disturbed, upon land he has no other title to, but only his making use of it. But, on the contrary, the inhabitants think themselves beholden to him, who by his industry on neglected and consequently waste land, has increased the stock of corn, which they wanted. But be this as it will, which I lay no stress on; this I dare boldly affirm, that the same *rule of propriety*, (*viz.*) that every man should have as much as he could make use of, would hold still in the world, without straitening any body, since there is land enough in the world to suffice double the inhabitants, had not the *invention of money*, and the tacit agreement of men to put a value on it, introduced (by consent) larger possessions, and a right to them; which, how it has done, I shall by and by shew more at large.

37. This is certain, that in the beginning, before the desire of having more than man needed had altered the intrinsic value of things, which depends only on their usefulness to the life of man; or had *agreed, that a little piece of yellow metal*, which would keep without wasting or decay, should be worth a great piece of flesh, or a whole heap of corn; though men had a right to appropriate, by their labour, each one to himself as much of the things of nature as he could use: yet this could not be much, nor to the prejudice of others, where the same plenty was still left to those who would use the same industry. To which let me add, that he who appropriates land to himself by his labour, does not lessen, but increase the common stock of mankind. For the provisions serving to the support of human life, produced by one acre of enclosed and cultivated land, are (to speak much within compass) ten times more than those which are yielded by an acre of land of an equal richness lying waste in common. And therefore he that encloses land, and has a greater plenty of the conveniencies of life from ten acres, than he could have from an hundred left to nature, may truly be said to give ninety acres to mankind. For his labour now supplies him with provisions out of ten acres, which were by the product of an hundred lying in common. I have here rated the improved land very low, in making its product but as ten to one, when it is much nearer an hundred to one. For I ask, whether in the wild woods and uncultivated waste of America, left to nature, without any improvement, tillage, or husbandry, a thousand acres yield the needy and wretched inhabitants as many conveniencies of life, as ten acres equally fertile land do in Devonshire, where they are well cultivated?

Before the appropriation of land, he who gathered as much of the wild fruit, killed, caught, or tamed, as many of the beasts as he could; he that so employed his pains about any of the spontaneous products of nature, as any way to alter them from the state which nature put them in, *by* placing any of his *labour* on them, did thereby *acquire a propriety in them:* but if they perished, in his possession, without their due use; if the fruits rotted, or the venison putrified, before he could spend it, he offended against the common law of nature, and was liable to be punished; he invaded his neighbour's share, for he had *no right, farther than his use* called for any of them, and they might serve to afford him conveniencies of life.

38. The same *measures* governed the *possession of land* too: whatsoever he tilled and reaped, laid up and made use of, before it spoiled, that was his peculiar right;

whatsoever he enclosed, and could feed, and make use of, the cattle and product was also his. But if either the grass of his inclosure rotted on the ground, or the fruit of his planting perished without gathering, and laying up, this part of the earth, notwithstanding his inclosure, was still to be looked on as waste, and might be the possession of any other. Thus at the beginning, Cain might take as much ground as he could till, and make it his own land, and yet leave enough to Abel's sheep to feed on; a few acres would serve for both their possessions. But as families increased, and industry enlarged their stocks, their *possessions enlarged* with the need of them; but yet it was commonly *without any fixed property in the ground* they made use of, till they incorporated, settled themselves together, and built cities, and then, by consent, they came in time to set out the *bounds of their distinct territories*, and agree on limits between them and their neighbours; and by laws within themselves settled the *properties* of those of the same society. For we see, that in that part of the world which was first inhabited, and therefore like to be best peopled, even as low down as Abraham's time, they wandered with their flocks, and their herds, which was their substance, freely up and down; and this Abraham did, in a country where he was a stranger. Whence it is plain, that at least a great part of the *land lay in common;* that the inhabitants valued it not, nor claimed property in any more than they made use of. But when there was not room enough in the same place, for their herds to feed together, they by consent, as Abraham and Lot did, *Gen.* xiii. 5. separated and enlarged their pasture, where it best liked them. And for the same reason Esau went from his father, and his brother, and planted in Mount Seir, *Gen.* xxxvi. 6.

39. And thus, without supposing any private dominion, and property in Adam, over all the *world,* exclusive of all other men, which can no way be proved, nor any one's property be made out from it; but supposing the *world* given, as it was, to the children of men *in common,* we see how *labour* could make men distinct titles to several parcels of it, for their private uses; wherein there could be no doubt of right, no room for quarrel.

40. Nor is it so strange, as perhaps before consideration it may appear, that the *property of labour* should be able to over-balance the community of land. For it is *labour* indeed that *puts the difference of value* on every thing; and let any one consider what the difference is between an acre of land planted with tobacco or sugar, sown with wheat or barley, and an acre of the same land lying in common, without any husbandry upon it, and he will find, that the improvement of *labour makes* the far greater part of the value. I think it will be but a very modest computation to say, that of the *products* of the earth useful to the life of man, nine tenths are the *effects of labour:* nay, if we will rightly estimate things as they come to our use, and cast up the several expences about them, what in them is purely owing to *nature,* and what to *labour,* we shall find, that in most of them ninety-nine hundredths are wholly to be put on the account of *labour.*

41. There cannot be a clearer demonstration of any thing, than several nations of the Americans are of this, who are rich in land, and poor in all the comforts of life; whom nature having furnished as liberally as any other people, with the materials of plenty, i.e. a fruitful soil, apt to produce in abundance what might serve for food, raiment, and delight; yet *for want of improving it by labour,* have not one hundredth part of the conveniencies we enjoy: and a king of a large and fruitful territory there feeds, lodges, and is clad worse than a day labourer in England.

42. To make this a little clearer, let us but trace some of the ordinary provisions of life, through their several progresses, before they come to our use, and see how much they receive of their *value from human industry.* Bread, wine, and cloth, are things of daily use, and great plenty, yet notwithstanding, acorns, water, and leaves, or skins, must be our bread, drink, and cloathing, did not labour furnish us with these more useful commodities. For whatever bread is more worth than acorns, wine than water, and *cloth* or *silk,* than leaves, skins, or moss, that is *wholly owing to labour* and *industry.* The one of these being the food and raiment which unassisted nature furnishes us with; the other, provisions which our industry and pains prepare for us, which how much they exceed the other in value, when any one hath computed, he will then see how much *labour makes the far greatest part of the value* of things we enjoy in this world: and the ground which produces the materials, is scarce to be reckoned in, as any, or, at most, but a very small part of it: so little, that even amongst us, land that is left wholly to nature, that hath no improvement of pasturage, tillage, or planting, is called, as indeed it is, *waste;* and we shall find the benefit of it amount to little more than nothing.

This shews how much numbers of men are to be preferred to largeness of dominions; and that the increase of lands, and the right of employing of them, is the great art of government: and that prince, who shall be so wise and godlike, as by established laws of liberty to secure protection and encouragement to the honest industry of mankind, against the oppression of power and narrowness of party, will quickly be too hard for his neighbours; but this by the by. To return to the argument in hand.

43. An acre of land, that bears here twenty bushels of wheat, and another in America, which, with the same husbandry, would do the like, are, without doubt, of the same natural intrinsic value: but yet the benefit mankind receives from the one in a year, is worth 5 l. and from the other possibly not worth a penny, if all the profit an Indian received from it were to be valued, and sold here; at least, I may truly say, not one thousandth. It is *labour* then which *puts the greatest part of the value upon land,* without which it would scarcely be worth any thing: it is to that we owe the greatest part of all its useful products; for all that the straw, bran, bread, of that acre of wheat, is more worth than the product of an acre of as good land, which lies waste, is all the effect of labour. For it is not barely the ploughman's pains, the reaper's and thresher's toil, and the baker's sweat is to be counted into the *bread* we eat; the labour of those who broke the oxen, who digged and wrought the iron and stones, who felled and framed the timber employed about the plough, mill, oven, or any other utensils, which are a vast number requisite to this corn, from its being seed to be sown, to its being made bread, must all be *charged on* the account of *labour,* and received as an effect of that: nature and the earth furnished only the almost worthless materials, as in themselves. It would be a strange *catalogue of things, that industry provided and made use of, about every loaf of bread,* before it came to our use, if we could trace them; iron, wood, leather, bark, timber, stone, bricks, coals, lime, cloth, dying drugs, pitch, tar, masts, ropes, and all the materials made use of in the ship, that brought any of the commodities made use of by any of the workmen, to any part of the work, all which it would be almost impossible, at least too long, to reckon up.

44. From all which it is evident, that though the things of nature are given in common, yet man, by being master of himself, and *proprietor of his own person, and*

the actions or labour of it, had still in himself the great foundation of property; and that, which made up the great part of what he applied to the support or comfort of his being, when invention and arts had improved the conveniencies of life, was perfectly his own, and did not belong in common to others.

45. Thus *labour,* in the beginning, *gave a right of property,* wherever any one was pleased to employ it upon what was common, which remained a long while the far greater part, and is yet more than mankind makes use of. Men, at first, for the most part, contented themselves with what unassisted nature offered to their necessities: and though afterwards, in some parts of the world, (where the increase of people and stock, with the *use of money,* had made land scarce, and so of some value) the several *communities* settled the bounds of their distinct territories, and by laws within themselves regulated the properties of the private men of their society, and so, by *compact* and agreement, *settled the property* which labour and industry began; and the leagues that have been made between several states and kingdoms, either expressly or tacitly disowning all claim and right to the land in the others possession, have, by common consent, given up their pretences to their natural common right, which originally they had to those countries, and so have, by *positive agreement, settled a property* amongst themselves, in distinct parts and parcels of the earth; yet there are still *great tracts of ground* to be found, which (the inhabitants thereof not having joined with the rest of mankind, in the consent of the use of their common money) *lie waste,* and are more than the people who dwell on it do, or can make use of, and so still lie in common. Though this can scarce happen amongst that part of mankind that have consented to the use of money.

46. The greatest part of *things really useful* to the life of man, and such as the necessity of subsisting made the first commoners of the world look after, as it doth the Americans now, *are* generally things of *short duration;* such as, if they are not consumed by use, will decay and perish of themselves: gold, silver, and diamonds, are things that fancy or agreement hath put the value on, more than real use, and the necessary support of life. Now of those good things which nature hath provided in common, every one had a right, (as hath been said) to as much as he could use, and property in all that he could affect with his labour; all that his *industry* could extend to, to alter from the state nature had put it in, was his. He that *gathered* a hundred bushels of acorns or apples, had thereby a *property* in them, they were his goods as soon as gathered. He was only to look, that he used them before they spoiled, else he took more than his share, and robbed others. And indeed it was a foolish thing, as well as dishonest, to hoard up more than he could make use of. If he gave away a part to any body else, so that it perished not uselessly in his possession, these he also made use of. And if he also bartered away plums, that would have rotted in a week, for nuts that would last good for his eating a whole year, he did no injury; he wasted not the common stock; destroyed no part of the portion of goods that belonged to others, so long as nothing perished uselessly in his hands. Again, if he would give his nuts for a piece of metal, pleased with its colour; or exchange his sheep for shells, or wool for a sparkling pebble or a diamond, and keep those by him all his life, he invaded not the right of others, he might heap up as much of these durable things as he pleased; the *exceeding of the bounds of* his *just property* not lying in the largeness of his possession, but the perishing of any thing uselessly in it.

47. And thus *came in the use of money,* some lasting thing that men might keep without spoiling, and that by mutual consent men would take in exchange for the truly useful, but perishable supports of life.

48. And as different degrees of industry were apt to give men possessions in different proportions, so this *invention of money* gave them the opportunity to continue and enlarge them. For supposing an island, separate from all possible commerce with the rest of the world, wherein there were but an hundred families, but there were sheep, horses, and cows, with other useful animals, wholesome fruits, and land enough for corn for a hundred thousand times as many, but nothing in the island, either because of its commonness, or perishableness, fit to supply the place of *money:* What reason could any one have there to enlarge his possessions beyond the use of his family and a plentiful supply to its *consumption,* either in what their own industry produced, or they could barter for like perishable, useful commodities with others? Where there is not something, both lasting and scarce, and so valuable to be hoarded up, there men will not be apt to enlarge their *possessions of land,* were it never so rich, never so free for them to take. For I ask, what would a man value ten thousand, or an hundred thousand acres of excellent *land,* ready cultivated and well stocked too with cattle, in the middle of the inland parts of America, where he had no hopes of commerce with other parts of the world, to draw *money* to him by the sale of the product? It would not be worth the enclosing, and we should see him give up again to the wild common of nature, whatever was more than would supply the conveniencies of life to be had there for him and his family.

49. Thus in the beginning all the world was America, and more so than that is now; for no such thing as *money* was any where known. Find out something that hath the *use and value of money* amongst his neighbours, you shall see the same man will begin presently to *enlarge* his possessions.

50. But since gold and silver, being little useful to the life of man in proportion to food, raiment, and carriage, has its *value* only from the consent of men, whereof *labour* yet *makes,* in great part, the *measure,* it is plain, that men have agreed to a disproportionate and unequal *possession of the earth,* they having, by a tacit and voluntary consent, found out a way how a man may fairly possess more land than he himself can use the product of, by receiving in exchange for the overplus, gold and silver, which may be hoarded up without injury to any one; these metals not spoiling or decaying in the hands of the possessor. This partage of things in an inequality of private possessions, men have made practicable out of the bounds of society, and without compact, only by putting a value on gold and silver, and tacitly agreeing in the use of money. For in governments, the laws regulate the right of property, and the possession of land is determined by positive constitutions.

51. And thus, I think, it is very easy to conceive, without any difficulty *how labour could at first begin a title of property* in the common things of nature, and how the spending it upon our uses bounded it. So that there could then be no reason of quarrelling about title, nor any doubt about the largeness of possession it gave. Right and conveniency went together; for as a man had a right to all he could employ his labour upon, so he had no temptation to labour for more than he could make use of. This left no room for controversy about the title, nor for encroachment on the right of others; what portion a man carved to himself, was easily seen; and it was useless, as well as dishonest, to carve himself too much, or take more than he needed.

CHAPTER VI
Of Paternal Power

52. It may perhaps be censured as an impertinent criticism, in a discourse of this nature, to find fault with words and names, that have obtained in the world: and yet

possibly it may not be amiss to offer new ones, when the old are apt to lead men into mistakes, as this of *paternal power* probably has done, which seems so to place the power of parents over their children wholly in the *father,* as if the *mother* had no share in it, whereas, if we consult reason or revelation, we shall find she hath an equal title. This may give one reason to ask, whether this might not be more properly called *parental power.* For whatever obligation nature and the right of generation lays on children, it must certainly bind them equally to both concurrent causes of it. And accordingly we see the positive law of God every where joins them together without distinction, when it commands the obedience of children: "Honour thy father and thy mother," *Exod.* xx. 12. "Whosoever curseth his father or his mother," *Lev.* xx. 9. "Ye shall fear every man his mother and his father," *Lev.* xix. 5. "Children, obey your parents," &c. *Eph.* vi. 1, is the style of the Old and New Testament.

53. Had but this one thing been well considered, without looking any deeper into the matter, it might perhaps have kept men from running into those gross mistakes they have made, about this power of parents; which, however it might, without any great harshness, bear the name of absolute dominion, and regal authority, when under the title of *paternal power* it seemed appropriated to the father, would yet have sounded but oddly, and in the very name shewn the absurdity, if this supposed absolute power over children had been called *parental;* and thereby have discovered, that it belonged to the *mother* too. For it will but very ill serve the turn of those men, who contend so much for the absolute power and authority of the fatherhood, as they call it, that the mother should have any share in it. And it would have but ill supported the monarchy they contend for, when by the very name it appeared that that fundamental authority, from whence they would derive their government of a single person only, was not placed in one, but two persons jointly. But to let this of names pass.

54. Though I have said above, chap. ii. "That all men by nature are equal," I cannot be supposed to understand all sorts of *equality: age* or *virtue* may give men a just precedency: *excellency of parts* and *merit* may place others above the common level: *birth* may subject some, and *alliance* or *benefits* others, to pay an observance to those whom nature, gratitude, or other respects, may have made it due; and yet all this consists with the *equality,* which all men are in, in respect of jurisdiction or dominion one over another; which was the *equality* I there spoke of, as proper to the business in hand, being that *equal right,* that every man hath, *to his natural freedom,* without being subjected to the will or authority of any other man.

55. *Children,* I confess, are not born in this state of *equality,* though they are born to it. Their parents have a sort of rule and jurisdiction over them, when they come into the world, and for some time after, but it is but a temporary one. The bonds of this subjection are like the swaddling clothes they are wrapt up in, and supported by, in the weakness of their infancy: Age and reason, as they grow up, loosen them, till at length they drop quite off, and leave a man at his own free disposal.

56. Adam was created a perfect man, his body and mind in full possession of their strength and reason, and so was capable from the first instant of his being to provide for his own support and preservation; and govern his actions according to the dictates of the law of reason which God had implanted in him. From him the world is peopled with his descendants, who are all born infants, weak and helpless, without knowledge or understanding: But to supply the defects of this imperfect state, till the improvement of growth and age hath removed them, Adam and Eve, and after

them all *parents* were, by the law of nature, *under an obligation to preserve, nourish, and educate the children,* they had begotten; not as their own workmanship, but the workmanship of their own maker, the Almighty, to whom they were to be accountable for them.

57. The law, that was to govern Adam, was the same that was to govern all his posterity, the *law of reason.* But his offspring having another way of entrance into the world, different from him, by a natural birth, that produced them ignorant and without the use of *reason,* they were not presently *under that law;* for no body can be under a law, which is not promulgated to him: and this law being promulgated or made known by *reason* only, he that is not come to the use of his *reason,* cannot be said to be *under this law;* and Adam's children, being not presently as soon as born, *under this law of reason,* were not presently free. For law, in its true notion, *is* not so much the limitation, *as the direction of a free and intelligent agent* to his proper interest, and prescribes no farther than is for the general good of those under that law. Could they be happier without it, the law, as an useless thing, would of it self vanish: and that ill deserves the name of confinement which hedges us in only from bogs and precipices. So that, however it may be mistaken, *the end of law* is not to abolish or restrain, but *to preserve and enlarge freedom.* For in all the states of created beings capable of laws, *where there is no law, there is no freedom.* For liberty is to be free from restraint and violence from others which cannot be where there is no law: but freedom is not, as we are told, "a liberty for every man to do what he lists:" (for who could be free, when every other man's humour might domineer over him?) but a liberty to dispose, and order as he lists, his person, actions, possessions, and his whole property, within the allowance of those laws under which he is, and therein not to be subject to the arbitrary will of another, but freely follow his own.

58. The *power,* then, *that parents have* over their children, arises from that duty which is incumbent on them, to take care of their offspring during the imperfect state of childhood. To inform the mind, and govern the actions of their yet ignorant nonage, till reason shall take its place, and ease them of that trouble, is what the children want, and the parents are bound to. For God having given man an understanding to direct his actions, has allowed him a freedom of will, and liberty of acting, as properly belonging thereunto, within the bounds of that law he is under. But whilst he is in an estate, wherein he has not understanding of his own to direct his will, he is not to have any will of his own to follow: he that understands for him, must will for him too; he must prescribe to his will, and regulate his actions: but when he comes to the estate that made his *father a freeman,* the *son is a freeman* too.

59. This holds in all the laws a man is under, whether natural or civil. Is a man under the law of nature? *What made him free* of that law? What gave him a free disposing of his property according to his own will, within the compass of that law? I answer, a state of maturity, wherein he might be supposed capable to know that law, that so he might keep his actions within the bounds of it. When he has acquired that state, he is presumed to know how far that law is to be his guide, and how far he may make use of his *freedom,* and so comes to have it; till then, some body else must guide him, who is presumed to know how far the law allows a liberty. If such a state of reason, such an age of discretion *made him free,* the same shall make his son free too. Is a man under the law of England? *What made him free* of that law? That is, to have the liberty to dispose of his actions and possessions according to his own will within the permission of that law? A capacity of knowing that law. Which is

supposed by that law, at the age of one and twenty years, and in some cases sooner. If this made the father free, it shall make the son free too. Till then we see the law allows the son to have no will, but he is to be guided by the will of his father or guardian, who is to understand for him. And if the father die, and fail to substitute a deputy in his trust; if he hath not provided a tutor to govern his son, during his minority, during his want of understanding; the law takes care to do it; some other must govern him, and be a will to him, till he hath *attained to a state of freedom*, and his understanding be fit to take the government of his will. But after that, the father and son are equally free as much as tutor and pupil after nonage: equally subjects of the same law together, without any dominion left in the father over the life, liberty, or estate of his son, whether they be only in the state and under the law of nature, or under the positive laws of an established government.

60. But if, through defects that may happen out of the ordinary course of nature, any one comes not to such a degree of reason, wherein he might be supposed capable of knowing the law, and so living within the rules of it; he is *never capable of being a free man*, he is never let loose to the disposure of his own will (because he knows no bounds to it, has not understanding, its proper guide) but is continued under the tuition and government of others, all the time his own understanding is incapable of that charge. And so *lunatics* and *idiots* are never set free from the government of their parents. "Children, who are not as yet come into those years whereat they may have; and innocents which are excluded by a natural defect from ever having; thirdly, madmen, which for the present cannot possibly have the use of right reason to guide themselves; have for their guide the reason that guideth other men, which are tutors over them, to seek and procure their good for them," says Hooker, Eccl. Pol. Lib. I. Sect. 7. All which seems no more than that duty which God and nature has laid on man, as well as other creatures, to preserve their offspring, till they can be able to shift for themselves, and will scarce amount to an instance or proof of parents regal authority.

61. Thus we are *born free*, as we are born rational; not that we have actually the exercise of either: age, that brings one, brings with it the other too. And thus we see how *natural freedom and subjection to parents* may consist together, and are both founded on the same principle. A *child* is *free* by his father's title, by his father's understanding, which is to govern him till he hath it of his own. The *freedom of a man at years of discretion*, and the *subjection* of a child *to* his parents, whilst yet short of that age, are so consistent, and so distinguishable, that the most blinded contenders for monarchy, *by right of fatherhood*, cannot miss this difference; the most obstinate cannot but allow their consistency. For were their doctrine all true, were the right heir of Adam now known, and by that title settled a monarch in his throne, invested with all the absolute unlimited power, Sir Robert Filmer talks of; if he should die as soon as his heir were born, must not the child, notwithstanding he were never so free, never so much sovereign, be in subjection to his mother and nurse, to tutors and governors, till age and education brought him reason and ability to govern himself and others? The necessities of his life, the health of his body, and the information of his mind, would require him to be directed by the will of others, and not his own; and yet will any one think, that this restraint and subjection were inconsistent with, or spoiled him of, that liberty or sovereignty he had a right to, or gave away his empire to those who had the government of his nonage? This government over him only prepared him the better and sooner for it. If any body should ask me when my son is of *age to be free?* I shall answer, just when his monarch is of

age to govern. "But at what time," says the judicious Hooker, Eccl. Pol. Lib. I. Sect. 6 "a man may be said to have attained so far forth the use of reason, as sufficeth to make him capable of those laws whereby he is then bound to guide his actions: this is a great deal more easy for sense to discern, than for any one by skill and learning to determine."

62. Commonwealths themselves take notice of, and allow, that there is *a time when men* are to *begin to act like free men*, and therefore till that time require not oaths of fealty, or allegiance, or other public owning of, or submission to, the government of their countries.

63. The *freedom* then of man, and liberty of acting according to his own will, is *grounded* on his having *reason*, which is able to instruct him in that law he is to govern himself by, and make him know how far he is left to the freedom of his own will. To turn him loose to an unrestrained liberty, before he has reason to guide him, is not the allowing him the privilege of his nature to be free; but to thrust him out amongst brutes, and abandon him to a state as wretched, and as much beneath that of a man, as theirs. This is that which puts the *authority* into the *parents* hands to govern the *minority* of their children. God hath made it their business to employ this care on their offspring, and hath placed in them suitable inclinations of tenderness and concern to temper this power, to apply it, as his wisdom designed it, to the children's good as long as they should need to be under it.

64. But what reason can hence advance this care of the *parents* due to their offspring into an *absolute arbitrary dominion* of the father, whose power reaches no farther than, by such a discipline as he finds most effectual, to give such strength and health to their bodies, such vigour and rectitude to their minds, as may best fit his children to be most useful to themselves and others; and, if it be necessary to his condition, to make them work, when they are able, for their own subsistence. But in this power the *mother* too has her share with the *father*.

65. Nay, *this* power so little belongs to the father by any peculiar right of nature, but only as he is guardian of his children, that when he quits his care of them, he loses his power over them, which goes along with their nourishment and education, to which it is inseparably annexed; and it belongs as much to the foster-father of an exposed child, as to the natural father of another. So little power does the bare *act of begetting* give a man over his issue; if all his care ends there, and this be all the title he hath to the name and authority of a father. And what will become of this *paternal power* in that part of the world, where one woman hath more than one husband at a time? or in those parts of America, where, when the husband and wife part, which happens frequently, the children are all left to the mother, follow her, and are wholly under her care and provision? If the father die whilst the children are young, do they not naturally every where owe the same obedience to their mother, during their minority, as to their father were he alive? And will any one say, that the mother hath a legislative power over her children? that she can make standing rules, which shall be of perpetual obligation, by which they ought to regulate all the concerns of their property, and bound their liberty all the course of their lives? or can she enforce the observation of them with capital punishments? For this is the proper *power of the magistrate*, of which the father hath not so much as the shadow. His command over his children is but temporary, and reaches not their life or property: it is but a help to the weakness and imperfection of their nonage, a discipline necessary to their education: and though a father may dispose of his own possessions

as he pleases, when his children are out of danger of perishing for want, yet his power extends not to the lives or goods, which either their own industry, or another's bounty has made theirs; nor to their liberty neither, when they are once arrived to the infranchisement of the years of discretion. The *father's empire* then ceases, and can from thence forwards no more dispose of the liberty of his son, than that of any other man: and it must be far from an absolute or perpetual jurisdiction, from which a man may withdraw himself, having licence from divine authority to *leave father and mother, and cleave to his wife*.

66. But though there be a time when a child comes to be as free from subjection to the will and command of his father, as the father himself is free from subjection to the will of any body else, and they are each under no other restraint but that which is common to them both, whether it be the law of nature, or municipal law of their country; yet this freedom exempts not a son from that honour which he ought, by the law of God and nature, to pay his parents. God having made the parents instruments in his great design of continuing the race of mankind, and the occasions of life to their children; as he hath laid on them an obligation to nourish, preserve, and bring up their offspring; so he has laid on the children a perpetual obligation of *honouring their parents,* which containing in it an inward esteem and reverence to be shewn by all outward expressions, ties up the child from any thing that may ever injure or affront, disturb or endanger, the happiness or life of those from whom he received his; and engages him in all actions of defence, relief, assistance, and comfort of those, by whose means he entered into being, and has been made capable of any enjoyments of life. From this obligation no state, no freedom can absolve children. But this is very far from giving parents a power of command over their children, or an authority to make laws and dispose as they please of their lives and liberties. It is one thing to owe honour, respect, gratitude, and assistance; another to require an absolute obedience and submission. The *honour due to parents,* a monarch in his throne owes his mother, and yet this lessens not his authority, nor subjects him to her government.

67. The subjection of a minor places in the father a temporary government, which terminates with the minority of the child: and the *honour due from a child,* places in the parents a perpetual right to respect, reverence, support and compliance too, more or less, as the father's care, cost, and kindness in his education, have been more or less. This ends not with minority, but holds in all parts and conditions of a man's life. The want of distinguishing these two powers, viz. that which the father hath in the right of *tuition,* during minority, and the right of honour all his life, may perhaps have caused a great part of the mistakes about this matter. For to speak properly of them, the first of these is rather the privilege of children, and duty of parents, than any prerogative of paternal power. The nourishment and education of their children is a charge so incumbent on parents for their children's good, that nothing can absolve them from taking care of it. And though the *power of commanding and chastising* them go along with it, yet God hath woven into the principles of human nature such a tenderness for their offspring, that there is little fear that parents should use their power with too much rigour; the excess is seldom on the severe side, the strong bias of nature drawing the other way. And therefore God Almighty, when he would express his gentle dealing with the Israelites, he tells them, that though he chastened them, "he chastened them as a man chastens his son," *Deut.* viii. 5. i.e. with tenderness and affection, and kept them under no severer discipline than what was absolutely best for them, and had been less kindness to have slackened.

This is that power to which children are commanded obedience, that the pains and care of their parents may not be increased, or ill rewarded.

68. On the other side, *honour* and *support,* all that which gratitude requires to return for the benefits received by and from them, is the indispensable duty of the child, and the proper privilege of the parents. This is intended for the parents advantage, as the other is for the child's; though education, the parents duty, seems to have most power, because the ignorance and infirmities of childhood stand in need of restraint and correction; which is a visible exercise of rule, and a kind of dominion. And that duty which is comprehended in the word *honour,* requires less obedience, though the obligation be stronger on grown than younger children. For who can think the command, "Children, obey your parents," requires in a man that has children of his own the same submission to his father, as it does in his yet young children to him; and that by this precept he were bound to obey all his father's commands, if, out of a conceit of authority, he should have the indiscretion to treat him still as a boy?

69. The first part then of *paternal power,* or rather duty, which is *education,* belongs so to the father, that it terminates at a certain season; when the business of education is over, it ceases of itself, and is also alienable before. For a man may put the tuition of his son in other hands; and he that has made his son an *apprentice* to another, has discharged him, during that time, of a great part of his obedience both to himself and to his mother. But all the *duty of honour,* the other part, remains nevertheless entire to them; nothing can cancel that: It is so inseparable from them both, that the father's authority cannot dispossess the mother of this right, nor can any man discharge his son from *honouring* her that bore him. But both these are very far from a power to make laws, and enforcing them with penalties that may reach estate, liberty, limbs, and life. The power of commanding ends with nonage; and though after that, *honour* and respect, support and defence, and whatsoever gratitude can oblige a man to, for the highest benefits he is naturally capable of, be always due from a son to his parents; yet all this puts no sceptre into the father's hand, no sovereign power of commanding. He has no dominion over his son's property, or actions; nor any right that his will should prescribe to his son's in all things; however it may become his son in many things not very inconvenient to him and his family, to pay a deference to it.

70. A man may owe *honour* and respect to an ancient, or wise man; defence to his child or friend; relief and support to the distressed; and gratitude to a benefactor, to such a degree, that all he has, all he can do, cannot sufficiently pay it: but all these give no authority, no right to any one, of making laws over him from whom they are owing. And it is plain, all this is due not only to the bare title of father; not only because, as has been said, it is owing to the mother too, but because these obligations to parents, and the degrees of what is required of children, may be varied by the different care and kindness, trouble and expense, which is often employed upon one child more than another.

71. This shews the reason how it comes to pass, that *parents in societies,* where they themselves are subjects, retain a *power over their children,* and have as much right to their subjection as those who are in the state of nature. Which could not possibly be, if all political power were only paternal, and that in truth they were one and the same thing. For then, all paternal power being in the prince, the subject could naturally have none of it. But these two *powers, political* and *paternal,* are so perfectly

distinct and separate, are built upon so different foundations, and given to so different ends, that every subject that is a father, has as much a paternal power over his children, as the prince has over his: and every prince, that has parents, owes them as much filial duty and obedience, as the meanest of his subjects do to theirs; and cannot therefore contain any part or degree of that kind of dominion which a prince or magistrate has over his subject.

72. Though the obligation on the parents to bring up their children, and the obligation on children to honour their parents, contain all the power on the one hand, and submission on the other, which are proper to this relation, yet there is *another power* ordinary *in the father,* whereby he has a tie on the obedience of his children; which though it be common to him with other men, yet the occasions of shewing it almost constantly happening to fathers in their private families, and the instances of it elsewhere being rare, and less taken notice of, it passes in the world for a part of paternal jurisdiction. And this is the power men generally have to *bestow their estates* on those who please them best. The possession of the father being the expectation and inheritance of the children, ordinarily in certain proportions, according to the law and custom of each country; yet it is commonly in the father's power to bestow it with a more sparing or liberal hand, according as the behaviour of this or that child hath comported with his will and humour.

73. This is no small tie on the obedience of children: and there being always annexed to the enjoyment of land a submission to the government of the country, of which that land is a part; it has been commonly supposed, that a father could *oblige his posterity to that government,* of which he himself was a subject, and that his compact held them; whereas it being only a necessary condition annexed to the land, and the inheritance of an estate which is under that government, reaches only those who will take it on that condition, and so is no natural tie or engagement, but a voluntary submission. For *every man's children* being by nature as free as himself, or any of his ancestors ever were, may, whilst they are in that freedom, choose what society they will join themselves to, what commonwealth they will put themselves under. But if they will enjoy the inheritance of their ancestors, they must take it on the same terms their ancestors had it, and submit to all the conditions annexed to such a possession. By this power indeed fathers oblige their children to obedience to themselves, even when they are past minority, and most commonly too subject them to this or that political power. But neither of these by any peculiar right of fatherhood, but by the reward they have in their hands to enforce and recompence such a compliance; and is no more power than what a Frenchman has over an Englishman, who, by the hopes of an estate he will leave him, will certainly have a strong tie on his obedience: and if, when it is left him, he will enjoy it, he must certainly take it upon the conditions annexed to the *possession of land* in that country where it lies, whether it be France or England.

74. To conclude then, though the father's power of commanding extends no farther than the minority of his children, and to a degree only fit for the discipline and government of that age; and though that honour and respect, and all that which the Latins called piety, which they indispensably owe to their parents all their life-time, and in all estates, with all that support and defence which is due to them, gives the father no power of governing, i.e. making laws and enacting penalties on his children; though by all this he has no dominion over the property or actions of his son; yet it is obvious to conceive how easy it was, in the first ages of the world, and

in places still, where the thinness of people gives families leave to separate into unpossessed quarters, and they have room to remove or plant themselves in yet vacant habitations, for the *father of the family* to become the prince[1] of it; he had been a ruler from the beginning of the infancy of his children: and since without some government it would be hard for them to live together, it was likeliest it should, by the express or tacit consent of the children when they were grown up, be in the father, where it seemed without any change barely to continue; when indeed nothing more was required to it, than the permitting the father to exercise alone, in his family, that executive power of the law of nature, which every free man naturally hath, and by that permission resigning up to him a monarchical power, whilst they remained in it. But that this was not by any *paternal right*, but only by the consent of his children, is evident from hence, that no body doubts, but if a stranger, whom chance or business had brought to his family, had there killed any of his children, or committed any other fact, he might condemn and put him to death, or otherwise punish him, as well as any of his children: which it was impossible he should do by virtue of any paternal authority over one who was not his child, but by virtue of that executive power of the law of nature, which, as a man, he had a right to: and he alone could punish him in his family, where the respect of his children had laid by the exercise of such a power, to give way to the dignity and authority they were willing should remain in him, above the rest of his family.

75. Thus it was easy, and almost natural for children, by a tacit, and scarce avoidable consent, to make way for the *father's authority and government*. They had been accustomed in their childhood to follow his direction, and to refer their little differences to him; and when they were men, who fitter to rule them? Their little properties, and less covetousness, seldom afforded greater controversies; and when any should arise, where could they have a fitter umpire than he, by whose care they had every one been sustained and brought up, and who had a tenderness for them all? It is no wonder that they made no distinction betwixt minority and full age; nor looked after one and twenty, or any other age that might make them the free disposers of themselves and fortunes, when they could have no desire to be out of their pupilage. The government they had been under during it, continued still to be more their protection than restraint: and they could no where find a greater security to their peace, liberties, and fortunes, than in the *rule of a father*.

76. Thus the natural *fathers of families* by an insensible change became the *politic monarchs* of them too: and as they chanced to live long, and leave able and worthy heirs, for several successions, or otherwise; so they laid the foundations of hereditary, or elective kingdoms, under several constitutions and manners, according as chance, contrivance, or occasions happened to mould them. But if princes have their

---

1. It is no improbable opinion therefore, which the arch-philosopher was of, "That the chief person in every household was always, as it were, a king: so when numbers of households joined themselves in civil societies together, kings were the first kind of governors amongst them, which is also, as it seemeth, the reason why the name of fathers continued still in them, who, of fathers, were made rulers; as also the ancient custom of governors to do as Melchizedeck, and being kings, to exercise the office of priests, which fathers did, at the first grew perhaps by the same occasion. Howbeit, this is not the only kind of regiment that has been received in the world. The inconveniences of one kind have caused sundry others to be devised; so that in a word, all public regiment of what kind soever, seemeth evidently to have risen from the deliberate advice, consultation and composition between men, judging it convenient and behoveful; there being no impossibility in nature considered by itself, but that man might have lived without any public regiment." Hooker's Eccl. P. L. I. Sect. 10.

titles in their fathers right, and it be a sufficient proof of the natural *right of fathers* to political authority, because they commonly were those in whose hands we find, *de facto,* the exercise of government: I say, if this argument be good, it will as strongly prove, that all princes, nay princes only, ought to be priests, since it is as certain, that in the beginning, *the father of the family was priest, as that he was ruler in his own household.*

CHAPTER VII
Of Political or Civil Society

77. God having made man such a creature, that in his own judgment, it was not good for him to be alone, put him under strong obligations of necessity, convenience, and inclination, to drive him into society, as well as fitted him with understanding and language to continue and enjoy it. The first society was between man and wife, which gave beginning to that between parents and children; to which, in time, that between master and servant came to be added; and though all these might, and commonly did meet together, and make up but one family, wherein the master or mistress of it had some sort of rule proper to a family; each of these, or all together, came short of *political society,* as we shall see, if we consider the different ends, ties, and bounds of each of these.

78. *Conjugal society* is made by a voluntary compact between man and woman; and though it consist chiefly in such a communion and right in one another's bodies as is necessary to its chief end, procreation; yet it draws with it mutual support and assistance, and a communion of interests too, as necessary not only to unite their care and affection, but also necessary to their common offspring, who have a right to be nourished and maintained by them, till they are able to provide for themselves.

79. For the end of *conjunction between male and female* being not barely procreation, but the continuation of the species; this conjunction betwixt male and female ought to last, even after procreation, so long as is necessary to the nourishment and support of the young ones, who are to be sustained by those that got them, till they are able to shift and provide for themselves. This rule, which the infinite wise Maker hath set to the works of his hands, we find the inferior creatures steadily obey. In those viviparous animals which feed on grass, the *conjunction between male and female* lasts no longer than the very act of copulation; because the teat of the dam being sufficient to nourish the young, till it be able to feed on grass, the male only begets, but concerns not himself for the female or young, to whose sustenance he can contribute nothing. But in beasts of prey the conjunction lasts longer: because the dam not being able well to subsist herself, and nourish her numerous offspring by her own prey alone, a more laborious, as well as more dangerous way of living, than by feeding on grass; the assistance of the male is necessary to the maintenance of their common family, which cannot subsist till they are able to prey for themselves, but by the joint care of male and female. The same is to be observed in all birds (except some domestic ones, where plenty of food excuses the cock from feeding, and taking care of the young brood), whose young needing food in the nest, the cock and hen continue mates, till the young are able to use their wing, and provide for themselves.

80. And herein I think lies the chief, if not the only reason, *why the male and female in mankind are tied to a longer conjunction* than other creatures, viz. because the female is capable of conceiving, and *de facto* is commonly with child again, and brings forth

too a new birth, long before the former is out of a dependency for support on his parents help, and able to shift for himself, and has all the assistance that is due to him from his parents: whereby the father, who is bound to take care for those he hath begot, is under an obligation to continue in conjugal society with the same woman longer than other creatures, whose young being able to subsist of themselves before the time of procreation returns again, the conjugal bond dissolves of itself, and they are at liberty, till Hymen at his usual anniversary season summons them again to choose new mates. Wherein one cannot but admire the wisdom of the great Creator, who having given to man foresight, and an ability to lay up for the future, as well as to supply the present necessity, hath made it necessary, that *society of man and wife should be more lasting,* than of male and female amongst other creatures; that so their industry might be encouraged, and their interest better united, to make provision and lay up goods for their common issue, which uncertain mixture, or easy and frequent solutions of conjugal society, would mightily disturb.

81. But though these are ties upon *mankind,* which make the *conjugal bonds* more firm and lasting in man, than the other species of animals; yet it would give one reason to inquire, why this compact, where procreation and education are secured, and inheritance taken care for, may not be made determinable, either by consent, or at a certain time, or upon certain conditions, as well as any other voluntary compacts, there being no necessity in the nature of the thing, nor to the ends of it, that it should always be for life; I mean, to such as are under no restraint of any positive law, which ordains all such contracts to be perpetual.

82. But the husband and wife, though they have but one common concern, yet having different understandings, will unavoidably sometimes have different wills too; it therefore being necessary that the last determination, i.e. the rule, should be placed somewhere; it naturally falls to the man's share, as the abler and the stronger. But this reaching but to the things of their common interest and property, leaves the wife in the full and free possession of what by contract is her peculiar right, and gives the husband no more power over her life than she has over his. The *power of the husband* being so far from that of an absolute monarch, that the *wife* has in many cases a liberty to separate from him, where natural right or their contract allows it; whether that contract be made by themselves in the state of nature, or by the customs or laws of the country they live in; and the children upon such separation fall to the father's or mother's lot, as such contract does determine.

83. For all the ends of *marriage* being to be obtained under politic government, as well as in the state of nature, the civil magistrate doth not abridge the right or power of either naturally necessary to those ends, viz. procreation and mutual support and assistance whilst they are together; but only decides any controversy that may arise between man and wife about them. If it were otherwise, and that absolute sovereignty and power of life and death naturally belonged to the husband, and were *necessary to the society between man and wife,* there could be no matrimony in any of those countries where the husband is allowed no such absolute authority. But the ends of matrimony requiring no such power in the husband, the condition of conjugal society put it not in him, it being not at all necessary to that state. Conjugal society could subsist and attain its ends without it; nay, community of goods, and the power over them, mutual assistance and maintenance, and other things belonging to conjugal society, might be varied and regulated by that contract which unites man

and wife in that society, as far as may consist with procreation and the bringing up of children till they could shift for themselves; nothing being necessary to any society, that is not necessary to the ends for which it is made.

84. The *society betwixt parents and children,* and the distinct rights and powers belonging respectively to them, I have treated of so largely, in the foregoing chapter, that I shall not here need to say any thing of it. And I think it is plain, that it is far different from a politic society.

85. *Master* and *servant* are names as old as history, but given to those of far different condition; for a free man makes himself a servant to another, by selling him, for a certain time, the service he undertakes to do, in exchange for wages he is to receive: and though this commonly puts him into the family of his master, and under the ordinary discipline thereof: yet it gives the master but a temporary power over him, and no greater than what is contained in the *contract* between them. But there is another sort of servants, which by a peculiar name we call *slaves,* who being captives taken in a just war, are by the right of nature subjected to the absolute dominion and arbitrary power of their masters. These men having, as I say, forfeited their lives, and with it their liberties, and lost their estates; and being in the *state of slavery,* not capable of any property, cannot in that state be considered as any part of *civil society;* the chief end whereof is the preservation of property,

86. Let us therefore consider a *master of a family* with all these subordinate relations of *wife, children, servants,* and *slaves,* united under the domestic rule of a family; which, what resemblance soever it may have in its order, offices, and number too, with a little commonwealth, yet is very far from it, both in its constitution, power, and end: or if it must be thought a monarchy, and the *paterfamilias* the absolute monarch in it, absolute monarchy will have but a very shattered and short power, when it is plain by what has been said before, that the *master of the family* has a very distinct and differently limited power, both as to time and extent, over those several persons that are in it. For excepting the slave (and the family is as much a family, and his power as *paterfamilias* as great, whether there be any slaves in his family or no) he has no legislative power of life and death over any of them, and none too but what a *mistress of a family* may have as well as he. And he certainly can have no absolute power over the whole family, who has but a very limited one over every individual in it. But how a family, or any other society of men, differ from that which is properly political society, we shall best see by considering wherein political society itself consists.

87. Man being born, as has been proved, with a title to perfect freedom, and an uncontrolled enjoyment of all the rights and privileges of the law of nature, equally with any other man, or number of men in the world, hath by nature a power, not only to preserve his property, that is, his life, liberty, and estate, against the injuries and attempts of other men; but to judge of and punish the breaches of that law in others, as he is persuaded the offence deserves, even with death itself, in crimes where the heinousness of the fact, in his opinion, requires it. But because no *political* society can be, nor subsist, without having in itself the power to preserve the property, and, in order thereunto, punish the offences of all those of that society; there and there only is *political society,* where every one of the members hath quitted his natural power, resigned it up into the hands of the community in all cases that excludes him not from appealing for protection to the law established by it. And thus all private judgment of every particular member being excluded, the commu-

nity comes to be umpire by settled standing rules, indifferent, and the same to all parties; and by men having authority from the community, for the execution of those rules, decides all the differences that may happen between any members of that society concerning any matter of right; and punishes those offences which any member hath committed against the society, with such penalties as the law has established, whereby it is easy to discern, who are, and who are not, in *political society* together. Those who are united into one body, and have a common established law and judicature to appeal to, with authority to decide controversies between them, and punish offenders, *are in civil society* one with another: but those who have no such common appeal, I mean on earth, are still in the state of nature, each being, where there is no other, judge for himself, and executioner: which is, as I have before shewed, the perfect *state of nature*.

88. And thus the commonwealth comes by a power to set down what punishment shall belong to the several transgressions which they think worthy of it, committed amongst the members of that society, (which is the *power of making laws*) as well as it has the power to punish any injury done unto any of its members, by any one that is not of it, (which is the power of war and peace,) and all this for the preservation of the property of all the members of that society, as far as is possible. But though every man who has entered into civil society, and is become a member of any commonwealth, has thereby quitted his power to punish offences against the law of nature, in prosecution of his own private judgment; yet with the judgment of offences, which he has given up to the legislative in all cases, where he can appeal to the magistrate, he has given a right to the commonwealth to employ his force, for the execution of the judgments of the commonwealth whenever he shall be called to it; which indeed are his own judgments, they being made by himself, or his representative. And herein we have the original of the legislative and executive power of civil society, which is to judge by standing laws, how far offences are to be punished, when committed within the commonwealth; and also to determine, by occasional judgments founded on the present circumstances of the fact, how far injuries from without are to be vindicated; and in both these to employ all the force of all the members, when there shall be need.

89. Whenever therefore any number of men are so united into one society, as to quit every one his executive power of the law of nature, and to resign it to the public, there and there only is a political, or civil society. And this is done, wherever any number of men, in the state of nature, enter into society to make one people, one body politic, under one supreme government; or else when any one joins himself to, and incorporates with any government already made. For hereby he authorizes the society, or, which is all one, the legislative thereof, to make laws for him, as the public good of the society shall require; to the execution whereof, his own assistance (as to his own degrees) is due. And this puts men out of a state of nature into that of a commonwealth, by setting up a judge on earth, with authority to determine all the controversies, and redress the injuries that may happen to any member of the commonwealth: which judge is the legislative, or magistrate appointed by it. And wherever there are any number of men, however associated, that have no such decisive power to appeal to, there they are still in the state of nature.

90. Hence it is evident, that absolute monarchy, which by some men is counted the only government in the world, is indeed inconsistent with civil society, and so can be no form of civil government at all; for the end of civil society being to avoid

and remedy these inconveniencies of the state of nature, which necessarily follow from every man's being judge in his own case, by setting up a known authority, to which every one of that society may appeal upon any injury received, or controversy that may arise, and which every one of the[2] society ought to obey; wherever any persons are, who have not such an authority to appeal to for the decision of any difference between them, there those persons are still *in the state of nature*. And so is every *absolute prince*, in respect of those who are under his dominion.

91. For he being supposed to have all, both legislative and executive power in himself alone, there is no judge to be found, no appeal lies open to any one, who may fairly, and indifferently, and with authority decide, and from whose decision relief and redress may be expected of any injury or inconveniency that may be suffered from the prince, or by his order: so that such a man, however intitled, *czar*, or *grand seignior*, or how you please, is as much *in the state of nature*, with all under his dominion, as he is with the rest of mankind. For wherever any two men are, who have no standing rule, and common judge to appeal to on earth, for the determination of controversies of right betwixt them, there they are still *in the state of*[3] *nature*, and under all the inconveniencies of it, with only this woful difference to the subject, or rather slave of an absolute prince; that whereas in the ordinary state of nature he has a liberty to judge of his right, and, according to the best of his power, to maintain it; now, whenever his property is invaded by the will and order of his monarch, he has not only no appeal, as those in society ought to have, but, as if he were degraded from the common state of rational creatures, is denied a liberty to judge of, or to defend his right; and so is exposed to all the misery and inconveniencies that a man can fear from one, who being in the unrestrained state of nature, is yet corrupted with flattery, and armed with power.

92. For he that thinks *absolute power purifies men's blood*, and corrects the baseness of human nature, need read but the history of this or any other age, to be convinced of the contrary. He that would have been so insolent and injurious in the woods of America, would not probably be much better in a throne; where perhaps learning and religion shall be found out to justify all that he shall do to his subjects, and the sword presently silence all those that dare question it. For what the *protection of absolute monarchy* is, what kind of fathers of their countries it makes princes to be, and to what a degree of happiness and security it carries civil society, where this sort

2. The public power of all society is above every soul contained in "the same society; and the principal use of that power is, to give laws unto all that are under it, which laws in such cases we must obey," unless there be reason shewed which may necessarily inforce, that the law of reason, or of God, doth enjoin the contrary." Hook. Eccl. Pol. L. I. Sect. 16.

3. "To take away all such mutual grievances, injuries and wrongs," i.e. such as attend men in the state of nature, "there was no way but only by growing into composition and agreement amongst themselves, by ordaining some kind of government public, and by yielding themselves subject thereunto, that unto whom they granted authority to rule and govern, by them the peace, tranquillity, and happy state of the rest might be procured. Men always knew that where force and injury was offered, they might be defenders of themselves; they knew that however men may seek their own commodity; yet if this were done with injury unto others, it was not to be suffered, but by all men, and all good means to be withstood. Finally, they knew that no man might in reason take upon him to determine his own right, and according to his own determination proceed in maintenance thereof, in as much as every man is towards himself, and whom he greatly affects, partial; and therefore that strifes and troubles would be endless, except they gave their common consent, all to be ordered by some, whom they should agree upon, without which consent there would be no reason that one man should take upon him to be lord or judge over another." Hooker's Eccl. Pol. L. I. Sect. 10.

of government is grown to perfection; he that will look into the late relation of Ceylon, may easily see.

93. *In absolute monarchies,* indeed, as well as other governments of the world, the subjects have an appeal to the law, and judges to decide any controversies, and restrain any violence that may happen betwixt the subjects themselves, one amongst another. This every one thinks necessary, and believes he deserves to be thought a declared enemy to society and mankind, who should go about to take it away. But whether this be from a true love of mankind and society, and such a charity as we all owe one to another, there is reason to doubt. For this is no more than what every man, who loves his own power, profit, or greatness, may and naturally must do, keep those animals from hurting, or destroying one another, who labour and drudge only for his pleasure and advantage; and so are taken care of, not out of any love the master has for them, but love of himself, and the profit they bring him. For if it be asked, what security, what fence is there, in such a state, *against the violence and oppression of this absolute ruler?* the very question can scarce be borne. They are ready to tell you, that it deserves death only to ask after safety. Betwixt subject and subject, they will grant, there must be measures, laws, and judges, for their mutual peace and security: but as for the ruler he ought to be *absolute,* and is above all such circumstances; because he has power to do more hurt and wrong, it is right when he does it. To ask how you may be guarded from harm, or injury, on that side where the strongest hand is to do it, is presently the voice of faction and rebellion: as if when men quitting the state of nature entered into society, they agreed that all of them but one should be under the restraint of laws, but that he should still retain all the liberty of the state of nature, increased with power, and made licentious by impunity. This is to think, that men are so foolish, that they take care to avoid what mischiefs may be done them by *pole cats,* or *foxes;* but are content, nay think it safety, to be devoured by *lions.*

94. But whatever flatterers may talk to amuse people's understandings, it hinders not men from feeling; and when they perceive, that any man, in what station soever, is out of the bounds of the civil society which they are of, and that they have no appeal on earth against any harm they may receive from him, they are apt to think themselves in the state of nature, in respect of him whom they find to be so: and to take care, as soon as they can, to have that *safety and security in civil society,* for which it was instituted, and for which only they entered into it. And therefore, though perhaps at first, (as shall be shewed more at large hereafter in the following part of this discourse) some one good and excellent man having got a pre-eminence amongst the rest, had this deference paid to his goodness and virtue, as to a kind of natural authority, that the chief rule, with arbitration of their differences, by a tacit consent devolved into his hands, without any other caution, but the assurance they had of his uprightness and wisdom; yet when time, giving authority, and (as some men would persuade us) sacredness to customs, which the negligent and unforeseen innocence of the first ages began, had brought in successors of another stamp, the people finding their properties not secure under the government, as then it was, (whereas government has no other end but the preservation of[4] property) could

4. "At the first, when some certain kind of regiment was once appointed, it may be that nothing was then farther thought upon for the manner of governing, but all permitted unto their wisdom and discretion, which were to rule, till by experience they found this for all parts very inconvenient, so as the thing which they had devised for a remedy, did indeed but increase the sore, which it should have cured. They saw, that to live by

never be safe nor at rest, *nor think themselves in civil society,* till the legislature was placed in collective bodies of men, call them senate, parliament, or what you please. By which means every single person became subject, equally with other the meanest men, to those laws, which he himself, as part of the legislative, had established; nor could any one, by his own authority, avoid the force of the law, when once made; nor by any pretence of superiority plead exemption, thereby to license his own, or the miscarriages of any of his dependents.[5] *No man in civil society can be exempted from the laws of it.* For if any man may do what he thinks fit, and there be no appeal on earth, for redress or security against any harm he shall do; I ask, whether he be not perfectly still in the state of nature, and so can be *no part or member of that civil society:* unless any one will say, the state of nature and civil society are one and the same thing, which I have never yet found any one so great a patron of anarchy as to affirm.

CHAPTER VIII
Of the Beginning of Political Societies

95. Men being, as has been said, by nature, all free, equal, and independent, no one can be put out of this estate, and subjected to the political power of another, without his own consent. The only way, whereby any one divests himself of his natural liberty, and puts on the *bonds of civil society,* is by agreeing with other men to join and unite into a community, for their comfortable, safe, and peaceable living one amongst another, in a secure enjoyment of their properties, and a greater security against any, that are not of it. This any number of men may do, because it injures not the freedom of the rest; they are left as they were in the liberty of the state of nature. When any number of men have so *consented to make one community or government,* they are thereby presently incorporated, and make *one body politic,* wherein the *majority* have a right to act and conclude the rest.

96. For when any number of men have, by the consent of every individual, made a *community,* they have thereby made that *community* one body, with a power to act as one body, which is only by the will and determination of the majority. For that which acts any community, being only the *consent* of the individuals of it, and it being necessary to that which is one body to move one way; it is necessary the body should move that way whither the greater force carries it, which is the *consent of the majority:* or else it is impossible it should act or continue one body, one community, which the consent of every individual that united into it, agreed that it should; and so every one is bound by that consent to be concluded by the majority. And therefore we see, that in assemblies, impowered to act by positive laws, where no number is set by that positive law which impowers them, the *act of the majority* passes for the act of the whole, and of course determines, as having, by the law of nature and reason, the power of the whole.

97. And thus every man, by consenting with others to make one body politic under one government, puts himself under an obligation, to every one of that society, to

---

one man's will, became the cause of all men's misery. This constrained them to come into laws, wherein all men might see their duty beforehand, and know the penalties of transgressing them." Hooker's Eccl. Pol. L. I. Sect. 10.

5. "Civil law, being the act of the whole body politic, doth therefore over-rule each several part of the same body." Hooker, ibid.

submit to the determination of the majority, and to be concluded by it; or else this *original compact,* whereby he with others incorporate into one society, would signify nothing, and be no compact, if he be left free, and under no other ties than he was in before in the state of nature. For what appearance would there be of any compact? What new engagement if he were no farther tied by any decrees of the society, than he himself thought fit, and did actually consent to? This would be still as great a liberty, as he himself had before his compact, or any one else in the state of nature hath, who may submit himself, and consent to any acts of it if he thinks fit.

98. For if *the consent of the majority* shall not, in reason, be received as *the act of the whole,* and conclude every individual; nothing but the consent of every individual can make any thing to be the act of the whole: But such a consent is next to impossible ever to be had, if we consider the infirmities of health, and avocations of business, which in a number, though much less than that of a commonwealth, will necessarily keep many away from the public assembly. To which if we add the variety of opinions, and contrariety of interests, which unavoidably happen in all collections of men, the coming into society upon such terms would be only like Cato's coming into the theatre, only to go out again. Such a constitution as this would make the mighty *leviathan* of a shorter duration, than the feeblest creatures, and not let it outlast the day it was born in: which cannot be supposed, till we can think, that rational creatures should desire and constitute societies only to be dissolved. For where the majority cannot conclude the rest, there they cannot act as one body, and consequently will be immediately dissolved again.

99. Whosoever therefore out of a state of nature unite into a community, must be understood to give up all the power, necessary to the ends for which they unite into society, to the majority of the community, unless they expressly agreed in any number greater than the majority. And this is done by barely agreeing to *unite into one political society,* which is *all the compact* that is, or needs be, between the individuals, that enter into, or make up a commonwealth. And thus that, which begins and actually *constitutes any political society,* is nothing, but the consent of any number of freemen capable of a majority, to unite and incorporate into such a society. And this is that, and that only, which did, or could give beginning to any lawful government in the world.

100. To this I find two objections made.

First, *That there are no instances to be found in story, of a company of men independent and equal one amongst another, that met together, and in this way began and set up a government.*

Secondly, *It is impossible of right, that men should do so, because all men being born under government, they are to submit to that, and are not at liberty to begin a new one.*

101. To the first there is this to answer, That it is not at all to be wondered, that *history* gives us but a very little account of *men, that lived together in the state of nature.* The inconveniencies of that condition and the love and want of society, no sooner brought any number of them together, but they presently united and incorporated, if they designed to continue together. And if we may not suppose men ever to have been *in the state of nature,* because we hear not much of them in such a state, we may as well suppose the armies of Salmanasser or Xerxes were never children, because we hear little of them, till they were men, and embodied in armies. Government is every where antecedent to records, and letters seldom come in amongst a people till a long continuation of civil society has, by other more necessary arts, provided for

their safety, ease, and plenty. And then they begin to look after the history of their founders, and search into their original, when they have outlived the memory of it. For it is with commonwealths, as with particular persons, they are commonly *ignorant of their own births and infancies:* and if they know any thing of their original, they are beholden for it to the accidental records that others have kept of it. And those that we have of the beginning of any politics in the world, excepting that of the Jews, where God himself immediately interposed, and which favours not at all paternal dominion, are all either plain instances of such a beginning as I have mentioned, or at least have manifest footsteps of it.

102. He must shew a strange inclination to deny evident matter of fact, when it agrees not with his hypothesis, who will not allow, that the *beginning* of Rome and Venice were by the uniting together of several men free and independent one of another, amongst whom there was no natural superiority or subjection. And if Josephus Acosta's word may be taken, he tells us, that in many parts of America there was no government at all. "There are great and apparent conjectures," says he, "that these men, speaking of those of Peru, for a long time had neither kings nor commonwealths, but lived in troops, as they do this day in Florida, the Cheriquanas, those of Brasil, and many other nations, which have no certain kings, but as occasion is offered, in peace or war, they choose their captains as they please," l. I. c. 25. If it be said, that every man there was born subject to his father, or the head of his family. That the subjection due from a child to a father took not away his freedom of uniting into what political society he thought fit, has been already proved. But be that as it will, these men, it is evident, were actually free; and whatever superiority some politicians now would place in any of them, they themselves claimed it not, but by consent were all equal, till by the same consent they set rulers over themselves. So that their politic societies all began from a voluntary union, and the mutual agreement of men freely acting in the choice of their governors, and forms of government.

103. And I hope those who went away from Sparta with Palantus, mentioned by Justin, l. iii. c. 4, will be allowed to have been freemen, *independent* one of another, and to have set up a government over themselves, by their own consent. Thus I have given several examples out of history, of *people free and in the state of nature,* that being met together, incorporated and *began a commonwealth.* And if the want of such instances be an argument to prove that governments were not, nor could not be so begun, I suppose the contenders for paternal empire were better let it alone, than urge it against natural liberty. For if they can give so many instances out of history, of governments begun upon paternal right, I think (though at best an argument from what has been, to what should of right be, has no great force) one might, without any great danger, yield them the cause. But if I might advise them in the case, they would do well not to search too much into the *original of governments,* as they have begun *de facto;* lest they should find, at the foundation of most of them, something very little favourable to the design they promote, and such a power as they contend for.

104. But to conclude, reason being plain on our side, that men are naturally free, and the examples of history shewing, that the governments of the world, that were begun in peace, had their beginning laid on that foundation, and were *made by the consent of the people;* there can be little room for doubt, either where the right is,

or what has been the opinion, or practice of mankind, about the *first erecting of governments*.

105. I will not deny, that if we look back as far as history will direct us, towards the *original of commonwealths*, we shall generally find them under the government and administration of one man. And I am also apt to believe, that where a family was numerous enough to subsist by itself, and continued entire together, without mixing with others, as it often happens, where there is much land, and few people, the government commonly began *in the father*. For the father having, by the law of nature, the same power with every man else to punish, as he thought fit, any offences against that law, might thereby punish his transgressing children, even when they were men, and out of their pupilage; and they were very likely to submit to his punishment, and all join with him against the offender, in their turns, giving him thereby power to execute his sentence against any transgression, and so in effect make him the law maker, and governour over all that remained in conjunction with his family. He was fittest to be trusted; paternal affection secured their property and interest under his care; and the custom of obeying him, in their childhood, made it easier to submit to him, rather than to any other. If, therefore, they must have one to rule them, as government is hardly to be avoided amongst men that live together; who so likely to be the man as he that was their common father; unless negligence, cruelty, or any other defect of mind or body made him unfit for it? But when either the father died, and left his next heir, for want of age, wisdom, courage, or any other qualities, less fit for rule; or where several families met, and consented to continue together; there, it is not to be doubted, but they used their natural freedom to set up him whom they judged the ablest, and most likely to rule well over them. Conformable hereunto we find the people of America, who (living out of the reach of the conquering swords, and spreading domination of the two great empires of Peru and Mexico) enjoyed their own natural freedom, though, *caeteris paribus*, they commonly prefer the heir of their deceased king; yet, if they find him any way weak, or incapable, they pass him by, and set up the stoutest and bravest man for their ruler.

106. Thus, though looking back as far as records give us any account of peopling the world, and the history of nations, we commonly find the government to be in one hand; yet it destroys not that which I affirm, viz. that the *beginning of politic society* depends upon the consent of the individuals, to join into, and make one society; who, when they are thus incorporated, might set up what form of government they thought fit. But this having given occasion to men to mistake, and think, that by nature government was monarchical, and belonged to the father; it may not be amiss here to consider, why people in the beginning generally pitched upon this form; which though perhaps the father's pre-eminency might, in the first institution of some commonwealth give rise to, and place in the beginning the power in one hand; yet it is plain that the reason, that continued the form of *government in a single person*, was not any regard or respect to paternal authority; since all petty monarchies, that is, almost all monarchies, near their original, have been commonly, at least upon occasion, *elective*.

107. First then, in the beginning of things, the father's government of the childhood of those sprung from him, having accustomed them to the *rule of one man*, and taught them that where it was exercised with care and skill, with affection and love to those

under it, it was sufficient to procure and preserve to men all the political happiness they sought for in society. It was no wonder that they should pitch upon, and naturally run into that form of government, which from their infancy they had been all accustomed to; and which, by experience, they had found both easy and safe. To which, if we add, that monarchy being simple, and most obvious to men, whom neither experience had instructed in forms of government, nor the ambition or insolence of empire had taught to beware of the encroachments of prerogative, or the inconveniencies of absolute power, which monarchy in succession was apt to lay claim to, and bring upon them; it was not at all strange, that they should not much trouble themselves to think of methods of restraining any exorbitancies of those to whom they had given the authority over them, and of balancing the power of government, by placing several parts of it in different hands. They had neither felt the oppression of tyrannical dominion, nor did the fashion of the age, nor their possessions, or way of living, (which afforded little matter for covetousness or ambition) give them any reason to apprehend or provide against it; and therefore it is no wonder they put themselves into such a *frame of government*, as was not only, as I said, most obvious and simple, but also best suited to their present state and condition; which stood more in need of defence against foreign invasions and injuries, than of multiplicity of laws. The equality of a simple poor way of living, confining their desires within the narrow bounds of each man's small property, made few controversies, and so no need of many laws to decide them, or variety of officers to superintend the process, or look after the execution of justice, where there were but few trespasses, and few offenders. Since then those, who liked one another so well as to join into society, cannot but be supposed to have some acquaintance and friendship together, and some trust one in another; they could not but have greater apprehensions of others, than of one another: and therefore their first care and thought cannot but be supposed to be, how to secure themselves against foreign force. It was natural for them to put themselves under a *frame of government* which might best serve to that end, and choose the wisest and bravest man to conduct them in their wars, and lead them out against their enemies, and in this chiefly be their *ruler*.

108. Thus we see, that the *kings* of the Indians in America, which is still a pattern of the first ages in Asia and Europe, whilst the inhabitants were too few for the country, and want of people and money gave men no temptation to enlarge their possessions of land, or contest for wider extent of ground, are little more than *generals of their armies;* and though they command absolutely in war, yet at home and in time of peace they exercise very little dominion, and have but a very moderate sovereignty; the resolutions of peace and war being ordinarily either in the people, or in a council. Though the war itself, which admits not of plurality of governors, naturally devolves the command into the *king's sole authority*.

109. And thus, in Israel itself, the *chief business of their judges, and first kings*, seems to have been *to be captains in war*, and leaders of their armies; which (besides what is signified by *going out and in before the people*, which was to march forth to war, and home again at the heads of their forces) appears plainly in the story of Jephthah. The Ammonites making war upon Israel, the Gileadites in fear sent to Jephthah, a bastard of their family whom they had cast off, and article with him, if he will assist them against the Ammonites, to make him their ruler; which they do in these words, "And the people made him head and captain over them," *Judg.* xi. 11. which was, as it seems, all one as to be judge. "And he judged Israel," *Judg.* xii. 7. that is, was

their captain-general, *six years*. So when Jotham upbraids the Shechemites with the obligation they had to Gideon, who had been their judge and ruler, he tells them, "He fought for you, and adventured his life far, and delivered you out of the hands of Midian," *Judg.* ix. 17. Nothing is mentioned of him, but what he did as a *general:* and indeed that is all is found in his history, or in any of the rest of the judges. And Abimelech particularly is called *king*, though at most he was but their *general*. And when, being weary of the ill conduct of Samuel's sons, the children of Israel desired a king, "like all the nations, to judge them, and to go out before them, and to fight their battles," *1 Sam.* viii. 20. God granting their desire, says to Samuel. "I will send thee a man, and thou shalt anoint him to be captain over my people Israel, that he may save my people out of the hands of the Philistines," c. ix. 16. As if the only *business of a king* had been to lead out their armies, and fight in their defence; and accordingly at his inauguration, pouring a vial of oil upon him, declares to Saul, that "the Lord had anointed him to be captain over his inheritance," c. x. 1. And therefore those who, after Saul's being solemnly chosen and saluted *king* by the *tribes* of Mispah, were unwilling to have him their king, made no other objection but this, "How shall this man save us?" v. 27. as if they should have said, this man is unfit to be our *king*, not having skill and conduct enough in war to be able to defend us. And when God resolved to transfer the government to David, it is in these words, "But now thy kingdom shall not continue: the Lord hath sought him a man after his own heart, and the Lord hath commanded him to be captain over his people," c. xiii. 14. As if the whole kingly authority were nothing else but to be their general: and therefore the tribes who had stuck to Saul's family, and opposed David's reign, when they came to Hebron with terms of submission to him, they tell him, amongst other arguments, they had to submit to him as their king, that he was in effect their king in Saul's time, and therefore they had no reason but to receive him as their king now. "Also" (say they,) "in time past, when Saul was king over us, thou wast he that leddest out, and broughtest in Israel, and the Lord said unto thee, Thou shalt feed my people Israel, and thou shalt be a captain over Israel."

110. Thus, whether a family by degrees *grew up into a commonwealth*, and the fatherly authority being continued on to the elder son, every one in his turn growing up under it, tacitly submitted to it; and the easiness and equality of it not offending any one, every one acquiesced, till time seemed to have confirmed it, and settled a right of succession by prescription: or whether several families, or the descendants of several families, whom chance, neighbourhood, or business brought together, *uniting into society*, the need of a general, whose conduct might defend them against their enemies in war, and the great confidence the innocence and sincerity of that poor but virtuous age (such as are almost all those which begin governments, that ever come to last in the world), gave men of one another, made the first beginners of commonwealths generally put the rule into one man's hand, without any other express limitation or restraint, but what the nature of the thing and the end of government required: Whichever of those it was that at first put the rule into the hands of a single person, certain it is that no body was entrusted with it but for the public good and safety, and to those ends, in the infancies of commonwealths, those who had it, commonly used it. And unless they had done so, young societies could not have subsisted; without such nursing fathers tender and careful of the public weal, all governments would have sunk under the weakness and infirmities of their infancy, and the prince and the people had soon perished together.

111. But though the *golden age* (before vain ambition, and *amor sceleratus habendi*, evil concupiscence, had corrupted men's minds into a mistake of true power and honour) had more virtue, and consequently better governors, as well as less vicious subjects; and there was then *no stretching prerogative* on the one side, to oppress the people; nor consequently on the other, any *dispute about privilege*, to lessen or restrain the power of the magistrate; and so no contest betwixt rulers and people about governors or government: yet when ambition and luxury in future ages[6] would retain and increase the power, without doing the business for which it was given; and, aided by flattery, taught princes to have distinct and separate interests from their people; men found it necessary to examine more carefully the original and rights of government, and to find out ways to *restrain the exorbitancies*, and prevent the abuses of that power, which they having entrusted in another's hands only for their own good, they found was made use of to hurt them.

112. Thus we may see how probable it is, that people that were naturally free, and by their own consent either submitted to the government of their father, or united together out of different families to make a government, should generally put the *rule into one man's hands*, and choose to be under the conduct of a single person, without so much as by express conditions limiting or regulating his power, which they thought safe enough in his honesty and prudence. Though they never dreamed of monarchy being *jure divino*, which we never heard of among mankind, till it was revealed to us by the divinity of this last age; nor ever allowed paternal power to have a right to dominion, or to be the foundation of all government. And thus much may suffice to shew, that, as far as we have any light from history, we have reason to conclude, that all peaceful beginnings of government have been *laid in the consent of the people*. I say peaceful, because I shall have occasion in another place to speak of conquest, which some esteem a way of beginning of governments.

The other objection I find urged against the beginning of polities, in the way I have mentioned, is this, viz.

113. *That all men being born under government, some or other, it is impossible any of them should ever be free, and at liberty to unite together, and begin a new one, or ever be able to erect a lawful government.*

If this argument be good, I ask, how came so many lawful monarchies into the world? for if any body, upon this supposition, can shew me any one man in any age of the world free to begin a lawful monarchy, I will be bound to shew him ten other *free men* at liberty at the same time to unite and begin a new government under a regal or any other form. It being demonstration, that if any one, *born under the dominion* of another, may be so free as to have a right to command others in a new and distinct empire, every one that is *born under the dominion* of another may be so free too, and may become a ruler, or subject of a distinct separate government. And so by this their own principle, either all men, however born, are free, or else there is but one lawful prince, one lawful government in the world. And then they have

---

6. "At first, when some certain kind of regiment was once approved, it may be nothing was then farther thought upon for the manner of governing, but all permitted unto their wisdom and discretion which were to rule, till by experience they found this for all parts very inconvenient, so as the thing which they had devised for a remedy, did indeed but increase the sore which it should have cured. They saw, that to live by one man's will, became the cause of all men's misery. This constrained them to come unto laws wherein all men might see their duty beforehand, and know the penalties of transgressing them." Hooker's Eccl. Pol. L. I. Sect. 10.

nothing to do, but barely to shew us which that is; which when they have done, I doubt not but all mankind will easily agree to pay obedience to him.

114. Though it be a sufficient answer to their objection, to shew that it involves them in the same difficulties that it doth those they use it against; yet I shall endeavour to discover the weakness of this argument a little farther.

"All men," say they, "are born under government, and therefore they cannot be at liberty to begin a new one. Every one is born a subject to his father, or his prince, and is therefore under the perpetual tie of subjection and allegiance." It is plain mankind never owned nor considered any such natural *subjection that they were born in,* to one or to the other, that tied them, without their own consents, to a subjection to them and their heirs.

115. For there are no examples so frequent in history, both sacred and profane, as those of men withdrawing themselves, and their obedience from the jurisdiction they were born under, and the family or community they were bred up in, and *setting up new governments* in other places, from whence sprang all that number of petty commonwealths in the beginning of ages, and which always multiplied as long as there was room enough, till the stronger, or more fortunate, swallowed the weaker; and those great ones again breaking to pieces, dissolved into lesser dominions. All which are so many testimonies against paternal sovereignty, and plainly prove, that it was not the natural right of the father descending to his heirs, that made governments in the beginning, since it was impossible, upon that ground, there should have been so many little kingdoms; all must have been but only one universal monarchy, if men had not been *at liberty to separate themselves* from their families, and the government, be it what it will, that was set up in it, and go and make distinct commonwealths and other governments, as they thought fit.

116. This has been the practice of the world from its first beginning to this day; nor is it now any more hindrance to the freedom of mankind, that they are *born under constituted and ancient polities,* that have established laws, and set forms of government, than if they were born in the woods, amongst the unconfined inhabitants, that run loose in them. For those who would persuade us, that, *by being born under any government, we are naturally subjects to it,* and have no more any title or pretence to the freedom of the state of nature; have no other reason (bating that of paternal power, which we have already answered) to produce for it, but only, because our fathers or progenitors passed away their natural liberty, and thereby bound up themselves and their posterity to a perpetual subjection to the government which they themselves submitted to. It is true, that whatever engagements or promises any one has made for himself, he is under the obligation of them, but cannot, by any compact whatsoever, bind his children or posterity. For his son, when a man, being altogether as free as the father, any *act of the father can no more give away the liberty of the son,* than it can of any body else: he may indeed annex such conditions to the land he enjoyed as a subject of any commonwealth, as may oblige his son to be of that community, if he will enjoy those possessions which were his father's; because that estate being his father's property, he may dispose, or settle it, as he pleases.

117. And this has generally given the occasion to mistake in this matter; because commonwealths not permitting any part of their dominions to be dismembered, nor to be enjoyed by any but those of their community, the son cannot ordinarily enjoy the possessions of his father, but under the same terms his father did, by becoming a member of the society; whereby he puts himself presently under the government

he finds there established, as much as any other subject of that commonwealth. And thus *the consent of freemen, born under government, which only makes them members of it,* being given separately in their turns, as each comes to be of age, and not in a multitude together; people take no notice of it, and thinking it not done at all, or not necessary, conclude they are naturally subjects as they are men.

118. But, it is plain, governments themselves understand it otherwise; they claim *no power over the son, because of that they had over the father;* nor look on children as being their subjects, by their fathers being so. If a subject of England have a child, by an English woman in France, whose subject is he? Not the king of England's; for he must have leave to be admitted to the privileges of it. Nor the king of France's: for how then has his father a liberty to bring him away, and breed him as he pleases? And who ever was judged as a traitor or deserter, if he left, or warred against a country, for being barely born in it of parents that were aliens there? It is plain then, by the practice of governments themselves, as well as by the law of right reasons, that *a child is born a subject of no country or government.* He is under his father's tuition and authority, till he comes to age of discretion; and then he is a freeman, at liberty what government he will put himself under, what body politic he will unite himself to. For if an Englishman's son, born in France, be at liberty, and may do so, it is evident there is no tie upon him by his father's being a subject of this kingdom; nor is he bound up by any compact of his ancestors. And why then hath not his son, by the same reason, the same liberty, though he be born any where else? Since the power that a father hath naturally over his children is the same, wherever they be born, and the ties of natural obligations are not bounded by the positive limits of kingdoms and commonwealths.

119. Every man being, as has been shewed, naturally free, and nothing being able to put him into subjection to any earthly power, but only his own consent; it is to be considered, what shall be understood to be a *sufficient declaration of* a man's *consent, to make him subject* to the laws of any government. There is a common distinction of an express and a tacit consent, which will concern our present case. No body doubts but an express consent, of any man entering into any society, makes him a perfect member of that society, a subject of that government. The difficulty is, what ought to be looked upon as a *tacit consent,* and how far it binds, i.e. how far any one shall be looked on to have consented, and thereby submitted to any government, where he has made no expressions of it at all. And to this I say, that every man, that hath any possessions, or enjoyment of any part of the dominions of any government, doth thereby give his *tacit consent,* and is as far forth obliged to obedience to the laws of that government, during such enjoyment, as any one under it; whether this his possession be of land, to him and his heirs for ever, or a lodging only for a week; or whether it be barely travelling freely on the highway: and, in effect, it reaches as far as the very being of any one within the territories of that government.

120. To understand this the better, it is fit to consider, that every man, when he at first incorporates himself into any commonwealth, he, by his uniting himself thereunto, annexed also, and submits to the community, those possessions which he has, or shall acquire, that do not already belong to any other government. For it would be a direct contradiction, for any one to enter into society with others for the securing and regulating of property, and yet to suppose, his land, whose property is to be regulated by the laws of the society, should be exempt from the jurisdiction of that government, to which he himself, the proprietor of the land, is a subject. By

the same act therefore, whereby any one unites his person, which was before free, to any commonwealth; by the same he unites his possessions, which were before free, to it also: and they become, both of them, person and possession, subject to the government and dominion of that commonwealth, as long as it hath a being. Whoever therefore, from thenceforth, by inheritance, purchase, permission, or otherways, *enjoys any part of the land* so annexed to, and under the government *of that commonwealth, must take it with the condition* it is under; that is, *of submitting to the government of the commonwealth,* under whose jurisdiction it is, as far forth as any subject of it.

121. But since the government has a direct jurisdiction only over the land, and reaches the possessor of it, (before he has actually incorporated himself in the society) only as he dwells upon, and enjoys that; the obligation any one is under, by virtue of such enjoyment, to *submit to the government, begins and ends with the enjoyment:* so that whenever the owner, who has given nothing but such a tacit consent to the government, will, by donation, sale, or otherwise, quit the said possession, he is at liberty to go and incorporate himself into any other commonwealth; or to agree with others to begin a new one, *in vacuis locis,* in any part of the world they can find free and unpossessed: whereas he, that has once, by actual agreement, and any express declaration, given his *consent* to be of any commonwealth, is perpetually and indispensably obliged to be, and remain unalterably a subject to it, and can never be again in the liberty of the state of nature; unless, by any calamity, the government he was under comes to be dissolved, or else by some public act cuts him off from being any longer a member of it.

122. But submitting to the laws of any country, living quietly, and enjoying privileges and protection under them, *makes not a man a member of that society:* this is only a local protection and homage due to and from all those, who, not being in a state of war, come within the territories belonging to any government, to all parts whereof the force of its laws extends. But this no more *makes a man a member of that society,* a perpetual subject of that commonwealth, than it would make a man a subject to another, in whose family he found it convenient to abide for some time, though, whilst he continued in it, he were obliged to comply with the laws, and submit to the government he found there. And thus we see, that foreigners, by living all their lives under another government, and enjoying the privileges and protection of it, though they are bound, even in conscience, to submit to its administration, as far forth as any denison; yet do not thereby come to be *subjects or members of that commonwealth.* Nothing can make any man so, but his actually entering into it by positive engagement, and express promise and compact. This is that, which I think, concerning the beginning of political societies, and that *consent which makes any one a member of any commonwealth.*

CHAPTER IX
Of the Ends of Political Society and Government

123. If man in the state of nature be so free, as has been said; if he be absolute lord of his own person and possessions, equal to the greatest, and subject to no body, why will he part with his freedom? why will he give up this empire, and subject himself to the dominion and control of any other power? To which it is obvious to answer, that though in the state of nature he hath such a right, yet the enjoyment of it is very uncertain, and constantly exposed to the invasion of others. For all being

kings as much as he, every man his equal, and the greater part no strict observers of equity and justice, the enjoyment of the property he has in this state is very unsafe, very unsecure. This makes him willing to quit this condition, which, however free, is full of fears and continual dangers: and it is not without reason, that he seeks out, and is willing to join in society with others, who are already united, or have a mind to unite, for the mutual preservation of their lives, liberties, and estates, which I call by the general name, property.

124. The great and *chief end,* therefore, of men's uniting into commonwealths, and putting themselves under government, *is the preservation of their property.* To which in the state of nature there are many things wanting.

First, There wants an established, settled, known law, received and allowed by common consent to be the standard of right and wrong, and the common measure to decide all controversies between them. For though the law of nature be plain and intelligible to all rational creatures; yet men being biassed by their interest, as well as ignorant for want of studying it, are not apt to allow of it as a law binding to them in the application of it to their particular cases.

125. Secondly, In the state of nature there wants *a known and indifferent judge,* with authority to determine all differences according to the established law. For every one in that state being both judge and executioner of the law of nature, men being partial to themselves, passion and revenge is very apt to carry them too far, and with too much heat, in their own cases; as well as negligence, and unconcernedness, to make them too remiss in other men's.

126. Thirdly, In the state of nature, there often wants power to back and support the sentence when right, and to give it due execution. They who by any injustice offended, will seldom fail, where they are able, by force to make good their injustice; such resistance many times makes the punishment dangerous, and frequently destructive, to those who attempt it.

127. Thus mankind, notwithstanding all the privileges of the state of nature, being but in an ill condition, while they remain in it, are quickly driven into society. Hence it comes to pass that we seldom find any number of men live any time together in this state. The inconveniencies that they are therein exposed to, by the irregular and uncertain exercise of the power every man has of punishing the transgressions of others, make them take sanctuary under the established laws of government, and therein seek *the preservation of their property.* It is this makes them so willingly give up every one his single power of punishing, to be exercised by such alone, as shall be appointed to it amongst them; and by such rules as the community, or those authorized by them to that purpose, shall agree on. And in this we have the original *right and rise of both the legislative and executive power,* as well as of the governments and societies themselves.

128. For in the state of nature, to omit the liberty he has of innocent delights, a man has two powers.

The first is to do whatsoever he thinks fit for the preservation of himself and others within the permission of the *law of nature:* by which law, common to them all, he and all the rest of *mankind are one community,* make up one society, distinct from all other creatures. And, were it not for the corruption and viciousness of degenerate men, there would be no need of any other; no necessity that men should separate from this great and natural community, and by positive agreements combine into smaller and divided associations.

The other power a man has in the state of nature, is the *power to punish the crimes committed against that law.* Both these he gives up, when he joins in a private, if I may so call it, or particular politic society, and incorporates into any commonwealth, separate from the rest of mankind.

129. The first *power,* viz. *of doing whatsoever he thought fit for the preservation of himself,* and the rest of mankind, *he gives up* to be regulated by laws made by the society, so far forth as the preservation of himself and the rest of that society shall require; which laws of the society in many things confine the liberty he had by the law of nature.

130. *Secondly,* The *power of punishing he wholly gives up,* and engages his natural force, (which he might before employ in the execution of the law of nature, by his own single authority, as he thought fit) to assist the executive power of the society, as the law thereof shall require. For being now in a new state, wherein he is to enjoy many conveniencies, from the labour, assistance, and society of others in the same community, as well as protection from its whole strength; he is to part also, with as much of his natural liberty, in providing for himself, as the good, prosperity, and safety of the society shall require; which is not only necessary, but just, since the other members of the society do the like.

131. But though men, when they enter into society, give up the equality, liberty, and executive power they had in the state of nature, into the hands of the society, to be so far disposed of by the legislative, as the good of the society shall require; yet it being only with an intention in every one the better to preserve himself, his liberty and property; (for no rational creature can be supposed to change his condition with an intention to be worse) the power of the society, or legislative constituted by them, *can never be supposed to extend farther, than the common good;* but is obliged to secure every one's property, by providing against those three defects above mentioned, that made the state of nature so unsafe and uneasy. And so whoever has the legislative or supreme power of any commonwealth, is bound to govern by established standing laws, promulgated and known to the people, and not by extemporary decrees; by indifferent and upright judges, who are to decide controversies by those laws; and to employ the force of the community at home, *only in the execution of such laws;* or abroad to prevent or redress foreign injuries, and secure the community from inroads and invasion. And all this to be directed to no other *end,* but the *peace, safety,* and *public good* of the people.

CHAPTER X
Of the Forms of a Commonwealth

132. The majority having, as has been shewed, upon men's first uniting into society, the whole power of the community naturally in them, may employ all that power in making laws for the community from time to time, and executing those laws by officers of their own appointing; and then the *form* of the government is a perfect *democracy:* or else may put the power of making laws into the hands of a few select men, and their heirs or successors; and then it is an *oligarchy:* or else into the hands of one man, and then it is a *monarchy:* if to him and his heirs, it is an *hereditary monarchy:* if to him only for life, but upon his death the power only of nominating a successor to return to them; an *elective monarchy.* And so accordingly of these the community may make compounded and mixed forms of government, as they think good. And if the legislative power be at first given by the majority to one or more

persons only for their lives, or any limited time, and then the supreme power to revert to them again; when it is so reverted, the community may dispose of it again anew into what hands they please, and so constitute a new form of government. For the *form of government depending upon the placing* the supreme power, which is the *legislative* (it being impossible to conceive that an inferiour power should prescribe to a superiour, or any but the supreme make laws), according as the power of making laws is placed, such is the *form of the commonwealth*.

133. By commonwealth, I must be understood all along to mean, not a democracy, or any form of government, but *any independent community,* which the Latines signified by the word *civitas;* to which the word which best answers in our language, is *commonwealth,* and most properly expresses such a society of men, which community or city in English does not. For there may be subordinate communities in government; and city amongst us has quite a different notion from commonwealth: and therefore, to avoid ambiguity, I crave leave to use the word *commonwealth* in that sense, in which I find it used by King *James the first:* and I take it to be its genuine signification; which if any body dislike, I consent with him to change it for a better.

CHAPTER XI
Of the Extent of the Legislative Power

134. The great end of men's entering into society being the enjoyment of their properties in peace and safety, and the great instrument and means of that being the laws established in that society; the *first and fundamental positive law* of all commonwealths *is the establishing of the legislative* power; as the *first and fundamental natural law,* which is to govern even the legislative itself, *is the preservation of the society,* and (as far as will consist with the public good) of every person in it. This *legislative* is not only *the supreme power* of the commonwealth, but sacred and unalterable in the hands where the community have once placed it; nor can any edict of any body else, in what form soever conceived, or by what power soever backed, have the force and obligation of a law, which has not its *sanction from* that *legislative* which the public has chosen and appointed; for without this the law could not have that, which is absolutely necessary to its being a *law,*[7] *the consent of the society;* over whom no body can have a power to make laws, but by their own consent, and by authority received from them; and therefore all the obedience, which by the most solemn ties any one can be obliged to pay, ultimately terminates in this supreme power, and is directed by those laws which it enacts; nor can any oaths to any foreign power whatsoever, or any domestic subordinate power, discharge any member of the society from his *obedience to the legislative,* acting pursuant to their trust; nor oblige him to any obedience contrary to the laws so enacted, or farther than they do allow; it being

---

7. "The lawful power of making laws to command whole politic societies of men, belonging so properly unto the same entire societies, that for any prince or potentate of what kind soever upon earth, to exercise the same of himself, and not by express commission immediately and personally received from God, or else by authority derived at the first from their consent, upon whose persons they impose laws, it is no better than mere tyranny. Laws they are not therefore which public approbation hath not made so." Hooker's Eccl. Pol. L. I. Sect. 10. "Of this point therefore we are to note, that sith men naturally have no full and perfect power to command whole politic multitudes of men, therefore utterly without our consent, we could in such sort be at no man's commandment living. And to be commanded we do consent when that society, whereof we be a part, hath at any time before consented, without revoking the same after by the like universal agreement.

Laws therefore human, of what kind so ever, are available by consent." Ibid.

ridiculous to imagine one can be tied ultimately to obey any power in the society, which is not the supreme.

135. Though the legislative, whether placed in one or more, whether it be always in being, or only by intervals, though it be the supreme power in every commonwealth; yet,

First, It is *not*, nor can possibly be absolutely *arbitrary* over the lives and fortunes of the people. For it being but the joint power of every member of the society given up to that person, or assembly, which is legislator, it can be no more than those persons had in a state of nature before they entered into society, and gave up to the community. For no body can transfer to another more power than he has in himself; and no body has an absolute arbitrary power over himself, or over any other, to destroy his own life, or take away the life or property of another. A man, as has been proved, cannot subject himself to the arbitrary power of another; and having in the state of nature no arbitrary power over the life, liberty, or possession of another, but only so much as the law of nature gave him for the preservation of himself and the rest of mankind; this is all he doth, or can give up to the commonwealth, and by it to the legislative power, so that the legislative can have no more than this. Their power, in the utmost bounds of it, is *limited to the public good* of the society. It is a power, that hath no other end but preservation, and therefore can never[8] have a right to destroy, enslave, or designedly to impoverish the subjects. The obligations of the law of nature cease not in society, but only in many cases are drawn closer, and have by human laws known penalties annexed to them, to enforce their observation. Thus the law of nature stands as an eternal rule to all men, legislators as well as others. The rules that they make for other men's actions, must, as well as their own and other men's actions, be conformable to the law of nature, i.e. to the will of God, of which that is a declaration; and the *fundamental law of nature being the preservation of mankind*, no human sanction can be good or valid against it.

136. Secondly,[9] The legislative or supreme authority cannot assume to itself a power to rule, by extemporary, arbitrary decrees, but *is bound to dispense justice*, and decide the rights of the subject, *by promulgated, standing laws, and known authorised judges*. For the law of nature being unwritten, and so no-where to be found, but in the minds of men; they who through passion, or interest, shall miscite, or misapply it, cannot so easily be convinced of their mistake, where there is no established judge: and so it serves not, as it ought, to determine the rights, and fence the

---

8. "Two foundations there are which bear up public societies, the one a natural inclination, whereby all men desire sociable life and fellowship; the other an order, expressly or secretly agreed upon, touching the manner of their union in living together: the latter is that which we call the law of a commonweal, the very soul of a politic body, the parts whereof are by law animated, held together, and set on work in such actions as the common good requireth. Laws politic, ordained for external order and regiment amongst men, are never framed as they should be, unless presuming the will of man to be inwardly obstinate, rebellious, and averse from all obedience to the sacred laws of his nature; in a word, unless presuming man to be, in regard of his depraved mind, little better than a wild beast, they do accordingly provide notwithstanding, so to frame his outward actions, that they be no hindrance unto the common good, for which societies are instituted. Unless they do this, they are not perfect." Hooker's Eccl. Pol. L. I. Sect. 10.

9. "Human laws are measures in respect of men whose actions they must direct, howbeit such measures they are as have also their higher rules to be measured by, which rules are two, the law of God, and the law of nature; so that laws human must be made according to the general laws of nature, and without contradiction to any positive law of scripture, otherwise they are ill made." Hooker's Eccl. Pol. L. 3. Sect. 9.

"To constrain men to any thing inconvenient doth seem unreasonable." Ibid. L. I. Sect. 10.

properties of those that live under it; especially where every one is judge, interpreter, and executioner of it too, and that in his own case: and he that has right on his side, having ordinarily but his own single strength, hath not force enough to defend himself from injuries, or to punish delinquents. To avoid these inconveniencies, which disorder men's properties in the state of nature, men unite into societies, that they may have the united strength of the whole society to secure and defend their properties, and may have standing rules to bound it, by which every one may know what is his. To this end it is that men give up all their natural power to the society which they enter into, and the community put the legislative power into such hands as they think fit: with this trust, that they shall be governed by *declared laws*, or else their peace, quiet, and property will still be at the same uncertainty, as it was in the state of nature.

137. Absolute arbitrary power, or governing without *settled standing laws,* can neither of them consist with the ends of society and government, which men would not quit the freedom of the state of nature for, and tie themselves up under, were it not to preserve their lives, liberties, and fortunes, and by *stated rules* of right and property to secure their peace and quiet. It cannot be supposed that they should intend, had they a power so to do, to give to any one, or more, an *absolute arbitrary power* over their persons and estates, and put a force into the magistrate's hand to execute his unlimited will arbitrarily upon them. This were to put themselves into a worse condition than the state of nature, wherein they had a liberty to defend their right against the injuries of others, and were upon equal terms of force to maintain it, whether invaded by a single man, or many in combination. Whereas by supposing they have given up themselves to the absolute arbitrary power and will of a legislator, they have disarmed themselves, and armed him, to make a prey of them when he pleases. He being in a much worse condition, who is exposed to the arbitrary power of one man, who has the command of 100,000, than he that is exposed to the arbitrary power of 100,000 single men; no body being secure, that his will, who has such a command, is better than that of other men, though his force be 100,000 times stronger. And therefore, whatever form the commonwealth is under, the ruling power ought to govern by declared and received laws, and not by extemporary dictates and undetermined resolutions. For then mankind will be in a far worse condition than in the state of nature, if they shall have armed one or a few men with the joint power of a multitude, to force them to obey at pleasure the exorbitant and unlimited decrees of their sudden thoughts, or unrestrained, and till that moment unknown wills, without having any measures set down which may guide and justify their actions; for all the power the government has, being only for the good of the society, as it ought not to be arbitrary and at pleasure, so it ought to be exercised by *established and promulgated laws;* that both the people may know their duty, and be safe and secure within the limits of the law, and the rulers too kept within their bounds, and not to be tempted, by the power they have in their hands, to employ it to such purposes, and by such measures, as they would not have known, and own not willingly.

138. *Thirdly,* The *supreme power cannot take* from any man part of his property without his own consent. For the preservation of property being the end of government, and that for which men enter into society, it necessarily supposes and requires, that the people should *have property,* without which they must be supposed to lose that, by entering into society, which was the end for which they entered into it; too gross an absurdity for any man to own. *Men* therefore *in society having property,* they have such right to the goods, which by the law of the community are theirs, that no

body hath a right to take their substance or any part of it from them, without their own consent; without this they have no property at all. For I have truly no property in that, which another can by right take from me, when he pleases, against my consent. Hence it is a mistake to think, that the *supreme or legislative power* of any commonwealth can do what it will, and dispose of the estates of the subject arbitrarily, or take any part of them at pleasure. This is not much to be feared in governments where the legislative consists, wholly or in part, in assemblies which are variable, whose members, upon the dissolution of the assembly, are subjects under the common laws of their country, equally with the rest. But in governments, where the legislative is in one lasting assembly always in being, or in one man, as in absolute monarchies, there is danger still, that they will think themselves to have a distinct interest from the rest of the community; and so will be apt to increase their own riches and power by taking what they think fit from the people. For a man's property is not at all secure, though there be good and equitable laws to set the bounds of it between him and his fellow subjects, if he who commands those subjects, have power to take from any private man, what part he pleases of his property, and use and dispose of it as he thinks good.

139. But government, into whatsoever hands it is put, being, as I have before shewed, intrusted with this condition, and *for this end,* that men might have and secure their properties; the prince, or senate, however it may have power to make laws, for the regulating of property between the subjects one amongst another, yet can never have a power to take to themselves the whole, or any part of the subject's property, without their own consent. For this would be in effect to leave them no property at all. And to let us see, that even absolute power where it is necessary, is not arbitrary by being absolute, but is still limited by that reason, and confined to those ends, which required it in some cases to be absolute, we need look no farther than the common practice of martial discipline. For the preservation of the army, and in it of the whole commonwealth, requires an absolute obedience to the command of every superiour officer, and it is justly death to disobey or dispute the most dangerous or unreasonable of them; but yet we see, that neither the serjeant, that could command a soldier to march up to the mouth of a cannon, or stand in a breach, where he is almost sure to perish, can command that soldier to give him one penny of his money; nor the general, that can condemn him to death for deserting his post, or for not obeying the most desperate orders, can yet, with all his absolute power of life and death, dispose of one farthing of that soldier's estate, or seize one jot of his goods; whom yet he can command any thing, and hang for the least disobedience: because such a blind obedience is necessary to that end, for which the commander has his power, viz. the preservation of the rest; but the disposing of his goods has nothing to do with it.

140. It is true, governments cannot be supported without great charge, and it is fit every one who enjoys his share of the protection, should pay out of his estate his proportion for the maintenance of it. But still it must be with his own consent, i.e. the consent of the majority, giving it either by themselves, or their representatives chosen by them. For if any one shall claim a *power to lay* and levy *taxes* on the people, by his own authority, and without such consent of the people, he thereby invades the *fundamental law of property,* and subverts the end of government. For what property have I in that, which another may by right take when he pleases, to himself?

141. *Fourthly,* The *legislative cannot transfer the power of making laws* to any other hands. For it being but a delegated power from the people, they who have it cannot pass it over to others. The people alone can appoint the form of the commonwealth,

which is by constituting the legislative, and appointing in whose hands that shall be. And when the people have said, we will submit to rules, and be governed by laws made by such men, and in such forms, no body else can say other men shall make laws for them; nor can the people be bound by any laws, but such as are enacted by those whom they have chosen, and authorized to make laws for them. The power of the legislative being derived from the people by a positive voluntary grant and institution, can be no other than what that positive grant conveyed, which being only to make laws, and not to make legislators, the legislative can have no power to transfer their authority of making laws and place it in other hands.

142. These are the bounds which the trust, that is put in them by the society and the law of God and nature, have *set to the legislative* power of every commonwealth, in all forms of government.

First, They are to govern by *promulgated established laws,* not to be varied in particular cases, but to have one rule for rich and poor, for the favourite at court, and the countryman at plough.

Secondly, These laws also ought to be designed for no other end ultimately, but *the good of the people.*

Thirdly, They must *not raise taxes* on the *property of the people, without the consent of the people,* given by themselves or their deputies. And this properly concerns only such governments where the legislative is always in being, or at least where the people have not reserved any part of the legislative to deputies, to be from time to time chosen by themselves.

Fourthly, The legislative neither must *nor can transfer the power of making laws* to any body else, or place it any where, but where the people have.

CHAPTER XII
Of the Legislative, Executive, and Federative Power of the Commonwealth

143. The legislative power is that, which has a right *to direct how the force of the commonwealth* shall be employed for preserving the community and the members of it. But because those laws which are constantly to be executed, and whose force is always to continue, may be made in a little time; therefore there is no need, that the legislative should be always in being, not having always business to do. And because it may be too great a temptation to human frailty, apt to grasp at power, for the same persons, who have the power of making laws, to have also in their hands the power to execute them, whereby they may exempt themselves from obedience to the laws they make, and suit the law, both in its making and execution, to their own private advantage, and thereby come to have a distinct interest from the rest of the community, contrary to the end of society and government: therefore in well ordered commonwealths, where the good of the whole is so considered, as it ought, the legislative power is put into the hands of divers persons, who, duly assembled, have by themselves, or jointly with others, a power to make laws; which when they have done, being separated again, they are themselves subject to the laws they have made; which is a new and near tie upon them, to take care that they make them for the public good.

144. But because the laws, that are at once, and in a short time made, have a constant and lasting force, and need a *perpetual execution,* or an attendance thereunto: therefore it is necessary there should be a *power always in being,* which should see to

the execution of the laws that are made, and remain in force. And thus the legislative and executive power come often to be separated.

145. There is another power in every commonwealth, which one may call *natural,* because it is that which answers to the power every man naturally had before he entered into society. For though in a commonwealth, the members of it are distinct persons still in reference to one another, and as such are governed by the laws of the society; yet in reference to the rest of mankind, they make one body, which is, as every member of it before was, still in the state of nature with the rest of mankind. Hence it is, that the controversies that happen between any man of the society with those that are out of it, are managed by the public; and an injury done to a member of their body engages the whole in the reparation of it. So that, under this consideration, the whole community is one body in the state of nature, in respect of all other states or persons out of its community.

146. This therefore contains the power of war and peace, leagues and alliances, and all the transactions, with all persons and communities without the commonwealth; and may be called federative, if any one pleases. So the thing be understood, I am indifferent as to the name.

147. These two powers, executive and federative, though they be really distinct in themselves, yet one comprehending the execution of the municipal laws of the society within itself, upon all that are parts of it; the other the management of the *security and interest of the public without,* with all those that it may receive benefit or damage from; yet they are always almost united. And though this *federative power* in the well or ill management of it be of great moment to the commonwealth, yet it is much less capable to be directed by antecedent, standing, positive laws, than the executive; and so must necessarily be left to the prudence and wisdom of those whose hands it is in, to be managed for the public good. For the laws that concern subjects one amongst another, being to direct their actions, may well enough precede them. But what is to be done in reference to foreigners, depending much upon their actions, and the variation of designs, and interests, must be left in great part to the prudence of those who have this power committed to them, to be managed by the best of their skill, for the advantage of the commonwealth.

148. Though, as I said, the executive and federative power of every community be really distinct in themselves, yet they are hardly to be separated, and placed at the same time in the hands of distinct persons. For both of them requiring the force of the society for their exercise, it is almost impracticable to place the force of the commonwealth in distinct, and not subordinate hands; or that the executive and federative power should be placed in persons that might act separately, whereby the force of the public would be under different commands: which would be apt some time or other to cause disorder and ruin.

CHAPTER XIII
Of the Subordination of the Powers of the Commonwealth

149. Though in a constituted commonwealth, standing upon its own basis, and acting according to its own nature, that is, acting for the preservation of the community, there can be but *one supreme power,* which is the *legislative,* to which all the rest are and must be subordinate; yet the legislative being only a fiduciary power to act for certain ends, there remains still *in the people a supreme power to remove or alter the*

legislative, when they find the legislative act contrary to the trust reposed in them. For all *power given with trust* for the attaining an end, being limited by that end; whenever that end is manifestly neglected or opposed, the trust must necessarily be forfeited, and the power devolve into the hands of those that gave it, who may place it anew where they shall think best for their safety and security. And thus the *community* perpetually *retains a supreme power* of saving themselves from the attempts and designs of any body, even of their legislators, whenever they shall be so foolish, or so wicked, as to lay and carry on designs against the liberties and properties of the subject. For no man, or society of men, having a power to deliver up their preservation, or consequently the means of it, to the absolute will and arbitrary dominion of another; whenever any one shall go about to bring them into such a slavish condition, they will always have a right to preserve what they have not a power to part with; and to rid themselves of those who invade this fundamental, sacred, and unalterable law of self-preservation, for which they entered into society. And thus the community may be said in this respect to be *always the supreme power,* but not as considered under any form of government, because this power of the people can never take place till the government be dissolved.

150. In all cases, whilst the government subsists, the *legislative is the supreme power.* For what can give laws to another, must needs be superiour to him; and since the legislative is no otherwise legislative of the society, but by the right it has to make laws for all the parts, and for every member of the society, prescribing rules to their actions, and giving power of execution, where they are transgressed; the legislative must needs be the supreme, and all other powers, in any members or parts of the society, derived from and subordinate to it.

151. In some commonwealths, where the legislative is not always in being, and the executive is vested in a single person, who has also a share in the legislative; there that single person in a very tolerable sense may also be called supreme; not that he has in himself all the supreme power, which is that of law-making; but because he has in him the supreme execution, from whom all inferiour magistrates derive all their several subordinate powers, or at least the greatest part of them: having also no legislative superiour to him, there being no law to be made without his consent, which cannot be expected should ever subject him to the other part of the legislative, he is properly enough in this sense *supreme.* But yet it is to be observed, that though *oaths of allegiance* and fealty are taken to him, it is not to him as supreme legislator, but as *supreme executor* of the law, made by a joint power of him with others: allegiance being nothing but an *obedience according to law,* which when he violates, he has no right to obedience, nor can claim it otherwise, than as the public person invested with the power of the law; and so is to be considered as the image, phantom, or representative of the commonwealth, acted by the will of the society, declared in its laws; and thus he has no will, no power, but that of the law. But when he quits this representation, this public will, and acts by his own private will, he degrades himself, and is but a single private person without power, and without will, that has no right to obedience; the members owing no obedience but to the public will of the society.

152. The *executive power,* placed any where but in a person that has also a share in the legislative, is visibly subordinate and accountable to it, and may be at pleasure changed and displaced; so that it is not the *supreme executive power* that is exempt from subordination, but the *supreme executive power* vested in one, who having a share in the legislative, has no distinct superiour legislative to be subordinate and

accountable to, farther than he himself shall join and consent; so that he is no more subordinate than he himself shall think fit, which one may certainly conclude will be but very little. Of other ministerial and subordinate powers in a commonwealth, we need not speak, they being so multiplied with infinite variety in the different customs and constitutions of distinct commonwealths, that it is impossible to give a particular account of them all. Only thus much, which is necessary to our present purpose, we may take notice of concerning them, that they have no manner of authority, any of them, beyond what is by positive grant and commission delegated to them, and are all of them accountable to some other power in the commonwealth.

153. It is not necessary, no, nor so much as convenient, that the *legislative* should be *always in being*. But absolutely necessary that the executive power should; because there is not always need of new laws to be made, but always need of execution of the laws that are made. When the legislative hath put the execution of the laws they make into other hands, they have a power still to resume it out of those hands, when they find cause, and to punish for any mall-administration against the laws. The same holds also in regard of the federative power, that and the executive being both *ministerial and subordinate to the legislative,* which, as has been shewed, in a constituted commonwealth is the supreme. The legislative also in this case being supposed to consist of several persons, (for if it be a single person, it cannot but be always in being, and so will, as supreme, naturally have the supreme executive power, together with the legislative) may *assemble, and exercise their legislature,* at the times that either their original constitution, or their own adjournment, appoints, or when they please; if neither of these hath appointed any time, or there be no other way prescribed to convoke them. For the supreme power being placed in them by the people, it is always in them, and they may exercise it when they please, unless by their original constitution they are limited to certain seasons, or by an act of their supreme power they have adjourned to a certain time; and when that time comes, they have a right to assemble and act again.

154. If the legislative, or any part of it, be made up of representatives chosen for that time by the people, which afterwards return into the ordinary state of subjects, and have no share in the legislature but upon a new choice, this power of choosing must also be exercised by the people, either at certain appointed seasons, or else when they are summoned to it; and in this latter case the power of convoking the legislative is ordinarily placed in the executive, and has one of these two limitations in respect of time: that either the original constitution requires their assembling and acting at certain intervals, and then the executive power does nothing but ministerially issue directions for their electing and assembling according to due forms; or else it is left to his prudence to call them by new elections, when the occasions, or exigencies of the public require the amendment of old, or making of new laws, or the redress or prevention of any inconveniencies, that lie on, or threaten the people.

155. It may be demanded here, What if the executive power, being possessed of the force of the commonwealth, shall make use of that force to hinder the *meeting* and *acting of the legislative;* when the original constitution, or the public exigencies require it? I say, using force upon the people without authority, and contrary to the trust put in him that does so, is a state of war with the people, who have a right to *reinstate* their *legislative in the exercise* of their power. For having erected a legislative, with an intent they should exercise the power of making laws, either at certain set

times, or when there is need of it; when they are hindered by any force from what is so necessary to the society, and wherein the safety and preservation of the people consists, the people have a right to remove it by force. In all states and conditions, the true remedy of force without authority, is to oppose force to it. The use of force without authority, always puts him that uses it into a *state of war*, as the aggressor; and renders him liable to be treated accordingly.

156. The *power of assembling and dismissing the legislative*, placed in the executive, gives not the executive a superiority over it, but is a fiduciary trust placed in him for the safety of the people, in a case where the uncertainty and variableness of human affairs could not bear a steady fixed rule. For it not being possible that the first framers of the government should, by any foresight, be so much masters of future events as to be able to prefix so just periods of return and duration to the *assemblies of the legislative,* in all times to come, that might exactly answer all the exigencies of the commonwealth; the best remedy could be found for this defect was to trust this to the prudence of one who was always to be present, and whose business it was to watch over the public good. Constant *frequent meetings of the legislative,* and long continuations of their assemblies, without necessary occasion, could not but be burdensome to the people, and must necessarily in time produce more dangerous inconveniencies, and yet the quick turn of affairs might be sometimes such as to need their present help: any delay of their convening might endanger the public; and sometimes too their business might be so great, that the limited time of their sitting might be too short for their work, and rob the public of that benefit which could be had only from their mature deliberation. What then could be done in this case to prevent the community from being exposed some time or other to eminent hazard, on one side or the other, by fixed intervals and periods, set to the *meeting and acting of the legislative;* but to intrust it to the prudence of some, who being present, and acquainted with the state of public affairs, might make use of this prerogative for the public good? And where else could this be so well placed as in his hands, who was intrusted with the execution of the laws for the same end? Thus supposing the regulation of times for the *assembling and sitting of the legislative* not settled by the original constitution, it naturally fell into the hands of the executive, not as an arbitrary power depending on his good pleasure, but with this trust always to have it exercised only for the public weal, as the occurrences of times and change of affairs might require. Whether *settled periods of their convening,* or *a liberty* left to the prince for *convoking the legislative,* or perhaps a mixture of both, hath the least inconvenience attending it, it is not my business here to inquire; but only to shew, that though the executive power may have the prerogative of *convoking* and *dissolving* such *conventions of the legislative,* yet it is not thereby superior to it.

157. Things of this world are in so constant a flux, that nothing remains long in the same state. Thus people, riches, trade, power, change their stations, flourishing mighty cities come to ruin, and prove in time neglected desolate corners, whilst other unfrequented places grow into populous countries, filled with wealth and inhabitants. But things not always changing equally, and private interest often keeping up customs and privileges, when the reasons of them are ceased; it often comes to pass, that in governments, where part of the legislative consists of representatives chosen by the people, that in tract of time this representation becomes very unequal and disproportionate to the reasons it was at first established upon. To what gross absurdities the following of custom, when reason has left it, may lead, we may be satisfied, when we see the bare name of a town, of which there remains not so

much as the ruins, where scarce so much housing as a sheepcote, or more inhabitants than a shepherd is to be found, sends *as many representatives* to the grand assembly of law-makers, as a whole county numerous in people, and powerful in riches. This strangers stand amazed at, and every one must confess needs a remedy. Though most think it hard to find one; because the constitution of the legislative being the original and supreme act of the society, antecedent to all positive laws in it, and depending wholly on the people, no inferiour power can alter it. And therefore the people, when the legislative is once constituted, having, in such a government as we have been speaking of, no power to act as long as the government stands; this inconvenience is thought incapable of a remedy.

158. *Salus populi suprema lex,* is certainly so just and fundamental a rule, that he, who sincerely follows it, cannot dangerously err. If therefore the executive, who has the power of convoking the legislative, observing rather the true proportion than fashion of representation, regulates not by old custom, but true reason, the *number of members* in all places that have a right to be distinctly represented, which no part of the people, however incorporated, can pretend to, but in proportion to the assistance which it affords to the public; it cannot be judged to have set up a new legislative, but to have restored the old and true one, and to have rectified the disorders which succession of time had insensibly, as well as inevitably introduced. For it being the interest as well as intention of the people, to have a fair and equal representative; whoever brings it nearest to that, is an undoubted friend to, and establisher of the government, and cannot miss the consent and approbation of the community. Prerogative being nothing but a power in the hands of the prince to provide for the public good, in such cases, which depending upon unforeseen and uncertain occurrences, certain and unalterable laws could not safely direct; whatsoever shall be done manifestly for the good of the people, and the establishing the government upon its true foundations, is, and always will be, just *prerogative.* The power of erecting new corporations, and therewith *new representatives,* carries with it a supposition that in time the *measures of representation* might vary, and those places have a just right to be represented which before had none; and by the same reason, those cease to have a right, and be too inconsiderable for such a privilege, which before had it. It is not a change from the present state, which perhaps corruption or decay has introduced, that makes an inroad upon the government; but the tendency of it to injure or oppress the people, and to set up one part or party, with a distinction from, and an unequal subjection of the rest. Whatsoever cannot but be acknowledged to be of advantage to the society, and people in general, upon just and lasting measures, will always, when done, justify itself; and whenever the people shall choose their *representatives upon* just and undeniably *equal measures,* suitable to the original frame of the government, it cannot be doubted to be the will and act of the society, whoever permitted or caused them so to do.

CHAPTER XIV
Of Prerogative

159. Where the legislative and executive power are in distinct hands, (as they are in all moderated monarchies and well-framed governments) there the good of the society requires, that several things should be left to the discretion of him that has the executive power. For the legislators not being able to foresee, and provide by laws, for all that may be useful to the community, the executor of the laws having

the power in his hands, has by the common law of nature a right to make use of it for the good of the society, in many cases, where the municipal law has given no direction, till the legislative can conveniently be assembled to provide for it. Many things there are, which the law can by no means provide for; and those must necessarily be left to the discretion of him that has the executive power in his hands, to be ordered by him as the public good and advantage shall require: nay, it is fit that the laws themselves should in some cases give way to the executive power, or rather to this fundamental law of nature and government, viz. That, as much as may be, all the members of the society are to be preserved. For since many accidents may happen, wherein a strict and rigid observation of the laws may do harm; (as not to pull down an innocent man's house to stop the fire, when the next to it is burning) and a man may come sometimes within the reach of the law, which makes no distinction of persons, by an action that may deserve reward and pardon; it is fit the ruler should have a power, in many cases, to mitigate the severity of the law, and pardon some offenders. For the *end of government* being the *preservation of all,* as much as may be, even the guilty are to be spared, where it can prove no prejudice to the innocent.

160. This power to act according to discretion, for the public good, without the prescription of the law, and sometimes even against it, is that which is called *prerogative.* For since in some governments the lawmaking power is not always in being, and is usually too numerous, and so too slow for the dispatch requisite to execution; and because also it is impossible to foresee, and so by laws to provide for all accidents and necessities that may concern the public, or to make such laws as will do no harm, if they are executed with an inflexible rigour on all occasions, and upon all persons that may come in their way; therefore there is a latitude left to the executive power, to do many things of choice which the laws do not prescribe.

161. This power, whilst employed for the benefit of the community, and suitably to the trust and ends of the government, *is undoubted prerogative,* and never is questioned. For the people are very seldom or never scrupulous or nice in the point; they are far from examining prerogative, whilst it is in any tolerable degree employed for the use it was meant; that is, for the good of the people, and not manifestly against it. But if there comes to be a *question* between the executive power and the people, about a thing claimed as a *prerogative,* the tendency of the exercise of such prerogative to the good or hurt of the people will easily decide that question.

162. It is easy to conceive, that in the infancy of governments, when commonwealths differed little from families in number of people, they differed from them too but little in number of laws: and the governors being as the fathers of them, watching over them, for their good, the government was almost all prerogative. A few established laws served the turn, and the discretion and care of the ruler supplied the rest. But when mistake or flattery prevailed with weak princes to make use of this power for private ends of their own, and not for the public good, the people were fain by express laws to get prerogative determined in those points wherein they found disadvantage from it: and thus declared *limitations of prerogative* were by the people found necessary in cases which they and their ancestors had left, in the utmost latitude, to the wisdom of those princes who made no other but a right use of it; that is, for the good of their people.

163. And therefore they have a very wrong notion of government, who say, that the people have *encroached upon the prerogative,* when they have got any part

of it to be defined by positive laws. For in so doing they have not pulled from the prince any thing that of right belonged to him, but only declared, that that power which they indefinitely left in his or his ancestors hands, to be exercised for their good, was not a thing which they intended him when he used it otherwise. For the end of government being the good of the community, whatsoever alterations are made in it, tending to that end, cannot be an encroachment upon any body, since no body in government can have a right tending to any other end: and those only are encroachments which prejudice or hinder the public good. Those who say otherwise, speak as if the prince had a distinct and separate interest from the good of the community, and was not made for it; the root and source from which spring almost all those evils and disorders which happen in kingly governments. And indeed, if that be so, the people under his government are not a society of rational creatures, entered into a community for their mutual good; they are not such as have set rulers over themselves, to guard and promote that good; but are to be looked on as an herd of inferior creatures under the dominion of a master, who keeps them and works them for his own pleasure or profit. If men were so void of reason, and brutish, as to enter into society upon such terms, prerogative might indeed be, what some men would have it, an arbitrary power to do things hurtful to the people.

164. But since a rational creature cannot be supposed, when free, to put himself into subjection to another, for his own harm; (though, where he finds a good and wise ruler, he may not perhaps think it either necessary or useful to set precise bounds to his power in all things) prerogative can be nothing but the people's permitting their rulers to do several things, of their own free choice, where the law was silent, and sometimes too against the direct letter of the law, for the public good; and their acquiescing in it when so done. For as a good prince, who is mindful of the trust put into his hands, and careful of the good of his people, cannot have too much prerogative, that is, power to do good; so a weak and ill prince, who would claim that power which his predecessors exercised without the direction of the law, as a prerogative belonging to him by right of his office, which he may exercise at his pleasure, to make or promote an interest distinct from that of the public, gives the people an occasion to claim their right, and limit that power, which, whilst it was exercised for their good, they were content should be tacitly allowed.

165. And therefore he that will look into the *history of England,* will find, that prerogative was always *largest* in the hands of our wisest and best princes; because the people, observing the whole tendency of their actions to be the public good, contested not what was done without law to that end: or, if any human frailty or mistake (for princes are but men, made as others) appeared in some small declinations from that end; yet it was visible, the main of their conduct tended to nothing but the care of the public. The people therefore, finding reason to be satisfied with these princes, whenever they acted without, or contrary to the letter of the law, acquiesced in what they did, and without the least complaint, let them enlarge their prerogative as they pleased; judging rightly, that they did nothing herein to the prejudice of their laws, since they acted conformably to the foundation and end of all laws, the public good.

166. Such God-like princes indeed had some title to arbitrary power by that argument, that would prove absolute monarchy the best government, as that which God himself governs the universe by; because such kings partook of his wisdom and

goodness. Upon this is founded that saying, That the reigns of good princes have been always most dangerous to the liberties of their people. For when their successors, managing the government with different thoughts, would draw the actions of those good rulers into precedent, and make them the standard of their prerogative, as if what had been done only for the good of the people was a right in them to do, for the harm of the people, if they so pleased; it has often occasioned contest, and sometimes public disorders, before the people could recover their original right, and get that to be declared not to be prerogative, which truly was never so: since it is impossible that any body in the society should ever have a right to do the people harm; though it be very possible, and reasonable, that the people should not go about to set any bounds to the prerogative of those kings, or rulers, who themselves transgressed not the bounds of the public good. For *prerogative is nothing but the power of doing public good without a rule.*

167. The power of calling parliaments in England, as to precise time, place, and duration, is certainly a prerogative of the king, but still with this trust, that it shall be made use of for the good of the nation, as the exigencies of the times, and variety of occasions, shall require. For it being impossible to foresee which should always be the fittest place for them to assemble in, and what the best season, the choice of these was left with the executive power, as might be most subservient to the public good, and best suit the ends of parliaments.

168. The old question will be asked in this matter of prerogative, "But who shall be judge when this power is made a right use of?" I answer: between an executive power in being, with such a prerogative, and a legislative that depends upon his will for their convening, there can be no *judge on earth;* as there can be none between the legislative and the people, should either the executive or the legislative, when they have got the power in their hands, design, or go about to enslave or destroy them. The people have no other remedy in this, as in all other cases where they have no judge on earth, but to *appeal to heaven.* For the rulers, in such attempts, exercising a power the people never put into their hands, (who can never be supposed to consent that any body should rule over them for their harm) do that which they have not a right to do. And where the body of the people, or any single man, is deprived of their right, or is under the exercise of a power without right, and have no appeal on earth, then they have a liberty to appeal to heaven, whenever they judge the cause of sufficient moment. And therefore, *though the people cannot* be *judge,* so as to have, by the constitution of that society, any superior power to determine and give effective sentence in the case; yet they have, by a law antecedent and paramount to all positive laws of men, reserved that ultimate determination to themselves which belongs to all mankind, where there lies no appeal on earth, viz. to judge, whether they have just cause to make their appeal to heaven. And this judgment they cannot part with, it being out of a man's power so to submit himself to another, as to give him a liberty to destroy him; God and nature never allowing a man so to abandon himself, as to neglect his own preservation: and since he cannot take away his own life, neither can he give another power to take it. Nor let any one think, this lays a perpetual foundation for disorder; for this operates not, till the inconveniency is so great, that the majority feel it, and are weary of it, and find a necessity to have it amended. But this the executive power, or wise princes, never need come in the danger of: and it is the thing, of all others, they have most need to avoid, as of all others the most perilous.

CHAPTER XV
Of Paternal, Political, and Despotical Power, Considered Together

169. Though I have had occasion to speak of these separately before, yet the great mistakes of late about government having, as I suppose, arisen from confounding these distinct powers one with another, it may not, perhaps, be amiss to consider them here together.

170. *First*, then, *Paternal* or *parental power* is nothing but that which parents have over their children, to govern them for the children's good, till they come to the use of reason, or a state of knowledge, wherein they may be supposed capable to understand that rule, whether it be the law of nature, or the municipal law of their country, they are to govern themselves by: capable, I say, to know it, as well as several others, who live as freemen under that law. The affection and tenderness which God hath planted in the breast of parents towards their children, makes it evident that this is not intended to be a severe arbitrary government, but only for the help, instruction, and preservation of their offspring. But happen it as it will, there is, as I have proved, no reason why it should be thought to extend to life and death, at any time, over their children, more than over any body else; neither can there be any pretence why this *parental power* should keep the child, when grown to a man, in subjection to the will of his parents, any farther than having received life and education from his parents, obliges him to respect, honour, gratitude, assistance and support, all his life, to both father and mother. And thus, it is true, the paternal is a natural government, but not at all extending itself to the ends and jurisdictions of that which is political. The *power of the father doth not reach* at all to the *property* of the child, which is only in his own disposing.

171. *Secondly, Political power* is that power which every man having in the state of nature, has given up into the hands of the society, and therein to the governors, whom the society hath set over itself, with this express or tacit trust, that it shall be employed for their good, and the preservation of their property: now this *power,* which every man has *in the state of nature,* and which he parts with to the society in all such cases where the society can secure him, is to use such means for the preserving of his own property, as he thinks good, and nature allows him; and to punish the breach of the law of nature in others, so as (according to the best of his reason) may most conduce to the preservation of himself, and the rest of mankind. So that the *end and measure of this power,* when in every man's hands in the state of nature, being the preservation of all of his society, that is, all mankind in general; it can have no other *end or measure,* when in the hands of the magistrate, but to preserve the members of that society in their lives, liberties, and possessions; and so cannot be an absolute arbitrary power, over their lives and fortunes, which are as much as possible to be preserved; but a *power to make laws,* and annex such penalties to them, as may tend to the preservation of the whole, by cutting off those parts, and those only, which are so corrupt, that they threaten the sound and healthy, without which no severity is lawful. And this *power has its original only from compact* and agreement, and the mutual consent of those who make up the community.

172. Thirdly, Despotical power is an absolute, arbitrary power; one man has over another, to take away his life, whenever he pleases. This is a power, which neither nature gives, for it has made no such distinction between one man and another; nor compact can convey. For man not having such an arbitrary power over his own life,

cannot give another man such a power over it; but it is *the effect only of forfeiture* which the aggressor makes of his own life, when he puts himself into the state of war with another. For having quitted reason, which God hath given to be the rule betwixt man and man, and the common bond whereby human kind is united into one fellowship and society; and having renounced the way of peace which that teaches, and made use of the force of war, to compass his unjust ends upon another, where he has no right; and so revolting from his own kind to that of beasts, by making force, which is theirs, to be his rule of right; he renders himself liable to be destroyed by the injured person, and the rest of mankind, that will join with him in the execution of justice, as any other wild beast, or noxious brute, with whom mankind can have neither society nor security.[10] And thus *captives*, taken in a just and lawful war, and such only, are *subject to a despotical power;* which, as it arises not from compact, so neither is it capable of any, but is the state of war continued. For what compact can be made with a man that is not master of his own life? What condition can he perform? And if he be once allowed to be master of his own life, the *despotical arbitrary power* of his master ceases. He that is master of himself; and his own life, has a right too to the means of preserving it; so that, *as soon as compact enters, slavery ceases,* and he so far quits his absolute power, and puts an end to the state of war, who enters into conditions with his captive.

173. Nature gives the first of these, viz. *paternal power, to parents* for the benefit of their children during their minority, to supply their want of ability and understanding how to manage their property. (By property I must be understood here, as in other places, to mean that property which men have in their persons as well as goods.) *Voluntary agreement gives* the second, *viz. political power to governors* for the benefit of their subjects, to secure them in the possession and use of their properties. And *forfeiture gives* the third *despotical power to lords,* for their own benefit, over those who are stripped of all property.

174. He, that shall consider the distinct rise and extent, and the different ends of these several powers, will plainly see, that *paternal power* comes as far short of that of the *magistrate,* as *despotical* exceeds it; and that *absolute dominion,* however placed, is so far from being one kind of civil society, that it is as inconsistent with it, as slavery is with property. *Paternal power* is only where minority makes the child incapable to manage his property; *political,* where men have property in their own disposal; and *despotical,* over such as have no property at all.

CHAPTER XVI
Of Conquest

175. Though governments can originally have no other rise than that beforementioned, nor *polities* be *founded* on any thing but *the consent of the people;* yet such have been the disorders ambition has filled the world with, that in the noise of war, which makes so great a part of the history of mankind, *this consent* is little taken notice of: and therefore many have mistaken the force of arms for the consent of the people, and reckon conquest as one of the originals of government. But conquest is as far from setting up any government, as demolishing an house is from building a new one in the place. Indeed, it often makes way for a new frame of a common-

---

10. Another copy, corrected by Mr. Locke, has it thus, "Noxious brute that is destructive to their being."

wealth, by destroying the former; but, without the consent of the people, can never erect a new one.

176. That the *aggressor*, who puts himself into the state of war with another, and *unjustly invades* another man's right, can, by such an unjust war, *never* come to *have a right over the conquered*, will be easily agreed by all men, who will not think, that robbers and pirates have a right of empire over whomsoever they have force enough to master; or that men are bound by promises, which unlawful force extorts from them. Should a robber break into my house, and with a dagger at my throat, make me seal deeds to convey my estate to him, would this give him any title? Just such a title, by his sword, has an *unjust conqueror,* who forces me into submission. The injury and the crime are equal, whether committed by the wearer of the crown, or some petty villain. The title of the offender, and the number of his followers, make no difference in the offence, unless it be to aggravate it. The only difference is, great robbers punish little ones, to keep them in their obedience; but the great ones are rewarded with laurels and triumphs; because they are too big for the weak hands of justice in this world, and have the power in their own possession, which should punish offenders. What is my remedy against a robber, that so broke into my house? Appeal to the law for justice. But perhaps justice is denied, or I am crippled and cannot stir, robbed and have not the means to do it. If God has taken away all means of seeking remedy, there is nothing left but patience. But my son, when able, may seek the relief of the law, which I am denied: he or his son may renew his appeal, till he recover his right. But the conquered, or their children, have no court, no arbitrator on earth to appeal to. Then they may appeal, as Jephthah did, to heaven, and repeat their appeal till they have recovered the native right of their ancestors, which was, to have such a legislative over them, as the majority should approve, and freely acquiesce in. If it be objected, this would cause endless trouble; I answer, no more than justice does, where she lies open to all that appeal to her. He that troubles his neighbour without a cause, is punished for it by the justice of the court he appeals to. And he that *appeals to heaven* must be sure he has right on his side; and a right too that is worth the trouble and cost of the appeal, as he will answer at a tribunal that cannot be deceived, and will be sure to retribute to every one according to the mischiefs he hath created to his fellow-subjects; that is, any part of mankind: from whence it is plain, that he that *conquers in an unjust war, can thereby have no title to the subjection and obedience of the conquered.*

177. But supposing victory favours the right side, let us consider *a conqueror in a lawful war,* and see what power he gets, and over *whom.*

First, it is plain, *he gets no power by his conquest over those that conquered with him.* They that fought on his side cannot suffer by the conquest, but must at least be as much freemen as they were before. And most commonly they serve upon terms, and on conditions to share with their leader, and enjoy a part of the spoil, and other advantages that attended the conquering sword; or at least have a part of the subdued country bestowed upon them. And *the conquering people are not, I hope, to be slaves by conquest,* and wear their laurels only to shew they are sacrifices to their leader's triumph. They that found absolute monarchy upon the title of the sword, make their heroes, who are the founders of such monarchies, arrant Drawcansirs, and forget they had any officers and soldiers that fought on their side in the battles they won, or assisted them in the subduing, or shared in possessing, the countries they mastered. We are told by some, that the English monarchy is founded in the

Norman conquest, and that our princes have thereby a title to absolute dominion: which if it were true, (as by the history it appears otherwise) and that William had a right to make war on this island; yet his dominion by conquest could reach no farther than to the Saxons and Britons, that were then inhabitants of this country. The Normans that came with him, and helped to conquer, and all descended from them, are freemen, and no subjects by conquest, let that give what dominion it will. And if I, or any body else, shall claim freedom, as derived from them, it will be very hard to prove the contrary; and it is plain, the law, that has made no distinction between the one and the other, intends not there should be any difference in their freedom or privileges.

178. But supposing, which seldom happens, that the conquerors and conquered never incorporate into one people, under the same laws and freedom. Let us see next *what power a lawful conqueror has over the subdued;* and that I say is purely despotical. He has an absolute power over the lives of those who by an unjust war have forfeited them; but not over the lives or fortunes of those who engaged not in the war, nor over the possessions even of those who were actually engaged in it.

179. Secondly, I say then the conqueror gets no power but only over those who have actually assisted, concurred, or consented to that unjust force that is used against him. For the people having given to their governors no power to do an unjust thing, such as is to make an unjust war, (for they never had such a power in themselves) they ought not to be charged as guilty of the violence and injustice that is committed in an unjust war, any farther than they actually abet it; no more than they are to be thought guilty of any violence or oppression their governors should use upon the people themselves, or any part of their fellow-subjects, they having impowered them no more to the one than to the other. Conquerors, it is true, seldom trouble themselves to make the distinction, but they willingly permit the confusion of war to sweep all together: but yet this alters not the right; for the conqueror's power over the lives of the conquered being only because they have used force to do, or maintain an injustice, he can have that power only over those who have concurred in that force; all the rest are innocent; and he has no more title over the people of that country, who have done him no injury, and so have made no forfeiture of their lives, than he has over any other, who without any injuries or provocations, have lived upon fair terms with him.

180. *Thirdly,* The *power a conqueror gets* over those he overcomes *in a just war, is perfectly despotical:* he has an absolute power over the lives of those, who, by putting themselves in a state of war, have forfeited them; but he has not thereby a right and title to their possessions. This I doubt not but at first sight will seem a strange doctrine, it being so quite contrary to the practice of the world; there being nothing more familiar in speaking of the dominion of countries, than to say such an one conquered it. As if conquest, without any more ado, conveyed a right of possession. But when we consider, that the practice of the strong and powerful, how universal soever it may be, is seldom the rule of right, however it be one part of the subjection of the conquered, not to argue against the conditions cut out to them by the conquering sword.

181. Though in all war there be usually a complication of force and damage, and the aggressor seldom fails to harm the estate, when he uses force against the persons of those he makes war upon; yet it is the use of force only that puts a man into the state of war. For whether by force he begins the injury, or else, having quietly, and

by fraud, done the injury, he refuses to make reparation, and by force maintains it, (which is the same thing, as at first to have done it by force) it is the unjust use of force that makes the war. For he that breaks open my house, and violently turns me out of doors; or, having peaceably got in, by force keeps me out; does in effect the same thing; supposing we are in such a state, that we have no common judge on earth, whom I may appeal to, and to whom we are both obliged to submit. For of such I am now speaking. It is the *unjust use of force then, that puts a man into the state of war* with another; and thereby he that is guilty of it makes a forfeiture of his life. For quitting reason, which is the rule given between man and man, and using force, the way of beasts, he becomes liable to be destroyed by him he uses force against as any savage ravenous beast, that is dangerous to his being.

182. But because the miscarriages of the father are no faults of the children, and they may be rational and peaceable, notwithstanding the brutishness and injustice of the father; the father, by his miscarriages and violence, can forfeit but his own life, but involves not his children in his guilt or destruction. His goods, which nature, that willeth the preservation of all mankind as much as is possible, hath made to belong to the children, to keep them from perishing, do still continue to belong to his children. For supposing them not to have joined in the war, either through infancy, absence, or choice, they have done nothing to forfeit them: *nor has the conqueror any right* to take them away, by the bare title of having subdued him that by force attempted his destruction; though perhaps he may have some right to them, to repair the damages he has sustained by the war, and the defence of his own right; which how far it reaches to the possessions of the conquered, we shall see by and by. So that he that *by conquest has a right over a man's person* to destroy him if he pleases, has not thereby a right *over his estate* to possess and enjoy it. For it is the brutal force the aggressor has used, that gives his adversary a right to take away his life, and destroy him if he pleases as a noxious creature; but it is damage sustained that alone gives him title to another man's goods. For, though I may kill a thief that sets on me in the highway, yet I may not (which seems less) take away his money and let him go: this would be robbery on my side. His force, and the state of war he put himself in, made him forfeit his life, but gave me no title to his goods. The *right* then *of conquest extends only to the lives* of those who joined in the war, *not to their estates*, but only in order to make reparation for the damages received, and the charges of the war; and that too with reservation of the right of the innocent wife and children.

183. Let the conqueror have as much justice on his side as could be supposed, he has no right to seize more than the vanquished could forfeit: his life is at the victor's mercy; and his service and goods he may appropriate, to make himself reparation; but he cannot take the goods of his wife and children: they too had a title to the goods he enjoyed, and their shares in the estate he possessed. For example, I in the state of nature (and all commonwealths are in the state of nature one with another) have injured another man, and refusing to give satisfaction it comes to a state of war, wherein my defending by force what I had gotten unjustly makes me the aggressor. I am conquered: my life, it is true, as forfeit, is at mercy, but not my wife's and children's. They made not the war, nor assisted in it. I could not forfeit their lives; they were not mine to forfeit. My wife had a share in my estate; that neither could I forfeit. And my children also, being born of me, had a right to be maintained out of my labour or substance. Here then is the case: the conqueror has a title to reparation for damages received, and the children have a title to their father's estate for their subsistence. For as to the wife's share, whether her own labour, or compact,

gave her a title to it, it is plain, her husband could not forfeit what was hers. What must be done in the case? I answer; the fundamental law of nature being, that all, as much as may be, should be preserved, it follows, that if there be not enough fully to satisfy both, viz. for the conqueror's losses, and children's maintenance, he that hath, and to spare, must remit something of his full satisfaction, and give way to the pressing and preferable title of those who are in danger to perish without it.

184. But supposing the *charge* and *damages of the war* are to be made up to the conqueror, to the utmost farthing; and that the children of the vanquished, spoiled of all their father's goods, are to be left to starve and perish; yet the satisfying of what shall, on this score, be due to the conqueror, will scarce give him a *title to any country he shall conquer*. For the damages of war can scarce amount to the value of any considerable tract of land, in any part of the world, where all the land is possessed, and none lies waste. And if I have not taken away the conqueror's land, which, being vanquished, it is impossible I should; scarce any other spoil I have done him can amount to the value of mine, supposing it equally cultivated, and of an extent any way coming near what I had over-run of his. The destruction of a year's product or two (for it seldom reaches four or five) is the utmost spoil that usually can be done. For as to money, and such riches and treasure taken away, these are none of nature's goods, they have but a fantastical imaginary value: nature has put no such upon them: they are of no more account by her standard, than the wampompeke of the Americans to an European prince, or the silver money of Europe would have been formerly to an American. And five years product is not worth the perpetual inheritance of land, where all is possessed, and none remains waste, to be taken up by him that is disseized: which will be easily granted, if one do but take away the imaginary value of money, the disproportion being more than between five and five hundred; though, at the same time, half a year's product is more worth than the inheritance, where there being more land than the inhabitants possess and make use of, any one has liberty to make use of the waste: but there conquerors take little care to possess themselves of the *lands of the vanquished*. No damage therefore, that men in the state of nature (as all princes and governments are in reference to one another) suffer from one another, can give a conqueror power to dispossess the posterity of the vanquished, and turn them out of that inheritance which ought to be the possession of them and their descendants to all generations. The conqueror indeed will be apt to think himself master: and it is the very condition of the subdued not to be able to dispute their right. But if that be all, it gives no other title than what bare force gives to the stronger over the weaker. And, by this reason, he that is strongest will have a right to whatever he pleases to seize on.

185. Over those then that joined with him in the war, and over those of the subdued country that opposed him not, and the posterity even of those that did, the conqueror, even in a just war, hath, by his conquest, no *right of dominion:* they are free from any subjection to him, and if their former government be dissolved, they are at liberty to begin and erect another to themselves.

186. The conqueror, it is true, usually, by the force he has over them, compels them, with a sword at their breasts, to stoop to his conditions, and submit to such a government as he pleases to afford them; but the inquiry is, what right he has to do so? If it be said, they submit by their own consent, then this allows their own *consent* to be *necessary to give the conqueror a title to rule* over them. It remains only to be

considered, whether *promises extorted by force,* without right, can be thought consent, and *how far they bind.* To which I shall say, they *bind not at all;* because whatsoever another gets from me by force, I still retain the right of, and he is obliged presently to restore. He that forces my horse from me, ought presently to restore him, and I have still a right to retake him. By the same reason, he that *forced a promise* from me, ought presently to restore it, i.e. quit me of the obligation of it: or I may resume it myself, i.e. choose whether I will perform it. For the law of nature laying an obligation on me only by the rules she prescribes, cannot oblige me by the violation of her rules: such is the extorting any thing from me by force. Nor does it at all alter the case to say, "I gave my promise," no more than it excuses the force, and passes the right, when I put my hand in my pocket and deliver my purse myself to a thief, who demands it with a pistol at my breast.

187. From all which it follows, that the *government of a conqueror,* imposed by force, on the subdued, against whom he had no right of war, or who joined not in the war against him, where he had right, *has no obligation* upon them.

188. But let us suppose that all the men of that community, being all members of the same body politic, may be taken to have joined in that unjust war, wherein they are subdued, and so their lives are at the mercy of the conqueror.

189. I say this concerns not their children who are in their minority. For since a father hath not, in himself, a power over the life or liberty of his child, no act of his can possibly forfeit it. So that the children, whatever may have happened to the fathers, are freemen, and the absolute power of the conqueror reaches no farther than the persons of the men that were subdued by him, and dies with them: and should he govern them as slaves subjected to his absolute arbitrary power, he *has* no *such right of dominion over their children.* He can have no power over them but by their own consent, whatever he may drive them to say or do; and he has no lawful authority, whilst force, and not choice, compels them to submission.

190. Every man is born with a double right: *first, a right of freedom to his person,* which no other man has a power over, but the free disposal of it lies in himself. *Secondly, a right,* before any other man, *to inherit with* his brethren his *father's goods.*

191. By the first of these, a man is *naturally free* from subjection to any government, though he be born in a place under its jurisdiction. But if he disclaim the lawful government of the country he was born in, he must also quit the right that belonged to him by the laws of it, and the possessions there descending to him from his ancestors, if it were a government made by their consent.

192. By the second, the inhabitants of any country, who are descended, and derive a title to their estates from those who are subdued, and had a government forced upon them against their free consents, *retain a right to the possession of their ancestors,* though they consent not freely to the government, whose hard conditions were by force imposed on the possessors of that country. For, the first *conqueror never having had a title to the land* of that country, the people who are the descendants of, or claim under those who were forced to submit to the yoke of a government by constraint, have always a right to shake it off, and free themselves from the usurpation or tyranny which the sword hath brought in upon them, till their rulers put them under such a frame of government as they willingly and of choice consent to. Who doubts but the Grecian christians, descendants of the ancient possessors of that country, may justly cast off the Turkish yoke, which they have so long groaned under, whenever they have an opportunity to do it? For no government can have a right to

obedience from a people who have not freely consented to it; which they can never be supposed to do, till either they are put in a full state of liberty to choose their government and governors, or at least till they have such standing laws, to which they have by themselves or their representatives given their free consent; and also till they are allowed their due property, which is, so to be proprietors of what they have, that no body can take away any part of it without their own consent, without which, men under any government are not in the state of freemen, but are direct slaves under the force of war.

193. But granting that the *conqueror* in a just war has a right to the estates, as well as power over the persons of the conquered; which, it is plain, he *hath* not: nothing of absolute power will follow from hence, in the continuance of the government. Because the descendants of these being all freemen, if he grants them estates and possessions to inhabit his country (without which it would be worth nothing) whatsoever he grants them, they have, so far as it is granted, property in. The nature whereof is, that *without a man's own consent, it cannot be taken from him.*

194. Their *persons* are *free* by a native right, and their properties, be they more or less, are *their own, and at their own dispose,* and not at his; or else it is no property. Supposing the conqueror gives to one man a thousand acres, to him and his heirs for ever; to another he lets a thousand acres for his life, under the rent of 50*l.* or 500*l.* per annum, has not the one of these a right to his thousand acres for ever, and the other during his life, paying the said rent? and hath not the tenant for life a property in all that he gets over and above his rent, by his labour and industry during the said term, supposing it to be double the rent? Can any one say, the king, or conqueror, after his grant, may, by his power of conqueror, take away all, or part of the land from the heirs of one, or from the other during his life, he paying the rent? Or can he take away from either the goods or money they have got upon the said land, at his pleasure? If he can, then all free and voluntary contracts cease, and are void in the world; there needs nothing to dissolve them at any time but power enough: and all the grants and *promises* of *men in power* are but mockery and collusion. For can there be any thing more ridiculous than to say, I give you and yours this for ever, and that in the surest and most solemn way of conveyance can be devised; and yet it is to be understood, that I have a right, if I please, to take it away from you again to-morrow?

195. I will not dispute now, whether princes are exempt from the laws of their country; but this I am sure, they owe subjection to the laws of God and nature. No body, no power, can exempt them from the obligations of that eternal law. Those are so great, and so strong, in the case of *promises,* that omnipotency itself can be tied by them. *Grants, promises,* and *oaths,* are *bonds* that *hold the Almighty:* whatever some flatterers say to princes of the world, who all together, with all their people joined to them, are in comparison of the great God, but as a drop of the bucket, or a dust on the balance, inconsiderable, nothing!

196. The short of the *case in conquest* is this. The conqueror, if he have a just cause, has a despotical right over the persons of all that actually aided, and concurred in the war against him, and a right to make up his damage and cost out of their labour and estates, so he injure not the right of any other. Over the rest of the people, if there were any that consented not to the war, and over the children of the captives themselves, or the possessions of either, he has no power and so can have, *by virtue of conquest, no lawful title* himself *to dominion* over them, or derive it to his posterity;

but is an aggressor, if he attempts upon their properties, and thereby puts himself in a state of war against them: and has no better a right of principality, he, nor any of his successors, than Hingar, or Hubba, the Danes, had here in England; or Spartacus had he conquered Italy, would have had; which is to have their yoke cast off, as soon as God shall give those under their subjection courage and opportunity to do it. Thus, notwithstanding whatever title the kings of Assyria had over Judah, by the sword, God assisted Hezekiah to throw off the dominion of that conquering empire. "And the Lord was with Hezekiah, and he prospered; wherefore he went forth, and he rebelled against the king of Assyria, and served him not," *2 Kings,* xviii. 7. Whence it is plain, that shaking off a power, which force, and not right, hath set over any one, though it hath the name of *rebellion,* yet is no offence before God, but is that which he allows and countenances, though even promises and covenants, when obtained by force, have intervened. For it is very probable, to any one that reads the story of Ahaz and Hezekiah attentively, that the Assyrians subdued Ahaz, and deposed him, and made Hezekiah king in his father's life-time; and that Hezekiah by agreement had done him homage, and paid him tribute all this time.

CHAPTER XVII
Of Usurpation

197. As conquest may be called a foreign usurpation, so usurpation is a kind of domestic conquest; with this difference, that an usurper can never have right on his side, it being no *usurpation* but where one is got into the *possession of what another has right to.* This, so far as it is *usurpation,* is a change only of persons, but not of the forms and rules of the government; for if the usurper extend his power beyond what of right belonged to the lawful princes, or governors of the commonwealth, it is *tyranny* added to *usurpation.*

198. In all lawful governments, the designation of the persons, who are to bear rule, is as natural and necessary a part, as the form of the government itself, and is that which had its establishment originally from the people; the anarchy being much alike to have no form of government at all, or to agree, that it shall be monarchical, but to appoint no way to design the person that shall have the power, and be the monarch. Hence all commonwealths, with the form of government established, have rules also of appointing those who are to have any share in the public authority, and settled methods of conveying the right to them. For the anarchy is much alike to have no form of government at all, or to agree that it shall be monarchical, but to appoint no way to know or design the person that shall have the power and be the monarch. Whoever gets into the exercise of any part of the power, by other ways than what the laws of the community have prescribed, hath no right to be obeyed, though the form of the commonwealth be still preserved; since he is not the person the laws have appointed, and consequently not the person the people have consented to. Nor can such an *usurper,* or any deriving from him, ever have a title, till the people are both at liberty to consent, and have actually consented to allow, and confirm in him the power he hath till then usurped.

CHAPTER XVIII
Of Tyranny

199. As usurpation is the exercise of power, which another hath a right to, so *tyranny is the exercise of power beyond right,* which no body can have a right to. And this

is making use of the power any one has in his hands, not for the good of those who are under it, but for his own private separate advantage.—When the governor, however intitled, makes not the law, but his will, the rule; and his commands and actions are not directed to the preservation of the properties of his people, but the satisfaction of his own ambition, revenge, covetousness, or any other irregular passion.

200. If one can doubt this to be truth, or reason, because it comes from the obscure hand of a subject, I hope the authority of a king will make it pass with him. King James the first, in his speech to the parliament, 1603, tells them thus: "I will ever prefer the weal of the public, and of the whole commonwealth, in making of good laws and constitutions, to any particular and private ends of mine. Thinking ever the wealth and weal of the commonwealth to be my greatest weal and worldly felicity; a point wherein a lawful king doth directly differ from a tyrant. For I do acknowledge, that the special and greatest point of difference that is between a rightful king and an usurping tyrant, is this, that whereas the proud and ambitious tyrant doth think his kingdom and people are only ordained for satisfaction of his desires and unreasonable appetites, the righteous and just king doth by the contrary acknowledge himself to be ordained for the procuring of the wealth and property of his people." And again, in his speech to the parliament, 1609, he hath these words: "The king binds himself by a double oath to the observation of the fundamental laws of his kingdom; tacitly, as by being a king, and so bound to protect as well the people, as the laws of his kingdom; and expressly, by his oath at his coronation; so as every just king, in a settled kingdom, is bound to observe that paction made to his people by his laws, in framing his government agreeable thereunto, according to that paction which God made with Noah after the deluge: Hereafter, seed-time and harvest, and cold and heat, and summer and winter, and day and night, shall not cease while the earth remaineth. And therefore a king governing in a settled kingdom, leaves to be a king, and degenerates into a tyrant, as soon as he leaves off to rule according to his laws." And a little after, "Therefore all kings that are not tyrants, or perjured, will be glad to bound themselves within the limits of their laws; and they that persuade them the contrary, are vipers, and pests, both against them and the commonwealth." Thus that learned king, who well understood the notions of things, makes the difference betwixt a *king* and a *tyrant* to consist only in this, that one makes the laws the bounds of his power, and the good of the public the end of his government; the other makes all give way to his own will and appetite.

201. It is a mistake to think this fault is proper only to monarchies; other forms of government are liable to it, as well as that. For wherever the power, that is put in any hands for the government of the people, and the preservation of their properties, is applied to other ends, and made use of to impoverish, harass, or subdue them to the arbitrary and irregular commands of those that have it; there it presently becomes tyranny, whether those that thus use it are one or many. Thus we read of the thirty tyrants at Athens, as well as one at Syracuse; and the intolerable dominion of the decemviri at Rome was nothing better.

202. *Wherever law ends, tyranny begins*, if the law be transgressed to another's harm; and whosoever in authority exceeds the power given him by the law, and makes use of the force he has under his command, to compass that upon the subject, which the law allows not, ceases in that to be a magistrate; and, acting without authority, may be opposed as any other man, who by force invades the right of another. This

is acknowledged in subordinate magistrates. He that hath authority to seize my person in the street, may be opposed as a thief and a robber if he endeavours to break into my house to execute a writ, notwithstanding that I know he has such a warrant, and such a legal authority, as will impower him to arrest me abroad. And why this should not hold in the highest, as well as in the most inferiour magistrate, I would gladly be informed. Is it reasonable that the eldest brother, because he has the greatest part of his father's estate, should thereby have a right to take away any of his younger brother's portions? Or, that a rich man, who possessed a whole country, should from thence have a right to seize, when he pleased, the cottage and garden of his poor neighbour? The being rightfully possessed of great power and riches, exceedingly beyond the greatest part of the sons of Adam, is so far from being an excuse, much less a reason for rapine and oppression, which the endamaging another without authority is, that it is a great aggravation of it. For the exceeding the bounds of authority is no more a right in a great, than in a petty officer; no more justifiable in a king than a constable; but is so much the worse in him, in that he has more trust put in him, has already a much greater share than the rest of his brethren, and is supposed, from the advantages of his education, employment, and counsellors, to be more knowing in the measures of right or wrong.

203. May the *commands* then *of a prince be opposed?* may he be resisted as often as any one shall find himself aggrieved, and but imagine he has not right done him? This will unhinge and overturn all polities, and, instead of government and order, leave nothing but anarchy and confusion.

204. To this I answer, that *force* is to be *opposed* to nothing but to unjust and unlawful *force;* whoever makes any opposition in any other case, draws on himself a just condemnation both from God and man; and so no such danger or confusion will follow, as is often suggested. For,

205. *First,* As, in some countries, the person of the prince by the law is sacred; and so, whatever he commands or does, his person is still free from all question or violence, not liable to force, or any judicial censure or condemnation. But yet opposition may be made to the illegal acts of any inferiour officer, or other commissioned by him; unless he will, by actually putting himself into a state of war with his people, dissolve the government, and leave them to that defence which belongs to every one in the state of nature. For of such things who can tell what the end will be? And a neighbour kingdom has shewed the world an odd example. In all other cases the *sacredness* of the *person exempts him from all inconveniencies,* whereby he is secure, whilst the government stands, from all violence and harm whatsoever; than which there cannot be a wiser constitution. For the harm he can do in his own person not being likely to happen often, nor to extend itself far; nor being able by his single strength to subvert the laws, nor oppress the body of the people, should any prince have so much weakness and ill-nature as to be willing to do it, the inconveniency of some particular mischiefs that may happen sometimes, when a heady prince comes to the throne, are well recompensed by the peace of the public, and security of the government, in the person of the chief magistrate, thus set out of the reach of danger: it being safer for the body that some few private men should be sometimes in danger to suffer, than that the head of the republic should be easily, and upon slight occasions, exposed.

206. *Secondly,* But this privilege belonging only to the king's person, hinders not, but they may be questioned, opposed, and resisted, who use unjust force, though

they pretend a commission from him, which the law authorizes not. As is plain in the case of him that has the king's writ to arrest a man, which is a full commission from the king; and yet he that has it cannot break open a man's house to do it, nor execute this command of the king upon certain days, nor in certain places, though this commission have no such exception in it, but they are the limitations of the law, which if any one transgress, the king's commission excuses him not. For the king's authority being given him only by the law, he cannot impower any one to act against the law, or justify him, by his commission, in so doing. The *commission* or *command of any magistrate, where he has no authority,* being as void and insignificant, as that of any private man. The difference between the one and the other being that the magistrate has some authority so far, and to such ends, and the private man has none at all. For it is not the commission, but the authority, that gives the right of acting; and *against the laws there can be no authority.* But notwithstanding such resistance, the king's person and authority are still both secured, and so *no danger to governor or government.*

207. *Thirdly,* supposing a government wherein the person of the chief magistrate is not thus sacred; yet this *doctrine* of the lawfulness of *resisting* all unlawful exercises of his power, *will not* upon every slight occasion endanger him, or *embroil the government.* For where the injured party may be relieved, and his damages repaired by appeal to the law, there can be no pretence for force, which is only to be used where a man is intercepted from appealing to the law. For nothing is to be accounted hostile force, but where it leaves not the remedy of such an appeal. And it is such force alone, that puts him that uses it *into a state of war,* and makes it lawful to resist him. A man with a sword in his hand, demands my purse in the highway, when perhaps I have not twelve-pence in my pocket: this man I may lawfully kill. To another I deliver £100 to hold only whilst I alight, which he refuses to restore me, when I am got up again, but draws his sword to defend the possession of it by force, if I endeavour to retake it. The mischief this man does me is an hundred, or possibly a thousand times more than the other perhaps intended me (whom I killed before he really did me any;) and yet I might lawfully kill the one, and cannot so much as hurt the other lawfully. The reason whereof is plain; because the one using force, which threatened my life, I could not have *time to appeal* to the law to secure it: and when it was gone, it was too late to appeal. The law could not restore life to my dead carcass, the loss was irreparable: which to prevent, the law of nature gave me a right to destroy him, who had put himself into a state of war with me, and threatened my destruction. But in the other case, my life not being in danger, I may have the *benefit of appealing* to the law, and have reparation for my £100 that way.

208. *Fourthly,* But if the unlawful acts done by the magistrate be maintained (by the power he has got) and the remedy which is due by law, be by the same power obstructed: yet the *right of resisting,* even in such manifest acts of tyranny, will not suddenly, or on slight occasions, disturb the government. For if it reach no farther than some private men's cases, though they have a right to defend themselves, and to recover by force what by unlawful force is taken from them: yet the right to do so will not easily engage them in a contest, wherein they are sure to perish; it being as impossible for one, or a few oppressed men to *disturb the government,* where the body of the people do not think themselves concerned in it, as for a raving madman, or heady malecontent, to overturn a well-settled state, the people being as little apt to follow the one, as the other.

209. But if either these illegal acts have extended to the majority of the people; or if the mischief and oppression has lighted only on some few, but in such cases, as the precedent and consequences seem to threaten all; and they are persuaded in their consciences, that their laws, and with them their estates, liberties, and lives are in danger, and perhaps their religion too: how they will be hindered from resisting illegal force, used against them, I cannot tell. This is an *inconvenience,* I confess, that *attends all governments* whatsoever, when the governors have brought it to this pass, to be generally suspected of their people; the most dangerous state which they can possibly put themselves in; wherein they are the less to be pitied, because it is so easy to be avoided; it being as impossible for a governor, if he really means the good of his people, and the preservation of them, and their laws together, not to make them see and feel it, as it is for the father of a family, not to let his children see he loves and takes care of them.

210. But if all the world shall observe pretences of one kind, and actions of another; arts used to elude the law, and the trust of prerogative, (which is an arbitrary power in some things left in the prince's hand to do good, not harm, to the people) employed contrary to the end for which it was given: if the people shall find the ministers and subordinate magistrates chosen suitable to such ends, and favoured, or laid by, proportionably as they promote or oppose them: if they see several experiments made of arbitrary power, and that religion underhand favoured (though publicly proclaimed against) which is readiest to introduce it; and the operators in it supported, as much as may be; and when that cannot be done, yet approved still, and liked the better: if a *long train of actions shew the councils* all tending that way; how can a man any more hinder himself from being persuaded in his own mind, which way things are going; or from casting about how to save himself, than he could from believing the captain of the ship he was in, was carrying him, and the rest of the company, to Algiers, when he found him always steering that course, though cross winds, leaks in his ship, and want of men and provisions did often force him to turn his course another way for some time, which he steadily returned to again, as soon as the wind, weather, and other circumstances would let him?

CHAPTER XIX
Of the Dissolution of Government

211. He that will with any clearness speak of the *dissolution of government,* ought in the first place to distinguish between the *dissolution of the society* and the *dissolution of the government.* That which makes the community, and brings men out of the loose state of nature into *one politic society,* is the agreement which every one has with the rest to incorporate, and act as one body, and so be one distinct commonwealth. The usual, and almost only way whereby *this union is dissolved,* is the inroad of foreign force making a conquest upon them. For in that case, (not being able to maintain and support themselves, as *one entire* and *independent body*) the union belonging to that body which consisted therein, must necessarily cease, and so every one return to the state he was in before, with a liberty to shift for himself, and provide for his own safety, as he thinks fit, in some other society. Whenever the *society is dissolved,* it is certain the government of that society cannot remain. Thus conquerors swords often cut up governments by the roots, and mangle societies to pieces, separating the subdued or scattered multitude from the protection of, and dependence on,

that society which ought to have preserved them from violence. The world is too well instructed in, and too forward to allow of, this way of dissolving of governments, to need any more to be said of it; and there wants not much argument to prove, that where the *society is dissolved*, the government cannot remain; that being as impossible, as for the frame of a house to subsist when the materials of it are scattered and dissipated by a whirlwind, or jumbled into a confused heap by an earthquake.

212. Besides this overturning from without, *governments are dissolved from within.*

First, When the *legislative* is *altered.* Civil society being a state of peace, amongst those who are of it, from whom the state of war is excluded by the umpirage, which they have provided in their legislative, for the ending all differences that may arise amongst any of them; it is in their legislative, that the members of a commonwealth are united, and combined together into one coherent living body. This *is the soul that gives form, life, and unity* to the commonwealth: from hence the several members have their mutual influence, sympathy, and connexion; and therefore, when the legislative is broken, or dissolved, dissolution and death follows. For, *the essence and union of the society* consisting in having one will, the legislative, when once established by the majority, has the declaring, and as it were keeping of that will. The *constitution of the legislative* is the first and fundamental act of society, whereby provision is made for the *continuation of their union*, under the direction of persons, and bonds of laws, made by persons authorized thereunto, by the consent and appointment of the people; without which no one man, or number of men, amongst them, can have authority of making laws that shall be binding to the rest. When any one, or more, shall take upon them to make laws, whom the people have not appointed so to do, they make laws without authority, which the people are not therefore bound to obey; by which means they come again to be out of subjection, and may constitute to themselves a new legislative, as they think best, being in full liberty to resist the force of those, who without authority would impose any thing upon them. Every one is at the disposure of his own will, when those who had, by the delegation of the society, the declaring of the public will, are excluded from it, and others usurp the place, who have no such authority or delegation.

213. This being usually brought about by such in the commonwealth who misuse the power they have, it is hard to consider it aright, and know at whose door to lay it, without knowing the form of government in which it happens. Let us suppose then the legislative placed in the concurrence of three distinct persons.

1. A single hereditary person, having the constant, supreme, executive power, and with it the power of convoking and dissolving the other two, within certain periods of time.
2. An assembly of hereditary nobility.
3. An assembly of representatives chosen *pro tempore*, by the people. Such a form of government supposed, it is evident,

214. First, That when such a single person, or prince, sets up his own arbitrary will in place of the laws, which are the will of the society, declared by the legislative, then the *legislative is changed.* For that being in effect the legislative, whose rules and laws are put in execution, and required to be obeyed; when other laws are set up, and other rules pretended, and enforced, than what the legislative, constituted by the society, have enacted, it is plain that the *legislative is changed.* Whoever introduces new laws, not being thereunto authorized, by the fundamental appointment of the

society, or subverts the old, disowns and overturns the power by which they were made, and so sets up a *new legislative*.

215. Secondly, When the prince hinders the legislative from assembling in its due time, or from acting freely, pursuant to those ends for which it was constituted, the *legislative is altered:* for it is not a certain number of men, no, nor their meeting, unless they have also freedom of debating, and leisure of perfecting, what is for the good of the society, wherein the legislative consists: when these are taken away or altered, so as to deprive the society of the due exercise of their power, the legislative is truly altered. For it is not names that constitute governments, but the use and exercise of those powers that were intended to accompany them; so that he, who takes away the freedom, or hinders the acting of the legislative in its due seasons, in effect *takes away the legislative,* and *puts an end to the government.*

216. Thirdly, When, by the arbitrary power of the prince, the electors, or ways of election, are altered, without the consent, and contrary to the common interest of the people, there also the *legislative is altered.* For, if others than those whom the society hath authorized thereunto, do choose, or in another way than what the society hath prescribed, those chosen are not the legislative appointed by the people.

217. Fourthly, The delivery also of the people into the subjection of a foreign power, either by the prince, or by the legislative, is certainly a *change of the legislative,* and so a *dissolution of the government.* For the end why people entered into society being to be preserved one intire, free, independent society, to be governed by its own laws; this is lost, whenever they are given up into the power of another.

218. Why, in such a constitution as this, the *dissolution of the government* in these cases is to be imputed to the prince, is evident; because he, having the force, treasure, and offices of the state to employ, and often persuading himself, or being flattered by others, that as supreme magistrate, he is uncapable of control; he alone is in a condition to make great advances toward such changes, under pretence of lawful authority, and has it in his hands to terrify or suppress opposers, as factious, seditious, and enemies to the government: whereas no other part of the legislative, or people, is capable by themselves to attempt any alteration of the legislative, without open and visible rebellion, apt enough to be taken notice of; which, when, it prevails, produces effects very little different from foreign conquest. Besides, the prince in such a form of government having the power of dissolving the other parts of the legislative, and thereby rendering them private persons, they can never in opposition to him, or without his concurrence, alter the legislative by a law, his consent being necessary to give any of their decrees that sanction. But yet, so far as the other parts of the legislative any way contribute to any attempt upon the government, and do either promote, or not, what lies in them, hinder such designs; they are guilty, and partake in this, which is certainly the greatest crime men can be guilty of one towards another.

219. There is one way more whereby such a government may be dissolved, and that is, when he who has the supreme executive power neglects and abandons that charge, so that the laws already made can no longer be put in execution. This is demonstratively to reduce all to anarchy, and so effectually to *dissolve the government.* For laws not being made for themselves, but to be, by their execution, the bonds of the society, to keep every part of the body politic in its due place and function; when that totally ceases, the *government* visibly *ceases,* and the people become a confused multitude, without order or connexion. Where there is no longer the administration

of justice, for the securing of men's rights, nor any remaining power within the community to direct the force, or provide for the necessities of the public; there certainly is *no government left*. Where the laws cannot be executed, it is all one as if there were no laws; and a government without laws is, I suppose, a mystery in politics, inconceivable to human capacity, and inconsistent with human society.

220. In these and the like cases, *when the government is dissolved,* the people are at liberty to provide for themselves, by erecting a new legislative, differing from the other, by the change of persons, or form, or both, as they shall find it most for their safety and good. For the *society* can never, by the fault of another, lose the native and original right it has to preserve itself; which can only be done by a settled legislative, and a fair and impartial execution of the laws made by it. But the state of mankind is not so miserable that they are not capable of using this remedy, till it be too late to look for any. To tell *people* they *may provide for themselves,* by erecting a new legislative, when by oppression, artifice, or being delivered over to a foreign power, their old one is gone, is only to tell them, they may expect relief when it is too late, and the evil is past cure. This is in effect no more, than to bid them first be slaves, and then to take care of their liberty; and when their chains are on, tell them, they may act like freemen. This, if barely so, is rather mockery than relief; and men can never be secure from tyranny, if there be no means to escape it, till they are perfectly under it: And therefore it is, that they have not only a right to get out of it, but to prevent it.

221. There is, therefore, secondly, another way whereby *governments are dissolved,* and that is, when the legislative, or the prince either of them, act contrary to their trust.

First, The *legislative acts against the trust* reposed in them, when they endeavour to invade the property of the subject, and to make themselves, or any part of the community, masters, or arbitrary disposers of the lives, liberties, or fortunes of the people.

222. The reason why men enter into society, is the preservation of their property; and the end why they choose and authorize a legislative, is, that there may be laws made, and rules set, as guards and fences to the properties of all the members of the society: to limit the power, and moderate the dominion, of every part and member of the society. For since it can never be supposed to be the will of the society, that the legislative should have a power to destroy that, which every one designs to secure, by entering into society, and for which the people submitted themselves to legislators of their own making, whenever the *legislators endeavour to take away and destroy the property of the people,* or to reduce them to slavery under arbitrary power, they put themselves into a state of war with the people, who are thereupon absolved from any farther obedience, and are left to the common refuge, which God hath provided for all men, against force and violence. Whensoever therefore the *legislative* shall transgress this fundamental rule of society; and either by ambition, fear, folly or corruption, *endeavour to grasp* themselves, *or put into the hands of any other an absolute power* over the lives, liberties, and estates of the people; by this breach of trust they *forfeit the power,* the people had put into their hands, for quite contrary ends, and it devolves to the people, who have a right to resume their original liberty, and, by the establishment of a new legislative, (such as they shall think fit) provide for their own safety and security, which is the end for which they are in society. What I have said here, concerning the legislative in general, holds true also concerning the supreme

executor, who having a double trust put in him, both to have a part in the legislative, and the supreme execution of the law, acts against both, when he goes about to set up his own arbitrary will, as the law of the society. He *acts* also *contrary to his trust*, when he either employs the force, treasure, and offices of the society to corrupt the *representatives*, and gain them to his purposes; or openly pre-engages the *electors*, and prescribes to their choice, such, whom he has by solicitations, threats, promises, or otherwise, won to his designs: and employs them to bring in such, who have promised before-hand, what to vote, and what to enact. Thus to regulate candidates and electors, and new model the ways of election, what is it but to cut up the government by the roots, and poison the very fountain of public security? for the people having reserved to themselves the choice of their *representatives*, as the fence to their properties, could do it for no other end, but that they might always be freely chosen, and so chosen, freely act, and advise, as the necessity of the commonwealth, and the public good should, upon examination and mature debate, be judged to require. This, those who give their votes before they hear the debate, and have weighed the reasons on all sides, are not capable of doing. To prepare such an assembly as this, and endeavour to set up the declared abettors of his own will, for the true representatives of the people, and the law-makers of the society, is certainly as great a *breach of trust,* and as perfect a declaration of a design to subvert the government, as is possible to be met with. To which if one shall add rewards and punishments visibly employed to the same end, and all the arts of perverted law made use of, to take off and destroy all that stand in the way of such a design, and will not comply and consent to betray the liberties of their country, it will be past doubt what is doing. What power they ought to have in the society, who thus employ it contrary to the trust that went along with it in its first institution, is easy to determine; and one cannot but see, that he, who has once attempted any such thing as this, cannot any longer be trusted.

223. To this perhaps it will be said, that the people being ignorant, and always discontented, to lay the foundation of government in the unsteady opinion and uncertain humour of the people, is to expose it to certain ruin; and *no government will be able long to subsist,* if the people may set up a new legislative, whenever they take offence at the old one. To this I answer, quite the contrary. People are not so easily got out of their old forms as some are apt to suggest. They are hardly to be prevailed with to amend the acknowledged faults in the frame they have been accustomed to. And if there be any original defects, or adventitious ones introduced by time, or corruption: it is not an easy thing to get them changed, even when all the world sees there is an opportunity for it. This slowness and aversion in the people to quit their old constitutions, has in the many revolutions which have been seen in this kingdom, in this and former ages, still kept us to, or, after some interval of fruitless attempts, still brought us back again to, our old legislative of king, lords, and commons: and whatever provocations have made the crown be taken from some of our princes heads, they never carried the people so far as to place it in another line.

224. But it will be said, this *hypothesis* lays a *ferment for* frequent *rebellion.* To which I *answer,*

First, no more than any other *hypothesis:* for when the people are made miserable, and find themselves *exposed to the ill usage of arbitrary power,* cry up their governors as much as you will, for *sons of Jupiter;* let them be sacred or divine, descended, or authorized from heaven; give them out for whom or what you please, the same will happen. *The people generally ill treated,* and contrary to right, will be ready upon any occasion to ease themselves of a burden that sits heavy upon them. They will wish, and seek for the opportunity, which in the change, weakness, and accidents of human affairs, seldom delays long to offer itself. He must have lived but a little while in the world, who has not seen examples of this in his time; and he must have read very little, who cannot produce examples of it in all sorts of governments in the world.

225. *Secondly,* I answer, such *revolutions happen* not upon every little mismanagement in public affairs. *Great mistakes* in the ruling part, many wrong and inconvenient laws, and all the slips of human frailty, will be *borne by the people* without mutiny or murmur. But if a long train of abuses, prevarications and artifices, all tending the same way, make the design visible to the people, and they cannot but feel what they lie under, and see whither they are going; it is not to be wondered, that they should then rouse themselves, and endeavour to put the rule into such hands which may secure to them the ends for which government was at first erected; and without which, ancient names, and specious forms, are so far from being better, that they are much worse, than the state of nature, or pure anarchy; the inconveniencies being all as great and as near, but the remedy farther off and more difficult.

226. *Thirdly,* I answer, that *this doctrine* of a power in the people of providing for their safety anew, by a new legislative, when their legislators have acted contrary to their trust, by invading their property, is the *best fence against rebellion,* and the probablest means to hinder it. For *rebellion* being an opposition, not to persons, but authority, which is founded only in the constitutions and laws of the government; those, whoever they be, who by force break through, and by force justify their violation of them, are truly and properly *rebels.* For when men, by entering into society and civil government, have excluded force, and introduced laws for the preservation of property, peace, and unity amongst themselves; those who set up force again in opposition to the laws, do *rebellare,* that is, bring back again the state of war, and are properly rebels: Which they who are in power, (by the pretence they have to authority, the temptation of force they have in their hands, and the flattery of those about them) being likeliest to do; the properest way to prevent the evil, is to shew them the danger and injustice of it, who are under the greatest temptation to run into it.

227. In both the forementioned cases, when either the legislative is changed, or the legislators act contrary to the end for which they were constituted, those who are guilty are *guilty of rebellion;* for if any one by force takes away the established legislative of any society, and the laws by them made pursuant to their trust, he thereby takes away the umpirage, which every one had consented to, for a peaceable decision of all their controversies, and a bar to the state of war amongst them. They who remove, or change the legislative, take away this decisive power, which no body can have but by the appointment and consent of the people; and so destroying the authority which the people did, and no body else can set up, and introducing a power which the people hath not authorized, they actually *introduce a state of war,* which is that of force without authority; and thus by removing the legislative established by the society, (in whose decisions the people acquiesced and united, as to that of their own will) they untie the knot, and *expose the people anew to the state of war.* And if those, who by force take away the legislative, are *rebels,* the *legislators*

themselves, as has been shewn, can be no less esteemed so; when they, who were set up for the protection and preservation of the people, their liberties and properties, shall by force invade and endeavour to take them away; and so they putting themselves into a state of war with those who made them the protectors and guardians of their peace, are properly, and with the greatest aggravation, *rebellantes*, rebels.

228. But if they, who say, "it lays a foundation for rebellion," mean that it may occasion civil wars, or intestine broils, to tell the people they are absolved from obedience when, illegal attempts are made upon their liberties or properties, and may oppose the unlawful violence of those who were their magistrates, when they invade their properties contrary to the trust put in them; and that therefore this doctrine is not to be allowed, being so destructive to the peace of the world: they may as well say, upon the same ground, that honest men may not oppose robbers or pirates, because this may occasion disorder or bloodshed. If any *mischief* come in such cases, it is not to be charged upon him who defends his own right, but *on him that invades* his neighbour's. If the innocent honest man must quietly quit all he has, for peace sake, to him who will lay violent hands upon it, I desire it may be considered, what a kind of peace there will be in the world, which consists only in violence and rapine; and which is to be maintained only for the benefit of robbers and oppressors. Who would not think it an admirable peace betwixt the mighty and the mean, when the lamb, without resistance, yielded his throat to be torn by the imperious wolf? Polyphemus's den gives us a perfect pattern of such a peace, and such a government, wherein Ulysses and his companions had nothing to do, but quietly to suffer themselves to be devoured. And no doubt Ulysses, who was a prudent man, preached up *passive obedience,* and exhorted them to a quiet submission, by representing to them of what concernment peace was to mankind; and by shewing the inconveniencies might happen, if they should offer to resist Polyphemus, who had now the power over them.

229. The end of government is the good of mankind: and which is *best for mankind,* that the people should be always exposed to the boundless will of tyranny; or that the rulers should be sometimes liable to be opposed, when they grow exorbitant in the use of their power, and employ it for the destruction, and not the preservation of the properties of their people?

230. Nor let any one say, that mischief can arise from hence, as often as it shall please a busy head, or turbulent spirit, to desire the alteration of the government. It is true, such men may stir, whenever they please; but it will be only to their own just ruin and perdition. For till the mischief be grown general, and the ill designs of the rulers become visible, or their attempts sensible to the greater part, the people, who are more disposed to suffer than right themselves by resistance, are not apt to stir. The examples of particular injustice or oppression, of here and there an unfortunate man, moves them not. But if they universally have a persuasion, grounded upon manifest evidence, that designs are carrying on against their liberties, and the general course and tendency of things cannot but give them strong suspicions of the evil intention of their governors, who is to be blamed for it? Who can help it, if they, who might avoid it, bring themselves into this suspicion? Are the people to be blamed, if they have the sense of rational creatures, and can think of things no otherwise than as they find and feel them? And is it not rather *their fault,* who put things into such a posture, that they would not have them thought to be as they are? I grant, that the pride, ambition, and turbulency of private men, have

sometimes caused great disorders in commonwealths, and factions have been fatal to states and kingdoms. But whether *the mischief* hath *oftener* begun *in the peoples wantonness,* and a desire to cast off the lawful authority of their rulers, or in *the rulers insolence,* and endeavours to get and exercise an arbitrary power over their people; whether oppression, or disobedience, gave the first rise to the disorder; I leave it to impartial history to determine. This I am sure, whoever, either ruler or subject, by force goes about to invade the rights of either prince or people, and lays the foundation for *overturning* the constitution and frame of *any just government;* is highly guilty of the greatest crime, I think, a man is capable of; being to answer for all those mischiefs of blood, rapine, and desolation, which the breaking to pieces of governments bring on a country. And he who does it, is justly to be esteemed the common enemy and pest of mankind, and is to be treated accordingly.

231. That *subjects* or *foreigners,* attempting by force on the properties of any people, may be resisted with force, is agreed on all hands. But that *magistrates,* doing the same thing, may be *resisted,* hath of late been denied: as if those who had the greatest privileges and advantages by the law, had thereby a power to break those laws, by which alone they were set in a better place than their brethren: whereas their offence is thereby the greater, both as being ungrateful for the greater share they have by the law, and breaking also that trust which is put into their hands by their brethren.

232. Whosoever uses *force without right,* as every one does in society, who does it without law, puts himself into a *state of war* with those against whom he so uses it; and in that state all former ties are cancelled, all other rights cease, and every one has a right to defend himself, and to *resist the aggressor.* This is so evident, that Barclay himself, that great assertor of the power and sacredness of kings, is forced to confess, that it is lawful for the people, in some cases, to resist their king; and that too in a chapter, wherein he pretends to shew, that the divine law shuts up the people from all manner of rebellion. Whereby it is evident, even by his own doctrine, that, since they may in some cases resist, all resisting of *princes* is not rebellion. His words are these. "Quod siquis dicat, Ergone populus tyrannicae crudelitati & furori jugulum semper praebebit? Ergone multitudo civitates suas fame, ferro, & flamma vastari, seque, conjuges, & liberos fortunae ludibrio & tyranni libidini exponi, inque omnia vitae pericula omnesque miserias & molestias a rege de luci patientur? Num illis quod omni animantium generi est a natura tributum, denegari debet, ut sc. vim vi repellant, seseq; ab injuria tueantur? Huic brevitur responsum sit, Populo universo negari defensionem, quae juris naturalis est, neque ultionem quae praeter naturam est adversus regem concedi debere. Quapropter si rex non in singulares tantum personas aliquot privatum odium exerceat, sed corpus etiam reipublicae, cujus ipse caput est, i.e. totum populum, vel insignem aliquam ejus partem immani & intoleranda saevitia seu tyrannide divexet; populo quidem hoc casu resistendi ac tuendi se ab injuria potestas competit; sed tuendi se tantum, non enim in principem invadendi: & restituendae injuriae illatae, non recedendi a debita reverentia propter acceptam injuriam. Praesentem denique impetum propulsandi non vim praeteritam ulciscendi jus habet. Horum enim alterum a natura est, ut vitam scilicet corpusque tueamur. Alterum vero contra naturam, ut inferior de superiori supplicium sumat. Quod itaque populus malum, antequam factum sit, impedire potest, ne fiat; id postquam factum est, in regem authorem sceleris vindicare non potest: populus igitur hoc amplius quam privatus quispiam habet: quod huic, vel ipsis adversariis judicibus, excepto Buchanano, nullum nisi in patientia remedium superest. Cum

ille si intolerabilis tyrannus est (modicum enim ferre omnino debet) resistere cum reverentia possit." Barclay *contra Monarchom.* l. iii. c. 8.

In English thus:

233. "But if any one should ask, Must the people then always lay themselves open to, the cruelty and rage of tyranny? Must they see their cities pillaged and laid in ashes, their wives and children exposed to the tyrant's lust and fury, and themselves and families reduced by their king to ruin, and all the miseries of want and oppression; and yet sit still? Must men alone be debarred the common privilege of opposing force with force, which nature allows so freely to all other creatures for their preservation from injury? I answer: Self-defence is a part of the law of nature; nor can it be denied the community, even against the king himself: but to revenge themselves upon him, must by no means be allowed them; it being not agreeable to that law. Wherefore if the king should shew an hatred, not only to some particular persons, but sets himself against the body of the commonwealth, whereof he is the head, and shall, with intolerable ill-usage, cruelly tyrannize over the whole, or a considerable part of the people, in this case the people have a right to resist and defend themselves from injury: but it must be with this caution, that they only defend themselves, but do not attack their prince: they may repair the damages received, but must not for any provocation exceed the bounds of due reverence and respect. They may repulse the present attempt, but must not revenge past violences. For it is natural for us to defend life and limb, but that an inferiour should punish a superiour, is against nature. The mischief which is designed them the people may prevent before it be done; but when it is done, they must not revenge it on the king, though author of the villainy. This therefore is the privilege of the people in general, above what any private person hath; that particular men are allowed by our adversaries themselves (Buchanan only excepted) to have no other remedy but patience; but the body of the people may with reverence resist intolerable tyranny; for, when it is but moderate, they ought to endure it."

234. Thus far that great advocate of monarchical power allows of *resistance.*

235. It is true, he has annexed two limitations to it, to no *purpose:*

First, He says, it must be with reverence.

Secondly, It must be without retribution, or punishment; and the reason he gives is, "Because an inferiour cannot punish a superiour."

First, *How to resist force without striking again,* or how to *strike with reverence,* will need some skill to make intelligible. He that shall oppose an assault only with a shield to receive the blows, or in any more respectful posture, without a sword in his hand, to abate the confidence and force of the assailant, will quickly be at an end of his *resistance,* and will find such a defence serve only to draw on himself the worse usage. This is as ridiculous a way of resisting, as Juvenal thought it of fighting; "ubi tu pulsas, ego vapulo tantum." And the success of the combat will be unavoidably the same he there describes it:

> Libertas pauperis haec est:
> Pulsatus rogat, & pugnis concisus, adorat,
> Ut liceat paucis cum dentibus inde reverti.

This will always be the event of such an imaginary *resistance*, where men may not strike again. He therefore *who may resist, must be allowed to strike*. And then let our author, or any body else, join a knock on the head, or a cut on the face, with as much *reverence* and *respect* as he thinks fit. He that can reconcile blows and reverence, may, for aught I know, deserve for his pains a civil, respectful cudgelling, wherever he can meet with it.

Secondly, as to his second, "An inferiour cannot punish a superiour;" that is true, generally speaking, whilst he is his superiour. But to resist force with force, being the *state of war* that *levels the parties,* cancels all former relation of reverence, respect, and *superiority:* And then the odds that remains, is, that he, who opposes the unjust aggressor, has this *superiority* over him, that he has a right when he prevails, to punish the offender, both for the breach of the peace, and all the evils that followed upon it. Barclay therefore, in another place, more coherently to himself, denies it to be lawful to *resist* a king in any case. But he there assigns two cases, whereby a king may un-king himself. His words are,

"Quid ergo, nulline casus incidere possunt quibus populo sese erigere atque in regem impotentius dominantem arma capere & invadere jure suo suaque authoritate liceat? Nulli certe quamdiu rex manet. Semper enim ex divinis id obstat, Regem honorificato; & qui potestati resistit, Dei ordinationi resistit: non alias igitur in eum populo potestas est quam si id committat propter quod ipso jure rex esse desinat. Tunc enim se ipse principatu exuit atque in privatis constituit liber: hoc modo populus & superior efficitur, reverso ad eum sc. jure illo quod ante regem inauguratum in interregno habuit. At sunt paucorum generum commissa ejusmodi quae hunc effectum pariunt. At ego cum plurima animo perlustrem, duo tantam invenio, duos, inquam, casus quibus rex ipso facto ex rege non regem se facit & omni honore & dignitate regali atque in subditos potestate destituit; quorum etiam meminit Winzerus. Horum unus est, Si regnum disperdat, quemadmodum de Nerone fertur, quod is nempe senatum populumque Romanum, atque adeo urbem ipsam ferro flammaque vastare, ac novas sibi sedes quaerere, decrevisset. Et de Caligula, quod palam denunciarit se neque civem neque principem senatui amplius fore, inque animo habuerit interempto utriusque ordinis electissimo quoque Alexandriam commigrare, ac ut populum uno ictu interimeret, unam ei cervicem optavit. Talia cum rex aliquis meditatur & molitur serio, omnem regnandi curam & animum ilico abjicit, ac proinde imperium in subditos amittit, ut dominus servi pro derelicto habiti dominium."

236. "Alter casus est, Si rex in alicujus clientelam se contulit, ac regnum quod liberum a majoribus & populo traditum accepit, alienae ditioni mancipavit. Nam tunc quamvis forte non ea mente id agit populo plane ut incommodet: tamen quia quod praecipuum est regiae dignitatis amisit, ut summus scilicet in regno secundum Deum sit, & solo Deo inferior, atque populum etiam totum ignorantem vel invitum, cujus libertatem sartam & tectam conservare debuit in alterius gentis ditionem & potestatem dedidit, hac velut quadam regni ab alienatione effecit, ut nec quod ipse in regno imperium habuit retineat, nec in eum cui collatum voluit, juris quicquam transferat; atque ita eo facto liberum jam & suae potestatis populum relinquit, cujus rei exemplum unum annales Scotici suppeditant." Barclay *contra Monarchom.* l. iii. c. 16.

Which in English runs thus:

237. "What then, can there no case happen wherein the people may of right, and by their own authority, help themselves, take arms, and set upon their king

imperiously domineering over them? None at all, whilst he remains a king. Honour the king, and he that resists the power, resists the ordinance of God; are divine oracles that will never permit it. The people therefore can never come by a power over him, unless he does something that makes him cease to be a king. For then he divests himself of his crown and dignity, and returns to the state of a private man, and the people become free and superiour, the power which they had in the interregnum, before they crowned him king, devolving to them again. But there are but few miscarriages which bring the matter to this state. After considering it well on all sides, I can find but two. Two cases there are, I say, whereby a king, ipso facto, becomes no king, and loses all power and regal authority over his people; which are also taken notice of by Winzerus.

The first is, If he endeavour to overturn the government, that is, if he have a purpose and design to ruin the kingdom and commonwealth; as it is recorded of Nero, that he resolved to cut off the senate and people of Rome, lay the city waste with fire and sword, and then remove to some other place. And of Caligula, that he openly declared, that he would be no longer a head to the people or senate, and that he had it in his thoughts to cut off the worthiest men of both ranks, and then retire to Alexandria: and he wished that the people had but one neck, that he might dispatch them all at a blow. Such designs as these, when any king harbours in his thoughts, and seriously promotes, he immediately gives up all care and thought of the commonwealth; and consequently forfeits the power of governing his subjects, as a master does the dominion over his slaves whom he hath abandoned."

238. "The other case is, When a king makes himself the dependent of another, and subjects his kingdom which his ancestors left him, and the people put free into his hands, to the dominion of another. For however perhaps it may not be his intention to prejudice the people, yet because he has hereby lost the principal part of regal dignity, viz. to be next and immediately under God supreme in his kingdom; and also because he betrayed or forced his people, whose liberty he ought to have carefully preserved, into the power and dominion of a foreign nation. By this, as it were, alienation of his kingdom, he himself loses the power he had in it before, without transferring any the least right to those on whom he would have bestowed it; and so by this act sets the people free, and leaves them at their own disposal. One example of this is to be found in the Scotch Annals."

239. In these cases Barclay, the great champion of absolute monarchy, is forced to allow, that a king may be *resisted*, and *ceases to be a king*. That is, in short, not to multiply cases, in whatsoever he has no authority, there he is no king, and may be resisted. For wheresoever the *authority ceases, the king ceases too*, and becomes like other men who have no *authority*. And these two cases the instances differ little from those above-mentioned, to be destructive to governments, only that he has omitted the principle from which his doctrine flows; and that is, the breach of trust, in not preserving the form of government agreed on, and in not intending the end of government itself, which is the public good and preservation of property. When a king has dethroned himself, and put himself in a state of war with his people, what shall hinder them from prosecuting him who is no king, as they would any other man, who has put himself into a state of war with them; Barclay and those of his opinion would do well to tell us. This farther I desire may be taken notice of out of Barclay, that he says, "The mischief that is designed them, the people may prevent before it be done"; whereby he allows "resistance" when tyranny is but in design.

"Such designs as these" (says he) "when any king harbours in his thoughts and seriously promotes, he immediately gives up all care and thought of the commonwealth;" so that, according to him, the neglect of the public good is to be taken as an evidence of such "design," or at least for a sufficient cause of "resistance." And the reason of all, he gives in these words, "Because he betrayed or forced his people, whose liberty he ought carefully to have preserved." What he adds, "into the power and dominion of a foreign nation," signifies nothing, the fault and forfeiture lying in the loss of their "liberty," which he "ought to have preserved," and not in any distinction of the persons to whose dominion they were subjected. The people's right is equally invaded, and their liberty lost, whether they are made slaves to any of their own, or a foreign nation; and in this lies the injury, and against this only have they the right of defence. And there are instances to be found in all countries, which shew, that it is not the change of nations in the persons of their governors, but the change of government, that gives the offence. Bilson, a bishop of our church, and a great stickler for the power and prerogative of princes, does, if I mistake not, in his treatise of christian subjection, acknowledge, *that princes may forfeit their power,* and their title to the obedience of their subjects; and if there needed authority in a case where reason is so plain, I could send my reader to Bractan, Fortescue, and the author of the Mirrour, and others, writers that cannot be suspected to be ignorant of our government, or enemies to it. But I thought Hooker alone might be enough to satisfy those men, who relying on him for their ecclesiastical polity, are by a strange fate carried to deny those principles upon which he builds it. Whether they are herein made the tools of cunninger workmen, to pull down their own fabric, they were best look. This I am sure, their civil policy is so new, so dangerous, and so destructive to both rulers and people, that as former ages never could bear the broaching of it; so it may be hoped, those to come, redeemed from the impositions of these Egyptian under taskmasters, will abhor the memory of such servile flatterers, who, whilst it seemed to serve their turn, resolved all government into absolute tyranny, and would have all men born to, what their mean souls fitted them for, slavery.

240. Here, it is like, the common question will be made, *Who shall be judge,* whether the prince or legislative act contrary to their trust? This, perhaps, ill-affected and factious men may spread amongst the people, when the prince only makes use of his due prerogative. To this I reply, "The people shall be judge;" for who shall be *judge* whether his trustee or deputy acts well, and according to the trust reposed in him, but he who deputes him, and must by having deputed him, have still a power to discard him, when he fails in his trust? If this be reasonable in particular cases of private men, why should it be otherwise in that of the greatest moment, where the welfare of millions is concerned, and also where the evil, if not prevented, is greater, and the redress very difficult, dear, and dangerous?

241. But farther, this question, ("Who shall be judge?") cannot mean that there is no judge at all. For where there is no judicature on earth, to decide controversies amongst men, God in heaven is judge. He alone, it is true, is judge of the right. But *every man* is *judge* for himself, as in all other cases, so in this, whether another hath put himself into a state of war with him, and whether he should appeal to the supreme judge, as Jephthah did.

242. If a controversy arise betwixt a prince and some of the people, in a matter where the law is silent, or doubtful, and the thing be of great consequence, I should

think the proper *umpire*, in such a case, should be the body of the *people:* for in cases where the prince hath a trust reposed in him, and is dispensed from the common ordinary rules of the law; there, if any men find themselves aggrieved, and think the prince acts contrary to, or beyond that trust, who so proper to *judge* as the body of the *people*, (who, at first, lodged that trust in him) how far they meant it should extend? But if the prince, or whoever they be in the administration, decline that way of determination, the appeal then lies no where but to heaven; force between either persons, who have no known superior on earth, or which permits no appeal to a judge on earth, being properly a state of war, wherein the appeal lies only to heaven; and in that state the *injured party must judge* for himself, when he will think fit to make use of that appeal, and put himself upon it.

243. To conclude, The *power that every individual gave the society*, when he entered into it, can never revert to the individuals gain, as long as the society lasts, but will always remain in the community; because without this there can be no community, no commonwealth, which is contrary to the original agreement: so also when the society hath placed the legislative in any assembly of men, to continue in them and their successors, with direction and authority for providing such successors, the *legislative can never revert to the people* whilst that government lasts: Because, having provided a legislative with power to continue for ever, they have given up their political power to the legislative, and cannot resume it. But if they have set limits to the duration of their legislative, and made this supreme power in any person, or assembly, only temporary; or else, when by the miscarriages of those in authority, it is forfeited; upon the forfeiture, or at the determination of the time set, *it reverts to the society*, and the people have a right to act as supreme, and continue the legislative in themselves; or erect a new form, or under the old form place it in new hands, as they think good.

DAVID HUME

The philosophical writings of David Hume (1711–1776) reflect the confluence of a number of important traditions and controversies of the early modern period. Hume was widely read and a powerful intellect; this combination placed him at a critical juncture in eighteenth-century philosophy.

Hume was attracted, for example, to the scientific method exemplified in the work of Isaac Newton, and at the same time he was passionately committed to the humanistic study of Cicero, Seneca, and Virgil, among other classical authors. Furthermore, Hume's greatest insight was that Thomas Hobbes, René Descartes, Baruch Spinoza, and others had trusted too much in reason and its powers, and, in order to show their error, he embraced the modes of skeptical attack found in the writings of Sextus Empiricus and employed by Pierre Bayle, one of his favorite authors. Among other doubts that Hume had about the role and authority of reason, one concerned morality. He admired the moral philosophy of the First Earl of Shaftesbury, Francis Hutcheson, and Bishop Butler, with its focus on the sentiments and on benevolence; he saw in this tradition a response to the pessimism and otherworldliness of Scottish Calvinism and other modes of Christian thought. Hume was also a vigorous opponent of religion but a devoted friend of the good life as lived in this world. In his own day, he sought "literary fame" but achieved it only in measured degree and then only for his historical and political writings. His philosophy influenced but a few until after his death, when its powerful impact on diverse schools of thought established Hume as a member of the pantheon of early modern philosophers.

Hume was born on April 26, 1711, in Edinburgh, Scotland, near the family estate of Ninewells. In 1722 he entered the University of Edinburgh ostensibly to pursue a law degree. After spending four years at the university but refusing to prepare for a law career, he returned home in 1726 for a period of intense reading and studying. In 1734 Hume took a position in Bristol, which was not a success, and in the same year travelled to France, where, from 1734 to 1737, he completed the composition of his great systematic work, *A Treatise of Human Nature*. The first two books were published anonymously in London in 1739, the third book in 1740.

Although the book received some critical notice, it was, in Hume's eyes, largely ignored. He always treated it as a failure. It stimulated no debate and did nothing to cultivate its author's fame. Hume thought that the *Treatise*'s problems stemmed from his literary style. He chose to rewrite the first and third parts and to publish them separately. The *Philosophical Essays* (later *An Inquiry*) *Concerning the Human*

Understanding appeared in 1748 and then in a revised version in 1758. *An Enquiry Concerning the Principles of Morals* was published in 1751.

During the decades following the publication of the *Treatise*, Hume held a number of minor positions, private and public, and wrote extensively. Twice he was passed over for academic positions, in 1745 at Edinburgh and again in 1751 in Glasgow. His *Essays Moral and Political*, published in 1741–42, were very well received, and his six-volume history of England, which appeared from 1754 to 1762, made Hume a celebrity in France and at home. His most famous critique of religion, *Dialogues Concerning Natural Religion*, was begun in 1751 but published only three years after his death in 1776. He died in Scotland, where he had lived since 1769. By that time, Hume's secular treatment of morality, his attack on rational religion and deism, and his criticism of Calvinism had made him so notorious that his friend Adam Smith, to whom he had entrusted the manuscript of the *Dialogues*, feared arranging for its publication. When it appeared in 1779, it did so without a publisher's imprint.

Hume's great contribution to moral theory rests on his attack on the primacy and self-sufficiency of reason and on his development of the moral sense tradition of Shaftesbury and Hutcheson. Morality rests not on reason, as Spinoza and Locke had argued, and not on the commands of God, as religious thinkers claimed. Rather, morality is based on our feelings of approval and disapproval and on the benevolence that such feeling positively endorses. Reason does of course play important roles in such a moral view, ordering the sentiments and elsewhere, but ultimately, for Hume, morality is grounded in our sentiments or feelings and not in faith or reason, and its goal is not divine reward or an otherworldly salvation but rather the best and most enjoyable life here on earth. Unlike Hobbes, then, Hume saw human nature as fundamentally good and human life as desirable.

Moreover, Hume's moral thinking is not simply an attempt to understand morality. It is also a vehicle for moral conduct and practice. In his own words: "Be a philosopher; but, amidst all your philosophy, be still a man."

Recommended readings

Broad, C. D. *Five Types of Ethical Theory*. London: Routledge, 1930.

Chappell, V. (ed.). *Hume*. Garden City: Doubleday, 1966.

Livingston, Donald. *Hume's Philosophy of Common Life*. Chicago: University of Chicago Press, 1984.

MacIntyre, Alasdair. *Whose Justice? Which Rationality?* Notre Dame: University of Notre Dame Press, 1988.

Norton, David Fate. *David Hume: Common Sense Moralist, Sceptical Metaphysician*. Princeton: Princeton University Press, 1982.

Smith, Norman Kemp. *The Philosophy of David Hume*. London: Macmillan, 1941, 1964.

Stroud, Barry. *Hume*. London: Routledge, 1978.

TREATISE OF HUMAN NATURE

BOOK III: OF MORALS

PART I: Of virtue and vice in general
1. Moral distinctions not derived from reason
2. Moral distinctions derived from a moral sense

PART II: Of justice and injustice
1. Justice, whether a natural or artificial virtue?
2. Of the origin of justice and property

BOOK III
OF MORALS

PART I
OF VIRTUE AND VICE IN GENERAL

SECTION I

Moral Distinctions Not Derived from Reason

There is an inconvenience which attends all abstruse reasoning, that it may silence, without convincing an antagonist, and requires the same intense study to make us sensible of its force, that was at first requisite for its invention. When we leave our closet, and engage in the common affairs of life, its conclusions seem to vanish like the phantoms of the night on the appearance of the morning; and it is difficult for us to retain even that conviction which we had attained with difficulty. This is still more conspicuous in a long chain of reasoning, where we must preserve to the end the evidence of the first propositions, and where we often lose sight of all the most received maxims, either of philosophy or common life. I am not, however, without hopes, that the present system of philosophy will acquire new force as it advances; and that our reasonings concerning *morals* will corroborate whatever has been said concerning the *understanding* and the *passions*. Morality is a subject that interests us above all others; we fancy the peace of society to be at stake in every decision concerning it; and it is evident that this concern must make our speculations appear more real and solid, than where the subject is in a great measure indifferent to us. What affects us, we conclude, can never be a chimera; and, as our passion is engaged on the one side or the other, we naturally think that the question lies within human

[From the *Hume* database in the PAST MASTERS series. Copyright © 1990 by Intelex Corporation. The text of *A Treatise of Human Nature* was drawn from the Everyman's Library edition, edited by Ernest Rhys, E. P. Dutton, 1911. Corrections were introduced from *Essays Moral, Political, and Literary*, edited by T. H. Green and T. H. Grose, Longmans, Green, and Co., 1898.]

comprehension; which, in other cases of this nature, we are apt to entertain some doubt of. Without this advantage, I never should have ventured upon a third volume of such abstruse philosophy, in an age wherein the greatest part of men seem agreed to convert reading into an amusement, and to reject every thing that requires any considerable degree of attention to be comprehended.

It has been observed, that nothing is ever present to the mind but its perceptions; and that all the actions of seeing, hearing, judging, loving, hating, and thinking, fall under this denomination. The mind can never exert itself in any action which we may not comprehend under the term of *perception;* and consequently that term is no less applicable to those judgments by which we distinguish moral good and evil, than to every other operation of the mind. To approve of one character, to condemn another, are only so many different perceptions.

Now, as perceptions resolve themselves into two kinds, viz. *impressions* and *ideas,* this distinction gives rise to a question, with which we shall open up our present enquiry concerning morals, *whether it is by means of our* ideas *or* impressions *we distinguish betwixt vice and virtue, and pronounce an action blamable or praiseworthy?* This will immediately cut off all loose discourses and declamations, and reduce us to something precise and exact on the present subject.

Those who affirm that virtue is nothing but a conformity to reason; that there are eternal fitnesses and unfitnesses of things, which are the same to every rational being that considers them; that the immutable measures of right and wrong impose an obligation, not only on human creatures, but also on the Deity himself: all these systems concur in the opinion, that morality, like truth, is discerned merely by ideas, and by their juxtaposition and comparison. In order, therefore, to judge of these systems, we need only consider whether it be possible from reason alone, to distinguish betwixt moral good and evil, or whether there must concur some other principles to enable us to make that distinction.

If morality had naturally no influence on human passions and actions, it were in vain to take such pains to inculcate it; and nothing would be more fruitless than that multitude of rules and precepts with which all moralists abound. Philosophy is commonly divided into *speculative* and *practical;* and as morality is always comprehended under the latter division, it is supposed to influence our passions and actions, and to go beyond the calm and indolent judgments of the understanding. And this is confirmed by common experience, which informs us that men are often governed by their duties, and are deterred from some actions by the opinion of injustice, and impelled to others by that of obligation.

Since morals, therefore, have an influence on the actions and affections, it follows that they cannot be derived from reason; and that because reason alone, as we have already proved, can never have any such influence. Morals excite passions, and produce or prevent actions. Reason of itself is utterly impotent in this particular. The rules of morality, therefore, are not conclusions of our reason.

No one, I believe, will deny the justness of this inference; nor is there any other means of evading it, than by denying that principle on which it is founded. As long as it is allowed, that reason has no influence on our passions and actions, it is in vain to pretend that morality is discovered only by a deduction of reason. An active principle can never be founded on an inactive; and if reason be inactive in itself, it must remain so in all its shapes and appearances, whether it exerts itself in natural or moral subjects, whether it considers the powers of external bodies, or the actions of rational beings.

It would be tedious to repeat all the arguments by which I have proved[1] that reason is perfectly inert, and can never either prevent or produce any action or affection. It will be easy to recollect what has been said upon that subject. I shall only recall on this occasion one of these arguments, which I shall endeavour to render still more conclusive, and more applicable to the present subject.

Reason is the discovery of truth or falsehood. Truth or falsehood consists in an agreement or disagreement either to the *real* relations of ideas, or to *real* existence and matter of fact. Whatever therefore is not susceptible of this agreement or disagreement, is incapable of being true or false, and can never be an object of our reason. Now, it is evident our passions, volitions, and actions, are not susceptible of any such agreement or disagreement; being original facts and realities, complete in themselves, and implying no reference to other passions, volitions, and actions. It is impossible, therefore, they can be pronounced either true or false, and be either contrary or conformable to reason.

This argument is of double advantage to our present purpose. For it proves *directly*, that actions do not derive their merit from a conformity to reason, nor their blame from a contrariety to it; and it proves the same truth more *indirectly*, by shewing us, that as reason can never immediately prevent or produce any action by contradicting or approving of it, it cannot be the source of moral good and evil, which are found to have that influence. Actions may be laudable or blamable; but they cannot be reasonable or unreasonable: laudable or blamable, therefore, are not the same with reasonable or unreasonable. The merit and demerit of actions frequently contradict, and sometimes control our natural propensities. But reason has no such influence. Moral distinctions, therefore, are not the offspring of reason. Reason is wholly inactive, and can never be the source of so active a principle as conscience, or a sense of morals.

But perhaps it may be said, that though no will or action can be immediately contradictory to reason, yet we may find such a contradiction in some of the attendants of the action, that is, in its causes or effects. The action may cause a judgment, or may be *obliquely* caused by one, when the judgment concurs with a passion; and by an abusive way of speaking, which philosophy will scarce allow of, the same contrariety may, upon that account, be ascribed to the action. How far this truth or falsehood may be the source of morals, it will now be proper to consider.

It has been observed that reason, in a strict and philosophical sense, can have an influence on our conduct only after two ways: either when it excites a passion, by informing us of the existence of something which is a proper object of it; or when it discovers the connexion of causes and effects, so as to afford us means of exerting any passion. These are the only kinds of judgment which can accompany our actions, or can be said to produce them in any manner; and it must be allowed, that these judgments may often be false and erroneous. A person may be affected with passion, by supposing a pain or pleasure to lie in an object which has no tendency to produce either of these sensations, or which produces the contrary to what is imagined. A

---

1. Book II. Part III. Sect. 3.

person may also take false measures for the attaining his end, and may retard, by his foolish conduct, instead of forwarding the execution of any project. These false judgments may be thought to affect the passions and actions, which are connected with them, and may be said to render them unreasonable, in a figurative and improper way of speaking. But though this be acknowledged, it is easy to observe, that these errors are so far from being the source of all immorality, that they are commonly very innocent, and draw no manner of guilt upon the person who is so unfortunate as to fall into them. They extend not beyond a mistake of *fact*, which moralists have not generally supposed criminal, as being perfectly involuntary. I am more to be lamented than blamed, if I am mistaken with regard to the influence of objects in producing pain or pleasure, or if I know not the proper means of satisfying my desires. No one can ever regard such errors as a defect in my moral character. A fruit, for instance, that is really disagreeable, appears to me at a distance, and, through mistake, I fancy it to be pleasant and delicious. Here is one error. I choose certain means of reaching this fruit, which are not proper for my end. Here is a second error; nor is there any third one, which can ever possibly enter into our reasonings concerning actions. I ask, therefore, if a man in this situation, and guilty of these two errors, is to be regarded as vicious and criminal, however unavoidable they might have been? Or if it be possible to imagine that such errors are the sources of all immorality?

And here it may be proper to observe, that if moral distinctions be derived from the truth or falsehood of those judgments, they must take place wherever we form the judgments; nor will there be any difference, whether the question be concerning an apple or a kingdom, or whether the error be avoidable or unavoidable.

For as the very essence of morality is supposed to consist in an agreement or disagreement to reason, the other circumstances are entirely arbitrary, and can never either bestow on any action the character of virtuous or vicious, or deprive it of that character. To which we may add, that this agreement or disagreement, not admitting of degrees, all virtues and vices would of course be equal.

Should it be pretended, that though a mistake of *fact* be not criminal, yet a mistake of *right* often is; and that this may be the source of immorality: I would answer, that it is impossible such a mistake can ever be the original source of immorality, since it supposes a real right and wrong; that is, a real distinction in morals, independent of these judgments. A mistake, therefore, of right, may become a species of immorality; but it is only a secondary one, and is founded on some other antecedent to it.

As to those judgments which are the *effects* of our actions, and which, when false, give occasion to pronounce the actions contrary to truth and reason; we may observe, that our actions never cause any judgment, either true or false, in ourselves, and that it is only on others they have such an influence. It is certain that an action, on many occasions, may give rise to false conclusions in others; and that a person, who, through a window, sees any lewd behaviour of mine with my neighbour's wife, may be so simple as to imagine she is certainly my own. In this respect my action resembles somewhat a lie or falsehood; only with this difference, which is material, that I perform not the action with any intention of giving rise to a false judgment in another, but merely to satisfy my lust and passion. It causes, however, a mistake and false judgment by accident; and the falsehood of its effects may be ascribed, by some odd figurative way of speaking, to the action itself. But still I can see no pretext of reason for asserting, that the tendency to cause such an error is the first spring or original source of all immorality.[2]

Thus, upon the whole, it is impossible that the distinction betwixt moral good and evil can be made by reason; since that distinction has an influence upon our actions, of which reason alone is incapable. Reason and judgment may, indeed, be the mediate cause of an action, by prompting or by directing a passion; but it is not pretended that a judgment of this kind, either in its truth or falsehood, is attended with virtue or vice. And as to the judgments, which are caused by our judgments, they can still less bestow those moral qualities on the actions which are their causes.

But, to be more particular, and to shew that those eternal immutable fitnesses and unfitnesses of things cannot be defended by sound philosophy, we may weigh the following considerations.

2. One might think it were entirely superfluous to prove this, if a late author, who has had the good fortune to obtain some reputation, had not seriously affirmed, that such a falsehood is the foundation of all guilt and moral deformity. That we may discover the fallacy of his hypothesis, we need only consider, that a false conclusion is drawn from an action, only by means of an obscurity of natural principles, which makes a cause be secretly interrupted in its operation, by contrary causes, and renders the connexion betwixt two objects uncertain and variable. Now, as a like uncertainty and variety of causes take place, even in natural objects, and produce a like error in our judgment, if that tendency to produce error were the very essence of vice and immorality, it should follow, that even inanimate objects might be vicious and immoral.

It is in vain to urge, that inanimate objects act without liberty and choice. For as liberty and choice are not necessary to make an action produce in us an erroneous conclusion, they can be, in no respect essential to morality; and I do not readily perceive, upon this system how they can ever come to be regarded by it. If the tendency to cause error be the origin of immorality, that tendency and immorality would in every case be inseparable.

Add to this, that if I had used the precaution of shutting the window while I indulged myself in those liberties with my neighbour's wife, I should have been guilty of no immorality; and that because my action, being perfectly concealed, would have had no tendency to produce any false conclusion.

For the same reason, a thief, who steals in by a ladder at a window, and takes all imaginable care to cause no disturbance, is in no respect criminal. For either he will not be perceived, or if he be it is impossible he can produce any error, nor will any one, from these circumstances, take him to be other than what he really is.

It is well known, that those who are squint-sighted do very readily cause mistakes in others, and that we imagine they salute or are talking to one person, while they address themselves to another. Are they, therefore, upon that account, immoral?

Besides, we may easily observe, that in all those arguments there is an evident reasoning in a circle. A person who takes possession of *another's* goods, and uses them as his *own*, in a manner declares them to be his own; and this falsehood is the source of the immorality of injustice. But is property, or right, or obligation, intelligible without an antecedent morality?

A man that is ungrateful to his benefactor, in a manner affirms that he never received any favours from him. But in what manner? Is it because it is his duty to be grateful? But this supposes that there is some antecedent rule of duty and morals. Is it because human nature is generally grateful, and makes us conclude that a man who does any harm, never receives any favour from the person he harmed? But human nature is not so generally grateful as to justify such a conclusion; or, if it were, is an exception to a general rule in every case criminal, for no other reason than because it is an exception?

But what may suffice entirely to destroy this whimsical system is, that it leaves us under the same difficulty to give a reason why truth is virtuous and falsehood vicious, as to account for the merit or turpitude of any other action. I shall allow, if you please, that all immorality is derived from this supposed falsehood in action, provided you can give me any plausible reason why such a falsehood is immoral. If you consider rightly of the matter, you will find yourself in the same difficulty as at the beginning.

This last argument is very conclusive; because, if there be not an evident merit or turpitude annexed to this species of truth or falsehood, it can never have any influence upon our actions. For who ever thought of forbearing any action, because others might possibly draw false conclusions from it? Or who ever performed any, that he might give rise to true conclusions?

If the thought and understanding were alone capable of fixing the boundaries of right and wrong, the character of virtuous and vicious either must lie in some relations of objects, or must be a matter of fact which is discovered by our reasoning. This consequence is evident. As the operations of human understanding divide themselves into two kinds, the comparing of ideas, and the inferring of matter of fact, were virtue discovered by the understanding, it must be an object of one of these operations; nor is there any third operation of the understanding which can discover it. There has been an opinion very industriously propagated by certain philosophers, that morality is susceptible of demonstration; and though no one has ever been able to advance a single step in those demonstrations, yet it is taken for granted that this science may be brought to an equal certainty with geometry or algebra. Upon this supposition, vice and virtue must consist in some relations; since it is allowed on all hands, that no matter of fact is capable of being demonstrated. Let us therefore begin with examining this hypothesis, and endeavour, if possible, to fix those moral qualities which have been so long the objects of our fruitless researches; point out distinctly the relations which constitute morality or obligation, that we may know wherein they consist, and after what manner we must judge of them.

If you assert that vice and virtue consist in relations susceptible of certainty and demonstration, you must confine yourself to those *four* relations which alone admit of that degree of evidence; and in that case you run into absurdities from which you will never be able to extricate yourself. For as you make the very essence of morality to lie in the relations, and as there is no one of these relations but what is applicable, not only to an irrational but also to an inanimate object, it follows that even such objects must be susceptible of merit or demerit. *Resemblance, contrariety, degrees in quality, and proportions in quantity and number;* all these relations belong as properly to matter as to our actions, passions, and volitions. It is unquestionable, therefore, that morality lies not in any of these relations, nor the sense of it in their discovery.[3]

Should it be asserted, that the sense of morality consists in the discovery of some relation distinct from these, and that our enumeration was not complete when we comprehended all demonstrable relations under four general heads; to this I know not what to reply, till some one be so good as to point out to me this new relation. It is impossible to refute a system which has never yet been explained. In such a manner of fighting in the dark, a man loses his blows in the air, and often places them where the enemy is not present.

I must therefore, on this occasion, rest contented with requiring the two following conditions of any one that would undertake to clear up this system. *First*, as moral

3. As a proof how confused our way of thinking on this subject commonly is, we may observe, that those who assert that morality is demonstrable, do not say that morality lies in the relations, and that the relations are distinguishable by reason. They only say, that reason can discover such an action, in such relations, to be virtuous, and such another vicious. It seems they thought it sufficient if they could bring the word Relation into the proposition, without troubling themselves whether it was to the purpose or not. But here, I think, is plain argument. Demonstrative reason discovers only relations. But that reason, according to this hypothesis, discovers also vice and virtue. These moral qualities, therefore, must be relations. When we blame any action, in any situation, the whole complicated object of action and situation must form certain relations, wherein the essence of vice consists. This hypothesis is not otherwise intelligible. For what does reason discover, when it pronounces any action vicious? Does it discover a relation or a matter of fact? These questions are decisive, and must not be eluded.

good and evil belong only to the actions of the mind, and are derived from our situation with regard to external objects, the relations from which these moral distinctions arise must lie only betwixt internal actions and external objects, and must not be applicable either to internal actions, compared among themselves, or to external objects, when placed in opposition to other external objects. For as morality is supposed to attend certain relations, if these relations could belong to internal actions considered singly, it would follow, that we might be guilty of crimes in ourselves, and independent of our situation with respect to the universe; and in like manner, if these moral relations could be applied to external objects, it would follow that even inanimate beings would be susceptible of moral beauty and deformity. Now, it seems difficult to imagine that any relation can be discovered betwixt our passions, volitions, and actions, compared to external objects, which relation might not belong either to these passions and volitions, or to these external objects, compared among *themselves*.

But it will be still more difficult to fulfil the *second* condition, requisite to justify this system. According to the principles of those who maintain an abstract rational difference betwixt moral good and evil, and a natural fitness and unfitness of things, it is not only supposed, that these relations, being eternal and immutable, are the same, when considered by every rational creature, but their *effects* are also supposed to be necessarily the same; and it is concluded they have no less, or rather a greater, influence in directing the will of the Deity, than in governing the rational and virtuous of our own species. These two particulars are evidently distinct. It is one thing to know virtue, and another to conform the will to it. In order, therefore, to prove that the measures of right and wrong are eternal laws, *obligatory* on every rational mind, it is not sufficient to shew the relations upon which they are founded: we must also point out the connexion betwixt the relation and the will; and must prove that this connexion is so necessary, that in every well-disposed mind, it must take place and have its influence; though the difference betwixt these minds be in other respects immense and infinite. Now, besides what I have already proved, that even in human nature no relation can ever alone produce any action; besides this, I say, it has been shewn, in treating of the understanding, that there is no connexion of cause and effect, such as this is supposed to be, which is discoverable otherwise than by experience, and of which we can pretend to have any security by the simple consideration of the objects. All beings in the universe, considered in themselves, appear entirely loose and independent of each other. It is only by experience we learn their influence and connexion; and this influence we ought never to extend beyond experience.

Thus it will be impossible to fulfil the *first* condition required to the system of eternal rational measures of right and wrong; because it is impossible to shew those relations, upon which such a distinction may be founded: and it is as impossible to fulfil the *second* condition; because we cannot prove *a priori*, that these relations, if they really existed and were perceived, would be universally forcible and obligatory.

But to make these general reflections more clear and convincing, we may illustrate them by some particular instances, wherein this character of moral good or evil is the most universally acknowledged. Of all crimes that human creatures are capable of committing, the most horrid and unnatural is ingratitude, especially when it is committed against parents, and appears in the more flagrant instances of wounds and death. This is acknowledged by all mankind, philosophers as well as the people: the question only arises among philosophers, whether the guilt or moral deformity of this action be discovered by demonstrative reasoning, or be felt by an internal sense, and by means of some sentiment, which the reflecting on such an action naturally occasions. This question will soon be decided against the former opinion, if we can shew the same relations in other objects, without the notion of any guilt or iniquity attending them. Reason or science is nothing but the comparing of ideas, and the discovery of their relations; and if the same relations have different characters, it must evidently follow, that those characters are not discovered merely by reason. To put the affair, therefore, to this trial, let us choose any inanimate object, such as an oak or elm; and let us suppose, that, by the dropping of its seed, it produces a sapling below it, which, springing up by degrees, at last overtops and destroys the parent tree: I ask, if, in this instance, there be wanting any relation which is discoverable in parricide or ingratitude? Is not the one tree the cause of the other's existence, and the latter the cause of the destruction of the former, in the same manner as when a child murders his parent? It is not sufficient to reply, that a choice or will is wanting. For in the case of parricide, a will does not give rise to any *different* relations, but is only the cause from which the action is derived; and consequently produces the *same* relations, that in the oak or elm arise from some other principles. It is a will or choice that determines a man to kill his parent: and they are the laws of matter and motion that determine a sapling to destroy the oak from which it sprung. Here then the same relations have different causes; but still the relations are the same: and as their discovery is not in both cases attended with a notion of immorality, it follows, that that notion does not arise from such a discovery.

But to choose an instance still more resembling; I would fain ask any one, why incest in the human species is criminal, and why the very same action, and the same relations in animals, have not the smallest moral turpitude and deformity? If it be answered, that this action is innocent in animals, because they have not reason sufficient to discover its turpitude; but that man, being endowed with that faculty, which *ought* to restrain him to his duty, the same action instantly becomes criminal to him. Should this be said, I would reply, that this is evidently arguing in a circle. For, before reason can perceive this turpitude, the turpitude must exist; and consequently is independent of the decisions of our reason, and is their object more properly than their effect. According to this system, then, every animal that has sense and appetite and will, that is, every animal must be susceptible of all the same virtues and vices, for which we ascribe praise and blame to human creatures. All the difference is, that our superior reason may serve to discover the vice or virtue, and by that means may augment the blame or praise: but still this discovery supposes a separate being in these moral distinctions, and a being which depends only on the will and appetite, and which, both in thought and reality, may be distinguished from the reason. Animals are susceptible of the same relations with respect to each other as the human species, and therefore would also be susceptible of the same morality, if the essence of morality consisted in these relations. Their want of a sufficient degree of reason may hinder them from perceiving the duties and obligations of morality, but can never hinder these duties from existing; since they must antecedently exist, in order to their being perceived. Reason must find them, and can never produce them. This argument deserves to be weighed, as being, in my opinion, entirely decisive.

Nor does this reasoning only prove, that morality consists not in any relations that are the objects of science; but if examined, will prove with equal certainty, that it consists not in any *matter of fact,* which can be discovered by the understanding. This is the *second* part of our argument; and if it can be made evident, we may conclude that morality is not an object of reason. But can there be any difficulty in proving that vice and virtue are not matters of fact, whose existence we can infer by reason? Take any action allowed to be vicious; wilful murder, for instance. Examine it in all lights, and see if you can find that matter of fact, or real existence, which you call *vice.* In whichever way you take it, you find only certain passions, motives, volitions, and thoughts. There is no other matter of fact in the case. The vice entirely escapes you, as long as you consider the object. You never can find it, till you turn your reflection into your own breast, and find a sentiment of disapprobation, which arises in you, towards this action. Here is a matter of fact; but it is the object of feeling, not of reason. It lies in yourself, not in the object. So that when you pronounce any action or character to be vicious, you mean nothing, but that from the constitution of your nature you have a feeling or sentiment of blame from the contemplation of it. Vice and virtue, therefore, may be compared to sounds, colours, heat, and cold, which, according to modern philosophy, are not qualities in objects, but perceptions in the mind: and this discovery in morals, like that other in physics, is to be regarded as a considerable advancement of the speculative sciences; though, like that too, it has little or no influence on practice. Nothing can be more real, or concern us more, than our own sentiments of pleasure and uneasiness; and if these be favourable to virtue, and unfavourable to vice, no more can be requisite to the regulation of our conduct and behaviour.

I cannot forbear adding to these reasonings an observation, which may, perhaps, be found of some importance. In every system of morality which I have hitherto met with, I have always remarked, that the author proceeds for some time in the ordinary way of reasoning, and establishes the being of a God, or makes observations concerning human affairs; when of a sudden I am surprized to find, that instead of the usual copulations of propositions, *is,* and *is not,* I meet with no proposition that is not connected with an *ought,* or an *ought not.* This change is imperceptible; but is, however, of the last consequence. For as this *ought,* or *ought not,* expresses some new relation or affirmation, it is necessary that it should be observed and explained; and at the same time that a reason should be given, for what seems altogether inconceivable, how this new relation can be a deduction from others, which are entirely different from it. But as authors do not commonly use this precaution, I shall presume to recommend it to the readers; and am persuaded, that this small attention would subvert all the vulgar systems of morality, and let us see that the distinction of vice and virtue is not founded merely on the relations of objects, nor is perceived by reason.

SECTION II
Moral Distinctions Derived from a Moral Sense

Thus the course of the argument leads us to conclude, that since vice and virtue are not discoverable merely by reason, or the comparison of ideas, it must be by means of some impression or sentiment they occasion, that we are able to mark the difference betwixt them. Our decisions concerning moral rectitude and depravity are evidently perceptions; and as all perceptions are either impressions or ideas, the exclusion of the one is a convincing argument for the other. Morality therefore, is more properly felt than judged of; though this feeling or sentiment is commonly so soft and gentle that we are apt to confound it with an idea, according to our common custom of taking all things for the same which have any near resemblance to each other.

The next question is, of what nature are these impressions, and after what manner do they operate upon us? Here we cannot remain long in suspense, but must pronounce the impression arising from virtue to be agreeable, and that proceeding from vice to be uneasy. Every moment's experience must convince us of this. There is no spectacle so fair and beautiful as a noble and generous action; nor any which gives us more abhorrence than one that is cruel and treacherous. No enjoyment equals the satisfaction we receive from the company of those we love and esteem; as the greatest of all punishments is to be obliged to pass our lives with those we hate or contemn. A very play or romance may afford us instances of this pleasure which virtue conveys to us; and pain, which arises from vice.

Now, since the distinguishing impressions by which moral good or evil is known, are nothing but *particular* pains or pleasures, it follows, that in all enquiries concerning these moral distinctions, it will be sufficient to shew the principles which make us feel a satisfaction or uneasiness from the survey of any character, in order to satisfy us why the character is laudable or blamable. An action, or sentiment, or character, is virtuous or vicious; why? because its view causes a pleasure or uneasiness of a particular kind. In giving a reason, therefore, for the pleasure or uneasiness, we sufficiently explain the vice or virtue. To have the sense of virtue, is nothing but to *feel* a satisfaction of a particular kind from the contemplation of a character. The very *feeling* constitutes our praise or admiration. We go no further; nor do we enquire into the cause of the satisfaction. We do not infer a character to be virtuous, because it pleases; but in feeling that it pleases after such a particular manner, we in effect feel that it is virtuous. The case is the same as in our judgments concerning all kinds of beauty, and tastes, and sensations. Our approbation is implied in the immediate pleasure they convey to us.

I have objected to the system which establishes eternal rational measures of right and wrong, that it is impossible to shew, in the actions of reasonable creatures, any relations which are not found in external objects; and therefore, if morality always attended these relations, it were possible for inanimate matter to become virtuous or vicious. Now it may, in like manner, be objected to the present system, that if virtue and vice be determined by pleasure and pain, these qualities must, in every case, arise from the sensations; and consequently any object, whether animate or inanimate, rational or irrational, might become morally good or evil, provided it can excite a satisfaction or uneasiness. But though this objection seems to be the very same, it has by no means the same force in the one case as in the other. For, *first*, it is evident that, under the term *pleasure*, we comprehend sensations, which are very different from each other, and which have only such a distant resemblance as is requisite to make them be expressed by the same abstract term. A good composition of music and a bottle of good wine equally produce pleasure; and, what is more, their goodness is determined merely by the pleasure. But shall we say, upon that account, that the wine is harmonious, or the music of a good flavour? In like manner, an inanimate object, and the character or sentiments of any person, may, both of them, give satisfaction; but, as the satisfaction is different, this keeps our sentiments concerning them from being confounded, and makes us ascribe virtue to the one and not to the other. Nor is every sentiment of pleasure or pain, which arises from characters and actions, of that *peculiar* kind which makes us praise or condemn. The good qualities of an enemy are hurtful to us, but may still command our esteem and respect. It is only when a character is considered in general, without reference to our particular interest, that it causes such a feeling or sentiment as denominates it morally good or evil. It is true, those sentiments from interest and morals are apt to be confounded, and naturally run into one another. It seldom happens that we do not think an enemy vicious, and can distinguish betwixt his opposition to our interest and real villainy or baseness. But this hinders not but that the sentiments are in themselves distinct; and a man of temper and judgment may preserve himself from these illusions. In like manner, though it is certain a musical voice is nothing but one that naturally gives a *particular* kind of pleasure; yet it is difficult for a man to be sensible that the voice of an enemy is agreeable, or to allow it to be musical. But a person of a fine ear, who has the command of himself, can separate these feelings, and give praise to what deserves it.

Secondly, we may call to remembrance the preceding system of the passions, in order to remark a still more considerable difference among our pains and pleasures. Pride and humility, love and hatred, are excited, when there is any thing presented to us that both bears a relation to the object of the passion, and produces a separate sensation, related to the sensation of the passion. Now, virtue and vice are attended with these circumstances. They must necessarily be placed either in ourselves or others, and excite either pleasure or uneasiness; and therefore must give rise to one of these four passions, which clearly distinguishes them from the pleasure and pain arising from inanimate objects, that often bear no relation to us; and this is, perhaps, the most considerable effect that virtue and vice have upon the human mind.

It may now be asked, *in general,* concerning this pain or pleasure that distinguishes moral good and evil, *From what principles is it derived, and whence does it arise in the human mind?* To this I reply, *first,* that it is absurd to imagine that, in every particular instance, these sentiments are produced by an *original* quality and *primary* constitution. For as the number of our duties is in a manner infinite, it is impossible that our original instincts should extend to each of them, and from our very first infancy impress on the human mind all that multitude of precepts which are contained in the completest system of ethics. Such a method of proceeding is not conformable to the usual maxims by which nature is conducted, where a few principles produce all that variety we observe in the universe, and every thing is carried on in the easiest and most simple manner. It is necessary, therefore, to abridge these primary impulses, and find some more general principles upon which all our notions of morals are founded.

But, in the *second* place, should it be asked, whether we ought to search for these principles in *nature,* or whether we must look for them in some other origin? I would reply, that our answer to this question depends upon the definition of the word Nature, than which there is none more ambiguous and equivocal. If *nature* be opposed to miracles, not only the distinction betwixt vice and virtue is natural, but also every event which has ever happened in the world, *excepting those miracles on which our religion is founded.* In saying, then, that the sentiments of vice and virtue are natural in this sense, we make no very extraordinary discovery.

But *nature* may also be opposed to rare and unusual; and in this sense of the word, which is the common one, there may often arise disputes concerning what is natural or unnatural; and one may in general affirm, that we are not possessed of any very precise standard by which these disputes can be decided. Frequent and rare depend upon the number of examples we have observed; and as this number may gradually encrease or diminish, it will be impossible to fix any exact boundaries betwixt them. We may only affirm on this head, that if ever there was any thing which could be called natural in this sense, the sentiments of morality certainly may; since there never was any nation of the world, nor any single person in any nation, who was utterly deprived of them, and who never, in any instance, showed the least approbation or dislike of manners. These sentiments are so rooted in our constitution and temper, that, without entirely confounding the human mind by disease or madness, it is impossible to extirpate and destroy them.

But *nature* may also be opposed to artifice, as well as to what is rare and unusual; and in this sense it may be disputed, whether the notions of virtue be natural or not. We readily forget that the designs, and projects, and views of men are principles as necessary in their operation as heat and cold, moist and dry; but, taking them to be free and entirely our own, it is usual for us to set them in opposition to the other principles of nature. Should it therefore be demanded, whether the sense of virtue be natural or artificial, I am of opinion that it is impossible for me at present to give any precise answer to this question. Perhaps it will appear afterwards that our sense of some virtues is artificial, and that of others natural. The discussion of this question will be more proper, when we enter upon an exact detail of each particular vice and virtue.[4]

Mean while, it may not be amiss to observe, from these definitions of *natural* and *unnatural*, that nothing can be more unphilosophical than those systems which assert that virtue is the same with what is natural, and vice with what is unnatural. For, in the first sense of the word, nature, as opposed to miracles, both vice and virtue are equally natural; and, in the second sense, as opposed to what is unusual, perhaps virtue will be found to be the most unnatural. At least it must be owned, that heroic virtue, being as unusual, is as little natural as the most brutal barbarity. As to the third sense of the word, it is certain that both vice and virtue are equally artificial and out of nature. For, however it may be disputed, whether the notion of a merit or demerit in certain actions, be natural or artificial, it is evident that the actions themselves are artificial, and are performed with a certain design and intention; otherwise they could never be ranked under any of these denominations. It is impossible, therefore, that the character of natural and unnatural can ever, in any sense, mark the boundaries of vice and virtue.

Thus we are still brought back to our first position, that virtue is distinguished by the pleasure, and vice by the pain, that any action, sentiment, or character, gives us by the mere view and contemplation. This decision is very commodious; because it reduces us to this simple question, *Why any action or sentiment, upon the general view or survey, gives a certain satisfaction or uneasiness*, in order to shew the origin of its moral rectitude or depravity, without looking for any incomprehensible relations and qualities, which never did exist in nature, nor even in our imagination, by any clear and distinct conception. I flatter myself I have executed a great part of my present design by a state of the question, which appears to me so free from ambiguity and obscurity.

---

4. In the following discourse, *natural* is also opposed sometimes to *civil*, sometimes to *moral*. The opposition will always discover the sense in which it is taken.

PART II
OF JUSTICE AND INJUSTICE

SECTION I
Justice, Whether A Natural or Artificial Virtue?

I have already hinted, that our sense of every kind of virtue is not natural; but that there are some virtues that produce pleasure and approbation by means of an artifice or contrivance, which arises from the circumstances and necessity of mankind. Of this kind I assert *justice* to be; and shall endeavour to defend this opinion by a short, and, I hope, convincing argument, before I examine the nature of the artifice, from which the sense of that virtue is derived.

It is evident that, when we praise any actions, we regard only the motives that produced them, and consider the actions as signs or indications of certain principles in the mind and temper. The external performance has no merit. We must look within to find the moral quality. This we cannot do directly; and therefore fix our attention on actions, as on external signs. But these actions are still considered as signs; and the ultimate object of our praise and approbation is the motive that produced them.

After the same manner, when we require any action, or blame a person for not performing it, we always suppose that one in that situation should be influenced by the proper motive of that action, and we esteem it vicious in him to be regardless of it. If we find, upon enquiry, that the virtuous motive was still powerful over his breast, though checked in its operation by some circumstances unknown to us, we retract our blame, and have the same esteem for him, as if he had actually performed the action which we require of him.

It appears, therefore, that all virtuous actions derive their merit only from virtuous motives, and are considered merely as signs of those motives. From this principle I conclude, that the first virtuous motive which bestows a merit on any action, can never be a regard to the virtue of that action, but must be some other natural motive or principle. To suppose that the mere regard to the virtue of the action, may be the first motive which produced the action, and rendered it virtuous, is to reason in a circle. Before we can have such a regard, the action must be really virtuous; and this virtue must be derived from some virtuous motive: and, consequently, the virtuous motive must be different from the regard to the virtue of the action. A virtuous motive is requisite to render an action virtuous. An action must be virtuous before we can have a regard to its virtue. Some virtuous motive, therefore, must be antecedent to that regard.

Nor is this merely a metaphysical subtilty; but enters into all our reasonings in common life, though perhaps we may not be able to place it in such distinct philosophical terms. We blame a father for neglecting his child. Why? because it shews a want of natural affection, which is the duty of every parent. Were not natural affection a duty, the care of children could not be a duty; and it were impossible we could have the duty in our eye in the attention we give to our offspring. In this case, therefore, all men suppose a motive to the action distinct from a sense of duty.

Here is a man that does many benevolent actions; relieves the distressed, comforts the afflicted, and extends his bounty even to the greatest strangers. No character can be more amiable and virtuous. We regard these actions as proofs of the greatest humanity. This humanity bestows a merit on the actions. A regard to this merit is, therefore, a secondary consideration, and derived from the antecedent principle of humanity, which is meritorious and laudable.

In short, it may be established as an undoubted maxim, *that no action can be virtuous, or morally good, unless there be in human nature some motive to produce it distinct from the sense of its morality.*

But may not the sense of morality or duty produce an action, without any other motive? I answer, it may: but this is no objection to the present doctrine. When any virtuous motive or principle is common in human nature, a person who feels his heart devoid of that motive, may hate himself upon that account, and may perform the action without the motive, from a certain sense of duty, in order to acquire, by practice, that virtuous principle, or at least to disguise to himself, as much as possible, his want of it. A man that really feels no gratitude in his temper, is still pleased to perform grateful actions, and thinks he has, by that means, fulfilled his duty. Actions are at first only considered as signs of motives: but it is usual, in this case, as in all others, to fix our attention on the signs, and neglect, in some measure, the thing signified. But though, on some occasions, a person may perform an action merely out of regard to its moral obligation, yet still this supposes in human nature some distinct principles, which are capable of producing the action, and whose moral beauty renders the action meritorious.

Now, to apply all this to the present case; I suppose a person to have lent me a sum of money, on condition that it be restored in a few days; and also suppose, that after the expiration of the term agreed on, he demands the sum: I ask, *What reason or motive have I to restore the money?* It will perhaps be said, that my regard to justice, and abhorrence of villainy and knavery, are sufficient reasons for me, if I have the least grain of honesty, or sense of duty and obligation. And this answer, no doubt, is just and satisfactory to man in his civilized state, and when trained up according to a certain discipline and education. But in his rude and more natural condition, if you are pleased to call such a condition natural, this answer would be rejected as perfectly unintelligible and sophistical. For one in that situation would immediately ask you, *Wherein consists this honesty and justice, which you find in restoring a loan, and abstaining from the property of others?* It does not surely lie in the external action. It must, therefore, be placed in the motive from which the external action is derived. This motive can never be a regard to the honesty of the action. For it is a plain fallacy to say, that a virtuous motive is requisite to render an action honest, and, at the same time, that a regard to the honesty is the motive of the action. We can never have a regard to the virtue of an action, unless the action be antecedently virtuous. No action can be virtuous, but so far as it proceeds from a virtuous motive. A virtuous motive, therefore, must precede the regard to the virtue; and it is impossible that the virtuous motive and the regard to the virtue can be the same.

It is requisite, then, to find some motive to acts of justice and honesty, distinct from our regard to the honesty; and in this lies the great difficulty. For should we say, that a concern for our private interest or reputation, is the legitimate motive to all honest actions: it would follow that wherever that concern ceases, honesty can no longer have place. But it is certain that self-love, when it acts at its liberty, instead of engaging us to honest actions, is the source of all injustice and violence; nor can a man ever correct those vices, without correcting and restraining the *natural* movements of that appetite.

But should it be affirmed that the reason or motive of such actions is the *regard to public interest,* to which nothing is more contrary than examples of injustice and dishonesty; should this be said, I would propose the three following considerations as worthy of our attention. *First,* Public interest is not naturally attached to the observation of the rules of justice; but is only connected with it, after an artificial convention for the establishment of these rules, as shall be shewn more at large hereafter. *Secondly,* If we suppose that the loan was secret, and that it is necessary for the interest of the person, that the money be restored in the same manner (as when the lender would conceal his riches), in that case the example ceases, and the public is no longer interested in the actions of the borrower; though I suppose there is no moralist who will affirm that the duty and obligation ceases. *Thirdly,* Experience sufficiently proves that men, in the ordinary conduct of life, look not so far as the public interest, when they pay their creditors, perform their promises, and abstain from theft, and robbery, and injustice of every kind. That is a motive too remote and too sublime to affect the generality of mankind, and operate with any force in actions so contrary to private interest as are frequently those of justice and common honesty.

In general, it may be affirmed, that there is no such passion in human minds as the love of mankind, merely as such, independent of personal qualities, of services, or of relation to ourself. It is true, there is no human, and indeed no sensible creature, whose happiness or misery does not, in some measure, affect us, when brought near to us, and represented in lively colours: but this proceeds merely from sympathy, and is no proof of such an universal affection to mankind, since this concern extends itself beyond our own species. An affection betwixt the sexes is a passion evidently implanted in human nature; and this passion not only appears in its peculiar symptoms, but also in inflaming every other principle of affection, and raising a stronger love from beauty, wit, kindness, than what would otherwise flow from them. Were there an universal love among all human creatures, it would appear after the same manner. Any degree of a good quality would cause a stronger affection than the same degree of a bad quality would cause hatred; contrary to what we find by experience. Men's tempers are different, and some have a propensity to the tender, and others to the rougher affections: but in the main, we may affirm, that man in general, or human nature, is nothing but the object both of love and hatred, and requires some other cause, which, by a double relation of impressions and ideas, may excite these passions. In vain would we endeavour to elude this hypothesis. There are no phenomena that point out any such kind affection to men, independent of their merit, and every other circumstance. We love company in general; but it is as we love any other amusement. An Englishman in Italy is a friend; a European in China; and perhaps a man would be beloved as such, were we to meet him in the moon. But this proceeds only from the relation to ourselves; which in these cases gathers force by being confined to a few persons.

If public benevolence, therefore, or a regard to the interests of mankind, cannot be the original motive to justice, much less can *private benevolence, or a regard to the interests of the party concerned,* be this motive. For what if he be my enemy, and has given me just cause to hate him? What if he be a vicious man, and deserves the hatred of all mankind? What if he be a miser, and can make no use of what I would deprive him of? What if he be a profligate debauchee, and would rather receive harm than benefit from large possessions? What if I be in necessity, and have urgent motives to acquire something to my family? In all these cases, the original motive to justice would fail; and consequently the justice itself, and along with it all property, right, and obligation.

A rich man lies under a moral obligation to communicate to those in necessity a share of his superfluities. Were private benevolence the original motive to justice a man would not be obliged to leave others in the possession of more than he is obliged to give them. At least, the difference would be very inconsiderable. Men generally fix their affections more on what they are possessed of, than on what they never enjoyed: for this reason, it would be greater cruelty to dispossess a man of any thing, than not to give it him. But who will assert that this is the only foundation of justice?

Besides, we must consider, that the chief reason why men attach themselves so much to their possessions, is, that they consider them as their property, and as secured to them inviolably by the laws of society. But this is a secondary consideration, and dependent on the preceding notions of justice and property.

A man's property is supposed to be fenced against every mortal, in every possible case. But private benevolence is, and ought to be, weaker in some persons than in others: and in many, or indeed in most persons, must absolutely fail. Private benevolence, therefore, is not the original motive of justice.

From all this it follows, that we have no real or universal motive for observing the laws of equity, but the very equity and merit of that observance; and as no action can be equitable or meritorious, where it cannot arise from some separate motive, there is here an evident sophistry and reasoning in a circle. Unless, therefore, we will allow that nature has established a sophistry, and rendered it necessary and unavoidable, we must allow, that the sense of justice and injustice is not derived from nature, but arises artificially, though necessarily, from education and human conventions.

I shall add, as a corollary to this reasoning, that since no action can be laudable or blamable, without some motives or impelling passions, distinct from the sense of morals, these distinct passions must have a great influence on that sense. It is according to their general force in human nature that we blame or praise. In judging of the beauty of animal bodies, we always carry in our eye the economy of a certain species; and where the limbs and features observe that proportion which is common to the species, we pronounce them handsome and beautiful. In like manner, we always consider the *natural* and *usual* force of the passions, when we determine concerning vice and virtue; and if the passions depart very much from the common measures on either side, they are always disapproved as vicious. A man naturally loves his children better than his nephews, his nephews better than his cousins, his cousins better than strangers, where every thing else is equal. Hence arise our common measures of duty, in preferring the one to the other. Our sense of duty always follows the common and natural course of our passions.

To avoid giving offence, I must here observe, that when I deny justice to be a natural virtue, I make use of the word *natural*, only as opposed to *artificial*. In another sense of the word, as no principle of the human mind is more natural than a sense of virtue, so no virtue is more natural than justice. Mankind is an inventive species; and where an invention is obvious and absolutely necessary, it may as properly be said to be natural as any thing that proceeds immediately from original principles, without the intervention of thought or reflection. Though the rules of justice be *artificial*, they are not *arbitrary*. Nor is the expression improper to call them *Laws of*

Nature; if by natural we understand what is common to any species, or even if we confine it to mean what is inseparable from the species.

SECTION II

Of the Origin of Justice and Property

We now proceed to examine two questions, viz. *concerning the manner in which the rules of justice are established by the artifice of men;* and *concerning the reasons which determine us to attribute to the observance or neglect of these rules a moral beauty and deformity.* These questions will appear afterwards to be distinct. We shall begin with the former.

Of all the animals with which this globe is peopled, there is none towards whom nature seems, at first sight, to have exercised more cruelty than towards man, in the numberless wants and necessities with which she has loaded him, and in the slender means which she affords to the relieving these necessities. In other creatures, these two particulars generally compensate each other. If we consider the lion as a voracious and carnivorous animal, we shall easily discover him to be very necessitous; but if we turn our eye to his make and temper, his agility, his courage, his arms, and his force, we shall find that his advantages hold proportion with his wants. The sheep and ox are deprived of all these advantages; but their appetites are moderate, and their food is of easy purchase. In man alone this unnatural conjunction of infirmity and of necessity may be observed in its greatest perfection. Not only the food which is required for his sustenance flies his search and approach, or at least requires his labour to be produced, but he must be possessed of cloaths and lodging to defend him against the injuries of the weather; though, to consider him only in himself, he is provided neither with arms, nor force, nor other natural abilities which are in any degree answerable to so many necessities.

It is by society alone he is able to supply his defects, and raise himself up to an equality with his fellow-creatures, and even acquire a superiority above them. By society all his infirmities are compensated; and though in that situation his wants multiply every moment upon him, yet his abilities are still more augmented, and leave him in every respect more satisfied and happy than it is possible for him, in his savage and solitary condition, ever to become. When every individual person labours apart, and only for himself, his force is too small to execute any considerable work; his labour being employed in supplying all his different necessities, he never attains a perfection in any particular art; and as his force and success are not at all times equal, the least failure in either of these particulars must be attended with inevitable ruin and misery. Society provides a remedy for these three inconveniences. By the conjunction of forces, our power is augmented; by the partition of employments, our ability encreases; and by mutual succour, we are less exposed to fortune and accidents. It is by this additional *force, ability,* and *security,* that society becomes advantageous.

But, in order to form society, it is requisite not only that it be advantageous, but also that men be sensible of these advantages; and it is impossible, in their wild uncultivated state, that by study and reflection alone they should ever be able to attain this knowledge. Most fortunately, therefore, there is conjoined to those necessities, whose remedies are remote and obscure, another necessity, which, having a present and more obvious remedy, may justly be regarded as the first and original principle of human society. This necessity is no other than that natural appetite betwixt the sexes, which unites them together, and preserves their union, till a new tie takes place in their concern for their common offspring. This new concern becomes also a principle of union betwixt the parents and offspring, and forms a more numerous society, where the parents govern by the advantage of their superior strength and wisdom, and at the same time are restrained in the exercise of their authority by that natural affection which they bear their children. In a little time, custom and habit, operating on the tender minds of the children, makes them sensible of the advantages which they may reap from society, as well as fashions them by degrees for it, by rubbing off those rough corners and untoward affections which prevent their coalition.

For it must be confessed, that however the circumstances of human nature may render a union necessary, and however those passions of lust and natural affection may seem to render it unavoidable, yet there are other particulars in our *natural temper*, and in our *outward circumstances*, which are very incommodious, and are even contrary to the requisite conjunction. Among the former we may justly esteem our *selfishness* to be the most considerable. I am sensible that, generally speaking, the representations of this quality have been carried much too far; and that the descriptions which certain philosophers delight so much to form of mankind in this particular, are as wide of nature as any accounts of monsters which we meet with in fables and romances. So far from thinking that men have no affection for any thing beyond themselves, I am of opinion that, though it be rare to meet with one who loves any single person better than himself, yet it is as rare to meet with one in whom all the kind affections, taken together, do not overbalance all the selfish. Consult common experience; do you not see, that though the whole expence of the family be generally under the direction of the master of it, yet there are few that do not bestow the largest part of their fortunes on the pleasures of their wives and the education of their children, reserving the smallest portion for their own proper use and entertainment. This is what we may observe concerning such as have those endearing ties; and may presume, that the case would be the same with others, were they placed in a like situation.

But though this generosity must be acknowledged to the honour of human nature, we may at the same time remark, that so noble an affection, instead of fitting men for large societies, is almost as contrary to them as the most narrow selfishness. For while each person loves himself better than any other single person, and in his love to others bears the greatest affection to his relations and acquaintance, this must necessarily produce an opposition of passions, and a consequent opposition of actions, which cannot but be dangerous to the new-established union.

It is, however, worth while to remark, that this contrariety of passions would be attended with but small danger, did it not concur with a peculiarity in our *outward circumstances*, which affords it an opportunity of exerting itself. There are three different species of goods which we are possessed of; the internal satisfaction of our minds; the external advantages of our body; and the enjoyment of such possessions as we have acquired by our industry and good fortune. We are perfectly secure in the enjoyment of the first. The second may be ravished from us, but can be of no advantage to him who deprives us of them. The last only are both exposed to the violence of others, and may be transferred without suffering any loss or alteration; while at the same time there is not a sufficient quantity of them to supply every one's desires and necessities. As the improvement, therefore, of these goods is the chief advantage of society, so the *instability* of their possession, along with their *scarcity,* is the chief impediment.

In vain should we expect to find, in *uncultivated nature,* a remedy to this inconvenience; or hope for any inartificial principle of the human mind which might control those partial affections, and make us overcome the temptations arising from our circumstances. The idea of justice can never serve to this purpose, or be taken for a natural principle, capable of inspiring men with an equitable conduct towards each other. That virtue, as it is now understood, would never have been dreamed of among rude and savage men. For the notion of injury or injustice implies an immorality or vice committed against some other person: And as every immorality is derived from some defect or unsoundness of the passions, and as this defect must be judged of, in a great measure, from the ordinary course of nature in the constitution of the mind, it will be easy to know whether we be guilty of any immorality with regard to others, by considering the natural and usual force of those several affections which are directed towards them. Now, it appears that, in the original frame of our mind, our strongest attention is confined to ourselves; our next is extended to our relations and acquaintance; and it is only the weakest which reaches to strangers and indifferent persons. This partiality, then, and unequal affection, must not only have an influence on our behaviour and conduct in society, but even on our ideas of vice and virtue; so as to make us regard any remarkable transgression of such a degree of partiality, either by too great an enlargement or contraction of the affections, as vicious and immoral. This we may observe in our common judgments concerning actions, where we blame a person who either centers all his affections in his family, or is so regardless of them as, in any opposition of interest, to give the preference to a stranger or mere chance acquaintance. From all which it follows, that our natural uncultivated ideas of morality, instead of providing a remedy for the partiality of our affections, do rather conform themselves to that partiality, and give it an additional force and influence.

The remedy, then, is not derived from nature, but from *artifice;* or, more properly speaking, nature provides a remedy, in the judgment and understanding, for what is irregular and incommodious in the affections. For when men, from their early education in society, have become sensible of the infinite advantages that result from it, and have besides acquired a new affection to company and conversation, and when they have observed that the principal disturbance in society arises from those goods, which we call external, and from their looseness and easy transition from one person to another, they must seek for a remedy, by putting these goods, as far as possible, on the same footing with the fixed and constant advantages of the mind and body. This can be done after no other manner, than by a convention entered into by all the members of the society to bestow stability on the possession of those external goods, and leave every one in the peaceable enjoyment of what he may acquire by his fortune and industry. By this means every one knows what he may safely possess; and the passions are restrained in their partial and contradictory motions. Nor is such a restraint contrary to these passions; for, if so, it could never be entered into nor maintained; but it is only contrary to their heedless and impetuous movement. Instead of departing from our own interest, or from that of our nearest friends, by abstaining from the possessions of others, we cannot better consult both these interests than by such a convention; because it is by that means we maintain society, which is so necessary to their well-being and subsistence, as well as to our own.

This convention is not of the nature of a *promise;* for even promises themselves, as we shall see afterwards, arise from human conventions. It is only a general sense of common interest; which sense all the members of the society express to one another, and which induces them to regulate their conduct by certain rules. I observe, that it will be for my interest to leave another in the possession of his goods, *provided* he will act in the same manner with regard to me. He is sensible of a like interest in the regulation of his conduct. When this common sense of interest is mutually expressed, and is known to both, it produces a suitable resolution and behaviour. And this may properly enough be called a convention or agreement betwixt us, though without the interposition of a promise; since the actions of each of us have a reference to those of the other, and are performed upon the supposition that something is to be performed on the other part. Two men who pull the oars of a boat, do it by an agreement or convention, though they have never given promises to each other. Nor is the rule concerning the stability of possession the less derived from human conventions, that it arises gradually, and acquires force by a slow progression, and by our repeated experience of the inconveniences of transgressing it. On the contrary, this experience assures us still more, that the sense of interest has become common to all our fellows, and gives us a confidence of the future regularity of their conduct; and it is only on the expectation of this, that our moderation and abstinence are founded. In like manner are languages gradually established by human conventions, without any promise. In like manner do gold and silver become the common measures of exchange, and are esteemed sufficient payment for what is of a hundred times their value.

After this convention, concerning abstinence from the possessions of others, is entered into, and every one has acquired a stability in his possessions, there immediately arise the ideas of justice and injustice; as also those of *property, right,* and *obligation.* The latter are altogether unintelligible, without first understanding the former. Our property is nothing but those goods, whose constant possession is established by the laws of society; that is, by the laws of justice. Those, therefore, who make use of the words *property,* or *right,* or *obligation,* before they have explained the origin of justice, or even make use of them in that explication, are guilty of a very gross fallacy, and can never reason upon any solid foundation. A man's property is some object related to him. This relation is not natural, but moral, and founded on justice. It is very preposterous, therefore, to imagine that we can have any idea of property, without fully comprehending the nature of justice, and shewing its origin in the artifice and contrivance of men. The origin of justice explains that of property. The same artifice gives rise to both. As our first and most natural sentiment of morals is founded on the nature of our passions, and gives the preference to ourselves and friends above strangers, it is impossible there can be naturally any such thing as a fixed right or property, while the opposite passions of men impel them in contrary directions, and are not restrained by any convention or agreement.

No one can doubt that the convention for the distinction of property, and for the stability of possession, is of all circumstances the most necessary to the establishment of human society, and that, after the agreement for the fixing and observing of this rule, there remains little or nothing to be done towards settling a perfect harmony and concord. All the other passions, beside this of interest, are either easily restrained, or are not of such pernicious consequence when indulged. *Vanity* is rather to be esteemed a social passion, and a bond of union among men. *Pity* and *love* are to be considered in the same light. And as to *envy* and *revenge,* though pernicious, they operate only by intervals, and are directed against particular persons, whom we consider as our superiors or enemies. This avidity alone, of acquiring goods and possessions for ourselves and our nearest friends, is insatiable, perpetual, universal, and directly destructive of society. There scarce is any one who is not actuated by it; and there is no one who has not reason to fear from it, when it acts without any restraint, and gives way to its first and most natural movements. So that, upon the whole, we are to esteem the difficulties in the establishment of society to be greater or less, according to those we encounter in regulating and restraining this passion.

It is certain, that no affection of the human mind has both a sufficient force and a proper direction to counterbalance the love of gain, and render men fit members of society, by making them abstain from the possessions of others. Benevolence to strangers is too weak for this purpose; and as to the other passions, they rather inflame this avidity, when we observe, that the larger our possessions are, the more ability we have of gratifying all our appetites. There is no passion, therefore, capable of controlling the interested affection, but the very affection itself, by an alteration of its direction. Now, this alteration must necessarily take place upon the least reflection, since it is evident that the passion is much better satisfied by its restraint than by its liberty, and that, in preserving society, we make much greater advances in the acquiring possessions, than in the solitary and forlorn condition which must follow upon violence and an universal licence. The question, therefore, concerning the wickedness or goodness of human nature, enters not in the least into that other question concerning the origin of society; nor is there any thing to be considered but the degrees of men's sagacity or folly. For whether the passion of self-interest be esteemed vicious or virtuous, it is all a case, since itself alone restrains it; so that if it be virtuous, men become social by their virtue; if vicious, their vice has the same effect.

Now, as it is by establishing the rule for the stability of possession that this passion restrains itself, if that rule be very abstruse and of difficult invention, society must be esteemed in a manner accidental, and the effect of many ages. But if it be found that nothing can be more simple and obvious than that rule; that every parent, in order to preserve peace among his children, must establish it; and that these first rudiments of justice must every day be improved, as the society enlarges: if all this appear evident, as it certainly must, we may conclude that it is utterly impossible for men to remain any considerable time in that savage condition which precedes society, but that his very first state and situation may justly be esteemed social. This, however, hinders not but that philosophers may, if they please, extend their reasoning to the supposed *state of nature;* provided they allow it to be a mere philosophical fiction, which never had, and never could have, any reality. Human nature being composed of two principal parts, which are requisite in all its actions, the affections and understanding, it is certain that the blind motions of the former, without the direction of the latter, incapacitate men for society; and it may be allowed us to consider separately the effects that result from the separate operations of these two component parts of the mind. The same liberty may be permitted to moral, which is allowed to natural philosophers; and it is very usual with the latter to consider any motion as compounded and consisting of two parts separate from each other, though at the same time they acknowledge it to be in itself uncompounded and inseparable.

This *state of nature,* therefore, is to be regarded as a mere fiction, not unlike that of the *golden age* which poets have invented; only with this difference, that the former is described as full of war, violence, and injustice; whereas the latter is painted out to us as the most charming and most peaceable condition that can possibly be imagined. The seasons, in that first age of nature, were so temperate, if we may believe the poets, that there was no necessity for men to provide themselves with cloaths and houses as a security against the violence of heat and cold. The rivers flowed with wine and milk; the oaks yielded honey; and nature spontaneously produced her greatest delicacies. Nor were these the chief advantages of that happy age. The storms and tempests were not alone removed from nature; but those more furious tempests were unknown to human breasts, which now cause such uproar, and engender such confusion. Avarice, ambition, cruelty, selfishness, were never heard of: cordial affection, compassion, sympathy, were the only movements with which the human mind was yet acquainted. Even the distinction of *mine* and *thine* was banished from that happy race of mortals, and carried with them the very notions of property, and obligation, justice and injustice.

This, no doubt, is to be regarded as an idle fiction; but yet deserves our attention, because nothing can more evidently shew the origin of those virtues, which are the subjects of our present enquiry. I have already observed, that justice takes its rise from human conventions; and that these are intended as a remedy to some inconveniences, which proceed from the concurrence of certain *qualities* of the human mind with the *situation* of external objects. The qualities of the mind are *selfishness* and *limited generosity:* and the situation of external objects is their *easy change,* joined to their *scarcity* in comparison of the wants and desires of men. But however philosophers may have been bewildered in those speculations, poets have been guided more infallibly, by a certain taste or common instinct, which, in most kinds of reasoning, goes further than any of that art and philosophy with which we have been yet acquainted. They easily perceived, if every man had a tender regard for another, or if nature supplied abundantly all our wants and desires, that the jealousy of interest, which justice supposes, could no longer have place; nor would there be any occasion for those distinctions and limits of property and possession, which at present are in use among mankind. Encrease to a sufficient degree the benevolence of men, or the bounty of nature, and you render justice useless, by supplying its place with much nobler virtues, and more valuable blessings. The selfishness of men is animated by the few possessions we have, in proportion to our wants; and it is to restrain this selfishness, that men have been obliged to separate themselves from the community, and to distinguish betwixt their own goods and those of others.

Nor need we have recourse to the fictions of poets to learn this; but, beside the reason of the thing, may discover the same truth by common experience and observation. It is easy to remark, that a cordial affection renders all things common among friends; and that married people, in particular, mutually lose their property, and are unacquainted with the mine and thine, which are so necessary, and yet cause such disturbance in human society. The same effect arises from any alteration in the circumstances of mankind; as when there is such a plenty of any thing as satisfies all the desires of men: in which case the distinction of property is entirely lost, and every thing remains in common. This we may observe with regard to air and water, though the most valuable of all external objects; and may easily conclude, that if men were supplied with every thing in the same abundance, or if *every one* had the same affection and tender regard for *every one* as for himself, justice and injustice would be equally unknown among mankind.

Here then is a proposition, which, I think, may be regarded as certain, *that it is only from the selfishness and confined generosity of men, along with the scanty provision nature has made for his wants, that justice derives its origin.* If we look backward we shall find, that this proposition bestows an additional force on some of those observations which we have already made on this subject.

First, We may conclude from it, that a regard to public interest, or a strong extensive benevolence, is not our first and original motive for the observation of the rules of justice; since it is allowed, that if men were endowed with such a benevolence, these rules would never have been dreamed of.

Secondly, We may conclude from the same principle, that the sense of justice is not founded on reason, or on the discovery of certain connexions and relations of ideas, which are eternal, immutable, and universally obligatory. For since it is confessed, that such an alteration as that above mentioned, in the temper and circumstances of mankind, would entirely alter our duties and obligations, it is necessary upon the common system, *that the sense of virtue is derived from reason,* to shew the change which this must produce in the relations and ideas. But it is evident, that the only cause why the extensive generosity of man, and the perfect abundance of every thing, would destroy the very idea of justice, is, because they render it useless; and that, on the other hand, his confined benevolence, and his necessitous condition, give rise to that virtue, only by making it requisite to the public interest, and to that of every individual. It was therefore a concern for our own and the public interest which made us establish the laws of justice; and nothing can be more certain, than that it is not any relation of ideas which gives us this concern, but our impressions and sentiments, without which every thing in nature is perfectly indifferent to us, and can never in the least affect us. The sense of justice, therefore, is not founded on our ideas, but on our impressions.

Thirdly, We may further confirm the foregoing proposition, *that those impressions, which give rise to this sense of justice, are not natural to the mind of man, but arise from artifice and human conventions.* For, since any considerable alteration of temper and circumstances destroys equally justice and injustice; and since such an alteration has an effect only by changing our own and the public interest, it follows that the first establishment of the rules of justice depends on these different interests. But if men pursued the public interest naturally, and with a hearty affection, they would have never dreamed of restraining each other by these rules; and if they pursued their own interest, without any precaution, they would run headlong into every kind of injustice and violence. These rules, therefore, are artificial, and seek their end in an oblique and indirect manner; nor is the interest which gives rise to them of a kind that could be pursued by the natural and inartificial passions of men.

To make this more evident, consider, that, though the rules of justice are established merely by interest, their connexion with interest is somewhat singular, and is different from what may be observed on other occasions. A single act of justice is frequently contrary to *public interest;* and were it to stand alone, without being followed by other acts, may, in itself, be very prejudicial to society. When a man of merit, of a beneficent disposition, restores a great fortune to a miser, or a seditious bigot, he has acted justly and laudably; but the public is a real sufferer. Nor is every single act of justice, considered apart, more conducive to private interest than to public; and it is easily conceived how a man may impoverish himself by a signal instance of integrity, and have reason to wish, that, with regard to that single act, the laws of justice were for a moment suspended in the universe. But, however single acts of justice may be contrary, either to public or private interest, it is certain that the whole plan or scheme is highly conducive, or indeed absolutely requisite, both to the support of society, and the well-being of every individual. It is impossible to separate the good from the ill. Property must be stable, and must be fixed by general rules. Though in one instance the public be a sufferer, this momentary ill is amply compensated by the steady prosecution of the rule, and by the peace and order which it establishes in society. And even every individual person must find himself a gainer on balancing the account; since, without justice, society must immediately dissolve, and every one must fall into that savage and solitary condition, which is infinitely worse than the worst situation that can possibly be supposed in society. When, therefore, men have had experience enough to observe, that, whatever may be the consequence of any single act of justice, performed by a single person, yet the whole system of actions concurred in by the whole society, is infinitely advantageous to the whole, and to every part, it is not long before justice and property take place. Every member of society is sensible of this interest: every one expresses this sense to his fellows, along with the resolution he has taken of squaring his actions by it, on condition that others will do the same. No more is requisite to induce any one of them to perform an act of justice, who has the first opportunity. This becomes an example to others; and thus justice establishes itself by a kind of convention or agreement, that is, by a sense of interest, supposed to be common to all, and where every single act is performed in expectation that others are to perform the like. Without such a convention, no one would ever have dreamed that there was such a virtue as justice, or have been induced to conform his actions to it. Taking any single act, my justice may be pernicious in every respect; and it is only upon the supposition that others are to imitate my example, that I can be induced to embrace that virtue; since nothing but this combination can render justice advantageous, or afford me any motives to conform myself to its rules.

We come now to the *second* question we proposed, viz. *Why we annex the idea of virtue to justice, and of vice to injustice.* This question will not detain us long after the principles which we have already established. All we can say of it at present will be despatched in a few words: and for further satisfaction, the reader must wait till we come to the third part of this book. The *natural* obligation to justice, viz. interest, has been fully explained; but as to the *moral* obligation, or the sentiment of right and wrong, it will first be requisite to examine the natural virtues, before we can give a full and satisfactory account of it.

After men have found by experience, that their selfishness and confined generosity, acting at their liberty, totally incapacitate them for society; and at the same time have observed that society is necessary to the satisfaction of those very passions, they are naturally induced to lay themselves under the restraint of such rules, as may render their commerce more safe and commodious. To the imposition, then, and observance of these rules, both in general, and in every particular instance, they are at first induced only by a regard to interest; and this motive, on the first formation of society, is sufficiently strong and forcible. But when society has become numerous, and has encreased to a tribe or nation, this interest is more remote; nor do men so readily perceive that disorder and confusion follow upon every breach of these rules, as in a more narrow and contracted society. But though, in our own actions, we may frequently lose sight of that interest which we have in maintaining order, and may follow a lesser and more present interest, we never fail to observe the prejudice we receive, either mediately or immediately, from the injustice of others; as not being in that case either blinded by passion, or biassed by any contrary temptation. Nay, when the injustice is so distant from us as no way to affect our interest, it still displeases us; because we consider it as prejudicial to human society, and pernicious to every one that approaches the person guilty of it. We partake of their uneasiness by *sympathy;* and as every thing which gives uneasiness in human actions, upon the general survey, is called Vice, and whatever produces satisfaction, in the same manner, is denominated Virtue, this is the reason why the sense of moral good and evil follows upon justice and injustice. And though this sense, in the present case, be derived only from contemplating the actions of others, yet we fail not to extend it even to our own actions. The *general rule* reaches beyond those instances from which it arose; while, at the same time, we naturally *sympathize* with others in the sentiments they entertain of us. *Thus self-interest is the original motive to the* establishment *of justice: but a sympathy with public interest is the source of the* moral approbation, *which attends that virtue.*

Though this progress of the sentiments be *natural,* and even necessary, it is certain that it is here forwarded by the artifice of politicians, who, in order to govern men more easily, and preserve peace in human society, have endeavoured to produce an esteem for justice, and an abhorrence of injustice. This, no doubt, must have its effect; but nothing can be more evident than that the matter has been carried too far by certain writers on morals, who seem to have employed their utmost efforts to extirpate all sense of virtue from among mankind. Any artifice of politicians may assist nature in the producing of those sentiments, which she suggests to us, and may even, on some occasions, produce alone an approbation or esteem for any particular action; but it is impossible it should be the sole cause of the distinction we make betwixt vice and virtue. For if nature did not aid us in this particular, it would be in vain for politicians to talk of *honourable* or *dishonourable, praiseworthy* or *blamable.* These words would be perfectly unintelligible, and would no more have any idea annexed to them, than if they were of a tongue perfectly unknown to us. The utmost politicians can perform, is to extend the natural sentiments beyond their original bounds; but still nature must furnish the materials, and give us some notion of moral distinctions.

As public praise and blame encrease our esteem for justice, so private education and instruction contribute to the same effect. For as parents easily observe, that a man is the more useful, both to himself and others, the greater degree of probity and honour he is endowed with, and that those principles have greater force when custom and education assist interest and reflection: for these reasons they are induced to inculcate on their children, from their earliest infancy, the principles of probity, and teach them to regard the observance of those rules by which society is maintained, as worthy and honourable, and their violation as base and infamous. By this means the sentiments of honour may take root in their tender minds, and acquire such firmness and solidity, that they may fall little short of those principles which are the most essential to our natures, and the most deeply radicated in our internal constitution.

What further contributes to encrease their solidity, is the interest of our reputation, after the opinion, *that a merit or demerit attends justice or injustice,* is once firmly established among mankind. There is nothing which touches us more nearly than our reputation, and nothing on which our reputation more depends than our conduct with relation to the property of others. For this reason, every one who has any regard to his character, or who intends to live on good terms with mankind, must fix an inviolable law to himself, never, by any temptation, to be induced to violate those principles which are essential to a man of probity and honour.

I shall make only one observation before I leave this subject, viz. that, though I assert that, in the *state of nature*, or that imaginary state which preceded society, there be neither justice nor injustice, yet I assert not that it was allowable, in such a state, to violate the property of others. I only maintain, that there was no such thing as property; and consequently could be no such thing as justice or injustice. I shall have occasion to make a similar reflection with regard to *promises*, when I come to treat of them; and I hope this reflection, when duly weighed, will suffice to remove all odium from the foregoing opinions, with regard to justice and injustice.

JEAN-JACQUES ROUSSEAU

Writing in 1764, Immanuel Kant acknowledged his debt to Jean-Jacques Rousseau (1712–1778), whose "noble sweep of genius" had uncovered for Kant "the deeply hidden nature of man." This debt is not surprising. Kant was only one among many who benefitted from Rousseau's critique of culture, his commitment to freedom and the natural character of human goodness, and his respect for the new science. Flamboyant, controversial, unorthodox, complex, and brilliant, Rousseau employed his self-taught intelligence in diverse ways and for diverse purposes, from musical theory, drama, and operatic composition, to cultural criticism and political analysis. His mind wandered as he himself did, and while his heart remained bound to Geneva, his birthplace, it was as ambivalent a fidelity as that which characterized many other relationships of his life.

Born in Geneva in 1712, Rousseau had an unhappy childhood. His mother died a week after his birth, and his father, ambitious but irresponsible, was eventually forced to leave Geneva. His younger son, whom his father had educated at home, was at thirteen apprenticed to a harsh, insensitive engraver. In 1728, returning late from a country walk, Rousseau found the city gates locked and, rather than face the man's anger, fled Geneva.

By 1742 Rousseau had become richly educated, encouraged by Madame de Warens, with whom he lived as a guest and then as a lover. In that year he moved to Paris and became secretary to the Comte de Montaigu, the French ambassador to Venice. After a bitter dispute with the ambassador in Venice, Rousseau returned to Paris and was befriended by Denis Diderot, Jean Le Rond d'Alembert, and other *philosophes* of the French Enlightenment. They recognized in Rousseau a rare intellect, with range and fascinating depth. He had already written a play, developed a new system of musical notation, and begun a major work on political institutions.

In 1750, ironically at the urging of Diderot, Rousseau submitted an essay for the prize of the Academy of Dijon on the question: "Has the progress of the sciences and arts contributed to the purification of morals?" In his *Discourse on the Sciences and the Arts*, which won the competition, Rousseau extolled those in antiquity who, like the Spartans, were strong as a result of military discipline, and he assailed moderns who were weak and effeminate because of their lack of such discipline. Furthermore, Rousseau praised the modern scientists, like Francis Bacon and Isaac Newton, who remained independent of court intrigue and corruption and were capable of employing modern science for public benefit. He developed similar themes in a political context and by means of a *scientific* examination of people living in primitive, natural societies in his *Discourse on the Origin of Inequality*, published in 1755.

This second Discourse failed to win the Dijon prize, but it did win Rousseau international fame and recognition. But not by all. By the mid-1750s Rousseau had become estranged from many of his intellectual friends, in part as a result of his vigorous attack on modern culture and the scientific spirit that supported it. At about this time, he converted back to Protestantism and returned to Geneva, only to be compelled to return to France by a dispute with Voltaire and fears of repression in Geneva. It is ironic that for all his devotion to the ideal of Geneva as a small participatory democracy, he never enjoyed life in his birthplace. In 1755 he had dedicated his *Discourse on the Origin of Inequality* to the sovereign citizens of Geneva, but by the 1760s he was to indict the city as an "odious and lawless despotism."

In 1762 Rousseau published *Émile*, his famous account of a mode of education consonant with natural growth and conducted with respect for the child's kinship with nature. In the same year, drawing on his long-term project on political institutions, Rousseau published *On The Social Contract*. In this short work, he grounded sovereignty in the freedom of the citizen and the general will that expresses the common well-being of the people. Both works generated great debate until, on June 9, 1762, the Parlemant of Paris authorized Rousseau's arrest, and, a short time later, both books were condemned. Simultaneously, the two books were burned in Geneva and his arrest was decreed. From then until his death in 1778, Rousseau lived a fitful life, in ill health, constantly moving, and forever defending his views on the corrupting influence of culture, the purity of nature, and the centrality of freedom and equality. It was during this period that Rousseau wrote his famous autobiographical *Confessions*, a work which was completed by 1775 but which remained unpublished until after his death.

Recommended readings

Cassirer, Ernst. *The Question of Jean-Jacques Rousseau*. Bloomington: Indiana University Press, 1963.

Chavet, John. *The Social Problem in the Philosophy of Rousseau*. Cambridge: Cambridge University Press, 1974.

Cranston, Maurice, and R. Peters (eds.). *Hobbes and Rousseau*. Garden City: Doubleday, 1972.

Gildin, Hilail. *Rousseau's Social Contract*. Chicago: University of Chicago Press, 1982.

Hendel, Charles. *Jean-Jacques Rousseau: Moralist*. Oxford: Oxford University Press, 1936.

Masters, Roger D. *The Political Philosophy of Rousseau*. Princeton: Princeton University Press, 1968.

Okin, Susan Moller. *Women in Western Political Thought*. Princeton: Princeton University Press, 1979.

Shklar, Judith. *Men and Citizens: A Study of Rousseau's Social Theory*. Cambridge: Cambridge University Press, 1969.

DISCOURSE ON THE ORIGIN AND FOUNDATIONS OF INEQUALITY AMONG MEN

by

Jean-Jacques Rousseau,
Citizen of Geneva

"Not in depraved things but in those well oriented according to nature, are we to consider what is natural."

—Aristotle, *Politics*, II.

To
The Republic
of Geneva

Magnificent, Most Honored and Sovereign Lords:

Convinced that only a virtuous man may bestow on his homeland those honors which it can acknowledge, I have labored for thirty years to earn the right to offer you public homage. And since this happy occasion supplements to some extent what my efforts have been unable to accomplish, I believed I might be allowed here to give heed to the zeal that urges me on, instead of the right that ought to have given me authorization. Having had the good fortune to be born among you, how could I meditate on the equality which nature has established among men and upon the inequality they have instituted without thinking of the profound wisdom with which both, felicitously combined in this state, cooperate in the manner that most closely approximates the natural law and that is most favorable to society, to the maintenance of public order and to the happiness of private individuals? In searching for the best maxims that good sense could dictate concerning the constitution of a government, I have been so struck on seeing them all in operation in your own, that even if I had not been born within your walls, I would have believed myself incapable of dispensing with offering this picture of human society to that people which, of all peoples, seems to me to be in possession of the greatest advantages, and to have best prevented its abuses.

If I had had to choose my birthplace, I would have chosen a society of a size limited by the extent of human faculties, that is to say, limited by the possibility of being well governed, and where, with each being sufficient to his task, no one would have been forced to relegate to others the functions with which he was charged; a

[Reprinted from *The Basic Political Writings*, translated by Donald A. Cress (Indianapolis: Hackett Publishing Company, 1987), by permission of the publisher.]

state where, with all private individuals being known to one another, neither the obscure maneuvers of vice nor the modesty of virtue could be hidden from the notice and the judgment of the public, and where that pleasant habit of seeing and knowing one another turned love of homeland into love of the citizens rather than into love of the land.

I would have wanted to be born in a country where the sovereign and the people could have but one and the same interest, so that all the movements of the machine always tended only to the common happiness. Since this could not have taken place unless the people and the sovereign were one and the same person, it follows that I would have wished to be born under a democratic government, wisely tempered.

I would have wanted to live and die free, that is to say, subject to the laws in such wise that neither I nor anyone else could shake off their honorable yoke: that pleasant and salutary yoke, which the most arrogant heads bear with all the greater docility, since they are made to bear no other.

I would therefore have wanted it to be impossible for anyone in the state to say that he was above the law and for anyone outside to demand that the state was obliged to give him recognition. For whatever the constitution of a government may be, if a single man is found who is not subject to the law, all the others are necessarily at his discretion.[1] And if there is a national leader and a foreign leader as well, whatever the division of authority they may make, it is impossible for both of them to be strictly obeyed and for the state to be well governed.

I would not have wanted to dwell in a newly constituted republic, however good its laws may be, out of fear that, with the government perhaps constituted otherwise than would be required for the moment and being unsuited to the new citizens or the citizens to the new government, the state would be subject to being overthrown and destroyed almost from its inception. For liberty is like those solid and tasty foods or those full-bodied wines which are appropriate for nourishing and strengthening robust constitutions that are used to them, but which overpower, ruin and intoxicate the weak and delicate who are not suited for them. Once peoples are accustomed to masters, they are no longer in a position to get along without them. If they try to shake off the yoke, they put all the more distance between themselves and liberty, because, in mistaking for liberty an unbridled license which is its opposite, their revolutions nearly always deliver them over to seducers who simply make their chains heavier. The Roman people itself—that model of all free peoples—was in no position to govern itself when it emerged from the oppression of the Tarquins. Debased by slavery and the ignominious labors the Tarquins had imposed on it, at first it was but a stupid rabble that needed to be managed and governed with the greatest wisdom, so that, as it gradually became accustomed to breathe the salutary air of liberty, these souls, enervated or rather brutalized under tyranny, acquired by degrees that severity of mores and that high-spirited courage which eventually made them, of all the peoples, most worthy of respect. I would therefore have sought for my homeland a happy and tranquil republic, whose antiquity was somehow lost in the dark recesses of time, which had experienced only such attacks as served to manifest and strengthen in its inhabitants courage and love of homeland, and where the citizens, long accustomed to a wise independence, were not only free but worthy of being so.

I would have wanted to choose for myself a homeland diverted by a fortunate impotence from the fierce love of conquest, and protected by an even more fortunate position from the fear of becoming itself the conquest of another state; a free city, situated among several peoples none of whom had any interest in invading it, while each had an interest in preventing the others from invading it themselves; in a word, a republic that did not tempt the ambition of its neighbors and that could reasonably count on their assistance in time of need. It follows that in so fortunate a position, it would have had nothing to fear except from itself; and that, if its citizens were trained in the use of arms, it would have been more to maintain in them that martial fervor and that high-spirited courage that suit liberty so well and whet the appetite for it, than out of the necessity to provide for their defense.

I would have searched for a country where the right of legislation was common to all citizens, for who can know better than they the conditions under which it suits them to live together in a single society? But I would not have approved of plebiscites like those of the Romans where the state's leaders and those most interested in its preservation were excluded from the deliberations on which its safety often depended, and where, by an absurd inconsistency, the magistrates were deprived of the rights enjoyed by ordinary citizens.

On the contrary, I would have desired that, in order to stop the self-centered and ill-conceived projects and the dangerous innovations that finally ruined Athens, no one would have the power to propose new laws according to his fancy; that this right belonged exclusively to the magistrates; that even they used it with such caution that the populace, for its part, was so hesitant about giving its consent to these laws, and that their promulgation could only be done with such solemnity that before the constitution was overturned one had time to be convinced that it is above all the great antiquity of the laws that makes them holy and venerable; that the populace soon holds in contempt those laws that it sees change daily; and that in becoming accustomed to neglect old usages on the pretext of making improvements, great evils are often introduced in order to correct the lesser ones.

Above all, I would have fled, as necessarily ill-governed, a republic where the people, believing it could get along without its magistrates or permit them but a precarious authority, would imprudently have held on to the administration of civil affairs and the execution of its own laws. Such must have been the rude constitution of the first governments immediately emerging from the state of nature, and such too was one of the vices which ruined the republic of Athens.

But I would have chosen that republic where private individuals, being content to give sanction to the laws and to decide as a body and upon the recommendation of their leaders the most important public affairs, would establish respected tribunals, distinguish with care their various departments, annually elect the most capable and most upright of their fellow citizens to administer justice and to govern the state; and where, with the virtue of the magistrates thus bearing witness to the wisdom of the people, they would mutually honor one another. Thus if some fatal misunderstandings were ever to disturb public concord, even those periods of blindness and errors were marked by indications of moderation, reciprocal esteem, and a common respect for the laws: presages and guarantees of a sincere and perpetual reconciliation.

Such, MAGNIFICENT, MOST HONORED, AND SOVEREIGN LORDS, are the advantages that I would have sought in the homeland that I would have chosen for myself. And if in addition providence had joined to it a charming location, a temperate climate, a fertile country and the most delightful appearance there is under the heavens, to complete my happiness I would have desired only to enjoy all these goods in the bosom of that happy homeland, living peacefully in sweet society with my fellow citizens, and practicing toward them (following their own example), humanity, friendship, and all the virtues; and leaving behind me the honorable memory of a good man and a decent and virtuous patriot.

If, less happy or too late grown wise, I had seen myself reduced to end an infirm and languishing career in other climates, pointlessly regretting the repose and peace of which an imprudent youth deprived me, I would at least have nourished in my soul those same sentiments I could not have used in my native country; and penetrated by a tender and disinterested affection for my distant fellow citizens, I would have addressed them from the bottom of my heart more or less along the following lines:

My dear fellow citizens, or rather my brothers, since the bonds of blood as well as the laws unite almost all of us, it gives me pleasure to be incapable of thinking of you without at the same time thinking of all the good things you enjoy, and of which perhaps none of you appreciates the value more deeply than I who have lost them. The more I reflect upon your political and civil situation, the less I am capable of imagining that the nature of human affairs could admit of a better one. In all other governments, when it is a question of assuring the greatest good of the state, everything is always limited to imaginary projects, and at most to simple possibilities. As for you, your happiness is complete; it remains merely to enjoy it. And to become perfectly happy you are in need of nothing more than to know how to be satisfied with being so. Your sovereignty, acquired or recovered at the point of a sword, and preserved for two centuries by dint of valor and wisdom, is at last fully and universally recognized. Honorable treaties fix your boundaries, secure your rights and strengthen your repose. Your constitution is excellent, since it is dictated by the most sublime reason and is guaranteed by friendly powers deserving of respect. Your state is tranquil; you have neither wars nor conquerors to fear. You have no other masters but the wise laws you have made, administered by upright magistrates of your own choosing. You are neither rich enough to enervate yourself with softness and to lose in vain delights the taste for true happiness and solid virtues, nor poor enough to need more foreign assistance than your industry procures for you. And this precious liberty, which in large nations is maintained only by exorbitant taxes, costs you almost nothing to pursue.

For the happiness of its citizens and the examples of the peoples, may a republic so wisely and so happily constituted last forever! This is the only wish left for you to make, and the only precaution left for you to take. From here on, it is for you alone, not to bring about your own happiness, your ancestors having saved you the trouble, but to render it lasting by the wisdom of using it well. It is upon your perpetual union, your obedience to the laws, your respect for their ministers that your preservation depends. If there remains among you the slightest germ of bitterness or distrust, hasten to destroy it as a ruinous leaven that sooner or later results in your misfortunes and the ruin of the state. I beg you all to look deep inside your hearts and to heed the secret voice of your conscience. Is there anyone among you who knows of a body that is more upright, more enlightened, more worthy of respect than that of your magistracy? Do not all its members give you the example of moderation, of simplicity of mores, of respect for the laws, and of the most sincere reconciliation? Then freely give such wise chiefs that salutary confidence that reason owes to virtue. Bear in mind that they are of your choice, that they justify it, and that the honors due to those whom you have established in dignity necessarily reflect back upon yourselves. None of you is so unenlightened as to be ignorant of the fact that where the vigor of laws and the authority of their defenders cease, there can be neither security nor freedom for anyone. What then is the point at issue among you except to do wholeheartedly and with just confidence what you should always be obliged to do by a true self-interest, by duty and for the sake of reason? May a sinful and ruinous indifference to the maintenance of the constitution never make you neglect in time of need the wise teachings of the most enlightened and most zealous among you. But may equity, moderation, and the most respectful firmness continue to regulate all your activities and display in you, to the entire universe, the example of a proud and modest people, as jealous of its glory as of its liberty. Above all, beware (and this will be my last counsel) of ever listening to sinister interpretations and venomous speeches, whose secret motives are often more dangerous than the actions that are their object. An entire household awakens and takes warning at the first cries of a good and faithful watchdog who never barks except at the approach of burglars. But people hate the nuisance caused by those noisy animals that continually disturb the public repose and whose continual and ill-timed warnings are not heeded even at the moment when they are necessary.

And you, MAGNIFICENT AND MOST HONORED LORDS, you upright and worthy magistrates of a free people, permit me to offer you in particular my compliments and my respects. If there is a rank in the world suited to conferring honor on those who hold it, it is without doubt the one that is given by talents and virtue, that of which you have made yourselves worthy, and to which your fellow citizens have raised you. Their own merit adds still a new luster to yours. And I that find you, who were chosen by men capable of governing others in order that they themselves may be governed, are as much above other magistrates as a free people; and above all that the one which you have the honor of leading, is, by its enlightenment and reason, above the populace of the other states.

May I be permitted to cite an example of which better records ought to remain, and which will always be near to my heart. I never call to mind without the sweetest emotion the memory of the virtuous citizen to whom I owe my being, and who often spoke to me in my childhood of the respect that was owed you. I still see him living from the work of his hands, and nourishing his soul on the most sublime truths. I see Tacitus, Plutarch and Grotius mingled with the instruments of his craft before him. I see at his side a beloved son receiving with too little profit the tender instruction of the best of fathers. But if the aberrations of foolish youth made me forget such wise lessons for a time, I have the happiness to sense at last that whatever the inclination one may have toward vice, it is difficult for an education in which the heart is involved to remain forever lost.

Such, MAGNIFICENT AND MOST HONORED LORDS, are the citizens and even the simple inhabitants born in the state you govern. Such are those educated and sensible men concerning whom, under the name of workers and people, such base and false ideas are entertained in other nations. My father, I gladly acknowledge, was in no way distinguished among his fellow citizens; he was only what they all are; and such as he was, there was no country where his company would not have been sought after, cultivated, and profitably too, by the most upright men. It does not behoove me, nor, thank heaven, is it necessary to speak to you of the regard which men of that stamp can expect from you: your equals by education as well as by the rights of nature and of birth; your inferiors by their will and by the preference they owe your merit, which they have granted to it, and for which you in turn owe them some sort of gratitude. It is with intense satisfaction that I learn how much, in your dealings with them, you temper with gentleness and cooperativeness the gravity suited to the ministers of the law; how much you repay them in esteem and attention for the obedience and respect they owe you; conduct full of justice and wisdom, suited to putting at a greater and greater distance the memory of unhappy events which must be forgotten so as never to see them again; conduct all the more judicious because this equitable and generous people makes a pleasure out of its duty, because it naturally loves to honor you, and because those who are most zealous in upholding their rights are the ones who are most inclined to respect yours.

It should not be surprising that the leaders of a civil society love its glory and happiness; but, unfortunately for the tranquility of men, that those who consider themselves as the magistrates, or rather as the masters, of a more holy and more sublime homeland manifest some love for the earthly homeland which nourishes them. How sweet it is for me to be able to make such a rare exception in our favor, and to place in the rank of our best citizens those zealous trustees of the sacred dogmas authorized by the laws, those venerable pastors of souls, whose lively and sweet eloquence the better instills the maxims of the Gospel into people's hearts as they themselves always begin by practicing them. Everyone knows the success with which the great art of preaching is cultivated in Geneva. But since people are too accustomed to seeing things said in one way and done in another, few of them know the extent to which the spirit of Christianity, the saintliness of mores, severity to oneself and gentleness to others reign in the body of our ministers. Perhaps it behooves only the city of Geneva to provide the edifying example of such a perfect union between a society of theologians and of men of letters. It is in large part upon their wisdom and their acknowledged moderation and upon their zeal for the prosperity of the state that I base my hopes for its eternal tranquility. And I note, with a pleasure mixed with amazement and respect, how much they abhor the atrocious maxims of those sacred and barbarous men of whom history provides more than one example, and who, in order to uphold the alleged rights of God— that is to say, their own interests—were all the less sparing of human blood because they hoped their own would always be respected.

Could I forget that precious half of the republic which produces the happiness of the other and whose gentleness and wisdom maintain peace and good mores? Amiable and virtuous women citizens, it will always be the fate of your sex to govern ours. Happy it is when your chaste power, exercised only within the conjugal union, makes itself felt only for the glory of the state and the public happiness! Thus it was that in Sparta women were in command, and thus it is that you deserve to be in command in Geneva. What barbarous man could resist the voice of honor and reason in the mouth of an affectionate wife? And who would not despise vain luxury on seeing your simple and modest attire, which, from the luster it derives from you, seems the most favorable to beauty? It is for you to maintain always, by your amiable and innocent dominion and by your insinuating wit, the love of laws in the state and concord among the citizens; to reunite, by happy marriages, divided families; and above all, to correct, by the persuasive sweetness of your lessons and by the modest graces of your conversation, those extravagances which our young people come to acquire in other countries, whence, instead of the many useful things they could profit from, they bring back, with a childish manner and ridiculous airs adopted among fallen women, nothing more than an admiration for who knows what pretended grandeurs, frivolous compensations for servitude, which will never be worth as much as august liberty. Therefore always be what you are, the chaste guardians of mores and the gentle bonds of peace; and continue to assert on every occasion the rights of the heart and of nature for the benefit of duty and virtue.

I flatter myself that events will not prove me wrong in basing upon such guarantees hope for the general happiness of the citizens and for the glory of the republic. I admit that with all these advantages it will not shine with that brilliance which dazzles most eyes; and the childish and fatal taste for this is the deadliest enemy of happiness and liberty. Let a dissolute youth go elsewhere in search of easy pleasures and lengthy repentances. Let the alleged men of taste admire someplace else the grandeur of palaces, the beauty of carriages, the sumptuous furnishings, the pomp of spectacles, and all the refinements of softness and luxury. In Geneva we will find only men; but such a sight has a value of its own, and those who seek it are well worth the admirers of the rest.

May you all, MAGNIFICENT, MOST HONORED AND SOVEREIGN LORDS, deign to receive with the same goodness the respectful testimonies of the interest I take in your common prosperity. If I were unfortunate enough to be guilty of some indiscreet rapture in this lively effusion of my heart, I beg you to pardon it as the tender affection of a true patriot, and to the ardent and legitimate zeal of a man who envisages no greater happiness for himself than that of seeing all of you happy.

With the most profound respect, I am, MAGNIFICENT, MOST HONORED AND SOVEREIGN LORDS, your most humble and most obedient servant and fellow citizen.

Jean-Jacques Rousseau

Chambéry
12 June 1754

PREFACE

Of all the branches of human knowledge, the most useful and the least advanced seems to me to be that of man;[2] and I dare say that the inscription on the temple at Delphi alone contained a precept more important and more difficult than all the huge tomes of the moralists. Thus I regard the subject of this discourse as one of the most interesting questions that philosophy is capable of proposing, and unhappily for us, one of the thorniest that philosophers can attempt to resolve. For how can the source of the inequality among men be known unless one begins by knowing men themselves? And how will man be successful in seeing himself as nature formed him, through all the changes that the succession of time and things must have produced in his original constitution, and in separating what he derives from his own wherewithal from what circumstances and his progress have added to or changed in his primitive state? Like the statue of Glaucus, which time, sea and storms had disfigured to such an extent that it looked less like a god than a wild beast, the human soul, altered in the midst of society by a thousand constantly recurring causes, by the acquisition of a multitude of bits of knowledge and of errors, by changes that took place in the constitution of bodies, by the constant impact of the passions, has, as it were, changed its appearance to the point of being nearly unrecognizable. And instead of a being active always by certain and invariable principles, instead of that heavenly and majestic simplicity whose mark its author had left on it, one no longer finds anything but the grotesque contrast of passion which thinks it reasons and an understanding in a state of delirium.

What is even more cruel is that, since all the progress of the human species continually moves away from its primitive state, the more we accumulate new knowledge, the more we deprive ourselves of the means of acquiring the most important knowledge of all. Thus, in a sense, it is by dint of studying man that we have rendered ourselves incapable of knowing him.

It is easy to see that it is in these successive changes of the human constitution that we must seek the first origin of the differences that distinguish men, who, by common consensus, are naturally as equal among themselves as were the animals of each species before various physical causes had introduced into certain species the varieties we now observe among some of them. In effect, it is inconceivable that these first changes, by whatever means they took place, should have altered all at once and in the same manner all the individuals of the species. But while some improved or declined and acquired various good or bad qualities which were not inherent in their nature, the others remained longer in their original state. And such was the first source of inequality among men, which it is easier to demonstrate thus in general than to assign with precision its true causes.

Let my readers not imagine, then, that I dare flatter myself with having seen what appears to me so difficult to see. I have begun some lines of reasoning; I have hazarded some guesses, less in the hope of resolving the question than with the intention of clarifying it and of reducing it to its true state. Others will easily be able to go farther on this same route, though it will not be easy for anyone to reach the end of it. For it is no light undertaking to separate what is original from what is artificial in the present nature of man, and to have a proper understanding of a state which no longer exists, which perhaps never existed, which probably never will exist, and yet about which it is necessary to have accurate notions in order to judge properly our own present state. He who would attempt to determine precisely which precautions to take in order to make solid observations on this subject would need even more philosophy than is generally supposed; and a good solution of the following problem would not seem to me unworthy of the Aristotles and Plinys of our century: *What experiments would be necessary to achieve knowledge of natural man? And what are the means of carrying out these experiments in the midst of society?* Far from undertaking to resolve this problem, I believe I have meditated sufficiently on the subject to dare respond in advance that the greatest philosophers will not be too good to direct these experiments, nor the most powerful sovereigns to carry them out. It is hardly reasonable to expect such a combination, especially with the perseverance or rather the succession of understanding and good will needed on both sides in order to achieve success.

These investigations, so difficult to carry out and so little thought about until now, are nevertheless the only means we have left of removing a multitude of difficulties that conceal from us the knowledge of the real foundations of human society. It is this ignorance of the nature of man which throws so much uncertainty and obscurity on the true definition of natural right. For the idea of right, says M. Burlamaqui, and even more that of natural right, are manifestly ideas relative to the nature of man. Therefore, he continues, the principles of this science must be deduced from this very nature of man from man's constitution and state.

It is not without surprise and a sense of outrage that one observes the paucity of agreement that prevails among the various authors who have treated it. Among the most serious writers one can hardly find two who are of the same opinion on this point. The Roman jurists—not to mention the ancient philosophers who seem to have done their best to contradict each other on the most fundamental principles—subject man and all other animals indifferently to the same natural law, because they take this expression to refer to the law that nature imposes on itself rather than the law she prescribes, or rather because of the particular sense in which those jurists understood the word "law," which on this occasion they seem to have taken only for the expression of the general relations established by nature among all animate beings for their common preservation. The moderns, in acknowledging under the word "law" merely a rule prescribed to a moral being, that is to say, intelligent, free and considered in his relations with other beings, consequently limit the competence of the natural law to the only animal endowed with reason, that is, to man. But with each one defining this law in his own fashion, they all establish it on such metaphysical principles that even among us there are very few people in a position to grasp these principles, far from being able to find them by themselves. So that all the definitions of these wise men, otherwise in perpetual contradiction with one another, agree on this alone, that it is impossible to understand the law of nature and consequently to obey it without being a great reasoner and a profound metaphysician, which means precisely that for the establishment of society, men must have used enlightenment which develops only with great difficulty and by a very small number of people within the society itself.

Knowing nature so little and agreeing so poorly on the meaning of the word "law," it would be quite difficult to come to some common understanding regarding a good definition of natural law. Thus all those definitions that are found in books have, over and above a lack of uniformity, the added fault of being drawn from several branches of knowledge which men do not naturally have, and from advantages the idea of which they cannot conceive until after having left the state of nature. Writers begin by seeking the rules on which, for the common utility, it would be appropriate for men to agree among themselves; and then they give the name *natural law* to the collection of these rules, with no other proof than the good which presumably would result from their universal observance. Surely this is a very convenient way to compose definitions and to explain the nature of things by virtually arbitrary views of what is seemly.

But as long as we are ignorant of natural man, it is futile for us to attempt to determine the law he has received or which is best suited to his constitution. All that we can see very clearly regarding this law is that, for it to be law, not only must the will of him who is obliged by it be capable of knowing submission to it, but also, for it to be natural, it must speak directly by the voice of nature.

Leaving aside therefore all the scientific books which teach us only to see men as they have made themselves, and meditating on the first and most simple operations of the human soul, I believe I perceive in it two principles that are prior to reason, of which one makes us ardently interested in our well-being and our self-preservation, and the other inspires in us a natural repugnance to seeing any sentient being, especially our fellow man, perish or suffer. It is from the conjunction and combination that our mind is in a position to make regarding these two principles, without the need for introducing that of sociability, that all the rules of natural right appear to me to flow; rules which reason is later forced to reestablish on other foundations, when, by its successive developments, it has succeeded in smothering nature.

In this way one is not obliged to make a man a philosopher before making him a man. His duties toward others are not uniquely dictated to him by the belated lessons of wisdom; and as long as he does not resist the inner impulse of compassion, he will never harm another man or even another sentient being, except in the legitimate instance where, if his preservation were involved, he is obliged to give preference to himself. By this means, an end can also be made to the ancient disputes regarding the participation of animals in the natural law. For it is clear that, lacking intelligence and liberty, they cannot recognize this law; but since they share to some extent in our nature by virtue of the sentient quality with which they are endowed, one will judge that they should also participate in natural right, and that man is subject to some sort of duties toward them. It seems, in effect, that if I am obliged not to do any harm to my fellow man, it is less because he is a rational being than because he is a sentient being: a quality that, since it is common to both animals and men, should at least give the former the right not to be needlessly mistreated by the latter.

This same study of original man, of his true needs and the fundamental principles of his duties, is also the only good means that can be used to remove those multitudes of difficulties which present themselves regarding the origin of moral inequality, the true foundations of the body politic, the reciprocal rights of its members, and a thousand other similar questions that are as important as they are poorly explained.

In considering human society from a tranquil and disinterested point of view it seems at first to manifest merely the violence of powerful men and the oppression of the weak. The mind revolts against the harshness of the former; one is inclined to deplore the blindness of the latter. And since nothing is less stable among men than those external relationships which chance brings about more often than wisdom, and which are called weakness or power, wealth or poverty, human establishments appear at first glance to be based on piles of shifting sand. It is only in examining them closely, only after having cleared away the dust and sand that surround the edifice, that one perceives the unshakeable base on which it is raised and one learns to respect its foundations. Now without a serious study of man, of his natural faculties and their successive developments, one will never succeed in making these distinctions and in separating, in the present constitution of things, what the divine will has done from what human art has pretended to do. The political and moral investigations occasioned by the important question I am examining are therefore useful in every way; and the hypothetical history of governments is an instructive lesson for man in every respect. In considering what we would have become, left to ourselves, we ought to learn to bless him whose beneficent hand, in correcting our institutions and giving them an unshakeable foundation, has prevented the disorders that must otherwise result from them, and has brought about our happiness from the means that seemed likely to add to our misery.

Learn whom God has ordered you to be, and in what part of human affairs you have been placed.

NOTICE ON THE NOTES

I have added some notes to this work, following my indolent custom of working in fits and starts. Occasionally these notes wander so far from the subject that they are not good to read with the text. I therefore have consigned them to the end of the Discourse, in which I have tried my best to follow the straightest path. Those who have the courage to begin again will be able to amuse themselves the second time as they beat the bushes and try to run through the notes. There will be little harm done if others do not read them at all.

[Translator's note: These notes are presented on p. 896. Additions to the text, made by Rousseau in the 1782 edition, are translated here and enclosed by brackets.]

QUESTION

Proposed by the Academy of Dijon
What is the Origin of Inequality
Among Men, and is it Authorized
by the Natural Law?

DISCOURSE ON THE ORIGIN AND FOUNDATIONS OF INEQUALITY AMONG MEN

It is of man that I have to speak, and the question I am examining indicates to me that I am going to be speaking to men, for such questions are not proposed by those who are afraid to honor the truth. I will therefore confidently defend the cause of humanity before the wise men who invite me to do so, and I will not be displeased with myself if I make myself worthy of my subject and my judges.

I conceive of two kinds of inequality in the human species: one which I call natural or physical, because it is established by nature and consists in the difference of age, health, bodily strength, and qualities of mind or soul. The other may be called moral or political inequality, because it depends on a kind of convention and is established, or at least authorized, by the consent of men. This latter type of inequality consists in the different privileges enjoyed by some at the expense of others, such as being richer, more honored, more powerful than they, or even causing themselves to be obeyed by them.

There is no point in asking what the source of natural inequality is, because the answer would be found enunciated in the simple definition of the word. There is still less of a point in asking whether there would not be some essential connection between the two inequalities, for that would amount to asking whether those who command are necessarily better than those who obey, and whether strength of body or mind, wisdom or virtue are always found in the same individuals in proportion to power or wealth. Perhaps this is a good question for slaves to discuss within earshot of their masters, but it is not suitable for reasonable and free men who seek the truth.

Precisely what, then, is the subject of this discourse? To mark, in the progress of things, the moment when, right taking the place of violence, nature was subjected to the law. To explain the sequence of wonders by which the strong could resolve to serve the weak, and the people to buy imaginary repose at the price of real felicity.

The philosophers who have examined the foundations of society have all felt the necessity of returning to the state of nature, but none of them has reached it. Some have not hesitated to ascribe to man in that state the notion of just and unjust, without bothering to show that he had to have that notion, or even that it was useful to him. Others have spoken of the natural right that everyone has to preserve what belongs to him, without explaining what they mean by "belonging." Others started out by giving authority to the stronger over the weaker, and immediately brought about government, without giving any thought to the time that had to pass before the meaning of the words "authority" and "government" could exist among men. Finally, all of them, speaking continually of need, avarice, oppression, desires, and pride, have transferred to the state of nature the ideas they acquired in society. They spoke about savage man, and it was civil man they depicted. It did not even occur to most of our philosophers to doubt that the state of nature had existed, even though it is evident from reading the Holy Scriptures that the first man, having received enlightenment and precepts immediately from God, was not himself in that state; and if we give the writings of Moses the credence that every Christian owes them, we must deny that, even before the flood, men were ever in the pure state of nature, unless they had fallen back into it because of some extraordinary event: a paradox that is quite awkward to defend and utterly impossible to prove.

Let us therefore begin by putting aside all the facts, for they have no bearing on the question. The investigations that may be undertaken concerning this subject should not be taken for historical truths, but only for hypothetical and conditional reasonings, better suited to shedding light on the nature of things than on pointing out their true origin, like those our physicists make everyday with regard to the formation of the world. Religion commands us to believe that since God himself drew men out of the state of nature, they are unequal because he wanted them to be so; but it does not forbid us to form conjectures, drawn solely from the nature of man and the beings that surround him, concerning what the human race could have become, if it had been left to itself. That is what I am asked, and what I propose to examine in this discourse. Since my subject concerns man in general, I will attempt to speak in terms that suit all nations, or rather, forgetting times and places in order to think only of the men to whom I am speaking, I will imagine I am in the Lyceum in Athens, reciting the lessons of my masters, having men like Plato and Xenocrates for my judges, and the human race for my audience.

O man, whatever country you may be from, whatever your opinions may be, listen: here is your history, as I have thought to read it, not in the books of your fellowmen, who are liars, but in nature, who never lies. Everything that comes from nature will be true; there will be nothing false except what I have unintentionally added. The times about which I am going to speak are quite remote: how much you have changed from what you were! It is, as it were, the life of your species that I am about to describe to you according to the qualities you have received, which your education and your habits have been able to corrupt but have been unable to destroy. There is, I feel, an age at which an individual man would want to stop. You will seek the age at which you would want your species to have stopped. Dissatisfied with your present state for reasons that portend even greater grounds for dissatisfaction for your unhappy posterity, perhaps you would like to be able to go backwards in time. This feeling should be a hymn in praise of your first ancestors, the criticism of your contemporaries, and the dread of those who have the unhappiness of living after you.

PART ONE

However important it may be, in order to render sound judgments regarding the natural state of man, to consider him from his origin and to examine him, so to speak, in the first embryo of the species, I will not follow his nature through its successive developments. I will not stop to investigate in the animal kingdom what he might have been at the beginning so as eventually to become what he is. I will not examine whether, as Aristotle thinks, man's elongated nails were not at first hooked claws, whether man was not furry like a bear, and whether, if man walked on all fours,[3] his gaze, directed toward the ground and limited to a horizon of a few steps—did not provide an indication of both the character and the limits of his ideas. On this subject I could form only vague and almost imaginary conjectures. Comparative anatomy has as yet made too little progress; the observations of naturalists are as yet too uncertain for one to be able to establish the basis of solid reasoning on such foundations. Thus, without having recourse to the supernatural knowledge we have on this point, and without taking note of the changes that must have occurred in the internal as well as the external conformation of man, as he applied his limbs to new purposes and nourished himself on new foods, I will suppose him to have been formed from all time as I see him today: walking on two feet, using his hands as we use ours, directing his gaze over all of nature, and measuring with his eyes the vast expanse of the heavens.

When I strip that being, thus constituted, of all the supernatural gifts he could have received and of all the artificial faculties he could have acquired only through long progress; when I consider him, in a word, as he must have left the hands of nature, I see an animal less strong than some, less agile than others, but all in all, the most advantageously organized of all. I see him satisfying his hunger under an oak tree, quenching his thirst at the first stream, finding his bed at the foot of the same tree that supplied his meal; and thus all his needs are satisfied.

When the earth is left to its natural fertility[4] and covered with immense forests that were never mutilated by the axe, it offers storehouses and shelters at every step to animals of every species. Men, dispersed among the animals, observe and imitate their industry, and thereby raise themselves to the level of animal instinct, with the advantage that, whereas each species has only its own instincts, man, who may perhaps have none that belongs to him, appropriates all of them to himself, feeds himself equally well on most of the various foods[5] which the other animals divide among themselves, and consequently finds his sustenance more easily than any of the rest can.

Accustomed from childhood to inclement weather and the rigors of the seasons, acclimated to fatigue, and forced, naked and without arms, to defend their lives and their prey against other ferocious beasts, or to escape them by taking flight, men develop a robust and nearly unalterable temperament. Children enter the world with the excellent constitution of their parents and strengthen it with the same exercises that produced it, thus acquiring all the vigor that the human race is capable of having. Nature treats them precisely the way the law of Sparta treated the children of its citizens: it renders strong and robust those who are well constituted and makes all the rest perish, thereby differing from our present-day societies, where the state, by making children burdensome to their parents, kills them indiscriminately before their birth.

Since the savage man's body is the only instrument he knows, he employs it for a variety of purposes that, for lack of practice, ours are incapable of serving. And our industry deprives us of the force and agility that necessity obliges him to acquire. If he had had an axe, would his wrists break such strong branches? If he had had a sling, would he throw a stone with so much force? If he had had a ladder, would he climb a tree so nimbly? If he had had a horse, would he run so fast? Give a civilized man time to gather all his machines around him, and undoubtedly he will easily overcome a savage man. But if you want to see an even more unequal fight, pit them against each other naked and disarmed, and you will soon realize the advantage of constantly having all of one's forces at one's disposal, of always being ready for any event, and of always carrying one's entire self, as it were, with one.[6]

Hobbes maintains that man is naturally intrepid and seeks only to attack and to fight. On the other hand, an illustrious philosopher thinks, and Cumberland and Pufendorf also affirm, that nothing is as timid as man in the state of nature, and that he is always trembling and ready to take flight at the slightest sound he hears or at the slightest movement he perceives. That may be the case with regard to objects with which he is not acquainted. And I do not doubt that he is frightened by all the new sights that present themselves to him every time he can neither discern the physical good and evil he may expect from them nor compare his forces with the dangers he must run: rare circumstances in the state of nature, where everything takes place in such a uniform manner and where the face of the earth is not subject to those sudden and continual changes caused by the passions and inconstancy of peoples living together. But since a savage man lives dispersed among the animals and, finding himself early on in a position to measure himself against them, he soon makes the comparison; and, aware that he surpasses them in skillfulness more than they surpass him in strength, he learns not to fear them any more. Pit a bear or a wolf against a savage who is robust, agile, and courageous, as they all are, armed with stones and a hefty cudgel, and you will see that the danger will be at least equal on both sides, and that after several such experiences, ferocious beasts, which do not like to attack one another, will be quite reluctant to attack a man, having found him to be as ferocious as themselves. With regard to animals that actually have more strength than man has skillfulness, he is in the same position as other weaker species, which nevertheless subsist. Man has the advantage that, since he is no less adept than they at running and at finding almost certain refuge in trees, he always has the alternative of accepting or leaving the encounter and the choice of taking flight or entering into combat. Moreover, it appears that no animal naturally attacks man, except in the case of self-defense or extreme hunger, or shows evidence of those violent antipathies toward him that seem to indicate that one species is destined by nature to serve as food for another.

[No doubt these are the reasons why negroes and savages bother themselves so little about the ferocious beasts they may encounter in the woods. In this respect, the Caribs of Venezuela, among others, live in the most profound security and without the slightest inconvenience. Although they are practically naked, says Francisco Coreal, they boldly expose themselves in the forest, armed only with bow and arrow, but no one has ever heard of one of them being devoured by animals.]

There are other, more formidable enemies, against which man does not have the same means of self-defense: natural infirmities, childhood, old age, and illnesses of all kinds—sad signs of our weakness, of which the first two are common to all animals, with the last belonging principally to man living in society. On the subject of childhood, I even observe that a mother, by carrying her child everywhere with her, can feed it much more easily than females of several animal species, which are forced to be continually coming and going, with great fatigue, to seek their food and to suckle or feed their young. It is true that if a woman were to perish, the child runs a considerable risk of perishing with her. But this danger is common to a hundred other species, whose young are for quite some time incapable of going off to seek their nourishment for themselves. And although childhood is longer among us, our lifespan is also longer; thus things are more or less equal in this respect,[7] although there are other rules, not relevant to my subject, which are concerned with the duration of infancy and the number of young.[8] Among the elderly, who are less active and perspire little, the need for food diminishes with the faculty of providing for it. And since savage life shields them from gout and rheumatism, and since old age is, of all ills, the one that human assistance can least alleviate, they eventually die without anyone being aware that they are ceasing to exist, and almost without being aware of it themselves.

With regard to illnesses, I will not repeat the vain and false pronouncements made against medicine by the majority of people in good health. Rather, I will ask whether there is any solid observation on the basis of which one can conclude that the average lifespan is shorter in those countries where the art of medicine is most neglected than in those where it is cultivated most assiduously. And how could that be the case, if we give ourselves more ills than medicine can furnish us remedies? The extreme inequality in our lifestyle: excessive idleness among some, excessive labor among others; the ease with which we arouse and satisfy our appetites and our sensuality; the overly refined foods of the wealthy, which nourish them with irritating juices and overwhelm them with indigestion; the bad food of the poor, who most of the time do not have even that, and who, for want of food, are inclined to stuff their stomachs greedily whenever possible; staying up until all hours, excesses of all kinds, immoderate outbursts of every passion, bouts of fatigue and mental exhaustion; countless sorrows and afflictions which are felt in all levels of society and which perpetually gnaw away at souls: these are the fatal proofs that most of our ills are of our own making, and that we could have avoided nearly all of them by preserving the simple, regular and solitary lifestyle prescribed to us by nature. If nature has destined us to be healthy, I almost dare to affirm that the state of reflection is a state contrary to nature and that the man who meditates is a depraved animal. When one thinks about the stout constitutions of the savages, at least of those whom we have not ruined with our strong liquors; when one becomes aware of the fact that they know almost no illnesses but wounds and old age, one is strongly inclined to believe that someone could easily write the history of human maladies by following the history of civil societies. This at least was the opinion of Plato, who believed that, from certain remedies used or approved by Podalirius and Machaon at the siege of Troy, various illnesses which these remedies should exacerbate were as yet unknown among men. [And Celsus reports that diet, so necessary today, was only an invention of Hippocrates.]

With so few sources of ills, man in the state of nature hardly has any need therefore of remedies, much less of physicians. The human race is in no worse condition than all the others in this respect; and it is easy to learn from hunters whether in their chases they find many sick animals. They find quite a few that have received serious wounds that healed quite nicely, that have had bones or even limbs broken and reset with no other surgeon than time, no other regimen than their everyday life, and that are no less perfectly cured for not having been tormented with incisions, poisoned with drugs, or exhausted with fasting. Finally, however correctly adminis-tered medicine may be among us, it is still certain that although a sick savage, abandoned to himself, has nothing to hope for except from nature, on the other hand, he has nothing to fear except his illness. This frequently makes his situation preferable to ours.

Therefore we must take care not to confuse savage man with the men we have before our eyes. Nature treats all animals left to their own devices with a predilection that seems to show how jealous she is of that right. The horse, the cat, the bull, even the ass, are usually taller, and all of them have a more robust constitution, more vigor, more strength, and more courage in the forests than in our homes. They lose half of these advantages in becoming domesticated; it might be said that all our efforts at feeding them and treating them well only end in their degeneration. It is the same for man himself. In becoming habituated to the ways of society and a slave, he becomes weak, fearful, and servile; his soft and effeminate lifestyle completes the enervation of both his strength and his courage. Let us add that the difference between the savage man and the domesticated man should be still greater than that between the savage animal and the domesticated animal; for while animal and man have been treated equally by nature, man gives more comforts to himself than to the animals he tames, and all of these comforts are so many specific causes that make him degenerate more noticeably.

It is therefore no great misfortune for those first men, nor, above all, such a great obstacle to their preservation, that they are naked, that they have no dwelling, and that they lack all those useful things we take to be so necessary. If they do not have furry skin, they have no need for it in warm countries, and in cold countries they soon learn to help themselves to the skins of animals they have vanquished. If they have but two feet to run with, they have two arms to provide for their defense and for their needs. Perhaps their children learn to walk late and with difficulty, but mothers carry them easily: an advantage that is lacking in other species, where the mother, on being pursued, finds herself forced to abandon her young or to conform her pace to theirs. [It is possible there are some exceptions to this. For example, the animal from the province of Nicaragua which resembles a fox and which has feet like a man's hands, and, according to Coreal, has a pouch under its belly in which the mother places her young when she is forced to take flight. No doubt this is the same animal that is called *tlaquatzin* in Mexico; the female of the species Laët describes as having a similar pouch for the same purpose.] Finally, unless we suppose those singular and fortuitous combinations of circumstances of which I will speak later, and which might very well have never taken place, at any rate it is clear that the first man who made clothing or a dwelling for himself was giving himself things that were hardly necessary, since he had done without them until then and since it is not clear why, as a grown man, he could not endure the kind of life he had endured ever since he was a child.

Alone, idle, and always near danger, savage man must like to sleep and be a light sleeper like animals which do little thinking and, as it were, sleep the entire time they are not thinking. Since his self-preservation was practically his sole concern, his best trained faculties ought to be those that have attack and defense as their principal object, either to subjugate his prey or to prevent his becoming the prey of another animal. On the other hand, the organs that are perfected only by softness and sensuality must remain in a state of crudeness that excludes any kind of refinement in him. And with his senses being divided in this respect, he will have extremely crude senses of touch and taste; those of sight, hearing and smell will have the greatest subtlety. Such is the state of animals in general, and, according to the reports of travellers, such also is that of the majority of savage peoples. Thus we should not be surprised that the Hottentots of the Cape of Good Hope can sight ships with the naked eye as far out at sea as the Dutch can with telescopes; or that the savages of America were as capable of trailing Spaniards by smell as the best dogs could have done; or that all these barbarous nations endure their nakedness with no discomfort, whet their appetites with hot peppers, and drink European liquors like water.

So far I have considered only physical man. Let us now try to look at him from a metaphysical and moral point of view.

In any animal I see nothing but an ingenious machine to which nature has given senses in order for it to renew its strength and to protect itself, to a certain point, from all that tends to destroy or disturb it. I am aware of precisely the same things in the human machine, with the difference that nature alone does everything in the operations of an animal, whereas man contributes, as a free agent, to his own operations. The former chooses or rejects by instinct and the later by an act of freedom. Hence an animal cannot deviate from the rule that is prescribed to it, even when it would be advantageous to do so, while man deviates from it, often to his own detriment. Thus a pigeon would die of hunger near a bowl filled with choice meats, and so would a cat perched atop a pile of fruit or grain, even though both could nourish themselves quite well with the food they disdain, if they were of a mind to try some. And thus dissolute men abandon themselves to excesses which cause them fever and death, because the mind perverts the senses and because the will still speaks when nature is silent.

Every animal has ideas, since it has senses; up to a certain point it even combines its ideas, and in this regard man differs from an animal only in degree. Some philosophers have even suggested that there is a greater difference between two given men than between a given man and an animal. Therefore it is not so much understanding which causes the specific distinction of man from all other animals as it is his being a free agent. Nature commands every animal, and beasts obey. Man feels the same impetus, but he knows he is free to go along or to resist; and it is above all in the awareness of this freedom that the spirituality of his soul is made manifest. For physics explains in some way the mechanism of the senses and the formation of ideas; but in the power of willing, or rather of choosing, and in the feeling of this power, we find only purely spiritual acts, about which the laws of mechanics explain nothing.

But if the difficulties surrounding all these questions should leave some room for dispute on this difference between man and animal, there is another very specific quality which distinguishes them and about which there can be no argument: the faculty of self-perfection, a faculty which, with the aid of circumstances, successively develops all the others, and resides among us as much in the species as in the individual. On the other hand, an animal, at the end of a few months, is what it will be all its life; and its species, at the end of a thousand years, is what it was in the first of those thousand years. Why is man alone subject to becoming an imbecile? Is it not that he thereby returns to his primitive state, and that, while the animal which has acquired nothing and which also has nothing to lose, always retains its instinct, man, in losing through old age or other accidents all that his *perfectibility* has enabled him to acquire, thus falls even lower than the animal itself? It would be sad for us to be forced to agree that this distinctive and almost unlimited faculty is the source of all man's misfortunes; that this is what, by dint of time, draws him out of that original condition in which he would pass tranquil and innocent days; that this is what, through centuries of giving rise to his enlightenment and his errors, his vices and his virtues, eventually makes him a tyrant over himself and nature.[9] It would be dreadful to be obliged to praise as a beneficent being the one who first suggested to the inhabitant on the banks of the Orinoco the use of boards which he binds to his children's temples, and which assure them of at least part of their imbecility and their original happiness.

Savage man, left by nature to instinct alone, or rather compensated for the instinct he is perhaps lacking by faculties capable of first replacing them and then of raising him to the level of instinct, will therefore begin with purely animal functions.[10] Perceiving and feeling will be his first state, which he will have in common with all animals. Willing and not willing, desiring, and fearing will be the first and nearly the only operations of his soul until new circumstances bring about new developments in it.

Whatever the moralists may say about it, human understanding owes much to the passions, which, by common consensus, also owe a great deal to it. It is by their activity that our reason is perfected. We seek to know only because we desire to find enjoyment; and it is impossible to conceive why someone who had neither desires nor fears would go to the bother of reasoning. The passions in turn take their origin from our needs, and their progress from our knowledge. For one can desire or fear things only by virtue of the ideas one can have of them, or from the simple impulse of nature; and savage man, deprived of every sort of enlightenment, feels only the passion of this latter sort. His desires do not go beyond his physical needs.[11] The only goods he knows in the universe are nourishment, a woman and rest; the only evils he fears are pain and hunger. I say pain and not death because an animal will never know what it is to die; and knowledge of death and its terrors is one of the first acquisitions that man has made in withdrawing from the animal condition.

Were it necessary, it would be easy for me to support this view with facts and to demonstrate that, among all the nations of the world, the progress of the mind has been precisely proportionate to the needs received by peoples from nature or to those needs to which circumstances have subjected them, and consequently to the passions which inclined them to provide for those needs. I would show the arts coming into being in Egypt and spreading with the flooding of the Nile. I would follow their progress among the Greeks, where they were seen to germinate, grow and rise to the heavens among the sands and rocks of Attica, though never being able to take root on the fertile banks of the Eurotas. I would point out that in general the peoples of the north are more industrious than those of the south, because they cannot get along as well without being so, as if nature thereby wanted to equalize things by giving to their minds the fertility it refuses their soil.

But without having recourse to the uncertain testimony of history, does anyone fail to see that everything seems to remove savage man from the temptation and the means of ceasing to be savage? His imagination depicts nothing to him; his heart asks nothing of him. His modest needs are so easily found at hand, and he is so far from the degree of knowledge necessary to make him desire to acquire greater knowledge, that he can have neither foresight nor curiosity. The spectacle of nature becomes a matter of indifference to him by dint of its becoming familiar to him. It is always the same order, always the same succession of changes. He does not have a mind for marveling at the greatest wonders; and we must not seek in him the philosophy that a man needs in order to know how to observe once what he has seen everyday. His soul, agitated by nothing, is given over to the single feeling of his own present existence, without any idea of the future, however, near it may be, and his projects, as limited as his views, hardly extend to the end of the day. Such is, even today, the extent of the Carib's foresight. In the morning he sells his bed of cotton and in the evening he returns in tears to buy it back, for want of having foreseen that he would need it that night.

The more one meditates on this subject, the more the distance from pure sensations to the simplest knowledge increases before our eyes; and it is impossible to conceive how a man could have crossed such a wide gap by his forces alone, without the aid of communication and without the provocation of necessity. How many centuries have perhaps gone by before men were in a position to see any fire other than that from the heavens? How many different risks did they have to run before they learned the most common uses of that element? How many times did they let it go out before they had acquired the art of reproducing it? And how many times perhaps did each of these secrets die with the one who had discovered it? What will we say about agriculture, an art that requires so much labor and foresight, that depends on so many other arts, that quite obviously is practicable only in a society which is at least in its beginning stages, and that serves us not so much to derive from the earth food it would readily provide without agriculture, as to force from it those preferences that are most to our taste? But let us suppose that men multiplied to the point where the natural productions were no longer sufficient to nourish them: a supposition which, it may be said in passing, would show a great advantage for the human species in that way of life. Let us suppose that, without forges or workshops, farm implements had fallen from the heavens into the hands of the savages; that these men had conquered the mortal hatred they all have for continuous work; that they had learned to foresee their needs far enough in advance; that they had guessed how the soil is to be cultivated, grains sown, and trees planted;

that they had discovered the arts of grinding wheat and fermenting grapes: all things they would need to have been taught by the gods, for it is inconceivable how they could have picked these things up on their own. Yet, after all this, what man would be so foolish as to tire himself out cultivating a field that will be plundered by the first comer, be it man or beast, who takes a fancy to the crop? And how could each man resolve to spend his life in hard labor, when, the more necessary to him the fruits of his labor may be, the surer he is of not realizing them? In a word, how could this situation lead men to cultivate the soil as long as it is not divided among them, that is to say, as long as the state of nature is not wiped out?

Were we to want to suppose a savage man as skilled in the art of thinking as our philosophers make him out to be; were we, following their example, to make him a full-fledged philosopher, discovering by himself the most sublime truths, and, by chains of terribly abstract reasoning, forming for himself maxims of justice and reason drawn from the love of order in general or from the known will of his creator; in a word, were we to suppose there was as much intelligence and enlightenment in his mind as he needs, and is in fact found to have been possessed of dullness and stupidity, what use would the species have for all that metaphysics, which could not be communicated and which would perish with the individual who would have invented it? What progress could the human race make, scattered in the woods among the animals? And to what extent could men mutually perfect and enlighten one another, when, with neither a fixed dwelling nor any need for one another, they would hardly encounter one another twice in their lives, without knowing or talking to one another.

Let us consider how many ideas we owe to the use of speech; how much grammar trains and facilitates the operations of the mind. And let us think of the inconceivable difficulties and the infinite amount of time that the first invention of languages must have cost. Let us join their reflections to the preceding ones, and we will be in a position to judge how many thousands of centuries would have been necessary to develop successively in the human mind the operations of which it was capable.

May I be permitted to consider for a moment the obstacles to the origin of languages. I could be content here to cite or repeat the investigations that the Abbé de Condillac has made on this matter, all of which completely confirm my view, and may perhaps have given me the idea in the first place. But since the way in which this philosopher resolves the difficulties he himself raises concerning the origin of conventional signs shows that he assumed what I question (namely, a kind of society already established among the inventors of language), I believe that, in referring to his reflections, I must add to them my own, in order to present the same difficulties from a standpoint that is pertinent to my subject. The first that presents itself is to imagine how languages could have become necessary; for since men had no communication among themselves nor any need for it, I fail to see either the necessity of this invention or its possibility, if it were not indispensable. I might well say, as do many others, that languages were born in the domestic intercourse among fathers, mothers, and children. But aside from the fact that this would not resolve the difficulties, it would make the mistake of those who, reasoning about the state of nature, intrude into it ideas taken from society. They always see the family gathered in one and the same dwelling, with its members maintaining among themselves a union as intimate and permanent as exists among us, where so many common interests unite them. But the fact of the matter is that in that primitive state, since nobody had houses or huts or property of any kind, each one bedded down in some random spot and often for only one night. Males and females came together fortuitously as a result of chance encounters, occasion, and desire, without there being any great need for words to express what they had to say to one another. They left one another with the same nonchalance.[12] The mother at first nursed her children for her own need; then, with habit having endeared them to her, she later nourished them for their own need. Once they had the strength to look for their food, they did not hesitate to leave the mother herself. And since there was practically no other way of finding one another than not to lose sight of one another, they were soon at the point of not even recognizing one another. It should also be noted that, since the child had all his needs to explain and consequently more things to say to the mother than the mother to the child, it is the child who must make the greatest effort toward inventing a language, and that the language he uses should in large part be of his own making, which multiplies languages as many times as there are individuals to speak them. This tendency was abetted by a nomadic and vagabond life, which does not give any idiom time to gain a foothold. For claiming that the mother teaches her child the words he ought to use in asking her for this or that is a good way of showing how already formed languages are taught, but it does not tell us how languages are formed.

Let us suppose this first difficulty has been overcome. Let us disregard for a moment the immense space that there must have been between the pure state of nature and the need for languages. And, on the supposition that they are necessary,[13] let us inquire how they might have begun to be established. Here we come to a new difficulty, worse still than the preceding one. For if men needed speech in order to learn to think, they had a still greater need for knowing how to think in order to discover the art of speaking. And even if it were understood how vocal sounds had been taken for the conventional expressions of our ideas, it would still remain for us to determine what could have been the conventional expressions for ideas that, not having a sensible object, could not be indicated either by gesture or by voice. Thus we are scarcely able to form tenable conjectures regarding the birth of this art of communicating thoughts and establishing intercourse between minds, a sublime art which is already quite far from its origin, but which the philosopher still sees at so prodigious a distance from its perfection that there is no man so foolhardy as to claim that it will ever achieve it, even if the sequences of change that time necessarily brings were suspended in its favor, even if prejudices were to be barred from the academies or be silent before them, and even if they were able to occupy themselves with that thorny problem for whole centuries without interruption.

Man's first language, the most universal, the most energetic and the only language he needed before it was necessary to persuade men assembled together, is the cry of nature. Since this cry was elicited only by a kind of instinct in pressing circumstances, to beg for help in great dangers, or for relief of violent ills, it was not used very much in the ordinary course of life, where more moderate feelings prevail. When the ideas of men begin to spread and multiply, and closer communication was established among them, they sought more numerous signs and a more extensive language. They multiplied vocal inflections and combined them with gestures, which, by their nature, are more expressive, and whose meaning is less dependent on a prior determination. They therefore signified visible and mobile objects by means of gestures, and audible ones by imitative sounds. But since a gesture indicates hardly anything more than present or easily described objects and visible actions; since its use is not universal, because darkness or the interposition of a body renders it useless; and since it requires rather than stimulates attention, men finally thought of replacing them with vocal articulations, which, while not having the same relationship to certain ideas, were better suited to represent all ideas as conventional signs. Such a substitution could only be made by a common consent and in a way rather difficult to practice for men whose crude organs had as yet no exercise, and still more difficult to conceive in itself, since that unanimous agreement had to have had a motive, and speech appears to have been necessary in order to establish the use of speech.

We must infer that the first words men used had a much broader meaning in their mind than do those used in languages that are already formed; and that, being ignorant of the division of discourse into its constitutive parts, at first they gave each word the meaning of a whole sentence. When they began to distinguish subject from attribute and verb from noun, which was no mean effort of genius, substantives were at first only so many proper nouns; the [present] infinitive was the only verb tense; and the notion of adjectives must have developed only with considerable difficulty, since every adjective is an abstract word, and abstractions are difficult and not particularly natural operations.

At first each object was given a particular name, without regard to genus and species which those first founders were not in a position to distinguish; and all individual things presented themselves to their minds in isolation, as they are in the spectacle of nature. If one oak tree was called A, another was called B. [For the first idea one draws from two things is that they are not the same; and it often requires quite some time to observe what they have in common.] Thus the more limited the knowledge, the more extensive becomes the dictionary. The difficulty inherent in all this nomenclature could not easily be alleviated, for in order to group beings under various common and generic denominations, it was necessary to know their properties and their differences. Observations and definitions were necessary, that is to say, natural history and metaphysics, and far more than men of those times could have had.

Moreover, general ideas can be introduced into the mind only with the aid of words, and the understanding grasps them only through sentences. That is one reason why animals cannot form such ideas or even acquire the perfectibility that depends on them. When a monkey moves unhesitatingly from one nut to another, does anyone think the monkey has the general idea of that type of fruit and that he compares its archetype with these two individuals? Undoubtedly not; but the sight of one of these nuts recalls to his memory the sensations he received of the other; and his eyes, modified in a certain way, announce to his sense of taste the modification it is about to receive. Every general idea is purely intellectual. The least involvement of the imagination thereupon makes the idea particular. Try to draw for yourself the image of a tree in general; you will never succeed in doing it. In spite of yourself, it must be seen as small or large, barren or leafy, light or dark; and if you were in a position to see in it nothing but what you see in every tree, this image would no longer resemble a tree. Purely abstract beings are perceived in the same way, or are conceived only through discourse. The definition of a triangle alone gives you the true idea of it. As soon as you behold one in your mind, it is a particular triangle and not some other one, and you cannot avoid making its lines to be perceptible or its plane to have color. It is therefore necessary to utter sentences, and thus to speak, in order to have general ideas. For as soon as the imagination stops, the mind proceeds no further without the aid of discourse. If, then, the first inventors of language could give names only to ideas they already had, it follows that the first substantives could not have been anything but proper nouns.

But when, by means I am unable to conceive, our new grammarians began to extend their ideas and to generalize their words, the ignorance of the inventors must have subjected this method to very strict limitations. And just as they had at first unduly multiplied the names of individual things, owing to their failure to know the genera and species, they later made too few species and genera, owing to their failure to have considered beings in all their differences. Pushing these divisions far enough would have required more experience and enlightenment than they could have had, and more investigations and work than they were willing to put into it. Now if even today new species are discovered everyday that until now had escaped all our observations, just imagine how many species must have escaped the attention of men who judged things only on first appearance! As for primary classes and the most general notions, it is superfluous to add that they too must have escaped them. How, for example, would they have imagined or understood the words "matter," "mind," "substance," "mode," "figure," and "movement," when our philosophers, who for so long have been making use of them, have a great deal of difficulty understanding them themselves; and when, since the ideas attached to these words are purely metaphysical, they found no model of them in nature?

I stop with these first steps, and I implore my judges to suspend their reading here to consider, concerning the invention of physical substantives alone, that is to say, concerning the easiest part of the language to discover, how far language still had to go in order to express all the thoughts of men, assume a durable form, be capable of being spoken in public, and influence society. I implore them to reflect upon how much time and knowledge were needed to discover numbers,[14] abstract words, aorists, and all the tenses of verbs, particles, syntax, the connecting of sentences, reasoning, and the forming of all the logic of discourse. As for myself, being shocked by the unending difficulties and convinced of the almost demonstrable impossibility that languages could have arisen and been established by merely human means, I leave to anyone who would undertake it the discussion of the following difficult problem: which was the more necessary: an already formed society for the invention of languages, or an already invented language for the establishment of society?

Whatever these origins may be, it is clear, from the little care taken by nature to bring men together through mutual needs and to facilitate their use of speech, how little she prepared them for becoming habituated to the ways of society, and how little she contributed to all that men have done to establish the bonds of society. In fact, it is impossible to imagine why, in that primitive state, one man would have a greater need for another man than a monkey or a wolf has for another of its respective species; or, assuming this need, what motive could induce the other man to satisfy it; or even, in this latter instance, how could they be in mutual agreement regarding the conditions. I know that we are repeatedly told that nothing would have been so miserable as man in that state; and if it is true, as I believe I have proved, that it is only after many centuries that men could have had the desire and the opportunity to leave that state, that would be a charge to bring against nature, not against him whom nature has thus constituted. But if we understand the word *miserable* properly, it is a word which is without meaning or which signifies merely a painful privation and suffering of the body or the soul. Now I would very much like someone to explain to me what kind of misery can there be for a free being whose heart is at peace and whose body is in good health? I ask which of the two, civil or natural life, is more likely to become insufferable to those who live it? We see about us practically no people who do not complain about their existence; many even deprive themselves of it to the extent they are able, and the combination of divine and human laws is hardly enough to stop this disorder. I ask if anyone has ever heard tell of a savage who was living in liberty ever dreaming of complaining about his life and of killing himself. Let the judgment therefore be made with less pride on which side real misery lies. On the other hand, nothing would have been so miserable as savage man, dazzled by enlightenment, tormented by passions, and reasoning about a state different from his own. It was by a very wise providence that the latent faculties he possessed should develop only as the occasion to exercise them presents itself, so that they would be neither superfluous nor troublesome to him beforehand, nor underdeveloped and useless in time of need. In instinct alone, man had everything he needed in order to live in the state of nature; in a cultivated reason, he has only what he needs to live in society.

At first it would seem that men in that state, having among themselves no type of moral relations or acknowledged duties, could be neither good nor evil, and had neither vices nor virtues, unless, if we take these words in a physical sense, we call those qualities that can harm an individual's preservation "vices" in him, and those that can contribute to it "virtues." In that case it would be necessary to call the one who least resists the simple impulses of nature the most virtuous. But without departing from the standard meaning of these words, it is appropriate to suspend the judgment we could make regarding such a situation and to be on our guard against our prejudices, until we have examined with scale in hand whether there are more virtues than vices among civilized men; or whether their virtues are more advantageous than their vices are lethal; or whether the progress of their knowledge is sufficient compensation for ills they inflict on one another as they learn of the good they ought to do; or whether, all things considered, they would not be in a happier set of circumstances if they had neither evil to fear nor good to hope for from anyone, rather than subjecting themselves to a universal dependence and obliging themselves to receive everything from those who do not oblige themselves to give them anything.

Above all, let us not conclude with Hobbes that because man has no idea of goodness he is naturally evil; that he is vicious because he does not know virtue; that he always refuses to perform services for his fellow men he does not believe he owes them; or that, by virtue of the right, which he reasonably attributes to himself, to those things he needs, he foolishly imagines himself to be the sole proprietor of the entire universe. Hobbes has very clearly seen the defect of all modern definitions of natural right, but the consequences he draws from his own definition show that he takes it in a sense that is no less false. Were he to have reasoned on the basis of the principles he establishes, this author should have said that since the state of nature is the state in which the concern for our self-preservation is the least prejudicial to that of others, that state was consequently the most appropriate for peace and the best suited for the human race. He says precisely the opposite, because he had wrongly injected into the savage man's concern for self-preservation the need to satisfy a multitude of passions which are the product of society and which have made laws necessary. The evil man, he says, is a robust child. It remains to be seen whether savage man is a robust child. Were we to grant him this, what would we conclude from it? That if this man were as dependent on others when he is robust as he is when he is weak, there is no type of excess to which he would not tend: he would beat his mother if she were too slow in offering him her breast; he would strangle one of his younger brothers, should he find him annoying; he would bite someone's leg, should he be assaulted or aggravated by him. But being robust and being dependent are two contradictory suppositions in the state of nature. Man is weak when he is dependent, and he is emancipated from that dependence before he is robust. Hobbes did not see that the same cause preventing savages from using their reason, as our jurists claim, is what prevents them at the same time from abusing their faculties, as he himself maintains. Hence we could say that savages are not evil precisely because they do not know what it is to be good; for it is neither the development of enlightenment nor the restraint imposed by the law, but the calm of the passions and the ignorance of vice which prevents them from doing evil. *So much more profitable to these is the ignorance of vice than the knowledge of virtue is to those.* Moreover, there is another principle that Hobbes failed to notice, and which, having been given to man in order to mitigate, in certain circumstances, the ferocity of his egocentrism or the desire for self-preservation before this egocentrism of his came into being,[15] tempers the ardor he has for his own well-being by an innate repugnance to seeing his fellow men suffer. I do not believe I have any contradiction to fear in granting the only natural virtue that the most excessive detractor of human virtues was forced to recognize. I am referring to pity, a disposition that is fitting for beings that are as weak and as subject to ills as we are; a virtue all the more universal and all the more useful to man in that it precedes in him any kind of reflection, and so natural that even animals sometimes show noticeable signs of it. Without speaking of the tenderness of mothers for their young and of the perils they have to brave in order to protect them, one daily observes the repugnance that horses have for trampling a living body with their hooves. An animal does not go undisturbed past a dead animal of its own species. There are even some animals that give them a kind of sepulchre; and the mournful lowing of cattle entering a slaughterhouse voices the impression they receive of the horrible spectacle that strikes them. One notes with pleasure the author of *The Fable of the Bees,* having been forced to acknowledge man as a compassionate and sensitive being, departing from his cold and subtle style in the example he gives, to offer us the pathetic image of an imprisoned man who sees outside his cell a ferocious animal tearing a child from its mother's breast, mashing its frail limbs with its murderous teeth, and ripping with its claws the child's quivering entrails. What horrible agitation must be felt by this witness of an event in which he has no personal interest! What anguish must he suffer at this sight, being unable to be of any help to the fainting mother or to the dying child?

Such is the pure movement of nature prior to all reflection. Such is the force of natural pity, which the most depraved mores still have difficulty destroying, since everyday one sees in our theaters someone affected and weeping at the ills of some unfortunate person, and who, were he in the tyrant's place, would intensify the torments of his enemy still more; [like the bloodthirsty Sulla, so sensitive to ills he had not caused, or like Alexander of Pherae, who did not dare attend the performance of any tragedy, for fear of being seen weeping with Andromache and Priam, and yet who listened impassively to the cries of so many citizens who were killed everyday on his orders. *Nature, in giving men tears, bears witness that she gave the human race the softest hearts.*] Mandeville has a clear awareness that, with all their mores, men would never have been anything but monsters, if nature had not given them pity to aid their reason; but he has not seen that from this quality alone flow all the social virtues that he wants to deny in men. In fact, what are generosity, mercy, and humanity, if not pity applied to the weak, to the guilty, or to the human species in general. Benevolence and even friendship are, properly understood, the products of a constant pity fixed on a particular object; for is desiring that someone not suffer anything but desiring that he be happy? Were it true that commiseration were merely a sentiment that puts us in the position of the one who suffers, a sentiment that is obscure and powerful in savage man, developed but weak in man dwelling in civil society, what importance would this idea have to the truth of what I say, except to give it more force? In fact, commiseration will be all the more energetic as the witnessing animal identifies itself more intimately with the suffering animal. Now it is evident that this identification must have been infinitely closer in the state of nature than in the state of reasoning. Reason is what engenders egocentrism, and reflection strengthens it. Reason is what turns man in upon himself. Reason is what separates him from all that troubles him and afflicts him. Philosophy is what isolates him and what moves him to say in secret, at the sight of a suffering man, "Perish if you will; I am safe and sound." No longer can anything but danger to the entire society trouble the tranquil slumber of the philosopher and yank him from his bed. His fellow man can be killed with impunity underneath his window. He has merely to place his hands over his ears and argue with himself a little in order to prevent nature, which rebels within him, from identifying him with the man being assassinated. Savage man does not have this admirable talent, and for lack of wisdom and reason he is always seen thoughtlessly giving in to the first sentiment of humanity. When there is a riot or a street brawl, the populace gathers together; the prudent man withdraws from the scene. It is the rabble, the women of the marketplace, who separate the combatants and prevent decent people from killing one another.

It is therefore quite certain that pity is a natural sentiment, which, by moderating in each individual the activity of the love of oneself, contributes to the mutual preservation of the entire species. Pity is what carries us without reflection to the aid of those we see suffering. Pity is what, in the state of nature, takes the place of laws, mores, and virtue, with the advantage that no one is tempted to disobey its sweet voice. Pity is what will prevent every robust savage from robbing a weak child or an infirm old man of his hard-earned subsistence, if he himself expects to be able to find his own someplace else. Instead of the sublime maxim of reasoned justice, *Do unto others as you would have them do unto you,* pity inspires all men with another maxim of natural goodness, much less perfect but perhaps more useful than the preceding one: *Do what is good for you with as little harm as possible to others.* In a word, it is in this natural sentiment, rather than in subtle arguments that one must search for the cause of the repugnance at doing evil that every man would experience, even independently of the maxims of education. Although it might be appropriate for Socrates and minds of his stature to acquire virtue through reason, the human race would long ago have ceased to exist, if its preservation had depended solely on the reasonings of its members.

With passions so minimally active and such a salutary restraint, being more wild than evil, and more attentive to protecting themselves from the harm they could receive than tempted to do harm to others, men were not subject to very dangerous conflicts. Since they had no sort of intercourse among themselves; since, as a consequence, they knew neither vanity, nor deference, nor esteem, nor contempt; since they had not the slightest notion of mine and thine, nor any true idea of justice; since they regarded the acts of violence that could befall them as an easily redressed evil and not as an offense that must be punished; and since they did not even dream of vengeance except perhaps as a knee-jerk response right then and there, like the dog that bites the stone that is thrown at him, their disputes would rarely have had bloody consequences, if their subject had been no more sensitive than food. But I see a more dangerous matter that remains for me to discuss.

Among the passions that agitate the heart of man, there is an ardent, impetuous one that renders one sex necessary to the other; a terrible passion which braves all dangers, overcomes all obstacles, and which, in its fury, seems fitted to destroy the human race it is destined to preserve. What would become of men, victimized by this unrestrained and brutal rage, without modesty and self-control, fighting everyday over the object of their passion at the price of their blood?

There must first be agreement that the more violent the passions are, the more necessary the laws are to contain them. But over and above the fact that the disorders and the crimes these passions cause daily in our midst show quite well the insufficiency of the laws in this regard, it would still be good to examine whether these disorders did not come into being with the laws themselves; for then, even if they were capable of repressing them, the least one should expect of them would be that they call a halt to an evil that would not exist without them.

Let us begin by distinguishing between the moral and the physical aspects of the sentiment of love. The physical aspect is that general desire which inclines one sex to unite with another. The moral aspect is what determines this desire and fixes it exclusively on one single object, or which at least gives it a greater degree of energy for this preferred object. Now it is easy to see that the moral aspect of love is an artificial sentiment born of social custom, and extolled by women with so much skill and care in order to establish their hegemony and make dominant the sex that ought to obey. Since this feeling is founded on certain notions of merit or beauty that a savage is not in a position to have, and on comparisons he is incapable of making, it must be almost non-existent for him. For since his mind could not form abstract ideas of regularity and proportion, his heart is not susceptible to sentiments of admiration and love, which, even without its being observed come into being from the application of these ideas. He pays exclusive attention to the temperament he has received from nature, and not the taste [aversion] he has been unable to acquire; any woman suits his purpose.

Limited merely to the physical aspect of love, and fortunate enough to be ignorant of those preferences which stir up the feeling and increase the difficulties in satisfying it, men must feel the ardors of their temperament less frequently and less vividly, and consequently have fewer and less cruel conflicts among themselves. Imagination, which wreaks so much havoc among us, does not speak to savage hearts; each man peacefully awaits the impetus of nature, gives himself over to it without choice, and with more pleasure than frenzy; and once the need is satisfied, all desire is snuffed out.

Hence it is incontestable that love itself, like all other passions, had acquired only in society that impetuous ardor which so often makes it lethal to men. And it is all the more ridiculous to represent savages as continually slaughtering each other in order to satisfy their brutality, since this opinion is directly contrary to experience; and since the Caribs, of all existing peoples, are the people that until now has wandered least from the state of nature, they are the people least subject to jealousy, even though they live in a hot climate which always seems to occasion greater activity in these passions.

As to any inferences that could be drawn, in the case of several species of animals, from the clashes between males that bloody our poultry yards throughout the year, and which make our forests resound in the spring with their cries as they quarrel over a female, it is necessary to begin by excluding all species in which nature has manifestly established, in the relative power of the sexes, relations other than those that exist among us. Hence cockfights do not form the basis for an inference regarding the human species. In species where the proportion is more closely observed, these fights can have for their cause only the scarcity of females in relation to the number of males, or the exclusive intervals during which the female continually rejects the advances of the male, which adds up to the cause just cited. For if each female receives the male for only two months a year, in this respect it is as if the number of females were reduced by five-sixths. Now neither of these two cases is applicable to the human species where the number of females generally surpasses the number of males, and where human females, unlike those of other species, have never been observed to have periods of heat and exclusion, even among savages. Moreover, among several of these animal species, where the entire species goes into heat simultaneously, there comes a terrible moment of common ardor, tumult, disorder and combat: a moment that does not happen in the human species where love is never periodic. Therefore one cannot conclude from the combats of certain animals for the possession of females that the same thing would happen to man in the state of nature. And even if one could draw that conclusion, given that these conflicts do not destroy the other species, one should conclude that they would not be any more lethal for ours. And it is quite apparent that they would wreak less havoc in the state of nature than in society, especially in countries where mores still count for something and where the jealousy of lovers and the vengeance of husbands every day give rise to duels, murders and still worse things; where the duty of eternal fidelity serves merely to create adulterers; and where even the laws of continence and honor necessarily spread debauchery and multiply the number of abortions.

Let us conclude that, wandering in the forests, without industry, without speech, without dwelling, without war, without relationships, with no need for his fellow men, and correspondingly with no desire to do them harm, perhaps never even recognizing any of them individually, savage man, subject to few passions and self-sufficient, had only the sentiments and enlightenment appropriate to that state; he felt only his true needs, took notice of only what he believed he had an interest in seeing; and that his intelligence made no more progress than his vanity. If by chance he made some discovery, he was all the less able to communicate it to others because he did not even know his own children. Art perished with its inventor. There was neither education nor progress; generations were multiplied to no purpose. Since each one always began from the same point, centuries went by with all the crudeness of the first ages; the species was already old, and man remained ever a child.

If I have gone on at such length about the supposition of that primitive condition, it is because, having ancient errors and inveterate prejudices to destroy, I felt I should dig down to the root and show, in the depiction of the true state of nature how far even natural inequality is from having as much reality and influence in that state as our writers claim.

In fact, it is easy to see that, among the differences that distinguish men, several of them pass for natural ones which are exclusively the work of habit and of the various sorts of life that men adopt in society. Thus a robust or delicate temperament, and the strength or weakness that depend on it, frequently derive more from the harsh or effeminate way in which one has been raised than from the primitive constitution of bodies. The same holds for mental powers; and not only does education make a difference between cultivated minds and those that are not, it also augments the difference among the former in proportion to their culture; for were a giant and a dwarf walking on the same road, each step they both take would give a fresh advantage to the giant. Now if one compares the prodigious diversity of educations and lifestyles in the different orders of the civil state with the simplicity and uniformity of animal and savage life, where all nourish themselves from the same foods live in the same manner, and do exactly the same things, it will be understood how much less the difference between one man and another must be in the state of nature than in that of society, and how much natural inequality must increase in the human species through inequality occasioned by social institutions.

But even if nature were to affect, in the distribution of her gifts, as many preferences as is claimed, what advantage would the most favored men derive from them, to the detriment of others, in a state of things that allowed practically no sort of relationships among them? Where there is no love, what use is beauty? What use is wit for people who do not speak, and ruse to those who have no dealing with others? I always hear it repeated that the stronger will oppress the weaker. But let me have an explanation of the meaning of the word "oppression." Some will dominate with violence; others will groan, enslaved to all their caprices. That is precisely what I observe among us; but I do not see how this could be said of savage men, to whom it would be difficult even to explain what servitude and domination are. A man could well lay hold of the fruit another has gathered, the game he has killed, the cave that served as his shelter. But how will he ever succeed in making himself be obeyed? And what can be the chains of dependence among men who possess nothing? If someone chases me from one tree, I am free to go to another; if someone torments me in one place, who will prevent me from going elsewhere? Is there a man with strength sufficiently superior to mine and who is, moreover, sufficiently depraved, sufficiently lazy and sufficiently ferocious to force me to provide for his subsistence while he remains idle? He must resolve not to take his eyes off me for a single instant, to keep me carefully tied down while he sleeps, for fear that I may escape or that I would kill him. In other words, he is obliged to expose himself voluntarily to a much greater hardship than the one he wants to avoid and gives me. After all that, were his vigilance to relax for an instant, were an unforeseen noise to make him turn his head, I take twenty steps into the forest; my chains are broken, and he never sees me again for the rest of his life.

Without needlessly prolonging these details, anyone should see that, since the bonds of servitude are formed merely from the mutual dependence of men and the reciprocal needs that unite them, it is impossible to enslave a man without having first put him in the position of being incapable of doing without another. This being a situation that did not exist in the state of nature, it leaves each person free of the yoke, and renders pointless the law of the strongest.

After having proved that inequality is hardly observable in the state of nature, and that its influence there is almost nonexistent, it remains for me to show its origin and progress in the successive developments of the human mind. After having shown that *perfectibility*, social virtues, and the other faculties that natural man had received in a state of potentiality could never develop by themselves, that to achieve this development they required the chance coming together of several unconnected causes that might never have come into being and without which he would have remained eternally in his primitive constitution, it remains for me to consider and to bring together the various chance happenings that were able to perfect human reason while deteriorating the species, make a being evil while rendering it habituated to the ways of society, and, from so distant a beginning, finally bring man and the world to the point where we see them now.

I admit that, since the events I have to describe could have taken place in several ways, I cannot make a determination among them except on the basis of conjecture. But over and above the fact that these conjectures become reasons when they are the most probable ones that a person can draw from the nature of things and the sole means that a person can have of discovering the truth, the consequences I wish to deduce from mine will not thereby be conjectural, since, on the basis of the principles I have just established, no other system is conceivable that would not furnish me with the same results, and from which I could not draw the same conclusions.

This will excuse me from expanding my reflections on the way in which the lapse of time compensates for the slight probability of events; concerning the surprising power that quite negligible causes may have when they act without interruption; concerning the impossibility, on the one hand, of a person's destroying certain hypotheses, even though, on the other hand, one is not in a position to accord them the level of factual certitude; concerning a situation in which two facts given as real are to be connected by a series of intermediate facts that are unknown or regarded as such, it belongs to history, when it exists, to provide the facts that connect them; it belongs to philosophy, when history is unavailable, to determine similar facts that can connect them; finally, concerning how, with respect to events, similarity reduces the facts to a much smaller number of different classes than one might imagine. It is enough for me to offer these objects to the consideration of my judges; it is enough for me to have seen to it that ordinary readers would have no need to consider them.

PART TWO

The first person who, having enclosed a plot of land, took it into his head to say *this is mine* and found people simple enough to believe him, was the true founder of civil society. What crimes, wars, murders, what miseries and horrors would the human race have been spared, had someone pulled up the stakes or filled in the ditch and cried out to his fellow men: "Do not listen to this impostor. You are lost if you forget that the fruits of the earth belong to all and the earth to no one!" But it is quite likely that by then things had already reached the point where they could no longer continue as they were. For this idea of property, depending on many prior ideas which could only have arisen successively, was not formed all at once in the human mind. It was necessary to make great progress, to acquire much industry and enlightenment, and to transmit and augment them from one age to another, before arriving at this final stage in the state of nature. Let us therefore take things farther back and try to piece together under a single viewpoint that slow succession of events and advances in knowledge in their most natural order.

Man's first sentiment was that of his own existence; his first concern was that of his preservation. The products of the earth provided him with all the help he needed; instinct led him to make use of them. With hunger and other appetites making him experience by turns various ways of existing, there was one appetite that invited him to perpetuate his species; and this blind inclination, devoid of any sentiment of the heart, produced a purely animal act. Once this need had been satisfied, the two sexes no longer took cognizance of one another, and even the child no longer meant anything to the mother once it could do without her.

Such was the condition of man in his nascent stage; such was the life of an animal limited at first to pure sensations, and scarcely profiting from the gifts nature offered him, far from dreaming of extracting anything from her. But difficulties soon presented themselves to him; it was necessary to learn to overcome them. The height of trees, which kept him from reaching their fruits, the competition of animals that sought to feed themselves on these same fruits, the ferocity of those animals that wanted to take his own life: everything obliged him to apply himself to bodily exercises. It was necessary to become agile, fleet-footed and vigorous in combat. Natural arms, which are tree branches and stones, were soon found ready at hand. He learned to surmount nature's obstacles, combat other animals when necessary, fight for his subsistence even with men, or compensate for what he had to yield to those stronger than himself.

In proportion as the human race spread, difficulties multiplied with the men. Differences in soils, climates and seasons could force them to inculcate these differences in their lifestyles. Barren years, long and hard winters, hot summers that consume everything required new resourcefulness from them. Along the seashore and the riverbanks they invented the fishing line and hook, and became fishermen and fish-eaters. In the forests they made bows and arrows, and became hunters and warriors. In cold countries they covered themselves with the skins of animals they had killed. Lightning, a volcano, or some fortuitous chance happening acquainted them with fire: a new resource against the rigors of winter. They learned to preserve this element, then to reproduce it, and finally to use it to prepare meats that previously they devoured raw.

This repeated appropriation of various beings to himself, and of some beings to others, must naturally have engendered in man's mind the perceptions of certain relations. These relationships which we express by the words "large," "small," "strong," "weak," "fast," "slow," "timorous," "bold," and other similar ideas, compared when needed and almost without thinking about it, finally produced in him a kind of reflection, or rather a mechanical prudence which pointed out to him the precautions that were most necessary for his safety.

The new enlightenment which resulted from this development increased his superiority over the other animals by making him aware of it. He trained himself to set traps for them; he tricked them in a thousand different ways. And although several surpassed him in fighting strength or in swiftness in running, of those that could serve him or hurt him, he became in time the master of the former and the scourge of the latter. Thus the first glance he directed upon himself produced within him the first stirring of pride; thus, as yet hardly knowing how to distinguish the ranks, and contemplating himself in the first rank by virtue of his species, he prepared himself from afar to lay claim to it in virtue of his individuality.

Although his fellowmen were not for him what they are for us, and although he had hardly anything more to do with them than with other animals, they were not forgotten in his observations. The conformities that time could make him perceive among them, his female, and himself, made him judge those he did not perceive. And seeing that they all acted as he would have done under similar circumstances, he concluded that their way of thinking and feeling was in complete conformity with his own. And this important truth, well established in his mind, made him follow, by a presentiment as sure as dialectic and more prompt, the best rules of conduct that it was appropriate to observe toward them for his advantage and safety.

Taught by experience that love of well-being is the sole motive of human actions, he found himself in a position to distinguish the rare occasions when common interest should make him count on the assistance of his fellowmen, and those even rarer occasions when competition ought to make him distrust them. In the first case, he united with them in a herd, or at most in some sort of free association, that obligated no one and that lasted only as long as the passing need that had formed it. In the second case, everyone sought to obtain his own advantage, either by overt force, if he believed he could, or by cleverness and cunning, if he felt himself to be the weaker.

This is how men could imperceptibly acquire some crude idea of mutual commitments and of the advantages to be had in fulfilling them, but only insofar as present and perceptible interests could require it, since foresight meant nothing to them, and far from concerning themselves about a distant future, they did not even give a thought to the next day. Were it a matter of catching a deer, everyone was quite aware that he must faithfully keep to his post in order to achieve this purpose; but if a hare happened to pass within reach of one of them, no doubt he would have pursued it without giving it a second thought, and that, having obtained his prey, he cared very little about causing his companions to miss theirs.

It is easy to understand that such intercourse did not require a language much more refined than that of crows or monkeys, which flock together in practically the same way. Inarticulate cries, many gestures, and some imitative noises must for a long time have made up the universal language. By joining to this in each country a few articulate and conventional sounds, whose institution, as I have already said, is not too easy to explain, there were individual languages, but crude and imperfect ones, quite similar to those still spoken by various savage nations today. Constrained by the passing of time, the abundance of things I have to say, and the practically imperceptible progress of the beginnings, I am flying like an arrow over the multitudes of centuries. For the slower events were in succeeding one another, the quicker they can be described.

These first advances enabled man to make more rapid ones. The more the mind was enlightened, the more industry was perfected. Soon they ceased to fall asleep under the first tree or to retreat into caves, and found various types of hatchets made of hard, sharp stones, which served to cut wood, dig up the soil, and make huts from branches they later found it useful to cover with clay and mud. This was the period of a first revolution which formed the establishment of the distinction among families and which introduced a kind of property, whence perhaps there already arose many quarrels and fights. However, since the strongest were probably the first to make themselves lodgings they felt capable of defending, presumably the weak found it quicker and safer to imitate them than to try to dislodge them; and as for those who already had huts, each of them must have rarely sought to appropriate that of his neighbor, less because it did not belong to him than because it was of no use to him, and because he could not seize it without exposing himself to a fierce battle with the family that occupied it.

The first developments of the heart were the effect of a new situation that united the husbands and wives, fathers and children in one common habitation. The habit of living together gave rise to the sweetest sentiments known to men: conjugal love and paternal love. Each family became a little society all the better united because mutual attachment and liberty were its only bonds; and it was then that the first difference was established in the lifestyle of the two sexes, which until then had had only one. Women became more sedentary and grew accustomed to watch over the hut and the children, while the man went to seek their common subsistence. With their slightly softer life the two sexes also began to lose something of their ferocity and vigor. But while each one separately became less suited to combat savage beasts, on the other hand it was easier to assemble in order jointly to resist them.

In this new state, with a simple and solitary life, very limited needs, and the tools they had invented to provide for them, since men enjoyed a great deal of leisure time, they used it to procure for themselves many types of conveniences unknown to their fathers; and that was the first yoke they imposed on themselves without realizing it, and the first source of evils they prepared for their descendants. For in addition to their continuing thus to soften body and mind (those conveniences having through habit lost almost all their pleasure, and being at the same time degenerated into true needs), being deprived of them became much more cruel than possessing them was sweet; and they were unhappy about losing them without being happy about possessing them.

At this point we can see a little better how the use of speech was established or imperceptibly perfected itself in the bosom of each family; and one can further conjecture how various particular causes could have extended the language and accelerated its progress by making it more necessary. Great floods or earthquakes surrounded the inhabited areas with water or precipices. Upheavals of the globe detached parts of the mainland and broke them up into islands. Clearly among men thus brought together and forced to live together, a common idiom must have been formed sooner than among those who wandered freely about the forests of the mainland. Thus it is quite possible that after their first attempts at navigation, the islanders brought the use of speech to us; and it is at least quite probable that society and languages came into being on islands and were perfected there before they were known on the mainland.

Everything begins to take on a new appearance. Having previously wandered about the forests and having assumed a more fixed situation, men slowly came together and united into different bands, eventually forming in each country a particular nation, united by mores and characteristic features, not by regulations and laws, but by the same kind of life and foods and by the common influence of the climate. Eventually a permanent proximity cannot fail to engender some intercourse among different families. Young people of different sexes live in neighboring huts; the passing intercourse demanded by nature soon leads to another, through frequent contact with one another, no less sweet and more permanent. People become accustomed to consider different objects and to make comparisons. Imperceptibly they acquire the ideas of merit and beauty which produce feelings of preference. By dint of seeing one another, they can no longer get along without seeing one another again. A sweet and tender feeling insinuates itself into the soul and at the least opposition becomes an impetuous fury. Jealousy awakens with love; discord triumphs, and the sweetest passion receives sacrifices of human blood.

In proportion as ideas and sentiments succeed one another and as the mind and heart are trained, the human race continues to be tamed, relationships spread and bonds are tightened. People grew accustomed to gather in front of their huts or around a large tree; song and dance, true children of love and leisure, became the amusement or rather the occupation of idle men and women who had flocked together. Each one began to look at the others and to want to be looked at himself, and public esteem had a value. The one who sang or danced the best, the handsomest, the strongest, the most adroit or the most eloquent became the most highly regarded. And this was the first step toward inequality and, at the same time, toward vice. From these first preferences were born vanity and contempt on the one hand, and shame and envy on the other. And the fermentation caused by these new leavens eventually produced compounds fatal to happiness and innocence.

As soon as men had begun mutually to value one another, and the idea of esteem was formed in their minds, each one claimed to have a right to it, and it was no longer possible for anyone to be lacking it with impunity. From this came the first duties of civility, even among savages; and from this every voluntary wrong became an outrage, because along with the harm that resulted from the injury, the offended party saw in it contempt for his person, which often was more insufferable than the harm itself. Hence each man punished the contempt shown him in a manner proportionate to the esteem in which he held himself; acts of revenge became terrible, and men became bloodthirsty and cruel. This is precisely the stage reached by most of the savage people known to us; and it is for want of having made adequate distinctions among their ideas or of having noticed how far these peoples already were from the original state of nature that many have hastened to conclude that man is naturally cruel, and that he needs civilization in order to soften him. On the contrary, nothing is so gentle as man in his primitive state, when, placed by nature at an equal distance from the stupidity of brutes and the fatal enlightenment of civil man, and limited equally by instinct and reason to protecting himself from the harm that threatens him, he is restrained by natural pity from needlessly harming anyone himself, even if he has been harmed. For according to the axiom of the wise Locke, *where there is no property, there is no injury.*

But it must be noted that society in its beginning stages and the relations already established among men required in them qualities different from those they derived from their primitive constitution; that, with morality beginning to be introduced into human actions, and everyone, prior to the existence of laws, being sole judge and avenger of the offenses he had received, the goodness appropriate to the pure state of nature was no longer what was appropriate to an emerging society; that it was necessary for punishments to become more severe in proportion as the occasions for giving offense became more frequent; and that it was for the fear of vengeance to take the place of the deterrent character of laws. Hence although men had become less forebearing, and although natural pity had already undergone some alteration, this period of the development of human faculties, maintaining a middle position between the indolence of our primitive state and the petulant activity of our egocentrism, must have been the happiest and most durable epoch. The more one reflects on it, the more one finds that this state was the least subject to upheavals and the best for man,[16] and that he must have left it only by virtue of some fatal chance happening that, for the common good, ought never have happened. The example of savages, almost all of whom have been found in this state, seems to confirm that the human race had been made to remain in it always; that this state is the veritable youth of the world; and that all the subsequent progress has been in appearance so many steps toward the perfection of the individual, and in fact toward the decay of the species.

As long as men were content with the rustic huts, as long as they were limited to making their clothing out of skins sewn together with thorns or fish bones, adorning themselves with feathers and shells, painting their bodies with various colors, perfecting or embellishing their bows and arrows, using sharp-edged stones to make some fishing canoes or some crude musical instruments; in a word, as long as they applied themselves exclusively to tasks that a single individual could do and to the arts that did not require the cooperation of several hands, they lived as free, healthy, good and happy as they could in accordance with their nature; and they continued to enjoy among themselves the sweet rewards of independent intercourse. But as soon as one man needed the help of another, as soon as one man realized that it was useful for a single individual to have provisions for two, equality disappeared, property came into existence, labor became necessary. Vast forests were transformed into smiling fields which had to be watered with men's sweat, and in which slavery and misery were soon seen to germinate and grow with the crops.

Metallurgy and agriculture were the two arts whose invention produced this great revolution. For the poet, it is gold and silver; but for the philosopher, it is iron and wheat that have civilized men and ruined the human race. Thus they were both unknown to the savages of America, who for that reason have always remained savages. Other peoples even appear to have remained barbarous, as long as they practiced one of those arts without the other. And perhaps one of the best reasons why Europe has been, if not sooner, at least more constantly and better governed than the other parts of the world, is that it is at the same time the most abundant in iron and the most fertile in wheat.

It is very difficult to guess how men came to know and use iron, for it is incredible that by themselves they thought of drawing the ore from the mine and performing the necessary preparations on it for smelting it before they knew what would result. From another point of view, it is even less plausible to attribute this discovery to some accidental fire, because mines are set up exclusively in arid places devoid of trees and plants, so that one would say that nature had taken precautions to conceal this deadly secret from us. Thus there remains only the extraordinary circumstance of some volcano that, in casting forth molten metal, would have given observers the idea of imitating this operation of nature. Even still we must suppose them to have had a great deal of courage and foresight to undertake such a difficult task and to have envisaged so far in advance the advantages they could derive from it. This is hardly suitable for minds already better trained than theirs must have been.

As for agriculture, its principle was known long before its practice was established, and it is hardly possible that men, constantly preoccupied with deriving their subsistence from trees and plants, did not rather quickly get the idea of the methods used by nature to grow plant life. But their industry probably did not turn in that direction until very late either because trees, which, along with hunting and fishing, provided their nourishment, had no need of their care; or for want of knowing how to use wheat; or for want of tools with which to cultivate it; or for want of foresight regarding future needs; or, finally, for want of the means of preventing others from appropriating the fruits of their labors. Having become more industrious, it is believable that, with sharp stones and pointed sticks, they began by cultivating some vegetables or roots around their huts long before they knew how to prepare wheat and had the tools necessary for large-scale cultivation. Moreover, to devote oneself to that occupation and to sow the lands, one must be resolved to lose something at first in order to gain a great deal later: a precaution quite far removed from the mind of the savage man, who, as I have said, finds it quite difficult to give thought in the morning to what he will need at night.

The invention of the other arts was therefore necessary to force the human race to apply itself to that of agriculture. Once men were needed in order to smelt and forge the iron, other men were needed in order to feed them. The more the number of workers increased, the fewer hands there were to obtain food for the common subsistence, without there being fewer mouths to consume it; and since some needed foodstuffs in exchange for their iron, the others finally found the secret of using iron to multiply foodstuffs. From this there arose farming and agriculture, on the one hand, and the art of working metals and multiplying their uses, on the other.

From the cultivation of land, there necessarily followed the division of land; and from property once recognized, the first rules of justice. For in order to render everyone what is his, it is necessary that everyone can have something. Moreover, as men began to look toward the future and as they saw that they all had goods to lose, there was not one of them who did not have to fear reprisals against himself for wrongs he might do to another. This origin is all the more natural as it is impossible to conceive of the idea of property arising from anything but manual labor, for it is not clear what man can add, beyond his own labor, in order to appropriate things he has not made. It is labor alone that, in giving the cultivator a right to the product of the soil he has tilled, consequently gives him a right, at least until the harvest, and thus from year to year. With this possession continuing uninterrupted, it is easily transformed into property. When the ancients, says Grotius, gave Ceres the epithet of legislatrix, gave the name Thesmophories to a festival celebrated in her honor, they thereby made it apparent that the division of lands has produced a new kind of right: namely, the right of property, different from that which results from the natural law.

Things in this state could have remained equal, if talents had been equal, and if the use of iron and the consumption of foodstuffs had always been in precise balance. But this proportion, which was not maintained by anything, was soon broken. The strongest did the most work; the most adroit turned theirs to better advantage: the most ingenious found ways to shorten their labor. The farmer had a greater need for iron, or the blacksmith had a greater need for wheat; and in laboring equally, the one earned a great deal while the other barely had enough to live. Thus it is that natural inequality imperceptibly manifests itself together with inequality occasioned by the socialization process. Thus it is that the differences among men, developed by those of circumstances, make themselves more noticeable, more permanent in their effects, and begin to influence the fate of private individuals in the same proportion.

With things having reached this point, it is easy to imagine the rest. I will not stop to describe the successive invention of the arts, the progress of languages, the testing and use of talents, the inequality of fortunes, the use or abuse of wealth, nor all the details that follow these and that everyone can easily supply. I will limit myself exclusively to taking a look at the human race placed in this new order of things.

Thus we find here all our faculties developed, memory and imagination in play, egocentrism looking out for its interests, reason rendered active, and the mind having nearly reached the limit of the perfection of which it is capable. We find here all the natural qualities put into action, the rank and fate of each man established not only on the basis of the quantity of goods and the power to serve or harm, but also on the basis of mind, beauty, strength or skill, on the basis of merit or talents. And since these qualities were the only ones that could attract consideration, he was soon forced to have them or affect them. It was necessary, for his advantage, to show himself to be something other than what he in fact was. Being something and appearing to be something became two completely different things; and from this distinction there arose grand ostentation, deceptive cunning, and all the vices that follow in their wake. On the other hand, although man had previously been free and independent, we find him, so to speak, subject, by virtue of a multitude of fresh needs, to all of nature and particularly to his fellowmen, whose slave in a sense he becomes even in becoming their master; rich, he needs their services; poor, he needs their help; and being midway between wealth and poverty does not put him in a position to get along without them. It is therefore necessary for him to seek incessantly to interest them in his fate and to make them find their own profit, in fact or in appearance, in working for his. This makes him two-faced and crooked with some, imperious and harsh with others, and puts him in the position of having to abuse everyone he needs when he cannot make them fear them and does not find it in his interests to be of useful service to them. Finally, consuming ambition, the zeal for raising the relative level of his fortune, less out of real need than in order to put himself above others, inspires in all men a wicked tendency to harm one another, a secret jealousy all the more dangerous because, in order to strike its blow in greater safety, it often wears the mask of benevolence; in short, competition and rivalry on the one hand, opposition of interest[s] on the other, and always the hidden desire to profit at the expense of someone else. All these ills are the first effect of property and the inseparable offshoot of incipient inequality.

Before representative signs of wealth had been invented, it could hardly have consisted of anything but lands and livestock, the only real goods men can possess. Now when inheritances had grown in number and size to the point of covering the entire landscape and of all bordering on one another, some could no longer be enlarged except at the expense of others; and the supernumeraries, whom weakness or indolence had prevented from acquiring an inheritance in their turn, became poor without having lost anything, because while everything changed around them, they alone had not changed at all. Thus they were forced to receive or steal their subsistence from the hands of the rich. And from that there began to arise, according to the diverse characters of the rich and the poor, domination and servitude, or violence and thefts. For their part, the wealthy had no sooner known the pleasure of domination, than before long they disdained all others, and using their old slaves to subdue new ones, they thought of nothing but the subjugation and enslavement of their neighbors, like those ravenous wolves which, on having once tasted human flesh, reject all other food and desire to devour only men.

Thus, when both the most powerful or the most miserable made of their strength or their needs a sort of right to another's goods, equivalent, according to them, to the right of property, the destruction of equality was followed by the most frightful disorder. Thus the usurpations of the rich, the acts of brigandage by the poor, the unbridled passions of all, stifling natural pity and the still weak voice of justice, made men greedy, ambitious and wicked. There arose between the right of the strongest and the right of the first occupant a perpetual conflict that ended only in fights and murders.[17] Emerging society gave way to the most horrible state of war; since the human race, vilified and desolated, was no longer able to retrace its steps or give up the unfortunate acquisitions it had made, and since it labored only toward its shame by abusing the faculties that honor it, it brought itself to the brink of its ruin. *Horrified by the newness of the ill, both the poor man and the rich man hope to flee from wealth, hating what they once had prayed for.*

It is not possible that men should not have eventually reflected upon so miserable a situation and upon the calamities that overwhelm them. The rich in particular must have soon felt how disadvantageous to them it was to have a perpetual war in which they alone paid all the costs, and in which the risk of losing one's life was common to all and the risk of losing one's goods was personal. Moreover, regardless of the light in which they tried to place their usurpations, they knew full well that they were established on nothing but a precarious and abusive right, and that having been acquired merely by force, force might take them away from them without their having any reason to complain. Even those enriched exclusively by industry could hardly base their property on better claims. They could very well say: "I am the one who built that wall; I have earned this land with my labor." In response to them it could be said: "Who gave you the boundary lines? By what right do you claim to exact payment at our expense for labor we did not impose upon you? Are you unaware that a multitude of your brothers perish or suffer from need of what you have in excess, and that you needed explicit and unanimous consent from the human race for you to help yourself to anything from the common subsistence that went beyond your own?" Bereft of valid reasons to justify himself and sufficient forces to defend himself; easily crushing a private individual, but himself crushed by troops of bandits; alone against all and unable on account of mutual jealousies to unite with his equals against enemies united by the common hope of plunder, the rich, pressed by necessity, finally conceived the most thought-out project that ever entered the human mind. It was to use in his favor the very strength of those who attacked him, to turn his adversaries into his defenders, to instill in them other maxims, and to give them other institutions which were as favorable to him as natural right was unfavorable to him.

With this end in mind, after having shown his neighbors the horror of a situation which armed them all against each other and made their possessions as burdensome as their needs, and in which no one could find safety in either poverty or wealth, he easily invented specious reasons to lead them to his goal. "Let us unite," he says to them, "in order to protect the weak from oppression, restrain the ambitious, and assure everyone of possessing what belongs to him. Let us institute rules of justice and peace to which all will be obliged to conform, which will make special exceptions for no one, and which will in some way compensate for the caprices of fortune by subjecting the strong and the weak to mutual obligations. In short, instead of turning our forces against ourselves, let us gather them into one supreme power that governs us according to wise laws, that protects and defends all the members of the association, repulses common enemies, and maintains us in an eternal concord."

Considerably less than the equivalent of this discourse was needed to convince crude, easily seduced men who also had too many disputes to settle among themselves to be able to get along without arbiters, and too much greed and ambition to be able to get along without masters for long. They all ran to chain themselves, in the belief that they secured their liberty, for although they had enough sense to realize the advantages of a political establishment, they did not have enough experience to foresee its dangers. Those most capable of anticipating the abuses were precisely those who counted on profiting from them; and even the wise saw the need to be resolved to sacrifice one part of their liberty to preserve the other, just as a wounded man has his arm amputated to save the rest of his body.

Such was, or should have been, the origin of society and laws, which gave new fetters to the weak and new forces to the rich,[18] irretrievably destroyed natural liberty, established forever the law of property and of inequality, changed adroit usurpation into an irrevocable right, and for the profit of a few ambitious men henceforth subjected the entire human race to labor, servitude and misery. It is readily apparent how the establishment of a single society rendered indispensable that of all the others, and how, to stand head to head against the united forces, it was necessary to unite in turn. Societies, multiplying or spreading rapidly, soon covered the entire surface of the earth; and it was no longer possible to find a single corner in the universe where someone could free himself from the yoke and withdraw his head from the often ill-guided sword which everyone saw perpetually hanging over his own head. With civil right thus having become the common rule of citizens, the law of nature no longer was operative except between the various societies, when, under the name of the law of nations, it was tempered by some tacit conventions in order to make intercourse possible and to serve as a substitute for natural compassion which, losing between one society and another nearly all the force it had between one man and another, no longer resides anywhere but in a few great cosmopolitan souls, who overcome the imaginary barriers that separate peoples, and who, following the example of the sovereign being who has created them, embrace the entire human race in their benevolence.

Remaining thus among themselves in the state of nature, the bodies politic soon experienced the inconveniences that had forced private individuals to leave it; and that state became even more deadly among these great bodies than that state had among the private individuals of whom they were composed. Whence came the national wars, battles, murders, and reprisals that make nature tremble and offend reason, and all those horrible prejudices that rank the honor of shedding human blood among the virtues. The most decent people learned to consider it one of their duties to kill their fellow men. Finally, men were seen massacring one another by the thousands without knowing why. More murders were committed in a single day of combat and more horrors in the capture of a single city than were committed in the state of nature during entire centuries over the entire face of the earth. Such are the first effects one glimpses of the division of mankind into different societies. Let us return to the founding of these societies.

I know that many have ascribed other origins to political societies, such as conquests by the most powerful, or the union of the weak; and the choice among these causes is indifferent to what I want to establish. Nevertheless, the one I have just described seems to me the most natural, for the following reasons. 1. In the first case, the right of conquest, since it is not a right, could not have founded any other, because the conqueror and conquered peoples always remain in a state of war with one another, unless the nation, returned to full liberty, were to choose voluntarily its conqueror as its leader. Until then, whatever the capitulations that may have been made, since they have been founded on violence alone and are consequently null by this very fact, on this hypothesis there can be neither true society nor body politic, nor any other law than that of the strongest. 2. These words *strong* and *weak* are equivocal in the second case, because in the interval between the establishment of the right of property or of the first occupant and that of political governments, the meaning of these terms is better rendered by the words *poor* and *rich*, because, before the laws, man did not in fact have any other means of placing his equals in subjection except by attacking their goods or by giving them part of his. 3. Since the poor had nothing to lose but their liberty, it would have been utter folly for them to have voluntarily surrendered the only good remaining to them, gaining nothing in return. On the contrary, since the rich men were, so to speak, sensitive in all parts of their goods, it was much easier to do them harm, and consequently they had to take greater precautions to protect themselves. And finally it is reasonable to believe that a thing was invented by those to whom it is useful rather than by those to whom it is harmful.

Incipient government did not have a constant and regular form. The lack of philosophy and experience permitted only present inconveniences to be perceived, and there was thought of remedying the others only as they presented themselves. Despite all the labors of the wisest legislators, the political state always remained imperfect, because it was practically the work of chance and, because it had been badly begun, time, in discovering faults and suggesting remedies, could never repair the vices of the constitution. People were continually patching it up, whereas they should have begun by clearing the air and putting aside all the old materials, as Lycurgus did in Sparta, in order to raise a good edifice later on. At first, society consisted merely of some general conventions that all private individuals promised to observe, and concerning which the community became the guarantor for each of them. Experience had to demonstrate how weak such a constitution was, and how easy it was for lawbreakers to escape conviction or punishment for faults of which the public alone was to be witness and judge. The law had to be evaded in a thousand ways; inconveniences and disorders had to multiply continually in order to make them finally give some thought to confiding to private individuals the dangerous trust of public authority, and to make them entrust to magistrates the care of enforcing the observance of the deliberations of the people. For to say that the leaders were chosen before the confederation was brought about and that the ministers of the laws existed before the laws themselves is a supposition that does not allow of serious debate.

It would be no more reasonable to believe that initially the peoples threw themselves unconditionally and for all time into the arms of an absolute master, and that the first means of providing for the common security dreamed up by proud and unruly men was to rush headlong into slavery. In fact, why did they give themselves over to superiors, if not to defend themselves against oppression and to protect their goods, their liberties and their lives, which are, as it were, the constitutive elements of their being? Now, since, in relations between men, the worst that can happen to someone is for him to see himself at the discretion of someone else, would it not have been contrary to good sense to begin by surrendering into the hands of a leader the only things for whose preservation they needed his help? What equivalent could he have offered them for the concession of so fine a right? And if he had dared to demand it on the pretext of defending them, would he not have immediately received the reply given in the fable: "what more will the enemy do to us?" It is therefore incontestable, and it is a fundamental maxim of all political right, that peoples have given themselves leaders in order to defend their liberty and not to enslave themselves. *If we have a prince,* Pliny said to Trajan, *it is so that he may preserve us from having a master.*

[Our] political theorists produce the same sophisms about the love of liberty that [our] philosophers have made about the state of nature. By the things they see they render judgments about very different things they have not seen; and they attribute to men a natural inclination to servitude owing to the patience with which those who are before their eyes endure their servitude, without giving a thought to the fact that it is the same for liberty as it is for innocence and virtue: their value is felt only as long as one has them oneself, and the taste for them is lost as soon as one has lost them. "I know the delights of your country," said Brasidas to a satrap who compared the life of Sparta to that of Persepolis, "but you cannot know the pleasures of mine."

As an unbroken steed bristles his mane, paws the ground with his hoof, and struggles violently at the mere approach of the bit, while a trained horse patiently endures the whip and the spur, barbarous man does not bow his head for the yoke that civilized man wears without a murmur, and he prefers the most stormy liberty to tranquil subjection. Thus it is not by the degradation of enslaved peoples that man's natural dispositions for or against servitude are to be judged, but by the wonders that all free peoples have accomplished to safeguard themselves from oppression. I know that enslaved peoples do nothing but boast of the peace and tranquillity they enjoy in their chains and that *they give the name 'peace' to the most miserable slavery.* But when I see free peoples sacrificing pleasures, tranquillity, wealth, power, and life itself for the preservation of this sole good which is regarded so disdainfully by those who have lost it; when I see animals born free and abhorring captivity break their heads against the bars of their prison; when I see multitudes of utterly naked savages scorn European pleasures and brave hunger, fire, sword and death, simply to preserve their independence, I sense that it is inappropriate for slaves to reason about liberty.

As for paternal authority, from which several have derived absolute government and all society, it is enough, without having recourse to the contrary proofs of Locke and Sidney, to note that nothing in the world is farther from the ferocious spirit of despotism than the gentleness of that authority which looks more to the advantage of the one who obeys than to the utility of the one who commands; that by the law of nature, the father is master of the child as long as his help is necessary for him; that beyond this point they become equals, and the son, completely independent of the father, then owes him merely respect and not obedience; for gratitude is clearly a duty that must be rendered, but not a right that can be demanded. Instead of saying that civil society derives from paternal power, on the contrary it must be said that it is from civil society that this power draws its principal force. An individual was not recognized as the father of several children until the children remained gathered about him. The goods of the father, of which he is truly the master, are the goods that keep his children in a state of dependence toward him, and he can cause their receiving a share in his estate to be consequent upon the extent to which they will have well merited it from him by continuous deference to his wishes. Now, far from having some similar favor to expect from their despot (since they belong to him as personal possessions—they and all they possess—or at least he claims this to be the case), subjects are reduced to receiving as a favor what he leaves them of their goods. He does what is just when he despoils them; he does them a favor when he allows them to live.

In continuing thus to examine facts from the viewpoint of right, no more solidity than truth would be found in the belief that the establishment of tyranny was voluntary; and it would be difficult to show the validity of a contract that would obligate only one of the parties, where all the commitments would be placed on one side with none on the other, and that it would turn exclusively to the disadvantage of the one making the commitments. This odious system is quite far removed from being, even today, that of wise and good monarchs, and especially of the kings of France, as may be seen in various places in their edicts, and particularly in the following passage of a famous writing published in 1667 in the name of and by order of Louis XIV: *Let it not be said therefore that the sovereign is not subject to the laws of his state, for the contrary statement is a truth of the law of nations, which flattery has on occasion attacked, but which good princes have always defended as a tutelary divinity of their states. How much more legitimate is it to say, with the wise Plato, that the perfect felicity of a kingdom is that a prince be obeyed by his subjects, that the prince obey the law, and that the law be right and always directed to the public good.* I will not stop to investigate whether, with liberty being the most noble of man's faculties, he degrades his nature, places himself on the level of animals enslaved by instinct, offends even his maker, when he unreservedly renounces the most precious of all his gifts, and allows himself to commit all the crimes he forbids us to commit, in order to please a ferocious or crazed master; nor whether this sublime workman should be more irritated at seeing his finest work destroyed rather than at seeing it dishonored. [I will disregard, if you will, the authority of Barbeyrac, who flatly declares, following Locke, that no one can sell his liberty to the point of submitting himself to an arbitrary power that treats him according to its fancy. *For,* he adds, *this would be selling his own life, of which he is not the master.*] I will merely ask by what right those who have not been afraid of debasing themselves to this degree have been able to subject their posterity to the same ignominy and to renounce for it goods that do not depend on their liberality, and without which life itself is burdensome to all who are worthy of it.

Pufendorf says that just as one transfers his goods to another by conventions and contracts, one can also divest himself of his liberty in favor of someone. That, it seems to me, is very bad reasoning; for, in the first place, the goods I give away become something utterly foreign to me, and it is a matter of indifference to me whether or not these goods are abused; but it is important to me that my liberty is not abused, and I cannot expose myself to becoming the instrument of crime without making myself guilty of the evil I will be forced to commit. Moreover, since the right of property is merely the result of convention and human institution, every man can dispose of what he possesses as he sees fit. But it is not the same for the essential gifts of nature such as life and liberty, which everyone is allowed to enjoy, and of which it is at least doubtful that one has the right to divest himself. In giving up the one he degrades his being; in giving up the other he annihilates that being insofar as he can. And because no temporal goods can compensate for the one or the other, it would offend at the same time both nature and reason to renounce them, regardless of the price. But even if one could give away his liberty as he does his goods, the difference would be very great for the children who enjoy the father's goods only by virtue of a transmission of his right; whereas, since liberty is a gift they receive from nature in virtue of being men, their parents had no right to divest them of it. Thus, just as violence had to be done to nature in order to establish slavery, nature had to be changed in order to perpetuate this right. And the jurists, who have gravely pronounced that the child of a slave woman is born a slave, have decided, in other words, that a man is not born a man.

Thus it appears certain to me not only that governments did not begin with arbitrary power, which is but their corruption and extreme limit, and which finally brings them back simply to the law of the strongest, for which they were initially to have been the remedy; but also that even if they had begun thus, this power, being illegitimate by its nature, could not have served as a foundation for the rights of society, nor, as a consequence, for the inequality occasioned by social institutions.

Without entering at present into the investigations that are yet to be made into the nature of the fundamental compact of all government, I restrict myself, in following common opinion, to considering here the establishment of the body politic as a true contract between the populace and the leaders it chooses for itself: a contract by which the two parties obligate themselves to observe the laws that are stipulated in it and that form the bonds of their union. Since, with respect to social relations, the populace has united all its wills into a single one, all the articles on which this will is explicated become so many fundamental laws obligating all the members of the state without exception, and one of these regulates the choice and power of the magistrates charged with watching over the execution of the others. This power extends to everything that can maintain the constitution, without going so far as to change it. To it are joined honors that make the laws and their ministers worthy of respect, and, for the ministers personally, prerogatives that compensate them for the troublesome labors that a good administration requires. The magistrate, for his part, obligates himself to use the power entrusted to him only in accordance with the intention of the constituents, to maintain each one in the peaceful enjoyment of what belongs to him, and to prefer on every occasion the public utility to his own interest.

Before experience had shown or knowledge of the human heart had made men foresee the inevitable abuses of such a constitution, it must have seemed all the better because those who were charged with watching over its preservation were themselves the ones who had the greatest interest in it. For since the magistracy and its rights were established exclusively on fundamental laws, were they to be destroyed, the magistracy would immediately cease to be legitimate; the people would no longer be bound to obey them. And since it was not the magistrate but the law that had constituted the essence of the state, everyone would rightfully return to his natural liberty.

The slightest attentive reflection on this point would confirm this by new reasons, and by the nature of the contract it would be seen that it could not be irrevocable.

For were there no superior power that could guarantee the fidelity of the contracting parties or force them to fulfill their reciprocal commitments, the parties would remain sole judges in their own case, and each of them would always have the right to renounce the contract as soon as he should find that the other party violated the conditions of the contract, or as soon as the conditions should cease to suit him. It is on this principle that it appears the right to abdicate can be founded. Now to consider, as we are doing, only what is of human institution, if the magistrate, who has all the power in his hands and who appropriates to himself all the advantages of the contract, nevertheless had the right to renounce the authority, a fortiori the populace, which pays for all the faults of the leaders, should have the right to renounce their dependence. But the horrible dissensions, the infinite disorders that this dangerous power would necessarily bring in its wake, demonstrate more than anything else how much need human governments had for a basis more solid than reason alone, and how necessary it was for public tranquillity that the divine will intervened to give to sovereign authority a sacred and inviolable character which took from the subjects the fatal right to dispose of it. If religion had brought about this good for men, it would be enough to oblige them to cherish and adopt it, even with its abuses, since it spares even more blood than fanaticism causes to be shed. But let us follow the thread of our hypothesis.

The various forms of government take their origin from the greater or lesser differences that were found among private individuals at the moment of institution. If a man were eminent in power, virtue, wealth or prestige, he alone was elected magistrate, and the state became monarchical. If several men, more or less equal among themselves, stood out over all the others, they were elected jointly, and there was an aristocracy. Those whose fortune or talents were less disproportionate, and who least departed from the state of nature, kept the supreme administration and formed a democracy. Time made evident which of these forms was the most advantageous to men. Some remained in subjection only to the laws; the others soon obeyed masters. Citizens wanted to keep their liberty; the subjects thought only of taking it away from their neighbors, since they could not endure others enjoying a good they themselves no longer enjoyed. In a word, on the one hand were riches and conquests, and on the other were happiness and virtue.

In these various forms of government all the magistratures were at first elective; and when wealth did not prevail, preference was given to merit, which gives a natural ascendancy, and to age, which gives experience in conducting business and cool-headedness in deliberation. The elders of the Hebrews, the gerontes of Sparta, the senate of Rome, and even the etymology of our word *seigneur* show how much age was respected in former times. The more elections fell upon men of advanced age, the more frequent elections became, and the more their difficulties were made to be felt. Intrigues were introduced; factions were formed; parties became embittered; civil wars flared up. Finally, the blood of citizens was sacrificed to the alleged happiness of the state, and people were on the verge of falling back into the anarchy of earlier times. The ambition of the leaders profited from these circumstances to perpetuate their offices within their families. The people, already accustomed to dependence, tranquillity and the conveniences of life, and already incapable of breaking their chains, consented to let their servitude increase in order to secure their tranquillity. Thus it was that the leaders, having become hereditary, grew accustomed to regard their magistratures as family property, to regard themselves as the proprietors of the state (of which at first they were but the officers), to call their fellow citizens their slaves, to count them like cattle in the number of things that belonged to them, and to call themselves equals of the gods and kings of kings.

If we follow the progress of inequality in these various revolutions, we will find that the first stage was the establishment of the law and of the right of property, the second stage was the institution of the magistracy, and the third and final stage was the transformation of legitimate power into arbitrary power. Thus the class of rich and poor was authorized by the first epoch, that of the strong and the weak by the second, and that of master and slave by the third: the ultimate degree of inequality and the limit to which all the others finally lead, until new revolutions completely dissolve the government or bring it nearer to its legitimate institution.

To grasp the necessity of this progress, we must consider less the motives for the establishment of the body politic than the form it takes in its execution and the disadvantages that follow in its wake. For the vices that make social institutions necessary are the same ones that make their abuses inevitable. And with the sole exception of Sparta, where the law kept watch chiefly over the education of children, and where Lycurgus established mores that nearly dispensed with having to add laws to them, since laws are generally less strong than passions and restrain men without changing them, it would be easy to prove that any government that always moved forward in conformity with the purpose for which it was founded without being corrupted or altered, would have been needlessly instituted, and that a country where no one eluded the laws and abused the magistrature would need neither magistracy nor laws.

Political distinctions necessarily lend themselves to civil distinctions. The growing inequality between the people and its leaders soon makes itself felt among private individuals, and is modified by them in a thousand ways according to passions, talents and events. The magistrate cannot usurp illegitimate power without producing protégés for himself to whom he is forced to yield some part of it. Moreover, citizens allow themselves to be oppressed only insofar as they are driven by blind ambition; and looking more below than above them, domination becomes more dear to them than independence, and they consent to wear chains in order to be able to give them in turn to others. It is very difficult to reduce to obedience someone who does not seek to command; and the most adroit politician would never succeed in subjecting men who wanted merely to be free. But inequality spreads easily among ambitious and cowardly souls always ready to run the risks of fortune and, almost indifferently, to dominate or serve, according to whether it becomes favorable or unfavorable to them. Thus it is that there must have come a time when the eyes of people were beguiled to such an extent that its leaders merely had to say to the humblest men, "Be great, you and all your progeny," and he immediately appeared great to everyone as well as in his own eyes, and his descendants were elevated even more in proportion as they were at some remove from him. The more remote and uncertain the cause, the more the effect increased; the more loafers one could count in a family, the more illustrious it became.

If this were the place to go into detail, I would easily explain how [even without government involvement] the inequality of prestige and authority becomes inevitable among private individuals,[19] as soon as they are united in one single society and are forced to make comparisons among themselves and to take into account the differences they discover in the continual use they have to make of one another.

These differences are of several sorts, but in general, since wealth, nobility or rank, power and personal merit are the principal distinctions by which someone is measured in society, I would prove that the agreement or conflict of these various forces is the surest indication of a well- or ill-constituted state. I would make it apparent that among these four types of inequality, since personal qualities are the origin of all the others, wealth is the last to which they are ultimately reduced, because it readily serves to buy all the rest, since it is the most immediately useful to well-being and the easiest to communicate. This observation enables one to judge rather precisely the extent to which each people is removed from its primitive institution, and of the progress it has made toward the final stage of corruption. I would note how much that universal desire for reputation, honors, and preferences, which devours us all, trains and compares our talents and strengths; how much it excites and multiplies the passions; and, by making all men competitors, rivals, or rather enemies, how many setbacks, successes and catastrophes of every sort it causes every day, by making so many contenders run the same course. I would show that it is to this ardor for making oneself the topic of conversation, to this furor to distinguish oneself which nearly always keeps us outside ourselves, that we owe what is best and worst among men, our virtues and vices, our sciences and our errors, our conquerors and our philosophers, that is to say, a multitude of bad things against a small number of good ones. Finally, I would prove that if one sees a handful of powerful and rich men at the height of greatness and fortune while the mob grovels in obscurity and misery, it is because the former prize the things they enjoy only to the extent that the others are deprived of them; and because, without changing their position, they would cease to be happy, if the people ceased to be miserable.

But these details alone would be the subject of a large work in which one would weigh the advantages and the disadvantages of every government relative to the rights of the state of nature, and where one would examine all the different faces under which inequality has appeared until now and may appear in [future] ages, according to the nature of these governments and the upheavals that time will necessarily bring in its wake. We would see the multitude oppressed from within as a consequence of the very precautions it had taken against what menaced it from without. We would see oppression continually increase, without the oppressed ever being able to know where it would end or what legitimate means would be left for them to stop it. We would see the rights of citizens and national liberties gradually die out, and the protests of the weak treated like seditious murmurs. We would see politics restrict the honor of defending the common cause to a mercenary portion of the people. We would see arising from this the necessity for taxes, the discouraged farmer leaving his field, even during peacetime, and leaving his plow in order to gird himself with a sword. We would see the rise of fatal and bizarre rules in the code of honor. We would see the defenders of the homeland sooner or later become its enemies, constantly holding a dagger over their fellow citizens, and there would come a time when we would hear them say to the oppressor of their country: "*If you order me to plunge my sword into my brother's breast or my father's throat, and into my pregnant wife's entrails, I will do so, even though my right hand is unwilling.*"

From the extreme inequality of conditions and fortunes, from the diversity of passions and talents, from useless arts, from pernicious arts, from frivolous sciences there would come a pack of prejudices equally contrary to reason, happiness and virtue. One would see the leaders fomenting whatever can weaken men united together by disuniting them; whatever can give society an air of apparent concord while sowing the seeds of real division; whatever can inspire defiance and hatred in the various classes through the opposition of their rights and interests, and can as a consequence strengthen the power that contains them all.

It is from the bosom of this disorder and these upheavals that despotism, by gradually raising its hideous head and devouring everything it had seen to be good and healthy in every part of the state, would eventually succeed in trampling underfoot the laws and the people, and in establishing itself on the ruins of the republic. The times that would precede this last transformation would be times of troubles and calamities; but in the end everything would be swallowed up by the monster, and the peoples would no longer have leader or laws, but only tyrants. Also, from that moment on, there would no longer be any question of mores and virtue, for wherever despotism, *in which decency affords no hope,* reigns, it tolerates no other master. As soon as it speaks, there is neither probity nor duty to consult, and the blindest obedience is the only virtue remaining for slaves.

Here is the final stage of inequality, and the extreme point that closes the circle and touches the point from which we started. Here all private individuals become equals again, because they are nothing. And since subjects no longer have any law other than the master's will, nor the master any rule other than his passions, the notions of good and the principles of justice again vanish. Here everything is returned solely to the law of the strongest, and consequently to a new state of nature different from the one with which we began, in that the one was the state of nature in its purity, and this last one is the fruit of an excess of corruption. Moreover, there is so little difference between these two states, and the governmental contract is so utterly dissolved by despotism, that the despot is master only as long as he is the strongest; and as soon as he can be ousted, he has no cause to protest against violence. The uprising that ends in the strangulation or the dethronement of a sultan is as lawful an act as those by which he disposed of the lives and goods of his subjects the day before. Force alone maintained him; force alone brings him down. Thus everything happens in accordance with the natural order, and whatever the outcome of these brief and frequent upheavals may be, no one can complain about someone else's injustice, but only of his own imprudence or his misfortune.

In discovering and following thus the forgotten and lost routes that must have led man from the natural state to the civil state; in reestablishing, with the intermediate positions I have just taken note of, those that time constraints on me have made me suppress or that the imagination has not suggested to me, no attentive reader can fail to be struck by the immense space that separates these two states. It is in this slow succession of things that he will see the solution to an infinity of moral and political problems which the philosophers are unable to resolve. He will realize that, since the human race of one age is not the human race of another age, the reason why Diogenes did not find his man is because he searched among his contemporaries for a man who no longer existed. Cato, he will say, perished with Rome and liberty because he was out of place in his age; and this greatest of men merely astonished the world, which five hundred years earlier he would have governed. In short, he will explain how the soul and human passions are imperceptibly altered and, as it were, change their nature; why, in the long run, our needs and our pleasures change their objects; why, with original man gradually disappearing, society no longer offers to the eyes of the wise man anything but an assemblage of artificial men and factitious passions which are the work of all these new relations and have no true foundation in nature. What reflection teaches us on this subject is perfectly confirmed by observation: savage man and civilized man differ so greatly in the depths of their hearts and in their inclinations, that what constitutes the supreme happiness of the one would reduce the other to despair. Savage man breathes only tranquillity and liberty; he wants simply to live and rest easy; and not even the unperturbed tranquillity of the Stoic approaches his profound indifference for any other objects. On the other hand, the citizen is always active and in a sweat, always agitated, and unceasingly tormenting himself in order to seek still more laborious occupations. He works until he dies; he even runs to his death in order to be in a position to live, or renounces life in order to acquire immortality. He pays court to the great whom he hates and to the rich whom he scorns. He stops at nothing to obtain the honor of serving them. He proudly crows about his own baseness and their protection; and proud of his slavery, he speaks with disdain about those who do not have the honor of taking part in it. What a spectacle for the Carib are the difficult and envied labors of the European minister! How many cruel deaths would that indolent savage not prefer to the horror of such a life, which often is not mollified even by the pleasure of doing good. But in order to see the purpose of so many cares, the words *power* and *reputation* would have to have a meaning in his mind; he would have to learn that there is a type of men who place some value on the regard the rest of the world has for them, and who know how to be happy and content with themselves on the testimony of others rather than on their own. Such, in fact, is the true cause of all these differences; the savage lives in himself; the man accustomed to the ways of society is always outside himself and knows how to live only in the opinion of others. And it is, as it were, from their judgment alone that he draws the sentiment of his own existence. It is not pertinent to my subject to show how, from such a disposition, so much indifference for good and evil arises, along with such fine discourse on morality; how, with everything reduced to appearances, everything becomes factitious and bogus: honor, friendship, virtue, and often even our vices, about which we eventually find the secret of boasting; how, in a word, always asking others what we are and never daring to question ourselves on this matter, in the midst of so much philosophy, humanity, politeness, and sublime maxims, we have merely a deceitful and frivolous exterior: honor without virtue, reason without wisdom, and pleasure without happiness. It is enough for me to have proved that this is not the original state of man, and that this is only the spirit of society, and the inequality that society engenders, which thus change and alter all our natural inclinations.

I have tried to set forth the origin and progress of inequality, the establishment and abuse of political societies, to the extent that these things can be deduced from the nature of man by the light of reason alone, and independently of the sacred dogmas that give to sovereign authority the sanction of divine right. It follows from this presentation that, since inequality is practically non-existent in the state of nature, it derives its force and growth from the development of our faculties and the progress of the human mind, and eventually becomes stable and legitimate through the establishment of property and laws. Moreover, it follows that moral inequality, authorized by positive right alone, is contrary to natural right whenever it is not combined in the same proportion with physical inequality: a distinction that is sufficient to determine what one should think in this regard about the sort of inequality that reigns among all civilized people, for it is obviously contrary to the law of nature, however it may be defined, for a child to command an old man, for an imbecile to lead a wise man, and for a handful of people to gorge themselves on superfluities while the starving multitude lacks necessities.

Rousseau's Notes to
Discourse on the Origin of Inequality

1. Herodotus relates that after the murder of the false Smerdis, the seven liberators of Persia being assembled to deliberate on the form of government they would give the state, Otanes was fervently in support of a republic: an opinion all the more extraordinary in the mouth of a satrap, since, over and above the claim he could have to the empire, a grandee fears more than death a type of government that forces him to respect men. Otanes, as may readily be believed, was not listened to; and seeing that things were progressing toward the election of a monarch, he, who wanted neither to obey nor command, voluntarily yielded to the other rivals his right to the crown, asking as his sole compensation that he and his descendants be free and independent. This was granted him. If Herodotus did not inform us of the restriction that was placed on this privilege, it would be necessary to suppose it, otherwise Otanes, not acknowledging any sort of law and not being accountable to anyone, would have been all powerful in the state and more powerful than the king himself. But there was hardly any likelihood that a man capable of contenting himself, in similar circumstances, with such a privilege, was capable of abusing it. In fact, there is no evidence that this right ever caused the least trouble in the kingdom, either from wise Otanes or from any of his descendants.

2. From the start I rely with confidence on one of those authorities that are respectable for philosophers, because they come from a solid and sublime reason, which they alone know how to find and perceive.

"Whatever interest we may have in knowing ourselves, I do not know whether we do not have a better knowledge of everything that is not us. Provided by nature with organs uniquely destined for our preservation, we use them merely to receive impressions of external things; we seek merely to extend ourselves outward and to exist outside ourselves. Too much taken with multiplying the functions of our senses and with increasing the external range of our being, we rarely make use of that internal sense which reduces us to our true dimensions, and which separates us from all that is not us. Nevertheless, this is the sense we must use if we wish to know ourselves. It is the only one by which we can judge ourselves. But how can this sense be activated and given its full range? How can our soul, in which it resides, be rid of all the illusions of our mind? We have lost the habit of using it; it has remained unexercised in the midst of the tumult of our bodily sensations; it has been dried out by the fire of our passions; the heart, the mind, the senses, everything has worked against it." *Hist. Nat.*, Vol. IV: *de la Nat. de l'homme*, p. 151.

3. The changes that a long-established habit of walking on two feet could have brought about in the conformation of man, the relations that are still observed between his arms and the forelegs of quadrupeds, and the induction drawn from their manner of walking, could have given rise to doubts about the manner that must have been the most natural to us. All children begin by walking on all fours, and need our example and our lessons to learn to stand upright. There are even savage nations, such as the Hottentots, who, greatly neglecting their children, allow them to walk on their hands for so long that they then have a great deal of trouble getting them to straighten up. The children of the Caribs of the Antilles do the same thing. There are various examples of quadruped men, and I could cite among others that of the child who was found in 1344 near Hesse, where he had been raised by wolves, and who said afterward at the court of Prince Henry that, had the decision been left exclusively to him, he would have preferred to return to the wolves than to live among men. He had embraced to such an extent the habit of walking like those animals, that wooden boards had to be attached to him to force him to stand upright and maintain his balance on two feet. It was the same with the child who was found in 1694, in the forests of

Lithuania, and who lived among bears. He did not give, says M. de Condillac, any sign of reason, walked on his hands and feet, had no language, and formed sounds that bore no resemblance whatever to those of a man. The little savage of Hanover, who was brought to the court of England several years ago, had all sorts of trouble getting himself to walk on two feet. And in 1719, two other savages, who were found in the Pyrenees, ran about the mountains in the manner of quadrupeds. As for the objection one might make that this deprives one of the use of one's hands from which we derive so many advantages, over and above the fact that the example of monkeys shows that the hand can be used quite well in both ways, this would prove only that man can give his limbs a destination more congenial than that of nature, and not that nature has destined man to walk otherwise than it teaches him.

But there are, it seems to me, much better reasons to state in support of the claim that man is a biped. First, if it were shown that he could have originally been formed otherwise than we see him and yet finally become what he is, this would not suffice to conclude that this is how it happened; for, after having shown the possibility of these changes, it would still be necessary, prior to granting them, to demonstrate at least their probability. Moreover, if man's arms seem as if they could have served as legs when needed, it is the sole observation favorable to that system, out of a great number of others which are contrary to it. The chief ones are that the manner in which man's head is attached to his body, instead of directing his view horizontally (as is the case for all other animals and for man himself when he walks upright), would have kept him, while walking on all fours, with his eyes fixed directly on the ground, a situation hardly conducive to the preservation of the individual; that the tail he is lacking, and for which he has no use when walking on two feet, is useful to quadrupeds, and none of them is deprived of one; that the breast of a woman, very well located for a biped who holds her child in her arms, is so poorly located for a quadruped that none has it located in that way; that, since the hind part is of an excessive height in proportion to the forelegs (which causes us to crawl on our knees when walking on all fours), the whole would have made an animal that was poorly proportioned and that walked uncomfortably; that if he had placed his foot as well as his hand down flat, he would have had one less articulation in the hind leg than do other animals, namely the one that joins canon to the tibia; and that by setting down only the tip of the foot, as doubtlessly he would have been forced to do, the tarsus (not to mention the plurality of bones that make it up) appears too large to take the place of the canon, and its articulations with the metatarsus and the tibia too close together to give the human leg in this situation the same flexibility as those of quadrupeds. Since the example of children is taken from an age when natural forces are not yet developed nor the members strengthened, it proves nothing whatever. I might just as well say that dogs are not destined to walk because several weeks after their birth they merely crawl. Particular facts also have little force against the universal practice of all men; even nations that have had no communication with others could not have imitated anything about them. A child abandoned in a forest before he is able to walk, and nourished by some beast, will have followed the example of his nurse in training himself to walk like her. Habit could have given him capabilities he did not have from nature, and just as one-armed men are successful, by dint of exercise, at doing with their feet whatever we do with our hands, he will finally have succeeded in using his hands as feet.

4. Should there be found among my readers a scientist nasty enough to cause me difficulties regarding the supposition of this natural fertility of the earth, I am going to answer him with the following passage:

"As plants derive much more substance from air and water for their sustenance than they do from the earth, it happens that when they rot they return to the earth more than they have derived from it. Moreover, a forest determines the amount of rainwater by stopping vapors. Thus, in a wooded area that was preserved for a long time without being touched, the bed of earth that serves for vegetation would increase considerably. But since animals return to the soil less than they derive from it, and since men take in huge quantities of wood and plants for fire and other uses, it follows that the bed of vegetative earth of an inhabited country must always diminish and finally become like the terrain of Arabia Petraea, and like that of so many other provinces of the

Orient (which in fact is the region that has been inhabited from the most ancient times), where only salt and sand are found. For the fixed salt of plants and animals remains, while all the other parts are volatized." M. de Buffon, *Hist. Nat.*

To this can be added the factual proof based on the quantity of trees and plants of every sort, which filled almost all the uninhabited islands that have been discovered in the last few centuries, and on what history teaches us about the immense forests all over the earth that had to be cut down to the degree that it was populated or civilized. On this I will also make the following three remarks. First, if there is a kind of vegetation that can make up for the loss of vegetative matter which was occasioned by animals, according to M. de Buffon's reasoning, it is above all the wooded areas, where the treetops and the leaves gather and appropriate more water and vapors than do other plants. Second, the destruction of the soil, that is, the loss of the substance that is appropriate for vegetation, should accelerate in proportion as the earth is more cultivated and as the more industrious inhabitants consume in greater abundance its products of every sort. My third and most important remark is that the fruits of trees supply animals with more abundant nourishment than is possible for other forms of vegetation: an experiment I made myself, by comparing the products of two land masses of equal size and quality, the one covered with chestnut trees and the other sown with wheat.

5. Among the quadrupeds, the two most universal distinguishing traits of voracious species are derived, on the one hand, from the shape of the teeth, and, on the other, from the conformation of the intestines. Animals that live solely on vegetation have all flat teeth, like the horse, ox, sheep and hare, but voracious animals have pointed teeth, like the cat, dog, wolf and fox. And as for the intestines, the frugivorous ones have some, such as the colon, which are not found in voracious animals. It appears therefore that man, having teeth and intestines like frugivorous animals, should naturally be placed in that class. And not only do anatomical observations confirm this opinion, but the monuments of antiquity are also very favorable to it. "Dicaearchus," says St. Jerome, "relates in his books on Greek antiquities that under the reign of Saturn, when the earth was still fertile by itself, no man ate flesh, but that all lived on fruits and vegetables that grew naturally." (*Adv. Jovinian.*, Bk. II) [This opinion can also be supported by the reports of several modern travelers. François Corréal, among others, testifies that the majority of inhabitants of the Lucayes, whom the Spaniards transported to the islands of Cuba, Santo Domingo, and elsewhere, died from having eaten flesh.] From this one can see that I am neglecting several advantageous considerations that I could turn to account. For since prey is nearly the exclusive subject of fighting among carnivorous animals, and since frugivorous animals live among themselves in continual peace, if the human species were of this latter genus, it is clear that it would have had a much easier time subsisting in the state of nature, and much less need and occasion to leave it.

6. All the kinds of knowledge that demand reflection, all those acquired only by the concatenation of ideas and perfected only successively, appear to be utterly beyond the grasp of savage man, owing to the lack of communication with his fellow-men, that is to say, owing to the lack of the instrument which is used for that communication, and to the lack of the needs that make it necessary. His understanding and his industry are limited to jumping, running, fighting, throwing a stone, climbing a tree. But if he knows only those things, in return he knows them much better than we, who do not have the same need for them as he. And since they depend exclusively on bodily exercise and are not capable of any communication or progress from one individual to another, the first man could have been just as adept at them as his last descendants.

The reports of travelers are full of examples of the force and vigor of men of barbarous and savage nations. They praise scarcely less their adroitness and nimbleness. And since eyes alone are needed to observe these things, nothing hinders us from giving credence to what eyewitnesses certify on the matter. I draw some random examples from the first books that fall into my hands.

"The Hottentots," says Kolben, "understand fishing better than the Europeans at the Cape. Their skill is equal when it comes to the net, the hook and the spear, in coves as well as in rivers. They catch fish by hand no less skillfully. They are incomparably good at swimming. Their style of swimming has something surprising about it, something entirely unique to them. They swim with their body upright and their hands stretched out of the water, so that they appear to be walking on land. In the greatest agitation of the sea, when the waves form so many mountains, they somehow dance on the top of the waves, rising and falling like a piece of cork.

"The Hottentots," says the same author further, "are surprisingly good at hunting, and the nimbleness of their running surpasses the imagination." He is amazed that they did not put their agility to ill use more often, which, however, sometimes happens, as can be judged from the example he gives. "A Dutch sailor," he says, "on disembarking at the Cape, charged a Hottentot to follow him to the city with a roll of tobacco that weighed about twenty pounds. When they were both some distance from the crew, the Hottentot asked the sailor if he knew how to run. Run! answered the Dutchman; yes, very well. Let us see, answered the African. And fleeing with the tobacco, he disappeared almost immediately. The sailor, confounded by such marvelous quickness, did not think of following him, and he never again saw either his tobacco or his porter.

"They have such quick sight and such a sure hand that Europeans cannot go near them. At a hundred paces they will hit with a stone a mark the size of a halfpenny. And what is more amazing, instead of fixing their eyes on the target as we do, they make continuous movements and contortions. It appears that their stone is carried by an invisible hand."

Father du Tertre says about the savages of the Antilles nearly the same things that have just been read about the Hottentots of the Cape of Good Hope. He praises, above all, their accuracy in shooting with their arrows birds in flight and swimming fish, which they then catch by diving for them. The savages of North America are no less famous for their strength and adroitness, and here is an example that will lead us to form a judgment about those qualities in the Indians of South America.

In the year 1746, an Indian from Buenos Aires, having been condemned to the galleys of Cadiz, proposed to the governor that he buy back his liberty by risking his life at a public festival. He promised that by himself he would attack the fiercest bull with no other weapon in his hand but a rope; that he would bring him to the ground, seize him with his rope by whatever part they would indicate, saddle him, bridle him, mount him, and so mounted he would fight two other of the fiercest bulls to be released from the Torillo, and that he would put all of them to death, one after the other, the moment they would command him to do so, and without anyone's help. This was granted him. The Indian kept his word and succeeded in everything he had promised. On the way in which he did it and on the details of the fight, one can consult M. Gautier, *Observations sur l'Histoire Naturelle*, Vol. I (in-12°), p. 262, whence this fact is taken.

7. "The lifespan of horses," says M. de Buffon, "is, as in all other species of animals, proportionate to the length of their growth period. Man, who takes fourteen years to grow, can live six or seven times as long, that is to say, ninety or a hundred years. The horse, whose growth period is four years, can live six or seven times as long, that is to say, twenty-five or thirty years. The examples that could be contrary to this rule are so rare, that they should not even be regarded as an exception from which conclusions can be drawn. And just as large horses achieve their growth in less time than slender horses, they also have a shorter lifespan and are old from the age of fifteen."

8. I believe I see another difference between carnivorous and frugivorous animals still more general than the one I have remarked upon in Note 5, since this one extends to birds. This difference consists in the number of young, which never exceeds two in each litter for the species that lives exclusively on plant life, and which ordinarily exceeds this number for voracious animals. It is easy to know nature's plan in this regard by the number of teats, which is only two in each female of the first species, like the mare, the cow, the goat, the doe, the ewe, etc., and which is always six or eight in the other females, such as the dog, the cat, the wolf, the tigress, etc. The hen, the goose, the duck, which are all voracious birds (as are the eagle, the sparrow hawk, the screech owl), also lay and hatch a large number of eggs, which never happens to the pigeon, the turtle-dove, or to birds that eat nothing but grain, which lay and hatch scarcely more than two eggs at a time. The reason that can be given for this difference is that the animals that live exclusively on grass and plants, remaining nearly the entire day grazing and being forced to spend considerable time feeding themselves, could not be up to the task of nursing several young; whereas the voracious animals, taking their meal almost in an instant, can more easily and more

often return to their young and to their hunting, and can compensate for the loss of so large a quantity of milk. There would be many particular observations and reflections to make on all this, but this is not the place to make them, and it is enough for me to have shown in this part the most general system of nature, a system which furnishes a new reason to remove man from the class of carnivorous animals and to place him among the frugivorous species.

9. A famous author, on calculating the goods and evils of human life and comparing the two sums, has found that the latter greatly exceeded the former, and that, all things considered, life was a pretty poor present for man. I am not surprised by his conclusion; he has drawn all of his arguments from the constitution of civil man. Had he gone back as far as natural man, the judgment can be made that he would have found very different results, that he would have realized that man has scarcely any evils other than those he has given himself, and that nature would have been justified. It is not without trouble that we have managed to make ourselves so unhappy. When, on the one hand, one considers the immense labors of men, so many sciences searched into, so many arts invented, and so many forces employed, abysses filled up, mountains razed, rocks broken, rivers made navigable, lands cleared, lakes dug, marshes drained, enormous buildings raised upon the earth, the sea covered with ships and sailors; and when, on the other hand, one searches with a little meditation for the true advantages that have resulted from all this for the happiness of the human species, one cannot help being struck by the astonishing disproportion that obtains between these things, and to deplore man's blindness, which, to feed his foolish pride and who knows what vain sense of self-importance, makes him run ardently after all the miseries to which he is susceptible, and which beneficent nature has taken pains to keep from him.

Men are wicked; a sad and continual experience dispenses us from having to prove it. Nevertheless, man is naturally good; I believe I have demonstrated it. What therefore can have depraved him to this degree, if not the changes that have befallen his constitution, the progress he has made, and the sorts of knowledge he has acquired? Let human society be admired as much as one wants; it will be no less true for it that it necessarily brings men to hate one another to the extent that their interests are at cross-purposes with one another, to render mutually to one another apparent services and in fact do every evil imaginable to one another. What is one to think of an interaction where the reason of each private individual dictates to him maxims directly contrary to those that public reason preaches to the body of society, and where each finds his profit in the misfortune of another? Perhaps there is not a wealthy man whose death is not secretly hoped for by greedy heirs and often by his own children; not a ship at sea whose wreck would not be good news to some merchant; not a firm that a debtor of bad faith would not wish to see burn with all the papers it contains; not a people that does not rejoice at the disasters of its neighbors. Thus it is that we find our advantage in the setbacks of our fellow-men, and that one person's loss almost always brings about another's prosperity. But what is even more dangerous is that public calamities are anticipated and hoped for by a multitude of private individuals. Some want diseases, others death, others war, others famine. I have seen ghastly men weep with the sadness at the likely prospects of a fertile year. And the great and deadly fire of London, which cost the life or the goods of so many unfortunate people, made the fortunes of perhaps more than ten thousand people. I know that Montaigne blames the Athenian Demades for having had a worker punished, who, by selling coffins at a high price, made a great deal from the death of the citizens. But since the reason Montaigne proposes is that everyone would have to be punished, it is evident that it confirms my own. Let us therefore penetrate, through our frivolous demonstration of good will, to what happens at the bottom of our hearts; and let us reflect on what the state of things must be where all men are forced to caress and destroy one another, and where they are born enemies by duty and crooks by interest. If someone answers me by claiming that society is constituted in such a manner that each man gains by serving others, I will reply that this would be very well and good, provided he did not gain still more by harming them. There is no profit, however legitimate, that is not surpassed by one that can be made illegitimately, and wrong done to a neighbor is always more lucrative than services. It is therefore no longer a question of anything but finding the means of being assured of impunity. And this is what the powerful spend all their forces on, and the weak all their ruses.

Savage man, when he has eaten, is at peace with all nature, and the friend of all his fellow-men. Is it sometimes a question of his disputing over his meal? He never comes to blows without having first compared the difficulty of winning with that of finding his sustenance elsewhere. And since pride is not involved in the fight, it is ended by a few swings of the fist. The victor eats; the vanquished is on his way to seek his fortune, and everything is pacified. But for man in society, these are quite different affairs. It is first of all a question of providing for the necessary and then for the superfluous; next come delights, and then immense riches, and then subjects, and then slaves. He has not a moment's respite. What is most singular is that the less natural and pressing the needs, the more the passions increase and, what is worse, the power to satisfy them; so that after long periods of prosperity, after having swallowed up many treasures and ruined many men, my hero will end by butchering everything until he is the sole master of the universe. Such in brief is the moral portrait, if not of human life, then at least of the secret pretensions of the heart of every civilized man.

Compare, without prejudices, the state of civil man with that of savage man and seek, if you can, how many new doors to suffering and death (other than his wickedness, his needs and his miseries) the former has opened. If you consider the emotional turmoil that consumes us, the violent passions that exhaust and desolate us, the excessive labors with which the poor are overburdened, the still more dangerous softness to which the rich abandon themselves, and which cause the former to die of their needs and the latter of their excesses; if you call to mind the monstrous combinations of foods, their pernicious seasonings, the corrupted foodstuffs, tainted drugs, the knavery of those who sell them, the errors of those who administer them, the poison of the vessels in which they are prepared; if you pay attention to the epidemic diseases engendered by the bad air among the multitudes of men gathered together, to the illnesses occasioned by the effeminacy of our lifestyle, by the coming and going from the inside of our houses to the open air, the use of garments put on or taken off with too little precaution, and all the cares that our excessive sensuality has turned into necessary habits, the neglect or privation of which then costs us our life or our health; if you take into account fires and earthquakes, which, in consuming or turning upside down whole cities, cause their inhabitants to die by the thousands; in a word, if you unite the dangers that all these causes continually gather over our heads, you will realize how dearly nature makes us pay for the scorn we have shown for its lessons.

I will not repeat here what I have said elsewhere about war, but I wish that informed men would, for once, want or dare to give the public the detail of the horrors that are committed in armies by provisions and hospital suppliers. One would see that their not too secret maneuvers, on account of which the most brilliant armies dissolve into less than nothing, cause more soldiers to perish than are cut down by enemy swords. Moreover, no less surprising is the calculation of the number of men swallowed up by the sea every year, either by hunger, or scurvy, or pirates, or fire, or shipwrecks. It is clear that we must also put to the account of established property, and consequently to that of society, the assassinations, the poisonings, the highway robberies, and even the punishments of these crimes, punishments necessary to prevent greater ills, but which, costing the lives of two or more for the murder of one man, do not fail really to double the loss to the human species. How many are the shameful ways to prevent the birth of men or to fool nature: either by those brutal and depraved tastes which insult its most charming work, tastes that neither savages nor animals ever knew, and that have arisen in civilized countries only as the result of a corrupt imagination; or by those secret abortions, worthy fruits of debauchery and vicious honor; or by the exposure or the murder of a multitude of infants, victims of the misery of their parents or of the barbarous shame of their mothers; or, finally by the mutilation of those unfortunates, part of whose existence and all of whose posterity are sacrificed to vain songs, or what is worse still, to the brutal jealousy of a few men: a mutilation which, in this last case, doubly outrages nature, both by the treatment received by those who suffer it and by the use to which they are destined.

[But are there not a thousand more frequent and even more dangerous cases where paternal rights overtly offend humanity? How many talents are buried and inclinations are forced by the imprudent constraint of fathers! How many men would have distinguished themselves in a suitable station who die unhappy and dishonored in another station for which they have no taste! How many happy but unequal marriages have been broken or disturbed, and how many chaste wives dishonored by this order of conditions always in contradiction with that of nature! How many other bizarre unions formed by interests and disavowed by love and by reason! How many even honest and virtuous couples cause themselves torment because they were ill-matched! How many young and unhappy victims of their parent's greed plunge into vice or pass their sorrowful days in tears, and moan in indissoluble chains which the heart rejects and which gold alone has formed! Happy sometimes are those whose courage and even virtue tear them from life before a barbarous violence forces them into crime or despair. Forgive me, father and mother forever deplorable. I regrettably worsen your sorrows; but may they serve as an eternal and terrible example to whoever dares, in the name of nature, to violate the most sacred of its rights!

If I have spoken only of those ill-formed relationships that are the result of our civil order, is one to think that those where love and sympathy have presided are themselves exempt from drawbacks?]

What would happen if I were to undertake to show the human species attacked in its very source, and even in the most holy of all bonds, where one no longer dares to listen to nature until after having consulted fortune, and where, with civil disorder confounding virtues and vices, continence becomes a criminal precaution, and the refusal to give life to one's fellow-man an act of humanity? But without tearing away the veil that covers so many horrors, let us content ourselves with pointing out the evil, for which others must supply the remedy.

Let us add to all this that quantity of unwholesome trades which shorten lives or destroy one's health, such as work in mines, various jobs involving the processing of metals, minerals, and especially lead, copper, mercury, cobalt, arsenic, realgar; those other perilous trades which every-day cost the lives of a number of workers, some of them roofers, others carpenters, others masons, others working in quarries; let us bring all of these objects together, I say, and we will be able to see in the establishment and the perfection of societies the reasons for the diminution of the species, observed by more than one philosopher.

Luxury, impossible to prevent among men who are greedy for their own conveniences and for the esteem of others, soon completes the evil that societies have begun; and on the pretext of keeping the poor alive (which it was not necessary to do), luxury impoverishes everyone else, and sooner or later depopulates the state.

Luxury is a remedy far worse than the evil it means to cure; or rather it is itself the worst of all evils in any state, however large or small it may be, and which, in order to feed the hordes of lackeys and wretches it has produced, crushes and ruins the laborer and the citizen—like those scorching south winds that, by covering grass and greenery with devouring insects, take sustenance away from useful animals, and bring scarcity and death to all the places where they make themselves felt.

From society and the luxury it engenders, arise the liberal and mechanical arts, commerce, letters, and all those useless things that make industry flourish, enriching and ruining states. The reason for this decay is quite simple. It is easy to see that agriculture, by its nature, must be the least lucrative of all the arts, because, with its product being of the most indispensable use to all men, its price must be proportionate to the abilities of the poorest. From the same principle can be drawn this rule: that, in general, the arts are lucrative in inverse proportion to their usefulness, and that the most necessary must finally become the most neglected. From this it is clear what must be thought of the true advantages of industry and of the real effect that results from its progress.

Such are the discernible causes of all the miseries into which opulence finally brings down the most admired nations. To the degree that industry and the arts expand and flourish, the scorned farmer, burdened with taxes necessary to maintain luxury and condemned to spend his life between toil and hunger, abandons his fields to go to the cities in search of the bread he ought to be carrying there. The more the capital cities strike the stupid eyes of the people as wonderful, the more it will be necessary to groan at the sight of countrysides abandoned, fields fallow, and main roads jammed with unhappy citizens who have become beggars or thieves, destined to end their misery one day on the rack or on a dung-heap. Thus it is that the state, enriching itself on the one hand, weakens and depopulates itself on the other; and that the most powerful monarchies, after much labor to become opulent and deserted, end by becoming the prey of poor nations which succumb to the deadly temptation to invade them, and which enrich and enfeeble themselves in their turn, until they are themselves invaded and destroyed by others.

Let someone deign to explain to us for once what could have produced those hordes of barbarians which for so many centuries have overrun Europe, Asia and Africa. Was it to the industry of their arts, the wisdom of their laws, the excellence of their civil order that they owed that prodigious population? Would our learned ones be so kind as to tell us why, far from multiplying to that degree, those ferocious and brutal men, without enlightenment, without restraint, without education, did not all kill one another at every moment to argue with one another over their food or game? Let them explain to us how these wretches even had the gall to look right in the eye such capable people as we were, with such fine military discipline, such fine codes, and such wise laws, and why, finally, after society was perfected in the countries of the north, and so many pains were taken there to teach men their mutual duties and the art of living together agreeably and peaceably, nothing more is seen to come from them like those multitudes of men it produced formerly. I am very much afraid that someone might finally get it into his head to reply to me that all these great things, namely the arts, sciences, and laws, have been very wisely invented by men as a salutary plague to prevent the excessive multiplication of the species, out of fear that this world, which is destined for us, might finally become too small for its inhabitants.

What then! Must we destroy societies, annihilate thine and mine, and return to live in the forests with bears?—a conclusion in the style of my adversaries, which I prefer to anticipate, rather than leave to them the shame of drawing it. Oh you, to whom the heavenly voice has not made itself heard, and who recognize for your species no other destination except to end this brief life in peace; you who can leave in the midst of the cities your deadly acquisitions, your troubled minds, your corrupt hearts and your unbridled desires. Since it depends on you, retake your ancient and first innocence; go into the woods to lose sight and memory of the crimes of your contemporaries, and have no fear of cheapening your species in renouncing its enlightenment in order to renounce its vices. As for men like me, whose passions have forever destroyed their original simplicity, who can no longer feed on grass and acorn[s], nor get by without laws and chiefs; those who were honored in their first father with supernatural lessons; those who will see, in the intention of giving human actions from the beginning a morality they would not have acquired for a long time, the reason for a precept indifferent in itself and inexplicable in any other system; those, in a word, who are convinced that the divine voice called the entire human race to the enlightenment and the happiness of the celestial intelligences; all those latter ones will attempt, through the exercise of virtues they oblige themselves to practice while learning to know them, to merit the eternal reward that they ought to expect for them. They will respect the sacred bonds of the societies of which they are members; they will love their fellow-men and will serve them with all their power; they will scrupulously obey the laws and the men who are their authors and their ministers; they will honor above all the good and wise princes who will know how to prevent, cure or palliate that pack of abuses and evils always ready to overpower us; they will animate the zeal of these worthy chiefs by showing them without fear or flattery the greatness of their task and the rigor of their duty. But they will despise no less for it a constitution that can be maintained only with the help of so many respectable people, who are desired more often than they are obtained, and from which, despite all their care, always arise more real calamities than apparent advantages.

10. Among the men we know, whether by ourselves, or from historians, or from travelers, some are black, others white, others red. Some wear their hair long; others have merely curly wool. Some are almost entirely covered with hair; others do not even have a beard. There have been and perhaps there still are nations of men of gigantic size; and apart from the fable of the

Pygmies (which may well be merely an exaggeration), we know that the Laplanders and above all the Greenlanders are considerably below the average size of man. It is even maintained that there are entire peoples who have tails like quadrupeds. And without putting blind faith in the accounts of Herodotus and Ctesias, we can at least draw from them the very likely opinion that had one been able to make good observations in those ancient times when various peoples followed lifestyles differing more greatly among themselves than do those of today, one would have also noted in the shape and posture of the body, much more striking varieties. All these facts, for which it is easy to furnish incontestable proofs, are capable of surprising only those who are accustomed to look solely at the objects that surround them and who are ignorant of the powerful effects of the diversity of climates, air, foods, lifestyle, habits in general, and especially the astonishing force of the same causes when they act continually for long successions of generations. Today, when commerce, voyages and conquests reunite various peoples further, and their lifestyles are constantly approximating one another through frequent communication, it is evident that certain national differences have diminished; and, for example, everyone can take note of the fact that today's Frenchmen are no longer those large, colorless and blond-haired bodies described by Latin historians, although time, together with the mixture of the Franks and the Normans, themselves colorless and blond-haired, should have reestablished what commerce with the Romans could have removed from the influence of the climate in the natural constitution and complexion of the inhabitants. All of these observations on the varieties that a thousand causes can produce and have in fact produced in the human species cause me to wonder whether the various animals similar to men, taken without much scrutiny by travelers for beasts, either because of some differences they noticed in their outward structure or simply because these animals did not speak, would not in fact be veritable savage men, whose race, dispersed in the woods during olden times, had not had an occasion to develop any of its virtual faculties, had not acquired any degree of perfection, and was still found in the primitive state of nature. Let us give an example of what I mean.

"There are found in the kingdom of the Congo," says the translator of the *Histoire des Voyages*, "many of those large animals called *orangutans* in the East Indies, which occupy a middle ground between the human species and the baboons. Battel relates that in the forests of Mayomba, in the kingdom of Loango, one sees two kinds of monsters, the larger of which are called *pongos* and the others *enjocos*. The former bear an exact resemblance to man, except they are much larger and very tall. With a human face, they have very deep-set eyes. Their hands, cheeks and ears are without hair, except for their eyebrows, which are very long. Although the rest of their body is quite hairy, the hair is not very thick; the color of the hair is brown. Finally, the only part that distinguishes them from men is their leg, which has no calf. They walk upright, grasping the hair of their neck with their hand. Their retreat is in the woods. They sleep in the trees, and there they make a kind of roof which offers them shelter from the rain. Their foods are fruits or wild nuts; they never eat flesh. The custom of the Negroes who cross the forests is to light fires during the night. They note that in the morning, at their departure, the pongos take their place around the fire, and do not withdraw until it is out; because, for all their cleverness, they do not have enough sense to lay wood on the fire to keep it going.

"They occasionally walk in groups and kill the Negroes who cross the forests. They even fall upon elephants who come to graze in the places they inhabit, and they irritate the elephants so much with punches or with whacks of a stick that they force them howling to take flight. Pongos are never taken alive, because they are so strong that ten men would not be enough to stop them. But the Negroes take a good many young ones after having killed the mother, to whose body the young stick very closely. When one of these animals dies, the others cover its body with a pile of branches or leaves. Purchass adds that, in the conversations he has had with Battel, he had learned from him also that a pongo abducted a little Negro who passed an entire month in the society of these animals, for they do not harm men they take by surprise, at least when these men do not pay any attention to them, as the little Negro had observed. Battel had not described the second species of monster.

"Dapper confirms that the kingdom of the Congo is filled with those animals which in the Indies bear the name orangutans, that is to say, inhabitants of the woods, and which the Africans call *quojas-*

morros. This beast, he says, is so similar to man, that it has occurred to some travelers that it could have issued from a woman and a monkey: a myth which even the Negroes reject. One of these animals was transported from the Congo to Holland and presented to the Prince of Orange, Frederick Henry. It was the height of a three-year old child, moderately stocky, but square and well-proportioned, very agile and lively; its legs fleshy and robust; the entire front of the body naked, but the rear covered with black hairs. At first sight, its face resembled that of a man, but it had a flat and turned up nose; its ears were also those of the human species; its breast (for it was a female), was plump, its navel sunken, its shoulders very well joined, its hands divided into fingers and thumbs, its calves and heels fat and fleshy. It often walked upright on its legs; it was capable of lifting and carrying heavy burdens. When it wanted to drink, it took the cover of the pot in one hand, and held the base with the other; afterward it graciously wiped its lips. It lay down to sleep with its head on a cushion, covering itself with such skill that it would have been taken for a man in bed. The Negroes tell strange stories about this animal. They assert not only that it takes women and girls by force, but that it dares to attack armed men. In a word, there is great likelihood that it is the satyr of the ancients. Perhaps Merolla is speaking only of these animals whom he relates that Negroes sometimes lay hold of savage men and women in their hunts."

These species of anthropomorphic animals are again discussed in the third volume of the same *Histoire des Voyages* under the name of *beggos* and *mandrills*. But sticking to the preceding accounts, we find in the description of these alleged monsters striking points of conformity with the human species and lesser differences than those that would be assigned between one man and another. From these pages it is not clear what the reasons are that the authors have for refusing to give the animals in question the name "savage men"; but it is easy to conjecture that it is on account of their stupidity and also because they did not speak—feeble reasons for those who know that although the organ of speech is natural to man, nevertheless speech itself is not natural to him, and who knows to what point his perfectibility can have elevated civil man above his original state. The small number of lines these descriptions contain can cause us to judge how badly these animals have been observed and with what prejudices they have been viewed. For example, they are categorized as monsters, and yet there is agreement that they reproduce. In one place, Battel says that the pongos kill the Negroes who cross the forests; in another place, Purchass adds that they do not do any harm, even when they surprise them, at least when the Negroes do not fix their gaze upon them. The pongos gather around fires lit by the Negroes upon the Negroes' withdrawal, and withdraw in their turn when the fire is out. There is the fact. Here now is the commentary of the observer: *because, for all their cleverness, they do not have enough sense to lay wood on the fire to keep it going.* I would like to hazard a guess how Battel, or Purchass, his compiler, could have known that the withdrawal of the pongos was an effect of their stupidity rather than their will. In a climate such as Loango, fire is not something particularly necessary for the animals; and if the Negroes light a fire, it is less against the cold than to frighten ferocious beasts. It is therefore a very simple matter that, after having been for some time delighted with the flame or being well warmed, the pongos grow tired of always remaining in the same place and go off to graze, which requires more time than if they ate flesh. Moreover, we know that most animals, man not excluded, are naturally lazy, and that they refuse all sorts of cares which are not absolutely necessary. Finally, it seems very strange that pongos, whose adroitness and strength are praised, the pongos who know how to bury their dead and to make themselves roofs out of branches, should not know how to push fagots into the fire I recall having seen a monkey perform the same maneuver that people deny the pongos can do. It is true that since my ideas were not oriented in this direction, I myself committed the mistake for which I reproach our travelers; I neglected to examine whether the intention of the monkey was actually to sustain the fire or simply, as I believe is the case, to imitate the actions of a man. Whatever the case may be, it is well demonstrated that the monkey is not a variety of man: not only because he is deprived of the faculty of speech, but above all because it is certain that his species does not have the faculty of perfecting itself, which is the specific characteristic of the human species: experiments that do not seem to have been made on the pongos and the orangutan with sufficient care to enable one to draw the same conclusion in their case. However, there would be a means by which, if the orangutan or others were of the human species, even the least sophisticated observers could assure themselves of it by means of demonstration. But beyond the fact that a single generation would not be sufficient for this experiment, it should pass as unworkable, since it would be necessary that what is merely a supposition be demonstrated to be true, before the test that should establish the fact could be innocently tried.

Precipitous judgments, which are not the fruit of an enlightened reason, are prone to be excessive. Without any fanfare, our travelers made into beasts, under the names *pongos, mandrills, orangutans,* the same beings that the ancients, under the names *satyrs, fauns, sylvans,* made into divinities. Perhaps, after more precise investigations it will be found that they are [neither beasts nor gods but] men. Meanwhile, it would seem to me that there is as much reason to defer on this point to Merolla, an educated monk, an eyewitness, and one who, with all his naïveté, did not fail to be a man of wit, as to the merchant Battel, Dapper, Purchass, and the other compilers.

What judgment do we think such observers would have made regarding the child found in 1694, of whom I have spoken before, who gave no indication of reason, walked on his feet and hands, had no language, and made sounds that bore no resemblance whatever to those of a man? It took a long time, continues the same philosopher who provided me with this fact, before he could utter a few words, and then he did it in a barbarous manner. Once he could speak, he was questioned about his first state, but he did not recall it any more than we recall what happened to us in the cradle. If, unhappily* for him, this child had fallen into the hands of our travelers, there can be no doubt that after having observed his silence and stupidity, they would have resolved to send him back to the woods or lock him up in a menagerie; after which they would have spoken eruditely about him in their fine accounts as a very curious beast who looked rather like a man.

For the three or four hundred years since the inhabitants of Europe inundated the other parts of the world and continually published new collections of travels and stories, I am convinced that we know no other men but the Europeans alone. Moreover, it would appear, from the ridiculous prejudices that have not been extinguished even among men of letters, that everybody does hardly anything under the pompous name of "the study of man" except study the men of his country. Individuals may well come and go; it seems that philosophy travels nowhere; moreover, the philosophy of one people is little suited to another. The reason for this is manifest, at least for distant countries. There are hardly more than four sorts of men who make long voyages: sailors, merchants, soldiers, and missionaries. Now we can hardly expect the first three classes to provide good observers; and as for those in the fourth, occupied by the sublime vocation that calls them, even if they were not subject to the prejudices of social position as are all the rest, we must believe that they would not voluntarily commit themselves to investigations that would appear to be sheer curiosity, and which would sidetrack them from the more important works to which they are destined. Besides, to preach the Gospel in a useful manner, zeal alone is needed, and God gives the rest. But to study men, talents are needed which God is not required to give anyone, and which are not always the portion of saints. One does not open a book of voyages where one does not find descriptions of characters and mores. But one is utterly astonished to see that these people who have described so many things have said merely what everyone already knew, that, at the end of the world, they knew how to understand only what it was for them to notice without leaving their street; and that those true qualities which characterize nations and strike eyes made to see have almost always escaped theirs. Whence this fine moral slogan, so bandied about by the philosophizing rabble: that men are everywhere the same; that, since everywhere they have the same passions and the same vices, it is rather pointless to seek to characterize different peoples— which is about as well reasoned as it would be for someone to say that Peter and James cannot be distinguished from one another, because they both have a nose, a mouth and eyes.

Will we never see those happy days reborn when the people did not dabble in philosophizing, but when a Plato, a Thales, a Pythagoras, taken with an ardent desire to know, undertook the greatest voyages merely to inform themselves, and went far away to shake off the yoke of national prejudices, in order to learn to know men by their similarities and their differences, and to acquire

[*In the copy of the Discourse *sent to Richard Davenport, Rousseau inserts here:* or perhaps happily.]

those sorts of universal knowledge that are exclusively those of a single century or country, but which, since they are of all times and all places, are, as it were, the common science of the wise?

We admire the splendor of some curious men who, at great expense, made or caused to be made voyages to the Orient with learned men and painters, in order to sketch hovels and to decipher or copy inscriptions. But I have trouble conceiving how, in a century where people take pride in fine sorts of knowledge, there are not to be found two closely united men—rich, one in money, the other in genius, both loving glory and aspiring for immortality—one of whom sacrifices twenty thousand crowns of his goods and the other ten years of his life for a famous voyage around the world, in order to study, not always rocks and plants, but, for once, men and mores, and who, after so many centuries used to measure and examine the house, would finally be of a mind to want to know its inhabitants.

The academicians who have traveled through the northern parts of Europe and the southern parts of America had for their object to visit them more as geometers than as philosophers. Nevertheless, since they were both simultaneously, we cannot regard as utterly unknown the regions that have been seen and described by La Condamine and Maupertuis. The jeweler Chardin, who has traveled like Plato, has left nothing to be said about Persia. China appeared to have been well observed by the Jesuits. Kempfer gives a passable idea of what little he has seen in Japan. Except for these reports, we know nothing about the peoples of the East Indies, who have been visited exclusively by Europeans interested more in filling their purses than their heads. All of Africa and its numerous inhabitants, as unique in character as in color, are yet to be examined. The entire earth is covered with nations of which we know only the names, and we dabble in judging the human race! Let us suppose a Montesquieu, a Buffon, a Diderot, a Duclos, a d'Alembert, a Condillac, or men of that ilk traveling in order to inform their compatriots, observing and describing as they know how to do, Turkey, Egypt, Barbary, the empire of Morocco, Guinea, the land of the Bantus, the interior of Africa and its eastern coastlines, the Malabars, Mogul, the banks of the Ganges, the kingdoms of Siam, Pegu, and Ava, China, Tartary, and especially Japan; then in the other hemisphere, Mexico, Peru, Chile, the straits of Magellan, not to forget the Patagonias true or false, Tucuman, Paraguay (if possible), Brazil; finally the Caribbean Islands, Florida, and all the savage countries—the most important voyage of all and the one that should be embarked upon with the greatest care. Let us suppose that these new Hercules, back from these memorable treks, then wrote at leisure the natural, moral, and political history of what they would have seen; we ourselves would see a new world sally forth from their pen, and we would thus learn to know our own. I say that when such observers will affirm of an animal that it is a man and of another that it is a beast, we will have to believe them. But it would be terribly simpleminded to defer in this to unsophisticated travelers, concerning whom we will sometimes be tempted to put the same question that they dabble at resolving concerning other animals.

11. That appears utterly evident to me and I am unable to conceive whence our philosophers can derive all the passions they ascribe to natural man. With the single exception of the physically necessary which nature itself demands, all our other needs are such merely out of habit (previous to which they were not needs), or by our own desires; and we do not desire what we are not in a position to know. Whence it follows that since savage man desires only the things he knows and knows only those things whose possession is in his power or easily acquired, nothing should be so tranquil as his soul and nothing so limited as his mind.

12. I find in Locke's *Civil Government* an objection which seems to me too specious for me to be permitted to hide it. "Since the purpose of the society between male and female," says this philosopher, "is not merely to procreate, but to continue the species, this society should last, even after procreation, at least as long as it is necessary for the nurture and support of the procreated, that is to say, until they are capable of seeing to their needs on their own. This rule, which the infinite wisdom of the creator has established upon the works of his hands, we see creatures inferior to man observing constantly and strictly. In those animals which live on grass, the society between male and female lasts no longer than each act of copulation, because, the teats of the mother being sufficient to feed the young until they are able to feed on grass, the male is content to beget and no longer mingles with the female or the young, to whose sustenance he has nothing

to contribute. But as far as beasts of prey are concerned, the society lasts longer, because, with the mother being unable to see to her own sustenance and at the same time feed her young by means of her prey alone (which is a more laborious and more dangerous way of taking in nourishment than by feeding on grass), the assistance of the male is utterly necessary for the maintenance of their common family (if one may use that term), which is able to subsist to the point where it can go hunt for prey only through the efforts of the male and the female. We note the same thing in all the birds (with the exception of some domestic birds which are found in places where the continual abundance of nourishment exempts the male from the effort of feeding the young). It is clear that when the young in their nest need food, the male and female bring it to them until the young there are capable of flying and seeing to their own sustenance.

"And, in my opinion, herein lies the principal, if not the only reason why the male and the female in mankind are bound to a longer period of society than is undertaken by other creatures: namely, that the female is capable of conceiving and is ordinarily pregnant again and has a new child long before the previous child is in a position to do without the help of its parents and can take care of itself. Thus, since the father is bound to take care of those he has produced, and to take that care for a long time, he is also under an obligation to continue in conjugal society with the same woman by whom he has had them, and to remain in that society much longer than other creatures, whose young being capable of subsisting by themselves before the time comes for a new procreation, the bond of the male and female breaks of its own accord, and they are both at complete liberty, until such time as that season, which usually solicits the animals to join with one another, obliges them to choose new mates. And here we cannot help admiring the wisdom of the creator, who, having given to man the qualities needed to provide for the future as well as for the present, has willed and has brought it about that the society of man should last longer than that of the male and female among other creatures, so that thereby the industry of man and woman might be stimulated more, and that their interests might be better united, with a view to making provisions for their children and to leaving them their goods—nothing being more to the detriment of the children than an uncertain and vague conjunction, or an easy and frequent dissolution of the conjugal society."*

The same love of truth which has made me to set forth sincerely this objection, moves me to accompany it with some remarks, if not to resolve it, at least to clarify it.

1. I will observe first that moral proofs do not have great force in matters of physics, and that they serve more to explain existing facts than to establish the real existence of those facts. Now such is the type of proof that M. Locke employs in the passage I have just quoted; for although it may be advantageous to the human species for the union between man and woman to be permanent, it does not follow that it has been thus established by nature; otherwise it would be necessary to say that it also instituted civil society, the arts, commerce, and all that is asserted to be useful to men.

2. I do not know where M. Locke has found that among animals of prey, the society of the male and female lasts longer than does the society of those that live on grass, and that the former assists the latter to feed the young; for it is not manifest that the dog, the cat, the bear, or the wolf recognize their female better than the horse, the ram, the bull, the stag, or all the other quadruped animals do theirs. On the contrary, it seems that if the assistance of the male were necessary to the female to preserve her young, it would be particularly in the species that live only on grass, because a long period of time is needed by the mother to graze, and during that entire interval she is forced to neglect her brood, whereas the prey of a female bear or wolf is devoured in an instant, and, without suffering hunger, she has more time to nurse her young. This line of reasoning is confirmed by an observation upon the relative number of teats and young which distinguishes carnivorous from frugivorous species, and of which I have spoken in Note 8. If this observation is accurate and general, since a woman has only two teats and rarely has more than one child at a time, this is one more strong reason for doubting that the human species is naturally carnivorous. Thus it seems that, in order to draw Locke's conclusion, it would be necessary to

reverse completely his reasoning. There is no more solidity in the same distinction when it is applied to birds. For who could be persuaded that the union of the male and the female is more durable among vultures and crows than among turtle-doves? We have two species of domestic birds, the duck and the pigeon, which furnish us with examples directly contrary to the system of this author. The pigeon, which lives solely on grain, remains united to its female, and they feed their young in common. The duck, whose voraciousness is known, recognizes neither his female nor his young, and provides no help in their sustenance. And among hens, a species hardly less carnivorous, we do not observe that the rooster bothers himself in the least with the brood. And if in the other species the male shares with the female the care of feeding the young, it is because birds, which at first are unable to fly and which the mother cannot nurse, are much less in a position to get along without the help of the father than are quadrupeds, for which the mother's teat is sufficient, at least for a time.

3. There is much uncertainty about the principal fact that serves as a basis for all of M. Locke's reasoning; for in order to know whether, as he asserts, in the pure state of nature the female ordinarily is pregnant again and has a new child long before the preceding one could see to its needs for itself, it would be necessary to perform experiments that M. Locke surely did not perform and that no one is in a position to perform. The continual cohabitation of husband and wife is so near an occasion for being exposed to a new pregnancy that it is very difficult to believe that the chance encounter or the mere impulsion of temperament produced such frequent effects in the pure state of nature as in that of conjugal society: a slowness that would contribute perhaps toward making the children more robust, and that, moreover, might be compensated by the power to conceive, prolonged to a greater age in the women who would have abused it less in their youth. As to children, there are several reasons for believing that their forces and their organs develop much later among us than they did in the primitive state of which I am speaking. The original weakness which they derive from the constitution of the parents, the cares taken to envelop and constrain all of their members, the softness in which they are raised, perhaps the use of milk other than that of their mother, everything contradicts and slows down in them the initial progress of nature. The heed they are forced to pay to a thousand things on which their attention is continually fixed, while no exercise is given to their bodily forces, can also bring about considerable deflection from their growth. Thus, if, instead of first overworking and exhausting their minds in a thousand ways, their bodies were allowed to be exercised by the continual movements that nature seems to demand of them, it is to be believed that they would be in a much better position to walk and to provide for their needs by themselves.

4. Finally, M. Locke at most proves that there could well be in a man a motive for remaining attached to a woman when she has a child but in no way does he prove that the man must have been attached to her before the childbirth and during the nine months of pregnancy. If a given woman is indifferent to the man during those nine months, if she even becomes unknown to him, why will he help her after childbirth? Why will he help her to raise a child that he does not know belongs to him alone, and whose birth he has neither decided upon nor foreseen? Evidently M. Locke presumes what is in question, for it is not a matter of knowing why the man will remain attached to the woman after childbirth, but why he will be attached to her after conception. Once his appetite is satisfied, the man has no further need for a given woman, nor the woman for a given man. The man does not have the least care or perhaps the least idea of the consequences of his action. The one goes off in one direction, the other in another, and there is no likelihood that at the end of nine months they have the memory of having known one another. For this type of memory, by which one individual gives preference to another for the act of generation, requires, as I prove in the text, more progress or corruption in human understanding than may be supposed in man in the state of animality we are dealing with here. Another woman can therefore satisfy the new desires of the man as congenially as the one he has already known, and another man in the same manner satisfy the woman, supposing she is impelled by the same appetite during the time of pregnancy, about which one can reasonably be in doubt. And if in the state of nature the woman no longer feels the passion of love after the conception of the child, the obstacle to her society with the man thus becomes much greater still, since she then has no further need either for the man who has made her pregnant or for anyone else. There is not, therefore, in the man any reason to seek the same woman, or in the woman any reason to seek the same man. Thus

Locke's reasoning falls in ruin, and all the dialectic of this philosopher has not shielded him from the mistake committed by Hobbes and others. They had to explain a fact of the state of nature, that is to say, of a state where men lived in isolation and where a given man did not have any motive for living in proximity to another given man, nor perhaps did a given group of men have a motive for living in proximity to another given group of men, which is much worse. And they gave no thought to transporting themselves beyond the centuries of society, that is to say, of those times when men always have a reason for living in proximity to one another, and when a given man often has a reason for living in proximity to a given man or woman.

13. I will hold back from embarking on the philosophical reflections that there would be to engage in concerning the advantages and disadvantages of this institution of languages. It is not for me to be permitted to attack vulgar errors; and educated people respect their prejudices too much to abide patiently my alleged paradoxes. Let us therefore allow men to speak, to whom it has not been made a crime to risk sometimes taking the part of reason against the opinion of the multitude. *Nor would anything disappear from the happiness of the human race, if, when the disaster and confusion of so many languages has been cast out, mortals should cultivate one art, and if it should be allowed to explain anything by means of signs, movements and gestures. But now it has been so established that the condition of animals commonly believed to be brutes is considerably better than ours in this respect, inasmuch as they articulate their feelings and their thoughts without an interpreter more readily and perhaps more felicitously than any mortals can, especially if they use a foreign language.** Is. Vossius *de Poëmat. Cant. et Viribus Rythmi*, p. 66.

14. In showing how ideas of discrete quantity and its relationships are necessary in the humblest of the arts, Plato mocks with good reason the authors of his time who alleged that Palamedes had invented numbers at the siege of Troy, as if, says this philosopher, Agamemnon could have been ignorant until then of how many legs he had. In fact, one senses the impossibility that society and the arts should have arrived at the point where they already were at the time of the siege of Troy, unless men had the use of numbers and arithmetic. But the necessity for knowing numbers, before acquiring other types of knowledge, does not make their invention easier to imagine. Once the names of the numbers are known, it is easy to explain their meaning and to elicit the ideas which these names represent; but in order to invent them, it was necessary, prior to conceiving of these same ideas, to be, as it were, on familiar terms with philosophical meditations, to be trained to consider beings by their essence alone and independently of all other perception—a very difficult, very metaphysical, hardly natural abstraction, and yet one without which these ideas could never have been transported from one species or genus to another, nor could numbers have become universal. A savage could consider separately his right leg and his left leg, or look at them together under the indivisible idea of a pair without ever thinking that he had two of them; for the representative idea that portrays for us an object is one thing, and the numerical idea which determines it is another. Even less was he able to count to five. And although, by placing his hands one on top of the other, he could have noticed that the fingers corresponded exactly, he was far from thinking of their numerical equality. He did not know the sum of his fingers any more than that of his hairs. And if, after having made him understand what numbers are, someone had said to him that he had as many fingers as toes, he perhaps would have been quite surprised, in comparing them, to find that this was true.

15. We must not confuse egocentrism with love of oneself, two passions very different by virtue of both their nature and their effects. Love of oneself is a natural sentiment which moves every animal to be vigilant in its own preservation and which, directed in man by reason and modified by pity, produces humanity and virtue. Egocentrism is merely a sentiment that is relative, artificial and born in society, which moves each individual to value himself more than anyone else, which inspires in men all the evils they cause one another, and which is the true source of honor.

With this well understood, I say that in our primitive state, in the veritable state of nature, egocentrism does not exist; for since each particular man regards himself as the only spectator who observes him, as the only being in the universe that takes an interest in him, as the only judge of his own merit, it is impossible that a sentiment which has its source in comparisons that he is not in a position to make could germinate in his soul. For the same reason, this man could not have either hatred or desire for revenge, passions which can arise only from the belief that offense has been received. And since what constitutes the offense is scorn or the intention to harm and not the harm, men who know neither how to appraise nor to compare themselves can do considerable violence to one another when it returns them some advantage for doing it, without ever offending one another. In a word, on seeing his fellow-men hardly otherwise than he would see animals of another species, each man can carry away the prey of the weaker or yield his own to the stronger, viewing these lootings as merely natural events, without the least stirring of insolence or resentment, and without any other passion but the sadness or the joy of a good or bad venture.

16. It is something extremely remarkable that, for the many years that the Europeans torment themselves in order to acclimate the savages of various countries to their lifestyle, they have not yet been able to win over a single one of them, not even by means of Christianity; for our missionaries sometimes turn them into Christians, but never into civilized men. Nothing can overcome the invincible repugnance they have against appropriating our mores and living in our way. If these poor savages are as unhappy as is alleged, by what inconceivable depravity of judgment do they constantly refuse to civilize themselves in imitation of us, or to learn to live happily among us; whereas one reads in a thousand places that the French and other Europeans have voluntarily taken refuge among those nations, and have spent their entire lives there, no longer able to leave so strange a lifestyle; and whereas we even see level-headed missionaries regret with tenderness the calm and innocent days they have spent among those much scorned peoples? If one replies that they do not have enough enlightenment to make a sound judgment about their state and ours, I will reply that the reckoning of happiness is less an affair of reason than of sentiment. Moreover, this reply can be turned against us with still greater force; for there is a greater distance between our ideas and the frame of mind one needed to be in in order to conceive the taste which the savages find in their lifestyle, than between the ideas of savages and those that can make them conceive our lifestyle. In fact, after a few observations it is easy for them to see that all our labors are directed toward but two objects: namely, the conveniences of life for oneself and esteem among others. But what are the means by which we are to imagine the sort of pleasure a savage takes in spending his life alone amidst the woods, or fishing, or blowing into a sorry-looking flute, without ever knowing how to derive a single tone from it and without bothering himself to learn?

Savages have frequently been brought to Paris, London and other cities; people have been eager to display our luxury, our wealth, and all our most useful and curious arts. None of this has ever excited in them anything but a stupid admiration, without the least stirring of covetousness. I recall, among others, the story of a chief of some North Americans who was brought to the court of England about thirty years ago. A thousand things were made to pass before his eye in an attempt to give him some present that could please him, but nothing was found about which he seemed to care. Our weapons seemed heavy and cumbersome to him, our shoes hurt his feet, our clothes restricted him; he rejected everything. Finally, it was noticed that, having taken a wool blanket, he seemed to take some pleasure in wrapping it around his shoulders. You will agree at least, someone immediately said to him, on the usefulness of this furnishing? Yes, he replies, this seems to me to be nearly as good as an animal skin. However, he would not have said that, had he worn them both in the rain.

Perhaps someone will say to me that it is habit which, in attaching everyone to his lifestyle, prevents savages from realizing what is good in ours. And at that rate, it must at least appear quite extraordinary that habit has more force in maintaining the savages in the taste for their misery than the Europeans in the enjoyment of their felicity. But to give to this last objection a reply to which there is not a word to make in reply, without adducing all the young savages that people have tried in vain to civilize, without speaking of the Greenlanders and the inhabitants of Iceland, whom people have tried to raise and feed in Denmark, and all of whom sadness and despair caused to perish, whether from languor or in the sea when they attempted to regain their homeland by swimming back to it, I will be content to cite a single, well-documented example, which I give to the admirers of European civilization to examine.

"All the efforts of the Dutch missionaries at the Cape of Good Hope have never been able to convert a single Hottentot. Van der Stel, Governor of the Cape, having taken one from infancy, had raised him in the principles of the Christian religion and in the practice of the customs of Europe. He was richly clothed; he was taught several languages and his progress corresponded very closely to the care that was taken for his education. Having great hopes for his wit, the Governor sent him to the Indies with a commissioner general who employed him usefully in the affairs of the company. He returned to the Cape after the death of the commissioner. A few days after his return, on a visit he made to some of his Hottentot relatives, he made the decision to strip himself of his European dress in order to clothe himself with a sheepskin. He returned to the fort in this new outfit, carrying a bundle containing his old clothes, and, on presenting them to the Governor, he made the following speech to him: *Please, sir, be so kind as to pay heed to the fact that I forever renounce this clothing. I also renounce the Christian religion for the rest of my life. My resolution is to live and die in the religion, ways and customs of my ancestors. The only favor I ask of you is that you let me keep the necklace and cutlass I am wearing. I will keep them for love of you.* Thereupon, without waiting for Van der Stel's reply, he escaped by taking flight and was never seen again at the Cape." *Histoire des Voyages,* Vol. V, p. 175.

17. One could raise against me the objection that, in such a disorder, men, instead of willfully murdering one another, would have dispersed, had there been no limits to their dispersion. But first, these limits would at least have been those of the world. And if one thinks about the excessive population that results from the state of nature, one will judge that the earth in that state would not have taken long to be covered with men thus forced to keep together. Besides, they would have dispersed, had the evil been rapid, and had it been an overnight change. But they were born under the yoke; they were in the habit of carrying it when they felt its weight, and they were content to wait for the opportunity to shake it off. Finally, since they were already accustomed to a thousand conveniences which forced them to keep together, dispersion was no longer so easy as in the first ages, when, since no one had need for anyone but himself, everyone made his decision without waiting for someone else's consent.

18. Marshal de V*** related that, on one of his campaigns, when the excessive knavery of a provisions supplier had made the army suffer and complain, he gave him a severe dressing down and threatened to have him hanged. "This threat has no effect on me," the knave boldly replied to him, "and I am quite pleased to tell you that nobody hangs a man with a hundred thousand crowns at his disposal." I do not know how it happened, the Marshal added naïvely, but in fact he was not hanged, even though he deserved to be a hundred times over.

19. Distributive justice would still be opposed to this rigorous equality of the state of nature, if it were workable in civil society. And since all the members of the state owe it services proportionate to their talents and forces, the citizens for their part should be distinguished and favored in proportion to their services. It is in this sense that one must understand a passage of Isocrates, in which he praises the first Athenians for having known well how to distinguish which of the two sorts of equality was the more advantageous, one of which consists in portioning out indifferently to all citizens the same advantages, and the other in distributing them according to each one's merit. These able politicians, adds the orator, in banishing that unjust equality that makes no differentiation between wicked and good men, adhered inviolably to that equality which rewards and punishes each according to one's merit. But first, no society has ever existed, regardless of the degree of corruption they could have achieved, in which no differentiation between wicked and good men was made. And in the matter of mores, where the law cannot set a sufficiently precise measurement to serve as a rule for the magistrate, the law very wisely prohibits him from the judgment of persons, leaving him merely the judgment of actions, in order not to leave the fate or the rank of citizens to his discretion. Only mores as pure as those of the ancient Romans could withstand censors; such tribunals would soon have overturned everything among us. It is for public esteem to differentiate between wicked and good men. The magistrate is judge only of strict law [*droit*]; but the populace is the true judge of mores—an upright and even enlightened judge on this point, occasionally deceived but never corrupted. The ranks of citizens ought therefore to be regulated not on the basis of their personal merit, which would be to leave to the magistrate the means of making an almost arbitrary application of the law, but upon the real services which they render to the state and which lend themselves to a more precise reckoning.

ON THE
SOCIAL CONTRACT,
OR
PRINCIPLES OF
POLITICAL RIGHT

By J.-J. Rousseau,
Citizen of Geneva

—foederis aequas
Dicamus leges
—*Aeneid,* XI

FOREWORD

This little treatise is part of a longer work I undertook some time ago without taking stock of my abilities, and have long since abandoned. Of the various selections that could have been drawn from what had been completed, this is the most considerable, and, it appears to me, the one least unworthy of being offered to the public. The rest no longer exists.

ON THE SOCIAL CONTRACT

BOOK I

I want to inquire whether there can be some legitimate and sure rule of administration in the civil order, taking men as they are and laws as they might be. I will always try in this inquiry to bring together what right permits with what interest prescribes, so that justice and utility do not find themselves at odds with one another.

I begin without demonstrating the importance of my subject. It will be asked if I am a prince or a legislator that I should be writing about politics. I answer that I am neither, and that is why I write about politics. Were I a prince or a legislator, I would not waste my time saying what ought to be done. I would do it or keep quiet.

Reprinted from *The Basic Political Writings,* translated by Donald A. Cress (Indianapolis: Hackett Publishing Company, 1987), by permission of the publisher.

Born a citizen of a free state and a member of the sovereign, the right to vote is enough to impose upon me the duty to instruct myself in public affairs, however little influence my voice may have in them. Happy am I, for every time I meditate on governments, I always find new reasons in my inquiries for loving that of my country.

CHAPTER I
Subject of the First Book

Man is born free, and everywhere he is in chains. He who believes himself the master of others does not escape being more of a slave than they. How did this change take place? I have no idea. What can render it legitimate? I believe I can answer this question.

Were I to consider only force and the effect that flows from it, I would say that so long as a people is constrained to obey and does obey, it does well. As soon as it can shake off the yoke and does shake it off, it does even better. For by recovering its liberty by means of the same right that stole it, either the populace is justified in getting it back or else those who took it away were not justified in their actions. But the social order is a sacred right which serves as a foundation for all other rights. Nevertheless, this right does not come from nature. It is therefore founded upon convention. Before coming to that, I ought to substantiate what I just claimed.

CHAPTER II
Of the First Societies

The most ancient of all societies and the only natural one, is that of the family. Even so children remain bound to their father only so long as they need him to take care of them. As soon as the need ceases, the natural bond is dissolved. Once the children are freed from the obedience they owed the father and their father is freed from the care he owed his children, all return equally to independence. If they continue to remain united, this no longer takes place naturally but voluntarily, and the family maintains itself only by means of convention.

This common liberty is one consequence of the nature of man. Its first law is to see to his maintenance; its first concerns are those he owes himself; and, as soon as he reaches the age of reason, since he alone is the judge of the proper means of taking care of himself, he thereby becomes his own master.

The family therefore is, so to speak, the prototype of political societies; the leader is the image of the father, the populace is the image of the children, and, since all are born equal and free, none give up their liberty except for their utility. The entire difference consists in the fact that in the family the love of the father for his children repays him for the care he takes for them, while in the state, where the leader does not have love for his peoples, the pleasure of commanding takes the place of this feeling.

Grotius denies that all human power is established for the benefit of the governed, citing slavery as an example. His usual method of reasoning is always to present fact as a proof of right.[1] A more logical method could be used, but not one more favorable to tyrants.

---

1. "Learned research on public right is often nothing more than the history of ancient abuses, and taking a

According to Grotius, it is therefore doubtful whether the human race belongs to a hundred men, or whether these hundred men belong to the human race. And throughout his book he appears to lean toward the former view. This is Hobbes' position as well. On this telling, the human race is divided into herds of cattle, each one having its own leader who guards it in order to devour it.

Just as a herdsman possesses a nature superior to that of his herd, the herdsmen of men who are the leaders, also have a nature superior to that of their peoples. According to Philo, Caligula reasoned thus, concluding quite properly from this analogy that kings were gods, or that the peoples were beasts.

Caligula's reasoning coincides with that of Hobbes and Grotius. Aristotle, before all the others, had also said that men are by no means equal by nature, but that some were born for slavery and others for domination.

Aristotle was right, but he took the effect for the cause. Every man born in slavery is born for slavery; nothing is more certain. In their chains slaves lose everything, even the desire to escape. They love their servitude the way the companions of Ulysses loved their degradation.[2] If there are slaves by nature, it is because there have been slaves against nature. Force has produced the first slaves; their cowardice has perpetuated them.

I have said nothing about King Adam or Emperor Noah, father of three great monarchs who partitioned the universe, as did the children of Saturn, whom some have believed they recognize in them. I hope I will be appreciated for this moderation, for since I am a direct descendent of these princes, and perhaps of the eldest branch, how am I to know whether, after the verification of titles, I might not find myself the legitimate king of the human race? Be that as it may, we cannot deny that Adam was the sovereign of the world, just as Robinson Crusoe was sovereign of his island, so long as he was its sole inhabitant. And the advantage this empire had was that the monarch, securely on his throne, had no rebellions, wars or conspirators to fear.

CHAPTER III
On the Right of the Strongest

The strongest is never strong enough to be master all the time, unless he transforms force into right and obedience into duty. Hence the right of the strongest, a right that seems like something intended ironically and is actually established as a basic principle. But will no one explain this word to me? Force is a physical power; I fail to see what morality can result from its effects. To give in to force is an act of necessity, not of will. At most, it is an act of prudence. In what sense could it be a duty?

Let us suppose for a moment that there is such a thing as this alleged right. I maintain that all that results from it is an inexplicable mish-mash. For once force produces the right, the effect changes places with the cause. Every force that is superior to the first succeeds to its right. As soon as one can disobey with impunity, one can do so legitimately; and since the strongest is always right, the only thing to

---

lot of trouble to study them too closely gets one nowhere." *Treatise on the Interests of France Along With Her Neighbors*, by the Marquis d'Argenson. This is just what Grotius has done.

2. See a short treatise of Plutarch entitled "That Animals Reason."

do is to make oneself the strongest. For what kind of right is it that perishes when the force on which it is based ceases? If one must obey because of force, one need not do so out of duty; and if one is no longer forced to obey one is no longer obliged. Clearly then, this word "right" adds nothing to force. It is utterly meaningless here.

Obey the powers that be. If that means giving in to force, the precept is sound, but superfluous. I reply it will never be violated. All power comes from God—I admit it—but so does every disease. Does this mean that calling in a physician is prohibited? If a brigand takes me by surprise at the edge of a wooded area, is it not only the case that I must surrender my purse, but even that I am in good conscience bound to surrender it, if I were able to withhold it? After all, the pistol he holds is also a power.

Let us then agree that force does not bring about right, and that one is obliged to obey only legitimate powers. Thus my original question keeps returning.

CHAPTER IV
On Slavery

Since no man has a natural authority over his fellow man, and since force does not give rise to any right, conventions therefore remain the basis of all legitimate authority among men.

If, says Grotius, a private individual can alienate his liberty and turn himself into the slave of a master, why could not an entire people alienate its liberty and turn itself into the subject of a king? There are many equivocal words here which need explanation, but let us confine ourselves to the word *alienate*. To alienate is to give or to sell. A man who makes himself the slave of someone else does not give himself; he sells himself, at least for his subsistence. But why does a people sell itself? Far from furnishing his subjects with their subsistence, a king derives his own from them alone, and, according to Rabelais, a king does not live cheaply. Do subjects then give their persons on the condition that their estate will also be taken? I fail to see what remains for them to preserve.

It will be said that the despot assures his subjects of civil tranquility. Very well. But what do they gain, if the wars his ambition drags them into, if his insatiable greed, if the oppressive demands caused by his ministers occasion more grief for his subjects than their own dissensions would have done? What do they gain, if this very tranquility is one of their miseries? A tranquil life is also had in dungeons; is that enough to make them desirable? The Greeks who were locked up in the Cyclops' cave lived a tranquil existence as they awaited their turn to be devoured.

To say that a man gives himself gratuitously is to say something absurd and inconceivable. Such an act is illegitimate and null, if only for the fact that he who commits it does not have his wits about him. To say the same thing of an entire populace is to suppose a populace composed of madmen. Madness does not bring about right.

Even if each person can alienate himself, he cannot alienate his children. They are born men and free. Their liberty belongs to them; they alone have the right to dispose of it. Before they have reached the age of reason, their father can, in their name, stipulate conditions for their maintenance and for their well-being. But he cannot give them irrevocably and unconditionally, for such a gift is contrary to the ends of nature and goes beyond the rights of paternity. For an arbitrary government to be legitimate, it would therefore be necessary in each generation for the people to be master of its acceptance or rejection. But in that event this government would no longer be arbitrary.

Renouncing one's liberty is renouncing one's dignity as a man, the rights of humanity and even its duties. There is no possible compensation for anyone who renounces everything. Such a renunciation is incompatible with the nature of man. Removing all morality from his actions is tantamount to taking away all liberty from his will. Finally, it is a vain and contradictory convention to stipulate absolute authority on one side and a limitless obedience on the other. Is it not clear that no commitments are made to a person from whom one has the right to demand everything? And does this condition alone not bring with it, without equivalent or exchange, the nullity of the act? For what right would my slave have against me, given that all he has belongs to me, and that, since his right is my right, my having a right against myself makes no sense?

Grotius and others derive from war another origin for the alleged right of slavery. Since, according to them, the victor has the right to kill the vanquished, these latter can repurchase their lives at the price of their liberty—a convention all the more legitimate, since it turns a profit for both of them.

But clearly this alleged right to kill the vanquished does not in any way derive from the state of war. Men are not naturally enemies, for the simple reason that men living in their original state of independence do not have sufficiently constant relationships among themselves to bring about either a state of peace or a state of war. It is the relationship between things and not that between men that brings about war. And since this state of war cannot come into existence from simple personal relations, but only from real [proprietary] relations, a private war between one man and another can exist neither in the state of nature, where there is no constant property, nor in the social state, where everything is under the authority of the laws.

Fights between private individuals, duels, encounters are not acts which produce a state. And with regard to private wars, authorized by the ordinances of King Louis IX of France and suspended by the Peace of God, they are abuses of feudal government, an absurd system if there ever was one, contrary to the principles of natural right and to all sound polity.

War is not therefore a relationship between one man and another, but a relationship between one state and another. In war private individuals are enemies only incidentally: not as men or even as citizens,[3] but as soldiers; not as members of the homeland but as its defenders. Finally, each state can have as enemies only other

---

3. [*At this point the following passage was added to the 1782 edition:* The Romans, who had a better understanding of and a greater respect for the right of war than any other nation, carried their scruples so far in this regard that a citizen was not allowed to serve as a volunteer unless he had expressly committed himself against the enemy and against a specifically named enemy. When a legion in which Cato the Younger first served had been reorganized, Cato the Elder wrote Popilius that if he wanted his son to continue to serve under him, he would have to make him swear the military oath afresh, since, with the first one having been annulled, he could no longer take up arms against the enemy. And this very same Cato wrote his son to take care to avoid going into battle without swearing this military oath afresh. I know the siege of Clusium and other specific cases can be raised as counter-examples to this, but for my part I cite laws and customs. The Romans were the ones who transgressed their laws least often, and are the only ones to have had such noble laws.]

states and not men, since there can be no real relationship between things of disparate natures.

This principle is even in conformity with the established maxims of all times and with the constant practice of all civilized peoples. Declarations of war are warnings not so much to powers as to their subjects. The foreigner (be he king, private individual, or a people) who robs, kills or detains subjects of another prince without declaring war on the prince, is not an enemy but a brigand. Even in the midst of war a just prince rightly appropriates to himself everything in an enemy country belonging to the public, but respects the person and goods of private individuals. He respects the rights upon which his own rights are founded. Since the purpose of war is the destruction of the enemy state, one has the right to kill the defenders of that state so long as they bear arms. But as soon as they lay down their arms and surrender, they cease to be enemies or instruments of the enemy. They return to being simply men; and one no longer has a right to their lives. Sometimes a state can be killed without a single one of its members being killed. For war does not grant a right that is unnecessary to its purpose. These principles are not those of Grotius. They are not based on the authority of poets. Rather they are derived from the nature of things; they are based on reason.

As to the right of conquest, the only basis it has is the law of the strongest. If war does not give the victor the right to massacre the vanquished peoples, this right (which he does not have) cannot be the basis for the right to enslave them. One has the right to kill the enemy only when one cannot enslave him. The right to enslave him does not therefore derive from the right to kill him. Hence it is an iniquitous exchange to make him buy his life, to which no one has any right, at the price of his liberty. In establishing the right of life and death on the right of slavery, and the right of slavery on the right of life and death, is it not clear that one falls into a vicious circle?

Even if we were to suppose that there were this terrible right to kill everyone, I maintain that neither a person enslaved during wartime nor a conquered people bears any obligation whatever toward its master, except to obey him for as long as it is forced to do so. In taking the equivalent of his life, the victor has done him no favor. Instead of killing him unprofitably he kills him usefully. Hence, far from the victor having acquired any authority over him beyond force, the state of war subsists between them just as before. Their relationship itself is the effect of war, and the usage of the right to war does not suppose any peace treaty. They have made a convention. Fine. But this convention, far from destroying the state of war, presupposes its continuation.

Thus, from every point of view, the right of slavery is null, not simply because it is illegitimate, but because it is absurd and meaningless. These words, *slavery* and *right,* are contradictory. They are mutually exclusive. Whether it is the statement of one man to another man, or one man to a people, the following sort of talk will always be equally nonsensical. *I make a convention with you which is wholly at your expense and wholly to my advantage; and, for as long as it pleases me, I will observe it and so will you.*

CHAPTER V
That It Is Always Necessary to Return to a First Convention

Even if I were to grant all that I have thus far refuted, the supporters of despotism would not be any better off. There will always be a great difference between subduing a multitude and ruling a society. If scattered men, however many they may be, were successively enslaved by a single individual, I see nothing there but a master and slaves; I do not see a people and its leader. It is, if you will, an aggregation, but not an association. There is neither a public good nor a body politic there. Even if that man had enslaved half the world, he is always just a private individual. His interest, separated from that of others, is never anything but a private interest. If this same man is about to die, after his passing his empire remains scattered and disunited, just as an oak tree dissolves and falls into a pile of ashes after fire has consumed it.

A people, says Grotius, can give itself to a king. According to Grotius, therefore, a people is a people before it gives itself to a king. This gift itself is a civil act; it presupposes a public deliberation. Thus, before examining the act whereby a people chooses a king, it would be well to examine the act whereby a people is a people. For since this act is necessarily prior to the other, it is the true foundation of society.

In fact, if there were no prior convention, then, unless the vote were unanimous, what would become of the minority's obligation to submit to the majority's choice, and where do one hundred who want a master get the right to vote for ten who do not? The law of majority rule is itself an established convention, and presupposes unanimity on at least one occasion.

CHAPTER VI
On the Social Compact

I suppose that men have reached the point where obstacles that are harmful to their maintenance in the state of nature gain the upper hand by their resistance to the forces that each individual can bring to bear to maintain himself in that state. Such being the case, that original state cannot subsist any longer, and the human race would perish if it did not alter its mode of existence.

For since men cannot engender new forces, but merely unite and direct existing ones, they have no other means of maintaining themselves but to form by aggregation a sum of forces that could gain the upper hand over the resistance, so that their forces are directed by means of a single moving power and made to act in concert.

This sum of forces cannot come into being without the cooperation of many. But since each man's force and liberty are the primary instruments of his maintenance, how is he going to engage them without hurting himself and without neglecting the care that he owes himself? This difficulty, seen in terms of my subject, can be stated in the following terms:

"Find a form of association which defends and protects with all common forces the person and goods of each associate, and by means of which each one, while uniting with all, nevertheless obeys only himself and remains as free as before?" This is the fundamental problem for which the social contract provides the solution.

The clauses of this contract are so determined by the nature of the act that the least modification renders them vain and ineffectual, that, although perhaps they have never been formally promulgated, they are everywhere the same, everywhere tacitly accepted and acknowledged. Once the social compact is violated, each person then regains his first rights and resumes his natural liberty, while losing the conventional liberty for which he renounced it.

These clauses, properly understood, are all reducible to a single one, namely the total alienation of each associate, together with all of his rights, to the entire community. For first of all, since each person gives himself whole and entire, the condition is equal for everyone; and since the condition is equal for everyone, no one has an interest in making it burdensome for the others.

Moreover, since the alienation is made without reservation, the union is as perfect as possible, and no associate has anything further to demand. For if some rights remained with private individuals, in the absence of any common superior who could decide between them and the public, each person would eventually claim to be his own judge in all things, since he is on some point his own judge. The state of nature would subsist and the association would necessarily become tyrannical or hollow.

Finally, in giving himself to all, each person gives himself to no one. And since there is no associate over whom he does not acquire the same right that he would grant others over himself, he gains the equivalent of everything he loses, along with a greater amount of force to preserve what he has.

If, therefore, one eliminates from the social compact whatever is not essential to it, one will find that it is reducible to the following terms. Each of us places his person and all his power in common under the supreme direction of the general will; and as one we receive each member as an indivisible part of the whole.

At once, in place of the individual person of each contracting party, this act of association produces a moral and collective body composed of as many members as there are voices in the assembly, which receives from this same act its unity, its common *self*, its life and its will. This public person, formed thus by union of all the others formerly took the name *city*,[4] and at present takes the name *republic* or *body politic*, which is called *state* by its members when it is passive, *sovereign* when it is active, *power* when compared to others like itself. As to the associates, they collectively take the name *people;* individually they are called *citizens,* insofar as participants in the sovereign authority, and *subjects,* insofar as they are subjected to the laws of the state. But these terms are often confused and mistaken for one another. It is enough to know how to distinguish them when they are used with absolute precision.

CHAPTER VII
On the Sovereign

This formula shows that the act of association includes a reciprocal commitment between the public and private individuals, and that each individual, contracting, as it were, with himself, finds himself under a twofold commitment: namely as a member of the sovereign to private individuals, and as a member of the state toward the sovereign. But the maxim of civil law that no one is held to commitments made

---

4. The true meaning of this word is almost entirely lost on modern men. Most of them mistake a town for a city and a townsman for a citizen. They do not know that houses make a town but citizens make a city. Once this mistake cost the Carthaginians dearly. I have not found in my reading that the title of *citizen* has ever been given to the subjects of a prince, not even in ancient times to the Macedonians or in our own time to the English, although they are closer to liberty than all the others. Only the French adopt this name *citizen* with complete familiarity, since they have no true idea of its meaning, as can be seen from their dictionaries. If this were not the case, they would become guilty of treason for using it. For them, this name expresses a virtue and not a right. When Bodin wanted to speak about our citizens and townsmen, he committed a terrible blunder when he mistook the one group for the other. M. d'Alembert was not in error, and in his article entitled *Geneva* he has carefully distinguished the four orders of men (even five, counting ordinary foreigners) who are in our towns, and of whom only two make up the republic. No other French author I am aware of has grasped the true meaning of the word *citizen*.

to himself cannot be applied here, for there is a considerable difference between being obligated to oneself, or to a whole of which one is a part.

It must be further noted that the public deliberation that can obligate all the subjects to the sovereign, owing to the two different relationships in which each of them is viewed, cannot, for the opposite reason, obligate the sovereign to itself, and that consequently it is contrary to the nature of the body politic that the sovereign impose upon itself a law it could not break. Since the sovereign can be considered under but one single relationship, it is then in the position of a private individual contracting with himself. Whence it is apparent that there neither is nor can be any type of fundamental law that is obligatory for the people as a body, not even the social contract. This does not mean that the whole body cannot perfectly well commit itself to another body with respect to things that do not infringe on this contract. For in regard to the foreigner, it becomes a simple being, an individual.

However, since the body politic or the sovereign derives its being exclusively from the sanctity of the contract, it can never obligate itself, not even to another power, to do anything that derogates from the original act, such as alienating some portion of itself or submitting to another sovereign. Violation of the act whereby it exists would be self-annihilation, and whatever is nothing produces nothing.

As soon as this multitude is thus united in a body, one cannot harm one of the members without attacking the whole body. It is even less likely that the body can be harmed without the members feeling it. Thus duty and interest equally obligate the two parties to come to one another's aid, and the same men should seek to combine in this two-fold relationship all the advantages that result from it.

For since the sovereign is formed entirely from the private individuals who make it up, it neither has nor could have an interest contrary to theirs. Hence, the sovereign power has no need to offer a guarantee to its subjects, since it is impossible for a body to want to harm all of its members, and, as we will see later, it cannot harm any one of them in particular. The sovereign, by the mere fact that it exists, is always all that it should be.

But the same thing cannot be said of the subjects in relation to the sovereign, for which, despite their common interest, their commitments would be without substance if it did not find ways of being assured of their fidelity.

In fact, each individual can, as a man, have a private will contrary to or different from the general will that he has as a citizen. His private interest can speak to him in an entirely different manner than the common interest. His absolute and naturally independent existence can cause him to envisage what he owes the common cause as a gratuitous contribution, the loss of which will be less harmful to others than its payment is burdensome to him. And in viewing the moral person which constitutes the state as a being of reason because it is not a man, he would enjoy the rights of a citizen without wanting to fulfill the duties of a subject, an injustice whose growth would bring about the ruin of the body politic.

Thus, in order for the social compact to avoid being an empty formula, it tacitly entails the commitment—which alone can give force to the others—that whoever refuses to obey the general will will be forced to do so by the entire body. This means merely that he will be forced to be free. For this is the sort of condition that, by giving each citizen to the homeland, guarantees him against all personal dependence—a condition that produces the skill and the performance of the political machine, and which alone bestows legitimacy upon civil commitments. Without it such commitments would be absurd, tyrannical and subject to the worst abuses.

CHAPTER VIII
On the Civil State

This passage from the state of nature to the civil state produces quite a remarkable change in man, for it substitutes justice for instinct in his behavior and gives his actions a moral quality they previously lacked. Only then, when the voice of duty replaces physical impulse and right replaces appetite, does man, who had hitherto taken only himself into account, find himself forced to act upon other principles and to consult his reason before listening to his inclinations. Although in this state he deprives himself of several of the advantages belonging to him in the state of nature, he regains such great ones. His faculties are exercised and developed, his ideas are broadened, his feelings are ennobled, his entire soul is elevated to such a height that, if the abuse of this new condition did not often lower his status to beneath the level he left, he ought constantly to bless the happy moment that pulled him away from it forever and which transformed him from a stupid, limited animal into an intelligent being and a man.

Let us summarize this entire balance sheet so that the credits and debits are easily compared. What man loses through the social contract is his natural liberty and an unlimited right to everything that tempts him and that he can acquire. What he gains is civil liberty and the proprietary ownership of all he possesses. So as not to be in error in these compensations, it is necessary to draw a careful distinction between natural liberty (which is limited solely by the force of the individual involved) and civil liberty (which is limited by the general will), and between possession (which is merely the effect of the force or the right of the first occupant) and proprietary ownership (which is based solely on a positive title).

To the preceding acquisitions could be added the acquisition in the civil state of moral liberty, which alone makes man truly the master of himself. For to be driven by appetite alone is slavery, and obedience to the law one has prescribed for oneself is liberty. But I have already said too much on this subject, and the philosophical meaning of the word *liberty* is not my subject here.

CHAPTER IX
On the Real [i.e., Proprietary] Domain

Each member of the community gives himself to it at the instant of its constitution, just as he actually is, himself and all his forces, including all the goods in his possession. This is not to say that by this act possession changes its nature as it changes hands and becomes property in the hands of the sovereign. Rather, since the forces of the city are incomparably greater than those of a private individual, public possession is by that very fact stronger and more irrevocable, without being more legitimate, at least to strangers. For with regard to its members, the state is master of all their goods in virtue of the social contract, which serves in the state as the basis of all rights. But with regard to other powers, the state is master only in virtue of the right of the first occupant, which it derives from private individuals.

The right of first occupant, though more real than the right of the strongest, does not become a true right until after the establishment of the right of property. Every man by nature has a right to everything he needs; however, the positive act whereby he becomes a proprietor of some goods excludes him from all the rest. Once his lot has been determined, he should limit himself thereto, no longer having any right against the community. This is the reason why the right of the first occupant, so weak in the state of nature, is able to command the respect of every man living in the civil state. In this right, one respects not so much what belongs to others as what does not belong to oneself.

In general, the following rules must obtain in order to authorize the right of the first occupant on any land. First, this land may not already be occupied by anyone. Second, no one may occupy more than the amount needed to subsist. Third, one is to take possession of it not by an empty ceremony, but by working and cultivating it—the only sign of property that ought, in the absence of legal titles, to be respected by others.

In fact, by according to need and work the right of the first occupant, is it not extended as far as it can go? Is it possible to avoid setting limits to this right? Will setting one's foot on a piece of common land be sufficient to claim it at once as one's own? Will having the force for a moment to drive off other men be sufficient to deny them the right ever to return? How can a man or a people seize a vast amount of territory and deprive the entire human race of it except by a punishable usurpation, since this seizure deprives all other men of the shelter and sustenance that nature gives them in common? When Nuñez Balboa stood on the shoreline and took possession of the South Sea and all of South America in the name of crown of Castille, was this enough to dispossess all the inhabitants and to exclude all the princes of the world? On that basis, those ceremonies would be multiplied quite in vain. All the Catholic King had to do was to take possession of the universe all at once from his private room, excepting afterwards from his empire only what already belonged to other princes.

One can imagine how the combined and contiguous lands of private individuals became public territory; and how the right of sovereignty, extending from subjects to the land they occupied, becomes at once real and personal. This places its owners in a greater dependence, turning their very own forces into guarantees of their loyalty. This advantage does not seem to have been fully appreciated by the ancient monarchs, who, calling themselves merely King of the Persians, the Scythians, and the Macedonians, appeared to regard themselves merely as the leaders of men rather than the masters of the country. Today's monarchs more shrewdly call themselves King of France, Spain, England, and so on. In holding the land thus, they are quite sure of holding the inhabitants.

What is remarkable about this alienation is that, in accepting the goods of private individuals, the community is far from despoiling them; rather, in so doing, it merely assures them of legitimate possession, changing usurpation into a true right, and enjoyment into proprietary ownership. In that case, since owners are considered trustees of the public good, and since their rights are respected by all members of the state and maintained with all its force against foreigners, through an advantageous surrender to the public and still more so to themselves, they have, so to speak, acquired all they have given. This paradox is easily explained by the distinction between the rights of the sovereign and those of the proprietor to the same store, as will be seen later.

It can also happen, as men begin to unite before possessing anything and later appropriate a piece of land sufficient for everyone, that they enjoy it in common or divide it among themselves either in equal shares or according to proportions laid down by the sovereign. In whatever way this acquisition is accomplished, each private individual's right to his very own store is always subordinate to the community's right to all, without which there could be neither solidity in the social fabric nor real force in the exercise of sovereignty.

I will end this chapter and this book with a remark that should serve as a basis for every social system. It is that instead of destroying natural equality, the fundamental compact, on the contrary, substitutes a moral and legitimate equality to whatever physical inequality nature may have been able to impose upon men, and that, however, unequal in force or intelligence they may be, men all become equal by convention and by right.[5]

END OF THE FIRST BOOK

BOOK II

CHAPTER I
That Sovereignty Is Inalienable

The first and most important consequence of the principles established above is that only the general will can direct the forces of the state according to the purpose for which it was instituted, which is the common good. For if the opposition of private interests made necessary the establishment of societies, it is the accord of these same interests that made it possible. It is what these different interests have in common that forms the social bond, and, were there no point of agreement among all these interests, no society could exist. For it is utterly on the basis of this common interest that society ought to be governed.

I therefore maintain that since sovereignty is merely the exercise of the general will, it can never be alienated, and that the sovereign, which is only a collective being, cannot be represented by anything but itself. Power can perfectly well be transmitted, but not the will.

In fact, while it is not impossible for a private will to be in accord on some point with the general will, it is impossible at least for this accord to be durable and constant. For by its nature the private will tends toward having preferences, and the general will tends toward equality. It is even more impossible for there to be a guarantee of this accord even if it ought always to exist. This is not the result of art but of chance. The sovereign may well say, "Right now I want what a certain man

---

5. Under bad governments this equality is only apparent and illusory. It serves merely to maintain the poor man in his misery and the rich man in his usurpation. In actuality, laws are always useful to those who have possessions and harmful to those who have nothing. Whence it follows that the social state is advantageous to men only insofar as they all have something and none of them has too much.

wants or at least what he says he wants." But it cannot say, "What this man will want tomorrow I too will want," since it is absurd for the will to tie its hands for the future and since it does not depend upon any will's consenting to anything contrary to the good of the being that wills. If, therefore, the populace promises simply to obey, it dissolves itself by this act, it loses its standing as a people. The very moment there is a master, there no longer is a sovereign, and thenceforward the body politic is destroyed.

This is not to say that the commands of the leaders could not pass for manifestations of the general will, so long as the sovereign, who is free to oppose them, does not do so. In such a case, the consent of the people ought to be presumed on the basis of universal silence. This will be explained at greater length.

CHAPTER II
That Sovereignty Is Indivisible

Sovereignty is indivisible for the same reason that it is inalienable. For either the will is general,[6] or it is not. It is the will of either the people as a whole or of only a part. In the first case, this declared will is an act of sovereignty and constitutes law. In the second case, it is merely a private will, or an act of magistracy. At most it is a decree.

However, our political theorists, unable to divide sovereignty in its principle, divide it in its object. They divide it into force and will, into legislative and executive power, into rights of imposing taxes, of justice and of war, into internal administration and power to negotiate with foreigners. Occasionally they confuse all these parts and sometimes they separate them. They turn the sovereign into a fantastic being made of interconnected pieces. It is as if they built a man out of several bodies, one of which had eyes, another had arms, another feet, and nothing more. Japanese sleight-of-hand artists are said to dismember a child before the eyes of spectators, then, throwing all the parts in the air one after the other, they make the child fall back down alive and all in one piece. These conjuring acts of our political theorists are more or less like these performances. After having taken apart the social body by means of a sleight-of-hand worthy of a carnival, they put the pieces back together who knows how.

This error comes from not having formed precise notions of sovereign authority, and from having taken for parts of that authority what were merely emanations from it. Thus, for example, the acts of declaring war and making peace have been viewed as acts of sovereignty, which they are not, since each of these acts is not a law but merely an application of the law, a particular act determining the legal circumstances, as will be clearly seen when the idea attached to the word *law* comes to be defined.

In reviewing the other divisions in the same way, one would find that one is mistaken every time one believes one sees sovereignty divided, and that the rights one takes to be the parts of this sovereignty are all subordinated to it and always presuppose supreme wills which these rights merely put into effect.

---

6. For a will to be general, it need not always be unanimous; however, it is necessary for all the votes to be counted. Any formal exclusion is a breach of generality.

It would be impossible to say how much this lack of precision has obscured the decisions of authors who have written about political right when they wanted to judge the respective rights of kings and peoples on the basis of the principles they had established. Anyone can see, in Chapters III and IV of Book I of Grotius, how this learned man and his translator, Barbeyrac, become entangled and caught up in their sophisms, for fear of either saying too much or too little according to their perspectives, and of offending the interests they needed to reconcile. Grotius, taking refuge in France, unhappy with his homeland and desirous of paying court to Louis XIII (to whom his book is dedicated), spares no pain to rob the people of all their rights and to invest kings with them by every possible artifice. This would also have been the wish of Barbeyrac, who dedicated his translation to King George I of England. But unfortunately the expulsion of James II (which he calls an abdication) forced him to be evasive and on his guard and to beat around the bush, in order to avoid making William out to be a usurper. If these two writers had adopted the true principles, all their difficulties would have been alleviated and they would always have been consistent. However, sad to say, they would have told the truth and paid court only to the people. For truth does not lead to fortune, and the populace grants neither ambassadorships, university chairs nor pensions.

CHAPTER III
Whether the General Will Can Err

It follows from what has preceded that the general will is always right and always tends toward the public utility. However, it does not follow that the deliberations of the people always have the same rectitude. We always want what is good for us, but we do not always see what it is. The populace is never corrupted, but it is often tricked, and only then does it appear to want what is bad.

There is often a great deal of difference between the will of all and the general will. The latter considers only the general interest, whereas the former considers private interest and is merely the sum of private wills. But remove from these same wills the pluses and minuses that cancel each other out,[7] and what remains as the sum of the differences is the general will.

If, when a sufficiently informed populace deliberates, the citizens were to have no communication among themselves, the general will would always result from the large number of small differences, and the deliberation would always be good. But when intrigues and partial associations come into being at the expense of the large association, the will of each of these associations becomes general in relation to its members and particular in relation to the state. It can be said, then, that there are no longer as many voters as there are men, but merely as many as there are associations. The differences become less numerous and yield a result that is less general. Finally, when one of these associations is so large that it dominates all the others, the result is no longer a sum of minor differences, but a single difference. Then there is no longer a general will, and the opinion that dominates is merely a private opinion.

---

7. *Each interest,* says the Marquis d'Argenson, *has different principles. The accord of two private interests is formed in opposition to that of a third.* He could have added that the accord of all the interests is found in the opposition to that of each. If there were no different interests, the common interest, which would never encounter any obstacle, would scarcely be felt. Everything would proceed on its own and politics would cease being an art.

For the general will to be well articulated, it is therefore important that there should be no partial society in the state and that each citizen make up his own mind.[8] Such was the unique and sublime institution of the great Lycurgus. If there are partial societies, their number must be multiplied and inequality among them prevented, as was done by Solon, Numa and Servius. These precautions are the only effective way of bringing it about that the general will is always enlightened and that the populace is not tricked.

CHAPTER IV
On the Limits of Sovereign Power

If the state or the city is merely a moral person whose life consists in the union of its members, and if the most important of its concerns is that of its own conservation, it ought to have a universal compulsory force to move and arrange each part in the manner best suited to the whole. Just as nature gives each man an absolute power over all his members, the social compact gives the body politic an absolute power over all its members, and it is the same power which, as I have said, is directed by the general will and bears the name sovereignty.

But over and above the public person, we need to consider the private persons who make it up and whose life and liberty are naturally independent of it. It is, therefore, a question of making a rigorous distinction between the respective rights of the citizens and the sovereign,[9] and between the duties the former have to fulfill as subjects and the natural right they should enjoy as men.

We grant that each person alienates, by the social compact, only that portion of his power, his goods, and liberty whose use is of consequence to the community; but we must also grant that only the sovereign is the judge of what is of consequence.

A citizen should render to the state all the services he can as soon as the sovereign demands them. However, for its part, the sovereign cannot impose on the subjects any fetters that are of no use to the community. It cannot even will to do so, for under the law of reason nothing takes place without a cause, any more than under the law of nature.

The commitments that bind us to the body politic are obligatory only because they are mutual, and their nature is such that in fulfilling them one cannot work for someone else without also working for oneself. Why is the general will always right, and why do all constantly want the happiness of each of them, if not because everyone applies the word *each* to himself and thinks of himself as he votes for all? This proves that the quality of right and the notion of justice it produces are derived from the preference each person gives himself, and thus from the nature of man; that the general will, to be really such, must be general in its object as well as in its essence; that it must derive from all in order to be applied to all; and that it loses its natural

---

8. "*It is true*," says Machiavelli, "*that some divisions are harmful to the republic while others are helpful to it. Those that are accompanied by sects and partisan factions are harmful. Since, therefore, a ruler of a republic cannot prevent enmities from arising within it, he at least ought to prevent them from becoming sects,*" *The History of Florence*, Book VII. [Rousseau here quotes the Italian.]

9. Attentive readers, please do not rush to accuse me of contradiction here. I have been unable to avoid it in my choice of words, given the poverty of the language. But wait.

rectitude when it tends toward any individual, determinate object. For then, judging what is foreign to us, we have no true principle of equity to guide us.

In effect, once it is a question of a state of affairs or a particular right concerning a point that has not been regulated by a prior, general convention, the issue becomes contentious. It is a suit in which the interested private individuals are one of the parties and the public the other, but in which I fail to see either what law should be followed or what judge should render the decision. In these circumstances it would be ridiculous to want to defer to an express decision of the general will, which can only be the conclusion reached by one of its parts, and which, for the other party, therefore, is merely an alien, particular will, inclined on this occasion to injustice and subject to error. Thus, just as a private will cannot represent the general will, the general will, for its part, alters its nature when it has a particular object; and as general, it is unable to render a decision on either a man or a state of affairs. When, for example, the populace of Athens appointed or dismissed its leaders, decreed that honors be bestowed on one or inflicted penalties on another, and by a multitude of particular decrees, indiscriminately exercised all the acts of government, the people in this case no longer had a general will in the strict sense. It no longer functioned as sovereign but as magistrate. This will appear contrary to commonly held opinions, but I must be given time to present my own.

It should be seen from this that what makes the will general is not so much the number of votes as the common interest that unites them, for in this institution each person necessarily submits himself to the conditions he imposes on others, an admirable accord between interest and justice which bestows on common deliberations a quality of equity that disappears when any particular matter is discussed, for lack of a common interest uniting and identifying the role of the judge with that of the party.

From whatever viewpoint one approaches this principle, one always arrives at the same conclusion, namely that the social compact establishes among the citizens an equality of such a kind that they all commit themselves under the same conditions and should all enjoy the same rights. Thus by the very nature of the compact, every act of sovereignty (that is, every authentic act of the general will) obligates or favors all citizens equally, so that the sovereign knows only the nation as a body and does not draw distinctions between any of those members that make it up. Strictly speaking, then, what is an act of sovereignty? It is not a convention between a superior and an inferior, but a convention of the body with each of its members. This convention is legitimate, because it has the social contract as a basis; equitable, because it is common to all; useful, because it can have only the general good for its object; and solid, because it has the public force and the supreme power as a guarantee. So long as the subjects are subordinated only to such convention, they obey no one but their own will alone. And asking how far the respective rights of the sovereign and the citizens extend is asking how far the latter can commit themselves to one another, each to all and all to each.

We can see from this that the sovereign power, absolute, wholly sacred and inviolable as it is, does not and cannot exceed the limits of general conventions, and that every man can completely dispose of such goods and freedom as has been left to him by these conventions. This results in the fact that the sovereign never has the right to lay more charges on one subject than on another, because in that case the matter becomes particular, no longer within the range of the sovereign's competence.

Once these distinctions are granted, it is so false that there is, in the social contract, any genuine renunciation on the part of private individuals that their situation, as a result of this contract, is really preferable to what it was beforehand; and, instead of an alienation, they have merely made an advantageous exchange of an uncertain and precarious mode of existence for another that is better and surer. Natural independence is exchanged for liberty; the power to harm others is exchanged for their own security; and their force, which others could overcome, for a right which the social union renders invincible. Their life itself, which they have devoted to the state, is continually protected by it; and when they risk their lives for its defense, what are they then doing but returning to the state what they have received from it? What are they doing, that they did not do more frequently and with greater danger in the state of nature, when they would inevitably have to fight battles, defending at the peril of their lives the means of their preservation? It is true that everyone has to fight, if necessary, for the homeland; but it also is the case that no one ever has to fight on his own behalf. Do we not still gain by running, for something that brings about our security, a portion of the risks we would have to run for ourselves once our security is taken away?

CHAPTER V
On the Right of Life or Death

The question arises how private individuals who have no right to dispose of their own lives can transfer to the sovereign this very same right which they do not have. This question seems difficult to resolve only because it is poorly stated. Every man has the right to risk his own life in order to preserve it. Has it ever been said that a person who jumps out a window to escape a fire is guilty of committing suicide? Has this crime ever been imputed to someone who perishes in a storm, unaware of its danger when he embarked?

The social treaty has as its purpose the conservation of the contracting parties. Whoever wills the end also wills the means, and these means are inseparable from some risks, even from some losses. Whoever wishes to preserve his life at the expense of others should also give it up for them when necessary. For the citizen is no longer judge of the peril to which the law wishes he be exposed, and when the prince has said to him, "it is expedient for the state that you should die," he should die. Because it is under this condition alone that he has lived in security up to then, and because his life is not only a kindness of nature, but a conditional gift of the state.

The death penalty inflicted on criminals can be viewed from more or less the same point of view. It is in order to avoid being the victim of an assassin that a person consents to die, were he to become one. According to this treaty, far from disposing of his own life, one thinks only of guaranteeing it. And it cannot be presumed that any of the contracting parties is then planning to get himself hanged.

Moreover, every malefactor who attacks the social right becomes through his transgressions a rebel and a traitor to the homeland; in violating its laws, he ceases to be a member, and he even wages war with it. In that case the preservation of the state is incompatible with his own. Thus one of the two must perish; and when the guilty party is put to death, it is less as a citizen than as an enemy. The legal proceeding and the judgment are the proofs and the declaration that he has broken the social treaty, and consequently that he is no longer a member of the state. For since he has acknowledged himself to be such, at least by his living there, he ought to be removed from it by exile as a violator of the compact, or by death as a public enemy. For such an enemy is not a moral person, but a man, and in this situation the right of war is to kill the vanquished.

But it will be said that the condemnation of a criminal is a particular act. Fine. So this condemnation is not a function of the sovereign. It is a right the sovereign can confer without itself being able to exercise it. All of my opinions are consistent, but I cannot present them all at once.

In addition, frequency of physical punishment is always a sign of weakness or of torpor in the government. There is no wicked man who could not be made good for something. One has the right to put to death, even as an example, only someone who cannot be preserved without danger.

With regard to the right of pardon, or of exempting a guilty party from the penalty decreed by the law and pronounced by the judge, this belongs only to one who is above the judge and the law, that is, to the sovereign. Still its right in this regard is not clearly defined, and the cases in which it is used are quite rare. In a well governed state, there are few punishments, not because many pardons are granted, but because there are few criminals. When a state is in decline, the sheer number of crimes insures impunity. Under the Roman Republic, neither the senate nor the consuls ever tried to grant pardons. The people itself did not do so, even though it sometimes revoked its own judgment. Frequent pardons indicate that transgressions will eventually have no need of them, and everyone sees where that leads. But I feel that my heart murmurs and holds back my pen. Let us leave these questions to be discussed by a just man who has not done wrong and who himself never needed pardon.

CHAPTER VI
On Law

Through the social compact we have given existence and life to the body politic. It is now a matter of giving it movement and will through legislation. For the primitive act whereby this body is formed and united still makes no determination regarding what it should do to preserve itself.

Whatever is good and in conformity with order is such by the nature of things and independently of human conventions. All justice comes from God; he alone is its source. But if we knew how to receive it from so exalted a source, we would have no need for government or laws. Undoubtedly there is a universal justice emanating from reason alone; but this justice, to be admitted among us, ought to be reciprocal. Considering things from a human standpoint, the lack of a natural sanction causes the laws of justice to be without teeth among men. They do nothing but good to the wicked and evil to the just, when the latter observes them in his dealings with everyone while no one observes them in their dealings with him. There must therefore be conventions and laws to unite rights and duties and to refer justice back to its object. In the state of nature where everything is commonly held, I owe nothing to those to whom I have promised nothing. I recognize as belonging to someone else only what is not useful to me. It is not this way in the civil state where all rights are fixed by law.

But what then is a law? So long as we continue to be satisfied with attaching only metaphysical ideas to this word, we will continue to reason without coming to any understanding. And when they have declared what a law of nature is, they will not thereby have a better grasp of what a law of the state is.

I have already stated that there is no general will concerning a particular object. In effect, this particular object is either within or outside of the state. If it is outside of the state, a will that is foreign to it is not general in relation to it. And if this object is within the state, that object is part of it; in that case, a relationship is formed between the whole and its parts which makes two separate beings, one of which is the part, and the other is the whole less that same part. But the whole less a part is not the whole, and so long as this relationship obtains, there is no longer a whole, but rather two unequal parts. Whence it follows that the will of the one is not more general in relation to the other.

But when the entire populace enacts a statute concerning the entire populace, it considers only itself, and if in that case a relationship is formed, it is between the entire object seen from one perspective and the entire object seen from another, without any division of the whole. Then the subject matter about which a statute is enacted is general like the will that enacts it. It is this act that I call a law.

When I say that the object of the laws is always general, I have in mind that the law considers subjects as a body and actions in the abstract, never a man as an individual or a particular action. Thus the law can perfectly well enact a statute to the effect that there be privileges, but it cannot bestow them by name on anyone. The law can create several classes of citizens, and even stipulate the qualifications that determine membership in these classes, but it cannot name specific persons to be admitted to them. It can establish a royal government and a hereditary line of succession, but it cannot elect a king or name a royal family. In a word, any function that relates to an individual does not belong to the legislative power. On this view, it is immediately obvious that it is no longer necessary to ask who is to make the laws, since they are the acts of the general will; nor whether the prince is above the laws, since he is a member of the state; nor whether the law can be unjust, since no one is unjust to himself; nor how one is both free and subject to the laws, since they are merely the record of our own wills.

Moreover, it is apparent that since the law combines the universality of the will and that of the object, what a man, whoever he may be, decrees on his own authority is not a law. What even the sovereign decrees concerning a particular object is no closer to being a law; rather, it is a decree. Nor is it an act of sovereignty but of magistracy.

I therefore call every state ruled by laws a republic, regardless of the form its administration may take. For only then does the public interest govern, and only then is the "public thing" [in Latin: *res publica*] something real. Every legitimate government is republican.[10] I will explain later on what government is.

---

10. By this word I do not have in mind merely an aristocracy or a democracy, but in general every government guided by the general will, which is the law. To be legitimate, the government need not be made indistinguishable from the sovereign, but it must be its minister. Then the monarchy itself is a republic. This will become clear in the next Book.

Strictly speaking, laws are merely the conditions of civil association. The populace that is subjected to the laws ought to be their author. The regulating of the conditions of a society belongs to no one but those who are in association with one another. But how will they regulate these conditions? Will it be by a common accord, by a sudden inspiration? Does the body politic have an organ for making known its will? Who will give it the necessary foresight to formulate acts and to promulgate them in advance, or how will it announce them in time of need? How will a blind multitude, which often does not know what it wants (since it rarely knows what is good for it), carry out on its own an enterprise as great and as difficult as a system of legislation? By itself the populace always wants the good, but by itself it does not always see it. The general will is always right, but the judgment that guides it is not always enlightened. It must be made to see objects as they are, and sometimes as they ought to appear to it. The good path it seeks must be pointed out to it. It must be made safe from the seduction of private wills. It must be given a sense of time and place. It must weigh present, tangible advantages against the danger of distant, hidden evils. Private individuals see the good they reject. The public wills the good that it does not see. Everyone is equally in need of guides. The former must be obligated to conform their wills to their reason; the latter must learn to know what it wants. Then public enlightenment results in the union of the understanding and the will in the social body; hence the full cooperation of the parts, and finally the greatest force of the whole. Whence there arises the necessity of having a legislator.

CHAPTER VII
On the Legislator

Discovering the rules of society best suited to nations would require a superior intelligence that beheld all the passions of men without feeling any of them; who had no affinity with our nature, yet knew it through and through; whose happiness was independent of us, yet who nevertheless was willing to concern itself with ours; finally, who, in the passage of time, procures for himself a distant glory, being able to labor in one age and find enjoyment in another.[11] Gods would be needed to give men laws.

The same reasoning used by Caligula regarding matters of fact was used by Plato regarding right in defining the civil or royal man he looks for in his dialogue *The Statesman*. But if it is true that a great prince is a rare man, what about a great legislator? The former merely has to follow the model the latter should propose to him. The latter is the engineer who invents the machine; the former is merely the workman who constructs it and makes it run. At the birth of societies, says Montesquieu, it is the leaders of republics who bring about the institution, and thereafter it is the institution that forms the leaders of the republic.

He who dares to undertake the establishment of a people should feel that he is, so to speak, in a position to change human nature, to transform each individual (who by himself is a perfect and solitary whole), into a part of a larger whole from which this individual receives, in a sense, his life and his being; to alter man's constitution in order to strengthen it; to substitute a partial and moral existence for

---

11. A people never becomes famous except when its legislation begins to decline. It is not known for how many centuries the institution established by Lycurgus caused the happiness of the Spartans before the rest of Greece took note of it.

the physical and independent existence we have all received from nature. In a word, he must deny man his own forces in order to give him forces that are alien to him and that he cannot make use of without the help of others. The more these natural forces are dead and obliterated, and the greater and more durable are the acquired forces, the more too is the institution solid and perfect. Thus if each citizen is nothing and can do nothing except in concert with all the others, and if the force acquired by the whole is equal or superior to the sum of the natural forces of all the individuals, one can say that the legislation has achieved the highest possible point of perfection.

The legislator is in every respect an extraordinary man in the state. If he ought to be so by his genius, he is no less so by his office, which is neither magistracy nor sovereignty. This office, which constitutes the republic, does not enter into its constitution. It is a particular and superior function having nothing in common with the dominion over men. For if he who has command over men must not have command over laws, he who has command over the laws must no longer have any authority over men. Otherwise, his laws, ministers of his passions, would often only serve to perpetuate his injustices, and he could never avoid private opinions altering the sanctity of his work.

When Lycurgus gave laws to his homeland, he began by abdicating the throne. It was the custom of most Greek cities to entrust the establishment of their laws to foreigners. The modern republics of Italy often imitated this custom. The republic of Geneva did the same and things worked out well.[12] In its finest age Rome saw the revival within its midst of all the crimes of tyranny and saw itself on the verge of perishing as a result of having united the legislative authority and the sovereign power in the same hands.

Nevertheless, the decemvirs themselves never claimed the right to have any law passed on their authority alone. *Nothing we propose,* they would tell the people, *can become law without your consent. Romans, be yourselves the authors of the laws that should bring about your happiness.*

He who frames the laws, therefore, does not or should not have any legislative right. And the populace itself cannot, even if it wanted to, deprive itself of this incommunicable right, because, according to the fundamental compact, only the general will obligates private individuals, and there can never be any assurance that a private will is in conformity with the general will until it has been submitted to the free vote of the people. I have already said this, but it is not a waste of time to repeat it.

Thus we find together in the work of legislation two things that seem incompatible: an undertaking that transcends human force, and, to execute it, an authority that is nil.

Another difficulty deserves attention. The wise men who want to speak to the common masses in the former's own language rather than in the common vernacular cannot be understood by the masses. For there are a thousand kinds of ideas that are impossible to translate in the language of the populace. Overly general perspec-

---

12. Those who view Calvin simply as a theologian fail to grasp the extent of his genius. The codification of our wise edicts, in which he had a large role, does him as much honor as his *Institutes*. Whatever revolution time may bring out in our cult, so long as the love of homeland and of liberty is not extinguished among us, the memory of this great man will never cease to be held sacred.

tives and overly distant objects are equally beyond its grasp. Each individual, in having no appreciation for any other plan of government but the one that relates to his own private interest, finds it difficult to realize the advantages he ought to draw from the continual privations that good laws impose. For an emerging people to be capable of appreciating the sound maxims of politics and to follow the fundamental rules of statecraft, the effect would have to become the cause. The social spirit which ought to be the work of that institution, would have to preside over the institution itself. And men would be, prior to the advent of laws, what they ought to become by means of laws. Since, therefore, the legislator is incapable of using either force or reasoning, he must of necessity have recourse to an authority of a different order, which can compel without violence and persuade without convincing.

This is what has always forced the fathers of nations to have recourse to the intervention of heaven and to credit the gods with their own wisdom, so that the peoples, subjected to the laws of the state as to those of nature and recognizing the same power in the formation of man and of the city, might obey with liberty and bear with docility the yoke of public felicity.

It is this sublime reason, which transcends the grasp of ordinary men, whose decisions the legislator puts in the mouth of the immortals in order to compel by divine authority those whom human prudence could not move.[13] But not everybody is capable of making the gods speak or of being believed when he proclaims himself their interpreter. The great soul of the legislator is the true miracle that should prove his mission. Any man can engrave stone tablets, buy an oracle, or feign secret intercourse with some divinity, or train a bird to talk in his ear, or find other crude methods of imposing his beliefs on the people. He who knows no more than this may perchance assemble a troupe of lunatics, but he will never found an empire and his extravagant work will soon die with him. Pointless sleights-of-hand form a fleeting connection; only wisdom can make it lasting. The Judaic Law, which still exists, and that of the child of Ishmael, which has ruled half the world for ten centuries, still proclaim today the great men who enunciated them. And while pride-ridden philosophy or the blind spirit of factionalism sees in them nothing but lucky impostors, the true political theoretician admires in their institutions that great and powerful genius which presides over establishments that endure.

We should not, with Warburton, conclude from this that politics and religion have a common object among us, but that in the beginning stages of nations the one serves as an instrument of the other.

CHAPTER VIII
On the People

Just as an architect, before putting up a large building, surveys and tests the ground to see if it can bear the weight, the wise teacher does not begin by laying down laws that are good in themselves. Rather he first examines whether the people for whom they are destined are fitted to bear them. For this reason, Plato refused

---

13. *And in truth*, says Machiavelli, *there has never been among a people a single legislator who, in proposing extraordinary laws, did not have recourse to God, for otherwise they would not be accepted, since there are many benefits known to a prudent man that do not have in themselves evident reasons enabling him to persuade others. Discourses on Titus Livy*, Book I, Ch. XI. [Rousseau here quotes the Italian.]

to give laws to the Arcadians and to the Cyrenians, knowing that these two peoples were rich and could not abide equality. For this reason, one finds good laws and evil men in Crete, because Minos had disciplined nothing but a vice-ridden people.

A thousand nations have achieved brilliant earthly success that could never have abided good laws; and even those that could have would have been able to have done so for a very short period of their entire existence. Peoples,[14] like men, are docile only in their youth. As they grow older they become incorrigible. Once customs are established and prejudices have become deeply rooted, it is a dangerous and vain undertaking to want to reform them. The people cannot abide having even their evils touched in order to eliminate them, just like those stupid and cowardly patients who quiver at the sight of a physician.

This is not to say that, just as certain maladies unhinge men's minds and remove from them the memory of the past, one does not likewise sometimes find in the period during which states have existed violent epochs when revolutions do to peoples what certain crises do to individuals, when the horror of the past takes the place of forgetfulness, and when the state, set afire by civil wars, is reborn, as it were, from its ashes and takes on again the vigor of youth as it escapes death's embrace. Such was Sparta at the time of Lycurgus; such was Rome after the Tarquins; and such in our time have been Holland and Switzerland after the expulsion of the tyrants.

But these events are rare. They are exceptions whose cause is always to be found in the particular constitution of the states in question. They cannot take place even twice to the same people, for it can make itself free so long as it is merely barbarous; but it can no longer do so when civil strength is exhausted. At that point troubles can destroy it with revolutions being unable to reestablish it. And as soon as its chains are broken, it falls apart and exists no longer. Henceforward a master is needed, not a liberator. Free peoples, remember this axiom: Liberty can be acquired, but it can never be recovered.

For nations, as for men, there is a time of maturity that must be awaited before subjecting them to the laws.[15] But the maturity of a people is not always easily recognized; and if it is foreseen, the work is ruined. One people lends itself to discipline at its inception; another, not even after ten centuries. The Russians will never be truly civilized, since they have been civilized too early. Peter had a genius for imitation. He did not have true genius, the kind that creates and makes everything out of nothing. Some of the things he did were good; most of them were out of place. He saw that his people was barbarous; he did not see that it was not ready for civilization. He wanted to civilize it when all it needed was toughening. First he wanted to make Germans and Englishmen, when he should have made Russians. He prevented his subjects from ever becoming what they could have been by persuading them that they were something they are not. This is exactly how a French tutor trains his pupil to shine for a short time in his childhood, and afterwards never to amount to a thing. The Russian Empire would like to subjugate Europe and will itself be subjugated. The Tartars, its subjects or its neighbors, will become its masters

14. [*In the 1782 edition, this sentence was revised to read:* "Most people, like men. . . ."]

15. [*In the 1782 edition, this sentence was revised to read:* "Youth is not childhood. For nations, as for men, maturity must be awaited. . . ."]

and ours. This revolution appears inevitable to me. All the kings of Europe are working in concert to hasten its occurrence.

CHAPTER IX
The People (continued)

Just as nature has set limits to the status of a well-formed man, beyond which there are but giants or dwarfs, so too, with regard to the best constitution of a state, there are limits to the size it can have, so as not to be too large to be capable of being well governed, nor too small to be capable of preserving itself on its own. In every body politic there is a *maximum* force that it cannot exceed, and which has often fallen short by increasing in size. The more the social bond extends the looser it becomes, and in general a small state is proportionately stronger than a large one.

A thousand reasons prove this maxim. First, administration becomes more difficult over great distances, just as a weight becomes heavier at the end of a longer lever. It also becomes more onerous as the number of administrative levels multiplies, because first each city has its own administration which the populace pays for; each district has its own, again paid for by the people; next each province has one and then the great governments, the satrapies and vice royalties, requiring a greater cost the higher you go, and always at the expense of the unfortunate people. Finally, there is the supreme administration which weights down on everyone. All these surcharges continually exhaust the subjects. Far from being better governed by these different orders, they are worse governed than if there were but one administration over them. Meanwhile, hardly any resources remain for meeting emergencies; and when recourse must be made to them, the state is always on the verge of its ruin.

This is not all. Not only does the government have less vigor and quickness in enforcing the observance of the laws, preventing nuisances, correcting abuses and foreseeing the seditious undertakings that can occur in distant places, but also the populace has less affection for its leaders when it never sees them, for the homeland, which, to its eyes, is like the world, and for its fellow citizens, the majority of whom are foreigners to it. The same laws cannot be suitable to so many diverse provinces which have different customs, live in contrasting climates, and which are incapable of enduring the same form of government. Different laws create only trouble and confusion among the peoples who live under the same rulers and are in continuous communication. They intermingle and intermarry, and, being under the sway of other customs, never know whether their patrimony is actually their own. Talents are hidden; virtues are unknown; vices are unpunished in this multitude of men who are unknown to one another which the seat of supreme administration brings together in one place. The leaders, overwhelmed with work, see nothing for themselves; clerks govern the state. Finally, the measures that need to be taken to maintain the general authority, which so many distant officials want to avoid or harass, absorb all the public attention. Nothing more remains for the people's happiness, and there barely remains enough for its defense in time of need. And thus a body which is too big for its constitution collapses and perishes, crushed by its own weight.

On the other hand, the state ought to provide itself with a firm foundation to give it solidity, to resist the shocks it is bound to experience, as well as the efforts it will have to make to sustain itself. For all the peoples have a kind of centrifugal force, by which they continually act one against the other and tend to expand at the expense of their neighbors, like Descartes' vortices. Thus the weak risk being soon swallowed up; scarcely any people can preserve itself except by putting itself in a kind of equilibrium with all, which nearly equalizes the pressure on all sides.

It is clear from this that there are reasons for expanding and reasons for contracting, and it is not the least of the political theorist's talents to find, between these and other reasons, the proportion most advantageous to the preservation of the state. In general, it can be said that the former reasons, being merely external and relative, should be subordinated to the latter reasons, which are internal and absolute. A strong, healthy constitution is the first thing one needs to look for, and one should count more on the vigor born of a good government than on the resources furnished by a large territory.

Moreover, there have been states so constituted that the necessity for conquests entered into their very constitution, and that, to maintain themselves, they were forced to expand endlessly. Perhaps they congratulated themselves greatly on account of this happy necessity, which nevertheless showed them, together with the limit of their size, the inevitable moment of their fall.

CHAPTER X
The People (continued)

A body politic can be measured in two ways: namely, by the size of its territory and by the number of its people. And between these measurements there is a relationship suitable for giving the state its true greatness. Men are what make up the state and land is what feeds men. This relationship therefore consists in there being enough land for the maintenance of its inhabitants and as many inhabitants as the land can feed. It is in this proportion that the *maximum* force of a given population size is found. For if there is too much land, its defense is onerous, its cultivation inadequate, and its yield surplus. This is the proximate cause of defensive wars. If there is not enough land, the state finds itself at the discretion of its neighbors for what it needs as a supplement. This is the proximate cause of offensive wars. Any people whose position provides it an alternative merely between commerce and war is inherently weak. It depends on its neighbors; it depends on events. It never has anything but an uncertain and brief existence. Either it conquers and changes the situation, or it is conquered and obliterated. It can keep itself free only by means of smallness or greatness.

No one can provide in mathematical terms a fixed relationship between the size of land and the population size which are sufficient for one another, as much because of the differences in the characteristics of the terrain, its degrees of fertility, the nature of its crops, the influence of its climates, as because of the differences to be noted in the temperaments of the men who inhabit them, some of whom consume little in a fertile country, while others consume a great deal on a barren soil. Again, attention must be given to the greater or lesser fertility of women, to what the country can offer that is more or less favorable to the population, to the number of people that the legislator can hope to bring together through his institutions. Thus, the legislator should not base his judgment on what he sees but on what he foresees. And he should dwell less upon the present state of the population as upon the state it should naturally attain. Finally, there are a thousand situations where the idiosyncrasies of a place require or permit the assimilation of more land than appears necessary. Thus, there is considerable expansion in mountainous country, where the natural crops—namely, woods and pastures—demand less work; where experience shows that women are more fertile than on the plains; and where a large amount of sloping soil provides only a very small amount of flat land, the only thing that can be counted on for vegetation. On the other hand, people can draw closer to one another at the seashore, even on rocks and nearly barren sand, because fishing can make up to a great degree for the lack of land crops, since men should be more closely gathered together in order to repulse pirates, and since in addition it is easier to unburden the country of surplus inhabitants by means of colonies.

To these conditions for instituting a people must be added one that cannot be a substitute for any other, but without which all the rest are useless: the enjoyment of the fullness of peace. For the time when a state is organized, like the time when a battalion is formed, is the instant when the body is the least capable of resisting and easiest to destroy. There would be better resistance at a time of absolute disorder than at a moment of fermentation, when each man is occupied with his own position rather than with the danger. Were a war, famine, or sedition to arise in this time of crisis the state inevitably is overthrown.

This is not to say that many governments are not established during such storms; but in these instances it is these governments themselves that destroy the state. Usurpers always bring about or choose these times of trouble to use public terror to pass destructive laws that the people never adopt when they have their composure. The choice of the moment of a government's institution is one of the surest signs by which the work of a legislator can be distinguished from that of a tyrant.

What people, therefore, is suited for legislation? One that, finding itself bound by some union of origin, interest or convention, has not yet felt the true yoke of laws. One that has no custom or superstitions that are deeply rooted. One that does not fear being overpowered by sudden invasion. One that can, without entering into the squabbles of its neighbors, resist each of them single-handed or use the help of one to repel another. One where each member can be known to all, and where there is no need to impose a greater burden on a man than a man can bear. One that can get along without peoples and without which every other people can get along.[16] One that is neither rich nor poor and can be sufficient unto itself; finally, one that brings together the stability of an ancient people and the docility of a new people. What makes the work of legislation trying is not so much what must be established or what must be destroyed. And what makes success so rare is the impossibility of finding the simplicity of nature together with the needs of society. All these conditions, it is true, are hard to find in combination. Hence few well constituted states are to be seen.

In Europe there is still one country capable of receiving legislation. It is the island of Corsica. The valor and constancy with which this brave people has regained and defended its liberty would well merit having some wise man teaching them how to preserve it. I have a feeling that some day that little island will astonish Europe.

---

16. If there were two neighboring peoples, one being unable to get along without the other, it would be a very tough situation for the former and very dangerous for the latter. In such a case, every wise nation will work very quickly to free the other of its dependency. The republic of Thlascala, enclosed within the Mexican empire, preferred to do without salt, rather than buy it from the Mexicans or even take it from them for nothing. The wise Thlascalans saw the trap hidden beneath this generosity. They kept themselves free, and this small state, enclosed within this great empire, was finally the instrument of its ruin.

CHAPTER XI

On the Various Systems of Legislation

If one enquires into precisely wherein the greatest good of all consists, which should be the purpose of every system of legislation, one will find that it boils down to the two principal objects, *liberty* and *equality*. Liberty, because all particular dependence is that much force taken from the body of the state; equality, because liberty cannot subsist without it.

I have already said what civil liberty is. Regarding equality, we need not mean by this word that degrees of power and wealth are to be absolutely the same, but rather that, with regard to power, it should transcend all violence and never be exercised except by virtue of rank and laws; and, with regard to wealth, no citizen should be so rich as to be capable of buying another citizen, and none so poor that he is forced to sell himself. This presupposes moderation in goods and credit on the part of the great, and moderation in avarice and covetousness[17] on the part of the lowly.

This equality is said to be a speculative fiction that cannot exist in practice. But if abuse is inevitable, does it follow that it should not at least be regulated? It is precisely because the force of things tends always to destroy equality that the force of legislation should always tend to maintain it.

But these general objects of every good institution should be modified in each country in accordance with the relationships that arise as much from the local situation as from the temperament of the inhabitants. And it is on the basis of these relationships that each people must be assigned a particular institutional system that is the best, not perhaps in itself, but for the state for which it is destined. For example, is the soil barren and unproductive, or the country too confining for its inhabitants? Turn to industry and crafts, whose products you will exchange for the foodstuffs you lack. On the other hand, do you live in rich plains and fertile slopes? Do you lack inhabitants on a good terrain? Put all your effort into agriculture, which increases the number of men, and chase out the crafts that seem only to achieve the depopulation of the country by grouping in a few sectors what few inhabitants there are.[18] Do you occupy long, convenient coastlines? Cover the sea with vessels; cultivate commerce and navigation. You will have a brilliant and brief existence. Does the sea wash against nothing on your coasts but virtually inaccessible rocks? Remain barbarous and fish-eating. You will live in greater tranquillity, better perhaps and certainly happily. In a word, aside from the maxims common to all, each people has within itself some cause that organizes them in a particular way and renders its legislation proper for it alone. Thus it was that long ago the Hebrews and recently the Arabs have had religion as their main object; the Athenians had letters; Carthage and Tyre, commerce; Rhodes, seafaring; Sparta, war; and Rome, virtue. The author of *The Spirit of the Laws* has shown with a large array of examples the art by which the legislator directs the institution toward each of its objects.

---

17. Do you therefore want to give constancy to the State? Bring the extremes as close together as possible. Tolerate neither rich men nor beggars. These two estates, which are naturally inseparable, are equally fatal to the common good. From the one come the fomenters of tyranny, and from the other the tyrants. It is always between them that public liberty becomes a matter of commerce. The one buys it and the other sells it.

18. Any branch of foreign trade, says the Marquis d'Argenson, creates hardly anything more than a false utility for a kingdom in general. It can enrich some private individuals, even some towns, but the nation as a whole gains nothing and the populace is none the better for it.

What makes the constitution of a state truly solid and lasting is that proprieties are observed with such fidelity that the natural relations and the laws are always in agreement on the same points, and that the latter serve only to assure, accompany and rectify them. But if the legislator is mistaken about his object and takes a principle different from the one arising from the nature of things (whether the one tends toward servitude and the other toward liberty; the one toward riches, the other toward increased population; the one toward peace, the other toward conquests), the laws will weaken imperceptibly, the constitution will be altered, and the state will not cease being agitated until it is destroyed or changed, and invincible nature has regained her empire.

CHAPTER XII
Classification of the Laws

To set the whole in order or to give the commonwealth the best possible form, there are various relations to consider. First, the action of the entire body acting upon itself, that is, the relationship of the whole to the whole, or of the sovereign to the state, and this relationship, as we will see later, is composed of relationships of intermediate terms.

The laws regulating this relationship bear the name political laws, and are also called fundamental laws, not without reason if these laws are wise. For there is only one way of organizing in each state. The people who have found it should stand by it. But if the established order is evil, why should one accept as fundamental, laws that prevent it from being good? Besides, a people is in any case always in a position to change its laws, even the best laws. For if it wishes to do itself harm, who has the right to prevent it from doing so?

The second relation is that of the members to each other or to the entire body. And this relationship should be as small as possible in regard to the former and as large as possible in regard to the latter, so that each citizen would be perfectly independent of all the others and excessively dependent upon the city. This always takes place by the same means, for only the force of the state brings about the liberty of its members. It is from this second relationship that civil laws arise.

We may consider a third sort of relation between man and law, namely that of disobedience and penalty. And this gives rise to the establishment of criminal laws, which basically are not so much a particular kind of law as the sanction for all the others.

To these three sorts of law is added a fourth, the most important of all. It is not engraved on marble or bronze, but in the hearts of citizens. It is the true constitution of the state. Everyday it takes on new forces. When other laws grow old and die away, it revives and replaces them, preserves a people in the spirit of its institution and imperceptibly substitutes the force of habit for that of authority. I am speaking of mores, customs, and especially of opinion, a part of the law unknown to our political theorists but one on which depends the success of all the others; a part with which the great legislator secretly occupies himself, though he seems to confine himself to the particular regulations that are merely the arching of the vault, whereas mores, slower to arise, form in the end its immovable keystone.

Among these various classes, only political laws, which constitute the form of government, are relevant to my subject.

END OF THE SECOND BOOK

BOOK III

Before speaking of the various forms of government, let us try to determine the precise meaning of this word, which has not as yet been explained very well.

CHAPTER I
On Government in General

I am warning the reader that this chapter should be read carefully and that I do not know the art of being clear to those who do not want to be attentive.

Every free action has two causes that come together to produce it. The one is moral, namely the will that determines the act; the other is physical, namely the power that executes it. When I walk toward an object, I must first want to go there. Second, my feet must take me there. A paralyzed man who wants to walk or an agile man who does not want to walk will both remain where they are. The body politic has the same moving causes. The same distinction can be made between force and the will; the one under the name *legislative power* and the other under the name *executive power*. Nothing is done and ought to be done without their concurrence.

We have seen that legislative power belongs to the people and can belong to it alone. On the contrary, it is easy to see, by the principles established above, that executive power cannot belong to the people at large in its role as legislator or sovereign, since this power consists solely of particular acts that are not within the province of the law, nor consequently of the sovereign, none of whose acts can avoid being laws.

Therefore the public force must have an agent of its own that unifies it and gets it working in accordance with the directions of the general will, that serves as a means of communication between the state and the sovereign, and that accomplishes in the public person just about what the union of soul and body accomplishes in man. This is the reason for having government in the state, something often badly confused with the sovereign, of which it is merely the minister.

What then is the government? An intermediate body established between the subjects and the sovereign for their mutual communication, and charged with the execution of the laws and the preservation of liberty, both civil and political.

The members of this body are called magistrates or *kings*, that is to say, *governors*, and the entire body bears the name *prince*.[19] Therefore those who claim that the act by which a people submits itself to leaders is not a contract are quite correct. It is absolutely nothing but a commission, an employment in which the leaders, as simple officials of the sovereign, exercise in its own name the power with which it has entrusted them. The sovereign can limit, modify, or appropriate this power as it pleases, since the alienation of such a right is incompatible with the nature of the social body and contrary to the purpose of the association.

Therefore, I call *government* or supreme administration the legitimate exercise of executive power; I call prince or magistrate the man or the body charged with that administration.

---

19. Thus in Venice the College is given the name *Most Serene Prince* even when the Doge is not present.

In government one finds the intermediate forces whose relationships make up that of the whole to the whole or of the sovereign to the state. This last relationship can be represented as one between the extremes of a continuous proportion, whose proportional mean is the government. The government receives from the sovereign the orders it gives the people, and, for the state to be in good equilibrium, there must, all things considered, be an equality between the output or the power of the government, taken by itself, and the output or power of the citizens, who are sovereigns on the one hand and subjects on the other.

Moreover, none of these three terms could be altered without the simultaneous destruction of the proportion. If the sovereign wishes to govern, or if the magistrate wishes to give laws, or if the subjects refuse to obey, disorder replaces rule, force and will no longer act in concert, and thus the state dissolves and falls into despotism or anarchy. Finally, since there is only one proportional mean between each relationship, there is only one good government possible for a state. But since a thousand events can change the relationships of a people, not only can different governments be good for different peoples, but also for the same people at different times.

In trying to provide an idea of the various relationships that can obtain between these two extremes, I will take as an example the number of people, since it is a more easily expressed relationship.

Suppose the state is composed of ten thousand citizens. The sovereign can only be considered collectively and as a body. But each private individual in his position as a subject is regarded as an individual. Thus the sovereign is to the subject as ten thousand is to one. In other words, each member of the state has as his share only one ten-thousandth of the sovereign authority, even though he is totally in subjection to it. If the populace is made up of a hundred thousand men, the condition of the subjects does not change, and each bears equally the entire dominion of the laws, while his vote, reduced to one hundred-thousandth, has ten times less influence in the drafting of them. In that case, since the subject always remains one, the ratio of the sovereign to the subject increases in proportion to the number of citizens. Whence it follows that the larger the state becomes, the less liberty there is.

When I say that the ratio increases, I mean that it places a distance between itself and equality. Thus the greater the ratio is in the sense employed by geometricians, the less relationship there is in the everyday sense of the word. In the former sense, the ratio, seen in terms of quantity, is measured by the quotient; in the latter sense, ratio, seen in terms of identity, is reckoned by similarity.

Now the less relationship there is between private wills and the general will, that is, between mores and the laws, the more repressive force ought to increase. Therefore, in order to be good, the government must be relatively stronger in proportion as the populace is more numerous.

On the other hand, as the growth of the state gives the trustees of the public authority more temptations and the means of abusing their power, the more the force the government must have in order to contain the people, the more the force the sovereign must have in order to contain the government. I am speaking here not of an absolute force but of the relative force of the various parts of the state.

It follows from this twofold relationship that the continuous proportion between the sovereign, the prince and the people, is in no way an arbitrary idea, but a necessary consequence of the nature of the body politic. It also follows that since one of the extremes, namely the people as subject, is fixed and represented by unity, whenever the doubled ratio increases or decreases, the simple ratio increases or decreases in like fashion, and that as a consequence the middle term is changed. This makes it clear that there is no unique and absolute constitution of government, but that there can be as many governments of differing natures as there are states of differing sizes.

If, in ridiculing this system, someone were to say that in order to find this proportional mean and to form the body of the government, it is necessary merely, in my opinion, to derive the square root of the number of people, I would reply that here I am taking this number only as an example; that the relationships I am speaking of are not measured solely by the number of men, but in general by the quantity of action, which is the combination of a multitude of causes; and that, in addition, if to express myself in fewer words I borrow for the moment the terminology of geometry, I nevertheless am not unaware of the fact that geometrical precision has no place in moral quantities.

The government is on a small scale what the body politic which contains it is on a large scale. It is a moral person endowed with certain faculties, active like the sovereign and passive like the state, and capable of being broken down into other similar relationships whence there arises as a consequence a new proportion and yet again another within this one according to the order of tribunals, until an indivisible middle term is reached; that is, a single leader or supreme magistrate, who can be represented in the midst of this progression as the unity between the series of fractions and that of whole numbers.

Without involving ourselves in this multiplication of terms, let us content ourselves with considering the government as a new body in the state, distinct from the people and sovereign, and intermediate between them.

The essential difference between these two bodies is that the state exists by itself, while the government exists only through the sovereign. Thus the dominant will of the prince is not and should not be anything other than the general will or the law. His force is merely the public force concentrated in him. As soon as he wants to derive from himself some absolute and independent act, the bond that links everything together begins to come loose. If it should finally happen that the prince had a private will more active than that of the sovereign, and that he had made use of some of the public force that is available to him in order to obey this private will, so that there would be, so to speak, two sovereigns—one de jure and the other de facto, at that moment the social union would vanish and the body politic would be dissolved.

However, for the body of the government to have an existence, a real life that distinguishes it from the body of the state, and for all its members to be able to act in concert and to fulfill the purpose for which it is instituted, there must be a particular *self*, a sensibility common to all its members, a force or will of its own that tends toward its preservation. This particular existence presupposes assemblies, councils, a power to deliberate and decide, rights, titles and privileges that belong exclusively to the prince and that render the condition of the magistrate more honorable in proportion as it is more onerous. The difficulties lie in the manner in which this subordinate whole is so organized within the whole, that it in no way alters the general constitution by strengthening its own, that it always distinguishes its particular force, which is intended for its own preservation, from the public force intended for the preservation of the state, and that, in a word, it is always ready to sacrifice the government to the people and not the people to the government.

In addition, although the artificial body of the government is the work of another artificial body and has, in a sense, only a borrowed and subordinate life, this does not prevent it from being capable of acting with more or less vigor or speed, or from enjoying, so to speak, more or less robust health. Finally, without departing directly from the purpose of its institution, it can deviate more or less from it, according to the manner in which it is constituted.

From all these differences arise the diverse relationships that the government should have with the body of the state, according to the accidental and particular relationships by which the state itself is modified. For often the government that is best in itself will become the most vicious, if its relationships are not altered according to the defects of the body politic to which it belongs.

CHAPTER II
On the Principle that Constitutes the Various Forms of Government

In order to lay out the general cause of these differences, a distinction must be made here between the prince and the government, as I had done before between the state and the sovereign.

The body of the magistrates can be made up of a larger or smaller number of members. We have said that the ratio of the sovereign to the subjects was greater in proportion as the populace was more numerous, and by a manifest analogy we can say the same thing about the government in relation to the magistrates.

Since the total force of the government is always that of the state, it does not vary. Whence it follows that the more of this force it uses on its own members, the less that is left to it for acting on the whole populace.

Therefore, the more numerous the magistrates, the weaker the government. Since this maxim is fundamental, let us attempt to explain it more clearly.

We can distinguish in the person of the magistrate three essentially different wills. First, the individual's own will, which tends only to its own advantage. Second, the common will of the magistrates which is uniquely related to the advantage of the prince. This latter can be called the corporate will, and is general in relation to the government, and particular in relation to the state, of which the government forms a part. Third, the will of the people or the sovereign will, which is general both in relation to the state considered as the whole and in relation to the government considered as a part of the whole.

In a perfect act of legislation, the private or individual will should be nonexistent; the corporate will proper to the government should be very subordinate; and consequently the general or sovereign will should always be dominant and the unique rule of all the others.

According to the natural order, on the contrary, these various wills become more active in proportion as they are the more concentrated. Thus the general will is always the weakest, the corporate will has second place, and the private will is first of all, so that in the government each member is first himself, then a magistrate, and then a citizen—a gradation directly opposite to the one required by the social order.

Granting this, let us suppose the entire government is in the hands of one single man. In that case the private will and the corporate will are perfectly united, and consequently the latter is at the highest degree of intensity it can reach. But since the use of force is dependent upon the degree of will, and since the absolute force of the government does not vary one bit, it follows that the most active of governments is that of one single man.

On the other hand, let us suppose we are uniting the government to the legislative authority. Let us make the sovereign the prince and all the citizens that many magistrates. Then the corporate will, confused with the general will, will have no more activity than the latter, and will leave the private will all its force. Thus the government, always with the same absolute force, will have its *minimum* relative force or activity.

These relationships are incontestable, and there are still other considerations that serve to confirm them. We see, for example, that each magistrate is more active in his body than each citizen is in his, and consequently that the private will has much more influence on the acts of the government than on those of the sovereign. For each magistrate is nearly always charged with the responsibility for some function of government, whereas each citizen, taken by himself, exercises no function of sovereignty. Moreover, the more the state is extended, the more its real force increases, although it does not increase not in proportion to its size. But if the state remains the same, the magistrates may well be multiplied without the government acquiring any greater real force, since this force is that of the state, whose size is always equal. Thus the relative force or activity of the government diminishes without its absolute or real force being able to increase.

It is also certain that the execution of public business becomes slower in proportion as more people are charged with the responsibility for it; that in attaching too much importance to prudence, too little importance is attached to fortune, opportunities are missed, and the fruits of deliberation are often lost by dint of deliberation.

I have just proved that the government becomes slack in proportion as the magistrates are multiplied; and I have previously proved that the more numerous the people, the greater should be the increase of repressive force. Whence it follows that the ratio of the magistrate to the government should be the inverse of the ratio of the subjects to the sovereign; that is to say, the more the state increases in size, the more the government should shrink, so that the number of leaders decreases in proportion to the increase in the number of people.

I should add that I am speaking here only about the relative force of the government and not about its rectitude. For, on the contrary, the more numerous the magistrates, the more closely the corporate will approaches the general will, whereas under a single magistrate, the same corporate will is, as I have said, merely a particular will. Thus what can be gained on the one hand is lost on the other, and the art of the legislator is to know how to determine the point at which the government's will and force, always in a reciprocal proportion, are combined in the relationship that is most advantageous to the state.

CHAPTER III
Classification of Governments

We have seen in the previous chapter why the various kinds or forms of government are distinguished by the number of members that compose them. It remains to be seen in this chapter how this classification is made.

In the first place, the sovereign can entrust the government to the entire people or to the majority of the people, so that there are more citizens who are magistrates than who are ordinary private citizens. This form of government is given the name *democracy*.

Or else it can restrict the government to the hands of a small number, so that there are more ordinary citizens than magistrates; and this form is called *aristocracy*.

Finally, it can concentrate the entire government in the hands of a single magistrate from whom all the others derive their power. This third form is the most common and is called *monarchy* or royal government.

It should be noted that all these forms, or at least the first two, can be had in greater or lesser degrees, and even have a rather wide range. For democracy can include the entire populace or be restricted to half. Aristocracy, for its part, can be indeterminately restricted from half the people down to the smallest number. Even royalty can be had in varying levels of distribution. Sparta always had two kings, as required by its constitution; and the Roman Empire is known to have had up to eight emperors at a time, without it being possible to say that the empire was divided. Thus there is a point at which each form of government is indistinguishable from the next, and it is apparent that, under just three names, government can take on as many diverse forms as the state has citizens.

Moreover, since this same government can, in certain respects, be subdivided into other parts, one administered in one way, another in another, there can result from the combination of these three forms a multitude of mixed forms, each of which can be multiplied by all the simple forms.

There has always been a great deal of argument over the best form of government, without considering that each one of them is best in certain cases and the worst in others.

If the number of supreme magistrates in the different states ought to be in inverse ratio to that of the citizens, it follows that in general democratic government is suited to small states, aristocratic government to states of intermediate size, and monarchical government to large ones. This rule is derived immediately from the principle; but how is one to count the multitude of circumstances that can furnish exceptions?

CHAPTER IV
On Democracy

He who makes the law knows better than anyone else how it should be executed and interpreted. It seems therefore to be impossible to have a better constitution than one in which the executive power is united to the legislative power. But this is precisely what renders such a government inadequate in certain respects, since things that should be distinguished are not, and the prince and sovereign, being merely the same person, form, as it were, only a government without a government.

It is not good for the one who makes the laws to execute them, nor for the body of the people to turn its attention away from general perspectives in order to give it particular objects. Nothing is more dangerous than the influence of private interests on public affairs; and the abuse of the laws by the government is a lesser evil than the corruption of the legislator, which is the inevitable outcome of particular perspectives. In such a situation, since the state is being substantially altered, all reform becomes impossible. A people that would never misuse the government would never misuse independence. A people that would always govern well would not need to be governed.

Taking the term in the strict sense, a true democracy has never existed and never will. It is contrary to the natural order that the majority govern and the minority is governed. It is unimaginable that the people would remain constantly assembled to handle public affairs; and it is readily apparent that it could not establish commissions for this purpose without changing the form of administration.

In fact, I believe I can lay down as a principle that when the functions of the government are shared among several tribunals, those with the fewest members sooner or later acquire the greatest authority, if only because of the facility in expediting public business which brings this about naturally.

Besides, how many things that are difficult to unite are presupposed by this government? First, a very small state where it is easy for the people to gather together and where each citizen can easily know all the others. Second, a great simplicity of mores, which prevents the multitude of public business and thorny discussions. Next, a high degree of equality in ranks and fortunes, without which equality in rights and authority cannot subsist for long. Finally, little or no luxury, for luxury either is the effect of wealth or it makes wealth necessary. It simultaneously corrupts both the rich and the poor, the one by possession, the other by covetousness. It sells the homeland to softness and vanity. It takes all its citizens from the state in order to make them slaves to one another, and all of them to opinion.

This is why a famous author has made virtue the principle of the republic. For all these conditions could not subsist without virtue. But owing to his failure to have made the necessary distinctions, this great genius often lacked precision and sometimes clarity. And he did not realize that since the sovereign authority is everywhere the same, the same principle should have a place in every well constituted state, though in a greater or lesser degree, it is true, according to the form of government.

Let us add that no government is so subject to civil wars and internal agitations as a democratic or popular one, since there is none that tends so forcefully and continuously to change its form, or that demands greater vigilance and courage to be maintained in its own form. Above all, it is under this constitution that the citizen ought to arm himself with force and constancy, and to say each day of his life from the bottom of his heart what a virtuous Palatine[20] said in the Diet of Poland: *Better to have liberty fraught with danger than servitude in peace.*

Were there a people of gods, it would govern itself democratically. So perfect a government is not suited to men.

CHAPTER V
On Aristocracy

We have here two very distinct moral persons, namely the government and the sovereign, and consequently two general wills, one in relation to all the citizens, the other only for the members of the administration. Thus, although the government

---

20. The Palatine of Posen, father of the King of Poland, Duke of Lorraine. [Rousseau quotes in Latin the maxim which follows.]

can regulate its internal administration as it chooses, it can never speak to the people except in the name of the sovereign, that is to say, in the name of the populace itself. This is something not to be forgotten.

The first societies governed themselves aristocratically. The leaders of families deliberated among themselves about public affairs. Young people deferred without difficulty to the authority of experience. This is the origin of the words *priests*, *ancients, senate* and *elders*. The savages of North America still govern themselves that way to this day, and are very well governed.

But to the extent that inequality occasioned by social institutions came to prevail over natural inequality, wealth or power[21] was preferred to age, and aristocracy became elective. Finally, the transmission of the father's power, together with his goods, to his children created patrician families; the government was made hereditary, and we know of senators who were only twenty years old.

There are therefore three sorts of aristocracy: natural, elective and hereditary. The first is suited only to simple people; the third is the worst of any government. The second is the best; it is aristocracy properly so-called.

In addition to the advantage of the distinction between the two powers, aristocracy has that of the choice of its members. For in popular government all the citizens are born magistrates; however, this type of government limits them to a small number, and they become magistrates only through election,[22] a means by which probity, enlightenment, experience, and all the other reasons for public preference and esteem are so many new guarantees of being well governed.

Furthermore, assemblies are more conveniently held, public business better discussed and carried out with more orderliness and diligence, the reputation of the state is better sustained abroad by venerable senators than by a multitude that is unknown or despised.

In a word, it is the best and most natural order for the wisest to govern the multitude, when it is certain that they will govern for its profit and not for their own. There is no need for multiplying devices uselessly or for doing with twenty thousand men what one hundred hand-picked men can do even better. But it must be noted here that the corporate interest begins to direct the public force in less strict a conformity with the rule of the general will, and that another inevitable tendency removes from the laws a part of the executive power.

With regard to the circumstances that are specifically suitable, a state must not be so small, nor its people so simple and upright that the execution of the laws follows immediately from the public will, as is the case in a good democracy. Nor must a nation be so large that the leaders, scattered about in order to govern it, can each play the sovereign in his own department, and begin by making themselves independent in order finally to become the masters.

But if aristocracy requires somewhat fewer virtues than popular government, it also demands others that are proper to it, such as moderation among the wealthy

---

21. It is clear that among the ancients the word *optimates* does not mean the best, but the most powerful.

22. It is of great importance that laws should regulate the form of the election of magistrates, for if it is left to the will of the prince, it is impossible to avoid falling into a hereditary aristocracy, as has taken place in the Republics of *Venice* and *Berne*. Thus the former has long been a state in dissolution, while the latter maintains itself through the extreme wisdom of its senate. It is a very honorable and very dangerous exception.

and contentment among the poor. For it appears that rigorous equality would be out of place here. It was not observed even in Sparta.

Moreover, if this form of government carries with it a certain inequality of fortune, this is simply in order that in general the administration of public business may be entrusted to those who are best able to give all their time to it, but not, as Aristotle claims, in order that the rich may always be given preference. On the contrary, it is important that an opposite choice should occasionally teach the people that more important reasons for preference are to be found in a man's merit than in his wealth.

CHAPTER VI
On Monarchy

So far, we have considered the prince as a moral and collective person, united by the force of laws, and as the trustee of the executive power in the state. We have now to consider this power when it is joined together in the hands of a natural person, of a real man, who alone has the right to dispose of it in accordance with the laws. Such a person is called a monarch or a king.

In utter contrast with the other forms of administration where a collective entity represents an individual, in this form of administration an individual represents a collective entity; so that the moral unity constituting the prince is at the same time a physical unity, in which all the faculties which are combined by the law in the other forms of administration with such difficulty are found naturally combined.

Thus the will of the people, the will of the prince, the public force of the state, and the particular force of the government, all respond to the same moving agent; all the springs of the machine are in the same hand; everything moves toward the same end; there are no opposing movements which are at cross purposes with one another; and no constitution is imaginable in which a lesser effort produces a more considerable action. Archimedes sitting serenely on the shore and effortlessly launching a huge vessel is what comes to mind when I think of a capable monarch governing his vast states from his private study, and making everything move while appearing himself to be immovable.

But if there is no government that has more vigor, there is none where the private will has greater sway and more easily dominates the others. Everything moves toward the same end, it is true; but this end is not that of public felicity, and the very force of the administration unceasingly operates to the detriment of the state.

Kings want to be absolute, and from a distance one cries out to them that the best way to be so is to make themselves loved by their peoples. This maxim is very noble and even very true in certain respects. Unfortunately it will always be an object of derision in courts. The power that comes from the peoples' love is undoubtedly the greatest, but it is precarious and conditional. Princes will never be satisfied with it. The best kings want to be able to be wicked if it pleases them, without ceasing to be the masters. A political sermonizer might well say to them that since the people's force is their force, their greatest interest is that the people should be flourishing, numerous and formidable. They know perfectly well that this is not true. Their personal interest is first of all that the people should be weak and miserable and incapable of ever resisting them. I admit that, assuming the subjects were always in perfect submission, the interest of the prince would then be for the people to be powerful, so that this power, being his own, would render him formidable in the eyes of his neighbors. But since this interest is merely secondary and subordinate, and since the two suppositions are incompatible, it is natural that the princes should always give preference to the maxim that is the most immediately useful to them. This is the point that Samuel made so forcefully to the Hebrews, and that Machiavelli has made apparent. Under the pretext of teaching kings, he has taught important lessons to the peoples. Machiavelli's *The Prince* is the book of republicans.[23]

We have found, through general relationships, that the monarchy is suited only to large states, and we find this again in examining the monarchy itself. The more numerous the public administration, the more the ratio of the prince to subject diminishes and approaches equality, so that this ratio increases in proportion as the government is restricted, and is at its *maximum* when the government is in the hands of a single man. Then there is too great a distance between the prince and the people, and the state lacks cohesiveness. In order to bring about this cohesiveness, there must therefore be intermediate orders; there must be princes, grandees, and a nobility to fill them. Now none of this is suited to a small state, which is ruined by all these social levels.

But if it is difficult for a large state to be well governed, it is much harder still for it to be well governed by just one man, and everyone knows what happens when the king appoints substitutes.

An essential and inevitable defect, which will always place the monarchical form of government below the republican form, is that in the latter form the public voice hardly ever raises to the highest positions men who are not enlightened and capable and who would not fill their positions with honor. On the other hand, those who attain these positions in monarchies are most often petty bunglers, petty swindlers, petty intriguers, whose petty talents, which cause them to attain high positions at court, serve only to display their incompetence to the public as soon as they reach these positions. The populace is much less often in error in its choice than the prince, and a man of real merit in the ministry is almost as rare as a fool at the head of a republican government. Thus, when by some happy chance one of these men who are born to govern takes the helm of public business in a monarchy that has nearly been sunk by this crowd of fine managers, there is utter amazement at the resources he finds, and his arrival marks an era in the history of the country.

For a monarchical state to be capable of being well governed, its size or extent must be proportionate to the faculties of the one who governs. It is easier to conquer than to rule. With a long enough lever it is possible for a single finger to make the world shake; but holding it in place requires the shoulders of Hercules. However small a state may be, the prince is nearly always too small for it. When, on the contrary, it happens that the state is too small for its leader, which is quite rare, it is still poorly governed, since the leader, always pursuing his grand schemes, forgets the interests of the peoples, making them no less wretched through the abuse of talents he has too much of than does a leader who is limited for want of what he

---

23. [The following was inserted in the 1782 edition: "Machiavelli was a decent man and a good citizen. But since he was attached to the house of Medici, he was forced during the oppression of his homeland to disguise his love of liberty. The very choice of his execrable hero makes clear enough his hidden intention. And the contrast between the maxims of his book *The Prince* and those of his *Discourses on Titus Livy* and of his *History of Florence* shows that this profound political theorist has until now had only superficial or corrupt readers. The court of Rome has sternly prohibited his book. I can well believe it; it is the court he most clearly depicts."]

lacks. A kingdom must, so to speak, expand or contract with each reign, depending on the ability of the prince. On the other hand, since the talents of a senate have a greater degree of stability, the state can have permanent boundaries without the administration working any less well.

The most obvious disadvantage of the government of just one man is the lack of that continuous line of succession which forms an unbroken bond of unity in the other two forms of government. When one king dies, another is needed. Elections leave dangerous intervals and are stormy. And unless the citizens have a disinterestedness and integrity that seldom accompanies this form of government, intrigue and corruption enter the picture. It is difficult for one to whom the state has sold itself not to sell it in turn, and reimburse himself at the expense of the weak for the money extorted from him by the powerful. Sooner or later everything becomes venal under such an administration, and in these circumstances, the peace enjoyed under kings is worse than the disorders of the interregna.

What has been done to prevent these ills? In certain families, crowns have been made hereditary, and an order of succession has been established which prevents all dispute when kings die. That is to say, by substituting the disadvantage of regencies for that of elections, an apparent tranquillity has been preferred to a wise administration, the risk of having children, monsters, or imbeciles for leaders has been preferred to having to argue over the choice of good kings. No consideration has been given to the fact that in being thus exposed to the risk of the alternative, nearly all the odds are against them. There was a lot of sense in what Dionysius the Younger said in reply to his father, who, while reproaching his son for some shameful action, said "Have I given you such an example?" "Ah," replied the son, "but your father was not king."

When a man has been elevated to command others, everything conspires to deprive him of justice and reason. A great deal of effort is made, it is said, to teach young princes the art of ruling. It does not appear that this education does them any good. It would be better to begin by teaching them the art of obeying. The greatest kings whom history celebrates were not brought up to reign. It is a science one is never less in possession of than after one has learned too much, and that one acquires it better in obeying than in commanding. *For the most useful as well as the shortest method of finding out what is good and what is bad is to consider what you would have wished or not wished to have happened under another prince.*[24]

One result of this lack of coherence is the instability of the royal form of government, which, now regulated by one plan now by another according to the character of the ruling prince or of those who rule for him, cannot have a fixed object for very long or a consistent policy. This variation always causes the state to drift from maxim to maxim, from project to project, and does not take place in the other forms of government, where the prince is always the same. It is also apparent that in general, if there is more cunning in a royal court, there is more wisdom in a senate; and that republics proceed toward their objectives by means of policies that are more consistent and better followed. On the other hand, each revolution in the ministry produces a revolution in the state, since the maxim common to all ministers and nearly all kings is to do the reverse of their predecessor in everything.

---

24. Tacitus, *Histories*, Book I. [Rousseau here quotes the Latin.]

From this same incoherence we derive the solution to a sophism that is very familiar to royalist political theorists. Not only is civil government compared to domestic government and the prince to the father of the family (an error already refuted), but this magistrate is also liberally given all the virtues he might need, and it is always presupposed that the prince is what he ought to be. With the help of this presupposition, the royal form of government is obviously preferable to any other, since it is unquestionably the strongest; and it lacks only a corporate will that is more in conformity with the general will in order to be the best as well.

But if according to Plato,[25] a king by nature is such a rare person, how many times will nature and fortune converge to crown him; and if a royal education necessarily corrupts those who receive it, what is to be hoped from a series of men who have been brought up to reign? Surely then it is deliberate self-deception to confuse the royal form of government with that of a good king. To see what this form of government is in itself, we need to consider it under princes who are incompetent or wicked, for either they come to the throne wicked or incompetent, or else the throne makes them so.

These difficulties have not escaped the attention of our authors, but they have not been troubled by them. The remedy, they say, is to obey without a murmur. God in his anger gives us bad kings, and they must be endured as punishments from heaven. No doubt this sort of talk is edifying, however I do not know but that it belongs more in a pulpit than in a book on political theory. What is to be said of a physician who promises miracles, and whose art consists entirely of exhorting his sick patient to practice patience? It is quite obvious that we must put up with a bad government when that is what we have. The question would be how to find a good one.

CHAPTER VII
On Mixed Government

Strictly speaking, there is no such thing as a simple form of government. A single leader must have subordinate magistrates; a popular government must have a leader. Thus in the distribution of the executive power there is always a gradation from the greater to the lesser number, with the difference that sometimes the greater number depends on the few, and sometimes the few depend on the greater number.

At times the distribution is equal, either when the constitutive parts are in a state of mutual dependence, as in the government of England; or when the authority of each part is independent but imperfect, as in Poland. This latter form is bad, since there is no unity in the government and the state lacks a bond of unity.

Which one is better, a simple or a mixed form of government? A question much debated among political theorists, to which the same reply must be given that I gave above regarding every form of government.

In itself the simple form of government is the best, precisely because it is simple. But when the executive power is not sufficiently dependent upon the legislative power, that is to say, when there is more of a ratio between the prince and the sovereign than between the people and the prince, this defect in the proportion must be remedied by dividing the government; for then all of its parts have no less

---

25. *The Statesman.*

authority over the subjects, and their division makes all of them together less forceful against the sovereign.

The same disadvantage can also be prevented through the establishment of intermediate magistrates, who, by being utterly separate from the government, serve merely to balance the two powers and to maintain their respective rights. In that case, the government is not mixed; it is tempered.

The opposite difficulty can be remedied by similar means. And when the government is too slack, tribunals can be set up to give it a concentrated focus. This is done in all democracies. In the first case the government is divided in order to weaken it, and in the second to strengthen it. For the *maximum* of force and weakness are found equally in the simple forms of government, while the mixed forms of government provide an intermediate amount of strength.

CHAPTER VIII
That Not All Forms of Government Are Suited to All Countries

Since liberty is not a fruit of every climate, it is not within the reach of all peoples. The more one meditates on this principle established by Montesquieu, the more one is aware of its truth. The more one contests it, the more occasions there are for establishing it by means of new proofs.

In all the governments in the world, the public person consumes, but produces nothing. Whence therefore does it get the substance it consumes? It is from the labor of its members. It is the surplus of private individuals that produces what is needed by the public. Whence it follows that the civil state can subsist only so long as men's labor produces more than they need.

Now this surplus is not the same in every country in the world. In many countries it is considerable; in others it is moderate; in others it is nil; in still others it is negative.

This ratio depends on the fertility of the climate, the sort of labor the land requires, the nature of its products, the force of its inhabitants, the greater or lesser consumption they need, and many other similar ratios of which it is composed.

On the other hand, not all governments are of the same nature. They are more or less voracious; and the differences are founded on this added principle that the greater the distance the public contributions are from their source, the more onerous they are. It is not on the basis of the amount of the taxes that this burden is to be measured, but on the basis of the path they have to travel in order to return to the hands from which they came. When this circulation is prompt and well established, it is unimportant whether one pays little or a great deal. The populace is always rich and the finances are always in good shape. On the contrary, however little the populace gives, when this small amount does not return, it is soon wiped out by continual giving. The state is never rich and the populace is always destitute.

It follows from this that the greater the distance between the people and the government, the more onerous the taxes become. Thus in a democracy the populace is the least burdened; in an aristocracy it is more so; in a monarchy it bears the heaviest weight. Monarchy, therefore, is suited only to wealthy nations; aristocracy to states of moderate wealth and size; democracy to states that are small and poor.

In fact, the more one reflects on it, the more one finds in it the difference between free and monarchical states. In the former, everything is used for the common utility. In the latter, the public and private forces are reciprocal, the one being augmented by the weakening of the other. Finally, instead of governing subjects in order to make them happy, despotism makes them miserable in order to govern them.

Thus in each climate there are natural causes on the basis of which one can assign the form of government that the force of the climate requires, and can even say what kind of inhabitants it should have. Barren and unproductive lands, where the product is not worth the labor, ought to remain uncultivated and deserted, or peopled only by savages. Places where men's labor yields only what is necessary ought to be inhabited by barbarous peoples; in places such as these all polity would be impossible. Places where the surplus of products over labor is moderate are suited to free peoples. Those where an abundant and fertile soil produces a great deal in return for a small amount of labor require a monarchical form of government, in order that the subject's excess of surplus may be consumed by the prince's luxurious living. For it is better for this excess to be absorbed by the government than dissipated by private individuals. I realize that there are exceptions; but these exceptions themselves prove the rule, in that sooner or later they produce revolutions that restore things to the order of nature.

General laws should always be distinguished from the particular causes that can modify their effect. Even if the entire south were covered with republics and the entire north with despotic states, it would still be no less true that the effect of climate makes despotism suited to hot countries, barbarism to cold countries, and good polity to intermediate regions. I also realize that, while granting the principle, disputes may arise over its application. It could be said that there are cold countries that are very fertile and southern ones that are quite barren. But this poses a difficulty only for those who have not examined the thing in all its relationships. As I have said, it is necessary to take into account those of labor, force, consumption, and so on.

Let us suppose that there are two parcels of land of equal size, one of which yields five units and the other yields ten. If the inhabitants of the first parcel consume four units and the inhabitants of the second consume nine, the excess of the first will be one-fifth and that of the other will be one-tenth. Since the ratio of these two excesses is therefore the inverse of that of the products, the parcel of land that produces only five units will yield a surplus that is double that of the parcel of land that produces ten.

But it is not a question of a double product, and I do not believe that anyone dares, as a general rule, to place the fertility of a cold country even on an equal footing with that of hot countries. Nevertheless, let us assume that this equality does obtain. Let us, if you will, reckon England to be the equal of Sicily, and Poland the equal of Egypt. Further south we have Africa and the Indies; further north we have nothing at all. To achieve this equality of product, what difference must there be in agricultural techniques? In Sicily one needs merely to scratch the soil; in England what efforts it demands to work it! Now where more hands are needed to obtain the same product, the surplus ought necessarily to be less.

Consider too that the same number of men consumes much less in hot countries. The climate demands that a person keep sober in order to be in good health. Europeans wanting to live there just as they do at home would all die of dysentery and indigestion. *We are,* says Chardin, *carnivorous beasts, wolves, in comparison with the*

Asians. Some attribute the sobriety of the Persians to the fact that their land is less cultivated. On the contrary, I believe that this country is less abundant in commodities because the inhabitants need less. If their frugality, he continues, *were an effect of the country's scarcity, only the poor would eat little; however, it is generally the case that everyone does so. And more or less would be eaten in each province according to the fertility of the country; however, the same sobriety is found throughout the kingdom. They take great pride in their lifestyle, saying that one has only to look at their complexions to recognize how far it excels that of the Christians. In fact, the complexion of the Persians is clear. They have fair skin, fine and polished, whereas the complexion of their Armenian subjects, who live in the European style, is coarse and blotchy, and their bodies are fat and heavy.*

The closer you come to the equator, the less people live on. They rarely eat meat; rice, maize, couscous, millet and cassava are their usual diet. In the Indies there are millions of men whose sustenance costs less than a penny a day. In Europe itself we see noticeable differences in appetite between the peoples of the north and the south. A Spaniard will live for eight days on a German's dinner. In countries where men are the most voracious, luxury too turns toward things edible. In England, luxury is shown in a table loaded with meats; in Italy you are regaled on sugar and flowers.

Luxury in clothing also offers similar differences. In the climate where the seasonal changes are sudden and violent, people have better and simpler clothing. In climates where people clothe themselves merely for ornamental purposes, flashiness is more sought after than utility. The clothes themselves are a luxury there. In Naples you see men strolling everyday along the Posilippo decked out in gold-embroidered coats and bare legged. It is the same with buildings; magnificence is the sole consideration when there is nothing to fear from the weather. In Paris or London, people want to be housed warmly and comfortably. In Madrid, there are superb salons, but no windows that close, and people sleep in rat holes.

In hot countries foodstuffs are considerably more substantial and succulent. This is a third difference which cannot help but influence the second. Why do people eat so many vegetables in Italy? Because there they are good, nourishing, and have an excellent flavor. In France, where they are fed nothing but water, they are not nourishing at all, and are nearly counted for nothing at table. Be that as it may, they occupy no less land and cost at least as much effort to cultivate. It is a known fact that the wheats of Barbary, in other respects inferior to those of France, yield far more flour, and that those of France, for their part, yield more wheats than those of the north. It can be inferred from this that a similar gradation in the same direction is generally observed from the equator to the pole. Now is it not a distinct disadvantage to have a smaller quantity of food in an equal amount of produce?

To all these different considerations, I can add one which depends on and strengthens them. It is that hot countries have less of a need for inhabitants than do cold countries, and yet could feed more of them. This produces a double surplus, always to the advantage of despotism. The greater the area occupied by the same number of inhabitants, the more difficult it becomes to revolt, since concerted action cannot be taken promptly and secretly; and it is always easy for the government to discover plots and cut off communications. But the closer together a numerous people is drawn, the less the government can usurp from the sovereign. The leaders deliberate as safely in their rooms as the prince does in his council; and the crowd assembles as quickly in public squares as do troops in their quarters. In this regard, the advantage of a tyrannical government, therefore, is that of acting over great distances. With the help of the points of support it establishes, its force increases with distance like that of levers.[26] On the other hand, the strength of the people acts only when concentrated; it evaporates and is lost as it spreads, like the effect of gunpowder scattered on the ground, which catches fire only one grain at a time. The least populated countries are thus the best suited for tyranny. Ferocious animals reign only in deserts.

CHAPTER IX
On the Signs of a Good Government

When the question arises which one is absolutely the best government, an insoluble question is being raised because it is indeterminate. Or, if you wish, it has as many good answers as there are possible combinations in the absolute and relative positions of peoples.

But if it is asked by what sign it is possible to know that a given people is well or poorly governed, this is another matter, and the question of fact could be resolved.

However, nothing is answered, since each wants to answer it in his own way. The subjects praise public tranquillity; the citizens praise the liberty of private individuals. The former prefers the security of possessions; the latter that of persons. The former has it that the best government is the one that is most severe; the latter maintains that the best government is the one that is mildest. This one wants crimes to be punished, and that one wants them prevented. The former think it a good thing to be feared by their neighbors; the latter prefer to be ignored by them. The one is content so long as money circulates; the other demands that the people have bread. Even if agreement were had on these and similar points, would we be any closer to an answer? Since moral quantities do not allow of precise measurement, even if there were agreement regarding the sign, how could there be agreement regarding the evaluation.

For my part, I am always astonished that such a simple sign is overlooked or that people are of such bad faith as not to agree on it. What is the goal of the political association? It is the preservation and prosperity of its members. And what is the surest sign that they are preserved and prospering? It is their number and their population. Therefore do not go looking elsewhere for this much disputed sign. All other things being equal, the government under which, without external means, without naturalizations, without colonies, the citizens become populous and multiply the most, is infallibly the best government. That government under which a populace diminishes and dies out is the worst. Calculators, it is now up to you. Count, measure, compare.[27]

---

26. This does not contradict what I said earlier in Book II, Chapter IX, regarding the disadvantages of large states, for there it was a question of the authority of the government over its members, and here it is a question of its force against the subjects. Its scattered members serve it as points of support for acting from a distance upon the people, but it has no support for acting directly on these members themselves. Thus in the one case the length of the lever causes its weakness, and in the other case its force.

27. We should judge on this same principle the centuries that merit preference with respect to the prosperity of the human race. Those in which letters and arts are known to have flourished have been admired too much, without penetrating the secret object of their cultivation, and without considering its devastating effect, *and this was called humanity by the inexperienced, when it was a part of servitude.* [Rousseau here quotes Tacitus, *Agricola*, 21, in Latin.] Will we never see in the maxims of books the crude interest that causes the authors to speak? No.

CHAPTER X

On the Abuse of Government and Its Tendency to Degenerate

Just as the private will acts constantly against the general will, so the government makes a continual effort against sovereignty. The more this effort increases, the more the constitution is altered. And since there is here no other corporate will which, by resisting the will of the prince, would create an equilibrium with it, sooner or later the prince must finally oppress the sovereign and break the social treaty. That is the inherent and inevitable vice which, from the birth of the body politic, tends unceasingly to destroy it, just as old age and death destroy the human body.

There are two general ways in which a government degenerates, namely, when it shrinks, or when the state dissolves.

The government shrinks when it passes from a large to a small number, that is to say, from democracy to aristocracy, and from aristocracy to royalty. That is its natural inclination.[28] If it were to go backward from a small number to a large number, it could be said to slacken, but this reverse progression is impossible.

Whatever they may say, when a country is depopulated, it is not true, despite its brilliance, that all goes well; and the fact that a poet has an income of a hundred thousand livres is not sufficient to make his century the best of all. The apparent calm and tranquillity of the leader ought to be less of an object of consideration than the well-being of whole nations and especially of the most populous states. A hailstorm may devastate a few cantons, but it rarely causes famine. Riots and civil wars may greatly disturb the leaders, but they are not the true misfortunes of the people, who may even have a reprieve while people argue over who will tyrannize them. It is their permanent condition that causes real periods of prosperity or calamity. It is when everything remains crushed under the yoke that everything decays. It is then that the leaders destroy them at will, *where they bring about solitude they call it peace.*

[Rousseau here quotes Tacitus, *Agricola,* 31, in Latin.] When the quarrels of the great disturbed the kingdom of France, and the Coadjutor of Paris brought with him to the Parliament a knife in his pocket, this did not keep the French people from living happily and in great numbers in a free and decent ease. Long ago, Greece flourished in the midst of the cruelest wars. Blood flowed in waves, and the whole country was covered with men. It seemed, says Machiavelli, that in the midst of murders, proscriptions, and civil wars, our republic became more powerful; the virtue of its citizens, their mores, and their independence did more to reinforce it than all its dissensions did to weaken it. A little agitation gives strength to souls, and what truly brings about prosperity for the species is not so much peace as liberty.

28. The slow formation and the progress of the Republic of Venice in its lagoons offers a notable example of this succession. And it is rather astonishing that after more than twelve hundred years the Venetians seem to be no further than the second stage, which began with *Serrar di Consiglio* in 1198. As for the ancient dukes, for whom the Venetians are reproached, whatever the *squitinio della libertà veneta* may say about them, it has been proved that they were not their sovereigns.

The Roman Republic does not fail to be brought forward as an objection against me, which, it will be said, followed a completely opposite course, passing from monarchy to aristocracy to democracy. I am quite far from thinking of it in this way.

The first establishment of Romulus was a mixed government that promptly degenerated into despotism. For some particular reasons, the state perished before its time, just as one sees a newborn die before reaching manhood. The expulsion of the Tarquins was the true epoch of the birth of the republic. But it did not at first take on a constant form, because in failing to abolish the patriciate, only half the work was completed. For in this way, since hereditary aristocracy, which is the worst of all forms of legitimate administration, remained in conflict with democracy, a form of government that is always uncertain and adrift, it was not determined, as Machiavelli has proved, until the establishment of the tribunes. It was only then that there was a true government and a veritable democracy. In fact, the populace then was not merely sovereign but also magistrate and judge. The senate was merely a subordinate tribunal whose purpose was to temper and concentrate the government; and the consuls themselves, though they were patricians, magistrates, and absolute generals in war, in Rome were merely presidents of the people.

From that point on, the government was also seen to follow its natural inclination and to tend strongly toward aristocracy. With the patriciate having abolished itself, as it were, the aristocracy was no longer in the body of patricians, as it was in Venice and Genoa, but in the body of the senate which was composed of patricians and

In fact, the government never changes its form except when its exhausted energy leaves it too enfeebled to be capable of preserving what belongs to it. Now if it were to become still more slack while it expanded, its force would become entirely nil; it would be still less likely to subsist. It must therefore wind up and tighten its force in proportion as it gives way; otherwise the state it sustains would fall into ruin.

The dissolution of the state can come about in two ways.

First, when the prince no longer administers the state in accordance with the laws and usurps the sovereign power. In that case a remarkable change takes place, namely that it is not the government but the state that shrinks. I mean that the state as a whole is dissolved, and another is formed inside it, composed exclusively of the members of the government, and which is no longer anything for the rest of the populace but its master and tyrant. So that the instant that the government usurps sovereignty, the social compact is broken, and all ordinary citizens, on recovering by right their natural liberty, are forced but not obliged to obey.

The same thing happens also when the members of the government separately usurp the power they should only exercise as a body. This is no less an infraction of the laws, and produces even greater disorder. Under these circumstances, there are, so to speak, as many princes as magistrates, and the state, no less divided than the government, perishes or changes its form.

When the state dissolves, the abuse of government, whatever it is, takes the common name *anarchy*. To distinguish, democracy degenerates into *ochlocracy,* aristocracy into *oligarchy*. I would add that royalty degenerates into *tyranny,* however this latter term is equivocal and requires an explanation.

In the ordinary sense a tyrant is a king who governs with violence and without regard for justice and the laws. In the strict sense, a tyrant is a private individual who arrogates to himself royal authority without having any right to it. This is how the Greeks understood the word tyrant. They gave the name indifferently to good and bad princes whose authority was not legitimate.[29] Thus *tyrant* and *usurper* are two perfectly synonymous words.

To give different names to different things, I call the usurper of royal authority a *tyrant,* and the usurper of sovereign power a *despot*. The tyrant is someone who intrudes himself, contrary to the laws, in order to govern according to the laws. The despot is someone who places himself above the laws themselves. Thus the tyrant cannot be a despot, but the despot is always a tyrant.

CHAPTER XI
On the Death of the Body Politic

Such is the natural and inevitable tendency of the best constituted governments. If Sparta and Rome perished, what state can hope to last forever? If we wish to form

---

plebeians, and even in the body of the tribunes when they began to usurp an active power. For words do not affect things, and when the populace has leaders who govern for it, it is always an aristocracy, regardless of the name these leaders bear.

The abuse of aristocracy gave birth to civil wars and the triumvirate. Sulla, Julius Caesar, and Augustus became in fact veritable monarchs, and finally, under the despotism of Tiberius, the state was dissolved. Roman history therefore does not invalidate my principle; it confirms it.

29. *For all are considered and are called tyrants who use perpetual power in a city accustomed to liberty.* [Rousseau here quotes the Latin.] Cornelius Nepos, *Life of Miltiades*. It is true that Aristotle, *Nicomachean Ethics,* Book XVIII, Chapter 10, distinguishes between a tyrant and a king, in that the former governs for his own utility and the

a durable establishment, let us then not dream of making it eternal. To succeed, one must not attempt the impossible or flatter oneself with giving to the work of men a solidity that things human do not allow.

The body politic, like the human body, begins to die from the very moment of its birth, and carries within itself the causes of its destruction. But both can have a constitution that is more or less robust and suited to preserve them for a longer or shorter time. The constitution of man is the work of nature; the constitution of the state is the work of art. It is not within men's power to prolong their lives; it is within their power to prolong the life of the state as far as possible, by giving it the best constitution it can have. The best constituted state will come to an end, but later than another, if no unforeseen accident brings about its premature fall.

The principle of political life is in the sovereign authority. Legislative power is the heart of the state; the executive power is the brain, which gives movement to all the parts. The brain can fall into paralysis and yet the individual may still live. A man may remain an imbecile and live. But once the heart has ceased its functions, the animal is dead.

It is not through laws that the state subsists; it is through legislative power. Yesterday's law does not obligate today, but tacit consent is presumed from silence, and the sovereign is taken to be giving incessant confirmation to the laws it does not abrogate while having the power to do so. Whatever it has once declared it wants, it always wants, unless it revokes its declaration.

Why then is so much respect paid to ancient laws? For just this very reason. We must believe that nothing but the excellence of the ancient wills that could have preserved them for so long. If the sovereign had not constantly recognized them to be salutary, it would have revoked them a thousand times. This is why, far from growing weak, the laws continually acquire new force in every well constituted state. The prejudice in favor of antiquity each day renders them more venerable. On the other hand, wherever the laws weaken as they grow old, this proves that there is no longer a legislative power, and that the state is no longer alive.

CHAPTER XII
How the Sovereign Authority Is Maintained

The sovereign, having no other force than legislative power, acts only through the laws. And since the laws are only authentic acts of the general will, the sovereign can act only when the populace is assembled. With the populace assembled, it will be said: what a chimera! It is a chimera today, but two thousand years ago it was not. Have men changed their nature?

The boundaries of what is possible in moral matters are less narrow than we think. It is our weaknesses, our vices and our prejudices that shrink them. Base souls do not believe in great men; vile slaves smile with an air of mockery at the word liberty.

Let us consider what can be done in the light of what has been done. I will not speak of the ancient republics of Greece; however, the Roman Republic was, to my mind, a great state, and the town of Rome was a great town. The last census in Rome

---

latter governs only for the utility of his subjects. But besides the fact that generally all the Greek authors used the word tyrant in another sense, as appears most clearly in Xenophon's *Hiero*, it would follow from Aristotle's distinction that there has not yet been a single king since the beginning of the world.

gave four thousand citizens bearing arms, and the last census count of the empire gave four million citizens, not counting subjects, foreigners, women, children, and slaves.

What difficulty might not be imagined in frequently calling assemblies of the immense populace of that capital and its environs. Nevertheless, few weeks passed by without the Roman people being assembled, and even several times in one week. It exercised not only the rights of sovereignty but also a part of those of the government. It took care of certain matters of public business; it tried certain cases; and this entire populace was in the public meeting place hardly less often as magistrate than as citizen.

In looking back to the earliest history of nations, one would find that most of the ancient governments, even the monarchical ones such as those of the Macedonians and the Franks, had similar councils. Be that as it may, this lone contestable fact answers every difficulty: arguing from the actual to the possible seems like good logic to me.

CHAPTER XIII
Continuation

It is not enough for an assembled people to have once determined the constitution of the state by sanctioning a body of laws. It is not enough for it to have established a perpetual government or to have provided once and for all for the election of magistrates. In addition to the extraordinary assemblies that unforeseen situations can necessitate, there must be some fixed, periodic assemblies that nothing can abolish or prorogue, so that on a specified day the populace is rightfully convened by law, without the need for any other formal convocation.

But apart from these assemblies which are lawful by their date alone, any assembly of the people that has not been convened by the magistrates appointed for that task and in accordance with the prescribed forms should be regarded as illegitimate, and all that takes place there should be regarded as null, since the order itself to assemble ought to emanate from the law.

As to the question of the greater or lesser frequency of legitimate assemblies, this depends on so many considerations that no precise rules can be given about it. All that can be said is that in general the more force a government has, the more frequently the sovereign ought to show itself.

I will be told that this may be fine for a single town, but what is to be done when the state includes several? Will the sovereign authority be divided, or will it be concentrated in a single town with all the rest made subject to it?

I answer that neither should be done. In the first place, the sovereign authority is simple and one; it cannot be divided without being destroyed. In the second place, a town cannot legitimately be in subjection to another town, any more than a nation can be in subjection to another nation, since the essence of the body politic consists in the harmony of obedience and liberty; and the words *subject* and *sovereign* are identical correlatives, whose meaning is combined in the single word "citizen."

I answer further that it is always an evil to unite several towns in a single city, and that anyone wanting to bring about this union should not expect to avoid its natural disadvantages. The abuses of large states should not be raised as an objection against someone who wants only small ones. But how are small states to be given enough force to resist the large ones, just as the Greek cities long ago resisted a great king, and more recently Holland and Switzerland have resisted the house of Austria?

Nevertheless, if the state cannot be reduced to appropriate boundaries, one expedient still remains: not to allow a fixed capital, to make the seat of government move from one town to another, and to assemble the estates of the country in each of them in their turn.

Populate the territory uniformly, extend the same rights everywhere, spread abundance and life all over. In this way the state will become simultaneously as strong and as well governed as possible. Recall that town walls are made from the mere debris of rural houses. With each palace I see being erected in the capital, I believe I see an entire countryside turned into hovels.

CHAPTER XIV
Continuation

Once the populace is legitimately assembled as a sovereign body, all jurisdiction of the government ceases; the executive power is suspended, and the person of the humblest citizen is as sacred and inviolable as that of the first magistrate, for where those who are represented are found, there is no longer any representative. Most of the tumults that arose in the comitia in Rome were due to ignorance or neglect of this rule. On such occasions the consuls were merely the presidents of the people; the tribunes, ordinary speakers;[30] the senate, nothing at all.

These intervals of suspension, during which the prince recognizes or ought to recognize an actual superior, have always been disturbing to him. And these assemblies of the people, which are the aegis of the body politic and the curb on the government, have at all times been the horror of leaders. Thus they never spare efforts, objections, difficulties, or promises to keep the citizens from having them. When the citizens were greedy, cowardly, and pusillanimous, more enamored of repose than with liberty, they do not hold out very long against the redoubled efforts of the government. Thus it is that, as the resisting force constantly grows, the sovereign authority finally vanishes, and the majority of the cities fall and perish prematurely.

But between the sovereign authority and arbitrary government, there sometimes is introduced an intermediate power about which we must speak.

CHAPTER XV
On Deputies or Representatives

Once public service ceases to be the chief business of the citizens, and they prefer to serve with their wallet rather than with their person, the state is already near its ruin. Is it necessary to march off to battle? They pay mercenary troops and stay at home. Is it necessary to go to the council? They name deputies and stay at home. By dint of laziness and money, they finally have soldiers to enslave the country and representatives to sell it.

---

30. In nearly the same sense as is given this word in English Parliament. The similarity between these activities would have put the consuls and the tribunes in conflict, even if all jurisdiction had been suspended.

The hustle and bustle of commerce and the arts, the avid interest in profits, softness and the love of amenities: these are what change personal services into money. A person gives up part of his profit in order to increase it at leisure. Give money and soon you will be in chains. The word *finance* is a slave's word. It is unknown in the city. In a truly free state the citizens do everything with their own hands and nothing with money. Far from paying to be exempted from their duties, they would pay to fulfill them themselves. Far be it from me to be sharing commonly held ideas. I believe that forced labor is less opposed to liberty than are taxes.

The better a state is constituted, the more public business takes precedence over private business in the minds of the citizens. There even is far less private business, since, with the sum of common happiness providing a more considerable portion of each individual's happiness, less remains for him to look for through private efforts. In a well run city everyone flies to the assemblies; under a bad government no one wants to take a step to get to them, since no one takes an interest in what happens there, for it is predictable that the general will will not predominate, and that in the end domestic concerns absorb everything. Good laws lead to making better laws; bad laws bring about worse ones. Once someone says *what do I care?* about the affairs of state, the state should be considered lost.

The cooling off of patriotism, the activity of private interest, the largeness of states, conquests, the abuse of government: these have suggested the route of using deputies or representatives of the people in the nation's assemblies. It is what in certain countries is called the third estate. Thus the private interest of two orders is given first and second place; the public interest is given merely third place.

Sovereignty cannot be represented for the same reason that it cannot be alienated. It consists essentially in the general will, and the will does not allow of being represented. It is either itself or something else; there is nothing in between. The deputies of the people, therefore, neither are nor can be its representatives; they are merely its agents. They cannot conclude anything definitively. Any law that the populace has not ratified in person is null; it is not a law at all. The English people believes itself to be free. It is greatly mistaken; it is free only during the election of the members of Parliament. Once they are elected, the populace is enslaved; it is nothing. The use the English people makes of that freedom in the brief moments of its liberty certainly warrants their losing it.

The idea of representatives is modern. It comes to us from feudal government, that iniquitous and absurd government in which the human race is degraded and the name of man is in dishonor. In the ancient republics and even in monarchies, the people never had representatives. The word itself was unknown. It is quite remarkable that in Rome where the tribunes were so sacred, no one even imagined that they could usurp the functions of the people, and that in the midst of such a great multitude, they never tried to pass a single plebiscite on their own authority. However, we can size up the difficulties that were sometimes caused by the crowd by what took place in the time of the Gracchi, when part of the citizenry voted from the rooftops.

Where right and liberty are everything, inconveniences are nothing. In the care of this wise people, everything was handled correctly. It allowed its lictors to do what its tribunes would not have dared to do. It had no fear that its lictors would want to represent it.

However, to explain how the tribunes sometimes represented it, it is enough to conceive how the government represents the sovereign. Since the law is merely the declaration of the general will, it is clear that the people cannot be represented in the legislative power. But it can and should be represented in the executive power, which is merely force applied to the law. This demonstrates that, on close examination, very few nations would be found to have laws. Be that as it may, it is certain that, since they have no share in the executive power, the tribunes could never represent the Roman people by the rights of their office, but only by usurping those of the senate.

Among the Greeks, whatever the populace had to do, it did by itself. It was constantly assembled at the public square. It inhabited a mild climate; it was not greedy; its slaves did the work; its chief item of business was its liberty. No longer having the same advantages, how are the same rights to be preserved? Your harsher climates cause you to have more needs;[31] six months out of the year the public square is uninhabitable; your muted tongues cannot make themselves understood in the open air; you pay more attention to your profits than to your liberty; and you are less fearful of slavery than you are of misery.

What! Can liberty be maintained only with the support of servitude? Perhaps. The two extremes meet. Everything that is not in nature has its drawbacks, and civil society more so than all the rest. There are some unfortunate circumstances where one's liberty can be preserved only at the expense of someone else's, and where the citizen can be perfectly free only if the slave is completely enslaved. Such was the situation in Sparta. As for you, modern peoples, you do not have slaves, but you yourselves are slaves. You pay for their liberty with your own. It is in vain that you crow about that preference. I find more cowardice in it than humanity.

I do not mean by all this that having slaves is necessary, nor that the right of slavery is legitimate, for I have proved the contrary. I am merely stating the reasons why modern peoples who believe themselves free have representatives, and why ancient peoples did not have them. Be that as it may, the moment a people gives itself representatives, it is no longer free; it no longer exists.

All things considered, I do not see that it is possible henceforth for the sovereign to preserve among us the exercise of its rights, unless the city is very small. But if it is very small, will it be subjugated? No. I will show later[32] how the external power of a great people can be combined with the ease of administration and the good order of a small state.

CHAPTER XVI
That the Institution of Government Is Not a Contract

Once the legislative power has been well established, it is a matter of establishing the executive power in the same way. For this latter, which functions only by means of particular acts, not being of the essence of the former, is naturally separate from

31. To adopt in cold countries the luxury and softness of the orientals is to desire to be given their chains; it is submitting to these with even greater necessity than they did.

32. This is what I intended to do in the rest of this work, when in treating external relations I would have come to confederations. An entirely new subject, and its principles have yet to be established.

it. Were it possible for the sovereign, considered as such, to have the executive power, right and fact would be so completely confounded that we would no longer know what is law and what is not. And the body politic, thus denatured, would soon fall prey to the violence against which it was instituted.

Since the citizens are all equal by the social contract, what everyone should do can be prescribed by everyone. On the other hand, no one has the right to demand that someone else do what he does not do for himself. Now it is precisely this right, indispensable for making the body politic live and move, that the sovereign gives the prince in instituting the government.

Several people have claimed that this act of establishment was a contract between the populace and the leaders it gives itself, a contract by which are stipulated between the two parties the conditions under which the one obliges itself to command and the other to obey. It will be granted, I am sure, that this is a strange way of entering into a social contract! But let us see if this opinion is tenable.

First, the supreme authority cannot be modified any more than it can be alienated; to limit it is to destroy it. It is absurd and contradictory for the sovereign to acquire a superior. To obligate oneself to obey a master is to return to full liberty.

Moreover, it is evident that this contract between the people and some or other persons would be a particular act. Whence it follows that this contract could be neither a law nor an act of sovereignty, and that consequently it would be illegitimate.

It is also clear that the contracting parties would, in relation to one another, be under only the law of nature and without any guarantee of their reciprocal commitments, which is contrary in every way to the civil state. Since the one who has force at his disposal is always in control of its employment, it would come to the same thing if we were to give the name contract to the act of a man who would say to another, "I am giving you all my goods, on the condition that you give me back whatever you wish."

There is only one contract in the state, that of the association, and that alone excludes any other. It is impossible to imagine any public contract that was not a violation of the first contract.

CHAPTER XVII
On the Institution of the Government

What should be the terms under which we should conceive the act by which the government is instituted? I will begin by saying that this act is complex or composed of two others, namely the establishment of the law and the execution of the law.

By the first, the sovereign decrees that there will be a governing body established under some or other form. And it is clear that this act is a law.

By the second, the people names the leaders who will be placed in charge of the established government. And since this nomination is a particular act, it is not a second law, but merely a consequence of the first and a function of the government.

The problem is to understand how there can be an act of government before a government exists, and how the people, which is only sovereign or subject, can in certain circumstances become prince or magistrate.

Moreover, it is here that we discover one of those remarkable properties of the body politic, by which it reconciles seemingly contradictory operations. For this takes place by a sudden conversion of sovereignty into democracy, so that, without any noticeable change, and solely by a new relation of all to all, the citizens, having become magistrates, pass from general to particular acts, and from the law to its execution.

This change of relation is not a speculative subtlety without exemplification in practice. It takes place everyday in the English Parliament, where the lower chamber on certain occasions turns itself into a committee of the whole in order to discuss better the business of the sovereign court, thus becoming the simple commission of the sovereign court (the latter being what it was the moment before), so that it later reports to itself, as the House of Commons, the result of what it has just settled in the committee of the whole, and deliberates all over again under one title about what it had already settled under another.

The peculiar advantage to democratic government is that it can be established in actual fact by a simple act of the general will. After this, the provisional government remains in power, if this is the form adopted, or establishes in the name of the sovereign the government prescribed by the law; and thus everything is in accordance with the rule. It is not possible to institute the government in any other legitimate way without renouncing the principles established above.

CHAPTER XVIII
The Means of Preventing Usurpations of the Government

From these clarifications, it follows, in confirmation of Chapter XVI, that the act that institutes the government is not a contract but a law; that the trustees of the executive power are not the masters of the populace but its officers; that it can establish and remove them when it pleases; that for them there is no question of contracting, but of obeying; and that in taking on the functions the state imposes on them, they merely fulfill their duty as citizens, without in any way having the right to dispute over the conditions.

Thus, when it happens that the populace institutes a hereditary government, whether it is monarchical within a single family or aristocratic within a class of citizens, this is not a commitment it is entering. It is a provisional form that it gives the administration, until the populace is pleased to order it otherwise.

It is true that these changes are always dangerous, and that the established government should never be touched except when it becomes incompatible with the public good. But this circumspection is a maxim of politics and not a rule of law [*droit*], and the state is no more bound to leave civil authority to its leaders than it is to leave military authority to its generals.

Again, it is true that in such cases it is impossible to be too careful about observing all the formalities required in order to distinguish a regular and legitimate act from a seditious tumult, and the will of an entire people from the clamor of a faction. And it is here above all that one must not grant anything to odious cases except what cannot be refused according to the full rigor of the law [*droit*]. And it is also from this obligation that the prince derives a great advantage in preserving his power in spite of the people, without anyone being able to say that he has usurped it. For in appearing to use only his rights, it is quite easy for him to extend them, and under the pretext of public peace, to prevent assemblies destined to reestablish good order. Thus he avails himself of a silence he keeps from being broken, or of irregularities he causes to be committed, to assume that the opinion of those who are silenced by fear is supportive of him, and to punish those who dare to speak. This is how the decemvirs, having been first elected for one year and then continued for another year, tried to retain their power in perpetuity by no longer permitting the comitia to assemble. And it is by this simple means that all the governments of the world, once armed with the public force, sooner or later usurp the public authority.

The periodic assemblies I have spoken of earlier are suited to the prevention or postponement of this misfortune, especially when they have no need for a formal convocation. For then the prince could not prevent them without openly declaring himself a violator of the laws and an enemy of the state.

The opening of these assemblies, which have as their sole object the preservation of the social treaty, should always take place through two propositions which can never be suppressed, and which are voted on separately:

The first: *Does it please the sovereign to preserve the present form of government?*

The second: *Does it please the people to leave its administration to those who are now in charge of it?*

I am presupposing here what I believe I have demonstrated, namely that in the state there is no fundamental law that cannot be revoked, not even the social compact. For if all the citizens were to assemble in order to break this compact by common agreement, no one could doubt that it was legitimately broken. Grotius even thinks that each person can renounce the state of which he is a member and recover his natural liberty and his goods by leaving the country.[33] But it would be absurd that all the citizens together could not do what each of them can do separately.

END OF THE THIRD BOOK

BOOK IV

CHAPTER I

That the General Will Is Indestructible

So long as several men together consider themselves to be a single body, they have but a single will, which is concerned with their common preservation and the general well-being. Then all the energies of the state are vigorous and simple; its maxims are clear and luminous; there are no entangled, contradictory interests; the common good is clearly apparent everywhere, demanding only good sense in order to be perceived. Peace, union, equality are enemies of political subtleties. Upright and simple men are difficult to deceive on account of their simplicity. Traps and clever pretexts do not fool them. They are not even clever enough to be duped. When, among the happiest people in the world, bands of peasants are seen regulating their affairs of state under an oak tree, and always acting wisely, can one help scorning

---

33. On the understanding that one does not leave in order to evade one's duty and to be exempt from serving the homeland the moment it needs us. In such circumstances, taking flight would be criminal and punishable; it would no longer be withdrawal, but desertion.

the refinements of other nations, which make themselves illustrious and miserable with so much art and mystery?

A state thus governed needs very few laws; and in proportion as it becomes necessary to promulgate new ones, this necessity is universally understood. The first to propose them merely says what everybody has already felt; and there is no question of either intrigues or eloquence to secure the passage into law of what each has already resolved to do, once he is sure the others will do likewise.

What misleads argumentative types is the fact that, since they take into account only the states that were badly constituted from the beginning, they are struck by the impossibility of maintaining such an administration. They laugh when they imagine all the foolishness a clever knave or a sly orator could get the people of Paris or London to believe. They do not know that Cromwell would have been sentenced to hard labor by the people of Berne, and the Duc de Beaufort imprisoned by the Genevans.

But when the social bond begins to relax and the state to grow weak, when private interests begin to make themselves felt and small societies begin to influence the large one, the common interest changes and finds opponents. Unanimity no longer reigns in the votes; the general will is no longer the will of all. Contradictions and debates arise, and the best advice does not pass without disputes.

Finally, when the state, on the verge of ruin, subsists only in an illusory and vain form, when the social bond of unity is broken in all hearts, when the meanest interest brazenly appropriates the sacred name of the public good, then the general will becomes mute. Everyone, guided by secret motives, no more express their opinions as citizens than if the state had never existed; and iniquitous decrees having as their sole purpose the private interest are falsely passed under the name of laws.

Does it follow from this that the general will is annihilated or corrupted? No, it is always constant, unalterable and pure; but it is subordinate to other wills that prevail over it. Each man, in detaching his interest from the common interest, clearly sees that he cannot totally separate himself from it; but his share of the public misfortune seems insignificant to him compared to the exclusive good he intends to make his own. Apart from this private good, he wants the general good in his own interest, just as strongly as anyone else. Even in selling his vote for money he does not extinguish the general will in himself; he evades it. The error he commits is that of changing the thrust of the question and answering a different question from the one he was asked. Thus, instead of saying through his vote *it is advantageous to the state, he says it is advantageous to this man or that party that this or that view should pass.* Thus the law of the public order in the assemblies is not so much to maintain the general will, as to bring it about that it is always questioned and that it always answers.

I could present here a number of reflections about the simple right to vote in every act of sovereignty, a right that nothing can take away from the citizens; and on the right to state an opinion, to offer proposals, to divide, to discuss, which the government always takes great care to allow only to its members. But this important subject would require a separate treatise, and I cannot say everything in this one.

CHAPTER II
On Voting

It is clear from the preceding chapter that the manner in which general business is taken care of can provide a rather accurate indication of the present state of mores and of the health of the body politic. The more harmony reigns in the assemblies, that is to say, the closer opinions come to unanimity, the more dominant too is the general will. But long debates, dissensions, and tumult betoken the ascendance of private interests and the decline of the state.

This seems less evident when two or more orders enter into its constitution, as had been done in Rome by the patricians and the plebeians, whose quarrels often disturbed the comitia, even in the best of times in the Republic. But this exception is more apparent than real. For then, by the vice inherent in the body politic, there are, as it were, two states in one. What is not true of the two together is true of each of them separately. And indeed even in the most tumultuous times, the plebiscites of the people, when the senate did not interfere with them, always passed quietly and by a large majority of votes. Since the citizens have but one interest, the people had but one will.

At the other extreme of the circle, unanimity returns. It is when the citizens, having fallen into servitude, no longer have either liberty or will. Then fear and flattery turn voting into acclamations. People no longer deliberate; either they adore or they curse. Such was the vile manner in which the senate expressed its opinions under the emperors; sometimes it did so with ridiculous precautions. Tacitus observes that under Otho, the senators, while heaping curses upon Vitellius, contrived at the same time to make a frightening noise, so that, if by chance he became master, he would be unable to know what each of them had said.

From these various considerations there arise the maxims by which the manner of counting votes and comparing opinions should be regulated, depending on whether the general will is more or less easy to know and the state more or less in decline.

There is but one law that by its nature requires unanimous consent. This is the social compact. For civil association is the most voluntary act in the world. Since every man is born free and master of himself, no one can, under any pretext whatever, place another under subjection without his consent. To decide that the son of a slave is born a slave is to decide that he was not a man.

If, therefore, at the time of the social compact, there are opponents to it, their opposition does not invalidate the contract; it merely prevents them from being included in it. They are foreigners among citizens. Once the state is instituted, residency implies consent. To inhabit the territory is to submit to sovereignty.[34]

Aside from this primitive contract, the vote of the majority always obligates all the others. This is a consequence of the contract itself. But it is asked how a man can be both free and forced to conform to wills that are not his own. How can the opponents be both free and be placed in subjection to laws to which they have not consented?

I answer that the question is not put properly. The citizen consents to all the laws, even to those that pass in spite of his opposition, and even to those that punish him when he dares to violate any of them. The constant will of all the members of the state is the general will; through it they are citizens and free.[35] When a law is

34. This should always be understood in connection with a free state, for otherwise the family, goods, the lack of shelter, necessity, or violence can keep an inhabitant in a country in spite of himself; and then his sojourn alone no longer presupposes his consent to the contract or to the violation of the contract.

35. In Genoa, the word *libertas* [liberty] can be read on the front of prisons and on the chains of galley-slaves. This application of the motto is fine and just. Indeed it is only malefactors of all social classes who prevent the

proposed in the people's assembly, what is asked of them is not precisely whether they approve or reject, but whether or not it conforms to the general will that is theirs. Each man, in giving his vote, states his opinion on this matter, and the declaration of the general will is drawn from the counting of votes. When, therefore, the opinion contrary to mine prevails, this proves merely that I was in error, and that what I took to be the general will was not so. If my private opinion had prevailed, I would have done something other than what I had wanted. In that case I would not have been free.

This presupposes, it is true, that all the characteristics of the general will are still in the majority. When they cease to be free, there is no longer any liberty regardless of the side one takes.

In showing earlier how private wills were substituted for the general will in public deliberations, I have given an adequate indication of the possible ways of preventing this abuse. I will discuss this again at a later time. With respect to the proportional number of votes needed to declare this will, I have also given the principles on the basis of which it can be determined. The differences of a single vote breaks a tie vote; a single opponent destroys a unanimous vote. But between a unanimous and a tie vote there are several unequal divisions, at any of which this proportionate number can be fixed in accordance with the condition and needs of the body politic.

Two general maxims can serve to regulate these ratios. One, that the more important and serious the deliberations are, the closer the prevailing opinion should be to unanimity. The other, that the more the matter at hand calls for alacrity, the smaller the prescribed difference in the division of opinion should be. In decisions that must be reached immediately, a majority of a single vote should suffice. The first of these maxims seems more suited to the laws, and the second to public business. Be that as it may, it is the combination of the two that establishes the ratios that best help the majority to render its decision.

CHAPTER III
On Elections

With regard to the elections of the prince and the magistrates, which are, as I have said, complex acts, there are two ways to proceed, namely by choice or by lots. Both of these have been used in various republics, and at present we still see a very complicated mixture of the two in the election of the Doge of Venice.

Voting by lot, says Montesquieu, *is of the essence of democracy.* I agree, but why is this the case? *Drawing lots,* he continues, *is a way of electing that harms no one; it leaves each citizen a reasonable hope of serving the homeland.* These are not reasons.

If we keep in mind that the election of leaders is a function of government and not of the sovereignty, we will see why the method of drawing lots is more in the nature of democracy, where the administration is better in proportion as its acts are less numerous.

In every true democracy the magistrature is not an advantage but a heavy responsibility that cannot justly be imposed on one private individual rather than another. The law alone can impose this responsibility on the one to whom it falls by lot. For

___
citizen from being free. In a country where all such people were in the galleys, the most perfect liberty would be enjoyed.

in that case, with the condition being equal for all and the choice not depending on any human will, there is no particular application that alters the universality of the law.

In any aristocracy, the prince chooses the prince; the government is preserved by itself, and it is there that voting is appropriate.

The example of the election of the Doge of Venice, far from destroying this distinction, confirms it. This mixed form suits a mixed government. For it is an error to regard the government of Venice as a true aristocracy. For although the populace there has no part in the government, the nobility is itself the people. A multitude of poor Barnabites never came near any magistrature, have nothing to show for their nobility but the vain title of excellency and the right to be present at the grand council. Since this grand council is as numerous as our general council in Geneva, its illustrious members have no more privileges than our single citizens. It is certain that, aside from the extreme disparity between the two republics, the bourgeoisie of Geneva exactly corresponds to the Venetian patriciate. Our natives and inhabitants correspond to the townsmen and people of Venice. Our peasants correspond to the subjects on the mainland. Finally, whatever way one considers this Republic, apart from its size, its government is no more aristocratic than ours. The whole difference lies in the fact that, since we do not have leaders who serve for life, we do not have the same need to draw lots.

Elections by lot would have few disadvantages in a true democracy where, all things being equal both in mores and talents as well as in maxims and fortunes, the choice would become almost indifferent. But I have already said there is no such thing as a true democracy.

When choice and lots are mixed, the former should fill the position requiring special talents, such as military posts. The latter is suited to those positions, such as the responsibilities of judicature, where good sense, justice, and integrity are enough, because in a well constituted state these qualities are common to all the citizens.

Neither the drawing of lots nor voting have any place in a monarchical government. Since the monarch is by right the only prince and sole magistrate, the choice of his lieutenants belongs to him alone. When the Abbé de St. Pierre proposed multiplying the Councils of the King of France and electing the members by ballot, he did not realize that he was proposing to change the form of government.

It remains for me to speak of the manner in which the votes are cast and gathered in the people's assembly. But perhaps in this regard the history of the Roman system of administration will explain more clearly all the maxims I could establish. It is not beneath the dignity of a judicious reader to consider in some detail how public and private business was conducted in a council made of two hundred thousand men.

CHAPTER IV
On the Roman Comitia

We have no especially reliable records of the earliest period of Rome's history. It even appears quite likely that most of the things reported about it are fables.[36] And

---

36. The name *Rome*, which presumably comes from *Romulus*, is Greek, and means *force*. The name *Numa* is also Greek, and means *law*. What is the likelihood that the first two kings of that town would have borne in advance names so clearly related to what they did?

in general the most instructive part of the annals of peoples, which is the history of their founding, is the part we most lack. Experience teaches us every day the causes that lead to the revolutions of empires. But since peoples are no longer being formed, we have almost nothing but conjecture to explain how they were formed.

The customs we find established attest at the very least to the fact that these customs had an origin. Of the traditions that go back to these origins, those that are supported by the greatest authorities and that are confirmed by the strongest reasons should pass for the most certain. These are the maxims I have tried to follow in attempting to find out how the freest and most powerful people on earth exercised its supreme power.

After the founding of Rome, the new-born Republic, that is, the army of the founder, composed of Albans, Sabines, and foreigners, was divided into three classes, which took the name *tribus* [tribes] by nature of this division. Each of these tribes was divided into ten curiae, and each curia into decuriae, at the head of which were placed leaders called *curiones* and *decuriones*.

Moreover, from each tribe was drawn a body of one hundred horsemen or knights, called a *century*. It is clear from this that these divisions, being hardly necessary in a market-town, originally were exclusively military. But it appears that an instinct for greatness led the small town of Rome to provide itself in advance with a system of administration suited to the capital of the world.

One disadvantage soon resulted from this initial division. With the tribes of the Albans[37] and the Sabines[38] always remaining constant, while that of the foreigners[39] grew continually, thanks to their perpetual influx, this latter group soon outnumbered the other two. The remedy that Servius found for this dangerous abuse was to change the division and, in place of the division based on race, which he abolished, to substitute another division drawn from the areas of the town occupied by each tribe. In place of the three tribes, he made four. Each of them occupied one of the hills of Rome and bore its name. Thus, in remedying the inequality of the moment, he also prevented it from happening in the future. And in order that this division might not be merely one of localities but of men, he prohibited the inhabitants of one quarter from moving into another, which prevented the races from mingling with one another.

He also doubled the three ancient centuries of horsemen and he added to them twelve others, but always under the old names, a simple and judicious means by which he achieved the differentiation of the body of knights from that of the people, without causing the latter to murmur.

To the four urban tribes, Servius added fifteen others called rural tribes because they were formed from the inhabitants of the countryside, divided into the same number of cantons. Subsequently, the same number of new ones were brought into being, and the Roman people finally found itself divided into thirty-five tribes, a number at which they remained fixed until the end of the Republic.

37. Ramnenses.

38. Tatienses.

39. Luceres.

There resulted from this distinction between the tribes of the city and those of the countryside an effect worth noting, because there is no other example of it, and because Rome owed it both the preservation of its mores and the growth of its empire. One might have thought that the urban tribes soon would have arrogated to themselves power and honors, and wasted no time in vilifying the rural tribes. What took place was quite the opposite. The early Romans' taste for country life is well known. They inherited this taste from the wise founder who united liberty with rural and military labors, and, so to speak, relegated to the town arts, crafts, intrigue, fortune and slavery.

Thus, since all the illustrious men in Rome lived in the country and tilled the soil, people became accustomed to look only there for the mainstays of the Republic. Since this condition was that of the worthiest patricians, it was honored by everyone. The simple and laborious life of the townsmen was preferred to the lazy and idle life of the bourgeois of Rome. And someone who would have been merely a miserable proletarian in the town, became a respected citizen as a field worker. It was not without reason, said Varro, that our great-souled ancestors established in the village the nursery of those robust and valiant men who defended them in time of war and nourished them in time of peace. Pliny says positively that the tribes of the fields were honored on account of the men who made them up; on the other hand, cowards whom men wished to vilify were transferred in disgrace to the tribes of the town. When the Sabine Appius Claudius came to settle in Rome, he was decked with honors and inscribed in a rural tribe that later took the name of his family. Finally, freedmen all entered the urban tribes, never the rural ones. And during the entire period of the Republic, there was not a single example of any of these freedmen reaching any magistrature, even if he had become a citizen.

This maxim was excellent, but it was pushed so far that it finally resulted in a change and certainly an abuse in the administration.

First, the censors, after having long arrogated to themselves the right to transfer citizens arbitrarily from one tribe to another, permitted most of them to have themselves inscribed in whatever tribe they pleased. Certainly this permission served no useful purpose and deprived the censorship of one of its greatest resources. Moreover, with the great and the powerful having themselves inscribed in the tribes of the countryside, and the freedmen who had become citizens remaining with the populace in the tribes of the town, the tribes in general no longer had either place or territory. On the contrary, they all found themselves so intermixed that the number of each could no longer be identified except by the registers, so that in this way the idea of the word *tribe* passed from being proprietary to personal, or rather, it became almost a chimera.

In addition, it happened that since the tribes of the town were nearer at hand, they were often the strongest in the comitia, and sold the state to those who deigned to buy the votes of the mob that made them up.

Regarding the curiae, since the founder had created ten curiae in each tribe, the entire Roman people, which was then contained within the town walls, was composed of thirty curiae, each of which had its temples, its gods, its officials, its priests and its feasts called *compitalia,* similar to the *paganalia* later held by the rural tribes.

When Servius established this new division, since this number thirty could not be divided equally among his four tribes, and since he did not want to alter it, the curiae became another division of the inhabitants of Rome, independent of the tribes. But there was no question of the curiae either in the rural tribes or among the people that make them up, for since the tribes had become a purely civil establishment and another system of administration had been introduced for the raising of troops, the military divisions of Romulus were found to be superfluous. Thus, even though every citizen was inscribed in a tribe, there were quite a few who were not inscribed in a curia.

Servius established still a third division which bore no relationship to the two preceding ones and which became, in its effects, the most important of all. He divided the entire Roman people into six classes, which he distinguished neither by place nor by person, but by wealth. Thus the first classes were filled by the rich, the last by the poor, and the middle ones by those who enjoyed a moderate fortune. These six classes were subdivided into one hundred ninety-three other bodies called centuries, and these bodies were divided in such wise that the first class alone contained more than half of them, and the last contained only one. Thus it was that the class with the smallest number of men was the one with the greatest number of centuries, and that the entire last class counted only as a subdivision, even though it alone contained more than half the inhabitants of Rome.

In order that the people might have less of a grasp of the consequences of this last form, Servius feigned giving it a military air. He placed in the second class two centuries of armorers, and two instruments of war in the fourth. In each class, with the exception of the last, he made a distinction between the young and the old, that is to say, between those who were obliged to carry arms and those whose age exempted them by law. This distinction, more than that of wealth, produced the necessity for frequently retaking the census or counting. Finally, he wished the assembly to be held in the Campus Martius, and that all those who were of age to serve should come there with their arms.

The reason he did not follow this same division of young and old in the last division is that the populace of which it was composed was not accorded the honor of bearing arms for the homeland. It was necessary to possess a hearth in order to obtain the right to defend it. And of the innumerable troops of beggars who today grace the armies of kings, there is perhaps no one who would not have been disdainfully chased from a Roman cohort, when the soldiers were the defenders of liberty.

There still is a distinction in the last class between the *proletarians* and those that are called *capite censi*. The former, not completely reduced to nothing, at least gave citizens to the state, sometimes even soldiers in times of pressing need. As for those who possessed nothing at all and could be reckoned only by counting heads, they were reckoned to be absolutely worthless, and Marius was the first who deigned to enroll them.

Without deciding here whether this third method of reckoning was good or bad in itself, I believe I can affirm that it could be made practicable only by the simple mores of the early Romans, their disinterestedness, their taste for agriculture, their dislike for commerce and for the passion for profits. Where is the modern people among whom their devouring greed, their unsettled spirit, their intrigue, their continual displacements, their perpetual revolutions of fortunes could allow such an establishment to last twenty years without overturning the entire state? It must also be duly noted that the mores and the censorship, which were stronger than this institution, corrected its defects in Rome, and that a rich man found himself relegated to the class of the poor for having made too much of a show of his wealth.

From all this, it is easy to grasp why mention is almost never made of more than five classes, even though there actually were six. The sixth, since it furnished neither soldiers for the army nor voters for the Campus Martius[40] and was of virtually no use in the Republic, was hardly ever counted for anything.

Such were the various divisions of the Roman people. Let us now look at the effect these divisions had on the assemblies. When legitimately convened, these assemblies were called *comitia*. Ordinarily they were held in the Roman forum or in the Campus Martius, and were distinguished as comitia curiata, comitia centuriata, and comitia tributa, according to which of the three forms was the basis on which they were organized. The comitia curiata were based on the institution of Romulus, the comitia centuriata on that of Servius, and the comitia tributa on that of the tribunes of the people. No law received sanction, no magistrate was elected save in the comitia. And since there was no citizen who was not inscribed in a curia, in a century, or in a tribe, it followed that no citizen was excluded from the right of suffrage, and that the Roman people was truly sovereign both de jure and de facto.

For the comitia to be legitimately assembled and for what took place to have the force of law, three conditions had to be met: first, the body or the magistrate who called these assemblies had to be invested with the necessary authority to do so; second, the assembly had to be held on one of the days permitted by law; third, the auguries had to be favorable.

The reason for the first regulation needs no explanation. The second is an administrative matter. Thus the comitia were not allowed to be held on holidays and market days, when people from the country, coming to Rome on business, did not have time to spend the day in the public forum. By means of the third rule, the senate held in check a proud and restless people, and appropriately tempered the ardor of seditious tribunes. But these latter found more than one way of getting around this constraint.

The laws and the election of leaders were not the only matters submitted to the judgment of the comitia. Since the Roman people had usurped the most important functions of government, it can be said that the fate of Europe was decided in its assemblies. This variety of objects gave rise to the various forms these assemblies took on according to the matters on which they had to pronounce.

In order to judge these various forms, it is enough to compare them. In instituting the curiae, Romulus had intended to contain the senate by means of the people and the people by means of the senate, while he dominated both equally. He therefore gave the people, by means of this form, all the authority of number to balance that of power and wealth which he left to the patricians. But in conformity with the spirit of the monarchy, he nevertheless left a greater advantage to the patricians through their clients' influence on the majority of the votes. This admirable institution of patrons and clients was a masterpiece of politics and humanity, without which the patriciate, so contrary to the spirit of the Republic, could not have subsisted. Only Rome had the honor of giving the world this fine example, which never led to any abuse, and which, for all that, has never been followed.

---

40. I say *Campus Martius* because it was here that the comitia centuriata gathered. In the two other forms of assembly, the people gathered in the *forum* or elsewhere, and then the *capite censi* had as much influence and authority as the first citizens.

Since this same form of curiae had subsisted under the kings until Servius, and since the reign of the last Tarquin was not considered legitimate, royal laws were generally known by the name *leges curiatae*.

Under the Republic, the curiae, always limited to the four urban tribes and including no more than the populace of Rome, was unable to suit either the senate, which was at the head of the patricians, or the tribunes, who, plebeians though they were, were at the head of the citizens who were in comfortable circumstances. The curiae therefore fell into discredit and their degradation was such that their thirty assembled lictors together did what the comitia curiata should have done.

The division by centuries was so favorable to the aristocracy, that at first difficult it is to see how the senate did not always prevail in the comitia which bears this name, and by which the consuls, the censors, and other crurale magistrates were elected. In fact, of the one hundred ninety-three centuries that formed the six classes of the entire Roman people, the first class contained ninety-eight, and, since the voting was counted by centuries only, this first class alone prevailed in the number of votes over all the rest. When all its centuries were in agreement, they did not even continue to gather the votes. Decisions made by the smallest number passed for a decision of the multitude; and it can be said that in the comitia centuriata business was regulated more by the majority of money than by one of votes.

But this extreme authority was tempered in two ways. First, since ordinarily the tribunes, and always a large number of plebeians, were in the class of the rich, they balanced the credit of the patricians in this first class.

The second way consisted in the following. Instead of at the outset making the centuries vote according to their order, which would have meant always beginning with the first, one century was chosen by lot, and that one[41] alone proceeded to the election. After this, all the centuries were called on another day according to their rank, repeated the same election and usually confirmed it. Thus the authority of example was removed from rank in order to give it to lot, in accordance with the principle of democracy.

There resulted from this custom still another advantage; namely that the citizens from the country had time between the two elections to inform themselves of the merit of the provisionally named candidate, so as to give their votes only on condition of their having knowledge of the issue. But on the pretext of speeding things up, this custom was finally abolished and the two elections were held on the same day.

Strictly speaking, the comitia tributa were the council of the Roman people. They were convened only by the tribunes. The tribunes were elected and passed their plebiscites there. Not only did the senate hold no rank in them, it did not even have the right to be present. And since the senators were forced to obey the laws upon which they could not vote, they were less free in this regard than the humblest citizens. This injustice was altogether ill-conceived, and was by itself enough to invalidate the decrees of a body to which all its members were not admitted. If all the patricians had been present at these comitia in virtue of the right they had as citizens, having then become simple private individuals, they would not have had a

---

41. This century, having been chosen thus by lot, was called *prae rogativa*, on account of the fact that it was the first to be asked for its vote, and it is from this that the word *prerogative* is derived.

great deal of influence on a form of voting that was tallied by counting heads, and where the humblest proletarian had as much clout as the prince of the senate.

Thus it can be seen that besides the order that resulted from these various distributions for gathering the votes of so great a people, these distributions were not reducible to forms indifferent in themselves, but each one had effects relative to the viewpoints that caused it to be preferred.

Without going further into greater detail here, it is a consequence of the preceding clarifications that the comitia tributa were the most favorable to the popular government, and the comitia centuriata more favorable to the aristocracy. Regarding the comitia curiata, in which the populace of Rome alone formed the majority, since these were good only for favoring tyranny and evil designs, they fell of their own weight into disrepute, and even the seditious abstained from using a means that gave too much exposure to their projects. It is certain that all the majesty of the Roman people is found only in the curia centuriata, which alone were complete, for the comitia curiata excluded the rural tribes, and the comitia tributa the senate and the patricians.

As to the manner of counting the votes, among the early Romans it was as simple as their mores, though not so simple as in Sparta. Each gave his vote in a loud voice, and a clerk marked it down accordingly. The majority vote in each tribe determined the tribe's vote; the majority vote of the tribes determined the people's vote; and the same went for the curia and the centuries. This custom was good so long as honesty reigned among the citizens and each was ashamed to give his vote publicly in favor of an unjust proposal or an unworthy subject. But when the people became corrupt and votes were bought, it was fitting that they should give their votes in secret in order to restrain the buyers through distrust and to provide scoundrels the means of not being traitors.

I know that Cicero condemns this change and attributes the ruin of the Republic partly to it. But although I am aware of the weight that Cicero's authority should have here, I cannot agree with him. On the contrary, I think that, by having made not enough of these changes, the fall of the state was accelerated. Just as the regimen of healthy people is not suitable for the sick, one should not want to govern a corrupt people by means of the same laws that are suited to a good people. Nothing proves this maxim better than the long life of the Republic of Venice, whose shadow still exists, solely because its laws are suited only to wicked men.

Tablets were therefore distributed to the citizens by mean of which each man could vote without anyone knowing what his opinion was. New formalities were also established for collecting the tablets, counting the votes, comparing the numbers, and so on. None of this prevented the integrity of the officials in charge of these functions[42] from often being under suspicion. Finally, to prevent intrigue and vote trafficking, edicts were passed whose sheer multiplicity is proof of their uselessness.

Toward the end of the period of the Republic, it was often necessary to have recourse to extraordinary expedients in order to make up for the inadequacy of the law. Sometimes miracles were alleged. But this means, which could deceive the populace, did not deceive those who governed it. Sometimes an assembly was unexpectedly convened before the candidates had time to carry out their intrigues.

42. Custodes, diribitores, rogatores suffragiorum.

Sometimes an entire session was spent on talk, when it was clear that the populace was won over and ready to take the wrong side on an issue. But finally ambition eluded everything; and what is unbelievable is that in the midst of so much abuse, this immense people, by virtue of its ancient regulations, did not cease to choose magistrates, pass laws, judge cases, or expedite private and public business, almost as easily as the senate itself could have done.

CHAPTER V
On the Tribunate

When it is not possible to establish an exact proportion between the constitutive parts of the state, or when indestructible causes continually alter the relationships between them, a special magistrature is then established that does not make up a larger body along with them. This magistrature restores each term to its true relationship to the others, and which creates a link or a middle term either between the prince and the people or between the prince and the sovereign, or on both sides at once, if necessary.

This body, which I will call the *tribunate,* is the preserver of the laws and the legislative power. It serves sometimes to protect the sovereign against the government, as the tribunes of the people did in Rome; sometimes to sustain the government against the people, as the Council of Ten now does in Venice; and sometimes to maintain equilibrium between the two, as the ephors did in Sparta.

The tribunate is not a constitutive part of the city and it should have no share in either the legislative or the executive power. But this is precisely what makes its own power the greater. For although it is unable to do anything, it can prevent everything. It is more sacred and more revered as a defender of the laws than the prince who executes them and the sovereign who gives them. This was very clearly apparent in Rome when the proud patricians, who always scorned the entire populace, were forced to bow before a humble official of the people, who had neither auspices nor jurisdiction.

A well tempered tribunate is the firmest support of a good constitution. But if it has the slightest bit too much force, it undermines everything. As to weakness, there is none in its nature; and provided it is something, it is never less than it ought to be.

It degenerates into tyranny when it usurps the executive power, of which it is merely the moderator, and when it wants to dispense the laws it ought only protect. The enormous power of the ephors, which was without danger so long as Sparta preserved its mores, hastened corruption once it had begun. The blood of Agis, who was slaughtered by these tyrants, was avenged by his successor. The crime and the punishment of the ephors equally hastened the fall of the republic; and after Cleomenes Sparta was no longer anything. Rome also perished in the same way, and the excessive power of the tribunes, which they had gradually usurped, finally served, with the help of the laws that were made to protect liberty, as a safeguard for the emperors who destroyed it. As for the Council of Ten in Venice, it is a tribunal of blood, equally horrible to the patricians and the people, and which, far from proudly protecting the laws, no longer serves any purpose, after their degradation, beyond that of delivering blows in the dark which no one dares notice.

Just like the government, the tribunate weakened as a result of the multiplication of its members. When the tribunes of the Roman people, who at first were two in number, then five, wanted to double this number, the senate let them do so, certain that one part would hold the others in check; and this did not fail to happen.

The best way to prevent usurpations by so formidable a body, one that no government has yet made use of, would be not to make this body permanent, but to regulate the intervals during which it would be suppressed. These intervals, which ought not be so long as to allow abuses time to grow in strength, can be fixed by law in such a way that it is easy to shorten them, as needed, by means of extraordinary commissions.

This way seems to me to have no disadvantage, for since, as I have said, the tribunate is not part of the constitution, it can be set aside without doing the constitution any harm, because a newly established magistrate begins not with the power his predecessor had, but with the power the law gives him.

CHAPTER VI
On Dictatorship

The inflexibility of the laws, which prevents them from adapting to circumstances, can in certain instances make them harmful and render them the instrument of the state's downfall in time of crisis. The order and the slowness of formal procedures require a space of time which circumstances sometimes do not permit. A thousand circumstances can present themselves which the legislator has not foreseen, and it is a very necessary bit of foresight to realize that not everything can be foreseen.

It is therefore necessary to avoid the desire to strengthen political institutions to the point of removing the power to suspend their effect. Sparta itself allowed its laws to lie dormant.

But only the greatest dangers can counterbalance the danger of altering the public order, and the sacred power of the laws should never be suspended except when it is a question of the safety of the homeland. In these rare and obvious cases, public safety can be provided for by a special act which confers the responsibility for it on someone who is most worthy. This commission can be carried out in two ways, according to the type of danger.

If increasing the activity of government is enough to remedy the situation, it is concentrated in one or two members. Thus it is not the authority of the laws that is altered, but merely the form of their administration. But if the peril is such that the apparatus of the laws is an obstacle to their being protected, then a supreme leader is named who silences all the laws and briefly suspends the sovereign authority. In such a case, the general will is not in doubt, and it is evident that the first intention of the people is that the state should not perish. In this manner, the suspension of legislative authority does not abolish it. The magistrate who silences it cannot make it speak; he dominates it without being able to represent it. He can do anything but make laws.

The first way was used by the Roman senate when, by a sacred formula, it entrusted the consuls with the responsibility for providing for the safety of the Republic. The second took place when one of the two consuls named a dictator,[43] a custom for which Alba had provided Rome the precedent.

---

43. This nomination was made at night and in secret, as if it were shameful to place a man beyond the laws.

In the beginning days of the Republic, there was frequent recourse to dictatorship, since the state did not yet have a sufficiently stable basis to be capable of sustaining itself by the force of its constitution. Since the mores at that time made many of the precautions superfluous that would have been necessary in other times, there was no fear either that a dictator would abuse his authority or that he would try to hold on to it beyond his term of office. On the contrary, it seemed that such a great power was a burden to the one in whom it was vested, so quickly did he hasten to rid himself of it, as if a position that took the place of the laws would have been too troublesome and dangerous!

Thus it is not so much the danger of its being abused as it is that of its being degraded which makes one criticize the injudicious use of this supreme magistrature in the early days of the Republic. For while it was being wasted on elections, dedications and purely formal proceedings, there was reason to fear that it would become less formidable in time of need, and that people would become accustomed to regard as empty a title that was used exclusively in empty ceremonies.

Toward the end of the Republic, the Romans, having become more circumspect, were as unreasonably sparing in their use of the dictatorship as they had formerly been lavish. It was easy to see that their fear was ill-founded; that the weakness of the capital then protected it against the magistrates who were in its midst; that a dictator could, under certain circumstances, defend the public liberty without ever being able to make an attack on it; and that Rome's chains would not be forged in Rome itself, but in its armies. The weak resistance that Marius offered Sulla and Pompey offered Caesar clearly demonstrated what could be expected of internal authority in the face of external force.

This error caused them to make huge mistakes; for example, failing to name a dictator in the Catalinian affair. For since this was a question merely of the interior of the town and, at most, of some province in Italy, with the unlimited authority that the laws give the dictator, he would have easily quelled the conspiracy, which was stifled only by a coming together of favor chance happenings, which human prudence has no right to expect.

Instead of that, the senate was content to entrust all its power to the consuls. Whence it happened that, in order to act effectively, Cicero was forced to exceed this power on a crucial point. And although the first transports of joy indicated approval of his conduct, eventually Cicero was justly called to account for the blood of citizens shed against the laws, a reproach that could not have been delivered against a dictator. But the eloquence of the consul carried the day. And since even he, Roman though he was, preferred his own glory to his homeland, he sought not so much the most legitimate and safest way of saving the state as he did the way that would get him all the honor for settling this affair.[44] Thus he was justly honored as the liberator of Rome and justly punished as a law-breaker. However brilliant his recall may have been, it undoubtedly was a pardon.

For the rest, whatever the manner in which this important commission was conferred, it is important to limit a dictatorship's duration to a very short period of time which cannot be prolonged. In the crises that call for its being established, the state

---

44. He could not have been sure of this, had he proposed a dictator, since he did not dare name himself, and he could not be sure that his colleague would name him.

is soon either destroyed or saved; and once the pressing need has passed, the dictatorship becomes tyrannical or needless. In Rome, where the dictators had terms of six months only, most of them abdicated before their terms had expired. If the term had been longer, perhaps they would have been tempted to prolong it further, as did the decemvirs with a one year term. The dictator only had time enough to see to the need that got him elected. He did not have time to dream up other projects.

CHAPTER VII
On the Censorship

Just as the declaration of the general will takes place through the law, the declaration of the public judgment takes place through the censorship. Public opinion is the sort of law whose censor is the minister, and which he only applies to particular cases, after the example of the prince.

Thus the censorial tribunal, far from being the arbiter of the people's opinion, is merely its spokesman; and as soon as it deviates from this opinion, its decisions are vain and futile.

It is useless to distinguish the mores of a nation from the objects of its esteem, for all these things derive from the same principle and are necessarily intermixed. Among all the peoples of the world, it is not nature but opinion which decides the choice of their pleasures. Reform men's opinions, and their mores will soon become purified all by themselves. Men always love what is good or what they find to be so; but it is in this judgment that they make mistakes. Hence this is the judgment whose regulation is the point at issue. Whoever judges mores judges honor; and whoever judges honor derives his law from opinion.

The opinions of a people arise from its constitution. Although the law does not regulate mores, legislation is what gives rise to them. When legislation weakens, mores degenerate; but then the judgment of the censors will not do what the force of the laws has not done.

It follows from this that the censorship can be useful for preserving mores, but never for reestablishing them. Establish censors while the laws are vigorous. Once they have lost their vigor, everything is hopeless. Nothing legitimate has any force once the laws no longer have force.

The censorship maintains mores by preventing opinions from becoming corrupt, by preserving their rectitude through wise applications, and sometimes even by making a determination on them when they are still uncertain. The use of seconds in duels, which had been carried to the point of being a craze in the kingdom of France, was abolished by the following few words of the king's edict: *as for those who are cowardly enough to call upon seconds.* This judgment anticipated that of the public and suddenly made a determination. But when the same edicts tried to declare that it was also an act of cowardice to fight duels (which of course is quite true, but contrary to common opinion), the public mocked this decision; it concerned a matter about which its mind was already made up.

I have said elsewhere[45] that since public opinion is not subject to constraint, there should be no vestige of it in the tribunal established to represent it. It is impossible to show too much admiration for the skill with which this device, entirely lost among

---

45. I merely call attention in this chapter to what I have treated at greater length in my *Letter to D'Alembert.*

us moderns, was put into effect among the Romans and even better among the Lacedaemonians.

When a man of bad mores put forward a good proposal in the council of Sparta, the ephors ignored it and had the same proposal put forward by a virtuous citizen. What honor for the one, what shame for the other; and without having given praise or blame to either of the two! Certain drunkards of Samos[46] defiled the tribunals of the ephors. The next day, a public edict gave the Samians permission to be filthy. A true punishment would have been less severe than impunity such as this. When Sparta made a pronouncement on what was or was not decent, Greece did not appeal its judgments.

CHAPTER VIII
On Civil Religion

At first men had no other kings but the gods, and no other government than a theocratic one. They reasoned like Caligula, and then they reasoned correctly. A lengthy alteration of feelings and ideas is necessary before men can be resolved to accept a fellow man as a master, in the hope that things will turn out well for having done so.

By the mere fact that a god was placed at the head of every political society, it followed that there were as many gods as there were peoples. Two peoples who were alien to one another and nearly always enemies, could not recognize the same master for very long. Two armies in combat with one another could not obey the same leader. Thus national divisions led to polytheism, and this in turn led to theological and civil intolerance which are by nature the same, as will be stated later.

The fanciful notion of the Greeks that they had rediscovered their gods among the beliefs of barbarian peoples arose from another notion they had of regarding themselves as the natural sovereigns of these peoples. But in our day it is a ridiculous bit of erudition which equates the gods of different nations: as if Moloch, Saturn, and Chronos could have been the same god; as if the Phoenicians' Baal, the Greeks' Zeus, and the Romans' Jupiter could have been the same; as if there could be anything in common among chimerical beings having different names!

But if it is asked how in pagan cultures, where each state has its own cult and its own gods, there are no wars of religion, I answer that it was for this very reason that each state, having its own cult as well as its own government, did not distinguish its gods from its laws. Political war was theological as well. The departments of the gods were, so to speak, fixed by national boundaries. The gods of one people had no rights over other peoples. The gods of the pagans were not jealous gods. They divided dominion over the world among themselves. Moses himself and the Hebrew people sometimes countenanced this idea in speaking of the god of Israel. It is true they regarded as nothing the gods of the Canaanites, a proscribed people destined for destruction, and whose land they were to occupy. But note how they spoke of the divinities of neighboring peoples whom they were forbidden to attack! *Is not th[e] possession of what belongs to your god Chamos*, said Jephthah to the Ammonites, *l[awf]ul for*

---

46. [Rousseau adds the following in the 1782 edition: "They are from another i[sland] our language prohibits me from naming at this time."]

yours? By the same right we possess the lands our victorious god has acquired for himself.[47] It appears to me that here was a clear recognition of the parity between the rights of Chamos and those of the god of Israel.

But when the Jews, while in subjection to the kings of Babylon and later to the kings of Syria, wanted to remain steadfast in not giving recognition to any other god but their own, their refusal, seen as rebellion against the victor, brought them the persecutions we read of in their history, and of which there is no other precedent prior to Christianity.[48]

Since, therefore, each religion was uniquely tied to the laws of the state which prescribed it, there was no other way of converting a people except by enslaving it, nor any other missionaries than conquerors. And with the obligation to change cult being the law of the vanquished, it was necessary to begin by conquering before talking about it. Far from men fighting for the gods, it was, as it was in Homer, the gods who fought for men; each asked his own god for victory and paid for it with new altars. Before taking an area, the Romans summoned that area's gods to leave it. And when they allowed the Tarentines to keep their angry gods, it was because at that point they considered these gods to be in subjection to their own and forced to do them homage. They left the vanquished their gods, just as they left them their laws. A wreath to the Capitoline Jupiter was often the only tribute they imposed.

Finally, the Romans having spread this cult and their gods, along with their empire, and having themselves often adopted the gods of the vanquished by granting the right of the city to both alike, the peoples of this vast empire gradually found themselves to have multitudes of gods and cults, which were nearly the same everywhere. And that is how paganism finally became a single, identical religion in the known world.

Such were the circumstances under which Jesus came to establish a spiritual kingdom on earth. In separating the theological system from the political system, this made the state to cease being united and caused internal divisions that never ceased to agitate Christian peoples. But since this new idea of an otherworldly kingdom had never entered the heads of the pagans, they always regarded the Christians as true rebels who, underneath their hypocritical submission, were only waiting for the moment when they would become independent and the masters, and adroitly usurp the authority they pretended in their weakness to respect. This is the reason for the persecutions.

What the pagans feared happened. Then everything changed its appearance. The humble Christians changed their language, and soon this so-called otherworldly kingdom became, under a visible leader, the most violent despotism in this world.

However, since there has always been a prince and civil laws, this double power has given rise to a perpetual jurisdictional conflict that has made all good polity impossible in Christian states, and no one has ever been able to know whether it is the priest or the master whom one is obliged to obey.

Nevertheless, several peoples, even in Europe or nearby have wanted to preserve or reestablish the ancient system, but without success. The spirit of Christianity has won everything. The sacred cult has always remained or again become independent of the sovereign and without any necessary link to the state. Mohammed had very sound opinions. He tied his political system together very well, and so long as the form of his government subsisted under his successors, the caliphs, this government was utterly unified, and for that reason it was good. But as the Arabs became prosperous, lettered, polished, soft and cowardly, they were subjugated by barbarians. Then the division between the two powers began again. Although it is less apparent among the Mohammedans than among the Christians, it is there all the same, especially in the sect of Ali; and there are states, such as Persia, where it never ceases to be felt.

Among us, the kings of England have established themselves as heads of the Church, and the czars have done the same. But with this title, they became less its masters than its ministers. They have acquired not so much the right to change it as the power to maintain it. They are not its legislators; they are merely its princes. Wherever the clergy constitutes a body,[49] it is master and legislator in its own realm. Thus there are two powers, two sovereigns, in England and in Russia, just as there are everywhere else.

Of all the Christian writers, the philosopher Hobbes is the only one who clearly saw the evil and the remedy, who dared to propose the reunification of the two heads of the eagle and the complete restoration of political unity, without which no state or government will ever be well constituted. But he should have seen that the dominating spirit of Christianity was incompatible with his system, and that the interest of the priest would always be stronger than that of the state. It is not so much what is horrible and false in his political theory as what is just and true that has caused it to be hated.[50]

I believe that if the facts of history were developed from this point of view, it would be easy to refute the opposing sentiments of Bayle and Warburton, the one holding that no religion is useful to the body politic, while the other maintains, to the contrary, that Christianity is its firmest support. We could prove to the first that no state has ever been founded without religion serving as its base, and to the second that Christian law is at bottom more injurious than it is useful for the strong constitution of the state. To succeed in making myself understood, I need only give a bit more precision to the excessively vague ideas about religion that are pertinent to my subject.

49. It should be carefully noted that it is not so much the formal assemblies, such as those of France, which bind the clergy together into a body, as it is the communion of the churches. Communion and excommunication are the social compact of the clergy, one with which it will always be the master of the peoples and the kings. All the priests who communicate together are citizens, even if they should be from the opposite ends of the world. This invention is a political masterpiece. There is nothing like this among the pagan priests; thus they never made up a body of clergy.

50. Notice, among other things, in Grotius' letter to his brother, dated April 11, 1643, what this learned man approves of and what he criticizes in his book *De Cive*. It is true that, prone to being indulgent, he appears to forgive the author for his good points for the sake of his bad ones. But not everyone is so merciful.

When considered in relation to society, which is either general or particular, religion can also be divided into two kinds, namely the religion of the man and that of the citizen. The first—without temples, altars or rites, and limited to the purely internal cult of the supreme God and to the eternal duties of morality—is the pure and simple religion of the Gospel, the true theism, and what can be called natural divine law [*droit*]. The other, inscribed in a single country, gives it its gods, its own titulary patrons. It has its dogmas, its rites, its exterior cult prescribed by laws. Outside the nation that practices it, everything is infidel, alien and barbarous to it. It extends the duties and rights of man only as far as its altars. Such were all the religions of the early peoples, to which the name of civil or positive divine law [*droit*] can be given.

There is a third sort of religion which is more bizarre. In giving men two sets of legislation, two leaders, and two homelands, it subjects them to contradictory duties and prevents them from being simultaneously devout men and citizens. Such is the religion of the Lamas and of the Japanese, and such is Roman Christianity. It can be called the religion of the priest. It leads to a kind of mixed and unsociable law [*droit*] which has no name.

Considered from a political standpoint, these three types of religion all have their faults. The third is so bad that it is a waste of time to amuse oneself by proving it. Whatever breaks up social unity is worthless. All institutions that place man in contradiction with himself are of no value.

The second is good in that it unites the divine cult with love of the laws, and that, in making the homeland the object of its citizens' admiration, it teaches them that all service to the state is service to its tutelary god. It is a kind of theocracy in which there ought to be no pontiff other than the prince and no priests other than the magistrates. To die for one's country is then to become a martyr; to violate its laws is to be impious. To subject a guilty man to public execration is to deliver him to the wrath of the gods: *sacer estod*.

On the other hand, it is bad in that, being based on error and lies, it deceives men, makes them credulous and superstitious, and drowns the true cult of the divinity in an empty ceremony. It is also bad when, on becoming exclusive and tyrannical, it makes a people bloodthirsty and intolerant, so that men breathe only murder and massacre, and believe they are performing a holy action in killing anyone who does not accept its gods. This places such a people in a natural state of war with all others, which is quite harmful to its own security.

Thus there remains the religion of man or Christianity (not that of today, but that of the Gospel, which is completely different). Through this holy, sublime, true religion, men, in being the children of the same God, all acknowledge one another as brothers, and the society that unites them is not dissolved even at death.

But since this religion has no particular relation to the body politic, it leaves laws with only the force the laws derive from themselves, without adding any other force to them. And thus one of the great bonds of a particular society remains ineffectual. Moreover, far from attaching the hearts of the citizens to the state, it detaches them from it as from all the other earthly things. I know of nothing more contrary to the social spirit.

We are told that a people of true Christians would form the most perfect society imaginable. I see but one major difficulty in this assumption, namely that a society of true Christians would no longer be a society of men.

I even say that this supposed society would not, for all its perfection, be the strongest or the most durable. By dint of being perfect, it would lack a bond of union; its destructive vice would be in its very perfection.

Each man would fulfill his duty; the people would be subject to the laws; the leaders would be just and moderate, the magistrates would be upright and incorruptible; soldiers would scorn death; there would be neither vanity nor luxury. All of this is very fine, but let us look further.

Christianity is a completely spiritual religion, concerned exclusively with things heavenly. The homeland of the Christian is not of this world. He does his duty, it is true, but he does it with a profound indifference toward the success or failure of his efforts. So long as he has nothing to reproach himself for, it matters little to him whether anything is going well or poorly down here. If the state is flourishing, he hardly dares to enjoy the public felicity, for fear of becoming puffed up with his country's glory. If the state is in decline, he blesses the hand of God that weighs heavily on his people.

For the society to be peaceful and for harmony to be maintained, every citizen without exception would have to be an equally good Christian. But if, unhappily, there is a single ambitious man, a single hypocrite, a Cataline, for example, or a Cromwell, he would quite undoubtedly gain the upper hand on his pious compatriots. Christian charity does not readily allow one to think ill of his neighbors. Once he has discovered by some ruse the art of deceiving them and of laying hold of a part of the public authority, behold a man established in dignity! God wills that he be respected. Soon, behold a power! God wills that he be obeyed. Does the trustee of his power abuse it? He is the rod with which God punishes his children. It would be against one's conscience to expel the usurper. It would be necessary to disturb the public tranquillity, use violence and shed blood. All this accords ill with the meekness of a Christian. And after all, what difference does it make whether one is a free man or a serf in this vale of tears? The essential thing is getting to heaven, and resignation is but another means to that end.

What if a foreign war breaks out? The citizens march without reservation into combat; none among them dreams of deserting. They do their duty, but without passion for victory; they know how to die better than how to be victorious. What difference does it make whether they are the victors or the vanquished? Does not providence know better than they what they need? Just imagine the advantage a fierce, impetuous and passionate enemy could draw from their stoicism! Set them face to face with those generous peoples who were devoured by an ardent love of glory and homeland. Suppose your Christian republic is face to face with Sparta or Rome. The pious Christians will be beaten, crushed and destroyed before they realize where they are, or else they will owe their safety only to the scorn their enemies will conceive for them. To my way of thinking, the oath taken by Fabius' soldiers was a fine one. They did not swear to die or to win; they swore to return victorious. And they kept their promise. Christians would never have taken such an oath; they would have believed they were tempting God.

But I am deceiving myself in talking about a Christian republic; these terms are mutually exclusive. Christianity preaches only servitude and dependence. Its spirit is too favorable to tyranny for tyranny not to take advantage of it at all times. True Christians are made to be slaves. They know it and are hardly moved by this. This brief life has too little value in their eyes.

Christian troops, we are told, are excellent. I deny this. Is someone going to show me some? For my part, I do not know of any Christian troops. Someone will mention the crusades. Without disputing the valor of the crusaders, I will point out that quite far from being Christians, they were soldiers of the priest; they were citizens of the church; they were fighting for its spiritual country which the church, God knows how, had made temporal. Properly understood, this is a throwback to paganism. Since the Gospel does not establish a national religion, no holy war is possible among Christians.

Under the pagan emperors, Christian soldiers were brave. All the Christian authors affirm this, and I believe it. This was a competition for honor against the pagan troops. Once the emperors were Christians, this competition ceased. And when the cross expelled the eagle, all Roman valor disappeared.

But leaving aside political considerations, let us return to right and determine the principles that govern this important point. The right which the social compact gives the sovereign over the subjects does not, as I have said, go beyond the limits of public utility.[51] The subjects, therefore, do not have to account to the sovereign for their opinions, except to the extent that these opinions are of importance to the community. For it is of great importance to the state that each citizen have a religion that causes him to love his duties. But the dogmas of that religion are of no interest either to the state or its members, except to the extent that these dogmas relate to morality and to the duties which the one who professes them is bound to fulfill toward others. Each man can have in addition such opinions as he pleases, without it being any of the sovereign's business to know what they are. For since the other world is outside the province of the sovereign, whatever the fate of subjects in the life to come, it is none of its business, so long as they are good citizens in this life.

There is, therefore, a purely civil profession of faith, the articles of which it belongs to the sovereign to establish, not exactly as dogmas of religion, but as sentiments of sociability, without which it is impossible to be a good citizen or a faithful subject.[52] While not having the ability to obligate anyone to believe them, the sovereign can banish from the state anyone who does not believe them. It can banish him not for being impious but for being unsociable, for being incapable of sincerely loving the laws and justice, and of sacrificing his life, if necessary, for his duty. If, after having publicly acknowledged these same dogmas, a person acts as if he does not believe them, he should be put to death; he has committed the greatest of crimes: he has lied before the laws.

The dogmas of the civil religion ought to be simple, few in number, precisely worded, without explanations or commentaries. The existence of a powerful, intelligent, beneficent divinity that foresees and provides; the life to come; the happiness

51. *In the Republic,* says the Marquis d'Argenson, *each man is perfectly free with respect to what does not harm others.* This is the invariable boundary. It cannot be expressed more precisely. I have been unable to deny myself the pleasure of occasionally citing this manuscript, even though it is unknown to the public, in order to pay homage to the memory of a famous and noteworthy man, who, even as a minister, retained the heart of a citizen, along with just and sound opinions on the government of his country.

52. By pleading for Cataline, Caesar tried to establish the dogma of the mortality of the soul. To refute him, Cato and Cicero did not waste time philosophizing. They contented themselves with showing that Caesar spoke like a bad citizen and advanced a doctrine that was injurious to the state. In fact, this was what the Roman senate had to judge, and not a question of theology.

of the just; the punishment of the wicked; the sanctity of the social contract and of the laws. These are the positive dogmas. As for the negative dogmas, I am limiting them to just one, namely intolerance. It is part of the cults we have excluded.

Those who distinguish between civil and theological intolerance are mistaken, in my opinion. Those two types of intolerance are inseparable. It is impossible to live in peace with those one believes to be damned. To love them would be to hate God who punishes them. It is absolutely necessary either to reclaim them or torment them. Whenever theological intolerance is allowed, it is impossible for it not to have some civil effect;[53] and once it does, the sovereign no longer is sovereign, not even over temporal affairs. Thenceforward, priests are the true masters; kings are simply their officers.

Now that there no longer is and never again can be an exclusive national religion, tolerance should be shown to all those that tolerate others, so long as their dogmas contain nothing contrary to the duties of a citizen. But whoever dares to say *outside the church there is no salvation* ought to be expelled from the state, unless the state is the church and the prince is the pontiff. Such a dogma is good only in a theocratic government; in all other forms of government it is ruinous. The reason why Henry IV is said to have embraced the Roman religion should make every decent man, and above all any prince who knows how to reason, leave it.

CHAPTER IX

Conclusion

After laying down the true principles of political right and attempting to establish the state on this basis, it remains to support the state by means of its external relations, which would include the laws of nations, commerce, the right of war and conquest, public law, leagues, negotiations, treaties, and so on. But all that forms a new subject which is too vast for my nearsightedness. I should always set my sights on things that are nearer at hand to me.

END

53. Marriage, for example, being a civil contract, has civil effects without which it is impossible for a society even to subsist. Suppose then that a clergy reaches the point where it ascribes to itself alone the right to permit this act (a right that must necessarily be usurped in every intolerant religion). In that case, is it not clear that in establishing the authority of the church in this matter, it will render ineffectual that of the prince, who will have no more subjects than those whom the clergy wishes to give him? Is it not also clear that the clergy—if master of whether to marry or not to marry people according to whether or not they accept this or that doctrine, according to whether they accept or reject this or that formula, according to whether they are more or less devout—in behaving prudently and holding firm, will alone dispose of inheritance, offices, the citizens, the state itself, which could not subsist, if composed solely of bastards? But, it will be said, abuses will be appealed; summonses and decrees will be issued; temporal holdings will be seized. What a pity! If it has a little—I will not say courage—but good sense, the clergy will serenely allow the appeals, the summonses, the decrees and the seizures, and it will end up master. It is not, it seems to me, a big sacrifice to abandon a part when one is sure of securing the whole.

IMMANUEL KANT

By 1784, the movement known as the Enlightenment was virtually dead in Germany. The Leibniz-Wolffian rationalism of earlier decades would not survive the century. Moses Mendelssohn, its clearest expositor, would die in 1785, embroiled in debate about the Spinozism of his friend Gotthold Ephraim Lessing. Yet, in 1784, Mendelssohn published in the *Berlinische Monatsschrift* an essay in which he answered the question: "What is Enlightenment?" In the next issue, another answer to the same question was published by Mendelssohn's younger contemporary and associate Immanuel Kant (1724–1804), and yet while Kant's answer clearly underlines the themes of the period, it is written by a philosopher whose work and whose thinking had already superseded it. To be sure, Kant would never abandon the themes of rationality and freedom; they are the core of his thinking. But in 1781 he had already published a work that dramatically altered the terms of discussion. Kant and the German Romantics—Johann Gottfried Herder, Johann Georg Hamann, Novalis, and others—set the Enlightenment and dogmatic rationalism to rest in the 1780s and 1790s, and yet in 1784 Kant's differences with the past were perhaps hard to discern.

Kant lived all of his life in or near Königsberg, in East Prussia, where he was born on April 22, 1724. His father was a harnessmaker; the family were devoted Pietists, committed to moral conduct and inner purity as the primary modes of religious worship. In his youth Kant learned to dislike the trappings of religious ritual and formality. In 1750 he enrolled at the University of Königsberg, where he studied with Martin Knutzen, a Leibniz-Wolffian who introduced him to mathematics, physics, and astronomy, as well as logic and metaphysics. After leaving the university, Kant served as a private tutor and returned to town in 1754, when he published the *Universal Natural History and Theory of the Heavens*. It was an attempt, now considered original, to apply Newtonian physics and its principles to the problem of the generation of the solar system.

By 1755 Kant was qualified as a *Privatdozent* (lecturer) at the university, where he lectured on mathematics, philosophy, scientific subjects, and much more. Until this time Newton and the new science, along with the current rationalist philosophy, were the major influences on Kant. In 1762, however, another powerful influence was added to them. When Kant received his copy of Rousseau's *Émile*, for two days he interrupted his rigorous routine of afternoon walks in order to finish reading the book. It was Rousseau who taught him "to honor man" and to make the cultural and political defense of human dignity his primary task. In the same year Kant submitted an essay to the Berlin Academy on the subject whether the principles of natural theology and morality can be proven like those of geometry. Although Mendelssohn's essay won the prize, both were published together in 1764.

In 1770 the University of Königsberg appointed Kant Professor of Logic and Metaphysics, and Kant delivered his Inaugural Dissertation, in which he first adumbrated the "critical" philosophy that would shape the remainder of his career. The following decade Kant published nothing. He was deep at work on his classic, the *Critique of Pure Reason*, which would appear in 1781. This was followed by a flood of publications: the *Prolegomena to Any Future Metaphysics*, the revisions of the First Critique in 1787, the *Critique of Practical Reason* in 1787, the *Critique of Judgment* in 1790, and the *Grounding for the Metaphysics of Morals* in 1785. In this last, extraordinary work, Kant presented his defense of rational morality, of autonomy, and of human dignity in a book that is one of the classic texts of Western moral philosophy.

During these years Kant's life was filled with teaching, writing, conversation, and occasional public controversy. In his public writings and discussions, he defended the rule of law, argued against the right of rebellion, and yet praised the French Revolution. In 1793 Kant published *Religion within the Limits of Reason Alone* and with this strange and difficult work drew the severe censure of Frederick William II and his royal cabinet. Kant was forbidden to write or lecture on any religious subject. He weighed the dilemma, to heed his sovereign or to acknowledge his deepest convictions, and on October 12, 1794, Kant chose to submit as an obedient subject. It was an act that generated widespread criticism.

In 1795 Kant published *Perpetual Peace*, his first work after the ban and his defense of an international league of nations. The book was especially praised in France; in it Kant gives fullest expression to his political views. In 1797 he chose no longer to lecture but continued to write until his death, on February 12, 1804. Heine once said that no one could write a life of Kant because Kant had no life. This is a harsh judgment. Having read Plato since 1768, Kant had assimilated the Socratic commitment to truth. His life was a quest for it, and hence to write the tale of that life would be to write the story of his thought, a story of reason, freedom, and human dignity.

Kant's critical philosophy is a watershed in modern metaphysics, epistemology, and moral theory. His goal was to acknowledge the supremacy of science, to revise the role of metaphysics, and yet to ground morality in rationality. All subsequent Western philosophy and moral theory is indebted to his work and to the strategies which he employed for confronting the challenges of science, philosophy, ethics, and religion in the modern world.

Recommended readings

Allison, Henry. *Kant's Theory of Freedom*. Cambridge: Cambridge University Press, 1990.

Arendt, Hannah. *Lectures on Kant's Political Philosophy*. Chicago: University of Chicago Press, 1982.

Beck, Lewis White. *A Commentary on Kant's Critique of Practical Reason*. Chicago: University of Chicago Press, 1960.

Booth, James. *Interpreting the World: Kant's Philosophy of History and Politics*. Toronto: University of Toronto Press, 1987.

O'Neill, Onora. *Acting on Principle*. New York: Columbia University Press, 1975.

O'Neill, Onora. *Constructions of Reason: Explorations of Kant's Practical Philosophy.* Cambridge: Cambridge University Press, 1989.

Paton, H. J. *The Categorical Imperative.* 3rd ed. London: Hutcheson, 1958.

Reiss, Hans (ed.). *Kant's Political Writings.* Cambridge: Cambridge University Press, 1970.

Wolf, Robert Paul. *The Autonomy of Reason.* New York: Harper & Row, 1973.

Wolf, Robert Paul. *In Defense of Anarchism.* New York: Harper & Row, 1970.

Wolf, Robert Paul (ed.). *Kant.* Garden City: Doubleday, 1967.

Wolf, Robert Paul (ed.). *Kant's Foundation and Critical Essays.* Indianapolis: Bobbs-Merrill, 1969.

Wood, Alan. *Kant's Moral Religion.* Ithaca: Cornell University Press, 1970.

Yovel, Y. *Kant and the Philosophy of History.* Princeton: Princeton University Press, 1968.

GROUNDING
FOR THE
METAPHYSICS OF MORALS

PREFACE

Ancient Greek philosophy was divided into three sciences: physics, ethics, and logic. This division is perfectly suitable to the nature of the subject, and the only improvement that can be made in it is perhaps only to supply its principle so that there will be a possibility on the one hand of insuring its completeness and on the other of correctly determining its necessary subdivisions.

All rational knowledge is either material and concerned with some object, or formal and concerned only with the form of understanding and of reason themselves and with the universal rules of thought in general without regard to differences of its objects. Formal philosophy is called logic. Material philosophy, however, has to do with determinate objects and with the laws to which these objects are subject; and such philosophy is divided into two parts, because these laws are either laws of nature or laws of freedom. The science of the former is called physics, while that of the latter is called ethics; they are also called doctrine of nature and doctrine of morals respectively.

Logic cannot have any empirical part, i.e., a part in which the universal and necessary laws of thought would be based on grounds taken from experience; for in that case it would not be logic, i.e., a canon for understanding and reason, which is valid for all thinking and which has to be demonstrated.[1] Natural and moral philosophy, on the contrary, can each have an empirical part. The former has to because it must determine the laws of nature as an object of experience, and the latter because it must determine the will of man insofar as the will is affected by nature. The laws of the former are those according to which everything does happen, while the laws of the latter are those according to which everything ought to happen, although these moral laws also consider the conditions under which what ought to happen frequently does not.

All philosophy insofar as it is founded on experience may be called empirical, while that which sets forth its doctrines as founded entirely on a priori principles may be called pure. The latter, when merely formal, is called logic; but when limited to determinate objects of the understanding, it is called metaphysics.

Reprinted by permission of the translator, James W. Ellington, from Kant, *Grounding for the Metaphysics of Morals* (Indianapolis, Hackett Publishing Company, 1981).

---

1. [Kant's *Logic* was first published in 1800 in a version edited by Gottlob Benjamin Jäsche, who was one of Kant's students. —J.W.E.]

In this way there arises the idea of a twofold metaphysics: a metaphysics of nature and a metaphysics of morals.[2] Physics will thus have its empirical part, but also a rational one. Ethics will too, though here the empirical part might more specifically be called practical anthropology,[3] while the rational part might properly be called morals.

All industries, crafts, and arts have gained by the division of labor, viz., one man does not do everything, but each confines himself to a certain kind of work that is distinguished from all other kinds by the treatment it requires, so that the work may be done with the highest perfection and with greater ease. Where work is not so distinguished and divided, where everyone is a jack of all trades, there industry remains sunk in the greatest barbarism. Whether or not pure philosophy in all its parts requires its own special man might well be in itself a subject worthy of consideration. Would not the whole of this learned industry be better off if those who are accustomed, as the public taste demands, to purvey a mixture of the empirical with the rational in all sorts of proportions unknown even to themselves and who style themselves independent thinkers, while giving the name of hair-splitters to those who apply themselves to the purely rational part, were to be given warning about pursuing simultaneously two jobs which are quite different in their technique, and each of which perhaps requires a special talent that when combined with the other talent produces nothing but bungling? But I only ask here whether the nature of science does not require that the empirical part always be carefully separated from the rational part. Should not physics proper (i.e., empirical physics) be preceded by a metaphysics of nature, and practical anthropology by a metaphysics of morals? Both

389   of these metaphysics must be carefully purified of everything empirical in order to know how much pure reason can accomplish in each case and from what sources it draws its a priori teaching, whether such teaching be conducted by all moralists (whose name is legion) or only by some who feel a calling thereto.

Since I am here primarily concerned with moral philosophy, the foregoing question will be limited to a consideration of whether or not there is the utmost necessity for working out for once a pure moral philosophy that is wholly cleared of everything which can only be empirical and can only belong to anthropology. That there must be such a philosophy is evident from the common idea of duty and of moral laws. Everyone must admit that if a law is to be morally valid, i.e., is to be valid as a ground of obligation, then it must carry with it absolute necessity. He must admit that the command, "Thou shalt not lie," does not hold only for men, as if other rational beings had no need to abide by it, and so with all the other moral laws properly so called; and he must concede that the ground of obligation here must therefore be sought not in the nature of man nor in the circumstances of the world in which man is placed, but must be sought a priori solely in the concepts of pure reason; he must grant that every other precept which is founded on principles of mere experience — even a precept that may in certain respects be universal — insofar as it rests in the least on empirical grounds — perhaps only in its motive — can indeed be called a practical rule, but never a moral law.

Thus not only are moral laws together with their principles essentially different from every kind of practical cognition in which there is anything empirical, but all

2. [*The Metaphysical Foundations of Natural Science* was published in 1786. *The Metaphysics of Morals* appeared in 1797.]

3. [*Anthropology from a Pragmatic Point of View* first appeared in 1798.]

moral philosophy rests entirely on its pure part. When applied to man, it does not in the least borrow from acquaintance with him (anthropology) but gives a priori laws to him as a rational being. To be sure, these laws require, furthermore, a power of judgment sharpened by experience, partly in order to distinguish in what cases they are applicable, and partly to gain for them access to the human will as well as influence for putting them into practice. For man is affected by so many inclinations that, even though he is indeed capable of the idea of a pure practical reason, he is not so easily able to make that idea effective *in concreto* in the conduct of his life.

A metaphysics of morals is thus indispensably necessary, not merely because of motives of speculation regarding the source of practical principles which are present a priori in our reason, but because morals themselves are liable to all kinds of corruption as long as the guide and supreme norm for correctly estimating them are missing. For in the case of what is to be morally good, that it conforms to the moral law is not enough; it must also be done for the sake of the moral law. Otherwise that conformity is only very contingent and uncertain, since the non-moral ground may now and then produce actions that conform with the law but quite often produces actions that are contrary to the law. Now the moral law in its purity and genuineness (which is of the utmost concern in the practical realm) can be sought nowhere but in a pure philosophy. Therefore, pure philosophy (metaphysics) must precede; without it there can be no moral philosophy at all. That philosophy which mixes pure principles with empirical ones does not deserve the name of philosophy (for philosophy is distinguished from ordinary rational knowledge by its treatments in a separate science of what the latter comprehends only confusedly). Still less does it deserve the name of moral philosophy, since by this very confusion it spoils even the purity of morals and counteracts its own ends.

390

There must be no thought that what is required here is already contained in the propaedeutic that precedes the celebrated Wolff's moral philosophy, i.e., in what he calls *Universal Practical Philosophy*,[4] and that hence there is no need to break entirely new ground. Just because his work was to be a universal practical philosophy, it has not taken into consideration any special kind of will, such as one determined solely by a priori principles without any empirical motives and which could be called a pure will, but has considered volition in general, together with all the actions and conditions belonging to it under this general signification. And thereby does his propaedeutic differ from a metaphysics of morals in the same way that general logic, which expounds the acts and rules of thinking in general, differs from transcendental philosophy, which treats merely of the particular acts and rules of pure thinking, i.e., of that thinking whereby objects are cognized completely a priori. For the metaphysics of morals has to investigate the idea and principles of a possible pure will and not the actions and conditions of human volition as such, which are for the most part drawn from psychology. Moral laws and duty are discussed in this universal practical philosophy (though quite improperly), but this is no objection to what has been said about such philosophy. For the authors of this science remain true to their idea of it on the following point also: they do not distinguish the motives which, as such, are presented completely a priori by reason alone and are properly moral, from the empirical motives which the understanding raises to general concepts merely by the comparison of experiences. Rather, they consider motives irrespective of any dif-

391

4. [This work of Christian Wolff was published in 1738–39; this and other of his works served for many years as the standard philosophy textbooks in German universities. Wolff's philosophy was founded on that of Leibniz.]

ference in their source; and inasmuch as they regard all motives as being homogeneous, they consider nothing but their relative strength or weakness. In this way they frame their concept of obligation, which is certainly not moral, but is all that can be expected from a philosophy which never decides regarding the origin of all possible practical concepts whether they are a priori or merely a posteriori.

I intend some day to publish a metaphysics of morals,[5] but as a preliminary to that I now issue this *Grounding* [1785]. Indeed there is properly no other foundation for such a metaphysics than a critical examination of pure practical reason, just as there is properly no other foundation for a metaphysics [of nature] than the critical examination of pure speculative reason, which has already been published.[6] But, in the first place, the former critique is not so absolutely necessary as the latter one, because human reason can, even in the most ordinary mind, be easily brought in moral matters to a high degree of correctness and precision, while on the other hand in its theoretical but pure use it is wholly dialectical. In the second place, if a critical examination of pure practical reason is to be complete, then there must, in my view, be the possibility at the same time of showing the unity of practical and speculative reason in a common principle; for in the final analysis there can be only one and the same reason, which is to be differentiated solely in its application. But there is no possibility here of bringing my work to such completeness, without introducing considerations of an entirely different kind and without thereby confusing the reader. Instead of calling the present work a *Critique of Pure Practical Reason*, I have, therefore, adopted the title *Grounding for the Metaphysics of Morals* [*Grundlegung zur Metaphysik der Sitten.*][7]

But, in the third place, since a metaphysics of morals, despite the forbidding title, is nevertheless capable of a high degree of popularity and adaptation to the ordinary understanding, I find it useful to separate from the aforementioned metaphysics this preliminary work on its foundation [*Grundlage*] in order later to have no need to introduce unavoidable subtleties into doctrines that are easier to grasp.

392

The present *Grounding* [*Grundlegung*] is, however, intended for nothing more than seeking out and establishing the supreme principle of morality. This constitutes by itself a task which is complete in its purpose and should be kept separate from every other moral inquiry. The application of this supreme principle to the whole ethical system would, to be sure, shed much light on my conclusions regarding this central question, which is important but has not heretofore been at all satisfactorily discussed; and the adequacy manifested by the principle throughout such application would provide strong confirmation for the principle. Nevertheless, I must forego this advantage, which after all would be more gratifying for myself than helpful for others, since ease of use and apparent adequacy of a principle do not provide any certain proof of its soundness, but do awaken, rather, a certain bias which prevents any rigorous examination and estimation of it for itself, without any regard to its consequences.

5. [This appeared in 1797.]

6. [The first edition of the *Critique of Pure Reason* appeared in 1781, while the second edition appeared in 1787. The *Critique of Practical Reason* was published in 1788.]

7. [This might be translated as *Laying the Foundation for the Metaphysics of Morals.* But for the sake of brevity *Grounding for the Metaphysics of Morals* has been chosen.]

The method adopted in this work is, I believe, one that is most suitable if we proceed analytically from ordinary knowledge to a determination of the supreme principle and then back again synthetically from an examination of this principle and its sources to ordinary knowledge where its application is found. Therefore, the division turns out to be the following:

1. *First Section*. Transition from the Ordinary Rational Knowledge of Morality to the Philosophical.
2. *Second Section*. Transition from Popular Moral Philosophy to a Metaphysics of Morals.
3. *Third Section*. Final Step from a Metaphysics of Morals to a Critique of Pure Practical Reason.

FIRST SECTION

393

*Transition from the Ordinary Rational Knowledge
of Morality to the Philosophical*

There is no possibility of thinking of anything at all in the world, or even out of it, which can be regarded as good without qualification, except a *good will*. Intelligence, wit, judgment, and whatever talents of the mind one might want to name are doubtless in many respects good and desirable, as are such qualities of temperament as courage, resolution, perseverance. But they can also become extremely bad and harmful if the will, which is to make use of these gifts of nature and which in its special constitution is called character, is not good. The same holds with gifts of fortune; power, riches, honor, even health, and that complete well-being and contentment with one's condition which is called happiness make for pride and often hereby even arrogance, unless there is a good will to correct their influence on the mind and herewith also to rectify the whole principle of action and make it universally conformable to its end. The sight of a being who is not graced by any touch of a pure and good will but who yet enjoys an uninterrupted prosperity can never delight a rational and impartial spectator. Thus a good will seems to constitute the indispensable condition of being even worthy of happiness.

Some qualities are even conducive to this good will itself and can facilitate its work. Nevertheless, they have no intrinsic unconditional worth; but they always presuppose, rather, a good will, which restricts the high esteem in which they are otherwise rightly held, and does not permit them to be regarded as absolutely good. Moderation in emotions and passions, self-control, and calm deliberation are not only good in many respects but even seem to constitute part of the intrinsic worth of a person. But they are far from being rightly called good without qualification (however unconditionally they were commended by the ancients). For without the principles of a good will, they can become extremely bad; the coolness of a villain makes him not only much more dangerous but also immediately more abominable in our eyes than he would have been regarded by us without it.

394

A good will is good not because of what it effects or accomplishes, nor because of its fitness to attain some proposed end; it is good only through its willing, i.e., it is good in itself. When it is considered in itself, then it is to be esteemed very much higher than anything which it might ever bring about merely in order to favor some inclination, or even the sum total of all inclinations. Even if, by some especially unfortunate fate or by the niggardly provision of stepmotherly nature, this will should be wholly lacking in the power to accomplish its purpose; if with the greatest effort it should yet achieve nothing, and only the good will should remain (not, to be sure, as a mere wish but as the summoning of all the means in our power), yet would it, like a jewel, still shine by its own light as something which has its full value in itself. Its usefulness or fruitlessness can neither augment nor diminish this value. Its usefulness would be, as it were, only the setting to enable us to handle it in ordinary dealings or to attract to it the attention of those who are not yet experts, but not to recommend it to real experts or to determine its value.

But there is something so strange in this idea of the absolute value of a mere will, in which no account is taken of any useful results, that in spite of all the agreement received even from ordinary reason, yet there must arise the suspicion that such an idea may perhaps have as its hidden basis merely some high-flown fancy, and that we may have misunderstood the purpose of nature in assigning to reason the governing 395 of our will. Therefore, this idea will be examined from this point of view.

In the natural constitution of an organized being, i.e., one suitably adapted to the purpose of life, let there be taken as a principle that in such a being no organ is to be found for any end unless it be the most fit and the best adapted for that end. Now if that being's preservation, welfare, or in a word its happiness, were the real end of nature in the case of a being having reason and will, then nature would have hit upon a very poor arrangement in having the reason of the creature carry out this purpose. For all the actions which such a creature has to perform with this purpose in view, and the whole rule of his conduct would have been prescribed much more exactly by instinct; and the purpose in question could have been attained much more certainly by instinct than it ever can be by reason. And if in addition reason had been imparted to this favored creature, then it would have had to serve him only to contemplate the happy constitution of his nature, to admire that nature, to rejoice in it, and to feel grateful to the cause that bestowed it; but reason would not have served him to subject his faculty of desire to its weak and delusive guidance nor would it have served him to meddle incompetently with the purpose of nature. In a word, nature would have taken care that reason did not strike out into a practical use nor presume, with its weak insight, to think out for itself a plan for happiness and the means for attaining it. Nature would have taken upon herself not only the choice of ends but also that of the means, and would with wise foresight have entrusted both to instinct alone.

And, in fact, we find that the more a cultivated reason devotes itself to the aim of enjoying life and happiness, the further does man get away from true contentment. Because of this there arises in many persons, if only they are candid enough to admit it, a certain degree of misology, i.e., hatred of reason. This is especially so in the case of those who are the most experienced in the use of reason, because after calculating all the advantages they derive, I say not from the invention of all the arts of common luxury, but even from the sciences (which in the end seem to them to be also a luxury of the understanding), they yet find that they have in fact only brought more trouble 396 on their heads than they have gained in happiness. Therefore, they come to envy, rather than despise, the more common run of men who are closer to the guidance of mere natural instinct and who do not allow their reason much influence on their conduct. And we must admit that the judgment of those who would temper, or even reduce below zero, the boastful eulogies on behalf of the advantages which reason is supposed to provide as regards the happiness and contentment of life is by no means morose or ungrateful to the goodness with which the world is governed. There lies at the root of such judgments, rather, the idea that existence has another and much more worthy purpose, for which, and not for happiness, reason is quite properly intended, and which must, therefore, be regarded as the supreme condition to which the private purpose of men must, for the most part, defer.

Reason, however, is not competent enough to guide the will safely as regards its objects and the satisfaction of all our needs (which it in part even multiplies); to this end would an implanted natural instinct have led much more certainly. But inasmuch as reason has been imparted to us as a practical faculty, i.e., as one which is to have influence on the will, its true function must be to produce a will which is not merely good as a means to some further end, but is good in itself. To produce a will good in itself reason was absolutely necessary, inasmuch as nature in distributing her capacities has everywhere gone to work in a purposive manner. While such a will may not indeed be the sole and complete good, it must, nevertheless, be the highest good and the condition of all the rest, even of the desire for happiness. In this case there is nothing inconsistent with the wisdom of nature that the cultivation of reason, which is requisite for the first and unconditioned purpose, may in many ways restrict, at least in this life, the attainment of the second purpose, viz., happiness, which is always conditioned. Indeed happiness can even be reduced to less than nothing, without nature's failing thereby in her purpose; for reason recognizes as its highest practical function the establishment of a good will, whereby in the attainment of this end reason is capable only of its own kind of satisfaction, viz., that of fulfilling a purpose which is in turn determined only by reason, even though such fulfilment should often interfere with the purposes of inclination.

The concept of a will estimable in itself and good without regard to any further end   397
must now be developed. This concept already dwells in the natural sound understanding and needs not so much to be taught as merely to be elucidated. It always holds first place in estimating the total worth of our actions and constitutes the condition of all the rest. Therefore, we shall take up the concept of *duty*, which includes that of a good will, though with certain subjective restrictions and hindrances, which far from hiding a good will or rendering it unrecognizable, rather bring it out by contrast and make it shine forth more brightly.

I here omit all actions already recognized as contrary to duty, even though they may be useful for this or that end; for in the case of these the question does not arise at all as to whether they might be done from duty, since they even conflict with duty. I also set aside those actions which are really in accordance with duty, yet to which men have no immediate inclination, but perform them because they are impelled thereto by some other inclination. For in this [second] case to decide whether the action which is in accord with duty has been done from duty or from some selfish purpose is easy. This difference is far more difficult to note in the [third] case where the action accords with duty and the subject has in addition an immediate inclination to do the action. For example,[1] that a dealer should not overcharge an inexperienced purchaser certainly accords with duty; and where there is much commerce, the prudent merchant does not overcharge but keeps to a fixed price for everyone in general, so that a child may buy from him just as well as everyone else may. Thus customers are honestly served, but this is not nearly enough for making us believe that the merchant has acted this way from duty and from principles of honesty; his own advantage

---

1. [The ensuing example provides an illustration of the second case.]

required him to do it. He cannot, however, be assumed to have in addition [as in the third case] an immediate inclination toward his buyers, causing him, as it were, out of love to give no one as far as price is concerned any advantage over another. Hence the action was done neither from duty nor from immediate inclination, but merely for a selfish purpose.

398

On the other hand,[2] to preserve one's life is a duty; and, furthermore, everyone has also an immediate inclination to do so. But on this account the often anxious care taken by most men for it has no intrinsic worth, and the maxim of their action has no moral content. They preserve their lives, to be sure, in accordance with duty, but not from duty. On the other hand,[3] if adversity and hopeless sorrow have completely taken away the taste for life, if an unfortunate man, strong in soul and more indignant at his fate than despondent or dejected, wishes for death and yet preserves his life without loving it — not from inclination or fear, but from duty — then his maxim indeed has a moral content.[4]

To be beneficent where one can is a duty; and besides this, there are many persons who are so sympathetically constituted that, without any further motive of vanity or self-interest, they find an inner pleasure in spreading joy around them and can rejoice in the satisfaction of others as their own work. But I maintain that in such a case an action of this kind, however dutiful and amiable it may be, has nevertheless no true moral worth.[5] It is on a level with such actions as arise from other inclinations, e.g., the inclination for honor, which if fortunately directed to what is in fact beneficial and accords with duty and is thus honorable, deserves praise and encouragement, but not esteem; for its maxim lacks the moral content of an action done not from inclina-

2. [This next example illustrates the third case.]

3. [The ensuing example illustrates the fourth case.]

4. [Four different cases have been distinguished in the two foregoing paragraphs. Case 1 involves those actions which are contrary to duty (lying, cheating, stealing, etc.). Case 2 involves those which accord with duty but for which a person perhaps has no immediate inclination, though he does have a mediate inclination thereto (one pays his taxes not because he likes to but in order to avoid the penalties set for delinquents, one treats his fellows well not because he really likes them but because he wants their votes when at some future time he runs for public office, etc.). A vast number of so-called "morally good" actions actually belong to this case 2 — they accord with duty because of self-seeking inclinations. Case 3 involves those which accord with duty and for which a person does have an immediate inclination (one does not commit suicide because all is going well with him, one does not commit adultery because he considers his wife to be the most desirable creature in the whole world, etc.). Case 4 involves those actions which accord with duty but are contrary to some immediate inclination (one does not commit suicide even when he is in dire distress, one does not commit adultery even though his wife has turned out to be an impossible shrew, etc.). Now case 4 is the crucial test case of the will's possible goodness — but Kant does not claim that one should lead his life in such a way as to encounter as many such cases as possible in order constantly to test his virtue (deliberately marry a shrew so as to be able to resist the temptation to commit adultery). Life itself forces enough such cases upon a person without his seeking them out. But when there is a conflict between duty and inclination, duty should always be followed. Case 3 makes for the easiest living and the greatest contentment, and anyone would wish that life might present him with far more of these cases than with cases 2 or 4. But yet one should not arrange his life in such a way as to avoid case 4 at all costs and to seek out case 3 as much as possible (become a recluse so as to avoid the possible rough and tumble involved with frequent association with one's fellows, avoid places where one might encounter the sick and the poor so as to spare oneself the pangs of sympathy and the need to exercise the virtue of benefiting those in distress, etc.). For the purpose of philosophical analysis Kant emphasizes case 4 as being the test case of the will's possible goodness, but he is not thereby advocating puritanism.]

5. [This is an example of case 3.]

tion but from duty. Suppose then the mind of this friend of mankind to be clouded over with his own sorrow so that all sympathy with the lot of others is extinguished, and suppose him still to have the power to benefit others in distress, even though he is not touched by their trouble because he is sufficiently absorbed with his own; and now suppose that, even though no inclination moves him any longer, he nevertheless tears himself from this deadly insensibility and performs the action without any inclination at all, but solely from duty—then for the first time his action has genuine moral worth.[6] Further still, if nature has put little sympathy in this or that man's heart, if (while being an honest man in other respects) he is by temperament cold and indifferent to the sufferings of others, perhaps because as regards his own sufferings he is endowed with the special gift of patience and fortitude and expects or even requires that others should have the same; if such a man (who would truly not be nature's worst product) had not been exactly fashioned by her to be a philanthropist, would he not yet find in himself a source from which he might give himself a worth far higher than any that a good-natured temperament might have? By all means, because just here does the worth of the character come out; this worth is moral and incomparably the highest of all, viz., that he is beneficent, not from inclination, but from duty.[7]

399

To secure one's own happiness is a duty (at least indirectly); for discontent with one's condition under many pressing cares and amid unsatisfied wants might easily become a great temptation to transgress one's duties. But here also do men of themselves already have, irrespective of duty, the strongest and deepest inclination toward happiness, because just in this idea are all inclinations combined into a sum total.[8] But the precept of happiness is often so constituted as greatly to interfere with some inclinations, and yet men cannot form any definite and certain concept of the sum of satisfaction of all inclinations that is called happiness. Hence there is no wonder that a single inclination which is determinate both as to what it promises and as to the time within which it can be satisfied may outweigh a fluctuating idea; and there is no wonder that a man, e.g., a gouty patient, can choose to enjoy what he likes and to suffer what he may, since by his calculation he has here at least not sacrificed the enjoyment of the present moment to some possibly groundless expectations of the good fortune that is supposed to be found in health. But even in this case, if the universal inclination to happiness did not determine his will and if health, at least for him, did not figure as so necessary an element in his calculations; there still remains here, as in all other cases, a law, viz., that he should promote his happiness not from inclination but from duty, and thereby for the first time does his conduct have real moral worth.[9]

Undoubtedly in this way also are to be understood those passages of Scripture which command us to love our neighbor and even our enemy. For love as an inclination cannot be commanded; but beneficence from duty, when no inclination impels

6. [This is an example of case 4.]

7. [This is an even more extreme example of case 4.]

8. [This is an example of case 3.]

9. [This example is a weak form of case 4; the action accords with duty but is not contrary to some immediate inclination.]

us[10] and even when a natural and unconquerable aversion opposes such beneficence,[11] is practical, and not pathological, love. Such love resides in the will and not
in the propensities of feeling, in principles of action and not in tender sympathy; and
only this practical love can be commanded.

The second proposition[12] is this: An action done from duty has its moral worth, not
in the purpose that is to be attained by it, but in the maxim according to which the
action is determined. The moral worth depends, therefore, not on the realization of
400   the object of the action, but merely on the principle of volition according to which,
without regard to any objects of the faculty of desire, the action has been done. From
what has gone before it is clear that the purposes which we may have in our actions,
as well as their effects regarded as ends and incentives of the will, cannot give to actions any unconditioned and moral worth. Where, then, can this worth lie if it is not
to be found in the will's relation to the expected effect? Nowhere but in the principle
of the will, with no regard to the ends that can be brought about through such action.
For the will stands, as it were, at a crossroads between its a priori principle, which is
formal, and its a posteriori incentive, which is material; and since it must be determined by something, it must be determined by the formal principle of volition, if the
action is done from duty—and in that case every material principle is taken away
from it.

The third proposition, which follows from the other two, can be expressed thus:
Duty is the necessity of an action done out of respect for the law. I can indeed have an
inclination for an object as the effect of my proposed action; but I can never have
respect for such an object, just because it is merely an effect and is not an activity of
the will. Similarly, I can have no respect for inclination as such, whether my own or
that of another. I can at most, if my own inclination, approve it; and, if that of
another, even love it, i.e., consider it to be favorable to my own advantage. An object
of respect can only be what is connected with my will solely as ground and never as effect—something that does not serve my inclination but, rather, outweighs it, or at
least excludes it from consideration when some choice is made—in other words, only
the law itself can be an object of respect and hence can be a command. Now an action done from duty must altogether exclude the influence of inclination and
therewith every object of the will. Hence there is nothing left which can determine the
will except objectively the law and subjectively pure respect for this practical law, i.e.,
the will can be subjectively determined by the maxim[13] that I should follow such a law
401   even if all my inclinations are thereby thwarted.

Thus the moral worth of an action does not lie in the effect expected from it nor in
any principle of action that needs to borrow its motive from this expected effect. For
all these effects (agreeableness of one's condition and even the furtherance of other
people's happiness) could have been brought about also through other causes and
would not have required the will of a rational being, in which the highest and

10. [This is case 4 in its weak form.]

11. [This is case 4 in its strong form.]

12. [The first proposition of morality says that an action must be done from duty in order to have any
moral worth. It is implicit in the preceding examples but was never explicitly stated.]

13. A maxim is the subjective principle of volition. The objective principle (i.e., one which would serve
all rational beings also subjectively as a practical principle if reason had full control over the faculty of
desire) is the practical law. [See below Kant's footnote at Ak. 420-21.]

unconditioned good can alone be found. Therefore, the pre-eminent good which is called moral can consist in nothing but the representation of the law in itself, and such a representation can admittedly be found only in a rational being insofar as this representation, and not some expected effect, is the determining ground of the will. This good is already present in the person who acts according to this representation, and such good need not be awaited merely from the effect.[14]

But what sort of law can that be the thought of which must determine the will   402
without reference to any expected effect, so that the will can be called absolutely good without qualification? Since I have deprived the will of every impulse that might arise for it from obeying any particular law, there is nothing left to serve the will as principle except the universal conformity of its actions to law as such, i.e., I should never act except in such a way that I can also will that my maxim should become a universal law.[15] Here mere conformity to law as such (without having as its basis any law determining particular actions) serves the will as principle and must so serve it if duty is not to be a vain delusion and a chimerical concept. The ordinary reason of mankind in its practical judgments agrees completely with this, and always has in view the aforementioned principle.

For example, take this question. When I am in distress, may I make a promise with the intention of not keeping it? I readily distinguish here the two meanings which the question may have; whether making a false promise conforms with prudence or with duty. Doubtless the former can often be the case. Indeed I clearly see that escape from some present difficulty by means of such a promise is not enough. In addition I must carefully consider whether from this lie there may later arise far greater inconvenience for me than from what I now try to escape. Furthermore, the consequences of my false promise are not easy to forsee, even with all my supposed cunning; loss of confidence in me might prove to be far more disadvantageous than the misfortune which I now try to avoid. The more prudent way might be to act according to a universal maxim and to make it a habit not to promise anything without intending to keep it. But that such a maxim is, nevertheless, always based on nothing but a fear of consequences becomes clear to me at once. To be truthful from duty is, however, quite different from being truthful from fear of disadvantageous consequences; in the first case the concept of the action itself contains a law for me, while

---

14. There might be brought against me here an objection that I take refuge behind the word "respect" in an obscure feeling, instead of giving a clear answer to the question by means of a concept of reason. But even though respect is a feeling, it is not one received through any outside influence but is, rather, one that is self-produced by means of a rational concept; hence it is specifically different from all feelings of the first kind, which can all be reduced to inclination or fear. What I recognize immediately as a law for me, I recognize with respect; this means merely the consciousness of the subordination of my will to a law without the mediation of other influences upon my sense. The immediate determination of the will by the law, and the consciousness thereof, is called respect, which is hence regarded as the effect of the law upon the subject and not as the cause of the law. Respect is properly the representation of a worth that thwarts my self-love. Hence respect is something that is regarded as an object of neither inclination nor fear, although it has at the same time something analogous to both. The object of respect is, therefore, nothing but the law—indeed that very law which we impose on ourselves and yet recognize as necessary in itself. As law, we are subject to it without consulting self-love; as imposed on us by ourselves, it is a consequence of our will. In the former aspect, it is analogous to fear; in the latter, to inclination. All respect for a person is properly only respect for the law (of honesty, etc.) of which the person provides an example. Since we regard the development of our talents as a duty, we think of a man of talent as being also a kind of example of the law (the law of becoming like him by practice), and that is what constitutes our respect for him. All so-called moral interest consists solely in respect for the law.

15. [This is the first time in the *Grounding* that the categorical imperative is stated.]

in the second I must first look around elsewhere to see what are the results for me that might be connected with the action. For to deviate from the principle of duty is quite certainly bad; but to abandon my maxim of prudence can often be very advantageous for me, though to abide by it is certainly safer. The most direct and infallible way, however, to answer the question as to whether a lying promise accords with duty is to ask myself whether I would really be content if my maxim (of extricating myself from difficulty by means of a false promise) were to hold as a universal law for myself as well as for others, and could I really say to myself that everyone may promise falsely when he finds himself in a difficulty from which he can find no other way to extricate himself. Then I immediately become aware that I can indeed will the lie but can not at all will a universal law to lie. For by such a law there would really be no promises at all, since in vain would my willing future actions be professed to other people who would not believe what I professed, or if they over-hastily did believe, then they would pay me back in like coin. Therefore, my maxim would necessarily destroy itself just as soon as it was made a universal law.[16]

Therefore, I need no far-reaching acuteness to discern what I have to do in order that my will may be morally good. Inexperienced in the course of the world and incapable of being prepared for all its contingencies, I only ask myself whether I can also will that my maxim should become a universal law. If not, then the maxim must be rejected, not because of any disadvantage accruing to me or even to others, but because it cannot be fitting as a principle in a possible legislation of universal law, and reason exacts from me immediate respect for such legislation. Indeed I have as yet no insight into the grounds of such respect (which the philosopher may investigate). But I at least understand that respect is an estimation of a worth that far outweighs any worth of what is recommended by inclination, and that the necessity of acting from pure respect for the practical law is what constitutes duty, to which every other motive must give way because duty is the condition of a will good in itself, whose worth is above all else.

Thus within the moral cognition of ordinary human reason we have arrived at its principle. To be sure, such reason does not think of this principle abstractly in its universal form, but does always have it actually in view and does use it as the standard of judgment. It would here be easy to show how ordinary reason, with this compass in hand, is well able to distinguish, in every case that occurs, what is good or evil, in accord with duty or contrary to duty, if we do not in the least try to teach reason anything new but only make it attend, as Socrates did, to its own principle — and thereby do we show that neither science nor philosophy is needed in order to know what one must do to be honest and good, and even wise and virtuous. Indeed we might even have conjectured beforehand that cognizance of what every man is obligated to do, and hence also to know, would be available to every man, even the most ordinary. Yet we cannot but observe with admiration how great an advantage the power of practical judgment has over the theoretical in ordinary human understanding. In the theoretical, when ordinary reason ventures to depart from the laws of experience and the perceptions of sense, it falls into sheer inconceivabilities and self-contradictions, or at least into a chaos of uncertainty, obscurity, and instability. In the practical, however, the power of judgment first begins to show itself to advantage

16. [This means that when you tell a lie, you merely take exception to the general rule that says everyone should always tell the truth and believe that what you are saying is true. When you lie, you do not thereby will that everyone else lie and not believe that what you are saying is true, because in such a case your lie would never work to get you what you want.]

when ordinary understanding excludes all sensuous incentives from practical laws. Such understanding then becomes even subtle, whether in quibbling with its own conscience or with other claims regarding what is to be called right, or whether in wanting to determine correctly for its own instruction the worth of various actions. And the most extraordinary thing is that ordinary understanding in this practical case may have just as good a hope of hitting the mark as that which any philosopher may promise himself. Indeed it is almost more certain in this than even a philosopher is, because he can have no principle other than what ordinary understanding has, but he may easily confuse his judgment by a multitude of foreign and irrelevant considerations and thereby cause it to swerve from the right way. Would it not, therefore, be wiser in moral matters to abide by the ordinary rational judgment or at most to bring in philosophy merely for the purpose of rendering the system of morals more complete and intelligible and of presenting its rules in a way that is more convenient for use (especially in disputation), but not for the purpose of leading ordinary human understanding away from its happy simplicity in practical matters and of bringing it by means of philosophy into a new path of inquiry and instruction?

Innocence is indeed a glorious thing; but, unfortunately, it does not keep very well and is easily led astray. Consequently, even wisdom—which consists more in doing and not doing than in knowing—needs science, not in order to learn from it, but in order that wisdom's precepts may gain acceptance and permanence. Man feels within himself a powerful counterweight to all the commands of duty, which are presented to him by reason as being so pre-eminently worthy of respect; this counterweight consists of his needs and inclinations, whose total satisfaction is summed up under the name of happiness. Now reason irremissibly commands its precepts, without thereby promising the inclinations anything; hence it disregards and neglects these impetuous and at the same time so seemingly plausible claims (which do not allow themselves to be suppressed by any command). Hereby arises a natural dialectic, i.e., a propensity to quibble with these strict laws of duty, to cast doubt upon their validity, or at least upon their purity and strictness, and to make them, where possible, more compatible with our wishes and inclinations. Thereby are such laws corrupted in their very foundations and their whole dignity is destroyed—something which even ordinary practical reason cannot in the end call good.

Thus is ordinary human reason forced to go outside its sphere and take a step into the field of practical philosophy, not by any need for speculation (which never befalls such reason so long as it is content to be mere sound reason) but on practical grounds themselves. There it tries to obtain information and clear instruction regarding the source of its own principle and the correct determination of this principle in its opposition to maxims based on need and inclination, so that reason may escape from the perplexity of opposite claims and may avoid the risk of losing all genuine moral principles through the ambiguity into which it easily falls. Thus when ordinary practical reason cultivates itself, there imperceptibly arises in it a dialectic which compels it to seek help in philosophy. The same thing happens in reason's theoretical use; in this case, just as in the other, peace will be found only in a thorough critical examination of our reason.

405

406

SECOND SECTION

Transition from Popular Moral Philosophy
to a Metaphysics of Morals

If we have so far drawn our concept of duty from the ordinary use of our practical reason, one is by no means to infer that we have treated it as a concept of experience. On the contrary, when we pay attention to our experience of the way human beings act, we meet frequent and — as we ourselves admit — justified complaints that there cannot be cited a single certain example of the disposition to act from pure duty; and we meet complaints that although much may be done that is in accordance with what duty commands, yet there are always doubts as to whether what occurs has really been done from duty and so has moral worth. Hence there have always been philosophers who have absolutely denied the reality of this disposition in human actions and have ascribed everything to a more or less refined self-love. Yet in so doing they have not cast doubt upon the rightness of the concept of morality. Rather, they have spoken with sincere regret as to the frailty and impurity of human nature, which they think is noble enough to take as its precept an idea so worthy of respect but yet is too weak to follow this idea: reason, which should legislate for human nature, is used only to look after the interest of inclinations, whether singly or, at best, in their greatest possible harmony with one another.

407

In fact there is absolutely no possibility by means of experience to make out with complete certainty a single case in which the maxim of an action that may in other respects conform to duty has rested solely on moral grounds and on the representation of one's duty. It is indeed sometimes the case that after the keenest self-examination we can find nothing except the moral ground of duty that could have been strong enough to move us to this or that good action and to such great sacrifice. But there cannot with certainty be at all inferred from this that some secret impulse of self-love, merely appearing as the idea of duty, was not the actual determining cause of the will. We like to flatter ourselves with the false claim to a more noble motive; but in fact we can never, even by the strictest examination, completely plumb the depths of the secret incentives of our actions. For when moral value is being considered, the concern is not with the actions, which are seen, but rather with their inner principles, which are not seen.

Moreover, one cannot better serve the wishes of those who ridicule all morality as being a mere phantom of human imagination getting above itself because of self-conceit than by conceding to them that the concepts of duty must be drawn solely from experience (just as from indolence one willingly persuades himself that such is the case as regards all other concepts as well). For by so conceding, one prepares for them a sure triumph. I am willing to admit out of love for humanity that most of our actions are in accordance with duty; but if we look more closely at our planning and striving, we everywhere come upon the dear self, which is always turning up, and upon which the intent of our actions is based rather than upon the strict command of duty (which would often require self-denial). One need not be exactly an enemy of virtue, but only a cool observer who does not take the liveliest wish for the good to be straight off its realization, in order to become doubtful at times whether any true virtue is actually to be found in the world. Such is especially the case when years increase and one's power of judgment is made shrewder by experience and keener in observation. Because of these things nothing can protect us from a complete falling away from our ideas of duty and preserve in the soul a well-grounded respect for duty's law

except the clear conviction that, even if there never have been actions springing from
such pure sources, the question at issue here is not whether this or that has happened
but that reason of itself and independently of all experience commands what ought to
happen. Consequently, reason unrelentingly commands actions of which the world
has perhaps hitherto never provided an example and whose feasibility might well be
doubted by one who bases everything upon experience; for instance, even though
there might never yet have been a sincere friend, still pure sincerity in friendship is
nonetheless required of every man, because this duty, prior to all experience, is contained as duty in general in the idea of a reason that determines the will by means of a
priori grounds.

There may be noted further that unless we want to deny to the concept of morality
all truth and all reference to a possible object, we cannot but admit that the moral
law is of such widespread significance that it must hold not merely for men but for all
rational beings generally, and that it must be valid not merely under contingent conditions and with exceptions but must be absolutely necessary. Clearly, therefore, no
experience can give occasion for inferring even the possibility of such apodeictic laws.
For with what right could we bring into unlimited respect as a universal precept for
every rational nature what is perhaps valid only under the contingent conditions of
humanity? And how could laws for the determination of our will be regarded as laws
for the determination of a rational being in general and of ourselves only insofar as we
are rational beings, if these laws were merely empirical and did not have their source
completely a priori in pure, but practical, reason?

Moreover, worse service cannot be rendered morality than that an attempt be
made to derive it from examples. For every example of morality presented to me must
itself first be judged according to principles of morality in order to see whether it is fit
to serve as an original example, i.e., as a model. But in no way can it authoritatively
furnish the concept of morality. Even the Holy One of the gospel must first be compared with our ideal of moral perfection before he is recognized as such. Even he says
of himself, "Why do you call me (whom you see) good? None is good (the archetype of
the good) except God only (whom you do not see)." But whence have we the concept
of God as the highest good? Solely from the idea of moral perfection, which reason
frames a priori and connects inseparably with the concept of a free will. Imitation has
no place at all in moral matters. And examples serve only for encouragement, i.e.,
they put beyond doubt the feasibility of what the law commands and they make visible what the practical rule expresses more generally. But examples can never justify
us in setting aside their true original, which lies in reason, and letting ourselves be
guided by them.

If there is then no genuine supreme principle of morality that must rest merely on
pure reason, independently of all experience, I think it is unnecessary even to ask
whether it is a good thing to exhibit these concepts generally (*in abstracto*), which,
along with the principles that belong to them, hold a priori, so far as the knowledge
involved is to be distinguished from ordinary knowledge and is to be called
philosophical. But in our times it may well be necessary to do so. For if one were to
take a vote as to whether pure rational knowledge separated from everything empirical, i.e., metaphysics of morals, or whether popular practical philosophy is to be
preferred, one can easily guess which side would be preponderant.

This descent to popular thought is certainly very commendable once the ascent to
the principles of pure reason has occurred and has been satisfactorily accomplished.
That would mean that the doctrine of morals has first been grounded on metaphysics

and that subsequently acceptance for morals has been won by giving it a popular character after it has been firmly established. But it is quite absurd to try for popularity in the first inquiry, upon which depends the total correctness of the principles. Not only can such a procedure never lay claim to the very rare merit of a true philosophical popularity, inasmuch as there is really no art involved at all in being generally intelligible if one thereby renounces all basic insight, but such a procedure turns out a disgusting mishmash of patchwork observations and half-reasoned principles in which shallowpates revel because all this is something quite useful for the chitchat of everyday life. Persons of insight, on the other hand, feel confused by all this and turn their eyes away with a dissatisfaction which they nevertheless cannot cure. Yet philosophers, who quite see through the delusion, get little hearing when they summon people for a time from this pretended popularity in order that they may be rightfully popular only after they have attained definite insight.

411

One need only look at the attempts to deal with morality in the way favored by popular taste. What he will find in an amazing mixture is at one time the particular constitution of human nature (but along with this also the idea of a rational nature in general), at another time perfection, at another happiness; here moral feeling, and there the fear of God; something of this, and also something of that. But the thought never occurs to ask whether the principles of morality are to be sought at all in the knowledge of human nature (which can be had only from experience). Nor does the thought occur that if these principles are not to be sought here but to be found, rather, completely a priori and free from everything empirical in pure rational concepts only, and are to be found nowhere else even to the slightest extent—then there had better be adopted the plan of undertaking this investigation as a separate inquiry, i.e., as pure practical philosophy or (if one may use a name so much decried) as a metaphysics[1] of morals. It is better to bring this investigation to full completeness entirely by itself and to bid the public, which demands popularity, to await the outcome of this undertaking.

But such a completely isolated metaphysics of morals, not mixed with any anthropology, theology, physics, or hyperphysics, and still less with occult qualities (which might be called hypophysical), is not only an indispensable substratum of all theoretical and precisely defined knowledge of duties, but is at the same time a desideratum of the highest importance for the actual fulfillment of their precepts. For the pure thought of duty and of the moral law generally, unmixed with any extraneous addition of empirical inducements, has by the way of reason alone (which first becomes aware hereby that it can of itself be practical) an influence on the

411

human heart so much more powerful than all other incentives[2] which may be derived from the empirical field that reason in the consciousness of its dignity despises such

---

1. Pure philosophy of morals (metaphysics) may be distinguished from the applied (viz., applied to human nature) just as pure mathematics is distinguished from applied mathematics and pure logic from applied logic. By this designation one is also immediately reminded that moral principles are not grounded on the peculiarities of human nature but must subsist a priori of themselves, and that from such principles practical rules must be derivable for every rational nature, and accordingly for human nature.

2. I have a letter from the late excellent Sulzer [Johann Georg Sulzer (1720-1779), an important Berlin savant, who translated Hume's *Inquiry Concerning the Principles of Morals* into German in 1755] in which he asks me why it is that moral instruction accomplishes so little, even though it contains so much that is convincing to reason. My answer was delayed so that I might make it complete. But it is just that the teachers themselves have not purified their concepts: since they try to do too well by looking everywhere for motives for being morally good, they spoil the medicine by trying to make it really strong. For the most or-

incentives and is able gradually to become their master. On the other hand, a mixed moral philosophy, compounded both of incentives drawn from feelings and inclinations and at the same time of rational concepts, must make the mind waver between motives that cannot be brought under any principle and that can only by accident lead to the good but often can also lead to the bad.

It is clear from the foregoing that all moral concepts have their seat and origin completely a priori in reason, and indeed in the most ordinary human reason just as much as in the most highly speculative. They cannot be abstracted from any empirical, and hence merely contingent, cognition. In this purity of their origin lies their very worthiness to serve us as supreme practical principles; and to the extent that something empirical is added to them, just so much is taken away from their genuine influence and from the absolute worth of the corresponding actions. Moreover, it is not only a requirement of the greatest necessity from a theoretical point of view, when it is a question of speculation, but also of the greatest practical importance, to draw these concepts and laws from pure reason, to present them pure and unmixed, and indeed to determine the extent of this entire practical and pure rational cognition, i.e., to determine the whole faculty of pure practical reason. The principles should not be made to depend on the particular nature of human reason, as speculative philosophy may permit and even sometimes finds necessary; but, rather, the principles should be derived from the universal concept of a rational being in general, since moral laws should hold for every rational being as such. In this way all morals, which require anthropology in order to be applied to humans, must be entirely expounded at first independently of anthropology as pure philosophy, i.e., as metaphysics (which can easily be done in such distinct kinds of knowledge). One knows quite well that unless one is in possession of such a metaphysics, then the attempt is futile, I shall not say to determine exactly for speculative judgment the moral element of duty in all that accords with duty, but that the attempt is impossible, even in ordinary and practical usage, especially in that of moral instruction, to ground morals on their genuine principles and thereby to produce pure moral dispositions and engraft them on men's minds for the promotion of the highest good in the world.

412

In this study we must advance by natural stages not merely from ordinary moral judgment (which is here ever so worthy of respect) to philosophical judgment, as has already been done, but also from popular philosophy, which goes no further than it can get by groping about with the help of examples, to metaphysics (which does not permit itself to be held back any longer by what is empirical, and which, inasmuch as it must survey the whole extent of rational knowledge of this kind, goes right up to ideas, where examples themselves fail us). In order to make such an advance, we must follow and clearly present the practical faculty of reason from its universal rules of determination to the point where the concept of duty springs from it.

Everything in nature works according to laws. Only a rational being has the power to act according to his conception of laws, i.e., according to principles, and thereby has he a will. Since the derivation of actions from laws requires reason, the will is

---

dinary observation shows that when a righteous act is represented as being done with a steadfast soul and sundered from all view to any advantage in this or another world, and even under the greatest temptations of need or allurement, it far surpasses and eclipses any similar action that was in the least affected by any extraneous incentive; it elevates the soul and inspires the wish to be able to act in this way. Even moderately young children feel this impression, and duties should never be represented to them in any other way.

nothing but practical reason. If reason infallibly determines the will, then in the case of such a being actions which are recognized to be objectively necessary are also subjectively necessary, i.e., the will is a faculty of choosing only that which reason, independently of inclination, recognizes as being practically necessary, i.e., as good. But if reason of itself does not sufficiently determine the will, and if the will submits also to subjective conditions (certain incentives) which do not always agree with objective conditions; in a word, if the will does not in itself completely accord with reason (as is actually the case with men), then actions which are recognized as objectively necessary are subjectively contingent, and the determination of such a will according to objective laws is necessitation. That is to say that the relation of objective laws to a will not thoroughly good is represented as the determination of the will of a rational being by principles of reason which the will does not necessarily follow because of its own nature.

The representation of an objective principle insofar as it necessitates the will is called a command (of reason), and the formula of the command is called an imperative.

All imperatives are expressed by an *ought* and thereby indicate the relation of an objective law of reason to a will that is not necessarily determined by this law because of its subjective constitution (the relation of necessitation). Imperatives say that something would be good to do or to refrain from doing, but they say it to a will that does not always therefore do something simply because it has been represented to the will as something good to do. That is practically good which determines the will by means of representations of reason and hence not by subjective causes, but objectively, i.e., on grounds valid for every rational being as such. It is distinguished from the pleasant as that which influences the will only by means of sensation from merely subjective causes, which hold only for this or that person's senses but do not hold as a principle of reason valid for everyone.[3]

A perfectly good will would thus be quite as much subject to objective laws (of the good), but could not be conceived as thereby necessitated to act in conformity with law, inasmuch as it can of itself, according to its subjective constitution, be determined only by the representation of the good. Therefore no imperatives hold for the divine will, and in general for a holy will; the *ought* is here out of place, because the *would* is already of itself necessarily in agreement with the law. Consequently, imperatives are only formulas for expressing the relation of objective laws of willing in general to the subjective imperfection of the will of this or that rational being, e.g., the human will.

---

3. The dependence of the faculty of desire on sensations is called inclination, which accordingly always indicates a need. The dependence of a contingently determinable will on principles of reason, however, is called interest. Therefore an interest is found only in a dependent will which is not of itself always in accord with reason; in the divine will no interest can be thought. But even the human will can take an interest in something without thereby acting from interest. The former signifies practical interest in the action, while the latter signifies pathological interest in the object of the action. The former indicates only dependence of the will on principles of reason by itself, while the latter indicates the will's dependence on principles of reason for the sake of inclination, i.e., reason merely gives the practical rule for meeting the need of inclination. In the former case the action interests me, while in the latter case what interests me is the object of the action (so far as this object is pleasant for me). In the First Section we have seen that in the case of an action done from duty regard must be given not to the interest in the object, but only to interest in the action itself and in its rational principle (viz., the law).

Now all imperatives command either hypothetically or categorically. The former represent the practical necessity of a possible action as a means for attaining something else that one wants (or may possibly want). The categorical imperative would be one which represented an action as objectively necessary in itself, without reference to another end.

Every practical law represents a possible action as good and hence as necessary for a subject who is practically determinable by reason; therefore all imperatives are formulas for determining an action which is necessary according to the principle of a will that is good in some way. Now if the action would be good merely as a means to something else, so is the imperative hypothetical. But if the action is represented as good in itself, and hence as necessary in a will which of itself conforms to reason as the principle of the will, then the imperative is categorical.

An imperative thus says what action possible by me would be good, and it presents the practical rule in relation to a will which does not forthwith perform an action simply because it is good, partly because the subject does not always know that the action is good and partly because (even if he does know it is good) his maxims might yet be opposed to the objective principles of practical reason.

A hypothetical imperative thus says only that an action is good for some purpose, 415 either possible or actual. In the first case it is a problematic practical principle; in the second case an assertoric one. A categorical imperative, which declares an action to be of itself objectively necessary without reference to any purpose, i.e., without any other end, holds as an apodeictic practical principle.

Whatever is possible only through the powers of some rational being can be thought of as a possible purpose of some will. Consequently, there are in fact infinitely many principles of action insofar as they are represented as necessary for attaining a possible purpose achievable by them. All sciences have a practical part consisting of problems saying that some end is possible for us and of imperatives telling us how it can be attained. These can, therefore, be called in general imperatives of skill. Here there is no question at all whether the end is reasonable and good, but there is only a question as to what must be done to attain it. The prescriptions needed by a doctor in order to make his patient thoroughly healthy and by a poisoner in order to make sure of killing his victim are of equal value so far as each serves to bring about its purpose perfectly. Since there cannot be known in early youth what ends may be presented to us in the course of life, parents especially seek to have their children learn many different kinds of things, and they provide for skill in the use of means to all sorts of arbitrary ends, among which they cannot determine whether any one of them could in the future become an actual purpose for their ward, though there is always the possibility that he might adopt it. Their concern is so great that they commonly neglect to form and correct their children's judgment regarding the worth of things which might be chosen as ends.

There is, however, one end that can be presupposed as actual for all rational beings (so far as they are dependent beings to whom imperatives apply); and thus there is one purpose which they not merely can have but which can certainly be assumed to be such that they all do have by a natural necessity, and this is happiness. A hypothetical imperative which represents the practical necessity of an action as means for the promotion of happiness is assertoric. It may be expounded not simply as necessary to an uncertain, merely possible purpose, but as necessary to a purpose 416 which can be presupposed a priori and with certainty as being present in everyone because it belongs to his essence. Now skill in the choice of means to one's own greatest well-being can be called prudence[4] in the narrowest sense. And thus the imperative that refers to the choice of means to one's own happiness, i.e., the precept of prudence, still remains hypothetical; the action is commanded not absolutely but only as a means to a further purpose.

Finally, there is one imperative which immediately commands a certain conduct without having as its condition any other purpose to be attained by it. This imperative is categorical. It is not concerned with the matter of the action and its intended result, but rather with the form of the action and the principle from which it follows; what is essentially good in the action consists in the mental disposition, let the consequences be what they may. This imperative may be called that of morality.

Willing according to these three kinds of principles is also clearly distinguished by dissimilarity in the necessitation of the will. To make this dissimilarity clear I think that they are most suitably named in their order when they are said to be either *rules of skill, counsels of prudence,* or *commands (laws) of morality.* For law alone involves the concept of a necessity that is unconditioned and indeed objective and hence universally valid, and commands are laws which must be obeyed, i.e., must be followed even in opposition to inclination. Counsel does indeed involve necessity, but involves such necessity as is valid only under a subjectively contingent condition, viz., whether this or that man counts this or that as belonging to his happiness. On the other hand, the categorical imperative is limited by no condition, and can quite properly be called a command since it is absolutely, though practically, necessary. The first kind of imperatives might also be called technical (belonging to art), the second kind pragmatic[5] (belonging to welfare), the third kind moral (belonging to free conduct as such, i.e., to morals).

417

The question now arises: how are all of these imperatives possible?[6] This question does not seek to know how the fulfillment of the action commanded by the imperative can be conceived, but merely how the necessitation of the will expressed by the imperative in setting a task can be conceived. How an imperative of skill is possible requires no special discussion. Whoever wills the end, wills (so far as reason has decisive influence on his actions) also the means that are indispensably necessary to his actions and that lie in his power. This proposition, as far as willing is concerned, is analytic. For in willing an object as my effect there is already thought the causality of myself as an acting cause, i.e., the use of means. The imperative derives the concept of actions necessary to this end from the concept of willing this end. (Synthetic propositions are indeed required for determining the means to a proposed end; but such propositions are concerned not with the ground, i.e., the act of the will, but only with the way to

---

4. The word "prudence" is used in a double sense: firstly, it can mean worldly wisdom, and, secondly, private wisdom. The former is the skill of someone in influencing others so as to use them for his own purposes. The latter is the sagacity to combine all these purposes for his own lasting advantage. The value of the former is properly reduced to the latter, and it might better be said of one who is prudent in the former sense but not in the latter that he is clever and cunning, but on the whole imprudent.

5. It seems to me that the proper meaning of the word "pragmatic" could be defined most accurately in this way. For those sanctions are called pragmatic which properly flow not from the law of states as necessary enactments but from provision for the general welfare. A history is pragmatically written when it teaches prudence, i.e., instructs the world how it can provide for its interests better than, or at least as well as, has been done in former times.

6. [That is, why should one let his actions be determined at various times by one or the other of these three kinds of imperatives?]

realize the object of the will.) Mathematics teaches by nothing but synthetic propositions that in order to bisect a line according to a sure principle I must from each of its extremities draw arcs such that they intersect. But when I know that the proposed result can come about only by means of such an action, then the proposition (if I fully will the effect, then I also will the action required for it) is analytic. For it is one and the same thing to conceive of something as an effect that is possible in a certain way through me and to conceive of myself as acting in the same way with regard to the aforesaid effect.

If it were only as easy to give a determinate concept of happiness, then the imperatives of prudence would exactly correspond to those of skill and would be likewise analytic. For there could be said in this case just as in the former that whoever wills the end also wills (necessarily according to reason) the sole means thereto which are in his power. But, unfortunately, the concept of happiness is such an indeterminate one that even though everyone wishes to attain happiness, yet he can never say definitely and consistently what it is that he really wishes and wills. The reason for this is that all the elements belonging to the concept of happiness are unexceptionally empirical, i.e., they must be borrowed from experience, while for the idea of happiness there is required an absolute whole, a maximum of well-being in my present and in every future condition. Now it is impossible for the most insightful and at the same time most powerful, but nonetheless finite, being to frame here a determinate concept of what it is that he really wills. Does he want riches? How much anxiety, envy, and intrigue might he not thereby bring down upon his own head! Or knowledge and insight? Perhaps these might only give him an eye that much sharper for revealing that much more dreadfully evils which are at present hidden but are yet unavoidable, or such an eye might burden him with still further needs for the desires which already concern him enough. Or long life? Who guarantees that it would not be a long misery? Or health at least? How often has infirmity of the body kept one from excesses into which perfect health would have allowed him to fall, and so on? In brief, he is not able on any principle to determine with complete certainty what will make him truly happy, because to do so would require omniscience. Therefore, one cannot act according to determinate principles in order to be happy, but only according to empirical counsels, e.g., of diet, frugality, politeness, reserve, etc., which are shown by experience to contribute on the average the most to well-being. There follows from this that imperatives of prudence, strictly speaking, cannot command at all, i.e., present actions objectively as practically necessary. They are to be taken as counsels (*consilia*) rather than as commands (*praecepta*) of reason. The problem of determining certainly and universally what action will promote the happiness of a rational being is completely insoluble. Therefore, regarding such action no imperative that in the strictest sense could command what is to be done to make one happy is possible, inasmuch as happiness is not an ideal of reason but of imagination. Such an ideal rests merely on empirical grounds; in vain can there be expected that such grounds should determine an action whereby the totality of an infinite series of consequences could be attained. This imperative of prudence would, nevertheless, be an analytic practical proposition if one assumes that the means to happiness could with certainty be assigned; for it differs from the imperative of skill only in that for it the end is given while for the latter the end is merely possible. Since both, however, command only the means to what is assumed to be willed as an end, the imperative commanding him who wills the end to will likewise the means thereto is in both cases analytic. Hence there is also no difficulty regarding the possibility of an imperative of prudence.

On the other hand, the question as to how the imperative of morality is possible is undoubtedly the only one requiring a solution. For it is not at all hypothetical; and hence the objective necessity which it presents cannot be based on any presupposition, as was the case with the hypothetical imperatives. Only there must never here be forgotten that no example can show, i.e., empirically, whether there is any such imperative at all. Rather, care must be taken lest all imperatives which are seemingly categorical may nevertheless be covertly hypothetical. For instance, when it is said that you should not make a false promise, the assumption is that the necessity of this avoidance is no mere advice for escaping some other evil, so that it might be said that you should not make a false promise lest you ruin your credit when the falsity comes to light. But when it is asserted that an action of this kind must be regarded as bad in itself, then the imperative of prohibition is therefore categorical. Nevertheless, it cannot with certainty be shown by means of an example that the will is here determined solely by the law without any other incentive, even though such may seem to be the case. For it is always possible that secretly there is fear of disgrace and perhaps also obscure dread of other dangers; such fear and dread may have influenced the will. Who can prove by experience that a cause is not present? Experience only shows that a cause is not perceived. But in such a case the so-called moral imperative, which as such appears to be categorical and unconditioned, would actually be only a pragmatic precept which makes us pay attention to our own advantage and merely teaches us to take such advantage into consideration.

420

We shall, therefore, have to investigate the possibility of a categorical imperative entirely a priori, inasmuch as we do not here have the advantage of having its reality given in experience and consequently of thus being obligated merely to explain its possibility rather than to establish it. In the meantime so much can be seen for now: the categorical imperative alone purports to be a practical law, while all the others may be called principles of the will but not laws. The reason for this is that whatever is necessary merely in order to attain some arbitrary purpose can be regarded as in itself contingent, and the precept can always be ignored once the purpose is abandoned. Contrariwise, an unconditioned command does not leave the will free to choose the opposite at its own liking. Consequently, only such a command carries with it that necessity which is demanded from a law.

Secondly, in the case of this categorical imperative, or law of morality, the reason for the difficulty (of discerning its possibility) is quite serious. The categorical imperative is an a priori synthetic practical proposition;[7] and since discerning the possibility of propositions of this sort involves so much difficulty in theoretic knowledge, there may readily be gathered that there will be no less difficulty in practical knowledge.

In solving this problem, we want first to inquire whether perhaps the mere concept of a categorical imperative may not also supply us with the formula containing the proposition that can alone be a categorical imperative. For even when we know the

---

7. I connect a priori, and therefore necessarily, the act with the will without presupposing any condition taken from some inclination (though I make such a connection only objectively, i.e., under the idea of a reason having full power over all subjective motives). Hence this is a practical proposition which does not analytically derive the willing of an action from some other willing already presupposed (for we possess no such perfect will) but which connects the willing of an action immediately with the concept of the will of a rational being as something which is not contained in this concept.

purport of such an absolute command, the question as to how it is possible will still require a special and difficult effort, which we postpone to the last section.[8]

If I think of a hypothetical imperative in general, I do not know beforehand what it will contain until its condition is given. But if I think of a categorical imperative, I know immediately what it contains. For since, besides the law, the imperative contains only the necessity that the maxim[9] should accord with this law, while the law contains no condition to restrict it, there remains nothing but the universality of a law as such with which the maxim of the action should conform. This conformity alone is properly what is represented as necessary by the imperative.

Hence there is only one categorical imperative and it is this: Act only according to that maxim whereby you can at the same time will that it should become a universal law.[10]

Now if all imperatives of duty can be derived from this one imperative as their principle, then there can at least be shown what is understood by the concept of duty and what it means, even though there is left undecided whether what is called duty may not be an empty concept.

The universality of law according to which effects are produced constitutes what is properly called nature in the most general sense (as to form), i.e., the existence of things as far as determined by universal laws. Accordingly, the universal imperative of duty may be expressed thus: Act as if the maxim of your action were to become through your will a universal law of nature.[11]

We shall now enumerate some duties, following the usual division of them into duties to ourselves and to others and into perfect and imperfect duties.[12]

1. A man reduced to despair by a series of misfortunes feels sick of life but is still so far in possession of his reason that he can ask himself whether taking his own life would not be contrary to his duty to himself.[13] Now he asks whether the maxim of his action could become a universal law of nature. But his maxim is this: from self-love I make as my principle to shorten my life when its continued duration threatens more evil than it promises satisfaction. There only remains the question as to whether this

421

422

---

8. [See below Ak. 446-63.]

9. A maxim is the subjective principle of acting and must be distinguished from the objective principle, viz., the practical law. A maxim contains the practical rule which reason determines in accordance with the conditions of the subject (often his ignorance or his inclinations) and is thus the principle according to which the subject does act. But the law is the objective principle valid for every rational being, and it is the principle according to which he ought to act, i.e., an imperative.

10. [This formulation of the categorical imperative is often referred to as the formula of universal law.]

11. [This is often called the formula of the law of nature.]

12. There should be noted here that I reserve the division of duties for a future *Metaphysics of Morals* [in Part II of the *Metaphysics of Morals*, entitled *The Metaphysical Principles of Virtue*, Ak. 417-474]. The division presented here stands as merely an arbitrary one (in order to arrange my examples). For the rest, I understand here by a perfect duty one which permits no exception in the interest of inclination. Accordingly, I have perfect duties which are external [to others], while other ones are internal [to oneself]. This classification runs contrary to the accepted usage of the schools, but I do not intend to justify it here, since there is no difference for my purpose whether this classification is accepted or not.

13. [Not committing suicide is an example of a perfect duty to oneself. See *Metaphysical Principles of Virtue*, Ak. 422-24.]

principle of self-love can become a universal law of nature. One sees at once a contradiction in a system of nature whose law would destroy life by means of the very same feeling that acts so as to stimulate the furtherance of life, and hence there could be no existence as a system of nature. Therefore, such a maxim cannot possibly hold as a universal law of nature and is, consequently, wholly opposed to the supreme principle of all duty.

2. Another man in need finds himself forced to borrow money. He knows well that he won't be able to repay it, but he sees also that he will not get any loan unless he firmly promises to repay it within a fixed time. He wants to make such a promise, but he still has conscience enough to ask himself whether it is not permissible and is contrary to duty to get out of difficulty in this way. Suppose, however, that he decides to do so. The maxim of his action would then be expressed as follows: when I believe myself to be in need of money, I will borrow money and promise to pay it back, although I know that I can never do so. Now this principle of self-love or personal advantage may perhaps be quite compatible with one's entire future welfare, but the question is now whether it is right.[14] I then transform the requirement of self-love into a universal law and put the question thus: how would things stand if my maxim were to become a universal law? He then sees at once that such a maxim could never hold as a universal law of nature and be consistent with itself, but must necessarily be self-contradictory. For the universality of a law which says that anyone believing himself to be in difficulty could promise whatever he pleases with the intention of not keeping it would make promising itself and the end to be attained thereby quite impossible, inasmuch as no one would believe what was promised him but would merely laugh at all such utterances as being vain pretenses.

3. A third finds in himself a talent whose cultivation could make him a man useful in many respects. But he finds himself in comfortable circumstances and prefers to indulge in pleasure rather than to bother himself about broadening and improving his fortunate natural aptitudes. But he asks himself further whether his maxim of neglecting his natural gifts, besides agreeing of itself with his propensity to indulgence, might agree also with what is called duty.[15] He then sees that a system of nature could indeed always subsist according to such a universal law, even though every man (like South Sea Islanders) should let his talents rust and resolve to devote his life entirely to idleness, indulgence, propagation, and, in a word, to enjoyment. But he cannot possibly will that this should become a universal law of nature or be implanted in us as such a law by a natural instinct. For as a rational being he necessarily wills that all his faculties should be developed, inasmuch as they are given him for all sorts of possible purposes.

4. A fourth man finds things going well for himself but sees others (whom he could help) struggling with great hardships; and he thinks: what does it matter to me? Let everybody be as happy as Heaven wills or as he can make himself; I shall take nothing from him nor even envy him; but I have no desire to contribute anything to his well-being or to his assistance when in need. If such a way of thinking were to become a universal law of nature, the human race admittedly could very well subsist and doubtless could subsist even better than when everyone prates about sympathy and benevolence and even on occasions exerts himself to practice them but, on the other

14. [Keeping promises is an example of a perfect duty to others. See *ibid.*, Ak. 423–31.]

15. [Cultivating one's talents is an example of an imperfect duty to oneself. See *ibid.*, Ak. 444–46.]

hand, also cheats when he can, betrays the rights of man, or otherwise violates them. But even though it is possible that a universal law of nature could subsist in accordance with that maxim, still it is impossible to will that such a principle should hold everywhere as a law of nature.[16] For a will which resolved in this way would contradict itself, inasmuch as cases might often arise in which one would have need of the love and sympathy of others and in which he would deprive himself, by such a law of nature springing from his own will, of all hope of the aid he wants for himself.

These are some of the many actual duties, or at least what are taken to be such, whose derivation from the single principle cited above is clear. We must be able to will that a maxim of our action become a universal law; this is the canon for morally estimating any of our actions. Some actions are so constituted that their maxims cannot without contradiction even be thought as a universal law of nature, much less be willed as what should become one. In the case of others this internal impossibility is indeed not found, but there is still no possibility of willing that their maxim should be raised to the universality of a law of nature, because such a will would contradict itself. There is no difficulty in seeing that the former kind of action conflicts with strict or narrow [perfect] (irremissible) duty, while the second kind conflicts only with broad [imperfect] (meritorious) duty.[17] By means of these examples there has thus been fully set forth how all duties depend as regards the kind of obligation (not the object of their action) upon the one principle. 424

If we now attend to ourselves in any transgression of a duty, we find that we actually do not will that our maxim should become a universal law—because this is impossible for us—but rather that the opposite of this maxim should remain a law universally.[18] We only take the liberty of making an exception to the law for ourselves (or just for this one time) to the advantage of our inclination. Consequently, if we weighed up everything from one and the same standpoint, namely, that of reason, we would find a contradiction in our own will, viz., that a certain principle be objectively necessary as a universal law and yet subjectively not hold universally but should admit of exceptions. But since we at one moment regard our action from the standpoint of a will wholly in accord with reason and then at another moment regard the very same action from the standpoint of a will affected by inclination, there is really no contradiction here. Rather, there is an opposition (*antagonismus*) of inclination to the precept of reason, whereby the universality (*universalitas*) of the principle is changed into a mere generality (*generalitas*) so that the practical principle of reason may meet the maxim halfway. Although this procedure cannot be justified in our own impartial judgment, yet it does show that we actually acknowledge the validity of the categorical imperative and (with all respect for it) merely allow ourselves a few exceptions which, as they seem to us, are unimportant and forced upon us.

We have thus at least shown that if duty is a concept which is to have significance and real legislative authority for our actions, then such duty can be expressed only in categorical imperatives but not at all in hypothetical ones. We have also—and this is 425

16. [Benefiting others is an example of an imperfect duty to others. See *ibid.*, Ak. 452-54.]

17. [Compare *ibid.*, Ak. 390-94, 410-11, 421-51.]

18. [This is to say, for example, that when you tell a lie, you do so on the condition that others are truthful and believe that what you are saying is true, because otherwise your lie will never work to get you what you want. When you tell a lie, you simply take exception to the general rule that says everyone should always tell the truth.]

already a great deal—exhibited clearly and definitely for every application what is the content of the categorical imperative, which must contain the principle of all duty (if there is such a thing at all). But we have not yet advanced far enough to prove a priori that there actually is an imperative of this kind, that there is a practical law which of itself commands absolutely and without any incentives, and that following this law is duty.

In order to attain this proof there is the utmost importance in being warned that we must not take it into our mind to derive the reality of this principle from the special characteristics of human nature. For duty has to be a practical, unconditioned necessity of action; hence it must hold for all rational beings (to whom alone an imperative is at all applicable) and for this reason only can it also be a law for all human wills. On the other hand, whatever is derived from the special natural condition of humanity, from certain feelings and propensities, or even, if such were possible, from some special tendency peculiar to human reason and not holding necessarily for the will of every rational being—all of this can indeed yield a maxim valid for us, but not a law. This is to say that such can yield a subjective principle according to which we might act if we happen to have the propensity and inclination, but cannot yield an objective principle according to which we would be directed to act even though our every propensity, inclination, and natural tendency were opposed to it. In fact, the sublimity and inner worth of the command are so much the more evident in a duty, the fewer subjective causes there are for it and the more they oppose it; such causes do not in the least weaken the necessitation exerted by the law or take away anything from its validity.

Here philosophy is seen in fact to be put in a precarious position, which should be firm even though there is neither in heaven nor on earth anything upon which it depends or is based. Here philosophy must show its purity as author of its laws, and not as the herald of such laws as are whispered to it by an implanted sense or by who knows what tutelary nature. Such laws may be better than nothing at all, but they can never give us principles dictated by reason. These principles must have an origin that is completely a priori and must at the same time derive from such origin their authority to command. They expect nothing from the inclination of men but, rather, expect everything from the supremacy of the law and from the respect owed to the law. Without the latter expectation, these principles condemn man to self-contempt and inward abhorrence.

Hence everything empirical is not only quite unsuitable as a contribution to the principle of morality, but is even highly detrimental to the purity of morals. For the proper and inestimable worth of an absolutely good will consists precisely in the fact that the principle of action is free of all influences from contingent grounds, which only experience can furnish. This lax or even mean way of thinking which seeks its principle among empirical motives and laws cannot too much or too often be warned against, for human reason in its weariness is glad to rest upon this pillow. In a dream of sweet illusions (in which not Juno but a cloud is embraced) there is substituted for morality some bastard patched up from limbs of quite varied ancestry and looking like anything one wants to see in it but not looking like virtue to him who has once beheld her in her true form.[19]

426

---

19. To behold virtue in her proper form is nothing other than to present morality stripped of all admixture of what is sensuous and of every spurious adornment of reward or self-love. How much she then eclipses all else that appears attractive to the inclinations can be easily seen by everyone with the least effort of his reason, if it be not entirely ruined for all abstraction.

Therefore, the question is this: is it a necessary law for all rational beings always to judge their actions according to such maxims as they can themselves will that such should serve as universal laws? If there is such a law, then it must already be connected (completely a priori) with the concept of the will of a rational being in general. But in order to discover this connection we must, however reluctantly, take a step into metaphysics, although into a region of it different from speculative philosophy, i.e., we must enter the metaphysics of morals. In practical philosophy the concern is not with accepting grounds for what happens but with accepting laws of what ought to happen, even though it never does happen—that is, the concern is with objectively practical laws. Here there is no need to inquire into the reasons as to why something pleases or displeases, how the pleasure of mere sensation differs from taste, and whether taste differs from a general satisfaction of reason, upon what does the feeling of pleasure and displeasure rest, and how from this feeling desires and inclinations arise, and how, finally, from these there arise maxims through the cooperation of reason. All of this belongs to an empirical psychology, which would constitute the second part of the doctrine of nature, if this doctrine is regarded as the philosophy of nature insofar as this philosophy is grounded on empirical laws. But here the concern is with objectively practical laws, and hence with the relation of a will to itself insofar as it is determined solely by reason. In this case everything related to what is empirical falls away of itself, because if reason entirely by itself determines conduct (and the possibility of such determination we now wish to investigate), then reason must necessarily do so a priori.

427

The will is thought of as a faculty of determining itself to action in accordance with the representation of certain laws, and such a faculty can be found only in rational beings. Now what serves the will as the objective ground of its self-determination is an end; and if this end is given by reason alone, then it must be equally valid for all rational beings. On the other hand, what contains merely the ground of the possibility of the action, whose effect is an end, is called the means. The subjective ground of desire is the incentive; the objective ground of volition is the motive. Hence there arises the distinction between subjective ends, which rest on incentives, and objective ends, which depend on motives valid for every rational being. Practical principles are formal when they abstract from all subjective ends; they are material, however, when they are founded upon subjective ends, and hence upon certain incentives. The ends which a rational being arbitrarily proposes to himself as effects of this action (material ends) are all merely relative, for only their relation to a specially constituted faculty of desire in the subject gives them their worth. Consequently, such worth cannot provide any universal principles, which are valid and necessary for all rational beings and, furthermore, are valid for every volition, i.e., cannot provide any practical laws. Therefore, all such relative ends can be grounds only for hypothetical imperatives.

428

But let us suppose that there were something whose existence has in itself an absolute worth, something which as an end in itself could be a ground of determinate laws. In it, and in it alone, would there be the ground of a possible categorical imperative, i.e., of a practical law.

Now I say that man, and in general every rational being, exists as an end in himself and not merely as a means to be arbitrarily used by this or that will. He must in all his actions, whether directed to himself or to other rational beings, always be regarded at the same time as an end. All the objects of inclinations have only a conditioned value; for if there were not these inclinations and the needs founded on them, then their object would be without value. But the inclinations themselves, being sources of needs, are so far from having an absolute value such as to render them desirable for their own sake that the universal wish of every rational being must be, rather, to be wholly free from them. Accordingly, the value of any object obtainable by our action is always conditioned. Beings whose existence depends not on our will but on nature have, nevertheless, if they are not rational beings, only a relative value as means and are therefore called things. On the other hand, rational beings are called persons inasmuch as their nature already marks them out as ends in themselves, i.e., as something which is not to be used merely as means and hence there is imposed thereby a limit on all arbitrary use of such beings, which are thus objects of respect. Persons are, therefore, not merely subjective ends, whose existence as an effect of our actions has a value for us; but such beings are objective ends, i.e., exist as ends in themselves. Such an end is one for which there can be substituted no other end to which such beings should serve merely as means, for otherwise nothing at all of absolute value would be found anywhere. But if all value were conditioned and hence contingent, then no supreme practical principle could be found for reason at all.

If then there is to be a supreme practical principle and, as far as the human will is concerned, a categorical imperative, then it must be such that from the conception of what is necessarily an end for everyone because this end is an end in itself it constitutes an objective principle of the will and can hence serve as a practical law. The ground 429 of such a principle is this: rational nature exists as an end in itself. In this way man necessarily thinks of his own existence; thus far is it a subjective principle of human actions. But in this way also does every other rational being think of his existence on the same rational ground that holds also for me;[20] hence it is at the same time an objective principle, from which, as a supreme practical ground, all laws of the will must be able to be derived. The practical imperative will therefore be the following: Act in such a way that you treat humanity, whether in your own person or in the person of another, always at the same time as an end and never simply as a means.[21] We now want to see whether this can be carried out in practice.

Let us keep to our previous examples.[22]

First, as regards the concept of necessary duty to oneself, the man who contemplates suicide will ask himself whether his action can be consistent with the idea of humanity as an end in itself. If he destroys himself in order to escape from a difficult situation, then he is making use of his person merely as a means so as to maintain a tolerable condition till the end of his life. Man, however, is not a thing and hence is not something to be used merely as a means; he must in all his actions always be regarded as an end in himself. Therefore, I cannot dispose of man in my own person by mutilating, damaging, or killing him. (A more exact determination of this principle so as to avoid all misunderstanding, e.g., regarding the amputation of limbs in order to save oneself, or the exposure of one's life to danger in order to save it, and so on, must here be omitted; such questions belong to morals proper.)

Second, as concerns necessary or strict duty to others, the man who intends to make

20. This proposition I here put forward as a postulate. The grounds for it will be found in the last section. [See below Ak. 446-63.]

21. [This oft-quoted version of the categorical imperative is usually referred to as the formula of the end in itself.]

22. [See above Ak. 422-23.]

a false promise will immediately see that he intends to make use of another man merely as a means to an end which the latter does not likewise hold. For the man whom I want to use for my own purposes by such a promise cannot possibly concur 430 with my way of acting toward him and hence cannot himself hold the end of this action. This conflict with the principle of duty to others becomes even clearer when instances of attacks on the freedom and property of others are considered. For then it becomes clear that a transgressor of the rights of men intends to make use of the persons of others merely as a means, without taking into consideration that, as rational beings, they should always be esteemed at the same time as ends, i.e., be esteemed only as beings who must themselves be able to hold the very same action as an end.[23]

Third, with regard to contingent (meritorious) duty to oneself, it is not enough that the action does not conflict with humanity in our own person as an end in itself; the action must also harmonize with this end. Now there are in humanity capacities for greater perfection which belong to the end that nature has in view as regards humanity in our own person. To neglect these capacities might perhaps be consistent with the maintenance of humanity as an end in itself, but would not be consistent with the advancement of this end.

Fourth, concerning meritorious duty to others, the natural end that all men have is their own happiness. Now humanity might indeed subsist if nobody contributed anything to the happiness of others, provided he did not intentionally impair their happiness. But this, after all, would harmonize only negatively and not positively with humanity as an end in itself, if everyone does not also strive, as much as he can, to further the ends of others. For the ends of any subject who is an end in himself must as far as possible be my ends also, if that conception of an end in itself is to have its full effect in me.

This principle of humanity and of every rational nature generally as an end in itself 431 is the supreme limiting condition of every man's freedom of action. This principle is not borrowed from experience, first, because of its universality, inasmuch as it applies to all rational beings generally, and no experience is capable of determining anything about them; and, secondly, because in experience (subjectively) humanity is not thought of as the end of men, i.e., as an object that we of ourselves actually make our end which as a law ought to constitute the supreme limiting condition of all subjective ends (whatever they may be); and hence this principle must arise from pure reason [and not from experience]. That is to say that the ground of all practical legislation lies objectively in the rule and in the form of universality, which (according to the first principle) makes the rule capable of being a law (say, for example, a law of nature). Subjectively, however, the ground of all practical legislation lies in the end; but (according to the second principle) the subject of all ends is every rational being as an end in himself. From this there now follows the third practical principle of the will as the supreme condition of the will's conformity with universal practical reason, viz., the idea of the will of every rational being as a will that legislates universal law.[24]

---

23. Let it not be thought that the trivial *quod tibi non vis fieri, etc.* [do not do to others what you do not want done to yourself] can here serve as a standard or principle. For it is merely derived from our principle, although with several limitations. It cannot be a universal law, for it contains the ground neither of duties to oneself nor of duties of love toward others (for many a man would gladly consent that others should not benefit him, if only he might be excused from benefiting them). Nor, finally, does it contain the ground of strict duties toward others, for the criminal would on this ground be able to dispute with the judges who punish him; and so on.

24. [This is usually called the formula of autonomy.]

According to this principle all maxims are rejected which are not consistent with the will's own legislation of universal law. The will is thus not merely subject to the law but is subject to the law in such a way that it must be regarded also as legislating for itself and only on this account as being subject to the law (of which it can regard itself as the author).

In the previous formulations of imperatives, viz., that based on the conception of the conformity of actions to universal law in a way similar to a natural order and that based on the universal prerogative of rational beings as ends in themselves, these imperatives just because they were thought of as categorical excluded from their legislative authority all admixture of any interest as an incentive. They were, however, only assumed to be categorical because such an assumption had to be made if the concept of duty was to be explained. But that there were practical propositions which commanded categorically could not itself be proved, nor can it be proved anywhere in this section. But one thing could have been done, viz., to indicate that in willing from duty the renunciation of all interest is the specific mark distinguishing a categorical imperative from a hypothetical one and that such renunciation was expressed in the imperative itself by means of some determination contained in it. This is done in the present (third) formulation of the principle, namely, in the idea of the will of every rational being as a will that legislates universal law.

432

When such a will is thought of, then even though a will which is subject to law may be bound to this law by means of some interest, nevertheless a will that is itself a supreme lawgiver is not able as such to depend on any interest. For a will which is so dependent would itself require yet another law restricting the interest of its self-love to the condition that such interest should itself be valid as a universal law.

Thus the principle that every human will as a will that legislates universal law in all its maxims,[25] provided it is otherwise correct, would be well suited to being a categorical imperative in the following respect: just because of the idea of legislating universal law such an imperative is not based on any interest, and therefore it alone of all possible imperatives can be unconditional. Or still better, the proposition being converted, if there is a categorical imperative (i.e., a law for the will of every rational being), then it can only command that everything be done from the maxim of such a will as could at the same time have as its object only itself regarded as legislating universal law. For only then are the practical principle and the imperative which the will obeys unconditional, inasmuch as the will can be based on no interest at all.

When we look back upon all previous attempts that have been made to discover the principle of morality, there is no reason now to wonder why they one and all had to fail. Man was viewed as bound to laws by his duty; but it was not seen that man is subject only to his own, yet universal, legislation and that he is bound only to act in accordance with his own will, which is, however, a will purposed by nature to legislate universal laws. For when man is thought as being merely subject to a law (whatever it might be), then the law had to carry with it some interest functioning as an attracting stimulus or as a constraining force for obedience, inasmuch as the law did not arise as a law from his own will. Rather, in order that his will conform with law, it had to be necessitated by something else to act in a certain way. By this absolutely necessary conclusion, however, all the labor spent in finding a supreme ground for duty was ir-

433

---

25. I may here be excused from citing instances to elucidate this principle inasmuch as those which were first used to elucidate the categorical imperative and its formula can all serve the same purpose here. [See above Ak. 421-23, 429-30.]

retrievably lost; duty was never discovered, but only the necessity of acting from a certain interest. This might be either one's own interest or another's, but either way the imperative had to be always conditional and could never possibly serve as a moral command. I want, therefore, to call my principle the principle of the autonomy of the will, in contrast with every other principle, which I accordingly count under heteronomy.

The concept of every rational being as one who must regard himself as legislating universal law by all his will's maxims, so that he may judge himself and his actions from this point of view, leads to another very fruitful concept, which depends on the aforementioned one, viz., that of a kingdom of ends.

By "kingdom" I understand a systematic union of different rational beings through common laws. Now laws determine ends as regards their universal validity; therefore, if one abstracts from the personal differences of rational beings and also from all content of their private ends, then it will be possible to think of a whole of all ends in systematic connection (a whole both of rational being as ends in themselves and also of the particular ends which each may set for himself); that is, one can think of a kingdom of ends that is possible on the aforesaid principles.

For all rational beings stand under the law that each of them should treat himself and all others never merely as means but always at the same time as an end in himself. Hereby arises a systematic union of rational beings through common objective laws, i.e., a kingdom that may be called a kingdom of ends (certainly only an ideal), inasmuch as these laws have in view the very relation of such beings to one another as ends and means.[26]

A rational being belongs to the kingdom of ends as a member when he legislates in it universal laws while also being himself subject to these laws. He belongs to it as sovereign, when as legislator he is himself subject to the will of no other.

A rational being must always regard himself as legislator in a kingdom of ends rendered possible by freedom of the will, whether as member or as sovereign. The position of the latter can be maintained not merely through the maxims of his will but only if he is a completely independent being without needs and with unlimited power adequate to his will.

434

Hence morality consists in the relation of all action to that legislation whereby alone a kingdom of ends is possible. This legislation must be found in every rational being and must be able to arise from his will, whose principle then is never to act on any maxim except such as can also be a universal law and hence such as the will can thereby regard itself as at the same time the legislator of universal law. If now the maxims do not by their very nature already necessarily conform with this objective principle of rational beings as legislating universal laws, then the necessity of acting on that principle is called practical necessitation, i.e., duty. Duty does not apply to the sovereign in the kingdom of ends, but it does apply to every member and to each in the same degree.

The practical necessity of acting according to this principle, i.e., duty, does not rest at all on feelings, impulses, and inclinations, but only on the relation of rational beings to one another, a relation in which the will of a rational being must always be regarded at the same time as legislative, because otherwise he could not be thought of as an end in himself. Reason, therefore, relates every maxim of the will as legislating

---

26. [This is usually called the formula of the kingdom of ends.]

universal laws to every other will and also to every action toward oneself; it does so not on account of any other practical motive or future advantage but rather from the idea of the dignity of a rational being who obeys no law except what he at the same time enacts himself.

In the kingdom of ends everything has either a price or a dignity. Whatever has a price can be replaced by something else as its equivalent; on the other hand, whatever is above all price, and therefore admits of no equivalent, has a dignity.

435 Whatever has reference to general human inclinations and needs has a market price; whatever, without presupposing any need, accords with a certain taste, i.e., a delight in the mere unpurposive play of our mental powers,[27] has an affective price; but that which constitutes the condition under which alone something can be an end in itself has not merely a relative worth, i.e., a price, but has an intrinsic worth, i.e., dignity.

Now morality is the condition under which alone a rational being can be an end in himself, for only thereby can he be a legislating member in the kingdom of ends. Hence morality and humanity, insofar as it is capable of morality, alone have dignity. Skill and diligence in work have a market price; wit, lively imagination, and humor have an affective price; but fidelity to promises and benevolence based on principles (not on instinct) have intrinsic worth. Neither nature nor art contain anything which in default of these could be put in their place; for their worth consists, not in the effects which arise from them, nor in the advantage and profit which they provide, but in mental dispositions, i.e., in the maxims of the will which are ready in this way to manifest themselves in action, even if they are not favored with success. Such actions also need no recommendation from any subjective disposition or taste so as to meet with immediate favor and delight; there is no need of any immediate propensity or feeling toward them. They exhibit the will performing them as an object of immediate respect; and nothing but reason is required to impose them upon the will, which is not to be cajoled into them, since in the case of duties such cajoling would be a contradiction. This estimation, therefore, lets the worth of such a disposition be recognized as dignity and puts it infinitely beyond all price, with which it cannot in the least be brought into competition or comparison without, as it were, violating its sanctity.

Now there follows incontestably from this that every rational being as an end in himself must be able to regard himself with reference to all laws to which he may be subject as being at the same time the legislator of universal law, for just this very fitness of his maxims for the legislation of universal law distinguishes him as an end in himself. There follows also that his dignity (prerogative) of being above all the mere things of nature implies that his maxims must be taken from the viewpoint that regards himself, as well as every other rational being, as being legislative beings (and hence are they called persons). In this way there is possible a world of rational beings (*mundus intelligibilis*) as a kingdom of ends, because of the legislation belonging to all persons as members. Therefore, every rational being must so act as if he were through his maxim always a legislating member in the universal kingdom of ends. The formal principle of these maxims is this: So act as if your maxims were to serve at the same time as a universal law (for all rational beings). Thus a kingdom of ends is possible only on the analogy of a kingdom of nature; yet the former is possible only through maxims, i.e., self-imposed rules, while the latter is possible only through laws

27. [See Kant, *Critique of Aesthetic Judgment*, §'s 1–5.]

of efficient causes necessitated from without. Regardless of this difference and even though nature as a whole is viewed as a machine, yet insofar as nature stands in a relation to rational beings as its ends, it is on this account given the name of a kingdom of nature. Such a kingdom of ends would actually be realized through maxims whose rule is prescribed to all rational beings by the categorical imperative, if these maxims were universally obeyed. But even if a rational being himself strictly obeys such a maxim, he cannot for that reason count on everyone else's being true to it, nor can he expect the kingdom of nature and its purposive order to be in harmony with him as a fitting member of a kingdom of ends made possible by himself, i.e., he cannot expect the kingdom of nature to favor his expectation of happiness. Nevertheless, the law: Act in accordance with the maxims of a member legislating universal laws for a merely possible kingdom of ends, remains in full force, since it commands categorically. And just in this lies the paradox that merely the dignity of humanity as rational nature without any further end or advantage to be thereby gained—and hence respect for a mere idea—should yet serve as an inflexible precept for the will; and that just this very independence of the maxims from all such incentives should constitute the sublimity of maxims and the worthiness of every rational subject to be a legislative member in the kingdom of ends, for otherwise he would have to be regarded as subject only to the natural law of his own needs. And even if the kingdom of nature as well as the kingdom of ends were thought of as both united under one sovereign so that the latter kingdom would thereby no longer remain a mere idea but would acquire true reality, then indeed the kingdom of ends would gain the addition of a strong incentive, but never any increase in its intrinsic worth. For this sole absolute legislator must, in spite of all this, always be thought of as judging the worth of rational beings solely by the disinterested conduct prescribed to themselves by means of this idea alone. The essence of things is not altered by their external relations; and whatever without reference to such relations alone constitutes the absolute worth of man is also what he must be judged by, whoever the judge may be, even the Supreme Being. Hence morality is the relation of actions to the autonomy of the will, i.e., to the possible legislation of universal law by means of the maxims of the will. That action which is compatible with the autonomy of the will is permitted; that which is not compatible is forbidden. That will whose maxims are necessarily in accord with the laws of autonomy is a holy, or absolutely good, will. The dependence of a will which is not absolutely good upon the principle of autonomy (i.e., moral necessitation) is obligation, which cannot therefore be applied to a holy will. The objective necessity of an action from obligation is called duty.

What then is it that entitles the morally good disposition, or virtue, to make such lofty claims? It is nothing less than the share which such a disposition affords the rational being of legislating universal laws, so that he is fit to be a member in a possible kingdom of ends, for which his own nature has already determined him as an end in himself and therefore as a legislator in the kingdom of ends. Thereby is he free as regards all laws of nature, and he obeys only those laws which he gives to himself. Accordingly, his maxims can belong to a universal legislation to which he at the same time subjects himself. For nothing can have any worth other than what the law determines. But the legislation itself which determines all worth must for that very reason have dignity, i.e., unconditional and incomparable worth; and the word "respect" alone provides a suitable expression for the esteem which a rational being must have for it. Hence autonomy is the ground of the dignity of human nature and of every rational nature.

436

The aforementioned three ways of representing the principle of morality are at bottom only so many formulas of the very same law: one of them by itself contains a combination of the other two. Nevertheless, there is a difference in them, which is subjectively rather than objectively practical, viz., it is intended to bring an idea of reason closer to intuition (in accordance with a certain analogy) and thereby closer to feeling. All maxims have, namely,

1. A form, which consists in universality; and in this respect the formula of the moral imperative is expressed thus: maxims must be so chosen as if they were to hold as universal laws of nature.

2. A matter, viz., an end; and here the formula says that a rational being, in-asmuch as he is by his very nature an end and hence an end in himself, must serve in every maxim as a condition limiting all merely relative and arbitrary ends.

3. A complete determination of all maxims by the formula that all maxims pro-ceeding from his own legislation ought to harmonize with a possible kingdom of ends as a kingdom of nature.[28] There is a progression here through the categories of the *unity* of the form of the will (its universality), the *plurality* of its matter (its objects, i.e., its ends), and the *totality* or completeness of its system of ends. But one does bet-ter if in moral judgment he follows the rigorous method and takes as his basis the universal formula of the categorical imperative: Act according to that maxim which can at the same time make itself a universal law. But if one wants also to secure ac-ceptance for the moral law, it is very useful to bring one and the same action under the three aforementioned concepts and thus, as far as possible, to bring the moral law nearer to intuition.

We can now end where we started in the beginning, viz., the concept of an uncon-ditionally good will. That will is absolutely good which cannot be evil, i.e., whose maxim, when made into a universal law, can never conflict with itself. This principle is therefore also its supreme law: Act always according to that maxim whose univer-sality as a law you can at the same time will. This is the only condition under which a will can never be in conflict with itself, and such an imperative is categorical. In-asmuch as the validity of the will as a universal law for possible actions is analogous to the universal connection of the existence of things in accordance with universal laws, which is the formal aspect of nature in general, the categorical imperative can also be expressed thus: Act according to maxims which can at the same time have for their object themselves as universal laws of nature. In this way there is provided the for-mula for an absolutely good will.

Rational nature is distinguished from the rest of nature by the fact that it sets itself an end. This end would be the matter of every good will. But in the idea of an ab-solutely good will—good without any qualifying condition (of attaining this or that end) —complete abstraction must be made from every end that has to come about as an effect (since such would make every will only relatively good). And so the end must here be conceived, not as an end to be effected, but as an independently existing end. Hence it must be conceived only negatively, i.e., as an end which should never be acted against and therefore as one which in all willing must never be regarded merely

28. Teleology considers nature as a kingdom of ends; morals regards a possible kingdom of ends as a kingdom of nature. In the former the kingdom of ends is a theoretical idea for explaining what exists. In the latter it is a practical idea for bringing about what does not exist but can be made actual by our conduct, i.e., what can be actualized in accordance with this very idea.

as means but must always be esteemed at the same time as an end. Now this end can be nothing but the subject of all possible ends themselves, because this subject is at the same time the subject of a possible absolutely good will; for such a will cannot without contradiction be subordinated to any other object. The principle: So act in regard to every rational being (yourself and others) that he may at the same time count in your maxim as an end in himself, is thus basically the same as the principle: Act on a maxim which at the same time contains in itself its own universal validity for every rational being. That in the use of means for every end my maxim should be restricted to the condition of its universal validity as a law for every subject says just the same as that a subject of ends, i.e., a rational being himself, must be made the ground for all maxims of actions and must thus be used never merely as means but as the supreme limiting condition in the use of all means, i.e., always at the same time as an end.

Now there follows incontestably from this that every rational being as an end in himself must be able to regard himself with reference to all laws to which he may be subject as being at the same time the legislator of universal law, for just this very fitness of his maxims for the legislation of universal law distinguishes him as an end in himself. There follows also that his dignity (prerogative) of being above all the mere things of nature implies that his maxims must be taken from the viewpoint that regards himself, as well as every other rational being, as being legislative beings (and hence are they called persons). In this way there is possible a world of rational beings (*mundus intelligibilis*) as a kingdom of ends, because of the legislation belonging to all persons as members. Therefore, every rational being must so act as if he were through his maxim always a legislating member in the universal kingdom of ends. The formal principle of these maxims is this: So act as if your maxims were to serve at the same time as a universal law (for all rational beings). Thus a kingdom of ends is possible only on the analogy of a kingdom of nature; yet the former is possible only through maxims, i.e., self-imposed rules, while the latter is possible only through laws of efficient causes necessitated from without. Regardless of this difference and even though nature as a whole is viewed as a machine, yet insofar as nature stands in a relation to rational beings as its ends, it is on this account given the name of a kingdom of nature. Such a kingdom of ends would actually be realized through maxims whose rule is prescribed to all rational beings by the categorical imperative, if these maxims were universally obeyed. But even if a rational being himself strictly obeys such a maxim, he cannot for that reason count on everyone else's being true to it, nor can he expect the kingdom of nature and its purposive order to be in harmony with him as a fitting member of a kingdom of ends made possible by himself, i.e., he cannot expect the kingdom of nature to favor his expectation of happiness. Nevertheless, the law: Act in accordance with the maxims of a member legislating universal laws for a merely possible kingdom of ends, remains in full force, since it commands categorically. And just in this lies the paradox that merely the dignity of humanity as rational nature without any further end or advantage to be thereby gained—and hence respect for a mere idea—should yet serve as an inflexible precept for the will; and that just this very independence of the maxims from all such incentives should constitute the sublimity of maxims and the worthiness of every rational subject to be a legislative member in the kingdom of ends, for otherwise he would have to be regarded as subject only to the natural law of his own

438

439

needs. And even if the kingdom of nature as well as the kingdom of ends were thought of as both united under one sovereign so that the latter kingdom would thereby no longer remain a mere idea but would acquire true reality, then indeed the kingdom of ends would gain the addition of a strong incentive, but never any increase in its intrinsic worth. For this sole absolute legislator must, in spite of all this, always be thought of as judging the worth of rational beings solely by the disinterested conduct prescribed to themselves by means of this idea alone. The essence of things is not altered by their external relations; and whatever without reference to such relations alone constitutes the absolute worth of man is also what he must be judged by, whoever the judge may be, even the Supreme Being. Hence morality is the relation of actions to the autonomy of the will, i.e., to the possible legislation of universal law by means of the maxims of the will. That action which is compatible with the autonomy of the will is permitted; that which is not compatible is forbidden. That will whose maxims are necessarily in accord with the laws of autonomy is a holy, or absolutely good, will. The dependence of a will which is not absolutely good upon the principle of autonomy (i.e., moral necessitation) is obligation, which cannot therefore be applied to a holy will. The objective necessity of an action from obligation is called duty.

440   From what has just been said, there can now easily be explained how it happens that, although in the concept of duty we think of subjection to the law, yet at the same time we thereby ascribe a certain dignity and sublimity to the person who fulfills all his duties. For not insofar as he is subject to the moral law does he have sublimity, but rather has it only insofar as with regard to this very same law he is at the same time legislative, and only thereby is he subject to the law. We have also shown above[29] how neither fear nor inclination, but solely respect for the law, is the incentive which can give an action moral worth. Our own will, insofar as it were to act only under the condition of its being able to legislate universal law by means of its maxims—this will, ideally possible for us, is the proper object of respect. And the dignity of humanity consists just in its capacity to legislate universal law, though with the condition of humanity's being at the same time itself subject to this very same legislation.

Autonomy of the Will
As the Supreme Principle of Morality

Autonomy of the will is the property that the will has of being a law to itself (independently of any property of the objects of volition). The principle of autonomy is this: Always choose in such a way that in the same volition the maxims of the choice are at the same time present as universal law. That this practical rule is an imperative, i.e., that the will of every rational being is necessarily bound to the rule as a condition, cannot be proved by merely analyzing the concepts contained in it, since it is a synthetic proposition. For proof one would have to go beyond cognition of objects to a critical examination of the subject, i.e. go to a critique of pure practical reason, since this synthetic proposition which commands apodeictically must be capable of being cognized completely a priori. This task, however, does not belong to the present section. But that the above principle of autonomy is the sole principle of morals can

29. [Ak. 400-402.]

quite well be shown by mere analysis of the concepts of morality; for thereby the principle of morals is found to be necessarily a categorical imperative, which commands nothing more nor less than this very autonomy.

441

Heteronomy of the Will
As the Source of All Spurious Principles of Morality

If the will seeks the law that is to determine it anywhere but in the fitness of its maxims for its own legislation of universal laws, and if it thus goes outside of itself and seeks this law in the character of any of its objects, then heteronomy always results. The will in that case does not give itself the law, but the object does so because of its relation to the will. This relation, whether it rests on inclination or on representations of reason, admits only of hypothetical imperatives: I ought to do something because I will something else. On the other hand, the moral, and hence categorical, imperative says that I ought to act in this way or that way, even though I did not will something else. For example, the former says that I ought not to lie if I would maintain my reputation; the latter says that I ought not to lie even though lying were to bring me not the slightest discredit. The moral imperative must therefore abstract from every object to such an extent that no object has any influence at all on the will, so that practical reason (the will) may not merely minister to an interest not belonging to it but may merely show its own commanding authority as the supreme legislation. Thus, for example, I ought to endeavor to promote the happiness of others, not as though its realization were any concern of mine (whether by immediate inclination or by any satisfaction indirectly gained through reason), but merely because a maxim which excludes it cannot be comprehended as a universal law in one and the same volition.

Classification of All Possible Principles of Morality
Founded upon the Assumed Fundamental Concept of Heteronomy

Here as elsewhere human reason in its pure use, so long as it lacks a critical examination, first tried every possible wrong way before it succeeded in finding the only right way.

All principles that can be taken from this point of view are either empirical or rational. The first kind, drawn from the principle of happiness, are based upon either physical or moral feeling. The second kind, drawn from the principle of perfection, are based upon either the rational concept of perfection as a possible effect of our will or else upon the concept of an independent perfection (the will of God) as a determining cause of our will.

442

Empirical principles are wholly unsuited to serve as the foundation for moral laws. For the universality with which such laws ought to hold for all rational beings without exception (the unconditioned practical necessity imposed by moral laws upon such beings) is lost if the basis of these laws is taken from the particular constitution of human nature or from the accidental circumstances in which such nature is placed. But the principle of one's own happiness is the most objectionable. Such is the case not merely because this principle is false and because experience contradicts the supposition that well-being is always proportional to well-doing, nor yet merely because this principle contributes nothing to the establishment of morality, inasmuch as making a man happy is quite different from making him good and making him prudent and sharp-sighted for his own advantage quite different from making him virtuous. Rather, such is the case because this principle of one's own happiness bases morality upon incentives that undermine it rather than establish it and that totally destroy its sublimity, inasmuch as motives to virtue are put in the same class as motives to vice and inasmuch as such incentives merely teach one to become better at calculation, while the specific difference between virtue and vice is entirely obliterated. On the other hand, moral feeling, this alleged special sense,[30] remains closer to morality than does the aforementioned principle of one's own happiness. Yet the appeal to the principle of moral feeling is superficial, since men who cannot think believe that they will be helped out by feeling, even when the question is solely one of universal laws. They do so even though feelings naturally differ from one another by an infinity of degrees, so that feelings are not capable of providing a uniform measure of good and evil; furthermore, they do so even though one man cannot by his feeling judge validly at all for other men. Nevertheless, the principle of moral feeling is closer to morality and its dignity than is the principle of one's own happiness inasmuch as the former principle pays virtue the honor of ascribing to her directly the satisfaction and esteem that is held for her, and does not, as it were, tell her to her face that our attachment to her rests not on her beauty but only on our advantage.

443

Among the rational principles of morality (or those arising from reason rather than from feeling) there is the ontological concept of perfection. It is empty, indeterminate, and hence of no use for finding in the immeasurable field of possible reality the maximum sum suitable for us. Furthermore, in attempting to distinguish specifically between the reality just mentioned and every other, it exhibits an inevitable tendency for turning about in a circle and cannot avoid tacitly presupposing the morality that it has to explain. Nevertheless, it is better than the theological concept, whereby morality is derived from a divine and most perfect will. It is better not merely because we cannot intuit divine perfection but can only derive it from our own concepts, among which morality is foremost; but also because if it is not so derived (and being thus derived would involve a crudely circular explanation), then the only remaining concept of God's will is drawn from such characteristics as desire for glory and dominion combined with such frightful representations as those of might and vengeance. Any system of morals based on such notions would be directly opposed to morality.

But if I had to choose between the concept of moral sense and that of perfection in general (both of which at least do not weaken morality, even though they are not at all capable of serving as its foundation), I would decide for the latter because it at least withdraws the decision of the question from sensibility and brings it to the court

---

30. I count the principle of moral feeling under that of happiness, because every empirical interest promises to contribute to our well-being through the amenity afforded by something, whether immediately and without any reference to advantage or with reference to advantage. Similarly, the principle of sympathy for the happiness of others must with Hutcheson be counted along with the principle of moral sense as adopted by him. [Francis Hutcheson (1694–1747) was Professor of Moral Philosophy in the University of Glasgow, Scotland. He was the main proponent of the doctrine of moral sense.]

of pure reason, though it does not even here get any decision. Furthermore, I would choose the concept of perfection in general because it preserves the indeterminate idea (of a will good in itself) free from falsity until it can be more precisely determined.

For the rest, I believe that I may be excused from a lengthy refutation of all these doctrines. Such a refutation would be merely superfluous labor, since it is so easy and is presumably so well understood even by those whose office requires them to declare themselves for one of these theories (since their hearers would not tolerate suspension of judgment). But what interests us more here is to know that these principles never lay down anything but heteronomy of the will as the first ground of morality and that they must, consequently, necessarily fail in their purpose.

In every case where an object of the will must be laid down as the foundation for prescribing a rule to determine the will, there the rule is nothing but heteronomy. The imperative is then conditioned, viz., if or because one wills this object, one should act thus or so. Hence the imperative can never command morally, i.e., categorically. Now the object may determine the will by means of inclination, as in the case of the principle of one's own happiness, or by means of reason directed to objects of our volition in general, as in the case of the principle of perfection. Yet in both cases the will never determines itself immediately by the thought of an action, but only by the incentive that the anticipated effect of the action has upon the will: I ought to do something because I will something else. And here must yet another law be assumed in me the subject, whereby I necessarily will this something else; this other law in turn requires an imperative to restrict this maxim. For the impulse which the representation of an object that is possible by means of our powers is to exert upon the will of a subject in accordance with his natural constitution belongs to the nature of the subject, whether to his sensibility (his inclination and taste) or to his understanding and reason, whose employment on an object is by the particular arrangement of their nature attended with satisfaction; consequently, the law would, properly speaking, be given by nature. This law, insofar as it is a law of nature, must be known and proved through experience and is therefore in itself contingent and hence is not fit to be an apodeictic practical rule, such as a moral rule must be. The law of nature under discussion is always merely heteronomy of the will; the will does not give itself the law, but a foreign impulse gives the law to the will by means of the subject's nature, which is adapted to receive such an impulse.

An absolutely good will, whose principle must be a categorical imperative, will therefore be indeterminate as regards all objects and will contain merely the form of willing; and indeed that form is autonomy. This is to say that the fitness of the maxims of every good will to make themselves universal laws is itself the only law that the will of every rational being imposes on itself, without needing to assume any incentive or interest as a basis.

How such a synthetic practical a priori proposition is possible and why it is necessary are problems whose solution does not lie any longer within the bounds of a metaphysics of morals. Furthermore, we have not here asserted the truth of this proposition, much less professed to have within our power a proof of it. We simply showed by developing the universally accepted concept of morality that autonomy of the will is unavoidably bound up with it, or rather is its very foundation. Whoever, then, holds morality to be something real, and not a chimerical idea without any truth, must also admit the principle here put forward. Hence this section, like the first, was

444

445

merely analytic. To show that morality is not a mere phantom of the brain, which morality cannot be if the categorical imperative, and with it the autonomy of the will, is true and absolutely necessary as an a priori principle, we require a possible synthetic use of pure practical reason. But we must not venture on this use without prefacing it with a critical examination of this very faculty of reason. In the last section we shall give the main outlines of this critical examination as far as sufficient for our purpose.[31]

446

THIRD SECTION

TRANSITION FROM A METAPHYSICS OF MORALS TO A CRITIQUE OF PURE PRACTICAL REASON

The Concept of Freedom Is the Key for an Explanation of the Autonomy of the Will

The will is a kind of causality belonging to living beings insofar as they are rational; freedom would be the property of this causality that makes it effective independent of any determination by alien causes. Similarly, natural necessity is the property of the causality of all non-rational beings by which they are determined to activity through the influence of alien causes.

The foregoing explanation of freedom is negative and is therefore unfruitful for attaining an insight regarding its essence; but there arises from it a positive concept, which as such is richer and more fruitful. The concept of causality involves that of laws according to which something that we call cause must entail something else—namely, the effect. Therefore freedom is certainly not lawless, even though it is not a property of will in accordance with laws of nature. It must, rather, be a causality in accordance with immutable laws, which, to be sure, is of a special kind; otherwise a free will would be something absurd. As we have already seen [in the preceding

447   paragraph], natural necessity is a heteronomy of efficient causes, inasmuch as every effect is possible only in accordance with the law that something else determines the efficient cause to exercise its causality. What else, then, can freedom of the will be but autonomy, i.e., the property that the will has of being a law to itself? The proposition that the will is in every action a law to itself expresses, however, nothing but the principle of acting according to no other maxim than that which can at the same time have itself as a universal law for its object. Now this is precisely the formula of the categorical imperative and is the principle of morality. Thus a free will and a will subject to moral laws are one and the same.

Therefore if freedom of the will is presupposed, morality (together with its principle) follows by merely analyzing the concept of freedom. However, the principle of morality is, nevertheless, a synthetic proposition: viz., an absolutely good will is one

---

31. [The ensuing Third Section is difficult to grasp. Kant expressed himself more clearly regarding the topics discussed there in the *Critique of Practical Reason*, Part I, Book I ("Analytic of Pure Practical Reason").]

whose maxim can always have itself as content when such maxim is regarded as a universal law; it is synthetic because this property of the will's maxim can never be found by analyzing the concept of an absolutely good will. Now such synthetic propositions are possible only as follows — two cognitions are bound together through their connection with a third in which both of them are to be found. The positive concept of freedom furnishes this third cognition, which cannot, as is the case with physical causes, be the nature of the world of sense (in whose concept is combined the concept of something as cause in relation to something else as effect). We cannot here yet show straight away what this third cognition is which freedom indicates to us and of which we have an a priori idea, nor can we as yet conceive of the deduction of the concept of freedom from pure practical reason and therewith also the possibility of a categorical imperative. Rather, we require some further preparation.

Freedom Must Be Presupposed as a Property of the Will of All Rational Beings

It is not enough to ascribe freedom to our will, on whatever ground, if we have not also sufficient reason for attributing it to all rational beings. For inasmuch as morality serves as a law for us only insofar as we are rational beings, it must also be valid for all rational beings. And since morality must be derived solely from the property of freedom, one must show that freedom is also the property of the will of all rational beings. It is not enough to prove freedom from certain alleged experiences of human nature (such a proof is indeed absolutely impossible, and so freedom can be proved only a priori). Rather, one must show that freedom belongs universally to the activity of rational beings endowed with a will. Now I say that every being who cannot act in any way other than under the idea of freedom is for this very reason free from a practical point of view. This is to say that for such a being all the laws that are inseparably bound up with freedom are valid just as much as if the will of such a being could be declared to be free in itself for reasons that are valid for theoretical philosophy.[1] Now I claim that we must necessarily attribute to every rational being which has a will also the idea of freedom, under which only can such a being act. For in such a being we think of a reason that is practical, i.e., that has causality in reference to its objects. Now we cannot possibly think of a reason that consciously lets itself be directed from outside as regards its judgments; for in that case the subject would ascribe the determination of his faculty of judgment not to his reason, but to an impulse. Reason must regard itself as the author of its principles independent of foreign influences. Therefore as practical reason or as the will of a rational being must reason regard itself as free. This is to say that the will of a rational being can be a will of its own only under the idea of freedom, and that such a will must therefore, from a practical point of view, be attributed to all rational beings.

448

---

1. I adopt this method of assuming as sufficient for our purpose that freedom is presupposed merely as an idea by rational beings in their actions in order that I may avoid the necessity of having to prove freedom from a theoretical point of view as well. For even if this latter problem is left unresolved, the same laws that would bind a being who was really free are valid equally for a being who cannot act otherwise than under the idea of its own freedom. Thus we can relieve ourselves of the burden which presses on the theory.

Concerning the Interest Attached
to the Ideas of Morality

We have finally traced the determinate concept of morality back to the idea of freedom, but we could not prove freedom to be something actual in ourselves and in human nature. We saw merely that we must presuppose it if we want to think of a being as rational and as endowed with consciousness of its causality as regards actions, i.e., as endowed with a will. And so we find that on the very same ground we must attribute to every being endowed with reason and a will this property of determining itself to action under the idea of its own freedom.

Now there resulted from the presupposition of this idea of freedom also the consciousness of a law of action: that the subjective principles of actions, i.e., maxims, must always be so adopted that they can also be valid objectively, i.e., universally, as principles, and can therefore serve as universal laws of our own legislation. But why, then, should I subject myself to this principle simply as a rational being and by so doing also subject to this principle all other beings endowed with reason? I am willing to grant that no interest impels me to do so, because this would not give a categorical imperative. But nonetheless I must necessarily take an interest in it and discern how this comes about, for this *ought* is properly a *would* which is valid for every rational being, provided that reason is practical for such a being without hindrances. In the case of beings who, like ourselves, are also affected by sensibility, i.e., by incentives of a kind other than the purely rational, and who do not always act as reason by itself would act, this necessity of action is expressed only as an *ought,* and the subjective necessity is to be distinguished from the objective.

It therefore seems as if we have in the idea of freedom actually only presupposed the moral law, namely, the principle of the autonomy of the will, and as if we could not prove its reality and objective necessity independently. In that case we should indeed still have gained something quite considerable by at least determining the genuine principle more exactly than had previously been done. But as regards its validity and the practical necessity of subjecting oneself to it, we would have made no progress. We could give no satisfactory answer if asked the following questions: why must the universal validity of our maxim taken as a law be a condition restricting our actions; upon what do we base the worth that we assign to this way of acting—a worth that is supposed to be so great that there can be no higher interest; how does it happen that by this alone does man believe that he feels his own personal worth, in comparison with which that of an agreeable or disagreeable condition is to be regarded as nothing.

Indeed we do sometimes find that we can take an interest in a personal characteristic which involves no interest in any [external] condition but only makes us capable of participating in the condition in case reason were to effect the allotment. This is to say that the mere worthiness of being happy can of itself be of interest even without the motive of participating in this happiness. This judgment, however, is in fact only the result of the importance that we have already presupposed as belonging to moral laws (when by the idea of freedom we divorce ourselves from all empirical interest). However, in this way we are not as yet able to have any insight into why it is that we should divorce ourselves from such interest, i.e., that we should consider ourselves as free in action and yet hold ourselves as subject to certain laws so as to find solely in our own person a worth that can compensate us for the loss of everything that gives worth to our condition. We do not see how this is possible and hence how the moral law can obligate us.

One must frankly admit that there is here a sort of circle from which, so it seems, there is no way to escape. In the order of efficient causes we assume that we are free so that we may think of ourselves as subject to moral laws in the order of ends. And we then think of ourselves as subject to these laws because we have attributed to ourselves freedom of the will. Freedom and self-legislation of the will are both autonomy and are hence reciprocal concepts. Since they are reciprocal, one of them cannot be used to explain the other or to supply its ground, but can at most be used only for logical purposes to bring seemingly different conceptions of the same object under a single concept (just as different fractions of the same value are reduced to lowest terms).

However, one recourse still remains open to us, namely, to inquire whether we do not take one point of view when by means of freedom we think of ourselves as a priori efficient causes, and another point of view when we represent ourselves with reference to our actions as effects which we see before our eyes.

No subtle reflection is required for the following observation, which even the commonest understanding may be supposed to make, though it does so in its own fashion through some obscure discrimination of the faculty of judgment which it calls feeling: all representations that come to us without our choice (such as those of the senses) enable us to know objects only as they affect us; what they may be in themselves remains unknown to us. Therefore, even with the closest attention and the greatest clarity that the understanding can bring to such representations, we can attain to a mere knowledge of appearances but never to knowledge of things in themselves. Once this distinction is made (perhaps merely as a result of observing the difference between representations which are given to us from without and in which we are passive from those which we produce entirely from ourselves and in which we show our own activity), then there follows of itself that we must admit and assume that behind the appearances there is something else which is not appearance, namely, things in themselves. Inasmuch as we can never cognize them except as they affect us [through our senses], we must admit that we can never come any nearer to them nor ever know what they are in themselves. This must provide a distinction, however crude, between a world of sense and a world of understanding; the former can vary considerably according to the difference of sensibility [and sense impressions] in various observers, while the latter, which is the basis of the former, remains always the same. Even with regard to himself, a man cannot presume to know what he is in himself by means of the acquaintance which he has through internal sensation. For since he does not, as it were, create himself and since he acquires the concept of himself not a priori but empirically, it is natural that he can attain knowledge even about himself only through inner sense and therefore only through the appearance of his nature and the way in which his consciousness is affected. But yet he must necessarily assume that beyond his own subject's constitution as composed of nothing but appearances there must be something else as basis, namely, his ego as constituted in itself. Therefore with regard to mere perception and the receptivity of sensations, he must count himself as belonging to the world of sense; but with regard to whatever there may be in him of pure activity (whatever reaches consciousness immediately and not through affecting the senses) he must count himself as belonging to the intellectual world, of which he has, however, no further knowledge.

451

452 Such a conclusion must be reached by a reflective man regarding all the things that may be presented to him. It is presumably to be found even in the most ordinary understanding, which, as is well known, is quite prone to expect that behind objects of the senses there is something else invisible and acting of itself. But such understanding spoils all this by making the invisible again sensible, i.e., it wants to make the invisible an object of intuition; and thereby does it become not a bit wiser.

Now man really finds in himself a faculty which distinguishes him from all other things and even from himself insofar as he is affected by objects. That faculty is reason, which as pure spontaneity is elevated even above understanding. For although the latter is also spontaneous and does not, like sense, merely contain representations that arise only when one is affected by things (and is therefore passive), yet understanding can produce by its activity no other concepts than those which merely serve to bring sensuous representations [intuitions] under rules and thereby to unite them in one consciousness. Without this use of sensibility, understanding would think nothing at all. Reason, on the other hand, shows such a pure spontaneity in the case of what are called ideas that it goes far beyond anything that sensibility can offer and shows its highest occupation in distinguishing the world of sense from the world of understanding, thereby prescribing limits to the understanding itself.

Therefore a rational being must regard himself qua intelligence (and hence not from the side of his lower powers) as belonging not to the world of sense but to the world of understanding. Therefore he has two standpoints from which he can regard himself and know laws of the use of his powers and hence of all his actions: first, insofar as he belongs to the world of sense subject to laws of nature (heteronomy); secondly, insofar as he belongs to the intelligible world subject to laws which, independent of nature, are not empirical but are founded only on reason.

As a rational being and hence as belonging to the intelligible world, can man never think of the causality of his own will except under the idea of freedom; for independence from the determining causes of the world of sense (an independence which reason must always attribute to itself) is freedom. Now the idea of freedom is inseparably connected with the concept of autonomy, and this in turn with the 453 universal principle of morality, which ideally is the ground of all actions of rational beings, just as natural law is the ground of all appearances.

The suspicion that we raised earlier is now removed, viz., that there might be a hidden circle involved in our inference from freedom to autonomy, and from this to the moral law — this is to say that we had perhaps laid down the idea of freedom only for the sake of the moral law in order subsequently to infer this law in its turn from freedom, and that we had therefore not been able to assign any ground at all for this law but had only assumed it by begging a principle which well-disposed souls would gladly concede us but which we could never put forward as a demonstrable proposition. But now we see that when we think of ourselves as free, we transfer ourselves into the intelligible world as members and know the autonomy of the will together with its consequence, morality; whereas when we think of ourselves as obligated, we consider ourselves as belonging to the world of sense and yet at the same time to the intelligible world.

How Is a Categorical Imperative Possible?

The rational being counts himself, qua intelligence, as belonging to the intelligible world, and only insofar as he is an efficient cause belonging to the intelligible world does he call his causality a will. But on the other side, he is conscious of himself as being also a part of the world of sense, where his actions are found as mere appearances of that causality. The possibility of these actions cannot, however, be discerned through such causality, which we do not know; rather, these actions as belonging to the world of sense must be viewed as determined by other appearances, namely, desires and inclinations. Therefore, if I were solely a member of the intelligible world, then all my actions would perfectly conform to the principle of the autonomy of a pure will; if I were solely a part of the world of sense, my actions would have to be taken as in complete conformity with the natural law of desires and inclinations, i.e., with the heteronomy of nature. (My actions would in the first case rest on the supreme principle of morality, in the second case on that of happiness.) But the intelligible world contains the ground of the world of sense and therefore also the ground of its laws; consequently, the intelligible world is (and must be thought of as) directly legislative for my will (which belongs wholly to the intelligible world). Therefore, even though on the one hand I must regard myself as a being belonging to the world of sense, yet on the other hand shall I have to know myself as an intelligence and as subject to the law of the intelligible world, i.e., to reason, which contains this law in the idea of freedom, and hence to know myself as subject to the autonomy of the will. Consequently, I must regard the laws of the intelligible world as imperatives for me, and the actions conforming to this principle as duties.

454

And thus are categorical imperatives possible because the idea of freedom makes me a member of an intelligible world. Now if I were a member of only that world, all my actions *would* always accord with autonomy of the will. But since I intuit myself at the same time as a member of the world of sense, my actions *ought* so to accord. This categorical *ought* presents a synthetic a priori proposition, whereby in addition to my will as affected by sensuous desires there is added further the idea of the same will, but as belonging to the intelligible world, pure and practical of itself, and as containing the supreme condition of the former will insofar as reason is concerned. All this is similar to the way in which concepts [categories] of the understanding, which of themselves signify nothing but the form of law in general, are added to intuitions of the world of sense and thus make possible synthetic a priori propositions, upon which all knowledge of nature rests.

The practical use of ordinary human reason bears out the correctness of this deduction. There is no one, not even the meanest villain, provided only that he is otherwise accustomed to the use of reason, who, when presented with examples of honesty of purpose, of steadfastness in following good maxims, and of sympathy and general benevolence (even when involved with great sacrifices of advantages and comfort) does not wish that he might also possess these qualities. Yet he cannot attain these in himself only because of his inclinations and impulses; but at the same time he wishes to be free from such inclinations which are a burden to him. He thereby proves that by having a will free of sensuous impulses he transfers himself in thought into an order of things entirely different from that of his desires in the field of sensibility. Since he cannot expect to obtain by the aforementioned wish any gratification of his desires or any condition that would satisfy any of his actual or even conceivable inclinations (inasmuch as through such an expectation the very idea that elicited the wish would be deprived of its preeminence) he can only expect a greater intrinsic worth of his own person. This better person he believes himself to be when he transfers himself to the standpoint of a member of the intelligible world, to which he is involuntarily forced by the idea of freedom, i.e., of being independent of deter-

455

mination by causes of the world of sense. From this standpoint he is conscious of having a good will, which by his own admission constitutes the law for the bad will belonging to him as a member of the world of sense—a law whose authority he acknowledges even while he transgresses it. The moral *ought* is, therefore, a necessary *would* insofar as he is a member of the intelligible world, and is thought by him as an *ought* only insofar as he regards himself as being at the same time a member of the world of sense.

Concerning the Extreme Limit of All Practical Philosophy

All men think of themselves as free as far as their will is concerned. Hence arise all judgments upon actions as being such as ought to have been done, even though they were not done. But this freedom is not a concept of experience, nor can it be such, since it always holds, even though experience shows the opposite of those requirements represented as necessary under the presupposition of freedom. On the other hand, it is just as necessary that whatever happens should be determined without any exception according to laws of nature; and this necessity of nature is likewise no concept of experience, just because it involves the concept of necessity and thus of a priori knowledge. But this concept of nature is confirmed by experience and must inevitably be presupposed if there is to be possible experience, which is coherent knowledge of the objects of sense in accordance with universal laws. Freedom is, therefore, only an idea of reason whose objective reality is in itself questionable; but nature is a concept of the understanding, which proves, and necessarily must prove, its reality by examples from experience.

There arises from this a dialectic of reason, since the freedom attributed to the will seems to contradict the necessity of nature. And even though at this parting of the ways reason for speculative purposes finds the road of natural necessity much better worn and more serviceable than that of freedom, yet for practical purposes the foot-path of freedom is the only one upon which it is possible to make use of reason in our conduct. Therefore, it is just as impossible for the most subtle philosophy as for the most ordinary human reason to argue away freedom. Hence philosophy must assume that no real contradiction will be found between freedom and natural necessity in the same human actions, for it cannot give up the concept of nature any more than that of freedom.

Nevertheless, even though one might never be able to comprehend how freedom is possible, yet this apparent contradiction must at least be removed in a convincing manner. For if the thought of freedom contradicts itself or nature, which is equally necessary, then freedom would have to be completely given up in favor of natural necessity.

It would, however, be impossible to escape this contradiction if the subject, deeming himself free, were to think of himself in the same sense or in the very same relationship when he calls himself free as when he assumes himself subject to the law of nature regarding the same action. Therefore, an unavoidable problem of speculative philosophy is at least to show that its illusion regarding the contradiction rests on our thinking of man in a different sense and relation when we call him free from when we regard him as being a part of nature and hence as subject to the laws of nature. Hence it must show not only that both can coexist very well, but that both must be thought of as necessarily united in the same subject; for otherwise no explanation could be given as to why reason should be burdened with an idea which involves us in a perplexity that is sorely embarrassing to reason in its theoretic use, even though it may without contradiction be united with another idea that is sufficiently established. This duty, however, is incumbent solely on speculative philosophy in order that it may clear the way for practical philosophy. Thus the philosopher has no option as to whether he will remove the apparent contradiction or leave it untouched; for in the latter case the theory regarding this could be *bonum vacans*,[2] into the possession of which the fatalist can justifiably enter and chase all morality out of its supposed property as occupying it without title.

Nevertheless, one cannot here say as yet that the boundary of practical philosophy begins. For the settlement of the controversy does not belong to practical philosophy; the latter only requires speculative reason to put an end to the dissension in which it is entangled as regards theoretical questions in order that practical reason may have rest and security from external attacks that might make disputable the ground upon which it wants to build.

457

The just claim to freedom of the will made even by ordinary human reason is founded on the consciousness and the admitted presupposition that reason is independent of mere subjective determination by causes which together make up what belongs only to sensation and comes under the general designation of sensibility. Regarding himself in this way as intelligence, man thereby puts himself into another order of things. And when he thinks of himself as intelligence endowed with a will and consequently with causality, he puts himself into relation with determining grounds of a kind altogether different from the kind when he perceives himself as a phenomenon in the world of sense (as he really is also) and subjects his causality to external determination according to laws of nature. Now he soon realizes that both can—and indeed must—hold good at the same time. For there is not the slightest contradiction involved in saying that a thing as appearance (belonging to the world of sense) is subject to certain laws, while it is independent of those laws when regarded as a thing or being in itself. That man must represent and think of himself in this two-fold way rests, on the one hand, upon the consciousness of himself as an object affected through the senses and, on the other hand, upon the consciousness of himself as intelligence, i.e., as independent of sensuous impulses in his use of reason (and hence as belonging to the intelligible world).

And hence man claims that he has a will which reckons to his account nothing that belongs merely to his desires and inclinations, and which, on the contrary, thinks of actions that can be performed only by disregarding all desires and sensuous incitements as being possible and as indeed being necessary for him. The causality of such actions lies in man as intelligence and lies in the laws of such effects and actions as are in accordance with principles of an intelligible world, of which he knows nothing more than that in such a world reason alone, and indeed pure reason independent of sensibility, gives the law. Furthermore, since he is in such a world his proper self only as intelligence (whereas regarded as a human being he is merely an appearance of himself), those laws apply to him immediately and categorically. Consequently, incitements from inclinations and impulses (and hence from the whole

2. [vacant property]

458 nature of the world of sense) cannot impair the laws of his willing insofar as he is intelligence. Indeed he does not even hold himself responsible for such inclinations and impulses or ascribe them to his proper self, i.e., his will, although he does ascribe to his will any indulgence which he might extend to them if he allowed them any influence on his maxims to the detriment of the rational laws of his will.

When practical reason thinks itself into an intelligible world, it does not in the least thereby transcend its limits, as it would if it tried to enter it by intuition or sensation. The thought of an intelligible world is merely negative as regards the world of sense. The latter world does not give reason any laws for determining the will and is positive only in this single point, viz., it simultaneously combines freedom as negative determination with a positive faculty and even a causality of reason. This causality is designated as a will to act in such a way that the principle of actions may accord with the essential character of a rational cause, i.e., with the condition that the maxim of these actions have universal validity as a law. But if practical reason were to bring in an object of the will, i.e., a motive of action, from the intelligible world, then it would overstep its boundaries and pretend to be acquainted with something of which it knows nothing. The concept of an intelligible world is thus only a point of view which reason sees itself compelled to take outside of appearances in order to think of itself as practical. If the influences of sensibility were determining for man, reason would not be able to take this point of view, which is nonetheless necessary if he is not to be denied the consciousness of himself as intelligence and hence as a rational cause that is active through reason, i.e., free in its operation. This thought certainly involves the idea of an order and a legislation different from that of the mechanism of nature which applies to the world of sense; and it makes necessary the concept of an intelligible world (i.e., the whole of rational beings as things in themselves). But it makes not the slightest claim to anything more than to think of such a world as regards merely its formal condition—i.e., the universality of the will's maxims as laws and thus the will's autonomy, which alone is consistent with freedom. On the contrary, all laws determined by reference to an object yield heteronomy, which can be found only in laws of nature and can apply only to the world of sense.

459 But reason would overstep all its bounds if it undertook to explain how pure reason can be practical. This is exactly the same problem as explaining how freedom is possible.

For we can explain nothing but what we can reduce to laws whose object can be given in some possible experience. But freedom is a mere idea, whose objective reality can in no way be shown in accordance with laws of nature and consequently not in any possible experience. Therefore, the idea of freedom can never admit of comprehension or even of insight, because it cannot by any analogy have an example falling under it. It holds only as a necessary presupposition of reason in a being who believes himself conscious of a will, i.e., of a faculty distinct from mere desire (namely, a faculty of determining himself to action as intelligence and hence in accordance with laws of reason independently of natural instincts). But where determination according to laws of nature ceases, there likewise ceases all explanation and nothing remains but defense, i.e., refutation of the objections of those who profess to have seen deeper into the essence of things and thereupon boldly declare freedom to be impossible. One can only show them that their supposed discovery of a contradiction lies nowhere but here: in order to make the law of nature applicable to human actions, they have necessarily had to regard man as an appearance; and now when they are required to think of man qua intelligence as thing in himself as well, they still persist in regarding him as appearance. In that case, to be sure, the exemption of man's causality (i.e., his will) from all the natural laws of the world of sense would, as regards one and the same subject, give rise to a contradiction. But this disappears if they would but bethink themselves and admit, as is reasonable, that behind appearances there must lie as their ground also things in themselves (though hidden) and that the laws of their operations cannot be expected to be the same as those that govern their appearances.

The subjective impossibility of explaining freedom of the will is the same as the impossibility of discovering and explaining an interest[3] which man can take in moral laws. Nevertheless, he does indeed take such an interest, the basis of which in us is called moral feeling. Some people have falsely construed this feeling to be the standard of our moral judgment, whereas it must rather be regarded as the subjective effect that the law exercises upon the will, while reason alone furnishes the objective grounds of such moral feeling. 460

In order to will what reason alone prescribes as an *ought* for sensuously affected rational beings, there certainly must be a power of reason to infuse a feeling of pleasure or satisfaction in the fulfillment of duty, and hence there has to be a causality of reason to determine sensibility in accordance with rational principles. But it is quite impossible to discern, i.e., to make a priori conceivable, how a mere thought which itself contains nothing sensuous can produce a sensation of pleasure or displeasure. For here is a special kind of causality regarding which, as with all causality, we can determine nothing a priori but must consult experience alone. However, experience can provide us with no relation of cause and effect except between two objects of experience. But in this case pure reason by means of mere ideas (which furnish no object at all for experience) is to be the cause of an effect that admittedly lies in experience. Consequently, there is for us men no possibility at all for an explanation as to how and why the universality of a maxim as a law, and hence morality, interests us. This much only is certain: the moral law is valid for us not because it interests us (for this is heteronomy and the dependence of practical reason on sensibility, viz., on an underlying feeling whereby reason could never be morally legislative); but, rather, 461 the moral law interests us because it is valid for us as men, since it has sprung from our will as intelligence and hence from our proper self. But what belongs to mere appearance is necessarily subordinated by reason to the nature of the thing in itself.

Thus the question as to how a categorical imperative is possible can be answered to the extent that there can be supplied the sole presupposition under which such an im-

---

3. Interest is that by which reason becomes practical, i.e., a cause determining the will. Therefore one says of rational beings only that they take an interest in something; non-rational creatures feel only sensuous impulses. Reason takes an immediate interest in the action only when the universal validity of the maxim of the action is a sufficient determining ground of the will. Such an interest alone is pure. But when reason is able to determine the will only by means of another object of desire or under the presupposition of some special feeling in the subject, then reason takes only a mediate interest in the action. And since reason of itself alone without the help of experience can discover neither objects of the will nor a special feeling underlying the will, the latter interest would be only empirical and not a pure rational interest. The logical interest of reason (viz., to extend its insights) is never immediate, but presupposes purposes for which reason might be used.

perative is alone possible—namely, the idea of freedom. The necessity of this presupposition is discernible, and this much is sufficient for the practical use of reason, i.e., for being convinced as to the validity of this imperative, and hence also of the moral law; but how this presupposition itself is possible can never be discerned by any human reason. However, on the presupposition of freedom of the will of an intelligence, there necessarily follows the will's autonomy as the formal condition under which alone the will can be determined. To presuppose this freedom of the will (without involving any contradiction with the principle of natural necessity in the connection of appearances in the world of sense) is not only quite possible (as speculative philosophy can show), but is without any further condition also necessary for a rational being conscious of his causality through reason and hence conscious of a will (which is different from desires) as he makes such freedom in practice, i.e., in idea, the underlying condition of all his voluntary actions. But how pure reason can be practical by itself without other incentives taken from whatever source—i.e., how the mere principle of the universal validity of all reason's maxims as laws (which would certainly be the form of a pure practical reason) can by itself, without any matter (object) of the will in which some antecedent interest might be taken, furnish an incentive and produce an interest which could be called purely moral; or, in other words, how pure reason could be practical: to explain all this is quite beyond the power of human reason, and all the effort and work of seeking such an explanation is wasted.

462   It is just the same as if I tried to find out how freedom itself is possible as causality of a will. For I thereby leave the philosophical basis of explanation, and I have no other basis. Now I could indeed flutter about in the world of intelligences, i.e., in the intelligible world still remaining to me. But even though I have an idea of such a world—an idea which has its own good grounds—yet I have not the slightest acquaintance with such a world and can never attain such acquaintance by all the efforts of my natural faculty of reason. This intelligible world signifies only a something that remains over when I have excluded from the determining grounds of my will everything that belongs to the world of sense, so as to restrict the principle of having all motives come from the field of sensibility. By so doing I set bounds to this field and show that it does not contain absolutely everything within itself but that beyond it there is still something more, regarding which, however, I have no further acquaintance. After the exclusion of all matter, i.e., cognition of objects, from pure reason which thinks this ideal, nothing remains over for me except such reason's form, viz., the practical law of the universal validity of maxims; and in conformity with this law I think of reason in its relation to a pure intelligible world as a possible efficient cause, i.e., as a cause determining the will. An incentive must in this case be wholly absent; this idea of an intelligible world would here have to be itself the incentive or have to be that in which reason originally took an interest. But to make this conceivable is precisely the problem that we cannot solve.

Here then is the extreme limit of all moral inquiry. To determine this limit is of great importance for the following considerations. On the one hand, reason should not, to the detriment of morals, search around in the world of sense for the supreme motive and for some interest that is conceivable but is nonetheless empirical. On the other hand, reason should not flap its wings impotently, without leaving the spot, in a space that for it is empty, namely, the space of transcendent concepts that is called the intelligible world, and thereby lose itself among mere phantoms of the brain. Furthermore, the idea of a pure intelligible world regarded as a whole of all intelligences to which we ourselves belong as rational beings (even though we are from another standpoint also members of the world of sense) remains always a useful and permissible idea for the purpose of a rational belief, although all knowledge ends at its boundary. This idea produces in us a lively interest in the moral law by means of the splendid ideal of a universal kingdom of ends in themselves (rational beings), to which we can belong as members only if we careful- ly conduct ourselves according to maxims of freedom as if they were laws of nature.

463

Concluding Remark

The speculative use of reason with regard to nature leads to the absolute necessity of some supreme cause of the world. The practical use of reason with reference to freedom leads also to absolute necessity, but only to the necessity of the laws of the actions of a rational being as such. Now it is an essential principle of all use of our reason to push its knowledge to a consciousness of its necessity (for without necessity there would be no rational knowledge). But there is an equally essential restriction of the same reason that it cannot have insight into the necessity either of what is or what does happen or of what should happen, unless there is presupposed a condi- tion under which it is or does happen or should happen. In this way, however, the satisfaction of reason is only further and further postponed by the continual inquiry after the condition. Reason, therefore, restlessly seeks the unconditionally necessary and sees itself compelled to assume this without having any means of making such necessity conceivable; reason is happy enough if only it can find a concept which is compatible with this assumption. Hence there is no fault in our deduction of the supreme principle of morality, but rather a reproach which must be made against human reason generally, involved in the fact that reason cannot render conceivable the absolute necessity of an unconditioned practical law (such as the categorical im- perative must be). Reason cannot be blamed for not being willing to explain this necessity by means of a condition, namely, by basing it on some underlying interest, because in that case the law would no longer be moral, i.e., a supreme law of freedom. And so even though we do not indeed grasp the practical unconditioned necessity of the moral imperative, we do nevertheless grasp its inconceivability. This is all that can be fairly asked of a philosophy which strives in its principles to reach the very limit of human reason.

JOHN STUART MILL

John Stuart Mill (1806–1873) was born in London on May 20, 1806. His father, James Mill, was a journalist and an official of the East India Company. Two years after John Stuart Mill's birth, his father met the philosopher and reformer Jeremy Bentham; for the remainder of his life he was Bentham's devoted friend, disciple, and spokesman. His commitment to the utilitarian creed involved his son, whom James Mill chose to educate at home in order to cultivate the perfect utilitarian individual.

Mill tells the story of his remarkable education in his *Autobiography*, published after his death by his stepdaughter Helen Taylor in 1873. By age three, Mill had studied Greek and, by eight, Latin. He began philosophy and logic at twelve, spent a year in France, and returned to England at fifteen to study law with the famous legal thinker John Austin. Throughout this process Mill conversed with his father's Benthamite friends on philosophical, political, and economic issues and engaged in drills, recitations, and debates under his father's severe direction.

In 1823 Mill completed his education and was employed by the East India Company, where he remained until his retirement in 1858. In 1856 he was appointed to the office of Chief Examiner, the company's second highest post, and two years later refused government employment when the company was dissolved by Act of Parliament.

In 1826, at the age of twenty, Mill was the victim of an intellectual crisis. Later he would recall the event as the beginning of his intellectual independence from Bentham. He had once been so totally committed to Bentham's utilitarianism that it served for him as a virtual religion; he was student, disciple, and even evangelist of this rational, humanistic faith, founding the Utilitarian Society, editing the Benthamite journal, the *Westminster Review*, and leading the "Philosophical Radicals," the young Benthamite organization. But at twenty he came to recognize his lack of emotion and feeling; he had become a pawn of reason, without tenderness or sensitivity. He turned to Wordsworth and Coleridge, the great romantic poets, for guidance in those feelings without which life could not be whole and fulfilled.

In 1831 Mill met Mrs. Harriet Taylor, the young wife of a wealthy merchant; she became his closest friend and confidant. As the years passed, the Platonic relationship deepened, and eventually, shortly after her husband's death in 1849, the two married. Mill's praise for Harriet Taylor's intelligence, imagination, and tenderness of soul was boundless; he was devoted to her and acknowledged her profound influence on his thinking and his life. To her, Mill would say, should be ascribed the human element in his writings and the sensitive application of principle to the issues of the day. In 1858 she died in Avignon, while on a vacation.

Perhaps the outstanding result of their collaboration—and Mill's most famous political work—is *On Liberty*, published in 1859. At least from 1854 they had worked on this account of the significance of individual self-development, enriched by Mill's study of Wordsworth and Coleridge, and the limitations of social and governmental control over the individual. In it Mill famously argues that creative self-development is central to personal character and that only self-protection justifies limitations on individual freedom. As one modern commentator has put it, *On Liberty* "is such a deeply felt defence of the right of individuals to be left alone unless they are causing real damage to other people that hardly anyone puts it down without reading it straight through." When Harriet died, the book had not received its final revisions, but Mill sent it to the publisher, without further alteration and dedicated to her.

After Harriet's death and his retirement, Mill wrote extensively, bringing to fruition many projects that he had begun during the eight years of their marriage. Among these were the *Considerations on Representative Government*, published in 1861, and *The Subjection of Women*, his revolutionary defense of women's capacity for self-development, which was written in 1861 but appeared only in 1869.

In October, November, and December of 1861 Mill published three essays in a prominent intellectual monthly, *Fraser's Magazine*. It was his attempt to appeal to an educated lay audience about some fundamental matters concerning morality, religion, reason, pleasure, and duty. These essays, reworked into five chapters and published in book form as *Utilitarianism* in 1863, are an act of radical reform, an effort to defend the integrity of a benevolent, rational moral view that was humane and that would encourage positive change. The book was also an attack—on Kant and intuitionist moral theorists and on Bentham, whose conception of the goal of utility was too narrow and intellectualist for Mill. It remains to this day a classic formulation of instrumentalist moral theory.

Two years later Mill was elected to Parliament from Westminster, serving three years, until 1868. From then until his death on May 8, 1873, he wrote and avoided those who sought him. Tended in these last years by his stepdaughter Helen, Mill died quietly and was buried in Avignon, alongside his beloved Harriet.

Recommended readings

Berger, Fred. *Happiness, Justice and Freedom*. Berkeley: University of California Press, 1985.

Gorowitz, S. (ed.). *Utilitarianism and Critical Essays*. Indianapolis: Bobbs-Merrill, 1971.

Gray, John. *Mill on Liberty: A Defence*. London: Routledge, 1983.

Okin, Susan Moller. *Women in Western Political Thought*. Princeton: Princeton University Press, 1979.

Ryan, Alan. *Mill*. London: Routledge, 1974.

Thomas, William. *J. S. Mill*. Oxford: Oxford University Press, 1985.

ON LIBERTY

Contents

Chapter I.   Introductory.
Chapter II.   Of the Liberty of Thought and Discussion.
Chapter III. Of Individuality, as One of the Elements of Well-Being.
Chapter IV. Of the Limits to the Authority of Society over the Individual.
Chapter V.   Applications.

The grand, leading principle, towards which every argument unfolded in these pages directly converges, is the absolute and essential importance of human development in its richest diversity.

—Wilhelm von Humboldt: *Sphere and Duties of Government.*

To the beloved and deplored memory of her who was the inspirer, and in part the author, of all that is best in my writings—the friend and wife whose exalted sense of truth and right was my strongest incitement, and whose approbation was my chief reward—I dedicate this volume. Like all that I have written for many years, it belongs as much to her as to me; but the work as it stands has had, in a very insufficient degree, the inestimable advantage of her revision; some of the most important portions having been reserved for a more careful re-examination, which they are now never destined to receive. Were I but capable of interpreting to the world one half the great thoughts and noble feelings which are buried in her grave, I should be the medium of a greater benefit to it, than is ever likely to arise from anything that I can write, unprompted and unassisted by her all but unrivalled wisdom.

ON LIBERTY

CHAPTER I

Introductory

The subject of this Essay is not the so-called Liberty of the Will, so unfortunately opposed to the misnamed doctrine of Philosophical Necessity; but Civil, or Social Liberty: the nature and limits of the power which can be legitimately exercised by society over the individual. A question seldom stated, and hardly ever discussed, in general terms, but which profoundly influences the practical controversies of the age by its latent presence, and is likely soon to make itself recognised as the vital question of the future. It is so far from being new, that, in a certain sense, it has divided mankind, almost from the remotest ages; but in the stage of progress into which the more civilized portions of the species have now entered, it presents itself under new conditions, and requires a different and more fundamental treatment.

This edition of *On Liberty* was drawn from the 1869 4th edition Longmans, Green, Reader, and Dyer.

The struggle between Liberty and Authority is the most conspicuous feature in the portions of history with which we are earliest familiar, particularly in that of Greece, Rome, and England. But in old times this contest was between subjects, or some classes of subjects, and the Government. By liberty, was meant protection against the tyranny of the political rulers. The rulers were conceived (except in some of the popular governments of Greece) as in a necessarily antagonistic position to the people whom they ruled. They consisted of a governing One, or a governing tribe or caste, who derived their authority from inheritance or conquest, who, at all events, did not hold it at the pleasure of the governed, and whose supremacy men did not venture, perhaps did not desire, to contest, whatever precautions might be taken against its oppressive exercise. Their power was regarded as necessary, but also as highly dangerous; as a weapon which they would attempt to use against their subjects, no less than against external enemies. To prevent the weaker members of the community from being preyed upon by innumerable vultures, it was needful that there should be an animal of prey stronger than the rest, commissioned to keep them down. But as the king of the vultures would be no less bent upon preying on the flock than any of the minor harpies, it was indispensable to be in a perpetual attitude of defence against his beak and claws. The aim, therefore, of patriots was to set limits to the power which the ruler should be suffered to exercise over the community; and this limitation was what they meant by liberty. It was attempted in two ways. First, by obtaining a recognition of certain immunities, called political liberties or rights, which it was to be regarded as a breach of duty in the ruler to infringe, and which if he did infringe, specific resistance, or general rebellion, was held to be justifiable. A second, and generally a later expedient, was the establishment of constitutional checks, by which the consent of the community, or of a body of some sort, supposed to represent its interests, was made a necessary condition to some of the more important acts of the governing power. To the first of these modes of limitation, the ruling power, in most European countries, was compelled, more or less, to submit. It was not so with the second; and, to attain this, or when already in some degree possessed, to attain it more completely, became everywhere the principal object of the lovers of liberty. And so long as mankind were content to combat one enemy by another, and to be ruled by a master, on condition of being guaranteed more or less efficaciously against his tyranny, they did not carry their aspirations beyond this point.

A time, however, came, in the progress of human affairs, when men ceased to think it a necessity of nature that their governors should be an independent power, opposed in interest to themselves. It appeared to them much better that the various magistrates of the State should be their tenants or delegates, revocable at their pleasure. In that way alone, it seemed, could they have complete security that the powers of government would never be abused to their disadvantage. By degrees this new demand for elective and temporary rulers became the prominent object of the exertions of the popular party, wherever any such party existed; and superseded, to a considerable extent, the previous efforts to limit the power of rulers. As the struggle proceeded for making the ruling power emanate from the periodical choice of the ruled, some persons began to think that too much importance had been attached to the limitation of the power itself. *That* (it might seem) was a resource against rulers whose interests were habitually opposed to those of the people. What was now wanted was, that the rulers should be identified with the people; that their interest and will should be the interest and will of the nation. The nation did not need to be protected against its own will. There was no fear of its tyrannizing over itself. Let the rulers be effectually responsible to it, promptly removable by it, and it could afford to trust them with power of which it could itself dictate the use to be made. Their power was but the nation's own power, concentrated, and in a form convenient for exercise. This mode of thought, or rather perhaps of feeling, was common among the last generation of European liberalism, in the Continental section of which it still apparently predominates. Those who admit any limit to what a government may do, except in the case of such governments as they think ought not to exist, stand out as brilliant exceptions among the political thinkers of the Continent. A similar tone of sentiment might by this time have been prevalent in our own country, if the circumstances which for a time encouraged it, had continued unaltered.

But, in political and philosophical theories, as well as in persons, success discloses faults and infirmities which failure might have concealed from observation. The notion, that the people have no need to limit their power over themselves, might seem axiomatic, when popular government was a thing only dreamed about, or read of as having existed at some distant period of the past. Neither was that notion necessarily disturbed by such temporary aberrations as those of the French Revolution, the worst of which were the work of an usurping few, and which, in any case, belonged, not to the permanent working of popular institutions, but to a sudden and convulsive outbreak against monarchical and aristocratic despotism. In time, however, a democratic republic came to occupy a large portion of the earth's surface, and made itself felt as one of the most powerful members of the community of nations; and elective and responsible government became subject to the observations and criticisms which wait upon a great existing fact. It was now perceived that such phrases as 'self-government,' and 'the power of the people over themselves,' do not express the true state of the case. The 'people' who exercise the power are not always the same people with those over whom it is exercised; and the 'self-government' spoken of is not the government of each by himself, but of each by all the rest. The will of the people, moreover, practically means the will of the most numerous or the most active *part* of the people; the majority, or those who succeed in making themselves accepted as the majority; the people, consequently, *may* desire to oppress a part of their number; and precautions are as much needed against this as against any other abuse of power. The limitation, therefore, of the power of government over individuals loses none of its importance when the holders of power are regularly accountable to the community, that is, to the strongest party therein. This view of things, recommending itself equally to the intelligence of thinkers and to the inclination of those important classes in European society to whose real or supposed interests democracy is adverse, has had no difficulty in establishing itself; and in political speculations 'the tyranny of the majority' is now generally included among the evils against which society requires to be on its guard.

Like other tyrannies, the tyranny of the majority was at first, and is still vulgarly, held in dread, chiefly as operating through the acts of the public authorities. But reflecting persons perceived that when society is itself the tyrant—society collectively, over the separate individuals who compose it—its means of tyrannizing are not restricted to the acts which it may do by the hands of its political functionaries. Society can and does execute its own mandates: and if it issues wrong mandates instead of right, or any mandates at all in things with which it ought not to meddle, it practises a social tyranny more formidable than many kinds of political oppression, since, though not usually upheld by such extreme penalties, it leaves fewer means of escape, penetrating much more deeply into the details of life, and enslaving the soul itself. Protection, therefore, against the tyranny of the magistrate is not enough: there needs protection also against the tyranny of the prevailing opinion and feeling; against the tendency of society to impose, by other means than civil penalties, its own ideas and practices as rules of conduct on those who dissent from them; to fetter the development, and, if possible, prevent the formation, of any individuality not in harmony with its ways, and compel all characters to fashion themselves upon the model of its own. There is a limit to the legitimate interference of collective opinion with individual independence: and to find that limit, and maintain it against encroachment, is as indispensable to a good condition of human affairs, as protection against political despotism.

But though this proposition is not likely to be contested in general terms, the practical question, where to place the limit—how to make the fitting adjustment between individual independence and social control—is a subject on which nearly everything remains to be done. All that makes existence valuable to any one, depends on the enforcement of restraints upon the actions of other people. Some rules of conduct, therefore, must be imposed, by law in the first place, and by opinion on many things which are not fit subjects for the operation of law. What these rules should be, is the principal question in human affairs; but if we except a few of the most obvious cases, it is one of those which least progress has been made in resolving. No two ages, and scarcely any two countries, have decided it alike; and the decision of one age or country is a wonder to another. Yet the people of any given age and country no more suspect any difficulty in it, than if it were a subject on which mankind had always been agreed. The rules which obtain among themselves appear to them self-evident and self-justifying. This all but universal illusion is one of the examples of the magical influence of custom, which is not only, as the proverb says, a second nature, but is continually mistaken for the first. The effect of custom, in preventing any misgiving respecting the rules of conduct which mankind impose on one another, is all the more complete because the subject is one on which it is not generally considered necessary that reasons should be given, either by one person to others, or by each to himself. People are accustomed to believe, and have been encouraged in the belief by some who aspire to the character of philosophers, that their feelings, on subjects of this nature, are better than reasons, and render reasons unnecessary. The practical principle which guides them to their opinions on the regulation of human conduct, is the feeling in each person's mind that everybody should be required to act as he, and those with whom he sympathizes, would like them to act. No one, indeed, acknowledges to himself that his standard of judgment is his own liking; but an opinion on a point of conduct, not supported by reasons, can only count as one person's preference; and if the reasons, when given, are a mere appeal to a similar preference felt by other people, it is still only many people's liking instead of one. To an ordinary man, however, his own preference, thus supported, is not only a perfectly satisfactory reason, but the only one he generally has for any of his notions of morality, taste, or propriety, which are not expressly written in his religious creed; and his chief guide in the interpretation even of that. Men's opinions, accordingly, on what is laudable or blameable, are affected by all the multifarious causes which influence their wishes in regard to the conduct of others, and which are as numerous as those which determine their wishes on any other subject. Sometimes their reason—at other times their prejudices or superstitions: often their social affections, not seldom their antisocial ones, their envy or jealousy, their arrogance or contemptuousness: but most commonly, their desires or fears for themselves—their legitimate or illegitimate self-interest. Wherever there is an ascendant class, a large portion of the morality of the country emanates from its class interests, and its feelings of class superiority. The morality between Spartans and Helots, between planters and negroes, between princes and subjects, between nobles and roturiers, between men and women, has been for the most part the creation of these class interests and feelings: and the sentiments thus generated, react in turn upon the moral feelings of the members of the ascendant class, in their relations among themselves. Where, on the other hand, a class, formerly ascendant, has lost its ascendancy, or where its ascendancy is unpopular, the prevailing moral sentiments frequently bear the impress of an impatient dislike of superiority. Another grand determining principle of the rules of conduct, both in act and forbearance, which have been enforced by law or opinion, has been the servility of mankind towards the supposed preferences or aversions of their temporal masters, or of their gods. This servility, though essentially selfish, is not hypocrisy; it gives rise to perfectly genuine sentiments of abhorrence; it made men burn magicians and heretics. Among so many baser influences, the general and obvious interests of society have of course had a share, and a large one, in the direction of the moral sentiments: less, however, as a matter of reason, and on their own account, than as a consequence of the sympathies and antipathies which grew out of them: and sympathies and antipathies which had little or nothing to do with the interests of society, have made themselves felt in the establishment of moralities with quite as great force.

The likings and dislikings of society, or of some powerful portion of it, are thus the main thing which has practically determined the rules laid down for general observance, under the penalties of law or opinion. And in general, those who have been in advance of society in thought and feeling, have left this condition of things unassailed in principle, however they may have come into conflict with it in some of its details. They have occupied themselves rather in inquiring what things society ought to like or dislike, than in questioning whether its likings or dislikings should be a law to individuals. They preferred endeavouring to alter the feelings of mankind on the particular points on which they were themselves heretical, rather than make common cause in defence of freedom, with heretics generally. The only case in which the higher ground has been taken on principle and maintained with consistency, by any but an individual here and there, is that of religious belief: a case instructive in many ways, and not least so as forming a most striking instance of the fallibility of what is called the moral sense: for the *odium theologicum,* in a sincere bigot, is one of the most unequivocal cases of moral feeling. Those who first broke the yoke of what called itself the Universal Church, were in general as little willing to permit difference of religious opinion as that church itself. But when the heat of the conflict was over, without giving a complete victory to any party, and each church or sect was reduced to limit its hopes to retaining possession of the ground it already occupied; minorities, seeing that they had no chance of becoming majorities, were under the necessity of pleading to those whom they could not convert, for permission to differ. It is accordingly on this battle field, almost solely, that the rights of the individual against society have been asserted on broad grounds of principle, and the claim of society to exercise authority over dissentients, openly controverted. The great writers to whom the world owes what religious liberty it possesses, have mostly asserted freedom of conscience as an indefeasible right, and denied absolutely that a human being is accountable to others for his religious belief. Yet so natural to mankind is intolerance in whatever they really care about, that religious freedom has hardly anywhere been practically realized, except where religious indifference, which dislikes to have its peace disturbed by theological quarrels, has added its weight to the scale. In the minds of almost all religious persons, even in the most tolerant countries, the duty of toleration is admitted with tacit reserves. One person will bear with dissent in matters of church government, but not of dogma; another can tolerate everybody, short of a Papist or an Unitarian; another, every one who believes in revealed religion; a few extend their charity a little further, but stop at the belief in a God and in a future state. Wherever the sentiment of the majority is still genuine and intense, it is found to have abated little of its claim to be obeyed.

In England, from the peculiar circumstances of our political history, though the yoke of opinion is perhaps heavier, that of law is lighter, than in most other countries of Europe; and there is considerable jealousy of direct interference, by the legislative or the executive power, with private conduct; not so much from any just regard for the independence of the individual, as from the still subsisting habit of looking on the government as representing an opposite interest to the public. The majority have not yet learnt to feel the power of the government their power, or its opinions their opinions. When they do so, individual liberty will probably be as much exposed to invasion from the government, as it already is from public opinion. But, as yet, there is a considerable amount of feeling ready to be called forth against any attempt of the law to control individuals in things in which they have not hitherto been accustomed to be controlled by it; and this with very little discrimination as to whether the matter is, or is not, within the legitimate sphere of legal control; insomuch that the feeling, highly salutary on the whole, is perhaps quite as often misplaced as well grounded in the particular instances of its application. There is, in fact, no recognised principle by which the propriety or impropriety of government interference is customarily tested. People decide according to their personal preferences. Some, whenever they see any good to be done, or evil to be remedied, would willingly instigate the government to undertake the business; while others prefer to bear almost any amount of social evil, rather than add one to the departments of human interests amenable to governmental control. And men range themselves on one or the other side in any particular case, according to this general direction of their sentiments; or according to the degree of interest which they feel in the particular thing which it is proposed that the government should do, or according to the belief they entertain that the government would, or would not, do it in the manner they prefer; but very rarely on account of any opinion to which they consistently adhere, as to what things are fit to be done by a government. And it seems to me that in consequence of this absence of rule or principle, one side is at present as often wrong as the other; the interference of government is, with about equal frequency, improperly invoked and improperly condemned.

The object of this Essay is to assert one very simple principle, as entitled to govern absolutely the dealings of society with the individual in the way of compulsion and control, whether the means used be physical force in the form of legal penalties, or the moral coercion of public opinion. That principle is, that the sole end for which mankind are warranted, individually or collectively, in interfering with the liberty of action of any of their number, is self-protection. That the only purpose for which power can be rightfully exercised over any member of a civilized community, against his will, is to prevent harm to others. His own good, either physical or moral, is not a sufficient warrant. He cannot rightfully be compelled to do or forbear because it will be better for him to do so, because it will make him happier, because, in the opinions of others, to do so would be wise, or even right. These are good reasons for remonstrating with him, or reasoning with him, or persuading him, or entreating him, but not for compelling him, or visiting him with any evil in case he do otherwise. To justify that, the conduct from which it is desired to deter him, must be calculated to produce evil to some one else. The only part of the conduct of any one, for which he is amenable to society, is that which concerns others. In the part which merely concerns himself, his independence is, of right, absolute. Over himself, over his own body and mind, the individual is sovereign.

It is, perhaps, hardly necessary to say that this doctrine is meant to apply only to human beings in the maturity of their faculties. We are not speaking of children, or of young persons below the age which the law may fix as that of manhood or womanhood. Those who are still in a state to require being taken care of by others, must be protected against their own actions as well as against external injury. For the same reason, we may leave out of consideration those backward states of society in which the race itself may be considered as in its nonage. The early difficulties in the way of spontaneous progress are so great, that there is seldom any choice of means for overcoming them; and a ruler full of the spirit of improvement is warranted in the use of any expedients that will attain an end, perhaps otherwise unattainable. Despotism is a legitimate mode of government in dealing with barbarians, provided the end be their improvement, and the means justified by actually effecting that end. Liberty, as a principle, has no application to any state of things anterior to the time when mankind have become capable of being improved by free and equal discussion. Until then, there is nothing for them but implicit obedience to an Akbar or a Charlemagne, if they are so fortunate as to find one. But as soon as mankind have attained the capacity of being guided to their own improvement by conviction or persuasion (a period long since reached in all nations with whom we need here concern ourselves), compulsion, either in the direct form or in that of pains and penalties for non-compliance, is no longer admissible as a means to their own good, and justifiable only for the security of others.

It is proper to state that I forego any advantage which could be derived to my argument from the idea of abstract right, as a thing independent of utility. I regard utility as the ultimate appeal on all ethical questions; but it must be utility in the largest sense, grounded on the permanent interests of man as a progressive being. Those interests, I contend, authorize the subjection of individual spontaneity to external control, only in respect to those actions of each, which concern the interest of other people. If any one does an act hurtful to others, there is a *prima facie* case for punishing him, by law, or, where legal penalties are not safely applicable, by general disapprobation. There are also many positive acts for the benefit of others which he may rightfully be compelled to perform; such as, to give evidence in a court of justice; to bear his fair share in the common defence, or in any other joint work necessary to the interest of the society of which he enjoys the protection; and to perform certain acts of individual beneficence, such as saving a fellow-creature's

life, or interposing to protect the defenceless against ill-usage, things which whenever it is obviously a man's duty to do, he may rightfully be made responsible to
society for not doing. A person may cause evil to others not only by his actions but
by his inaction, and in either case he is justly accountable to them for the injury.
The latter case, it is true, requires a much more cautious exercise of compulsion
than the former. To make any one answerable for doing evil to others, is the rule;
to make him answerable for not preventing evil, is, comparatively speaking, the
exception. Yet there are many cases clear enough and grave enough to justify that
exception. In all things which regard the external relations of the individual, he is
de jure amenable to those whose interests are concerned, and if need be, to society
as their protector. There are often good reasons for not holding him to the responsibility; but these reasons must arise from the special expediencies of the case: either
because it is a kind of case in which he is on the whole likely to act better, when left
to his own discretion, than when controlled in any way in which society have it in
their power to control him; or because the attempt to exercise control would produce
other evils, greater than those which it would prevent. When such reasons as these
preclude the enforcement of responsibility, the conscience of the agent himself
should step into the vacant judgment seat, and protect those interests of others
which have no external protection; judging himself all the more rigidly, because the
case does not admit of his being made accountable to the judgment of his fellow-
creatures.

But there is a sphere of action in which society, as distinguished from the individual, has, if any, only an indirect interest; comprehending all that portion of a
person's life and conduct which affects only himself, or if it also affects others, only
with their free, voluntary, and undeceived consent and participation. When I say
only himself, I mean directly, and in the first instance: for whatever affects himself,
may affect others through himself; and the objection which may be grounded on this
contingency, will receive consideration in the sequel. This, then, is the appropriate
region of human liberty. It comprises, first, the inward domain of consciousness;
demanding liberty of conscience, in the most comprehensive sense; liberty of
thought and feeling; absolute freedom of opinion and sentiment on all subjects,
practical or speculative, scientific, moral, or theological. The liberty of expressing
and publishing opinions may seem to fall under a different principle, since it belongs
to that part of the conduct of an individual which concerns other people; but, being
almost of as much importance as the liberty of thought itself, and resting in great
part on the same reasons, is practically inseparable from it. Secondly, the principle
requires liberty of tastes and pursuits; of framing the plan of our life to suit our
own character; of doing as we like, subject to such consequences as may follow:
without impediment from our fellow-creatures, so long as what we do does not harm
them, even though they should think our conduct foolish, perverse, or wrong.
Thirdly, from this liberty of each individual, follows the liberty, within the same
limits, of combination among individuals; freedom to unite, for any purpose not
involving harm to others: the persons combining being supposed to be of full age,
and not forced or deceived.

No society in which these liberties are not, on the whole, respected, is free,
whatever may be its form of government; and none is completely free in which they
do not exist absolute and unqualified. The only freedom which deserves the name,
is that of pursuing our own good in our own way, so long as we do not attempt to
deprive others of theirs, or impede their efforts to obtain it. Each is the proper

guardian of his own health, whether bodily, or mental and spiritual. Mankind are greater gainers by suffering each other to live as seems good to themselves, than by compelling each to live as seems good to the rest.

Though this doctrine is anything but new, and, to some persons, may have the air of a truism, there is no doctrine which stands more directly opposed to the general tendency of existing opinion and practice. Society has expended fully as much effort in the attempt (according to its lights) to compel people to conform to its notions of personal, as of social excellence. The ancient commonwealths thought themselves entitled to practise, and the ancient philosophers countenanced, the regulation of every part of private conduct by public authority, on the ground that the State had a deep interest in the whole bodily and mental discipline of every one of its citizens; a mode of thinking which may have been admissible in small republics surrounded by powerful enemies, in constant peril of being subverted by foreign attack or internal commotion, and to which even a short interval of relaxed energy and self-command might so easily be fatal, that they could not afford to wait for the salutary permanent effects of freedom. In the modern world, the greater size of political communities, and above all, the separation between spiritual and temporal authority (which placed the direction of men's consciences in other hands than those which controlled their worldly affairs), prevented so great an interference by law in the details of private life; but the engines of moral repression have been wielded more strenuously against divergence from the reigning opinion in self-regarding, than even in social matters; religion, the most powerful of the elements which have entered into the formation of moral feeling, having almost always been governed either by the ambition of a hierarchy, seeking control over every department of human conduct, or by the spirit of Puritanism. And some of those modern reformers who have placed themselves in strongest opposition to the religions of the past, have been noway behind either churches or sects in their assertion of the right of spiritual domination: M. Comte, in particular, whose social system, as unfolded in his *Système de Politique Positive,* aims at establishing (though by moral more than by legal appliances) a despotism of society over the individual, surpassing anything contemplated in the political ideal of the most rigid disciplinarian among the ancient philosophers.

Apart from the peculiar tenets of individual thinkers, there is also in the world at large an increasing inclination to stretch unduly the powers of society over the individual, both by the force of opinion and even by that of legislation: and as the tendency of all the changes taking place in the world is to strengthen society, and diminish the power of the individual, this encroachment is not one of the evils which tend spontaneously to disappear, but, on the contrary, to grow more and more formidable. The disposition of mankind, whether as rulers or as fellow-citizens, to impose their own opinions and inclinations as a rule of conduct on others, is so energetically supported by some of the best and by some of the worst feelings incident to human nature, that it is hardly ever kept under restraint by anything but want of power; and as the power is not declining, but growing, unless a strong barrier of moral conviction can be raised against the mischief, we must expect, in the present circumstances of the world, to see it increase.

It will be convenient for the argument, if, instead of at once entering upon the general thesis, we confine ourselves in the first instance to a single branch of it, on which the principle here stated is, if not fully, yet to a certain point, recognised by the current opinions. This one branch is the Liberty of Thought: from which it is impossible to separate the cognate liberty of speaking and of writing. Although these liberties, to some considerable amount, form part of the political morality of all countries which profess religious toleration and free institutions, the grounds, both philosophical and practical, on which they rest, are perhaps not so familiar to the general mind, nor so thoroughly appreciated by many even of the leaders of opinion, as might have been expected. Those grounds, when rightly understood, are of much wider application than to only one division of the subject, and a thorough consideration of this part of the question will be found the best introduction to the remainder. Those to whom nothing which I am about to say will be new, may therefore, I hope, excuse me, if on a subject which for now three centuries has been so often discussed, I venture on one discussion more.

CHAPTER II
Of the Liberty of Thought and Discussion

The time, it is to be hoped, is gone by, when any defence would be necessary of the 'liberty of the press' as one of the securities against corrupt or tyrannical government. No argument, we may suppose, can now be needed, against permitting a legislature or an executive, not identified in interest with the people, to prescribe opinions to them, and determine what doctrines or what arguments they shall be allowed to hear. This aspect of the question, besides, has been so often and so triumphantly enforced by preceding writers, that it needs not be specially insisted on in this place. Though the law of England, on the subject of the press, is as servile to this day as it was in the time of the Tudors, there is little danger of its being actually put in force against political discussion, except during some temporary panic, when fear of insurrection drives ministers and judges from their propriety;[1] and, speaking generally, it is not, in constitutional countries, to be apprehended, that the government, whether completely responsible to the people or not, will often attempt to control the expression of opinion, except when in doing so it makes itself the organ of the general intolerance of the public. Let us suppose, therefore, that the government is entirely at one with the people, and never thinks of exerting any power of coercion unless in agreement with what it conceives to be their voice. But

---

1. These words had scarcely been written, when, as if to give them an emphatic contradiction, occurred the Government Press Prosecutions of 1858. That ill-judged interference with the liberty of public discussion has not, however, induced me to alter a single word in the text, nor has it at all weakened my conviction that, moments of panic excepted, the era of pains and penalties for political discussion has, in our own country, passed away. For, in the first place, the prosecutions were not persisted in; and, in the second, they were never, properly speaking, political prosecutions. The offence charged was not that of criticising institutions, or the acts or persons of rulers, but of circulating what was deemed an immoral doctrine, the lawfulness of Tyrannicide.

If the arguments of the present chapter are of any validity, there ought to exist the fullest liberty of professing and discussing, as a matter of ethical conviction, any doctrine, however immoral it may be considered. It would, therefore, be irrelevant and out of place to examine here, whether the doctrine of Tyrannicide deserves that title. I shall content myself with saying that the subject has been at all times one of the open questions of morals; that the act of a private citizen in striking down a criminal, who, by raising himself above the law, has placed himself beyond the reach of legal punishment or control, has been accounted by whole nations, and by some of the best and wisest of men, not a crime, but an act of exalted virtue; and that, right or wrong, it is not of the nature of assassination, but of civil war. As such, I hold that the instigation to it, in a specific case, may be a proper subject of punishment, but only if an overt act has followed, and at least a probable connexion can be established between the act and the instigation. Even then, it is not a foreign government, but the very government assailed, which alone, in the exercise of self-defence, can legitimately punish attacks directed against its own existence.

I deny the right of the people to exercise such coercion, either by themselves or by their government. The power itself is illegitimate. The best government has no more title to it than the worst. It is as noxious, or more noxious, when exerted in accordance with public opinion, than when in opposition to it. If all mankind minus one, were of one opinion, and only one person were of the contrary opinion, mankind would be no more justified in silencing that one person, than he, if he had the power, would be justified in silencing mankind. Were an opinion a personal possession of no value except to the owner; if to be obstructed in the enjoyment of it were simply a private injury, it would make some difference whether the injury was inflicted only on a few persons or on many. But the peculiar evil of silencing the expression of an opinion is, that it is robbing the human race; posterity as well as the existing generation; those who dissent from the opinion, still more than those who hold it. If the opinion is right, they are deprived of the opportunity of exchanging error for truth: if wrong, they lose, what is almost as great a benefit, the clearer perception and livelier impression of truth, produced by its collision with error.

It is necessary to consider separately these two hypotheses, each of which has a distinct branch of the argument corresponding to it. We can never be sure that the opinion we are endeavouring to stifle is a false opinion; and if we were sure, stifling it would be an evil still.

First: the opinion which it is attempted to suppress by authority may possibly be true. Those who desire to suppress it, of course deny its truth; but they are not infallible. They have no authority to decide the question for all mankind, and exclude every other person from the means of judging. To refuse a hearing to an opinion, because they are sure that it is false, is to assume that *their* certainty is the same thing as *absolute* certainty. All silencing of discussion is an assumption of infallibility. Its condemnation may be allowed to rest on this common argument, not the worse for being common.

Unfortunately for the good sense of mankind, the fact of their fallibility is far from carrying the weight in their practical judgment, which is always allowed to it in theory; for while every one well knows himself to be fallible, few think it necessary to take any precautions against their own fallibility, or admit the supposition that any opinion, of which they feel very certain, may be one of the examples of the error to which they acknowledge themselves to be liable. Absolute princes, or others who are accustomed to unlimited deference, usually feel this complete confidence in their own opinions on nearly all subjects. People more happily situated, who sometimes hear their opinions disputed, and are not wholly unused to be set right when they are wrong, place the same unbounded reliance only on such of their opinions as are shared by all who surround them, or to whom they habitually defer: for in proportion to a man's want of confidence in his own solitary judgment, does he usually repose, with implicit trust, on the infallibility of 'the world' in general. And the world, to each individual, means the part of it with which he comes in contact; his party, his sect, his church, his class of society: the man may be called, by comparison, almost liberal and large-minded to whom it means anything so comprehensive as his own country or his own age. Nor is his faith in this collective authority at all shaken by his being aware that other ages, countries, sects, churches, classes, and parties have thought, and even now think, the exact reverse. He devolves upon his own world the responsibility of being in the right against the dissentient worlds of other people; and it never troubles him that mere accident has decided which of these numerous worlds is the object of his reliance, and that the same causes which make him a Churchman in London, would have made him a Buddhist or a Confucian in Pekin. Yet it is as evident in itself, as any amount of argument can make it, that ages are no more infallible than individuals; every age having held many opinions which subsequent ages have deemed not only false but absurd; and it is as certain that many opinions, now general, will be rejected by future ages, as it is that many, once general, are rejected by the present.

The objection likely to be made to this argument, would probably take some such form as the following. There is no greater assumption of infallibility in forbidding the propagation of error, than in any other thing which is done by public authority on its own judgment and responsibility. Judgment is given to men that they may use it. Because it may be used erroneously, are men to be told that they ought not to use it at all? To prohibit what they think pernicious, is not claiming exemption from error, but fulfilling the duty incumbent on them, although fallible, of acting on their conscientious conviction. If we were never to act on our opinions, because those opinions may be wrong, we should leave all our interests uncared for, and all our duties unperformed. An objection which applies to all conduct, can be no valid objection to any conduct in particular. It is the duty of governments, and of individuals, to form the truest opinions they can; to form them carefully, and never impose them upon others unless they are quite sure of being right. But when they are sure (such reasoners may say), it is not conscientiousness but cowardice to shrink from acting on their opinions, and allow doctrines which they honestly think dangerous to the welfare of mankind, either in this life or in another, to be scattered abroad without restraint, because other people, in less enlightened times, have persecuted opinions now believed to be true. Let us take care, it may be said, not to make the same mistake: but governments and nations have made mistakes in other things, which are not denied to be fit subjects for the exercise of authority: they have laid on bad taxes, made unjust wars. Ought we therefore to lay on no taxes, and, under whatever provocation, make no wars? Men, and governments, must act to the best of their ability. There is no such thing as absolute certainty, but there is assurance sufficient for the purposes of human life. We may, and must, assume our opinion to be true for the guidance of our own conduct: and it is assuming no more when we forbid bad men to pervert society by the propagation of opinions which we regard as false and pernicious.

I answer, that it is assuming very much more. There is the greatest difference between presuming an opinion to be true, because, with every opportunity for contesting it, it has not been refuted, and assuming its truth for the purpose of not permitting its refutation. Complete liberty of contradicting and disproving our opinion, is the very condition which justifies us in assuming its truth for purposes of action; and on no other terms can a being with human faculties have any rational assurance of being right.

When we consider either the history of opinion, or the ordinary conduct of human life, to what is it to be ascribed that the one and the other are no worse than they are? Not certainly to the inherent force of the human understanding; for, on any matter not self-evident, there are ninety-nine persons totally incapable of judging of it, for one who is capable; and the capacity of the hundredth person is only comparative; for the majority of the eminent men of every past generation held many opinions now known to be erroneous, and did or approved numerous things which no one will now justify. Why is it, then, that there is on the whole a preponderance among mankind of rational opinions and rational conduct? If there really is this preponderance—which there must be unless human affairs are, and have always been, in an almost desperate state—it is owing to a quality of the human mind, the source of everything respectable in man either as an intellectual or as a moral being, namely, that his errors are corrigible. He is capable of rectifying his mistakes, by discussion and experience. Not by experience alone. There must be discussion, to show how experience is to be interpreted. Wrong opinions and practices gradually yield to fact and argument: but facts and arguments, to produce any effect on the mind, must be brought before it. Very few facts are able to tell their own story, without comments to bring out their meaning. The whole strength and value, then, of human judgment, depending on the one property, that it can be set right when it is wrong, reliance can be placed on it only when the means of setting it right are kept constantly at hand. In the case of any person whose judgment is really deserving of confidence, how has it become so? Because he has kept his mind open to criticism of his opinions and conduct. Because it has been his practice to listen to all that could be said against him; to profit by as much of it as was just, and expound to himself, and upon occasion to others, the fallacy of what was fallacious. Because he has felt, that the only way in which a human being can make some approach to knowing the whole of a subject, is by hearing what can be said about it by persons of every variety of opinion, and studying all modes in which it can be looked at by every character of mind. No wise man ever acquired his wisdom in any mode but this; nor is it in the nature of human intellect to become wise in any other manner. The steady habit of correcting and completing his own opinion by collating it with those of others, so far from causing doubt and hesitation in carrying it into practice, is the only stable foundation for a just reliance on it: for, being cognisant of all that can, at least obviously, be said against him, and having taken up his position against all gainsayers—knowing that he has sought for objections and difficulties, instead of avoiding them, and has shut out no light which can be thrown upon the subject from any quarter—he has a right to think his judgment better than that of any person, or any multitude, who have not gone through a similar process.

It is not too much to require that what the wisest of mankind, those who are best entitled to trust their own judgment, find necessary to warrant their relying on it, should be submitted to by that miscellaneous collection of a few wise and many foolish individuals, called the public. The most intolerant of churches, the Roman Catholic Church, even at the canonization of a saint, admits, and listens patiently to, a 'devil's advocate.' The holiest of men, it appears, cannot be admitted to posthumous honours, until all that the devil could say against him is known and weighed. If even the Newtonian philosophy were not permitted to be questioned, mankind could not feel as complete assurance of its truth as they now do. The beliefs which we have most warrant for, have no safeguard to rest on, but a standing invitation to the whole world to prove them unfounded. If the challenge is not accepted, or is accepted and the attempt fails, we are far enough from certainty still; but we have done the best that the existing state of human reason admits of; we have neglected nothing that could give the truth a chance of reaching us: if the lists are kept open, we may hope that if there be a better truth, it will be found when the human mind is capable of receiving it; and in the meantime we may rely on having attained such approach to truth, as is possible in our own day. This is the amount of certainty attainable by a fallible being, and this the sole way of attaining it.

Strange it is, that men should admit the validity of the arguments for free discussion, but object to their being 'pushed to an extreme;' not seeing that unless the reasons are good for an extreme case, they are not good for any case. Strange that they should imagine that they are not assuming infallibility, when they acknowledge that there should be free discussion on all subjects which can possibly be *doubtful*, but think that some particular principle or doctrine should be forbidden to be questioned because it is so *certain*, that is, because *they are certain* that it is certain. To call any proposition certain, while there is any one who would deny its certainty if permitted, but who is not permitted, is to assume that we ourselves, and those who agree with us, are the judges of certainty, and judges without hearing the other side.

In the present age—which has been described as 'destitute of faith, but terrified at scepticism'—in which people feel sure, not so much that their opinions are true, as that they should not know what to do without them—the claims of an opinion to be protected from public attack are rested not so much on its truth, as on its importance to society. There are, it is alleged, certain beliefs, so useful, not to say indispensable to well-being, that it is as much the duty of governments to uphold those beliefs, as to protect any other of the interests of society. In a case of such necessity, and so directly in the line of their duty, something less than infallibility may, it is maintained, warrant, and even bind, governments, to act on their own opinion, confirmed by the general opinion of mankind. It is also often argued, and still oftener thought, that none but bad men would desire to weaken these salutary beliefs; and there can be nothing wrong, it is thought, in restraining bad men, and prohibiting what only such men would wish to practise. This mode of thinking makes the justification of restraints on discussion not a question of the truth of doctrines, but of their usefulness; and flatters itself by that means to escape the responsibility of claiming to be an infallible judge of opinions. But those who thus satisfy themselves, do not perceive that the assumption of infallibility is merely shifted from one point to another. The usefulness of an opinion is itself matter of opinion: as disputable, as open to discussion, and requiring discussion as much, as the opinion itself. There is the same need of an infallible judge of opinions to decide an opinion to be noxious, as to decide it to be false, unless the opinion condemned has full opportunity of defending itself. And it will not do to say that the heretic may be allowed to maintain the utility or harmlessness of his opinion, though forbidden to maintain its truth. The truth of an opinion is part of its utility. If we would know whether or not it is desirable that a proposition should be believed, is it possible to exclude the consideration of whether or not it is true? In the opinion, not of bad men, but of the best men, no belief which is contrary to truth can be really useful: and can you prevent such men from urging that plea, when they are charged with culpability for denying some doctrine which they are told is useful, but which they believe to be false? Those who are on the side of received opinions, never fail to take all possible advantage of this plea; you do not find *them* handling the question of utility as if it could be completely abstracted from that of truth: on the contrary, it is, above all, because their doctrine is the 'truth,' that the knowledge or the belief of it is held to be so indispensable. There can be no fair discussion of the question of usefulness, when an argument so vital may be employed on one side, but not on the other. And in point of fact, when law or public feeling do not permit the truth of an opinion to be disputed, they are just as little tolerant of a denial of its usefulness. The utmost they allow is an extenuation of its absolute necessity, or of the positive guilt of rejecting it.

In order more fully to illustrate the mischief of denying a hearing to opinions because we, in our own judgment, have condemned them, it will be desirable to fix down the discussion to a concrete case; and I choose, by preference, the cases which are least favourable to me—in which the argument against freedom of opinion, both on the score of truth and on that of utility, is considered the strongest. Let the opinions impugned be the belief in a God and in a future state, or any of the commonly received doctrines of morality. To fight the battle on such ground, gives a great advantage to an unfair antagonist; since he will be sure to say (and many who have no desire to be unfair will say it internally), Are these the doctrines which you do not deem sufficiently certain to be taken under the protection of law? Is the belief in a God one of the opinions, to feel sure of which, you hold to be assuming infallibility? But I must be permitted to observe, that it is not the feeling sure of a doctrine (be it what it may) which I call an assumption of infallibility. It is the undertaking to decide that question *for others*, without allowing them to hear what can be said on the contrary side. And I denounce and reprobate this pretension not the less, if put forth on the side of my most solemn convictions. However positive any one's persuasion may be, not only of the falsity but of the pernicious consequences—not only of the pernicious consequences, but (to adopt expressions which I altogether condemn) the immorality and impiety of an opinion; yet if, in pursuance of that private judgment, though backed by the public judgment of his country or his cotemporaries, he prevents the opinion from being heard in its defence, he assumes infallibility. And so far from the assumption being less objectionable or less dangerous because the opinion is called immoral or impious, this is the case of all others in which it is most fatal. These are exactly the occasions on which the men of one generation commit those dreadful mistakes, which excite the astonishment and horror of posterity. It is among such that we find the instances memorable in history, when the arm of the law has been employed to root out the best men and the noblest doctrines; with deplorable success as to the men, though some of the doctrines have survived to be (as if in mockery) invoked, in defence of similar conduct towards those who dissent from *them*, or from their received interpretation.

Mankind can hardly be too often reminded, that there was once a man named Socrates, between whom and the legal authorities and public opinion of his time, there took place a memorable collision. Born in an age and country abounding in individual greatness, this man has been handed down to us by those who best knew both him and the age, as the most virtuous man in it; while we know him as the head and prototype of all subsequent teachers of virtue, the source equally of the lofty inspiration of Plato and the judicious utilitarianism of Aristotle, '*i maestri di color che sanno*,' the two headsprings of ethical as of all other philosophy. This acknowledged master of all the eminent thinkers who have since lived—whose fame, still growing after more than two thousand years, all but outweighs the whole remainder of the names which make his native city illustrious—was put to death by his countrymen, after a judicial conviction, for impiety and immorality. Impiety, in denying the gods recognised by the State; indeed his accuser asserted (see the Apologia) that he believed in no gods at all. Immorality, in being, by his doctrines and instructions, a 'corruptor of youth.' Of these charges the tribunal, there is every ground for believing, honestly found him guilty, and condemned the man who probably of all then born had deserved best of mankind, to be put to death as a criminal.

To pass from this to the only other instance of judicial iniquity, the mention of which, after the condemnation of Socrates, would not be an anti-climax: the event which took place on Calvary rather more than eighteen hundred years ago. The man who left on the memory of those who witnessed his life and conversation, such an impression of his moral grandeur, that eighteen subsequent centuries have done homage to him as the Almighty in person, was ignominiously put to death, as what? As a blasphemer. Men did not merely mistake their benefactor; they mistook him for the exact contrary of what he was, and treated him as that prodigy of impiety, which they themselves are now held to be, for their treatment of him. The feelings with which mankind now regard these lamentable transactions, especially the later of the two, render them extremely unjust in their judgment of the unhappy actors. These were, to all appearance, not bad men—not worse than men commonly are, but rather the contrary; men who possessed in a full, or somewhat more than a full measure, the religious, moral, and patriotic feelings of their time and people: the very kind of men who, in all times, our own included, have every chance of passing through life blameless and respected. The high-priest who rent his garments when the words were pronounced, which, according to all the ideas of his country, constituted the blackest guilt, was in all probability quite as sincere in his horror and indignation, as the generality of respectable and pious men now are in the religious and moral sentiments they profess; and most of those who now shudder at his conduct, if they had lived in his time, and been born Jews, would have acted precisely as he did. Orthodox Christians who are tempted to think that those who stoned to death the first martyrs must have been worse men than they themselves are, ought to remember that one of those persecutors was Saint Paul.

Let us add one more example, the most striking of all, if the impressiveness of an error is measured by the wisdom and virtue of him who falls into it. If ever any one, possessed of power, had grounds for thinking himself the best and most enlightened among his cotemporaries, it was the Emperor Marcus Aurelius. Absolute monarch of the whole civilized world, he preserved through life not only the most unblemished justice, but what was less to be expected from his Stoical breeding, the tenderest heart. The few failings which are attributed to him, were all on the side of indulgence: while his writings, the highest ethical product of the ancient mind, differ scarcely perceptibly, if they differ at all, from the most characteristic teachings of Christ. This man, a better Christian in all but the dogmatic sense of the word, than almost any of the ostensibly Christian sovereigns who have since reigned, persecuted Christianity. Placed at the summit of all the previous attainments of humanity, with an open, unfettered intellect, and a character which led him of himself to embody in his moral writings the Christian ideal, he yet failed to see that Christianity was to be a good and not an evil to the world, with his duties to which he was so deeply penetrated. Existing society he knew to be in a deplorable state. But such as it was, he saw, or thought he saw, that it was held together, and prevented from being worse, by belief and reverence of the received divinities. As a ruler of mankind, he deemed it his duty not to suffer society to fall in pieces; and saw not how, if its existing ties were removed, any others could be formed which could again knit it together. The new religion openly aimed at dissolving these ties: unless, therefore, it was his duty to adopt that religion, it seemed to be his duty to put it down. Inasmuch then as the theology of Christianity did not appear to him true or of divine origin; inasmuch as this strange history of a crucified God was not credible to him, and a system which purported to rest entirely upon a foundation to him so wholly unbelievable, could not be foreseen by him to be that renovating agency which, after all abatements, it has in fact proved to be; the gentlest and most amiable of philosophers and rulers, under a solemn sense of duty, authorized the persecution of Christianity. To my mind this is one of the most tragical facts in all history. It is a bitter thought, how different a thing the Christianity of the world might have been, if the Christian faith had been adopted as the religion of the empire under the auspices of Marcus Aurelius instead of those of Constantine. But it would be equally unjust to him and false to truth, to deny, that no one plea which can be urged for punishing anti-Christian teaching, was wanting to Marcus Aurelius for punishing, as he did, the propagation of Christianity. No Christian more firmly believes that Atheism is false, and tends to the dissolution of society, than Marcus Aurelius believed the same things of Christianity; he who, of all men then living, might have been thought the most capable of appreciating it. Unless any one who approves of punishment for the promulgation of opinions, flatters himself that he is a wiser and better man than Marcus Aurelius—more deeply versed in the wisdom of his time, more elevated in his intellect above it—more earnest in his search for truth, or more single-minded in his devotion to it when found;—let him abstain from that assumption of the joint infallibility of himself and the multitude, which the great Antoninus made with so unfortunate a result.

Aware of the impossibility of defending the use of punishment for restraining irreligious opinions, by any argument which will not justify Marcus Antoninus, the enemies of religious freedom, when hard pressed, occasionally accept this consequence, and say, with Dr. Johnson, that the persecutors of Christianity were in the right; that persecution is an ordeal through which truth ought to pass, and always passes successfully, legal penalties being, in the end, powerless against truth, though sometimes beneficially effective against mischievous errors. This is a form of the argument for religious intolerance, sufficiently remarkable not to be passed without notice.

A theory which maintains that truth may justifiably be persecuted because persecution cannot possibly do it any harm, cannot be charged with being intentionally hostile to the reception of new truths; but we cannot commend the generosity of its dealing with the persons to whom mankind are indebted for them. To discover to the world something which deeply concerns it, and of which it was previously ignorant; to prove to it that it had been mistaken on some vital point of temporal or spiritual interest, is as important a service as a human being can render to his fellow-creatures, and in certain cases, as in those of the early Christians and of the Reformers, those who think with Dr. Johnson believe it to have been the most precious gift which could be bestowed on mankind. That the authors of such splendid benefits should be requited by martyrdom; that their reward should be to be dealt with as the vilest of criminals, is not, upon this theory, a deplorable error and misfortune, for which humanity should mourn in sackcloth and ashes, but the normal and justifiable state of things. The propounder of a new truth, according to this doctrine, should stand, as stood, in the legislation of the Locrians, the proposer of a new law, with a halter round his neck, to be instantly tightened if the public assembly did not, on hearing his reasons, then and there adopt his proposition. People who defend this mode of treating benefactors, cannot be supposed to set much value on the benefit; and I believe this view of the subject is mostly confined to the sort of persons who think that new truths may have been desirable once, but that we have had enough of them now.

But, indeed, the dictum that truth always triumphs over persecution, is one of those pleasant falsehoods which men repeat after one another till they pass into commonplaces, but which all experience refutes. History teems with instances of truth put down by persecution. If not suppressed for ever, it may be thrown back for centuries. To speak only of religious opinions: the Reformation broke out at least twenty times before Luther, and was put down. Arnold of Brescia was put down. Fra Dolcino was put down. Savonarola was put down. The Albigeois were put down. The Vaudois were put down. The Lollards were put down. The Hussites were put down. Even after the era of Luther, wherever persecution was persisted in, it was successful. In Spain, Italy, Flanders, the Austrian empire, Protestantism was rooted out; and, most likely, would have been so in England, had Queen Mary lived, or Queen Elizabeth died. Persecution has always succeeded, save where the heretics were too strong a party to be effectually persecuted. No reasonable person can doubt that Christianity might have been extirpated in the Roman Empire. It spread, and became predominant, because the persecutions were only occasional, lasting but a short time, and separated by long intervals of almost undisturbed propagandism. It is a piece of idle sentimentality that truth, merely as truth, has any inherent power denied to error, of prevailing against the dungeon and the stake. Men are not more zealous for truth than they often are for error, and a sufficient application of legal or even of social penalties will generally succeed in stopping the propagation of either. The real advantage which truth has, consists in this, that when an opinion is true, it may be extinguished once, twice, or many times, but in the course of ages there will generally be found persons to rediscover it, until some one of its reappearances falls on a time when from favourable circumstances it escapes persecution until it has made such head as to withstand all subsequent attempts to suppress it.

It will be said, that we do not now put to death the introducers of new opinions: we are not like our fathers who slew the prophets, we even build sepulchres to them. It is true we no longer put heretics to death; and the amount of penal infliction which modern feeling would probably tolerate, even against the most obnoxious opinions, is not sufficient to extirpate them. But let us not flatter ourselves that we are yet free from the stain even of legal persecution. Penalties for opinion, or at least for its expression, still exist by law; and their enforcement is not, even in these times, so unexampled as to make it at all incredible that they may some day be revived in full force. In the year 1857, at the summer assizes of the county of Cornwall, an unfortunate man,[2] said to be of unexceptionable conduct in all relations of life, was sentenced to twenty-one months' imprisonment, for uttering, and writing on a gate, some offensive words concerning Christianity. Within a month of the same time, at the Old Bailey, two persons, on two separate occasions,[3] were rejected as jurymen, and one of them grossly insulted by the judge and by one of the counsel, because they honestly declared that they had no theological belief; and a third, a

2. Thomas Pooley, Bodmin Assizes, July 31, 1857. In December following, he received a free pardon from the Crown.

3. George Jacob Holyoake, August 17, 1857; Edward Truelove, July, 1857.

foreigner,[4] for the same reason, was denied justice against a thief. This refusal of redress took place in virtue of the legal doctrine, that no person can be allowed to give evidence in a court of justice, who does not profess belief in a God (any god is sufficient) and in a future state; which is equivalent to declaring such persons to be outlaws, excluded from the protection of the tribunals; who may not only be robbed or assaulted with impunity, if no one but themselves, or persons of similar opinions, be present, but any one else may be robbed or assaulted with impunity, if the proof of the fact depends on their evidence. The assumption on which this is grounded, is that the oath is worthless, of a person who does not believe in a future state; a proposition which betokens much ignorance of history in those who assent to it (since it is historically true that a large proportion of infidels in all ages have been persons of distinguished integrity and honour); and would be maintained by no one who had the smallest conception how many of the persons in greatest repute with the world, both for virtues and for attainments, are well known, at least to their intimates, to be unbelievers. The rule, besides, is suicidal, and cuts away its own foundation. Under pretence that atheists must be liars, it admits the testimony of all atheists who are willing to lie, and rejects only those who brave the obloquy of publicly confessing a detested creed rather than affirm a falsehood. A rule thus self-convicted of absurdity so far as regards its professed purpose, can be kept in force only as a badge of hatred, a relic of persecution; a persecution, too, having the peculiarity, that the qualification for undergoing it, is the being clearly proved not to deserve it. The rule, and the theory it implies, are hardly less insulting to believers than to infidels. For if he who does not believe in a future state, necessarily lies, it follows that they who do believe are only prevented from lying, if prevented they are, by the fear of hell. We will not do the authors and abettors of the rule the injury of supposing, that the conception which they have formed of Christian virtue is drawn from their own consciousness.

These, indeed, are but rags and remnants of persecution, and may be thought to be not so much an indication of the wish to persecute, as an example of that very frequent infirmity of English minds, which makes them take a preposterous pleasure in the assertion of a bad principle, when they are no longer bad enough to desire to carry it really into practice. But unhappily there is no security in the state of the public mind, that the suspension of worse forms of legal persecution, which has lasted for about the space of a generation, will continue. In this age the quiet surface of routine is as often ruffled by attempts to resuscitate past evils, as to introduce new benefits. What is boasted of at the present time as the revival of religion, is always, in narrow and uncultivated minds, at least as much the revival of bigotry; and where there is the strong permanent leaven of intolerance in the feelings of a people, which at all times abides in the middle classes of this country, it needs but little to provoke them into actively persecuting those whom they have never ceased to think proper objects of persecution.[5] For it is this—it is the opinions men entertain,

4. Baron de Gleichen, Marlborough-street Police Court, August 4, 1857.

5. Ample warning may be drawn from the large infusion of the passions of a persecutor, which mingled with the general display of the worst parts of our national character on the occasion of the Sepoy insurrection. The ravings of fanatics or charlatans from the pulpit may be unworthy of notice; but the heads of the Evangelical party have announced as their principle for the government of Hindoos and Mahomedans, that no schools be supported by public money in which the Bible is not taught, and by necessary consequence that no public employment be given to any but real or pretended Christians. An Under-Secretary of State, in a speech delivered

and the feelings they cherish, respecting those who disown the beliefs they deem important, which makes this country not a place of mental freedom. For a long time past, the chief mischief of the legal penalties is that they strengthen the social stigma. It is that stigma which is really effective, and so effective is it, that the profession of opinions which are under the ban of society is much less common in England, than is, in many other countries, the avowal of those which incur risk of judicial punishment. In respect to all persons but those whose pecuniary circumstances make them independent of the good will of other people, opinion, on this subject, is as efficacious as law; men might as well be imprisoned, as excluded from the means of earning their bread. Those whose bread is already secured, and who desire no favours from men in power, or from bodies of men, or from the public, have nothing to fear from the open avowal of any opinions, but to be ill-thought of and ill-spoken of, and this it ought not to require a very heroic mould to enable them to bear. There is no room for any appeal *ad misericordiam* in behalf of such persons. But though we do not now inflict so much evil on those who think differently from us, as it was formerly our custom to do, it may be that we do ourselves as much evil as ever by our treatment of them. Socrates was put to death, but the Socratic philosophy rose like the sun in heaven, and spread its illumination over the whole intellectual firmament. Christians were cast to the lions, but the Christian church grew up a stately and spreading tree, overtopping the older and less vigorous growths, and stifling them by its shade. Our merely social intolerance kills no one, roots out no opinions, but induces men to disguise them, or to abstain from any active effort for their diffusion. With us, heretical opinions do not perceptibly gain, or even lose, ground in each decade or generation; they never blaze out far and wide, but continue to smoulder in the narrow circles of thinking and studious persons among whom they originate, without ever lighting up the general affairs of mankind with either a true or a deceptive light. And thus is kept up a state of things very satisfactory to some minds, because, without the unpleasant process of fining or imprisoning anybody, it maintains all prevailing opinions outwardly undisturbed, while it does not absolutely interdict the exercise of reason by dissentients afflicted with the malady of thought. A convenient plan for having peace in the intellectual world, and keeping all things going on therein very much as they do already. But the price paid for this sort of intellectual pacification, is the sacrifice of the entire moral courage of the human mind. A state of things in which a large portion of the most active and inquiring intellects find it advisable to keep the general principles and grounds of their convictions within their own breasts, and attempt, in what they address to the public, to fit as much as they can of their own conclusions to premises which they have internally renounced, cannot send forth the open, fearless characters, and logical, consistent intellects who once adorned the thinking world. The

---

to his constituents on the 12th of November, 1857, is reported to have said: 'Toleration of their faith' (the faith of a hundred millions of British subjects), 'the superstition which they called religion, by the British Government, had had the effect of retarding the ascendancy of the British name, and preventing the salutary growth of Christianity. . . . Toleration was the great corner-stone of the religious liberties of this country; but do not let them abuse that precious word toleration. As he understood it, it meant the complete liberty to all, freedom of worship, *among Christians, who worshipped upon the same foundation.* It meant toleration of all sects and denominations of *Christians who believed in the one mediation.*' I desire to call attention to the fact, that a man who has been deemed fit to fill a high office in the government of this country, under a liberal Ministry, maintains the doctrine that all who do not believe in the divinity of Christ are beyond the pale of toleration. Who, after this imbecile display, can indulge the illusion that religious persecution has passed away, never to return?

sort of men who can be looked for under it, are either mere conformers to common-place, or time-servers for truth, whose arguments on all great subjects are meant for their hearers, and are not those which have convinced themselves. Those who avoid this alternative, do so by narrowing their thoughts and interest to things which can be spoken of without venturing within the region of principles, that is, to small practical matters, which would come right of themselves, if but the minds of mankind were strengthened and enlarged, and which will never be made effectually right until then: while that which would strengthen and enlarge men's minds, free and daring speculation on the highest subjects, is abandoned.

Those in whose eyes this reticence on the part of heretics is no evil, should consider in the first place, that in consequence of it there is never any fair and thorough discussion of heretical opinions; and that such of them as could not stand such a discussion, though they may be prevented from spreading, do not disappear. But it is not the minds of heretics that are deteriorated most, by the ban placed on all inquiry which does not end in the orthodox conclusions. The greatest harm done is to those who are not heretics, and whose whole mental development is cramped, and their reason cowed, by the fear of heresy. Who can compute what the world loses in the multitude of promising intellects combined with timid characters, who dare not follow out any bold, vigorous, independent train of thought, lest it should land them in something which would admit of being considered irreligious or immoral? Among them we may occasionally see some man of deep conscientiousness, and subtle and refined understanding, who spends a life in sophisticating with an intellect which he cannot silence, and exhausts the resources of ingenuity in attempting to reconcile the promptings of his conscience and reason with orthodoxy, which yet he does not, perhaps, to the end succeed in doing. No one can be a great thinker who does not recognise, that as a thinker it is his first duty to follow his intellect to whatever conclusions it may lead. Truth gains more even by the errors of one who, with due study and preparation, thinks for himself, than by the true opinions of those who only hold them because they do not suffer themselves to think. Not that it is solely, or chiefly, to form great thinkers, that freedom of thinking is required. On the contrary, it is as much and even more indispensable, to enable average human beings to attain the mental stature which they are capable of. There have been, and may again be, great individual thinkers, in a general atmosphere of mental slavery. But there never has been, nor ever will be, in that atmosphere, an intellectually active people. When any people has made a temporary approach to such a character, it has been because the dread of heterodox speculation was for a time suspended. Where there is a tacit convention that principles are not to be disputed; where the discussion of the greatest questions which can occupy humanity is considered to be closed, we cannot hope to find that generally high scale of mental activity which has made some periods of history so remarkable. Never when controversy avoided the subjects which are large and important enough to kindle enthusiasm, was the mind of a people stirred up from its foundations, and the impulse given which raised even persons of the most ordinary intellect to something of the dignity of thinking beings. Of such we have had an example in the condition of Europe during the times immediately following the Reformation; another, though limited to the Continent and to a more cultivated class, in the speculative movement of the latter half of the eighteenth century; and a third, of still briefer duration, in the intellectual fermentation of Germany during the Goethian and Fichtean period. These periods differed widely in the particular opinions which they developed; but were alike in this, that during all three the yoke of authority was broken. In each, an old mental despotism had been thrown off, and no new one had yet taken its place. The impulse given at these three periods has made Europe what it now is. Every single improvement which has taken place either in the human mind or in institutions, may be traced distinctly to one or other of them. Appearances have for some time indicated that all three impulses are well nigh spent; and we can expect no fresh start, until we again assert our mental freedom.

Let us now pass to the second division of the argument, and dismissing the supposition that any of the received opinions may be false, let us assume them to be true, and examine into the worth of the manner in which they are likely to be held, when their truth is not freely and openly canvassed. However unwillingly a person who has a strong opinion may admit the possibility that his opinion may be false, he ought to be moved by the consideration that however true it may be, if it is not fully, frequently, and fearlessly discussed, it will be held as a dead dogma, not a living truth.

There is a class of persons (happily not quite so numerous as formerly) who think it enough if a person assents undoubtingly to what they think true, though he has no knowledge whatever of the grounds of the opinion, and could not make a tenable defence of it against the most superficial objections. Such persons, if they can once get their creed taught from authority, naturally think that no good, and some harm, comes of its being allowed to be questioned. Where their influence prevails, they make it nearly impossible for the received opinion to be rejected wisely and considerately, though it may still be rejected rashly and ignorantly; for to shut out discussion entirely is seldom possible, and when it once gets in, beliefs not grounded on conviction are apt to give way before the slightest semblance of an argument. Waving, however, this possibility—assuming that the true opinion abides in the mind, but abides as a prejudice, a belief independent of, and proof against, argument— this is not the way in which truth ought to be held by a rational being. This is not knowing the truth. Truth, thus held, is but one superstition the more, accidentally clinging to the words which enunciate a truth.

If the intellect and judgment of mankind ought to be cultivated, a thing which Protestants at least do not deny, on what can these faculties be more appropriately exercised by any one, than on the things which concern him so much that it is considered necessary for him to hold opinions on them? If the cultivation of the understanding consists in one thing more than in another, it is surely in learning the grounds of one's own opinions. Whatever people believe, on subjects on which it is of the first importance to believe rightly, they ought to be able to defend against at least the common objections. But, some one may say, 'Let them be *taught* the grounds of their opinions. It does not follow that opinions must be merely parroted because they are never heard controverted. Persons who learn geometry do not simply commit the theorems to memory, but understand and learn likewise the demonstrations; and it would be absurd to say that they remain ignorant of the grounds of geometrical truths, because they never hear any one deny, and attempt to disprove them.' Undoubtedly: and such teaching suffices on a subject like mathematics, where there is nothing at all to be said on the wrong side of the question. The peculiarity of the evidence of mathematical truths is, that all the argument is on one side. There are no objections, and no answers to objections. But on every subject on which difference of opinion is possible, the truth depends on a balance to be struck between two sets of conflicting reasons. Even in natural philosophy, there is always some other explanation possible of the same facts; some geocentric theory instead of heliocentric, some phlogiston instead of oxygen; and it has to be shown why that other theory cannot be the true one: and until this is shown, and until we know how it is shown, we do not understand the grounds of our opinion. But when we turn to subjects infinitely more complicated, to morals, religion, politics, social relations, and the business of life, three-fourths of the arguments for every disputed opinion consist in dispelling the appearances which favour some opinion different from it. The greatest orator, save one, of antiquity, has left it on record that he always studied his adversary's case with as great, if not with still greater, intensity than even his own. What Cicero practised as the means of forensic success, requires to be imitated by all who study any subject in order to arrive at the truth. He who knows only his own side of the case, knows little of that. His reasons may be good, and no one may have been able to refute them. But if he is equally unable to refute the reasons on the opposite side; if he does not so much as know what they are, he has no ground for preferring either opinion. The rational position for him would be suspension of judgment, and unless he contents himself with that, he is either led by authority, or adopts, like the generality of the world, the side to which he feels most inclination. Nor is it enough that he should hear the arguments of adversaries from his own teachers, presented as they state them, and accompanied by what they offer as refutations. That is not the way to do justice to the arguments, or bring them into real contact with his own mind. He must be able to hear them from persons who actually believe them; who defend them in earnest, and do their very utmost for them. He must know them in their most plausible and persuasive form; he must feel the whole force of the difficulty which the true view of the subject has to encounter and dispose of; else he will never really possess himself of the portion of truth which meets and removes that difficulty. Ninety-nine in a hundred of what are called educated men are in this condition; even of those who can argue fluently for their opinions. Their conclusion may be true, but it might be false for anything they know: they have never thrown themselves into the mental position of those who think differently from them, and considered what such persons may have to say; and consequently they do not, in any proper sense of the word, know the doctrine which they themselves profess. They do not know those parts of it which explain and justify the remainder; the considerations which show that a fact which seemingly conflicts with another is reconcilable with it, or that, of two apparently strong reasons, one and not the other ought to be preferred. All that part of the truth which turns the scale, and decides the judgment of a completely informed mind, they are strangers to; nor is it ever really known, but to those who have attended equally and impartially to both sides, and endeavoured to see the reasons of both in the strongest light. So essential is this discipline to a real understanding of moral and human subjects, that if opponents of all important truths do not exist, it is indispensable to imagine them, and supply them with the strongest arguments which the most skilful devil's advocate can conjure up.

To abate the force of these considerations, an enemy of free discussion may be supposed to say, that there is no necessity for mankind in general to know and understand all that can be said against or for their opinions by philosophers and theologians. That it is not needful for common men to be able to expose all the misstatements or fallacies of an ingenious opponent. That it is enough if there is always somebody capable of answering them, so that nothing likely to mislead uninstructed persons remains unrefuted. That simple minds, having been taught the obvious grounds of the truths inculcated on them, may trust to authority for the rest, and being aware that they have neither knowledge nor talent to resolve every difficulty which can be raised, may repose in the assurance that all those which have been raised have been or can be answered, by those who are specially trained to the task.

Conceding to this view of the subject the utmost that can be claimed for it by those most easily satisfied with the amount of understanding of truth which ought to accompany the belief of it; even so, the argument for free discussion is no way weakened. For even this doctrine acknowledges that mankind ought to have a rational assurance that all objections have been satisfactorily answered; and how are they to be answered if that which requires to be answered is not spoken? or how can the answer be known to be satisfactory, if the objectors have no opportunity of showing that it is unsatisfactory? If not the public, at least the philosophers and theologians who are to resolve the difficulties, must make themselves familiar with those difficulties in their most puzzling form; and this cannot be accomplished unless they are freely stated, and placed in the most advantageous light which they admit of. The Catholic Church has its own way of dealing with this embarrassing problem. It makes a broad separation between those who can be permitted to receive its doctrines on conviction, and those who must accept them on trust. Neither, indeed, are allowed any choice as to what they will accept; but the clergy, such at least as can be fully confided in, may admissibly and meritoriously make themselves acquainted with the arguments of opponents, in order to answer them, and may, therefore, read heretical books; the laity, not unless by special permission, hard to be obtained. This discipline recognises a knowledge of the enemy's case as beneficial to the teachers, but finds means, consistent with this, of denying it to the rest of the world: thus giving to the *élite* more mental culture, though not more mental freedom, than it allows to the mass. By this device it succeeds in obtaining the kind of mental superiority which its purposes require; for though culture without freedom never made a large and liberal mind, it can make a clever *nisi prius* advocate of a cause. But in countries professing Protestantism, this resource is denied; since Protestants hold, at least in theory, that the responsibility for the choice of a religion must be borne by each for himself, and cannot be thrown off upon teachers. Besides, in the present state of the world, it is practically impossible that writings which are read by the instructed can be kept from the uninstructed. If the teachers of mankind are to be cognisant of all that they ought to know, everything must be free to be written and published without restraint.

If, however, the mischievous operation of the absence of free discussion, when the received opinions are true, were confined to leaving men ignorant of the grounds of those opinions, it might be thought that this, if an intellectual, is no moral evil, and does not affect the worth of the opinions, regarded in their influence on the character. The fact, however, is, that not only the grounds of the opinion are forgotten in the absence of discussion, but too often the meaning of the opinion itself. The words which convey it, cease to suggest ideas, or suggest only a small portion of those they were originally employed to communicate. Instead of a vivid conception and a living belief, there remain only a few phrases retained by rote; or, if any part, the shell and husk only of the meaning is retained, the finer essence being lost. The great chapter in human history which this fact occupies and fills, cannot be too earnestly studied and meditated on.

It is illustrated in the experience of almost all ethical doctrines and religious creeds. They are all full of meaning and vitality to those who originate them, and to the direct disciples of the originators. Their meaning continues to be felt in undiminished strength, and is perhaps brought out into even fuller consciousness, so long as the struggle lasts to give the doctrine or creed an ascendancy over other creeds. At last it either prevails, and becomes the general opinion, or its progress stops; it keeps possession of the ground it has gained, but ceases to spread further. When either of these results has become apparent, controversy on the subject flags, and gradually dies away. The doctrine has taken its place, if not as a received opinion, as one of the admitted sects or divisions of opinion: those who hold it have generally inherited, not adopted it; and conversion from one of these doctrines to another, being now an exceptional fact, occupies little place in the thoughts of their professors. Instead of being, as at first, constantly on the alert either to defend themselves against the world, or to bring the world over to them, they have subsided into acquiescence, and neither listen, when they can help it, to arguments against their creed, nor trouble dissentients (if there be such) with arguments in its favour. From this time may usually be dated the decline in the living power of the doctrine. We often hear the teachers of all creeds lamenting the difficulty of keeping up in the minds of believers a lively apprehension of the truth which they nominally recognise, so that it may penetrate the feelings, and acquire a real mastery over the conduct. No such difficulty is complained of while the creed is still fighting for its existence: even the weaker combatants then know and feel what they are fighting for, and the difference between it and other doctrines; and in that period of every creed's existence, not a few persons may be found, who have realized its fundamental principles in all the forms of thought, have weighed and considered them in all their important bearings, and have experienced the full effect on the character, which belief in that creed ought to produce in a mind thoroughly imbued with it. But when it has come to be an hereditary creed, and to be received passively, not actively— when the mind is no longer compelled, in the same degree as at first, to exercise its vital powers on the questions which its belief presents to it, there is a progressive tendency to forget all of the belief except the formularies, or to give it a dull and torpid assent, as if accepting it on trust dispensed with the necessity of realizing it in consciousness, or testing it by personal experience; until it almost ceases to connect itself at all with the inner life of the human being. Then are seen the cases, so frequent in this age of the world as almost to form the majority, in which the creed remains as it were outside the mind, incrusting and petrifying it against all other influences addressed to the higher parts of our nature; manifesting its power by not suffering any fresh and living conviction to get in, but itself doing nothing for the mind or heart, except standing sentinel over them to keep them vacant.

To what an extent doctrines intrinsically fitted to make the deepest impression upon the mind may remain in it as dead beliefs, without being ever realized in the imagination, the feelings, or the understanding, is exemplified by the manner in which the majority of believers hold the doctrines of Christianity. By Christianity I here mean what is accounted such by all churches and sects—the maxims and precepts contained in the New Testament. These are considered sacred, and accepted as laws, by all professing Christians. Yet it is scarcely too much to say that not one Christian in a thousand guides or tests his individual conduct by reference to those laws. The standard to which he does refer it, is the custom of his nation, his class, or his religious profession. He has thus, on the one hand, a collection of ethical maxims, which he believes to have been vouchsafed to him by infallible wisdom as rules for his government; and on the other, a set of every-day judgments and practices, which go a certain length with some of those maxims, not so great a length with others, stand in direct opposition to some, and are, on the whole, a compromise between the Christian creed and the interests and suggestions of worldly life. To the first of these standards he gives his homage; to the other his real allegiance. All Christians believe that the blessed are the poor and humble, and those who are ill-used by the world; that it is easier for a camel to pass through the eye of a needle than for a rich man to enter the kingdom of heaven; that they should judge not, lest they be judged; that they should swear not at all; that they should love their neighbour as themselves; that if one take their cloak, they should give him their coat also; that they should take no thought for the morrow; that if they would be perfect, they should sell all that they have and give it to the poor. They are not insincere when they say that they believe these things. They do believe them, as people believe what they have always heard lauded and never discussed. But in the sense of that living belief which regulates conduct, they believe these doctrines just up to the point to which it is usual to act upon them. The doctrines in their integrity are serviceable to pelt adversaries with; and it is understood that they are to be put forward (when possible) as the reasons for whatever people do that they think laudable. But any one who reminded them that the maxims require an infinity of things which they never even think of doing, would gain nothing but to be classed among those very unpopular characters who affect to be better than other people. The doctrines have no hold on ordinary believers—are not a power in their minds. They have an habitual respect for the sound of them, but no feeling which spreads from the words to the things signified, and forces the mind to take *them* in, and make them conform to the formula. Whenever conduct is concerned, they look round for Mr. A and B to direct them how far to go in obeying Christ.

Now we may be well assured that the case was not thus, but far otherwise, with the early Christians. Had it been thus, Christianity never would have expanded from an obscure sect of the despised Hebrews into the religion of the Roman empire. When their enemies said, 'See how these Christians love one another' (a remark not likely to be made by anybody now), they assuredly had a much livelier feeling of the meaning of their creed than they have ever had since. And to this cause, probably, it is chiefly owing that Christianity now makes so little progress in extending its domain, and after eighteen centuries, is still nearly confined to Europeans and the descendants of Europeans. Even with the strictly religious, who are much in earnest about their doctrines, and attach a greater amount of meaning to many of them than people in general, it commonly happens that the part which is thus compara-tively active in their minds is that which was made by Calvin, or Knox, or some such person much nearer in character to themselves. The sayings of Christ coexist passively in their minds, producing hardly any effect beyond what is caused by mere listening to words so amiable and bland. There are many reasons, doubtless, why doctrines which are the badge of a sect retain more of their vitality than those common to all recognised sects, and why more pains are taken by teachers to keep their meaning alive; but one reason certainly is, that the peculiar doctrines are more questioned, and have to be oftener defended against open gainsayers. Both teachers and learners go to sleep at their post, as soon as there is no enemy in the field.

The same thing holds true, generally speaking, of all traditional doctrines—those of prudence and knowledge of life, as well as of morals or religion. All languages and literatures are full of general observations on life, both as to what it is, and how to conduct oneself in it; observations which everybody knows, which everybody repeats, or hears with acquiescence, which are received as truisms, yet of which most people first truly learn the meaning, when experience, generally of a painful kind, has made it a reality to them. How often, when smarting under some unforeseen misfortune or disappointment, does a person call to mind some proverb or common saying, familiar to him all his life, the meaning of which, if he had ever before felt it as he does now, would have saved him from the calamity. There are indeed reasons for this, other than the absence of discussion: there are many truths of which the full meaning *cannot* be realized, until personal experience has brought it home. But much more of the meaning even of these would have been understood, and what was understood would have been far more deeply impressed on the mind, if the man had been accustomed to hear it argued *pro* and *con* by people who did understand it. The fatal tendency of mankind to leave off thinking about a thing when it is no longer doubtful, is the cause of half their errors. A cotemporary author has well spoken of 'the deep slumber of a decided opinion.'

But what! (it may be asked) Is the absence of unanimity an indispensable condition of true knowledge? Is it necessary that some part of mankind should persist in error, to enable any to realize the truth? Does a belief cease to be real and vital as soon as it is generally received—and is a proposition never thoroughly understood and felt unless some doubt of it remains? As soon as mankind have unanimously accepted a truth, does the truth perish within them? The highest aim and best result of improved intelligence, it has hitherto been thought, is to unite mankind more and more in the acknowledgment of all important truths: and does the intelligence only last as long as it has not achieved its object? Do the fruits of conquest perish by the very completeness of the victory?

I affirm no such thing. As mankind improve, the number of doctrines which are no longer disputed or doubted will be constantly on the increase: and the well-being of mankind may almost be measured by the number and gravity of the truths which have reached the point of being uncontested. The cessation, on one question after another, of serious controversy, is one of the necessary incidents of the consolidation of opinion; a consolidation as salutary in the case of true opinions, as it is dangerous and noxious when the opinions are erroneous. But though this gradual narrowing of the bounds of diversity of opinion is necessary in both senses of the term, being at once inevitable and indispensable, we are not therefore obliged to conclude that all its consequences must be beneficial. The loss of so important an aid to the intelligent and living apprehension of a truth, as is afforded by the necessity of explaining it to, or defending it against, opponents, though not sufficient to out-weigh, is no trifling drawback from, the benefit of its universal recognition. Where this advantage can no longer be had, I confess I should like to see the teachers of mankind endeavouring to provide a substitute for it; some contrivance for making the difficulties of the question as present to the learner's consciousness, as if they were pressed upon him by a dissentient champion, eager for his conversion.

But instead of seeking contrivances for this purpose, they have lost those they formerly had. The Socratic dialectics, so magnificently exemplified in the dialogues of Plato, were a contrivance of this description. They were essentially a negative discussion of the great questions of philosophy and life, directed with consummate skill to the purpose of convincing any one who had merely adopted the common-places of received opinion, that he did not understand the subject—that he as yet attached no definite meaning to the doctrines he professed; in order that, becoming aware of his ignorance, he might be put in the way to attain a stable belief, resting on a clear apprehension both of the meaning of doctrines and of their evidence. The school disputations of the middle ages had a somewhat similar object. They were intended to make sure that the pupil understood his own opinion, and (by necessary correlation) the opinion opposed to it, and could enforce the grounds of the one and confute those of the other. These last-mentioned contests had indeed the incurable defect, that the premises appealed to were taken from authority, not from reason; and, as a discipline to the mind, they were in every respect inferior to the powerful dialectics which formed the intellects of the 'Socratici viri:' but the modern mind owes far more to both than it is generally willing to admit, and the present modes of education contain nothing which in the smallest degree supplies the place either of the one or of the other. A person who derives all his instruction from teachers or books, even if he escape the besetting temptation of contenting himself with cram, is under no compulsion to hear both sides; accordingly it is far from a frequent accomplishment, even among thinkers, to know both sides; and the weakest part of what everybody says in defence of his opinion, is what he intends as a reply to antagonists. It is the fashion of the present time to disparage negative logic—that which points out weaknesses in theory or errors in practice, without establishing positive truths. Such negative criticism would indeed be poor enough as an ultimate result; but as a means to attaining any positive knowledge or conviction worthy the name, it cannot be valued too highly; and until people are again systemati-cally trained to it, there will be few great thinkers, and a low general average of intellect, in any but the mathematical and physical departments of speculation. On any other subject no one's opinions deserve the name of knowledge, except so far as he has either had forced upon him by others, or gone through of himself, the same mental process which would have been required of him in carrying on an active controversy with opponents. That, therefore, which when absent, it is so indispensable, but so difficult, to create, how worse than absurd it is to forego, when spontaneously offering itself! If there are any persons who contest a received opinion, or who will do so if law or opinion will let them, let us thank them for it, open our minds to listen to them, and rejoice that there is some one to do for us what we otherwise ought, if we have any regard for either the certainty or the vitality of our convictions, to do with much greater labour for ourselves.

It still remains to speak of one of the principal causes which make diversity of opinion advantageous, and will continue to do so until mankind shall have entered a stage of intellectual advancement which at present seems at an incalculable dis-tance. We have hitherto considered only two possibilities: that the received opinion may be false, and some other opinion, consequently, true; or that, the received opinion being true, a conflict with the opposite error is essential to a clear apprehen-sion and deep feeling of its truth. But there is a commoner case than either of these; when the conflicting doctrines, instead of being one true and the other false, share the truth between them; and the nonconforming opinion is needed to supply the remainder of the truth, of which the received doctrine embodies only a part. Popular opinions, on subjects not palpable to sense, are often true, but seldom or never the whole truth. They are a part of the truth; sometimes a greater, sometimes a smaller part, but exaggerated, distorted, and disjoined from the truths by which they ought to be accompanied and limited. Heretical opinions, on the other hand, are generally some of these suppressed and neglected truths, bursting the bonds which kept them down, and either seeking reconciliation with the truth contained in the common opinion, or fronting it as enemies, and setting themselves up, with similar exclusiveness, as the whole truth. The latter case is hitherto the most frequent, as, in the human mind, one-sidedness has always been the rule, and many-sidedness the exception. Hence, even in revolutions of opinion, one part of the truth usually sets while another rises. Even progress, which ought to superadd, for the most part only substitutes, one partial and incomplete truth for another; improvement consisting chiefly in this, that the new fragment of truth is more wanted, more adapted to the needs of the time, than that which it displaces. Such being the partial character of prevailing opinions, even when resting on a true foundation, every opinion which embodies somewhat of the portion of truth which the common opinion omits, ought to be considered precious, with whatever amount of error and confusion that truth may be blended. No sober judge of human affairs will feel bound to be indignant because those who force on our notice truths which we should otherwise have overlooked, overlook some of those which we see. Rather, he will think that so long as popular truth is one-sided, it is more desirable than otherwise that unpopular truth should have one-sided asserters too; such being usually the most energetic, and the most likely to compel reluctant attention to the fragment of wisdom which they proclaim as if it were the whole.

Thus, in the eighteenth century, when nearly all the instructed, and all those of the uninstructed who were led by them, were lost in admiration of what is called civilization, and of the marvels of modern science, literature, and philosophy, and while greatly overrating the amount of unlikeness between the men of modern and those of ancient times, indulged the belief that the whole of the difference was in their own favour; with what a salutary shock did the paradoxes of Rousseau explode like bombshells in the midst, dislocating the compact mass of one-sided opinion, and forcing its elements to recombine in a better form and with additional ingredients. Not that the current opinions were on the whole farther from the truth than Rousseau's were; on the contrary, they were nearer to it; they contained more of positive truth, and very much less of error. Nevertheless there lay in Rousseau's doctrine, and has floated down the stream of opinion along with it, a considerable amount of exactly those truths which the popular opinion wanted; and these are the deposit which was left behind when the flood subsided. The superior worth of simplicity of life, the enervating and demoralizing effect of the trammels and hypocrisies of artificial society, are ideas which have never been entirely absent from cultivated minds since Rousseau wrote; and they will in time produce their due effect, though at present needing to be asserted as much as ever, and to be asserted by deeds, for words, on this subject, have nearly exhausted their power.

In politics, again, it is almost a commonplace, that a party of order or stability, and a party of progress or reform, are both necessary elements of a healthy state of political life; until the one or the other shall have so enlarged its mental grasp as to be a party equally of order and of progress, knowing and distinguishing what is fit to be preserved from what ought to be swept away. Each of these modes of thinking derives its utility from the deficiencies of the other; but it is in a great measure the opposition of the other that keeps each within the limits of reason and sanity. Unless opinions favourable to democracy and to aristocracy, to property and to equality, to co-operation and to competition, to luxury and to abstinence, to sociality and individuality, to liberty and discipline, and all the other standing antagonisms of practical life, are expressed with equal freedom, and enforced and defended with equal talent and energy, there is no chance of both elements obtaining their due; one scale is sure to go up, and the other down. Truth, in the great practical concerns of life, is so much a question of the reconciling and combining of opposites, that very few have minds sufficiently capacious and impartial to make the adjustment with an approach to correctness, and it has to be made by the rough process of a struggle between combatants fighting under hostile banners. On any of the great open questions just enumerated, if either of the two opinions has a better claim than the other, not merely to be tolerated, but to be encouraged and countenanced, it is the one which happens at the particular time and place to be in a minority. That is the opinion which, for the time being, represents the neglected interests, the side of human well-being which is in danger of obtaining less than its share. I am aware that there is not, in this country, any intolerance of differences of opinion on most of these topics. They are adduced to show, by admitted and multiplied examples, the universality of the fact, that only through diversity of opinion is there, in the existing state of human intellect, a chance of fair play to all sides of the truth. When there are persons to be found, who form an exception to the apparent unanimity of the world on any subject, even if the world is in the right, it is always probable that dissentients have something worth hearing to say for themselves, and that truth would lose something by their silence.

It may be objected, 'But *some* received principles, especially on the highest and most vital subjects, are more than half-truths. The Christian morality, for instance, is the whole truth on that subject, and if any one teaches a morality which varies from it, he is wholly in error.' As this is of all cases the most important in practice, none can be fitter to test the general maxim. But before pronouncing what Christian morality is or is not, it would be desirable to decide what is meant by Christian morality. If it means the morality of the New Testament, I wonder that any one who derives his knowledge of this from the book itself, can suppose that it was announced, or intended, as a complete doctrine of morals. The Gospel always refers to a pre-existing morality, and confines its precepts to the particulars in which that morality was to be corrected, or superseded by a wider and higher; expressing itself, more-over, in terms most general, often impossible to be interpreted literally, and pos-sessing rather the impressiveness of poetry or eloquence than the precision of legislation. To extract from it a body of ethical doctrine, has never been possible without eking it out from the Old Testament, that is, from a system elaborate indeed, but in many respects barbarous, and intended only for a barbarous people. St. Paul, a declared enemy to this Judaical mode of interpreting the doctrine and filling up the scheme of his Master, equally assumes a pre-existing morality, namely that of the Greeks and Romans; and his advice to Christians is in a great measure a system of accommodation to that; even to the extent of giving an apparent sanction to slavery. What is called Christian, but should rather be termed theological, morality, was not the work of Christ or the Apostles, but is of much later origin, having been gradually built up by the Catholic church of the first five centuries, and though not implicitly adopted by moderns and Protestants, has been much less modified by them than might have been expected. For the most part, indeed, they have contented themselves with cutting off the additions which had been made to it in the middle ages, each sect supplying the place by fresh additions, adapted to its own character and tendencies. That mankind owe a great debt to this morality, and to its early teachers, I should be the last person to deny; but I do not scruple to say of it, that it is, in many important points, incomplete and one-sided, and that unless ideas and feelings, not sanctioned by it, had contributed to the formation of European life and character, human affairs would have been in a worse condition than they now are. Christian morality (so called) has all the characters of a reaction; it is, in great part, a protest against Paganism. Its ideal is negative rather than positive; passive rather than active; Innocence rather than Nobleness; Abstinence from Evil, rather than energetic Pursuit of Good: in its precepts (as has been well said) 'thou shalt not' predominates unduly over 'thou shalt.' In its horror of sensuality, it made an idol of asceticism, which has been gradually compromised away into one of legality. It holds out the hope of heaven and the threat of hell, as the appointed and appropriate motives to a virtuous life: in this falling far below the best of the ancients, and doing what lies in it to give to human morality an essentially selfish character, by disconnecting each man's feelings of duty from the interests of his fellow-creatures, except so far as a self-interested inducement is offered to him for consulting them. It is essentially a doctrine of passive obedience; it inculcates submission to all authorities found established; who indeed are not to be actively obeyed when they command what religion forbids, but who are not to be resisted, far less rebelled against, for any amount of wrong to ourselves. And while, in the morality of the best Pagan nations, duty to the State holds even a disproportionate place, infringing on the just liberty of the individual; in purely Christian ethics, that grand department of duty is scarcely noticed or acknowledged. It is in the Koran, not the New Testament, that we read the maxim—'A ruler who appoints any man to an office, when there is in his dominions another man better qualified for it, sins against God and against the State.' What little recognition the idea of obligation to the public obtains in modern morality, is derived from Greek and Roman sources, not from Christian; as, even in the morality of private life, whatever exists of magnanimity, highmindedness, personal dignity, even the sense of honour, is derived from the purely human, not the religious part of our education, and never could have grown out of a standard of ethics in which the only worth, professedly recognised, is that of obedience.

I am as far as any one from pretending that these defects are necessarily inherent in the Christian ethics, in every manner in which it can be conceived, or that the many requisites of a complete moral doctrine which it does not contain, do not admit of being reconciled with it. Far less would I insinuate this of the doctrines and precepts of Christ himself. I believe that the sayings of Christ are all, that I can see any evidence of their having been intended to be; that they are irreconcilable with nothing which a comprehensive morality requires; that everything which is excellent in ethics may be brought within them, with no greater violence to their language than has been done to it by all who have attempted to deduce from them any practical system of conduct whatever. But it is quite consistent with this, to believe that they contain, and were meant to contain, only a part of the truth; that many essential elements of the highest morality are among the things which are not provided for, nor intended to be provided for, in the recorded deliverances of the Founder of Christianity, and which have been entirely thrown aside in the system of ethics erected on the basis of those deliverances by the Christian Church. And this being so, I think it a great error to persist in attempting to find in the Christian doctrine that complete rule for our guidance, which its author intended it to sanction and enforce, but only partially to provide. I believe, too, that this narrow theory is becoming a grave practical evil, detracting greatly from the value of the moral training and instruction, which so many well-meaning persons are now at length exerting themselves to promote. I much fear that by attempting to form the mind and feelings on an exclusively religious type, and discarding those secular standards (as for want of a better name they may be called) which heretofore co-existed with and supplemented the Christian ethics, receiving some of its spirit, and infusing into it some of theirs, there will result, and is even now resulting, a low, abject, servile type of character, which, submit itself as it may to what it deems the Supreme Will, is incapable of rising to or sympathizing in the conception of Supreme Goodness. I believe that other ethics than any which can be evolved from exclusively Christian sources, must exist side by side with Christian ethics to produce the moral regeneration of mankind; and that the Christian system is no exception to the rule, that in an imperfect state of the human mind, the interests of truth require a diversity of opinions. It is not necessary that in ceasing to ignore the moral truths not contained in Christianity, men should ignore any of those which it does contain. Such prejudice, or oversight, when it occurs, is altogether an evil; but it is one from which we cannot hope to be always exempt, and must be regarded as the price paid for an inestimable good. The exclusive pretension made by a part of the truth to be the whole, must and ought to be protested against; and if a reactionary impulse should make the protestors unjust in their turn, this one-sidedness, like the other, may be lamented, but must be tolerated. If Christians would teach infidels to be just to Christianity, they should themselves be just to infidelity. It can do truth no service to blink the fact, known to all who have the most ordinary acquaintance with literary history, that a large portion of the noblest and most valuable moral teaching has been the work, not only of men who did not know, but of men who knew and rejected, the Christian faith.

I do not pretend that the most unlimited use of the freedom of enunciating all possible opinions would put an end to the evils of religious or philosophical sectarianism. Every truth which men of narrow capacity are in earnest about, is sure to be asserted, inculcated, and in many ways even acted on, as if no other truth existed in the world, or at all events none that could limit or qualify the first. I acknowledge that the tendency of all opinions to become sectarian is not cured by the freest discussion, but is often heightened and exacerbated thereby; the truth which ought to have been, but was not, seen, being rejected all the more violently because proclaimed by persons regarded as opponents. But it is not on the impassioned partisan, it is on the calmer and more disinterested bystander, that this collision of opinions works its salutary effect. Not the violent conflict between parts of the truth, but the quiet suppression of half of it, is the formidable evil; there is always hope when people are forced to listen to both sides; it is when they attend only to one that errors harden into prejudices, and truth itself ceases to have the effect of truth, by being exaggerated into falsehood. And since there are few mental attributes more rare than that judicial faculty which can sit in intelligent judgment between two sides of a question, of which only one is represented by an advocate before it, truth has no chance but in proportion as every side of it, every opinion which embodies any fraction of the truth, not only finds advocates, but is so advocated as to be listened to.

We have now recognised the necessity to the mental well-being of mankind (on which all their other well-being depends) of freedom of opinion, and freedom of the expression of opinion, on four distinct grounds; which we will now briefly recapitulate.

First, if any opinion is compelled to silence, that opinion may, for aught we can certainly know, be true. To deny this is to assume our own infallibility.

Secondly, though the silenced opinion be an error, it may, and very commonly does, contain a portion of truth; and since the general or prevailing opinion on any subject is rarely or never the whole truth, it is only by the collision of adverse opinions that the remainder of the truth has any chance of being supplied.

Thirdly, even if the received opinion be not only true, but the whole truth; unless it is suffered to be, and actually is, vigorously and earnestly contested, it will, by most of those who receive it, be held in the manner of a prejudice, with little comprehension or feeling of its rational grounds. And not only this, but, fourthly, the meaning of the doctrine itself will be in danger of being lost, or enfeebled, and deprived of its vital effect on the character and conduct: the dogma becoming a mere formal profession, inefficacious for good, but cumbering the ground, and preventing the growth of any real and heartfelt conviction, from reason or personal experience.

Before quitting the subject of freedom of opinion, it is fit to take some notice of those who say, that the free expression of all opinions should be permitted, on condition that the manner be temperate, and do not pass the bounds of fair discussion. Much might be said on the impossibility of fixing where these supposed bounds are to be placed; for if the test be offence to those whose opinion is attacked, I think experience testifies that this offence is given whenever the attack is telling and powerful, and that every opponent who pushes them hard, and whom they find it difficult to answer, appears to them, if he shows any strong feeling on the subject, an intemperate opponent. But this, though an important consideration in a practical point of view, merges in a more fundamental objection. Undoubtedly the manner of asserting an opinion, even though it be a true one, may be very objectionable, and may justly incur severe censure. But the principal offences of the kind are such as it is mostly impossible, unless by accidental self-betrayal, to bring home to conviction. The gravest of them is, to argue sophistically, to suppress facts or arguments, to misstate the elements of the case, or misrepresent the opposite opinion. But all this, even to the most aggravated degree, is so continually done in perfect good faith, by persons who are not considered, and in many other respects may not deserve to be considered, ignorant or incompetent, that it is rarely possible on adequate grounds conscientiously to stamp the misrepresentation as morally culpable; and still less could law presume to interfere with this kind of controversial misconduct. With regard to what is commonly meant by intemperate discussion, namely invective, sarcasm, personality, and the like, the denunciation of these weapons would deserve more sympathy if it were ever proposed to interdict them equally to both sides; but it is only desired to restrain the employment of them against the prevailing opinion: against the unprevailing they may not only be used without general disapproval, but will be likely to obtain for him who uses them the praise of honest zeal and righteous indignation. Yet whatever mischief arises from their use, is greatest when they are employed against the comparatively defenceless; and whatever unfair advantage can be derived by any opinion from this mode of asserting it, accrues almost exclusively to received opinions. The worst offence of this kind which can be committed by a polemic, is to stigmatize those who hold the contrary opinion as bad and immoral men. To calumny of this sort, those who hold any unpopular opinion are peculiarly exposed, because they are in general few and uninfluential, and nobody but themselves feels much interested in seeing justice done them; but this weapon is, from the nature of the case, denied to those who attack a prevailing opinion: they can neither use it with safety to themselves, nor, if they could, would it do anything but recoil on their own cause. In general, opinions contrary to those commonly received can only obtain a hearing by studied moderation of language, and the most cautious avoidance of unnecessary offence, from which they hardly ever deviate even in a slight degree without losing ground: while unmeasured vituperation employed on the side of the prevailing opinion, really does deter people from professing contrary opinions, and from listening to those who profess them. For the interest, therefore, of truth and justice, it is far more important to restrain this employment of vituperative language than the other; and, for example, if it were necessary to choose, there would be much more need to discourage offensive attacks on infidelity, than on religion. It is, however, obvious that law and authority have no business with restraining either, while opinion ought, in every instance, to determine its verdict by the circumstances of the individual case; condemning every one, on whichever side of the argument he places himself, in whose mode of advocacy either want of candour, or malignity, bigotry, or intolerance of feeling manifest themselves; but not inferring these vices from the side which a person takes, though it be the contrary side of the question to our own: and giving merited honour to every one, whatever opinion he may hold, who has calmness to see and honesty to state what his opponents and their opinions really are, exaggerating nothing to their discredit, keeping nothing back which tells, or can be supposed to tell, in their favour. This is the real morality of public discussion: and if often violated, I am happy to think that there are many controversialists who to a great extent observe it, and a still greater number who conscientiously strive towards it.

CHAPTER III
Of Individuality, as One of the Elements of Well-Being

Such being the reasons which make it imperative that human beings should be free to form opinions, and to express their opinions without reserve; and such the baneful consequences to the intellectual, and through that to the moral nature of man, unless this liberty is either conceded, or asserted in spite of prohibition; let us next examine whether the same reasons do not require that men should be free to act upon their opinions—to carry these out in their lives, without hindrance, either physical or moral, from their fellow-men, so long as it is at their own risk and peril. This last proviso is of course indispensable. No one pretends that actions should be as free as opinions. On the contrary, even opinions lose their immunity, when the circumstances in which they are expressed are such as to constitute their expression a positive instigation to some mischievous act. An opinion that corn-dealers are starvers of the poor, or that private property is robbery, ought to be unmolested when simply circulated through the press, but may justly incur punishment when delivered orally to an excited mob assembled before the house of a corn-dealer, or when handed about among the same mob in the form of a placard. Acts, of whatever kind, which, without justifiable cause, do harm to others, may be, and in the more important cases absolutely require to be, controlled by the unfavourable sentiments, and, when needful, by the active interference of mankind. The liberty of the individual must be thus far limited; he must not make himself a nuisance to other people. But if he refrains from molesting others in what concerns them, and merely acts according to his own inclination and judgment in things which concern himself, the same reasons which show that opinion should be free, prove also that he should be allowed, without molestation, to carry his opinions into practice at his own cost. That mankind are not infallible; that their truths, for the most part, are only half-truths; that unity of opinion, unless resulting from the fullest and freest comparison of opposite opinions, is not desirable, and diversity not an evil, but a good, until mankind are much more capable than at present of recognising all sides of the truth, are principles applicable to men's modes of action, not less than to their opinions. As it is useful that while mankind are imperfect there should be different opinions, so is it that there should be different experiments of living; that free scope should be given to varieties of character, short of injury to others; and that the worth of different modes of life should be proved practically, when any one thinks fit to try them. It is desirable, in short, that in things which do not primarily concern others, individuality should assert itself. Where, not the person's own character, but the traditions or customs of other people are the rule of conduct, there is wanting one of the principal ingredients of human happiness, and quite the chief ingredient of individual and social progress.

In maintaining this principle, the greatest difficulty to be encountered does not lie in the appreciation of means towards an acknowledged end, but in the indifference of persons in general to the end itself. If it were felt that the free development of individuality is one of the leading essentials of well-being; that it is not only a co-ordinate element with all that is designated by the terms civilization, instruction, education, culture, but is itself a necessary part and condition of all those things; there would be no danger that liberty should be undervalued, and the adjustment of the boundaries between it and social control would present no extraordinary difficulty. But the evil is, that individual spontaneity is hardly recognised by the common modes of thinking, as having any intrinsic worth, or deserving any regard on its own account. The majority, being satisfied with the ways of mankind as they now are (for it is they who make them what they are), cannot comprehend why those ways should not be good enough for everybody; and what is more, spontaneity forms no part of the ideal of the majority of moral and social reformers, but is rather looked on with jealousy, as a troublesome and perhaps rebellious obstruction to the general acceptance of what these reformers, in their own judgment, think would be best for mankind. Few persons, out of Germany, even comprehend the meaning of the doctrine which Wilhelm Von Humboldt, so eminent both as a *savant* and as a politician, made the text of a treatise—that 'the end of man, or that which is prescribed by the eternal or immutable dictates of reason, and not suggested by vague and transient desires, is the highest and most harmonious development of his powers to a complete and consistent whole;' that, therefore, the object 'towards which every human being must ceaselessly direct his efforts, and on which especially those who design to influence their fellow-men must ever keep their eyes, is the individuality of power and development;' that for this there are two requisites, 'freedom, and variety of situations;' and that from the union of these arise 'individual vigour and manifold diversity,' which combine themselves in 'originality.'[6]

Little, however, as people are accustomed to a doctrine like that of Von Humboldt, and surprising as it may be to them to find so high a value attached to individuality, the question, one must nevertheless think, can only be one of degree. No one's idea of excellence in conduct is that people should do absolutely nothing but copy one another. No one would assert that people ought not to put into their mode of life, and into the conduct of their concerns, any impress whatever of their own judgment, or of their own individual character. On the other hand, it would be absurd to pretend that people ought to live as if nothing whatever had been known in the world before they came into it; as if experience had as yet done nothing towards showing that one mode of existence, or of conduct, is preferable to another. Nobody denies that people should be so taught and trained in youth, as to know and benefit by the ascertained results of human experience. But it is the privilege and proper condition of a human being, arrived at the maturity of his faculties, to use and interpret experience in his own way. It is for him to find out what part of recorded experience is properly applicable to his own circumstances and character. The traditions and customs of other people are, to a certain extent, evidence of what their experience has taught *them;* presumptive evidence, and as such, have a claim to his deference: but, in the first place, their experience may be too narrow; or they may not have interpreted it rightly. Secondly, their interpretation of experience may be correct, but unsuitable to him. Customs are made for customary circumstances, and customary characters; and his circumstances or his character may be uncustomary. Thirdly, though the customs be both good as customs, and suitable to him, yet to conform to custom, merely as custom, does not educate or develop in him any of the qualities which are the distinctive endowment of a human being. The human faculties of perception, judgment, discriminative feeling, mental activity, and even moral preference, are exercised only in making a choice. He who does anything because it is the custom, makes no choice. He gains no practice either in discerning or in desiring what is best. The mental and moral, like the muscular powers, are improved only by being used. The faculties are called into no exercise by doing a thing merely because others do it, no more than by believing a thing only because others believe it. If the grounds of an opinion are not conclusive to the person's own reason, his reason cannot be strengthened, but is likely to be weakened, by his adopting it: and if the inducements to an act are not such as are consentaneous to his own feelings and character (where affection, or the rights of others, are not concerned) it is so much done towards rendering his feelings and character inert and torpid, instead of active and energetic.

He who lets the world, or his own portion of it, choose his plan of life for him, has no need of any other faculty than the ape-like one of imitation. He who chooses his plan for himself, employs all his faculties. He must use observation to see, reasoning and judgment to foresee, activity to gather materials for decision, discrimination to decide, and when he has decided, firmness and self-control to hold to his deliberate decision. And these qualities he requires and exercises exactly in proportion as the part of his conduct which he determines according to his own

---

6. *The Sphere and Duties of Government,* from the German of Baron Wilhelm von Humboldt, pp. 11–13.

judgment and feelings is a large one. It is possible that he might be guided in some good path, and kept out of harm's way, without any of these things. But what will be his comparative worth as a human being? It really is of importance, not only what men do, but also what manner of men they are that do it. Among the works of man, which human life is rightly employed in perfecting and beautifying, the first in importance surely is man himself. Supposing it were possible to get houses built, corn grown, battles fought, causes tried, and even churches erected and prayers said, by machinery—by automatons in human form—it would be a considerable loss to exchange for these automatons even the men and women who at present inhabit the more civilized parts of the world, and who assuredly are but starved specimens of what nature can and will produce. Human nature is not a machine to be built after a model, and set to do exactly the work prescribed for it, but a tree, which requires to grow and develope itself on all sides, according to the tendency of the inward forces which make it a living thing.

It will probably be conceded that it is desirable people should exercise their understandings, and that an intelligent following of custom, or even occasionally an intelligent deviation from custom, is better than a blind and simply mechanical adhesion to it. To a certain extent it is admitted, that our understanding should be our own: but there is not the same willingness to admit that our desires and impulses should be our own likewise; or that to possess impulses of our own, and of any strength, is anything but a peril and a snare. Yet desires and impulses are as much a part of a perfect human being, as beliefs and restraints: and strong impulses are only perilous when not properly balanced; when one set of aims and inclinations is developed into strength, while others, which ought to co-exist with them, remain weak and inactive. It is not because men's desires are strong that they act ill; it is because their consciences are weak. There is no natural connexion between strong impulses and a weak conscience. The natural connexion is the other way. To say that one person's desires and feelings are stronger and more various than those of another, is merely to say that he has more of the raw material of human nature, and is therefore capable, perhaps of more evil, but certainly of more good. Strong impulses are but another name for energy. Energy may be turned to bad uses; but more good may always be made of an energetic nature, than of an indolent and impassive one. Those who have most natural feeling, are always those whose culti- vated feelings may be made the strongest. The same strong susceptibilities which make the personal impulses vivid and powerful, are also the source from whence are generated the most passionate love of virtue, and the sternest self-control. It is through the cultivation of these, that society both does its duty and protects its interests: not by rejecting the stuff of which heroes are made, because it knows not how to make them. A person whose desires and impulses are his own—are the expression of his own nature, as it has been developed and modified by his own culture—is said to have a character. One whose desires and impulses are not his own, has no character, no more than a steam-engine has a character. If, in addition to being his own, his impulses are strong, and are under the government of a strong will, he has an energetic character. Whoever thinks that individuality of desires and impulses should not be encouraged to unfold itself, must maintain that society has no need of strong natures—is not the better for containing many persons who have much character—and that a high general average of energy is not desirable.

In some early states of society, these forces might be, and were, too much ahead of the power which society then possessed of disciplining and controlling them.

There has been a time when the element of spontaneity and individuality was in excess, and the social principle had a hard struggle with it. The difficulty then was, to induce men of strong bodies or minds to pay obedience to any rules which required them to control their impulses. To overcome this difficulty, law and discipline, like the Popes struggling against the Emperors, asserted a power over the whole man, claiming to control all his life in order to control his character—which society had not found any other sufficient means of binding. But society has now fairly got the better of individuality; and the danger which threatens human nature is not the excess, but the deficiency, of personal impulses and preferences. Things are vastly changed, since the passions of those who were strong by station or by personal endowment were in a state of habitual rebellion against laws and ordinances, and required to be rigorously chained up to enable the persons within their reach to enjoy any particle of security. In our times, from the highest class of society down to the lowest, every one lives as under the eye of a hostile and dreaded censorship. Not only in what concerns others, but in what concerns only themselves, the individual or the family do not ask themselves—what do I prefer? or, what would suit my character and disposition? or, what would allow the best and highest in me to have fair play, and enable it to grow and thrive? They ask themselves, what is suitable to my position? what is usually done by persons of my station and pecuniary circumstances? or (worse still) what is usually done by persons of a station and circumstances superior to mine? I do not mean that they choose what is customary, in preference to what suits their own inclination. It does not occur to them to have any inclination, except for what is customary. Thus the mind itself is bowed to the yoke: even in what people do for pleasure, conformity is the first thing thought of; they like in crowds; they exercise choice only among things commonly done: peculiarity of taste, eccentricity of conduct, are shunned equally with crimes: until by dint of not following their own nature, they have no nature to follow: their human capacities are withered and starved: they become incapable of any strong wishes or native pleasures, and are generally without either opinions or feelings of home growth, or properly their own. Now is this, or is it not, the desirable condition of human nature?

It is so, on the Calvinistic theory. According to that, the one great offence of man is self-will. All the good of which humanity is capable, is comprised in obedience. You have no choice; thus you must do, and no otherwise: 'whatever is not a duty, is a sin.' Human nature being radically corrupt, there is no redemption for any one until human nature is killed within him. To one holding this theory of life, crushing out any of the human faculties, capacities, and susceptibilities, is no evil: man needs no capacity, but that of surrendering himself to the will of God: and if he uses any of his faculties for any other purpose but to do that supposed will more effectually, he is better without them. This is the theory of Calvinism; and it is held, in a mitigated form, by many who do not consider themselves Calvinists; the mitigation consisting in giving a less ascetic interpretation to the alleged will of God; asserting it to be his will that mankind should gratify some of their inclinations; of course not in the manner they themselves prefer, but in the way of obedience, that is, in a way prescribed to them by authority; and, therefore, by the necessary conditions of the case, the same for all.

In some such insidious form there is at present a strong tendency to this narrow theory of life, and to the pinched and hidebound type of human character which it patronizes. Many persons, no doubt, sincerely think that human beings thus cramped and dwarfed, are as their Maker designed them to be; just as many have thought that trees are a much finer thing when clipped into pollards, or cut out into figures of animals, than as nature made them. But if it be any part of religion to believe that man was made by a good Being, it is more consistent with that faith to believe, that this Being gave all human faculties that they might be cultivated and unfolded, not rooted out and consumed, and that he takes delight in every nearer approach made by his creatures to the ideal conception embodied in them, every increase in any of their capabilities of comprehension, of action, or of enjoyment. There is a different type of human excellence from the Calvinistic; a conception of humanity as having its nature bestowed on it for other purposes than merely to be abnegated. 'Pagan self-assertion' is one of the elements of human worth, as well as 'Christian self-denial.'[7] There is a Greek ideal of self-development, which the Platonic and Christian ideal of self-government blends with, but does not supersede. It may be better to be a John Knox than an Alcibiades, but it is better to be a Pericles than either; nor would a Pericles, if we had one in these days, be without anything good which belonged to John Knox.

It is not by wearing down into uniformity all that is individual in themselves, but by cultivating it and calling it forth, within the limits imposed by the rights and interests of others, that human beings become a noble and beautiful object of contemplation; and as the works partake the character of those who do them, by the same process human life also becomes rich, diversified, and animating, furnishing more abundant aliment to high thoughts and elevating feelings, and strengthening the tie which binds every individual to the race, by making the race infinitely better worth belonging to. In proportion to the development of his individuality, each person becomes more valuable to himself, and is therefore capable of being more valuable to others. There is a greater fulness of life about his own existence, and when there is more life in the units there is more in the mass which is composed of them. As much compression as is necessary to prevent the stronger specimens of human nature from encroaching on the rights of others, cannot be dispensed with; but for this there is ample compensation even in the point of view of human development. The means of development which the individual loses by being prevented from gratifying his inclinations to the injury of others, are chiefly obtained at the expense of the development of other people. And even to himself there is a full equivalent in the better development of the social part of his nature, rendered possible by the restraint put upon the selfish part. To be held to rigid rules of justice for the sake of others, developes the feelings and capacities which have the good of others for their object. But to be restrained in things not affecting their good, by their mere displeasure, developes nothing valuable, except such force of character as may unfold itself in resisting the restraint. If acquiesced in, it dulls and blunts the whole nature. To give any fair play to the nature of each, it is essential that different persons should be allowed to lead different lives. In proportion as this latitude has been exercised in any age, has that age been noteworthy to posterity. Even despotism does not produce its worst effects, so long as individuality exists under it; and whatever crushes individuality is despotism, by whatever name it may be called, and whether it professes to be enforcing the will of God or the injunctions of men.

---

7. Sterling's *Essays.*

Having said that individuality is the same thing with development, and that it is only the cultivation of individuality which produces, or can produce, well-developed human beings, I might here close the argument: for what more or better can be said of any condition of human affairs, than that it brings human beings themselves nearer to the best thing they can be? or what worse can be said of any obstruction to good, than that it prevents this? Doubtless, however, these considerations will not suffice to convince those who most need convincing; and it is necessary further to show, that these developed human beings are of some use to the undeveloped—to point out to those who do not desire liberty, and would not avail themselves of it, that they may be in some intelligible manner rewarded for allowing other people to make use of it without hindrance.

In the first place, then, I would suggest that they might possibly learn something from them. It will not be denied by anybody, that originality is a valuable element in human affairs. There is always need of persons not only to discover new truths, and point out when what were once truths are true no longer, but also to commence new practices, and set the example of more enlightened conduct, and better taste and sense in human life. This cannot well be gainsaid by anybody who does not believe that the world has already attained perfection in all its ways and practices. It is true that this benefit is not capable of being rendered by everybody alike: there are but few persons, in comparison with the whole of mankind, whose experiments, if adopted by others, would be likely to be any improvement on established practice. But these few are the salt of the earth; without them, human life would become a stagnant pool. Not only is it they who introduce good things which did not before exist; it is they who keep the life in those which already existed. If there were nothing new to be done, would human intellect cease to be necessary? Would it be a reason why those who do the old things should forget why they are done, and do them like cattle, not like human beings? There is only too great a tendency in the best beliefs and practices to degenerate into the mechanical; and unless there were a succession of persons whose ever-recurring originality prevents the grounds of those beliefs and practices from becoming merely traditional, such dead matter would not resist the smallest shock from anything really alive, and there would be no reason why civilization should not die out, as in the Byzantine Empire. Persons of genius, it is true, are, and are always likely to be, a small minority; but in order to have them, it is necessary to preserve the soil in which they grow. Genius can only breathe freely in an *atmosphere* of freedom. Persons of genius are, *ex vi termini, more* individual than any other people—less capable, consequently, of fitting themselves, without hurtful compression, into any of the small number of moulds which society provides in order to save its members the trouble of forming their own character. If from timidity they consent to be forced into one of these moulds, and to let all that part of themselves which cannot expand under the pressure remain unexpanded, society will be little the better for their genius. If they are of a strong character, and break their fetters, they become a mark for the society which has not succeeded in reducing them to commonplace, to point at with solemn warning as 'wild,' 'erratic,' and the like; much as if one should complain of the Niagara river for not flowing smoothly between its banks like a Dutch canal.

I insist thus emphatically on the importance of genius, and the necessity of allowing it to unfold itself freely both in thought and in practice, being well aware that no one will deny the position in theory, but knowing also that almost every one, in reality, is totally indifferent to it. People think genius a fine thing if it enables a man to write an exciting poem, or paint a picture. But in its true sense, that of originality in thought and action, though no one says that it is not a thing to be admired, nearly all, at heart, think that they can do very well without it. Unhappily this is too natural to be wondered at. Originality is the one thing which unoriginal minds cannot feel the use of. They cannot see what it is to do for them: how should they? If they could see what it would do for them, it would not be originality. The first service which originality has to render them, is that of opening their eyes: which being once fully done, they would have a chance of being themselves original. Meanwhile, recollecting that nothing was ever yet done which some one was not the first to do, and that all good things which exist are the fruits of originality, let them be modest enough to believe that there is something still left for it to accomplish, and assure themselves that they are more in need of originality, the less they are conscious of the want.

In sober truth, whatever homage may be professed, or even paid, to real or supposed mental superiority, the general tendency of things throughout the world is to render mediocrity the ascendant power among mankind. In ancient history, in the middle ages, and in a diminishing degree through the long transition from feudality to the present time, the individual was a power in himself; and if he had either great talents or a high social position, he was a considerable power. At present individuals are lost in the crowd. In politics it is almost a triviality to say that public opinion now rules the world. The only power deserving the name is that of masses, and of governments while they make themselves the organ of the tendencies and instincts of masses. This is as true in the moral and social relations of private life as in public transactions. Those whose opinions go by the name of public opinion, are not always the same sort of public: in America they are the whole white population; in England, chiefly the middle class. But they are always a mass, that is to say, collective mediocrity. And what is a still greater novelty, the mass do not now take their opinions from dignitaries in Church or State, from ostensible leaders, or from books. Their thinking is done for them by men much like themselves, addressing them or speaking in their name, on the spur of the moment, through the newspapers. I am not complaining of all this. I do not assert that anything better is compatible, as a general rule, with the present low state of the human mind. But that does not hinder the government of mediocrity from being mediocre government. No government by a democracy or a numerous aristocracy, either in its political acts or in the opinions, qualities, and tone of mind which it fosters, ever did or could rise above mediocrity, except in so far as the sovereign. Many have let themselves be guided (which in their best times they always have done) by the counsels and influence of a more highly gifted and instructed One or Few. The initiation of all wise or noble things, comes and must come from individuals; generally at first from some one individual. The honour and glory of the average man is that he is capable of following that initiative; that he can respond internally to wise and noble things, and be led to them with his eyes open. I am not countenancing the sort of 'hero-worship' which applauds the strong man of genius for forcibly seizing on the government of the world and making it do his bidding in spite of itself. All he can claim is, freedom to point out the way. The power of compelling others into it, is not only inconsistent with the freedom and development of all the rest, but corrupting to the strong man himself. It does seem, however, that when the opinions of masses of merely average men are everywhere become or becoming the dominant power, the counterpoise and corrective to that tendency would be, the more and more pronounced individuality of those who stand on the higher eminences of thought. It is in these circumstances most especially, that exceptional individuals, instead of being deterred, should be encouraged in acting differently from the mass. In other times there was no advantage in their doing so, unless they acted not only differently, but better. In this age, the mere example of nonconformity, the mere refusal to bend the knee to custom, is itself a service. Precisely because the tyranny of opinion is such as to make eccentricity a reproach, it is desirable, in order to break through that tyranny, that people should be eccentric. Eccentricity has always abounded when and where strength of character has abounded; and the amount of eccentricity in a society has generally been proportional to the amount of genius, mental vigour, and moral courage which it contained. That so few now dare to be eccentric, marks the chief danger of the time.

I have said that it is important to give the freest scope possible to uncustomary things, in order that it may in time appear which of these are fit to be converted into customs. But independence of action, and disregard of custom, are not solely deserving of encouragement for the chance they afford that better modes of action, and customs more worthy of general adoption, may be struck out; nor is it only persons of decided mental superiority who have a just claim to carry on their lives in their own way. There is no reason that all human existence should be constructed on some one or some small number of patterns. If a person possesses any tolerable amount of common sense and experience, his own mode of laying out his existence is the best, not because it is the best in itself, but because it is his own mode. Human beings are not like sheep; and even sheep are not undistinguishably alike. A man cannot get a coat or a pair of boots to fit him, unless they are either made to his measure, or he has a whole warehouseful to choose from: and is it easier to fit him with a life than with a coat, or are human beings more like one another in their whole physical and spiritual conformation than in the shape of their feet? If it were only that people have diversities of taste, that is reason enough for not attempting to shape them all after one model. But different persons also require different conditions for their spiritual development; and can no more exist healthily in the same moral, than all the variety of plants can in the same physical, atmosphere and climate. The same things which are helps to one person towards the cultivation of his higher nature, are hindrances to another. The same mode of life is a healthy excitement to one, keeping all his faculties of action and enjoyment in their best order, while to another it is a distracting burthen, which suspends or crushes all internal life. Such are the differences among human beings in their sources of pleasure, their susceptibilities of pain, and the operation on them of different physical and moral agencies, that unless there is a corresponding diversity in their modes of life, they neither obtain their fair share of happiness, nor grow up to the mental, moral, and aesthetic stature of which their nature is capable. Why then should tolerance, as far as the public sentiment is concerned, extend only to tastes and modes of life which extort acquiescence by the multitude of their adherents? Nowhere (except in some monastic institutions) is diversity of taste entirely unrecognised; a person may, without blame, either like or dislike rowing, or smoking, or music, or athletic exercises, or chess, or cards, or study, because both those who like each of these things, and those who dislike them, are too numerous to be put down. But the man, and still more the woman, who can be accused either of doing 'what nobody does,' or of not doing 'what everybody does,' is the subject of as much depreciatory remark as if he or she had committed some grave moral delinquency.

Persons require to possess a title, or some other badge of rank, or of the consideration of people of rank, to be able to indulge somewhat in the luxury of doing as they like without detriment to their estimation. To indulge somewhat, I repeat: for whoever allow themselves much of that indulgence, incur the risk of something worse than disparaging speeches—they are in peril of a commission *de lunatico,* and of having their property taken from them and given to their relations.[8]

There is one characteristic of the present direction of public opinion, peculiarly calculated to make it intolerant of any marked demonstration of individuality. The general average of mankind are not only moderate in intellect, but also moderate in inclinations: they have no tastes or wishes strong enough to incline them to do anything unusual, and they consequently do not understand those who have, and class all such with the wild and intemperate whom they are accustomed to look down upon. Now, in addition to this fact which is general, we have only to suppose that a strong movement has set in towards the improvement of morals, and it is evident what we have to expect. In these days such a movement has set in; much has actually been effected in the way of increased regularity of conduct, and discouragement of excesses; and there is a philanthropic spirit abroad, for the exercise of which there is no more inviting field than the moral and prudential improvement of our fellow-creatures. These tendencies of the times cause the public to be more disposed than at most former periods to prescribe general rules of conduct, and endeavour to make every one conform to the approved standard. And that standard, express or tacit, is to desire nothing strongly. Its ideal of character is to be without any marked character; to maim by compression, like a Chinese lady's foot, every part of human nature which stands out prominently, and tends to make the person markedly dissimilar in outline to commonplace humanity.

As is usually the case with ideals which exclude one-half of what is desirable, the present standard of approbation produces only an inferior imitation of the other half. Instead of great energies guided by vigorous reason, and strong feelings strongly controlled by a conscientious will, its result is weak feelings and weak energies, which therefore can be kept in outward conformity to rule without any strength either of will or of reason. Already energetic characters on any large scale are becoming merely traditional. There is now scarcely any outlet for energy in this country except business. The energy expended in this may still be regarded as considerable. What little is left from that employment, is expended on some hobby;

8. There is something both contemptible and frightful in the sort of evidence on which, of late years, any person can be judicially declared unfit for the management of his affairs; and after his death, his disposal of his property can be set aside, if there is enough of it to pay the expenses of litigation—which are charged on the property itself. All the minute details of his daily life are pried into, and whatever is found which, seen through the medium of the perceiving and describing faculties of the lowest of the low, bears an appearance unlike absolute commonplace, is laid before the jury as evidence of insanity, and often with success; the jurors being little, if at all, less vulgar and ignorant than the witnesses; while the judges, with that extraordinary want of knowledge of human nature and life which continually astonishes us in English lawyers, often help to mislead them. These trials speak volumes as to the state of feeling and opinion among the vulgar with regard to human liberty. So far from setting any value on individuality—so far from respecting the right of each individual to act, in things indifferent, as seems good to his own judgment and inclinations, judges and juries cannot even conceive that a person in a state of sanity can desire such freedom. In former days, when it was proposed to burn atheists, charitable people used to suggest putting them in a madhouse instead: it would be nothing surprising now-a-days were we to see this done, and the doers applauding themselves, because, instead of persecuting for religion, they had adopted so humane and Christian a mode of treating these unfortunates, not without a silent satisfaction at their having thereby obtained their deserts.

which may be a useful, even a philanthropic hobby, but is always some one thing, and generally a thing of small dimensions. The greatness of England is now all collective: individually small, we only appear capable of anything great by our habit of combining; and with this our moral and religious philanthropists are perfectly contented. But it was men of another stamp than this that made England what it has been; and men of another stamp will be needed to prevent its decline.

The despotism of custom is everywhere the standing hindrance to human advancement, being in unceasing antagonism to that disposition to aim at something better than customary, which is called, according to circumstances, the spirit of liberty, or that of progress or improvement. The spirit of improvement is not always a spirit of liberty, for it may aim at forcing improvements on an unwilling people; and the spirit of liberty, in so far as it resists such attempts, may ally itself locally and temporarily with the opponents of improvement; but the only unfailing and permanent source of improvement is liberty, since by it there are as many possible independent centres of improvement as there are individuals. The progressive principle, however, in either shape, whether as the love of liberty or of improvement, is antagonistic to the sway of Custom, involving at least emancipation from that yoke; and the contest between the two constitutes the chief interest of the history of mankind. The greater part of the world has, properly speaking, no history, because the despotism of Custom is complete. This is the case over the whole East. Custom is there, in all things, the final appeal; justice and right mean conformity to custom; the argument of custom no one, unless some tyrant intoxicated with power, thinks of resisting. And we see the result. Those nations must once have had originality; they did not start out of the ground populous, lettered, and versed in many of the arts of life; they made themselves all this, and were then the greatest and most powerful nations of the world. What are they now? The subjects or dependents of tribes whose forefathers wandered in the forests when theirs had magnificent palaces and gorgeous temples, but over whom custom exercised only a divided rule with liberty and progress. A people, it appears, may be progressive for a certain length of time, and then stop: when does it stop? When it ceases to possess individuality. If a similar change should befall the nations of Europe, it will not be in exactly the same shape: the despotism of custom with which these nations are threatened is not precisely stationariness. It proscribes singularity, but it does not preclude change, provided all change together. We have discarded the fixed costumes of our forefathers; every one must still dress like other people, but the fashion may change once or twice a year. We thus take care that when there is change it shall be for change's sake, and not from any idea of beauty or convenience; for the same idea of beauty or convenience would not strike all the world at the same moment, and be simultaneously thrown aside by all at another moment. But we are progressive as well as changeable: we continually make new inventions in mechanical things, and keep them until they are again superseded by better; we are eager for improvement in politics, in education, even in morals, though in this last our idea of improvement chiefly consists in persuading or forcing other people to be as good as ourselves. It is not progress that we object to; on the contrary, we flatter ourselves that we are the most progressive people who ever lived. It is individuality that we war against: we should think we had done wonders if we had made ourselves all alike; forgetting that the unlikeness of one person to another is generally the first thing which draws the attention of either to the imperfection of his own type, and the superiority of another, or the possibility, by combining the advantages of both, of producing something better than either. We have a warning example in China—a nation of much talent, and, in some respects, even wisdom, owing to the rare good fortune of having been provided at an early period with a particularly good set of customs, the work, in some measure, of men to whom even the most enlightened European must accord, under certain limitations, the title of sages and philosophers. They are remarkable, too, in the excellence of their apparatus for impressing, as far as possible, the best wisdom they possess upon every mind in the community, and securing that those who have appropriated most of it shall occupy the posts of honour and power. Surely the people who did this have discovered the secret of human progressiveness, and must have kept themselves steadily at the head of the movement of the world. On the contrary, they have become stationary—have remained so for thousands of years; and if they are ever to be farther improved, it must be by foreigners. They have succeeded beyond all hope in what English philanthropists are so industriously working at—in making a people all alike, all governing their thoughts and conduct by the same maxims and rules; and these are the fruits. The modern *régime* of public opinion is, in an unorganized form, what the Chinese educational and political systems are in an organized; and unless individuality shall be able successfully to assert itself against this yoke, Europe, notwithstanding its noble antecedents and its professed Christianity, will tend to become another China.

What is it that has hitherto preserved Europe from this lot? What has made the European family of nations an improving, instead of a stationary portion of mankind? Not any superior excellence in them, which, when it exists, exists as the effect, not as the cause; but their remarkable diversity of character and culture. Individuals, classes, nations, have been extremely unlike one another: they have struck out a great variety of paths, each leading to something valuable; and although at every period those who travelled in different paths have been intolerant of one another, and each would have thought it an excellent thing if all the rest could have been compelled to travel his road, their attempts to thwart each other's development have rarely had any permanent success, and each has in time endured to receive the good which the others have offered. Europe is, in my judgment, wholly indebted to this plurality of paths for its progressive and many-sided development. But it already begins to possess this benefit in a considerably less degree. It is decidedly advancing towards the Chinese ideal of making all people alike. M. de Tocqueville, in his last important work, remarks how much more the Frenchmen of the present day resemble one another, than did those even of the last generation. The same remark might be made of Englishmen in a far greater degree. In a passage already quoted from Wilhelm von Humboldt, he points out two things as necessary conditions of human development, because necessary to render people unlike one another; namely, freedom, and variety of situations. The second of these two conditions is in this country every day diminishing. The circumstances which surround different classes and individuals, and shape their characters, are daily becoming more assimilated. Formerly, different ranks, different neighbourhoods, different trades and professions, lived in what might be called different worlds; at present, to a great degree in the same. Comparatively speaking, they now read the same things, listen to the same things, see the same things, go to the same places, have their hopes and fears directed to the same objects, have the same rights and liberties, and the same means of asserting them. Great as are the differences of position which remain, they are nothing to those which have ceased. And the assimilation is still proceeding. All the political changes of the age promote it, since they all tend to raise the low and to lower the high. Every extension of education promotes it, because education brings people under common influences, and gives them access to the general stock of facts and sentiments. Improvements in the means of communication promote it, by bringing the inhabitants of distant places into personal contact, and keeping up a rapid flow of changes of residence between one place and another. The increase of commerce and manufactures promotes it, by diffusing more widely the advantages of easy circumstances, and opening all objects of ambition, even the highest, to general competition, whereby the desire of rising becomes no longer the character of a particular class, but of all classes. A more powerful agency than even all these, in bringing about a general similarity among mankind, is the complete establishment, in this and other free countries, of the ascendancy of public opinion in the State. As the various social eminences which enabled persons entrenched on them to disregard the opinion of the multitude, gradually become levelled; as the very idea of resisting the will of the public, when it is positively known that they have a will, disappears more and more from the minds of practical politicians; there ceases to be any social support for nonconformity—any substantive power in society, which, itself opposed to the ascendancy of numbers, is interested in taking under its protection opinions and tendencies at variance with those of the public.

The combination of all these causes forms so great a mass of influences hostile to Individuality, that it is not easy to see how it can stand its ground. It will do so with increasing difficulty, unless the intelligent part of the public can be made to feel its value—to see that it is good there should be differences, even though not for the better, even though, as it may appear to them, some should be for the worse. If the claims of Individuality are ever to be asserted, the time is now, while much is still wanting to complete the enforced assimilation. It is only in the earlier stages that any stand can be successfully made against the encroachment. The demand that all other people shall resemble ourselves, grows by what it feeds on. If resistance waits till life is reduced *nearly* to one uniform type, all deviations from that type will come to be considered impious, immoral, even monstrous and contrary to nature. Mankind speedily become unable to conceive diversity, when they have been for some time unaccustomed to see it.

CHAPTER IV
Of the Limits to the Authority of Society over the Individual

What, then, is the rightful limit to the sovereignty of the individual over himself? Where does the authority of society begin? How much of human life should be assigned to individuality, and how much to society?

Each will receive its proper share, if each has that which more particularly concerns it. To individuality should belong the part of life in which it is chiefly the individual that is interested; to society, the part which chiefly interests society.

Though society is not founded on a contract, and though no good purpose is answered by inventing a contract in order to deduce social obligations from it, every one who receives the protection of society owes a return for the benefit, and the fact of living in society renders it indispensable that each should be bound to observe a certain line of conduct towards the rest. This conduct consists first, in not injuring the interests of one another; or rather certain interests, which, either by express legal provision or by tacit understanding, ought to be considered as rights; and secondly, in each person's bearing his share (to be fixed on some equitable principle) of the labours and sacrifices incurred for defending the society or its members from injury and molestation. These conditions society is justified in enforcing at all costs to those who endeavour to withhold fulfilment. Nor is this all that society may do. The acts of an individual may be hurtful to others, or wanting in due consideration for their welfare, without going the length of violating any of their constituted rights. The offender may then be justly punished by opinion, though not by law. As soon as any part of a person's conduct affects prejudicially the interests of others, society has jurisdiction over it, and the question whether the general welfare will or will not be promoted by interfering with it, becomes open to discussion. But there is no room for entertaining any such question when a person's conduct affects the interests of no persons besides himself, or needs not affect them unless they like (all the persons concerned being of full age, and the ordinary amount of understanding). In all such cases there should be perfect freedom, legal and social, to do the action and stand the consequences.

It would be a great misunderstanding of this doctrine to suppose that it is one of selfish indifference, which pretends that human beings have no business with each other's conduct in life, and that they should not concern themselves about the well-doing or well-being of one another, unless their own interest is involved. Instead of any diminution, there is need of a great increase of disinterested exertion to promote the good of others. But disinterested benevolence can find other instruments to persuade people to their good, than whips and scourges, either of the literal or the metaphorical sort. I am the last person to undervalue the self-regarding virtues; they are only second in importance, if even second, to the social. It is equally the business of education to cultivate both. But even education works by conviction and persuasion as well as by compulsion, and it is by the former only that, when the period of education is past, the self-regarding virtues should be inculcated. Human beings owe to each other help to distinguish the better from the worse, and encouragement to choose the former and avoid the latter. They should be for ever stimulating each other to increased exercise of their higher faculties, and increased direction of their feelings and aims towards wise instead of foolish, elevating instead of degrading, objects and contemplations. But neither one person, nor any number of persons, is warranted in saying to another human creature of ripe years, that he shall not do with his life for his own benefit what he chooses to do with it. He is the person most interested in his own well-being: the interest which any other person, except in cases of strong personal attachment, can have in it, is trifling, compared with that which he himself has; the interest which society has in him individually (except as to his conduct to others) is fractional, and altogether indirect: while, with respect to his own feelings and circumstances, the most ordinary man or woman has means of knowledge immeasurably surpassing those that can be possessed by any one else. The interference of society to overrule his judgment and purposes in what only regards himself, must be grounded on general presumptions; which may be altogether wrong, and even if right, are as likely as not to be misapplied to individual cases, by persons no better acquainted with the circumstances of such cases than those are who look at them merely from without. In this department, therefore, of human affairs, Individuality has its proper field of action. In the conduct of human beings towards one another, it is necessary that general rules should for the most part be observed, in order that people may know what they have to expect; but in each person's own concerns, his individual spontaneity is entitled to free exercise. Considerations to aid his judgment, exhortations to strengthen his will, may be offered to him, even obtruded on him, by others; but he himself is the final judge. All errors which he is likely to commit against advice and warning, are far outweighed by the evil of allowing others to constrain him to what they deem his good.

I do not mean that the feelings with which a person is regarded by others, ought not to be in any way affected by his self-regarding qualities or deficiencies. This is neither possible nor desirable. If he is eminent in any of the qualities which conduce to his own good, he is, so far, a proper object of admiration. He is so much the nearer to the ideal perfection of human nature. If he is grossly deficient in those qualities, a sentiment the opposite of admiration will follow. There is a degree of folly, and a degree of what may be called (though the phrase is not unobjectionable) lowness or depravation of taste, which, though it cannot justify doing harm to the person who manifests it, renders him necessarily and properly a subject of distaste, or, in extreme cases, even of contempt: a person could not have the opposite qualities in due strength without entertaining these feelings. Though doing no wrong to any one, a person may so act as to compel us to judge him, and feel to him, as a fool, or as a being of an inferior order: and since this judgment and feeling are a fact which he would prefer to avoid, it is doing him a service to warn him of it beforehand, as of any other disagreeable consequence to which he exposes himself. It would be well, indeed, if this good office were much more freely rendered than the common notions of politeness at present permit, and if one person could honestly point out to another that he thinks him in fault, without being considered unmannerly or presuming. We have a right, also, in various ways, to act upon our unfavourable opinion of any one, not to the oppression of his individuality, but in the exercise of ours. We are not bound, for example, to seek his society; we have a right to avoid it (though not to parade the avoidance), for we have a right to choose the society most acceptable to us. We have a right, and it may be our duty, to caution others against him, if we think his example or conversation likely to have a pernicious effect on those with whom he associates. We may give others a preference over him in optional good offices, except those which tend to his improvement. In these various modes a person may suffer very severe penalties at the hands of others, for faults which directly concern only himself; but he suffers these penalties only in so far as they are the natural, and, as it were, the spontaneous consequences of the faults themselves, not because they are purposely inflicted on him for the sake of punishment. A person who shows rashness, obstinacy, self-conceit—who cannot live within moderate means—who cannot restrain himself from hurtful indulgences—who pursues animal pleasures at the expense of those of feeling and intellect—must expect to be lowered in the opinion of others, and to have a less share of their favourable sentiments; but of this he has no right to complain, unless he has merited their favour by special excellence in his social relations, and has thus established a title to their good offices, which is not affected by his demerits towards himself.

What I contend for is, that the inconveniences which are strictly inseparable from the unfavourable judgment of others, are the only ones to which a person should ever be subjected for that portion of his conduct and character which concerns his own good, but which does not affect the interests of others in their relations with him. Acts injurious to others require a totally different treatment. Encroachment on their rights; infliction on them of any loss or damage not justified by his own rights; falsehood or duplicity in dealing with them; unfair or ungenerous use of advantages over them; even selfish abstinence from defending them against injury—these are fit objects of moral reprobation, and, in grave cases, of moral retribution and punishment. And not only these acts, but the dispositions which lead to them, are properly immoral, and fit subjects of disapprobation which may rise to abhorrence. Cruelty of disposition; malice and ill-nature; that most anti-social and odious of all passions, envy; dissimulation and insincerity; irascibility on insufficient cause, and resentment disproportioned to the provocation; the love of domineering over others; the desire to engross more than one's share of advantages (the *pleonexia* of the Greeks); the pride which derives gratification from the abasement of others; the egotism which thinks self and its concerns more important than everything else, and decides all doubtful questions in its own favour;—these are moral vices, and constitute a bad and odious moral character: unlike the self-regarding faults previously mentioned, which are not properly immoralities, and to whatever pitch they may be carried, do not constitute wickedness. They may be proofs of any amount of folly, or want of personal dignity and self-respect; but they are only a subject of moral reprobation when they involve a breach of duty to others, for whose sake the individual is bound to have care for himself. What are called duties to ourselves are not socially obligatory, unless circumstances render them at the same time duties to others. The term duty to oneself, when it means anything more than prudence, means self-respect or self-development; and for none of these is any one accountable to his fellow creatures, because for none of them is it for the good of mankind that he be held accountable to them.

The distinction between the loss of consideration which a person may rightly incur by defect of prudence or of personal dignity, and the reprobation which is due to him for an offence against the rights of others, is not a merely nominal distinction. It makes a vast difference both in our feelings and in our conduct towards him, whether he displeases us in things in which we think we have a right to control him, or in things in which we know that we have not. If he displeases us, we may express our distaste, and we may stand aloof from a person as well as from a thing that displeases us; but we shall not therefore feel called on to make his life uncomfortable. We shall reflect that he already bears, or will bear, the whole penalty of his error; if he spoils his life by mismanagement, we shall not, for that reason, desire to spoil it still further: instead of wishing to punish him, we shall rather endeavour to alleviate his punishment, by showing him how he may avoid or cure the evils his conduct tends to bring upon him. He may be to us an object of pity, perhaps of dislike, but not of anger or resentment; we shall not treat him like an enemy of society: the worst we shall think ourselves justified in doing is leaving him to himself, if we do not interfere benevolently by showing interest or concern for him. It is far otherwise if he has infringed the rules necessary for the protection of his fellow-creatures, individually or collectively. The evil consequences of his acts do not then fall on himself, but on others; and society, as the protector of all its members, must retaliate on him; must inflict pain on him for the express purpose of punishment, and must take care that it be sufficiently severe. In the one case, he is an offender at our bar, and we are called on not only to sit in judgment on him, but, in one shape or another, to execute our own sentence: in the other case, it is not our part to inflict any suffering on him, except what may incidentally follow from our using the same liberty in the regulation of our own affairs, which we allow to him in his.

The distinction here pointed out between the part of a person's life which concerns only himself, and that which concerns others, many persons will refuse to admit. How (it may be asked) can any part of the conduct of a member of society be a matter of indifference to the other members? No person is an entirely isolated being; it is impossible for a person to do anything seriously or permanently hurtful to himself, without mischief reaching at least to his near connexions, and often far beyond them. If he injures his property, he does harm to those who directly or indirectly derived support from it, and usually diminishes, by a greater or less amount, the general resources of the community. If he deteriorates his bodily or mental faculties, he not only brings evil upon all who depended on him for any portion of their happiness, but disqualifies himself for rendering the services which he owes to his fellow creatures generally; perhaps becomes a burthen on their affection or benevolence; and if such conduct were very frequent, hardly any offence that is committed would detract more from the general sum of good. Finally, if by his vices or follies a person does no direct harm to others, he is nevertheless (it may be said) injurious by his example; and ought to be compelled to control himself, for the sake of those whom the sight or knowledge of his conduct might corrupt or mislead.

And even (it will be added) if the consequences of misconduct could be confined to the vicious or thoughtless individual, ought society to abandon to their own guidance those who are manifestly unfit for it? If protection against themselves is confessedly due to children and persons under age, is not society equally bound to afford it to persons of mature years who are equally incapable of self-government? If gambling, or drunkenness, or incontinence, or idleness, or uncleanliness, are as injurious to happiness, and as great a hindrance to improvement, as many or most of the acts prohibited by law, why (it may be asked) should not law, so far as is consistent with practicability and social convenience, endeavour to repress these also? And as a supplement to the unavoidable imperfections of law, ought not opinion at least to organize a powerful police against these vices, and visit rigidly with social penalties those who are known to practise them? There is no question here (it may be said) about restricting individuality, or impeding the trial of new and original experiments in living. The only things it is sought to prevent are things which have been tried and condemned from the beginning of the world until now; things which experience has shown not to be useful or suitable to any person's individuality. There must be some length of time and amount of experience, after which a moral or prudential truth may be regarded as established: and it is merely desired to prevent generation after generation from falling over the same precipice which has been fatal to their predecessors.

I fully admit that the mischief which a person does to himself may seriously affect, both through their sympathies and their interests, those nearly connected with him, and in a minor degree, society at large. When, by conduct of this sort, a person is led to violate a distinct and assignable obligation to any other person or persons, the case is taken out of the self-regarding class, and becomes amenable to moral disapprobation in the proper sense of the term. If, for example, a man, through intemperance or extravagance, becomes unable to pay his debts, or, having under-taken the moral responsibility of a family, becomes from the same cause incapable of supporting or educating them, he is deservedly reprobated, and might be justly punished; but it is for the breach of duty to his family or creditors, not for the extravagance. If the resources which ought to have been devoted to them, had been diverted from them for the most prudent investment, the moral culpability would have been the same. George Barnwell murdered his uncle to get money for his mistress, but if he had done it to set himself up in business, he would equally have been hanged. Again, in the frequent case of a man who causes grief to his family by addiction to bad habits, he deserves reproach for his unkindness or ingratitude; but so he may for cultivating habits not in themselves vicious, if they are painful to those with whom he passes his life, or who from personal ties are dependent on him for their comfort. Whoever fails in the consideration generally due to the interests and feelings of others, not being compelled by some more imperative duty, or justified by allowable self-preference, is a subject of moral disapprobation for that failure, but not for the cause of it, nor for the errors, merely personal to himself, which may have remotely led to it. In like manner, when a person disables himself, by conduct purely self-regarding, from the performance of some definite duty incumbent on him to the public, he is guilty of a social offence. No person ought to be punished simply for being drunk; but a soldier or a policeman should be punished for being drunk on duty. Whenever, in short, there is a definite damage, or a definite risk of damage, either to an individual or to the public, the case is taken out of the province of liberty, and placed in that of morality or law.

But with regard to the merely contingent, or, as it may be called, constructive injury which a person causes to society, by conduct which neither violates any specific duty to the public, nor occasions perceptible hurt to any assignable individual except himself; the inconvenience is one which society can afford to bear, for the sake of the greater good of human freedom. If grown persons are to be punished for not taking proper care of themselves, I would rather it were for their own sake, than under pretence of preventing them from impairing their capacity of rendering to society benefits which society does not pretend it has a right to exact. But I cannot consent to argue the point as if society had no means of bringing its weaker members up to its ordinary standard of rational conduct, except waiting till they do something irrational, and then punishing them, legally or morally, for it. Society has had absolute power over them during all the early portion of their existence: it has had the whole period of childhood and nonage in which to try whether it could make them capable of rational conduct in life. The existing generation is master both of the training and the entire circumstances of the generation to come; it cannot indeed make them perfectly wise and good, because it is itself so lamentably deficient in goodness and wisdom; and its best efforts are not always, in individual cases, its most successful ones; but it is perfectly well able to make the rising generation, as a whole, as good as, and a little better than, itself. If society lets any considerable number of its members grow up mere children, incapable of being acted on by rational consideration of distant motives, society has itself to blame for the consequences. Armed not only with all the powers of education, but with the ascendancy which the authority of a received opinion always exercises over the minds who are least fitted to judge for themselves; and aided by the natural penalties which cannot be prevented from falling on those who incur the distaste or the contempt of those who know them; let not society pretend that it needs, besides all this, the power to issue commands and enforce obedience in the personal concerns of individuals, in which, on all principles of justice and policy, the decision ought to rest with those who are to abide the consequences. Nor is there anything which tends more to discredit and frustrate the better means of influencing conduct, than a resort to the worse. If there be among those whom it is attempted to coerce into prudence or temperance, any of the material of which vigorous and independent characters are made, they will infallibly rebel against the yoke. No such person will ever feel that others have a right to control him in his concerns, such as they have to prevent him from injuring them in theirs; and it easily comes to be considered a mark of spirit and courage to fly in the face of such usurped authority, and do with ostentation the exact opposite of what it enjoins; as in the fashion of grossness which succeeded, in the time of Charles II., to the fanatical moral intolerance of the Puritans. With respect to what is said of the necessity of protecting society from the bad example set to others by the vicious or the self-indulgent; it is true that bad example may have a pernicious effect, especially the example of doing wrong to others with impunity to the wrong-doer. But we are now speaking of conduct which, while it does no wrong to others, is supposed to do great harm to the agent himself: and I do not see how those who believe this, can think otherwise than that the example, on the whole, must be more salutary than hurtful, since, if it displays the misconduct, it displays also the painful or degrading consequences which, if the conduct is justly censured, must be supposed to be in all or most cases attendant on it.

But the strongest of all the arguments against the interference of the public with purely personal conduct, is that when it does interfere, the odds are that it interferes wrongly, and in the wrong place. On questions of social morality, of duty to others, the opinion of the public, that is, of an overruling majority, though often wrong, is likely to be still oftener right; because on such questions they are only required to judge of their own interests; of the manner in which some mode of conduct, if allowed to be practised, would affect themselves. But the opinion of a similar majority, imposed as a law on the minority, on questions of self-regarding conduct, is quite as likely to be wrong as right; for in these cases public opinion means, at the best, some people's opinion of what is good or bad for other people; while very often it does not even mean that; the public, with the most perfect indifference, passing over the pleasure or convenience of those whose conduct they censure, and considering only their own preference. There are many who consider as an injury to themselves any conduct which they have a distaste for, and resent it as an outrage to their feelings; as a religious bigot, when charged with disregarding the religious feelings of others, has been known to retort that they disregard his feelings, by persisting in their abominable worship or creed. But there is no parity between the feeling of a person for his own opinion, and the feeling of another who is offended at his holding it; no more than between the desire of a thief to take a purse, and the desire of the right owner to keep it. And a person's taste is as much his own peculiar concern as his opinion or his purse. It is easy for any one to imagine an ideal public, which leaves the freedom and choice of individuals in all uncertain matters undisturbed, and only requires them to abstain from modes of conduct which universal experience has condemned. But where has there been seen a public which set any such limit to its censorship? or when does the public trouble itself about universal experience? In its interferences with personal conduct it is seldom thinking of anything but the enormity of acting or feeling differently from itself; and this standard of judgment, thinly disguised, is held up to mankind as the dictate of religion and philosophy, by nine-tenths of all moralists and speculative writers. These teach that things are right because they are right; because we feel them to be so. They tell us to search in our own minds and hearts for laws of conduct binding on ourselves and on all others. What can the poor public do but apply these instructions, and make their own personal feelings of good and evil, if they are tolerably unanimous in them, obligatory on all the world?

The evil here pointed out is not one which exists only in theory; and it may perhaps be expected that I should specify the instances in which the public of this age and country improperly invests its own preferences with the character of moral laws. I am not writing an essay on the aberrations of existing moral feeling. That is too weighty a subject to be discussed parenthetically, and by way of illustration. Yet examples are necessary, to show that the principle I maintain is of serious and practical moment, and that I am not endeavouring to erect a barrier against imaginary evils. And it is not difficult to show, by abundant instances, that to extend the bounds of what may be called moral police, until it encroaches on the most unquestionably legitimate liberty of the individual, is one of the most universal of all human propensities.

As a first instance, consider the antipathies which men cherish on no better grounds than that persons whose religious opinions are different from theirs, do not practise their religious observances, especially their religious abstinences. To cite a rather trivial example, nothing in the creed or practice of Christians does more to envenom the hatred of Mahomedans against them, than the fact of their eating pork. There are few acts which Christians and Europeans regard with more unaffected disgust, than Mussulmans regard this particular mode of satisfying hunger. It is, in the first place, an offence against their religion; but this circumstance by no means explains either the degree or the kind of their repugnance; for wine also is forbidden by their religion, and to partake of it is by all Mussulmans accounted wrong, but not disgusting. Their aversion to the flesh of the 'unclean beast' is, on the contrary, of that peculiar character, resembling an instinctive antipathy, which the idea of uncleanness, when once it thoroughly sinks into the feelings, seems always to excite even in those whose personal habits are anything but scrupulously cleanly, and of which the sentiment of religious impurity, so intense in the Hindoos, is a remarkable example. Suppose now that in a people, of whom the majority were Mussulmans, that majority should insist upon not permitting pork to be eaten within the limits of the country. This would be nothing new in Mahomedan countries.[9] Would it be a legitimate exercise of the moral authority of public opinion? and if not, why not? The practice is really revolting to such a public. They also sincerely think that it is forbidden and abhorred by the Deity. Neither could the prohibition be censured as religious persecution. It might be religious in its origin, but it would not be persecution for religion, since nobody's religion makes it a duty to eat pork. The only tenable ground of condemnation would be, that with the personal tastes and self-regarding concerns of individuals the public has no business to interfere.

To come somewhat nearer home: the majority of Spaniards consider it a gross impiety, offensive in the highest degree to the Supreme Being, to worship him in

9. The case of the Bombay Parsees is a curious instance in point. When this industrious and enterprising tribe, the descendants of the Persian fire-worshippers, flying from their native country before the Caliphs, arrived in Western India, they were admitted to toleration by the Hindoo sovereigns, on condition of not eating beef. When those regions afterwards fell under the dominion of Mahomedan conquerors, the Parsees obtained from them a continuance of indulgence, on condition of refraining from pork. What was at first obedience to authority became a second nature, and the Parsees to this day abstain both from beef and pork. Though not required by their religion, the double abstinence has had time to grow into a custom of their tribe; and custom, in the East, is a religion.

any other manner than the Roman Catholic; and no other public worship is lawful on Spanish soil. The people of all Southern Europe look upon a married clergy as not only irreligious, but unchaste, indecent, gross, disgusting. What do Protestants think of these perfectly sincere feelings, and of the attempt to enforce them against non-Catholics? Yet, if mankind are justified in interfering with each other's liberty in things which do not concern the interests of others, on what principle is it possible consistently to exclude these cases? or who can blame people for desiring to suppress what they regard as a scandal in the sight of God and man? No stronger case can be shown for prohibiting anything which is regarded as a personal immorality, than is made out for suppressing these practices in the eyes of those who regard them as impieties; and unless we are willing to adopt the logic of persecutors, and to say that we may persecute others because we are right, and that they must not persecute us because they are wrong, we must beware of admitting a principle of which we should resent as a gross injustice the application to ourselves.

The preceding instances may be objected to, although unreasonably, as drawn from contingencies impossible among us: opinion, in this country, not being likely to enforce abstinence from meats, or to interfere with people for worshipping, and for either marrying or not marrying, according to their creed or inclination. The next example, however, shall be taken from an interference with liberty which we have by no means passed all danger of. Wherever the Puritans have been sufficiently powerful, as in New England, and in Great Britain at the time of the Commonwealth, they have endeavoured, with considerable success, to put down all public, and nearly all private, amusements: especially music, dancing, public games, or other assemblages for purposes of diversion, and the theatre. There are still in this country large bodies of persons by whose notions of morality and religion these recreations are condemned; and those persons belonging chiefly to the middle class, who are the ascendant power in the present social and political condition of the kingdom, it is by no means impossible that persons of these sentiments may at some time or other command a majority in Parliament. How will the remaining portion of the community like to have the amusements that shall be permitted to them regulated by the religious and moral sentiments of the stricter Calvinists and Methodists? Would they not, with considerable peremptoriness, desire these intrusively pious members of society to mind their own business? This is precisely what should be said to every government and every public, who have the pretension that no person shall enjoy any pleasure which they think wrong. But if the principle of the pretension be admitted, no one can reasonably object to its being acted on in the sense of the majority, or other preponderating power in the country; and all persons must be ready to conform to the idea of a Christian commonwealth, as understood by the early settlers in New England, if a religious profession similar to theirs should ever succeed in regaining its lost ground, as religions supposed to be declining have so often been known to do.

To imagine another contingency, perhaps more likely to be realized than the one last mentioned. There is confessedly a strong tendency in the modern world towards a democratic constitution of society, accompanied or not by popular political institutions. It is affirmed that in the country where this tendency is most completely realized—where both society and the government are most democratic—the United States—the feeling of the majority, to whom any appearance of a more showy or costly style of living than they can hope to rival is disagreeable, operates as a tolerably effectual sumptuary law, and that in many parts of the Union it is really difficult for a person possessing a very large income, to find any mode of spending it, which will not incur popular disapprobation. Though such statements as these are doubtless much exaggerated as a representation of existing facts, the state of things they describe is not only a conceivable and possible, but a probable result of democratic feeling, combined with the notion that the public has a right to a veto on the manner in which individuals shall spend their incomes. We have only further to suppose a considerable diffusion of Socialist opinions, and it may become infamous in the eyes of the majority to possess more property than some very small amount, or any income not earned by manual labour. Opinions similar in principle to these, already prevail widely among the artizan class, and weigh oppressively on those who are amenable to the opinion chiefly of that class, namely, its own members. It is known that the bad workmen who form the majority of the operatives in many branches of industry, are decidedly of opinion that bad workmen ought to receive the same wages as good, and that no one ought to be allowed, through piecework or otherwise, to earn by superior skill or industry more than others can without it. And they employ a moral police, which occasionally becomes a physical one, to deter skilful workmen from receiving, and employers from giving, a larger remuneration for a more useful service. If the public have any jurisdiction over private concerns, I cannot see that these people are in fault, or that any individual's particular public can be blamed for asserting the same authority over his individual conduct, which the general public asserts over people in general.

But, without dwelling upon supposititious cases, there are, in our own day, gross usurpations upon the liberty of private life actually practised, and still greater ones threatened with some expectation of success, and opinions propounded which assert an unlimited right in the public not only to prohibit by law everything which it thinks wrong, but in order to get at what it thinks wrong, to prohibit any number of things which it admits to be innocent.

Under the name of preventing intemperance, the people of one English colony, and of nearly half the United States, have been interdicted by law from making any use whatever of fermented drinks, except for medical purposes: for prohibition of their sale is in fact, as it is intended to be, prohibition of their use. And though the impracticability of executing the law has caused its repeal in several of the States which had adopted it, including the one from which it derives its name, an attempt has notwithstanding been commenced, and is prosecuted with considerable zeal by many of the professed philanthropists, to agitate for a similar law in this country. The association, or 'Alliance' as it terms itself, which has been formed for this purpose, has acquired some notoriety through the publicity given to a correspondence between its Secretary and one of the very few English public men who hold that a politician's opinions ought to be founded on principles. Lord Stanley's share in this correspondence is calculated to strengthen the hopes already built on him, by those who know how rare such qualities as are manifested in some of his public appearances, unhappily are among those who figure in political life. The organ of the Alliance, who would 'deeply deplore the recognition of any principle which could be wrested to justify bigotry and persecution,' undertakes to point out the 'broad and impassable barrier' which divides such principles from those of the association. 'All matters relating to thought, opinion, conscience, appear to me,' he says, 'to be without the sphere of legislation; all pertaining to social act, habit, relation, subject only to a discretionary power vested in the State itself, and not in the individual, to be within it.' No mention is made of a third class, different from either of these, viz. acts and habits which are not social, but individual; although it is to this class, surely, that the act of drinking fermented liquors belongs. Selling fermented liquors, however, is trading, and trading is a social act. But the infringement complained of is not on the liberty of the seller, but on that of the buyer and consumer; since the State might just as well forbid him to drink wine, as purposely make it impossible for him to obtain it. The Secretary, however, says, 'I claim, as a citizen, a right to legislate whenever my social rights are invaded by the social act of another.' And now for the definition of these 'social rights.' 'If anything invades my social rights, certainly the traffic in strong drink does. It destroys my primary right of security, by constantly creating and stimulating social disorder. It invades my right of equality, by deriving a profit from the creation of a misery I am taxed to support. It impedes my right to free moral and intellectual development, by surrounding my path with dangers, and by weakening and demoralizing society, from which I have a right to claim mutual aid and intercourse.' A theory of 'social rights,' the like of which probably never before found its way into distinct language: being nothing short of this—that it is the absolute social right of every individual, that every other individual shall act in every respect exactly as he ought; that whosoever fails thereof in the smallest particular, violates my social right, and entitles me to demand from the legislature the removal of the grievance. So monstrous a principle is far more dangerous than any single interference with liberty; there is no violation of liberty which it would not justify; it acknowledges no right to any freedom whatever, except perhaps to that of holding opinions in secret, without ever disclosing them: for, the moment an opinion which I consider noxious passes any one's lips, it invades all the 'social rights' attributed to me by the Alliance. The doctrine ascribes to all mankind a vested interest in each other's moral, intellectual, and even physical perfection, to be defined by each claimant according to his own standard.

Another important example of illegitimate interference with the rightful liberty of the individual, not simply threatened, but long since carried into triumphant effect, is Sabbatarian legislation. Without doubt, abstinence on one day in the week, so far as the exigencies of life permit, from the usual daily occupation, though in no respect religiously binding on any except Jews, is a highly beneficial custom. And inasmuch as this custom cannot be observed without a general consent to that effect among the industrious classes, therefore, in so far as some persons by working may impose the same necessity on others, it may be allowable and right that the law should guarantee to each the observance by others of the custom, by suspending the greater operations of industry on a particular day. But this justification, grounded on the direct interest which others have in each individual's observance of the practice, does not apply to the self-chosen occupations in which a person may think fit to employ his leisure; nor does it hold good, in the smallest degree, for legal restrictions on amusements. It is true that the amusement of some is the day's work of others; but the pleasure, not to say the useful recreation, of many, is worth the labour of a few, provided the occupation is freely chosen, and can be freely resigned. The operatives are perfectly right in thinking that if all worked on Sunday, seven days' work would have to be given for six days' wages: but so long as the great mass of employments are suspended, the small number who for the enjoyment of others must still work, obtain a proportional increase of earnings; and they are not obliged to follow those occupations, if they prefer leisure to emolument. If a further remedy is sought, it might be found in the establishment by custom of a holiday on some other day of the week for those particular classes of persons. The only ground, therefore, on which restrictions on Sunday amusements can be defended, must be that they are religiously wrong; a motive of legislation which never can be too earnestly protested against. '*Deorum injuriae Diis curae.*' It remains to be proved that society or any of its officers holds a commission from on high to avenge any supposed offence to Omnipotence, which is not also a wrong to our fellow creatures. The notion that it is one man's duty that another should be religious, was the foundation of all the religious persecutions ever perpetrated, and if admitted, would fully justify them. Though the feeling which breaks out in the repeated attempts to stop railway travelling on Sunday, in the resistance to the opening of Museums, and the like, has not the cruelty of the old persecutors, the state of mind indicated by it is fundamentally the same. It is a determination not to tolerate others in doing what is permitted by their religion, because it is not permitted by the persecutor's religion. It is a belief that God not only abominates the act of the misbeliever, but will not hold us guiltless if we leave him unmolested.

I cannot refrain from adding to these examples of the little account commonly made of human liberty, the language of downright persecution which breaks out from the press of this country, whenever it feels called on to notice the remarkable phenomenon of Mormonism. Much might be said on the unexpected and instructive fact, that an alleged new revelation, and a religion founded on it, the product of palpable imposture, not even supported by the *prestige* of extraordinary qualities in its founder, is believed by hundreds of thousands, and has been made the foundation of a society, in the age of newspapers, railways, and the electric telegraph. What here concerns us is, that this religion, like other and better religions, has its martyrs; that its prophet and founder was, for his teaching, put to death by a mob; that others of its adherents lost their lives by the same lawless violence; that they were forcibly expelled, in a body, from the country in which they first grew up; while, now that they have been chased into a solitary recess in the midst of a desert, many in this country openly declare that it would be right (only that it is not convenient) to send an expedition against them, and compel them by force to conform to the opinions of other people. The article of the Mormonite doctrine which is the chief provocative to the antipathy which thus breaks through the ordinary restraints of religious tolerance, is its sanction of polygamy; which, though permitted to Mahomedans, and Hindoos, and Chinese, seems to excite unquenchable animosity when practised by persons who speak English, and profess to be a kind of Christians. No one has a deeper disapprobation than I have of this Mormon institution; both for other reasons, and because, far from being in any way countenanced by the principle of liberty, it is a direct infraction of that principle, being a mere rivetting of the chains of one half of the community, and an emancipation of the other from reciprocity of obligation towards them. Still, it must be remembered that this relation is as much voluntary on the part of the women concerned in it, and who may be deemed the sufferers by it, as is the case with any other form of the marriage institution; and however surprising this fact may appear, it has its explanation in the common ideas and customs of the world, which teaching women to think marriage the one thing needful, make it intelligible that many a woman should prefer being one of several wives, to not being a wife at all. Other countries are not asked to recognise such unions, or release any portion of their inhabitants from their own laws on the score of Mormonite opinions. But when the dissentients have conceded to the hostile sentiments of others, far more than could justly be demanded; when they have left the countries to which their doctrines were unacceptable, and established themselves in a remote corner of the earth, which they have been the first to render habitable to human beings; it is difficult to see on what principles but those of tyranny they can be prevented from living there under what laws they please, provided they commit no aggression on other nations, and allow perfect freedom of departure to those who are dissatisfied with their ways. A recent writer, in some respects of considerable merit, proposes (to use his own words) not a crusade, but a *civilizade*, against this polygamous community, to put an end to what seems to him a retrograde step in civilization. It also appears so to me, but I am not aware that any community has a right to force another to be civilized. So long as the sufferers by the bad law do not invoke assistance from other communities, I cannot admit that persons entirely unconnected with them ought to step in and require that a condition of things with which all who are directly interested appear to be satisfied, should be put an end to because it is a scandal to persons some thousands of miles distant, who have no part or concern in it. Let them send missionaries, if they please, to preach against it; and let them, by any fair means (of which silencing the teachers is not one,) oppose the progress of similar doctrines among their own people. If civilization has got the better of barbarism when barbarism had the world to itself, it is too much to profess to be afraid lest barbarism, after having been fairly got under, should revive and conquer civilization. A civilization that can thus succumb to its vanquished enemy, must first have become so degenerate, that neither its appointed priests and teachers, nor anybody else, has the capacity, or will take the trouble, to stand up for it. If this be so, the sooner such a civilization receives notice to quit, the better. It can only go on from bad to worse, until destroyed and regenerated (like the Western Empire) by energetic barbarians.

CHAPTER V
Applications

The principles asserted in these pages must be more generally admitted as the basis for discussion of details, before a consistent application of them to all the various departments of government and morals can be attempted with any prospect of advantage. The few observations I propose to make on questions of detail, are designed to illustrate the principles, rather than to follow them out to their consequences. I offer, not so much applications, as specimens of application; which may serve to bring into greater clearness the meaning and limits of the two maxims which together form the entire doctrine of this Essay, and to assist the judgment in holding the balance between them, in the cases where it appears doubtful which of them is applicable to the case.

The maxims are, first, that the individual is not accountable to society for his actions, in so far as these concern the interests of no person but himself. Advice, instruction, persuasion, and avoidance by other people if thought necessary by them for their own good, are the only measures by which society can justifiably express its dislike or disapprobation of his conduct. Secondly, that for such actions as are prejudicial to the interests of others, the individual is accountable, and may be subjected either to social or to legal punishment, if society is of opinion that the one or the other is requisite for its protection.

In the first place, it must by no means be supposed, because damage, or probability of damage, to the interests of others, can alone justify the interference of society, that therefore it always does justify such interference. In many cases, an individual, in pursuing a legitimate object, necessarily and therefore legitimately causes pain or loss to others, or intercepts a good which they had a reasonable hope of obtaining. Such oppositions of interest between individuals often arise from bad social institutions, but are unavoidable while those institutions last; and some would be unavoidable under any institutions. Whoever succeeds in an overcrowded profession, or in a competitive examination; whoever is preferred to another in any contest for an object which both desire, reaps benefit from the loss of others, from their wasted exertion and their disappointment. But it is, by common admission, better for the general interest of mankind, that persons should pursue their objects undeterred by this sort of consequences. In other words, society admits no right, either legal or moral, in the disappointed competitors, to immunity from this kind of suffering; and feels called on to interfere, only when means of success have been employed which it is contrary to the general interest to permit—namely, fraud or treachery, and force.

Again, trade is a social act. Whoever undertakes to sell any description of goods to the public, does what affects the interest of other persons, and of society in general; and thus his conduct, in principle, comes within the jurisdiction of society: accordingly, it was once held to be the duty of governments, in all cases which were considered of importance, to fix prices, and regulate the processes of manufacture. But it is now recognised, though not till after a long struggle, that both the cheapness and the good quality of commodities are most effectually provided for by leaving the producers and sellers perfectly free, under the sole check of equal freedom to the buyers for supplying themselves elsewhere. This is the so-called doctrine of Free Trade, which rests on grounds different from, though equally solid with, the principle of individual liberty asserted in this Essay. Restrictions on trade, or on production for purposes of trade, are indeed restraints; and all restraint, qua restraint, is an evil: but the restraints in question affect only that part of conduct which society is competent to restrain, and are wrong solely because they do not really produce the results which it is desired to produce by them. As the principle of individual liberty is not involved in the doctrine of Free Trade, so neither is it in most of the questions which arise respecting the limits of that doctrine; as for example, what amount of public control is admissible for the prevention of fraud by adulteration; how far sanitary precautions, or arrangements to protect workpeople employed in dangerous occupations, should be enforced on employers. Such questions involve considerations of liberty, only in so far as leaving people to themselves is always better, caeteris paribus, than controlling them: but that they may be legitimately controlled for these ends, is in principle undeniable. On the other hand, there are questions relating to interference with trade, which are essentially questions of liberty; such as the Maine Law, already touched upon; the prohibition of the importation of opium into China; the restriction of the sale of poisons; all cases, in short, where the object of the interference is to make it impossible or difficult to obtain a particular commodity. These interferences are objectionable, not as infringements on the liberty of the producer or seller, but on that of the buyer.

One of these examples, that of the sale of poisons, opens a new question; the proper limits of what may be called the functions of police; how far liberty may legitimately be invaded for the prevention of crime, or of accident. It is one of the undisputed functions of government to take precautions against crime before it has been committed, as well as to detect and punish it afterwards. The preventive function of government, however, is far more liable to be abused, to the prejudice of liberty, than the punitory function; for there is hardly any part of the legitimate freedom of action of a human being which would not admit of being represented, and fairly too, as increasing the facilities for some form or other of delinquency. Nevertheless, if a public authority, or even a private person, sees any one evidently preparing to commit a crime, they are not bound to look on inactive until the crime is committed, but may interfere to prevent it. If poisons were never bought or used for any purpose except the commission of murder, it would be right to prohibit their manufacture and sale. They may, however, be wanted not only for innocent but for useful purposes, and restrictions cannot be imposed in the one case without operating in the other. Again, it is a proper office of public authority to guard against accidents. If either a public officer or any one else saw a person attempting to cross a bridge which had been ascertained to be unsafe, and there were no time to warn him of his danger, they might seize him and turn him back, without any real infringement of his liberty; for liberty consists in doing what one desires, and he does not desire to fall into the river. Nevertheless, when there is not a certainty, but only a danger of mischief, no one but the person himself can judge of the sufficiency of the motive which may prompt him to incur the risk: in this case, therefore, (unless he is a child, or delirious, or in some state of excitement or absorption incompatible with the full use of the reflecting faculty) he ought, I conceive, to be only warned of the danger; not forcibly prevented from exposing himself to it. Similar considerations, applied to such a question as the sale of poisons, may enable us to decide which among the possible modes of regulation are or are not contrary to principle. Such a precaution, for example, as that of labelling the drug with some word expressive of its dangerous character, may be enforced without violation of liberty: the buyer cannot wish not to know that the thing he possesses has poisonous qualities. But to require in all cases the certificate of a medical practitioner, would make it sometimes impossible, always expensive, to obtain the article for legitimate uses. The only mode apparent to me, in which difficulties may be thrown in the way of crime committed through this means, without any infringement, worth taking into account, upon the liberty of those who desire the poisonous substance for other purposes, consists in providing what, in the apt language of Bentham, is called 'preappointed evidence.' This provision is familiar to every one in the case of contracts. It is usual and right that the law, when a contract is entered into, should require as the condition of its enforcing performance, that certain formalities should be observed, such as signatures, attestation of witnesses, and the like, in order that in case of subsequent dispute, there may be evidence to prove that the contract was really entered into, and that there was nothing in the circumstances to render it legally invalid: the effect being, to throw great obstacles in the way of fictitious contracts, or contracts made in circumstances which, if known, would destroy their validity. Precautions of a similar nature might be enforced in the sale of articles adapted to be instruments of crime. The seller, for example, might be required to enter in a register the exact time of the transaction, the name and address of the buyer, the precise quality and quantity sold; to ask the purpose for which it was wanted, and record the answer he received. When there was no medical prescription, the presence of some third person might be required, to bring home the fact to the purchaser, in case there should afterwards be reason to believe that the article had been applied to criminal purposes. Such regulations would in general be no material impediment to obtaining the article, but a very considerable one to making an improper use of it without detection.

The right inherent in society, to ward off crimes against itself by antecedent precautions, suggests the obvious limitations to the maxim, that purely self-regarding misconduct cannot properly be meddled with in the way of prevention or punishment. Drunkenness, for example, in ordinary cases, is not a fit subject for legislative interference; but I should deem it perfectly legitimate that a person, who had once been convicted of any act of violence to others under the influence of drink, should be placed under a special legal restriction, personal to himself; that if he were afterwards found drunk, he should be liable to a penalty, and that if when in that state he committed another offence, the punishment to which he would be liable for that other offence should be increased in severity. The making himself drunk, in a person whom drunkenness excites to do harm to others, is a crime against others. So, again, idleness, except in a person receiving support from the public, or except when it constitutes a breach of contract, cannot without tyranny be made a subject of legal punishment; but if, either from idleness or from any other avoidable cause, a man fails to perform his legal duties to others, as for instance to support his children, it is no tyranny to force him to fulfil that obligation, by compulsory labour, if no other means are available.

Again, there are many acts which, being directly injurious only to the agents themselves, ought not to be legally interdicted, but which, if done publicly, are a violation of good manners, and coming thus within the category of offences against others, may rightfully be prohibited. Of this kind are offences against decency; on which it is unnecessary to dwell, the rather as they are only connected indirectly with our subject, the objection to publicity being equally strong in the case of many actions not in themselves condemnable, nor supposed to be so.

There is another question to which an answer must be found, consistent with the principles which have been laid down. In cases of personal conduct supposed to be blameable, but which respect for liberty precludes society from preventing or punishing, because the evil directly resulting falls wholly on the agent; what the agent is free to do, ought other persons to be equally free to counsel or instigate? This question is not free from difficulty. The case of a person who solicits another to do an act, is not strictly a case of self-regarding conduct. To give advice or offer inducements to any one, is a social act, and may, therefore, like actions in general which affect others, be supposed amenable to social control. But a little reflection corrects the first impression, by showing that if the case is not strictly within the definition of individual liberty, yet the reasons on which the principle of individual liberty is grounded, are applicable to it. If people must be allowed, in whatever concerns only themselves, to act as seems best to themselves at their own peril, they must equally be free to consult with one another about what is fit to be so done; to exchange opinions, and give and receive suggestions. Whatever it is permitted to do, it must be permitted to advise to do. The question is doubtful, only when the instigator derives a personal benefit from his advice; when he makes it his occupation, for subsistence or pecuniary gain, to promote what society and the State consider to be an evil. Then, indeed, a new element of complication is introduced; namely, the existence of classes of persons with an interest opposed to what is considered as the public weal, and whose mode of living is grounded on the counter-action of it. Ought this to be interfered with, or not? Fornication, for example, must be tolerated, and so must gambling; but should a person be free to be a pimp, or to keep a gambling-house? The case is one of those which lie on the exact boundary line between two principles, and it is not at once apparent to which of the two it properly belongs. There are arguments on both sides. On the side of toleration it may be said, that the fact of following anything as an occupation, and living or profiting by the practice of it, cannot make that criminal which would otherwise be admissible; that the act should either be consistently permitted or consistently prohibited; that if the principles which we have hitherto defended are true, society has no business, as society, to decide anything to be wrong which concerns only the individual; that it cannot go beyond dissuasion, and that one person should be as free to persuade, as another to dissuade. In opposition to this it may be contended, that although the public, or the State, are not warranted in authoritatively deciding, for purposes of repression or punishment, that such or such conduct affecting only the interests of the individual is good or bad, they are fully justified in assuming, if they regard it as bad, that its being so or not is at least a disputable question: That, this being supposed, they cannot be acting wrongly in endeavouring to exclude the influence of solicitations which are not disinterested, of instigators who cannot possibly be impartial—who have a direct personal interest on one side, and that side the one which the State believes to be wrong, and who confessedly promote it for personal objects only. There can surely, it may be urged, be nothing lost, no sacrifice of good, by so ordering matters that persons shall make their election, either wisely or foolishly, on their own prompting, as free as possible from the arts of persons who stimulate their inclinations for interested purposes of their own. Thus (it may be said) though the statutes respecting unlawful games are utterly indefensible—though all persons should be free to gamble in their own or each other's houses, or in any place of meeting established by their own subscriptions, and open only to the members and their visitors—yet public gambling-houses should not be permitted. It is true that the prohibition is never effectual, and that, whatever amount of tyrannical power may be given to the police, gambling-houses can always be maintained under other pretences; but they may be compelled to conduct their operations with a certain degree of secrecy and mystery, so that nobody knows anything about them but those who seek them; and more than this, society ought not to aim at. There is considerable force in these arguments. I will not venture to decide whether they are sufficient to justify the moral anomaly of punishing the accessary, when the principal is (and must be) allowed to go free; of fining or imprisoning the procurer, but not the fornicator, the gambling-house keeper, but not the gambler. Still less ought the common operations of buying and selling to be interfered with on analogous grounds. Almost every article which is bought and sold may be used in excess, and the sellers have a pecuniary interest in encouraging that excess; but no argument can be founded on this, in favour, for instance, of the Maine Law; because the class of dealers in strong drinks, though interested in their abuse, are indispensably required for the sake of their legitimate use. The interest, however, of these dealers in promoting intemperance is a real evil, and justifies the State in imposing restrictions and requiring guarantees which, but for that justification, would be infringements of legitimate liberty.

A further question is, whether the State, while it permits, should nevertheless indirectly discourage conduct which it deems contrary to the best interests of the agent; whether, for example, it should take measures to render the means of drunkenness more costly, or add to the difficulty of procuring them by limiting the number of the places of sale. On this as on most other practical questions, many distinctions require to be made. To tax stimulants for the sole purpose of making them more difficult to be obtained, is a measure differing only in degree from their entire prohibition; and would be justifiable only if that were justifiable. Every increase of cost is a prohibition, to those whose means do not come up to the augmented price; and to those who do, it is a penalty laid on them for gratifying a particular taste. Their choice of pleasures, and their mode of expending their income, after satisfying their legal and moral obligations to the State and to individuals, are their own concern, and must rest with their own judgment. These considerations may seem at first sight to condemn the selection of stimulants as special subjects of taxation for purposes of revenue. But it must be remembered that taxation for fiscal purposes is absolutely inevitable; that in most countries it is necessary that a considerable part of that taxation should be indirect; that the State, therefore, cannot help imposing penalties, which to some persons may be prohibitory, on the use of some articles of consumption. It is hence the duty of the State to consider, in the imposition of taxes, what commodities the consumers can best spare; and *a fortiori*, to select in preference those of which it deems the use, beyond a very moderate quantity, to be positively injurious. Taxation, therefore, of stimulants, up to the point which produces the largest amount of revenue (supposing that the State needs all the revenue which it yields) is not only admissible, but to be approved of.

The question of making the sale of these commodities a more or less exclusive privilege, must be answered differently, according to the purposes to which the restriction is intended to be subservient. All places of public resort require the restraint of a police, and places of this kind peculiarly, because offences against society are especially apt to originate there. It is, therefore, fit to confine the power of selling these commodities (at least for consumption on the spot) to persons of known or vouched-for respectability of conduct; to make such regulations respecting hours of opening and closing as may be requisite for public surveillance, and to withdraw the licence if breaches of the peace repeatedly take place through the connivance or incapacity of the keeper of the house, or if it becomes a rendezvous for concocting and preparing offences against the law. Any further restriction I do not conceive to be, in principle, justifiable. The limitation in number, for instance, of beer and spirit houses, for the express purpose of rendering them more difficult of access, and diminishing the occasions of temptation, not only exposes all to an inconvenience because there are some by whom the facility would be abused, but is suited only to a state of society in which the labouring classes are avowedly treated as children or savages, and placed under an education of restraint, to fit them for future admission to the privileges of freedom. This is not the principle on which the labouring classes are professedly governed in any free country; and no person who sets due value on freedom will give his adhesion to their being so governed, unless after all efforts have been exhausted to educate them for freedom and govern them as freemen, and it has been definitively proved that they can only be governed as children. The bare statement of the alternative shows the absurdity of supposing that such efforts have been made in any case which needs be considered here. It is only because the institutions of this country are a mass of inconsistencies, that things find admittance into our practice which belong to the system of despotic, or what is called paternal, government, while the general freedom of our institutions precludes the exercise of the amount of control necessary to render the restraint of any real efficacy as a moral education.

It was pointed out in an early part of this Essay, that the liberty of the individual, in things wherein the individual is alone concerned, implies a corresponding liberty in any number of individuals to regulate by mutual agreement such things as regard them jointly, and regard no persons but themselves. This question presents no difficulty, so long as the will of all the persons implicated remains unaltered; but since that will may change, it is often necessary, even in things in which they alone are concerned, that they should enter into engagements with one another; and when they do, it is fit, as a general rule, that those engagements should be kept. Yet, in the laws, probably, of every country, this general rule has some exceptions. Not only persons are not held to engagements which violate the rights of third parties, but it is sometimes considered a sufficient reason for releasing them from an engagement, that it is injurious to themselves. In this and most other civilized countries, for example, an engagement by which a person should sell himself, or allow himself to be sold, as a slave, would be null and void; neither enforced by law nor by opinion. The ground for thus limiting his power of voluntarily disposing of his own lot in life, is apparent, and is very clearly seen in this extreme case. The reason for not interfering, unless for the sake of others, with a person's voluntary acts, is consideration for his liberty. His voluntary choice is evidence that what he so chooses is desirable, or at the least endurable, to him, and his good is on the whole best provided for by allowing him to take his own means of pursuing it. But by selling himself for a slave, he abdicates his liberty; he foregoes any future use of it beyond that single act. He therefore defeats, in his own case, the very purpose which is the justification of allowing him to dispose of himself. He is no longer free; but is thenceforth in a position which has no longer the presumption in its favour, that would be afforded by his voluntarily remaining in it. The principle of freedom cannot require that he should be free not to be free. It is not freedom, to be allowed to alienate his freedom. These reasons, the force of which is so conspicuous in this peculiar case, are evidently of far wider application; yet a limit is everywhere set to them by the necessities of life, which continually require, not indeed that we should resign our freedom, but that we should consent to this and the other limitation of it. The principle, however, which demands uncontrolled freedom of action in all that concerns only the agents themselves, requires that those who have become bound to one another, in things which concern no third party, should be able to release one another from the engagement: and even without such voluntary release, there are perhaps no contracts or engagements, except those that relate to money or money's worth, of which one can venture to say that there ought to be no liberty whatever of retractation. Baron Wilhelm von Humboldt, in the excellent essay from which I have already quoted, states it as his conviction, that engagements which involve personal relations or services, should never be legally binding beyond a limited duration of time; and that the most important of these engagements, marriage, having the peculiarity that its objects are frustrated unless the feelings of both the parties are in harmony with it, should require nothing more than the declared will of either party to dissolve it. This subject is too important, and too complicated, to be discussed in a parenthesis, and I touch on it only so far as is necessary for purposes of illustration. If the conciseness and generality of Baron Humboldt's dissertation had not obliged him in this instance to content himself with enunciating his conclusion without discussing the premises, he would doubtless have recognised that the question cannot be decided on grounds so simple as those to which he confines himself. When a person, either by express promise or by conduct, has encouraged another to rely upon his continuing to act in a certain way—to build expectations and calculations, and stake any part of his plan of life upon that supposition—a new series of moral obligations arises on his part towards that person, which may possibly be overruled, but cannot be ignored. And again, if the relation between two contracting parties has been followed by consequences to others; if it has placed third parties in any peculiar position, or, as in the case of marriage, has even called third parties into existence, obligations arise on the part of both the contracting parties towards those third persons, the fulfilment of which, or at all events the mode of fulfilment, must be greatly affected by the continuance or disruption of the relation between the original parties to the contract. It does not follow, nor can I admit, that these obligations extend to requiring the fulfilment of the contract at all costs to the happiness of the reluctant party; but they are a necessary element in the question; and even if, as Von Humboldt maintains, they ought to make no difference in the *legal* freedom of the parties to release themselves from the engagement (and I also hold that they ought not to make *much* difference), they necessarily make a great difference in the *moral* freedom. A person is bound to take all these circumstances into account, before resolving on a step which may affect such important interests of others; and if he does not allow proper weight to those interests, he is morally responsible for the wrong. I have made these obvious remarks for the better illustration of the general principle of liberty, and not because they are at all needed on the particular question, which, on the contrary, is usually discussed as if the interest of children was everything, and that of grown persons nothing.

I have already observed that, owing to the absence of any recognised general principles, liberty is often granted where it should be withheld, as well as withheld where it should be granted; and one of the cases in which, in the modern European world, the sentiment of liberty is the strongest, is a case where, in my view, it is altogether misplaced. A person should be free to do as he likes in his own concerns; but he ought not to be free to do as he likes in acting for another, under the pretext that the affairs of the other are his own affairs. The State, while it respects the liberty of each in what specially regards himself, is bound to maintain a vigilant control over his exercise of any power which it allows him to possess over others. This obligation is almost entirely disregarded in the case of the family relations, a case, in its direct influence on human happiness, more important than all others taken together. The almost despotic power of husbands over wives needs not be enlarged upon here, because nothing more is needed for the complete removal of the evil, than that wives should have the same rights, and should receive the protection of law in the same manner, as all other persons; and because, on this subject, the defenders of established injustice do not avail themselves of the plea of liberty, but stand forth openly as the champions of power. It is in the case of children, that misapplied notions of liberty are a real obstacle to the fulfilment by the State of its duties. One would almost think that a man's children were supposed to be literally, and not metaphorically, a part of himself, so jealous is opinion of the smallest interference of law with his absolute and exclusive control over them; more jealous than of almost any interference with his own freedom of action: so much less do the generality of mankind value liberty than power. Consider, for example, the case of education. Is it not almost a self-evident axiom, that the State should require and compel the education, up to a certain standard, of every human being who is born its citizen? Yet who is there that is not afraid to recognise and assert this truth? Hardly any one indeed will deny that it is one of the most sacred duties of the parents (or, as law and usage now stand, the father), after summoning a human being into the world, to give to that being an education fitting him to perform his part well in life towards others and towards himself. But while this is unanimously declared to be the father's duty, scarcely anybody, in this country, will bear to hear of obliging him to perform it. Instead of his being required to make any exertion or sacrifice for securing education to the child, it is left to his choice to accept it or not when it is provided gratis! It still remains unrecognised, that to bring a child into existence without a fair prospect of being able, not only to provide food for its body, but instruction and training for its mind, is a moral crime, both against the unfortunate offspring and against society; and that if the parent does not fulfil this obligation, the State ought to see it fulfilled, at the charge, as far as possible, of the parent.

Were the duty of enforcing universal education once admitted, there would be an end to the difficulties about what the State should teach, and how it should teach, which now convert the subject into a mere battle-field for sects and parties, causing the time and labour which should have been spent in educating, to be wasted in quarrelling about education. If the government would make up its mind to *require* for every child a good education, it might save itself the trouble of *providing* one. It might leave to parents to obtain the education where and how they pleased, and content itself with helping to pay the school fees of the poorer classes of children, and defraying the entire school expenses of those who have no one else to pay for them. The objections which are urged with reason against State education, do not apply to the enforcement of education by the State, but to the State's taking upon itself to direct that education: which is a totally different thing. That the whole or any large part of the education of the people should be in State hands, I go as far as any one in deprecating. All that has been said of the importance of individuality of character, and diversity in opinions and modes of conduct, involves, as of the same unspeakable importance, diversity of education. A general State education is a mere contrivance for moulding people to be exactly like one another: and as the mould in which it casts them is that which pleases the predominant power in the government, whether this be a monarch, a priesthood, an aristocracy, or the majority of the existing generation in proportion as it is efficient and successful, it establishes a despotism over the mind, leading by natural tendency to one over the body. An education established and controlled by the State should only exist, if it exist at all, as one among many competing experiments, carried on for the purpose of example and stimulus, to keep the others up to a certain standard of excellence. Unless, indeed, when society in general is in so backward a state that it could not or would not provide for itself any proper institutions of education, unless the government undertook the task: then, indeed, the government may, as the less of two great evils, take upon itself the business of schools and universities, as it may that of joint stock companies, when private enterprise, in a shape fitted for undertaking great works of industry, does not exist in the country. But in general, if the country contains a sufficient number of persons qualified to provide education under government auspices, the same persons would be able and willing to give an equally good education on the voluntary principle, under the assurance of remuneration afforded by a law rendering education compulsory, combined with State aid to those unable to defray the expense.

The instrument for enforcing the law could be no other than public examinations, extending to all children, and beginning at an early age. An age might be fixed at which every child must be examined, to ascertain if he (or she) is able to read. If a child proves unable, the father, unless he has some sufficient ground of excuse, might be subjected to a moderate fine, to be worked out, if necessary, by his labour, and the child might be put to school at his expense. Once in every year the examination should be renewed, with a gradually extending range of subjects, so as to make the universal acquisition, and what is more, retention, of a certain minimum of general knowledge, virtually compulsory. Beyond that minimum, there should be voluntary examinations on all subjects, at which all who come up to a certain standard of proficiency might claim a certificate. To prevent the State from exercising, through these arrangements, an improper influence over opinion, the knowledge required for passing an examination (beyond the merely instrumental parts of knowledge, such as languages and their use) should, even in the higher classes of examinations, be confined to facts and positive science exclusively. The examinations on religion, politics, or other disputed topics, should not turn on the truth or falsehood of opinions, but on the matter of fact that such and such an opinion is held, on such grounds, by such authors, or schools, or churches. Under this system, the rising generation would be no worse off in regard to all disputed truths, than they are at present; they would be brought up either churchmen or dissenters as they now are, the State merely taking care that they should be instructed churchmen, or instructed dissenters. There would be nothing to hinder them from being taught religion, if their parents chose, at the same schools where they were taught other things. All attempts by the State to bias the conclusions of its citizens on disputed subjects, are evil; but it may very properly offer to ascertain and certify that a person possesses the knowledge, requisite to make his conclusions, on any given subject, worth attending to. A student of philosophy would be the better for being able to stand an examination both in Locke and in Kant, whichever of the two he takes up with, or even if with neither: and there is no reasonable objection to examining an atheist in the evidences of Christianity, provided he is not required to profess a belief in them. The examinations, however, in the higher branches of knowledge should, I conceive, be entirely voluntary. It would be giving too dangerous a power to governments, were they allowed to exclude any one from professions, even from the profession of teacher, for alleged deficiency of qualifications: and I think, with Wilhelm von Humboldt, that degrees, or other public certificates of scientific or professional acquirements, should be given to all who present themselves for examination, and stand the test; but that such certificates should confer no advantage over competitors, other than the weight which may be attached to their testimony by public opinion.

It is not in the matter of education only, that misplaced notions of liberty prevent moral obligations on the part of parents from being recognised, and legal obligations from being imposed, where there are the strongest grounds for the former always, and in many cases for the latter also. The fact itself, of causing the existence of a human being, is one of the most responsible actions in the range of human life. To undertake this responsibility—to bestow a life which may be either a curse or a blessing—unless the being on whom it is to be bestowed will have at least the ordinary chances of a desirable existence, is a crime against that being. And in a country either over-peopled or threatened with being so, to produce children, beyond a very small number, with the effect of reducing the reward of labour by their competition, is a serious offence against all who live by the remuneration of their labour. The laws which, in many countries on the Continent, forbid marriage unless the parties can show that they have the means of supporting a family, do not exceed the legitimate powers of the State: and whether such laws be expedient or not (a question mainly dependent on local circumstances and feelings), they are not objectionable as violations of liberty. Such laws are interferences of the State to prohibit a mischievous act—an act injurious to others, which ought to be a subject of reprobation, and social stigma, even when it is not deemed expedient to superadd legal punishment. Yet the current ideas of liberty, which bend so easily to real infringements of the freedom of the individual in things which concern only himself, would repel the attempt to put any restraint upon his inclinations when the consequence of their indulgence is a life or lives of wretchedness and depravity to the offspring, with manifold evils to those sufficiently within reach to be in any way affected by their actions. When we compare the strange respect of mankind for liberty, with their strange want of respect for it, we might imagine that a man had an indispensable right to do harm to others, and no right at all to please himself without giving pain to any one.

I have reserved for the last place a large class of questions respecting the limits of government interference, which, though closely connected with the subject of this Essay, do not, in strictness, belong to it. These are cases in which the reasons against interference do not turn upon the principle of liberty: the question is not about restraining the actions of individuals, but about helping them: it is asked whether the government should do, or cause to be done, something for their benefit, instead of leaving it to be done by themselves, individually, or in voluntary combination.

The objections to government interference, when it is not such as to involve infringement of liberty, may be of three kinds.

The first is, when the thing to be done is likely to be better done by individuals than by the government. Speaking generally, there is no one so fit to conduct any business, or to determine how or by whom it shall be conducted, as those who are personally interested in it. This principle condemns the interferences, once so common, of the legislature, or the officers of government, with the ordinary processes of industry. But this part of the subject has been sufficiently enlarged upon by political economists, and is not particularly related to the principles of this Essay.

The second objection is more nearly allied to our subject. In many cases, though individuals may not do the particular thing so well, on the average, as the officers of government, it is nevertheless desirable that it should be done by them, rather than by the government, as a means to their own mental education—a mode of strengthening their active faculties, exercising their judgment, and giving them a familiar knowledge of the subjects with which they are thus left to deal. This is a principal, though not the sole, recommendation of jury trial (in cases not political); of free and popular local and municipal institutions; of the conduct of industrial and philanthropic enterprises by voluntary associations. These are not questions of liberty, and are connected with that subject only by remote tendencies; but they are questions of development. It belongs to a different occasion from the present to dwell on these things as parts of national education; as being, in truth, the peculiar training of a citizen, the practical part of the political education of a free people, taking them out of the narrow circle of personal and family selfishness, and accustoming them to the comprehension of joint interests, the management of joint concerns—habituating them to act from public or semi-public motives, and guide their conduct by aims which unite instead of isolating them from one another. Without these habits and powers, a free constitution can neither be worked nor preserved; as is exemplified by the too-often transitory nature of political freedom in countries where it does not rest upon a sufficient basis of local liberties. The management of purely local business by the localities, and of the great enterprises of industry by the union of those who voluntarily supply the pecuniary means, is further recommended by all the advantages which have been set forth in this Essay as belonging to individuality of development, and diversity of modes of action. Government operations tend to be everywhere alike. With individuals and voluntary associations, on the contrary, there are varied experiments, and endless diversity of experience. What the State can usefully do, is to make itself a central depository, and active circulator and diffuser, of the experience resulting from many trials. Its business is to enable each experimentalist to benefit by the experiments of others; instead of tolerating no experiments but its own.

The third, and most cogent reason for restricting the interference of government, is the great evil of adding unnecessarily to its power. Every function superadded to those already exercised by the government, causes its influence over hopes and fears to be more widely diffused, and converts, more and more, the active and ambitious part of the public into hangers-on of the government, or of some party which aims at becoming the government. If the roads, the railways, the banks, the insurance offices, the great joint-stock companies, the universities, and the public charities, were all of them branches of the government; if, in addition, the municipal corporations and local boards, with all that now devolves on them, became departments of the central administration; if the employees of all these different enterprises were appointed and paid by the government, and looked to the government for every rise in life; not all the freedom of the press and popular constitution of the legislature would make this or any other country free otherwise than in name. And the evil would be greater, the more efficiently and scientifically the administrative machinery was constructed—the more skilful the arrangements for obtaining the best qualified hands and heads with which to work it. In England it has of late been proposed that all the members of the civil service of government should be selected by competitive examination, to obtain for those employments the most intelligent and instructed persons procurable; and much has been said and written for and against this proposal. One of the arguments most insisted on by its opponents, is that the occupation of a permanent official servant of the State does not hold out sufficient prospects of emolument and importance to attract the highest talents, which will always be able to find a more inviting career in the professions, or in the service of companies and other public bodies. One would not have been surprised if this argument had been used by the friends of the proposition, as an answer to its principal difficulty. Coming from the opponents it is strange enough. What is urged as an objection is the safety-valve of the proposed system. If indeed all the high talent of the country *could* be drawn into the service of the government, a proposal tending to bring about that result might well inspire uneasiness. If every part of the business of society which required organized concert, or large and comprehensive views, were in the hands of the government, and if government offices were universally filled by the ablest men, all the enlarged culture and practised intelligence in the country, except the purely speculative, would be concentrated in a numerous bureaucracy, to whom alone the rest of the community would look for all things: the multitude for direction and dictation in all they had to do; the able and aspiring for personal advancement. To be admitted into the ranks of this bureaucracy, and when admitted, to rise therein, would be the sole objects of ambition. Under this regime, not only is the outside public ill-qualified, for want of practical experience, to criticize or check the mode of operation of the bureaucracy, but even if the accidents of despotic or the natural working of popular institutions occasionally raise to the summit a ruler or rulers of reforming inclinations, no reform can be effected which is contrary to the interest of the bureaucracy. Such is the melancholy condition of the Russian empire, as shown in the accounts of those who have had sufficient opportunity of observation. The Czar himself is powerless against the bureaucratic body; he can send any one of them to Siberia, but he cannot govern without them, or against their will. On every decree of his they have a tacit veto, by merely refraining from carrying it into effect. In countries of more advanced civilization and of a more insurrectionary spirit, the public, accustomed to expect everything to be done for them by the State, or at least to do nothing for themselves without asking from the State not only leave to do it, but even how it is to be done, naturally hold the State responsible for all evil which befals them, and when the evil exceeds their amount of patience, they rise against the government and make what is called a revolution; whereupon somebody else, with or without legitimate authority from the nation, vaults into the seat, issues his orders to the bureaucracy, and everything goes on much as it did before; the bureaucracy being unchanged, and nobody else being capable of taking their place.

A very different spectacle is exhibited among a people accustomed to transact their own business. In France, a large part of the people having been engaged in military service, many of whom have held at least the rank of non-commissioned officers, there are in every popular insurrection several persons competent to take the lead, and improvise some tolerable plan of action. What the French are in military affairs, the Americans are in every kind of civil business; let them be left without a government, every body of Americans is able to improvise one, and to carry on that or any other public business with a sufficient amount of intelligence, order, and decision. This is what every free people ought to be: and a people capable of this is certain to be free; it will never let itself be enslaved by any man or body of men because these are able to seize and pull the reins of the central administration. No bureaucracy can hope to make such a people as this do or undergo anything that they do not like. But where everything is done through the bureaucracy, nothing to which the bureaucracy is really adverse can be done at all. The constitution of such countries is an organization of the experience and practical ability of the nation, into a disciplined body for the purpose of governing the rest; and the more perfect that organization is in itself, the more successful in drawing to itself and educating for itself the persons of greatest capacity from all ranks of the community, the more complete is the bondage of all, the members of the bureaucracy included. For the governors are as much the slaves of their organization and discipline, as the governed are of the governors. A Chinese mandarin is as much the tool and creature of a despotism as the humblest cultivator. An individual Jesuit is to the utmost degree of abasement the slave of his order, though the order itself exists for the collective power and importance of its members.

It is not, also, to be forgotten, that the absorption of all the principal ability of the country into the governing body is fatal, sooner or later, to the mental activity and progressiveness of the body itself. Banded together as they are—working a system which, like all systems, necessarily proceeds in a great measure by fixed rules—the official body are under the constant temptation of sinking into indolent routine, or, if they now and then desert that mill-horse round, of rushing into some half-examined crudity which has struck the fancy of some leading member of the corps: and the sole check to these closely allied, though seemingly opposite, tendencies, the only stimulus which can keep the ability of the body itself up to a high standard, is liability to the watchful criticism of equal ability outside the body. It is indispensable, therefore, that the means should exist, independently of the government, of forming such ability, and furnishing it with the opportunities and experience necessary for a correct judgment of great practical affairs. If we would possess permanently a skilful and efficient body of functionaries—above all a body able to originate and willing to adopt improvements; if we would not have our bureaucracy degenerate into a pedantocracy, this body must not engross all the occupations which form and cultivate the faculties required for the government of mankind.

To determine the point at which evils, so formidable to human freedom and advancement, begin, or rather at which they begin to predominate over the benefits attending the collective application of the force of society, under its recognised chiefs, for the removal of the obstacles which stand in the way of its well-being; to secure as much of the advantages of centralized power and intelligence, as can be had without turning into governmental channels too great a proportion of the general activity—is one of the most difficult and complicated questions in the art of government. It is, in a great measure, a question of detail, in which many and various considerations must be kept in view, and no absolute rule can be laid down. But I believe that the practical principle in which safety resides, the ideal to be kept in view, the standard by which to test all arrangements intended for overcoming the difficulty, may be conveyed in these words: the greatest dissemination of power consistent with efficiency; but the greatest possible centralization of information, and diffusion of it from the centre. Thus, in municipal administration, there would be, as in the New England States, a very minute division among separate officers, chosen by the localities, of all business which is not better left to the persons directly interested; but besides this, there would be, in each department of local affairs, a central superintendence, forming a branch of the general government. The organ of this superintendence would concentrate, as in a focus, the variety of information and experience derived from the conduct of that branch of public business in all the localities, from everything analogous which is done in foreign countries, and from the general principles of political science. This central organ should have a right to know all that is done, and its special duty should be that of making the knowledge acquired in one place available for others. Emancipated from the petty prejudices and narrow views of a locality by its elevated position and comprehensive sphere of observation, its advice would naturally carry much authority; but its actual power, as a permanent institution, should, I conceive, be limited to compelling the local officers to obey the laws laid down for their guidance. In all things not provided for by general rules, those officers should be left to their own judgment, under responsibility to their constituents. For the violation of rules, they should be responsible to law, and the rules themselves should be laid down by the legislature; the central administrative authority only watching over their execution, and if they were not properly carried into effect, appealing, according to the nature of the case, to the tribunals to enforce the law, or to the constituencies to dismiss the functionaries who had not executed it according to its spirit. Such, in its general conception, is the central superintendence which the Poor Law Board is intended to exercise over the administrators of the Poor Rate throughout the country. Whatever powers the Board exercises beyond this limit, were right and necessary in that peculiar case, for the cure of rooted habits of maladministration in matters deeply affecting not the localities merely, but the whole community; since no locality has a moral right to make itself by mismanagement a nest of pauperism, necessarily overflowing into other localities, and impairing the moral and physical condition of the whole labouring community. The powers of administrative coercion and subordinate legislation possessed by the Poor Law Board (but which, owing to the state of opinion on the subject, are very scantily exercised by them), though perfectly justifiable in a case of first-rate national interest, would be wholly out of place in the superintendence of interests purely local. But a central organ of information and instruction for all the localities, would be equally valuable in all departments of administration. A government cannot have too much of the kind of activity which does not impede, but aids and stimulates, individual exertion and development. The mischief begins when, instead of calling forth the activity and powers of individuals and bodies, it substitutes its own activity for theirs; when, instead of informing, advising, and, upon occasion, denouncing, it makes them work in fetters, or bids them stand aside and does their work instead of them. The worth of a State, in the long run, is the worth of the individuals composing it; and a State which postpones the interests of *their* mental expansion and elevation, to a little more of administrative skill, or of that semblance of it which practice gives, in the details of business; a State which dwarfs its men, in order that they may be more docile instruments in its hands even for beneficial purposes—will find that with small men no great thing can really be accomplished; and that the perfection of machinery to which it has sacrificed everything, will in the end avail it nothing, for want of the vital power which, in order that the machine might work more smoothly, it has preferred to banish.

UTILITARIANISM

Contents

Chapter I.   General Remarks.
Chapter II.   What Utilitarianism Is.
Chapter III. Of the Ultimate Sanction of the Principle of Utility.
Chapter IV. Of What Sort of Proof the Principle of Utility Is Susceptible.
Chapter V.   Of the Connexion between Justice and Utility.

CHAPTER I
General Remarks

There are few circumstances among those which make up the present condition of human knowledge, more unlike what might have been expected, or more significant of the backward state in which speculation on the most important subjects still lingers, than the little progress which has been made in the decision of the controversy respecting the criterion of right and wrong. From the dawn of philosophy, the question concerning the *summum bonum,* or, what is the same thing, concerning the foundation of morality, has been accounted the main problem in speculative thought, has occupied the most gifted intellects, and divided them into sects and schools, carrying on a vigorous warfare against one another. And after more than two thousand years the same discussions continue, philosophers are still ranged under the same contending banners, and neither thinkers nor mankind at large seem nearer to being unanimous on the subject, than when the youth Socrates listened to the old Protagoras, and asserted (if Plato's dialogue be grounded on a real conversation) the theory of utilitarianism against the popular morality of the so-called sophist.

It is true that similar confusion and uncertainty, and in some cases similar discordance, exist respecting the first principles of all the sciences, not excepting that which is deemed the most certain of them, mathematics; without much impairing, generally indeed without impairing at all, the trustworthiness of the conclusions of those sciences. An apparent anomaly, the explanation of which is, that the detailed doctrines of a science are not usually deduced from, nor depend for their evidence upon, what are called its first principles. Were it not so, there would be no science more precarious, or whose conclusions were more insufficiently made out, than algebra; which derives none of its certainty from what are commonly taught to learners as its elements, since these, as laid down by some of its most eminent teachers, are as full of fictions as English law, and of mysteries as theology. The truths which are ultimately accepted as the first principles of a science, are really the last results of metaphysical analysis, practised on the elementary notions with which the science is conversant; and their relation to the science is not that of foundations to an edifice, but of roots to a tree, which may perform their office equally well though they be never dug down to and exposed to light. But though in science the particular truths precede the general theory, the contrary might be expected to be the case with a practical art, such as morals or legislation. All action is for the sake of some end, and rules of action, it seems natural to suppose, must

This edition of *Utilitarianism* was drawn from the 4th edition 1871 Longmans, Green, Reader, and Dyer.

take their whole character and colour from the end to which they are subservient. When we engage in a pursuit, a clear and precise conception of what we are pursuing would seem to be the first thing we need, instead of the last we are to look forward to. A test of right and wrong must be the means, one would think, of ascertaining what is right or wrong, and not a consequence of having already ascertained it.

The difficulty is not avoided by having recourse to the popular theory of a natural faculty, a sense or instinct, informing us of right and wrong. For—besides that the existence of such a moral instinct is itself one of the matters in dispute—those believers in it who have any pretensions to philosophy, have been obliged to abandon the idea that it discerns what is right or wrong in the particular case in hand, as our other senses discern the sight or sound actually present. Our moral faculty, according to all those of its interpreters who are entitled to the name of thinkers, supplies us only with the general principles of moral judgments; it is a branch of our reason, not of our sensitive faculty; and must be looked to for the abstract doctrines of morality, not for perception of it in the concrete. The intuitive, no less than what may be termed the inductive, school of ethics, insists on the necessity of general laws. They both agree that the morality of an individual action is not a question of direct perception, but of the application of a law to an individual case. They recognise also, to a great extent, the same moral laws; but differ as to their evidence, and the source from which they derive their authority. According to the one opinion, the principles of morals are evident *a priori*, requiring nothing to command assent, except that the meaning of the terms be understood. According to the other doctrine, right and wrong, as well as truth and falsehood, are questions of observation and experience. But both hold equally that morality must be deduced from principles; and the intuitive school affirm as strongly as the inductive, that there is a science of morals. Yet they seldom attempt to make out a list of the *a priori* principles which are to serve as the premises of the science; still more rarely do they make any effort to reduce those various principles to one first principle, or common ground of obligation. They either assume the ordinary precepts of morals as of *a priori* authority, or they lay down as the common groundwork of those maxims, some generality much less obviously authoritative than the maxims themselves, and which has never succeeded in gaining popular acceptance. Yet to support their pretensions there ought either to be some one fundamental principle or law, at the root of all morality, or if there be several, there should be a determinate order of precedence among them; and the one principle, or the rule for deciding between the various principles when they conflict, ought to be self-evident.

To inquire how far the bad effects of this deficiency have been mitigated in practice, or to what extent the moral beliefs of mankind have been vitiated or made uncertain by the absence of any distinct recognition of an ultimate standard, would imply a complete survey and criticism of past and present ethical doctrine. It would, however, be easy to show that whatever steadiness or consistency these moral beliefs have attained, has been mainly due to the tacit influence of a standard not recognised. Although the non-existence of acknowledged first principle has made ethics not so much a guide as a consecration of men's actual sentiments, still, as men's sentiments, both of favour and of aversion, are greatly influenced by what they suppose to be the effects of things upon their happiness, the principle of utility, or as Bentham latterly called it, the greatest happiness principle, has had a large share in forming the moral doctrines even of those who most scornfully reject its authority. Nor is there any school of thought which refuses to admit that the influence of actions on happiness is a most material and even predominant consideration in many of the details of morals, however unwilling to acknowledge it as the fundamental principle of morality, and the source of moral obligation. I might go much further, and say that to all those *a priori* moralists who deem it necessary to argue at all, utilitarian arguments are indispensable. It is not my present purpose to criticize these thinkers; but I cannot help referring, for illustration, to a systematic treatise by one of the most illustrious of them, the *Metaphysics of Ethics,* by Kant. This remarkable man, whose system of thought will long remain one of the landmarks in the history of philosophical speculation, does, in the treatise in question, lay down an universal first principle as the origin and ground of moral obligation; it is this:— 'So act, that the rule on which thou actest would admit of being adopted as a law by all rational beings.' But when he begins to deduce from this precept any of the actual duties of morality, he fails, almost grotesquely, to show that there would be any contradiction, any logical (not to say physical) impossibility, in the adoption by all rational beings of the most outrageously immoral rules of conduct. All he shows is that the *consequences* of their universal adoption would be such as no one would choose to incur.

On the present occasion, I shall, without further discussion of the other theories, attempt to contribute something towards the understanding and appreciation of the Utilitarian or Happiness theory, and towards such proof as it is susceptible of. It is evident that this cannot be proof in the ordinary and popular meaning of the term. Questions of ultimate ends are not amenable to direct proof. Whatever can be proved to be good, must be so by being shown to be a means to something admitted to be good without proof. The medical art is proved to be good, by its conducing to health; but how is it possible to prove that health is good? The art of music is good, for the reason, among others, that it produces pleasure; but what proof is it possible to give that pleasure is good? If, then, it is asserted that there is a comprehensive formula, including all things which are in themselves good, and that whatever else is good, is not so as an end, but as a mean, the formula may be accepted or rejected, but is not a subject of what is commonly understood by proof. We are not, however, to infer that its acceptance or rejection must depend on blind impulse, or arbitrary choice. There is a larger meaning of the word proof, in which this question is as amenable to it as any other of the disputed questions of philosophy. The subject is within the cognizance of the rational faculty; and neither does that faculty deal with it solely in the way of intuition. Considerations may be presented capable of determining the intellect either to give or withhold its assent to the doctrine; and this is equivalent to proof.

We shall examine presently of what nature are these considerations; in what manner they apply to the case, and what rational grounds, therefore, can be given for accepting or rejecting the utilitarian formula. But it is a preliminary condition of rational acceptance or rejection, that the formula should be correctly understood. I believe that the very imperfect notion ordinarily formed of its meaning, is the chief obstacle which impedes its reception; and that could it be cleared, even from only the grosser misconceptions, the question would be greatly simplified, and a large proportion of its difficulties removed. Before, therefore, I attempt to enter into the philosophical grounds which can be given for assenting to the utilitarian standard, I shall offer some illustrations of the doctrine itself; with the view of showing more clearly what it is, distinguishing it from what it is not, and disposing of such of the practical objections to it as either originate in, or are closely connected with, mistaken interpretations of its meaning. Having thus prepared the ground, I shall afterwards endeavour to throw such light as I can upon the question, considered as one of philosophical theory.

CHAPTER II
What Utilitarianism Is

A passing remark is all that needs be given to the ignorant blunder of supposing that those who stand up for utility as the test of right and wrong, use the term in that restricted and merely colloquial sense in which utility is opposed to pleasure. An apology is due to the philosophical opponents of utilitarianism, for even the momentary appearance of confounding them with any one capable of so absurd a misconception; which is the more extraordinary, inasmuch as the contrary accusation, of referring everything to pleasure, and that too in its grossest form, is another of the common charges against utilitarianism: and, as has been pointedly remarked by an able writer, the same sort of persons, and often the very same persons, denounce the theory 'as impracticably dry when the word utility precedes the word pleasure, and as too practicably voluptuous when the word pleasure precedes the word utility.' Those who know anything about the matter are aware that every writer, from Epicurus to Bentham, who maintained the theory of utility, meant by it, not something to be contradistinguished from pleasure, but pleasure itself, together with exemption from pain; and instead of opposing the useful to the agreeable or the ornamental, have always declared that the useful means these, among other things. Yet the common herd, including the herd of writers, not only in newspapers and periodicals, but in books of weight and pretension, are perpetually falling into this shallow mistake. Having caught up the word utilitarian, while knowing nothing whatever about it but its sound, they habitually express by it the rejection, or the neglect, of pleasure in some of its forms; of beauty, of ornament, or of amusement. Nor is the term thus ignorantly misapplied solely in disparagement, but occasionally in compliment; as though it implied superiority to frivolity and the mere pleasures of the moment. And this perverted use is the only one in which the word is popularly known, and the one from which the new generation are acquiring their sole notion of its meaning. Those who introduced the word, but who had for many years discontinued it as a distinctive appellation, may well feel themselves called upon to resume it, if by doing so they can hope to contribute anything towards rescuing it from this utter degradation.[1]

The creed which accepts as the foundation of morals, Utility, or the Greatest Happiness Principle, holds that actions are right in proportion as they tend to promote happiness, wrong as they tend to produce the reverse of happiness. By happiness is intended pleasure, and the absence of pain; by unhappiness, pain, and the privation of pleasure. To give a clear view of the moral standard set up by the theory, much more requires to be said; in particular, what things it includes in the

---

1. The author of this essay has reason for believing himself to be the first person who brought the word utilitarian into use. He did not invent it, but adopted it from a passing expression in Mr. Galt's *Annals of the Parish*. After using it as a designation for several years, he and others abandoned it from a growing dislike to anything resembling a badge or watchword of sectarian distinction. But as a name for one single opinion, not a set of opinions—to denote the recognition of utility as a standard, not any particular way of applying it—the term supplies a want in the language, and offers, in many cases, a convenient mode of avoiding tiresome circumlocution.

ideas of pain and pleasure; and to what extent this is left an open question. But these supplementary explanations do not affect the theory of life on which this theory of morality is grounded—namely, that pleasure, and freedom from pain, are the only things desirable as ends; and that all desirable things (which are as numerous in the utilitarian as in any other scheme) are desirable either for the pleasure inherent in themselves, or as means to the promotion of pleasure and the prevention of pain.

Now, such a theory of life excites in many minds, and among them in some of the most estimable in feeling and purpose, inveterate dislike. To suppose that life has (as they express it) no higher end than pleasure—no better and nobler object of desire and pursuit—they designate as utterly mean and grovelling; as a doctrine worthy only of swine, to whom the followers of Epicurus were, at a very early period, contemptuously likened; and modern holders of the doctrine are occasionally made the subject of equally polite comparisons by its German, French, and English assailants.

When thus attacked, the Epicureans have always answered, that it is not they, but their accusers, who represent human nature in a degrading light; since the accusation supposes human beings to be capable of no pleasures except those of which swine are capable. If this supposition were true, the charge could not be gainsaid, but would then be no longer an imputation; for if the sources of pleasure were precisely the same to human beings and to swine, the rule of life which is good enough for the one would be good enough for the other. The comparison of the Epicurean life to that of beasts is felt as degrading, precisely because a beast's pleasures do not satisfy a human being's conceptions of happiness. Human beings have faculties more elevated than the animal appetites, and when once made conscious of them, do not regard anything as happiness which does not include their gratification. I do not, indeed, consider the Epicureans to have been by any means faultless in drawing out their scheme of consequences from the utilitarian principle. To do this in any sufficient manner, many Stoic, as well as Christian elements require to be included. But there is no known Epicurean theory of life which does not assign to the pleasures of the intellect, of the feelings and imagination, and of the moral sentiments, a much higher value as pleasures than to those of mere sensation. It must be admitted, however, that utilitarian writers in general have placed the superiority of mental over bodily pleasures chiefly in the greater permanency, safety, uncostliness, &c., of the former—that is, in their circumstantial advantages rather than in their intrinsic nature. And on all these points utilitarians have fully proved their case; but they might have taken the other, and, as it may be called, higher ground, with entire consistency. It is quite compatible with the principle of utility to recognise the fact, that some *kinds* of pleasure are more desirable and more valuable than others. It would be absurd that while, in estimating all other things, quality is considered as well as quantity, the estimation of pleasures should be supposed to depend on quantity alone.

If I am asked, what I mean by difference of quality in pleasures, or what makes one pleasure more valuable than another, merely as a pleasure, except its being greater in amount, there is but one possible answer. Of two pleasures, if there be one to which all or almost all who have experience of both give a decided preference, irrespective of any feeling of moral obligation to prefer it, that is the more desirable pleasure. If one of the two is, by those who are competently acquainted with both, placed so far above the other that they prefer it, even though knowing it to be attended with a greater amount of discontent, and would not resign it for any quantity of the other pleasure which their nature is capable of, we are justified in ascribing to the preferred enjoyment a superiority in quality, so far outweighing quantity as to render it, in comparison, of small account.

Now it is an unquestionable fact that those who are equally acquainted with, and equally capable of appreciating and enjoying, both, do give a most marked preference to the manner of existence which employs their higher faculties. Few human creatures would consent to be changed into any of the lower animals, for a promise of the fullest allowance of a beast's pleasures; no intelligent human being would consent to be a fool, no instructed person would be an ignoramus, no person of feeling and conscience would be selfish and base, even though they should be persuaded that the fool, the dunce, or the rascal is better satisfied with his lot than they are with theirs. They would not resign what they possess more than he, for the most complete satisfaction of all the desires which they have in common with him. If they ever fancy they would, it is only in cases of unhappiness so extreme, that to escape from it they would exchange their lot for almost any other, however undesirable in their own eyes. A being of higher faculties requires more to make him happy, is capable probably of more acute suffering, and is certainly accessible to it at more points, than one of an inferior type; but in spite of these liabilities, he can never really wish to sink into what he feels to be a lower grade of existence. We may give what explanation we please of this unwillingness; we may attribute it to pride, a name which is given indiscriminately to some of the most and to some of the least estimable feelings of which mankind are capable; we may refer it to the love of liberty and personal independence, an appeal to which was with the Stoics one of the most effective means for the inculcation of it; to the love of power, or to the love of excitement, both of which do really enter into and contribute to it: but its most appropriate appellation is a sense of dignity, which all human beings possess in one form or other, and in some, though by no means in exact, proportion to their higher faculties, and which is so essential a part of the happiness of those in whom it is strong, that nothing which conflicts with it could be, otherwise than momentarily, an object of desire to them. Whoever supposes that this preference takes place at a sacrifice of happiness—that the superior being, in anything like equal circumstances, is not happier than the inferior—confounds the two very different ideas, of happiness, and content. It is indisputable that the being whose capacities of enjoyment are low, has the greatest chance of having them fully satisfied; and a highly-endowed being will always feel that any happiness which he can look for, as the world is constituted, is imperfect. But he can learn to bear its imperfections, if they are at all bearable; and they will not make him envy the being who is indeed unconscious of the imperfections, but only because he feels not at all the good which those imperfections qualify. It is better to be a human being dissatisfied than a pig satisfied; better to be Socrates dissatisfied than a fool satisfied. And if the fool, or the pig, is of a different opinion, it is because they only know their own side of the question. The other party to the comparison knows both sides.

It may be objected, that many who are capable of the higher pleasures, occasionally, under the influence of temptation, postpone them to the lower. But this is quite compatible with a full appreciation of the intrinsic superiority of the higher. Men often, from infirmity of character, make their election for the nearer good, though they know it to be the less valuable; and this no less when the choice is between two bodily pleasures, than when it is between bodily and mental. They pursue sensual indulgences to the injury of health, though perfectly aware that health is the greater good. It may be further objected, that many who begin with youthful enthusiasm for everything noble, as they advance in years sink into indolence and selfishness. But I do not believe that those who undergo this very common change, voluntarily choose the lower description of pleasures in preference to the higher. I believe that before they devote themselves exclusively to the one, they have already become incapable of the other. Capacity for the nobler feelings is in most natures a very tender plant, easily killed, not only by hostile influences, but by mere want of sustenance; and in the majority of young persons it speedily dies away if the occupations to which their position in life has devoted them, and the society into which it has thrown them, are not favourable to keeping that higher capacity in exercise. Men lose their high aspirations as they lose their intellectual tastes, because they have not time or opportunity for indulging them; and they addict themselves to inferior pleasures, not because they deliberately prefer them, but because they are either the only ones to which they have access, or the only ones which they are any longer capable of enjoying. It may be questioned whether any one who has remained equally susceptible to both classes of pleasures, ever knowingly and calmly preferred the lower; though many, in all ages, have broken down in an ineffectual attempt to combine both.

From this verdict of the only competent judges, I apprehend there can be no appeal. On a question which is the best worth having of two pleasures, or which of two modes of existence is the most grateful to the feelings, apart from its moral attributes and from its consequences, the judgment of those who are qualified by knowledge of both, or, if they differ, that of the majority among them, must be admitted as final. And there needs be the less hesitation to accept this judgment respecting the quality of pleasures, since there is no other tribunal to be referred to even on the question of quantity. What means are there of determining which is the acutest of two pains, or the intensest of two pleasurable sensations, except the general suffrage of those who are familiar with both? Neither pains nor pleasures are homogeneous, and pain is always heterogeneous with pleasure. What is there to decide whether a particular pleasure is worth purchasing at the cost of a particular pain, except the feelings and judgment of the experienced? When, therefore, those feelings and judgment declare the pleasures derived from the higher faculties to be preferable *in kind*, apart from the question of intensity, to those of which the animal nature, disjoined from the higher faculties, is susceptible, they are entitled on this subject to the same regard.

I have dwelt on this point, as being a necessary part of a perfectly just conception of Utility or Happiness, considered as the directive rule of human conduct. But it is by no means an indispensable condition to the acceptance of the utilitarian standard; for that standard is not the agent's own greatest happiness, but the greatest amount of happiness altogether; and if it may possibly be doubted whether a noble character is always the happier for its nobleness, there can be no doubt that it makes other people happier, and that the world in general is immensely a gainer by it. Utilitarianism, therefore, could only attain its end by the general cultivation of nobleness of character, even if each individual were only benefited by the nobleness of others, and his own, so far as happiness is concerned, were a sheer deduction from the benefit. But the bare enunciation of such an absurdity as this last, renders refutation superfluous.

According to the Greatest Happiness Principle, as above explained, the ultimate end, with reference to and for the sake of which all other things are desirable (whether we are considering our own good or that of other people), is an existence exempt as far as possible from pain, and as rich as possible in enjoyments, both in point of quantity and quality; the test of quality, and the rule for measuring it against quantity, being the preference felt by those who in their opportunities of experience, to which must be added their habits of self-consciousness and self-observation, are best furnished with the means of comparison. This, being, according to the utilitarian opinion, the end of human action, is necessarily also the standard of morality; which may accordingly be defined, the rules and precepts for human conduct, by the observance of which an existence such as has been described might be, to the greatest extent possible, secured to all mankind; and not to them only, but, so far as the nature of things admits, to the whole sentient creation.

Against this doctrine, however, arises another class of objectors, who say that happiness, in any form, cannot be the rational purpose of human life and action; because, in the first place, it is unattainable: and they contemptuously ask, What right hast thou to be happy? a question which Mr. Carlyle clenches by the addition, What right, a short time ago, hadst thou even *to be*? Next, they say, that men can do *without* happiness; that all noble human beings have felt this, and could not have become noble but by learning the lesson of *Entsagen,* or renunciation; which lesson, thoroughly learnt and submitted to, they affirm to be the beginning and necessary condition of all virtue.

The first of these objections would go to the root of the matter were it well founded; for if no happiness is to be had at all by human beings, the attainment of it cannot be the end of morality, or of any rational conduct. Though, even in that case, something might still be said for the utilitarian theory; since utility includes not solely the pursuit of happiness, but the prevention or mitigation of unhappiness; and if the former aim be chimerical, there will be all the greater scope and more imperative need for the latter, so long at least as mankind think fit to live, and do not take refuge in the simultaneous act of suicide recommended under certain conditions by Novalis. When, however, it is thus positively asserted to be impossible that human life should be happy, the assertion, if not something like a verbal quibble, is at least an exaggeration. If by happiness be meant a continuity of highly pleasurable excitement, it is evident enough that this is impossible. A state of exalted pleasure lasts only moments, or in some cases, and with some intermissions, hours or days, and is the occasional brilliant flash of enjoyment, not its permanent and steady flame. Of this the philosophers who have taught that happiness is the end of life were as fully aware as those who taunt them. The happiness which they meant was not a life of rapture; but moments of such, in an existence made up of few and transitory pains, many and various pleasures, with a decided predominance of the active over the passive, and having as the foundation of the whole, not to expect more from life than it is capable of bestowing. A life thus composed, to those who have been fortunate enough to obtain it, has always appeared worthy of the name of happiness. And such an existence is even now the lot of many, during some considerable portion of their lives. The present wretched education, and wretched social arrangements, are the only real hindrance to its being attainable by almost all.

The objectors perhaps may doubt whether human beings, if taught to consider happiness as the end of life, would be satisfied with such a moderate share of it. But great numbers of mankind have been satisfied with much less. The main constituents of a satisfied life appear to be two, either of which by itself is often found sufficient for the purpose: tranquillity, and excitement. With much tranquillity, many find that they can be content with very little pleasure: with much excitement, many can reconcile themselves to a considerable quantity of pain. There is assuredly no inherent impossibility in enabling even the mass of mankind to unite both; since the two are so far from being incompatible that they are in natural alliance, the prolongation of either being a preparation for, and exciting a wish for, the other. It is only those in whom indolence amounts to a vice, that do not desire excitement after an interval of repose; it is only those in whom the need of excitement is a disease, that feel the tranquillity which follows excitement dull and insipid, instead of pleasurable in direct proportion to the excitement which preceded it. When people who are tolerably fortunate in their outward lot do not find in life sufficient enjoyment to make it valuable to them, the cause generally is, caring for nobody but themselves. To those who have neither public nor private affections, the excitements of life are much curtailed, and in any case dwindle in value as the time approaches when all selfish interests must be terminated by death: while those who leave after them objects of personal affection, and especially those who have also cultivated a fellow-feeling with the collective interests of mankind, retain as lively an interest in life on the eve of death as in the vigour of youth and health. Next to selfishness, the principal cause which makes life unsatisfactory is want of mental cultivation. A cultivated mind—I do not mean that of a philosopher, but any mind to which the fountains of knowledge have been opened, and which has been taught, in any tolerable degree, to exercise its faculties—finds sources of inexhaustible interest in all that surrounds it; in the objects of nature, the achievements of art, the imaginations of poetry, the incidents of history, the ways of mankind past and present, and their prospects in the future. It is possible, indeed, to become indifferent to all this, and that too without having exhausted a thousandth part of it; but only when one has had from the beginning no moral or human interest in these things, and has sought in them only the gratification of curiosity.

Now there is absolutely no reason in the nature of things why an amount of mental culture sufficient to give an intelligent interest in these objects of contemplation, should not be the inheritance of every one born in a civilized country. As little is there an inherent necessity that any human being should be a selfish egotist, devoid of every feeling or care but those which centre in his own miserable individuality. Something far superior to this is sufficiently common even now, to give ample earnest of what the human species may be made. Genuine private affections, and a sincere interest in the public good, are possible, though in unequal degrees, to every rightly brought up human being. In a world in which there is so much to interest, so much to enjoy, and so much also to correct and improve, every one who has this moderate amount of moral and intellectual requisites is capable of an existence which may be called enviable; and unless such a person, through bad laws, or subjection to the will of others, is denied the liberty to use the sources of happiness within his reach, he will not fail to find this enviable existence, if he escape the positive evils of life, the great sources of physical and mental suffering—such as indigence, disease, and the unkindness, worthlessness, or premature loss of objects of affection. The main stress of the problem lies, therefore, in the contest with these calamities, from which it is a rare good fortune entirely to escape; which, as things now are, cannot be obviated, and often cannot be in any material degree mitigated. Yet no one whose opinion deserves a moment's consideration can doubt that most of the great positive evils of the world are in themselves removable, and will, if human affairs continue to improve, be in the end reduced within narrow limits. Poverty, in any sense implying suffering, may be completely extinguished by the wisdom of society, combined with the good sense and providence of individuals. Even that most intractable of enemies, disease, may be indefinitely reduced in dimensions by good physical and moral education, and proper control of noxious influences; while the progress of science holds out a promise for the future of still more direct conquests over this detestable foe. And every advance in that direction relieves us from some, not only of the chances which cut short our own lives, but, what concerns us still more, which deprive us of those in whom our happiness is wrapt up. As for vicissitudes of fortune, and other disappointments connected with worldly circumstances, these are principally the effect either of gross imprudence, of ill-regulated desires, or of bad or imperfect social institutions. All the grand sources, in short, of human suffering are in a great degree, many of them almost entirely, conquerable by human care and effort; and though their removal is grievously slow—though a long succession of generations will perish in the breach before the conquest is completed, and this world becomes all that, if will and knowledge were not wanting, it might easily be made—yet every mind sufficiently intelligent and generous to bear a part, however small and unconspicuous, in the endeavour, will draw a noble enjoyment from the contest itself, which he would not for any bribe in the form of selfish indulgence consent to be without.

And this leads to the true estimation of what is said by the objectors concerning the possibility, and the obligation, of learning to do without happiness. Unquestionably it is possible to do without happiness; it is done involuntarily by nineteen-twentieths of mankind, even in those parts of our present world which are least deep in barbarism; and it often has to be done voluntarily by the hero or the martyr, for the sake of something which he prizes more than his individual happiness. But this something, what is it, unless the happiness of others, or some of the requisites of happiness? It is noble to be capable of resigning entirely one's own portion of happiness, or chances of it: but, after all, this self-sacrifice must be for some end; it is not its own end; and if we are told that its end is not happiness, but virtue, which is better than happiness, I ask, would the sacrifice be made if the hero or martyr did not believe that it would earn for others immunity from similar sacrifices? Would it be made if he thought that his renunciation of happiness for himself would produce no fruit for any of his fellow creatures, but to make their lot like his, and place them also in the condition of persons who have renounced happiness? All honour to those who can abnegate for themselves the personal enjoyment of life, when by such renunciation they contribute worthily to increase the amount of happiness in the world; but he who does it, or professes to do it, for any other purpose, is no more deserving of admiration than the ascetic mounted on his pillar. He may be an inspiriting proof of what men *can* do, but assuredly not an example of what they *should*.

Though it is only in a very imperfect state of the world's arrangements that any one can best serve the happiness of others by the absolute sacrifice of his own, yet so long as the world is in that imperfect state, I fully acknowledge that the readiness to make such a sacrifice is the highest virtue which can be found in man. I will add, that in this condition of the world, paradoxical as the assertion may be, the conscious ability to do without happiness gives the best prospect of realizing such happiness as is attainable. For nothing except that consciousness can raise a person above the chances of life, by making him feel that, let fate and fortune do their worst, they have not power to subdue him: which, once felt, frees him from excess of anxiety concerning the evils of life, and enables him, like many a Stoic in the worst times of the Roman Empire, to cultivate in tranquillity the sources of satisfaction accessible to him, without concerning himself about the uncertainty of their duration, any more than about their inevitable end.

Meanwhile, let utilitarians never cease to claim the morality of self-devotion as a possession which belongs by as good a right to them, as either to the Stoic or to the Transcendentalist. The utilitarian morality does recognise in human beings the power of sacrificing their own greatest good for the good of others. It only refuses to admit that the sacrifice is itself a good. A sacrifice which does not increase, or tend to increase, the sum total of happiness, it considers as wasted. The only self-renunciation which it applauds, is devotion to the happiness, or to some of the means of happiness, of others; either of mankind collectively, or of individuals within the limits imposed by the collective interests of mankind.

I must again repeat, what the assailants of utilitarianism seldom have the justice to acknowledge, that the happiness which forms the utilitarian standard of what is right in conduct, is not the agent's own happiness, but that of all concerned. As between his own happiness and that of others, utilitarianism requires him to be as strictly impartial as a disinterested and benevolent spectator. In the golden rule of Jesus of Nazareth, we read the complete spirit of the ethics of utility. To do as one would be done by, and to love one's neighbour as oneself, constitute the ideal perfection of utilitarian morality. As the means of making the nearest approach to this ideal, utility would enjoin, first, that laws and social arrangements should place the happiness, or (as speaking practically it may be called) the interest, of every individual, as nearly as possible in harmony with the interest of the whole; and secondly, that education and opinion, which have so vast a power over human character, should so use that power as to establish in the mind of every individual an indissoluble association between his own happiness and the good of the whole; especially between his own happiness and the practice of such modes of conduct, negative and positive, as regard for the universal happiness prescribes: so that not only he may be unable to conceive the possibility of happiness to himself, consistently with conduct opposed to the general good, but also that a direct impulse to promote the general good may be in every individual one of the habitual motives of action, and the sentiments connected therewith may fill a large and prominent place in every human being's sentient existence. If the impugners of the utilitarian morality represented it to their own minds in this its true character, I know not what recommendation possessed by any other morality they could possibly affirm to be wanting to it: what more beautiful or more exalted developments of human nature any other ethical system can be supposed to foster, or what springs of action, not accessible to the utilitarian, such systems rely on for giving effect to their mandates.

The objectors to utilitarianism cannot always be charged with representing it in a discreditable light. On the contrary, those among them who entertain anything like a just idea of its disinterested character, sometimes find fault with its standard as being too high for humanity. They say it is exacting too much to require that people shall always act from the inducement of promoting the general interests of society. But this is to mistake the very meaning of a standard of morals, and to confound the rule of action with the motive of it. It is the business of ethics to tell us what are our duties, or by what test we may know them; but no system of ethics requires that the sole motive of all we do shall be a feeling of duty; on the contrary, ninety-nine hundredths of all our actions are done from other motives, and rightly so done, if the rule of duty does not condemn them. It is the more unjust to utilitarianism that this particular misapprehension should be made a ground of objection to it, inasmuch as utilitarian moralists have gone beyond almost all others in affirming that the motive has nothing to do with the morality of the action, though much with the worth of the agent. He who saves a fellow creature from drowning does what is morally right, whether his motive be duty, or the hope of being paid for his trouble: he who betrays the friend that trusts him, is guilty of a crime, even if his object be to serve another friend to whom he is under greater obligations.[2] But to speak only of actions done from the motive of duty, and in direct obedience to principle: it is a misapprehension of the utilitarian mode of thought, to conceive it as implying that people should fix their minds upon so wide a generality as the world, or society at large. The great majority of good actions are intended, not for the benefit of the world, but for that of individuals, of which the good of the world is made up; and the thoughts of the most virtuous man need not on these occasions travel beyond the particular persons concerned, except so far as is necessary to assure himself that in benefiting them he is not violating the rights—that is, the legitimate and authorized expectations—of any one else. The multiplication of happiness is, according to the utilitarian ethics, the object of virtue: the occasions on which any person (except one in a thousand) has it in his power to do this on an extended scale, in other words, to be a public benefactor, are but exceptional; and on these occasions alone is he called on to consider public utility; in every other case, private utility, the interest or happiness of some few persons, is all he has to attend to. Those alone the influence of whose actions extends to society in general, need concern themselves habitually about so large an object. In the case of abstinences

---

2. An opponent, whose intellectual and moral fairness it is a pleasure to acknowledge (the Rev. J. Llewellyn Davies), has objected to this passage, saying, "Surely the rightness or wrongness of saving a man from drowning does depend very much upon the motive with which it is done. Suppose that a tyrant, when his enemy jumped into the sea to escape from him, saved him from drowning simply in order that he might inflict upon him more exquisite tortures, would it tend to clearness to speak of that rescue as 'a morally right action?' Or suppose again, according to one of the stock illustrations of ethical inquiries, that a man betrayed a trust received from a friend, because the discharge of it would fatally injure that friend himself or some one belonging to him, would utilitarianism compel one to call the betrayal 'a crime' as much as if it had been done from the meanest motive?"

I submit, that he who saves another from drowning in order to kill him by torture afterwards, does not differ only in motive from him who does the same thing from duty or benevolence; the act itself is different. The rescue of the man is, in the case supposed, only the necessary first step of an act far more atrocious than leaving him to drown would have been. Had Mr. Davies said, "The rightness or wrongness of saving a man from drowning does depend very much"—not upon the motive, but—"upon the *intention*," no utilitarian would have differed from him. Mr. Davies, by an oversight too common not to be quite venial, has in this case confounded the very different ideas of Motive and Intention. There is no point which utilitarian thinkers (and Bentham pre-eminently) have taken more pains to illustrate than this. The morality of the action depends entirely upon the intention—that is, upon what the agent *wills to do*. But the motive, that is, the feeling which makes him will so to do, when it makes no difference in the act, makes none in the morality: though it makes a great difference in our moral estimation of the agent, especially if it indicates a good or a bad habitual *disposition*—a bent of character from which useful, or from which hurtful actions are likely to arise.

indeed—of things which people forbear to do, from moral considerations, though the consequences in the particular case might be beneficial—it would be unworthy of an intelligent agent not to be consciously aware that the action is of a class which, if practised generally, would be generally injurious, and that this is the ground of the obligation to abstain from it. The amount of regard for the public interest implied in this recognition, is no greater than is demanded by every system of morals; for they all enjoin to abstain from whatever is manifestly pernicious to society.

The same considerations dispose of another reproach against the doctrine of utility, founded on a still grosser misconception of the purpose of a standard of morality, and of the very meaning of the words right and wrong. It is often affirmed that utilitarianism renders men cold and unsympathizing; that it chills their moral feelings towards individuals; that it makes them regard only the dry and hard consideration of the consequences of actions, not taking into their moral estimate the qualities from which those actions emanate. If the assertion means that they do not allow their judgment respecting the rightness or wrongness of an action to be influenced by their opinion of the qualities of the person who does it, this is a complaint not against utilitarianism, but against having any standard of morality at all; for certainly no known ethical standard decides an action to be good or bad because it is done by a good or a bad man, still less because done by an amiable, a brave, or a benevolent man, or the contrary. These considerations are relevant, not to the estimation of actions, but of persons; and there is nothing in the utilitarian theory inconsistent with the fact that there are other things which interest us in persons besides the rightness and wrongness of their actions. The Stoics, indeed, with the paradoxical misuse of language which was part of their system, and by which they strove to raise themselves above all concern about anything but virtue, were fond of saying that he who has that has everything; that he, and only he, is rich, is beautiful, is a king. But no claim of this description is made for the virtuous man by the utilitarian doctrine. Utilitarians are quite aware that there are other desirable possessions and qualities besides virtue, and are perfectly willing to allow to all of them their full worth. They are also aware that a right action does not necessarily indicate a virtuous character, and that actions which are blameable often proceed from qualities entitled to praise. When this is apparent in any particular case, it modifies their estimation, not certainly of the act, but of the agent. I grant that they are, notwithstanding, of opinion, that in the long run the best proof of a good character is good actions; and resolutely refuse to consider any mental disposition as good, of which the predominant tendency is to produce bad conduct. This makes them unpopular with many people; but it is an unpopularity which they must share with every one who regards the distinction between right and wrong in a serious light; and the reproach is not one which a conscientious utilitarian need be anxious to repel.

If no more be meant by the objection than that many utilitarians look on the morality of actions, as measured by the utilitarian standard, with too exclusive a regard, and do not lay sufficient stress upon the other beauties of character which go towards making a human being loveable or admirable, this may be admitted. Utilitarians who have cultivated their moral feelings, but not their sympathies nor their artistic perceptions, do fall into this mistake; and so do all other moralists under the same conditions. What can be said in excuse for other moralists is equally available for them, namely, that if there is to be any error, it is better that it should be on that side. As a matter of fact, we may affirm that among utilitarians as among adherents of other systems, there is every imaginable degree of rigidity and of laxity in the application of their standard: some are even puritanically rigorous, while others are as indulgent as can possibly be desired by sinner or by sentimentalist. But on the whole, a doctrine which brings prominently forward the interest that mankind have in the repression and prevention of conduct which violates the moral law, is likely to be inferior to no other in turning the sanctions of opinion against such violations. It is true, the question, What does violate the moral law? is one on which those who recognise different standards of morality are likely now and then to differ. But difference of opinion on moral questions was not first introduced into the world by utilitarianism, while that doctrine does supply, if not always an easy, at all events a tangible and intelligible mode of deciding such differences.

It may not be superfluous to notice a few more of the common misapprehensions of utilitarian ethics, even those which are so obvious and gross that it might appear impossible for any person of candour and intelligence to fall into them: since persons, even of considerable mental endowments, often give themselves so little trouble to understand the bearings of any opinion against which they entertain a prejudice, and men are in general so little conscious of this voluntary ignorance as a defect, that the vulgarest misunderstandings of ethical doctrines are continually met with in the deliberate writings of persons of the greatest pretensions both to high principle and to philosophy. We not uncommonly hear the doctrine of utility inveighed against as a *godless* doctrine. If it be necessary to say anything at all against so mere an assumption, we may say that the question depends upon what idea we have formed of the moral character of the Deity. If it be a true belief that God desires, above all things, the happiness of his creatures, and that this was his purpose in their creation, utility is not only not a godless doctrine, but more profoundly religious than any other. If it be meant that utilitarianism does not recognise the revealed will of God as the supreme law of morals, I answer, that an utilitarian who believes in the perfect goodness and wisdom of God, necessarily believes that whatever God has thought fit to reveal on the subject of morals, must fulfil the requirements of utility in a supreme degree. But others besides utilitarians have been of opinion that the Christian revelation was intended, and is fitted, to inform the hearts and minds of mankind with a spirit which should enable them to find for themselves what is right, and incline them to do it when found, rather than to tell them, except in a very general way, what it is: and that we need a doctrine of ethics, carefully followed out, to *interpret* to us the will of God. Whether this opinion is correct or not, it is superfluous here to discuss; since whatever aid religion, either natural or revealed, can afford to ethical investigation, is as open to the utilitarian moralist as to any other. He can use it as the testimony of God to the usefulness or hurtfulness of any given course of action, by as good a right as others can use it for the indication of a transcendental law, having no connexion with usefulness or with happiness.

Again, Utility is often summarily stigmatized as an immoral doctrine by giving it the name of Expediency, and taking advantage of the popular use of that term to contrast it with Principle. But the Expedient, in the sense in which it is opposed to the Right, generally means that which is expedient for the particular interest of the agent himself; as when a minister sacrifices the interest of his country to keep himself in place. When it means anything better than this, it means that which is expedient for some immediate object, some temporary purpose, but which violates a rule whose observance is expedient in a much higher degree. The Expedient, in this sense, instead of being the same thing with the useful, is a branch of the hurtful. Thus, it would often be expedient, for the purpose of getting over some momentary embarrassment, or attaining some object immediately useful to ourselves or others, to tell a lie. But inasmuch as the cultivation in ourselves of a sensitive feeling on the subject of veracity, is one of the most useful, and the enfeeblement of that feeling one of the most hurtful, things to which our conduct can be instrumental; and inasmuch as any, even unintentional, deviation from truth, does that much towards weakening the trustworthiness of human assertion, which is not only the principal support of all present social well-being, but the insufficiency of which does more than any one thing that can be named to keep back civilization, virtue, everything on which human happiness on the largest scale depends; we feel that the violation, for a present advantage, of a rule of such transcendant expediency, is not expedient, and that he who, for the sake of a convenience to himself or to some other individual, does what depends on him to deprive mankind of the good, and inflict upon them the evil, involved in the greater or less reliance which they can place in each other's word, acts the part of one of their worst enemies. Yet that even this rule, sacred as it is, admits of possible exceptions, is acknowledged by all moralists; the chief of which is when the withholding of some fact (as of information from a malefactor, or of bad news from a person dangerously ill) would preserve some one (especially a person other than oneself) from great and unmerited evil, and when the withholding can only be effected by denial. But in order that the exception may not extend itself beyond the need, and may have the least possible effect in weakening reliance on veracity, it ought to be recognised, and, if possible, its limits defined; and if the principle of utility is good for anything, it must be good for weighing these conflicting utilities against one another, and marking out the region within which one or the other preponderates.

Again, defenders of utility often find themselves called upon to reply to such objections as this—that there is not time, previous to action, for calculating and weighing the effects of any line of conduct on the general happiness. This is exactly as if any one were to say that it is impossible to guide our conduct by Christianity, because there is not time, on every occasion on which anything has to be done, to read through the Old and New Testaments. The answer to the objection is, that there has been ample time, namely, the whole past duration of the human species. During all that time mankind have been learning by experience the tendencies of actions; on which experience all the prudence, as well as all the morality of life, is dependent. People talk as if the commencement of this course of experience had hitherto been put off, and as if, at the moment when some man feels tempted to meddle with the property or life of another, he had to begin considering for the first time whether murder and theft are injurious to human happiness. Even then I do not think that he would find the question very puzzling; but, at all events, the matter is now done to his hand. It is truly a whimsical supposition that if mankind were agreed in considering utility to be the test of morality, they would remain without any agreement as to what is useful, and would take no measures for having their notions on the subject taught to the young, and enforced by law and opinion. There is no difficulty in proving any ethical standard whatever to work ill, if we suppose universal idiocy to be conjoined with it; but on any hypothesis short of that, mankind must by this time have acquired positive beliefs as to the effects of some actions on their happiness; and the beliefs which have thus come down are the rules of morality for the multitude, and for the philosopher until he has succeeded in finding better. That philosophers might easily do this, even now, on many subjects; that the received code of ethics is by no means of divine right; and that mankind have still much to learn as to the effects of actions on the general happiness, I admit, or rather, earnestly maintain. The corollaries from the principle of utility, like the precepts of every practical art, admit of indefinite improvement, and, in a progressive state of the human mind, their improvement is perpetually going on. But to consider the rules of morality as improvable, is one thing; to pass over the intermediate generalizations entirely, and endeavour to test each individual action directly by the first principle, is another. It is a strange notion that the acknowledgment of a first principle is inconsistent with the admission of secondary ones. To inform a traveller respecting the place of his ultimate destination, is not to forbid the use of landmarks and direction-posts on the way. The proposition that happiness is the end and aim of morality, does not mean that no road ought to be laid down to that goal, or that persons going thither should not be advised to take one direction rather than another. Men really ought to leave off talking a kind of nonsense on this subject, which they would neither talk nor listen to on other matters of practical concernment. Nobody argues that the art of navigation is not founded on astronomy, because sailors cannot wait to calculate the Nautical Almanack. Being rational creatures, they go to sea with it ready calculated; and all rational creatures go out upon the sea of life with their minds made up on the common questions of right and wrong, as well as on many of the far more difficult questions of wise and foolish. And this, as long as foresight is a human quality, it is to be presumed they will continue to do. Whatever we adopt as the fundamental principle of morality, we require subordinate principles to apply it by: the impossibility of doing without them, being common to all systems, can afford no argument against any one in particular: but gravely to argue as if no such secondary principles could be had, and as if mankind had remained till now, and always must remain, without drawing any general conclusions from the experience of human life, is as high a pitch, I think, as absurdity has ever reached in philosophical controversy.

The remainder of the stock arguments against utilitarianism mostly consist in laying to its charge the common infirmities of human nature, and the general difficulties which embarrass conscientious persons in shaping their course through life. We are told that an utilitarian will be apt to make his own particular case an exception to moral rules, and, when under temptation, will see an utility in the breach of a rule, greater than he will see in its observance. But is utility the only creed which is able to furnish us with excuses for evil doing, and means of cheating our own conscience? They are afforded in abundance by all doctrines which recognise as a fact in morals the existence of conflicting considerations; which all doctrines do, that have been believed by sane persons. It is not the fault of any creed, but of the complicated nature of human affairs, that rules of conduct cannot be so framed as to require no exceptions, and that hardly any kind of action can safely be laid down as either always obligatory or always condemnable. There is no ethical creed which does not temper the rigidity of its laws, by giving a certain latitude, under the moral responsibility of the agent, for accommodation to peculiarities of circumstances; and under every creed, at the opening thus made, self-deception and dishonest casuistry get in. There exists no moral system under which there do not arise unequivocal cases of conflicting obligation. These are the real difficulties, the knotty points both in the theory of ethics, and in the conscientious guidance of personal conduct. They are overcome practically with greater or with less success according to the intellect and virtue of the individual; but it can hardly be pretended that any one will be the less qualified for dealing with them, from possessing an ultimate standard to which conflicting rights and duties can be referred. If utility is the ultimate source of moral obligations, utility may be invoked to decide between them when their demands are incompatible. Though the application of the standard may be difficult, it is better than none at all: while in other systems, the moral laws all claiming independent authority, there is no common umpire entitled to interfere between them; their claims to precedence one over another rest on little better than sophistry, and unless determined, as they generally are, by the unacknowledged influence of considerations of utility, afford a free scope for the action of personal desires and partialities. We must remember that only in these cases of conflict between secondary principles is it requisite that first principles should be appealed to. There is no case of moral obligation in which some secondary principle is not involved; and if only one, there can seldom be any real doubt which one it is, in the mind of any person by whom the principle itself is recognised.

CHAPTER III
Of the Ultimate Sanction of the Principle of Utility

The question is often asked, and properly so, in regard to any supposed moral standard—What is its sanction? what are the motives to obey it? or more specifically, what is the source of its obligation? whence does it derive its binding force? It is a necessary part of moral philosophy to provide the answer to this question; which, though frequently assuming the shape of an objection to the utilitarian morality, as if it had some special applicability to that above others, really arises in regard to all standards. It arises, in fact, whenever a person is called on to *adopt* a standard, or refer morality to any basis on which he has not been accustomed to rest it. For the customary morality, that which education and opinion have consecrated, is the only one which presents itself to the mind with the feeling of being *in itself* obligatory; and when a person is asked to believe that this morality *derives* its obligation from some general principle round which custom has not thrown the same halo, the assertion is to him a paradox; the supposed corollaries seem to have a more binding force than the original theorem; the superstructure seems to stand better without, than with, what is represented as its foundation. He says to himself, I feel that I am bound not to rob or murder, betray or deceive; but why am I bound to promote the general happiness? If my own happiness lies in something else, why may I not give that the preference?

If the view adopted by the utilitarian philosophy of the nature of the moral sense be correct, this difficulty will always present itself, until the influences which form moral character have taken the same hold of the principle which they have taken of some of the consequences—until, by the improvement of education, the feeling of unity with our fellow creatures shall be (what it cannot be doubted that Christ intended it to be) as deeply rooted in our character, and to our own consciousness as completely a part of our nature, as the horror of crime is in an ordinarily well-brought up young person. In the mean time, however, the difficulty has no peculiar application to the doctrine of utility, but is inherent in every attempt to analyse morality and reduce it to principles; which, unless the principle is already in men's minds invested with as much sacredness as any of its applications, always seems to divest them of a part of their sanctity.

The principle of utility either has, or there is no reason why it might not have, all the sanctions which belong to any other system of morals. Those sanctions are either external or internal. Of the external sanctions it is not necessary to speak at any length. They are, the hope of favour and the fear of displeasure from our fellow creatures or from the Ruler of the Universe, along with whatever we may have of sympathy or affection for them, or of love and awe of Him, inclining us to do his will independently of selfish consequences. There is evidently no reason why all these motives for observance should not attach themselves to the utilitarian morality, as completely and as powerfully as to any other. Indeed, those of them which refer to our fellow creatures are sure to do so, in proportion to the amount of general intelligence; for whether there be any other ground of moral obligation than the general happiness or not, men do desire happiness; and however imperfect may be their own practice, they desire and commend all conduct in others towards themselves, by which they think their happiness is promoted. With regard to the religious motive, if men believe, as most profess to do, in the goodness of God, those who think that conduciveness to the general happiness is the essence, or even only the criterion, of good, must necessarily believe that it is also that which God approves. The whole force therefore of external reward and punishment, whether physical or moral, and whether proceeding from God or from our fellow men, together with all that the capacities of human nature admit, of disinterested devotion to either, become available to enforce the utilitarian morality, in proportion as that morality is recognised; and the more powerfully, the more the appliances of education and general cultivation are bent to the purpose.

So far as to external sanctions. The internal sanction of duty, whatever our standard of duty may be, is one and the same—a feeling in our own mind; a pain, more or less intense, attendant on violation of duty, which in properly-cultivated moral natures rises, in the more serious cases, into shrinking from it as an impossibility. This feeling, when disinterested, and connecting itself with the pure idea of duty, and not with some particular form of it, or with any of the merely accessory circumstances, is the essence of Conscience; though in that complex phenomenon as it actually exists, the simple fact is in general all encrusted over with collateral associations, derived from sympathy, from love, and still more from fear; from all the forms of religious feeling; from the recollections of childhood and of all our past life; from self-esteem, desire of the esteem of others, and occasionally even self-abasement. This extreme complication is, I apprehend, the origin of the sort of mystical character which, by a tendency of the human mind of which there are many other examples, is apt to be attributed to the idea of moral obligation, and which leads people to believe that the idea cannot possibly attach itself to any other objects than those which, by a supposed mysterious law, are found in our present experience to excite it. Its binding force, however, consists in the existence of a mass of feeling which must be broken through in order to do what violates our standard of right, and which, if we do nevertheless violate that standard, will probably have to be encountered afterwards in the form of remorse. Whatever theory we have of the nature or origin of conscience, this is what essentially constitutes it.

The ultimate sanction, therefore, of all morality (external motives apart) being a subjective feeling in our own minds, I see nothing embarrassing to those whose standard is utility, in the question, what is the sanction of that particular standard? We may answer, the same as of all other moral standards—the conscientious feelings of mankind. Undoubtedly this sanction has no binding efficacy on those who do not possess the feelings it appeals to; but neither will these persons be more obedient to any other moral principle than to the utilitarian one. On them morality of any kind has no hold but through the external sanctions. Meanwhile the feelings exist, a fact in human nature, the reality of which, and the great power with which they are capable of acting on those in whom they have been duly cultivated, are proved by experience. No reason has ever been shown why they may not be cultivated to as great intensity in connexion with the utilitarian, as with any other rule of morals.

There is, I am aware, a disposition to believe that a person who sees in moral obligation a transcendental fact, an objective reality belonging to the province of 'Things in themselves,' is likely to be more obedient to it than one who believes it to be entirely subjective, having its seat in human consciousness only. But whatever a person's opinion may be on this point of Ontology, the force he is really urged by is his own subjective feeling, and is exactly measured by its strength. No one's belief that Duty is an objective reality is stronger than the belief that God is so; yet the belief in God, apart from the expectation of actual reward and punishment, only operates on conduct through, and in proportion to, the subjective religious feeling. The sanction, so far as it is disinterested, is always in the mind itself; and the notion therefore of the transcendental moralists must be, that this sanction will not exist *in* the mind unless it is believed to have its root out of the mind; and that if a person is able to say to himself, This which is restraining me, and which is called my conscience, is only a feeling in my own mind, he may possibly draw the conclusion that when the feeling ceases the obligation ceases, and that if he find the feeling inconvenient, he may disregard it, and endeavour to get rid of it. But is this danger confined to the utilitarian morality? Does the belief that moral obligation has its seat outside the mind make the feeling of it too strong to be got rid of? The fact is so far otherwise, that all moralists admit and lament the ease with which, in the generality of minds, conscience can be silenced or stifled. The question, Need I obey my conscience? is quite as often put to themselves by persons who never heard of the principle of utility, as by its adherents. Those whose conscientious feelings are so weak as to allow of their asking this question, if they answer it affirmatively, will not do so because they believe in the transcendental theory, but because of the external sanctions.

It is not necessary, for the present purpose, to decide whether the feeling of duty is innate or implanted. Assuming it to be innate, it is an open question to what objects it naturally attaches itself; for the philosophic supporters of that theory are now agreed that the intuitive perception is of principles of morality, and not of the details. If there be anything innate in the matter, I see no reason why the feeling which is innate should not be that of regard to the pleasures and pains of others. If there is any principle of morals which is intuitively obligatory, I should say it must be that. If so, the intuitive ethics would coincide with the utilitarian, and there would be no further quarrel between them. Even as it is, the intuitive moralists, though they believe that there are other intuitive moral obligations, do already believe this to be one; for they unanimously hold that a large *portion* of morality turns upon the consideration due to the interests of our fellow creatures. Therefore, if the belief in the transcendental origin of moral obligation gives any additional efficacy to the internal sanction, it appears to me that the utilitarian principle has already the benefit of it.

On the other hand, if, as is my own belief, the moral feelings are not innate, but acquired, they are not for that reason the less natural. It is natural to man to speak, to reason, to build cities, to cultivate the ground, though these are acquired faculties. The moral feelings are not indeed a part of our nature, in the sense of being in any perceptible degree present in all of us; but this, unhappily, is a fact admitted by those who believe the most strenuously in their transcendental origin. Like the other acquired capacities above referred to, the moral faculty, if not a part of our nature, is a natural outgrowth from it; capable, like them, in a certain small degree, of springing up spontaneously; and susceptible of being brought by cultivation to a high degree of development. Unhappily it is also susceptible, by a sufficient use of the external sanctions and of the force of early impressions, of being cultivated in almost any direction: so that there is hardly anything so absurd or so mischievous that it may not, by means of these influences, be made to act on the human mind with all the authority of conscience. To doubt that the same potency might be given by the same means to the principle of utility, even if it had no foundation in human nature, would be flying in the face of all experience.

But moral associations which are wholly of artificial creation, when intellectual culture goes on, yield by degrees to the dissolving force of analysis: and if the feeling of duty, when associated with utility, would appear equally arbitrary; if there were no leading department of our nature, no powerful class of sentiments, with which that association would harmonize, which would make us feel it congenial, and incline us not only to foster it in others (for which we have abundant interested motives), but also to cherish it in ourselves; if there were not, in short, a natural basis of sentiment for utilitarian morality, it might well happen that this association also, even after it had been implanted by education, might be analysed away.

But there *is* this basis of powerful natural sentiment; and this it is which, when once the general happiness is recognised as the ethical standard, will constitute the strength of the utilitarian morality. This firm foundation is that of the social feelings of mankind; the desire to be in unity with our fellow creatures, which is already a powerful principle in human nature, and happily one of those which tend to become stronger, even without express inculcation, from the influences of advancing civilization. The social state is at once so natural, so necessary, and so habitual to man, that, except in some unusual circumstances or by an effort of voluntary abstraction, he never conceives himself otherwise than as a member of a body; and this association is riveted more and more, as mankind are further removed from the state of savage independence. Any condition, therefore, which is essential to a state of society, becomes more and more an inseparable part of every person's conception of the state of things which he is born into, and which is the destiny of a human being. Now, society between human beings, except in the relation of master and slave, is manifestly impossible on any other footing than that the interests of all are to be consulted. Society between equals can only exist on the understanding that the interests of all are to be regarded equally. And since in all states of civilization, every person, except an absolute monarch, has equals, every one is obliged to live on these terms with somebody; and in every age some advance is made towards a state in which it will be impossible to live permanently on other terms with anybody. In this way people grow up unable to conceive as possible to them a state of total disregard of other people's interests. They are under a necessity of conceiving themselves as at least abstaining from all the grosser injuries, and (if only for their own protection) living in a state of constant protest against them. They are also familiar with the fact of co-operating with others, and proposing to themselves a collective, not an individual, interest, as the aim (at least for the time being) of their actions. So long as they are co-operating, their ends are identified with those of others; there is at least a temporary feeling that the interests of others are their own interests. Not only does all strengthening of social ties, and all healthy growth of society, give to each individual a stronger personal interest in practically consulting the welfare of others; it also leads him to identify his *feelings* more and more with their good, or at least with an ever greater degree of practical consideration for it. He comes, as though instinctively, to be conscious of himself as a being who *of course* pays regard to others. The good of others becomes to him a thing naturally and necessarily to be attended to, like any of the physical conditions of our existence. Now, whatever amount of this feeling a person has, he is urged by the strongest motives both of interest and of sympathy to demonstrate it, and to the utmost of his power encourage it in others; and even if he has none of it himself, he is as greatly interested as any one else that others should have it. Consequently the smallest germs of the feeling are laid hold of and nourished by the contagion of sympathy and the influences of education; and a complete web of corroborative association is woven round it, by the powerful agency of the external sanctions. This mode of conceiving ourselves and human life, as civilization goes on, is felt to be more and more natural. Every step in political improvement renders it more so, by removing the sources of opposition of interest, and levelling those inequalities of legal privilege between individuals or classes, owing to which there are large portions of mankind whose happiness it is still practicable to disregard. In an improving state of the human mind, the influences are constantly on the increase, which tend to generate in each individual a feeling of unity with all the rest; which feeling, if perfect, would make him never think of, or desire, any beneficial condition for himself, in the benefits of which they are not included. If we now suppose this feeling of unity to be taught as a religion, and the whole force of education, of institutions, and of opinion, directed, as it once was in the case of religion, to make every person grow up from infancy surrounded on all sides both by the profession and by the practice of it, I think that no one, who can realize this conception, will feel any misgiving about the sufficiency of the ultimate sanction for the Happiness morality. To any ethical student who finds the realization difficult, I recommend, as a means of facilitating it, the second of M. Comte's two principal works, the *Système de Politique Positive*. I entertain the strongest objections to the system of politics and morals set forth in that treatise; but I think it has superabundantly shown the possibility of giving to the service of humanity, even without the aid of belief in a Providence, both the psychical power and the social efficacy of a religion; making it take hold of human life, and colour all thought, feeling, and action, in a manner of which the greatest ascendancy ever exercised by any religion may be but a type and foretaste; and of which the danger is, not that it should be insufficient, but that it should be so excessive as to interfere unduly with human freedom and individuality.

Neither is it necessary to the feeling which constitutes the binding force of the utilitarian morality on those who recognise it, to wait for those social influences which would make its obligation felt by mankind at large. In the comparatively early state of human advancement in which we now live, a person cannot indeed feel that entireness of sympathy with all others, which would make any real discordance in the general direction of their conduct in life impossible; but already a person in whom the social feeling is at all developed, cannot bring himself to think of the rest of his fellow creatures as struggling rivals with him for the means of happiness, whom he must desire to see defeated in their object in order that he may succeed in his. The deeply-rooted conception which every individual even now has of himself as a social being, tends to make him feel it one of his natural wants that there should be harmony between his feelings and aims and those of his fellow creatures. If differences of opinion and of mental culture make it impossible for him to share many of their actual feelings—perhaps make him denounce and defy those feelings—he still needs to be conscious that his real aim and theirs do not conflict; that he is not opposing himself to what they really wish for, namely, their own good, but is, on the contrary, promoting it. This feeling in most individuals is much inferior in strength to their selfish feelings, and is often wanting altogether. But to those who have it, it possesses all the characters of a natural feeling. It does not present itself to their minds as a superstition of education, or a law despotically imposed by the power of society, but as an attribute which it would not be well for them to be without. This conviction is the ultimate sanction of the greatest happiness morality. This it is which makes any mind, of well-developed feelings, work with, and not against, the outward motives to care for others, afforded by what I have called the external sanctions; and when those sanctions are wanting, or act in an opposite direction, constitutes in itself a powerful internal binding force, in proportion to the sensitiveness and thoughtfulness of the character; since few but those whose mind is a moral blank, could bear to lay out their course of life on the plan of paying no regard to others except so far as their own private interest compels.

CHAPTER IV
Of What Sort of Proof the Principle of Utility Is Susceptible

It has already been remarked, that questions of ultimate ends do not admit of proof, in the ordinary acceptation of the term. To be incapable of proof by reasoning is common to all first principles; to the first premises of our knowledge, as well as to those of our conduct. But the former, being matters of fact, may be the subject of a direct appeal to the faculties which judge of fact—namely, our senses, and our internal consciousness. Can an appeal be made to the same faculties on questions of practical ends? Or by what other faculty is cognizance taken of them?

Questions about ends are, in other words, questions what things are desirable. The utilitarian doctrine is, that happiness is desirable, and the only thing desirable, as an end; all other things being only desirable as means to that end. What ought to be required of this doctrine—what conditions is it requisite that the doctrine should fulfil—to make good its claim to be believed?

The only proof capable of being given that an object is visible, is that people actually see it. The only proof that a sound is audible, is that people hear it: and so of the other sources of our experience. In like manner, I apprehend, the sole evidence it is possible to produce that anything is desirable, is that people do actually desire it. If the end which the utilitarian doctrine proposes to itself were not, in theory and in practice, acknowledged to be an end, nothing could ever convince any person that it was so. No reason can be given why the general happiness is desirable, except that each person, so far as he believes it to be attainable, desires his own happiness. This, however, being a fact, we have not only all the proof which the case admits of, but all which it is possible to require, that happiness is a good: that each person's happiness is a good to that person, and the general happiness, therefore, a good to the aggregate of all persons. Happiness has made out its title as *one* of the ends of conduct, and consequently one of the criteria of morality.

But it has not, by this alone, proved itself to be the sole criterion. To do that, it would seem, by the same rule, necessary to show, not only that people desire happiness, but that they never desire anything else. Now it is palpable that they do desire things which, in common language, are decidedly distinguished from happiness. They desire, for example, virtue, and the absence of vice, no less really than pleasure and the absence of pain. The desire of virtue is not as universal, but it is as authentic a fact, as the desire of happiness. And hence the opponents of the utilitarian standard deem that they have a right to infer that there are other ends of human action besides happiness, and that happiness is not the standard of approbation and disapprobation.

But does the utilitarian doctrine deny that people desire virtue, or maintain that virtue is not a thing to be desired? The very reverse. It maintains not only that virtue is to be desired, but that it is to be desired disinterestedly, for itself. Whatever may be the opinion of utilitarian moralists as to the original conditions by which virtue is made virtue; however they may believe (as they do) that actions and dispositions are only virtuous because they promote another end than virtue; yet this being granted, and it having been decided, from considerations of this description, what is virtuous, they not only place virtue at the very head of the things which are good as means to the ultimate end, but they also recognise as a psychological fact the possibility of its being, to the individual, a good in itself, without looking to any end beyond it; and hold, that the mind is not in a right state, not in a state conformable to Utility, not in the state most conducive to the general happiness, unless it does love virtue in this manner—as a thing desirable in itself, even although, in the individual instance, it should not produce those other desirable consequences which it tends to produce, and on account of which it is held to be virtue. This opinion is not, in the smallest degree, a departure from the Happiness principle. The ingredients of happiness are very various, and each of them is desirable in itself, and not merely when considered as swelling an aggregate. The principle of utility does not mean that any given pleasure, as music, for instance, or any given exemption from pain, as for example health, are to be looked upon as means to a collective something termed happiness, and to be desired on that account. They are desired and desirable in and for themselves; besides being means, they are a part of the end. Virtue, according to the utilitarian doctrine, is not naturally and originally part of the end, but it is capable of becoming so; and in those who love it disinterestedly it has become so, and is desired and cherished, not as a means to happiness, but as a part of their happiness.

To illustrate this farther, we may remember that virtue is not the only thing, originally a means, and which if it were not a means to anything else, would be and remain indifferent, but which by association with what it is a means to, comes to be desired for itself, and that too with the utmost intensity. What, for example, shall we say of the love of money? There is nothing originally more desirable about money than about any heap of glittering pebbles. Its worth is solely that of the things which it will buy; the desires for other things than itself, which it is a means of gratifying. Yet the love of money is not only one of the strongest moving forces of human life, but money is, in many cases, desired in and for itself; the desire to possess it is often stronger than the desire to use it, and goes on increasing when all the desires which point to ends beyond it, to be compassed by it, are falling off. It may be then said truly, that money is desired not for the sake of an end, but as part of the end. From being a means to happiness, it has come to be itself a principal ingredient of the individual's conception of happiness. The same may be said of the majority of the great objects of human life—power, for example, or fame; except that to each of these there is a certain amount of immediate pleasure annexed, which has at least the semblance of being naturally inherent in them; a thing which cannot be said of money. Still, however, the strongest natural attraction, both of power and of fame, is the immense aid they give to the attainment of our other wishes; and it is the strong association thus generated between them and all our objects of desire, which gives to the direct desire of them the intensity it often assumes, so as in some characters to surpass in strength all other desires. In these cases the means have become a part of the end, and a more important part of it than any of the things which they are means to. What was once desired as an instrument for the attainment of happiness, has come to be desired for its own sake. In being desired for its own sake it is, however, desired as *part* of happiness. The person is made, or thinks he would be made, happy by its mere possession; and is made unhappy by failure to obtain it. The desire of it is not a different thing from the desire of happiness, any more than the love of music, or the desire of health. They are included in happiness. They are some of the elements of which the desire of happiness is made up. Happiness is not an abstract idea, but a concrete whole; and these are some of its parts. And the utilitarian standard sanctions and approves their being so. Life would be a poor thing, very ill provided with sources of happiness, if there were not this provision of nature, by which things originally indifferent, but conducive to, or otherwise associated with, the satisfaction of our primitive desires, become in themselves sources of pleasure more valuable than the primitive pleasures, both in permanency, in the space of human existence that they are capable of covering, and even in intensity.

Virtue, according to the utilitarian conception, is a good of this description. There was no original desire of it, or motive to it, save its conduciveness to pleasure, and especially to protection from pain. But through the association thus formed, it may be felt a good in itself, and desired as such with as great intensity as any other good; and with this difference between it and the love of money, of power, or of fame, that all of these may, and often do, render the individual noxious to the other members of the society to which he belongs, whereas there is nothing which makes him so much a blessing to them as the cultivation of the disinterested love of virtue. And consequently, the utilitarian standard, while it tolerates and approves those other acquired desires, up to the point beyond which they would be more injurious to the general happiness than promotive of it, enjoins and requires the cultivation of the love of virtue up to the greatest strength possible, as being above all things important to the general happiness.

It results from the preceding considerations, that there is in reality nothing desired except happiness. Whatever is desired otherwise than as a means to some end beyond itself, and ultimately to happiness, is desired as itself a part of happiness, and is not desired for itself until it has become so. Those who desire virtue for its own sake, desire it either because the consciousness of it is a pleasure, or because the consciousness of being without it is a pain, or for both reasons united; as in truth the pleasure and pain seldom exist separately, but almost always together, the same person feeling pleasure in the degree of virtue attained, and pain in not having attained more. If one of these gave him no pleasure, and the other no pain, he would not love or desire virtue, or would desire it only for the other benefits which it might produce to himself or to persons whom he cared for.

We have now, then, an answer to the question, of what sort of proof the principle of utility is susceptible. If the opinion which I have now stated is psychologically true—if human nature is so constituted as to desire nothing which is not either a part of happiness or a means of happiness, we can have no other proof, and we require no other, that these are the only things desirable. If so, happiness is the sole end of human action, and the promotion of it the test by which to judge of all human conduct; from whence it necessarily follows that it must be the criterion of morality, since a part is included in the whole.

And now to decide whether this is really so; whether mankind do desire nothing for itself but that which is a pleasure to them, or of which the absence is a pain; we have evidently arrived at a question of fact and experience, dependent, like all similar questions, upon evidence. It can only be determined by practised self-consciousness and self-observation, assisted by observation of others. I believe that these sources of evidence, impartially consulted, will declare that desiring a thing and finding it pleasant, aversion to it and thinking of it as painful, are phenomena entirely inseparable, or rather two parts of the same phenomenon; in strictness of language, two different modes of naming the same psychological fact: that to think of an object as desirable (unless for the sake of its consequences), and to think of it as pleasant, are one and the same thing; and that to desire anything, except in proportion as the idea of it is pleasant, is a physical and metaphysical impossibility.

So obvious does this appear to me, that I expect it will hardly be disputed: and the objection made will be, not that desire can possibly be directed to anything ultimately except pleasure and exemption from pain, but that the will is a different thing from desire; that a person of confirmed virtue, or any other person whose purposes are fixed, carries out his purposes without any thought of the pleasure he has in contemplating them, or expects to derive from their fulfilment; and persists in acting on them, even though these pleasures are much diminished, by changes in his character or decay of his passive sensibilities, or are outweighed by the pains which the pursuit of the purposes may bring upon him. All this I fully admit, and have stated it elsewhere, as positively and emphatically as any one. Will, the active phenomenon, is a different thing from desire, the state of passive sensibility, and though originally an offshoot from it, may in time take root and detach itself from the parent stock; so much so, that in the case of an habitual purpose, instead of willing the thing because we desire it, we often desire it only because we will it. This, however, is but an instance of that familiar fact, the power of habit, and is nowise confined to the case of virtuous actions. Many indifferent things, which men originally did from a motive of some sort, they continue to do from habit. Sometimes this is done unconsciously, the consciousness coming only after the action: at other times with conscious volition, but volition which has become habitual, and is put into operation by the force of habit, in opposition perhaps to the deliberate preference, as often happens with those who have contracted habits of vicious or hurtful indulgence. Third and last comes the case in which the habitual act of will in the individual instance is not in contradiction to the general intention prevailing at other times, but in fulfilment of it; as in the case of the person of confirmed virtue, and of all who pursue deliberately and consistently any determinate end. The distinction between will and desire thus understood, is an authentic and highly important psychological fact; but the fact consists solely in this—that will, like all other parts of our constitution, is amenable to habit, and that we may will from habit what we no longer desire for itself, or desire only because we will it. It is not the less true that will, in the beginning, is entirely produced by desire; including in that term the repelling influence of pain as well as the attractive one of pleasure. Let us take into consideration, no longer the person who has a confirmed will to do right, but him in whom that virtuous will is still feeble, conquerable by temptation, and not to be fully relied on; by what means can it be strengthened? How can the will to be virtuous, where it does not exist in sufficient force, be implanted or awakened? Only by making the person *desire* virtue—by making him think of it in a pleasurable light, or of its absence in a painful one. It is by associating the doing right with pleasure, or the doing wrong with pain, or by eliciting and impressing and bringing home to the person's experience the pleasure naturally involved in the one or the pain in the other, that it is possible to call forth that will to be virtuous, which, when confirmed, acts without any thought of either pleasure or pain. Will is the child of desire, and passes out of the dominion of its parent only to come under that of habit. That which is the result of habit affords no presumption of being intrinsically good; and there would be no reason for wishing that the purpose of virtue should become independent of pleasure and pain, were it not that the influence of the pleasurable and painful associations which prompt to virtue is not sufficiently to be depended on for unerring constancy of action until it has acquired the support of habit. Both in feeling and in conduct, habit is the only thing which imparts certainty; and it is because of the importance to others of being able to rely absolutely on one's feelings and conduct, and to oneself of being able to rely on one's own, that the will to do right ought to be cultivated into this habitual independence. In other words, this state of the will is a means to good, not intrinsically a good; and does not contradict the doctrine that nothing is a good to human beings but in so far as it is either itself pleasurable, or a means of attaining pleasure or averting pain.

But if this doctrine be true, the principle of utility is proved. Whether it is so or not, must now be left to the consideration of the thoughtful reader.

CHAPTER V
On the Connexion between Justice and Utility

In all ages of speculation, one of the strongest obstacles to the reception of the doctrine that Utility or Happiness is the criterion of right and wrong, has been drawn from the idea of Justice. The powerful sentiment, and apparently clear perception, which that word recalls with a rapidity and certainty resembling an instinct, have seemed to the majority of thinkers to point to an inherent quality in things; to show that the Just must have an existence in Nature as something absolute, generically distinct from every variety of the Expedient, and, in idea, opposed to it, though (as is commonly acknowledged) never, in the long run, disjoined from it in fact.

In the case of this, as of our other moral sentiments, there is no necessary connexion between the question of its origin, and that of its binding force. That a feeling is bestowed on us by Nature, does not necessarily legitimate all its promptings. The feeling of justice might be a peculiar instinct, and might yet require, like our other instincts, to be controlled and enlightened by a higher reason. If we have intellectual instincts, leading us to judge in a particular way, as well as animal instincts that prompt us to act in a particular way, there is no necessity that the former should be more infallible in their sphere than the latter in theirs: it may as well happen that wrong judgments are occasionally suggested by those, as wrong actions by these. But though it is one thing to believe that we have natural feelings of justice, and another to acknowledge them as an ultimate criterion of conduct, these two opinions are very closely connected in point of fact. Mankind are always predisposed to believe that any subjective feeling, not otherwise accounted for, is a revelation of some objective reality. Our present object is to determine whether the reality, to which the feeling of justice corresponds, is one which needs any such special revelation; whether the justice or injustice of an action is a thing intrinsically peculiar, and distinct from all its other qualities, or only a combination of certain of those qualities, presented under a peculiar aspect. For the purpose of this inquiry, it is practically important to consider whether the feeling itself, of justice and injustice, is *sui generis* like our sensations of colour and taste, or a derivative feeling, formed by a combination of others. And this it is the more essential to examine, as people are in general willing enough to allow, that objectively the dictates of justice coincide with a part of the field of General Expediency; but inasmuch as the subjective mental feeling of Justice is different from that which commonly attaches to simple expediency, and, except in extreme cases of the latter, is far more imperative in its demands, people find it difficult to see, in Justice, only a particular kind or branch of general utility, and think that its superior binding force requires a totally different origin.

To throw light upon this question, it is necessary to attempt to ascertain what is the distinguishing character of justice, or of injustice: what is the quality, or whether there is any quality, attributed in common to all modes of conduct designated as unjust (for justice, like many other moral attributes, is best defined by its opposite), and distinguishing them from such modes of conduct as are disapproved, but without having that particular epithet of disapprobation applied to them. If in everything which men are accustomed to characterize as just or unjust, some one common attribute or collection of attributes is always present, we may judge whether this particular attribute or combination of attributes would be capable of gathering round it a sentiment of that peculiar character and intensity by virtue of the general laws of our emotional constitution, or whether the sentiment is inexplicable, and requires to be regarded as a special provision of Nature. If we find the former to be the case, we shall, in resolving this question, have resolved also the main problem: if the latter, we shall have to seek for some other mode of investigating it.

To find the common attributes of a variety of objects, it is necessary to begin by surveying the objects themselves in the concrete. Let us therefore advert successively to the various modes of action, and arrangements of human affairs, which are classed, by universal or widely spread opinion, as Just or as Unjust. The things well known to excite the sentiments associated with those names, are of a very multifarious character. I shall pass them rapidly in review, without studying any particular arrangement.

In the first place, it is mostly considered unjust to deprive any one of his personal liberty, his property, or any other thing which belongs to him by law. Here, therefore, is one instance of the application of the terms just and unjust in a perfectly definite sense, namely, that it is just to respect, unjust to violate, the *legal rights* of any one.

But this judgment admits of several exceptions, arising from the other forms in which the notions of justice and injustice present themselves. For example, the person who suffers the deprivation may (as the phrase is) have *forfeited* the rights which he is so deprived of: a case to which we shall return presently. But also,

Secondly; the legal rights of which he is deprived, may be rights which *ought* not to have belonged to him; in other words, the law which confers on him these rights, may be a bad law. When it is so, or when (which is the same thing for our purpose) it is supposed to be so, opinions will differ as to the justice or injustice of infringing it. Some maintain that no law, however bad, ought to be disobeyed by an individual citizen; that his opposition to it, if shown at all, should only be shown in endeavouring to get it altered by competent authority. This opinion (which condemns many of the most illustrious benefactors of mankind, and would often protect pernicious institutions against the only weapons which, in the state of things existing at the time, have any chance of succeeding against them) is defended, by those who hold it, on grounds of expediency; principally on that of the importance, to the common interest of mankind, of maintaining inviolate the sentiment of submission to law. Other persons, again, hold the directly contrary opinion, that any law, judged to be bad, may blamelessly be disobeyed, even though it be not judged to be unjust, but only inexpedient; while others would confine the licence of disobedience to the case of unjust laws: but again, some say, that all laws which are inexpedient are unjust; since every law imposes some restriction on the natural liberty of mankind, which restriction is an injustice, unless legitimated by tending to their good. Among these diversities of opinion, it seems to be universally admitted that there may be unjust laws, and that law, consequently, is not the ultimate criterion of justice, but may give to one person a benefit, or impose on another an evil, which justice condemns. When, however, a law is thought to be unjust, it seems always to be regarded as being so in the same way in which a breach of law is unjust, namely, by infringing somebody's right; which, as it cannot in this case be a legal right, receives a different appellation, and is called a moral right. We may say, therefore, that a second case of injustice consists in taking or withholding from any person that to which he has a *moral right*.

Thirdly, it is universally considered just that each person should obtain that (whether good or evil) which he *deserves;* and unjust that he should obtain a good, or be made to undergo an evil, which he does not deserve. This is, perhaps, the clearest and most emphatic form in which the idea of justice is conceived by the general mind. As it involves the notion of desert, the question arises, what constitutes desert? Speaking in a general way, a person is understood to deserve good if he does right, evil if he does wrong; and in a more particular sense, to deserve good from those to whom he does or has done good, and evil from those to whom he does or has done evil. The precept of returning good for evil has never been regarded as a case of the fulfilment of justice, but as one in which the claims of justice are waived, in obedience to other considerations.

Fourthly, it is confessedly unjust to *break faith* with any one: to violate an engagement, either express or implied, or disappoint expectations raised by our own conduct, at least if we have raised those expectations knowingly and voluntarily. Like the other obligations of justice already spoken of, this one is not regarded as absolute, but as capable of being overruled by a stronger obligation of justice on the other side; or by such conduct on the part of the person concerned as is deemed to absolve us from our obligation to him, and to constitute a *forfeiture* of the benefit which he has been led to expect.

Fifthly, it is, by universal admission, inconsistent with justice to be *partial;* to show favour or preference to one person over another, in matters to which favour and preference do not properly apply. Impartiality, however, does not seem to be regarded as a duty in itself, but rather as instrumental to some other duty; for it is admitted that favour and preference are not always censurable, and indeed the cases in which they are condemned are rather the exception than the rule. A person would be more likely to be blamed than applauded for giving his family or friends no superiority in good offices over strangers, when he could do so without violating any other duty; and no one thinks it unjust to seek one person in preference to another as a friend, connexion, or companion. Impartiality where rights are concerned is of course obligatory, but this is involved in the more general obligation of giving to every one his right. A tribunal, for example, must be impartial, because it is bound to award, without regard to any other consideration, a disputed object to the one of two parties who has the right to it. There are other cases in which impartiality means, being solely influenced by desert; as with those who, in the capacity of judges, preceptors, or parents, administer reward and punishment as such. There are cases, again, in which it means, being solely influenced by consideration for the public interest; as in making a selection among candidates for a government employment. Impartiality, in short, as an obligation of justice, may be said to mean, being exclusively influenced by the considerations which it is supposed ought to influence the particular case in hand; and resisting the solicitation of any motives which prompt to conduct different from what those considerations would dictate.

Nearly allied to the idea of impartiality, is that of *equality;* which often enters as a component part both into the conception of justice and into the practice of it, and, in the eyes of many persons, constitutes its essence. But in this, still more than in any other case, the notion of justice varies in different persons, and always conforms in its variations to their notion of utility. Each person maintains that equality is the dictate of justice, except where he thinks that expediency requires inequality. The justice of giving equal protection to the rights of all, is maintained by those who support the most outrageous inequality in the rights themselves. Even in slave countries it is theoretically admitted that the rights of the slave, such as they are, ought to be as sacred as those of the master; and that a tribunal which fails to enforce them with equal strictness is wanting in justice; while, at the same time, institutions which leave to the slave scarcely any rights to enforce, are not deemed unjust, because they are not deemed inexpedient. Those who think that utility requires distinctions of rank, do not consider it unjust that riches and social privileges should be unequally dispensed; but those who think this inequality inexpedient, think it unjust also. Whoever thinks that government is necessary, sees no injustice in as much inequality as is constituted by giving to the magistrate powers not granted to other people. Even among those who hold levelling doctrines, there are as many questions of justice as there are differences of opinion about expediency. Some Communists consider it unjust that the produce of the labour of the community should be shared on any other principle than that of exact equality; others think it just that those should receive most whose needs are greatest; while others hold that those who work harder, or who produce more, or whose services are more valuable to the community, may justly claim a larger quota in the division of the produce.

And the sense of natural justice may be plausibly appealed to in behalf of every one of these opinions.

Among so many diverse applications of the term Justice, which yet is not regarded as ambiguous, it is a matter of some difficulty to seize the mental link which holds them together, and on which the moral sentiment adhering to the term essentially depends. Perhaps, in this embarrassment, some help may be derived from the history of the word, as indicated by its etymology.

In most, if not in all, languages, the etymology of the word which corresponds to Just, points to an origin connected either with positive law, or with that which was in most cases the primitive form of law—authoritative custom. *Justum* is a form of *jussum,* that which has been ordered. *Jus* is of the same origin. *Dikaion* comes from *dike,* of which the principal meaning, at least in the historical ages of Greece, was a suit at law. Originally, indeed, it meant only the mode or *manner* of doing things, but it early came to mean the *prescribed* manner; that which the recognised authorities, patriarchal, judicial, or political, would enforce. *Recht,* from which came *right* and *righteous,* is synonymous with law. The original meaning indeed of *recht* did not point to law, but to physical straightness; as *wrong* and its Latin equivalents meant twisted or *tortuous;* and from this it is argued that right did not originally mean law, but on the contrary law meant right. But however this may be, the fact that *recht* and *droit* became restricted in their meaning to positive law, although much which is not required by law is equally necessary to moral straightness or rectitude, is as significant of the original character of moral ideas as if the derivation had been the reverse way. The courts of justice, the administration of justice, are the courts and the administration of law. *La justice,* in French, is the established term for judicature. There can, I think, be no doubt that the *idée mère,* the primitive element, in the formation of the notion of justice, was conformity to law. It constituted the entire idea among the Hebrews, up to the birth of Christianity; as might be expected in the case of a people whose laws attempted to embrace all subjects on which precepts were required, and who believed those laws to be a direct emanation from the Supreme Being. But other nations, and in particular the Greeks and Romans, who knew that their laws had been made originally, and still continued to be made, by men, were not afraid to admit that those men might make bad laws; might do, by law, the same things, and from the same motives, which, if done by individuals without the sanction of law, would be called unjust. And hence the sentiment of injustice came to be attached, not to all violations of law, but only to violations of such laws as *ought* to exist, including such as ought to exist but do not; and to laws themselves, if supposed to be contrary to what ought to be law. In this manner the idea of law and of its injunctions was still predominant in the notion of justice, even when the laws actually in force ceased to be accepted as the standard of it.

It is true that mankind consider the idea of justice and its obligations as applicable to many things which neither are, nor is it desired that they should be, regulated by law. Nobody desires that laws should interfere with the whole detail of private life; yet every one allows that in all daily conduct a person may and does show himself to be either just or unjust. But even here, the idea of the breach of what ought to be law, still lingers in a modified shape. It would always give us pleasure, and chime in with our feelings of fitness, that acts which we deem unjust should be punished, though we do not always think it expedient that this should be done by the tribunals. We forego that gratification on account of incidental inconveniences. We should be glad to see just conduct enforced and injustice repressed, even in the minutest details, if we were not, with reason, afraid of trusting the magistrate with so unlimited an amount of power over individuals. When we think that a person is bound in justice to do a thing, it is an ordinary form of language to say, that he ought to be compelled to do it. We should be gratified to see the obligation enforced by anybody who had the power. If we see that its enforcement by law would be inexpedient, we lament the impossibility, we consider the impunity given to injustice as an evil, and strive to make amends for it by bringing a strong expression of our own and the public disapprobation to bear upon the offender. Thus the idea of legal constraint is still the generating idea of the notion of justice, though undergoing several transformations before that notion, as it exists in an advanced state of society, becomes complete.

The above is, I think, a true account, as far as it goes, of the origin and progressive growth of the idea of justice. But we must observe, that it contains, as yet, nothing to distinguish that obligation from moral obligation in general. For the truth is, that the idea of penal sanction, which is the essence of law, enters not only into the conception of injustice, but into that of any kind of wrong. We do not call anything wrong, unless we mean to imply that a person ought to be punished in some way or other for doing it; if not by law, by the opinion of his fellow creatures; if not by opinion, by the reproaches of his own conscience. This seems the real turning point of the distinction between morality and simple expediency. It is a part of the notion of Duty in every one of its forms, that a person may rightfully be compelled to fulfil it. Duty is a thing which may be *exacted* from a person, as one exacts a debt. Unless we think that it might be exacted from him, we do not call it his duty. Reasons of prudence, or the interest of other people, may militate against actually exacting it; but the person himself, it is clearly understood, would not be entitled to complain. There are other things, on the contrary, which we wish that people should do, which we like or admire them for doing, perhaps dislike or despise them for not doing, but yet admit that they are not bound to do; it is not a case of moral obligation; we do not blame them, that is, we do not think that they are proper objects of punishment. How we come by these ideas of deserving and not deserving punishment, will appear, perhaps, in the sequel; but I think there is no doubt that this distinction lies at the bottom of the notions of right and wrong; that we call any conduct wrong, or employ, instead, some other term of dislike or disparagement, according as we think that the person ought, or ought not, to be punished for it; and we say that it would be right to do so and so, or merely that it would be desirable or laudable, according as we would wish to see the person whom it concerns, compelled, or only persuaded and exhorted, to act in that manner.[3]

This, therefore, being the characteristic difference which marks off, not justice, but morality in general, from the remaining provinces of Expediency and Worthiness; the character is still to be sought which distinguishes justice from other branches of morality. Now it is known that ethical writers divide moral duties into two classes, denoted by the ill-chosen expressions, duties of perfect and of imperfect obligation; the latter being those in which, though the act is obligatory, the particular occasions of performing it are left to our choice; as in the case of charity or benefi-

---

3. See this point enforced and illustrated by Professor Bain, in an admirable chapter (entitled "The Ethical Emotions, or the Moral Sense"), of the second of the two treatises composing his elaborate and profound work on the Mind.

cence, which we are indeed bound to practise, but not towards any definite person, nor at any prescribed time. In the more precise language of philosophic jurists, duties of perfect obligation are those duties in virtue of which a correlative *right* resides in some person or persons; duties of imperfect obligation are those moral obligations which do not give birth to any right. I think it will be found that this distinction exactly coincides with that which exists between justice and the other obligations of morality. In our survey of the various popular acceptations of justice, the term appeared generally to involve the idea of a personal right—a claim on the part of one or more individuals, like that which the law gives when it confers a proprietary or other legal right. Whether the injustice consists in depriving a person of a possession, or in breaking faith with him, or in treating him worse than he deserves, or worse than other people who have no greater claims, in each case the supposition implies two things—a wrong done, and some assignable person who is wronged. Injustice may also be done by treating a person better than others; but the wrong in this case is to his competitors, who are also assignable persons. It seems to me that this feature in the case—a right in some person, correlative to the moral obligation—constitutes the specific difference between justice, and generosity or beneficence. Justice implies something which it is not only right to do, and wrong not to do, but which some individual person can claim from us as his moral right. No one has a moral right to our generosity or beneficence, because we are not morally bound to practise those virtues towards any given individual. And it will be found with respect to this as with respect to every correct definition, that the instances which seem to conflict with it are those which most confirm it. For if a moralist attempts, as some have done, to make out that mankind generally, though not any given individual, have a right to all the good we can do them, he at once, by that thesis, includes generosity and beneficence within the category of justice. He is obliged to say, that our utmost exertions are *due* to our fellow creatures, thus assimilating them to a debt; or that nothing less can be a sufficient *return* for what society does for us, thus classing the case as one of gratitude; both of which are acknowledged cases of justice. Wherever there is a right, the case is one of justice, and not of the virtue of beneficence: and whoever does not place the distinction between justice and morality in general, where we have now placed it, will be found to make no distinction between them at all, but to merge all morality in justice.

Having thus endeavoured to determine the distinctive elements which enter into the composition of the idea of justice, we are ready to enter on the inquiry, whether the feeling, which accompanies the idea, is attached to it by a special dispensation of nature, or whether it could have grown up, by any known laws, out of the idea itself; and in particular, whether it can have originated in considerations of general expediency.

I conceive that the sentiment itself does not arise from anything which would commonly, or correctly, be termed an idea of expediency; but that though the sentiment does not, whatever is moral in it does.

We have seen that the two essential ingredients in the sentiment of justice are, the desire to punish a person who has done harm, and the knowledge or belief that there is some definite individual or individuals to whom harm has been done.

Now it appears to me, that the desire to punish a person who has done harm to some individual, is a spontaneous outgrowth from two sentiments, both in the highest degree natural, and which either are or resemble instincts; the impulse of self-defence, and the feeling of sympathy.

It is natural to resent, and to repel or retaliate, any harm done or attempted against ourselves, or against those with whom we sympathize. The origin of this sentiment it is not necessary here to discuss. Whether it be an instinct or a result of intelligence, it is, we know, common to all animal nature; for every animal tries to hurt those who have hurt, or who it thinks are about to hurt, itself or its young. Human beings, on this point, only differ from other animals in two particulars. First, in being capable of sympathizing, not solely with their offspring, or, like some of the more noble animals, with some superior animal who is kind to them, but with all human, and even with all sentient, beings. Secondly, in having a more developed intelligence, which gives a wider range to the whole of their sentiments, whether self-regarding or sympathetic. By virtue of his superior intelligence, even apart from his superior range of sympathy, a human being is capable of apprehending a community of interest between himself and the human society of which he forms a part, such that any conduct which threatens the security of the society generally, is threatening to his own, and calls forth his instinct (if instinct it be) of self-defence. The same superiority of intelligence, joined to the power of sympathizing with human beings generally, enables him to attach himself to the collective idea of his tribe, his country, or mankind, in such a manner that any act hurtful to them rouses his instinct of sympathy, and urges him to resistance.

The sentiment of justice, in that one of its elements which consists of the desire to punish, is thus, I conceive, the natural feeling of retaliation or vengeance, rendered by intellect and sympathy applicable to those injuries, that is, to those hurts, which wound us through, or in common with, society at large. This sentiment, in itself, has nothing moral in it; what is moral is, the exclusive subordination of it to the social sympathies, so as to wait on and obey their call. For the natural feeling tends to make us resent indiscriminately whatever any one does that is disagreeable to us; but when moralized by the social feeling, it only acts in the directions conformable to the general good: just persons resenting a hurt to society, though not otherwise a hurt to themselves, and not resenting a hurt to themselves, however painful, unless it be of the kind which society has a common interest with them in the repression of.

It is no objection against this doctrine to say, that when we feel our sentiment of justice outraged, we are not thinking of society at large, or of any collective interest, but only of the individual case. It is common enough certainly, though the reverse of commendable, to feel resentment merely because we have suffered pain; but a person whose resentment is really a moral feeling, that is, who considers whether an act is blameable before he allows himself to resent it—such a person, though he may not say expressly to himself that he is standing up for the interest of society, certainly does feel that he is asserting a rule which is for the benefit of others as well as for his own. If he is not feeling this—if he is regarding the act solely as it affects him individually—he is not consciously just; he is not concerning himself about the justice of his actions. This is admitted even by anti-utilitarian moralists. When Kant (as before remarked) propounds as the fundamental principle of morals, 'So act, that thy rule of conduct might be adopted as a law by all rational beings,' he virtually acknowledges that the interest of mankind collectively, or at least of mankind indiscriminately, must be in the mind of the agent when conscientiously deciding on the morality of the act. Otherwise he uses words without a meaning: for, that a rule even of utter selfishness could not *possibly* be adopted by all rational beings—that there is any insuperable obstacle in the nature of things to its adoption—cannot be even plausibly maintained. To give any meaning to Kant's principle, the sense put upon it must be, that we ought to shape our conduct by a rule which all rational beings might adopt *with benefit to their collective interest.*

To recapitulate: the idea of justice supposes two things; a rule of conduct, and a sentiment which sanctions the rule. The first must be supposed common to all mankind, and intended for their good. The other (the sentiment) is a desire that punishment may be suffered by those who infringe the rule. There is involved, in addition, the conception of some definite person who suffers by the infringement; whose rights (to use the expression appropriated to the case) are violated by it. And the sentiment of justice appears to me to be, the animal desire to repel or retaliate a hurt or damage to oneself, or to those with whom one sympathizes, widened so as to include all persons, by the human capacity of enlarged sympathy, and the human conception of intelligent self-interest. From the latter elements, the feeling derives its morality; from the former, its peculiar impressiveness, and energy of self-assertion.

I have, throughout, treated the idea of a *right* residing in the injured person, and violated by the injury, not as a separate element in the composition of the idea and sentiment, but as one of the forms in which the other two elements clothe themselves. These elements are, a hurt to some assignable person or persons on the one hand, and a demand for punishment on the other. An examination of our own minds, I think, will show, that these two things include all that we mean when we speak of violation of a right. When we call anything a person's right, we mean that he has a valid claim on society to protect him in the possession of it, either by the force of law, or by that of education and opinion. If he has what we consider a sufficient claim, on whatever account, to have something guaranteed to him by society, we say that he has a right to it. If we desire to prove that anything does not belong to him by right, we think this done as soon as it is admitted that society ought not to take measures for securing it to him, but should leave it to chance, or to his own exertions. Thus, a person is said to have a right to what he can earn in fair professional competition; because society ought not to allow any other person to hinder him from endeavouring to earn in that manner as much as he can. But he has not a right to three hundred a-year, though he may happen to be earning it; because society is not called on to provide that he shall earn that sum. On the contrary, if he owns ten thousand pounds three per cent stock, he *has* a right to three hundred a-year; because society has come under an obligation to provide him with an income of that amount.

To have a right, then, is, I conceive, to have something which society ought to defend me in the possession of. If the objector goes on to ask why it ought, I can give him no other reason than general utility. If that expression does not seem to convey a sufficient feeling of the strength of the obligation, nor to account for the peculiar energy of the feeling, it is because there goes to the composition of the sentiment, not a rational only but also an animal element, the thirst for retaliation; and this thirst derives its intensity, as well as its moral justification, from the extraordinarily important and impressive kind of utility which is concerned. The interest involved is that of security, to every one's feelings the most vital of all interests. Nearly all other earthly benefits are needed by one person, not needed by another; and many of them can, if necessary, be cheerfully foregone, or replaced by something else; but security no human being can possibly do without; on it we depend for all our immunity from evil, and for the whole value of all and every good, beyond the passing moment; since nothing but the gratification of the instant could be of any worth to us, if we could be deprived of everything the next instant by whoever was momentarily stronger than ourselves. Now this most indispensable of all necessaries, after physical nutriment, cannot be had, unless the machinery for providing it is kept unintermittedly in active play. Our notion, therefore, of the claim we have on our fellow creatures to join in making safe for us the very groundwork of our existence, gathers feelings round it so much more intense than those concerned in any of the more common cases of utility, that the difference in degree (as is often the case in psychology) becomes a real difference in kind. The claim assumes that character of absoluteness, that apparent infinity, and incommensurability with all other considerations, which constitute the distinction between the feeling of right and wrong and that of ordinary expediency and inexpediency. The feelings concerned are so powerful, and we count so positively on finding a responsive feeling in others (all being alike interested), that *ought* and *should* grow into *must,* and recognised indispensability becomes a moral necessity, analogous to physical, and often not inferior to it in binding force.

If the preceding analysis, or something resembling it, be not the correct account of the notion of justice; if justice be totally independent of utility, and be a standard *per se*, which the mind can recognise by simple introspection of itself; it is hard to understand why that internal oracle is so ambiguous, and why so many things appear either just or unjust, according to the light in which they are regarded.

We are continually informed that Utility is an uncertain standard, which every different person interprets differently, and that there is no safety but in the immutable, ineffaceable, and unmistakeable dictates of Justice, which carry their evidence in themselves, and are independent of the fluctuations of opinion. One would suppose from this that on questions of justice there could be no controversy; that if we take that for our rule, its application to any given case could leave us in as little doubt as a mathematical demonstration. So far is this from being the fact, that there is as much difference of opinion, and as fierce discussion, about what is just, as about what is useful to society. Not only have different nations and individuals different notions of justice, but in the mind of one and the same individual, justice is not some one rule, principle, or maxim, but many, which do not always coincide in their dictates, and in choosing between which, he is guided either by some extraneous standard, or by his own personal predilections.

For instance, there are some who say, that it is unjust to punish any one for the sake of example to others; that punishment is just, only when intended for the good of the sufferer himself. Others maintain the extreme reverse, contending that to punish persons who have attained years of discretion, for their own benefit, is despotism and injustice, since if the matter at issue is solely their own good, no one has a right to control their own judgment of it; but that they may justly be punished to prevent evil to others, this being an exercise of the legitimate right of self-defence. Mr. Owen, again, affirms that it is unjust to punish at all; for the criminal did not make his own character; his education, and the circumstances which surround him, have made him a criminal, and for these he is not responsible. All these opinions are extremely plausible; and so long as the question is argued as one of justice simply, without going down to the principles which lie under justice and are the source of its authority, I am unable to see how any of these reasoners can be refuted.

For in truth every one of the three builds upon rules of justice confessedly true. The first appeals to the acknowledged injustice of singling out an individual, and making him a sacrifice, without his consent, for other people's benefit. The second relies on the acknowledged justice of self-defence, and the admitted injustice of forcing one person to conform to another's notions of what constitutes his good. The Owenite invokes the admitted principle, that it is unjust to punish any one for what he cannot help. Each is triumphant so long as he is not compelled to take into consideration any other maxims of justice than the one he has selected; but as soon as their several maxims are brought face to face, each disputant seems to have exactly as much to say for himself as the others. No one of them can carry out his own notion of justice without trampling upon another equally binding. These are difficulties; they have always been felt to be such; and many devices have been invented to turn rather than to overcome them. As a refuge from the last of the three, men imagined what they called the freedom of the will; fancying that they could not justify punishing a man whose will is in a thoroughly hateful state, unless it be supposed to have come into that state through no influence of anterior circumstances. To escape from the other difficulties, a favourite contrivance has been the fiction of a contract, whereby at some unknown period all the members of society engaged to obey the laws, and consented to be punished for any disobedience to them; thereby giving to their legislators the right, which it is assumed they would not otherwise have had, of punishing them, either for their own good or for that of society. This happy thought was considered to get rid of the whole difficulty, and to legitimate the infliction of punishment, in virtue of another received maxim of justice, *Volenti non fit injuria;* that is not unjust which is done with the consent of the person who is supposed to be hurt by it. I need hardly remark, that even if the consent were not a mere fiction, this maxim is not superior in authority to the others which it is brought in to supersede. It is, on the contrary, an instructive specimen of the loose and irregular manner in which supposed principles of justice grow up. This particular one evidently came into use as a help to the coarse exigencies of courts of law, which are sometimes obliged to be content with very uncertain presumptions, on account of the greater evils which would often arise from any attempt on their part to cut finer. But even courts of law are not able to adhere consistently to the maxim, for they allow voluntary engagements to be set aside on the ground of fraud, and sometimes on that of mere mistake or misinformation.

Again, when the legitimacy of inflicting punishment is admitted, how many conflicting conceptions of justice come to light in discussing the proper apportionment of punishment to offences. No rule on this subject recommends itself so strongly to the primitive and spontaneous sentiment of justice, as the *lex talionis,* an eye for an eye and a tooth for a tooth. Though this principle of the Jewish and of the Mahomedan law has been generally abandoned in Europe as a practical maxim, there is, I suspect, in most minds, a secret hankering after it; and when retribution accidentally falls on an offender in that precise shape, the general feeling of satisfaction evinced, bears witness how natural is the sentiment to which this repayment in kind is acceptable. With many the test of justice in penal infliction is that the punishment should be proportioned to the offence; meaning that it should be exactly measured by the moral guilt of the culprit (whatever be their standard for measuring moral guilt): the consideration, what amount of punishment is necessary to deter from the offence, having nothing to do with the question of justice, in their estimation: while there are others to whom that consideration is all in all; who maintain that it is not just, at least for man, to inflict on a fellow creature, whatever may be his offences, any amount of suffering beyond the least that will suffice to prevent him from repeating, and others from imitating, his misconduct.

To take another example from a subject already once referred to. In a co-operative industrial association, is it just or not that talent or skill should give a title to superior remuneration? On the negative side of the question it is argued, that whoever does the best he can, deserves equally well, and ought not in justice to be put in a position of inferiority for no fault of his own; that superior abilities have already advantages more than enough, in the admiration they excite, the personal influence they command, and the internal sources of satisfaction attending them, without adding to these a superior share of the world's goods; and that society is bound in justice rather to make compensation to the less favoured, for this unmerited inequality of advantages, than to aggravate it. On the contrary side it is contended, that society receives more from the more efficient labourer; that his services being more useful, society owes him a larger return for them; that a greater share of the joint result is actually his work, and not to allow his claim to it is a kind of robbery; that if he is only to receive as much as others, he can only be justly required to produce as much, and to give a smaller amount of time and exertion, proportioned to his superior efficiency. Who shall decide between these appeals to conflicting principles of justice? Justice has in this case two sides to it, which it is impossible to bring into harmony, and the two disputants have chosen opposite sides; the one looks to what it is just that the individual should receive, the other to what it is just that the community should give. Each, from his own point of view, is unanswerable; and any choice between them, on grounds of justice, must be perfectly arbitrary. Social utility alone can decide the preference.

How many, again, and how irreconcileable, are the standards of justice to which reference is made in discussing the repartition of taxation. One opinion is, that payment to the State should be in numerical proportion to pecuniary means. Others think that justice dictates what they term graduated taxation; taking a higher percentage from those who have more to spare. In point of natural justice a strong case might be made for disregarding means altogether, and taking the same absolute sum (whenever it could be got) from every one: as the subscribers to a mess, or to a club, all pay the same sum for the same privileges, whether they can all equally afford it or not. Since the protection (it might be said) of law and government is afforded to, and is equally required by all, there is no injustice in making all buy it at the same price. It is reckoned justice, not injustice, that a dealer should charge to all customers the same price for the same article, not a price varying according to their means of payment. This doctrine, as applied to taxation, finds no advocates, because it conflicts strongly with men's feelings of humanity and perceptions of social expediency; but the principle of justice which it invokes is as true and as binding as those which can be appealed to against it. Accordingly, it exerts a tacit influence on the line of defence employed for other modes of assessing taxation. People feel obliged to argue that the State does more for the rich than for the poor, as a justification for its taking more from them: though this is in reality not true, for the rich would be far better able to protect themselves, in the absence of law or government, than the poor, and indeed would probably be successful in converting the poor into their slaves. Others, again, so far defer to the same conception of justice, as to maintain that all should pay an equal capitation tax for the protection of their persons (these being of equal value to all), and an unequal tax for the protection of their property, which is unequal. To this others reply, that the all of one man is as valuable to him as the all of another. From these confusions there is no other mode of extrication than the utilitarian.

Is, then, the difference between the Just and the Expedient a merely imaginary distinction? Have mankind been under a delusion in thinking that justice is a more sacred thing than policy, and that the latter ought only to be listened to after the former has been satisfied? By no means. The exposition we have given of the nature and origin of the sentiment, recognises a real distinction; and no one of those who profess the most sublime contempt for the consequences of actions as an element in their morality, attaches more importance to the distinction than I do. While I dispute the pretensions of any theory which sets up an imaginary standard of justice not grounded on utility, I account the justice which is grounded on utility to be the chief part, and incomparably the most sacred and binding part, of all morality. Justice is a name for certain classes of moral rules, which concern the essentials of human well-being more nearly, and are therefore of more absolute obligation, than any other rules for the guidance of life; and the notion which we have found to be of the essence of the idea of justice, that of a right residing in an individual, implies and testifies to this more binding obligation.

The moral rules which forbid mankind to hurt one another (in which we must never forget to include wrongful interference with each other's freedom) are more vital to human well-being than any maxims, however important, which only point out the best mode of managing some department of human affairs. They have also the peculiarity, that they are the main element in determining the whole of the social feelings of mankind. It is their observance which alone preserves peace among human beings: if obedience to them were not the rule, and disobedience the exception, every one would see in every one else a probable enemy, against whom he must be perpetually guarding himself. What is hardly less important, these are the precepts which mankind have the strongest and the most direct inducements for impressing upon one another. By merely giving to each other prudential instruction or exhortation, they may gain, or think they gain, nothing: in inculcating on each other the duty of positive beneficence they have an unmistakeable interest, but far less in degree: a person may possibly not need the benefits of others; but he always needs that they should not do him hurt. Thus the moralities which protect every individual from being harmed by others, either directly or by being hindered in his freedom of pursuing his own good, are at once those which he himself has most at heart, and those which he has the strongest interest in publishing and enforcing by word and deed. It is by a person's observance of these, that his fitness to exist as one of the fellowship of human beings, is tested and decided; for on that depends his being a nuisance or not to those with whom he is in contact. Now it is these moralities primarily, which compose the obligations of justice. The most marked cases of injustice, and those which give the tone to the feeling of repugnance which character-izes the sentiment, are acts of wrongful aggression, or wrongful exercise of power over some one; the next are those which consist in wrongfully withholding from him something which is his due; in both cases, inflicting on him a positive hurt, either in the form of direct suffering, or of the privation of some good which he had reasonable ground, either of a physical or of a social kind, for counting upon.

The same powerful motives which command the observance of these primary moralities, enjoin the punishment of those who violate them; and as the impulses

of self-defence, of defence of others, and of vengeance, are all called forth against
such persons, retribution, or evil for evil, becomes closely connected with the sentiment of justice, and is universally included in the idea. Good for good is also one of
the dictates of justice; and this, though its social utility is evident, and though it
carries with it a natural human feeling, has not at first sight that obvious connexion
with hurt or injury, which, existing in the most elementary cases of just and unjust,
is the source of the characteristic intensity of the sentiment. But the connexion,
though less obvious, is not less real. He who accepts benefits, and denies a return of
them when needed, inflicts a real hurt, by disappointing one of the most natural and
reasonable of expectations, and one which he must at least tacitly have encouraged,
otherwise the benefits would seldom have been conferred. The important rank,
among human evils and wrongs, of the disappointment of expectation, is shown in
the fact that it constitutes the principal criminality of two such highly immoral acts
as a breach of friendship and a breach of promise. Few hurts which human beings
can sustain are greater, and none wound more, than when that on which they
habitually and with full assurance relied, fails them in the hour of need; and few
wrongs are greater than this mere withholding of good; none excite more resentment, either in the person suffering, or in a sympathizing spectator. The principle,
therefore, of giving to each what they deserve, that is, good for good as well as evil
for evil, is not only included within the idea of Justice as we have defined it, but is
a proper object of that intensity of sentiment, which places the Just, in human
estimation, above the simply Expedient.

Most of the maxims of justice current in the world, and commonly appealed to in
its transactions, are simply instrumental to carrying into effect the principles of
justice which we have now spoken of. That a person is only responsible for what he
has done voluntarily, or could voluntarily have avoided; that it is unjust to condemn
any person unheard; that the punishment ought to be proportioned to the offence,
and the like, are maxims intended to prevent the just principle of evil for evil from
being perverted to the infliction of evil without that justification. The greater part
of these common maxims have come into use from the practice of courts of justice,
which have been naturally led to a more complete recognition and elaboration than
was likely to suggest itself to others, of the rules necessary to enable them to fulfil
their double function, of inflicting punishment when due, and of awarding to each
person his right.

That first of judicial virtues, impartiality, is an obligation of justice, partly for the
reason last mentioned; as being a necessary condition of the fulfilment of the other
obligations of justice. But this is not the only source of the exalted rank, among
human obligations, of those maxims of equality and impartiality, which, both in
popular estimation and in that of the most enlightened, are included among the
precepts of justice. In one point of view, they may be considered as corollaries from
the principles already laid down. If it is a duty to do to each according to his deserts,
returning good for good as well as repressing evil by evil, it necessarily follows that
we should treat all equally well (when no higher duty forbids) who have deserved
equally well of us, and that society should treat all equally well who have deserved
equally well of it, that is, who have deserved equally well absolutely. This is the
highest abstract standard of social and distributive justice; towards which all institutions, and the efforts of all virtuous citizens, should be made in the utmost possible
degree to converge. But this great moral duty rests upon a still deeper foundation,
being a direct emanation from the first principle of morals, and not a mere logical

corollary from secondary or derivative doctrines. It is involved in the very meaning of Utility, or the Greatest-Happiness Principle. That principle is a mere form of words without rational signification, unless one person's happiness, supposed equal in degree (with the proper allowance made for kind), is counted for exactly as much as another's. Those conditions being supplied, Bentham's dictum, 'everybody to count for one, nobody for more than one,' might be written under the principle of utility as an explanatory commentary.[4] The equal claim of everybody to happiness in the estimation of the moralist and the legislator, involves an equal claim to all the means of happiness, except in so far as the inevitable conditions of human life, and the general interest, in which that of every individual is included, set limits to the maxim; and those limits ought to be strictly construed. As every other maxim of justice, so this, is by no means applied or held applicable universally; on the contrary, as I have already remarked, it bends to every person's ideas of social expediency. But in whatever case it is deemed applicable at all, it is held to be the dictate of justice. All persons are deemed to have a *right* to equality of treatment, except when some recognised social expediency requires the reverse. And hence all social inequalities which have ceased to be considered expedient, assume the character not of simple inexpediency, but of injustice, and appear so tyrannical, that people are apt to wonder how they ever could have been tolerated; forgetful that they themselves perhaps tolerate other inequalities under an equally mistaken notion of expediency, the correction of which would make that which they approve seem quite as monstrous as what they have at last learnt to condemn. The entire history of social improvement has been a series of transitions, by which one custom or institution after another, from being a supposed primary necessity of social existence, has passed into the rank of an universally stigmatized injustice and tyranny. So it has been with the distinctions of slaves and freemen, nobles and serfs, patricians and plebeians; and so it will be, and in part already is, with the aristocracies of colour, race, and sex.

4. This implication, in the first principle of the utilitarian scheme, of perfect impartiality between persons, is regarded by Mr. Herbert Spencer (in his 'Social Statics') as a disproof of the pretensions of utility to be a sufficient guide to right; since (he says) the principle of utility presupposes the anterior principle, that everybody has an equal right to happiness. It may be more correctly described as supposing that equal amounts of happiness are equally desirable, whether felt by the same or by different persons. This, however, is not a presupposition; not a premise needful to support the principle of utility, but the very principle itself; for what is the principle of utility, if it be not that 'happiness' and 'desirable' are synonymous terms? If there is any anterior principle implied, it can be no other than this, that the truths of arithmetic are applicable to the valuation of happiness, as of all other measurable quantities.

[Mr. Herbert Spencer, in a private communication on the subject of the preceding Note, objects to being considered an opponent of Utilitarianism, and states that he regards happiness as the ultimate end of morality; but deems that end only partially attainable by empirical generalizations from the observed results of conduct, and completely attainable only by deducing, from the laws of life and the conditions of existence, what kinds of action necessarily tend to produce happiness, and what kinds to produce unhappiness. With the exception of the word "necessarily," I have no dissent to express from this doctrine; and (omitting that word) I am not aware that any modern advocate of utilitarianism is of a different opinion. Bentham, certainly, to whom in the *Social Statics* Mr. Spencer particularly referred, is, least of all writers, chargeable with unwillingness to deduce the effect of actions on happiness from the laws of human nature and the universal conditions of human life. The common charge against him is of relying too exclusively upon such deductions, and declining altogether to be bound by the generalizations from specific experience which Mr. Spencer thinks that utilitarians generally confine themselves to. My own opinion (and, as I collect, Mr. Spencer's) is, that in ethics, as in all other branches of scientific study, the consilience of the results of both these processes, each corroborating and verifying the other, is requisite to give to any general proposition the kind and degree of evidence which constitutes scientific proof.]

It appears from what has been said, that justice is a name for certain moral requirements, which, regarded collectively, stand higher in the scale of social utility, and are therefore of more paramount obligation, than any others; though particular cases may occur in which some other social duty is so important, as to overrule any one of the general maxims of justice. Thus, to save a life, it may not only be allowable, but a duty, to steal, or take by force, the necessary food or medicine, or to kidnap, and compel to officiate, the only qualified medical practitioner. In such cases, as we do not call anything justice which is not a virtue, we usually say, not that justice must give way to some other moral principle, but that what is just in ordinary cases is, by reason of that other principle, not just in the particular case. By this useful accommodation of language, the character of indefeasibility attributed to justice is kept up, and we are saved from the necessity of maintaining that there can be laudable injustice.

The considerations which have now been adduced resolve, I conceive, the only real difficulty in the utilitarian theory of morals. It has always been evident that all cases of justice are also cases of expediency: the difference is in the peculiar sentiment which attaches to the former, as contradistinguished from the latter. If this characteristic sentiment has been sufficiently accounted for; if there is no necessity to assume for it any peculiarity of origin; if it is simply the natural feeling of resentment, moralized by being made coextensive with the demands of social good; and if this feeling not only does but ought to exist in all the classes of cases to which the idea of justice corresponds; that idea no longer presents itself as a stumbling-block to the utilitarian ethics. Justice remains the appropriate name for certain social utilities which are vastly more important, and therefore more absolute and imperative, than any others are as a class (though not more so than others may be in particular cases); and which, therefore, ought to be, as well as naturally are, guarded by a sentiment not only different in degree, but also in kind; distinguished from the milder feeling which attaches to the mere idea of promoting human pleasure or convenience, at once by the more definite nature of its commands, and by the sterner character of its sanctions.

KARL MARX

Western ideologies have often been philosophical, combining critical reflection with systematic boldness. But few philosophies have been social or political ideologies. Marxism is almost unique in this regard. Arising out of the thinking of a German philosopher, it became first a comprehensive conception of human nature, history, society, and salvation, and then the mobilizing ideology of nations. Marxism warns us not to forget that our thinking about human beings and their lives arises out of history and is capable of being realized in history. Moreover, it was no accident that Marxism became the framework of commitments and of conduct for millions. For its turn away from abstract, theoretical thinking to practice and action is part of its very understanding of history, society, thought, and the ultimate goals of human life.

Marxism arises out of the life and work of Karl Heinrich Marx (1818–1883), who was born on May 5, 1818, in Trier, in Prussia. Marx's father, Heinrich, was a lawyer of Jewish descent who converted to Christianity in 1824. He expected his son to practise law also, and Karl Marx entered the University of Bonn in 1836 with this intention. But a year later, he transferred to Berlin, became associated with Bruno Bauer and the young left-wing Hegelians, and turned to philosophy. These disciples of Georg Wilhelm Friedrich Hegel had traded in Hegel's reverence for religion, morality, philosophy, and the spiritual character of history for a humanistic critique in which religion, morality, and traditional politics were viewed as distortions of what is genuinely human and ultimately as sources of alienation. According to Ludwig Feuerbach, a young theologian and a leader of the movement, Hegel had been wrong to see all things, including human culture, society, and morality, as expressions of Spirit or the divine; rather, all things, even God, are in truth expressions of human interests and human productivity.

After completing his doctoral dissertation, on the ancient atomists and critics of religion, Democritus and Epicurus, at the University of Jena in 1841, Marx turned to journalism. He edited the radical newspaper the *Rheinische Zeitung* in Cologne until 1843, when government censorship led him to resign. During this period Marx completed his critique of the *Philosophy of Right*, Hegel's central work on ethics and politics, and wrote his famous review-essay of Bauer's *The Jewish Question*, with its important treatment of political alienation, the primacy of social existence, and the relation between money and labor.

In June of 1843 Marx married his childhood love, Jenny von Westphalen, and together they moved to Paris, as Marx joined Arnold Ruge, another young left-wing Hegelian, in editing the *Deutsch-Französische Jahrbücher* (*German-French Yearbooks*). In

France Marx became reacquainted with Friedrich Engels, who became his closest friend and collaborator. By the end of 1844, the two had completed their first project, *The Holy Family*, a critique of young Hegelian philosophy on the basis of a new humanism, a critical analysis of the Hegelian treatment of property, and an attack on the hidden theology of the young radicals.

In 1845 Marx was banished from Paris and moved to Brussels. He and Engels joined the Communist League in 1847 and in February 1848, on the eve of the revolutions in France, published their famous *Manifesto*. Then, after moving back and forth across Western Europe, Marx was finally expelled from all Prussian territories; he set sail for London, where he settled in 1849 and lived for virtually all of his remaining years.

The 1850s and 1860s were extremely difficult decades for Marx and his family. Poverty and illness filled their lives with suffering and grief. By 1856 three of the six Marx children had died. Marx worked steadily, even fanatically, ten hours a day in the British Museum studying economics and the analysis of political economy, and then writing at home long into the night. The results were the *Critique of Political Economy* of 1859; the long unpublished draft on political economy called the *Grundrisse* (1857–58); and, most important, the critical analysis of capitalism, *Capital*, the first volume of which was published in 1867. The final two volumes were published by Engels in 1885 and 1894, after Marx's death.

During the 1850s Marx wrote articles for the *New York Daily Tribune*, but the American Civil War put an end to even such modest employment. Fortunately, by the end of the decade, a small bequest to Jenny and Engels's support from his company in Manchester bettered the Marx family's situation. By this time, however, Marx's health was very bad.

In 1864 Marx helped found the International Working Men's Association in London and served on its General Council for seven years. But his health deteriorated steadily. Physically debilitated, Marx was increasingly less productive in what would be his last decade. In 1881 Jenny died of cancer; ill since 1878, she had been less and less able to help decipher his notorious handwriting. Then, on March 14, 1883, Marx too died, leaving to Engels the task of editing the remaining volumes of *Capital*. Less than forty years later, in the Russian Revolution of 1917, history would seek to confirm Marx's understanding of it in a rare, if not unique, celebration of the efficacy of philosophical thought to change the world—and not merely to understand it.

Recommended readings

Avineri, Shlomo. *The Social and Political Thought of Karl Marx*. Cambridge: Cambridge University Press, 1968.

Ball, Terence, and James Farr (eds.). *After Marx*. Cambridge: Cambridge University Press, 1984.

Cohen, Gerald. *Karl Marx's Theory of History*. Oxford: Oxford University Press, 1978.

Elster, Jon. *Making Sense of Marx*. Cambridge: Cambridge University Press, 1985.

Lukes, S. *Marxism and Morality*. Oxford: Oxford University Press, 1984.

Tucker, Robert C. *Philosophy and Myth in Karl Marx*. 2nd ed. Cambridge: Cambridge University Press, 1972.

Wood, Alan. *Karl Marx*. London: Routledge, 1981.

ESTRANGED LABOUR

We have proceeded from the premises of political economy. We have accepted its language and its laws. We presupposed private property, the separation of labour, capital and land, and of wages, profit of capital and rent of land—likewise division of labour, competition, the concept of exchange-value, etc. On the basis of political economy itself, in its own words, we have shown that the worker sinks to the level of a commodity and becomes indeed the most wretched of commodities; that the wretchedness of the worker is in inverse proportion to the power and magnitude of his production; that the necessary result of competition is the accumulation of capital in a few hands, and thus the restoration of monopoly in a more terrible form; that finally the distinction between capitalist and land-rentier, like that between the tiller of the soil and the factory-worker, disappears and that the whole of society must fall apart into the two classes—the property-*owners* and the propertyless *workers*.

Political economy proceeds from the fact of private property, but it does not explain it to us. It expresses in general, abstract formulae the *material* process through which private property actually passes, and these formulae it then takes for *laws*. It does not *comprehend* these laws—i.e., it does not demonstrate how they arise from the very nature of private property. Political economy does not disclose the source of the division between labour and capital, and between capital and land. When, for example, it defines the relationship of wages to profit, it takes the interest of the capitalists to be the ultimate cause; i.e., it takes for granted what it is supposed to evolve. Similarly, competition comes in everywhere. It is explained from external circumstances. As to how far these external and apparently fortuitous circumstances are but the expression of a necessary course of development, political economy teaches us nothing. We have seen how, to it, exchange itself appears to be a fortuitous fact. The only wheels which political economy sets in motion are *avarice* and the *war amongst the avaricious—competition*.

Precisely because political economy does not grasp the connections within the movement, it was possible to counterpose, for instance, the doctrine of competition to the doctrine of monopoly, the doctrine of craft-liberty to the doctrine of the corporation, the doctrine of the division of landed property to the doctrine of the big estate—for competition, craft-liberty and the division of landed property were explained and comprehended only as fortuitous, premeditated and violent consequences of monopoly, the corporation, and feudal property, not as their necessary, inevitable and natural consequences.

Now, therefore, we have to grasp the essential connection between private property, avarice, and the separation of labour, capital and landed property; between exchange and competition, value and the devaluation of men, monopoly and competition, etc.; the connection between this whole estrangement and the *money*-system.

Do not let us go back to a fictitious primordial condition as the political economist does, when he tries to explain. Such a primordial condition explains nothing. He merely pushes the question away into a grey nebulous distance. He assumes in the form of fact, of an event, what he is supposed to deduce—namely, the necessary

1. [From *Economic and Philosophic Manuscripts of 1844.*]

relationship between two things—between, for example, division of labour and exchange. Theology in the same way explains the origin of evil by the fall of man: that is, it assumes as a fact, in historical form, what has to be explained.

We proceed from an *actual* economic fact.

The worker becomes all the poorer the more wealth he produces, the more his production increases in power and range. The worker becomes an ever cheaper commodity the more commodities he creates. With the *increasing value* of the world of things proceeds in direct proportion the *devaluation* of the world of men. Labour produces not only commodities; it produces itself and the worker as a *commodity*— and does so in the proportion in which it produces commodities generally.

This fact expresses merely that the object which labour produces—labour's product—confronts it as *something alien,* as a *power independent* of the producer. The product of labour is labour which has been congealed in an object, which has become material: it is the *objectification* of labour. Labour's realization is its objectification. In the conditions dealt with by political economy this realization of labour appears as *loss of reality* for the workers; objectification as *loss of the object* and *object-bondage;* appropriation as *estrangement,* as *alienation.*[2]

So much does labour's realization appear as loss of reality that the worker loses reality to the point of starving to death. So much does objectification appear as loss of the object that the worker is robbed of the objects most necessary not only for his life but for his work. Indeed, labour itself becomes an object which he can get hold of only with the greatest effort and with the most irregular interruptions. So much does the appropriation of the object appear as estrangement that the more objects the worker produces the fewer can he possess and the more he falls under the dominion of his product, capital.

All these consequences are contained in the definition that the worker is related to the *product of his labour* as to an *alien* object. For on this premise it is clear that the more the worker spends himself, the more powerful the alien objective world becomes which he creates over-against himself, the poorer he himself—his inner world—becomes, the less belongs to him as his own. It is the same in religion. The more man puts into God, the less he retains in himself. The worker puts his life into the object; but now his life no longer belongs to him but to the object. Hence, the greater this activity, the greater is the worker's lack of objects. Whatever the product of his labour is, he is not. Therefore the greater this product, the less is he himself. The *alienation* of the worker in his product means not only that his labour becomes an object, an *external* existence, but that it exists *outside him,* independently, as something alien to him, and that it becomes a power of its own confronting him; it means that the life which he has conferred on the object confronts him as something hostile and alien.

Let us now look more closely at the *objectification,* at the production of the worker; and therein at the *estrangement,* the *loss* of the object, his product.

The worker can create nothing without *nature,* without the *sensuous external world.* It is the material on which his labour is manifested, in which it is active, from which and by means of which it produces.

2. ["Alienation"—*Entäusserung.*]

But just as nature provides labour with the *means of life* in the sense that labour cannot *live* without objects on which to operate, on the other hand, it also provides the *means of life* in the more restricted sense—i.e., the means for the physical subsistence of the *worker* himself.

Thus the more the worker by his labour *appropriates* the external world, sensuous nature, the more he deprives himself of *means of life* in the double respect: first, that the sensuous external world more and more ceases to be an object belonging to his labour—to be his labour's *means of life;* and secondly, that it more and more ceases to be *means of life* in the immediate sense, means for the physical subsistence of the worker.

Thus in this double respect the worker becomes a slave of his object, first, in that he receives an *object of labour,* i.e., in that he receives *work;* and secondly, in that he receives *means of subsistence.* Therefore, it enables him to exist, first, as a *worker;* and, second, as a *physical subject.* The extremity of this bondage is that it is only as a *worker* that he continues to maintain himself as a *physical subject,* and that it is only as a *physical subject* that he is a *worker.*

(The laws of political economy express the estrangement of the worker in his object thus: the more the worker produces, the less he has to consume; the more values he creates, the more valueless, the more unworthy he becomes; the better formed his product, the more deformed becomes the worker; the more civilized his object, the more barbarous becomes the worker; the mightier labour becomes, the more powerless becomes the worker; the more ingenious labour becomes, the duller becomes the worker and the more he becomes nature's bondsman.)

Political economy conceals the estrangement inherent in the nature of labour by not consider-ing the direct relationship between the worker (labour) *and production.* It is true that labour produces for the rich wonderful things—but for the worker it produces privation. It produces palaces—but for the worker, hovels. It produces beauty—but for the worker, deformity. It replaces labour by machines—but some of the workers it throws back to a barbarous type of labour, and the other workers it turns into machines. It produces intelligence—but for the worker idiocy, cretinism.

The direct relationship of labour to its produce is the relationship of the worker to the objects of his production. The relationship of the man of means to the objects of production and to production itself is only a *consequence* of this first relationship—and confirms it. We shall consider this other aspect later.

When we ask, then, what is the essential relationship of labour we are asking about the relationship of the *worker* to production.

Till now we have been considering the estrangement, the alienation of the worker only in one of its aspects, i.e., the worker's *relationship to the products of his labour.* But the estrangement is manifested not only in the result but in the *act of production*—within the *producing activity* itself. How would the worker come to face the product of his activity as a stranger, were it not that in the very act of production he was estranging himself from himself? The product is after all but the summary of the activity of production.

If then the product of labour is alienation, production itself must be active alien-ation, the alienation of activity, the activity of alienation. In the estrangement of the object of labour is merely summarized the estrangement, the alienation, in the activity of labour itself.

What, then, constitutes the alienation of labour?

First, the fact that labour is *external* to the worker, i.e., it does not belong to his essential being; that in his work, therefore, he does not affirm himself but denies himself, does not feel content but unhappy, does not develop freely his physical and mental energy but mortifies his body and ruins his mind. The worker therefore only feels himself outside his work, and in his work feels outside himself. He is at home when he is not working, and when he is working he is not at home. His labour is therefore not voluntary, but coerced; it is *forced labour*. It is therefore not the satisfaction of a need; it is merely a *means* to satisfy needs external to it. Its alien character emerges clearly in the fact that as soon as no physical or other compulsion exists, labour is shunned like the plague. External labour, labour in which man alienates himself, is a labour of self-sacrifice, of mortification. Lastly, the external character of labour for the worker appears in the fact that it is not his own, but someone else's, that it does not belong to him, that in it he belongs, not to himself, but to another. Just as in religion the spontaneous activity of the human imagination, of the human brain and the human heart, operates independently of the individual—that is, operates on him as an alien, divine or diabolical activity—in the same way the worker's activity is not his spontaneous activity. It belongs to another; it is the loss of his self.

As a result, therefore, man (the worker) no longer feels himself to be freely active in any but his animal functions—eating, drinking, procreating, or at most in his dwelling and in dressing-up, etc.; and in his human functions he no longer feels himself to be anything but an animal. What is animal becomes human and what is human becomes animal.

Certainly eating, drinking, procreating, etc., are also genuinely human functions. But in the abstraction which separates them from the sphere of all other human activity and turns them into sole and ultimate ends, they are animal.

We have considered the act of estranging practical human activity, labour, in two of its aspects. (1) The relation of the worker to the *product of labour* as an alien object exercising power over him. This relation is at the same time the relation to the sensuous external world, to the objects of nature as an alien world antagonistically opposed to him. (2) The relation of labour to the *act of production* within the *labour* process. This relation is the relation of the worker to his own activity as an alien activity not belonging to him; it is activity as suffering, strength as weakness, begetting as emasculating, the worker's *own* physical and mental energy, his personal life or what is life other than activity—as an activity which is turned against him, neither depends on nor belongs to him. Here we have *self-estrangement*, as we had previously the estrangement of the *thing*.

We have yet a third aspect of *estranged labour* to deduce from the two already considered.

Man is a species being, not only because in practice and in theory he adopts the species as his object (his own as well as those of other things), but—and this is only another way of expressing it—but also because he treats himself as the actual, living species; because he treats himself as a *universal* and therefore a free being.

The life of the species, both in man and in animals, consists physically in the fact that man (like the animal) lives on inorganic nature; and the more universal man is compared with an animal, the more universal is the sphere of inorganic nature on which he lives. Just as plants, animals, stones, the air, light, etc., constitute a part of human consciousness in the realm of theory, partly as objects of natural science, partly as objects of art—his spiritual inorganic nature, spiritual nourishment which he must first prepare to make it palatable and digestible—so too in the realm of practice they constitute a part of human life and human activity. Physically man lives only on these products of nature, whether they appear in the form of food, heating, clothes, a dwelling, or whatever it may be. The universality of man is in practice manifested precisely in the universality which makes all nature his *inorganic body*—both inasmuch as nature is (1) his direct means of life, and (2) the material, the object, and the instrument of his life-activity. Nature is man's *inorganic body*—nature, that is, in so far as it is not itself the human body. Man *lives* on nature—means that nature is his *body,* with which he must remain in continuous intercourse if he is not to die. That man's physical and spiritual life is linked to nature means simply that nature is linked to itself, for man is a part of nature.

In estranging from man (1) nature, and (2) himself, his own active functions, his life-activity, estranged labour estranges the *species* from man. It turns for him the *life of the species* into a means of individual life. First it estranges the life of the species and individual life, and secondly it makes individual life in its abstract form the purpose of the life of the species, likewise in its abstract and estranged form.

For in the first place labour, *life-activity, productive life* itself, appears to man merely as a *means* of satisfying a need—the need to maintain the physical existence. Yet the productive life is the life of the species. It is life-engendering life. The whole character of a species—its species character—is contained in the character of its life-activity; and free, conscious activity is man's species character. Life itself appears only as *a means to life.*

The animal is immediately identical with its life-activity. It does not distinguish itself from it. It is *its life-activity.* Man makes his life-activity itself the object of his will and of his consciousness. He has conscious life-activity. It is not a determination with which he directly merges. Conscious life-activity directly distinguishes man from animal life-activity. It is just because of this that he is a species being. Or it is only because he is a species being that he is a Conscious Being, i.e., that his own life is an object for him. Only because of that is his activity free activity. Estranged labour reverses this relationship, so that it is just because man is a conscious being that he makes his life-activity, his *essential* being, a mere means to his *existence.*

In creating an *objective world* by his practical activity, in *working-up* inorganic nature, man proves himself a conscious species being, i.e., as a being that treats the species as its own essential being, or that treats itself as a species being. Admittedly animals also produce. They build themselves nests, dwellings, like the bees, beavers, ants, etc. But an animal only produces what it immediately needs for itself or its young. It produces one-sidedly, whilst man produces universally. It produces only under the dominion of immediate physical need, whilst man produces even when he is free from physical need and only truly produces in freedom therefrom. An animal produces only itself, whilst man reproduces the whole of nature. An animal's product belongs immediately to its physical body, whilst man freely confronts his product. An animal forms things in accordance with the standard and the need of the species to which it belongs, whilst man knows how to produce in accordance with the standard of every species, and knows how to apply everywhere the inherent standard to the object. Man therefore also forms things in accordance with the laws of beauty.

It is just in the working-up of the objective world, therefore, that man first really proves himself to be a *species being*. This production is his active species life. Through and because of this production, nature appears as *his* work and his reality. The object of labour is, therefore, the *objectification of man's species life:* for he duplicates himself not only, as in consciousness, intellectually, but also actively, in reality, and therefore he contemplates himself in a world that he has created. In tearing away from man the object of his production, therefore, estranged labour tears from him his *species life,* his real species objectivity, and transforms his advantage over animals into the disadvantage that his inorganic body, nature, is taken from him. Similarly, in degrading spontaneous activity, free activity, to a means, estranged labour makes man's species life a means to his physical existence. The consciousness which man has of his species is thus transformed by estrangement in such a way that the species life becomes for him a means. Estranged labour turns thus:

(3) *Man's species being,* both nature and his spiritual species property, into a being *alien* to him, into a *means* to his *individual existence*. It estranges man's own body from him, as it does external nature and his spiritual essence, his *human* being.

(4) An immediate consequence of the fact that man is estranged from the product of his labour, from his life-activity, from his species being is the *estrangement of man* from *man*. If a man is confronted by himself, he is confronted by the *other* man. What applies to a man's relation to his work, to the product of his labour and to himself, also holds of a man's relation to the other man, and to the other man's labour and object of labour.

In fact, the proposition that man's species nature is estranged from him means that one man is estranged from the other, as each of them is from man's essential nature.[3]

The estrangement of man, and in fact every relationship in which man stands to himself, is first realized and expressed in the relationship in which a man stands to other men.

Hence within the relationship of estranged labour each man views the other in accordance with the standard and the position in which he finds himself as a worker.

We took our departure from a fact of political economy—the estrangement of the worker and his production. We have formulated the concept of this fact—*estranged, alienated* labour. We have analysed this concept—hence analysing merely a fact of political economy.

Let us now see, further, how in real life the concept of estranged, alienated labour must express and present itself.

If the product of labour is alien to me, if it confronts me as an alien power, to whom, then, does it belong?

If my own activity does not belong to me, if it is an alien, a coerced activity, to whom, then, does it belong?

---

3. ["Species nature" (and, earlier, "species being")—*Gattungswesen;* "man's essential nature"—*menschlichen Wesen.*]

To a being *other* than me.

Who is this being?

The *gods?* To be sure, in the earliest times the principal production (for example, the building of temples, etc., in Egypt, India and Mexico) appears to be in the service of the gods, and the product belongs to the gods. However, the gods on their own were never the lords of labour. No more was *nature.* And what a contradiction it would be if, the more man subjugated nature by his labour and the more the miracles of the gods were rendered superfluous by the miracles of industry, the more man were to renounce the joy of production and the enjoyment of the produce in favour of these powers.

The *alien* being, to whom labour and the produce of labour belongs, in whose service labour is done and for whose benefit the produce of labour is provided, can only be *man* himself.

If the product of labour does not belong to the worker, if it confronts him as an alien power, this can only be because it belongs to some *other man than the worker.* If the worker's activity is a torment to him, to another it must be *delight* and his life's joy. Not the gods, not nature, but only man himself can be this alien power over man.

We must bear in mind the above-stated proposition that man's relation to himself only becomes *objective* and *real* for him through his relation to the other man. Thus, if the product of his labour, his labour *objectified,* is for him an *alien,* hostile, powerful object independent of him, then his position towards it is such that someone else is master of this object, someone who is alien, hostile, powerful, and independent of him. If his own activity is to him an unfree activity, then he is treating it as activity performed in the service, under the dominion, the coercion and the yoke of another man.

Every self-estrangement of man from himself and from nature appears in the relation in which he places himself and nature to men other than and differentiated from himself. For this reason religious self-estrangement necessarily appears in the relationship of the layman to the priest, or again to a mediator, etc., since we are here dealing with the intellectual world. In the real practical world self-estrangement can only become manifest through the real practical relationship to other men. The medium through which estrangement takes place is itself *practical.* Thus through estranged labour man not only engenders his relationship to the object and to the act of production as to powers that are alien and hostile to him; he also engenders the relationship in which other men stand to his production and to his product, and the relationship in which he stands to these other men. Just as he begets his own production as the loss of his reality, as his punishment; just as he begets his own product as a loss, as a product not belonging to him; so he begets the dominion of the one who does not produce over production and over the product. Just as he estranges from himself his own activity, so he confers to the stranger activity which is not his own.

Till now we have only considered this relationship from the standpoint of the worker and later we shall be considering it also from the standpoint of the non-worker.

Through *estranged, alienated labour,* then, the worker produces the relationship to this labour of a man alien to labour and standing outside it. The relationship of the worker to labour engenders the relation to it of the capitalist, or whatever one chooses to call the master of labour. *Private property* is thus the product, the result, the necessary consequence, of *alienated labour,* of the external relation of the worker to nature and to himself.

Private property thus results by analysis from the concept of *alienated labour*—i.e., of *alienated man,* of estranged labour, of estranged life, of *estranged* man.

True, it is as a result of the *movement of private property* that we have obtained the concept of *alienated labour (of alienated life)* from political economy. But on analysis of this concept it becomes clear that though private property appears to be the source, the cause of alienated labour, it is really its consequence, just as the gods *in the beginning* are not the cause but the effect of man's intellectual confusion. Later this relationship becomes reciprocal.

Only at the very culmination of the development of private property does this, its secret, re-emerge, namely, that on the one hand it is the *product* of alienated labour, and that secondly it is the *means* by which labour alienates itself, the *realization of this alienation.*

This exposition immediately sheds light on various hitherto unsolved conflicts.

(1) Political economy starts from labour as the real soul of production; yet to labour it gives nothing, and to private property everything. From this contradiction Proudhon has concluded in favour of labour and against private property. We understand, however, that this apparent contradiction is the contradiction of *estranged labour* with itself, and that political economy has merely formulated the laws of estranged labour.

We also understand, therefore, that *wages* and *private property* are identical: where the product, the object of labour pays for labour itself, the wage is but a necessary consequence of labour's estrangement, for after all in the wage of labour, labour does not appear as an end in itself but as the servant of the wage. We shall develop this point later, and meanwhile will only deduce some conclusions.

A *forcing-up of wages* (disregarding all other difficulties, including the fact that it would only be by force, too, that the higher wages, being an anomaly, could be maintained) would therefore be nothing but *better payment for the slave,* and would not conquer either for the worker or for labour their human status and dignity.

Indeed, even the *equality of wages* demanded by Proudhon only transforms the relationship of the present-day worker to his labour into the relationship of all men to labour. Society is then conceived as an abstract capitalist.

Wages are a direct consequence of estranged labour, and estranged labour is the direct cause of private property. The downfall of the one aspect must therefore mean the downfall of the other.

(2) From the relationship of estranged labour to private property it further follows that the emancipation of society from private property, etc., from servitude, is expressed in the *political* form of the *emancipation of the workers;* not that *their* emancipation alone was at stake but because the emancipation of the workers contains universal human emancipation—and it contains this, because the whole of human servitude is involved in the relation of the worker to production, and every relation of servitude is but a modification and consequence of this relation.

Just as we have found the concept of *private property* from the concept of *estranged, alienated labour* by *analysis,* in the same way every *category* of political economy can be evolved with the help of these two factors; and we shall find again in each category, e.g., trade, competition, capital, money, only a *definite* and *developed expression* of the first foundations.

Before considering this configuration, however, let us try to solve two problems.

(1) To define the general *nature of private property*, as it has arisen as a result of estranged labour, in its relation to *truly human, social property*.

(2) We have accepted the *estrangement of labour*, its *alienation*, as a fact, and we have analysed this fact. How, we now ask, does *man* come to *alienate*, to estrange, *his labour*? How is this estrangement rooted in the nature of human development? We have already gone a long way to the solution of this problem by *transforming* the question as to the *origin of private property* into the question as to the relation of *alienated labour* to the course of humanity's development. For when one speaks of *private property*, one thinks of being concerned with something external to man. When one speaks of labour, one is directly concerned with man himself. This new formulation of the question already contains its solution.

As to *(1): The general nature of private property and its relation to truly human property.*

Alienated labour has resolved itself for us into two elements which mutually condition one another, or which are but different expressions of one and the same relationship. *Appropriation* appears as *estrangement*, as *alienation*; and *alienation* appears as *appropriation, estrangement* as true *enfranchisement*.

We have considered the one side—*alienated labour* in relation to the *worker* himself, i.e., *the relation of alienated labour to itself*. The *property-relation of the non-worker to the worker and to labour* we have found as the product, the necessary outcome of this relation of alienated labour. *Private property*, as the material, summary expression of alienated labour, embraces both relations—the *relation of the worker to work, to the product of his labour and to the non-worker*, and the relation of the *non-worker to the worker and to the product of his labour*.

Having seen that in relation to the worker who *appropriates* nature by means of his labour, this appropriation *appears* as estrangement, his own spontaneous activity as activity for another and as activity of another, vitality as a sacrifice of life, production of the object as loss of the object to an alien power, to an *alien* person—we shall now consider the relation to the worker, to labour and its object of this person who is alien to labour and the worker.

First it has to be noticed, that everything which appears in the worker as an *activity of alienation, of estrangement*, appears in the non-worker as a *state of alienation, of estrangement*.

Secondly, that the worker's *real, practical attitude* in production and to the product (as a state of mind) appears in the non-worker confronting him as a *theoretical* attitude.

Thirdly, the non-worker does everything against the worker which the worker does against himself; but he does not do against himself what he does against the worker.

Let us look more closely at these three relations.[4]

---

4. [At this point the first manuscript breaks off unfinished.]

ON THE JEWISH QUESTION

1. Bruno Bauer, *Die Judenfrage*[1]

The German Jews seek emancipation. What kind of emancipation do they want? *Civic, political* emancipation.

Bruno Bauer replies to them: In Germany no one is politically emancipated. We ourselves are not free. How then could we liberate you? You Jews are *egoists* if you demand for yourselves, as Jews, a special emancipation. You should work, as Germans, for the political emancipation of Germany, and as men, for the emancipation of mankind. You should feel the particular kind of oppression and shame which you suffer, not as an exception to the rule but rather as a confirmation of the rule.

Or do the Jews want to be placed on a footing of equality with the *Christian subjects?* If they recognize the *Christian state* as legally established they also recognize the régime of general enslavement. Why should their particular yoke be irksome when they accept the general yoke? Why should the German be interested in the liberation of the Jew, if the Jew is not interested in the liberation of the German?

The *Christian* state recognizes nothing but *privileges.* The Jew himself, in this state, has the privilege of being a Jew. As a Jew he possesses rights which the Christians do not have. Why does he want rights which he does not have but which the Christians enjoy?

In demanding his emancipation from the Christian state he asks the Christian state to abandon its *religious* prejudice. But does he, the Jew, give up *his* religious prejudice? Has he then the right to insist that someone else should forswear his religion?

The *Christian* state, *by its very nature,* is incapable of emancipating the Jew. But, adds Bauer, the Jew, by his very nature, cannot be emancipated. As long as the state remains Christian, and as long as the Jew remains a Jew, they are equally incapable, the one of conferring emancipation, the other of receiving it.

With respect to the Jews the Christian state can only adopt the attitude of a Christian state. That is, it can permit the Jew, as a matter of privilege, to isolate himself from its other subjects; but it must then allow the pressures of all the other spheres of society to bear upon the Jew, and all the more heavily since he is in *religious* opposition to the dominant religion. But the Jew likewise can only adopt a Jewish attitude, i.e. that of a foreigner, towards the state, since he opposes his illusory nationality to actual nationality, his illusory law to actual law. He considers it his right to separate himself from the rest of humanity; as a matter of principle he takes no part in the historical movement and looks to a future which has nothing in common with the future of mankind as a whole. He regards himself as a member of the Jewish people, and the Jewish people as the chosen people.

On what grounds, then, do you Jews demand emancipation? On account of your religion? But it is the mortal enemy of the state religion. As citizens? But there are no citizens in Germany. As men? But you are not men any more than are those to whom you appeal.

---

1. [The Jewish question.] Braunschweig, 1843.—Marx.

Bauer, after criticizing earlier approaches and solutions, formulates the question of Jewish emancipation in a new way. What, he asks, is the nature of the Jew who is to be emancipated, and the *nature* of the Christian state which is to emancipate him? He replies by a critique of the Jewish religion, analyses the religious opposition between Judaism and Christianity, explains the essence of the Christian state; and does all this with dash, clarity, wit and profundity, in a style which is as precise as it is pithy and vigorous.

How then does Bauer resolve the Jewish question? What is the result? To formulate a question is to resolve it. The critical study of the Jewish question is the answer to the Jewish question. Here it is in brief: we have to emancipate ourselves before we can emancipate others.

The most stubborn form of the opposition between Jew and Christian is the *religious* opposition. How is an opposition resolved? By making it impossible. And how is *religious* opposition made impossible? By abolishing *religion*. As soon as Jew and Christian come to see in their respective religions nothing more than *stages in the development of the human mind*—snake skins which have been cast off by *history,* and *man* as the snake who clothed himself in them—they will no longer find themselves in religious opposition, but in a purely critical, *scientific* and human relationship. *Science* will then constitute their unity. But scientific oppositions are resolved by science itself.

The *German* Jew, in particular, suffers from the general lack of political freedom and the pronounced Christianity of the state. But in Bauer's sense the Jewish question has a general significance, independent of the specifically German conditions. It is the question of the relations between religion and the state, of the *contradiction between religious prejudice and political emancipation.* Emancipation from religion is posited as a condition, both for the Jew who wants political emancipation, and for the state which should emancipate him and itself be emancipated.

"Very well, it may be said (and the Jew himself says it) but the Jew should not be emancipated because he is a Jew, because he has such an excellent and universal moral creed; the *Jew* should take second place to the citizen, and he will be a *citizen* although he is and desires to remain a Jew. In other words, he is and remains a *Jew,* even though he is a *citizen* and as such lives in a universal human condition; his restricted Jewish nature always finally triumphs over his human and political obligations. The bias persists even though it is overcome by general principles. But if it persists, it would be truer to say that it overcomes all the rest." "It is only in a sophistical and superficial sense that the Jew could remain a Jew in political life. Consequently, if he wanted to remain a Jew, this would mean that the superficial became the essential and thus triumphed. In other words, his life *in the state* would be only a semblance, or a momentary exception to the essential and normal."[2]

Let us see also how Bauer establishes the role of the state.

"France," he says, "has provided us recently,[3] in connexion with the Jewish question (and for that matter all other *political* questions), with the spectacle of a life

2. Bauer, "Die Fähigkeit der heutigen Juden und Christen, frei zu werden," *Einundzwanzig Bogen,* p. 57.— *Marx.* [Emphases added by Marx.]

3. Chamber of Deputies. Debate of 26th December, 1840.—*Marx.*

which is free but which revokes its freedom by law and so declares it to be merely an appearance; and which, on the other hand, denies its free laws by its acts."[4]

"In France, universal liberty is not yet established by law, nor is the *Jewish question as yet resolved,* because legal liberty, i.e. the equality of all citizens, is restricted in actual life, which is still dominated and fragmented by religious privileges, and because the lack of liberty in actual life influences law in its turn and obliges it to sanction the division of citizens who are by nature free into oppressors and oppressed."[5]

When, therefore, would the Jewish question be resolved in France?

"The Jew would really have ceased to be Jewish, for example, if he did not allow his religious code to prevent his fulfilment of his duties towards the state and his fellow citizens; if he attended and took part in the public business of the Chamber of Deputies on the sabbath. It would be necessary, further, to abolish all *religious privilege,* including the monopoly of a privileged church. If, thereafter, some or many or *even the overwhelming majority felt obliged to fulfil their religious duties,* such practices should be left *to them as an absolutely* private matter."[6] "There is no longer any religion when there is no longer a privileged religion. Take away from religion its power to excommunicate and it will no longer exist."[7] "Mr. Martin du Nord has seen, in the suggestion to omit any mention of Sunday in the law, a proposal to declare that Christianity has ceased to exist. With equal right (and the right is well founded) the declaration that the law of the sabbath is no longer binding upon the Jew would amount to proclaiming the end of Judaism."[8]

Thus Bauer demands, on the one hand, that the Jew should renounce Judaism, and in general that man should renounce religion, in order to be emancipated as a citizen. On the other hand, he considers, and this follows logically, that the political abolition of religion is the abolition of all religion. The state which presupposes religion is not yet a true or actual state. "Clearly, the religious idea gives some assurances to the state. But to what state? *To what kind of state?*"[9]

At this point we see that the Jewish question is considered only from one aspect.

It was by no means sufficient to ask: who should emancipate? who should be emancipated? The critic should ask a third question: *what kind of emancipation is involved?* What are the essential conditions of the emancipation which is demanded? The criticism of *political emancipation* itself was only the final criticism of the Jewish question and its genuine resolution into the *"general question of the age."*

Bauer, since he does not formulate the problem at this level, falls into contradictions. He establishes conditions which are not based upon the nature of *political* emancipation. He raises questions which are irrelevant to his problem, and he

4. Bauer, *Die Judenfrage*, p. 64.—*Marx.*

5. Ibid., p. 65.—*Marx.*

6. Loc. cit.—*Marx.*

7. Ibid., p. 71.—*Marx.*

8. Bauer, *Die Judenfrage*, p. 66.—*Marx.*

9. Ibid., p. 97.—*Marx.*

resolves problems which leave his question unanswered. When Bauer says of the opponents of Jewish emancipation that "Their error was simply to assume that the Christian state was the only true one, and not to subject it to the same criticism as Judaism,"[10] we see his own error in the fact that he subjects only the "Christian state," and not the "state as such" to criticism, that he does not examine *the relation between political emancipation and human emancipation,* and that he, therefore, poses conditions which are only explicable by his lack of critical sense in confusing political emancipation and universal human emancipation. Bauer asks the Jews: Have you, from your standpoint, the right to demand *political emancipation?* We ask the converse question: from the standpoint of *political* emancipation can the Jew be required to abolish Judaism, or man be asked to abolish religion?

The Jewish question presents itself differently according to the state in which the Jew resides. In Germany, where there is no political state, no state as such, the Jewish question is purely *theological*. The Jew finds himself in *religious* opposition to the state, which proclaims Christianity as its foundation. This state is a theologian *ex professo*. Criticism here is criticism of theology; a double-edged criticism, of Christian and of Jewish theology. And so we move always in the domain of theology, however *critically* we may move therein.

In France, which is a *constitutional* state, the Jewish question is a question of constitutionalism, of the incompleteness of *political emancipation*. Since the *semblance* of a state religion is maintained here, if only in the insignificant and self-contradictory formula of a *religion of the majority*, the relation of the Jews to the state also retains a semblance of religious, theological opposition.

It is only in the free states of North America, or at least in some of them, that the Jewish question loses its *theological* significance and becomes a truly *secular* question. Only where the state exists in its completely developed form can the relation of the Jew, and of the religious man in general, to the political state appear in a pure form, with its own characteristics. The criticism of this relation ceases to be theological criticism when the state ceases to maintain a *theological* attitude towards religion, that is, when it adopts the attitude of a state, i.e. a *political* attitude. Criticism then becomes *criticism of the political* state. And at this point, where the question ceases to be *theological*, Bauer's criticism ceases to be critical.

"There is not, in the United States, either a state religion or a religion declared to be that of a majority, or a predominance of one religion over another. The state remains aloof from all religions."[11] There are even some states in North America in which "the constitution does not impose any religious belief or practice as a condition of political rights."[12] And yet, "no one in the United States believes that a man without religion can be an honest man."[13] And North America is pre-eminently the

---

10. Bauer, *Die Judenfrage*, p. 3.—*Marx.*

11. Gustave de Beaumont, *Marie ou l'esclavage aux États-Unis Bruxelles*, 1835, 2 vols., II, p. 207.—*Marx.* [Marx refers to another edition, Paris, 1835.]

12. Ibid., p. 216. [Beaumont actually refers to *all* the States of North America.]

13. Ibid., p. 217.—*Marx.*

country of religiosity, as Beaumont,[14] Tocqueville[15] and the Englishman, Hamilton,[16] assure us in unison. However, the states of North America only serve as an example. The question is: what is the relation between *complete* political emancipation and religion? If we find in the country which has attained full political emancipation, that religion not only continues to *exist* but is *fresh* and *vigorous*, this is proof that the existence of religion is not at all opposed to the perfection of the state. But since the existence of religion is the existence of a defect, the source of this defect must be sought in the *nature* of the state itself. Religion no longer appears as the basis, but as the *manifestation* of secular narrowness. That is why we explain the religious constraints upon the free citizens by the secular constraints upon them. We do not claim that they must transcend their religious narrowness in order to get rid of their secular limitations. We claim that they will transcend their religious narrowness once they have overcome their secular limitations. We do not turn secular questions into theological questions; we turn theological questions into secular ones. History has for long enough been resolved into superstition; but we now resolve superstition into history. The question of the *relation between political emancipation and religion* becomes for us a question of the *relation between political emancipation and human emancipation*. We criticize the religious failings of the political state by criticizing the political state in its *secular* form, disregarding its religious failings. We express in human terms the contradiction between the state and a *particular religion,* for example Judaism, by showing the contradiction between the state and particular *secular elements,* between the state and *religion in general* and between the state and its general *presuppositions.*

The *political* emancipation of the Jew or the Christian—of the *religious* man in general—is the *emancipation of* the state from Judaism, Christianity, and *religion* in general. The *state* emancipates itself from religion in its own particular way, in the mode which corresponds to its nature, by emancipating itself from the *state religion;* that is to say, by giving recognition to no religion and affirming itself purely and simply as a state. To be *politically* emancipated from religion is not to be finally and completely emancipated from religion, because political emancipation is not the final and absolute form of *human* emancipation.

The limits of political emancipation appear at once in the fact that the *state* can liberate itself from a constraint without man himself being *really* liberated; that a state may be a *free state* without man himself being a *free man*. Bauer himself tacitly admits this when he makes political emancipation depend upon the following condition—

"It would be necessary, moreover, to abolish all religious privileges, including the monopoly of a privileged church. If some people, or even the *immense majority, still felt obliged to fulfil their religious duties,* this practice should be left to them as a *completely private matter*." Thus the state may have emancipated itself from religion, even though the *immense majority* of people continue to be religious. And the immense majority do not cease to be religious by virtue of being religious *in private*.

---

14. G. de Beaumont, op. cit.—*Marx.*

15. A. de Tocqueville, *De la démocratie en Amérique.*—*Marx.*

16. Thomas Hamilton, *Men and Manners in North America,* Edinburgh, 1833, 2 vols.—*Marx.* [Marx quotes from the German translation, Mannheim, 1834.]

The attitude of the state, especially the *free state,* towards religion is only the attitude towards religion of the individuals who compose the state. It follows that man frees himself from a constraint in a *political* way, through the state, when he transcends his limitations, in contradiction with himself, and in an *abstract, narrow* and partial way. Furthermore, by emancipating himself *politically,* man emancipates himself in a *devious way,* through an intermediary, however *necessary* this intermediary may be. Finally, even when he proclaims himself an atheist through the intermediary of the state, that is, when he declares the state to be an atheist, he is still engrossed in religion, because he only recognizes himself as an atheist in a roundabout way, through an intermediary. Religion is simply the recognition of man in a roundabout fashion; that is, through an intermediary. The state is the intermediary between man and human liberty. Just as Christ is the intermediary to whom man attributes all his own divinity and all his *religious* bonds, so the state is the intermediary to which man confides all his non-divinity and all his *human freedom.*

The *political* elevation of man above religion shares the weaknesses and merits of all such political measures. For example, the state as a state abolishes *private property* (i.e. man decrees by *political* means the *abolition* of private property) when it abolishes the *property qualification* for electors and representatives, as has been done in many of the North American States. Hamilton interprets this phenomenon quite correctly from the political standpoint: *The masses have gained a victory over property owners and financial wealth.*[17] Is not private property ideally abolished when the nonowner comes to legislate for the owner of property? The *property qualification* is the last *political* form in which private property is recognized.

But the political suppression of private property not only does not abolish private property; it actually presupposes its existence. The state abolishes, after its fashion, the distinctions established by birth, *social rank, education, occupation,* when it decrees that birth, social rank, education, occupation are *non-political* distinctions; when it proclaims, without regard to these distinctions, that every member of society is an *equal* partner in popular sovereignty, and treats all the elements which compose the real life of the nation from the standpoint of the state. But the state, none the less, allows private property, education, occupation, to *act* after *their* own fashion, namely as private property, education, occupation, and to manifest their *particular* nature. Far from abolishing these *effective* differences, it only exists so far as they are presupposed; it is conscious of being a *political state* and it manifests its *universality* only in opposition to these elements. Hegel, therefore, defines the relation of the political state to religion quite correctly when he says: "In order for the state to come in to existence as the *self-knowing* ethical actuality of spirit, it is essential that it should be distinct from the forms of authority and of faith. But this distinction emerges only in so far as divisions occur within the ecclesiastical sphere itself. It is only in this way that the state, above the *particular* churches, has attained to the universality of thought—its formal principle—and is bringing this universality into existence."[18] To be sure! Only in this manner, *above* the *particular* elements, can the state constitute itself as universality.

---

17. Hamilton, op. cit., I, pp. 288, 306, 309.—*Marx.*

18. Hegel, *Grundlinien der Philosophie des Rechts, I"' Aufgabe,* 1821, p. 346.—*Marx.* [See the English translation by T. M. Knox, *Hegel's Philosophy of Right,* Oxford, 1942, p. 173.]

The perfected political state is, by its nature, the *species-life*[19] of man as *opposed* to his material life. All the presuppositions of this egoistic life continue to exist in *civil society outside* the political sphere, as qualities of civil society. Where the political state has attained to its full development, man leads, not only in thought, in consciousness, but in *reality*, in *life*, a double existence—celestial and terrestrial. He lives in the *political community*, where he regards himself as a *communal being*, and in *civil society* where he acts simply as a *private individual*, treats other men as means, degrades himself to the role of a mere means, and becomes the plaything of alien powers. The political state, in relation to civil society, is just as spiritual as is heaven in relation to earth. It stands in the same opposition to civil society, and overcomes it in the same manner as religion overcomes the narrowness of the profane world; i.e. it has always to acknowledge it again, re-establish it, and allow itself to be dominated by it. Man, in his *most intimate* reality, in civil society, is a profane being. Here, where he appears both to himself and to others as a real individual he is an *illusory* phenomenon. In the state, on the contrary, where he is regarded as a species-being,[20] man is the imaginary member of an imaginary sovereignty, divested of his real, individual life, and infused with an unreal universality.

The conflict in which the individual, as the professor of a *particular* religion, finds himself involved with his own quality of citizenship and with other men as members of the community, may be resolved into the *secular* schism between the *political* state and *civil society*. For man as a *bourgeois*[21] "life in the state is only an appearance or a fleeting exception to the normal and essential." It is true that the *bourgeois*, like the Jew, participates in political life only in a sophistical way, just as the *citoyen*[22] is a Jew or a *bourgeois* only in a sophistical way. But this sophistry is not personal. It is the *sophistry of the political state* itself. The difference between the religious man and the citizen is the same as that between the shopkeeper and the citizens, between the day-labourer and the citizen, between the landed proprietor and the citizen, between the *living individual* and the *citizen*. The contradiction in which the religious man finds himself with the political man, is the same contradiction in which the *bourgeois* finds himself with the citizen, and the member of civil society with his *political lion's skin*.

This secular opposition, to which the Jewish question reduces itself—the relation between the political state and its presuppositions, whether the latter are material elements such as private property, etc., or spiritual elements such as culture or

---

19. [The terms "species-life" (*Gattungsleben*) and "species-being" (*Gattungswesen*) are derived from Feuerbach. In the first chapter of *Das Wesen des Christentums* [*The Essence of Christianity*], Leipzig, 1841, Feuerbach discusses the nature of man, and argues that man is to be distinguished from animals not by "consciousness" as such, but by a particular kind of consciousness. Man is not only conscious of himself as an individual; he is also conscious of himself as a member of the human species, and so he apprehends a "human essence" which is the same in himself and in other men. According to Feuerbach this ability to conceive of "species" is the fundamental element in the human power of reasoning: "Science is the consciousness of species." Marx, while not departing from this meaning of the terms, employs them in other contexts; and he insists more strongly than Feuerbach that since this "species-consciousness" defines the nature of man, man is only living and acting authentically (i.e. in accordance with his nature) when he lives and acts deliberately as a "species-being," that is, as a *social* being.]

20. [See previous note.]

21. [I.e. as a member of civil society.]

22. [I.e. the individual with political rights.]

religion, the conflict between the *general interest* and *private interest*, the schism between the *political* state and *civil society*—these profane contradictions, Bauer leaves
intact, while he directs his polemic against their *religious* expression. "It is precisely
this basis—that is, the needs which assure the existence of *civil society* and *guarantee
its necessity*—which exposes its existence to continual danger, maintains an element
of uncertainty in civil society, produces this continually changing compound of
wealth and poverty, of prosperity and distress, and above all generates change."[23]
Compare the whole section entitled "Civil society,"[24] which follows closely the distinctive features of Hegel's philosophy of right. Civil society, in its opposition to this
political state, is recognized as necessary because the political state is recognized as
necessary.

Political emancipation certainly represents a great progress. It is not, indeed, the
final form of human emancipation, but it is the final form of human emancipation
within the framework of the prevailing social order. It goes without saying that we
are speaking here of real, practical emancipation.

Man emancipates himself *politically* from religion by expelling it from the sphere
of public law to that of private law. Religion is no longer the spirit of the state, in
which man behaves, albeit in a specific and limited way and in a particular sphere,
as a species-being, in community with other men. It has become the spirit of *civil
society*, of the sphere of egoism and of the *bellum omnium contra omnes*. It is no longer
the essence of *community*, but the essence of *differentiation*. It has become what it was
at the *beginning*, an expression of the fact that man is *separated* from the *community*,
from himself and from other men. It is now only the abstract avowal of an individual
folly, a private whim or caprice. The infinite fragmentation of religion in North
America, for example, already gives it the *external* form of a strictly private affair.
It has been relegated among the numerous private interests and exiled from the life
of the community as such. But one should have no illusions about the scope of
political emancipation. The division of man into the *public person* and the *private
person*, the *displacement* of religion from the state to civil society—all this is not a stage
in political emancipation but its consummation. Thus political emancipation does
not abolish, and does not even strive to abolish, man's *real* religiosity.

The *decomposition* of man into Jew and citizen, Protestant and citizen, religious
man and citizen, is not a deception practised *against* the political system nor yet an
evasion of political emancipation. It is *political emancipation itself*, the *political* mode
of emancipation from religion. Certainly, in periods when the political state as such
comes violently to birth in civil society, and when men strive to liberate themselves
through political emancipation, the state can, and must, proceed to *abolish and destroy
religion;* but only in the same way as it proceeds to abolish private property, by
declaring a maximum, by confiscation, or by progressive taxation, or in the same
way as it proceeds to abolish life, by the *guillotine*. At those times when the state is
most aware of itself, political life seeks to stifle its own prerequisites—civil society
and its elements—and to establish itself as the genuine and harmonious species-life
of man. But it can only achieve this end by setting itself in *violent* contradiction
with its own conditions of existence, by declaring a *permanent* revolution. Thus the

23. Bauer, *Die Judenfrage*, p. 8.—*Marx.*

24. Ibid., pp. 8–9.—*Marx.*

political drama ends necessarily with the restoration of religion, of private property, of all the elements of civil society, just as war ends with the conclusion of peace.

In fact, the perfected Christian state is not the so-called *Christian* state which acknowledges Christianity as its basis, as the state religion, and thus adopts an exclusive attitude towards other religions; it is, rather, the *atheistic* state, the democratic state, the state which relegates religion among the other elements of civil society. The state which is still theological, which still professes officially the Christian creed, and which has not yet dared to declare itself a *state*, has not yet succeeded in expressing in a human and *secular* form, in its political *reality*, the human basis of which Christianity is the transcendental expression. The so-called Christian state is simply a *non-state;* since it is not Christianity as a religion, but only the *human core* of the Christian religion which can realize itself in truly human creations.

The so-called Christian state is the Christian negation of the state, but not at all the political realization of Christianity. The state which professes Christianity as a religion does not yet profess it in a political form, because it still has a religious attitude towards religion. In other words, such a state is not the *genuine realization* of the human basis of religion, because it still accepts the *unreal, imaginary* form of this human core. The so-called Christian state is an *imperfect* state, for which the Christian religion serves as the *supplement* and *sanctification* of its imperfection. Thus religion becomes necessarily one of its *means;* and so it is the *hypocritical* state. There is a great difference between saying: (i) that the *perfect* state, owing to a deficiency in the general *nature* of the state, counts religion as one of its *prerequisites*, or (ii) that the *imperfect* state, owing to a deficiency in its *particular existence* as an imperfect state, declares that religion is its *basis*. In the latter, religion becomes *imperfect politics*. In the former, the imperfection even of perfected *politics* is revealed in religion. The so-called Christian state needs the Christian religion in order to complete itself *as a state*. The democratic state, the real state, does not need religion for its political consummation. On the contrary, it can dispense with religion, because in this case the human core of religion is realized in a profane manner. The so-called Christian state, on the other hand, has a political attitude towards religion, and a religious attitude towards politics. It reduces political institutions and religion equally to mere appearances.

In order to make this contradiction clearer we shall examine Bauer's model of the Christian state, a model which is derived from his study of the German-Christian state.

"Quite recently," says Bauer, "in order to demonstrate the *impossibility* or the *non-existence* of a Christian state, those passages in the Bible have been frequently quoted with which the state *does not conform* and *cannot conform unless it wishes to dissolve itself entirely*."

"But the question is not so easily settled. What do these Biblical passages demand? Supernatural renunciation, submission to the authority of revelation, turning away from the state, the abolition of profane conditions. But the Christian state proclaims and accomplishes all these things. It has assimilated the *spirit of the Bible,* and if it does not reproduce it exactly in the terms which the Bible uses, that is simply because it expresses this spirit in political forms, in forms which are borrowed from the political system of this world but which, in the religious rebirth which they are obliged to undergo, are reduced to simple appearances. Man turns away from the state and by this means realizes and completes the political institutions."[25]

Bauer continues by showing that the members of a Christian state no longer constitute a nation with a will of its own. The nation has its true existence in the leader to whom it is subjected, but this leader is, by his origin and nature, alien to it since he has been imposed by God without the people having any part in the matter. The laws of such a nation are not its own work, but are direct revelations. The supreme leader, in his relations with the real nation, the masses, requires privileged intermediaries; and the nation itself disintegrates into a multitude of distinct spheres which are formed and determined by chance, are differentiated from each other by their interests and their specific passions and prejudices, and acquire as a privilege the permission to isolate themselves from each other, etc.[26]

But Bauer himself says: "Politics, if it is to be nothing more than religion, should not be politics; any more than the scouring of pans, if it is treated as a religious matter, should be regarded as ordinary housekeeping."[27] But in the German-Christian state religion is an "economic matter" just as "economic matters" are religion. In the German-Christian state the power of religion is the religion of power.

The separation of the "spirit of the Bible" from the "letter of the Bible" is an *irreligious* act. The state which expresses the Bible in the letter of politics, or in any letter other than that of the Holy Ghost, commits sacrilege, if not in the eyes of men at least in the eyes of its own religion. The state which acknowledges the Bible as its charter and Christianity as its supreme rule must be assessed according to the words of the Bible; for even the language of the Bible is sacred. Such a state, as well as the *human rubbish* upon which it is based, finds itself involved in a painful contradiction, which is insoluble from the standpoint of religious consciousness, when it is referred to those words of the Bible "with which it does not conform and *cannot conform unless it wishes to dissolve itself entirely.*" And why does it not wish to dissolve itself entirely? The state itself cannot answer either itself or others. In its own consciousness the official Christian state is an "ought" whose realization is impossible. It cannot affirm the *reality* of its own existence without lying to itself, and so it remains always in its own eyes an object of doubt, an uncertain and problematic object. Criticism is, therefore, entirely within its rights in forcing the state, which supports itself upon the Bible, into a total disorder of thought in which it no longer knows whether it is *illusion* or *reality;* and in which the infamy of its *profane* ends (for which religion serves as a cloak) enter into an insoluble conflict with the probity of its *religious* consciousness (for which religion appears as the goal of the world). Such a state can only escape its inner torment by becoming the *myrmidon* of the Catholic Church. In the face of this Church, which asserts that secular power is entirely subordinate to its commands, the state is powerless; powerless the secular power which claims to be the rule of the religious spirit.

What prevails in the so-called Christian state is not man but alienation. The only man who counts—the *King*—is specifically differentiated from other men and is still

25. Bauer, *Die Judenfrage*, p. 55.—*Marx.*

26. Ibid., p. 56.—*Marx.*

27. Ibid., p. 108.—*Marx.*

a religious being associated directly with heaven and with God. The relations which exist here are relations still based upon *faith*. The religious spirit is still not really secularized.

But the religious spirit cannot be *really* secularized. For what is it but the *non-secular* form of a stage in the development of the human spirit? The religious spirit can only be realized if the stage of development of the human spirit which it expresses in religious form, manifests and constitutes itself in its *secular* form. This is what happens in the *democratic* state. The basis of this state is not Christianity but the *human basis* of Christianity. Religion remains the ideal, non-secular consciousness of its members, because it is the ideal form of the *stage of human development* which has been attained.

The members of the political state are religious because of the dualism between individual life and species-life, between the life of civil society and political life. They are religious in the sense that man treats political life, which is remote from his own individual existence, as if it were his true life; and in the sense that religion is here the spirit of civil society, and expresses the separation and withdrawal of man from man. Political democracy is Christian in the sense that man, not merely one man but every man, is there considered a sovereign being, a supreme being; but it is uneducated, unsocial man, man just as he is in his fortuitous existence, man as he has been corrupted, lost to himself, alienated, subjected to the rule of inhuman conditions and elements, by the whole organization of our society—in short man who is not yet a *real* species-being. Creations of fantasy, dreams, the postulates of Christianity, the sovereignty of man—but of man as an alien being distinguished from the real man—all these become, in democracy, the tangible and present reality, secular maxims.

In the perfected democracy, the religious and theological consciousness appears to itself all the more religious and theological in that it is apparently without any political significance or terrestrial aims, is an affair of the heart withdrawn from the world, an expression of the limitations of reason, a product of arbitrariness and fantasy, a veritable life in the beyond. Christianity here attains the *practical* expression of its universal religious significance, because the most varied views are brought together in the form of Christianity, and still more because Christianity does not ask that anyone should profess Christianity, but simply that he should have some kind of religion (*see* Beaumont, op. cit.). The religious consciousness runs riot in a wealth of contradictions and diversity.

We have shown, therefore, that political emancipation from religion leaves religion in existence, although this is no longer a privileged religion. The contradiction in which the adherent of a particular religion finds himself in relation to his citizenship is only *one aspect* of the universal *secular contradiction between the political state and* civil society. The consummation of the Christian state is a state which acknowledges itself simply as a state and ignores the religion of its members. The emancipation of the state from religion is not the emancipation of the real man from religion.

We do not say to the Jews, therefore, as does Bauer: you cannot be emancipated politically without emancipating yourselves completely from Judaism. We say rather: it is because you can be emancipated politically, without renouncing Judaism completely and absolutely, that *political emancipation* itself is not *human emancipation*. If you want to be politically emancipated, without emancipating yourselves humanly, the inadequacy and the contradiction is not entirely in yourselves but in the *nature* and the *category* of political emancipation. If you are preoccupied with this category you share the general prejudice. Just as the state *evangelizes* when, although it is a state, it adopts a Christian attitude towards the Jews, the Jew *acts politically* when, though a Jew, he demands civil rights.

But if a man, though a Jew, can be emancipated politically and acquire civil rights, can he claim and acquire what are called the *rights of man*? Bauer *denies* it. "The question is whether the Jew as such, that is, the Jew who himself avows that he is constrained by his true nature to live eternally separate from men, is able to acquire and to concede to others the *universal rights of man.*"

"The idea of the rights of man was only discovered in the Christian world, in the last century. It is not an innate idea; on the contrary, it is acquired in a struggle against the historical traditions in which man has been educated up to the present time. The rights of man are not, therefore, a gift of nature, nor a legacy from past history, but the reward of a struggle against the accident of birth and against the privileges which history has hitherto transmitted from generation to generation. They are the results of culture, and only he can possess them who has merited and earned them."

"But can the Jew really take possession of them? As long as he remains Jewish the limited nature which makes him a Jew must prevail over the human nature which should associate him, as a man, with other men; and it will isolate him from everyone who is not a Jew. He declares, by this separation, that the particular nature which makes him Jewish is his true and supreme nature, before which human nature has to efface itself."

"Similarly, the Christian as such cannot grant the rights of man."[28]

According to Bauer man has to sacrifice the *"privilege of faith"* in order to acquire the general rights of man. Let us consider for a moment the so-called rights of man; let us examine them in their most authentic form, that which they have among those who *discovered* them, the North Americans and the French! These rights of man are, in part, *political rights,* which can only be exercised if one is a member of a community. Their content is *participation* in the *community* life, in the *political* life of the community, the life of the state. They fall in the category of *political liberty,* of *civil rights,* which as we have seen do not at all presuppose the consistent and positive abolition of religion; nor consequently, of Judaism. It remains to consider the other part, namely the *rights of man* as distinct from the *rights of the citizen.*

Among them is to be found the freedom of conscience, the right to practise a chosen religion. The *privilege of faith* is expressly recognized, either as a *right of man* or as a consequence of a right of man, namely liberty. *Declaration of the Rights of Man and of the Citizen,* 1791, Article 10: "No one is to be disturbed on account of his opinions, even religious opinions." There is guaranteed, as one of the rights of man, "the liberty of every man to practise the *religion* to which he adheres."

The Declaration of the Rights of Man, etc. 1793, enumerates among the rights of man (Article 7): "The liberty of religious observance." Moreover, it is even stated, with respect to the right to express ideas and opinions, to hold meetings, to practise a religion, that: "The necessity of enunciating these *rights* presupposes either the

---

28. Bauer, *Die Judenfrage,* pp. 19–20.—*Marx.*

existence or the recent memory of despotism." Compare the Constitution of 1795, Section XII, Article 354.

Constitution of Pennsylvania, Article 9, §3: "All men have received from nature the imprescriptible *right* to worship the Almighty according to the dictates of their conscience, and no one can be legally compelled to follow, establish or support against his will any religion or religious ministry. No human authority can, in any circumstances, intervene in a matter of conscience or control the forces of the soul."

Constitution of New Hampshire, Articles 5 and 6: "Among these natural rights some are by nature inalienable since nothing can replace them. The rights of conscience are among them."[29]

The incompatibility between religion and the rights of man is so little manifest in the concept of the rights of man that the *right to be religious,* in one's own fashion, and to practise one's own particular religion, is expressly included among the rights of man. The privilege of faith is a *universal right of man.*

A distinction is made between the rights of man and the rights of the citizen. Who is this *man* distinct from the *citizen?* No one but the *member of civil society.* Why is the member of civil society called "man," simply man, and why are his rights called the "rights of man"? How is this fact to be explained? By the relation between the political state and civil society, and by the nature of political emancipation.

Let us notice first of all that the so-called *rights of man,* as distinct from the *rights of the citizen,* are simply the rights of a *member of civil society,* that is, of egoistic man, of man separated from other men and from the community. The most radical constitution, that of 1793, says: *Declaration of the Rights of Man and of the Citizen:* Article 2. "These rights, etc. (the natural and imprescriptible rights) are: *equality, liberty, security, property.*

What constitutes liberty?

Article 6. "Liberty is the power which man has to do everything which does not harm the rights of others."

Liberty is, therefore, the right to do everything which does not harm others. The limits within which each individual can act without harming others are determined by law, just as the boundary between two fields is marked by a stake. It is a question of the liberty of man regarded as an isolated monad, withdrawn into himself. Why, according to Bauer, is the Jew not fitted to acquire the rights of man? "As long as he remains Jewish the limited nature which makes him a Jew must prevail over the human nature which should associate him, as a man, with other men; and it will isolate him from everyone who is not a Jew." But liberty as a right of man is not founded upon the relations between man and man, but rather upon the separation of man from man. It is the right of such separation. The right of the *circumscribed* individual, withdrawn into himself.

The practical application of the right of liberty is the right of private property. What constitutes the right of private property?

Article 16 (Constitution of 1793). "The right of *property* is that which belongs to every citizen of enjoying and disposing *as he will* of his goods and revenues, of the fruits of his work and industry."

---

29. Beaumont, op. cit., II, pp. 206–7.—*Marx.*

The right of property is, therefore, the right to enjoy one's fortune and to dispose of it as one will; without regard for other men and independently of society. It is the right of self-interest. This individual liberty, and its application, form the basis of civil society. It leads every man to see in other men, not the *realization,* but rather the *limitation* of his own liberty. It declares above all the right "to enjoy and to dispose *as one will,* one's goods and revenues, the fruits of one's work and industry."

There remain the other rights of man, equality and security.

The term "equality" has here no political significance. It is only the equal right to liberty as defined above; namely that every man is equally regarded as a self-sufficient monad. The Constitution of 1795 defines the concept of liberty in this sense.

Article 5 (*Constitution* of 1795). "Equality consists in the fact that the law is the same for all, whether it protects or punishes."

And security?

Article 8 (*Constitution* of 1793). "Security consists in the protection afforded by society to each of its members for the preservation of his person, his rights, and his property."

Security is the supreme social concept of civil society; the concept of the police. The whole society exists only in order to guarantee for each of its members the preservation of his person, his rights and his property. It is in this sense that Hegel calls civil society "the state of need and of reason."

The concept of security is not enough to raise civil society above its egoism. Security is, rather, the *assurance* of its egoism.

None of the supposed rights of man, therefore, go beyond the egoistic man, man as he is, as a member of civil society; that is, an individual separated from the community, withdrawn into himself, wholly preoccupied with his private interest and acting in accordance with his private caprice. Man is far from being considered, in the rights of man, as a species-being; on the contrary, species-life itself—society—appears as a system which is external to the individual and as a limitation of his original independence. The only bond between men is natural necessity, need and private interest, the preservation of their property and their egoistic persons.

It is difficult enough to understand that a nation which has just begun to liberate itself, to tear down all the barriers between different sections of the people and to establish a political community, should solemnly proclaim (*Declaration* of 1791) the rights of the egoistic man, separated from his fellow men and from the community, and should renew this proclamation at a moment when only the most heroic devotion can save the nation (and is, therefore, urgently called for), and when the sacrifice of all the interests of civil society is in question and egoism should be punished as a crime. (*Declaration of the Rights of Man, etc.* 1793). The matter becomes still more incomprehensible when we observe that the political liberators reduce citizenship, the *political community,* to a mere *means* for preserving these so-called rights of man; and consequently, that the citizen is declared to be the servant of egoistic "man," that the sphere in which man functions as a species-being is degraded to a level below the sphere where he functions as a partial being, and finally that it is man as a bourgeois and not man as a citizen who is considered the *true* and *authentic* man.

"The end of every *political association* is the *preservation* of the natural and impre-scriptible rights of man." (*Declaration of the Rights of Man, etc.* 1791, Article 2.)

"Government is instituted in order to guarantee man's enjoyment of his natural and imprescriptible rights." (*Declaration, etc.* 1793, Article 1.) Thus, even in the period of its youthful enthusiasm, which is raised to fever pitch by the force of circumstances, political life declares itself to be only a *means*, whose end is the life of civil society. It is true that its revolutionary practice is in flagrant contradiction with its theory. While, for instance, security is declared to be one of the rights of man, the violation of the privacy of correspondence is openly considered. While the "unlimited freedom of the Press" (*Constitution* of 1793, Article 122), as a corollary of the right of individual liberty, is guaranteed, the freedom of the Press is completely destroyed, since "the freedom of the Press should not be permitted when it endangers public liberty."[30] This amounts to saying: the right to liberty ceases to be a right as soon as it comes into conflict with *political* life, whereas in theory political life is no more than the guarantee of the rights of man—the rights of the individual man—and should, therefore, be suspended as soon as it comes into contradiction with its *end*, these rights of man. But practice is only the exception, while theory is the rule. Even if one decided to regard revolutionary practice as the correct expression of this relation, the problem would remain as to why it is that in the minds of political liberators the relation is inverted, so that the end appears as the means and the means as the end? This optical illusion of their consciousness would always remain a problem, though a psychological and theoretical one.

But the problem is easily solved.

Political emancipation is at the same time the *dissolution* of the old society, upon which the sovereign power, the alienated political life of the people, rests. Political revolution is a revolution of civil society. What was the nature of the old society? It can be characterized in one word: *feudalism.* The old civil society had a *directly political* character; that is, the elements of civil life such as property, the family, and types of occupation had been raised, in the form of lordship, caste and guilds, to elements of political life. They determined, in this form, the relation of the individual to the *state as a whole;* that is, his *political* situation, or in other words, his separation and exclusion from the other elements of society. For this organization of national life did not constitute property and labour as social elements; it rather succeeded in *separating* them from the body of the state, and made them *distinct* societies within society. Nevertheless, at least in the feudal sense, the vital functions and conditions of civil society remained political. They excluded the individual from the body of the state, and transformed the *particular* relation which existed between his corporation and the state into a general relation between the individual and social life, just as they transformed his specific civil activity and situation into a general activity and situation. As a result of this organization, the state as a whole and its consciousness, will and activity—the general political power—also necessarily appeared as the *private* affair of a ruler and his servants, separated from the people.

The political revolution which overthrew this power of the ruler, which made state affairs the affairs of the people, and the political state a matter of *general* concern, i.e. a real state, necessarily shattered everything—estates, corporations, guilds, privileges—which expressed the separation of the people from community life. The political revolution therefore *abolished* the *political character of civil society.*

---

30. Buchez et Roux, "Robespierre jeune," *Histoire parlementaire de la Révolution française,* Tome XXVIII, p. 159.—*Marx.*

It dissolved civil society into its basic elements, on the one hand *individuals,* and on the other hand the *material and cultural elements* which formed the life experience and the civil situation of these individuals. It set free the political spirit which had, so to speak, been dissolved, fragmented and lost in the various culs-de-sac of feudal society; it reassembled these scattered fragments, liberated the political spirit from its connexion with civil life and made of it the community sphere, the *general* concern of the people, in principle independent of these particular elements of civil life. A *specific* activity and situation in life no longer had any but an individual significance. They no longer constituted the general relation between the individual and the state as a whole. Public affairs as such became the general affair of each individual, and political functions became general functions.

But the consummation of the idealism of the state was at the same time the consummation of the materialism of civil society. The bonds which had restrained the egoistic spirit of civil society were removed along with the political yoke. Political emancipation was at the same time an emancipation of civil society from politics and from even the *semblance* of a general content.

Feudal society was dissolved into its basic element, *man;* but into *egoistic* man who was its real foundation.

Man in this aspect, the member of civil society, is now the foundation and presupposition of the *political* state. He is recognized as such in the rights of man.

But the liberty of egoistic man, and the recognition of this liberty, is rather the recognition of the *frenzied* movement of the cultural and material elements which form the content of his life.

· Thus man was not liberated from religion; he received religious liberty. He was not liberated from property; he received the liberty to own property. He was not liberated from the egoism of business; he received the liberty to engage in business.

· The *formation of the political state,* and the dissolution of civil society into independent *individuals* whose relations are regulated by *law,* as the relations between men in the corporations and guilds were regulated by *privilege,* are accomplished by *one and the same act.* Man as a member of civil society—*non-political* man—necessarily appears as the *natural* man. The rights of man appear as natural rights because *conscious* activity is concentrated upon political *action. Egoistic* man is the *passive, given* result of the dissolution of society, an object of *direct apprehension* and consequently a *natural* object. The *political revolution* dissolves civil society into its elements without *revolutionizing* these elements themselves or subjecting them to criticism. This revolution regards civil society, the sphere of human needs, labour, private interests and civil law, as the *basis of its own existence,* as a self-subsistent *precondition,* and thus as its *natural basis.* Finally, man as a member of civil society is identified with *authentic man,* man as distinct from citizen, because he is man in his sensuous, individual and *immediate* existence, whereas *political* man is only abstract, artificial man, man as an *allegorical, moral* person. Thus man as he really is, is seen only in the form of *egoistic* man, and man in his *true* nature only in the form of the *abstract citizen.*

The abstract notion of political man is well formulated by Rousseau: "Whoever dares undertake to establish a people's institutions must feel himself capable of *changing,* as it were, *human nature* itself, of *transforming* each individual who, in isolation, is a complete but solitary whole, into a *part* of something greater than himself, from which in a sense, he derives his life and his being; [of changing man's nature in order to strengthen it;] of substituting a limited and moral existence for the physical and independent life [with which all of us are endowed by nature]. His task, in short, is to take from *a man his own powers,* and to give him in exchange alien powers which he can only employ with the help of other men."[31]

Every emancipation is a *restoration* of the human world and of human relationships to *man himself.*

Political emancipation is a reduction of man, on the one hand to a member of civil society, an *independent* and *egoistic* individual, and on the other hand, to a *citizen,* to a moral person.

Human emancipation will only be complete when the real, individual man has absorbed into himself the abstract citizen; when as an individual man, in his everyday life, in his work, and in his relationships, he has become a *species-being;* and when he has recognized and organized his own powers (*forces propres*) as *social* powers so that he no longer separates this social power from himself as *political* power.

2. Bruno Bauer, "Die Fähigkeit der heutigen Juden und Christen frei zu werden"[32]

It is in this form that Bauer studies the relation between the *Jewish and Christian religions,* and also their relation with modern criticism. This latter relation is their relation with "the capacity to become free."

He reaches this conclusion: "The Christian has only to raise himself one degree, to rise above his religion, in order to abolish religion in general," and thus to become free; but "the Jew, on the contrary, has to break not only with his Jewish nature, but also with the process towards the consummation of his religion, a process which has remained alien to him."[33]

Thus Bauer here transforms the question of Jewish emancipation into a purely religious question. The theological doubt about whether the Jew or the Christian has the better chance of attaining salvation is reproduced here in the more enlightened form: which of the two is more *capable of emancipation?* It is indeed no longer asked: which makes free—Judaism or Christianity? On the contrary, it is now asked: which makes free—the negation of Judaism or the negation of Christianity?

"If they wish to become free the Jews should not embrace Christianity as such, but Christianity in dissolution, religion in dissolution; that is to say, the Enlightenment, criticism, and its outcome, a free humanity."[34]

It is still a matter, therefore, of the Jews professing some kind of faith; no longer Christianity as such, but Christianity in dissolution.

Bauer asks the Jews to break with the essence of the Christian religion, but this demand does not follow, as he himself admits, from the development of the Jewish nature.

---

31. J. J. Rousseau, *Du contrat social,* Book II. Chapter VII, "The Legislator." [Marx quoted this passage in French, and added the emphases; he omitted the portions enclosed in square brackets.]

32. [The capacity of the present-day Jews and Christians to become free.] In *Einundzwanzig Bogen aus der Schweiz* (Ed. G. Herwegh), pp. 56–71.—*Marx.*

33. Loc. cit., p. 71.—*Marx.*

34. Ibid., p. 70.—*Marx.*

From the moment when Bauer, at the end of his *Judenfrage,* saw in Judaism only a crude religious criticism of Christianity, and, therefore, attributed to it only a religious significance, it was to be expected that he would transform the emancipation of the Jews into a philosophico-theological act.

Bauer regards the *ideal* and abstract essence of the Jew—his *religion*—as the *whole* of his nature. He, therefore, concludes rightly that "The Jew contributes nothing to mankind when he disregards his own limited law," when he renounces all his Judaism.[35]

The relation between Jews and Christians thus becomes the following: the only interest which the emancipation of the Jew presents for the Christian is a general human and *theoretical* interest.

Judaism is a phenomenon which offends the religious eye of the Christian. As soon as the Christian's eye ceases to be religious the phenomenon ceases to offend it. The emancipation of the Jew is not in itself, therefore, a task which falls to the Christian to perform.

The Jew, on the other hand, if he wants to emancipate himself has to undertake, besides his own work, the work of the Christian—the "criticism of the gospels," of the "life of Jesus," etc.[36]

"It is for them to arrange matters; they will decide their own destiny. But history does not allow itself to be mocked."[37]

We will attempt to escape from the theological formulation of the question. For us, the question concerning the capacity of the Jew for emancipation is transformed into another question: what specific *social* element is it necessary to overcome in order to abolish Judaism? For the capacity of the present-day Jew to emancipate himself expresses the relation of Judaism to the emancipation of the contemporary world. The relation results necessarily from the particular situation of Judaism in the present enslaved world.

Let us consider the real Jew: not the *sabbath* Jew, whom Bauer considers, but the *everyday Jew.*

Let us not seek the secret of the Jew in his religion, but let us seek the secret of the religion in the real Jew.

What is the profane basis of Judaism? *Practical* need, *self-interest.* What is the worldly cult of the Jew? *Huckstering.* What is his worldly god? *Money.*

Very well: then in emancipating itself from *huckstering* and *money,* and thus from real and practical Judaism, our age would emancipate itself.

An organization of society which would abolish the preconditions and thus the very possibility of huckstering, would make the Jew impossible. His religious consciousness would evaporate like some insipid vapour in the real, life-giving air of society. On the other hand, when the Jew recognizes his *practical* nature as invalid

35. Loc. cit., p. 65.—*Marx.*

36. [Marx alludes here to Bruno Bauer, *Kritik der evangelischen Geschichte der Synoptiker,* Vols. I–II, Leipzig, 1841; Vol. III, Braunschweig, 1842, and David Friedrich Strauss, *Das Leben Jesu,* 2 vols. Tübingen, 1835–6. An English translation of Strauss's book by Marian Evans (George Eliot) was published in 1846 under the title *Life of Jesus Critically Examined.*]

37. Bauer, "Die Fähigkeit . . . etc.," p. 71.—*Marx.*

and endeavours to abolish it, he begins to deviate from his former path of development, works for general *human emancipation* and turns against the *supreme practical*
expression of human self-estrangement.

We discern in Judaism, therefore, a universal *antisocial* element of the *present time*,
whose historical development, zealously aided in its harmful aspects by the Jews,
has now attained its culminating point, a point at which it must necessarily begin to
disintegrate.

In the final analysis, the *emancipation of* the Jews is the emancipation of mankind
from *Judaism*.

The Jew has already emancipated himself in a Jewish fashion. "The Jew, who is
merely tolerated in Vienna for example, determines the fate of the whole Empire
by his financial power. The Jew, who may be entirely without rights in the smallest
German state, decides the destiny of Europe. While the corporations and guilds
exclude the Jew, or at least look on him with disfavour, the audacity of industry
mocks the obstinacy of medieval institutions."[38]

This is not an isolated instance. The Jew has emancipated himself in a Jewish
manner, not only by acquiring the power of money, but also because *money* has
become, through him and also apart from him, a world power, while the practical
Jewish spirit has become the practical spirit of the Christian nations. The Jews have
emancipated themselves in so far as the Christians have become Jews.

Thus, for example, Captain Hamilton reports that the devout and politically free
inhabitant of New England is a kind of Laocoon who makes not the least effort to
escape from the serpents which are crushing him. *Mammon* is his idol which he
adores not only with his lips but with the whole force of his body and mind. In his
view the world is no more than a Stock Exchange, and he is convinced that he has
no other destiny here below than to become richer than his neighbour. Trade has
seized upon all his thoughts, and he has no other recreation than to exchange
objects. When he travels he carries, so to speak, his goods and his counter on his
back and talks only of interest and profit. If he loses sight of his own business for
an instant it is only in order to pry into the business of his competitors.[39]

In North America, indeed, the effective domination of the Christian world by
Judaism has come to be manifested in a common and unambiguous form; the
preaching of the Gospel itself, Christian preaching, has become an article of commerce,
and the bankrupt trader in the church behaves like the prosperous clergyman in
business. "This man whom you see at the head of a respectable congregation began
as a trader; his business having failed he has become a minister. This other began
as a priest, but as soon as he had accumulated some money he abandoned the
priesthood for trade. In the eyes of many people the religious ministry is a veritable
industrial career."[40]

According to Bauer, it is "a hypocritical situation when, in theory, the Jew is
deprived of political rights, while in practice he wields tremendous power and

---

38. Bauer, *Die Judenfrage*, p. 14.—*Marx.*

39. Hamilton, op. cit., I, p. 213.—*Marx.* [Marx paraphrases this passage.]

40. Beaumont, op. cit., II, p. 179.—*Marx.*

exercises on a wholesale scale the political influence which is denied him in minor matters."[41]

The contradiction which exists between the effective political power of the Jew and his political rights, is the contradiction between politics and the power of money in general. Politics is in principle superior to the power of money, but in practice it has become its bondsman.

Judaism has maintained itself *alongside* Christianity, not only because it constituted the religious criticism of Christianity and embodied the doubt concerning the religious origins of Christianity, but equally because the practical Jewish spirit—Judaism or commerce[42]—has perpetuated itself in Christian society and has even attained its highest development there. The Jew, who occupies a distinctive place in civil society, only manifests in a distinctive way the Judaism of civil society.

Judaism has been preserved, not in spite of history, but by history.

It is from its own entrails that civil society ceaselessly engenders the Jew.

What was, in itself, the basis of the Jewish religion? Practical need, egoism.

The monotheism of the Jews is, therefore, in reality, a polytheism of the numerous needs of man, a polytheism which makes even the lavatory an object of divine regulation. *Practical need, egoism,* is the principle of *civil society,* and is revealed as such in its pure form as soon as civil society has fully engendered the political state. The god of *practical need and self-interest is money.*

Money is the jealous god of Israel, beside which no other god may exist. Money abases all the gods of mankind and changes them into commodities. Money is the universal and self-sufficient *value* of all things. It has, therefore, deprived the whole world, both the human world and nature, of their own proper value. Money is the alienated essence of man's work and existence; this essence dominates him and he worships it.

The god of the Jews has been secularized and has become the god of this world. The bill of exchange is the real god of the Jew. His god is only an illusory bill of exchange.

The mode of perceiving nature, under the rule of private property and money, is a real contempt for, and a practical degradation of, nature, which does indeed exist in the Jewish religion but only as a creature of the imagination.

It is in this sense that Thomas Münzer declares it intolerable "that every creature should be transformed into property—the fishes in the water, the birds of the air, the plants of the earth: the creature too should become free."[43]

That which is contained in an abstract form in the Jewish religion—contempt for theory, for art, for history, and for man as an end in himself—is the *real, conscious* standpoint and the virtue of the man of money. Even the species-relation itself, the

---

41. Bauer, *Die Judenfrage,* p. 14.—*Marx.*

42. [The German word *Judentum* had, in the language of the time, the secondary meaning of "commerce," and in this and other passages Marx exploits the two senses of the word.]

43. Quoted from Thomas Münzer's pamphlet against Luther, "Hochverrusachte Schutzrede und Antwort wider das geistlose, sanftlebende Fleisch zu Wittenberg, welches mit verkehrter Weise durch den Diebstahl der heiligen Schrift die erbärmliche Christenheit also ganz jammerlich besudelt hat." (p. B. iii. 1524.)—*Marx.*

relation between man and woman, becomes an object of commerce. Woman is bartered away.

The *chimerical* nationality of the Jew is the nationality of the trader, and above all of the financier.

The law, without basis or reason, of the Jew, is only the religious caricature of morality and right in general, without basis or reason; the purely *formal* rites with which the world of self-interest encircles itself.

Here again the supreme condition of man is his *legal* status, his relationship to laws which are valid for him, not because they are the laws of his own will and nature, but because they are dominant and any infraction of them will be *avenged*.

Jewish Jesuitism, the same practical Jesuitism which Bauer discovers in the Talmud, is the relationship of the world of self-interest to the laws which govern this world, laws which the world devotes its principal arts to circumventing.

Indeed, the operation of this world within its framework of laws is impossible without the continual supersession of law.

Judaism could not develop further as a *religion*, in a theoretical form, because the world view of practical need is, by its very nature, circumscribed, and the delineation of its characteristics soon completed.

The religion of practical need could not, by its very nature, find its consummation in theory, but only in *practice*, just because practice is its truth.

Judaism could not create a new world. It could only bring the new creations and conditions of the world within its own sphere of activity, because practical need, the spirit of which is self-interest, is always passive, cannot expand at will, but *finds* itself extended as a result of the continued development of society.

Judaism attains its apogee with the perfection of civil society; but civil society only reaches perfection in the *Christian* world. Only under the sway of Christianity, which *objectifies all* national, natural, moral and theoretical relationships, could civil society separate itself completely from the life of the state, sever all the species-bonds of man, establish egoism and selfish need in their place, and dissolve the human world into a world of atomistic, antagonistic individuals.

Christianity issued from Judaism. It has now been re-absorbed into Judaism.

From the beginning, the Christian was the theorizing Jew; consequently, the Jew is the practical Christian. And the practical Christian has become a Jew again.

It was only in appearance that Christianity overcame real Judaism. It was too *refined*, too spiritual to eliminate the crudeness of practical need except by raising it into the ethereal realm.

Christianity is the sublime thought of Judaism; Judaism is the vulgar practical application of Christianity. But this practical application could only become universal when Christianity as perfected religion had accomplished, in a *theoretical* fashion, the alienation of man from himself and from nature.

It was only then that Judaism could attain universal domination and could turn alienated man and alienated nature into *alienable*, saleable objects, in thrall to egoistic need and huckstering.

Objectification is the practice of alienation. Just as man, so long as he is engrossed in religion, can only objectify his essence by an *alien* and fantastic being; so under the sway of egoistic need, he can only affirm himself and produce objects in practice by subordinating his products and his own activity to the domination of an alien entity, and by attributing to them the significance of an alien entity, namely money.

In its perfected practice the spiritual egoism of Christianity necessarily becomes the material egoism of the Jew, celestial need is transmuted into terrestrial need, subjectivism into self-interest. The tenacity of the Jew is to be explained, not by his religion, but rather by the human basis of his religion—practical need and egoism.

It is because the essence of the Jew was universally realized and secularized in civil society, that civil society could not convince the Jew of the *unreality* of his *religious* essence, which is precisely the ideal representation of practical need. It is not only, therefore, in the Pentateuch and the Talmud, but also in contemporary society, that we find the essence of the present-day Jew; not as an abstract essence, but as one which is supremely empirical, not only as a limitation of the Jew, but as the Jewish narrowness of society.

As soon as society succeeds in abolishing the *empirical* essence of Judaism—huckstering and its conditions—the Jew becomes *impossible,* because his consciousness no longer has an object. The subjective basis of Judaism—practical need—assumes a human form, and the conflict between the individual, sensuous existence of man and his species-existence, is abolished.

The *social* emancipation of the Jew is the *emancipation of society from Judaism.*

MANIFESTO OF THE COMMUNIST PARTY

Preface to the German Edition of 1872

The Communist League, an international association of workers, which could of course be only a secret one under the conditions obtaining at the time, commissioned the undersigned, at the Congress held in London in November 1847, to draw up for publication a detailed theoretical and practical programme of the Party. Such was the origin of the following Manifesto, the manuscript of which travelled to London, to be printed, a few weeks before the February Revolution.[1] First published in German, it has been republished in that language in at least twelve different editions in Germany, England and America. It was published in English for the first time in 1850 in the *Red Republican,* London, translated by Miss Helen Macfarlane, and in 1871 in at least three different translations in America. A French version first appeared in Paris shortly before the June insurrection of 1848 and recently in *Le Socialiste* of New York. A new translation is in the course of preparation. A Polish version appeared in London shortly after it was first published in German. A Russian translation was published in Geneva in the sixties. Into Danish, too, it was translated shortly after its first appearance.

However much the state of things may have altered during the last twenty-five years, the general principles laid down in this Manifesto are, on the whole, as correct today as ever. Here and there some detail might be improved. The practical application of the principles will depend, as the Manifesto itself states, everywhere and at all times, on the historical conditions for the time being existing, and, for that reason, no special stress is laid on the revolutionary measures proposed at the end of Section II. That passage would, in many respects, be very differently worded today. In view of the gigantic strides of Modern Industry in the last twenty-five years, and of the accompanying improved and extended party organisation of the working class, in view of the practical experience gained, first in the February Revolution, and then, still more, in the Paris Commune, where the proletariat for the first time held political power for two whole months, this programme has in some details become antiquated. One thing especially was proved by the Commune, *viz.,* that "the working class cannot simply lay hold of the ready-made State machinery, and wield it for its own purposes." (See *The Civil War in France; Address of the General Council of the International Working Men's Association,* London, Trulove, 1871, p. 15, where this point is further developed.) Further, it is self-evident that the criticism of socialist literature is deficient in relation to the present time, because it comes down only to 1847; also, that the remarks on the relation of the Communists to the various opposition parties (Section IV), although in principle still correct, yet

1. [The February Revolution in France, 1848.]

in practice are antiquated, because the political situation has been entirely changed, and the progress of history has swept from off the earth the greater portion of the political parties there enumerated.

But, then, the Manifesto has become a historical document which we have no longer any right to alter. A subsequent edition may perhaps appear with an introduction bridging the gap from 1847 to the present day; this reprint was too unexpected to leave us time for that.

London, June 24, 1872   *Karl Marx   Friedrich Engels*

Preface to the Russian Edition of 1882

The first Russian edition of the *Manifesto of the Communist Party*, translated by Bakunin, was published early in the sixties[2] by the printing office of the *Kolokol*. Then the West could see in it (the *Russian* edition of the Manifesto) only a literary curiosity. Such a view would be impossible today.

What a limited field the proletarian movement still occupied at that time (December 1847) is most clearly shown by the last section of the Manifesto: the position of the Communists in relation to the various opposition parties in the various countries. Precisely Russia and the United States are missing here. It was the time when Russia constituted the last great reserve of all European reaction, when the United States absorbed the surplus proletarian forces of Europe through immigration. Both countries provided Europe with raw materials and were at the same time markets for the sale of its industrial products. At that time both were, therefore, in one way or another, pillars of the existing European order.

How very different today! Precisely European immigration fitted North America for a gigantic agricultural production, whose competition is shaking the very foundations of European landed property—large and small. In addition it enabled the United States to exploit its tremendous industrial resources with an energy and on a scale that must shortly break the industrial monopoly of Western Europe, and especially of England, existing up to now. Both circumstances react in revolutionary manner upon America itself. Step by step the small and middle landownership of the farmers, the basis of the whole political constitution, is succumbing to the competition of giant farms; simultaneously, a mass proletariat and a fabulous concentration of capitals are developing for the first time in the industrial regions.

And now Russia! During the Revolution of 1848–49 not only the European princes, but the European bourgeois as well, found their only salvation from the proletariat, just beginning to awaken, in Russian intervention. The tsar was proclaimed the chief of European reaction. Today he is a prisoner of war of the revolution, in Gatchina, and Russia forms the vanguard of revolutionary action in Europe.

---

2. [The date is not correct; the edition referred to appeared in 1869.]

The Communist Manifesto had as its object the proclamation of the inevitably impending dissolution of modern bourgeois property. But in Russia we find, face to face with the rapidly developing capitalist swindle and bourgeois landed property, just beginning to develop, more than half the land owned in common by the peasants. Now the question is: Can the Russian *obshchina*,[3] though greatly undermined, yet a form of the primeval common ownership of land, pass directly to the higher form of communist common ownership? Or, on the contrary, must it first pass through the same process of dissolution as constitutes the historical evolution of the West?

The only answer to that possible today is this: If the Russian Revolution becomes the signal for a proletarian revolution in the West, so that both complement each other, the present Russian common ownership of land may serve as the starting-point for a communist development.

London, January 21, 1882   *Karl Marx   Friedrich Engels*

Preface to the German Edition of 1883

The preface to the present edition I must, alas, sign alone. Marx, the man to whom the whole working class of Europe and America owes more than to anyone else, rests at Highgate Cemetery and over his grave the first grass is already growing. Since his death, there can be even less thought of revising or supplementing the Manifesto. All the more do I consider it necessary again to state here the following expressly:

The basic thought running through the Manifesto—that economic production and the structure of society of every historical epoch necessarily arising therefrom constitute the foundation for the political and intellectual history of that epoch; that consequently (ever since the dissolution of the primeval communal ownership of land) all history has been a history of class struggles, of struggles between exploited and exploiting, between dominated and dominating classes at various stages of social development; that this struggle, however, has now reached a stage where the exploited and oppressed class (the proletariat) can no longer emancipate itself from the class which exploits and oppresses it (the bourgeoisie), without at the same time forever freeing the whole of society from exploitation, oppression and class struggles—this basic thought belongs solely and exclusively to Marx.

I have already stated this many times; but precisely now it is necessary that it also stand in front of the Manifesto itself.

London, June 28, 1883   *Friedrich Engels*

---

3. [Village community.]

MANIFESTO
OF THE COMMUNIST PARTY

A spectre is haunting Europe—the spectre of Communism. All the Powers of old Europe have entered into a holy alliance to exorcise this spectre: Pope and Czar, Metternich and Guizot, French Radicals and German police-spies.

Where is the party in opposition that has not been decried as Communistic by its opponents in power? Where the Opposition that has not hurled back the branding reproach of Communism, against the more advanced opposition parties, as well as against its reactionary adversaries?

Two things result from this fact.

I. Communism is already acknowledged by all European Powers to be itself a Power.

II. It is high time that Communists should openly, in the face of the whole world, publish their views, their aims, their tendencies, and meet this nursery tale of the Spectre of Communism with a Manifesto of the party itself.

To this end, Communists of various nationalities have assembled in London, and sketched the following Manifesto, to be published in the English, French, German, Italian, Flemish and Danish languages.

I. Bourgeois and Proletarians[4]

The history of all hitherto existing society[5] is the history of class struggles.

Freeman and slave, patrician and plebeian, lord and serf, guild-master[6] and journeyman, in a word, oppressor and oppressed, stood in constant opposition to one another, carried on an uninterrupted, now hidden, now open fight, a fight that each

---

4. By bourgeoisie is meant the class of modern Capitalists, owners of the means of social production and employers of wage-labour. By proletariat, the class of modern wage-labourers who, having no means of production of their own, are reduced to selling their labour-power in order to live.—*Engels, English edition of 1888.*

5. That is, all *written* history. In 1847, the pre-history of society, the social organisation existing previous to recorded history, was all but unknown. Since then, Haxthausen discovered common ownership of land in Russia, Maurer proved it to be the social foundation from which all Teutonic races started in history, and by and by village communities were found to be, or to have been the primitive form of society everywhere from India to Ireland. The inner organisation of this primitive Communistic society was laid bare, in its typical form, by Morgan's crowning discovery of the true nature of the *gens* and its relation to the *tribe*. With the dissolution of these primaeval communities society begins to be differentiated into separate and finally antagonistic classes. I have attempted to retrace this process of dissolution in: "Der Ursprung der Familie, des Privateigenthums und des Staats" [*The Origin of the Family, Private Property and the State*], 2nd edition, Stuttgart 1886.—*Engels, English edition of 1888.*

6. Guild-master, that is, a full member of a guild, a master within, not a head of a guild.—*Engels, English edition of 1888.*

time ended, either in a revolutionary re-constitution of society at large, or in the common ruin of the contending classes.

In the earlier epochs of history, we find almost everywhere a complicated arrangement of society into various orders, a manifold gradation of social rank. In ancient Rome we have patricians, knights, plebeians, slaves; in the Middle Ages, feudal lords, vassals, guild-masters, journeymen, apprentices, serfs; in almost all of these classes, again, subordinate gradations.

The modern bourgeois society that has sprouted from the ruins of feudal society has not done away with clash antagonisms. It has but established new classes, new conditions of oppression, new forms of struggle in place of the old ones.

Our epoch, the epoch of the bourgeoisie, possesses, however, this distinctive feature: it has simplified the class antagonisms: Society as a whole is more and more splitting up into two great hostile camps, into two great classes directly facing each other: Bourgeoisie and Proletariat.

From the serfs of the Middle Ages sprang the chartered burghers of the earliest towns. From these burgesses the first elements of the bourgeoisie were developed.

The discovery of America, the rounding of the Cape, opened up fresh ground for the rising bourgeoisie. The East-Indian and Chinese markets, the colonisation of America, trade with the colonies, the increase in the means of exchange and in commodities generally, gave to commerce, to navigation, to industry, an impulse never before known, and thereby, to the revolutionary element in the tottering feudal society, a rapid development.

The feudal system of industry, under which industrial production was monopolised by closed guilds, now no longer sufficed for the growing wants of the new markets. The manufacturing system took its place. The guild-masters were pushed on one side by the manufacturing middle class; division of labour between the different corporate guilds vanished in the face of division of labour in each single workshop.

Meantime the markets kept ever growing, the demand ever rising. Even manufacture no longer sufficed. Thereupon, steam and machinery revolutionised industrial production. The place of manufacture was taken by the giant, Modern Industry, the place of the industrial middle class, by industrial millionaires, the leaders of whole industrial armies, the modern bourgeois.

Modern industry has established the world-market, for which the discovery of America paved the way. This market has given an immense development to commerce, to navigation, to communication by land. This development has, in its turn, reacted on the extension of industry; and in proportion as industry, commerce, navigation, railways extended, in the same proportion the bourgeoisie developed, increased its capital, and pushed into the background every class handed down from the Middle Ages.

We see, therefore, how the modern bourgeoisie is itself the product of a long course of development, of a series of revolutions in the modes of production and of exchange.

Each step in the development of the bourgeoisie was accompanied by a corresponding political advance of that class. An oppressed class under the sway of the feudal nobility, an armed and self-governing association in the mediaeval commune;[7] here independent urban republic (as in Italy and Germany), there taxable "third estate" of the monarchy (as in France), afterwards, in the period of manufacture proper, serving either the semi-feudal or the absolute monarchy as a counterpoise against the nobility, and, in fact, corner-stone of the great monarchies in general, the bourgeoisie has at last, since the establishment of Modern Industry and of the world-market, conquered for itself, in the modern representative State, exclusive political sway. The executive of the modern State is but a committee for managing the common affairs of the whole bourgeoisie.

The bourgeoisie, historically, has played a most revolutionary part.

The bourgeoisie, wherever it has got the upper hand, has put an end to all feudal, patriarchal, idyllic relations. It has pitilessly torn asunder the motley feudal ties that bound man to his "natural superiors," and has left remaining no other nexus between man and man than naked self-interest, than callous "cash payment." It has drowned the most heavenly ecstasies of religious fervour, of chivalrous enthusiasm, of philistine sentimentalism, in the icy water of egotistical calculation. It has resolved personal worth into exchange value, and in place of the numberless indefeasible chartered freedoms, has set up that single, unconscionable freedom—Free Trade. In one word, for exploitation, veiled by religious and political illusions, it has substituted naked, shameless, direct, brutal exploitation.

The bourgeoisie has stripped of its halo every occupation hitherto honoured and looked up to with reverent awe. It has converted the physician, the lawyer, the priest, the poet, the man of science, into its paid wage-labourers.

The bourgeoisie has torn away from the family its sentimental veil, and has reduced the family relation to a mere money relation.

The bourgeoisie has disclosed how it came to pass that the brutal display of vigour in the Middle Ages, which Reactionists so much admire, found its fitting complement in the most slothful indolence. It has been the first to show what man's activity can bring about. It has accomplished wonders far surpassing Egyptian pyramids, Roman aqueducts, and Gothic cathedrals; it has conducted expeditions that put in the shade all former Exoduses of nations and crusades.

The bourgeoisie cannot exist without constantly revolutionising the instruments of production, and thereby the relations of production, and with them the whole relations of society. Conservation of the old modes of production in unaltered form, was, on the contrary, the first condition of existence for all earlier industrial classes. Constant revolutionising of production, uninterrupted disturbance of all social conditions, everlasting uncertainty and agitation distinguish the bourgeois epoch from all earlier ones. All fixed, fast-frozen relations, with their train of ancient and venerable prejudices and opinions, are swept away, all new-formed ones become antiquated before they can ossify. All that is solid melts into air, all that is holy is

---

7. "Commune" was the name taken, in France, by the nascent towns even before they had conquered from their feudal lords and masters local self-government and political rights as the "Third Estate." Generally speaking, for the economical development of the bourgeoisie, England is here taken as the typical country; for its political development, France.—*Engels, English edition of 1888.*

This was the name given their urban communities by the townsmen of Italy and France, after they had purchased or wrested their initial rights of self-government from their feudal lords.—*Engels, German edition of 1890.*

profaned, and man is at last compelled to face with sober senses, his real conditions of life, and his relations with his kind.

The need of a constantly expanding market for its products chases the bourgeoisie over the whole surface of the globe. It must nestle everywhere, settle everywhere, establish connexions everywhere.

The bourgeoisie has through its exploitation of the world-market given a cosmopolitan character to production and consumption in every country. To the great chagrin of Reactionists, it has drawn from under the feet of industry the national ground on which it stood. All old-established national industries have been destroyed or are daily being destroyed. They are dislodged by new industries, whose introduction becomes a life and death question for all civilised nations, by industries that no longer work up indigenous raw material, but raw material drawn from the remotest zones; industries whose products are consumed, not only at home, but in every quarter of the globe. In place of the old wants, satisfied by the productions of the country, we find new wants, requiring for their satisfaction the products of distant lands and climes. In place of the old local and national seclusion and self-sufficiency, we have intercourse in every direction, universal inter-dependence of nations. And as in material, so also in intellectual production. The intellectual creations of individual nations become common property. National one-sidedness and narrow-mindedness become more and more impossible, and from the numerous national and local literatures, there arises a world literature.

The bourgeoisie, by the rapid improvement of all instruments of production, by the immensely facilitated means of communication, draws all, even the most barbarian, nations into civilisation. The cheap prices of its commodities are the heavy artillery with which it batters down all Chinese walls, with which it forces the barbarians' intensely obstinate hatred of foreigners to capitulate. It compels all nations, on pain of extinction, to adopt the bourgeois mode of production; it compels them to introduce what it calls civilisation into their midst, *i.e.*, to become bourgeois themselves. In one word, it creates a world after its own image.

The bourgeoisie has subjected the country to the rule of the towns. It has created enormous cities, has greatly increased the urban population as compared with the rural, and has thus rescued a considerable part of the population from the idiocy of rural life. Just as it has made the country dependent on the towns, so it has made barbarian and semi-barbarian countries dependent on the civilised ones, nations and peasants on nations of bourgeois, the East on the West.

The bourgeoisie keeps more and more doing away with the scattered state of the population, of the means of production, and of property. It has agglomerated population, centralised means of production, and has concentrated property in a few hands. The necessary consequence of this was political centralisation. Independent, or but loosely connected provinces, with separate interests, laws, governments and systems of taxation, became lumped together into one nation, with one government, one code of laws, one national class-interest, one frontier and one customs-tariff. The bourgeoisie, during its rule of scarce one hundred years, has created more massive and more colossal productive forces than have all preceding generations together. Subjection of Nature's forces to man, machinery, application of chemistry to industry and agriculture, steam-navigation, railways, electric telegraphs, clearing of whole continents for cultivation, canalisation of rivers, whole populations conjured out of the ground—what earlier century had even a presentiment that such productive forces slumbered in the lap of social labour?

We see then: the means of production and of exchange, on whose foundation the bourgeoisie built itself up, were generated in feudal society. At a certain stage in the development of these means of production and of exchange, the conditions under which feudal society produced and exchanged, the feudal organisation of agriculture and manufacturing industry, in one word, the feudal relations of property became no longer compatible with the already developed productive forces; they became so many fetters. They had to be burst asunder; they were burst asunder.

Into their place stepped free competition, accompanied by a social and political constitution adapted to it, and by the economical and political sway of the bourgeois class.

A similar movement is going on before our own eyes. Modern bourgeois society with its relations of production, of exchange and of property, a society that has conjured up such gigantic means of production and of exchange, is like the sorcerer, who is no longer able to control the powers of the nether world whom he has called up by his spells. For many a decade past the history of industry and commerce is but the history of the revolt of modern productive forces against modern conditions of production, against the property relations that are the conditions for the existence of the bourgeoisie and of its rule. It is enough to mention the commercial crises that by their periodical return put on its trial, each time more threateningly, the existence of the entire bourgeois society. In these crises a great part not only of the existing products, but also of the previously created productive forces, are periodically destroyed. In these crises there breaks out an epidemic that, in all earlier epochs, would have seemed an absurdity—the epidemic of over-production. Society suddenly finds itself put back into a state of momentary barbarism; it appears as if a famine, a universal war of devastation had cut off the supply of every means of subsistence; industry and commerce seem to be destroyed; and why? Because there is too much civilisation, too much means of subsistence, too much industry, too much commerce. The productive forces at the disposal of society no longer tend to further the development of the conditions of bourgeois property; on the contrary, they have become too powerful for these conditions, by which they are fettered, and so soon as they overcome these fetters, they bring disorder into the whole of bourgeois society, endanger the existence of bourgeois property. The conditions of bourgeois society are too narrow to comprise the wealth created by them. And how does the bourgeoisie get over these crises? On the one hand by enforced destruction of a mass of productive forces; on the other, by the conquest of new markets, and by the more thorough exploitation of the old ones. That is to say, by paving the way for more extensive and more destructive crises, and by diminishing the means whereby crises are prevented.

The weapons with which the bourgeoisie felled feudalism to the ground are now turned against the bourgeoisie itself.

But not only has the bourgeoisie forged the weapons that bring death to itself; it has also called into existence the men who are to wield these weapons—the modern working class—the proletarians.

In proportion as the bourgeoisie, *i.e.*, capital, is developed, in the same proportion is the proletariat, the modern working class, developed—a class of labourers, who live only so long as they find work, and who find work only so long as their labour increases capital. These labourers, who must sell themselves piece-meal, are a commodity, like every other article of commerce, and are consequently exposed to all the vicissitudes of competition, to all the fluctuations of the market.

Owing to the extensive use of machinery and to division of labour, the work of the proletarians has lost all individual character, and consequently, all charm for the workman. He becomes an appendage of the machine, and it is only the most simple, most monotonous, and most easily acquired knack, that is required of him. Hence, the cost of production of a workman is restricted, almost entirely, to the means of subsistence that he requires for his maintenance, and for the propagation of his race. But the price of a commodity, and therefore also of labour,[8] is equal to its cost of production. In proportion, therefore, as the repulsiveness of the work increases, the wage decreases. Nay more, in proportion as the use of machinery and division of labour increases, in the same proportion the burden of toil also increases, whether by prolongation of the working hours, by increase of the work exacted in a given time or by increased speed of the machinery, etc.

Modern industry has converted the little workshop of the patriarchal master into the great factory of the industrial capitalist. Masses of labourers, crowded into the factory, are organised like soldiers. As privates of the industrial army they are placed under the command of a perfect hierarchy of officers and sergeants. Not only are they slaves of the bourgeois class, and of the bourgeois State; they are daily and hourly enslaved by the machine, by the over-looker, and, above all, by the individual bourgeois manufacturer himself. The more openly this despotism proclaims gain to be its end and aim, the more petty, the more hateful and the more embittering it is.

The less the skill and exertion of strength implied in manual labour, in other words, the more modern industry becomes developed, the more is the labour of men superseded by that of women. Differences of age and sex have no longer any distinctive social validity for the working class. All are instruments of labour, more or less expensive to use, according to their age and sex.

No sooner is the exploitation of the labourer by the manufacturer, so far, at an end, that he receives his wages in cash, than he is set upon by the other portions of the bourgeoisie, the landlord, the shopkeeper, the pawnbroker, etc.

The lower strata of the middle class—the small tradespeople, shopkeepers, and retired tradesmen generally, the handicraftsmen and peasants—all these sink gradually into the proletariat, partly because their diminutive capital does not suffice for the scale on which Modern Industry is carried on, and is swamped in the competition with the large capitalists, partly because their specialised skill is rendered worthless by new methods of production. Thus the proletariat is recruited from all classes of the population.

The proletariat goes through various stages of development. With its birth begins its struggle with the bourgeoisie. At first the contest is carried on by individual labourers, then by the workpeople of a factory, then by the operatives of one trade, in one locality, against the individual bourgeois who directly exploits them. They direct their attacks not against the bourgeois conditions of production, but against

---

8. [Subsequently Marx pointed out that the worker sells not his labour but his labour power.]

the instruments of production themselves; they destroy imported wares that compete with their labour, they smash to pieces machinery, they set factories ablaze, they seek to restore by force the vanished status of the workman of the Middle Ages.

At this stage the labourers still form an incoherent mass scattered over the whole country, and broken up by their mutual competition. If anywhere they unite to form more compact bodies, this is not yet the consequence of their own active union, but of the union of the bourgeoisie, which class, in order to attain its own political ends, is compelled to set the whole proletariat in motion, and is moreover yet, for a time, able to do so. At this stage, therefore, the proletarians do not fight their enemies, but the enemies of their enemies, the remnants of absolute monarchy, the landowners, the non-industrial bourgeois, the petty bourgeoisie. Thus the whole historical movement is concentrated in the hands of the bourgeoisie; every victory so obtained is a victory for the bourgeoisie.

But with the development of industry the proletariat not only increases in number; it becomes concentrated in greater masses, its strength grows, and it feels that strength more. The various interests and conditions of life within the ranks of the proletariat are more and more equalised, in proportion as machinery obliterates all distinctions of labour, and nearly everywhere reduces wages to the same low level. The growing competition among the bourgeois, and the resulting commercial crises, make the wages of the workers ever more fluctuating. The unceasing improvement of machinery, ever more rapidly developing, makes their livelihood more and more precarious; the collisions between individual workmen and individual bourgeois take more and more the character of collisions between two classes. Thereupon the workers begin to form combinations (Trades Unions) against the bourgeois; they club together in order to keep up the rate of wages; they found permanent associations in order to make provision beforehand for these occasional revolts. Here and there the contest breaks out into riots.

Now and then the workers are victorious, but only for a time. The real fruit of their battles lies, not in the immediate result, but in the ever-expanding union of the workers. This union is helped on by the improved means of communication that are created by modern industry and that place the workers of different localities in contact with one another. It was just this contact that was needed to centralise the numerous local struggles, all of the same character, into one national struggle between classes. But every class struggle is a political struggle. And that union, to attain which the burghers of the Middle Ages, with their miserable highways, required centuries, the modern proletarians, thanks to railways, achieve in a few years.

This organisation of the proletarians into a class, and consequently into a political party, is continually being upset again by the competition between the workers themselves. But it ever rises up again, stronger, firmer, mightier. It compels legislative recognition of particular interests of the workers, by taking advantage of the divisions among the bourgeoisie itself. Thus the ten-hours' bill in England was carried.

Altogether collisions between the classes of the old society further, in many ways, the course of development of the proletariat. The bourgeoisie finds itself involved in a constant battle. At first with the aristocracy; later on, with those portions of the bourgeoisie itself, whose interests have become antagonistic to the progress of industry; at all times, with the bourgeoisie of foreign countries. In all these battles it sees itself compelled to appeal to the proletariat, to ask for its help, and thus, to drag it into the political arena. The bourgeoisie itself, therefore, supplies the proletariat with its own elements of political and general education, in other words, it furnishes the proletariat with weapons for fighting the bourgeoisie.

Further, as we have already seen, entire sections of the ruling classes are, by the advance of industry, precipitated into the proletariat, or are at least threatened in their conditions of existence. These also supply the proletariat with fresh elements of enlightenment and progress.

Finally, in times when the class struggle nears the decisive hour, the process of dissolution going on within the ruling class, in fact within the whole range of society, assumes such a violent, glaring character, that a small section of the ruling class cuts itself adrift, and joins the revolutionary class, the class that holds the future in its hands. Just as, therefore, at an earlier period, a section of the nobility went over to the bourgeoisie, so now a portion of the bourgeoisie goes over to the proletariat, and in particular, a portion of the bourgeois ideologists, who have raised themselves to the level of comprehending theoretically the historical movement as a whole.

Of all the classes that stand face to face with the bourgeoisie today, the proletariat alone is a really revolutionary class. The other classes decay and finally disappear in the face of Modern Industry; the proletariat is its special and essential product.

The lower middle class, the small manufacturer, the shopkeeper, the artisan, the peasant, all these fight against the bourgeoisie, to save from extinction their existence as fractions of the middle class. They are therefore not revolutionary, but conservative. Nay more, they are reactionary, for they try to roll back the wheel of history. If by chance they are revolutionary, they are so only in view of their impending transfer into the proletariat, they thus defend not their present, but their future interests, they desert their own standpoint to place themselves at that of the proletariat.

The "dangerous class," the social scum, that passively rotting mass thrown off by the lowest layers of old society, may, here and there, be swept into the movement by a proletarian revolution; its conditions of life, however, prepare it far more for the part of a bribed tool of reactionary intrigue.

In the conditions of the proletariat, those of old society at large are already virtually swamped. The proletarian is without property; his relation to his wife and children has no longer anything in common with the bourgeois family-relations; modern industrial labour, modern subjection to capital, the same in England as in France, in America as in Germany, has stripped him of every trace of national character. Law, morality, religion, are to him so many bourgeois prejudices, behind which lurk in ambush just as many bourgeois interests.

All the preceding classes that got the upper hand, sought to fortify their already acquired status by subjecting society at large to their conditions of appropriation. The proletarians cannot become masters of the productive forces of society, except by abolishing their own previous mode of appropriation, and thereby also every other previous mode of appropriation. They have nothing of their own to secure and to fortify; their mission is to destroy all previous securities for, and insurances of, individual property.

All previous historical movements were movements of minorities, or in the interests of minorities. The proletarian movement is the self-conscious, independent movement of the immense majority, in the interests of the immense majority. The proletariat, the lowest stratum of our present society, cannot stir, cannot raise itself up, without the whole superincumbent strata of official society being sprung into the air.

Though not in substance, yet in form, the struggle of the proletariat with the bourgeoisie is at first a national struggle. The proletariat of each country must, of course, first of all settle matters with its own bourgeoisie.

In depicting the most general phases of the development of the proletariat, we traced the more or less veiled civil war, raging within existing society, up to the point where that war breaks out into open revolution, and where the violent overthrow of the bourgeoisie lays the foundation for the sway of the proletariat.

Hitherto, every form of society has been based, as we have already seen, on the antagonism of oppressing and oppressed classes. But in order to oppress a class, certain conditions must be assured to it under which it can, at least, continue its slavish existence. The serf, in the period of serfdom, raised himself to membership in the commune, just as the petty bourgeois, under the yoke of feudal absolutism, managed to develop into a bourgeois. The modern labourer, on the contrary, instead of rising with the progress of industry, sinks deeper and deeper below the conditions of existence of his own class. He becomes a pauper, and pauperism develops more rapidly than population and wealth. And here it becomes evident, that the bourgeoisie is unfit any longer to be the ruling class in society, and to impose its conditions of existence upon society as an over-riding law. It is unfit to rule because it is incompetent to assure an existence to its slave within his slavery, because it cannot help letting him sink into such a state, that it has to feed him, instead of being fed by him. Society can no longer live under this bourgeoisie, in other words, its existence is no longer compatible with society.

The essential condition for the existence, and for the sway of the bourgeois class, is the formation and augmentation of capital; the condition for capital is wage-labour. Wage-labour rests exclusively on competition between the labourers. The advance of industry, whose involuntary promoter is the bourgeoisie, replaces the isolation of the labourers, due to competition, by their revolutionary combination, due to association. The development of Modern Industry, therefore, cuts from under its feet the very foundation on which the bourgeoisie produces and appropriates products. What the bourgeoisie, therefore, produces, above all, is its own grave-diggers. Its fall and the victory of the proletariat are equally inevitable.

II. Proletarians and Communists

In what relation do the Communists stand to the proletarians as a whole?

The Communists do not form a separate party opposed to other working-class parties.

They have no interests separate and apart from those of the proletariat as a whole.

They do not set up any sectarian principles of their own, by which to shape and mould the proletarian movement.

The Communists are distinguished from the other working-class parties by this only: (1) In the national struggles of the proletarians of the different countries, they point out and bring to the front the common interests of the entire proletariat, independently of all nationality. (2) In the various stages of development which the struggle of the working class against the bourgeoisie has to pass through, they always and everywhere represent the interests of the movement as a whole.

The Communists, therefore, are on the one hand, practically, the most advanced and resolute section of the working-class parties of every country, that section which pushes forward all others; on the other hand, theoretically, they have over the great mass of the proletariat the advantage of clearly understanding the line of march, the conditions, and the ultimate general results of the proletarian movement.

The immediate aim of the Communists is the same as that of all the other proletarian parties: formation of the proletariat into a class, overthrow of the bourgeois supremacy, conquest of political power by the proletariat.

The theoretical conclusions of the Communists are in no way based on ideas or principles that have been invented, or discovered, by this or that would-be universal reformer.

They merely express, in general terms, actual relations springing from an existing class struggle, from a historical movement going on under our very eyes. The abolition of existing property relations is not at all a distinctive feature of Communism.

All property relations in the past have continually been subject to historical change consequent upon the change in historical conditions.

The French Revolution, for example, abolished feudal property in favour of bourgeois property.

The distinguishing feature of Communism is not the abolition of property generally, but the abolition of bourgeois property. But modern bourgeois private property is the final and most complete expression of the system of producing and appropriating products, that is based on class antagonisms, on the exploitation of the many by the few.

In this sense, the theory of the Communists may be summed up in the single sentence: Abolition of private property.

We Communists have been reproached with the desire of abolishing the right of personally acquiring property as the fruit of a man's own labour, which property is alleged to be the groundwork of all personal freedom, activity and independence.

Hard-won, self-acquired, self-earned property! Do you mean the property of the petty artisan and of the small peasant, a form of property that preceded the bourgeois form? There is no need to abolish that; the development of industry has to a great extent already destroyed it, and is still destroying it daily.

Or do you mean modern bourgeois private property?

But does wage-labour create any property for the labourer? Not a bit. It creates capital, *i.e.,* that kind of property which exploits wage-labour, and which cannot increase except upon condition of begetting a new supply of wage-labour for fresh exploitation. Property, in its present form, is based on the antagonism of capital and wage-labour. Let us examine both sides of this antagonism.

To be a capitalist, is to have not only a purely personal, but a social *status* in production. Capital is a collective product, and only by the united action of many members, nay, in the last resort, only by the united action of all members of society, can it be set in motion.

Capital is, therefore, not a personal, it is a social power.

When, therefore, capital is converted into common property, into the property of all members of society, personal property is not thereby transformed into social property. It is only the social character of the property that is changed. It loses its class-character.

Let us now take wage-labour.

The average price of wage-labour is the minimum wage, *i.e.*, that quantum of the means of subsistence, which is absolutely requisite to keep the labourer in bare existence as a labourer. What, therefore, the wage-labourer appropriates by means of his labour, merely suffices to prolong and reproduce a bare existence. We by no means intend to abolish this personal appropriation of the products of labour, an appropriation that is made for the maintenance and reproduction of human life, and that leaves no surplus wherewith to command the labour of others. All that we want to do away with, is the miserable character of this appropriation, under which the labourer lives merely to increase capital, and is allowed to live only in so far as the interest of the ruling class requires it.

In bourgeois society, living labour is but a means to increase accumulated labour. In Communist society, accumulated labour is but a means to widen, to enrich, to promote the existence of the labourer.

In bourgeois society, therefore, the past dominates the present; in Communist society, the present dominates the past. In bourgeois society capital is independent and has individuality, while the living person is dependent and has no individuality.

And the abolition of this state of things is called by the bourgeois, abolition of individuality and freedom! And rightly so. The abolition of bourgeois individuality, bourgeois independence, and bourgeois freedom is undoubtedly aimed at.

By freedom is meant, under the present bourgeois conditions of production, free trade, free selling and buying.

But if selling and buying disappears, free selling and buying disappears also. This talk about free selling and buying, and all the other "brave words" of our bourgeoisie about freedom in general, have a meaning, if any, only in contrast with restricted selling and buying, with the fettered traders of the Middle Ages, but have no meaning when opposed to the Communistic abolition of buying and selling, of the bourgeois conditions of production, and of the bourgeoisie itself.

You are horrified at our intending to do away with private property. But in your existing society, private property is already done away with for nine-tenths of the population; its existence for the few is solely due to its non-existence in the hands of those nine-tenths. You reproach us, therefore, with intending to do away with a form of property, the necessary condition for whose existence is the non-existence of any property for the immense majority of society.

In one word, you reproach us with intending to do away with your property. Precisely so; that is just what we intend.

From the moment when labour can no longer be converted into capital, money, or rent, into a social power capable of being monopolised, *i.e.*, from the moment when individual property can no longer be transformed into bourgeois property, into capital, from that moment, you say, individuality vanishes.

You must, therefore, confess that by "individual" you mean no other person than the bourgeois, than the middle-class owner of property. This person must, indeed, be swept out of the way, and made impossible.

Communism deprives no man of the power to appropriate the products of society; all that it does is to deprive him of the power to subjugate the labour of others by means of such appropriation.

It has been objected that upon the abolition of private property all work will cease, and universal laziness will overtake us.

According to this, bourgeois society ought long ago to have gone to the dogs through sheer idleness; for those of its members who work, acquire nothing, and those who acquire anything, do not work. The whole of this objection is but another expression of the tautology: that there can no longer be any wage-labour when there is no longer any capital.

All objections urged against the Communistic mode of producing and appropriating material products, have, in the same way, been urged against the Communistic modes of producing and appropriating intellectual products. Just as, to the bourgeois, the disappearance of class property is the disappearance of production itself, so the disappearance of class culture is to him identical with the disappearance of all culture.

That culture, the loss of which he laments, is, for the enormous majority, a mere training to act as a machine.

But don't wrangle with us so long as you apply, to our intended abolition of bourgeois property, the standard of your bourgeois notions of freedom, culture, law, &c. Your very ideas are but the outgrowth of the conditions of your bourgeois production and bourgeois property, just as your jurisprudence is but the will of your class made into a law for all, a will, whose essential character and direction are determined by the economical conditions of existence of your class.

The selfish misconception that induces you to transform into eternal laws of nature and of reason, the social forms springing from your present mode of production and form of property—historical relations that rise and disappear in the progress of production—this misconception you share with every ruling class that has preceded you. What you see clearly in the case of ancient property, what you admit in the case of feudal property, you are of course forbidden to admit in the case of your own bourgeois form of property.

Abolition of the family! Even the most radical flare up at this infamous proposal of the Communists.

On what foundation is the present family, the bourgeois family, based? On capital, on private gain. In its completely developed form this family exists only among the bourgeoisie. But this state of things finds its complement in the practical absence of the family among the proletarians, and in public prostitution.

The bourgeois family will vanish as a matter of course when its complement vanishes, and both will vanish with the vanishing of capital.

Do you charge us with wanting to stop the exploitation of children by their parents? To this crime we plead guilty.

But, you will say, we destroy the most hallowed of relations, when we replace home education by social.

And your education! Is not that also social, and determined by the social conditions under which you educate, by the intervention, direct or indirect, of society, by means of schools, &c.? The Communists have not invented the intervention of society in education; they do but seek to alter the character of that intervention, and to rescue education from the influence of the ruling class.

The bourgeois clap-trap about the family and education, about the hallowed co-relation of parent and child, becomes all the more disgusting, the more, by the action of Modern Industry, all family ties among the proletarians are torn asunder, and their children transformed into simple articles of commerce and instruments of labour.

But you Communists would introduce community of women, screams the whole bourgeoisie in chorus.

The bourgeois sees in his wife a mere instrument of production. He hears that the instruments of production are to be exploited in common, and, naturally, can come to no other conclusion than that the lot of being common to all will likewise fall to the women.

He has not even a suspicion that the real point aimed at is to do away with the status of women as mere instruments of production.

For the rest, nothing is more ridiculous than the virtuous indignation of our bourgeois at the community of women which, they pretend, is to be openly and officially established by the Communists. The Communists have no need to intro-duce community of women; it has existed almost from time immemorial.

Our bourgeois, not content with having the wives and daughters of their proletari-ans at their disposal, not to speak of common prostitutes, take the greatest pleasure in seducing each other's wives.

Bourgeois marriage is in reality a system of wives in common and thus, at the most, what the Communists might possibly be reproached with, is that they desire to introduce, in substitution for a hypocritically concealed, an openly legalised community of women. For the rest, it is self-evident that the abolition of the present system of production must bring with it the abolition of the community of women springing from that system, *i.e.*, of prostitution both public and private.

The Communists are further reproached with desiring to abolish countries and nationality.

The working men have no country. We cannot take from them what they have not got. Since the proletariat must first of all acquire political supremacy, must rise to be the leading class of the nation, must constitute itself *the* nation, it is, so far, itself national, though not in the bourgeois sense of the word.

National differences and antagonisms between peoples are daily more and more vanishing, owing to the development of the bourgeoisie, to freedom of commerce, to the world-market, to uniformity in the mode of production and in the conditions of life corresponding thereto.

The supremacy of the proletariat will cause them to vanish still faster. United action, of the leading civilised countries at least, is one of the first conditions for the emancipation of the proletariat.

In proportion as the exploitation of one individual by another is put an end to, the exploitation of one nation by another will also be put an end to. In proportion as the antagonism between classes within the nation vanishes, the hostility of one nation to another will come to an end.

The charges against Communism made from a religious, a philosophical, and, generally, from an ideological standpoint, are not deserving of serious examination.

Does it require deep intuition to comprehend that man's ideas, views and conceptions, in one word, man's consciousness, changes with every change in the conditions of his material existence, in his social relations and in his social life?

What else does the history of ideas prove, than that intellectual production changes its character in proportion as material production is changed? The ruling ideas of each age have ever been the ideas of its ruling class.

When people speak of ideas that revolutionise society, they do but express the fact, that within the old society, the elements of a new one have been created, and that the dissolution of the old ideas keeps even pace with the dissolution of the old conditions of existence.

When the ancient world was in its last throes, the ancient religions were overcome by Christianity. When Christian ideas succumbed in the 18th century to rationalist ideas, feudal society fought its death battle with the then revolutionary bourgeoisie. The ideas of religious liberty and freedom of conscience merely gave expression to the sway of free competition within the domain of knowledge.

"Undoubtedly," it will be said, "religious, moral, philosophical and juridical ideas have been modified in the course of historical development. But religion, morality, philosophy, political science, and law, constantly survived this change."

"There are, besides, eternal truths, such as Freedom, Justice, etc., that are common to all states of society. But Communism abolishes eternal truths, it abolishes all religion, and all morality, instead of constituting them on a new basis; it therefore acts in contradiction to all past historical experience."

What does this accusation reduce itself to? The history of all past society has consisted in the development of class antagonisms, antagonisms that assumed different forms at different epochs.

But whatever form they may have taken, one fact is common to all past ages, viz., the exploitation of one part of society by the other. No wonder, then, that the social consciousness of past ages, despite all the multiplicity and variety it displays, moves within certain common forms, or general ideas, which cannot completely vanish except with the total disappearance of class antagonisms.

The Communist revolution is the most radical rupture with traditional property relations; no wonder that its development involves the most radical rupture with traditional ideas.

But let us have done with the bourgeois objections to Communism.

We have seen above, that the first step in the revolution by the working class, is to raise the proletariat to the position of ruling class, to win the battle of democracy.

The proletariat will use its political supremacy to wrest, by degrees, all capital from the bourgeoisie, to centralise all instruments of production in the hands of the State, i.e., of the proletariat organised as the ruling class; and to increase the total of productive forces as rapidly as possible.

Of course, in the beginning, this cannot be effected except by means of despotic inroads on the rights of property, and on the conditions of bourgeois production;

by means of measures, therefore, which appear economically insufficient and untenable, but which, in the course of the movement, outstrip themselves, necessitate further inroads upon the old social order, and are unavoidable as a means of entirely revolutionising the mode of production.

These measures will of course be different in different countries.

Nevertheless in the most advanced countries, the following will be pretty generally applicable.

1. Abolition of property in land and application of all rents of land to public purposes.
2. A heavy progressive or graduated income tax.
3. Abolition of all right of inheritance.
4. Confiscation of the property of all emigrants and rebels.
5. Centralisation of credit in the hands of the State, by means of a national bank with State capital and an exclusive monopoly.
6. Centralisation of the means of communication and transport in the hands of the State.
7. Extension of factories and instruments of production owned by the State; the bringing into cultivation of waste-lands, and the improvement of the soil generally in accordance with a common plan.
8. Equal liability of all to labour. Establishment of industrial armies, especially for agriculture.
9. Combination of agriculture with manufacturing industries; gradual abolition of the distinction between town and country, by a more equable distribution of the population over the country.
10. Free education for all children in public schools. Abolition of children's factory labour in its present form. Combination of education with industrial production, &c., &c.

When, in the course of development, class distinctions have disappeared, and all production has been concentrated in the hands of a vast association of the whole nation, the public power will lose its political character. Political power, properly so called, is merely the organised power of one class for oppressing another. If the proletariat during its contest with the bourgeoisie is compelled, by the force of circumstances, to organise itself as a class, if, by means of a revolution, it makes itself the ruling class, and, as such, sweeps away by force the old conditions of production, then it will, along with these conditions, have swept away the conditions for the existence of class antagonisms and of classes generally, and will thereby have abolished its own supremacy as a class.

In place of the old bourgeois society, with its classes and class antagonisms, we shall have an association, in which the free development of each is the condition for the free development of all.

III. Socialist and Communist Literature

1. REACTIONARY SOCIALISM

A. Feudal Socialism

Owing to their historical position, it became the vocation of the aristocracies of France and England to write pamphlets against modern bourgeois society. In the

French revolution of July 1830, and in the English reform agitation, these aristocracies again succumbed to the hateful upstart. Thenceforth, a serious political contest
was altogether out of the question. A literary battle alone remained possible. But
even in the domain of literature the old cries of the restoration period[9] had become
impossible.

In order to arouse sympathy, the aristocracy were obliged to lose sight, apparently,
of their own interests, and to formulate their indictment against the bourgeoisie in
the interest of the exploited working class alone. Thus the aristocracy took their
revenge by singing lampoons on their new master, and whispering in his ears sinister
prophecies of coming catastrophe.

In this way arose Feudal Socialism: half lamentation, half lampoon; half echo of
the past, half menace of the future; at times, by its bitter, witty and incisive criticism,
striking the bourgeoisie to the very heart's core; but always ludicrous in its effect,
through total incapacity to comprehend the march of modern history.

The aristocracy, in order to rally the people to them, waved the proletarian alms-
bag in front for a banner. But the people, so often as it joined them, saw on their
hindquarters the old feudal coats of arms, and deserted with loud and irreverent
laughter.

One section of the French Legitimists[10] and "Young England"[11] exhibited this
spectacle.

In pointing out that their mode of exploitation was different to that of the bourgeoisie, the feudalists forget that they exploited under circumstances and conditions
that were quite different, and that are now antiquated. In showing that, under their
rule, the modern proletariat never existed, they forget that the modern bourgeoisie
is the necessary offspring of their own form of society.

For the rest, so little do they conceal the reactionary character of their criticism
that their chief accusation against the bourgeoisie amounts to this, that under the
bourgeois *régime* a class is being developed, which is destined to cut up root and
branch the old order of society.

What they upbraid the bourgeoisie with is not so much that it creates a proletariat,
as that it creates a *revolutionary* proletariat.

In political practice, therefore, they join in all coercive measures against the
working class; and in ordinary life, despite their high falutin phrases, they stoop to
pick up the golden apples dropped from the tree of industry, and to barter truth,
love, and honour for traffic in wool, beetroot-sugar, and potato spirits.[12]

---

9. Not the English Restoration 1660 to 1689, but the French Restoration 1814 to 1830.—*Engels, English edition of 1888.*

10. [The party of the noble landowners, who advocated the restoration of the Bourbon dynasty.]

11. [A group of British Conservatives—aristocrats and men of politics and literature—formed about 1842. Prominent among them were Disraeli, Thomas Carlyle, and others.]

12. This applies chiefly to Germany where the landed aristocracy and squire-archy have large portions of their estates cultivated for their own account by stewards, and are, moreover, extensive beetroot-sugar manufacturers and distillers of potato spirits. The wealthier British aristocracy are, as yet, rather above that: but they, too, know how to make up for declining rents by lending their names to floaters of more or less shady joint-stock companies.—*Engels, English edition of 1888.*

As the parson has ever gone hand in hand with the landlord, so has Clerical Socialism with Feudal Socialism.

Nothing is easier than to give Christian asceticism a Socialist tinge. Has not Christianity declaimed against private property, against marriage, against the State? Has it not preached in the place of these, charity and poverty, celibacy and mortification of the flesh, monastic life and Mother Church? Christian Socialism is but the holy water with which the priest consecrates the heart-burnings of the aristocrat.

B. *Petty-Bourgeois Socialism*

The feudal aristocracy was not the only class that was ruined by the bourgeoisie, not the only class whose conditions of existence pined and perished in the atmosphere of modern bourgeois society. The mediaeval burgesses and the small peasant proprietors were the precursors of the modern bourgeoisie. In those countries which are but little developed, industrially and commercially, these two classes still vegetate side by side with the rising bourgeoisie.

In countries where modern civilisation has become fully developed, a new class of petty bourgeois has been formed, fluctuating between proletariat and bourgeoisie and ever renewing itself as a supplementary part of bourgeois society. The individual members of this class, however, are being constantly hurled down into the proletariat by the action of competition, and, as modern industry develops, they even see the moment approaching when they will completely disappear as an independent section of modern society, to be replaced, in manufactures, agriculture and commerce, by overlookers, bailiffs and shopmen.

In countries like France, where the peasants constitute far more than half of the population, it was natural that writers who sided with the proletariat against the bourgeoisie, should use, in their criticism of the bourgeois *régime,* the standard of the peasant and petty bourgeois, and from the standpoint of these intermediate classes should take up the cudgels for the working class. Thus arose petty-bourgeois Socialism. Sismondi was the head of this school, not only in France but also in England.

This school of Socialism dissected with great acuteness the contradictions in the conditions of modern production. It laid bare the hypocritical apologies of economists. It proved, incontrovertibly, the disastrous effects of machinery and division of labour; the concentration of capital and land in a few hands; overproduction and crises; it pointed out the inevitable ruin of the petty bourgeois and peasant, the misery of the proletariat, the anarchy in production, the crying inequalities in the distribution of wealth, the industrial war of extermination between nations, the dissolution of old moral bonds, of the old family relations, of the old nationalities.

In its positive aims, however, this form of Socialism aspires either to restoring the old means of production and of exchange, and with them the old property relations, and the old society, or to cramping the modern means of production and of exchange, within the framework of the old property relations that have been, and were bound to be, exploded by those means. In either case, it is both reactionary and Utopian.

Its last words are: corporate guilds for manufacture, patriarchal relations in agriculture.

Ultimately, when stubborn historical facts had dispersed all intoxicating effects of self-deception, this form of Socialism ended in a miserable fit of the blues.

C. German, or "True," Socialism

The Socialist and Communist literature of France, a literature that originated under the pressure of a bourgeoisie in power, and that was the expression of the struggle against this power, was introduced into Germany at a time when the bourgeoisie, in that country, had just begun its contest with feudal absolutism.

German philosophers, would-be philosophers, and *beaux esprits*, eagerly seized on this literature, only forgetting, that when these writings immigrated from France into Germany, French social conditions had not immigrated along with them. In contact with German social conditions, this French literature lost all its immediate practical significance, and assumed a purely literary aspect. Thus, to the German philosophers of the eighteenth century, the demands of the first French Revolution were nothing more than the demands of "Practical Reason" in general, and the utterance of the will of the revolutionary French bourgeoisie signified in their eyes the law of pure Will, of Will as it was bound to be, of true human Will generally.

The work of the German *literati* consisted solely in bringing the new French ideas into harmony with their ancient philosophical conscience, or rather, in annexing the French ideas without deserting their own philosophic point of view.

This annexation took place in the same way in which a foreign language is appropriated, namely, by translation.

It is well known how the monks wrote silly lives of Catholic Saints *over* the manuscripts on which the classical works of ancient heathendom had been written. The German *literati* reversed this process with the profane French literature. They wrote their philosophical nonsense beneath the French original. For instance, beneath the French criticism of the economic functions of money, they wrote "Alienation of Humanity," and beneath the French criticism of the bourgeois State they wrote "dethronement of the Category of the General," and so forth.

The introduction of these philosophical phrases at the back of the French historical criticisms they dubbed "Philosophy of Action," "True Socialism," "German Science of Socialism," "Philosophical Foundation of Socialism," and so on.

The French Socialist and Communist literature was thus completely emasculated. And, since it ceased in the hands of the German to express the struggle of one class with the other, he felt conscious of having overcome "French one-sidedness" and of representing, not true requirements, but the requirements of truth; not the interests of the proletariat, but the interests of Human Nature, of Man in general, who belongs to no class, has no reality, who exists only in the misty realm of philosophical fantasy.

This German Socialism, which took its schoolboy task so seriously and solemnly, and extolled its poor stock-in-trade in such mountebank fashion, meanwhile gradually lost its pedantic innocence.

The fight of the German, and especially, of the Prussian bourgeoisie, against feudal aristocracy and absolute monarchy, in other words, the liberal movement, became more earnest.

By this, the long wished-for opportunity was offered to "True" Socialism of confronting the political movement with the Socialist demands, of hurling the traditional anathemas against liberalism, against representative government, against bourgeois competition, bourgeois freedom of the press, bourgeois legislation, bourgeois liberty and equality, and of preaching to the masses that they had nothing to gain, and everything to lose, by this bourgeois movement. German Socialism forgot, in the nick of time, that the French criticism, whose silly echo it was, presupposed the existence of modern bourgeois society, with its corresponding economic conditions of existence, and the political constitution adapted thereto, the very things whose attainment was the object of the pending struggle in Germany.

To the absolute governments, with their following of parsons, professors, country squires and officials, it served as a welcome scarecrow against the threatening bourgeoisie.

It was a sweet finish after the bitter pills of floggings and bullets with which these same governments, just at that time, dosed the German working-class risings.

While this "True" Socialism thus served the governments as a weapon for fighting the German bourgeoisie, it, at the same time, directly represented a reactionary interest, the interest of the German Philistines. In Germany the *petty-bourgeois* class, a relic of the sixteenth century, and since then constantly cropping up again under various forms, is the real social basis of the existing state of things.

To preserve this class is to preserve the existing state of things in Germany. The industrial and political supremacy of the bourgeoisie threatens it with certain destruction; on the one hand, from the concentration of capital; on the other, from the rise of a revolutionary proletariat. "True" Socialism appeared to kill these two birds with one stone. It spread like an epidemic.

The robe of speculative cobwebs, embroidered with flowers of rhetoric, steeped in the dew of sickly sentiment, this transcendental robe in which the German Socialists wrapped their sorry "eternal truths," all skin and bone, served to wonderfully increase the sale of their goods amongst such a public.

And on its part, German Socialism recognised, more and more, its own calling as the bombastic representative of the petty-bourgeois Philistine.

It proclaimed the German nation to be the model nation, and the German petty Philistine to be the typical man. To every villainous meanness of this model man it gave a hidden, higher, Socialistic interpretation, the exact contrary of its real character. It went to the extreme length of directly opposing the "brutally destructive" tendency of Communism, and of proclaiming its supreme and impartial contempt of all class struggles. With very few exceptions, all the so-called Socialist and Communist publications that now (1847) circulate in Germany belong to the domain of this foul and enervating literature.[13]

2. CONSERVATIVE, OR BOURGEOIS, SOCIALISM

A part of the bourgeoisie is desirous of redressing social grievances, in order to secure the continued existence of bourgeois society.

To this section belong economists, philanthropists, humanitarians, improvers of the condition of the working class, organisers of charity, members of societies for the

---

13. The revolutionary storm of 1848 swept away this whole shabby tendency and cured its protagonists of the desire to dabble further in Socialism. The chief representative and classical type of this tendency is Herr Karl Grün.—*Engels, German edition of 1890.*

prevention of cruelty to animals, temperance fanatics, hole-and-corner reformers of every imaginable kind. This form of Socialism has, moreover, been worked out into complete systems.

We may site Proudhon's *Philosophie de la Misère* as an example of this form.

The Socialistic bourgeois want all the advantages of modern social conditions without the struggles and dangers necessarily resulting therefrom. They desire the existing state of society minus its revolutionary and disintegrating elements. They wish for a bourgeoisie without a proletariat. The bourgeoisie naturally conceives the world in which it is supreme to be the best; and bourgeois Socialism develops this comfortable conception into various more or less complete systems. In requiring the proletariat to carry out such a system, and thereby to march straightway into the social New Jerusalem, it but requires in reality, that the proletariat should remain within the bounds of existing society, but should cast away all its hateful ideas concerning the bourgeoisie.

A second and more practical, but less systematic, form of this Socialism sought to depreciate every revolutionary movement in the eyes of the working class, by showing that no mere political reform, but only a change in the material conditions of existence, in economical relations, could be of any advantage to them. By changes in the material conditions of existence, this form of Socialism, however, by no means understands abolition of the bourgeois relations of production, an abolition that can be effected only by a revolution, but administrative reforms, based on the continued existence of these relations; reforms, therefore, that in no respect affect the relations between capital and labour, but, at the best, lessen the cost, and simplify the administrative work, of bourgeois government.

Bourgeois Socialism attains adequate expression, when, and only when, it becomes a mere figure of speech.

Free trade: for the benefit of the working class. Protective duties: for the benefit of the working class. Prison Reform: for the benefit of the working class. This is the last word and the only seriously meant word of bourgeois Socialism.

It is summed up in the phrase: the bourgeois is a bourgeois—for the benefit of the working class.

3. CRITICAL-UTOPIAN SOCIALISM AND COMMUNISM

We do not here refer to that literature which, in every great modern revolution, has always given voice to the demands of the proletariat, such as the writings of Babeuf and others.

The first direct attempts of the proletariat to attain its own ends, made in times of universal excitement, when feudal society was being overthrown, these attempts necessarily failed, owing to the then undeveloped state of the proletariat, as well as to the absence of the economic conditions for its emancipation, conditions that had yet to be produced, and could be produced by the impending bourgeois epoch alone. The revolutionary literature that accompanied these first movements of the proletariat had necessarily a reactionary character. It inculcated universal asceticism and social levelling in its crudest form.

The Socialist and Communist systems properly so called, those of Saint-Simon, Fourier, Owen and others, spring into existence in the early undeveloped period, described above, of the struggle between proletariat and bourgeoisie (see Section I. Bourgeois and Proletarians).

The founders of these systems see, indeed, the class antagonisms, as well as the action of the decomposing elements, in the prevailing form of society. But the proletariat, as yet in its infancy, offers to them the spectacle of a class without any historical initiative or any independent political movement.

Since the development of class antagonism keeps even pace with the development of industry, the economic situation, as they find it, does not as yet offer to them the material conditions for the emancipation of the proletariat. They therefore search after a new social science, after new social laws, that are to create these conditions.

Historical action is to yield to their personal inventive action, historically created conditions of emancipation to fantastic ones, and the gradual, spontaneous class-organisation of the proletariat to the organisation of society specially contrived by these inventors. Future history resolves itself, in their eyes, into the propaganda and the practical carrying out of their social plans.

In the formation of their plans they are conscious of caring chiefly for the interests of the working class, as being the most suffering class. Only from the point of view of being the most suffering class does the proletariat exist for them.

The undeveloped state of the class struggle, as well as their own surroundings, causes Socialists of this kind to consider themselves far superior to all class antagonisms. They want to improve the condition of every member of society, even that of the most favoured. Hence, they habitually appeal to society at large, without distinction of class; nay, by preference, to the ruling class. For how can people, when once they understand their system, fail to see in it the best possible plan of the best possible state of society?

Hence, they reject all political, and especially all revolutionary, action; they wish to attain their ends by peaceful means, and endeavour, by small experiments, necessarily doomed to failure, and by the force of example, to pave the way for the new social Gospel.

Such fantastic pictures of future society, painted at a time when the proletariat is still in a very undeveloped state and has but a fantastic conception of its own position correspond with the first instinctive yearnings of that class for a general reconstruction of society.

But these Socialist and Communist publications contain also a critical element. They attack every principle of existing society. Hence they are full of the most valuable materials for the enlightenment of the working class. The practical measures proposed in them—such as the abolition of the distinction between town and country, of the family, of the carrying on of industries for the account of private individuals, and of the wage system, the proclamation of social harmony, the conversion of the functions of the State into a mere superintendence of production, all these proposals, point solely to the disappearance of class antagonisms which were, at that time, only just cropping up, and which, in these publications, are recognised in their earliest, indistinct and undefined forms only. These proposals, therefore, are of a purely Utopian character.

The significance of Critical-Utopian Socialism and Communism bears an inverse relation to historical development. In proportion as the modern class struggle develops and takes definite shape, this fantastic standing apart from the contest, these

fantastic attacks on it, lose all practical value and all theoretical justification. Therefore, although the originators of these systems were, in many respects, revolutionary,
their disciples have, in every case, formed mere reactionary sects. They hold fast
by the original views of their masters, in opposition to the progressive historical
development of the proletariat. They, therefore, endeavour, and that consistently,
to deaden the class struggle and to reconcile the class antagonisms. They still dream
of experimental realisation of their social Utopias, of founding isolated "*phalanstères*," of establishing "Home Colonies," of setting up a "Little Icaria"[14]—duodecimo
editions of the New Jerusalem—and to realise all these castles in the air, they are
compelled to appeal to the feelings and purses of the bourgeois. By degrees they
sink into the category of the reactionary conservative Socialists depicted above,
differing from these only by more systematic pedantry, and by their fanatical and
superstitious belief in the miraculous effects of their social science.

They, therefore, violently oppose all political action on the part of the working
class; such action, according to them, can only result from blind unbelief in the new
Gospel.

The Owenites in England, and the Fourierists in France, respectively, oppose the
Chartists and the *Réformistes*.[15]

IV. Position of the Communists in Relation to the Various Existing Opposition Parties

Section II has made clear the relations of the Communists to the existing working-
class parties, such as the Chartists in England and the Agrarian Reformers in
America.

The Communists fight for the attainment of the immediate aims, for the enforcement of the momentary interests of the working class; but in the movement of the
present, they also represent and take care of the future of that movement. In
France the Communists ally themselves with the Social-Democrats,[16] against the
conservative and radical bourgeoisie, reserving, however, the right to take up a

14. *Phalanstères* were Socialist colonies on the plan of Charles Fourier; *Icaria* was the name given by Cabet to
his Utopia and, later on, to his American Communist colony.—*Engels, English edition of 1888.*
   "Home colonies" were what Owen called his Communist model societies. *Phalanstères* was the name of the
public palaces planned by Fourier. *Icaria* was the name given to the Utopian land of fancy, whose Communist
institutions Cabet portrayed.—*Engels, German edition of 1890.*

15. [This refers to the adherents of the newspaper *La Réforme* which was published in Paris from 1843 to
1850.]

16. The party then represented in Parliament by Ledru-Rollin, in literature by Louis Blanc, in the daily press
by the *Réforme*. The name of Social-Democracy signified, with these its inventors, a section of the Democratic
or Republican party more or less tinged with Socialism.—*Engels, English edition of 1888.*
   The party in France which at that time called itself Socialist-Democratic was represented in political life by
Ledru-Rollin and in literature by Louis Blanc; thus it differed immeasurably from present-day German Social-
Democracy.—*Engels, German edition of 1890.*

critical position in regard to phrases and illusions traditionally handed down from the great Revolution.

In Switzerland they support the Radicals, without losing sight of the fact that this party consists of antagonistic elements, partly of Democratic Socialists, in the French sense, partly of radical bourgeois.

In Poland they support the party that insists on an agrarian revolution as the prime condition for national emancipation, that party which fomented the insurrection of Cracow in 1846.

In Germany they fight with the bourgeoisie whenever it acts in a revolutionary way, against the absolute monarchy, the feudal squire-archy, and the petty bourgeoisie.[17]

But they never cease, for a single instant, to instil into the working class the clearest possible recognition of the hostile antagonism between bourgeoisie and proletariat, in order that the German workers may straightway use, as so many weapons against the bourgeoisie, the social and political conditions that the bourgeoisie must necessarily introduce along with its supremacy, and in order that, after the fall of the reactionary classes in Germany, the fight against the bourgeoisie itself may immediately begin.

The Communists turn their attention chiefly to Germany, because that country is on the eve of a bourgeois revolution that is bound to be carried out under more advanced conditions of European civilisation, and with a much more developed proletariat, than that of England was in the seventeenth, and of France in the eighteenth century, and because the bourgeois revolution in Germany will be but the prelude to an immediately following proletarian revolution.

In short, the Communists everywhere support every revolutionary movement against the existing social and political order of things.

In all these movements they bring to the front, as the leading question in each, the property question, no matter what its degree of development at the time.

Finally, they labour everywhere for the union and agreement of the democratic parties of all countries.

The Communists disdain to conceal their views and aims. They openly declare that their ends can be attained only by the forcible overthrow of all existing social conditions. Let the ruling classes tremble at a Communistic revolution. The proletarians have nothing to lose but their chains. They have a world to win.

WORKING MEN OF ALL COUNTRIES, UNITE!

---

17. [*Kleinbürgerei* in the German original. Marx and Engels used this term to describe the reactionary elements of the urban petty bourgeoisie.]

CRITIQUE OF THE GOTHA PROGRAM

1. "Labour is the source of all wealth and all culture, *and since* useful labour is possible only in society and through society, the proceeds of labour belong undiminished with equal right to all members of society."

First Part of the Paragraph: "Labour is the source of all wealth and all culture."

Labour is *not the source* of all wealth. *Nature* is just as much the source of use values (and it is surely of such that material wealth consists!) as labour, which itself is only the manifestation of a force of nature, human labour power. The above phrase is to be found in all children's primers and is correct in so far as it is *implied* that labour is performed with the appurtenant subjects and instruments. But a socialist programme cannot allow such bourgeois phrases to pass over in silence the *conditions* that alone give them meaning. And in so far as man from the beginning behaves towards nature, the primary source of all instruments and subjects of labour, as an owner, treats her as belonging to him, his labour becomes the source of use values, therefore also of wealth. The bourgeois have very good grounds for falsely ascribing *supernatural creative power* to labour; since precisely from the fact that labour depends on nature it follows that the man who possesses no other property than his labour power must, in all conditions of society and culture, be the slave of other men who have made themselves the owners of the material conditions of labour. He can work only with their permission, hence live only with their permission.

Let us now leave the sentence as it stands, or rather limps. What would one have expected in conclusion? Obviously this:

"Since labour is the source of all wealth, no one in society can appropriate wealth except as the product of labour. Therefore, if he himself does not work, he lives by the labour of others and also acquires his culture at the expense of the labour of others."

Instead of this, by means of the verbal rivet *"and since"* a second proposition is added in order to draw a conclusion from this and not from the first one.

Second Part of the Paragraph: "Useful labour is possible only in society and through society."

According to the first proposition, labour was the source of all wealth and all culture; therefore no society is possible without labour. Now we learn, conversely, that no "useful" labour is possible without society.

One could just as well have said that only in society can useless and even socially harmful labour become a branch of gainful occupation, that only in society can one live by being idle, etc., etc.—in short, one could just as well have copied the whole of Rousseau.

And what is "useful" labour? Surely only labour which produces the intended useful result. A savage—and man was a savage after he had ceased to be an ape— who kills an animal with a stone, who collects fruits, etc., performs "useful" labour.

Thirdly. The Conclusion: "And since useful labour is possible only in society and through society, the proceeds of labour belong undiminished with equal right to all members of society."

A fine conclusion! If useful labour is possible only in society and through society, the proceeds of labour belong to society—and only so much therefrom accrues to the individual worker as is not required to maintain the "condition" of labour, society.

In fact, this proposition has at all times been made use of by the champions of the *state of society prevailing at any given time.* First come the claims of the government and everything that sticks to it, since it is the social organ for the maintenance of the social order; then come the claims of the various kinds of private property, for the various kinds of private property are the foundations of society, etc. One sees that such hollow phrases can be twisted and turned as desired.

The first and second parts of the paragraph have some intelligible connection only in the following wording:

"Labour becomes the source of wealth and culture only as social labour," or, what is the same thing, "in and through society."

This proposition is incontestably correct, for although isolated labour (its material conditions presupposed) can create use values, it can create neither wealth nor culture.

But equally incontestable is this other proposition:

"In proportion as labour develops socially, and becomes thereby a source of wealth and culture, poverty and destitution develop among the workers, and wealth and culture among the non-workers."

This is the law of all history hitherto. What, therefore, had to be done here, instead of setting down general phrases about "labour" and "society," was to prove concretely how in present capitalist society the material, etc., conditions have at last been created which enable and compel the workers to lift this social curse.

In fact, however, the whole paragraph, bungled in style and content, is only there in order to inscribe the Lassallean catchword of the "undiminished proceeds of labour" as a slogan at the top of the party banner. I shall return later to the "proceeds of labour," "equal right," etc., since the same thing recurs in a somewhat different form further on.

2. "In present-day society, the instruments of labour are the monopoly of the capitalist class; the resulting dependence of the working class is the cause of misery and servitude in all its forms."

This sentence, borrowed from the Rules of the International, is incorrect in this "improved" edition.

In present-day society the instruments of labour are the monopoly of the landowners (the monopoly of property in land is even the basis of the monopoly of capital) *and* the capitalists. In the passage in question, the Rules of the International do not mention either the one or the other class of monopolists. They speak of the "*monopoliser of the means of labour, that is, the sources of life.*" The addition, "*sources of life,*" makes it sufficiently clear that land is included in the instruments of labour.

The correction was introduced because Lassalle, for reasons now generally known, attacked *only* the capitalist class and not the landowners. In England, the capitalist is usually not even the owner of the land on which his factory stands.

3. "The emancipation of labour demands the promotion of the instruments of labour to the common property of society and the co-operative regulation of the total labour with a fair distribution of the proceeds of labour."

"Promotion of the instruments of labour to the common property" ought obviously to read their "conversion into the common property"; but this only in passing.

What are "proceeds of labour"? The product of labour or its value? And in the latter case, is it the total value of the product or only that part of the value which labour has newly added to the value of the means of production consumed?

"Proceeds of labour" is a loose notion which Lassalle has put in the place of definite economic conceptions.

What is "a fair distribution"?

Do not the bourgeois assert that the present-day distribution is "fair"? And is it not, in fact, the only "fair" distribution on the basis of the present-day mode of production? Are economic relations regulated by legal conceptions or do not, on the contrary, legal relations arise from economic ones? Have not also the socialist sectarians the most varied notions about "fair" distribution?

To understand what is implied in this connection by the phrase "fair distribution," we must take the first paragraph and this one together. The latter presupposes a society wherein "the instruments of labour are common property and the total labour is cooperatively regulated," and from the first paragraph we learn that "the proceeds of labour belong undiminished with equal right to all members of society."

"To all members of society"? To those who do not work as well? What remains then of the "undiminished proceeds of labour"? Only to those members of society who work? What remains then of the equal right" of all members of society?

But "all members of society" and "equal right" are obviously mere phrases. The kernel consists in this, that in this communist society every worker must receive the "undiminished" Lassallean "proceeds of labour."

Let us take first of all the words "proceeds of labour" in the sense of the product of labour; then the co-operative proceeds of labour are the *total social product*.

From this must now be deducted:

First, cover for replacement of the means of production used up.

Secondly, additional portion for expansion of production.

Thirdly, reserve or insurance funds to provide against accidents, dislocations caused by natural calamities, etc.

These deductions from the "undiminished proceeds of labour" are an economic necessity and their magnitude is to be determined according to available means and forces, and partly by computation of probabilities, but they are in no way calculable by equity.

There remains the other part of the total product, intended to serve as means of consumption.

Before this is divided among the individuals, there has to be deducted again, from it:

First, the general costs of administration not belonging to production.

This part will, from the outset, be very considerably restricted in comparison with present-day society and it diminishes in proportion as the new society develops.

Secondly, that which is intended for the common satisfaction of needs, such as schools, health services, etc.

From the outset this part grows considerably in comparison with present-day society and it grows in proportion as the new society develops.

Thirdly, funds for those unable to work, etc., in short, for what is included under so-called official poor relief today.

Only now do we come to the "distribution" which the programme, under Lassallean influence, alone has in view in its narrow fashion, namely, to that part of the means of consumption which is divided among the individual producers of the co-operative society.

The "undiminished proceeds of labour" have already unnoticeably become converted into the "diminished" proceeds, although what the producer is deprived of in his capacity as a private individual benefits him directly or indirectly in his capacity as a member of society.

Just as the phrase of the "undiminished proceeds of labour" has disappeared, so now does the phrase of the "proceeds of labour" disappear altogether.

Within the co-operative society based on common ownership of the means of production, the producers do not exchange their products; just as little does the labour employed on the products appear here *as the value* of these products, as a material quality possessed by them, since now, in contrast to capitalist society, individual labour no longer exists in an indirect fashion but directly as a component part of the total labour. The phrase "proceeds of labour," objectionable also today on account of its ambiguity, thus loses all meaning.

What we have to deal with here is a communist society, not as it has *developed* on its own foundations, but, on the contrary, just as it *emerges* from capitalist society; which is thus in every respect, economically, morally and intellectually, still stamped with the birth marks of the old society from whose womb it emerges. Accordingly, the individual producer receives back from society—after the deductions have been made—exactly what he gives to it. What he has given to it is his individual quantum of labour. For example, the social working day consists of the sum of the individual hours of work; the individual labour time of the individual producer is the part of the social working day contributed by him, his share in it. He receives a certificate from society that he has furnished such and such an amount of labour (after deducting his labour for the common funds), and with this certificate he draws from the social stock of means of consumption as much as costs the same amount of labour. The same amount of labour which he has given to society in one form he receives back in another.

Here obviously the same principle prevails as that which regulates the exchange of commodities, as far as this is exchange of equal values. Content and form are changed, because under the altered circumstances no one can give anything except his labour, and because, on the other hand, nothing can pass to the ownership of individuals except individual means of consumption. But, as far as the distribution of the latter among the individual producers is concerned, the same principle prevails as in the exchange of commodity equivalents: a given amount of labour in one form is exchanged for an equal amount of labour in another form.

Hence, *equal right* here is still in principle—*bourgeois right,* although principle and practice are no longer at loggerheads, while the exchange of equivalents in commodity exchange only exists *on the average* and not in the individual case.

In spite of this advance, this *equal right* is still constantly stigmatised by a bourgeois limitation. The right of the producers is *proportional* to the labour they supply; the equality consists in the fact that measurement is made with an *equal standard*, labour.

But one man is superior to another physically or mentally and so supplies more labour in the same time, or can labour for a longer time; and labour, to serve as a measure, must be defined by its duration or intensity, otherwise it ceases to be a standard of measurement. This *equal* right is an unequal right for unequal labour. It recognises no class differences, because everyone is only a worker like everyone else; but it tacitly recognises unequal individual endowment and thus productive capacity as natural privileges. *It is, therefore, a right of inequality, in its content, like every right.* Right by its very nature can consist only in the application of an equal standard; but unequal individuals (and they would not be different individuals if they were not unequal) are measurable only by an equal standard in so far as they are brought under an equal point of view, are taken from one *definite* side only, for instance, in the present case, are regarded *only as workers* and nothing more is seen in them, everything else being ignored. Further, one worker is married, another not; one has more children than another, and so on and so forth. Thus, with an equal performance of labour, and hence an equal share in the social consumption fund, one will in fact receive more than another, one will be richer than another, and so on. To avoid all these defects, right instead of being equal would have to be unequal.

But these defects are inevitable in the first phase of communist society as it is when it has just emerged after prolonged birth pangs from capitalist society. Right can never be higher than the economic structure of society and its cultural development conditioned thereby.

In a higher phase of communist society, after the enslaving subordination of the individual to the division of labour, and therewith also the antithesis between mental and physical labour, has vanished; after labour has become not only a means of life but life's prime want; after the productive forces have also increased with the all-round development of the individual, and all the springs of cooperative wealth flow more abundantly—only then can the narrow horizon of bourgeois right be crossed in its entirety and society inscribe on its banner: From each according to his ability, to each according to his needs!

I have dealt more at length with the "undiminished proceeds of labour," on the one hand, and with "equal right" and "fair distribution," on the other, in order to show what a crime it is to attempt, on the one hand, to force on our Party again, as dogmas, ideas which in a certain period had some meaning but have now become obsolete verbal rubbish, while again perverting, on the other, the realistic outlook, which it cost so much effort to instil into the Party but which has now taken root in it, by means of ideological nonsense about right and other trash so common among the democrats and French Socialists.

Quite apart from the analysis so far given, it was in general a mistake to make a fuss about so-called *distribution* and put the principal stress on it.

Any distribution whatever of the means of consumption is only a consequence of the distribution of the conditions of production themselves. The latter distribution, however, is a feature of the mode of production itself. The capitalist mode of production, for example, rests on the fact that the material conditions of production are in the hands of non-workers in the form of property in capital and land, while the masses are only owners of the personal condition of production, of labour power.

If the elements of production are so distributed, then the present-day distribution of the means of consumption results automatically. If the material conditions of production are the co-operative property of the workers themselves, then there likewise results a distribution of the means of consumption different from the present one. Vulgar socialism (and from it in turn a section of the democracy) has taken over from the bourgeois economists the consideration and treatment of distribution as independent of the mode of production and hence the presentation of socialism as turning principally on distribution. After the real relation has long been made clear, why retrogress again?

4. "The emancipation of labour must be the work of the working class, relatively to which all other classes are *only one reactionary mass*."

The first strophe is taken from the introductory words of the Rules of the International, but "improved." There it is said: "The emancipation of the working class must be the act of the workers themselves"; here, on the contrary, the "working class" has to emancipate—what? "Labour." Let him understand who can.

In compensation, the antistrophe, on the other hand, is a Lassallean quotation of the first water: "relatively to which (the working class) all other classes are *only one reactionary mass*."

In the *Communist Manifesto* it is said: "Of all the classes that stand face to face with the bourgeoisie today, the proletariat alone is a *really revolutionary class*. The other classes decay and finally disappear in the face of modern industry; the proletariat is its special and essential product."

The bourgeoisie is here conceived as a revolutionary class—as the bearer of large-scale industry—relatively to the feudal lords and the lower middle class, who desire to maintain all social positions that are the creation of obsolete modes of production. Thus they do not form *together* with the *bourgeoisie* only one reactionary mass.

On the other hand, the proletariat is revolutionary relatively to the bourgeoisie because, having itself grown up on the basis of large-scale industry, it strives to strip off from production the capitalist character that the bourgeoisie seeks to perpetuate. But the *Manifesto* adds that the "lower middle class" is becoming revolutionary "in view of [its] impending transfer into the proletariat."

From this point of view, therefore, it is again nonsense to say that it, together with the bourgeoisie, and with the feudal lords into the bargain, "form only one reactionary mass" relatively to the working class.

Has one proclaimed to the artisans, small manufacturers, etc., and *peasants* during the last elections: Relatively to us you, together with the bourgeoisie and feudal lords, form only one reactionary mass?

Lassalle knew the *Communist Manifesto* by heart, as his faithful followers know the gospels written by him. If, therefore, he has falsified it so grossly, this has occurred only to put a good colour on his alliance with absolutist and feudal opponents against the bourgeoisie.

In the above paragraph, moreover, his oracular saying is dragged in by main force without any connection with the botched quotation from the Rules of the International. Thus is it here simply an impertinence, and indeed not at all displeasing to Herr Bismarck, one of those cheap pieces of insolence in which the Marat of Berlin[1] deals.

5. "The working class strives for its emancipation first of all *within the framework of the present-day national state,* conscious that the necessary result of its efforts, which are common to the workers of all civilised countries, will be the international brotherhood of peoples."

Lassalle, in opposition to the *Communist Manifesto* and to all earlier socialism, conceived the workers' movement from the narrowest national standpoint. He is being followed in this—and that after the work of the International!

It is altogether self-evident that, to be able to fight at all, the working class must organise itself at home *as a class* and that its own country is the immediate arena of its struggle. In so far its class struggle is national, not in substance, but, as the *Communist Manifesto* says, "in form." But the "framework of the present-day national state," for instance, the German Empire, is itself in its turn economically "within the framework" of the world market, politically "within the framework" of the system of states. Every businessman knows that German trade is at the same time foreign trade, and the greatness of Herr Bismarck consists, to be sure, precisely in his pursuing a kind of *international* policy.

And to what does the German workers' party reduce its internationalism? To the consciousness that the result of its efforts will be "*the international brotherhood of peoples*"—a phrase borrowed from the bourgeois League of Peace and Freedom[2] which is intended to pass as equivalent to the international brotherhood of the working classes in the joint struggle against the ruling classes and their governments. Not a word, therefore, *about the international functions* of the German working class! And it is thus that it is to challenge its own bourgeoisie—which is already linked up in brotherhood against it with the bourgeois of all other countries—and Herr Bismarck's international policy of conspiracy!

In fact, the internationalism of the programme stands even *infinitely below* that of the Free Trade Party. The latter also asserts that the result of its efforts will be "the international brotherhood of peoples." But it also *does* something to make trade international and by no means contents itself with the consciousness—that all peoples are carrying on trade at home.

The international activity of the working classes does not in any way depend on the existence of the *International Working Men's Association.* This was only the first attempt to create a central organ for that activity; an attempt which was a lasting success on account of the impulse which it gave but which was no longer realisable in its *first historical form* after the fall of the Paris Commune.

Bismarck's *Norddeutsche* was absolutely right when it announced, to the satisfaction of its master, that the German workers' party had sworn off internationalism in the new programme.[3]

---

1. [A reference to Hasselmann, the chief editor of the *Neuer Sozial-Demokrat,* the central organ of the Lassalleans.]

2. [The International League of Peace and Freedom was organized in Geneva in 1867 by liberals and pacifists.]

3. [Marx refers to the editorial which appeared in No. 67 of the *Norddeutsche Allgemeine Zeitung* (*North German General Newspaper*) of March 20, 1875. It stated with regard to Article 5 of the Social-Democratic Programme

II

"Starting from these basic principles, the German workers' party strives by all legal means for the *free state—and*—socialist society: the abolition of the wage system *together with* the *iron law of wages*—and—exploitation in every form; the elimination of all social and political inequality."

I shall return to the "free" state later.

So, in future, the German workers' party has got to believe in Lassalle's "iron law of wages"! That this may not be lost, the nonsense is perpetrated of speaking of the "abolition of the wage system" (it should read: system of wage labour) *"together with* the iron law of wages." If I abolish wage labour, then naturally I abolish its laws also, whether they are of "iron" or sponge. But Lassalle's attack on wage labour turns almost solely on this so-called law. In order, therefore, to prove that Lassalle's sect has conquered, the "wage system" must be abolished *"together with* the iron law of wages" and not without it.

It is well known that nothing of the "iron law of wages" is Lassalle's except the word "iron" borrowed from Goethe's "great eternal iron laws." The word *iron* is a label by which the true believers recognise one another. But if I take the law with Lassalle's stamp on it and, consequently, in his sense, then I must also take it with his substantiation for it. And what is that? As Lange already showed, shortly after Lassalle's death, it is the Malthusian theory of population (preached by Lange himself). But if this theory is correct, then again I *cannot* abolish the law even if I abolish wage labour a hundred times over, because the law then governs not only the system of wage labour but *every* social system. Basing themselves directly on this, the economists have been proving for fifty years and more that socialism cannot abolish poverty, *which has its basis in nature,* but can only make it *general,* distribute it simultaneously over the whole surface of society!

But all this is not the main thing. *Quite apart* from the *false* Lassallean formulation of the law, the truly outrageous retrogression consists in the following.

Since Lassalle's death there has asserted itself in *our* Party the scientific understanding that wages are not what they *appear* to be, namely, the *value,* or *price, of labour,* but only a masked form for the *value,* or *price, of labour power.* Thereby the whole bourgeois conception of wages hitherto, as well as all the criticism hitherto directed against this conception, was thrown overboard once for all and it was made clear that the wage-worker has permission to work for his own subsistence, that is, *to live,* only in so far as he works for a certain time gratis for the capitalist (and hence also for the latter's co-consumers of surplus value); that the whole capitalist system of production turns on the increase of this gratis labour by extending the working day or by developing the productivity, that is, increasing the intensity of labour power, etc; that, consequently, the system of wage labour is a system of slavery, and indeed of a slavery which becomes more severe in proportion as the social productive forces of labour develop, whether the worker receives better or worse payment. And after this understanding has gained more and more ground in our Party, one returns to Lassalle's dogmas, although one must have known that Lassalle *did not know*

that "Social-Democratic agitation had in many respects become more prudent" and that it was "repudiating the International."]

what wages were, but following in the wake of the bourgeois economists took the appearance for the essence of the matter.

It is as if, among slaves who have at last got behind the secret of slavery and broken out in rebellion, a slave still in thrall to obsolete notions were to inscribe on the programme of the rebellion: Slavery must be abolished because the feeding of slaves in the system of slavery cannot exceed a certain low maximum!

Does not the mere fact that the representatives of our Party were capable of perpetrating such a monstrous attack on the understanding that has spread among the mass of our Party prove by itself with what criminal levity and with what lack of conscience they set to work in drawing up this compromise programme!

Instead of the indefinite concluding phrase of the paragraph, "the elimination of all social and political inequality," it ought to have been said that with the abolition of class distinctions all social and political inequality arising from them would disappear of itself.

III

"The German workers' party, in order *to pave the way to the solution of the social question,* demands the establishment of producers' co-operative societies *with state aid under the democratic control of the toiling people.* The producers' co-operative societies *are to be called into being* for industry and agriculture on such a scale *that the socialist organisation of the total labour will arise from them.*"

After the Lassallean "iron law of wages," the physic of the prophet. The way to it is "paved" in worthy fashion. In place of the existing class struggle appears a newspaper scribbler's phrase: "the social *question,*" to the "*solution*" of which one "paves the way." Instead of arising from the revolutionary process of transformation of society, the "socialist organisation of the total labour" "arises" from the "state aid" that the state gives to the producers' co-operative societies and which the *state,* not the worker, "*calls into being.*" It is worthy of Lassalle's imagination that with state loans one can build a new society just as well as a new railway!

From the remnants of a sense of shame, "state aid" has been put—under the democratic control of the "toiling people."

In the first place, the majority of the "toiling people" in Germany consists of peasants, and not of proletarians.

Secondly, "democratic" means in German "*volksherrschaftlich*" ["by the rule of the people"]. But what does "control by the rule of the people of the toiling people" mean? And particularly in the case of a toiling people which, through these demands that it puts to the state, expresses its full consciousness that it neither rules nor is ripe for ruling!

It would be superfluous to deal here with the criticism of the recipe prescribed by Buchez in the reign of Louis Philippe in *opposition* to the French Socialists and accepted by the reactionary workers of the *Atelier.*[4] The chief offence does not lie in having inscribed this specific nostrum in the programme, but in taking, in general,

4. [*Atelier* (Workshop): A workers' monthly which appeared in Paris in 1840–50. It was under the influence of the Catholic socialism of Buchez.]

a retrograde step from the standpoint of a class movement to that of a sectarian movement.

That the workers desire to establish the conditions for co-operative production on a social scale, and first of all on a national scale in their own country, only means that they are working to revolutionise the present conditions of production, and it has nothing in common with the foundation of co-operative societies with state aid. But as far as the present co-operative societies are concerned, they are of value *only* in so far as they are the independent creations of the workers and not protégés either of the government or of the bourgeois.

IV

I come now to the democratic section.

A. *"The free basis of the state."*

First of all, according to II, the German workers' party strives for "the free state."

Free state—what is this?

It is by no means the aim of the workers, who have got rid of the narrow mentality of humble subjects, to set the state free. In the German Empire the "state" is almost as "free" as in Russia. Freedom consists in converting the state from an organ superimposed upon society into one completely subordinate to it, and today, too, the forms of state are more free or less free to the extent that they restrict the "freedom of the state."

The German workers' party—at least if it adopts the programme—shows that its socialist ideas are not even skin-deep; in that, instead of treating existing society (and this holds good for any future one) as the *basis* of the existing state (or of the future state in the case of future society), it treats the state rather as independent entity that possesses its own *intellectual, ethical and libertarian bases.*

And what of the riotous misuse which the programme makes of the words *"present-day state," "present-day society,"* and of the still more riotous misconception it creates in regard to the state to which it addresses its demands?

"Present-day society" is capitalist society, which exists in all civilised countries, more or less free from medieval admixture, more or less modified by the special historical development of each country, more or less developed. On the other hand, the "present-day state" changes with a country's frontier. It is different in the Prusso-German Empire from what it is in Switzerland, it is different in England from what it is in the United States. The "present-day state" is, therefore, a fiction.

Nevertheless, the different states of the different civilised countries, in spite of their manifold diversity of form, all have this in common, that they are based on modern bourgeois society, only one more or less capitalistically developed. They have, therefore, also certain essential features in common. In this sense it is possible to speak of the "present-day state," in contrast with the future, in which its present root, bourgeois society, will have died off.

The question then arises: what transformation will the state undergo in communist society? In other words, what social functions will remain in existence there that are analogous to present functions of the state? This question can only be answered scientifically, and one does not get a flea-hop nearer to the problem by a thousandfold combination of the word people with the word state.

Between capitalist and communist society lies the period of the revolutionary transformation of the one into the other. There corresponds to this also a political transition period in which the state can be nothing but *the revolutionary dictatorship of the proletariat.*

Now the programme does not deal with this nor with the future state of communist society.

Its political demands contain nothing beyond the old democratic litany familiar to all: universal suffrage, direct legislation, popular rights, a people's militia, etc. They are a mere echo of the bourgeois People's Party, of the League of Peace and Freedom. They are all demands which, in so far as they are not exaggerated in fantastic presentation, have already been *realised*. Only the state to which they belong does not lie within the borders of the German Empire, but in Switzerland, the United States, etc. This sort of "state of the future" is a present-day state, although existing outside the "framework" of the German Empire.

But one thing has been forgotten. Since the German workers' party expressly declares that it acts within "the present-day national state," hence within *its own* state, the Prusso-German Empire—its demands would indeed otherwise be largely meaningless, since one only demands what one has not got—it should not have forgotten the chief thing, namely, that all those pretty little gewgaws rest on the recognition of the so-called sovereignty of the people and hence are appropriate only in a *democratic republic.*

Since one has not the courage—and wisely so, for the circumstances demand caution—to demand the democratic republic, as the French workers' programmes under Louis Philippe and under Louis Napoleon did, one should not have resorted, either, to the subterfuge, neither "honest"[5] nor decent, of demanding things which have meaning only in a democratic republic from a state which is nothing but a police-guarded military despotism, embellished with parliamentary forms, alloyed with a feudal admixture, already influenced by the bourgeoisie and bureaucratically carpentered, and then to assure this state into the bargain that one imagines one will be able to force such things upon it "by legal means."

Even vulgar democracy, which sees the millennium in the democratic republic and has no suspicion that it is precisely in this last form of state of bourgeois society that the class struggle has to be fought out to a conclusion—even it towers mountains above this kind of democratism which keeps within the limits of what is permitted by the police and not permitted by logic.

That, in fact, by the word "state" is meant the government machine, or the state in so far as it forms a special organism separated from society through division of labour, is shown by the words "the German worker's party demands *as the economic basis of the state:* a single progressive income tax," etc. Taxes are the economic basis of the government machinery and of nothing else. In the state of the future, existing in Switzerland, this demand has been pretty well fulfilled. Income tax presupposes various sources of income of the various social classes, and hence capitalist society. It is, therefore, nothing remarkable that the Liverpool financial reformers, bourgeois

---

5. ["*Honest*" was the epithet applied to the Eisenachers. Here a play upon words.]

headed by Gladstone's brother, are putting forward the same demand as the programme.

B. "The German workers' party demands as the intellectual and ethical basis of the state:

"1. Universal and *equal elementary education* by the state. Universal compulsory school attendance. Free instruction."

Equal elementary education? What idea lies behind these words? Is it believed that in present-day society (and it is only with this one has to deal) education can be *equal* for all classes? Or is it demanded that the upper classes also shall be compulsorily reduced to the modicum of education—the elementary school—that alone is compatible with the economic conditions not only of the wage-workers but of the peasants as well?

"Universal compulsory school attendance. Free instruction." The former exists even in Germany, the second in Switzerland and in the United States in the case of elementary schools. If in some states of the latter country higher educational institutions are also "free" that only means in fact defraying the cost of the education of the upper classes from the general tax receipts. Incidentally, the same holds good for "free administration of justice" demanded under A, 5. The administration of criminal justice is to be had free everywhere; that of civil justice is concerned almost exclusively with conflicts over property and hence affects almost exclusively the possessing classes. Are they to carry on their litigation at the expense of the national coffers?

The paragraph on the schools should at least have demanded technical schools (theoretical and practical) in combination with the elementary school.

"*Elementary education by the state*" is altogether objectionable. Defining by a general law the expenditures on the elementary schools, the qualifications of the teaching staff, the branches of instruction, etc., and, as is done in the United States, supervising the fulfilment of these legal specifications by state inspectors, is a very different thing from appointing the state as the educator of the people! Government and Church should rather be equally excluded from any influence on the school. Particularly, indeed, in the Prusso-German Empire (and one should not take refuge in the rotten subterfuge that one is speaking of a "state of the future"; we have seen how matters stand in this respect) the state has need, on the contrary, of a very stern education by the people.

But the whole programme, for all its democratic clang, is tainted through and through by the Lassallean sect's servile belief in the state, or, what is no better, by a democratic belief in miracles, or rather it is a compromise between these two kinds of belief in miracles, both equally remote from socialism.

"*Freedom of science*" says a paragraph of the Prussian Constitution. Why, then, here?

"*Freedom of conscience*"! If one desired at this time of the *Kulturkampf*[6] to remind liberalism of its old catchwords, it surely could have been done only in the following form: Everyone should be able to attend to his religious as well as his bodily needs

---

6. [*Kulturkampf* (Struggle for culture): Bismarck's struggle in the seventies against the German Catholic Party, the Party of the "Centre," by means of police persecution of Catholicism.]

without the police sticking their noses in. But the workers' party ought at any rate in this connection to have expressed its awareness of the fact that bourgeois "freedom of conscience" is nothing but the toleration of all possible kinds of *religious freedom of conscience,* and that for its part it endeavours rather to liberate the conscience from the witchery of religion. But one chooses not to transgress the "bourgeois" level.

I have now come to the end, for the appendix that now follows in the programme does not constitute a characteristic component part of it. Hence I can be very brief here.

2. *"Normal working day."*

In no other country has the workers' party limited itself to such an indefinite demand, but has always fixed the length of the working day that it considers normal under the given circumstances.

3. "Restriction of female labour and prohibition of child labour."

The standardisation of the working day must include the restriction of female labour, in so far as it relates to the duration, intermissions, etc., of the working day; otherwise it could only mean the exclusion of female labour from branches of industry that are especially unhealthy for the female body or are objectionable morally for the female sex. If that is what was meant, it should have been said so: *"Prohibition of child labour."* Here it was absolutely essential to state the age limit.

A *general prohibition* of child labour is incompatible with the existence of large-scale industry and hence an empty, pious wish. Its realisation—if it were possible— would be reactionary, since, with a strict regulation of the working time according to the different age groups and other safety measures for the protection of children, an early combination of productive labour with education is one of the most potent means for the transformation of present-day society.

4. "State supervision of factory, workshop and domestic industry."

In consideration of the Prusso-German state it should definitely have been demanded that the inspectors are to be removable only by a court of law; that any worker can have them prosecuted for neglect of duty; that they must belong to the medical profession.

5. "Regulation of prison labour."

A petty demand in a general workers' programme. In any case, it should have been clearly stated that there is no intention from fear of competition to allow ordinary criminals to be treated like beasts, and especially that there is no desire to deprive them of their sole means of betterment, productive labour. This was surely the least one might have expected from Socialists.

6. "An effective liability law."

It should have been stated what is meant by an "effective" liability law.

Be it noted, incidentally, that in speaking of the normal working day the part of factory legislation that deals with health regulations and safety measures, etc., has been overlooked. The liability law only comes into operation when these regulations are infringed.

In short, this appendix also is distinguished by slovenly editing.

Dixi et salvavi animam meam.[7]

7. ["I have spoken and saved my soul."]

FRIEDRICH NIETZSCHE

From Plato and Aristotle to Locke and Kant, moral and political theorists build their theories on the founding principle that human beings are especially valuable, somehow preeminent in the natural order, usually by virtue of reason or intellect, possessing thereby a nobility and grandeur that singles them out. Other thinkers, however, begin with a different estimate of the human and its place in nature; to them the proper way to understand humankind is to appreciate the impulses, desires, and instincts that ground all animal behavior and hence human action as well. Morality and political conduct, on such a view, are manifestations of these desires and drives, e.g., the desire for self-preservation. On this view, human beings are to be considered like any other natural beings. Among such thinkers are Hobbes, Spinoza, Freud, and, perhaps the most bold and dramatic of all, Friedrich Nietzsche (1844–1900).

In an unpublished fragment of 1873, Nietzsche expresses this view about human intelligence with a powerful image:

> In some remote corner of the universe, poured out and glittering in innumerable solar systems, there once was a star on which clever animals invented knowledge. . . . After nature had drawn a few breaths the star grew cold, and the clever animals had to die. . . . how wretched, how shadowy and flighty, how aimless and arbitrary, the human intellect appears in nature. There have been eternities when it did not exist; and when it is done for again, nothing will have happened.
>
> (from *On Truth and Lie in an Extra-Moral Sense*)

According to Nietzsche, then, reason or intellect is no special capacity. It comes and goes like other natural abilities, as do knowledge, truth, and morality, too. All are tools of nature and must be studied historically, almost anthropologically or biologically, as devices that manifest the deepest drives of human nature. Western morality and religion incorporate many traditions, some that repress such central drives and others that enable them to flourish. Philosophy works to unearth these various traditions, to clarify them, and to enhance the lives of the philosophers and artists who do so. The proper way to study morality is not to seek to ground a special set of principles in some universal or transcendent source; rather, it is to examine and expose the features of various moralities as they have functioned in societies throughout history, that is, to study moralities historically and to see how some do and some do not repress the natural drives that characterize the human animal.

Such a conception—of morality as a historical, natural phenomenon and not as a set of universal principles—is one teaching of a powerful, influential set of works written by Nietzsche in the second half of the nineteenth century. These works are the products of a brilliant student of classical philology who broke out of the bonds of technical scholarship and welded a deep affinity with ancient culture to rare literary ability. Nietzsche was once attacked as a source of Nazi ideology; more recently, he is frequently cited as an inspiration for deconstructionists. But in his own day he was famous and controversial on a variety of fronts, not least of all for his bold style and his withering critique of Christianity and religion.

Nietzsche was born on October 15, 1844, in Rocken, Germany, where his father was a Lutheran pastor. In 1849, when he was nearly five, his father died, and Nietzsche spent his youth surrounded by his mother, his sister Elisabeth, who was two years younger than Nietzsche, his grandmother, and two maiden aunts. In 1864 he entered the University of Bonn to study theology. By the next year, however, Nietzsche had transferred to Leipzig to study classical philology and was hard at work on a dissertation on the classical Greek poet Theognis. The results were a lecture, an essay, and, as Nietzsche put it, his "birth as a philologist." During the next few years he was deeply involved with a variety of projects, from essays on Diogenes Laertius and on Democritus to studies of history and teleology.

In 1869 the brilliant young scholar was appointed to a professorship at Basel University in Switzerland. At about this time, he first met the composer Richard Wagner, who became a powerful influence on his work. With the outbreak of the Franco-Prussian War in 1870, Nietzsche volunteered and served for a short time as a medical orderly. When he contracted dysentary and diphtheria, however, he was forced to return home. His deteriorating health and insomnia accompanied him for the rest of his life. By 1872, his first book, *The Birth of Tragedy*, was published; in it he explored the emergence of Greek tragedy out of music and its ruin at the hands of the rational philosophy of Socrates.

Nietzsche's health was constantly bad. By 1876 his painful physical condition mirrored his relationship with Wagner, which finally fell apart. Wagner had become a commercial success and the center of a cult at the opera center at Bayreuth. Wagner's self-importance, insensitivity, anti-Semitism, and total neglect of Nietzsche's work repelled Nietzsche, whose physical pain and psychological torment was expressed in his writings. During this period, his work, no longer scholarly, appeared at a steady rate—essays on David Strauss, the New Testament scholar and young radical Hegelian, on philosophy and Greek tragedy, on the uses and disadvantages of history, on Schopenhauer, and much else. Several of these essays were published, from 1873 to 1876, as *Untimely Meditations*. In 1878, *Human, All Too Human* appeared, then the *Gay Science* in 1882, *Thus Spoke Zarathustra* (Parts One and Two) in 1883, *Beyond Good and Evil* in 1886, *Toward a Geneology of Morals* in 1887, and the *Twilight of the Idols* in 1889.

During these extraordinarily productive but pain-racked years, Nietzsche was rarely at rest. His bad health forced him to clinics and convalescence, and illness interrupted his teaching. By 1876 he had stopped teaching altogether at the university, and in 1879 he formally resigned. The decade of the 1880s was filled with suffering, sickness, writing, and the interminable moving, mostly in Switzerland and

Italy, in a vain effort to find a comfortable climate and peaceful surroundings. For much of these years Nietzsche and his entourage traveled from Genoa to Sils-Maria, back and forth, with occasional trips to Venice, Nice, Naumburg, and elsewhere. Then, in January of 1889, Nietzsche collapsed in the street in Turin, Italy, hopelessly insane. After brief periods in clinics, Nietzsche was released into the care of his mother, in whose home in Jena he lived until his death on August 25, 1900. His autobiographical work, *Ecce Homo*, written in 1888, was published in 1908.

Recommended readings

Danto, Arthur. *Nietzsche as Philosopher*. New York: Macmillan, 1965.

MacIntyre, Alasdair. *After Virtue*. Notre Dame: University of Notre Dame Press, 1981.

Nehamas, Alexander. *Nietzsche: Life as Literature*. Cambridge: Harvard University Press, 1985.

Schacht, Richard. *Nietzsche*. London: Routledge, 1983.

Solomon, Robert (ed.). *Nietzsche*. Garden City: Doubleday, 1973.

Thiele, Paul. *Friedrich Nietzsche and the Politics of the Soul*. Princeton: Princeton University Press, 1990.

Warren, Mark. *Nietzsche and Political Thought*. Cambridge: M.I.T. Press, 1988.

ON THE GENEALOGY OF MORALS

Preface

1

We are unknown to ourselves, we men of knowledge—and with good reason. We have never sought ourselves—how could it happen that we should ever *find* ourselves? It has rightly been said: "Where your treasure is, there will your heart be also";[1] *our* treasure is where the beehives of our knowledge are. We are constantly making for them, being by nature winged creatures and honey-gatherers of the spirit; there is one thing alone we really care about from the heart—"bringing something home." Whatever else there is in life, so-called "experiences"—which of us has sufficient earnestness for them? Or sufficient time? Present experience has, I am afraid, always found us "absent-minded": we cannot give our hearts to it—not even our ears! Rather, as one divinely preoccupied and immersed in himself into whose ear the bell has just boomed with all its strength the twelve beats of noon suddenly starts up and asks himself: "what really was that which just struck?" so we sometimes rub our ears *afterward* and ask, utterly surprised and disconcerted, "what really was that which we have just experienced?" and moreover: "who *are* we really?" and, afterward as aforesaid, count the twelve trembling bell-strokes of our experience, our life, our *being*—and alas! miscount them.—So we are necessarily strangers to ourselves, we do not comprehend ourselves, we *have* to misunderstand ourselves, for us the law "Each is furthest from himself" applies to all eternity—we are not "men of knowledge" with respect to ourselves.

2

My ideas on the *origin* of our moral prejudices—for this is the subject of this polemic—received their first, brief, and provisional expression in the collection of aphorisms that bears the title *Human, All-Too-Human. A Book for Free Spirits.* This book was begun in Sorrento during a winter when it was given to me to pause as a wanderer pauses and look back across the broad and dangerous country my spirit had traversed up to that time. This was in the winter of 1876–77; the ideas themselves are older. They were already in essentials the same ideas that I take up again in the present treatises—let us hope the long interval has done them good, that they have become riper, clearer, stronger, more perfect! *That* I still cleave to them today, however, that they have become in the meantime more and more firmly attached to one another, indeed entwined and interlaced with one another, strengthens my joyful assurance that they might have arisen in me from the first not as isolated, capricious, or sporadic things but from a common root, from a *fundamental will* of knowledge, pointing imperiously into the depths, speaking more and more precisely, demanding greater and greater precision. For this alone is fitting for a philosopher. We have no right to *isolated* acts of any kind: we may not make isolated errors or hit

1. [Matthew 6:21.—W.K.]

upon isolated truths. Rather do our ideas, our values, our yeas and nays, our ifs and buts, grow out of us with the necessity with which a tree bears fruit—related and each with an affinity to each, and evidence of *one* will, *one* health, *one* soil, *one* sun.— Whether *you* like them, these fruits of ours?—But what is that to the trees! What is that to *us,* to us philosophers!

3

Because of a scruple peculiar to me that I am loth to admit to—for it is concerned with *morality,* with all that has hitherto been celebrated on earth as morality—a scruple that entered my life so early, so uninvited, so irresistibly, so much in conflict with my environment, age, precedents, and descent that I might almost have the right to call it my "*a priori*"—my curiosity as well as my suspicions were bound to halt quite soon at the question of where our good and evil really *originated.* In fact, the problem of the origin of evil pursued me even as a boy of thirteen: at an age in which you have "half childish trifles, half God in your heart,"[2] I devoted to it my first childish literary trifle, my first philosophical effort—and as for the "solution" of the problem I posed at that time, well, I gave the honor to God, as was only fair, and made him the *father* of evil. Was *that* what my "*a priori*" demanded of me? that new immoral, or at least unmoralistic "*a priori*" and the alas! so anti-Kantian, enigmatic "categorical imperative" which spoke through it and to which I have since listened more and more closely, and not merely listened?

Fortunately I learned early to separate theological prejudice from moral prejudice and ceased to look for the origin of evil *behind* the world. A certain amount of historical and philological schooling, together with an inborn fastidiousness of taste in respect to psychological questions in general, soon transformed my problem into another one: under what conditions did man devise these value judgments good and evil? *and what value do they themselves possess?* Have they hitherto hindered or furthered human prosperity? Are they a sign of distress, of impoverishment, of the degeneration of life? Or is there revealed in them, on the contrary, the plenitude, force, and will of life, its courage, certainty, future?

Thereupon I discovered and ventured divers answers; I distinguished between ages, peoples, degrees of rank among individuals; I departmentalized my problem; out of my answers there grew new questions, inquiries, conjectures, probabilities— until at length I had a country of my own, a soil of my own, an entire discrete, thriving, flourishing world, like a secret garden the existence of which no one suspected.—Oh how *fortunate* we are, we men of knowledge, provided only that we know how to keep silent long enough!

4

The first impulse to publish something of my hypotheses concerning the origin of morality was given me by a clear, tidy, and shrewd—also precocious—little book in which I encountered distinctly for the first time an upside-down and perverse species of genealogical hypothesis, the genuinely *English* type, that attracted me— with that power of attraction which everything contrary, everything antipodal possesses. The title of the little book was *The Origin of the Moral Sensations;* its author

---

2. [Goethe's *Faust,* lines 3781f.]

Dr. Paul Rée; the year in which it appeared 1877. Perhaps I have never read anything to which I would have said to myself No, proposition by proposition, conclusion by conclusion, to the extent that I did to this book: yet quite without ill-humor or impatience. In the above-mentioned work, on which I was then engaged, I made opportune and inopportune reference to the propositions of that book, not in order to refute them—what have I to do with refutations!—but, as becomes a positive spirit, to replace the improbable with the more probable, possibly one error with another. It was then, as I have said, that I advanced for the first time those genealogical hypotheses to which this treatise is devoted—ineptly, as I should be the last to deny, still constrained, still lacking my own language for my own things and with much backsliding and vacillation. One should compare in particular what I say in *Human, All-Too-Human,* section 45, on the twofold prehistory of good and evil (namely, in the sphere of the noble and in that of the slaves); likewise, section 136, on the value and origin of the morality of asceticism; likewise, sections 96 and 99 and volume II, section 89, on the "morality of mores," that much older and more primitive species of morality which differs *toto caelo* [diametrically: literally, by the whole heavens] from the altruistic mode of evaluation (in which Dr. Rée, like all English moral genealogists, sees moral evaluation *as such*); likewise, section 92, *The Wanderer,* section 26, and *Dawn,* section 112, on the origin of justice as an agreement between two approximately equal powers (equality as the presupposition of all compacts, consequently of all law); likewise *The Wanderer,* sections 22 and 33, on the origin of punishment, of which the aim of intimidation is neither the essence nor the source (as Dr. Rée thinks—it is rather only introduced, under certain definite circumstances, and always as an incidental, as something added).[3]

5

Even then my real concern was something much more important than hypothesis-mongering, whether my own or other people's, on the origin of morality (or more precisely: the latter concerned me solely for the sake of a goal to which it was only one means among many). What was at stake was the *value* of morality—and over this I had to come to terms almost exclusively with my great teacher Schopenhauer, to whom that book of mine, the passion and the concealed contradiction of that book, addressed itself as if to a contemporary (—for that book, too, was a "polemic"). What was especially at stake was the value of the "unegoistic," the instincts of pity, self-abnegation, self-sacrifice, which Schopenhauer had gilded, deified, and projected into a beyond for so long that at last they became for him "value-in-itself," on the basis of which he *said No* to life and to himself. But it was against precisely *these* instincts that there spoke from me an ever more fundamental mistrust, an ever more corrosive skepticism! It was precisely here that I saw the *great* danger to mankind, its sublimest enticement and seduction—but to what? to nothingness?— it was precisely here that I saw the beginning of the end, the dead stop, a retrospective weariness, the will turning *against* life, the tender and sorrowful signs of the ultimate illness: I understood the ever spreading morality of pity that had seized even on philosophers and made them ill, as the most sinister symptom of a European culture

---

3. [Nietzsche always gives page references to the first editions. I have substituted section numbers, which are the same in all editions and translations. For Nietzsche's relation to Rée see Rudolph Binion, *Frau Lou,* Princeton, N.J., Princeton University Press, 1968.]

that had itself become sinister, perhaps as its by-pass to a new Buddhism? to a Buddhism for Europeans? to—*nihilism?*

For this overestimation of and predilection for pity on the part of modern philosophers is something new: hitherto philosophers have been at one as to the *worthlessness* of pity. I name only Plato, Spinoza, La Rochefoucauld and Kant—four spirits as different from one another as possible, but united in one thing: in their low estimation of pity.

6

This problem of the *value* of pity and of the morality of pity (—I am opposed to the pernicious modern effeminacy of feeling—) seems at first to be merely something detached, an isolated question mark; but whoever sticks with it and *learns* how to ask questions here will experience what I experienced—a tremendous new prospect opens up for him, a new possibility comes over him like a vertigo, every kind of mistrust, suspicion, fear leaps up, his belief in morality, in all morality, falters—finally a new demand becomes audible. Let us articulate this *new demand:* we need a *critique* of moral values, *the value of these values themselves must first be called in question*—and for that there is needed a knowledge of the conditions and circumstances in which they grew, under which they evolved and changed (morality as consequence, as symptom, as mask, as tartufferie, as illness, as misunderstanding; but also morality as cause, as remedy, as stimulant, as restraint, as poison), a knowledge of a kind that has never yet existed or even been desired. One has taken the *value* of these "values" as given, as factual, as beyond all question; one has hitherto never doubted or hesitated in the slightest degree in supposing "the good man" to be of greater value than "the evil man," of greater value in the sense of furthering the advancement and prosperity of man in general (the future of man included). But what if the reverse were true? What if a symptom of regression were inherent in the "good," likewise a danger, a seduction, a poison, a narcotic, through which the present was possibly living *at the expense of the future?* Perhaps more comfortably, less dangerously, but at the same time in a meaner style, more basely?—So that precisely morality would be to blame if the *highest power and splendor* actually possible to the type man was never in fact attained? So that precisely morality was the danger of dangers?

7

Let it suffice that, after this prospect had opened up before me, I had reasons to look about me for scholarly, bold, and industrious comrades (I am still looking). The project is to traverse with quite novel questions, and as though with new eyes, the enormous, distant, and so well hidden land of morality—of morality that has actually existed, actually been lived; and does this not mean virtually to *discover* this land for the first time?

If I considered in this connection the above-mentioned Dr. Rée, among others, it was because I had no doubt that the very nature of his inquiries would compel him to adopt a better method for reaching answers. Have I deceived myself in this? My desire, at any rate, was to point out to so sharp and disinterested an eye as his a better direction in which to look, in the direction of an actual *history of morality*, and to warn him in time against gazing around haphazardly in the blue after the English fashion. For it must be obvious which color is a hundred times more vital for a genealogist of morals than blue: namely *gray*, that is, what is documented, what can actually be confirmed and has actually existed, in short the entire long hieroglyphic record, so hard to decipher, of the moral past of mankind!

This was unknown to Dr. Rée; but he had read Darwin—so that in his hypotheses, and after a fashion that is at least entertaining, the Darwinian beast and the ultra-modern unassuming moral milksop who "no longer bites" politely link hands, the latter wearing an expression of a certain good-natured and refined indolence, with which is mingled even a grain of pessimism and weariness, as if all these things— the problems of morality—were really not worth taking quite so seriously. But to me, on the contrary, there seems to be nothing *more* worth taking seriously, among the rewards for it being that some day one will perhaps be allowed to take them *cheerfully.* For cheerfulness—or in my own language *gay science*—is a reward: the reward of a long, brave, industrious, and subterranean seriousness, of which, to be sure, not everyone is capable. But on the day we can say with all our hearts, "On-wards! our old morality too is part *of the comedy!*" we shall have discovered a new complication and possibility for the Dionysian drama of "The Destiny of the Soul"— and one can wager that the grand old eternal comic poet of our existence will be quick to make use of it!

8

If this book is incomprehensible to anyone and jars on his ears, the fault, it seems to me, is not necessarily mine. It is clear enough, assuming, as I do assume, that one has first read my earlier writings and has not spared some trouble in doing so: for they are, indeed, not easy to penetrate. Regarding my *Zarathustra,* for example, I do not allow that anyone knows that book who has not at some time been profoundly wounded and at some time profoundly delighted by every word in it; for only then may he enjoy the privilege of reverentially sharing in the halcyon element out of which that book was born and in its sunlight clarity, remoteness, breadth, and certainty. In other cases, people find difficulty with the aphoristic form: this arises from the fact that today this form is *not taken seriously enough.* An aphorism, properly stamped and molded, has not been "deciphered" when it has simply been read; rather, one has then to begin its *exegesis,* for which is required an art of exegesis. I have offered in the third essay of the present book an example of what I regard as "exegesis" in such a case—an aphorism is prefixed to this essay, the essay itself is a commentary on it. To be sure, one thing is necessary above all if one is to practice reading as an *art* in this way, something that has been unlearned most thoroughly nowadays—and therefore it will be some time before my writings are "readable"— something for which one has almost to be a cow and in any case *not* a "modern man": *rumination.*

Sils-Maria, Upper Engadine,
July 1887

First Essay
"Good and Evil," "Good and Bad"

1

These English psychologists, whom one has also to thank for the only attempts hitherto to arrive at a history of the origin of morality—they themselves are no easy riddle; I confess that, as living riddles, they even possess one essential advantage over their books—*they are interesting!* These English psychologists—what do they really want? One always discovers them voluntarily or involuntarily at the same task, namely at dragging the *partie honteuse* [shame] of our inner world into the foreground and seeking the truly effective and directing agent, that which has been decisive in its evolution, in just that place where the intellectual pride of man would least *desire* to find it (in the *vis inertiae* [inertia] of habit, for example, or in forgetfulness, or in a blind and chance mechanistic hooking-together of ideas, or in something purely passive, automatic, reflexive, molecular, and thoroughly stupid)—what is it really that always drives these psychologists in just *this* direction? Is it a secret, malicious, vulgar, perhaps self-deceiving instinct for belittling man? Or possibly a pessimistic suspicion, the mistrustfulness of disappointed idealists grown spiteful and gloomy? Or a petty subterranean hostility and rancor toward Christianity (and Plato) that has perhaps not even crossed the threshold of consciousness? Or even a lascivious taste for the grotesque, the painfully paradoxical, the questionable and absurd in existence? Or finally—something of each of them, a little vulgarity, a little gloominess, a little anti-Christianity, a little itching and need for spice?

But I am told they are simply old, cold, and tedious frogs, creeping around men and into men as if in their own proper element, that is, in a *swamp*. I rebel at that idea; more, I do not believe it; and if one may be allowed to hope where one does not know, then I hope from my heart they may be the reverse of this—that these investigators and microscopists of the soul may be fundamentally brave, proud, and magnanimous animals, who know how to keep their hearts as well as their sufferings in bounds and have trained themselves to sacrifice all desirability to truth, *every* truth, even plain, harsh, ugly, repellent, unchristian, immoral truth.—For such truths do exist.—

2

All respect then for the good spirits that may rule in these historians of morality! But it is, unhappily, certain that the *historical spirit* itself is lacking in them, that precisely all the good spirits of history itself have left them in the lurch! As is the hallowed custom with philosophers, the thinking of all of them is *by nature* unhistorical; there is no doubt about that. The way they have bungled their moral genealogy comes to light at the very beginning, where the task is to investigate the origin of the concept and judgment "good." "Originally"—so they decree—"one approved unegoistic actions and called them good from the point of view of those to whom they were done, that is to say, those to whom they were *useful;* later one *forgot* how this approval originated and, simply because unegoistic actions were always *habitually* praised as good, one also felt them to be good—as if they were something good in themselves." One sees straightaway that this primary derivation already contains all the typical traits of the idiosyncrasy of the English psychologists—we have "utility," "forgetting," "habit," and finally "error," all as the basis of an evaluation of which the higher man has hitherto been proud as though it were a kind of prerogative of man as such. This pride *has* to be humbled, this evaluation disvalued: has that end been achieved?

Now it is plain to me, first of all, that in this theory the source of the concept "good" has been sought and established in the wrong place: the judgment "good" did *not* originate with those to whom "goodness" was shown! Rather it was "the good" themselves, that is to say, the noble, powerful, high-stationed and high-minded, who felt and established themselves and their actions as good, that is, of the first rank, in contradistinction to all the low, low-minded, common and plebeian. It was out of this *pathos of distance*[4] that they first seized the right to create values and to coin names for values: what had they to do with utility! The viewpoint of utility is as remote and inappropriate as it possibly could be in face of such a burning eruption of the highest rank-ordering, rank-defining value judgments: for here feeling has attained the antithesis of that low degree of warmth which any calculating prudence, any calculus of utility, presupposes—and not for once only, not for an exceptional hour, but for good. The pathos of nobility and distance, as aforesaid, the protracted and domineering fundamental total feeling on the part of a higher ruling order in relation to a lower order, to a "below"—*that* is the origin of the antithesis "good" and "bad." (The lordly right of giving names extends so far that one should allow oneself to conceive the origin of language itself as an expression of power on the part of the rulers: they say "this *is* this and this," they seal every thing and event with a sound and, as it were, take possession of it.) It follows from this origin that the word "good" was definitely *not* linked from the first and by necessity to "unegoistic" actions, as the superstition of these genealogists of morality would have it. Rather it was only when aristocratic value judgments *declined* that the whole antithesis "egoistic" "unegoistic" obtruded itself more and more on the human conscience—it is, to speak in my own language, the *herd instinct* that through this antithesis at last gets its word (and its *words*) in. And even then it was a long time before that instinct attained such dominion that moral evaluation was actually stuck and halted at this antithesis (as, for example, is the case in contemporary Europe: the prejudice that takes "moral," "unegoistic," "*désintéressé*" as concepts of equivalent value already rules today with the force of a "fixed idea" and brain-sickness).

3

In the second place, however: quite apart from the historical untenability of this hypothesis regarding the origin of the value judgment "good," it suffers from an inherent psychological absurdity. The utility of the unegoistic action is supposed to be the source of the approval accorded it, and this source is supposed to have been *forgotten*—but how is this forgetting *possible?* Has the utility of such actions come to an end at some time or other? The opposite is the case: this utility has rather been an everyday experience at all times, therefore something that has been underlined again and again: consequently, instead of fading from consciousness, instead of becoming easily forgotten, it must have been impressed on the consciousness more and more clearly. How much more reasonable is that opposing theory (it is not for that reason more true—) which Herbert Spencer,[5] for example, espoused: that the concept "good" is essentially identical with the concept "useful," "practical," so that in the judgments "good" and "bad" mankind has summed up and sanctioned precisely its *unforgotten* and *unforgettable* experiences regarding what is useful-practical and what is harmful-impractical. According to this theory, that which has always proved itself useful is good: therefore it may claim to be "valuable in the highest

---

4. [Cf. *Beyond Good and Evil*, section 257.]

5. [Herbert Spencer (1820–1903) was probably the most widely read English philosopher of his time. He applied the principle of evolution to many fields, including sociology and ethics.]

degree," "valuable in itself." This road to an explanation is, as aforesaid, also a wrong one, but at least the explanation is in itself reasonable and psychologically tenable.

4

The signpost to the *right* road was for me the question: what was the real etymological significance of the designations for "good" coined in the various languages? I found they all led back to the *same conceptual transformation*—that everywhere "noble," "aristocratic" in the social sense, is the basic concept from which "good" in the sense of "with aristocratic soul," "noble," "with a soul of a high order," "with a privileged soul" necessarily developed: a development which always runs parallel with that other in which "common," "plebeian," "low" are finally transformed into the concept "bad." The most convincing example of the latter is the German word *schlecht* [bad] itself: which is identical with *schlicht* [plain, simple]—compare *schlechtweg* [plainly], *schlechterdings* [simply]—and originally designated the plain, the common man, as yet with no inculpatory implication and simply in contradistinction to the nobility. About the time of the Thirty Years' War, late enough therefore, this meaning changed into the one now customary.[6]

With regard to a moral genealogy this seems to me a *fundamental* insight; that it has been arrived at so late is the fault of the retarding influence exercised by the democratic prejudice in the modern world toward all questions of origin. And this is so even in the apparently quite objective domain of natural science and physiology, as I shall merely hint here. But what mischief this prejudice is capable of doing, especially to morality and history, once it has been unbridled to the point of hatred is shown by the notorious case of Buckle;[7] here the *plebeianism* of the modern spirit, which is of English origin, erupted once again on its native soil, as violently as a mud volcano and with that salty, noisy, vulgar eloquence with which all volcanos have spoken hitherto.—

5

With regard to *our* problem, which may on good grounds be called a *quiet* problem and one which fastidiously directs itself to few ears, it is of no small interest to ascertain that through those words and roots which designate "good" there frequently still shines the most important nuance by virtue of which the noble felt themselves to be men of a higher rank. Granted that, in the majority of cases, they designate themselves simply by their superiority in power (as "the powerful," "the masters," "the commanders") or by the most clearly visible signs of this superiority, for example, as "the rich," "the possessors" (this is the meaning of arya; and of corresponding words in Iranian and Slavic). But they also do it by a *typical character trait:* and this is the case that concerns us here. They call themselves, for instance, "the truthful"; this is so above all of the Greek nobility, whose mouthpiece is the

---

6. [Cf. *Dawn*, section 231.]

7. [Henry Thomas Buckle (1821–1862), English historian, is known chiefly for his *History of Civilization* (1857ff.). The suggestion in the text is developed more fully in section 876 of *The Will to Power*.]

Megarian poet Theognis.[8] The root of the word coined for this, *esthlos* [Greek: good, brave], signifies one who *is*, who possesses reality, who is actual, who is true; then, with a subjective turn, the true as the truthful: in this phase of conceptual transformation it becomes a slogan and catchword of the nobility and passes over entirely into the sense of "noble," as distinct from the *lying* common man, which is what Theognis takes him to be and how he describes him—until finally, after the decline of the nobility, the word is left to designate nobility of soul and becomes as it were ripe and sweet. In the word *kakos* [Greek: bad, ugly, ill-born, mean, craven], as in *deilos* [Greek: cowardly, worthless, vile, wretched] (the plebeian in contradistinction to the *agathos* [Greek: good, well-born, gentle, brave, capable]), cowardice is emphasized: this perhaps gives an indication in which direction one should seek the etymological origin of *agathos,* which is susceptible of several interpretations. The Latin *malus* [bad] (beside which I set *melas* [Greek: black, dark]) may designate the common man as the dark-colored, above all as the black-haired man (*"hic niger est"*[9]—), as the pre-Aryan occupant of the soil of Italy who was distinguished most obviously from the blond, that is Aryan, conqueror race by his color; Gaelic, at any rate, offers us a precisely similar case—*fin* (for example in the name *Fin-Gal*), the distinguishing word for nobility, finally for the good, noble, pure, originally meant the blond-headed, in contradistinction to the dark, black-haired aboriginal inhabitants.

The Celts, by the way, were definitely a blond race; it is wrong to associate traces of an essentially dark-haired people which appear on the more careful ethnographical maps of Germany with any sort of Celtic origin or blood-mixture, as Virchow[10] still does: it is rather the *pre-Aryan* people of Germany who emerge in these places. (The same is true of virtually all Europe: the suppressed race has gradually recovered the upper hand again, in coloring, shortness of skull, perhaps even in the intellectual and social instincts: who can say whether modern democracy, even more modern anarchism and especially that inclination for "*commune,*" for the most primitive form of society, which is now shared by all the socialists of Europe, does not signify in the main a tremendous *counterattack*—and that the conqueror and *master race,* the Aryan, is not succumbing physiologically, too?

I believe I may venture to interpret the Latin *bonus* [good] as "the warrior," provided I am right in tracing *bonus* back to an earlier *duonus*[11] (compare *bellum* = *duellum* = *duen-lum,* which seems to me to contain *duonus*). Therefore *bonus* as the man of strife, of dissention (*duo*), as the man of war: one sees what constituted the "goodness" of a man in ancient Rome. Our German *gut* [good] even: does it not

---

8. [Nietzsche's first publication, in 1867 when he was still a student at the University of Leipzig, was an article in a leading classical journal, *Rheinisches Museum,* on the history of the collection of the maxims of Theognis ("Zur Geschichte der Theognideischen Spruchsammlung"). Theognis of Megara lived in the sixth century B.C.]

9. [Quoted from Horace's *Satires,* I.4, line 85: "He that backbites an absent friend . . . and cannot keep secrets, is black, O Roman, beware!" *Niger,* originally "black," also came to mean unlucky and, as in this quotation, wicked. Conversely, *candidus* means white, bright, beautiful, pure, guileless, candid, honest, happy, fortunate. And in *Satires,* I.5, 41, Horace speaks of "the whitest souls earth ever bore" (*animae qualis neque candidiores terra tulit*).]

10. [Rudolf Virchow (1821–1902) was one of the greatest German pathologists, as well as a liberal politician, a member of the German Reichstag (parliament), and an opponent of Bismarck.]

11. [Listed in Harper's Latin Dictionary as the old form of *bonus,* with the comment: "for *duonus,* cf. *bellum.*" And *duellum* is identified as an early and poetic form of *bellum* (war).]

signify "the godlike," the man of "godlike race"? And is it not identical with the popular (originally noble) name of the Goths? The grounds for this conjecture cannot be dealt with here.—

6

To this rule that a concept denoting political superiority always resolves itself into a concept denoting superiority of soul it is not necessarily an exception (although it provides occasions for exceptions) when the highest caste is at the same time the *priestly* caste and therefore emphasizes in its total description of itself a predicate that calls to mind its priestly function. It is then, for example, that "pure" and "impure" confront one another for the first time as designations of station; and here too there evolves a "good" and a "bad" in a sense no longer referring to station. One should be warned, moreover, against taking these concepts "pure" and "impure" too ponderously or broadly, not to say symbolically: all the concepts of ancient man were rather at first incredibly uncouth, coarse, external, narrow, straightforward, and altogether *unsymbolical* in meaning to a degree that we can scarcely conceive. The "pure one" is from the beginning merely a man who washes himself, who forbids himself certain foods that produce skin ailments, who does not sleep with the dirty women of the lower strata, who has an aversion to blood—no more, hardly more! On the other hand, to be sure, it is clear from the whole nature of an essentially priestly aristocracy why antithetical valuations could in precisely this instance soon become dangerously deepened, sharpened, and internalized; and indeed they finally tore chasms between man and man that a very Achilles of a free spirit would not venture to leap without a shudder. There is from the first something *unhealthy* in such priestly aristocracies and in the habits ruling in them which turn them away from action and alternate between brooding and emotional explosions, habits which seem to have as their almost invariable consequence that intestinal morbidity and neurasthenia which has afflicted priests at all times; but as to that which they themselves devised as a remedy for this morbidity—must one not assert that it has ultimately proved itself a hundred times more dangerous in its effects than the sickness it was supposed to cure? Mankind itself is still ill with the effects of this priestly naïveté) in medicine! Think, for example, of certain forms of diet (abstinence from meat), of fasting, of sexual continence, of flight "into the wilderness" (the Weir Mitchell isolation cure[12]—without, to be sure, the subsequent fattening and overfeeding which constitute the most effective remedy for the hysteria induced by the ascetic ideal): add to these the entire antisensualistic metaphysic of the priests that makes men indolent and overrefined, their autohypnosis in the manner of fakirs and Brahmins—Brahma used in the shape of a glass knob and a fixed idea— and finally the only-too-comprehensible satiety with all this, together with the radical cure for it, *nothingness* (or God—the desire for a *unio mystica* with God is the desire of the Buddhist for nothingness, Nirvana—and no more!). For with the priests *everything* becomes more dangerous, not only cures and remedies, but also arrogance, revenge, acuteness, profligacy, love, lust to rule, virtue, disease—but it is only fair to add that it was on the soil of this *essentially dangerous* form of human existence, the priestly form, that man first became an *interesting animal,* that only here did the

---

12. [The cure developed by Dr. Silas Weir Mitchell (1829–1914, American) consisted primarily in isolation, confinement to bed, dieting, and massage.]

human soul in a higher sense acquire *depth* and become *evil*—and these are the two basic respects in which man has hitherto been superior to other beasts!

7

One will have divined already how easily the priestly mode of valuation can branch off from the knightly-aristocratic and then develop into its opposite; this is particularly likely when the priestly caste and the warrior caste are in jealous opposition to one another and are unwilling to come to terms. The knightly-aristocratic value judgments presupposed a powerful physicality, a flourishing, abundant, even overflowing health, together with that which serves to preserve it: war, adventure, hunting, dancing, war games, and in general all that involves vigorous, free, joyful activity. The priestly-noble mode of valuation presupposes, as we have seen, other things: it is disadvantageous for it when it comes to war! As is well known, the priests are the *most evil enemies*—but why? Because they are the most impotent. It is because of their impotence that in them hatred grows to monstrous and uncanny proportions, to the most spiritual and poisonous kind of hatred. The truly great haters in world history have always been priests; likewise the most ingenious [*geistreich*] haters: other kinds of spirit [*Geist*] hardly come into consideration when compared with the spirit of priestly vengefulness. Human history would be altogether too stupid a thing without the spirit that the impotent have introduced into it—let us take at once the most notable example. All that has been done on earth against "the noble," "the powerful," "the masters," "the rulers," fades into nothing compared with what the *Jews* have done against them; the Jews, that priestly people, who in opposing their enemies and conquerors were ultimately satisfied with nothing less than a radical revaluation of their enemies' values, that is to say, an act of the *most spiritual revenge*. For this alone was appropriate to a priestly people, the people embodying the most deeply repressed [*zurückgetretensten*] priestly vengefulness. It was the Jews who, with awe-inspiring consistency, dared to invert the aristocratic value-equation (good = noble = powerful = beautiful = happy = beloved of God) and to hang on to this inversion with their teeth, the teeth of the most abysmal hatred (the hatred of impotence), saying "the wretched alone are the good; the poor, impotent, lowly alone are the good; the suffering, deprived, sick, ugly alone are pious, alone are blessed by God, blessedness is for them alone—and you, the powerful and noble, are on the contrary the evil, the cruel, the lustful, the insatiable, the godless to all eternity; and you shall be in all eternity the unblessed, accursed, and damned!" . . . One knows *who* inherited this Jewish revaluation . . . In connection with the tremendous and immeasurably fateful initiative provided by the Jews through this most fundamental of all declarations of war, I recall the proposition I arrived at on a previous occasion (*Beyond Good and Evil*, section 195)—that with the Jews there begins *the slave revolt in morality:* that revolt which has a history of two thousand years behind it and which we no longer see because it—has been victorious.

8

But you do not comprehend this? You are incapable of seeing something that required two thousand years to achieve victory?—There is nothing to wonder at in that: all *protracted* things are hard to see, to see whole. *That,* however, is what has happened: from the trunk of that tree of vengefulness and hatred, Jewish hatred—the profoundest and sublimest kind of hatred, capable of creating ideals and reversing values, the like of which has never existed on earth before—there grew something equally incomparable, a *new love*, the profoundest and sublimest kind of love—and from what other trunk could it have grown?

One should not imagine it grew up as the denial of that thirst for revenge, as the opposite of Jewish hatred! No, the reverse is true! That love grew out of it as its crown, as its triumphant crown spreading itself farther and farther into the purest brightness and sunlight, driven as it were into the domain of light and the heights in pursuit of the goals of that hatred—victory, spoil, and seduction—by the same impulse that drove the roots of that hatred deeper and deeper and more and more covetously into all that was profound and evil. This Jesus of Nazareth, the incarnate gospel of love, this "Redeemer" who brought blessedness and victory to the poor, the sick, and the sinners—was he not this seduction in its most uncanny and irresistible form, a seduction and bypath to precisely those *Jewish* values and new ideals? Did Israel not attain the ultimate goal of its sublime vengefulness precisely through the bypath of this "Redeemer," this ostensible opponent and disintegrator of Israel? Was it not part of the secret black art of truly *grand* politics of revenge, of a farseeing, subterranean, slowly advancing, and premeditated revenge, that Israel must itself deny the real instrument of its revenge before all the world as a mortal enemy and nail it to the cross, so that "all the world," namely all the opponents of Israel, could unhesitatingly swallow just this bait? And could spiritual subtlety imagine any *more dangerous* bait than this? Anything to equal the enticing, intoxicating, overwhelming, and undermining power of that symbol of the "holy cross," that ghastly paradox of a "God on the cross," that mystery of an unimaginable ultimate cruelty and self-crucifixion of God *for the salvation of man?*

What is certain, at least, is that *sub hoc signo* [under this sign] Israel, with its vengefulness and revaluation of all values, has hitherto triumphed again and again over all other ideals, over all *nobler* ideals.—

9

"But why are you talking about *nobler* ideals! Let us stick to the facts: the people have won—or 'the slaves' or 'the mob' or 'the herd' or whatever you like to call them—if this has happened through the Jews, very well! in that case no people ever had a more world-historic mission. 'The masters' have been disposed of; the morality of the common man has won. One may conceive of this victory as at the same time a blood-poisoning (it has mixed the races together)—I shan't contradict; but this intoxication has undoubtedly been *successful*. The 'redemption' of the human race (from 'the masters,' that is) is going forward; everything is visibly becoming Judaized, Christianized, mob-ized (what do the words matter!). The progress of this poison through the entire body of mankind seems irresistible, its pace and tempo may from now on even grow slower, subtler, less audible, more cautious—there is plenty of time.—To this end, does the church today still have any *necessary* role to play? Does it still have the right to exist? Or could one do without it? *Quaeritur* [One asks]. It seems to hinder rather than hasten this progress. But perhaps that is its usefulness.— Certainly it has, over the years, become something crude and boorish, something repellent to a more delicate intellect, to a truly modern taste. Ought it not to become at least a little more refined?—Today it alienates rather than seduces.—Which of us would be a free spirit if the church did not exist? It is the church, and not its poison, that repels us.—Apart from the church, we, too, love the poison.—"

This is the epilogue of a "free spirit" to my speech; an honest animal, as he has abundantly revealed, and a democrat, moreover; he had been listening to me till then and could not endure to listen to my silence. For at this point I have much to be silent about.

10

The slave revolt in morality begins when *ressentiment* [resentment] itself becomes creative and gives birth to values: the *ressentiment* of natures that are denied the true reaction, that of deeds, and compensate themselves with an imaginary revenge. While every noble morality develops from a triumphant affirmation of itself, slave morality from the outset says No to what is "outside," what is "different," what is "not itself"; and *this* No is its creative deed. This inversion of the value-positing eye—this *need* to direct one's view outward instead of back to oneself—is of the essence of *ressentiment:* in order to exist, slave morality always first needs a hostile external world; it needs, physiologically speaking, external stimuli in order to act at all—its action is fundamentally reaction.

The reverse is the case with the noble mode of valuation: it acts and grows spontaneously, it seeks its opposite only so as to affirm itself more gratefully and triumphantly—its negative concept "low," "common," "bad" is only a subsequently-invented pale, contrasting image in relation to its positive basic concept—filled with life and passion through and through—"we noble ones, we good, beautiful, happy ones!" When the noble mode of valuation blunders and sins against reality, it does so in respect to the sphere with which it is *not* sufficiently familiar, against a real knowledge of which it has indeed inflexibly guarded itself: in some circumstances it misunderstands the sphere it despises, that of the common man, of the lower orders; on the other hand, one should remember that, even supposing that the affect of contempt, of looking down from a superior height, *falsifies* the image of that which it despises, it will at any rate still be a much less serious falsification than that perpetrated on its opponent—*in effigie* of course—by the submerged hatred, the vengefulness of the impotent. There is indeed too much carelessness, too much taking lightly, too much looking away and impatience involved in contempt, even too much joyfulness, for it to be able to transform its object into a real caricature and monster.

One should not overlook the almost benevolent nuances that the Greek nobility, for example, bestows on all the words it employs to distinguish the lower orders from itself; how they are continuously mingled and sweetened with a kind of pity, consideration, and forbearance, so that finally almost all the words referring to the common man have remained as expressions signifying "unhappy," "pitiable" (campore *deilos* [cowardly, worthless, vile],[13] *deilaios* [paltry], *ponēros* [oppressed by toils, good for nothing, worthless, knavish, base, cowardly], *mochthēros* [suffering hardship, knavish], the last two of which properly designate the common man as work-slave and beast of burden)—and how on the other hand "bad," "low," "un-happy" have never ceased to sound to the Greek ear as one note with a tone-color in which "unhappy" preponderates: this as an inheritance from the ancient nobler aristocratic mode of evaluation, which does not belie itself even in its contempt

---

13. [All of the footnoted words in this section are Greek. The first four mean *wretched*, but each has a separate note to suggest some of its other connotations.]

(—philologists should recall the sense in which *oïzyros* [woeful, miserable, toilsome; wretch], *anolbos* [unblest, wretched, luckless, poor], *tlēmōn* [wretched, miserable], *dystychein* [to be unlucky, unfortunate], *xymphora* [misfortune] are employed). The "well-born" *felt* themselves to be the "happy"; they did not have to establish their happiness artificially by examining their enemies, or to persuade themselves, *deceive* themselves, that they were happy (as all men of *ressentiment* are in the habit of doing); and they likewise knew, as rounded men replete with energy and therefore *necessarily* active, that happiness should not be sundered from action—being active was with them necessarily a part of happiness (whence *eu prattein* [to do well in the sense of faring well] takes its origin)—all very much the opposite of "happiness" at the level of the impotent, the oppressed, and those in whom poisonous and inimical feelings are festering, with whom it appears as essentially narcotic, drug, rest, peace, "sabbath," slackening of tension and relaxing of limbs, in short *passively*.

While the noble man lives in trust and openness with himself (*gennaios* [high-born, noble, high-minded] "of noble descent" underlines the nuance "upright" and probably also "naïve"), the man of *ressentiment* is neither upright nor naive nor honest and straightforward with himself. His soul *squints;* his spirit loves hiding places, secret paths and back doors, everything covert entices him as *his* world, *his* security, *his* refreshment; he understands how to keep silent, how not to forget, how to wait, how to be provisionally self-deprecating and humble. A race of such men of *ressentiment* is bound to become eventually *cleverer* than any noble race; it will also honor cleverness to a far greater degree: namely, as a condition of existence of the first importance; while with noble men cleverness can easily acquire a subtle flavor of luxury and subtlety—for here it is far less essential than the perfect functioning of the regulating *unconscious* instincts or even than a certain imprudence, perhaps a bold recklessness whether in the face of danger or of the enemy, or that enthusiastic impulsiveness in anger, love, reverence, gratitude, and revenge by which noble souls have at all times recognized one another. *Ressentiment* itself, if it should appear in the noble man, consummates and exhausts itself in an immediate reaction, and therefore does not *poison:* on the other hand, it fails to appear at all on countless occasions on which it inevitably appears in the weak and impotent.

To be incapable of taking one's enemies, one's accidents, even one's misdeeds seriously for very long—that is the sign of strong, full natures in whom there is an excess of the power to form, to mold, to recuperate and to forget (a good example of this in modern times is Mirabeau,[14] who had no memory for insults and vile actions done him and was unable to forgive simply because he—forgot). Such a man shakes off with a *single* shrug many vermin that eat deep into others; here alone genuine "love of one's enemies" is possible—supposing it to be possible at all on earth. How much reverence has a noble man for his enemies!—and such reverence is a bridge to love.—For he desires his enemy for himself, as his mark of distinction; he can endure no other enemy than one in whom there is nothing to despise and *very much* to honor! In contrast to this, picture "the enemy" as the man of *ressentiment* conceives him—and here precisely is his deed, his creation: he has conceived "the evil enemy," "*the Evil One,*" and this in fact is his basic concept, from which he then evolves, as an afterthought and pendant, a "good one"—himself!

14. [Honoré Gabriel Riqueti, Comte de Mirabeau (1749–1791), was a celebrated French Revolutionary statesman and writer.]

11

This, then, is quite the contrary of what the noble man does, who conceives the basic concept "good" in advance and spontaneously out of himself and only then creates for himself an idea of "bad"! This "bad" of noble origin and that "evil" out of the cauldron of unsatisfied hatred—the former an after-production, a side issue, a contrasting shade, the latter on the contrary the original thing, the beginning, the distinctive *deed* in the conception of a slave morality—how different these words "bad" and "evil" are, although they are both apparently the opposite of the same concept "good." But it is *not* the same concept "good": one should ask rather precisely *who* is "evil" in the sense of the morality of *ressentiment*. The answer, in all strictness, is: precisely the "good man" of the other morality, *precisely* the noble, powerful man, the ruler, but dyed in another color, interpreted in another fashion, seen in another way by the venomous eye of *ressentiment.*

Here there is one thing we shall be the last to deny: he who knows these "good men" only as enemies knows only *evil enemies*, and the same men who are held so sternly in check *inter pares* [among equals] by custom, respect, usage, gratitude, and even more by mutual suspicion and jealousy, and who on the other hand in their relations with one another show themselves so resourceful in consideration, self-control, delicacy, loyalty, pride, and friendship—once they go outside, where the strange, the *stranger* is found, they are not much better than uncaged beasts of prey. There they savor a freedom from all social constraints, they compensate themselves in the wilderness for the tension engendered by protracted confinement and enclosure within the peace of society, they go *back* to the innocent conscience of the beast of prey, as triumphant monsters who perhaps emerge from a disgusting [*scheusslichen*] procession of murder, arson, rape, and torture, exhilarated and undisturbed of soul, as if it were no more than a students' prank, convinced they have provided the poets with a lot more material for song and praise. One cannot fail to see at the bottom of all these noble races the beast of prey, the splendid *blond beast* prowling about avidly in search of spoil and victory; this hidden core needs to erupt from time to time, the animal has to get out again and go back to the wilderness: the Roman, Arabian, Germanic, Japanese nobility, the Homeric heroes, the Scandinavian Vikings—they all shared this need.

It is the noble races that have left behind them the concept "barbarian" wherever they have gone; even their highest culture betrays a consciousness of it and even a pride in it (for example, when Pericles says to his Athenians in his famous funeral oration "our boldness has gained access to every land and sea, everywhere raising imperishable monuments to its goodness *and wickedness*"). This "boldness" of noble races, mad, absurd, and sudden in its expression, the incalculability, even incredibility of their undertakings—Pericles specially commends the *rhathymia*[15] of the Athenians—their indifference to and contempt for security, body, life, comfort, their hair-raising [*entsetzliche*] cheerfulness and profound joy in all destruction, in all the voluptuousness of victory and cruelty—all this came together, in the minds of those who suffered from it, in the image of the "barbarian," the "evil enemy," perhaps as

---

15. [Thucydides, 2.39. In *A Historical Commentary on Thucydides,* vol. II (Oxford, Clarendon Press, 1956; corrected imprint of 1966), p. 118, A. W. Gomme comments on this word: "in its original sense, 'ease of mind,' 'without anxiety' . . . But ease of mind can in certain circumstances become carelessness, remissness, frivolity: Demosthenes often accused the Athenians of *rhathymia* . . ."]

the "Goths," the "Vandals." The deep and icy mistrust the German still arouses today whenever he gets into a position of power is an echo of that inextinguishable horror with which Europe observed for centuries that raging of the blond Germanic beast (although between the old Germanic tribes and us Germans there exists hardly a conceptual relationship, let alone one of blood).

I once drew attention to the dilemma in which Hesiod found himself when he concocted his succession of cultural epochs and sought to express them in terms of gold, silver, and bronze: he knew no way of handling the contradiction presented by the glorious but at the same time terrible and violent world of Homer except by dividing one epoch into two epochs, which he then placed one behind the other— first the epoch of the heroes and demigods of Troy and Thebes, the form in which that world had survived in the memory of the noble races who were those heroes' true descendants; then the bronze epoch, the form in which that same world appeared to the descendants of the downtrodden, pillaged, mistreated, abducted, enslaved: an epoch of bronze, as aforesaid, hard, cold, cruel, devoid of feeling or conscience, destructive and bloody.

Supposing that what is at any rate believed to be the "truth" really is true, and the *meaning of all culture* is the reduction of the beast of prey "man" to a tame and civilized animal, a *domestic animal,* then one would undoubtedly have to regard all those instincts of reaction and *ressentiment* through whose aid the noble races and their ideals were finally confounded and overthrown as the actual *instruments of culture;* which is not to say that the *bearers* of these instincts themselves represent culture. Rather is the reverse not merely probable—no! today it is *palpable!* These bearers of the oppressive instincts that thirst for reprisal, the descendants of every kind of European and non-European slavery, and especially of the entire pre-Aryan populace—they represent the *regression* of mankind! These "instruments of culture" are a disgrace to man and rather an accusation and counterargument against "culture" in general! One may be quite justified in continuing to fear the blond beast at the core of all noble races and in being on one's guard against it: but who would not a hundred times sooner fear where one can also admire than *not* fear but be permanently condemned to the repellent sight of the ill-constituted, dwarfed, atrophied, and poisoned? And is that not *our* fate? What today constitutes *our* antipathy to "man"?—for we *suffer* from man, beyond doubt.

Not fear; rather that we no longer have anything left to fear in man; that the maggot[16] "man" is swarming in the foreground; that the "tame man," the hopelessly mediocre and insipid [*unerquicklich*] man, has already learned to feel himself as the goal and zenith, as the meaning of history, as "higher man"—that he has indeed a certain right to feel thus, insofar as he feels himself elevated above the surfeit of ill-constituted, sickly, weary and exhausted people of which Europe is beginning to stink today, as something at least relatively well-constituted, at least still capable of living, at least affirming life.

12

At this point I cannot suppress a sigh and a last hope. What is it that I especially find utterly unendurable? That I cannot cope with, that makes me choke and faint?

---

16. [*Gewürm* suggests wormlike animals; *wimmelt* can mean swarm or crawl but is particularly associated with maggots—in a cheese, for example.]

Bad air! Bad air! The approach of some ill-constituted thing; that I have to smell the entrails of some ill-constituted soul!

How much one is able to endure: distress, want, bad weather, sickness, toil, solitude. Fundamentally one can cope with everything else, born as one is to a subterranean life of struggle; one emerges again and again into the light, one experiences again and again one's golden hour of victory—and then one stands forth as one was born, unbreakable, tensed, ready for new, even harder, remoter things, like a bow that distress only serves to draw tauter.

But grant me from time to time—if there are divine goddesses in the realm beyond good and evil—grant me the sight, but *one* glance of something perfect, wholly achieved, happy, mighty, triumphant, something still capable of arousing fear! Of a man who justifies *man,* of a complementary and redeeming lucky hit on the part of man for the sake of which one may still *believe in man!*

For this is how things are: the diminution and leveling of European man constitutes *our* greatest danger, for the sight of him makes us weary.—We can see nothing today that wants to grow greater, we suspect that things will continue to go down, down, to become thinner, more good-natured, more prudent, more comfortable, more mediocre, more indifferent, more Chinese, more Christian—there is no doubt that man is getting "better" all the time.

Here precisely is what has become a fatality for Europe—together with the fear of man we have also lost our love of him, our reverence for him, our hopes for him, even the will to him. The sight of man now makes us weary—what is nihilism today if it is not *that?*—We are weary *of man.*

13

But let us return: the problem of the *other* origin of the "good," of the good as conceived by the man of *ressentiment,* demands its solution.

That lambs dislike great birds of prey does not seem strange: only it gives no ground for reproaching these birds of prey for bearing off little lambs. And if the lambs say among themselves: "these birds of prey are evil; and whoever is least like a bird of prey, but rather its opposite, a lamb—would he not be good?" there is no reason to find fault with this institution of an ideal, except perhaps that the birds of prey might view it a little ironically and say: "*we* don't dislike them at all, these good little lambs; we even love them: nothing is more tasty than a tender lamb."

To demand of strength that it should *not* express itself as strength, that it should *not* be a desire to overcome, a desire to throw down, a desire to become master, a thirst for enemies and resistances and triumphs, is just as absurd as to demand of weakness that it should express itself as strength. A quantum of force is equivalent to a quantum of drive, will, effect—more, it is nothing other than precisely this very driving, willing, effecting, and only owing to the seduction of language (and of the fundamental errors of reason that are petrified in it) which conceives and misconceives all effects as conditioned by something that causes effects, by a "subject," can it appear otherwise. For just as the popular mind separates the lightning from its flash and takes the latter for an *action,* for the operation of a subject called lightning, so popular morality also separates strength from expressions of strength, as if there were a neutral substratum behind the strong man, which was *free* to express strength or not to do so. But there is no such substratum; there is no "being" behind doing, effecting, becoming; "the doer" is merely a fiction added to the deed—the deed is everything. The popular mind in fact doubles the deed; when it sees the lightning flash, it is the deed of a deed: it posits the same event first as cause and then a second time as its effect. Scientists do no better when they say "force moves," "force causes," and the like—all its coolness, its freedom from emotion notwithstanding, our entire science still lies under the misleading influence of language and has not disposed of that little changeling, the "subject" (the atom, for example, is such a changeling, as is the Kantian "thing-in-itself"); no wonder if the submerged, darkly glowering emotions of vengefulness and hatred exploit this belief for their own ends and in fact maintain no belief more ardently than the belief that *the strong man is free* to be weak and the bird of prey to be a lamb—for thus they gain the right to make the bird of prey *accountable* for being a bird of prey.

When the oppressed, downtrodden, outraged exhort one another with the vengeful cunning of impotence: "let us be different from the evil, namely good! And he is good who does not outrage, who harms nobody, who does not attack, who does not requite, who leaves revenge to God, who keeps himself hidden as we do, who avoids evil and desires little from life, like us, the patient, humble, and just"—this, listened to calmly and without previous bias, really amounts to no more than: "we weak ones are, after all, weak; it would be good if we did nothing *for which we are not strong enough*"; but this dry matter of fact, this prudence of the lowest order which even insects possess (posing as dead, when in great danger, so as not to do "too much"), has, thanks to the counterfeit and self-deception of impotence, clad itself in the ostentatious garb of the virtue of quiet, calm resignation, just as if the weakness of the weak—that is to say, their *essence*, their effects, their sole ineluctable, irremovable reality—were a voluntary achievement, willed, chosen, a *deed*, a *meritorious* act. This type of man *needs* to believe in a neutral independent "subject," prompted by an instinct for self-preservation and self-affirmation in which every lie is sanctified. The subject (or, to use a more popular expression, the *soul*) has perhaps been believed in hitherto more firmly than anything else on earth because it makes possible to the majority of mortals, the weak and oppressed of every kind, the sublime self-deception that interprets weakness as freedom, and their being thus-and-thus as a *merit*.

14

Would anyone like to take a look into the secret of how *ideals are made* on earth? Who has the courage?—Very well! Here is a point we can see through into this dark workshop. But wait a moment or two, Mr. Rash and Curious: your eyes must first get used to this false iridescent light.—All right! Now speak! What is going on down there? Say what you see, man of the most perilous kind of inquisitiveness—now I am the one who is listening.—

—"I see nothing, but I hear the more. There is a soft, wary, malignant muttering and whispering coming from all the corners and nooks. It seems to me one is lying; a saccharine sweetness clings to every sound. Weakness is being lied into something *meritorious*, no doubt of it—so it is just as you said"—

—Go on!

—"and impotence which does not requite into 'goodness of heart'; anxious lowliness into 'humility'; subjection to those one hates into 'obedience' (that is, to one of whom they say he commands this subjection—they call him God). The inoffensiveness of the weak man, even the cowardice of which he has so much, his lingering at the door, his being ineluctably compelled to wait, here acquire flattering names, such as 'patience,' and are even called virtue itself; his inability for revenge is called unwillingness to revenge, perhaps even forgiveness ('for *they* know not what they do—we alone know what *they* do!'). They also speak of 'loving one's enemies'—and sweat as they do so."

—Go on!

—"They are miserable, no doubt of it, all these mutterers and nook counterfeiters, although they crouch warmly together—but they tell me their misery is a sign of being chosen by God; one beats the dogs one likes best; perhaps this misery is also a preparation, a testing, a schooling, perhaps it is even more—something that will one day be made good and recompensed with interest, with huge payments of gold, no! of happiness. This they call 'bliss.'"

—Go on!

—"Now they give me to understand that they are not merely better than the mighty, the lords of the earth whose spittle they have to lick (*not* from fear, not at all from fear! but because God has commanded them to obey the authorities)[17]— that they are not merely better but are also 'better off,' or at least will be better off someday. But enough! enough! I can't take any more. Bad air! Bad air! This work- shop where *ideals are manufactured*—it seems to me it stinks of so many lies."

—No! Wait a moment! You have said nothing yet of the masterpiece of these black magicians, who make whiteness, milk, and innocence of every blackness—haven't you noticed their perfection of refinement, their boldest, subtlest, most ingenious, most mendacious artistic stroke? Attend to them! These cellar rodents full of venge- fulness and hatred—what have they made of revenge and hatred? Have you heard these words uttered? If you trusted simply to their words, would you suspect you were among men of *ressentiment*? . . .

—"I understand; I'll open my ears again (oh! oh! oh! and *close* my nose). Now I can really hear what they have been saying all along: 'We good men—*we are the just*'—what they desire they call, not retaliation, but 'the triumph of *justice*'; what they hate is not their enemy, no! they hate 'injustice,' they hate 'godlessness'; what they believe in and hope for is not the hope of revenge, the intoxication of sweet revenge (—'sweeter than honey' Homer called it), but the victory of God, of the *just* God, over the godless; what there is left for them to love on earth is not their brothers in hatred but their 'brothers in love,' as they put it, all the good and just on earth."

—And what do they call that which serves to console them for all the suffering of life—their phantasmagoria of anticipated future bliss?

—"What? Do I hear aright? They call that 'the Last Judgment,' the coming of *their* kingdom, of the 'Kingdom of God'—meanwhile, however, they live 'in faith,' 'in love,' 'in hope.'"

—Enough! Enough!

17. [Allusion to Romans 13:1–2.]

15

In faith in what? In love of what? In hope of what?—These weak people—some day or other *they* too intend to be the strong, there is no doubt of that, some day *their* "kingdom" too shall come—they term it "the kingdom of God," of course, as aforesaid: for one is so very humble in all things! To experience *that* one needs to live a long time, beyond death—indeed one needs eternal life, so as to be eternally indemnified in the "kingdom of God" for this earthly life "in faith, in love, in hope." Indemnified for what? How indemnified?

Dante, I think, committed a crude blunder when, with a terror-inspiring ingenuity, he placed above the gateway of his hell the inscription "I too was created by eternal love"—at any rate, there would be more justification for placing above the gateway to the Christian Paradise and its "eternal bliss" the inscription "I too was created by eternal *hate*"—provided a truth may be placed above the gateway to a lie! For *what* is it that constitutes the bliss of this Paradise?

We might even guess, but it is better to have it expressly described for us by an authority not to be underestimated in such matters, Thomas Aquinas, the great teacher and saint. *"Beati in regno coelesti,"* he says, meek as a lamb, *"videbunt poenas damnatorum,* **ut beatitudo illis magis complaceat."**[18] Or if one would like to hear it in a stronger key, perhaps from the mouth of a triumphant Church Father, adjuring his Christians to avoid the cruel pleasures of the public games—but why? "For the faith offers us much more"—he says, *De Spectaculis,* chs. 29f.—*something much stronger;* thanks to the Redemption, quite other joys are at our command; in place of athletes we have our martyrs; if we crave blood, we have the blood of Christ . . . But think of what awaits us on the day of his return, the day of his triumph!"—and then he goes on, the enraptured visionary.[19] *"At enim supersunt alia spectacula, ille*

18. The blessed in the kingdom of heaven will see the punishments of the damned, *in order that their bliss be more delightful for them.*—To be precise, what we find in *Summa Theologiae,* III, *Supplementum,* Q. 94, An. 1, is this: "In order that the bliss of the saints may be more delightful for them and that they may render more copious thanks to God for it, it is given to them to see perfectly the punishment of the damned." *Ut beatitudo sanctorum eis magis complaceat, et de ea uberiores gratias Deo agant, datur eis ut poenam impiorum perfecte intueantur.*

19. [Nietzsche quotes Tertullian in the original Latin.

"Yes, and there are other sights: that last day of judgment, with its everlasting issues; that day unlooked for by the nations, the theme of their derision, when the world hoary with age, and all its many products, shall be consumed in one great flame! How vast a spectacle then bursts upon the eye! *What there excites my admiration? what my derision? Which sight gives me joy? which rouses me to exultation?*—as I see so many illustrious monarchs, whose reception into the heavens was publicly announced, groaning now in the lowest darkness with great Jove himself, and those, too, who bore witness of their exultation; governors of provinces, too, who persecuted the Christian name, in fires more fierce than those with which in the days of their pride they raged against the followers of Christ. What world's wise men besides, the very philosophers, in fact, who taught their followers that God had no concern in aught that is sublunary, and were wont to assure them that either they had no souls, or that they would never return to the bodies which at death they had left, now covered with shame before the poor deluded ones, as one fire consumes them! Poets also, trembling not before the judgment-seat of Rhadamanthus or Minos, but of the unexpected Christ! I shall have a better opportunity then of hearing the tragedians, louder-voiced in their own calamity; of viewing the play-actors, much more 'dissolute' [another translation has "much lither of limb"] in the dissolving flame; of looking upon the charioteer, all glowing in his chariot of fire; of beholding the wrestlers, not in their gymnasia, but tossing in the fiery billows; unless even then I shall not care to attend to such ministers of sin, in my eager wish rather to fix a gaze *insatiable* on those whose fury vented itself against the Lord. 'This,' I shall say, 'this is that carpenter's or hireling's son, that Sabbath-breaker, that Samaritan and devil-possessed! This is He whom you purchased from Judas! [*Quaestuaria* means prostitute, not carpenter: see Nietzsche's parenthesis above.] This is He whom you struck with reed and fist, whom you contemptuously spat upon, to whom you gave gall and vinegar to drink! This is He whom His

ultimus et perpetuus judicii dies, ille nationibus insperatus, ille derisus, cum tanta saeculi vetustas et tot ejus nativitates uno igne haurientur. Quae tunc spectaculi latitudo! **Quid admirer! Quid rideam! Ubi gaudeam! Ubi exultem,** *spectans tot et tantos reges, qui in coelum recepti nuntiabantur, cum ipso Jove et ipsis suis testibus in imis tenebris congemescentes! Item praesides"* (the provincial governors) *"persecutores dominici nominis saevioribus quam ipsi flammis saevierunt insultantibus contra Christianos liquescentes! Quos praeterea sapientes illos philosophos coram discipulis suis una conflagrantibus erubescentes, quibus nihil ad deum pertinere suadebant, quibus animas aut nullas aut non in pristina corpora redituras affirmabant! Etiam poetas non ad Rhadamanti nec ad Minois, sed ad inopinati Christi tribunal palpitantes! Tunc magis tragoedi audiendi, magis scilicet vocales"* (in better voice, yet worse screamers) *"in sua propria calamitate; tunc histriones cognoscendi, solutiores multo per ignem; tunc spectandus auriga in flammea rota totus rubens, tunc xystici contemplandi non in gymnasiis, sed in igne jaculati, nisi quod ne tunc quidem illos velim vivos, ut qui malim ad eos potius conspectum* **insatiabilem** *conferre, qui in dominum desaevierunt.* *'Hic est ille,' dicam, 'fabri aut quaestuariae filius'"* (what follows, and especially this term for the mother of Jesus, which is found in the Talmud, shows that from here on Tertullian is referring to the Jews), *"'sabbati destructor, Samarites et daemonium habens. Hic est, quem a Juda redemistis, hic est ille arundine et colaphis diverberatus, sputamentis dedecoratus, felle et aceto potatus. Hic est, quem clam discentes subripuerunt, ut resurrexisse dicatur vel hortulanus detraxit, ne lactucae suae frequentia commeantium laederentur.' Ut talia spectes,* **ut talibus exultes,** *quis tibi praetor aut consul aut guaestor aut sacerdos de sua liberalitate praestabit? Et tamen haec jam habemus quodammodo* **per fidem** *spiritu imaginante repraesentata. Ceterum qualia illa sunt, quae nec oculus vidit nec auris audivit nec in cor hominis ascenderunt?"* (1 Cor. 2,9.) *"Credo circo et utraque cavea"* (first and fourth rank or, according to others, the comic and tragic stage) *"et omni stadio gratiora."*—**Per fidem:** thus is it written.

16

Let us conclude. The two *opposing* values "good and bad," "good and evil" have been engaged in a fearful struggle on earth for thousands of years; and though the latter value has certainly been on top for a long time, there are still places where the struggle is as yet undecided. One might even say that it has risen ever higher and thus become more and more profound and spiritual: so that today there is perhaps no more decisive mark of a *"higher nature,"* a more spiritual nature, than that of being divided in this sense and a genuine battleground of these opposed values.

The symbol of this struggle, inscribed in letters legible across all human history, is "Rome against Judea, Judea against Rome":—there has hitherto been no greater event than *this* struggle, *this* question, *this* deadly contradiction. Rome felt the Jew to be something like anti-nature itself, its antipodal monstrosity as it were: in Rome the Jew stood *"convicted* of hatred for the whole human race"; and rightly, provided

---

disciples secretly stole away, that it might be said He had risen again, or the gardener abstracted, that his lettuces might come to no harm from the crowds of visitants!' What quaestor or priest in his munificence will bestow on you the favour of seeing and *exulting in such things as these*? And yet even now we in a measure have them *by faith* in the picturings of imagination. But what are the things which eye has not seen, ear has not heard, and which have not so much as dimly dawned upon the human heart? Whatever they are, they are nobler, I believe, than circus, and both theatres, and every race-course." [Translation by the Rev. S. Thelwall in *The Ante-Nicene Fathers: Translations of The Writings of the Fathers down to A.D. 325*, edited by the Rev. Alexander Roberts, D.D. and James Donaldson, LL.D., in volume III: *Latin Christianity: Its Founder, Tertullian* (American Reprint of the Edinburgh Edition, Grand Rapids, Mich., Wm. B. Eerdmans Publishing Company, 1957).]

one has a right to link the salvation and future of the human race with the unconditional dominance of aristocratic values, Roman values.

How, on the other hand, did the Jews feel about Rome? A thousand signs tell us; but
it suffices to recall the Apocalypse of John, the most wanton of all literary outbursts
that vengefulness has on its conscience. (One should not underestimate the profound
consistency of the Christian instinct when it signed this book of hate with the name of
the disciple of love, the same disciple to whom it attributed that amorous-enthusiastic
Gospel: there is a piece of truth in this, however much literary counterfeiting might
have been required to produce it.) For the Romans were the strong and noble, and
nobody stronger and nobler has yet existed on earth or even been dreamed of: every
remnant of them, every inscription gives delight, if only one divines *what* it was that
was there at work. The Jews, on the contrary, were the priestly nation of *ressentiment
par excellence*, in whom there dwelt an unequaled popular-moral genius: one only has
to compare similarly gifted nations—the Chinese or the Germans, for instance—with
the Jews, to sense which is of the first and which of the fifth rank.

Which of them has won *for the present,* Rome or Judea? But there can be no doubt:
consider to whom one bows down in Rome itself today, as if they were the epitome of
all the highest values—and not only in Rome but over almost half the earth, everywhere that man has become tame or desires to become tame: *three Jews,* as is known,
and *one Jewess* (Jesus of Nazareth, the fisherman Peter, the rug weaver Paul, and the
mother of the aforementioned Jesus, named Mary). This is very remarkable: Rome
has been defeated beyond all doubt.

There was, to be sure, in the Renaissance an uncanny and glittering reawakening
of the classical ideal, of the noble mode of evaluating all things; Rome itself, oppressed by the new superimposed Judaized Rome that presented the aspect of an
ecumenical synagogue and was called the "church," stirred like one awakened from
seeming death: but Judea immediately triumphed again, thanks to that thoroughly
plebeian (German and English) *ressentiment* movement called the Reformation, and
to that which was bound to arise from it, the restoration of the church—the restoration too of the ancient sepulchral repose of classical Rome.

With the French Revolution, Judea once again triumphed over the classical ideal,
and this time in an even more profound and decisive sense: the last political noblesse
in Europe, that of the *French* seventeenth and eighteenth century, collapsed beneath
the popular instincts of *ressentiment*—greater rejoicing, more uproarious enthusiasm
had never been heard on earth! To be sure, in the midst of it there occurred the
most tremendous, the most unexpected thing: the ideal of antiquity itself stepped
incarnate and in unheard-of splendor before the eyes and conscience of mankind—
and once again, in opposition to the mendacious slogan of *ressentiment,* "supreme
rights of the majority," in opposition to the will to the lowering, the abasement, the
leveling and the decline and twilight of mankind, there sounded stronger, simpler,
and more insistently than ever the terrible and rapturous counterslogan "supreme
rights of the few"! Like a last signpost to the *other* path, Napoleon appeared, the
most isolated and late-born man there has ever been, and in him the problem of the
noble ideal as such made flesh—one might well ponder *what* kind of problem it is:
Napoleon, this synthesis of the *inhuman* and *superhuman.*

17

Was that the end of it? Had that greatest of all conflicts of ideals been placed *ad
acta* [disposed of] for all time? Or only adjourned, indefinitely adjourned?

Must the ancient fire not some day flare up much more terribly, after much longer preparation? More: must one not desire it with all one's might? even will it? even promote it?

Whoever begins at this point, like my readers, to reflect and pursue his train of thought will not soon come to the end of it—reason enough for me to come to an end, assuming it has long since been abundantly clear what my *aim* is, what the aim of that dangerous slogan is that is inscribed at the head of my last book *Beyond Good and Evil.*—At least this does *not* mean "Beyond Good and Bad."—

Note [*Anmerkung*]. I take the opportunity provided by this treatise to express publicly and formally a desire I have previously voiced only in occasional conversation with scholars; namely, that some philosophical faculty might advance *historical* studies of *morality* through a series of academic prize-essays—perhaps this present book will serve to provide a powerful impetus in this direction. In case this idea should be implemented, I suggest the following question: it deserves the attention of philologists and historians as well as that of professional philosophers:

"What light does linguistics, and especially the study of etymology, throw on the history of the evolution of moral concepts?"

On the other hand, it is equally necessary to engage the interest of physiologists and doctors in these problems (of the *value* of existing evaluations); it may be left to academic philosophers to act as advocates and mediators in this matter too, after they have on the whole succeeded in the past in transforming the originally so reserved and mistrustful relations between philosophy, physiology, and medicine into the most amicable and fruitful exchange. Indeed, every table of values, every "thou shalt" known to history or ethnology, requires first a *physiological* investigation and interpretation, rather than a psychological one; and every one of them needs a critique on the part of medical science. The question: what is the *value* of this or that table of values and "morals"? should be viewed from the most divers perspectives; for the problem "value *for what?*" cannot be examined too subtly. Something, for example, that possessed obvious value in relation to the longest possible survival of a race (or to the enhancement of its power of adaptation to a particular climate or to the preservation of the greatest number) would by no means possess the same value if it were a question, for instance, of producing a stronger type. The well-being of the majority and the well-being of the few are opposite viewpoints of value: to consider the former *a priori* of higher value may be left to the naïveté of English biologists.— *All* the sciences have from now on to prepare the way for the future task of the philosophers: this task understood as the solution of the *problem of value*, the determination of the *order of rank among values.*

Second Essay
"Guilt," "Bad Conscience,"[20] and the Like

1

To breed an animal *with the right to make promises*—is not this the paradoxical task that nature has set itself in the case of man? is it not the real problem regarding man?

---

20. *Schlechtes Gewissen* is no technical term but simply the common German equivalent of "bad conscience."

That this problem has been solved to a large extent must seem all the more remarkable to anyone who appreciates the strength of the opposing force, that of *forgetfulness*. Forgetting is no mere *vis inertiae* [inertia] as the superficial imagine; it is rather an active and in the strictest sense positive faculty of repression [*positives Hemmungsvermögen*], that is responsible for the fact that what we experience and absorb enters our consciousness as little while we are digesting it (one might call the process "inpsychation") as does the thousandfold process, involved in physical nourishment—so-called "incorporation." To close the doors and windows of consciousness for a time; to remain undisturbed by the noise and struggle of our underworld of utility organs working with and against one another; a little quietness, a little *tabula rasa* [clean slate] of the consciousness, to make room for new things, above all for the nobler functions and functionaries, for regulation, foresight, premeditation (for our organism is an oligarchy)—that is the purpose of active forgetfulness, which is like a doorkeeper, a preserver of psychic order, repose, and etiquette: so that it will be immediately obvious how there could be no happiness, no cheerfulness, no hope, no pride, no *present*, without forgetfulness. The man in whom this apparatus of repression is damaged and ceases to function properly may be compared (and more than merely compared) with a dyspeptic—he cannot "have done" with anything.

Now this animal which needs to be forgetful, in which forgetting represents a force, a form of *robust* health, has bred in itself an opposing faculty, a memory, with the aid of which forgetfulness is abrogated in certain cases—namely in those cases where promises are made. This involves no mere passive inability to rid oneself of an impression, no mere indigestion through a once-pledged word with which one cannot "have done," but an active *desire* not to rid oneself, a desire for the continuance of something desired once, a real *memory of the will:* so that between the original "I will," "I shall do this" and the actual discharge of the will, its *act*, a world of strange new things, circumstances, even acts of will may be interposed without breaking this long chain of will. But how many things this presupposes! To ordain the future in advance in this way, man must first have learned to distinguish necessary events from chance ones, to think causally, to see and anticipate distant eventualities as if they belonged to the present, to decide with certainty what is the goal and what the means to it, and in general be able to calculate and compute. Man himself must first of all have become *calculable, regular, necessary*, even in his own image of himself, if he is to be able to stand security for *his own future*, which is what one who promises does!

2

This precisely is the long story of how *responsibility* originated. The task of breeding an animal with the right to make promises evidently embraces and presupposes as a preparatory task that one first *makes* men to a certain degree necessary, uniform, like among like, regular, and consequently calculable. The tremendous labor of that which I have called "morality of mores" (*Dawn*, sections 9, 14, 16)[21]—the labor performed by man upon himself during the greater part of the existence of the

21. [See also *Human, All-Too-Human*, section 96; *Mixed Opinions and Maxims*, section 89; and *The Dawn*, section 18. Dawn, section 16, is included in *The Portable Nietzsche*, p. 76. The German phrase is *die Sittlichkeit der Sitte*, the morality of mores.]

human race, his entire *prehistoric* labor, finds in this its meaning, its great justification, notwithstanding the severity, tyranny, stupidity, and idiocy involved in it: with the aid of the morality of mores and the social straitjacket, man was actually *made* calculable.

If we place ourselves at the end of this tremendous process, where the tree at last brings forth fruit, where society and the morality of custom at last reveal *what* they have simply been the means to: then we discover that the ripest fruit is the *sovereign individual,* like only to himself, liberated again from morality of custom, autonomous and supramoral (for "autonomous" and "moral" are mutually exclusive), in short, the man who has his own independent, protracted will and the *right to make promises*— and in him a proud consciousness, quivering in every muscle, of *what* has at length been achieved and become flesh in him, a consciousness of his own power and freedom, a sensation of mankind come to completion. This emancipated individual, with the actual *right* to make promises, this master of a *free* will, this sovereign man— how should he not be aware of his superiority over all those who lack the right to make promises and stand as their own guarantors, of how much trust, how much fear, how much reverence he arouses—he *"deserves"* all three—and of how this mastery over himself also necessarily gives him mastery over circumstances, over nature, and over all more short-willed and unreliable creatures? The "free" man, the possessor of a protracted and unbreakable will, also possesses his *measure of value:* looking out upon others from himself, he honors or he despises; and just as he is bound to honor his peers, the strong and reliable (those with the *right* to make promises)—that is, all those who promise like sovereigns, reluctantly, rarely, slowly, who are chary of trusting, whose trust is a mark of *distinction,* who give their word as something that can be relied on because they know themselves strong enough to maintain it in the face of accidents, even "in the face of fate"—he is bound to reserve a kick for the feeble windbags who promise without the right to do so, and a rod for the liar who breaks his word even at the moment he utters it. The proud awareness of the extraordinary privilege of *responsibility,* the consciousness of this rare freedom, this power over oneself and over fate, has in his case penetrated to the profoundest depths and become instinct, the dominating instinct. What will he call this dominating instinct, supposing he feels the need to give it a name? The answer is beyond doubt: this sovereign man calls it his *conscience.*

3

His conscience?—It is easy to guess that the concept of "conscience" that we here encounter in its highest, almost astonishing, manifestation, has a long history and variety of forms behind it. To possess the right to stand security for oneself and to do so with pride, thus to possess also the *right to affirm oneself*—this, as has been said, is a ripe fruit, but also a *late* fruit: how long must this fruit have hung on the tree, unripe and sour! And for a much longer time nothing whatever was to be seen of any such fruit: no one could have promised its appearance, although everything in the tree was preparing for and growing toward it!

"How can one create a memory for the human animal? How can one impress something upon this partly obtuse, partly flighty mind, attuned only to the passing moment, in such a way that it will stay there?"

One can well believe that the answers and methods for solving this primeval problem were not precisely gentle; perhaps indeed there was nothing more fearful and uncanny in the whole prehistory of man than his *mnemotechnics*. "If something is to stay in the memory it must be burned in: only that which never ceases to *hurt* stays in the memory"—this is a main clause of the oldest (unhappily also the most enduring) psychology on earth. One might even say that wherever on earth solemnity, seriousness, mystery, and gloomy coloring still distinguish the life of man and a people, something of the terror that formerly attended all promises, pledges, and vows on earth is *still effective:* the past, the longest, deepest and sternest past, breathes upon us and rises up in us whenever we become "serious." Man could never do without blood, torture, and sacrifices when he felt the need to create a memory for himself; the most dreadful sacrifices and pledges (sacrifices of the first-born among them), the most repulsive mutilations (castration, for example), the cruelest rites of all the religious cults (and all religions are at the deepest level systems of cruelties)— all this has its origin in the instinct that realized that pain is the most powerful aid to mnemonics.

In a certain sense, the whole of asceticism belongs here: a few ideas are to be rendered inextinguishable, ever-present, unforgettable, "fixed," with the aim of hypnotising the entire nervous and intellectual system with these "fixed ideas"— and ascetic procedures and modes of life are means of freeing these ideas from the competition of all other ideas, so as to make them "unforgettable." The worse man's memory has been, the more fearful has been the appearance of his customs; the severity of the penal code provides an especially significant measure of the degree of effort needed to overcome forgetfulness and to impose a few primitive demands of social existence as *present realities* upon these slaves of momentary affect and desire.

We Germans certainly do not regard ourselves as a particularly cruel and hard-hearted people, still less as a particularly frivolous one, living only for the day; but one has only to look at our former codes of punishments to understand what effort it costs on this earth to breed a "nation of thinkers" (which is to say, *the* nation in Europe in which one still finds today the maximum of trust, seriousness, lack of taste, and matter-of-factness—and with these qualities one has the right to breed every kind of European mandarin). These Germans have employed fearful means to acquire a memory, so as to master their basic mob-instinct and its brutal coarseness. Consider the old German punishments; for example, stoning (the sagas already have millstones drop on the head of the guilty), breaking on the wheel (the most characteristic invention and speciality of the German genius in the realm of punishment!), piercing with stakes, tearing apart or trampling by horses ("quartering"), boiling of the criminal in oil or wine (still employed in the fourteenth and fifteenth centuries), the popular flaying alive ("cutting straps"), cutting flesh from the chest, and also the practice of smearing the wrongdoer with honey and leaving him in the blazing sun for the flies. With the aid of such images and procedures one finally remembers five or six "I will not's," in regard to which one had given one's *promise* so as to participate in the advantages of society—and it was indeed with the aid of this kind of memory that one at last came "to reason"! Ah, reason, seriousness, mastery over the affects, the whole somber thing called reflection, all these prerogatives and showpieces of man: how dearly they have been bought! how much blood and cruelty lie at the bottom of all "good things"!

4

But how did that other "somber thing," the consciousness of guilt, the "bad conscience," come into the world?—And at this point we return to the genealogists of morals. To say it again—or haven't I said it yet?—they are worthless. A brief span of experience that is merely one's own, merely modern; no knowledge or will to knowledge of the past; even less of historical instinct, of that "second sight" needed here above all—and yet they undertake history of morality: it stands to reason that their results stay at a more than respectful distance from the truth. Have these genealogists of morals had even the remotest suspicion that, for example, the major moral concept *Schuld* [guilt] has its origin in the very material concept *Schulden* [debts]?[22] Or that punishment, as requital, evolved quite independently of any presupposition concerning freedom or nonfreedom of the will?—to such an extent, indeed, that a *high* degree of humanity had to be attained before the animal "man" began even to make the much more primitive distinctions between "intentional," "negligent," "accidental," "accountable," and their opposites and to take them into account when determining punishments. The idea, now so obvious, apparently so natural, even unavoidable, that had to serve as the explanation of how the sense of justice ever appeared on earth—"the criminal deserves punishment *because* he could have acted differently"—is in fact an extremely late and subtle form of human judgment and inference: whoever transposes it to the beginning is guilty of a crude misunderstanding of the psychology of more primitive mankind. Throughout the greater part of human history punishment was *not* imposed *because* one held the wrongdoer responsible for his deed, thus *not* on the presupposition that only the guilty one should be punished: rather, as parents still punish their children, from anger at some harm or injury, vented on the one who caused it—but this anger is held in check and modified by the idea that every injury has its *equivalent* and can actually be paid back, even if only through the *pain* of the culprit. And whence did this primeval, deeply rooted, perhaps by now ineradicable idea draw its power— this idea of an equivalence between injury and pain? I have already divulged it: in the contractual relationship between *creditor* and *debtor,* which is as old as the idea of "legal subjects" and in turn points back to the fundamental forms of buying, selling, barter, trade, and traffic.

5

When we contemplate these contractual relationships, to be sure, we feel consider- able suspicion and repugnance toward those men of the past who created or permit- ted them. This was to be expected from what we have previously noted. It was here that *promises* were made; it was here that a memory had to be *made* for those who promised; it is here, one suspects, that we shall find a great deal of severity, cruelty, and pain. To inspire trust in his promise to repay, to provide a guarantee of the seriousness and sanctity of his promise, to impress repayment as a duty, an obligation upon his own conscience, the debtor made a contract with the creditor and pledged that if he should fail to repay he would substitute something else that he "possessed," something he had control over; for example, his body, his wife, his freedom, or even his life (or, given certain religious presuppositions, even his bliss after death, the salvation of his soul, ultimately his peace in the grave: thus it was in Egypt, where the debtor's corpse found no peace from the creditor even in the grave—and among the Egyptians such peace meant a great deal). Above all, however, the creditor could inflict every kind of indignity and torture upon the body of the debtor; for example,

22. The German equivalent of "guilt" is *Schuld;* and the German for "debt(s)" is *Schuld(en).* "Innocent" is *unschuldig;* "debtor" is *Schuldner;* and so forth.

cut from it as much as seemed commensurate with the size of the debt—and everywhere and from early times one had exact evaluations, *legal* evaluations, of the individual limbs and parts of the body from this point of view, some of them going into horrible and minute detail. I consider it as an advance, as evidence of a freer, more generous, *more Roman* conception of law when the Twelve Tables of Rome decreed it a matter of indifference how much or how little the creditor cut off in such cases: "*si plus minusve secuerunt, ne fraude esto* [if they have secured more or less, let that be no crime]."

Let us be clear as to the logic of this form of compensation: it is strange enough. An equivalence is provided by the creditor's receiving, in place of a literal compensation for an injury (thus in place of money, land, possessions of any kind), a recompense in the form of a kind of *pleasure*—the pleasure of being allowed to vent his power freely upon one who is powerless, the voluptuous pleasure "*de faire le mal pour le plaisir de le faire* [of doing evil for the pleasure of doing it]," the enjoyment of violation. This enjoyment will be the greater the lower the creditor stands in the social order, and can easily appear to him as a most delicious morsel, indeed as a foretaste of higher rank. In "punishing" the debtor, the creditor participates in a *right of the masters:* at last he, too, may experience for once the exalted sensation of being allowed to despise and mistreat someone as "beneath him"—or at least, if the actual power and administration of punishment has already passed to the "authorities," to *see* him despised and mistreated. The compensation, then, consists in a warrant for and title to cruelty.—

6

It was in *this* sphere then, the sphere of legal obligations, that the moral conceptual world of "guilt," "conscience," "duty," "sacredness of duty" had its origin: its beginnings were, like the beginnings of everything great on earth, soaked in blood thoroughly and for a long time. And might one not add that, fundamentally, this world has never since lost a certain odor of blood and torture? (Not even in good old Kant: the categorical imperative smells of cruelty.) It was here, too, that that uncanny intertwining of the ideas "guilt and suffering" was first effected—and by now they may well be inseparable. To ask it again: to what extent can suffering balance debts or guilt ["debts or guilt": "*Schulden*"]? To the extent that to *make* suffer was in the highest degree pleasurable, to the extent that the injured party exchanged for the loss he had sustained, including the displeasure caused by the loss, an extraordinary counterbalancing pleasure: that of *making* suffer—a genuine *festival,* something which, as aforesaid, was prized the more highly the more violently it contrasted with the rank and social standing of the creditor. This is offered only as a conjecture; for the depths of such subterranean things are difficult to fathom, besides being painful; and whoever clumsily interposes the concept of "revenge" does not enhance his insight into the matter but further veils and darkens it (—for revenge merely leads us back to the same problem: "how can making suffer constitute a compensation?").

It seems to me that the delicacy and even more the tartuffery of tame domestic animals (which is to say modern men, which is to say us) resists a really vivid comprehension of the degree to which *cruelty* constituted the great festival pleasure of more primitive men and was indeed an ingredient of almost every one of their pleasures; and how naïvely, how innocently their thirst for cruelty manifested itself, how, as a matter of principle, they posited "disinterested malice" (or, in Spinoza's words, *sympathia malevolens*) as a *normal* quality of man—and thus as something to which the conscience cordially *says Yes!* A more profound eye might perceive enough of this oldest and most fundamental festival pleasure of man even in our time; in *Beyond Good and Evil*, section 229[23] (and earlier in *The Dawn*, sections 18, 77, 113) I pointed cautiously to the ever-increasing spiritualization and "deification" of cruelty which permeates the entire history of higher culture (and in a significant sense actually constitutes it). In any event, it is not long since princely weddings and public festivals of the more magnificent kind were unthinkable without executions, torturings, or perhaps an auto-da-fé, and no noble household was without creatures upon whom one could heedlessly vent one's malice and cruel jokes. (Consider, for instance, *Don Quixote* at the court of the Duchess. Today we read Don Quixote with a bitter taste in our mouths, almost with a feeling of torment, and would thus seem very strange and incomprehensible to its author and his contemporaries: they read it with the clearest conscience in the world as the most cheerful of books, they laughed themselves almost to death over it.) To see others suffer does one good, to make others suffer even more: this is a hard saying but an ancient, mighty, human, all-too-human principle to which even the apes might subscribe; for it has been said that in devising bizarre cruelties they anticipate man and are, as it were, his "prelude." Without cruelty there is no festival: thus the longest and most ancient part of human history teaches—and in punishment there is so much that is *festive!*—

7

With this idea, by the way, I am by no means concerned to furnish our pessimists with more grist for their discordant and creaking mills of life-satiety. On the contrary, let me declare expressly that in the days when mankind was not yet ashamed of its cruelty, life on earth was more cheerful than it is now that pessimists exist. The darkening of the sky above mankind has deepened in step with the increase in man's feeling of shame *at man*. The weary pessimistic glance, mistrust of the riddle of life, the icy No of disgust with life—these do not characterize the most *evil* epochs of the human race: rather do they first step into the light of day as the swamp weeds they are when the swamp to which they belong comes into being—I mean the morbid softening and moralization through which the animal "man" finally learns to be ashamed of all his instincts. On his way to becoming an "angel" (to employ no uglier word) man has evolved that queasy stomach and coated tongue through which not only the joy and innocence of the animal but life itself has become repugnant to him—so that he sometimes holds his nose in his own presence and, with Pope Innocent the Third, disapprovingly catalogues his own repellent aspects ("impure begetting, disgusting means of nutrition in his mother's womb, baseness of the matter out of which man evolves, hideous stink, secretion of saliva, urine, and filth").

Today, when suffering is always brought forward as the principal argument *against* existence, as the worst question mark, one does well to recall the ages in which the opposite opinion prevailed because men were unwilling to refrain from *making* suffer and saw in it an enchantment of the first order, a genuine seduction *to* life.

23. Nietzsche, as usual, furnishes a page reference to the first edition—in this instance, pp. 117ff., which would take us to the middle of section 194 and the following section(s); and German editors, down to Karl Schlechta, give the equivalent page reference. But 117 is plainly a misprint for 177, which takes us to section 229—beyond a doubt, the passage Nietzsche means.

Perhaps in those days—the delicate may be comforted by this thought—pain did not hurt as much as it does now; at least that is the conclusion a doctor may arrive at who has treated Negroes (taken as representatives of prehistoric man—) for severe internal inflammations that would drive even the best constituted European to distraction—in the case of Negroes they do *not* do so. (The curve of human susceptibility to pain seems in fact to take an extraordinary and almost sudden drop as soon as one has passed the upper ten thousand or ten million of the top stratum of culture; and for my own part, I have no doubt that the combined suffering of all the animals ever subjected to the knife for scientific ends is utterly negligible compared with *one* painful night of a single hysterical bluestocking.) Perhaps the possibility may even be allowed that this joy in cruelty does not really have to have died out: if pain hurts more today, it simply requires a certain sublimation and subtilization, that is to say it has to appear translated into the imaginative and psychical and adorned with such innocent names that even the tenderest and most hypocritical conscience is not suspicious of them ("tragic pity" is one such name; "*les nostalgies de la croix* [the nostalgia of the cross]" is another).

What really arouses indignation against suffering is not suffering as such but the senselessness of suffering: but neither for the Christian, who has interpreted a whole mysterious machinery of salvation into suffering, nor for the naive man of more ancient times, who understood all suffering in relation to the spectator of it or the causer of it, was there any such thing as *senseless* suffering. So as to abolish hidden, undetected, unwitnessed suffering from the world and honestly to deny it, one was in the past virtually compelled to invent gods and genii of all the heights and depths, in short something that roams even in secret, hidden places, sees even in the dark, and will not easily let an interesting painful spectacle pass unnoticed. For it was with the aid of such inventions that life then knew how to work the trick which it has always known how to work, that of justifying itself, of justifying its "evil." Nowadays it might require other auxiliary inventions (for example, life as a riddle, life as an epistemological problem). "Every evil the sight of which edifies a god is justified": thus spoke the primitive logic of feeling—and was it, indeed, only primitive? The gods conceived of as the friends of *cruel* spectacles—oh how profoundly this ancient idea still permeates our European humanity! Merely consult Calvin and Luther. It is certain, at any rate, that the *Greeks* still knew of no tastier spice to offer their gods to season their happiness than the pleasures of cruelty. With what eyes do you think Homer made his gods look down upon the destinies of men? What was at bottom the ultimate meaning of Trojan Wars and other such tragic terrors? There can be no doubt whatever: they were intended as *festival plays* for the gods; and, insofar as the poet is in these matters of a more "godlike" disposition than other men, no doubt also as festival plays for the poets.

It was in the same way that the moral philosophers of Greece later imagined the eyes of God looking down upon the moral struggle, upon the heroism and self-torture of the virtuous: the "Herakles of duty" was on a stage and knew himself to be; virtue without a witness was something unthinkable for this nation of actors. Surely, that philosophers' invention, so bold and so fateful, which was then first devised for Europe, the invention of "free will," of the absolute spontaneity of man in good and in evil, was devised above all to furnish a right to the idea that the interest of the gods in man, in human virtue, *could never be exhausted*. There must never be any lack of real novelty, of really unprecedented tensions, complications, and catastrophes on the stage of the earth: the course of a completely deterministic world would have been predictable for the gods and they would have quickly grown weary of it—reason enough for those *friends of the gods,* the philosophers, not to inflict such a deterministic world on their gods! The entire mankind of antiquity is full of tender regard for "the spectator," as an essentially public, essentially visible world which cannot imagine happiness apart from spectacles and festivals.—And, as aforesaid, even in great *punishment* there is so much that is festive!

8

To return to our investigation: the feeling of guilt, of personal obligation, had its origin, as we saw, in the oldest and most primitive personal relationship, that between buyer and seller, creditor and debtor: it was here that one person first encountered another person, that one person first *measured himself* against another. No grade of civilization, however low, has yet been discovered in which something of this relationship has not been noticeable. Setting prices, determining values, contriving equivalences, exchanging—these preoccupied the earliest thinking of man to so great an extent that in a certain sense they constitute thinking *as such:* here it was that the oldest kind of astuteness developed; here likewise, we may suppose, did human pride, the feeling of superiority in relation to other animals, have its first beginnings. Perhaps our word "man" (*manas*) still expresses something of precisely *this* feeling of self-satisfaction: man designated himself as the creature that measures values, evaluates and measures, as the "valuating animal as such."

Buying and selling, together with their psychological appurtenances, are older even than the beginnings of any kind of social forms of organization and alliances: it was rather out of the most rudimentary form of personal legal rights that the budding sense of exchange, contract, guilt, right, obligation, settlement, first *transferred* itself to the coarsest and most elementary social complexes (in their relations with other similar complexes), together with the custom of comparing, measuring, and calculating power against power. The eye was now focused on this perspective; and with that blunt consistency characteristic of the thinking of primitive mankind, which is hard to set in motion but then proceeds inexorably in the same direction, one forthwith arrived at the great generalization, "everything has its price; *all* things can be paid for"—the oldest and naïvest moral canon of *justice,* the beginning of all "good-naturedness," all "fairness," all "good will," all "objectivity" on earth. Justice on this elementary level is the good will among parties of approximately equal power to come to terms with one another, to reach an "understanding" by means of a settlement—and to *compel* parties of lesser power to reach a settlement among themselves.—

9

Still retaining the criteria of prehistory (this prehistory is in any case present in all ages or may always reappear): the community, too, stands to its members in that same vital basic relation, that of the creditor to his debtors. One lives in a community, one enjoys the advantages of a communality (oh what advantages! we sometimes underrate them today), one dwells protected, cared for, in peace and trustfulness, without fear of certain injuries and hostile acts to which the man *outside,* the "man without peace," is exposed—a German will understand the original connotations of *Elend* [misery; originally, exile]—since one has bound and pledged oneself to the community precisely with a view to injuries and hostile acts. What will happen *if this pledge is broken?* The community, the disappointed creditor, will get what repayment it can, one may depend on that. The direct harm caused by the culprit is here a minor matter; quite apart from this, the lawbreaker is above all a "breaker," a breaker of his contract and his word *with the whole* in respect to all the benefits and comforts of communal life of which he has hitherto had a share. The lawbreaker is a debtor who has not merely failed to make good the advantages and advance payments bestowed upon him but has actually attacked his creditor: therefore he is not only deprived henceforth of all these advantages and benefits, as is fair—he is also reminded *what these benefits are really worth.* The wrath of the disappointed creditor, the community, throws him back again into the savage and outlaw state against which he has hitherto been protected: it thrusts him away—and now every kind of hostility may be vented upon him. "Punishment" at this level of civilization is simply a copy, a *mimus,* of the normal attitude toward a hated, disarmed, prostrated enemy, who has lost not only every right and protection, but all hope of quarter as well; it is thus the rights of war and the victory celebration of the *vae victis!* [Woe to the losers!] in all their mercilessness and cruelty—which explains why it is that war itself (including the warlike sacrificial cult) has provided all the *forms* that punishment has assumed throughout history.

10

As its power increases, a community ceases to take the individual's transgressions so seriously, because they can no longer be considered as dangerous and destructive to the whole as they were formerly: the malefactor is no longer "set beyond the pale of peace" and thrust out; universal anger may not be vented upon him as unrestrainedly as before—on the contrary, the whole from now on carefully defends the malefactor against this anger, especially that of those he has directly harmed, and takes him under its protection. A compromise with the anger of those directly injured by the criminal; an effort to localize the affair and to prevent it from causing any further, let alone a general, disturbance; attempts to discover equivalents and to settle the whole matter (*compositio*); above all, the increasingly definite will to treat every crime as in some sense *dischargeable,* and thus at least to a certain extent to *isolate* the criminal and his deed from one another—these traits become more and more clearly visible as the penal law evolves. As the power and self-confidence of a community increase, the penal law always becomes more moderate; every weakening or imperiling of the former brings with it a restoration of the harsher forms of the latter. The "creditor" always becomes more humane to the extent that he has grown richer; finally, how much injury he can endure without suffering from it becomes the actual *measure* of his wealth. It is not unthinkable that a society might attain such a *consciousness of power* that it could allow itself the noblest luxury possible to it— letting those who harm it go *unpunished.* "What are my parasites to me?" it might say. "May they live and prosper: I am strong enough for that!"

The justice which began with, "everything is dischargeable, everything must be discharged," ends by winking and letting those incapable of discharging their debt go free: it ends, as does every good thing on earth, by *overcoming itself.*[24] This self-

24. *Sich selbst aufhebend.* And in the next sentence *Selbstaufhebung* has been translated as self-overcoming. Similarly, *aufzuheben* in the middle of section 13, below, and *aufgehoben* in section 8 of the third essay have been rendered "overcome." *Aufheben* is a very troublesome word, though common in ordinary German. Literally, it means "pick up"; but it has two derivative meanings that are no less common: "cancel" and "preserve" or "keep."

overcoming of justice: one knows the beautiful name it has given itself—*mercy;* it goes without saying that mercy remains the privilege of the most powerful man, or better, his—beyond the law.

11

Here a word in repudiation of attempts that have lately been made to seek the origin of justice in quite a different sphere—namely in that of *ressentiment.* To the psychologists first of all, presuming they would like to study *ressentiment* close up for once, I would say: this plant blooms best today among anarchists and anti-Semites—where it has always bloomed, in hidden places, like the violet, though with a different odor. And as like must always produce like, it causes us no surprise to see a repetition in such circles of attempts often made before—see above, section 14—to sanctify *revenge* [Rache] under the name of *justice* [*Gerechtigkeit*]—as if justice were at bottom merely a further development of the feeling of being aggrieved—and to rehabilitate not only revenge but all *reactive* affects in general. To the latter as such I would be the last to raise any objection: in respect to the entire biological problem (in relation to which the value of these affects has hitherto been underrated) it even seems to me to constitute a *service.* All I draw attention to is the circumstance that it is the spirit of *ressentiment* itself out of which this new nuance of scientific fairness (for the benefit of hatred, envy, jealousy, mistrust, rancor, and revenge) proceeds. For this "scientific fairness" immediately ceases and gives way to accents of deadly enmity and prejudice once it is a question of dealing with another group of affects, affects that, it seems to me, are of even greater biological value than those reactive affects and consequently deserve even more to be *scientifically* evaluated and esteemed: namely, the truly *active* affects, such as lust for power, avarice, and the like. (E. Dühring:[25] *The Value of Life; A Course in Philosophy;* and, fundamentally, *passim.*)

So much against this tendency in general: as for Dühring's specific proposition that the home of justice is to be sought in the sphere of the reactive feelings, one is obliged for truth's sake to counter it with a blunt antithesis: the *last* sphere to be conquered by the spirit of justice is the sphere of the reactive feelings! When it really happens that the just man remains just even toward those who have harmed him (and not merely cold, temperate, remote, indifferent: being just is always a *positive* attitude), when the exalted, clear objectivity, as penetrating as it is mild, of the eye of justice and *judging* is not dimmed even under the assault of personal injury, derision, and calumny, this is a piece of perfection and supreme mastery on earth—something it would be prudent not to expect or to *believe* in too readily. On the average, a small dose of aggression, malice, or insinuation certainly suffices to drive the blood into the eyes—and fairness out of the eyes—of even the most upright people. The active, aggressive, arrogant man is still a hundred steps closer to justice than the reactive man; for he has absolutely no need to take a false and prejudiced view of the object before him in the way the reactive man does and is bound to do. For that reason the aggressive man, as the stronger, nobler, more courageous, has

---

Something picked up is no longer there, but the point of picking it up may be to keep it. Hegel made much of this term.

25. Eugen Dühring (1833–1901), a prolific German philosopher and political economist, was among other things an impassioned patriot and anti-Semite and hated the cosmopolitan Goethe and the Greeks. He is remembered chiefly as the butt of polemical works by Karl Marx and Friedrich Engels and of scattered hostile remarks in Nietzsche's writings.

in fact also had at all times a *freer* eye, a *better* conscience on his side: conversely, one can see who has the invention of the "bad conscience" on his conscience—the man of *ressentiment!*

Finally, one only has to look at history: in which sphere has the entire administration of law [*Recht*] hitherto been at home—also the need for law? In the sphere of reactive men, perhaps? By no means: rather in that of the active, strong, spontaneous, aggressive. From a historical point of view, law represents on earth—let it be said to the dismay of the above-named agitator (who himself once confessed: "the doctrine of revenge is the red thread of justice that runs through all my work and efforts")—the struggle *against* the reactive feelings, the war conducted against them on the part of the active and aggressive powers who employed some of their strength to impose measure and bounds upon the excesses of the reactive pathos and to compel it to come to terms. Wherever justice is practiced and maintained one sees a stronger power seeking a means of putting an end to the senseless raging of *ressentiment* among the weaker powers that stand under it (whether they be groups or individuals)—partly by taking the object of *ressentiment* out of the hands of revenge, partly by substituting for revenge the struggle against the enemies of peace and order, partly by devising and in some cases imposing settlements, partly by elevating certain equivalents for injuries into norms to which from then on *ressentiment* is once and for all directed. The most decisive act, however, that the supreme power performs and accomplishes against the predominance of grudges and rancor—it always takes this action as soon as it is in any way strong enough to do so—is the institution of *law* [*Gesetz*], the imperative declaration of what in general counts as permitted, as just [*recht*], in its eyes, and what counts as forbidden, as unjust [*unrecht*]: once it has instituted the law, it treats violence and capricious acts on the part of individuals or entire groups as offenses against the law, as rebellion against the supreme power itself, and thus leads the feelings of its subjects away from the direct injury caused by such offenses; and in the long run it thus attains the reverse of that which is desired by all revenge that is fastened exclusively to the viewpoint of the person injured: from now on the eye is trained to an ever more *impersonal* evaluation of the deed, and this applies even to the eye of the injured person himself (although last of all, as remarked above).

"Just" and "unjust" exist, accordingly, only after the institution of the law (and *not,* as Dühring would have it, after the perpetration of the injury). To speak of just or unjust *in itself* is quite senseless; *in itself,* of course, no injury, assault, exploitation, destruction can be "unjust," since life operates *essentially,* that is in its basic functions, through injury, assault, exploitation, destruction and simply cannot be thought of at all without this character. One must indeed grant something even more unpalatable: that, from the highest biological standpoint, legal conditions can never be other than *exceptional conditions,* since they constitute a partial restriction of the will of life, which is bent upon power, and are subordinate to its total goal as a single means: namely, as a means of creating *greater* units of power. A legal order thought of as sovereign and universal, not as a means in the struggle between power-complexes but as a means of *preventing* all struggle in general—perhaps after the communistic cliché of Dühring, that every will must consider every other will its equal—would be a principle *hostile to life,* an agent of the dissolution and destruction of man, an attempt to assassinate the future of man, a sign of weariness, a secret path to nothingness.—

12

Yet a word on the origin and the purpose of punishment—two problems that are separate, or ought to be separate: unfortunately, they are usually confounded. How have previous genealogists of morals set about solving these problems? Naïvely, as has always been their way: they seek out some "purpose" in punishment, for example, revenge or deterrence, then guilelessly place this purpose at the beginning as *causa fiendi* [the cause of the origin] of punishment, and—have done. The "purpose of law," however, is absolutely the last thing to employ in the history of the origin of law: on the contrary, there is for historiography of any kind no more important proposition than the one it took such effort to establish but which really *ought to be* established now: the cause of the origin of a thing and its eventual utility, its actual employment and place in a system of purposes, lie worlds apart; whatever exists, having somehow come into being, is again and again reinterpreted to new ends, taken over, transformed, and redirected by some power superior to it; all events in the organic world are a subduing, a *becoming master,* and all subduing and becoming master involves a fresh interpretation, an adaptation through which any previous "meaning" and "purpose" are necessarily obscured or even obliterated. However well one has understood the *utility* of any physiological organ (or of a legal institution, a social custom, a political usage, a form in art or in a religious cult), this means nothing regarding its origin: however uncomfortable and disagreeable this may sound to older ears—for one had always believed that to understand the demonstrable purpose, the utility of a thing, a form, or an institution, was also to understand the reason why it originated—the eye being made for seeing, the hand being made for grasping.

Thus one also imagined that punishment was devised for punishing. But purposes and utilities are only *signs* that a will to power has become master of something less powerful and imposed upon it the character of a function; and the entire history of a "thing," an organ, a custom can in this way be a continuous sign-chain of ever new interpretations and adaptations whose causes do not even have to be related to one another but, on the contrary, in some cases succeed and alternate with one another in a purely chance fashion. The "evolution" of a thing, a custom, an organ is thus by no means its *progressus* toward a goal, even less a logical *progressus* by the shortest route and with the smallest expenditure of force—but a succession of more or less profound, more or less mutually independent processes of subduing, plus the resistances they encounter, the attempts at transformation for the purpose of defense and reaction, and the results of successful counteractions. The form is fluid, but the "meaning" is even more so.

The case is the same even within each individual organism: with every real growth in the whole, the "meaning" of the individual organs also changes; in certain circumstances their partial destruction, a reduction in their numbers (for example, through the disappearance of intermediary members) can be a sign of increasing strength and perfection. It is not too much to say that even a partial *diminution of utility,* an atrophying and degeneration, a loss of meaning and purposiveness—in short, death—is among the conditions of an actual *progressus,* which always appears in the shape of a will and way to *greater power* and is always carried through at the expense of numerous smaller powers. The magnitude of an "advance" can even be measured by the mass of things that had to be sacrificed to it; mankind in the mass sacrificed to the prosperity of a single *stronger* species of man—that *would* be an advance.

I emphasize this major point of historical method all the more because it is in fundamental opposition to the now prevalent instinct and taste which would rather be reconciled even to the absolute fortuitousness, even the mechanistic senselessness of all events than to the theory that in all events a *will to power* is operating. The democratic idiosyncracy which opposes everything that dominates and wants to dominate, the modern *misarchism* [hatred of rule or government] (to coin an ugly word for an ugly thing) has permeated the realm of the spirit and disguised itself in the most spiritual forms to such a degree that today it has forced its way, has acquired the *right* to force its way into the strictest, apparently most objective sciences; indeed, it seems to me to have already taken charge of all physiology and theory of life—to the detriment of life, as goes without saying, since it has robbed it of a fundamental concept, that of *activity*. Under the influence of the above-mentioned idiosyncracy, one places instead "adaptation" in the foreground, that is to say, an activity of the second rank, a mere reactivity; indeed, life itself has been defined as a more and more efficient inner adaptation to external conditions (Herbert Spencer). Thus the essence of life, its *will to power*, is ignored; one overlooks the essential priority of the spontaneous, aggressive, expansive, form-giving forces that give new interpretations and directions, although "adaptation" follows only after this; the dominant role of the highest functionaries within the organism itself in which the will to life appears active and form-giving is denied. One should recall what Huxley[26] reproached Spencer with—his "administrative nihilism": but it is a question of rather *more* than mere "administration."

13

To return to our subject, namely *punishment,* one must distinguish two aspects: on the one hand, that in it which is relatively enduring, the custom, the act, the "drama," a certain strict sequence of procedures; on the other, that in it which is *fluid,* the meaning, the purpose, the expectation associated with the performance of such procedures. In accordance with the previously developed major point of historical method, it is assumed without further ado that the procedure itself will be something older, earlier than its employment in punishment, that the latter is *projected* and interpreted *into* the procedure (which has long existed but been employed in another sense), in short, that the case is not as has hitherto been assumed by our naive genealogists of law and morals, who have one and all thought of the procedure as *invented* for the purpose of punishing, just as one formerly thought of the hand as invented for the purpose of grasping.

As for the other element in punishment, the fluid element, its "meaning," in a very late condition of culture (for example, in modern Europe) the concept "punishment" possesses in fact not *one* meaning but a whole synthesis of "meanings": the previous history of punishment in general, the history of its employment for the most various purposes, finally crystallizes into a kind of unity that is hard to disentangle, hard to analyze and, as must be emphasized especially, totally *indefinable*. (Today it is impossible to say for certain *why* people are really punished: all concepts

---

26. Thomas Henry Huxley (1825–95), the English biologist and writer, fought tirelessly for the acceptance of Darwinism. In 1869 he coined the word *agnosticism*, which Spencer took over from him. Aldous Huxley (1894–1963), the author of *Brave New World* (1932), and Julian Huxley (1887–1975), the biologist, are T. H. Huxley's grandsons.

in which an entire process is semiotically concentrated elude definition; only that which has no history is definable.) At an earlier stage, on the contrary, this synthesis of "meanings" can still be disentangled, as well as changed; one can still perceive how in each individual case the elements of the synthesis undergo a shift in value and rearrange themselves accordingly, so that now this, now that element comes to the fore and dominates at the expense of the others; and under certain circumstances one element (the purpose of deterrence perhaps) appears to overcome all the remaining elements.

To give at least an idea of how uncertain, how supplemental, how accidental "the meaning" of punishment is, and how one and the same procedure can be employed, interpreted, adapted to ends that differ fundamentally, I set down here the pattern that has emerged from consideration of relatively few chance instances I have noted. Punishment as a means of rendering harmless, of preventing further harm. Punishment as recompense to the injured party for the harm done, rendered in any form (even in that of a compensating affect). Punishment as the isolation of a disturbance of equilibrium, so as to guard against any further spread of the disturbance. Punishment as a means of inspiring fear of those who determine and execute the punishment. Punishment as a kind of repayment for the advantages the criminal has enjoyed hitherto (for example, when he is employed as a slave in the mines). Punishment as the expulsion of a degenerate element (in some cases, of an entire branch, as in Chinese law: thus as a means of preserving the purity of a race or maintaining a social type). Punishment as a festival, namely as the rape and mockery of a finally defeated enemy. Punishment as the making of a memory, whether for him who suffers the punishment—so-called "improvement"—or for those who witness its execution. Punishment as payment of a fee stipulated by the power that protects the wrongdoer from the excesses of revenge. Punishment as a compromise with revenge in its natural state when the latter is still maintained and claimed as a privilege by powerful clans. Punishment as a declaration of war and a war measure against an enemy of peace, of the law, of order, of the authorities, whom, as a danger to the community, as one who has broken the contract that defines the conditions under which it exists, as a rebel, a traitor, and breaker of the peace, one opposes with the means of war.—

14

This list is certainly not complete; it is clear that punishment is overdetermined [*überladen*] by utilities of all kinds. All the more reason, then, for deducting from it a *supposed* utility that, to be sure, counts in the popular consciousness as the most essential one—belief in punishment, which for several reasons is tottering today, always finds its strongest support in this. Punishment is supposed to possess the value of awakening the *feeling of guilt* in the guilty person; one seeks in it the actual *instrumentum* of that psychical reaction called "bad conscience," "sting of conscience." Thus one misunderstands psychology and the reality of things even as they apply today: how much more as they applied during the greater part of man's history, his prehistory!

It is precisely among criminals and convicts that the sting of conscience is extremely rare; prisons and penitentiaries are *not* the kind of hotbed in which this species of gnawing worm is likely to flourish: all conscientious observers are agreed on that, in many cases unwillingly enough and contrary to their own inclinations.

Generally speaking, punishment makes men hard and cold; it concentrates; it sharpens the feeling of alienation; it strengthens the power of resistance. If it happens that punishment destroys the vital energy and brings about a miserable prostration and self-abasement, such a result is certainly even less pleasant than the usual effects of punishment—characterized by dry and gloomy seriousness.

If we consider those millennia *before* the history of man, we may unhesitatingly assert that it was precisely through punishment that the development of the feeling of guilt was most powerfully *hindered*—at least in the victims upon whom the punitive force was vented. For we must not underrate the extent to which the sight of the judicial and executive procedures prevents the criminal from considering his deed, the type of his action *as such,* reprehensible: for he sees exactly the same kind of actions practiced in the service of justice and approved of and practiced with a good conscience: spying, deception, bribery, setting traps, the whole cunning and underhand art of police and prosecution, plus robbery, violence, defamation, imprisonment, torture, murder, practiced as a matter of principle and without even emotion to excuse them, which are pronounced characteristics of the various forms of punishment—all of them therefore actions which his judges in no way condemn and repudiate *as such,* but only when they are applied and directed to certain particular ends.

The "bad conscience," this most uncanny and most interesting plant of all our earthly vegetation, did *not* grow on this soil; indeed, during the greater part of the past the judges and punishers themselves were *not at all* conscious of dealing with a "guilty person." But with an instigator of harm, with an irresponsible piece of fate. And the person upon whom punishment subsequently descended, again like a piece of fate, suffered no "inward pain" other than that induced by the sudden appearance of something unforeseen, a dreadful natural event, a plunging, crushing rock that one cannot fight.

15

This fact once came insidiously into the mind of Spinoza (to the vexation of his interpreters, Kuno Fischer,[27] for example, who make a real *effort* to misunderstand him on this point), when one afternoon, teased by who knows what recollection, he mused on the question of what really remained to him of the famous *morsus conscientiae* [sting of conscience]—he who had banished good and evil to the realm of human imagination and had wrathfully defended the honor of his "free" God against those blasphemers who asserted that God effected all things *sub ratione boni* [for a good reason] ("but that would mean making God subject to fate and would surely be the greatest of all absurdities"). The world, for Spinoza, had returned to that state of innocence in which it had lain before the invention of the bad conscience: what then had become of the *morsus conscientiae?*

"The opposite of *gaudium* [joy]" he finally said to himself—"a sadness accompanied by the recollection of a past event that flouted all of our expectations." *Eth. III, propos. XVIII, schol. I. II.* Mischief-makers overtaken by punishments have for thousands of years felt in respect of their "transgressions" *just as Spinoza did:* "here something has

---

27. Kuno Fischer (1824–1907), professor at Heidelberg, made a great reputation with a ten-volume history of modern philosophy that consists of imposing monographs on selected modern philosophers. One of the volumes is devoted to Spinoza.

unexpectedly gone wrong," *not:* "I ought not to have done that." They submitted to punishment as one submits to an illness or to a misfortune or to death, with that stout-hearted fatalism without rebellion through which the Russians, for example, still have an advantage over us Westerners in dealing with life.

If there existed any criticism of the deed in those days, it was prudence that criticized the deed: the actual *effect* of punishment must beyond question be sought above all in a heightening of prudence, in an extending of the memory, in a will henceforth to go to work more cautiously, mistrustfully, secretly, in the insight that one is definitely too weak for many things, in a kind of improvement in self-criticism. That which can in general be attained through punishment, in men and in animals, is an increase of fear, a heightening of prudence, mastery of the desires: thus punishment *tames* men, but it does not make them "better"—one might with more justice assert the opposite. ("Injury makes one prudent," says the proverb: insofar as it makes one prudent it also makes one bad. Fortunately, it frequently makes people stupid.)

16

At this point I can no longer avoid giving a first, provisional statement of my own hypothesis concerning the origin of the "bad conscience": it may sound rather strange and needs to be pondered, lived with, and slept on for a long time. I regard the bad conscience as the serious illness that man was bound to contract under the stress of the most fundamental change he ever experienced—that change which occurred when he found himself finally enclosed within the walls of society and of peace. The situation that faced sea animals when they were compelled to become land animals or perish was the same as that which faced these semi-animals, well adapted to the wilderness, to war, to prowling, to adventure: suddenly all their instincts were disvalued and "suspended." From now on they had to walk on their feet and "bear themselves" whereas hitherto they had been borne by the water: a dreadful heaviness lay upon them. They felt unable to cope with the simplest undertakings; in this new world they no longer possessed their former guides, their regulating, unconscious and infallible drives: they were reduced to thinking, inferring, reckoning, co-ordinating cause and effect, these unfortunate creatures; they were reduced to their "consciousness," their weakest and most fallible organ! I believe there has never been such a feeling of misery on earth, such a leaden discomfort—and at the same time the old instincts had not suddenly ceased to make their usual demands! Only it was hardly or rarely possible to humor them: as a rule they had to seek new and, as it were, subterranean gratifications.

All instincts that do not discharge themselves outwardly *turn inward*—this is what I call the *internalization* [*Verinnerlichung*] of man: thus it was that man first developed what was later called his "soul." The entire inner world, originally as thin as if it were stretched between two membranes, expanded and extended itself, acquired depth, breadth, and height, in the same measure as outward discharge was *inhibited*. Those fearful bulwarks with which the political organization protected itself against the old instincts of freedom—punishments belong among these bulwarks—brought about that all those instincts of wild, free, prowling man turned backward *against man himself.* Hostility, cruelty, joy in persecuting, in attacking, in change, in destruction—all this turned against the possessors of such instincts: *that* is the origin of the "bad conscience."

The man who, from lack of external enemies and resistances and forcibly confined to the oppressive narrowness and punctiliousness of custom, impatiently lacerated, persecuted, gnawed at, assaulted, and maltreated himself; this animal that rubbed itself raw against the bars of its cage as one tried to "tame" it; this deprived creature, racked with homesickness for the wild, who had to turn himself into an adventure, a torture chamber, an uncertain and dangerous wilderness—this fool, this yearning and desperate prisoner became the inventor of the "bad conscience." But thus began the gravest and uncanniest illness, from which humanity has not yet recovered, man's suffering *of man, of himself*—the result of a forcible sundering from his animal past, as it were a leap and plunge into new surroundings and conditions of existence, a declaration of war against the old instincts upon which his strength, joy, and terribleness had rested hitherto.

Let us add at once that, on the other hand, the existence on earth of an animal soul turned against itself, taking sides against itself, was something so new, profound, unheard of, enigmatic, contradictory, *and pregnant with a future* that the aspect of the earth was essentially altered. Indeed, divine spectators were needed to do justice to the spectacle that thus began and the end of which is not yet in sight—a spectacle too subtle, too marvelous, too paradoxical to be played senselessly unobserved on some ludicrous planet! From now on, man is *included* among the most unexpected and exciting lucky throws in the dice game of Heraclitus' "great child," be he called Zeus or chance; he gives rise to an interest, a tension, a hope, almost a certainty, as if with him something were announcing and preparing itself, as if man were not a goal but only a way, an episode, a bridge, a great promise.—

17

Among the presuppositions of this hypothesis concerning the origin of the bad conscience is, first, that the change referred to was not a gradual or voluntary one and did not represent an organic adaptation to new conditions but a break, a leap, a compulsion, an ineluctable disaster which precluded all struggle and even all *ressentiment*. Secondly, however, that the welding of a hitherto unchecked and shapeless populace into a firm form was not only instituted by an act of violence but also carried to its conclusion by nothing but acts of violence—that the oldest "state" thus appeared as a fearful tyranny, as an oppressive and remorseless machine, and went on working until this raw material of people and semi-animals was at last not only thoroughly kneaded and pliant but also *formed*.

I employed the word "state": it is obvious what is meant—some pack of blond beasts of prey [*irgendein Rudel blonder Raubtiere, eine Eroberer- und Herren-Rasse*], a conqueror and master race which, organized for war and with the ability to organize, unhesitatingly lays its terrible claws upon a populace perhaps tremendously superior in numbers but still formless and nomad. That is after all how the "state" began on earth: I think that sentimentalism which would have it begin with a "contract" has been disposed of. He who can command, he who is by nature "master," he who is violent in act and bearing—what has he to do with contracts! One does not reckon with such natures; they come like fate, without reason, consideration, or pretext; they appear as lightning appears, too terrible, too sudden, too convincing, too "different" even to be hated. Their work is an instinctive creation and imposition of forms; they are the most involuntary, unconscious artists there are—wherever they appear something new soon arises, a ruling structure that *lives*, in which parts and functions are delimited and coordinated, in which nothing whatever finds a place that has not first been assigned a "meaning" in relation to the whole. They do not know what guilt, responsibility, or consideration are, these born organizers; they exemplify that terrible artists' egoism that has the look of bronze and knows itself justified to all eternity in its "work," like a mother in her child. It is not in *them* that the "bad conscience" developed, that goes without saying—but it would not have developed *without them*, this ugly growth, it would be lacking if a tremendous quantity of freedom had not been expelled from the world, or at least from the visible world, and made as it were *latent* under their hammer blows and artists' violence. This *instinct for freedom* forcibly made latent—we have seen it already—this instinct for freedom pushed back and repressed, incarcerated within and finally able to discharge and vent itself only on itself: that, and that alone, is what the *bad conscience* is in its beginnings.

18

One should guard against thinking lightly of this phenomenon merely on account of its initial painfulness and ugliness. For fundamentally it is the same active force that is at work on a grander scale in those artists of violence and organizers who build states, and that here, internally, on a smaller and pettier scale, directed backward, in the "labyrinth of the breast," to use Goethe's expression, creates for itself a bad conscience and builds negative ideals—namely, the *instinct for freedom* (in my language: the will to power); only here the material upon which the form-giving and ravishing nature of this force vents itself is man himself, his whole ancient animal self—and not, as in that greater and more obvious phenomenon, some *other* man, *other* men. This secret self-ravishment, this artists' cruelty, this delight in imposing a form upon oneself as a hard, recalcitrant, suffering material and in burning a will, a critique, a contradiction, a contempt, a No into it, this uncanny, dreadfully joyous labor of a soul voluntarily at odds with itself that makes itself suffer out of joy in making suffer—eventually this entire *active* "bad conscience"—you will have guessed it—as the womb of all ideal and imaginative phenomena, also brought to light an abundance of strange new beauty and affirmation, and perhaps beauty itself.—After all, what would be "beautiful" if the contradiction had not first become conscious of itself, if the ugly had not first said to itself: "I am ugly"?

This hint will at least make less enigmatic the enigma of how contradictory concepts such as *selflessness, self-denial, self-sacrifice* can suggest an ideal, a kind of beauty; and one thing we know henceforth—I have no doubt of it—and that is the nature of the *delight* that the selfless man, the self-denier, the self-sacrificer feels from the first: this delight is tied to cruelty.

So much for the present about the origin of the moral value of the "unegoistic," about the soil from which this value grew: only the bad conscience, only the will to self-maltreatment provided the conditions for the *value* of the unegoistic.—

19

The bad conscience is an illness, there is no doubt about that, but an illness as pregnancy is an illness. Let us seek out the conditions under which this illness has reached its most terrible and most sublime height; we shall see what it really was that thus entered the world. But for that one needs endurance—and first of all we must go back again to an earlier point of view.

The civil-law relationship between the debtor and his creditor, discussed above, has been interpreted in an, historically speaking, exceedingly remarkable and dubious manner into a relationship in which to us modern men it seems perhaps least to belong: namely into the relationship between the present generation and its ancestors.

Within the original tribal community—we are speaking of primeval times—the living generation always recognized a juridical duty toward earlier generations, and especially toward the earliest, which founded the tribe (and by no means a merely sentimental obligation: there are actually reasons for denying the existence of the latter for the greater part of human history). The conviction reigns that it is only through the sacrifices and accomplishments of the ancestors that the tribe *exists*— and that one has to *pay them back* with sacrifices and accomplishments: one thus recognizes a *debt* that constantly grows greater, since these forebears never cease, in their continued existence as powerful spirits, to accord the tribe new advantages and new strength. In vain, perhaps? But there is no "in vain" for these rude and "poor-souled" ages. What can one give them in return? Sacrifices (initially as food in the coarsest sense), feasts, music, honors; above all, obedience—for all customs, as works of the ancestors, are also their statutes and commands: can one ever give them enough? This suspicion remains and increases; from time to time it leads to a wholesale sacrifice, something tremendous in the way of repayment to the "creditor" (the notorious sacrifice of the first-born, for example; in any case blood, human blood).

The *fear* of the ancestor and his power, the consciousness of indebtedness to him, increases, according to this kind of logic, in exactly the same measure as the power of the tribe itself increases, as the tribe itself grows ever more victorious, independent, honored, and feared. By no means the other way round! Every step toward the decline of a tribe, every misfortune, every sign of degeneration, of coming disintegration always *diminishes* fear of the spirit of its founder and produces a meaner impression of his cunning, foresight, and present power. If one imagines this rude kind of logic carried to its end, then the ancestors of the *most powerful* tribes are bound eventually to grow to monstrous dimensions through the imagination of growing fear and to recede into the darkness of the divinely uncanny and unimaginable: in the end the ancestor must necessarily be transfigured into a *god*. Perhaps this is even the origin of gods, an origin therefore out of *fear!* . . . And whoever should feel obliged to add, "but out of piety also!" would hardly be right for the greater part of the existence of man, his prehistory. To be sure, he would be quite right for the *intermediate* age, in which the noble tribes developed—who indeed paid back their originators, their ancestors (heroes, gods) with interest all the qualities that had become palpable in themselves, the *noble* qualities. We shall take another look later at the ennoblement of the gods (which should not be confused with their becoming "holy"); let us first of all follow to its end the course of this whole development of the consciousness of guilt.

20

History shows that the consciousness of being in debt [*Schulden zu haben*] to the deity did not by any means come to an end together with the organization of communities on the basis of blood relationship. Even as mankind inherited the concepts "good and bad" from the tribal nobility (along with its basic psychological propensity to set up orders of rank), it also inherited, along with the tribal and family divinities, the burden of still unpaid debts and of the desire to be relieved of them. (The transition is provided by those numerous slave and dependent populations who, whether through compulsion or through servility and mimicry, adapted themselves to their masters' cult of the gods: this inheritance then overflows from them in all directions.) The guilty feeling of indebtedness [*das Schuldgefühl*] to the divinity continued to grow for several millennia—always in the same measure as the concept of God and the feeling for divinity increased on earth and was carried to the heights. (The entire history of ethnic struggle, victory, reconciliation, fusion, everything that precedes the definitive ordering of rank of the different national elements in every great racial synthesis, is reflected in the confused genealogies of their gods, in the sagas of the gods' struggles, victories, and reconciliations; the advance toward universal empires is always also an advance toward universal divinities; despotism with its triumph over the independent nobility always prepares the way for some kind of monotheism.)

The advent of the Christian God, as the maximum god attained so far, was therefore accompanied by the maximum feeling of guilty indebtedness [*des Schuldgefühls*] on earth. Presuming we have gradually entered upon the *reverse* course, there is no small probability that with the irresistible decline of faith in the Christian God there is now also a considerable decline in mankind's feeling of guilt [*Schuldbewusstseins*]; indeed, the prospect cannot be dismissed that the complete and definitive victory of atheism might free mankind of this whole feeling of guilty indebtedness [*Gefühl, Schulden . . . zu haben*] toward its origin, its *causa prima* [first cause]. Atheism and a kind of *second innocence* [*Unschuld*] belong together.—

21

So much for a first brief preliminary on the connection of the concepts "guilt" and "duty" with religious presuppositions: I have up to now deliberately ignored the moralization of these concepts (their pushing back into the conscience; more precisely, the involvement of the *bad* conscience with the concept of god); and at the end of the last section I even spoke as if this moralization had not taken place at all, and as if these concepts were now necessarily doomed since their presupposition, the faith in our "creditor" [*der Glaube an unsern "Gläubiger"*: the creed in our "creditor"—or: that one credits our "creditor"], in God, had disappeared. The reality is, to a fearful degree, otherwise.

The moralization of the concepts guilt and duty, their being pushed back into the *bad* conscience, actually involves an attempt to *reverse* the direction of the development described above, or at least to bring it to a halt: the *aim* now is to preclude pessimistically, once and for all, the prospect of a final discharge; the *aim* now is to make the glance recoil disconsolately from an iron impossibility; the *aim* now is to turn back the concepts "guilt" and "duty"—back against whom? There can be no doubt: against the "debtor" first of all, in whom from now on the bad conscience is firmly rooted, eating into him and spreading within him like a polyp, until at last the irredeemable debt gives rise to the conception of irredeemable penance, the idea that it cannot be discharged ("*eternal* punishment"). Finally, however, they are turned back against the "creditor," too: whether we think of the *causa prima* of man, the beginning of the human race, its primal ancestor who is from now on burdened with a curse ("Adam," "original sin," "unfreedom of the will"), or of nature from whose womb mankind arose and into whom the principle of evil is projected from now on ("the diabolizing of nature"), or of existence in general, which is now considered *worthless as such* (nihilistic withdrawal from it, a desire for nothingness or a desire for its antithesis, for a different mode of being, Buddhism and the like)— suddenly we stand before the paradoxical and horrifying expedient that afforded temporary relief for tormented humanity, that stroke of genius on the part of Christianity: God himself sacrifices himself for the guilt of mankind, God himself makes payment to himself, God as the only being who can redeem man from what has become unredeemable for man himself—the creditor sacrifices himself for his debtor, out of *love* (can one credit that?), out of love for his debtor!—

22

You will have guessed *what* has really happened here, *beneath* all this: that will to self-tormenting, that repressed cruelty of the animal-man made inward and scared back into himself, the creature imprisoned in the "state" so as to be tamed, who invented the bad conscience in order to hurt himself after the *more natural* vent for this desire to hurt had been blocked—this man of the bad conscience has seized upon the presupposition of religion so as to drive his self-torture to its most gruesome pitch of severity and rigor. Guilt before *God:* this thought becomes an instrument of torture to him. He apprehends in "God" the ultimate antithesis of his own ineluctable animal instincts; he reinterprets these animal instincts themselves as a form of guilt before God (as hostility, rebellion, insurrection against the "Lord," the "father," the primal ancestor and origin of the world); he stretches himself upon the contradiction "God" and "Devil"; he ejects from himself all his denial of himself, of his nature, naturalness, and actuality, in the form of an affirmation, as something existent, corporeal, real, as God, as the holiness of God, as God the Judge, as God the Hangman, as the beyond, as eternity, as torment without end, as hell, as the immeasurability of punishment and guilt.

In this psychical cruelty there resides a madness of the will which is absolutely unexampled: the *will* of man to find himself guilty and reprehensible to a degree that can never be atoned for; his *will* to think himself punished without any possibility of the punishment becoming equal to the guilt; his *will* to infect and poison the fundamental ground of things with the problem of punishment and guilt so as to cut off once and for all his own exit from this labyrinth of "fixed ideas"; his *will* to erect an ideal—that of the "holy God"—and in the face of it to feel the palpable certainty of his own absolute unworthiness. Oh this insane, pathetic beast—man! What ideas he has, what unnaturalness, what paroxysms of nonsense, what *bestiality of thought* erupts as soon as he is prevented just a little from being a *beast in deed!*

All this is interesting, to excess, but also of a gloomy, black, unnerving sadness, so that one must forcibly forbid oneself to gaze too long into these abysses. Here is *sickness*, beyond any doubt, the most terrible sickness that has ever raged in man; and whoever can still bear to hear (but today one no longer has ears for this!) how in this night of torment and absurdity there has resounded the cry of *love*, the cry of the most nostalgic rapture, of redemption through *love*, will turn away, seized by invincible horror.—There is so much in man that is hideous!—Too long, the earth has been a madhouse!—

23

This should dispose once and for all of the question of how the "holy God" originated.

That the conception of gods *in itself* need not lead to the degradation of the imagination that we had to consider briefly, that there are *nobler* uses for the invention of gods than for the self-crucifixion and self-violation of man in which Europe over the past millennia achieved its distinctive mastery—that is fortunately revealed even by a mere glance at the *Greek gods*, those reflections of noble and autocratic men, in whom *the animal* in man felt deified and did *not* lacerate itself, did *not* rage against itself! For the longest time these Greeks used their gods precisely so as to ward off the "bad conscience," so as to be able to rejoice in their freedom of soul— the very opposite of the use to which Christianity put its God. They went *very far* in this direction, these splendid and lionhearted children; and no less an authority than the Homeric Zeus himself occasionally gives them to understand that they are making things too easy for themselves. "Strange!" he says once—the case is that of Aegisthus, a *very* bad case—

> Strange how these mortals so loudly complain of the gods!
> We alone produce evil, *they say; yet themselves*
> Make themselves wretched through folly, even counter to fate.[28]

Yet one can see and hear how even this Olympian spectator and judge is far from holding a grudge against them or thinking ill of them on that account: "how *foolish* they are!" he thinks when he observes the misdeeds of mortals—and "foolishness," "folly," a little "disturbance in the head," this much even the Greeks of the strongest, bravest age conceded of themselves as the reason for much that was bad and calamitous—foolishness, *not* sin! do you grasp that?

Even this disturbance in the head, however, presented a problem: "how is it possible? how could it actually have happened to heads such as *we* have, we men of aristocratic descent, of the best society, happy, well-constituted, noble, and virtuous?"—thus noble Greeks asked themselves for centuries in the face of every incomprehensible atrocity or wantonness with which one of their kind had polluted himself. "He must have been deluded by a *god*," they concluded finally, shaking their heads . . . This expedient is *typical* of the Greeks . . . In this way the gods served in those days to justify man to a certain extent even in his wickedness, they served as the originators of evil—in those days they took upon themselves, not the punishment but, what is *nobler*, the guilt.

24

I end up with three question marks; that seems plain. "What are you really doing, erecting an ideal or knocking one down?" I may perhaps be asked.

But have you ever asked yourselves sufficiently how much the erection of *every* ideal on earth has cost? How much reality has had to be misunderstood and slandered, how

---

28. *Odyssey*, I, line 32ff.

many lies have had to be sanctified, how many consciences disturbed, how much "God" sacrificed every time? If a temple is to be erected *a temple must be destroyed:* that is the law—let anyone who can show me a case in which it is not fulfilled!

We modern men are the heirs of the conscience-vivisection and self-torture[29] of millennia: this is what we have practiced longest, it is our distinctive art perhaps, and in any case our subtlety in which we have acquired a refined taste. Man has all too long had an "evil eye" for his natural inclinations, so that they have finally become inseparable from his "bad conscience." An attempt at the reverse would *in itself* be possible—but who is strong enough for it?—that is, to wed the bad conscience to all the *unnatural* inclinations, all those aspirations to the beyond, to that which runs counter to sense, instinct, nature, animal, in short all ideals hitherto, which are one and all hostile to life and ideals that slander the world. To whom should one turn today with *such* hopes and demands?

One would have precisely the *good* men against one; and, of course, the comfortable, the reconciled, the vain, the sentimental, the weary.

What gives greater offense, what separates one more fundamentally, than to reveal something of the severity and respect with which one treats oneself? And on the other hand—how accommodating, how friendly all the world is toward us as soon as we act as all the world does and "let ourselves go" like all the world!

The attainment of this goal would require a *different* kind of spirit from that likely to appear in this present age: spirits strengthened by war and victory, for whom conquest, adventure, danger, and even pain have become needs; it would require habituation to the keen air of the heights, to winter journeys, to ice and mountains in every sense; it would require even a kind of sublime wickedness, an ultimate, supremely self-confident mischievousness in knowledge that goes with great health; it would require, in brief and alas, precisely this *great health!*

Is this even possible today?—But some day, in a stronger age than this decaying, self-doubting present, he must yet come to us, the *redeeming* man of great love and contempt, the creative spirit whose compelling strength will not let him rest in any aloofness or any beyond, whose isolation is misunderstood by the people as if it were flight *from* reality—while it is only his absorption, immersion, penetration *into* reality, so that, when he one day emerges again into the light, he may bring home the redemption of this reality: its *redemption* from the curse that the hitherto reigning ideal has laid upon it. This man of the future, who will redeem us not only from the hitherto reigning ideal but also from that which was bound to grow out of it, the great nausea, the will to nothingness, nihilism; this bell-stroke of noon and of the great decision that liberates the will again and restores its goal to the earth and his hope to man; this Antichrist and antinihilist; this victor over God and nothingness— *he must come one day.*—

25

But what am I saying? Enough! Enough! At this point it behooves me only to be silent; or I shall usurp that to which only one younger, "heavier with future," and stronger than I has a right—that to which only *Zarathustra* has a right, *Zarathustra the godless.*—

29. [*Selbsttierquälerei: Tierquälerei* really means cruelty to animals or, literally, animal torture; hence Nietzsche's coinage suggests that this kind of self-torture involves mortification of the animal nature of man.]